GOOD HOUSEKEEPING

FAMILY
HEALTH
&
MEDICAL
GUIDE

GOOD HOUSEKEEPING

FAMILY HEALTH & MEDICAL GUIDE

HEARST BOOKS

NEW YORK, NEW YORK

Published by Hearst Books, A Division of The Hearst Corporation

Designed and produced by
Reference International Publishers Ltd.

Copyright © 1979, 1980 by The Hearst Corporation

Manufactured in the United States of America.
All rights reserved. No part of this book
may be reproduced in any manner whatsoever
without the written permission of the publisher.

ISBN 0-87851-023-0

Library of Congress Catalog Card Number 78-51129

Contributors

Graham H. Barker M.B., B.S., A.K.C., M.R.C.O.G., Lecturer, Institute of Cancer Research, Royal Marsden Hospital; Medical Officer, Department of Family Planning, Queen Charlotte's Maternity Hospital, London.

Michael Hastin Bennett M.A., M.B., F.R.C.S., formerly Resident Surgical Officer, National Hospital, London and Wolfson Foundation Research Fellow in Neurosurgery.

Arthur J. Berman M.D., Attending Gastroenterologist. Lawrence Hospital, Bronxville, New York; Associate Attending Gastroenterologist, Montefiore Hospital, Bronx, New York.

Richard J. Bing M.D., F.A.C.P., Professor of Medicine, University of Southern California; Director of Experimental Cardiology and Scientific Development, Huntington Memorial Hospital; Visiting Associate, California Institute of Technology.

John H. Bland M.D., F.A.C.P., Professor of Medicine, University of Vermont College of Medicine; Attending Physician, Medical Center Hospital of Vermont, Burlington, Vermont.

Gordon Bourne F.R.C.S., F.R.C.O.G., Head of Department of Obstetrics and Gynecology, St. Bartholomew's Hospital; Gynecologist, Royal Masonic Hospital, London.

William T. Bowles M.D., F.A.C.S., Associate Professor of Clinical Urology, Washington University School of Medicine; Assistant Surgeon, Barnes Hospital, St. Louis, Missouri.

Frank M. Calia M.D., F.A.C.P., Professor of Medicine, University of Maryland School of Medicine; Chief of Medical Service, Baltimore Veterans Administration Hospital.

Rachmel Cherner M.D., F.A.C.P., Associate Clinical Professor of Medicine, Jefferson Medical College of Thomas Jefferson University, Philadelphia; formerly Chief of Endocrinology, Albert Einstein Medical Center (Southern Division), Philadelphia.

David N. Danforth M.D., Ph.D., F.A.C.S., F.A.C.O.G., Thomas J. Watkins Professor of Obstetrics and Gynecology, Northwestern University Medical School, Chicago; Attending Obstetrician and Gynecologist, Evanston Hospital, Evanston, Illinois.

Joseph A. DeJulia D.D.S., Associate Clinical Professor of Dentistry, School of Dentistry and Oral Surgery, Columbia University, New York City.

Stephen Engel M.D., F.A.C.S., Associate Clinical Professor of Surgery, University of Colorado School of Medicine.

Robert A. Glick M.D., Assistant Clinical Professor of Psychiatry, Columbia University; Physician-in-Charge, Emergency and Acute Care Psychiatric Services, Columbia-Presbyterian Medical Center, New York City.

Arlene N. Heyman M.D., formerly Robert Wood Johnson Clinical Scholar and Instructor in Clinical Psychiatry, College of Physicians and Surgeons, Columbia University; currently in private practice in New York City.

Robert M. Hui M.D., Attending Otolaryngologist, Presbyterian Hospital; Professor of Clinical Otolaryngology, College of Physicians and Surgeons, Columbia University, New York City.

Ginette Betty Jacob M.D., formerly Assistant Professor of Medicine, Columbia-Presbyterian Medical Center and Director, Hemodialysis Unit, Presbyterian Hospital, New York City.

Mark A. Jacobs M.D., Resident, Department of Obstetrics and Gynecology, Baylor College of Medicine.

Warren M. Jacobs M.D., F.A.C.S., F.A.C.O.G., Clinical Professor of Obstetrics and Gynecology, Baylor College of Medicine.

Judith K. Jones M.D., Ph.D., Director, Division of Drug Experience, U.S. Food and Drug Administration, Rockville, Maryland;* formerly Assistant Clinical Professor of Medicine, University of California, San Francisco.

---

*The opinions expressed in the article "Drugs and Medicines" are the author's; they do not necessarily represent the official position of the U.S. Food and Drug Administration.

Acknowledgments

The publishers are grateful to the following individuals and companies for assistance in the preparation of this book:

The staff of Reference International Publishers, Ltd.:

Edward R. Brace, Medical Editor; Winfred Van Atta, Associate Medical Editor; Martin Self, Editorial Director; Stephen Jones, Managing Editor; Anthony Pearce, Executive Editor; Dr. Tony Smith and Dr. Michael Hastin Bennett, Special Editorial Consultants; Dr. Andrew Brown, Picture research and captions; Julian Holland, Art director and design; Richard Bonson, Andrew Popkiewicz, Sidney Woods, Roger Twinn and George Angelini, Artists; John Cleary, Production Manager; and Robert Crocker, Production Assistant.

Robert M. Liles, Medical Editor of *Good Housekeeping* magazine.

Richard Bonson, who drew many of the illustrations throughout the book, and also produced all the full-color artwork.

Dr. Ian Starke and Dr. Grahame Howard for help with text for the full-color illustrations, and Sally Walters for picture research on the full-color illustrations.

Medtronic (U.K.) Ltd.
Technicon Instruments Co. Ltd.
EMI Medical Ltd.
Philips Medical Systems
GEC Medical Equipment Ltd.
for technical assistance in preparing certain illustrations.

Dr. William K. Frankenburg and the LADOCA Project and Publishing Foundation, Denver, Colorado, for permission to reproduce the Denver Prescreening Developmental Questionnaire.

Several illustrations in the full-color section on "The Immune System" are based on drawings in *Immunology II* by Joseph A. Bellanti; this is by kind permission of the publishers, W. B. Saunders Company, Philadelphia, PA.

Tables in the *The Primary Care Physician* and *Infectious Diseases* are based on material published in "The Task of Medicine", by William H. Glazier, in *Scientific American*.

Contents

Thomas Kalchthaler D.O., Professor of Medicine, New York Medical College; Medical Director and Chief of Geriatrics, St. Joseph's Hospital Nursing Home, Yonkers, New York.

Lenore S. Katkin M.D., F.A.A.P., Associate Professor of Clinical Pediatrics, Cornell Medical College; Director of Pediatric Ambulatory Services and Community Medicine, North Shore University Hospital, Long Island, New York.

Margaret M. Kilcoyne M.D., Assistant Professor of Medicine in the Department of Medicine (Division of Cardiovascular Diseases), College of Physicians and Surgeons, Columbia University; Assistant Attending Physician, Presbyterian Hospital, New York City.

Robert Lewy M.D., Director, Employee Health Services, Presbyterian Hospital; Adjunct Assistant Professor of Public Health, Columbia University School of Public Health, New York City.

Henry O. Marsh M.D., Associate Clinical Professor of Orthopedics, Kansas University School of Medicine; Chief, Orthopedic Section, St. Francis Hospital, Wichita, Kansas.

Marceline Meyerriecks R.N., B.S.N., Memorial Sloan-Kettering Cancer Center, New York City.

Lawrence G. Pape M.D., Ph.D., Instructor in Clinical Ophthalmology, College of Physicians and Surgeons, Columbia University; Attending Ophthalmologist, Edward S. Harkness Eye Institute, Columbia-Presbyterian Medical Center, New York City.

Christopher S. Pitcher D.M., F.R.C.Path., Consultant Hematologist, Stoke Mandeville Hospital, Buckinghamshire (England).

Alexander S. Playfair M.R.C.S., L.R.C.P., D.Obst.R.C.O.G., Member of Council of the British Red Cross Society and Medical Officer of its Cambridgeshire Branch.

John L. Roglieri M.D., Vice President, Ambulatory Services, Presbyterian Hospital; Assistant Professor of Clinical Medicine, College of Physicians and Surgeons, Columbia University; Assistant Attending Physician, Medical Service, Presbyterian Hospital, New York City.

Saul L. Sanders M.D., Clinical Professor of Dermatology, College of Physicians and Surgeons, Columbia University; Attending Dermatologist, Presbyterian Hospital, New York City.

Lawrence Scharer M.D., F.A.C.P., Associate Clinical Professor of Medicine, College of Physicians and Surgeons, Columbia University; Attending Physician, Roosevelt Hospital; Visiting Lecturer in Medicine, Cornell University, New York.

Tony Smith B.M., M.A., Deputy Editor, *British Medical Journal;* Medical Correspondent, *The Times,* London.

Joseph E. Snyder M.D., Director of Medical Affairs, Presbyterian Hospital; Lecturer in Public Health, College of Physicians and Surgeons, Columbia University, New York City.

Paul S. Stein M.D., Clinical Associate, Department of Surgery, University of Kansas School of Medicine; Member of Surgical Teaching Staff, Wesley Medical Center, Wichita, Kansas.

Richard D. Sweet M.D., Chief of Neurology Service, Veterans Administration Hospital, Bronx; Associate Professor of Neurology, Mount Sinai School of Medicine, New York City.

John Yudkin M.D., Ph.D., F.R.C.P., F.R.I.C., Emeritus Professor of Nutrition and Dietetics, London University.

Jonathan E. Zucker M.D., Chief of Allergy and Immunology Service, Southern Maryland Hospital Center, Clinton, Maryland.

Preface

The Good Housekeeping Family Health & Medical Guide **is the most comprehensive medical reference available today for family use. More than forty highly qualified and professionally respected experts in all fields of the medical and health sciences (covering thousands of subjects) have contributed their knowledge and experience to the book. Some 500 medical drawings were specially commissioned, and years of research were also invested to produce the Guide.**

No one wants to be an amateur doctor when his own or his family's health hangs in the balance. Medicine is clearly a business of life and death. But, today, the subject is becoming so specialized, technical, complex, and expensive that a comprehensive guide on the subject is virtually a necessity. We need to understand what doctors are trying to do, and we need to be better judges of the results they achieve. We also need to be in a postion to provide physicians with our informed consent or refusal in a crisis. And our knowledge must be as current and free of prejudice as we can make it.

By using straightforward layman's terms and with hundreds of drawings, diagrams, and charts, this reference makes modern medicine and health care readily understandable. It answers a wide variety of needs by providing both general and specific information about every facet of health care. And its format is designed for easy use. The pages of the encyclopedia and first aid sections are tinted in different shades so they can be quickly found, and extensive cross-referencing between sections has been achieved by setting important topics in italics, small capital letters, or bold face type to indicate how they have been handled in the text.

With proper information, such as this guide provides, we can make medicine more effective by asking intelligent questions and by taking proper care of ourselves and our loved ones. We will also be better equipped to make the difficult decisions that are left to us as patients and parents.

The Good Housekeeping Family Health & Medical Guide, which is specially bound for lasting use, is an outstanding reference for education, family health, and emergency care.

How to use this book

The Good Housekeeping Family Health & Medical Guide **surveys the entire complex subject of medical knowledge and care today. It presents information clearly and comprehensively by approaching the subject from three points of view: that of the doctor, that of the interested layman, and that of the family looking for medical guidance. As a result, the Guide has been divided into three major sections, preceded by a four-color atlas of the body. These are described below.**

A Color Atlas of the Body
103 full-color, detailed anatomical drawings show what the body looks like inside, what its component structures and organs are called, where they are located, and, most important, brief descriptions explain how each body system functions. The atlas serves as a valuable reference for the entire Guide.

Section I: A Survey of Medical Specialities
This section presents the state of the art in the most important fields of modern medicine. It is composed of 23 essays, each written by an expert currently practicing in a specific area of medicine. Each doctor reviews his or her specialty, discussing major breakthroughs that have been made, current treatment, and future prospects for improved care. He or she describes the area of the body treated, its function, and the symptoms and illnesses connected with it.

Section II: The A-Z of Medicine
The core of the book, this section is a complete encyclopedia of medical topics, including diseases, symptoms, procedures, conditions, and technical terms. Its tinted pages are designed for easy recognition.

Section III: The Complete Family Health Guide
Up-to-the-minute medical knowledge translated into practical, easy-to-understand information, advice, and instructions that can be applied to everyday situations by ordinary, untrained laymen. Here you will find expert advice on how to keep in good physical shape, eat sensibly, and reduce the health risks of living in our age. You will also find articles on how to care for members of your family of any age who become ill or need special help, such as that of a nursing home. Pregnancy, childbirth, and family planning are covered, too.

Other features of this section include a guide to medications with a full survey of the current uses and actions of the major prescription and over-the-counter drugs; discussions on preventive medicine; psychotherapy and examination, diagnosis, and therapy; and a fifty-five page section presenting a doctor's answers to questions frequently asked by patients.

The Family Health Guide section assembles in one place the kind of practical, down-to-earth help everyone needs sooner or later for self-care or the care of another.

Section: IV: First Aid
With its tinted pages, this complete, illustrated course in emergency first aid can be located quickly in a crisis. The drawings and diagrams make emergency procedures easy to follow, even under the worst circumstances. A separate table of contents at the beginning of this section directs the reader quickly to the specific information required.

Cross-references: Throughout the book you will find certain words printed in SMALL CAPITAL LETTERS. These subjects are listed alphabetically in Section II, "The A-Z of Medicine." Subjects printed in bold type refer to major articles in the Guide. If you are unable to find the entry you are looking for in Section II, consult the comprehensive fifty-page index at the back of the book for the appropriate page(s).

carcinoma

Any of various types of malignant cancerous growths composed of epithelial cells—the cells which line the body's organs and ducts.

See CANCER and the major article on **Oncology**.

cardiac massage

A technique used in the attempt to restore function to a heart which has stopped suddenly.

Direct cardiac massage is massage of the heart itself; it is only performed by doctors, usually after heart surgery.

6. Most patients with cardiac arrest also stop breathing and need artificial respiration. This is best performed by an assistant at one forced breath for every five to eight cardiac massages, but the two procedures can be performed by the same person if essential.
7. Keep going. Recovery may occur after an hour or more of cardiac massage, although this is uncommon.
8. Other measures are urgently required but must await medical assistance.

When resuscitating children, care must be taken not to use excessive force.

See *Resuscitation* in the **First Aid** section.

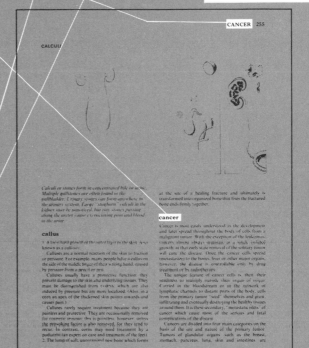

Oncology
Dr. Graham H. Barker

The modern approach to the treatment of cancer involves the "multimodal" use of new chemotherapeutic agents, radiation therapy and the surgical removal of tumors which have not yet begun to spread their cells to other parts of the body. The following article discusses what we know about the various forms of this dreaded disease and the outlook for the future.

Early cancer research

callus

cancer

ASTHMA

HEART ATTACKS

Coronary occlusion

Acute congestive heart failure

RESUSCITATION

How to use the subject locator system

These sample pages illustrate how related or identical subjects are keyed for easy reference throughout the *Family Health and Medical Guide.* The quickest way to locate any subject is to check the index that begins on page 877. But once you start reading, you will see that closely related topics, covered elsewhere in the book, are italized. For example, the discussion on cardiac massage refers to *Resuscitation,* which is described in the First Aid section. Words set in **bold type** direct you to a section or major article on that subject in Section I, "A Survey of Medical Specialties," or Section III, "The Complete Family Health Care Guide." Subjects set in SMALL CAPITAL LETTERS can be found in Section II, "The A-Z of Medicine," a medical encyclopedia.

A Color Atlas of the Body

The color illustrations on the following pages show the exact location, shape, and important details of each of the body's organs and major systems, and the brief descriptions that accompany them explain the remarkable way these systems function.

To make the descriptions as clear and comprehensive as possible, the pages have been organized so that both general as well as microscopically detailed drawings of each system appear together, on facing pages. For example, on the lefthand page of color plate IV, "Muscles," you can see how the muscles protect and interact with nerves, bones, inner organs, and the circulatory system. On the opposite page, the micro-anatomy of muscles is made clear in drawings that picture the incredible complexity of a single muscle fiber, the interface of muscles with the nervous system (which makes movement possible), and the detailed structure of different kinds of muscle.

Contents

The Head

The bones of the skull determine the shape of the head and also give protection to the brain and special sense organs. This view shows the intimate relationships between the various organs of the head; this compactness is one of the marvels of human evolution. The brain is by far the most complex structure in the body, and a great deal still remains to be learned about its function. With the spinal cord, it constitutes the central nervous system. The neck conveys major blood vessels, the respiratory and digestive passages and the spinal cord, and also permits extensive movement of the head around the first two cervical vertebrae.

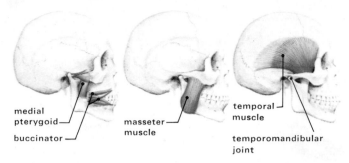

medial pterygoid
buccinator
masseter muscle
temporal muscle
temporomandibular joint

Biting and chewing muscles
Biting and chewing depend on movements at the temporomandibular joint between the lower jaw (mandible) and the rest of the skull. These movements are produced by contractions of the powerful muscles of mastication shown in the illustration above.

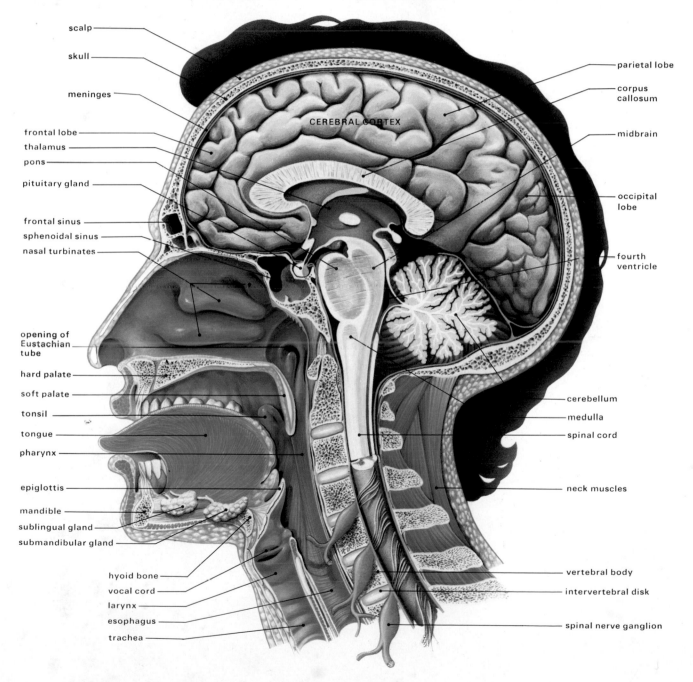

scalp
skull
meninges
frontal lobe
thalamus
pons
pituitary gland
frontal sinus
sphenoidal sinus
nasal turbinates
opening of Eustachian tube
hard palate
soft palate
tonsil
tongue
pharynx
epiglottis
mandible
sublingual gland
submandibular gland
hyoid bone
vocal cord
larynx
esophagus
trachea

CEREBRAL CORTEX

parietal lobe
corpus callosum
midbrain
occipital lobe
fourth ventricle
cerebellum
medulla
spinal cord
neck muscles
vertebral body
intervertebral disk
spinal nerve ganglion

The Bones and Joints

The skeleton gives form, support and protection to the body. It consists of about 206 bones, supplemented by pieces of cartilage. The bones, especially the long bones of the limbs, act as levers operated by the muscles (the joints forming fulcrums), thus allowing movement. Some bones (e.g., the ribs and skull) serve to protect the organs they enclose. Bones are also a reservoir of vital minerals, and some contain bone marrow, where blood cells are formed. Joints between bones are of three types: *fibrous* (allowing no movement), *cartilaginous* (limited movement) and *synovial* (freely movable).

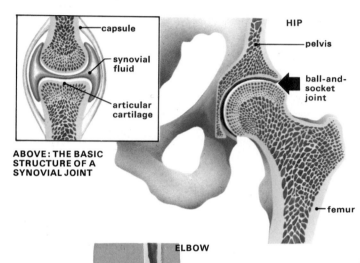

ABOVE: THE BASIC STRUCTURE OF A SYNOVIAL JOINT

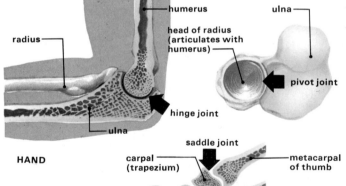

Free movement around **synovial joints** is permitted by the smooth *articular cartilage* coating the ends of the bones and the lubricating *synovial fluid* which fills the joint. The joint is enclosed by a fibrous capsule. Six different types of synovial joint are shown above. Ball-and-socket joints (hip and shoulder) allow a wide range of movement; hinge joints (elbow) allow movement in one plane only; pivot joints allow rotation—the radius/humerus pivot allows the hand to be turned palm up or down; ovoid or egg-shaped joints (wrist) and saddle joints (thumb) allow both side-to-side and back-and-forth motion, and gliding joints (carpals of the hand) permit similar but more restricted movements.

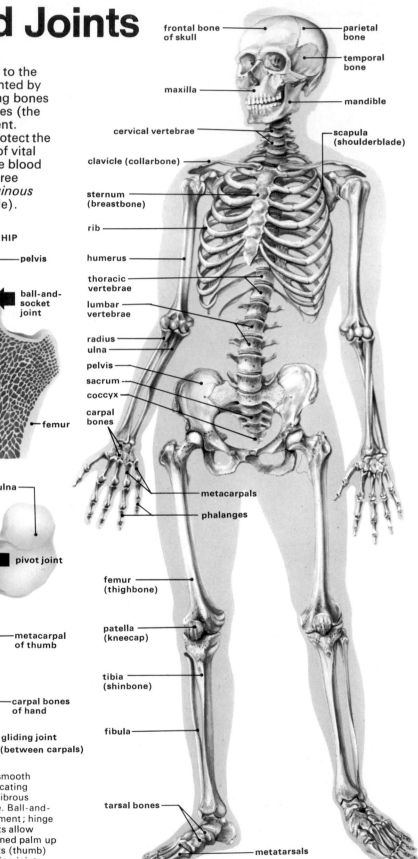

II

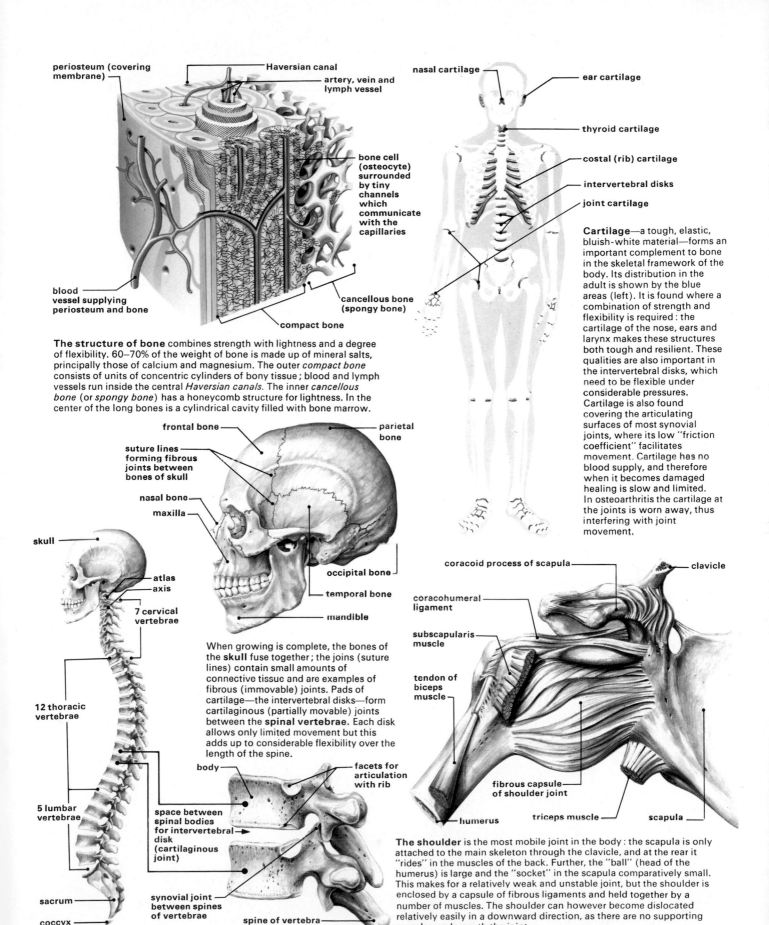

periosteum (covering membrane)

Haversian canal

artery, vein and lymph vessel

bone cell (osteocyte) surrounded by tiny channels which communicate with the capillaries

blood vessel supplying periosteum and bone

cancellous bone (spongy bone)

compact bone

The structure of bone combines strength with lightness and a degree of flexibility. 60–70% of the weight of bone is made up of mineral salts, principally those of calcium and magnesium. The outer *compact bone* consists of units of concentric cylinders of bony tissue; blood and lymph vessels run inside the central *Haversian canals*. The inner *cancellous bone* (or *spongy bone*) has a honeycomb structure for lightness. In the center of the long bones is a cylindrical cavity filled with bone marrow.

frontal bone

parietal bone

suture lines forming fibrous joints between bones of skull

nasal bone

maxilla

skull

atlas

axis

7 cervical vertebrae

occipital bone

temporal bone

mandible

12 thoracic vertebrae

When growing is complete, the bones of the **skull** fuse together; the joins (suture lines) contain small amounts of connective tissue and are examples of fibrous (immovable) joints. Pads of cartilage—the intervertebral disks—form cartilaginous (partially movable) joints between the **spinal vertebrae**. Each disk allows only limited movement but this adds up to considerable flexibility over the length of the spine.

5 lumbar vertebrae

body

facets for articulation with rib

space between spinal bodies for intervertebral disk (cartilaginous joint)

synovial joint between spines of vertebrae

sacrum

coccyx

spine of vertebra

nasal cartilage

ear cartilage

thyroid cartilage

costal (rib) cartilage

intervertebral disks

joint cartilage

Cartilage—a tough, elastic, bluish-white material—forms an important complement to bone in the skeletal framework of the body. Its distribution in the adult is shown by the blue areas (left). It is found where a combination of strength and flexibility is required: the cartilage of the nose, ears and larynx makes these structures both tough and resilient. These qualities are also important in the intervertebral disks, which need to be flexible under considerable pressures. Cartilage is also found covering the articulating surfaces of most synovial joints, where its low "friction coefficient" facilitates movement. Cartilage has no blood supply, and therefore when it becomes damaged healing is slow and limited. In osteoarthritis the cartilage at the joints is worn away, thus interfering with joint movement.

coracoid process of scapula

clavicle

coracohumeral ligament

subscapularis muscle

tendon of biceps muscle

fibrous capsule of shoulder joint

humerus

triceps muscle

scapula

The shoulder is the most mobile joint in the body: the scapula is only attached to the main skeleton through the clavicle, and at the rear it "rides" in the muscles of the back. Further, the "ball" (head of the humerus) is large and the "socket" in the scapula comparatively small. This makes for a relatively weak and unstable joint, but the shoulder is enclosed by a capsule of fibrous ligaments and held together by a number of muscles. The shoulder can however become dislocated relatively easily in a downward direction, as there are no supporting muscles underneath the joint.

The Muscles

Muscle is a tissue with a unique property : it can shorten (contract) when stimulated by a supplying nerve. There are three types of muscle in the body : *skeletal* or *voluntary muscle* (the "meat" of the body), *smooth* or *involuntary muscle* (found in the digestive tract, blood vessels and elsewhere) and *cardiac muscle* (found only in the heart). Skeletal muscles are attached at both ends to bones, cartilage, ligaments, skin or other muscles. When a muscle contracts, one attachment will remain static, and the other will therefore move. Muscle fibers do not increase in number with use, but each fiber becomes thicker, causing the muscles to swell and bulge.

A CROSS SECTION THROUGH THE NECK

front

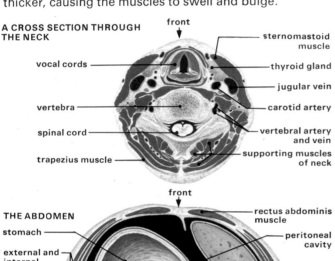

- sternomastoid muscle
- vocal cords
- thyroid gland
- jugular vein
- vertebra
- carotid artery
- spinal cord
- vertebral artery and vein
- trapezius muscle
- supporting muscles of neck

THE ABDOMEN

front

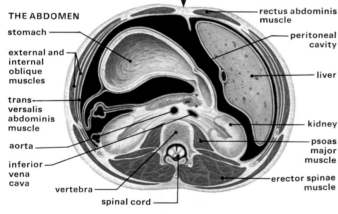

- stomach
- rectus abdominis muscle
- external and internal oblique muscles
- peritoneal cavity
- trans-versalis abdominis muscle
- liver
- aorta
- kidney
- inferior vena cava
- psoas major muscle
- vertebra
- spinal cord
- erector spinae muscle

THE UPPER ARM

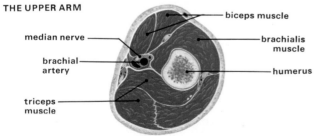

- biceps muscle
- median nerve
- brachialis muscle
- brachial artery
- humerus
- triceps muscle

The arrangement of skeletal muscles in different parts of the body is shown by the cross sections above. The neck is crowded with important structures passing from the trunk to the head, including the windpipe, esophagus, spinal cord and major blood vessels supplying the brain. The many different muscles permit a wide range of head movements. The abdomen has three layers of superficial muscles giving support to the abdominal contents. Several important muscles support the spine and govern its movements, maintaining our upright posture. The section through the upper arm shows the arrangement of muscles around the humerus.

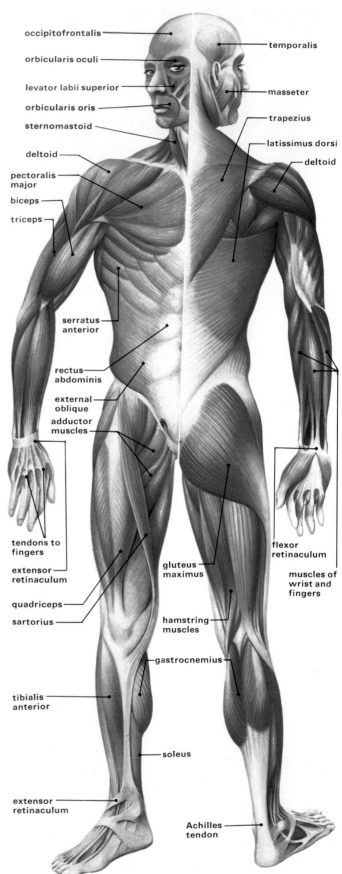

- occipitofrontalis
- temporalis
- orbicularis oculi
- levator labii superior
- masseter
- orbicularis oris
- trapezius
- sternomastoid
- latissimus dorsi
- deltoid
- deltoid
- pectoralis major
- biceps
- triceps
- serratus anterior
- rectus abdominis
- external oblique
- adductor muscles
- tendons to fingers
- extensor retinaculum
- gluteus maximus
- flexor retinaculum
- muscles of wrist and fingers
- quadriceps
- sartorius
- hamstring muscles
- gastrocnemius
- tibialis anterior
- soleus
- extensor retinaculum
- Achilles tendon

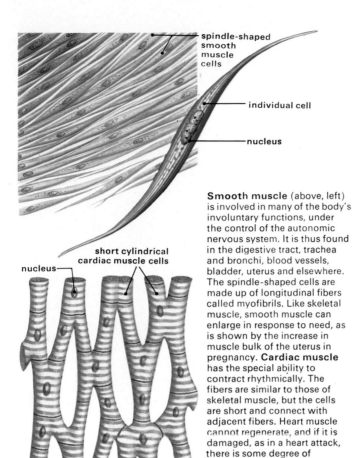

spindle-shaped smooth muscle cells

individual cell

nucleus

nucleus

short cylindrical cardiac muscle cells

Smooth muscle (above, left) is involved in many of the body's involuntary functions, under the control of the autonomic nervous system. It is thus found in the digestive tract, trachea and bronchi, blood vessels, bladder, uterus and elsewhere. The spindle-shaped cells are made up of longitudinal fibers called myofibrils. Like skeletal muscle, smooth muscle can enlarge in response to need, as is shown by the increase in muscle bulk of the uterus in pregnancy. **Cardiac muscle** has the special ability to contract rhythmically. The fibers are similar to those of skeletal muscle, but the cells are short and connect with adjacent fibers. Heart muscle cannot regenerate, and if it is damaged, as in a heart attack, there is some degree of functional loss.

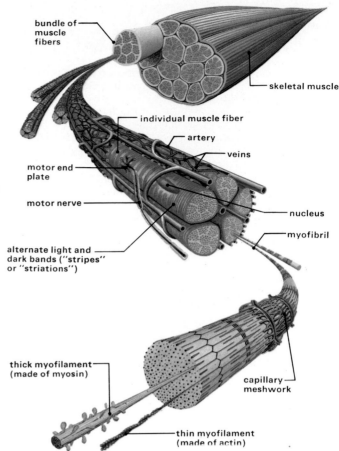

bundle of muscle fibers

skeletal muscle

individual muscle fiber

artery

veins

motor end plate

motor nerve

nucleus

myofibril

alternate light and dark bands ("stripes" or "striations")

thick myofilament (made of myosin)

capillary meshwork

thin myofilament (made of actin)

Skeletal muscle (or striated muscle) is made up of bundles of muscle fibers grouped together. Motor nerves, which stimulate the muscle to contract, are attached to the fibers at *motor end plates*. There is a rich blood supply, able to cope with the enormous demand for blood during vigorous activity. The fibers themselves are made up of *myofibrils* which in turn contain two types of *myofilament*, thick and thin. During contraction, these interact, sliding between each other and causing the muscle fibers to shorten.

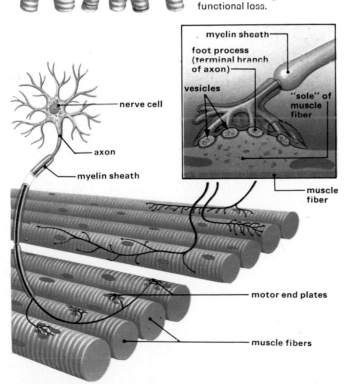

nerve cell

axon

myelin sheath

myelin sheath

foot process (terminal branch of axon)

vesicles

"sole" of muscle fiber

muscle fiber

motor end plates

muscle fibers

A motor end plate is the junction between a motor nerve and skeletal muscle fibers. The nerve terminates in several "feet" attached to a swelling or "sole" on the muscle fiber. The nervous signal is relayed to the fibers by a biochemical "transmitter" substance, thought to be stored in vesicles near the junction.

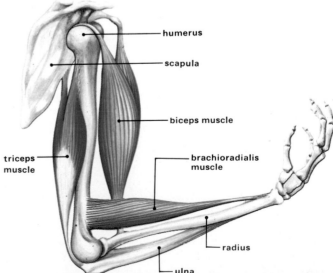

humerus

scapula

biceps muscle

brachioradialis muscle

triceps muscle

radius

ulna

Movement of joints usually involves contraction of some muscles and relaxation of others (skeletal muscles are generally arranged in opposing groups). Thus flexing the elbow to raise the forearm involves contraction of the biceps and brachioradialis muscles and relaxation of the triceps ; to straighten the elbow, the process is reversed.

The Circulatory System

The many vital functions of the blood depend on its continuous circulation to all parts of the body. Blood is pumped by the right side of the heart through the pulmonary artery into the lungs, where it absorbs oxygen. It then returns via the pulmonary veins to the left side of the heart to be pumped through the aorta and the arterial system. It gives up oxygen – necessary for all vital bodily processes – to every tissue in the body. The deoxygenated blood returns through the veins to enter the right side of the heart once again.

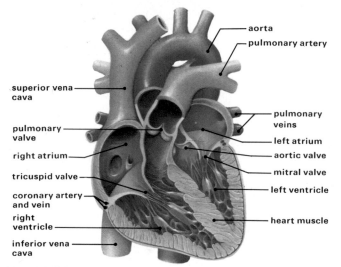

Labels: aorta, pulmonary artery, superior vena cava, pulmonary valve, right atrium, tricuspid valve, coronary artery and vein, right ventricle, inferior vena cava, pulmonary veins, left atrium, aortic valve, mitral valve, left ventricle, heart muscle

CARDIAC CYCLE

venous blood fills atria | atria contract to fill ventricles | ventricles contract to expel blood | relaxed atria are filled again

The heart is a double-sided pump with four chambers; valves ensure the correct flow of blood. Venous blood enters the right atrium, passes into the right ventricle and is pumped along the pulmonary artery into the lungs. Blood returns from the lungs via the pulmonary veins into the left atrium, passes into the left ventricle and is forced out through the aorta. The sequence of these events is shown in the center diagram.

ANTERIOR SURFACE OF HEART   **POSTERIOR SURFACE OF HEART**

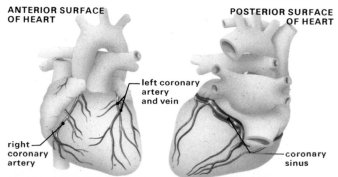

Labels: left coronary artery and vein, right coronary artery, coronary sinus

The heart muscle receives its oxygen supply from the right and left **coronary arteries.** If either of these vessels becomes blocked, a "heart attack" occurs—with muscle damage, chest pain and possibly death. The **coronary veins** drain into the right atrium via the coronary sinus.

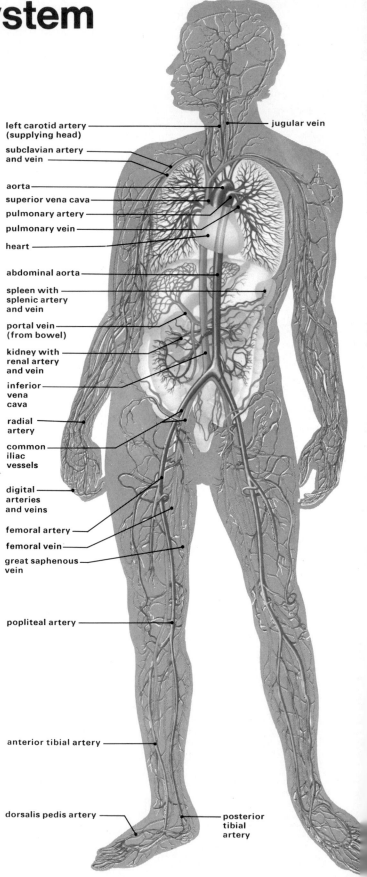

Labels: left carotid artery (supplying head), subclavian artery and vein, aorta, superior vena cava, pulmonary artery, pulmonary vein, heart, abdominal aorta, spleen with splenic artery and vein, portal vein (from bowel), kidney with renal artery and vein, inferior vena cava, radial artery, common iliac vessels, digital arteries and veins, femoral artery, femoral vein, great saphenous vein, popliteal artery, anterior tibial artery, dorsalis pedis artery, jugular vein, posterior tibial artery

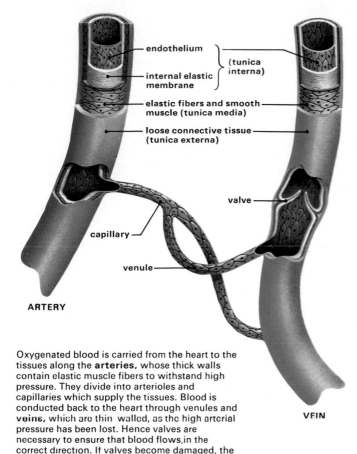

- endothelium
- internal elastic membrane
  } (tunica interna)
- elastic fibers and smooth muscle (tunica media)
- loose connective tissue (tunica externa)
- valve
- capillary
- venule

ARTERY

VEIN

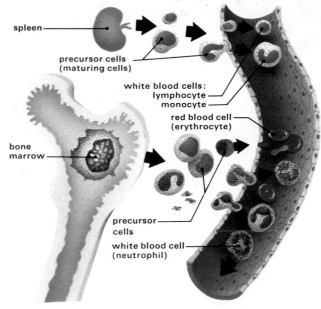

- spleen
- precursor cells (maturing cells)
- white blood cells: lymphocyte monocyte
- red blood cell (erythrocyte)
- bone marrow
- precursor cells
- white blood cell (neutrophil)

Oxygenated blood is carried from the heart to the tissues along the **arteries,** whose thick walls contain elastic muscle fibers to withstand high pressure. They divide into arterioles and capillaries which supply the tissues. Blood is conducted back to the heart through venules and **veins,** which are thin walled, as the high arterial pressure has been lost. Hence valves are necessary to ensure that blood flows in the correct direction. If valves become damaged, the back pressure can cause varicose veins.

The principal blood-forming organs are the bone marrow, the lymph nodes and the spleen. The active bone marrow tissue is found at the ends of most long bones, and in the ribs, breastbone, skull and vertebrae. Red blood cells (which transport oxygen and are by far the most numerous type of blood cell) are formed in the bone marrow, passing through various stages of maturation before they are released into the bloodstream. The bone marrow also manufactures certain types of white blood cells and platelets (important in clotting). The lymphatic tissues (including the spleen) form other types of white blood cells, which similarly pass through several stages before reaching maturity. White blood cells defend the body against infection.

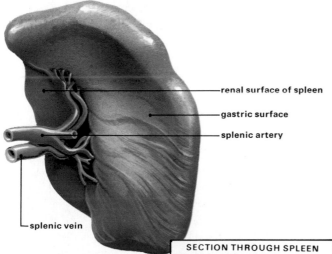

- renal surface of spleen
- gastric surface
- splenic artery
- splenic vein

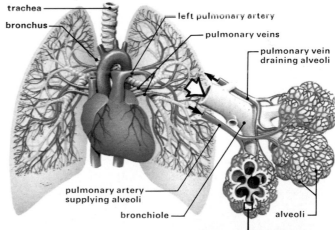

- trachea
- bronchus
- left pulmonary artery
- pulmonary veins
- pulmonary vein draining alveoli
- pulmonary artery supplying alveoli
- bronchiole
- alveoli

SECTION THROUGH SPLEEN

- capsule
- splenic pulp
- venous sinusoids
- branch of splenic artery
- branch of splenic vein
- lymphatic nodule

The spleen is a complex organ with several functions. It acts as a filter for the blood, removing old or damaged red blood cells. This takes place largely in the spaces known as the venous sinusoids. The spleen also contains lymphatic nodules which form part of the body's immune system; they also manufacture and release white blood cells into the circulation.

Gaseous interchange—the uptake by the blood of oxygen and the release of carbon dioxide—takes place in the alveoli of the lungs. There are about 300 million alveoli, each surrounded by a mesh of blood capillaries which lie very close to the air-filled space (lumen) inside the alveolus. Oxygen diffuses into the oxygen-poor blood vessels from the oxygen-rich air in the lumen, while carbon dioxide similarly diffuses from the blood into the alveoli.

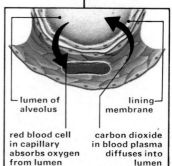

- lumen of alveolus
- lining membrane
- red blood cell in capillary absorbs oxygen from lumen
- carbon dioxide in blood plasma diffuses into lumen

The Digestive System

Digestion consists of first reducing food to its constituent parts and then absorbing the essential nutrients. Food is broken down in the stomach and duodenum by the action of enzymes released from glands in the mouth, stomach and pancreas. The absorption of nutrients into the bloodstream occurs mainly in the small intestine. In the large intestine, water is absorbed to leave semisolid waste which is passed via the rectum as feces. The liver — the largest gland in the body — is responsible for utilizing the products of digestion absorbed into the blood.

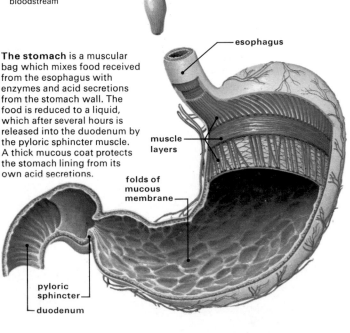

liver processes the products of digestion

gallbladder stores bile

stomach mixes food with enzymes and acid

pancreas secretes further digestive enzymes and neutralizes stomach acid

small intestine absorbs nutrients into the bloodstream

large intestine absorbs water from waste material

The stomach is a muscular bag which mixes food received from the esophagus with enzymes and acid secretions from the stomach wall. The food is reduced to a liquid, which after several hours is released into the duodenum by the pyloric sphincter muscle. A thick mucous coat protects the stomach lining from its own acid secretions.

esophagus

muscle layers

folds of mucous membrane

pyloric sphincter

duodenum

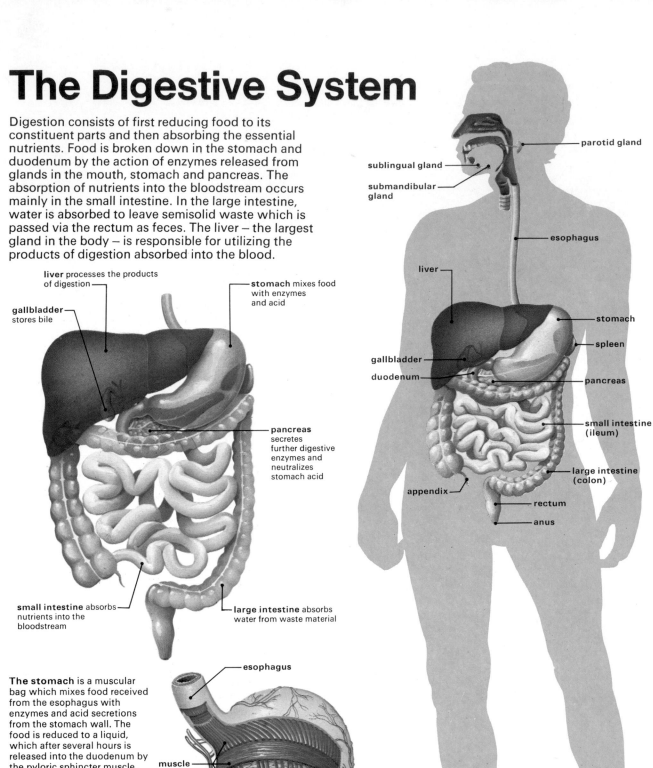

parotid gland

sublingual gland

submandibular gland

esophagus

liver

stomach

spleen

gallbladder

duodenum

pancreas

small intestine (ileum)

large intestine (colon)

appendix

rectum

anus

A CROSS SECTION THROUGH THE LIVER

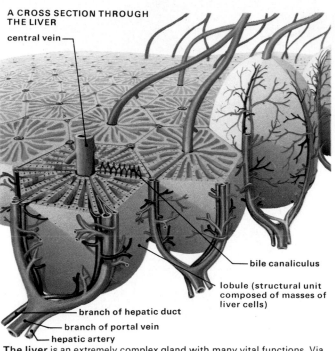

central vein

branch of hepatic duct
branch of portal vein
hepatic artery

bile canaliculus

lobule (structural unit composed of masses of liver cells)

The liver is an extremely complex gland with many vital functions. Via the portal vein it receives nutrients absorbed from the intestines. It converts poisonous ammonia compounds into nontoxic urea; it stores sugar for release into the bloodstream when necessary; it synthesizes complex proteins from simple ones absorbed from food; it makes bile which is stored in the gallbladder and is essential for fat absorption.

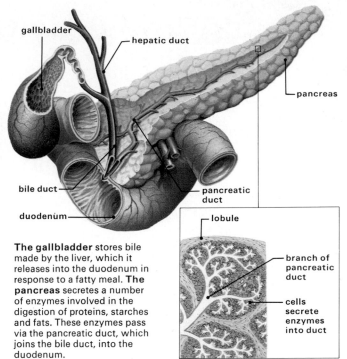

gallbladder

hepatic duct

pancreas

bile duct

pancreatic duct

duodenum

lobule

branch of pancreatic duct

cells secrete enzymes into duct

The gallbladder stores bile made by the liver, which it releases into the duodenum in response to a fatty meal. **The pancreas** secretes a number of enzymes involved in the digestion of proteins, starches and fats. These enzymes pass via the pancreatic duct, which joins the bile duct, into the duodenum.

TRANSPORTATION OF NUTRIENTS

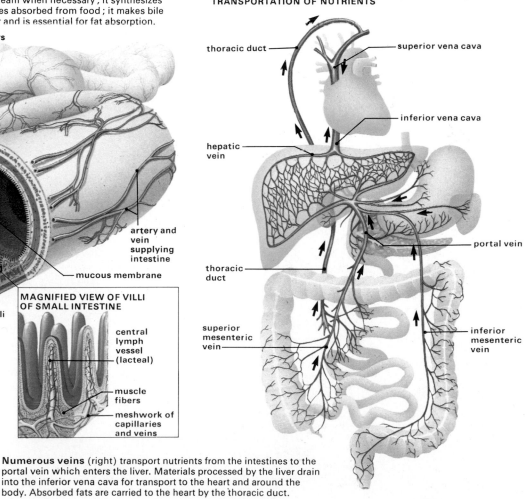

thoracic duct

superior vena cava

hepatic vein

inferior vena cava

thoracic duct

portal vein

superior mesenteric vein

inferior mesenteric vein

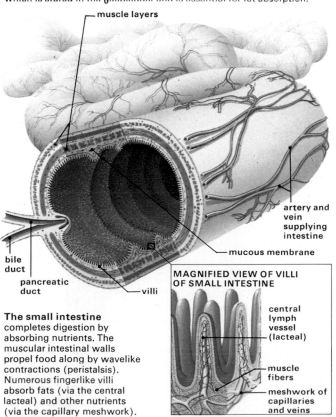

muscle layers

artery and vein supplying intestine

mucous membrane

bile duct
pancreatic duct

villi

MAGNIFIED VIEW OF VILLI OF SMALL INTESTINE

central lymph vessel (lacteal)

muscle fibers

meshwork of capillaries and veins

The small intestine completes digestion by absorbing nutrients. The muscular intestinal walls propel food along by wavelike contractions (peristalsis). Numerous fingerlike villi absorb fats (via the central lacteal) and other nutrients (via the capillary meshwork).

Numerous veins (right) transport nutrients from the intestines to the portal vein which enters the liver. Materials processed by the liver drain into the inferior vena cava for transport to the heart and around the body. Absorbed fats are carried to the heart by the thoracic duct.

The Nervous System

Nerves are complex fibers which conduct electrochemical impulses. Nerves to and from all parts of the body are grouped together within the spinal cord and conveyed to the brain, which controls and coordinates the nervous signals involved in any bodily function—innumerable in even the simplest activity. The nervous system can be divided into the *motor system* (muscular control), the *sensory system* (information from the senses to the brain) and the *autonomic nervous system* (bodily functions not under conscious control, e.g., digestion).

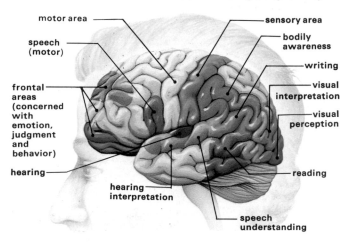

- motor area
- sensory area
- speech (motor)
- bodily awareness
- writing
- frontal areas (concerned with emotion, judgment and behavior)
- visual interpretation
- visual perception
- hearing
- reading
- hearing interpretation
- speech understanding

Each area of the **cerebral cortex** (outer layer of the brain) is concerned with a particular function. For example, voluntary movements are initiated in the motor area, while sensations of pain and touch are processed in the sensory area. Complex incoming signals may be collected together and processed in more than one area—for example, visual signals are perceived in one area and interpreted in another.

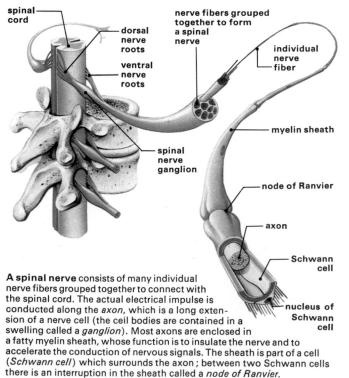

- spinal cord
- dorsal nerve roots
- ventral nerve roots
- nerve fibers grouped together to form a spinal nerve
- individual nerve fiber
- spinal nerve ganglion
- myelin sheath
- node of Ranvier
- axon
- Schwann cell
- nucleus of Schwann cell

A spinal nerve consists of many individual nerve fibers grouped together to connect with the spinal cord. The actual electrical impulse is conducted along the *axon*, which is a long extension of a nerve cell (the cell bodies are contained in a swelling called a *ganglion*). Most axons are enclosed in a fatty myelin sheath, whose function is to insulate the nerve and to accelerate the conduction of nervous signals. The sheath is part of a cell (*Schwann cell*) which surrounds the axon; between two Schwann cells there is an interruption in the sheath called a *node of Ranvier*.

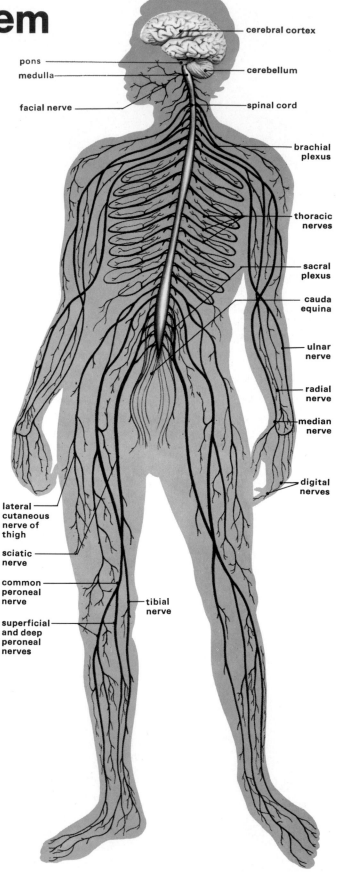

- cerebral cortex
- pons
- medulla
- cerebellum
- facial nerve
- spinal cord
- brachial plexus
- thoracic nerves
- sacral plexus
- cauda equina
- ulnar nerve
- radial nerve
- median nerve
- digital nerves
- lateral cutaneous nerve of thigh
- sciatic nerve
- common peroneal nerve
- superficial and deep peroneal nerves
- tibial nerve

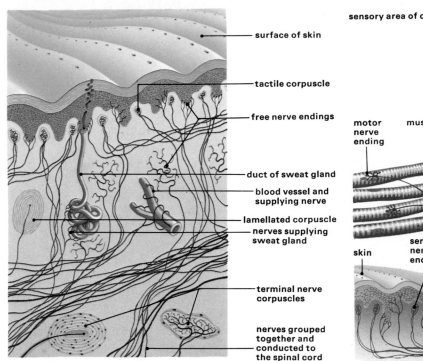

surface of skin

tactile corpuscle

free nerve endings

duct of sweat gland

blood vessel and supplying nerve

lamellated corpuscle
nerves supplying sweat gland

terminal nerve corpuscles

nerves grouped together and conducted to the spinal cord

sensory area of cerebral cortex

motor area

thalamus

motor nerve ending

muscle fibers

sensory fibers carry information from nerve endings to brain

motor fibers carry instruct-ions from brain to muscles

medulla

motor nerve

spino-thalamic tract

skin

sensory nerve endings

spinal nerve

synapse

sensory nerve

spinal cord

Nerve supply of the skin

Both motor and sensory nerves are to be found in and just below the skin. The autonomic nervous system supplies nerve fibers to the sweat glands and capillaries; these control sweating and constriction or dilatation of the capillaries and thus heat loss from the body through the skin. Sensory nerve fibers supplying the skin may terminate in various types of structures called corpuscles. It is not certain whether a particular type is concerned with a particular sensation, though the lamellated corpuscle is thought to be sensitive to vibration and pressure. Other sensory nerves have free nerve endings, which may be concerned with the sensation of pain. Where there are hairs, the hair follicle is also supplied by nerves from the autonomic and sensory systems.

Motor and sensory nervous system

Sensory nerves carrying stimuli of pain, temperature, touch, etc., join the spinal cord via a spinal nerve. Those fibers carrying pain and temperature sensations (blue line) cross over to the other side of the cord; this involves the transfer of the stimulus from one nerve cell to another at a *synapse*. (Other sensations, e.g. touch, are conducted along a different route.) The fibers then ascend the spinal cord in the spinothalamic tract to the thalamus, and from there to the sensory cortex. Here, with the aid of other parts of the brain, the stimulus is interpreted. Motor nerves carrying signals from the motor cortex to the voluntary muscles (red line) cross in the medulla of the brain stem before descending the spinal cord to leave via a spinal nerve.

THE PARASYMPATHETIC NERVOUS SYSTEM

THE SYMPATHETIC NERVOUS SYSTEM

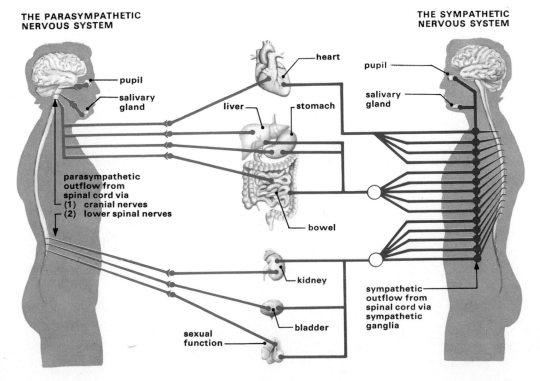

pupil

salivary gland

heart

liver

stomach

pupil

salivary gland

parasympathetic outflow from spinal cord via
(1) cranial nerves
(2) lower spinal nerves

bowel

kidney

bladder

sexual function

sympathetic outflow from spinal cord via sympathetic ganglia

The autonomic nervous system regulates the automatic functions of the body and is composed of the sympathetic and parasympathetic systems, which have opposing effects. The sympathetic system prepares the body for emergency action by reducing nonessential activities such as digestion. The sympathetic nerves are relayed from the sympathetic ganglia which form a chain along either side of the vertebral column. Stimulation of these nerves leads to increases in heart and respiration rate, blood supply to the muscles and dilatation of the pupils, while salivation, urine production and digestive activity are reduced. Ejaculation is also mediated by the sympathetic system, though penile erection is a parasympathetic function. The parasympathetic system involves the 3rd, 7th, 9th and 10th cranial nerves and the lower spinal nerves and comes into play during rest and sleep—slowing the heart and breathing, constricting the pupils and increasing digestion.

The Endocrine System

The endocrine glands (ductless glands) secrete hormones directly into the bloodstream. Hormones are complex chemical "messenger" substances; they are released in tiny amounts, yet they can produce dramatic changes in the activity of body cells. In this way they control basic body functions such as growth, metabolism and sexual development; they are also responsible for maintaining the correct levels in the blood of certain vital substances (e.g. sugar and salt).

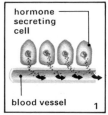
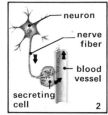
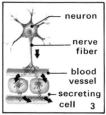

Hormones can be released into the bloodstream in a number of different ways. They may be released directly by a secreting cell (1) or when such a cell is stimulated by a nerve impulse (2). In the posterior lobe of the pituitary, nerve fibers themselves release hormones directly into the blood, which stimulate another hormone-producing cell (3).

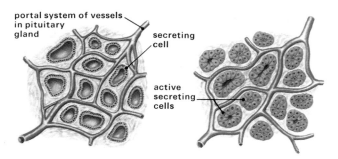

The anterior pituitary has a rich network of blood vessels connecting it to the hypothalamus. It is thought that "neurosecretions" from the hypothalamus stimulate the hormone-secreting cells.

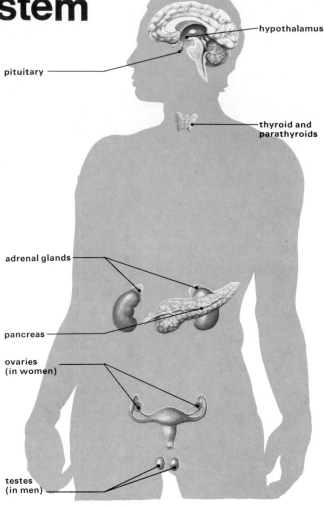

The secretion of hormones is controlled by a complex feedback mechanism in which the nervous system is closely involved. The **hypothalamus** and **pituitary** play particularly important roles.

The pituitary gland (right) is situated at the base of the brain and is about the size of a pea; it is divided into two lobes. It is subject to the influence of the hypothalamus, to which it is connected by a slender stalk. It releases a variety of hormones which act on several "target" organs. The hormones of the anterior lobe, with the exception of somatotropin and MSH, stimulate other glands. The hypothalamus is thought to monitor the level of the hormones released by these glands and to direct the pituitary to cut off the stimulating hormone once the correct level is reached.

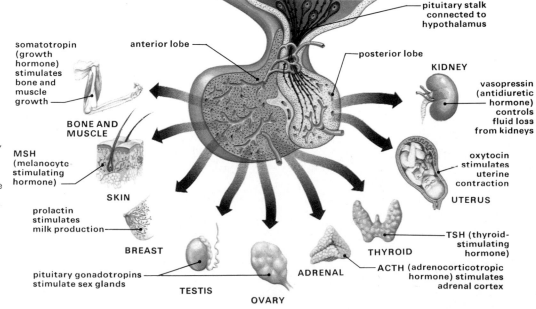

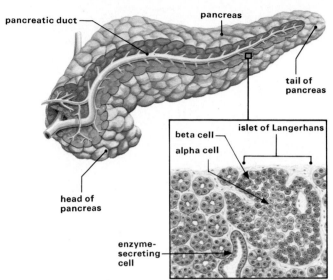

pancreatic duct | pancreas | tail of pancreas

head of pancreas

beta cell
alpha cell
islet of Langerhans

enzyme-secreting cell

The pancreas, which lies behind and under the stomach, is a mixed-function gland; as well as containing cells which secrete digestive enzymes, it has clumps of cells known as the *islets of Langerhans* which secrete hormones. These are most numerous toward the tail or pointed end of the pancreas. The islets contain two types of cells—*alpha* and *beta* cells. The alpha cells produce the hormone glucagon which raises the level of sugar in the blood; the beta cells secrete insulin which lowers blood sugar. A lack of this hormone as the result of disease or damage to the pancreas produces diabetes.

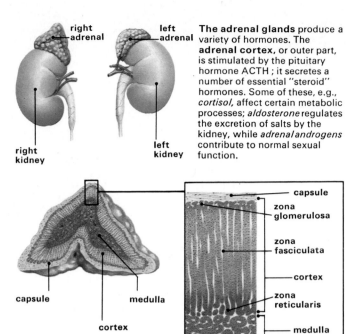

right adrenal | left adrenal

right kidney | left kidney

The adrenal glands produce a variety of hormones. The **adrenal cortex,** or outer part, is stimulated by the pituitary hormone ACTH; it secretes a number of essential "steroid" hormones. Some of these, e.g., *cortisol,* affect certain metabolic processes; *aldosterone* regulates the excretion of salts by the kidney, while *adrenal androgens* contribute to normal sexual function.

capsule | zona glomerulosa | zona fasciculata | cortex | zona reticularis | medulla

capsule | medulla | cortex

The adrenal medulla, or inner part of the adrenal glands, is entirely separate in function from the cortex and is not influenced by the pituitary gland. It secretes the hormones epinephrine and norepinephrine (adrenaline and noradrenaline) in response to fear, anger or sexual desire; these prepare the body for instant action by increasing the heart rate and the blood supply to the muscles.

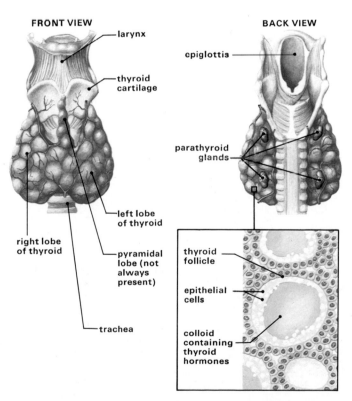

FRONT VIEW — larynx, thyroid cartilage, left lobe of thyroid, right lobe of thyroid, pyramidal lobe (not always present), trachea

BACK VIEW — epiglottis, parathyroid glands

thyroid follicle
epithelial cells
colloid containing thyroid hormones

The thyroid gland is situated at the base of the neck on either side of the trachea, just below the larynx. It is made up of follicles containing a fluid called colloid, in which the two thyroid hormones thyroxine and tri-iodothyronine (T_4 and T_3) are stored for release into the bloodstream as necessary. These hormones control the body's metabolic rate. There are four small **parathyroid glands** situated behind the thyroid. These secrete parathyroid hormone (or parathormone), which controls the level of calcium and phosphorus in the blood.

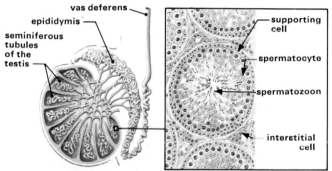

vas deferens
epididymis
seminiferous tubules of the testis

supporting cell
spermatocyte
spermatozoon
interstitial cell

The tubules of **the testes** contain cells called spermatocytes which, under the influence of gonadotropic hormones, mature into spermatozoa. These are stored in the tubules and epididymis until they are conducted to the penis at ejaculation by the vas deferens. The interstitial cells between the tubules also produce the male hormone testosterone, responsible for secondary sexual characteristics.

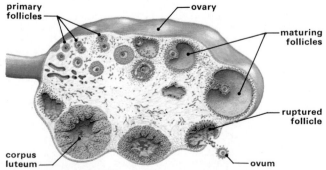

primary follicles | ovary | maturing follicles | ruptured follicle | ovum | corpus luteum

At birth, **the ovaries** contain numerous primary follicles; after puberty, these develop under complex hormonal control. At the mid-point of each menstrual cycle an ovum (egg cell) is released from a mature follicle, which then becomes a corpus luteum. If pregnancy occurs, this secretes hormones which interrupt the menstrual cycle.

The Immune System

The immune system defends the body against invasion by disease-producing organisms and against toxins they produce. It can distinguish between what belongs in the body ("self") and what does not ("non-self"), and reacts against any cells that are not recognized as "self." This reaction may be either to produce antibodies (*humoral immunity*) or to activate cells which attack the invader directly (*cell-mediated immunity*). In both cases the outcome is to make the foreign cell or invading organism subject to *phagocytosis* — destruction by certain white blood cells.

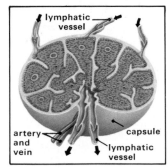

lymphatic vessel

artery and vein

capsule

lymphatic vessel

Lymph nodes (above) are pea-sized structures situated in groups at strategic points in the lymphatic vessels—the network of channels which drain the tissues and return excess fluid to the bloodstream. Foreign particles, such as bacteria, are trapped in the lymph nodes, which are inhabited by *macrophages* (white blood cells which can phagocytose, i.e. engulf and destroy, foreign particles) and *lymphocytes* (white blood cells which mount immune reactions).

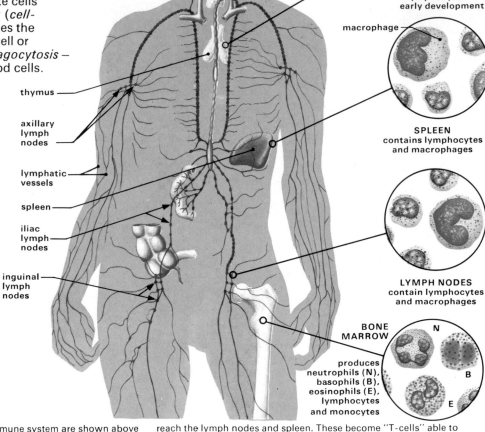

thymus
axillary lymph nodes
lymphatic vessels
spleen
iliac lymph nodes
inguinal lymph nodes

lymphocyte

THYMUS GLAND "processes" some lymphocytes in early development

macrophage

SPLEEN contains lymphocytes and macrophages

LYMPH NODES contain lymphocytes and macrophages

BONE MARROW produces neutrophils (N), basophils (B), eosinophils (E), lymphocytes and monocytes

N
B
E

The main components of the body's immune system are shown above (right). The lymphatic system and lymphoid tissues represent the basic structural framework. The magnified cells shown are all different types of white blood cell. Lymphocytes are concentrated in the lymph nodes and spleen: they are of two types—"T-lymphocytes" and "B-lymphocytes"—which inhabit different regions of the nodes and spleen and play different roles in the immune response. In early development, the thymus gland "processes" some circulating lymphocytes before they reach the lymph nodes and spleen. These become "T-cells" able to mount a cell-mediated immune response. Others, called "B-cells," are not processed in this way, but are capable of responding to antigens by producing antibodies. The bone marrow manufactures a variety of white blood cells: *monocytes,* which eventually become phagocytic macrophages; *neutrophils,* which are also mainly phagocytic, *basophils* (called Mast cells outside the bloodstream), which produce histamine, and *eosinophils,* which limit the effects of histamine release.

TWO METHODS OF ANTIBODY FUNCTION

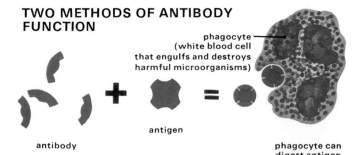

phagocyte (white blood cell that engulfs and destroys harmful microorganisms)

antibody

+ antigen = phagocyte can digest antigen more easily

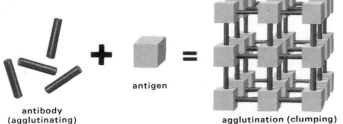

antibody (agglutinating)

+ antigen = agglutination (clumping) immobilizes antigens

The above diagrams illustrate two ways in which antibodies act to render the corresponding antigen harmless. **Left:** antibodies coat the surface of the antigen. As a result of this process, certain other enzymes in the blood are activated which, if the antigen is a cell or micro-organism, damage the cell wall, killing the cell. In addition, coating makes the antigen more readily destroyed by phagocytic cells: specific sites on the phagocytes attract the antibody molecules. **Right:** the antibody can combine with two molecules of antigen, thereby binding the antigen into clumps. This process of agglutination immobilizes the antigens, which can again be ingested by the phagocytes.

PHAGOCYTOSIS AND THE INFLAMMATORY RESPONSE

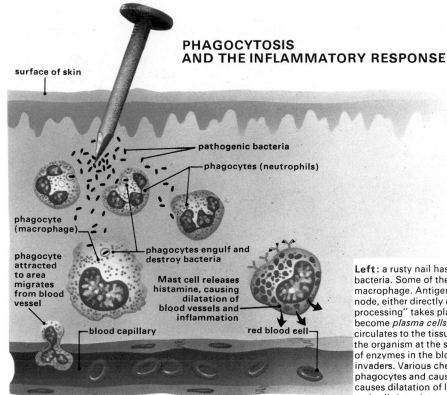

surface of skin

pathogenic bacteria

phagocytes (neutrophils)

phagocyte (macrophage)

phagocytes engulf and destroy bacteria

phagocyte attracted to area migrates from blood vessel

Mast cell releases histamine, causing dilatation of blood vessels and inflammation

blood capillary

red blood cell

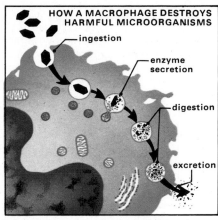

HOW A MACROPHAGE DESTROYS HARMFUL MICROORGANISMS

ingestion

enzyme secretion

digestion

excretion

Left: a rusty nail has broken the skin, carrying in with it pathogenic bacteria. Some of these are ingested by phagocytic neutrophils and by a macrophage. Antigen from the organism will reach the local lymph node, either directly or carried within the macrophage, and "antigen processing" takes place (see below). Lymphocytes are stimulated to become *plasma cells* which make the appropriate antibody ; this then circulates to the tissue and combines with the antigen on the surface of the organism at the site of the wound. This reaction causes activation of enzymes in the blood, causing damage to the cell walls of the invaders. Various chemical substances are released ; these attract phagocytes and cause secretion of histamine by Mast cells. Histamine causes dilatation of local blood vessels and increased migration of fluid and cells into the area, leading to the familiar features of inflammation.

DEVELOPMENT OF CELL-MEDIATED AND HUMORAL IMMUNITY

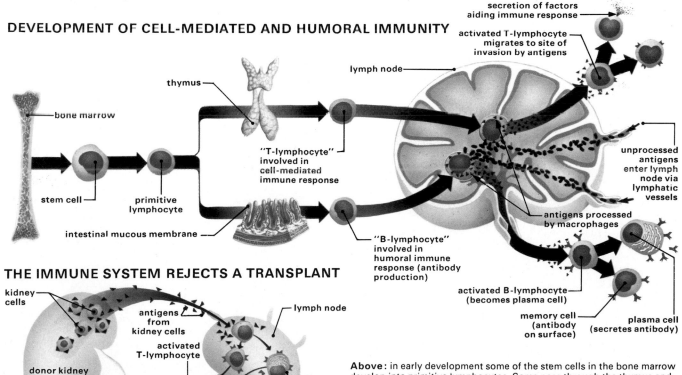

bone marrow

thymus

lymph node

stem cell

primitive lymphocyte

"T-lymphocyte" involved in cell-mediated immune response

intestinal mucous membrane

"B-lymphocyte" involved in humoral immune response (antibody production)

secretion of factors aiding immune response

activated T-lymphocyte migrates to site of invasion by antigens

unprocessed antigens enter lymph node via lymphatic vessels

antigens processed by macrophages

activated B-lymphocyte (becomes plasma cell)

memory cell (antibody on surface)

plasma cell (secretes antibody)

THE IMMUNE SYSTEM REJECTS A TRANSPLANT

kidney cells

antigens from kidney cells

lymph node

activated T-lymphocyte

donor kidney

plasma cell (secretes antibody)

antibodies

humoral attack

cell-mediated attack on donor kidney

The immune system can recognize the cells of a transplanted organ as "non-self" and attacks the organ. Both types of immune response are involved, though cell-mediated immunity plays the greater part. The rejection process can be countered by immunosuppressive drugs, or by closely matching the "tissue types" of donor and recipient.

Above: in early development some of the stem cells in the bone marrow develop into primitive lymphocytes. Some pass through the thymus and become "T-lymphocytes." Others become "B-lymphocytes." (It is possible that these are processed by the intestine.) Both types of lymphocytes are stimulated by antigen : activated T-lymphocytes migrate to the point where the antigen has arisen and may destroy foreign cells themselves or activate local macrophages to do so. These lymphocytes secrete factors which "arm" macrophages and attract other white blood cells. Activated B-lymphocytes divide, and some become plasma cells. Plasma cells make large quantities of antibody ; they are found in lymph nodes and bone marrow and may continue to produce low levels of antibody for many years. In addition some activated T- and B-lymphocytes become "memory cells," able to respond again if the same antigen presents itself.

The Major Sense Organs

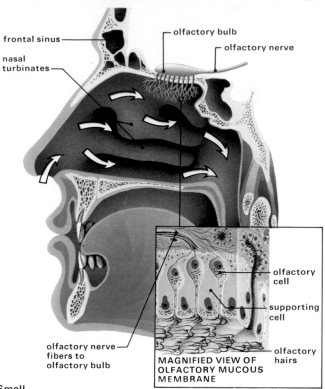

frontal sinus
nasal turbinates
olfactory bulb
olfactory nerve

olfactory cell
supporting cell
olfactory hairs

olfactory nerve fibers to olfactory bulb

MAGNIFIED VIEW OF OLFACTORY MUCOUS MEMBRANE

Smell
The olfactory mucous membrane, a small area in the nasal cavity, contains 10–20 million olfactory cells, each tipped by 10–20 tiny hairs. When air containing odorous molecules reaches the olfactory cells, certain molecules fit certain receptors on the hairs; nervous signals are then sent to the brain, where they are interpreted as odors.

Sight
Rays of light enter the eyeball through the cornea, pass through the lens and vitreous humor to the fovea centralis—the most sensitive region of the retina. This pathway is called the visual axis. By means of a complex system of muscles and nerves, the brain insures that the two visual axes remain parallel. The exception is when the eyes converge to read or study a close object.

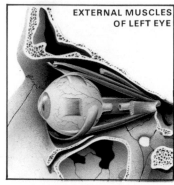

EXTERNAL MUSCLES OF LEFT EYE

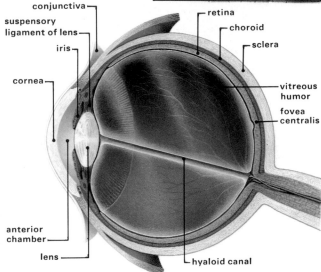

conjunctiva
suspensory ligament of lens
iris
cornea
anterior chamber
lens

retina
choroid
sclera
vitreous humor
fovea centralis
hyaloid canal

CROSS SECTION THROUGH RIGHT EYEBALL

Hearing

auditory nerve
cochlear nerve
vestibular nerve
semicircular canals
cochlea
temporal bone
auricle
ossicles
tympanic membrane (eardrum)
middle ear
Eustachian tube
external auditory meatus

cochlear nerve fibers
organ of Corti
duct of the cochlea

Hearing begins when sound waves reach the eardrum; the vibrations pass through the ossicles and displace fluid within the cochlea. The fluid stimulates hair cells of the organ of Corti to send signals to the brain. The semicircular canals monitor balance by a similar mechanism.

Taste
The nervous signals responsible for our sense of taste originate in the taste buds. These microscopic structures are most numerous in the grooves around the vallate papillae of the tongue. Any substance tasted must first dissolve in saliva and then percolate through tiny pores to the hair receptors of the taste bud. There are thought to be specialized receptors for each of the basic tastes: sweet, sour, salty and bitter. All flavors are made up of combinations of these four tastes.

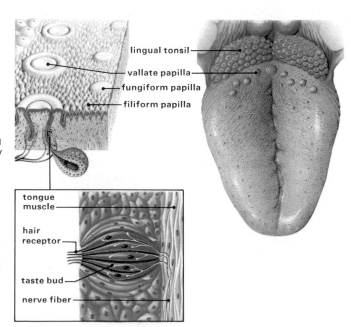

lingual tonsil
vallate papilla
fungiform papilla
filiform papilla

tongue muscle
hair receptor
taste bud
nerve fiber

XVI

Section I

A Survey of
Medical Specialties

The Primary Care Physician

Dr. John L. Roglieri

The primary care physician, who knows us and our medical history, has the diagnostic skill and wide clinical experience to deal directly with most of our problems. For most people, primary care is what medicine is all about.

Because of my close involvement in the education and clinical training of future physicians—including those qualifying for the major specialties and subspecialties of medicine—I was invited to introduce this most important section. In it I will try to describe the role of the primary care physician, who is expected to play an important part in meeting our nation's future health care needs, both in providing general family medical care and in administering preventive measures to avoid disease.

A common question asked today is, "What has happened to that revered family doctor who used to take care of all our medical problems, who came when needed—at all hours of the day and night— and who is remembered by most of us with respect and affection?" Well, he's still around in many areas of the country, caring for entire communities. But he's getting along in years now and when he retires or passes on to his well-earned rest, he is expected to be replaced by the primary care physician, whose specialty training prepares him to look after patients and families when they are in good health as well as when they are sick, and to coordinate and integrate the care provided by other specialists when specific expertise is required. This modern family practitioner is expected to combine the best of the fondly remembered general practitioner with the scientific know-how of modern medicine—together with special insights into the functioning of patients within their families and their communities. An increasing number of young doctors are now choosing this emerging specialty, which offers challenges and rewards that may not be found in the specialties which deal with a single organ system of the body.

The term "primary care" was not widely used during my clinical training years. During that period I vividly remember being rudely awakened at 4 a.m. to care for a pleasant middle-aged woman whose gastrointestinal problems, after three days, had brought her to our emergency service. She told me how pleased she was with the care she received from Dr. J, one of our senior attending physicians in private practice. When I asked why she had not called him about her recent symptoms, she seemed quite surprised at my ignorance. She said, "But Dr. J is my heart doctor, Dr. R looks after my arthritic hip, and Dr. B is my gynecologist. I never bother them with my other problems; I just come here to the emergency room."

Each of the above doctors, if asked, would have—with lesser or greater enthusiasm—taken care of this woman's minor gastrointestinal (GI) problem; but she, like so many patients today, thought of the specialist only in connection with the organ system which is his main area of practice. When dealing with any of the specialists described, you should keep in mind that he was first trained in all areas of general medicine and is qualified to recognize and treat disorders that may or may not be related to his major field of interest. Indeed, with intimate knowledge of his patient and her major physical problems, he may be the best person available to ask for help. The emergency room can be the best place to go when there is a true emergency, but a tired and sleepy resident physician—who is seeing a patient for the first time and may not have her medical records immediately available—will often call her attending specialist and ask for help. At 4 a.m., this will not, I assure you, endear him to the rudely awakened senior physician; but each will know that he is acting in the best interest of the patient.

Why so many specialists?

Another question frequently asked is, "Why must there be so many specialists?" A careful reading of the following articles, each written by a representative of the specialty described, will help answer this question. Perhaps an additional explanation will help you better to understand medicine as it is practiced today.

Most of the development of medical specialization has occurred in this century, following the now famous reports of Sir William Osler (1905) and Abraham Flexner (1910) on the state of American medical education. At that time there were more medical schools than were required and academic standards in many schools were woefully lax or nonexistent. Following these reports, the many "proprietary" (i.e., privately owned) medical schools were closed in short order and the remaining medical schools became affiliated with universities which established and monitored standards for medical education. Thereafter, essentially all medical education took place within university classrooms and laboratories and at the affiliated teaching hospitals. General practitioners could no longer be full-time faculty members and the decline in availability and adequate training of general practitioners and primary care physicians began. The faculties of newly created academic departments comprised increasing numbers of specialists and the effort to achieve scientific excellence took priority over provision of coordinated and comprehensive care.

In the years following World War II, the research model for medical education was given further impetus by the emergence of the National Institutes of Health (NIH) and the growing financial support of medical schools through this federal agency. Medical school faculties became increasingly supported by the NIH research grants and physicians-in-training were also encouraged to pursue research careers by NIH-supported research fellowships. Because most medical research is highly technical and specialized, the trend toward specialization gained increasing strength. Further, the spectacular successes of many of these research projects led to the creation of such an

The physician is a practical scientist working to relieve suffering with all the means available. In this sense his role through the centuries has remained remarkably unchanged.

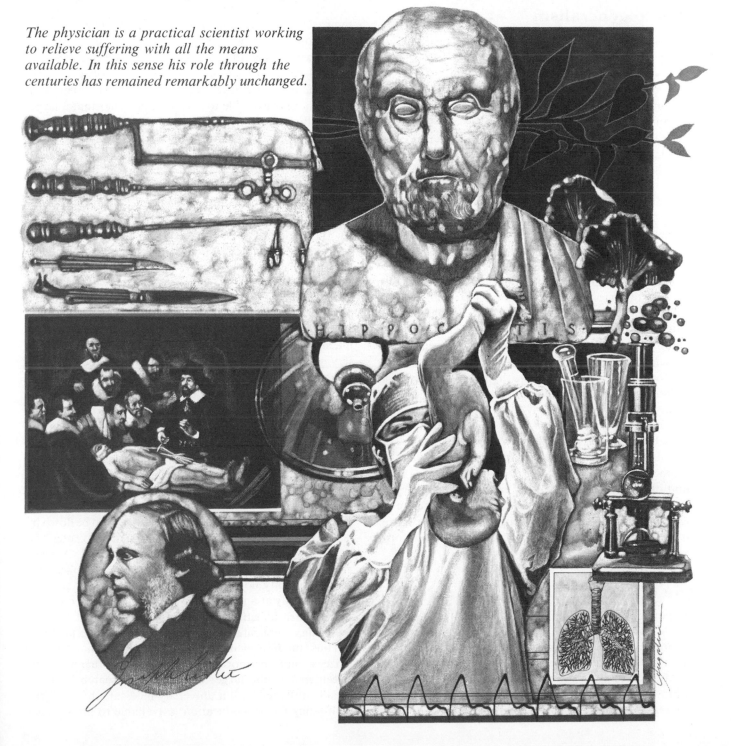

extensive body of medical knowledge that only a specialist or a subspecialist could hope to master and keep abreast of the continuing developments in each clinical area. A succession of increasingly specialized physicians evolved—for example, *internists* (who defined their area of expertise as that comprising all nonsurgical adult medical problems), followed by *endocrinologists* (disturbances of hormonal or "glandular" function), followed by subspecialists in a single gland, such as the thyroid.

Back to generalism

The rise of specialism appears to have peaked and a resurgence of generalism begun in the mid-1960s. Several reports (most notably that of the Millis Commission) called for a renewed emphasis on the preparation of physicians committed to the provision of *primary care* with a personal or family orientation. In the late 1960s the specialty of *family medicine* was approved under the leadership of the American Academy of General Practice. The provision of federal funds which began in 1971 for programs in family medicine spurred medical schools and teaching hospitals to develop training programs for primary care physicians. By 1972, there were over 100 recognized family medicine residency programs; by 1975, there were 259 such programs. It is of interest that during these major swings in professional and academic philosophy the attitudes of patients toward primary care physicians, especially general practitioners, did not substantially change. In the late 1950s when status, privilege, working conditions and income all favored specialization for physicians, an Opinion Research Corporation study found general practitioners were held in the highest esteem by patients.

What does "primary care" really mean? This term and the term "primary medicine" have become common within recent years due, in large part, to the events described above. Because so many commentators have applied the terms in so many ways to differentiate between physicians engaged in general practice, their meanings have become obscured. This could lead to confusion in the mind of the average patient not only about primary care but about the roles of the various specialists to whom they may be referred for special treatment. It would be a simple matter to explain health care today if it were uniformly practiced in all areas of our country.

The distribution of medical care

As many of you know, there are entire counties in our rural areas with no doctor at all, or only one or two physicians to provide medical care for all the residents of the community. The nearest hospital may be many miles away. In our large cities where once there was a general practitioner within two or three blocks to serve his own specific community, there are now few neighborhood doctors at all.

The people—mostly the poor—must depend upon the outpatient departments of general hospitals and medical centers for all of their medical care, often waiting their turn in line to see a doctor, seldom if ever getting the same one twice in a row. In the exurban communities, to which large segments of the middle and upper classes have fled from the cities, doctors are plentiful—often serving in group practices, with specialists in all disciplines of medicine and surgery located in a single setting. Thus, as our national health care planners see it, our problem is not so much a lack of physicians as it is their uneven distribution and thus reduced availability to many of our citizens. The goal, from their point of view, is to make better use of medical manpower so that all of our citizens can receive adequate medical care, with as great an emphasis on preventive medicine as on treating illness after it occurs. This goal seems more reasonable today, if we consider that a larger part of the cost of all medical care is paid for out of public funds—through Medicare, Medicaid and welfare agencies. The broad plan for total medical care now emerging can be broken down into three broad divisions, as follows:

1. *Primary care:* provided by general physicians (family doctors, general practitioners, general internists, primary care physicians), who are capable of diagnosing and treating a majority of the medical problems of individuals and families, referring to the specialist only those patients with problems beyond their competence to diagnose and treat adequately.

2. *Specialized (secondary) care:* provided by the physicians in the various disciplines of medicine and surgery, who are often in private or group practice and do much of their treatment in local community hospitals. In serving many rural areas these physicians will be located in the nearest small city with a hospital. Perhaps several surrounding counties will be served.

3. *Tertiary care* (the third phase of modern medicine): the application of the most advanced techniques in the treatment of disease, which may be found only at large medical centers and teaching hospitals. There, sophisticated equipment and the new knowledge constantly evolving from basic and clinical research is first available. For example, a badly burned person might receive emergency treatment in his local community hospital, then be flown by helicopter or rushed by ambulance to the burn center of a university medical center or teaching hospital. A heart attack victim might develop life-threatening complications in a community hospital and require open-heart surgery, available only at a tertiary care center. The same could be said of rare infectious diseases or neurological diseases requiring complicated neurosurgery and backup facilities.

Thus, modern medicine—if it is to be on hand for all citizens—must be coordinated in such a way that its "hub" is centered in the large teaching and research hospital, usually affiliated with a university medical school. There, continuing medical education is available to physicians.

Nonphysician specialists

The nurse-midwives, long accepted as legitimate and important members of the health care team in Europe, are now gaining recognition in the United States. Today, most of them serve in outpatient clinics of general hospitals and medical centers. They work directly under the supervision of the obstetrician-gynecologist, but are prepared by general medical educational programs and clinical training and experience to provide prenatal care and, in uncomplicated pregnancies, to take their patients through delivery. When they recognize possible complications during a pregnancy, the obstetrician is called in to direct prenatal care and eventually deliver the baby. Midwives may also direct classes in nutrition, in the techniques of relaxation and special exercises, in preparing both husband and wife for the experience in the delivery room and in the proper care of their baby after it is taken home. As stated, most nurse-midwives now work in clinics and hospitals, but it is expected that more and more will be accepted by physicians, by insurance companies who provide maternal benefit coverage, and by the public. Such "physicians' assistants" can greatly extend the busy obstetrician's capabilities in areas where a few such specialists must be responsible for many patients and where their greater skills can be used in the care of women with detected complications and a predictable risk at the time of delivery.

In primary care, especially in pediatric primary care, the office nurse has long been "unofficial doctor" on an informal basis to the regular patients needing brief telephone advice or reassurance. What is new is the *formalization* of the "sole provider" status for nurses, not only in office-based practices but in free-standing clinics, in hospital walk-in facilities and especially in the innovative prepaid health insurance plans. Many schools of nursing have established master's degree programs in adult medicine, pediatrics and geriatric nursing. The nurses are qualified by clinical training and experience to take medical histories, perform physical examinations and order required x-rays and laboratory tests for their patients. At this time, physicians must review and sign all prescriptions for drugs.

The nurse practitioner works in cooperation with one or more physicians, freeing them from routine duties. The National Board of Medical Examiners has recently developed an examination and certification program for eligible nurse practitioners. The value of such specially trained personnel in the future of health care programs not only lies in extending the capabilities of physicians in their daily practices: in doctor-shortage areas they can also serve in screening programs as county nurses and in inner-city visiting nurse programs.

As previously mentioned, similar systems have been developed in the European continent and in the United Kingdom with great success.

PROPORTIONS OF SPECIALIST AND PRIMARY CARE PRACTITIONERS

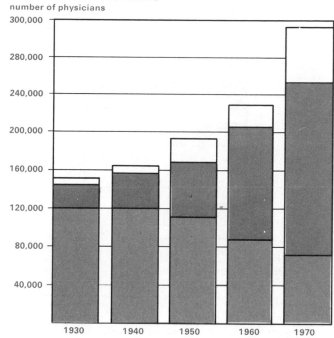

Here we can see the increasing proportion of U.S. physicians active in specialty practice (gray) rather than general practice (color). This trend has made it more difficult for people to obtain primary care, but there are now signs that it is being slowly reversed. The white portions of the bars represent hospital physicians (interns and residents).

The Medex program

Most nonnursing, nonphysician primary care providers are graduates of the *Medex program*. The need for such paramedical personnel was early recognized by Dr. Eugene Stead, who initiated the Medex program at the University of North Carolina. This two-year program is designed to accommodate nurses as well as nonnursing individuals who have had some medical background. The largest pool of such "nonprofessional" personnel has been the group of young men and women who became medics while on active military duty. Many have had extensive experience in the most serious and difficult of all medical situations—the various theaters of war in which our forces have been involved. Until the Medex program was initiated, these experienced medics were unable to make use of their hard-earned clinical skills in any meaningful civilian role. While certified Medex physicians' assistants perform the same tasks as nurse practitioners, many have taken positions in remote areas, and as members of paramedical teams who deal at the scene with trauma victims.

In addition to these nonphysician specialists who are now engaging in various aspects of primary care, and the general physicians who engage in family practice, primary

DISTRIBUTION OF PHYSICIANS

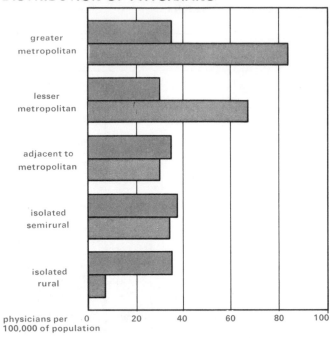

physicians per 100,000 of population

This chart shows the distribution of active physicians according to type of community, with specialists represented by gray bars and primary care practitioners by colored bars. Whereas specialists are concentrated in cities, the number of general practitioners per head of population is relatively constant in all types of communities.

care is also given by many of the specialists and subspecialists. For example, many young and healthy mothers—by choice or necessity—have had no "health maintenance" or "preventive medicine" contact with any physician until the time of their pregnancy. Following childbirth they return to their obstetricians for checkups or because of routine medical problems, and are usually accommodated by them. The same can be said of patients with chronic diseases who have been referred to a specialist for diagnosis and treatment and who subsequently return to him rather than to their referring doctor for future medical care.

Thus, with all of the many types of medical personnel now engaged in providing primary care, it is difficult to pinpoint the role of the primary care physician. For the sake of this discussion, I shall outline what primary medical care *should* include, whether it is provided by a general practitioner, family doctor, general internist, or by a specialist who may also engage in various aspects of general practice. Generally, he will be referred to in the following sections as a "family doctor" or "general practitioner." In years to come, as more and more young doctors qualify in this specialty, the title "primary care physician" may replace most of the other titles used today. But good medical care is the important point, not the titles.

What is a primary care physician?

Perhaps the role of primary care has been best described for lay readers by The American Academy of Family Practice, but it also applies to general physicians who may not be members of this growing professional organization: "Family Practice is comprehensive medical care with particular emphasis on the family unit, in which the physician's continuing responsibility for health care is neither limited by the patient's age or sex nor by a particular organ system or disease entity. Family Practice is the specialty in breadth which builds upon a core of knowledge derived from other disciplines—drawing most heavily upon internal medicine, pediatrics, obstetrics and gynecology, surgery and psychiatry—and which establishes a cohesive unit, combining the behavioral sciences. The core of knowledge encompassed by the discipline of Family Practice prepares the family physician for a unique role in patient management, problem solving, counseling and as a personal physician who coordinates total health care delivery."

In less formal terms, the primary care physician is trained in his specialty to provide total medical care, being personally able to treat all general diseases and injuries within his competence. But he will refer patients to the proper specialists when their particular knowledge and skills are required; he will resume the medical management of his patients when the specialist is no longer needed. The primary care physician is concerned with individual needs and with a family's special needs, and is the counselor and friend who is concerned with preventive medicine as well as with the treatment of disease. He not only lances boils, excises splinters, sets simple fractures, treats sore throats, hemorrhoids, childhood diseases and special complaints of the aged, but provides prenatal care, delivers babies (if an obstetrician is not consulted), treats diabetes and heart problems and, if needed, lends an ear to let a parent talk about the problems of a nonconforming child who is not doing well at home or in school. He takes steps to see that proper vaccinations and booster shots are given, sets dates for physical checkups and is available by telephone if any special problems arise. In brief, he exemplifies all of the virtues and skills that most of us associate with that revered old family doctor we knew and trusted—who was there when needed and knew exactly what to do when we brought our problems to him.

Your doctor's training

Perhaps a word should be given here about a doctor's training for the practice of medicine—past and present. The right to practice medicine is based upon qualifying for a medical license. The conditions for licensing are determined by each of the states. However, on a nationwide basis, the minimal requirements for the practice of medicine include graduation from an approved medical school, one year of postgraduate clinical training, and the passing of a state licensing examination. (Graduates of foreign medical schools are required to pass a special additional test which is standard across the country.) Most states will accept in place of their own examination the successful completion of the uniform examination administered by the National Board of Medical Examiners.

The year of required postgraduate clinical hospital training was until recently known as the "internship" or the "first postgraduate year." The year may be one of concentration in a single branch of medicine (such as surgery, pediatrics or internal medicine), or it may be equally divided between internal medicine, pediatrics, surgery and obstetrics-gynecology. The divided year, or rotating internship was the one most preferred by our older physicians who, usually, had only one postgraduate year of training prior to entering the general (nonspecialized) practice of medicine. Most general practitioners took only the one required year, but some elected a second year of general preparation. Specialists, on the other hand, usually took a specialized year of internship (straight medical, surgical or pediatric year) and then were required to complete two to six years of residency training to qualify for certification by a specialty board, such as the American Board of Internal Medicine or the American Board of General Surgery.

General practice as a "specialty"

Until the 1950s, physicians going into general practice most often took the minimum clinical training to qualify for general practice. In fact, in the early 1960s when 783 positions in the 165 general practice residency programs were offered to physicians who wanted to specialize in general practice, more than half were left vacant. A majority of those who accepted the positions were graduates of foreign medical schools. At the same time, residency programs in the other major specialties were oversubscribed. Obviously, general practice was not considered attractive enough to young doctors about to embark on lifetime careers. For general practice to remain alive as a medical specialty, it would have to compete—both in clinical training programs and in public esteem—with the other highly regarded specialties. To this end was established (in September 1964) the Ad Hoc Committee on Education for Family Practice of the Council of Medical Education of the American Medical Association. This committee developed five basic guidelines for the specialty of family practice:

1. Extension of the classical rotating internship was insufficient preparation; teaching should stress continuing and comprehensive patient responsibility rather than episodic handling of acute conditions.

2. Experience in emergency care and in the care of patients prior and subsequent to surgery should be included.

3. There should be an additional new body of knowledge taught to trainees to enable them to deal with the patient in relation to the social pressures that have a bearing on his or her health and emotional adjustment.

4. The various graduate programs should provide an opportunity for individual variations in the teaching curriculum.

5. The level of training should be on a par with other specialties. A two-year graduate program would not be sufficient; to equate this new specialty with the others in medicine, a specialty board with certifying examinations and diplomate status should be established.

Within a decade the concept of the family practitioner as a specialist became so popular that 278 residency programs had been established and filled with candidates for qualification in family practice. While the individual programs which were offered in various teaching hospitals and medical centers varied considerably in format, all had three characteristic features that separated them from other specialties: training in behavioral sciences, participation in a model practice unit, and training in community medicine.

The behavioral sciences training gives the young doctor an understanding of the basic principles of sociology, anthropology and psychology, permitting him to integrate the physical, social and emotional components of a patient's illness and his needs.

In the model practice unit the resident assumes progressive responsibility for the management of a socioeconomic cross section of families for whom he provides comprehensive and continuous care, with emphasis placed on "ambulatory patients, upon diseases of high incidence, chronic diseases, health maintenance and rehabilitation." The family practice resident rotates through the other major clinical services, but retains the model practice unit throughout his training as his "home base."

Community medicine training includes exposure to the related fields of epidemiology, biostatistics and environmental health. In addition to developing a greater sense of the appropriate allocation of regional health resources, this exposure is helping the physician to understand better what is most needed for patients within a community he might serve.

From the above, it seems obvious that a new breed of that respected and appreciated old family doctor is beginning to emerge to take his place in modern medicine. His instinct and commitment to serve the family had, in most cases, to be there to influence his choice of specialty, but he emerges with several years of clinical training and experience behind him, possessing the skills and judgment that our older doctors often had to learn empirically from several years of actual practice. How do you find such a doctor?

You may already have him in your present trusted and experienced family doctor or general practitioner. Or you may have several primary care physicians, a pediatrician caring for your children, an obstetrician-gynecologist caring for the women in the family, and an internist for the men. If so, there may be no advantage in seeking a single physician to care for all members of the family, especially if these physicians know the problems of each individual well and have been caring for them over a long period of time.

However, if your family has only loose ties with a physician who is not involved specifically in primary care, or if you are moving to a new community, as so many are doing these days, you might be wise to consider a family doctor who is certified in family practice as your primary care physician. Important considerations in choosing such a doctor should include his convenient location, his hospital affiliations, his availability, your emotional reactions to him as a person, and his willingness to make emergency house calls in case there is an invalid or immobile older person in the family—all of which may well be of greater importance to you than his certification as a family physician.

Choosing your primary care physician

A call to your county medical society is all that is necessary to obtain names of several primary care physicians in your area. This service provides the names of physicians on a master index without regard to availability, qualifications, or range of services offered. A friend or neighbor may be able to offer some useful information based on personal experience with local doctors. However, his or her needs and preferences in physicians may be quite different from your own. If you are not in immediate need of a physician, you might want to write to the American Academy of Family Physicians at 1740 West 92nd Street, Kansas City, Missouri 64114, asking for names of its members practicing in your vicinity. To check the educational and clinical training credentials of any physician you are considering, you can use a national physicians directory that may be available at your local library, or you can write for such information to the American Medical Association, 535 Dearborn Street, Chicago, Illinois 60610.

The choosing of a family primary care physician is generally important enough that you may wish to "interview" two or three different doctors. Whether you decide on one or consider several, there are some very basic questions you should be prepared to ask:

Will he treat all members of your family? Does he have admitting privileges at the nearest accredited hospital? Will he make emergency house calls or come to see a bedridden patient? In the event of pregnancy, does he provide prenatal care and perform the delivery, referring to the obstetrician only the high-risk mothers who require his special experience and training? What (if any) types of surgery does he perform? Does he, as a matter of routine, practice preventive medicine, sending notices for needed annual physical checkups, booster inoculations, repeat tests for breast and cervical cancer, and other follow-up checks and tests that are due? Does he maintain office hours that will permit your children and working members of the family to be seen without loss of work or school times? What are his fees for routine and special visits? Does he charge for telephone consultations? And of special importance: What doctor, or doctors, cover for him when he is away or not available?

You should also use this opportunity to ask any specific question you might have about any member of your family. A good doctor will not resent your asking these questions, but will recognize you as a person who does not take your doctor or his medical services lightly.

Consultation and referral

There is also one other aspect of the patient-physician relationship which patients are often reluctant to discuss: the question of consultation and referral. By definition, the family doctor is broadly experienced in many branches of medicine, while the specialist is deeply experienced in but one, much smaller area. The real test of a good family physician is his judgment of when and to whom to refer patients for consultation. Too many referrals will result in great expense and inconvenience for you, perhaps with no benefit to your overall health. On the other hand, reluctance to use consultants, when appropriate, could result in an undue delay in scheduling a needed operation or in arranging other needed treatment. It is sometimes difficult to determine whether your primary care physician's referrals are appropriate or are too frequent or inadequate. However, you should insist upon your right to seek a "second opinion," to be facilitated by your physician whenever you feel the need. You should steer clear of any physician who would be affronted by such a request.

The family physician is a specialist in breadth rather than a specialist in depth. While other specialists and subspecialists are vitally needed to attend to the less common, more serious diseases (which, fortunately, afflict relatively few patients), the public also appears to want a more broadly based physician to attend to less serious but more common vexations of modern life. To meet this greater challenge, the family physician must be proficient in many basic techniques and sensitive to the patient's need for more sophisticated skills as he assumes comprehensive and continuing responsibility for the health of the family.

Urology

Dr. William T. Bowles

The modern urologist deals with the organs concerned with the elimination of urine. In men, these also include the genital tract. Bladder infections in women and prostrate troubles in men are the most common of the many conditions he sees.

Urology, as a specialty, is as old as the art of medicine itself. In his venerable oath, Hippocrates stated, "I will not cut persons laboring under the stone, but will leave this to be done by practitioners of this work." In those days in ancient Greece, and for more than two thousand years, about the only operation performed on the urinary tract, except for the lancing of abscesses and circumcision, was that of lithotomy (Greek *lithos* = "stone")—the surgical removal of a stone in the bladder or urinary tract. To appreciate the great strides medical science has taken in the last century or so, one has only to read the early descriptions of this formerly brutal operation. The patient, who was not anesthetized, was laid flat on a table and the arms and legs were bound securely—the legs being flexed and pulled back against the abdomen. The surgeon then inserted two fingers or (in some cases) the entire hand into the rectum and forced the bladder and its stone down into the perineal area (the area between the anus and scrotum or the anus and vulva). Then, with great speed, a sharp knife was used to stab through the perineum into the bladder and, after a gush of urine proved the placement of the incision to be in the correct plane, hooks were inserted into the incision and the stone was extracted. The patient would recover if he did not bleed to death or die of infection soon after the operation. Hippocrates left this operation to others, usually itinerant surgeons who would travel from town to town and depart soon after the operation, placing the responsibility for subsequent care of the patient with the local doctors. The death rate following this operation was so high that these "lithotomists" were frequently looked upon with some disfavor.

Modern methods of examination

It was not until the beginning of the 20th century that urologists were able to diagnose and treat diseases not only of the bladder but the entire urinary tract. This capability was made possible by the development of the incandescent light, the x-ray, electrical cautery, aseptic surgical techniques and general anesthesia. With these inventions in hand, progress came rapidly. By the 1920s, physicians were able to make an exact diagnosis of many urologic disorders that previously could be diagnosed only at the autopsy table. The kidneys and ureters were outlined on x-ray films by means of iodine-containing fluids which were opaque to x-rays; they could delineate the internal structure of these organs when injected into the ureters. This was made possible by the invention of the cystoscope, a thin tube containing lenses and a small electric light on the tip. This instrument also allowed direct examination of the interior of the bladder, the prostate and the urethra. Soon after these improvements became widely used, it was found that some iodine compounds could be injected directly into a vein and, when excreted by the kidneys, could also delineate these structures by x-ray. This development, the "intravenous pyelogram," allowed the physician to examine the entire urinary tract, often without any passage of instruments.

The urologist today is a physician highly trained in surgical techniques and an expert in the use of the cystoscope and related instruments. Training includes a one-year internship, a year of residency training in general surgery, and a minimum of three years in an approved urologic training program. Certification in the Board of Urology is possible two years after the completion of residency training, dependent upon the satisfactory completion of a rigorous written and a detailed oral examination.

Why see a urologist?

A patient usually seeks out a urologist because of some problem arising in the passage of urine or some disorder related to the male sex organs. These include a burning sensation on urination, the passage of bloody urine, the sudden development of severe pain in the back, or a total inability to urinate. A complete examination, which should include a microscopic examination of the urinary sediment, a urine culture, an intravenous pyelogram, a rectal examination, and, in some cases, a cystoscopic examination, will usually pinpoint the source of the trouble.

In my practice, the most frequently encountered conditions are acute bladder infection in women and chronic prostate infection in men. These usually respond rapidly to proper medical treatment; a complete examination may not be necessary unless the condition recurs.

Chronic prostatitis

Inflammation of the prostate gland is usually seen in younger men. They complain of vague pain in the genital region, occasional sexual dysfunction and, in some cases, urinary symptoms. The urologist makes the diagnosis by massaging the prostate gland with a gloved finger in the patient's rectum. This produces a small amount of prostatic secretion which is then examined under the microscope. Treatment with antibiotics is continued until the secretion remains clear.

Many patients are seen who exhibit all the symptoms of prostatitis, but who show no infection. They may suffer from simple congestion of the prostate due to decreased sexual activity and may note marked improvement after the gland is massaged.

There are others who continue to complain, and I feel many of these patients have some form of psychiatric cause for their complaints. They usually go from doctor to doctor and are always dissatisfied with their treatment.

Male sexual problems

Another common problem is decreased sexual performance in males, or impotence. Some decline in sexual activity is normal as a man reaches his 50s, but I often see males in their 40s with this complaint. We must rule out causes such as diabetes, vascular diseases, spinal cord disorders and prostate infections. In about 90% of these cases, I find nothing to explain the impotence and feel it is probably secondary to depression or some unexpressed marital discord. Though I frequently recommend a psychiatric consultation, few patients will accept a psychiatric cause for their complaints. Many will demand injections of hormone shots, as they have heard from others how well they work. I believe the effect is mainly that of a placebo, as the only real indication for testosterone replacement is a

The urinary tract consists of the kidneys, ureters, bladder and urethra. In the male, the urethra also has a sexual function since sperm and seminal fluid are propelled along it. The urinary tract is subject to infection, trauma, stone formation and cancer.

URINARY SYSTEM
female

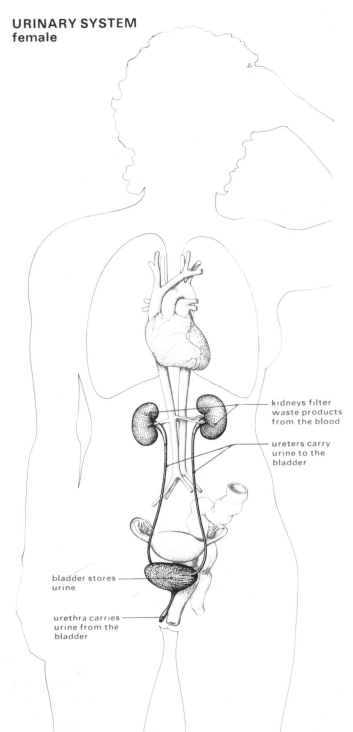

kidneys filter waste products from the blood

ureters carry urine to the bladder

bladder stores urine

urethra carries urine from the bladder

URINARY AND GENITAL TRACT
male

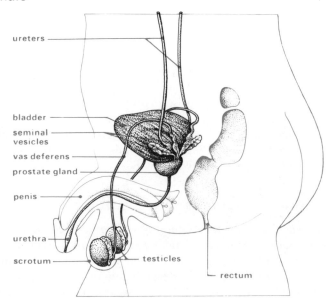

ureters

bladder

seminal vesicles

vas deferens

prostate gland

penis

urethra

scrotum

testicles

rectum

patient's true lack of the hormone associated with damaged or poorly developed testicles. A blood testosterone level will objectively indicate those who would benefit from added hormones.

Another problem is male sterility. Usually the patient will have some sperm in a specimen of ejaculate, but the number is way below the 100,000,000 seen in each cubic centimeter of a normal specimen. Small doses of thyroid hormone may sometimes be helpful in increasing the number of sperm. Some patients with infertility will show a varicocele, a large collection of dilated veins around the left testicle. Surgical correction of a varicocele will often restore low sperm counts to normal levels in a matter of months.

Mysterious symptoms

About half the patients in an afternoon's office session are women, complaining of pelvic pressure, urinary frequency, occasional burning on urination and backache. Examination frequently reveals nothing but tenderness and a little redness of the urethra (the passage through which urine is voided). These complaints respond temporarily to stretching of the urethra with graduated dilators and instillation of some antiseptic solution such as silver nitrate. The symptoms usually recur and subsequent treatments are often necessary. It is difficult to assume, with the paucity of findings, that many of these complaints are not functional or hypochondriacal in origin; but I am always amazed when a few dilation treatments seem to help the problem dramatically. Some urologists have even claimed that the complaints of these women are mostly symptomatic of sexual frustration and that dilation of the urethra serves as a substitute for sexual intercourse. I don't accept this theory, even though I find it hard to explain the symptoms with so few findings on examination.

Bladder infection

A true bladder infection in women is another story. The symptoms usually start suddenly and consist of frequent, extremely painful urination, sometimes associated with bloody urine. There is no doubt about the diagnosis in these women when the urine is checked under the microscope. In recent years it has become apparent that frequent bladder infections in women of childbearing age are caused by contamination of the bladder by bacteria-laden vaginal secretions introduced into the urethra during intercourse. It has been shown by culture techniques that women prone to such infections have frequently experienced a transfer of disease-producing bacteria from the rectum to their vaginas. In many cases, small prophylactic doses of an antibacterial drug before or after intercourse will ward off such attacks. A relatively new drug combination, which contains trimethoprim and sulfamethoxazole, is available. This chemical has the property of being secreted in the

PROSTATE GLAND

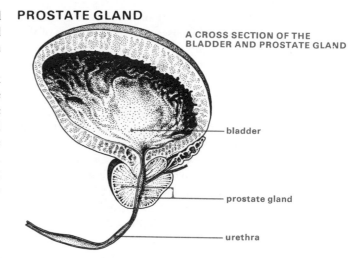

A CROSS SECTION OF THE BLADDER AND PROSTATE GLAND

bladder

prostate gland

urethra

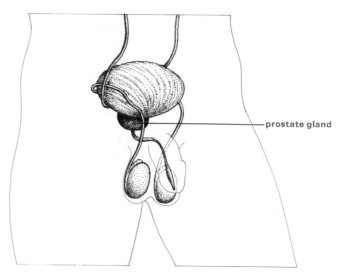

prostate gland

The prostate sits at the base of the bladder and secretes fluid into the urethra during sexual excitement. Most prostates enlarge after middle age and may cause urinary symptoms. Partial or total removal of the gland (prostatectomy) may then be necessary. The two methods most widely used are to remove the gland through a small abdominal incision or to extract the core of the gland through the urethra—a technique known as transurethral resection.

vaginal fluids and is highly effective in preventing rectal bacteria from surviving in the vagina. As little as half a tablet taken daily has been shown to be quite effective in knocking out the distressing recurrences of infection or cystitis.

Enlargement of the prostate

Another urologic problem, common in males around the age of retirement, is increasing difficulty in passing urine. This condition is usually due to an abnormal enlargement of the prostate gland which encircles the urethra right at the neck of the bladder. The cause of such enlargement is not fully understood; but, in the cases not due to cancer of the prostate, some changes in body hormone levels are thought to be responsible. Since the prostate surrounds the urethra, its enlargement produces an external constriction and slows the flow of urine (much as a clamp applied to the outside of a garden hose would diminish the flow). In most cases, the enlarged portion of the gland can be removed through an instrument similar to a cystoscope but also incorporating a small wire which acts as a "knife" when a specific electric current is passed through it. With this device, the enlarged gland is removed piece by piece and the small chips of tissue are then irrigated out of the bladder. Bleeding is controlled with a slightly different electric current applied directly to the severed blood vessels. The patient is required to wear a catheter for a few days and then is usually sent home after five to seven days in the hospital. The patient experiences almost no pain, and there is no incision to heal. Sometimes the patient does not seek relief until the prostate gland (which normally is the size of a walnut) has reached the size of a small orange. In these patients an operation through the urethra is impossible; a surgical incision and removal of the gland under direct vision is necessary. The approach to the prostate can be made through the lower part of the abdomen or through the perineal area as in the old lithotomy operation.

Cancer of the prostate

Cancer of the prostate gland may sometimes cause obstruction of the urethra and difficult urination. But more often it causes few if any symptoms in its early stages and is usually discovered by rectal examination during a routine physical examination. When the tumor is small and seems to be confined to the prostate itself, the urologist may remove the gland surgically or recommend radiotherapy. When the prostate tumor is first discovered, however, it has often already spread beyond the prostate—either into surrounding tissues and lymph nodes, or to distant areas such as the skull and spinal column. This stage of the tumor is often treated with hormones, as the tumor seems to depend on male hormones for its continued growth. With small doses of the female hormone estrogen (or a synthetic substitute known as *diethylstilbestrol*) remarkable regressions have been noted. In some patients, the female hormones would not be tolerated and a simple removal of both testicles—thus removing the source of the male hormone, testosterone—will often achieve a similar remission. This treatment is not curative, merely palliative, but one often sees complete regression of the cancer for periods of up to ten years.

In order to find these prostatic cancers when they are small and potentially curable, the physician must examine the patient regularly. I recommend that every man over the age of 50 have a rectal examination at least once a year.

CYSTOSCOPY

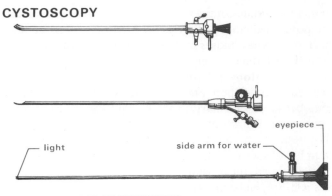

THREE VARIETIES OF CYSTOSCOPE

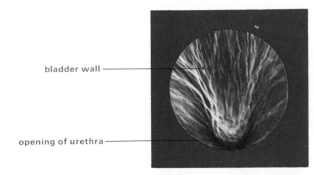

VIEW THROUGH A CYSTOSCOPE

Urologists use cystoscopes primarily for examining the interior of the bladder. Essentially a cystoscope consists of a telescope with a light at its far end and a side arm through which water can be introduced. Cystoscopy may be performed under general or local anesthetic and care must be taken to avoid infection. The cystoscope is carefully pushed along the urethra into the bladder, which is then inflated with sterile water.

Blood in the urine

Aside from inability to urinate, the most distressing sign to the patient is the sudden appearance of bright red, bloody urine. There are many causes of bloody urine (hematuria). In almost all cases the cause can be found with a complete urologic investigation. Apart from infection of the bladder, which is generally associated with *painful* urination, many episodes of bleeding are painless. If the blood is only at the start or end of urination, it is usually coming from an area below the bladder (such as the prostate or the urethra) and is rarely of a serious nature. Sometimes this type of bleeding is accompanied by blood in the semen, another usually innocuous sign. If the blood is equally distributed throughout the urination, it is referred to as *total hematuria* and may originate anywhere from the kidneys down to the bladder. In children, the appearance of bloody urine sometimes indicates the onset of an inflammatory disease of the kidneys (nephritis, Bright's disease, glomerulonephritis, etc.). Such diseases are often treated by specialists in internal medicine, pediatricians, or "super-specialists" in nephritis-type diseases referred to as nephrologists, and are not considered urological problems. (See the major article on **Nephrology**.) Urologic conditions associated with bleeding are legion and include many cancers, stones, benign prostatic enlargement and trauma.

Cancer of the urinary tract

In addition to the prostate gland, the urinary tract is the site of many primary cancers. Modern medical technology has resulted in increasing cure rates, especially if these tumors are discovered early. For this reason, an episode of bleeding should be investigated promptly in case it is indeed due to a tumor somewhere in the urinary tract. Cancers of the kidney are usually treated by a complete removal of the affected kidney if there is no sign of spread to the rest of the body. If the tumor involves the lining of the kidney, the entire ureter (the tube that conveys urine to the bladder) on that side may be removed as well, as it is frequently the site of recurrences in this type of tumor. A person can live a completely normal life with one kidney, provided the remaining kidney is healthy. Tumors of the ureter usually require removal of the kidney as well as the involved ureter for cure.

Cancers of the bladder occur in various stages of malignancy. Those which are of "low grade" malignancy and involve minor penetration of the bladder wall can frequently be removed with the same instrument used in removal of the prostate. If a highly malignant tumor is found, cure may necessitate heavy radiation treatment or complete surgical removal of the bladder. In such cases, a substitute for the bladder must be provided. The urine is collected in an inconspicuous bag attached to the skin.

In the male, the treatment of tumors involving the testicles and penis come under the domain of the urologist. It is interesting to note that the most common malignant tumor of the penis is a carcinoma and that these tumors are never seen in patients who were circumcised at birth. This would seem to me to be a good argument for routine circumcision in newborns.

Urinary stones

The field of urology also includes the diagnosis, location and treatment of urinary stones or calculi. The bladder stone treated by the roving lithotomists of old usually was a complaint of children. It is rarely ever seen today in the industrialized nations, although it is still a major problem in India, Thailand, Indonesia and surrounding countries. It has long been suspected that this type of stone is caused by dietary factors; years of research indicate that it occurs mainly in well-nourished children who derive most of their protein intake from vegetable or cereal sources rather than animal protein. In essence, it is a problem among rice eaters. In the United States, the most frequently encountered stones are small kidney stones seen in adult patients. These form "silently" in the collecting ducts of the kidney and then suddenly cause pain as they drop down into the narrow ureter and begin their passage into the bladder. The stones themselves do not cause the pain. The pain is the result of distension of the tract above the stone by trapped urine. The pain of stones passing down the ureter can be excruciating and may require heavy doses of morphine for relief. An immediate intravenous pyelogram (an x-ray of the kidneys and ureters) will usually show the location and size of the stone and allow the urologist to plan the appropriate treatment. Fortunately, most of these stones will pass by themselves in a few hours, but may take as long as several months. The decision to intervene is made when the urologist feels that there is little hope that the stone will pass by itself or if the obstruction caused by the stone is also associated with infection. If the stone is relatively small and has lodged in the lower part of the ureter, it can sometimes be extracted through the cystoscope—using a basket-like device which is passed up the ureter and then retracted. Stones in the kidney itself or stones lodged in the upper part of the ureter may require a surgical incision for removal. Patients often ask whether it is possible to dissolve stones. The majority of stones contain calcium and are not soluble in urine; however, there are certain stones which are composed purely of uric acid (a waste product of metabolism). This substance dissolves slowly in an alkaline urine, and it may be possible to dissolve these stones merely by adding alkali (such as common baking soda) to the diet.

Children's problems

Although all urology residents are thoroughly trained in the treatment of childhood disorders, in larger medical centers this field has developed into the subspecialty of *pediatric urology*. These subspecialists take extra training in childhood disorders and limit their practice to the urologic problems of children, which are mainly disorders of fetal development. These include hypospadias (an abnormal opening of the urethra on the undersurface of the penis), congenitally obstructed kidneys and bladders, and nerve dysfunction of the bladder associated with such spinal cord problems as meningocele (a congenital hernia of the membranes surrounding the spinal cord, caused by a failure of the spine to fuse during the fetal period). The pediatric urologist is also concerned with the treatment of undescended testicles. The testicles develop inside the abdomen of the male fetus near the kidneys, and normally descend into the scrotum before birth. However, sometimes the descent is imperfect. If the affected testis cannot be manipulated into its correct position, surgery may be required. (See UNDESCENDED TESTIS.)

Venereal diseases (VD)

The urologist specializes in the diagnosis and treatment of diseases and disorders affecting the urinary tract in both males and females, and the genital tract as well in males (disorders of the female genital tract are usually treated by a gynecologist). Although the treatment of syphilis is usually undertaken by specialists in internal medicine, other venereal diseases of men may be diagnosed and treated by the urologist.

Gonorrhea in the male is usually suspected with the onset of a puslike discharge from the penis, associated with a burning sensation on urination. Symptoms of the disease typically appear about three days after sexual intercourse with an infected partner. A simple test in the office can often make the distinction between gonorrhea and a urethral infection of nonvenereal cause. The distinction is important because the treatment of gonorrhea differs from that of *nonspecific urethritis (NSU)* and also because in the case of gonorrhea the infected partner ("contact") should be identified and treated, to prevent the continued spread of the disease. In some cases a bacterial culture may

> **If you have any suspicious signs or symptoms of venereal disease (VD)—especially syphilis or gonorrhea—see your doctor or consult a special VD clinic at once. Your case will be treated in the strictest confidence. Modern diagnostic techniques and treatment with antibiotics early in the course of the disease guarantee a cure in almost every instance. Be assured that a patient with VD is no longer looked upon as a social outcast or someone with atypical sexual habits.**

be needed to substantiate the diagnosis of gonorrhea. In the male, *syphilis* is usually suspected when the patient develops a raised, firm ulcerated sore (*chancre*) on the penis. The diagnosis at this point depends on a special microscopic examination of scrapings taken from the sore, as the blood test for syphilis does not reveal positive results until a few weeks after the onset of the disease. Without treatment, the sore will heal. The disease then enters a quiescent phase until about six to eight weeks later, when the skin will break out in what is known as secondary syphilis. This stage is also associated with general ill-feeling, fever, and enlargement of the lymph nodes.

Treatment is still simple and effective at this point. Without treatment, the secondary phase will likewise pass. Then, years later, a third stage will sometimes occur which can be associated with heart disease, severe mental deterioration and many other severe consequences. In order to find unsuspected cases before they progress to the tertiary stage, all adult patients are given a blood test for syphilis on admission to a hospital. In many cases a test for syphilis will also be given in conjunction with an employment physical examination.

Conclusion

Advances in the field of urology, both in diagnosis and treatment, continue to be made. Recent developments include silicone implants to aid the patient with organic impotence and urinary incontinence, together with improvements in the success rate for kidney transplants with the use of new immunosuppressive drugs (see the major article on **Nephrology**).

In medicine it has always been easy to say that we have come as far as we can go—I'm sure Hippocrates felt so in his time. But seeing the great progress in just the last ten years, it is not improbable that cures will be found for many conditions now considered hopeless and that much will be learned about the successful treatment of many diseases whose causes are now only suspected or unknown.

Nephrology

Dr. Ginette Betty Jacob

The nephrologist is concerned with the diagnosis and treatment of diseases and disorders which affect the kidneys—the paired organs at the back of the abdominal cavity, near the spine, which filter out waste substances in the blood. The kidneys also form and excrete urine and help maintain the delicate salt and water balance of the body.

In her science class, my 14-year-old daughter had just learned about the heart, the lungs, the blood and the digestive system. To her, it all seemed to fit into a logical scheme, in proper sequence. Then the teacher introduced the kidneys. They were described as "vital organs," but to my daughter they did not seem to fit into the scheme she had understood about the other vital organ systems.

The crucial question was saved for me, at the dinner table, when my daughter asked, "Where do the kidneys fit in? Before the heart, after the intestines or in between?" Her question was not profound, but it gave me, as a nephrologist, a great opportunity to expound on this magnificently structured organ system.

Nephrology is the branch of medical science concerned with the study of the structure and function of the kidneys and the diagnosis and treatment of diseases and disorders which affect them. To place nephrology in its proper perspective, we must first identify the *nephrologist*. This specialist completes two years of residency training in internal medicine, followed by a minimum of two years of training in nephrology. These latter two years are generally divided into "subrotations" which include clinical work as well as investigational work, each one under the supervision of experienced senior staff members. The clinical rotation exposes the doctor to the various diseases encountered by the practicing nephrologist, which I'll cover in some detail later in this article. The nephrologist's investigational work, generally initiated by a senior research worker, pertains to some aspect of renal (kidney) function.

First and foremost, the nephrologist is a medical internist. He must be able to assess the function of all organ systems as well as their intimate interrelationships. No organ anywhere can be treated as an isolated entity—nor can the specialist confine himself to the examination of "his" organ system only. Even as a consultant, he must integrate his clinical findings with those of the referring physician. Only by means of such open lines of medical communication can the patient fully benefit from today's medical expertise.

Certain anatomic considerations are necessary to understand renal function.

The kidneys are two matched organs, located toward the back of the abdominal cavity near the spinal column, one on each side of the midline. Traditionally described as "bean-shaped," they measure approximately 4 in. (12 cm) in their longest axis, with their lower edge extending just below the rib cage.

Kidneys grow in size with normal body growth, probably to meet the increasing demands made upon them. They reach their full size when bone growth is completed, in the mid-teens.

Each kidney has approximately one million functioning units, known as *nephrons*. Because of this tremendous functional reserve, the presence of kidney disease may not become evident until 60–70% of these functioning units are diseased.

Equally significant is the ability of a healthy solitary kidney to meet all the metabolic needs of the body. This important observation has proved to be crucial in the field of kidney transplantation, for two reasons: (1) a healthy person with two normally functioning kidneys can donate one to a relative who has renal failure without compromising his own well-being. After a period of about six weeks, the donor's measured kidney function will have returned to normal; (2) the recipient of a single kidney—whether it comes from a live related donor or from a cadaver—can hopefully expect to have normal kidney function restored.

Kidney diseases

The most common complaints brought to the physician's attention are poor appetite, irritability, frequent urination, or—at the other extreme—decreased urine output, with swelling of the face, abdomen and extremities These symptoms can be caused by underdeveloped kidneys, inadequate drainage to the kidneys caused by partial blockage, gradual replacement of the kidneys by enlarging cysts, or unusual losses of chemically important substances in the urine (such as salt and protein). Early diagnosis and treatment of these problems permit the preservation of maximum kidney function.

Some structural abnormalities are documented only in adult life. They may be detected only by chance in the course of a routine medical examination and generally require no specific treatment. They include the congenital

THE KIDNEYS AND URINARY SYSTEM - male

absence of one kidney, a kidney abnormally supplied by several blood vessels rather than the customary single one, or the *mobile kidney* that seems to "fall" on standing. They are all benign (basically harmless) conditions.

On the other hand, kidneys which become larger and larger, as they develop enlarging cysts, often come to the physician's attention because of associated pain, fullness, infection or bleeding. Specific treatment is essential.

A brief review of the body's demands on our urinary system, and the effectiveness with which it meets them, will help us understand the disease states that can develop.

The kidneys maintain normal *water balance:* they regulate the urinary output to compensate for variations in fluid intake and for water losses through perspiration— as well as for intestinal losses in cases of severe diarrhea or vomiting. Failure of this regulatory mechanism can lead either to water excess or deficit, both of which are potentially life threatening. Intimately related to water balance is the maintenance of *electrolyte balance*—that is, the chemical environment that insures proper cell function. The kidneys, through very precise "sensing" mechanisms,

The kidney consists of a fairly thick outer layer (the renal cortex) and a much larger inner portion (the renal medulla). In the adult the kidney measures approximately 4 in. long, 2 in. wide and 1 in. thick and is surrounded by a tough fibrous membrane. The entire kidney is covered with a mass of protective fatty tissue.

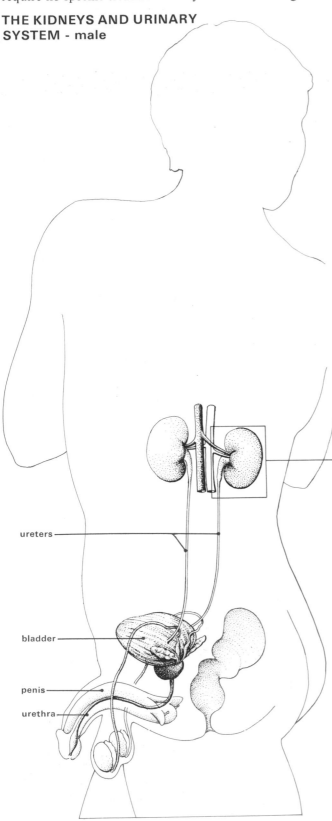

- ureters
- bladder
- penis
- urethra

A CROSS SECTION THROUGH THE KIDNEY

The kidneys filter out waste products in the blood to produce urine; each kidney contains about 1 million functional units called *nephrons*.

- cortex
- renal artery
- renal vein
- renal pelvis
- medulla
- ureter

excrete or retain an appropriate amount of salt to compensate again for changes in intake.

The kidneys have the added burden of eliminating the waste products of metabolism—the by-products that are not used as sources of energy or as "building blocks" for the body. We have not yet identified all these substances. Those that are best known and most readily measured include urea, creatinine, phosphate and uric acid. All of these substances gradually become concentrated in the blood as the kidneys lose their ability to excrete them.

Our kidneys also play an important role in the regulation of blood pressure, by their ability to produce a specific hormone (called *renin*) in varying amounts to meet the body's needs. The "renin-angiotensin system," as this mechanism is called, is triggered by changes in pressure within the kidney. Unfortunately, this response may become exaggerated and produce high blood pressure (*renovascular hypertension*) or it may be triggered by a lesion within the artery supplying the kidney and therefore not respond to the body's needs; this situation will also lead to renovascular hypertension.

Another hormone produced by the kidney is *erythropoietin*, which controls the total number of circulating red blood cells by regulating their manufacture in the bone marrow.

The kidneys have also been recently implicated in the regulation of bone metabolism, through their action on vitamin D.

With disease of the kidneys, all kidney functions are compromised to varying degrees; this leads to the signs and symptoms the nephrologist will see. Kidney disease, like disease in any other organ, falls into four distinct categories:

(1) inflammatory; (2) hemodynamic (pertaining to blood circulation); (3) obstructive; (4) cancerous.

By far the most common condition which can progress to kidney failure is inflammation of the kidneys.

Inflammation

Inflammation often affects both kidneys, to nearly the same extent. Its exact cause cannot always be found. The general technical name for kidney inflammation is *nephritis*. When the inflammation primarily affects the kidneys' filtering units (glomeruli) it is called GLOMERULONEPHRITIS.

Glomerulonephritis is most often associated with a previous bacterial infection, especially certain strains of streptococcus. The disease commonly starts with a moderately severe "strep throat"; two to three weeks later there is generalized weakness, puffiness of the face (especially the eyelids), headache, an almost rusty color to the urine and, in the more extreme form, a marked decrease in urine output.

Upon physical examination, the patient, usually a child, appears obviously sick. He may have an elevation in blood

pressure and some congestion in his lungs. The most consistent laboratory finding is blood in the urine (hematuria)—sometimes it is only visible when a specimen is examined under a microscope.

For most patients, hospitalization is advisable. Treatment consists primarily of prevention and management of possible complications. No method of treatment available today is able to change the course of the renal lesion itself. It is important to emphasize that most children with "post-streptococcal glomerulonephritis" make a complete recovery; the length of time varies. The adult with this disease, however, doesn't fare as well; but this is partly compensated for by a lower incidence of the disease in adult life.

Glomerulonephritis may also be associated with a general (systemic) infection or infection of the heart valves. The manifestations are similar, but treatment here must be aimed at eradicating the underlying infection. The renal lesion is usually reversible with successful treatment of the primary infection.

Less common, but very important, is *hereditary nephritis*. It occurs in both males and females, with males generally being more seriously affected. The disease is associated with hearing loss and, less frequently, certain eye abnormalities. There is no specific treatment.

Some systemic diseases can, and often do, affect the kidneys. Most frequently diagnosed is *systemic lupus erythematosus*. The associated nephritis may be minimal and undetectable by routine means, or be severe and life threatening—the degrees vary. Much progress is being made in our understanding of systemic lupus erythematosus. Its treatment consists primarily of "immunosuppression" with corticosteroids. If the kidney lesion is in an active phase at the time of diagnosis, some improvement can be expected. If the kidney involvement is found to be very advanced, no method of treatment has yet proved to be ultimately successful.

Another systemic disease often encountered is DIABETES MELLITUS. For practical purposes, we can say that the kidneys are always affected, but to very different degrees. Strict regulation of the blood sugar is absolutely essential; however, it is not yet clear whether such control affects the progress of the kidney disease. What does definitely help is the prompt diagnosis and treatment of any kidney infection.

Infections of the urinary tract occur with great frequency; they can affect any part of the urinary system, with each kind carrying its own prognosis. (See also the major article on **Urology**.)

The most benign infection is that which occurs in inflammation of the bladder: CYSTITIS. This is found more frequently in the female, due to anatomic differences which make entrance to the urinary tract by bacteria more accessible. Cystitis causes very distinct symptoms— burning on urination, a frequent need to pass small

INFLAMMATION OF THE URINARY TRACT

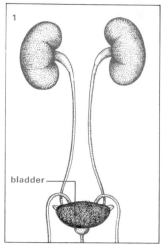

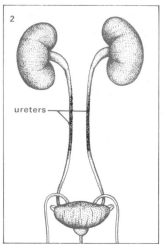

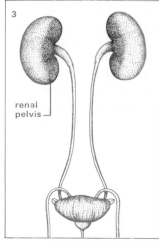

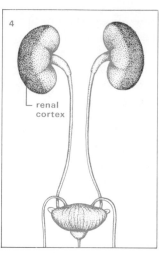

CYSTITIS   URETER INFLAMMATION   PYELONEPHRITIS   GLOMERULONEPHRITIS

In females, cystitis (1) mainly results from bacteria which have climbed up the urethra; in males, it is often associated with obstruction due to a large prostate. The bladder can usually clear itself of infection, but in some cases the bacteria ascend the ureters (2) to infect the kidneys, causing pyelonephritis (3). Glomerulonephritis (4), inflammation of the kidney cortex, is most often the result of infection elsewhere in the body.

amounts of urine and sometimes blood in the urine. Occasionally there is a low-grade fever. The usual cause of cystitis is a bacterial infection; the administration of some drugs has also been found to be associated with a "chemical cystitis."

Appropriate investigation consists of microscopic examination and analysis of a specimen of voided urine and bacterial culture of a very clean urine specimen. In addition, the physician will order a blood count and perhaps a test to determine the level of blood sugar (this is because cystitis is a frequent complication in the diabetic patient).

A single episode of cystitis usually requires no further medical investigation. However, when the condition recurs a further evaluation by a urologist will be necessary. He'll probably want to look into the bladder with a cystoscope to rule out a local cause for the problem.

Treatment of cystitis will depend on its cause. In the case of bacterial infection, antibiotics must be chosen appropriately to reflect the drug sensitivity of the infecting microorganism. "Chemical cystitis" is typically brought under control when administration of the responsible drug is discontinued.

Infection of the main substance of the kidney itself, called PYELONEPHRITIS, is usually accompanied by more severe systemic symptoms: chills, fever and pain in the small of the back (usually one-sided only); it is made worse by pressure over the involved side. The diagnosis here depends on a thorough physical examination which will

confirm the tenderness over the inflamed, infected kidney, and analysis and culture of a urine specimen. The culture results will usually identify the responsible microorganism (usually a single species of bacteria) and thereby dictate the choice of antibiotic treatment. Since there is a 24 to 48 hour delay in obtaining these results, the physician may elect to begin antibiotic treatment pending the laboratory results. The justification for this is the high frequency with which certain specific bacteria are found in this condition. A great deal of controversy exists around the extent of the infection, as measured by a number of bacteria found in the urine. It is fair to say, however, that irrespective of this count, should the patient show signs and symptoms suggestive of this disease, and there is bacterial growth in his urine, he should receive the appropriate antibiotics.

As I stated previously, pyelonephritis is usually confined to one kidney only; but if it is recurrent, the other kidney may become involved. Recurrence is often a complication of diabetes mellitus and may actually be the main presenting symptom. In such cases, the careful regulation of the level of blood sugar may decrease the incidence of pyelonephritis. Structural abnormalities of the kidneys or ureters (the slender tubes which convey urine from the kidneys to the bladder) have also been associated with a higher frequency of recurrent pyelonephritis.

While recurrent cystitis by itself never affects kidney function, recurrent pyelonephritis is the second most common cause of kidney failure (an inability of the kidneys to eliminate toxic waste products from the blood). It therefore warrants vigorous care, as its progression seems to be influenced by the adequacy or inadequacy of treatment.

Primary infection of the ureters is not common. It can occur with ureteral stones, especially those which cause obstruction of a ureter. Treatment in this case is removal of the stone and the administration of appropriate antibiotics. The disease cannot be dismissed quite this easily, unfortunately, because it can lead to kidney failure; therefore, it warrants all possible therapeutic efforts.

Kidney stones

In at least 50% of patients with kidney stones, no specific cause can be found, making prevention of stone formation in such cases naturally difficult.

Among the manageable causes of stones is an increased excretion of calcium in the urine, as the result of a very high level of calcium in the blood. This, in turn, can be associated with an excessive calcium intake in the patient's diet, or to a benign or malignant tumor of the parathyroid glands. These glands meticulously regulate the amount of calcium we absorb from our intestinal tract and the amount we excrete in our urine. When these glands are diseased, they can lose their regulatory function and permit a dangerous rise in blood levels of calcium.

Cancer, with involvement of bone, is often associated with the release of large amounts of calcium into the bloodstream. This will lead to increased loads for the kidney to handle.

Not all stones are made of calcium. Uric acid—a waste product of metabolism which, when present in the bloodstream in abnormally large amounts, can cause gout—can also lead to stone formation.

Kidney stones, and their attempted passage through the narrow ureters, lead to signs and symptoms the patient can easily recognize: a crampy, sudden sharp pain in the mid-back flank or groin, fever, malaise (a general feeling of being unwell) and, in many cases, blood in the urine. The symptoms may last only a few hours, or may not go away at all until after treatment is well underway.

Larger stones may get stuck in the ureter, causing complete obstruction on that side. The symptoms will persist until the stone is removed. A small stone, formed within the kidney, will readily pass down the ureter and into the bladder. At this point, the symptoms usually subside. But stones remaining in the bladder may cause irritation and possibly bladder infection.

Every patient who has or is suspected of having kidney stones deserves a thorough medical evaluation. A few causes of stone formation—such as a benign or malignant tumor of the parathyroid gland, which is easily removed—are curable. Other causes, such as an abnormal accumulation in the blood of uric acid, are not curable but can be effectively controlled by appropriate medication. Because of the high incidence of infection in these patients, diagnosis and treatment must be initiated at the earliest possible time.

Hemodynamic diseases

Hemodynamic diseases make up an admittedly "muddy" category which aims at encompassing those factors which adversely affect the blood flow or blood pessure (or both) with regard to the kidneys.

If you keep in mind that the driving force to urine production is the amount of blood presented to the kidneys, and the pressure under which it is filtered, it is easy to see how kidney function can be compromised. At one extreme is the hypertension (high blood pressure) occasionally generated by the kidney itself. This condition represents less than 1% of all causes of hypertension, but its curability deserves recognition.

The renin the kidney produces is a very potent enzyme which helps to maintain normal blood pressure. Certain vascular lesions can cause a partial closing of the renal artery, thus reducing the quantity and pressure of blood flow beyond the lesion. The kidney "senses" this as a reduction in systemic pressure and responds to it by an increased production of renin. This partly restores the blood flow to the kidney, but at the price of a significant increase in the systemic blood pressure. This problem, *renovascular hypertension,* is now relatively easy to diagnose and the results of corrective surgery are usually excellent.

Essential hypertension (high blood pressure in which the underlying cause is unknown) progressively reduces the diameter of the blood vessels of the kidneys and thus reduces the amount of blood the kidneys can filter. Controlling the blood pressure adequately by appropriate medications on a chronic or long-term basis is needed to preserve as much kidney function as possible.

At the other extreme is the situation where the blood pressure is too low to maintain an adequate flow to the kidneys. This can occur in the presence of high fever, infection, bleeding, advanced liver disease or advanced heart disease. Needless to say, this condition needs to be corrected as soon as possible to protect the kidney from irreversible damage. If the problem goes unrecognized for several days, acute kidney failure may occur.

Obstructive diseases

Obstruction of the urinary tract can significantly damage kidney function. The most common such problem in the male is prostate gland obstruction. The bladder cannot empty adequately; urine continues to form for a time until the entire urinary system is fully dilated and no longer functioning. If relief of the obstruction comes early enough, normal function will return.

Obstruction of one ureter may go unnoticed, because the other (nonobstructed) kidney can carry on with its tasks. But eventually the obstructed kidney will become infected, and the symptoms of pyelonephritis will be noted.

Obstruction to both ureters, by such processes as cancer that is spreading, gives no initial warning and is difficult to treat. The physician must bypass the ureters so that the patient's urine drains directly from his kidneys. Sometimes the disease regresses enough through treatment to permit the normal flow of urine to resume. Antibiotics are administered to treat any associated infection.

Cancer

Malignant diseases of the kidney are, fortunately, fairly rare.

In children, *Wilms' tumor* is the most common. Its most telltale sign is usually a mass in the abdomen, with few accompanying symptoms. The tumor must be treated as early as possible, before it has spread to other parts of the body. Excising the tumor totally by means of surgical removal of the affected kidney (nephrectomy) has proved to be satisfactory in many cases. Multiple chemotherapy regimens, still being evaluated, have had various results in controlling the spread of the cancer.

In the adult, *renal cell carcinoma* (or *clear cell carcinoma*) is the most frequent kind of cancer of the kidney. It occurs twice as often in men as in women. The most frequent symptoms are blood in the urine, flank pain and fever. During the medical examination the patient is often found to have hypertension.

If the tumor is large enough, it may be felt by hand; the mass is generally not tender. The physician has many useful diagnostic procedures at his disposal, including the ability to get an x-ray outline of the tumor by means of *arteriography*. The treatment of choice is surgical removal of the affected kidney.

While tumors of the ureters are very rare, tumors of the bladder are not uncommon. They mimic all the signs and symptoms of cystitis, and are often associated with it. Treatment here often requires removal of the entire bladder and diverting the urine flow. Excision of just the tumor itself can be performed, but in such cases there is a risk of recurrence.

Kidney failure

Significant loss of kidney function leads to dramatic changes in body physiology and chemistry. Complete loss of kidney function, if untreated, leads to death.

Considering the many intricate functions of the kidney, you can easily understand the state of chaos the body's "economy" finds itself in when this vital organ system fails.

Fluid and electrolyte balance is no longer adequately regulated. Often there is fluid overload, signaled by shortness of breath, ankle swelling and weakness. Occasionally there will be fluid deficit—the kidney will continue to put out a large volume of urine, irrespective of the body's needs. The patient will feel weak, lose his appetite and become dizzy on standing.

Electrolyte imbalance is a frequent companion to fluid abnormalitites. The most notorious and threatening is the accumulation of potassium in the blood. At high levels, this can cause irregularities in heart rhythm, ultimately leading to a stopping of the heart (*cardiac standstill* or *cardiac arrest*). Because of the presence of potassium in practically all foods, this abnormality requires prompt attention because of its progressive nature.

Blood pressure monitoring by the kidney is no longer effective; often hypertension results. The hypertension seems to be mediated by at least two known factors—one is the relative excess of renin production, and the other is the true salt and water retention of kidney failure. Red cell production is slowed if not completely suppressed, due to the decrease in erythropoietin, leading to a progressive anemia.

The metabolic waste products accumulate in the blood. They act as systemic toxins (poisons) and lead to what we have learned to recognize as the *uremic syndrome*. This total loss of renal function has been referred to as "Bright's disease" in the older medical literature. It is to be distinguished from *acute kidney failure*, which, as the name implies, is reversible. Acute renal failure is seen with the ingestion of certain poisons, with SHOCK (circulatory collapse), and with vascular catastrophies such as a ruptured ANEURYSM (a ballooning out of a weakened blood vessel). (See also KIDNEY DISEASES.)

Regardless of the reasons for kidney failure, supportive measures are essential to maintain the patient's life. Medical technology has progressed remarkably in the past two decades, and we now have several approaches of treatment that can imitate normal kidney function.

Dialysis

The "artificial kidney machine" is known technically as a *hemodialyzer*. Dialysis is the process of separating or extracting certain substances from a solution by means of a porous membrane. Removal of waste products from the blood can be performed either by *hemodialysis* or by means of *peritoneal dialysis*.

Hemodialysis, the removal of waste products through the bloodstream, is accomplished by inserting a needle into the patient's vein, usually in the arm. The blood is conducted to the dialysis machine, where the waste products diffuse out across a thin cellophane membrane into the surrounding fluid. The blood is then returned to the patient through another needle into a different vein. Hemodialysis is generally performed three times a week, for sessions usually lasting four to five hours each.

Peritoneal dialysis makes use of the large lining (peritoneum) that covers our abdominal organs. This lining allows diffusion of the metabolic wastes into the peritoneal cavity. The cavity is filled with fluid or dialysate which is changed every 30 to 45 minutes to allow for maximum diffusion. This process takes longer than hemodialysis (48 to 72 hours every week), but because of its slower rate it simulates the actions of the normal kidney much more closely.

Either form of dialysis can be performed in the home, at any time of the day or night. This allows the patient to design his own schedule.

The "artificial kidney machine"—known technically as a hemodialyzer—filters waste products from the bloodstream into a circulating saline solution. The waste particles, dissolved in the blood, pass through a semipermeable membrane in the machine which is just porous enough to permit them through.

Kidney transplants

The best treatment for kidney failure is a new kidney. One healthy kidney, successfully transplanted, will meet all the body's needs.

Several criteria must be met before transplantation is performed:

1. Age limit is set today at about 55; there is no lower limit—transplants have even been performed on infants. Exceptions to the age limit are being constantly made, based on a total evaluation of all the patient's organ systems and his overall suitability.

2. The patient must be free from any other life-threatening illness. This includes previous heart attacks, strokes or cancer.

3. The patient must be able to follow the recommended medical regimen, with assistance if necessary.

The crucial issue today is the source of the kidney used for transplantation. The kidney obtained from a living relative usually has a better success rate than the kidney obtained from an unrelated cadaver. However, a great many patients do not have a relative who is suitable or willing to give a kidney; thus they must wait until a suitable cadaver kidney becomes available.

There is a tremendous shortage of cadaver kidneys, one that could be met easily through public education and cooperation. The *uniform donor card,* legalized by the Uniform Anatomical Gift Act, is a wallet-sized card that each one of us should sign and carry at all times. In case of accidental sudden death, it authorizes the attending physician to remove our kidneys (and any other organ we specify) for transplantation. There is no financial reward for such donation, but the contribution thus made is priceless.

Since cadaver kidneys become available at the most unexpected times, it is vital that the patient be well-motivated and informed about the experience so that little hesitation is made when the awaited kidney arrives.

What the transplant patient needs to know. First of all, the chance of success is about 50% and has not changed significantly since the mid-1970s. Secondly, the means to prevent rejection, the "immunosuppressive" drugs, must usually be taken for as long as the kidney remains—even if it is functioning perfectly. Thirdly, some rejections do occur in spite of all preventive measures known. Many rejections, especially those occurring within the first three to six months of the transplant, can be reversed. Fourthly, the corticosteroids used in immunosuppression often cause some changes in physical appearance: puffy cheeks, obesity. These side effects are reversible as the dose of corticosteroid drugs is reduced and as the patient learns to modify his eating habits.

On a more ethical level, one has to deal with the issue of which treatment is best for whom. This is usually and most appropriately answered by the patient himself, after he has been duly informed about his alternatives. Is every patient a candidate for these heroic measures? This must be a team decision, especially when the patient is elderly and already incapacitated by other handicaps—such as strokes, blindness caused by diabetes, or loss of limbs due to vascular insufficiency. The family, the social worker, a member of the clergy *and* the attending physicians should participate in making the decision.

Conclusion

Nephrology is a rapidly developing specialty. Through improved diagnostic procedures, we can deal much more effectively with a particular kidney disease and try to cure it or at least arrest its progression. We have learned how to prevent certain diseases of the kidney. And we are able to offer substitutes for the failed kidney. The therapeutic gains are usually improved by early diagnosis and treatment.

Working in close cooperation with the nephrologist are specialists in treating diseases and disorders of the lower part of the urinary system—the bladder and urethra. Such specialists are known as urologists (see the major article on **Urology**). In effect, the nephrologist and urologist are concerned with many of the same diagnostic problems and in many cases their interests overlap. This is understandable, since they are both concerned with different aspects of the same organ system.

Cardiology

Dr. Richard J. Bing

The cardiologist deals with a wide range of diseases and disorders that affect the heart and its associated blood vessels. No branch of medical science has seen greater diagnostic, therapeutic and surgical advances within recent years than this important specialty.

When I was a medical student, in the 1930s, I vividly remember a professor demonstrating a patient with inflammation of the heart valves, calling our attention to the murmur heard over the heart and the telltale spots on the skin. I remember also his somber conclusion—that there was little anyone could do for the patient, who must soon succumb to his illness. The outlook then was equally grim for many children born with heart defects and for adults with high blood pressure. Best of all, I remember that as a student I was not even taught to recognize a heart attack and the signs and symptoms that often predict it, even though the clinical picture had been clearly described 18 years earlier. It was many years later that we learned to recognize myocardial infarction (death of heart muscle tissue from lack of oxygenated blood), and later still that we learned to cope with it.

I dwell on these memories only because they point up how far medicine has advanced in this relatively short period, especially in the diagnosis and treatment of heart disease. Today, the patients described above are almost routinely treated with effective drugs or with open-heart surgery. It is also significant that during this same period the incidence of heart disease has continued to rise, until today it has become our number one killer—with the average age of the heart attack victim continuing to drop.

Heart diseases and disorders can be broken down into several categories: coronary heart disease, hypertensive heart disease, rheumatic heart disease, infectious heart disease, heart defects present at birth, and others. I will discuss some of the major ones in this short article; but first let me outline the role of the cardiologist in modern medicine.

Role of the heart specialist

The cardiologist must first be a good general physician, familiar with all of the body's organ systems, the diseases which afflict them, and the effective treatment methods that are available today. Thus, following graduation from medical school, he will spend at least three years of residency training in Internal Medicine at an accredited teaching hospital, which qualifies him to take the extensive oral and written examinations to become certified as competent in Internal Medicine. Following this, he may put in additional time in residency training in cardiology.

As a practitioner, the cardiologist sees a majority of his patients by referral from general physicians and sometimes from other specialists. I would point out that today the primary care physician is quite capable of recognizing and treating early HEART DISEASE; he refers patients to the cardiologist only after he recognizes a need for the specialist's broader experience and knowledge and sophisticated diagnostic testing techniques. After the cardiologist has completed his examination and tests to evaluate the extent of the disease and the specific structures involved, he most often refers the patient back to his regular physician, with a complete report of his findings and his recommendations for continuing treatment. If surgery is indicated, he will work with the regular physician in preparing the patient for such treatment.

The cardiologist is also usually involved in some area of research, and is deeply concerned with public education in the prevention of heart disease—especially coronary heart disease, hypertensive cardiovascular disease (associated with high blood pressure), and heart disorders caused by infections. Prevention is important in all areas of medicine, but especially in heart disease. In this respect I am sure that fear and ignorance of what preventive measures can accomplish and of how the various disease processes finally result in catastrophic illness keep many patients from seeking help—even though they know something is wrong with them.

The above is understandable, if we take into account the constant announcements of deaths due to heart attacks (usually of "newsworthy" individuals), the frightening statistics that are released almost weekly, and personal knowledge of family and friends who have become incapacitated. Above all other advice I might offer, I would ask you to understand today's statistics for what they are: simply the number of deaths for which heart disease is statistically given as the specific cause. Although heart attacks are now striking down many men in their 30s and 40s, a great majority of those who die from heart disease are elderly; many others suffer severe diseases that terminate in a heart attack. Bear in mind that we all must die sometime, of something. Millions who once would have died of infectious diseases and other serious illnesses, now live to die eventually of heart or other diseases. That is why life expectancy today is almost 20 years longer than it was

ELECTROCARDIOGRAM (ECG)

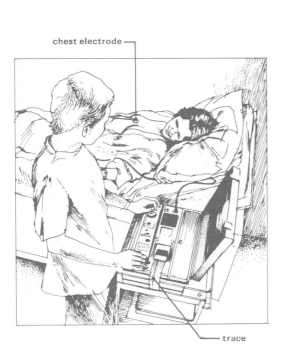

chest electrode

trace

RECORDING THE ELECTROCARDIOGRAM

V1 V2 V3 V4 V5 V6

NORMAL ECG TRACINGS

Electrocardiogram (ECG) recordings of the electrical activity of the heart are made from standard points (V1 to V6) on the chest wall. The tracing from each point is different, but should conform to a normal pattern. Abnormalities in the tracing can indicate a variety of heart diseases.

only a few decades ago. Equally important for the layman to understand is that today the vast majority of patients do not die during the acute stage of a heart attack. Properly treated during the acute stage and following preventive measures afterwards, a large percentage return to almost normal living—even at a relatively advanced age—and some live to extreme old age following a heart attack. Many patients recover from two or more attacks; but how much better it is to take preventive measures *before* a heart attack strikes to avoid or delay it and the inevitable damage to heart muscle.

Risk factors of cardiovascular disease

It is very important that every adult should know the high risk factors that are associated not only with heart disease but with many other diseases, including stroke. We know that people who are overweight have a shorter life expectancy; the degree of overweight is carefully judged by

life insurance companies who have kept precise medical statistics over many years and base their rates on them. The seriously overweight person who reduces to a normal weight and maintains it, even though once refused insurance or given it only at a special rate, can now obtain it at regular rates if there are no other health factors involved. Insurance companies are governed by a profit motive, so their evaluation of overweight as a health hazard is realistic. SMOKING is dangerous for heart patients, because chemicals in tobacco smoke may increase the work of the heart—necessitating an additional oxygen supply to the heart muscle. Other known factors include the presence of DIABETES MELLITUS, GOUT, excessive fats or fatlike substances carried in the blood (including CHOLESTEROL), lack of adequate physical exercise and unrelieved ANXIETY or emotional stress. High blood pressure (hypertension) is a most dangerous symptom of vascular disease, but it can now be effectively controlled by special drugs. All adults should periodically be checked for this potentially dangerous condition, because it usually develops and progresses without signs or symptoms.

Coronary heart disease

Coronary heart disease (*or coronary occlusion, coronary thrombosis, coronary insufficiency, myocardial infarction*) is due to what commonly is called "hardening of the arteries" but medically is called *atherosclerosis* (or *arteriosclerosis*). All of us, as we age, develop some degree of this condition; but it progresses more rapidly in some, suggesting a variance in internal bodily function—especially in the metabolism of blood fats. Some of these fatty substances accumulate in the blood and may be deposited in the walls of the large arteries.

In ATHEROSCLEROSIS the fatty deposits may accumulate and harden into scar-like patches. In coronary heart disease these deposits (which are also known as *atheromas* or *plaques*) gradually form in the coronary arteries which provide the heart with its own vital blood supply. With time, the plaques can become natural lodging places for additional fat deposits, calcium and blood clots—which may be carried in the blood from an inflammation elsewhere in the body. Eventually, the plaques protrude into the channel of the vessel, much as lime forms in water pipes, to impede the flow within. When the point is reached where heart muscle tissue is denied enough blood to do its work, the need is expressed in chest pain (*angina pectoris*), usually during strenuous exercise. The pain of angina pectoris is characteristically relieved when the patient stops to rest, or when a drug such as nitroglycerin is taken. This distinguishes it diagnostically from other causes of chest pain. Angina pectoris is an indication of heart disease, and at this point the cardiologist is most likely to be called in as a consultant. Medical treatment and changes in the patient's way of living may permit him to function almost normally within his limitation for many years. Heart attack may be due to a blood clot that totally blocks blood flow to tissue served by the artery involved (coronary thrombosis). In many cases, however, the atherosclerotic process develops until it occludes the flow of blood.

Heart attacks and their treatment

Symptoms of a heart attack vary greatly, but the most common are: severe sensation of pain and pressure in the front of the chest, sometimes spreading to the left arm, often lasting for hours. Some attacks are accompanied by nausea and vomiting and are mistaken for indigestion. Sweating is common, as is sudden intense shortness of breath, and loss of consciousness occasionally occurs.

What should you do when you observe a heart attack? First, call a doctor at once. Help the patient take a position that is most comfortable to him. This will usually be halfway between lying and sitting, which aids breathing. *Do not* carry or lift the patient without the supervision of a doctor, nurse or other medically trained person. Loosen tight clothing, such as collar and belt. See that the patient does not become chilled, but do not induce sweating by too many blankets. Do not give the patient anything to drink, except under a doctor's instructions. In most cities, firemen, policemen and mobile resuscitation teams are specially trained to deal with heart attack victims and, if available, should be called when a doctor cannot be immediately reached. In any event, if possible, the patient should be safely and quickly transported to a hospital, where he will be placed under intensive care.

Medical treatment is first given to relieve pain and its attendant anxiety, most often by injections of morphine. From the moment the patient reaches an intensive care unit his "vital signs" (respiration, pulse, temperature and heart action) will be continuously monitored to detect possible complications—the most dangerous being *cardiac arrest* (sudden stopping of the heart) and *ventricular fibrillation* (abnormally rapid, uncoordinated and ineffective contractions of the ventricular chambers of the heart). Hospital resuscitation teams, on duty 24 hours a day, have become more and more successful in restarting hearts that have suddenly stopped and in restoring normal rhythm to a fibrillating heart, in which the heart beats in an uncoordinated manner from many points simultaneously—each side working against the other, resulting in complete failure of the heart to work as a pump. Electric shocks and drugs are both used to restore normal rhythm and *artificial pacemakers* may be implanted to control the heartbeat in patients who suffer certain disturbances of rhythm (see PACEMAKER). Most of those patients who now die in the early stages of a heart attack are victims of sudden heart arrest, usually as the result of VENTRICULAR FIBRILLATION.

Recovery period

During the first most critical week following a heart attack, treatment is directed toward relieving in every possible way any unnecessary demands upon the heart. Oxygen is provided and the continuing pain is controlled. Pain continues for as long as damaged heart muscle struggles to do its contractions without oxygenated blood. This damaged area, which may range in size from a small nut to a golf ball (depending upon whether a large or a branch artery is blocked), acts somewhat like an inflammation, causing fever. Toward the end of the first week and in the early days of the second, the heart wall near the site of infarction is at its weakest and the danger of rupture, hemorrhage and sudden death is greatest. Thus, rest is essential during this critical period. During the second week the heart's remarkable ability for self-repair begins. Fibroblasts (building cells) appear along with tiny new blood vessels and the debris of dead tissue is carried away by special white cells (phagocytes), to be replaced by scar tissue. By the end of the fourth week the scar is firmer and during the second month it becomes solid. If the healed area is small or moderate in size, the patient is able to resume ordinary living during the third month.

Modern chemistry has provided accurate new blood tests that are most useful to cardiologists in the diagnosis of heart attack. Tests performed on the day following an attack of severe chest pain accurately confirm a heart attack that has occurred (but rule it out if the pain was due to other causes).

During the healing process, "collateral circulation" is developed in muscle tissue surrounding the infarct. Just as a bone fracture heals with proper time and care, so does the heart in most cases; but complications, in a few, may delay the healing process. In those who have not suffered much cardiac enlargement and are without angina pectoris (either of which may follow myocardial infarction) the future life may need little or no restriction. It is true that future attacks may occur months or years after the first; but they, too, may be resolved like the first. Once healing has occurred, drugs are seldom required, except to control complications or other chronic diseases.

Proper exercise is something every cardiac patient should take seriously. It is started as early during the healing stage of a heart attack as possible—first, by gentle leg and foot movements (to avoid pooling of blood in the extremities with the risk of clots forming), followed by short periods sitting in a chair, then by walking (see also THROMBOSIS/THROMBUS). Once a patient resumes normal living he should—under his doctor's guidance—follow a sensible program of diet control and physical exercise. At the same time, however, the patient should attempt to pursue a life style that avoids excessive emotional stress, fatigue and anything that interferes with needed rest.

There are many coronary rehabilitation centers, established throughout the country, where patients with heart disease are trained to cope with their problems and are instructed in specific exercises and diet. There are also "Mended Heart Clubs" to which patients who have undergone heart surgery are eligible for membership. These members also play a most important role in supporting patients who face such surgery.

THE HEART-LUNG MACHINE

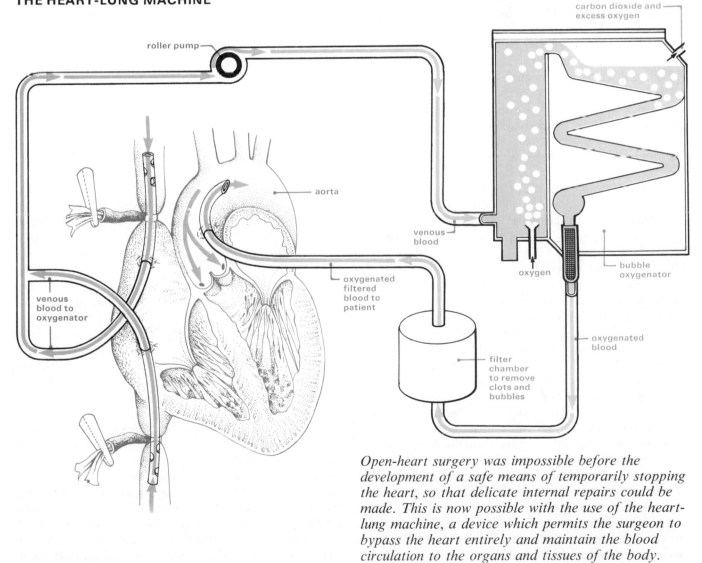

roller pump — carbon dioxide and excess oxygen — aorta — venous blood — oxygen — bubble oxygenator — oxygenated filtered blood to patient — venous blood to oxygenator — filter chamber to remove clots and bubbles — oxygenated blood

Open-heart surgery was impossible before the development of a safe means of temporarily stopping the heart, so that delicate internal repairs could be made. This is now possible with the use of the heart-lung machine, a device which permits the surgeon to bypass the heart entirely and maintain the blood circulation to the organs and tissues of the body.

Common assumptions about coronary heart disease: true or false?

1. One's genetic inheritances and personality are closely associated with one's liability to heart attacks. This is true. Cardiologists and all physicians are most careful to obtain a complete family history. Those who have a history of heart disease or stroke in their families, on either side, are more prone than those who do not. Persons with aggressive, competitive personalities, and those who have a low tolerance for emotional stress, also seem to have more heart attacks.

Individuals with a certain type of personality, called "Type A," have been found to be particularly prone to coronary artery disease. Such individuals are highly strung, competitive and "success-oriented"—very often the executive type found in business. However, one's specific occupation is not as important as the ability to cope with emotional stress. City bus drivers, for example, as a group, have a very high incidence of heart attacks and stroke. Consider these obvious facts: the driver sits throughout his work day, fights congested traffic and is often a victim of passenger abuse. He has, or develops, an aggressive personality and is usually primed for "fight or flight." Unrelieved stress often leads to excessive eating and drinking. Studies made of personnel at various levels of business have shown that the top executive has fewer heart attacks than those stuck in frustrating jobs in middle management who cannot, or dare not, leave them. Perhaps the top executive is better equipped to handle stress on his way up the success ladder, and once there can make his own rules and better control his work situation.

2. Men have more heart attacks than women. This is true, but only with qualifications. Until the menopause is reached, women have far fewer heart attacks than men do. After the menopause, women are as vulnerable as men, with the age of onset being higher—proving that the female endocrine system plus a special composition of lipids (fats or fatlike substances) in the blood provide women with extra protection during the childbearing years. A study of very young women who had their ovaries removed at an early age showed them to have about the same rate of heart attacks as men.

3. The wife of a heart attack victim can be of great help in his recovery and the prevention of future attacks. This is most certainly true, and she should have important reasons for doing it. Heart attack frequently strikes her husband when he is most needed, at an age when his children may be in college, when he is usually at or near the top of his career and earning power, and at a time when she herself may find it most difficult to find a second life partner. She can plan and prepare proper menus and is usually the first to detect the results of stress, overwork and excessive fatigue. She, better than anyone else, can reinforce the doctor's recommendations.

4. How can doctors be so sure about the part diet and lack of exercise play in coronary heart disease? They reach their conclusions from information gathered from the study of large groups of patients who have the disease, finding the similarities among them as a group and the variances that set them apart from those who do not have it. We know, for example, that individuals who have a history of heart disease, or stroke, in their immediate family (on one or both sides) are far more likely to suffer an attack than those who don't. Many studies of large populations in various parts of the world, especially with regard to diet and living habits, provide much valuable information. In undeveloped countries, where food is hard to come by and survival depends upon a constant effort to avoid starvation, coronary heart disease is hardly known. Among the people living in the developed nations of Finland and Norway—which had a high incidence of heart disease prior to World War II—there was a radical change during the war when their rich diet of meat and dairy products was reduced, when walking rather than riding was a necessity, and when the struggle for existence was constant. The incidence of heart attack and stroke dropped greatly, but in the years following 1945 this has returned to prewar levels. Many studies of groups of heart attack victims are currently being followed; evidence continues to grow which shows that those who pay strict attention to diet, exercise and a sensible life style have fewer second attacks than those who soon go back to their old habit patterns.

Other diseases of the heart

Heart tissues and the tissues of the blood vessels serving it are, like other parts of the body, vulnerable to infectious agents which may invade them and set up an inflammatory process. Untreated, they can cause great damage and result in invalidism or death. The invading organisms include staphylococcal, streptococcal and other bacteria, viruses such as those responsible for measles, influenza, mumps and others, and the spirochetes responsible for syphilis.

Bacterial endocarditis is an infection of a heart valve. It may start elsewhere in the body and be carried to the heart, or it may start within the heart from invasion of bacteria that may ordinarily be tolerated. Most often the latter type of infection starts in a valve already damaged from previous attacks of rheumatic fever or congenital heart disease. Until the discovery of penicillin, the infection was fatal in more than 98% of all cases. The symptoms are high fever, chills, weakness, loss of appetite and great fatigue. Red spots appear on the skin and mucous membranes. Old heart murmurs may change and new ones develop as the valve is affected. Blood clots may break away and lodge in the brain or vessels in other parts of the body. Treatment calls for massive injections of antibiotics as soon as possible and continued over a period of weeks. Again, prevention is the best treatment. Those with congenital heart disorders should be protected from all infections as soon as possible with adequate doses of antibiotics. When great damage is done to a heart valve in the absence of early or effective treatment, the cardiologist may recommend valve replacement by open-heart surgery.

Acute pericarditis can develop much as the above from bacteria or viruses, but the inflammation is in the pericardium—the membranous sac that envelops the heart. Symptoms are moderate fever, chest pain that is increased by coughing, heavy breathing and a general feeling of being unwell (malaise). A physician hears a rubbing sound through his stethoscope, produced by friction as the membranes rub against each other during breathing. If the infection is of bacterial origin, antibiotic drugs are effective. There are no effective drugs for viral infections, but the body's immunological system will ordinarily counteract the infection in time—usually within two or three weeks—so that the patient fully recovers.

Chronic constrictive pericarditis develops when the pericardium thickens and loses its flexibility, constricting expansion of the heart within. In many cases the cause is unknown, but it may be due to inflammation from bacteria or viruses, or result from tuberculosis. The condition is three times more common in men than in women. The flow of blood in veins back to the heart is impeded; pressure builds up within them and the veins in the neck often become enlarged. Other signs include the accumulation of fluid in the legs and enlargement of the liver. Weakness, loss of appetite and weight loss are common. The treatment for chronic constrictive pericarditis is usually surgical, which may require sophisticated studies (such as catheterization and angiocardiography) to evaluate the condition and differentiate it from other disorders with similar signs and symptoms.

Acute myocarditis is an inflammation of heart muscle, which may be caused by infection with bacteria, viruses or other microorganisms that travel to the heart from other parts of the body. It may also be a complication of rheumatic fever. The symptoms are heart enlargement, palpitations, heavy breathing, fever and changes in heart sounds. Strict bed rest is important during the active stages; appropriate antibiotic drugs are prescribed when indicated. Most patients recover and regain normal function (see MYOCARDITIS).

Rheumatic fever deserves special mention, because it causes so much heart damage in so many people. It usually starts with a sore throat and the symptoms common to inflammatory infections. All of us suffer from sore throats, especially children. Such infections usually run a short course and end; but a single type of bacteria, *Grade A hemolytic streptococcus*, is responsible for the rheumatic fever that may follow weeks later, with inflammation of the knee, wrist, elbow or other body joints. These symptoms may be so mild that they go unnoticed in children, or are blamed as "growing pains." The most serious effects are not in the joints but in the valves of the heart. A first attack may do only minor damage; but repeated attacks often occur in the susceptible child, with extensive damage. *Thus, every sore throat in a child deserves a doctor's attention.* When he identifies the Grade A hemolytic streptococcus, he will carefully treat the patient with antibiotic drugs to kill the microorganisms before they can damage the heart. Drugs are not usually effective once the damaging process is underway, which indicates that the bacteria in time produce the by-products to which the body reacts, much like an allergic process. In most children valve damage may be minor and they can live with their handicap; but when valve damage is so great that function is grossly disturbed, open-heart surgery and valve replacement may be the only way to save the patient from invalidism or, in severe cases, early death. (See RHEUMATIC FEVER.)

Hypertensive heart disease. Heart failure may ensue from unrelieved high blood pressure. When our BLOOD PRESSURE remains at an abnormally high level, the condition is called *hypertension*. Normally, the blood pressure goes down slightly when we sleep or are at rest; it goes up when we are physically active, excited or frightened. Thus, when we suffer from unrelieved stress, anxiety or fear, we are said to be primed for "fight or flight." At such times our heart beats faster and the blood pressure rises; this places increased pressure on the arterial walls, much in the same manner that pressure goes up within a hose as its nozzle is slowly closed. There are many diseases and conditions that produce high blood pressure. Whatever the cause, it can, in most cases, be controlled today by effective new drugs. Unrelieved, the heart muscle must continue to work under stress and gradually enlarges under its increased load. Because hypertension is so often without obvious symptoms, all people should have their blood pressure checked at periodic intervals—especially older people, who are most prone to strokes and heart disease. Such checks are imperative for people with known arterial disease.

See also the major article on **Hypertension.**

Congenital heart defects

Not too long ago, various congenital defects of the heart doomed many children to invalidism and early death. Today they are being corrected by open-heart surgery, which restores many victims to full health and a normal life expectancy. The causes of congenital defects are not yet fully understood, but German measles and other viral diseases suffered by the mother during the early months of pregnancy are known to cause some congenital defects. The use of certain drugs, chemicals and other agents in the environment are also suspected. Corrective surgery is indicated when gross dysfunction of the heart results from such defects, which include the following:

1. Patent ductus arteriosus is present in every infant at

birth. It is a duct, or channel, which transports blood between the pulmonary artery and aorta. This channel is needed before birth, because it provides blood from the mother to the fetus. After birth, the infant's own lungs function to provide oxygenated blood and the channel is no longer needed; but in some it fails to close and some of the oxygenated blood from the aorta is shunted back to the lungs. The heart must then increase its contractions to provide needed fresh blood to the body. Over a period of time the heart may suffer damage and lose its ability to provide enough needed blood. Surgical closure of the ductus completely restores normal circulation (see PATENT DUCTUS ARTERIOSUS). Because the ductus lies outside the heart, this operation is relatively simple and the heart-lung machine and other equipment are not required. I should add that nonsurgical treatment of this condition in the newborn is now being used effectively in some cases. Newly discovered substances (*prostaglandins*) may be effective in closing the ductus by medical means. (Prostaglandins are a class of physiologically potent substances present naturally in many tissues and most heavily concentrated in human semen. Their various potentially useful therapeutic effects are being carefully evaluated.)

2. Atrial septal defect is an abnormal opening in the upper septum, the wall that separates the two upper chambers (atria) of the heart, allowing fresh blood to flow from the left atrium to the right and back to the lungs. The amount of blood lost to general circulation with each heartbeat depends upon the size of the hole. Open-heart surgery, with the heart-lung machine taking over the body's circulation, is required to correct the condition. If the opening is small it can be stitched and closed; if large, a patch may be needed to close it. The patient remains in the hospital from 10 to 14 days, if there are no complications, and is back in school within a month or so, with normal life expectancy when correction has been made before gross damage to the heart has occurred.

3. Ventricular septal defect is similar to the atrial defect, except the hole is between the two lower chambers (ventricles) of the heart. The corrective surgical procedure and outlook is similar to the above.

4. Pulmonary stenosis describes a congenital defect of the pulmonary valve, which controls blood flow from heart to lungs. When the valve is too narrow, blood flow is impeded and the body receives less than its needed supply of oxygenated blood. The heart must work harder and in time enlarges on the right side. If the stenosis is minor, no treatment is needed; if major, surgery is indicated, preferably in childhood.

5. Aortic stenosis may also be a congenital defect. It describes an abnormal narrowing of the major artery (aorta)—the "trunk line" of the body. Aortic stenosis can exist in various shapes and forms. The narrowing may be at the valve, above the valve, or below it. Thus, wherever the

CONGENITAL HEART DEFECTS

TETRALOGY OF FALLOT

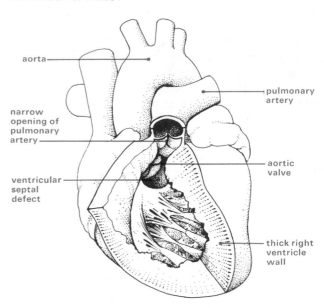

TRANSPOSITION OF THE GREAT ARTERIES

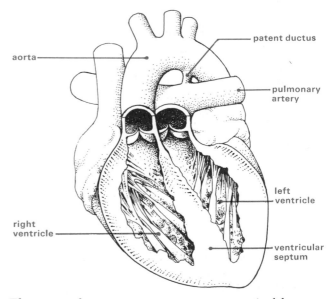

These are the two most common congenital heart defects causing cyanosis ("blue babies"). The four abnormalities of Fallot's tetralogy are shown above: (1) large ventricular septal defect; (2) the aorta lies above what is left of the septum; (3) thickened right ventricle wall; (4) small pulmonary artery. In transposition, the aorta arises from the right ventricle and the pulmonary trunk from the left instead of vice versa; to survive at all these babies must have an additional abnormality (patent ductus) to allow the two circulations to mix. Surgical correction of both conditions is now possible.

narrowing is located, normal flow of oxygenated blood is impeded to the body and functions of the heart are affected. Many times an operation is helpful and may even be life-saving, but drugs may also be helpful in controlling some of these conditions.

6. *Tetralogy of Fallot* describes a defect of the heart which results in the mixture of fresh (arterial) and "used" (venous) blood that flows throughout the body. Because the oxygen content is reduced, the blood is bluish-red in color, causing CYANOSIS—the "blue baby" syndrome (so-called because of the blueness that appears in lips, fingernails, tip of the nose and other areas). This is the most common form of congenital cyanotic heart disease. In the majority of children a complete cure is possible through surgery, which is best done in older children or young adults. If a child is too ill to wait, a palliative operation may be performed to bypass the damaged valve and provide more oxygenated blood. Later, open-heart surgery can be performed to repair the valve. (See TETRALOGY OF FALLOT.)

7. *Transposition of the great vessels* is another type of congenital cyanotic disorder, in which the pulmonary artery and aorta are transposed in position. Infants suffering this defect are blue at birth or soon afterwards; until quite recently they did not survive unless they had additional defects that permitted a mixture of fresh and used blood. Survival depends upon the circulation of an adequate amount of oxygenated blood throughout the body. It is a tribute to modern research and surgical techniques that correction of this defect is now being accomplished in selected cases.

There are other less common congenital heart defects, but space does not permit description here. However, the cardiologist will identify them and recommend proper treatment, when evidence of heart malfunction calls for his evaluation.

Diagnostic tests

Armed with the information provided by the referring physician—which will combine medical records of past illnesses, family history and treatments—the cardiologist will carry out his diagnostic procedures in a step-by-step fashion. Depending on the underlying disorder, he will perform various laboratory tests and radiological procedures, take his own history of the case and give the patient a careful physical examination. If necessary, he will then perform elaborate tests, including *heart catheterization*—which involves the insertion of a special catheter (tube) into the heart through a vein or an artery. The catheter tip may be introduced into the right or left coronary artery and contrast (radiopaque) material injected. This permits the outline of these arteries to be seen on a film and shown as moving pictures; it reveals the presence and location (or absence) of possible obstructions within the vessels. Catheterization also permits internal evaluation of heart action, pressure, valve function and the size and location of congenital defects. Provided with the specific information obtained by catheterization, the cardiologist uses his knowledge and experience with the many types of heart patient he has dealt with to determine the best medical treatment for specific patients, or whether cardiac surgery should be performed.

Heart surgery

When surgery is being considered, the cardiologist works in close cooperation with the heart surgeon to weigh risks against possible advantages and decide when surgery may be essential to maintain life.

HEART SURGERY has made tremendous advances in recent years—although the much discussed "bypass" operation for coronary heart disease was first carried out in the dog by Dr. Alexis Carrel at the beginning of this century, and the present efficient heart-lung machine was developed over several decades. Use of the heart-lung machine, which permits the surgeon to work on a bloodless and quiescent heart, with adequate time for careful surgery, has greatly reduced risks and permits procedures that were impossible only a short time ago. Damaged valves and abnormalities within the heart can now be visually inspected, repaired or replaced. The skilled anesthesiologist can monitor bodily functions and correct many abnormalities before they become life-threatening. Hearts can be stopped and restarted almost at will. The bypass operation, using a graft (a connection with a vein or artery taken from another part of the body to bypass an occluded coronary artery), is now being done safely to provide adequate oxygenated blood to the heart muscle. Although it is too early to make a final assessment of the value of this operation, in many cases it has been life-saving. (See the illustration at BYPASS.)

Although great progress has been made in medicine and surgery since I was a medical student, I know that we are at the brink of new discoveries which will come from a better understanding of disease processes. Of particular interest at the moment is the promising research that is being done in laboratories and research centers to find ways of salvaging damaged heart tissue before it is totally destroyed during the period immediately following a heart attack. Many new drugs are being studied and there is hope that a new type of therapy can be provided for heart attack victims. In the meantime, we should take advantage of all that is known to prevent, correct or delay the progress of all types of heart disease. Future developments should reduce the death toll for many cardiovascular problems.

Hypertension

Dr. Margaret M. Kilcoyne*

The fatal complications associated with hypertension—severe high blood pressure—constitute the major cause of death each year. With sensible precautions and regular medical checkups, many of these deaths could be avoided. The following article discusses how physicians deal with this important health problem.

When we stop to think about the superb living machine that we have in our own body, it is a wonder that we so often give it less care and attention than we would an automobile—which, unlike our body, can be replaced for new each year.

Diseases of the heart and blood vessels (cardiovascular diseases) kill more people each year in the United States than any other single cause. The truly tragic fact, however, is that many of these deaths could have been avoided with a sensible program of "preventive maintenance" by the victims themselves. A better understanding of some of the basic requirements of the body may help to change the grim statistics.

Consider first the single cell: it has the capacity to carry out the most complex biological and biochemical functions. To achieve this it must have a source of energy and nutrition. The human cell depends for energy, and for the nutrients that permit it to function properly, on the constant flow of blood throughout the body. Quite simply, this is a matter of life and death.

Both the heart and the blood vessels are extremely responsive to the demands of the body for variations in blood flow from moment to moment. If we suddenly begin to run, for example, our heart will beat faster in order to supply more blood to satisfy the increased energy demands of the muscles, including the heart muscle itself. The blood vessels are designed at every level of the branching vascular system to provide for the delivery of blood to the cells (and thus, of course, to the organs and tissues) in the most efficient possible way. As the arteries approach the cells, their walls contain more muscle fibers; this enables them to alter their diameter to allow more or less blood to enter a particular organ or part. This is most pronounced in the smallest of the arterial vessels, the *arterioles*, which are tiny channels leading to the capillaries.

*Research Career Award, National Institutes of Health, National Heart, Lung and Blood Institute # 5K 04 HL 00183–02

The *capillaries* form a link between the arterial and venous systems and constitute the most delicate of all the blood vessels. It is by diffusion through their extremely thin walls that oxygen from the lungs is given up to the cells of the body, together with nutrients and certain other substances (such as hormones).

The proper functioning of each of these sets of blood vessels is obviously critical to the delivery of the appropriate blood flow *at the appropriate pressure* so that damage to the blood vessels does not occur—which would interfere with the source of energy and nutrition for the cells, with the ultimate threat of cellular death.

Regulation of blood flow

In order to assist in the distribution of blood throughout the system, there are circulating substances which influence the capacity of the blood vessels to alter their internal diameter or bore. Just as in many delicately balanced systems, there are "push-pull" factors which allow a *constrictor* for narrowing the internal diameter of the blood vessels, balanced by a *dilator* for expanding their internal diameter.

The most familiar *vasoconstrictors* (substances which narrow blood vessels) are epinephrine and norepinephrine, released largely by the adrenal glands and the nerve endings. An even more powerful vasoconstrictor is *angiotensin*, a peptide sent into the bloodstream from the kidneys when the amount of blood or salt in the body is inadequate. *Vasodilators* (substances which dilate blood vessels) such as *prostaglandin* and *bradykinin* are distributed widely in order to enhance the delivery of blood to the cells.

A number of such substances are recognized now, but we are quite certain that additional circulating substances await discovery. Many such vasoactive substances have been recognized in recent years because of incredible advances in biochemical methods and sophisticated instruments which permit their detection and measurement. They are present in such minute quantities that

Extremely complex mechanisms (right) interact to maintain and regulate the blood pressure, volume and flow throughout the body's vast network of blood vessels. In addition to the pumping action of the heart, which forces blood through the arterial system, the blood pressure is influenced by nerve impulses to and from the heart and by hormonal control mechanisms.

SOME OF THE FACTORS INVOLVED IN BLOOD PRESSURE CONTROL

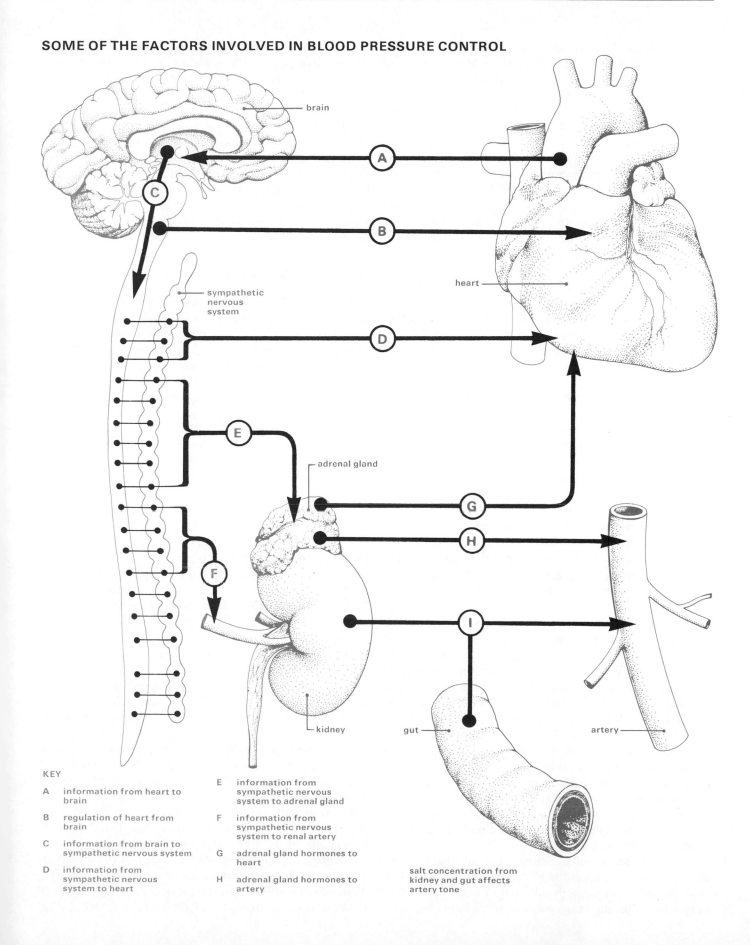

brain

A

C

B

sympathetic
nervous
system

heart

D

E

adrenal gland

G

H

F

kidney

I

gut

artery

KEY

A   information from heart to
    brain

B   regulation of heart from
    brain

C   information from brain to
    sympathetic nervous system

D   information from
    sympathetic nervous
    system to heart

E   information from
    sympathetic nervous
    system to adrenal gland

F   information from
    sympathetic nervous
    system to renal artery

G   adrenal gland hormones to
    heart

H   adrenal gland hormones to
    artery

    salt concentration from
    kidney and gut affects
    artery tone

previous methods were inadequate for the task. For example, one measures the amount of blood sugar (or glucose) in *milligram* (one-thousandth of a gram) quantities. In contrast, angiotensin, a substance that is particularly critical in the management of blood flow and blood pressure, is measured in *picogram* (one-trillionth of a gram) quantities.

Pioneer work has been done in recent years. Extremely important is the radioimmunoassay devised by Dr. Rosalyn Yalow, a winner of the Nobel Prize for this work. This procedure has allowed us to measure many of these circulating hormones or peptides which have such significant control over the amount of blood available for individual cells. Other substances which are not normal for the circulation, but are imposed on it, create an imbalance. Nicotine, for example, constricts all blood vessels and reduces blood flow indiscriminately. In healthy young individuals, smoking cigarettes is thus an abuse of a fine machine and is especially dangerous in those with diseases of the heart and blood vessels.

Abnormally high arterial pressure (hypertension)

You may be wondering why so much emphasis is being placed on blood flow when the topic is called hypertension. Hypertension is frequently thought of as a condition of high blood pressure *due* to high tension in the body or a particularly tense life situation. There is no question that a variety of factors influence the blood pressure, including the stimulus to increase blood pressure when critical situations produce stress for the individual. But stress does not in itself explain this very complicated disease. It is only one factor among many that are now recognized; how many others remain to be discovered is obviously unknown.

What, then, is hypertension or high blood pressure? It is a condition in which the delivery of blood to the cells is obstructed by constriction of the blood vessels, which requires the heart to generate more pressure to force an adequate (normal) amount of blood through the vessels. If one had the ideal means of measuring blood flow, as simply as one is able to measure blood pressure, then blood flow would be the first choice of measurement of adequacy of the cardiovascular system. However, such a measurement requires either entering the blood vessels with instruments or using radioactive substances. These are sophisticated techniques which are indicated when serious threats to blood flow are present, such as in coronary artery disease or for research purposes, but they are not really practical for everyday checking.

A simpler means of measuring the adequacy of the cardiovascular system is the blood pressure reading. This information, however, tells only the pressure required to propel blood through the system to reach individual cells.

It may seem to be within the normal range found in large numbers of people, or it may seem to be higher than what is recognized as a reasonable or "normal" blood pressure at a given age. Under rare circumstances, such as shock or massive hemorrhage, it may be too low. The circumstances under which the blood pressure is being measured need to be known since the blood pressure may, for instance, normally be higher after exercise or stress than the "normal" level for the individual when seated at rest. Conversely, at rest—particularly during sleep when the body is requiring very little energy except for the repair and replenishment of cells—the blood pressure should be lower.

Factors that influence blood pressure

A number of factors exist which appear to influence whether one individual develops high blood pressure compared with another. A definite genetic pattern of blood pressure levels has not been demonstrated, nor have we been able to identify at the molecular level the genes responsible for blood flow and blood pressure regulation. Nevertheless, it is clear that high blood pressure tends to occur in certain families. It is important to know the kinds of diseases that appear within an individual's family tree, because of the greater likelihood of developing diseases frequently seen within the family. This is not to say that these diseases are all hereditary or based on genetic factors, but rather that we are so aware of the importance of early detection of disease and, if possible, its prevention, that all individuals are well advised to learn what patterns of disease are present within their families and to keep this in their chronologic health history.

Numerous environmental factors appear to influence whether or not an individual develops high blood pressure. Members of the black population develop high blood pressure two to three times more frequently than members of the white population. The quantity of salt in the diet seems to be one strong contributor to the high rate of hypertension in the black population, in addition to the high stress factors and often strong family history of the disease. Since our diets contain large amounts of ions, such as sodium or salt, potassium and other such substances, the body must be able to rid itself of excess ions; the kidney is largely responsible for this task. Ordinarily, any amount of excess salt or potassium can be excreted by the kidneys. If this were not so, that familiar steak dinner would be the last meal remembered!

Sensitive cells are present within the kidneys for detection of the quantity of salt in the blood passing through them. Adjustments are made swiftly. In addition, the kidneys are very sensitive to the quantity of blood flow and the pressure under which it is being delivered. When a reduction of blood flow or salt (or both) develops, a threat to the normal environment of the body is detected. The kidneys release hormones which stimulate the release of hormones that retain salt and water in the body rather than excrete it into the urine. Vasoconstrictor substances are also released to cause the blood vessels to constrict around whatever amount of blood is in the system until balance returns. This function can alter each minute because the maintenance of the proper environment for cells is critical at all times.

A person with high blood pressure seems to handle the salt in his or her body differently from a person with normal blood pressure. The reason for this is not completely understood and considerable research continues in this area. One factor that may be important is an increase in salt and water in the walls of the blood vessels, which can contribute to a greater degree of vascular constriction or narrowing with a normal stimulus. The blood vessels also appear to be changed in their basic structure; whether or not this is the cause or the result of the high pressure pounding against their walls is still not definitely known.

Every age seems to think that the stress level for the society is the highest in history. The current statistics for violent crime in our society make a good case for our own era. The blood pressure does increase with stress but decreases again when stress is reduced. It is possible that the same apparent degree of stress will cause one person to develop hypertension and another to remain normal. It seems likely that the explanation is in the combination of factors against which the stress is operating in each person. For example, if one has a strong family history of hypertension and coronary artery disease, and has eaten large quantities of salt from infancy onward and reacts strongly even to minor stresses, the natural vulnerability plus the repeated stimuli to push up the blood pressure may eventually cause it to remain high.

Excess weight is another risk factor for the development of high blood pressure. Like all other factors acting alone, however, excess weight is not associated with hypertension in all persons. Nicotine, like stress, causes the blood pressure to rise directly since it is a constrictor of blood vessels. Each time a dose of nicotine is given, the blood pressure goes up and when the nicotine is gone, the blood pressure goes down. Delivery of blood to the cells is low during the "nicotine load." If the coronary arteries are already narrowed by plaques of cholesterol, fats and other material build up, sections of the heart may temporarily lose most of the blood supply. The pain in the chest that results from this loss is known as ANGINA PECTORIS. So lifestyle can be modified to help create an optimal operating environment on the inside if not on the outside.

Complications of untreated hypertension

For years it was thought that there was no reason to worry about high blood pressure because early studies had shown that those patients who had hypertension lived as long as those who did not. Even in extreme cases, where it seemed necessary to bring the blood pressure to reasonable levels, there were very few drugs available for the purpose.

The question of why the blood pressure should be high still remained and Kempner, who originated the "rice diet," wanted to test whether or not blood pressure could be lowered by removing all salt from the diet. The diet consisted of rice, fruit and sugar only. From personal experience on that diet in medical school for five days, I can attest to the fact that the blood pressure declines; but one's interest in life declines equally, so that as a plan of treatment for high blood pressure few enthusiastic participants could be found. Nevertheless, it was clear from these studies that salt was important and that removal of salt was effective in lowering blood pressure, at least among the patients evaluated after accepting this very strict diet.

A few patients with very high blood pressure were treated by cutting some of the nerves leaving the spinal cord (*sympathectomy*), but the results varied. Finally, studies were undertaken which were to bring about a great change in the treatment of hypertension, by showing that it did indeed have many serious effects on the body. As more drugs for the treatment of extremely high blood pressure become available one important research study was performed by the Veterans Administration Cooperative Study Group. Patients who had hypertension who wanted to participate in the study were divided into two groups: one group had full treatment for hypertension with three different drugs and the second group had no treatment for hypertension. The results clearly showed that a number of serious complications developed in patients with high blood pressure. This could be seen if they were observed closely for months to years. Furthermore, those who were treated had far fewer complications than those who were not treated.

Each of the major complications develops in an organ system critical for normal bodily functioning: the brain, heart and kidneys. We now know that patients who have high blood pressure and who are not receiving treatment are vulnerable to the development of a poor blood supply to the brain, resulting in stroke, poor blood supply to the kidney, resulting in kidney failure, enlargement of the heart (cardiomegaly), and a greater risk of coronary artery disease.

When the work of the heart is increased because of the high blood pressure it must overcome to pump blood into the arterial tree, it tries to accommodate the extra load by enlarging the heart muscle itself. Unfortunately, the enlargement of the heart muscle only helps to some degree because as the muscle of the heart thickens, the chance for the energy supplies in the blood to diffuse into the innermost cells of the heart muscle becomes smaller. Eventually, malfunction develops because the thickened and weakened heart muscle can no longer contract properly and is unable to eject the blood out of the heart in normal amounts. Heart failure then occurs. When the pump fails, delivery of blood to all cells fails. It must be corrected or cell death will inevitably occur.

When the blood supply to the brain is reduced because of high blood pressure there is a danger of paralysis. There may be a brief loss of consciousness and a temporary loss of speech or use of arms or legs, or there may be continued disturbance of some of these functions because of cell death in one part of the brain.

The most common underlying cause of stroke is high blood pressure. The number of strokes developing in patients whose hypertension is treated satisfactorily is one quarter the number found in untreated or insufficiently treated hypertensive patients.

Treatment of hypertension

When hypertension is diagnosed and treatment is advised, a "partnership" must be established between the patient and physician. Physicians who try to be both doctor and patient for themselves are warned that in such cases there is "a fool at both ends of the stethoscope." Patients who try to treat their hypertension are obviously even worse off.

The first four to six weeks of drug treatment are most important. Modification of the lifestyle is often advised before drugs are administered for patients with moderate elevations of blood pressure. In those with severe hypertension the two modes of treatment are employed together. Modification of some of the patterns of his or her life is the patient's responsibility; appropriate factors for the patient to alter are individual. In some cases weight reduction, increased exercise and salt reduction will be needed; in others, a reduction of stress and removal of nicotine. The physician will analyze the needs and recommend methods, supportive groups and techniques of relaxation.

During the first four to six weeks of treatment the patient is quite likely to feel worse as a consequence of this program to improve health than he did with the disease. Two things have happened: (1) foreign chemicals have been poured into his complicated physiological system, and (2) the body, having been forced to adapt to a high-pressure internal environment, is temporarily unbalanced with the drop in pressure. Readjustments will be made gradually until the blood pressure reaches desirable levels and is held there for some time without interruption. If the patient is forewarned of this and if the prescribed drugs (and *only* the prescribed drugs) are taken under close control of both the patient and physician, with modifications in dosage as needed, the result will often surprise even the most pessimistic of persons. The patient must come to realize the importance of following his physician's instructions to the letter regarding dosage.

Drugs prescribed

Three main classes of drugs are commonly prescribed in the treatment of hypertension. *Diuretics* ("water pills") act on the kidneys to allow more water and salt to be excreted in the urine. There is also an effect on the blood vessels in some diuretics. *Sympathetic inhibitors* lower the neural stimulus for high blood pressure or lower the effectiveness of circulating epinephrine. *Vasodilators* relax the blood vessels. (See also *Drugs for high blood pressure* in the major article **Drugs and Medicines.**)

The diuretic drugs function adequately for the control of blood pressure in approximately 25–30% of patients. A diuretic may be all that is needed to return the blood pressure to normal levels. As a group of drugs, diuretics have a variety of potential adverse reactions in the body, usually quite mild; but all require that patients be under the supervision of their physician to avoid possible complications of the drug. In particular, most diuretics lower potassium in the body so that either a dietary replacement or a potassium supplement will be required in either liquid or pill form. However, patients who take diuretics and have not been prescribed potassium supplements, or who have failed to follow the recommended diet for replacing potassium, begin to feel extremely weak (particularly in the legs) as the potassium stores diminish. (See also *Diuretics* in the major article on **Drugs and Medicines.**)

Generally, the second drug added to the diuretic—when that drug alone fails to control the blood pressure at the appropriate level—is a sympathetic inhibitor. Several drugs are available, from the oldest—which was the first drug found to have antihypertensive properties (reserpine) —to the newest drugs now available which selectively block sites on the blood vessels where epinephrine and similar substances of the nervous system act. These are known as *alpha-adrenergic* and *beta-adrenergic blocking agents.*

Most patients who begin treatment with one of the sympathetic inhibitors feel fatigued (even to the point of falling asleep) with the sudden drop in nervous activity. This will gradually be replaced by a sense of renewed vigor when the blood pressure is controlled and the body begins to adjust to the drug. As with diuretics, the sympathetic inhibitors can produce a number of unwanted effects, some more extreme than others. Baseline blood tests are usually conducted routinely before drugs for the control of high blood pressure are administered and these must be repeated at intervals, depending upon the reports of the patient and the observation of the physician.

Vasodilators are usually prescribed in combination with one of the other classes of drugs. Recently, powerful new vasodilators have been developed and tested which add still more potential for blood pressure control with minimal side effects.

As with any prescription drug, vasodilators must be used only under close medical supervision.

Referral to a specialist

Patients who are under the care of a family practitioner or internist ordinarily have their blood pressure managed by their own physician because this is optimal for the patient and because referral to the specialist can be made when appropriate. There may be evidence of unusual or complicated hypertensive disease which makes referral or cooperative management advisable with physicians who are actively performing research in the area. The physician who specializes in hypertension and cardiovascular disease is usually a board qualified or certified cardiologist. In some centers in the United States, a nephrologist (kidney specialist) or an endocrinologist (expert in the hormonal system) may provide consultation.

It is not necessary after the initial evaluation to have a physician measure the blood pressure routinely but it is important that it be evaluated by a *physician*. This is true also when blood pressure is measured in screening centers in the community. As has been mentioned repeatedly, the blood pressure normally fluctuates somewhat in response to appropriate stimuli. Some individuals are troubled and apprehensive about having their blood pressures measured. Apprehension may cause the blood pressure to rise, but it will usually return to normal.

Persons who have abnormal blood pressures may also overreact in apprehension but their blood pressure will continue to be elevated after repeated measurements even under quiet circumstances. If there is evidence of any abnormality, the patient may be tempted to deny it; but denying the early signals that the body gives may prevent appropriate and timely medical treatment to maintain or promote the health of the individual. To understand the truth of this you only have to experience the sadness of observing young individuals in the cardiac intensive care unit with advanced disease which could have been modified or prevented had the patient attended to the early signals. Again and again the doctor is in the position of having to encourage modification in the customary way of life for the patient *after* the tragic event has occurred. In instances of heart failure because of hypertension or concomitant coronary artery disease, the changes will certainly be beneficial—but what a shame it is that a damaged heart had to occur before the patient responded to the signal.

The obvious time to begin appropriate treatment is while you still have an illness amenable to treatment. Still, there is an inertia in each of us which combines early denial that something is wrong with delay in seeking medical attention, followed by an irresolute adherence to the plan of treatment which ends in failure to follow through because the patient feels better, or hasn't the time.

Unfortunately, hypertension is one of the diseases that is most insidious and patients gradually become accustomed to the fatigue, to the borderline irritability, to the high pounding pressure within the blood vessels, and to the fact

that they know so many others with this disease that it could hardly be of monumental importance. Strangely enough, it is the rare patient who—with advance infor-

THE ARTERIAL AND VENOUS SYSTEMS

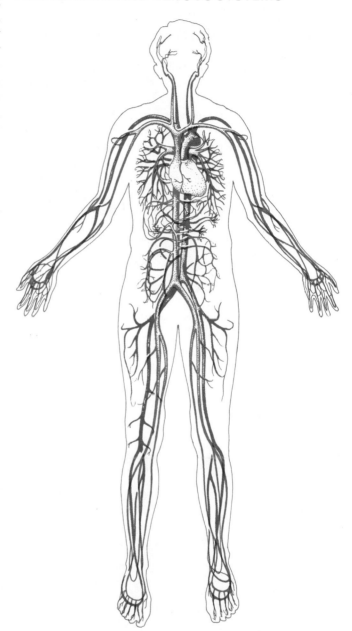

There are three main types of blood vessel: arteries, veins and capillaries. Arteries carry oxygen-rich blood to the tissues and organs of the body; veins transport oxygen-depleted blood back to the heart, where it is pumped into the lungs for a fresh supply of oxygen. The capillaries are microscopically small blood vessels, with walls only a single cell thick. Through these walls oxygen is given up to the tissues and waste material—such as carbon dioxide—diffuses back to be carried via the veins to the lungs, where it is exhaled.

mation about a potential stroke, heart attack, or failure of the kidneys—will actually bring himself to believe that the condition will affect him.

Medical Research

In conclusion, a few words must be said about research in cardiovascular disease. Our understanding of hypertension and cardiovascular disease today is certainly far advanced, even compared with 10 years ago. Sophisticated techniques for better diagnosis of diseases of the heart and blood vessels are available and major advances have been made in cellular physiology which have favorably altered the treatment of coronary artery disease and hypertension. Centers have been established throughout the United States for basic and clinical research in hypertension and cardiovascular disease. Major programs have been established for the detection, follow-up and treatment of hypertension in many communities all over the U.S.A.

In the research laboratories, intensive study of cellular mechanisms and circulating substances which affect them is going forward. Nevertheless, the complexity of human physiology and the subtlety of the interactions with which it is maintained virtually dwarf the most advanced technology in our society. It is obvious that much more work will be required before our understanding reaches the level which will permit the elimination of major cardiovascular diseases.

The preservation of health with modification of risk factors and adherence to prescribed treatment is therefore a responsibility which each of us must share with our physician on a daily basis.

See also ANEURYSM, ANGIOGRAPHY, ATHEROSCLEROSIS, BLOOD PRESSURE, CHOLESTEROL, HEART DISEASE, SPHYGMOMANOMETER, STROKE and the major article on **Cardiology.**

Ophthalmology

Dr. Lawrence G. Pape

The ophthalmologist is concerned with the diagnosis and treatment of diseases and disorders which affect the eyes. Sight is one of man's most precious gifts, without which many of the joys of life would be impossible. Although the eye functions much like a camera, it is millions of times more complex.

Poets and romanticists throughout the ages have often looked upon the eyes as the "portals of the soul." Physicians look upon them as portals through which the general health of their patients can be assessed, as well as those diseases and abnormalities within the eye itself that affect vision. The eyes and their surrounding tissues are among the body's most delicate structures, the anatomy and physiology of which are extremely complex.

The eyes are subject to most of the diseases that affect muscles, nerves, tissues and blood vessels in other parts of the body—in addition to ocular diseases which are unique to the special structures of the eye. Infections, degenerative diseases, circulatory disorders, congenital defects, abnormal growths all can affect the eyes directly to disturb vision or be associated with systemic diseases elsewhere in the body—especially in the neurological, endocrinological and vascular systems.

Although the eyes are protected within their bony sockets, they are highly vulnerable to injuries. Lacerations, abrasions and the entry into the eye of foreign bodies may sever vital nerves, muscles, connective tissue and blood vessels and may also open interior structures to microorganisms capable of causing serious infections. Burns, especially those caused by chemicals, can result in blindness. Much remains to be learned about some eye diseases to control or cure them, but great progress has been made in recent years not only in prevention but in treating many conditions considered hopeless only a short time ago.

Most of us value our gift of sight above all other senses, and the loss of it is too frightening for many of us to even consider. Perhaps that is why people with obvious signs and symptoms of serious eye problems sometimes delay seeking medical help until gross damage has occurred. If this article accomplishes nothing more than to make readers aware of the urgent need for early detection and treatment of serious eye disease, it will have been well worthwhile. Early diagnosis and treatment of potentially serious eye problems are essential.

Role of the ophthalmologist

Thus, we are concerned here with the *ophthalmologist*—whose role in modern medicine is to diagnose and treat abnormalities of the eye, both medically and surgically. He should not be confused with the *optometrist*, who is licensed (in many states) only to examine the eyes and prescribe corrective lenses. His training and experience may qualify him to recognize evidence of serious disease, in which case he should make a referral to a qualified medical doctor, usually an ophthalmologist. The *optician* is a highly skilled technician who is qualified to fill specific lens prescriptions. The *orthoptist* and *ophthalmic assistant*, seen in many ophthalmologists' offices these days, are specially trained persons who are qualified to relieve the ophthalmologist of many routine and time-consuming duties. Such personnel must work under the ophthalmologist's direct supervision; they may apply eyedrops required for special tests and examinations and may conduct vision testing using standard eye charts. Orthoptists may also instruct patients in special eye exercises, prescribed to strengthen the muscles which move the eyeball.

The qualified ophthalmologist must have a broad knowledge of general medicine and also years of vigorous clinical training and experience in the diagnosis and treatment, both medical and surgical, of the diseases and injuries that affect vision. After receiving the M.D. degree from an accredited medical school, he must complete four years of postgraduate clinical training. The first year is spent as an intern in general medicine and surgery, followed by three years of residency training in an approved program, usually at an eye facility within a medical center or teaching hospital. Here he will gain experience in diagnosing and treating all types of eye disorder, using medical and surgical techniques as needed. After completing residency training, he must practice his specialty for at least one year to be eligible to take the written and oral examinations necessary for certification by the American Board of Ophthalmology. If he should choose to specialize in one specific area of ophthalmology, he may devote an additional year or two after residency to fellowship training in the subspecialty of his choice.

A substantial number of the ophthalmologist's patients seek him out only after their vision has been impaired significantly or when their eyes hurt severely. Very serious damage may have taken place by then. Thus, it pays to heed early warning signs and to seek out expert advice promptly. Some of these signs are: fuzzy vision; double vision; halos; crossed eyes; "cobwebs," "floaters" and flashes of light;

THE EYE

The eye is actually a direct extension of the brain. The retina, *the light-sensitive structure at the back of the eye, contains millions of* rods *and* cones—*specialized nerve endings which convert light into electrical impulses. These impulses are then conveyed by the* optic nerve *to the* visual center *at the back of the brain, where the individual interprets them as specific images.*

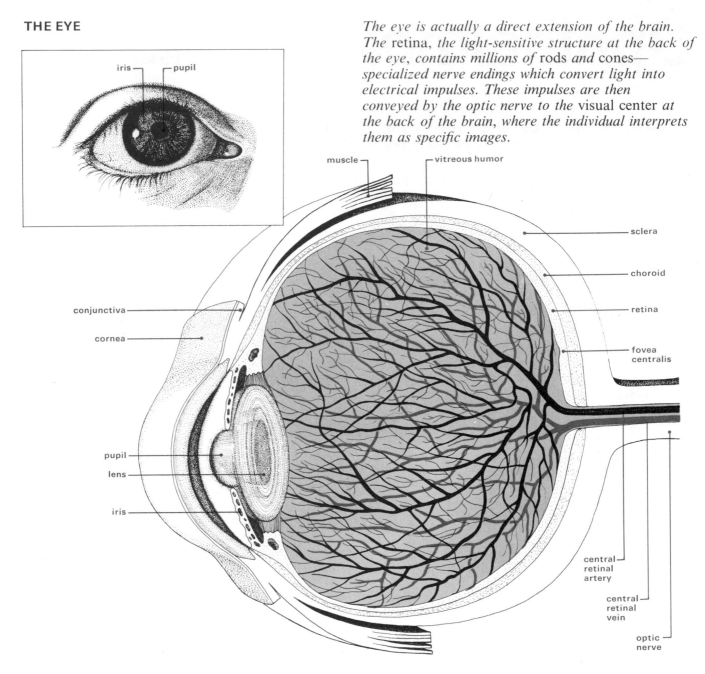

sensitivity to light; inflamed eyes; white pupil; and "cat's-eye" pupil (a slit-like, elongated pupil).

The majority of these complaints are correctible, but checking them out is the only way to spot the serious cases. It is always advisable for adults past the age of 40 to have periodic checkups for glaucoma and, in later years, checkups for cataracts every two years. Patients with sickle cell anemia or diabetes should have their eyes examined at six-month intervals.

Diagnostic procedures

A discussion of the initial examination of the eyes gives the best indication of the wide range of diagnostic testing performed by the modern ophthalmologist.

After taking a specific and general history, the ophthalmologist may position the patient in front of a reading chart to find out if his vision deviates from the standard 20/20. A reading of 20/70 in a given patient means, for instance, that the patient can discern letters at 20 feet that a normally sighted person could see at 70 feet.

The phoropter. Seated behind this device or behind a simple wire trial frame, the patient looks through various combinations of lenses. The combination resulting in the sharpest image is called the *refractive error* and shows whether the patient is near-sighted, far-sighted or astigmatic. ASTIGMATISM is a visual defect caused by a deviation of the cornea from its typical spherical surface.

The retinoscope. Success with the phoropter depends on reliable responses and choices by the patient. Non-cooperative adults and children can be evaluated with a retinoscope, a highly precise instrument that projects predetermined streaks of light into the patient's eye and establishes the refractive error from the behavior of the reflected image of the projected light.

Lens fitting. Once the refractive error is known, the patient can be fitted with either a spectacle lens or a contact lens. Irregular types of astigmatism can be corrected only with a contact lens, the fitting of which must include measurement of the curves of the cornea with an instrument known as a keratometer. Soft CONTACT LENSES will not correct pronounced astigmatism; in these cases, hard contact lenses are prescribed.

Visual field testing. Having the patient fix his gaze on one spot is of key importance in determining his peripheral vision and the location of his normal blind spot (an area at the back of the eye where the optic nerve enters and the light-sensitive rods and cones are absent) or of abnormal blind spots.

Physical examination. The thorough ophthalmologist will check all the external structures of the eye. He will have the patient look in all the directions of gaze and evaluate the action of each eye muscle. He will test the reaction of each pupil to light and to focusing on near objects.

The slit lamp. The slit lamp biomicroscope provides highly magnified views of ocular structures. The patient keeps his head steady on a chin and head rest while the examiner looks at the cornea, anterior chamber, iris, lens or the front part of the vitreous (the transparent gelatin-like substance that fills most of the eyeball). He may place special contact lenses on the anesthetized cornea to look into the angle of the anterior chamber of the eye or to obtain a magnified view of the retina and vitreous cavity.

Tonometers. Measurement of the pressure inside the eyeball (intraocular pressure) is of paramount importance for the detection of GLAUCOMA. The intraocular pressure can be measured painlessly at the slit lamp with an *applanation tonometer* or the pressure can be measured with the patient in the recumbent position by use of the *Schiötz tonometer.* Unlike the other types of tonometer, the *air-blast tonometer* does not require corneal anesthesia, since it does not touch the eyeball.

The *direct ophthalmoscope* is the most frequently used instrument for viewing the central part of the retina at the back of the eye. The *binocular indirect ophthalmoscope* affords an overview of the entire retina and is particularly valuable in detecting retinal tears and detachments. The light emanating from this instrument is quite powerful and can cause some stress to the patient, who should be assured that the examination cannot cause harm to the eye in any way.

In addition to these techniques, the ophthalmologist may order more specialized procedures. They include: (1)

x-rays of the skull and orbit to locate metallic foreign objects or fractures of the bony casing. Other foreign bodies and growths not detectable by ordinary x-rays can be visualized with ultrasound or computerized axial tomography (CAT scan). (For a discussion of the CAT scan, see the appropriate section in the major article on **Examination, Diagnosis and Therapy.**) (2) *Ultrasound studies* of the inner eye, in case the view inside is obstructed, as with dense cataracts or vitreous hemorrhage. (3) *Fluorescein angiography* to locate retinal lesions and degenerations. This technique involves rapid-sequence photographs of the passage of injected fluorescein dye through the retinal blood vessel network. (4) The radioactive P^{32} isotope (radiophosphorus) accumulates in malignant eye tumors and can thus be used to differentiate them from benign tumors. (5) A number of electro-diagnostic techniques, such as the *electroretinogram* and *electro-oculogram,* enable the ophthalmologist to pinpoint otherwise undiagnosable conditions of the retina, choroid and the optic nerve.

Diseases and disorders of the eye

Having listed most of the diagnostic procedures which a patient may encounter today, we will briefly survey some of the major eye abnormalities and their treatment.

Injuries

The eye and the surrounding structures are among the most delicate of the body and can be easily injured.

An injury to the eyelid may result in a drooping upper lid or a lid that won't close. In addition, an inward or outward turning of the margin of an eyelid is sometimes caused by scar formation. All these lid abnormalities, which may also be caused by a preceding illness or degenerative changes, can be helped with reconstructive surgery. Severe lacerations of the lower eyelid may lead to interruptions of the tear-drainage system.

The sudden appearance of a red spot on the white of the eye usually signals the rupture of a superficial blood vessel. The spot, which fades in about two weeks, is of no consequence unless systemic hypertension (high blood pressure) or a clotting disorder is present, in which case the ocular problem could be an indicator of an underlying medical disorder.

Probably the most common eye injury is an abrasion of the cornea (the clear outer covering or "front window" of the eye). The symptoms include a feeling of a foreign body in the eye and a sharp pain every time the eyelid is blinked. The ophthalmologist may outline the abrasion with fluorescein dye and will instill antibiotics prior to immobilizing the eye with a pressure patch. A gritty sensation and a burning feeling in the eye can also be caused by inadequate tear production. These symptoms of the "dry eye" can be treated with artificial tear substitutes.

Foreign bodies deeply embedded in the cornea and corneal lacerations are serious matters and must be treated by an experienced ophthalmic surgeon. (See also KERATITIS.)

Retinal tears and detachments can occur spontaneously or may be associated with trauma. Statistically, retinal tears or detachments are more likely to occur in significantly near-sighted persons. Victims may report flashes, floaters, loss of vision or a "veil" over part or all of the visual field. In most cases, the floaters will turn out to be a benign indication of contraction of the vitreous (the inner gelatinous part of the eye), but examination is still necessary to exclude sight-threatening disorders. If only a peripheral tear is diagnosed, it can be sealed by inducing a scar to surround the tear. The scar can be produced by several techniques, including freezing, heat or laser coagulation. In case of a retinal detachment, the surgical repair becomes much more involved and its outcome most difficult to predict. (See DETACHED RETINA.)

Infectious and inflammatory conditions

Any laceration or abrasion of the eye can be very serious because it opens the route for invading bacteria, viruses and fungi. The cornea itself can be the site of ulcer formation, an extremely painful condition requiring immediate treatment. Infections of the eye caused by *herpes simplex* and *herpes zoster* viruses run a protracted course and can result in extensive visual loss.

Probably the single most frequent inflammatory condition of the eye is CONJUNCTIVITIS. It may be caused by a bacterial or viral infection or by an allergic reaction and is characterized by redness, discharge, itching, burning and a foreign-body sensation about the eyeball and the eyelid. Treatment is directed toward eliminating the offending agent, which in some cases can be determined by taking a culture from the eye.

A STY or a CHALAZION on an eyelid can also be caused by a bacterial infection. Treatment usually involves the administration of antibiotics in combination with hot soaks.

Infections of the tear sac should be treated aggressively with the administration of systemic and local antibiotics, as well as hot soaks, to prevent obstruction to tear drainage by scarring.

Inflammations of the *uvea* (the pigmented vascular layer of the eye, consisting of the iris, ciliary body and choroid) are classified by their specific location, such as IRITIS, cyclitis, iridocyclitis and chorioretinitis. Although the causative organism in pus-forming infections of the uvea may be identified, even rapid and intensive antibiotic treament may not prevent extensive loss of vision in many cases. The specific causes of the much more frequent nonpurulent UVEITIS (inflammation of the uvea) are clouded in mystery, but this affliction is sometimes associated with certain systemic conditions, such as rheumatoid arthritis and ankylosing spondylitis.

In the absence of a systemic association, the uveal inflammation is treated empirically with drops that dilate the pupil and with corticosteroids. Complete cure may never be possible, although treatment may prevent complications such as glaucoma, cataracts and retinal degeneration.

Keratitis is an inflammation of the cornea, the transparent "window" at the front of the eye which bends incoming light into a narrow cone and directs it to the lens. The condition may be associated with conjunctivitis or follow minor injury or damage to the surface of the cornea, when microorganisms become established in the damaged tissue and set up an infection. The major complication is an ulcer of the cornea. Prompt medical treatment is required to prevent the loss of sight; this usually involves the use of tetracycline ointment, atropine eyedrops and the application of hot compresses. (See KERATITIS.)

Degenerative and aging conditions

The cornea is subject to a wide variety of degenerations and dystrophies, some of which will be mentioned here. Note should be made, though, of *Fuchs' dystrophy*, or the inability of the cornea to maintain its normal thickness and clarity. This condition—named after the German ophthalmologist Ernst Fuchs (1851–1930)—may require a corneal transplant.

LASER SURGERY

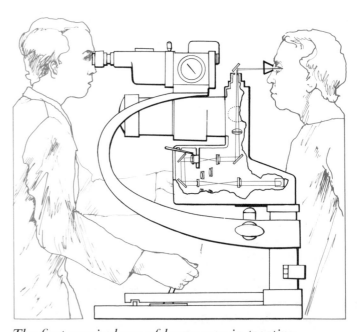

The first surgical use of lasers was in treating certain types of eye disorders, particularly the repair of a detached retina. The intense beam of light is directed into a pinpoint and focused for a split second on the detached part of the retina, producing an inflammation reaction which causes the tissues to fuse together.

In *bullous keratopathy* there is swelling of the cornea, loss of its normal transparency and development of constantly rupturing blisters on the outer corneal layer. A therapeutic soft contact lens may relieve the severe pain from the blisters. In some cases a corneal transplant may be necessary although the procedure is not always successful in curing the condition. Consequently, patients considering a corneal transplant for this condition should review with their ophthalmologists the long-term outlook in their individual cases. (See CORNEAL GRAFTING.)

Still another corneal abnormality, *keratoconus*, is characterized by a conical protrusion of the corneal surface; it produces such a high degree of astigmatism in its advanced stage that it cannot be corrected even with hard contact lenses. Fortunately, visual improvement is possible following a corneal transplant—perhaps one of the most beautiful and refined of all operations. In it, a circular disk of the diseased cornea is replaced with a corresponding disk of clear healthy corneal tissue from a deceased human donor (the cornea must be removed from the donor within 12 hours following death).

Cataracts

A CATARACT is defined as a painless progressive clouding over of the lens of the eye. The vast majority of cataracts are "senile cataracts," but some are congenital or associated with trauma or such diseases as uveitis, diabetes mellitus, hypothyroidism and atopic dermatitis.

Because there is approximately a 2% incidence of retinal detachment following cataract surgery, cataract removal is a serious step, not to be embarked upon lightly or without good indications. Congenital cataracts in one eye are best left untouched in children, since good results cannot be guaranteed in this age group.

As a general rule, in children and young adults up to 30 years of age the back part of the capsule membrane covering the lens is not removed—instead, an "extracapsular extraction" is performed. In persons over 30, the entire capsule sac and the sac contents are removed at one time; this is called an "intracapsular cataract extraction." With the advent of fine sutures and the use of an operating microscope, the latter operation now produces excellent results. This is the standard form of cataract extraction performed today. The day after surgery the patient can be out of bed and can even be discharged.

Within the past several years, *phacoemulsification* has gained some acceptance within the field of ophthalmology as a presumably better method of cataract extraction. In this method, which is a form of extracapsular extraction, the lens is broken up within the eye by an ultrasonic probe that vibrates approximately 40,000 times a second. The probe suctions off the emulsified material while irrigating the chamber. There is no well-controlled study published in the scientific literature to date which demonstrates convincingly that the visual results obtained from phacoemulsification are superior to those of routine intracapsular surgery. It would seem to some surgeons that potential complications from surgery might be more difficult to remedy after phacoemulsification than after intracapsular extraction.

Yet another decision exists which the patient must make with his physician prior to cataract surgery. During the 1970s, there was a resurgence in the implantation of an artificial intraocular lens at the time of cataract extraction. With this lens in place, there is no need for contact lens correction or for special "cataract glasses." It must be kept in mind, however, that lens implantation does increase somewhat the risk of postoperative complications. Thus, the choice of the intraocular lens versus the use of contact lenses or cataract glasses must be weighed carefully.

Diseases of the optic nerve

These are particularly important not only because they can impair vision but also because they may indicate problems in the central nervous system. Increased pressure within the skull, for example, may cause swelling and congestion of the nerve, resulting in an enlarged blind spot. An impediment of the circulation in the optic nerve, characterized by a marked loss of vision, may be the result of arteriosclerotic degeneration or of temporal arteritis. The latter condition is usually treated with high doses of corticosteroids to prevent total loss of vision. Blood studies and temporal artery biopsy can be performed which will substantiate the diagnostic possibility of temporal arteritis.

Optic atrophy, evidenced by a loss of nerve fibers and of nerve substance, can be the end result of many disease processes. It may be associated with loss of the visual field, loss of visual acuity and deficient color perception. The finding of optic atrophy, not fully explained by a disease process within the eye, demands a thorough medical and neurological evaluation.

Retinal Disorders. Disorders of the circulatory system can become manifest in the retinal circulation. Systemic hypertension, for example, can affect the circulation through the blood vessels of the retina. Small chips breaking off the walls of arteriosclerotic blood vessels elsewhere in the body can lodge in the central retinal artery. Aspiration of fluid from the anterior chamber of the eye, if performed promptly (i.e., within 30 minutes of the occlusion), may restore some vision, but this is virtually always impossible and so the general outcome of central retinal occlusion is complete and permanent visual loss. The occlusion of the central retinal vein can result in profound loss of vision, but some return of visual function can be expected.

Diabetic retinopathy

An important population group which should be concerned about retinal degeneration are diabetics, who

THE RETINA

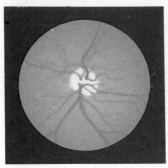
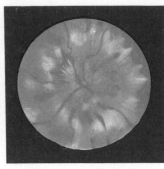

Normal retina as seen through an ophthalmoscope

Hypertensive retinopathy as seen through an ophthalmoscope

Examination of the retina and its blood vessels is a routine feature of most general medical examinations. The ophthalmoscope is a simple optical instrument with a light source, by means of which the general physician—as well as the ophthalmologist—can detect not only primary disorders of the eye but also signs of various bodily disorders, including evidence of high blood pressure and changes associated with diabetes.

number approximately 5 million in the United States. Diabetes damages retinal circulation with the development of hemorrhages and leakage of edema fluid into the retina, which can be responsible for loss of clear vision. The effect on the retina tends not to be as severe in patients who have reasonably good control of their diabetes. (See DIABETES MELLITUS.)

In patients with diabetes, and especially in those with juvenile-onset diabetes, there is often a gradual proliferation of new fragile blood vessels ("neovascularization"). This may occur on the head of the optic nerve and on the retina, sometimes extending even into the vitreous cavity. These new vessels are prone to rupture with the production of potentially sight-threatening vitreous hemorrhages.

The argon laser has emerged as the mainstay of treatment for diabetic retinopathy. It must be emphasized, however, that not all diabetics can be helped with laser therapy (which, incidentally, is in no way painful). Scientifically controlled studies show that laser treatments may be of some benefit in retarding proliferation of the new blood vessels and in preserving macular function. In general, it should be remembered that the earlier the retinal signs of diabetes are detected and treated, the better is the prognosis for sight preservation in any given patient. Consequently, it is imperative for all patients with histories of diabetes to have thorough baseline eye examinations at periodic intervals.

One of the more disastrous complications of diabetic retinopathy (damage to the retina associated with diabetes mellitus) is persistent vitreous hemorrhage, which was surgically untreatable until a few years ago. Today, some patients can be helped with *vitrectomy*, a procedure in which a very fine nibbling device (guided with the aid of a microscope into the vitreous cavity) chews up and flushes out debris and blood residue.

Macular degeneration

This process can occur at any age, but is most common in the elderly, who report a slowly progressive loss of reading vision and of sharp distance vision. Treatment of macular degeneration has not proved remarkably successful to date, and laser therapy of this condition is still in its very early stages.

It is most important for the patient with this condition to keep in mind that this is not a blinding disease. While he may not be able to read, the patient will, in all likelihood, retain good peripheral vision and will be able to walk about and function well enough to take care of himself.

Glaucoma

This is one of the most common of the serious eye ailments. GLAUCOMA is defined as a condition in which loss of visual field and damage to the optic nerve have occurred due to abnormally high pressure within the eye. The most common form of glaucoma is chronic simple glaucoma, which can be found in 1–2% of all adults over the age of 40. It is symptomless until very late in its course. The cornerstone of therapy for glaucoma is the use of *miotic drugs* (which cause the pupil of the eye to contract) to facilitate the drainage of the aqueous humor. Miotic drops, such as pilocarpine, may cause brow ache and eyestrain and tend to dim the patient's vision, especially in the presence of cataracts.

In the vast majority of patients with glaucoma, miotics alone or in combination with epinephrine and carbonic anhydrase inhibitor pills will control the pressure. For the small minority, a drainage pathway has to be created surgically to allow the aqueous humor to leave the eye. With modern refinements, "filtering surgery" is successful in approximately 80% of cases; in the unsuccessful cases, the pathway becomes occluded through scarring.

Another type of operation, called *peripheral iridectomy*, is used to correct *angle-closure glaucoma*—a much less common but still potentially devastating form of adult glaucoma. The first manifestation of this condition may be an acute crisis, when the pressure within the eyeball rises suddenly, causing severe pain with accompanying redness and a decrease in vision. The patient typically reports seeing halos around lights and may complain of nausea. Initially, the eye pressure must be controlled with drugs. Once pressure has been stabilized, a small piece of the iris (the colored aperture near the front of the eye) is removed at the base, allowing free flow of the aqueous from the posterior chamber into the anterior chamber.

The secondary glaucomas comprise a wide spectrum of disease entities. In these abnormalities, high pressure within the eye develops as a complication of trauma or such diverse conditions as uveitis, cataracts, tumors or diabetic retinopathy, to mention only a few.

Congenital defects

Strabismus. Strabismus (crossed eyes) occurs when one eye deviates from its normally expected position as the other eye fixes upon an object. The condition is found in approximately 1–2% of children. It is a potentially serious abnormality because the brain suppresses signals from the deviating eye in order to avoid double vision. The visual acuity in that eye deteriorates because of disuse and the deterioration may become irreversible if not detected and treated early enough. (See STRABISMUS.)

The basic corrective measure is to place a patch over the sound eye, forcing the child to use the deviating eye. Glasses are prescribed as indicated. Once the deviating eye can hold fixation indefinitely, its outer muscles can be adjusted surgically to improve ocular alignment. The operation is a cosmetic one and has no effect on the vision itself.

Tumors. Arising from the retina, *retinoblastoma* is the most common malignant intraocular tumor in children. The condition is bilateral in about 30% of such patients. Its presenting signs include a yellow or a white pupillary reflex or a misalignment of the affected eye. In unilateral cases, the usual preferred treatment is to remove the affected eye; in bilateral cases, the usual approach is to remove the worse eye and to treat the better eye with some combination of chemotherapy, radiation and light coagulation.

Tumors of the uveal tract are of great clinical importance in adult ophthalmology. They include benign lesions; for example, certain types of benign melanomas of the iris and the choroid. However, the uveal tract is also subject to malignant melanomas—of the choroid, ciliary body and the iris, in order of decreasing frequency. The uveal tract can also harbor cancer cells spread from a site elsewhere in the body, including the breast and lungs.

On occasion, when a malignant melanoma of the choroid is diagnosed, removal of the affected eye is usually advised. The advice is usually met with an extreme amount of emotional distress by the patient, and understandably so. However, it is important for the patient to realize that the removal of the eye may save his life. Furthermore, with modern surgical techniques and the fitting of an artificial eye, very favorable cosmetic results are obtained.

Ophthalmology and the future

Cornea

One of the most serious and emergent conditions in all of ophthalmic practice is posed by chemical burns to the eye. The tragic aspect of these burns is that, despite timely emergency measures, extreme corneal damage can occur quickly and inexorably. Attempts to graft a new cornea on the damaged eye often fail, despite the most sophisticated of modern corneal transplant techniques.

This state of affairs has stimulated the development of a "keratoprosthesis," or plastic cornea, which can be sutured to the front of the eye. The long-term success of these plastic implants has been superior in chemical burns to the results obtained with standard corneal transplants. The keratoprosthesis remains, however, a new and controversial procedure; this is because ophthalmologists are still undecided about whether it should be employed as a primary procedure in certain cases or whether the more conventional corneal transplantation should be performed first and keratoprosthesis considered only when this fails.

At any rate, the keratoprosthesis exemplifies the bright, innovative future of corneal surgery. Problems still remain, however, including the occurrence of extrusion many years after surgery. Many technological advances for smoother and more successful results in hitherto inoperable cases are in the offing. *Ocular immunology* is also rapidly developing and will ultimately provide new insights into the immune mechanism governing the anterior segment of the eye. These insights may give us increasing control over the corneal rejection process.

The use of a relatively new type of microscope, the *corneal endothelial specular microscope*, for the study of the corneal endothelium will afford ophthalmologists a most sophisticated view of the response of this most critical corneal layer to various medical and surgical procedures. One hopes these techniques will lead to breakthroughs in the diagnosis and management of corneal disorders.

Uvea

For future developments in the treatment of disorders of the uveal tract—a most frustrating and bewildering group—we will also have to look to the work of ocular immunologists. Their studies on animal models of uveitis may ultimately lead us to the cause and to an effective management of human uveitis of unknown cause.

Cataracts

Ideally, it may be possible to translate the results of many scientifically controlled studies of cataract formation into the development of a medical regimen for the prevention or dissolution of cataracts. In the meantime, further refinements in cataract surgery will undoubtedly emerge. Newer, safer and more sophisticated methods of intraocular lens implantation will be the procedure of choice for some patients. For others, the ideal solution will be a continuous-wear contact lens which provides good visual acuity even in the presence of significant astigmatism. The *silicone lens*, which is currently under investigation, may be the prototype of such contact lenses.

Very early trials would indicate that it may also be possible to reshape the cornea surgically following cataract extraction so that neither cataract glasses, contact lenses, nor intraocular lens implantation is required.

Retina

The future of retino-vitreal studies promises to be a very active one. New microsurgical techniques are constantly being developed to treat heretofore inoperable cases of retinal detachment, as well as inoperable cases of severe proliferative retinopathy with vitreal complications.

More advanced types of retinal and choroidal angiography may allow us to map out, even in greater detail than now possible, the precise blood vessel abnormalities responsible for retinal disorders, particularly macular degenerations. This, we hope, will lead us to new and more fruitful applications of laser therapy.

Glaucoma

We may look forward to the general widespread use of new drugs that will more effectively regulate inside-the-eye pressure in this disorder, but will not have the unpleasant side effects associated with the current use of miotics or epinephrine.

Strabismus

In the future we hope to have ever more predictable guidelines for the surgical treatment of strabismus. We may witness the application of special electrophysiological and computer programming techniques to help design appropriate treatment for the more complicated ocular deviations, particularly those requiring multiple reoperations.

Conclusion

We have briefly reviewed the major diagnostic techniques, specific problems and therapeutic approaches as practiced in modern ophthalmology. And we have allowed ourselves glimpses into the future to perceive the paths that ophthalmologic research will probably follow during the next decade. The future of ophthalmology is indeed a bright one, from which many people will benefit.

One word in conclusion. As in other areas of modern medicine in which transplantation of healthy organs from a deceased person is possible, the donation of such organs at death can provide great happiness and, in many cases, a return to normal life for many people. This is especially true of healthy corneas from eyes donated for transplantation. Such gifts surely must represent the highest expression of human concern for one's fellowman. (You can discuss this possibility with your physician.)

See also ACCOMMODATION, BLINDNESS, COLOR BLINDNESS, MYOPIA, NIGHT BLINDNESS, VISION.

Otolaryngology Dr. Robert M. Hui

Most people have had some problem with their ears, nose or throat that demanded prompt medical attention; children are particularly vulnerable. In most cases the family physician is able to treat such problems successfully. In particularly troublesome or persistent cases, however, it may be necessary to seek the advice of an expert who specializes in this part of the body—the otolaryngologist.

Otolaryngology is the branch of medical science concerned with the diagnosis and treatment of diseases and disorders of the ear, nose and throat. It thus includes the basic organs of communication—the larynx and related structures for creating meaningful sounds, and the ear for receiving them.

In addition, otolaryngology is concerned with the organs that maintain the sense of balance and with those that govern the senses of smell and taste. Not long ago, the specialty of ear, nose and throat disorders was known as "oto*rhino*laryngology"—the dropped two syllables accounting for the nose—but the term proved to be too much of a tongue twister for everyone concerned.

Although Celsus, the 1st-century Roman physician-writer, mentioned tonsillectomy and uvulotomy in his records, otolaryngology remained at an undefined stage until the 16th and 17th centuries. During this period, advances were made in understanding the anatomy of the ear, the nasal sinuses and the throat muscles. These advances were mainly anatomical, dependent as they were on the development of special mirrors and lights with which to inspect the eardrums, the internal part of the nose and the throat.

In the 18th century, the ear structures were studied further and better understood, but the physiology of the ear was not. This period contributed the insight that the apparently separate structures—the ear, nose and throat—are an interconnected network of passages that should be regarded, from a clinical point of view, as one system. During this century the *Eustachian catheter* was tested and a surgical technique was introduced for the removal of the bony process behind the ear (mastoidectomy) as a way of limiting middle-ear infections. Brain abscesses were recognized as a possible complication of ear infections.

The reader should keep in mind that in human evolutionary development, the ear, nose and throat had to share the narrow confines of the head with the developing brain—and in the neck with the vital channels of nerves and blood vessels connecting the head to the trunk. As a result, the otolaryngologist must deal with small and delicate organs or organs that are tightly packed, much like lines in a coaxial cable.

The 19th century witnessed the emergence of some surgical techniques capable of dealing with these sensitive structures. Because of their unique qualities, otolaryngology received early recognition as a separate surgical specialty. In the United States, in fact, the demanding qualifications of a doctor required to treat these highly specialized structures were accorded specialty status (just after those of ophthalmology were recognized).

Today's otolaryngologist—who is certified by the American Board of Otolaryngology—has had a year of internship, a year's training as a general surgical resident and three years of advanced training. In the last-named stage of preparation, he or she has chosen one anatomical area to be at home with, such as the nose or the ear, or one problem area to be proficient in, such as allergic reactions, cancer or plastic surgery. Such specialization is not surprising, given the delicacy and the minuteness of the organs.

The ear

The structures which conduct sound are extremely fragile and deserving of the greatest expertise and circumspection.

The deep end of the external ear canal, which is a little more than one inch long, is closed off by the three-layered eardrum, of which much the larger part is taut; the flaccid part accommodates pressure variations of the middle ear. Braced against the tense drum on the inside is the footlike end of the first of three minute bones, suspended in the empty cavity by ligaments. The bones—called the hammer *(malleus)*, the anvil *(incus)* and the stirrup *(stapes)*—conduct vibrations picked up by the eardrum across the middle ear, amplifying them 17-fold.

Attached to the "oval window" separating the middle ear from the inner ear, the stirrup makes waves in the liquid filling the mazelike labyrinth—which consists of the *vestibule*, the *semicircular canals* and the *cochlea* ("snail shell"). The cochlea accommodates along its convoluted length a spiral tube containing special hair cells connected to the endings of the auditory nerve. The hair cells are sandwiched by two membranes, one of which—the *basilar membrane*—is extremely taut. When vibrations of the liquid in the inner ear reach that membrane, its tension

THE EAR

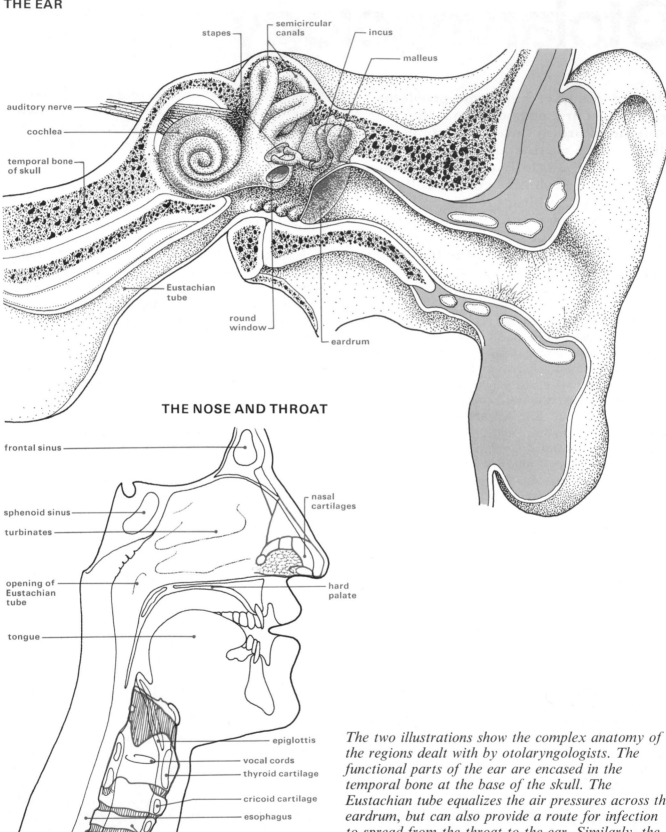

stapes

semicircular canals

incus

malleus

auditory nerve

cochlea

temporal bone of skull

Eustachian tube

round window

eardrum

THE NOSE AND THROAT

frontal sinus

nasal cartilages

sphenoid sinus

turbinates

opening of Eustachian tube

hard palate

tongue

epiglottis

vocal cords

thyroid cartilage

cricoid cartilage

esophagus

trachea

The two illustrations show the complex anatomy of the regions dealt with by otolaryngologists. The functional parts of the ear are encased in the temporal bone at the base of the skull. The Eustachian tube equalizes the air pressures across the eardrum, but can also provide a route for infection to spread from the throat to the ear. Similarly, the air sinuses in the skull communicate with the nose through openings under the turbinates.

creates a shearing force many times stronger than the impulse from the stirrup. The rubbing action of the membranes on the hair cells generates electrical signals that travel to the brain and are translated there into perceived sounds.

I must mention also that the hair cells, part of the *organ of Corti*, can be stimulated by vibrations received by bone conduction—such as the sound of one's chewing or humming. The ability to perceive sounds through the bone of the skull but not through the ear points to an obstruction in the middle ear or external ear as the cause of the deafness.

Of the other parts of the labyrinth, the three semicircular canals help the brain keep track of the head's movements while the vestibule reports to the brain on the body's position. These structures are traversed by nerve fibers ending with bunches of hair cells. All head movements or changes in the body's position cause fluctuations in the inner ear's fluid, which bend the hair cells.

The nose

The external nose covers the beginning of a complex cavity divided into halves by a thin wall called the *nasal septum* and filled with three or four fleshy, streamlined ridges. These ridges—called *turbinates*—are attached to the side wall of the nose and run almost its whole length.

Located in bones adjacent to the nose and connected to the main cavity are about two dozen air cavities called the *sinuses*. The walls of both the sinuses and the nasal cavity are covered with a layer of special hair cells, which propagate a sticky lining of mucus.

The streamlined passageways inside the nose break up the inhaled air, so that it passes the sticky lining in thin steady streams. The size of the streams can be adjusted to outside temperature by erectile tissue. During its passage through the nose, lasting a quarter of a second, the inspired air is humidified and its temperature usually raised to the body's internal temperature by contact with the fleshy protuberances. Mucus-secreting glands in the sticky lining also contribute to the humidity, if the air is too dry. Thus the nose acts as a "homeostatic" mechanism for the body.

The work of the body's most efficient air-processing plant would not be complete without the removal of air-borne bacteria and air pollutants. Probably because of its opposite electric polarity, most of the inhaled foreign matter is trapped by the sticky mucus, which covers all the crannies and recesses of the nose, sinuses, Eustachian tubes, the pharynx and the whole bronchial network. The mucus contains *lysozyme* (also known as *muramidase)*, the enzyme that zeroes in on bacteria and dissolves them. The unique hair cells (or *cilia*), bending in wavelike unison, constantly move the mucus containing the debris of pollutants and trapped bacteria to the throat entrance, where the mucus is automatically swallowed. Stomach acids then dissolve the bacteria that have managed to survive the lysozyme line of defense. The system is so efficient in most people that barely a battalion from the entire armies of bacteria entering through the nostrils reaches the pharynx alive.

Our sense of smell is derived from a patch of *olfactory receptor cells* in the roof of the nose. Distributed evenly in a layer of supporting cells, the receptor ends of the olfactory cells protrude from the surface of the nasal cavity and are supplied by half a dozen or more cilia. It is believed that particles or molecules in the air start a chemical reaction when they brush against the receptor cells, which is interpreted in the brain as a specific smell.

The throat

The throat is an expressway into the body and has two main access routes, the nose and the mouth. It is furthermore connected with the ears via the Eustachian tubes. In its nether reaches, the throat divides into the windpipe and the esophagus (gullet). Concerned with the production of articulated sounds and with swallowing, the throat is encircled by rings of muscle and cartilage.

At the turn-off for the windpipe, which is in front of the esophagus, the throat has a lidlike protuberance called the *epiglottis*. During swallowing, the epiglottic lid combines with the valvelike action of the *false vocal cords* to deflect all solid and liquid matter into the esophagus.

Located at the top end of the windpipe, the *larynx* is more than a mere "voice box." The larynx is operated by five muscles, used for opening and closing the airway and for tensing the vocal cords in the production of sound. In addition to their protective function, the closing muscles of the larynx rhythmically change the atmospheric pressure in the lungs, thus creating a pumping effect on the blood circulating through that organ. The muscles of the larynx also help expel foreign substances or accumulated impurities from the bronchial tree.

The other noteworthy areas of the throat include the *tonsils*—attachments of lymphoid tissue on the throat wall—and the taste buds—chemical receptors for taste—in the back of the tongue. Depending on your age, there are usually more than 200 taste buds on *each* of the nipple-like elevations on the top of the tongue; with advancing age this number is greatly reduced. The taste buds can distinguish among only four basic sensations—sweet, sour (or acid), salty and bitter. Nuances of flavor are registered by our sense of *smell*—and this is why food often "tastes" different (or even seems tasteless) when our nose is blocked during a common cold.

The otolaryngological examination

When to visit an otolaryngologist. Many of the reasons for going to an ear, nose and throat (E.N.T.) specialist are self-evident, for example, heavy nosebleeds or a sharp earache, but there are a number of warning signs and symptoms that also call for an E.N.T. consultation. They include:

Oozing from the ear; the sensation of hissing, buzzing, or ringing sounds in the head; episodes of diminished hearing; persistent dizziness with vomiting and an inability to maintain balance; discomfort in swallowing; a feeling of obstruction in the nose, or an unpleasant secretion from one nostril; enlargement or hardening of lymph nodes in the neck, and a sore throat and persistent hoarseness of the voice, accompanied by an inability to completely "clear the throat." Abnormalities in facial structure—both congenital or traumatic—are treated as well.

Critical information. The thorough otolaryngologist will have a multitude of questions to ask before the start of the actual examination. Besides the details of the specific complaint and of past illnesses, the patient should volunteer information about any of the above-mentioned signs and symptoms.

The checkup. The examination itself will take place with the patient in a sitting position. Besides the ever-present head mirror, which directs a reflected light beam at the area being examined, the otolaryngologist will use a hand-held otoscope to view the eardrum, having first cleared the canal of any excess earwax. The basic equipment of the ear, nose and throat specialist also consists of an ear speculum and a nasal speculum to widen the passageways and of small, round mirrors attached to thin handles for viewing the larynx and the internal part of the nose.

Using the small mirrors, the otolaryngologist will gently inspect the back part of the patient's nose and the throat. The examiner may apply a mild anesthetic to minimize the patient's discomfort or to preclude a pronounced gag reflex. The larynx can be seen with a "laryngeal mirror" while the otolaryngologist holds down the patient's tongue.

The condition of the patient's sinuses can be determined by directing a strong light source through them in the dark (a technique known as *transillumination*).

The initial tool for testing a person's hearing is a tuning fork, but if there is any evidence of hearing loss or any disturbance of the balance apparatus, more extensive tests are in order. They include *audiometry* (which is itself a specialized diagnostic area) with a sound-producing electronic device connected to the patient by earphones. The patient's sensitivity to loudness, prolonged noise, small changes in sound intensity and to an interrupted tone helps the discerning audiologist determine where the patient's trouble lies.

Disorders of the patient's balance apparatus in the inner ear are studied by evaluating rapid eye movements and other reactions after irrigating the patient's ears, one after the other, with cold or warm water. Although the cold douche is a bit unpleasant, the test is advisable because the results very often pinpoint the trouble.

Finally, the otolaryngologist will incorporate into the general examination a search of the patient's neck for enlarged lymph nodes or other abnormalities of gross structure.

Diseases of the head and neck

Otolaryngological conditions range from those that are merely annoying to conditions which can be life threatening. Many require immediate attention; others can be taken care of at the mutual convenience of the patient and the doctor.

The external ear

The ear canal on the outer side of the eardrum is open to all manner of irritants—from alcohol, cotton swabs and hairpins to earplugs or water. If they are applied often enough (mostly in well-meant attempts to practice good hygiene), they result in either too little earwax or in its impaction at the end of the canal. In the former case, the normally acid environment of the canal becomes alkaline, permitting some dangerous bacteria to take hold. In the latter case, water trapped by the plug of earwax leads to maceration of the canal's sensitive skin. In either event, the canal can become inflamed (OTITIS EXTERNA), with accompanying pain or fever.

Very often, a period of intermittent itching in the canal serves as a harbinger of the inflammation to follow. The condition clears up after removal of the byproducts of the inflammation, such as pus, and the instillation of antibiotic drops.

The prognosis is equally favorable in inflammations of the eardrum itself which are caused by injury from hairpins and the like or by pathogenic organisms as a complication of an upper respiratory infection. The intense pain characteristic of this condition can be lessened with analgesic eardrops. If the eardrum has been accidentally punctured, the edges of the wound can be approximated under the microscope to assist spontaneous healing.

Middle-ear disease

Conditions of the middle ear are often predicated on a blockage of the Eustachian tube or on an invasion of the middle-ear cavity by microorganisms via the tube.

Serous effusion. A blockage of the tube, caused most frequently by an infectious or an allergic process in the throat, sets up negative pressure within the closed-off chamber of the middle ear, drawing forth a serous effusion of fluid from surrounding structures. The fluid, appearing through a mechanical effect rather than a disease process, results in reduced hearing and sometimes in some pain or the sensation of noises in the head.

The treatment of this condition, which is seen mostly in young children, is directed at removing the blockage of the Eustachian tube. In obstinate cases, a small, fast-healing incision can be made in the eardrum to relieve the middle ear of the accumulated fluid with placement of a plastic drainage tube. Antibiotics should be prescribed if the fluid contains microorganisms, which it very well might.

When a throat infection has traveled up the Eustachian tube to the middle ear, the most frequent complaints are a mild earache and fever. This stage of middle-ear disease is called *acute serous otitis media* and may develop into the purulent stage if proper antibiotic therapy is not instituted.

Acute purulent otitis media. This development may follow the serous stage by only a few hours and is characterized by the buildup of gas and pus inside the middle ear. The pressure inside changes from negative to positive, threatening rupture of the eardrum. In contrast with the mild pain of serous otitis media, the pain in this stage tends to be pronounced, with an accompanying sense of fullness in the ear, buzzing, chills, malaise (a general feeling of being unwell) and vomiting. The modern otolaryngologist relies primarily on the administration of antibiotics and sulfonamides to combat the infection. An incision of the eardrum to withdraw the pus from the middle-ear cavity should be undertaken if the drug therapy does not yield prompt results.

Chronic purulent otitis media. Certain inherited structural weaknesses, such as a poorly aerated mastoid process or childhood infections that made the mucous membranes less resistant to bacteria, favor the development of chronic middle-ear disease. The chronic form is likely to develop if the underlying problem—the blockage of the Eustachian tube—is itself caused by a chronic inflammation in the nasal cavity or by a chronic allergy.

Today's otolaryngologist will try to counteract the principal danger of chronic purulent otitis media—slow loss of hearing—by eliminating the conditions which favor it. The countermeasures include surgical removal of the infected tissue in the throat or a defective, fluid-permeated mastoid process.

The chronic purulent form of middle-ear disease varies in severity from mild cases involving an odorless discharge and no destructive changes, to infections with a foul discharge and with damage to the inner ear, brain, or the facial nerve.

Frequently seen in the chronic purulent form, cystlike formations called *cholesteatomas* may erode the delicate sound-conducting bones in the middle ear. Some cholesteatomas arise from the upper part of the eardrum due to repeated negative pressure and contribute to the development of chronic purulent otitis media. Other cholesteatomas are secondary to the disease, developing from infectious changes in the eardrum. Those cholesteatomas that are secondary to the disease are more likely to interfere with sound conduction.

A total loss of hearing in this condition usually indicates that the disease has spread to the inner ear. Another alarming symptom is the presence of pain, dizziness, or facial paralysis.

The less serious cases of purulent otitis media should be treated conservatively, although it must be understood that such approaches may include (if necessary) surgery to insure continued drainage of the cavity and to guarantee an open Eustachian tube.

Modern surgical techniques permit the restoration of hearing even in ears extensively ravaged by chronic middle-ear disease, once the suppurative process has been stopped.

These procedures are: in severe cases, the removal of the mastoid to eliminate all traces of the infection, followed by extensive muscle grafting to fill the empty space; the reconstruction of the eardrum through sophisticated grafting of the patient's own vein tissue or fascia; the attachment of the eardrum to any of the three bones after the removal of the bones damaged by disease; the substitution of the damaged bone-conduction chain with a prosthesis made of Teflon or stainless steel, or with cartilage. (See also OTITIS MEDIA, STAPEDECTOMY.)

Inner-ear disease

The most frequent complaints suggesting an inner-ear problem are vertigo (spinning sensation) and ear noises, but they may also signal any one of a combination of other problems, such as cardiovascular disease, hypertension, arteriosclerosis, meningitis and even overexposure to certain chemicals or to alcohol or tobacco.

In the presence of chronic middle-ear disease, these symptoms—especially if they are accompanied by fever—may indicate an extension of the infectious process into the labyrinth, a development meriting prompt surgical intervention. (See also OTITIS INTERNA.)

Ménière's disease. The most common type of inner-ear disorder is Ménière's disease, in which an excess of the inner ear's lymphatic fluid presses on the sensitive structures of the labyrinth.

Two diagnostic points are worth remembering in this disorder. (1) the excess fluid may be triggered by a period of stress; and (2) the first symptoms are all kinds of ear noises and problems with sound perception, followed (a few moments or even years later) by vertigo.

Attacks of dizziness and nausea are the more easily treated aspects of MÉNIÈRE'S DISEASE. Attempts to control the overproduction of the internal lymph, or the absorption of the fluid, are among other treatment approaches. However, neither approach has met with consistent success.

Other conditions that lead to a loss of hearing include OTOSCLEROSIS and damage to the hair cells in the cochlea or of the nerve connection between the inner ear and the brain. Otosclerosis, which is most common in women between the ages of 18 and 40, is characterized by a change in the bone that immobilizes the stirrup (stapes). Today most patients can have satisfactory hearing restored with a stapes prosthesis, which I mentioned earlier.

An alarming source of gradual hearing loss through the wearing down of hair cells in the cochlea must be mentioned here. Many industries have introduced measures to protect their workers from excessive noise levels, which wear down the hair cells. While we do not yet know exactly how this happens, we do know that high noise levels can lead to a loss of hearing. The fans of modern rock groups remain exposed to dangerously high levels of sound—both at live concerts and at home in the privacy of their earphones. The degree of hearing loss in the nation remains to be estimated, but it is certain that the hearing of many teenagers will turn out to have been impaired.

Diseases of the nose

The Eustachian tube should be kept free of obstructions at its opening in the back of the nasal cavity, as previously mentioned. Unfortunately, the nose is an open house to many noxious invaders from airborne, allergens to cold viruses. The inflammations they cause can easily obstruct the tube. (See also the major article on **Allergy and Immunology.**)

Allergic rhinitis. Allergic inflammations of the nasal membranes can be seasonal, as in hay fever, or perennial, if the allergen is present the year round. If the substance cannot be avoided, the patient is given antihistamine therapy and drugs to reduce nasal congestion. Persons with allergic rhinitis are statistically more likely to develop *nasal polyps*, soft appendages arising from the mucous membrane of the nose. Although they are otherwise harmless, they should be removed if they obstruct breathing or sinus drainage.

Nasal obstruction. Blockages of the efficient ventilation system predispose patients to upper respiratory infections. The types of obstructive defect and their causes are too numerous to mention here, but it can be said that most all structural defects (such as a deviated septum) can be corrected by surgery.

Acute rhinitis. The best advice for the common cold sufferer seems to be bed rest for a couple of days. If a persistent runny nose is troublesome, nasal decongestants may be prescribed.

Chronic rhinitis. Of the several types of chronic rhinitis, one should note the *hypertrophic* kind, which develops in many patients from repeated infections of the nose or of the sinuses. In others it seems to follow endocrine changes. The treatment should focus on loosening the secretions, which tend to be thicker than in the acute form.

Atrophic rhinitis. The other type of chronic inflammation is characterized by a dry membrane and the formation of foul-smelling crusts. Of unknown cause, atrophic rhinitis does not have a specific treatment. Palliative measures consist of irrigations and emollient sprays containing estrogen. (See RHINITIS.)

Sinusitis. The air chambers surrounding the nasal cavity are exposed to practically the same pathogens as the nose.

SINUSITIS usually disappears along with the nasal inflammation that caused it. The chronic type of sinusitis is often accompanied by an ache, whose location indicates which sinuses are involved. While acute sinusitis can be treated with judicious doses of vasoconstrictor drugs and sinus drainage, the chronic form may require enzyme therapy, suction to relieve the pain, surgical repair of any obstructive deformities and a rational use of antibiotics.

Nosebleeds. Repeated nosebleeds (epistaxis) may be a warning flag for any number of conditions, or they may be an innocent consequence of a local disturbance. In any case, the "garden-variety" type of bleeding can usually be stopped by having the patient sit up and tilt the head forward. Applications of a cold compress or ice pack to the bridge of the nose and to the neck are helpful. Heavy bleeding may require packing and cautery of the bleeding vessel. (See NOSEBLEED.)

Throat disease

The structures of the throat are tightly packed in a limited space, just below the base of the skull and adjacent to vital vascular and nerve connections. Apparently local symptoms in the throat area may mask the beginning of a benign tumor or of malignant lesions, which are not uncommon in the throat tissues and which can easily spread to organs

TONSILLITIS

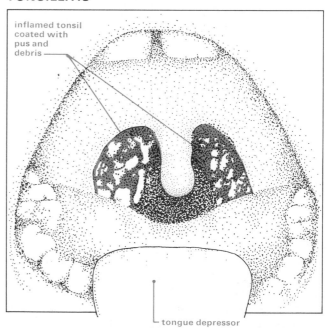

inflamed tonsil coated with pus and debris

tongue depressor

Tonsillitis occurs most often in children and may be caused by bacteria or viruses. The child has a high fever and if old enough will complain of a sore throat and difficulty in swallowing. If the fever does not abate after two days rest with regular doses of aspirin and plenty of fluids, a course of penicillin is necessary. Repeated attacks may require tonsillectomy.

nearby. If discovered early, these cancers may be tackled with deep-radiation therapy or excision. This is why it is important to have all seemingly innocuous complaints—such as nosebleeds, earache, or any neck swelling—thoroughly investigated.

In addition, the tonsils and adenoids, which form a defense perimeter around the main corridor into the body, are the potential sites of acute and chronic infections, which account for a sizeable percentage of complaints about "sore throats."

Acute tonsillitis. Despite the customary high fever and difficulty in swallowing, an inflammation of the tonsils is usually transitory. A return to normal can be speeded by the administration of appropriate antibiotics and the relief of symptoms by the use of moderately hot throat irrigations or gargles.

Chronic tonsillitis. The most frequently encountered of all throat diseases, chronic tonsil inflammation more often than not also involves the adenoids. The patients have a sore throat, nasal discharge, low-grade fever, susceptibility to colds and a fetid breath. Although surgical removal of the tonsils (TONSILLECTOMY) is not performed as routinely as it was years ago, the operation may be advised in persistently troublesome cases. (See TONSILLITIS.)

Acute pharyngitis. This condition, a frequent "satellite" infection of the tonsils, can be diagnosed from a feeling of burning dryness and scratchiness in the throat, in addition to signs of fever and difficult swallowing. The treatment of this condition resembles that of acute tonsillitis. A chronic inflammation of the pharynx may follow persistent strain of the voice or smoking and an excessive consumption of hard liquor.

The first step toward rectifying this condition is to avoid the irritants that led to the inflammation in the first place. Throat swabs and gentle irrigations may be tried in helping the throat membrane to recover.

Acute laryngitis. This complication can follow any inflammation of the throat, nose and sinuses, as well as a host of illnesses not discussed here (for example, bronchitis, influenza, measles and pneumonia). While fever, difficulty in swallowing and throat pain may occur in the more serious cases, LARYNGITIS can be recognized from hoarseness or an inability to speak above a whisper. Treatment is aimed at eliminating the causative agent with drug therapy. The voice must not be used at all, and a cough syrup and anesthetic lozenges are helpful.

If the hoarseness of the voice persists for more than a month, the otolaryngologist should investigate the reason for this abnormality. While the list of possible causes for hoarseness is quite long and includes benign polyps of the vocal cords, the possibility exists that a cancerous lesion on a vocal cord has begun. If found early, it can often be treated with x-rays without removing the cord and without damaging the voice.

The latest in otolaryngology

As in other disciplines of medicine, new treatments and diagnostic advances have emerged as a result of refinements of technology. New microsurgical techniques permitted the attachment of the tiny piston-shaped substitute for a diseased stirrup (stapes). The operation led to a significant advance in restoring hearing in patients disabled by otosclerosis.

The most recent applications of microsurgery by otolaryngologists have been to make minute excisions or repairs on the vocal cords. In one such procedure, normal voice has been restored in patients with vocal cord paralysis by diverting another nerve fiber and another muscle to the cord muscle.

In head and neck surgery, increasing sophistication of microsurgical techniques allows the removal of deep-seated growths at the junction of the head and neck with minimal damage to vital tissues. Cosmetic reconstruction (plastic surgery) is a prominent part of the training and capabilities of otolaryngologists for tissue replacement and repair.

A quiet revolution in head and neck surgery has invalidated a tenet of many decades—that the surgical removal of a malignant lesion must be followed by radiation or drug therapy. The latest thinking, based on some very encouraging results, is that drug therapy and radiation therapy should *precede* the surgery.

Lastly, a word about hearing aids. It is eminently human not to want people to know that you are wearing one. By striving to make them "invisible," modern technology favors increased reliance on hearing aids. With more and more patients opting for the smallest devices—of which we certainly haven't seen the last!—the otolaryngologist should be consulted before their acquisition, lest the patient spend his hard-earned money on one that is not suited to his particular type of hearing problem. The type of hearing aid chosen—either a bone-conduction type or air-conduction type—and the sound frequency being intensified are important considerations, which should be weighed by a specialist before the final decision is made.

Dermatology

Dr. Saul L. Sanders

The dermatologist is primarily concerned with the diagnosis and treatment of diseases and disorders that affect the essential protective covering of the body. Our skin is extremely sensitive not only to various external stimuli, but to internal ones as well. Disorders that involve the entire body, or a part of it, can often be recognized by a change in this complex "organ."

Dermatology is that specialty of medicine which deals with diseases and abnormalities of the skin and mucous membranes, including its specialized structures: hair, nails, sweat glands and sebaceous glands. Because the skin is a large and complex organ and is continuously "open to inspection" by others, it is a frequent source of complaint by patients of all ages—especially by the young, who are so sensitive about their appearance. Recent surveys indicate that from 10% to 15% of all patients seen by general practitioners seek help because of primary skin problems.

Structure and function of the skin

To understand the things that can go wrong with the skin, it is important to know something about what it does and how it does it. Its most important functions are to protect us from our external environment and help us maintain a normal functioning internal environment (homeostasis). These functions are becoming increasingly more difficult as we are subjected to an ever-widening range of potentially irritating and disease-producing chemicals.

The skin is composed of two types of tissue which do an effective job of protecting us. The outer tissue of the skin is called the *epidermis;* the tissue underlying it is called the *dermis.* Each type of tissue has specific functions. Understanding its basic physiology is important to patients if they are to understand various skin disorders; equally important, such knowledge will help them to cooperate with the dermatologist and follow his instructions exactly.

The epidermis

The epidermis is composed of cells (keratinocytes) whose function is to form a highly specialized protein membrane (stratum corneum) which forms the outer lining of the skin and which is invisibly shed continuously. Shedding or scaling becomes visible only when the stratum corneum is dry or is produced in excessive quantities, usually in response to chronic irritation. This lining is surprisingly thin (only 0.1 mm) except in the palms and soles where it is 0.5 mm to provide added protection from irritation in these areas. It must remain intact to perform adequately its function of preventing the diffusion of water and chemicals in the environment. Disorders affecting this lining layer of the skin account for about a third of all skin problems—all are associated with a loss of its "barrier" function. Regardless of the initial cause of the problem, the inability of this area to protect itself from chemicals and infection in the environment can, and often does, prolong what should have been a minor self-limited disease. This is a concept to be stressed in this short discussion of skin diseases, because it is one of the most common and occasionally most easily preventable causes of prolonged chronic skin disease. The axiom "heal thyself" should be interpreted here to mean rest and protection of the injured area, thus shielding it from a potentially hostile environment as it heals. If a bone is broken, the part is put to rest in a cast for approximately six weeks; but when the lining of the skin is damaged, resting and protecting the injured skin lining is rarely even considered.

Keratinocytes represent almost 95% of the cells of the epidermis. The remaining 5%, the melanocytes, are also of great importance, because they manufacture and distribute *melanin* (a black protein pigment) throughout the epidermis. Interestingly, it is not the *number* of these cells that determines our skin color, but how the protein is packaged within the cell. Melanin protects us from many of the damaging effects of the sun's ultraviolet rays. Disorders of this pigment and the cells that produce it account for a significant number of skin problems.

Hair and nails

Two highly specialized forms of the "lining protein" keratin—hair and nails—are also a frequent source of patient complaints. The hair's protective and warming functions, so well developed in animal fur, have been replaced by its predominately cosmetic function in humans. Normal hair grows about 1 cm each week.

In skin cancers (see basal cell carcinoma *and* squamous cell carcinoma, *illustrated right) the malignant growth disrupts the tissues and the cells escape from their normal anatomical boundaries. By contrast,* psoriasis *and the* common wart *(see illustration) are not malignant conditions and the abnormalities of cell growth cause only a thickening or outgrowth of the skin.*

STRUCTURE OF NORMAL SKIN

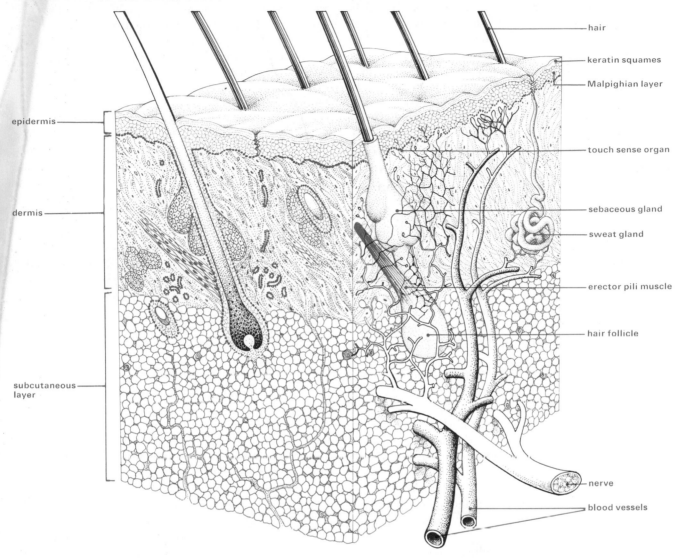

hair

keratin squames

Malpighian layer

epidermis

touch sense organ

dermis

sebaceous gland

sweat gland

erector pili muscle

hair follicle

subcutaneous layer

nerve

blood vessels

SKIN DISEASES

PSORIASIS

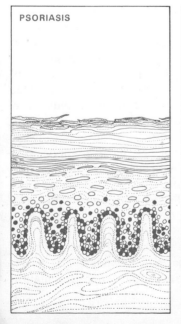

COMMON WART

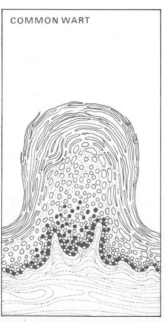

BASAL CELL CARCINOMA

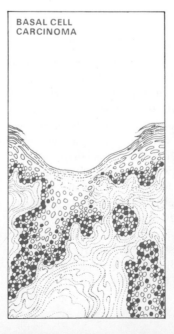

SQUAMOUS CELL CARCINOMA

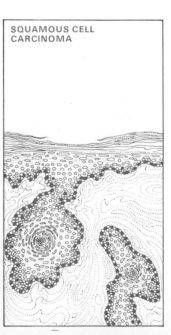

This growth phase continues normally for a two-year period; then the hair-forming organ, the hair bulb, goes into a resting phase and the hair is shed and new hair begins to grow. Since each human scalp hair is on a slightly different time cycle, we lose hair gradually. When hair cycles are synchronized (as in dogs) there is a period of excessive shedding, when large amounts of hair are lost. In humans it is normal to lose as many as 100 scalp hairs daily; when even this amount of loss is noticed by those who do not know that it is being replaced, grave concern often results. For this reason, readers should know more about hair problems.

Hair loss. The normal hair cycle is a delicate balance of genetic and environmental factors. Metabolic changes or stresses such as pregnancy, high fever, anemia, thyroid disease, drugs (such as birth control pills, anticoagulants and anticancer drugs) and toxic chemicals (such as thallium in rat poisons) may produce rapid and widespread hair loss (but usually completely reversible). Genetic and hormonal factors acting in concert produce the most common (and, unfortunately, both irreversible and untreatable) types of "pattern baldness"(alopecia) in both males and females. This type of permanent hair loss evolves slowly and intermittently over many years.

In female pattern baldness, hair loss is less extensive; only rarely do completely bald areas develop. In women there is usually a mild diffuse thinning of the hairs, which is in contrast to pattern baldness in men, who may develop a recession of the scalp hairline until the top of the scalp is totally bald. I should also emphasize that nutritional factors probably do not influence hair loss patterns until marked deficiencies have occurred along with other signs of nutritional disease. Although local factors (such as skin disease of the scalp) may affect hair loss, these are rare and minor and easily diagnosed.

It seems obvious from the above that any person concerned about hair loss should consult his physician rather than respond to advertising appeals for lotions and concoctions that are both expensive and useless. A physician can readily diagnose and treat reversible forms of alopecia, but nothing presently known to modern medicine (or to those who continue to huckster their proprietary concoctions to the gullible) will influence the progress of baldness due to genetic inheritances. (It has been said that anyone who thinks *anyone* can cure male pattern baldness should go look around at a dermatologists' convention!)

Nails. Our nails are another form of specialized keratin. They give protection and allow for manipulatory functions of the ends of our fingers and toes. Nails grow much slower than hair (about 0.1 cm a week) and are less susceptible to many of the conditions that affect hair growth. Nail growth is more affected by local factors, such as diseases of the skin or changes in the blood supply in the area of the nail. These conditions can result in "ridging" and thickening of the nails. The role of nutrition in nail growth and strength has not been well-defined, but there is good evidence that gelatin (once frequently prescribed to help strengthen nails) is of little value. The most common problems of brittleness and peeling of the nails are usually secondary to drying of this protein by strong soap, detergents, and the formalin base of nail polish.

The dermis

The dermis, or tissue underlying the epidermal layer, makes up the largest part of the skin; it varies in thickness from 1 mm on the scalp to 4 mm on the back. It is a highly complex structure formed predominately of fibers and a gel that give strength, mobility and elasticity to our body covering. It also forms an encasement for the blood vessels of our skin, which not only bring nutrients to the epidermis but also play an important role in heat regulation. An extensive network of nerves which provide sensory and regulatory function is also found in the dermis. Thus, these connecting links with the "internal milieu" can provide valuable information for the examining physician in diagnosing internal diseases.

The dermis contains important excretory glands. About 3 million *eccrine sweat glands* are found scattered over the entire body surface and are essential to the control of body temperature. They produce a solution of water with a lower concentration of salt than other body fluids. This solution both conserves salt in the body and cools the skin surface by evaporation. When this system cannot adequately adjust to a rapid or prolonged increase in temperature, severe heat stroke may result. Interestingly, unlike eccrine glands in most parts of the body, those on the palms and soles react almost exclusively to emotions rather than to temperature changes. Thus, sweaty palms are a frequent sign of emotional stress.

The *sebaceous glands*, also contained in the dermis, are of great importance to normal body function. They are widely dispersed throughout the skin, but are most concentrated on the face, back and chest. They secrete an oily substance called *sebum*, which coats the skin and is essential for preventing evaporation of water from the stratum corneum. These glands are exquisitely sensitive to hormonal stimulation of testosterone in the male and progesterone and androgenic hormones in the female. Due to hormonal stimulation, the sebaceous glands grow rapidly during puberty. Because of such growth, sebum drainage from the skin during this period is not always adequate, resulting in one of the most common skin disorders, *acne vulgaris* (common acne). Because acne is so widespread and causes so much distress, especially to the sensitive adolescent, I will discuss it in some detail here.

Acne

This disorder of adolescence is produced by plugging and inflammation of the sebaceous glands and pores. Associated with rapid growth and hormonal stimulation during puberty is the poor drainage of sebum, which dries in the pores causing blackheads (*comedones*) and a good growth medium for bacteria—ever present on the skin, but especially on the face. As the bacteria increase in number they break down sebum into irritating "free fatty acids," which produce the inflammation that results in the red bumps and cysts seen in the more severe forms of acne. At the end of puberty, when sebum drainage is again normally established, the acne usually disappears. However, the anguish and emotional stress suffered in these important formative years should be dealt with professionally.

At one time diet was believed to be one of the most important factors in acne, but recent controlled studies do not substantiate this. Today, the dermatologist and family physician prescribe the antibiotics tetracycline and erythromycin to control bacterial growth in the sebaceous glands and suppress the inflammation process. This has proved to be a safe, effective, long-term treatment; started early it can prevent significant scarring. Vitamin A acid, a local peeling agent, along with Benzoyl Peroxide, a peeling and antibacterial agent, have proved helpful in removing the plugging comedones of the sebaceous glands. Keeping the face clean and the scalp and hair free of excess oil is also important. However, *excessive* washing and the continued use of abrasive cleaners can cause irritation of the face and subsequent exacerbations of acne. Picking at and manipulation of the spots or pimples should be avoided, because it makes the problem worse and can cause significant scarring.

General management

In reading the above review of the anatomy and physiology of the skin, it should be apparent that the reason for the large number of skin complaints is due both to the complex structure of the skin and its ability to react to disease-producing factors both from within and without.

Many skin diseases can be adequately managed by the primary care physician. In fact, one of the major commitments of the American Board of Dermatology is to improve the training of all general physicians in diseases of the skin. The Board evaluates and periodically gives accreditation to training programs in dermatology, and administers the certifying examination to those who have qualified to take it. If a physician is qualified to take it ("board eligible"), it means he has completed at least four years of resident training in a teaching hospital, three of which must be in dermatology. Partial credit toward residency requirements is now allowed for completion of residency training in pediatrics or internal medicine, because knowledge of systemic disease and general medical concepts is required to practice dermatology. A Board-certified dermatologist has passed the extensive oral and written examinations and is a "diplomate" of the Board. The Board has also developed guidelines and is encourag-

ing training programs to insure the continued medical education of dermatologists.

Usually the dermatologist will evaluate and treat patients on referral from other physicians; but in many parts of the country, because of a shortage of primary care physicians, many patients with skin problems come directly to the dermatologist.

Two common skin complaints

Two of the most common complaints heard by the dermatologist are itching (pruritus) and dry skin (xerosis).

Itching

Itching is a subjective symptom caused by stimulation of nerve endings in the skin. The normal response is to scratch the itch. This causes damage to the skin, but brings temporary relief. Any skin disease can cause itching, but the most typical ones associated with the symptom are *dermatitis* ("eczema"), an inflammation of the upper layers of the dermis and epidermis, and *urticaria* ("hives"), an inflammation of the dermis with a leakage of fluids into the surrounding tissues. Treatment of the diseases that cause the itching brings relief without skin damage. The best way to obtain temporary relief from abnormal itching without further injury to the skin is to apply cool to cold tapwater compresses to the affected areas. Aspirin can also bring temporary relief, but it should be realized that in some people this common drug can cause hives.

SCABIES, a relatively rare disease until the recent pandemic in the United States and many parts of Europe, is characterized by intense itching, usually most troublesome at bedtime. It is caused by infestation with a mite (*Sarcoptes scabeii*) which burrows into the upper layer of the skin. Warmth of the covers at night stimulates movement of the mite and associated intense itching. Scabies spreads by close, direct and usually prolonged contact with infected individuals and should always be suspected if itching becomes a family symptom. Characteristic skin changes with small blisters and scratch marks on the hands (usually between the fingers), breasts, buttocks and on wrists and genitalia will be found by close inspection of the afflicted. The physician makes his definite diagnosis by microscopic examination of scraping taken from the base of a blister, in which the mite is revealed. Treatment with local medications (such as Kwell or Eurax) have proved effective in curing this troublesome problem, but complete decontamination of all clothing and bed coverings is necessary to avoid recurrent infestations.

Dry skin

Dry skin is also associated with pruritus. It is caused by a loss of water from the stratum corneum with secondary scaling, peeling and occasionally superficial cracking of the tissue. It can be associated with certain inherited skin conditions (ichthyosis), and with eczema. It is also seen frequently as part of the normal aging process in the elderly. Frequent or prolonged washing of the skin, especially in winter, can remove the protective oil coating and cause dry skin. Living in a relatively low-humidity environment will cause increased evaporation of water, adding to the problem. The most effective treatment for dry skin is to decrease washing and lubricate the skin with oils or ointments that replace the protective coating.

Common problems specific to the skin

Although diseases which can involve the skin encompass all fields of medicine, certain problems are specific to the skin or occur so frequently that they deserve special attention.

Dermatitis

The skin will react to a wide variety of stresses in only a few limited ways. Thus, although one rash may look exactly like another, each may be due to an entirely different cause. This is particularly true of dermatitis. The skin, in the more acute types of dermatitis, is red, blistered and swollen; in the chronic stages it is dry, scaly and thickened and almost always itchy. An accurate history of when and how the rash started and spread, family background and past history of skin problems, possible chemicals and other irritants to which the patient might have been exposed, and the distribution of the rash offers the physician clues to its cause. The two most common causes of dermatitis are chemicals which come in contact with the skin and infection of the skin with fungi.

Contact dermatitis develops when the epidermis is irritated by chemicals, detergents or soap (common causes of industrial disability and "housewife's eczema"), or the skin develops an allergic reaction to such agents. As our environment becomes more complex, so have the chemicals which come in contact with our skin. The most common sources of contact dermatitis are plants (poison ivy), metals (often nickel), paraphenylene diamine (hair and clothing dye), cosmetics, rubber and leather. Ironically, one of the most common sources of allergic contact dermatitis is the ointments purchased at drugstores to help clear a rash or control itching. Local antihistamines and drugs containing procaine (used in many of the anti-itch medications) are frequently a cause of dermatitis. Neomycin, an antibiotic used to treat infections, is also a common cause. Therefore, it is important to read the labels on all medications, because often the same active agent is used in many brand-name products; once you are sensitized to it you will continue to be allergic to it, whatever its commercial name.

When contact dermatitis is suspected, it is important to discontinue using all drugs, lotions, ointments and medications not prescribed by your doctor. This is true even of products that you have been using over long periods without ill effects. Inflamed skin is most susceptible to allergic reactions, even from substances that have previously been used safely.

The use of cortisone has revolutionized the treatment of contact dermatitis. This powerful drug, applied locally or taken by mouth, is most effective (whatever the cause of dermatitis) but it does not *cure*. Unless the cause of the rash is identified and treated, the rash will return upon withdrawal of cortisone.

Dermatitis due to fungi commonly involves the feet ("athlete's foot"), groin ("jock itch"), body and scalp ("ringworm"). Fungi are simple nonflowering plants. They are widespread in nature and unfortunately they infect the skin. These infections become chronic unless adequately treated. Effective topical antifungal agents are available as

Many people break out in a rash or experience other allergic reactions to specific substances in soaps, face creams, lotions, lipsticks and other cosmetics. It is often possible to avoid such problems by changing brands or selecting one of several "hypoallergenic" cosmetics or soaps.

well as an oral fungicide to cure these problems. However, once the nails are involved, complete clearing (even with long-term treatment) is rare.

Hives

Like dermatitis, hives (urticaria) can be due to many causes: ingested food (especially shellfish, nuts and berries), the drugs we take (such as penicillin, eyedrops, nosedrops, stomach and bowel preparations, nerve tonics, lozenges—in fact, *anything we ingest should be suspected when hives appear*. Physical agents (such as heat, cold and sunlight), various infections, insect bites and emotional stress are also known to cause hives. A careful history and physical examination, and sometimes extensive laboratory testing, are necessary to find the cause of this reaction. Oral antihistamines can control the symptoms until the source of the problem is found.

Psoriasis

This is another common skin disease. Its exact cause is unknown, but it is related to a defect in the production of the lining layer of the skin. Rather than taking 14 days to form the stratum corneum in normal people, the process is accomplished in about four days in the psoriasis patient. This results in an abnormal stratum corneum. Red patches of skin covered with whitish scales result. The scalp, elbows, knees, palms and soles are most frequently involved. Psoriasis is a chronic disease with a genetic factor and it has no known cure; but two-thirds of the afflicted will have temporary or even permanent remission during the course of the disease. Any agent which can slow the rapid production of the stratum corneum can help control the problem. Certain anticancer drugs, although dangerous unless given under careful supervision, are effective in the treatment of some cases. Ultraviolet light, especially when combined with local application of coal tar, is also helpful. A relatively recent treatment, combining an oral drug (psoralen) which sensitizes the skin to long-wave ultraviolet light, and the subsequent exposure of the skin to measured doses of this light, is giving encouraging results in the control of psoriasis. Local treatment with various cortisone preparations is also proving useful.

Warts

These are benign growths on the skin caused by viral infection of the keratinocytes. (The technical name for a wart is a *verruca*.) They are most commonly found on the back of the hands, or around the nails of children and adolescents. If they involve the palms or soles, they tend to be smooth rather than raised and are called PLANTAR WARTS. Unless painful, they represent only a cosmetic problem and usually disappear spontaneously within two years in most cases. Resolution seems to occur when patients develop immunity to the wart virus. Since no effective antiviral agents are presently available, treatment involves the destruction of the warts by burning, freezing or the use of chemicals. Experimental treatment with chemicals which produce an allergic reaction at the site of the wart has shown promising results. See also MOLES, NEVUS.

Herpes simplex

This is a virus which causes the common fever blister ("cold sore") and is one of the most widespread viruses found in man. Almost all adults have been infected at some time, although the infection may be "subclinical" (no apparent symptoms evident). The infection is usually marked by recurrent episodes of grouped blisters associated with burning pain on the lips or oral mucosa. It may be triggered by such factors as fever, emotional stress, or sun exposure. A variant of herpes simplex, causing a similar disease on the genitalia, has become one of our most common venereal diseases. Even though genital herpes appears to be easily transferred by direct contact, the type involving the lips only appears to spread rapidly to infants, people taking immunosuppressive drugs, and those with widespread dermatitis. When herpes involves the eyes, an ophthalmologist should be seen. Scarring of the cornea can be a serious complication, which proper treatment can prevent. There is no treatment at present to permanently eradicate this virus from the skin, but each episode of blistering is self-limited, lasting from one to two weeks. Mild local treatment, such as cool water compresses, and drying agents, such as alcohol and spirits of camphor, may shorten the course of recurrent episodes.

Skin cancers

Of all the organ systems of the body the skin is most vulnerable to environmentally induced diseases—not only dermatitis but also cancers, some of which appear to be related to exposure to certain chemicals and various forms of radiation, including sunlight and x-rays.

The first description of an environmentally induced cancer in man was given by Sir Percival Pott in 1775; he noted that soot was responsible for the high incidence of skin cancer found on the scrotums of chimney sweeps. Today, the incidence of skin cancer can be closely correlated with the amount of exposure to the sun (the lighter the complexion, the greater the danger) and other sources of radiation.

As people age they develop many benign growths on the skin, but three types of skin cancer are also frequently seen. Two of these—*basal cell carcinoma* and *squamous cell carcinoma*—tend to develop most frequently on areas exposed to the sun, especially the face and hands. Warty growths in these areas or any ulcerated or bleeding lesions should be evaluated by a physician. Basal cell carcinomas (by far the most frequent) do not spread throughout the body (metastasize); therefore, they have a high rate of cure when removed by excision, electrosurgery, or by radiotherapy. Squamous cell carcinomas, although more serious, also are curable if detected and treated early.

MELANOMAS, the third type of skin cancer and by far the most dangerous, are pigmented skin cancers and carry a most serious prognosis. Unless widely excised at an early stage they can spread rapidly and widely throughout the body by means of the lymphatic system and the blood vessels. *Most melanomas do not, as we once suspected, arise in moles; they develop spontaneously.* The danger signals to watch for in pigmented lesions are irregularity in the pigment—shades of red, white and blue—and irregularity in the borders of the lesion and on its surface. When these signs are seen, consult a physician immediately. The lesion, whether benign or malignant, can be identified by study of cells taken by biopsy and examined under a microscope. Even though melanomas have shown an alarming increased incidence in recent years, studies in the immunology and biochemistry of pigment cell formation have given hope for effective medical treatment.

Venereal diseases

SYPHILLIS, the great imitator of many skin diseases in its early stages, was once responsible for many patients seen by dermatologists; but it declined rapidly with the advent of effective antibiotic drugs. However, during the last decade the incidence of syphilis has increased significantly. Untreated, it is a most devastating disease and everyone should know its earliest symptoms because it is curable. The first symptom is a small ulcer, usually not tender, found most often on the genitalia. The diagnosis can be made at this stage by a "dark-field" microscopic examination of a scraping from the base of the ulcer. Even if untreated, the ulcer disappears; but the disease will continue to "smoulder" and in a significant number of its victims the *secondary stage* develops, its signs being a wide variety of rashes. If syphilis is suspected at this time, the diagnosis can be determined by a specific blood test. Cure is achieved with the administration of penicillin, or other antibiotics for those who are allergic to penicillin. If the disease is not treated during the primary and secondary stages, 25% of those infected will develop *tertiary syphilis;* this stage begins 10 to 30 years after the initial infection, resulting in major changes in the cardiovascular and central nervous systems. See also VENEREAL DISEASES, GONORRHEA.

The future

The practice of dermatology has advanced and changed along with the other specialties of medicine. New and powerful drugs make the treatment of infection and allergy more effective. But it is becoming apparent that the medicine of tomorrow will be more involved with the effects of the complex chemicals in our environment and in drugs used to treat disease. Today, 5% of all hospitalizations are due to adverse reactions ("side effects") to medications. (For a further discussion of diseases that affect the skin, see the source list at SKIN DISEASES.)

How to deal with your skin problems

In summary, the following suggestions should be helpful in dealing with your skin problems:

1. When a skin problem develops, first consult with your family physician. He will be a more helpful physician if he is familiar with all of your health problems. Often he will be able to treat your skin disease without specialist consultation, saving you unnecessary expense.

2. Try to rest the injured area to allow normal healing. Do not complicate the problem by using your friend's ointment. If it works dramatically for him, it probably contained a cortisone derivative or an antibiotic. *Cortisone creams help all rashes, cure none and can allow infection to spread.* Antibiotics may further sensitize an inflamed skin. The same holds true for "over-the-counter" topical medications, which can also be potent sensitizers.

3. If you go to a dermatologist, give an accurate account of your problem. If you have seen other physicians or specialists and they have done diagnostic tests and prescribed medications, this is important information. A good history is essential for proper diagnosis and treatment; withholding information makes for a "guessing game"—which wastes time and money.

4. Take oral and topical medications as directed. Never overuse medication, even local ointments, which can also be harmful. Ask if a rash should be covered. Sometimes it is helpful, other times it is contraindicated.

5. *Don't be afraid to ask questions!* Patients who understand the nature of their problem, and why certain methods of treatment are used, tend to follow instructions more carefully.

6. Don't always expect dramatic results from treatment: sometimes the healing process takes a long time. If your problem is a chronic one, without a known cure, expect the dermatologist to set reasonable goals to be reached.

7. If the doctor's expectations are not what you feel are reasonable, or if you do not seem to be reaching established goals, do not hesitate to ask whether further consultation might not be useful.

8. When referred to a dermatologist, or if you go to one directly, ask him to send a summary of his diagnosis and treatment to your regular doctor. The lack of centralization of medical records has become a serious problem in this age of specialization.

Gastroenterology Dr. Arthur J. Berman

The way to a man's heart may sometimes be through his stomach, but unfortunately this route is often abused by too much traffic—overindulgence in food and drink. Indigestion and ulcers are fairly common problems with the body's digestive system. When more serious problems occur, examination by a specialist may be indicated.

A gastroenterologist is a physician, usually qualified in internal medicine, who specializes in gastroenterology—the branch of medical science concerned with the study of the digestive system and the diagnosis and treatment of diseases and disorders which affect it.

After food is chewed in the mouth the particles, moistened by saliva, are pushed to the back of the throat by the action of the tongue and are swallowed. The food particles thus enter the esophagus ("gullet") where they are quickly conveyed to the stomach by wavelike muscular contractions of the esophageal walls. After the food particles have been further broken down into more simple chemical compounds by the action of the digestive juices of the stomach, and have been transformed into a liquid state known as *chyme*, the material is passed in brief spurts into the first and shortest part of the small intestine (the *duodenum:* approximately 12 in. in length). There it is mixed with incoming bile from the gallbladder and digestive juices from the pancreas—both of which are conveyed through specific ducts to the inner wall of the duodenum.

As the liquid passes through the remaining sections of the small intestine (the *jejunum* and *ileum*, which together with the duodenum form a coiled loop approximately 20 ft. in length), the nutrients are gradually absorbed into the bloodstream. The waste products of digestion pass into the large intestine (*colon*) where they are eventually deprived of most of their liquid content (which is reabsorbed) and are formed—together with other waste material such as bile, pigment, cellular debris, mucus and bacteria—into stools (feces). These enter the rectum and are expelled from the body at the *anus*. This, in the main, is the system of particular interest to the gastroenterologist.

Referral to a gastroenterologist

When I first see a patient it is usually because of one or more symptoms which suggest a disorder or some other problem in this system. What follows is a disciplined diagnostic procedure.

After taking the patient's full medical history, I will proceed to examine his digestive tract. (Basic approaches are shared by virtually all branches of medicine in their studies of any organ system, and they are often crucial to an accurate diagnosis.) Results of these primary steps may lead to further examination using the specialized tools and tests available to the gastroenterologist. What information would make him suspect a gastrointestinal problem? Much depends upon his knowledge of normal structures and functions and his experience in dealing with their abnormal functions. Questions he will pursue are: Is the symptom caused by some problem in or near the structures of the digestive tract? Is it a symptom of the type related to the digestive process? Is it associated with physical abnormalities detected during the physical examination?

Signs and symptoms of gastrointestinal disorders commonly include one or more of the following: a history of nausea or vomiting; "heartburn" (pyrosis); pain brought on by swallowing, by the ingestion of food or by the avoidance of food; abnormalities in bowel function (such as DIARRHEA, severe CONSTIPATION or the passage of blood or black stools); crampy abdominal pain; jaundice and certain abdominal swellings. Changes in appetite, weakness, malaise (a general feeling of being unwell), depression and other symptoms may also be related to such disorders, but would have to be further investigated to demonstrate their association.

Diagnostic procedures

Let's take an example. A patient may complain of recurring and persistent pain in the upper part of the abdomen. It has been going on for three months, it is "burning" in quality, but temporarily relieved by eating or taking common antacid drugs, only to return within a few hours. Pain often awakens the patient at night, and he has recently begun to feel it in his back too. The patient admits he has been under tension on his job, but other functions are normal (such as bowel movements) and there has been no loss or gain of weight. The examination reveals only some tenderness (on pressure by the physician's fingers) in a small area of the upper part of the abdomen. The results of blood count tests and urinalysis are normal, as are the results of various other tests of the body's chemistry.

The "G.I. series"

The gastroenterologist could elect to study the stomach

acid, but more likely would go directly to a "G.I. series," which is a series of x-rays and fluoroscopy of the stomach and adjacent portions of the esophagus and duodenum, using a contrast material to outline organs which would otherwise be invisible on x-rays. This contrast material is *barium sulfate*, an inert and insoluble salt in the form of a fine white powder which is mixed with water to form a milky suspension. It has no taste, but its chalky consistency may be disguised with flavoring. (See BARIUM MEAL/BARIUM ENEMA.)

The patient fasts overnight before the G.I. series, except in certain emergencies. After a preliminary x-ray of the abdomen, the patient is examined by fluoroscopy (often while standing and then lying down) as the doctor instructs him to swallow small amounts of the barium mixture (known as a "barium meal"). It outlines the walls of the esophagus, stomach and duodenum and shows defects and irregularities in the shape, size and position of the outlined organs.

After fluoroscopic studies of the organs in action, the patient is given more barium sulfate to drink and several additional x-ray films are taken in standardized positions. Delayed films may be taken to visualize the small intestine further along the tract, or to determine how well the stomach empties. Occasionally, gas may be introduced within the tract in the form of club soda or other means to add more contrast to the films. This entire procedure is not uncomfortable to most people and there are usually no after-effects.

Indications for the G.I. series
These are many. Unexplained or uncertain conditions associated with symptoms related to the digestive tract are the most common. Ulcers, tumors, and hiatus hernias (see HERNIA) are among the most common problems found. Distortions of the stomach or intestine produced by masses in surrounding tissues pressing on these organs may also be found. One fairly common condition may be suspected in certain cases of JAUNDICE in which the cause is a tumor in or near the "head" of the pancreas. The head of the pancreas, not visible on a G.I. series, is cradled next to the duodenum just past the stomach. We may detect a tumor mass in this organ by seeing its pressure effect on the duodenum. A more elaborate way of accomplishing this is by injecting medicines to relax the duodenum and make it lie flabbily against any encroaching mass. A G.I. series is not usually done if perforation or an obstruction is present or strongly suspected; but when uncertainty exists it may occasionally be accomplished using a water-soluble contrast agent containing organic iodine rather than barium. If a patient is unconscious, uncooperative, or has persistent nausea and vomiting, a G.I. series cannot usually be done.

A "small bowel series" is an extension of a G.I. series. A much larger amount of barium is swallowed and its passage through the small intestine is awaited and followed with serial x-rays. Iced barium or a hormone called *cholecysto-kinin* may be added to hurry it along. Masses (inside or

THE DIGESTIVE SYSTEM

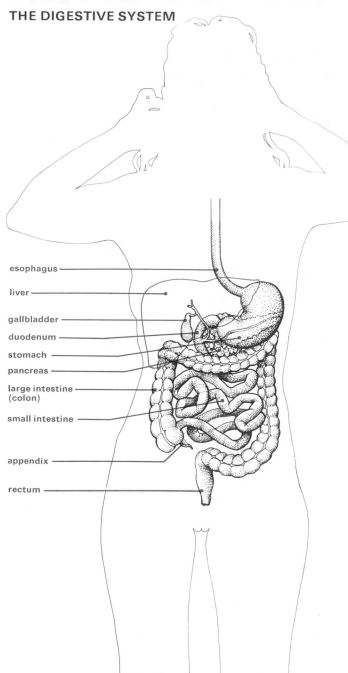

esophagus
liver
gallbladder
duodenum
stomach
pancreas
large intestine (colon)
small intestine
appendix
rectum

The digestive tract is basically a hollow tube which extends from the mouth to the rectum, at the end of the large intestine. Inside this tube, nutrients are digested and assimilated into the body and waste products are formed into a semisolid mass for elimination from the body. Usually nothing serious happens to the automatic working of this complex system. When it does, your physician may refer you to a gastroenterologist.

pressing on the intestine), inflammations, strictures, diverticula (small abnormal outpouchings of the intestine) and malabsorption problems are studied in this manner. Occasionally an intestinal obstruction may be located by passing a long tube via the nose or mouth into the intestine. When an obstruction blocks further passage of the tube, a small amount of contrast material is ejected through the tube and x-rays are taken.

In the example given, the patient is most likely to have a peptic ulcer revealed by the G.I. series, located in the first part of the duodenum (duodenal bulb). If this is the case, often no additional tests will be necessary. The patient will usually be treated nonsurgically; he will be instructed to eliminate from his diet certain acid-stimulating or irritating foods, advised to do something about the job stress which is probably contributing to his problem told that he should give up smoking, and treated with medicines to neutralize or control acid.

Endoscopy

If no ulcer is seen, or one is seen but is unusual in some way, or if another type of lesion is detected, the next step may well be *upper intestinal endoscopy.*

Although begun over a hundred years ago with straight tubes, swallowed like a sword, the modern era of ENDOSCOPY began in 1957 with the introduction into medical practice of the flexible *fiberoptic gastroscope.* The instrument contains two or three fiberoptic bundles, which are cable-like clusters of glass fibers with unique optical properties. They have the ability to transmit light (and therefore an image) from one end to the other, even when bent or twisted into a knot. One bundle is used to transmit the image. The others carry light from an outside source to illuminate the organ under study. This remarkable instrument (and its later variations) is used to look into the stomach, small intestine and large intestine (colon). It can be passed through the natural curves of the gastrointestinal

tract while the endoscopist maintains an excellent view. Under direct visualization, dye can be injected into the bile and pancreatic ducts for x-raying these ductal systems. More recently, a "miniscope" has been developed which can be threaded through the larger duct and then directly into the bile and pancreatic ducts, where possible lesions may be inspected.

Benign tumors may be removed through the endoscope and other lesions, including those suspected of being malignant, may be biopsied (see BIOPSY). The instrument is also used to cut open the end of the common bile duct to allow the removal of stones and to cauterize bleeding lesions, using an electric current or (more recently) laser beams. Progress is still very active and new techniques continue to be developed.

Most modern endoscopes look remarkably alike, often having the diameter of a finger, and may be of variable length (up to several feet). There is a hand-held control head and handle, with an eyepiece through which the endoscopist looks. An "umbilical" connects the head to a light source, air pump and suction apparatus.

The swallowing of a tube may seem a fearsome prospect to some people. Actually, it is accomplished with relative ease and little or no discomfort. A local anesthetic may be gargled, sprayed or painted on throat tissues to minimize discomfort, and some form of sedation may also be given. Because the instrument is flexible, endoscopy is usually performed with the patient lying comfortably on his left side, although he may be asked to sit up or take other positions.

The patient's head is bent forward. The endoscopist's finger guides the scope into the throat and he asks the

The fiberoptic endoscope shown here permits direct visual examination of the esophagus, stomach and duodenum. It is a quick and safe procedure in experienced hands and the patient requires only mild sedation beforehand. The long tube, which is swallowed, contains thousands of fibers which project light and also act as a telescope.

FIBEROPTIC ENDOSCOPE

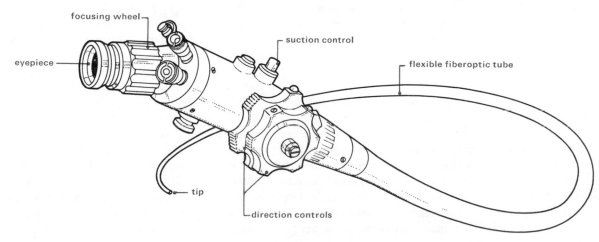

focusing wheel

eyepiece

suction control

flexible fiberoptic tube

tip

direction controls

patient to swallow. If the patient is relaxed there is little or no tendency to gag as the tube is introduced into the esophagus ("gullet"). Once there, the endoscope is advanced by the operator looking through its optical system. If there was any discomfort, it usually subsides at this point. As the scope advances through the stomach and into the small intestine, any abnormalities present can be directly observed. By introducing a small cable with a tiny "jaw" at the tip through an open channel of the endoscope. tiny bits of tissue can be removed for study by the pathologist. POLYPS may be removed with an electric cautery snare ("wire lasso"), also painlessly. Obstructing rings of tissue may be broken away or stretched. Foreign bodies can often be visualized and removed using biopsy forceps or other modified instruments.

The endoscope has eliminated the need for much exploratory surgery, once common in gastroenterology. When there is a history of internal bleeding, or when evidence of abnormalities show up on x-ray studies, the endoscope can then be used for direct visualization, biopsy and evaluation. Conditions best investigated by this technique are duodenal or gastric ulcers (*peptic ulcers*), erosive gastritis (inflammation of the stomach lining), cancer, benign tumors, esophageal varicose veins (see ESOPHAGEAL VARICES), esophagitis (inflammation of the esophagus) and tears at the lower end of the esophagus. Perhaps one of the most important uses of the instrument is the ease and speed of obtaining biopsy specimens. About 10% of gastric ulcers are actually ulcerating malignant tumors, which can often be identified and treated early.

Rectal bleeding

Another common problem seen by the gastroenterologist is rectal bleeding, always a fearful sign to patients—so fearful, in fact, that at times they arbitrarily or subconsciously attribute it to HEMORRHOIDS ("piles") and ignore it, which is always a potentially dangerous thing to do. Although cancers can bleed, the source of blood may be other lesions that should be treated as early as possible, including polyps, diverticula, inflammations, and, yes, hemorrhoids. Rectal bleeding calls for immediate medical evaluation, with consideration of blood replacement (transfusion) and studies of blood clotting time high on the priority list.

Sigmoidoscopy

The physical examination may or may not reveal diagnostic findings such as an abdominal or rectal mass, an enlarged nodular liver, or tenderness. In any event, the doctor is likely to perform a *sigmoidoscopy*, a procedure often done even in routine physical examinations. It consists of inserting a straight metal or plastic tubular instrument into the rectum and slightly beyond; then, with the help of a light source, internal tissues of the lower colon and rectum can be visually examined as the instrument is slowly withdrawn. Biopsies and other procedures can be performed through the sigmoidoscope.

In our example, a polyp or other abnormal growth may be seen to be bleeding, or blood may be seen although the source of the bleeding is not visible; this would suggest that it comes from above the viewing limit of the scope. If the bleeding stops, or is not severe, the next step is likely to be a *barium enema*.

The colon (large intestine) must be thoroughly cleaned out before the barium enema is given. Strong laxatives and cleansing enemas are usually required; castor oil is a traditional laxative, but others may be used. If harsh laxatives are contraindicated, a strict diet of clear liquids may be given for three days or more before the examination. They produce virtually no stools. Cleansing enemas may also be used. A recent and somewhat novel approach to cleansing involves the rapid drinking of several quarts of fluids, which eventually induces diarrhea.

Once prepared, the patient lies supine on the x-ray table, the enema tip is inserted into the rectum, and the fluoroscopist monitors the barium sulfate suspension as it flows in, filling the entire colon from the rectum to the cecum (using perhaps one to two quarts of fluid). The "ileocecal valve" normally prevents the barium from traveling beyond the cecum (the blind pouch which forms the first portion of the colon) into the small intestine, but this may be overcome by gentle pressure if this area needs to be evaluated. "Spot films" are taken during fluoroscopy. Then x-rays are taken in several positions while the patient retains the barium. The enema is then passed, either into the toilet or back into the original container, followed by the taking of postevacuation x-ray films. Air may also be introduced through a rectal tube and together with the leftover barium may give additional information, especially regarding masses.

Colonoscopy

If the results of the x-rays taken after a barium enema are negative or leave unanswered questions, and if bleeding has stopped, a *colonoscopy* may be ordered. Fiberoptic colonoscopy, first described in 1963, has become widely used in recent years to diagnose colonic lesions and to treat some of them. The instrument closely resembles the gastroscope (discussed previously), but it has several lengths; the longest is used to reach the cecum, the farthest part of the colon from the rectum.

Once again, the patient must have a thoroughly clean colon. The procedure itself is usually performed with the patient lying comfortably on his left side. An intravenous line may be used to administer medications, usually sedatives or analgesics ("painkillers"). An x-ray table is preferred by some physicians because of the occasional need for fluoroscopy to determine the precise position of the scope inside. It requires considerably more skill and patience to pass a colonoscope up through the winding colon than it does to pass a gastroscope down into the upper part of the digestive tract. There may be some discomfort as the intestine and its attachments are stretched to negotiate certain curves, but medication is usually very helpful in minimizing discomfort and relaxing the patient.

Indications for colonoscopy include suspicious x-ray findings following a barium enema, unexplained bleeding, inflammatory bowel disease (where the type or extent must be determined or an abnormal change explained), DIVERTICULOSIS where cancer or other additional diseases may be present, and in COLOSTOMY and ILEOSTOMY investigations. Tumors, inflammation and other lesions may be biopsied, malformed blood vessels (a source of bleeding) may be found, and artifacts, revealed on x-rays, ruled out.

Removal of polyps

A well-established procedure associated with colonoscopy is *polypectomy*. Development of the wire snare and electrocautery technique has all but replaced the need for transabdominal surgery to remove polyps from the colon. Electrical connections are made to a wire loop inserted through the endoscope; the wire loop is slipped over the polyp, drawn snugly around its stalk-like "neck," and the current applied—severing the polyp. The polyp can then be grasped by the instrument and withdrawn with the endoscope.

Tumors without a neck may also be removed, large ones in sections. Colonic polyps often bleed and are generally considered to be "premalignant" lesions. Removing them without the need for abdominal surgery adds significantly to the usefulness of this versatile instrument; however, this technique is not used for the removal of a *cancerous* growth. When cancer is diagnosed, major surgical removal is the usual approach, so that the margins of tissue which are free of malignancy may also be removed (to minimize or prevent the possible spread of cancer cells). Not infrequently, early cancerous changes may be found in a polyp removed during colonoscopy. If additional treatment is required for such patients it is determined individually in each case. Colonoscopy is generally a safe procedure, but it is occasionally associated with perforation of the colon or bleeding.

Arteriography

In the presence of severe bleeding which does not stop, none of the above techniques is helpful. Blood vessels nourishing the gastrointestinal tract are not normally visible on x-rays. However, when they are injected with a contrast material containing iodine they become visible on x-rays—a procedure known as *arteriography*. It not only is helpful in diagnosing diseases of the blood vessels but is also useful to diagnose massive bleeding, trauma, pancreatic disease, certain tumors, specific lesions, problems of

the circulation leading to the liver, and in demonstration of the vascular anatomy.

Displacement, distortion and abrupt termination of blood vessels, new blood vessel formation, and abnormally late or early filling of veins and vascular shunts ("filling defects") with the contrast material are among the abnormalities sought in arteriography. Risks include allergic reactions, bleeding and dislodging of a clot or plaque with the danger of an embolism. However, the incidence of such complications is low and the procedure has become widely accepted.

Gallbladder and bile tract investigation

Biliary tract problems may become apparent in several different ways. A patient, typically a middle-aged woman, may complain of indigestion (dyspepsia) after meals or of bloating and "gassiness," particularly after eating certain foods. She may or may not have some tenderness in the upper part of the abdomen. If the physician suspects gallbladder disease he will usually order a "gallbladder series" (oral cholecystogram). This x-ray procedure is based on an iodide contrast agent, which after being swallowed eventually ends up in the liver and then the gallbladder, where it may be seen on the x-ray film as a pale gray shadow. Indications for the procedure usually revolve around the search for inflammation of the gallbladder or the formation of GALLSTONES. In severe cases the gallbladder may have to be removed surgically (see illustration overleaf).

Most gallstones are made predominantly of CHOLESTEROL. A few are made of calcium bilirubinate (a yellow pigment). Either type may have a rim of calcium within the stone, making them visible on a *plain x-ray* of the abdomen (that is, an x-ray taken without the use of a contrast agent). Pure cholesterol stones, however, are not visible on x-rays, but may be seen as dark "holes" in the contrast material. The gallbladders series is usually not uncomfortable for the patient and is not likely to be followed by after-effects. However, it does require the use of a contrast agent, which may occasionally produce side effects such as diarrhea, cramps, nausea, vomiting, or a rash. Contraindications for its use include jaundice or known or suspected allergy to the contrast agent.

Some of my patients when first seen may have jaundice, with or without additional symptoms. If not obviously associated with HEPATITIS (inflammation of the liver), jaundice may represent a more challenging diagnostic problem; it may be more difficult to diagnose because the usual tests and x-rays either are not often helpful or may not be done. The treatment may or may not be surgical; the decision about whether to operate is a serious one.

Diagnostic use of sound waves

Several new tests have come into use in the diagnosis of this type of problem, but they are still being evaluated for

CHOLECYSTECTOMY

Cholecystectomy, removal of the gallbladder, is usually performed because of gallstones. The surgeon first divides the cystic artery and then ties off the cystic duct (1). The cystic duct is cut and the gallbladder removed (2). Any bleeding vessels are coagulated using a diathermy probe (3).

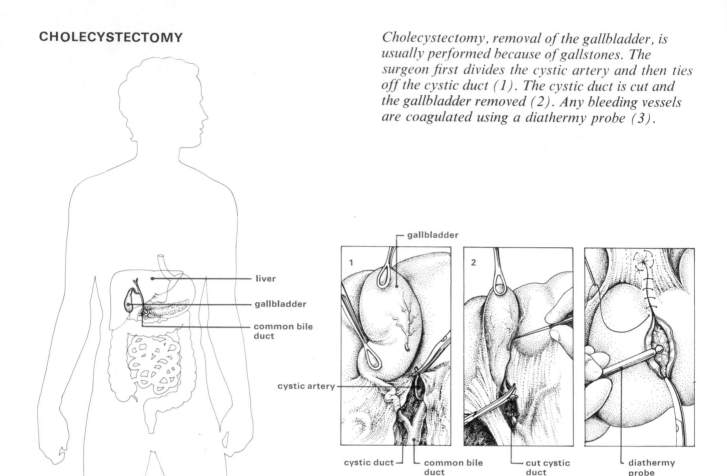

overall usefulness. Frequently, however, an *ultrasound test* (ultrasonography, echogram) will be performed early. This basic technique, developed by the U.S. Navy to locate submerged submarines, is now being applied to the human body and refinements have turned it into a useful "noninvasive" diagnostic tool. Echoes increase at an "interface"—that is, in this case, the coming together of two tissues. Fluid-filled organs or masses produce fewer echoes. The resulting echoes, when sound is directed into specific areas, are converted into a series of lighted dots on a screen, which form a picture resembling a radar weather map. This technique is used by specialists in many branches of medicine; it is especially useful to the gastroenterologist in detecting abdominal masses, enlarged organs, aneurysms of great vessels, fluid-filled organs, cavities, cysts and even large gallstones. The procedure is simple and painless and appears to have no after-effects.

CAT scan

Another noninvasive diagnostic tool, the *CAT scan* (computerized axial tomography), is now coming into use. (For details of this technique, see the major section on **Examination and Diagnosis.**) The potential applications of this technique are changing rapidly. In general, it is useful to the gastroenterologist in detecting deep-seated

masses (particularly in the pancreas), enlargement of organs and even dilated bile ducts. The method is not particularly useful in most conditions involving the stomach and intestines.

X-ray of the bile ducts

Intravenous cholangiography is an x-ray of the bile ducts accomplished by first giving the patient an intravenous injection of a contrast agent, which is taken up by the liver and secreted in the bile. It usually works within 20 to 60 minutes, but may at times be extended up to three hours in hopes of visualizing the gallbladder on the x-ray film as well. The technique is most often used to visualize the major bile ducts after the gallbladder has been removed and subsequent blockage of bile flow is suspected, even though jaundice is absent or minimal. It is also useful in ruling out a diagnosis of acute inflammation of the gallbladder (cholecystitis) when this possible condition is thought to exist. It is also used at times to help distinguish the cause of acute inflammation of the pancreas (pancreatitis). Intravenous cholangiography is contraindicated in the presence of severe liver or kidney disease, sensitivity to compounds containing iodine, or any condition in which an acute lowering of blood pressure (hypotension) could be dangerous.

ULTRASOUND SCANNING

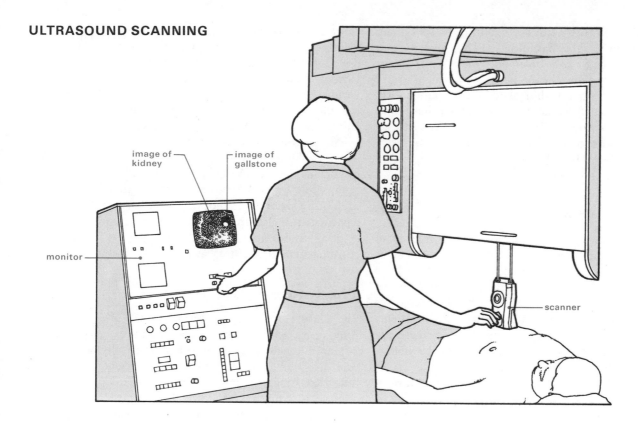

image of kidney

image of gallstone

monitor

scanner

Ultrasound scanning is a technique which measures the reflections of low-intensity, high-frequency sound waves by the soft tissues of the body. Unlike x-rays, ultrasound is not dangerous and can be used in pregnancy. It has also proved valuable in gastroenterology where it can display the abdominal organs and reveal abnormalities such as gallstones.

Liver biopsy

If the doctor suspects that jaundice is due to hepatitis, infections, or is induced by drugs or alcoholism, or if there is an accessible tumor in the liver, a liver biopsy may be ordered. Introduced in the 1880s, the *needle biopsy* became somewhat more common from the 1940s. The introduction of a "one-second" liver biopsy needle in the late 1950s made the procedure safer, and it has become a principal means of making a specific diagnosis of liver disease. The procedure is usually performed in the hospital, with the patient's blood count and clotting time determined in advance. Blood may be cross-matched and held for possible transfusion, and sedative drugs may be administered to allay anxiety. The patient lies on his back, the needle is placed in an anesthetized spot between the ribs and then, as the patient holds his breath, the one-second biopsy is performed. Suction is applied to the attached syringe and a tiny piece of liver is drawn into the hollow needle and then removed for examination by the pathologist. The patient is kept in bed for several hours to observe for any possible complications.

Other diagnostic tests

A test often performed (but of more limited usefulness) is the *liver scan*. Using an injected radioisotope trace, the scan produces a crude picture of the liver and spleen. If foreign tissue is present, such as a tumor or scar, it may show up as a "hole" in the radioactive pattern. The size, shape and position of the liver and spleen can usually be determined with this technique. Liver scans are simple, painless and acceptably safe.

Another typical diagnostic problem of the gastroenterologist is the patient with diarrhea and unexpected weight loss. If the stools are bulky or greasy, or they float, they usually contain excessive amounts of fat or gas, and the gastroenterologist may suspect MALABSORPTION. If so, he may request a 72-hour stool collection to determine the precise amount of fat and order x-ray studies of the small intestine. In addition, he may perform a biopsy of the small intestine.

The lining cells inside the small intestine are intimately involved in the process of absorption of the products of digestion. In disease involving malabsorption, changes in the "architecture" of these cells may be diagnostic or otherwise helpful. In certain diseases the cells lose their height and become flattened. In some parasitic diseases the actual organism may be found in the biopsied specimen of tissue from the small intestine; in certain other rare diseases, characteristic changes occur in the cells.

Biopsy of the small intestine is accomplished by having the patient swallow a thin flexible tube with a small device at its end which removes a tiny section of the bowel's lining for examination by the pathologist. This procedure is simple, safe and can be done on an outpatient basis (that is, the patient need not stay in the hospital overnight).

Tests of the blood for shortages of materials poorly absorbed (such as folic acid, iron and calcium) and procedures in which test substances are swallowed to see how they are absorbed may also be performed. Newer tests analyzing the exhaled breath have also been developed and are gradually coming into use.

Cancer detection

The early detection of cancer of the digestive tract is an awesome responsibility of the gastroenterologist as well as all physicians. Cancer of the colon and rectum have become the most common internal malignancy in the United States, with approximately 100,000 new cases reported each year, of which an estimated 49,000 patients will die. It is generally accepted that because these are usually slow-growing tumors, at least half of the victims could be saved by early diagnosis and treatment.

If I have gone on at length to explain the various techniques of gastrointestinal diagnosis, it was to familiarize you with the methods used to detect most forms of disease, especially malignancies. The precise, step-by-step discipline followed by gastroenterologists for any complaint is always in the patient's best interest, because it is often a means of detecting malignancies before their symptoms are noticed by a patient—thus making early treatment and cure possible.

What has been most needed in cancer detection is an inexpensive and reliable SCREENING test applicable to large population groups. A test is now available which fulfills some essential criteria. It takes advantage of the tendency of tumors to shed blood cells into the stools, even in the early stages of development. Such cells do not usually discolor the stools, but they may be detected chemically. Several stools must be tested, because there are sometimes "false positive" and "false negative" results and there are other conditions which may cause bleeding. But it is a useful procedure, in general, and if used for mass screenings could detect many early curable cancers.

The Japanese, who also have a high incidence of stomach cancer, have taken to mass screening to detect this disease. They have pioneered in the use of endoscopy, have improved on methods of performing a G.I. series, and have developed a device called the *gastrocamera*. This is a swallowable camera on the end of a tube, which takes flash pictures of the inflated stomach, permitting multiple views at different angles. The procedure takes only a few minutes, is inexpensive, and is applicable to large groups. There are "blind spots" to the lens of the camera, but it nevertheless remains a useful diagnostic method.

The gastroenterologist performs many other procedures.

He tests esophageal function with swallowed tubes which measure pressures, and he may treat certain esophageal disorders (such as uncontrolled bleeding) with dilators of various kinds. He may study gastric acidity, measure various gastrointestinal hormones, pass small tubes into the intestine to collect bile and pancreatic secretions and culture bacteria from the small intestine.

The gastroenterologist is, of necessity, a well-trained general physician with many special skills. Like all physicians, his most important skill is the reasoning and good clinical and diagnostic judgment that he brings to each of his patients. It should be emphasized that a good gastroenterologist typically works in close association with a good abdominal surgeon, in terms of diagnosis, consultation, studies, treatment and follow-up care.

The future

The future of gastroenterology is bright indeed. Endoscopy, with its spectacular advances, is still in its infancy and new developments may hopefully be expected year by year. The leap forward represented by computerized axial tomography (the CAT scan) and ultrasonography is certain to be followed by new developments and new applications. Advances in understanding of the gastrointestinal tract have led to new treatments: hepatitis B immune globulin for passive protection against hepatitis B; cimetidine to reduce gastric acidity and help heal ulcers; chenodeoxycholic acid and ursodeoxycholic acid which in preliminary studies have been shown to dissolve gallstones, but which are still under investigation; and there is hope that an effective vaccine for hepatitis B will soon be available. The cause of ULCERATIVE COLITIS and CROHN'S DISEASE is unknown, but a great deal of investigational work is going on in this area, revolving largely around a possible infectious agent.

It would have been next to impossible 20 years ago to have predicted the revolutionary changes in gastroenterology which now seem commonplace. If current progress is any indication, future developments are almost certain to be equally exciting. One of the satisfactions of being a gastroenterologist today is the ability to watch the step-by-step unfolding of this advance.

See also ACUTE ABDOMEN, APPENDICITIS/APPENDECTOMY, BARIUM MEAL/BARIUM ENEMA, BOWEL AND BOWEL MOVEMENTS, CELIAC DISEASE, CHOLECYSTECTOMY, CHOLECYSTITIS, CIRRHOSIS, COLONIC CANCER, DIGESTION, DIVERTICULITIS, DUODENAL ULCER, ENTERITIS, ESOPHAGITIS, FECALITH, FECES, GASTRECTOMY, GASTRIC ULCER, GASTROENTERITIS, HEARTBURN, HEPATOMA, HIRSCHSPRUNG'S DISEASE, INDIGESTION, IRRITABLE BOWEL SYNDROME, MALNUTRITION, NECROTIZING ENTEROCOLITIS, SIGMOIDECTOMY, STARVATION, TUBE FEEDING, ULCER.

Pulmonary diseases

Dr. Lawrence Scharer

In the majority of cases, your family physician can deal with the diagnosis and treatment of problems that affect the respiratory system—primarily the lungs and bronchial tubes, but also including the nose, pharynx and larynx. However, in particularly severe cases or when confronted with a troublesome diagnostic problem, he may refer you to a pulmonary specialist.

Recently while examining a patient, I asked him to breathe deeply for a few breaths and then asked him to breathe normally. He replied, "If I could breathe normally, Doc, I wouldn't be here."

Many patients seen by the pulmonary specialist have breathing difficulty as their primary complaint. Breathing is normally an unconscious effort for most of us and we pay it little attention. Breathlessness may not be alarming if it is expected as a result of exercise; but when it becomes unreasonably uncomfortable, it is frightening. Physicians use the word *dyspnea* to describe this sensation, and we say a patient is "dyspneic" if he has unexpected shortness of breath.

Symptoms

Symptoms which suggest pulmonary disease include dyspnea, cough, chest pain and HEMOPTYSIS (the spitting of blood or blood-stained sputum from the lungs or major air passages). Cough is normally a mechanism to clear the air passages when normal ciliary motion is not enough. (*Cilia* are rhythmically beating hairlike processes which project from the inner lining of the larger air passages of the lungs—*bronchi*—and propel mucus, dust particles, etc., upwards.) This may or may not occur with expulsion of sputum. (See PULMONARY DISEASES.)

Shortness of breath (DYSPNEA) may be a sign of something wrong the first time it happens, but usually comes on gradually. It is not just rapid breathing, which is normal with exercise. When it occurs without exertion it is never normal and can be especially serious if combined with certain other symptoms. When it is not caused by organic disease, it may be related to anxiety—a common complaint. The patient feels that he cannot take a deep enough breath and resorts to deep "sighing" respirations. This condition is often present with inactivity.

In some cases, chest pain associated with disease of the respiratory system may be made worse by coughing but not by breathing (as when the trachea, or "windpipe" is inflamed); such pain may appear to originate behind the breastbone. In other cases the pain may be made much worse by both deep breathing and coughing. It may be experienced as a sharp, stabbing sensation on either side of the chest, on the shoulder, under the arms or sometimes in the back. This is suggestive of an inflammation of the *pleural membrane* or *pleura*, the fluid-coated membrane which covers each lung and lines the chest wall and diaphragm. (See PLEURISY.)

The pulmonary specialist

Any symptoms which persist might cause the general physician to refer a patient to the pulmonary specialist. Sometimes a patient may be referred on the basis of an abnormal chest x-ray. In today's society of annual check-ups, heavy cigarette smoking and great publicity about lung cancer, a routine chest x-ray may reveal serious early pulmonary disease before symptoms are noticed.

The pulmonary specialist is fully trained in internal medicine, then must complete an additional two years of clinical training in pulmonary diseases. During this time he learns the essential principles of diagnosis and treatment of diseases of the chest. The American Thoracic Society is the national organization of physicians and other professionals interested in pulmonary diseases. It has chapters in every state and is the medical component of the American Lung Association, a voluntary organization of individuals interested in lung disease (each year they sell Christmas seals to raise funds for educational programs).

There has been some concern in recent years about a proper name for this new but growing subspecialty of medicine. "Pulmonology" has been suggested and someday may be adopted; or, who knows, perhaps "Lungology"? Until the early 1950s, the main concern of internists interested in diseases of the chest was tuberculosis; such physicians were usually known as "phthisiologists." The specialty changed dramatically when its practitioners developed an increasing interest in the study of pulmonary function and all diseases which can affect breathing.

Physicians trained today in internal medicine can diagnose and treat most routine pulmonary problems. The normal functioning of the lungs—"ventilation" to oxygenate blood and remove carbon dioxide—is of great

PULMONARY DISEASES

The lungs and respiratory passages can be affected by many pulmonary diseases. Smoking and air pollution are important causes of chronic bronchitis, in which the glands lining the bronchi enlarge, producing excess phlegm and difficulty in breathing. Emphysema is a condition where the air sacs become greatly expanded, and it often accompanies chronic bronchitis. Most lung cancers grow in the larger bronchi; the most important single cause of lung cancer is cigarette smoking.

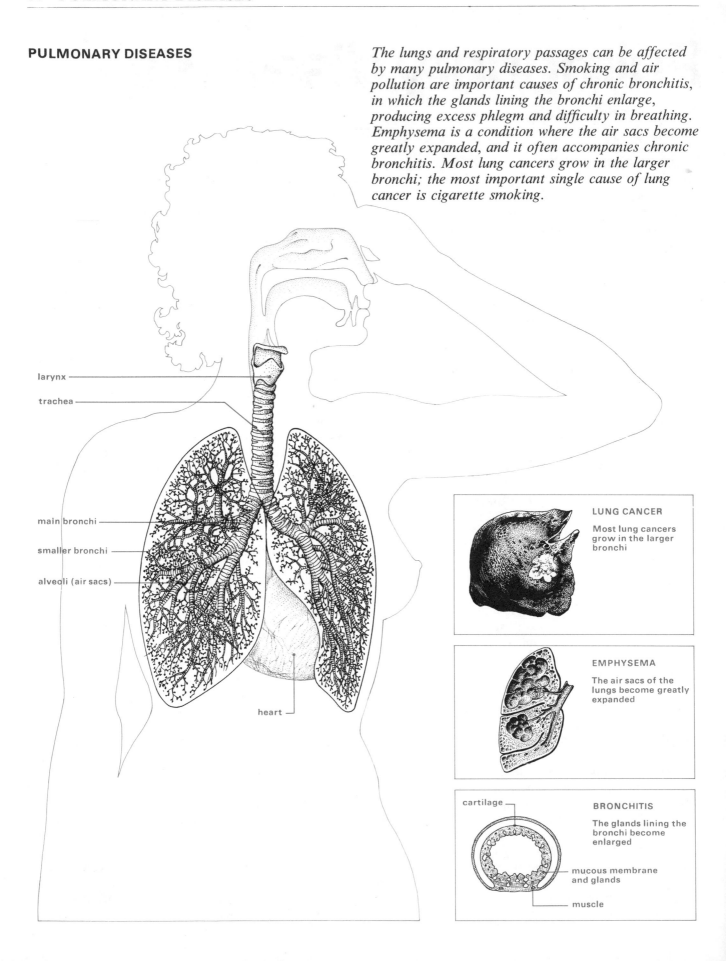

larynx

trachea

main bronchi

smaller bronchi

alveoli (air sacs)

heart

LUNG CANCER

Most lung cancers grow in the larger bronchi

EMPHYSEMA

The air sacs of the lungs become greatly expanded

cartilage

BRONCHITIS

The glands lining the bronchi become enlarged

mucous membrane and glands

muscle

importance to all physicians and surgeons, because success or failure in the treatment of many diseases depends on healthy lungs. Some internists may have a primary interest in pulmonary diseases, but also serve as general internists. When a general physician refers his patients to the specialist in pulmonary diseases, it will usually be in the patient's best interest and come about as a result of one of the following conditions: (1) symptoms are more prolonged than expected for the particular illness; (2) complications of respiratory insufficiency develop; (3) specialized diagnostic tests are necessary; (4) pulmonary surgery is being contemplated; (5) the illness is rare and expert care is warranted.

Diagnostic steps in pulmonary evaluation

A complete medical history and physical examination are the initial steps, as in all areas of clinical medicine. This is of particular importance in cases of suspected pulmonary disease, because the diagnosis can often be made from the patient's history alone. For example, there are areas in the United States which are endemic for certain fungal diseases (our Southwestern states for COCCIDIOIDOMYCOSIS; the Ohio Valley for HISTOPLASMOSIS). Travel or residence in these areas suggests that these diseases may be contributing to or causing the pulmonary symptoms of some patients. A history of excessive smoking or exposure to other pollutants raises the possibility of cancer of the lung. An occupational history which reveals exposure to known lung irritants also often points to a diagnosis without additional testing. Symptoms such as fever, weight loss or other constitutional signs are always important. The family history may suggest possible exposure to tuberculosis and other contagious diseases, as well as reveal inherited tendencies toward certain diseases. In pulmonary disease, previous lung x-rays, the results of certain laboratory tests and a history of other illnesses and their treatment are of great importance to the doctor.

The physical examination of the pulmonary patient is not limited to the chest cavity; much information can be obtained from examination of other parts of the body. Rounding and swelling of the ends of the fingers and curving of the fingernails, called *clubbing*, is common in cancer of the lung as well as in suppurative (pus-producing) lung diseases. In addition to changes in the nails, there may be *osteoarthropathy*, causing pain above finger joints, which is especially suggestive of lung cancer. There may be *cyanosis* (blueness of the lips, tongue, etc.) indicating an oxygen shortage in arterial blood. Neurologic findings which indicate a lack of oxygen, or excessive carbon dioxide retention, are important findings; peripheral EDEMA raises the possibility of HEART FAILURE.

(See also HEART DISEASE and the major article on **Cardiology**.)

X-ray studies

In addition to obtaining the patient's medical history and performing a thorough physical examination, there are a number of laboratory techniques and procedures which are of considerable help to the physician in the diagnosis and management of pulmonary diseases. The first is the standard chest x-ray. Most physicians will take both a back-to-front or "posterior-anterior" x-ray (PA) and one lateral (side) view in order to see as much of the chest area as possible. Fluoroscopy has been widely used in the past; but because of the excessive risk of radiation exposure, the routine use of fluoroscopy is no longer widely practiced. It is particularly helpful in certain situations, however, especially in evaluating the motions of the heart and diaphragm and diagnosing diseases of the esophagus ("gullet"). Special x-rays of the chest may be obtained by rotating the patient into various positions, using *tomography*—which allows the radiologist to separate the chest radiographically into different levels. The new development of *computerized axial tomography* ("CAT scans") provides an even more advanced diagnostic tool (for a description of this technique, see the appropriate section in the major article **Examination, Diagnosis and Therapy**). In addition, the older technique of *bronchography* is especially useful in patients with suspected BRONCHIECTASIS (abnormal and sometimes permanent widening of the larger or smaller air passages). In this procedure, a contrast material which is opaque to x-rays is placed into the bronchial "tree" to better outline possible disease states. Pulmonary vessels can best be identified by the techniques of *pulmonary angiography*, in which a substance opaque to x-rays is injected into the right side of the heart. This procedure has been especially helpful in the diagnosis of PULMONARY EMBOLISM (blockage of one of the pulmonary arteries).

Examination of sputum and skin tests

Other routine tests performed in patients with pulmonary disease include examination of expectorated mucus (which is not saliva but a thicker "cough sputum"). This can be smeared on a glass slide and examined under a microscope as well as "cultured" to detect the possible presence of infecting microorganisms. Furthermore, it can be examined for the possible presence of cancer cells; therefore, an examination of the patient's sputum is of great usefulness in the diagnosis of many pulmonary diseases. Skin testing for tuberculosis as well as various fungal diseases can be very helpful in the evaluation of a pulmonary patient. Positive results from skin tests indicate that the individual has had exposure and probably infection with a particular microorganism but in no way necessarily proves the presence of an active infection.

If the disease process involves the pleural membrane (pleura) and causes the abnormal collection of pleural fluid, aspiration of this fluid and careful examination will often provide a diagnosis of the underlying disease which is causing the fluid to accumulate. Furthermore, needle BIOPSY of the pleural lining can be performed at the same time. Positive biopsy results are quite diagnostic and often allow the physician to initiate appropriate therapy without more extensive procedures.

Testing pulmonary function

Physiologic studies of the lung are performed at all hospitals and can be done in a limited way as an office procedure. This allows the physician to analyze compartments of the lung and describe various lung volumes such as the *vital capacity* (the maximum volume of air which can be exhaled after a maximal inspiration). We use predicted normal values which are dependent on age, height and sex; deviations from these normal values are suggestive of specific disease states. In addition to the lung volumes, we also look at the speed with which a patient can exhale.

Abnormalitites of pulmonary function are often divided into two major categories: *obstructive*, which include those conditions in which there is prolongation of air flow; and *restrictive*, in which there is a reduction in the volume of air which can be inspired and exhaled. The first group of diseases includes ASTHMA, BRONCHITIS and EMPHYSEMA; the second group includes those diseases associated with abnormalities of the chest wall, as seen in patients with polio and in those in whom biopsied specimens of lung

PNEUMOTHORAX

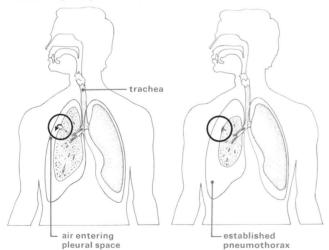

trachea

air entering pleural space

established pneumothorax

The pleural space—between the lung and chest wall—normally contains a partial vacuum. Pneumothorax occurs when air enters this space from the lung or air passages. This may be caused by a penetrating chest wound, a congenital lung weakness, or emphysema. The abnormal pressure of air in the pleural space prevents the lung on that side from expanding effectively, and in time may impede the function of the other lung. Pneumothorax may be treated by inserting a drain through the chest wall to release the air.

tissue show evidence of diseases which cause extensive scarring. In recent years much of this testing has been computerized; but the basic principles remain and the tests continue to be helpful in both diagnosing restrictive and obstructive conditions as well as monitoring improvement or deterioration in these disease states.

Special studies

One of the great advances in pulmonary medicine has been the increasing availability of *arterial blood gas* studies. These allow the physician to measure the actual amount of oxygen present in the blood as well as the level of carbon dioxide and whether the blood is abnormally acidic. Lower than normal oxygen saturation in the blood can be caused by a variety of disease states, including both heart and lung diseases. Carbon dioxide retention in the arterial blood is a very specific indication of some problem of ventilation; although there are many situations in which carbon dioxide retention may occur, they all are serious and often life threatening. Thus, this information can be very helpful in the assessment of the severity and management of the condition. *Arterial puncture* for collection of blood samples is somewhat more difficult than simple aspiration of blood from the veins, but is a routine test today in most hospitals and is often performed repeatedly.

Direct examination of the major air passages

Of particular interest to the pulmonary physician in the last few years is the development and widespread use of the *fiberoptic bronchoscope*. This instrument has made direct visualization of the bronchial tree under local anesthesia a fairly simple procedure. In addition to direct visualization, the physician can now collect specimens for culture or for analysis from deep within the lung, without relying only on expectorated material (which may be diluted or contaminated). Furthermore, fine brushes or biopsy forceps can be pushed through the instrument and even further into the lung so that specific tissue can be removed for microscopic examination. This instrument has dramatically changed the routine evaluation in many disease states since it is relatively easy to use, safe and well tolerated by the patient; in addition, it may provide material which, otherwise, could only be obtained by a major surgical operation. The risks of this procedure are minimal in the hands of an experienced physician.

Biopsy of lung tissue is often necessary to give a definitive diagnosis. This may be possible through the bronchoscope, but may also be performed directly through the chest wall with a biopsy needle. Finally, for diagnostic purposes, an open-lung biopsy may be indicated (which is a major operation, although it may involve the removal of only a small portion of lung tissue). An operation is, of course, indicated to remove a growth or any other substance which is locally interfering with the normal function of the lung.

Common pulmonary diseases

Diseases caused by infection are the most common, because they include complications of the common cold involving inflammation of the major air passages (tracheobronchial tree). Such illnesses are typically of short duration; complications of PNEUMONIA may occur, but not often. Treatment is usually symptomatic and adequate rest probably helps the patient recover more quickly than if the cold is ignored.

Influenza and the common cold

Whereas the common cold is caused by any of over 100 different types of viruses, INFLUENZA is caused by a specific virus and the resulting illness is considerably more debilitating. It is an infectious, epidemic disease characterized by high fever, muscle aches and a variety of constitutional symptoms. The virus has a special affinity for the respiratory tract; as a result, a severe and persisting cough is a characteristic sign of the illness. Because of damage to the surface lining, there is a good possibility of secondary bacterial infections of the lung, which may be severe enough to cause death in older and more debilitated people. Immunization with vaccines has been widely used in recent years and is quite effective in preventing the disease.

In both the common cold and influenza, there has been much debate about the routine use of antibiotics. Physicians generally agree that they do not affect the viral illness but it is debated whether "broad-spectrum" drugs (such as tetracycline) protect or adequately treat secondary bacterial infections. In general, it is probably best for them not to be used routinely except in patients with a known predisposition to recurrent bacterial infections, such as chronic obstructive pulmonary diseases.

Pneumonia

Pneumonia is a general term for an inflammation of the lungs. It is usually a primary disease but may be a complication of another illness. It can be caused by a variety of microorganisms, including some viruses, bacteria and fungi. It can also be caused by chemical irritants. The most common bacterial pneumonia is caused by infection with the pneumococcus; recently a new vaccine to provide some protection against this organism has been developed. Antibiotics are usually quite effective; but patients weakened by age, malnutrition or other complicating illnesses (such as cancer) still have a high mortality rate because of a low resistance not helped by drug therapy. The new vaccine will, hopefully, provide some protection in these special groups of patients.

The bacteria and viruses which cause pneumonia may be present in the nose or throat and not cause disease. For reasons not well understood, often when body defenses are reduced, these germs are inhaled into the lungs and cause inflammation in the small air sacs (the alveoli). Multiplication of the organisms is usually rapid and they may invade the bloodstream and carry the infection to other parts of the body.

Bacterial pneumonias can be treated with antibiotics. Penicillin is often used since it is effective against pneumococcal infections, which are the most common. Identification of the infecting organism from sputum or blood is important, however, so that the most appropriate antibiotic can be administered.

The treatment of pneumonia caused by infection with bacteria of the species *Mycoplasma pneumoniae* is relatively straightforward because this organism is quite sensitive to tetracycline and erythromycin. The problem, however, is making the diagnosis; the patients have a variable illness which usually includes a severe dry cough, high fever, but few findings on physical examination. Chest x-rays show various abnormalities but there are specific serologic blood tests available to confirm the diagnosis.

LEGIONNAIRE'S DISEASE is a newly recognized cause of pneumonia and has been widely publicized because of its infectious nature and high mortality rate. Erythromycin appears to be effective and since it also works with mycoplasmas and some bacteria, it has become a frequently used drug in the early treatment of patients with pneumonia prior to isolation of a specific causative agent or when the infectious agent is not apparent.

Pneumonia caused by a fungus, usually COCCIDIOIDO-MYCOSIS in the Southwestern United States and HISTOPLASMOSIS in the Ohio and Mississippi Valley areas, does not normally require treatment. These diseases can be diagnosed by a history of exposure, serologic tests and skin tests.

Tuberculosis

Perhaps the best-known lung infection—and still a great problem in some areas of the world—is TUBERCULOSIS, which invariably occurs by inhalation of the causative organism (the *tubercle bacillus*) carried on droplets of saliva or sputum expelled by the coughs and sneezes of a person with the active disease. When the organism gets into the small lung units (alveoli) it causes an activation of the body's defenses, both cellular and immunologic. Usually the tubercle bacilli are walled off where they originally arrive, but they may overwhelm local defenses and spread in the lung and throughout the body. In most healthy individuals the bacilli do not cause disease because they are controlled by the development of an immune response. Unfortunately, this protection is not always adequate and the disease can develop—especially in children and adolescents and in any patient with lowered resistance.

Fortunately, with the discovery of drugs to kill the tuberculous organisms, this infection is no longer the dreaded disease it was earlier in this century. Once it is discovered it can be treated effectively, but still requires close observation and patient cooperation for a relatively long period of time (usually two years). In 1977 there were approximately 30,000 new cases in the United States and probably about 250,000 cases under medical supervision. In recent years, public health officials have also concentrated their efforts on trying to identify individuals infected with tubercle bacilli, but who show no symptoms of the disease. Once the germ has entered the body and caused even an unnoticed reaction, hypersensitivity to the organism develops which can be demonstrated by a *tuberculin skin test*. Individuals with positive results from this skin test (done by the Mantoux or Tine methods) are at greater risk of developing tuberculosis in the future, especially if the infection occurs below the age of 25, if their test results have recently changed from negative to positive ("converters"), or if they have impaired defenses because of other medical problems. Treatment of these groups of patients with antituberculous medication reduces their chances of ever developing the active form of the disease.

Chronic obstructive lung diseases: asthma, bronchitis and emphysema.

These diseases are quite distinct clinically (the way they affect the patients) and pathologically (the way they affect the lung tissues), but there may be considerable overlap so that for purposes of study they are often grouped together. They all cause airway obstruction and share common symptoms of cough, wheezing and shortness of breath (dyspnea).

Asthma

Asthma is best characterized by its reversibility; between attacks the patient is usually without symptoms. Sometimes the disease may be chronic and more difficult to identify. There is an abnormal responsiveness of the bronchial tree and the smaller air passages become obstructed by muscle spasm, swelling of the lining mucosa and the accumulation of thick secretions. An identifiable allergy may cause attacks, but more often the attacks are not caused by any well-defined factors. Allergies, infection, irritation and emotional factors may all play a role. The disease can affect people of all ages; an estimated 1% of the population has asthma.

Severe shortness of breath is the most common and distressing symptom, usually associated with a dry cough and wheezing. The attacks may follow exercise, inhalation of an irritant such as cigarette smoke, or, most often, may occur for no apparent reason. They may subside without treatment or require emergency treatment and hospitalization.

Prevention of the attacks, whenever possible, is most important. Identification of possible allergic factors, avoidance of known irritants, removing house pets, and reducing house dust as much as possible may be quite helpful. Once attacks have started, therapy is directed at relieving spasm of the air passages to the lungs (bronchospasm) and shrinking swollen mucosa (the lining of the air passages). Effective drugs can be given by various routes, from orally to intravenously, in severe attacks. These will be discussed later in this section.

Bronchitis

The term "chronic bronchitis" describes an illness with chronic cough (usually "productive"—that is, with the expectoration of thick sputum), which is present for at least several months over a period of about two years. It is usually the result of prolonged irritation of the bronchial lining, which causes an increase in the secretion of mucus and some reduction in the effectiveness of the cleaning mechanisms of the cilia. It is most commonly seen in cigarette smokers, but prolonged air pollution from any cause may be a contributing factor. Weather and season may also play a role, with cold winter air or fog often related to an increased severity of the disease.

The treatment is to remove the source of irritation; but, unfortunately, many individuals with this disease prefer to continue smoking and coughing, rather than give up cigarettes. Since infection (especially in winter months) may contribute to the disease, antibiotics are used both prophylactically and freely any time there is a possibility they might be effective. *Bronchodilators* (drugs which open up the air passages to the lungs)—in the form of an aerosol spray, tablets, capsules or liquids—are often used as well, especially if there is a question of bronchospasm. Patients who appear to have acute intermittent asthmatic attacks superimposed on chronic cough and the abnormal production of sputum are often said to have "asthmatic bronchitis."

Emphysema

Pulmonary emphysema is the most disabling of this group, for it results from actual destruction of lung tissue. The cause is unknown, but since it is often associated with chronic bronchitis, it has been assumed that recurrent infection and irritation of the smaller branches of the bronchial tree is the most likely cause. It is rare for asthma to progress to emphysema unless the patient has symptoms of bronchitis as well. A small group of patients has been shown to have an inherited deficiency of a specific blood plasma protein (alpha$_1$-antitrypsin) which predisposes them to develop emphysema.

Shortness of breath is the predominant symptom, which becomes increasingly severe and fixed as opposed to a daily variability seen in patients with asthma and bronchitis. Cough, excess production of sputum and wheezing may all be present, but are usually the result of associated bronchitis. Treatment with bronchodilators may provide some relief. If the disease is severe and progressive, the patient will develop increasing cyanosis (lack of oxygen) and carbon dioxide retention, both causing increasing

EMPHYSEMA

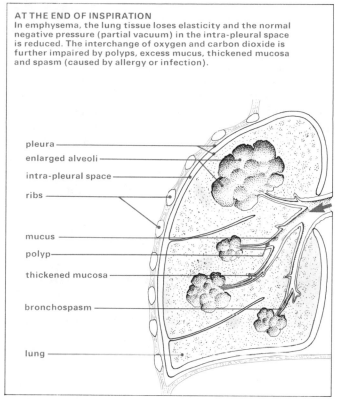

AT THE END OF INSPIRATION
In emphysema, the lung tissue loses elasticity and the normal negative pressure (partial vacuum) in the intra-pleural space is reduced. The interchange of oxygen and carbon dioxide is further impaired by polyps, excess mucus, thickened mucosa and spasm (caused by allergy or infection).

pleura
enlarged alveoli
intra-pleural space
ribs
mucus
polyp
thickened mucosa
bronchospasm
lung

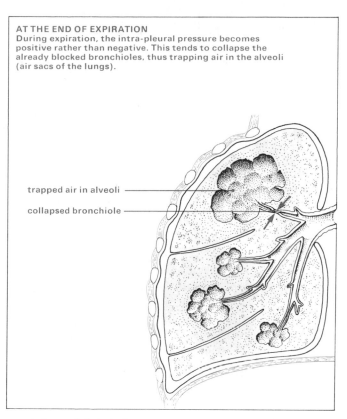

AT THE END OF EXPIRATION
During expiration, the intra-pleural pressure becomes positive rather than negative. This tends to collapse the already blocked bronchioles, thus trapping air in the alveoli (air sacs of the lungs).

trapped air in alveoli
collapsed bronchiole

Emphysema is a progressive disease in which the air sacs (alveoli) of the lungs become overdistended or inflated with trapped air. The condition may be associated with an inherited weakness of the lungs, an infection of the lung tissue, or the prolonged inhalation of polluted air (including smoking).

heart strain secondary to high blood pressure in the lungs (pulmonary hypertension) and often heart failure. Treatment of the heart disease (COR PULMONALE) helps to control symptoms, but the disease is slowly progressive and disabling. Pulmonary hypertension cannot be treated with the same drugs used to treat systemic hypertension, and once it develops it is usually progressive.

The treatment of emphysema is unfortunately inadequate; thus, physicians and public health workers are devoting much effort to *prevention* of the disease. Widespread publicity is now being given to the association of bronchitis and emphysema with cigarette smoking, air pollution and exposure to certain occupational dusts and fumes. Certainly, once the diagnosis is suggested, patients must avoid bronchial irritants whenever possible.

Treatment of emphysema is similar to that for bronchitis and asthma, for it is directed at relieving bronchial obstruction and bronchospasm when they are present. The drugs used fall into the following categories:

(1) *Sympathomimetic agents*, such as epinephrine, isoproterenol and terbutaline. These act by stimulating receptors in bronchial smooth muscle which allow relaxation and bronchodilation. They are often adminis-

tered through inhaled aerosols or by injections beneath the skin (subcutaneous injections), but they can also be given by mouth (orally). They are fast acting and often give dramatic relief. Side effects, which are unfortunately common, include tremor, rapid pulse, headache, nervousness and hypertension.

(2) *Methylxanthines*, such as theophylline and aminophylline. These act by inhibiting chemical mediators which cause constriction of the bronchial tree (bronchoconstriction). They can be given by mouth or by rectum in suppository form and are often administered intravenously in critically ill patients. They work synergistically (that is, by combining and enhancing therapeutic effects) with the sympathomimetic agents and are thus often administered together. Side effects are less common, but include gastrointestinal upsets, palpitations, irritability and insomnia.

(3) *Corticosteroids*, such as prednisone, relax bronchial smooth muscle and reduce swelling of the lining membranes of the air passages. High dosage and prolonged use may lead to numerous side effects, including peptic ulcer, fluid retention, weight gain, hypertension, mental changes and thinning of the bones. They have usually been given orally, but recently inhaled topical steroid aerosols have become available; these appear to be effective without giving rise to numerous side effects (except local irritation), since their absorption into the bloodstream is minimal.

(4) *Antibiotics*, such as penicillin or tetracycline, are often used whenever there is a question of an associated bacterial infection. Many patients take them, especially

during the winter months, in the hope of preventing infections from occurring.

(5) *Expectorants*, especially water, are used to thin secretions and make expectoration easier. Cough suppressants, however, are avoided since any mucus present will block the airflow if allowed to remain in the bronchial tree.

Physical conditioning and breathing exercises have become popular treatment in patients with emphysema. This disease begins insidiously and is slowly progressive. Many patients are not diagnosed until a fairly late stage in the disease. They can be taught controlled breathing and energy conservation techniques at any time to give them greater breathing capacity. Patients are taught to use pursed lip breathing to prolong expiration to prevent collapse of bronchioles (the smallest air passages of the bronchial tree). They can be shown various physical maneuvers to aid in production of sputum.

In rare situations, it may be necessary to consider surgical treatment. Some patients have large air-containing sacs called *bullae*, which compress normal adjacent lung tissue; removal of these nonfunctioning areas improves overall lung function.

Lung tumors

Primary tumors of the lung may be benign, but are usually removed surgically because of the possibility that they may be or become malignant. When we speak of lung cancer, we usually mean *bronchogenic carcinoma*, which is a malignant growth arising in the bronchial mucous membrane.

There are several types which have different clinical and pathologic characteristics. The most common is *epidermoid* or *squamous cell* carcinoma. This often occurs in cigarette smokers, is located close to the root of the lung and causes complications because of obstruction of the bronchial tree beyond the tumor. Fortunately, such cancers are slow-growing and slow to metastasize (spread to other parts of the body) and, therefore, have a somewhat better prognosis if discovered early in their course. Also more common among smokers is the undifferentiated or "oat-cell" carcinoma, but this type of cancer is rapid in growth and early to metastasize. Because of their very aggressive nature, treatment today is with special drugs (chemotherapy) rather than surgery, since the tumor is usually inoperable once discovered. Another type of tumor is the *adenocarcinoma*, which looks quite different to the pathologist because it appears to contain glandular tissue. These tumors often arise on the outer edge of the lung and are confused clinically and pathologically with glandular tumors from elsewhere (especially the gastrointestinal tract) which spread to the lung by means of the bloodstream. The final group of tumors are called *bronchiolar* or *alveolar cell* since they arise in the terminal lung units (alveoli). These are often misdiagnosed since

they may behave like a pneumonic process or may arise multicentrically. Both adenocarcinomas and *alveolar cell* cancers tend to spread before being diagnosed.

If the patient appears to have a tumor which has not spread beyond the lung and it is not known to be of the "oat-cell" type, surgical excision remains the treatment of choice. The best prognosis is with small, asymptomatic lesions discovered on routine chest x-rays.

If surgery is not feasible because of evidence of spread of the tumor, or if it is known to be of the "oat-cell" type, or if the patient's medical condition rules out surgery, other treatment is available. Depending on the individual case, radiotherapy (with cobalt) or chemotherapy may control symptoms but may not significantly prolong life.

See also the major article on **Oncology.**

Diseases caused by dust inhalation

Dust diseases of the lungs (pneumoconioses) are named after the dusts which cause them. SILICOSIS is caused by the inhalation of silica in crystalline form small enough to be retained in the bronchial tree. This results in progressive scarring of the lung tissues and interferes with lung function. It develops in proportion to the amount of silica inhaled and the length of time a worker is exposed to it—whether in mining, sandblasting or in various foundry jobs where workers are exposed to quartz rock.

ASBESTOSIS is a diffuse fibrosis of the lung caused by prolonged exposure to airborne asbestos fibers. Increasing evidence points to the fact that cancer of the lung and intestinal tract are more common in workers exposed to fine asbestos fibers which are both inhaled and swallowed.

"Black lung" (or *coal-worker's pneumoconiosis*) is well known to most readers as an occupational disease of coal miners. It is caused by the accumulation of coal dust in the lungs. In recent years there have been attempts to link shortness of breath (dyspnea), chronic cough and the excessive production of sputum to this exposure and to distinguish it from bronchitis caused by cigarette smoking in this same population. If the exposure is extensive and prolonged—especially if the patient is also exposed to silica dust—then massive progressive fibrosis (the abnormal formation of fibrous tissue) may occur as a late stage of the disease. In such cases, more objective evidence of interference with lung function can be demonstrated.

Workers in other occupations also have their share of lung disease. For example: *Berylliosis* is caused by inhaling beryllium dust and can be most serious. *Bagassosis* is caused by breathing dust from the pressed stalks of sugar cane. *Farmer's lung* is caused by inhaling fungal spores in moldy hay; it is more an allergic sensitivity, which can be quite disabling during the acute exposure stage. *Byssinosis* is caused by the inhalation of cotton dust.

Retention of dust in the lungs does not invariably lead to disease, but it may cause suspicious shadows on a lung

x-ray if the dust is sufficiently dense. The doctor can usually make the diagnosis from a careful history.
(See also PNEUMOCONIOSIS.)

Pulmonary embolism and infarction

An *embolism* means the plugging of an artery, usually by a blood clot carried from another part of the body. The clot (embolus) may start in the heart and go to the brain or an extremity, or it may start in a peripheral vein and travel to the heart and then to the lung. An *infarction* is a localized area of tissue death (necrosis) secondary to the obstruction, caused by a loss of blood supply to the affected area.

It is estimated that 90% of pulmonary emboli originally arise in the veins of the legs or pelvis. They usually develop in the following situations: (1) conditions which predispose to poor blood flow and even stagnation, such as in persons confined to bed; (2) patients with a disorder of the normal blood-clotting mechanism with a tendency to clotting, such as occasionally occurs in some women taking birth control pills; or (3) inflammation of a vein (PHLEBITIS) which causes a local irritation resulting in increased clotting and THROMBOSIS (a blood clot which remains at its site of formation).

If a pulmonary embolism is very large, it may cause sudden death. The majority of clots which reach the lungs are probably very small and cause no symptoms. Only about 10% are large enough to cause obstruction and pulmonary infarction. The most common symptoms are breathlessness, pleuritic chest pain, cough with the production of bloody sputum (hemoptysis), and a rapid heartbeat.

Pulmonary embolisms usually occur in bedridden patients; they may also occur following major surgery, accidents, or during medical treatment for heart failure or pneumonia. The symptoms may initially be misinterpreted, but a sudden change in the patient's condition usually alerts the doctor to the complication. Treatment is primarily directed toward prevention of more emboli forming and causing further lung injury. If drug therapy is ineffective or impractical, and there is reliable evidence of repeated embolization, surgical interruption of the *vena cava* (the large vein which brings blood to the heart from the legs and pelvis) usually will control the problem.

Conclusion

In conclusion, I would point out that we have made great progress in diagnosing and treating many lung diseases, especially the infectious diseases. However, as we succeed in controlling infections, we seem to be seeing more and more diseases related to cigarette smoking and other forms of air pollution. Cancer of the lung is now the most common malignancy in men, and emphysema is becoming a significant cause of death and disability in both sexes (especially between the ages of 50 and 70).

The relationship of these diseases to cigarette smoking is well known and we must find some effective way to get patients to stop smoking. Earlier diagnosis of any disease will always permit a better chance for successful treatment, but the statistics for cancer of the lung are still quite depressing with currently available forms of treatment.

The defense of the lung against smoking and all forms of air pollution is the primary objective of the American Lung Association, as well as being a major concern of all public health workers. Once lung disease has occurred, we can usually diagnose and sometimes treat, but prevention makes the most sense.

Orthopedics Dr. Henry O. Marsh

The modern orthopedist is primarily concerned with the diagnosis and treatment of injuries and diseases that affect the bones and joints and with correcting skeletal deformities. His tasks range from the resetting of a dislocated shoulder (which any physician can do) to the highly skilled surgical replacement of a diseased hip joint with an artificial ball-and-socket joint or even surgical repair of a slipped disk (an ability he shares with the neurosurgeon).

Orthopedics is one of the oldest specialties of Medicine. It dates back to 1741, when Dr. Nicholas André, Professor of Medicine at the University of Paris, coined the word "orthopedics" to describe that area of medicine concerned with the treatment and prevention of deformities in children. Modern orthopedics goes far beyond this narrow definition and now encompasses all conditions that affect the musculoskeletal system, which consists of bones, joints, muscles, cartilage, tendons, nerves, ligaments and related structures of the body.

How do you choose an orthopedist and how can you know that he is competent? Most often you will be referred to one by your personal physician, who may be able to judge which orthopedist is best qualified to deal with you as a patient and to treat your particular problem. You might also meet an orthopedist for the first time if you are an accident victim and are brought to the emergency room of a hospital, or you might seek one out on the recommendation of a friend who has a similar problem.

The certified orthopedist qualifies by graduation from medical school, followed by five years of postgraduate clinical training and experience. The first year may be a revolving internship in general medicine; or it can, by choice, be entirely in surgery: the second year will be in surgery (plastic surgery, neurosurgery, general surgery, etc.) with the last three years devoted entirely to gaining knowledge and experience in all areas of orthopedics and orthopedic surgery, including pediatric, hand, total joint replacement and all forms of reconstructive surgery. He or she must then practice for at least three years before seeking membership in the American Academy of Orthopedic Surgery, a society devoted to the continuing education of its members, the encouragement of orthopedic research and the maintenance of a standard of excellence in orthopedic practice.

The orthopedist works in close cooperation with family doctors, rheumatologists and other specialists who refer patients to him. When he has made his examination and diagnosis and decided upon what treatments are indicated, he should discuss his findings with the referring physician. This might be done by telephone, letter, or in personal conversation, and it is important for several reasons. A family doctor may be able, especially in chronic conditions, to carry on treatments that have been recommended. If surgery is required and the patient or parents may be apprehensive about it, the referring physician can be of great help in discussing, explaining and reinforcing the specialist's recommendations and in preparing the patient for surgery (emotionally and perhaps physically). Equally important, when there is close cooperation between doctors seeing the same patient, the patient cannot "play off" one against the other to obtain drugs from each, especially those which are required for sedation and to relieve pain and which can become addictive.

If one orthopedist should refer you to another, you should accept his recommendation as being in your best interest. As in other specialties, some orthopedists limit their practice to specific surgical procedures and treatments.

Such referrals are often made in certain diseases and high-risk surgical cases which the general orthopedist may see only two or three times a year; he knows that the patient will be better served by an orthopedist who deals with such patients regularly.

Diagnostic procedures

Unless a severe injury calls for emergency action, the orthopedist starts by obtaining a careful family and personal medical history and the details of the specific complaint that has brought you to him. He may order various laboratory tests following a thorough physical examination of the bodily parts affected. He must know about drugs to which you are allergic, the clotting time of

The bones of the skeleton (right) are living tissues, quite unlike the brittle and bleached collection of bones seen wired together in museums or biology classes. The skeleton is composed of 50% water and 50% inorganic salts (mainly calcium and phosphorus) and begins to form in the fetus during the second month of pregnancy. It is the supporting and protective framework of the body and provides points of attachment for the muscles.

THE SKELETON

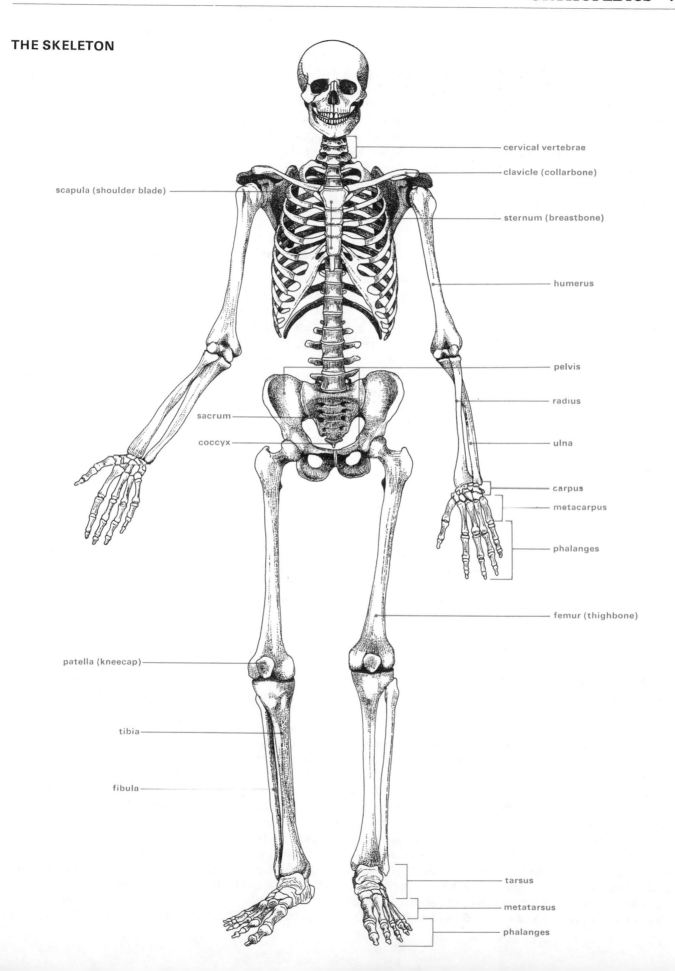

cervical vertebrae

clavicle (collarbone)

scapula (shoulder blade)

sternum (breastbone)

humerus

pelvis

radius

sacrum

coccyx

ulna

carpus

metacarpus

phalanges

femur (thighbone)

patella (kneecap)

tibia

fibula

tarsus

metatarsus

phalanges

your blood and the existence of any systemic diseases. Many patients have problems which involve displacement and injury to bones, ligaments and other parts of the musculoskeletal system; therefore part of his diagnosis and evaluation of a complaint is based on "visualization."

The discovery of x-rays in 1895 provided a tremendous impetus to all of medical science, but in particular to orthopedics. For the first time broken bones could be visualized and properly set. The position of displaced joints, the extent of abnormal bone growths and other conditions could actually be seen. Without x-rays and the sophisticated radiological techniques that have continued to evolve, we would still be working blind—a situation almost impossible to comprehend today.

Many sophisticated radiological tests exist which the orthopedist relies on for diagnosis and evaluation:

Arthrograms
Arthrograms may be used to evaluate the internal condition of a joint, often to learn if an implanted artificial hip joint has loosened, or to diagnose the dislocation of a child's hip. Dye is injected into the joint to provide contrast on x-rays. The dye shows up white on the film and clearly outlines internal structures and abnormalities that may be present. The dye is quickly absorbed by the body and causes no ill effects.

Myelograms
Myelograms may be used to determine if a ruptured or herniated intervertebral disk is present in the lumbar part of the spine to cause low back pain, if bony spurs are pressing upon nerves, or if a tumor is present. In this test the contrast material is injected (by means of a lumbar puncture) into the cerebrospinal fluid which surrounds the spinal cord. The patient is placed upon a special x-ray table that can be tilted, much like a playground teeter-totter. This causes the contrast material to flow up and down within the spinal canal. If there is a ruptured disk, the material flows around it and reveals obstructions on the x-ray film. Obstructions may also be caused by tumors and other "space-occupying" lesions.

Bone scans
The bone scan is performed by injecting a small amount of radioactive material into the bloodstream. A sophisticated Geiger counter is then passed over the body to determine where the radioactive material has concentrated. If the machine shows significant concentrations in the musculo-skeletal system, this may indicate infection, bone tumor, "wear-and-tear" arthritis, or other abnormalities which can usually be identified on the basis of additional tests and the patient's medical history. One of the most useful applications of this technique is to determine, as early as possible, the spread of cancer cells (metastasis) to bones from a known primary site—such as the breast or lung.

CAT scans
The newest diagnostic tool of use in orthopedics is the *CAT scan* (computerized axial tomography). This modern-age miracle takes thin cross section x-rays of the body as it passes over it, much as one cuts thin slices of bologna. The computer collates the many x-rays into a three-dimensional picture. If a tumor is present, or if the spinal canal is narrowed to pinch or "choke off" a nerve, this can be visualized. The clinical application of this special technique is just now being thoroughly studied and all possible areas in which it might be useful are not yet known.

Problems of concern to the orthopedist

The orthopedist treats patients of all ages, with problems that can be grouped into several broad categories—such as hereditary and congenital defects (present at birth or evident shortly thereafter), developmental disorders, degenerative diseases, infections, tumors and other abnormal growths, and a wide range of injuries due to trauma. He may make use of medical, mechanical or surgical methods or (when required) combinations of all three. We will discuss these categories of problem in order.

Hereditary and congenital defects
Hereditary defects are those which are passed on to children in the sex cells (ovum and sperm) of the parents. They may result in defects of bone and growth, but may also affect other organ systems of the body and have secondary effects in the musculoskeletal system. *Osteochondromatosis*, for example, is a known hereditary disease, characterized by warty bony growths that appear over the skeleton. Such growths are surgically removed if they are deforming, cosmetically objectionable, or if there is any question of malignancy.

HEMOPHILIA is a hereditary disease in which the clotting of blood is impaired and hemorrhage occurs which may be difficult to control. This condition is usually treated by the hematologist (an expert in diagnosing and treating blood disorders), but it can also cause destructive changes in joints and require surgical intervention. In such cases the orthopedist and hematologist work in close cooperation, with the latter closely monitoring the blood and supplying it with the missing substances to make it clot during surgery and during the early healing period.

There are many other hereditary diseases that affect bones and its connective tissues directly, and systemic diseases that affect them indirectly. DIABETES MELLITUS, for example, runs in families and in advanced stages may cause circulatory blockage of blood in the lower extremities with the possible complication of GANGRENE; the ortho-pedic surgeon may be called in to perform an amputation above the dead tissue as a life-saving measure.

Congenital defects usually develop within the fetus as it matures and may be due to environmental factors affecting the mother—for example, reactions to drugs such as thalidomide; infectious diseases, such as rubella (German measles); radiation exposure and other environmental factors not yet fully understood. Defects may result from a combination of hereditary, developmental and environmental factors.

Hip dislocation

A congenital hip dislocation may be present at birth or develop shortly thereafter and may be due to both hereditary and *developmental disorders*. It is seen five times more often in girls than in boys, and is more likely to be found in the infant of a mother who has suffered the same condition; but it is also seen in infants whose mothers did not have the disorder. In either case, treatment is best undertaken immediately after birth. Nonsurgical treatment, much like that advocated by Hippocrates centuries ago, is frequently used by orthopedists today. Hippocrates recommended that the bones be bandaged into their correct positions. Modern methods involve the application of corrective plaster casts to hold the hip in place while muscles and ligaments are developing during the first few months. If correction is not achieved in this fashion, then surgical correction is usually performed within the first year of life. If the young child is allowed to walk for several years with the dislocation, gross deformity occurs and surgical treatment becomes complex: in such cases complete correction may not always be possible. This condition is becoming less common as routine examinations are carried out on infants soon after birth. Nevertheless, orthopedists see too many young girls who walk with the typical "duck-waddling gait" which, when seen, can be diagnosed from across the room.

Clubfoot

Clubfoot (talipes) is a congenital defect which in most cases can be successfully treated by nonsurgical methods. Immediately following birth the feet are gently stretched at periodic intervals back toward their proper position and held there so they can grow normally. (See CLUBFOOT.)

Other congenital defects include too many or too few fingers and toes, the absence of a hand and other gross deformities. Surgical treatment is always directed toward obtaining the best functional and cosmetic results possible. Extra appendages can be amputated. Reconstructive surgery can permit a finger to function as a thumb, providing the child with grasping ability, so important to everyday living.

Scoliosis

Scoliosis is a disorder in which there is an abnormal curvature of the spine in a side-to-side direction (the natural curves of the spine are from front to back). It is much more common in girls than boys and may arise from a variety of causes including hereditary, developmental, or

environmental influences and other factors not yet known. The condition usually is seen at about junior high school age and is frequently first detected in school screening programs; it can often be successfully treated by special exercises and posture training. If the curvature is well advanced, braces are required and must be worn day and night for the remainder of the growth period. The "Milwaukee brace" is uncomfortable, often embarrassing to the young person who must wear it, and requires frequent adjustments. But in most cases (if the condition is detected and treated at an early stage) it can eliminate the need for complex surgery, such as spinal fusion and the insertion of a steel rod to hold the spine in proper

ARTIFICIAL JOINTS

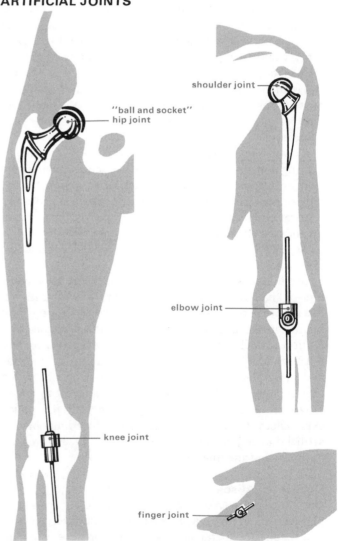

shoulder joint

"ball and socket" hip joint

elbow joint

knee joint

finger joint

Artificial joints are used to replace joints which have been severely damaged by arthritis. The most successful and widely performed replacement operations are to implant artificial hip joints. The ball and socket is made up of a metal strut and a metal or plastic cup.

alignment. This is an example of a condition that the general orthopedist often refers to a colleague who specializes in spinal deformities. (See also SPINAL CURVATURE.)

Degenerative diseases

Degenerative diseases—such as OSTEOARTHRITIS, RHEUMATOID ARTHRITIS and other forms of rheumatic disease which may eventually become disabling—are usually treated in their early stages by general physicians and rheumatologists (see the major article on **Rheumatology**). They are referred to the orthopedist when joint pain and musculoskeletal deformity require his special skills. Conservative (nonsurgical) treatments are almost always tried first and these include special exercises and application of casts, splints, or other forms of bracing. If pain is not relieved and deformity continues to progress, surgery may be necessary. Fusion of the affected joints in the proper position may improve function and relieve pain and is an extremely useful procedure—as is the "rerouting" of tendons to improve their functional capabilities, especially in joints of the hand. Total *joint replacement* may be necessary.

As we grow older our joints—especially the weight-bearing joints—tend to "wear out," much as moving parts do in an automobile. When other treatments fail, total joint replacement can produce dramatic results and quickly restore mobility, relieve pain and permit many semi-invalids to return to nearly normal living. This is one of the most rewarding satisfactions an orthopedic surgeon can experience.

The first successful total joint replacement involved the hip—a "ball-and-socket" joint which readily lends itself to this type of surgery. The knee is also a weight-bearing joint, but its replacement is not as successful; this is because knee motion is much more complicated and artificial knees have not been able to duplicate natural movements. The stress and strain placed on the implanted joint, when the patient tries to achieve natural motion, often causes it to loosen. However, if the knee is badly worn and the patient experiences disabling pain that keeps him immobile, an artificial knee joint may bring relief and greatly improve mobility and the quality of life.

Deficiency diseases

DEFICIENCY DISEASES are treated medically by general physicians, but they may affect the musculoskeletal system and require the therapeutic skill of the orthopedist. When bones become soft, porous and deformed, or become hard and brittle (subject to frequent fractures), the patient is often referred to the orthopedist for specialized treatment such as bracing to prevent deformity, the application of casts, or surgical procedures.

Infections can occur in bones, joints and connective tissue, as in other parts of the body; the infecting microorganisms may be carried in the blood from inflammations in other organ systems. Before the advent of antibiotics, a large part of orthopedic practice involved treatment of "acute hematogenous (blood-borne) osteomyelitis." Hospital wards were once filled with children suffering from this painful, crippling infectious disease. Now it is rare, but is still occasionally seen and can be serious if not diagnosed and treated early.

Tumors and other bone growths

Bones are subject to tumors, cysts and other abnormal growths, most of which are benign (relatively harmless or not a threat to life). The first indication of their presence may be a fracture, or pain may develop suddenly in an affected area. A BIOPSY of suspicious growths should be obtained as soon as possible to rule out malignancy. *Benign* growths can often be surgically removed. Primary *malignant* bone tumors (malignancies originating in bone) are quite rare. Secondary bone malignancies are much more common. In these tumors the cancer cells spread (metastasize) to the bones from primary sites in other parts of the body, especially from the breast, lung, prostate, kidney or thyroid.

Pain is an important first symptom. A bone scan or biopsy may detect and confirm the presence of cancer that has spread from a primary site elsewhere in the body. Treatment of primary bone cancer at present is unsatisfactory. Amputation above the lesion has been the standard procedure for years, but this is being replaced in selected cases by a combination treatment with anticancer (cytotoxic) drugs, radiation therapy and, as the last resort, with surgery. Research in this field is active today and we have hopes that more effective treatments for malignant disease will be available in the not too distant future. When the orthopedist detects cancer in one of his patients, he often seeks the assistance of an *oncologist*, a physician who specializes in treating all types of malignant disease (see the major article on **Oncology**).

Bursitis and other inflammatory disorders

Among the inflammatory disorders seen most often by the orthopedist, excluding those related to the various chronic rheumatic diseases, are the following:

Bursitis. This painful, sometimes disabling condition can first appear in its acute form following injury, or it may develop slowly without a known cause and become chronic. It may be caused by repeated friction, resulting from a person's occupation (*olecranon bursitis* is a medical word used to describe "miner's elbow"; *prepatellar bursitis* describes "housemaid's knee"; *ischial bursitis* describes "tailor's bottom" or "weaver's bottom"; *subdeltoid* and *subacromial bursitis* are used to describe arthritis of the shoulder bursas).

Bursas are padlike sacs in connective tissues. Their function, generally, is to reduce friction between tendon and bone and tendon and ligament. When injury or friction causes them to become inflamed, the result is pain, swelling and limitation of movement. The acute phase is treated with rest of the extremity (a sling or splint) until the pain has been reduced in supporting muscles and exercises can be started to prevent adhesions. Analgesics (painkillers, such as aspirin), heat and massage help relieve symptoms, which usually pass in a week or two.

In chronic BURSITIS the cause or causes should be identified, if possible, and corrected, especially if they are related to occupation or sports activities. Localized treatments, as described above, give temporary relief. Relief over long periods is often obtained by injections of drugs directly into the affected bursa (hydrocortisone or prednisolone with procaine). At the same time calcium deposits, if present, may be broken up with the needle. Disabling adhesions may be treated by careful manipulation of affected joints. If muscle wasting has occurred from the prolonged inactivity caused by chronic pain, specific exercises must be carried out to strengthen them.

Tendonitis and *tenosynovitis* are often associated with various forms of arthritis, or may follow injury. There are no infectious microorganisms to explain the inflammatory process which affects the tenosynovium (tendon sheath) and tendons, causing intense pain and limitation of movements. The cause may be obscure and adults of both sexes may be affected. Splinting, local applications of heat, and anti-inflammatory drugs may provide symptomatic relief. The injection of corticosteroid drugs directly into the affected area provides rapid, definitive treatment. In severe cases, surgical incision of the tendon sheath may be done to relieve constricting pressure and irritation.

Backache

Backache may result from inflammatory disease processes—but can be caused by almost as many things as there are people; it is in a class all by itself. It is probably the most common complaint seen by general physicians, neurologists and orthopedists, and is the cause of more lost work days in business and industry than any other work-related disorder. (See BACKACHE.)

A comprehensive study was recently made in California of more than a million patients who, during a single year, suffered back pain severe enough to require hospitalization. This study, based on information derived from the patients' hospital discharge records, suggests that about 10 million Americans are hospitalized each year for back pain, at a cost of about $1.38 billion (or 1.4% of all health care dollars spent in the United States). This cost does not include the expense of outpatient care, or the cost to patients and employers of time lost from work.

Almost all of us, at least once in our lifetimes, will suffer some form of back disability—such as a pulled or inflamed muscle, LUMBAGO, SCIATICA, or a ruptured or herniated intervertebral disk (SLIPPED DISK). The problem is so widespread and its manifestations are so diverse that it becomes a fertile field for charlatans, hucksters of proprietary medicines, and unsolicited advice over the backyard fence. This fact of life can readily be verified by reading almost any newspaper or magazine which accepts advertising or by watching television. The most sensible approach to the problem is to seek competent medical attention which can prove to be less costly in the end. Most patients with sprained backs or pulled muscles may require only time, heat and simple medications for complete recovery; but some patients with sprained backs already afflicted with "wear-and-tear" arthritis can never be expected to recover fully.

A small percentage of people with ruptured intervertebral disks may require surgery, but I must emphasize that this is a *small* percentage. Most back problems are responsive to nonoperative treatment—corrective exercise, proper posture, a firm mattress, special medications and control of weight. For short periods, the wearing of a back support may be required.

Orthopedic surgery

The gray-haired lady entered my office on crutches, accompanied by her two devoted daughters and grandchildren. She complained of almost constant pain from degeneration of one hip due to "wear-and-tear" arthritis. Any twist of the hip or misstep sent a jab of pain through her, and restful sleep had become impossible. Her family doctor had referred her for consideration of a new total hip. However, she was a poor surgical risk, with a history of blood clots in the leg after childbirth, high blood pressure and diabetes. She was also a little on the heavy side. We sat and talked about the risks of surgery and explained that complications such as infection or dislocation could follow the actual surgery. She listened to all this, then said, "I don't care—I am ready to go, if necessary. I can't go on living like this."

She was carefully prepared for surgery and the operation was successful. A few months later she returned to the office and was positively beaming, walking without crutches, a truly transformed grandmother. Her gratitude was actually embarrassing, both to her family doctor and to me.

Orthoplasty (joint remodeling or replacement) is today done quite successfully in carefully selected patients (see the major article on **Rheumatology**). Total hip replacement involves the use of an acrylic cement which permits the gluing of prosthetic plastic-metal joint parts to natural bone. A plastic socket is "glued" into the old deformed bony socket and a stainless steel ball replaces the bony ball. Usually the patient's former pain is gone and the hip is capable of supporting the body a few weeks after surgery. Because of the patient's age, care must be taken to control other medical conditions that may be present and to employ the most careful guards against infections. Such surgery may be performed in *laminar flow-rooms*, in which the air of the surgery constantly flows out and no infectious agents can be "sucked" into the carefully disinfected operating room.

Knock-knees may be due to deformity of the hip in certain cases, but the common type develops spontaneously. In young children it may correct spontaneously with growth, or a wedge may be fitted to the heel of shoes to change the angle of weight-bearing. If the condition continues beyond the age of 10 or 11, surgery may be indicated to remove a wedge of bone from the femur (thigh bone) or tibia (leg bone). One-sided retardation of bone growth is quite effective and this allows future growth to straighten the legs. (See KNOCK-KNEES.)

Recurrent kneecap dislocation may require corrective surgery by surgically transposing a tendon to correct the alignment of the kneecap with the axis of the leg. This problem is often congenital but can be due to injury.

Ligament damage is often due to sports injuries or perhaps from a person's particular occupation. If the knee ligaments are only sprained, they can be treated by immobilization in a cast or by careful wrapping with bandages. If completely torn this is a serious condition and requires surgical repair. Postoperative muscle wasting (atrophy) must be minimized by special exercises which are carried out to strengthen them and provide future protection of the joint.

Degenerative wrist changes. The wrist is not a weight-bearing joint and therefore arthritis of the wrist is not as common or as disabling. Nevertheless, arthritis of the wrist can be of great concern to its victims because the wrist is used in almost all activities. The pain and tenderness can be quite disabling if present in both wrists. Symptoms may be relieved with specially molded plastic or leather splints to give rest to the joint, but most patients will not wear them over prolonged periods. Surgery can be either to completely stiffen the wrist or to insert a new mechanical joint in some patients. The same can be said of involved thumb and finger joints.

Herniated intervertebral disk—also referred to as *ruptured*, *prolapsed* or *slipped* disk—causes painful, often disabling symptoms in the back. As stated before, most backaches are *not* due to this condition. However, when the diagnosis is confirmed by radiologic examination (myelogram), surgery may be required.

The intervertebral disks are made of cartilage-like substances which act as shock absorbers between the vertebrae. Degenerative changes in the disk may not produce symptoms in the early stages. At the first sign of symptoms, proper exercises to improve posture and strengthen the muscles (especially those of the abdomen) will often control the condition. However, when the pulpy part of the disk herniates (protrudes through a surrounding ligament to press on nerves), surgery with the removal of the offending parts of the disk will relieve the pain. I would emphasize, this operation is very seldom required to relieve back pain.

Accident victims

The treatment of the injuries caused by trauma make up a large part of orthopedic practice and are due, in part, to high-speed transportation. Traffic accidents in the United States account for about 55,000 deaths annually, in addition to countless serious injuries which leave many victims partially or permanently disabled. Other serious injuries result from modern, highly mechanized farm equipment. Industrial accidents account for many more, as do sports—in which people of all ages participate often without proper physical conditioning. More accidents occur within the home than anywhere else, but these are usually less serious than those caused by traffic, industrial and job-related accidents.

Injuries caused by trauma range from simple sprains and strains (which are usually treated by taping, splinting or the application of plaster casts) to multiple fractures—with the crushing of joints and the tearing or severing of ligaments, tendons, muscles and connective tissue. Such serious injuries require extensive surgical reconstruction and usually weeks of treatment in a hospital. Bones have a remarkable capacity for self-repair if properly treated and aligned before splinting or casting.

Treating broken bones or fractures

A bone fracture is "reduced" (set) by manipulation, such as pulling and bending, until the ends of the fracture are in the best position for healing. *Closed reduction* (not requiring surgery to open tissues for direct viewing of the injured bone or joint) is possible in most fractures, but *open reductions* may be required in the treatment of badly damaged bones, joints, tendons and ligaments.

The orthopedist uses many kinds of devices to hold bones together until they can heal—pins, nails, metal plates, rods—all of which are made of special alloy metals that do not cause tissue reaction. Some are left in the body permanently; others are later removed.

Compound ("open") fractures which penetrate the skin always require the most careful treatment because the bone marrow, muscles and tissues have been directly exposed to infectious agents, and dirt may be mashed into the exposed tissue. The wound is usually left open for days before final reduction is undertaken, so that infections and drainage may be dealt with directly. In some cases, badly damaged parts of tissue and muscle may have to be surgically removed.

Hip fractures are common in older patients. These once required casting and long periods of immobilization in bed, with a high risk of infections (such as pneumonia) and the development of bed sores; unfortunately, the treatment

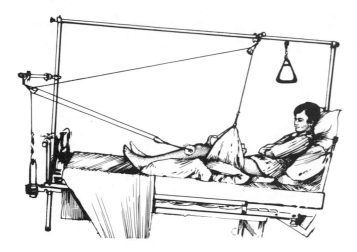

Traction aids the healing of fractures by maintaining the proper alignment of the broken bones and minimizing the pull of muscles.

was often more dangerous than the injury. Today, hips are pinned or nailed into place and the patient can usually be up in a chair and use a walker in a relatively short time. (See also *Fractures* in the **First Aid** section.)

Fitting artificial limbs

When damage to a limb from trauma or disease is so great that it cannot be repaired or treated, *amputation* may become necessary. This does not often happen; but when it does the orthopedist performs the surgery in a manner to permit the fitting of a *prosthetic device* (an artificial limb or other part) that will permit maximum function. Such devices have greatly improved in recent years and rehabilitation training in their use permits most patients to lead almost normal lives.

Preventing accidents

Because orthopedists treat so many victims of traffic and industrial accidents, their professional organizations have campaigned aggressively for compulsory safety regulations. Seat belts, head rests, safety glass and padded interiors of automobiles *do* save lives and prevent serious injuries. Well-enforced legal speed limits *do* prevent many accidents and help to minimize the possibility of serious injuries. In addition, close inspection for maintenance of safety standards within industrial plants and public housing can reduce the incidence of injuries.

(See also the major article on **Preventive Medicine**.)

Seeking help for orthopedic problems

Many specific diseases, disorders and anomalies are common to various parts of the musculoskeletal system—shoulder, neck, hands, feet and limbs—but space does not permit a detailed discussion of them. If you have persistent symptoms of pain, swelling, impairment of movement, or unexplained fever, seek medical help from your family doctor. He will be able to treat most of these problems. If there is a potentially serious musculoskeletal problem he will refer you to a qualified orthopedist.

Should you seek an orthopedist out on your own, I would suggest that you take with you a list of recent diagnostic procedures that were performed by other doctors, and the names of laboratories or hospitals where they were done. If performed recently they may save you the expense of new ones. If they are not recent, they can offer information that will be helpful in evaluating changes that might have taken place in the time since they were done.

Points to keep in mind

I would like to caution that healing time in fractures depends upon which bones are involved, how badly the bones have been damaged, and the age of the patient. Don't become too anxious—follow your doctors advice.

I would also like to caution that recovery from almost any orthopedic problem requires time. Patients should remember that it takes a considerable time to heal a fractured femur (thigh bone) or to recover from a severe back injury. Sad, indeed, are patients who become impatient and seek help from charlatans and faith healers—often running from one to another, squandering their money on implausible cures. This is not only true of patients suffering from cancer but of those with painful arthritis and other orthopedic problems. Too often such patients end up broke and wards of the state, and the charlatan ends up rich.

Most of the serious diseases and disorders treated by orthopedists require rehabilitation counseling and treatment. One cannot put a new hip or knee into a patient or provide him with a prosthetic leg and foot and expect him to go out and use them properly without encouragement and instruction to help him become proficient in their use. Orthopedists must treat the whole patient with understanding, compassion and psychological support during the period of readjustment and recovery to obtain the best possible results.

Obstetrics and Gynecology

Dr. Warren M. Jacobs and Dr. Mark A. Jacobs

Obstetrics is the branch of medical science concerned with the care of women during pregnancy, childbirth and the period immediately thereafter. For some years now this has often been combined with gynecology, which involves the diagnosis and treatment of the diseases of women—particularly those relating to the sexual organs. The modern obstetrician-gynecologist plays an essential role in the health care of women.

The obstetrician-gynecologist is primarily concerned with human reproduction and the diseases and disorders that affect the female reproductive system. However, because he may be the only physician a woman will see during much of her lifetime, he must also be qualified to serve as her primary care physician. For example, in the management of a complicated pregnancy he may have to deal with diabetes, hypertension, cardiovascular disease, kidney disease and other problems usually managed by the internist or general physician.

At times, when a pediatrician is not readily available, he must manage the care of a newborn infant. Thus, the approved residency programs for the "ob-gyn" candidate must include, over a four-year period following graduation from medical school, broad experience in internal medicine, pediatrics, anesthesiology, urology, nephrology, as well as obstetrics and gynecology, including gynecological surgery. At the conclusion of a year of practice of his specialty, he can take the written and oral examinations given by the American Board of Obstetrics and Gynecology. When he successfully passes such examinations he will become a "diplomate" of the board, certified as competent in all areas of his specialty. He may then choose to practice as a general ob-gyn specialist, or may continue an extra two years of fellowship training to qualify in one of the subspecialties.

Among the subspecialties are *perinatology*, which is concerned with the complicated pregnancy; *gynecological oncology*, which is concerned with cancers of the reproductive tract; and *gynecological endocrinology*, which is concerned with hormonal and fertility problems. The subspecialist may then choose to practice his subspecialty exclusively, serving as a consultant to the general ob-gyn practitioner.

Obstetrics and gynecology were once practiced as separate disciplines, but were merged into a single specialty because the problems of each were so closely related. Though it might appear so, the ob-gyn practitioner does not wear two hats. From his first contact with a patient, whether she suspects pregnancy or has symptoms of a gynecological disorder, he will be concerned with the total woman—who may range in age from adolescence to advanced old age. He will be interested in her personal and family medical history, her general health, emotional makeup and marital situation—all of which may have a bearing on her present complaint and possible future problems. Although obstetrics and gynecology is a single discipline today, we will for the sake of clarity in this short article discuss the gynecological and obstetrical problems separately.

THE GYNECOLOGICAL PATIENT
Family Planning

The advent of oral contraceptives must be one of the greatest advances of all time in gynecology. With the exception of those women in whom they are contraindicated—those over 40, those who have a history of liver disease, cardiovascular disease, phlebitis and migraine—the oral contraceptive pills are relatively safe, easy to take and effective. They are synthetic compounds of naturally occurring human hormones (estrogen and progesterone) and they act by preventing ovulation (the release of a mature egg from the ovary). The pills also have therapeutic uses other than for contraception.

Intrauterine devices (IUD) have also been improved. They are mechanical devices which are placed in the uterus to set up an irritation of its inner lining to block implantation of a fertilized ovum. Recent improvements in IUDs have reduced undesirable side effects related to the irritation.

"Barrier methods" of contraception, such as spermicidal foams, diaphragms and condoms are still being used today, but to a lesser degree.

A surgical procedure, using the *laparoscope*, provides permanent sterilization when this means of contraception is desired for health or personal reasons.

Equally important in family planning is the great progress that has been made in the field of fertility, permitting many women to have healthy babies who had thought such happy events were impossible for them. This progress has been made possible by better understanding of the body's hormonal (endocrine) system.

PREGNANCY
— the fetus at full term

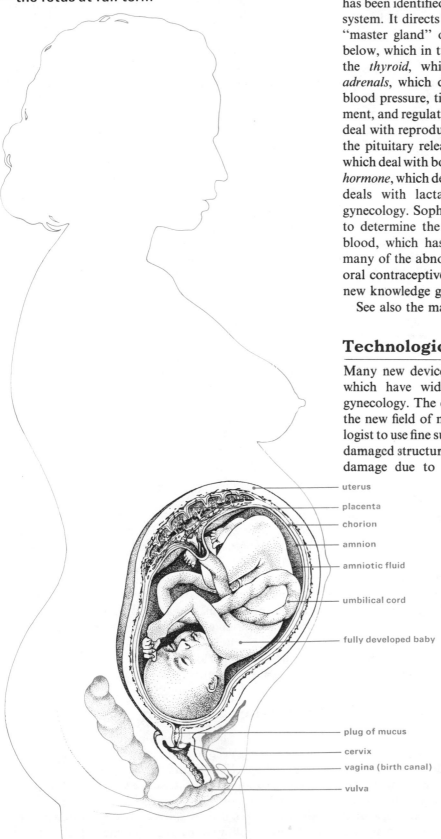

uterus

placenta

chorion

amnion

amniotic fluid

umbilical cord

fully developed baby

plug of mucus

cervix

vagina (birth canal)

vulva

The hypothalamus, located near the base of the brain, has been identified as the regulator of the body's hormonal system. It directs the function of the pituitary gland (the "master gland" of the hormonal system), lying directly below, which in turn directs the function of other glands: the *thyroid*, which deals with body metabolism; the *adrenals*, which deal with the body's reaction to stress, blood pressure, tissue growth and repair, sexual development, and regulation of body fluids; and the *ovaries*, which deal with reproduction and sexual responses. In addition, the pituitary releases HORMONES directly into the blood which deal with body growth and development: *antidiuretic hormone*, which deals with body fluids; and *prolactin*, which deals with lactation and has other implications in gynecology. Sophisticated tests have now been developed to determine the levels of the various hormones in the blood, which has made possible specific treatments for many of the abnormalities responsible for infertility. The oral contraceptive pills were, of course, a direct result of new knowledge gained about hormonal functions.

See also the major article on **Family Planning.**

Technological advances

Many new devices have been developed in recent years which have wide diagnostic and therapeutic uses in gynecology. The operating microscope has made possible the new field of microsurgery, which permits the gynecologist to use fine surgical thread when operating on severely damaged structures, such as the Fallopian tube, to correct damage due to disease, greatly reducing the scarring

The average duration of human pregnancy is 280 days (40 weeks), as calculated from the beginning of the woman's last menstrual period. At full term, as shown in the illustration, the fetus normally lies in the uterus with its head directed downward.

which one finds quite often associated with surgery.

The laparoscope contains a fiberoptic lighting system which permits the gynecologist to see within the abdominal cavity. Only a small opening in the abdomen is needed, through which the instrument is introduced. This instrument not only permits direct viewing of the internal genitalia, which include the uterus, ovaries and Fallopian tubes, but permits minor surgical procedures and BIOPSY of suspicious tissue. Prior to insertion of the laparoscope, the abdominal cavity is inflated with carbon dioxide gas to protect its structures from the instrument. The value of this instrument as a diagnostic tool and for minor surgery, such as tubal sterilization, is immeasurable. Its use has greatly reduced the exploratory operations once required. Laparoscopy permits the patient to have this procedure done in the morning and to return home the same evening with only a small adhesive bandage over her navel.

Ultrasonography is an important new technique which bounces sound waves off structures within the pelvis, printing a picture of its contents which permits the detection of abnormalities that might not be found by physical examination or on x-rays. It is an invaluable technique for examining women who may be pregnant and for evaluating the developing fetus, avoiding the risks of radiation damage associated with exposure to x-rays. (See also ULTRASOUND.)

The *colposcope* is a magnifying instrument used for vaginal examinations, allowing the gynecologist to detect lesions in the uterine cervix (neck of the womb) that routine examinations might not reveal.

The *hysteroscope* enables the physician to look directly inside the uterus for diagnostic purposes and permits him to treat minor abnormalities, often on an outpatient basis (that is, without the need for an overnight admission to the hospital).

The use of *laser beams* as "optical scalpels" is now coming into use and holds great promise for controlling lesions of a suspicious nature found early during routine examinations. Laser surgery is so precise that gynecologists can now remove tiny areas of tissue and even decide how many layers of cells they want to destroy without damage to adjacent healthy tissue. There is no pain resulting from such procedures; the beams cauterize (seal the blood vessels) as they remove suspicious tissue, thus reducing bleeding.

Common gynecological problems

Complaints of gynecological significance which make a woman seek gynecological help include irregularity in uterine bleeding patterns, pelvic pain, vaginal discharge, urinary and bowel symptoms, infertility, a protrusion from the vagina and suspected pregnancy. Some women, alerted by public education programs, will come for a complete gynecological examination after deciding to start a family.

Many women will come by referral from their family doctor when he has recognized a need for the gynecologist's experience and surgical skills.

What can you expect when you visit the gynecologist? If it is a first visit, he will want a detailed personal and family medical history—past illnesses and operations you have had; your menstrual patterns, starting with the menarche (age at which your menstrual periods began); past pregnancies and abortions, spontaneous or elected; and medicines you may be taking. He will ask you about any diseases which seem to run in your family, such as diabetes, cardiovascular diseases, liver and kidney diseases, cancer and others. Have there been multiple births in your family? Your cooperation in giving complete and accurate information is of utmost importance, because his maneuvers in reaching a specific diagnosis will usually be based upon information he obtains from your history.

Age, for example, is always a factor in helping to diagnose the cause of a specific complaint in the patients treated by the gynecologist; his patients range in age from adolescence to the elderly. Abnormal vaginal bleeding in a woman of childbearing age suggests pregnancy and a threatened spontaneous abortion; in an elderly woman it may suggest cancer; and in an adolescent girl it may suggest an endocrine imbalance, which is benign and readily treatable, or pregnancy and threatened spontaneous abortion.

The gynecologist will be particularly interested in the specific complaint that brings you to him. If it is pain, which may be due to many different causes, he will want to know its precise location and date of onset. Is it in one area, such as the vagina, abdomen, pelvis, lower back, or is it diffuse, starting in one area and spreading to another? Is it sharp or dull, constant or intermittent? Did it come suddenly or gradually? Were there precipitating events? Have there been chills or fever? Have you taken self-medication, such as aspirin, and with what results?

The same type of specific information will be required regarding urinary and bowel symptoms, vaginal discharge, abnormal protrusions, or a lump or mass. From broad experience in dealing with such complaints, the gynecologist will have a good idea of what is causing your problem and will be alerted to look for specific abnormalities during his physical examination.

Physical examination

The thorough physical examination, which a patient coming to the gynecologist for the first time will receive, is a step-by-step procedure, carried out in the examining room with a nurse present to assist the physician and provide emotional support for the often anxious patient. The examination will usually start with careful examination of the breasts, followed by the abdomen, pelvis and the rectovaginal structures.

Throughout the examination, the doctor will be feeling and looking for abnormalities. Direct viewing of external structures will tell him much, and the new illuminated instruments will permit internal visualization. Palpation of breasts and abdomen will permit him to discover or rule out the presence of abnormal lumps and masses and areas of tenderness, abnormal bladder and bowel retentions and an enlarged liver. Taking the blood pressure and listening to the heart through a stethoscope will help alert him to any abnormal cardiovascular problems.

The *pelvic examination* involves inspection of the internal genitals within the pelvis, specifically the interior of the vagina and the neck of the uterus (cervix). This is typically performed by the gynecologist first inserting his rubber-gloved index finger into the vagina; he will feel around for any unusual lumps or masses and assess the texture and position of the cervix. Visual examination of these structures is then made by inserting a vaginal speculum, which gently separates the walls of the vagina so that a light source will reveal the tissues of the vagina and cervix. The gynecologist will be looking for abnormal discoloration, lesions, areas of bleeding, abnormal growths, old scars and tears of internal structures, abnormal protrusions and evidence of infection.

During the pelvic examination he will take a "Pap smear" from the neck of the uterus and its entrance (the cervix and cervical canal) for laboratory examination, which permits the early detection and treatment of cervical cancer. He may also remove tiny bits of tissue from abnormal growths to be examined for possible malignancy. If he finds an abscess of purulent (pus-filled) infection, he will take a pus specimen so that the invading micro-organisms responsible can be identified and the appropriate antibiotic or other drug prescribed immediately.

At the conclusion of his examination, the gynecologist will usually have arrived at a specific diagnosis, but may order laboratory and radiological (x-ray) tests to confirm it. If he has discovered evidence of systemic disease in other organ systems, he may refer the patient to an internist or urologist for their evaluation and management.

What are the common gynecological disorders the gynecologist is most likely to find from his examination? Perhaps they can be more readily understood if we present them by the signs and symptoms they have produced.

Pelvic pain

High on the list is pelvic pain. Common causes include ENDOMETRIOSIS, or the abnormal implantation of fragments of the inner lining of the uterus on an ovary or within the lower part of the abdominal cavity; *pelvic inflammatory disease (PID)*, in which bacterial infection has spread from the cervix to the Fallopian tubes and abdomen; *fibroid tumors*, which are growths of a benign nature that originate in the muscular layer of the uterus (see FIBROIDS); and pain

of a more physiologic nature which may be associated with abnormal menstruation or ovulation. Of serious consequence is pain associated with PID in which the bacterial infection spreads to the Fallopian tubes, or pain associated with an *ectopic pregnancy*, in which a fertilized ovum becomes attached to and begins its growth in the Fallopian tube. In such patients, the diagnosis might require a series of diagnostic laboratory tests or surgical procedures.

Fortunately for the patient, and to the great satisfaction of the gynecologist, many of the underlying conditions which cause pelvic pain have a ready treatment and, in many cases, a cure. For example: the patient with endometriosis often responds favorably to low dosage of oral contraceptive pills. They act by suppressing the growth of the endometrial tissue implants, which are responsible for the pain. In the case of inflammation of the Fallopian tubes—if treated before gross scarring or abscess formation develops—the condition usually responds quite rapidly to the administration of appropriate antibiotics. Those who do suffer scarring or abscess formation can often expect relief of their pain as a result of surgery. Following the early diagnosis of ectopic pregnancy, the proper timing of surgery may not only save a life and relieve

FEMALE REPRODUCTIVE ORGANS

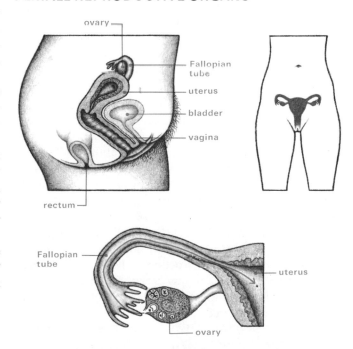

The reproductive system of the female, unlike that of the male, undergoes regular cyclic changes which revolve around ovulation—the release of an egg from the ovary. The egg passes along the Fallopian tube into the cavity of the uterus. If it has been fertilized, the egg embeds itself in the lining of the uterus; if not, the egg and the lining of the uterus are shed at menstruation.

future pain, but in some cases will result in preservation of the diseased tube.

Bleeding

Abnormal bleeding includes the absence of regular menstrual periods, bleeding between periods, bleeding in response to sexual intercourse, or prolonged heavy bleeding. The absence of menstruation, of course, is often due to an unsuspected pregnancy, stress, hormonal disease, a reaction to drugs, or an underlying gynecological disease. The withdrawal of certain drugs may control bleeding, which is why the patient's drug-taking history is so important to the gynecologist, including the high and regular intake of aspirin and major tranquilizers. The pelvic examination may reveal pregnancy, which can be confirmed by specific tests.

Abnormal increased bleeding from the vagina may be caused by a spontaneous abortion ("miscarriage") following an unsuspected pregnancy, the increasing dysfunction of the ovaries near the onset of the menopause, or cancer. Although it is always hoped that the bleeding can be controlled medically, some cases (such as spontaneous abortion) require a DILATATION AND CURETTAGE (D & C). Bleeding may be an indication for surgical diagnostic procedures, such as taking tissue specimens from the endometrium (lining of the uterus) for microscopic examination to confirm or rule out cancer—especially in an older woman, who is most susceptible to it.

Cancer

The gynecologist who today detects CANCER in its early stages of development takes great satisfaction in knowing that this frightening condition is now treatable and in many cases curable. His great advantage over other specialists is that the sites of gynecological cancer are anatomically accessible for simple and accurate diagnostic procedures, such as the "Pap smear" or biopsy. The yearly or six-monthly "Pap smear"—started from about the age of 25 and continued regularly—can in many cases of cervical cancer lead to selective destruction of the cancer tissue with preservation of the underlying cervix. We would add that this approach is used mainly in the patient in whom future pregnancies are desired.

(See also CERVICAL SMEAR, BREAST CANCER and the major article on **Oncology**.)

In women with early signs of cervical cancer who are beyond childbearing age, treatment is often the surgical removal of the uterus (hysterectomy). Many cervical and uterine cancers which, before they are detected, have spread beyond the stage where surgical treatment is possible, are still treatable with radiation therapy. Much of the evaluation at this stage requires determination of the extent of the spread (metastasis) of the cancer cells, a

process that may require consultation with the urologist and proctologist.

The great future challenge in gynecological oncology is the development of ways to initiate an early, accurate diagnosis of ovarian cancer. The ovaries, which lie hidden within the pelvis, are not as accessible for visual examination as are other gynecological organs.

Infertility

Only a short time ago, INFERTILITY (the inability or impaired ability to produce offspring) was more accepted than treated. Today, however, it has become a clinical problem that can be systematically evaluated and often successfully treated. A comparatively new subspecialty of gynecology is *andrology*, which is concerned with male infertility and spontaneous abortions which can be traced to the male. Thus, treatment of infertility starts with a collection of the husband's sperm for inspection of abnormalities, shape, number and movement. From the wife is elicited a careful history of menstruation, previous pregnancies, use of medications and the presence or history of disease associated with infertility—including previous severe pelvic infections and endometriosis. The pelvic examination may also reveal ovarian enlargement, some-times associated with hormonal disease, scarring of the Fallopian tubes and, in some cases, abnormal development of the reproductive tract—which is usually congenital.

Further evaluation may include x-rays of the uterus and Fallopian tubes, blood tests to measure the level of certain hormones critical in reproduction, or even laparoscopy. Treatment may involve a medical approach with drugs to correct underlying endocrine disease, such as HYPER-THYROIDISM, or surgical treatment to correct identified abnormalities. Sometimes simply identifying the causes of emotional stress and its resultant anxiety, then helping the couple to understand and avoid them will enhance the possibility of a wanted pregnancy.

The vast spectrum of hormonal disorders may produce any of the previously mentioned common symptoms of bleeding, pain or infertility, and a myriad of other symptoms. Diseases involving the hormonal system often present syndromes (a collection of signs and symptoms) that are seemingly unrelated. A common example seen by gynecologists is the young woman who is slightly obese, has an abnormal distribution of body hair, acne and AMENORRHEA (a history of absent menstrual periods), and is infertile. Examination of these young women often reveals an abnormally enlarged and poorly functioning ovary, which is often responsive to certain types of drug therapy. Another common syndrome is the woman who presents with amenorrhea and galactorrhea (the expression of milk from her breast without pregnancy). Some of these women are found to have tumors of the pituitary gland, usually benign, a condition that may be very responsive to treatment. Evaluation of some endocrinological (hormonal) abnormalities identified by the gynecologist may require evaluation by an endocrinologist.

See also the section on *Infertility* in the major article on **Family Planning.**

Venereal diseases

The gynecologist is always on the alert for venereal diseases today, because the incidence of such infections has been steadily rising in recent years. This is sad indeed, because specific cures are readily possible when treatment is sought before the infection spreads or is passed to others. GONORRHEA is one of the most frequently reported infections in the United States. In women, gonorrhea begins as an infection in the cervix and spreads upward through the uterus to the Fallopian tubes, where it causes pelvic inflammatory disease (PID). Of this process, two statements can be made: the early stage of cervical infection is without symptoms, and its spread to the uterus and Fallopian tubes is among the most common causes of

> **Venereal diseases (VD) are those transmitted during sexual intercourse with an infected partner. Despite the effectiveness of antibiotics, the incidence of gonorrhea and syphilis—the major venereal diseases—is slowly on the rise again. Prompt medical attention, involving both partners, is essential to prevent serious damage.**

serious pelvic inflammatory disease seen today. When detected by bacterial culture in its cervical stage, it is readily treated with antibiotics. Once it has progressed to involve the Fallopian tubes, antibiotics may not always suffice and surgery may be required, with its possible consequence of infertility. An ominous development is the relatively recent discovery of strains of the microorganisms which cause gonorrhea which apparently are resistant to many forms of widely used antibiotics.

SYPHILIS, if untreated, is the venereal disease with the most far-reaching consequences, including disease of the heart, brain and spinal cord. Its early signs of a chancre (sore), usually on the membranes of the external genitalia, sometimes followed by a body rash, should warn its victims (male and female alike) to seek immediate medical attention. This is essential, because these early signs disappear without treatment and the disease continues its silent, insidious course, resulting in catastrophic damage to the central nervous system and other vital organ systems. Identified before gross damage is done, it is readily treated with currently available antibiotics.

Another rapidly increasing form of venereal disease is that caused by the *herpes virus*, resulting in inflammation of the vagina with possible involvement of the opening of the urethra (the tube that empties the bladder). The only treatment available at this time for herpes is pain-relieving drugs and rest until the body's immunological system permits recovery by production of specific antibodies. The herpes virus, however, remains within the infected individual and may flare up during periods of stress. Once a woman has had such an infection, it should be reported to her obstetrician, because it can, during a flare-up, infect an infant as it passes through the birth canal—with a resultant death rate of approximately 80%. The woman who has had a herpes infection within a month of her time of delivery is therefore delivered by Cesarean section in order to avoid the risk to her baby.

Special examinations and tests

From the foregoing, the value of periodic gynecological checkups should be apparent, but especially to women of childbearing age. In addition to taking the patient's medical history, physical examination, a "Pap smear" and tests to diagnose specific abnormalities discovered during the examination, the regular checkup should include such routine laboratory tests as a complete blood count (which may detect anemia, common in menstruating women); a test to determine blood levels of sugar (to detect diabetes, thought to be present in 10% of the population); and a urinalysis (which may detect urinary tract infection, also quite common in women).

Specialized lab work ordered by the obstetrician-gynecologist most commonly includes a *pregnancy test*, which is performed on urine to detect the presence of a hormone secreted into the blood from the placenta. The test becomes valuable approximately from the 6th through the 12th week of pregnancy, when the hormonal level is high enough to be detected. At the time of this writing, there are reports of a newer test that is said to detect pregnancy before the woman has missed her first period.

The *VDRL blood test* is used to screen women for syphilis. It is nonspecific, because a positive result can be caused by other conditions. However, if syphilis has been present for six weeks or more it will produce a positive result. Thus, if a negative result is obtained the patient can be fairly certain that she does not have the disease. If positive, more tests will be made to confirm or rule out syphilis.

If a nonsyphilitic infection is present, a smear will be taken from tissue involved and its bacterial contents grown in a special culture medium. The bacteria will then be tested against various antibiotics to find which is the most effective against it. In the office this procedure is useful in identifying and treating urinary tract infections or gonorrhea.

The *hysterosalpingogram* is an x-ray taken through the pelvis after the uterus has been injected with a contrast substance (i.e., one opaque to x-rays) passed through a tube placed in the pelvis. The contrast substance outlines the shape of the uterus and Fallopian tubes, permitting the physician to detect abnormalities in the anatomy of the uterus and scarring of the tubes; both conditions may be a cause of infertility.

Ultrasonography, previously described, can also pick up ovarian and tubal abnormalities that are suspected but cannot be felt on pelvic examination. Such tests prevent much unnecessary surgery and also permit effective early surgery when such abnormalities as tumors, abscesses and ectopic pregnancies are found. (See also ULTRASOUND.)

The menopause marks that period in a woman's life when the reproductive process ends, commonly and accurately described as "the change of life." The menstrual periods end and there are hormonal changes (in estrogen production) which may be accompanied by a variety of symptoms—hot flushes, heart palpitations, sweating, depression, insomnia, headache, itching of the external genitalia, aching joints and bladder irritation, often accompanied by urinary incontinence. This condition was once looked upon by physicians as a naturally occurring event which women had to pass through until the body made its physiological adjustments. Today, however, management includes the careful replacement of estrogen (hormone replacement therapy), with dosage adjusted to control bleeding. Such treatment relieves the physiological symptoms, and psychological support by the physician relieves many of the emotional symptoms due to anxiety. (See MENOPAUSE.)

Gynecological surgery

Gynecological surgery, like other forms of surgery, has received much public criticism in recent years by a society which is questioning the standards of practice of its health professionals. A major complaint is being made against unnecessary surgery. In gynecological surgery, the most maligned procedure, and perhaps the least understood, is the hysterectomy—which is the treatment of choice for some gynecological problems and can be life-saving when evidence of cancer and other serious diseases cannot be medically treated.

Hysterectomy

Hysterectomy involves removal of the uterus and cervix (its neck), which may be done through the abdomen or through the vagina. The vaginal hysterectomy is quicker, has fewer complications and is the preferred approach when it is not contraindicated by the disease being treated. Indications for abdominal hysterectomy are pelvic infection with formation of an abscess, ovarian cancer and very large fibroids, all of which require that the surgeon have greater access provided by the abdominal approach.

Regardless of the method, hysterectomy is indicated in a variety of situations which cannot be defined by a simple list of rules. Diseases and disorders not generally understood by the public and which are best treated surgically would include *adenomyosis* (a painful growth of gland tissue within the muscle area of the uterus); *pelvic relaxation*, which describes collapse of the uterus into the vagina, usually resulting from multiple births; and sometimes hysterectomy must be performed when a situation normally controlled by medication becomes unmanageable. For example, a woman in her 30s or early 40s suffers prolonged menstrual periods, with heavy bleeding, that are not responsive to medication. Without surgical intervention, this condition leads to serious anemia with resultant adverse cardiovascular effects. The same is true of serious pelvic infection that cannot be controlled with antibiotics.

Ovaries and Fallopian tubes

Other surgical procedures include the removal of the ovaries and Fallopian tubes. The presence of cancer or an uncontrollable abscess are obvious indications for such surgery, but sometimes it must also be performed in the presence of an ectopic pregnancy in the tube. Without surgical intervention, the Fallopian tube may rupture, causing heavy bleeding which can be fatal. Sometimes the ovary must be removed because it is compromised by scar tissue from previous pelvic surgery and causes severe debilitating pain. Another indication for surgery is severe endometriosis with destruction of the ovary. However, it is often possible to remove endometrial tissue selectively and save the ovary.

D and C

Dilatation and curettage (D & C) is a procedure performed under general anesthesia, during which the cervix (neck of the womb) is dilated with the use of a series of metal rods. A curette (a sharp spoonlike instrument) is then passed through the opened cervix and across the surface of the uterus to remove a fraction of the lining endometrium for microscopic study. This can confirm or rule out suspected cancer that has not been demonstrated by endometrial biopsy; in addition, it can help determine whether or not a woman is ovulating, if infertility is a problem. The D & C may also be used for elective termination of pregnancy, to remove small growths called POLYPS, and to remove tissue that may remain following a spontaneous abortion (miscarriage).

Other surgical procedures are performed by the gynecologist to correct *cystocele* (sagging bladder) and *rectocele* (sagging rectum). Such operations may become necessary when the muscles that support these structures stretch and weaken, often due to aging. The procedure involves the shortening and tightening of the muscles; it may be done in combination with vaginal hysterectomy or independently, depending upon the age of the patient and the seriousness of the problem. If the uterus is removed, its ligaments can be used to support the bladder and rectum.

Other surgical procedures

The newest field of gynecological surgery incorporates a variety of procedures within the field of fertility, the most common being surgical removal of endometrial implants from the ovary, the pelvic wall, the uterus and its supporting ligaments. The nerve supply to the uterus may also be severed to alleviate pain and uterine spasm, and the uterus suspended to prevent further passage of endometrial fragments from the lining of the uterus through the Fallopian tubes and into the abdominal cavity. Other procedures are carried out to repair anatomical defects of the uterus. Microscopic surgery (extremely delicate surgery performed with the aid of a low-power microscope) holds great promise for the successful repair of Fallopian tubes that in the past were thought to be hopelessly destroyed by infections and other diseases or previous tubal ligation (tying off of the Fallopian tubes).

The gynecologist, it should be mentioned, plays an active role in the detection of benign and malignant tumors of the breast, but medical, radiological (x-ray) and surgical treatment are in the province of the oncologist, radiologist and general surgeon (see the major article on **Oncology**).

THE OBSTETRICAL PATIENT

Much progress has also been made in the art and practice of obstetrics in recent years, during which the incidence of maternal and fetal death has been reduced to its present low incidence. This is due in great part to public education programs and to the availability of modern hospital facilities and well-trained obstetricians and supporting personnel. It should be pointed out, however, that although obstetrical and gynecological services available to most American women rank with the world's best, many women do not take advantage of them, either through ignorance of their importance, or because in sparsely populated areas such specialists and hospital facilities are not readily available. One of the saddest sights an obstetrician-gynecologist sees is the young teenager who arrives at the emergency room in the early stages of labor to be seen by a doctor for the first time, or a mature woman suffering spontaneous abortion that might have been avoided by proper early care.

Educating the parents

Modern obstetrics not only calls for careful management of mother and fetus throughout pregnancy, but for educating both mother and father in their responsibilities during and following pregnancy. Today, in maternity hospitals and medical centers, clinics are maintained for such purposes. Usually a nurse-nutritionist gives specific instructions regarding proper diet, especially when there is a problem of malnourishment, overweight, or a diet-related complication such as diabetes or hypertension (high blood pressure).

A nurse-midwife conducts classes to prepare mother and father for what to expect during the delivery, to instruct the mother in the techniques of relaxation and exercises and to prepare her for proper care of the baby after it is taken home. With such preparation, the husband may be invited into the delivery room as a participant, where he can be of great help in providing emotional support for his wife.

Today, when young couples are concerned with making the birth experience a shared one, great emphasis is being placed on "natural birth" techniques. Much of this popular movement is productive, but the expectant mother can benefit fully only if she receives adequate education about her pregnancy and the process of birth. Those parents who wish delivery without the help of professionals or the use of hospital facilities are, in the opinion of the authors, taking an unwarranted risk with the health of both mother and infant.

BREECH PRESENTATION

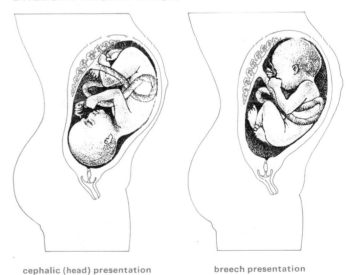

cephalic (head) presentation   breech presentation

At about the 28th week of pregnancy most babies are in the breech *position, with the bottom directed toward the pelvic floor and the head upward. From about the 32nd to the 34th week of pregnancy the baby spontaneously turns around inside the uterus, so that its head is directed downward toward the opening of the birth canal (*cephalic presentation*); however, approximately 4% of all babies fail to turn around at this time and at the beginning of labor remain in the* breech presentation.

Early identification of risk factors

The obstetrician's goal today is to deliver not only a live baby at the end of nine months, but also a healthy one. To accomplish this, in many cases, he must be permitted to monitor a pregnancy through each trimester (3-month period), during which complications associated with fetal development can be detected and treated. The best age range for childbearing is between 18 and 30; women who are older or younger than this age range require more special care, and each trimester presents potential dangers. Some problems either are initially without symptoms or else so subtle in onset that they may be detected only by examination or laboratory tests.

Following confirmation of pregnancy and a thorough gynecological examination, the physician will know much about the risk factors of his patient—the presence of diabetes, hypertension and endocrine (hormonal) problems—which require careful medical control. In addition, a knowledge of her physical reproductive anatomy may alert him to problems to be expected at the time of delivery. He will impart to his patient the new knowledge that has evolved about the adverse effects of smoking, alcohol and various drugs on the developing fetus, warning her that she must take no drugs which he has not approved. Throughout the course of pregnancy his attention will be focused upon the developing fetus.

Studies of certain hormones excreted in the maternal urine provide information concerning the uterine fetal environment and is of great help in identifying the fetus at risk for disease. Monitoring the fetus under conditions of artificial stress, carried out in a carefully controlled hospital environment, can also identify the fetus at risk. Ultrasonography is of great diagnostic value in establishing fetal age, aiding the physician in making important decisions for the mother and her potential child. If there is a question of fetal death within the womb, ultrasound can detect possible fetal movement.

Amniocentesis

This is a procedure that involves needle puncture of the fetal sac to withdraw amniotic fluid. Examination of this fluid can provide valuable information—fetal age, which is most important when the date of gestation is in doubt near the expected date of delivery and decisions must be made about inducing labor; the presence of certain enzyme abnormalities which are incompatible with fetal life; and chromosomal abnormalities detected in fetal cells which can identify genetic disorders, such as mongolism (Down's syndrome). Detected during the early stages of pregnancy, a fetus known to be developing in an abnormal way can be aborted. A new instrument, the *fetoscope*, can be inserted into the uterus for direct observation of the fetus and to remove fetal blood and tissue for study.

Toxemia of pregnancy

A potentially dangerous complication of pregnancy is *toxemia* (or PREECLAMPSIA), seen most often in younger women pregnant for the first time. This disease presents with elevated blood pressure, edema (swelling), and the presence of protein in the urine. It cannot be detected until the 20th week of pregnancy and may occur at any time from the 20th week through delivery. Mild forms may be controlled by bed rest alone, but serious cases may require hospitalization and special medication. Untreated, preeclampsia may progress to *eclampsia*, which is characterized by seizures; it can be fatal for both mother and child. Eclampsia is seen much less frequently in mothers who have received proper early treatment.

Spontaneous abortion (miscarriage)

Another possible complication of pregnancy is miscarriage. A distinction exists between miscarriage and premature labor based upon the survival potential of the fetus, which in turn is based on its size. Generally speaking, the delivery of any fetus less than 24 weeks of age will weigh less than 500 g (1lb. 2oz.) with no chance of survival. A baby born weighing from 500 to 1000 grams has a decreased chance of survival; it will range from 24 to 30 weeks of age, but will be considered a premature birth.

Because of advances made in pediatrics and neonatal care, a fetus delivered between 30 and 36 weeks of age has an increasingly good prognosis. These distinctions are important in terms of management. Bleeding occurring in the first trimester is a sign of impending miscarriage and may progress to the stage of incomplete abortion with a need for immediate dilatation and curettage (D & C) to halt bleeding that may become life threatening. Detected early, however, the process may be arrested by bed rest and the use of intravenous alcohol drips which, in many cases, will save the fetus. After the 12th week of pregnancy, incomplete abortion is not treated by surgery alone. Drugs may be given to accelerate abortion, then be followed by a D & C.

Infections

Infections can be initially symptomless and result in serious complications during pregnancy. Urinary tract infections are common because of changes in urine flow, resulting in the inhibition of the emptying mechanism of the system. Undetected and untreated, urinary tract infections may lead to premature labor or spontaneous abortion. They can be detected by routine urine testing throughout pregnancy. When they progress to the symptomatic stage they produce burning sensations during urination, but can still be successfully treated at this stage. Without treatment, the infection may ascend to the kidneys to produce symptoms of high fever, abdominal pain and marked illness. Vigorous treatment at this stage is mandatory if infection of the fetus is to be avoided.

Some patients experience premature rupture of membranes surrounding the fetus as the time of delivery nears, with resultant leakage of fluid from the vagina. This situation must be carefully followed, because prolonged rupture can lead to infection of the amniotic cavity (which is the "home" of the fetus). This complication can lead to infection and death of the fetus, or infections serious enough to require hysterectomy. It should be quickly added, however, that most cases of vaginal leakage are not due to premature rupture of the membranes, but all should have immediate medical investigation.

Bleeding

In the third trimester, bleeding also always requires immediate medical evaluation. One of the two dangerous cases is *placenta previa*, a condition in which the placenta precedes the fetus. It can occur at any time during the last three months and during delivery itself. Untreated, it may result in serious bleeding and abnormalities of clotting. This problem is diagnosed by an ultrascan. The other cause of dangerous bleeding in the last trimester is *abruptio placentae*, a condition in which the placenta separates from the uterus before delivery has occurred. Like placenta previa, it requires immediate management.

Among the modern technological advances in obstetrics has been the development of sophisticated monitoring equipment which permits the obstetrician to evaluate mother and fetus during the delivery process. The monitor records, both on an electronic screen and a paper roll, the contractions of the uterus and the heartbeat of the fetus. This permits immediate detection of potential disasters such as fetal distress which may be due to compression of the umbilical cord or to an insufficient blood supply through the placenta. Therapy includes positional maneuvers of the fetus to relieve the stress, which, if unsuccessful, may be followed by Cesarean section.

Prolonged labor can be safely speeded up by the use of a drug which augments labor contractions. Labor character ized by adequate uterine contractions without descent of the fetus into the birth canal can also be accurately diagnosed by the monitor. It is a disproportion between the size of the fetus and the pelvis making normal delivery mechanically impossible; delivery by Cesarean section then becomes mandatory.

Although in women who have had proper prenatal care, vaginal delivery is usually without complications, they do sometimes occur. Such complications include *dystocia* (halting of the delivery process in its midportion), unsuspected multiple births, and protrusion of the uterus from the vagina with resultant heavy bleeding. All are readily treated.

Erythroblastosis fetalis

This condition, once a most serious complication of pregnancy and a serious threat to the life of the fetus and newborn infants, is a disease resulting from "hostile antibodies" passed in the mother's blood to the fetus to destroy red cells in fetal blood. Once the cause of 10,000 infant deaths a year in the United States, it is now controlled by special vaccines given to the mother. On the rare occasions when it does occur today, a total blood exchange in the infant must be carried out immediately after birth. Perinatal teams can now do the blood exchange while the fetus is being carried by the mother. (See also RH FACTOR.)

Cesarean section

Surgical delivery, involving the opening of the abdomen, then the uterus, to remove the baby and placenta. The procedure may be carried out under general or spinal anesthesia. Once a woman has had one Cesarean section her future babies should be delivered by this method, because the first surgical scar of the uterus is susceptible to rupture and bleeding during the labor of a vaginal delivery.

Postnatal complications

Complications following delivery of the baby are usually relatively minor ones. They include bleeding, which is well treated in most cases by medications; infection, which is treated by appropriate antibiotics; and breast engorgement, which is treated by ice packs and hormones. Of potentially serious consequence following childbirth, however, can be *postpartum depression;* it may progress to impair the functioning ability of the mother and, like other severe forms of depression, can carry the threat of suicide. In such cases the obstetrician relies on consultation by the psychiatrist.

Health check of the newborn

In the absence of a pediatrician or family physician at the time of birth, the obstetrician provides initial management of the infant. This includes careful checking of several parameters, expressed in terms of what is known as the *Apgar score*—established by Dr. Virginia Apgar (U.S. anesthesiologist, born 1909) to identify dangerous stress factors in the newborn. This provides a quantitative evaluation of the baby within one to five minutes following birth. Points are assigned to the quality of the heartbeat, respiratory effort, muscle tone, color and reflex action (determined as the response to stimulation). A perfectly healthy baby has an Apgar score of 10. A low Apgar score is usually found in infants born following complicated pregnancies and complicated prolonged labors. Infants found to have three or more Apgar stress factors are usually sent immediately to neonatal intensive care nurseries, if available, where they receive special care.

Conclusion

In this article we have sought to give the reader a better understanding of the role of the obstetrician-gynecologist in modern medicine. All women should learn to recognize the more common signs and symptoms that point to some gynecological problem, so that expert medical help can be obtained at the earliest possible time. Not only will the treatment then have a better chance of success, but its course may be considerably shortened. Likewise, it is sensible to seek competent medical care at the first sign of pregnancy, and have periodic checkups.

Neurology

Dr. Richard D. Sweet

No electronic computer ever made or conceived can remotely approach the marvelous complexity of the human brain and its associated nerve tracts, which supply every part of the body. When something goes wrong with this system, as the result of a specific disease or disorder, it is the neurologist who is best qualified to deal with the problem.

At a time of great happiness one might say, "How great to be alive!" But a neurologist might say, "How great to have a healthy nervous system!" The brain, eyes, ears, spinal cord and peripheral nerves are included in the nervous system and enable us to think, see, hear, speak, walk, feel pain and experience pleasure.

A neurologist is a specially trained physician who treats diseases and disorders of the nervous system. (For a discussion of the surgical treatment of such problems, see the major article on **Neurosurgery**.) He sees patients who have headaches, back pain, dizziness, muscular weakness, poor balance, impaired sensation, poor memory, lapses of consciousness and convulsive seizures. Like most doctors, he tries to diagnose the cause of such complaints by looking at (examining) his patient, asking him questions and performing or requesting various laboratory tests. However, compared with other specialists, he is at a distinct disadvantage—because he cannot see, feel, hear or sample the body parts which concern him. A cardiologist listens to the sounds of a heartbeat, the hematologist removes a sample of blood and studies it through a microscope. An orthopedist looks at and can feel the movements and structures of bones and joints. Unfortunately, none of these methods is so readily available to a neurologist, who must diagnose disorders in nerve tissue encased by bones of the skull and spine or concealed deep within the trunk or limbs.

The neurologist must thus resort to an indirect method of examining the nervous system, by observing the functions it performs. He takes advantage of the highly specialized way the nervous system acts and the location of certain functions in particular parts of the system. For example, a person may have trouble moving the right side of his face and hand. The neurologist knows that impulses for such movements originate in the *left* side of the brain. He also knows that impulses to the right leg originate near the top of the *left* side of the brain and that impulses to the face and hand originate (more precisely) next to each other near the bottom of the left side of the brain. His knowledge of nervous system structures and functions allows him to deduce that the person in the example given has a disorder of the lower part of the left half of the brain. In daily practice, he deals with many more complicated problems in pinpointing a neurological disorder, but the principle is always the same. He pieces together changes in the patient's thinking, vision, strength, coordination, sensation, reflexes, and thereby forms an idea of where in the nervous system a disorder might lie.

The neurological examination

This examination is always an "experience" for the patient. The doctor watches you walk "normally," then with one foot in front of the other on a straight line. He has you move your eyes in all directions, grimace, stick out your tongue, bend and straighten limbs against resistance and smell and describe different substances. He tests how far to the side you can see with your eyes looking straight ahead, how well you feel the touch of a cotton wisp, the light prick of a pin, the movement of a finger or toe, and hear the vibrations of a tuning fork. He shines light into your eyes and mouth, taps muscle tendons around elbows, wrists, knees and ankles with a rubber hammer to produce reflex jerks and, finally, he scratches the bottom of your feet with a stick or key to elicit another reflex movement in your big toe. This may seem like a silly game or pointless ritual to the uninformed, but each such maneuver tests a particular pathway in the nervous system, enabling the neurologist to localize a specific problem.

Confirming tests

Once a tentative diagnosis has been made, the neurologist can request simple or complicated laboratory tests to confirm or rule out conclusions reached as a result of the neurological examination. These tests also help to discover the kind of disorder that is causing the problem, such as a STROKE, tumor or injury. Electrical tests are made to measure the small amounts of electricity that nerves and muscles use to send messages within the nervous system— the patterns of which can be measured in one person and compared with similar patterns of many "normal" persons. This is the same technique used for an *electrocardiogram* (see ECG) of the heart (which is a specialized muscle). The patterns picked up by many electrodes placed on the scalp overlying the brain produce an *electroencephalogram* (see EEG). The brain's electrical pattern

THE HUMAN NERVOUS SYSTEM

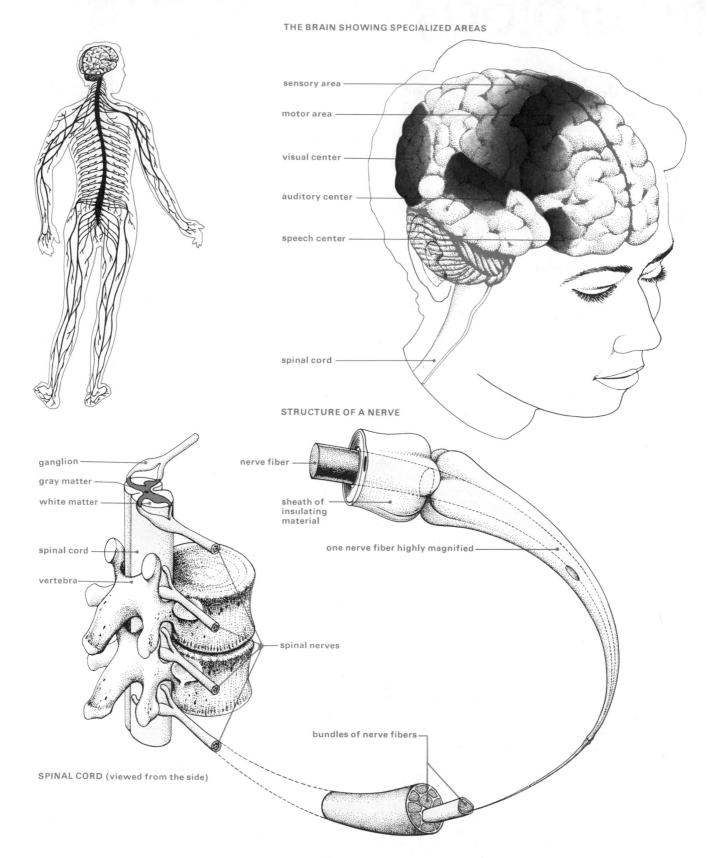

THE BRAIN SHOWING SPECIALIZED AREAS

sensory area

motor area

visual center

auditory center

speech center

spinal cord

STRUCTURE OF A NERVE

nerve fiber

sheath of insulating material

one nerve fiber highly magnified

ganglion

gray matter

white matter

spinal cord

vertebra

spinal nerves

bundles of nerve fibers

SPINAL CORD (viewed from the side)

at the back of the brain is called the "alpha" rhythm, consisting of 8–13 waves per second. Brain rhythms are slower and less well organized in children than in adults. The rhythm patterns are usually slowed by brain disease and the changes in rhythm are localized in infectious "focal" disorders. The electroencephalogram or EEG is best at showing abnormal electrical discharges of the brain, or seizures, which produce very fast waves or "spikes on the moving paper record."

Nerve conduction times

These are measured by applying a small electric current to a nerve high up in an arm or leg and measuring the time it takes this impulse to reach a muscle supplied by that nerve. Normally, the rate of electrical conduction in nerves is very fast, but it is slowed by pressure on or injury to the nerve. The site of the pressure or injury can be determined by finding the place where slow conduction starts. For example, a person with pressure on a nerve at the elbow will have a normal electrical conduction time from a current applied *below* the elbow but a slow conduction from a similar current applied *above* the elbow.

Electromyograms

An electromyogram (EMG) is obtained by putting a very thin needle through the skin into a muscle. A wire connects the needle to a special machine (electromyograph) to measure electricity; the electrical activity of the muscle is observed with the muscle relaxed and then contracted. It sounds like popping corn or a distant motorboat when listened to in a loudspeaker; the electrical activity can be seen when the signal is fed into an oscilloscope. This test tells about the condition of the muscle and also about the nerve supplying it. It can be of great diagnostic value when used in combination with other tests.

The human nervous system (left) can be broadly divided into two parts: the central nervous system (the brain and spinal cord) and the peripheral nervous system (the branching network which supplies our skin, muscles and internal organs). The brain acts as the controlling center, interpreting all incoming information from the senses and adapting our behavior accordingly. Specific areas on its surface are responsible for the special senses and for generating speech and movement. All the signals between the brain and the body flow up and down pathways in the spinal cord, and this vital structure is well protected by the bony vertebrae. Pairs of spinal nerves attach to the spinal cord at regular intervals and they contain motor and sensory fibers which supply muscles and skin, respectively.

Examining the cerebrospinal fluid

Spinal tap (or, more properly, *lumbar puncture*) is a most important test to the neurologist. After an injection of Novocain, a needle is inserted between the bones of the lower spine into a sac which contains cerebrospinal fluid. The pressure of this fluid is first measured, then a small amount of the fluid is removed and the needle is withdrawn. A sample of the cerebrospinal fluid, which bathes the surface of the spinal cord and brain, can show evidence of infection (pus cells), bleeding (blood cells), or tumor (abnormally high pressure or the presence of protein) in the

LUMBAR PUNCTURE

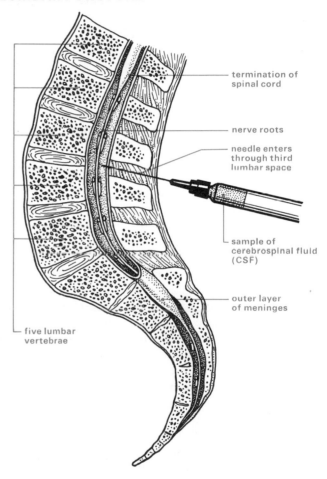

termination of spinal cord

nerve roots

needle enters through third lumbar space

sample of cerebrospinal fluid (CSF)

outer layer of meninges

five lumbar vertebrae

Lumbar punctures are performed by neurologists and other specialists in order to obtain samples of cerebrospinal fluid (CSF). This fluid bathes the brain and spinal cord and is contained between two layers of their enveloping membranes, the meninges. The appearance and chemical composition of CSF changes in diseases such as meningitis, cerebral hemorrhage and multiple sclerosis; it is therefore an important aid to diagnosis. The lumbar puncture needle is introduced between the third and fourth lumbar vertebrae to avoid damaging the spinal cord.

nervous system. Many patients unjustifiably fear a lumbar puncture because they have listened to "horror tales" about it. In fact, it is one of the fastest, safest and easiest tests a neurologist does. The major side effect, experienced by some patients for one or two days, is a headache on standing. It is always sad when a patient denies his doctor access to this valuable information in spinal fluid because of unfounded fears.

X-rays and special scans

Although nerve tissue does not show up on x-rays, the neurologist can still use them to gain useful information. Bones of the skull and spinal column enclose the soft brain and spinal cord, and disorders of these bones can cause neurological disorders. Tumors within the nervous system may also erode or alter surrounding bones. Therefore, the neurologist carefully examines x-rays of the skull and spine for evidence of fractures, degeneration, displacement or tumor of the bones.

Because the neurologist actually wants and needs to know the structure of nerve tissue itself, he uses a substance which contrasts with nerve tissue, revealing its structure on x-rays taken of brain or cord and vessels leading to them.

Arteriograms (angiograms)

These are obtained by injecting an oily liquid contrast material (containing iodine) into a particular artery; this flows to the part of the nervous system to be studied. X-rays of this part are taken rapidly, usually one every half second, and the blood vessels (first arteries and then veins) of the part are outlined on the x-rays by the contrast material within them. Since the position of the vessels corresponds closely to the structure of the brain, an arteriogram is one of the most accurate diagnostic tools of neurology. Having one taken involves minor discomfort; the patient must have a needle puncture of a blood vessel, usually numbed with Novocain. He may feel intense flushing as the contrast material is injected.

Myelogram

X-rays of the spinal cord can be obtained by injecting contrast liquid into the narrow space surrounding the spinal cord (the "spinal sac") through a lumbar puncture needle. On the x-ray, the contrast material outlines the spinal cord, the nerves connected to it, and the spinal canal formed by the bones around it. Ruptured intervertebral disks show up well with this technique. As with other lumbar punctures, some patients have a headache on standing for one or two days after the test.

Pneumoencephalogram

This test outlines the brain on x-rays after air is injected into the spinal sac through a lumbar puncture needle. Air is useful because it rises through heavier spinal fluid to the brain if the person is sitting up. However, it causes fever and severe headache. The pneumoencephalogram used to be one of the most accurate ways of outlining the brain, but it has largely been abandoned during the past few years in favor of the computerized scan.

Radioisotope brain scan

In this test a radioactive material is injected into a vein and soon circulates throughout the body. As it passes through the blood vessels of the head, a "scanner" is used to detect the pattern of radioactivity. Disorders such as tumors, strokes or blood clots show up as "hot spots" on the scan. Since the amount of radioactive material used is very small and disappears in several hours, the test is not dangerous. However, it is not as accurate as x-rays taken after the intravenous injections of contrast material (opaque to x-rays).

Computerized axial tomography

This procedure (also known as the CAT scan) provides the equivalent of x-ray vision. It gives a detailed "three-dimensional" picture of the structure of the brain and its surroundings within the skull without any injections or invasion of the body. This is accomplished by having a computer correlate thousands of very tiny x-ray pictures taken at angles all around the head. Very slight differences in the x-ray patterns given by brain, spinal cord and diseased tissues are magnified by the computer into a recognizable picture. Since its introduction in 1972 the CAT scan has changed neurological practice, helping many patients to avoid admission to hospitals for x-rays that necessitate the injection of a contrast substance. Most neurologists today use the CAT scan instead of a pneumoencephalogram but arteriograms may still be needed to show changes in blood vessels (which do not show on the CAT scan).

Limits of diagnostic tests

Although diagnostic tests are increasingly more accurate today, the neurologist is needed to select, interpret and correlate these tests in relationship with a patient's problem. For example, the performance of three or four very accurate tests on the brain can be avoided if a clinical neurological examination localizes the problem to the spinal cord. A skilled neurologist uses all the information he can gather from speaking to and examining the patient to direct the choice of tests which will help him to make the diagnosis quickly and safely.

NEUROLOGICAL ILLNESSES

Most patients seen by neurologists have persistent or recurrent pain (especially headaches), dizziness or trouble moving their limbs.

Headache and migraine

Headache is a common symptom which may be due to tension, the effect of an illness outside the nervous system (such as high blood pressure, poor eyesight or an infection), migraine or other disorders of the blood vessels of the face and scalp, pressure on individual nerves supplying the head, or increased pressure within the skull. A physical examination is required to find the cause of headache or any pain, but many clues come from the patient's description of his problem. When describing it to a physician, you should ask yourself if your headache involves the whole head or only a part of it. Is the pain steady, like a vice, throbbing like a hammer or sticking like a pin? Does it occur at any one time of day or during any particular activity? Recall any injuries to your head or neck and the occurrence of any similar headaches in other members of your family. Your accurate answers to such questions are invaluable to the doctor.

Tension headaches result from tightening of muscles of the neck and head during mental stress. A dull ache at the back of the head extends around both temples to the forehead like a tight band and lasts most of the day. Relief of anxiety or stress is the best treatment, but aspirin and a mild sedative may give temporary relief.

Prolonged high blood pressure can cause headaches and no examination is complete without accurate measurement of blood pressure. A need for eyeglasses and visual strain may cause headaches, but less often than is commonly believed. Infection in the sinuses around the nose produces facial or forehead pain. Sudden headache and fever are possible evidence of meningitis (an inflammation of the membranes that surround the brain and spinal cord), which calls for immediate professional care.

MIGRAINE is the most common vascular headache disorder; it is produced by changes in the walls of blood vessels supplying the scalp, eyes and face. At first, the blood vessel walls tighten and the reduced blood flow to the eyes may cause shimmering lights to appear in a patient's vision. After a few minutes, the walls relax and the vessels expand enough to cause headache which throbs with the pulsebeat, often only on one side of the head at a time. Migraine usually starts in childhood or young adulthood and may affect several members of a family. Some attacks of

The illustration (right) shows how the central nervous system (brain and spinal cord) connects with the peripheral nervous system—in this case a spinal nerve supplying the fingers. When receptors in the skin are stimulated, signals travel up the sensory nerve fibers to the spinal cord and brain. The brain processes this incoming information and then sends a return message down a parallel motor pathway to the muscles of the fingers so that an appropriate movement is made.

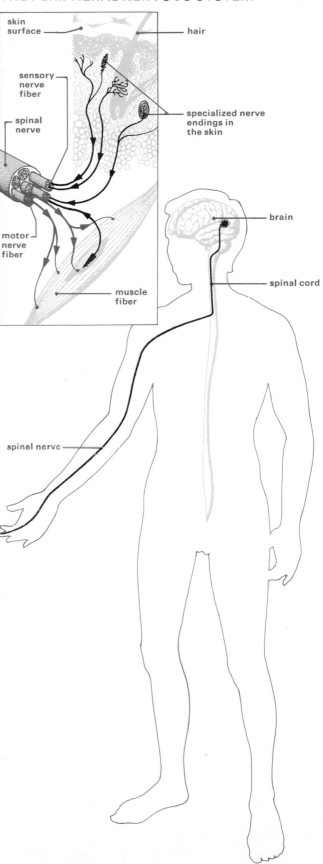

THE PERIPHERAL NERVOUS SYSTEM

skin surface

hair

sensory nerve fiber

specialized nerve endings in the skin

spinal nerve

motor nerve fiber

muscle fiber

brain

spinal cord

spinal nerve

migraine are triggered by foods such as chocolate, cheese or fish. It is treated with medicines which constrict the blood vessels at the start of an attack, preventing their painful expansion.

Pain about the temple or forehead

Severe pain and tenderness of the temple or forehead in an older person may be caused by inflammation in a blood vessel due to *temporal arteritis*. This illness may suddenly stop the blood flow to an eye, causing blindness. Because the administration of cortisone rapidly reverses the inflammation and forestalls the loss of vision, active temporal arteritis is a true medical emergency that requires immediate medical attention.

Pressure on structures around the brain can cause headache. A nerve "complains" about pressure on it by causing sticking or jabbing pain in the area it supplies, most often the face or back of the head. Pressure from within the skull from a tumor causes dull, steady pain which may be worse in the morning and is usually accompanied by nausea and drowsiness.

Most headaches are temporary and are not caused by serious illness. But a new unexplained type of headache should always be looked into by a doctor, especially in a person who "never has a headache."

Dizziness

Dizziness (loss of orientation in space) is of two types. VERTIGO, a spinning sensation, is caused by disorders of the inner ear or its connections within the brain. Lightheadedness ("giddiness") is associated with a condition which decreases the flow of blood to the brain. Vertigo is the sensation of spinning you feel after turning around and around rapidly, and is often accompanied by nausea and worsened by a sudden change of position. The typical illness of the middle ear, labyrinthitis (see OTITIS MEDIA), starts suddenly with vertigo, nausea and jumping vision. These symptoms last for days at a time. You can experience lightheadedness after breathing as fast and hard as possible for a minute. Giddiness usually results from a fall in blood pressure with sudden standing or an irregular heartbeat.

Stroke and other vascular disorders

Stroke is a problem in the brain caused by a block of blood flow in a cerebral blood vessel or a leak from or rupture of the vessel. Most strokes start suddenly, reach their worst within hours, and resolve much more slowly over days or months. Brain damage from strokes often resists treatment. Thus, much emphasis is placed on STROKE *prevention*.

Block of flow in a blood vessel to the brain is very much like a log jam in a river. The "logs" are usually small blood clots which form "upstream" on rough patches (plaques) in the walls of neck arteries. The clots break loose into the bloodstream and lodge "downstream" in smaller vessels within the brain, stopping or seriously impairing the circulation beyond. The victim experiences sudden weakness, incoordination, changes in vision, or dizziness—depending on which part of the brain is involved. These symptoms change as the blood clot changes: they disappear if the clot dissolves; if the clot enlarges, however, the condition becomes progressively worse.

Transient ischemic attack (TIA)

Some people have occlusion of a blood vessel to the brain which disappears completely within minutes or hours. Such an episode is called a *transient ischemic attack* (TIA) and may be a warning of an impending stroke. About one in five people who suffer such attacks have a stroke within the next year. Some of these strokes can be prevented by surgically removing plaques in the neck vessels or by the use of blood-thinning medicines. Especially encouraging is the finding that common aspirin seems to interfere with blood clotting enough to provide a small degree of protection against stroke. However, aspirin for this purpose should be taken only under a doctor's supervision, because it can have dangerous side effects. This important fact should be kept in mind: *temporary weakness, incoordination, change in vision or dizziness may signal an impending stroke and should always be brought to your doctor's attention.*

The rough plaques mentioned above are caused by hardening of the arteries (ARTERIOSCLEROSIS) which in turn is linked to high blood pressure, diabetes, blood fats and smoking. Therefore, control of these factors throughout adult life is very important in stroke prevention.

Some "logs" which "jam" in arteries to the brain are from the heart rather than from vessels in the neck. Infection of heart valves (such as that associated with RHEUMATIC HEART DISEASE) or the presence of certain congenital or acquired heart disorders tends to release some clots into the bloodstream. In addition, certain diseases of the blood (such as SICKLE CELL ANEMIA) predispose to formation of clots within blood vessels in the brain. Recognition and treatment of such conditions are also important in stroke prevention.

Hemorrhage

Bleeding from vessels within the brain is often a catastrophe, causing severe neurological damage or sudden death. Hemorrhage may be a result of injury but spontaneous bleeding can be caused by high blood pressure, abnormalities in blood vessels or impaired blood clotting.

High blood pressure predisposes healthy appearing middle-aged people to suffer sudden bleeding deep within the brain. There is severe headache ("like a bolt from the blue") followed by paralysis of one side of the body or loss of consciousness, or both. No treatment is truly effective and the patient often dies or is left severely handicapped. *The remedy for hypertensive brain hemorrhage lies in prevention by control of high blood pressure before bleeding occurs.* (See also BLOOD PRESSURE and the major article on **Hypertension.**)

Aneurysms

Much as a weak spot on a tire's inner tube bulges out, weak spots in blood vessels within the head form berry-like bulges called aneurysms. Once formed, there is always a danger they may burst from increased blood pressure and release blood into the brain's lining. The patient may then suffer a severe headache or a stiff neck and may lose consciousness. Aneurysms, which can be seen on arteriograms, can very often be "clipped off" by the neurosurgeon to prevent rupture and massive hemorrhage. (See ANEURYSM.)

Convulsions

Convulsions (SEIZURES, or "fits") are the result of excessive electrical discharges by the brain and cause shaking or loss of consciousness. Generalized seizures start suddenly as the patient falls unconscious, stiffens, and then repeatedly shakes both arms and legs for about a minute. Clenched teeth often cause tongue biting and the person may pass urine or feces during the spell. "Focal" seizures result from the electrical discharge of one part of the brain; they may be accompanied by twitching of one arm or automatic lip smacking and chewing and loss of awareness. *Absence spells* occur mostly in children, who stare or blink for a short time and for a few seconds are out of contact with their surroundings.

Seizures may result from the scar of an old brain injury or stroke, from a brain tumor or from infection. Again, the story of how a seizure developed is very important to the neurologist. The patient should recall any prelude ("aura") to the seizure, such as flashing lights or a strange feeling in one part of the body. A witness to the seizure should note where the shaking first started.

EPILEPSY is a term for the tendency to have repeated seizures without obvious cause. A person who develops seizures for the first time in his life does not necessarily have epilepsy. In fact, it is the doctor's job to search for a separate cause rather than automatically settle for a diagnosis of epilepsy.

Seizures can be controlled today with medicines called anticonvulsants, commonly phenytoin (Dilantin) or phenobarbital. *These medicines work well only if they are taken faithfully every day; the prime cause of poor seizure control is inadequate dosage.* However, too much of an anticonvulsant causes drowsiness and unsteadiness.

Analysis of blood samples for content of anticonvulsants is most helpful to the doctor in adjusting the dose or in determining if the patient is neglecting to take enough of his medicine.

Brain tumor

Many people who seek neurological consultation are afraid they have a brain tumor. *In most cases this is highly unlikely!* Brain tumors typically cause steadily progressive symptoms rather than sudden ones—including headache, nausea (especially in the morning), lethargy and focal weakness. These symptoms, often due to high pressure within the brain caused by swelling around the tumor, can be relieved by cortisone medication. Many tumors within the head lie outside the brain and can be surgically removed. Even tumors within the brain can be partially removed and the remaining parts treated with x-rays and special medicine. (See the major article on **Neurosurgery.**)

Parkinson's disease

Because the nervous system is so highly organized and specialized, it is vulnerable to deterioration of specific functions such as movement, coordination or feeling. Among the many "systems degenerations" of the central nervous system, the commonest and one of the most treatable today is PARKINSON'S DISEASE. This illness affects middle-aged or older people and causes slowness of movement, stiff limbs, a bending posture, a slow, short-stepped walk and shaking of the limbs. Without treatment, symptoms steadily progress and the person may become incapacitated by his difficulty in moving. Fortunately, there are several medicines which improve the symptoms, the strongest being L-DOPA. L-DOPA is converted into a vital chemical messenger, dopamine—missing in the brains of persons with Parkinson's disease. The use of L-DOPA often enables a patient with difficulty in writing, dressing, walking and rising from a chair or bed to do all of these things with relative ease. L-DOPA and newer medicines which incorporate or mimic it, especially Sinemet, must be given on schedule and in doses that are individualized. Such treatment often results in the addition of years of useful function to the lives of those with Parkinson's disease.

Mental disturbances

Dementia is one of the most important problems faced by a neurologist. The symptoms are confusion and poor memory, usually linked to disease of the brain. A sudden deterioration of mental abilities is almost always due to a physical illness affecting the brain rather than to a psychiatric cause. An example is the elderly person who develops fever and is suddenly very excited and confused. When the fever is reduced the confusion abates.

Disorders of the thyroid gland, deficiency of certain vitamins, or disease of the liver or kidneys may also underlie mental deterioration; specific treatment of the

BRAIN TUMOR

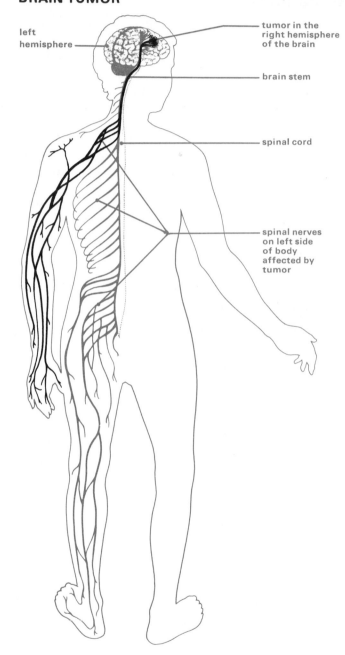

left hemisphere

tumor in the right hemisphere of the brain

brain stem

spinal cord

spinal nerves on left side of body affected by tumor

A tumor or some other disorder such as a stroke affecting the right hemisphere of the brain causes effects on the left side of the body. The reason is that the nerve fibers connecting the limbs and trunk to the brain cross over in the spinal cord or in the brain stem. Depending on the size of the tumor, paralysis or loss of sensation may result in part or all of the opposite side of the body.

primary disease solves the mental problem. Medications are also often linked to confusion because of overdose, undue sensitivity to them (especially in young children and the elderly), or sudden stopping of sedatives (sleeping pills, tranquilizers or alcohol) by individuals who habitually use them in large amounts.

Reversible confusion is also caused by disorders within the head. Inflammation of the membranes that surround the brain (meningitis) or bleeding beneath the innermost of these membranes (subarachnoid hemorrhage) may cause initial symptoms of confusion or lethargy as well as headache, fever and a stiff neck. Blood clots or tumors pressing upon or within the brain typically change personality, alertness and memory. Blockage of cerebrospinal fluid circulation in the head leads to trouble in walking and dementia which is sometimes relieved by a tube (shunt) to let some of the fluid out of the head.

Although the neurologist searches for each of these treatable causes of dementia, a substantial number of patients have none of them. Their gradually worsening confusion, memory loss (especially for recent events) and change in personality is due to disease of the brain cells themselves resulting in cerebral atrophy (shrinkage of the brain). These people become senile, some of them very prematurely. Popular myths link senility to "hardening of the arteries" but such an association is probably infrequent.

Multiple sclerosis (MS)

MULTIPLE SCLEROSIS causes episodes of neurological trouble, usually starting between the ages of 15 and 45. Common symptoms are dizziness, staggering gait, slurred speech, double vision or diminished vision in one eye, leg weakness and loss of urinary control. One or several of these symptoms last a few weeks. The symptoms may then disappear or persist fully or partially. This disease results from disruption of the insulating white myelin sheath around nerve fibers in the brain and spinal cord, perhaps due to an "autoimmune" reaction. Multiple sclerosis is episodic with variable symptoms; several therapeutic approaches seem to provide some degree of relief. Cortisone medication is sometimes helpful, but no one treatment is always effective.

Other common neurological disorders

All the diseases discussed above affect the central nervous system. A neurologist also sees patients who have disorders of the nerves outside the spinal cord or of the muscles supplied by those nerves.

The roots of nerves just outside the spinal cord are vulnerable to compression as they pass between bones of the spine to reach the limbs or trunk. The pressure often comes from a *herniated* ("slipped") disk, the cushioning cartilage which lies between bones of the spine. Disks slip most frequently in the neck or lower part of the back, causing pain which radiates from the spine into an arm or hand or down the outside of the buttock, thigh and leg ("sciatica"). Prolonged pressure causes weakness and shrinkage (atrophy) of the muscles served by the nerve root, or numbness and tingling in the areas supplied by sensor nerves from that root. The symptoms of a slipped disk often disappear with several days or weeks of bed rest (one should use a hard mattress or bed board). If the symptoms persist, especially if weakness or numbness stays the same or worsens, the doctor may perform a *myelogram* to confirm his diagnosis and the exact location of the involved disk (which may have to be surgically removed).

The symptoms of *peripheral nerve disorders* are also weakness, muscle shrinkage, or numbness and tingling. If one nerve is affected, such as compression of the median nerve to the hand by a tight band of cartilage in the wrist (CARPAL TUNNEL SYNDROME), the symptoms will be limited to the area served by the nerve, in this case the hand. However, generalized illnesses affect many nerves at the same time to cause weakness, numbness and tingling in the hands and feet. Diabetes mellitus is the most frequent underlying disease, along with malnutrition (most often associated with alcoholism in the United States).

Diseases of muscles cause weakness of areas close to the trunk. The affected person may have trouble brushing his hair, getting out of bed or a chair, or climbing steps. Many disorders of muscles are hereditary (muscular dystrophies) and their causes are unknown. Inflammation of muscles (polymyositis) couples weakness with some tenderness and often improves with cortisone treatment.

MYASTHENIA GRAVIS causes changeable muscle weakness in eye movements, face and limbs which is treatable with medicine or by surgical removal of the thymus gland. Electromyography tests and a muscle biopsy (in which a small piece of muscle is removed surgically and examined under a microscope) help the doctor in his diagnosis of muscle disorders.

Points to remember

Several important points deserve to be emphasized again:
1. A new severe or persistent headache should be evaluated by your doctor.
2. The best treatment for stroke is *prevention* by control of high blood pressure, diabetes, obesity and smoking.
3. Temporary weakness or loss of feeling in a body part and blindness in one eye may be a warning of stroke.
4. Sudden loss of consciousness with convulsive-like symptoms is not necessarily caused by epilepsy. An observer's detailed description of the episode helps the doctor make a correct diagnosis.

5. "Senility" has many causes, some of them curable.

Conclusion

In conclusion, I would point out that the neurologist is a consultant who works best in cooperation with other doctors. He pinpoints new neurological problems for primary care physicians and supplies suggestions for treatment. He refers patients who need surgical treatment to a neurosurgeon. He may himself become the primary doctor for patients with chronic neurological illnesses (seizures, multiple sclerosis, Parkinson's disease) but he still remembers to coordinate his care with a general doctor and with specialists in rehabilitation and urology. A major complaint about neurologists by both doctors and patients is that they produce much diagnosis but little treatment. Leaving treatment aside, accurate diagnosis by the neurologist helps the general physician to choose his treatment, save unnecessary "shotgun" testing (performing a wide variety of diagnostic tests) and relieves anxiety by at least quickly naming the disorder affecting a patient. That is why nine out of ten patients come to the neurologist by referral from other doctors.

A neurologist, before he can apply for board certification by the American Board of Psychiatry and Neurology, must have completed at least four years of postgraduate training and experience; then he must successfully pass the Board's extensive written and oral examinations to be certified.

Neurological research in the past 30 years has greatly expanded treatments available to the neurologist and general physician. Knowledge of the chemicals which transmit messages from one cell to another has helped to develop anticonvulsants to prevent seizures, and L-DOPA for the treatment of Parkinsonism. Studies of the way nerves send messages to muscles have improved the treatment of myasthenia gravis. Dogged inquiry into abnormalities of blood vessels has led to operations and medicines which at least improve the odds for stroke victims. Recent work on viruses and allergies within the nervous system may lead to better treatment for multiple sclerosis.

There is much yet to be learned, and one may well ask if man can even hope to completely understand the organ system which contains his own mind. The practicing neurologist must constantly continue the educational process to keep abreast of all new knowledge that continues to evolve. His job is to use his examination and tests to find the diagnosis and point the way to whatever treatment is appropriate.

Some neurologists are engaged in basic research to discover more about how the brain handles information and how it makes use of various chemicals. Early "models" of the brain resulted in the development of the modern electronic computer, which even now remains millions of times less complex than our nervous system.

Neurosurgery Dr. Paul S. Stein

The modern neurosurgeon is highly skilled in the diagnosis and surgical treatment of a wide variety of conditions that affect the brain, spinal cord and other parts of the nervous system. One of his most dramatic procedures is to expose the living brain (as in the removal of a brain tumor or an accessible blood clot). The following article discusses some of his diagnostic tools and techniques and the major conditions with which he deals.

Neurosurgery is the medical specialty which consists of the evaluation, diagnosis and surgical treatment of diseases involving the nervous system (brain, spinal cord and nerves). Because of the highly specialized nature of his field, the neurosurgeon generally sees patients on a consultation basis. That is, most of his patients are referred to him by other physicians who suspect their patients may have a disorder of the nervous system amenable to surgical treatment. (See also the major article on **Neurology.**)

Because the evaluation of such disorders is a highly intricate and sophisticated process, many patients do not have a definitive diagnosis made prior to his consultation. Therefore, the neurosurgeon must be completely trained as a neurological diagnostician as well as a surgical technician. Like a three-legged stool, his ability to function rests on three legs. These are knowledge, surgical skill and judgment. If any of these "legs" is deficient, shorter than the others, the neurosurgeon does not function with maximum efficiency.

Preparation and training

All of the accredited training programs in the United States are geared toward providing these skills. To enter such a program, one must be a graduate of an accredited medical school and have completed at least one year of formal training in general surgery. The actual residency program in neurological surgery will be a minimum of four years, but may be as many as seven depending upon the institution chosen. Almost all neurosurgical training programs in the United States are affiliated with medical schools. During the latter part of his residency, the individual may take the written examination given by the American Board of Neurological Surgeons. However, the final examination cannot be taken until the candidate has

successfully completed his formal training program and has been in practice for two years in one location. At that time he must submit the case histories and records of all the patients he cared for in those two years as well as recommendations by his colleagues and training institution. He must then successfully complete an oral examination by the American Board of Neurological Surgeons before they will give him a diploma of certification. This rigorous process is designed to provide the public with the best possible care in a highly specialized field of surgery. If your neurosurgeon is "Board Certified" you can be assured that he has gone through the entire process and has accomplished all of these objectives. A "Board Eligible" neurosurgeon is one who has fulfilled all the basic requirements but has not yet completed the oral examination.

Diagnostic approach

Like the sleuth of detective fiction, the neurosurgeon listens, looks and investigates for clues in order to make his diagnosis. The "history taking," in which he discusses the symptoms and complaints with the patient, is of utmost importance. It is at this time that details are extracted regarding what the patient is actually experiencing and what the pattern of symptoms has been. For example, if the patient's problem is pain, it is necessary for the doctor to know where the pain is, how long it has been present, whether it is improving or getting worse, what kinds of activity make it worse, what makes it better, and so on. This information may be pivotal in making the diagnosis, since many disorders of the nervous system follow a specific pattern in terms of timing, progress and anatomical distribution. Therefore, the more accurate the information given by the patient, the more accurate is the diagnosis.

Based upon this information, the neurosurgeon frequently knows what to look for during the physical examination. The neurological examination is designed to test and evaluate those bodily functions which are related to the activity of the nerves, spinal cord and brain. These include movement and strength of all extremities, reflex activity, sensation in all extremities and on the face and trunk, balance and coordination, thinking ability, speech, and the special senses of sight, smell and hearing. This information is correlated with that obtained during the history taking, and the diagnostic possibilities are thereby narrowed down to the most likely few; diagnostic tests are then selected to confirm the physician's impressions and provide specialized information needed to plan treatment.

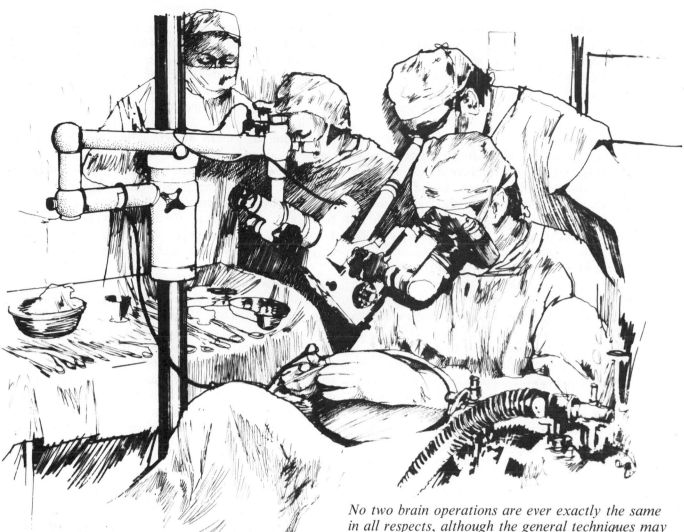

No two brain operations are ever exactly the same in all respects, although the general techniques may be similar. A section of the cranium is first removed to expose the appropriate area of the cerebral cortex. In the above illustration the chief neurosurgeon and his surgical assistant are viewing an exposed area of the brain of a patient concealed by surgical drapes under a low-power microscope. A camera attached to the lens system of the microscope permits the taking of photographs for partial documentation of the procedure.

Diagnostic tools and techniques

Modern neurosurgeons and their patients are fortunate indeed to have at their disposal many excellent diagnostic tools. The most recent and most revolutionary of these is the *computerized axial tomographic scan* (*CAT scan,* or *CT scan*). By combining a special x-ray unit with a computer, this machine very quickly takes many thousands of x-ray pictures through the skull at different angles. It puts all of this together on a screen where it can be seen by the doctor as a cross-sectional picture of the brain and those structures related to it. This test has the advantage of being "non-invasive" (no needles or materials are injected into sensitive and vital areas of the body). The pictures provided are very useful in the diagnosis or exclusion of brain tumors, bleeding in and around the brain, blockages to the normal flow of cerebrospinal fluid and many other disorders of the brain.

Angiography (or arteriography)

This technique provides special information concerning the blood vessels in the brain. In this test, a needle or plastic tube is placed in the blood vessels supplying blood to the brain and a dye is injected. Rapid serial x-ray pictures are taken which show this dye being carried through the blood vessels. This test carries with it less than one chance in a hundred for serious complications. However, it does have some risks and is frequently reserved for those patients in whom the CAT scan has shown a problem and in whom more specific information is required. Sometimes this test is done before or instead of the CAT scan when the physician feels that the primary problem is related to the blood vessels in and around the brain. Many of these types of abnormality will not show up on the CAT scan, but will be shown by angiography. Not infrequently the diagnosis will have been made by other tests prior to angiography, but the angiogram is needed to provide specific information to the surgeon in order to plan his operative procedure.

Pneumoencephalography

This is a diagnostic test in which the neurosurgeon performs a "spinal tap" (lumbar puncture) and injects air into the space between the spinal cord and the arachnoid, one of its three covering membranes (the "subarachnoid space") with the patient sitting in a special chair. The air will bubble up around the spinal cord and enter the *cerebral ventricles* and other spaces filled with cerebrospinal fluid in and around the brain. X-ray pictures taken at this time will show the air very well as a result of the large difference in density between the air and the brain tissue. Because the air outlines the shape of the brain and the cerebral ventricles (cavities within the brain which contain cerebrospinal fluid), it gives a relatively good picture of major structures inside the head. This test is sometimes needed for specific information about certain areas inside the brain. However, it is not done as frequently as it was in the past, because the CAT scan now provides much of this information. This particular test causes the patient a certain amount of discomfort (generally in the form of headache and nausea) and has a similar risk factor to the angiograms discussed above. In some cases, when the pressure inside the head is significantly elevated, a slightly different procedure may be used. Because lumbar puncture in this case might be dangerous, the air is introduced directly into the fluid spaces within the brain by drilling a small hole in the skull and placing a needle through the brain into the fluid area. Some of the fluid is then replaced with a small amount of air (as with the pneumoencephalogram). This procedure is called a *ventriculogram* because the fluid-filled spaces inside the brain are called the ventricles.

Myelography

This is frequently performed in the process of evaluating a patient for disease involving the spinal cord or the nerve roots as they leave the spinal cord. Lumbar puncture is performed with the patient lying on the x-ray table; a small amount of cerebrospinal fluid is replaced with an oily appearing liquid dye which is opaque to x-rays. The dye (or "contrast medium") will appear white on the x-rays in contrast to the dark bony structures and will outline the spinal cord and the nerves. It is heavier than the cerebrospinal fluid and so the examiner can make it travel up and down the spinal axis by tilting the patient up and down on the x-ray table. In this manner the entire spinal axis can be examined, if necessary. Myelography is one of the most frequently performed diagnostic tests done by a neurosurgeon. It is used in the diagnosis of pinched nerves

in the back and neck as the result of a "slipped disk" (a herniated, ruptured or prolapsed intervertebral disk). For some reason, myelograms have a very bad reputation among patients and there are many rumors regarding this test. The truth is that this is a relatively safe test and generally is only mildly uncomfortable. About two or three patients out of ten will have some headache following the myelogram, particularly when they stand up. Occasionally this will linger for some time, but in most cases is gone within a few days. Some back discomfort may linger for a few days, but also is generally short-lived. The major risk of myelography is an internal reaction to the dye, which can result in severe scarring around the spine and nerves. Luckily, this is an extremely rare occurrence; it happens only about once out of several thousand tests.

Brain scans

Radioactive brain scans are often used in the process of neurological diagnosis. The patient receives an injection of radioactive material in a vein, and then lies under a scan machine which safely and painlessly traces the distribution of radioactive material within the head. There is no danger from the minimal amount of radioactivity used in this test either to the patient or examiner. It is often used as a screening test to help decide if more definitive tests (such as angiography or pneumoencephalography) are needed.

CEREBRAL ANGIOGRAM

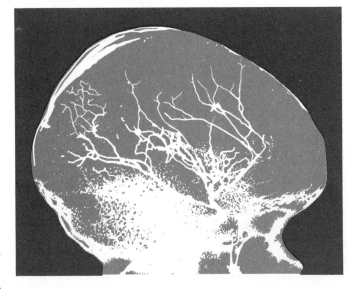

Cerebral angiography is an x-ray technique for displaying the arteries which supply the brain. The normal pattern can be altered by a congenital malformation of the vessels, an aneurysm, blockage with a blood clot or a brain tumor. The neurosurgeon needs precise information about the location of these abnormalities if he is to operate.

Other tests

Several other tests exist which may be used to aid in the diagnosis of neurological disease. A lumbar puncture to obtain some cerebrospinal fluid for examination may be required. This is a simpler procedure than the myelogram; the side effects are very similar, except that there is no risk of reaction to the dye since none is injected. An electroencephalogram (EEG) involves pasting several wires to the skull and recording the electrical activity of the brain. It is useful in evaluating convulsive disorders (epileptic attacks) and for a variety of other problems. Similarly, the electrical activity of nerves and muscles can be measured and evaluated by use of electrodes taped to the skin or by use of small needles placed into a muscle through the skin. This is known as an *electromyogram*, and provides information regarding a variety of problems which primarily affect the nerves outside the spinal cord and the muscles.

The decision to operate

When the clinical investigation is completed, the neurosurgeon will often know if surgery can be helpful in a given patient. At this point an intelligent discussion can be held regarding the diagnosis, the type of surgical procedure indicated, and its expectations and risks. The surgeon will make his recommendations to the patient and his family based upon his knowledge, experience and judgment. Patients and their families should not be afraid to ask any questions that come to mind. Frequently the decision to have an operation is a balance between the hoped for (but not guaranteed) results and the potential dangers of the procedure. Many cases are quite clear-cut, such as a brain tumor that might be cured by surgery, but in others the decision for surgery may be elective. Except in dire emergencies, permission to proceed lies with the patient and family, thereby requiring them to be properly informed and prepared to make important decisions.

Preparing for surgery

The day of surgery is often full of new and sometimes frightening experiences for the patient. Some understanding of these activities may help allay the fear. It is necessary not to eat for at least 6 to 8 hours prior to the administration of a general anesthetic. Frequently, the patient will not be fed from about midnight of the day before surgery. This is done to protect the occasional patient who might be sensitive to the anesthetic and vomit during surgery. It is essential that the stomach be empty so that no gastric material is vomited and then (while unconscious) inhaled into the lungs—an extremely serious complication. A rubber or plastic tube (called a "Foley catheter") may be placed through the urinary opening into the bladder to allow free drainage of urine during the

procedure. This is done in some brain operations where special medicines may be given which cause increased urine output. It is also done during long operations to prevent the bladder from becoming overdistended. A needle will generally be placed in a vein to give the patient some fluids and sustenance during the procedure. It also provides a means for the anesthesiologist to give needed medicines or administer blood during the operation.

Some neurosurgical procedures, particularly delicate brain operations, require the neurosurgeon to have very accurate information about vital bodily functions at all times. Therefore, certain monitoring devices may be attached to the patient prior to the procedure—for example, a needle in an artery or vein to provide information about blood pressure, blood contents, etc., or electrodes attached to the chest to give information about the heart, or to the scalp to give electrical information about brain activity during the operation. One should not be concerned by all of these devices when it is realized that they are designed to give the anesthesiologist and surgeon information about the patient's well-being throughout the procedure and for some time afterward. This is an extra measure of protection that the patient has in undergoing modern surgery. Likewise, the family should understand that a significant part of the time that their loved one is in the operating room is involved not only with the surgery itself but with these preparations.

Typical neurosurgical procedures

The initial operation done in preparing a patient for brain surgery is called a *craniotomy*. The hair is removed and the scalp shaved. Incision is made in the scalp in such a manner as to expose the bone of the skull over the appropriate area of the brain. The scalp incision is made above the hairline, if at all possible, so that no scar will be visible when the hair grows back. A portion of the skull in the surgical area is removed using a special saw. The heavy, fabric-like covering over the brain is then opened in such a manner that it can be sewn shut again after the operation. The brain is thus exposed and the surgeon proceeds with the specific operation planned. Afterward the piece of skull which has been removed is replaced in its normal position and attached to the surrounding skull by several wire sutures, which hold it in place until healing can occur. After suturing the scalp closed, a sterile bandage is applied in a manner resembling an Indian turban. The amount of postoperative discomfort for this kind of procedure is surprisingly small (there are no pain receptors in the brain itself) and most patients are quite comfortable with just some aspirin and a small amount of codeine.

In approaching lesions of the spinal cord or nerves leaving the spinal cord, a procedure called *laminectomy* is frequently performed. Incision is made in the skin over the appropriate area of the spine. The muscles attached to the spine are carefully elevated from the bone on either side and are held apart, thus exposing the bone over the spinal cord. This bone is then removed in small pieces by a sharp biting type of instrument called a "rongeur." Enough bone is removed to expose the operating area and the covering over the spinal cord and nerves is then opened. After the operation, this covering is sewn back together. The bone cannot be replaced in this instance, however, since it was removed in many small pieces. The spinal muscles are quite thick and strong, and provide adequate covering and protection for this area after they have been sewn back together. Often the amount of bone actually removed is relatively small and these procedures do not generally affect the stability and strength of the spine. There is generally more postoperative discomfort with this type of procedure than with craniotomy; thus, stronger post-operative medication is ordered by the physician.

Brain tumors

Tumors affecting the brain represent a large part of a neurosurgeon's practice. Although they may be found at any age, such tumors are common in early adult life and in middle age. Their presence may manifest itself in a variety of symptoms or groups of symptoms. It is important to remember that most of the symptoms caused by brain tumors are also seen in many other less serious conditions. For example, although headache is a very common presenting complaint in patients with a BRAIN TUMOR, by far the vast majority of severe headaches have nothing whatever to do with the development of a tumor. Likewise, seizures or convulsions can be caused by brain tumors, but most people with convulsions do not have brain tumors.

The symptoms of brain tumors are caused either by irritation of the brain or by pressure on the brain from the growing tumor. Irritation and stretching of the pain nerves around the coverings of the brain (membranes known as *meninges*) can cause headache. There is no simple diagnostic way to distinguish the headaches caused by a brain tumor from many other causes of headache. However, if an individual with no previous history of headaches suddenly begins to have them, and they become progressively more frequent and more severe, further investigation is warranted. Headaches that are more severe in the morning, associated with vomiting, or brought on by mild stress (such as bending over to tie one's shoelaces) should also be discussed with your physician.

Seizures and convulsions

Another symptom caused by irritation of the brain is seizure. SEIZURES are periods of excessive, uncontrolled brain activity—rather like an avalanche as compared with gently falling snow. Convulsions are the most common form of seizure activity. In other instances, there may be only twitching or jumping movements of one extremity or of one side of the body. Seizures of the *petit mal* variety rarely involve any motor activity. The patient simply seems to lose contact with the environment for a few seconds (usually less than a minute) and tends to stare off into space. Occasionally strange kinds of repetitive behavioral activity will be seen. Even outbursts of temper and uncontrollable rage may represent seizure activity, particularly if it is not typical of the patient's usual personality and if the activity appears to become repetitive. Many times it is very difficult even for a trained neurologist or neurosurgeon to know if certain kinds of activity are simply "neurotic" or represent a form of seizure. This is where the EEG (electroencephalogram) as well as other diagnostic tests might be helpful.

Other evidence of brain tumors

Other symptoms that may be related to brain tumors are progressive weakness involving one side of the body, difficulty with coordination and balance, mental changes, and visual problems. Visual difficulties associated with brain tumors may often not be recognized as such in the beginning. Occasionally, patients will find that they are tending to bump into objects such as lampposts and doorposts while they are walking. They may note that in reading a newspaper there is no difficulty finishing the line, but finding the new line sometimes represents a bit of a problem. That is because brain tumors will frequently affect the peripheral vision first, and usually on one side or the other. This is often not noticed as visual difficulty at first because the "straight ahead vision" is unaffected; the only initial difficulty is when peripheral vision is needed. A proper neurological examination will often demonstrate what the visual problem is and what part of the brain is probably involved.

If symptoms and signs on examination indicate the possible presence of a brain tumor, further diagnostic tests will be ordered. Usually the safe "screening tests"(such as the radioactive brain scan, CAT scan and EEG) will be done first. Further testing—such as angiography or pneumoencephalography—may follow in order to give more specific information regarding the possible presence of a tumor, its location, its blood supply, and the nature of the growth. Although these tests will help the neurosurgeon considerably in making the diagnosis and planning his surgical approach, the type of tumor present may not be established until some tissue can be obtained at surgery for microscopic examination.

Meningiomas

One common lesion which can potentially be cured surgically is the *meningioma*. Meningiomas account for about 15% of all tumors arising inside the skull. This growth originates from the covering tissues of the brain (meninges) or from similar tissue lining the fluid spaces within the brain. Because it is separate from the brain tissue itself, the meningioma can often be completely removed. It is frequently a very slow-growing tumor and may attain a very large size before causing enough symptoms to be recognized. If the tumor has wrapped itself around delicate structures such as the carotid artery (main artery to the brain) or the optic nerve, complete removal may be impossible. However, even in these instances removal of most of the tumor tissue can be quite beneficial. The pressure from the large growth will have been removed and further growth of the tumor may be very slow—in some cases taking several years before symptoms are noticed again. If the entire tumor has been removed it is unlikely, though possible, that it will recur and grow again in the same area. About 10–15% of patients with meningiomas may later develop one in another area. Overall the prognosis for this type of tumor is relatively good, particularly if complete removal can be accomplished, although even partial removal can be important.

> **Brain tumors may be malignant, but those that are occasionally found are very often benign. The major concern with tumors of the brain is that, as they slowly grow larger, they exert pressure on the surrounding brain tissue—thus causing a wide variety of potentially serious neurological disturbances. Total surgical removal is often possible.**

Acoustic neuromas
Another relatively benign tumor is the *acoustic neuroma*. Arising from the nerve to the ear on either side, this growth may cause buzzing or ringing in the ear, progressive loss of hearing and difficulty with balance and walking. The nerve to the muscles of the face is located in this area and may be compressed by the tumor, causing sagging of the cheek and inability to close the eye on that side. Removal of an acoustic neuroma is an extremely delicate, tedious and difficult operation because of the many important structures in the area. However, if complete removal can be accomplished, the ultimate prognosis may be quite good.

Tumors of the pituitary gland
The PITUITARY gland lies in a bony case at the base of the brain just behind the nerve to the eyes (optic nerve). Tumors in this gland are frequently benign, but difficult to cure surgically because of their location. Occasionally they will be treated by radiation without surgery if there is no evidence of pressure on the optic nerves. If there has been loss of vision due to the tumor an attempt will generally be made to remove the bulk of the tumor surgically and subsequently to destroy the rest with irradiation. By operating with the aid of a microscope (which allows the surgeon to use direct lighting and magnified vision in a

small space), a new approach to these tumors has developed. This is called the "trans-sphenoidal" procedure. The tumor in the gland is approached without disturbing the brain by going through the nose and removing the bony case underneath the gland. This procedure is gaining more acceptance among modern neurosurgeons and may prove to allow better surgical treatment of this tumor.

Craniopharyngiomas
Another tumor found in this area, called a *craniopharyngioma*, may cause symptoms which are similar to a pituitary tumor. It can cause glandular disturbances by compression and destruction of the pituitary gland, and can cause visual difficulty by compression of the nearby optic nerve. Craniopharyngiomas are generally found in children and young adults and are quite uncommon in middle age or beyond. Despite the fact that these tumors are considered "benign," they are difficult to remove because of attachments to the gland and base of the brain and optic nerve. Unfortunately, they are not generally sensitive to radiation therapy (as are the pituitary tumors) and the ultimate outlook (prognosis) may be poor in many instances. (See CRANIOPHARYNGIOMA.)

Tumors involving the brain tissue
The most difficult tumors to treat surgically are those which arise from the brain tissue itself. Called *gliomas* or *astrocytomas*, these growths are graded from I to IV by the pathologist in order of increasing growth rate and malignancy. Except for one example which will be mentioned, even the grades I and II gliomas cannot be cured surgically. However, their slow growth patterns may make them compatible with many years of relatively normal life. The grade III and IV tumors (sometimes called *glioblastoma multiforme*) are quite "aggressive" and are frequently associated with a life span of less than one to two years. Because one cannot always diagnose these tumors without actually looking at the tissue under the microscope, surgery may be necessary even though ultimately a cure cannot be obtained. Radiation treatment will sometimes slow down the growth of the tumor, but is not curative. Gliomas represent almost half of all brain tumors and a great deal of research is being done to try to find a cure for this devastating problem.

Tumors of the cerebellum
Occasionally, in children, a tumor will be found called a "grade I cystic cerebellar astrocytoma." Located in the cerebellum (the balance and coordination center of the brain), these tumors have a big fluid-filled cyst associated with a small nodule of tumor. Sometimes this cyst can be drained and the tumor nodule completely removed. This type of removal may be compatible with a very long life span and even possibly a cure. However, most of the

astrocytoma tumors found in this part of the brain are of the type discussed in the preceding paragraph and not this more benign form.

Tumors of the spinal cord

Spinal tumors are less common than those affecting the brain. Initial symptoms include pain either in the spinal area or affecting the nerves to the arm or legs, disturbance or loss of sensation to the extremities, progressive difficulty with strength and coordination, and loss of bladder control. These symptoms are caused by pressure on the spinal cord and the nerves arising from it. The most common tumor in this situation is cancer which has spread by means of the bloodstream from another part of the body (metastasis) and invaded the bones of the spine. The prognosis in tumors of this kind, as might be expected, is relatively poor. However, surgery to take the pressure off the spinal cord and nerves may sometimes save the use of the arms and legs and thus make the time remaining to the patient much more pleasant.

GLIOMAS arise in the spinal cord as they do in the brain. In this location they do not pose the great threat to life as those previously discussed, but most of them still cannot be removed or cured surgically. Radiation treatments may slow down the growth considerably, but ultimate loss of spinal cord function and the onset of paralysis is all too often the end result. Luckily, many tumors in the spine are benign and can be removed before destruction of the spinal cord occurs. About half of these are MENINGIOMAS similar to those found in the brain. The others are called NEUROFIBROMAS and are quite similar to the acoustic neuroma described previously, but these arise from the spinal nerves rather than the auditory nerve. Even when there has been a great deal of damage to the spinal cord by pressure, removal of these tumors may result in dramatic improvement of neurological function in the months and years following surgery.

Pain

One of the most common symptoms for which neurosurgical consultation is obtained is PAIN. Because the nervous system carries the messages of pain to the brain, disease or injury of the nerves can (in itself) result in discomfort. One of the most severe types of nerve pain is called *trigeminal neuralgia* (or *tic douloureux*). The underlying cause for this condition is unknown (see TIC). The patient experiences severe lightning-like jabs of pain in one or more parts of the face. The jabs of pain last only a second or two but may come so frequently that they seem to be causing minutes or even hours of relatively continuous pain. The patient is frequently unable to eat because the act of chewing or touching certain parts of the face or cheek may trigger the pain. Some medications exist which will often control the pain of trigeminal neuralgia, but many times side effects will require the administration of the painkiller to be discontinued. If the medicine fails, an operation may be necessary to cut the nerve carrying pain from the face to provide relief. A procedure called "radiofrequency rhizotomy" can also be done in some cases. This involves placing a needle into the nerve through an opening in the base of the skull. A special device then causes radio waves to heat the tip of the needle, thus destroying the nerve without a major operation. This relatively new procedure has significantly altered the treatment of trigeminal neuralgia.

Neck and back pain

Pinching of a spinal nerve in the neck or the lower part of the back is a very common cause of pain in these areas. The pain frequently radiates into an arm or leg. The nerve is usually pinched by a piece of intervertebral disk material which is bulging or has herniated out of its normal place between the bones of the spine. This bulging piece of disk (SLIPPED DISK) presses the nerve against the bone of the spine. When other forms of treatment (such as rest, a brace for support of the neck or back, and traction) have failed, a myelogram may be done to outline the problem. Laminectomy with subsequent removal of the bulging disk material may be required to provide lasting pain relief. If a great part of the pain is thought to be associated with arthritic changes in the spine, or related to instability of the spine, a *fusion* may be planned in addition. This simply means that some bone will be taken from another part of the body (generally the hip bone) and placed in the neck or back in such a way that the bones will be expected to grow together. This limits movement at the place where the bone fusion is made and provides extra support in this area. Because it takes 2 to 5 months for the bone fusion to heal solidly, the recovery period from this type of surgery is longer than from a laminectomy alone. In addition, the patient may be required to wear a brace or support for some time after the surgery. These operations, no matter how well performed, are unfortunately not always successful in relieving the patient's pain.

Back pain is still an area of neurosurgery in which we do not have a complete knowledge of all the underlying problems. Chronic back pain which does not respond to any type of operation, or any number of operations, is one of the most frustrating areas of neurosurgery for both the patient and the physician.

Pain in the arm and hand

Nerves may be trapped in areas other than the spine. The *ulnar nerve* runs under the elbow and is the reason for the strange shock-like feeling in your hand when you hit your "funny bone." If the tissues that surround the nerve and hold it near the bones of the elbow become very thickened, the nerve can be irritated and cause pain in the arm and numbness and tingling in the small finger and adjacent finger. Removing the surrounding scar from the nerve and moving the nerve from behind the elbow to the front of the elbow often alleviates this discomfort. The *median nerve* (which supplies feeling to the remaining fingers of the hand) can be trapped at the wrist where it travels under a thick ligament called the "carpal ligament." Thickening of this ligament can cause numbness and tingling of these fingers as well as pain in the hand, wrist and forearm. This is called the CARPAL TUNNEL SYNDROME. Cutting the ligament and relieving the pressure on the nerve will often be successful in alleviating the pain.

Other sources of pain

Sometimes the cause of the pain for which a patient is referred does not originate within the central nervous system (the brain and spinal cord). The patient may be sent to a neurosurgeon for an operation to cut fibers carrying pain messages to the brain in a variety of diseases. For instance, a person with cancer in the bones of one leg may have severe and disabling pain, and cannot cope. Even the strongest medication may not relieve this discomfort. Interrupting the pathway carrying the pain from the leg through the spinal cord to the brain may be helpful. Various operations have been devised to destroy parts of a nerve, parts of the spinal cord or specific areas of the brain related to pain transmission. Cutting of the nerve roots as they enter the spine is called *rhizotomy* and destruction of the pain pathways in the spine is called *cordotomy*. The chief drawback of these procedures is that they may result in destruction of adjacent nerves or associated tissues, causing impairment of other bodily functions; for example, weakness of the extremities and difficulty with urine control may result. Additionally, the relief given by these procedures does not always last beyond 6 to 12 months. This is because the pain pathways in the nervous system are extremely complex and difficult to destroy selectively. Much research is currently being conducted at special centers using very fine needles (placed under x-ray control) to destroy selectively these pathways more efficiently.

Vascular diseases

Diseases of the blood vessels to the brain are extremely common. Hardening of the arteries (arteriosclerosis) in the neck is a very common cause of stroke, with its resultant severe disability. Some patients will have a warning of impending stroke in the form of a "transient ischemic attack" (TIA). This occurs when a small bit of material on

The spinal cord (right) runs inside the spinal column from the base of the skull down to a level approximately opposite the navel. Thus it is only about 18 inches long, and during this short course 31 pairs of spinal nerves sprout from its sides. They supply the skin and muscles of the trunk and limbs.

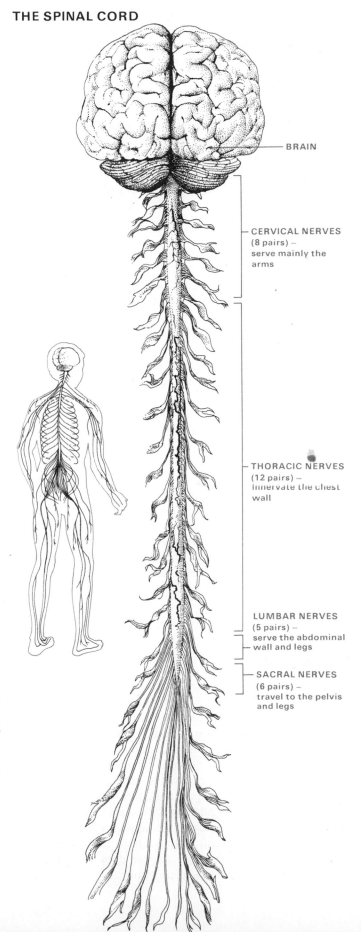

THE SPINAL CORD

BRAIN

CERVICAL NERVES
(8 pairs) –
serve mainly the
arms

THORACIC NERVES
(12 pairs) –
innervate the chest
wall

LUMBAR NERVES
(5 pairs) –
serve the abdominal
wall and legs

SACRAL NERVES
(6 pairs) –
travel to the pelvis
and legs

the inner wall of the hardened artery breaks loose and temporarily blocks an artery in the brain. The patient will have the symptoms of a stroke (such as paralysis on one side, difficulty with speech, numbness or weakness); but these are usually temporary, often lasting less than 24 hours. When the physician can make a diagnosis of such vascular disease before a serious stroke has occurred, an operation may be performed to clean out the obstructing material from the arteries. This is called an ENDARTERECTOMY. New procedures using healthy vessels to bypass severely diseased ones which cannot be cleaned out are just recently being proven successful and will most likely be more common in the future.

Intracranial bleeding

Bleeding may occur in or around the brain from a variety of reasons—such as high blood pressure, hardening of the arteries, or rupture of a "berry" ANEURYSM. In the first two instances, surgery may be performed to remove a blood clot which is putting pressure on the brain; but there is no surgical treatment for the underlying disease process. In the case of a berry aneurysm the situation is quite different. A berry aneurysm is a weak spot on the wall of a blood vessel which pouches out much like an inner tube pouches through a worn spot on a tire. If the patient recovers from the initial episode of bleeding, he is at risk of subsequent hemorrhage from this weak spot. For this reason, surgery is frequently recommended to place a metal clip on this area—thus preventing the possibility of hemorrhage.

Bleeding from an aneurysm in the brain generally starts as a very sudden, severe headache which may be associated with stiff neck and other neurological signs. The diagnosis is usually confirmed by a spinal tap (lumbar puncture) which shows blood in the spinal fluid and subsequently by angiography which shows the weak spot on the blood vessel. Surgery for this problem has been vastly improved in recent years by the use of the operating microscope and improved anesthetic techniques allowing better control of blood pressure during surgery.

Spina bifida

SPINA BIFIDA occurs when the spinal cord coverings and the bone and skin over the spinal cord have not formed properly in the development of a newborn infant. The child is born with an opening over the spine and there is generally a fluid-filled sac protruding from this area. Parts of the spinal cord and nerves are frequently present in this sac and are not capable of functioning. Depending on the location and severity of the opening, the child will suffer mild to severe impairment of function in the legs and of urinary and bowel control. Closure of the defect and coverage with skin is necessary as soon as possible to prevent infection and loss of life. This surgery, however, does not restore any of the impaired neurological function.

Hydrocephalus

Hydrocephalus ("water on the brain") occurs when the normal pathways for cerebrospinal fluid from inside the brain are blocked. This frequently occurs in patients who are born with a myelomeningocele but may occur in infants who have no other neurological abnormality. It is usually noticed that the infant's head is larger than it should be and is growing at an abnormal rate. The most serious danger of HYDROCEPHALUS is pressure on the brain by accumulation of cerebrospinal fluid, resulting in mental retardation. The placement of a small plastic tube into the fluid space of the brain and running this tube under the skin into the abdomen "shunts" the spinal fluid from the blocked area into the abdominal cavity. This shunting procedure is the only adequate treatment for hydrocephalus known today. There are many potential complications to this operation, but the most common problem is subsequent blockage of the shunt tube. This may occur because of tissue in the spinal fluid which blocks the tubing, or because of scarring in the abdomen around the tip of the tube which blocks it. These obstructions necessitate the changing of the tube and another operation. Sometimes a shunt will function quite well for many years without difficulty, but in other cases it will require changing several times in one year. Despite these problems, many children who would otherwise have had deformed heads and been severely retarded are now living relatively normal lives with good intelligence.

The bones of a baby's skull are somewhat loose and allow for growth in all directions. Occasionally, there will be premature fusion of one of these growth areas causing the remainder of the head to grow in an abnormal direction. This is called "premature closure of the sutures," or *craniosynostosis*. When this occurs the problem is predominantly a cosmetic one. If it is recognized early enough, the strip of fused bone can be removed surgically, thus allowing for expansion of the head in the normal direction once again.

Head and spinal injuries

The treatment of injuries to the head and spine is within the province of the neurosurgeon. Surgical intervention will sometimes be necessary to relieve pressure on the brain or spinal cord from a blood clot or depressed fragments of bone. Often, however, the injury to the nervous tissues will occur at the moment of impact and a certain amount of irreversible damage will be incurred. By supporting and caring for the metabolic needs of the nervous system, the goal is to minimize the amount of irreversible injury and maximize the potential for recovery. Early treatment of such secondary effects as swelling of the brain tissue (much as an ankle will swell when severely twisted) may be of major importance to the patient. Because the nervous system is encased in bone, the neurosurgeon cannot visualize the amount of damage done or see the secondary processes occurring. There have been some recent major advances in monitoring devices attempting to provide such information to the neurosurgeon. This may allow earlier treatment of developing complications in severe head and spinal cord trauma. Hopefully, the prognosis in some of these disastrous injuries will be better in the future.

Neurosurgical advances and the future

Today's neurosurgeon has at his disposal many techniques and much specialized equipment unavailable to previous generations. Some of these have been mentioned in this section. Others are either in or just coming out of the research phase. These advances, coupled with the knowledge, surgical skill and judgment gained in years of training and experience are the offerings of the modern neurosurgeon to his patient. Hopefully, some understanding of these processes will foster a stronger and more positive relationship between patient and physician in reaching their common goal.

As the result of the pioneering work of the late Dr. Wilder Penfield, of Montreal, much is now known about the localization of function of the cerebral cortex. This, in turn, has encouraged the development of many new neurosurgical techniques.

Dentistry

Dr. Joseph A. DeJulia

Modern American dental care is with little doubt the finest in the world. This reputation goes hand in hand with the efforts by dentists to educate their patients in the techniques of good oral hygiene—thus minimizing the risk of tooth decay and gum diseases. The following article discusses the various aspects of dentistry and how you can help save your own teeth with just a little additional effort each day.

Among all diseases affecting mankind throughout history, dental diseases are by far the most prevalent. It is estimated that only about 1 person out of 10,000 escapes the destruction of this widespread disease. Because of the historical "track record," a large segment of the human race tends to believe that as we age the loss of teeth is inevitable. This common belief is simply not true. Barring any unavoidable traumatic incidents, one does not have to lose any or all of one's permanent teeth.

Cavities and gum problems, technically known as *caries* and *periodontal disease*, make up the bulk of dental diseases responsible for the loss of teeth. In attempting to explain the reason for this widespread acceptance of losing one's teeth, you might compare the encompassing nature of dental disease to the prevalence of the common cold. We accept the fact that we "catch a cold" and most of us are not too worried about it. However, the similarity stops there. With proper rest and diet, and with the help of our immune system (the body's defense mechanism against foreign substances such as bacteria and viruses), the illness will most likely be uneventful and will cure itself. This, however, is not so for CARIES and periodontal disease—at least not at present. (See also PERIODONTICS.)

Caries and periodontal disease will not cure themselves, even though the immune system is present and normal in most people. Small cavities can only get bigger and are never arrested or eliminated with neglect. Unless you give proper attention to your mouth, the chances are that the service you will eventually require will be more expensive and time consuming. A small cavity will eventually progress into the nerve center (dental pulp) of the tooth; this causes extreme discomfort and will generally lead to swelling and infections (dental abscess) which could lead to the loss of the tooth. Other physical illness may cause pain in their early stage; pain in dental disease is most likely, in the later stage. Therefore, don't wait until pain compels you to visit the dentist; seek dental service regularly—at least every six months—to avoid complex dental problems.

The dental examination and patients at risk

The famous Canadian physician and medical historian Sir William Osler (1849–1919), who wrote *Principles and Practices of Medicine*, a most prestigious medical textbook, stated: "The oral cavity is the mirror which reflects the health of the entire body." When a dentist examines your mouth he will be looking for many things besides "holes" in your teeth. He will note the color and tone of the surrounding tissue, which could be indicative of more serious and possibly even life-threatening diseases.

After looking into many, many mouths, he begins to form a composite picture in his mind's eye of what a healthy mouth should represent. He will also compile a past and present medical history, which is necessary for his diagnosis and planned treatment. The treatment must be compatible with any ailments, allergies, sensitivities or abnormalities that exist or have existed. This precaution is essential to avoid any untoward reaction that might otherwise develop during and after dental treatment. For example, certain patients with disease of the cardiovascular system require special consideration. It may be advisable for your dentist to consult with your physician prior to any dental procedure; excessive apprehension, worry or long fatiguing dental procedures must certainly be minimized in such cases. Patients with certain valvular heart involvements, artificial heart valves or a history of rheumatic fever are predisposed to further damage of the heart valves and may require properly prescribed antibiotic therapy before certain dental procedures are undertaken. The prophylactic benefit of the antibiotic may prevent bacteria that are inadvertently forced into the bloodstream from becoming attached to the irregularities of the heart valves (natural or artificial) and ultimately prevent a condition known as *subacute bacterial endocarditis (SBE)*. (See ENDOCARDITIS.)

An uncontrolled diabetic patient presents with a risk of not being able to undergo a stressful situation, and normal healing is impaired after surgical procedures. The dentist needs to know whether a patient may be sensitive to certain local anesthetics in order to prevent or minimize the possibility of an allergic response.

The dentist must determine the obstetrical status of the adult female patient before the possible use of x-rays or tetracyclines. The injection of certain tetracyclines during

PERMANENT AND PRIMARY DENTITION

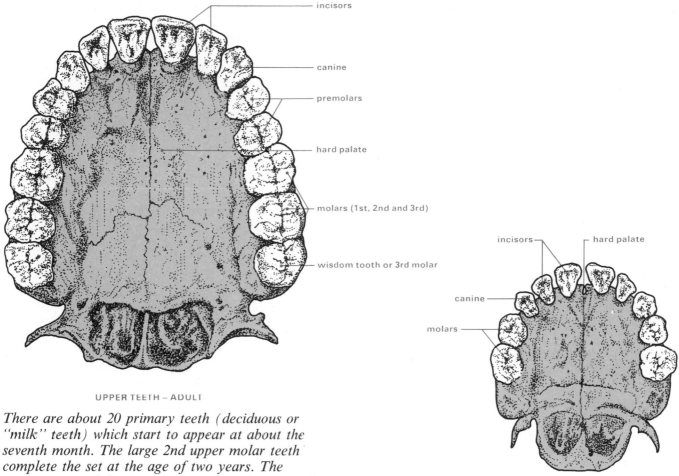

UPPER TEETH – ADULT

There are about 20 primary teeth (deciduous or "milk" teeth) which start to appear at about the seventh month. The large 2nd upper molar teeth complete the set at the age of two years. The permanent teeth begin to replace the primary teeth at the age of six but are not complete until the 3rd molars ("wisdom teeth") erupt in early adulthood.

UPPER TEETH – YOUNG CHILD

the last three months of pregnancy, or during infancy or early childhood, may produce a permanent discoloration of the teeth. The exposure to x-rays must be cautiously monitored and precisely controlled during the first three months of pregnancy, at which time the fetus is particularly vulnerable. Many authorities advise that all drugs be avoided, except in the treatment of any life-threatening situation, during this period.

Occasionally, the dentist may be the first to detect any malfunctioning of vital organs such as the liver. Upon examining the oral cavity, the color of the soft tissues surrounding the teeth may reveal an initial jaundice hue that upon further investigation by your family physician may disclose a condition such as HEPATITIS.

Oral cancer detection

The American Cancer Society has continually sponsored programs on cancer throughout the nation. Pamphlets and other handouts are widely distributed by the various health professions, thus making it one of the most widely discussed diseases. Because the dentist sees more apparently well patients than any other health professional, he has a particular responsibility in the detection of oral cancer.

It has been estimated that approximately 30% of the incidence of this disease is located in the region of the head and neck. Early diagnosis and treatment can in many cases lead to a cure for this dreaded disease. A complete oral examination should include both visual inspection and digital palpation of the facial and neck areas as well as of various structures within the mouth. Since the earlier stages of cancer can be painless, one might have the tendency to overlook it, or suspect it as being a "cold sore" that will go away. Ulceration of the lip, tongue, inside of cheeks and adjacent soft tissues should be brought to the attention of a trained health professional. Numbness, tingling and loss of feeling in any area of the mouth, jaws, lips and face should be thoroughly investigated by a physician immediately.

Introduction to dental care

The best time to be introduced to the world of dental care is at an early and formative age. On the average, a child is ready to accept the environment of a dental office ("dental chair acceptance") at the age of four years. However, this does not mean that a child cannot be taken with a parent or guardian to the dental office earlier than four years as a guest or observer. Children two to three years old should accompany the parent or guardian so as to familiarize themselves with the general surroundings. This will help to instill the conception that going to the dental office is as important to healthy living as going to the medical office.

Up to this point in the child's life, all or most of his or her dental education would have been derived by observation of the habits and practices of the parents regarding dental care. If the parents have a negative outlook toward dental care it is quite conceivable that the very young will detect this attitude and come to accept it. Therefore, it is important when in earshot of small children to take extreme care when discussing past and present dental experience, so as not to influence them wrongly. An extreme example would be to say, within earshot, that "the dentist nearly killed me drilling my tooth." A mature mind can readily accept the dramatic aura of this comment, but a young impressionable mind associates this statement with a true life or death consequence.

Also, a definite "must" in the dental education of the young is to refrain from using the health professional as a reward or punishment exercise. A patient once said that when a child his grandmother had threatened: "If you're not good, I'll take you to the dentist and have all your teeth pulled out." Understandably, such threats can have very serious consequences; it was said that at the age of 35 this individual could not make himself go to a dental office—he broke out in a "cold sweat" just talking over the telephone asking for proper dental advice.

Nutrition

Dietary standards and habits are important adjuncts to proper dental development: they have a direct bearing on the formation of healthy bodies and healthy teeth. It is very important to consider recommended dietary allowances for all women of childbearing ages, since often two or three months go by before there is more than an inkling of pregnancy. Pregnant and lactating women should have dietary counseling by their physicians as to proper intake of essential vitamins and nutrients. This can insure optimal development of the oral tissue of the fetus during this critical period.

(See also the major articles on **Nutrition** and **Pregnancy and Childbirth.**)

Fluoride and fluoridation

By the time children are brought to the dental office the parents will ideally have had counseling by the pediatrician on the proper use of the nursing bottle, appropriate supplementation of vitamins and fluorides, and proper diet. Fluorides and vitamins should be encouraged as a diet supplement in the developing child. The Food and Nutrition Board, a few years back, accepted fluoride as an essential nutrient. Accordingly, almost all dental experts now agree that the most effective method to insure the building of sound, healthy teeth during their development is by administering fluoride during tooth mineralization—from birth to eight or nine years of age. Some advocate fluoride supplements into the early teens.

Most of the key researchers and clinicians in the field of fluorides have been extolling the benefits of different fluoride programs. Presently, FLUORIDATION—the addition of fluoride to a community water supply—has received the approval of most major health organizations together with the American Dental Association. Convincing documentation, accumulated over a period of 30 years, clearly demonstrates that the benefits of fluoride are not merely hypothetical. Dental benefits from fluoridated water are not limited to children alone; protection against caries persists throughout the adult years.

Topical fluorides applied directly on the teeth by dental personnel can be beneficial to those living in nonfluoridated communities and to some patients who continue to show a high susceptibility to dental decay in spite of optimal fluorides in the water. In most dental offices, topical fluoride is applied in a paste, gel or solution. Studies conducted by the military showed *stannous fluoride* is very effective when used as a three-point program that includes:

(1) 9% stannous fluoride prophylactic paste with zuconium silicate or a compatible cleansing paste;
(2) 10% stannous fluoride solution applied to air-dried teeth for 15 to 30 seconds;
(3) the home use (toothbrushing) of a dentifrice containing 0.4% stannous fluoride.

It has also been suggested that patients undergoing orthodontic treatments, where all or most teeth are covered with bands (braces), should use a fluoride gel applied with a toothbrush after thorough brushing; best results are realized when this is done at bedtime. Fluoride gels are beneficial to patients undergoing radiation therapy of the mouth, nose and throat areas to prevent the development of *root caries* (decay of the roots of the teeth). Acidulated phosphate fluorides (APF) solutions and gels when used simultaneously by patients in nonfluoridated communities have reduced their rate of decay by 30–50%.

Recommended concentrations of fluoridation range from 0.7 ppm (parts per million) to 1.2 ppm. Presently, in the United States, approximately 100 million people

SECTIONS OF TEETH

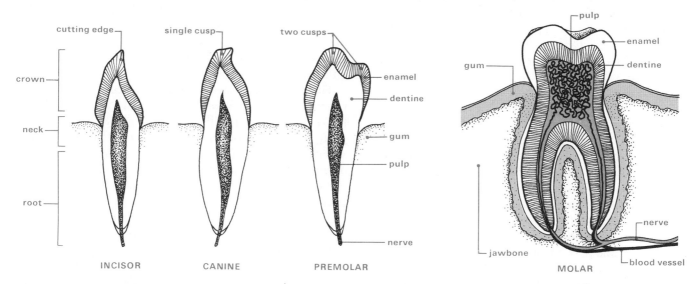

Incisor teeth have sharp cutting edges which allow us to bite off chunks of food. Human canine, or "eye," teeth are small compared to those of other meat-eating animals, but are still the longest teeth in the mouth. The premolar teeth each have two cusps and are used in chewing. The molar teeth have a surface that permits the grinding of food particles.

consume water containing optimal levels of fluoride and benefit from a reduction in tooth decay amounting to 50–65%. Protection from tooth decay is derived both from systemic and topical exposure to fluorides. In one study where preschool children received fluoride supplements, their tooth decay rate was lowered 50–75%. When a fluoride supplement program is started at six or seven years of age, the decay rate is reduced 20–45%.

Your dentist is equipped to provide you with the proper dosage and appropriate type of fluoride supplement, which is only available to patients by prescription. Proper dosage is related to the patient's exposure to fluoridated water and his or her age. Fluoride supplements are available as a liquid, tablets, and in combination with vitamin preparations. Parents should understand the frequency and method of administration, which should appear both on the prescription and the label.

How tooth decay (caries) develops

An abundance of evidence strongly suggests that the incidence of caries is in direct relation to the availability and individual consumption of sugar. Studies conducted on Eskimos some time ago revealed that the closer the Eskimo resided to a candy store, the higher the number of cavities.

While there is more than one reason for the occurrence of tooth decay, it is firmly believed that one of the most common causes arises from bacteria normally present in the mouth. By fermenting dietary sugars they produce acids that dissolve the hard protective enamel covering of the teeth. The colonies of bacteria, chiefly *Streptococcus*, accumulate in and around the teeth as sticky masses (dental plaque) within 20 to 30 minutes of food ingestion. Acids formed by these bacteria dissolve microscopic openings in the surface of a tooth which continue to enlarge with the production of more and more acids.

If left unattended, the microscopic holes will progress to larger and deeper holes that eventually penetrate the softer dentin layer which lies beneath the hard outer enamel layer. Since dentin is by nature a softer material than enamel, the decay will travel at a faster rate and ultimately strike the pulp tissues (commonly referred to as the "dental nerve") and sound the alarm of infection by pain, swelling and occasionally a dental abscess. Consequently, this is one of the reasons for regular dental checkups and periodic x-ray examinations. Small cavities can then be filled to stop further dental destruction.

The speed of tooth destruction varies from individual to individual, from adults to children and from healthy people to sickly people. Consequently, your dentist should determine the frequency for dental checkups for each patient. The range can be three, four, six, nine or twelve months in between visits depending on the above criteria.

In addition to cavities, bacterial plaque can be demonstrated to initiate gingival (gum) irritations by producing chemicals and toxins that cause *gingivitis*, an inflammation of the gums. When plaque accumulates for a long period it may harden and become *calculus* (tartar). Calculus is a hard irregular mass attached to the smooth surface of the teeth, near the junction of teeth and gums; it can eventually become a constant source of irritation. This irritation can lead to further irritation and inflammation can progress to the more advanced condition known as *periodontitis*. In such cases not only are soft tissues affected but the harder underlying structure of bone also becomes involved. Crevices (periodontal pockets) are formed which gradually extend toward the root tip and eventually weaken and loosen the entire supporting structures of the tooth. This represents another good reason for regular dental checkups.

Cleaning the teeth

In conjunction with regular dental visits, thorough and efficient cleaning of your teeth is the most important thing that you, as a patient, can do to prevent dental problems and keep your teeth and gums healthy for a lifetime. Although this sounds rather simple, effectively cleaning one's teeth is probably one of the most dexterous assignments one may encounter and should not be taken lightly.

We have all probably heard the old saying "a clean tooth doesn't decay" and it sounds as if it might have some logic. The crux of the matter, however, is that it is very difficult and time consuming to get teeth properly cleaned— especially when you have anything up to 16 teeth side by side in both upper and lower jaws. It has been said that you only have to brush your teeth effectively once a day, preferably at bedtime. The idea has some value: but if you rely on this approach you must develop expertise in the art of brushing and flossing all the five major surfaces of 28 to

32 teeth—or 5 x 32 surfaces, equal to 160 major surfaces. If there were enough spaces between teeth they would be much easier to clean; but we are all aware that teeth, with the exception of the most distal (the last teeth in the row), are touching a neighboring tooth very tightly, and it is very difficult if not impossible to brush between them.

The most effective way to clean between teeth is by the rubbing action of *dental floss*. About 18 inches of dental floss is wrapped around the middle finger of each hand, and gently eased through the space between the teeth with a sawing motion. The floss is moved toward the gums with an up and down and back and forth sideways movement, with pressure placed on the tooth surface being flossed. Floss the back surface of one tooth and then the front surface of the adjacent tooth for about six to twelve strokes. Once this is done, remove the floss by pulling it in an outward direction, not back up through the teeth contacting area.

It is these hard-to-reach areas that need to be emphasized when cleaning your teeth, since these are the areas which are most prone to cavities and gum problems as the result of the accumulation of dental plaque. A thorough demonstration should be requested from your dental personnel. Unwaxed dental floss is recommended because of its enhanced ability to pick up and remove plaque. Healthy gums do not generally bleed unless the floss is suddenly snapped through the contacting teeth. Some bleeding may occur at first because of these areas being missed, but bleeding should disappear after a week of

DENTAL CARIES

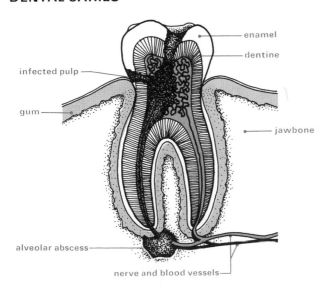

The molar tooth pictured here is in an advanced state of decay. Poor dental hygiene has allowed bacteria to penetrate the tooth enamel; further neglect has permitted extensive involvement of the tooth pulp and a alveolar abscess has formed at the root. Such a tooth, having caused severe pain, would now have to be extracted.

DENTAL HYGIENE

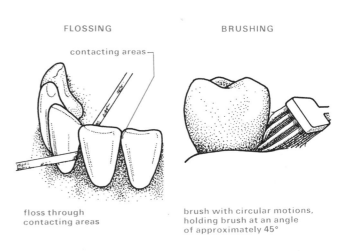

Without adequate dental hygiene, bacteria collect in the crevices and fissures of teeth, setting up caries or tooth decay. Regular brushing helps prevent tooth and gum disease, while twice weekly use of dental floss helps clear bacteria and debris from between the teeth, particularly the "contacting areas." Your dentist will offer special advice.

correct flossing. If bleeding persists, you should ask your dentist about these problem areas.

Toothbrushes come in many sizes, shapes and bristle stiffnesses, and should be recommended by your dentist for your specific needs. In general, toothbrushing is accomplished with the toothbrush held downward at an acute angle (45°) where your teeth and gums meet. A vibrating or circular motion, brushing between the teeth and under the gum crevice, produces a slight tingling sensation. Red *disclosing solution* (or tablets) can be obtained from your dentist to assist in determining how effectively you are able to clean your teeth; it contains a harmless red food coloring that will stain the missed areas of plaque.

The growth and development of teeth

At birth there are usually no teeth visible in the baby's tiny mouth. Hidden away under the gums are tiny *tooth buds* situated in different stages of development and ready to erupt into the oral cavity at their proper time. At about three months of age the gums begin to harden and appear blanched along their crest; around six months (± 2 months) the *central incisors* appear in the front of the mouth. Next come the *lateral incisors*. At one year (± 3 months) the first molars appear. Usually, by the time the child reaches its second birthday, all the primary teeth have erupted.

There are 20 *deciduous teeth;* ten in the upper and ten in the lower jaw. In general, a lower tooth precedes its mate in the upper arch—e.g., lower central incisors erupt first, followed by the upper central incisors. If the order is reversed, upper teeth erupting before lower teeth, and the time elapsed is relatively the same, then there are usually little or no consequences. If there is a large discrepancy in the time of eruption it may be an indication of congenitally missing teeth. There are usually more congenitally missing teeth in the permanent dentitious teeth than in the primary teeth. In the case of a child having one or more permanent teeth absent, your dentist may request that an *orthodontist* be consulted.

Many parents are quite concerned about spaces between the primary teeth. Spaces between primary teeth generally provide a good indication that there will be more room for the larger, permanent teeth and should be beneficial, leading to less crowding of the permanent teeth. However, this does not mean to imply that *not* having spaces will lead to crowding. There are many other factors that come into play in deciding the outcome of the arch forms of the permanent dentition.

Through a biological process known as *exfoliation*, the roots of the deciduous teeth ("baby teeth") are completely resorbed (melted away); this makes the tooth loose and able to fall out. In many cases the child will sense the looseness of the tooth and "tug and rock" it until the tooth is lifted away. It is very important that temporary teeth remain until this time of looseness, since the normal exfoliation pattern will help guide the eruption of the permanent teeth.

Sometimes your dentist will advise the extraction of a deciduous tooth when there appears to be sinking or submerging of the primary tooth into the gums. A little understood condition known as *ankylosis* may be present: the tooth and bone around it seem to be firmly attached to each other, which will unfortunately influence the eruption of the underlying permanent tooth. Extraction may also be recommended when a permanent tooth erupts alongside a deciduous tooth and both teeth are vying for the same space; if the baby tooth is not loose it is usually necessary to extract it to provide space for the permanent tooth.

Malocclusion

It is estimated that between 30% and 50% of all children seen in the dental office have some sort of *malocclusion*. Malocclusion is basically an abnormal arrangement and improper positioning of the upper and lower teeth when the jaws are closed, ranging from minor to major disharmonies. This is commonly referred to as a person's *bite*— for example, among the descriptive terms are *overbite*, *underbite*, *crossbite*, *open bite*, etc.

It is very important to preserve the arch form and space that can result from early loss of primary teeth as the result of trauma or severe tooth decay. There is a tendency toward space closure with the premature loss of primary teeth, especially with loss of the first and second primary molars. The permanent first molars (six-year molars) will not have the primary molars to guide them in their proper place. The dentist will want to control this space closure by suggesting a *space maintainer*. As the name implies, this device maintains the space until the permanent tooth erupts into it.

"Tongue thrusting"

It has been estimated that 50–70% of the population have an abnormal swallowing habit known as *tongue thrusting*. The tongue placed between the teeth when swallowing can cause an open bite that will not allow the teeth to fit together properly with their opposing mates. There are various techniques and exercises that the dentist or the *myofunctional therapist* (one who treats problems of incorrect swallowing) can suggest to help retrain the individual to proper placement of the tongue during the act of swallowing. It has been estimated that an individual may very likely swallow 1,500 times a day. By this count, one can see the magnitude of force that can be delivered by the tongue if it is incorrectly placed against the teeth instead of the hard palate. (During normal swallowing the front part of the tongue braces up against the hard palate, the teeth come together and the middle and back part of the tongue forces the bolus of food or liquid down into the back of the throat.) Problems of the temporomandibular joint (the joint between the upper and lower jaws) such as pain and clicking, can be caused as the result of this improper placement of the tongue during swallowing.

Discouraging bad habits

Habits such as thumb sucking and lip biting should be firmly discouraged so that hopefully by age four or five they will be discontinued. Abnormal mouth breathing habits should be be checked by the physician for any obstruction of the nose or throat that can be corrected early in life.

The child progresses from the deciduous dentition into the mixed dentition between the ages of 6 and 12 years. The mixed dentition results from a combination of the loss of the primary teeth and the erupting of the permanent teeth. During this phase of development, one must caution against choking on stringy foods (such as celery, etc.), because of the reduced opposing grinding surfaces which have not, as yet, come into contact. Special protective attention should be given to the erupting permanent teeth if the child's activities include contact sports (boxing, football, hockey, etc.); properly fitted mouth guards should be worn to prevent any unnecessary trauma to the teeth. During the mixed dentition years, the child should be examined every six months for any abnormal alignment and crowding of teeth.

Your dentist may request a consultation with a dentist specializing in the treatment of major malocclusion (orthodontist). Many times early interceptive techniques can be instituted that may prevent many types of malocclusion and improper jaw relationships. If the need arises that a child will undergo orthodontic treatment, particular attention must be given to the total cleansing of the teeth because of the ability of the bands (braces) and other appliances to trap food debris. Routine dental checkups and fluoride treatments must coincide with the orthodontic treatment phase to detect and treat cavities and gum problems.

Permanent dentition is generally complete by the age of 12 (± 6 months). If the proper habits of routine flossing, brushing, proper diet, timely dental checkups and early treatment are firmly implanted, the child is on his or her way to having a healthier mouth. The effort of instilling these habits is more than repaid by the end results.

Periodontal disease

Periodontal disease—that which affects the gums and other tissues surrounding and supporting the teeth—is the major reason for the loss of teeth after age 35 and its prevention is one of the dentist's primary concerns. In certain areas of the mouth and at one age or another, periodontal disease afflicts an estimated 95% of the adult population. Generally speaking, it can begin in the mid-20s; if no attempt is made to correct it, it will result in the loss of teeth in the middle or late 30s and 40s.

Periodontal disease is a slowly progressive and virtually painless type of affliction, especially in the early stage, and may therefore go unnoticed by the sufferer. Because of its insidious nature, pain does not occur until extensive damage has been done. Treatment of periodontal disease, especially after marked loss of bone has occurred, is at best difficult and not without treatment problems. Prevention, through early detection and correction, is therefore essential.

Prevention of periodontal disease involves the periodic removal of all local irritants to the tissues (plaque and calculus, or tartar) along with the correction of any traumatic occlusion. The surfaces of the teeth are scraped clean and polished to yield a highly glazed surface that is less irritable to the soft tissues and less attractive to mineral deposits and bacterial colonies. These treatments need repeating over a prescribed period, generally determined by your dentist. If the condition is permitted to go beyond the soft tissue irritation stage, then a more sophisticated type of treatment may be required.

Dentists are reasonably successful if the disease is detected and treated in the early soft tissue stages. Factors such as medical problems, lack of dental care, poor diet, etc., play a role in determining the fate of your teeth and must be carefully scrutinized and controlled before any success can be expected. In the more advanced periodontal case the main thrust of therapy is directed toward eliminating the periodontal lesion, commonly referred to

PERIODONTAL DISEASE

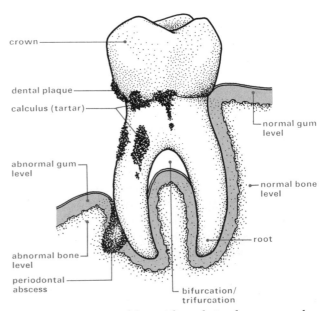

crown

dental plaque

calculus (tartar)

normal gum level

abnormal gum level

normal bone level

abnormal bone level

root

periodontal abscess

bifurcation/ trifurcation

The major cause of loss of teeth in those over the age of 35 is disease of the gums and other tissues which surround and support the teeth. Prevention of periodontal disease is possible with proper care and attention to oral hygiene.

as the "periodontal pocket." In order to restore the supporting tissues to a healthier environment, surgical removal of the inflamed tissue (gingivectomy) may be required in addition to repairing and building up bony defects (osteoplasty).

Bruxism

One of the most common forms of occlusal trauma in periodontal patients can also come about through some disorder of jaw movement, such as clenching, clamping and grinding of the teeth—known as *bruxism*. Bruxism is an unnatural grinding of the teeth, either while awake or asleep, which produces destructive lateral forces on the teeth. Recent electromyographic studies (tests to measure muscle activity) of the neuromuscular mechanism of the jaws have demonstrated that there is an intimate relationship between occlusal irregularities and emotional tension. This destruction, seen in the form of broken teeth and bone loss around the teeth, is much more severe during sleep; this is because during sleep our *proprioceptors* (protective feedback mechanisms) are not functioning fully, or possibly not at all.

Treatment consists of relieving or relaxing these emotional tensions through counseling or medication. In addition, your dentist can make a protective plastic guard; this appliance is inserted over the teeth and may be worn during sleep or during waking hours to prevent spontaneous grinding and clenching of the teeth.

Trench mouth

There are a few common acute periodontal diseases that some people will experience at one time or another. These afflictions usually come on suddenly and are moderately painful, as opposed to the chronic painless type of periodontal disease. As far back as the turn of the 19th century, an epidemic of gum infections was experienced by soldiers of the French Army and was appropriately named *trench mouth*. Today this condition is also referred to as *Vincent's angina* or *acute necrotizing ulcerative gingivitis*. The condition is characterized by excessive bleeding of the gums on the slightest pressure. It occurs primarily in young adults between the ages 18 and 30. Some of the factors implicated are poor oral hygiene, inadequate diet, alcohol, tobacco and emotional and physical stress. The disease is often observed in college students during examination times. Treatment consists of gentle DEBRIDEMENT of the affected tissues around the teeth and gums, the hourly use of an oxygenating mouth rinse, and the immediate institution of plaque control with a soft toothbrush. If required, an appropriate antibiotic may also be prescribed.

Other common problems

Another acute condition affecting the periodontal tissues is *herpetic gingivostomatitis*. As the name implies, the chief offender is the *herpes simplex virus*. Characteristically, this disease can become manifest anywhere in or around the mouth. The severity generally depends on whether or not it is the first encounter with the virus or a subsequent bout. Most adults have circulating antibodies against the herpes simplex virus and therefore do not experience much discomfort from one or more areas of involvement. The child who is exposed to this virus and does not have the neutralizing antibodies may become extremely ill. There is usually fever, malaise (a general feeling of being unwell), generalized pain throughout the entire mouth and lips and tender lymph nodes in the neck. Within a few days yellowish vesicles appear on the lips, tongue, inside the cheeks and on the roof of the mouth. As these rupture they form reddish, painful ulcers which will eventually become crusted and bleed easily. Treatment involves keeping the person comfortable with a soft, bland diet (since spicy foods are painful), bed rest (if fever and listlessness exist) and, if required, antibiotics to control secondary infections. The disease is typically self-limiting and subsides within 7–14 days.

Another quite common problem among those over the age of about 17 is inflammation and infection of the area around the third molars (wisdom teeth) during their partial eruption. This condition is known as *acute periocoronitis*. It starts with the collection and accumulation of food debris and plaque under the flap of tissue around the erupting third molar; this area is practically inaccessible in some mouths and a greater effort in brushing the wisdom teeth is needed. If left unattended too long, the condition may be further aggravated and will limit the opening of the jaws (TRISMUS). Treatment consists of draining the area, hourly rinses of warm saline solution (1 tablespoon of table salt in a glass of water), antibiotics if required, and adequate plaque control in this area. In some cases it may be necessary to remove the tooth to prevent recurrence.

Restorative dentistry

Along with regular annual and six-monthly dental checkups, people will visit the dental office for the restoring of tooth structures and replacement of missing teeth. Once a cavity has developed, the dentist will prepare the tooth by removing all the caries and proceed to restore (fill) the tooth to its natural shape and form. He can choose from a wide variety of approved materials. In general, the size and location of the cavity determines which material is used.

Cavity classification can range from simple to complex depending on its location and ultimate size. If a cavity involves only one surface of a normal five-surface tooth, and penetrates only a short distance into the tooth, then it is usually a simple one. If the decay process is extensive, and destruction involves three or more of the five surfaces, then one can assume the cavity to be complex. Accordingly, most dentists base their fee on the number of surfaces involved. Teeth in the back part of the mouth (bicuspids and molars) are the most likely candidates for using *amalgam restorations*, known as "silver fillings."

Amalgam restorations have been widely used for over 100 years because of their relatively low cost, ease of manipulation (completed in one visit) and durability. Amalgam is sufficiently strong to resist the forces of chewing and maintain its integrity as long as it is supported by sound tooth structure. Generally, amalgam is not used in the front teeth because of its unesthetic grayish appearance. Because of cosmetic considerations, front teeth are generally restored with tooth-colored materials. One of the materials most widely used to fill front teeth is a *composite resin*, which was developed in the early 1960s. Composite resin restorations are completed in one visit and have a "chameleon" effect that produces favorable color matching with the tooth. In many instances, pure gold fillings (gold foil) will also be used in front teeth if the cavity is toward the tongue side of the tooth. If the cavity is large and extensive (complex) and in the back teeth, then the material of choice would be a *cast gold restoration* (gold inlay). Gold has been used for dental restorations since the inception of the dental arts and makes all other dental materials relative newcomers.

If a tooth is badly broken down, as when a complete cusp is fractured, then the most effective restoration is probably a *gold crown* (cap). Crowns, essentially, are cast gold restorations that can be veneered with plastic or porcelain. A durable crown restoration for the front teeth can also be made solely from porcelain and this is referred to as a *porcelain jacket*. Missing teeth between existing teeth can be replaced by joining the crowns (with gold solder) and this restoration is known as a *fixed bridge*.

Prosthodontics

When a large number of teeth are missing, the replacement of these teeth can be supported by a denture base; such an appliance is known as a *removable partial denture*. As the name implies, the denture can be removed by the patient; it is supported and retained in the mouth by some of the remaining teeth and the underlying soft and bony tissues. When all of the natural teeth are missing in the upper or lower jaw, or both, then one must consider the wearing of a *complete denture*.

There is a misconception bandied about that when all of the teeth are extracted and replaced by complete dentures (the "third set" of teeth) all of their teeth problems will cease to exist. First, let's make it clear that properly fitted complete dentures are at best only about 25% as efficient as natural teeth. Many adjust nicely, but some people find it difficult to adapt and learn to use their complete dentures properly. Along with the preservation of natural oral structures, this is another reason why today's dentistry is geared to maintaining the integrity of all the teeth.

The mouth tissues of the *edentulous* mouth (having no

teeth) are constantly undergoing changes, which may result in loose or ill-fitting dentures. Such dentures can cause damage to the oral tissues; therefore, everyone who wears dentures must continue to see their dentist for regular annual checkups. Patients who wear complete dentures must understand the importance of oral hygiene; the supporting soft tissues need thorough cleansing (three or four times daily) by a soft mouth brush in addition to cleansing of the dentures.

Endodontics (root canal therapy)

With the concept of preservation of the teeth gaining greater acceptance, more and more teeth are being saved by the application of endodontics—or *root canal therapy*.

If a tooth is subjected to the ravages of the decay process long enough, or is severely damaged, its blood and nerve supply (within the pulp of the tooth) will eventually become nonvital ("dead" tooth). Most likely, this nonvitality of pulpal tissues (pulpal necrosis) will lead to an acute or chronic abscess. Once this condition occurs the treatment made of choice is endodontics.

Endodontics, essentially, involves the removal of all nonvital tissue and infectious debris from within the root of a tooth. The root canal is then made sterile and hermetically sealed (made airtight).

Root canal therapy is highly successful (in up to 90% of cases) and can obviate the need for extraction.

Dental specialists

The following list contains the major dental specialists, together with a brief description of their particular area of interest in the health care of the teeth, etc.

Endodontist—A dentist who limits his practice to the treatment of the dental pulp and periapical tissues, (i.e., root canal therapy).

Oral diagnostician—A dentist who limits his practice to the diagnosis of soft-tissue diseases of the oral cavity, including tumors.

Oral surgeon—A dentist who limits his practice to the surgical corrections of the mouth, which include extractions, repair of fractured jaws, removal of tumors, etc.

Orthodontist—A dentist who limits his practice to the correction of malocclusion (abnormal tooth position and alignment) and abnormal jaw relationships.

Pedodontist—A dentist who limits his practice to the treatment of children.

Periodontist—A dentist who limits his practice to the treatment of the supporting structures of the teeth (gums and bones).

Prosthodontist—A dentist who limits his practice to the restoration of teeth and contiguous oral structures through the use of artificial substitutes, complete and partial dentures, and bridges.

Surgery
Dr. Stephen Engel

Surgery first became a distinct scientific discipline over 2,000 years ago in ancient Greece. However, it was not until the introduction of general anesthesia in the 19th century that complicated surgical techniques could be developed. This article discusses the role of the modern general surgeon and mentions those subspecialties of surgery not dealt with elsewhere.

The mention of "surgery" or "surgeon" will normally elicit two types of reaction from the listener, depending on the circumstances of the conversation. In a social gathering, it is likely that the mind of a nonmedical person will conjure up images, based on past reading and television viewing, that endow the surgeon with an aura of mystery and magical powers that are not always realistic. In the setting of the physician's office when the recommendation of surgery for a person or a member of his family is made, the reaction is entirely different. The elements of fear and doubt often wipe out past images of a surgeon's infallibility, and the patient becomes realistic in his judgment of those who propose invasion of his own body or the body of a loved one. This, of course, is a sensible reaction. The image and reputation of the surgeon, as of physicians in general, have had their peaks and troughs in history.

Doctors in prerecorded times had to practice varying amounts of surgery to salvage victims of the injuries of war and trauma. Reputations of individual surgeons varied, according to their skills and (often) luck. Later, in the Middle Ages, physicians first began to disassociate themselves from surgeons. Unfortunately, it was often the least trained and skilled persons who ventured to perform surgery; thus, the general esteem of surgeons and surgery was not very high. In the later 18th and 19th centuries, virtuoso surgeons performed with such daring and such theatrical skill that the public image of surgeons was nearly at an all-time high. The great European surgical clinics, with their secrecy and almost total neglect of communication with patients and their families, were responsible for much of the aura and mystery that surrounded surgery.

Modern surgery

The real breakthrough in surgery came relatively recently with the advent of anesthesia, the understanding of infection, and the development of better surgical instruments. Following World War II, antibiotics, availability of solutions for transfusion, donor blood and blood products, and great strides in the understanding of disease have made the surgeon better equipped and more successful than ever before. The improved education of the general public and the demand for more communicative physicians have diminished the stature of surgeons. The removal of the veil of secrecy from medicine has also paradoxically diminished the aura in which physicians and surgeons are held; and rightly so. It is imperative to have an understanding and be informed about surgery (and surgeons in particular) in order to be able to confront intelligently the necessary decisions at that moment when surgery becomes a personal concern.

Surgeons today are better and more uniformly trained than ever before. The establishment of "Boards" in the various specialties has done much to insure the competence and uniformity of training. The Board of General Surgery was established in 1937. Initially, it was not mandatory to become certified by the Board, but today nearly every hospital requires its staff to have certification in order to perform surgery. This has become such an important issue recently that surgeons certified after 1974 are only awarded their certificates for ten years and then must be reexamined. The Boards also prescribe training standards. Normally this means a minimum of five years specialty training after completion of four years of medical school and three to four years of college training. Upon completion of the above, and after one to two years of practice, the certification exam can be applied for and taken.

Subspecialties of surgery

Today the expansion of medical knowledge is so great that numerous subspecialties have branched off from general surgery and established their own examinations, training programs and societies. What once constituted General Surgery is now divided into such branches as Orthopedic Surgery, Urology, Otolaryngology, Pediatric Surgery, Plastic Surgery, Neurosurgery, Gynecology and others. Subspecialization in the above fields is also common, so that thoracic surgery has been further compartmentalized into cardiac surgery; plastic and orthopedic surgery have given rise to surgery of the hand as a subunit, and there is a drive to form a board of abdominal surgery within what is now General Surgery. "Colorectal surgery" (involving the large bowel and rectum) is practiced as a subspecialty by many as well. The general surgeon as defined today

The above illustration shows a typical operation in progress. On the left, the anesthesiologist monitors the patient's breathing and heart rate and regulates the flow of anesthesia to maintain the appropriate depth of unconsciousness. The bank of lights above the operating table provides shadow-free illumination of the operative site as the surgeon makes his intitial incision. In the foreground, the surgical nurse stands ready to hand the surgeon the instruments he requires at each stage of the operation.

concerns himself with surgery of the *head and neck* area, such as parotid gland, thyroid gland and neck cancer; surgery of the *abdominal cavity*, including gallbladder, appendix, stomach, intestines, liver and spleen; and *vascular surgery*, such as repair or reconstruction of arteries and veins. In general, the subspecialties of surgery are well defined in most areas, and within the medical community

the primary care physician and internist will be aware of what surgeons are well qualified to do the procedures required by their patients.

Meeting the surgeon

When a need for surgery has been established, usually following a complete medical workup, the primary physician will probably suggest referral to a surgeon he knows and trusts to carry out the procedure required. If there is an emergency, or if there is only one hospital and few surgeons on its staff, the choice of local surgeons is obviously limited. However, surgery is always a serious matter and may be hard for the patient to accept. If it is elective surgery, when time is not an immediate factor, the patient should understand that he has every right not only to seek a second opinion from an internist or general physician to confirm the need for surgery but to get his recommendation of a surgeon. If two surgeons of equal qualifications are available, the patient might want to talk with each and choose the one with whom he feels most comfortable. Confidence in and rapport with the surgeon, or any physician, may be as important to the patient's response to treatment as are his doctors' medical and surgical qualifications.

The initial visit with the surgeon—depending upon his personality and methods of practice and, often, the amount of time he has to give to a patient—should help reinforce the referring physician's recommendation for surgery. Once the patient has agreed to surgery, the surgeon should answer all his questions and explain the operation to be done. It is my practice to explain the procedure and use diagrams to illustrate how it will be carried out. The patient should be told the risks as well as the benefits to be expected from surgery. If it is extremely high-risk surgery, alternate methods of management should also be carefully explained to him.

Admission to the hospital

If the referring physician has done a complete medical workup on the patient and found his general condition compatible with the surgical procedure to be performed, and has made this information available to the surgeon, the patient will usually be admitted to the hospital the night before the scheduled surgery. However, if there are complicating factors—such as respiratory, cardiac, endocrine and other diseases present that have not been recently evaluated—the responsible surgeon may admit the patient to the hospital two or three days prior to surgery for a new medical evaluation. This may require consultations with an internist and other specialists. If indicated, special tests will be made, such as blood studies, x-rays, electrocardiogram, lung reserve studies, and others that may be required. The surgeon will be especially concerned with the blood's clotting mechanism, which is most important for the establishment of proper clotting during surgery and prevention of excessive clotting in the postoperative period. When needed, special medications such as insulin, cortisone, antibiotics, vitamins, and donor blood and blood products will be given to provide adequate body reserve and preserve homeostasis (maintenance of the body's physiological equilibrium).

Prior to surgery, preparation for the postoperative recuperative period is begun. Special devices which may be needed after the operation are explained to the patient by qualified personnel. These might include crutches and walkers, appliances for colostomies, and artificial limbs when amputations are to be done. Following throat surgery, the patient may require speech therapy. If a patient is elderly and has no family to care for him during recuperation, or if a prolonged recuperative period is anticipated, the need for limited nursing and medical care in an extended-care facility will be explained. The patient, if properly prepared for what to expect following surgery, is less likely to be upset when such devices and special care become necessary.

Prior to surgery, the surgeon will ask you to sign a "consent form" giving your permission for surgery. Today most hospitals have prepared a very detailed and complete consent form, which gives the possible complications and risks of surgery in clear, understandable language. As a patient, you should read the form very carefully before signing it. This is also the time to discuss with your surgeon any questions that may remain unanswered in your mind. He should never avoid giving honest answers to your questions about major risks involved. But he should also stress the benefits to be gained from the operation, weighing one against the other, so that you have a clear understanding of what may happen before you sign the consent form, which your surgeon will witness with his own signature.

Preparation for surgery

When shaving of an operative site is required, this will usually be done in your hospital room. Enemas and laxatives may be ordered, intravenous fluids may be administered, and required catheters and tubes may be placed just prior to surgery. For example, if abdominal surgery is to be performed, the doctor may order a liquid supper on the evening before surgery, an enema, and a sleeping pill to help you relax and get a good night's rest. Breakfast the following morning will be skipped. A stomach tube will be inserted through the nose and into the stomach to drain digestive fluids that have accumulated in your stomach during the night. Removal of such fluids and emptying the stomach of food particles is important just prior to surgery because of possible vomiting, during which food particles might be aspirated into the windpipe and obstruct breathing—a dangerous event for a patient highly sedated or under an anesthetic (when the cough reflex is damped). Prior to leaving for the operating room for any major procedure the patient is given an injection of a potent sedative, so that his anxiety will be relieved and he will arrive there totally relaxed. The relaxed, medically sedated patient will require less anesthetic for the operation.

The surgical team

In addition to the surgeon, the surgical team will usually include an assistant doctor (often a resident who is being trained in surgery), the anesthesiologist, two scrub nurses or operating-room technicians to handle instruments and a circulating nurse, who provides sterile materials that may be required from the nearby sterilizing room. If surgery is being performed in a teaching hospital, surgical resident physicians may be admitted to the operating room to observe the surgery; in addition, medical students may watch from the glass-enclosed amphitheater above as the surgeon explains his steps through a microphone.

The anesthesiologist may be selected by the surgeon, who has worked with him and trusts his competence and judgment, or he may be an approved member of the hospital's anesthesiology staff. The modern anesthesiologist not only administers the anesthetic but has medicine as well as anesthesiology. His presence in operating rooms today has contributed much to reducing serious operating risks, which now are much less during surgery than in the postoperative period. The anesthesiologist not only administers the anesthetic, but has sophisticated *ventilation monitors* which automatically monitor the mixture of anesthetic gases and assure their uniform delivery from moment to moment. Modern operating rooms also have electronic equipment which permits the anesthesiologist continuous monitoring of heart action, respiration, blood pressure and pulse beats. By this means he can detect at once any developing abnormality in the patient's vital signs so that corrective measures can be taken immediately. (See also *The Anesthesiologist* in the major article on **Specialists You Seldom See.**)

The anesthesiologist, like the surgeon, should ideally visit the patient prior to surgery and administration of sedatives. He should answer any questions asked about the role he plays and dispel any fears the patient may have about the period of unconsciousness. Although he may visit with you only a few minutes, you can be sure he has studied your medical records and will be prepared to anticipate any complications that might occur during surgery, because he knows that anesthetic risks today are much greater than the actual surgical risks.

After the operation

The recovery room to which the patient is taken immediately after surgery is an area seldom remembered by patients, but it is one of the most highly specialized and equipped areas of the hospital, containing sophisticated monitoring and resuscitative equipment. The personnel here are highly trained and serve a most vital role. As in flying, where takeoff and landing are the most precarious, the immediate postoperative period is one of the most important phases of the surgery drama. Vital signs (respiration rate, blood pressure and pulse) are monitored continuously. Urine output is closely checked. Drainage from tubes placed in the stomach or other area is checked for evidence of internal bleeding. The wound area is also observed for excessive bleeding or fluid drainage. Most importantly, the adequate and smooth transition from unconsciousness to consciousness is closely monitored.

Adverse reactions to drugs or anesthetic agents (if they are to be experienced at all) usually occur during the time a patient is in the recovery room. Return of normal respiration, avoidance of obstruction of the windpipe and lungs, and stabilization of the heart rate and blood pressure are carefully monitored until the patient has passed the critical stage of recovery.

The intensive care unit

This is really an extension of the recovery unit. Here will be found the same monitoring equipment and highly trained personnel and physicians who are experienced in providing intensive care. The INTENSIVE CARE UNIT is usually reserved for those patients who are acutely ill and whose conditions are unstable, but who have emerged from the anesthetic stage. The unit is a hub of activity and can be frightening to the now conscious patient.

The stay in the intensive care unit may vary from 24 hours to several weeks. There is no denying that this is a psychologically traumatic experience, but it has saved more lives than almost any other hospital improvement in care made in the past two decades.

Postoperative recovery

Postoperative recovery, although mainly smooth and without incident, can involve complications. Again, the competence of the surgeon is largely responsible for the type of recovery made. It is essential to be able to recognize and resolve problems early in the postoperative period—before they become irreversible and before they cause major complications. Possible complications and special

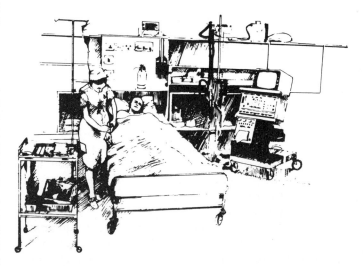

Following a major operation the patient is usually wheeled into a postoperative recovery room, where specially trained nurses monitor his respiratory rate, blood pressure and pulse. They keep a watchful eye until consciousness is regained; the patient is then moved from the recovery room to his bed in the surgical ward or a private room.

problems in the postoperative period include: (1) problems of the wound: infection, breakdown, hemorrhage; (2) chest problems: incomplete expansion of the lungs, accumulation of secretions, pneumonia; (3) abdominal problems: distention, infection or abscess formation, peptic ulcers, adhesions and intestinal obstruction, or clotting problems; (4) fever of various origins. Early medical attention will eliminate most, if not all, such problems. The possibilities of these problems occurring will have been explained at the time of the initial consultation.

Hospital stay following surgery has been significantly shortened. Early ambulation (even to the extent of being out of bed on the night of the surgical procedure) has been one of the factors responsible for faster recovery. Attention to nutrition and hydration has helped to make the average hospital stay much shorter. The average stay for such conditions as gallbladder disease, stomach ulcers, bowel obstruction, or cancer of the bowel or liver, is 10 to 14 days unless some complication supervenes. For relatively minor operations (such as appendectomy, hernia repair or surgical treatment of varicose veins) the stay may be only 5 to 7 days or less. Three to four weeks following discharge from the hospital should be allowed for resumption of activity and regaining of preoperative strength.

It is important, at this time, to mention the patient's mental attitude—which can aid or hinder his recovery from surgery. Certainly, all of the potential difficulties must be explained and fears allayed; but the patient's well-being is often determined by his own mental outlook even if no complications occur. This, of course, is an intangible element, but we surgeons continue to marvel at its tremendous impact. All of us are aware of patients with grave illnesses who manage to survive when all hope seems lost; conversely, some patients become increasingly worse when their future should be optimistic. Naturally, these cases remain enigmatic; but there is no doubt that the sheer willpower and determination of the patient (or the lack of same) are largely responsible.

Following almost any kind of surgery, severe pain can be expected for 24 to 48 hours, although this is always attended to and minimized by the appropriate medication. The amount of pain will gradually decrease and the patient will be given less medication, so that a drug dependency does not occur by the time he leaves the hospital. There *can* be discomfort for weeks following surgery (rarely severe or disabling), but this will diminish so that ideally by 4 to 6 weeks after the operation the patient should really be functioning at his optimum level once again. Many patients expect resumption of normal activities before they are physically and emotionally ready, and in some cases the consequences of resuming strenuous tasks too soon can result in a major setback. It is important to realize the limitations of activity during the healing period and take advantage of the opportunity to rest.

Special postoperative problems

A few words about some special problems that may pose physical and psychological stress.

Drains
Thin rubber drains are left in wounds if infection, bleeding or fluid accumulation is anticipated. These are painless, emerge from the abdomen near the area of the incision and can be removed with little or no discomfort.

Catheters
Tubes are inserted through the urethra into the bladder if major surgery is anticipated. This obviates the need to get out of bed as often and allows for accurate measurement of urine output. When surgery is done in the vicinity of the bladder, a catheter keeps it out of the way and allows for function of the bladder to return more promptly. There is minimal discomfort while the catheter is in place. Removal is painless.

Nasogastric tube
This is usually a plastic or rubber tube leading into the stomach through the nose and throat. There is discomfort because the tube feels very large as it courses through the pharynx (throat). It is usually placed after anesthesia is achieved, but may be inserted prior to surgery if "decompression" of the stomach and intestines is required. It also avoids gas pains in the postoperative period. Removal of the tube is simple and painless.

Other tubes
A small rubber tube is left in place when the major bile ducts are opened or explored. The tube is then connected to a bag or bottle and drains bile. It serves to decompress the biliary system and is left in place for seven to ten days on the average. Before removal, the tube is clamped; if this is well tolerated for 24 hours, it can be removed at the bedside in a few seconds. Tubes in the stomach or intestine are introduced at times for feeding purposes. These are lodged during surgery and are perfectly painless. Removal usually presents no problems and is performed at the bedside.

Intravenous catheters and needles
Intravenous feeding is quite commonplace and is familiar to everyone. A needle (or often a plastic catheter) is inserted into a vein and may be left in place for prolonged periods. The catheters are painless but do become uncomfortable if the area is infected or if the solution leaks around the catheter site. Prompt removal under these circumstances solves the problem. Occasionally catheters are placed in the neck area for measurement of venous pressure in or near the heart. The care of these is more meticulous but there is no increased discomfort for the patient.

Colostomy

Occasionally, in a case of serious bowel disease, it is necessary to remove the lower part of the colon and the rectum, so that normal passage of feces is impossible. There are also times when temporary interruption of the normal bowel function may be required. In these circumstances, a portion of the healthy bowel is brought out through an opening made in the abdominal wall. Feces can be eliminated through this opening (COLOSTOMY) into a plastic bag or container. In either circumstance, new appliances, deodorants, adhesive and belts are now available which make the colostomy quite acceptable. There is no need for apprehension about leakage or odor. The major hurdle is the psychological adjustment that needs to be made.

In the foregoing I have discussed the role of the general surgeon, and the patient-surgeon relationship—most of which is appropriate for all forms of surgery. Most of the specialized surgery has been covered in other articles in this section of the book, but I have been asked to describe briefly those surgeons not otherwise covered but who play vital roles in modern medicine.

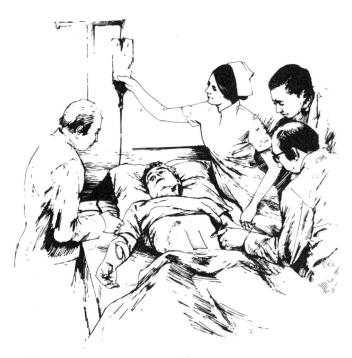

Intravenous fluids are commonly given following major surgery. They prevent the dehydration that might otherwise occur from the inevitable loss of blood and other body fluids during the operation. In the above illustration a nurse checks the flow of fluid from its plastic bag, while the surgeon inspects the operative site to make sure the wound is healing properly and that the sutures or clips are still holding its outer edges together.

Plastic surgery

When we think of the *plastic surgeon*, many of us think immediately of cosmetic surgery, performed to enhance the appearance of our aging population—such as the removal of sagging tissues and unseemly wrinkles, or the reconstruction of a large or mishaped nose, ears and other visible parts of the anatomy. Don't be misled by the publicity you read of movie stars and other newsworthy individuals whose cosmetic surgery often receives coverage in the press. Cosmetic surgery is an important part of the plastic surgeon's practice, but it is not all performed just to improve the image of people conscious of naturally occurring changes in their appearances. Often there is a real psychological need for such surgery, but a person's appearance may also be his "bread and butter" and help extend his or her career—whether it be in show business or in a regular job. When several candidates of equal qualifications are being considered for promotion, personal appearance is too often a deciding factor. Qualified young people may also sometimes be passed over for jobs because a potential boss does not like their looks.

Most cosmetic plastic surgery carried out today is performed on accident victims, young and old, who may need new ears, new noses, a chin, or the removal of disfiguring scar tissue.

One of the plastic surgeon's most important contributions is in the treatment and rehabilitation of burn victims. Once, and only a short time ago, the person who suffered third-degree burns on more than a third of his body could be expected to die. Today, because of many new techniques developed by plastic surgeons and others, patients are recovering from serious burns that cover much of their bodies. Such a badly burned person may have to undergo plastic surgery many times over a period of months; the grafting of new skin over burned areas—whether taken from the victim's own body, from donors, or even from cadavers—is necessary to avoid life-threatening infections and the loss of body heat. When total healing of serious burns has been accomplished, the plastic surgeon then may perform cosmetic surgery to replace remaining scar tissue that is disfiguring.

The plastic surgeon must undergo the longest period of training of all physicians and surgeons before he can be certified in his specialty by the American Board of Plastic Surgery. Following graduation from medical school (four years) he will serve a one-year internship, followed by three years of residency training in general surgery, followed by an additonal two years of residency in plastic surgery—a total of ten years of postgraduate training.

Thoracic surgery

This once included any type of surgery within the chest cavity (thorax), which contains the heart, lungs, esophagus and their associated structures. In major teaching hospitals and medical centers today, however, this specialty is generally subdivided into two subspecialties: *cardiovascular surgery* and *pulmonary surgery*.

Cardiovascular surgery

The cardiovascular surgeon (or "open-heart" surgeon)—with his large team of physicians and specially trained nurses and technicians—may be better known to laymen than any other surgical specialist. This is largely due to the vast publicity given in the press and on national television to the drama associated with early heart transplant operations, the replacement of diseased or damaged heart valves with artificial pacemakers to govern the rhythmic beating of the heart—seriously affected in certain types of heart disease. (See also the major article on **Cardiology**.)

Being able to stop the heart while it is being surgically repaired—let alone while it is removed and replaced with a donor or artificial heart—is awe-inspiring to virtually everyone. This was largely made possible by the development of the *heart-lung machine*, a device which permits the heart to be bypassed and which temporarily takes over the responsibility of maintaining the oxygenation and circulation of the blood to all the organs and tissues. The greatest contributions of open-heart surgeons are not the rare cases of total heart transplants—which, in any case, are rather controversial and far from ideal in terms of patient survival. More important is their ability to repair congenital or acquired heart defects in children and adults who only a short time ago faced early death or lives of invalidism. Little in surgery or medicine is more heart-warming than to watch a previously blue-lipped (cyanosed) child, grossly handicapped, who a short time after corrective heart surgery is able to romp and play with other children. (See also CYANOSIS.)

Pulmonary surgery

The pulmonary surgeon, though less publicized, is also making great contributions at a time when lung cancer, respiratory disorders and other handicapping pulmonary diseases are on the increase from excessive smoking and other chemical pollutants in the environment. Many victims of lung cancer, receiving surgical treatment following early detection, are free of the disease after several years. Many other pulmonary problems unresponsive to medical treatment are being corrected by surgery. As new knowledge of the body's immunological system becomes available, it is not unreasonable to predict that total lung transplants will become more successful than they are at present. (See also PULMONARY DISEASES and the major article on **Pulmonary Diseases.**)

Advances in surgery and surgical technology

Progress continues at a phenomenal pace. In addition to the numerous advances of the past 15 to 20 years—some of which have been enumerated—the explosion of knowledge continues. Exciting new developments which are in the forefront of surgery today are rapidly advancing to become routine procedures. These include the correction of heart defects, the correction of poor coronary circulation to the heart (i.e., coronary BYPASS) and heart transplants. Liver and kidney transplantation is now almost routine, but still done primarily in large medical centers. Corneal transplants, artificial joints and artificial artery replacements are all performed almost daily.

The advances are indeed astonishing and marvelous, but they did not evolve in a vacuum. The cost of research that made them possible, and the expenditures that make them available to almost every region of the country, are astronomical. It is the combination of the sophistication of the equipment, the evolution of the myriads of diagnostic tests and procedures, and the need to make these universally available, that have accounted for the breathtaking rise in medical costs.

The future

What of the future? The basic problems of heart disease, cancer and aging are still an enigma. Tremendous amounts of energy and money are being expended in these areas and a breakthrough should be forthcoming. Although it is not yet possible to guess whether this will be in the area of basic science, or within the medical or surgical fields, it is safe to assume that all the areas will contribute. It is a most exciting time to be practicing surgery today. Great strides are being made, new developments are coming at a rapid pace and we are doing more to alleviate pain and suffering more effectively than ever before. There are bigger and greater breakthroughs ahead, however, and the answers to the unsolved riddles promise to be even more stupendous than the events leading up to the present.

Today's surgeon is better equipped, both with technical knowledge and instrumentation, than ever before in history.

Specialists you seldom see
The radiologist, anesthesiologist, pathologist and hematologist

Dr. Joseph E. Snyder and Dr. Christopher S. Pitcher

Many medical specialists are never seen by patients because they work behind the scenes in hospitals and laboratories. The following article discusses the important contributions of four of these indispensable experts.

One of the most upsetting experiences a patient can face during or following a period of hospitalization is the delivery of bills from doctors he has never seen. Equally disturbing is a bill from a doctor who might have stopped at his bedside for a few minutes to ask a question or two, then departed—not to be heard from again until his bill arrived. Such experiences quite understandably can make a patient wonder whether he was being exploited at a time when he was in no position to question the services his doctor might have ordered for him. This is especially true today, when the news media are questioning the high cost of medical care, citing "patient swapping" among doctors as one of the contributing causes.

Most often, the unseen or seldom seen specialist has been called in as a consultant because your doctor recognized a need for his special knowledge and experience. Such consultations can often save you an unnecessary operation, or lead you to early treatment and surgery that might be life saving. This article, therefore, is being written to describe briefly the roles of those specialists who often work in the background, but may bill the patient directly for services his attending doctor has ordered. They include the radiologist, anesthesiologist, pathologist and hematologist.

THE RADIOLOGIST

The most common medical procedure done today, along with the blood count and urinalysis, is the x-ray examination. Although many x-rays are taken by highly trained technicians, they are always seen and their meanings interpreted by the radiologist, who sends his reports to the doctors who ordered them. Thus, the radiologist is for the

most part a "doctor's doctor." Few physicians will undertake treatment of serious disease or recommend surgery without his consultation. The modern radiologist can visually explore every nook and cranny in every organ system of the body. He may work within the hospital, serving its staff and patients, or he may have an office practice to which patients are sent by their physicians for examinations or treatments required.

Diagnostic and therapeutic use of radiant energy

The radiologist is not only a master diagnostician but is also a *radiotherapist* who uses radiant energy to irradiate malignant tumors and treat other conditions with irradiation. He or she is first trained in general medicine and surgery, then spends a minimum of four years in postgraduate training to become proficient in all areas of radiology, including those that require invasion of the body to introduce dyes, air and other contrast materials that are x-rayed as they pass through blood vessels and the organs they serve.

Radiology, a comparatively new specialty, was not recognized as a distinct medical discipline until 1934, when it established its own examining board and became responsible for the educational and clinical training programs of future radiologists, as well as their examination for competence and certification.

There are three types of ionizing radiation, which are the radiologist's basic tools: *x-rays*, discovered in 1895 by William Conrad Roentgen; *radium*, discovered by Pierre and Marie Curie in 1899; and *radioactive isotopes*, which are products of nuclear energy.

Discovery of radiation hazards

Modern radiology has developed highly sophisticated equipment and standards for the use of radiant energy which now make it safe for both patients and doctors. In the early days, when improperly shielded equipment was used and protective garments were not worn by those

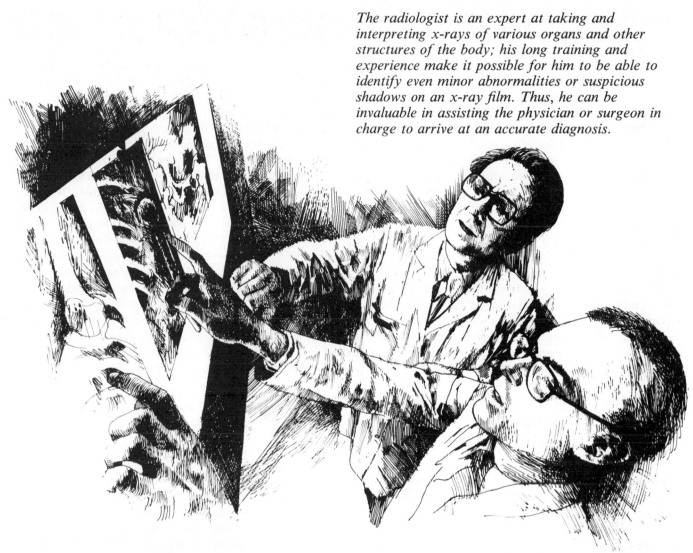

The radiologist is an expert at taking and interpreting x-rays of various organs and other structures of the body; his long training and experience make it possible for him to be able to identify even minor abnormalities or suspicious shadows on an x-ray film. Thus, he can be invaluable in assisting the physician or surgeon in charge to arrive at an accurate diagnosis.

operating it, there were high risks for both patients and doctors. Radiation damage is due to the accumulation of radiation exposure. The pioneers in the use of x-rays suffered severe radiation sickness from continued exposure. Some died and many lost fingers and hands and became sterile. Until rigid standards were established, doctors and dentists used x-rays indiscriminately. Shoe stores used it on children and adults to fit shoes. Until very recent times, doctors themselves used it to treat conditions that were better treated conventionally.

Today, diagnostic procedures and radiation therapy are carried out with minimal amounts of radiation exposure. Hospitals require their equipment to be regularly checked and calibrated. The rooms in which powerful x-ray and other radiation equipment are used has protective lead shielding, which absorbs radiation, to protect people working nearby. Radiologists and their technicians wear monitoring devices on their white coats which accurately evaluate undue exposure. X-ray examinations are seldom given to pregnant women because of risks to the developing fetus. *Ultrasonography*, which uses sound waves to

visualize internal structures, is now widely used for examining expectant mothers and this technique usually lies in the province of the radiologist. (See ULTRASOUND.)

Modern developments in radiology

Recent progress in radiology has been due to the development of new products and equipment made possible by the nuclear age and to the discovery of new ways to use old principles. Knowledge that the body's naturally trapped gases were useful in x-ray examinations led to the deliberate injection or ingestion of many substances to increase opacity and contrast on the x-ray film. Among these substances are air, barium sulfate solutions, watery iodides, iodinated oils and phenolphthalein compounds. The success of such substances in providing contrast led to new ways of introducing them into the body.

A most difficult organ to x-ray internally was the heart; contrast media introduced through the large vessels were diluted before they reached their target. Modern heart catheterization is a technique used to introduce a small catheter through an arm vessel directly into the heart for the introduction of contrast dyes. Contrast materials introduced into the brain permit the detection of tumors, blood clots, hemorrhagic spots, plugged vessels and ballooning aneurysms. The availability of manmade radioactive isotopes opened an entirely new concept in radiology. Various elements known to concentrate in specific organs of the body are made radioactive in atomic piles. They are introduced into the body and when they concentrate in the target area are studied by a computerized scanner, which prints out a picture that the radiologist can interpret meaningfully in relationship to abnormalities that may or may not be present. For example, radioactive gold and sulfur colloid concentrate in the liver, red blood cells tagged with chromium concentrate in the spleen, phosphorus and strontium concentrate in the bones and iodine concentrates in the thyroid. Radiation exposure from such substances is minimal.

An especially difficult target area once difficult to evaluate was the delicate LYMPHATIC SYSTEM, which is frequently attacked by cancer. Today, a needle is inserted into the lymph channel in the foot and an iodinated oil is injected. After several hours the oil travels through the system, making the lymphatics visible to x-rays. Iodinated oils can also be dropped into the trachea ("windpipe") to trickle down to reveal the tiny bronchial tubes. Once a very uncomfortable procedure for the patient, the oil can now be introduced to specific areas through a tiny metal-tipped catheter that is guided by a magnet moved on the outside of the body.

Tomography

Abnormalities involving the tiny structures of the middle and inner ear can now be evaluated by *tomography*. This procedure, which focuses on tissue no thicker than 1/25 of an inch, can save the patient with hearing loss or facial palsy the expense and risk of an exploratory operation.

Mammography

A comparatively new radiological technique, which is being questioned by many experts today, is MAMMOGRAPHY; this uses very low energy radiation and super-sensitive film to detect cancer of the breast, often before it can be felt or detected by other methods. Many radiologists now feel that healthy young women should forgo the routine six-month or annual mammographic examination. However, all women over 40 and those with a history of breast cancer in their family (the most vulnerable groups), can benefit from such examinations. This is because radiation risks are not as important as the early discovery of a developing cancer that can be removed by "conservative" rather than "radical" surgery.

(See also BREAST CANCER.)

Thermography

In addition to ultrasonography, a new diagnostic technique called THERMOGRAPHY is coming into use. Its diagnostic value lies in catching, recording and interpreting the meaning of radiant heat thrown off by diseased tissues.

CAT scan

Perhaps the most exciting new advance in diagnostic radiology has been the recent development of *computerized axial tomography (CAT scan)*. Used first to evaluate abnormalities of the brain and inner eye structures, new scanners (*whole-body scanners*) can now evaluate the entire body. The procedure combines the use of a programmed computer and special x-ray equipment. The patient simply lies on a table and the scanner passes slowly across his entire body, photographing thin "slices"—which the computer collates into three-dimensional pictures. This technique requires no invasion of the body, avoids the risks associated with some radiological techniques, especially those used to evaluate the brain, and it can be done on an outpatient basis. (For a further discussion of the CAT scan, see the appropriate section in the major article on **Examination, Diagnosis and Therapy**.)

Preparing for an x-ray

The inexperienced patient being prepared for radiological examination for the first time may wonder why he or she must disrobe, remove false teeth, jewelry and hairpins, and wear only a string-tie down in the examining room—then lie on a hard, unpadded table. Buttons, dentures, jewelry and padding show up on x-rays and can obliterate or distort underlying shadows cast by body structures.

It should perhaps be explained that all doctors now have had training and experience in taking and interpreting x-rays, and many have x-ray equipment in their office, as most of you know. They are competent to identify obvious abnormalities, but only the experienced radiologist is qualified to evaluate those subtle variations in the intensity of x-ray shadows. He will have studied thousands just like the ones other doctors may send to him for interpretation. If he is in doubt about a diagnosis, he will order additional x-rays to be taken (perhaps taken from different angles) to confirm or rule out his tentative diagnosis.

In each of the specialties and subspecialties of medicine and surgery described in this section of the book, the various radiological diagnostic studies that are made of the various organ systems are explained in some detail, so I will not repeat them here. But readers who wonder about procedures their doctor orders for them for their particular medical problem might want to read the individual articles to better understand why the x-rays are needed. In addition, your own doctor will usually be pleased to take the time to answer specific questions.

(See also X-RAYS.)

Radiation therapy

A radiologist may practice both diagnostic radiology and radiation therapy (radiotherapy), or specialize in only one area. The radiotherapist may use any of the three sources of radiant energy in his treatments, or a combination of them. In most cases his therapy will be part of a treatment plan that combines surgery, the administration of drugs, and irradiation.

The radiotherapist will evolve his own plan for irradiation—based upon consultation with the referring doctor, his study of the patient's medical record, and his own careful physical examination. The plan will be individualized for each patient, because several patients having the same type of cancer, located in the same structures, may have it in different stages of development. Based on past experience, the therapist can usually inform the patient in advance of the number of treatments he is likely to receive.

There is no pain or sensation felt when radiation is being directed into the body, whether the tissue being irradiated lies on or near the surface of the skin or deep within the body. Redness and slight irritation on the outer surface of the skin may develop as treatments are continued; but, like sunburn, this passes when treatments are stopped. During prolonged therapy some patients may suffer symptoms of radiation sickness, nausea or vomiting, feelings of fatigue and lassitude, and loss of body hair. These effects also pass after treatments are completed.

Radiation therapy, used in combination with other types of therapy, can cure many conditions and control others. In HYPERTHYROIDISM, for example, which is caused by an overactive thyroid, the patient may be given an "atomic cocktail" containing radioactive iodine. This will concentrate in the thyroid to give off a steady stream of beta and gamma rays, which can slow down overactive thyroid cells and bring the thyroid back to normal functioning. Radioactive gold, which produces beta rays that penetrate only short distances, can be introduced into the chest and abdominal cavities to control fluid formations that may occur in cancer patients. Irradiation is also used to shrink swollen brain tissue that is causing dangerous neurological symptoms.

Radioactive materials, such as radium and cobalt 60, may be contained in hollow needles and wires that are directly inserted into tumors to produce their effects. Cobalt 60 "bombs" and multi-million voltage x-rays may be directed by special machines to pinpoint sites located deep within the body to destroy malignant tissue or retard its growth.

Whatever the condition being treated, the radiotherapist will use the technique and type of radiation needed in the smallest possible amounts required for therapeutic results.

The basic principle upon which therapeutic irradiation depends is that carefully directed rays to specific diseased sites can destroy diseased cells, while only damaging nearby healthy cells—permitting them to recover, multiply and replace the dead cells. Thus, the skill of the radiotherapist is as important in treatment as the type of radiation he uses.

Controlled use of radiant energy

Today, irradiation treatment of benign conditions (those not cancerous) is being abandoned, except when no other treatment is available. X-rays are no longer justified for treating common skin problems (such as acne, eczema and fungus infections) or for shrinking a suspected enlarged thymus. The same can be said for bursitis, peritendonitis and arthritis in women of childbearing age, as well as other conditions formerly treated with x-rays. For the patient's benefit, most of these conditions could be better controlled by available conservative methods.

The *fluoroscopic examination*, which plays such an important part in modern radiology, but which requires longer exposure and more radiation than still x-rays, should not be used when still x-rays can give the same diagnostic information. However, it is indispensable as a diagnostic tool when movement of internal structures is necessary to evaluate abnormalities. Incidentally, the patient may only see the fluoroscopist when he is in a darkened room, wearing colored glasses, a shielding apron and protective gloves. The glasses are worn to intensify his vision and are removed just before the examination begins.

Radiology is one of the most important specialties in medicine and is now highly safe and effective, both for diagnosis and therapy. Its practitioners are responsible for much of the progress that has been made in recent years to detect and control many of the diseases that afflict us. The radiologist is well worth his fee, even though he only interprets an x-ray taken by a technician and is never seen by you.

THE ANESTHESIOLOGIST

Anesthesiology was recognized as a distinct medical specialty in 1937, and is concerned with the administration of local and general anesthesia and with monitoring surgical patients safely through the period of unconsciousness to consciousness.

The anesthesiologist is a physician well-trained in general medicine and surgery who spends an additional four to five years in postgraduate clinical training. During this long training period he becomes proficient in all areas of anesthesiology, including the techniques of resuscitation, which may be required for surgical patients who develop life-threatening complications while under deep anesthesia. He is also concerned with research to develop better anesthetics and better techniques for administering them.

Because of the well-trained anesthesiologist and the various techniques and support systems available to him, many high-risk patients—who only a short time ago could not be recommended for surgery—are now routinely operated on and come safely through even long procedures.

Medicine's search for some method to relax patients and control pain is as old as surgery itself—which dates back to the ancient Greeks and Egyptians. Throughout at least six centuries, this quest was unsuccessful; millions upon millions had to undergo the sting of the surgeon's knife, while tied down by thongs. The only method of combating pain was the ingestion of great amounts of alcohol, or a well-placed blow to the head, each potentially as dangerous as the operation itself. The pain suffered by mankind down through the centuries is incalculable, especially if we remember that the only effective weapon against hemorrhage and infection was cauterization with a red-hot iron.

Early use of general anesthesia

The first known successful use of a general anesthesia for surgery was by a young American doctor, Crawford Williamson Long (1815–1878). While sniffing sulfuric ether, with other young men in Jefferson, Georgia—much as young people experiment with mood-altering drugs

General anesthesia was first administered in the 19th century by dropping chloroform or ether onto a cloth held over the patient's face. Modern inhalation anesthesia is administered by temperature-controlled vaporizers which accurately supply a known concentration of the anesthetic agent and a mixture of oxygen. An airtight seal between the patient and the anesthesia machine may be achieved either by the use of a face mask or the positioning of an endotracheal tube (see illustration) into the patient's trachea (windpipe) through the mouth.

today—he noted that while under the effects of ether they often fell and suffered bruises without any feeling of pain. In 1842, he let a patient breathe the ether through a towel until the patient was totally unconscious, then removed a tumor from his neck. When the patient regained consciousness, he said he had felt no pain whatever. Dr. Long missed his niche in medical history by not publishing the results of his experiment until 1849, from fear of what his colleagues might say about such an "unethical" action.

In 1846, Dr. William Thomas Green Morton (1819–1868), a Boston dentist, successfully used ether to extract teeth. After prolonged pestering for an opportunity to demonstrate ether as an anesthetic for surgery, Morton was finally given an opportunity to do his demonstration at Massachussetts General Hospital by Dr. Charles Warren, Chief of Surgery—who mostly wanted to disprove his ridiculous claims. Morton, late for his appointment, was greeted with derision by the doctors who had gathered to witness the upstart's humiliation. Morton set up his equipment, rendered the patient unconscious, and Dr. Warren removed a tumor from his patient's jaw. On that October 16, 1846, when Dr. Warren turned to his colleagues and said, "Gentlemen, this is no humbug," modern anesthesiology was born. From that small operating room, known today as the "ether dome," knowledge of ether anesthesia spread throughout the civilized world. Ether, however, proved to have many disadvantages. It was highly flammable and explosive and could not be used for extended periods. The search for new anesthetics began.

Modern developments in anesthesiology

Today's anesthesiologist has a variety of anesthetics from which to choose, both for local and general anesthesia. In *general anesthesia*, which causes loss of consciousness, the patient inhales carefully controlled amounts of vapor or gas anesthetics, such as ether, nitrous oxide and methoxyflurane. For *local anesthesia*, during which the patient remains fully conscious, he may inject alcohol into a nerve trunk to deaden all feeling in the area it serves. In *caudal block* a needle is inserted into the sacrococcygeal notch (an area between the sacrum and coccyx) into the epidural space (just outside the spinal cord), killing in the area below the blockage all sensation of nerve impulses to the brain. Promising research points toward the development of anesthetics that can produce general anesthesia by the injection of drugs, which would greatly reduce the high risk of inhalant gases for patients with potentially dangerous respiratory problems.

In the recent past and in many doctors' offices and some hospitals today, a specially trained nurse may act as the anesthetist. In 1970, however, the Joint Commission for the Accreditation of Hospitals ruled that, for a hospital to be eligible for accreditation, all of its anesthesiology services must be under the supervision of a physician.

Most patients, I know, quite logically assume that anesthesiologists work entirely within hospitals as full-time staff members. About a third do; but two-thirds have office practices, often as members of a group practice. They serve in various hospitals, but will usually see their patients only after they have been admitted—often the night before surgery is scheduled. He may stop for only a brief visit, to explain the procedures he will carry out and give you a chance to meet him. This is a good time to ask him any questions that may still be bothering you. Although the anesthesiologist may ask you only a few general questions, you can be certain that he or she knows a great deal about you—various drugs to which you may be sensitive and other allergies, your blood count, respiratory efficiency and the presence of other diseases that might be complicating factors during surgery. It is essential for him to know all that your medical records contain, because anesthetic risks today are greater than the actual surgical risks. He will be "breathing" for you during the period when you are unconscious and will be prepared to deal with even the slightest variation in your vital functions.

Most patients, wisely I think, usually accept the anesthesiologist their surgeon recommends, who will usually be someone with whom he has worked and whose judgment and competence he trusts. He has every right and reason to be careful, because he, rather than the anesthesiologist, is most likely to be blamed if the patient dies. However, patients should know that it is their right to choose their own anesthesiologist, except in an emergency situation. In *elective surgery*, in which time is not a factor, you can always check a recommended anesthesiologist's credentials, perhaps through the county Medical Society, the information office at the hospital(s) with which he is affiliated, or in the Medical Specialty Index, which can usually be found in your library.

Administration of general anesthesia

When you arrive at the operating room on a mobile stretcher, you will be sedated and relaxed, requiring less anesthetic than if you were anxious and rigid. During the first stage of general anesthesia you will likely become euphoric and excited, but this quickly passes as voluntary control passes; your last sensory perception to go will be hearing. In the last stages, you will be totally relaxed, without rigidity, and your breathing will become deep and regular. The anesthesiologist, bending over you at the head of the operating table—where he will remain throughout the operation—will be flashing lights into your eyes, touching the corneal surface with a soft sterile object to test corneal reflexes, which will be one of his guides to judge the deepness of anesthesia. He tells the surgeon when he may begin the operation.

Throughout the operation the minimal amount of anesthetic needed will be provided by respiratory machines, which assure a uniform mixture of the inhalants and moment-to-moment delivery. The anesthesiologist will constantly monitor the state of your vital functions on instruments previously connected to your body—your heart action on a continuous electrocardiogram, blood pressure, respiratory efficiency and pulse beat. At the first indication of an abnormality, he will be prepared to take measures to counteract it. He may provide additional oxygen or warn the surgeon to inject certain drugs. In acute situations, such as heart arrest or respiratory failure, he will participate in resuscitation measures.

Because of the anesthesiologist's special skills and experience, only a few patients die during surgery today. The most dangerous period may be in the recovery room, where careful monitoring of all vital signs is continued until the patient passes safely from unconsciousness to consciousness. If you become a surgical patient, your anesthesiologist, perhaps never seen in an emergency situation and only briefly in any event, will be one of your most important doctors. He is well worth his fee, which today will be billed directly and not included in your hospital charges, as was once a common practice.

THE PATHOLOGIST

When we think of the pathologist, many of us remember that rustic, acerbic, sloppily dressed old curmudgeon we came to know from movies and books. He was that different kind of doctor, who spent his time in his basement laboratory, surrounded by his specimen cases, technicians and their lab tables. He never had to put on a front for patients he would never see, or court doctors who might refer patients to him. He was the "watchdog" who monitored other doctors' work and missed few opportunities to point out their mistakes, which he could prove by microscopic examination of healthy tissue and organs needlessly removed, or at his marble autopsy table.

Role of the modern pathologist

The basic role of pathologists remains unchanged in some ways, but modern pathology, like other disciplines, has splintered into subspecialties with the explosion of medical knowledge and the proliferation of dozens of new pathological tests that continue to evolve. He has sophisticated analyzing machines which can now perform in minutes tests that once took hours of differential testing, the powerful electron microscope which can visualize the tiniest microorganisms, including viruses, and computer installations to instantly relay his diagnostic decisions in printouts that go simultaneously to doctors, the medical record room and to nursing stations on hospital floors.

Much has changed, indeed, but many of the

pathologist's responsibilities remain the same. His decisions, made from pathological studies, still remain the final diagnoses upon which physicians and surgeons will act. He still serves as the hospital's watchdog. If a surgeon performs too many operations that were needless, if medical doctors make too many mistakes in diagnosis and treatments, the pathologist will catch them and they will have to answer for their errors. Disciplinary actions may be taken; if they continue to make mistakes, they can lose their admitting privileges to the hospital. The Joint Commission on Hospital Accreditation requires that all tissue removed from patients be examined microscopically, and that is why a patient is wise to choose a doctor who has admitting privileges at an accredited hospital.

Background, training and subspecialties

The pathologist is first educated and trained in all areas of general medicine, then spends a minimum of four years in residency training to be eligible for certification in his specialty. He may choose to practice in the two primary divisions of pathology, or in both; these include *anatomic pathology*, responsible for studying structural changes in tissues; and *clinical pathology*, concerned with the chemical and physiologic changes in body fluids and tissues. If a pathologist is interested in a particular organ system, he may limit his practice to that subspecialty, such as hematologic pathology, neuropathology and others. Pathologists may work in hospitals, or maintain private laboratories to which doctors send specimens for study.

The anatomic pathologist's basic tool is the microscope. He quickly freezes tissue specimens, then removes a thin slice which he places upon a glass slide and then stains it to make its structures more distinct under the microscope. The big question he must always answer is, "Is it cancer?" And if it is, "What kind?" It is just as important to know that it is not cancerous. Only the pathologist who has studied thousands of tissue specimens can make the distinction between the many types of cancers, which may be in different stages of development and require different approaches to treatment. He will make few mistakes, even though his decisions must often be made quickly during exploratory operations while the patient remains under anesthesia. His diagnosis, "malignant" or "benign," can mean the difference between radical surgery to remove large areas of tissue or complete organs, or the comparatively simple excision of a benign growth.

The clinical pathologist, assisted by technicians, must evaluate all of the body fluids, such as blood, urine, hormones, enzymes, sputum and saliva. He studies stool specimens and tissue specimens. He must detect and identify the wide range of infectious microorganisms—which include bacteria, viruses, protozoa, fungi, rickettsiae, spirochetes and larger parasites, each of which may require different treatments. He will grow microorganisms in appropriate culture broths, then test them against different drugs, or a combination of drugs, to see which are most effective. Such determinations are becoming increasingly more important since bacteria continue to produce strains that become resistant to antibiotics that once destroyed them with a single injection. He often determines not only the proper drugs to be used, but the dosage to be given and the length of time it should be continued. This not only assures proper treatment for the individual patient but helps prevent the development of resistant strains of bacteria. That is why a patient taking oral antibiotics at home should continue to take them for the number of days prescribed by his doctor, even though his symptoms may disappear after only a day or two.

THE HEMATOLOGIST

The hematologist specializes in disorders affecting the blood and, to some extent, in those affecting the closely associated lymphatic system. He is also concerned with the provision of blood for transfusion and of blood products for the treatment of a variety of disorders.

Historically, his specialty developed in much the same way as those of his laboratory colleagues and he was

The pathologist examines tissue specimens obtained at biopsy· or removed during the course of a surgical procedure. If he confirms, for example, that they show evidence of cancerous changes the surgeon may then decide to remove the tumor or affected part.

essentially a "backroom boy." Indeed, it is only in recent years that increasing specialization has separated his work from that of the microbiologist (who deals with the organisms of infectious disease), the chemical pathologist (who concerns himself with changes in the body's chemistry), and the histopathologist (who performs autopsies and examines tissues removed by the surgeon). At one stage, all these roles were concentrated in a single individual who was referred to simply as a pathologist or one who studied the nature of disease processes.

The earliest pathologists were confined to the dissection of the dead body and observation with the naked eye of the changes present in disease. The invention of the microscope then allowed the histopathologist to study the microscopic changes in diseased tissues; the appearance of the hematologist coincides with the use of this instrument to examine the blood. Initially this was done by examining either dried or wet films of the patient's blood on glass slides. The red and white blood cells could be observed and later made more prominent by staining them with aniline dyes; changes in the size and shape of the red cells and in the number of white cells were noted in certain diseases.

Modern developments and techniques

More quantitative techniques were soon demanded and methods of counting the red and white cells and of determining the concentration of hemoglobin pigment in the blood were devised. Until quite recently, all measurements of red and white cell numbers were made by diluting the blood and placing the diluted sample on a microscope slide divided into squares of known area, enabling the cells to be counted visually under the microscope. In the last 20 years, rapid advances in these techniques have been made so that visual counting has been eliminated and manual manipulation of the samples reduced to a minimum. Modern electronic blood-count analyzers can, in a few seconds, determine from a small sample of blood the red cell count, white cell count, hemoglobin concentration, hematocrit (volume of red cells in a unit volume of blood) and a set of calculated indices showing red cell size and hemoglobin content. The number of platelets, which are important in blood clotting, can be determined at the same time and a machine can even routinely determine the relative numbers of the different types of white blood cells present. (An illustration of a modern blood-count analyzer can be found in the major article on **Examination, Diagnosis and Therapy**.)

Other body tissues—such as the bone marrow, where the blood cells are formed, or lymphatic glands, removed by a surgeon for examination under the microscope—are also accessible to the hematologist; he also has available an increasing list of chemical, isotopic and radiologic tests that bear on the establishment of purely hematologic diagnoses in his patients.

The changing role of the hematologist

The original concept of the hematologist as a doctor who merely supervises a laboratory department, producing test results on which his clinical colleagues base their diagnoses, is now becoming outmoded. The lab naturally still produces results that are of great importance to his clinical colleagues, because the blood in many ways reflects the presence of disease processes elsewhere in the body. For example, a common laboratory procedure is the measurement of the rate at which red blood cells settle to the bottom in a tall, narrow tube (see ERYTHROCYTE SEDIMENTATION RATE). An increased rate is a valuable indication of the presence of disease, though quite nonspecific in terms of diagnosis, while a normal figure reassures the clinician that little is amiss. An anemia is similarly a common accompaniment of major diseases, while changes in the white cell count and unusual changes in the size or shape of red cells may all be valuable evidence of particular disorders which are not themselves primary diseases of the blood. Thus, red cells that are larger than normal may suggest not only a common primary blood disorder such as pernicious

The modern hematologist can now quickly provide valuable diagnostic information to physicians on a wide variety of blood disorders and other conditions which are suggested by abnormal blood chemistry and blood cell counts. For example, a small sample of blood can now be analyzed in seconds by an electronic device to provide evidence of anemia (low hemoglobin levels), general infection (high white cell counts) and many other conditions that can be detected by lab tests on the blood and bone marrow.

anemia but also the presence of such diverse conditions as liver disease, defective thyroid function, alcohol abuse, or drug overdosage.

The modern clinical hematologist, however, might object to his inclusion among "specialists you seldom see." The increasing scope of his specialty means that his clinical colleagues often feel unable to master all its complexities themselves. The hematologist has therefore undergone a transformation from a laboratory worker who produced data for others to use, to a skilled clinician who not only supervises his laboratory but comes more and more into direct contact with patients suffering from primary blood diseases, carrying out his own diagnostic procedures and, when a diagnosis is reached, personally supervising the increasingly complex treatments now available.

A patient might thus approach a hematologist directly for advice, or be referred directly to him by his family doctor or indirectly via a specialist colleague. If referred via a specialist colleague or his family doctor, an initial blood count will probably already be available, although the patient's symptoms alone might lead to his direct referral to a hematologist without preliminary blood counts. This would be particularly true in cases of unusual bruising or bleeding, and in patients with obvious and severe anemia or enlarged lymph glands.

Like other specialists, the hematologist will take a careful history from the patient since—when taken in conjunction with even a basic blood count—this may be sufficient to suggest a fairly certain diagnosis. The ease and speed with which the basic blood count figures can be obtained, however, make it possible for him to look for the type and degree of anemia and changes in the red cell, white cells and platelets even before taking the history. The patient should not therefore feel that this essential step is being omitted if the hematologist collects a blood sample at the beginning of the consultation and studies the results before questioning the patient about his symptoms.

Armed with the basic blood count result and the history, he will then examine the patient, paying particular attention to pallor, bruising or bleeding, and enlargement of the lymph nodes in the neck, armpits or groin. Abdominal examination may detect enlargement of the spleen (under the margin of the left rib) or the liver (similarly placed on the right side). He will look carefully at the mouth and throat for evidence of infection or hemorrhage in the lips, gums or throat.

Diagnosis of blood disorders

At this stage the history, clinical examination, and the basic blood count may already clearly indicate the likely diagnosis. Examination of a stained blood film, taking a little longer to prepare, may provide all the confirmation necessary. In many cases, however, further tests will be required. The changes seen in the blood reflect changes occurring in the bone marrow—where the red cells, white cells and platelets are produced. Examination of the bone marrow itself—by means of a BIOPSY—is therefore valuable if the changes in the blood count are not themselves diagnostic.

A marrow sample is usually obtained under local anesthetic, either in the hematologist's office or in a hospital bed if the patient has been admitted. The sample is obtained by aspiration of a very small quantity of marrow into a special hollow needle inserted through the skin into the breastbone or sternum (*sternal puncture*) or into the upper margin of the pelvic bone at the hip (*iliac puncture*). It is a minor procedure and not usually more than momentarily uncomfortable. It is often an unavoidable necessity in the confirmation of the diagnosis of serious disorders such as leukemia, but it should not be assumed that anything so serious is being considered in every case in which it is performed. Many patients with common types of anemia require a marrow puncture to confirm the diagnosis.

Even with the history, examination, blood count and marrow, the diagnosis may remain unconfirmed. The hematologist will then turn to other blood tests, performed on the samples he has taken. These may include the measurement of iron levels in the blood or the levels of vitamins important to the blood, such as vitamin B_{12} and folic acid. In cases of abnormal bleeding or bruising, assays of blood clotting factors are made. As the diagnostic possibilities increase, other biochemical tests or more specialized procedures may be required, such as the measurement of vitamin B_{12} absorption, determination of red cell life span, or measurement of the blood volume using radioactive isotopes. In anemia, x-rays of the bowel or the testing of stool samples may be necessary to detect sites from which blood might be lost. Endoscopic procedures to detect changes in the stomach or bowel wall may be required and urine samples may also be examined.

Treatment

Lastly, the diagnosis established, the hematologist often takes personal charge of the treatment. This may be as simple as a course of iron tablets, followed by a repeat blood count to ensure that an anemia has been fully corrected. It may, however, be complex, as in acute leukemia, requiring admission to the hospital, the provision of blood and platelets for transfusion, antibiotics for control of infection and, under blood count surveillance, specific therapy for the leukemia itself. In disorders such as HEMOPHILIA, the care of the patient may need to be lifelong.

In many cases, once the diagnosis has been established and the appropriate treatment has been approved, the family physician will resume full responsibility for the patient's medical care and periodic evaluation.

Infectious diseases

Dr. Frank M. Calia

The vast majority of cases of infectious diseases can now be successfully cured with early diagnosis and treatment. Most microorganisms are harmless or even beneficial to man. Those few which are not, can have devastating effects if uncontrolled, and are of special interest to the expert on infectious diseases. The following article discusses some of the features of infectious diseases and how modern medical science has learned to control them.

As part of the human condition, man must live in an environment inhabited by many living organisms. Some are so small as to be invisible to the naked eye; because of their size, they are known as *microorganisms* or *microbes*. For the most part, man lives in harmony with these microorganisms, many of which colonize his skin and gastrointestinal and respiratory tracts. Indeed, the majority are beneficial—producing antibiotics or vitamins, or contributing to many of the biological processes on which human survival depends. Only a very small percentage are capable of causing diseases and are therefore called *pathogenic;* the diseases they cause are known as infectious diseases. These organisms invade our bodies from the surrounding environment, either from other infected individuals, animals, insects or inanimate objects (for example, contaminated needles, bed linen or water).

A multitude of infectious diseases, some currently rare, such as plague, smallpox and yellow fever, as well as more common ones such as measles, tuberculosis, malaria and cholera, have literally determined the course of history; the outcome of critical battles has often been decided by the number of combatants brought down by these diseases. The potential effect on population migrations, national economies and work forces is obvious.

The development of the microscope and its application to clinical medicine finally led scientists to the cause of many of these infectious illnesses. In the 1800s, men such as Louis Pasteur and Robert Koch clarified the role of microorganisms in causing this group of diseases.

Early contributions of microbiology

Despite the identification of the infectious nature of many of these illnesses, initially the only means of control were public health measures. In 1847, a Hungarian physician, Ignaz Semmelweis, demonstrated that physicians could dramatically reduce the incidence of puerperal fever (caused by a bacterium known as the *Streptococcus*) by washing their hands prior to delivering infants. Puerperal fever was almost invariably fatal and was a leading cause of maternal mortality. It was a common practice for physicians to go from the autopsy table to the maternity ward without so much as a hand wash. In 1854, John Snow removed the handle of a commonly used water pump in London and was able to abate a major epidemic of cholera. The local water supply had been heavily contaminated by the microbe that causes that disease.

The process of vaccination was developed by Edward Jenner in 1796, and this was a major breakthrough in control of infectious diseases. He noted that dairy maids who acquired a minor illness (cowpox) from cows were protected from smallpox. Both diseases are caused by closely related viruses. Infection with cowpox induced immunity in the individual to the smallpox virus. This same process is used today in many types of vaccines; the microbe is weakened (attenuated) or killed, or a closely related one, as with smallpox, is used to induce immunity. Occasionally a product of the organism is used, rather than the organism itself, to induce immunity. Such products are usually involved in the pathologic disease process and are called *toxins;* prior to use in a vaccine they are altered chemically so as not to induce diseases. These altered toxins, called *toxoids*, are still capable of inducing immunity. It was not until the early 1900s that the requisite technology was available to allow medical investigators to develop a variety of vaccines.

Discovery of drugs to combat bacterial infection

In 1935, Domagk discovered the first major sulfa drug. He noted that this drug could kill microbes that cause certain infections. This major discovery ushered in the era of *antimicrobials*, drugs that killed or stopped the growth of microbes, so that infected patients could recuperate. In 1929, penicillin was discovered in a British laboratory by Sir Alexander Fleming, but it was not until 1940 that it was used to treat a patient—an English policeman who was infected with a bacterium known as *Staphylococcus aureus*. Although he eventually died of his infection, it was clear that the drug had a salutary effect. At present, there are several dozen antimicrobials available that have been developed to combat many of the infectious diseases of man and these drugs have revolutionized the practice of medicine. (See also *Drugs to treat infections* in the major article **Drugs and Medicines**.)

The subspecialty of infectious diseases, an offshoot of the specialty of internal medicine, is a relatively recent development. Physicians trained in this subspecialty are skilled in identifying specific infectious agents, diagnosing infectious diseases, and tailoring treatment of these illnesses.

DEATHS DUE TO INFECTIOUS DISEASES

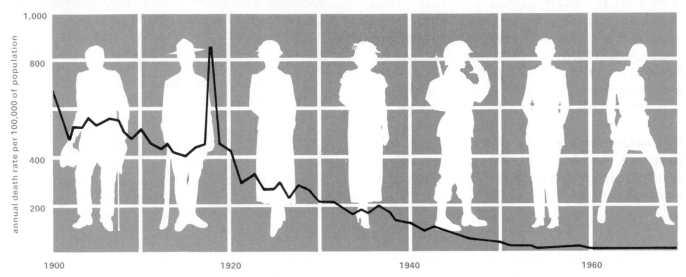

The graph shows the dramatic decline in the importance of infectious diseases as a cause of death in the United States during this century. This decline owes more to improvements in sanitation than it does to advances in medicine—antibiotics were not in general use before 1940. The 1918 peak was due to the "Swine flu" pandemic.

MAJOR CAUSES OF DEATH

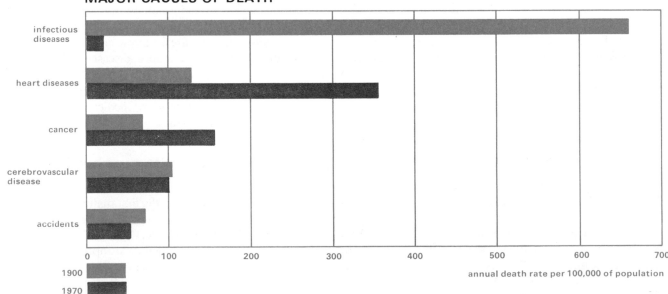

This chart compares the principal causes of death in the United States in 1900 and 1970. Longer life expectancy, which in part results from the control of infectious diseases, means that more people now reach the age where they are at risk of dying from heart diseases and cancer. Strict comparisons between 1900 and 1970 are impossible because public records and diagnostic categories have changed over the years: this probably accounts for the apparent decrease in the incidence of cerebrovascular disease.

Types of microorganism

The classification of microbes is based on size of the organism, its morphology or shape, the way it reproduces and the place within the host in which it commonly resides. The following group of organisms contain certain ones which may be pathogenic for man.

PARASITES include a number of members of the animal kingdom including *helminths* (worms) and *protozoa* (single-celled organisms). Common examples of helminthic infections include tapeworm infestation (teniasis), schistosomiasis and trichinosis. Malaria and amoebic dysentery are examples of protozoan diseases.

BACTERIA account for many infectious diseases, including streptococcal sore throat, typhoid fever, cholera, bacillary dysentery, tuberculosis, many of the pneumonias, meningitis, whooping cough, tetanus, diphtheria, boils, rheumatic fever, middle-ear infections, etc.

Examples of *fungi* which cause disease in man are organisms such as *Candida albicans* (see CANDIDA) which causes thrush and *Coccidioides immitis* (see COCCIDIOIDOMYCOSIS), the cause of valley fever.

RICKETTSIAE are very small organisms, intermediate in size between bacteria and viruses, which live within the cells of infected individuals. Diseases caused by these microbes include Rocky Mountain spotted fever and typhus fever.

Three different genera of *spirochetes* (spiral-shaped microbes) can cause disease in man: *Borrelia*, *Treponema* and *Leptospira*. Various species of *Borrelia* cause relapsing fever; the species *Treponema pallidum* causes syphilis; organisms of the genus *Leptospira* cause leptospirosis.

The smallest microbes known to infest man are the VIRUSES, which may cause the common cold, influenza, yellow fever, smallpox, chickenpox, measles, rubella, polio, hepatitis, etc. The latter organisms are so small that they cannot be seen with the commonly used light microscope. Only with the development of the electron microscope have these organisms been identified in infected tissue.

Currently available antimicrobials have activity against many of these microbes, including parasites, bacteria, rickettsiae, spirochetes and fungi. Only recently have drugs been developed that are active against viruses; for the most part, however, these drugs remain experimental. The commonly used antibiotics are ineffective against these organisms.

The specialty of infectious diseases

The classification of an infectious disease may be based on the *causative organism* (e.g., measles—caused by the measles virus) or on the *organ involved* (e.g., pneumonia—infection of the lung which may be caused by certain bacteria, viruses, rickettsiae, protozoa or fungi). Specialists in infectious diseases, therefore, encounter a great variety of clinical syndromes. Such physicians must be capable of using a number of sophisticated procedures, must be intimately familiar with the large number of antimicrobials available, must be able to select the optimal drug for the specific organism involved, must decide the duration of therapy and must try to anticipate and prevent potential side effects of any drugs used.

The specialty of infectious diseases has a relatively small membership and most experts in this field are concentrated at referral hospitals, the majority being in university hospitals. Usually they are not involved in primary patient care but serve as consultants. Typically, an infectious diseases specialist following medical school serves an internship and two years of residency training in internal medicine. This is followed by two more years of subspecialty training in infectious diseases. Trainees in the subspecialty gain clinical experience and learn to perform and interpret laboratory procedures to aid in the diagnosis and treatment of infectious illnesses. Following this training, they are eligible for board certification in both internal medicine and infectious diseases. Because the subspecialty is a very rapidly changing one—as a consequence of the ongoing development of new pharmacologic agents, the identification of previously unknown pathogenic microbes (as in LEGIONNAIRE'S DISEASE) and the refinement of diagnostic procedures—the specialist must keep abreast of these changes.

A number of continuing education activities are offered throughout the year and most subspecialists in this field attend meetings sponsored by the American Society of Microbiology and the Infectious Diseases Society of America. Papers are presented at these meetings by investigators from universities, research foundations and the pharmaceutical industry. In this way, newly generated information in the subspecialty is rapidly disseminated to the practicing subspecialist.

Referral to a specialist

A patient may be referred to an infectious diseases specialist under a number of circumstances. Typical patients may have a life-threatening infectious illness, have an illness which appears to be infectious but in which the cause is not readily apparent or may be infected with an organism that requires the use of very potent antibiotics. Consultation may also be requested when a serious drug side effect is suspected or is anticipated. On occasion, patients may have to receive potent and potentially toxic drugs and endure their side effects because the disease itself is devastating and poses a direct threat to life.

Initially, the subspecialist will repeat the process of history taking and perform a physical examination. In order to be a competent subspecialist, the "infectionist" must first be a very skilled internist. Many noninfectious diseases mimic infectious ones. A subspecialist in infectious diseases must be able to make this distinction in the patient.

If the illness is indeed infectious, he must carry out or recommend the necessary diagnostic laboratory procedures to identify the causative organism. An analysis and examination of various body fluids under the microscope—such as spinal fluid, urine, blood or pus, which have been stained with one of several bacterial stains—may identify the causative microbe. Identification of organisms by their microscopic appearance must always be confirmed in the laboratory by growing (culturing) the microbe on specific laboratory material (culture media) or in animals. Because the growth requirements of microbes vary, the specialists must recommend specific culture media or animals depending on the species of organism suspected.

Diagnosis and treatment

A number of blood tests measure the body's response to infection, usually indicated by a rise in certain blood proteins called *antibodies* (see ANTIBODY/ANTIGEN). The specialist may suggest specific antibody tests and then interpret their results. Occasionally, the laboratory depends on the subspecialist to identify an isolated organism with unusual growth characteristics or to assist in pinning down an organism which is difficult to isolate. Blood levels of antimicrobials are occasionally measured, especially when there is any question that they may accumulate in the blood and reach toxic levels.

All drugs are potentially dangerous; this is especially true of antibiotics. Patients with kidney or liver disease may accumulate drugs in gross excess of the therapeutic level

Starting in the latter part of the 19th century, immigrants to the United States began to be checked routinely for any evidence of infectious diseases. These early control measures were often ineffective, however, except in the most obvious cases. Doctors at the time were aware of the causes of many infectious diseases, but sophisticated diagnostic techniques had yet to be developed.

required. This may lead to the development of side effects, including hearing loss, vertigo, kidney damage, anemia, etc. The subspecialist may recommend sampling of the blood to measure levels of drug for this reason, or in order to ensure that the drugs administered are reaching a proper or therapeutic level. An inadequate dose of antibiotic may be a cause of treatment failure. Occasionally, patients will have reactions to drugs other than from the direct toxic effects. These reactions are idiosyncratic and cannot be predicted; they are usually allergic in nature and are called *hypersensitivity reactions*. The subspecialist may be called upon to identify and treat these reactions, which can range from relatively trivial ones such as minor drug rashes to the life-threatening state known as ANAPHYLACTIC SHOCK.

Typically, when a patient is referred to him, the subspecialist assists in making the diagnosis and recommending appropriate therapy, including antibiotics, if indicated. The actual treatment is usually administered by the referring physician. Occasionally the patient has a change in the infecting organism. This is called a *superinfection;* it must be identified early in the course of therapy and necessary changes in antibiotic therapy made.

Signs and symptoms

The symptoms of infection are numerous, but perhaps fever is the most common. Rashes also are common and may be specific for the causative organism, e.g., measles or chickenpox. Most symptoms are related to the organ system involved. For example, patients with pneumonia commonly have a cough which produces a rust-colored sputum, and sharp chest pain which worsens on coughing and unusually deep breathing. Patients with infections of the urinary tract frequently have an increase in urinary frequency, burning on urination and may have blood or pus in their urine. In addition to high fever, patients with meningitis have severe headache, a stiff neck and, occasionally, seizures.

The majority of infectious diseases respond well to early diagnosis and treatment and are easily handled by a primary care physician. It is only the more complicated or esoteric ones that require a subspecialist. Obviously any patient with a very high fever, with or without a headache or a stiff neck, severe chest or abdominal pain or a rash should immediately consult his physician. Newborn infants do not manifest the same response to infection as older children and adults. Severe infection may merely be reflected by failure to eat, listlessness, or regurgitation of food. When these symptoms occur in the first few weeks of life, a pediatrician should be consulted immediately.

Prevention and control

The patient and his family may help in many ways in controlling infectious illnesses. Diseases which may easily be prevented and controlled—such as polio, whooping cough, measles and German measles (rubella)—continue to plague the United States because people still fail to insure that all family members are appropriately vaccinated. Effective vaccines are currently available that will prevent diphtheria, whooping cough, tetanus, measles, mumps and rubella. Smallpox has finally been controlled and vaccination against the causative organism is no longer recommended in the United States. Travelers to foreign countries may be exposed to diseases that are uncommon in the United States but are endemic in those countries. Such people should consult their physician well in advance of the trip and receive appropriate vaccinations. Diseases such as yellow fever occasionally infect the traveler, but may be prevented with an effective vaccine. International travelers may also be exposed to malaria, which is easily prevented. Although a vaccine directed against this organism is not available, low doses of the drugs used to treat this infection will prevent the disease (prophylaxis). Finally, travelers should exert discretion in their eating habits while in foreign countries.

Patients and their families may help in other ways as well. A common cause of treatment failure is simply failure of the patient to take a prescribed medication; careful compliance is especially important in infected patients for whom antibiotics have been prescribed.

Finally, patients and their families should practice simple measures of public health, which will often prevent the spread of infection within the family. In the main, tuberculosis may be treated in the home rather than the sanatorium because powerful drugs are available to cure the disease and prevent the spread of infection. The patient must take care when coughing (cover his mouth) and dispose carefully of any sputum produced during the infection. Since many diseases are transmitted by fecal contamination, including the infectious diarrheas, salmonellosis and hepatitis, patients so infected should take special care to wash their hands following bowel movements and should not be involved in food handling.

Choice of antibiotics

The most commonly used antibiotics are the *penicillins*—several types exist. Each type has a specific spectrum of activity directed against specific bacteria. These are widely used and are among the safest of drugs; however, some patients are allergic to the penicillins and occasionally the allergic patient may have a severe reaction. Rashes are common reactions to the penicillins and for the most part are minor irritations. The presence of URTICARIA ("hives"), on the other hand, may signal a potentially serious drug reaction and warrants immediate cessation of the drug and prompt consultation with a physician. *Cephalosporins* are a closely related family of drugs and are also relatively safe. The *tetracyclines* are commonly used to

treat a number of infectious illnesses and are considered to be "broad-spectrum" drugs. Drug rashes and occasionally vertigo have been the most common side effects of this family of drugs. *Chloramphenicol* is no longer commonly used, although it is a very powerful and effective drug when used for the proper indications. Because it occasionally causes an unusual form of bone marrow depression, it should be used only in severe infections.

A family of potent antimicrobials called *aminoglycosides* are commonly used in the moderately to severely ill patient. These drugs include *streptomycin*; *neomycin, kanamycin, gentamycin* and *tobramycin*. The reaction rate is low when dosage is determined with care, but occasionally damage may occur to hearing and to the kidneys. Previous kidney disease may predispose to these complications. However, if the dose is carefully adjusted and the blood level maintained at a nontoxic range, these drugs can be given with relative safety.

Clindamycin is a drug that is now commonly used in the United States. In a small percentage of cases its use has been identified with a syndrome called *pseudomembranous colitis*. Any patient receiving this drug who develops diarrhea should immediately contact his physician.

ANTIBIOTIC TEST DISK

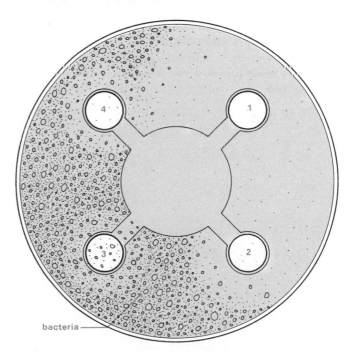

bacteria

This is a simple technique for testing the effectiveness of new antibiotic drugs against specific bacteria. The plate is "seeded" with bacteria and the four disks are impregnated with different antibiotics. An effective antibiotic (1) clears the surrounding bacterial growth, while the bacteria are relatively undisturbed by an ineffective drug (3). Other drugs (2, 4) are only partially successful.

Isoniazid, a drug which is extremely effective in treating tuberculosis, may rarely induce hepatitis. Patients who develop weakness, fatigue, listlessness and diarrhea or jaundice while taking this drug should immediately contact their physician.

When possible, the causative organism should be identified because not all antibiotics have the same spectrum of activity. For example, penicillin may be effective in treating pneumonia but it is not effective in treating tuberculosis. Medicine in general has been a victim of its own success. It is not uncommon for patients to have some familiarity with drugs and demand them of their physician despite the fact that their use would be totally inappropriate for the infection that the patient has. A common practice is for a patient with a cold to demand a "shot of penicillin" from his family physician. Penicillin is totally ineffective against the viruses that cause the common cold. In addition, this practice exposes the patient needlessly to penicillin and might ultimately sensitize him to this drug. The danger in such cases is that in the event he eventually needs penicillin to treat a more serious infection, he cannot receive this group of drugs because he is allergic to them.

Research and development

Much research on infectious diseases is being conducted at universities, foundations and pharmaceutical houses. Ways are now being developed to facilitate their diagnosis, to identify more rapidly their causative organisms and to aid in selecting appropriate antimicrobials. New drugs are being evaluated, although the major breakthrough has to be the development of drugs directed against viral infections.

Antiviral drugs currently available tend to be very toxic and for that reason are only used in the most grave of situations. Certain well-localized viral infections (such as infections of the cornea) may be treated with these drugs topically, as they are not absorbed. However, major generalized viral infections must be treated with drugs administered in such a way that adequate blood levels are achieved and, unfortunately, these drugs tend to be too toxic. Encouraging preliminary work has been published that would suggest that safe antiviral drugs are on the horizon.

Follow the exact instructions of your physician

One final word about the use of oral antibiotics that your doctor prescribes and you take at home. Often symptoms disappear within a day or two and patients feel they are no longer needed. Many antibiotics prescribed today have been tested against specific microorganisms and the time determined that is required for the drug to totally destroy them. If they are only partially killed your symptoms may go away, but many of the organisms may still be alive to survive and develop resistance to that particular antibiotic. This is thought to account for the many strains of bacteria that are unaffected by drugs that formerly used to destroy them in a single injected dose. Thus, it is essential to follow your physician's instructions to the letter.

Rheumatology   Dr. John H. Bland

Painful diseases of the bones, joints and muscles—while rarely fatal—affect an estimated 20 million people in the United States alone. The rheumatologist is concerned with the diagnosis and treatment of these diseases.

Rheumatology is that subspecialty of internal medicine concerned with the body's bones, joints and muscles, with the 104 officially recognized diseases that afflict them, and with research to find better ways to treat, cure or control these diseases. The rheumatologist is concerned not only with diagnosis, treatment and research, but also with public education to help people recognize the symptoms and dangers of rheumatic diseases, which now afflict 20 million Americans, with a new victim claimed every 52 seconds.

Few die as a result of rheumatic disease, but many without early and adequate treatment may face a lifetime of pain and increasing disability as well as emotional and economic disaster. A young mother afflicted with rheumatoid arthritis may develop pain and swelling of her joints, her muscles become weak, wasting occurs, deformity follows in the absence of proper medical treatment, and her marriage may dissolve because she can no longer manage her home and children. A young girl may be afflicted with systemic LUPUS ERYTHEMATOSUS and develop fever, painful joints and skin symptoms, and her family faces the ordeal of raising a child doomed to invalidism and a lifetime of suffering. A 70-year-old man becomes incapacitated with OSTEOARTHRITIS and sees his life's savings wiped out. A skilled craftsman develops crippling ARTHRITIS of his hands, loses his job, and must go on welfare. Disease alone does not create these social casualties; their already bleak future is compounded by the socioeconomic impact of chronic illness (see also the major article on **Health Care of the Elderly**).

Arthritis

Arthritis—which by common consent among doctors is the term now officially used to describe the 104 known diseases that affect bone, muscle and joint—has now replaced the word "rheumatism," used for centuries. It is not used to designate a specific disease, but means inflammation of a joint resulting from any cause.

By whatever name it is known, arthritis is probably one of the most ancient diseases known to man and animals. It has been recognized in the bones of dinosaurs and swimming reptiles that lived 180 million years ago, and in the bones of Neanderthal man. From the time before Hippocrates until the late 19th century, all rheumatic disease was regarded by doctors as GOUT. In 1787 William Hyde Wollaston (1766–1828) first connected uric acid with gout. In 1848 Alfred Baring Garrod thought there were differences among rheumatic diseases, and he developed the first test for gout that clearly separated it from a disease he called "rheumatic gout." In 1857 he proposed the term *rheumatoid arthritis* to describe this other kind of gout. For centuries the victims of arthritic disease looked upon their afflictions as another burden to be accepted, hoping for the periods of remission that sometimes came.

It was not until the end of World War II that modern rheumatology was born, when doctors began to understand the differences between the various forms of arthritis, due to a wide variety of disease processes, including degenerative, inflammatory, infectious, biochemical, metabolic and allergic reactions. It was learned that trauma could lead to arthritis, and that genetic inheritances might make some people more prone to certain types of arthritis.

We now know that of the 20 million Americans who suffer arthritis requiring medical attention, 15 per 1,000 are under age 45 and 154 per 1,000 are between 45 and 65. The prevalence is higher among women of all ages, higher among blacks than whites, and higher among low-income groups than high-income groups.

Background and training of rheumatologists

There are presently only about 1,000 certified rheumatologists practicing in the United States (or 1 for every 20,000 patients), most of them serving in teaching hospitals, medical centers, and as members of a group practice. Some rheumatologists may practice both internal medicine and rheumatology.

The rheumatologist qualifies for certification in his specialty by four years of medical college, four years of internship and residency training and experience in internal medicine, followed by an additional two years or more of clinical training and experience in all areas of rheumatology. He can then seek certification by passing the extensive oral and written examinations given by the American Board of Rheumatology, in which case he becomes a diplomate of that examining board.

Because of the limited number of rheumatologists available, patients with arthritis must look to the family

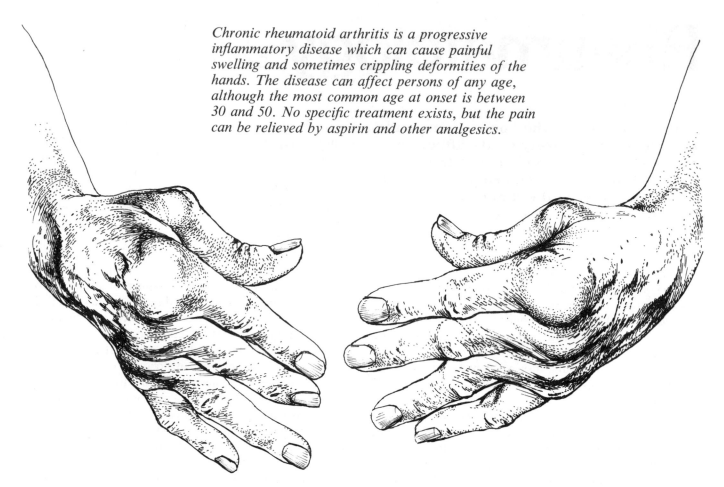

Chronic rheumatoid arthritis is a progressive inflammatory disease which can cause painful swelling and sometimes crippling deformities of the hands. The disease can affect persons of any age, although the most common age at onset is between 30 and 50. No specific treatment exists, but the pain can be relieved by aspirin and other analgesics.

doctor for most of their professional care. Family doctors see so much arthritis among their patients that they become competent in diagnosing and treating most of their patients. However, in more serious cases, the general physician may recognize a need for diagnostic and management assistance and refer his patient to a rheumatologist for his evaluation and recommendations. The rheumatologist's role is to examine the patient carefully, carry out special diagnostic tests and studies, then formulate an individualized treatment plan. In most cases, this will be sent to the referring doctor, who will usually resume management of the patient. In more serious cases the patient's regular doctor may want the rheumatologist to provide specialized treatment until the patient improves. The relationship between the rheumatologist and the referring physician should be a free and understanding one, with the patient understanding that it is quite proper to ask for referral back to the rheumatologist, should the patient feel that his course is not progressing satisfactorily.

Diagnostic procedures

The most important aspects of diagnosis in arthritic disease are a detailed medical history and a careful physical examination, with emphasis on bones, muscles and joints. A review of body systems—gastrointestinal, cardiopulmonary, musculoskeletal, and neurological—is made. Of particular interest will be past illnesses that have required medical treatment, drugs you have taken and are currently taking (some drugs can cause arthritis and need only be withdrawn or changed to effect a cure), recent and past infections, metabolic and familial diseases, and your socioeconomic situation. You should be prepared to present in detail the history of your first symptoms of arthritis, and then describe their progress to the present time.

Many routine blood tests and pathological studies will be carried out; typical routine tests include a complete blood count, urinalysis, and ERYTHROCYTE SEDIMENTATION RATE. Special blood studies of cells and tissues, hormonal levels, enzymes, joint fluid and antibodies may be done; all will help confirm or rule out specific diseases the doctor might suspect from the history and physical examination. The presence of "rheumatoid factor," though not always specific, will help confirm a diagnosis of rheumatoid arthritis, the most crippling and deforming of all arthritic diseases.

The presence of too many or too few red and white blood cells, antibodies, hormonal imbalances and many other factors will not only offer strong diagnostic clues for specific diseases, but identify systemic conditions that may be complicating factors and must be dealt with. Tests for the presence of two types of crystal—*monosodium urate* (which secures a diagnosis of gout) and *calcium pyrophosphate dihydrate* (which confirms the diagnosis of CHONDROCALCINOSIS or "pseudogout") will usually be made.

A part of the body's immunological system contains 14 proteins, which can be measured in blood serum, and they tell the physician much about the severity of a disease process. An *electromyogram* may be used to evaluate muscle disease and strength potential. A small specimen of muscle tissue may also be removed for microscopic examination and other tests.

Radiological examinations are of utmost importance for evaluating bone diseases and anatomical deformities. A technique called *scanning* may be used to identify early inflammatory disease. Dyes are sometimes instilled into joints to obtain an x-ray called an *arthrogram*, which can tell much about their structures. ARTHROSCOPY—direct viewing of an inner joint with an illuminated light instrument—is sometimes used, but is rarely necessary. THERMOGRAPHY may be used to measure joint temperature, which normally is much lower than in other parts of the body, ranging from about 88° to 92°F.

The nature of connective tissues

Connective tissues—the materials that hold our bodies together: skin, bone, muscle, tendon, cartilage and fascia—are mechanical and living systems that provide environment for cells, and all provide support, mechanical strength and compliance in proper proportion to the parts of the body. Thus, we are all made of "composite materials," a term used by engineers that means a mixture of fiber, stuffing and binding material, as in prestressed concrete.

In living tissue the fiber is a protein called *collagen*, which, when its molecules are aggregated, has high tensile strength (tendons have a tensile strength equal to that of a steel wire of similar size). The other component is a gel material made of large molecules called *polysaccharides*, which are rich in water and salt. The gel-fiber ratio in a given tissue is equal to its functional needs. For example, a tendon requiring great strength will be mostly fiber, but cartilage (a "bearing") which is required to take tremendous loads, will contain more polysaccharide in which the water is so tightly bound that it makes an ideal slippery bearing surface. (See also COLLAGEN DISEASES.)

The muscles
MUSCLE is a most remarkable tissue. Its cells are able to shorten on demand and propel bones and joints in appropriate directions. Muscles are normally maintained in good running order, even with a great deal of abuse and mistreatment. Their efficiency depends very much upon tiny amounts of calcium being pumped in and out with each contraction.

We are born with our total number of muscle cells and will receive no more, because they cannot divide once they are established as muscles. Muscles have the ability to increase in size with hard use and exercise, but of great importance to arthritis patients is knowledge that they can also waste away (atrophy) when not adequately used. Many problems of arthritis and the process of aging are a result of the inadequate use of muscles day to day.

The bones
BONE can be described as constructed like a lattice, with its meshlike spaces filled in with a special kind of collagen, into which minerals are deposited—calcium and a calcium salt called *hydroxyapatite*. These give bone its hardness and compliance. Bone is constantly being formed (remodeled) and degraded. Bone is much more dynamic, metabolically and biochemically, than is generally appreciated; it has plasticity but, like muscle, is maintained at its required strength only by use. Wolff's old law says that bone will alter its size and shape in compliance with the mechanical forces exerted upon it. That is a fact we take advantage of in the maintenance of normal bone. Three hormones are also essential to normal bone maintenance (parathyroid hormone, calcitonin and vitamin D, a hormone-like substance); deficiencies of these substances, complicated by disuse, can cause bone to thin and atrophy.

A joint is made up of cartilage, one half collagen and the other half polysaccharide; the *synovium* (the membrane lining of the joint) and the *articular capsule* (a high tensile strength tissue that holds together the bones) make up a joint.

Cartilage
CARTILAGE contains comparatively few cells and has no blood supply, nor does it need one. In fact, if it does receive blood it can no longer function as cartilage. However, it has unique chemical and biological properties which permit it to function as joint bearings over the years, with a slippery surface that is superior to any produced by man-made lubricants. A major goal in therapy is to maintain cartilage efficiency, because once it is destroyed it cannot be replaced. Synovium has a massive blood supply and its small blood vessels are frequent sites of inflammatory disease. Bone and joints normally have a remarkable ability to repair themselves and new cells are produced as needed within the bone marrow.

Signs and symptoms of arthritis

The signs and symptoms of most forms of arthritis are quite similar, and in some only the rheumatologist can differentiate between them. Many of the following symptoms common in arthritis are also common in other conditions unrelated to arthritis. However, a good policy to follow is to seek medical evaluation of any symptom, or combination of symptoms, that does not go away within a few days or, at most, a few weeks. A painful, red and swollen joint calls for immediate medical attention.

Fever, ease of fatigue, loss of appetite and weight, accompanied by joint pain, if not otherwise explained, suggest arthritis. Important signs are: *hair changes* (thinning, fineness and silkiness of texture); *skin changes* (rashes, dryness and tightness, diffused deposits, and patches of discoloration); *anemia* (present in most forms of arthritis); and disturbances of vision accompanied by redness, swelling and deposits in the cornea. Loss of balance and dizziness is also common in developing and advanced arthritis.

Pain, however, is the most common symptom. Recurring pain in the back, especially in its lower area; SCIATICA (pain at the back of the thighs and buttocks, often radiating down the legs); stiffness of joints upon awakening, but passing as the patient becomes active, are all important symptoms. The same is true of disturbances in sleep patterns, due in most cases to discomfort or pain upon changing positions. Pain in the neck and shoulders are common in "soft tissue rheumatism." Pain over the balls of the feet and during the fine movements of the hands when sewing, writing, or using tools are often the first symptoms arthritic patients may notice, because all are so important in daily activities.

Therapeutic approaches

Just as the symptoms of arthritis are similar in many diseases, so are methods of treatment. Many forms of arthritis are of unknown origin and have no cure, but can be controlled with careful, lifelong management. Patients must never be led to believe that treatment can accomplish more than is possible to attain, and they must be made to understand why certain things must be done—however painful, annoying, or disruptive to normal routines they may be. The major goals of therapy are to cure when possible, to induce and maintain remissions, and maintain maximum treatment during acute periods to avoid deformities and crippling. Some diseases, such as gout, can be effectively controlled simply by taking regular medications; even the most crippling diseases can now be satisfactorily managed, if we do everything we now know how to do.

Physical and emotional rest is a most important part of therapy. Home and family situations must be examined, then every effort made to make parents and spouses aware of how important their support of the patient is to successful treatment. If physical and emotional rest cannot be provided at home, the patient may have to be hospitalized to make certain it is received. Hospitalization may also be required in acute phases of disease, when physical therapy and occupational therapy must be carried out with the use of special equipment by trained personnel.

In no other area of medicine is the "do-it-yourself" principle more important than in arthritis. The patient must follow rest prescriptions (rest one hour for every four hours of activity, but when up and about, go as hard as you can); medicines must be taken exactly as prescribed, and any adverse effects resulting from them must be reported to the doctor immediately. Prescribed exercises, just as important as rest, must be carried out exactly as ordered, no matter how painful they may be at times.

All forms of heat are used in treating arthritis, moist and dry heat, using tub baths, infrared lamps and Hubbard tanks. Ultrasound treatments are also useful. Certain posture exercises may be ordered to bring into play specific joints and muscles. Splints and braces are used, if needed, to ease pain and prevent deformities. In acute phases of a disease, canes, walkers, wheelchairs and other aids may be provided, but generally are used only until therapy reaches a point where they will no longer be needed.

Drug therapy

Aspirin and sodium salicylate are the most widely prescribed and the most effective drugs used in arthritis. About 15% of patients may suffer stomach irritation from the required dosage levels, but this is often overcome by crushing the tablets in milk and then blending them in a mixer before taking them. Dosage is established by increasing dosage until tinnitus (ringing in the ears) develops. The dosage is then decreased, one tablet at a time, until the tinnitus is relieved. Fortunately, this commonly coincides with the proper level to provide effective pharmacologic action. The tablets are taken in divided doses at six-hour intervals—the time it takes for the chemical ingredients to be removed naturally from the blood. (See also *Drugs for the relief of pain or inflammation* in the major article **Drugs and Medicines**.)

Gold compounds, long used in the treatment of arthritis, are still among the most effective for inducing and maintaining remissions in rheumatoid arthritis and other types of progressive disease. However, they are contraindicated in patients with kidney or liver disease, because of their high potential toxicity.

Antimalarial drugs are effectively used in the treatment of rheumatoid arthritis and lupus erythematosus.

Indomethacin is an effective analgesic and anti-inflammatory agent, but may produce side effects in some patients.

Phenylbutazone (Butazolidin) is an effective anti-inflammatory agent and is used intermittently, but it may produce potentially serious side effects. Periodic blood tests are given to patients on long-term therapy.

The *corticosteroid* family of drugs (e.g., prednisone) are among the most effective anti-inflammatory agents and are cautiously used in small doses for short periods to maintain joint motion, especially during acute episodes of a disease.

There are several new noncortisone drugs now being

used experimentally as anti-inflammatory agents, but their place in therapy is not yet firmly established.

Most of the drugs now commonly used are well-understood; so if one cannot be tolerated because of side effects, another can be substituted.

Orthopedic surgery also plays an important role in the treatment of arthritis. Removal of the joint lining membrane is the most commonly performed procedure, and this may improve function in a severely damaged joint. Total joint replacements, especially of hips and knees, are done successfully today; they can often return mobility and an improved quality of life to patients in whom all other treatments have failed and in whom there is no hope that a joint can regain function. Prosthetic joints for other parts of the body are also being developed and coming into use. (See the major article on **Orthopedics**.)

Most of the arthritic diseases can be separated into several broad groups, but space permits only a brief discussion of those major diseases which are most commonly seen.

Diseases of unknown cause

Rheumatoid arthritis (RA)
This disease is thought to afflict about 2% of the world's population, but only 10% suffer its most incapacitating manifestations. There are no climatic, cultural or environmental factors to explain its prevalence worldwide. It is a generalized disease, involving many organ systems, but is manifested locally in joints. It afflicts women three times more often than men, and is progressive in its course, leading to crippling and deformities if treatment is not carried out and maintained throughout life.

It may come on suddenly in its most acute phase, with fever, swelling of the joint and intense pain; but most often it progresses silently and insidiously, with vague aches and pains, chronic tiredness, stiffness of joints which is relieved with activity, and loss of both appetite and weight. Anemia is present in 90% of RA patients and is an important early diagnostic sign. The disease may strike at any age, but the acute phase usually occurs between the ages of 20 and 35, often during or following a period of great physical stress. It is usually symmetrical, affecting the same joints on both sides of the body—hands, wrists, elbows, hips, knees, feet.

The diagnosis is based upon the history and physical examination, and confirmed by the presence of the *rheumatoid factor* and other abnormalities to be found in the blood and joint fluids.

Treatment is directed toward controlling the patient's general health, maintaining joint function during acute phases, and inducing and prolonging remissions. Aspirin and other anti-inflammatory drugs are used in adequate dosages to control pain. Gold compounds are used to induce and prolong remissions. One or a combination of the anti-inflammatory drugs may be used, with sub-stitutions made as needed when side effects develop. Splints and braces may be used, as required, to relieve pain and prevent contractures. Prescribed periods of rest, alternated with periods of exercise and physical therapy, will be a major part of therapy. In advanced stages of the disease, orthopedic surgery may be indicated to model or remodel joint bones, with or without prosthetic replacements.

Juvenile rheumatoid arthritis
This disease, sometimes known as *Still's disease*, afflicts children and is similar in most respects to the adult form of rheumatoid arthritis; but its prognosis is much more favorable, with remissions obtained in about 75% of the children afflicted. Characteristic signs are abnormalities in growth and development. A typical birdlike facial expression is the result of improper development of bone in the lower jaw. Most commonly only the larger joints of the body are involved. The rheumatoid factor is usually negative. Anemia, infections and involvement of the spleen and lymphatic system are often complicating factors.

Because of the high incidence of remissions, treatment is directed toward providing optimal relief during the acute stage, with the application of splints when needed to prevent deformities, and physical therapy, exercises, and the use of heat to insure joint movements. Because children generally have a greater tolerance of the corticosteroid drugs, they can be used with more effectiveness in children than adults. Management following remissions calls for careful attention to infections, rest, adequate exercise, and the avoidance of stress and overactivity.

Ankylosing spondylitis
This is a chronic, progressive disease of the small joints of the spine. It is similar in its symptoms to rheumatoid arthritis (RA), but is a distinct disease entity. In contrast to RA, it most commonly afflicts young men and is truly *ankylosing* (steadily progressing toward immobility of the spine). If not detected and treated in time, it will result in gross deformity of the spine and its supporting muscles. (See ANKYLOSING SPONDYLITIS.)

The most common early symptom is pain in the lower part of the back. The diagnosis is confirmed by x-rays of the sacroiliac joints, where erosion of the bones can first be seen. It then spreads progressively to the spinal joints. If proper measures are not taken, fusion of the joints occurs and the ligaments become calcified, presenting the picture of the typical "bamboo spine." In a few patients the disease may progress until the entire spine becomes "frozen" (immobile). The results of tests for rheumatoid factor are always negative, but general treatment of the disease is similar to that of rheumatoid arthritis—the primary goal is to prevent deformity before it can occur.

Posture-maintaining exercises must be started early and continued throughout life. Gold therapy is not effective. Aspirin and salicylates are effective analgesics, and

Butazolidin is most effective in controlling symptoms, with only small doses required. Maintaining proper posture is of greatest importance, even though braces may be required; if this is accomplished, patients can expect a reasonably functional life.

Psoriatic arthritis

This condition is also similar to rheumatoid arthritis, both in symptoms and treatment, but it is found only in people who have PSORIASIS. Its active phase parallels the psoriatic activity, and controlling the psoriasis often brings a remission of arthritis symptoms. Untreated, the disease can be just as crippling as rheumatoid arthritis. The test for *rheumatoid factor* is almost always negative. The anti-malarial drugs are contraindicated because they induce peeling of the skin. Otherwise, treatment is the same as for rheumatoid arthritis. New improved therapies for controlling psoriasis offer new hope for the victims of this chronic disease.

Connective tissue disorders

Systemic lupus erythematosus

This is a most serious collagen-vascular disease, which occurs most often in young women, but can also occur in older adults as well as children. Its effects can be detected in various organs of the body as "fibrinoid deposits," but it is most obvious in the skin and joints—in which case the prognosis is much better than if its major effects are localized in the kidneys, heart, or other vital organs. (See LUPUS ERYTHEMATOSUS.)

The disease may begin abruptly, with fever and other symptoms typical of an infection. When it involves joints its effects are similar to rheumatoid arthritis. It often develops insidiously over a period of months or years, with periods of fever and general feelings of fatigue and malaise, but it eventually involves major organ systems. Inflammation of the skin, especially of the face, is common; a typical "butterfly pattern" under the eyes and over the bridge of the nose is seen in some patients.

The cause of systemic lupus erythematosus is unknown, but it is suspected to be an AUTOIMMUNE DISEASE (one in which the body becomes "allergic" to its own tissues). The diagnosis is based on the history and physical examination and is confirmed by blood studies and abnormal immuno-logical reactions. Once considered to be always fatal, new knowledge and optimal medical management started early is permitting many patients to live almost normal lives. Even those with the more serious forms of the disease are living longer and with less incapacitating periods of acute illness. Treatment for the arthritis symptoms are similar to those for rheumatoid arthritis, with general medical management of the systemic involvements. The cortico-steroid drugs are most effective, and the antimalarial drugs are helpful against skin symptoms.

Scleroderma

This disease, also known as *progressive systemic sclerosis*, is of unknown origin and characterized by thickening of the skin and involvement of the subcutaneous tissue of internal organs and joints. The skin thickens, seems to become attached to underlying structures, and may be hard to pinch up. It takes on a smooth, shiny appearance amd may become so rigid that it affects movements of the eyelids, mouth, throat and digestive tract. In its arthritis involve-ment it affects joint tendons, synovium and muscles. (See SCLERODERMA.)

The disease usually develops slowly, first showing in the skin after the age of 40, with progressive involvement of other organs. Women are afflicted more often than men. RAYNAUD'S DISEASE (in which the fingers and toes turn white upon exposure to cold) is often an early sign of scleroderma. Its usual course is marked by periods of remissions and flare-ups.

ANKYLOSING SPONDYLITIS

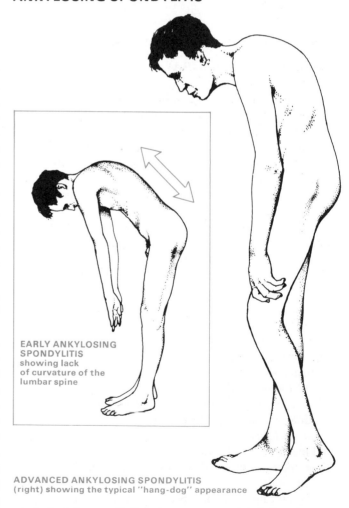

EARLY ANKYLOSING SPONDYLITIS showing lack of curvature of the lumbar spine

ADVANCED ANKYLOSING SPONDYLITIS (right) showing the typical "hang-dog" appearance

Ankylosing spondylitis is a progressive inflammatory disease that affects the spinal column. Movement is gradually limited and in severe cases the backbone may become totally rigid.

There is no known cure for the disease, but arthritis symptoms are treated much as those in rheumatoid arthritis, with special attention given to avoid deformities of the lower extremities, which results from skin contractures and inflammation of muscles, tendons and synovium. Gold and antimalarial drugs are not effective, but the corticosteroids may produce dramatic results. Physical therapy is useful, but orthopedic surgery may be required to minimize or correct contractures.

Polymyositis and dermatomyositis

These terms describe aspects of a systemic disorder of connective tissue that results in inflammatory and degenerative changes in the skin and voluntary muscles. If skeletal muscles are predominately involved the condition is called *polymyositis*. If skin symptoms predominate it is called DERMATOMYOSITIS. The cause is unknown but the condition often follows serious infections. It most often occurs in females between the ages of 10 and 50. Onset is often abrupt, with fever, skin rashes and painfully inflamed muscles; or it may develop slowly, with feelings of chronic tiredness, gradual weakening of muscle groups, and mild scaling of the skin and slight evidence of pigmentation.

The similarity between this disorder and others (especially systemic lupus erythematosus) makes the diagnosis difficult and patients are often referred to a rheumatologist for evaluation. Studies of muscle tissue, muscle enzymes and muscle electrical activity help to confirm the diagnosis.

Treatment is directed toward inducing remissions, which are sometimes permanent. Heat therapy and splinting to immobilize painful muscles are carried out. Anti-inflammatory drugs are prescribed, together with aspirin and sedatives to control pain, but care is taken to avoid dependence upon sedatives. Rest is of great importance.

Osteoarthritis

This form of arthritis is the most common in man and other animals. Often accurately described as "wear and tear arthritis," it was once thought to be due entirely to aging, but we now know it to be a progressive degenerative disease. Most of us have signs of it in our bones by age 30, but unless there is serious injury to a joint, symptoms do not usually appear before age 40. Women are affected more than men, most often after the menopause. One form of the disease may occur in young adults and is thought to be associated with genetic inheritances.

The degenerative process involves a steady thinning of the joint cartilage which provides the slippery weight-bearing surface of the leg joints. There are no nerve receptors in cartilage, so the degenerative process goes on unnoticed until the cartilage is worn away and the bones overgrow and rub together. Trauma affecting cartilage, obesity, aging and perhaps some types of occupation are predisposing factors. Unlike rheumatoid arthritis and ankylosing spondylitis, it is not totally crippling, unless hip joint function is totally destroyed.

Symptoms

The most common symptoms are stiffness and pain, which is greater during rest than during exercise. The pain may become especially troublesome at night. If severe degeneration continues the pain may eventually become constant and be intensified by muscle spasms. The process is not marked by flare-ups and remissions. Involvement of spinal joints, especially those in the neck and lower spine, may cause much pain and impair movements of turning and bending as the result of the formation of bony spurs that may press on nerve roots.

Treatment

Weight reduction is very important in overweight patients who have an involvement of the weight-bearing joints. Aspirin is the most effective analgesic and should be given in maximum dosage to control pain. Indomethacin (Indocin) is also helpful in some patients in relieving pain and improving movements. The application of heat, either dry or moist, is effective in providing temporary relief. Hot and cold applications are helpful to control pain in the hands. The hands should be placed in warm water for four minutes then cold water for one minute, with the procedure continued for 15 minutes; this should be repeated two or three times a day.

Although there is no known way to restore an osteoarthritic joint to its once youthful function, much can be done to retard progress of the disease. Physical therapy, followed by regular exercises, strengthens muscles and prevents their wasting. Adequate rest and avoidance of stress are also important. Injections of cortisone directly into joints can relieve pain for long periods, but corticosteroid drugs should not be taken orally, because of their systemic effects. Bracing devices for the knees and spine are helpful. Neck collars and traction may relieve pain that radiates from pinched nerves in neck joints (*cervical radiculitis, cervical neuralgia*).

Most of us with OSTEOARTHRITIS learn to live with it, using simple measures to control pain and stiffness. But in some persons the disease process, especially in hip and knee joints, may progress to the point of total incapacitation. An estimated 65,000 Americans are so afflicted that they are unable to use the bathroom on their own. Others are unable to continue in their jobs. For many of these patients, *arthroplasty* (surgery to remodel joint bones, or replace them with prosthetic equivalents) is providing dramatic results. Total hip joint replacements in carefully selected patients are today returning many of them to almost normal functioning, adding greatly to their quality of life. Total knee joints are also replaced, but not as often and with less dramatic results.

Other arthritic diseases

Gout

Gout is a disorder with which most of us are familiar, usually associating it with an inflamed, "red hot" big toe; but it may affect other joints of the body, usually starting in the knee or foot. It afflicts men much more often than women, usually after the age of 30, and tends to run in families. It is caused by the overaccumulation of uric acid in the body, when the kidneys cannot remove the excess from the blood as quickly as it is produced. It is deposited in joints as tiny crystals (urate), which produce inflammation and intense pain. The pain typically comes on at night, starting with vague discomfort and progressing in intensity until no change in body position brings relief.

During the acute phase, the affected leg should be elevated and supported by pillows. Colchicine, an old but very effective drug, is used by injection to induce

ACUTE GOUT

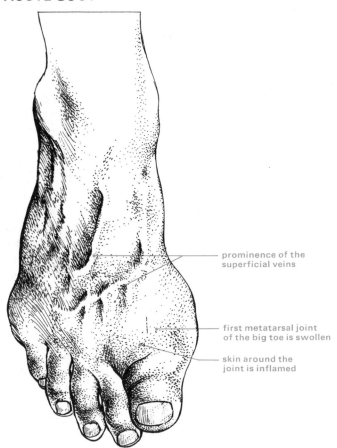

prominence of the superficial veins

first metatarsal joint of the big toe is swollen

skin around the joint is inflamed

In acute cases of gout (or gouty arthritis) the joint of the big toe is commonly affected, causing a characteristic inflammatory reaction and excruciating pain. Other joints may also be affected. The development of modern drugs has made it possible to relieve the symptoms and in most cases to avoid subsequent attacks.

remissions, which can be maintained by two drugs, probenecid (Benemid) or allopurinol (Zyloprim), taken in tablet form. The old belief that overindulgence in food and alcohol is the main cause of gout has generally been disproved.

Infectious-related arthritis

This may be caused by a broad variety of infectious microorganisms, is diagnosed and treated by identifying the organism responsible, growing it in a culture broth, then testing various antibiotics against it to find which is most effective. The arthritis usually disappears when the infectious agent is destroyed.

Allergic-related arthritis

This condition is also readily curable when the substance causing the immunological reaction is identified and withdrawn. A common reaction is to drugs, especially penicillin; other causes are hypersensitivity to foods, cosmetics, airborne substances such as pollens, animal dander, house dust and others.

There is a large group of miscellaneous arthritic disorders that are associated with cancer, diseases of the blood, *avascular necrosis,* and juvenile osteochondritis, (cartilage and bone diseases that afflict young people).

Fraud and quackery in arthritis

Because arthritis afflicts so many people and its most common symptom is pain, its victims (understandably) may seek relief from any type of medication or quack diet that is advertised by "pitchmen"—who convincingly elucidate their effectiveness. Victims of arthritis should understand that of all drugs that can be obtained without prescriptions, common aspirin, Bufferin or Ascriptin are the best analgesics obtainable and are most predictable in their pharmacologic effects; they are also the least expensive. *Do not take any other drugs except those prescribed by your doctor.*

What does the future offer?

Only a few years ago little was known about the causes of arthritis, but enormous advances have been made—more during the past 20 years than in all the previous centuries of civilization. Today, we are fairly certain of the basic mechanism responsible for most arthritic diseases—an infectious agent or an abnormal immunological response.

By knowing the mechanism responsible for the damage that results from progressive stages of arthritis, we can now favorably influence the course of the disease. We are optimistic about the possibility of a cure, or at least very effective control, of most arthritic diseases in the not too distant future. However, when major advances are made in medicine you can be certain that the basic knowledge involved had to accumulate over a period of many years. Such was the case with our victory over polio and the discovery of antibiotics.

I firmly believe that past basic and clinical research has brought us to a point where we need only a concentrated effort to make a major breakthrough. There is no longer justification for a pessimistic attitude by patients, the medical profession, government, industry and insurance companies. We can and should mount a responsible, realistic and aggressive effort in order that our second most costly and disabling group of diseases can be added to the growing list of illnesses conquered by medicine.

Endocrinology

Dr. Rachmel Cherner

Special problems that relate to hormone imbalance or growth and development are often referred to an expert for precise diagnosis and treatment. The endocrinologist is concerned with the study and function, in health and disease, of the dozens of different hormones secreted directly into the bloodstream by the endocrine (or ductless) glands. They exert a powerful influence on the way we act, think and respond to the stresses of life.

Endocrinology is the branch of medical science concerned with those glands in the body, known as *endocrine glands* or *ductless glands*, that secrete the substances they produce—HORMONES—directly into the bloodstream.

The major endocrine glands include the *pituitary gland* (traditionally known as the "master gland" because of its great influence on the other endocrine glands), *parathyroid glands, thyroid gland, adrenal glands*, the *islets of Langerhans* (specialized groups of cells in the pancreas which secrete the hormone insulin), *ovaries* and *testes*. In addition, hormones or hormone-like substances are secreted by other specialized tissues in the body (such as the hormones secretin, gastrin and cholecystokinin which are produced in the gastrointestinal tract; they are commonly known as *local hormones*).

The body has two complex control systems which make it possible for an individual to respond quickly and efficiently to changes in the environment: the nervous system and the endocrine (or hormonal) system. Hormones are ordinarily released into the bloodstream following a specific stimulus of an endocrine gland—such as a nerve impulse or a change in the concentration of a specific substance carried to the gland in the blood. In a normal, healthy person the activity of the hormonal system is kept in delicate balance, but sometimes things can go wrong. This is where the endocrinologist comes in.

The endocrinologist deals with diseases that are caused by hormone imbalance or by growth problems. Thus, you are not likely to see an endocrinologist if you have a "garden variety" type of ailment such as a cold, or a sore throat, or a strained back. You may get to see him (or her) if you have a goiter that won't regress, or if your physician suspects that your pituitary gland is out of kilter, or if he cannot control your diabetes.

The endocrinologist deals with the internal environment of the body. The stability of this internal environment depends on the healthy and efficient working of both of the two major control systems of the body.

How hormones work

The endocrine system consists of specialized cells that, as we have noted, put out chemicals called hormones. These hormones are carried in the bloodstream to various parts of the body and influence the activity of specifically sensitive *target cells*. Hormones regulate metabolism in their target cells by influencing the rate at which enzymes and other proteins are manufactured.

The hormone is the "first messenger." It conveys its message to the interior of the cell by interacting with the cell membrane to form the "second messenger," *cyclic AMP* (cyclic adenosine monophosphate: a chemical which mediates many of the actions of a wide variety of hormones). In this way the low level "signal"—presented by the hormone outside the cell—can be amplified many thousands of times by the manufacture of cyclic AMP, stimulating the cell to produce proteins, enzymes and other factors necessary for cell maintenance, function and growth.

Hormones are of two types. The *steroid hormones* are all derived from CHOLESTEROL. They include the stress hormone, *cortisol;* the male sex hormone, *testosterone*, and the female sex hormone, *estradiol*. The other hormones are derived from peptides, such as INSULIN, or from amino acids, such as epinephrine (adrenalin) and norepinephrine (noradrenalin). These hormones are unable to penetrate the cell membrane because of their size or molecular configuration. They must attach themselves to specialized receptor sites on the cell surface and thus influence the biochemical "machinery" from outside the cell.

A group of nerve centers at the base of the brain (in the hypothalamus) produce both releasing and inhibitory hormones. These travel by means of the blood circulation to the PITUITARY GLAND. The pituitary gland, under control of the various hypothalamic hormones, produces other hormones which eventually stimulate the target glands—that is, the adrenals, ovaries, testes and thyroid gland. These glands, in turn, release the hormones which influence and control metabolism. The pituitary gland produces thyroid stimulating hormone, adrenal gland stimulating hormone, follicle stimulating hormone (in the male this stimulates the production of sperm; in the female it stimulates egg development), growth hormone, luteinizing hormone (responsible for the stimulation of the sex-

THE PITUITARY GLAND – effects of the hormones it secretes into the bloodstream

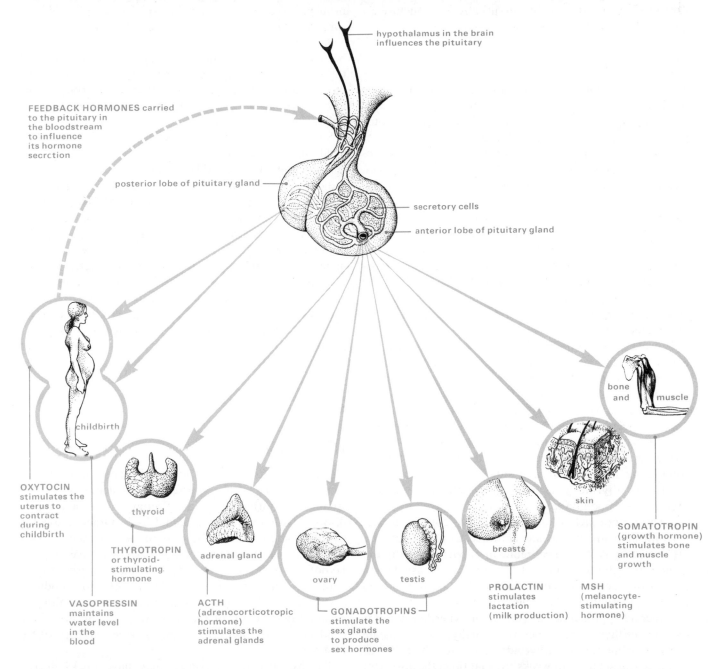

hypothalamus in the brain influences the pituitary

FEEDBACK HORMONES carried to the pituitary in the bloodstream to influence its hormone secrction

posterior lobe of pituitary gland

secretory cells

anterior lobe of pituitary gland

childbirth

bone and muscle

skin

OXYTOCIN stimulates the uterus to contract during childbirth

thyroid

VASOPRESSIN maintains water level in the blood

THYROTROPIN or thyroid-stimulating. hormone

adrenal gland

ACTH (adrenocorticotropic hormone) stimulates the adrenal glands

ovary

GONADOTROPINS stimulate the sex glands to produce sex hormones

testis

breasts

PROLACTIN stimulates lactation (milk production)

MSH (melanocyte-stimulating hormone)

SOMATOTROPIN (growth hormone) stimulates bone and muscle growth

hormone producing portions of the ovary and testes), and prolactin (responsible for milk production in the nursing mother). The posterior part of the pituitary gland produces antidiuretic hormone (responsible for water absorption by the kidney).

Pituitary hormones—constantly oozing out into the bloodstream, controlled by various complex stimuli—cause the release of cortisol (stress hormone), androgens and estrogen, triiodothyronine and thyroxine—as well as many other hormones—responsible for the intricate interrelationships in cellular communication.

Glandular underactivity or overactivity may cause such

The pituitary is the "master gland" of the body's hormonal system and influences the activities of the other endocrine glands. It is about the size of a pea and is attached to the base of the brain by a slender stalk-like process. The above illustration indicates the names and actions of the various hormones it releases into the bloodstream.

characteristic physical changes that they quickly point to the correct cause of the symptoms. Sometimes, however, the clear changes of endocrine disturbance are over-shadowed by more prominent mental or emotional symptoms severe enough to cause difficulty with diagnosis. Fortunately, the diagnosis can usually be conclusively established with well-chosen laboratory tests.

Hyperthyroidism

The most common cause for excess thyroid hormone production is HYPERTHYROIDISM. This disorder typically causes enlargement of the thyroid gland (goiter), nervousness, emotional lability and restlessness. The patient's eyes may be extraordinarily prominent with a staring appearance (exophthalmos). Weight loss, muscle weakness, increased fatigue and insomnia, increased sweating, increased frequency of bowel movements, changes in menstrual cycling and libido may occur.

The diagnosis of hyperthyroidism is usually made from thyroid blood tests including radioimmunoassay of thyroxine and triiodothyronine, the major thyroid hormones in blood (T-3 RIA, T-4 RIA). The radioactive iodine uptake and scan also indicate whether the gland is greedily taking up the isotope—thus, indicating the degree of hyperactivity.

However, the endocrinologist must differentiate between hyperthyroidism and less common causes for the excessive production or release of thyroid hormones—including a "toxic" or hyperfunctioning nodule of the thyroid gland, THYROIDITIS, and an increase in thyroid hormone release secondary to cancers of the uterus and testes (HYDATIDIFORM MOLES or CHORIOCARCINOMA). Other rare causes include increased release of thyroid stimulating hormone by a pituitary tumor, widespread metastatic thyroid cancer and, sometimes, excessive thyroid hormone intake.

Several approaches are possible to control hyperthyroidism. Some physicians continue to prefer subtotal THYROIDECTOMY (surgical removal of part of the thyroid gland) as definitive surgical therapy. It is usually an extremely effective procedure that quickly controls thyroid gland overactivity in about 90% of cases.

A second approach to the control of hyperthyroidism is specific antithyroid drug therapy. Usually, a normal state of thyroid function ("euthyroid" state) may be achieved within about six to eight weeks. At that time, the dosage of medication is gradually reduced to a maintenance dosage. One of the side effects of therapy, however, is that the thyroid gland may enlarge. The physician may elect to supplement the antithyroid drug with small doses of thyroid hormone to try to decrease the thyroid size.

Also, radioactive iodine may be used to destroy some of the thyroid cells and thus reduce the production of thyroid hormone. In many centers around the country, this has become the treatment of choice for adults. It is convenient, usually amounting to taking a small tasteless drink or a small capsule, and can be given on an "outpatient" basis (that is, not requiring an overnight stay in the hospital).

The treatment is usually curative and it avoids most of the problems of anesthesia and the possible complications of surgical treatment.

The first clinical effects of radioactive iodine therapy become evident in about six to eight weeks: the enlarged thyroid gland usually diminishes in size. About 80% of the patients become "euthyroid" (the thyroid function returns to normal) after one dose, while the remainder may require only a smaller second dose.

Special consideration must be paid to the treatment of children; generally, antithyroid drug therapy is preferred in children and adolescents. However, in some centers, since radioactive iodine has been found to be safe and effective, this form of therapy is also suggested for children without restriction. But radioactive iodine is absolutely contraindicated in pregnancy because the thyroid gland of the infant concentrates iodine after the 12th week of pregnancy. Care must be taken in giving *any* radioactive isotope to pregnant women. Hyperthyroidism during pregnancy is generally treated with antithyroid drugs, although these drugs easily cross the placenta and may produce a GOITER or hypothyroidism in the fetus. For this reason, dosages of antithyroid drugs are usually kept to a minimum and thyroid hormone is usually added to the treatment schedule to avoid these possible complications. (See also *Drugs for thyroid disorders* in the major article on **Drugs and Medicines**.)

Hypothyroidism

Underactivity of the thyroid gland (HYPOTHYROIDISM) can occur as the result of decreased production of thyroid stimulating hormone by the pituitary or by a primary disorder within the thyroid gland itself. Other causes for hypothyroidism include failure of development of the thyroid gland or its abnormal embryologic development. Hypothyroidism may be due in many cases to an "autoimmune" phenomenon—that is, the body produces destructive antibodies against the thyroid cells, resulting in eventual destruction of the cells and a falling off of the production of thyroid hormone (see AUTOIMMUNE DISEASE).

The hypothyroid individual may have thick, slurred speech and a deep hoarse voice. He or she may be lethargic, forgetful, slow, clumsy and depressed.

Diagnosis can usually be confirmed with thyroid blood tests and possibly a study of the uptake by the thyroid of radioactive iodine. The values of the test results for all these studies are usually far below normal. Probably the most sensitive test (although somewhat more expensive) is the level of thyroid stimulating hormone (TSH). The pituitary gland pushes out TSH in an attempt to stimulate or "whip" the thyroid gland into producing more hormone. The TSH level, as measured by a specific immunoassay, is usually significantly elevated in primary hypothyroidism.

The treatment ordinarily involves thyroid hormone replacement. Gradual improvement and reversal of symptoms may take as long as several months. The patient can be considered normal when symptoms have completely disappeared and when the test results are within normal limits and the TSH level decreases to normal.

Probably one of the most common causes for thyroid gland enlargement is simple (or "colloid") GOITER. The cause is unknown, but it appears to be familial (principally, on the female side of the family). Eventually, under hormonal stimulation, the thyroid gland becomes thickened with increased growth and nodular formation. Simple goiters may also occur in people who live in areas where iodine and iodide consumption is low. These goiters are usually benign.

Treatment depends upon gland size, consistency and the results of thyroid function studies. If the gland is small and cosmetically acceptable, the endocrinologist may decide just to observe it over a long time. If the gland is unusually large and interferes with swallowing, suppression with thyroid hormones may be attempted with larger doses of thyroid hormone than needed for mere thyroid replacement. If the gland is very much enlarged, surgical removal of part of the thyroid gland may be necessary; this should be followed by thyroid hormone medication to suppress the gland and prevent enlargement. (See also *Drugs for thyroid disorders* in the major article on **Drugs and Medicines.**)

Thyroiditis

HASHIMOTO'S DISEASE (or *Hashimoto's thyroiditis*), a chronic form of inflammation of the thyroid, may occur in people with a family history of thyroid disorders. The diagnosis is usually made by measuring antithyroid antibodies in the blood. A thyroid scan and other tests may also help in making a firm diagnosis.

Other forms of thyroiditis may be caused by upper respiratory viruses that attack and destroy the thyroid cells. Cell material is discharged into the bloodstream and the body fails to recognize this material as belonging to itself and prepares antibodies against it. The antibodies recirculate and attack the thyroid gland, which, again, results in destruction of enough of the gland to produce hypothyroidism.

Usually the early stages of thyroiditis can be treated with aspirin alone. If aspirin is not effective, cortisone or prednisone may diminish the inflammation. If tenderness and discomfort recur, the patient may be given large doses of a preparation of thyroid hormone (obtained from the thyroid gland of certain animals) to suppress the gland.

Disorders of the adrenal glands

Many conditions and diseases result in adrenal gland destruction (ADDISON'S DISEASE) and impaired production of cortisol, aldosterone, and male and female sex hormones. A rare cause may be adrenal gland atrophy (wasting away) because the pituitary gland does not produce enough adrenocorticotropic hormone (ACTH).

The definitive diagnosis of Addison's disease may be made by injecting ACTH, measuring plasma cortisol levels before and after injection. Patients with Addison's disease show no rise in cortisol levels following this ACTH stimulation.

The patient with Addison's disease is maintained on replacement therapy with hydrocortisone (a pharmaceutical product with the same actions and uses as cortisol). Since hormone requirements are increased during stress, in severe stress such as bleeding, surgery, or any life-threatening infection, large doses of steroids are usually given intravenously.

Cortisol overproduction can also occur, leading to what is known as CUSHING'S SYNDROME. This may result from conditions such as a benign or malignant tumor of the adrenal glands, or from excessive stimulation of the adrenals by ACTH by an overactive pituitary gland; it may also be associated with the prolonged therapeutic administration of large doses of cortisol (hydrocortisone) or other hormones derived from the adrenal cortex or related drugs manufactured synthetically. The adrenal cortex may also be stimulated to produce excessive amounts of cortisol as the result of a nonpituitary tumor, such as one involving the lungs, thymus, pancreas, or other organs.

The symptoms of full-blown Cushing's syndrome include marked obesity, usually restricted to the trunk; in contrast, the arms and legs are usually somewhat thin and wasted. The face is typically rounded ("mooning") and usually somewhat red due to thinning of the skin from protein malnutrition. Purple stripes may be noted over the abdomen, thigh, arms and chest. There is a tendency to easy bruising and wound healing is poor. Bone pain and fractures of the spine are common. Because of increased androgen production, signs of masculinization appear—such as loss of scalp hair, increase in hair growth over the body and arms and legs, increase in oiliness of the skin (with ACNE) and, in women, changes in the menstrual cycle. Hypertension (high blood pressure) and mild diabetes are common. Many times other associated symptoms of recurrent headache and a marked change in personality occur.

Diagnosis is usually based on the patient's physical appearance and high cortisol levels and loss of usual hormone diurnal variation (that is, it is not highest in the morning and lowest in midafternoon). Bilateral total adrenalectomy (surgical removal of both adrenal glands) appears to be the most effective treatment.

In addition to abnormalities of the adrenal cortex (the outer part of the gland), abnormalities may occur also in the adrenal medulla or "core tissue." The adrenal medulla produces the hormones norepinephrine and epinephrine (called "catecholamines"). These hormones have rather dramatic effects; they can produce contraction of gastrointestinal smooth muscle, increased sweating and spasm of peripheral blood vessels (vasoconstriction). They may also have an effect in causing dilation of peripheral blood vessels (vasodilation), stimulation of the heart, relaxation of the muscles of the lungs and decreased motility of the muscle of the gastrointestinal tract. These compounds may produce an increase in the levels of blood sugar (glucose) by causing an increased release of glucose from the liver. They also cause an increased breakdown of fat. These hormones seem to function as "emergency hormones" to insure that sufficient glucose will be supplied to the brain and other organs and tissues under periods of stress.

Tumors of the adrenal glands

Rarely, a tumor which produces catecholamines is found in the adrenal gland. They are probably most important in their effect in producing hypertension. With appropriate diagnosis and treatment this form of hypertension is usually curable.

The symptoms of tumor of the adrenal medulla (PHEOCHROMOCYTOMA) include hypertension, headache, perspiration, heart palpitation, tremor of the fingers, episodes of flushing of the face, weakness, dizziness, and, occasionally, chest pain. All these symptoms are caused by the release of catecholamines. The production of these hormones may be either chronic or episodic. The episodes are usually quite dramatic, sudden in onset, and occasionally precipitated by eating, activity, changes in body position, or anxiety. Between the episodes, the patient may be asymptomatic (experience no symptoms) and have a normal blood pressure. In some families the tumor can be inherited. In this case, tumors are frequently found in both adrenal glands. Occasionally, a pheochromocytoma can be found in association with other endocrine tumors— including cancer of the thyroid, parathyroid tumors, or pituitary tumors.

Diagnosis rests on the demonstration of increased production of the catecholamines (epinephrine and norepinephrine). The usual tests used for the determination of a pheochromocytoma include a 24-hour urine collection. The urine is subjected to a test for the measurement of VMA (vanillylmandelic acid), and metanephrines (metabolic products of catecholamines) as well as direct measurement of norepinephrine and epinephrine.

Surgical intervention is the treatment of choice for pheochromocytoma. Careful administration of anesthesia with preoperative medication, consisting of agents which block the effects of epinephrine and norepinephrine, are generally used. With these compounds, the risk of surgery has been considerably reduced. Although most of the tumors are benign, occasionally pheochromocytoma

undergoes a malignant change. Also, recurrence is possible. Various chemical compounds to block the effects of catecholamines may then be used to keep the patient as comfortable and symptom-free as possible.

Pituitary gland disorders

Although it is considered to be the "master gland" of the body, the pituitary is directly under the control of various releasing and inhibiting hormones produced by the hypothalamus (a part of the brain). Examination of the anterior pituitary tissue indicates three different types of cells. There are cells that can be stained with a red dye (*eosinophilic* cells), cells that take up blue dye (*basophilic*), and cells that do not take up any dye (*chromophobe*). The eosinophilic cells produce growth hormone and prolactin. Basophilic cells secrete thyroid stimulating hormone (TSH), adrenal stimulating hormone or "adrenocorticotropin" (ACTH), and gonadotropins (LH and TSH) that stimulate the sex organs. Chromophobe cells produce ACTH and other pituitary hormones.

The endocrinologist is interested in disorders of the pituitary such as eosinophilic cell tumors that cause GIGANTISM and ACROMEGALY; basophilic cell tumors that cause Cushing's syndrome; chromophobe cell tumors that may cause menstrual changes, loss of sex drive, hypothyroidism, adrenal insufficiency, or loss of vision. It is his responsibility to discover and pinpoint them and to determine whether treatment should be surgery or hormone replacement therapy.

By far the greatest number of pituitary tumors is produced by abnormalities of the chromophobe cells. These cells, which are now known to produce ACTH as well as other pituitary hormones, usually produce their effects by local increase in size. As the tumor grows, normal pituitary tissue is compressed and the production of normal amounts of pituitary hormones is impaired. This may result in changes in the menstrual period or loss of sex drive due to loss of gonadotropic hormones, hypothyroidism due to the loss of TSH, and adrenal insufficiency due to decreased ACTH production. The tumor, by extending upward, may cause pressure on the optic nerve and cause loss of vision. Occasionally, milk may leak from the male and female breast due to increased release of prolactin, the milk-producing hormone.

Tests for a pituitary tumor include skull x-rays to evaluate the size of the bony recess in which the pituitary gland rests, as well as tests of pituitary and target hormones (including growth hormone, TSH, and prolactin levels). Determination of plasma cortisol levels, estrogen and testosterone levels are also helpful. Other studies may include a radioactive brain scan, computerized axial tomography (CAT scan), a pneumoencephalogram (x-ray study of the ventricles—the fluid-filled chambers of the brain—and other areas of the brain following withdrawal

MALE AND FEMALE SEX HORMONES

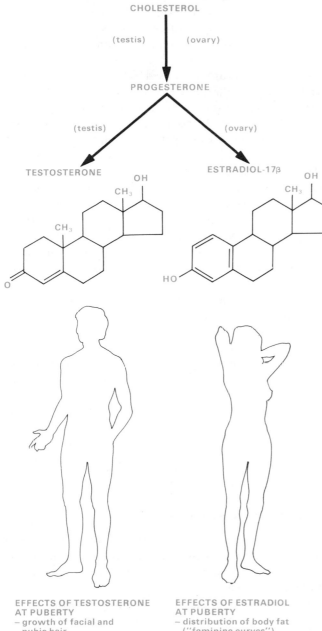

EFFECTS OF TESTOSTERONE AT PUBERTY
- growth of facial and pubic hair
- deepening of the voice
- sexual response (erection of the penis)
- muscular development

EFFECTS OF ESTRADIOL AT PUBERTY
- distribution of body fat ("feminine curves")
- breast development
- changes in vaginal and uterine lining during menstruation
- distribution of body hair

Testosterone is the male sex hormone and estradiol and estrone are the two major female sex hormones (estrogens); they play important roles in the development and function of the adult. Both testosterone and estradiol are manufactured by the body from cholesterol, and as the illustration shows, the molecular structure of these hormones is remarkably similar. Both the male and female sex hormones—testosterone and estrogens—can be prepared synthetically for therapeutic use.

of some cerebrospinal fluid and replacement with an injection of air or gas), or cerebral arteriogram. Treatment is usually surgical removal of the pituitary gland (hypophysectomy) with follow-up radiation if necessary. Because of the extensive loss of tropic hormones usually produced by the pituitary gland, replacement medication consisting of estrogens or androgens, cortisol, and thyroid hormone may be necessary. All patients with symptoms of hypopituitarism should have a medical alert card and bracelet (or necklace) to indicate what replacement hormones are required.

The endocrinologist must also consider disorders of the posterior part of the pituitary gland. This gland produces antidiuretic hormone (which causes the reabsorption of water) and oxytocin (needed to bring on labor in pregnancy).

Antidiuretic hormone is active on the kidney, causing the reabsorption of water. In the absence of satisfactory amounts of this hormone, the patient develops distressing symptoms of frequent urination of large volumes of urine, and increasing thirst. Treatment is replacement with antidiuretic hormone obtained from animal pituitary glands.

Sexual development and infertility

The endocrinologist is especially active in the field of sexuality. The major problems he deals with are physical development of the pubertal child, fertility control in the adult population (see FERTILITY), and treatment of the infertile couple with pituitary hormones. In some cases, of course, infertility or sexual maldevelopment may result from chromosomal abnormalities (see KLINEFELTER'S SYNDROME) rather than hormonal problems. Then an analysis of the patient's chromosomes may help in evaluating the condition.

In addition to disorders of the endocrine glands, the endocrinologist is also involved in treating metabolic disorders including obesity, lipid (fat) disturbances, and diabetes mellitus (both the maturity-onset type of adulthood and the more dangerous juvenile-diabetes).

Diabetes mellitus

It is believed that up to 5% of the population of the United States either has diagnosed or undiagnosed DIABETES MELLITUS. It is also believed that 25% of the population of the United States carries some form of genetic predisposition to diabetes ("pre-diabetes"). Basic to the cause of diabetes is either a disorder of insulin production by the cells of the pancreas that secrete insulin (islets of Langerhans) or interference with the effect of insulin at the cellular level.

Sometimes an individual may not even have an elevated blood sugar level, as determined by the results of tests commonly known as a "fasting blood sugar" or a "postprandial blood sugar" (sugar after eating). Nevertheless, a family history of obesity, lipid disturbance, premature cardiovascular disease, or eye or kidney disease may often give a clue to underlying diabetes.

By far the most common type of diabetes is that which occurs in older, obese individuals (usually after the age of 40). These individuals have a normal supply of insulin in the pancreas. The islets of Langerhans appear to be normal and, indeed, insulin levels may even be higher than normal in response to a glucose "challenge." There appears to be some resistance to the action of insulin by the peripheral cells which contributes to the rise in blood sugar. Because of this inability of insulin to exert its normal metabolic effect of inhibiting protein breakdown, the blood sugar rises and the individual is said to be diabetic. The disorder in these individuals can often be controlled by weight reduction and diet alone. Unfortunately, adherence to a proper diet is difficult for most patients. The endocrinologist may then suggest one of the oral agents to control the elevated blood sugar. (See also *Drugs for diabetes* in the major article on **Drugs and Medicines**.)

Juvenile-onset diabetes

The other form of diabetes is known as "juvenile-onset diabetes," though it may affect older individuals. Those affected are usually young and, for whatever reason, lack the ability to produce a sufficient quantity of insulin. Why the insulin-secreting cells of the pancreas should be defective is not clear. Various theories have been advanced to explain this phenomenon—including hereditary factors, viral infections, or an autoimmune phenomenon.

Patients with juvenile-onset diabetes cannot be controlled with oral agents but require insulin replacement. If they do not obtain it in sufficient amounts, they begin to burn fats instead of sugar (the usual "fuel"). As a result of this, certain products of fat breakdown (*ketone bodies*) accumulate in the blood and spill over in the urine. The accumulation of these compounds causes a severe acidosis and dehydration and may lead to diabetic coma (*ketoacidosis*). Diabetic patients who require insulin are best "custom treated" with a tailored prescription of insulin. Many times the endocrinologist is able to adjust the daily dosage of insulin so that the level of sugar in both the blood and urine is well controlled throughout an entire 24-hour period.

Hypoglycemia

In addition to problems in which the blood sugar is elevated, such as diabetes mellitus, the endocrinologist also deals with problems of HYPOGLYCEMIA (in which the blood sugar is abnormally low).

Hypoglycemia can occur as a result of other endocrine deficiencies. These include adrenal insufficiency and pituitary insufficiency. Hypoglycemia may occur as the first symptom in symptom-free diabetes of the maturity-onset type. This probably represents an initial overproduction of insulin by the stimulated pancreas. Hypoglycemia can also be caused by a tumor of the insulin-secreting cells of the pancreas (an "islet cell adenoma") which produces insulin in large amounts. Hypoglycemia can also be accidentally induced in a diabetic patient when too much insulin or oral agent is taken, which causes an abnormal drop in the level of sugar in the circulating blood.

Hypoglycemia can also accompany alcohol intake as well as ingestion of various drugs. Many times it occurs as a reaction to large amounts of glucose, occurring several hours after eating a high carbohydrate meal. This form of true "reactive hypoglycemia" is probably relatively rare. It is unfortunate that so many people attribute their symptoms of depression, tiredness and anxiety to a low blood sugar. This has led to an almost "cult" attitude among many people who neglect the real reason for their symptoms.

Symptoms of hypoglycemia are many, including sweating, headache, nausea, palpitation, mental fuzziness and disorientation. Severe hypoglycemia may result in unconsciousness and, at times, convulsive seizures. If hypoglycemia is suspected, sugar should be immediately given by mouth (if the patient is conscious and able to swallow) or glucose can be administered under the tongue or intravenously under medical direction. It is most important that the reason for the hypoglycemia be adequately diagnosed.

Parathyroid glands

The endocrinologist is also concerned with disorders of calcium metabolism, with which the parathyroid glands are involved. Too high a level of calcium (*hypercalcemia*) can be life-threatening.

Single or multiple *adenomas* (benign growths) of the parathyroid glands may produce large amounts of parathyroid hormone that cause an elevation of the serum calcium level and produce many clinical symptoms. *Hyperplasia* (excessive proliferation of normal cells), caused by overstimulation of the parathyroid glands, may also produce a similar calcium elevation. HYPERPARATHYROIDISM can also be found secondary to chronic kidney disease, associated with childhood RICKETS, or OSTEOMALACIA in adults, cancer of the parathyroid gland, or parathyroid hormone-like material produced by various cancers.

The most common symptoms are those which usually drive the patient to the urologist because of recurrent kidney stones or kidney infections (see the major article on **Urology**). The patient may also consult his family physician or gastroenterologist with signs and symptoms of a duodenal ulcer or inflammation of the pancreas. The patient with hyperparathyroidism may complain of bone pain and diffuse joint pains. Indeed, he may have severe pain secondary to a fracture of bone with minimal trauma such as rolling over in bed. Most often, with laboratory testing, the diagnosis is first made with the discovery of hypercalcemia.

A definite diagnosis may be difficult in many patients because it depends primarily on the finding of an elevated serum calcium level and, indeed, elevated calcium levels can be found in other conditions—including metastatic malignancy (the spread of cancer cells to other parts of the body from the site of an original or primary tumor), SARCOIDOSIS, vitamin D intoxication and other metabolic disturbances. A radioimmunoassay for serum parathyroid hormone can be very valuable in confirming the diagnosis.

Other tests besides repeated tests of calcium levels (expected to be high in this condition) and phosphorus levels (usually found to be lower than normal) are the findings of loss of calcium from bone on x-ray examination, the finding of a duodenal ulcer or a kidney stone, or calcification within the joint spaces of the body. Because of difficulty in localizing the parathyroid glands (in the neck), various techniques have been tried in an attempt to overcome this problem. The technique of introducing a catheter (a special flexible tube) into the blood vessels draining the parathyroid glands has been useful in localizing the tumor. Arteriography (an x-ray technique in which a contrast material is first injected into the blood vessels) of the parathyroid glands has also had some limited success. However, consistently elevated calcium levels with low phosphorus levels, and an elevated parathyroid hormone immunoassay, with other signs and symptoms, usually allow a diagnosis of overactivity of the parathyroid glands.

The treatment of hyperparathyroidism is that of surgical removal of one or more of the enlarged and hyperfunctioning glands.

Hypocalcemia

Just as dangerous as hypercalcemia is HYPOCALCEMIA— an abnormally low calcium level. (This occurs when the serum level of calcium falls below 8.5 milligrams percent.) Hypocalcemia secondary to underactivity of the parathyroid glands can occur in all age groups, from the newborn to the elderly. In the newborn infant, neuromuscular symptoms such as twisting, irritability, tremors or actual convulsions can take place. The baby may show difficulty in breathing, with gasping respiration due to spasm of the larynx.

A similar spasm of the larynx with "crowing" (labored respiration) may occur in older children as well as adults. TETANY may also occur: this consists of generalized muscle contractions, particularly involving the small muscles of the hands. Tetany (not to be confused with TETANUS) may be associated with a sensation of numbness and tingling in the fingers and toes. Adult patients may show various neurologic deficits. Emotionally, they may be hysterical or show fear, depression, neurosis, or sometimes even psychosis. Some of these patients complain of abdominal pains. Many times they have scaling of the skin, eczema, loss of body hair, and a secondary growth of fungus of the nails. The eyes may be affected with CATARACT formation and sometimes EDEMA of the back of the eye (usually in hypocalcemia of many years duration). X-rays sometimes reveal changes in the long bones and in certain areas of the brain.

Another cause of hypocalcemia is gastrointestinal disease. This may be secondary to CELIAC DISEASE in childhood, SPRUE in adults or chronic inflammation of the pancreas. A low calcium level can also occur in chronic kidney disease (congenital or acquired). Chronic nutritional lack of vitamin D can also produce hypocalcemia.

Relatively symptom-free chronic hypocalcemia is best treated with a combination of oral calcium salts, a vitamin D preparation and a low phosphate diet. A low phosphate diet usually *excludes* milk, butter and cheese. Patients given this combination of therapy must have periodic checks of their calcium levels. It is as important to avoid the dangerous state of hypercalcemia resulting from overtreatment, as it is to avoid a chronic state of tetany due to a *low* calcium level.

Summary

As I have said, hormones are the special field of the endocrinologist, and hormones are involved with every part of the body. Moreover, just within the past several years, a whole variety of *hypothalamic releasing hormones* have been described. A brand new hormone, *somatostatin*, has been discovered whose effects are not completely known. And startling facts are reported almost monthly regarding the "old" hormones such as insulin, cortisol and thyroid hormone. The endocrinologist must keep up with all this new information.

Hormones are the messengers of the body; thus, the endocrinologist must understand the complexities of the human body in both health and disease.

Oncology Dr. Graham H. Barker

The modern approach to the treatment of cancer involves the "multimodal" use of new chemotherapeutic agents, radiation therapy and the surgical removal of tumors which have not yet begun to spread their cells to other parts of the body. The following article discusses what we know about the various forms of this dreaded disease and the outlook for the future.

Oncology is the study of tumors or CANCER and the word comes from the Greek *onkos*, meaning "a mass." However, not all "cancers" are solid tumors; a significant proportion in fact are leukemias, lymphomas, etc. The word *cancer* (Latin for "crab") has been used in medical literature since at least the time of Hippocrates. Galen (A.D. 131–201), probably in writing about breast cancer, stated: "Just as a crab's feet extend from every part of its body, so in this disease the veins are distended, forming a similar figure." Other early writers noted the appearance of breast tumors invading a female breast with claw-like projections. This can be misleading, for many tumors do not behave like this. Some doctors use the word *malignancy*. However, not all tumors are malignant or invasive, some are benign. Probably the most satisfactory term is *neoplasm* ("new growth"), which correctly implies that from ordered original tissue comes forth a new growth, be it benign or malignant, solid or not, and that is the essential basis of cancer.

Despite the great prevalence of the disease (about 20% of all deaths in the United States result from cancer), the study of neoplasms as an entity by specialist oncologists is relatively young. Oncologists usually qualify as specialists in internal medicine, then undergo an additional fellowship of clinical training in oncology which will include radiation therapy, chemotherapy and hematology. Working usually in a medical center, the oncologist will also coordinate the other specialists involved in the management of cancer, such as the surgeons, gynecologists and radiologists. He or she may well further specialize to become expert in a subdivision such as colorectal, gynecological, or head and neck tumors; others become involved in research, publicity and prevention programs.

There is much yet to be discovered about the nature of cancer, but essentially cells (or a cell) within a group at a particular time in life begin to multiply and either produce an enlarged mass of the original tissue (a benign tumor) or lose their differentiation (i.e., become "wilder") and grow continuously (malignant)—possibly invading adjacent structures or throwing off cells to form colonies elsewhere in the body (known as secondaries or metastases). What causes this change is not completely known for each tumor, but several cancer-causing stimuli (carcinogens) are now known to provoke this change.

Early cancer research

Probably the earliest and most significant discovery was by the Englishman Sir Percival Pott who (in 1775) noticed that chimney sweeps were particularly susceptible to scrotal cancers associated with repeated exposure to soot. By the end of the 19th century tar, pitch, shale oil, certain dyes and arsenic were all recognized as carcinogens. However, it was not until 1916—when two Japanese scientists, Yamagiwa and Ichikawa, successfully produced cancer in rabbits experimentally by painting their skins with tar products—that a realistic approach through scientific investigation was possible.

As early as 1847, the celebrated German pathologist Rudolf Virchow made the observation that cancer could be caused by local irritation. He suggested that irritation subsequent to clay pipe smoking (causing tongue and lip cancer), sunburn (causing skin cancer) and friction from leather harnesses set up local inflammatory processes causing epithelial changes that may become malignant. Later experiments by Berenblum on the role of irritants led him to propose (in 1947) the thesis of a two-stage carcinogenesis—process initiation and promotion— suggesting that tumors arise by a multistage mechanism.

In 1908 the experimental induction of leukemia in chickens was reported by Ellermann and Bang. Viral origin of a sarcoma was first demonstrated in 1911 when Rous reported evidence of the transmittability of cell-free filtrates in chickens. Shope further demonstrated this transmission in 1932 in rabbit papilloma, and in 1936 Vittaer demonstrated the infective milk factors in mammary cancer in mice. In the early 1950s, Gross demonstrated the transmission of a mouse leukemia virus which in other mice produced not only leukemia but parotid gland tumors. Repeating Gross's experiments Stewart and Eddy discovered the polyoma virus capable of producing multiple kinds of cancer not only in mice but in other laboratory animals as well. At London's Royal Cancer Hospital (now called the Royal Marsden Hospital), Kennaway devoted major efforts to a study of exogenous factors in the cause of cancer. In 1928 he isolated the first

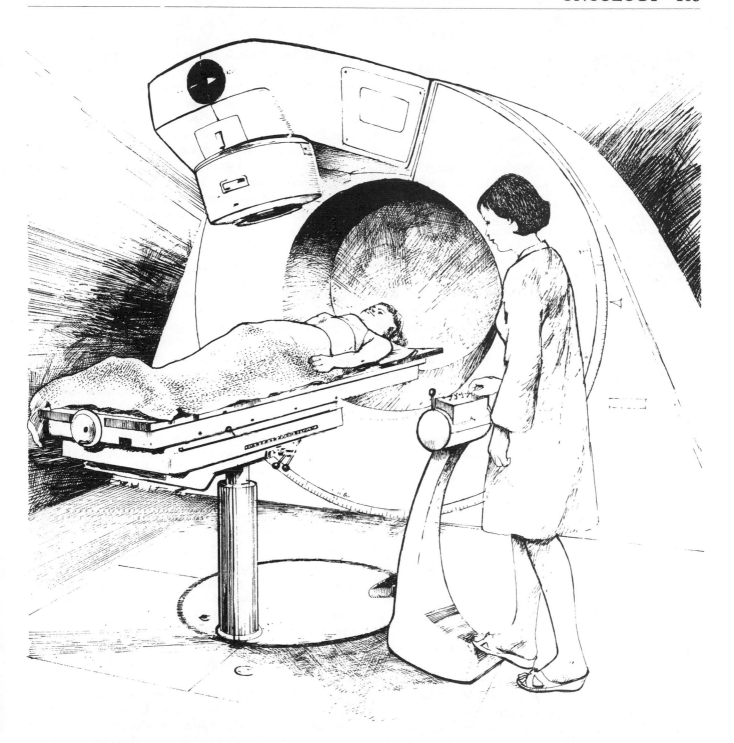

pure individual chemical to manifest pronounced carcino-genic properties; in 1933 he identified the active substance in carcinogenic pitch followed by, in 1955, the identifi-cation of the carcinogenic compound in coal tar. Rehn, in 1895, reported for the first time the possible relationship of other tumors to aniline byproducts.

The association of exposure to radiation in the production of cancer became clinically suspect soon after the use of irradiation in medical therapeutics was instituted at the beginning of this century, and was confirmed experimentally by Clunet in 1910 in a rabbit.

Radiation therapy dates from the late 19th century, with the discovery of x-rays (1895) and the radioactive properties of radium (1898). Modern advances in radiation therapy now make it possible, in selected cases, to expose a tumor to controlled doses of high-voltage x-rays in an attempt to retard tumor growth and prevent the spread of cancer cells (metastasis) to other parts of the body. The illustration depicts one type of machine used to generate high-voltage radiation for use in cancer treatment.

Modern cancer research

The theory of carcinogenesis based on immunological differences was advanced by Green in 1954. Discovery of cell transformation in a test tube outside a living body without the stimulus of a carcinogen was reported by Earle in 1943.

Thus, the cause of cancer is gradually being understood, but it is obvious that there is more than one cause and the trigger mechanisms for many cancers remain a mystery. Intense research is currently geared to explaining why the body allows a cancer to develop. It is thought that abnormal cells are being produced frequently throughout life but that these abnormal cells or parts of cells are discarded by a sort of "quality control" mechanism. This process may well be linked to the cells and organs of the body which are known to provide immunity from diseases such as bacterial infections, and this knowledge may provide a possible future line of treatment. Furthermore, increased knowledge of how cells normally divide and multiply—and in particular what happens to the gene-carrying parts of a cell's nucleus—may give further clues about how cancers begin and possibly help with their treatment.

Assuming that as an individual goes through life he or she becomes progressively more exposed to cancer-inducing aspects of the environment, it is not surprising that the risk of developing cancer increases with age. In ethnic groups with low expectations of life, malnutrition often replaces cancer or heart attacks as the greatest threat to life. It must not, however, be forgotten that children and babies may also develop forms of cancer; indeed, cancer is second only to automobile accidents as the biggest killer of children in the United States.

Classification of tumors

There are a large variety of names which can be applied to any specific tumor, depending upon its behavior, site of origin, microscopic appearance, etc. As has been stated, the terms *benign* and *malignant* are applied depending on the tumor's tendency to remain localized or its tendency to invade adjacent tissue or spread via the bloodstream or lymph system. The other very important consideration is the tumor's site of origin. If it arises from the lining cells of an organ (epithelium), such as the inner surface of the intestine, the malignant tumor produced is called a *carcinoma*. A malignant growth arising from connective tissue (e.g., bone, muscle) is called a SARCOMA (from the Greek word *sarx*, meaning "flesh").

Surface cells tend to be flat, overlapping plates, rather like the sides of a ship, and these are called *squamous*. Cells of glands, such as those which secrete digestive juices in the stomach, are termed *adeno*. Thus, malignant tumors of the skin become possible *squamous cell carcinomas*, while a

tumor of the stomach might well be described as an ADENOCARCINOMA. Sometimes the appearance of the growth lends itself to pathological description and we might have a fluid-filled tumor of a gland with finger-like projections described as a *papillary cystadenocarcinoma* (e.g., from the ovary). It is interesting to note that the sarcomas are, broadly speaking, more aggressive, more difficult to treat and occur in younger patients. Benign tumors are often designated by the addition of *-oma* to the end of the word; for example, fibrous tissue becomes a *benign fibroma* or a *malignant fibrosarcoma* (see FIBROMA, FIBROSARCOMA).

Symptoms and signs

It is difficult to be specific about the sign any particular type of tumor may produce. However, symptoms they initiate may be roughly divided into general and specific types. Broadly speaking, patients with cancer often lose weight, their appetites become depressed and they develop a pale, leathery appearance, which in association with the severe weight loss, in the advanced stages, doctors call CACHEXIA. It is not fully understood why patients who have a small-sized tumor should have such severe weight loss in some cases, even when the patient has a good appetite and is eating well. It is obvious in some cases that these tumors can have profound effects on the nutrition of a patient.

In all stages of cancer illness, a patient may sometimes "switch off" to the seriousness of the disease, and become indifferent to, or even oblivious of, the life-threatening condition. Like every doctor who has worked in the field of cancer, I have often been told by middle-aged women that they "have a little lump in the bosom which might be a bit serious"—only to find, when they undress, that one breast is entirely replaced with a very advanced tumor that must have been growing for many months! Perpetual tiredness and apathy often accompany widespread malignant disease; but do not, for one minute, think that anyone who is frequently lethargic is undoubtedly suffering from cancer.

The localized signs and symptoms vary with the site of the tumor and the hazards it causes. Bladder tumors often bleed and produce bloodstained urine (HEMATURIA); lung tumors similarly produce bloodstained sputum (HEMOPTYSIS). Often the sheer increase in size of the tumor produces symptoms such as an enlarging abdominal girth, or swelling of the lymph nodes in the neck.

The skin is one of the easier places to observe cancer growth. A simple mole (or NEVUS) may subsequently become malignant, particularly if stimulated by excessive sunlight, and the local signs of this are a change in size, a tendency to bleed, or a change in color. Sometimes a sore which is slow or fails to heal may suggest that a malignant process is at work.

A vaginal discharge, especially if bloodstained, or

vaginal bleeding after the menopause or coitus may herald a gynecological cancer. Cancers of the large bowel may cause changes in bowel habit, either constipation or diarrhea. Cancers of the stomach or esophagus (gullet) may cause difficulty in swallowing or even obstruction and vomiting. Needless to say, any abnormal lump appearing anywhere in the body, especially the breast, needs prompt investigation by a doctor. Occasionally, the pressure caused by the local growth of a tumor may cause symptoms, such as a cancer of the larynx causing a hoarse voice. Certain types of tumors may uncommonly produce abnormal hormones which will cause unusual effects. Cancers of the lung can cause the bones of the limbs to swell, cancers of the pancreas predispose to the formation of clots (THROMBOSIS) in the veins of the legs and pelvis, while some rare tumors of the ovary (arrhenoblastomas) produce male hormones causing a gradual masculinization in appearance of the affected woman.

Age and geographical distribution

It is curious how certain neoplastic disorders affect specific age groups. For instance, certain types of kidney cancer (Wilms' tumor) affect young children, leave young adults alone and attack the later middle-age to old-age groups (hypernephroma). It is not known why young adults are relatively spared in this way. It may be that some develop the kidney cancer at the beginning of their lives from an inherited chromosome abnormality, while those who suffer in later life have been, perhaps, exposed to carcinogens which cause kidney tumors. On the other hand, brain tumors can attack at any time, but have a predilection for young adults.

The proportions of deaths from various tumors vary from country to country. In Japan, for instance, there is a much higher incidence of stomach cancer (thought to be related to the amount of raw fish eaten) than there is in the United States or Britain. Similarly, tumors arising from the fetal membranes in the womb (CHORIOCARCINOMA) are much more common in the Far East than in the West. However, when these people emigrate to the West and adopt the local life style and diet, after a generation or two their proportion of cancers soon matches that of the new surroundings. Cancer of the large bowel is the most common cancer in men and women of the Western world and is believed to be related to our diet and its relative lack of roughage and other ingredients. In other poorer countries, such as parts of Africa, the diet is unrefined and bowel cancer is much less prevalent. Conversely, certain bean crops are frequently contaminated by a fungus (*Aspergillus flavus*) in areas within Africa. This fungus produces "aflatoxins" which are known to stimulate primary cancers of the liver (HEPATOMA) in great numbers—a tumor which is, in contrast, quite rare in Europe and the United States.

Local conditions can have a great influence on the incidence of cancer. In regions of high sunshine levels (e.g., Australia, South Africa and the southern United States) the incidence of skin cancers is much higher than in, say, the damp, cloudy British Isles. If you work in or around an asbestos mine you will have a higher chance of developing a growth of the lung lining (pleura) called a MESOTHELIOMA than one who does not. Survivors of the atomic bomb blasts in Nagasaki and Hiroshima who were irradiated have a high incidence of leukemia and other malignancies. However, the time between exposure to a carcinogen and the development of the cancer may be a very long time, of about 10 to 20 years, and a firm association may be very difficult to prove, until many have suffered the disease.

Making the diagnosis

Often the clue to the disease is given in a patient's history. Marked weight loss, decreased appetite, blood in the sputum, localized back pain all can add up to a lung tumor (and many benign conditions too). It is essential to establish the correct diagnosis before the often tragic news is imparted, and before the correct treatment can be commenced.

The usual way of establishing the identity of a solid tumor is for a surgeon either to remove it completely or to take a small piece (BIOPSY) for investigation under the microscope by an expert (histopathologist). Occasionally, removal of fluid in the chest may be helpful (pleural aspiration) in making a diagnosis, or an accumulation of malignant fluid in the abdomen can be tapped off (paracentesis) and sent for analysis. By looking at the type of tumor cells in this fluid a specialist (cytologist) can often suggest the site of origin of the tumor—e.g., a cancer of the ovary producing fluid in the abdomen. It usually takes an actual biopsy of the tumor to confirm those findings.

The malignant blood disorders (leukemias) are usually suggested by the results of blood tests and confirmed by an examination of the active bone marrow aspirated either from the sternum (breastbone) or from a pelvic bone. (See also *The Pathologist* in the major article **Specialists You Seldom See**.)

Investigations

There is a tremendous range of investigations available to the oncologist to enable him to detect cancer within the body, aside from the traditional x-rays, especially in the last few years with the addition of improved diagnostic methods and techniques. Having established the presence of a tumor the oncologist will attempt to discover if it has invaded elsewhere and perhaps spread through the body. By knowing how advanced the tumor is, the oncologist can allot it to a particular stage of development. International medical agreement regarding staging allows the effectiveness of treatments to be compared in cancer centers throughout the world. A tumor in the abdomen may have spread to the lungs, carried by the bloodstream, and this may be detected by a simple chest x-ray. Advanced breast cancers not infrequently send a secondary deposit to the brain. The confirmation of this may be more difficult to establish, often requiring an isotope brain scan, ultrasonography, or even computerized axial tomography (CAT scan).

An *isotope scan* involves the injection into the bloodstream of a normal body substance which has radioactive particles attached to it. The labeled substance is actively absorbed by the organ you wish to show up (e.g., brain, spleen, liver) and the body is then scanned for radioactivity. In this way a "map" of the organ can be produced on paper or on a TV screen. Organs invaded by a tumor have abnormal appearances. The amount of radioactivity is always very small.

An *ultrasound scan* is very similar to submarine detection by the Navy. Beams of sound waves are passed through the body and as they meet organ surfaces the beams are reflected back. By knowing how quickly the sound waves are reflected back in an echo at various depths through the body, a picture can be built up on a TV screen. Ultrasound is used extensively to measure the growth of a baby in the mother's womb; it can also be used to detect abnormal masses in the body cavities, such as the skull, abdomen and pelvis. (See ULTRASOUND.)

The CAT scan is the latest help in mapping and measuring tumor masses. The system is based upon a circle of tiny x-ray cameras producing a three-dimensional "slice" picture at different levels throughout the head, if required, or nowadays any region of the body (the "Whole Body Scanner"). The individual pictures are formed into an overall picture by a computer. Very small tumors, undetectable by other means, can now often be demonstrated by this technique, which has been particularly useful in the diagnosis of brain tumors.

Psychological aspects

Having made the diagnosis, staged the extent of the tumor, and planned treatment, the oncological team will wish to convey these findings and their meanings to the patient in the kindest possible way. As those involved with the patient—doctors, nurses, paramedicals, etc.—get to know him or her, it usually becomes obvious how best to convey these facts. Many patients will want to know from A to Z—tumor, treatment, prognosis, the lot—in cold hard facts. Many ask some questions but obviously imply that the information they require is limited, and some patients just do not want to know at all. "I'll leave it all to you, doctor; do your best." It is as cruel to present bare unqualified facts to an unprepared patient as it is to withhold facts from a patient who genuinely wants to know them and can make

vital rearrangements to his or her life in time if the prognosis is poor.

As an understanding and trust build up between the oncological team and the patient, often the full impact of the diagnosis and prognosis can be achieved gradually in a rational and sensitive manner without needless alarm or, on the other hand, inappropriate optimism. It is usual to inform a close relative or next of kin of the precise nature of the disease and prognosis if the patient has made it clear he or she does not want to know much about what is really wrong. Much time, however, is frequently spent dispelling preconceived myths and folklore before giving the true facts.

Often the term "cancer" causes patients to think they are immediately doomed; they must be told the correct facts about the chances of cure (or, at least, the chances of considerable prolongation of life) which can be achieved with modern treatments of even the severest tumors. Conversely, in cases where treatments have failed, the doctors and their teams will not abandon the terminal patient but continue to support him or her mentally and to reassure the patient that when death comes it will be painfree and with dignity.

Treatments

There are three major forms of treatment available: surgery, radiation therapy and chemotherapy. Often these different approaches are used in combination or in sequence. In addition, *immunotherapy* is currently being introduced at an experimental stage. The idea behind immunotherapy is that if you stimulate the patient's own internal protective systems against disease into action by, say, injecting bacteria into a patient's bloodstream, the stimulated host defense against the bacterial or other insult may then attempt to destroy the cancer as well. As more becomes known of the immune defense systems of the body—normal, in disease, and in the presence of malignancy—then the closer we come to harnessing that knowledge in order to stimulate a body to eradicate its own cancers, or possibly prevent them from occurring in the first place. (See IMMUNE SYSTEM.)

Surgery

Excision of a tumor is the oldest treatment. It sounds logical that if you have an abnormal lump you can cut it out. Unfortunately, the situation is often not that simple. In many cases the tumor may have encircled or invaded vital structures such as the spinal cord or major blood vessels—the removal of which would be fatal—so that complete surgical clearance is prevented.

Before contemplating excision, a surgeon would like to be sure that the lump he removes will be a *complete* removal, before the tumor cells have spread elsewhere through the body. It is pointless removing a whole breast in a radical MASTECTOMY if the tumor has spread to the other breast, spine and brain. Curative cancer surgery is usually preceded by intensive investigation (or "work-up") with scans and x-rays to discover the full extent of the disease process. However, even if complete excision is prevented, removing as much as possible of some tumors may assist the subsequent efforts of eradication by radiation therapy or chemotherapy, or both.

Spread (METASTASIS) is often facilitated through the natural filtration and drainage system of the body—the lymphatics. These chains have filter stations along their routes called lymph nodes; spreading cancer cells can be trapped in these and the surgeon will endeavor to remove invaded nodes with the rest of the tumor. (See LYMPHATIC SYSTEM.)

> Surgical removal of a malignant tumor can be successful if the cancer cells have not already spread to other parts of the body (metastasis). Thus, it is essential to seek prompt medical attention at the first sign of a suspicious lump or new growth. In women, this is particularly true if they discover a lump in the breast.

Surgery plays an important part in palliation and improvement in the life quality of patients with advanced cancer. A bleeding, tumor-filled breast is often better removed even if the operation is not curative, so that the scar can dry and heal, whereas the tumor-invaded breast would continue to discharge and bleed. Uncontrollable intra-abdominal cancers may block the bowel, causing obstruction and vomiting. Bypassing the blockage by bringing the bowel out onto the abdominal surface (colostomy or ileostomy) will often relieve the obstruction and allow the patient to lead a reasonably useful life, despite the tumor which may be growing in the pelvis but is not causing any immediate harm.

Limbs invaded by advanced tumors may become extremely painful, only to be relieved by a palliative amputation. It is, however, the surgeon's hope that by catching the tumor early enough he will be able to remove it easily and completely with an excellent chance of cure. Of course, individual tumor cells are too small to be seen by the naked eye at operation, and it is not difficult for a surgeon unknowingly to leave microscopic deposits of tumor behind when a full clearance is thought to have been achieved.

Radiation therapy

The phenomenon of radioactivity was discovered by the French physicist Antoine Henri Becquerel in 1896 as a natural occurrence in uranium. The later work of Pierre and Marie Curie led to the discovery and isolation of the radioactive element radium. For many years the only known radioactive elements were those occurring naturally; but in 1932 it was found to be possible to cause previously stable atoms to become radioactive. Radium, because of its steady slow rate of decay and radioactive emission, has been used extensively in the treatment of localized cancers where high dosage at short range is required, such as cancer of the neck of the womb (cervix).

The radiations used in cancer treatment are divided into two groups: *electromagnetic* and *particulate* radiation. The terms "x-rays" and "gamma rays" are both used for the former. Although these radiations are of an identical nature, the difference in terminology has grown up because x-rays can be produced by electrical generators, but gamma rays are radiations emitted spontaneously by radioactive materials undergoing nuclear reactions. As far as the particulate radiations are concerned, *Beta particles* are of greatest interest in therapy. Beta particles are electrons which are emitted from atoms in the process of radioactive decay. Standard x-ray machines produce energies of 10 to 1,000 kVolts, ranging from diagnostic x-rays (10 to 20 kV) to radiotherapeutic x-rays (150 to 1,000 kV). Cobalt 60 and cesium 137 isotope teletherapy machines produce gamma rays of 1,000 to 2,000 kV. Linear accelerator supervoltage machines (4,000 to 10,000 kV) produce tumor-killing levels of radiation even at deep levels within the body.

After the discovery of diagnostic x-rays at the turn of the century, doctors soon discovered the therapeutic effects of radiation in curing a wide variety of diseases, but, in particular, cancers. Initial treatments were unplanned and occasionally did more harm than good. As the development of physics offered greater understanding and accuracy of radiation, the treatments produced became more precise and effective, until the present time when radiation therapy is now used extensively in highly organized medical centers throughout the world.

The aim of radiation therapy is to kill all cells of the tumor, or to render them incapable of further cell division, but without producing excessive damage to surrounding normal tissues. All the malignant cells in all types of tumor could be killed if a sufficiently high dose of radiation was given—however, this amount of radiation would nearly always cause severe damage to the surrounding healthy tissues and possibly kill the patient. The sensitivity of any particular tumor or tissue varies a great deal; for example, bone marrow cells and the intestinal lining are very radiosensitive, whereas kidneys, liver, muscle and bone cells are relatively insensitive. Tumor radiosensitivity also depends on many factors; but, on the whole, the more wild and rapidly growing the tumor is, the more damaged it will be by radiation. However, the more rapidly growing tumors frequently spread early in the disease and it is difficult to irradiate every part of the body safely where the spread of the tumor may have already taken place.

It has been realized for many years that the response of a tumor to a given dose of radiation depends on the length of time during which the radiation is delivered, and that the longer the time the less the effect. Despite the fact that an increased total dose of radiation is needed, radiation therapy is usually *fractionated;* that is, the required dose of radiation is given in daily treatments over a given period, usually several weeks, in order to decrease many of the undesirable side effects of radiation treatment. After a single dose of radiation, a fraction of the tumor cells dies immediately. The remainder of the cells recover, as they receive sublethal damage, and then respond to further irradiation in the next 24 hours as if they were normal, previously unirradiated cells.

Despite the drawbacks, fractionated radiation therapy has many advantages: the radiotolerance of the normal tissues surrounding the tumor is increased, the risk of radiation damage and NECROSIS (death) of these tissues is decreased, and the cosmetic appearance of irradiated areas is improved as the damage to the skin is minimized. In addition, since all cells are more sensitive to radiation when undergoing cell division, and since at any one time only a small proportion of the total number of malignant cells will be dividing, it is preferable to fractionate treatment so that the chance of irradiating dividing cells is greatly increased.

Many factors, therefore, affect the "radiocurability" of cancers: the radiosensitivity of malignant cells, which in turn partly depends upon the rate of cell division and the degree of oxygenation; the radiosensitivity of the normal tissue surrounding the tumor, which may limit the dose used; and the size of the tumor mass—for, if a large volume of tissue is irradiated, the integral dose will be high and patients often cannot tolerate the symptoms of the resulting radiation sickness. If large areas of bowel have been irradiated, diarrhea may well ensue and possibly internal holes (fistulae) may form between bowel loops causing many problems. A potential danger is the effect of radiation on active bone marrow, which can cause a failure of blood cell production resulting in anemia.

Chemotherapy

Since many cancers have occupied more than one site in the body by the time the patients have consulted the doctor, and the site, extent or invasion of some tumors prevent complete treatment by radiation therapy or surgery, there is an obvious need for anticancer drugs which can be injected into the bloodstream, or taken by mouth, to be carried to all parts of the body and kill even disseminated cancers. Drugs have already been prepared which are able to eradicate completely certain tumors and others have been used to shrink solid tumors significantly to render a previously inoperable tumor smaller and more easily removed surgically.

Doctors throughout history have tried to treat tumors using compounds such as arsenic, usually rubbed on the affected part, mostly with little success. In 1942 Gilman noted anemia occurring in servicemen who had been exposed to mustard gas after the sinking of a military transport vessel. This was quickly followed by screening of many related chemicals and in 1945 the first nitrogen-mustard antitumor drugs were produced. These were shown to have some activity against lymphomas (see LYMPHOMA). Two years later a whole range of antitumor drugs was produced whose activity interfered with the nutrition of tumor cells (the antimetabolites) and were shown to have great efficacy in the treatment of a wide spectrum of tumors. Since that time, the Western world research laboratories have produced a steady flow of new antitumor drugs. Approximately 600,000 compounds have been screened using animals in the past 30 years, and 6,000 of them have antitumor activity. However, only 75 have

> For well over 30 years various chemical compounds have been investigated for their effectiveness in destroying cancer cells. Very few of these drugs have been ideal for clinical use, largely because—although they successfully attacked malignant growths— they also produced undesirable toxic side effects on the patients.

progressed beyond preliminary testing on humans and of these about 30 are in general use.

The results of chemotherapy in the treatment of non-solid tumors (leukemias and lymphomas) are exciting and gratifyingly good, but a greater problem lies with the management of solid tumors (which are vastly the more common). Much of the earliest treatment was given in the absence of any real understanding of tumor behavior. Even now we do not understand enough completely to rationalize treatment. Early therapy consisted of single drugs used continuously or in sporadic doses, sufficient to induce temporary remissions. Eventually tumor resistance occurred and another drug was substituted. This method of sequential administration has largely been superseded by high dose intermittent therapy with combination agents.

The whole range of drugs available can be divided into several big groups. The *alkylating agents*, such as the nitrogen mustards, form cross linkages in DNA molecules (in the tumor cell nucleus or organizing center) and therefore stop manufacture of more DNA for replication of cells. *Antimetabolites*, such as methotrexate, act by blocking the formation of the DNA and stop new cell production. *Antitumor antibiotics*, such as Adriamycin, produce DNA strand breaks and immobilize the active cell. *Plant products*, such as vincristine, which comes from a little blue-flowered plant (the periwinkle), interfere with the actual mechanical division of the cell. *Enzymes*, such as L-asparaginase, inhibit cells by starving them of protein building blocks (essential aminoacids). Some *hormones* have antitumor effects, for example in the management of cancers of the breast and womb. The remaining drugs available do not fit into the above categories but have potent antitumor properties, such as the platinum-based group of compounds.

In an "ideal" tumor where all cells are sensitive to the drug, antitumor agents kill a fixed proportion of the cell population with each dose given. If we assume that most clinically evident tumors contain 10^{11} cells initially, and that 50% are killed by each dose of therapy, then approximately three to four years of intensive treatment is potentially required if such doses are given monthly as is usually the case. The bulk of tumor to be removed by chemotherapy may have already been reduced by surgery or radiation therapy. However, once tumor cell numbers fall to about 10^9 (equivalent to a mass 1 cm in diameter) the disease is no longer clinically detectable, even with ultrasound and other scans. Therefore, apparent clearance of the disease does not mean that treatment can be stopped at this time but often requires *maintenance therapy*. The question of when it is safe to stop medication is often raised by the patient (and doctor too) and is extremely difficult to answer. Blood tests and other tests which are able to give an accurate assessment of whether or not there is tumor left in the body are, at the moment, largely unreliable, although they are being improved gradually.

The doses used are often limited by a particular drug's toxicity and side effects. As with radiation therapy, the normal tissues most at risk are those undergoing rapid division and growth, including the blood-forming bone marrow, the lining of the intestine, the gonads (ovaries and testes) and the hair follicles. Certain drugs have selective toxicity (for example, they can damage the heart or lungs). Most of these powerful antitumor drugs cause nausea and vomiting, and it is possible patients may require hospitalization for short periods while they are receiving the drugs.

Assessment of new cancer treatments

When drugs have been shown to have suitable antitumor properties without severe problems in their administration or tolerance, they can be assessed in clinical trials. Before being used on humans these drugs will have been tested extensively on animals. Often human tumors are grown in immunosuppressed mice (xenografting) and the effectiveness or otherwise of the drug is then assessed. Side effects and toxicity are demonstrated in a wide variety of animal experiments, e.g. showing nausea in dogs. The Food and Drug Administration (FDA) may then grant permission for carefully supervised trials in selected major cancer treatment centers; such trials are usually divided into three progressive phases.

Phase I: This involves the administration of the drugs to patients with tumors that are not amenable to, or have failed to respond to, other established regimes, i.e. last ditch attempts to save essentially doomed patients with a new drug. The antitumor activity and side effects are then assessed.

Phase II: This attempts to establish the range of cancer influenced; approximately 20 patients are treated and usually include the common "signal" tumors, e.g. of colon, bronchus, breast, leukemias, lymphomas and malignant melanomas of the skin.

Phase III: This defines the place of an active drug in a specific cancer; comparisons are made with other agents in random studies.

This information is documented for the world literature and response to treatment is graded as complete, partial or nonresponse. This is usually related to measurements of clinically assessable disease. Complete response indicates the disappearance of all known tumor. Partial responses are often subdivided into those where regression of 50% or more is obtained and those achieving less than this. Nonresponse describes static or progressive disease. Highly variable response rates reported by different groups of workers using the agents may indicate the difficulties encountered in obtaining reproducible objective measurements. Often a multicenter study is the only means of rapidly obtaining large numbers of patients with an uncommon tumor. Ethical considerations—including the rights and desires of patients—remain of paramount importance and may limit the design of such studies.

Combined treatment

Failure of drug treatments alone is often caused by excessive tumor size. The results of experimental studies suggest that if the majority of the cancer is removed by surgery or radiation therapy then drugs may erradicate the main tumor. This has given rise to the concept of *adjuvant chemotherapy* and combinations of treatments. As an illustration of this let us consider a Wilms' tumor—a cancer of the kidney arising in children. This disease, previously treated by surgery and radiation therapy, used to be associated with only a 30% cure rate even when apparently localized (with no obvious spread) when first seen. Since the advent of the drugs vincristine and actinomycin D, used in combination with local treatment, the cure rate is in the region of 80–90%, if there is no obvious spread. Even in the presence of spread (metastasis) the combined approach can probably save at least 60% of such children.

The future

The current principal strategies for improving the results

from cancer treatment are concerned with developing new drugs and learning to use the existing ones, in conjunction with surgery and radiation therapy, in a more efficient manner.

As mentioned earlier, there are many immunological techniques under investigation which include the non-specific stimulation of the immune system of the patient suffering from cancer—using the simple BCG vaccination, injections of *Corynebacterium parvum* bacteria and a drug specifically designed to stimulate the immune system. Some evidence has been presented to suggest that chemotherapy may be more effective under these circumstances.

Unfortunately, patients with cancer frequently fall prey to quacks and charlatans throughout the world who offer completely useless, often bizarre, forms of treatment for large sums of money. Spontaneous cures of even advanced cancers are not uncommonly reported, e.g., after a visit to the Shrine at Lourdes in France, and are often "confirmed" with x-rays and other sound evidence. It is possible that, perhaps, the body's own defense mechanisms in a few very fortunate patients suddenly become sufficiently active enough to overthrow the tumor spontaneously, with regrowth of the normal tissue. It may be that doctors will be able to stimulate this process more effectively in the future. In the meantime, it is sincerely hoped that the tragedy of suffering from an incurable terminal cancer will not be made worse by participation in a despicable confidence trick at the hands of medical charlatans.

SOME COMMON TUMORS

Gastrointestinal tract

Tumors of the gastrointestinal tract form the largest cause of deaths due to cancer (about 100,000 people in the United States every year), equally divided between men and women. They usually affect elderly patients and current research is endeavoring to establish carcinogens (substances which stimulate cancer) amongst the many varied compounds and elements which pass through the gastrointestinal tract during a person's life—a formidable task.

Recent evidence indicates that lack of roughage (e.g., bran) in a diet may enhance the exposure to these carcinogens, for it is known that primitive peoples who eat basically unrefined foods, such as unpolished rice, tend not to develop colon or rectal (large bowel) cancers. However, these people's expectation of life does not usually extend up to the peak age for acquiring these cancers.

The principal treatment for gastrointestinal cancers is usually surgical, preceded or followed by radiation therapy or chemotherapy, or both. The outlook for those who develop cancer of the esophagus and stomach is, with a few exceptions, rather poor. As mentioned before, people whose diet tends to contain a high proportion of raw fish (e.g., Japan, Iceland) are more susceptible. In Finland the

disease is also common, and the diet has a high proportion of milk and milk products. The prevalence of iron deficiency is also marked. About a quarter of the population are tapeworm carriers and often exhibit an anemia due to vitamin B_{12} deficiency. Cancer of the esophagus often presents with difficulty in swallowing and is treated by surgical removal of the tumor; the stomach is then either brought up into the chest to link up to the esophageal remnant, or a piece of large bowel is cut out and used to "bridge the gap."

Tumors too advanced to be removed are usually irradiated. Cancer of the stomach produces symptoms of weight loss and occasional vomiting of blood, or the passage of altered blood in the stools. It is often difficult to decide whether an ulcer in the stomach is benign, peptic, or malignant until a piece is removed for analysis. This is simply and swiftly performed nowadays using a fiberoptic gastroscope: a flexible lighted tube is swallowed into the stomach and duodenum allowing the surgeon to examine the ulcer for the appearance of malignancy, and to take a biopsy using a tiny pair of forceps operated via a long wire. Removal of the stomach (gastrectomy) is the usual treatment in such cases.

When tumors arise in the lower part of the large bowel patients often have a change in bowel habit—sometimes constipation, sometimes diarrhea. Some tumors will block the bowel completely and cause obstruction with vomiting. Occasionally a patient will pass fresh blood with the stools. Every time this happens a full investigation is required. It may just be piles (hemorrhoids) or possibly, in elderly patients, a tumor. The large bowel can be examined with a finger, a short metal hollow tube (proctoscope), a longer hollow metal tube (sigmoidoscope), or a flexible lighted fiberoptic colonoscope, which also permits the taking of biopsies. Barium studies are also very helpful in the x-ray diagnosis of gastrointestinal tumors. (See BARIUM MEAL/BARIUM ENEMA.)

Large bowel tumors are usually removed surgically and frequently have a very good prognosis. If there is sufficient bowel still attached to the anus, the two ends of the bowel where the tumor was removed can be joined together. If there is insufficient bowel to do a join-up (as in the case of cancer very near the anus), the anus will be closed surgically and the remaining bowel opened out onto the surface of the abdomen to form a manageable, artificial anus (COLOSTOMY).

Lung

Just behind the number of gastrointestinal cancers sits the vast quantity of people dying from lung cancer each year. Men outnumber women but the proportion of women is gradually increasing. In addition to the great number of primary cancers beginning in the lungs, the chest is a frequent site for secondary deposits of other tumors. The outlook on the whole for these patients with primary lung tumors is generally bleak. The tumors are often aggressive and rapidly spreading long before the first symptoms appear (e.g. cough, blood in the sputum, weight loss, constant rib pain).

Extensive evidence now shows that by far the majority of lung cancers are caused by excessive cigarette smoking. The typical male candidate for lung cancer is between 60 and 70 years old (although it can strike as early as 30 years of age) and has been smoking one or two packs of cigarettes a day for 20 years or more, and probably began smoking when he was fairly young. The risk of dying from lung cancer for these smokers is 15–20 times greater than for men who have never smoked. The typical female candidate is between 55 and 65 years old and has been smoking one or more packs of cigarettes a day for 20 years, and began smoking before she was 20. Her chance of dying of lung cancer is five times greater than that of a woman who has never smoked. Pipe and cigar smokers have a greater risk of lung cancer than nonsmokers, but much less so than cigarette smokers. However, they do have three to five times the risk of developing mouth and esophageal cancers than nonsmokers.

After a smoker stops the habit, the risk of developing lung cancer decreases with each year that a once heavy smoker avoids smoking; after 10 years of abstinence the risks are no greater than for a person who has never smoked.

The diagnosis is usually suspected by a shadow appearing on a chest x-ray, and confirmed by a biopsy, frequently made nowadays using another fiberoptic instrument—the bronchoscope. Sometimes cancer cells can also be detected in the patient's sputum. If, after extensive investigation, the disease is found to be localized (e.g., to one lobe of the lung), it is occasionally possible to remove the tumor entirely by opening the chest (thoracotomy) and removing part or all of the affected lung (pneumonectomy). However, the majority of tumors have spread by the time the diagnosis is made and major surgery at this time would be pointless.

Palliation with radiation therapy and chemotherapy may well prolong life for a few months or longer but death usually rapidly relieves the patient of a miserable terminal illness, often accompanied by perpetual chest pain, frequent coughing or vomiting of blood and usually profound weight loss (cachexia). There can be no stronger incentive to stop smoking than to witness the sad demise of these often strong young men rapidly reduced to a leathery crisp—a shadow of their former self. Statistics gathered after British doctors gave up smoking on a national scale (now only one in six smokes at all—not even an occasional cigar) have shown a marked drop recently in the incidence of lung cancer among them. So if you are dying for a smoke—don't.

(See also the major article on **Pulmonary Diseases**.)

Breast

BREAST CANCER is the most common cancer among women in both the United States and Britain: 34,000 American women die each year out of the 90,000 new cases. The predisposing factors for this disease are: an immediate family history of breast cancer, never having borne a child, having had the first child when over 30 years of age, and women who have had their breast feeding suppressed with estrogen tablets. Of course, these only represent *trends;* it is quite possible for a woman to acquire breast cancer even if she has had ten children before the age of 30 and no one in her family has ever had the disease before.

The chance of developing a malignant breast lump increases with age. Roughly speaking, the outlook is worse for women who develop the tumor before the menopause.

The signs and symptoms are usually a lump found in (or swelling of) the breast, recent nipple retraction, local skin tethering, nipple bleeding or discharge. Occasionally women present with back pain and an x-ray of the spine reveals a secondary deposit from a small previously undetected tumor of the breast. The diagnosis may be established by one or more of the following investigations: (1) *mammography:* low-dose x-rays of the breasts; (2) *xeroradiography:* x-ray examination producing pictures of the breast on coated paper (rather than film), like a dry copier; (3) *thermography,* which depicts heat patterns of the skin of the breast, showing tumors which have different temperatures than the rest of the breast tissue; and (4) *fine needle aspiration:* a few cells in the lump are looked at by a cytologist after being sucked out using a fine needle.

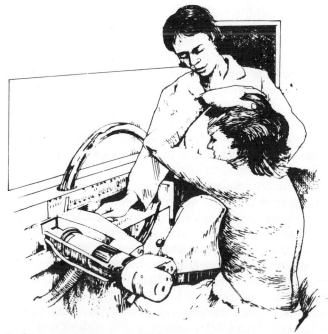

Soft tissue x-rays of the breasts (mammograms), taken in two planes, can aid in the diagnosis of both benign and cancerous tumors of the breast.

The diagnosis is usually confirmed by biopsy under general anesthesia. Despite all the sophisticated diagnostic facilities available, 80% of all breast lumps biopsied at the present time are found to be benign. Routine self-examination and screening in Early Diagnostic Units will help detect breast cancers in their earlier stages, and the chance of complete cure for early stage disease is excellent. However, many women, fearing cancer, do not bring their breast lumps to the attention of their doctors until it is too late to help them.

The correct treatment for advanced breast cancer remains an enigma. In the early stages of advanced disease, surgical removal, usually by removing the whole breast, can be curative. In more advanced cases, treatment is not so well established. The mortality rate for breast cancer is the same today as it was when records began in the first English cancer hospital well over a hundred years ago. Modern treatment has increased survival length but not improved the mortality rates. Many multicenter trials throughout the world are taking place to discover the best form of management.

Some oncologists believe that if the lymph node drainage system of the breast is involved and the tumor cannot be shown to have spread elsewhere in the body, a *radical mastectomy*—removing the breast and chest muscles underneath (along with all the nearby lymph nodes)—should be performed. Others would give postoperative radiation therapy. Some just remove the malignant lump ("lumpectomy") and then irradiate the remaining breast. Chemotherapy used in conjunction with surgery or radiation therapy (or both) can benefit some patients, but it is far from being completely satisfactory.

It is well established that some cancers of the breast are hormone sensitive, so that if the patient's sex hormone status is changed the tumor may well regress. This can be achieved by giving anti-estrogen tablets or by removing the ovaries of premenopausal women (oophorectomy) with or without removing their adrenal glands (adrenalectomy) and pituitary gland (hypophysectomy).

Advanced breast tumors frequently spread to bone and lungs, and local radiation therapy to these deposits can bring temporary relief of pain.

The mastectomized woman is usually supported by trained personnel who will ensure that she is fitted with a false breast (prosthesis) shortly after the operation; later on, in some cases, it is possible to insert a plastic prosthesis under the skin. Despite the immediate support of her nurses, mastectomy counselors, husband and family, the mastectomized woman will often feel mutilated and that feeling may never leave her. In the majority of cases, however, as her confidence returns, the scar fades; and the initial resentment fades with it as she realizes that, with each passing year of survival, she has cheated this dreadful killing disease.

Every oncologist will have many sad stories to tell of women who left it too late for seeking help from a doctor after they have found breast lumps, and my own saddest was the sight of two tearful girls, aged six and eight, being led away by a nurse from the deathbed of their 33-year-old mother. It is hoped that these daughters—and all women—will learn to check their breasts for lumps routinely and to seek prompt medical advice the moment they detect something suspicious.

The leukemias

The leukemias are a variety of neoplastic diseases in which the white blood cell types proliferate wildly, and often almost replace the natural proportion of white cells to red cells (which are vastly in excess in health) to a virtual total domination by the malignant white cells. The blood-forming bone marrow becomes infiltrated with these abnormal cells preventing it from performing its normal task of producing all blood elements. About 22,000 new cases occur each year in the United States and the disease causes about 15,000 deaths per year. There are two basic types: a rapid form (acute) and a prolonged form (chronic).

Acute leukemia can attack at any age and the child or adult might find difficulty in getting over simple infections, or have persistent bleeding from the nose or gums. The liver and spleen can often be felt to be enlarged and as the disease progresses the patient becomes easily fatigued and frequently pale. As the bone marrow becomes infiltrated, bone pain may commence. *Chronic leukemias* have more insidious symptoms and are occasionally diagnosed after routine blood tests for unconnected indications.

The prognosis in many leukemias is improving every year. Improved chemotherapy is lengthening survival time impressively; at least temporary initial remissions are almost the rule nowadays. In 1960, few patients survived for five years following diagnosis; but with optimum treatment nearly 50% of children with acute leukemia can now expect to live at least five years after diagnosis.

Chronic leukemia is usually treated with tablets and frequently patients live long periods and die of something else. Occasionally the chronic form can become acute and these may well be extremely difficult to treat. (See also LEUKEMIA.)

Lymphomas

Lymphomas, of which HODGKIN'S DISEASE is the most common, are produced by malignant change in the cells of the body's natural tissue drainage system—the lymphatics. The "junction boxes" of these systems, the lymph nodes, often swell up to produce chains of lumps in the neck, groins, or sometimes within the abdomen and intestine. Specially selected combinations of radiation therapy and chemotherapy are producing very encouraging results in these diseases; 10-to-15-year remission rates are being achieved in 85% of all Hodgkin's disease sufferers treated early in the course of the disease. (See LYMPHOMA.)

Lymphomas also include the *lymphosarcomas*, among which is grouped BURKITT'S LYMPHOMA, thought to be caused by a virus.

Skin

Skin tumors are reasonably common, but because they are easy to detect, deaths from them are fortunately infrequent. Excessive exposure to sunlight and other causative factors have already been mentioned. Treatment is usually by surgical excision or radiation therapy and is usually curative, although similar tumors may arise near the same site later on.

One skin tumor worthy of mention is the *malignant melanoma*. This begins as a brown or black mole anywhere on the body, is never hairy, and is called a junctional nevus. After stimulation, believed to be by sunlight, this mole may increase in size, change color, become painful, bleed (one or more of these things) and if not removed send malignant melanoma cells off to distant sites in the body via the bloodstream and produce similar black tumors on the skin locally (known as "satellites"). If the original tumor is not widely removed surgically, the dissemination of this tumor is frequently fatal. No chemotherapy has yet produced any spectacular results in cases of advanced malignant melanoma, although immunotherapy with BCG is very promising. Of course, not every mole on your body will become malignant, but should any changes occur to them as described above—e.g., change in color or increase in size—consult your doctor immediately. (See MELANOMA.)

Brain

Tumors of the central nervous system cause about 10,000 deaths each year and render great sorrow because they commonly attack children and young adults in the prime of life. The brain is not infrequently the site of the blood-borne spread of other tumors, such as the breast and lung. The presence of even a small, benign tumor within the skull's enclosed boxlike structure causes pressure on delicate nerve centers, so that gross handicaps, paralyses, etc., can be produced by the havoc wrought. (See also the major article on **Neurosurgery.**)

Surgical removal and radiation, while successfully removing the tumor, may cause irreversible brain damage in the process. The prognosis of each brain tumor depends a great deal on the histological type. Some, like the *meningiomas* (a benign growth of the brain coverings), do extremely well after surgical removal; others, like high-grade *astrocytomas*, kill within a matter of months. Few chemotherapeutic agents are effective and none can be relied upon to produce cures at the present time. (See MENINGIOMA.)

Sarcomas

These relatively uncommon tumors arise from the connective tissue in the body—bone, muscle, fibrous tissue, joints and their lining membranes (synovial), etc. They are frequently highly aggressive cancers, often attacking the young, and their equally aggressive treatment often requires amputation of whole limbs. Radiation therapy can be of use in some cases, but so far chemotherapy has been disappointing. (See SARCOMA.)

Ovary

Cancer of the ovaries claims approximately 10,000 lives each year. Women usually complain of increased abdominal girth and lower abdominal pain; occasionally a bloodstained vaginal discharge or postmenopausal bleed-

> Of all cancers that attack women, those involving the ovaries constitute 18%. Most of the 10,000 women who die each year from cancer of the ovaries are in their 50s or 60s—the ages at which the incidence of this relatively common malignancy is at its peak. An affected ovary may grow to a considerable size before it is discovered.

ing heralds the malignancy, but approximately 70% of ovarian cancers are in an advanced stage before treatment can be started. The cause of these tumors is not fully known and they do not appear to be hormone dependent. It is curious to note that they are relatively uncommon in Japan but are much more prevalent in Denmark.

The early stages of the disease, e.g., an unruptured malignant ovarian cyst, are often completely cured by surgical excision with or without radiation therapy. Later stages present problems as spread throughout the abdominal cavity takes place. Recently, exciting developments in the chemotherapy of this malignancy—with agents such as the platinum group of compounds—are producing improved prognoses for these unfortunate women.

Body of the uterus

Cancer arising in the body of the uterus (womb) tends to present as postmenopausal vaginal bleeding in typically obese, diabetic women around the age of 60 to 65 years. The administration of estrogen hormone to prevent menopausal symptoms such as hot flashes causes an active growth of the uterine lining *(endometrial hyperplasia)* which, if very prolonged, can become malignant in some cases. This problem can usually be overcome by the intermittent administration of estrogens, inducing a withdrawal bleeding each month, or performing endometrial aspirates or a D & C at intervals. Recent evidence shows that the addition of a small amount of the natural pregnancy hormone, PROGESTERONE, greatly reduces the risk of malignancy.

Such tumors are frequently cured by removing the uterus (HYSTERECTOMY), ovaries and Fallopian tubes. Secondary spread and advanced local invasion are not the rule but when they do occur they frequently respond to radiation therapy or progesterone hormone therapy (or both).

Cervix

Cancer of the neck of the womb kills almost as many women as cancer of the ovary, but the death rate is falling: in the United States, from 26.8 per 100,000 in 1935 down to 11.9 per 100,000 in 1965. This is almost certainly due in great part to earlier detection using the Papanicolaou smear test ("Pap smear" or CERVICAL SMEAR). The predisposing factors are an early age of first sexual intercourse, a low social class, immediate family history, and possibly certain genital infections (e.g., Herpes virus). The lower incidence found among Jewish women was initially thought to be due to the practice of circumcising their men. However, the results of studies on other ethnic groups who also practice circumcision show that these women do not seem to benefit from this protection. Opinion now rests on the relatively low incidence of cervical cancer among Jewish women as being attributable to generally higher standards of social class, good hygienic standards and sexual conservatism.

The incidence of new cases has shown a recent sharp rise paralleling the current pandemic of venereal disease. It is postulated that exposure of the early teenage cervix to carcinogens, perhaps contained in semen or smegma, induces initial "premalignant changes." These premalignant changes in the cervical cells, called *dysplasia*, may remain static for up to 20 years. They may eventually return to normal, but some, upon an unknown stimulus, rapidly grow, become aggressive and turn into a very small cancer—*carcinoma in situ*. The "Pap smear" removes cells from the cervix and allows an expert microscopist to look for these early changes of premalignancy. Should they be found, a wedge of abnormal tissue can be removed surgically—a *cone biopsy*—before the cancers begin to invade into the womb and nearby bladder and rectum.

Unfortunately, a small proportion of the cancers pass through the premalignant stage to the invasive stage quite rapidly and these patients may first see their doctors with an advanced tumor. The early changes do not produce any symptoms, but the advanced tumors appear as a nasty-looking ulcer (easily seen by a doctor using a small vaginal speculum) which will bleed after intercourse, or spontaneously, and cause intermenstrual or postmenopausal bleeding.

Untreated, the cancer frequently invades the bladder and rectum, often killing the patient by blocking off the drainage tracts of the kidneys (ureters) as they enter the bladder. The early stages of the advanced disease can be treated by an extended hysterectomy or with radiation therapy—which, in addition to external radiation, usually involves the local application of a radioactive pellet (usually cesium) against the cervix in order to deliver a very powerful radiation with short range to avoid damaging vital organs close by. Early diagnosis by means of cervical smears, taken at intervals throughout the life of every woman who has had sexual intercourse, will catch the greater proportion of these tumors in the early, curable stages. Chemotherapy, as yet, does not offer a great deal, and the survival rates of the advanced stages of this disease, which frequently attacks young mothers with families, are appalling.

The future

The gradual conquering of cancer is slowly taking place. Many medical centers throughout the world are performing intensive research into the cause, nature and treatment of tumors and are slowly unraveling the knot.

There are several points to be made before we can expect to open a newspaper and read the headline "Cancer Defeated." Firstly, as has been shown above, cancer is just a general term for hundreds of different types of tumor, with tremendous variations between their behavior. Secondly, although a tremendous amount of work has been done to understand how normal cells and cancer cells function, it has frequently been impossible to translate and make use of that information into rationalizing diagnosis and treatment—i.e., what the lab people tell the doctor *should* happen often does not take place in the patient. Thirdly, the cooperation of the public is hampered by an inbuilt fear of cancers (quite understandably), slowing down the chance of early diagnosis, and a reluctance to avoid known cancer-inducing substances such as cigarette tobacco.

At our present state of knowledge and treatment, cancer cure is most often assured in the early stages. Patients, through a rationalized understanding that cancer does not always mean death, must seek help immediately when they develop signs or symptoms, and not sit back and hope that the "whole damn thing will just go away on its own."

Allergy and Immunology

Dr. Jonathan E. Zucker

Allergies can range in severity from the relatively common but annoying symptoms of hay fever (allergic rhinitis) to skin rashes (contact dermatitis) and more distressing problems, such as allergic asthma and bronchitis. In rare cases an allergic reaction may even result in death from anaphylactic shock. The allergist is a specially trained physician concerned with the diagnosis and treatment of a wide range of allergies and allergic diseases.

A friend of mine was recently stung by a bee. Within ten minutes he was covered with hives and experienced a feeling of tightness in his chest. Luckily, he lived just around the corner from a hospital. When he arrived in its emergency room his breathing became difficult and he began to feel faint. He passed into unconsciousness as the doctor reached him. After treatment with epinephrine (adrenaline) and other medications he was resuscitated. He was both mystified and frightened by this truly life-threatening experience because he had been stung once before by a bee and nothing much happened. One of the important things to know about allergic reactions was explained to him; even those persons most prone to allergies must be exposed at least once to an allergenic substance (*allergen*) to become sensitized to it.

My friend's experience is not the usual reaction to an allergen, but it exemplifies an allergic reaction in its most dangerous expression and also the need for people to know the facts about allergy, its immunological mechanisms, symptoms and treatments. Such knowledge can sometimes be life saving.

An estimated 15–25% of Americans suffer from some form of allergy. Needless to say, most reactions are not as dramatic as the acute kind I have just described, but all allergies, if untreated, can become serious lifelong illnesses, often starting in infancy and early childhood. Clinical allergy and hypersensitivity embrace a wide range of disease states, including asthma, allergic rhinitis (hay fever), eczema, contact dermatitis, urticaria (hives) and angioedema (wheals and swelling of skin tissue), drug reactions, insect allergy, food hypersensitivity and many others—including an anaphylactic reaction, which my friend experienced.

Allergy and the immune mechanism

Allergy and immunology go hand-in-hand. In fact, allergy has been accurately defined as "untoward physiological events caused by a variety of immunologic reactions." Any organ of the body can be involved, but the most common "shock organs" are the nose, skin and lungs. In most cases, immunologic mechanisms (see IMMUNE SYSTEM) are protective and act as the body's natural defense against infections, ridding it of potentially dangerous substances which may disturb its normal internal environment. Such substances may be introduced from outside the body or generated from within. Allergy is the effect that results when the immune mechanism "backfires" to produce unwanted results. The allergist must, therefore, be qualified in immunology, be familiar with the structure and function of internal organ systems, know the methods of determining abnormal function and understand how different forms of treatment will affect various organs in different ways. This is especially true of the ever-growing list of drugs which may work in different ways to accomplish the same result.

Today's allergist-immunologist is qualified by many years of education and training. Following graduation from medical school he must complete a full three years of residency training in internal medicine or pediatrics. He may then be certified in the discipline he has chosen for his residency training by passing the examinations given by that examining board. Following this he must complete a full two-year (in-hospital) fellowship in clinical allergy and immunology, which qualifies him to take the examinations (oral and written) given by the American Board of Allergy and Immunology. When he passes them, he becomes a diplomate of that board. In addition, most states require yearly continuing medical education as a requirement for relicensure.

Referral to an allergist

Most patients today are referred to the allergist by their family doctors for diagnosis and treatment of a wide variety of allergenic disorders. Before discussing the most common problems in the allergist's daily practice, let me discuss briefly some of the basic mechanisms of the allergic reaction. Allergy or *hypersensitivity* is mediated immunologically by interaction between an allergen (antigen) and specific antibodies which are produced by specialized cells

Some individuals seem to be born with a constitutional tendency to acquire certain allergies. As depicted in the above illustration, the nature of the allergic response may change as the "atopic" person grows older. For example, during infancy the problem may be expressed as contact dermatitis (skin rash), followed after an interval of several years by allergic asthma and in adult life by hay fever.

in various organs or tissues or between circulating blood cells called *lymphocytes*, which have become sensitized to the allergen.

In order to diagnose a specific allergy, the allergist must do three things: identify the allergen, demonstrate that it produces clinical signs and symptoms and identify the immunologic mechanisms that are causing the problem. This is often difficult to do because there are certain diseases that mimic allergic (immunologically mediated) states but are actually caused by other mechanisms. Probably the best example of such a problem in diagnosis is to differentiate between *allergic rhinitis* (HAY FEVER) which may be caused by interaction between an allergen (ragweed pollen) and its specific antibody, and *vasomotor rhinitis*, caused by hyperactivity to a cold that affects the same small blood vessels in the mucous membrane lining the nose. Symptoms in both reactions are similar, but the specific cause must be determined if proper treatment is to be given.

Antibodies

An antibody is a protein substance produced by specialized cells within the body when they become sensitized to an antigen, which may be an infectious agent of a disease. Specific antibodies are produced in reaction to specific antigens (see ANTIBODY/ANTIGEN). For example, when the specialized cells become sensitized to certain germs and viruses of infectious diseases (smallpox, measles, polio, rubella and others) at the time of first exposure, specific antibodies are created to fight them during what is often a serious disease. Later, upon subsequent exposure to the same germs or viruses these cells go into immediate production of specific antibodies, which destroy the invading organisms before they can produce symptoms of the disease. Knowledge of this mechanism made possible the manufacture of vaccines which contain the same infectious agents in a weakened or attenuated form which produces the same sensitization and production of antibodies without causing disease symptoms. Some may provide immunity for life, but in most cases immunity must be maintained by periodic booster vaccinations.

The antibody associated most often with antibody-mediated allergic reactions in man is one of the gamma globulins. It is called *IgE (Immune Globulin E)*. The cell associated with cell-mediated hypersensitivity is the specifically sensitized small lymphocyte which circulates in the blood. The two immunological mechanisms are interrelated and interdependent and, in addition to producing specific antibodies, they may also produce chemical "factors" which are not antibodies but which function as part of the immunologic response. If the response leads to hypersensitivity, then the reaction is an allergic one. Histamine is probably the best known of these chemical factors because we hear so much about anti-histamine drugs used to counteract allergic responses. It should be understood that in most people the immunologic mechanisms control the antigens so that hypersensitivity develops in only 15–25% of those exposed to them.

Types of allergen

The allergens to which so many people react adversely can be almost anything they eat, touch, breathe or have injected into them. In addition, they can also become hypersensitized to such physical factors as heat, cold and the rays of the sun. The *contact allergens* must touch the skin to produce reactions. The most common *contact allergens* are poison ivy, poison oak and poison sumac. Others include perfumes, soaps, dyes, hair sprays and various kinds of metals. *Inhalant allergens* include airborne dust, mold spores, animal dander, various plant pollens, chemical fumes and vapors with pollens being the most common. They will produce asthma and allergic rhinitis (year round or seasonal). *Ingested allergens*—foods, drugs, artificial flavorings, colorings and preservatives—can cause a variety of symptoms, including gastrointestinal, respiratory, urologic and many others. *Allergens that are injected* often present the most life-threatening reactions. These include certain drugs (especially penicillin and its derivatives), contrast solutions ("dyes") used in many x-ray studies, hormones and insect venom.

It is now generally accepted that allergy is, in most cases, inherited. That does not mean that allergies caused by specific allergens are inherited (although in some recent family studies this would seem to be the case), but rather that the tendency to become sensitized to "foreign" substances is passed on in the genes. Exposure to these substances in the environment is then necessary to complete the allergy. What then are the most common problems referred to the allergist and how does he treat them?

Allergic rhinitis

This is probably the entity he sees most frequently. There are three patterns to the problem: perennial (year-round) symptoms, seasonal symptoms, and perennial symptoms with seasonal flare-ups. In any case the symptoms result from a specific allergic reaction of the lining of the nose. Sometimes the eyes are involved as well (allergic conjunctivitis). Symptoms include nasal congestion, rhinorrhea (runny nose), sneezing, and itching of the nose, eyes and sometimes the throat.

The perennial form of the condition is characterized by intermittent or continuous nasal symptoms with no seasonal variation. Seasonal allergic rhinitis is also known as *pollenosis*, "rose fever" when it occurs in the Spring, or "hay fever" when it occurs in the Fall. Actually, roses and hay are not the true causes of the problem. The names derived from the fact that before the true causes of the problem were known it was noted that symptoms occurred at about the time that roses were blooming or that the hay was being cut and stored. In reality, tree and grass pollens are the culprits in the Spring and weed pollens in the Fall.

Allergic rhinitis may begin at any age, but is seen to have its onset most frequently in children and young adults. Various studies have shown that 10–20% of the population suffers from this problem. The reaction is caused by an antibody-mediated reaction (occurring in the cells lining the nose), usually to an inhaled allergen.

The major allergens in perennial allergic rhinitis are house dust, mold spores and animal danders. In seasonal allergic rhinitis, pollens and mold spores are the main offenders. The pollens are usually from trees, grasses and weeds, all of which produce large amounts of lightweight pollen which is carried by the wind to provide cross-pollination for these plants. Plants, depending on insect pollination (most flowers), produce smaller quantities of "sticky" pollen and do not often cause allergic rhinitis. The most common pollen that produces nasal allergy in the United States is ragweed, followed by grass pollen and tree pollen.

Signs and symptoms

Symptoms are usually obvious. Children may tend to rub their noses and mouth breathe. The eyes may be involved: itching, redness and watering. Treatment consists of medication for relief of symptoms, avoidance of offending allergens wherever possible and *immunotherapy*—hyposensitization (desensitization) injections. Avoidance is usually only possible in patients allergic to animal dander—avoidance of pollens is not practical.

Treatment

Medications most often prescribed are *antihistamines* (to block the action of histamine, which is released by the cells in the nose and causes much of the sneezing, itching and watering) and *decongestants* (to reduce the swelling of the lining of the nose). These medications can be extremely effective but one must always be on guard against side effects (especially drowsiness) in the use of antihistamines and "nervousness" in the use of decongestants. Nose drops containing decongestants are often used and, unfortunately, often abused. They must only be used for short-term therapy because they can lead to a "rebound" effect in which the lining of the nose becomes increasingly more congested and inflamed.

Specific immunotherapy (hyposensitization injections) is usually part of the treatment of someone who has symptoms year-round or in many pollen seasons, or whose symptoms may be confined to one pollen season but are so severe that they cannot be controlled easily by medication. Just as knowledge of the immunological mechanisms was responsible for the development of vaccines that can protect us from many serious bacterial and viral diseases (polio, measles, smallpox, influenza and many others), the identification of specific antigens permits the allergist to inject them into the body in gradually increased doses until the body slowly builds up a tolerance to them.

Antigens for immunotherapy should be for those agents which cannot be avoided in daily living (house dust, mold spores, pollens). The injection therapy is given year-round and usually in aqueous vaccine (mixed with sterile water). The tolerance that develops is probably due to at least two factors: (1) the production of a new antibody, a "blocking antibody" which combines with the allergen before it can affect the target organ; and (2) an actual decrease in the amount of allergenic antibody (IgE). Many studies have shown that 75–80% of patients treated with injection therapy have shown marked symptomatic improvement.

Eczema

Eczema (chronic dermatitis) occurs in 1–3% of the population. Its cause is still largely unknown. It is a condition seen often by the allergist. About 75% of patients who have it also have a strong history of other allergic disorders, such as asthma and allergic rhinitis. Moreover, up to 30% of those with ECZEMA also have asthma and up to 60% have allergic rhinitis.

Signs and symptoms

Eczema may begin at any age, but is most commonly seen in infancy and early childhood. Infants characteristically develop a red, itchy, oozing DERMATITIS involving the cheeks, forehead, arms and legs. There is often a scaly scalp. The course in infants often improves gradually with spontaneous clearing by age five. Childhood eczema develops generally between two and four years of age; it may follow the infantile form but need not do so. It commonly involves the face, arms, legs and especially the creases of the elbows and behind the knees. Again, there may be intense itching. This phase may disappear (usually by puberty) or continue into adulthood.

About 60% of all childhood eczema disappears spontaneously by age six. The problems of treatment are due to the high association with other forms of allergic disease. Such patients are also highly susceptible to viral infections of the skin, especially HERPES SIMPLEX virus and the live virus used in SMALLPOX vaccination. Both of these viruses can spread rapidly on the skin of eczematous patients and cause serious (sometimes fatal) systemic disease. Thus, patients with eczema should not receive smallpox vaccination, nor come in contact with someone who has recently received such vaccination.

Treatment

Treatment of chronic dermatitis consists largely of topical medications (rubbed directly on the skin) and antihistamine drugs to relieve itching. A variety of topical agents can be used. Wet dressings are effective during the acute phase. Subacute eczema can be well controlled by topical steroid (cortisone) therapy, which produces only rare systemic effects. Systemic steroids should be reserved

for only the most severe cases. Coal tar preparations, which may stain clothing and have a bad odor, can also be very effective. Hypersensitization therapy is not indicated for eczema unless it is associated with asthma or hay fever, or both; in such cases, if the specific antigen is identified, such injections may be beneficial.

Allergic contact dermatitis

This is a condition frequently seen by the allergist. It is the clearest example of an allergy that is due to a cell-mediated mechanism, not to an allergen with a specific antibody as in allergic rhinitis, asthma or insect sting allergy. The reaction on the skin is brought about by previously sensitized lymphocytes and the offending allergen is bound to a receptor on the cell surface. The lymphocyte then produces a number of diverse substances ("factors") which are responsible for bringing about the inflammatory skin reaction.

Allergic contact dermatitis may be seen at any age, but it is no more prevalent in families with a history of allergy than in those without such a history. The causes are extremely diverse, the most common being plants such as poison ivy, poison oak and poison sumac; topical medications such as neomycin and merthiolate; metals such as nickel and chrome; rubber and rubber-based adhesives; and cosmetics, perfumes, hair dyes, deodorants and soaps.

Signs and symptoms

The interval between exposure and symptoms may be anywhere from 4 to 70 hours, but most often it is between 12 and 48 hours. The skin eruption in the acute phase is generally red and itchy, with many small raised areas (papules). It may often be oozing and later crust over with thickening of the skin and scaliness. Often the dermatitis is localized to the area of exposure, but it may be present in other areas as well. Sometimes the offending agent is obvious; often it is not. A careful, detailed history may be the best resource a physician has in such a case.

Diagnosis and treatment

If doubt exists, *patch testing* is a valuable tool in aid of diagnosis. The idea is a simple one: apply a number of possible offending substances to different sites on the skin, cover them and examine them 48 to 72 hours later. A small area of contact dermatitis at a given site will hopefully reveal the cause of the overall problem. By means of the PATCH TEST the disorder has been reproduced in miniature in order to uncover the cause. Treatment consists of cold, wet dressings in the weeping acute stage. In the subacute and chronic stages, topical steroids work quite well. Systemic steroids should be reserved for the extremely widespread or acute dermatitis. Of extreme importance is avoiding further contact with the offending substance, which in turn becomes the obvious cure for the disease.

There are commercial preparations (both oral preparations and injections) for desensitizing patients to poison ivy. Some success has been reported; but, final judgment is reserved these methods of treatment. Future controlled studies will be needed before such treatments become routine practice.

Food allergy

Food allergy is an extremely complex problem and is not easily covered in a short space. The effort here will be to deal with some of the most frequent problems, concerns and questions that arise when the allergist is dealing with a patient who may be allergic to specific food.

It is generally considered that true food allergy is not common (0.3–1.0% of children), with the incidence decreasing with age. Symptoms need not be confined to the gastrointestinal tract (cramps, nausea, vomiting and diarrhea). Other clinical manifestations of food allergy can be cutaneous (hives, rashes), neurologic (headache, especially migraine), respiratory (asthma, rhinitis, sinusitis) or systemic (ANAPHYLACTIC SHOCK). It is important to note that foods may produce symptoms (which mimic allergic symptoms) by a variety of mechanisms which do not represent true food hypersensitivity or allergy. Two of the most common of these other mechanisms would be: (1) contaminants in the food such as bacteria or chemicals (additives); and (2) lack of intestinal enzymes to digest the food. These mechanisms would lead to *intolerance* of a

PATCH TEST

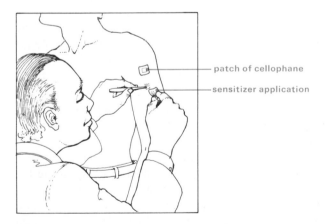

— patch of cellophane

— sensitizer application

Patch tests are performed in an attempt to identify the cause of allergic contact dermatitis. Possible sensitizers are made up in special creams, and each substance in turn is applied to an area of unaffected skin (usually on the arm). The area is then covered by a patch of impermeable material (cellophane) and left for 48 hours. A positive result, where the skin becomes inflamed, indicates the substance responsible for the dermatitis.

food but not true *allergy*—which depends, in this case, on an antigen-antibody interaction for symptoms to occur.

Diagnosis

How then can a diagnosis of food allergy be established? A detailed dietary history is a prerequisite. The patient or parent must keep a "diet diary" and stringently adhere to strict elimination diet trials. In some cases occasional ingestion of a certain food has been noted to cause a violent systemic reaction. In such cases, the patient usually does not need a physician to confirm the diagnosis. Such patients usually just avoid the offending food. However, in many cases the association between food and symptoms may not be readily apparent. This will occur with foods that are ingested daily and may thus be overlooked; or in cases where the onset of symptoms is delayed. The delayed onset of symptoms may be due to the fact that the allergen is one of the digestive breakdown products of the food in question and, thus, symptoms will not appear until hours after the food is ingested.

Skin testing is used as well to aid in the diagnosis. Careful *scratch testing* will often demonstrate true hypersensitivity to food, although there are always some "false positive" and some "false negative" reactions. The false positive reactions may, in reality, not be false at all. They do demonstrate the presence of an antibody (in the skin) specific for that allergen (food). Patients with such reactions may just be less hypersensitive and will, thus, not develop symptoms after eating that food. The false negative tests may represent those people who are allergic to a digestive breakdown product of the food being tested. This product might represent a different antigen and the patient would be "skin-test" negative, because he or she was not tested for that specific antigen.

The foods most commonly associated with food allergy are milk, eggs, shellfish, fish, nuts, peanuts (a vegetable in the pea and bean family), chocolate, strawberries and citrus fruits. Of course any food can become an allergen.

Treatment

When food hypersensitivity is detected, the only successful treatment is avoidance of the offending food or foods. This is often difficult, but almost always possible. An important point to remember is that many persons will gradually lose many clinical food allergies with time.

Insect stings

Insect sting allergy can be one of the most dramatic and frightening of all allergic reactions. While the bites or stings of many other insects (mosquito, flea, blackfly, deerfly, bedbug) can cause reactions (local or systemic) in man, it is the insects of the order *Hymenoptera* (bee, wasp, hornet, yellow jacket and fire ant) that cause the most frequent and severe problems. The wasp, hornet and yellow jacket can inflict multiple stings, while the bee can sting only once. It has a barbed stinger which cannot be withdrawn. As the bee attempts to withdraw after stinging, a portion of the abdomen and the venom sac are left behind and the bee dies.

As the venoms contain many irritative and toxic chemicals, local reactions are normal and do not necessarily represent allergy. Extremely large local reactions, usually defined as those extending two joints beyond the sting site (a sting on the hand with swelling past the wrist and elbow) may portend acute systemic reactions in some individuals. The most feared reaction after sting is the systemic reaction or ANAPHYLACTIC SHOCK. This is a true antigen-antibody reaction, mediated by antigen-specific IgE.

The majority of these reactions begin within 15 minutes of the sting, almost always within an hour (although serious reactions have been reported 24 to 48 hours following a sting). The symptoms can include generalized itching, hives, flushing, angioedema (swelling), difficulty in breathing (sometimes due to swelling of the larynx), nausea, abdominal cramps, wheezing, a drop in blood pressure and circulatory collapse (shock). If not treated promptly, an otherwise healthy patient can die from the sting. In fact, about 40 to 50 deaths from stings occur each year in the United States.

Treatment

Treatment for the anaphylactic attack consists first and foremost of epinephrine (adrenaline) given subcutaneously or intravenously, if necessary. Antihistamines can be helpful in milder reactions but are second-line medication in treating an anaphylactic reaction. Steroids are often administered but will take hours to exert their effects; thus they too are used only after epinephrine has been given. The person who has had a systemic reaction to an insect sting should always carry epinephrine with him for emergency use and should wear a bracelet identifying himself as allergic to insect stings. Local reactions may be treated by the application of ice packs to the area of the sting and the administration of oral antihistamines.

Skin testing and hyposensitization injections are presently used as part of the treatment for insect-allergic patients. At present, *whole body extract* is in general medical use. This is an extract of crushed whole bodies of a mixture of bee, wasp, hornet and yellow jacket. The skin testing (scratch and/or intradermal) is done to help determine the proper strength at which to begin treatment (in other words, to determine the degree of sensitivity). Desensitizing injections are then begun and the dose is gradually increased from a very dilute to a relatively potent one. The length of therapy is currently a subject of much debate. At present, lifetime treatment is still recommended by the Insect Allergy Committee of the American Academy of Allergy. This is because of the few disturbing cases involving patients who had years of adequate treatment following a systemic reaction to a sting, during which they were stung again and had no reaction of any consequence. Then, at some point after stopping treatment, they were stung yet again and had severe systemic reactions. Thus, until better methods of determining the "still-risk" patient are available, the recommendations remain the same.

There has also recently been much debate about using pure insect venoms for treatment, rather than whole body extract. The proponents of venom therapy argue that: (1) whole body extract contains little venom; and (2) whole body extract is not specific enough immunotherapy. This is because the bees are distinct enough from wasps, hornets and yellow jackets (in terms of their species-specific antigens) to warrant testing and treatment with individual venoms. These arguments may turn out to be valid in the end; however, for the present they are academic because only bee venom is commercially available. No means has yet been developed for obtaining large amounts of the wasp, hornet or yellow jacket venoms. It will probably be a long while before we have these venoms available in the quantities needed for hyposensitization therapy. In the meantime, it is reassuring to note that studies by the Insect Allergy Committee have shown that over 95% of patients who are allergic to stinging insects, and who received hyposensitization injections of whole body extract regularly and in adequate dosage, had very few if any symptoms when restung.

Drug reactions

Allergic drug reactions pose a complex problem. It should be noted that truly allergic drug reactions make up a small (10–20%) proportion of the total of all adverse drug reactions. However, adverse drug reactions are a major problem in many countries today because of the rapid development of so many drugs for diagnosis and treatment. In the United States, about one seventh of all patient-days in hospitals are for treatment of drug reactions.

In brief, *nonallergic* drug reactions are caused by the following:

(1) *Overdosage*. This may be due, at times, to an abnormality of kidney and liver functions preventing the elimination of medication from the patient's body in the normal time, permitting it to accumulate in the blood with repeated doses. It may also be due to carelessness in taking or giving a drug with doses repeated within too short a period of time. However it occurs, overdosage can give almost anyone a reaction—sometimes a most serious one.

(2) *Side effects*. These are due to a pharmacologic action of the drug different from the pharmacologic action which provides the result desired by the doctor and patient. The side effect may be undesirable, but unavoidable, in many cases. Side effects constitute by far the most frequent drug reactions, as most drugs have several pharmacologic

actions, only one of which may produce the desired effect. A good example of such an undesired side effect is the drowsiness caused by antihistamines. Often, drug dosage can be adjusted to produce more of the desired effect and less of the side effects. A subclass of side effects is represented by those drugs which cause direct histamine release and, thus, mimic many forms of allergic reaction. The most common drugs causing such a reaction include codeine and morphine.

(3) *Drug interactions.* Two different drugs, when administered simultaneously, may potentiate the adverse side effects of each. Many such adverse drug interactions are known and undoubtedly many more will be discovered as more new drugs come into use.

(4) *Intolerance.* A few individuals experience the expected pharmacologic effects of a drug (both desired and undesired) at unusually small doses. In such patients, the use of the drug will often have to be discontinued.

(5) *Idiosyncratic reactions.* These reactions are characterized by an abnormal response to a drug, differing from any known pharmacologic action of the drug. Many such reactions are due to inherited diseases involving enzyme systems. For example, some individuals develop a peripheral neuritis (a disorder involving the nerves in various parts of the body) after administration of isoniazid (a drug used in the treatment of tuberculosis). These patients lack an enzyme that normally inactivates the drug.

Allergic drug reactions are abnormal and are not related to the pharmacologic action of the drug. The risk of an allergic reaction during treatment is about 1–3% for most drugs. This figure includes skin rashes—some of which are not truly allergic in nature, but which are difficult to differentiate from allergic rashes. Allergic drug reactions require prior exposure to the drug (or a drug which is chemically related) in order for sensitization to take place. This involves, as has been noted many times, either production of antibodies or sensitized cells specific for the drug.

(See also *Problems with drugs: side effects* and *Factors increasing the likelihood of drug reactions* in the major article on **Drugs and Medicines**.)

Drugs most commonly involved

Penicillin (and its derivatives and analogs) and sulfa drugs account for the majority of allergic drug reactions. Other common drug allergens include: barbiturates, anticonvulsants, insulin, antithyroid drugs, local anesthetics, quinine, iodides, antituberculous drugs and phenolphthalein (in many laxatives). Aspirin, formerly thought to be the cause of many allergic drug reactions, is now the subject of much debate. Although aspirin can cause hives, nasal symptoms and asthma, no truly immunologic mechanism has now been proved for these reactions. Thus, many now classify aspirin reactions as idiosyncratic (see above).

Signs and symptoms

Skin rashes are the most common type of drug reaction (40–60%), followed by urticaria (hives). Anaphylactic reactions are extremely rare. Penicillin and animal serum (usually horse serum) innoculations—still used in the treatment of rabies, snake bites, botulism and diphtheria—can produce the *serum sickness* syndrome, characterized by fever, joint symptoms, skin eruptions (usually hives and swelling) and enlargement of many lymph glands. These symptoms appear 6–21 days after administration of the causative drug. Average duration is 7 days.

Allergic drug reactions appear to be more common in adults than in children. In addition, the route of administration of the drug seems to make a difference. Topical application of many drugs is the easiest way to induce sensitization. Moreover, oral administration of most drugs would seem to be a safer route than intramuscular or intravenous, although the oral route can also produce severe reactions.

> **Adverse reactions to prescription drugs are usually more troublesome than life-threatening. Nevertheless, any signs of skin rashes, hives, or other suspicious evidence of side effects should be reported right away to your family physician. He may be able to substitute another drug to which you are not sensitive.**

Diagnosis

The most important evidence that someone may be allergic to a given drug is a history of a previous reaction to that drug (or a chemically related drug).

Many patients are afraid that they will develop drug allergy because there is a family history of hypersensitivity to drugs. Although there is some disagreement on this point within the medical community, the consensus is that there is no hard evidence to support this idea.

All too often both the patient and the doctor may be uncertain as to whether or not true hypersensitivity to a drug exists. This is often the case with penicillin. Many patients have experienced a generalized skin eruption following administration of penicillin for the treatment of an infection. The rash might have been due either to the illness for which the patient was being treated or might have been due to the drug, but did not represent a true hypersensitivity reaction. The alternative often taken in such a situation is to treat with another antibiotic with the same antibacterial spectrum, such as erythromycin. In the case of penicillin, and a few other medications, skin testing can be a valuable diagnostic tool. Both scratch and intradermal testing can be done, although some of the antigens necessary for testing are still not generally available commercially.

Carefully done penicillin skin testing can accurately predict hypersensitivity in about 90–95% of patients. This gives no guarantee that a patient will not react, but is still an important aid to diagnosis. This type of testing is to detect a specific antibody of the IgE type. Such testing has also been used to detect hypersensitivity to insulin, egg-containing vaccines, equine antiserum and local anesthetics (in wide use in dentistry).

Desensitization

If a patient is allergic to a drug (such as penicillin) but must have this drug, a method of rapid *desensitization* can be used. This usually applies only to patients in a hospital with a life-threatening bacterial disease for which no alternative treatment is available. The method involves administration of the drug in extremely small doses at first and then increasing doses every 15 to 30 minutes, until a therapeutic dose is reached. There are, of course, many risks in such therapy, but, as noted above, it is used only in extreme situations and under the most carefully monitored conditions. Many successes have been reported. The mechanism of desensitization may be to deplete the body of its penicillin-specific IgE antibody. (The penicillin skin test often becomes negative during the desensitization process.)

Reactions to x-ray contrast medium

Another problem commonly facing the allergist as a consultant is the potential adverse reaction to injection of an iodinated (iodine-containing) contrast medium for an x-ray study in a patient with an allergic history. Skin testing has been tried, but is not reliable because the contrast media are irritative and can release histamine directly.

Many people feel that a history of allergy to seafood or inorganic iodine is associated with an increased risk in such x-ray studies. This is not the case. If there has been no previous reaction to contrast media, the risk of reaction is about 3–5%. *If there has been a previous reaction, however, the risk jumps to 15–20%.* In such patients, studies should be undertaken only when no alternative diagnostic procedure can be done. These patients should receive prophylactic steroid and antihistaminic therapy. The steroids should be started 18–24 hours prior to the procedure and continued for 12 hours after it. The number and severity of reactions are markedly reduced by this treatment.

Asthma

Asthma is a disease seen often by the allergist. It occurs in 2–4% of the population and is the major cause of hospitalization among the allergic diseases. It is a disease characterized by an increased responsiveness of the trachea and bronchi to various stimuli, only some of which are allergic.

There is no doubt that much ASTHMA is mediated by antigen-antibody (IgE) reactions in the lungs. there are, however, many other causes for the disease, including infection, exercise, emotions, and noxious physical and chemical stimuli (cold air, air pollution, sprays, drugs, etc.).

Signs and symptoms

The disease is characterized by episodes of wheezing, difficulty in breathing (shortness of breath) and increased bronchial mucus production. The wheezing and shortness of breath are caused by contraction of the bronchial smooth muscle and swelling of the cells lining the bronchi. All these changes are reversible, either spontaneously or with treatment.

Very few patients with asthma progress on to develop the irreversible destructive changes in the lungs characteristic of EMPHYSEMA. The mechanisms that bring about these changes occur at the cellular level in the lungs, are extremely complex, and are presently undergoing intensive study. There is a sequence of events which involves the nerve supply to the lungs; substances (known as "transmitters") which are released at the nerve endings (receptor sites for these transmitters on the smooth muscle and mucus-producing glandular cells lining the bronchi); and finally a "second messenger" produced within these cells that essentially regulates the function of the cells. This "second messenger" is called *cyclic AMP*; if its function is inhibited or defective then the cells will respond in an abnormal way, leading to release of mediators that cause constriction of the airway and increased mucus production—resulting in wheezing and difficulty in breathing.

Many of the medicines used to treat asthma work either to increase the production of cyclic AMP (Adrenalin and Isuprel) or to prevent its destruction (theophylline or aminophylline). It is the feeling of many experts that the basic defect in the asthmatic patient is at the bronchial cellular level, involving the nerve receptors and subsequent production of adequate levels of cyclic AMP. This defect is probably an inherited one, since a family history of allergic disease is common in patients with asthma.

Asthma in children

In children, bronchial asthma is the leading cause of both acute and chronic illness. It may occur at any age but usually begins by the age of five. Under the age of 10 there is a 2:1 ratio of boys to girls. Those developing asthma before age 25 are more likely to have allergic asthma, and many may have concurrent or antecedent allergic rhinitis or eczema. While it is a rare occurrence, death from asthma does occur.

Asthma in adults

In adults, asthma is a major cause of absence from work.

One study showed 14 days of restricted activity per asthmatic patient per year; five and a half of these days were spent in bed. Thus, asthma exerts a major economic impact.

When dealing with adult asthmatics, the physician is always faced with the problem of the possibility of other medical conditions that must be taken into consideration when treating the asthma. Therapy must be modified to meet the medical needs of each patient.

Nonallergic causes of asthma

As noted before, some asthma is allergic and skin testing will often reveal the causative allergens. These patients should have a course of hyposensitization injections as part of their therapy. Much asthma is not mediated by allergic mechanisms. Infection is a major cause of asthmatic attacks, especially in children. Emotions may play a dramatic role in bringing on wheezing. Physical and chemical noxious stimuli can directly affect the lungs and produce problems for the asthmatic patient.

Exercise-induced asthma (or bronchospasm) is a well-recognized entity, developing 1–10 minutes after the completion of strenuous physical activity. It may become worse for the next 5–10 minutes and then spontaneously abate; however, attacks can last much longer. These attacks can often be prevented by premedication (before exercise) with drugs that prevent the release of bronchospastic mediators.

Treatment

Treatment of asthma employs many drugs and modalities and requires an informed, understanding, supportive physician. Treatment includes:

(1) *Hyposensitization injections,* when indicated, as already mentioned.

(2) *Oral bronchodilators,* such as theophylline and aminophylline to block the destruction of cyclic AMP in bronchial cells; terbutaline, metaproterenol, salbutamol, to increase the production of cyclic AMP.

(3) *Cromolyn sodium,* an inhaled powder, useful in many cases of asthma, especially exercise-induced bronchospasm.

(4) *Fluids,* to help prevent dehydration and formation of mucus plugs in the lungs.

(5) *Expectorants,* which may help liquefy mucus in the lungs; iodides are most commonly used, but have many side effects. Their effectiveness is somewhat controversial.

(6) *Corticosteroids* are reserved for the minority of patients who do not respond sufficiently to the above measures and who continue to have severe, incapacitating, chronic wheezing. They have many side effects if used daily; they may be given every other day, in the morning, to minimize side effects. There is also a new corticosteroid aerosol which can be inhaled into the lungs—*beclomethasone dipropionate.* This drug, whose long-term benefits are being studied, appears to be extremely effective with minimal or no systemic effects; it is extremely helpful in the severe asthmatic or the asthmatic who is dependent upon oral steroids and has systemic side effects. Use of this new aerosol may permit the withdrawal of oral steroids.

(7) *Adrenalin* (epinephrine), administered by subcutaneous injection; excellent treatment for the acute attack, with a fast bronchodilator effect.

(8) *Other aerosols* (Isuprel, Adrenalin) can be effective, but often the patient will develop a dependence and stop taking oral medications; the result may be an actual worsening of the bronchospasm.

(9) *Antibiotics,* as indicated, for infections suffered by many asthmatics.

Treatment for asthma in some patients may involve round-the-clock medications for many months or even years; for others, medication, as needed, will suffice if started early enough in the attack. The key is to watch for early warning signs—cough, mild wheeze, infection—and begin therapy immediately. Such action may quickly terminate a serious acute attack. (See also *Drugs for asthma and lung diseases* in the major article on **Drugs and Medicines.**)

The Future

The field of allergy and immunology has undergone a rapid transformation in the last 15–20 years. What has happened is that advances in immunology have allowed us to understand better the function of perhaps man's most basic system, his immune mechanisms—the mechanisms through which he maintains his "self" against intrusion by a host of "foreign" invaders. We have learned to understand how specific injection therapy works and how many of the medications we use exert their actions.

New medications have been developed which can relieve symptoms and produce fewer side effects. New and practical laboratory procedures have been developed to aid the practicing allergist in diagnosis, such as the RadioAllergoSorbent (RAST) test, which allows us to draw a blood sample and measure specific antibodies against specific allergens, just as we do when we perform skin tests.

In the years to come, even better medications will almost certainly appear. Moreover, consider the fields of transplant immunology and tumor immunity: we are now able to transplant kidneys with a high rate of success and progress is being made each year toward the understanding of tumors and toward the eventual goal of suppressing their growth, or even their onset. Exciting work is just beginning to appear about suppressor cells and suppressor factor. In time, the clinical application of this work may enable us to prevent allergy, strengthen resistance to infection and even help protect against certain types of tumors.

Immunosuppressive drugs have greatly lowered the incidence of tissue rejection following organ transplants (such as a kidney transplant), where the body of the recipient "fights off" the transplant by the production of specific antibodies. The potential danger of immunosuppressive drugs, however, is that during the period of their administration (and for a time afterward) the body's ability to ward off infectious microorganisms is also lowered; thus, special precautions must be taken.

Immunotherapy has been proposed as one means of treating certain forms of cancer. Several new approaches are being explored, including the possibility that the injection into cancerous skin tissues of a vaccine known as BCG (Bacille Calmette-Guérin) will stimulate the patient's own immune mechanism to produce antibodies to destroy or control the growth of cancer cells.

The potetial contributions of within the field of immunology are among the most exciting in medical science.

Psychiatry

Dr. Robert A. Glick

The traditional view of psychiatry is changing rapidly. At one time many people considered the need for psychiatric consultation or treatment with a sense of fear or shame. Enlightened attitudes now prevail and it is common for emotional disorders to be looked upon in much the same way as physical illnesses. The following article discusses the role of the modern psychiatrist in diagnosing and treating a wide variety of emotional and mental disorders.

Psychiatry is concerned with the emotional and mental disorders that afflict mankind, with their diagnosis and treatment, and with research to find better ways to prevent, control or cure them.

In our daily lives, we are all aware of changing moods, feelings and attitudes as we cope with and adjust to life events. When do such changes represent an emotional disorder? At what point must we recognize that our reactions to such events are no longer "normal" and constitute a "problem" which requires professional treatment?

In a general way, an emotional disorder is a set of symptoms or impairments in day-to-day functioning that occurs when coping capacities are insufficient to deal with stress. Emotional disorders—like physical abnormalities—can include common, transient problems which, like a common cold, run their course and disappear without treatment; moderate conditions which require professional evaluation and treatment to prevent serious problems; and severe psychiatric conditions which represent serious emergencies and threats to life.

Uncertainty exists in many people's minds not only about what constitutes a true emotional or psychiatric problem but also about what a psychiatrist is supposed to know and do to deal with it. What is his training and how can you know if he is competent?

Background and training

A psychiatrist is a physician who, after completing medical school, has had at least a year of internship and three years of psychiatric residency training. During this period of clinical training he has studied and diagnosed a wide range of psychiatric, neurologic and medical problems. He has learned to recognize and treat major and less severe psychiatric disorders and psychological reactions to illness of all types—especially those which are chronic or disabling and call for a readjusted way of living. After completing his clinical training and two years of experience in psychiatric practice, he is eligible to take the comprehensive examinations given by the American Board of Psychiatry and Neurology. Certification of competency in psychiatry is given by the Board to those who successfully complete the extensive written and oral examinations.

Traditional views of the psychiatrist

To many people, the very idea of seeing a psychiatrist evokes fear and indignation. When the suggestion comes from a relative, the response is often rage and humiliation—"you think I'm crazy," which is equated with being worthless and hopeless. When it comes from the family doctor, the patient often feels that the doctor is rejecting him because "it's all in my head," as though he is faking. When recognition of need for professional help is reached by the patient alone, it is accompanied by grave concerns of helplessness, stigma and fear that the problem is incurable. The sources of such reactions come in part from the images of psychiatric treatment derived from the past: commitment to the "Asylum" or state hospital where patients are locked away for years or given shock treatments, rejected and often forgotten by family and friends. Today, with new knowledge and understanding of emotional illness, this pattern has changed radically for the better. Patients and doctors are learning that mental illness must be recognized and dealt with much like any other illness. The most important factors for successful treatment are early recognition and professional evaluation of a developing illness, followed by appropriate therapy. Today such treatment is largely provided in outpatient settings—private psychiatrists' offices, community mental health centers (which are now being provided throughout much of the nation) or psychiatric clinics in general hospitals. Inpatient treatment is used only for the most acutely ill, when there is a true emergency and the patient is a threat to himself or others, or is unable to care for himself.

Modern developments in psychiatry

An outgrowth of research in psychiatry during the past 30 years has provided psychiatrists with a broad spectrum of effective treatments. "Psychopharmacologic" research has

The vast majority of common sexual problems—such as impotence or premature ejaculation in men or frigidity in women—are the result of some underlying, often unexpressed, emotional conflict.

developed medications which can now effectively relieve anxiety, depression and psychotic reactions and stabilize manic-depressive illness. Psychotherapy as a tool for understanding human problems and constructive change has grown to include the knowledge gained from psychoanalysis and behaviour therapy. Briefer and more focused forms of PSYCHOTHERAPY are proving effective. "Crisis intervention teams" are widely available in clinics and general hospitals to deal with individual and family crises. Specialized treatment centers for specific problems now provide help in marital, family, drug, alcohol and sexual problems. (See also the major article on **Psychotherapy**.)

Perhaps the greatest resistance to seeking needed professional help today is the fear of getting "trapped" into treatment for several years. Such resistance is based on the virtually universal fear that exploring emotional problems is like wading into quicksand—one only gets in deeper and deeper, until there are only more problems and no solutions. We are all somewhat concerned about our limitations and weaknesses and about recognizing them and dealing with them realistically. Psychiatric treatment aims at relief of painful symptoms and adjustment to the tensions and anxieties of everyday life. The goal is not to interfere with strengths, nor to expect perfection or blissful happiness, but to accept and cope with the "ups and downs" that are a normal part of all our lives in a less than perfect world.

Facing the problem

In general, the greatest problem to be overcome by the patient in need of psychiatric treatment is his reluctance or inability to recognize and accept that he has an emotional disorder. This is true, even though the fact is often painfully obvious to those around him. Once he has accepted the problem realistically, he must overcome the attendant shame and fear that he unjustifiably associates with psychiatric treatment. Once the need for professional help is admitted, the next question is: "How do I go about it?"

Very often the family doctor will recognize the need for psychiatric treatment and help his patient to accept the situation. A few patients may know of a psychiatrist through friends and call directly for an appointment. Others—most people, in fact—may be uncertain where to turn for help. Today most general and community hospitals and all university medical centers have psychiatric clinics in their outpatient departments and provide immediate care in their emergency services. If there is no outpatient clinic, however, a call to the hospital or clinic will often provide the names of psychiatrists in private practice, or the location of the nearest community mental health center. If a crisis or emergency situation develops, it is best to go directly to the hospital and ask for psychiatric consultation at the Emergency Service or Walk-in Clinic.

Seeking professional help

Treatment of emotional and psychiatric disorders starts with a thorough psychiatric consultation, which may require one to six visits. During this period the psychiatrist will explore with the patient the precipitating problems in depth, the relevant past history and the overall psychological state. After a diagnosis has been made and the doctor and patient have clearly defined and recognized the problem areas (as well as probable triggers or stresses contributing to the present condition), a treatment plan will be developed and discussed. Special attention will be given to multiple factors that may underlie the main problem: marital and family conflicts, sexual maladjustments, job stresses, unemployment, heavy debts, loneliness, grief over the loss of a loved one, excessive drinking—in fact, any and all of the conditions that have accumulated to push the patient beyond his ability to cope with the realities of his everyday existence.

In the discussion which follows, the most common emotional and psychiatric disorders are explored and the appropriate treatments described.

Anxiety

Everyone is anxious at some time during his or her life. The stresses of work, family and interpersonal living cause periods of tension, uneasiness and apprehension. When the stress passes, or is alleviated, the attendant ANXIETY passes, usually having been recognized as a response to specific conditions. However, when anxiety is persistent or particularly intense, and is without clear or reasonable external cause, an anxiety state exists which requires professional evaluation.

Symptoms

Anxiety states are usually experienced as intermittent waves of tension and apprehension that can last for hours or days at a time. Although there may be a pervasive sense of fear about many things, there is no clear focus for this feeling of trepidation. Anxiety may interfere with concentration, productivity and (frequently) with sleep. Contact with other people often seems more stressful and is avoided. Irritability often develops and tearful outbursts may occur. Some people eat more; others lose their appetite completely. At times, anxiety may mount to a point of sheer dread or utter panic. Fears of "going crazy" or of dying can accompany this state. Physical symptoms are common in anxiety attacks: abdominal pain, hiccups, diarrhea and indigestion. As the attack intensifies, a set of extremely distressing symptoms appear: shortness of breath, tightness or pain in the chest, dizziness, palpitations, sweatiness, faintness and nausea.

At the height of an acute anxiety attack, there is often a sense of overwhelming terror and of impending death. This syndrome is called *hyperventilation* (a term which is also used medically to signify any instance of abnormally rapid breathing). Anxiety has triggered overbreathing, which causes physical symptoms by lowering blood bicarbonate level—symptoms which in turn are frightening and generate more anxiety, creating a vicious cycle. Numbness and tingling can develop in the hands and feet and around the mouth. Hyperventilation attacks are often mistaken for heart attacks, seizures or acute asthma attacks. The victim feels that the physical symptoms are the cause of his panic, but actually the reverse is true. The simplest and most effective emergency treatment for hyperventilation is to reverse the overbreathing reaction. This is accomplished by having the patient breathe slowly for 3 to 7 minutes (by the clock) into a paper bag held closely around the mouth and nose. By rebreathing the exhaled carbon dioxide, the blood bicarbonate level is raised and physical symptoms are reversed to relieve much of the immediate anxiety.

Anxiety states can also occur as a pervasive sense of uneasiness, or so-called "free-floating" anxiety at a constant but less intense level. Self-consciousness and a disconnected feeling with self and reality often occur as well. Concentration is impaired, work performance deteriorates and social withdrawal follows.

Treatment

A variety of effective medications are now available for the symptomatic treatment of anxiety: minor tranquilizers such as chlordiazepoxide and diazepam for mild to moderate reactions,and major tranquilizers such as the phenothiazines for severe reactions. These medications work in different brain centers to inhibit anxiety responses and produce a sense of calm. Major and minor tranquilizers produce an effect in from 20 to 30 minutes to a maximum of two to three hours, depending on dosage. Minor tranquilizers are usually prescribed on a schedule of three to four times daily when symptoms are moderate to severe and persistent, or on a more flexible basis for milder symptoms. Major tranquilizers are usually given three to four times daily and at bedtime for severe conditions.

(See also *Drugs for sleep disorders, etc.,* in the major article on **Drugs and Medicines.**)

For many people, simple symptomatic relief is sufficient for return to normal functioning and medication may not be required for more than a limited time. However, medication alone does not cure the cause of anxiety, because it does not deal with the often unrecognized emotional conflict responsible for the symptoms. When they persist, especially when increased dosage is required for relief, further consultation with the psychiatrist is helpful in uncovering the emotional concerns and conflicts responsible for the anxiety. Dependence upon medication can be a sign of serious underlying emotional conflicts which are best treated by psychotherapy. Habituation or dependence on even minor tranquilizers can occur after prolonged and high dose usage (see ADDICTION).

Phobias

Feeling afraid is part of our adaptive response to danger. From childhood we learn and unlearn to fear certain situations as our understanding of danger matures. These include fear of the dark, strangers, animals, thunder and lightning and many others. However, in certain people, irrational fears—uncorrected by experience—develop in adulthood or persist from childhood. Such fears, called *phobias*, are experienced as the compelling need to avoid certain situations or objects to prevent anxiety. Common examples of phobias are fear of heights, closed spaces, open spaces, water, trains, elevators and aircraft. Phobic objects can include bugs, animals, dirt and knives. Indeed, almost anything can be incorporated into a phobic reaction. These reactions are derived from unrecognized emotional fears or conflicts that are unconsciously transferred to something in the environment ("displaced"), as if to make the danger "external." This is true of persistent fears carried over from childhood as well as those developing later.

People with phobias do not usually complain about them. As long as they can avoid the "danger" they are fine. Often the PHOBIA poses more of a problem to others than to the victim, because they must accommodate to the phobia or accompany the victim into his "dangerous" situations. Thus, the "phobic partner" plays an important part in perpetuating the phobia as well as a potentially crucial role in its treatment. A wife, for example, may not be able to leave her house to shop, travel or see her doctor without her husband.

When phobias are well circumscribed they often go unrecognized. Life adjusts relatively easily to them and help is rarely sought, although it might well be. Major problems develop when new, additional phobic reactions appear and encroach on many areas of living, thus further restricting the victim's activities. This is usually an indication of some underlying emotional struggle that requires psychiatric help if the patient is to function well within his life situation. Consider the professional athlete, whose fear of flying inhibits his performance on the playing field and (without adequate help) may end his career; or the qualified person who repeatedly avoids promotions in his job because of his fear of "phobic situations" in a new environment or in new responsibilities.

Today, the treatment of phobias usually involves a combination of psychotherapy and what are known as *behavior modification* techniques to uncover the basic problems generating the phobia. Rarely is one sufficient without the other, although minor phobias can be overcome with behavioral approaches alone. Minor tranquilizers are occasionally used in conjunction with psychotherapy to increase anxiety tolerance while the patient is gaining mastery over his phobia.

Depression

All of us accept depressed moods as part of life, but many people (perhaps 10% of the population) suffer at least one significant DEPRESSION or depressive reaction during adult life. In contrast to common short periods of feeling "down," pessimistic or unhappy, true depression is characterized by a persistent depressed mood, a pessimistic outlook and self-doubt. Self-criticism becomes preoccupying. The victim finds no pleasure in any activity, has little initiative, is unable to make even minor decisions and sees no possibility of change in his future. His appetite diminishes and weight loss follows. Interest in sex wanes, sleep patterns are disrupted, with early awakening after only a few hours of sleep. To those around him, he appears sad, withdrawn and totally preoccupied with himself.

Physical symptoms develop: constipation, weakness, fatigue, vague aches and pains, abdominal discomfort,

Severe depression and suicidal tendencies are common features of many forms of mental illness. In addition to the therapeutic techniques of modern psychiatry, various mood-elevating drugs play an important role in relieving these feelings.

fears about cancer, senility (in older people) and other diseases intensify. At times the physical symptoms can be the first clues to developing depression, and family doctors are becoming skilled in recognizing and separating them from true physiologic illness.

Untreated, depressions can last for months. As the condition worsens the patient becomes less able to function in daily living and can progress to a state of total inertia and helplessness. He exaggerates his feelings of guilt and self-loathing. Punishment seems deserved and he may even wish for death. Suicidal ideas develop: "I'm worthless and hopeless, only a burden; I deserve to die." Never take such statements lightly; the person who threatens suicide may actually kill himself. Unrecognized and untreated, suicidal ideas often progress to plans and actions. Medication overdoses, wrist slashings and auto accidents (when not fatal) should be looked upon as "cries for help." When help does not come, a future attempt is often successful. Increased alcohol consumption is a common reaction, but only adds to the depression and increases the risk of suicide by impairment of judgment and control.

As depression deepens, immobility often occurs and contact with reality can be lost. The patient may sit for hours staring into space and avoiding food or contact with others. At times, severe agitation can develop with delusional beliefs of punishment, cancer or decay.

Treatment

When depression is suspected, treatment should be sought *at once*. Today, psychiatrists can treat the majority of depressed patients in clinics or offices, if seen soon after the development of symptoms. This is in marked contrast to images of the "back wards" of mental hospitals of decades past. New antidepressant medications can now usually relieve depression in a matter of weeks. Imipramine and amitriptyline are the most common drugs used, but take from ten days to two weeks to produce mood elevation; improvement in sleep, appetite and concentration often occurs days before mood is elevated. Common, nonserious side effects to medication (such as dry mouth, blurred vision or mild light-headedness) are the first signs that the drugs are reaching a therapeutic level and improvement soon follows.

The most difficult problem in this incapacitating illness is the decision for psychiatric hospitalization. When the person is severely depressed, unable to care for himself and—especially—when there is any risk of suicide, hospitalization is appropriate and necessary. Many people are fearful of "shock treatment" or electroconvulsive therapy (ECT). Although the antidepressant drugs have eliminated the need for ECT in most cases, it is the treatment of choice for those persons who fail to respond to medication or who are unable to take it for other reasons. It is no longer the violent, repugnant treatment we learn to fear from seeing it carried out in movies. It is safe and effective for the severely depressed and usually brings rapid relief of symptoms.

Manic-depressive illness

We have now learned a great deal about manic-depressive illness (or manic depression) and have developed a specific drug, lithium carbonate, to control it. Manic depression usually starts in young adulthood and is marked by episodes of severe depression and alternate episodes of mania. Sometimes the mania appears alone. The manic attack appears to be the opposite of depressive symptoms. The mood is abnormally elevated or intense and all activity is accelerated: thinking, speech and muscular activity. The victim feels more energy, needs little sleep and often stays up all night pursuing a variety of projects. Enthusiasm and excessive confidence interfere with judgment. Irritability and outbursts of rage alternate frequently with "infectious" elation. As judgment deteriorates, problems develop: money is spent extravagantly or given away; projects, jobs, courses are started and dropped capriciously. Any effort to reason, restrain or criticize manic behavior is met with arguments and often spiteful increased activity, while the patient seems oblivious to the chaos he is creating. Those around him suffer rather than the patient, which leads to resentment and difficulty in recognizing that the person is "sick" rather than just being impossible to live with.

Manic patients rarely accept that they are ill and refuse to seek help. Concerned, constructive family pressure is almost always necessary. If treatment is delayed, the condition worsens; judgment further deteriorates until contact with reality is lost, control of dangerous impulses diminishes and the risk to self and others grows. At this point hospitalization is imperative.

Treatment

Treatment combines the use of major tranquilizers and lithium carbonate to induce a "slowing down" reaction (which usually occurs within a few days) and full recovery can often be expected within a few weeks. Once over the acute episode, maintenance treatment with lithium carbonate is continued. Close medical follow-up is necessary to insure that the blood level of lithium remains within the therapeutic and nontoxic levels. Lithium carbonate is a salt, not a sedative or tranquilizer; thus it will cause no change of mood in those other than manic-depressives.

Some persons suffer from a milder form of mood disorder, called *cyclothymia*, in which mild mood swings from "high" to "low" occur in cycles unrelated to life events. Careful diagnosis by a psychiatrist is required to differentiate this condition from the normal mood variations experienced by most of us in response to life events.

(See also MANIA.)

Schizophrenia

This word was coined by a Swiss psychiatrist to describe one of the most serious of mental illnesses (actually, a variety of closely related conditions which have common symptoms). Its literal meaning is "split-mind." SCHIZOPHRENIA usually occurs in late adolescence or young adulthood and produces severe disorganization of the entire personality and (in many cases) loss of contact with reality. Its specific causes remain unknown, but current research has found evidence that strongly points to biochemical predispositions which are presumed to impair normal emotional development and lead to decompensation or "breakdown" under stress in young adults. Schizophrenic reactions usually begin with subjective feelings of tension, irritability, mistrust and a growing sense of strangeness and alienation. Thinking becomes disordered with racing and bizarrely connected ideas, often frightening in nature. Waking life takes on a progressive inexplicable, unpredictable, self-centered, nightmarish quality. Sleep is disturbed, voices are heard, plots are suspected. To others the schizophrenic victim appears increasingly bizarre, both in actions and conversation—often shifting from severe isolation and withdrawal to incoherent outbursts. He may appear to be talking to himself or responding with gestures to things not there. Impulsive and violent behavior is an increasing risk, especially suicide, as the condition worsens.

Many people still view this illness as hopeless, leading to lifelong hospitalization and a "vegetable-like" existence. Unfortunately, some individuals do develop severe chronic forms of schizophrenia, but psychiatrists know today that early recognition and treatment allow most patients to return to their communities to function with greater stability in society. Many recover and remain free of signs of illness.

Treatment

The prognosis for recovery or acceptable social functioning can be greatly improved by early treatment. Major tranquilizers, such as the phenothiazines, promptly decrease agitation and increase contact with reality and control of impulsive behavior. Depending on the overall clinical picture, particularly with self-destructive behavior, brief inpatient treatment is necessary to stabilize the patient on medication and to evaluate the stresses that are precipitating factors in abnormal behavior. Continuing outpatient treatment is essentially directed toward minimizing the possibility of further deterioration and recurrent acute episodes.

Alcoholism

In simple terms, we have a problem with alcohol when drinking becomes necessary for "normal functioning," or when consumption begins to interfere with or damage personal social adjustment and physical health. The telltale signs are often subtle. A drink or two in the evening may be normal for some of us, even therapeutic in "winding down" from a day of stress and tension; but is it only one or two? And how early does the evening drinking start? Drinking more with regularity and earlier in the evening are usually clues that alcohol is being used to deal with some emotional stress—"Just a few drinks to keep me going, or pick me up from the night before." If the problem goes unrecognized, the situation usually deteriorates. Drinking gradually increases, tolerance levels rise and there are no signs of drunkenness. But thinking dulls, memory slips, accidents happen, responsibilities pile up and drinking increases from more stress.

Serious signs of alcoholism follow: blackouts, confusional states, lost work days, irresponsible behavior at home and in public places. And heavier drinking continues. Once a physical addiction has developed, any period

Some patients who are undergoing psychiatric treatment for severe depression and certain other emotional disorders can benefit from occupational or recreational therapy. The objective is to help the patient relieve boredom, develop new interests, instill self-confidence and guide thinking into more desirable channels.

without alcohol induces withdrawal symptoms: irritability, morning shakes, tremors, then fever and delirium. Seizures and death occur in extreme cases. (See also ALCOHOL/ALCOHOLISM.)

Treatment

What to do? Medical and psychiatric consultation are essential; a complete physical examination to assess any toxic effects of alcohol on the liver or brain and psychiatric examination to determine contributing emotional problems (depression, job or family stresses, etc.). Treatment of underlying emotional problems will sometimes relieve the drinking symptom. When drinking has been a long and progressive problem and no clear precipitants can be found, which is more often the case, then the most successful approaches to dealing with chronic alcoholism are: (1) getting the patient to accept active membership in Alcoholics Anonymous and (2) regularly take the drug Antabuse. Antabuse is a medication which, when mixed with alcohol, causes acute physical distress. It is taken voluntarily by the alcoholic, who knows that if he mixes it with alcohol he will become very sick and could even possibly suffer a fatal reaction. This becomes a powerful reinforcement to abstinence.

Alcoholics Anonymous has helped millions overcome alcoholism and is respected by the medical profession. It works through an aggressive support system of recovered and recovering alcoholics. Membership is easily obtained through social agencies, clubs, doctors and hospitals—who are pleased to refer potential members. Alanon is an associated organization for spouses and families of alcoholics. Here not only is support given to those who are most affected by alcoholics but the members are educated to better understand the problem and perhaps modify their own reactions to it so that they can support the victim as he seeks recovery.

Drug abuse

This refers to the chronic overuse or misuse of medications or chemicals to alter mood—either without the advice of a physician or in doses not prescribed by a physician. It presents many of the problems caused by alcoholism and others that may be even more destructive—especially in the processes of addiction and withdrawal. Signs of drug abuse include mental dullness, forgetfulness, slurred speech, unsteady gait, confusional states, blackouts and marked mood fluctuation. In teenagers, a sudden deterioration of school performance is often the parent's first "clue." When drug addiction is suspected, treatment for it must always be under medical supervision; too rapid withdrawal from many types of drugs can cause seizures, coma and even death. As in alcoholism, good treatment must identify and relieve the emotional needs and stresses that have led to drug abuse. The patient must be motivated toward a sincere desire to overcome his problem and be given encouragement and support as he makes his painful way back to normalcy. (See ADDICTION, DRUG ABUSE.)

Sexual dysfunctions

Only in recent years have sexual problems been allowed "out of the closet." They have always been a source of great anguish, frustration and humiliation to many men and women, often leading to divorce. Victims and their physicians in years past usually avoided the problem. Today, the physiology and psychology of sexual responses are well understood. Courses on sexuality are now standard in the curricula of most medical schools. As embarrassment and stigma are lifted, it becomes easier to accept a sexual problem and face it, knowing that there is effective help available.

Common sexual problems affecting men

In men the most common forms of dysfunction are IMPOTENCE, PREMATURE EJACULATION and retarded ejaculation. Nearly all men have at times experienced a problem in getting an erection, usually as a result of fatigue, intoxication, illness or stress. With advancing age there is a normal decrease in the speed and firmness of an erection. These situations are not serious, though they may cause disappointment and embarrassment. There are certain organic causes of impotence, such as diabetic vascular disease which produces total inability of erection. However, the vast majority of sexual problems are the result of some underlying emotional conflict, unrecognized by the couple. Often there is a secret "power struggle" between husband and wife, with sex being only a part of the problem. But when a man feels sexually inadequate a vicious cycle develops; his painful embarrassment only makes him feel more of a failure, increasing anxiety until the bedroom becomes a "proving ground" to be avoided. Resentment develops on both sides, and most areas of the couple's relationship are affected negatively. Premature ejaculation most commonly happens just before or as penetration is attempted, and loss of erection usually follows. As with impotence, there is often some covert problem between the partners leading to anxiety and sexual dysfunction. Retarded ejaculation, although not rare, is a more unusual problem. Here the man finds himself unable to ejaculate after sufficient time; his anxiety increases and the sexual act becomes virtually pleasureless to him.

Common sexual problems affecting women

In women the most common sexual dysfunction is FRIGIDITY—which can mean total inability to experience any aspect of sexual arousal, or, more frequently, arousal but inhibition of orgasm. Invariably, such women feel themselves sexual failures, just as dysfunctional men do. They ask themselves such questions as, "What's wrong with me?" or "Am I a complete woman?" A common inhibiting factor in sexual pleasure among women is called DYSPAREUNIA—painful and difficult intercourse. There are many different causes, including a spasm of the vaginal muscles; this, in turn, may be a response to underlying anxiety or an intense fear of becoming pregnant.

One of the main difficulties between dysfunctional sexual partners is their inability to talk openly with one another about their problems, feeling that there is no hope. So it becomes a problem of just accepting and living with it. But as the communication gap widens, it is reflected in other ways and often leads to separation or divorce.

Treatment

Modern medical practice, fortunately, now has important therapeutic techniques for the treatment of sexual problems; many marriages and families are being saved because of them. Such programs are almost always directed toward the couple, rather than treating each individually. The goal is to instruct the partners about the physiological and psychological aspects of sexual response and to open communication channels that have perhaps been long closed. As the couple work through a series of therapeutic steps in a nonthreatening fashion, their anxiety and inhibitions diminish. Most couples eventually learn to function normally, with mutual pleasure and respect.

Sexual counseling clinics have now been established in many cities and communities throughout the nation; they are often connected with the outpatient departments of medical centers. Treatment does not necessarily require prolonged investigation of personalities. The greatest single factor for a successful outcome is motivation for treatment. However, some sexual problems are part of a complicated emotional disorder (such as depression) and require psychiatric evaluation as well.

Conclusion

In conclusion, it is important to mention the Community Mental Health Centers, for which federal funds are available in conjunction with local funding. Hopefully, such centers will become available to Americans throughout the entire nation. Their purpose is to deal with mental illness at the local level in collaboration with local hospital facilities—avoiding the stigma of state hospital commitments and the attending readjustment problems when a recovered patient is returned to his home and job. In addition, a primary goal of such centers is the education of not only the general public but also the clergy, police, school nurses and personnel managers in business and industry—so that those who have close contact with individuals and groups can learn to recognize the symptoms of mental illness and thus help victims to seek early treatment. Such centers deserve the support of individuals and communities.

Section II

The A-Z of Medicine

A

abduction/adduction

Two words used to describe the movements of limbs. Abduction is movement of a limb (or part of a limb) *away* from the midline of the body. Adduction is movement of a limb (or part of a limb) *toward* the midline.

When the arm is lifted away from the side and upwards toward a horizontal position, that is abduction. When it is brought down again to hang by the side, that movement is adduction. If you move your little toe outward you are abducting it; when you move it back in to lie alongside the other toes you are adducting it.

The practical importance of these terms is that they enable physicians to describe the actions of particular muscles with precision. Some body muscles are referred to as "abductors," while others are termed "adductors."

abortion

Loss of the fetus in early pregnancy.

Medically the terms "abortion" and "miscarriage" are generally synonymous, but in recent years there has been an increasing tendency for laymen to use the word "abortion" to mean deliberate termination of a pregnancy; "miscarriage" implies that the ending of a pregnancy has been accidental or spontaneous.

Deliberate abortion of pregnancy has been practiced for thousands of years, but was a very dangerous procedure until quite recently. Criminal, or "back-street" abortions are still highly dangerous and may result in loss of life or serious damage to health.

Legal abortion (carried out by trained medical practitioners, surgeons or gynecologists) is a relatively safe procedure, especially if performed very early in the pregnancy. Such abortions were rarely permitted before the mid-1960s, but are now carried out on a very wide scale in the United States and elsewhere. The Supreme Court decision of January 1973 made first trimester (first three months) abortions legal in any setting. Since then, an increasing number of abortions have been carried out in doctors' offices and medical centers.

The technique of an early abortion is relatively straightforward and usually involves aspirating the contents of the womb with a suction catheter. Later abortions (when pregnancy is advanced beyond 12 weeks) may involve more complex techniques and carry a much higher risk of side effects.

For a fuller discussion, see *Abortion* in the major article on **Family Planning.**

abruptio placentae

A condition of late pregnancy in which bleeding occurs within the womb as a result of partial premature separation (abruption) of the PLACENTA (afterbirth).

The cause of the placental separation is not known in most cases, although occasionally the bleeding follows an attempt at version (turning) of the fetus. Abruptio placentae is most common in women suffering from a toxic condition of pregnancy known as preeclampsia.

The features of abruptio placentae depend on whether the blood is retained within the womb ("concealed" hemorrhage) or escapes via the vagina ("revealed" hemorrhage). In the "concealed" variety, the mother suffers pain in the lower part of the abdomen and sometimes profound low blood pressure (shock). The same features are present in the "revealed" variety of the condition, but the diagnosis may be clarified by the additional presence of external bleeding.

Abruptio placentae is a danger to the mother (because of blood loss and shock) and to the baby, since severe hemorrhage may cause fetal death. Immediate admission to a hospital is thus essential. Intravenous fluid replacement and blood transfusion may be necessary. Once the condition of the mother is stabilized (and the diagnosis is differentiated from PLACENTA PREVIA) the obstetrician may attempt to deliver the baby—either by inducing labor or by carrying out a Cesarean operation.

abscess

A collection of pus formed anywhere in the body.

Abscesses are nearly always caused by bacterial infection, although occasionally they result from the presence of an irritating foreign body such as a splinter.

The usual response of the body to the stimulus of local irritation or damage by bacteria is the concentration of a large number of white blood cells (leukocytes) in the area affected. While the overall effect is beneficial, the reaction has certain local disadvantages: the infected part becomes hot, swollen, red and painful as the blood vessels dilate to carry leukocytes to the scene of action. The leukocytes pass through the walls of the blood vessels to "mop up" invading bacteria, and the area is walled off by the formation of fibrous tissue. Eventually the area of inflammation becomes localized and the collection of dead bacteria, dead leukocytes and exuded tissue fluid liquefies to form pus under tension.

The abscess so produced tends to find the line of least resistance in the surrounding tissues and "comes to a head" on the surface. If left to itself it bursts, but if possible the doctor hastens the process by making an incision to let out the pus and so ease the pain. It is dangerous to try to open an abscess before it is ready; an injudicious incision can only spread the infection.

ABSCESS

An abscess is a collection of pus in a cavity and is caused by infection with certain bacteria. Shown here are three ways in which an abscess might develop: (1) as a direct result of external infection, for example in a cut finger; (2) by local spread from a nearby site of infection, such as an alveolar abscess in the jawbone caused by a decayed tooth; (3) as a result of bacteria being transported in the bloodstream—for example, a brain abscess may follow from a lung infection.

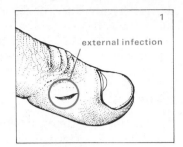

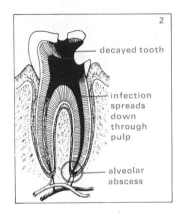

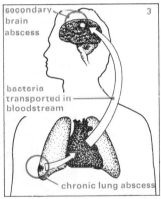

THREE ROUTES OF ABSCESS FORMATION

absorption

The process of absorbing food and other substances (including drugs) into the body.

Absorption may take place by means of a variety of routes. Medication may be given via all of them, but nutrients can be absorbed only through the gastrointestinal tract.

Food and drink are taken by mouth, pass down the esophagus, and reach the stomach. No significant absorption takes place in this organ, except in the case of alcohol and simple sugars such as glucose (which can be absorbed into the bloodstream through the stomach wall).

After a period of digestion in the stomach, nutrients move through the duodenum into the jejunum and ileum. (The duodenum, jejunum and ileum together make up the small intestine—one continuous tube about 22 ft. (6.5 meters) long.) The inside wall of the small intestine has a multitude of small finger-like projections with tiny blood vessels in them. It is in the small intestine that the absorption of food takes place: nutrients pass through the thin membrane covering the folds and enter the blood vessels lying underneath.

Many drugs are absorbed in precisely the same way, being taken by mouth and carried to the small intestine where they pass through the intestinal wall and enter the bloodstream. But drugs can also be absorbed through the skin as well as through mucous membranes of the eye, nose, mouth, vagina and rectum.

accommodation

The process that adjusts the lens of the eye for clear vision of objects either near to the eye or far from it.

If the lens of the eye were a solid immovable body (like glass and plastic lenses) it would not be able to provide a well-focused image of all objects; some would be out of focus because they were either too far away or too near. In a camera the problem is solved by moving the lens relative to the film. In the eye the distance is constant but the lens has its focal length changed. This is possible because the lens of the human eye is capable of changing its shape from moment to moment, depending on whether we are looking at objects near to us or far away.

When we look at a close object, the lens of the eye becomes thicker and more convex in order to focus the light from that object on the retina (the light-sensitive structure at the back of the eye). When we look at a distant object the lens becomes slimmer, so that the light from that object can be brought into focus. This alteration in the shape of the lens is the result of contraction of the *ciliary muscle*, which moves the circular ligament from which the lens is suspended and so alters its shape.

In middle age the lens loses a good deal of its elasticity, so reducing the range over which it can be focused. This loss of flexibility results in older people needing to hold a newspaper or other reading matter at arms' length or to use reading glasses. Anyone who has needed to wear glasses from childhood will probably need either two different pairs of glasses or bifocals as they grow older.

See also VISION and the major article on **Ophthalmology.**

achondroplasia

A congenital disorder in which the long bones of the limbs are much shorter than normal, resulting in dwarfism. The typical appearance—disproportionately short limbs and a prominent or bulging forehead—is seen in many circus dwarfs.

Achondroplasia (also known as chondrodystrophia fetalis) is an inherited form of dwarfism, although some cases occur as the result of new mutations. The disorder may affect either sex and is noted at birth.

The basic problem is retarded growth of cartilage and bone in the arms and legs (the trunk is commonly unaffected). The bones of the base of the skull also fail to develop normally, giving the appearance of a relatively large forehead. The bones that form the bridge of the nose fail to develop ("saddle nose"), giving a facial appearance that is virtually diagnostic of achondroplasia.

Muscular development is usually very good, which has helped many people with this condition to obtain employment as acrobats and tumblers over the ages. Mental ability is rarely affected and achondroplastics are sexually normal and capable of parenthood. However, achondroplastic women have abnormally small pelvises and their babies must be delivered by Cesarean section. Any person with achondroplasia should have genetic counseling before marriage.

There is no treatment. Nevertheless, the condition is compatible with a long, healthy and happy life, although it is obvious that psychological problems have to be overcome.

acidosis

An excess of acid in the body.

The human body's balance between acidity and excessive alkalinity is strictly maintained by a series of delicate control mechanisms. If this balance is disturbed the individual rapidly becomes extremely ill and, in the absence of medical treatment, may die.

The body fluids vary in their acidity. The most important fluid of all—the blood—is slightly alkaline. This mild alkalinity is due to the presence in the blood of the alkaline ion bicarbonate, which slightly outweighs the effect of the carbonic acid also present in the blood.

How then does acidosis occur? There are two principal mechanisms. The first is called respiratory acidosis and is mainly caused by respiratory disease— for instance, any disorder of the lungs that interferes with breathing. In such circumstances the carbon dioxide gas which should be exhaled in the breath tends to accumulate in the body and forms excess carbonic acid in the blood.

The second type of acidosis is called metabolic acidosis. This occurs when too many acid products accumulate in the body as a result of any metabolic or biochemical disease, such as uncontrolled DIABETES MELLITUS.

The symptoms of acidosis are ill-defined because they are usually overshadowed by those of the primary disease. Treatment is directed both toward correcting that primary disease process and (in many cases) toward correcting the body's acid-alkali balance by intravenous infusion of an alkaline solution.

acne

An extremely common inflammatory disorder of the sebaceous (oil-secreting) glands of the skin. Although several types of acne exist, described by various qualifying terms, when the term is used alone it usually refers to "common acne" (*acne vulgaris*).

Acne vulgaris can affect persons at any age, but it is especially troublesome among teenagers, where it can lead to extreme embarrassment about personal appearance or even severe emotional problems. During adolescence the sebaceous glands become particularly active and secrete large amounts of *sebum* (a fatty substance which ordinarily helps maintain the texture of the skin). This happens because of an increased production of *androgens* (sex hormones) in both males and females at the time of puberty. The sebum produced at this time is unusually thick and sticky and tends to

ACNE

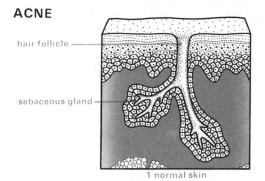

hair follicle

sebaceous gland

1 normal skin

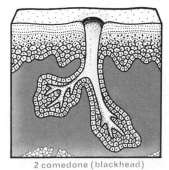

2 comedone (blackhead)

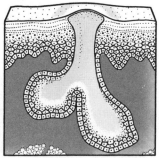

3 pustule

Normal skin has many microscopic hair follicles opening onto its surface (1). In acne, the mouth of the follicle is blocked by a plug of oily sebum (2). The sebaceous gland continues to secrete sebum so that the follicle becomes distended and inflamed. Bacteria then multiply in the follicle, and it becomes filled with pus (3).

block the sebaceous glands and their associated hair follicles. When this occurs, the follicles become dilated (stretched) with sebum and cellular debris.

If the plug of sebum extends to the skin surface, contact with the air causes its exposed surface to turn black—thus creating a *comedone* ("blackhead"). If the blockage does not extend to the surface, a "whitehead" is formed beneath the skin. Chemical changes within the blocked follicles result in the formation of irritating substances known as *free fatty acids* (FFA); retention of the secretions encourages the growth and multiplication of bacteria. As the follicles distend they form tiny cysts, which can eventually rupture and release the free fatty acids into the immediate area—inducing an inflammatory reaction. The affected follicles are typically filled with pus (papules, or "pimples") which can spread the infection if they are picked at or squeezed.

Acne vulgaris is further classified as *superficial* or *deep*, depending on the severity of the predominating lesions. The former is characterized by the formation of inflamed follicles filled with pus, which "come to a head" on the skin surface. *Deep acne*, as the term implies, affects deeper layers of the skin as well; pus-filled *cysts* may form beneath the skin, some of which discharge onto the skin surface. In severe cases, as these lesions heal they may leave permanent scarring. The main site involved in acne is the face, although the neck, chest, back and upper arms may also be involved.

At one time diet was implicated as a major cause of acne; however, modern medical opinion considers this to be unlikely in most cases. It is clear that hormonal factors during puberty are mostly responsible, although some experts believe that a hereditary influence may also contribute; this is almost impossible to document, however, since acne has a worldwide incidence and is undoubtedly the most common skin disorder of adolescence.

The treatment of acne depends largely on its severity. Often the only relief is brought by time, as the lesions tend to fade as the patient reaches adulthood (in many cases they last only two years or less). In the meantime, it is wise to wash the affected areas gently at least daily with mild soap and water. This helps by mechanically removing some of the blackheads, scales and bacteria. Medicated washes have proved effective in some mild cases, as has exposure to sunlight (which tends to dry up the lesions). Antibiotic ointments are generally not used, especially since they may produce further irritation of the skin in the form of a local allergic reaction. However, in selected cases a broad-spectrum antibiotic may be prescribed to be taken orally (by mouth); one of the most effective in such cases is tetracycline. Antibiotic treatment has no effect on the underlying cause of acne, but it may help reduce the number of bacteria responsible for much of the associated inflammation.

Acne strikes teenagers at a particularly sensitive time of life—when they are beginning to "discover" the opposite sex and are thus naturally concerned about personal appearance. Parents can be helpful in pointing out that acne is ordinarily of limited duration and that it is a nearly universal problem of those about to enter adulthood. This information may not help, of course, but there is really little else that can be done.

acromegaly

A glandular disorder characterized by great increase in size of hands, feet and head—producing a very typical coarse facial appearance with a large and jutting jaw.

Acromegaly is caused by excessive secretion of growth hormone in the anterior (front) part of the pituitary gland, which lies just underneath the brain. This excessive production is usually due to a tumor of the gland. (If the overactivity of the pituitary glands occurs before puberty—when the bones are still

ACROMEGALY

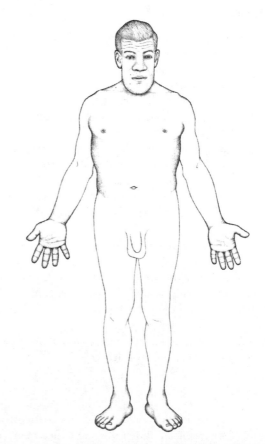

Acromegaly literally means "large extremities." This man shows the typical signs—enlarged hands and feet, massive chest, and coarse facial features with a characteristic jutting jaw. Acromegaly results from a benign tumor in the pituitary gland.

growing—the condition can result in GIGANTISM.)

Acromegaly is a relatively rare disease, although the fact that sufferers from it are so conspicuous has made it well known. The unusual facial appearance is illustrated in many medical textbooks, and people who are anxious about their health sometimes see such pictures and *unjustifiably* fear that they have the disease.

Early symptoms include headache or visual disturbances. The patient soon discovers that he has to take a larger size in shoes, gloves and sometimes hats. The fingers become square-ended and the tongue may enlarge. The facial features become rather coarse, with great prominence of the bony ridges above the eyes. Some patients also develop diabetes.

The disease usually runs a long course and it is not uncommon for some acromegalics to live to a great age. Treatment consists either in irradiation of the pituitary gland or surgical removal of the tumor. Unfortunately, therapy cannot reverse the changes that have already taken place in the hands, feet and skull, but it can arrest them.

acrophobia

An excessive and abnormal fear of high places. It is a natural part of human defense mechanisms to have some fear of heights because of the known danger of death or serious injury from a fall; acrophobia is merely an exaggeration of this normal fear. However, it has an element of unreason in it since the acrophobic subject will typically exhibit fear even in a room in a high building although the actual possibility of falling from it under these circumstances may be nil. It can be a very disabling condition since it may preclude the patient from going to work or attending social functions if these involve entering a building and going above the ground floor.

As with other phobias, therapy will involve analysis in an attempt to determine the possible cause of the phobia. Tranquilizing drugs may play a part and "deconditioning" the patient by teaching him to relax while in a real or imagined high place is sometimes helpful.

See also AGORAPHOBIA, CLAUSTROPHOBIA, PHOBIA and the major article on **Psychiatry.**

ACTH

ACTH is the abbreviation for adrenocorticotropic hormone, an essential hormone produced by the anterior (front) part of the pituitary gland, which lies at the base of the brain. It is also known as adrenocorticotropin or corticotropin. (The pituitary gland is the "master gland" of the endocrine system.) ACTH is of great importance because it provides the link between the pituitary and the cortex (covering) of the two tiny ADRENAL GLANDS—which lie at the back of the abdomen just above the kidneys. The cortex of the adrenal glands secretes steroid hormones such as cortisol (known pharmaceutically as hydrocortisone) and aldosterone, which are essential for maintaining the body's biochemical balance; without them we would die.

It is very important that the output of steroids is carefully controlled, since too much steroid production can be very harmful. It is the ACTH secreted by the pituitary which provides this control by means of a complex feedback mechanism.

What happens is that the pituitary secretes ACTH, which is carried in the bloodstream to the adrenal glands. There it stimulates them to produce steroids. But when the amount of steroids in the bloodstream reaches a certain level the production of ACTH by the pituitary is automatically shut off. This feedback mechanism produces a remarkably fine control of steroid production.

ACTH can be extracted from the pituitary glands of animals and given by injection in the treatment of certain diseases—such as asthma, rheumatoid arthritis and certain skin disorders.

Actinomyces/actinomycosis

Actinomyces is a genus of parasitic microorganisms formerly classified as fungi but now thought to be bacteria (some experts believe them to be intermediate between fungi and bacteria).

One species, *Actinomyces israelii*, is a common inhabitant of the mouth in persons with poor oral hygiene. The parasites cling to the teeth, gums and tonsils but rarely cause any problem—although they have been implicated as playing a role in the formation of dental plaque. However, the parasites *can* cause a severe infection if they gain entrance to the tissues, such as by means of a decayed tooth, following the extraction of a tooth, or an injury to the jaw. The resulting condition is known as *actinomycosis*.

Actinomycosis is characterized by painful, hard swellings that progress to the formation of abscesses (localized collections of pus). The sites most commonly affected are the jaws and neck, but if the parasites enter the bloodstream they may infect the lungs, intestines, kidneys and other organs. Early treatment with antibiotics, such as penicillin or tetracycline, is effective in most cases in limiting the progression of the disease.

acupuncture

The technique of producing anesthesia or attempting to treat disease by the insertion of the tips of long needles into the skin at certain special points. The needles are

ACUPUNCTURE

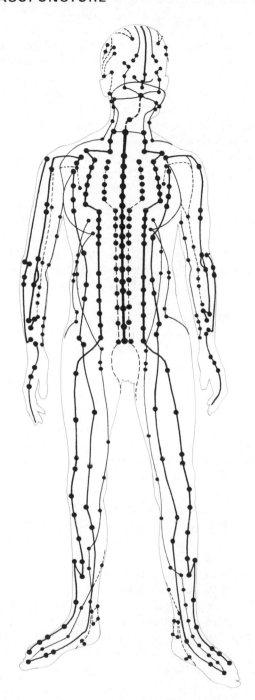

acupuncture points run along "meridians"

This is an acupuncturist's map of the body and shows the various points at which needles can be inserted through the skin in order to produce areas of anesthesia in other parts of the body. Many acupuncturists also claim that internal diseases can be cured by their skills. Contemporary Western science cannot explain how acupuncture works, and many conventional doctors are skeptical about its effectiveness.

then rotated back and forth by hand or charged with a small electric current for five minutes or so.

Acupuncture has been known in China for thousands of years, but until very recently it has been regarded by Western physicians as nothing more than one of the many forms of "quack" medicine. This view was also taken by orthodox (that is, Western-style) physicians in China itself until well into the 1950s.

However, Mao Tse-Tung's instruction to the medical profession in Communist China to "investigate the great treasure house of ancient Chinese medicine" led to a reappraisal of acupuncture. Chinese anesthesiologists were surprised to find that the technique could induce complete absence of pain during a wide range of surgical operations—although it was some years before they could convince their colleagues in the West of this.

In the 1960s Western physicians saw for themselves that operations could quite genuinely be performed under "acupuncture anesthesia" although not in all cases (some patients failed to respond to this method and continued to feel pain).

The value of acupuncture in treating disease is far less certain. Many Chinese doctors now accept the traditional oriental teaching that acupuncture can be used to treat a wide range of diseases. However, many American physicians are very doubtful of this, pointing out that the technique has never been subjected to the careful, scientifically designed clinical trials which are essential to prove that a method of therapy is actually effective. (Almost any procedure—no matter how bizarre and useless—will have a high apparent cure rate in some medical conditions as the result of what is known as a "placebo effect.")

The value of acupuncture in anesthesiology is documented, but its effectiveness as a form of treatment is still under investigation.

Why should it work at all? No Western or Chinese doctor has come up with a truly satisfactory explanation, although some have suggested that the insertion of the needles may in some way alter the balance between two important divisions of the nervous system, known respectively as the sympathetic and the parasympathetic systems. Western-style Chinese physicians have recently theorized that the needles may affect some minute structural network of the body which has not yet been discovered by anatomists. The traditional Chinese acupuncturists maintain that the insertion of the needles along certain "meridians" affects the inter-reaction of the two life-forces, which in their philosophy are termed "Yin" and "Yang."

acute abdomen

A jargon term used by many surgeons to signify any sudden, severe and continuing abdominal pain.

The diagnosis of the acute abdomen constitutes one of the major challenges to any general surgeon. Common causes include transient and harmless conditions like "gas" or "indigestion," as well as potentially more serious ones such as appendicitis, gastric ulcer, duodenal ulcer, gallbladder disease, pancreatitis, pyelitis (a form of kidney inflammation), and diverticulitis (inflammation of abnormal pouches in the large bowel).

In women, conditions such as ectopic pregnancy (pregnancy occurring in a Fallopian tube rather than the womb), miscarriage or abortion, and a twisted ovarian cyst have to be considered as possible causes of the acute abdomen.

Adams-Stokes syndrome

A condition which mostly affects the elderly, characterized by sudden episodes of unconsciousness. It can occur at any time of the day and is not dependent on bodily position. The cause is a disturbance in the heart's rhythm, such as VENTRICULAR FIBRILLATION or a temporary interruption of the heartbeat. Absence of the heartbeat (*asystole*) for 4 to 8 seconds will cause unconsciousness in the erect position; asystole of more than 12 seconds will cause unconsciousness in the recumbent position; asystole of up to 5 minutes leads to additional signs of CYANOSIS, fixed pupils, and neurological impairment (which may be permanent, if the patient survives).

Emergency treatment usually involves the intravenous administration of isoproterenol. This may be followed by the implantation of an artificial PACEMAKER.

See also ARRHYTHMIA, BRADYCARDIA.

addiction

Physical or mental dependence on a drug. Some experts make a distinction between *addiction* (physical dependence) and *habituation* (psychological dependence); both terms have traditionally been used to describe the adverse long-term effects of certain classes of drugs on the body and mind.

The World Health Organization, however, suggests that more meaningful diagnostic terms would be *drug dependence* and *drug abuse*. The essential feature of physical dependence is the occurrence of withdrawal symptoms if regular doses are not taken. Not all drugs which are responsible for extremely serious personality disruption cause a true physical dependence of this kind. LSD (lysergic acid diethylamide) is an example of an extremely potent drug (the use of which is now illegal except in medical research) which does not cause physical addiction, but which is nevertheless potentially dangerous for the mental changes it can cause (some of which can recur long after use of the drug has been abandoned).

The best known physically addictive drugs are the opiates or "narcotics," such as morphine and heroin. Even when prescribed legally for the relief of severe pain, prolonged treatment with opiates can lead to tolerance by the body of ever increasing doses of the drug. In these circumstances sudden withdrawal of the drug will cause cramping pains, sweating and acute mental distress. The need to relieve these symptoms by taking a further dose of the drug is the key feature of physical addiction. The fact that withdrawal symptoms occur indicates that the body's cells have themselves become dependent on regular supplies of the drug. This is why it is so difficult for a drug addict to "kick the habit"—he becomes physically ill if he does not get his regular "fix." A truly enormous amount of willpower is required over a very long period—usually with professional help—if he is to break the habit once and for all.

Other common drugs which may be addictive if abused include the amphetamines ("speed"), barbiturates and other types of sedatives ("sleeping pills"), and the major and minor tranquilizers such as chlorpromazine (Thorazine), meprobamate (Miltown) and diazepam (Valium). (See also the appropriate entries in the major article on **Drugs and Medicines.**)

There is still a great deal of misunderstanding about the drugs which cause addiction. Many people do not realize that CANNABIS (marijuana or "pot") is *not* physically addictive, but that nicotine *is* (witness the very considerable withdrawal symptoms which occur in the heavy cigarette smoker when he tries to give up the habit). ALCOHOL can also be addictive, although moderate amounts do not produce addiction in the majority of people.

The treatment of addiction is often best carried out by an experienced psychiatrist working in a drug addiction program. Analysis, group therapy, and the prescription of less harmful drugs to ease the withdrawal period may all help—together with the sympathetic support of family and friends, which is essential.

See also DRUG ABUSE.

Addison's disease

A disorder in which the adrenal glands cease to function adequately, and thus do not produce normal quantities of the hormones called steroids. Also known as *adrenal cortical hypofunction* or *chronic hypoadrenocorticism*. President Kennedy is believed to have been a sufferer.

These steroids are essential to life, since they maintain the biochemical balance of the body. Without them, the classical symptoms of Addison's disease (first described by the 19th-century English physician Thomas

Addison) soon appear. These symptoms include weakness, tiredness or even total collapse, vomiting, weight loss, low blood pressure, and a curious increase of dark pigmentation in the skin—so marked that in some cases a Caucasian may appear to be black.

In many instances the cause of the adrenal gland malfunction is unknown. Sometimes, however, it is due to a destruction of the adrenals by tuberculosis, or by a severe generalized infection associated with meningitis. Addison's disease is less common in the United States than it was, possibly because of the fall in the number of cases of T.B. However, it is estimated that one out of every 5,000 general hospital admissions is a case of this disorder.

Treatment of Addison's disease is usually very successful today, since it is possible for physicians to provide replacement of the missing hormones. Steroids are given by mouth, by injection, or by implantation under the skin; this therapy may well have to be maintained for life.

adduction

See ABDUCTION/ADDUCTION.

adenitis

Inflammation of a lymph gland (lymph node). These glands are scattered through various parts of the body, some of the main concentrations being at the side of the neck, in the armpits and in the groin. Their function is to help the body's defense against infection.

Unfortunately, there are times when the infection becomes sufficiently established to produce an intense inflammatory reaction in the lymph glands. These glands then become swollen and often painful. The inflammation may rarely proceed to such a stage that pus is formed in the glands.

Typically, adenitis of the glands in the groin is caused by some infection establishing itself in the leg, or in the sex organs. Adenitis of the glands in the armpits is caused by infection somewhere in the arm, or in the breast. Adenitis in the neck glands (cervical adenitis) is caused by infection in the throat, or ear, or sometimes infection of the scalp.

The type of infection causing adenitis varies greatly. At one time tuberculous adenitis was very common, but today most cases of adenitis are due to common bacteria such as streptococci (the organism found in many cases of sore throat) or to staphylococci (the organism found in boils). Also, adenitis of the neck glands is frequently due to viral infection—for instance, the viruses of infectious mononucleosis and German measles (rubella). Treatment of adenitis is basically treatment of the underlying infection (for instance, with antibiotics).

adenocarcinoma

A type of CANCER arising in glandular tissue.

Adenocarcinomas can be distinguished under the microscope from other types of tumor, and this differentiation is of some help in assessing the likely outcome of the disease and in deciding the best method of treatment.

Adenocarcinomas mainly arise in the stomach, large intestine (colon), gallbladder, pancreas, womb (uterus) and prostate gland. They can also arise in the breast and lungs.

These tumors may spread to other parts of the body (via the blood and lymphatic systems) if they are not detected and treated early enough. When such spread occurs, the secondary tumor which is formed at another site has the same "glandular" appearance under the microscope as that of the "primary" adenocarcinoma. This may be a help in diagnosis if the site of the primary tumor is not yet known.

adenoids

Masses of lymphatic glandular tissue found behind the nose on the back wall of the nasopharynx (that part of the throat which lies an inch or two above the area that is visible when the mouth is open). Doctors can inspect the adenoids by placing a small, upward-pointing mirror in the back of the throat.

ADENOIDS

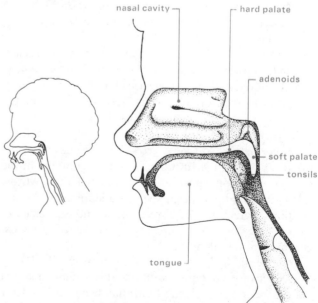

nasal cavity — hard palate — adenoids — soft palate — tonsils — tongue

The adenoids and tonsils form part of a ring of lymphoid tissue at the entrance to the throat. Their job is to form protective antibodies against any microorganisms which attempt to enter the respiratory and digestive tracts.

These glands are often referred to as the "nasopharyngeal tonsils" because they play a similar role to the tonsils in helping to protect a child against inhaled germs. Unfortunately, they sometimes become infected and grossly enlarged—in much the same way that tonsils often do—and when this happens they may cause symptoms of nasal obstruction, since they make it difficult for air to pass in through or out of the nose.

The symptoms of grossly enlarged adenoids include inability to breathe properly through the nose, a change in the quality of the voice ("adenoidal speech") and snoring.

Adenoids usually reach their maximum size at about the age of 6, when the child is being exposed to a wide range of respiratory germs through contact with other children at school. From about the age of 9 or 10 they tend to shrink away, They usually disappear entirely by the time of adolescence and it is rare to find any trace of adenoids in adults. In view of this natural tendency to shrink, surgeons are less keen to remove enlarged adenoids than they used to be.

adenoma

A benign swelling or tumor of glandular tissue (as opposed to ADENOCARCINOMA, which is a malignant tumor of the same type of tissue).

In contrast to adenocarcinoma, adenomas are basically harmless, although their presence may cause discomfort or slight pain. They do not invade other parts of the body, nor destroy bodily tissues, and they do not spread to distant regions of the body, producing "secondary" tumors.

Adenomas chiefly occur in such organs as the breast, stomach, bowel, pancreas, liver, thyroid gland, ovary, and the adrenal glands. They are characteristically firm swellings formed of cells which resemble those of the tissues in which the adenoma has developed.

In the stomach and bowel an adenoma commonly develops a stalk, so that it grows into the cavity of the organ like a POLYP. In other situations (notably in the ovary) an adenoma may become cystic—in other words, filled with fluid. In the breast, an adenoma frequently contains a great deal of fibrous tissue and is referred to as a FIBROADENOMA; this variety is one of the most common of all adenomas.

In general, adenomas are removed surgically. Partly this is because a *definite* diagnosis of a benign adenoma cannot be made until the lump has been removed for microscopic examination. In addition, a very small proportion of adenomas do become malignant (through changing into adenocarcinomas). Surgical excision therefore not only is a wise precaution but may be essential in treating those tumors which have undergone a malignant change.

adhesion

An abnormal band of tissue developing between two internal organs, especially in the abdominal cavity.

Adhesions occur as a result of inflammation and may develop following a severe infection, such as peritonitis. Very commonly, however, adhesions form after a surgical operation, like a sort of internal scar tissue. Some people seem to be much more likely to develop postoperative adhesions than others, but the reason for this is not known.

The great importance of adhesions is that they may interfere with the function of bodily organs. In many cases a person who has had an abdominal operation may develop an intestinal obstruction a few years later. When the surgeon opens the abdomen, the cause is found to be adhesions pressing on the intestine. Cutting through the adhesive bands relieves the situation, but there is always a small risk of recurrence later.

ADHESION

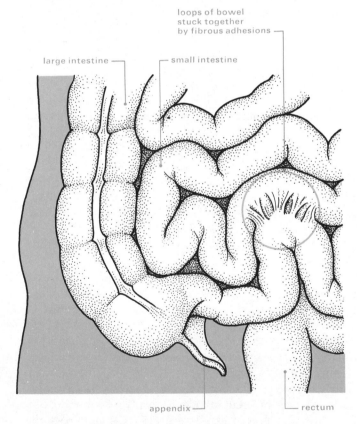

loops of bowel
stuck together
by fibrous adhesions

large intestine

small intestine

appendix

rectum

The loops of the bowel normally slide over each other freely, but occasionally become stuck together by fibrous adhesions. These may result from previous inflammation or from abdominal surgery. Adhesions may obstruct the passage of material along the bowel in which case further surgery is necessary to divide them.

adipose tissue

The layer of fat which mainly lies immediately under the skin; it acts both as an insulator and as a source of "fuel." Adipose tissue is also found in other parts of the body, but is not evenly distributed. It is quite thick in those parts most liable to sudden pressure, such as the buttocks and feet where it acts as a "shock absorber." It is also present in the bone marrow, where it supports the arteries and veins; around the heart and lungs, where it provides a cushion and support; around the intestines, to keep them warm; around the kidneys, for protection; and in the joints and muscles, where it prevents damage by sudden shock or jarring.

Excess formation of adipose tissue anywhere can be dangerous, especially around the heart—where it adds weight to that organ and impedes its movement. Heavy deposits around the lungs can restrict breathing and also affect the action of the heart. Excess fatty deposits can be avoided by the proper attention to diet and exercise. (See also the major article on **Nutrition.**)

ADIPOSE TISSUE

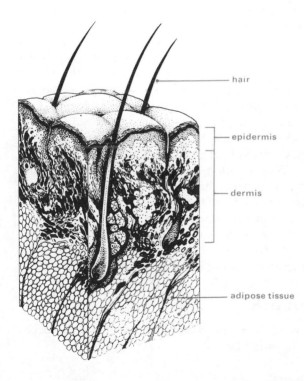

Adipose tissue is a collection of round cells full of fat; it is found throughout the body and acts as a reserve supply of energy. However, most Americans do not have to endure periods of starvation and tend to carry excess amounts of adipose tissue. The layer shown here beneath the skin is important for conserving body heat.

adrenal glands

Two tiny glandular masses which lie immediately above the kidneys, at the back of the abdominal cavity. They are also known as the *suprarenal glands.*

The adrenal glands have two quite separate functions, and this is reflected by the fact that each of them is

ADRENAL GLANDS

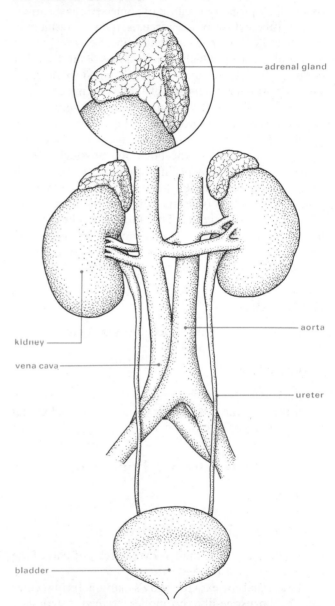

The adrenal glands sit on top of the kidneys like a pair of cocked hats. Although small, these glands are essential for life because of the hormones they produce: epinephrine and norepinephrine, which are secreted into the bloodstream when we are in stressful situations, cortisol and other stress hormones, and aldosterone, which plays an important role in regulating the blood pressure.

divided into two separate zones: an outer *cortex* and an inner *medulla*.

The cortex is absolutely essential to the body because it produces the cortisone-like hormones called "steroids," some of which play important roles in the metabolism of fats, carbohydrates, proteins, sodium and potassium, and others in sexual development and the maintenance of bodily strength. If the cortex is not functioning properly because of some serious disorder, such as tuberculosis of the adrenals, then the result may be ADDISON'S DISEASE—a condition of extreme weakness and lethargy which usually proved fatal until it became possible to provide replacement of adrenal steroid hormones by means of tablets or injections.

The medulla of the gland is entirely separate in function. It is part of the sympathetic nervous system, a division of the nerve communications network concerned with preparing the body for physical activity through release of epinephrine (adrenaline)—the chemical that prepares muscles, heart and blood vessels for instant action. It is often described as the hormone of "fight, flight, or fright." The adrenal medulla is the body's prime source of this important hormone, releasing it in bursts that are triggered off by stimuli such as excitement, fear, anger or sexual desire.

Adrenalin

A proprietary name for adrenaline (epinephrine).

adrenaline

Another word for epinephrine (a hormone secreted by the ADRENAL GLANDS). In the United States, Adrenalin is a trade name for epinephrine.

adrenocorticotropic hormone

See ACTH.

adrenogenital syndrome

A condition in which there is overactivity of part of the cortex of the ADRENAL GLANDS.

The adrenal cortex is the body's manufacturing center for the cortisone-like hormones termed "steriods," which are vitally important in maintaining the biochemical balance of our tissues. These hormones also have important effects on the sex organs, since some of them tend to promote the development of male characteristics. Overproduction of these hormones can result in the adrenogenital syndrome.

The characteristics of this condition depend on just which particular "mix" of hormones is being produced by the overactive adrenal gland. Chief symptoms,

however, tend to be masculinization in female children and adults (with excessive hairiness and enlargement of the clitoris), precocious puberty in boys (including abnormal enlargement of the penis), and sometimes high blood pressure.

The adrenogenital syndrome is fortunately rare, and the current use of hormone therapy is usually fairly effective.

African trypanosomiasis

African trypanosomiasis (also known as "African sleeping sickness") is an infection of the brain by specific protozoan parasites (*Trypanosoma gambiense* and *Trypanosoma rhodesiense*). The disease is spread by blood-sucking tsetse flies, which attack both men and animals over a broad region of central and southern Africa. In Rhodesia, Zaire, Zambia and Angola trypanosomiasis was the principal health problem until eradication campaigns controlled the numbers of tsetse flies.

The bite of the fly may pass unnoticed or it may cause a local inflammatory reaction of the skin which may develop into a characteristic hard sore. With the Rhodesian variety of the disease, symptoms develop within a week or two; elsewhere the incubation period may be months or even years. The early symptoms include a severe headache, difficulty in sleeping and a feeling of misery. If treatment is not given the disease progresses to cause weakness, apathy, increasing drowsiness and death (the mortality rate is close to 100% in untreated cases). However, drugs such as suramin and melarsoprol are capable of curing the disease in its later stages. Control of the disease depends on control of the tsetse flies; unfortunately, the political unrest and guerrilla wars in southern Africa have been followed by a huge increase in the population of flies and a resurgence of the disease.

South American trypanosomiasis (also known as CHAGAS' DISEASE) is caused by a different species of the trypanosome parasite (*Trypanosoma cruzi*).

afterbirth

The PLACENTA and associated membranes expelled after the birth of a child.

agglutination

Clumping or sticking together of numbers of small particles in a fluid. Particles or cells (for instance, red blood cells or bacteria) demonstrate this phenomenon when they are exposed to an antibody that reacts with an antigen they contain (see ANTIBODY/ANTIGEN).

The phenomenon is of considerable importance in

medical diagnosis, since it is used as the basis for many laboratory tests. For instance, if bacteria of unknown identity are obtained from a patient, they can be mixed with antibodies from laboratory animals. These antibodies are specific to a particular bacterium. If the bacteria taken from the patient clump (agglutinate) on contact with them, they can be positively identified as being the same organism and appropriate antibiotic treatment can then be prescribed.

Another variety of agglutination test uses the same principle in reverse. Serum (the amber fluid remaining after blood has clotted) of a patient who is suspected of having a particular infection is mixed with fluid containing bacteria which are known to cause that infection. If the bacteria agglutinate, this indicates that the patient has antibodies against them.

In practice, this does not mean that the patient currently has the disease but that he *has* had it at some time in the past. Often it is necessary to repeat the test after a period of time to see if the patient's titer of antibodies has risen. (The *agglutination titer* is the highest dilution of a serum which will cause clumping of the bacteria being tested.) If it has gone up, then this is strong evidence that the infection is a recent one.

Agglutination reactions are also used in the grouping of blood for transfusion, to ensure that the patient will not react adversely, and in the diagnosis of certain diseases (such as rheumatoid arthritis) where there is some unusual antibody present in the blood.

See also BLOOD.

aging

The process of aging begins much earlier than most people imagine. Even in childhood there are some slight changes caused by aging—for instance, an inability to perceive the very high notes which are detectable by young infants. By the age of 18, most American males have some evidence of degeneration in their coronary arteries.

By the late 20s, most people are already showing some decline in physical prowess (many athletes have passed their prime at this age). In the 30s, the aging process continues at a gradual rate—although to some extent it can be kept in check by careful attention to diet, regular exercise and avoidance of adverse health factors such as smoking, excessive alcohol consumption and obesity.

In the 40s and 50s, the pace of aging quickens somewhat. In women it may be accelerated by the relatively rapid loss of female hormone output at the menopause. And in the 60s and 70s the classical changes of aging become apparent in most people: white hair, wrinkled skin, stiffer joints and degeneration of the arteries (leading, very often, to coronary heart disease or impaired blood circulation in the brain). The effects of aging can to some extent be moderated by leading a healthy life, with an adequate amount of exercise and well-balanced meals. In some people (and in some isolated races of mankind) the process of aging is very much slower than normal: we are all familiar with people who appear to be in their 50s, but who in fact are 75 or more.

Medical science has yet to discover why aging occurs and how the "biological clock" works, which seems to determine that it will take place. (The clock sometimes malfunctions: there are a few tragic cases of children who became prematurely aged and wizened, dying in their teens or even earlier of "old age"—a condition known as "progeria.") All we can do at the moment is to try to stave off the effects of aging by keeping as fit as possible and by treating—or better still, preventing—the various diseases which are so often associated with age.

See also *Aging* in the major article on **The Health Care of the Elderly.**

agoraphobia

An irrational fear of open places.

Phobias are extremely common and agoraphobia is one of the most frequently encountered. On the most conservative of estimates, there must be tens of thousands of sufferers in the United States.

The reason why agoraphobia is so common is not known. Experts believe that many phobias are linked to frightening experiences that occur in early childhood, including excessively harsh or terrifying punishments by parents. It must be admitted, however, that this is still pure speculation.

The symptoms of agoraphobia are extremely distressing for the victim. When she (the disorder is much more common in women) attempts to go out into the open, there is a terrifying feeling of panic, often with racing heart, profuse sweating and trembling. The sufferer may be convinced that she is about to die, and this feeling cannot be alleviated until she gets back indoors again.

In variants of agoraphobia the victim may fear only a particular type of open space—for instance, a park or even a supermarket with a high roof. Agoraphobics often have other phobias as well, such as fear of cats, insects, or of talking to other people.

It cannot be denied that treatment of agoraphobia is difficult, partly because sufferers are unable to overcome their panic in order to visit a doctor's office. Even if a physician makes house calls, he is unlikely to be able to undertake the long-term therapy that is usually needed in such cases unless the patient can come to his office. However, some physicians specializing in this disorder have solved the problem by giving psychotherapy on the telephone.

Therapy may involve some form of analysis in an attempt to unravel the inner conflicts producing the panic (see DESENSITIZATION). Psychiatrists and psychologists use such techniques as desensitization (deconditioning) in which the patient is taught to relax while imagining herself in the feared situation. Tranquilizing drugs also have a small part to play in treatment, but do not solve the underlying problem.

Encouraging results have been achieved by doctors who have the knack of teaching agoraphobic patients that they have nothing to fear but fear itself—in other words, that if they can accept the symptoms of panic and not run for shelter when they occur, they will eventually triumph over the disorder.

See also PHOBIA; compare ACROPHOBIA and CLAUSTROPHOBIA.

agranulocytosis

A severe illness characterized by a gross deficiency of white blood cells. (The condition is also known as granulocytopenia.)

The white blood cells, mainly produced in the spongy center or marrow of the long bones, are of great importance in the defense of the body against infection. Unfortunately, the bone marrow is sometimes affected by disease or toxic substances (or both) and fails to produce an adequate number of white blood cells to replace those which are constantly being used up in the course of their protective work against invading microorganisms.

Failure of the bone marrow may occur as a complication of leukemia. More commonly it represents a toxic reaction to drugs such as sulfonamides, gold or arsenic preparations, phenylbutazone, chloramphenicol, or certain antiepileptic and antithyroid preparations. Industrial poisons (e.g., benzol) may have the same effects, as may exposure to radioactive material or x-rays. Occasionally, however, the bone marrow fails to produce white blood cells for no known reason ("idiopathic" agranulocytosis).

The symptoms of agranulocytosis include those that might be expected in an individual with no real defense against infection—fever and recurrent infective ulceration of the mouth and throat, with increasing ill health and (if the condition is unchecked) eventual death.

The treatment of agranulocytosis involves the administration of antibiotics to combat infection, blood transfusions to provide a temporary source of white blood cells, and steroid therapy (which is thought to encourage the bone marrow to resume its activity). In some cases the marrow will recover spontaneously once any toxic drugs have been withdrawn. Where it does not, it is occasionally possible to perform a bone marrow transplant, inserting marrow taken from a donor.

AID/AIH

Abbreviations used to indicate, respectively, *Artificial Insemination* [*by*] *Donor* and *Artificial Insemination* [*by*] *Husband*.

The term artificial insemination indicates the technique by means of which a man's seminal fluid is deposited in a woman's vagina or uterus under conditions other than sexual intercourse (usually with a special syringe) in the hope of achieving a pregnancy. AID and AIH, subjects of great controversy over the last few decades, have been extremely successful in providing previously childless couples with a much wanted baby.

Artificial insemination has been used by veterinarians for a very long time, but it is only since World War II that the technique has been widely used in women to overcome a chronic failure to become pregnant. Although some 10 to 15% of American marriages are relatively infertile (in other words, the couples concerned experience difficulty in conceiving), only a minority of couples can be helped by artificial insemination.

AIH involves taking a specimen of the husband's semen and introducing it into the wife's vagina or uterus. Ordinarily the physician is responsible for the procedure but sometimes he instructs the couple how to do this for themselves at home. It is important to realize that AIH is used only in appropriate cases: where the wife has some structural or—much more commonly—emotional problem that makes successful intercourse and impregnation very difficult; where the husband is unable to achieve or maintain an erection long enough to have sexual intercourse; and finally, where the concentration of sperms in the seminal fluid is abnormally low (the physician may then use special techniques to achieve a higher concentration of sperms before introducing the semen).

Much more controversial is AID, in which the seminal fluid is provided by a male donor, whose identity should be unknown to both husband and wife. The reason for this method is the situation where the wife is fertile but the husband is not. Today many husbands are happy to approve the technique of AID if (as is so often the case) it is the only means of ensuring that their wives will have the chance to have babies. This procedure should, of course, never be carried out without the husband's permission: in most states a legal agreement, signed by both husband and wife, is required in advance of the procedure.

An estimated 7,000 children are born each year in the United States as the result of artificial insemination, and the number is steadily increasing. Legislation pertaining to AID is rapidly changing too, with which the physician who carries out the procedure should be familiar.

albinism

Absence of the natural pigment from the skin, resulting in an unnaturally pale appearance.

Regardless of race, most people have a considerable amount of the dark pigment melanin in their skin; the concentration varies somewhat with the time of year. It increases greatly after sunbathing, and this is the mechanism responsible for suntan.

However, certain people have no melanin pigment whatever. This appears to occur as the result of an enzyme defect, which prevents the body from forming melanin from its biochemical precursor. This defect is hereditary, but is caused by a recessive gene—which means that it will appear only when two people who *both* carry the gene have children (even then it occurs in only about one in four of their children).

The incidence of albinism in the United States is estimated to be about one in 25,000 persons. The disorder can affect blacks as well as whites, and indeed in people of black descent the "washed out" appearance is very striking. The hair is white and the eyes are gray or pink.

Apart from the somewhat unusual appearance, the main problem for the person with albinism (known as an *albino*) is an excessive sensitivity of the skin to sunburn. In addition the eyes may not tolerate the light well.

There is no cure for the condition, although—if even a little melanin is present (as in the case with some atypical forms of albinism)—drugs can be given to stimulate melanin production. Otherwise sunscreening creams should be used to prevent sunburn. Good quality sunglasses are often helpful.

albumin

A natural protein, found in various forms in animals and plants. The best known form of albumin is egg white (the word *albumin* is derived from *albus*, the Latin for "white"). Other types of albumin are found in milk, beans and meat.

In the human body, albumin is one of the two major proteins of the blood, the other being globulin. It is formed in the liver from protein foods in the diet. Albumin has an important role in metabolism; it also maintains the osmotic pressure of the blood—that is, its water-holding capacity. If it were not present in an adequate concentration, excessive amounts of water would pass out of the blood and into the tissues, causing EDEMA. A low blood level of albumin is characteristic of protein malnutrition and is seen in certain disorders of the kidneys and liver.

There are several different kinds of laboratory tests to determine the abnormal presence of albumin in the urine—a condition known as ALBUMINURIA.

albuminuria

The presence of the protein ALBUMIN in the urine.

Albumin is one of the most important constituents of blood and is not usually found in urine. When blood passes through the kidneys, only impurities should be filtered out for excretion in the urine. When the kidney is malfunctioning, however, albumin may leak into the urine. That is why physicians make a regular practice of testing a urine specimen for albumin.

Albuminuria does not always indicate kidney disease. In women, for example, apparent albuminuria is frequently due to a small amount of vaginal secretion in the urine specimen. Other quite harmless causes of positive test results for urinary albumin include postural or orthostatic albuminuria (found in up to 5% of healthy college freshmen), in which albumin enters the urine only if the person has been standing up for some time.

Disorders which are of more significance include the various forms of nephritis (inflammation of the kidney), most types of fever, and toxemia of pregnancy.

The term PROTEINURIA (protein in the urine) is virtually synonymous with albuminuria, since albumin is the only protein ever found in significant quantities in the urine.

alcohol/alcoholism

Alcohol is the name of a type of chemical of which the most common is *ethyl alcohol*—the one obtained by the fermentation of sugar and enjoyed by man in beverages for thousands of years.

Alcoholic drinks are taken not only for their pleasant taste but because alcohol is a drug, albeit a socially acceptable one in most cultures. It is not a stimulant drug, as many people imagine, but a *selective depressant* of the central nervous system. It begins by depressing the frontal centers of the cerebrum; its effect slowly spreads back toward the cerebellum.

The effect of a small dose of alcohol is to depress the inhibitory or controlling centers of the brain, producing relaxation and a general loss of inhibitions. Larger quantities induce sedation and impair speech and muscular coordination. Very large quantities produce severe depression of the vital centers of the central nervous system and may be fatal.

Outside the central nervous system the physiologic effects of alcohol are less drastic. Small quantities increase the flow of gastric juices (thereby stimulating the appetite); larger amounts irritate the stomach lining, causing gastritis and even vomiting of blood. Alcohol also increases the flow of urine.

Unfortunately, chronic ingestion of fairly large quantities of alcohol can have highly deleterious effects on body tissues—particularly those of the liver.

CIRRHOSIS, a serious hardening and degeneration of liver tissue, kills many heavy drinkers. Cancer is especially likely to develop in a cirrhotic liver. Alcohol taken in excess over a long period may also cause a degeneration of the heart muscle (cardiomyopathy) and serious impairment of brain function. Alcoholic psychosis is one of the most common reasons for psychiatric hospitalization.

Alcoholism is a state of addiction to alcohol. Those who suffer from it are likely to develop the severe physical consequences of alcohol abuse which have been outlined above. Alcohol is not as addictive as heroin, morphine or nicotine; but research indicates that most humans (and mammals generally) can be habituated to it by prolonged, constant exposure. If a person drinks enough alcohol on a regular basis, there is a strong possibility that his body will become dependent upon it. Larger and larger doses may be required, as time goes by, to keep withdrawal symptoms at bay.

Although unhappiness and deprivation play a part in driving a man or woman to excessive drinking, it is quite untrue that only depraved and "worthless" people become alcoholics. Many Americans were astounded when the astronaut Buzz Aldrin was only one of many prominent persons to announce that he suffered from alcoholism. This brave declaration helped many people to realize that alcoholism is an *illness*, not a vice.

Treatment of alcoholism is difficult and fraught with disappointments. The alcoholic must first accept that he has the condition; he then needs caring support from his family, friends and personal physician. It may also be wise for the alcoholic to consult a psychiatrist who is thoroughly experienced in dealing with the condition.

The psychiatrist may employ analysis and may prescribe "antialcohol" drugs such as disulfiram (Antabuse), which produces a most violent and unpleasant physical reaction if alcohol is taken (including nausea and vomiting).

Other methods employed by psychiatrists include behaviorist techniques such as conditioning the patient to associate the sight and smell of alcohol with unpleasant sensations. Admission to a specialist alcoholic unit is often necessary so that the alcohol can be withdrawn completely ("drying out").

Alcoholics Anonymous is a leading organization whose supportive work in helping patients keep off alcohol has undoubtedly saved thousands of lives.

See also the major article on **Psychiatry.**

alkalosis

An excess of alkali in the blood and the tissue fluids of the body.

Metabolic alkalosis ordinarily arises as the result of an excessive loss of hydrochloric acid from the stomach through prolonged vomiting. It may also arise if a person takes excessive quantities of antacids for an ulcer or an upset stomach, and as a complication of treatment with diuretic drugs, which increase the acidity of the urine formed by the kidneys. In most cases, however, the condition will resolve provided enough fluid is taken to allow the kidneys to readjust the amount of alkali (bicarbonate) in the blood. In very severe cases, treatment with ammonium chloride will speed up the return to normal.

Respiratory alkalosis is caused by an excessive excretion of carbon dioxide gas in the exhaled breath. The most common reason is hysterical overbreathing, but the normal mechanisms that control the breathing rate may be disturbed in persons on respirators and in cases of aspirin poisoning. Symptoms include a form of spasmodic muscular contraction called tetany. Treatment may be no more complex than providing a paper bag for the patient to breath into, so ensuring that the carbon dioxide breathed out is breathed back in again. When the cause is biochemical it may be necessary to give fluids intravenously to restore the blood to normal.

alkaptonuria

A rare inborn error of metabolism, which causes the excretion in the urine of a substance called homogentisic acid. This causes the urine to become dark on exposure to the air, so that urine left overnight in a pot will become almost black. (The chemical defect is the absence of an enzyme termed homogentisate oxidase, which catalyzes an important step in the metabolism of the amino acid tyrosine.)

With modern sanitation an affected individual may be unaware of the abnormality unless other symptoms develop. These include a form of arthritis and stiffness and change in color of the cartilage in the ear and elsewhere due to deposition of a pigment formed as a result of the chemical defect. The arthritis, which typically develops at about the age of 30, affects the larger joints, and especially the spine. There is no specific treatment, but life expectancy is normal.

This defect is hereditary and will not appear unless both parents carry the gene. If they do, then the disease will appear in approximately one in four of their children. Fortunately, the gene is rare; the incidence of the disease in the United States is about one in 200,000. As with other recessively inherited diseases, alkaptonuria is much more likely to appear if the parents are related to each other; thus, the disease is more common in small, inbred communities. Genetic counseling is advisable for anyone with a relative with the disorder: the condition can be detected chemically before symptoms develop.

allergy

Allergy is the mechanism through which symptoms are caused by sensitivity to an *allergen*—an allergy-causing substance, such as pollen, feathers, fur or dust, or a chemical such as a detergent, cosmetic or drug. Allergy is the cause of hay fever and urticaria (hives) and underlies many cases of asthma and eczema.

Allergic reactions are exaggerations of the body's normal immune responses to bacteria and viruses and their toxins. Whenever an infecting organism penetrates the skin or enters the bloodstream the blood lymphocytes respond by forming antibodies. These are large protein molecules tailor-made to correspond to the chemical makeup of the bacteria or their toxins. The allergic response is essentially similar: antibodies are formed against pollen grains inhaled into the nose and lungs or against cosmetics coming into contact with the skin. However, whereas the normal immune response is designed to destroy bacteria and neutralize their toxins the allergic response causes symptoms rather than protecting against them. Characteristically, the first (sensitizing) exposure to an allergen causes no symptoms, but if the body responds by forming antibodies the stage is set for an allergic reaction on the next and subsequent exposures. Whether or not allergens such as pollen, dog hair, or strawberries provoke an allergic reaction depends on individual susceptibility. Some people are allergic to a whole range of common substances; others never develop sensitivities. Such tendencies often run in families.

The most common sites for allergic reactions are the respiratory tract and the skin. Inhaled allergens may stimulate the formation of antibodies which become fixed to the lining of the nose or lungs. Further exposure to the same allergen will cause the antibodies and antigens to react together, with the release of chemicals such as histamine from specialized immune cells (plasma cells and mast cells) in the surface membranes. It is the histamine release that causes the symptoms of hay fever such as the sneezing and eye-watering from swelling and inflammation of the conjunctiva and the nasal mucous membranes. In the lungs the predominant allergic response is spasm of the small air passages, causing asthma; in the skin the response causes swelling and irritation, though the scratching this induces may lead to secondary infection. Allergy may also affect the digestive system: allergy to gluten (wheat protein), for example, can damage the intestinal lining causing chronic diarrhea and stunted growth due to malabsorption of the food (CELIAC DISEASE).

Allergic responses may be immediate, in which exposure to the allergen causes symptoms within a few minutes, or delayed, in which there may be an interval of several days between contact with the allergen and the onset of symptoms. In delayed responses the illness may not be recognized as allergic unless careful attention is paid to the possibility.

Allergic reactions which cause troublesome symptoms may be treated either by antihistamine drugs which block the effects of histamine on the skin and blood vessels, or by drugs such as steroids or cromoglycate which suppress the formation of antibodies. Another approach is DESENSITIZATION: repeated injection of very small doses of the allergen responsible for symptoms eventually damps down the allergic response. This form of treatment is used most often for persons sensitive to only one or two specific dusts or pollens.

See also the major article on **Allergy and Immunology.**

alopecia

The technical term for BALDNESS.

alphafetoprotein

A substance that can help identify the presence of SPINA BIFIDA and similar deformities (such as ANENCEPHALY) in an unborn baby. Also referred to as *α-fetoprotein.*

Spina bifida and other "neural tube" defects are among the most common serious abnormalities occurring in pregnancy, with a rate as high as 4 per 1,000 births in some parts of the United States. Their cause is unknown and they are difficult to treat; many affected babies are stillborn and others die in the first few weeks of infancy. Even if the child survives he may have a miserable life, with partial paralysis, incontinence, and mental handicap. For these reasons, doctors have sought a test to identify the abnormalities before birth so that the mother could be offered a clinical abortion.

A test was eventually devised, during the 1960s, by Scottish doctors. They found that if they took fluid from around the baby in the womb, by the technique known as AMNIOCENTESIS, they could estimate the level of a substance, *alphafetoprotein* (*AFP*), in the fluid. High levels of AFP indicate an abnormality.

The test soon became routine in Britain for any mother known to be at special risk of producing a spina bifida baby—for example, one who had already had such a child. The test could not, however, be offered to all mothers because of its cost and its risks. Since few potential spina bifida mothers can be identified, its effect on the incidence of the condition was not great.

In 1975, however, the same Edinburgh team developed a further test for AFP in an ordinary blood sample—a much safer and easier technique. They found a good relationship between maternal blood levels of AFP and the likelihood of a deformed child, and as a result the number of affected children born in Scotland has now been dramatically reduced.

This test is now becoming more widely available and seems likely to prove to be one of the important medical advances of the 1970s.

altitude sickness

An illness occurring in persons on high mountains, or in unpressurized aircraft, as a result of the reduced quantity of oxygen in the air.

The proportion of oxygen in the atmosphere is the same at all altitudes (approximately 21%), but the atmosphere gets appreciably thinner at great heights so that less oxygen is available. At an altitude of 5,000 ft., the oxygen level is 80% of its value at sea level—a slight reduction that has little effect on a healthy person, except to make prolonged physical effort more difficult. At 10,000 ft., however, the partial pressure of oxygen falls to 69% of its value at sea level; at 15,000 ft..it is 56%, and at 20,000 ft. (say, around the summit of Mount McKinley) it is 45%. At the top of Mount Everest (29,000 ft.), it is 31%.

Man finds considerable difficulty in adapting to oxygen tensions which are 70% or less of normal—in other words, in adapting to altitudes of over 10,000 ft. The breathing rate has to be increased to permit the body to absorb the oxygen it needs, and this leads to an excessive loss of carbon dioxide from the bloodstream (see ALKALOSIS). Eventually the kidneys are able to readjust the acidity of the blood, but this process of acclimatization takes several weeks. Although small colonies of Andeans engage in quite strenuous work in their natural habitat at around 15,000 ft., it is highly doubtful if man could reside permanently at an altitude above 18,000 ft.

With careful, slow acclimatization it is possible for climbers to spend brief periods as high as the summit of Everest, even without carrying oxygen supplies. If a person does not take time to acclimatize himself, then altitude sickness is highly likely to develop at above 10,000 ft. Some people seem to be naturally much more sensitive or vulnerable than others—some cannot tolerate 7,000–8,000 ft. at all well.

Altitude sickness is best prevented by slowing the rate of ascent from sea level—the condition was rare in Everest expeditions when the climbers walked from the foothills into the Himalayas. It has become much more common now that tourists fly into mountainous regions and give their bodies no time to adjust.

Altitude sickness causes headache, shortness of breath, and coughing. In severe cases the lungs may be filled with a frothy fluid—pulmonary edema. Emergency treatment may be given with oxygen and the potent diuretic drug frusemide, but the key treatment is descent to a safe altitude.

Altitude sickness may recur on each occasion that an individual goes into the mountains: the speed of acclimatization is unpredictable and is not necessarily the same for one person on different occasions.

Alzheimer's disease

A presenile DEMENTIA

Most people suffer some degree of brain atrophy (wasting or shrinkage) as they get older, usually accompanied by a slowing of mental processes. Frequently the atrophy is so severe that the person suffers from senile dementia. Characteristically, this change takes place in some persons over the age of 70—sometimes much later.

In a small number of individuals, however, atrophy with resulting dementia occurs far earlier in life. Alzheimer's disease is caused by such an atrophy; the reasons why it occurs are not known. It tends to develop in the 30s or 40s, and the symptoms are precisely those of senile dementia: forgetfulness succeeded by irritability and then irrationality.

Unfortunately, there is no cure at present. Vasodilator drugs are prescribed in an attempt to improve the blood supply to the tissues of the brain. Psychotherapy and tranquilizers or antidepressants may be used, but "loving care" is probably the best therapy in this tragic affliction.

amaurosis

Blindness from some cause outside the eyes. Examples include the blindness sometimes associated with nephritis, toxemia of pregnancy, uremia, migraine, arteriosclerosis and Raynaud's disease.

In healthy persons, transient amaurosis sometimes occurs when standing up quickly from a prone position—caused simply by the draining of blood away from the head. There is also a hysterical variety of amaurosis. When amaurosis is of fairly short duration (as is often the case) it is referred to as *amaurosis fugax*.

The term "amaurotic family idiocy" refers to the inherited abnormality TAY-SACHS DISEASE (common in people of Jewish descent) in which blindness is a feature. The blindness, and indeed all the symptoms of the disease, are due to a lipoid degeneration of nerve ganglion cells.

amblyopia

Defective vision without any obvious disease of the eyeball. Amblyopia may be temporary or permanent and there are many possible causes; it may be partial or may progress to total blindness in the affected eye.

Poisons which may cause blindness include alcohol

and tobacco, lead, compounds that contain arsenic, and certain petroleum derivatives. *Bilateral toxic amblyopia* is common in alcoholics and is also seen in heavy smokers. Methyl alcohol ("meths") is far more dangerous than "ordinary" (ethyl) alcohol in this respect. Bilateral amblyopia may also occur as the result of poisoning with various drugs, chiefly the antimalarial agent quinine. Amblyopia can also occur as a result of damage to the region of the brain concerned with vision; some loss of vision is a common feature of strokes.

The most important preventable cause of amblyopia is strabismus ("cross-eye") in infancy. A child who develops strabismus has the eyes pointing in different directions, and his brain suppresses the image from one eye to prevent the confusion caused by double vision. If the squint is not treated the eye that is not used may become blind.

In general the treatment of amblyopia depends on the cause: cases of toxic amblyopia may improve if the source of poisoning is removed, but in cases due to brain damage or secondary to strabismus the blindness may be irreversible.

amenorrhea

Absence of menstrual periods. Amenorrhea may be primary or secondary. In primary amenorrhea, menstruation has never occurred at all; in secondary amenorrhea, a woman who has previously been menstruating ceases to do so.

Primary amenorrhea begins to give rise to some concern when a girls reaches 15 or 16 and has still not menstruated; she should then be taken to a physician for a gynecological evaluation of her condition. Primary amenorrhea at this age may be just a slight variation from normal; regular menstruation may commence shortly thereafter. But primary amenorrhea may be due to anemia, to disorders of the uterus, ovaries or pituitary gland, or to dysfunction of the thyroid or adrenal glands. Occasionally there is *false* primary amenorrhea (or cryptomenorrhea) in which a girl is menstruating but the menstrual blood is prevented from reaching the exterior by some obstacle, such as an *imperforate hymen* ("maidenhead" without an opening).

Secondary amenorrhea is common. Perhaps the most frequent causes are pregnancy and lactation. In almost any woman who has secondary amenorrhea the doctor will perform a pregnancy test. Secondary amenorrhea may also be due to anemia (often provoked by heavy menstrual blood loss in the past), by ovarian failure, by certain pituitary diseases, and by any kind of emotional disturbance or even a marked change in life style.

Amenorrhea may also occur on the contraceptive pill (or after coming off it) and in ANOREXIA NERVOSA. Treatment will depend on the underlying cause.

amnesia

Loss of MEMORY. Memories are held in the brain in short-term and long-term stores, and either or both functions may be impaired by disease or injury.

Typically, the adult has no memory for the events of infancy, but his recall of the rest of his lifetime is more or less continuous. In old age, however, the memory for recent events becomes impaired, while the events of childhood and early adult life are still well preserved. Loss of recent memory is also a feature of chronic alcoholism (in *Korsakoff's syndrome* the alcoholic invents stories to cover up his loss of memory) and some other brain diseases such as presenile DEMENTIA.

Head injuries that cause loss of consciousness—or even severe or frightening accidents that do not involve the head—may be associated with some loss of memory. Often there is a blank in the memory for some minutes or hours before the injury *(anterograde amnesia)* and for a variable period after the injury *(retrograde amnesia)*. The duration of both types of amnesia tends to diminish as the patient recovers from the injury, but often parts of memory are never recovered.

Sudden loss of memory without any injury or illness is most often due to a psychological disorder: the person who is found wandering far from home with no knowledge of his name or address is usually found to be suffering from *hysterical amnesia*, a condition provoked by emotional stress.

Despite claims to the contrary, no drug has yet been found to improve failing memory.

amniocentesis

A diagnostic test carried out in the first half of pregnancy. A needle is passed through the skin overlying the uterus to puncture the amniotic sac—the bag of membranes surrounding the developing fetus—and so to draw off into a syringe some of the amniotic fluid in which the fetus lies. The fluid can then be examined.

Amniocentesis is usually performed at about the 16th week of pregnancy under local anesthesia. When the needle is withdrawn, the tiny hole made in the amniotic sac seals itself promptly. Complications of amniocentesis are rare, although occasionally the technique may be followed by bleeding, persistent leakage of fluid or by miscarriage. It is very rare for the needle to injure the fetus accidentally, especially if the operator is guided by an ultrasound scan which enables him to locate the positions of the baby and the placenta.

Amniocentesis is one of the major diagnostic advances of recent years, since it enables the obstetrician to find out a great deal about the state of the fetus and to offer the woman termination of the pregnancy (therapeutic abortion) if a major abnormality is present.

The sample of fluid contains some cells from the fetus's skin, and these may be cultured in the laboratory. Tests on the cell culture will detect chromosomal abnormalities such as Down's syndrome (mongolism). Tests on the fluid itself will detect abnormalities such as SPINA BIFIDA and some forms of muscular dystrophy. Indeed, each year there is further growth in the number of fetal abnormalities that can be detected by amniocentesis and the related procedure of fetal blood sampling. The list includes blood abnormalities such as thalassemia, and brain disorders such as Tay-Sachs disease.

At present, however, the use of amniocentesis is restricted to cases in which there is already a higher than average risk of fetal abnormality. For instance, a woman whose last child was abnormal, or one with relatives with an inherited disease, might be referred for amniocentesis. Research is underway, however, to evaluate simple screening tests on blood samples taken early in pregnancy that can identify women at risk of an unsuspected fetal abnormality such as spina bifida and so enlarge the range of antenatal diagnosis by amniocentesis. Such diagnostic techniques require great skill in interpreting the results and the test is not available at all medical centers.

See also ALPHAFETOPROTEIN.

AMNIOCENTESIS

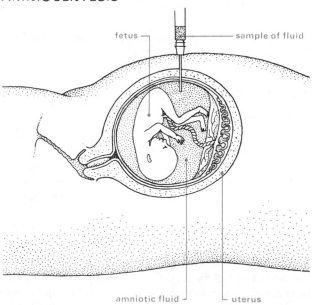

fetus — sample of fluid

amniotic fluid — uterus

Amniocentesis is a technique for removing a small sample of amniotic fluid from the uterus of a pregnant woman. Analysis of the fluid can show whether the fetus is affected by certain serious disorders such as Down's syndrome and spina bifida. In these cases the mother can be offered a therapeutic abortion; where the result of amniocentesis is normal, she is reassured.

AMOEBA

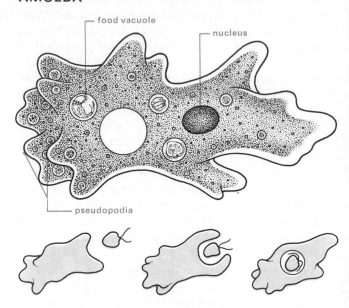

— food vacuole
— nucleus
— pseudopodia

free-living amoeba ingesting a flagellate

Amoebae are single-cell microorganisms which have changeable shape and move around on temporary projections called pseudopodia. They may be free-living or parasitic: certain species can infect humans, causing disease—for example, one type is responsible for amoebic dysentery.

amoeba

A simple type of protozoon, or single-celled living organism. Many species of amoeba are found throughout the world—living chiefly in ponds and stagnant water—and are well-known to biology students.

The medical importance of the amoeba is that certain species can infect man, usually through contamination of the water supply or of food. The most important is the species *Entamoeba histolytica* which causes amoebic DYSENTERY. (This should not be confused with bacillary dysentery, which is caused by entirely different organisms.)

E. histolytica is found throughout the world, especially in the tropics. According to some estimates, 10% of all Americans and Europeans are "carriers" of the organism, although other researchers doubt this figure. The amoeba exists in the bowel in both motile and nonmotile forms; it is usually the nonmotile forms (the cysts) that spread from person to person through fecal contamination of water or food.

Only a small percentage of people infected by *E. histolytica* actually become ill with dysentery. They develop either a chronic and relatively mild diarrhea or (much less commonly) a more acute illness with abdominal pain and profuse blood-stained diarrhea.

Possible complications include amoebic liver abscess.

The diagnosis is made by identifying the amoeba in the feces. Antiamoebic drugs such as Diodoquin cure the great majority of patients.

amputation

The removal of any part of the body, especially a limb or part of a limb.

Amputation may occur accidentally, as in automobile accidents or war injuries, or may have to be performed surgically because of severe injury or disease.

Accidental amputation of toes, fingers, legs and arms is fairly common, particularly in these days of frequent traffic accidents. Other cases occur in the home through mishaps with knives, fans, air-conditioning equipment, blenders and garbage disposal units. Amputations at work are also common, particularly if safety precautions are not observed while dealing with machinery.

In all these cases, surgical treatment is required to alleviate shock, arrest bleeding and remove the damaged tissues at the edges of the wound. The surgeon will suture (stitch up) and dress the wound and take precautions to ensure that tetanus (lockjaw) and other infections do not develop. In a few cases, it is possible by very skilled surgery to stitch back the amputated part— provided it is not too damaged and there has been little delay.

Deliberate surgical amputation is one of the oldest operations. It is commonly performed in cases of great trauma where a part of the body has been irreparably damaged (so that it would be dangerous if left in place), in cases of malignancy where a cancer—most frequently of bone—has developed in a limb, and in cases of gangrene due to trauma, exposure to cold, or vascular disease.

Before the development of anesthesia, amputation was a very rapid and crude procedure; the surgeon's main intention was to remove a limb or other part in a matter of seconds so that he would spare the unanesthetized patient pain. In the last 130 years however, since the introduction of anesthesia, techniques of amputation have become much more delicate, so that a reasonably good appearance is obtained. After a limb amputation an artificial limb can usually be fitted, but the psychological adjustment required after amputation may be more difficult than the physical adjustment.

See also PHANTOM LIMB SYNDROME.

amyloidosis

The infiltration of the liver, kidneys, heart and other internal organs with a starch-like protein substance known as amyloid. (The exact composition of amyloid is not known, and probably varies.)

Amyloidosis is a late complication of chronic infectious diseases such as tuberculosis and osteomyelitis; it also occurs in some cancers of the lymphatic system, such as Hodgkin's disease, and in the bone-marrow cancer multiple myeloma. Sometimes the amyloid infiltration occurs with no predisposing cause; this *primary amyloidosis* is often a familial disorder. Despite its recognition for over 100 years, the mechanism which leads to the deposition of amyloid remains unclear. The deposit itself consists of a mixture of protein and polysaccharides (complex carbohydrates of high molecular weight) and seems to be derived in part from the proteins in the bloodstream; the high rate of antibody formation in chronic infections is probably one of the underlying factors.

The importance of amyloidosis is that the infiltration of vital organs such as the kidneys may cause their progressive failure. Vigorous treatment of the underlying infection is sometimes followed by reabsorption of the amyloid, but there is no specific treatment for the infiltration itself.

amyotonia

A rare form of progressive muscular atrophy occurring in children, often known as Oppenheim's disease or "amyotonia congenita."

It is one of the milder forms of childhood muscular atrophy, although the condition is sometimes fatal and severe disability is common.

The symptoms may be present soon after birth. The most important is a widespread lack of muscle tone, so that the limbs can be readily moved into "contortionist" positions. Because of the weakness of the muscles, the child may find difficulty in supporting his head.

There is no specific treatment for amyotonia but there is a distinct tendency for the child to improve as he gets older. Therapy is largely directed at preventing spinal deformities and lung infections, both of which may occur because of the weakness of the musculature.

anabolism

The building-up by the body of relatively simple chemical substances into fats, proteins and carbohydrates. It is part of the total metabolic process of the body (the breaking-down of food into less complex substances is known as CATABOLISM).

In certain diseases there is an excess manufacture of some chemical substances as the result of faulty anabolism. Such situations occur in PORPHYRIA, in the overproduction of *serotonin* (a potent constrictor of blood vessels), in the "carcinoid syndrome," and in CYSTINURIA (an excess of amino acids—the "building blocks" of protein—in the urine). Most errors of metabolism, including faulty anabolism, are the result of rare hereditary conditions.

See also METABOLISM.

analgesia

Loss or reduction of the sensation of pain in the conscious individual.

Drugs which produce analgesia (*analgesics*) can be divided into three main groups: (1) those which act at the site of the pain; (2) those which act centrally on the brain; and (3) those which have a specific action.

Drugs in the first group are used in cases of fairly mild pain caused by arthritis, rheumatism and various muscular discomforts. Examples include acetaminophen (Exedrin, Tylenol) and aspirin (acetylsalicylic acid). Aspirin not only is effective against mild pain (analgesic action) but also reduces the body temperature in fever (antipyretic action) and has the effect of reducing inflammation (anti-inflammatory action) in rheumatic disease (such as rheumatoid arthritis). Unfortunately, in susceptible individuals it may produce dyspepsia (stomach upset) or even bleeding from the stomach lining, as well as sensitivity reactions. Acetaminophen, which is generally less noxious, is not as effective in reducing fever or controlling the symptoms of rheumatic disease.

Examples of the second group include the opiates (such as morphine), pethidine (Demerol), methadone and codeine. These analgesics, because of their potency and potential for abuse, are used only under medical supervision (that is, available only on prescription).

The third group includes *ergotamine tartrate*, which is specific in migraine; although it relieves headache, it does not help the visual symptoms or the nausea and vomiting which may accompany an attack. It also includes *carbamazepine*, which often reduces the number and the severity of attacks of *trigeminal neuralgia* (or *tic douloureux*).

Analgesia can also result from disease of the sensory nervous system, or from overdoses of alcohol.

anaphylactic shock

Anaphylatic shock is an antibody-antigen reaction in the body which may produce a state of profound collapse. This is characterized by increasing difficulty in breathing and failure of the circulation brought about by general dilation of the small blood vessels and the escape of plasma (the fluid component of the blood) into the tissue spaces. (See ANTIBODY/ANTIGEN.)

Anaphylactic shock may be caused by the injection of certain vaccines, antisera or antibiotics, or by insect stings; it is a desperate emergency in which "half-measures" or delay may prove fatal. Hydrocortisone is

given intravenously in large doses, accompanied perhaps by epinephrine or a similar drug. If respiratory distress is marked it is necessary to cut into the trachea (windpipe) to make an artificial opening (tracheostomy).

The condition is fortunately rare. Often undue sensitivity to injected substances can be demonstrated by the use of small test doses, but even a small test dose may trigger off anaphylactic shock in a "sensitized" individual. Patients receiving injections likely to produce this condition should stay within easy distance of medical aid for half an hour after the injection. Those who feel faint or start to swell in the face after an insect bite should at once seek a doctor's help, although neither of these reactions necessarily heralds anaphylactic shock.

See also the major article on **Allergy and Immunology.**

anemia

Anemia—literally, "lack of blood"—is a deficiency in the amount of the red pigment hemoglobin in the blood. Since men, women and children have different levels of hemoglobin, anemia must also be defined in terms of what the normal value for that group may be. Thus men have a hemoglobin level in the range of 13.5 to 18.5 g per 100 ml of blood; in men anemia is usually considered to be present when the hemoglobin value drops below 13.5 g. A corresponding figure for women would be 11.5 g and for a young child as low as 10 g. A similar lower figure would apply to a woman in the later stages of pregnancy.

Anemia has four basic causes. There may be a loss of red blood cells from the circulation through hemorrhage. There may be a deficiency of raw materials needed for the production of hemoglobin and red blood cells. The bone marrow itself may be diseased and therefore unable to produce sufficient red blood cells. Lastly, in the *hemolytic anemias*, production of red blood cells by the bone marrow is normal but the cells are destroyed unusually quickly and so do not survive for the normal period of 120 days in the circulation. Anemia may also occur as a presenting symptom of cancer, occurring for reasons that are not clearly understood and not necessarily related to any of these four causes.

Blood loss may be obvious, as in a patient with nosebleeds or a woman with heavy periods; but when it occurs internally, the patient may be unaware of it ("occult" blood loss).

The raw materials for the production of red cells include iron for hemoglobin production and vitamin B_{12} and folic acid (another B group vitamin). Deficiencies of these substances may be the result of dietary lack, failure to absorb them normally (though present in normal amounts in the diet), and, more rarely, an increased demand by the body (as with a need for more folic acid in pregnancy).

Diseases of the bone marrow causing a failure of red cell production include replacement of the marrow by cancer or leukemia cells and damage to the marrow by toxic drugs, chemicals and radiation. In many cases the marrow is depressed as an effect of a generalized disease—such as rheumatoid arthritis, tuberculosis or kidney failure ("secondary symptomatic anemia").

Anemia is a very common condition and in many cases goes undetected if it is not severe. For example, women, because of their menstrual blood loss, maintain their iron balance with difficulty; surveys have revealed that 5% or more of women who otherwise appear healthy are in fact anemic, while up to 30% have no reserves of iron and are thus in danger of developing iron-deficiency anemia.

The symptoms of anemia may be minimal; but if the condition is at all severe, the patient will be pale and will complain of tiredness and shortness of breath on exertion. In addition, specific types of anemia may produce characteristic symptoms.

Blood checks for the presence of anemia and other blood abnormalities form an important part of any comprehensive medical examination. Not only may the patient's symptoms be caused by anemia, but those who are in good health usually show normal numbers of red and white blood cells and the red cell sedimentation rate will be normal (see ERYTHROCYTE SEDIMENTATION RATE). All three measurements are usually included in a "blood count" test.

If a patient is found to be anemic, the fundamental problem for the doctor to resolve is whether the anemia is the result of a specific blood disease (such as pernicious anemia or leukemia) or whether it is a symptom of blood loss or an underlying disease (such as arthritis) or infection.

The treatment of anemia may be simple, as in the administration of iron tablets in iron-deficiency anemia; in other cases it may require initial blood transfusion or other measures, or treatment may be directed toward the underlying condition of which the anemia is a symptom.

See also the section on *The Hematologist* in the major article on **Specialists You Seldom See.**

anencephaly

A congenital condition in which a developing fetus has only a rudimentary or no brain. The child is born dead or, at most, lives for only a few hours after birth. A substance called ALPHAFETOPROTEIN (which is found in abnormally large amounts in the fluid surrounding the fetus in cases of anencephaly) is today used to screen for this congenital defect, as well as other congenital abnormalities such as SPINA BIFIDA, so that the mother may be offered a clinical termination of pregnancy.

See also AMNIOCENTESIS.

anesthesia

The loss of feeling, particularly the sensations of pain and touch. It can be produced by disease or damage to the nervous system, certain psychological states, or the action of drugs. The term is usually applied to the deliberate induction of insensibility (either *general* or *local*) to make it possible to perform surgical operations.

Up to the middle of the 19th century, surgery was often a brutal business, although drugs ranging from alcohol to opium were used to diminish the pain felt by the patient. After the introduction of *general anesthesia*—induced by ether, nitrous oxide ("laughing gas") and chloroform—life became more bearable both for patients and surgeons. In 1800, Sir Humphrey Davy noted the anesthetic effect of nitrous oxide and suggested its use in surgery; the similar effect of ether was noted both in the United States and Britain in 1818.

The first practical use of general anesthetics was introduced in 1842 by Crawford Long of Jefferson, Georgia, followed in 1844 by Horace Wells of Hartford, Connecticut. Dr. William Morton demonstrated the anesthetic effects of ether in Boston in 1846; in 1847 and 1848, J. Y. Simpson of Edinburgh used ether and chloroform to relieve the pains of childbirth. Up to fairly recent times, ether, chloroform, ethyl chloride and trichloroethylene were administered by inhalation through a mask to induce general anesthesia; but nowadays intravenous injections of drugs such as *Pentothal Sodium* are used to induce general anesthesia, which send the patient quietly and agreeably to sleep.

Modern anesthesiologists have many drugs available. They can induce temporary unconsciousness, temporary paralysis and temporary hypotension (low blood pressure) at will. New techniques have made modern surgery possible; a complicated surgical operation depends as much for its success on the skill of the anesthesiologist as on the skill of the surgeon.

Anesthesia of only a part of the body (without loss of consciousness) can be produced by drugs known as *local anesthetics*. *Cocaine* applied to the surface of mucous membranes renders them anesthetic; but the use of cocaine has now been abandoned in favor of synthetic compounds such as *tetracaine* (also known as *amethocaine*). Other synthetic compounds, such as *procaine* and *lidocaine*, are administered by injection; if they are injected into or under the skin they produce anesthesia of the immediate area, while if they are injected into sensory nerves they produce anesthesia of the particular region of the body supplied by the nerve.

It is possible to perform some types of major operations under local anesthesia or under *spinal anesthesia*. The latter is a technique in which the local anesthetic agent is introduced into the spinal canal under strict control to bring about temporary paralysis of the motor and sensory nerve roots as they leave the spinal cord. The height up the spinal canal to which the anesthetic solution is allowed to rise determines the area of anesthesia (which is nearly always confined to the lower part of the trunk and the legs). An alternative technique involves injecting the anesthetic into the space just outside the membranes covering the spinal cord (*extradural anesthesia*), and this method is widely used during labor and childbirth.

aneurysm

Swelling at a weak point in the wall of an artery, named according to its shape *fusiform, saccular, berry* or *dissecting* and classified as *congenital, inflammatory, degenerative,* or *traumatic.*

Common sites for aneurysms are the aorta (the largest artery of the body), the arteries at the base of the brain (the "circle of Willis"), and the artery behind the knee. Although aneurysms can produce symptoms by pressure on neighboring structures—one at the base of the brain can, for example, produce double vision by

ANEURYSM

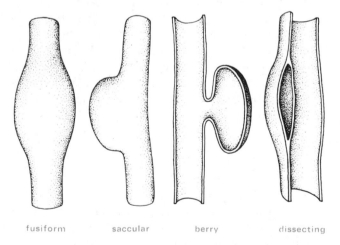

fusiform   saccular   berry   dissecting

Aneurysms form where a weak point in an artery wall is blown out by the pressure of blood. The weakness may be congenital, as with the small "berry" aneurysms in the brain which sometimes burst, causing hemorrhage. Most aneurysms, however, are due to atherosclerosis and are fusiform or saccular in shape. A dissecting aneurysm is one where blood actually runs between the layers of the arterial wall before reentering the true vessel.

interfering with nerves supplying the external muscles of the eye—the chief danger is rupture, which sets up internal bleeding with possibly fatal results.

Treatment depends on the site and nature of the aneurysm; surgery offers the only hope of cure and an operation may or may not be possible. Each case must be judged on its own merits. Saccular or berry aneurysms may have a "neck" that can be tied or clipped, and it is sometimes possible to carry out plastic reconstructions on dilated parts of the aorta.

angina pectoris

Angina pectoris (sometimes just called *angina*) is a characteristic type of chest pain caused by failure of the coronary arteries to supply enough oxygen to the heart muscle.

The pain is felt centrally in the chest but may radiate to the neck or down the left arm. It can be very severe or it may be described merely as a "tightness in the chest." A diagnostic feature is that the pain occurs during activity and will rapidly disappear if the patient stops and rests for a few minutes. Thus patients with chronic angina may come to recognize a characteristic degree or duration of exercise (walking a certain distance or exceeding a certain speed) which will bring on the pain and will learn to avoid it by keeping within their personal exercise tolerance. Emotional factors and cold may also contribute to the onset of pain.

Angina is most often caused by the narrowing of the coronary arteries by ATHEROSCLEROSIS so that the blood supply to the heart muscle is reduced. If the rate and strength of the heartbeat is increased by exercise, the blood flow required to keep the muscle adequately supplied is exceeded and the characteristic pain results. Reducing the requirement by reducing activity allows the blood flow to become adequate again. Less commonly the coronary arteries are normal but the heart muscle is "starved" of oxygen either because the blood is deficient in hemoglobin (ANEMIA) or the blood pressure is low from narrowing of the aortic valve (aortic STENOSIS). The diagnosis depends mainly on the patient's medical history, although the ECG will usually show characteristic abnormalities.

Angina is a serious disorder since its presence denotes diseased coronary arteries; all patients with angina should seek early medical advice. Under good medical care, however, many live a relatively normal life for many years with the condition.

Treatment consists of reducing the load on the heart by weight reduction, reduction of raised blood pressure, avoidance of smoking (which aggravates the condition) and possibly altering the diet to reduce blood levels of fat. Drugs which will relieve the symptoms include glyceryl trinitrate (nitroglycerin) which dilates the coronary arteries and reduces the work load of the heart, and drugs known as "beta-adrenergic blocking agents" which reduce the work load of the heart. In severe cases, coronary BYPASS surgery may be indicated.

See also the major article on **Cardiology.**

angiography

Radiological investigation in which a substance opaque to x-rays (radiopaque material) is injected into blood vessels to make them visible on the x-ray plate or viewing screen. The process of outlining arteries is called *arteriography;* that of outlining veins is known as *phlebography* or *venography.* The technique is used not only in demonstrating abnormalities or disease of the blood vessels but also in the diagnosis of tumors, particularly in the brain. Lymph vessels can also be outlined; the technique is then known as *lymphangiography.*

ankylosing spondylitis

A disease of the spine in which there is gradual loss of mobility in the joints between the vertebrae. It occurs mainly in males between the ages of 20 and 40 and is related to RHEUMATOID ARTHRITIS.

The illness results in a progressive stiffening of the spine as the normally flexible ligaments supporting the joints gradually harden and acquire the consistency of bone. The disease begins insidiously with stiffness of the back after a period of inactivity. The ability to expand the chest diminishes and there may be pain on breathing deeply, coughing or sneezing. Later the spine may become fixed in an upright position ("poker spine") or bent sideways. The neck may be bent forward and the head may eventually become fixed so that the patient is forced to look downward when walking.

When the symptoms first appear, aspirin or similar drugs are of use to control pain. X-ray therapy has been used with some success, but in a small number of cases (about 3%) it has provoked LEUKEMIA. For this reason, many doctors prefer to control the symptoms with *phenylbutazone* (an anti-inflammatory drug), at the same time ensuring that the patient sleeps with a board under the mattress and uses a supportive pillow for the neck. The great majority (approximately 75%) of patients with this disease are able to lead relatively normal lives.

anorexia nervosa

Anorexia nervosa is a disorder which mainly affects young girls aged 14 to 17 years, although older women and occasionally men may be affected. The patient is noted to be losing weight and, when attention is drawn

to this, it is usually explained as an intentional weight loss to avoid obesity or improve the figure. The dietary restriction, however, is then continued and carried to extremes, so that severe weight loss to the extent of emaciation follows. Multiple vitamin and mineral deficiencies may appear. Menstruation, if already established, usually ceases—a not uncommon effect of starvation whether voluntary or involuntary. If the condition is severe, the patient may resort to bizarre measures to increase her weight loss including self-induced vomiting, purgatives and excessive exercise. If untreated, the condition may prove fatal as the patient literally starves herself to death while continuing to assert that her food intake is adequate or even excessive.

The explanation of this curious situation is difficult to find. Physically, the patient will show only the expected findings in any case of starvation from any cause, which include changes in endocrine gland function (the pituitary, adrenal, thyroid and the sex glands).

Mentally, the patient is often depressed and hysterical; she may suffer from phobias or compulsive disorders and may be abnormally concerned about the manifestations of puberty (particularly about breast development). She may feel that any tendency to put on weight will exaggerate her breast or figure developments; it has even been suggested that the starvation is a deliberate attempt to suppress menstruation and that the patient wishes to delay puberty itself.

Treatment involves first obtaining the patient's cooperation in increasing her food intake; if this is done slowly, no problem usually arises, although she will usually also require psychiatric help to overcome her underlying psychological problems. The prognosis for restoration to normal physical health is excellent, but many patients have a subsequent relapse because the basic psychological problem remains.

anthrax

Infectious disease caused by *Bacillus anthracis,* which commonly infects cattle, goats or sheep. Humans contract the infection from the spores of the anthrax bacillus, which survive for a long time in contaminated wool, hair or hides; with increasingly hygienic methods of handling these raw materials the spread of the disease has diminished, and it is now rare in the West.

Infection can affect the skin, when it produces a severe localized reaction. The site of infection is marked by an itching "papule," which becomes surrounded by vesicles filled with blood-stained fluid. The center of the area dies as the infection spreads and becomes black, which gives the disease its name—anthrax—from the Greek word for coal.

Infection can also attack the lungs, to produce pneumonia, or it can advance to anthrax bacteremia (blood poisoning), with a high mortality rate if untreated. The old name for anthrax of the lung was "wool-sorter's disease," an illness which was usually fatal; but now anthrax of both the skin and the lungs responds to treatment with appropriate antibiotics.

antibody/antigen

When certain foreign and therefore potentially harmful substances enter the body, the body reacts to the threat of damage by producing antibodies. An antibody is a chemical compound, a protein, which has the ability to combine with and render harmless a specific foreign substance. The foreign material itself, which initiates the reaction leading to the formation of specific antibodies, is known as an *antigen*.

Most antigenic substances are protein. Proteins have a very complex and almost infinitely variable chemical composition and are constitutents of all living matter. For this reason, the antigens which cause the formation of antibodies are mostly substances derived directly or indirectly from living organisms. Common examples of antigens are the bacteria and viruses which cause human disease; "foreign" blood from an incompatible blood group, inadvertently given during a blood transfusion; and sera from other species injected into humans for the treatment or prevention of infectious diseases. Whatever the situation, the antibody formed in response to a particular antigen is unique to that antigen, reacting with no other (see illustration). The blood of an adult contains tens of thousands of individual antibodies directed against different antigens and together forming a distinct group of proteins in the serum, the *immunoglobulins*.

The basic purpose of antibody formation is defensive. One major role of antibodies is in overcoming attacks of infectious diseases and prevention of future recurrent attacks. Thus, when the patient who has never previously had an attack of whooping cough comes into contact with the whooping cough bacillus, he or she will develop symptoms of the disease. The defeat of the invading bacteria depends initially on the action of the *phagocytic blood cells* responsible for primary defense against bacterial invasion; these cells attack, kill and engulf the bacteria. As the disease runs its course, however, antibodies against the whooping cough bacilli start to appear in the blood and the final elimination of the infection is aided by their action. By the time the patient is convalescent, a good level of specific antibodies is present in the blood. In many diseases these antibodies persist at such a high level that the patient remains immune to a second attack of the disease throughout the rest of his life.

This natural phenomenon forms the basis of vaccination and inoculation against infectious diseases (see IMMUNIZATION). Antibodies are usually produced as the result of an infection with bacteria, viruses or other microorganisms; their production can also be stimulated artificially by the introduction into the body of a special preparation of these microorganisms or their products. In whooping cough and typhoid, for example, injection of dead bacteria (of the same species that can cause the respective disease) will evoke the identical kind of antibody formation as that seen in the actual disease

ANTIBODY AND ANTIGEN – how some antibodies work

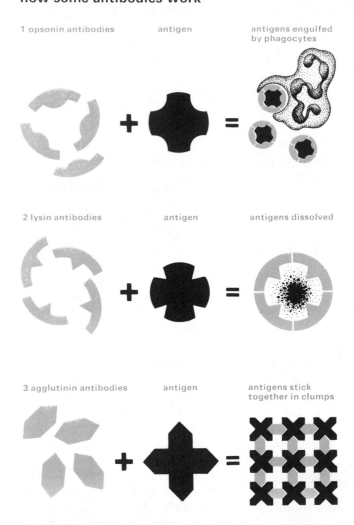

1 opsonin antibodies   antigen   antigens engulfed by phagocytes

2 lysin antibodies   antigen   antigens dissolved

3 agglutinin antibodies   antigen   antigens stick together in clumps

The diagrams show how antibodies produced by the body defend us against foreign substances (antigens). Each antibody can only combine with a specific antigen which has a complementary chemical "shape." Opsonin antibodies cling to antigens such as bacteria and make them more appetizing to certain white blood cells called phagocytes (1). Lysin antibodies kill bacteria directly by dissolving them (2). Agglutinin antibodies cause bacteria or viruses to clump together, rendering them ineffective (3).

and will confer lasting immunity. In diphtheria and tetanus, the bacteria produce their effects by means of the toxins (poisons) that they produce; injection of the toxin itself, suitably treated to render it no longer toxic though still antigenic, will enable the body to form antibodies against the toxin. Lastly, the inoculation of a specific living virus culture—which has been treated to weaken the virus to such a degree that it can no longer cause symptoms of the disease—will immunize the patient against smallpox, yellow fever, poliomyelitis and other diseases.

Most antibodies are thus acquired by contact with an antigen, but in a newborn baby some antibodies are already present that have been passively acquired from its mother and which persist for a few months after birth to provide an early protection against infections. The antibodies of the ABO blood group system are also present from birth and are not the result of antigenic stimulation.

In rare instances, antibodies may be formed against the body's own cells rather than against invading bacteria, viruses or other foreign material. In this case, damage to the tissue concerned results—a condition known as an AUTOIMMUNE DISEASE.

Transplanted organs or tissues, unless taken from an identical twin, are considered to be foreign invaders by the body and may be rejected unless immunosuppressive drugs are used (see TRANSPLANTATION).

See also the major article on **Allergy and Immunology.**

anxiety

Anxiety is a normal response to a crisis such as an impending examination or a new job; but excessive anxiety may be socially crippling and cause physical ill health.

In *anxiety neurosis* a perfectly normal concern about cleanliness, noise or any other everyday circumstance becomes magnified to dominate the thoughts. Typically this leads to obsessional behavior, with the sufferer returning repeatedly to his house to check that the door is shut and the gas turned off, or to a preoccupation with hand washing or some other ritual. In AGORAPHOBIA, anxiety about leaving the house and meeting strangers may lead to a self-imposed imprisonment in the home. However, the anxiety may be less specific. In such cases every minor event is seen as a threat and a cause for apprehension; again, the effect is to restrict behavior to a cautious, predictable routine.

Anxiety is a common component of the *depressive illnesses* which affect a high proportion of all men and women in middle and later life (see DEPRESSION). One third or more of all middle-aged women admit to episodes of depression, often including anxiety about

their family relationships and their worth. Anxiety is also frequently provoked in middle age by an episode of illness—such as a heart attack or a head injury—that impairs self-confidence.

The symptoms of recurrent anxiety include loss of appetite and weight, palpitations, headache, excessive sweating and difficulty in sleeping. These somatic symptoms may be suppressed readily following treatment with tranquilizing drugs: such treatment is often used to control the symptoms associated with isolated life-events, such as anxiety about flying or sea voyages. More intractable anxiety warrants treatment by PSYCHOTHERAPY. Many specific phobias—such as fear of dogs—can be treated effectively by techniques such as conditioning and behavior therapy, but individuals with anxiety as a prominent feature of their personalities are unlikely to undergo any dramatic change, whatever the treatment.

Apgar score

A system for assessing the state of the newborn infant.

At one minute and five minutes after birth, observations are made on the heart rate, respiratory effort, muscle tone, reflex irritability and color, and the results expressed as a score of 0, 1 or 2. For example, a blue or white color scores 0, blue extremities but pink body 1, and completely pink 2. The scores for each observation are added together; total scores of 0–2 are associated with a high mortality rate, 8–10 with a low mortality rate. It is said that the five-minute score is a more accurate prediction than the one-minute score.

The system was devised by the American anesthesiologist Virginia Apgar (b. 1909).

apnea

Absence or cessation of breathing. In newborn babies failure to breathe may be brought about by lack of oxygen caused by malfunction of the placental circulation (e.g., because of compression of the umbilical cord), a traumatic cerebral hemorrhage during delivery, or the presence in the baby's circulation of drugs administered to the mother during labor. Rarely it may be due to a congenital malformation.

It is essential in treating the condition to make sure that the baby's airways are open and free of mucus or other obstruction; it can then be given oxygen through a tube passed into the trachea (windpipe). If this is not possible, the baby's life may be saved by gentle mouth-to-mouth breathing. If time permits, the operator should cover the baby's mouth with a fold of clean cloth—a clean handkerchief will do. He then breathes into the mouth at a rate of 25 breaths a minute, with the operator using his cheek muscles only.

In later life, cessation of breathing may follow overoxygenation of the blood induced artificially or by overbreathing. When the blood chemistry returns to normal, breathing usually starts again. In severe disease, periods of overbreathing are sometimes followed by apnea, so that the pattern of respiration becomes periodic—a phenomenon first described by Drs. Cheyne and Stokes in the 19th century and now called *Cheyne-Stokes respiration*. It very often signals approaching death.

apoplexy

1. A sudden loss of consciousness, typically followed by paralysis, caused by bleeding from a ruptured blood vessel within the brain (CEREBRAL HEMORRHAGE) or blocking of an artery of the brain (cerebral thrombosis or CEREBRAL EMBOLISM). Also called *cerebral apoplexy*.
See also CEREBROVASCULAR DISEASE, STROKE.
2. A condition caused by the effusion of blood into an organ, such as the lung (*pulmonary apoplexy*).

appendicitis/appendectomy

Inflammation of the *vermiform appendix* (commonly called just the *appendix*), which is a small structure attached to the blind end of the large intestine (the *cecum*). It is about the size and shape of an earthworm.

Symptoms of acute appendicitis can vary widely and the condition is often difficult to diagnose. In the most typical case, the first symptom is diffuse discomfort felt in the area of the navel (umbilicus) with nausea and perhaps vomiting. There may be constipation or mild diarrhea. The discomfort turns into pain, and the pain settles in the lower right-hand part of the abdomen. The wall of the abdomen at first tightens when pressure is applied over the site of the pain ("guarding") and then in time becomes rigid. The patient's tongue is characteristically dry and the breath fetid. The temperature is usually only slightly raised.

Treatment is surgical removal of the appendix (*appendectomy*). If this can be carried out within the first 24 hours or so, convalescence is usually straightforward; but if the symptoms are not recognized, the appendix may become gangrenous and burst to produce PERITONITIS. Commonly this becomes localized, and an appendix abscess forms which can be drained after it has been sealed off by natural processes.

The appendix appears to be a useless (or "vestigial") organ. The operation for its removal is usually relatively easy; surgeons are therefore inclined to perform an appendectomy in most cases where they suspect inflammation of the organ, or remove it during the course of other scheduled abdominal surgery.

arrhythmia (dysrhythmia)

Any abnormality in the rhythm of the heartbeat, occurring in the normal healthy person or as a result of cardiac disease.

It can sometimes be felt as an "extra" beat of the heart, or it may only be detected by an electrocardiogram (ECG).

In the otherwise healthy person, occasional irregular beats are of no significance; many people experience extra beats, when anxious or after too much coffee or too many cigarettes. However, irregularity of the heartbeat may be a serious complication of a coronary thrombosis ("heart attack"); for that reason, patients are often admitted to a coronary care unit where the rhythm can be monitored electronically.

Dysrhythmias may also occur in diseases such as thyroid overactivity (HYPERTHYROIDISM) or as a side effect of drug treatment. Whatever the cause, the rhythm may be restored to normal either by drugs or by electric shock treatment (cardioversion); often, however, the change in rhythm is no cause for concern and no treatment may be needed.

See also BUNDLE BRANCH BLOCK; PACEMAKER; DEFIBRILLATION.

APPENDICITIS

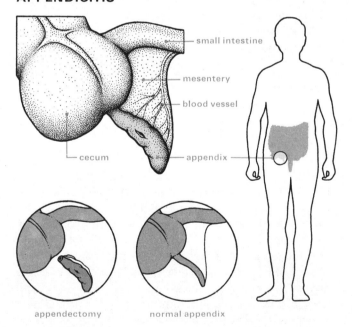

small intestine

mesentery

blood vessel

cecum

appendix

appendectomy

normal appendix

Appendicitis is the most common cause of acute abdominal pain and is a surgical emergency. In some unusual cases, accurate diagnosis may be impossible; a surgeon may then perform an appendectomy unnecessarily rather than risk leaving an inflamed appendix, which could lead to serious complications.

arteriosclerosis

The general term for any condition in which the walls of the arteries become thick, inelastic and hard. Popular name: *hardening of the arteries.*

The exact cause is unknown, but the condition is common and progressive from the middle years on. One particularly serious form of arteriosclerosis involves the deposition of fatty patches (atheromas) on the inner walls of the blood vessels.

See ATHEROSCLEROSIS.

arteritis

Inflammation of an artery. This may be incidental, that is, when an artery runs close to an area of infection (*nonspecific arteritis*), or it may be associated with a specific disease (of which the arterial inflammation represents only one manifestation).

In *temporal arteritis*, a serious illness which affects elderly persons, the arteries overlying the temples become swollen and painful. If the inflammation extends to the arteries supplying blood to the eyes it may cause sudden and permanent blindness. In most cases, treatment with corticosteroid drugs suppresses the inflammation and provides dramatic relief of symptoms.

Other forms of arteritis affect blood vessels in all parts of the body. These include LUPUS ERYTHEMATOSUS, POLYARTERITIS NODOSA and a number of less well defined disorders—such as POLYMYALGIA RHEUMATICA. The importance of the occurrence of arteritis in these disorders lies in what it does, since interruption of blood flow damages the organs or muscles supplied by the affected artery or arteries.

arthritis

Joints may be affected by inflammatory or degenerative changes, which cause pain and stiffness described as arthritis. The causes of arthritis range from infection after injury to the onset of age, and include rheumatic fever, rheumatoid processes which are poorly understood, gout, osteoarthritis, psoriasis, tumors and diseases of the nervous system.

Injury impairs the efficiency of a joint by damaging the smooth articular surface; age wears out the joint surface, particularly in the joints which have borne the weight of the body for many years—the hips and knees. Gout causes the deposition of crystals of uric acid in the joints, tumors derange the anatomy of the joint, and deficiency in nervous supply can lead to insensitivity of the joint or abnormality of muscular action; this may cause bizarre movements or repeated unnoticed injuries which produce mechanical derangement of the joint.

ARTHRITIS

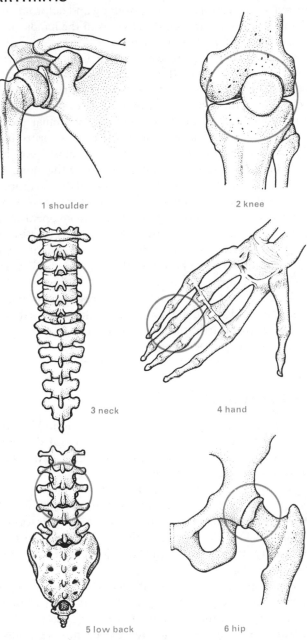

1 shoulder

2 knee

3 neck

4 hand

5 low back

6 hip

All joints in the body can be affected by arthritis. The illustration shows the joints most commonly involved, and the variety of conditions which can result. They are frozen shoulder (1); painful knee (2); pressure on spinal nerves (3); stiff fingers (4); low back pain (5); and painful hip (6).

The most common disease affecting joints in youth and maturity is RHEUMATOID ARTHRITIS, of which the cause is unknown. It attacks females three times more frequently than males, and occurs in at least 3% of the population of the United States. The lubricating lining of the joint (synovial membrane) suffers chronic inflammatory change with consequent irreversible damage to the joint capsule and cartilage and the formation of scar tissue. Pain, swelling and deformity of the joint ensues, particularly obvious in the hands, and there is limitation of movement.

Cases of arthritis are differentiated and diagnosed with the help of blood tests and x-rays. Treatment depends on the cause; there are specific drugs to treat gout, and antibiotics will be used in cases of infection. Anti-inflammatory drugs and aspirin (or similar pain-killers) are of help in cases of rheumatoid arthritis and degenerative arthritis in the elderly, but most have the drawback that they are inclined to irritate the lining of the stomach and must therefore be used with discretion. The surgical replacement of weight-bearing joints—hips in particular—has proved possible, and such operations relieve pain and restore movement. Steroids (cortisone derivatives) are used in rheumatoid disease, but their early promise has not been borne out. In nearly all cases physical therapy is invaluable.

Much research is currently in progress on these common and crippling conditions, and the patient suffering from arthritis has a much better prognosis today than in former years.

See also the major article on **Rheumatology.**

arthroplasty

Surgical technique used to create a new joint in place of one which has become stiffened and painful through disease or injury. Arthroplasty falls into two main classes: *excision* or *replacement.*

In *excision arthroplasty*, the diseased ends of the bones forming the joint are removed so that a gap is left. This gap can be filled with fibrous tissue as a scar forms. While such arthroplasties relieve pain and correct deformity, they leave an unstable joint unsuitable for weight-bearing.

However, in recent years it has become possible to replace diseased joints with artificial joints. Such *replacement arthroplasty* has proved very successful in treating arthritis and fractures of the hip. It is also possible to use artificial knee and elbow joints, although so far the success rate in such procedures has not been as good as it is in replacement of hip joints. Research in this field of orthopedic surgery is active and the advances are rapid. See also the major article on **Orthopedics.**

arthroscopy

The process of inspecting the interior of a joint through an optical instrument inserted into the joint cavity.

artificial insemination

See AID/AIH.

asbestosis

Asbestos is a substance made of a mixture of the silicates of iron, nickel, magnesium, aluminium and calcium; the name means "indestructible." It is used in making fire-resistant materials, brake and clutch linings, tiles and floor coverings, roofing felt, tires and many other products, including electrical insulation. Unfortunately, the lungs of workers in the asbestos industry sometimes suffer irritation from inhaled particles of asbestos and become fibrous. The patient becomes breathless, coughs, loses weight, feels tired and loses his appetite. Moreover, he is liable to contract tuberculosis and after a period (which may be as long as 20 to 40 years) to develop cancer of the lung.

Asbestos cannot easily be replaced in many of its applications, and the use of asbestos increases year by year. It is of the greatest importance that industrial processes should be rigorously controlled to prevent the inhalation of asbestos dust, for the only effective treatment of asbestosis is preventative.

See also the major article on **Pulmonary Diseases.**

ascites

The accumulation of fluid, mostly water, in the abdominal cavity, contained between the layer of *peritoneum* which covers the walls of the cavity and the layer covering the organs within the abdomen. As the fluid collects the abdomen swells and becomes uncomfortable, but it is possible to draw off the fluid through a needle passed through the abdominal wall.

Ascites occurs in a number of diseases, including heart failure, abdominal cancer, and some disorders of the liver and kidneys. Treatment is directed toward the underlying condition.

aspergillosis

Disease caused by the fungus *Aspergillus fumigatus.* This microorganism is found almost everywhere and does not normally cause disease in man; indeed, it often flourishes in the mouths of healthy people. It does, however, cause disease in birds and occasionally man, where it infects the lungs and sometimes the ear or the paranasal sinuses (sinuses which drain into the nasal cavities). Infection of the lung produces cough (which may be productive of blood) and fever; parts of the fungus may break off to set up infection in the heart, brain, kidneys or spleen (carried to these sites by means of the bloodstream). Sometimes a patient with aspergillosis may develop asthma.

Treatment involves the administration of antifungal drugs (such as amphotericin B). Except in cases where the infection is widely disseminated, the outlook is good.

asphyxia

Lack of oxygen in the blood due to the cessation of breathing or an obstruction to the entry of air into the lungs. If asphyxia is prolonged for more than a very few minutes, irreversible brain damage or death may occur.

One of the most common causes of asphyxia is drowning. The entry of water into the lungs leads to loss of consciousness and breathing stops. First aid—emptying the water out of the lungs and throat and giving artificial respiration—will restore normal breathing if given quickly. Electric shock is another fairly common cause of asphyxia, which can also be reversible by prompt artificial respiration.

Asphyxia may also be due to the inhalation of air containing too little oxygen (sometimes found at the bottom of disused wells) or poisonous gases, especially carbon monoxide. Among the mechanical obstructions to breathing are ligatures around the neck, as in suicidal hanging, and choking or the accidental inhalation of lumps of food; again, prompt first aid can be life-saving. The throat may also become blocked by swelling of the tissues secondary to infections such as diphtheria and by tumors; in such cases the obstruction may be bypassed by a surgeon making an opening in the trachea below the level of the blockage (TRACHEOSTOMY).

asthma

Air drawn into the lungs during breathing is conveyed to the small air sacs (alveoli) in the lungs. It is there that the exchange of oxygen and carbon dioxide (between the inspired air and the blood) takes place. To reach the alveoli, the inspired air must pass through a "tree" of air passages of ever-decreasing diameter (the *bronchi* and the *bronchioles*).

While the larger bronchi are of fixed diameter (their walls contain rigid rings of cartilage which permit no change in their "bore"), the smaller bronchioles have muscular walls and are capable of wide variation in their bore with contraction or relaxation of the muscle coat.

Changes in the bore of the bronchi are usually slight and occur in response to exercise or the secretion into the blood of certain chemically active compounds (hormones). In patients with asthma, however, the bronchioles are sensitive to stimulation by a variety of agents which produce marked contraction of the muscular wall, with narrowing of the bore to a degree that seriously obstructs the entry and exit of air in the lungs.

In an attack of asthma the breathing becomes difficult, expiration often being more affected than inspiration. The patient is short of breath and breathing may become audibly "wheezy," with coughing. The effort to draw breath increases, but despite this the movement of the chest is diminished. The patient may become agitated or confused and his skin color may change to a bluish tinge from insufficient oxygen (CYANOSIS). The attack may be short, lasting only a few minutes, or very long (*status asthmaticus*) and the patient may become exhausted by his efforts to obtain air.

There are numerous causes of the contraction of the muscular coat of the bronchioles. In some cases a frank allergy exists to a particular material; the patient responds to this by the onset of an attack of asthma, usually within minutes of exposure. Grass and tree pollens, molds and fungi, animal hair and dander, the minute "house-dust mite" (found in all areas of human habitation), and even some types of food may all provoke an asthmatic attack. In other cases a physical or chemical irritant (such as a smoky atmosphere, exhaust fumes, or acid fumes) may bring on an attack. Infections of the lungs, particularly those caused by viruses, may precipitate an attack in susceptible subjects. Prolonged exertion may also provoke an attack, as may a variety of emotional factors (such as stress, tension, or anxiety).

Treatment of an acute asthmatic attack involves the administration of drugs such as epinephrine or related compounds (in severe cases, injected subcutaneously), or the use of an aerosol spray (containing drugs such as isoproterenol or salbutamol). These cause relaxation of the contracted bronchioles. In most cases an impending attack can be controlled with the use of a nebulizing inhaler, which produces a fine mist of droplets that can be inhaled directly into the affected bronchioles. Regardless of whether a nebulizer or a pressurized aerosol is used, dosage must be cautiously restricted or the possibility of a dangerous overdosage may occur. Additional help may be obtained (especially if a marked allergic element is present) from the administration of a large dose of steroids (cortisone-like drugs) by mouth or injection. Oxygen may also be required.

For more long-term treatment, similar drugs may be given by mouth on a regular daily basis. In addition to the administration of epinephrine-like drugs and steroids, newer drugs are proving valuable for long-term treatment.

The prognosis is usually good although in very severe untreated cases death may occur rarely, especially in status asthmaticus. When the condition first occurs in early childhood, there may be a tendency to "grow out of it," but in adults the condition tends to recur.

See also the appropriate sections in the major articles on **Pulmonary Diseases** and **Allergy and Immunology**.

astigmatism

A defect in the refractive surfaces of the lens and cornea

ASTIGMATISM

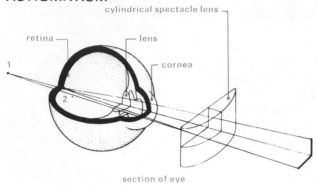

cylindrical spectacle lens

retina — lens

1

cornea

2

section of eye

Astigmatism is incorrect curvature of the cornea or the lens of the eye with the result that the image reaching the retina is not correctly focused (1), and appears blurred or distorted. The defect can be corrected by placing a cylindrical lens in front of the eye, thereby focusing the image on the retina (2).

of the eye, which causes the image falling on the retina to be partially out of focus. In the normal eye, objects are focused sharply onto all parts of the retina. When the refractive surfaces have an incorrect curvature the focusing is distorted and parts of the image appear blurred. A spherical ball, for instance, may seem egg-shaped or only partially clear.

Astigmatism is often associated with other sight defects in children, such as short-sightedness. To correct vision, glasses are prescribed in which the lens has the shape of a slice cut off a cylinder. It thus has one curved and one flat side and is able to bend the light rays so that they come to a correct focus on the retina. It is important that astigmatism—like any refractive error—should be corrected, since a child with such a handicap may otherwise develop permanently defective vision (see AMBLYOPIA).

See also VISION and the major article on **Ophthalmology.**

ataxia

Muscular incoordination, especially when attempting voluntary movements. The smoothness and precision of muscular action is impaired so that movements become unsteady, clumsy and inaccurate.

In general, ataxia is caused by lesions within the central nervous system (the brain and spinal cord). Ataxia can occur in childhood, usually as the result of congenital deficiency in the cerebellum or the nervous pathways connected with the cerebellum, although it can be caused by birth injury or subsequent disease. The child is not lacking in intelligence, but is "floppy"—when it first starts to reach out and handle objects it is

clumsy and shows a tremor (shaking). Such children are very late in starting to walk, and may be unsteady on their feet for some years. In some children ataxia is associated with the development of a spastic state of the lower limbs (spastic ataxia), a condition found in hydrocephalus and after severe meningitis or encephalitis.

In later life various diseases may affect the cerebellum to produce ataxia, which is described as "cerebellar ataxia" and is not influenced by visual guidance—unlike those forms of ataxia caused by damage to the sensory pathways of the spinal cord. Moreover, the incoordination of voluntary muscular movement results in speech disturbances so that words are slurred and produced slowly.

It is a matter of common observation that an overdose of alcohol can produce ataxia; chronic alcoholism can result in a permanent cerebellar type of ataxia. The most common causes of cerebellar ataxia, however, are the lesions of multiple sclerosis and tumors of the cerebellum. There are a number of rare conditions which involve the cerebellum and the spinal cord to produce ataxia, some of which show a family history, and various poisons such as organic mercurial salts and lead can render a patient ataxic.

Disease of the cerebellum interferes with a complicated central mechanism coordinating sensory and muscular nerve impulses to make smooth and purposeful movement possible; but ataxia will result if the sensory part of the circuit is deficient even though the central mechanism is healthy. Disease of the spinal cord may affect sensory nerve fibers running up the dorsal columns of the cord which carry impulses signaling the position of the limbs and the body. Possibly the best known example of such a disease is TABES DORSALIS (locomotor ataxia), a late manifestation of syphilis. The patient relies upon visual guidance to estimate the position of his limbs, and becomes completely ataxic when his eyes are closed or there is little or no light. Fortunately, the neurological manifestations of syphilis have become relatively rare since the introduction of penicillin.

atelectasis

Collapse of a segment or lobe of a lung (in infants, it is caused by faulty expansion of lung tissue at birth).

If an airway, large or small, in the lung is obstructed the air in the lung tissue beyond the obstruction is absorbed into the bloodstream and the lung air spaces collapse. Obstructions may be formed of sticky mucus, or brought about by the expansion of tumors or the inhalation of foreign bodies (e.g., a tooth).

Foreign bodies may often be removed through a bronchoscope; in the case of a tumor, both the tumor and the affected lung tissue must be removed by surgical operation, if possible. Bronchial secretions are excessive in conditions such as bronchitis; these tend to become dry and thick and may provoke atelectasis; to minimize the possibility of this complication, the air should be kept relatively humid.

Portions of the lung are liable to collapse after abdominal operations because the pain of the incision makes coughing (which expels bronchial secretions) an unpleasant experience to be avoided; postoperative patients thus have to be actively encouraged to clear their airways by coughing. Postoperative physical therapy is very important in the prevention of atelectasis.

At birth, one of the first duties of the obstetrician is to suck any mucus plugs out of the baby's airway through a small catheter and to make sure that the lungs expand properly.

Untreated areas of atelectasis may become infected and lead to the formation of a lung abscess.

atherosclerosis

Atherosclerosis (a form of ARTERIOSCLEROSIS, or "hardening of the arteries") is the condition underlying the current epidemic of coronary thrombosis ("heart attack") and STROKE. The smooth internal lining of the arteries becomes covered with yellowish fatty patches (atheromas) which narrow the caliber of the vessels. These patches (*plaques*) are often a focus for THROMBOSIS, further narrowing the arterial bore and eventually blocking the vessel completely.

Family history is probably the most important factor in the development of atherosclerosis, but the high incidence in the developed countries of the world suggests that it is also connected with some features of the Western way of life. Associated with atherosclerosis are excessive consumption of animal fats and refined carbohydrates, raised blood pressure (hypertension), tobacco smoking, and lack of physical exercise; the consequences—such as coronary thrombosis—are reaching epidemic proportions in Western societies and efforts are concentrated on prevention.

The treatment of established atherosclerosis is both unsatisfactory and controversial. Apart from the treatment of the major symptoms such as stroke or ANGINA PECTORIS, other important steps are reduction of raised blood pressure and weight reduction; a low intake of animal fat is generally advised in an attempt to lower blood levels of fat. Exercise should be increased and STRESS reduced. Surgical procedures to overcome failing blood supply in certain specific sites may be helpful (coronary BYPASS, arterial grafting and SYMPATHECTOMY). These measures may be of greater value in prevention than in treatment.

ATHEROSCLEROSIS

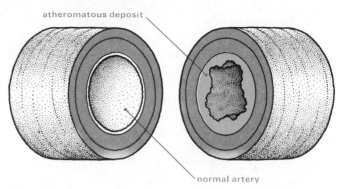

The illustration shows cross sections of a normal artery (left) and one in which atherosclerosis has formed. Atheroma is a fatty deposit of cholesterol which forms in the inner layer of the wall, narrowing the artery and reducing blood flow.

athetosis

A slow writhing movement of the limbs and facial muscles, a symptom of damage to the basal ganglia (nerve centers deep inside the brain). Most commonly athetosis is a feature of cerebral palsy or spastic paralysis, the combination of physical and mental defects caused by interference with the oxygen supply to the baby during and just after birth.

Athetosis may affect one or both sides of the body. The writhing movements are aggravated by emotion and when any voluntary action is attempted, so that they interfere with speech, eating and other daily activities. Occasionally, athetosis may develop in adult life as a symptom of tumors or infections affecting the basal ganglia.

The intensity of the movements may be reduced by treatment with drugs of the same kind used in Parkinson's disease, another disorder in which involuntary movements are caused by disease of the basal ganglia.

athlete's foot

A fungus infection of the foot. Also known as *tinea pedis, ringworm of the foot*. See TINEA.

atresia

The abnormal closure or congenital absence of a natural opening in the body. Among the sites where atresia may be present are the anus, vagina, or in organs such as the esophagus or duodenum. These defects need to be corrected by surgery (in the first few days of life in the case of congenital atresia). There are also various atresias of the heart and the neighboring arteries.

atrial fibrillation

A common consequence of ischemic and RHEUMATIC HEART DISEASE in which the normally coordinated action of the heart muscle forming the atria breaks down, allowing the muscle mass to contract and relax irregularly and rapidly. Waves of excitation pass through the muscle not at the normal rate of between 60 and 80, but at 500 to 600 a minute. Not all these waves of excitation are conducted to the ventricles, however, which beat in atrial fibrillation at about 100 to 150 a minute irregularly with much variation in force.

The patient in atrial fibrillation becomes breathless and may develop signs of HEART FAILURE. The state of atrial fibrillation is quite compatible with life, unlike the state of VENTRICULAR FIBRILLATION; but as circulation ceases in the atria because the muscle is virtually paralyzed, clots are liable to form and break off as emboli.

Treatment includes the administration of digitalis to slow down the ventricular rate of contraction, and possibly of quinidine to stop the irregular contraction. DEFIBRILLATION may be effective.

atrophy

The wasting away or reduction in size of a part of the body as the result of disease, inactivity or disuse, or interference with its blood or nerve supply.

auscultation

The act of listening to the sounds produced within the body, especially with the aid of a STETHOSCOPE. It is a valuable part of a physician's examination routine.

The stethoscope is most often used to listen to the sounds produced by the heart and lungs. The normal heart sounds can be approximately described by the words "lubb dupp," the first sound being produced by the contraction of the heart muscle and the second by the snapping shut of the valves, which prevents a return flow of blood from the arteries at the end of the contraction. In some forms of heart disease a variety of other sounds may also be heard which are generally known as "murmurs." These are usually produced by disease of the heart valves; many murmurs, however, may have no medical significance at all. Narrowing of the valve opening (*valvular stenosis*) obstructs the blood flow and produces a harsh murmur when blood is forced through the damaged valve. Laxity of the valves causes a leakage in a reverse direction (*incompetence* of the valve) and when the heart contraction is completed it tends to produce a softer *reflux murmur*. Disease of the *pericardium*, the membrane covering the surface of the heart, may roughen its normally smooth surface causing a "friction rub" to be heard in the stethoscope with each heart contraction.

The entry of air into the lungs also produces characteristic sounds, transmitted through the chest wall to the stethoscope. The presence of fluid in the lungs or obstruction to the airflow will produce additional sounds (*râles* and *rhonchi*). Sounds produced in the airways, as well as voice sounds, are conducted to the chest wall and are characteristically modified by changes in the intervening lung tissue. These sounds may be blocked by the accumulation of fluid in the space between the lung and the chest wall. Diseases which roughen the smooth surface of the membrane which covers the outside of the lungs and the inside of the ribs (*pleural membrane*) may produce a "pleural friction rub" with each breath (see PLEURISY), which can be heard on auscultation.

Australia antigen

A chemical substance first detected in the blood of an Australian aborigine (thus its name) and thought originally to be characteristic of the racial group. It is now known to be a "marker" for the presence of the virus causing one type of HEPATITIS (inflammation of the liver). The substance involved probably represents the virus itself and testing for it has become a valuable diagnostic aid; it is also used as one type of screening test before the transfusion of whole blood and other blood products.

autism

A psychosis in children of unknown cause, which may be related to the adult SCHIZOPHRENIA from which it differs in a number of respects.

The earliest signs are an indifference to parents and others who try to show affection and care for the child. The baby may not respond to being picked up and nursed, and may show ritualistic, repetitive play, even banging its head. It may rock to and fro. Although the child looks healthy and normal, feeding and toilet training become increasingly difficult and ineffective. The child learns to walk, but speaks late or stays mute. If it begins to speak, the words may be inappropriate, repeated and apparently spoken without meaning. Personal pronouns are used wrongly or not used at all, and words or phrases spoken to the child are echoed.

The afflicted children are not necessarily mentally deficient, and characteristically have an exceptional memory and high intelligence. They are upset by changes in their surroundings, for example, the rearrangement of furniture. In general, the children seem to behave as if they are alone in the world; they cannot perceive others as people, regarding them as inanimate objects, and they cannot understand that it is possible to communicate with them. Strangers will regard them as normal but very rude and ill-behaved, but it is possible to gain a little insight into their minds by imagining that they are unable to perceive the world in a normal way; somehow there is a distortion of the sensory impressions which go to make up a normal mental picture of everyday life, so that the autistic child's world is strange, incomprehensible and frightening. The natural reaction is to shut out external contacts and unfamiliar experiences, and to withdraw into surroundings which stay constant and closed.

A great deal can be done to help these children. Some suffer physical disabilities such as deafness or deficient vision which to a certain extent can be corrected; some suffer from mental deficiency; but many can be taught to communicate, although complete recovery is rare. About twice as many boys as girls are affected.

autoimmune disease

Many chronic, noninfectious diseases are due to a misdirection of the immune mechanisms which ordinarily protect the body against infections with bacteria and other microorganisms. Typically, antibodies are formed against vital structures such as the lining of the heart valves or the filtration units (glomeruli) in the kidneys, and the chronic inflammation that results causes fibrosis, scarring, and eventually failure of the organ concerned.

The body deals with microorganisms in two main ways: white blood cells engulf bacteria, destroying and digesting them and the lymphocytes and other immune cells form antibodies—protein molecules tailored to fit the organism or its toxin and so neutralize it (see ANTIBODY/ANTIGEN). Both mechanisms come into play in autoimmune diseases, although cellular infiltration is often less prominent than antibody formation. In some cases the misdirection of the immune system is easy to understand. For example, throat infections with one kind of bacterium, the streptococcus group B, are commonly followed after an interval of two or three weeks by rheumatic fever, an inflammation involving the heart valves among other parts of the body. In the individuals affected the chemical and physical makeup of the membranes lining the heart valves is very similar to the capsule of the bacterium, so that the antibodies formed against the infection also damage the heart. A similar mechanism applies to the *nephritis* (inflammation of the kidneys) that may also follow streptococcal throat infections.

However, no such bacterial infection seems to be involved in other autoimmune diseases in which antibodies are formed against structures in the liver (causing biliary cirrhosis) the thyroid (causing

Hashimoto's disease, autoimmune thyroiditis), the stomach (causing impairment of absorption of vitamin B_{12}, pernicious anemia) and the joints (causing rheumatoid arthritis). What these diseases have in common is their chronic course, often marked by episodes in which the symptoms improve or become worse for no obvious reason. Treatment with corticosteroid drugs (such as prednisone) is often effective in damping down symptoms, and immunosuppressive drugs (such as azathioprine) may also be useful, since they slow the formation of antibodies. More specific treatment will have to await a better understanding of the primary disease process in these disorders.

See also the major article on **Allergy and Immunology.**

autopsy

Examination of the body by dissection to determine the cause of death. Conducted by a pathologist, an autopsy (also known as a *necropsy* or *postmortem examination*) may be undertaken with the permission of the nearest relative if death has occurred in a hospital; but if violence or neglect has been the suspected cause of death, or the cause is not precisely known, an autopsy will usually be conducted in the absence of the relative's permission according to individual state laws.

First the pathologist (or Coroner's Medical Examiner) examines the external surface of the body and its orifices (natural openings) and notes any distinguishing marks, wounds, or evidence of disease. Then the abdomen, chest, neck and skull are opened and all the individual organs removed and examined. Specimens of tissue are taken for microscopic examination. The major blood vessels are opened to assess the state of the inner walls, and in particular the pathologist examines the arteries supplying the heart muscle (coronary arteries) and the arteries of the brain. The stomach and intestinal contents may be kept for analysis as well as specimens of blood and urine.

Where death has been caused by violence, identification of the precise cause is of the utmost importance since a criminal prosecution may rest on the proof established at autopsy. Wounds, injuries and poisons all leave particular signs that can be identified, and forensic scientists can nearly always determine with accuracy the cause of death even in bodies discovered after a considerable time has elapsed since death.

When a death has been fully investigated, the Medical Examiner will inform the appropriate authorities, who will issue a certificate for burial. If the cause is in doubt, or there is any dispute, the body will not be available for disposal until an inquest has been held.

After the autopsy the organs are replaced in the body and the incisions sewn up to render the body presentable for the funeral. More than a million autopsies are conducted every year in the United States for routine investigative procedures.

See also the section on *The Pathologist* in the major article on **Specialists You Seldom See**.

azoospermia

Absence from the semen of living spermatozoa. In normal semen there are about 60 million sperms per milliliter, about half of which will be motile—that is, able to move about and fertilize an ovum.

Azoospermia may be caused by disease, hormonal imbalance, or inborn abnormalities of the testicles; the possibility of treatment depends on the cause. Diagnosis of the condition involves the microscopic examination of at least two ejaculates.

B

Babinski's reflex

A reflex elicited on stroking the sole of the foot.

Josef Babinski (1857–1932) was a French neurologist after whom several signs of nervous system disorders were named. The sign most commonly referred to as Babinski's reflex (or *Babinski's sign*) is an abnormal reflex (except during infancy) diagnostic of some neurological disorder of the central nervous system (in a motor nerve pathway extending from the brain to the spinal cord). When the sole of the foot of a healthy person is sharply stroked the toes turn downward. When a certain neurological disorder exists, however, the big toe turns upward instead—eliciting Babinski's reflex.

In children under the age of about two, an upward movement of the toes is perfectly normal. Soon after the child learns to walk, a downward movement becomes the norm.

bacillus

Any rod-shaped bacterium.
See BACTERIA.

backache

Pain in the back may be caused by muscular strain, a "slipped" intervertebral disk, or it may be associated with some disease of the bones and joints of the spine.

The 24 vertebrae that make up the spinal column (7 cervical, 12 thoracic and 5 lumbar) extend from the base of the skull to the sacrum, the triangular "centerpiece"

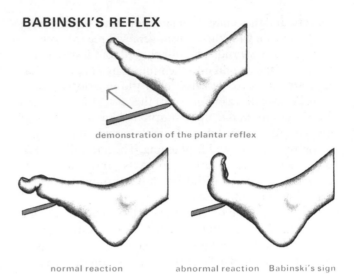

BABINSKI'S REFLEX

demonstration of the plantar reflex

normal reaction   abnormal reaction Babinski's sign

If the sole of the foot is gently stroked with a sharp pointer in the direction shown in the upper diagram, a plantar reflex will be seen with the toes curling down. Babinski's sign, where the toes curl up, is an indication of disease in either the brain or spinal cord. A positive Babinski's sign is normal in children under 2 years of age because their central nervous systems are still maturing.

of the pelvis. They are separated by pads of tough, elastic cartilage—the intervertebral disks—which give the spine its flexibility and also act as shock absorbers. The bones are also bound together by strong ligaments and by several groups of powerful muscles which mainly run in two bands on either side of the backbone. The spine acts as the central girder of the skeleton; it also provides a protective tunnel for the spinal cord (which reaches down from the brain to the level of the second lumbar vertebra) and the nerves which branch from it.

Most commonly, backache is caused by strain of the muscles around the lower part of the spine. This may be due to unaccustomed exercise—a weekend spent shoveling snow, for example—or to sitting for prolonged periods in an unsatisfactory posture. Strains on the spine are least when the back is straight; a chair which forces the spine into a curve is likely to provoke chronic back strain.

A separate, acutely painful type of backache also originating in the muscles is LUMBAGO. Here the pain is often localized to one extremely painful spot in the muscles, usually in the lower lumbar region and slightly to one side of the midline. Lumbago is often experienced after a combination of unaccustomed exercise and cold—digging the garden in spring, for example—and may be severe enough for the victim to be unable to move out of bed. The cause is believed to be spasm of a group of muscle fibers. Even with no treatment other than rest and simple pain-relieving drugs, such as aspirin, the condition resolves within a few days; but in some cases recovery may be hastened by injection of a mixture of a local anesthetic and a steroid drug into the "trigger spot."

The second common cause of sudden severe backache is damage to one of the intervertebral disks in the lumbar region of the spine. Damage is most likely to occur from lifting a heavy weight while the back is curved. Pressure on the disk, which consists of a tough capsule and a soft, elastic center, may rupture the capsule and allow part of the central nucleus to protrude. If this protrusion extends into the spinal canal it may press upon one of the spinal nerves or even the spinal cord. Typically, this pressure causes pain extending down the main sciatic nerve which runs from the buttock to the foot. The pain (SCIATICA) is made worse by coughing, straining, or bending the back. If the symptoms persist there may also be loss of feeling in the foot or the lower part of the leg and some muscular weakness.

The basic treatment of prolapsed disk (or "slipped disk") is rest, with the patient flat on his back in bed. Rest for two weeks, sometimes more, often allows the protrusion to be reabsorbed back into the disk and the damaged capsule to heal. If the symptoms from pressure on the spinal nerves are severe, or if they do not resolve with simple rest, TRACTION may be added—with weights attached to the legs pulling the vertebrae apart and so promoting return of the disk to its normal position. The most radical treatment, which may be necessary if the prolapse does not heal or in cases of recurrent prolapse, is surgical excision of the damaged portion of the disk.

Unfortunately, anyone who has suffered a prolapsed disk is at risk of recurrence; once the acute symptoms have settled, some program of preventive treatment is important. This will include exercises to strengthen the muscles which support the spine and instruction on posture and the safe, correct way to lift weights, tie the shoes, and other simple daily activities. Sometimes a physician may advise the wearing of a protective and supporting corset.

The third common cause of sudden backache is a minor displacement of the many small joints between the vertebrae. Just how frequent this sort of problem is is a matter of dispute within the medical profession. Some physicians (and all osteopaths and chiropractors) believe that most episodes of backache can be relieved by manipulation of the spine, thus encouraging the bones to return to their normal alignment. Without doubt spinal manipulation does often relieve symptoms, but it can be dangerous if the pain is due to one of the rarer causes of backache, such as a tumor or an infection such as tuberculosis.

More chronic backache may be caused by arthritis of the spinal joints. ANKYLOSING SPONDYLITIS is a severe form of spinal arthritis, especially common in young men and related to RHEUMATOID ARTHRITIS, which may also affect the spine: both diseases cause progressive pain and stiffness of the spine. The common degenerative OSTEOARTHRITIS also affects the spine; most people over the age of 50 have some stiffness of the back from minor arthritic changes. No specific treatment is needed for this form of arthritis unless specific symptoms develop.

Among the many other causes of backache are infections (tuberculosis was especially common in the last century and is still a major problem in developing countries), tumors of the bones and of the spinal cord and nerves, and secondary deposits from the spread of cancer cells elsewhere in the body. For that reason full investigation—including x-rays of the spine and blood tests—is needed before treatment is given in any case in which the cause of the pain is not obvious.

Most episodes of backache are preventable: with correct posture, care in lifting weights, and regular exercise to keep the muscles in trim, the joints in the back should remain as trouble free as those elsewhere in the body.

bacteremia

The presence in the blood of living bacteria, with or without a significant clinical response. Compare SEPTICEMIA.

bacteria

Living organisms, members of the kingdom Protista—which comprises animals and plants made up of one cell, smaller than yeasts but larger than viruses, found all over the surface of the globe in the air, soil, and water. Many live on or within larger living organisms, including man; some produce disease and are termed *pathogenic*, but not all are harmful. Some are actively useful—for example, the bacteria that produce nitrogen in the soil for plant growth.

Bacteria may be classified by their shape: round (*cocci*), straight rods (*bacilli*), curved (*vibrios*) and wavy (*spirilla*). Most are unable to move, but a few are motile by virtue of their flagellae (tails). Cocci are very often found in typical groups: *staphylococci* are gathered in bunches like grapes, *streptococci* form chains and *diplococci* are paired. All bacteria given the right circumstances can multiply very quickly, some doubling their numbers every half hour. In an unfavorable environment most die, but some can form spores—thick walled cells resistant to heat and drying out (dessication)—which lie dormant until conditions become favorable again.

BACTERIA

tuberculosis bacilli | tetanus bacilli | typhoid bacilli | anthrax bacilli | cocci | streptococci (rheumatic fever) | diplococci (pneumonia) | staphylococci (boils) | trypanosomes (sleeping sickness) | spirochete (syphilis)

Bacteria are single-cell microorganisms, classified according to their shapes into bacilli, cocci, spirilla and vibrios. Most are harmless— indeed many types are beneficial to us—but certain types of bacteria are responsible for infectious diseases, which were notorious killers before antibiotics were discovered.

Pathogenic bacteria cause disease in two basic ways. They may gain access to the tissues and there multiply to damage their surroundings, or they may release substances called *toxins* which poison remote parts of the body. *Endotoxins* are contained inside the bacteria to be released when they die, and *exotoxins* are produced by living bacteria. Usually the signs and symptoms of disease are produced by exotoxins—e.g., in tetanus, where the bacteria multiply in a dirty wound and produce an exotoxin which damages the nervous system.

Dangerous organisms are usually transmitted from man to man by direct contact, by breathing air exhaled from diseased air passages, by contact with contaminated excreta, or by insects. In most cases the body is able to deal with harmful bacteria, but if they gain a foothold and produce disease the defensive processes of inflammation and antibody formation can be aided by the use of drugs designed to kill pathogenic organisms or prevent their multiplication. These drugs, antibiotics, are called *bactericidal* if they kill bacteria or *bacteriostatic* if they inhibit their multiplication.

Antibiotics must not be used indiscriminately, because continued exposure to a particular antibiotic may result in the development of resistant strains.

Methods of controlling bacteria in the environment include the use of chemical disinfectants, the application of heat (as dry heat or steam) and irradiation.

See also the major article on **Infectious Diseases.**

bagassosis

A lung disease caused by the inhalation of the moldy fibrous waste (bagasse) of sugar cane.

See the major article on **Pulmonary Disease.**

Baker's cyst

A painless soft cyst at the back of the knee, commonly occurring when the knee joint is damaged by OSTEOARTHRITIS. The condition is named after William Morrant Baker (1839–1896), a 19th-century British surgeon.

The synovium (joint lining) produces an excessive amount of joint fluid, which escapes from the joint either by rupturing through the synovium or by pushing the synovium out ahead of it.

The size of the cyst may be reduced by drawing out the fluid with a needle and syringe, followed by an injection of hydrocortisone (a drug which reduces inflammation) into the affected area. Alternatively the whole cyst may be removed surgically.

balanitis

Inflammation of the tip of the penis. Balanitis is generally associated with PHIMOSIS—narrowing of the opening of the foreskin so that it cannot be pulled back.

In infancy the condition is usually of the type called *ammoniacal* balanitis. In such cases the inflammation is due to irritation caused by ammonia produced by the action of bacteria on the urine. It can usually be prevented by promptly changing wet diapers.

When balanitis occurs in older children and adults, it may be related to sugar in the urine and it may therefore be a warning sign of DIABETES MELLITUS. Other possible causes in adults are an underlying syphilitic sore (a chancre) or cancer of the penis.

Because the tip of the penis and the foreskin are in close contact, inflammation of one seldom occurs without inflammation of the other. Inflammation of both structures is called balanoposthitis.

In addition to the administration of an appropriate antibiotic (if required to control bacterial infection), treatment is directed at the primary or underlying cause.

baldness (alopecia)

The loss of hair on the head.

Hair grows from the base (bulb) of hair follicles, tiny tube-like structures in the skin. Although some hair is constantly being shed (as an actively growing hair expels an older one from its follicle), baldness does not usually occur.

Hair loss resulting in baldness may occur in disease or

in the normal individual as a hereditary phenomenon.

Skin infections which reach deep enough to affect the base of the hair follicles may cause temporary or permanent bald patches. Other skin diseases, burns, radiation injury, chemical injury, or any injury which causes scarring can lead to permanent bald patches. Some drugs cause an increased rate of shedding of the hair.

Increased shedding may also accompany several illnesses—such as prolonged fevers, certain malignancies, uncontrolled diabetes mellitus, or diseases of the thyroid, pituitary and adrenal glands. There is no special treatment for this type of baldness, which is often reversed as the underlying disease is treated.

Some women experience a temporarily increased rate of hair loss after pregnancy.

By far the most common type of baldness is *male-pattern baldness*—which starts around the temples and spreads to the crown, leaving behind a rim of hair at the sides and back. As in other types of baldness, the bald areas are seldom completely hairless but covered with a downy type of hair which is barely perceptible.

The tendency to male-pattern baldness is hereditary and nothing can prevent it. It usually occurs in middle

PATTERNS OF BALDNESS

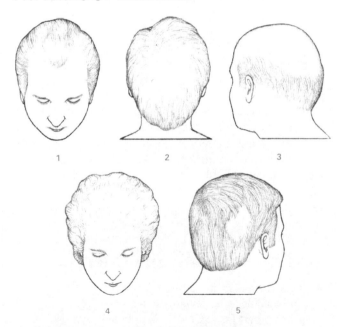

Male-pattern baldness is an inherited condition which usually starts in middle age around the temples (1) and the crown (2). In severe cases only a rim of hair remains around the back of the head (3). Baldness in women is uncommon but sometimes occurs after pregnancy (4). Patchy loss of hair (5) can either result from a skin infection (for example, ringworm of the scalp) or from a condition called alopecia areata.

age, although it may start as early as the late teens. It is irreversible and no successful form of treatment exists. In selected cases, however, a course of hair transplantation may improve appearance.

Hair loss of the male-pattern type may also occur in women, but usually results in severe thinning rather than actual baldness.

One type of baldness that can be very upsetting is *alopecia areata*—a patchy baldness which comes on suddenly. The bald patch may increase in size or new bald areas may form on the scalp, in the eyebrows, or in the beard region. Occasionally there is extensive loss of hair on both scalp and body.

The cause of alopecia areata is not known. Recovery usually occurs without treatment, especially if only a few areas are affected. The only treatment that may be of value is the injection of a corticosteroid drug.

Banti's syndrome

A condition (also known as *Banti's disease*) characterized by an enlarged spleen, anemia, leukopenia (an abnormal reduction in the number of circulating white blood cells), gastrointestinal bleeding and cirrhosis of the liver.

It was first described in 1898 by Guido Banti (1852–1925), an Italian pathologist. He thought that the disorder originated in the spleen, which produced a toxin causing cirrhosis of the liver. Doctors now know, however, that the primary disorder is obstruction of the blood circulation between the intestines and the liver (the "portal system"). The result is a condition known as portal hypertension (see LIVER DISEASE), leading to venous congestion in organs such as the spleen and stomach.

Blood cells are normally destroyed by the spleen, and the anemia and leukopenia are a consequence of a large and overactive spleen.

There are many causes of obstruction of the portal system, but cirrhosis of the liver accounts for about 70% of all cases.

barium meal/barium enema

X-ray studies of the digestive tract. In a barium meal, barium sulfate is swallowed before x-rays are taken; in a barium enema, barium sulfate is introduced into the rectum through a tube under gentle pressure.

X-rays do not pass through barium sulfate, so the barium sulfate shows up as an opaque mass on the x-ray picture. Like any liquid, the barium sulfate conforms to the shape of its container; a clear outline of the stomach and intestines can thus be obtained by taking x-rays as the barium sulfate passes along them.

A barium meal is used to diagnose abnormalities of

BARIUM MEAL/ENEMA

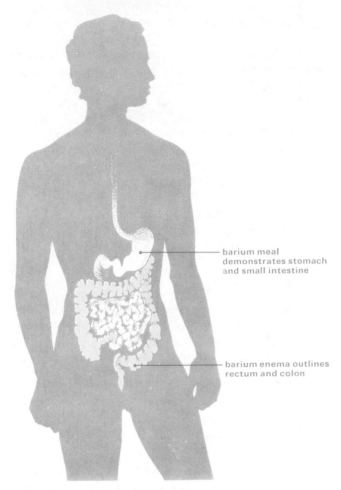

barium meal demonstrates stomach and small intestine

barium enema outlines rectum and colon

Barium sulfate is a radiopaque liquid (one which x-rays cannot pass through) and is extensively used by radiologists to outline the digestive tract. The barium is either swallowed as a meal or injected through the anus as an enema. Using these techniques the radiologist can diagnose peptic ulcers, cancers, pockets in the bowel wall, and other diseases of the bowel.

the upper gastrointestinal tract down to the small intestine, while a barium enema is used to study the large intestine.

battered-child syndrome

A condition in which young children, usually under the age of three, are deliberately injured (often repeatedly) by someone in a position of trust such as a parent or guardian.

The violence is totally inexcusable and occurs on the most trivial provocation. It results in bruising, fractures, injury to internal organs, burns and even death.

Besides being physically injured, the child may be deprived of food, care and affection; but battering can also occur in children who are otherwise well cared for.

It has been said that every parent is a potential child batterer; but no matter how exasperating a child's behavior may be, most parents fortunately do not resort to violence.

Child batterers come from all social classes and all levels of intelligence; some may be difficult to detect because they appear concerned over the child's injuries and extremely willing to cooperate with the doctor in every way. However, there are certain typical characteristics of child battering.

There may be a few hours' delay before the child is brought to a doctor. The explanation given is one of an accident, such as falling down the stairs or bumping into a crib or table. But examination reveals injuries incompatible with the history and may also reveal past injuries. Often there are similar injuries on opposite sides of the body, such as bruises on both legs or on both sides of the neck. The parent may try to explain away bruising by saying the child bleeds easily.

The child is very often an unplanned or unwanted child.

A greater proportion of child batterers come from the lower socioeconomic classes; there is usually a history of social, financial, or emotional problems within the family. Batterers are often in their twenties. In some cases the father is unemployed or may have a criminal record, and the mother may be pregnant or in the premenstrual period. Although generally one parent is the batterer, the other is usually aware that the battering is going on.

There may be no evidence of a psychopathic personality in batterers, but violence toward their children is considered to be a temporary psychosis resulting from emotional immaturity. In such cases treatment must be directed at both the child and the parents, who need all the help they can get for social rehabilitation. Otherwise, in more than half the cases, the child will be injured again.

BCG (bacille Calmette-Guérin)

A vaccine used in the control of tuberculosis.

The vaccine was developed by two French bacteriologists, Albert Léon Charles Calmette (1863–1933) and Camille Guérin (1872–1961). Their work began in 1906, with a painstaking series of culturing and subculturing of the causative organism of tuberculosis (the tubercle bacillus) until a stable and safe form of the vaccine was achieved. It was first used in the prevention of tuberculosis in 1921 (in a newborn baby whose mother had died of the disease). Culturing the organism in a succession of artificial media removes its virulence, so that while the vaccine can confer immunity or partial immunity against tuberculosis it does not produce the disease in the person vaccinated.

BCG both reduces the incidence of tuberculosis and results in a less progressive form of the disease when it occurs.

BCG is now being used experimentally to treat cancer. The rationale behind this is that the vaccine stimulates the production of antibodies which are thought to increase the body's general defense system. These antibodies may attack cancer cells and destroy them in the same way that they destroy the tubercle bacilli.

See also ANTIBODY/ANTIGEN, IMMUNIZATION.

bedsores

Sores caused by lying immobile in bed for long periods. They are also known as *pressure sores* or *decubitus ulcers.*

The skin and the tissues beneath it receive their nourishment from very small blood vessels. When these blood vessels are compressed for a sufficient length of time—for example, when the patient is lying down in bed—the skin becomes deprived of its nutrition and becomes vulnerable to death of cells in the area (necrosis). Continuing pressure is likely to progress to a large area of tissue destruction and the formation of an ulcer.

Healthy people do not get bedsores because they move about during sleep and because they shift position when pressure areas become uncomfortable. Pressure sores develop either because the person concerned is semiconscious and so does not feel the discomfort caused by pressure, or because weakness makes them unable to move. Anyone who is unconscious for more than a few hours may develop pressure sores if left unattended.

Bedsores usually begin as a reddening of the skin, which later assumes a bluish tinge. Once an ulcer forms, healing is difficult. It may become infected and so severe that the underlying bone becomes exposed. Treatment, like prevention, depends on relief of pressure: nursing the patient on an air bed or in a net hammock will allow the damaged skin to heal.

Prevention is the best method for coping with bedsores. People confined to bed should be helped to turn every two or three hours. Their skin should be washed regularly. Sheets should be clean and smooth, because movement against a crumpled sheet can hasten damage to the skin. Pressure points may be supported against soft cushions or pads, or on an air ring. Special air and water beds are now available to reduce the risk of pressure sores developing.

See also *Bedsores* in the major article **Guide to Home Nursing Care.**

bedwetting (enuresis)

There is no precise age at which bedwetting becomes abnormal. Most children are dry at night by the age of two or three, but others not until five or seven.

Even after good control is achieved, occasional bedwetting may occur up to the age of nine or ten or even older. These lapses of night-time control are usually associated with fatigue or emotional upset and should not be a cause for concern.

Most cases of bedwetting persist from infancy although sometimes regular bedwetting starts after a period of good control. There is usually a family pattern for the age at which control is achieved. As a rule, bedwetting does not require investigation until after the age of three or four.

Bedwetting is very rarely associated with nocturnal epilepsy, a disorder of the spinal cord, abnormality of the urinary tract, uncontrolled diabetes mellitus, or diabetes insipidus. But in most cases there is no obvious cause and the condition is thought to be a sign of a temporary emotional or psychological disorder.

The most common cause of persistent bedwetting extending from infancy is too vigorous and too early attempts at toilet training. In general children are not able to achieve voluntary daytime control before the age of 15 to 18 months.

Bedwetting may represent a desire for more parental attention. In contrast, some psychologists attribute the condition to unconscious resentment of the parents, while another proposed explanation is anxiety caused by an unconscious fear of injury to the genitals (associated with feelings of guilt due to sexual fantasies or activities such as masturbation).

Treatment is essentially training based on encouragement. Shaming, nagging, scolding or punishment should be avoided as they may only aggravate the problem. The parents' attitude is extremely important. They should not be overanxious about the bedwetting and should not make an undue fuss when carrying out measures aimed at preventing bedwetting.

These measures include restricting fluids for about two hours before bedtime and waking the child up so that he may empty his bladder before he wets the bed. Drugs are of doubtful value but a bell and pad may be helpful. This is a conditioning type of treatment in which a bell rings and wakens the child when the urine passed completes an electrical circuit in a pad placed beneath the child.

Another measure that may be worth a trial is based on the assumption that bedwetting is the result of a smaller than average bladder capacity. Some doctors believe that the bladder capacity can be increased by giving plenty of drinks during the day and encouraging the child to suppress the urge to go to the bathroom.

If a strong psychological disorder is the underlying cause of bedwetting, none of these measures will work and the help of a psychotherapist may be required.

Bell's palsy

A paralysis of the facial nerves resulting in a characteristic lopsided appearance of the face, due mainly to drooping of the angle of the mouth on the affected side.

There are several causes of facial nerve paralysis. Bell's palsy refers to cases of unknown cause, although exposure to cold has been implicated. The condition was first described in 1828 by Sir Charles Bell, a Scottish surgeon.

It has a rapid onset and mainly affects people aged 20 to 50. Recovery is usually spontaneous and begins within a week. About 75% of patients fully recover in several weeks. Occasionally, especially if the disease persists for a long time, the eventual recovery may be only partial. In such cases, facial spasms may accompany voluntary facial movement. It has been suggested that cortisone-like steroid drugs may help if prescribed early in the course of the disease.

bends

Pains experienced by deep-sea divers and compressed-air tunnel workers when they move too rapidly from areas of high pressure to areas of lower pressure. Bends are symptoms of decompression sickness (caisson disease).

Nitrogen, present in the air we breathe, can dissolve in the blood. As a person moves into areas of increasingly higher pressure, more nitrogen in the lungs dissolves in the blood and enters the circulation. However, the reverse process—when nitrogen moves from the blood to the lungs—takes longer. So if a diver surfaces too rapidly, nitrogen bubbles remain in the circulation where they form air locks and block the blood supply to various tissues.

The pain of bends is felt mainly in the muscles, bones and joints. It can range in severity from an ache to a severe cramp and may occur while the person is moving from high to low pressures, or within a few hours afterwards. Bends are relieved almost immediately if the person returns to high pressures again; a diver could go back into the deep sea or into a special recompression chamber.

Decompression—that is, moving from high to low pressure—should always be gradual because severe decompression sickness can cause immediate collapse, permanent brain damage or death. Repeated attacks of even mild decompression sickness can result in bone damage many years later. Modern diving procedures and special equipment minimize the risk of the bends.

beriberi

A disease caused by the dietary deficiency of vitamin B_1 (thiamine), seen especially in those parts of the world where the diet consists primarily of polished rice.

For a discussion of the signs and symptoms of beriberi, see the appropriate section in the major article on **Nutrition.**

berylliosis

A disease caused by poisoning from inhalation of the fumes or dust of beryllium or its compounds. (Beryllium is a white metallic element, formerly used in combination with other substances to coat the inner lining of fluorescent lamps and still widely used in industry in the form of beryllium-copper alloys because of its hardening qualities.)

Acute beryllium poisoning causes symptoms a few weeks after exposure, resembling those of bronchitis or pneumonia. Most cases are relatively mild and the patients usually recover within one to six months; corticosteroid drugs may be prescribed in moderate to severe cases.

Chronic berylliosis (also known as *beryllium granulomatosis*) mainly affects the lungs. It occurs after several months of exposure, although some cases have been reported decades later. In addition to progressive damage to the lungs, the disease may involve the heart and present a direct threat to life. The chronic form of the disease is characterized by the formation of small masses or nodules (known as granulomas) in the liver, kidneys, spleen and skin (often leading to ulceration of the skin).

Treatment and control of berylliosis involves the prescription of corticosteroids, which can be very effective if begun early during the course of the disease.

Up to 30 years ago, when beryllium was used to make fluorescent powders, excessive exposure to beryllium was quite common. Now it is used largely for making alloys or heat-resistant ceramics and there are strict controls on the amount that can be found in the factory environment.

bilharziasis

Another name for SCHISTOSOMIASIS.

biopsy

Removal of a small specimen of tissue from the living body for diagnostic purposes. Diagnosis is made by examining thin slices of the tissue under a microscope.

Since only very small pieces are required, tissues can be obtained from within the body by means of special instruments without a major surgical operation. To obtain tissue from the bronchi, intestines or bladder (all of which have natural openings onto the body surface) slender illuminated instruments are used known as *fiberoptic endoscopes:* bronchoscopes, gastroscopes, and cystoscopes—for viewing the bronchi, stomach and bladder, respectively. These are flexible tubes with special attachments which can be introduced into the appropriate body opening to the point at which a tissue specimen is to be taken. A gastroscope, for example, is passed via the mouth and esophagus into the stomach where the gastric lining can be viewed and a biopsy taken.

Biopsies of internal organs such as the liver and kidney are performed by means of a long hollow needle, which is passed through the skin and into the organ concerned.

Most biopsies are sent to the laboratory for processing before being examined under the microscope. This may take a day or two. But sometimes a biopsy is taken during an operation and an immediate result is required for the surgeon to decide how to proceed. In such cases a "frozen-section biopsy" is performed. This is a quick but less satisfactory means of processing the tissue by freezing before slices are made.

A diagnosis made on biopsy findings is generally a firm one. However, a disease may affect organs in a patchy manner; since only extremely tiny pieces are removed, these bits may not have come from the affected parts. To reduce the chance of missing affected parts, where possible several "bites" are taken at biopsy.

See also the major article on **Gastroenterology.**

bird breeder's lung

An allergy to substances contained in the excreta ("droppings") of birds. The condition is also known as *pigeon breeder's disease*—although it can be caused by other species of birds, such as parakeets.

The allergic reaction results in chills, fever, cough and shortness of breath. The attacks usually occur a few hours after handling or being otherwise closely associated with birds. Some patients experience only the breathlessness without fever and chills; others may have substantial weight loss as well. The chronic inflammation of the lungs (alveolitis) may cause progressive breathlessness and permanent lung damage.

Bird breeder's lung due to regular contact with pet parakeets (or other cage birds) is now recognized as an important cause of chronic respiratory disease. Removal of the birds will relieve symptoms. The allergic reaction may also be suppressed by desensitization or by the administration of antihistamines or steroid drugs.

birth injury

Damage to a baby at birth whether avoidable or unavoidable. Birth injuries may be either mechanical or due to a lack of oxygen at birth (anoxia).

Premature babies and those who lie in awkward positions in the uterus are most likely to suffer mechanical injuries, which include bruises, fractures and nerve injuries.

The most common life-threatening birth injury is hemorrhage into the brain. If the injury is severe, death may occur at birth or within a few days. Those who survive may recover fully, although they sometimes suffer permanent brain damage. It is often difficult to predict the effect the brain damage will have in later years.

The liver is another internal organ occasionally injured during birth. Injury may occur during delivery or as a result of external heart massage during attempts at resuscitation. The prognosis depends on the degree of injury.

Sufficient oxygen is essential because the brain can withstand only a few minutes of anoxia. Anoxia may result when the placental circulation has been inadequate during pregnancy, as in conditions such as PREECLAMPSIA (toxemia of pregnancy), multiple pregnancy or hemorrhage before the onset of labor.

Anoxia may also occur when the baby fails to breathe spontaneously at birth. Failure of spontaneous breathing (APNEA) is more likely following some complication of pregnancy such as premature birth, multiple pregnancy, toxemia or maternal diabetes mellitus. When these complications are present, however, apnea can be anticipated and skilled staff and specialized equipment for resuscitation can be prepared.

Sometimes, however, apnea is totally unexpected. As with brain hemorrhage, it is often difficult to predict how much and what kind of permanent brain damage, if any, will result.

birthmark

A skin blemish present at birth.
See NEVUS.

birth weight

The average weight of a baby at birth is approximately $7\frac{1}{2}$ lb. (3.4 kg) with boys being slightly heavier than girls. There is obviously great variation between newborn infants, but 95% weigh between $5\frac{1}{2}$ lb. (2.5 kg) and 10 lb. (4.6 kg).

The baby is often heavier than average if one of the parents is unusually large or if the mother is diabetic or prediabetic. Large size is not necessarily dependent on late delivery (that is, after a pregnancy lasting for more than 42 weeks).

Infants with unusually low birth weights are those under 5½ lb. (2.5 kg). Responsible factors can include a diminished length of pregnancy (less than 37 weeks from the first day of the last menstrual period, making them "premature") or the rate of intrauterine growth may be less than expected ("small-for-date"), although the baby is born perfectly healthy.

If an infant weighs 3.3 lb. (1.5 kg) or less at birth, it is likely to be both premature and small-for-date, a situation associated with ill health and a risk to life.

Although the length of pregnancy is relatively constant in different population groups, birth weight shows variation. The incidence of low birth weight in the United States is 7.2% for live-born white infants and 14% for non-white.

Premature birth resulting in a low birth weight is associated with several factors: disease in the mother during pregnancy, such as toxemia or nephritis; maternal age below 20 or above 35; and low social and economic status.

blackheads

Dried plugs of fatty material in the ducts of the sebaceous (oil-secreting) glands. Also known as *comedones*. The black color at the surface of the plugs is not dirt, as often believed; albinos (who lack the pigment melanin) have light-colored "blackheads."

The blackhead is produced by faulty functioning of the sebaceous follicle, which does not release the *sebum* (fatty secretion of the sebaceous glands) in a correct manner. The consequent obstruction to the gland leads to enlargement of the opening of the follicle. Infection by bacteria living on the skin may lead to inflammation and so to the characteristic papules, or "pimples," of ACNE.

Blackheads should never be squeezed; this increases the risk of infection. Gentle bathing with warm water and soap should release most of them.

blackout

A momentary loss of consciousness or vision, caused by an interruption of the blood supply to the brain.

See FAINTING.

bladder problems

Bladder problems can be separated into those arising from infection within the bladder, those due to growths within the bladder and those associated with loss of bladder control.

Inflammation of the bladder (CYSTITIS) is common

and is most often due to bacterial infection. The symptoms of burning pain on passing urine and increased frequency or urination may, however, also occur without any evidence of infection; this non-bacterial inflammation is especially common in women. Pregnancy and sexual intercourse both increase the likelihood of cystitis, which in women is often a consequence of infection spreading to the bladder from the genital organs. Treatment includes the drinking of large quantities of fluid and the administration of appropriate antibacterial drugs. Women who develop symptoms of cystitis in association with sexual intercourse need to pay special attention to regular washing of the genital region.

The bladder is occasionally the site of a growth. The most common is a benign wartlike tumor (apapilloma), but only specialist investigation can distinguish these from malignant tumors. In either case the first sign is blood in the urine, occasionally rather than constantly, without associated pain. Later the symptoms may resemble those of cystitis. Small bladder tumors can be removed through a tube passed into the bladder (cystoscope), but regular medical follow-up is needed to watch for any recurrence.

Urinary INCONTINENCE is involuntary urination; it may be caused by a defect in the nervous control of the bladder or a mechanical problem. Children often have episodes of urinary incontinence, especially during sleep (see BEDWETTING).

Stress incontinence—the leakage of a few drops of urine during coughing or straining—is common in women and is most often due to damage in childbirth to the muscles around the neck of the bladder. Surgical repair may be necessary in such cases. (Pregnant women sometimes experience stress incontinence merely as a result of the growing fetus pressing against the bladder.)

Inability to pass urine (retention) may be caused by an obstruction at the opening of the bladder from a tumor or a bladder stone; but in men the most common cause is enlargement of the prostate gland. The early symptoms of prostatic enlargement include increased frequency of urination, and slowness and hesitancy of the urinary stream. These symptoms can be relieved by a surgical operation to remove all or part of the prostate gland (PROSTATECTOMY). Inability to pass urine may also be due to an injury or disease of the spinal cord, such as MULTIPLE SCLEROSIS. In such cases the bladder may need to be emptied by passing a narrow tube (catheter) up through the urethra to the bladder.

See also URINARY TRACT INFECTION and the major article on **Urology.**

blepharitis

Inflammation of the margins of the eyelids, where the

skin joins the conjunctiva of the eye.

The symptoms are usually mild, but there may be heat, itching and grittiness resulting in considerable pain. The eyes may seem tired, unduly sensitive and intolerant to light, dust, or heat. Causes include allergies, bacterial infection, external irritants (such as foreign particles and wind) and eyestrain. The nature of the skin itself (pale-skinned people are generally more susceptible) may also influence the condition. (In addition, seborrhea of the scalp may also cause blepharitis.)

Squamous blepharitis is a superficial dermatitis in which the area is congested, swollen, inflamed and accompanied by scaling of the skin. The lid looks bleary and swollen as the result of congestion; the scaling skin forms yellow crusts as it adheres to the secretion produced. Later the margins become permanently swollen, thickened and disturbed in position.

The result is wetting of the lids; this induces rubbing, followed by eczema and eversion of the lid margin. Dirty handkerchiefs and fingers aggravate the infection.

If the condition is chronic the lashes become damaged and may be lost (usually temporarily, but sometimes permanently).

Follicular blepharitis is a less common but more serious form. The inflammation is deeper, pus is produced, and the inflammation may extend outside the hair follicles and form abscesses (resulting in destruction of tissue and ulceration). The lid margins are red and inflamed and the lashes matted. Healing eventually occurs with scarring.

The complications of blepharitis are chronic conjunctivitis, permanently red lids, loss of lashes and eversion of the lid (exposing its inner surface).

Treatment must include attention to general health and scrupulous cleanliness of the face. Antiseptics and soothing lotions may help. Where required, the doctor may prescribe antibiotics (to control any asociated bacterial infection) or ophthalmic steroid preparations.

See also the major article on **Ophthalmology.**

blindness

In the literal sense, blindness is the state or condition of being sightless. But in a legal or practical sense it also includes serious impairment of vision to the extent that certain types of activity or employment may be extremely difficult or impossible. Blindness may be permanent or transient and affect only one or both eyes. It may arise suddenly or develop gradually over months or years and may affect the entire field of vision or only part of it.

Blindness has many possible causes, but in each case one or more of four basic areas are affected: (1) the eye itself; (2) the blood supply which nourishes the *retina*

(the light-sensitive structure at the back of the eye); (3) the *optic nerve* (a bundle of over one million separate nerve fibers which conveys impulses from the retina to the brain); and (4) the *visual cortex* (an area toward the back of the brain which is primarily concerned with interpreting impulses from the retina as visual images).

Sudden loss of vision may affect only part of the visual field of one or both eyes. An unobservant person may at first remain unaware of visual loss in one eye until the other is inadvertently covered up. Total loss of vision that occurs suddenly may be caused by blockage of the artery or vein supplying the retina or by hemorrhage within the eye. Sudden loss of part of the visual field may occur when a part of the retina becomes detached from its normal position (see DETACHED RETINA) or when a blood clot forms in the blood vessels which supply the nerve tracts from the eye to the brain.

Several conditions may affect the arteries which supply blood to the eyes. These include: spasm of the vessels (which can cause temporary visual impairment); thickening of the arterial walls from the deposit of fatty material on their inner linings (ATHEROSCLEROSIS), which may seriously impede or block the flow of blood to the eye and cause a wasting away (atrophy) of the tissues of the retina and the optic nerve; and hemorrhage into the retina sometimes associated with high blood pressure (particularly as a complication of KIDNEY DISEASE or DIABETES MELLITUS).

Blindness can be caused by a congenital defect of the eye, optic nerve, or the visual cortex of the brain. Other causes include injuries or wounds affecting these areas, tumors of the eye or brain, meningitis (inflammation of the membranes which cover the brain), complications that occur as the result of chronic inflammation of the eye, CATARACT (an opacity of the crystalline lens of the eye), and GLAUCOMA (abnormally raised pressure within the eye, which can exert damaging pressure upon the optic nerve). The three major causes of a gradual loss of vision, mainly affecting the elderly, are cataract, glaucoma and senile macular degeneration (discussed below).

Cataract may be hereditary or a complication of German measles (rubella) in the mother during pregnancy. It may also follow injury (with or without rupture of the lens capsule) or inflammation within the eye.

Glaucoma is a disease of obscure cause, characterized by increased fluid pressure within the eye. It may arise suddenly or over a long period and is thought to be the result of an aging process in the vessels and tissues of the eye. The raised pressure of the internal watery fluid (aqueous humor) impairs the vision indirectly. Sight is gradually destroyed, beginning as a blind patch and gradually extending. Treatment involves controlling the pressure with drops or by surgical decompression.

Senile macular degeneration is the third main cause of blindness (after cataract and glaucoma). It is caused by degenerative changes in the retina associated with the general process of aging and is irreversible. Visual loss is gradual but progressive; older persons afflicted with this condition probably adapt better to a simple magnifying glass for reading than to elaborate aids such as telescopic glasses.

Blindness can occur as a complication of certain infectious diseases, including SYPHILIS, TUBERCULOSIS, MEASLES, DIPHTHERIA, SCARLET FEVER and the afore-mentioned German measles. At one time, babies born to mothers who harbored the microorganisms of GONORRHEA were frequently in danger of acquiring the infection—which often led to blindness. The practice of putting drops of silver nitrate or an antibiotic in the eyes of newborn babies has made this complication ex-tremely rare today, in addition to the fact that gonorrhea—because of its symptoms arising from acute inflammation of the Fallopian tubes—is commonly diagnosed and treated before a pregnant woman gives birth.

Some forms of blindness or severely impaired vision (such as cataract) can be corrected with prompt medical or surgical attention. Early treatment of other causes of defective eyesight (such as glaucoma and detached retina) can frequently limit or arrest the progress of impaired vision before blindness occurs.

Permanent blindness, whether present at birth or occurring later in life, is a condition which most sightless persons have learned to cope with successfully. It is important for sighted persons to realize that *the blind generally take great pride in being able to function with a minimum of outside assistance.* For example, even in such an apparently simple matter as offering to assist a blind person to cross a busy street it is important that the sighted person not "force" his help, but merely ask if he *may* help and then offer his arm as a guide. No one—sighted or not—likes being *dragged* across a road! A condescending manner should be rigorously avoided.

Various institutions and societies exist which offer valuable training and assistance for the blind, including those which provide guide dogs and others which teach the reading and printing of Braille (a system of raised dots, felt with the fingertips, used to represent letters and other characters).

See also the major article on **Ophthalmology.**

blisters

Outpouring of fluid under the outer layer of the skin as a result of local damage produces a blister. Blistering may be caused by repeated friction on tender skin (parti-cularly of the hands or feet), by heat (as in the case of burns and scalds), or by irritating chemicals.

Blisters caused by the friction of unaccustomed physical work on the hands or by ill-fitting shoes on the feet will heal easily if the source of friction is removed and the blister kept clean so that it cannot become infected. The extensive blistering and broken skin caused by burning or scalding needs careful treatment under medical supervision if infection and subsequent scarring are to be avoided.

blood

There are approximately $10\frac{1}{2}$ pints (5 liters) of blood in the circulation. Two-fifths of this volume consists of *erythrocytes* (red blood cells). The other cellular components, the *leukocytes* (white blood cells) and *platelets*, though equally important, are a thousand-fold less numerous and therefore occupy a relatively small proportion. The remaining three-fifths consists of *plasma*, a watery solution of proteins and salts in which the blood cells are suspended.

The basic concept of the blood as a vital body fluid is familiar enough to most people, and we know its appearance and consistency. We also know that it is pumped around the body by the heart, that it is under pressure in the arteries and that a cut artery bleeds profusely and possibly dangerously. It is also not difficult to imagine the failure of the pumping system if the bleeding leads to too great a reduction in the volume of blood in the circulation. We know that death follows because our "life blood" is gone.

The functions of the blood which make it so vital to life are less well known to the average person. These functions may be described under three main headings: (1) transport, (2) the maintenance of a stable internal environment and body temperature and (3) defense against infection and uncontrolled hemorrhage.

The fact that it is in constant movement around the body suggests that a principal function of the blood is as a *transport medium.* All the body's vital processes depend on a supply of oxygen to "burn" sugar and fat to produce energy. This oxygen is obtained from the air in the lungs and carried by the HEMOGLOBIN pigment in the red blood cells to all parts of the body; the unique properties of the pigment allow uptake of oxygen in the lungs and its subsequent release of the tissues. The principal waste product of energy production, carbon dioxide gas, is also carried in the blood—in both the red cells and the plasma—and is released in the lungs to be expelled in the expired air.

The food we eat, after digestion has reduced it to simpler chemical compounds, is absorbed mainly through the walls of the small intestine into the bloodstream. A variety of special transport mechanisms for individual compounds exists. Iron, for example, has its own "transporter protein" to which it is bound on entry into the circulation, to be "unloaded" when it reaches the red blood cells where it is needed for hemoglobin production. All the proteins, fats, sugars, vitamins and minerals required by the body tissues are similarly carried in the blood—either in simple solution, or attached to a transporter protein. This may involve the movement of absorbed food materials from the small intestine direct to the site where they are required or, if not immediately required for use, to storage in the liver or the "fat depots."

The processing of food materials and the replacement and repair of tissues produce waste products, which if allowed to accumulate would be harmful. These are transported either to the liver for further processing to render them less toxic or directly to the kidneys for excretion from the body.

Control of the body's functions depends to an important degree on "chemical messengers" (hormones) carried in the blood. These chemicals, produced by the endocrine glands (such as the pituitary and thyroid), are carried by the bloodstream to all parts of the body, giving a rapid and efficient control of its physical and chemical activities. (See also the major article on **Endocrinology**.)

The tissues of the body can function efficiently only if their physical and chemical environment remains constant within fairly narrow limits. The enzymes (ferments), which drive the chemical processes of the body, function optimally at 98.6°F (37°C) and the blood plays a vital role in maintaining all parts of the body reasonably close to this temperature. Heat produced from chemical processes occurring deep in the body is carried by the blood to warm the extremities. In hot conditions, excessive heat production by the body is controlled by increasing the flow of blood to these exposed parts; heat is dissipated through the skin (which is cooled by sweating). In cold conditions, however, the body prevents excessive heat loss by reducing the blood flow to the extremities.

The salt concentrations at which the body cells can function properly are similarly limited. The blood circulation ensures an even distribution of salts throughout the body, with excretion of any overall excess via the kidneys. This allows the tissues to maintain the correct balance of water and salts within their cells—without which the cells would collapse, or swell up and rupture or die.

In defense, the leukocytes (white blood cells), mostly produced together with the red cells and platelets in the bone marrow, are vital in combating infection. The *neutrophil leukocytes* directly attack bacteria invading the body and remove the debris of dead bacteria and damaged cells resulting from infection. The *lymphocytes* produce antibodies which act as specific chemical "antidotes" to invading bacteria and viruses and their

BLOOD FILM

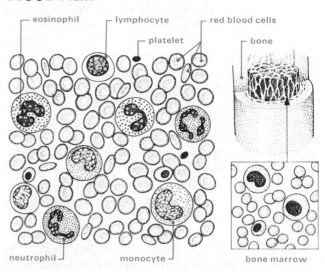

This drawing of a blood film gives an idea of the various cells a hematologist might see when he looks at blood under a microscope. In fact, not all the different types shown here would be present in any one sample. All these blood cells are derived from large primitive cells in the bone marrow.

products, helping to overcome their initial attack and to provide a lasting immunity to further attacks.

Finally, when body tissues are damaged and bleeding occurs, the blood flow through the tissues ensures a continuing supply of platelets and blood clotting factors carried in the plasma which will allow blood clotting to occur and thus control the bleeding.

See also AGGLUTINATION, AGRANULOCYTOSIS, ANEMIA, ANTIBODY, BLOOD CLOTTING, BLOOD GROUPS, BLOOD PRESSURE, BLOOD TRANSFUSION, CELL, CYANOSIS, ERYTHROCYTE SEDIMENTATION RATE, HEMORRHAGE, ISCHEMIA, LEUKEMIA, PHAGOCYTOSIS, PLATELETS, POLYCYTHEMIA, PULSE, RH FACTOR, SEPTICEMIA.

blood clotting

When a blood vessel is damaged, control of the resulting hemorrhage involves first the spontaneous contraction of the muscular wall of the vessel to reduce the flow and then clotting of the blood in the vessel and the wound.

The end result of clotting is the conversion of liquid blood to the familiar gelatinous, red material of a blood clot. This takes place by the conversion of a soluble protein material in the blood, *fibrinogen*, to insoluble *fibrin*—which is deposited in fine strands in which the red and white cells become enmeshed to form a clot.

The first step toward this end result is taken when the continuity of the wall of a blood vessel is interrupted by an injury (or when a blood sample removed from a vein is placed in a laboratory test tube). The lining membrane of the blood vessels allows blood to remain in close contact with it without change in its cells or chemical constituents. As soon as a vessel is damaged, however, contact is established between the blood and other tissues and blood clotting is initiated.

Platelets (cellular components of the blood which play an essential role in clotting) adhere to the damaged area and liberate chemical substances which set in motion a complex chain reaction involving a dozen or more protein constituents of the blood. (There are more than 15 million platelets in a single drop of blood.) Each of these constituents exists in two forms, an inactive precursor and an active material derived from it. The chain reaction is thus seen as a "cascade" or "domino" phenomenon in which activation of one factor by a chemical derived from damaged platelets leads to its conversion to its active form. This in turn will activate the next chemical in the chain, and so on, until the reaction is complete.

The final stages involve the conversion of the protein *prothrombin* to *thrombin;* this substance can convert fibrinogen to fibrin, leading to the formation of a blood clot as described above.

THROMBOSIS is a condition in which blood clots within an intact blood vessel. This may be associated with an abnormal slowing of the circulation (as in a patient restricted to bed following major surgery) or with various changes in the clotting factors or platelets. (See also EMBOLUS.)

The normal mechanism of blood clotting is disturbed in certain disorders (mostly notably HEMOPHILIA, an inherited defect of the clotting mechanism), which exposes the patient to the danger of uncontrolled bleeding—even after what in most people would be a relatively minor injury. Various diseases or disorders that affect the bone marrow (where blood cells are produced) may lead to an underproduction of platelets or an abnormally low quantity in the circulation (a condition known as THROMBOCYTOPENIA).

blood groups

The first human blood groups were discovered in 1900 by Karl Landsteiner (1868–1943). He described the separation of human blood cells into four classes, A, B, AB and O—which we now know as the *ABO blood groups.*

Characterization of these ABO blood groups depends not only on the detection of specific characteristics on the surface of the red cells of each group (*antigens*) but on the presence in the plasma (the liquid portion of the blood) of characteristic *antibodies* which are capable of clumping together (agglutinating) red cells of a specific group. Thus, persons of group A have in their plasma an

antibody (agglutinin) which agglutinates cells of group B (anti-B), while those of group B have the complementary agglutinin (anti-A) which reacts with A cells. Those of group O have both anti-A and anti-B in the plasma, but their cells are agglutinated by neither of these agglutinins. Those of group AB have no agglutinins in the plasma but their cells will obviously be agglutinated by both anti-A and anti-B agglutinins. In general, there will be no agglutinin in the plasma acting against the subject's own cells since the agglutination in circulation which would result from such a situation would be incompatible with life.

For many years it was thought that the ABO groups were the only groups that existed; but when, during World War I, some steps were taken to use Landsteiner's discovery to provide BLOOD TRANSFUSION to combat blood loss, it soon became apparent that the situation was more complex. While the ABO system remains the most important for transfusion purposes, many more blood group factors have now been demonstrated—including rare subgroups of the ABO system, the important "Rhesus groups" and others (such as the "MNS system"). The last two systems differ from the ABO system in that no corresponding agglutinins occur naturally in the blood but only appear as a result of blood transfusion or pregnancy involving a blood group differing from the patient's own group. Progress in understanding various blood group factors was initially slow; the Rhesus groups, for example, were not discovered until 1940. (See RH FACTOR.)

The blood groups are inheritable characteristics, passed from parents to their children and following the Mendelian laws of inheritance.

Today, the blood groups are of importance not only in blood transfusion work but also in the establishment of paternity and in forensic pathology. Lastly, since different blood groups have widely different frequencies in different races, they are of great interest to the anthropologist.

blood poisoning

See SEPTICEMIA.

blood pressure

Blood pressure is normally defined in terms of the *systolic* pressure, which is the maximum pressure produced in the larger arteries by each heartbeat (see SYSTOLE), and the *diastolic* pressure, which is the constant pressure maintained in the arteries between heartbeats (see DIASTOLE). The blood pressure, measured by means of a SPHYGMOMANOMETER, is expressed in millimeters of mercury. The "textbook normal" figure for the systolic pressure is 120 millimeters and for the diastolic 80 millimeters, usually expressed in abbreviated form as 120/80 ("one-twenty over eighty").

Many people have a blood pressure reading that is slightly below the average. This is normally no cause for concern.

It is important to realize that no fixed value exists for the blood pressure and that the "standard" figure of 120/80 is really the average of a fairly wide range. In a group of normal individuals, few will have a blood pressure of exactly 120/80. In a single individual, considerable fluctuations in blood pressure will occur from minute to minute, from hour to hour, and from day to day. The figure may be affected by rest, exercise, emotion or anxiety; the normal range typically widens with increasing age.

When a physician measures your blood pressure, he is unlikely to accept the first figure he obtains if it is at all raised, since anxiety about your visit to him may have considerably affected the reading. He may ask you to wait a few minutes (either sitting down or lying down) before taking it again, or may ask you to return on another day for a check. Only when he has decided that your blood pressure is constantly raised above an acceptable figure for your age, and that this is causing or is likely to cause symptoms, will he decide that you suffer from high blood pressure (hypertension) and initiate the appropriate treatment.

High blood pressure may be a primary disease entity (*essential hypertension*) or a symptom of a number of disorders affecting the kidneys (*renovascular hypertension*), blood vessels, or the adrenal glands. It may also be an unwanted side effect of drug treatment for other diseases.

Whatever the cause, the symptoms are extremely variable. In some cases, the pressure may be appreciably raised for many years without any notable symptoms. Headache, particularly in the early morning, may occur as well as giddiness—especially on a sudden change of posture. There may be palpitations and shortness of breath on exertion and changes in eyesight, with blurring of vision in one or both eyes. The patient may need to get up with increasing frequency during the night to pass urine. If the raised blood pressure is the result of another disease, such as kidney failure, the symptoms may be predominantly those of the underlying disease rather than a direct effect of the raised blood pressure.

The main effects of raised blood pressure involve the heart and blood vessels. High blood pressure is one of the major risk factors in the development of *coronary thrombosis* (also known as *myocardial infarction* or "heart attack") and coronary artery disease. It is also an important factor in the development of a STROKE, whether caused by brain hemorrhage or blood clots in the blood vessels of the brain. Taking the blood pressure is therefore an important part of any medical examination.

If treatment is necessary, the first step will involve tests to ensure that the disorder is not a symptom of kidney damage or some other disease. (If such a disease is found, obviously it will be treated.) Attention will then be given to other risk factors for the development of coronary artery disease, such as cigarette smoking, obesity or a high intake of animal fat in the diet (see CHOLESTEROL). Reduction in weight alone will often produce a fall in blood pressure and also a fall in blood levels of fat. If stress or anxiety is present, a change in life style or the use of tranquilizing drugs may be sufficient to control the disorder in mild cases.

If these measures fail to bring the blood pressure within normal limits for the individual, specific treatment will be required. Before any is given, it will be important to decide whether the patient has recently had a rise in blood pressure which is now causing symptoms or whether the blood pressure, particularly in elderly patients, has been raised for many years. In this latter group of patients there is frequently hardening and narrowing of the arteries (ARTERIOSCLEROSIS), particularly those supplying the brain, and the circulation is maintained at adequate levels only by the increased blood pressure. A sudden reduction in blood pressure may actually be harmful and the patient may become confused, unsteady and even mildly demented as the result of a poor blood supply to the brain.

The first line of treatment involves a simple reduction of the volume of circulating blood, which will in turn lower the blood pressure. This is achieved by giving a *diuretic* drug, which causes the kidneys to pass more urine. In some cases this, together with other measures (such as weight reduction), may be all that is required. If not, specific drugs that act to lower the blood pressure will be required. Many such drugs are now available and their action exerts a direct effect on the heart and blood vessels. They can often be usefully combined with a diuretic drug. The best choice of drugs is sometimes difficult and the physician may have to try several before he is satisfied that he has selected the one most suitable for an individual patient.

Unfortunately, these drugs are not always free from unwanted side effects. They may be responsible for producing giddiness on sudden changes of posture (postural hypotension), diarrhea, depression and (occasionally, in men) impotence. For this reason the decision to initiate treatment may be difficult; it is important for the doctor to ensure that the drug side effects have not been added to the patient's other symptoms without significant benefit in other ways.

See also the major articles on **Hypertension, Cardiology** and **Drugs and Medicines.**

blood transfusion

The discovery at the beginning of the 20th century of the ABO BLOOD GROUPS made possible for the first time the safe transfusion of blood to patients who would otherwise have died of hemorrhage. Previous attempts to give randomly selected blood had usually led to disastrous consequences, although occasional success had been achieved by chance.

Blood for transfusion is today provided by national blood transfusion organizations and by the blood banks of large hospitals, where it is collected from donors and stored. Blood is drawn from donors into sterile bottles or plastic bags containing chemicals to prevent clotting (anticoagulants). A maximum of 500 milliliters every six months is usually considered safe for donors.

Blood is administered through a special plastic bag (drip set) connected to a needle or plastic cannula placed in a vein in the arm. The rate of administration varies with the needs of the recipient, but in routine cases 500 milliliters will be given over two or three hours.

All blood for transfusion is ABO and Rhesus (RH) typed. Except in grave emergencies, blood of the patient's own ABO and Rhesus type is always used and direct compatibility tests performed between the blood of the donor and the recipient. See also RH FACTOR.

Modern transfusion practice involves much more than the routine provision of "whole" blood for transfusion. This is basically a wasteful procedure since whole blood contains many valuable components, only some of which are required by the individual patient. Thus a severely anemic patient may need red blood cells but not the plasma in which the cells are suspended and this can be separated before the blood is used, leaving "packed red cells." Other patients specifically require platelets or clotting factors from the plasma or specific protein fractions containing antibodies against infectious diseases (or whole plasma in the case of severe burns). It is increasingly likely that the individual patient will receive packed cells, platelet concentrates, plasma or clotting factor concentrates rather than whole donor blood. This results in a great economy in the use of this scarce and expensive material.

In some cases (as in the treatment of "hemolytic disease of the newborn") whole blood will be used in a procedure known as an *exchange transfusion*—in which all or most of the patient's blood is periodically replaced with donor blood.

See also *The Hematologist* in the major article on **Specialists You Seldom See.**

boil

A painful red swelling in the skin (also known as a *furuncle*) caused by bacterial infection of a hair follicle

BLOOD TRANSFUSION

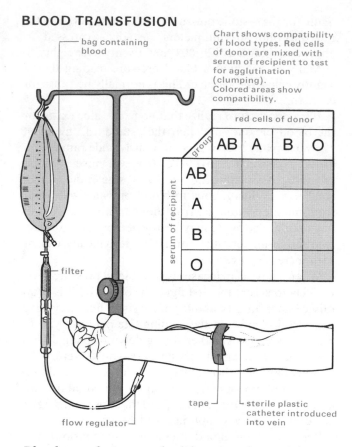

Chart shows compatibility of blood types. Red cells of donor are mixed with serum of recipient to test for agglutination (clumping). Colored areas show compatibility.

Blood transfusion can be lifesaving, but stringent checks are necessary before it is performed. The first step is to determine the patient's major blood group (AB, A, B, or O) and Rh (Rhesus) type so that possible donor blood can be selected. Before every transfusion, the blood is "cross matched" as an extra precaution—a sample of the recipient's serum is mixed with the donor's red blood cells to check that they do not agglutinate.

or sweat gland. Infection is usually caused by staphylococci, bacteria which are normally found on the skin. Boils are unusual unless there is some additional factor to provoke infection. This may be an underlying disease (such as diabetes) or it can be simple friction, which is why boils occur around the neck, on the forearms and on the seat.

The first sign of a boil is a red swelling which may be painful and cause itching. In some cases the boil will go no further and will subside after two or three days. But the more usual course is that after about six or seven days the swollen boil bursts and releases pus.

It is important to treat boils because an untreated one can lead to the development of further boils or to generalized septicemia (blood poisoning).

The new synthetic penicillins are the drugs of choice against staphylococcal infection.

bone

The substance of which the skeleton is made—a mixture of calcium carbonate, calcium phosphate and fibrous tissue. There are more than 200 bones in the human skeleton, made up of "compact" and "cancellous" bone. Compact bone, found in the shafts of the limb bones, consists of a hard tube surrounded by a membrane (*periosteum*) and enclosing a fatty substance (*bone marrow*). Cancellous bone forms the short bones and the ends of the long bones and has a fine lacework structure (it is also called "spongy" bone).

Bone is a living tissue and even the most dense is "tunneled" by fine canals in which there are small blood vessels, nerves and lymphatics, by which the bones are maintained and repaired. In children the bones include a plate of cartilage in which growth occurs; in the long bones (such as the femur and humerus) this "growth plate" is at one end only, the "growing end." At the end of puberty bone replaces the cartilage, the long bones cease growing, and the skeleton no longer increases in size.

Bone is repaired by cells of microscopic size. One type, the *osteoblast*, lays down strands of fibrous tissue between which calcium salts are deposited from the

BONE

section of femur

enlarged cross section of compact bone

Bone is a combination of mineral salts and fibrous material which is very resistant to mechanical stresses. The upper end of the femur, or thighbone, has a strongly developed meshwork of "spongy" bone designed to transmit the weight of the body. The shaft of the femur consists of "compact" bone, able to resist bending because of its structure—concentric rings of bony tissue.

blood. The other, the *osteoclast*, dissolves and breaks down dead or damaged bone. These processes occur when a bone is broken. The skeletal bones not only determine the body's "architecture," but are also vital because it is in the marrow of cancellous bone that new red blood cells are constantly formed.

botulism

A dramatic, life-threatening illness caused by the bacterium *Clostridium botulinum*. This microbe produces a toxin which is absorbed from the intestine.

Clostridium botulinum occurs in soil, in watery environments such as the sea bed, and in fish and many other animals. The disease is acquired from contaminated food which has not been heated to at least 250°F (121°C), the temperature at which the organism is killed. Thus, smoked or lightly cooked or raw food may be responsible. Home-preserved vegetables are the most frequent cause in the United States.

Outside the body, the organism is in spore form, which does not cause disease even when it contaminates fresh food; the spores must have germinated and actually produced toxin. The toxin is quickly absorbed from the intestine. Within 36 hours there are gastrointestinal symptoms of nausea, vomiting and abdominal pain, as well as weakness and unsteadiness. The nervous system is then attacked by the toxin resulting in blurred vision, difficulty in swallowing, muscular weakness of the arms and legs and potentially much more serious—paralysis of the muscles used in breathing.

Treatment of botulism is mainly directed toward preservation of lung function by use of a respirator, if necessary. Antitoxin is also given and a drug called guanidine has proved of some value. In spite of this, the disease is fatal in up to 65% of cases.

bowel and bowel movements

The intestinal tract—the basically hollow tube which extends from the stomach to the anus—has a total length of approximately 25 ft., although its length in life varies considerably with the contraction or relaxation of the muscle fibers in its wall. The main sections are the *small intestine*—comprising, from above downwards, the *duodenum*, *jejunum* and *ileum* (together, approximately 20 ft. in length) —and the *large intestine* or *colon* (about 5ft. in length).

The duodenum, the shortest section, is only 12 in. or so long; it is slightly wider in diameter (1½ in.) than the remainder of the small intestine. The jejunum forms about two-fifths of the small intestine (about 5 ft.) while the ileum is the longest segment (about 14 ft.); both are approximately 1 in. in diameter.

The colon ("large bowel") is the part of the intestinal

BOWEL

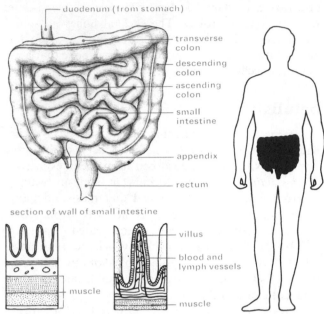

The bowel, or intestine, is a long muscular tube where food is digested and absorbed, and waste material travels to the rectum to be excreted as feces. The magnified sections of small intestine show the folds, or villi, which are important for absorption of nutrients into the blood.

tract usually referred to when the term "bowel" alone is used. It varies in diameter from about 1 to 3 in.

The whole of the small intestine and the greater part of the colon is supported in the abdomen by a membrane (*mesentery*), which is attached to the back wall of the abdominal cavity and carries in it the blood vessels and nerves which supply the intestines.

The function of the intestinal tract is to digest food particles introduced into it from the stomach, to allow the essential nutrients broken down into simpler compounds by the act of digestion to be absorbed into the bloodstream (this occurs mainly in the small intestine), and to excrete the unwanted residue from the body. Waste products are largely deprived of their water content in the large intestine (the water is reabsorbed into the body—and then formed into the semisolid mass known as feces (or "stools").

The intestinal tract has three coats: (1) the *mucosal membrane*, which lines it throughout; (2) the *muscular coat*, which surrounds the mucosa; and (3) the outer *serosal coat*, which is in fact part of the *peritoneum* (the smooth, moist membrane which lines the entire abdominal cavity).

The mucosal membrane both secretes digestive juices and allows absorption of the products of digestion to take place. Its surface area is greatly increased by its

being thrown into innumerable folds running around the bowel wall. In the small intestine, its surface can be seen under a microscope to be densely covered with minute "finger-like" processes (the *villi*), which measure about half a millimeter in length. The presence of these villi produces a further enormous increase in the surface area available for absorption—as is well seen when, as a result of disease, they are destroyed and absorption becomes severely impaired (see CELIAC DISEASE and MALABSORPTION). The mucosal cells also secrete digestive juices which act in combination with those produced by the salivary glands, stomach, liver and pancreas.

The muscular coat of the bowel consists of two layers—one of circular fibers, the other of longitudinal fibers. This allows it to contract both in diameter and in length. The essential wavelike movement of the bowel is called *peristalsis*; it moves food material down the bowel as digestion proceeds. A ring of contraction appears at one point in the bowel, producing a narrowing; this contraction ring then passes down· the length of the bowel, literally squeezing the fluid contents along before it, while the muscle wall relaxes again after the wave of contraction has passed. For the most part, we are not aware of this process; however, if there is gas as well as fluid in the bowel, we may be aware of gurgling noises or sensations of intestinal activity as peristalsis occurs. If the bowel is irritated or inflamed, the contractions become more vigorous and may be painful.

The contents of the small intestine are fluid; but on entering the colon, water is progressively absorbed until by the time the rectum is reached they are converted to semisolid (though normally soft) feces. These accumulate in the rectum until increasing distension produces a desire to open the bowels (defecation). The ring of muscle which controls the anus (anal sphincter) relaxes and contraction of the muscular walls of the rectum causes the feces to be passed. In most persons a bowel movement occurs once or sometimes twice daily, but there are wide variations dependent on diet and other factors. There is absolutely nothing abnormal about having a bowel movement only once every two or three days, providing this is regular and achieved without difficulty.

See also DIGESTION, CONSTIPATION, DIARRHEA and the major articles on **Nutrition** and **Gastroenterology.** For a discussion of appropriate drugs see also the sections on *Drugs for diarrhea* and *Drugs for constipation* in the major article on **Drugs and Medicines.**

bowleg

Bowleg is an outward bending of the legs. It is common during infancy and requires no treatment or undue concern unless the condition persists. A normal posture occurs after the child has been walking for about one year. But abnormal bowleg may arise in various conditions where growth is disturbed, such as rickets or OSTEOGENESIS IMPERFECTA.

If the bowlegged state of infancy does not improve spontaneously or if other disease is clearly evident, or if the infant is not developing normally, then further investigation is necessary.

There is a rare condition, the result of intrauterine deformity, in which congenital dislocation of the knee is present at birth. The resulting bowleg deformity is avoided by immediate treatment.

Another condition that causes severe bowing of the legs is known as *tibia vara*. It occurs mainly in infants but is sometimes seen in adolescents, particularly those from the West Indies and West Africa. The bone deformity, which is present at the upper end of the tibia (shinbone), may be due to the laxity of the ligaments in these races and their custom to walk earlier. The condition cannot be confused with the normal bowleg of infancy because it fails to improve and requires surgical correction.

See also KNOCK-KNEE.

BOWLEG AND KNOCK-KNEE

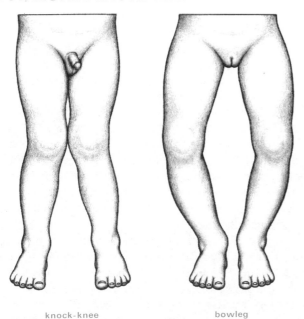

knock-knee   bowleg

Most young babies have bowleg but the condition corrects itself when they begin to walk. Very rarely, if the deformity persists, it may be necessary for the child to wear corrective splints at night. A mild degree of knock-knee is also very common in children under 6 years of age and only needs active treatment if it is severe. Either of these deformities in adults can result from trauma, rickets, and Paget's disease.

bradycardia

A slowing of the heart rate below 60 beats per minute. It can be a normal occurrence in fit young people at rest or during sleep (especially among well-trained athletes) and results from the inhibitory action of the vagus nerve (the Xth cranial nerve). In other circumstances bradycardia may be a sign of acute myocardial infarction ("heart attack"), depressant drug action (from the administration of drugs such as digitalis, morphine, reserpine, propranolol or prostigmine), low blood volume (as the result of internal bleeding or severe fluid depletion), heart block, or the ADAMS-STOKES SYNDROME.

In most cases bradycardia requires no treatment. However, in patients who have persistent symptoms of lightheadedness, fainting, angina pectoris, or congestive heart failure as the consequence of an abnormally low heart rate or insufficient acceleration of the heart under conditions of stress, an artificial PACEMAKER may be required. Compare TACHYCARDIA.

brain

The control center of the central nervous system, enclosed and protected by the skull.

More than 10 billion cells in the brain receive and transmit messages to and from all parts of the body; they filter, store and form associations between information received through the senses. The brain is often compared with a computer, but is thousands of times more complex than any existing electronic circuitry.

During fetal development the top end of the spinal cord thickens and expands to form distinct areas within the brain. Broadly speaking, the "higher" the center in the brain the more complex its function, culminating in intelligent or "cerebral" behavior.

A diffuse network of cells and fibers called the *reticular activating system* (RAS) extends through the core of the brain stem from the top of the spinal cord up into the hypothalamus. The RAS is the seat of consciousness and governs the states of sleep, arousal and attention. The RAS and the higher centers of the cerebral cortex have extensive two-way connections so that their levels of activity are mutually controlled.

At the back of the skull is the *cerebellum*, which coordinates reflex actions that control posture, balance and muscular activity. Deep within the brain, where the brain mass seems to tip forward, is the center for basic or "uncritical" appreciation of pain, temperature and crude touch—the *thalamus*. It is the main relay center for incoming sensory impulses (except those of smell), which it transmits to other parts of the brain, including those concerned with consciousness. Vital automatic functions, such as blood pressure, blood circulation, heartbeat, and hormone secretion are in part regulated by the *hypothalamus*, which is situated just below the thalamus (as its name implies). It also plays an important role in the experiencing of basic drives, such as hunger, thirst and sex.

Above and billowing out to fill the skull are the convoluted *cerebral hemispheres*, where the nerve centers exist that are responsible for conscious thought and action. In man, this part of the brain (the cerebrum) is larger in relation to total body weight than in any other animal. A dense layer of nerve cells—the *gray matter* of the cerebral cortex—forms the active "roof" of the brain. Deeper within the cerebrum are insulated nerve fibers of these cells, which intermingle to form the *white matter*.

Distinct areas have been mapped out for many voluntary movements and for sensations from most parts of the body. But the brain's "computer" activity, which is responsible for functions such as reason and memory, is basically a mystery. Indeed, experts still understand little about the phenomenon of consciousness itself.

See also the major article on **Neurology**.

BRAIN

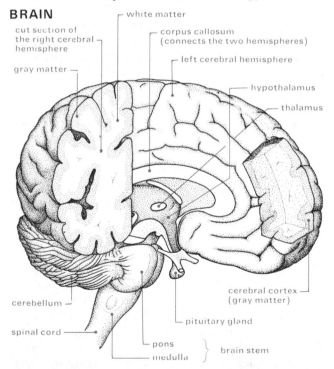

white matter

cut section of the right cerebral hemisphere

corpus callosum (connects the two hemispheres)

gray matter

left cerebral hemisphere

hypothalamus

thalamus

cerebral cortex (gray matter)

pituitary gland

cerebellum

spinal cord

pons
medulla } brain stem

The drawing shows the important structures of the human brain. Centers in the brain stem control the heart and breathing. The cerebellum smooths out our movements. The thalamus relays signals to and from the cerebral cortex, the thin layer of gray matter. The hypothalamus is concerned with "instinctive drives" and with emotions: it has intimate connections with the pituitary gland, controlling the body's hormones.

brain death

Brain death is a relatively new concept. It occurs when there is: (1) a prolonged failure of the brain to show any evidence of electrical activity (as indicated by electroencephalography); (2) absence of general neurological activity (manifested by fixed pupils, absence of spontaneous breathing, absence of any response to painful stimuli, etc.); (3) a prolonged state of deep unconsciousness. Head injury and brain hemorrhage are the most likely causes.

There has been deep public concern over brain death, especially accompanying controversial cases of patients in prolonged comas where relatives have wished to switch off life-support machines.

One view is that to switch off is to "allow" a patient to die, not that he has already died. Another is that indecision over death deprives people of dying with dignity, as when intensive care supports a vegetable-like body with an irreversibly damaged brain.

The informed consensus which now governs much of medical practice (although there are still controversial cases) is that if two or more doctors are convinced that brain death has occurred then the respirator (and other life-support equipment) should be switched off.

brain tumor

An abnormal growth in any part of the brain.

Brain tumors may be benign or malignant (cancerous). Unfortunately many are malignant, and these may be primary or secondary—that is, originating in the brain or caused by the spread of cancer cells from another part of the body.

The tumors may appear at any age. As they grow within the enclosed space of the skull they have little room for expansion against the delicate brain cells. Therefore, even quite small tumors in the brain may have serious consequences. As with many growths, the cause is usually unknown.

The gradually increasing pressure in the brain tissue causes many general symptoms. A dull nagging headache and vomiting are common. With some tumors, convulsions may sometimes precede other symptoms. Mental changes may occur, such as drowsiness, lethargy and possibly a change in the personality. Other symptoms depend on the part of the brain affected—for example, partial paralysis, dimming of vision or possibly speech problems.

Diagnosis involves specialized x-rays, lumbar puncture, and EEG tests. In recent years the advent of computerized x-ray scanning of the brain has improved diagnosis. It gives earlier diagnosis and a more accurate picture of the tumor than was possible in the past.

Treatment is mainly surgical; for benign tumors this

may be quite successful. In cases of malignant tumors, however, a permanent cure is difficult to achieve, although surgery may relieve the symptoms. Radiotherapy and drugs may play a subordinate therapeutic role.

See also the major article on **Neurosurgery.**

breast

The mammary, or milk-secreting, gland.

It was originally a sweat gland but has developed during evolution. It is also a potent sexual symbol with an important erotic function.

The breasts develop slowly under the influence of hormones during puberty. Each breast consists chiefly of fibrous tissue radiating from the nipple and dividing it into 15 to 20 lobes. Under hormonal control, these lobes produce milk following delivery of a baby. Each lobe has many small ducts draining into a main duct, which finally emerges as a tiny opening on the surface of the nipple. Just under the nipple these ducts dilate, forming reservoirs of milk during feeding. Pressure by the infant's mouth on the areola, the distinct circle of dark skin surrounding the nipple, causes milk to be ejected from the 15 to 20 ducts.

Surrounding the glandular tissue is a large pad of fat cells which give the breast its shape. The entire breast mass extends over a large area, reaching up into the armpit. (Thus, the importance of thorough feeling during self-examination of the breasts for early signs of cancer.)

There are no muscles in the breasts; if they lose their youthful firmness, exercise is unlikely to restore it. Despite the vagaries of fashion and the women's liberation movement, many women find that they do prefer to wear a brassiere—both for the sake of comfort and, hopefully, to ward off stretching and sagging. Support is especially important during pregnancy.

Throughout pregnancy the breasts become fuller. This and tingling nipples are, for many women, among the first indications of pregnancy. The areola itself may further darken, especially in dark-haired women.

Although boyish figures are promoted as fashionable, many women worry if their breasts are very small. Little can be done to enlarge breasts without expensive plastic surgery. Expensive creams and massage are virtually worthless. But size tends to increase after the age of 35 or so, chiefly due to fat being deposited in the breast.

Ideal size and shape of the breasts vary among different cultures as well as among individuals. Polynesians are said to admire small conical breasts, while North American Indians admire elongated drooping breasts.

See also BREAST CANCER, BREAST FEEDING, MAMMOPLASTY and MASTECTOMY.

breast cancer

Most of the great variety of tumors or growths which may occur in the female breast are not cancerous. Nevertheless, it is essential to seek immediate medical attention at the first sign of any suspicious changes or abnormalities in the breast since early diagnosis and treatment of breast cancer can be life-saving. Breast cancer continues to be the most common form of cancer in women—especially in those between the ages of about 40 to 45—and claims approximately 30,000 lives annually in the United States alone.

Despite massive worldwide research efforts to discover the possible causes of breast cancer in women and to evaluate the best methods of medical and surgical treatment, little significant progress has been made within the past 30 years. Indeed, great controversy still exists within the medical profession regarding the best method of treating various forms of breast cancer.

Experts are aware that the risk of breast cancer is highest among unmarried women with no pregnancies and who began their menstrual cycles at a relatively early age. But the obvious suggestion that this is definitely linked to prolonged exposure to high levels of ESTROGENS during menstrual cycles over many years (unrelieved by becoming pregnant) has not been substantiated scientifically. Objective evidence still does not exist that the female hormones contained in oral contraceptives (the "Pill") increase the incidence of breast cancer; indeed what evidence there is suggests that the Pill may even protect against breast cancer. Likewise, women receiving estrogen therapy have not been definitely proved to be more susceptible to cancer of the breast. In both cases, however, these possibilities are still being investigated in long-term research studies.

What *has* been shown to be true—even though the reasons are unclear—is that breast cancer is more common (1) in women in the higher socioeconomic classes; (2) in those with a family history of the disease; (3) in those with previous disease of the breast (regardless of the cause); (4) in single women who have not been pregnant; and (5) in those whose first menstrual cycles started at or before the age of 12. For some unexplained reason, breast cancer is also more common among Jewish women than among non-Jewish women. It is also more common in Western women than in Asiatics such as the Japanese. It is relatively rare in women below the age of 25, reaching its highest incidence just before, during, or after the MENOPAUSE (the "change of life").

Among the possible causes of breast cancer which have been extensively investigated is some form of viral infection. (Experiments have clearly demonstrated that certain viruses can cause mammary cancer in mice—animals which provide an important "model" of the

BREAST SELF-EXAMINATION

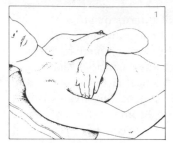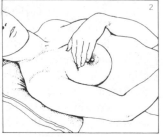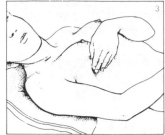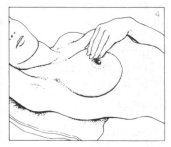

Most breast lumps are not cancerous, but any woman discovering a lump should consult a doctor. The correct method of self-examination is shown above. Feel with the flats of the fingers, not the tips (1). Start with the upper outer quadrant of the breast and remember it extends up into the armpit (2). Then examine the remainder of the outer half and underside of the breast (3). Feel around the nipple and gently roll the inner half of the breast over the ribs (4). Self-examination should be performed monthly because treatment is more successful in the early stages of breast cancer.

human form of the disease.) Another possibility under current investigation is the part played by diet. A popular belief exists among many women that a blow to the chest may be responsible for the subsequent development of breast cancer; this has never been substantiated, however, and it is generally thought that such a cause is most unlikely. (Breast cancer in men is an extremely rare disease.)

Warning signs. Among the warning signs of breast cancer are: (1) the appearance of any unusual lump or nodule in either breast (which may or may not be a harmless cyst or other benign growth); (2) changes in the nipple, either by alterations in position or by retraction ("inverted nipples"); (3) puckering of the skin on the breast; (4) bleeding or other discharges from the nipple; (5) an unusual rash on the breast or nipple; and (6) an unusual prominence of veins over the breast (however, in pregnant women this is fairly common). Many women may have one or more of these symptoms without having cancer. But because of the rapid growth of many breast cancers, medical attention must be obtained immediately—especially if any unusual lump is evident.

Self-examination. Many experts recommend monthly self-examination of the breasts. This can be performed while standing or sitting in front of a mirror or even while taking a shower. However, it is desirable to observe the shape of the breasts in a mirror in addition to feeling for any abnormal changes in the consistency of the breast tissues. The visual examination should be

made first with the arms raised and then with the arms hanging loosely by the sides. The light should fall evenly on the chest from the front, which will aid in recognizing any dimpling of the skin or changes in the size or shape of the breasts. About 95% of all women with breast cancer seek medical attention after discovering some abnormality or suspicious change as the result of self-examination. It is best to conduct this examination on or about the same day each month, preferably when the breasts are softest (after the menstrual period).

Note any changes of the shape with the arms upstretched, then feel every part of the breasts and up into the armpits for any lumps or changes (see illustration). Lumps may well be painless but should not be ignored.

Breast cancer may also be diagnosed at an early stage—before any lump can be detected—by regular screening using x-rays (MAMMOGRAPHY) or infrared imaging (THERMOGRAPHY). At present this form of SCREENING is recommended for women in high-risk groups and for all women aged over 50.

Treatment. Treatment of breast cancer may involve a combination of surgery (see MASTECTOMY), irradiation and drug therapy. The choice of therapy will depend largely on the extent of invasion of the breast and surrounding tissues with cancer cells. In some cases it may be possible to remove a small lump or nodule of cancerous tissue without removing the entire breast (a procedure known as a *lumpectomy*). In other cases, where the cancer cells have spread to involve the lymph nodes of the armpit and surrounding areas, it may be necessary to remove the breast and the underlying muscles, as well as tissues nearby which have become invaded by cancer cells (*radical mastectomy*). Between these two extremes, it may only be necessary to remove all or most of the affected breast without recourse to removing other tissues (*simple mastectomy*).

There is no general agreement regarding the best combination of therapy for the treatment of breast cancer. Some experts believe that the possible spread of cancer cells can be controlled following mastectomy by exposure of the tissues to x-rays (*irradiation therapy*). Other experts at treating breast cancers believe that the use of anticancer ("cytotoxic") drugs may be a possible alternative to radical mastectomy, although the research studies designed to answer that question are not yet complete. The aim of this *adjuvant chemotherapy* is the destruction of any small "satellites" of cancer cells in the bones, the liver or other organs remote from the breast.

Alternative means of treating breast cancer are currently being investigated, such as the administration of a vaccine ordinarily used for the prevention of tuberculosis. This vaccine, known as *BCG* (bacille Calmette-Guérin), stimulates the production of antibodies that in some cases are thought to destroy cancer cells. At present, however, such attempts to stimulate the body's immunological defense system (*immunotherapy*) in the control of breast cancer remains only a possibility.

The outlook for treatment of breast cancer remains guarded but there are some hopeful trends. Publicity and the growth of screening programs have encouraged women to seek treatment earlier, and the breast tumors removed by surgeons are now on average substantially smaller than ten years ago. The combination of early treatment and adjuvant chemotherapy should improve the cure rate in the next decade.

See also the major article on **Oncology**.

breast feeding

The natural way to feed small babies.

In this century breast feeding has largely been abandoned in affluent countries in favor of bottles. The use of a special formula of cow's milk, in bottles, is becoming widespread in developing nations. Pediatricians are trying to reverse this worrying trend. They are encouraging mothers to give their babies the advantages of breast milk for some time, even if only for a few weeks.

A chief advantage is that, not only does it give the baby some digestible milk proteins, but breast milk protects against infections such as gastroenteritis and pneumonia during the first few months of life when the baby's own immune system is immature. Immunity is passed from mother to baby through the milk. Breast-fed babies are also thought less likely to become overweight. There is some speculation that breast feeding may also protect against heart disease in later life. And it is also theorized that babies who have nonhuman milk early in life are more liable to develop allergies.

Suckling helps to develop close emotional links between mother and baby, demonstrated by the fact that a baby's cry a few rooms away will cause a "let down" of the mother's milk. Nursing also stimulates release of a hormone from the hypothalamus in the brain which aids the shrinking of the uterus back to normal size following childbirth.

Breast size is immaterial to successful feeding. Even quite flat-chested women may manage to feed twins. During pregnancy, the glandular tissue of the breast proliferates in readiness for lactation. When the baby suckles, the hormone oxytocin is released from the pituitary gland and stimulates milk production.

During the first few days, the breasts secrete small amounts of a thick yellow fluid known as colostrum—quite adequate for the baby, which has its own initial reserves of food—after which the milk "comes in."

The modern trend is to feed babies "on demand" and allow them to establish their own feeding pattern. A continued flow of milk depends upon the demands made by the baby. When the baby is weaned, the falloff in the sucking stimulus means that less milk is produced; eventually, the flow ceases.

Most women who want to feed successfully can do so. Worry, emotional upset and illness are major reasons why milk may fail. However, it is no failure if a woman is unable to feed her baby. Hundreds of thousands of happy adults were bottle fed.

Bright's disease

A somewhat vague or imprecise term for chronic inflammation of the kidney (nephritis), accompanied by proteinuria (the abnormal presence of protein in the urine). In modern medical terminology it is basically equivalent to GLOMERULONEPHRITIS.

The disease was named after the English physician Richard Bright (1789–1858), who described it in 1827.

bronchiectasis

A chronic condition in which one or more of the main airways in the lungs (bronchi) lose their elasticity and become permanently dilated. Mucus secretions collect in the damaged section of lung and secondary bacterial infection is a common complication. The disease is characterized by severe bouts of coughing early in the day as the sufferer tries to bring up the infected sputum.

Bronchiectasis may be associated with a congenital defect in the lung. More usually it occurs after pneumonia or some other infection, especially whooping cough. Bronchiectasis is also common in the genetic disorder CYSTIC FIBROSIS (mucoviscidosis), in which the mucus secreted by the lungs is excessively thick and sticky.

However, with antibiotic treatment readily available for prompt treatment of respiratory conditions, damage is less likely to occur than it once was. In very severe cases, but where damage is confined, an affected lobe of the lung may be removed surgically.

For additional information see also the major article on **Pulmonary Diseases**.

bronchitis

Inflammation of the air passages of the lung. Bronchitis may be acute or chronic.

Acute bronchitis very often follows a cold or an attack of influenza, for bacterial infection is facilitated by viral inflammation.

First the windpipe (trachea) becomes inflamed; then infection spreads through the bronchial tree to reach the larger air passages (bronchi) and so into the smaller bronchioles. In a severe or untreated case, inflammation may spread into the lung tissue itself to give rise to bronchopneumonia. There is no hard and fast line between these states.

Initially there is a hard and unproductive cough (i.e., no sputum is coughed up) with mild fever, malaise (a general feeling of being unwell), aching muscles and depression. After a day or two the patient begins to bring up sputum, and the cough is less painful. Treatment includes bed rest, warmth, steam inhalations and hot drinks; if necessary, antibiotics are given to cut short the duration of the illness and to prevent the development of bronchopneumonia, especially in the aged.

Chronic bronchitis is a different disease, the result of repeated irritation of the lining of the air passages by smoke, dust, fumes and general atmospheric pollution. It occurs in all industrial communities, and members of the managerial and professional classes are affected less than unskilled and semi-skilled workers. Men are more commonly affected than women.

The patient may be said to have chronic bronchitis when he continues to cough up sputum for at least three months in two years. Usually he becomes out of breath, because the disease is accompanied by EMPHYSEMA— enlargement of the bronchioles, the small terminal air passages, with dilation and destruction of the alveoli (air sacs) where gaseous exchange takes place during respiration. The basic process in chronic bronchitis is excessive secretion of mucus, which interferes with the proper drainage of the respiratory tract and aids the development of recurrent infection. Eventually the lung tissue loses is normal elasticity, the air spaces become disrupted, and there is interference with the blood circulation in the lung which may lead to increased pressure in the right side of the heart and its consequent failure.

Symptoms of chronic bronchitis include chronic productive cough, increasing breathlessness, wheezing and sometimes depression. The patient should stop smoking; usually it is impossible for him to change employment or to move into a more favorable climate without gross pollution of the air, but by doing so he may lengthen his life and diminish his discomfort. Acute flare-ups of the disease are treated with antibiotics, as

they are typically caused by added bacterial infection. Breathing exercises may help, and in very severe cases the administration of oxygen and the use of bronchodilator drugs under medical supervision may improve the condition.

See also the major article on **Pulmonary Diseases.**

bronchopneumonia

Inflammation of the lungs, usually beginning in the terminal air passages (bronchioles).

See PNEUMONIA.

brucellosis

A bacterial infection (also known as *undulent fever*) transmitted to man from cattle, hogs, and goats. It is mainly an occupational disease of those in contact with animals or meat, but it can also be contracted from unpasteurized milk.

The bacteria (of the genus *Brucella*) can enter the body through the nose, mouth or broken skin. The first symptoms usually appear within two weeks of infection, but the incubation period varies from about five days to several months. Symptoms include fever, headache, chills, fatigue and depression. Often there are no physical abnormalities except the high temperature and brucellosis can easily be mistaken for influenza. The fever sometimes recurs in repeated waves (or undulations) with intervening periods of several days without symptoms.

Even without therapy, the symptoms of acute brucellosis usually disappear within one year. However, nonspecific symptoms of chronic brucellosis may persist for many years. Treatment of acute brucellosis with tetracycline antibiotics reduces the chances of a relapse; once established, chronic brucellosis is difficult to cure and causes great personal misery.

bubonic plague

The most common variety of plague which—as the "Black Death"—killed an estimated 25 million people in Europe during the 14th century. Today it is more prevalent in insanitary areas of tropical countries, but limited outbreaks do occur occasionally in the western parts of the United States.

The infecting bacteria, *Yersinia pestis*, are transmitted to humans from the bite of infected rat fleas, which abandon rats dying of plague in favor of domestic animals such as cats and dogs.

The characteristic features of the disease are fever and swellings—buboes—of lymph glands in the armpits and groin. Bleeding into the skin results in dark blotches, which give rise to the historical name "Black Death."

The onset of the disease is very sudden. After a few sporadic cases, the disease may suddenly spread and reach epidemic proportions.

However, modern drugs have dramatically changed the outlook for plague victims. Treatment once used to consist of careful nursing and administration of antibubonic serum. Today a combination of sulfonamides and antibiotics is used with great success. Prevention of the disease involves the use of insect repellants to ward off the infective fleas and attempts to control the rodent population.

(*Pneumonic plague*, the other common form of plague, involves a severe infection of the lungs. In the absence of appropriate medical treatment it can prove fatal within two to five days of the onset of symptoms.)

Buerger's disease

Another name for THROMBOANGIITIS OBLITERANS.

bundle branch block

A defect in the electrical conduction system of the heart. There is a delay or block of the wave of electrical impulses that spreads out from the region of the heart's atrial chambers (responsible for controlling the heartbeat).

This causes one ventricle to contract before the other, resulting in an abnormal pattern of heart rhythm. The electrical impulses are conducted through a network of fibers known as the *bundle of His*. This bundle forms two branches: a block in the left branch usually means that heart disease is present, whereas a block in the right bundle (although linked with disorders of the heart) may occur in people with no evidence of abnormality.

Bundle branch block may occur in people suffering from arteriosclerosis, rheumatic heart disorders, or congenital heart disease.

Diagnosis is usually made with the help of electrocardiograph recordings. The outlook depends on the severity of the underlying disorder.

bunion

An unsightly deformity of the joint at the base of the big toe. It looks as if the joint has been pushed out of place and is the result of undue pressure on the joint over long periods.

Although injury which has not been treated satisfactorily may cause a bunion, badly fitting shoes are the most common cause. Pointed shoes which compress the feet push out the joint, as do shoes which throw the weight of the body onto the ball of the foot. As a result of pressure on the joint, the sac or bursa alongside the bones may also become inflamed and tender. Pus may be

BUNION

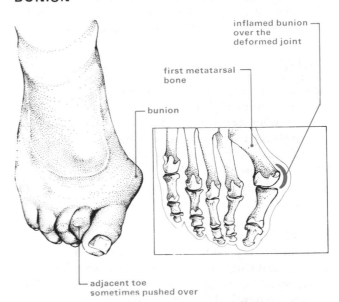

inflamed bunion over the deformed joint

first metatarsal bone

bunion

adjacent toe sometimes pushed over

A bunion is a painful swelling at the base of the big toe which results from tight shoes rubbing over a deformed joint. The primary cause is that the first metatarsal bone deviates away from the rest of the foot resulting in a prominent joint. A sac of fluid develops over this joint as a result of friction, and this sac may become inflamed and tender or even go septic (produce pus).

present.

Strapping, splinting and attention to wearing comfortable shoes may improve matters by reducing pressure. Once the damage is done, the only really effective treatment is surgical removal of the deformity. This operation is usually very successful.

Burkitt's lymphoma

A malignant tumor of the lymphatic tissue mainly affecting young children in certain parts of Africa, although it also occurs sporadically throughout the world.

It is named after Denis P. Burkitt, a 20th-century British surgeon who drew attention to the disease while working in Uganda. The characteristic feature is gross rapid swelling of the jaw. Many other bones and organs may be affected, and without treatment the disease is fatal in a few months.

Following Dr. Burkitt's interest in the disease, the tumor proved very amenable to powerful anticancer drugs. In Africa there are now many cases of complete cure. In other parts of the world, however, treatment has not been quite so successful.

There is very strong evidence to suggest that Burkitt's lymphoma is caused by the *Epstein-Barr virus* (the same microorganism which causes infectious mononucleosis). It is one of the very few human cancers in which a particular virus is so strongly implicated.

burns

Damage caused to the skin by either dry or wet heat (scalds). The biological properties of skin are destroyed just as when egg white is heated. Anything bringing about this change is said to cause burning—fire, boiling liquid, electricity, acids, alkalis and other corrosive fluids, or even excessive cold.

The severity of burns is assessed by considering the depth to which the skin is damaged and the surface area affected. A 1% burn would cover an area equivalent to that of the hand.

Fluid loss is a serious consequence of extensive burns. Plasma leaks out from blood vessels near the burned area. Small burns cause only a little leakage with local blisters, but very large burns (where skin is severely damaged) may interfere with the circulation to such an extent that large volumes of fluid are lost. There is a danger of a severe drop in blood pressure (shock) and the fluid loss requires prompt replacement with the transfusion of plasma, which may be immediately more important than treatment of the damaged tissue.

A 15% to 20% burn may well require transfusions. Burns over 25% of the body are virtually certain to require them; burns over 75% of the body are nearly always fatal. Children and the elderly are particularly at risk.

Burns are often divided roughly into three categories: first, second and third degree.

First degree burns involve superficial reddening of the skin with no blistering. This layer of the skin is usually shed and replaced naturally and healing is uncomplicated. Major treatment is unlikely to be necessary, although the patient may suffer some degree of shock.

In *second degree burns* the skin is actually destroyed and there may be extensive blistering as fluid seeps out of the blood vessels. But enough tissue is left for the surface layer to be fully replaced in time. The chief threat is from infection when the blisters burst.

In *third degree burns* the entire thickness of the skin is involved and cannot be renewed naturally. New skin will grow at the edges of the wound but destroyed skin must be replaced by skin grafts. These thin layers of skin—taken from other parts of the body—speed up the healing process, help prevent infection and reduce deformity. Grafts of pigskin are sometimes used to speed recovery when large areas are affected. Infection is the chief danger and badly burned patients are usually nursed in germ-free isolation units; they may be uncovered in the early stages. Devices such as air beds are used to prevent pressure on the damaged areas.

Although there is still some dispute over the first-aid treatment of burns, most experts advise cooling burns immediately. This certainly applies to minor household burns and scalds: the area should be cooled in running cold water for at least 10 minutes. Heat is retained in the skin following removal from the source of the burn and continues to "cook" unless cooled. Cooling also helps to relieve and prevent pain. However, concern with this should not prevent rapid removal to the hospital of more severely burned victims. Smoldering clothing should be peeled off but clothes adhering to damaged skin must be left.

Burns with acids or alkalis or other corrosive liquids should always be flushed with water. Acids should not be used to neutralize alkalis, or vice versa. Corrosive liquids in the eye should be flushed with water for some time and the patient encouraged to blink.

Blisters must be left strictly alone. Pricking them gives bacteria entry to a perfect breeding ground. Small trivial wounds may be covered with a sterile dressing, but larger burns should only be covered lightly if at all. A clean laundered sheet or handkerchief may be more suitable than gauze, which tends to stick. Ointments, creams or butter should *not* be applied.

Medical attention should be sought where there is any doubt. Burns caused by an electric current may be more serious than they look, as tissue below the surface can be damaged.

See also *Burns* in the **First Aid** section.

bursitis

A painful condition affecting certain joints, caused by inflammation of a bursa.

A bursa is a closed sac which helps muscles and tendons to move smoothly across places where bones are prominent, such as in the knee, shoulder, hip and bottom. Bursitis can be extremely painful; often the pain starts suddenly, especially in the shoulder—the most common joint to be affected.

The cause of bursitis in most cases is unknown, but it can be caused by injury, inflammatory arthritis, gout, rheumatoid arthritis, infection, or repeated friction. One popular name for bursitis involving the bursa in front of the kneecap is "housemaid's knee."

Acute bursitis often responds to injection into the affected bursa of hydrocortisone, following infiltration of 1% procaine. An anti-inflammatory drug such as phenylbutazone or indomethacin may also be helpful.

Once the worst is over, exercise of the joint will help to get it moving once more. This physical therapy, under proper supervision, is important to prevent any permanent loss of joint movement.

See also the major articles on **Orthopedics** and **Rheumatology**.

BURSITIS

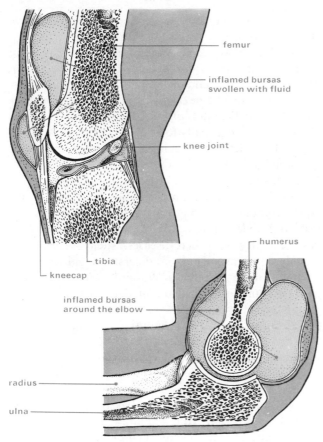

femur

inflamed bursas
swollen with fluid

knee joint

humerus

tibia

kneecap

inflamed bursas
around the elbow

radius

ulna

*Bursas are small, fluid-filled sacs which allow
tendons and skin to move freely over prominent
bones. Repeated trauma to these areas leads to
bursitis—painful, inflammatory swellings of the
bursa. This is particularly likely to occur in
bursas around the knee ("Housemaid's Knee")
and at the elbow ("Tennis Elbow.")*

bypass

When an artery becomes narrowed as a result of
ATHEROSCLEROSIS or other disease causing hardening
of the arteries, there may be harmful effects on the organ
or tissue supplied by the vessel. In addition, a narrowed
vessel is likely to become the site of a blood clot, which
may then completely stop the flow of blood. Narrowing
of the coronary arteries (which nourish the heart
muscle) may lead to ANGINA PECTORIS or to
CORONARY THROMBOSIS (myocardial infarction, or a
"heart attack"). In the limbs, a narrowed artery may
produce INTERMITTENT CLAUDICATION with pain
developing in the limb on exercise. In the brain,
narrowing of the blood vessels may cause mental
deterioration or confusion.

In certain sites, the problem may now be overcome by
the use of grafts to replace the narrowed portion of the
vessel or to bypass it. In the heart, narrowed coronary
arteries producing angina pectoris can be bypassed by
using a graft of a vein taken from the leg. Once the graft
has "taken," the vein soon assumes the structure of the
artery it replaces. In the leg and in the major blood
vessels at the lower end of the abdominal aorta (the main
artery from the heart carrying blood to the lower part of
the body), narrowed or obstructed vessels may be
replaced by a variety of plastic grafts, usually of woven
nylon or Teflon to give flexibility. Other bypass
procedures may shunt blood from the portal vein to the
vena cava in the abdomen, or may be done to provide
additional blood to the brain when a carotid artery is
obstructed. All these procedures demand a high level of
specialized surgical skill, but the results can be extremely
successful.

CORONARY BYPASS

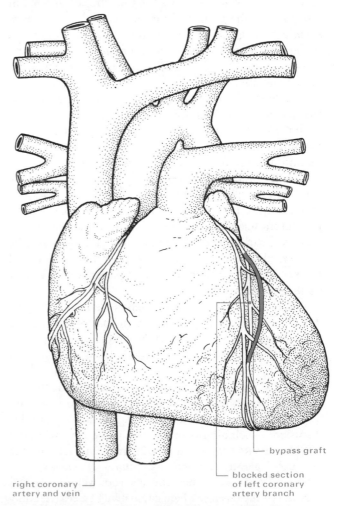

bypass graft

blocked section
of left coronary
artery branch

right coronary
artery and vein

*In principle the coronary bypass operation is
simple and involves bypassing the blocked section
of coronary artery with a length of vein taken
from the patient's leg. In practice, it calls for a
formidable surgical team and expensive
equipment.*

byssinosis

A lung disease caused by the inhalation of dust and foreign substances (including mold, fungi and bacteria) contained in cotton, flax and hemp. It primarily affects workers in industries where these materials are processed.

See *Diseases caused by dust inhalation* in the major article on **Pulmonary Diseases.**

C

cachexia

A severe wasting (atrophy) of the body produced as the consequence of disease. Wasting occurs, of course, in any patient who is starved for any reason; but the term *cachexia* is usually reserved for those in whom an underlying illness exists and in whom merely providing a well-balanced diet is usually ineffective in restoring normal health.

Simple starvation plays some part in many cases of true cachexia. For example, a patient with cancer of the esophagus ("gullet") or stomach may be quite unable, for purely mechanical reasons, to take in enough food to maintain health. In starvation, however, body fat is first lost; only when this has been consumed for energy production will essential tissue, such as muscles, be broken down. In some debilitating diseases, loss of body fat and muscle wasting often occur simultaneously as a relatively early sign of the disease and cannot always be easily explained by a loss of appetite or diminished food intake. This is particularly true of patients with cancer (*malignant cachexia*).

When a physician takes a patient's medical history he will often inquire about any recent loss of weight. He will sometimes be inclined to take a more serious view of the problem if there has been any significant weight loss over the preceding weeks or months. On the other hand, weight loss may simply be associated with a reduction in food intake as a result of anxiety or depression, without any underlying disease. Lastly, certain glandular disorders—including overactivity of the thyroid gland (HYPERTHYROIDISM) and a rare disorder of the pituitary gland (known as *pituitary cachexia* or *Simmond's disease*)—may cause severe weight loss and wasting of the tissues, which can usually be corrected by appropriate treatment of the glandular disorder.

caisson disease

A technical name (together with *decompression sickness*) for the BENDS.

calculus

An accumulation of solid material (a "stone") in any of the hollow organs or passages of the body.

Calculi commonly cause symptoms when they occur anywhere in the urinary tract—the kidney, ureter, bladder, prostate gland or urethra—or the biliary tract (GALLSTONES). The next most common sites for stone formation are the ducts of the salivary glands.

Urinary calculi usually form as a result of abnormally high blood levels of calcium or other metabolic abnormalities. Stasis of urine, infection and inadequate fluid intake are sometimes contributing factors.

Most *gallstones* are caused by an imbalance in the concentrations of cholesterol, phospholipid and bile salts in the bile; but infection·may contribute and a few cases are due to other diseases, such as hemolytic anemia. For reasons not yet understood, gallstones are becoming more common in Western societies; the most likely explanation is that the modern diet is especially rich in fats and proteins.

Calculi may cause no symptoms and their presence may first be recognized only on x-ray films taken during a routine health check. However, if symptoms do develop they may be severe. If a stone blocks the bile duct (leading from the liver to the duodenum) or the ureter (leading from the kidney to the bladder) the result is severe abdominal pain. The muscles of the blocked duct go into spasmodic contractions in an attempt to overcome the obstruction, causing repeated bouts of intense pain (colic).

Often an attack of colic will be short-lived as the calculus is passed into the bladder or the intestine. Sometimes, however, the obstruction may persist. In the case of a gallstone this will cause JAUNDICE. If the ureter is blocked the kidney cannot function and may be permanently damaged. Even if they do not cause obstruction, the presence of stones in the kidney or the gallbladder encourages inflammation.

When the cause of stone formation is known, as in some types of kidney stone associated with inborn biochemical defects (such as the presence of excessive quantities of uric acid in the circulating blood, which can lead to GOUT), treatment may be given with drugs such as allopurinol (Zyloprim) or with dietary modifications to reduce the chances of further stones being formed. Treatment with the drug *chenodeoxycholic acid* can cause the gradual dissolution of some types of gallstone. However, in most cases in which stones cause repeated symptoms the treatment is primarily surgical. Removal of the gallbladder (cholecystectomy) can provide a permanent cure of ill health from gallstones in many cases. Removal of kidney stones does not give a guarantee of cure either, but it is usually combined with dietary advice to reduce the risks of recurrence.

CALCULI

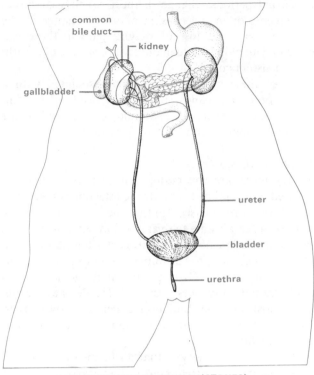

COMMON SITES FOR CALCULI (STONES)

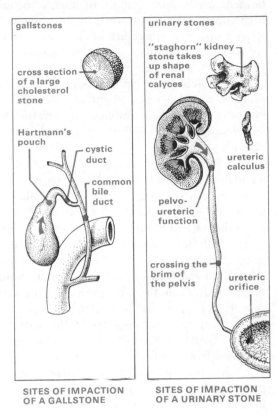

SITES OF IMPACTION OF A GALLSTONE

SITES OF IMPACTION OF A URINARY STONE

Calculi or stones form in concentrated bile or urine. Multiple gallstones are often found in the gallbladder. Urinary stones can form anywhere in the urinary system. Large "staghorn" calculi in the kidney may be unnoticed, but tiny stones passing along the ureter cause excruciating pain and blood in the urine.

callus

1. A local hard growth of the outer layer of the skin. Also known as a *callosity.*

Calluses are a normal reaction of the skin to friction or pressure. For example, many people have a callus on the side of the middle finger of their writing hand, caused by pressure from a pencil or pen.

Calluses usually have a protective function; they prevent damage to the skin and underlying tissues. They must be distinguished from CORNS, which are also induced by pressure but are more localized. (Also, in a corn an apex of the thickened skin points inwards and causes pain.)

Calluses rarely require treatment because they are painless and protective. They are occasionally removed for cosmetic reasons; this is pointless, however, unless the provoking factor is also removed, for they tend to recur. In contrast, corns may need treatment by a podiatrist (an expert on care and treatment of the feet). 2. The lump of soft, unorganized new bone which forms

at the site of a healing fracture and ultimately is transformed into organized bone that fixes the fractured bone ends firmly together.

cancer

Cancer is most easily understood as the development and later spread throughout the body of cells from a malignant tumor. With the exception of the leukemias, cancers almost always originate in a single isolated growth; at that early state removal of the solitary tumor will cure the disease. Once the cancer cells spread (metastasize) to the bones, liver or other major organs, however, the disease is controllable only by drug treatment or by radiotherapy.

The unique feature of cancer cells is, then, their readiness to multiply outside their organ of origin. Carried in the bloodstream or in the network of lymphatic channels to distant parts of the body, cells from the primary tumor "seed" themselves and grow, infiltrating and eventually destroying the healthy tissues around them. It is these secondary, "metastatic islets" of cancer which cause most of the serious and fatal complications of the disease.

Cancers are divided into four main categories on the basis of the site and nature of the primary tumor. Tumors of glandular organs—such as the breast, stomach, pancreas, lung, skin and intestines—are termed *carcinomas*. Tumors of muscle, bone and the other fibrous and supporting tissues of the body are termed *sarcomas:* these are often slower growing than carcinomas. Thirdly, the *lymphomas* (such as HODGKIN'S DISEASE) are tumors of the lymphatic system, affecting the lymph nodes in the neck, groin, armpits, and the liver and spleen; and similar in their symptoms and their response to treatment are the *leukemias*, the cancers of the blood-forming bone marrow.

The fundamental change in a cancer cell that distinguishes it from normal is in its *nuclear protein*. Seen beneath the microscope, cancer cells have large, often misshapen nuclei, and they often have two or three times the normal number of chromosomes. As the cells multiply those characteristics are passed on to each generation, perpetuating the abnormality in their growth pattern. What is not yet clearly understood is the nature of the event that changes a cell so that it becomes cancerous (malignant). It is clear, however, that most cancers originate as a response by the body to external factors. Some of these have been identified: nuclear radiation from substances such as radium, from atomic weapons, and from x-rays and radioactive isotopes used in medicine or industry; alcohol and tobacco smoke; industrial minerals and chemicals such as asbestos and polyvinyl chloride; and hormone drugs such as es-trogens. Others are only suspected: viruses in particular are believed to play a part. There also seems to be an association between intestinal tumors and a diet rich in meats and animal fats, but the constituent responsible has yet to be identified. Another equally important factor is the genetic and constitutional makeup of each individual: some cancers are found more commonly in racial groups such as the Japanese, and in other cases a tendency to one form of cancer may be found in successive generations of a family. Furthermore, while, for example, heavy cigarette smokers have a high risk of lung cancer, most of them (90%) do not develop the disease. This may be due to variations in the biochemical makeup of the individuals concerned, and much current cancer research is concerned with the identification of high-risk groups.

In their early stages cancerous tumors may be indistinguishable from other, benign growths such as warts, moles or cysts. Indeed, most lumps in the breast (for example) are not cancerous. Treatment is more likely to be curative, however, if it is given before the cancer has begun to spread, so that any lump or swelling in or beneath the skin in any part of the body, whether or not it is painful, must be suspected as potentially cancerous until proved to be benign. (See BREAST CANCER.) Warning signs of the possible presence of a malignant tumor in an internal organ include: the presence of blood in the urine or feces; abnormal bleeding from the vagina; change in the regularity of menstrual periods; change in the frequency of bowel movements or in the passing of urine; change in the voice; unexplained loss of weight; pain in the chest; coughing up blood; sudden onset of shortness of breath; or a persistent cough.

All of these symptoms may be associated with a disease other than cancer, but all may also be signs of an early cancer. Medical examination is needed for accurate diagnosis and effective treatment.

Treatment of cancer
Many cancers are now curable. Surgical removal of an isolated tumor in the breast or the intestine is successful in 60% or more of cases—in that there is no recurrence of the disease within a ten-year period. Radiotherapy is the best treatment for most early lymphomas; in Hodgkin's disease, for example, the cure rate is about 80% in such cases. Drug treatment for leukemia has made dramatic advances in the past decade; the cure rate in the most common childhood leukemia is now close to 50%, whereas a generation ago the disease was uniformly fatal.

It is still true, however, that all forms of cancer are most susceptible to treatment in their early stages and that in some cases the disease is widely spread before symptoms occur. Even in those circumstances a combination of drugs, radiotherapy and surgery may achieve a remission of symptoms for several years. One current research interest is the stimulation of the body's own defenses against cancer—*immunotherapy*—by injecting killed cancer cells or bacteria into the bloodstream; this and the development of new drugs are extending the survival—in reasonable health—of patients with widespread cancer.

Prevention
As more of the external causes of cancer are discovered, prevention of the disease becomes possible by protecting people from exposure to these "carcinogens" at work, in food and drink, and by education about the dangers of smoking.

The second branch of the preventive approach to cancer is the promotion of early diagnosis. Screening tests have been proved effective in a number of common cancers: the best known example is cancer of the cervix (neck of the womb), detected by a "Pap smear," and screening by mammography (x-rays of the breast) has been shown to achieve earlier diagnosis of breast cancer in women aged below 50. Screening is also valuable for people exposed to carcinogens at work and for those with a family history of the cancer. For the rest of us, however, the key to early diagnosis lies in alertness to the warning symptoms listed earlier.

See also the major article on **Oncology.**

Candida (Monilia)

A genus of yeastlike fungi (formerly known as *Monilia*), often harmlessly present in the mouths of healthy people. In some circumstances, however, the micro-organisms may proliferate to produce a symptomatic infection of the mouth, intestines, vagina, skin, or (rarely) the entire body. The species most often involved is *Candida albicans* and the infection is known as *candidiasis* (or, formerly, *moniliasis*). When the infection involves the mouth or the vagina the condition is commonly referred to as "thrush."

Thrush occurs particularly in babies, but it may also occur in debilitated adults or those with dentures. It usually forms a white curdlike deposit on the tongue, cheeks and palate which may cause severe discomfort.

Vaginal candidiasis is one of the most common causes of inflammation and itching of the vagina and vulva, typically producing a white, curdlike discharge. Vaginal candidiasis is becoming increasingly common, perhaps partly because of changes in vaginal acidity brought about by oral contraceptives. It is often seen in pregnant women and diabetics. The condition is not usually acquired during sexual intercourse but sometimes may cause a symptomatic infection in the male partner.

Candida albicans may occasionally infect the entire intestinal tract, causing anal itching and forming a reservoir for repeated accidental infection of the vagina.

The fungi may also infect the skin—particularly in moist areas, such as beneath the breasts of large women and in the finger webs of those working with water.

Infections with *Candida* are usually effectively treated with an antifungal drug such as nystatin—in the form of a mouthwash, lozenge, pessary, or a cream; intestinal infection is treated with nystatin tablets to prevent reinfection elsewhere.

Vaginal candidiasis tends to recur; avoidance of sexual intercourse during treatment reduces the recurrence rate.

Patients with reduced immune defenses (for example, those with any severe illness and those on drugs that suppress immunity) may get a generalized *Candida* infection involving most organs. This is a life-threatening condition that requires the intravenous administration of amphotericin B, a powerful (but quite toxic) antifungal agent used especially in the treatment of persistent deep-seated infections.

See also VAGINITIS.

cannabis

A drug derived from the flowering tips and shoots of *Cannabis sativa*, a plant which grows wild or cultivated all over the world.

The active substances in the drug are chemicals called

INDIAN HEMP (Cannabis Sativa)

flowering shoot of female plant

male flower

seed

female flower

fruit

Cannabis (marijuana) is obtained from the Indian hemp plant pictured above; it can be taken either by mouth (mixed with food or drink), or smoked in a pipe or cigarette. It is not considered to be an addictive drug, although heavy users may become psychologically dependent.

tetrahydrocannabinols. Cannabis is also known as hashish, Indian hemp, marijuana, grass, pot, tea, weed, ganja and many other names.

It is one of the oldest known drugs and was used in early surgery to produce drowsiness and euphoria. It has few legitimate medical uses today, but is widely consumed throughout the world—illegally, in most Western countries. The plant and its flowers are dried, ground up, and smoked in a cigarette (a "joint") (It has been used experimentally in the treatment of glaucoma and in the relief of symptoms in patients with terminal cancer.)

In the West, cannabis resin is smoked in a small pipe

("hash pipe"); in some parts of the world (e.g., the U.K.) it is mixed with tobacco and the smoke inhaled from a cigarette. It can also be drunk as an infusion (bhang), as in India, or eaten in food.

Cannabis has been widely used in the U.S. since the 1930s, when it was probably introduced from Mexico or from the Caribbean (perhaps into New Orleans). Originally its use was largely confined to urban minority groups, but since the 1960s it has spread to many millions of middle-class Americans. Its popularity is also growing in other Western countries.

The effects of cannabis vary with the individual. Mild intoxication is characterized by cheerfulness, giggling and easygoing extrovert behavior. With more severe intoxication there may be irritable outbursts, feelings of unreality, auditory and visual hallucinations, and even frank psychosis. The effect usually wears off within 12 hours or less.

Long-term use of cannabis has not been shown to have major dangers—but neither has it been shown to be safe. Chronic users often appear to be generally apathetic ("a motivational syndrome"), but this could be a reason for the long-term use rather than the result of it. Suggestions of brain damage due to prolonged use have not been confirmed, but decreased sexual function and potency seem to be a real, if slight, hazard.

Physical dependence on cannabis does not occur but psychological dependence may be severe. Cannabis does not directly lead the user toward "hard" drugs or crime, but the drug subculture in which it is often used may expose him to greater dangers, and its hallucinogenic activity may tempt him to seek the stronger effects of LSD or other drugs.

Cannabis is probably no more harmful than alcohol (many experts believe that it is much less so), but it is debatable whether this is a sufficient argument for its legalization.

carbohydrates

Natural compounds, relatively high in caloric value, of which sugars and starches are the best known examples. They are capable of producing energy or heat and form one of the three classes of nutrients (the others being protein and fat).

Carbohydrates make up the bulk of the organic matter on earth, occurring predominantly in plants—particularly, as the structural carbohydrate cellulose. In animals, including man, the principal structural material is protein; but carbohydrate (in the form of mucopolysaccharide) is an important part of skeletal and other connective tissue.

Carbohydrates provide energy for synthetic processes and other work undertaken by the cells; they also provide many of the simple starting materials required

for the synthesis of complex substances. The liver is an organ of particular importance in carbohydrate metabolism.

Carbohydrates may be classified into: (1) *monosaccharides*, simple sugars such as glucose and fructose; (2) *oligosaccharides*, compound sugars of two to ten monosaccharide units, such as sucrose and lactose; (3) *polysaccharides*, complex polymers of ten or more units, such as starch, glycogen, cellulose, dextran and mucopolysaccharides.

Carbohydrate yields four calories per gram; in developing countries it supplies up to 75% of the energy in the diet, mainly as unrefined cereal. In the United States 55% of dietary energy comes from carbohydrate, largely in the form of the refined carbohydrate sucrose (i.e., ordinary sugar). Sucrose contains none of the other nutrients found in unrefined carbohydrate sources and is thus a source of "empty calories." Most Americans eat too many calories, and sucrose intake should be reduced before that of more nutritious foods.

The carbohydrate cellulose is indigestible by man, but is of great importance in providing dietary fiber ("roughage"), which is important to health.

Excessive carbohydrate intake is the cause of obesity and dental caries. Carbohydrate intake must also be controlled in diabetes and in other more rare conditions where its metabolism is disturbed.

See also the major article on **Nutrition.**

carbuncle

A large boil with multiple openings.

Carbuncles may reach the size of an apple. They cause severe throbbing pain, associated with fever and a general feeling of being unwell (malaise).

Carbuncles usually occur where the skin is thick, especially on the back of the neck: extension beneath the skin is probably favored by its thickness, when elsewhere the infection would "come to a head." The infecting bacteria are usually *Staphylococcus aureus*. Carbuncles are particularly common in patients with reduced defense to infection due to other debilitating illness.

Treatment of carbuncles involves the administration of appropriate antibiotics. The application of local heat may relieve pain. Surgical drainage is sometimes performed, but is often ineffective since there is no single collection of pus.

Before antibiotic therapy was available carbuncles were potentially dangerous, often leading to septicemia (blood poisoning) and even death. With appropriate antibiotic therapy they are now usually cured, although in some cases the infecting microorganisms become resistant to one or more of the antibiotics, making successful treatment more difficult.

carcinoma

Any of various types of malignant cancerous growths composed of epithelial cells—the cells which line the body's organs and ducts.

See CANCER and the major article on **Oncology.**

cardiac massage

A technique used in the attempt to restore function to a heart which has stopped suddenly.

Direct cardiac massage is massage of the heart itself; it is only performed by doctors, usually after heart surgery.

External cardiac massage or compression is performed by means of pressure applied over the chest wall; this technique can save life when performed correctly by a fully trained person.

Cardiac massage should not be given to a patient dying of a general illness such as cancer, since it is ineffective and distressing for all concerned. Its main use is for otherwise healthy people whose hearts stop suddenly, usually following a heart attack (myocardial infarction), or after drug overdoses, electric shock, drowning, or other accidents.

Cardiac massage is appropriate *only* when the heart has stopped. It is unhelpful and dangerous in someone who has simply fainted, where a slow pulse can still be lightly felt.

The technique can lead to complications. Rib fractures are quite common, especially in the elderly. Although this is sometimes inevitable, such fractures are usually the result of excessive pressure and may allow air to enter the chest cavity. Excessive pressure may also rupture the liver, spleen, or the heart itself and cause death. It is thus considered best not to attempt external cardiac massage without the proper training.

What to do:

1. Note the time. Call for help and an ambulance. Act quickly—you have about three minutes only before brain death starts.
2. Confirm that the heart has stopped by feeling for the neck (carotid) or groin (femoral) pulse. If either is present cardiac massage is inappropriate.
3. Lay the patient on his back on a hard surface—usually the floor—and kneel beside him.
4. Thump the lower end of the sternum (breastbone) hard once with your fist; this is sometimes sufficient to restart the heart.
5. If not, put the heel of one hand on the lower end of the sternum, put the other hand on top of it, and compress the chest with all your weight. Effective massage produces a femoral pulse which can be felt by an assistant. Repeat 60 times a minute.
6. Most patients with cardiac arrest also stop breathing and need artificial respiration. This is best performed by an assistant at one forced breath for every five to eight cardiac massages, but the two procedures can be performed by the same person if essential.
7. Keep going. Recovery may occur after an hour or more of cardiac massage, although this is uncommon.
8. Other measures are urgently required but must await medical assistance.

When resuscitating children, care must be taken not to use excessive force.

See *Resuscitation* in the **First Aid** section.

caries

Decay and death of calcified tissue. Originally the term was applied to the death of bone, but it now always means *dental caries.*

CARIES

STRUCTURE OF TEETH

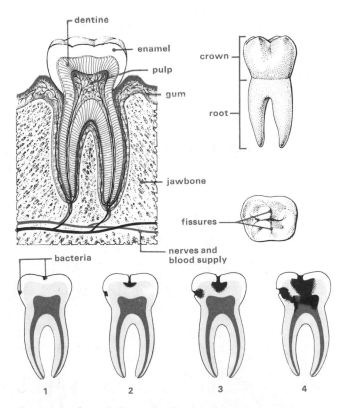

Caries or dental decay is the most common disease of Western man. Bacteria collect in the pits and fissures of the teeth and produce acid from refined sugar (1). The acid eats into the enamel (2). Decay then spreads more rapidly through the softer dentine (3). When the pulp becomes infected, irritation of the nerve leads to toothache (4).

Dental caries is the decalcification of a portion of a tooth, accompanied or followed by the disintegration of the living part of the tooth—resulting in the formation of "cavities."

Dental caries causes no symptoms during the early stages of decay, but when the living zones of the tooth are affected toothache results. The affected teeth eventually become visibly decayed and discolored.

Dental caries is a disease of modern Western man; the major cause is dietary. There are many relevant differences between a primitive unrefined diet and what most people eat today. But the most important is the consumption of refined sugar (sucrose), which adheres to the surface of teeth and encourages the growth of the bacteria which damage the teeth. The combination of sucrose, food debris and bacteria is known as *dental plaque*, which covers the area where caries develops. Sticky sweet foods are more likely to adhere to the teeth than granular ones; the more frequently the food is eaten, the worse the effects.

Almost all Americans have some caries, but its frequency and severity can be reduced by avoiding sweet foods, by regular use of a toothbrush and dental floss to remove plaque, by fluoridation of the water supply or fluoride supplements given to children, by the direct application of fluoride to the teeth as paints or in toothpaste, and by more modern techniques such as *fissure sealing*. Regular inspection by a dentist and the use of *disclosing tablets* help to reveal areas of plaque.

The development of caries can be arrested but not reversed; thus, the proper treatment of the resulting cavities is essential. If left untreated dental caries destroys teeth completely, with the added risk of serious infection (osteomyelitis) of the jawbones.

See also the major article on **Dentistry.**

carpal tunnel syndrome

The symptoms resulting from compression of a large nerve (the *median nerve*) as it passes through the tendinous "tunnel" in the wrist.

The carpal tunnel syndrome is fairly common. Symptoms include numbness, tingling and burning pain in the part of the hand supplied by the median nerve— that is, the thumb, index finger, middle finger and part of the ring finger. The symptoms typically first occur at night, often waking the patient; later they may also be experienced during the day and interfere with normal use of the hand. In advanced cases the thumb becomes quite weak.

The condition is seen in women more than men and is often a problem in pregnancy, although it disappears after delivery in nearly all cases. Sometimes there may be a demonstrable cause, such as acromegaly, myxedema, or arthritis; symptoms are often made worse by activities such as gardening, knitting, or typing. The common factor is *pressure on the median nerve* as it passes beneath a bridge of tough, tendinous tissue

CARPAL TUNNEL SYNDROME

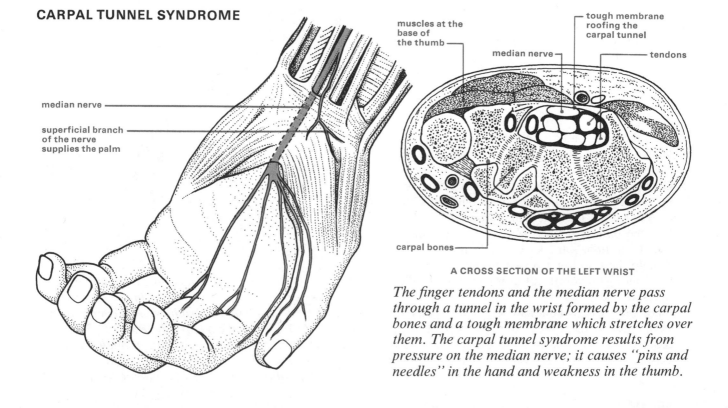

median nerve

superficial branch of the nerve supplies the palm

muscles at the base of the thumb

tough membrane roofing the carpal tunnel

median nerve

tendons

carpal bones

A CROSS SECTION OF THE LEFT WRIST

The finger tendons and the median nerve pass through a tunnel in the wrist formed by the carpal bones and a tough membrane which stretches over them. The carpal tunnel syndrome results from pressure on the median nerve; it causes "pins and needles" in the hand and weakness in the thumb.

underlying the skin creases at the wrist. Swelling of any of the other structures that pass through this "carpal tunnel" will compress the nerve.

The diagnosis is usually obvious, but if necessary it can be confirmed by special nerve conduction studies. Mild cases are relieved by rest or by splinting the wrist at night. Sometimes local injections of cortisone-type steroid drugs into the wrist will cure the condition; as a rule they at least produce some relief of the pain. The most effective and permanent treatment, however, is a minor surgical operation to reduce pressure in the carpal tunnel by dividing the wrist ligaments which lie above it.

cartilage

A tough, dense, elastic tissue which—together with bone—constitutes one of two main skeletal tissues of the body. Mature cartilage contains no blood supply of its own, but obtains nutrients for its living cells from the surrounding tissue fluids. (In meat, it is called "gristle.")

In the developing human embryo, the skeleton is formed of cartilage which is eventually transformed into bone by the process of *ossification* (the deposition of calcium within the cartilage). At this stage the cartilage is penetrated by small branching canals containing blood vessels. Cartilage persists until adolescence in the rapidly growing regions of the skeleton, and in particular at the ends of long bones (as *epiphyseal plates*). In adults, cartilage is restricted mainly to the frontal ends of the ribs (*costal cartilage*), the surfaces of joints, and certain areas outside of the skeletal system—such as the rim of the ear, in the nose, and in the respiratory passages (especially in the trachea and larynx).

The cartilage on the surfaces of most joints (articular cartilage) acts to reduce friction. The low "friction coefficient" of cartilage (three times more slippery than one ice cube moving across another) aids joint movement; it also has a cushioning effect.

Pads of cartilage mixed with tough fibrous tissue (fibrocartilage) are found as intervertebral disks between the bones of the spine. Fibrocartilage pads are also found in the knee, called "semilunar cartilages" because of their half-moon shape. These are sometimes injured in contact sports and have to be surgically removed (see MENISECTOMY).

Cartilage is occasionally the site of a benign tumor (CHONDROMA) or a malignant tumor (chondrosarcoma).

See also CHONDROCALCINOSIS and CHONDROMALACIA.

catabolism

The breaking down of complex chemical substances into

CARTILAGE OF THE KNEE

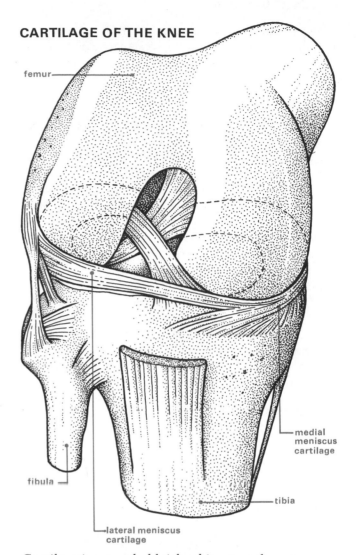

Cartilage is a tough, bluish-white, translucent material. Its perfect smoothness facilitates movement at joints. Thus at the knee, the contacting ends of the femur and tibia are covered with a thin layer of cartilage. In addition two crescent-shaped plates of cartilage, the menisci, help the bones to fit together snugly.

simpler ones by the living cells of the body, with the release of energy.

Catabolism occurs in all living cells, side by side with ANABOLISM (building up processes). The two processes in combination are known as METABOLISM.

The energy released in catabolism is used in maintaining body temperature, movement and other functions, as well as in the synthetic (anabolic) processes involved in energy storage, growth and repair.

The normal adult has a net equilibrium of catabolism and anabolism and is said to be in "metabolic balance." In severe illnesses, such as SEPTICEMIA, the patient may enter a "hypercatabolic state" in which catabolism predominates and the body tissues are broken down with a resulting rapid loss of weight. Unless this process is stopped with appropriate medical treatment it leads to severe wasting and eventually death.

cataract

An opacity in the lens of the eye causing defective vision.

Cataracts may be present in one or both eyes and may develop at any age. Fully developed cataracts cause BLINDNESS, but initially the symptoms include spots before the eyes (which do not move and can thus be distinguished from normal "floaters"), short sight (helped at first by glasses) and gradually diminishing vision. Cataracts do not cause pain or discomfort. Fully developed cataracts at birth may prevent the normal development of visual ability unless they are treated within a few months.

Cataracts in childhood may have no obvious cause or they may be caused by syphilis, German measles or abnormally low levels of calcium in the blood (hypocalcemia) in the mother during pregnancy.

Cataracts may also result from injury to the lens, including injury by heat or ionizing radiation. In adult life, cataracts occur in patients with diabetes but they are most common in the elderly (senile cataracts)—where they are considered to be an extreme case of the inevitable hardening of the lens that occurs with age.

The change that occurs in the lens in cases of cataract can be compared with the change that occurs in egg white when it is cooked. (Its protein is "denatured" and the opacity cannot be reversed.)

The only effective treatment is surgical. Operations for cataract have been performed as long ago as 1000 B.C. The modern operation for cataract extraction is a direct development of one first described in 1752.

The opaque lens is removed through the front of the eye under local or general anesthesia. Complications are

CATARACT

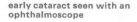

early cataract seen with an ophthalmoscope

mature senile cataract

A cataract is any opacity in the lens of the eye. Most cataracts are associated with aging ("senile cataract") and are present in both eyes, leading to progressively blurred vision and eventual blindness. However, surgical removal of the lens improves sight in over 90% of cases.

fairly uncommon and it is no longer necessary to wait until the patient is nearly blind before operating. It is safe to operate on both eyes at the same time, when necessary. Modern anesthesia has made the operation safe in many elderly patients who previously would have been considered unsuitable.

There is no possibility of recurrence in the same eye after the operation, but the patient needs an aid to vision in the absence of his own lens. Special glasses are commonly used but they may produce confusing visual images. Contact lenses—especially modern soft lenses worn permanently—give better results. An alternative is the implantation of an artificial lens within the eye (an intraocular lens implant), but this is not always possible.

See also the major article on **Ophthalmology.**

catarrh

A popular (not strictly medical) term for inflammation of the air passages of the nose and throat.

The symptoms under the general heading "catarrh" vary according to what the patient means by the word, but they usually include one or more of the following: a blocked nose, a runny nose, facial discomfort due to sinusitis, hearing difficulty due to obstruction, sore throat and a cough.

This range of symptoms may be caused by a number of nose and throat diseases, the most common of which is infection—especially the common cold and sinusitis. Allergy is also a common cause, while rarer possibilities are a deviated septum or nasal polyps.

Treatment depends on the exact cause. There is no cure for the common cold, although nasal symptoms may be relieved by the vasoconstrictor drugs (such as ephedrine) contained in many "cold cures" and nose drops. While these proprietary drugs are useful for short periods of symptomatic relief, they should not be used for long because they can damage the lining of the nose.

Sinusitis may need antibiotic treatment and sometimes surgical drainage of the affected sinuses.

Allergic causes of catarrh may sometimes be overcome by DESENSITIZATION or by removal of the allergen. Alternatively. drug treatment with vasoconstrictors or cortisone-like steriods may help in the short term.

A deviated nasal septum (wrong positioning of the cartilage that separates the two nostrils) and nasal polyps (growths) can be treated surgically if necessary.

In general, however, what people describe as catarrh is a simple and harmless infection which disappears rapidly without any treatment. The term "catarrh" is becoming obsolete in the United States, although the signs and symptoms represented are generally referred to under the medical phrase *chronic rhinitis.*

catatonia

A combination of mute withdrawal and abnormalities of movement and posture, found in some forms of schizophrenia.

The patient may be completely immobile and remain in any position in which his body is placed (a state known as *flexibilitas cerea*). For example, if his arm is lifted above his head he may leave it there until it is again moved for him. He may also obey verbal orders to move his body to an uncomfortable posture or he may precisely imitate the movements of another person.

Long-continued repetition of a meaningless word or phrase or the same movement (*perseveration*) is also common—for example, repeated eating motions with a knife and fork long after the food is finished. In extreme forms of catatonia the stupor may be extreme enough for there to be complete unresponsiveness, with failure to eat and drink (often necessitating tube feeding) and incontinence or retention of urine and feces. Such a phase may last from a few hours to several days.

The cause of catatonia—like that of schizophrenia—is unknown. Treatment is directed at the underlying schizophrenia and may include drugs, electroconvulsive therapy (see ECT), or psychotherapy.

catheter

A tube used to introduce fluids into or withdraw them from any of the body cavities or passages.

Early catheters were rigid and usually made of metal. The development of rubber and plastic catheters over the past few decades has greatly extended their uses.

Many catheters with special uses are now available—there is at least one specially made catheter for every space in the body. Some of the more common ones are as follows:

Urethral catheters are inserted through the urethra into the bladder to drain urine in cases of urethral obstruction (for example, when caused by an enlarged prostate gland). They are also needed in certain other medical and surgical situations, such as kidney failure or following gynecological surgery. Most patients require urethral catheters for only a short period, but patients with a paralyzed bladder may need permanent catheterization.

Intravenous catheters (or "cannulas") are inserted into a vein to take blood or administer fluids and drugs.

Cardiac catheters are passed via arteries and veins to the heart to measure cardiac function. Cardiac catheterization is often a routine preliminary to HEART SURGERY.

Vascular catheters of other kinds may be used—for example, to remove blood clots from the femoral and pelvic veins.

A *peritoneal dialysis catheter* is inserted through the abdominal wall into the peritoneal cavity to allow exchanges of fluid necessary for peritoneal DIALYSIS.

A *nasogastric tube* is a catheter passed via the nose to the stomach for the administration or removal of fluid.

An *epidural catheter* is used for the administration of anesthetics into the subarachnoid space surrounding the spinal cord during childbirth.

caudal anesthesia

An anesthetic injection into the lower back, especially used during CHILDBIRTH to produce painfree labor. (It is distinguished from *spinal anesthesia* in that the injection is made not into the dura, the outermost of the three membranes that surround the spinal cord, but into the "epidural space.")

Sensory nerves carrying pain impulses run from the uterus, vagina and perineal area (between the vagina and anus) to the spinal cord. Fortunately these nerves are much more sensitive to local anesthetic drugs than are the motor nerves which control movement in the same area. It is therefore possible to deaden the pain of childbirth while at the same time allowing muscle contraction and movement.

The spinal cord, which runs through the bony hole in the center of the vertebrae, is surrounded by a white membranous coat called the *dura*. The space between this coat and the vertebral bone (the *epidural space*) contains nerves running to and from the spinal cord, together with fatty tissues and blood vessels. An anesthetic injected into this space numbs pain sensations.

The injection is sometimes given near the beginning of labor at the stage when contractions start to become very painful. The woman usually lies on her side with her knees drawn up to her chin. The injection may be given by an anesthesiologist or by the obstetrician. With great care he inserts a needle between two vertebrae into the epidural space. He then pushes a fine tube, or catheter, through the needle into the space and withdraws the needle. The anesthetic drug is then injected through the tube. Its effect lasts for about two hours, after which it may be reinjected if necessary.

With some patients the injection may fail or may not be completely effective, sometimes for technical reasons. However, it is completely effective for about 90% of patients. The chief complications are a fall in blood pressure in about 5%, but this is easily corrected. Some women experience temporary sensations of heaviness or weakness in the legs after the anesthetic has worn off.

Epidural injections are expensive and time-consuming. Although many women can manage quite well without them, for difficult or prolonged labor they have been welcomed.

causalgia

A chronic, severe, burning pain of the skin that may occur after partial injury to a nerve. It occurs most often in the palm of the hand (after damage to the median nerve) or the foot (after sciatic nerve injury), although it may affect any part of the body. The pain is usually continuous and is often aggravated by pressure on the affected skin, which is typically shiny, thin and hairless. There may be excessive sweating, and the affected hand or foot is often abnormally cool. Ultimately, the muscles and bones in the area may waste away (atrophy) from lack of use.

The condition is common after gunshot wounds, traffic accidents and industrial injuries. It may also occur in patients with peripheral neuropathy (disease of the outlying nerves). Relief may be given by the application of local ice packs and by analgesics (pain-killers) and sedatives. The symptoms often improve without treatment, but in longstanding cases they may be suppressed by surgical division of the nerve fibers concerned.

cautery

The use of an agent to burn or destroy tissue. The term may also mean the agent used.

The main use of cautery is to prevent unwanted bleeding during surgical operations. Bleeding from small cut vessels can usually be stopped by cautery, thus obviating the need to tie off many vessels (which would delay the operation).

The most simple form of cautery is heat applied by a hot piece of metal, but this is seldom used in modern medicine. In surgery, cautery is usually achieved by an electric current which heats the tissues and produces hemostasis (localized arrest of blood flow). Electrocautery is also used for *surgical diathermy*, a common technique in which a heated blade is used to cut tissue, ensuring hemostasis as it cuts.

Extreme cold may also be used for cautery. Electrically cooled probes are used routinely in delicate operations (for example, in the eye) to destroy tissue by freezing. Cryocautery (cold cautery) may also be achieved by liquid nitrogen or solid carbon dioxide, as in the destruction of skin warts.

Chemocautery involves the use of caustic chemicals and is another technique used to destroy skin lesions.

celiac disease

A disease in which the small intestine fails to absorb fats, vitamins and other nutrients.

Although the condition was originally described in children, it is now clear that there is an adult counterpart ("nontropical sprue") which is probably common, though sometimes mild.

In the childhood form of the disease a previously healthy child loses weight, passes foul-smelling loose stools, and becomes irritable—usually at the age of six to nine months and always after solid feeding has started. Later the child's abdomen protrudes, his limbs waste, and ANEMIA and RICKETS may develop as the result of iron and vitamin deficiencies.

Adult celiac disease may develop at any age. Foul-smelling stools which are difficult to flush away (because they are frothy and light) are a prominent symptom; in addition weight loss, wasting and anemia often occur.

Celiac disease is caused by sensitivity to *gluten*, a protein found in wheat, rye and other grain. This was discovered during World War II, when it was noted that Dutch children with celiac disease improved when bread was unavailable. In some unknown way gluten leads to damage (fortunately reversible) in the lining of the small intestine, which results in the malabsorption of food.

Diagnosis usually involves BIOPSY of the lining of the small intestine by swallowing a small capsule on the end of a flexible tube. The treatment is to avoid all foods containing gluten. Special gluten-free flour, pasta and other foods are available. The restricted diet should probably be continued for life, but this is not yet certain. Vitamin supplements are required until the intestine has recovered.

Untreated celiac disease may lead to total wasting and eventual death, although milder forms of the disease are common. Treatment restores normal health. There is an increased risk of intestinal cancer in patients with this disease, but this is not great and the overall prognosis following the initiation of treatment is good.

cell

The functional unit of which all animals and plants are composed.

The human body contains an astronomical number of cells. The brain alone has billions of cells, and the total number of red cells in the blood is around 30 trillion (an average of 5 million in every cubic millimeter). Cells are quite variable in their size and shape. The average cell is around 7 microns (millionths of a meter) in diameter, but some are much smaller. Nerve cells are characteristically long and thin; in fact, some single nerve fibers stretch from the spinal cord to the tips of the toes.

A typical cell is composed of a *nucleus* (containing the genetic material DNA) and *cytoplasm* (which contains the enzymes necessary to translate the genetic information stored in the DNA into chemical action).

The cytoplasm contains a number of "organelles" in which the various metabolic processes are organized.

CELL

A GENERALIZED CELL

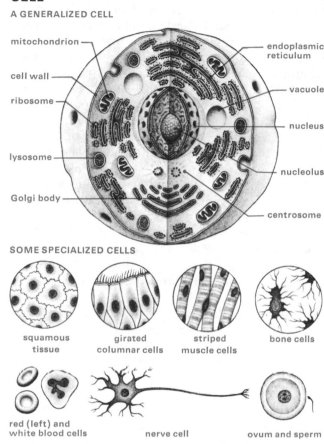

mitochondrion

cell wall

ribosome

lysosome

Golgi body

endoplasmic reticulum

vacuole

nucleus

nucleolus

centrosome

SOME SPECIALIZED CELLS

squamous tissue

girated columnar cells

striped muscle cells

bone cells

red (left) and white blood cells

nerve cell

ovum and sperm

Cells form the building blocks of all living tissue. Essentially, they consist of a sac of fluid enclosed by a membrane. Floating in the cell are smaller membranous sacs, or organelles, such as mitochondria and ribosomes, which are the sites of specialized activity. The varied shapes of the cells in the lower part of the drawing show how they adapt to perform many different jobs.

These can be clearly identified with the electron microscope and include the ribosomes, endoplasmic reticulum, mitochondria and lysosomes. The cytoplasm is surrounded by the cell membrane.

The internal environment of the cell is remarkably constant and differs greatly from the surrounding tissue fluid. This difference is maintained by active processes in the cell membrane. These processes, together with the other metabolic activities necessary for life, require a continuing supply of energy in the form of oxygen and nutrients.

All the cells in the body are derived by division from the original fertilized ovum. As the embryo develops, cells take on specialized functions; most remain capable of division in the event of injury. Nerve cells have no such potential, and mature red blood cells have lost their nuclei and are simply envelopes of cytoplasm. Most cells

are capable of regeneration if they are partially injured.

The study of individual types of cells has contributed to medical understanding of abnormalities in many diseases, including cancer and metabolic disorders.

cellulitis

A severe inflammation of the tissues just beneath the skin or certain deeper structures (such as the connective tissue that surrounds the uterus). The inflammation, usually caused by bacterial infection, typically spreads through the tissues producing sheets of pus.

In addition to the local pain and discomfort, toxins (poisons) released by the infection produce high fever and a general feeling of being unwell (malaise). The infecting bacteria probably enter the skin through a small scratch or wound.

ERYSIPELAS, in which there is little pus but the skin is raw, red, and painful, is a form of cellulitis caused by a specific streptococcus (*Streptococcus pyogenes*). It is usually cured by penicillin or similar antibiotics.

The bacteria that cause cellulitis are spread by the small lymph vessels. Patients with lymphatics blocked by disease or with congenital blockage of the lymph system are at particular risk of recurrent cellulitis.

cephalohematoma

A swelling on the head of a newborn baby, caused by bleeding under the membrane (pericranium) covering the bones of the skull. It is usually on one side of the head, but it may appear on both sides over the forehead or at the back of the head.

A cephalohematoma becomes obvious on the second or third day of life, when the normal molding of the head produced by birth disappears. It is soft and fluid-filled, and its borders are fixed to the edges of the affected bone. In about a week the rim of the swelling hardens and the softer center becomes depressed. At that stage it appears like a skull fracture, which may at first confuse the diagnosis.

A cephalohematoma needs no treatment, since it disappears completely within weeks or months. Attempts to aspirate it carry the risk of infection.

cerebral embolism

Embolism occurs when part of a blood clot, formed in a major artery or in the heart itself, separates and is carried by the circulation to a smaller artery. It lodges there, closing off the blood supply to the tissues beyond. Cerebral embolism—embolism in a blood vessel of the brain—can occur in patients whose cerebral blood vessels are otherwise normal.

When it happens in people aged under 50 years, there

is usually some heart disorder such as RHEUMATIC HEART DISEASE, or a "dead" segment of heart wall (myocardial infarction) following a heart attack.

In older patients, cerebral embolism may be a consequence of the breakup of areas of severe fatty degeneration of the aorta (the main artery leading from the heart) or its branches to the brain.

Emboli may be large, causing the catastrophic and irreversible changes of STROKE in which the brain tissue dies through lack of oxygen and nutrients. Small emboli, which pass briefly through the circulation, may cause transient symptoms such as dizziness or lapses of consciousness, without leaving permanent damage. These small emboli, collections of blood platelets or cholesterol crystals, may sometimes be seen during a medical examination passing along the blood vessels in the eyes of patients with such attacks.

Infected cerebral emboli may arise in patients with lung or heart infections, such as pneumonia and endocarditis, resulting in brain abscess and localized encephalitis.

The onset of illness in cerebral embolism is sudden. There is often a headache for a few hours before the signs of neurologic damage arise, such as paralysis or loss of feeling. Sometimes the illness starts with convulsions, which may be localized to a particular group of muscles before becoming generalized. About one quarter of patients become unconscious for some minutes, then return to consciousness in a confused state.

How much damage remains depends upon the site and size of the embolus. Embolism can occur in any major artery in the brain, so that residual damage varies from patient to patient.

Cerebral embolism is a minor cause of stroke. In a review of 873 stroke patients without cerebral hemorrhage in a large New York hospital (Bellevue), 8% were ascribed to cerebral embolism. The others were caused by blood clotting in the cerebral arteries themselves.

See also EMBOLISM/EMBOLUS.

cerebral hemorrhage

Leakage of blood inside the brain.

Cerebral hemorrhage is very serious, carrying a high death rate, and is the cause of about one in ten of all sudden circulatory disorders in the brain. Although its causes vary, the symptoms always follow the same pattern, arising from increased pressure within the skull and death of brain cells.

Cerebral hemorrhage starts with a sudden, very severe headache—much more intense than other headaches—which often extends to the neck and back. For a short initial period the patient may be able to feel the pain in one particular place, such as the front, back, or one side

of the head. This localization can be helpful in detecting the site of the lesion, as the pain quickly spreads throughout the head. Next, to add to the headache, come dizziness, vomiting, sweating and shivering, then progression from drowsiness to stupor and unconsciousness. In mild cases the patient recovers consciousness, but for many days or even weeks afterwards there is lethargy, clouding of intellect, confusion or delirium.

In the first 72 hours after the cerebral hemorrhage, the accumulation of blood around the surfaces of the brain and spinal cord leads to irritation of nerves and stiffness of the neck muscles.

At the same time, the brain damage causes various disturbances: unequal pupils, squint, paralysis, and loss of sensation. Fever lasts for several days.

Examination of the CEREBROSPINAL FLUID reveals traces of blood in 80% of patients with cerebral hemorrhage. The discovery of this blood rules out cerebral embolism or thrombosis as the cause of symptoms.

Most cerebral hemorrhages arise from a ruptured artery. In younger patients the most common cause is "berry" aneurysms—small balloonings of thinned arterial walls—usually on the system of arteries lying at the base of the brain. The aneurysms appear to form at points of weakness in the arterial wall which develop after infancy. Other causes of arterial rupture include high blood pressure, congenital abnormalities of the arteries and tumors involving the blood vessels.

cerebral palsy

Any disturbance of function of the muscular system associated with a congenital defect of the brain or birth injury. The term covers a wide range of disabilities, including paralysis of the muscles, inability to coordinate their movements and the occurrence of involuntary movements in an otherwise normal person.

Cerebral palsy affects two children in every thousand. Most cases are due to birth injury, either from instrumental or obstructed delivery or from lack of oxygen during labor or birth. Other causes include developmental defects of the brain, maternal infection during pregnancy, RHEUMATIC HEART DISEASE and JAUNDICE in the first few days of life. A quarter of all cases start in infancy, after a brain infection, thrombosis, embolus or injury. The condition is more common in first babies, particularly boys.

Patients may be hemiplegic—that is, with spastic paralysis (muscular rigidity accompanying partial paralysis) and poor growth of one side of the body. Arms are more severely affected than legs and the children walk with a "scissors" gait. Mental impairment sometimes occurs.

Forms of cerebral palsy with ATAXIA (awkwardness

of movement) vary from minor clumsiness to severe difficulties with coordination and balance. Such children may be of normal or even high intelligence. "Dyskinetic" patients are affected by involuntary muscle movements and changing muscle tone, which disappear only during sleep.

The outlook for the child with cerebral palsy depends on his reponse to help in overcoming the disability.

Physiotherapy, speech and behavior therapy, and mechanical aids may be useful.

cerebrospinal fluid

The clear, colorless fluid surrounding the brain and spinal cord and filling the spaces and channels (ventricles and aqueducts) within them. It is examined in the diagnosis of certain diseases.

Most of the cerebrospinal fluid (CSF) is formed in the ventricles of the brain from tufts of tiny blood vessels in their walls, called *choroid plexuses*. The CSF flows out over the surface of the brain through openings just above the base of the skull, and is later reabsorbed into the venous system by tongue-like processes. Some CSF flows downwards, within and around the spinal cord, and out into the nerve lymphatics. The CSF acts as a "water cushion" between the brain and skull and between the spinal cord and vertebrae.

CSF has a similar density to water. In a healthy person it is alkaline, almost protein-free, totally free of red blood cells, and with very few white blood cells. Its content of salts (such as sodium, chloride, bicarbonate and potassium) is similar to that of the blood.

Examination of CSF taken by needle from the lower back (*lumbar puncture*) or neck (*cysternal puncture*), helps in the diagnosis of neurologic disease. CSF pressure and protein levels may be raised in cancer; blood may be present in cerebrovascular disorders; white cells and bacteria are found in meningitis.

cerebrovascular disease

Any disorder of the circulation of blood in the brain. The most common is disease of the blood vessel wall or clotting of the blood within the vessels.

Cerebrovascular disease causes an estimated 200,000 deaths a year in the United States, and two million Americans suffer from some of the effects of the disease. Half a million become ill each year. Attacks are likely to recur and those who survive are often disabled and dependent on others.

The symptoms of paralysis, numbness, apathy and loss of intellect or memory arise from a reduction of the oxygen supply to the brain cells.

See also APOPLEXY, CEREBRAL HEMORRHAGE, CEREBRAL EMBOLISM, STROKE.

CEREBROSPINAL FLUID (CSF)

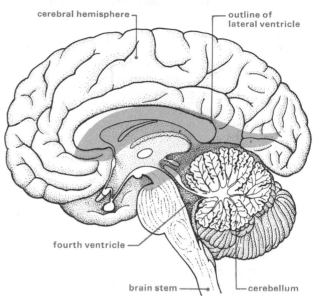

cerebral hemisphere — outline of lateral ventricle

fourth ventricle —

brain stem — cerebellum

Cerebrospinal fluid (CSF) is produced in the ventricles of the brain. It escapes through openings in the roof of the fourth ventricle to bathe the surface of the brain and spinal cord. If the flow of CSF through the ventricles is blocked, pressure builds up leading to the condition of hydrocephalus. The composition of CSF changes in meningitis and certain other diseases.

cerumen

The technical name for EARWAX.

cervical smear

A test in which the cells on the surface of the neck of the womb (cervix) are gently removed and examined microscopically. It was pioneered by Dr. George Papanicolaou (1883–1962) and is sometimes called a "Pap smear" or "Pap test."

Smear tests were originally aimed at early identification of cancer of the cervix—the second most common cancer in women after breast cancer—and this is still the main use of the technique. But its value has spread to include assessments of hormone imbalance in menstrual and menopausal disorders, infections and other nonmalignant changes in the tissues.

The technique is simple and painless and can be performed quickly without sedation or anesthesia. It has been adopted for mass screening of populations in developed countries, where experts in analyzing the smears are readily available. The tissues may be sucked into a round nozzled glass pipette (the original Papanicolaou method) or scraped away with a smooth wooden spatula. The latter is more likely to detect cancer cells, but is less useful for hormone studies.

When the material obtained is examined under the microscope, potential cancer cells can be detected by a skilled observer.

Since its first use in the 1940s, cervical smear testing has enabled doctors to prevent the onset and spread of cancer of the cervix. Detection and treatment of the disease in the early stages, before symptoms arise, has led to a significant reduction in the death rate among apparently healthy women. The test is advised for women entering their late twenties or early thirties, and for younger women whose family or personal history puts them at special risk.

Cesarean section

The delivery of a child through an incision made in the mother's abdomen, named after Julius Caesar who was said to have been born in this manner. For a full discussion of the subject see CHILDBIRTH.

Chagas' disease

An infectious disease caused by a species of parasitic protozoa (*Trypanosoma cruzi*). The disease (also known as *South American trypanosomiasis*) affects more than seven million people in Central and South America.

The infecting protozoa are transmitted to man by the bite of certain species of blood-sucking bugs known as *reduviids*, which are often found in the cracked walls of mud houses or in the thatch on the roofs. They deposit their contaminated feces on the skin of their victims, who then scratch the area and permit the protozoa to gain entrance to the body through the resulting abrasion.

The parasites eventually enter the blood circulation. Many of them are carried to the heart, where they invade the heart muscle (myocardium). As they undergo developmental changes they can cause inflammation of the heart muscle (MYOCARDITIS). In this stage of the disease there may be enlargement of the heart and eventual HEART FAILURE. Severe damage can also be caused if the parasites migrate to the digestive system, with consequent dilation of the esophagus, stomach and small and large intestine.

There is no specific treatment as yet for Chagas' disease, although research is being conducted into the possibility of developing an effective vaccine. Drugs are not available which can remove the parasites from the heart muscle and other tissues, but some drugs are effective in eliminating them from the blood circulation. Preventive measures involve control of the bugs that spread the disease (by means of insecticides) and improved domestic hygiene.

Compare AFRICAN TRYPANOSOMIASIS.

chalazion (meibomian cyst)

A cyst of the eyelid.

Chalazion is caused by blockage of an oil-secreting (sebaceous) gland in the eyelid (also known as a *meibomian gland*). The gland slowly enlarges, producing a lump in the eyelid which is more of a nuisance and a disfigurement than a source of pain or discomfort. Small chalazia are often not noticed until the finger is run over the eyelid. Everting the eyelid reveals a purple or red discoloration over the surface of the chalazion in the early stages, which later turns gray.

Pressure building up within the cyst may force the extrusion of the contents through the inner surface of the eyelid, giving rise to a chronic irritating discharge from the eye. If the gland becomes infected the swelling may be red and painful with a yellowish discharge. In *marginal chalazion* the inflammation affects only the duct of the gland.

The treatment is surgical removal of the cyst. There is no need for dressings or stitches.

chancroid

A sexually transmitted disease caused by infection with a bacterium called *Hemophilus ducreyi*. This germ is thought to enter the genitalia through a minor abrasion during sexual intercourse.

The first sign of chancroid, often not noticed by the patient, is a small pustule appearing on the external genital organs a few days after the contact. The pustule enlarges and erodes deeply into the tissues; it then bursts, leaving a shallow, painful purulent (pus-filled) ulcer with an irregular edge.

The center of the ulcer usually remains soft, a characteristic which distinguishes it from the firmly based chancre of syphilis. The ulcer is usually about 2 cm (less than an inch) in diameter and its base commonly settles to a clean granular appearance. But neglect and further infection with other bacteria may lead to destruction of the tissues and even gangrene.

Chancroid in women may lead to ulcers covering the genitalia, perineum and anus. (The perineum is the area between the opening of the vagina and the anus.) In men the ulcer is usually confined to the shaft of the penis rather than the tip. The disease may be caught from people who have no sign of it themselves but are "carriers" of the bacteria.

A common complication of chancroid, particularly in men, is painful swollen lymph glands in the groin. These may become greatly enlarged, rupture, and discharge foul pus (which may infect other areas of skin by contact).

A 10- to 20-day course of antibiotics such as tetracycline or sulfonamides usually cures chancroid.

cheilitis

Inflammation of the lips.

The lips, being particularly sensitive and often in contact with various irritants, are subject to inflammation—even when there is no inflammation in other organs.

In acute cheilitis the lips become swollen, tender and painful. In chronic cheilitis they are dry, cracked and peel easily. Patients with chronic cheilitis often pull or bite pieces of inflamed skin, thereby increasing the irritation and inflammation. As the lips become dry, cracked and sore, many patients resort to frequent licking in an attempt to ease the discomfort. Some cases of cheilitis are of nervous origin.

Cheilitis can be caused by allergy to chemicals in lipsticks, dentifrices, perfumes, and—particularly in young children—food. Deep fissures from chronic cheilitis may be persistent and annoying. "Splints" of gauze treated with collodion may be applied to them.

People with protruding lower lips constantly exposed to sunlight may develop "actinic" cheilitis, a condition which may later develop into cancer.

"Cold sore," or herpes simplex infection of the lip, is a common form of cheilitis. Repeated herpes attacks occur in the same places on the lip, suggesting that there may be a dormant virus which is reactivated at intervals, leaving minimal scarring. Such attacks are often precipitated by sunburn or fever. Nibbling at warts on the fingers may transfer the virus to the lips in warty cheilitis.

chest pain

Pain in the chest is a common complaint—so common, in fact, that it is mostly disregarded. Often only persistent or severe pains bring a patient to the doctor.

The pain may be a symptom of a potentially serious heart disease, or it may represent a relatively minor condition such as "heartburn" (pyrosis) brought on by the overindulgence in food or alcohol. In other cases a person may be unduly concerned about his or her heart and develop an anxiety state in which chest pains are experienced, or said to be experienced, without any physical cause (a condition known as *cardiac neurosis*).

Chest pain may arise from any of the organs in the chest or the upper part of the abdomen, or it may be "referred" from disease of the spine. A thorough physical examination, plus certain tests (which may include an electrocardiogram—a tracing of the electrical activity of the heart) will help in the diagnosis.

Most people when they suffer severe pain in the chest fear heart disease, and most physicians will first try to exclude the possibility of heart disease before they consider an alternative diagnosis. Pain that actually arises from the heart is produced by *ischemia* of the heart muscle—that is, a deficiency of the heart's blood supply brought about by disease of the coronary arteries (see ANGINA PECTORIS).

Peptic ulcers and gallbladder disease may both produce pain referred to the lower part of the chest, often associated with mealtimes. HIATUS HERNIA can cause pain or discomfort behind the sternum (breastbone).

In the process of making his diagnosis, the physician may wish to keep the patient at rest until his investigations are complete, rather than find too late that he is dealing with a condition that should have been treated with rest from the start.

Pain from the respiratory apparatus may be central, arising from the trachea ("windpipe") as a result of infection by viruses or bacteria, or it may be on the side—arising, for example, from inflammation of the membranes that cover the lungs (PLEURISY). Chest pain may be a consequence of lung inflammation secondary to pneumonia or it may be associated with a tumor of the lung; in such cases the pain is made worse during breathing in.

Occasionally, pain in the chest is caused by PNEUMOTHORAX or PULMONARY EMBOLISM, both conditions being accompanied by breathlessness. The skin of the chest may be affected by HERPES ZOSTER (shingles), a painful inflammation of the sensory nerves—characterized by blistering of the skin along the line of the nerve (in the case of the chest, one of the *intercostal nerves* which run around the body below each rib). In a number of cases no cause for chest pain can be found, and the physician may attribute it to "psychogenic tension."

In all cases, treatment of chest pain is directed at the underlying condition. Symptomatic relief can be given with analgesics such as aspirin or other drugs.

chickenpox

A highly infectious but rarely serious disease of childhood caused by the herpes virus. Also called *varicella*.

Chickenpox most commonly affects children during the early school years (between the ages of 5 and 10) and usually occurs in limited outbreaks in the winter and spring. It rarely attacks infants in the first six months of life, or adults. One attack virtually ensures permanent protection against future infections.

Chickenpox is passed on by close contact with a patient in the first week of the rash. The incubation period of 14 to 21 days is followed by a short period when the child feels generally unwell, perhaps with a mild fever and headache. Crops of spots appear during the next five days. They are thickest on the trunk and face and relatively sparse on the limbs. Some may appear inside the mouth and throat.

The rash develops from pink, flat spots into tiny single blisters which become dry and encrusted within two to four days. During the blister, or "vesicle," stage the patient is highly infectious, although he may not appear to be particularly unwell.

The rash often itches severely and younger children are strongly tempted to scratch. Scratching should always be discouraged because it can lead to bacterial infection of the skin and the subsequent formation of scars ("pockmarks"). Hygienic measures—such as close cutting and frequent cleaning of fingernails, and daily baths—are also useful in preventing infection.

Crusts may be removed from the skin by compresses or the use of carbolized oil. Once the last crop of blisters has become dry and encrusted, the patient is no longer a source of infection. There is no specific treatment for the disease. As a rule it is self-limiting and resolves completely with no adverse effects. Exceptions to that rule are children with leukemia or who are taking cortisone-like steroid drugs, who may develop pneumonia or liver problems. Chickenpox pneumonia may occur in adults, leaving many small lung scars which are seen on chest x-rays after the illness has cleared up.

The virus that causes chickenpox is the same as the one that causes HERPES ZOSTER (shingles). In fact, shingles—a disease mainly of adults—is thought to arise from reactivation of the virus which has remained dormant in the body since an attack of chickenpox during childhood.

chilblain

Hot, red, swollen patches of intensely itchy skin on the toes, feet, fingers and hands caused by exposure to cold and moisture.

Chilblain affects women and children more than men, especially those who are not well protected from exposure to the cold.

Acute chilblain usually disappears after a few days, but it can become chronic, with dull violet discoloration of the skin and the appearance of painful blisters containing blood-stained fluid. Ulceration may follow. Repeated exposure to cold may produce several areas of chronic chilblain which leave scars on healing.

The disease is much less common in the Northern United States than in parts of Europe with similar cold climates; the more widespread use of central heating in North America helps prevent it.

Prevention of chilblain is easier than cure; the condition hardly ever occurs in people provided with enough warm dry clothing (including gloves and footwear) in the colder seasons. High doses of various vitamins and vasodilators (drugs that dilate blood vessels) have been used in the management of chilblain, but their benefit has not been established.

childbed fever

Another name for PUERPERAL FEVER.

childbirth

The birth of a child, either by way of the vagina (vaginal birth) or by surgical means (*Cesarean section*).

Some 280 days after the beginning of the last menstrual period before conception, the term of pregnancy normally culminates in the birth of a child. While the child is developing in the uterus, the mother can prepare herself for the birth mentally as well as physically. In nearly every community, classes are available for prospective mothers—and fathers—where the mechanism of pregnancy and labor is fully described and discussed. The value of such classes is inestimable, for the knowledge that enables the mother to understand the changes in her body and the events that bring a child into the world can transform an event traditionally associated with anxiety and pain into one of complete fulfillment.

It is possible by using the methods of *psychoprophylaxis*—which teach the physiology and anatomy of childbirth and show the mother how to achieve good muscular relaxation by controlled respiration—to shorten labor, control pain and reduce muscular tension during labor to such an extent that a minimum of medication is needed—or in some cases no medication at all.

The individual mother's needs in the time of pregnancy will vary. Some are more affected emotionally than others, finding relaxation and confidence more difficult to attain. Some find themselves pregnant for the first time; others already have a family, so that preparation for the new birth will include particular attention to the siblings to help them accept the new baby with pleasure rather than jealousy. Increasing attention is now being paid to the manner in which the new arrival is welcomed into the world, for it is recognized that birth can be a traumatic experience to the baby as well as to the mother. The labor ward should ideally be a quiet place, without the glaring lights and sudden noises which contrast so alarmingly with the peace of the womb.

In a normal labor there are three stages. The first stage consists of a series of contractions of the muscles of the uterus to allow the cervix (neck of the uterus) to open. The baby starts to descend through the pelvis during the second stage when its presenting part, usually the back of the head, has passed through the fully opened cervix. At some time during this process the "bag of waters"

CHILDBIRTH

THE THREE STAGES OF LABOR

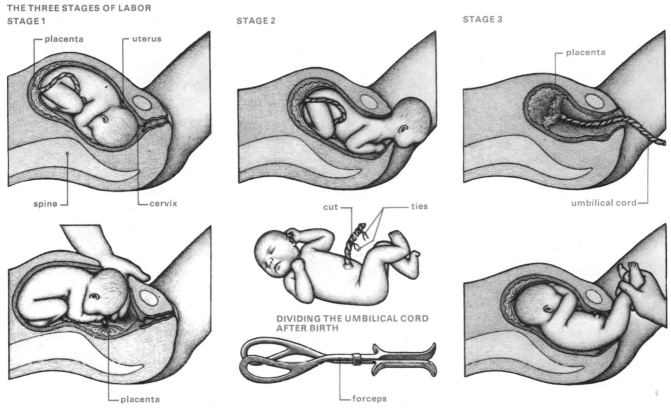

STAGE 1

placenta — — uterus

spine — — cervix

STAGE 2

cut — — ties

DIVIDING THE UMBILICAL CORD AFTER BIRTH

— forceps

STAGE 3

— placenta

umbilical cord —

CESAREAN SECTION
(delivery through a
lower abdominal incision)

— placenta

BREECH DELIVERY
(bottom or feet first)

During Stage 1 of labor, which often lasts as long as 12–16 hours, the cervix or exit from the uterus widens so that the baby can pass through. Stage 2, begins when the cervix is fully open and ends, in under an hour, with the delivery of the baby. Stage 3, expulsion of the placenta and umbilical cord, takes only five minutes. Cesarean section or forceps are sometimes necessary to assist childbirth.

within which the baby lies bursts and the fluid escapes.

After the beginning of the second stage of labor the mother is able to aid the delivery by pushing with her abdominal muscles in time with the frequent pains or contractions of the muscles of the uterus. As the baby's head descends through the pelvis it may press upon nerves, causing pain in the back and legs. Pressure of the head on the vaginal outlet gives a sensation of fullness in the anus and a flattening of the outlet. The appearance of the baby's head at the outlet is called "crowning."

In normal childbirth the nape of the baby's neck rests behind the mother's pubis. With the final push the head is expelled, the neck extending as it does so in order that the narrowest diameter of the skull will pass through the pelvic outlet. The back of the skull is delivered first, then the forehead, face and chin.

During a brief period of rest, the baby's head slowly rotates, to face one thigh. This allows an easy delivery of the shoulders with the next contraction, and the rest of the baby quickly follows. With the baby comes the remainder of the amniotic fluid and a little blood. The womb is now contracted and can be felt through the stomach wall as a firm, ball-shaped mass.

The umbilical cord is tied, clamped and cut. The baby should have gasped and cried on being born. It will be briefly checked by the obstetrician, nurse, or pediatrician, then passed to the cradling arms of the mother (if she is conscious).

When the baby is born it may at first appear quite ugly, with a swollen head, flattened nose and greasy skin. It may be partially covered by the remnants of the *amnion,* the membranous bag of waters which contains the fetus in the womb. But the swelling of the head usually begins to disappear in a matter of hours, and the greasy matter, or *vernix,* which covers the skin— composed of secretions from the sebaceous glands and cells shed from the surface of the skin—if left goes in a day.

Childbirth is not complete until the PLACENTA, or "afterbirth," is delivered, usually 10 to 15 minutes after the baby.

Normal childbirth depends on the infant's head being completely bent down, so that the chin rests on its chest. The blunt apex of the skull, pressing down into the pelvis, helps to open the cervix effectively. The shape of the mother's pelvis guides the head into the position in which the baby is born—facing the mother's back. Approximately one birth in ten occurs with the baby facing forward. Labor in such cases is usually slower, the stronger contractions are needed to bring the head into the lower part of the pelvis. The baby's position is much less flexible and the head is strikingly molded during delivery. Face-to-pubis deliveries are more exhausting for the mother, and the baby is at greater than normal risk of oxygen starvation. However, most infants entering the pelvis in this position rotate spontaneously to the safer backward position.

During a normal labor it is possible for the perineal tissues to be torn as the head passes through the vaginal outlet; the obstetrician often prevents the uncontrolled rupture of tissues by making an incision (EPISIOTOMY) through the stretched perineum extending backward and to the side, for by doing so he can ensure that the tissues part in the line which will make subsequent repair easy and efficient.

The use of obstetrical forceps—instruments designed to enable the obstetrician to guide and help the birth of the baby's head—is sometimes necessary in cases where the second stage of labor has been long, and the mother needs assistance in the birth of the head because she is becoming over-tired or the baby is showing signs of distress. The application of forceps is not as common as it once was, for the modern conduct of maternity cases is planned to avoid the occurrence of complications at birth. When applied properly, forceps do not injure the baby or the mother, and the obstetrician has the choice of a number of different types which are used for different purposes—some to rotate the head and some to apply gentle traction.

The relief of pain and anxiety in childbirth by drugs must be tempered by their effect on the fetus, for drugs administered to the mother will pass into the fetal circulation. Each obstetrician has his own well-tried favorite preparations and techniques. The risks of general anesthesia, particularly for the infant, have led to the use of regional local anesthesia. In the widely used technique of CAUDAL ANESTHESIA, the anesthetic agent is injected into the lower part of the spinal canal outside the membrane (dura mater) which contains the spinal cord and the nerve roots descending from it (cauda cquina), so that it anesthetizes the nerve roots as they emerge. Continuous caudal anesthesia ensures analgesia in 90% of patients, who remain alert and cooperative throughout delivery. The support of husband and family during labor is a source of great comfort and strength to the mother, and will help enable her to withstand the strain of labor without recourse to powerful analgesic drugs.

In a number of cases the obstetrician will consider that it is dangerous for the baby to be born through the natural birth passages, and will advise delivery by Cesarean section. In such cases an incision is made through the lower part of the abdomen and the lower part of the uterus, through which the child is delivered. Indications for the operation include disproportion between the size of the fetal head and the mother's pelvic outlet, malpresentation of the fetus, the most common of which is the breech presentation (although it is possible for a breech presentation to be delivered naturally), signs of fetal distress, and PLACENTA PREVIA, in which the placenta is implanted in such a position that it covers the internal opening of the cervix of the uterus.

Indications in the mother for Cesarean section include diabetes (where section is best undertaken in the 37th week of pregnancy), heart disease, and a bad obstetric history. Tumors in the pelvis may preclude normal delivery, and a failed induction of labor may make Cesarean section advisable. Many obstetricians will consider performing a section on the older mother who is having her first child. A mother who has been delivered by Cesarean section will almost always be advised to have her subsequent children in the same way.

See also the major articles on **Pregnancy and Childbirth** and **Obstetrics and Gynecology.**

chill

The popular name for an attack of shivering, accompanied by the sensation of being cold, resulting from a disturbance of the nerve centers in the brain which regulate body temperature. Despite the feeling of being cold, the patient may have a fever. Typically the chill occurs as the fever rises; when the fever breaks, the chill stops abruptly and the patient perspires profusely.

Most "chills" are due to minor virus infections of the nose, throat or chest; but an unexplained fever may be due, for example, to bacterial blood poisoning (septicemia), to infection of the kidneys or bladder, or to a protozoal infection such as malaria.

Whatever the cause of a fever, treatment should include plenty of fluids to replace those lost in sweat. If the temperature rises above 104°F the patient may be cooled by sponging the chest and forehead with cool but not ice cold water. Persistence of a fever for more than 48 hours or the development of further symptoms provides grounds for seeking medical advice.

chiropractic

A method of treatment which assumes that anatomical faults cause functional disturbances in the body and that, therefore, illnesses can be treated by "manipulation"—particularly of the spine. The specialty of chiropractic began (as did osteopathy) with the ancient techniques of "bonesetting." Eventually, chiropractors began to treat all types of strains, sprains and dislocations. Well before the end of World War II, the practitioners of spinal or skeletal manipulation considered themselves far more than mere bonesetters; they firmly believed that they had helped to develop a new system of medicine.

As probably the most successful form of "fringe medicine" (with about 40,000 practitioners in the United States alone), chiropractic has in the past been fiercely opposed by the American Medical Association (AMA). Nevertheless, it has prospered since it was founded a century ago by Daniel David Palmer, and an estimated 40 million Americans are receiving or have received treatment from a chiropractor, the great majority for back complaints.

Palmer believed that minor displacements of bones in the spine lead to nerve irritation and that this, in turn, leads to illness. The theory is that if the chiropractor then manipulates the spine to correct the anatomical faults, the pressure on the involved nerves is relieved. This is maintained to be beneficial on the course of the illness. In its basic philosophy it differs little from osteopathy, but some practitioners make wider and medically unjustified claims for it (including the ability to treat organic diseases such as cancer). This is one of the main reasons for the AMA's opposition; but, in virtually all states of the U.S., chiropractic is recognized by insurance companies as a legitimate form of medical treatment.

In addition to straightforward manipulation, chiropractors employ such orthopedic techniques as immobilization and traction. They also use a wide range of special electrical or mechanical devices in therapy, including those that employ ultrasonics, vibrotherapy and electric currents.

See also the major article on **Orthopedics**.

chloasma

A localized brown coloration in the skin associated with pregnancy or the MENOPAUSE.

Chloasma is most obvious on the face, where the areas affected are known as "liver spots," but it also occurs on the nipples and around the genitals. The cause is thought to be a disturbance in hormone production which leads to a rise in the amount of melanin (brown pigment) formed in the deeper layers of the skin. Although chloasma is sometimes disfiguring, it usually disappears at the end of pregnancy or after the menopause.

In severe or persistent cases, some success in reducing the pigment has been achieved with hydroquinone drugs. Surgical "planing" of the affected area is also sometimes performed to remove the discoloration.

Very rarely, chloasma is a sign of an ovarian tumor.

cholecystectomy

Surgical removal of the gallbladder.

The gallbladder is a reservoir for bile produced by the liver and destined for the small intestine. It can give rise to symptoms caused by inflammation, the formation of gallstones, or a tumor. Stones are usually associated with inflammation, although they may occur "silently." Cholecystectomy is performed when the illness has caused recurrent fever, pain or jaundice.

The risk of gallbladder disease increases with age. As the number of elderly people in the general population has increased, cholecystectomy has become a very common operation. Gallbladder problems are most common in overweight, middle-aged women, but they can affect both sexes of all ages and weights.

The symptoms of gallbladder disorders may be acute or chronic. In acute inflammation there is severe abdominal pain, usually under the border of the right ribs. It starts suddenly and persists for some hours; relief can usually be obtained only with the injection of a potent painkiller. The patient may appear pale, vomit bile, and have a rapid pulse and damp hands. The abdomen is often rigid and very tender; the pain can also radiate to the back and right shoulder. Cholecystectomy is performed only after the acute symptoms have subsided under special medical treatment. In the elderly, surgery may be considered earlier if the symptoms persist.

Chronic cholecystitis occurs as repeated attacks of indigestion with discomfort in the upper right part of the abdomen. Other features of the illness include intolerance to fatty foods, heartburn and flatulence. Repeated attacks of inflammation can reduce the gallbladder to a shriveled nonfunctioning sac contracted around gallstones. Treatment of chronic cholecystitis includes a low-fat diet and in obese patients may require weight reduction. Cholecystectomy is generally recommended if symptoms persist or if gallstones are a problem. (For an illustration, see the major article on **Gastroenterology**.)

Disagreement exists among medical experts regarding the most appropriate treatment for patients with gallstones but no symptoms. Some surgeons leave things alone; others remove the stones to prevent future problems. Research continues toward the development of drugs to dissolve some forms of gallstones. At present, however, surgical removal of the gallbladder is the only effective treatment in severe cases.

Tumors of the gallbladder are rare. They typically develop only in the presence of stones—perhaps because of chemical or mechanical irritation of the gallbladder wall. Unfortunately, such tumors have a tendency to spread to the liver, at which stage cholecystectomy is seldom successful.

cholecystitis

Inflammation of the gallbladder, usually associated with the presence of gallstones.

Acute cholecystitis is the most common form of the disease and may appear merely as "indigestion" along with tenderness and pain on the right side of the abdomen. More severe cases include spasm of the abdominal muscles. When gentle pressure on the spot is released, a flash of pain is experienced—a phenomenon called "rebound tenderness."

The body temperature is usually raised to over 102°F and nausea and vomiting are very common. Jaundice occurs in about 25% of patients.

The diagnosis can initially be confused with peptic ulcer or acute appendicitis, but is confirmed by the estimation of several enzymes in the blood and by ECG and x-ray investigations.

Treatment of acute cases is surgical removal of the gallbladder. Most surgeons prefer early operation; others like to wait a few days, during which time they administer intravenous fluids and antibiotics. Tube feeding may be given to rest the intestines.

Chronic cholecystitis is much less common. It is characterized by some tenderness and upper abdominal pain, but the symptoms are so general as to make the disease hard to diagnose. X-ray studies are essential for accurate diagnosis. Treatment commonly requires surgical removal of the gallbladder.

cholera

Cholera is caused by infection with comma-shaped bacteria known as *Vibrio cholerae* (or *Vibrio comma*). It occurs most often in India and other parts of Southeast Asia.

The usual picture is a sudden outbreak of a large number of cases in a particular locality. These epidemics arise when people come into contact with water or food contaminated by the feces of infected persons. Cholera epidemics are therefore a reflection of poor sanitation and living conditions. The severity of the disease can vary widely. On occasions it is fairly mild, but in some outbreaks up to 50% or more of those infected have died.

The symptomless incubation period may be as long as six days, but once the illness starts it is dramatic. The most prominent symptom is watery diarrhea, in which gray "rice water" stools are passed almost nonstop. Fluid loss may be as much as 20 quarts in a day. The liquid stools are flecked with mucus and there is little or no sign of fecal matter. There may also be vomiting, and the catastrophic loss of body fluid causes cramps and collapse. There is little or no output of urine and without prompt medical treatment death can occur within 48 hours. In the mild case, however, complete recovery typically occurs within one to three weeks.

The key to the treatment of cholera is replacement of the water and salts lost in the diarrhea. If treatment is given early the fluid may be taken by mouth, but in severe cases the fluid has to be given by direct infusion into a vein. Once the "drip" has been set up, an antibiotic such as tetracycline is given to overcome the bacteria. Vaccination every six months offers some protection for those who must remain in affected regions.

Control or prevention of cholera involves measures to purify public water supplies and the establishment of modern methods of sewage disposal. Also important is abandonment of the practice of fertilizing crops with human waste. Outbreaks in Western countries are rare and are usually confined to travelers returning from the Middle East, Central and South America.

cholesterol

A substance (technically known as a sterol) found in animal oils and fat, nervous tissue, bile, blood and egg yolks.

It has been found that those who suffer from arterial disease have a higher than average concentration of plasma cholesterol, and it has therefore been thought that a high level of cholesterol in the blood increases the risk of developing ATHEROSCLEROSIS. It has been shown that if animal fat in the diet is replaced by vegetable oil containing polyunsaturated fatty acids, the plasma cholesterol falls and remains low as long as animal fats are omitted from the diet. The relevance of a low cholesterol level, however, is still in doubt.

It is interesting to consider that man has been an omnivorous hunting animal for about two million years, during which time his natural diet must have been rich in animal fat. In fact the reasons behind the development of atherosclerosis remain obscure, although it is sensible for those who in middle age have any suspicion that they may have atherosclerosis to give up tobacco, take exercise and reduce their intake of fatty meat, butter, cream, salt and sugar. There are a number of drugs, such as clofibrate, which can reduce the concentration of cholesterol in the plasma.

The steroids, which include the sex hormones and the hormones of the adrenal glands, are derived from cholesterol—which is thus essential in limited amounts.

chondrocalcinosis

A disease, affecting the middle aged and elderly, which produces pain and swelling of one of the larger joints (for example, the knee). It is also known as *pseudo-gout*, for there are recurrent attacks of acute inflammation of one joint followed by chronic arthritis.

During the acute phase, crystals of calcium pyrophosphate are present in the synovial fluid of the affected joint and x-rays of the joints show calcification in cartilages and joint capsules.

Treatment includes aspiration of fluid from the joint, and perhaps the injection of steroids; pain is relieved with the use of phenylbutazone or large doses of aspirin.

chondroma

A benign tumor composed of cartilage.

chondromalacia

A rare disease of connective tissue especially involving cartilage, the white gristlelike substance that cushions the joints and plays a structural role (for example, in the nose and ear). Inflammation causes the cartilage to soften and produces deformities such as saddle nose and floppy ear. The windpipe, lungs and joint cartilages can all be affected.

Chondromalacia can occur in men and women of all ages. It is a chronic disease which from time to time flares up to produce pain, reddening of the overlying skin, and swelling of the affected cartilage. Fever and a raised white blood cell count are usually present. The softening effect mentioned above is the aftermath of acute attacks of this kind.

Regular administration of corticosteroid drugs may keep inflammatory episodes to a minimum.

chorditis

Inflammation of the vocal cords. Small inflamed fibrous nodules are found on the surface of one or both cords, and inflammation may extend to the membranes of the larynx in which the vocal cords are housed.

Chorditis is especially common in people such as professional singers and clergymen, who repeatedly subject their voices to considerable strain (a popular name for chorditis is "clergyman's throat"). Heavy smokers and drinkers are also at special risk.

Symptoms vary from slight huskiness or hoarseness of the voice to complete loss, together with pain on swallowing and difficulty in breathing. Diagnosis is helped by the use of the laryngoscope, which enables the doctor to obtain a direct view of the inflamed parts.

The first essential treatment is total rest of the voice; any attempt at its continued use makes things worse. Some doctors apply astringent solutions such as lactic acid and silver nitrate to the affected area, and the patient may be directed to inhale iodine or eucalyptus vapors. Alcohol, tobacco and spicy foods must be avoided. If necessary, thickened sections of the chords

can be removed by a minor but delicate operation.

In singers and public speakers there may be the underlying problems of incorrect voice production, in which case speech therapy may be required.

chorea

Disordered movements of the body due to lack of muscular control. In chorea normal movements are interrupted unpredictably: walking may suddenly be replaced by disorganized lurching, while the face may grimace and the eyes screw up. Interference with other muscles may affect breathing and speaking and the sufferer is unable to sit still. The power of the muscles cannot be sustained so that the grip squeezes and relaxes intermittently producing "milkmaid's grasp."

Huntington's chorea was first described in 1872 among families in Long Island by an American physician, George Huntington (1851–1916). It is a tragic condition which occurs worldwide with an incidence of between four and seven per 100,000 people. Since the condition is inherited and is genetically dominant, the incidence can rise to 50% in closed communities. The symptoms are those of chorea with progressive mental deterioration. They do not usually begin until the 30s or 40s but the disease is unsparingly progressive, terminating in death five to twenty years following onset.

To diagnose Huntington's chorea with certainty doctors need an honest family history, but concealment is common. Opinion in the medical profession is divided on the question of how much counseling affected parents should be given, but it is agreed that children at risk must be informed of the hazards ahead. At birth the child of a parent with Huntington's chorea has a 50% risk of developing the disease; by the age of 40 the risk has dropped to 33%—still a depressing statistic.

There are variations from this typical picture. When the onset is delayed until old age the condition is often not associated with mental impairment and in some cases there is muscle rigidity rather than the typical symptoms of chorea, although this presentation occurs in only about 6% of adult cases. Conversely, rigidity is found in half of the rare juvenile cases.

There is no cure and very little that can be done to relieve the symptoms.

Sydenham's chorea (also known as *St. Vitus' dance*) is a disease of childhood. It has become very rare since rheumatic fever, with which it is usually associated, has declined in incidence since World War II. Sydenham's chorea is one of the complications of previous infection with bacteria of the type known as group A hemolytic streptococcus.

The onset of the disease is usually insidious and progressive over a period of months, although about 20% of cases show acute dramatic symptoms. In half of the cases abnormal movements are restricted to one half of the body only. The age group most commonly affected is between 5 and 20 years. Psychological changes are common and the child typically becomes emotionally volatile, irritable and disobedient.

About a third of patients also show evidence of heart involvement at the same time, although this usually subsides within six months.

Treatment consists of rest and sedation. Penicillin may be given regularly until about the age of 20, to prevent further streptococcal infection. The chorea resolves within about six months; recurrences occur in about a third of cases but eventually the disease is self-limiting.

It is worth noting that women who have had Sydenham's chorea in childhood have been known to have a recurrence if they take the contraceptive pill. (It must be emphasized that this condition is not hereditary, does *not* involve mental deterioration and bears no relation whatsoever to Huntington's chorea.)

choriocarcinoma

A malignant tumor usually arising in the membranes surrounding the fetus in the womb, or occasionally in the testes, the ovary (where it is associated with a teratoma), or the pineal gland.

About half of the tumors follow the development of a HYDATIDIFORM MOLE in the uterus, another quarter follow abortions, and there have been some after an ECTOPIC PREGNANCY. About one third of these tumors occurs in women after the age of 40. The tumor appears a few months after pregnancy and induces vaginal bleeding. There may be abdominal pain and discomfort; the tumor may spread to produce secondary growths in the lungs or brain.

Diagnosis mainly depends on recognizing the possibility of choriocarcinoma. All cases of hydatidiform mole are watched very carefully. A firm decision is reached on the basis of repeated hormone measurements.

Today choriocarcinoma is treated with methotrexate and actinomycin D—a pairing of drugs which, most unusual for cancer, can have a devastating effect on this particular malignant growth: in one study, only 2 out of 87 patients failed to show substantial regression of the tumor if not complete recovery. Surgery tends to take a back seat, but may be tried in the occasional patient who fails to respond fully to drugs.

chromosomes

The blocks of genetic material in the nuclei of all cells in the body. They carry the *genes*—the units responsible for the transmission of parental characteristics to the offspring and also for passing on essential information with each cell division during the development of the embryo, during the growth of a baby to an adult, and throughout life. The material that makes up the chromosomes is *deoxyribonucleic acid (DNA)*, and it is this long-chain molecule which provides the "templates" for the formation of the protein building blocks of the cells of every tissue and organ in the body.

Human cells contain 23 pairs of chromosomes; 22 are identical pairs, but the 23rd pair, the sex chromosomes, are identical only in females, who have two X chromosomes. In males the 23rd pair contains only one X chromosome and a smaller Y chromosome. The sex cells themselves (the spermatozoa and ova) contain only half the normal number of chromosomes—one of each of the 23 pairs—so that when fertilization takes place the full complement of 46 is restored. All ova contain an X chromosome, but sperm may contain *either* an X or a Y; the sex of a child is thus determined by whether or not the sperm cell which fertilized the ovum carried an X chromosome (giving a girl) or a Y chromosome (giving a boy).

In the process of cell division in the sex organs which leads to a reduction of the 46 chromosomes to 23, the chromosomes are split and reformed so that each sperm or ovum contains a slightly different selection of the genetic characteristics of the parent. It is this "shuffling of the DNA pack" which insures that children are not carbon copies of each other or of their parents. However, the process is also susceptible to errors, and the resulting change or mutation may be either beneficial or harmful. Many congenital defects, such as DOWN'S SYNDROME (mongolism), are due to chromosomal abnormalities. Less obvious mutations are also responsible for disorders such as hemophilia and muscular dystrophy, which may then be passed on from one generation to the next.

To determine an individual's chromosome pattern, doctors take a cell sample from anywhere in the body—usually inside the mouth—and treat it so that the cells divide. On division the chromosomes become visible under the microscope: they are then photographed to be counted carefully later. The technique can be used for prenatal diagnosis of chromosomal abnormality by the examination of fetal cells taken from the womb by AMNIOCENTESIS.

circadian rhythm

Circadian rhythm describes an observed daily pattern in the behavior of body processes. Temperature, blood pressure, pulse, blood sugar levels, etc., change, rising and falling about every 24 hours. For example, body temperature drops at night by a degree or two and climbs during the morning to a plateau near which it

CHROMOSOMES

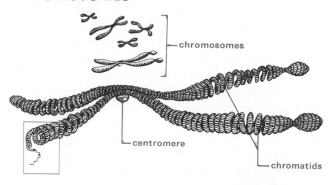

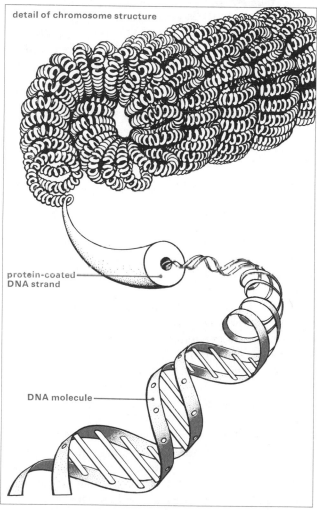

The chromosomes present in every cell nucleus in the body contain DNA and protein. Each DNA molecule consists of two long chains wound in a double helix. Genes, the units of inheritance derived from both parents, consist of long lengths of DNA chains. By controlling manufacture of the body's proteins, genes are ultimately responsible for each person's characteristics. Except for sex cells (spermatozoa and ova), all human cells contain 46 chromosomes (23 pairs).

remains throughout the rest of the day.

This "internal clock" usually continues to operate when people are kept in isolation. Individuals deprived of their wristwatches and natural sunlight have often continued to live a roughly 25-hour day. Studies of circadian rhythms in animals have led some enthusiasts to suggest that surgery, for instance, should be carried out when the body is at a physiological peak. The disabling effects of JET LAG have also been blamed on disruption of circadian rhythms.

circumcision

The minor surgical procedure of removing all or part of the foreskin (prepuce) of the penis. The historical basis of this practice is unknown, but it can be traced back to ancient times. When circumcision is performed for non-medical reasons—i.e., as a religious rite or as a routine hygienic measure—the operation is best done in the first one or two weeks of life.

In some ethnic groups circumcision is performed as a traditional religious rite—notably, among male Jewish babies on the eighth day after birth. But it is also practiced among Ethiopians, Muslims and some Christians for religious reasons. The Old Testament of the Bible refers to this practice as Abraham's Covenant with God (the "Law of Moses").

The main nonreligious reason for circumcision is the belief that it improves cleanliness. It would also appear to provide a significant degree of protection against cancer of the penis, as this is extremely rare in Jewish and other circumcised men. Cancer of the cervix (neck of the womb) is also said to be less common in women who are married to circumcised men. However in uncircumcised men, proper hygiene—by daily retracting the foreskin and washing the tip of the penis, to clean out the secretions which may have become trapped beneath it—is generally considered sufficient to minimize any health risks. Circumcision for specific medical rather than ritual reasons is performed in cases such as abnormal tightness of the foreskin which causes painful or difficult urination (see PHIMOSIS).

Some tribes (mostly African) ritually "circumcise" their women on reaching puberty. Varying amounts of genital tissues are removed, usually including the clitoris. This practice is becoming increasingly rare.

cirrhosis

A condition induced in the liver by scarring secondary to destruction of liver cells by infection, poisoning, or any other cause. The term was originally coined to describe the tawny color of the cirrhotic liver as seen after death. The essential feature of cirrhosis, however, is that much of the liver is replaced with a thick fibrous tissue; the relatively few remaining normal liver cells are left to cope with the vast biochemical functions of the organ.

Cirrhosis may follow virus hepatitis (infectious jaundice) and it is also commonly seen in association with alcoholism (*alcoholic cirrhosis*). Cirrhosis may also develop as a complication of heart failure (*cardiac cirrhosis*). Whatever the cause, the features of the disorder are due partly to the failure of the liver cells to carry out their normal functions and partly to *portal hypertension*—a raised pressure in the veins draining into the fibrotic liver from the intestinal tract.

In an attempt to compensate for the deficiency of normal liver cells the organ often initially increases in size; enlargement of the liver (hepatomegaly) is one of the early signs of the disease.

The liver cell failure leads to a whole range of biochemical defects. Accumulation of breakdown products causes the yellow discoloration of the skin (JAUNDICE). The amount of protein in the blood is reduced, leading to retention of fluid and swelling of the abdomen (ascites). Blood clotting may be slower than normal. In the later stages of the disorder the breath may have a characteristic sweet smell and an increase in the ammonia content of the blood may cause mental disturbances and eventually coma.

The portal hypertension causes the spleen to enlarge (splenomegaly), and the raised pressure may lead to bleeding into the stomach from engorged varicose veins at the lower end of the esophagus.

When cirrhosis is due to alcoholic poisoning the condition may be halted if drinking is stopped. In some other forms of cirrhosis the progress of the disease may be slowed by treatment with corticosteroid drugs. The symptoms may be relieved by a diet containing little protein; and fluid retention may be reduced by diuretic drugs. The complication of portal hypertension may require surgical treatment. In some cases the pressure in the portal vein may be lowered by diverting the blood flow into an alternative pathway, a surgical procedure known as a portocaval shunt.

claudication

The technical name for *limping*.
See INTERMITTENT CLAUDICATION.

claustrophobia

Fear of closed spaces or of being shut in. It is natural for us all to feel some fear of confined spaces, since there are circumstances in which one might be trapped in a narrow cave passage, a wrecked automobile, or a closet or small room where the door has swung shut and can be opened only from the outside. For the claustrophobic patient, however, even a closed room or the inside of a building will prove unbearable, even though he has only to open the door and walk out.

Such a phobic condition may prove severely disabling, preventing the patient from entering a vehicle to travel to work or from entering the building in which he works. In such circumstances he may develop shortness of breath, a rapid heartbeat with palpitations, sweating and other symptoms of a panic that he cannot control.

Treatment of all phobias is difficult. Psychotherapy may be useful if it can uncover the original reason for the development of the phobia, and it may be possible to relieve it by further analytical therapy. Another useful form of therapy is *desensitization*, in which the patient is either exposed to the feared situation or instructed to imagine himself in it while being continually reassured and encouraged by the therapist. This process may be assisted by the use of tranquilizing drugs. A cooperative and sympathetic relative may also help a great deal.

The prognosis, however, remains uncertain as many patients will subsequently relapse despite initially successful therapy.

See also ACROPHOBIA, AGORAPHOBIA, PHOBIA.

cleft lip/cleft palate

Cleft lip and cleft palate are developmental deformities present at birth. Besides the obvious and distressing physical disfigurement, there are often feeding problems as well as difficulties with speech and hearing. However, modern plastic surgery can usually provide remarkable repair of even the most severe deformities.

Clefts of the lip and palate arise because the processes of tissue fusion that normally take place early in the development of the fetus either fail or break down. Defects may vary from minor nasal and lip notching to deep splits running the full length of the roof of the mouth to the lip on both sides of the mouth.

Cleft lip and palate occur in two to three live-born babies in every thousand, with males affected more than females. The Japanese have a higher incidence than white Americans (black Americans have a lower incidence). There may be a family history of deformity.

The treatment of a child with cleft palate involves a team of surgical and other specialists, who follow his progress into adult life. Normally the lip is repaired at the age of 3 months and the palate at 12 to 15 months; major surgery involving the hard palate is usually postponed until late adolescence. In addition to correcting the deformity of the hard palate (which forms the roof of the mouth), the surgeon also examines the soft palate at the back for less obvious defects.

The child should return to the clinic for regular checkups and correction of any minor defects that may arise with growth. Speech, hearing, and dental problems require special attention and help.

CLEFT LIP/CLEFT PALATE

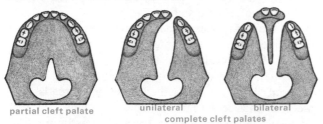

partial cleft palate | unilateral | bilateral
complete cleft palates

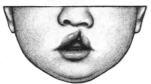

unilateral cleft lip

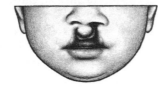

bilateral cleft lip

The face, lips, and palate normally form in the embryo by the fusion of many different components. About one baby in every 500 is born with a cleft deformity caused by failure of this fusion process. There is a wide spectrum of cleft defects ranging from minor lip notching to bilateral complete clefts of the lip and palate.

clonus

A rhythmic muscular spasm characterized by alternate contraction and relaxation. It is to be contrasted with *tonus*, in which the muscle is held in a partial but steady contraction.

Clonus of the ankle or foot is encountered in patients with spastic diseases such as paraplegia and paralytic hemiplegia. When the foot is forcibly flexed (tipped up) with the knee extended, rhythmic clonic movements occur at the ankle joint. This is one of the tests used in the examination of such patients.

Clonic facial spasm is nearly always confined to elderly people, usually women. Almost without exception it is restricted to one side of the face and the patient suffers from the embarrassing problem of involuntary winking. The only treatment in troublesome cases is surgical division of the upper fibers of the facial nerve.

Clonus is one of the possible signs of cramp, experienced as jerky painful muscular contractions. Cramp is usually brought on by poor blood circulation, as in cases of varicose veins, but may arise in healthy people engaged in strenuous physical activity. Treatment of the condition involves stretching the contracted muscles.

Clonus is sometimes found in people who are anxious, and it often affects healthy people who are under stress; they may notice rhythmic contractions of the calf muscles when the foot is pressed on the ground so as to stretch the Achilles tendon. In these cases clonus is of no significance.

clubbing

Clubbing of the fingers and sometimes the toes refers to an overgrowth of hard tissue in the region of the nailbed. It was first described by Hippocrates in the 5th century B.C. in patients with tuberculosis of the lung. Finger clubbing is present in approximately one third of patients with lung cancer but is also seen in an enormous variety of respiratory and other diseases.

The first stage in clubbing involves a filling in of the angle between the nail and the surrounding skin. The nailbed thickens and the top joint of the finger expands so that it resembles a drumstick. Rarely the nose may also thicken.

Besides the link with lung cancer, finger clubbing may be a sign of fungal infection of the nailbed or diseases of the heart, liver and thyroid gland; in some cases it may be an inherited trait and represent no cause for concern. Clubbing can arise in *pulmonary osteoarthropathy*, a condition which produces severe joint pain and in about 80% of cases is associated with lung cancer.

One theory about clubbing suggests that the tissue overgrowth is caused by an overly rich supply of oxygen through tumor-induced activation of the numerous short circuits between the arterial and venous circulations that are found in the finger. But this idea, like others, does not explain how clubbing can arise in such a diversity of diseases.

The treatment of clubbing necessarily involves treatment of the underlying disorder.

clubfoot

A deformity present at birth which prevents the foot being placed flat on the ground. Boys are affected twice as often as girls. Clubfoot may also be acquired as a result of paralytic disease such as poliomyelitis, or it may be associated with a hidden or obvious spinal abnormality.

The main defect is usually in the heel, which is pulled inward and upward so that the patient walks on his toes. Alternatively, the toes are pulled back and he walks on his heel. The foot itself may be twisted so that only either the outer or inner edge of the sole touches the ground. The foot arch is often abnormally high. Both feet are usually affected.

The structural faults in uncorrected clubfoot are due to defects in the shape and alignment of the bones of the foot. However, there may be secondary contractures in the soft tissues and shortening and tightening of the Achilles tendon and ligaments. Children with clubfoot can be divided into two main groups: (1) those with flexible clubfoot and less severe deformity and contracture, and (2) those with rigid clubfoot and poorly developed muscles, a small heel and deformed forefoot.

VARIETIES OF CLUBFOOT

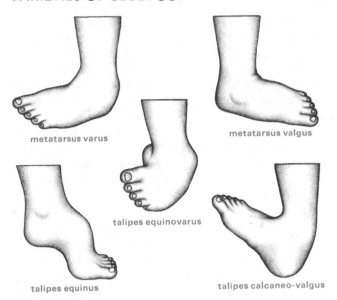

metatarsus varus

metatarsus valgus

talipes equinovarus

talipes equinus

talipes calcaneo-valgus

"Clubfoot" usually refers to talipes equinovarus (center, above)—a relatively common congenital deformity of unknown cause. The other varieties are much less common. The deformity can be corrected if treated immediately after birth.

The key to successful reversion of clubfoot is early treatment, particularly in cases of flexible clubfoot where the outlook is good. Manual manipulation of the deformed soft tissue should begin immediately after birth so that the various parts of the foot can be coaxed into proper alignment. If this is not done the rapidly developing bones of the foot may be irreversibly distorted. It is common for the surgeon to teach the various manipulative techniques to the parents so that therapy can continue at home. Correction is maintained by strapping and splinting the foot.

If manipulation is not completely successful, surgical correction of clubfoot is usually performed when the child is three months old. The foot is then kept in a plaster cast for about six weeks. Special boots are worn for at least two years thereafter.

Surgery in adolescence is usually reserved for the occasional patient with crippling painful deformity. Today such interventions are being carried out with decreasing frequency. This is evidence of the value of early manipulative treatment.

coccidioidomycosis

A fungal infection that first attacks the lungs and can spread to the skin, bones and brain. It consistently arises in people living in desert areas of the United States and Central America. The disease is picked up by breathing in dust from soil contaminated with microscopic spores of the fungus *Coccidioides immitis*. For this reason laborers are often affected.

Coccidioidomycosis usually produces a mild influenzalike illness (sometimes known as *valley fever* because of its prevalence in the San Joaquin Valley in California), which with adequate bed rest soon passes. In about 10% of cases the infection spreads and abscesses and deep-seated weeping wounds (sinuses) may result. It can also cause MENINGITIS (inflammation of the membranes which cover the brain and spinal cord). In such severe instances large doses of *amphotericin B* are necessary. The overall mortality rate is less than one in a thousand.

cold

1. See COMMON COLD.
2. See CHILBLAIN, FROSTBITE, HYPOTHERMIA.

cold sore

A blister on the lips caused by infection with a virus.
   See HERPES SIMPLEX.

colic

Any severe abdominal pain of a spasmodic nature, caused by contractions of the smooth muscle in the walls of a hollow organ under tension.

Biliary colic is the chief symptom of gallstones, caused by the gallbladder and bile duct dilating and contracting after a stone has lodged in the cystic duct. Attacks of pain usually begin abruptly several hours after a heavy meal. The pain is felt in short sharp bursts just below the rib cage. Each attack can last up to 30 minutes but may take up to a few hours before subsiding. The victim may be so distressed that he writhes and doubles up. Treatment involves the administration of powerful painkillers; surgical removal of the gallbladder may be necessary.

Renal colic is caused by a stone in the ureter, the tube linking the kidney to the urinary bladder. The excruciating pain of renal colic begins in the loin or flank and fans out downward to the inner surface of the thigh or the genitals. The urine commonly contains traces of blood. If the stone is small it may pass spontaneously, otherwise it may have to be removed surgically.

Intestinal colic produces widespread cramps, which are often worse just below the level of the navel. This type of pain may be caused by blockage or intestinal inflammation. If it is due to blockage the pain is accompanied by vomiting, swelling of the abdomen, and high-pitched gurgling sounds in the intestine.

Other forms of colic may be caused by lead poisoning, appendicitis, and difficulties in menstruation.

colitis

Inflammation of the lining of the large intestine (colon). It affects roughly 1 person in 2,000, begins most often in people in their 30s, and is a chronic condition characterized by sudden repeated attacks interspersed with periods of remission. Colitis should not be confused with the far less serious complaint of *spastic colon*, which is caused by emotional factors.

Among the possible causes of colitis are bacterial infection of the intestine, food allergies (especially milk) and genetic factors. In most cases, however, the cause is unknown or at least not documented.

Colitis may begin insidiously or suddenly. In about half the patients the first indications are malaise (a general feeling of being unwell), vague abdominal discomfort, and mild diarrhea or constipation. As more severe signs and symptoms appear, such as lower abdominal pain or bleeding from the rectum (indicative of a condition known as ULCERATIVE COLITIS), the patient is driven to seek medical advice. If the disease strikes abruptly there is worsening fever, bloody diarrhea, loss of appetite and weight loss. This happens in about a third of cases.

The first step in the diagnosis of colitis is direct visual inspection of the walls of the intestine with an endoscope (sigmoidoscope). A small sample of the diseased tissue is removed for further examination and to test for the presence of infection. X-rays of the intestine are also taken. Further tests may be needed to rule out diseases such as colonic cancer, diverticulitis and infectious enteritis which can coexist with colitis or produce similar symptoms.

Patients are classified on the basis of the severity of their symptoms. Those with mild disease can be treated at home and allowed a normal diet. A second "moderate" group are usually cared for in the hospital; in addition to the appropriate drug therapy they usually receive a high-protein diet with replacement of salts and fluids lost during bouts of diarrhea and bleeding. Seriously ill patients may require blood transfusions and surgical removal of all or part of the intestine and a COLOSTOMY.

collagen diseases

A group of poorly understood disorders affecting connective tissue, which is largely made up of collagen, a protein of exceptional strength. These diseases are thought to be due to some impairment of the IMMUNE SYSTEM, by means of which the body defends itelf against the introduction of foreign proteins.

There is evidence that the immune reaction can turn against the tissues it normally should protect, and that there are a number of diseases associated with this state (see AUTOIMMUNE DISEASES). Those affecting connective tissue include systemic lupus erythematosus (SLE), polyarteritis nodosa (PAN), rheumatoid arthritis (RA), and dermatomyositis.

Systemic lupus erythematosus occurs mainly in women between the age of 20 and 50, and is associated with complex disorders of the immune mechanism. It may start with symptoms of arthritis and pain in the muscles, pleurisy and pneumonia, the passage of protein in the urine, myocarditis (inflammation of the heart muscle), anemia, enlargement of the spleen, skin rashes, hepatitis or a combination of these. The diagnosis is made by specific tests on the blood. Treatment includes rest, analgesics, the administration of corticosteroids and chloroquine, and avoidance of exposure to strong sunlight. The patient should take as few drugs as possible.

In *polyarteritis nodosa* the lesion is thought to be due to hypersensitivity to an unknown antigen with a consequent reaction involving the arteries. The signs and symptoms are varied; they include loss of weight, fever, a high pulse rate, chronic bronchitis, recurrent pneumonia, abdominal pain, acute diarrhea, passage of protein in the urine, arthritis and pain in the muscles. The treatment resembles that used for SLE.

Women are affected more frequently than men by *rheumatoid arthritis;* the usual age at onset is between 20 and 50. It is fairly common, but the incidence is lower in the tropics than in temperate climates. Some studies put the incidence as high as 3% of the adult population, with a slight familial tendency. There is usually a preliminary illness lasting a number of weeks with raised pulse rate, fatigue, loss of weight, sweating and discomfort in the limbs. This is followed by the development of arthritis in the hands, which spreads to affect the wrists and elbows; the feet, ankles and knees may also be affected. The joints are hot and swollen and painful, and the muscles acting on the joints waste. There may be anemia, and nodules may be found in the skin. The most common complication in the lungs is pleurisy, with an effusion; patients with a long history of the disease develop an atrophied skin and ridged nails.

Treatment includes rest, with physical therapy directed at joints and muscles. The diet must be good. Salicylates and other anti-inflammatory drugs are usually prescribed; corticosteroids are of limited use, but may be introduced directly into affected joints. Gold salts by injection may be used under strict medical supervision, and the drug penicillamine is also useful, although research remains to be carried out in order to define its precise place in treatment. In chronic disease, orthopedic surgery may have much to offer; for example, hip joints crippled by chronic rheumatoid arthritis may be restored by HIP REPLACEMENT.

See also the major articles on **Orthopedics** and **Rheumatology.**

Colles' fracture

This fracture of the wrist is named after the Irish surgeon Abraham Colles (1773–1843) who described it in 1814, long before x-rays were available. It is quite common at all ages, but especially in women over 40. Colles' fracture is usually caused by a heavy fall on the outstretched hand.

The fractured bone is the *radius*, which runs from elbow to wrist and which "carries" the hand at the wrist. It is usually broken across, within one inch of the wrist. The force of the blow displaces the separated end a little sideways, toward the thumb side and backwards, taking the hand with it. This gives the typical "dinner fork deformity"—the forearm being the "handle" of the fork with a depression just before the wrist and the hand forming the curve of the "prongs" of the fork. Very often the other bone of the forearm (the *ulna*) is also involved, its lower and outer tip (the *styloid process*) being detached; the cartilage of the wrist joint may also be damaged.

Treatment generally demands an anesthetic, under which the bones are manipulated back to their correct

COLLES' FRACTURE

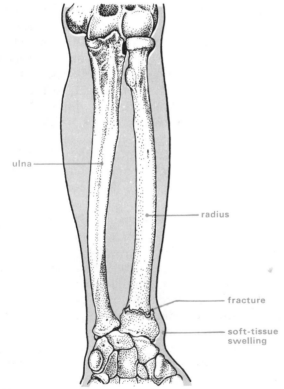

Colles' fractures of the lower end of the radius result from falling onto the outstretched hand and are very common in the elderly. This is partly because the elderly tend to fall heavily, but also because their bones are brittle.

positions. The wrist and the forearm to above the elbow are then immediately immobilized in a plaster cast. The fingers and the further end of the palm are left free so that the fingers can move fully. It is often necessary to take another x-ray soon after immobilization to make sure that correction has been maintained.

The cast has to be worn for up to six weeks, after which light work can be undertaken; heavy work should not be resumed for about another six weeks. While the wrist is "out of action" the patient is encouraged to exercise fingers and shoulder—with disuse they may stiffen up, especially in the elderly. Many housewives (common victims of Colles' fracture) find that they are able to continue their usual everyday tasks.

Once the cast is removed, strengthening and mobilizing exercises may be given for the wrist itself.

colonic cancer

Cancer of the large intestine (colon) accounts for about one sixth of all malignant tumors in the Western countries. It is extremely rare in Japan and Africa. Some 70% of the cancers occur in the rectum; if these are excluded, then 50% of cancers of the large intestine are found in the sigmoid, or pelvic, colon on the left of the abdomen—25% in the cecum or the ascending colon on the right side of the abdomen, and the other 25% in the transverse colon, descending colon and the flexures.

Predisposing factors include; ulcerative colitis and papillomatous conditions of the intestine. There may be a hereditary factor, and diet is thought to play a large part in the development of colonic tumors. It is interesting to note that the incidence of these tumors is four times as high in Japanese born and brought up in the United States as those born and brought up in Japan.

The most common warning symptom is an alteration in bowel habits. Growths occurring on the right do not often cause intestinal obstruction; they cause discomfort, loss of weight, anemia and fever. Those on the left often obstruct the passage of intestinal contents; there may be marked abdominal distension and pain. The tumor may sometimes be felt through the abdominal wall. Investigations include endoscopy and contrast radiography (scc BARIUM MEAL/BARIUM ENEMA).

The aim of the treatment is to remove the tumor completely with as many of the regional lymph glands as possible, and to restore the continuity of the bowel. It may be necessary during surgical treatment to use a temporary COLOSTOMY, but the end result of surgery is designed to avoid the necessity of permanent colostomy. Overall results are much better than those of surgery for cancer of the lung or the stomach, and about four out of every five patients make a good recovery.

See also the major article on **Gastroenterology.**

colostomy

An artificial opening in the large intestine so that it can discharge its contents through the abdominal wall. Colostomies can be temporary or permanent.

A *temporary colostomy* may be performed when cancer has attacked the bottom end of the intestine and the surgeon wishes to divert the bowel contents to facilitate treatment. Patients suffering from severe inflammation of the intestinal wall may also require a temporary colostomy. If the disease is so severe that the rectum must be removed, a permanent colostomy is unavoidable.

In the operation to form a temporary colostomy, the surgeon makes an opening in the abdomen and connects to it the tip of a loop of the transverse colon (the middle portion of the large bowel). Once the disease responsible for the temporary colostomy has been successfully treated, the opening is closed. It is usual to wait about three months before closure.

COLOSTOMY

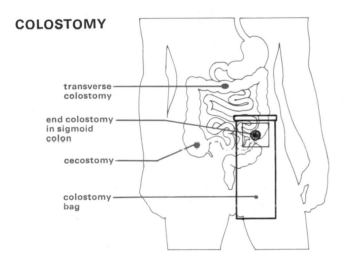

- transverse colostomy
- end colostomy in sigmoid colon
- cecostomy
- colostomy bag

colostomy bags can be held in place by magnets, adhesive tapes or belts

A colostomy is an opening (stoma) made into the large intestine in order to relieve an obstruction. It may either be temporary or permanent depending on the site. Cecostomies and transverse colostomies are both temporary diversions. End colostomies are permanent openings in the sigmoid colon.

In a *permanent colostomy* the lowest section of healthy intestine is fastened to the skin of the abdomen. The opening is positioned to one side of the midline so that the colostomy appliance (collection bag) is in a comfortable site.

In the first few days after the operation the effluent is fluid and is collected in a transparent disposable bag attached to the opening (stoma) by an adhesive seal. The bag is changed at least once daily. Later, when the feces become more solid, many patients switch to bags attached by a plastic flange. They need to be changed less often and problems of skin irritation are less common. Cosmetic factors are of great importance and "stoma therapists" advise on the use of medicaments to improve security of adhesion and reduce odor.

Once the immediate postoperative period is over, most patients find that their colostomy empties only two or three times a day. Often the timing is so regular that the bag can be emptied before the patient leaves home in the morning. Careful attention to diet can minimize problems with excess gas production or diarrhea, and a permanent colostomy need hardly restrict normal physical and social activities.

color blindness

An abnormality of the eye in which a person cannot distinguish colors. The most common forms are inability to distinguish between red, green and yellow or blue, green and yellow. Total blindness (monochromatism) is extremely rare.

About one man in eight suffers from some degree of red-green confusion, but the condition is far less common in women—only about one in 200 being affected. Overall, perhaps one person in 50 is afflicted to an appreciable extent.

Color blindness is usually present from birth and persists throughout life. It is believed to be inherited from the mother, who nearly always has normal color vision despite carrying a defective "color gene." Such congenital color blindness cannot be corrected. There have been reports of color blindness being acquired by people who drink or smoke heavily; cutting back on smoking has been known to restore normal color vision.

Color blindness is thought to be caused by deficiencies or defects of the color-sensitive cells (cones) in the retina. There are three kinds of cone, one for each of the primary colors: red, green and blue. All other colors are made up of combinations of these. Every color corresponds to light of a particular wavelength. Color confusion arises because cones that are tuned into one wavelength (or color) have some sensitivity to light of neighboring wavelengths. For instance, if someone has defective cones for green he may see this color as blue. The degree of color blindness in affected persons varies between a slight loss of brilliance at a distance to an inability to choose between vividly contrasting colors. Usually those with red-green blindness see these two colors as shades of gray or yellow.

The *Ishihara color test* (named after the Japanese ophthalmologist Shinobu Ishihara, b. 1879) is used to detect color blindness. This involves presenting the subject with a mosaic of colored dots in which there is a partly hidden symbol such as a number or letter. The color-blind person is unable to distinguish this symbol.

Color blindness may keep an affected person from holding certain jobs where color perception is essential (such as soldering color-coded wires), but it may not always be the handicap it appears. At a major scientific conference held in England in 1977, it was suggested that John Constable (1776–1837), one of the greatest landscape painters ever, was color blind.

See also BLINDNESS, VISION, and the major article on **Ophthalmology.**

coma

A state of unconsciousness so deep that the reflexes are lost and the eyeball can be touched without making the eye blink, while the most painful stimuli fail to have any effect.

Coma can be caused in a number of ways, all of which affect the higher functions of the brain while leaving the lower "vegetative" centers of the nervous system working (such as those which control breathing and the heartbeat). Direct damage to the brain sustained in head injuries or produced by intracranial bleeding, tumor or infection can result in coma. If part of the blood supply to the brain is cut off by a clot in one of the cerebral arteries (cerebral thrombosis), or if the blood pressure falls so that the blood flow to the brain becomes grossly impaired—as a result of surgical shock, massive loss of blood or a heart attack—the patient can become comatose.

Unconsciousness after an epileptic attack can be deep enough to be called coma. Other causes include electric shock and profound HYPOTHERMIA; biochemical changes in the blood may so interfere with the proper metabolism of the brain cells that coma ensues. The most common causes of such biochemical changes are diabetes, uremia and liver failure. Poisons can produce coma, perhaps the most common being the excessive ingestion of alcohol.

Treatment of coma is directed toward the underlying cause; but in all cases it is imperative that the airways be kept clear.

A patient who is comatose will require artificial feeding by means of an intravenous infusion of nutrients.

See also *Unconsciousness* in the **First Aid** section.

common cold

The common cold is a viral infection of the upper respiratory passages. It differs from other respiratory infections in that fever is most often absent and the symptoms are generally milder. Modern research has revealed that any one (or a combination) of over 100 different viruses can cause a cold. Colds are spread by direct person-to-person contact, although some people can become infected and spread the cold viruses without having any symptoms.

Colds tend to occur most frequently in the young. In the U.S., the preschool child has an average of six to twelve colds per year, parents with young children have about six colds a year, and older adults usually escape with two or three colds per year. (Some people, of course, have very few or none at all.) Colds are more widespread in the winter: about half the American population picks up a cold during the winter quarter. This figure drops to around 20% in the summer. The cold has a significant economic impact: among the American working population of 60 million, colds account for the loss of 1 million man years or roughly six days per person per year. This represents one quarter of the total time lost from work.

Contrary to popular belief, cold weather does not actually appear to *cause* colds. The results of studies in the Arctic and among volunteers exposed to cold weather have not shown any increase in the number of colds. The observed link between wintry conditions and colds remains unexplained. Colds tend to come in waves. In the U.S. the first outbreak is usually in the autumn a few weeks after the schools have opened, the second in midwinter, and the third in the spring.

The precise symptoms of the common cold vary from one individual to the next. Some people always seem to get "head" colds while others suffer from pharyngitis or cough. The first signs of a cold are usually sneezing, headache and a general feeling of ill health (malaise). Then come chilly sensations, a sore throat and heavy nasal discharge. Often, after a brief respite, the patient progresses to the classic symptoms of the common cold—chief of which is nasal congestion as the mucus changes from being clear and thin to become thick, tenacious and yellow-green in color. By this stage the sore throat has normally disappeared, but cough may become an increasing problem and last until the cold has completely resolved (generally one to two weeks).

Because so many viruses can cause a cold, and because the illness is short and readily dealt with by the body's natural defenses against infection, doctors usually recommend only supportive treatment. This means bed rest and warm clothing to make the patient feel more comfortable. If breathing difficulties occur drugs such as expectorants and nasal decongestants may be used. Aspirin is effective in relieving headache and malaise. Physicians tend to frown on the exotic "cocktails" of vitamins, multiple painkillers, antihistamines, tranquilizers, and so on, that are widely advertised as the remedy for colds. Antibiotic drugs are helpful only when a secondary bacterial infection follows "on the heels" of a cold—a relatively common event.

complex

An organized collection of emotions and ideas of which the individual may not be fully aware but which strongly influence attitudes and behavior.

The OEDIPUS COMPLEX is one of the main planks of PSYCHOANALYSIS, a method of psychiatric treatment originated by Sigmund Freud. It refers to a distinct group of linked ideas, instincts and fears which are most commonly observed in male children between three to six years and form a normal part of development. During this period a boy's sexuality is at a peak and is primarily directed toward his mother, accompanied by feelings of hostility toward his father. Baby girls go through a similar phase, but this time sexual interest is centered on the father and aggression on the mother. This is referred to as the *Electra complex*. At the age of five or six, sexuality wanes and the Oedipus complex normally passes.

In our society it is typical for parents to discourage overly intense expression of infant sexuality. This in itself is not wrong provided that it does not become an excuse for rigorous repression. With firm but loving direction, sexual and aggressive impulses can be channeled into constructive activities such as learning and play. Parents must certainly guard against viewing infant sexuality as abnormal or wicked.

A number of complexes relate to adolescent or adult life. One of the most widely known is the *inferiority complex*, in which the sufferer experiences an acute sense of inadequacy; this shows up as extreme shyness or compensatory aggressiveness. The *Cain complex* refers to excessive jealousy of a brother and the *Diana complex* to ideas leading to the adoption of masculine behavior by a female.

In everyday language the word "complex" is often used to describe feelings of apprehension or fear directed toward some particular object, person, or social situation. To some extent such tensions are normal, but if they become severe can cripple an individual's behavior. They are then more properly described as *anxiety states, phobias,* or *obsessions*—depending on their exact nature. (See ANXIETY, OBSESSION and PHOBIA.) Patients with these disorders usually need psychiatric help.

See also the major article on **Psychiatry**.

concussion

Cerebral concussion means a loss of consciousness immediately following a blow on the head. It is nearly always followed by loss of memory for the blow and the incidents leading up to it (retrograde amnesia). The extent of the amnesia is roughly related to the severity of the injury and the period of unconsciousness.

The mechanism is not properly understood, but it is thought that at the time of injury there is a wave of very high pressure inside the skull which is transmitted to the brain. This may produce many small pinpoint hemorrhages; the concussion is assumed to stop the higher centers of the brain from working for a while, although the lower centers continue to function. It is probable that the injury suffered by the brain in concussion differs in degree rather than in kind from the more severe injuries that result in coma.

Recovery from unconsciousness in concussion is followed by a period of minor confusion and headache; there should be no lasting effects other than the retrograde amnesia, which shortens in time and may eventually recover completely. A person who loses consciousness after a blow on the head should be put to bed under observation for 24 hours. Such a period of observation not only guards against insidious development of more severe complications to the injury but lessens the likelihood of postconcussion headaches and dizziness.

The presence or absence of scalp wounds or fractures of the skull has no influence on the state of concussion, although they may allow the surgeon to estimate the degree of violence involved in producing the concussion.

condyloma

A flat moist skin lesion raised from the surface like a wart. They usually affect the genital area of the body and can occur in both sexes at any age.

Condylomas are of two main types: those caused by a virus that is similar to that responsible for common warts (*condylomata acuminata*) and those that appear during the secondary stage of syphilis (*condylomata lata*).

Over the last few years viral condylomas have become increasingly common, possibly as a result of greater sexual freedom. They are moderately infectious and are transmitted by direct contact. They begin as tiny pinpoint spots which rapidly enlarge to form soft clusters of red or yellow warts. Condylomas thrive in moist regions of the body, which accounts for their tendency to infect the penis and the vulva. Small condylomas can be treated with applications such as podophyllin, but larger lesions may require surgical removal. Sometimes they tend to recur.

The condylomas of secondary syphilis are usually about half an inch or less in diameter and often appear in large numbers grouped closely together on the vulva and around the anus. They have a pink or violet color and may cause the skin surface to break down to form a shallow gray-pink ulcer which exudes a sticky puslike fluid. Examination of a sample of this fluid under a microscope reveals the presence of the highly mobile *Treponema* spirochete and enables the doctor to distinguish between these and viral condylomas. The lesions are highly infectious.

congenital dislocation of the hip

The hip is a ball and socket joint; if the socket (acetabulum) in the pelvis is abnormally shallow and the ball (the head of the femur) is small, the joint is unstable and easily dislocated.

Some babies, particularly those of Central European and North Italian descent, are found to have hips dislocated at birth; the deformity tends to run in families. Routine examination at birth includes examination of the hips for dislocation. If found, flexible metal splints are used to hold the legs abducted so that the head of the femur rests properly in the acetabulum.

The sooner treatment is started the better the results. If the deformity becomes apparent as the child starts to walk, a plaster cast is fitted to hold the joint in the right place, and it may be needed for six to nine months. Older children may need operative treatment to reduce the dislocation. If the deformity persists untreated into adult life, it is usually left unless the joint is affected by severe osteoarthritis, when suitable surgical treatment may be indicated.

See also the major article on **Orthopedics.**

conjunctivitis

Inflammation of the conjunctival membrane covering the outer aspect of the eyeball and the inner aspect of the eyelids. It is commonly the result of invasion by various microorganisms or allergies.

Acute conjunctivitis is often caused by *Staphylococcus aureus*, sometimes by *Streptococcus pneumoniae* or an adenovirus; classical epidemic "pink-eye" is caused by the *Koch-Weeks bacillus, (Haemophilus aegyptius)*, or the *Morax-Axenfeld bacillus (Moraxella lacunata)*. Gonococcus (*Neisseria gonorrhoeae*) may produce conjunctivitis, as may *Corynebacterium diphtheriae*. Chemicals splashed into the eye can produce severe inflammation, as can the irritating presence of an eyelash or other foreign body.

The affected eye feels gritty and burning, the discomfort being worse on movement and blinking. Both eyes soon become inflamed in most cases, and the discharge may become yellow and sticky. Antibiotic eyedrops are usually prescribed when bacterial infection is thought to be the cause of the inflammation. The patient is warned that the infection can be spread easily through contaminated towels, washcloths, etc., so that he or she must be very careful not to share toilet articles.

In some cases treatment is not immediately successful and the condition becomes chronic. This is sometimes the case in viral infections; or it may be that there is an allergic cause, for the conjunctiva can become sensitive to a number of cosmetics and drugs, including penicillin and atropine. A particular type of chronic conjunctivitis of great importance is TRACHOMA, which is due to a large virus-like organism. It occurs in all dry parts of the tropics and subtropics in communities afflicted by poverty; about 400 million poeple are affected. Trachoma is the chief cause of blindness in the world.

See also the major article on **Ophthalmology.**

constipation

The frequency with which bowel movements occur varies greatly (see BOWEL AND BOWEL MOVEMENTS). It is not necessary to have a bowel movement every day; some quite healthy people have bowel movements every two or three days or twice or more during the day. However, when emptying of the rectum is delayed there is increasing reabsorption of water from its contents so that the stools become excessively hard and dry. This in turn may lead to difficulty in passing them at all. The patient who has a bowel movement without difficulty every third day has no problem, but if difficulty results he suffers from constipation. In severe cases, the hard feces cannot be passed; but "paradoxical diarrhea" may occur with fluid feces from the large bowel being passed around the hardened mass of stool.

The causes of constipation include diseases of the bowel itself, an unsuitable diet containing too little roughage or dietary fiber (low-residue diet) and certain neurological disorders resulting in paralysis of the muscular walls of the bowel. Of much greater importance, however, is a failure by the patient to adhere to a regular bowel-opening habit. This may be due to inadequate toilet training as a child, to an unwillingness to open the bowels because of pain from piles or other anal conditions or, most important, a willful neglect of the urge to open the bowels because of lack of time, laziness or other factors.

Treatment of constipation depends on its cause. Any painful condition such as piles must be relieved. A diet containing plenty of dietary fiber should be taken and breakfast should be a meal of adequate bulk. If laxatives have been previously taken, they should be replaced by one of the bulk-producing preparations such as agar or mineral oil In severe cases, the bowel may have to be initially emptied by means of enemas or even by manual removal of the dry feces by the doctor or nurse.

Laxatives fall into three main categories: bulk-forming laxatives, stool softeners, and bowel stimulants or irritants (see the section on *Drugs for constipation* in the major article on **Drugs and Medicines**). It is important to note that prolonged or excessive use of chemical laxatives can lead to potassium depletion, muscle weakness and chronic diarrhea.

contact lenses

Contact lenses are molded to fit snugly over the cornea and sometimes the conjunctival surface of the eye. Over 99% are intended solely to correct refractive errors while allowing the user to dispense with glasses; in other words, their function is normally purely cosmetic.

The lenses are made of various plastics, most commonly an acrylic resin which is reliable and cheap, and are molded (unlike glass lenses, which must be ground). Softer plastics have also been introduced, which are permeable and therefore cause less irritation. In time they will doubtless replace the older type, but at present are considerably more expensive and have a relatively short life of about two to three years due to the fragility associated with their softness.

The period for which contact lenses can be worn without interruption depends on the individual; but, if they are fitted correctly, most people can wear them all day and need only remove them at night. Soft lenses can often be left in position longer.

Fitting lenses is liable to be uncomfortable, but the optometrist applies local anesthetic drops before beginning his assessment. In ordinary use no such preparation is necessary.

It should be remembered that about 15% of refractive errors (especially high degrees of astigmatism) are not suitable for correction by contact lenses because the corneal surface is too irregular. Certain medical conditions are greatly helped by contact lenses. One of these is congenital absence of the lens of the eye. Contact lenses are also beneficial in some cases following cataract removal. Rarer disorders, particularly those affecting the cornea, often benefit enormously from the use of contact lenses; but in these abnormal circumstances there can be hazards associated with their application. Very specialized medical advice is thus required.

Finally, it should not be forgotten how useful contact lenses are to some sportsmen and members of the armed forces—even though there have been occasional reports of injury from the lens itself.

Use of colored contact lenses for movie and television work is only worth mentioning to remind us that passport entries about eye color now seem pointless.

CONTACT LENS

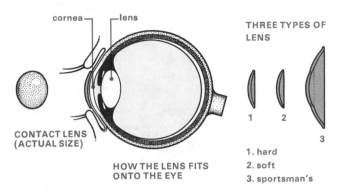

cornea — lens

THREE TYPES OF LENS

CONTACT LENS (ACTUAL SIZE)

HOW THE LENS FITS ONTO THE EYE

1
2
3

1. hard
2. soft
3. sportsman's

Most of the focusing of light rays takes place at the cornea in the front of the eye, with the lens making further adjustments. Contact lenses, which are placed directly onto the cornea, perform exactly the same function as glasses and are only preferred for reasons of appearance.

contagion

The spread of disease by direct contact.

contraception

Men and women have sought out ways to control conception since they began to understand the mechanism of reproduction, and measures such as douching, coitus interruptus and the use of tampons are very ancient. Curious objects and materials have been inserted into the vagina with varying results. The Egyptians put their faith in crocodile dung, and Casanova recommended the juice of half a lemon—the lemon skin being used as a Dutch cap (placed over the cervix).

In 1916, Margaret Sanger started the world's first birth control clinic in Brooklyn; in 1921 Marie Stopes opened a clinic in Britain. In the ensuing years the problems of population control, together with a more liberal outlook on the individual's needs, have brought the matter well into the open.

The simplest, but perhaps the least reliable, method of contraception is the observance of the "safe period." It is based on the belief that ovulation takes place midway in the menstrual cycle, and that the period during which fertilization of the ovum is possible is limited to the 10th to 17th days inclusive of a normal 28-day menstrual cycle. The method is allowable for Catholics, but while it decreases the risk of pregnancy it by no means precludes it. More effective is *coitus interruptus*, the technique of premature withdrawal of the penis from the vagina; but it is still unreliable and in some cases psychologically unsettling.

CONTRACEPTION

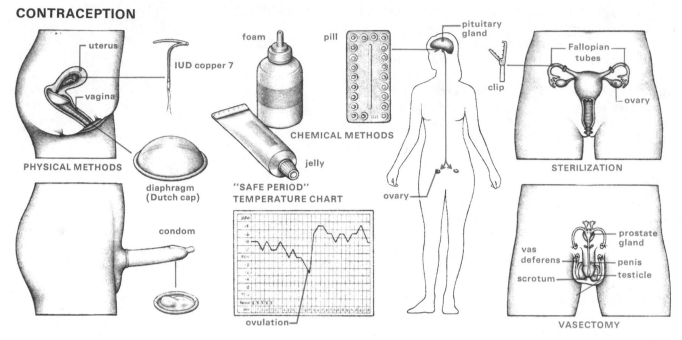

PHYSICAL METHODS · uterus · vagina · IUD copper 7 · diaphragm (Dutch cap) · condom · foam · jelly · "SAFE PERIOD" TEMPERATURE CHART · ovulation · CHEMICAL METHODS · pill · pituitary gland · ovary · clip · Fallopian tubes · ovary · STERILIZATION · vas deferens · scrotum · prostate gland · penis · testicle · VASECTOMY

Most contraceptives are either physical devices such as the condom and diaphragm, which act as barriers to the sperm, or chemical methods which either kill the sperm (foam or jelly) or prevent ovulation (the pill). The intrauterine device (IUD) occupies an intermediate position in that it probably works both by having a spermicidal coating of copper and by preventing implantation of a fertilized egg in the womb. Sterilization by dividing the Fallopian tubes or a vasectomy, in which the vasa deferentia are cut, provides permanent contraception.

Condoms ("safes," "prophylactics," or "rubbers") have been known since the 16th century. They were at first crude; but the invention of vulcanizing rubber in the 19th century made possible their manufacture on a large scale, and they were further improved by the use of latex about 50 years ago. Some are now made of plastic material. Their safety depends on their integrity, and many authorities recommend the use of chemical methods in addition to the condom. Nevertheless they form the most widely used method of birth control in the West, and are made and used in astronomical numbers.

Cervical occlusive devices for use by women have been known for many years. The modern vaginal *diaphragm* was introduced in Germany towards the end of the 19th century, and was enthusiastically promoted by Malthusians in Holland; it therefore became known as the Dutch cap. The vaginal diaphragm is made of thin rubber in the shape of a shallow dome, with a flat circular spring contained within the rim. When in place, it covers the uterine cervix, sloping from the vault of the vagina toward the pubic bone. It is effective if it is combined with a chemical contraceptive, and is quite harmless.

Chemical contraceptives in the form of gels, pessaries, foam and creams containing spermicidal compounds are not entirely reliable if used on their own, but form a strong reinforcement to the use of occlusive diaphragms and condoms.

The permanent intrauterine contraceptive device (IUD or IUCD) has been known for over a hundred years, but early devices were liable to introduce infection into the genital tract and therefore became unpopular. The introduction of plastic devices to a great extent prevented septic complications; at present there are a large number of designs available, some of which are covered by copper (which is said to increase the efficacy). Some authorities consider that they should not be used by women who have had no children, in cases with a history of pelvic infection, or in women who have painful or excessive periods. IUCDs are acceptable to about 75% of women; 25% tend to expel them. They are not completely effective, and rarely pregnancies can occur with the device in position. The precise mode of action is not understood.

The most effective method of contraception is the use of sex hormones—the oral contraceptive pill. The pill contains a combination of estrogen and a progestogen and is taken by mouth for 21 days with a gap of 7 days between courses, during which time there is withdrawal bleeding (which simulates the woman's menstrual period). There are a large number of preparations on the market; the choice is wide, but may be influenced by the observation that the incidence of thromboembolism may be related to the total amount of estrogen. It is therefore wise to use the lowest effective dose.

Disadvantages of the use of hormones are that some women tend to put on weight; some complain of headaches, nausea and a general feeling of being unwell (malaise); some may have discomfort in the breasts, and some become agitated and nervous. The greatest hazard to health is the risk of venous thrombosis, which is higher in those taking the contraceptive pill (but it should be remembered that there is also a risk of developing thromboembolism after childbirth).

Some evidence exists to suggest that there is an increased risk of developing hormone-dependent cancer after many years of taking the sex hormones, and it would seem that older women should be wary of the contraceptive pill. In any case, women taking the pill should have regular medical checkups and as they pass the age of 30 they may care to discuss alternative methods with their family physician.

See also STERILIZATION, VASECTOMY and the major article on **Family Planning**.

contracture

Abnormal shortening of the muscles or soft tissues surrounding a joint.

Most muscle contractures affect the hand, where they produce a clawlike deformity. Causes include nerve paralysis and scarring from burns. One of the most common contractures affects the fingers, the ring finger in particular. Named *Dupuytren's contracture*, it develops with age in some persons of European origin, a little more commonly in men than women. It may be inherited but is also associated with epilepsy and alcoholic cirrhosis of the liver. Often it progresses so slowly that it causes little disability. In several cases surgical treatment is possible.

Joint contracture usually affects the hips, knees and shoulders of elderly people. It is caused by lack of use of the joint, which the patient is eventually unable to flex freely.

convulsion

A sudden involuntary twitching or contraction of the body caused by an abnormal discharge of electrical activity in the brain. Convulsions are commonly associated with EPILEPSY, being the most disturbing feature of the major epileptic seizure or fit. But they can be brought on by many other disorders, such as stroke, meningitis, kidney disease, and heatstroke. In young children convulsions may be caused by high fever.

In the typical convulsive attack, as in the major form of epilepsy, the patient first loses consciousness and falls heavily to the ground, his muscles locked. For a brief period breathing may be impaired, which accounts for a temporary bluish discoloration of the skin. Next

comes a series of rapid, jerky and uncontrolled movements in the trunk and limbs. The jaw and tongue may also be affected, so that sometimes the patient lathers his saliva into a foam and appears to froth at the mouth. The tongue may be badly bitten. This period of frenzied activity usually lasts between two and three minutes. After a further few minutes of unconsciousness the patient generally regains consciousness, often to complain of a severe headache. He may remain in a state of confusion for several hours after an attack.

corneal grafting

This simple transplant technique is used to preserve the sight of people who are threatened with blindness when the cornea (the transparent area on the front of the eyeball) turns opaque.

With the exception of blood transfusions, corneal grafting is the most successful of all surgical operations involving the transfer of tissue from one person to another. The cornea can be removed from the eye of the donor up to six hours after death.

There are two main types of corneal graft: partial or full thickness. Some surgeons prefer not to replace the whole thickness of the cornea when only the outer layers of the recipient's cornea have turned opaque. Whole-thickness grafts are better optically than *lamella* or partial grafts. Partial grafts are sometimes performed because of special circumstances in individual cases.

About three quarters of corneal transplants are successful, but the failure of one operation does not necessarily doom the patient to blindness. In a few cases it has taken as many as six operations to restore vision.

It can take a month or so for a transplanted graft to "knit" naturally, during which time it is held in place by sutures or special disks. These have to withstand considerable pressure, since the pressure behind the cornea exceeds that of the atmosphere.

A major reason for the high success rate of corneal grafting is that the cornea contains no blood vessels, so that the body's defense system of rejection antibodies cannot get into it; these antibodies account for failure in many other transplant operations, in spite of the use of immunosuppressant drugs. (See ANTIBODY/ANTIGEN, IMMUNE SYSTEM.)

Few people are aware of the long history of corneal grafting. The first operation was performed in 1817 by Reisinger, a European surgeon, although the first successful graft was not performed until 1905. Inconsistent results thereafter underlined the need for better techniques, which were to emerge with better instruments and finer suture material. Even today there is a degree of mystery as to why corneal grafts sometimes fail.

See also the major article on **Ophthalmology**.

corns

A painful localized thickening of the skin of the foot. It is shaped like a cone, the point of which is directed inward, known as the eye or root of the corn. A CALLUS or callosity is a thickening over a wider area.

Corns on the upper part of the toes are caused by wearing tight or badly fitting shoes. Those on the underside of the foot are due to unevenness in the sole of the shoe. Where the skin is pinched or continually rubbed it grows more rapidly and, under the effect of pressure, gradually hardens. Corns between the toes are moist and are referred to as *soft corns*.

The first essential of treatment (despite the demands of fashion) is to start to wear sufficiently large and properly shaped shoes. These should not be pointed; the width of the sole at the level of the little toe should equal that of the bare foot when supporting the full weight of the body.

Corn plasters are circular pieces of felt which, when applied over a corn, give relief by spreading the unwelcome pressure of the shoe over a larger area.

Corns can be removed by soaking the foot in hot soapy water and then carefully cutting away the upper part of the softened corn. The affected area is dried and painted with a salicylic acid solution (included in many corn-removing lotions) to soften the corn even more and break it down. These lotions can damage healthy tissue surrounding the corn and should be used with great care. Finally, the eye of the corn may be picked out or rubbed away with a nail file, emery board or pumice stone. After complete removal of the corn, the foot should be washed or soaked in salt water every day to help return the skin to normal.

If foot problems continue, your physician may be able to recommend a foot specialist in your area.

coronary artery disease

See HEART DISEASE.

coronary bypass

See BYPASS.

coronary care unit

See INTENSIVE CARE UNIT.

coronary thrombosis

Blockage of one of the arteries that supplies the heart muscle (coronary artery) with a thrombus. Common name: *heart attack*.

See HEART DISEASE, THROMBOSIS.

CORN

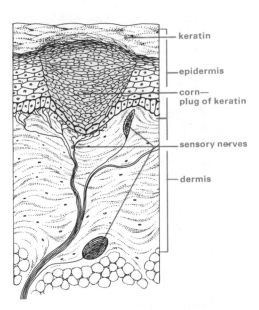

keratin

epidermis

corn—
plug of keratin

sensory nerves

dermis

A corn is a horny thickening in the skin, and may occur at any point of continued pressure. It consists of a compressed mass of keratin (dead skin cells), and usually has a conical shape with a broad base on the skin surface and a point extending down into the dermis. Pain is caused by pressure of the horny plug on nerve endings.

cor pulmonale

A heart condition that can afflict people suffering from lung diseases such as chronic bronchitis, emphysema and chronic asthma.

It is often brought on by a chest infection. This worsens an already poor respiratory performance and leads to a lack of oxygen in the capillary vessels of the lung. These constrict so that the right chamber of the heart has to pump harder to keep the blood moving. The overall result is an enlarged heart working under considerable strain—rather like a domestic water pump faced with clogged pipes.

The typical signs of cor pulmonale include a bluish discoloration of the skin, especially in the hands and feet (which are often warm to the touch). The pulse is usually full and easily detected and there may be swelling of the limbs and ankles.

Stethoscopic examination of the chest can reveal abnormal heart sounds. The electrocardiogram (ECG), which provides a graphic record of the heart rhythm, typically contains various abnormalities.

The main danger in cor pulmonale is failure of the overworked heart (see HEART FAILURE). Treatment is aimed at improving lung performance, and antibiotics such as tetracycline and ampicillin may be administered to overcome the chest infection. Patients with severe breathing difficulties frequently receive oxygen therapy.

cosmetic surgery

The stigma formerly attached to this small and highly specialized branch of surgery is gradually disappearing. It has become increasingly popular during the last 20 years and about a million Americans a year now have "image-enhancing" operations.

Disfiguring facial deformities sustained during World War I provided a great impetus to the development of *plastic surgery*, from which cosmetic, or "beauty," surgery has evolved. The public still tends to identify plastic surgery only with elective cosmetic surgery, but the subspecialty also deals with cosmetic repair following injuries like burns and removal of tumors. However, in this entry we will discuss only those operations designed to "beautify" or otherwise improve outward appearance and sought by the patient.

The work falls broadly into three categories: (1) removal of blemishes and scars; (2) repair of congenital defects; and (3) improvements in contour. Most cosmetic operations are designed to eliminate wrinkles and pouches of baggy tissue to provide a firmer skin and a more youthful appearance, although one procedure— breast enlargement through silicone implantation— *adds* rather than removes for its enhancing effect.

Theoretically, there is no limit to the amount of cosmetic surgery any one person can have. The effects of a procedure like a face lift usually last about seven years.

Many patients are afraid that cosmetic surgery will scar them. Scars are inevitable, but they can be hidden beyond the scrutiny of the eye. Any reputable surgeon will advise about treatment and the likelihood of noticeable postoperative scars.

The following are some of the more commonly performed cosmetic operations.

Rhytidectomy (standard face lift). The surgeon separates the facial skin and part of the skin of the neck through an incision just beyond the hairline. He then pulls the skin up to the temples and back toward the ear, cuts away all the excess and closes the incision. People such as film stars, to whom a youthful appearance is often particularly important, may have several operations over the years.

Rhinoplasty (alteration of the nose). One of the most common surgical procedures. A large nose can be reshaped with the removal of cartilage or bone. Conversely, a sunken or flat nose can be remodeled by implantation of a carved piece of bone or cartilage. No scars are visible, since incisions are made within the nasal cavity.

Blepharoplasty (eyelid correction). A basically simple technique to improve a tired-looking pair of eyes by removing excess skin from the upper and lower creases of the eyelids. Scars can be concealed in the remaining skin folds.

Supraorbital rhytidoplasty (eyebrow correction). Drooping eyebrows can give a tired look to the eyes. The incision is made above the brow, which is raised with the removal of an ellipse of skin. The suture line can be hidden within the upper hairline of the brow.

Mammoplasty (cosmetic breast surgery). Silicone implants can be used to restore the shape of the breasts after mastectomy; this is an extremely valuable procedure in making necessary mastectomy operations a more tolerable prospect to many women. Other operations can be performed to enhance or reduce the size of the breasts.

Many people have unrealistic expectations about what a change of looks will do for them; thus, any responsible plastic surgeon will subject a potential patient to searching questions about her motives. Some women seek cosmetic surgery fearing that their husbands are losing interest in them and are attracted to younger, more beautiful women. It must be fully understood that cosmetic surgery cannot perform miracles and cannot be used as a means of solving some deep-seated emotional problem, wrongly blamed on external appearance. Not all beautiful people have happy lives, by any stretch of the imagination!

See also the section on *Plastic Surgery* in the major article on **Surgery.**

cough

Sudden noisy explosive discharge of air from the lungs and air passages, which clears them of excessive mucus or irritating foreign matter.

Coughing depends on the integrity of a complicated reflex action during which (1) the chest first expands; (2) the glottis then closes; (3) the muscles of the chest contract, so that pressure builds up in the lungs; and (4) the glottis opens suddenly to release the air in a rush.

Any condition which increases the secretion of mucus in the lungs will produce a cough, for example, inflammation or a tumor; a dry, irritating cough typically follows infection of the upper air passages. Excessive secretions from the nose of the paranasal sinuses (which drain into the nasal cavities) may drip down the back of the throat and set up attacks of coughing ("postnasal drip"). The only cure for a cough is the cure of the condition which causes it. But coughing can be suppressed by drugs acting centrally on the cough reflex (codeine, pholcodine) or alleviated by drinking soothing liquids, one of the most effective (and inexpensive) being lemon juice and honey in warm water. Various compounds are said to loosen thick sputum, but none is unfailingly effective.

Persistent cough is rarely an early sign of a potentially serious underlying disease. Cough which produces blood requires immediate medical attention.

Coxsackie virus

Coxsackie viruses belong to the *enterovirus* group, which also includes the ECHO viruses and polioviruses. They are common infecting agents in humans and produce a wide variety of diseases. Thus, they may produce a condition resembling either the common cold or influenza, with a sore throat and painful neck glands. The sore throat may be accompanied by small blisterlike lesions in the back of the throat (a condition known as *herpangina*); a similar condition may involve the feet and hands as well (*hand, foot and mouth disease*). The pleura (the membrane lining the chest cavity and covering the outer surface of the lungs) may be affected to give a painful chest condition known as EPIDEMIC PLEURODYNIA or *Bornholm disease*. In both children and adults, the heart muscle may be affected (MYOCARDITIS) and the membranes surrounding the brain and spinal cord (MENINGITIS).

Infections produced by this group of viruses are usually not serious though they may be painful and distressing to the patient. Death is unusual except in young children.

cramp

A sudden, involuntary and prolonged spasm of the muscles causing severe pain.

It can occur in the abdominal muscles due to immersion in cold water (*swimmer's cramp*) or in groups of muscles used continually (e.g., *writer's cramp*). Hard physical labor in the heat leads to excessive salt losses by sweating and causes *heat cramps*. The elderly and the young, especially, also get cramps in the leg muscles while sleeping caused by impaired circulation that results from lying in one position too long.

The treatment of muscle cramp is to relax the spasm and improve the local circulation: keep the limb warm, rub and massage it, and avoid excessive fatigue. Heat cramps should be treated by drinking plenty of water with a little salt in it.

craniopharyngioma

A very rare tumor of the brain occurring only in children.

It is a congenital "leftover" piece of tissue at the base of the brain that should have evolved in the embryo into part of the mouth. As the child grows, this tissue grows and presses on the pituitary gland or the optic nerve. The result may be dwarfism, a rise in pressure in the skull, or progressive blindness. Craniopharyngioma is diagnosed by skull x-rays when any of the symptoms arise, usually in late childhood.

The only treatment is surgical removal of the tumor.

cretinism

A congenital condition characterized by retarded physical and mental development caused by a deficiency of thyroid hormone.

Inadequate or absent secretion of hormones by the THYROID GLAND in fetal or early neonatal life retards growth of the skeleton and the brain. This underactivity of the thyroid gland can be the result of inadequate nutrition and particularly the lack of iodine in the diet; it may occur when the mother has been taking antithyroid drugs before or during pregnancy; or it may be due to a biochemical abnormality in the thyroid (sporadic cretinism).

In the first months of life a cretin fails to feed properly and has a protruding tongue, thick dry skin, slow reflexes and poor muscle tone. These signs in a baby may lead to an early diagnosis. If not, then later, delayed dentition (development of the teeth), constipation, yellow scaling skin and retarded growth indicate the need for biochemical investigations. The tests will show depressed thryoid function and establish the diagnosis.

It is important to diagnose cretinism early before permanent brain damage occurs. Treatment with thyroid hormone has to be continued with increasing dosage as the child grows. Early treatment and good control can produce normal development and a complete cure.

Cretinism occurs endemically in areas of the world where the dietary intake of iodine is inadequate, especially in mountainous limestone districts, where rainfall has washed the iodine out of the soil. In such regions GOITER occurs in the adult population. Both conditions can be prevented by the dietary use of "iodized" salt.

See also the major article on **Nutrition.**

crib death

The sudden and unexpected death of an infant who was either well, or almost well, prior to death and whose death remains unexplained even after autopsy. The medical term is *sudden infant death syndrome.*

About 10,000 crib deaths occur every year in the United States. Throughout the world the incidence is consistently between 1 and 2 per 1,000 live births, with the highest frequency occurring in urban areas. Most cases involve infants of two to four months of age who die at home, in the night and unobserved.

More males than females are affected, and the children of minority groups and lower socioeconomic backgrounds experience a higher rate of crib death than others. The rate among siblings (brothers and sisters) of victims is four times higher than usual. The mother is often young, with a larger family than average, and inexperienced. The homes where crib deaths occur are frequently overcrowded. It is more common in winter.

The mechanism of crib death is unknown, although commonly a minor virus infection of the upper respiratory tract was present prior to the sudden tragedy. Since crib death invariably occurs in sleep, one theory links depression of respiration during sleep with the viral infection and perhaps a reduced immune response.

Sometimes autopsy reveals a severe virus infection, in which case it is not strictly a "crib death." There is no evidence to suggest that sleeping position is responsible, nor neglect on the part of the parents. It may be that an immature respiratory control center is responsible and prevention is difficult where this cannot be recognized.

The rate of crib deaths has been reduced somewhat by improvement in urban housing, education of the vulnerable parents by special classes and instruction on the subject of baby care. Even so, crib deaths do occur in well-educated, affluent families.

The parents suffer a desperate feeling of loss made worse by a sense of guilt, which is invariably unjustified. Parent groups have done much to alleviate this suffering through contact and useful literature. (One such group is the National Foundation for Sudden Infant Death, Inc., 1501 Broadway, New York, N.Y. 10036.)

Crohn's disease

A disorder of the intestines. It is characterized by recurrent episodes of abdominal pain (usually on the right lower side), diarrhea, fever, weight loss and appetite depression.

The disease was first described by the American gastroenterologist B. B. Crohn in 1932. It is also called *regional ileitis* and *regional enteritis.*

Crohn's disease mainly affects young adults and in the early acute attacks it is often misdiagnosed as appendicitis. The stools are loose, watery and continual. If the disease is not treated, serious complications such as peritonitis and abscesses may occur. It attacks both males and females and most ethnic groups, although it is unusually common among Jewish people.

The cause is unknown. Diet, infection and allergy have all been implicated, but without precise identification of the actual mechanism involved. Emotional stress undoubtedly leads to exacerbations and recurrences are seen at times of psychological disturbance.

The initial symptoms in most patients are nonspecific for this disease and include a low-grade fever with recurrent bouts of diarrhea over a period of months. Weakness and loss of weight become obvious and in former times tuberculosis of the intestines would be considered as a diagnosis. (It is now known that TB is not a cause of Crohn's disease.) As the attacks get worse

and more frequent, diagnosis requires investigation by x-rays (a barium enema—see BARIUM MEAL/BARIUM ENEMA) and biochemical analysis. The typical x-ray picture confirms the diagnosis.

In approximately a third of the cases the disease eventually resolves by itself and subsides. In the remainder it has to be treated by a high-calorie, high-protein diet and special drugs to relieve the stress and diarrhea. Cortisone-like steroid drugs help in overcoming the acute phase and bring about a remission; however, they are not a cure and the problems of continual medication with such powerful agents is considerable because of the side effects.

Surgery is usually necessary for severe cases and for patients over the age of about 50. Excision of the affected area of the intestine can bring short-term relief in all cases and long-term cure for some. The disease can recur after surgery, however; such patients are then treated with a combination of dietary care, medication and support.

croup

An inflammation of the larynx ("voice-box") leading to difficulty in breathing accompanied by a harsh croaking noise. The condition is virtually confined to small children.

Croup is usually a complication of a virus or bacterial infection of the upper respiratory tract. Inflammation in the larynx leads to the gap between the vocal cords being narrowed, so obstructing the breathing. The attack usually appears at night, when the child is lying down; the breathing becomes strident and difficult and the child will usually be frightened. Croup can be dangerous if the gap between the vocal cords is completely closed, and urgent treatment may be needed to overcome the obstruction either by passing a tube down the windpipe (intubation) or by making an opening through the neck into the windpipe (TRACHEOSTOMY).

Once a child has had an attack of croup it is liable to recur, so he should be guarded against cold and damp conditions which tend to encourage respiratory disorders. If a child suffers from an attack of croup and is having difficulty in breathing, a doctor should always be called. In the meantime, opening the window in a centrally heated house can bring relief, since hot dry air seems to encourage croup. For the same reason, a vaporizer should be placed in the bedroom. It is potentially dangerous to increase the humidity of the child's bedroom by means of a boiling kettle or pan, as scalding accidents are not uncommon. The parent should not panic, but be reassuring and assume a relaxed attitude.

See also *Lower respiratory infections* in the major article on **Health Care of Children.**

crush syndrome

A serious condition that can develop following a massive crushing injury to large groups of muscles, as in being trapped under heavy debris in a mining or industrial accident or being the victim of a traffic accident where part of the body (especially an arm or leg) is pinned. It has also occurred as the result of leaving a tourniquet on a limb for prolonged periods without relief.

The condition was first described by German physicians during World War I and was further investigated by British and American physicians during World War II (the falling debris from air strikes resulted in hundreds of military and civilian personnel being the victims of the crush syndrome). Even so, the underlying mechanisms are still unclear. Probably the kidneys are damaged by the complicated breakdown products of the injured and dead muscle cells that enter the circulation; the low blood pressure associated with SHOCK (circulatory collapse) is another factor.

Trouble typically starts two or three days after the injury, when the patient appears to have recovered reasonably well from the shock and the surgical treatment of the injuries. Urine production becomes scanty and eventually kidney function stops. The patient becomes apathetic, restless and delirious with the rise in blood concentrations of urea (the major nitrogenous waste product of metabolism) and other poisonous substances (toxins). (See UREMIA.)

Death was common before the invention of hemodialysis (the "artificial kidney") in people who had been severely crushed and trapped for prolonged periods. Despite modern surgical and medical advances, however, the condition still proves fatal in some cases. Early amputation of the crushed limb seems to be an important factor in reversing the kidney failure. The administration of intravenous fluids containing *mannitol* in the period immediately after the injury can also help to reduce the incidence of the crush syndrome. For those patients who experience the signs and symptoms of the condition, however, hemodialysis may be needed for a week or ten days before the kidneys begin to recover.

Cushing's syndrome

A disease with many symptoms, caused by excessive secretion of cortisone-like hormones by the adrenal glands. It was first recognized in 1932 by the Boston neurosurgeon Harvey Cushing (1869–1939).

Among the signs and symptoms of Cushing's syndrome are protein depletion causing muscle wasting and weakness, fragility of the blood vessels causing increased susceptibility to bruising, decalcification of the bones causing spinal curvature, occasional biochemical disorders such as diabetes, and—most obvious of all—the "moon face" and "buffalo hump" caused by facial obesity and redistribution of body fat. Women also suffer masculinization: excessive hair grows on the body, the voice deepens, and menstruation ceases.

Cushing's syndrome is relatively rare, more common in females than males, and most frequently develops in women over 30, particularly after a pregnancy.

The complicated disorders of the body seen in Cushing's syndrome—all due to an excess of cortisone-like hormones—are nowadays more commonly seen as a result of long-term or excessive treatment with cortisone or similar steroid drugs. People who depend on steroids to control such conditions as asthma, rheumatoid arthritis or colitis develop the characteristic "moon face" of Cushing's syndrome as an early sign of chronic overdosage.

Apart from excessive steroid treatment, the cause of Cushing's syndrome is usually a small tumor of one of the adrenal glands (which lie just above the kidneys). If the tumor cannot easily be identified and surgically removed, treatment consists of irradiation of the pituitary gland at the base of the brain—which controls many of the other hormone-producing glands.

The diagnosis is made by careful biochemical assessment of hormone output, and in particular measurement of the urinary excretion of cortisone breakdown products over a given period. Skull x-rays (to reveal a possible tumor of the pituitary gland) and complicated blood tests are also necessary. Once the diagnosis is made, drugs are necessary to compensate for the chemical, mineral and other hormonal deficiencies.

Then the diseased adrenal gland is removed surgically along with the tumor, the remaining gland is often found to be shrunken. Thus supplements of the correct amount of cortisone-like hormone are necessary until the other gland recovers function, and may be necessary for life.

See also the major article on **Endocrinology.**

cyanosis

Blue coloration of the skin due to lack of oxygen in the blood. Normally most of the pigment (HEMOGLOBIN) in the blood is combined with oxygen, giving it a bright red color. If for any reason the blood lacks oxygen a substantial proportion of the pigment is in its "reduced" form, giving the blood a dusky blue color. This is most noticeable in the patient's lips, face, fingernails, hands and feet.

Babies born with heart defects such as HOLE IN THE HEART, children and adults with diseases causing respiratory or cardiac failure, and the elderly with circulatory or cardiac inefficiency all show signs of cyanosis due to inadequate oxygenation of the blood. Poor circulation in the limbs may also cause cyanosis—for example, in RAYNAUD'S DISEASE, VARICOSE VEINS, or exposure to cold.

The condition is a *sign*—not a disease in itself—and may appear whenever an extra demand is made on a circulatory or respiratory system that cannot cope with more than its normal work. A "blue baby" is cyanosed because some of its blood bypasses the lungs and so is not oxygenated. A cardiac invalid may become cyanosed when he sustains a respiratory infection.

Treatment depends on the underlying cause, but if cyanosis appears during an illness, hospitalization and the provision of oxygen are usually necessary. Cardiac surgery may be required for the baby with congenital heart disease.

cyst

An abnormal sac or pouch within the body, usually filled with fluid, semifluid, or solid material (gas-filled cysts occasionally occur).

A common example is a SEBACEOUS CYST. Sebaceous glands in the skin secrete an oily material (sebum) essential to the maintenance of normal skin texture. Blockage of the opening of the gland leads to an accumulation of sebum in the duct of the gland. As it becomes greatly dilated, a rounded mass develops immediately beneath the skin, with its walls formed by the original lining of the duct. Such cysts are commonly half an inch in diameter but may occasionally be much larger.

Cysts may occur in any organ which produces a secretion if the duct becomes blocked while secretion continues. Cysts of this type may occur in the breast, mouth, genital tract, in the specialized sebaceous glands in the eyelid (CHALAZION) and in many of the internal organs, such as the ovaries, pancreas and kidneys. Other types of cyst may occur as the result of imperfect development of glands before birth, with the gland forming but its duct being absent. A *dermoid cyst* occurs when a portion of skin becomes buried in the tissues, either as a result of a penetrating injury or at the junction of two developing skin folds before birth. Occasionally, a tumor may develop a cystic area within itself and eventually come to resemble a cyst.

Cysts may also develop as a result of infection with parasitic worms, which form cystic structures in the tissues at certain stages of their life cycles (*hydatid cyst*).

Treatment of cysts may be unnecessary if they cause no symptoms. If they are unsightly, cause pressure on surrounding structures, or are suspected of originating in a tumor, surgical removal will be usually required. In some cases, simple aspiration of the cyst contents is performed to establish its nature.

cystadenoma

An ADENOMA containing cysts.

cystic fibrosis

An inherited disorder which primarily affects the PANCREAS (an organ in the abdominal cavity responsible for producing insulin and some enzymes essential for digestion).

The disease, also known as fibrocystic disease of the pancreas, causes obstruction of the gland's ducts and thus a deficiency or total absence of its secretions. In severe cases childhood development is severely retarded.

The pancreatic deficiency means that the patient cannot digest fats. This inability causes the bulky, offensive smelling stools consistently produced, and leads to malnutrition with shortened stature if the diagnosis is not made early and treatment started promptly.

Cystic fibrosis also effects the mucus-producing glands of the respiratory system. Chronic severe chest disease and proneness to chest infection are characteristic of cystic fibrosis.

Tests show that one in four of the immediate relatives of a child born with this disease has a partial tendency toward it. The test used is the "sweat-test," which indicates abnormality in the body's chemistry. The incidence of cystic fibrosis is one in a thousand Caucasian live births, while it is rare in blacks and never reported in Mongolian raccs.

Cystic fibrosis is diagnosed by measuring how well the patient digests fat from "test" meals. The fat content of the stool is analyzed. An increase of salt excretion in the sweat and a history of chronic lung disease are also diagnostic signs. Blood tests may confirm the diagnosis of the disease.

It is possible today to reduce fat intake through careful dietary control, to give pancreatic enzymes as a medication taken by mouth, and to replace the vitamin deficiencies. As a result, the outlook for patients has improved in recent years. The pancreas still produces insulin so diabetes does not occur. Control of the chest symptoms remains a problem: every minor infection presents the risk of bronchitis and chronic blockage of the air passages by excess mucus leads to permanent chest damage. Treatment involves the administration of antibiotics, physiotherapy to encourage the drainage of mucus, and nebulizers to promote the breakup of thickened secretions.

Survival used to be rare, but modern medical care and dietary control make the outlook for children born with cystic fibrosis more promising.

cystinuria

A rare inherited, or congenital, disorder of the kidneys in which the urine contains excessive amounts of an amino acid called cystine and related substances. This occurs because of an inability of the tubules of the kidneys to reabsorb these substances.

Cystine excretion poses no threat to life. The excess in the urine, however, may lead to stone formation in the kidneys or bladder and surgical treatment may then be necessary. Prevention of stones depends on the regular and frequent drinking of water as a lifetime habit for those who inherit cystinuria.

cystitis

Inflammation of the membrane lining the urinary bladder.

Urine is normally sterile and this freedom from infection is dependent on a number of factors. Firstly, the bladder lies wholly within the body and is connected with the exterior only by means of the narrow lower urinary passage (urethra). The external sites, in both male and female, at which the urethra opens teem with bacteria but their ascent up the urethra to reach the bladder is normally prevented by the constant downward flow of urine. Complete emptying of the bladder is important and obstruction to the outflow of urine, as by enlargement of the prostate gland in the male, or paralysis of the bladder, greatly increases the likelihood of ascending infection. The urine itself has antibacterial properties and the bladder membrane is resistant to the establishment of infection.

Infection of the bladder is much more common in women than in men since the urethra is much shorter in a woman and the infecting bacteria have less far to travel. The passage of instruments (*cystoscopy* or *catheters*) into the bladder will also tend to carry infection up the urethra. "Honeymoon cystitis" is a common condition in women following frequent sexual intercourse; both bruising of the urethra and bladder wall and a tendency to force infected material up the urethra play a part in its cause.

The symptoms of cystitis include pain in the lower part of the abdomen, a desire to pass urine frequently, pain on urination, and the passage of cloudy, blood-stained or foul-smelling urine. There may be more generalized symptoms with fever and lassitude. Examination of a urine sample in the laboratory will reveal the presence of pus cells and bacteria can be cultured from the urine. It may also contain protein and blood.

Treatment involves giving plenty of fluids to increase the urine flow and the administration of appropriate antibiotics for all but the mildest attacks. Recurrence of bladder infection in a woman (or, in a man, even a single attack) may indicate the need for further investigation to seek a local cause, such as an obstruction to urine flow. Recurrent bladder infections may, in some patients, give rise to more serious infections of the ureters (the passages from the kidneys to the bladder) or of the kidneys themselves (*pyelitis, pyelonephritis*) and the patient should always seek medical advice.

See also the major article on **Urology.**

cystocele

A herniation of the urinary bladder into the vagina sometimes occurring as a complication of multiple childbirth or as a complication of PROLAPSE of the uterus. In the latter case, weakening of the muscles which support the floor of the pelvis allows the uterus to descend from its normal position high in the pelvis so that it presses on the vagina from above, telescoping its walls and allowing the cervix (neck of the womb) to lie low in the vagina near its opening.

The uterus lies in the pelvis close to the bladder in front of it and the rectum behind. The distortion of the normal anatomy which occurs in prolapse of the uterus frequently causes the wall of the bladder to be forced downward as well so that it forms a pouch bulging down into the front wall of the vagina (cystocele). A similar situation may occur if the rectum herniates into the vagina (RECTOCELE).

In addition to the symptoms of a prolapse (vaginal discomfort, a dragging sensation in the pelvis and backache), a cystocele can produce its own specific symptoms. These include difficulty in emptying the bladder completely, with a resulting increase in the frequency of passing urine, a tendency to recurrent bladder infections and (most commonly) difficulty in preventing escape of urine when the bladder is full, especially on coughing or straining ("stress incontinence").

Treatment usually involves a surgical procedure known as *colporrhaphy*. The ligaments supporting the pelvic floor are tightened, the muscle layers repaired and the normal anatomic relationships of the bladder, uterus, vagina and rectum restored. In older women the procedure may be combined with surgical removal of the uterus (HYSTERECTOMY).

cytomegalovirus disease

A disease that attacks the salivary glands, liver, spleen and lungs. It was first recognized in the late 1950s; the name literally means "a large cell with a large virus inside."

In babies the unidentified virus—visible on microscopic study of tissue from the affected gland—causes pneumonia and a severe blood disorder which leads to hemorrhage in the tissues and death. Newborn babies are thought to be infected before birth via the placenta and they have insufficient immunity to fight the disease. Most adults have antibodies against the virus, suggesting that infection in a minor form has been encountered and overcome—perhaps as a misdiagnosed attack of a "mumps-like" disease. It is the occasional nonimmune mother who is infected by the virus in late pregnancy who will pass it to the fetus.

Cytomegalovirus disease of the newborn is thought to be responsible for a small proportion of CRIB DEATHS. In nonimmune adults some cases of virus pneumonia are due to infection with the cytomegalovirus, but they usually recover unless leukemic-type complications occur as a result of damage to the tissues that produce blood cells.

No treatment for the disease is known (immunity cannot yet be produced by vaccination) but the presence of antibodies in most of the adult population suggests that many attacks are relatively harmless.

D

dandruff

A dry scaly eruption of the scalp; it may also less commonly occur as thick greasy scales. It is thought to affect about 60% of people to some degree; the condition, although unsightly, is of little consequence except that those who suffer to a marked extent may develop skin disorders such as common ACNE and ROSACEA. They also incline to react more sharply than normal to contact with chemicals, developing sensitivity states, and are prone to superficial bacterial infection of the skin by *Staphylococcus aureus* and *Streptococcus pyogenes*.

There are a large number of preparations on the market designed to relieve this common condition. Among the most successful are shampoos containing cetrimide or selenium sulfide.

deafness

Loss or impairment of hearing. From about the age of 10 to 15 every person begins to lose the hearing acuity of childhood; thus every adult hears slightly less well than children, particularly in the higher frequencies.

The range of frequencies capable of being heard by the human ear are from 16 Hertz (i.e., cycles per second) to 20,000 Hz. Above 20,000 Hz lie the ultrasound frequencies, which are audible to dogs and certain other animals but not to man. The various types of deafness can best be explained by reference to the normal hearing apparatus of the healthy human.

Sounds come to us by means of vibrations of the air, which enter the ear through the external auditory meatus (earhole). The sound waves travel down the external ear canal and strike the eardrum, a tiny piece of specialized tissue about the size of a piece of confetti. The eardrum vibrates at the same frequency as the sound waves and passes on the vibrations to a tiny bone known as the *malleus* (or hammer) which fits into its rear surface. The malleus is jointed to a second tiny bone known as the *incus* (or anvil), which in turn is jointed to the smallest bone in the human body, the *stapes* (or stirrup; named because of its striking resemblance to a stirrup).

The base of the stapes fits into an oval window in the side of a highly specialized organ, about the size of a pea, known as the *cochlea* (literally, "snail"). The vibrations caused by the original sound waves, much intensified by the three bones—collectively known as the auditory ossicles—are passed by the stapes to the fluid in the cochlea (which forms part of the structures of the inner ear). Finally, within the cochlea is the *organ of Corti*, an elaborate center which transforms the fluid waves into impulses which pass to the brain through the *auditory nerve* (the nerve of hearing).

Specialists generally recognize four types of deafness:

1. *Conductive deafness* is caused by disease of or injury to some part of the hearing apparatus which conducts the sound waves from the eardrum to the fluid of the internal ear (that is, the eardrum or the auditory ossicles).

2. *Sensorineural deafness* (also known as *perceptive* or *nerve deafness*) is caused by damage to the part of the hearing apparatus that perceives the sound, from the cochlea to the brain.

3. *Mixed deafness* is a combination of the two above types.

4. *Functional*, or *psychogenic*, *deafness* is caused by psychological upset or shock in the absence of any organic disease.

Conductive deafness may be caused by a plug of wax in the external auditory meatus or by a direct blow to the ear which injures the eardrum or dislocates the auditory ossicles. A common cause in wartime is explosions that rupture the eardrum, but traffic accidents are now responsible for many cases. *Otic barotrauma* is the cause of a special type of conductive deafness caused by repeated changes in atmospheric pressure in air travel. *Otosclerosis* is a condition in which extra bone grows around the stapes and prevents conduction of sound to the cochlea; a surgical operation can correct this condition (see STAPEDECTOMY).

Sensorineural deafness can result from injury, and

also from constant subjection to loud noises, such as those made by machinery or loud rock music groups. Excessive alcohol consumption interferes with the absorption of vitamin B and this leads to sensorineural deafness. Drugs, in particular streptomycin, have also been involved in many cases of deafness.

About one in a thousand of all children are born deaf, either through heredity, maternal rubella (German measles) or drugs taken during pregnancy. Nearly all cases of congenital deafness are sensorineural.

A large proportion of people over the age of 65 complain of some degree of deafness, due to degenerative changes in the cells of the organs of hearing. This is usually permanent but it can be helped by appropriate hearing aids.

Some of the "miracle cures" of deafness arise from the fourth category, where the condition is caused by autosuggestion or the subconscious. These are often cured by psychotherapy.

See also HEARING and the major article on **Otolaryngology.**

debridement

The removal of foreign material, dead tissue and other debris from a wound. By keeping the wound as clean as possible, infection is discouraged and prompt healing is enhanced.

decompression sickness

A technical name for the BENDS.

defibrillation

The use of electrical energy to stop arrhythmias of the heart, particularly VENTRICULAR FIBRILLATION.

The ventricles are the two chambers which pump blood out of the heart into the arteries. In a normal heart the ventricles are controlled by the *pacemaker*, a bundle of fibers in the right atrium which sends out electrical impulses that control the rate of heartbeat.

In cases of heart disease, particularly where MYOCARDIAL INFARCTION kills part of the heart muscle, this normal rhythm can be disturbed. It is replaced by a form of excitation which causes the muscles of the ventricles to quiver rather than to contract regularly. The ventricles are then unable to perform their task of pumping blood around the body and death quickly follows if the fibrillation is not corrected.

Ventricular fibrillation is a common complication of coronary heart disease. Some 75 to 95% of patients in coronary care units suffer from arrhythmias. The first object of the medical team confronted with this condition is to stop the fibrillation and resume the normal rhythm.

This is done by applying electrodes to the chest (first placing on the skin a paste which increases electrical conductivity) and then passing an electric current through the chest wall to the heart. When open-heart surgery is being performed, the same procedure is carried out, but the electrodes are applied directly to the heart.

The defibrillator is a machine which gathers electrical charge in capacitors and then discharges it in a fraction of a second. The energy level is usually about 400 watts per second, which is sufficient to stop the heart quivering and give it a chance to resume its normal rhythm under the control of the pacemaker. Defibrillation is now a routine procedure in any well-equipped medical center; the overall success rate for termination of arrhythmias should approach 90%.

Complications are seen in about 15% of cases, but this figure does not include minor skin burns and transient arrhythmias. One of the most common complications is a change in concentration of enzymes in the body, which may be seen in one case out of ten.

deficiency diseases

Diseases caused by the shortage of an essential nutrient in the diet.

Humans require protein, carbohydrates, fat, vitamins and trace elements to maintain health; prolonged shortage of any one of these may cause a deficiency disease.

The most spectacular is deficiency of protein in children. This is uncommon in developed nations, but is a threat to life in the so-called Third World, where it is known as KWASHIORKOR.

Absence of vitamins in the diet can cause a variety of deficiency diseases. Vitamin A deficiency causes night blindness. Vitamin B_1 (thiamine) deficiency leads to beriberi. Vitamin B_2 (riboflavin) deficiency causes skin and eye troubles. One of the most serious deficiency diseases is pernicious anemia (see ANEMIA), which arises from a lack of vitamin B_{12}, and can be treated by regular injections of the vitamin. Pellagra is a deficiency disease caused by lack of niacin, another vitamin of the B complex. Rickets is caused by lack of vitamin D, and scurvy by a deficiency of vitamin C.

Among the trace elements, iron is the most commonly deficient; the result is ANEMIA.

See also the major article on **Nutrition.**

degenerative diseases

A group of disorders caused by aging of the structures of the body, with loss of elasticity, a reduction in the number of active cells and an increase in the proportion of fibrous connective tissue.

A major difficulty in the consideration of degenerative diseases lies in making the distinction between symptoms due to a disease and the universal effects of aging. If the rate of decline is faster in one organ than in the rest of the body, then the diagnosis is likely to be a degenerative disease. Doctors regard OSTEOARTHRITIS and ATHEROSCLEROSIS as diseases, whereas wrinkling of the skin and changes in the sex organs are accepted as normal processes. In part this is a difference of degree: while a family is likely to accept some forgetfulness, irritability and quirky behavior in an elderly grandparent, they will probably seek medical advice if his mental functioning falls below a certain level (and grandpa may well be diagnosed as having *senile dementia*). (See DEMENTIA.)

Although degenerative diseases most commonly afflict the aged, the underlying problem might have been progressing unnoticed for many years. For example, surveys in the United States and Britain have revealed that approximately 10% of people in their early 20s show the characteristic changes of osteoarthritis (noted by x-ray studies) in their joints; by the age of 50, such changes are present in over 80% of the population. However, *symptoms* of osteoarthritis are extremely rare in the 20s and affect only about 20% of people by the age of 50.

In many degenerative diseases there is a hereditary tendency. This factor is difficult to assess in common conditions such as osteoarthritis and atherosclerosis, but is striking in disorders such as CATARACT (which often seems to run in families).

The increasing proportion of old people in the populations of industrialized societies means that degenerative diseases are becoming more important in terms of human suffering and in the burden placed on health services. This has led belatedly to more research into the possible causes and treatment of degenerative disease. As a result, traditional ideas—like osteoarthritis being due to "wear and tear" and senile dementia resulting from atherosclerosis of the cerebral arteries—are now being critically reexamined and found to be inadequate.

The aim of research is to alleviate existing symptoms and possibly to arrest the progress of degenerative diseases. If successful, this would improve the quality of life—although it would probably not significantly increase the life span of man.

dehydration

The state produced by abnormal loss of body water; the deprivation or loss of water from the tissues.

Water at first may not appear to be a very important constituent of our relatively solid-looking bodies, but in fact it forms approximately 65% of the weight of the body. Most of this fluid (about 41% of the body weight) lies within the cells (intracellular fluid), from which it cannot be removed in any quantity without severe disturbance of their metabolic processes. The remaining fluid includes that which lies between the body cells (intercellular fluid), the liquid portion of the blood (blood plasma), the lymph and the fluid in certain cavities of the body (serous cavities). This *extracellular fluid* can be subject to greater variation than the *intracellular fluid*. The plasma component can to some extent use the intercellular water as a reservoir but, to maintain the circulation and other body functions, the total amount of extracellular fluid cannot be greatly reduced.

Dehydration may arise from deprivation of water or an inability to drink either because of difficulty in swallowing (as, for example, in cancer of the esophagus), or because the patient is weak, drowsy or comatose from any cause.

Vomiting may both prevent fluid from being taken and also increase loss of fluid from the body as the secretions of the stomach and intestine are lost. Diarrhea may act in the same way to increase water loss and a combination of vomiting and diarrhea will lead to rapid dehydration.

Dehydration may also be due to excessive secretion of urine despite falling body reserves of water; this occurs in both untreated DIABETES MELLITUS and DIABETES INSIPIDUS and in certain kidney disorders. Finally, excessive sweating in a hot climate will cause rapid dehydration if water is not freely available.

It is unusual for dehydration to occur as an uncomplicated problem. Vomiting, diarrhea, sweating and kidney disease frequently cause simultaneous excessive loss of salt from the body, the gross deficiency of which may be more serious than that of the water itself.

Symptoms of uncontrolled dehydration are thirst, followed by weakness, exhaustion and finally delirium and death.

While a healthy adult may survive weeks without food, complete deprivation of water and food may prove fatal within about three days. If food but not water is available the time will be longer, since most foods contain some water and additional water is produced during their metabolism in the body. Dehydration in small infants is more serious still and death may occur very quickly.

Treatment, if dehydration is the result of water deprivation alone, is by the cautious administration of fluids. If complicated by vomiting, diarrhea or sweating, laboratory tests to determine the extent of any salt deficiency and the administration of intravenous salt solutions may be required.

deja vu

A feeling that some event or experience has happened before; an apparent familiarity with what are in reality new events, strange surroundings or people.

Literally translated from the French, the expression means "already seen." Deja vu is experienced by normal individuals from time to time, especially when fatigued. However, it can be a prominent feature in the phobic anxiety type of neurosis or it may herald an attack of psychomotor EPILEPSY.

Deja vu usually occurs at a time of decreased consciousness and is often described as a dreamlike experience. It may be accompanied by other distorted perceptions, such as a feeling of depersonalization. The underlying mechanism of deja vu is not understood, but in epileptic cases an abnormality can frequently be demonstrated in the brain.

An analogous phenomenon of "jamais vu" (never seen), where objects appear unreal or very distant, can also be a symptom of temporal lobe epilepsy.

delirium

A clouding of consciousness in which attention and perception are disordered and the patient is extremely restless. Hallucinations frequently interrupt mental activity and add to the patient's general anxiety.

Usually the onset of delirium is abrupt and the condition lasts for a few days. There is remarkable variability in the patient's mental state from hour to hour, so that he might experience occasional islands of recognition in the sea of confusion and incomprehension.

Some individuals are thought to be more prone to delirium than others, but virtually anyone will develop delirium if subjected to certain intensive physical insults to the body—such as some infections, drugs, head trauma and destructive brain lesions (including hemorrhage).

In bacterial infections such as MENINGITIS, TYPHOID FEVER and PNEUMONIA, the accompanying delirium is thought to result from the action of toxins on certain parts of the brain. A similar "toxic" effect results from overdoses of amphetamines "speed" or certain antidepressants. By contrast, abrupt withdrawal of alcohol or barbiturates—drugs which have a strong inhibitory effect on the brain—leads to delirium.

The exact site of the brain's malfunction in delirium has not been identified, but there is strong evidence implicating the "reticular system" (which intricately controls the level of consciousness).

Treatment of delirium involves control of the underlying cause and reassurance by quiet, careful nursing; sedatives prevent self-injury or exhaustion.

delirium tremens (DTs)

A form of DELIRIUM due to sudden withdrawal of alcohol following a long period of intoxication. It is the most dramatic complication of ALCOHOLISM.

The condition is preceded by a generalized epileptic fit in about 25% of cases; there is often increasing tremulousness ("the shakes"), wakefulness and hallucination for a day or so beforehand.

In a full-blown attack the patient has many symptoms common to other types of delirium, but the special features of delirium tremens are (1) a fine tremor of the tongue, lips and hands; (2) an increased pulse rate and profuse sweating and (3) terrifying auditory and visual hallucinations (often of little animals).

In most cases, delirium tremens terminates in a deep sleep following three or four days of relentless activity. The patient normally awakes hungry, exhausted and clear minded—but with very little memory of the delirium.

Sedatives and anticonvulsants may be given during an attack, but they are only a prelude to the long-term treatment of chronic alcoholism. About 10% of cases of delirium tremens end fatally.

delusion

A false belief out of keeping with a person's educational, cultural and religious background.

A *primary* delusion occurs when a normal perception is abnormally interpreted so that it takes on an inexplicable personal meaning or significance. For example, a man sitting next to you in a bus lights a cigarette and this immediately conveys to you that he is having an affair with your wife. Such primary delusions appear suddenly and cannot be refuted by rational argument. They are one form of thought disorder typically encountered in schizophrenic patients.

In a *secondary* delusion, the false belief may be based on an abnormal initial perception (hallucination) or it might form part of an elaborate delusional system, the origin of which is not clear even to the patient. Secondary delusions are less specific to the diagnosis of schizophrenia than primary delusions because they are found in most other psychotic diseases, notably manic depressive psychosis.

A schizophrenic patient might construct a tortuous system of delusions on the basis of what voices in his head have told him. Often these delusions persecute the patient; they may have a political, erotic or religious theme. Delusions of grandeur also occur in schizophrenia, although historically they were associated with general paralysis of the insane (the final stage of syphilis).

In *depressive illness*, delusions are commonly hypochondriacal: the patient is convinced that his body is decomposing or that he has cancer. Alternatively delusions of guilt, unworthiness or poverty can haunt him. By contrast, in the *manic* phase of depression the delusions are of grandeur and omnipotence.

dementia

Literally "loss of mind."

Dementia can have many possible causes and mechanisms, but the constant feature is loss of memory, particularly for recent events.

The earliest signs of dementia are often very subtle and can be detected only by an observant relative or employer. There may be a mood change or a minor shortcoming at work, often attributed to depression by the doctor. However, as the underlying brain disease of dementia progresses over months or years, the patient loses all intellectual powers and emotional control, with the result that his personality is completely degraded. This total deterioration can be prevented in a few cases, so that it is important to try and establish the cause of every dementia.

Senile dementia is a degenerative condition of the nerve cells of the brain, particularly those of the cerebral cortex. The brain shrinks, the natural cavities (ventricles) within it enlarge and the surface convolutions begin to waste away (atrophy). Senile dementia is not just an exaggeration of the normal aging processes; its effects are more pronounced than the ordinary blunting of intellectual faculties.

ALZHEIMER'S DISEASE is an identical progressive dementia but it begins long before old age and results in early death.

In old people, disease of the brain's blood vessels causes *arteriosclerotic dementia*, which can be impossible to differentiate from senile dementia: indeed, the two conditions can coexist.

No specific therapy is available for the above dementias. Conditions such as subdural hematoma (a blood clot beneath the outer covering membrane of the brain), tumors of the frontal lobe of the brain, hypothyroidism and neurosyphilis can all give rise to a similar progressive intellectual deterioration, which is treatable by treatment of the underlying disease.

(*Dementia praecox* is an obsolete term for SCHIZOPHRENIA.)

See also *Senility* in the major article on **The Health Care of the Elderly.**

demyelination

Loss of the protective fatty coating of nerve fibers.

In order for the nervous system to function swiftly and efficiently, the nerves have to be insulated from each

DEMYELINATION

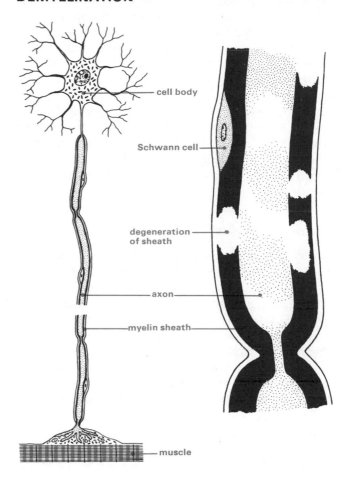

cell body

Schwann cell

degeneration of sheath

axon

myelin sheath

muscle

Nerve fibers are wrapped in a fatty myelin sheath which acts as an insulator and allows nerve impulses to travel at very high speeds. In certain diseases, for example, multiple sclerosis, the loss of insulation (demyelination) causes neurological disorders such as paralysis and numbness.

other. In many nerves this is achieved by a sheath of fatty material called myelin around each nerve fiber. (The "white matter" of the brain and spinal cord owes its appearance to this glistening myelin coating.) The loss of myelin is the common feature in "demyelinating diseases" of the central nervous system.

Such diseases may be acute (where the demyelination can occur within a few days) or chronic (where the condition progresses over several years).

Acute disseminated encephalomyelitis (see ENCEPHALOMYELITIS) can occur after various viral diseases (such as measles, chickenpox, smallpox and rubella) or after vaccination against smallpox or rabies. The vaccination-type tends to occur in older children and adults, about ten days after the vaccination. The outlook is grave because there is a high mortality rate and survivors usually have permanent neurological defects. The disease is thought to result from a type of allergic response or hypersensitivity reaction.

MULTIPLE SCLEROSIS—an example of a chronic demyelinating disease—shows a similar pattern of focal demyelination. Many experts believe that it, too, is caused by an allergic response to a viral infection, perhaps after a gap of several years.

Diffuse cerebral sclerosis—another chronic form of myelin loss—comprises a group of rare diseases (the leukodystrophies) which occasionally run in families. There is massive demyelination of the cerebral hemispheres due to defects in the metabolism of the myelin sheath fats.

dengue fever

An acute and often epidemic disease caused by infection with Arbor B group viruses. (The disease is also known as "breakbone fever.") It is transmitted to man by the *Aedes* mosquito and is found throughout the tropics, particularly in the mosquitoes' active season. When symptoms develop, 3 to 15 days after the bite, one of three broad clinical patterns may be seen: classical dengue, a mild atypical form or hemorrhagic fever.

In the *classical* form, a runny nose or conjunctivitis is followed within hours by a severe headache ("breakbone"), pain behind the eyes, backache, leg and joint pains and depression. The fever may be of a characteristic "saddle back" type: a raised temperature for about 3 days followed by several hours when the symptoms and fever disappear before returning for another day. During the second phase of fever, swollen glands and a characteristic berry-like rash are frequently present. Classical dengue fever usually lasts only 5 to 6 days and is never fatal. Treatment involves only the relief of symptoms (strong analgesics may be required). The patient commonly feels depressed and tired for several weeks.

The *atypical* mild form of dengue fever usually lasts less than 72 hours.

Dengue *hemorrhagic* fever occurs mainly in Southeast Asia, particularly in infants. The initial symptoms are similar to those of the classical fever, but damage to blood vessels leads to more severe problems. Again, treatment can only be supportive (relief of symptoms). Mortality rates of up to 20% have been reported in some epidemics.

dentistry

The profession that treats diseases of the teeth in particular and also supervises the general health of the mouth.

Common problems confronting dentists are caries (tooth decay), periodontitis (inflammation of surround-

DENTISTRY

PERMANENT TEETH OF RIGHT SIDE OF JAW

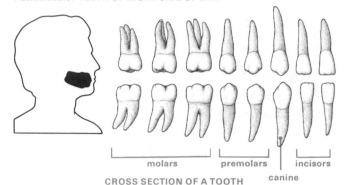

CROSS SECTION OF A TOOTH

The root of every tooth is securely fixed into a bony socket, and the blood vessels and nerve enter at this site. Enamel, the hardest substance in the body, covers each crown and allows it to endure years of biting, chewing and grinding of foodstuffs.

ing tissue, especially the gums) and malposition of teeth. Dental caries is the most common disease of man. In modern society, caries predominantly affects the tooth enamel, although the roots may be affected in adults when the gums have receded. Caries results from the acid dissolution of calcium salts in enamel and cement. Bacteria which colonize the mouth ferment sugars from food to produce various acids. These acids attack the enamel, especially where there are pits or fissures in the surface of the tooth. Although it is agreed that certain foodstuffs, such as cakes and candy, are more conducive to caries than others, there is no simple relationship between sugar composition and the amount of enamel demineralization. Free sucrose is removed from the mouth faster than sucrose combined with starch and seems to be less damaging to the enamel.

The treatment of dental caries has a long history. Extraction was practiced in ancient Greece, and the first attempts at restoring carious teeth were made in the Middle Ages. The earliest fillings used were resins and waxes; lead and gold fillings were introduced about 1450. Silver amalgam (a mixture of silver and other metals) appeared in 1828 and by 1910 had largely replaced gold because it was cheaper and easier to apply. There are now about 150 varieties of silver amalgam available, but subtle differences in composition are less important than correct manipulation of the amalgam by the dentist and his assistant. Over the years, silver amalgams have become smoother, faster setting and more durable.

Preventive dentistry has only been practiced since 1910, but is now recognized as being of fundamental importance. Fluoride is taken up by enamel and in dilute solutions has been shown to reduce caries significantly. Addition of fluoride in trace amounts to the water supply is the simplest method of giving this protection to the population. However, pressure groups have prevented fluoridation of water supplies in many areas because they fear it constitutes a health risk. To date there has been no convincing scientific evidence to support these fears, and surveys in America, England and Italy have found no relationship between fluoride and the incidence of cancer. Fluoride has also been shown to be effective when applied locally in toothpastes or mouthwashes. Fissures in the occlusal (chewing) surface of teeth have also been sealed as a measure to prevent caries. It has been appreciated for 900 years that removing calculus from the teeth improves the health of gums. We now know that removal of microbial plaque from teeth prevents periodontitis. Despite these facts, few people know how to use a toothbrush and dental floss effectively.

The American Dental Association (ADA) is the national organization which represents and regulates the dental profession. The wide range of work undertaken by dentists is reflected in the subspecialties recognized by the ADA. These include oral surgery, orthodontics, periodontics, pedodontics, prosthodontics, public health dentistry and oral pathology.

Oral surgeons carry out extractions of impacted teeth, treat facial trauma, reconstruct jaws, correct congenital abnormalities such as cleft palate and remove benign cysts and malignant tumors of the mouth. Orthodontists are concerned with the rectification of irregular teeth causing malocclusion; although traction by means of a dental brace is the most common treatment, severe cases may require surgical correction. Periodontists were originally concerned with the treatment of soft-tissue disease in the mouth, especially gingivitis (chronic, low-grade inflammation of the gums with painless bleeding).

Recently they have tended to become oral diagnosticians, since the gums can be affected by many systemic diseases and drugs.

Prosthodontics is the art of replacing natural teeth with artificial parts so that the functions of chewing and speech are preserved and the best esthetic result is obtained. Dentures may be fixed or removable, partial or a complete set. Crowns and bridges are fixed partial dentures. More extensive prostheses for the upper jaw can be constructed from acrylic resin and other materials, and are fitted after major surgery for oral cancer.

See also the major article on **Dentistry.**

deoxyribonucleic acid

See DNA/RNA.

depilation

The removal of unwanted body hair.

Unwanted hair is a common cosmetic problem, especially affecting women. If hair growth is excessive, a physician should examine the individual before any treatment is undertaken because there may occasionally be an underlying disorder of the ovaries, pituitary or adrenal glands. In most cases, however, no such problem exists and hormonal treatment is both ineffective and potentially dangerous.

A variety of local treatments are available to remove hairs without unnecessary damage to the skin. Depilatory pastes can be applied to the area but must be used in the correct concentration and not left on too long. Alternatively, the skin can be dusted with powder and hot wax applied. When the wax has hardened it is pulled off, bringing the hairs with it. Both depilatory creams and wax treatment are only temporary solutions; the hairs reappear within a month or so.

Permanent removal of superfluous hair may be achieved by electrolysis. This technique, first used by Hardaway of St. Louis in 1877, destroys the papilla which carries nutrients to the hair follicle in the skin. In the hands of a skilled operator, electrolysis should be virtually painless and not leave visible scars.

depression

Depression may be a normal reaction (probably experienced by everyone at some stage in life) or it may be a pathological state. There is no clear cut boundary between the two; a diagnosis of depressive illness is usually made when the degree or duration of symptoms is out of proportion to the apparent cause.

Depressive illness accounts for approximately 12% of all hospital admissions in the United States.

Psychiatrists have traditionally divided depression into three types. The first type, *reactive depression*, is precipitated by physical or emotional factors such as chronic illness or bereavement. These would sadden anyone, but some people become overwhelmed by them or even by an apparently trivial event.

In the second type, *endogenous depression*, there is no obvious precipitating cause but a family history of depression may exist. There may be pure depression or curious mood swings between despair and elation—the condition known as *manic-depressive psychosis*.

The third variety is *involutional melancholia*, an agitated depression which sometimes occurs in middle age or in the elderly.

Often these three conditions cannot be distinguished clinically and the diagnosis of involutional melancholia rather than endogenous depression is often made solely on the patient's age.

The main symptom of all depression is a persistent unhappy mood. According to a set of criteria established by psychiatrists in 1972, the patient should have in addition at least five of the following eight symptoms: poor appetite, sleep difficulty, loss of energy, slowness of thought, poor concentration, feelings of guilt, loss of interest in usual activities (particularly sex) and recurrent thoughts of death or suicide.

Treatment does not depend much on an exact psychiatric classification of the depression; both psychological support and drugs are important. There is some evidence that endogenous depression results from a depletion of substances called biogenic amines (particularly norepinephrine) in the nerve cells of the brain.

Two of the most widely used groups of antidepressant drugs—the tricyclics and the monoamine oxidase inhibitors—both conserve norepinephrine and this is thought to be the basis of their efficacy.

Lithium carbonate, a simple salt, has recently proved extremely useful in the treatment of manic-depressive psychosis. Electroconvulsive therapy is used by some psychiatrists in the treatment of depression that is refractory (unresponsive to any other treatment) and severe, but its use is controversial.

See also the major article on **Psychiatry.**

dermabrasion

A technique to scrape away areas of skin.

Dermabrasion is mostly used to remove the pitted scars of acne from the face. Sandpaper was the first abrasive employed, but it has been replaced by special high-speed, rotary steel brushes.

The aim of the treatment is to plane down the epidermis (the outer layer of skin) in the scarred area. As long as the glands in the underlying dermis are not damaged, the epidermis will soon grow again.

Local anesthesia is achieved by spraying the skin with a "freezing" fluid such as Freon. Skin abrasion then takes only a few minutes, although it is followed by superficial bleeding for 15 to 20 minutes. A dry dressing is applied for the first day but subsequently the wound is left open, so that dry crusts form and peel off after about 10 days. For the first month after the procedure, the skin should not be exposed to sunlight or cosmetics.

Dermabrasion has also been used to remove facial tattoos, some types of birthmarks and warts and (in selected cases) wrinkles.

dermatitis

An inflammation of the skin.

It may be the result of an infection or an allergic reaction or contact with a strong chemical or contact with the leaves of certain plants (such as poison ivy, poison oak or poison sumac). Although the term "dermatitis" covers a large number of conditions—which in themselves may arise from a bewildering number of causes—the pathological changes are remarkably constant.

Like any other inflammation, dermatitis can be classified as acute, subacute or chronic. The initial or acute stage is characterized by redness and swelling of the skin with the formation of vesicles (tiny blisters) in the outer layer. As the acute stage subsides, there are fewer vesicles and the skin becomes thickened and scaly. In chronic dermatitis, where the process has persisted for many weeks or months, there are usually no vesicles but the epidermis often becomes much thicker and leathery in appearance.

While the classification of many apparently different skin conditions under the heading of dermatitis is an oversimplification, it does avoid a multiplicity of terms which would otherwise be needed to denote minor variations.

Much confusion exists in the usage of the terms "dermatitis" and "eczema." In the United States, chronic recurrent skin inflammations are called "eczema" and more acute self-limited ones "dermatitis." In Britain, on the other hand, it has been customary to restrict the term "eczema" to those inflammatory skin conditions with no apparent external cause. The trend now is to regard the two terms as synonymous.

All of the individual types of dermatitis described below can be aggravated by the following factors: scratching; application of irritating medications which might have no effect on normal skin; infection due to a change in the bacterial population on an area of inflamed skin and blockage of the sweat ducts, which can cause a secondary heat rash.

Acute contact dermatitis—probably the single most

common type of dermatitis—is a reaction to external agents. The causative agent is often an irritant such as a strong acid or alkali; the skin reaction appears within 24 hours of contact. Alternatively, sensitizing agents such as nickel or rubber penetrate the epidermis and link with a tissue protein to form an antigen. The sensitized individual then experiences a delayed allergic response to this skin antigen over a period of days or years, leading eventually to dermatitis.

Primary irritants in sufficient concentrations will cause dermatitis in everyone, but sensitizing agents present in low concentrations over prolonged periods will cause a reaction only in susceptible individuals.

The sensitizing agent can be very difficult to identify, but the site of the dermatitis often gives a clue. For example, hair dyes and shampoo affect the scalp; airborne sprays or dusts, volatile chemicals and cosmetics involve the face; clothing and deodorants affect the armpits; and glue, industrial chemicals, plants and rubber produce a reaction on the hands. Many ointments, especially antibiotics, can cause contact dermatitis.

If dermatitis is recurrent and has no known cause, patch testing of the patient's skin with potential sensitizers can be carried out.

The first step in treatment is the removal of the offending agent. In severe cases a cortisone-like steroid drug, such as hydrocortisone, may be applied to the skin.

Atopic dermatitis runs in families and is closely associated with hay fever and asthma. About 10% of the population are *atopic* (that is allergic) because they are predisposed to form high concentrations of "IgE" type antibodies in their serum, although there is little evidence that these are directly responsible for the dermatitis.

Eczema usually starts in infancy and often disappears before adolescence. No cure is available but the intense itching can be relieved with creams.

Nummular (coin-shaped) eczema is a subacute dermatitis which begins in middle age.

Seborrheic dermatitis, often an inherited condition, is characterized by greasy scaling of the skin—not only of the scalp but around the eyebrows, behind the ears, between the shoulders and other skin folds. In mild cases the dandruff can be controlled by more frequent shampooing, but more extensive involvement may require steroid ointment. Since secondary bacterial infection may occur, an antibiotic is sometimes combined with the steroid.

See also the major article on **Dermatology.**

dermatofibroma

A FIBROMA affecting the skin.

dermatomyositis

Inflammation of the muscles accompanied by a rash over the eyelids, cheeks, chest and knuckles.

It affects females more commonly than males and may occur at any age, although two thirds of patients are over 30 years old.

A slowly progressive weakness develops during a period of 3 to 12 months, particularly affecting muscles around the shoulders and hips. The patient may notice difficulty in climbing stairs or in raising his arms above his head. The skin rash may appear before, during or after the onset of weakness.

Up to 50% of patients with dermatomyositis also show signs of a COLLAGEN DISEASE (rheumatoid arthritis, systemic lupus erythematosus or scleroderma). There is also some association with cancer, especially among older patients.

The exact cause of dermatomyositis is unknown but it is thought to be an autoimmune disorder (see AUTOIMMUNE DISEASE). Antibodies against their own muscle have been found in the blood of many patients. Most patients improve on high doses of corticosteroids and the chances of a cure are good in young patients.

dermatosis

A nonspecific name for any skin disorder.

Skin diseases are usually diagnosed by their visual appearance and the following terms are common.

A *macule* is a flat area of altered color, common to many rashes.

A round solid elevation of the skin is called a *papule* when it is less than 1 cm (2/5 inch) in diameter, and a *nodule* when over 1 cm.

A *plaque* is a raised flat patch of skin of any color; typical plaques occur in psoriasis.

A *vesicle* is a small fluid-containing blister, many of which are seen in the acute forms of dermatitis.

Bullae are larger fluid-filled spaces found in conditions such as pemphigus.

desensitization

1. A treatment used to suppress some forms of allergy such as hay fever or asthma. For uncontrollable hay fever, for example, after tests to determine which variety of pollen is responsible, repeated injections of minute doses are given for perhaps three to six months before the pollen season. It is unclear whether desensitization works by damping down the formation of antibodies to the allergen or by inducing "blocking antibodies" (which in effect neutralize pollen antigens before they reach the cells that produce the reaction). Desensitization is highly effective in some cases but it

needs to be repeated each year and the same result may not be obtained on later occasions. Some individuals find, however, that after several years of treatment their symptoms disappear completely.

See also the major article on **Dermatology.**

2. Desensitization is also the name of a method used by psychiatrists to reduce "phobic anxiety" by slowly accustoming the patient to the source of his fears while he is relaxed—often with the help of an intravenous injection of a tranquilizer.

In the first stage, the patient is asked to think of a small aspect of his phobia until it no longer provokes fear. For instance, if the phobia concerns air travel he might be asked to imagine himself taking a taxi to the airport. Then he has to imagine progressively more frightening situations until he can tolerate the whole idea of air travel. The next stage is to go through the same steps in real life. Desensitization is a painstaking and lengthy technique, but it can be effective in selected cases.

desquamation

Normal loss of the very outer layer of the skin (epidermis).

The epidermis consists of several layers of squamous (scale-like) cells covered by a layer of keratin. Squamous cells are thin flat cells which fit together to form a continuous membrane.

The cells in the deepest layer of the epidermis divide and move toward the surface. As they approach the surface, these cells are transformed into keratin—a tough waterproof protein, which forms a protective covering for the skin. Keratin is continuously being replaced from below and the superficial layer sloughs off. This sloughing of keratin is desquamation.

detached retina

In this condition there is not an actual detachment of the retina (the light-sensitive "screen" at the back of the eye) from the underlying tissues, but a collection of fluid between two layers of the retina. This fluid can come either from blood vessels or, more commonly, from the vitreous humor (fluid within the eye) through a hole in the retina.

When the detachment begins, the patient may notice flashes or streaks of light and clouding of vision. There has often been some recent injury; although this is directly responsible in only a small proportion of cases, it does accelerate detachment which has been developing over a long time.

Inflammation and tumors in the eye, high blood pressure, vitreous hemorrhage and myopia all predispose to retinal detachment.

DETACHED RETINA

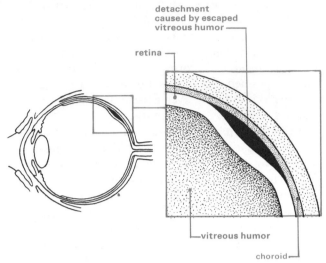

The retina is the film at the back of the eye which contains the light-sensitive receptors of the optic nerve. Detached retina results from a tear in this delicate film; the jellylike vitreous humor squeezes through the hole and separates the retina from the underlying choroid. Prompt treatment is vital.

The detached part of the retina can be "sealed" against the underlying tissues by means of an intense beam of light (such as a laser). It is directed into the eye in an extremely narrow column (about the size of a pinpoint), focused for a fraction of a second and automatically shut off. The inflammatory reaction this produces causes the detachment to fuse with the underlying tissues.

Unless surgery is undertaken quickly, the detachment extends progressively and sight in the affected eye may be irretrievably lost. Prophylactic surgery can be carried out in the unaffected eye if it is thought to be at risk of future detachment.

See also the major article on **Ophthalmology.**

diabetes insipidus

A rare condition in which the patient passes large quantities of urine and is constantly thirsty.

Part of the pituitary gland (at the base of the brain) normally secretes a hormone called vasopressin or *antidiuretic hormone* (ADH), which is carried by the blood to the kidneys; there it limits the outflow of water in the urine. Diabetes insipidus is caused by ADH deficiency and leads to the passage of large quantities of pale, dilute urine with consequent dehydration and excessive thirst.

The great majority of cases are due to a tumor or inflammation in the region of the pituitary gland, thereby suppressing ADH production. Trauma, whether a fracture of the base of the skull or surgery in the pituitary area, can also cause diabetes insipidus. In addition, there is a rare inherited form of diabetes insipidus where the production of ADH is normal but the kidneys do not respond to the circulating hormone.

The condition is unrelated to the more familiar form of diabetes (DIABETES MELLITUS).

diabetes mellitus

A syndrome in which the basic defect is absence or shortage of the pancreatic hormone *insulin*. There are two major types of diabetes—which are thought to differ in their cause, onset and response to treatment.

Juvenile-onset diabetes usually comes on very suddenly with excessive thirst and appetite and an unusually high daily output of urine. In addition to raised blood sugar levels, weight loss is often apparent. These children or young adults are totally dependent on regular insulin injections plus a strict diet to control their blood sugar levels. Unlike the grim and inevitable fate before insulin therapy became available in the 1920s, however, their life expectancy is not drastically shortened.

Maturity-onset diabetes has a slower onset, in middle age or later years, and can usually be controlled by diet alone or with special tablets. In fact the mild symptoms of maturity onset diabetes mean that it often goes unrecognized. It has been estimated that there are 4 million diabetics in the United States, up to 2 million of whom are undiagnosed.

Diabetes runs in families, although there is no simple pattern of inheritance. Close relatives of diabetics stand a two and a half times increased chance of developing diabetes. Recent studies on identical twins have tended to reverse the traditional ideas about the cause. Juvenile-onset diabetes was thought to be mainly genetic, but autoimmune processes and viral infections are now being postulated as causes. By contrast, maturity onset diabetes was long held to be the result of obesity and other environmental factors; it is now thought to have a stronger genetic basis than the juvenile type.

In a small number of patients diabetes mellitus is associated with some other predisposing disease—such as ACROMEGALY, CUSHING'S SYNDROME or HEMOCHROMATOSIS—or with the effects of drugs.

Although insulin primarily controls the metabolism of carbohydrates, fat metabolism is also disordered in diabetes. The latter defect leads to the appearance of ATHEROSCLEROSIS at an unusually early age in diabetics and may account for many of the complications (such as diseases of the kidneys and retina, gangrene of the feet, and nerve disorders).

A diabetic patient will lose consciousness if the level of sugar (glucose) in his blood is too high or too low.

Hyperglycemia (too much glucose) can occur in an undiagnosed diabetic or in one who has omitted to take his insulin; this can lead to a very dangerous condition marked by coma. Hypoglycemia (too little glucose) is very common and usually results from undereating or insulin overdose. It produces sweating, nervousness, weakness, irrational behavior and then rapid loss of consciousness. Sugar given by mouth during the brief period of warning symptoms will prevent the unconsciousness.

See also the major article on **Endocrinology**.

dialysis

A technique to remove waste products from the blood when the kidneys are unable to perform this task (also called *hemodialysis*).

The most important functions of the kidneys are to excrete the waste products of the body's metabolism and maintain the correct electrolyte balance of the blood. When both kidneys are failing, these functions have to be maintained artificially.

Dialysis is based on the simple principle of osmosis: many chemical substances will diffuse through a membrane from a strong to a weak solution.

Blood from a patient in renal failure contains high concentrations of urea and other toxic substances and low concentrations of essential electrolytes such as sodium. During dialysis the patient's blood and the dialyzing fluid (containing the correct concentrations of electrolytes) flow in opposite directions on either side of a membrane. The blood cells are too large to cross the membrane, but the toxic substances diffuse into the dialyzing fluid while electrolytes pass from the fluid into the blood.

In the familiar kidney machine (*hemodialyzer*) the membrane is made of a synthetic substance such as cellophane. In *peritoneal* dialysis the dialyzing fluid is introduced into the patient's peritoneal cavity where the peritoneal membrane serves as the barrier. It is only used in cases where the renal failure is expected to reverse quickly or as a holding operation until a kidney machine becomes available.

Although a kidney machine can maintain life for many years, it is not a perfect replacement for the natural kidney. A patient on long-term hemodialysis tends to develop ancillary medical problems and experience severe psychological stress. Successful kidney transplantation is the best treatment of chronic renal failure; most patients are maintained on dialysis only until a suitable donor kidney becomes available. In the event of transplantation failure, the patient can return to dialysis.

The treatment of chronic renal failure is governed by its enormous cost; unfortunately, the vast majority of patients die without being offered dialysis or transplantation. In an effort to reduce the expense, patients are now encouraged to dialyze at home rather than in the hospital. In addition, being at home means the patient can dialyze at convenient times; most choose to do so three nights a week during their sleep.

See also the major article on **Nephrology.**

diarrhea

The frequent passage of loose stools.

A sudden change in bowel habit to voluminous, watery stools, as in acute diarrhea, is an unmistakable symptom. Intermittent bouts of loose stools extending over a period of months (chronic diarrhea) usually presents a more difficult diagnostic problem.

Acute diarrhea in a previously healthy person is nearly always due to infection; it is occasionally possible to identify a particular meal as the source of infection, especially when other people contract the same illness. If diarrhea occurs within 24 hours of eating the meal, it is probably due to ingestion of a bacterial toxin. "Traveler's diarrhea," the scourge of tourists everywhere, is a self-limiting condition which lasts up to three days. It can be due to a pathogenic strain of the bacterium *Escherichia coli* or might result from the normal bacteria in the bowel being changed to unaccustomed strains.

If the diarrhea is bloodstained, dysentery due to *Shigella* bacteria or the protozoon *Entamoeba histolytica* may be responsible. The *Salmonella* group of bacteria produce either typical food poisoning with diarrhea about 72 hours after ingestion or the much more serious TYPHOID FEVER and PARATYPHOID FEVER, in which diarrhea is a late symptom.

The prevention of acute diarrhea by strict hygiene is more effective than its treatment, which in the self-limiting disease consists of salt and water replacement, perhaps with drugs such as Lomotil. Antibiotics are of value only in prolonged illnesses such as typhoid.

In chronic diarrhea it is the change in bowel habit which is important, rather than the number of visits to the bathroom daily or the consistency of the stools. Associated signs or symptoms might reveal that the diarrhea is one feature of a generalized disease, such as thyrotoxicosis. In the majority of patients, however, chronic diarrhea results from inflammation or irritation of the bowel. Such irritation occurs in ulcerative colitis, Crohn's disease, diverticular disease and tumors of the large bowel. In the absence of any positive physical findings, the diagnosis of IRRITABLE BOWEL SYNDROME is often made.

Some drugs can cause diarrhea as a side effect. See also *Drugs for diarrhea* in the major article on **Drugs and Medicines.**

diastole

Each of the four chambers of the heart acts as a pump, contracting and expanding alternately. Diastole is the period when a chamber expands and fills with blood.

The period of ventricular diastole corresponds to the period when the atria are contracting (SYSTOLE) and discharging blood into the ventricles.

When the ventricles contract to pump blood around the body, the atria are in diastole, the right filling up with blood from the general circulation and the left with blood from the lungs. Nonreturn valves between the atria and the ventricles prevent backflow.

When the term *diastolic blood pressure* is used, it refers to the pressure in large arteries during ventricular diastole.

See also BLOOD PRESSURE.

diathermy

The generation of heat in body tissues by means of an electric current. Diathermy is one form of CAUTERY.

The heat produced in tissues by the passage of the current may be sufficient to destroy them. This technique is used in surgery to seal blood vessels as they are cut and in the destruction of certain tumors.

Short wave diathermy uses current of a much higher frequency than that used in cauterization. It produces insufficient heat to destroy tissue but enough to dilate blood vessels and relax muscles. It is frequently used to relieve the pain and stiffness of rheumatic conditions of joints or muscles. Commonly the heat treatment is applied for about half an hour, several times a week.

digestion

The process whereby food is broken down into its constituent nutrients ready for absorption into the bloodstream.

Digestion of complex food molecules into smaller, absorbable molecules begins in the mouth and is completed by the time the food reaches the end of the small intestine. Apart from the mechanical processes of chewing and swallowing, the journey of food through the alimentary canal and its digestion take place without any voluntary control, but the activity of the digestive organs is very susceptible to emotion such as excitement, fear and anger.

Digestive juices are produced in the mouth, stomach, intestine and pancreas, under the control of nerves and hormones, and fat-embolizing bile is secreted by the liver and stored in the gallbladder. Enzymes in these juices encourage the breakdown of large molecules into smaller ones. Each digestive enzyme is responsible for the chemical splitting of a particular type of nutrient.

DIGESTIVE TRACT

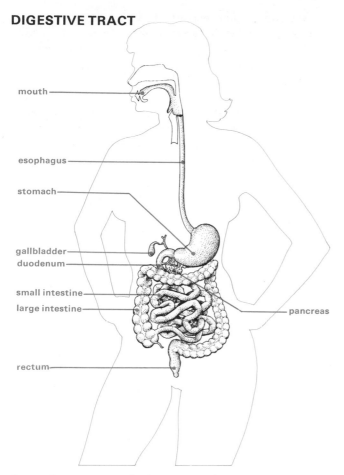

Digestion starts with chewing in the mouth; in the stomach the food is churned for several hours and mixed with acid and pepsin (a protein-breaking enzyme) so that it becomes liquid. Small amounts of this liquid are released into the duodenum where enzymes from the pancreas complete the digestive process.

Digestion of carbohydrates (starch and sugars) begins in the mouth under the influence of saliva and continues in the stomach and small intestine. The large molecules are split into smaller fragments, eventually yielding simple sugars such as glucose. In the same way, proteins are digested into their constituent amino acids by a series of enzymes secreted by the stomach, small intestine and pancreas.

Dietary fat is digested into smaller units in the small intestine, where these are mixed with bile salts which enable them to be absorbed as an emulsion.

Almost all the nutrients in the food—including minerals and vitamins as well as the end products of enzymatic digestion—are absorbed in the small intestine. The liquid waste is then passed into the large intestine (colon) where most of the water is absorbed and the solid feces stored in the lower part of the bowel (rectum) until it is convenient to discharge them.

Apart from the rare cases of absence of one or more of the digestive enzymes, most of the diseases of the gastrointestinal tract are due to physical damage to the organs concerned. The most common cause of indigestion is unwise eating or drinking—especially the excessive consumption of alcohol. The modern American diet is mostly made up of highly refined foods—white flour, white sugar—and contains few unrefined cereals or raw vegetables. The lack of vegetable fiber ("roughage") in such a diet is known to slow the transit of food through the intestines and is now thought to be largely responsible for chronic digestive disorders such as constipation and diverticular disease (see DIVERTICULITIS and DIVERTICULOSIS). The lining of the stomach and intestine may also be irritated and inflamed by virus and bacterial infections and by toxins (as in some forms of food poisoning). More serious digestive disorders may be due to ulceration of the stomach or the colon, to chronic inflammation of the intestine (as in CROHN'S DISEASE) and to tumors.

See also BOWEL AND BOWEL MOVEMENTS, METABOLISM and the major article on **Gastroenterology.**

dilatation

The expansion of a cavity or the widening of an opening, tube or passageway.

Dilatation may occur naturally under hormonal or nervous control. For example, blood vessels dilate in order to supply tissues with more blood when necessary; and the pupil of the eye dilates when it needs to admit more light in dim conditions.

Dilatation may also be part of a disease process or an adaptation to a disease. In heart failure the ventricles dilate as the heart is unable to pump blood out of them; again, when a tube such as the ureter is obstructed the part of the urinary tube before the obstruction is forced to dilate.

In some circumstances dilatation is used as a therapeutic procedure. A narrowed urethra, which makes passage of urine difficult, may be mechanically dilated; or the cervix may be dilated to provide access for a curette in the procedure of DILATATION AND CURETTAGE.

The opposite of dilatation is constriction.

dilatation and curettage (D & C)

A minor gynecological procedure performed to obtain tissue for examination or to treat certain disorders. The cervix (neck of the uterus) is dilated and a spoon-shaped scraping instrument (curette) passed in.

D & C is carried out under general anesthesia. A series of gradually widening dilators, metal rods of increasing

DILATATION AND CURETTAGE (D & C)

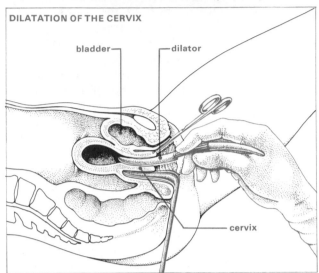

DILATATION OF THE CERVIX

bladder — — dilator

cervix

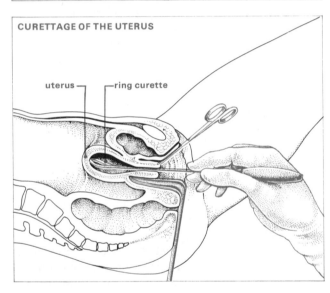

CURETTAGE OF THE UTERUS

uterus — — ring curette

A dilatation and curettage (D & C) is the most commonly performed gynecological operation. It is used both for diagnosis (in cases of abnormal bleeding from the uterus) and treatment (for example, after abortions). Progressively larger dilators are used to open the cervix, and then the lining of the uterus is scraped with a ring curette.

diameter, are passed via the vagina to dilate the cervix. When it is sufficiently dilated, a curette is passed into the uterine cavity.

A curette is a rod with a scraping device at one end, to scrape the lining of the womb (endometrium). A sample of endometrium is then sent to the laboratory for examination.

D & C is useful in establishing the diagnosis of menstrual disorders, pelvic tuberculosis and endometrial cancer, as well as for the investigation of infertility.

As a treatment procedure, D & C is sometimes used to procure abortion. When remnants of placenta are left in the uterus following childbirth or spontaneous or induced abortion, a D & C may be used to remove them and halt any associated bleeding. The technique is also used to remove POLYPS, for temporary relief in severe menstrual pain (dysmenorrhea) and to insert radioactive radium in the treatment of gynecological cancer.

See also the major article on **Obstetrics and Gynecology.**

discoid lupus erythematosus

See LUPUS ERYTHEMATOSUS.

disease

A condition in which the normal function of part of the body, or a bodily function, is impaired. It is not an entity, but the description of a pattern of symptoms and physical signs which enables the observer to foretell the probable course of events. Construction and identification of the pattern depends on degrees of probability in correlating the signs and symptoms; in some cases the data lead clearly to a diagnosis, in others there is no single discriminating factor.

The interpretation of signs and symptoms depends on knowledge of anatomy, physiology and pathology—the way the body is constructed, the way it works and the ways in which disease occur. In general, diseases are divided into four basic groups; congenital, traumatic, inflammatory and neoplastic. They may be acute (quickly appearing and soon over) or chronic (slow and long-lasting). They may be determined by genetic influences or by the environment (infections, injuries, reaction to chemicals or radiation, allergic reactions). They may have no known cause, as in the majority of new growths. Disease may be a consequence of genetic or environmental factors, or a combination of both.

Patterns of disease and the incidence of diseases alter in time, both because of advances in treatment and prevention (poliomyelitis and smallpox) and because of changes in the way people live. In the last century the prevalence of infectious disease, which had been by far the most common cause of sickness, began to give way to an increased incidence of chronic respiratory disease, heart disease and new growths (cancers). Infant mortality fell dramatically in the industrialized countries; but the incidence of road accidents as a cause of death and disability rose. It has been said that the occurrence of mental illness is no greater now than in the past; but as physical illnesses become less common, mental disturbances become more obvious.

Only about one third of illnesses occurring in the general population of industrialized countries receives medical attention, but most people see the doctor three or four times a year. The most common diseases are those affecting the respiratory system, which outnumber by far injuries and infections elsewhere which are the second most common acute conditions. The leading causes of death are heart disease, malignant growths and cerebrovascular disease.

dislocation

The displacement of a part of the body—most commonly a joint—from its normal position.

Injury is the usual cause of dislocation of a joint. The severity of the condition depends on whether the displaced joint presses on a neighboring artery or nerve.

The dislocated joint can be put back in position by skilled mechanical handling, a maneuver that is quick and safe in experienced hands but can cause great pain if attempted by the unskilled. The joint may afterwards be

DISLOCATION

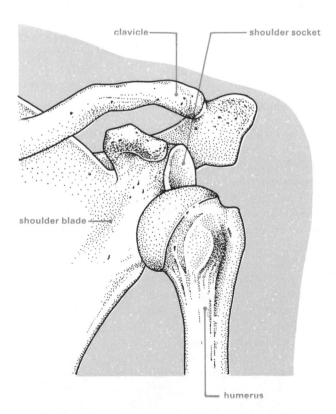

clavicle — shoulder socket

shoulder blade

humerus

Dislocation is due to trauma and results in the complete separation of the two bones which make up a joint. The shoulder joint becomes dislocated relatively frequently, because the socket into which the humerus fits is shallow. Because of the pull of the muscles, the humerus usually dislocates forwards and inwards as shown.

splinted to help it stabilize in the correct position. Joint dislocation sometimes tends to recur; in such cases an operation may be necessary to tighten the ligaments and thus help hold the joint in place.

CONGENITAL DISLOCATION OF THE HIP, as the name implies, is present from birth. It is due to a genetic or acquired structural deformity or to lax ligaments. All babies today are examined for "CDH" so that cases can be corrected immediately. Otherwise they might not be detected until the child attempts to walk, by which time irreversible damage may have occurred. Uncorrected CDH also carries an increased risk of osteoarthritis in later life.

Chronic inflammation may rarely cause joint dislocation.

disseminated lupus erythematosus

Another term for *systemic lupus erythematosus* (see LUPUS ERYTHEMATOSUS).

diuresis

The passing of abnormally large quantities of urine. It may be a symptom of disease, or it may be deliberately induced to treat certain conditions in which the body has too much water.

Urine is a concentrated solution of waste products which the body needs to excrete. Normally the amount of water in the solution is carefully controlled so the body is neither dehydrated nor waterlogged.

Diuresis occurs in certain diseases when the concentration mechanism in the kidney fails. It may also be a symptom of diabetes, since the kidney needs to excrete large quantities of water to carry the excess glucose out of the body.

Normally diuresis occurs if the body contains a lot of fluid—for example, if the person has drunk large quantities of fluid, especially alcoholic drinks.

Sometimes doctors give drugs called diuretics to remove excess fluid and salt from the body in conditions such as high blood pressure, heart failure or cirrhosis. Diuretics may also be used to flush out poisons or drugs when an overdose has been taken.

See also the section on *Diuretics ("water pills")* in the major article on **Drugs and Medicines.**

diverticulitis

Diverticula (small pouches which can form in the walls of any hollow organ) are commonly found in the large intestines of people after middle age. (This condition is known as DIVERTICULOSIS.) Diverticulitis is the term for an inflammation of these pouches.

The inflammation may affect one diverticulum or

many diverticula along a considerable length of the colon. Attacks tend to be recurrent. Symptoms are usually mild and consist of recurrent attacks of pain in the left side of the lower part of the abdomen, associated with constipation or bouts of diarrhea. This may continue for months or years.

Sometimes an acute attack supervenes, characterized by pain and tenderness in the left side of the lower part of the abdomen, often accompanied by fever. In an acute attack a diverticulum may perforate to produce a generalized PERITONITIS. One complication of recurrent attacks of inflammation is fibrosis and narrowing of the colon, which can result in complete obstruction of the colon.

Another complication is that the inflammation may extend to adjacent structures—most commonly the bladder, sometimes other parts of the small bowel, and rarely the uterus and vagina. The inflamed areas between these structures may break down resulting in abnormal passageways (fistulae) between the colon and the organs affected. Hemorrhage is another complication of diverticulitis and can sometimes be massive.

The diagnosis of diverticulitis is confirmed by a barium enema (see BARIUM MEAL/BARIUM ENEMA). Treatment consists of giving a bulk laxative to produce bulky and soft stools, while pain produced by spasm of the colon may be relieved by the administration of an antispasmodic drug. Acute attacks may require bed rest and broad-spectrum antibiotics. Surgery is indicated when attacks are frequent and crippling, when hemorrhage is severe or when other complications occur.

diverticulosis

Small pouches (diverticula) lined by mucous membrane in the walls of the large intestine, found in about a third of the population of industrialized countries after middle age. It is thought that contractions of the large bowel increase the pressure inside to a degree where the mucous membrane is forced through the muscular walls of the intestine at points of weakness where blood vessels run.

The condition is rare in countries where the normal diet contains much roughage (dietary fiber). The part of the large intestine most commonly affected is the sigmoid flexure of the colon, which lies in the lower left hand side of the abdominal cavity. Normally they give rise to no trouble, but in a minority of cases they become inflamed and give rise to the disease known as DIVERTICULITIS.

dizziness

Strictly, a sense of rotation—either of oneself or of the environment.

Such a symptom is also known as a true VERTIGO, indicating a disorder of parts of the nervous system concerned with maintaining balance: these are located in the eyes and the vestibular system of the ears, as well as in the brain.

Dizziness is often aggravated by movements of the head and in severe cases may be accompanied by nausea and vomiting.

Except for travel sickness, in which the cause is obvious, special tests are commonly required to establish the nervous fault responsible for the symptom.

People commonly use the term dizziness more loosely to mean any one of a range of symptoms including faintness, lightheadedness, a swimming sensation, uncertainty or strange feelings such as a sensation of walking on air. These symptoms are classified as "pseudovertigo" and are often experienced by neurotic or very introspective people. There is usually no underlying physical cause.

Dizziness of this type may, however, be a symptom of temporary lack of oxygen or nutrients to the brain. It is therefore common when a person suddenly gets up from a reclining to a standing position, during hunger, or as an accompaniment of anemia or disease of the heart or lungs. If dizziness is not associated with an obvious cause, and is unrelieved by rest, medical advice should be sought.

DNA/RNA

The chemical chains in all living cells which hold and activate the genetic code.

DNA (deoxyribonucleic acid) holds all the genetic information which ensures that the descendants of a cell—and thus the descendants of a whole plant or animal—are of the correct type for that species. Watson and Crick discovered in 1953 that the DNA molecule consists of two extremely long chains spiraled around each other to form a double helix. The arrangement of the chemicals called "bases" in each chain is the secret of the genetic code; it determines the exact order in which amino acids are joined together to form cell proteins, including enzymes.

RNA (ribonucleic acid) transfers the genetic information from the DNA in the chromosome to the part of the cell where protein is synthesized and also controls its synthesis.

double vision

Normally when an object is viewed with both eyes, a single image is seen because eye movements are coordinated by complex brain reflexes which ensure that light from an object falls on corresponding points on the two retinae. These reflexes involve several nerves and muscles. Any condition which affects these nerves or causes paralysis of one of the eye muscles can result in double vision (also known as *diplopia*).

Diplopia is rarely encountered in children under five, even if they have strabismus (cross-eye), because the brain is still able to ignore one of the images. Beyond this age it is difficult to suppress the second image.

If the cause of the diplopia is not treatable, the condition can be relieved by covering one eye with a patch.

DNA

THE CHEMICAL STRUCTURE OF DNA
—a double helix

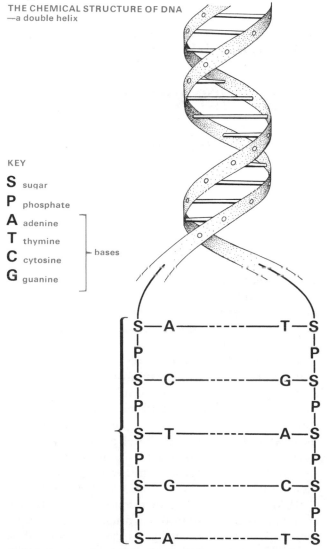

KEY

S sugar

P phosphate

A adenine

T thymine ⎤ bases

C cytosine

G guanine

DNA, a complex chemical substance, carries the genetic information which determines all the characteristics of an organism—bacteria, plants, insects and humans alike. Each molecule of DNA consists of two long strands, as shown above, which are held together by chemical bonds between pairs of base substances. The exact sequence of these bases along a strand of DNA forms the "genetic code."

Down's syndrome (mongolism)

A congenital disorder consisting of moderate to severe mental retardation accompanied by a variety of physical abnormalities.

It is also known as *trisomy 21*, because of the precise chromosomal abnormality which is responsible. The normal human complement of chromosomes is 23 pairs. A mongol, however, has an extra chromosome of the type known as number 21 (thus the term "trisomy 21") and a total of 47 chromosomes instead of 46.

In most cases this chromosomal abnormality occurs unpredictably rather than by inheritance, although there may sometimes be a familial tendency. The risk of producing a mongol child in a couple with some family history of the condition, or when the mother is relatively old (the risk increases with age), can be assessed by GENETIC COUNSELING. The overall incidence of the syndrome is 1 in 600 births, rising to 1 in 400 in mothers aged over 40, and 1 in 40 over the age of 45.

The mental deficiency in Down's syndrome does not make the sufferer aggressive or antisocial. Patients can mimic well and can be taught socially acceptable behavior. The average mental age attained is about eight years, a point to remember when dealing with adult mongols. Cases have been reported, however, of mongols given excellent parental help and encouragement who have attained almost normal intellectual capacity.

Physically, the best-known abnormality is the characteristic facial appearance with upward-slanting eyes. Other common physical abnormalities include a protruding tongue, small and badly aligned teeth, broad spade-like hands and feet, a short wide neck, short stature, dry skin, abnormal skin creases and cataracts. Congenital heart defects are also common.

The patient with Down's syndrome is especially prone to infection, and leukemia is at least ten times more common than in normal children. The mongol is also more likely to develop serum HEPATITIS, especially if he is raised in an institution in close contact with other mentally retarded children with poor hygiene.

There is no cure for Down's syndrome. Almost half of all sufferers die in infancy or in childhood, mainly from respiratory and gastrointestinal infections; but with proper care there is no reason why a mongol cannot survive into adulthood.

AMNIOCENTESIS can be used to determine whether a fetus is a mongol. The technique involves aspiration of a small quantity of the amniotic fluid surrounding the fetus in the womb. Fetal cells floating in the fluid are examined, and the presence of an extra chromosome detected. The mother may then be offered the opportunity of a clinical abortion.

Obviously this technique cannot be applied to all

DOWN'S SYNDROME (MONGOLISM)

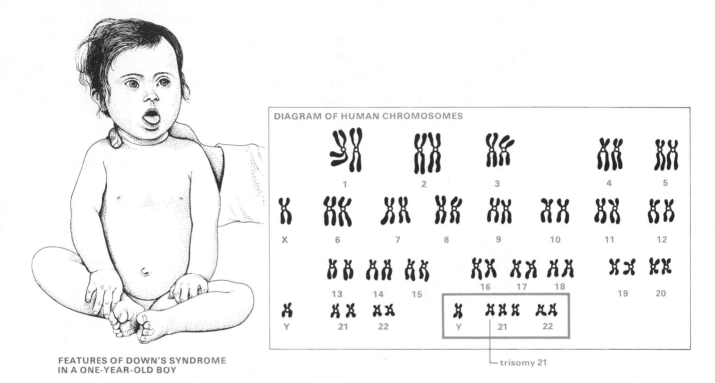

FEATURES OF DOWN'S SYNDROME
IN A ONE-YEAR-OLD BOY

DIAGRAM OF HUMAN CHROMOSOMES

└ trisomy 21

Down's syndrome, or mongolism, is a congenital condition which produces severe mental retardation as well as many physical abnormalities. The one-year-old boy pictured above shows the more obvious physical signs—slanting eyes, simple ears, large tongue, and squat hands with stubby fingers. All these effects are due to the child having an extra number 21 chromosome (trisomy 21) in his cells, giving him a total of 47 chromosomes.

pregnant mothers, for reasons of both cost and medical risk. It is, however, valuable for women at particular risk.

dreaming

Brain-wave studies have shown that sleep is accompanied by cycles of brain activity. One stage of sleep is called Rapid Eye Movement sleep (*REM sleep*), and it has been established that this is when dreaming occurs.

REM sleep comes on about every 90 minutes in the adult, and lasts for an average of 15 to 20 minutes each time. This represents, in total, up to a third of sleeping time. In infancy, a much greater proportion of sleep is REM sleep; the proportion gradually decreases until it reaches the adult level at about puberty.

REM sleep gets its name because it is characterized by rapid, jerky movements of the eyeballs under closed lids. During REM sleep the brain is active, the heart beats faster, the individual lies quite still with flaccid muscles, and he is more difficult to awaken. A number of other physical signs of REM sleep have been noted; for example, penile erection in the male.

If an individual is awakened during REM sleep he can usually remember his dream in vivid detail. If he is awakened some time after a period of REM sleep he will remember less of it.

Research on REM sleep has revealed several findings that indicate the importance of dreaming, although the exact reason for its importance is still not understood. If, for example, a person is consistently awakened at the start of periods of REM sleep he becomes irritable during the day, even if his total amount of sleep is normal. Moreover, when he is allowed to sleep undisturbed he will devote a greater proportion of the night to REM sleep, as if to make up for lost dreams.

REM sleep is depressed by alcohol, sleeping tablets, tranquilizers and certain other drugs. Again, when a person ceases to take such agents the proportion of his sleep devoted to REM sleep rises above normal for awhile. This is another indication that the body requires its REM sleep, and presumably also its dreams.

But just as the reason for the importance of dreams is not understood, neither is their physiological mechanism. It has been suggested that the characteristic pattern of a dream—a collection of related and unrelated random events strung into a semicoherent story—may reflect the work of the brain in ordering images into memory. There is, however, no real evidence for this or any other explanation, at least at a physiological level.

Psychologists have a special interest in dreams, interpreting them as messages of an individual's subconscious feelings. Freud, Jung and many others have classified dream images in terms of their sexual symbolism. Although modern psychologists are less prepared to accept such strict categorizations, there is little doubt that discussion and interpretation of dreams at least constitute a useful technique in exploring a person's mind through psychoanalysis (whether that is of ultimate value to the patient or not!).

dropsy

An obsolete term for generalized EDEMA.

drug abuse

In the the early years of this century, addiction to opium and hashish was prevalent in the Far East but rare (except in Chinese communities) in the United States and Europe. Sniffing cocaine was briefly fashionable in the 1920s, but drug abuse became a major social problem with the growth of heroin addiction. Heroin—an extract of opium which is usually taken by intravenous injection—is the most powerful and destructive of the drugs of addiction, and its use spread very rapidly in socially deprived areas of inner cities after World War II. Much of the growth of the problem was linked with organized crime.

The 1950s also saw an explosive growth in the prescription of sedatives and stimulants by doctors. As amphetamines, barbiturates and tranquilizers such as meprobamate (Miltown) came into ever wider legitimate use, their abuse also became common. At much the same time, opinion-formers such as Aldous Huxley began to write of the mind-enhancing potential of drugs such as mescaline (peyote), the active ingredient of the mescal cactus, and the current pattern of drug abuse became established.

Experimentation with drugs is now commonplace, especially among high-school children and college students. Many try cannabis (marijuana or "pot") or one of the many minor tranquilizers, especially if these are handed around at a weekend party; experimentation with injected barbiturates or opiates such as heroin or morphine is less common. Whether or not experimentation leads to addiction depends on many variables, including the addictive potential of the drug (high for heroin, amphetamine and tobacco; low or nonexistent for cannabis) and the personality and social environment of the individual. Hardcore addicts come mostly from socially deprived areas; in addition, many have

disturbed or unstable family backgrounds.

Psychological dependence on drugs is common. Most people are mildly dependent on coffee or tea; a similar but stronger dependence may develop on sleeping pills or tranquilizers. Dependence on cannabis is of this kind. But serious addiction is much more likely when the drug concerned causes physical dependence, when deprivation of the drug causes physical symptoms (see ADDICTION). In the case of heroin, for example, an addict who is deprived of the drug will within a few hours develop severe abdominal pains, sweating and tremors. Alcoholics have a similar strong physical dependence on their "drug."

Drug addiction causes problems partly from its socially disruptive effects, and in particular from the effects of chronic addiction on an individual's ability to live and work normally. Many addicts turn to crime to find money to pay for their supplies. Addiction to drugs such as heroin also carries a substantial hazard to health, particularly from intravenous injections given without sterile precautions. Addicts have a high mortality rate from hepatitis (inflammation of the liver) and blood poisoning, as well as from drug overdosage.

Treatment of established addiction is unrewarding. When heavy physical dependence exists, the risk of relapse is very high. The complex interactions of psychological and social factors which promote drug abuse are still little understood.

duodenal ulcer

The duodenum—the first and shortest part of the small intestine, connecting with the outlet of the stomach—is the most common site for *peptic ulcers*. Peptic ulcers include those that affect the lower part of the esophagus, the stomach and the first part of the duodenum. They are erosions of the lining of these structures produced by the action of digestive juices (acid and pepsin) secreted by the stomach. Normally the lining is able to withstand the action of these digestive secretions.

Duodenal ulcer affects about 10% of the population. Symptoms may start at any age, but usually begin in young adulthood. Males are affected four times as frequently as females. Symptoms may be vague, absent or atypical, but usually the patient complains of upper abdominal pain—which has variously been described as gnawing, burning, cramplike or boring. Typically the pain starts an hour or two after a meal and is relieved in about half an hour by food or milk. Diagnosis is confirmed by a barium meal or by gastroscopy. (See BARIUM MEAL/BARIUM ENEMA and the major article on **Gastroenterology**.) The aim of drug treatment is to reduce the secretion of the digestive juices, to neutralize the acid after it has been secreted or to increase the resistance of the gastrointestinal lining to the action of acid and pepsin. Stress and anxiety are thought to play a part in producing ulcers in some patients; thus, a sedative may also be prescribed.

It is no longer considered necessary to adhere strictly to a bland diet. Most patients would know what foods aggravate symptoms in their own cases, and these should be avoided. It is advisable to avoid foods which stimulate excessive acid secretion—such as tea, coffee, cola drinks and alcohol. Smoking encourages ulceration and delays healing and should be avoided. Meals, however, should be regular and frequent to neutralize the acid that is produced.

Symptoms tend to be recurrent despite treatment. In about 5–10% of cases, symptoms persist despite drug treatment and surgery may prove necessary. When complications such as hemorrhage, perforation of the duodenum or stenosis (narrowing or obstruction due to fibrosis) occur, the need for surgical treatment becomes urgent.

Dupuytren's contracture

An inherited deformity of the hand, almost exclusively affecting men of European descent.

Tendons of some finger muscles lie within the palm side of the hand. In Dupuytren's contracture, which usually starts after middle age, the covering of such a tendon contracts into a fibrous nodule. In doing so it causes the relevant finger to bend toward the palm. The fibrous nodule also causes a puckering of the skin of the palm.

In the early stages there is pain on grasping. Later the pain disappears but the grip becomes weak and the patient finds it difficult to release objects. In severe cases the fingernails dig into the palm.

Usually both hands are affected, one more severely than the other, and the condition may also afflict the feet.

Treatment is by surgical operation, which can produce reasonable results but does not always effect a complete correction of the deformity. Recurrence may take place (especially in younger patients) within a year or two of the operation.

Dupuytren's contracture is also associated with some cases of epilepsy and alcoholic cirrhosis of the liver.

dwarfism

See ACHONDROPLASIA.

dysentery

Dysentery is an infection of the colon which causes painful diarrhea with mucus and blood in the stools. It may be caused by bacterial or amoebic infection.

Bacillary dysentery is the result of infection of the large intestine by bacteria of the genus *Shigella*—*Shigella sonnei*, *Sh. flexneri*, *Sh. dysenteriae* and *Sh. boydii*, the last three flourishing in tropical and subtropical countries. Infection with *Sh. sonnei* is usually relatively mild, the other infections tending to produce severe loss of fluids and prostration. The incubation period of all is usually two or three days. Infection is spread by food contaminated by feces, being the result of poor standards of personal hygiene and sanitation. Flies may spread the infection. Diagnosis is made by isolation of the infecting organisms from the stools; treatment depends on the severity of the condition, ranging from simple kaolin mixtures in mild cases to suitable antibiotics and intravenous fluid therapy in those patients suffering from serious fluid loss.

Amoebic dysentery, also spread by faulty hygiene, results from infection with protozoa of the species *Entamoeba histolytica*. The disease is found all over the world, particularly in poor communities, and produces symptoms of varying severity ranging from mild abdominal discomfort with loose stools to severe and acute bloody diarrhea with frequent abdominal pain. The condition may become chronic, and may be mistaken for other gastric and intestinal disorders. But in time large numbers of amoebae may multiply in the liver and give rise to a dangerous abscess, which may burst into the abdominal cavity, the chest or through the wall of the abdomen or chest. Diagnosis is made by microscopic examination of the feces for *E. histolytica*, by endoscopy of the large bowel (which when infected shows typical ulceration) or by serological techniques. Treatment includes administration of diloxanide, injections of emetine and the use of tetracycline and chloroquine. Abscess formation in the liver may require surgical treatment.

It is important to note that both bacillary and amoebic infections can be spread by "carriers," infected persons who show no signs of having the disease but carry live organisms in their intestines. Unexplained outbreaks of dysentery in institutions are sometimes traced to such a carrier by examination of the stools of apparently healthy kitchen workers.

dyslexia

Word blindness; extreme difficulty in understanding the spoken or written word.

Dyslexia covers a wide range of language difficulties; in general, sufferers cannot grasp the meaning of sequences of letters, words or symbols or the concept of direction.

The condition can affect people of otherwise normal intelligence and of every socioeconomic group.

Sometimes there is a family history; sometimes the condition arises from brain damage. But often the cause is obscure.

In severe cases the dyslexic individual is unable to read, makes bizarre errors in spelling, cannot name colors or "left" and "right" and has difficulty putting a name to a picture. Milder cases show less extreme forms of the same difficulties and may go unrecognized.

Indeed, even severe dyslexia is often not diagnosed as the root of a person's problem; the sufferer may therefore be considered lazy, stupid, mentally handicapped, inattentive or obstinate. In fact he may be of normal intelligence but frustrated with his inability to comprehend words.

Signs that a child may be dyslexic include late language development, clumsiness, no preference for one hand or the other, a tendency to alter the sequence of syllables in words (like "efelant" for elephant) or of words in a sentence. Any of these signs in an otherwise bright child may raise the suspicion of dyslexia.

Treatment—which is most successful when the condition is diagnosed early—requires painstaking special teaching techniques.

dysmenorrhea

Pain associated with MENSTRUATION.

The most common type is *primary dysmenorrhea*, which is an extreme form of the discomfort most women feel in the first few hours or days of a period. The lower abdominal pain may be continuous or spasmodic and is sometimes accompanied by pain in the lower back or down the legs. In severe cases the woman may vomit or faint.

Dysmenorrhea is common in women who have not had a pregnancy. It is no reason to fear serious gynecological problems or eventual sterility. The pain is thought to be due to a reduction in blood supply to the uterus when its powerful contractions at the start of a period constrict the blood vessels. Childbirth usually cures the condition because extra blood vessels develop during pregnancy. Even in women who remain childless, dysmenorrhea tends to ease after the age of about 25 and disappear by 30.

A healthy active life helps prevent primary dysmenorrhea. Simple analgesics such as aspirin or acetaminophen can usually relieve the pain. Rest in bed with a hot-water bottle is a traditional and often successful treatment.

If such measures are ineffective, a doctor may prescribe the oral contraceptive pill for chronic sufferers, since it prevents ovulation (only periods following normal ovulation are painful). Temporary relief may be obtained by dilatation of the cervix, but ordinarily this maneuver would only be undertaken for

more serious gynecological disorders.

Secondary dysmenorrhea is a symptom of disease rather than a problem on its own. Diseases causing painful menstruation include chronic pelvic inflammatory disease, endometriosis, fibroids and many other gynecological conditions.

The pain usually starts about a week before menstruation and increases in intensity until the start of the period. It may then be relieved once bleeding starts or may worsen in some cases. Treatment is directed at the underlying disease.

Although many gynecological disorders produce dysmenorrhea, it should be stressed that dysmenorrhea does not necessarily indicate the presence of a disorder; very commonly it can be primary. Therefore it is not a symptom that should cause undue anxiety.

On the other hand, in persistent cases medical advice should be sought; the doctor may be able to relieve the pain and exclude the possibility of any underlying disorder.

dyspareunia

Difficult and painful sexual intercourse experienced by a woman. There is often incomplete vaginal penetration by the penis because of the pain or discomfort felt by the woman.

In most cases the embarrassment and sensitivity felt by the woman leads to frigidity. There are many causes of this condition, both physical and psychological.

Physical causes include extreme obesity of either partner, injuries of the hip joint leading to difficulty in wide separation of the legs, a thick hymen ("maidenhead"), a scarred vagina (as a result of episiotomies or gynecological surgery) and inelastic vaginal walls in those who marry relatively late in life.

Among psychological causes are clumsiness in the male, previous experience of pain and fear of pregnancy. In these circumstances the vaginal muscles can go into spasm (VAGINISMUS) and prevent entry of the penis.

Infections or inflammation of the pelvic organs (ovary, uterus, or Fallopian tubes), PROLAPSE of the uterus and ovarian cysts make intercourse painful. The complaint of dyspareunia may lead to the diagnosis of such conditions when they were previously asymptomatic.

Approximately 20% of women experience dyspareunia at some time in their lives. The treatment of physical causes is fairly simple: for example, eradicating the infection, correcting the prolapse or removing a cyst.

Psychologically, confidence may be less easily restored but education of both partners in sex techniques, and the use of lubricants and vaginal dilators, is necessary and usually successful.

dyspepsia

Literally, "difficulty in digesting."

Dyspepsia is experienced by most people at some time in their lives, since INDIGESTION is extremely common. It is ordinarily not a serious problem unless it is either constant or prolonged for many weeks. It can be associated with irregular meals, alcoholic excess or eating foods to which you are unaccustomed.

The symptoms include belching, a feeling of distension in the upper part of the abdomen, an acidic taste in the mouth, stomach pains and sometimes nausea. Common causes include eating fatty foods (especially when fried), foods which contain sulfur (such as eggs, cucumbers, onions and salads) or strongly acid foods (fruit and wines). Dyspepsia is sometimes associated with smoking on an empty stomach, skipping meals and chronic anxiety—thus provoking excess secretions of gastric acid.

If dyspepsia is continual, regularly causes disruption of sleep or occurs after every meal it may be a symptom of a developing ulcer (see GASTRIC ULCER and DUODENAL ULCER). Prompt medical attention should be sought to confirm the diagnosis and permit early treatment.

In mild cases the most effective treatment is the use of oral antacids—particularly the effervescent types—which will usually relieve the discomfort and bring up gas. A glass of milk is sometimes equally effective. Salicylate drugs such as aspirin, however, should never be taken because they can irritate the stomach lining; if an ulcer is the cause of the dyspepsia, aspirin can aggravate the condition or even lead to massive bleeding of the stomach lining. If the cause is related to dietary indiscretion, a change in the types of foods regularly eaten may be necessary to bring persistent dyspepsia under control.

dyspnea

Breathlessness or shortness of breath after slight physical effort, along with consciousness of the necessity to breathe.

The symptoms can occur in people who are otherwise healthy, often as a result of obesity, lack of physical fitness or excessive smoking. Respiratory or cardiac disease may be a cause, but as dyspnea is a subjective complaint it cannot be correlated closely with the extent of the disease.

In general the lungs have a diminished capacity to cope with the demands made of them—perhaps because of heart failure causing pulmonary congestion or chronic lung disease causing heart strain—but sufferers show a varying tolerance that depends on the anxiety level produced by the experience of breathlessness.

Rest, appropriate treatment of any underlying disease, dietary control and carefully graded physical training may improve the condition.

See also the major articles on **Pulmonary Diseases** and **Cardiology.**

dysuria

Painful or difficult urination.

See the major article on **Urology.**

E

earache

Pain in the ear may come from the hearing mechanisms themselves—the eardrum, inner ear, outer canal, or the deeper bone structure—whenever they are subject to trauma or inflammation.

For example, acute earache is felt when flying because of the unequal air pressure within the ear; cabin pressurization outside the ear stretches the eardrum. Similarly, coughs and colds may put pressure on the inner ear. Ear infections cause pain because of the swelling of the inflamed tissue and a consequent rise in pressure within the ear itself.

Because the cranial nerves of the neck, face, jaw and scalp all collect sensory branches from the ear, earache can be caused by disorders such as dental disease, tonsillitis, nasal congestion, jaw inflammation and cervical spine (neck) injury. Eruption of the wisdom teeth is often marked by coincident earache in adolescents and the growth of teeth of infants is frequently accompanied by earache.

Diagnosis of the cause is important to ensure there is no serious ear disease. Treatment, apart from relief of pain, may include the administration of antibiotic drops for the ear, removal of excess wax, or dental assessment. In young children otitis (inflammation of the ear) is a common cause of earache and appropriate treatment is necessary to prevent the complications of chronic infection that may damage hearing.

See also the major article on **Otolaryngology.**

earwax

Accumulated secretions of the minute glands in the skin which lines the external auditory canal of the ear. These secretions protect the eardrum and maintain elasticity. Excessive secretions, however, form a brownish-yellow mass which can block the canal and cause sudden or progressive impairment of hearing or even deafness. The wax then requires removal.

It is usually softened first with drops that dissolve fat (or with warm olive oil); later it can be gently and painlessly syringed out with warm water by a nurse or physician.

Working in a dusty, humid atmosphere or the frequent wearing of earphones increases wax secretion and some individuals require ear syringing regularly.

ecchymosis

A purplish-brown patch of flat bruising due to bleeding under the skin.

It may be due to fragility of the blood vessels, blood clotting defects, or minor trauma. Ecchymoses are very common in the elderly and are a normal part of aging—even where there is no evidence of other circulatory disorders, nutritional deficiency or blood disease.

In young people ecchymoses are rare unless they are associated with a serious blood defect, scurvy, hemophilia, or the effects of various drugs or chemicals.

Ecchymoses resolve themselves without treatment (by absorption of the "leaked" blood) usually within a week of their appearance. Frequent recurrence indicates the need for special blood tests.

ECG (or EKG; electrocardiogram)

A tracing that represents the contraction and relaxation of the heart muscle as it beats. The tracing is an electrocardio*gram;* the instrument used is an electro-cardio*graph.*

All muscular contraction emits very small electrical discharges. Over a hundred years ago it was discovered that heart muscle activity could be detected by electrodes placed on the chest wall and the limbs. Electronic sensitivity has improved dramatically since then, and nearly every physician now has access to an ECG machine. As a routine test to assess a patient's cardiac efficiency, the ECG is now a standard part of any comprehensive physical examination.

The ECG can alert physicians to a wide range of abnormalities: changes in heart size due to congenital defects or to hypertension; coronary thrombosis; arrhythmias; pericarditis; and many other conditions that alter the wave patterns of the electrical activity of the heart. However, the graph must always be interpreted in conjunction with a physical examination. An ECG may show various changes that are perfectly normal in some individuals but not in others.

The ECG can be traced either on paper or shown on an oscilloscope. The latter technique is an essential part of intensive care and major surgery, where doctors must constantly assess the state of the patient's heart. Some oscilloscopes sound an automatic early warning bell if there is any variation in the wave pattern, in order to alert the medical and nursing staff.

Fetal electrocardiography can be used before and during the induction of labor to assess the state of the baby's heart and give warning of FETAL DISTRESS. It is achieved by attaching electrodes across the mother's abdomen.

See also the major article on **Cardiology.**

ECHO viruses

A group of viruses responsible for several mild diseases such as summer flu, diarrhea of the newborn and certain skin rashes. (The name is derived from viruses which belong to the so-called *E*nteric *C*ytopathogenic *H*uman *O*rphan group.)

They attack young children mainly, although not exclusively, and are more active during the warm months of the year. Often they cause minor epidemics in which several children in a neighborhood become infected with the virus. The symptoms include a higher fever, headache, pains in the limbs and a sore throat.

One group of the ECHO viruses can produce blisters of the mouth or soft palate, while another causes chest pains similar to those seen in pleurisy; this is called *Bornholm disease*, after the island in the Baltic where the first epidemic was reported. Some other ECHO viruses produce ORCHITIS (inflammation of the testicles); a further group are responsible for a serious form of MENINGITIS (inflammation of the membranes that surround the brain).

This last type of ECHO virus infection is one of only two which require hospitalization, the other being the highly infectious diarrhea sometimes seen in newborn babies.

Many cases of ECHO virus infection go unrecognized. The patient tends to assume that it is a cold, chill, or sore throat. As a result of these mild infections, most people develop immunity to the ECHO viruses by the time they reach adulthood.

The treatment of mild infection is simple home nursing care. The illness seldom lasts more than a few days.

ECT (electroconvulsive therapy)

A form of psychiatric treatment to alleviate serious depressive illness.

A current of 85 to 110 volts A.C. is passed between electrodes placed on either side of the head for up to half a second. There are many technical variations, but usually a muscle-relaxant drug and a general anesthetic are given to spare the patient the distress produced by involuntary muscular convulsion.

ECT is usually given in courses of up to three a week, restricted to 10 to 12 treatments in all. It produces some damage to brain tissue and can impair memory and concentration (often for several weeks after the end of treatment). It can also dull both imagination and perception, but these effects may be beneficial if the patient has been disabled by fear, nightmares, delusions or desperate suicidal wishes.

ECT can be safely used on the old or the young, the physically fit or those with physical diseases. In all cases, however, it is now used only as a last resort since drug treatment of psychiatric disease has dramatically improved in recent years. Where drug treatment fails, the benefits of ECT can be helpful to the desperately disturbed psychiatric patient.

See also the major article on **Psychiatry.**

ectopic pregnancy

Pregnancy in which the fertilized egg is implanted somewhere other than the womb.

Normally the fertilized egg passes down the Fallopian tube and grows into a fetus in the wall of the uterine cavity. An ectopic pregnancy occurs when it fails to do so and starts to develop in another area, such as the abdominal cavity, Fallopian tube, ovary, ligaments of the uterus, or in a rudimentary "extra" cavity of a deformed uterus. By far the most common site for an ectopic pregnancy, however, is the Fallopian tube; this is alternatively called a "tubal" pregnancy. About one in every thousand pregnancies is ectopic.

The space for the embryo to grow is limited and the result is an acute surgical emergency at any time from the sixth week onwards. An ectopic pregnancy rarely proceeds beyond the 16th week without provoking a crisis.

The usual cause is blockage of the uterine tube as a result of a previous infection (SALPINGITIS), surgery, the use of an intrauterine contraceptive device, or ENDOMETRIOSIS.

The symptoms of early pregnancy are normal; then acute abdominal pain occurs, with shock (often because the tube has ruptured), collapse and vaginal bleeding. Surgery is then necessary to remove the damaged tissues and the fetus. Unfortunately, the tube usually has to be removed; only about 30% of women who suffer an ectopic pregnancy are subsequently able to conceive satisfactorily.

eczema

A noninfectious inflammatory disease of the skin that takes the form of redness, blistering, crusting and scaling.

The well-known type of eczema seen in infancy and childhood, medically called *atopic eczema*, tends to run in families where there is asthma, migraine or hay fever.

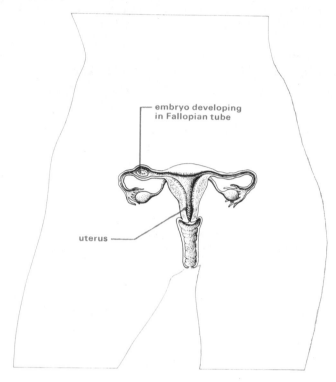

embryo developing
in Fallopian tube

uterus

An ectopic pregnancy occurs when a fertilized egg becomes implanted somewhere outside the uterus. A Fallopian tube pregnancy is the most common variety, and usually occurs following infection of the tube.

The skin typically breaks out in eczematous patches—particularly on the forearms, the backs of the knees and the face.

There are other types of eczema: *allergic eczema* is usually due to food allergy. Identification and avoidance of the cause, which may be anything from cow's milk to seafood, cures the problem. *Varicose eczema* occurs around varicose ulcers on the legs in people with circulatory deficiency. *Occupational eczema* may be caused by skin irritants such as mineral oils, detergents and degreasing agents. Liquid detergents and soap powders are a common cause of this type of eczema in housewives. In other cases the eczema may be caused by the application of ointments that produce a sensitivity reaction.

"Eczema" and "dermatitis" are often interchangeable words, especially in the sensitivity type of inflammation.

Eczema is fundamentally a reaction to irritants. Even atopic eczema may be due to an inherited metabolic disorder causing biochemical disturbance of the skin. Eczema is common, affecting 20% of the population at some time in their lives and is more frequent in whites than in blacks.

In treatment, the patient is advised to avoid any external skin irritants. At the same time, medications are used to suppress the inflammatory response in the skin. This is best achieved with creams, lotions and dressings which contain cortisone-like steroids.

Sedatives or antihistamines may be used to relieve the symptoms of itching and burning, and antibiotics prevent infection of the damaged skin.

Many young children with atopic eczema grow out of the worst manifestations of the disease by the time they reach puberty, but not everyone is completely cleared.

Successful treatment of the child with atopic eczema may require the frequent attention of a dermatologist.

See also the major article on **Dermatology.**

edema

Swelling of a part of the body due to congestion with an excess of retained tissue fluid.

If you press a finger into tissues that are excessively edematous, a "pit" mark remains afterwards. It is a sign of a disorder or disease rather than a disease itself.

Edema is most obviously seen in the legs of people with varicose veins or mild heart disease. Edematous swelling of the ankles can occur even in healthy people during hot weather or during pregnancy. Local edema is also seen around wounds or insect bites, or in eczema where the skin cells are injured and there is local "puffiness."

Excess body water is normally removed by the

ECZEMA

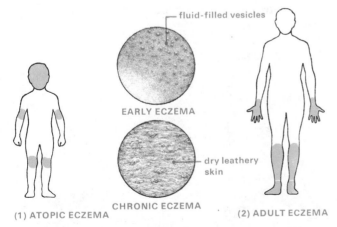

EARLY ECZEMA

fluid-filled vesicles

CHRONIC ECZEMA

dry leathery skin

(1) ATOPIC ECZEMA   (2) ADULT ECZEMA

Eczema may run in families ("atopic eczema") or result from an external irritant. Atopic eczema may start in infancy, when the face is particularly affected, and later tends to be confined to the hollows of the elbows and behind the knees (1). In adults, hands are often affected in certain occupations, and eczema over the legs develops with bad varicose veins (2).

EDEMA

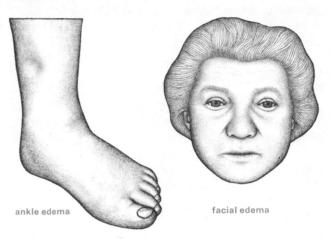

ankle edema   facial edema

Edema is the distension of the soft tissues by excess fluid which has seeped out of the circulation. Ankle edema usually results from poor drainage by the veins and is seen in congestive heart failure and pregnancy. Facial edema is a characteristic of kidney disease and is especially noticeable after a night's sleep.

circulation of the blood and excreted via the kidneys, so disease of either the heart or the kidneys characteristically results in edema. The patient may retain 10 to 20 pounds of excess water before edema is detectable. Ankle swelling is usually the first sign, although in bedbound patients the first swelling commonly appears in the lower back. The congestion impairs pulmonary efficiency since the lung tissue also becomes waterlogged; the patient then has difficulty in breathing.

Edema is often an early sign of toxemia of pregnancy, reflecting impaired kidney function and salt retention. It is also seen in severe malnutrition due to deficiencies of B vitamins or protein.

Edema does not cause pain, but it must be treated because it is a manifestation of some disorder and it can cause problems of its own. Drugs which stimulate kidney excretion (diuretics) are used to correct edema, in combination with cardiac muscle stimulants and a low-sodium diet. Potassium supplements have to be taken with some diuretics because they cause the kidneys to excrete this mineral along with the excess water.

The control of edema is an essential part of the treatment of chronic heart failure.

EEG (electroencephalogram)

A tracing of the brain's electrical activity obtained by the application of very sensitive electrodes to the skull. The instrument used is an electroencephalo*graph;* the tracing is an electroencephalo*gram.*

All the brain function involves electrical activity

which is detectable through the skull, in the same way that heart muscle activity is detectable by an ECG through the chest wall. The tracing of an EEG is very complicated and requires skilled interpretation. Changes from the normal can aid in the diagnosis of such conditions as brain tumors, brain injury and epilepsy.

Brain wave patterns of patients with seizures can indicate the type of disorder (petit mal or grand mal) by detecting the buildup of electrical discharge even when the patient has no symptoms, so the EEG is a common diagnostic method for those with a history of convulsions. The EEG has also been used to define BRAIN DEATH.

Attempts to interpret thought patterns by means of the EEG, so it could serve as a lie-detector or as a measurement of intellectual ability, have proved unsuccessful.

See also the major article on **Neurology.**

Electra complex

See OEDIPUS COMPLEX.

electric shock

The effect of the passage of an electric current through the body.

An electric shock with a voltage of 85 to 110 and a current of about half an ampere is commonly used to treat mental patients suffering from depression and other disorders. But in general electric shocks to the body, especially those caused by a higher current and voltage, can be dangerous and even fatal (electrocution); 110 volts is particularly dangerous in triggering cardiac arrhythmias. Every effort should be made at all times to avoid contact with live electrical wires, for the domestic supply can give a fatal shock, but even so a great deal can be done by way of first aid to bring help to victims.

The first measure to take is to switch off the supply as near to the main power line as possible, even if circuit breakers or fuses have blown. If this is not possible, stand on a rubber mat or other insulating material and maneuver the victim away from the source of the current with the aid of a nonconducting article such as a broomstick. Loosen the clothing to facilitate breathing. The victim may be unconscious and the heart may have stopped, so it will be necessary to give mouth to mouth resuscitation or (if you have received special training) external cardiac massage. Where the current entered and left the body there may be burns which will almost certainly be worse than they look. So even if an electric shock victim recovers quickly, medical aid should always be called. Where an overhead cable or industrial supply is involved, no move to rescue the victim should

be made until it is absolutely certain that the supply has been cut off.

See also *Electric Shock* in the **First Aid** section.

electrocardiogram

See ECG.

electrocution

Death by electric shock. See ELECTRIC SHOCK.

electroencephalogram

See EEG.

elephantiasis

Dramatic swelling of the tissues caused by severe blockage of the lymphatic vessels by tiny threadlike worms (filariae).

These microscopic worms are transmitted to humans in tropical and subtropical zones of the world largely by a particular species of mosquito *(Culex fatigans)*. Obstructive filariasis, to use its proper name, is commonly known as elephantiasis because it causes such marked and chronic swelling of the legs, scrotum, arms, breasts and vulva that the huge deformities look elephantine in their disproportion.

This severe form of filariasis develops slowly only after years of chronic reinfection and is seen in less than 0.2% of those infected with the worms. Treatment of the early infection is successful with drugs; once chronic obstruction has developed, however, surgical treatment may be necessary.

ELEPHANTIASIS

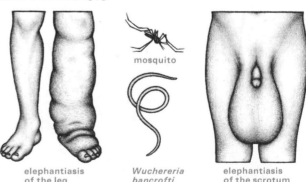

elephantiasis
of the leg

mosquito

*Wuchereria
bancrofti*

elephantiasis
of the scrotum

Elephantiasis is a state of severe swelling caused by the human filarial worm Wuchereria bancrofti, *which blocks the lymphatic channels draining the legs, arms, breast or scrotum. The worms enter the body as eggs which emerge from a mosquito's mouthparts when it bites.*

embolism/embolus

Blockage of a blood vessel by material transported in the blood circulation. The condition is called *embolism;* the blocking material is an *embolus.*

An embolus is often a piece of solid matter that forces its way through the circulatory system until it becomes wedged in and blocks a small blood vessel. It may be a clot of blood, a globule of fat, or a piece of tumor tissue that has eroded a blood vessel. Or it may be a bubble of air admitted during an intravenous injection.

The most common cause of embolism is the breaking away of a thrombus (the formation of a blood clot within the heart or blood vessels). It may occur in an artery, a vein, or the chambers of the heart. When a fragment of the thrombus breaks off it becomes the embolus, which eventually may lodge in a smaller blood vessel.

Pulmonary (lung) *embolism*—obstruction of the pulmonary artery or one of its branches—is so serious as to cause death in approximately 5% of cases. Most emboli arise from the veins of the legs and pelvis, and are a well-recognized complication of pregnancy, post-operative recovery, or extended bed rest.

Fat embolisms may occur after injury to the long bones and the consequent release of bone marrow fat into the bloodstream. *Air embolism,* as a consequence of unskilled intravenous injection, is commonly seen in drug addicts.

The effect of an embolism is to deprive the involved tissues of their blood supply (ISCHEMIA), which can cause irreparable damage or even death of those tissues. *Cerebral embolism*—where an embolus has lodged in an artery of the brain—may produce signs of a STROKE. In an arterial embolism (most often seen in the legs), the area beyond the blockage becomes white, cold and painful. If an air embolus lodges in the heart, cardiac arrest and death can occur instantly.

Vascular surgeons can often successfully remove an arterial thrombus (see THROMBOSIS/THROMBUS), especially if they operate soon after the diagnosis. Small venous embolisms may be bypassed in time with the development of new channels for the flow of blood. Their recurrence can be prevented by anticoagulant drugs.

EMBOLUS

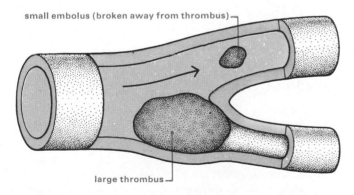

small embolus (broken away from thrombus)

large thrombus

An embolus is any abnormal particle circulating in the blood. The most common type is a fragment of blood clot which has broken off from a larger thrombus as pictured here. The embolus travels along until it blocks a small blood vessel, thus cutting off the supply to an area of tissue. Embolisms can be fatal, especially when they lodge in the circulation of the lung or brain.

emesis

The technical word for VOMITING.

emphysema

The abnormal presence of air in certain parts of the body, particularly in the lungs *(pulmonary emphysema).* Air may enter tissues by a variety of means, such as trauma or surgery; but in clinical practice the term emphysema is virtually confined to a lung condition characterized by distension of the air sacs (alveoli). This may occur as a consequence of other diseases, such as bronchitis or whooping cough, in which alveoli are damaged and merge into larger spaces. This results in a decrease in the efficiency of respiration, with a consequent strain on the heart, breathlessness and edema. The chest may become barrel-shaped and wheezy breathing is particularly common. Treatment of this basically irreversible condition is to protect the patient from infection and preserve general health as long as possible.

See also the major article on **Pulmonary diseases.**

empyema

A fluid-filled abscess in the chest.

It is a fairly rare complication of a primary infection of the lungs (e.g., pneumonia, tuberculosis, pulmonary abscess, or pleurisy). The inflamed tissue is "walled off" by the body's defense mechanisms and pus begins to accumulate within the chest.

The natural course of empyema is for the contained pus and fluid to burst and discharge itself outward through the chest wall or inward into the bronchus. Before this happens, however, the condition may be manifested by fever, sweating, and either lung collapse or visible fluid levels in the chest x-ray.

Empyema has been virtually eradicated by antibiotic therapy. Formerly it occurred in at least 5% of cases of severe pneumonia; the only treatment then available was surgical drainage.

encephalitis

Inflammation of the brain, usually caused by a viral infection (some cases are known to be bacterial in origin).

Certain viruses that attack man—a few of them transmitted by insects—show a tendency to localize their effects in the brain and the membranes surrounding the brain (meninges). All these tissues may become inflamed, swollen and edematous; the resulting vascular congestion sometimes leads to small hemorrhages. The patient is then suffering from encephalitis (sometimes called "brain fever").

Encephalitis can be a part of other virus diseases that have a developing stage of widespread viremia (viruses in the general blood circulation) before settling into their more obvious clinical manifestations. Examples are the early stages of measles, mumps, chickenpox and poliomyelitis. The symptoms are fever, headache, a stiff neck, photophobia (abnormal sensitivity of the eyes to light), irritability, and sometimes convulsions.

Epidemics of encephalitis have occurred in certain areas of the world, such as St. Louis, Japan, Russia and Australia's Murray Valley. These are spread by mosquitoes in the early spring and summer and mainly attack children. Adults are thought to develop immunity. The death rate is high, perhaps 20% in the undernourished and the very young. Attempts to produce a vaccine have been only partly successful. Thus, prevention of epidemics depends on public health measures to control insects and prevent them breeding.

The treatment of encephalitis is mainly careful nursing: control of fever, analgesics for the relief of headache, rest and prolonged convalescence.

encephalitis lethargica

A disease which first occurred in the wake of the pandemic of influenza during and for about 10 years after World War I. Nothing like this disease is recorded from before 1914 and few if any cases have been recorded in America and Western Europe since 1930. Also known as *von Economo's disease* and *sleeping sickness*.

Although the organism was never identified, the disease was typical of a viral infection. Patients usually suffered from pronounced somnolence together with ophthalmoplegia (paralysis of the eye muscles), although a minority were hyperactive. Disorders of movement, headache, insomnia, dizziness, tiredness and confusion were common. More than 20% of the victims died within a few weeks and a high proportion of the survivors developed PARKINSON'S DISEASE. Some children developed psychopathic personality with compulsive behavior.

encephalomyelitis

Diffuse inflammation of both the brain (ENCEPHALITIS) and spinal cord (MYELITIS). It can be caused by a number of agents, including viral infections and syphilis; bacterial encephalomyelitis rarely occurs.

endarterectomy

The surgical removal of part of the inner layers of an artery together with anything that is impairing the blood flow—such as a clot or fatty deposits (atheromas) on the arterial walls. Also called *thromboendarterectomy*.

The surgeon uses a "coring out" process which leaves behind the smooth inner lining of the arterial wall to act as the new channel for the blood circulation.

It was first performed in 1957 by American cardiac surgeons on the coronary arteries of the heart, in an attempt to increase blood flow to the heart muscle. But the entire length of the coronary artery is usually affected in patients with ATHEROSCLEROSIS and it is technically impossible to remove all of the lining of long, convoluted and tiny blood vessels. So endarterectomy did not prove successful for every patient with coronary artery disease. The technique is more successful with the larger arteries, such as those of the limbs.

It was not until the venous bypass operations on the coronary arteries became possible in the late 1960s, using grafts of leg vein tissue, that surgery for coronary atherosclerosis came into general favor. Since then a number of techniques have been combined: joining together blood vessels from inside the chest wall, bypass, and endarterectomy. Some 20,000 such operations for coronary disease are now undertaken annually in the U.S.A.

Carotid endarterectomy, to improve the blood flow to the brain by "coring out" the carotid arteries in the neck, has proved moderately successful.

endocarditis

Inflammation of the surface of the heart valves or of the lining of the heart chambers. Most often endocarditis is caused by bacterial infection; it may also be a complication of COLLAGEN DISEASES such as systemic lupus erythematosus or rheumatoid arthritis. *Thrombotic endocarditis* is a possible complication of the terminal stages of any fatal illness.

Infective endocarditis is usually an illness of slow onset, and weeks of unexplained ill health may pass before an accurate diagnosis is made. The initial symptoms include fever, sweating and loss of weight; later, small painful nodules may develop in the hands and feet and there may be bleeding beneath the fingernails. Untreated, the damage to the heart valves from multiplication of bacteria on their surface causes distortion of their shape, leading to heart failure. Treatment depends on recognition of the condition and laboratory culture of the microorganisms responsible from the bloodstream (which can include certain species of fungi in addition to bacteria). Prolonged therapy with an appropriate antibiotic should eradicate the infection, especially if begun at a relatively early stage in the disease.

Bacterial endocarditis is unusual in persons with normal hearts. The infection starts most often in persons with a heart defect associated with a congenital heart disease or in those with a heart valve which has been scarred by RHEUMATIC HEART DISEASE (a possible complication of RHEUMATIC FEVER during childhood).

Patients known to have a heart disease are usually given antibiotics to protect them from bacterial endocarditis on occasions (such as before a tooth extraction or other forms of dental surgery) when bacteria may be released into the bloodstream.

endocrine glands

The ductless glands of the body, which secrete HORMONES directly into the bloodstream.

See also the major article on **Endocrinology.**

endometriosis

The internal lining of the uterus, the *endometrium*, is normally confined to the cavity of the organ, but in some women "islands," or fragments, of endometrial tissue are to be found on the ovary or in various places within the abdominal cavity. These patches of endometrium respond in the same way as the normal lining of the uterus to the hormonal changes of each menstrual cycle. The internal bleeding that occurs with each cycle leads to the formation of blood-filled ("chocolate") cysts in the affected organs.

Endometriosis may be silent or it may produce symptoms, usually between the ages of 30 and 40. Lower abdominal discomfort or pain (worse at the time of the menstrual period), pain during sexual intercourse (dyspareunia), and disordered menstruation all suggest the possibility of endometriosis.

The condition may be one cause of infertility; but as it is often found in women who marry and conceive later in life, and less often in those who have early pregnancies (so that the pregnancy may be said to protect against endometriosis), the relationship is obscure. Symptoms certainly improve during pregnancy and disappear at the menopause.

Treatment includes surgical removal of the abnormally sited endometrial tissue or the administration of ovarian sex steroids.

endometritis

Inflammation of the endometrium (the lining of the uterus), usually caused by a bacterial infection.

The disease may occur spontaneously or follow a septic abortion or injury involving the pelvic organs. It may be acute or chronic; the chronic form of the disease is usually the result of repeated acute attacks.

Acute endometritis is characterized by pain in the lower part of the back, low abdominal pain and disorders of menstruation (such as DYSMENORRHEA and MENORRHAGIA).

Diagnosis may require DILATATION AND CURETTAGE (D & C), followed by microscopic examination of a sample of the affected tissues and culture and identification of the causative microorganisms. Once the cause of the inflammation of the endometrium is established, the appropriate antibiotic therapy can be initiated.

ENDOMETRITIS

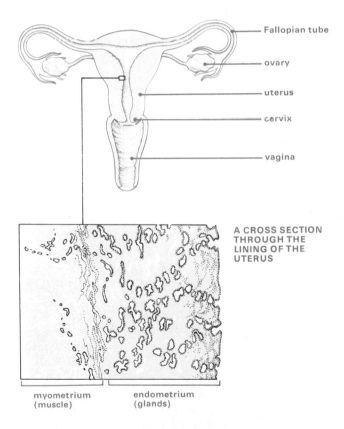

Fallopian tube
ovary
uterus
cervix
vagina

A CROSS SECTION
THROUGH THE
LINING OF THE
UTERUS

myometrium   endometrium
(muscle)   (glands)

The endometrium—the glandular lining of the uterus—grows rapidly in thickness under the influence of estrogens during every menstrual cycle, in preparation for a possible pregnancy.
Endometritis, inflammation of the endometrium, is rare but can occur after childbirth or in old age.

endoscopy

The examination of the interior of the body through optical instruments inserted into the interior of hollow organs by way of natural passages or, in some cases, through special incisions. It is possible through endoscopes to inspect the esophagus ("gullet"), stomach, large intestine, bladder, the air passages of the lungs (bronchi), the peritoneal cavity, the interior of joints and even the ventricles of the brain (cavities containing cerebrospinal fluid).

The basic technique was invented in the 19th century, but instruments were relatively clumsy because they depended on straight optical pathways demanding rigid shafts bearing an inspection lens and a light at the end. With the invention of fibers capable of conducting light (fiberoptics), the shaft of the endoscope no longer had to be rigid. Because of this flexibility, modern instruments make it possible to inspect structures formerly inaccessible. Photographs can be taken through the endoscope, and in many cases a fragment of suspected abnormal tissue can be removed through the endoscope for microscopic examination (BIOPSY).

Although the procedure is somewhat uncomfortable for the patient, endoscopy is not painful nor is it dangerous when performed by specially trained physicians. It does not require a general anesthetic and in many cases admission to the hospital is unnecessary.

See also the major article on **Gastroenterology.**

enema

A fluid introduced into the rectum through the anus. Water or oil may be used.

An enema may be necessary to: (1) clear the bowels of feces in severe constipation, or where the feces have become impacted, or before labor; (2) clean out the bowels before an operation on that part of the body; (3) replace body fluid in mild dehydration; and (4) administer drugs, as in the treatment of ulcerative colitis.

The enema nozzle is inserted up to three or four inches. As much as eight pints of fluid can be slowly introduced into the lower bowel. For a simple bowel evacuation the usual amount is two to four pints of soapy water.

enteritis

Inflammation of the intestines, particularly the small intestine.

There may be a number of causes. The most usual one is bacterial or viral infection after consuming contaminated food or water, as when on vacation in a strange country.

Outbreaks of food poisoning occasionally produce serious attacks of GASTROENTERITIS lasting a few days, with headaches, fever and severe diarrhea. Public health measures may be required to track down the offending organism, which often originates in a specific restaurant or institution. Gastroenteritis in babies is serious as it may cause rapid dehydration.

Acute gastroenteritis may also result from food allergies and excess alcohol.

Regional enteritis, or CROHN'S DISEASE, is an inflammatory disease of an isolated segment of the intestine, characterized by recurrent cramplike pains, weight loss and chronic diarrhea. Special diets and the elimination of stress may be required as well as steroid drugs, sulfonamides, or surgery.

enuresis

The technical name for BEDWETTING.

epidemic parotitis

The technical name for MUMPS.

epidemic pleurodynia

An infectious disease characterized by the sudden onset of severe abdominal pain or chest pain (or both), fever and headache. Also known as *epidemic myalgia, devil's grip* and *Bornholm disease* (after the Danish island of Bornholm where a study of an epidemic was made in 1930).

Epidemic pleurodynia usually occurs in outbreaks in the summer and fall, but it may also occur in single cases. It is most common in children and young adults and is caused by a virus of the Coxsackie B group. The first symptom is usually severe abdominal pain, made worse by movement, or pleuritic chest pain (see PLEURISY). A few patients have a preceding illness of a few days of a "head cold," with headaches and muscle pains—all eventually have headaches and a fever. The pattern of symptoms varies from one outbreak to another.

The diagnosis is easily made in an outbreak, but single cases are more difficult to diagnose and the condition may be initially confused with serious illnesses such as acute appendicitis or myocardial infarction ("heart attack").

There is no specific treatment. Bed rest, and the relief of pain and fever by drugs such as aspirin are all that can be offered. Death has never been reported and serious complications are very rare. The disease usually lasts for only a few days, but some patients may have lingering after effects of tiredness and weakness, with only a gradual return to full health.

epidural anesthesia

A form of regional anesthesia achieved by injecting the anesthetic agent between the spines of the vertebrae into the space (extradural space) just outside the outermost covering membrane (dura mater) of the spinal cord. Also called *peridural anesthesia.*

Compare CAUDAL ANESTHESIA.

epilepsy

Disorganized electrical activity in the brain leading to transient attacks of disturbed sensory or motor functions. Some forms of epilepsy are characterized by convulsions (epileptic seizures or "fits").

In what is known as *symptomatic* epilepsy, the convulsions may be traced to one of several definite causes. These include structural disorders of the brain, such as a tumor or abscess which causes pressure on sensitive brain tissue; disease of the blood vessels of the brain; poisoning by drugs, or injury to the brain. Children very often experience fits during infections in which there is a high fever.

More common, however, is *idiopathic* epilepsy where abnormal brain cell activity arises for no apparent reason. It is this condition which most people think of as epilepsy. Many physicians believe that this type may also be symptomatic but that the cause (a tiny scar in the brain tissue for instance) has gone unrecognized.

It is also possible that some people are more susceptible than others to minor irritation of brain cells. In support of this "lower threshold" theory is the fact that some children have childhood seizures which they grow out of, just as others grow out of having convulsions with high fevers.

Warning symptoms may be noticed: headaches, drowsiness, giddiness, yawning. These are followed by the "aura" which is really the beginning of the seizure. There may be tingling sensations in the limbs with disturbances of taste and smell.

The attack itself falls into one of three main types.

Petit mal attacks are quite difficult to recognize clinically, particularly in children, in whom they mainly occur. The child may simply appear to be vacantly daydreaming for a few seconds. If he is standing, he may sway slightly and fall to the ground. Observers are often unaware that anything has happened.

Grand mal attacks are usually preceded by warning symptoms and the aura. As consciousness is lost, the patient may fall and sometimes emits a characteristic "epileptic cry" as the larynx goes into spasm. The muscles contract rigidly and the jaws clamp shut with tremendous pressure. Sometimes the patient bites his tongue. Then the muscles start to jerk violently and the patient may look blue until the convulsion passes and normal breathing is resumed.

As the fit passes off the patient may fall into a deep sleep (from which he should not be disturbed) or may go into a trancelike state. It is important that epileptics are not left face downward or in a position where they could swallow their own vomit.

Focal seizures (or "Jacksonian seizures") usually result from organic disease or brain injury. The attack starts in a localized group of muscles and does not usually lead to loss of consciousness.

Many people are able to lead fully normal lives with their epilepsy controlled by special drugs. Epilepsy is not thought to be inherited, although there is sometimes a tendency for it to run in families. It is quite reasonable for epileptics to marry and have children.

Many jobs are open to epileptics. They cannot drive cars or operate dangerous machinery, unless the epilepsy is well controlled. Intellectual capacity is unimpaired in most epileptics. In only a small proportion, repeated attacks lead to mental deterioration.

Children tend to grow out of their epileptic seizures, although in some the condition may later recur. Many adults, especially those with a mild form of epilepsy, keep the seizures totally under control with drugs. Phenobarbital is used but is a potent sedative and leads to drowsiness. Other drugs are prescribed for the control of *grand mal;* after a period of trial and error the correct dose is worked out for each individual.

If the patient has not had a seizure after two years or so, the dose is slowly reduced. Some patients appear to be completely cured.

Because of general ignorance of the condition, epilepsy still has not lost its stigma. In earlier times the condition was thought to be associated with possession by evil or even divine spirits. Even in this century it has been erroneously linked with insanity. In fact it is a disease like any other; epileptics are otherwise as normal as people with high blood pressure or diabetes.

See also the major article on **Neurology.**

epinephrine

A hormone secreted by the ADRENAL GLANDS.

episiotomy

A small surgical incision in the perineal area (which lies between the back of the vagina and the anus) made to assist childbirth.

During delivery the perineal skin becomes very stretched, particularly if the baby's head is large; as a result, jagged tears of skin and muscles may occur. Many gynecologists believe it is better to prevent this by making a small incision to enlarge the entrance to the vagina just before delivery.

EPISIOTOMY

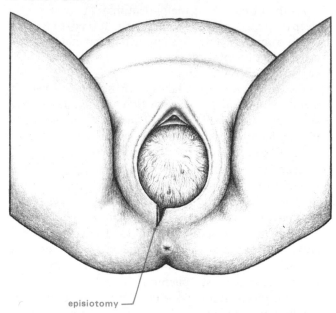

episiotomy

An episiotomy—a small cut made at the bottom of the vagina at the moment of delivery of the baby's head—is performed where there is a risk that the baby's head will tear the mother's perineal tissues. The cut is placed to avoid vital structures such as the anus and the supports of the uterus.

Little or no pain is felt because of the previously administered local anesthetic or general anesthesia. The surgical wound is stitched up following delivery. It heals rapidly, often with very little discomfort.

Episiotomies are essential to aid forceps or breech deliveries, although many experts do not think they should be a matter of routine for all births. Those in favor of the procedure point out that the stretching and damage (without the incision) may be severe enough to affect the future sex life of the mother and possibly predispose the woman to other gynecological complications.

epistaxis

The technical name for NOSEBLEED.

epithelioma

A type of tumor of the skin: there are various types with different degrees of severity.

Malignant ulcers may be caused by overexposure to sunlight; their incidence in such people as farmers, sportsmen and sun worshippers is directly linked with exposure to the sun. Fair-skinned people are more susceptible.

RODENT ULCERS are common and often occur on the face. There may be a small ulcer which heals centrally but continues its cancerous growth at the edges. Growth may be rapid or it may take several years for a spread of no more than one centimeter. But gradually deeper tissue will be invaded. The success of treatment of this condition by simple surgery is excellent.

Tumors known as *squamous cell epitheliomas* may suddenly start to grow after a long latent period. They look like papules or plaques which develop into crusted ulcers or fungal growths. The mucous membranes of the mouth, nose and vulva may be affected as well as the skin.

Unusual nodules, bumps and ulcers on the skin should always be reported to the doctor. After early diagnosis, treatment by surgery or irradiation is very successful.

Epstein-Barr virus

A virus, named after its discoverers, that is responsible for causing INFECTIOUS MONONUCLEOSIS and is strongly implicated as a cause of BURKITT'S LYMPHOMA. Also known as the *Ebb virus*.

ergotism

A serious but fortunately rare disease caused by eating bread made from rye that is contaminated with a certain parasitic fungus.

The symptoms are severe muscle pains, cold skin, vomiting, diarrhea, weakness and severe mental confusion.

The fungus contains a number of powerful chemicals called alkaloids, some of which are now used as therapeutic drugs. One, known as *ergometrine*, is used for the treatment of bleeding following childbirth. Another, *ergotamine*, is used for the relief of migraine. These ergot alkaloids are related chemically to the hallucinogenic drug lysergic acid diethylamide (LSD).

erysipelas

A dangerous skin disease, caused by infection with the bacterium *Streptococcus pyogenes*. Erysipelas (also known as "St. Anthony's fire") produces a bright red inflammation and swelling of the skin, together with fever, chills and sometimes nausea and vomiting.

The condition may originate from infection following a minor scratch or from contamination of a surgical wound. Infection with the streptococci causes a red, glistening swelling of the skin with a clearly demarcated edge. The inflammation may spread rapidly and in untreated cases may progress to collapse and death. Sulfa drugs or antibiotics are highly effective, however, and the disease is now rarely seen in its florid form.

erythema

Redness of the skin, caused by congestion of the tiny blood vessels (capillaries) near the surface. The capillaries may become dilated and congested with blood as the result of many factors, including some nervous mechanism or as the result of exposure to an external stimulus—such as heat, cold, ultraviolet rays (as in SUNBURN) or ionizing (high-energy) radiation—such as x-rays or gamma rays. Among other causes of erythema are reactions to certain drugs, insect bites or stings, and certain viral infections that produce an erythematous rash (such as MEASLES). Patchy erythema may also occur in chronic diseases such as systemic LUPUS ERYTHEMATOSUS.

Specific types of erythema are often indicated in medical practice by a modifying term: for example, *erythema nodosum* is an acute inflammatory skin disease, thought to be caused by various types of allergic reactions, characterized by the formation of red nodules.

erythrocyte sedimentation rate

If a sample of blood (treated with an anticoagulant to prevent clotting) is placed in a tall narrow tube which is set up in a vertical position, the red cells slowly settle toward the bottom of the tube. In a normal person, in good health, the process of sedimentation is slow; by the end of an hour the top of the red cell column will have dropped by only 5 to 10 millimeters.

In many diseases in which the blood proteins are abnormal the rate is increased—with figures as high as 100 to 150 millimeters per hour. This constitutes a simple but useful test for the presence of various organic diseases. However, since it provides little information about the *type* of disease present, it is quite nonspecific.

eschar

An area of dead tissue produced by the action of corrosive substances or by burning.

Escharotics are substances employed to treat warts, the most commonly used being trichloroacetic acid and nitric acid. Their action is unpredictable and the area burned may exceed that desired.

esophageal varices

Enlarged and tortuous veins in the lower part of the esophagus, found in association with raised blood pressure in the abdominal veins (*portal hypertension*)—a complication of CIRRHOSIS of the liver.

In the United States, portal hypertension is most commonly caused by alcoholic cirrhosis, but it may occur in cirrhosis secondary to HEPATITIS or to other causes. The branches of the veins in the esophagus near the stomach form links with the portal vein. The varices are potentially dangerous because they are often the site of bleeding. This may be massive and sudden or there may be minor bleeding for days before the condition is discovered.

It is often difficult to diagnose the source of this hemorrhage, since bleeding in the stomach may be due to an acute or chronic peptic ulcer. Treatment is also difficult. Injection of vasopressin, which causes the blood vessels to contract, is sometimes effective. If this fails it may be necessary to use "balloon tamponade," in which an inflatable device is inserted into the esophagus and pressed against the site of the bleeding. Finally, a surgical operation may be needed to seal the veins and so stop the bleeding directly. In cases of recurrent bleeding the portal hypertension may be treated by diverting the blood from the portal vein into the vena cava.

See also LIVER DISEASE.

esophagitis

Inflammation of the esophagus ("gullet"), often caused by the flow of small amounts of gastric juice up from the stomach. This reflux is sometimes known as "heartburn" and may appear after large meals or in the presence of a hiatus hernia—an abnormal protrusion into the chest cavity of the top part of the stomach through a gap, or "hiatus," in the diaphragm (see HERNIA). Because of the abnormal displacement and relaxation of the normally closed muscular ring at the base of the esophagus (known as the "cardiac sphincter"), some of the acid contents of the stomach may flow up to irritate and inflame the esophageal lining.

ESR

Abbreviation for ERYTHROCYTE SEDIMENTATION RATE.

estrogens

One of the two types of female sex hormone, secreted by the ovary. There have been more than 20 different estrogens identified biochemically but estrone, estradiol and estriol are the three main ones of clinical interest.

Estrogens are responsible for the regeneration of the uterine lining immediately after menstruation, and their withdrawal (as the ovarian follicle degenerates) provokes menstrual bleeding and the onset of a period. After the menopause the production of estrogens is considerably diminished; many of the unwanted symptoms of this time in a woman's life are related to the reduced amounts of estrogens circulating in the blood following the ovary's cessation of activity.

In pregnancy, estrogens are secreted by the placenta to stimulate breast growth and to maintain uterine growth and receptivity to the fetal demands. Measurements of plasma and urinary levels offer a useful assessment of placental efficiency where the baby is "small for dates," or where there is doubt about the prognosis for the pregnancy (i.e., after threatened labor or hemorrhage).

Estrogens, synthetically produced, are a constituent of the combination type of oral contraceptive used to suppress ovulation. Therapeutically they are used in hormonal creams or pessaries for the treatment of postmenopausal vaginitis, and as "depot" (i.e., long-acting) injections or as tablets in hormone replacement therapy ("HRT") for the menopausal woman. Used cosmetically to rejuvenate aging skin they have no value. Excessive doses are associated with an increase in blood-clotting and in recent years the dosage used in oral contraception has been reduced.

For a number of years replacement therapy with estrogens has been widely recommended in cases where the menopause is accompanied by troublesome symptoms, but recent work demonstrates that there is a slightly increased tendency for women who have taken estrogens for a long time to develop cancer of the endometrium (lining of the womb). It is also possible that the incidence of cancer of the breast could be similarly increased, but the evidence is not clear. The likely incidence of cancer of the womb has been given as 1 per thousand; the incidence with estrogen replacement 4 per thousand. The conclusion must be that it is unwise to use estrogens as a routine in women who are undergoing the menopause, and that if they are used it must only be under medical supervision.

See also *Estrogens and progestogens used in hormone therapy* in the major article on **Drugs and Medicines.**

exophthalmic goiter

HYPERTHYROIDISM accompanied by abnormal protrusion of the eyeballs (exophthalmos) and GOITER.

extrasystole

The heart normally beats in a regular rhythm which is controlled by specialized tissue in the heart known as the conducting system. The beat is generated by a small mass of tissue belonging to this system, which is known as the *sinoatrial node*. From there, an impulse spreads and travels along the rest of the conducting system and through heart muscle to cause other parts of the heart muscle to contract in a well-defined order.

However, impulses are sometimes generated outside the sinoatrial node so that extra beats (or extrasystoles)

occur. This may occur in normal health as a result of excessive stress or excitement, or it may be due to heart disease, or to drugs.

The patient may notice a "skipped beat," or a flutter, or extra beats. The significance of extrasystoles depends on the underlying cause of the extra beats and on their frequency; too many extra beats prevent the heart from pumping blood around the body efficiently. Treatment depends on the cause and on the type (site of origin) of extrasystole.

See also ARRHYTHMIA.

F

fainting

Complete or partial loss of consciousness due to a temporary lack of blood supply to the brain.

Fainting can be brought about by a physiological reaction to overwhelming pain, an emotional shock, or extreme fear. These cause stimulation and overactivity of the *vagus nerve*, resulting in a slow pulse and reduction of the output of the heart, accompanied by dilation of the blood vessels in the muscles and pooling of the blood (which thus fails to reach the brain in sufficient amounts).

The person about to faint feels weak and nauseated; the skin breaks out in a sweat and feels cold, and there is yawning or deep sighing. In a little while the complexion becomes deathly pale and consciousness slips away.

Some individuals may show small involuntary movements during a simple faint which can be mistaken for an epileptic attack. Fainting can also be induced by a close hot atmosphere, prolonged lack of food, or by standing still in one position too long so that the blood pools in the vessels of the legs. It is fairly common in young people.

Recovery quickly ensues once the patient's head is lowered in relation to the rest of the body, permitting a prompt return of blood to the brain.

See also *Unconsciousness* in the **First Aid** section.

Fallopian tube

The tube through which the female egg cell travels from the ovary to the uterus. There is one on each side of the uterus.

In each monthly cycle a *Graafian follicle* forms in an ovary and eventually ruptures, releasing an ovum into one of the tubes. It is during the passage of the ovum through the Fallopian tube (which takes several days) that fertilization by a sperm cell can occur. After fertilization the fertilized egg continues its journey through the tube to the uterus and is eventually implanted in the wall of the womb.

Sometimes the embryo remains in the tube and develops there—a condition known as ECTOPIC PREGNANCY.

Sterilization in women is most often performed by ligation of the tubes, which prevents ova from descending from the ovaries. The Fallopian tubes may be blocked by disease with the same effect, making the woman infertile.

farmer's lung

A disease associated with heavy exposure to organic dusts, particularly those given off by moldy hay, grain and other vegetable matter. It is also known as *acute interstitial pneumonitis* or "thresher's lung."

Characteristically it begins suddenly with night sweats, cough, fever, difficulty in breathing, headache and chest pains. Most sufferers recover soon after being removed from the environment in which they are exposed to hay and grain. With repeated attacks, however, more serious lung conditions such as emphysema may develop with potentially fatal consequences.

Farmer's lung is thought to be due to sensitivity to antigens in the molds.

fecalith

A concretion in the large intestine formed from hardened feces and calcium salts.

The condition is a relatively rare but potentially serious complication of chronic constipation. If the concretion blocks the intestine, surgical removal of the hardened mass may be necessary.

feces

The solid waste matter eliminated from the body after the digestion of food. Feces, like urine, are often a useful aid in the diagnosis of various diseases.

The process of digestion takes place in the stomach and small intestine. The indigestible residue passes through the large intestine, where its water content is largely reabsorbed, and collects in the rectum—together with large quantities of bacteria which have assisted in the process of digestion and coloring matter such as bile. The normal dark brown color of the feces is derived from a bile pigment known as stercobilin.

For most people, one daily bowel movement is normal; but the "normal" can range from several times a day to once every several days. A sudden change in bowel habits may be a warning sign of disease.

The shape of feces ("stools") should be cylindrical and the consistency should be firm without being hard. Many physicians believe that modern Western diets lack essential fiber ("roughage") and that added fiber is needed to ensure a healthy digestive system.

The two most common departures from the norm are diarrhea and constipation. Each can be a sign of a number of different diseases; if either is prolonged medical attention should be sought. Blood in the feces can be a sign of conditions as diverse as hemorrhoids and tumors, and is an even more important reason to seek medical attention.

Fecal fat is often measured during hospital laboratory investigations since it provides an indication of the efficiency of digestion and absorption.

felon

Any acute inflammation of the deep-seated tissues of the fingers, usually one that exudes pus. The term may also be applied to an inflammation of the toes. Also called *whitlow*.

The structure which is affected may be the root of the nail, the pulp of the finger or toe tip, the bone, or the sheaths of the tendons that run along the back and front of the fingers or toes. Usually, the felon begins either as a small abscess at the root of the nail or as an abscess in the tissues (both fatty and fibrous) that make up the pulp of the digit.

Inflammation of bones in the fingers or toes is rare, but a felon may originate in the sheath of the tendon.

Treatment involves incision and drainage of the lesion (usually by a surgeon who specializes in treating disorders of the hand) and the administration of antibiotics or other appropriate drugs.

fertility

Fertility—as measured by the number of children a couple have during the woman's reproductive lifetime—depends on a combination of biological and social factors. In societies such as the Hutterite communities, in which there are no social constraints on childbearing within marriage, couples commonly have 11 or 12 children. A woman's potential for childbearing is determined by her age at the MENARCHE (the onset of menstrual cycles) and at the MENOPAUSE, on the time spent recovering between pregnancies and on the frequency of sexual intercourse. A woman in good health in her 20s is estimated to have a 25% chance of conceiving from intercourse at the fertile midpoint of a single menstrual cycle.

Male fertility is less easily measured, but most men retain their fertility as long as they remain sexually potent, often well into the 70s or later. About one in every ten couples is infertile due to sterility in one or the other partner (see INFERTILITY). The infertile partner is just as likely to be the man as the woman.

In practice most societies have limited the number of children either by social means—late marriage and abstention from sexual intercourse within marriage—or by infanticide, abortion, or contraception. Even so, most countries in the world today have growing populations as the numbers of births exceed deaths. This is due to a dramatic fall in infant and childhood mortality worldwide with the control of diseases such as smallpox, malaria and tuberculosis, and better nutrition. Most couples in the developing world, however, still want a large family—especially of sons—to help work the land. Despite campaigns by the International Planned Parenthood Federation many communities are still slow to accept contraception.

See also *Infertility* in the major article on **Family Planning**.

fertilization

The process by which the egg cell (ovum) is fertilized by a sperm cell. It is believed to take place in a Fallopian

FERTILIZATION

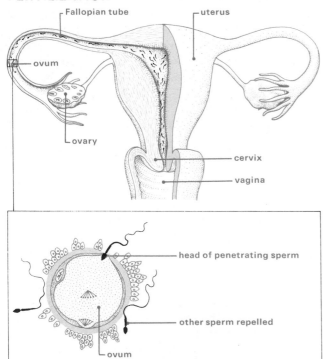

When a sperm meets the ovum, it releases enzymes which digest the membranes surrounding the egg allowing the head of the sperm to penetrate it. After successful union, no other sperm can penetrate this barrier; the fertilized egg implants in the uterine lining about one week after ovulation.

tube, down which the egg cell descends after ovulation. Sperm cells swim up through the uterus into the Fallopian tube to meet the egg. When they do so they release an enzyme to soften the outer layer of the ovum, thus making it possible for one sperm to penetrate it.

Of the millions of sperms produced during coitus, only one is required to fertilize the ovum: the first one to reach the goal immediately forms a barrier membrane around itself to prevent further penetrations. At this point, in a small minority of cases, the fertilized ovum may split in two and so bring about the conception of identical (homozygous) twins. Nonidentical (heterozygous) twins are conceived as a result of the simultaneous fertilization of two separate ova. (The release of more than one ovum, ordinarily a rare event, became more common with advent of the so-called *fertility drugs*.)

Upon fertilization, the nucleus of the sperm fuses with the nucleus of the ovum, forming a single cell which contains the 46 chromosomes necessary for human development. Division of the cell proceeds while the ovum is descending the tube into the uterus, where it arrives as a *blastocyst* containing many new cells. The process of fertilization may be said to be complete when the blastocyst implants itself into the lining of the uterus, where it will develop for the rest of the pregnancy.

fetal distress

The term used to describe the signs of lack of oxygen in the fetus during the process of labor. When the obstetrician detects evidence of fetal distress he will take steps to deliver the baby very quickly—by forceps or vacuum extraction, or by Cesarean section.

During the early stages of labor the obstetrician monitors the state of the fetus by recording its heartbeat, either by listening through a stethoscope or by an electronic instrument that records the fetal heartbeat continuously. The pattern of the change in the heart rate with each contraction can give an early warning of fetal distress.

Blood samples from the fetus may also be taken for direct measurement of its oxygen content and the acidity. When these techniques of fetal monitoring are used any lack of oxygen can be detected before any serious fetal distress occurs. Their introduction has led to a substantial fall in the numbers of stillbirths and of babies who have difficulty in breathing immediately after birth.

fever

A body temperature above the normal average of 98.6°F (about 37°C). The term is also used to describe a disease in which there is an elevation of body temperature above normal. Fever is one of the body's defense mechanisms against bacterial and viral infection: indeed as recently as 40 years ago patients with syphilis were treated by "fever therapy" in which they were deliberately given malaria to cause a high fever.

The autonomic nervous system, controlled by centers in the brainstem, regulates temperature in the body; the part of the brain called the *hypothalamus* is the biological "thermostat." On a hot day the hypothalamus senses the greater heat production and directs an increased flow of blood to the skin so that the capillaries dilate, sweat glands become active and heat is lost. On a cold day the hypothalamus directs the muscles to contract rapidly, or shiver, and heat production increases.

During an infection the thermostat sets itself at a higher level than normal, and thus may be enough to eliminate the microorganisms responsible for the illness. Fever may also be due to a noninfective cause—some brain diseases, neoplasms such as Hodgkin's disease, and metabolic disorders such as thyrotoxicosis may all cause a rise in body temperature, as may excessive exposure to heat.

The early symptoms of a fever may include a feeling of heat and discomfort, flushed skin or rash, increased pulse and respiration rates, nervous restlessness and insomnia. The simplest and most effective drug to control fever is aspirin, but if the fever rises above 104°F additional cooling may be provided by ice packs, fans, and sponging with tepid water.

fibrillation

The action of the heart muscle is normally coordinated so that the heart can pump blood efficiently. When the muscle relaxes, the chambers of the heart are filled by blood flowing into them—in the case of the right side, from the great veins, and on the left from the lungs.

Contraction normally occurs in an ordered sequence: the atria contract just before the ventricles to complete ventricular filling just before the ventricles themselves contract and expel the blood under pressure. Backward flow of blood is prevented by the heart valves.

There is a natural pacemaker in the wall of the right atrium, the *sinoatrial node*, from which a wave of excitation spreads through the muscle of the atria. A specialized bundle of fibers (Purkinje fibers) originates at another node, the *atrioventricular node* (also in the right atrium, but lower down and nearer the ventricle than the sinoatrial node). Through this bundle the wave of excitation is conducted at 400 to 500 centimeters per second to the right and left ventricular muscle. If contraction becomes disorganized the muscle contracts and relaxes irregularly throughout its mass and is effectively paralyzed. This condition is called *fibril-*

lation: the fibers going up to make the muscle mass contract and relax independently and circulation ceases in the part of the heart affected.

Fibrillation may affect the atria or the ventricles. In the latter case, death follows quickly unless treatment is immediate (see VENTRICULAR FIBRILLATION).

fibroadenoma

A benign tumor containing a mixture of fibrous and glandular tissue. Fibroadenomas may be found in many organs, but they are especially common in the breast.

The condition is probably much more common than is revealed by cases coming to the attention of surgeons: one study showed that even in "normal" breasts unsuspected fibroadenomas (often just visible to the naked eye) were present on biopsy in 25% of all patients.

Four out of every five women who have a lump removed from the breast are found *not* to have cancer, and fibroadenomas account for many of these benign tumors. Unfortunately they are sometimes recurrent, and some women have several removed over a period of years. Even so, any swelling or lump detected in the breast should be examined medically to exclude the possibility of cancer.

See also BREAST CANCER.

fibrocystic disease

Another term for CYSTIC FIBROSIS.

fibroids

Tumors of the womb consisting of muscle and some fibrous tissue.

Fibroids are benign and are the most common of all uterine tumors. Their cause is unknown.

They are more correctly known as *myomas*, since they rarely contain much fibrous material and consist almost entirely of smooth muscle. Fibroids are three times more common among black American women than among whites and are also more common in childless women. About one woman in five over the age of 35 has them, but the vast majority are benign and cause no symptoms. The fibroids range in size from microscopic lesions to multiple tumors weighing several pounds. Abnormal bleeding is the most common symptom.

In most cases the tumors require no treatment—particularly when there are no symptoms and when the patient is past the menopause. Once fibroids have been diagnosed the doctor will normally perform an examination every 6 or 12 months to make sure there is no increase in size. Some gynecologists have a rule that fibroids should be removed only when they are bigger than a pregnant uterus of 12 to 14 weeks. However, cervical myomas larger than $1\frac{1}{2}$ in. (3-4 cm) in diameter should usually be removed surgically.

Total hysterectomy is rarely necessary; it is performed only when the fibroids are large and multiple. Smaller fibroids may be removed by "shelling" them out (*myomectomy*).

Surgical removal is not normally attempted when a woman with fibroids is pregnant, unless there is a definite risk that the size of the fibroids may cause spontaneous abortion.

fibroma

A benign tumor composed principally of white fibrous connective tissue; almost any part of the body may be affected, but fibromas are especially common in the ovaries, nerves and skin. On the skin they can be seen as firm slowly growing nodules. They are reddish, yellow or bluish-black and found most often on the limbs.

Neurofibromas affect the nerve sheaths and contain nerve elements as well as fibrous tissue. When neurofibromas are present in large numbers the condition is known as *neurofibromatosis* (VON RECKLINGHAUSEN'S DISEASE). The tumors may cause symptoms from pressure on the nerves, especially in and around the spinal canal.

Odontogenic fibroma can lead to the development of benign tumors in the gums.

fibrosarcoma

A type of cancer in which the tumor contains collagen fibers.

Various kinds of fibrosarcoma affect different tissues, including the nerves, teeth and breast.

fibrosis

Damaged tissues are normally repaired by fibrosis, the formation of fibrous, or scar, tissue.

Fibrous repair restores the continuity of the damaged part, but fibrous tissue cannot function as part of the repaired organ; moreover, it contracts as the scar is formed and can interfere with normal function. Such contractures are often seen after the skin has been extensively damaged by burning, and may be severe enough to require plastic surgery.

Continued irritation of tissue may promote fibrosis. Examples include the fibrosis of lung substance produced by the inhalation of particles of silica in PNEUMOCONIOSIS, and the extensive fibrosis found in cases of ASBESTOSIS, when respiratory function is grossly impaired.

CYSTIC FIBROSIS is a condition found in about 1 in 2,500 live births. It is a disease affecting the exocrine glands, especially those which secrete mucus. (Exocrine glands, as opposed to endocrine glands, release their secretions onto the surface of epithelial tissue—either directly or by means of ducts; the endocrine glands are ductless.) The secretions from the glands are abnormally viscid, and there is a high concentration of chloride, potassium and sodium in the sweat. About 10% of babies affected die in the first few days from obstruction of the intestine. Later, the duct of the pancreas may become blocked with thick mucus; the substance of the gland becomes "cystic" because the secreting tubules dilate and a fibrous reaction follows. The children are very prone to develop infection of the lungs, and may suffer from repeated attacks of bronchitis and bronchopneumonia. Lack of normal intestinal secretions leads to constipation, and progressive destruction of pancreatic tissue may eventually produce diabetes. Diagnosis is made on analysis of the sweat and of pancreatic juice. Treatment may include a surgical operation to relieve obstruction, administration by mouth of pancreatic enzymes and fat-soluble vitamins, salt supplements, and the management of lung infections with wide-spectrum antibiotics and physical therapy. The disease is hereditary.

fibrositis

A general term for an aching condition of the muscles. (Also called *muscular rheumatism*.)

The condition was given the name because it was wrongly believed to result from inflammation ("–itis") of the fibrous tissue that binds the muscles together.

The pain described as fibrositis is sharp—particularly in the muscles of the back, shoulder and neck.

The connection between tension or stress and fibrositis is well known. It probably occurs because nervous tension can lead to tensed muscles. Cold is occasionally mentioned as a cause of fibrositis; this may also be due to the tensing of muscles, a natural reflex to cold conditions. Professional sportsmen, such as golfers and baseball players, seem to be particularly vulnerable but this may be an illusion—an attack is more costly and more widely noticed when a sportsman is involved.

Treatment consists of rest (with occasional moderate exercise if the pain is not too severe) and some form of heat treatment, which may be as simple as warming the affected area with hot towels.

fistula

An abnormal opening or passage between two hollow organs or structures, or between an organ or part and the exterior. The condition may be present from birth (congenital fistula) or may be a complication of an acquired disorder or disease process.

FISTULA

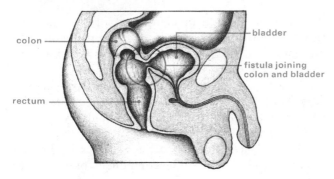

colon

bladder

fistula joining
colon and bladder

rectum

A fistula is an abnormal connection between any two hollow organs or between a hollow organ and the skin. Fistulas occur in Crohn's disease, cancers, as a result of inflammation (for example a rectal abscess) and as postoperative complications. A fistula between the colon and bladder, as pictured above, would let air and infecting bacteria into the bladder, and the patient might have the bizarre symptom of a whistling noise whenever he passes urine.

fits

See SEIZURES.

flatulence

The presence of gas in the stomach or intestines.

Swallowing air is a common cause. Flatulence may also be caused by bacterial fermentation of food. Cellulose in vegetables is broken down to produce methane and hydrogen, while eggs, peas and beans are responsible for sulfurated hydrogen and carbon disulfide.

Individuals who are particularly prone to flatulence should avoid foods that cause it.

Excessive swallowing of air (*aerophagia*) can occur when gulping down food or be associated with emotional stress. When the gas is in the stomach it is belched out through the mouth; in the bowels it causes rumbling, discomfort, and "breaking of wind."

Close control of the diet and attention to any air-swallowing habit are essential for the successful control of flatulence.

fleas

Wingless blood-sucking insects of the order Siphonaptera.

Several fleas are of medical importance because they can act as both host and transmitters of disease organisms.

The human flea, *Pulex irritans*, is parasitic on the skin of man. It is a host of the larval stage of *Dipylidium caninum*, the common tapeworm of dogs which can be passed on to man. It also transmits *Hymenolepis diminuta*, the dwarf tapeworm. The bites of *Pulex* can cause dermatitis and it may on occasions pass plague from one victim to another. Like all fleas, it is susceptible to DDT and to more recent insecticides such as malathion.

More important as a disease vector is the rat flea, *Xenopsylla cheopsis*. In addition to the dwarf tapeworm, it passes on to rats and man the microorganism that causes bubonic plague, *Pasteurella pestis*, and the cause of murine typhus, *Rickettsia mooseri*.

Two species of flea commonly infest pet animals: *Ctenocephalides canis* in dogs and *Ctenocephalides felis* in cats. Many pet owners find that these fleas, while normally confined to the coats of animals, make the transition to human hosts quite freely. Frequent use of flea-killing preparations on pets may be necessary to avoid the irritation and threat to health that infestation can bring.

Apart from the general undesirability of harboring a parasite that feeds on human blood, fleas should be eradicated because they are a common cause of papular urticaria in children. This condition—a rash of red blotches and white weals—is caused by animal fleas rather than *Pulex irritans* and is an allergic reaction to the protein of the fleas' bodies, whether dead or alive.

Any unduly sensitive child should not be allowed

FLEA

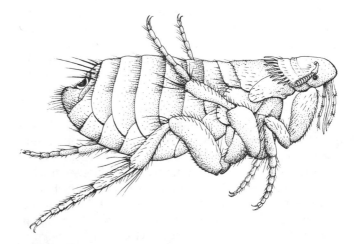

The flea is a wingless parasite which feeds solely on the blood of mammals and birds. Over 200 different species of flea are found in the United States, including the common rat flea (illustrated above). This little insect (length 0.1 in.) was responsible for millions of deaths in the Middle Ages, as it transmitted the bacteria which caused the Great Plague from rat to man.

close contact with pets that may be infested. Several proprietary preparations containing the latest effective pesticides against fleas are on sale at any drugstore.

Cat or dog fleas are rarely bothersome to humans where cats or dogs are around (since they really *prefer* cats or dogs); but when a cat or dog dies or is suddenly removed from the house, the house may suddenly appear massively infested and even become uninhabitable without the aid of professional pest control measures on two or three successive weeks. Also, fleas can stay active in an empty house for months without any host present.

flukes

Minute flatworms of the Trematoda family, which may infest man and other animals as parasites.

Flukes can invade many organs of the body and cause a number of diseases, the most important of which is SCHISTOSOMIASIS (or bilharziasis), which affects about 200 million of the world's population, most of them in Africa. Three types of fluke can cause the disease: *Schistosoma hematobium* and *S. mansoni* in Africa, Arabia and neighboring countries, and *S. japonicum* in China, Japan, the Phillipines, Taiwan and Indo-China. *S. hematobium* infestations mainly affect the bladder, *S. mansoni* and *S. japonicum* the intestinal tract.

Flukes have at least two hosts in their life cycle: as adults they live in vertebrates, while they develop in invertebrates, usually some sort of snail, often leaving the snail as free-swimming *cercariae* which lie in wait in the water until they are attracted to their next host by the agitation he produces by swimming or walking nearby. They penetrate his skin, leaving an irritating papule which blisters and then dries up in about two days. This is known as *swimmer's itch*. Fortunately, flukes do not multiply in the vertebrate host and the severity of the disease depends on the number of cercariae able to gain entry. Schistosomes become mature and mate in the veins of the liver; the eggs, which carry spines, are laid in the veins of the intestines or bladder where by ulceration they make their way into the cavity of the organ and pass to the exterior via the excreta. In water, the eggs develop into larval stage, known as a *miracidium*, which must gain entry into a suitable snail within 30 hours or die.

Flukes other than Schistosoma which cause human disease are *Clonorchis sinensis*, which may be eaten in raw or pickled freshwater fish in the Far East; *Opisthorchis felineus*, which also infects freshwater fish but is found in Southeastern Europe and parts of Asia; and the lung fluke *Paragonimus westermani*, which develops in crabs and crayfish. *Fasciola hepatica* is a liver fluke commonly found in cattle and sheep which may affect man, while a similar organism, *Fasciolopsis buski*, occurs in the Far East, usually in pigs.

fluoridation

Addition of fluoride (a compound of the chemical element fluorine) to the public water supply in order to prevent dental decay, especially in children. It is one of the simplest and most effective health measures available today, and it costs only a few cents per person a year. Yet it has been strongly resisted by some critics who maintain that it represents compulsory medical treatment and that fluoride is poisonous.

The incidence of dental caries is lower in districts where fluoride is a natural component of the water supply than in areas where it is not. Reputable scientific studies have established that adjustment of the fluoride level in water to one part per million can reduce caries by half: the reason is that the fluoride becomes incorporated in the mineral structure of the teeth and strengthens their resistance to caries.

Medical and dental authorities in favor of fluoridation agree that excessive levels of fluoride can cause mottling of teeth, but the proposed levels are not high enough to do so. Other alleged side effects, including even cancer, are easily dismissed.

An alternative way to obtain fluoride is in the form of toothpastes, mouthwashes, or tablets. For the maximum protection fluoride should be ingested with drinking water throughout tooth development.

folliculitis

Inflammation of the hair follicles of the skin or the scalp. It is usually caused by bacterial infection, the commonest organism being staphylococcus.

It may take a variety of forms. Acute infection originating in a hair follicle may develop into a boil or carbuncle. When the infection affects the hair follicles in the beard area, the patient has *sycosis barbae* or "barber's rash."

Pseudofolliculitis gives a similar appearance but is not directly due to infection. It is caused by damage to the surrounding tissues by the sharp tips of shaved hairs entering the skin around the follicle. Milder cases of folliculitis may occur on the legs or arms as a reddish rash corresponding to the distribution of hair follicles. This condition may be caused by infection, but irritants such as oil or chemicals coming into contact with the skin may also produce it.

Treatment is by attention to skin hygiene and, if severe, by the administration of antibiotics.

food poisoning

Food contaminated by bacteria or bacterial toxins can produce dramatic and swift intestinal disorders, characterized by vomiting and diarrhea.

Staphylococci growing on food—commonly dairy products, or cooked meat and fish—release a toxin which reduces the victim to a state of miserable shock in a few hours, but the attack passes off relatively quickly. Bacteria of the Salmonella group can contaminate various sorts of food; they produce symptoms which take longer to appear but which last longer. The patient may suffer from headache, shivering and prostration as well as diarrhea and vomiting. The illness may be extremely severe.

A rare but very dangerous disease—BOTULISM—is produced by the organism *Clostridium botulinis*, which grows without oxygen at low temperatures and can survive as spores resistant to boiling. The processes of home canning are often insufficiently stringent to kill this organism, which multiplies in preserved food and releases a toxin which can be absorbed by the intestine and taken up by the central nervous system. Botulism is characterized by double vision, dilated pupils, paralysis of the face, difficulty in swallowing and eventually paralysis of the muscles of respiration and arrest of the heart. Hospital treatment is essential, but even when this is provided the disease may prove fatal. A small but continuing number of cases have been recorded in recent years in the United States.

The treatment of staphylococcal food poisoning is directed toward relief of the symptoms, for the disease is not caused by the living organism itself. Salmonella food poisoning is a true infection, and severe cases may require the use of antibiotics.

Prevention is more important than cure. In tropical and subtropical climates it is important to remember that all food, particularly vegetables, may be contaminated and should only be eaten fresh after washing. Food must be stored in cool, well-ventilated places free from flies and dirt. All persons who handle food must be very careful in their personal hygiene. Home canned and preserved food must not be eaten if there is any suspicion that it has deteriorated, and processed food must not be kept too long.

foreign bodies

"Foreign body" is the term given to any extraneous object lodged in a part of the human body. This is generally accidental; occasionally it happens deliberately from ignorance or from abnormal action. Foreign bodies can range from bullets to badly swallowed food.

In the eyes dust, grit, hairs or filings flung from a lathe may move under the lids or become embedded in the eyeball. The condition is painful and may be a threat to sight unless expertly and promptly dealt with. Simple first-aid measures can be used for removal of those particles which are loose under the lids. See *Object in the*

eye in the **First Aid** section.

Ears and nostrils are sites where small children experimentally poke up beads or small toys, which they then cannot remove. They may forget about them or be too scared to tell their parents. If the objects remain, the subsequent inflammation and infection will eventually require medical attention, at which time the doctor will remove them. Sometimes insects can get inside these cavities and be unable to escape, especially if the region is hairy. The irritation they cause is out of proportion to their size. First-aid methods can help to extract insects from the ear (see *Object in the ear* in the **First Aid** section) but all other cases need a doctor's help. Probing is likely to drive objects further in.

Objects swallowed generally give little trouble, moving smoothly from the stomach through the bowel to be passed with the stools. This often can be helped by the doctor's prescription of smooth mucilaginous preparations. Surgery is very rarely needed, although it may be indicated if repeated x-ray checks show that the object appears stationary within the digestive tract.

In the throat and airways foreign bodies can cause great irritation and may constitute a serious medical emergency. The fishbone caught in the throat is painful, especially on swallowing movements; amateur attempts to dislodge it are likely to drive it back further. Larger objects—including hard candy, toys or small dentures—can cause severe choking and need rapid first aid. The most serious ASPHYXIA arises from a big bolus of food caught in the windpipe, blocking it entirely. This is a life-threatening emergency to be dealt with immediately by a technique of pressure on the abdomen just below the diaphragm to eject the object. The technique is known as the *Heimlich maneuver* and should be learned by everyone (see *Choking* in the **First Aid** section).

The urethra, bladder, rectum and vagina are occasionally the sites of foreign bodies lodged after having been inserted. They are unlikely to free themselves and may cause great trouble. There must be no hesitation in seeking medical help.

fracture

A break in a bone.

The signs and symptoms may include pain, swelling, deformity, shortening of the limb, loss of power, abnormal movement and a grating noise between the fractured ends. In severe cases there may be shock increased by loss of blood.

The obvious cause is direct violence, such as a blow from a heavy object. But there are indirect causes: for example, falling on the hand may cause a fracture of the collarbone; or a sudden violent contraction of muscles may fracture the kneecap. X-rays are used to confirm the diagnosis.

FOUR TYPES OF FRACTURE

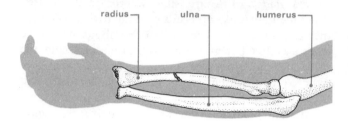

radius — ulna — humerus

1 simple—skin intact over fracture

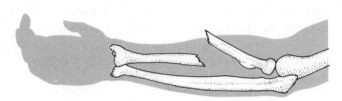

2 open—bone exposed to infection

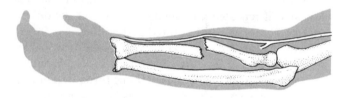

3 complicated—artery torn causing hemorrhage

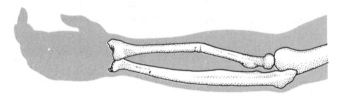

4 greenstick—incomplete break common in children

Bones may break in many different ways depending on the type of injury and on the age and general health of the person. Children have relatively soft, elastic bones which often break on one side only—a greenstick fracture (4). Elderly people have brittle bones which tend to be fractured by trivial forces. The most important complications of fractures are infection (2) and damage to structures adjacent to the fractured bone such as nerves, blood vessels (3), or internal organs.

In young children the break may be incomplete and is referred to as a *greenstick* fracture.

A *closed* fracture is one where the skin is not broken, while an *open,* or *compound,* fracture is one in which the broken bones pierce the skin. If the fractured end protrudes through the skin, bacteria may gain access.

The fracture is said to be *complicated* when it is associated with injury to an important structure such as the brain, major blood vessels, nerves, lungs, or liver; or when the fracture is associated with a dislocation of a joint.

Pathological fractures may be the result of bone disease; for example, a cyst or tumor may cause preliminary softening, which leads to a break.

An *impacted* fracture occurs when one fragment is driven into the other and locked into position.

In first aid, do not move the patient unless he is in immediate danger. After an accident the priorities are to make sure the patient is breathing and not bleeding heavily. Any wound should be dressed, using improvized bandages if necessary. The injured parts can be supported to prevent further damage.

The fracture and the joint (if any) on either side of it should be immobilized. This can be done by securing the broken part firmly to the nearest firm and convenient part of the patient's body. A broken leg is tied to the sound one, an arm to the chest wall. Whenever possible the uninjured part should be moved to the injured part and not the other way around.

If the fractured limb or other part has to be moved it should be given steady support so as to disturb it as little as possible. Padding is put between a limb and the part to which it is secured. Towels, belts and scarves make good emergency bandages.

In cases of a suspected fracture of the spine the patient must be kept absolutely still until experienced help is at hand.

See also *Fractures* in the **First Aid** section.

frigidity

Lack of sexual desire in women or failure to respond to sexual intercourse. This inability to experience sexual satisfaction may be a permanent feature or may persist for a time and then under favorable conditions be replaced by a more normal sexual response.

The cause is often psychological. Poor general health may also diminish sexual interest.

Ignorance of the basic techniques of sexual intercourse—especially, lack of knowledge by one or both partners of the essential role of the clitoris in governing the female sexual response—or poor communication about sexual needs may contribute to frigidity. Many women are aroused sexually more slowly than men and may be left unsatisfied and disappointed.

Concepts of feminity and masculinity, attitudes toward marriage, fear of pregnancy or genital injury can all affect sexual fulfillment.

If a teenage girl receives faulty sexual instruction she can come to believe that sexual matters are shameful or distasteful and this attitude of mind may be difficult to counter.

The time and energy a couple are able to devote to the sexual side of their relationship may also be significant. The pressures of life can seriously dampen a woman's response to intercourse.

Reassurance and education are essential in the treatment of frigidity. A sympathetic interview by a physician can frequently bring to light problems and mistaken attitudes. An alcoholic drink taken by the woman before intercourse can be relaxing and helpful, but despite popular belief there are no such things as aphrodisiacs.

In particularly severe cases of frigidity some form of psychiatric counseling or psychotherapy may be useful. In addition, many excellent books exist (which the family physician can recommend) that help dispel ignorance concerning sexual techniques and which have proved profitable to many more than the authors and publishers. However, one of the best treatment modes is patience, understanding and tenderness on the part of the male partner.

frostbite

Injury or death of a part of the body due to extreme cold.

Frostbite is caused by the direct effect of freezing on the tissues, made worse by the lack of blood to the area (ischemia). The ischemia itself is made worse by the effect of freezing, since blood clots form in the blood vessels and impede blood flow. *Wet* cold is more of a danger than *dry* cold in the induction of frostbite—which most commonly affects the ears, nose, chin, fingers and toes. The sufferer may not notice it, especially on the face, and companions in cold environments need to watch each other for frostbite.

The skin first takes on a pallid color, progressing later to reddish violet, and ultimately to black as the tissue dies. The black color is also derived from decomposition of hemoglobin from blood cells that have escaped from the circulation.

Skin and nails that slough off may regrow later, although there is often a permanent loss of movement.

Frostbite can be avoided by full protection of the face, hands and feet. Clothes should not be so tight as to restrict circulation. In any cold climate it is best to wear several layers of clothes to maintain body heat. The outer clothing should be waterproof to prevent the most damaging coldness induced by wet clothes.

Prevention of frostbite is better than treatment. As soon as it is noticed the area should be rewarmed by placing a fur glove over it. Cold hands and feet should be placed against a warm part of the body—either the victim's own body or a companion's.

The affected part must not be rubbed (especially not with snow!) and should be rewarmed gently, not rapidly.

See also *Frostbite* in the **First Aid** section.

furuncle

The technical name for a BOIL.

G

gallstones

Stones in the gallbladder or the bile ducts. They are present in 10–20% of all autopsies, and are more common in females than males below the age of 50. Women who have had children are more commonly affected than those who have not. The incidence increases with age; gallstones are very rare in infancy and childhood.

The mechanisms underlying the formation of gallstones are poorly understood, but they are often associated with infection of the gallbladder. There are three main types of stone; mixed stones, made of bile pigments, calcium and cholesterol; pure cholesterol stones; and those made up of bile pigments alone, which are rare. Cholesterol stones are usually solitary and large—up to $1\frac{1}{2}$ in. (4 cm) or more in diameter—while mixed stones and those composed of bile pigments are small and multiple.

The stones may be silent, producing no symptoms, or they may be associated with recurrent infection of the gallbladder following obstruction of the cystic duct. Obstruction of the common bile duct by a stone may lead to obstructive JAUNDICE. In obstruction of either duct the gallbladder first shows a noninfective inflammation of its wall secondary to the retention under pressure of bile, and then secondary infection by

GALLSTONES

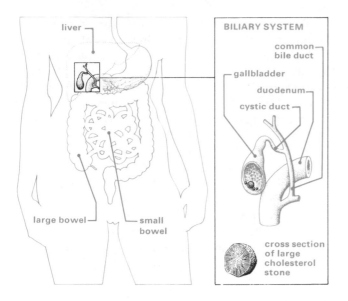

liver

BILIARY SYSTEM

common
bile duct

gallbladder

duodenum

cystic duct

large bowel — small
bowel

cross section
of large
cholesterol
stone

The gallbladder stores and concentrates bile, which is a mixture of substances manufactured in the liver. Most gallstones form because the concentration of cholesterol in the bile is too high, although the pure "cholesterol solitaire" shown above is unusual. If gallstones produce symptoms of jaundice, pain or fever, the gallbladder should be removed.

organisms from the intestines. The patient develops an acute pain in the upper part of the abdomen, usually traveling from the midline to become concentrated under the right ribs. Pain may be felt in the back and in the right shoulder, and may be accompanied by fever, nausea and vomiting.

Most cases settle with bed rest, a light fat-free diet and antibiotics. Subsequent plain x-rays may demonstrate radiopaque stones; but only about 10% of stones contain enough calcium to produce a strong shadow on the x-ray, and in most cases it is necessary to carry out "contrast radiography." If the gallbladder is shown to contain stones, and especially if its function is deficient, it may be necessary to remove the gallbladder and the stones by surgical operation. Some acute cases require urgent operation, but often surgery is best left until the acute attack has subsided and the inflammation died down.

ganglion

1. A swelling on a nerve at the site of the junction of nerve fibers. There are ganglions on the roots of each pair of sensory nerves as they emerge from the spinal cord; they also occur at major branching points of some of the cranial nerves.

2. A soft, painless swelling on the hand or foot due to a cyst developing from a tendon. The condition is harmless, but if the swelling causes inconvenience it may be removed surgically.

gangrene

Death of an area of tissue.

Gangrene may affect a small area, such as a fingertip or toe, or may spread to involve a whole limb.

Dry gangrene occurs without infection. It is caused by failure of the arterial blood supply to the affected part, as the result of injury to the artery, blockage due to disease, or frostbite. At first the area is painful and pale; later it becomes discolored and eventually black. There is a red line between the dead and living areas which moves as the gangrene spreads. Spread of dry gangrene is slow.

In *moist gangrene* infection plays a part and the changes are caused by tissue putrefaction. Poor blood supply is also a factor, perhaps due to infective thrombosis or pressure on blood vessels from a hernia. In addition to the unpleasant gangrenous area the patient may suffer all the signs of a generalized blood infection. Surgical removal of the gangrenous part may be necessary to save life.

Gangrene quite commonly develops in the legs of elderly people and of diabetics, because of an impaired blood supply. It should always be considered in people who have varicose ulcers or bedsores. If gangrene does occur the area must be kept free from infection.

Gas gangrene is due to infection with the bacterium *Clostridium*. It occurs as the result of entry of the bacteria into a wound, without any predisposing shortage of blood supply.

The bacteria are anaerobic—that is, they thrive in conditions where oxygen is absent. They are therefore found in dirty conditions as well as in cultivated soil. (Gas gangrene is a common complication of war wounds.) When they enter the body through a dirty wound they produce gas and toxins. The wound becomes green or black and has a very offensive discharge. The tissues crackle because of the presence of gas.

The infected tissue must be removed and the wound opened to admit oxygen. It may be irrigated with hydrogen peroxide to ensure oxygenation. In addition, *anti-gas gangrene serum* may be given by injection, together with local and systemic antibiotics.

gastrectomy

Surgical removal of all or part of the stomach. The extent of the operation depends on the condition for which it is being performed.

Gastrectomy may be indicated in cases of ulceration of the stomach and duodenum which have not responded to adequate medical treatment (see DUODENAL ULCER), in cases of uncontrollable bleeding from ulcers, in the treatment of cancer of the stomach, and for the relief of obstruction to the emptying of the stomach caused by old ulceration near the outlet of the stomach (pylorus)—scarring may narrow the passage from the stomach to the duodenum (the first part of the small intestine).

If the operation has been carried out in a suitable case the results are usually good, but there may be unwanted after effects such as loss of weight, anemia, recurrent ulcers, or the *dumping syndrome*. In the last-named, the patient either becomes faint and pale about five minutes after a meal and suffers from abdominal rumbling and distention with vomiting and diarrhea, or finds these symptoms coming on about half an hour after his meal. In the first case, symptoms are due to the rapid passage of food into the small intestine; in the latter case, which is far less common, the quick passage of food produces a sharp rise of blood sugar followed by an outpouring of insulin which leads to an abnormally low blood sugar (hypoglycemia). Relief may be obtained by taking small meals, lying down after meals and learning to take appropriate doses of glucose at the right time.

gastric ulcer

Ulceration of the lining of the stomach. Gastric ulcer most commonly occurs in the 60 to 70 age group, slightly more often in men than women. Gastric ulcers are slightly less common today than they were several years ago, but no one knows why. Whereas the "ulcer" was once the businessman's likely complaint through overwork, it has now been largely replaced by the "coronary."

Indigestion is present episodically with acute attacks lasting from two weeks to two months, with free intervals from two to twelve months. Pain usually occurs within two hours of eating. Weight loss is not uncommon and vomiting is a frequent feature.

X-ray examination following a BARIUM MEAL may assist the diagnosis. The ulcer may actually be seen directly on the stomach lining, however, through a *fiberoptic endoscope* (a special illuminated instrument passed into the stomach through the mouth and esophagus).

Bed rest in the hospital and refraining from smoking help gastric ulcers to heal. Milky diets and antacids do not speed healing but they may help to relieve the symptoms. There has been considerable controversy over the use of special diets. Many clinicians now feel that the patient himself is the best judge of what he should eat. But regular frequent meals which avoid highly seasoned and greasy foods may be of some benefit. Surgery (for example, GASTRECTOMY) may have to be considered in cases that do not respond to drugs.

Possible complications of gastric ulceration are hemorrhage, anemia, obstruction and perforation of the stomach wall.

gastroenteritis

Inflammation of the lining of the stomach and intestine.

It is usually due to infection and begins suddenly with a feeling of general discomfort, loss of appetite, vomiting, abdominal cramps and diarrhea. Persistent vomiting and diarrhea may result in severe dehydration and shock, requiring immediate medical attention. Acute alcoholism is also a frequent cause, as is overindulgence in highly spiced or other unsuitable foods. Other causes include food poisoning, arsenic or mercury poisoning and the excessive use of harsh laxatives or other drugs—such as aspirin or broad-spectrum antibiotics.

In adults the symptoms usually subside. All that may be necessary is bed rest with plenty of fluids to drink until diarrhea and vomiting have stopped; thereafter, a bland diet can be given. If symptoms do not disappear within 48 hours, stool examination and culture are needed to discover a possible causative organism.

Organisms called *rotaviruses* have recently been shown to account for about half the cases of gastroenteritis in children. Bacteria have been isolated from the stools in about 15% of infants with the acute form, which may be highly infective. Gastroenteritis often damages the villi (the absorptive cells of the intestine), preventing the absorption of milk sugar which then attracts water into the intestines and causes frequent and fluid stools.

The most serious danger in infants is that dehydration may lead to death, which can occur rapidly in a small baby. Signs of dehydration are failure to pass urine, sunken eyes, inelastic skin and a dry tongue.

Admission to the hospital is usually essential. Milk and solids are withheld from the diet initially; instead, clear fluids (such as 5% glucose solution) are given.

Gaucher's disease

An inherited disease seen most commonly in Ashkenazi Jews and due to an enzyme deficiency which results in the accumulation of a fatty compound in the liver, spleen and bone marrow. In a severe variant of the disease the brain is also affected, and the child dies in infancy. More commonly, however, the disease has a slow onset with the first symptoms coming on in adult life due to swelling of the spleen. Yellowish-brown discoloration of the skin is another frequent feature.

The effects on the spleen and bone marrow may lead to reduction in the number of blood cells: red cells, white cells and platelets. Nose bleeds and other hemorrhages tend to occur.

There is no specific treatment, although surgical removal of the spleen and blood transfusions may help correct the blood pattern.

genes

Geneticists use the word gene to signify a factor which controls the inheritance of a specific physical characteristic.

Genes are carried by structures in the cell nucleus called chromosomes, which are made up of deoxyribonucleic acid (DNA), and a gene may be regarded as a region of the very long spiral DNA molecule.

Each mammalian species has a characteristic number of chromosomes: in man the number is 46, arranged as 23 pairs. When cells divide the chromosomes split, so that each of the daughter cells still has 46. In the formation of the sex cells, or gametes, however, the chromosomes do not split, but go half to one cell and half to another; the ovum and the sperm thus have 23 chromosomes each, and the fertilized ovum the full 46. In this way characteristics are inherited from each parent in a very subtle and complicated way—studied by the science of genetics, initiated by the Austrian monk Gregor Mendel (1822-1884).

See also CHROMOSOMES, DNA/RNA.

genetic counseling

Advice to parents about inheritable diseases, especially concerning the likelihood of passing them on to their children. Genetic counselors also give information on alternatives to natural conception, such as artificial insemination and adoption.

They will also advise on AMNIOCENTESIS (a test on the uterine fluid to detect fetal abnormality) and ABORTION.

Counseling is commonly offered to a couple when either the man or woman is known to have a genetic disorder, or to a woman who becomes pregnant at a relatively old age (when the fetus is more at risk).

Part of the process of counseling consists of building up a family pedigree. Sometimes it is necessary to go back over the obstetric history and family history of several previous generations. Often the best results are obtained when patients acquire the family information they need, at the doctor's request, from the family "matriarch."

Medical records may also be consulted for details of earlier illnesses, and causes of death and stillbirths.

Conducted carefully, the procedure usually produces a realistic assessment of the risk of the genetic disorder recurring. This will be expressed as "odds." For example, the couple may have a one in ten risk of producing an abnormal child, which would obviously cause them to think carefully; on the other hand, a risk of one in several hundred would be worth taking, even though there is no guarantee of a normal child.

In simple dominant conditions such as Huntington's CHOREA, the risk of inheritance from one affected parent is as high as fifty-fifty. In recessive conditions such as CYSTIC FIBROSIS the risk may reach one in four if both parents are carriers.

With many common genetic diseases the mechanisms of inheritance are not simple to calculate; estimates must be made on the basis of past medical experience and observation.

genetic disorders

Any disease or malformation that may be passed from one generation to the next by inheritance.

In relatively straightforward diseases such as HEMOPHILIA, the risk of inheritance can be understood because the disease is known to be associated with a particular chromosome.

In many other diseases, however, only observation has established a tendency for families to suffer; in such cases the mechanisms of inheritance are not understood. They are certainly complicated and therefore difficult to quantify. Examples of this type include CLEFT LIP/CLEFT PALATE, SPINA BIFIDA, congenital heart defects, and CLUBFOOT.

Not all genetic disorders take the form of obvious physical malformation. Many are metabolic disorders, from the relatively common DIABETES MELLITUS to extremely rare enzyme defects.

Genetic disorder may not be the same as *congenital disorder,* which means any abnormality present from birth, whether inherited or not.

The risk of genetic disorders is assessed and the parents advised in the process of GENETIC COUNSELING.

genu valgum

The technical name for KNOCK-KNEE.

genu varum

The technical name for BOWLEG.

German measles

An acute viral disease, common in childhood, which is contagious but in most cases fairly mild. Also known as *rubella.* The importance of rubella as a public health problem is not in its effects on the sufferers but in the fact that if it is contracted by a pregnant woman during her pregnancy there may be congenital defects in the baby.

Defects can be multiple and include congenital CATARACT in both eyes, heart disease, deaf mutism, mental retardation and microcephaly (an abnormally small head).

No woman should embark on a pregnancy without natural immunity to the disease as a result of a previous infection, or vaccination. However, if infection occurs in pregnancy, an intramuscular injection of *gamma globulin* (a special protein formed in the blood, also available for therapeutic use, which is associated with the ability to resist infection) may be effective in diminishing the risk of abnormalities. The rubella virus appears to cause a major epidemic of the disease every seven years or so; formerly, in epidemic years before strong preventive measures were taken, there may have been as many as 20,000 abnormalities and fetal deaths in the United States.

In children, rubella is a mild disease with an incubation period of 14 to 21 days. Symptoms include slight fever, a moderate rash (which first appears on the face and neck and then spreads to the body and limbs), and some enlargement of the glands behind the ears. The child can infect others who have not had rubella until the fever and rash have subsided. The child should get plenty of rest and be given light meals and drinks. One attack of rubella usually provides immunity for life.

giardia

A common intestinal parasite, found especially in warm climates, which can cause acute attacks of diarrhea and abdominal pain.

The microorganism responsible, *Giardia lamblia*, is a pear-shaped protozoan parasite. The disease (known as *giardiasis*) is most prevalent in areas of poor sanitation and in institutions, but outbreaks have been reported due to contamination of water supplies. The carrier rate in different areas of America ranges from 1.5–20% depending on the community and the age group.

Infection leads to multiplication of the protozoa within the bowel. There may be no symptoms, but heavy infections produce diarrhea, abdominal cramps, bloating, anemia, fatigue and weight loss. Undigested fat may be present in the stools. Drugs such as metronidazole are highly effective in clearing up the condition.

gigantism

Overgrowth caused by excessive secretion of growth hormone before puberty (that is, before the long bones of the body have grown together naturally; their ends and shafts are originally separated by an area of cartilage).

Both the skeleton and the soft tissues hypertrophy with the result that there is an increase both in height and in overall size above the normal. The underlying cause is generally an ADENOMA of the anterior lobe of the PITUITARY GLAND, sometimes detectable in x-rays of the skull. At the beginning of the illness the patient is typically strong and alert, but later is likely to develop pituitary insufficiency with weakness and a tendency to tire easily. Later there may be the added complication of hypogonadism (underdevelopment of the genitalia) due to reduction in the amount of gonadotropin secreted.

Treatment is by surgery to remove the tumor (see ACROMEGALY) and the administration of adrenal, thyroid and gonadal hormones to combat hypopituitarism (underactivity of the pituitary gland).

See also the major article on **Endocrinology.**

Gilles de la Tourette disease

A bizarre psychiatric disorder of unknown cause, beginning in childhood and characterized by the tendency to swear obscenely, and progessively violent jerking movements of the face, shoulder and limbs. The patient grunts and makes explosive noises. The disease can be controlled with tranquilizing drugs.

gingivitis

Inflammation of the gums, causing pain and often minor bleeding when cleaning the teeth or eating hard food such as apples.

Gingivitis is the most common oral disease in adult life; children are more likely to have symptoms from caries ("cavities"). It is most often due to a combination of a soft, sugary diet and poor dental hygiene, but it may also occur as a complication of debilitating diseases and of vitamin deficiencies. Rarely a severe form of gingivitis (trench mouth) may result from infection with the organisms of VINCENT'S ANGINA.

Gingivitis is best treated by a dental surgeon, who may cut away damaged, overgrown portions of the gum (gingivectomy) in addition to giving advice on better dental hygiene and the use of a mouthwash.

glandular fever

Another name for INFECTIOUS MONONUCLEOSIS.

glaucoma

Impairment of vision due to a rise in the fluid pressure within the eye. One of the most important causes of blindness in middle age, it affects an estimated 0.5% of

GINGIVITIS

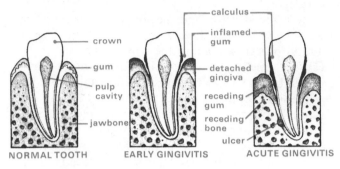

NORMAL TOOTH — crown, gum, pulp cavity, jawbone

EARLY GINGIVITIS — calculus, inflamed gum, detached gingiva, receding gum, receding bone, ulcer

ACUTE GINGIVITIS

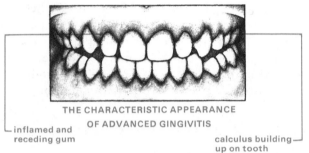

THE CHARACTERISTIC APPEARANCE OF ADVANCED GINGIVITIS

inflamed and receding gum

calculus building up on tooth

Gingivitis usually results from the buildup of calculus (tartar) near the junction of teeth and gums. It causes varying degrees of redness, swelling, and bleeding of the gums, as well as halitosis (bad breath). If left untreated, teeth may eventually become loose and fall out.

the adult population—1.5 million people in the United States.

There are several distinct types of glaucoma. The most common and most insidious is *chronic simple glaucoma,* in which the rise in pressure within the eye occurs over a period of months or years without causing any symptoms. The gradual narrowing of the field of vision (so that only objects directly in front of the eyes are visualized) may pass unnoticed unless the eyes are examined by an ophthalmologist. Without treatment chronic glaucoma eventually causes total blindness.

Acute glaucoma, in contrast, usually develops very suddenly, with severe pain in the eye, which becomes extremely hard, red and tender. Urgent treatment is needed to lower the pressure within the eye if vision is to be saved.

Glaucoma may also be *symptomatic,* in which the rise in pressure is secondary to some other disease in the eye.

Whatever the type of glaucoma, the underlying cause is a defect in the mechanism which removes fluid continuously formed in the front chamber of the eyeball. In acute glaucoma there is a physical block due to narrowing of the angle at the edge of the iris; in chronic glaucoma the blockage is thought to be in the meshwork of vessels that should absorb the fluid.

Treatment depends on the cause: *narrow angle*

glaucoma is usually relieved by a minor surgical operation, whereas *chronic glaucoma* is treated with drugs which reduce the rate of formation of fluid. Anyone with a family background of glaucoma should have the eyes examined regularly.

See also the major article on **Ophthalmology.**

glioma

A type of tumor of the brain or spinal cord.

Most gliomas are malignant (cancerous), but they seldom spread to other parts of the body. As with other brain tumors the symptoms include headache, vomiting and pressure upon the optic nerve (papilledema). There may be progressive mental or physical deterioration, such as deafness, partial blindness, or personality change. Other symptoms suggestive of tumor are giddiness and convulsions.

The diagnosis can be confirmed by skull x-rays, electroencephalography (see EEG) or brain scanning.

The intracranial pressure may be relieved by cutting into the skull (craniotomy). A glioma cannot usually be removed completely; the usual treatment is partial removal followed by radiotherapy.

globulin

The second major type of protein in the blood plasma. (The first is ALBUMIN.) Globulins are of several kinds. The types can be separated by modern methods of physicochemical analysis.

Alpha and *beta globulins* combine loosely with other important body chemicals to carry them around in the blood. *Alpha—1* globulin contains a fraction that binds bilirubin, and another responsible for the carriages of steroids and lipids. *Alpha—2* globulin combines with free hemoglobin in the plasma.

Beta globulins include some responsible for transporting lipids, and others that bind copper and iron for transport. Prothrombin, one of the blood-clotting factors, is a beta globulin.

The *gamma globulins* are extremely important in the body's IMMUNE SYSTEM; they are alternatively known as *immunoglobulins* and are subdivided into classes (IgA, IgE, IgM, etc.) according to their function.

The overall pattern of alpha, beta and gamma globulins may be measured to assess the progress of many different types of disease and treatment, since they are quite commonly affected. The specific immunoglobulins are also a useful diagnostic indicator.

glomerulonephritis

Inflammation of the glomeruli—the tiny clumps of blood vessels which act as filters to form the urine within the substance of the kidney. The condition may be acute or chronic and is an important cause of kidney failure: glomerular disease accounts for approximately two thirds of all patients dying of kidney disease.

Acute glomerulonephritis is most often a complication of infection of the throat or elsewhere in the body with one form of bacterium, a streptococcus. The immune defenses against the infection produce antibodies which also damage the glomeruli. This reaction usually occurs two to three weeks after the bacterial infection. The damage to the kidneys reduces the output of urine, which may become dark from the presence of blood. Typically, the ankles swell and the face becomes pale and puffy. Most often (in approximately 90% of cases in children) the symptoms of acute glomerulonephritis resolve within a few weeks. But in a minority of patients, the kidney failure may become total; without specific treatment by DIALYSIS or a kidney transplant the outcome is fatal. In another small proportion of cases, although the recovery appears complete, the inflammation within the kidneys grumbles on and the condition then becomes chronic. Over a period of years the kidneys become scarred and contracted, and again

GLOMERULONEPHRITIS

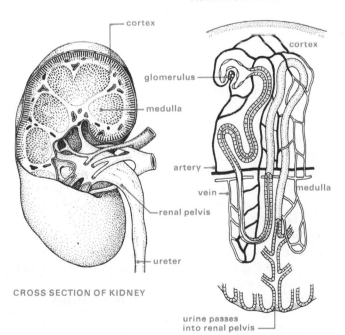

FILTRATION UNIT IN KIDNEY

cortex

glomerulus

medulla

cortex

artery

vein

medulla

renal pelvis

ureter

CROSS SECTION OF KIDNEY

urine passes
into renal pelvis

Glomerulonephritis is a complex disease resulting from the production of antibodies which damage the glomeruli in the kidney. Blood plasma passes through the glomeruli in the first stage of urine formation. In glomerulonephritis, proteins and red blood cells leak through as well so that the urine is said to resemble cola.

the end result may be kidney failure.

The glomeruli may also be damaged by chronic diseases such as diabetes mellitus, by high blood pressure, and by connective tissue disorders such as systemic lupus erythematosus. Whatever the underlying cause, loss of a substantial proportion of the two million glomeruli (one million in each kidney) leads to kidney failure.

See also KIDNEY DISEASES and the major article on **Nephrology.**

glossitis

Inflammation of the tongue.

Glossitis may be caused by an infection such as SCARLET FEVER, in which the red taste buds (papillae) protrude through a white coat or fur. Later the "fur" disappears, leaving the swollen papillae projecting from a bright red "strawberry tongue."

A smooth, bald tongue type of glossitis occurs in deficiency of some vitamins—for example, PELLAGRA (deficiency of niacin) and pernicious anemia (deficiency of vitamin B_{12}—see ANEMIA). A similar appearance is seen in CELIAC DISEASE and in the severe anemia of STARVATION.

Syphilis causes a chronic superficial glossitis. There are areas of opaque, white, thickened skin and in between a scarred surface without papillae.

Patchy tongue furring with smooth, well-defined red patches is known to doctors as "geographical tongue" because of its maplike appearance, and is not of any medical importance.

glycogen storage disease

The general name for a group of rare inherited diseases (about a dozen varieties are now known) in which the body is unable to store carbohydrate in the normal way.

Glucose, the body's principal carbohydrate, can only be stored in the liver and the muscle cells in the form of glycogen. A series of biochemical reactions is needed to control the formation and release of glycogen. Enzyme defects at various stages of this process account for the various subtypes of glycogen storage disease.

The symptoms of the disease vary widely, but the muscles are often weak—especially after exercise. Symptoms may begin immediately after birth or be delayed until the teens. Newborn infants may suffer convulsions because of a low blood sugar; in other cases the first sign may be an enlarged liver in a symptomless child several months old.

No treatment is possible for most varieties of the disease; when symptoms occur in infancy they may be reduced in severity by adjustment of the diet with frequent small feeds.

glycosuria

The presence of sugar (glucose) in the urine.

Glycosuria is the major sign of DIABETES MELLITUS, although not everyone with glycosuria necessarily has diabetes.

Doctors can detect glucose in a specimen of urine by means of a simple "dip" test. Similar tests are used by diabetics to detect and measure glucose in their own urine, thus permitting them to determine if their disease is under control.

Normal urine contains no glucose. It appears when the amount in the blood exceeds the "renal threshold"— that is, the quantity above which the kidneys cannot prevent it escaping in the urine. The threshold may be low, in which case glycosuria occurs in a nondiabetic. In diabetes the threshold is exceeded because of the high level of glucose in the blood.

Once glycosuria is detected, a test called a *glucose tolerance test* is used to determine whether the patient is diabetic or merely has a low renal threshold requiring no treatment. In a glucose tolerance test the patient drinks a standard amount of the sugar and the quantity remaining in the blood is measured hourly for a few hours.

goiter

A swelling of the thyroid gland on the neck.

It may be caused by too little iodine in the diet, or by an excess of certain foods (such as soya or cabbage) which prevent the gland from making the thyroid hormones, or it can arise without any known cause.

Iodine-deficiency goiter occurs in areas where the soil and water are virtually free of iodine. It is then called *endemic goiter*. In the United States at least 10% of the population once had obvious goiter in the areas around the Great Lakes, in Ohio, Minnesota and the Pacific Northwest. The introduction of iodized salt has caused this disease to die out. It is still seen, however, in the Austrian Tyrol and in many mountainous districts, including the Andes and the Himalayas.

The only sign of endemic goiter is a gradual enlargement of the neck. Where iodine deficiency is slight the disease is usually confined to young women. Men and preadolescent children are only affected when the deficiency is severe. In such areas CRETINISM is common.

Once formed, goiters do not respond to iodine treatment—indeed, iodine may make the condition worse by encouraging thyroid overactivity. Endemic goiter does not appear to lead to cancer of the gland.

Simple nonendemic goiter usually occurs in adolescent girls as a smooth swelling in the neck, which may disappear in a few years. but it may proceed slowly to

GOITER

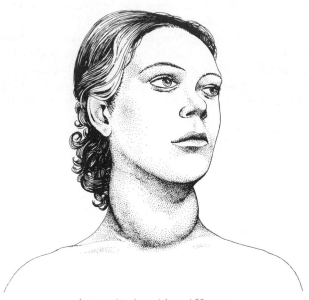

large goiter in a girl aged 20 years

A goiter is a swelling in the neck due to an enlarged thyroid gland. Surgical removal of goiters is only performed when drug treatment has failed, unless there is an acute emergency such as a respiratory obstruction due to a large goiter (above) or if it seems a cancer might develop.

become "nodular" (with small lumps) in middle age and finally "toxic" in old age, when signs of increased thyroid activity arise. Thyroid overactivity in the elderly with goiter often results in heart failure. In less than 2% of patients nonendemic goiter may become cancerous.

The treatment of early cases is by thyroid hormone preparations. Most cases of nonendemic simple goiter need no treatment, but follow-up is necessary. The thyroid enlargement may cause pressure on the windpipe or other structures in the neck, causing difficulty in breathing, swallowing or talking. Growth of a nodule may indicate a malignant (cancerous) change. Surgical removal is usually successful, although recurrent goiter is common after surgery. Surgeons give thyroid preparations postoperatively to prevent it.

See also the major article on **Endocrinology.**

gonadotropins

Any hormone capable of stimulating the gonads (sex glands); especially, certain female sex hormones.

The female reproductive system depends on these hormones, which are secreted from the pituitary gland at the base of the brain. Immediately after menstruation the first of the gonadotropins—*follicle-stimulating hormone* (FSH)—passes into the bloodstream. The ovary responds by ripening a small area on its surface, called a Graafian follicle, which contains an ovum.

The second gonadotropin—*luteinizing hormone* (LH)—starts flowing some days after FSH. The follicle then begins to produce the hormone *estrogen*.

After two weeks a sudden surge of LH induces the follicle to rupture, expelling the ovum from the ovary into the Fallopian tube. The follicle, now termed the "corpus luteum," produces the hormone *progesterone* which encourages correct implantation of the ovum into the uterine wall after fertilization.

The production of progesterone from the corpus luteum depends on continuous pituitary secretion of LH. If conception does not occur, the pituitary secretion of gonadotropins falls and the ovarian production of both estrogen and progesterone drops correspondingly. This results in the menstrual shedding of the uterine lining, which has responded to the hormones by thickening.

If fertilized, the ovum produces a third gonadotropin—called *chorionic gonadotropin*—which maintains the corpus luteum for the first three months of pregnancy and ensures the safe continuance of the pregnancy. It is this hormone which is detected in the urine in pregnancy tests.

In men, FSH promotes the growth of the sperm-forming tubes within the testicles and of the sperms themselves; LH ensures that the testicles produce androgens, the male sex hormones.

See also MENSTRUATION.

gonorrhea

A common venereal disease.

Gonorrhea is an infection of the genital organs and urinary outlet by the bacterium *Neisseria gonorrhoeae*. It can spread to other organs if the infection is left untreated—for example the joints, tendons, muscles, heart and brain—but this is relatively rare since the advent of antibiotics.

No one really knows the incidence of gonorrhea since the disease tends to be under-reported. Many patients treat themselves and many infected women have no symptoms. But one study showed that 6% of pregnant women in the United States were carriers of the disease. About 1.5 million new cases are believed to arise in America every year.

Who gets the disease? Most patients are between 15 and 25 years of age. Among men, gonorrhea tends to be seen in the armed forces, in men whose occupation requires a great deal of travel (such as migrant workers and seamen), and in homosexuals. In women, similar lifestyles may predispose to the disease; prostitutes are also commonly infected—it is estimated that between 10 and 35% are carriers of the disease.

Although sexual intercourse is by far the most common means of transmission, gonorrhea does spread in other ways. Babies can be infected at birth if the mother is infected. In such cases the disease causes a severe conjunctivitis which can lead to blindness. Until recently this was a principal cause of blindness, but it was largely eradicated when doctors began the routine procedure of instilling protective ointments into the eyes of the newborn.

In very rare cases infants and young children may contract the disease from their parents by close contact. In some institutions, outbreaks have occasionally been blamed on infected towels.

The incubation period of gonorrhea is between two and ten days. The illness starts suddenly in men, with a repeated urgent desire to pass urine and severe pain during urination. Considerable quantities of pus are discharged from the penis. At this stage infection is so obvious that the patient cannot fail to recognize the need for treatment. If the disease is not treated it can spread to the prostate gland and testicles, giving rise to fever and perhaps involuntary retention of urine. Eventually it will subside, even without treatment, but may leave strictures of the urinary outlet and cause sterility.

In women the disease is milder and may produce no symptoms at all—which is dangerous, since the woman may not realize she is infected. In other cases there may be urgency and pain on urination, discharge of pus and the formation of abscesses. Even when these resolve, the infecting bacteria remain to infect the woman's sexual partners unless she is properly treated with antibiotics.

Penicillin is the mainstay of treatment for patients with gonorrhea, although higher doses and longer courses have become necessary over the years as the gonococcus has developed resistance. Some strains now fail to respond to penicillin at all, in any dosage, and must be treated by other less effective antibiotics. In every case all sexual partners should be contacted and treated.

A condom provides some barrier to the spread of gonococcal infection, but is not completely protective.

gout

Almost everyone knows of gout as a cause of attacks of extremely painful arthritis (inflammation of a joint), but in fact the disease is essentially a chemical defect which causes the accumulation in the bloodstream of a waste product of metabolism known as *uric acid*. It is the deposition of crystals of uric acid (urate or sodium urate) in the skin, joints and kidneys which is responsible for the symptoms.

The disease has four major aspects: (1) gouty arthritis; (2) the formation of tophi (lumps of urate under the

GOUT

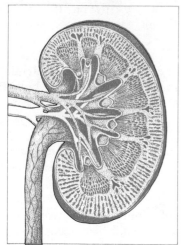

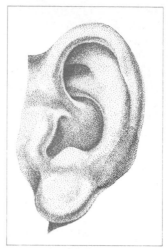

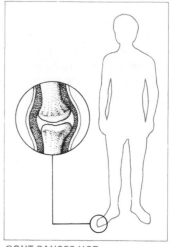

CRYSTALS CAN
DAMAGE KIDNEYS

URIC ACID CRYSTALS

CRYSTALS DEPOSITED
IN EARS AS "TOPHI"

GOUT CAUSES HOT,
SWOLLEN, PAINFUL JOINTS

Gout is an extremely painful condition which predominantly affects men. It is caused by an excess of uric acid which forms needle-sharp crystals in the joints, ears and kidneys. Gout is in part a hereditary disease, but is also exacerbated by high-protein food.

skin, especially in the fleshy rim of the ear); (3) the formation of kidney stones composed of crystals of uric acid; and (4) kidney failure (caused by blockage of the kidneys with stones).

Symptoms usually appear in men in middle age. The disease is much less common in women and rarely appears before the menopause. In the United States, gout affects about three people in every thousand and accounts for five in every 100 cases of arthritis. Gout is usually first manifest with a sudden and extremely painful attack affecting a single joint—mostly often the first joint of the big toe. The initial attack commonly occurs during sleep and may occur without warning or be precipitated by some stress such as the excessive consumption of alcohol a few hours earlier, or by unaccustomed exercise or an injury sustained earlier the same day.

An attack of gout can cause such severe pain that many sufferers are unable even to bear the weight of light sheets over the affected joint. The tissues around the joint are also inflamed in most cases—producing heat, swelling, redness and excruciating pain and tenderness. After the first attack, more can be expected—usually before a year has passed—in the absence of treatment.

Tophi, the second main feature of gout, develop in chronic untreated cases. They consist of creamy white lumps of insoluble sodium urate under the skin, seen (in addition to the rims of the outer ears) in the hands, feet and elbows. Tophi can become massive and disabling, sometimes ulcerating and discharging.

About 15-20% of patients with chronic gout have kidney stones, the symptoms of which are occasionally the first evidence of the disease. Urate crystals in the kidneys may lead to death as the result of kidney failure in untreated cases.

The treatment of gout used to be based on relief of symptoms by administration of the traditional herbal drug *colchicine*. Now that the underlying chemical cause of gout is clear, however, the treatment has changed. Although colchicine may still be used in acute attacks, the symptoms of an acute attack are now usually relieved by the administration of anti-inflammatory drugs such as phenylbutazone or indomethacin. (Both of these drugs can exert potentially serious side effects, especially if administered over prolonged periods; thus, their use must be under close medical supervision.) More important, once the acute attack has been controlled, is the prevention of future attacks. The drug allopurinol (Zyloprim) can prevent the formation of excess amounts of uric acid and thus prevent acute attacks. Other classes of drugs, known as *uricosurics*, can act to control the symptoms of gout by hastening the excretion of uric acid by the kidneys (however, they must not be used in the presence of known kidney damage). Allopurinol, which interferes with the production of uric acid, must usually be taken for years to control the blood levels of uric acid—the excessive production of which is known as *hyperuricemia*.

granuloma

A slowly growing inflammatory swelling, usually due to infection but sometimes arising from noninfectious foreign bodies.

Granulomas can cause various problems depending on their site and cause. They can vary from lumps in the skin following immunization (such as the triple vaccines given to infants) to masses within the brain.

Granulomas differ from abscesses in that they are solid—filled with inflammatory cells and tissue, but without pus. Diseases in which granulomas are common include tuberculosis, syphilis, fungal infections, sarcoidosis and parasitic disorders. They may be solitary or widespread.

Symptoms occur if the granuloma is in a vital area, such as the brain, or can be seen in the skin. Treatment of infective granuloma is directed toward eliminating the infecting organism, often by antibiotics. Surgery is sometimes necessary.

Lethal middle granuloma is a rare but terrible disease in which the tissues of the middle of the face are slowly eaten away by inflammation. The nose, eyelids, skin and finally the bones are destroyed and the patient (usually a man in early or middle adult life) succumbs eventually from infection. Radiation or anticancer drugs may help.

Wegener's granuloma, also rare, is another slowly progressive disease. It first affects the nose and sinuses, later spreading to the lungs and kidneys. Drugs to suppress immunity may be of help.

granuloma inguinale

A chronic bacterial disease, widespread in tropical and subtropical areas, in which an ulcerating infection spreads slowly over the skin of the genital organs and groin. The highest incidence is between the ages of 20 and 40.

It is thought to be transmitted during sexual intercourse or other close contact and is caused by microorganisms commonly known as *Donovan bodies* (technical name: *Calymmatobacterium granulomatis*). In rare cases the disease has been known to spread from the genitals to joints or bones in other parts of the body, due to invasion of the lymphatics and blood circulation.

Granuloma inguinale is usually not painful, but it is very destructive as it spreads over the genitals and the surrounding skin. Secondary infection with other bacteria is almost inevitable. Doctors can distinguish the disease from syphilis by microscopic identification of the Donovan bodies.

Two weeks of antibiotic treatment usually cures granuloma inguinale, although severe cases may take longer to heal. The disease can probably be prevented by washing the genital organs thoroughly after sexual intercourse.

Graves' disease

Another name for HYPERTHYROIDISM.

green monkey disease

Another name for MARBURG VIRUS DISEASE (also known as *green monkey fever*).

growth hormone

A hormone liberated by the anterior part of the pituitary gland, essential for the regulation of growth. Also called SOMATOTROPIN.

Guillain-Barré syndrome

An inflammation of the nerves and (less commonly) the spinal cord, of unknown cause. It usually follows 10 to 21 days after an infection of the upper respiratory tract (such as the common cold) or a gastrointestinal infection.

Guillain-Barré syndrome starts slowly with weakness of both legs. Later the weakness becomes a paralysis affecting muscles of the trunk, arms and occasionally the face. The condition was formerly thought to be caused by a viral infection of the nerves, but specific evidence is lacking.

Eventually the paralysis and accompanying loss of sensation reaches a plateau which may last for several weeks. Then a gradual return to normal health occurs, though this also may take weeks or even months.

About 10% of patients are left with some weakness.

Intensive care is given in the early stages of the condition because there is a risk of paralysis of the muscles that control breathing.

There was considerable interest in an outbreak of Guillain-Barré syndrome which appeared to follow the mass influenza vaccination program in the United States in the winter of 1976/77. About one in every 125,000 Americans vaccinated developed the syndrome—an incidence ten times the normal.

Other countries—for example, Britain and Holland—found no increase in Guillain-Barré cases after their vaccination campaigns in the same winter. The link between influenza, influenza vaccination and Guillain-Barré syndrome is therefore not established.

Guthrie test

A test for the disease PHENYLKETONURIA in newborn babies.

A few drops of blood taken from the baby's heel can ensure that the disorder of phenylketonuria is recognized early enough to prevent brain damage.

About one American child in 10,000 has phenylketonuria, an inherited disease in which an amino acid called phenylalanine accumulates in the blood. Untreated, it causes irreversible mental retardation by the fourth month of life. Early treatment with a special diet may allow the child to develop normally.

The test is performed when the baby is three to six days old. If the results are positive, other blood tests are performed to confirm the diagnosis. If the initial results are negative they should be confirmed by a follow-up urine test three to six weeks later.

gynecomastia

Excessive enlargement of the breasts in a boy or man.

Some enlargement of the breasts is a normal, transient occurence in newborn boys, whose breasts are engorged and swollen in response to their mothers' hormone levels. It may also be seen temporarily during adolescence, when it is of no significance except as a minor embarrassment. Fat boys may appear to have enlarged breasts—but this is not *true* gynecomastia, which is related to hormonal imbalance.

Boys with persisting gynecomastia may have the rare chromosomal abnormality known as KLINEFELTER'S SYNDROME—characterized by small testicles, disproportionately long limbs and a feminine body shape. Similar enlargement of the male breast occurs in some generalized skin disorders, malnutrition, overactivity of the pituitary or thyroid glands, lung and testicular tumors and failure of the liver or kidneys.

Gynecomastia also occurs occasionally as a side effect of certain drugs, including the heart drug digitalis, or estrogens given to control acne or breast cancer.

GYNECOMASTIA

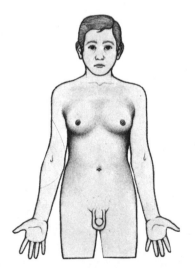

Gynecomastia results from an excess of the hormone estrogen. It is common in newborn boys, and the high estrogen levels in breast milk can prolong it for months. Gynecomastia is also normal around puberty, but at other ages it can be due to one of a number of diseases or drugs.

hair (diseases of)

The basic facts are that the growth of hair is cyclical, and that all the hair follicles are present at birth.

There are three types of hair: (1) *lanugo,* the hair which covers the fetus and is shed at about eight months; (2) *vellus,* fine hair up to 3 cm long which covers the body surface before puberty, except for the scalp, eyelashes and eyebrows; and (3) *terminal* hair, which appears on the scalp during childhood and in the pubic region at puberty; later it grows in the armpits and over the thighs, legs, forearms, chest, arms, shoulders and buttocks.

Loss of hair from the scalp (*alopecia*—see BALDNESS) may occur after general illness dampens down the activity of the hair follicles, in various specific illnesses such as hypothyroidism, in protein deficiency and in anemia. But the most common cause of patchy loss of hair is *alopecia areata,* where localized bald patches spread on the scalp for about three to six months, being followed by spontaneous recovery. The condition may recur, and the advice of a dermatologist is helpful.

Baldness in men is very common, and is due to a combination of factors—heredity, stimulation by the male hormone, and aging. The hair recedes, possibly starting soon after puberty, and the gradual loss proceeds until nearly all the scalp may be bald. No effective treatment is known except early castration (hardly an acceptable cure!), but there are many "cures" on the market. However, the only thing these products are definitely known to help is the manufacturers' needs to make money at the expense of a gullible public!

See also the major article on **Dermatology.**

halitosis

Bad-smelling breath arising either from the mouth or from the lungs.

Many people have a faint sweetish halitosis in the morning, accompanied by a bad taste in the mouth; both can be relieved by proper brushing of the teeth.

Halitosis can arise from poor oral hygiene (e.g., failure to brush away particles of food lodged between the teeth), decayed teeth, or pockets of diseased and overgrown gums. The breath is often foul after dental surgery, particularly when there is bleeding. Less often halitosis can be associated with an oral infection such as trench mouth.

Causes of halitosis outside the mouth include chronic infections of the sinuses or lungs (see BRONCHIECTASIS) or a lung abscess. More commonly halitosis results from foods such as garlic, whose chemical odors are excreted in the breath. Poor diabetic control leads to a characteristically sweet smell of acetone on the breath; kidney failure may cause a smell of ammonia. On corrective treatment the smell usually disappears.

hallucination

The perception of false sensations in the absence of any physical cause.

Hallucinations can affect any or all of the senses: they may be seen, heard, tasted, smelled or felt. They vary greatly, from simple flashes of light to sensations of highly specific and identifiable objects or sounds. Normal people under severe stress may share a hallucination, as when victims of a shipwreck together see a nonexistent shore.

Hallucinations may be a sign of a mental disorder, such as schizophrenia or severe depression, or may occur as a result of physical illness. Epileptics often experience hallucinations just before a seizure. In states of clouded consciousness—caused, for example, by high fever, chronic alcoholism, a head injury, liver failure, or senile brain degeneration—repeated and often terrifying hallucinations are common. Tumors of the brain can also cause hallucinations of taste, vision, or hearing, depending on the site of the brain tumor.

Some drugs, especially narcotics, can be powerful hallucinogens. The cocaine user may feel insects crawling under the skin. Drugs such as mescaline and LSD are classed as hallucinogenic because of the vivid and unpredictable nature of the visual hallucinations that they induce.

Hallucinations can best be suppressed by treating the underlying disease. The hallucinations seen in delirium associated with typhoid fever, for example, disappear as the body temperature returns to normal; the alcoholic with delirium tremens stops seeing terrifying animals following sedative treatment.

Hashimoto's disease

A chronic form of THYROIDITIS. Also known as *struma lymphomatosa* and *Hashimoto's struma*.

hay fever

An allergic disease of the membranes of the nose, throat and eyes, (also known as pollinosis). It is caused by increased sensitivity to airborne pollens and is therefore usually seasonal—occurring only when the air contains pollen of a specific type, not necessarily from hay.

Hay fever is an allergy similar to infantile eczema, asthma and some food allergies, all of which may be inherited.

Pollens that produce hay fever are usually light and scattered by the wind from grasses, weeds or trees. The pollen of plants pollinated by insects (which is heavy and sticky) rarely causes the disease.

In the United States and southern Canada hay fever is caused by tree pollens in April and May; by pollens of grasses, sorrels and plantain; and by weed pollens in August and September. The most southerly States are subjected to grass pollens throughout much of the year—thus, the hay fever season is correspondingly lengthened. Ragweed hay fever dominates States of the Midwest and those on the Eastern seaboard. Russian thistle, sage and amaranth are common causes of the allergy in mountain areas.

Hay fever affects about 10% of Americans, but many sufferers are only mildly affected and need no special treatment. The nose, eyes and throat itch and are congested and reddened, and the eyes water. Even the ears may itch. Most distressing are the bouts of uncontrollable sneezing. Coughing, breathlessness and wheezing often indicate that allergic ASTHMA is manifest.

The diagnosis is usually obvious: the seasonal timing, the worsening of symptoms on dry windy days and their relief during rain, and their onset in many fellow sufferers at the same time leave little doubt. The diagnosis can be confirmed by applying extremely weak extracts of pollens to the skin under strictly controlled conditions.

Patients with hay fever should avoid the provoking pollen. Certain drugs can prevent the reaction, or "desensitizing" injections of pollen extracts may be given three to four months before the season starts.

Hay fever, once contracted, is typically a lifelong problem but not a life-threatening one. Asthma may occur in up to one in three patients.

See also the major article on **Allergy and Immunology.**

headache

Most headaches arise in tissues outside the skull. Probably the most common type is the "tension" or "nervous" headache caused by contractions of the muscles of the scalp and the back of the neck. Pain spreads from the back of the head to the top of the eyes and is associated with feelings of pressure and tension. It is relieved when the muscle contractions cease.

MIGRAINE arises from dilation and constriction of blood vessels in the scalp, temple and face. Migrainous headaches are usually one-sided, sudden, very intense and associated with visual disturbances. Sufferers often know beforehand when an attack is imminent.

But not all migraines follow this pattern. Sometimes the headache is accompanied by temporary paralysis of one arm and leg, or of the eyes. *Cluster headache,* another migraine variant, combines one-sided headache with sweating, flushing, watering of the eyes and a runny nose. It lasts only a short time, but is nevertheless very unpleasant. Some "tension" and migraine headaches may occur together.

Congestion and inflammation of the nasal sinuses may give rise to headache in the forehead and face, usually with tightness and irritation in the nose. People often blame eye strain as a cause of headache, but it seldom is. Increase in pressure within the eye may cause headache—as in sudden-onset GLAUCOMA—and so may infection and inflammation of the eye. Poor light or prolonged reading are seldom responsible, in themselves, for headaches.

Headache may arise from disease of the teeth, ears, or nerves, and from the bones, muscles and joints of the neck and jaw.

Chronic severe headache may follow head injury— either because of tenderness at the point of injury or because of the contraction of muscles around it. Vascular (migraine-type) headaches are common after injury. Less common are "delusional" headaches, complained of when there is no damage. (They may miraculously disappear when financial compensation for the accident is paid!)

Trigeminal neuralgia is a stabbing, exceptionally severe pain in one side of the face, along the distribution of the fifth cranial nerve. It occurs sporadically, perhaps many times over a few hours, then disappears for a few months. Specific drugs are available to relieve trigeminal neuralgia; surgical interruption of the nerve is a last resort.

One form of headache in the elderly is particularly important, since failure to recognize and treat it early may lead to total and permanent blindness. In this condition, *cranial arteritis,* there is a structural change as well as inflammation in the major arteries of the temples. The patient has sudden severe pain in the temple and the scalp is particularly tender to the slightest touch. The tongue may be pale and tender. The artery itself is usually thickened and tortuous, but may be pulseless and difficult to locate. If the disease is allowed to continue, the artery to the retina may become blocked and blindness will inevitably follow. The condition can usually be arrested and blindness prevented by high doses of steroid drugs.

One condition popularly associated with headache is high blood pressure. Surprisingly, only one in ten patients with high blood pressure complains of headache (usually of the tension or migrainous type).

Headaches arising from within the skull are uncommon, but are often more important than those arising outside it. Headache in fevers and infectious diseases is caused by distension of the arteries in the brain. Tumors of the brain may press upon pain-sensitive nerve fibers.

Treatment of headache, if possible, should be directed at the cause. Where quick relief is required, most cases of simple headache respond quickly to aspirin or other analgesics.

head injury

Head injury is the most common cause of unconsciousness in patients seen in hospital emergency departments. The usual causes are violence and automobile accidents—often when under the influence of alcohol— and the outlook may be serious.

Anyone who witnesses a head injury should act quickly to obtain medical help, especially if the patient is unconscious. It may not be clear whether or not the patient is unconscious; if in doubt, assume that he is.

CONCUSSION is the state of mild confusion after a head injury, and can occur without loss of consciousness. A concussed person may answer questions quite reasonably or even volunteer information, but in other cases may be slow in his responses. The severely concussed patient repeats himself. On recovery, he usually cannot remember the incident or the events before and after it. Following a severe head injury consciousness may be dulled, but the patient can often answer questions in monosyllables and appreciate sound, touch and pain.

An annoying or aggressive "drunk" with a head injury may be merely drunk, or he may be suffering the effects of a concussion. Only overnight observation can distinguish between the two; thus the need for prompt medical attention.

The more deeply unconscious patient may still respond to painful stimuli—by attempting to push away the attendant's hand—and may blink when his eyelid is touched.

When even these responses are absent the outlook is grave, though not hopeless. Deep unconsciousness may be produced by hemorrhage within the brain, requiring surgical treatment.

A person found unconscious should be laid on his side and his tongue should be pulled forward: these maneuvers are to prevent the inhalation of vomit, which can be fatal. False teeth should be removed.

As well as performing these first aid measures and calling for medical help, the bystander who witnesses a head injury can be of considerable help if he has an accurate picture of the incident. The duration of loss of consciousness, the amount of blood lost, and the time of the incident can all be crucially important.

Since some head injuries follow fits or faints due to brain disease, particularly in the elderly, a description of the fall may be very important to the exact diagnosis.

See also *Head injuries* in the **First Aid** section.

HEARING

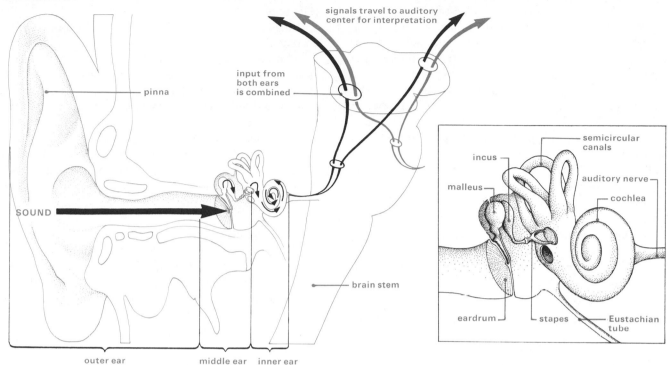

signals travel to auditory center for interpretation

input from both ears is combined

pinna

SOUND

brain stem

outer ear   middle ear   inner ear

semicircular canals

incus

malleus

auditory nerve

cochlea

eardrum   stapes   Eustachian tube

Hearing, the perception of sounds, involves mechanical and nervous mechanisms. Sound waves cause vibrations in the tense eardrum, which are transmitted and magnified by the chain of bones in the middle ear. The spiral cochlea contains delicate hair cells arranged along a membrane and they are stimulated by movements of the stapes to send signals up the auditory nerve to the brain.

hearing

Sound waves in the air are converted by the ear into impulses which travel in the auditory nerve to the brain, where they are perceived as sound. The outer ear canal *(external auditory meatus)* conducts the sound waves to the eardrum, on the inner side of which three small bones *(ossicles)* amplify the vibrations and conduct them to the organ of hearing *(cochlea)* in the inner ear. Nerve endings in the cochlea transmit the vibrations as impulses through the auditory nerve to the brain.

Hearing may be impaired by obstructions in the external ear canal such as wax, by disturbances in the middle ear (when the defect is called conductive deafness), or by disease of the inner ear (perceptive or sensorineural deafness).

Hearing is examined by a number of tests which vary from the simple one of whispering in the patient's ear while the other ear is covered up, through the use of the tuning fork, to the use of the audiometer (an instrument which produces sounds of selected frequency and pitch).

By the use of an audiometer the threshold of hearing can be measured at each desired frequency by reducing the intensity until it is inaudible. A recently introduced audiometric device can be used to measure brain waves to determine hearing deficit. This instrument, used while the patient is asleep, is particularly useful for very young children or mentally retarded patients.

Conduction through the air and through the bones of the skull can be measured. The degree of deafness is measured for both means of conduction in *decibels;* it represents the increased intensity of sound required for hearing in the deaf ear compared to a normal ear. Speech audiometry is very useful, as it measures the intensity of sound necessary for the understanding of recorded speech. It can be used to help in the diagnosis between conductive and perceptive deafness.

The range of sound technically capable of being heard by the normal ear is from about 16 to 20,000 Hertz (cycles per second). The discrimination of speech sounds primarily involves frequencies between about 500 and 5,000 Hertz; the loss of the ability to hear higher frequencies presents no communication problems.

See also DEAFNESS and the major article on **Otolaryngology.**

heartburn

A burning sensation felt behind the breastbone, sometimes radiating into the neck or the back. Technical name: *pyrosis.*

It is a common complaint, produced by the presence of gastric secretions in the lower part of the esophagus. It is usually made worse by bending down or lying down.

Normally the contents of the stomach do not regurgitate into the esophagus, both because of the shape of the upper part of the stomach and because the muscles of the diaphragm act as a sphincter. But in some cases, particularly where the patient is obese or pregnant, the upper part of the stomach may herniate upward through the opening of the diaphragm and form a hiatus HERNIA. In such cases heartburn is liable to follow a heavy meal, especially if the patient goes to bed; it may be relieved by sitting up.

The use of antacids (and the avoidance of heavy meals) is usually enough to relieve the symptoms, but in some cases surgical treatment may prove necessary. Hiatus hernia is present in about 50% of people over the age of 60, but in many it is "silent" (produces no discomfort).

heart disease

Heart disease affects persons of all ages: the baby born with congenital structural abnormalities of the heart, the teenager and young adult with rheumatic heart disease, the older patient with ischemic heart disease due to coronary artery blockage or high blood pressure. Ischemic heart disease (coronary artery disease) is now the most common cause of death in adult Americans.

Disorders of the heart affect its ability to pump blood around the body. Infants with mild congenital heart disease may show this by failing to grow as quickly as other children, or by becoming easily breathless or tired on exertion. More severe congenital heart disorders in which arterial and venous blood are mixed in "shunts" between the chambers of the heart, produce a blue coloration (CYANOSIS), of the lips and extremities. Infants with congenital heart disease may even be born with heart failure; they are pale, fretful infants unable to feed and constantly breathless. Their care is a surgical specialty in itself.

Congenital heart disease is not necessarily inherited. Maternal German measles infection during pregnancy may cause multiple heart abnormalities, and most children born with abnormal hearts have a normal genetic makeup. Their mothers can be reassured that future babies will be healthy.

Rheumatic heart disease in the older teenager and adult stems from throat infections with bacterium *Group A hemolytic streptococcus;* the body's reaction to this leads to rheumatic fever. Half the patients with rheumatic fever develop an acute heart illness which on subsiding leaves a slowly progressing disorder of the heart valves and the muscular walls of the heart. Heart failure from narrowing or incompetence of the valves may follow between 5 and 20 years after the attack of rheumatic fever.

Penicillin by mouth soon destroys the streptococcus, so that early and effective treatment of streptococcal sore throats prevents both rheumatic fever and the subsequent heart disease. Antibiotics have no effect on rheumatic fever itself. Its incidence has fallen steeply since the 1940s, so that rheumatic heart disease is becoming rare.

Even those with established rheumatic heart disease can take comfort from the great strides in heart surgery since the 1950s. Narrowed valves can often be reopened or replaced with artificial valves at minimal risk to the patient, and sophisticated drug therapy helps control possible complications.

The symptoms of ischemic heart disease arise from failure of the coronary arteries (which supply blood to the heart muscle itself) to deliver oxygen to the heart muscle. The result is ANGINA PECTORIS—a deep aching, crushing or vicelike pain in the chest, radiating perhaps to the arm, or the neck and jaw. It is fairly common in men in their 40s and older whose arteries have been seriously narrowed by ATHEROSCLEROSIS. The condition may progress to complete blockage of the arteries, and so to a myocardial infarction ("heart attack") with death or *infarction* of the muscle area supplied by the blocked vessel.

Factors leading to the present high death rate from ischemic heart disease have been investigated all over the world. The highest incidence is in Eastern Finland, where both blood fat levels and blood pressures are unusually high. Smoking, stress, lack of exercise and obesity are also considered to predispose to heart disease, but the evidence is less clear-cut. The Japanese male smokes as much and is subjected to as much stress as his American counterpart, but he has much lower blood cholesterol levels, and rarely has ischemic heart disease.

Widespread recognition that heart disease is the result of overindulgence, at least in the Western World, and can only be prevented by people themselves, has led already to fewer "heart" deaths. Americans are exercising more, smoking less, aware of their blood pressures and seek treatment sooner. Once severe ischemic heart disease is present, drugs or surgery can help, but prevention is far more effective than cure.

Heart disease may be secondary to other disorders, notably high blood pressure (hypertension). Because the left ventricle has an additional load placed on it by the high pressure in the arterial system, it may in time fail. At first it becomes enlarged, but then incapable of supporting the increased strain; the symptoms of left heart failure supervene, with breathlessness from edema of the lungs as the pressure in the venous circulation of the lungs, and eventual extravasation (escape) of fluid.

Moreover, the heart of a patient with an important degree of hypertension is liable to show the changes of ischemic disease which render it less able to withstand the increased arterial pressure.

Chronic bronchitis and emphysema may lead to such impairment of gaseous interchange in the lungs that there is a lack of oxygen in the blood (hypoxia) and an excess of carbon dioxide. Under these conditions, the function of the kidneys is impaired with retention of salt and water and an increase of blood volume. The hypoxia also produces constriction of the small arteries of the lungs; this, together with the circulatory changes, produces an increase of pressure in the vessels of the lungs. The right ventricle then is subject to increased strain, and may also be affected by the general low level of circulating oxygen; if it fails, there is increasing edema of the dependent parts and congestion of the veins. Cardiovascular disease secondary to disorder of the substance of the lung is called COR PULMONALE.

See also the major articles on **Cardiology** and **Hypertension.**

heart failure

The function of the heart is to pump the blood around the body, and to pump blood through the lungs. The left side of the heart is concerned with the systemic circulation, the right side with the pulmonary circulation.

Failure may be predominantly right- or left-sided, and may be caused by congenital or acquired disease. The most common kind of failure is left-sided heart failure following coronary artery disease, high blood pressure, or disease and incompetency of the mitral or aortic valves of the heart. Chronic disease of the lungs and congenital heart disease lead more often to right-sided failure.

The first symptom of left-sided failure is usually shortness of breath on exertion, which may progress so that the patient finds it difficult to make any exertion. He may find it easier to breathe sitting up rather than lying down. He feels tired and may complain of a feeling of tightness in the chest. There may be attacks of severe breathlessness at night. When the right side of the heart fails, the return of venous blood is impaired and the tissues tend to become waterlogged—the site of the swelling (edema) being determined by gravity. If the patient is up, the ankles swell; if he is in bed the swelling is most obvious over the sacrum (base of the spine). The liver may be swollen and the stomach and intestines congested so that there is discomfort in the abdomen and a sense of nausea.

The most important single factor in the treatment of heart failure is rest, which must be absolute in very severe cases but in milder cases proportionate to the

A CROSS SECTION THROUGH THE HEART

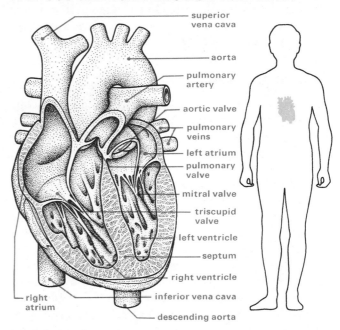

superior vena cava
aorta
pulmonary artery
aortic valve
pulmonary veins
left atrium
pulmonary valve
mitral valve
triscupid valve
left ventricle
septum
right ventricle
inferior vena cava
right atrium
descending aorta

BLOOD FLOW THROUGH THE HEART

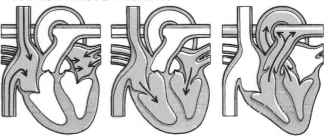

1 Relaxation: venous blood fills atria.

2 Contraction: phase 1– atria contract forcing blood into ventricles, which are still relaxed.

3 Contraction: phase 2– ventricles contract forcing blood into arteries.

The heart pumps out approximately $1\frac{1}{3}$ gallons of blood every minute, and it can double this amount when necessary during exercise. As the ventricles relax the valves open (1), allowing blood to flow down from the atria. When the ventricles contract (3), the valves are slammed shut, and blood from the right ventricle enters the pulmonary artery to go to the lungs, while the left ventricle pumps blood into the aorta; from there it is transported around the body in the arterial system.

degree of failure. It is dangerous to let old people become completely bedridden, as they may develop bedsores or infection of the lungs. The administration of digitalis is a major component of therapy in treating patients with chronic heart failure. Its primary effect is to increase the force of contraction of the heart muscle and slow the pulse rate. The excessive use of salt in the diet must be avoided, and in most cases the use of a diuretic helps in the excretion of excess water from the body tissues. The administration of morphine is specific in treating acute congestive heart failure. Other drugs (such as aminophylline and propranolol) are also useful.

See also the major article on **Cardiology.**

heart murmur

Two basic sounds can be heard through a stethoscope with each beat of the healthy heart. The first is the sound of the closure of the valves between the atria and the ventricles (the mitral and tricuspid valves), which is duller and longer than the second sound, produced by the shutting of the pulmonary and aortic valves.

Heart murmurs are extra sounds between, or even replacing, the usual sounds. They do not necessarily denote heart disease. *Functional murmurs,* arising from the flow of the blood through the heart, are not related to structural defects. *Organic murmurs* arise from obstruction to the flow of blood through a narrowed valve, or from regurgitation through an incompletely closed valve. Murmurs in childhood may arise from defects in the walls between the chambers of the heart (see HOLE IN THE HEART).

See also AUSCULTATION, STETHOSCOPE.

heart rhythms

See ARRHYTHMIA, FIBRILLATION and VENTRICULAR FIBRILLATION.

heart surgery

The first operation on the heart to relieve symptoms caused by a diseased heart valve was attempted on an aortic valve in 1894. An attempt was made to correct the action of a diseased mitral valve in 1924, but it was not until the 1950s that surgeons began to operate successfully for stenosis (abnormal constriction or narrowing) of the mitral valve.

At first, operations were carried out on the beating heart. But the development of heart-lung machines, capable of sustaining the circulation, made it possible to operate on the heart while the blood was bypassed. Techniques of "open-heart" surgery then advanced rapidly. (See the major article on **Cardiology**.)

It is now possible to replace heart valves with artificial valves, to carry out grafting operations on impaired coronary arteries, and to transplant complete hearts—although the problems associated with rejection of grafted heart muscle are far from solved. The correction of congenital heart malformations is in many cases possible, and there has been a remarkable improvement in mortality and morbidity figures.

Surgery involving opening the heart or the grafting of new vessels to its arterial tree requires use of heart-lung bypass technology. In babies with congenital heart malformations who would not survive their first year without surgery, techniques of surface cooling and total circulatory arrest (introduced in 1967, but not adopted generally until the 1970s), have enabled surgeons to operate on still hearts. This has allowed complete correction of complex abnormalities in a single operation, and led to dramatic improvements in results.

The less severely affected child, not requiring surgery in the first year, can wait until just before entering school before undergoing his or her one-stage surgical correction. The diagnosis and ongoing assessment of heart disorders not only have improved technically but are much more humane for the child, so that regular follow-up investigations are no longer a source of fear.

Surgery for valvular heart disease has shown a steady fall in operative deaths and very worthwhile improvement in deaths and illness from heart disease after operation. Surgeons are still searching for the perfect valve, but even the valves inserted in the early 1960s and now considered obsolete are associated with very good survival figures. The original artificial valves carried a higher risk of infection and clot formation on their surface than the newer ones. Nevertheless, patients undergoing replacement (particularly of a rheumatic mitral valve) are still given drugs to minimize the danger of blood clotting after the operation.

In the first decade of rheumatic valve replacement surgery, some deaths occurred from sudden heart attacks due to ischemic coronary artery disease. The recognition that both ischemic and rheumatic disease may occur together has led to routine x-ray examination of the coronary arteries before valve surgery. This has enabled surgeons to operate upon both valve and artery and has considerably reduced risk.

Replacement of diseased coronary arteries by vein grafts has become the most frequent heart operation in the United States. One 1976 report from Kansas City showed that 67.5% of heart operations performed in a community hospital unit were vein BYPASS procedures for coronary artery disease.

Coronary bypass surgery involves replacing a blocked artery with a length of vein taken from another part of the body. The precise area to be bypassed is measured by angiogram (x-ray of the artery) before surgery. Even in the most severe cases success (particularly in relieving pain) can be startling, and the opportunity it gives to remove areas of the heart wall that has become thinned by previous infarction may prolong life by years.

heat exhaustion

A serious disorder of the circulation following exposure to dry hot climatic conditions, caused by severe water and salt loss.

Symptoms start with headache, confusion, fatigue and drowsiness. The patient is pale, sweating profusely, with a low blood pressure, but usually no significant rise in body temperature. Loss of appetite, disturbance of vision and vomiting follow. If no treatment is given, the patient collapses into coma.

As the symptoms of the first stage are usually quickly obvious, a fatal outcome is almost always avoided by prompt, early treatment. The patient should be put to bed in cool surroundings and given copious amounts of salt and water. The vomiting or comatose patient has to be given saline solution by intravenous infusion.

(See *Heat effects* in the **First Aid** section.)

heat rash

A common name for MILIARIA.

Heberden's nodes

These common swellings of the last joints of the fingers affect ten times as many women as men, and involve both bone and cartilage. They are inherited, with sisters of affected women having twice the incidence of such nodes than the general population. Similar swellings can occur in baseball players and bowlers. They are commonly associated with generalized osteoarthritis.

Heberden's nodes develop without symptoms, over several years, but can arise suddenly and be painful and tender. They form on the top of the knuckles on each side of the midline. Only when the nodes are very large is the movement of the joint affected. Treatment is rarely needed, except to relieve pain. Aspirin reduces pain and inflammation, as does the application of heat.

hemangioma

A malformation made up of small blood vessels, which are distended and thin walled. They are seen in the skin of newborn infants as "port wine" stains, which tend to be permanent, or "strawberry" birthmarks or nevi, which commonly disappear as the child grows older.

Hemangiomas also occur in the brain, bone, liver, lungs, spleen and other organs. Patients may have multiple hemangiomas of the lips and intestines, which can cause bleeding, but most hemangiomas cause cosmetic rather than medical anxiety.

See also NEVUS.

hematemesis

The vomiting of blood. Hematemesis may be simply caused by irritation of the stomach (for example, by aspirin or alcohol) or be a sign of more serious illness, such as ulcers, cancer, or varicose veins at the lower end

of the esophagus often associated with liver disease (see ESOPHAGEAL VARICES).

About one third of hematemeses originates from chronic duodenal ulcers; another quarter is from acute ulcers of the stomach or duodenum. Bleeding from the junction of the stomach with the esophagus, or from the esophagus itself, is usually bright red; that from the stomach or duodenum is similar to coffee grounds in appearance. Endoscopy and x-ray studies are used to determine the site of bleeding.

Treatment depends on the diagnosis and may include blood transfusion, medical treatment or surgery

hematoma

A swelling composed of blood which has escaped from an injured, diseased or abnormally fragile vessel into the tissues—in other words, a bruise. The vast majority of hematomas subside in their own time, usually about a week, without need for treatment, changing color from

HEMATOMA

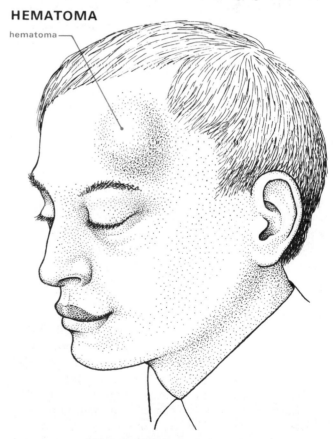

hematoma

Hematomas can become infected and this is particularly dangerous around the nose and eyes, because it can spread through the skull to cause meningitis. If somebody started to behave strangely or complain of severe headaches some days after an injury, he should be taken to the hospital for immediate medical evaluation.

purple to brown, to green-yellow, as the spilled hemoglobin is altered and taken back into the circulation.

Internal hematomas may follow severe injury, the effects depending on the site of the blow. After head injuries, hematomas may rarely occur over the surface of the brain or within its substance. A typical case involves a patient who recovers quickly from a knockout blow on the head, then some hours later develops headache, drowsiness, perhaps one-sided paralysis, then coma. This can occur in the absence of skull fracture, and even when the patient considers the blow to have been light and the resulting unconsciousness brief. Unless treated surgically, death can follow from pressure on the brain by the expanding hematoma. Injury-induced hematoma of the lung or kidney is much less serious, usually resolving without treatment in about three weeks.

hematuria

The passing of blood in the urine. Its cause, especially when painless, must always be fully investigated. It may vary from simple infection of the urethra, bladder, or kidneys, to more serious disease of any part of the urinary system. Rarely, it is a sign of inherited cysts of the kidneys or of disorders of bleeding or blood vessels. The presence of a stone in any part of the urinary system may cause hematuria—usually, but not always, in association with pain.

Investigation includes microscopic and bacteriological study of the urine, endoscopy and x-rays. In children nephritis and pyelonephritis are common findings; in adult life cystitis, pyelonephritis and stones; in the elderly, tumor and prostatic disease.

See also the major article on **Urology.**

hemianopia

Blindness for half the visual field. It may be *bitemporal,* in which both eyes are blind for the outer half of their field of vision; *nasal,* in which the eye cannot see the inner half of the visual field; or *homonymous,* in which each eye is blind for the same half visual field. The type of hemianopia depends on the site of interruption of the optic nerve pathway from the eye to the brain.

Light, received in the retina of each eye, is translated by receptor cells into electrical impulses which pass along the optic nerves—there is one for each eye—to the surface of the brain. Behind the eyes, on the floor of the skull just above the pituitary gland, the optic nerves meet, then part again in a cross-shaped structure, the optic *chiasma.* Here the fibers from the inner half of each retina, carrying perception of the outer half of the field of vision, cross over to the opposite sides of the brain.

Those from the outer half of the retina remain on the same side.

Interruption of either nerve between the eyeball and the optic chiasma will make that eye blind. A pituitary tumor, exerting pressure on the optic chiasma, produces bitemporal hemianopia. Interruption behind the chiasma leads to homonymous hemianopia. Hemianopias may arise from strokes, injuries, congenital abnormalities or tumor, and all require neurological investigation. Recovery of sight is rare.

hemiparesis

Weakness of the muscles on one side of the body, usually the sign of damage or disease affecting that part of the brain which controls the nerves which direct movement (motor nerves). The site of the damage is often the *internal capsule,* where the motor fibers run closely packed together on their way from the cerebral cortex to the spinal cord. The underlying cause of hemiparesis is usually cerebrovascular disease.

hemiplegia

Paralysis of one side of the body, as the result of damage or disease of the part of the brain that controls the motor nervous system; the left side of the brain controls the right side of the body, and the right side the left.

Damage can arise from injury, either at birth or as the consequence of accidents or wounds, and in such cases recovery is at best partial. The most common cause of hemiplegia is cerebrovascular disease leading to clotting of the cerebral arteries or bleeding from the diseased arterial wall. The most common site affected is the *internal capsule,* the part of the brain where nerve fibers descending from the cortex to the spinal cord are packed together. There are cases where the internal carotid arteries or the basilar artery are partially blocked, and here the paralysis may be transitory.

After a STROKE the limbs are at first limp, but they soon become stiff and may suffer cramps. The reflexes are exaggerated. Improvement may follow the most complete paralysis, and it is important to keep the limbs as flexible as possible and to avoid contractures. Some improvement is possible up to two years after the initial paralysis.

Slowly increasing paralysis of one side of the body is seen in cases where the brain is the seat of a tumor. Treatment depends on the nature of the growth.

See also the major article on **Neurology.**

hemochromatosis

A chronic illness in which iron is deposited in body tissues, causing FIBROSIS and malformation of the organs concerned. The liver and pancreas are mainly involved, their iron concentrations being between 50 and 100 times the normal level, but the heart muscle, endocrine glands and skin are also affected. The patient gets bronzed as the iron deposits become more dense.

Hemochromatosis is caused by the body's inability to prevent the absorption of large amounts of iron in the diet, a process usually controlled by the cells of the intestinal wall. Treatment aims at removing the iron by repeated blood letting or by injections of a chelating agent. Supplementary B vitamins may help.

hemodialysis

See DIALYSIS.

hemoglobin

Hemoglobin, the pigment carried in the red blood cells, is a complex protein containing iron; its specific function is to transport oxygen in the blood. Hemoglobin has a high affinity for oxygen and will absorb a large amount of the gas when the blood passes through the lungs. On reaching the tissues, where the oxygen level is much lower, hemoglobin is able to release its absorbed oxygen equally freely. Normal blood contains around 14 to 15 grams of hemoglobin in each 100 milliliters, although slightly lower levels are normal in women and children. A fall in hemoglobin below the normal lower limit for the individual constitutes ANEMIA.

In most persons, the hemoglobin is of a fixed and unvarying chemical composition and is referred to as *adult hemoglobin* (or *Hemoglobin A*). In newborn infants, a different chemical type of hemoglobin is present—better adapted to the needs of the baby while still in the womb—and is known as *fetal hemoglobin* (or *Hemoglobin F*). All normal blood also contains a trace of a third type of naturally occurring hemoglobin (*Hemoglobin A2*).

In certain individuals, however, a small but important chemical and structural abnormality is present in their hemoglobin molecule (*mutant* or *variant hemoglobin*).

In sickle cell disease, for example, most of the hemoglobin is in the form of *Hemoglobin S*. This causes the red cells to become distorted (sickle shaped when seen under the microscope) when they give up their oxygen, and they are easily destroyed. The symptoms of sickle cell disease include anemia and episodes of severe pain and fever due to the sickled cells blocking the small blood vessels in the bones and other organs. (See SICKLE CELL ANEMIA.)

Other hemoglobinopathies include thalassemia (affecting mainly peoples of Greek, Italian, or North African origin) and diseases associated with rarer abnormal hemoglobin such as Hemoglobins C, D and E.

hemophilia

Hemophilia is perhaps the best known of the inherited bleeding disorders. Although comparatively rare, it is still much more common than other similar disorders. In addition, its historical association with the royal families of Europe in the 19th and 20th centuries has made it familiar to many.

Hemophilia affects two to three people per 100,000 of the population. It is caused by an inherited deficiency of a specific clotting factor in the blood (*antihemophilic globulin,* also referred to as *Factor VIII*). The mode of inheritance of this clotting factor deficiency is unusual as it is a "sex-linked recessive" and carried on one of the chromosomes that determine sex (the X chromosome). Affected male hemophiliacs (XY) have only one X chromosome, the defective one; thus they have very low levels of Factor VIII and are susceptible to the fully developed disease. Female carriers of the disorder (XX) have one normal and one abnormal X chromosome and do not usually show any clinical abnormality, although they may have somewhat reduced levels of Factor VIII.

A male hemophiliac cannot pass the abnormality to his sons (to whom he passes only a Y chromosome). His daughters, however, must all receive his only X chromosome—a defective one—and must, therefore, become carriers of the disorder. A female carrier may transmit *either* one of her two X chromosomes (one of which is normal and one abnormal) to a son or a daughter. There is thus a 50/50 chance of a son being affected or a daughter being a carrier.

Clinically, the disorder may occur in either a mild or severe form; there may also be some variation within a family or a single generation. Patients bruise easily and large bruises characteristically occur in the deeper tissues rather than in the skin. Hemorrhage into joints may occur. Small injuries may result in excessive bleeding for long periods; the abnormality may first be revealed during surgery or the extraction of a tooth, although in many cases the problem will be discovered by means of preoperative tests to determine the clotting time. Severe cases may be identified for the first time in infancy when the baby starts to crawl (and is more prone to injuries). Diagnosis depends on the patient's medical history and on the results of specific blood tests which will reveal the absence of the clotting factor.

Treatment is now greatly improved but remains a complex problem which requires the supervision of a unit specializing in the management of bleeding disorders. Replacement of the missing factor with concentrated Factor VIII (obtained from human donor blood) is the mainstay of therapy. An effort is made to arrange home treatment so that the patient may lead a more normal life, especially with regard to education and job opportunities.

hemoptysis

The coughing or spitting up of blood. The amount of blood involved may vary from a small streak seen in a piece of phlegm coughed into a handkerchief, to a quantity that over even a limited period may be large enough to endanger life, to massive hemorrhage associated with tuberculosis or lung cancer.

Hemoptysis is a characteristic symptom in certain serious diseases, such as pulmonary tuberculosis or cancer of the lung; its occurrence should always be an indication to seek medical advice. It must be remembered, however, that hemoptysis can occur in much less serious conditions affecting the lungs, windpipe and larynx. It may also come from sites such as the nose and throat; the blood may trickle down the back of the throat and then appear to have been coughed up from within the chest (particularly in children).

hemorrhage

The technical term for bleeding.

In accidents and injuries the blood loss may occur from any tissue or part, but hemorrhage may also be caused by disease such as internal ulceration. Bleeding from the nose *(epistaxis)*, bleeding from the stomach and intestines with passage of blood in the stools *(melena)*, and bleeding from the kidney or urinary tract with passage of blood in the urine *(hematuria)* are all common examples of hemorrhage. In certain disorders—such as leukemia, hemophilia, or when there is a shortage of platelets in the blood *(thrombocytopenia)*—the blood-clotting mechanism is disturbed; in such cases bleeding may occur in any site, including bleeding into an internal organ (often with serious consequences).

The effects of hemorrhage depend on the site involved and the amount of blood loss. The loss of two or three pints of blood over a short period will produce a rapid pulse, palpitations, dizziness, faintness and often collapse and shock. The patient becomes pale, cold and sweaty; the blood pressure drops, the pulse rate rises, and, if the blood loss continues, death may occur.

The first-aid treatment of hemorrhage is pressure: a cloth pad pressed firmly over the bleeding point will usually halt the flow of blood. Anyone who is bleeding or has bled heavily should be admitted to the hospital, where (if necessary) the lost blood can be replaced by transfusion; if the bleeding continues it can be treated surgically either by ligation of the bleeding vessels or by electrocoagulation.

The chronic loss of small amounts of blood every day, possibly into the bowel or stomach (in which case it may pass unnoticed by the patient), can only be replaced by the body itself if the patient's reserve stores of iron are not exhausted. Men may have reserves of iron which will allow the natural replacement of several pints of blood, but many women of childbearing age may have little or no iron reserves because of their regular blood loss in menstruation. When reserves are exhausted, an *iron-deficiency anemia* appears; this will worsen unless iron is supplied, the bleeding is stopped, or transfusion blood is supplied.

hemorrhoids

Hemorrhoids (or "piles") is a condition in which the veins around the anus or in the anal canal are abnormally dilated. There is much argument about the cause. In certain cases, as in pregnancy, obstruction to the flow of blood in the veins of the rectum is the cause. In others, factors such as constipation, straining at stool, lack of dietary fiber, obesity, heavy lifting, athletic exertions and a hereditary predisposition have all been implicated.

Whatever the cause, the first symptom of hemorrhoids is usually bleeding from the anus, particularly during a bowel movement. Bleeding may be severe or only a slight trace of blood may be seen on the toilet

HEMORRHOIDS

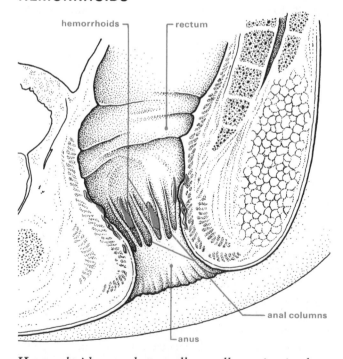

hemorrhoids — rectum — anal columns — anus

Hemorrhoids are abnormally swollen veins in the lining of the anal canal. They are extremely common in American adults but opinions vary as to their cause. Small hemorrhoids may go unnoticed while large ones protrude through the anus and require surgical removal.

paper. Irritation and itching commonly occur. The hemorrhoids, if large, may come to project through the anus *(prolapsed piles)*, where they are constricted by its contraction and become very painful.

Hemmorrhoids is a very common condition. The treatment is as controversial as the cause. In severe cases the dilated veins may be removed surgically and the remaining parts of the veins tied off *(hemorrhoidectomy)*; or, in less severe cases, the dilated veins may be injected with chemical solutions which will cause obliteration of the affected vessels by clot formation. The condition may also be treated by local freezing *(cryosurgery)* or the anus may be dilated and stretched under an anesthetic to relieve the pressure on the veins and allow them to return to normal.

All these methods of treatment are moderately successful, even though they are often uncomfortable for the patient. Surgical removal of the veins and cryosurgery usually require admission to the hospital, but injection and dilatation may be performed on an outpatient basis. Various suppositories and creams may provide temporary local relief but will not cure the condition, which may, however, regress by itself. Constipation and diarrhea both aggravate piles.

hepatitis

Inflammation of the liver; unless further qualified, the term is usually taken to refer to the virus infection of the liver referred to as "infectious hepatitis."

Virus hepatitis occurs in two basic forms, one of which is called *infectious hepatitis* (or *hepatitis A*) and the other *serum hepatitis* (or *hepatitis B*), which is also "infectious." It is fairly certain that these two conditions, although clinically similar, are caused by different viruses. There are other differences as well, including the length of the incubation period and the means by which the virus is spread. In hepatitis B, this appears to be mainly by the injection or transfusion of contaminated blood or blood products, or by accidental skin pricks or other injuries caused by contaminated needles or other sharp objects. Transmission also occurs from inadequately sterilized hypodermic needles, syringes, surgical and dental instruments, tattooing instruments and razors. It is common among narcotic addicts and others who use unsterile syringes for drug injections.

The virus which causes hepatitis A, by contrast, is present in the feces; although it can be spread by blood transfusion, the main route is from infective feces to the mouth via the hands or objects contaminated with feces.

The patient with hepatitis may notice little or nothing wrong, as many cases are very mild and occur without JAUNDICE (a yellowing of the skin). In more severe cases the patient will have fever, headache, nausea and vomiting, a severe loss of appetite and aching in the muscles. The jaundice, caused by an accumulation of yellow bile pigment in the blood, appears after a few days or, in some cases, a week or two from the onset of the symptoms. The liver may become enlarged and tender. With the appearance of jaundice, the symptoms may be temporarily increased but soon diminish. Convalescence may be prolonged and complicated by mental depression.

More acute or "fulminant" cases occasionally occur and may eventually lead to death from liver failure. A few patients will remain jaundiced, with an enlarged liver, for some months but in most cases they recover. Some patients may recover but ultimately develop CIRRHOSIS of the liver. This appears to be more common with hepatitis B, as is the condition of *chronic active hepatitis* in which liver damage continues over a long period and requires specific treatment.

An uncomplicated case requires only bed rest at home and care in the handling of infected excreta. Alcoholic beverages should be rigorously avoided. Injections of *gamma globulin* may temporarily protect against hepatitis A infections in those contemplating travel to high-risk areas.

Toxic hepatitis is caused by poisoning of the liver with various chemicals (such as industrial solvents), drugs, or (rarely) general anesthetics. Hepatitis is also occasionally caused as a result of a bacterial, protozoal, or other microbial infection. In such cases the treatment is directed toward the underlying cause.

hepatoma

A primary tumor of the liver, often malignant. It must be distinguished from the much more common secondary tumors of the liver which arise from the spread (metastasis) of cancer cells from other parts of the body, especially from organs within the abdominal cavity.

Primary tumors of the liver usually occur as a terminal complication of CIRRHOSIS of the liver. They are difficult to treat since the organ is already diseased and surgery rendered difficult. Tumors confined to one lobe of the liver, however, have been successfully removed and some anticancer ("cytotoxic") drugs may be useful. Liver transplantation has had a limited success.

Benign (nonmalignant) hepatomas that occur occasionally in women may be related to long-term use of oral contraceptives.

heredity

The transmission of physical and mental characteristics from parent to offspring. The study of heredity is known as genetics.

Each characteristic is carried by a gene—the basic unit of heredity. GENES, which are found in every cell, are fragments of a complex protein molecule known as DNA (see DNA/RNA). Genes are carried on chromosomes, rodlike structures found in the nuclei of cells. Each human cell (except ova and spermatozoa) normally has 46 chromosomes, arranged in 23 pairs. One pair consists of the sex chromosomes, which determine the sex of the individual; they may also carry genes for other characteristics. For example, the gene for hemophilia is carried on the female chromosome, and hemophilia is known as a sex-linked disease. The other 22 pairs are known as autosomes, which can be differentiated from each other under the microscope.

Genes are arranged along the chromosomes in linear order, each gene having its own position. Genes which occupy corresponding positions on a pair of chromosomes carry the trait for the same feature (for example, color of the eyes) and are known as *alleles* for that feature. If the alleles are identical—for example, both determine that the eyes should be brown—then the individual is *homozygous* for the color of the eyes, and will have brown eyes. If the alleles are not identical—for example, one gene dictates blue eyes and the other brown—the individual is *heterozygous* for that characteristic, and the color of his eyes will be that of the dominant gene (brown). Blue eyes are a recessive trait, and will only manifest themselves if the person is homozygous for blue eyes.

An individual gets half his genes from one parent and half from the other, because during the maturation of the sperm and the ovum the two halves of a pair of chromosomes separate from each other so that only one of a pair is transmitted to the offspring.

Not all features are determined in a clearcut manner by a single gene. Some have a familiar basis—for example, the tendency to develop diabetes mellitus or hypertension—but there is no clearly defined pattern of inheritance.

Genes may change spontaneously, a process known as *mutation*. If a mutation affects the gene in a sperm or ovum, the offspring that is produced may have characteristics carried by neither parent.

See GENETIC DISORDERS, GENETIC COUNSELING.

hernia

The protrusion of part of the abdominal contents through a defect in the wall of the abdominal cavity. The hernia, or rupture, may escape so that it lies under the skin or it may in the case of a diaphragmatic or *hiatus hernia* pass out of the abdominal cavity into the thorax.

The most common site for a hernia is the groin, at the point where the spermatic cord in a man or the round ligament of the uterus in a female passes out of the abdomen to enter the scrotum or the labium majus. This hernia is much commoner in men than women, and it may pass down into the scrotum itself to form a considerable swelling.

The hernias that follow the path of the spermatic cord are called *indirect inguinal hernias;* those which make their way through a weakened abdominal wall behind the cord to form a bulge are called *direct inguinal hernias.*

Commoner in women than men is a type of hernia which appears in the upper part of the thigh just below the groin; it makes its way out of the abdomen on the inner side of the canal through which the major blood vessels pass into the leg. This is called a *femoral hernia.*

Less common than inguinal or femoral hernias, a third type emerges at the navel—an *umbilical hernia*. It may be found at birth, caused by failure of part of the bowel to return within the abdominal cavity from its developmental position within the umbilical cord; or, more rarely, it may be the result of infection of the umbilicus soon after birth. Hernias are found in adults near the umbilicus, but they pass through a weak area of the abdominal wall just above or below the umbilicus itself and are called *para-umbilical hernias.*

Incisional hernias are the result of weakening or incomplete healing of a surgical wound in the abdominal wall, usually in the midline below the umbilicus. It may follow sepsis of the wound, and is more likely to

HERNIA

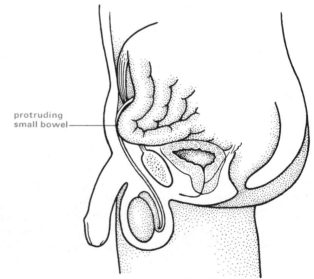

protruding small bowel

INGUINAL HERNIA

A hernia is any protrusion of an internal organ through the wall of the cavity which normally contains it. Most hernias involve the gut, the most common form being the inguinal hernia which causes a lump in the groin. Inguinal hernias should always be repaired by surgery.

develop in obese persons with weakened abdominal muscles.

The only common hernia in which the abdominal organs escape into another body cavity is the *diaphragmatic hernia*. Occasionally such a hernia forms in the newborn as a result of a developmental defect in the diaphragm, but in adults the protrusion of a part of the stomach through the esophageal opening of the diaphragm is often found, especially in those who are overweight. Usually, this *hiatus hernia* produces no symptoms, but it may mimic peptic ulcer and result in pain in the upper part of the abdomen or behind the lower part of the breastbone (sternum). It may also lead to an uncomfortable "heartburn," caused by the reflux of food or gastric juices into the esophagus, especially when the patient is lying down after a heavy meal.

Signs and symptoms of hernias in the abdominal wall include uncomfortable swelling and often pain on straining. It is often possible to return them with steady pressure into the abdominal cavity; if this cannot be achieved, it may mean that the hernia has become trapped. This is potentially dangerous, for once trapped the contents of the hernia tend to swell and if left unreduced may become gangrenous.

It follows that the best treatment for a hernia is a surgical operation designed to replace the herniated contents into the abdominal cavity and repair the defect in the abdominal wall. The attempt to hold a hernia in place with an old-fashioned truss is both insufficient and potentially dangerous.

Treatment for a hiatus hernia is much the same as that for peptic ulcer, except that it is reasonable to sleep with the head of the bed raised, and often possible to gain relief by sitting up when troubled at night. Only in severe cases is an operation justifiable.

herniated disk

Another name for SLIPPED DISK.

herpes simplex

A virus which causes crusted sores, commonly around the lips and mouth ("cold sores") and the genitalia. The infectious condition itself is also known as herpes simplex.

Many people suffer repeated attacks of cold sores whenever they have a fever, a rise in skin temperature, or are exposed to sunlight. Antibody studies have shown, however, that 90% of adults have immunity which prevents the spread of the virus in the body beyond the local site of attack. Herpes simplex is intermittently present in the mouths of healthy carriers and is spread by personal contact; genital herpes is spread by sexual contact with an infected person and is a venereal disease.

An attack begins with itching of the skin in the affected area, quickly followed by redness and swelling. Within a few hours fragile blisters (vesicles) appear and rupture to exude a sticky serum-like fluid which rapidly crusts. Unless secondary infection with bacteria occurs, the lesions heal without scarring within about a week.

The diagnosis can be confirmed by virus culture from the exudate, but this is both complicated and expensive. The appearance of the rash is so characteristic as to make the diagnosis obvious in most cases of herpes affecting the face. There are no serious complications of oral herpes simplex except for the unsightly appearance. When the conjunctiva is involved, however, there is a danger of corneal ulceration.

Antibiotics may be administered to prevent bacterial infection. Some success in reducing the spread of the virus has been achieved with the antiviral drug iododeoxyuridine (IDU), particularly in reducing the complications of conjunctivitis.

Genital herpes infections may cause a painful cervicitis (inflammation of the cervix) in women, with ulceration and a vaginal discharge. In men the genital infection is usually less severe. The results of recent research studies have suggested that women who develop herpes cervicitis may have an increased risk of developing cancer of the cervix in later years. The condition is now seen as a reason for regular screening by Pap smears, which can detect early cancerous changes at a stage when treatment is simple and curative.

herpes zoster (shingles)

A viral infection with the same virus (varicella-zoster virus) which causes chickenpox. It is characterized by a rash preceded by pain and skin irritation.

"Zoster" develops from reddened raised areas into blisters which join together and rapidly rupture and crust. The affected areas are always along the course of one or more of the spinal nerves beneath the skin. The rash typically progresses in a band around one side of the chest, trunk or abdomen. The virus may also attack the ophthalmic cranial nerve, causing a rash that stretches from the eyelid across the forehead into the hairline.

Once the rash appears, the diagnosis is obvious and needs no laboratory investigations. Zoster most commonly attacks adults between the ages of 40 and 70, often after contact with a child suffering from chickenpox. It can also arise in times of stress. One theory is that the virus may lie dormant in the body for many years before the infection erupts.

The main patient complaint following an attack of herpes zoster is pain (due to irritation of the affected nerve below the skin), which can be severe and particularly distressing in the elderly. The rash usually disappears within two weeks or so, although the pain can persist for many weeks thereafter. The patient may require frequent doses of analgesics (pain-killing drugs). As with most viral infections, there is no specific treatment for herpes zoster. Soothing dressings of calamine lotion help to dry up the crusts and antihistamines can relieve the itching. More commonly it is the pain that requires relief with strong analgesics. Recurrent attacks of shingles are very uncommon but do occur.

hiccup

Hiccup (or *hiccough*) is caused by an involuntary spasm of the muscle of the diaphragm, which separates the chest cavity from the abdomen.

This spasm sucks air down the windpipe, but the inhalation is checked by sudden closure of the glottis at the back of the throat. The result is the characteristic jerk and sound. As everyone has experienced, hiccups usually occur in repeated spasms and soon subside.

The reason for the spasm of the diaphragm is irritation of the nerve which supplies it (phrenic nerve), the irritation usually being provoked by eating or drinking too rapidly. Hiccup is of no medical significance unless it persists, in which case some disorder of the stomach, diaphragm, or chest may be responsible.

In a normal attack of hiccups the most effective cure is to hold the breath for as long as possible in order to suppress the response of the diaphragm. A number of treatments have been attempted for rare cases of very persistent hiccups, from dry sugar to numerous powerful drugs. A guaranteed treatment, if the hiccup is severe and persistent enough to merit it, is crushing of the phrenic nerve in a surgical operation.

high blood pressure

See BLOOD PRESSURE and the major article on **Hypertension.**

hip replacement

Osteoarthritis of the hip is a very common cause of severe disability, particularly in the elderly. It is caused by wear and tear, but any injury or disease that damages the joint surfaces tends to accelerate the development of osteoarthritis. Where the cartilage wears away there is considerable pain, made worse by walking, and increasing stiffness develops in the joint. For mild cases, medication and physical therapy may make life tolerable, but a worn-out joint cannot be regrown. However, there are two main types of operation for the surgical replacement of an artificial joint.

Cup arthroplasty is where the joint socket (acetabulum) on the pelvis is smoothed out and a highly polished metal cup (often of titanium) is placed over the head of the thighbone (femur) to serve as a replacement lining for the joint.

In *total replacement* the head of the femur is removed and replaced by a metal prosthesis permanently embedded in the shaft of the bone. The socket is deepened and a rigid plastic cup is cemented to the bone with an acrylic compound. This operation has fewer complications and is increasingly used. There is rapid convalescence, immediate pain relief and a dramatic improvement in movement range. Many thousands of hip replacements are now being performed each year in the United States and the duration of the new joint's activity is known to be at least a decade.

Hirschprung's disease (congenital megacolon)

A rare congenital disorder of the colon causing severe constipation in babies.

The baby, more commonly male than female, is born with a defect in the nerves that normally control the muscles of a specific area of the colon. That part of the colon therefore cannot relax to permit the passage of feces, so the intestine just above it becomes grossly distended.

The child may vomit and appear to have difficulty in passing feces soon after birth. For a while further trouble may be avoided since the baby is on a liquid diet, but as soon as he starts to eat solid food the bulkiness of the stools leads to more and more obstruction of the intestine; weeks may elapse without a bowel movement.

The disorder can be distinguished from a normal bout of persistent constipation because the latter responds to alterations in diet or to laxatives. Also, the abdomen of the baby with Hirschprung's disease becomes extremely distended and growth is retarded.

Once the diagnosis is confirmed by x-ray and biopsy (examination of a sample of colon tissue), the affected area of the colon is removed surgically and the remaining ends rejoined. The outcome of the operation is usually excellent.

hirsutism

The growth of unwanted hair on the body. The term is nearly always used to describe excessive hair growth in women, which creates upsetting cosmetic problems.

Typical of hirsutism are growth of the pubic hair up towards the navel, growth of hair around the nipples and hair in the "shaving" areas of the face. There may be some demonstrable hormone change that can be related to the woman's change of life (menopause), but such hormone problems are found only in about one case in a hundred.

Some rare genetic, hormonal and metabolic diseases cause hirsutism.

In the majority of cases, however, there is no explanation and little point in detailed hormonal investigations. What is required is skilled treatment for the cosmetic problem of the unwanted hair.

Hormone therapy cannot be used, as a rule, because it would cause too many other undesirable effects. The basis of treatment, therefore, is disguise or removal of the excessive growth of hair.

Unwanted hair can be disguised by bleaching or dyeing it a light color; shaving of the hair seems to encourage renewed growth. Removal can be effected by depilatory creams, abrasives, shaving waxes, or electrolysis. The advice of a skilled beautician is recommended.

Electrolysis—removal of the individual hairs by cautery of their roots—is expensive and in some cases can leave scars, but for small patches of strong growth it is ideal.

histocompatibility antigens

The antigens responsible for an individual's "tissue type," which is important in matching for transplantation.

An antigen is a protein substance that provokes an antibody response from the host through the mechanisms of the IMMUNE SYSTEM. All human cells have antigens on their surface, which can be recognized by the body as "self" but which, if transferred to another individual, would be recognized as "nonself." If too many of the antigens (termed "HL-A antigens" or "transplantation antigens") are dissimilar in the recipient of a donated organ his body is likely to reject it.

Unlike blood group matching—where A, B, AB and O groups can be accurately matched—histocompatibility antigens are far more complex.

When testing the suitability of a donor organ for transplantation, an attempt is usually made to match at least two of the four HL-A antigens. The chances of success are known to correspond to the closeness of the match. However, a minor degree of mismatching is not of crucial importance, since treatment with immunosuppressive drugs can damp down the rejection mechanisms.

histoplasmosis

A fungal disease of the lungs caused by the inhalation of contaminated dust.

The parasitic fungus responsible *(Histoplasma capsulatum)* is found particularly in the dust from chicken houses and other areas contaminated by bird dung.

Once inhaled it spreads through the lungs to cause a severe and persistent cough, shortness of breath, chest pain, fever and a general feeling of being unwell (malaise).

Fortunately histoplasmosis is usually a mild and self-limiting disease. However, some severe and untreated cases can be extremely serious. The treatment of choice is the antibiotic agent *amphotericin B,* usually administered intravenously.

X-ray and immunological tests have shown that as many as 80% of the population of the Eastern and Midwestern United States have been in contact with the disease at some time in their lives.

hives

A popular name for URTICARIA.

See also the major article on **Allergy and Immunology.**

HLA (human leukocyte antigens)

See HISTOCOMPATIBILITY ANTIGENS.

Hodgkin's disease

A malignant disease of the LYMPHATIC SYSTEM.

The lymph glands affected by this cancer, situated in many parts of the body and with an important role in immunity, enlarge and can eventually cause pressure on adjacent structures; cancer cells may also invade the spleen and liver and cause them to enlarge. The disease is not painful in the early stages, although there is fever, weight loss, malaise (a general feeling of being unwell), anemia and sometimes itching of the skin.

Hodgkin's disease affects twice as many males as females and is seen most often between the ages of 15 and 35 and after the age of 50. Modern treatment is prolonging the lives of many patients with this potentially fatal condition.

The reason why the whole lymphatic system is affected by malignant growth is unknown. A viral cause for Hodgkin's disease has been suspected but not proved.

The glands in the neck, groin and armpit first draw attention to the condition, usually because they do not settle after an infection in the normal way. Chest x-rays show lymph gland enlargement in the chest; superficial lymph glands feel tense and rubbery as they grow over a period of weeks and become entangled in neighboring glands.

The disease is treated by a combination of radiation and chemotherapy; newer combinations of anticancer drugs are being tried constantly with increasing success.

Survival is now often measured in years rather than months and there are many long-term survivors.

The prognosis is best if the disease is detected early, as with all types of malignant disease.

hole in the heart

A common name for a congenital heart defect in which two of the chambers of the heart are not properly separated.

The term "hole in the heart" is in fact an accurate description of the condition, which may occur on its own or with other congenital deformities in the cardiovascular system. The hole may be between the two upper chambers (an *atrial septal defect*) or the two lower chambers (*ventricular septal defect*). In either case the hole allows blood to pass directly from one side of the heart to the other, so that unoxygenated blood may pass around the circulation without going via the lungs. In consequence the sufferer may have a blue appearance due to the high proportion of unoxygenated blood in the circulation.

Congenital heart defects of this kind affect about one child in every thousand in America. The diagnosis is usually made by the pediatrician's detection of a heart murmur—although it must be stressed that not all heart murmurs are ominous. Occasionally a minor deformity may not be detected until much later in life, if at all.

If surgical treatment is planned, the diagnosis will be confirmed and the severity of the defect measured by cardiac catheterization: a thin flexible tube is passed via blood vessels into the chambers of the heart; the movement of blood within the heart is charted by the pressure in the chambers and by x-ray films. Many septal defects are isolated lesions, but in a minority of cases there are other anomalies in the heart, making surgical repair more difficult.

With advances in heart surgery such as the use of the heart-lung bypass to allow the surgeon time to work, most cases of hole in the heart can now be satisfactorily corrected. If the hole is large it is covered either by tissue taken from elsewhere in the patient's body or by an artificial fiber patch. Usually correction of the defect allows the child to return to normal or near normal life.

homeopathy

A system of medical treatment based on the principle that "like (in small doses) cures like."

Homeopathy was introduced in Europe at the beginning of the 19th century by a German physician, Samuel Hahnemann (1755–1843). Its basic tenet, quoted as "similia similibus curentur," was that the cure of a disease could be effected by very small amounts of a drug capable in larger doses of producing, in a healthy

HOLE IN THE HEART

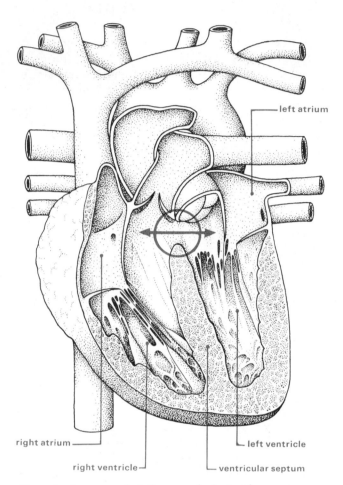

Ventricular septal defect—a hole in the septum between the two ventricles of the heart—is the most common type of congenital heart disease. Fortunately, most of these holes are small and close of their own accord, but larger defects and holes associated with other heart malformations require cardiac surgery to correct them.

subject, symptoms similar to those of the disease to be treated.

Dr. Hahnemann's original treatise, "Organon" (1796), provoked considerable controversy. It claimed that this type of therapy had been recommended by Hippocrates; its principles were contrary to those of its day. Minute doses were recommended, the agent being distilled and diluted until its final concentration might be less than a millionth part of the solution. Only a single drug was to be given at a time and many current practices were forbidden.

"Homeopathy," wrote Hahnemann, "sheds not a drop of blood, administers no emetics, purgatives or laxatives ... and applies no mustard plasters."

At the time, leeches were being applied by orthodox

doctors in cases of pneumonia, massive doses of opium were given to children, mercury was used as a teething powder and many other bizarre remedies—now known to be highly toxic—were prescribed by the most respected physicians.

In that context, it can be seen how the revolutionary philosophy of homeopathy as a purification of attitudes managed to attract its devotees. Hospitals for homeopathic treatment were established in Leipzig, Vienna and London.

The remedies have not, however, stood the test of modern scientific pharmacology. Some, like iodine for goiter, are established orthodox treatments today. But many others are regarded by a majority of the medical profession as pointless.

homocystinuria

A rare inherited disorder of metabolism.

Like other inborn errors of metabolism it is due to the deficiency of an enzyme, and is characterized by the appearance of an unusual substance—in this case homocystine—in the urine.

Patients are often mentally retarded and die young from THROMBOEMBOLISM. A diet low in the amino acid methionine may help if it is instituted virtually from birth.

hookworm

A human parasite endemic in certain parts of the United States.

The adult hookworm lives attached to the inside of the human intestine, from where it releases as many as 10,000 eggs daily which pass out with the feces. Eggs deposited on warm moist soil develop into larvae. Many weeks later the larvae may penetrate the skin of another person, enter a blood vessel and be carried to the lungs.

The larvae break out of the lung tissue and migrate up the bronchi to the throat, where they are swallowed and eventually reach the intestine to develop into adults. About six weeks elapse between skin penetration and the first appearance of eggs in the feces, but the adult can remain in the intestine for many years once it is established there.

Hookworm infection is endemic in many parts of the world where the climate is suitable; it is usually confined to rural areas where sanitation is relatively poor and many people go barefoot. The "hookworm belt" in the United States is along the Atlantic and Gulf coasts from Carolina to Texas; the disease is also endemic in parts of Virginia, Kentucky and Tennessee.

Since the hookworm feeds on blood it causes a severe ANEMIA. At the site of entry there is severe itching, with local redness and swelling. A heavy larval infestation will frequently cause symptoms of bronchitis.

Any inexplicable case of anemia, especially in someone who has returned from abroad or who lives in an endemic area, should be investigated for hookworms. The diagnosis is made by examination of the stools for egg cells.

A single dose of specific antihookworm drugs will kill all the adults in the intestine; it is usual to check the feces two weeks later to be sure. Thereafter, iron therapy progressively corrects anemia.

Prevention of hookworm infestation requires the proper disposal of human excreta, at least by deep burial, and the avoidance of any possibility of skin penetration by the wearing of shoes in all contaminated areas.

hormones

Hormones are very complex chemical substances, secreted by the ductless (endocrine) glands to serve as blood-borne "messengers" which regulate cell function elsewhere in the body. They form a communications system in the body and can bring about extraordinary changes in cell activity.

The transformation of a tadpole into a frog due to the influence of growth hormone is no more remarkable than the cure brought about in a person suffering from myxedema when treated with thyroid hormone. Similarly, the immature child of prepubertal years is changed by the influence of growth and sex hormones to become a sexually mature adult.

In therapy hormones are used as replacement where the patient is deficient (e.g., insulin for the diabetic), as treatment to overcome disease (e.g., cortisone for arthritis or asthma) and as controlling agents to divert natural functions (e.g., sex hormones as contraceptives). Synthetic compounds resembling the natural products, but achieving enhanced or differing affects, have gradually become available since the 1930s and in recent years an explosive increase in the knowledge of their benefits—and their disadvantages—in medicine has been achieved.

The nervous and endocrine systems of the body actually function as a single interrelated system. The central nervous system, particularly the hypothalamus, plays a crucial role in controlling hormone secretion; conversely, hormones markedly alter neural function. No hormone is secreted at a constant rate, and most hormones are either degraded by the liver or excreted by the kidneys. The investigation of endocrine disease therefore depends on assays of excretion rates (e.g., 24-hour urine samples) and circulating serum levels; but since many of these chemical messengers are bound to protein in the blood plasma, the diagnostic tests are particularly complicated and expensive.

Hormones exert their effects by altering the rates at which specific cellular processes proceed. For example, insulin promotes glucose (sugar) uptake by cells that require energy, follicle-stimulating hormone provokes the ovary into producing an ovum, and testosterone enhances the production of spermatozoa in the testes. They do this by combining with enzymes, or by enhancing enzyme production in the cell through a chemical effect on the RNA (ribonucleic acid) of the cell. The result in the body depends on the target organ cell of the hormone and its function: the table below illustrates some of the major hormones and their effects.

Disease in the endocrine system is revealed by a physiological defect in the expected effects of the target organ cells. For example, growth fails to occur, ovulation is inadequate, or myxedema occurs because of inadequate function of the thyroid gland. Less frequently the disorder may be that of excessive hormonal secretion, for example, virilization in a female from a pituitary tumor, or thyrotoxicosis from a thyroid tumor. The treatment of hormonal disorder is undertaken by an endocrinologist for it involves the achievement of balance in the supplements administered; diabetic control by the appropriate daily dosage of insulin is the clearest example of this.

Considerable improvements in the effectiveness of hormone treatment and replacement therapy have been achieved in recent years, but the accurate elucidation of each hormone's multiple influences on human physiology is a continued challenge.

See also the major article on **Endocrinology.**

Horner's syndrome

Dilatation of the pupil and drooping of the upper eyelid as a result of facial nerve damage.

Other features of the syndrome are a red face (due to vasodilatation) and often the absence of normal sweating. The eyeball seems more prominent than usual, probably because the patient is trying to overcome the effect of the droopy eyelid by contracting the forehead muscles.

Horner's syndrome almost always occurs only on one side of the face. The nerve damage causing it may arise for many reasons—including trauma, brain tumor, thrombosis, or neurological disease. Treatment is directed at the underlying disorder.

housemaid's knee

Inflammation and swelling of the bursa in front of the kneecap (a form of BURSITIS), caused by prolonged kneeling on a hard surface.

Hurler's syndrome (gargoylism)

A rare disease due to an error of metabolism which can be inherited.

The physical manifestations include a grotesque appearance due to a disproportionately large head and coarse facial expression, with a flat nose and thick lips. Bone changes lead to shortness of stature, chest deformities, marked limitation in the extensibility of

Gland	Hormone	Effect
anterior pituitary	growth hormone	increase in body size
	thyroid-stimulating hormone	enhanced metabolism
	adrenocorticotropic hormone (ACTH)	response to physical stress
	gonadotropic hormones	growth of gonads (sex glands)
	prolactin	breast development
posterior pituitary	oxytocin	uterine contraction
	antidiuretic hormone	excretion control
thyroid	thyroxine	metabolic rate increase
adrenal cortex	cortisone	defense against disease
	aldosterone	excretion rate control
ovary	estrogen	maintenance of
	progesterone	sexually reproductive
testes	testosterone	function
parathyroids	parathormone	calcium uptake by bone
pancreas	insulin	glucose uptake by cell

limbs and "spade-like" hands.

Other features include an enlarged tongue, liver and spleen, skin changes, mental deficiency, blindness, deafness, disease of the heart valves, congestive heart failure and angina pectoris.

No active treatment exists at present for Hurler's syndrome.

hyaline membrane disease

A disease of the newborn, also known as the *respiratory distress syndrome,* which usually develops within the first four hours after birth. It is characterized by difficulty in breathing, a bluish appearance of the skin caused by imperfect oxygenation of the blood (cyanosis), and easy collapsibility of the air sacs (alveoli) of

HORMONES

ENDOCRINE GLANDS WHICH PRODUCE THE BODY'S HORMONES

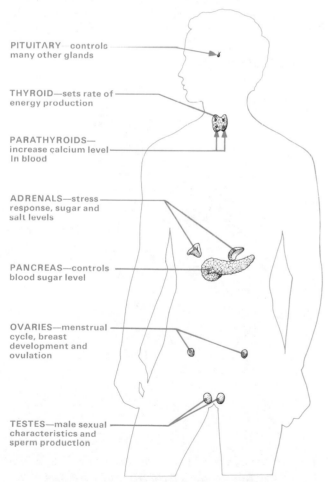

PITUITARY—controls many other glands

THYROID—sets rate of energy production

PARATHYROIDS— increase calcium level in blood

ADRENALS—stress response, sugar and salt levels

PANCREAS—controls blood sugar level

OVARIES—menstrual cycle, breast development and ovulation

TESTES—male sexual characteristics and sperm production

Hormones are chemical messenger substances secreted directly into the bloodstream by the endocrine glands shown above. They travel in the blood to different "target organs" where they control the rate of cell activity.

the lungs. It is due to a lack of *pulmonary surfactant,* a substance which normally serves to reduce "stickiness" within the air sacs.

When the disease persists for more than a few hours a thick *hyaline* (glassy or translucent) membrane is formed lining the air sacs and their ducts. Approximately 25,000 babies die each year in the United States from this disease, which has a mortality rate of from 30 to 50%.

Essentially, hyaline membrane disease is the result of premature birth. The lungs of a fetus do not contain enough surfactant for normal respiration until the last quarter of pregnancy. Prevention of the disease therefore depends on the prevention of premature births. When there are medical reasons (such as diabetes) for inducing labor prematurely, it is vital that this should be delayed until the fetal lungs contain surfactant. It is now possible to test the amniotic fluid (which surrounds the developing fetus) to determine whether or not the fetus is mature enough to avoid hyaline membrane disease; use of this test is reducing the incidence of the condition. When cases do occur, the infant may be treated by a special form of artificial respiration (intermittent positive pressure respiration) which helps support the lungs for the critical period until surfactant is formed normally. Even so, the condition remains the most important threat to the life of very small babies.

hydatidiform mole

An abnormality occurring about once in every 2,000 pregnancies, in which the ovum dies but does not miscarry. The placenta continues to grow, forming a swelling—or "mole"—which mimics a normal pregnancy. The condition is more common in Asian than in European women and the risk increases with age.

The first sign of hydatidiform mole is a rapid increase in the size of the womb shortly after conception—often much larger than it would normally grow at that stage of gestation. Other suspicious signs include vaginal bleeding and lack of fetal movement.

On investigation, the doctor will be unable to detect a fetal heartbeat; x-ray examination will fail to show bone formation after the 12th week, when it would normally be seen. Further tests, such as ultrasonic scanning, will confirm the diagnosis.

The mole will then be removed and the gynecologist will conduct further examinations at regular intervals to make sure that all fragments have been removed. The serious risk with a "molar pregnancy" is that the growth may be or become malignant: this variant, the CHORIOCARCINOMA, occurs about one in every 40 cases of hydatidiform mole.

If evacuation of the cyst reveals abnormal cells, or if

there is any suggestion of recurrence of the growth, then anticancer drugs such as methotrexate and dactinomycin may be administered. With early treatment the chances of cure of choriocarcinoma are close to 100%.

In view of the high risk of complications, many gynecologists advise more radical treatment of molar pregnancies, and in women over the age of 30 an immediate hysterectomy (surgical removal of the uterus) may be performed. However, in a younger woman such treatment may be unacceptable, since once recovery is complete—and followup for at least a year will be necessary—there is no reason why another, normal pregnancy should not follow.

hydatidosis

Formation of cysts *(hydatids)* in the internal organs due to infestation with the larval stages of the dog tapeworm *(Echinococcus granulosus)*. The condition occurs most often in agricultural communities where dogs mix closely with human families and where the dogs eat raw entrails.

The parasite is transmitted to man by the ingestion of food and water contaminated with the feces of infected animals, by hand-to-mouth transfer of dog feces and through objects soiled with feces. Eggs may survive for several years in farmland, gardens and households.

Ingested eggs hatch in the intestine and the larvae migrate to various organs to produce cysts, most often in the liver and lungs. Less commonly they occur in the kidney, heart, bone, central nervous system and thyroid gland. Humans do not harbor the adult tapeworm, which is about a quarter of an inch long and lives in the intestines of infected dogs.

The symptoms of hydatidosis are variable and depend on the location of the slowly growing cysts. Cysts in the liver may reach a considerable size without causing symptoms. Sometimes there is a "dragging pain" in the abdomen, and pressure on the bile duct may cause jaundice.

When the cyst is in the lungs there may again be no evidence of the disease, except perhaps for a cough and sometimes bloodstained sputum. Long-standing cysts may become calcified. In vital organs the cysts can cause severe symptoms, and may need to be removed surgically.

Effective preventive measures are education of schoolchildren and the public about the hazard and rigid control of the slaughter of herbivorous animals, so that dogs have no access to uncooked entrails.

hydrocele

A translucent swelling in the scrotum caused by the collection of fluid in the sac surrounding a testicle. The cause of hydroceles is not clearly understood; there may be some inflammation of the testicle and its appendages and consequent overproduction of fluid, or diminished resorption because of obstruction of the veins or lymphatics. The fluid is clear, slightly viscid and contains 6–10% of solids, including proteins, salts and sometimes cholesterol.

Surgical treatment may be necessary for a persistent hydrocele. Aspiration of the fluid is a temporary measure but may introduce secondary infection. Recurrence is common. In children, hydrocele is frequently associated with an inguinal hernia.

hydrocephalus

An abnormal collection of cerebrospinal fluid around the brain or in the brain cavities, leading to enlargement of the skull. The condition is known colloquially as "water on the brain." The clear, watery cerebrospinal fluid is normally formed within a cavity (ventricle) in the brain. It passes along a channel (the aqueduct) through the brain substance to reach its surface, where the fluid is

HYDROCEPHALUS

hydrocephalus in a nine-month-old baby

Hydrocephalus, or "water on the brain," is caused by obstruction to the circulation of cerebrospinal fluid in the brain. In babies, the resulting increase in pressure leads to expansion of the head. Hydrocephalus is often present at birth (usually combined with spina bifida), but may occur in an older infant due to a brain tumor (above).

absorbed into the bloodstream.

Hydrocephalus may be congenital due to a defect such as blocking of the aqueduct or acquired from inflammation of the membranes covering the brain. It is often associated with SPINA BIFIDA.

When hydrocephalus afflicts an infant the skull is still distensible and rapid enlargement of the head will take place in the first few weeks of life. The forehead bulges outward and the eyes turn down. If the circulation of cerebrospinal fluid is impaired in an adult the skull does not distend: instead the fluid pressure rises, causing damage to the brain and especially the eyes.

The condition can sometimes be relieved by a drainage operation. For instance, one end of a tube may be placed into a brain space and the other end into the jugular vein (in the neck). A device known as a Spitz-Holter valve (invented by an engineer whose child suffered from hydrocephalus) is included to permit the flow of cerebrospinal fluid out of the brain but prevent the flow of blood into it.

Without drainage, hydrocephalus causes progressive brain damage and may be fatal.

hydrops

The abnormal accumulation of clear fluid in body tissues or cavities.

See EDEMA.

hyperemesis gravidarum

A potentially serious form of MORNING SICKNESS in which excessive vomiting during pregnancy may lead to weight loss and complications such as ACIDOSIS.

Affected patients are typically (but not necessarily) of a highly sensitive or nervous disposition.

In most cases treatment involves only the administration of antiemetic drugs (to control vomiting), rest in bed, mild sedation and special dietary management.

hyperglycemia

The level of sugar in the blood, mainly in the form of glucose, is carefully controlled by a variety of mechanisms, including the action of insulin and other hormones. In DIABETES MELLITUS this control is defective and the blood sugar level rises beyond normal limits, a condition described as *hyperglycemia*.

Above a certain level of blood sugar, the sugar overflows into the urine, producing the condition of GLYCOSURIA; this can be detected with a common urine test. Measurement of the blood sugar level provides a confirmatory test for diabetes and is also valuable in adjusting treatment.

Compare HYPOGLYCEMIA.

hyperparathyroidism

Overactivity of the parathyroid glands, in which parathyroid hormone is produced in amounts greater than normal.

The hormone controls the level of calcium in the blood, and overactivity leads to a rise in blood calcium. If this is marked, the patient complains of lassitude, depression, loss of appetite, weakness, nausea, vomiting, constipation and occasionally excessive thirst. Calcium is removed from the bones; pain and tenderness may follow, and the bones (being fragile) are more prone to fracture. This may lead to diagnosis of the condition, for the x-ray appearances of the bones alter.

Increased excretion of calcium in the urine often leads to the formation of kidney stones; about 5% of patients with kidney stones are likely to show features of hyperparathyroidism.

There are four parathyroid glands, one pair situated on each side of the thyroid gland (see the illustration at THYROID) and are normally about the size of a pea. Overactivity may be due to the development of a tumor of one of the glands (primary hyperparathyroidism) or may be the result of a chronically low level of calcium in the blood—such as occurs in kidney disease or deficient absorption of calcium from the intestine. Treatment of primary hyperparathyroidism is surgical removal of the tumor; treatment of secondary hyperparathyroidism requires correction of the underlying condition. It is possible to raise the blood calcium level by reducing the phosphate level, so that in chronic kidney failure a diet low in protein and phosphorus, with added aluminum hydroxide and vitamin D, may be recommended.

hypertension

The technical name for high blood pressure.

See BLOOD PRESSURE and the major article on **Hypertension.**

hyperthyroidism

Excessive activity of the thyroid gland leading to over-secretion of the thyroid hormone. This produces a characteristic clinical picture first described by Dr. Parry in 1786, and later described independently by Graves and Basedow (who gave their names to the disease). It is also known as *thyrotoxicosis*, *exophthalmic goiter* or *toxic goiter*.

About five times as many women as men are affected; it can occur at any age, with a marked peak between the ages of 20 and 40. The onset of the disease is insidious. It may first be recognized when the condition is made worse by emotional stress, hot weather or an infection. The patient is hot, sweats excessively, and dislikes hot weather and heavy clothes. Sometimes he or she becomes very thirsty, loses weight, suffers from palpitations and breathlessness, becomes anxious and shows a fine tremor of the hands. Emotional instability is common, as is muscular weakness, and the patient may be subject to diarrhea or vomiting. The menstrual periods in female patients may be scanty or absent, and in many cases there is an obvious GOITER. The upper eyelids become drawn up to reveal more of the eye than normal, sometimes being so far retracted that the white of the eye is seen above the cornea. The eyeball itself may move forward in the orbit (its bony casing) and become unduly protuberant; this condition is called *exophthalmos*. Infiltration of the tissues behind the eyeball by white blood cells, as well as edema of the connective tissue, may produce partial paralysis of the muscles that move the eye. It may prove necessary to relieve the condition by a surgical operation to decompress the orbit.

Hyperthyroidism may be treated in three basic ways, all of which are designed to reduce the amount of thyroid hormone circulating in the bloodstream. Part of the thyroid gland may be removed surgically *(partial thyroidectomy)*; a proportion of the cells making up the thyroid gland may be destroyed by radioactive iodine (I^{131}) introduced into the body; or specific drugs can be administered which interfere with the synthesis of thyroid hormone. Antithyroid drugs are commonly tried first; but if they fail and the patient's condition relapses (as it does in about 50% of cases), it may be necessary to remove part of the thyroid surgically, particularly in people under the age of 40. In older patients, the physician may administer carefully calculated doses of radioactive iodine, which are taken up by the thyroid cells and produce partial destruction of the gland over a period of approximately one to three months.

See also HYPOTHYROIDISM.

hypnosis

A passive state of mind induced artificially without the use of drugs during which the subject shows increased obedience to suggestions or even commands.

The hypnotic state is brought about in susceptible subjects by placing them in a quiet environment at rest; they are asked to concentrate on a monotonous stimulus while listening to the voice of the hypnotist, who delivers his "patter" quietly and insistently. It is possible to hypnotize a subject by making him stare at a pin stuck into the wall while a tape recording of the hypnotist's voice is played through a loudspeaker.

About 15% of people cannot be hypnotized, and about 1 in 20 is exceptionally prone to hypnotic suggestion. It is not possible to make a person under hypnosis carry out any order or suggestion that conflicts with his or her conscious or unconscious wishes (although it may be possible to trick him or her into thinking that some harmful act is harmless).

Orthodox medicine makes relatively little use of hypnosis because the depth of hypnosis induced is variable and it takes a fairly long time to hypnotize the patient. Although hypnotic suggestion has produced suppression of pain sufficient to allow the extraction of teeth or the performance of certain surgical operations, it is not a reliable method of anesthesia.

Hypnosis is sometimes used to explore repressed memories in mentally disturbed patients, and it has been used for centuries in the treatment of warts. A carefully controlled series of cases concerned with the treatment of warts was recently published, in which it was suggested to patients that the warts on one side of the body would disappear while those on the other side would remain. Out of 14 patients, 9 showed disappearance of warts on one side of the body. It was thought that the phenomenon was related to the depth of hypnosis induced. In another recent scientific paper, a number of warts on a patient's hands were induced to disappear after treatment by hypnosis for about ten months. The reason for these results is not known.

hypocalcemia

An abnormal decrease in the concentration of free calcium ions in the blood circulation.

Although 98% of the calcium in the body is in the skeleton, the small proportion in the blood is essential to health. Results of hypocalcemia include increased neuromuscular irritability, which may lead to TETANY—cramplike involuntary muscle spasms which often spread to all but the eye muscles. Hypocalcemia may be a sign of HYPOPARATHYROIDISM (a deficiency of the parathyroid hormone), or may arise from kidney failure, OSTEOMALACIA, acute nutritional deficiency, MALABSORPTION and PANCREATITIS—although tetany does not appear in all these diseases. The aim of treatment is, first, to restore calcium to normal levels by supplementary dietary calcium and vitamin D, which relieves the symptoms of the neuromuscular irritability, and second, to correct the underlying cause of the hypocalcemia whenever possible.

See also the major article on **Endocrinology.**

hypochondria

A neurotic preoccupation by a person with his or her general state of health or the condition and function of a particular organ.

Hypochondria is often linked with obsession and depression, and may be a symptom of a specific mental illness. Complaints usually involve the abdominal organs; the patient insists that there is a malady, against all reassurance by the physician. Often he exaggerates the intensity of normal physical sensations, or describes bizarre discomforts. He cannot admit that his troubles are not due to physical lesions, and rarely agrees to seek psychiatric help. He is always liable to damage himself by excessive medication, and in some severe cases there is a risk of suicide.

Hypochondria is a personality disorder that may become manifest from adolescence onward. However, the origins of the disorder may lie in childhood experiences, particularly where illness may have been used successfully as "emotional blackmail" or a device to ensure attention.

hypoglycemia

The level of sugar in the blood, mainly in the form of glucose, is carefully controlled by a number of mechanisms including the action of insulin. In DIABETES MELLITUS lack of insulin causes a rise in the blood sugar level and a number of other disturbances of metabolism appear; treatment by the injection of daily doses of insulin is necessary in many cases.

A potential danger of this treatment, however, lies in the fact that too large a dose of insulin will produce an excessive fall in the blood sugar level, giving rise to a condition known as hypoglycemia. The patient becomes weak, shaky and confused and may, without further warning, lapse into coma.

Reversal of these symptoms may be obtained by giving sugar by mouth in the early stages, but hypoglycemic coma constitutes a serious emergency requiring immediate admission to the hospital in most cases.

Compare HYPERGLYCEMIA.

hypophysectomy

Surgical removal of the pituitary gland. An alternative name for the pituitary gland is the *hypophysis* (or *hypophysis cerebri*); thus the basis for the term *hypophysectomy* (surgical removal of the hypophysis).

The pituitary gland, the size of a pea, is situated beneath the brain behind the eyes. It acts as an intermediary between the brain and the major endocrine glands, controlling the secretion of sex hormones, thyroid hormone, and the adrenal corticosteroids. The pituitary also secretes growth hormone and hormones controlling lactation.

The pituitary may be removed surgically (hypophysectomy) if a tumor forms in the gland—though treatment by radiation therapy is often preferred. It is also removed in some cases of advanced breast cancer

when the tumor has been shown to be hormone-dependent. Whatever the cause, after removal of the pituitary the normal hormone balance of the body needs to be maintained by replacement therapy with synthetic hormones.

hypospadias

A congenital malformation in which the urinary opening is on the underside of the penis.

The urethra fails to extend the full length of the penis and therefore opens somewhere on the undersurface. The further back the opening, the more serious the condition.

Hypospadias occurs with an incidence of about one in every 200 male births.

In mild cases the urethral opening is just under the tip of the penis. No surgical treatment is necessary unless the presence of a fibrous band causes a severe downward curvature of the penis.

The main complication in such cases is the patient's difficulty in directing the urinary stream. He will be capable of normal sexual intercourse, although conception may be difficult since the semen is directed downwards instead of upwards.

When the urethral opening is further back, surgery is only indicated at birth if there is any obstruction to the passage of urine. Otherwise operation is delayed until about two years of age or later. The first procedure is to

HYPOSPADIAS

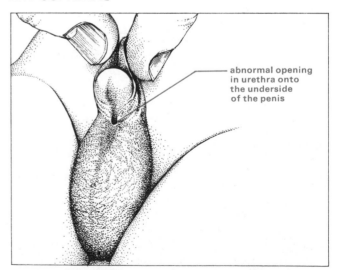

abnormal opening
in urethra onto
the underside
of the penis

During embryonic life the underside of the penis normally closes up like a zipper; hypospadias occurs where this closure is incomplete. Minor degrees of hypospadias do not require treatment, but an opening well down the shaft of the penis interferes with urinary and sexual functions and needs surgical correction.

straighten the shaft of the penis; later, plastic reconstruction of the urethra may be necessary.

Surgical complications include narrowing of the urethra and the development of abnormal routes for the passage of urine, which require further operation.

hypotension

The technical name for low blood pressure.
See BLOOD PRESSURE.

hypothalamus

A very important part of the brain which lies just above the pituitary gland. It is concerned with the vital functions and its integrity is essential for life, for it plays a major part in temperature regulation, sexual function, body weight, fluid balance and blood pressure.

Through the pituitary gland, which produces a wide range of hormones, it influences the activity of the thyroid gland, pancreas, parathyroids, adrenals and the sex glands. The pituitary also produces the growth hormone by which growth in childhood and adolescence is regulated.

It is thought that levels of hormones circulating in the blood are "sensed" by the hypothalamus, which keeps the balance as required through its controlling action on the pituitary. The hypothalamus has complex central connections in the nervous system, and is part of the *limbic system* that controls the physiologic expressions of emotion.

HYPOTHALAMUS

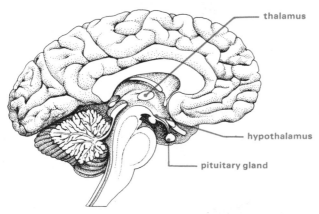

MIDLINE SECTION THROUGH THE BRAIN

The hypothalamus is a structure deep in the brain which regulates many bodily functions. It is linked to the higher centers via the thalamus and exerts its influence mainly by controlling the output of hormones from the pituitary gland. Tumors in the hypothalamus can disturb appetite, emotion, sexual behavior, blood pressure and sleep.

Disease rarely affects the hypothalamus, but it may be involved in tumors growing nearby or in injuries (sometimes surgical). In such cases there may be excessive thirst or water loss (DIABETES INSIPIDUS), excessive food intake, disorders of growth, loss of temperature control and somnolence.

hypothermia

Hypothermia means abnormally low body temperature. The normal body temperature is maintained at 98.6°F (37°C) and fluctuations around this figure are usually small. Falls in body temperature result from deficient heat production by the body or (more commonly) from excessive loss of body heat.

Patients who are in coma or suffering from extreme exhaustion, and in whom physical movement ceases, are in danger of hypothermia if the condition is prolonged and they are not kept warm. Hypothermia from heat loss occurs classically on immersion in cold water. Without protective clothing, a man in water at around 0°C (32°F) may lose consciousness in as little as five minutes and may be dead in 30 minutes; the actual time will vary with body build, movement and other factors. This has been well recognized in shipwreck victims in cold seas but is less well recognized among amateur sailors. Without protective clothing (a "wet suit," for example), the rescue of a crewman from even normal temperate seas is a matter of urgency. Hypothermia is also a threat to hikers, climbers and others who spend long periods outdoors during cold, damp weather.

Still another situation in which dangerous hypothermia occurs is *accidental hypothermia* in the elderly. This affects elderly persons in cold weather who live alone in underheated houses. Symptoms begin when body temperature falls to 95°F (35°C). The patient is listless and confused and makes little or no effort to keep warm. At 86°F (30°C), serious problems appear, with lowered respiration, pulse and blood pressure.

Treatment of hypothermia is by removing the patient to a warmer environment. If this is not possible, body heat must be conserved by wrapping the patient in insulating materials (e.g., "survival bag" for climbers). In serious cases restoration of body heat must be gradual, under medical supervision; sudden reheating, as in a hot bath, may be fatal.

See also *Hypothermia* in the **First Aid** section.

hypothyroidism

Underactivity of the thyroid gland leading to partial or complete deficiency of thyroid hormone in the circulating blood.

The condition may be the result of some congenital defect of the thyroid gland or be associated with a metabolic disorder. It may be divided into *juvenile* and *adult* types. Adult cases commonly occur in people between the ages of 40 and 60, and in the approximate proportion of six women to one man. Hypothyroidism may be accompanied by a GOITER, and it is common in those parts of the world where simple goiter is endemic because of lack of iodine in the diet. If the condition is not accompanied by a goiter, it is now thought to be due to an AUTOIMMUNE DISEASE. It may also occur as a result of radioactive iodine therapy or surgical removal of part of the thyroid gland in cases of overactivity of the thyroid gland (HYPERTHYROIDISM).

Symptoms of hypothyroidism, which are most likely to be felt when the weather is cold, consist of undue tiredness, a feeling of weakness, a hoarse voice and general slowing down of activity. The patient may experience an unusual weight gain, constipation, impaired memory and shortness of breath. Signs include a gradual change in appearance. The skin becomes thickened, particularly in the hands, feet and face (which typically becomes swollen and pale) and there is very little secretion of sweat. The hair becomes dry and coarse and tends to fall out. Occasionally, mental processes are affected and the patient becomes demented. The condition, when fully developed, is called MYXEDEMA; if medical treatment is not provided, the patient becomes cold and may eventually even fall into a coma. Fortunately, if the condition is not too far advanced, myxedema responds to adequate doses of *thyroxine,* the thyroid hormone.

Hypothyroidism in children is more difficult to recognize because the onset is insidious. Symptoms are similar to those found in adults, except that growth is retarded; at first the child may be thought lazy and careless.

Hypothyroid babies, if untreated, become *cretins:* the face is puffy, the nose snub and obstructed, the tongue too large for the mouth and the skin yellowish, cold and thick; the intelligence is diminished (see CRETINISM). Umbilical hernias are common in such babies and may aid in the diagnosis. The sooner treatment is begun with thyroid hormone, the more likely the infant is to recover; but in many cases lack of thyroid secretion in early development leads to permanent intellectual deficiency.

See also the major article on **Endocrinology.**

hypoxia

The condition produced by lack of oxygen. It may be due to lack of sufficient oxygen in the air breathed, as in mountain climbing, flying at high altitudes, or in other conditions where the oxygen supply is restricted.

Even if oxygen is present in normal amounts in the air, hypoxia may still occur if there is disease of the lungs preventing the oxygen from reaching the blood, or if the circulation to the lungs is reduced by heart failure or obstruction of the blood vessels in the lung.

The severely hypoxic patient will be short of breath and may show a bluish tinge to the skin (CYANOSIS) due to an increased proportion of unoxygenated hemoglobin in the blood.

Treatment involves the administration of oxygen by mask or oxygen tent, but the underlying condition must also be treated if lasting relief is to be obtained.

hysterectomy

Surgical removal of the uterus (womb), an operation which while classed as a major operative procedure is not considered dangerous. The uterus may be removed through an incision in the lower part of the abdomen or through the vagina. The most radical operations are carried out for cancer of the womb, and involve removal of not only the uterus but also the Fallopian tubes, the ovaries and the lymphatic glands which drain the area of malignancy. Such complete removals are best carried out through an abdominal incision, but in cases where a less radical clearance is indicated the vaginal approach is used.

The indications for such an operation include fibroid tumors, pelvic infections, endometriosis and excessive uterine hemorrhage. The operation may be advised for a number of other conditions, especially in women past childbearing age, for it is possible to argue that an organ which has no further function is useless and in many cases best removed. Opinion varies, and each case must be assessed on its own merits. Removal of the uterus clearly means that the patient will thereafter be sterile, but adverse physiological effects are kept to a minimum by the preservation of the ovaries where it is possible, and by the vaginal approach which leaves no scar. This approach is doubly indicated in some cases, for it is possible as part of the operation to carry out a repair to the pelvic floor where there is a degree of muscular weakness leading to a rectocele or cystocele. Contrary to popular opinion, sexual desire is not generally lost after the operation.

See also the major article on **Obstetrics and Gynecology.**

hysteria

In its widest definition, hysteria means any excessive emotional response. But psychiatrists prefer to define it as a disorder in which the patient develops symptoms of illness (mental, physical, or both) for subconscious reasons. Typically, the development of hysteria allows the patient to escape from an anxious or threatening life situation.

Hysterical illness may take the form of loss of memory, hysterical fits, or sleepwalking. *Conversion hysteria* takes the form of loss of function of some part of the body. There may be sudden and complete paralysis or loss of sensation in the legs or other parts of the body, blindness, deafness, or vomiting. Such symptoms are dramatic, but they are totally reversible—recovery is just as sudden as the onset of the disability.

The treatment of hysterical symptoms is often delayed while x-rays and laboratory investigations are performed to exclude the possibility that there is an underlying physical disease. Once the psychological basis is clear, treatment may be given with psychotherapy, tranquilizers, and more specific measures to remove the emotional stresses that precipitated the illness.

iatrogenic disorder

Any adverse mental or physical state or condition induced in a patient by his physician's or surgeon's attitudes, words, oversights, actions or treatments.

ichthyosis

A hereditary condition characterized by thick, scaly and very dry skin.

Keratin, the horny substance on the surface of the skin, is normally shed and replaced continuously throughout life. In ichthyosis, there seems to be an imbalance in the rates of replacement and shedding; that is, there is either an overproduction of keratin or it is shed relatively slowly.

The condition usually becomes apparent in the first few weeks or months of life. Mild cases may pass off as merely dry skin, but in severe cases the skin looks like fish skin or alligator hide. The scalp may also be affected, but usually not the palms and soles. Warm weather seems to have a beneficial effect.

Treatment consists of measures like protecting the skin against the cold, avoiding the handling of detergents, and lubricating the skin daily with lanolin or ointments based on petroleum jelly.

In winter it is advisable to have daily or twice daily baths in weak salt water to hydrate the skin, followed immediately by the application of ointments which impede the evaporation of water. Some people claim that vitamin A taken in the winter months is helpful.

All these measures may improve the condition of the skin, but a permanent cure is unlikely.

See also the major article on **Dermatology.**

icterus

Another word for JAUNDICE.

idiopathic disease

Any disease in which the cause is unknown or not clear.

ileitis

Inflammation of the ileum, the third and last part of the small intestine.

By far the most common cause of ileitis is a condition variously called *regional enteritis, regional ileitis* or *Crohn's disease.* Although the ileum is the site most frequently affected by Crohn's disease, any other part of the intestine may be affected, especially the colon.

In Crohn's disease, the inflammation characteristically affects one or more clearly demarcated segments of the intestine, producing rigidity and thickening of the affected length of bowel and a narrowing of the lumen.

The cause of the disease is unknown. It usually starts between the ages of 10 to 40 with intermittent bouts of right-sided lower abdominal pain, accompanied by a low-grade fever and diarrhea alternating with constipation. Sometimes the disease starts with a sudden flareup and may be mistaken for appendicitis, in which case the diagnosis is made at the time of surgical investigation (laparotomy).

In most cases the disease progresses, continuously or intermittently, producing mild to severe disability and complications such as perianal fistulas or fistulas into other organs. Rarely, perforation of the intestine or hemorrhage may occur. In severe and long-standing cases, malnutrition results.

Diagnosis rests on barium studies of the intestine. Treatment consists of rest in bed during the acute phase, with a high-calorie, high-protein and vitamin-rich diet, excluding raw fruit and vegetables. In severe cases, drugs may be given to suppress the inflammation; but if symptoms persist or worsen and complications occur, an operation may be required to remove the affected portions of the intestine.

See also the major article on **Gastroenterology.**

ileostomy

The surgical formation of an opening through the abdominal wall into the ileum (the lower part of the small intestine). The operation is performed whenever the colon has to be removed; the opening then acts as an artificial anus through which the contents of the small intestine are discharged instead of passing along the colon to the natural anus.

The opening does not have muscles like the opening of

ILEOSTOMY

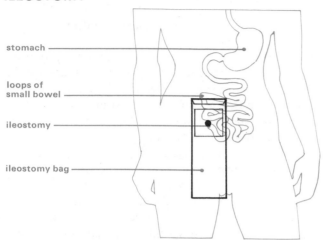

- stomach
- loops of small bowel
- ileostomy
- ileostomy bag

An ileostomy is an opening made in the ileum (the last part of the small bowel) in order to divert fecal material to the exterior, where it is collected in a bag. Ileostomies are necessary where the colon and rectum have been removed.

the natural anus, so patients with ileostomies have to wear a bag continually to collect the excreta. This sounds unpleasant, but in fact an ileostomy is perfectly compatible with a normal life.

The colon (large intestine) absorbs water from the intestinal contents. But the waste products discharged through an ileostomy have not passed along the colon; thus they are watery, especially when the colon is first removed. Later the body adapts and the excreta gradually become more formed, although never completely solid.

Minor dietary modifications, which vary from patient to patient, may be required to alter the consistency of the stools or to reduce odor.

Patients learn how to look after their ileostomies at the hospital where the operation is performed. Additional help may be obtained from the United Ostomy Association or its chapters which exist in all states of the United States.

See also the major article on **Gastroenterology.**

ileus

Paralysis of the intestine. Peristalsis, the wavelike rhythmic movement which propels food, along the gastrointestinal tract, ceases and the effect is a non-mechanical obstruction of the intestine.

The most common cause of ileus is PERITONITIS. Cessation of peristalsis in such a situation helps to localize infection, which could spread very rapidly if peristalsis continued. Another fairly common cause of ileus is an abdominal operation, which usually results in a temporary ileus lasting about 48 hours.

Ileus may also occur when the blood supply to the intestine is cut off, or following severe injuries to the abdomen or spine. Generally, when there is a mechanical obstruction the part of the intestine above the site of obstruction contracts vigorously in an attempt to overcome the obstruction; but if this persists an ileus may result.

The symptoms of ileus are abdominal distension and vomiting. Pain is not a prominent feature.

No food should be taken by mouth when there is an ileus. During this time, the patient is fed intravenously and a tube is passed into the stomach to remove the digestive juices which continue to be secreted. Salts lost in this way have to be replaced in the intravenous feeds. If there is peritonitis, antibiotics are essential. Otherwise treatment is that of the underlying cause of the ileus.

immune system

The body's defense mechanism against "foreign invaders."

The most common are infectious microorganisms, which are obviously a different species from humans. But human tissue may also be treated as foreign when it is introduced for medical reasons, such as occurs with blood transfusions (blood is technically one of the "tissues" of the body), skin grafting, or organ transplantation. This is because every individual is born with a set of "identification marks" or "immune markers" which makes his body regard any tissue that contains different markers as foreign or "non-self."

There are numerous possible combinations of the markers which make up an individual's set; that is why it is so difficult to find a suitable donor who is immunologically compatible with a patient who requires a transplant.

Since the markers are inherited, the chances of finding a compatible donor (or the least incompatible donor) are better among the patient's relatives. (The ideal donor would be the patient's identical twin.) Compatibility or a good match between two individuals is determined by tests known as tissue typing.

These markers, which are found on the surface of cells, are called *antigens*. An individual's immune system is quick to recognize any foreign marker and responds by the production of *antibodies*.

Antibodies are substances which counteract antigens; they are produced by lymphocytes (a type of white blood cell). Each type of antibody is formed in response to invasion by a particular antigen and is able to act only against that type of antigen.

In *circulating* or *humoral* immunity, antibodies are released into the circulation and travel around the body. Their primary role is defense against infection by bacteria, which they attack so that they can be more easily engulfed and digested by special cells known as phagocytes.

Some bacteria, such as the tubercle and leprosy bacilli, are able to live and grow within the cell which has engulfed them. In such cases the body has another immune mechanism, called *cellular* immunity, for dealing with them. In the newborn and during early childhood special lymphocytes are processed in the thymus gland (in the neck) to enable them to carry antibodies on their surface. They migrate to the area where they are needed, to surround and help to overcome the "invader."

This cellular (or "cell-mediated" or "delayed") immunity is responsible for rejecting transplants.

Several conditions arise from disorders of the immune system. Allergies, for example, are the result of an unusually sensitive immune system; people with allergies are more likely to react badly to immunization or to develop drug reactions.

On the other hand, those with abnormalities of the thymus or of the lymphocytes have a very poor immune response, the most important effect of which is a high susceptibility to infection.

The immune system may be depressed by a number of chronic debilitating diseases, including cancer and chronic kidney failure. It may also be suppressed by a number of drugs known collectively as *immunosuppressive* agents. These drugs are useful in the treatment of a variety of conditions, but patients receiving them become very prone to infections.

An abnormality of the immune system is believed to be responsible for a group of diseases known as the *autoimmune* disorders, which include the COLLAGEN DISEASES. They are currently thought to be due to an allergy to one's own tissues, but are not yet well understood.

IMMUNIZATION is the deliberate stimulation of antibody production. The infecting organism (in a modified form) is introduced into the body, which begins almost immediately to form antibodies against it. These antibodies, in common with those produced in response to natural invasion, remain in the circulation for some time (often for life) and are therefore ready in case the actual disease should attack.

It is a feature of the immune system that a second attack by an antigen is always repulsed more vigorously than the first attack—because the antibodies are ready and the body has "learned" to make more of that particular antibody quickly. Subsequent attacks are repulsed even more efficiently. This can be an advantage in that it prevents second attacks of certain diseases, but it can be a disadvantage in that allergies can produce increasingly severe attacks with every exposure.

See also the major article on **Allergy and Immunology.**

immunization

The process by which resistance to infection is artificially induced.

Normally the body resists infection by producing substances called antibodies, which act against infectious organisms. Each infectious organism has on its body surface a substance called an antigen which the body recognizes as "foreign." Whenever an infectious agent invades the body, the body starts to produce antibodies against this type of organism. The antibodies produced are released into the blood circulation so that they can reach the site of infection.

Each type of organism has its own particular type of antigen, and antibodies produced in response to infection by one type are specific only against that type of antigen. (See ANTIBODY/ANTIGEN.)

Often after recovery from an infection sufficient antibody remains in the circulation to protect against further infection by the same organism. This type of resistance is known as *naturally acquired immunity*.

Artificial immunization can be produced in two ways, active and passive. In active immunization the antibodies are produced in response to antigens deliberately introduced into the body, usually by injection but sometimes by swallowing. These antigens may come in the form of dead organisms, or organisms so weakened (by laboratory methods) that they cannot cause disease but can stimulate antibody production.

If the disease is caused by toxins (poisons) produced by infectious organisms, *antitoxin* production may be artificially stimulated by injecting chemically modified toxins, known as *toxoids*.

In *passive immunization*, ready-made antibodies against a particular organism are injected. These antibodies may have come from the blood of someone who has previously been infected or immunized, or from animals which have been deliberately immunized so that their antibodies can be harvested for use in passive immunization. Passive immunization provides quicker but only temporary immunity. Active immunization may require a few weeks before antibodies are produced, but the effect is longer-lasting, the degree and duration of immunity varying with different diseases. Sometimes the antigen has to be given in two or three doses to ensure the production of a reasonable quantity of antibody.

Immunization may sometimes produce unpleasant reactions, but this varies with the type of immunization. People who have allergies are more likely to suffer from adverse reactions.

Immunization against several specific diseases of childhood is advisable; not only does this protect the individual child, but it protects the whole community, because if a large proportion of the susceptible population is immune to a disease an epidemic cannot get under way—so that even those who are not, or cannot be, immunized are to some extent protected.

See also *Current immunization practices* in the major article on **The Health Care of Children.**

The age at which a child gives the best response to a vaccine varies with the type of immunization, and the following plan is one that is considered by the American Academy of Pediatricians to be suitable:

At two months: first dose of vaccine against diphtheria, tetanus and pertussis (whooping cough), all of which are given as a combined injection; and first dose of polio vaccine, which is usually given as a drop of liquid taken on a lump of sugar.

At four and six months, respectively: the second and third doses against diphtheria, tetanus, pertussis and polio.

At 15 months: immunize against measles, rubella and mumps.

At 18 months and between four and six years: booster doses against diphtheria, tetanus, pertussis and polio.

Between 14 and 16 years: combined tetanus and diphtheria toxoids, and then every ten years thereafter. However, if an open wound is sustained which is severe enough to justify additional tetanus toxoid booster at the time of injury, the subsequent ten-yearly doses can be calculated from the time a dose has been given following injury.

Smallpox vaccination should no longer be given routinely to all children in the United States. However, smallpox vaccination may still be required when traveling to certain other countries where there is a risk of infection (although the World Health Organization claims that smallpox has now been virtually eliminated throughout the world). Other infections for which immunization is required when traveling include cholera, yellow fever, plague and typhoid. The requirements vary from time to time and from country to country.

Prospective travelers may obtain information from shipping and airline offices, state and local health departments, or from branches of the U.S. Public Health Service. Inquiries should be made and vaccination obtained several weeks in advance of leaving the United States, partly because vaccination certificates become valid only 6–10 days after the vaccination (depending on type of vaccination) and because, if more than one vaccination is required, it might be wise to allow a two-week interval between vaccinations. It is also wise to inquire about what type of immunization is required for specific reentry into the United States.

impetigo

A highly contagious bacterial infection of the superficial layers of the skin. The organism most commonly re-

sponsible for the infection is the *Staphylococcus aureus;* less frequently, the infection is caused by streptococci. Impetigo may occur at any age, but is most common in the newborn and in children.

The lesions start as a reddening of the skin, but soon become clusters of blisters and pustules which break to leave sores with straw-colored or honey-colored crusts. The only symptom is itching. The lesions may be found anywhere on the body, but are most common over the face and limbs.

Treatment should be started promptly or the infection may spread rapidly to other areas of the skin. In babies, especially those who are ill or are premature, the infection may spread to other structures such as the bones or lungs. Occasionally, nephritis (inflammation of the kidneys) occurs a few weeks after the skin infection has settled.

Treatment consists of rupturing the blisters and pustules, and of removing the crusts by washing gently with water and an antiseptic agent. If necessary, the crusts may have to be soaked with wet dressings to make them easier to remove. Antibiotics are applied locally to the lesions, but if there is no improvement in three or four days, or if the infection is severe, antibiotics may have to be given by mouth or by injection.

To prevent the spread of infection to other areas of the skin or to other people, the patient should wash his hands frequently and take care not to touch or scratch the lesions.

impotence

The inability to attain or sustain erection of the penis in the presence of sexual desire.

Transient impotence is fairly common and does not imply a physical or psychological disorder. It is often related to mild degrees of anxiety, depression, preoccupation, or fatigue associated with ordinary problems of daily living.

Chronic impotence, on the other hand, is due to either physical or psychological reasons; emotional problems account for an estimated 90% of cases.

Physical factors should be ruled out first. These include aging (it has been estimated that 50% of men over the age of 65 are impotent), chronic debilitating disease, alcoholism, drug addiction, diabetic neuropathy, disease of the nervous system (such as spinal cord damage and multiple sclerosis), endocrine disorders (such as those of the pituitary gland, the thyroid or the gonads), damage to the urethra, and large hydroceles or hernias. Various drugs, including certain antihypertensive drugs, antidepressants and tranquilizers, may produce impotence in some men; the problem is solved when the drug is discontinued.

Whether or not impotence due to physical factors can

be treated depends on the underlying cause. If it is due to hormonal imbalance, improvement is usually possible; but if the nerves are affected, little can be done.

Psychological reasons for chronic impotence often include guilt and anxiety about the sexual act itself, hostility toward the partner, unwillingness to assume responsibility for all that goes with marriage and children, a mother fixation, or various neurotic tendencies. Psychosexual counseling may help.

incontinence

Lack of voluntary control over urination and bowel movements.

Incontinence is normal in young children, since voluntary control must be learned. It is usually achieved by the age of three, although some physically normal children do not become fully continent until five or six—or occasionally, in the case of urinary incontinence, not until the late teens. After this age urinary or fecal incontinence is often due to disease, such as cystitis, or to psychological reasons.

In adult life loss of control over urination may occur as a result of injuries to the mother during childbirth which weaken the muscles of the pelvic floor; this may also occur during pregnancy, or may be the result of surgical operations on the urethra or prostate gland. It may also occur when obstruction to the passage of urine leads to retention of urine in the bladder, with eventual overflow.

Neurological conditions and damage to the spinal cord may lead to loss of control over the passage of both urine and feces by interruption of the nervous pathways which control these functions. The elderly may become incontinent because of lack of sensation or confusion. In some cases severe constipation leads to the retention of hard masses of feces which cause irritation and obstruction, with the development of a paradoxical uncontrollable diarrhea. Such causes of apparent incontinence of feces are liable to be overlooked.

Treatment depends on the cause and may involve the administration of certain drugs, or surgery. When cure is not possible, incontinence bags may be used; however, no satisfactory bag has yet been devised for females. Sometimes mechanical or electronic devices are used to increase the pressure around the urethra to prevent the escape of urine, but all of these are still subject to various disadvantages.

See also BEDWETTING and the section on *The incontinent patient* in the **Guide to Home Nursing Care.**

indigestion

A popular term used to describe a multitude of vague symptoms thought to be associated with food intake or otherwise arising in the digestive system. Also called *dyspepsia.*

Indigestion is a nonspecific term that has a different meaning for different people. It may be used to mean abdominal discomfort, fullness, pressure, pain, heartburn, belching, distension, flatulence or nausea. Some even use it to mean constipation or diarrhea.

All these symptoms may be produced by disease in the gastrointestinal tract. Thus, if symptoms are severe or persist, a doctor should be consulted. Often, however, they are the result of consistently poor eating habits. They may also sometimes be psychogenic in origin, especially in those who always complain of "nervousness," or who are very bowel-conscious and frequently resort to laxatives. Eating habits which give rise to indigestion include overeating, gulping down food, or eating when the appetite is depressed by anger or worry.

A person may notice that certain foods bring on symptoms. There may be a reason for this. It could be that the person lacks the enzyme which deals with the digestion of that particular foodstuff; for example, people who lack lactase may get "indigestion" with milk which contains lactose. In such cases, which can be confirmed by special tests, the offending food should be avoided. But in most cases all that is necessary to avoid indigestion is to take regular, unhurried meals.

Often indigestion is due to increased quantities of gas in the gastrointestinal tract. Most of this gas is swallowed, the rest being produced by bacterial fermentation of carbohydrate and proteins—often from raw fruit and vegetables. Swallowing of air (aerophagia) is normal, but with chronic anxiety or poor eating habits more air tends to be swallowed. Fatty meals may aggravate symptoms due to gas because they slow down emptying of the stomach, so delaying the passage of gas down the gastrointestinal tract.

If there is no recognized disease causing the symptoms, and regulating the eating habits does not help, a number of drugs may relieve symptoms—usually those which neutralize gastric acid (antacids) or those which calm the gut. Rarely, psychotherapy may help.

induction of childbirth

The use of artificial means to start off the process of childbirth, or labor. This is sometimes carried out when it appears safer for the fetus or mother that pregnancy be terminated as soon as possible. The timing should be such that the fetus is mature enough to have at least as good a chance of survival outside the uterus (even if in an incubator) as inside it.

Sometimes labor is induced not for obstetric problems, but so that it can take place at a convenient time for both mother and doctor. The desirability of such induced abortions is highly debatable.

Labor can be induced in two basic ways. One is the use of drugs, given intravenously, to stimulate the uterus to contract. The other is artificial rupture of the membranes surrounding the fetus. The release of fluid produced by rupture of the membranes sets off uterine contractions. Sometimes artificial rupture of membranes is used in conjunction with induction by drugs.

Induction of labor carries some risk. The uterus may respond to induction by contracting too violently (in which case the uterus may even rupture), or it may not respond sufficiently. The fetus may turn out to be too premature, or it may not withstand the process of childbirth and show signs of FETAL DISTRESS. If the membranes have been ruptured, there is also a risk of infection. Thus, very careful observation of mother and fetus has to take place throughout an induced labor and, if necessary, a Cesarean section may have to be carried out if things do not go well.

See also CHILDBIRTH and the major article on **Pregnancy and Childbirth.**

infarct/infarction

An *infarct* is an area of dead tissue (see NECROSIS) surrounded by healthy tissue, caused by a blockage of blood flow to the affected area. In addition to meaning the same as infarct, *infarction* also refers to the formation of an infarct or the process which leads to it.

When the heart muscle is the site of the infarct, the condition is known as a *myocardial infarction* ("heart attack"). Most infarcts are caused by interruption of the blood flow by a thrombus or embolus (see EMBOLUS/EMBOLISM, THROMBOSIS/THROMBUS).

infectious mononucleosis

An acute viral infection, also known as *glandular fever.* It is caused by the *Epstein-Barr virus,* which is present worldwide. Some cases are associated with cytomegalovirus infection. Most infections with the Epstein-Barr virus occur in childhood and usually go unrecognized; the virus may be found in the throats of healthy people.

Infectious mononucleosis can affect any age group, but most commonly those between 10 and 35. The incubation period is uncertain but probably lies between four to seven weeks. The mode of spread is also uncertain, but there is evidence that it is transmitted in the saliva either by kissing or by sharing drinking vessels. The virus remains in the patient's throat for several months after recovery.

The disease affects many parts of the body and manifests itself in a number of ways. The typical patient has fever, a general feeling of being unwell (malaise), loss of appetite, aches and pains all over the body, enlarged lymph nodes felt as slightly painful lumps

(particularly around the neck) and a sore throat. Approximately half the patients have a rash; half may also have an enlarged spleen, which does not produce symptoms but which can be felt (palpated) by the doctor. About 5–25% have jaundice, and in a smaller proportion the heart, kidney or lungs may be affected without producing symptoms, although the involvement can be detected by laboratory tests. In a smaller proportion still, the nervous system is affected and patients may develop meningitis, encephalitis or neuritis.

Because of the wide variety of ways in which the disease presents itself, blood tests may be required before the diagnosis can be confirmed. As the name suggests, the blood contains atypical *mononuclear cells.*

There is no specific treatment for the disease. Bed rest is advisable until the fever disappears, and mild antipyretics and analgesics (such as aspirin) may be given to bring down the fever and to relieve aches and pains. Gargles may relieve the sore throat.

In uncomplicated cases, the fever settles in about ten days and the enlarged lymph nodes and enlarged spleen return to normal in about four weeks. In some cases the disease may linger on for months. Those who have had jaundice should avoid alcohol for about six months. Recovery is usually complete.

See also the major article on **Infectious Diseases.**

infertility

The inability to conceive. In general, infertility can be suspected if pregnancy has not occurred after a year of regular sexual intercourse (without the use of any form of contraception).

The cause of infertility may lie in the male or the female. There are numerous causes of infertility in each sex; sometimes no cause is ever found.

Investigations for causes in the male are safer and simpler; consequently, they are normally performed first to save the woman a series of tests if a cause can be found in the male. Doctors do not ordinarily rush through all the investigations but space them out over six months or so, because sometimes a pregnancy occurs for no apparent reason during the course of investigations.

The cause of infertility may be either structural or due to functions of the reproductive system. There may be no production of sperm or ova, or for some reason the two may not meet to bring about fertilization. Some causes are treatable, with varying degrees of success, by either surgery or drugs. Individual cases should be discussed with a medical expert, who will explain the possibility of any complications associated with the investigations and treatment and the chances of success.

General ill-health, especially chronic diseases or

endocrine abnormalities, can cause infertility. Where no cause can be found, simple measures like reducing obesity or improving physical fitness may help.

Sometimes the oral contraceptive pill produces a period of infertility in women when they stop taking it; this is nearly always temporary.

See also *Infertility* in the major article on **Family Planning**.

inflammation

The way in which living tissue responds to injury—usually to injury by an infectious agent, although the same response is seen with physical, chemical or radiation injuries. It is essentially a protective mechanism by which the tissues attempt to localize infection.

The blood vessels around the site of injury dilate and their walls become permeable, so that white blood cells can leave the vessel and migrate to the site of injury—where they either ingest the infecting organism or release chemical substances to digest damaged tissue.

Local inflammation produces swelling, heat, redness, pain and loss of function of the affected part. Sometimes the effects of inflammation are seen beyond the site of damage, as fever or as changes in the numbers and types of circulating white blood cells.

An acute inflammation usually heals completely, but sometimes a scar results.

influenza

An acute viral infection of the respiratory tract, with symptoms present elsewhere in the body. It can affect people at any age. The consequences in the very young, the elderly, the debilitated, and those with heart or lung disease are particularly dangerous. The infection is spread when infected droplets discharged by an infected person during speaking, coughing or sneezing are inhaled by an uninfected person. There is an incubation period of one to four days before symptoms appear.

Symptoms appear abruptly and include fever, chills, a dry cough, nasal stuffiness, a running nose, aches and pains all over the body, a sore throat, headache, loss of appetite, nausea, weakness and depression. Mild cases may resemble a common cold, although the weakness and depression are usually greater.

As with viral infections in general, there is no specific drug treatment for influenza. General measures include rest in bed during the acute phase, followed by a gradual resumption of normal activity. If required, a mild antipyretic and analgesic may be taken to relieve symptoms. In uncomplicated cases, symptoms usually subside within a week.

Influenza reduces the patient's resistance to bacterial infection; superimposed bacterial bronchitis is a com-

mon complication, which if untreated may lead to pneumonia. Other bacterial complications include sinusitis and infections of the middle ear (otitis media).

If the fever persists more than four days and purulent (pus-containing) sputum is brought up on coughing, it is advisable to see a doctor—who may prescribe antibiotics if he feels that a bacterial infection is imminent or is already established. Occasionally, the circulatory system is involved and the heart muscle (myocardium) or its outer covering (pericardium) may be inflamed—producing *myocarditis* or *pericarditis,* respectively.

The simplest way of minimizing the possibility of an attack is to avoid crowds during an epidemic. Some people claim that taking large doses of vitamin C regularly helps to prevent an attack and to reduce the severity of symptoms, but the consensus of medical opinion discredits this.

An attack of influenza confers immunity to the particular strain to which the infecting virus belongs. A temporary immunity to one or more strains can be acquired by injection of a vaccine prepared against those strains. Such vaccines take about two weeks after the injection to become effective; it is useless to have the injection once symptoms have appeared. Thus, immunization against influenza is usually given in the autumn to protect against attacks during the winter when influenza is most common.

Routine immunization is not generally advised for everyone, an exception being 1976 when it was feared in the United States that *Swine flu,* which caused a serious epidemic in the early part of the century, might re-emerge. Most doctors advise immunization only for those who are particularly susceptible. Unfortunately, immunization against known strains of influenza virus do not protect against new strains which crop up periodically and are responsible for the epidemics which appear every few years.

See also the major article on **Infectious Diseases**.

ingrowing nails

A condition in which the sides of the nail are more curved than usual and grow into the flesh of the nail groove. Although any nail may be affected, usually it is the nail of the big toe which becomes painful. The nail fold is unusually prominent and appears to ride up around the nail as pressure is placed on the toe.

Ingrowth is caused by badly fitting shoes or by cutting the nails too short. It can be prevented by cutting the nail carefully—so that the sides are a little longer than the middle, but without leaving a sharp spicule at the corner. The nail should be left just long enough to project from the nail groove.

If there is pain, the nail should be gently lifted out of the groove by elevating it with a sharp pair of scissors or

INGROWING TOENAIL

nail growing into skin fold

incorrect cutting— too short and curved

correct cutting— straight across, not too short

An ingrowing nail of the big toe results from a combination of sweaty feet, tight shoes and incorrect cutting. In most cases, correct cutting as shown above will relieve the condition. If unchecked, the top corner of the toenail grows into the skin fold which runs along the side of the nail; this can become infected.

the tip of a nail file placed just under the nail at the outer corner. This should be done for a few minutes each day to encourage the nail to grow out of the groove. Shoes should be roomy.

Toes with ingrown nails are very prone to chronic infection. The nail fold becomes intermittently swollen, red and painful and may discharge pus, while the nail lacks luster and becomes brownish and crumbly. This condition should be treated by a doctor. If antibiotics do not help, the nail may have to be removed. A complete nail will grow again in nine months to a year and should be carefully observed to see that it does not become ingrown again.

insulin

A hormone produced in the PANCREAS and responsible for the control of several body functions, especially carbohydrate metabolism.

Insulin helps the muscles and other tissues to obtain the sugar needed for their activity. A gross deficiency leads to DIABETES MELLITUS, in which the blood sugar is not used by the body and builds up to undesirable levels.

The existence of insulin as an essential component of metabolism was suspected as early as 1909. It was finally isolated in relatively pure form by the two Canadians, Banting and Best, in 1921.

Medical insulin is prepared from the pancreas of sheep or cattle and is injected daily in severe cases of diabetes. Many types of insulin are now available; they differ mainly in the duration of their action. It is estimated that insulin has saved over 30 million lives since it was introduced as a therapy for diabetics.

See also the major article on **Endocrinology.**

intelligence quotient (IQ)

A presumed measure of the intelligence of an individual as compared with the total population. The IQ of a person is obtained by means of a suitable series of tests to calculate his mental age, which is then divided by his chronological age and multiplied by 100 to give the IQ. Thus, a person whose mental age is 12 at a chronological age of 10 will be deemed to have an IQ of 120. This means that the IQ of a person of "normal" intelligence will naturally be taken as 100; about half the population score below 100 and the other half above.

Intelligence tests attempt to establish the mental ability of the subject in a number of different fields. Such matters as vocabulary, arithmetic, ability to reason, general knowledge and (somewhat less successfully) creativity are tested by the application of a battery of tests worked out by psychologists. Many intelligence tests now used in the United States and other Western countries have evolved from the pioneering work of the French psychologists Alfred Binet (1857–1911) and Théodore Simon (1873–1961).

In general, the IQ allocated to a child as a result of undergoing intelligence tests correlates well with later achievement in academic work. There is a less close correlation with achievement in later life, presumably because other qualities such as drive and acumen may be as important as sheer intelligence in one's working life.

IQ allocations are also under fire because some critics

INSULIN

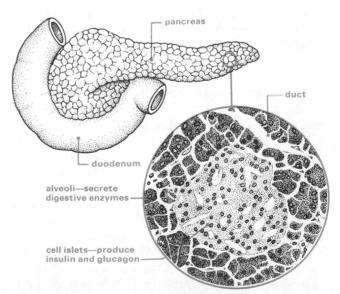

pancreas

duct

duodenum

alveoli—secrete digestive enzymes

cell islets—produce insulin and glucagon

The pancreas is a mixed-function gland. It secretes digestive enzymes through ducts into the duodenum where they break down fats and proteins. It also secretes hormones, most importantly insulin, directly into the bloodstream.

claim that the tests, having been designed by literate, numerate, middle-class white psychologists, do not adequately test the intelligence of children from other sectors of the community. In the most modern tests attempts are made to correct imbalances due to language barriers, reading disabilities or cultural differences. Nevertheless, the use of intelligence tests remains a somewhat controversial subject.

intensive care unit (ICU)

A unit in which especially intense surgical and medical care can be given to patients—widely used in caring for patients in the first few days after suffering from acute myocardial infarction ("heart attack").

Although the use of ICUs has been greatly increased by the application of the principle to the care of coronary patients, and in many people's minds ICUs are identified solely with heart attacks, their use is much more widespread.

ICUs are used to support surgical patients postoperatively, to keep accident victims alive until surgery can be performed on them, and to enable premature babies to survive the first few days of life. They also play a large part in the treatment of burns when the victims are critically ill and cannot undergo surgery until the crisis is over.

In general, it can be said that the objectives of an ICU are the initiation of resuscitation, the administration of electrolytes and fluids, and the prevention of contamination and cross-infection. ICUs designed to deal with coronary patients are usually equipped with a respirator and defibrillator as the basic equipment, and it has been observed that they have been helpful in decreasing the mortality rate from acute myocardial infarction due to the arrhythmias.

As an aid to the main task of keeping the patient alive, ICUs are commonly equipped with a number of monitoring devices; these are designed to keep the medical and nursing staff informed of the state of the patient's heart by displaying his ECG in various ways. An ICU will commonly have facilities for inserting pacemakers in cases where arrhythmias occur, and catheterization of the heart for diagnostic purposes is also common.

The proper use of ICUs has been an important factor in improving survival from heart attacks. The major problem which has arisen is a psychological one, called the "ICU syndrome." It is said to be a confused and agitated state of consciousness possibly related to sensory deprivation. A patient may become emotionally disturbed by the extensive electronic equipment around him, by being in a windowless room, or by hearing cardiac catastrophes occurring to nearby patients. Family and friends are advised to avoid business or other worrying discussions with patients, who should be given daily newspapers, possibly a radio, a clock and a calendar to prevent a feeling of isolation.

intermittent claudication

An intermittent cramp in the muscles of the leg brought on by exercise such as walking. It is caused by reduction in the blood supply of the muscles of the leg brought about by narrowing or obstruction of the arteries supplying the leg. The pain disappears swiftly with rest.

The disease affects nine times more men than women and is most common after the age of 50 to 55. Diabetics are particularly at risk, as are people with high levels of cholesterol in the blood.

The calf muscle is affected most often, but pain may also appear in the buttock and thigh. Other symptoms include tightness, numbness and severe fatigue in the muscles being exercised. The pain of claudication is due to the leg muscles not receiving sufficient oxygen via the blood to work properly. In severe cases the leg may become swollen with dry, shiny, tightly drawn skin. Ulceration may then become a problem.

Diagnosis is helped by the absence or lessening of pulses below the point of obstruction. X-rays usually enable the doctor to pinpoint the exact site of arterial damage. In mild cases the patient is advised to lose weight, walk more slowly (but more often), and give up smoking. If the intermittent claudication worsens, or the condition of the affected limb deteriorates, the diseased section of artery may be replaced surgically by a graft of the patient's own blood vessel or synthetic material. Considering the age of these patients, the outlook for prolonged survival is reasonably good.

intersexuality

The state of being intermediate between the sexes; having both male and female characteristics. (The term is descriptive rather than diagnostic.)

Sexual differentiation is determined in the fetus. In the sixth week of gestation the simple gonads begin to develop into testicles if the fetus has male chromosomes. Alternatively, they develop into ovaries in the twelfth week when the fetus has female chromosomes.

Various events may affect this process of differentiation and lead to intersexuality. In the ADRENOGENITAL SYNDROME, the male hormone testosterone is produced by abnormally functioning adrenocortical glands; a girl is born with either an enlarged clitoris or a normal penis with an empty scrotum. A female fetus may also be "virilized" when her mother has a tumor that produces male hormones, or is given progestin treatment (now obsolete). Lack of a specific substance in the fetus may result in a boy being born with a redundant uterus and Fallopian tubes.

Any condition in which the sexual anatomy is improperly or incompletely differentiated is an example of intersexuality. Treatment demands consideration of both psychological and physical factors. Experience over the past few decades has shown that it is not always correct to assign an individual to the sex indicated by the chromosomes. Surgery to correct the anomalies of the sexual organs may be performed at any time; a boy with abnormally small or underdeveloped genital organs (hypogonadism) may have been brought up as a girl and after surgical removal of the genitals may grow to maturity as a woman.

Every case of intersexuality is different and should receive the combined diagnostic and therapeutic expertise of a physician, an endocrinologist and a psychiatrist—as well as a surgeon, in selected patients.

intertrigo

Chafing of the skin where two surfaces, usually moist, rub together.

As a result of the chafing, erythema (redness) or dermatitis (skin inflammation) of the surfaces may occur. Intertrigo may be a particular problem in young infants, since the child does not detect the chafing. The most common sites are the natural folds of skin in the groin, armpits and elbows. Elderly obese people with a greater than normal overlap of tissues may also be especially susceptible.

In general, the condition may be encountered wherever clothes cause pressure or friction, or when individuals walk for long distances.

Retroauricular intertrigo is an inflammatory condition of the skin that develops in the fold where the ear joins the scalp. A painful crack may appear and is sometimes extremely persistent.

Seborrheic intertrigo, a condition similar to retroauricular intertrigo, arises from chafing under heavy breasts or in the folds of the buttocks. Between the scrotum and the thigh is another common site where intertrigo may appear.

Prevention of chafing is best accomplished by keeping the skin clean and dry. Warm water with "superfatted" soap should be used, after which the skin should be carefully dried and sprinkled with dusting powder, such as talcum powder or a mixture of starch, zinc and subnitrate of bismuth. Intertrigo may be aggravated by a fungus infection, which can later become complicated with a secondary bacterial infection.

intoxication

The condition produced by the presence of poison in the body. In everyday speech, intoxication usually refers to the effects of alcohol. In this condition the subject exhibits some or all of the classic symptoms of slurred speech, unsteadiness, nausea, vomiting, unconsciousness and amnesia, according to the stage reached.

Intoxication in severe cases may long outlast a night's sleep, so giving rise to the well-known hangover. It may be said to begin when the alcohol level reaches about 50 milligrams per 100 milliliters of blood, but some people tolerate alcohol more than others, so no universal rule can be applied.

In general terms, intoxication can be used to describe any case of poisoning in which either physical or mental symptoms appear. It may arise from the introduction of any poison externally administered, or in cases of *autointoxication* from toxins secreted by bacteria in the body.

Treatment for intoxication will obviously vary with the circumstances. For all but the most severe cases of alcohol intoxication an undisturbed night's sleep is probably the best treatment. However, alcohol can be fatal if taken in very large quantities. If it is suspected, for instance, that more than a fifth of whiskey has been consumed, it might be thought necessary to apply a stomach pump under medical supervision. In the case of a chronic alcoholic, even such large amounts might be easily tolerated, although not without deleterious long-term effects on the body and mind.

In other cases medical help should be sought and the doctor given all relevant information as to the poison ingested. Bottles, cans or other containers should be handed over to him for identification of their contents.

intrauterine device

A contraceptive device placed in the uterus, several types of which are available.

Also known as an *intrauterine contraceptive device,* an *IUD,* or an *IUCD.* See also CONTRACEPTION.

intrinsic factor

A substance produced by the lining of the stomach which is essential for the absorption of vitamin B_{12}. Intrinsic factor combines with the vitamin to produce an antianemic substance. Because the daily requirement of vitamin B_{12} is so small (1 or 2 micrograms or millionths of a gram), deficiency of this vitamin is almost invariably due to a breakdown of the absorption mechanism. This may be caused by a failure of the stomach to secrete intrinsic factor; or the cells that normally secrete the factor may be replaced by a tumor; or they may be cut out when part of the stomach is removed surgically.

Lack of intrinsic factor for any of these reasons is thought to lead to the type of ANEMIA known as *pernicious anemia*—which can be fatal if the patient is not treated with vitamin B_{12}, iron and a balanced diet.

intubation

The introduction of a tube into a body orifice. The term is usually used to mean the introduction of a tube through the mouth or nose into the windpipe in order to maintain an adequate air passage into the lungs. It is carried out in general anesthesia, in cases of unconsciousness due to other causes, and in cases where the breathing is obstructed.

Gastric intubation, the passage of a tube into the stomach through the esophagus, is necessary in some cases of obstruction to the esophagus or of paralysis of the mechanism of swallowing. It is used in cases of intestinal obstruction so that the contents of the stomach can be aspirated. It is also used to wash the stomach out in cases of poisoning. A gastric tube is passed before operation in many cases of abdominal surgery to guard against regurgitation of gastric contents into the lungs in an unconscious patient.

See also the major article on **Gastroenterology.**

intussusception

A condition in which one part of the intestine becomes pushed or telescoped into another portion.

It occurs mainly in infants under one year and usually starts at the lower end of the ileum. Overactive wave contractions (peristalsis) of the intestine may be the cause of the condition, driving a loop of the bowel into the one below. The same peristaltic movements may aggravate the condition so that more intestine becomes involved.

Intussusception results in sudden intestinal obstruction, causing severe abdominal pain. The infant has attacks of screaming and draws up its legs. The face becomes very pale when the pain is most intense and brightens in the intervals between spasms. Vomiting starts early and is severe and repeated. After the first bowel movement the infant passes only red jelly-like clots of pure blood and mucus from the bowel.

Examination of the abdomen by the doctor usually reveals a sausage-like mass.

Prompt surgical treatment is necessary to pull the telescoped portion of the intestine back to its normal position. If, as happens in some cases, the intestine is gangrenous, surgical removal of the affected part is necessary.

In adults, intussusception occasionally occurs due to ADENOMA or other abnormality.

iridectomy

Surgical removal of a portion of the iris of the eye. Several types of iridectomy are performed depending on the nature and state of the complaint.

The function of the iris is to act like the adjustable stop of a camera which controls the amount of light allowed to penetrate to the light-sensitive film; it lets in a controlled amount of light to the retina.

A portion of iris is removed to improve sight when for some reason the pupil becomes obscured, or when there is another disease which the procedure may improve.

There are a number of types of iridectomy operation: *basal* or *peripheral,* when a small portion of iris is removed from the base or periphery; *buttonhole,* when only a small portion is removed; *broad,* excision of a large area of the iris including the edge of the pupil, leaving a keyhole type of appearance; *complete,* when the section removed includes the entire width of the iris; *glaucoma* iridectomy, when a wide iridectomy is performed for the relief of congestive glaucoma; *optical* iridectomy, to shape a new pupil and improve vision in cases of central opacities of the cornea or lens; and finally *therapeutic* iridectomy, performed to prevent recurrence of IRITIS (inflammation of the iris).

iritis

Inflammation of the colored part of the eye, the iris. It is characterized by pain, contraction of the pupil and discoloration of the iris itself. Some temporary or permanent decrease in vision may also be involved.

The causes are varied and sometimes unclear. Possible causes include local infection or injury to the eye, tuberculosis, syphilis, collagen disease, REITER'S DISEASE and TOXOPLASMOSIS in infants.

Swelling of the upper eyelid and pain radiating to the temple are common symptoms. There may also be excessive production of tears, intolerance to bright light, blurring of vision and transient near-sightedness.

The eye becomes bloodshot and pus may appear in the anterior chamber of the eye or cover the surface of the lens. Adhesions may form between the iris and the lens, which may be permanent.

The acute form of the condition usually lasts several weeks and tends to recur. Chronic iritis may last considerably longer, with the outcome depending on the severity of the complications.

Early treatment is important. A drug called atropine is used to dilate the pupil so that adhesions are less likely to form between the iris and the lens. Cortisone-like steroid drugs frequently help to deal with the formation of exudates. Underlying causes of iritis are eliminated if possible.

iron

An essential constituent of the body necessary for blood formation and for certain chemical processes in living cells.

IRITIS

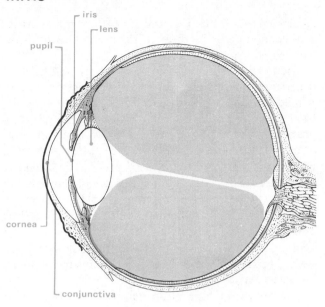

A CROSS SECTION THROUGH THE EYE

The iris is the colored part of the eye which surrounds the pupil. Iritis, inflammation of the iris, causes a painful red eye with a constricted pupil and blurred vision. Although iritis can occur in isolation, it can be a feature of many systemic diseases, for example rheumatoid arthritis, sarcoidosis and syphilis.

About two thirds of the body iron is to be found in hemoglobin—the oxygen-carrying component of red blood cells. The body of an adult contains some 3 to 4 grams of iron. It is lost in small quantities in the urine, feces and sweat, and in larger quantities during menstruation. Hemorrhage can obviously result in more serious loss.

Children require more dietary iron than adults, because of increased growth. Foods rich in iron include meat, eggs and green vegetables. Absorption in the intestine is aided by the presence of vitamin C.

Extra iron may be given to pregnant women as a precaution against ANEMIA and to ensure healthy supplies for the fetus.

See also the major article on **Nutrition.**

irritable bowel syndrome

The name given to a common syndrome of abdominal pain, alternating bouts of constipation and diarrhea, flatulence and distension of the abdomen. Typically, the stools are small and hard and there may be four to six bowel movements daily. Often the symptoms are made worse by tension, anxiety or emotional disturbances.

The syndrome sometimes appears after an episode of inflammation of the digestive tract (gastroenteritis), but more usually its onset is gradual. Symptoms usually start before the age of 30 and teenagers may be affected.

Although the cause of the irritable bowel syndrome is still disputed, its symptoms often respond dramatically to a change in the diet to one containing more vegetable fiber ("roughage"). The addition of two spoonfuls of bran to the daily food intake—or a switch to a diet containing wholemeal flour and a high proportion of cereals—will double the volume of feces passing through the colon (large intestine). The effect is a reduction in the episodes of spasm and abdominal pain and a return toward normal in the consistency of the stools. A substantial body of medical opinion now believes that the lack of fiber in the modern American diet is one of the main causes underlying the frequency of the syndrome.

ischemia

A reduction in blood supply to a part of the body or an organ, due either to an obstruction in the supplying artery or to a constriction in the diameter of the blood vessels serving the area.

An inadequate blood supply deprives the tissue of oxygen and leads to improper functioning.

Ischemia may give rise to transient symptoms including pain; in more severe cases it may lead to paralysis and death of the affected tissues. For example, the arteries carrying blood to the heart muscle often become narrowed with increasing age and are responsible for the symptoms of ANGINA PECTORIS. Similarly, DIABETES MELLITUS may lead to the narrowing of blood vessels in the legs so that changes occur in the toes which can become cold and ulcerated.

Cerebral ischemia, involving the blood vessels of the brain, can develop into a STROKE.

Control of the symptoms of angina pectoris with drugs can be rapid and effective, but the use of vasodilator drugs for other forms of ischemia is less certain. Surgeons sometimes remove an obstruction in an important blood vessel or bypass the blockage.

See also the major article on **Cardiology.**

Ishihara color test

A test devised by a Japanese ophthalmologist, S. Ishihara (b. 1879), to detect COLOR BLINDNESS.

The subject is asked to examine a set of cards upon which are printed round dots of various sizes, colors and combinations. On each card the dots of one color (or several shades of one color) form a number or letter, while other colors form the background. The numbers or letters can be easily read by those with normal sight. Those who are color blind cannot see them and may in fact detect other patterns which are built into the design.

The tests may be particularly useful in deciding whether a slightly color-blind person can safely be employed in a job where distinguishing between different colors is essential—such as driving a locomotive or connecting color-coded wires in electronic components.

islet cell tumor

A tumor of the insulin-secreting cells in the "islets of Langerhans" of the PANCREAS. These tumors are usually benign but may rarely be malignant. They may produce excess insulin for the body to cope with, or be nonfunctioning.

Associated with excess insulin production is the condition known as *hypoglycemia* (lowered blood sugar), which can have serious consequences for the patient unless treated promptly. Hypoglycemia brought about by the insulin from tumor cells occurs particularly when the patient is fasting, or after exercise.

If excess insulin production is a problem the tumor can be removed surgically. Drug treatment is an alternative if the tumor cannot be located or when surgery is inappropriate for other reasons.

See also the major article on **Endocrinology.**

isotopes

Radioactive isotopes are used widely in medicine in both diagnosis and treatment. The isotope of an element differs in its atomic weight but not in its chemical properties, so that a radioactive preparation of iodine, for example, behaves identically to the normal substance except for its emission of radiation.

When a dose of a chemical or drug containing a tiny proportion of the radioactive substance is given (by mouth or injection) it is possible for its pathway through the body to be followed by means of an apparatus similar to a Geiger counter. The extent of the uptake of radioactive iodine by the thyroid gland, for example, gives valuable information on the activity of the gland. Blood cells may be "tagged" with radioactive chromium to measure their survival in the bloodstream after injection. The amounts of radioactivity involved in tests of this kind are tiny—far too small to present any hazard to health.

Larger doses of radioactive isotopes are used in the treatment of some diseases: again, for example, overactivity of the thyroid gland may be treated in this way, as may excessive production of red blood cells by the bone marrow (polycythemia). Radioactive isotopes are also used to treat some tumors: needles of radioactive yttrium, for example, are used to treat some tumors of the pituitary gland.

itching

A sensation of tickling and irritation in the skin, producing a desire to scratch. Itching is known medically as *pruritus.*

The degree of itching can vary widely and may be experienced in only one place or as a general sensation. A mild itch can be almost pleasurable for some people; but, at the opposite extreme, severe and unrelenting pruritus may cause the sufferer to want to attempt suicide. The sensation arises in nerve endings in the skin which are stimulated by released proteolytic enzymes. Substances such as histamine and prostaglandins are thought to be involved. Itching can be caused by chemical, mechanical, thermal or electrical stimuli. For example, the rubbing of an insect bite may prolong itching for a considerable time after the original stimulus has been removed, as the skin remains in a state of increased excitability.

Vigorous scratching of an itch leads to an enlargement of the area involved so that the threshold is further lowered. The damage to the skin may lead to a secondary infection and the formation of fissures or crusts. Long-standing pruritus may be associated with hardening and pigmentation of the skin. Severe itching, often associated with redness and wealing, can be relieved by the administration of antihistamines.

Apart from outside stimuli, the root of the problem may be parasites or skin diseases such as ECZEMA, LICHEN PLANUS and PSORIASIS. Or there may be an underlying disease such as MYXEDEMA, JAUNDICE, KIDNEY DISEASE, LYMPHOMA or internal malignancy.

Pregnancy, the menopause, and drug and food allergies are other possible causes. Psychological elements are commonly associated with itching.

Treatment sometimes involves only the removal of a specific cause. In other cases more general measures may have to be used, such as the avoidance of very hot baths and a change in the brand of soap or cosmetics. Noninfected itching areas of skin can be treated with external steroid preparations. Drugs such as aspirin, antihistamines, tranquilizers or sedatives may also be valuable.

See also the major article on **Dermatology.**

J

jaundice

A yellow discoloration of the skin and other tissues as the result of deposition of the pigment bilirubin, which is derived from the breakdown of hemoglobin. Bilirubin is normally excreted by the liver in the bile.

There are three causes of jaundice: hepatic, obstructive and hemolytic.

In *hepatic jaundice,* damage to liver cells—as for example in yellow fever or poisoning by phosphorus—prevents normal formation of bile salts from bilirubin so that the level rises in the blood.

In *obstructive jaundice,* blockage of the bile ducts by stones, or tumors of the ducts or pancreas, prevents the normal excretion of bile into the intestine, so that it is reabsorbed into the bloodstream.

In *hemolytic jaundice,* increased breakdown of red blood cells and the release of hemoglobin in excessive amounts may swamp the liver so that the level of blood bilirubin rises.

In hepatic jaundice the urine becomes dark and the color of the stools slowly becomes lighter; in obstructive jaundice the urine is very dark and the stools are as light as clay; and in hemolytic jaundice the stools are dark but the urine is of normal color.

In all cases, it is not the jaundice itself that is treated but the underlying condition.

See also HEPATITIS, LIVER DISEASE.

jet lag

The symptoms which many people experience when they cross several time zones during international air travel.

During a long flight—such as one across the Atlantic—the physiological functions of the body become "desynchronized" from man's artificial time system.

When traveling from East to West, for instance, an airplane may leave one time zone at noon, fly for seven hours, and land in another time zone at 2 pm. The passenger will then usually resume his activities on the false assumption that only two hours have passed. He may carry out normal activities for the remainder of the day until he goes to bed; but in the evening his rhythms are those which would have been appropriate to the period between 7 pm and 3 am, rather than the 2 to 10 pm period of his new time zone. Symptoms include a dry mouth, racing pulse, disorientation, insomnia and often a loss of appetite.

There are certain types of rhythm in the biological system which operate on a period of approximately 24 hours. They include slight fluctuations of body temperature, minor changes in blood levels of salts such as potassium and sodium and changes in hormone secretion. The question of how long it takes to return to normal "circadian" rhythms is one that is still being debated by scientists; it is certainly true that some people are more adaptable than others. However, there is a rough rule of thumb that a passenger should rest for one

day after a flight lasting seven hours. West to East flights are more taxing than East to West because they result in a longer day; passengers therefore often lose sleep in addition to disturbing their circadian rhythm.

There is some evidence that performance is degraded after long flights. Some companies insist that executives should not make important decisions until the lapse of a few days after crossing a few time zones.

Passengers in pressurized airplanes tend to be dehydrated. This is associated both with the extremely dry atmosphere of the cabin and the consumption of alcoholic drinks. This aggravates the symptoms of jet lag. To minimize problems a passenger should have a high fluid intake without alcohol, sleep as much as possible (preferably without sedatives or sleeping pills) and retire to bed at the end of any long journey rather than undertake strenuous activity immediately.

keloid

A vascular, hypertrophied scar above the surface of the skin. Keloid is due to an excessive proliferation of the cells known as *fibroblasts* in a wound and it may invade the subcutaneous tissue as well as the skin. Keloid—from the Greek for "crab claw"—is an ugly pinkish elevated scar with clawlike processes.

Patients with burns often become victims of keloid when raw granulating surfaces in deep burns are not resurfaced with a skin graft. It also appears in accidental or operative wounds, or even in such slight traumas as the scar of a boil or abscess, a smallpox vaccination or an ear prick. It is more common in people with dark complexions, in tuberculosis patients and in pregnant women.

Keloid frequently itches and may ulcerate in places. Unlike more common forms of hypertrophied scars, it may grow for months or even years and it is notorious for recurring after surgical excision, but it rarely develops into a malignancy. In its early stages it may be relieved by the application of hydrocortisone ointment and solution. The conventional treatment is to subject the scar to deep x-rays in order to diminish the vascularity and to stop the proliferation of the fibroblasts. If surgical excision is undertaken it is usual to cover the area with skin grafts.

keratitis

Inflammation of the cornea (the transparent front layer of the eye). Worldwide, the most common cause is deficiency of vitamin A, but keratitis may also be due to chemical injury or to infection with viruses or bacteria. Exposure to sunlight or ultraviolet light may cause a transient keratitis.

Treatment clearly depends on the cause; correction of the vitamin deficiency will produce a dramatic cure if the condition is not too far advanced. Bacterial infections usually respond to the appropriate antibiotic, but viral infections do not respond to antibiotics or any other drugs. (In such cases a spontaneous remission can only be hoped for.) If the condition is allowed to progress untreated, however, it may eventually lead to blindness.

keratosis

Thickening of the outer horny layer of the skin. It may be caused by constant friction on the soles or the palms, or by pathological processes (particularly in the elderly).

In *senile keratosis*, multiple warty lesions covered by a hard scale form on the forehead, cheeks, lips and on the backs of the hands and forearms following prolonged exposure to sunlight. The condition is also called *actinic* or *solar* keratosis, and those who spend their lives working outdoors in prolonged sunshine may develop the lesions relatively early in life. Its main importance is that it may be precancerous; about 20% of these keratoses are liable to become malignant.

keratosis follicularis

A rare condition in which the outer layer of the skin is marked by overgrowths of the horny layer. Also known as *Darier's disease*, *White's disease*, or *keratosis vegetans*.

Keratosis follicularis is a form of ICHTHYOSIS, a skin disease in which the surface is very rough and presents a dry, cracked appearance like fish scales. The limbs, neck and face are particularly affected.

The condition appears to be hereditary, typically develops during childhood and is not contagious. No specific treatment or cure exists.

kernicterus

A condition in which the brain of infants suffering from severe jaundice becomes yellow, the nerve centers at the base of the brain (basal ganglia) in particular being susceptible.

If areas in the medulla oblongata are affected the baby may have difficulty in breathing and show twitching of the face and limbs; damage to the basal ganglia is manifest as abnormal writhing movement of the limbs and retarded psychomotor development, while mental defects may become apparent in consequence of damage to the higher cortical centers.

As there is no known treatment for the condition once it has occurred, excess of bile in the blood of an infant must be dealt with by exchange transfusion in the immediate neonatal period. About 75% of cases are due to hemolytic disease (see RH FACTOR), the others often being associated with birth before full term. Preventive treatment requires the early diagnosis and treatment of conditions in the newborn which can cause hemolysis.

Before the introduction of exchange transfusion about one in a thousand babies born alive was liable to develop kernicterus.

ketosis

The presence of excess ketones—a kind of chemical compound—in the body.

Ketones (of which acetone is an example) are normally produced in the liver through the partial oxidation of protein and fat foodstuffs. As a rule they are further oxidized in other tissues.

If, however, ketone production exceeds a certain level (known as the *ketone threshold*) the tissues are unable to cope with them and ketosis results.

The most common condition giving rise to ketosis is DIABETES MELLITUS. Unable to make use of its blood sugar in the normal way, the diabetic body metabolizes fat and produces ketones. It is sometimes possible to smell acetone on the breath of an uncontrolled diabetic; doctors can also test for ketones in the urine.

The patient has fast, panting breathing and may go into a coma. Injection of insulin resolves the diabetic emergency and, with it, the ketosis.

Ketosis is also a feature of starvation, because the body is metabolizing fat from its own stores.

kidney disease

Patients with kidney disease may either develop problems related to urine formation or present a more confusing picture in which the symptoms at first do not seem to involve the kidney.

The main signs and symptoms of disease of the urinary tract are the presence of abnormal constituents in the urine (such as blood and protein), a large increase or decrease in the volume of urine, frequency of urination and pain. The pain may either be a burning sensation on passing urine or low back pain (which has many causes other than kidney disease). Manifestations of kidney disease unrelated to the urinary system include anemia, hypertension, edema, loss of appetite, nausea, weakness, stunted growth in childhood, itching, convulsions, coma and bone disorders.

Apart from URINARY TRACT INFECTION (UTI), most of the kidney diseases mentioned in this article are uncommon. UTI is predominantly a disease of women and is caused by bacteria from the anus spreading up the urinary passages. If the infection is not effectively treated with antibiotics, the kidney is eventually involved in a PYELONEPHRITIS, marked by fever and lumbar pain. In low-grade pyelonephritis there may be no symptoms, yet the disease can progress insidiously to produce small scarred kidneys and chronic renal (kidney) failure.

Chronic renal failure. Chronic renal failure has many possible causes, pyelonephritis being the second most common. The chief cause in children and adults is GLOMERULONEPHRITIS—an inflammatory disease of the kidney which results from disorders in the body's immune defense mechanisms. Damage to the blood vessels of the kidneys, whether from atherosclerosis, hypertension or diabetes, can also result in chronic renal failure. Various congenital abnormalities such as POLYCYSTIC KIDNEY can produce chronic renal failure in adult life. Among the other causes, ingestion of large doses of analgesics such as aspirin over many years could often have been avoided.

Most patients developing chronic renal failure from whatever cause do not notice any symptoms until they have the equivalent of half a single kidney left functioning. The complications which then follow depend on a number of pathological mechanisms: (1) the failing kidney can no longer concentrate urine, leading to frequent voiding and imbalance in the blood levels of sodium, potassium and hydrogen; (2) at a later stage, urine formation falls dramatically so that toxins normally cleared from the blood by the kidney are retained; this state is called UREMIA and is marked by cardiac and neurological disorders; (3) the kidney normally activates vitamin D, which is important for calcium absorption, and when this process fails, bone disorders can occur; (4) hypertension is a common feature of chronic renal failure and the blood pressure may increase rapidly to cause fatal cerebral hemorrhage; (5) the healthy kidney secretes erythropoietin—a hormone which stimulates the bone marrow to produce red blood cells; this mechanism is depressed in chronic renal failure, causing anemia, which is further exacerbated by the state of uremia.

Until recent years the above complications of chronic renal failure were invariably fatal within a short time. Now with techniques of DIALYSIS and surgical TRANSPLANTATION it is possible to prolong life, often for many years, although the problems are formidable.

Acute renal failure. In contrast to the long, insidious buildup in chronic renal failure, acute renal failure is a state where the production of urine falls suddenly to less than a pint every 24 hours. An abrupt reduction in renal blood flow following hemorrhage, crushing muscle injuries (see CRUSH SYNDROME), burns or overwhelming infection can cause such a drop in urine output. If prompt action is taken to restore the blood pressure, the volume of urine produced soon returns to normal. Otherwise, prolonged lack of oxygen kills cells in the kidney tubules and acute renal failure is established. The same picture can result from a variety of drugs and toxins and from the transfusion of incompatible blood. A patient who suddenly stops producing urine completely probably has an obstruction in the urinary tract due to a CALCULUS (stone), blood clot or tumor.

If a patient with acute renal failure survives, he or she passes little urine for the first few weeks and then has a

THE KIDNEYS

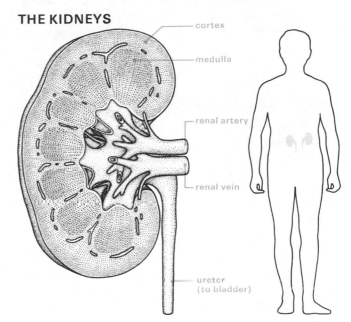

A CROSS SECTION THROUGH A KIDNEY

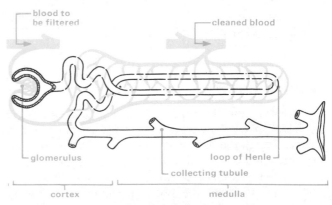

MAGNIFIED DIAGRAM OF A NEPHRON

The kidneys are paired organs, each about 4 in. long, lying alongside the backbone. Each kidney contains about 1 million functional units or nephrons. Blood is filtered through glomeruli in the cortex to produce urine, which then flows through the rest of the nephron to the collecting tubules, with great changes in its concentration and chemical composition being made on the way.

"diuretic phase" when the urine output increases to 6–8 pints per day. With good medical care, renal function usually returns to normal.

Cancer of the kidneys. There are two main types of kidney cancer. *Wilms' tumor* affects young children and in many cases is thought to originate in the fetus. Combination treatment with surgery, irradiation and drugs has recently improved the prognosis for these children. NEPHROMA accounts for less than 2% of all adult cancers and usually affects people over 45 years of age.

NEPHROTIC SYNDROME is mainly a disease of children and is caused by heavy loss of protein in the urine.

See also the major articles on **Nephrology** and **Urology.**

Klinefelter's syndrome

A chromosome disorder of men in which partly female characteristics occur.

The normal male has 46 chromosomes, including the two sex chromosomes XY. Females have 46 including XX. Men with Klinefelter's syndrome have 47 chromosomes, including three sex chromosomes XXY.

Patients often have female-type breasts (GYNECOMASTIA) and small testicles with a high output of hormones but which are unable to produce sperm (thus, such patients are infertile). They have a eunuchoid appearance, with long slender limbs, little body hair and low sex drive. Social and psychological disturbances are common.

About 75% of patients exhibit a positive chromatin pattern—that is, their cells contain chromatin, a genetic material normally found only in women.

knock-knee

A deformity of the lower limbs (also known as *genu valgum*) in which the knees turn inward and tend to knock together or touch when walking. When the inner surfaces of the knees are touching, as the child stands in a natural position, the condition leads to the appearance of a gap between the bony protuberances (medial malleoli) of the ankles. The size of this gap is commonly used as a measure of the degree of knock-knee.

After a child begins to walk and before it reaches the age of six years, slight knock-knee is so common that it may be ignored as part of normal development. If, however, it is particularly marked or if it persists to a later age, it may be due to faulty muscular tone. Obesity can aggravate the condition.

Rickets, caused by a deficiency of vitamin D, was formerly responsible for many cases of knock-knee, but

the occurrences of rickets are now relatively rare.

Up to the age of seven years, it is not considered necessary to treat knock-knee where the gap between the ankles is less than three inches. Most cases will have become corrected by that age. Splints are used to correct knock-knee in cases where the gap exceeds three inches; in exceptional cases, where it is as much as four inches, or the child is aged nine, an operation may be necessary.

See the illustration at BOWLEG.

kraurosis vulvae

A condition in which the vulva becomes dry, shriveled, red and sore.

Some atrophy of the vulva is normal after the menopause, and kraurosis vulvae probably represents an extreme degree of these normal changes. It is caused by a decrease in the level of circulating estrogens following the menopause; younger women are rarely affected.

Kraurosis vulvae needs treatment for two reasons: it may cause discomfort and it increases the risk of both vulval infections (with CANDIDA or bacteria) and vulval cancer. The treatment is with estrogen, best given in the form of a cream to reduce the risk of side effects.

kwashiorkor

Malnutrition due to a deficiency in the quality and quantity of dietary protein. The condition is common in children in all poor areas of the world.

Kwashiorkor usually develops in children after weaning; as the newborn child is put onto the breast the older baby runs short of food. The principal features are EDEMA of the legs (or even of the whole body), patches of peeling skin, dry and brittle hair, apathy, loss of appetite and failure to grow.

The liver becomes greatly enlarged due to its infiltration with fat and edema fluid collects in the peritoneal cavity, causing the child's abdomen to protrude. Diarrhea is common and usually leads to dehydration and salt imbalance in the body.

Kwashiorkor is treated by gradually restoring regular and well-balanced meals (including all the necessary vitamins), correction of fluid and salt balance, and by administration of antibiotics to control any accompanying infection.

Prevention of kwashiorkor depends upon provision of adequate protein in the diet and the education of parents to make proper use of such a diet for their children. Both of these requirements are lacking in most poor environments; kwashiorkor will continue to be a common disease until these problems are solved.

See also DEFICIENCY DISEASES, MALNUTRITION, and the major article on **Nutrition.**

kyphosis

An abnormal curvature of the spine, in which its normal curves are exaggerated (compare SCOLIOSIS). It results in the condition commonly referred to as *hunchback* or *humpback*.

See SPINAL CURVATURE.

labor

The process by which a baby is expelled from the uterus during childbirth; delivery.

See CHILDBIRTH.

labyrinthitis

A common name for OTITIS INTERNA.

lacrimation

The normal production and discharge of tears. The term is also sometimes used to imply excessive tear production.

Tears wash the eyeball constantly—removing dust, microorganisms and other particles. The composition of tears resembles blood plasma, but also contains an enzyme capable of killing many types of bacteria.

Tears are produced by the lacrimal glands, situated in the outer part of each upper eyelid. They flow over the eyeball to the inner part of each lower eyelid. From here they drain through tiny openings (the lacrimal canaliculi) into the lacrimal sac, which in turn drains through the "nasolacrimal" duct to the nose.

Excessive production of tears may be caused by emotional factors as well as by any condition which irritates the surface of the eyeball—such as conjunctivitis, foreign bodies, or irritant chemicals.

Tear production may appear to be excessive when the drainage apparatus is blocked—the tears spill over to run down the cheek (a condition known as "epiphora"). Blockage is commonly due to infection, but it may also occur from birth due to a failure of development of the drainage apparatus or may be due to a stone in the duct. Epiphora may be caused by paralysis or an outward turning of the lower lid, which prevents normal drainage.

Blocked ducts may be treated by syringing, antibiotics and eyedrops. Surgery is sometimes required; as a last resort, the production of tears may be reduced by injecting alcohol into the lacrimal gland.

Lacrimation is decreased in certain rare conditions. Damage to the surface of the eye may be avoided in such cases by the use of "artificial tear" eyedrops.

lactation

The production and secretion of milk by the female breasts.

See BREAST FEEDING.

laparoscopy

Examination of the contents of the abdominal cavity with an instrument known as a laparoscope (or peritoneoscope).

The patient is commonly given general anesthesia for the examination. Gas (usually carbon dioxide) is introduced into the abdomen through a needle to distend the abdominal cavity and provide room for maneuver of the instrument. A small incision is then made through the abdominal wall below the navel and the laparoscope is inserted through it.

Laparoscopy was first widely used by gynecologists to examine the ovaries, Fallopian tubes and uterus. A good view of these organs can be obtained, often avoiding the need for exploratory surgery. Minor operations can be performed through the laparoscope with special instruments. Female sterilization by cautery of the Fallopian tubes is often achieved in this way.

The laparoscope can be used to examine other abdominal organs—such as the liver, gallbladder and appendix—but the views obtained are often less complete than those of the reproductive organs.

Laparoscopy is relatively safe and has few complications. The minor wound heals rapidly, although the necessary introduction of gas may lead to mild abdominal distension and discomfort for a day or two.

See also the major article on **Gastroenterology.**

laparotomy

Any surgical operation in which an incision is made into the abdominal cavity.

Laparotomy may be performed in order to expose for operation any of the organs within the abdomen (stomach, gallbladder, colon, etc.) or for inspection of the abdominal contents (an "exploratory laparotomy"). Exploratory laparotomy is sometimes required to determine the nature of lumps felt in the abdomen, to inspect a suspected tumor and assess whether or not it is operable, and occasionally to seek the cause of an unexplained fever. Modern diagnostic techniques have made exploratory laparotomy a less common procedure than in the past.

See also LAPAROSCOPY.

laryngectomy

Surgical removal of the larynx, performed especially in cases of advanced cancer.

The larynx ("voice-box") is situated in the throat between the pharynx and the trachea. Laryngectomy destroys the power of normal speech, although following this procedure many patients can be taught "esophageal speech." The patient swallows air and then belches it up from the esophagus, moving his lips and tongue at the same time to form words. Artificial "voice-boxes," implanted in place of the removed larynx, have also been fairly successful in restoring speech.

LARYNX

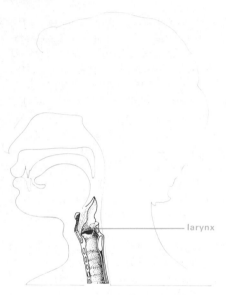

larynx

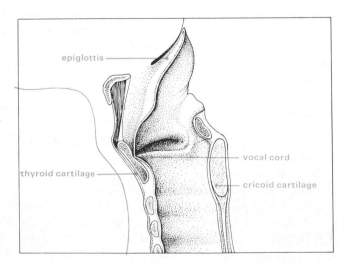

epiglottis

vocal cord

thyroid cartilage

cricoid cartilage

The larynx is the voice-box in the throat: it is an arrangement of cartilages which are connected by ligaments and muscles. Movements of the cartilages sets the tension in the vocal cords and this determines the pitch of the voice.

laryngitis

Inflammation of the larynx, especially the vocal cords, producing huskiness and weakness of the voice.

Acute laryngitis is caused by an infection (usually influenza or another virus) and often occurs in association with inflammation of the throat (pharyngitis) or tonsillitis. It usually causes a harsh dry cough; in young children it may cause obstructed noisy breathing and CROUP. As in most infections, the patient has a fever and feels unwell.

Humidified oxygen treatment may be necessary in very young children; steam inhalation may also help to relieve symptoms. A cough suppressant such as codeine may control the dry cough. Antibiotics are often prescribed, but are usually indicated only in the minority of cases where the infection is bacterial. Acute laryngitis commonly resolves spontaneously within a few days.

Chronic laryngitis most often results from overuse or abuse of the voice and is common in preachers, actors, politicians and singers; it is aggravated by smoking. Treatment is absolute rest of the voice for a few days. Rarely, chronic laryngitis may be due to infection with tuberculosis, and the symptoms may also be due to a tumor on the vocal cords. Anyone with persistent change or weakness of the voice should be seen by a laryngologist.

See also the major article on **Otolaryngology.**

Lassa fever

A serious viral disease, first reported from Lassa, Nigeria in 1969.

The virus is highly contagious and virulent. It can be transmitted to man from domestic rats (the natural host of the virus) and close personal contact with an infected patient. Airborne spread also occurs and infected patients must be treated in isolation.

The symptoms are quite variable. The fever sometimes takes several days to develop and early symptoms may include headache, backache, nausea and vomiting, cough, sore throat, abdominal pain and diarrhea. Examination usually shows inflammation of the throat and a variable range of other abnormalities. Laboratory tests often show a bleeding tendency and the virus can be isolated and identified from blood and other tissue fluids.

Most patients with Lassa fever die without treatment. A specific antiserum offers the best chance of cure and is available in limited supply from centers around the world. Intensive supportive treatment is also essential. Strict "barrier nursing" is necessary to protect doctors and nurses dealing with patients because no prophylactic vaccines or drugs are available.

As of early 1978, no cases of Lassa fever were contracted in the U.S., but rapid air travel makes its transmission by travelers from West Africa a real risk. All such travelers who develop a fever within 17 days (the longest known incubation period for the disease) should seek urgent medical attention.

See also the major article on **Infectious Diseases.**

lead poisoning

Lead may cause acute poisoning when someone swallows a relatively large amount of the metal or one of its compounds; but more commonly symptoms are due to chronic poisoning, since lead acts as a cumulative poison. Lead is not readily excreted in the urine or feces, so that anyone who regularly absorbs even traces of the metal slowly builds up the lead content of the body.

Lead poisoning occurs when water supplies are contaminated—and soft water will dissolve enough of the metal out of lead water pipes to cause problems. It is also common in ghetto areas, where buildings are still covered in lead-containing paints, and the dust from flaking paint work is swallowed, especially by children. Poisoning sometimes occurs from the use of lead-glazed pottery when used to store acidic fluids such as wine or hard cider. Pollution from industrial plants such as smelters may cause lead poisoning in communities around them. The extent of lead pollution from motor vehicle exhausts is disputed, but persons working in close contact with vehicles—traffic policemen, for example—have been shown to have raised blood levels of lead.

In adults mild lead poisoning causes anemia. More severe poisoning may cause cramping pains, especially in the intestines (*lead colic*), discoloration of the gums, and damage to the nerves causing weakness of the muscles, especially in the forearm. This weakness typically affects the muscles controlling the wrist, in which case it is known as "wrist-drop."

In children lead poisoning may cause mental irritability and (in severe cases) mental retardation, convulsions, and eventually death. There is medical disagreement about the effects on children's mental development of *minimal* degrees of lead poisoning: some authorities claim that the lead pollution from paint, vehicle exhausts and industry in inner city areas contributes to the poor intellectual performance of ghetto children (see also PICA).

Once suspected, lead poisoning is diagnosed by laboratory tests on the blood. Treatment—apart from prevention of further exposure—depends on removal of the lead from the body by *chelating agents*—drugs, such as calcium sodium edetate, which become chemically bound to the lead to form compounds which are readily excreted in the urine.

left ventricular failure

Failure of the left ventricle (left lower chamber) of the heart to pump blood adequately for the needs of the body.

Left ventricular failure (LVF) is most commonly caused by coronary artery disease, hypertension (high blood pressure), or disease of the heart valves.

The major symptom is breathlessness, caused by the pooling of blood and fluid in the lungs. At first the patient is short of breath only on exertion, but the condition gradually becomes worse. Shortness of breath is often worse when the patient is lying down and frightening attacks may occur during sleep. Ultimately, the untreated patient's lungs become so "waterlogged" that he can no longer breathe adequately and may lapse into a coma from lack of oxygen.

Acute or *severe LVF* requires urgent treatment with digoxin to aid heart function and diuretics to get rid of excess body fluid. The patient should sit up and receive oxygen. Other drugs are sometimes needed.

Chronic LVF requires treatment with the same drugs and an adjustment of the patient's life-style to suit his condition. Hypertension is controlled and diseased heart valves and blocked coronary arteries may require surgical treatment.

Effective treatment of hypertension has reduced the frequency of LVF and heart-valve disease associated with previous rheumatic fever is becoming far less common. Coronary artery disease, however, is frighteningly common, and is now the major cause of LVF in the Western world.

See also the major article on **Cardiology.**

legionnaire's disease

An acute infectious disease usually producing a form of pneumonia. It received its name from a large outbreak of the disease at an American Legion convention in Philadelphia in 1976, where 29 legionnaires died and scores of others were hospitalized. There had been reports of sporadic cases before that time, however; confirmation was made by the discovery of specific antibodies in blood samples that were stored for just such later tests.

The cause of the disease was at first a mystery, but it has now been identified as a previously unknown rod-shaped bacterium, initially referred to as *legionnaire's agent,* which can grow in the laboratory only under special conditions. The disease is more likely to affect those whose resistance to infection is already reduced. In the United States, one reservoir for the bacteria was found to be the stagnant water in cooling towers and commercial air-conditioning systems.

Symptoms, which are nonspecific but which first

resemble those of influenza, appear after an incubation period of two to ten days, usually with a high fever, malaise, muscle pains, headache and diarrhea. A severe and extensive pneumonia usually develops within a week and may produce symptoms like cough with blood-stained sputum or pain in the chest on coughing because of inflammation of the pleura. The diagnosis is made by finding the organism in specimens of the lung or from the pleural fluid or by detecting antibodies to legionnaire's agent in the blood. The disease has a high mortality rate. Most antibiotics are ineffective. So far, erythromycin seems to be the antibiotic of choice.

Leishmaniasis

A group of diseases caused by infection with protozoa (single-celled animals) of the genus *Leishmania*.

The organisms live within human body cells; they multiply until the cells ultimately burst, releasing a great number of new parasites to infect other cells. They are transmitted from one person to another by the bite of sandflies, in whose bodies further development and multiplication occurs. Animals such as dogs and rats act as "reservoirs" from which the sandflies can transmit the infection to man.

Visceral leishmaniasis ("kala-azar") occurs principally in India, the Near and Far East, around the Mediterranean, and in parts of South America. It has an incubation period of two to six months. The symptoms are often vague. There is usually an irregular fever of long duration and the patient gradually becomes emaciated. The spleen and often the liver enlarge greatly, and blood tests show anemia and high levels of globulins in the blood. Victims are very susceptible to other infections, which may cause additional symptoms and dangers.

The majority of patients with kala-azar die for lack of treatment (usually within two years of onset), although treatment with special drugs can slowly cure up to 98% of patients.

Cutaneous leishmaniasis ("oriental sore") is less serious than visceral leishmaniasis. It occurs in many tropical and subtropical regions and in every country in Central and South America except Chile. The main symptom is dry or moist ulcers of the skin, which may last for many months before healing spontaneously. Secondary infection of the ulcers may require treatment.

American mucocutaneous leishmaniasis is confined to Central and South America. It is similar to cutaneous leishmaniasis, but also causes ulcers of the nose, mouth and pharynx. Severe disfigurement may result from widespread destruction of the tissues of the nose and mouth, so early treatment is required. American mucocutaneous leishmaniasis is more resistant to treatment than the other varieties are, and prolonged treatment with several drugs is very often required.

All types of leishmaniasis are common in the areas in which they occur. The diseases can best be prevented by control of the sandfly vectors and by the individual use of insect repellants to prevent their bites. Elimination of "reservoir animals" has also succeeded in some areas. There are no specific preventive measures.

lens

Any device which causes a beam of light to converge or diverge as it passes through.

The lens of the eye (*crystalline lens*) consists of elongated fibers enclosed in a transparent elastic capsule, suspended by a ligament behind the iris. The ligament is attached to the circular ciliary muscle. Contraction and relaxation of the muscles change the shape of the lens, so altering its focusing power; this is the mechanism that allows us to make a sharp image of objects at variable distances from the eye.

The lens becomes stiffer with age and the range of focusing decreases. Most people over the age of 45 need glasses with weak convex lenses for reading to compensate for this. The lens normally becomes slightly opaque from the age of 60 onward, but impaired vision due to opacity of the lens (CATARACT) may occur at any age.

A penetrating injury of the lens can cause opacity. The lens may also be dislocated from its ligament by external injury to the eye.

Manmade lenses of glass or plastic are used in the manufacture of glasses and contact lenses. They compensate for inadequacies in the focusing ability of the lens of the eye (*presbyopia*), an uneven curvature of the cornea or lens (*astigmatism*), or for long or short sight caused by abnormalities in the shape of the eyeball.

See also the major article on **Ophthalmology.**

leprosy

A chronic but only mildly contagious disease caused by infection with bacteria of the species *Mycobacterium leprae*. Also known as Hansen's disease.

Leprosy occurs mainly in countries between the thirtieth parallels of latitude, but also in Japan, Korea, South China and South Africa. In the United States the disease occurs mainly in those states bordering the Gulf of Mexico and in Hawaii.

Leprosy damages the cooler tissues of the body: skin, superficial nerves, nose, pharynx, larynx and occasionally the eyes and testicles.

There are two main types of leprosy: lepromatous and tuberculoid.

In *lepromatous leprosy* the patient's resistance to infection is low. Many red painful swellings appear on the skin of the face and elsewhere. These harden and coalesce, causing the great disfigurement which has been feared and loathed since Biblical times. The patient has chronic ill-health; he rarely dies from leprosy itself, but death from a secondary infection is common.

In *tuberculoid leprosy* the patient's resistance is high. Unfortunately, his main reaction to the disease occurs in nerves. The "battle" itself causes numbness, tingling and loss of sensation in the areas these nerves supply. Deformities such as wrist-drop, foot-drop or claw-toes may result; the anesthetic areas may be painlessly damaged with ulceration and even the gradual disappearance of the ends of fingers and toes.

Tuberculoid leprosy is not contagious; even lepromatous sufferers are infectious only to those with whom they are in prolonged intimate contact. Contrary to popular belief, isolation of patients is unnecessary. The medical emphasis is now on early detection and treatment.

Leprosy is usually treated with dapsone, a relatively safe drug which may have to be taken for many years. Tuberculoid leprosy responds well, but lepromatous leprosy is not so predictable. Surgery may sometimes be required for some patients with leprosy to correct deformities.

leukemia

A progressive malignant disease (or cancer) of the white cells in the circulating blood and bone marrow. Proliferation of the cancerous cells crowds out the normal healthy white and red blood cells and blood platelets, causing anemia and bleeding disorders and lowering the natural defenses against infection.

Leukemia is still relatively rare, but has become somewhat more common over the past 50 years. Its causes are poorly understood. Exposure to ionizing radiation increases its incidence, but this cannot account for all cases. Viruses can cause leukemia in some animals, although there is no definite evidence of their role in man.

Leukemia is classified as *acute* (short course) or *chronic* (long course), as well as by the type of cells involved: *myeloid, lymphoid* (or *lymphatic*) and *monocytic*.

Acute leukemia occurs most commonly in children and, at any age, is commoner in males than females. Usually the onset of the disease is sudden, with fever, sore throat and often bleeding from the nose or mouth: it quickly becomes apparent that the patient is very ill. Examination of the blood and a bone marrow BIOPSY confirm the diagnosis.

Without treatment death usually occurs within a few days or weeks in all types of acute leukemia. Steady progress in treatment has occurred over the past 20

years, however; a remission of the disease can now be induced in most patients, especially in children, by a combination of anticancer drugs and radiation therapy.

Many patients relapse after a period of remission, but further treatment may then be effective. Some patients may be permanently cured by modern treatment, and in the most common leukemia of childhood, *acute lymphoblastic leukemia,* the cure rate is now approaching 50% of all cases.

Chronic myeloid leukemia (CML) occurs most commonly in adult males. Its onset is much more gradual than that of acute leukemia. Symptoms include tiredness caused by anemia and abdominal discomfort associated with massive enlargement of the spleen. Diagnosis is again confirmed from the results of blood tests and a biopsy of the bone marrow. Busulfan is the main drug used for treatment. Patients with CML may survive for several years, but the disease often leads to fatal acute leukemia despite treatment.

Chronic lymphatic leukemia (CLL) occurs particularly in men of late middle age. Symptoms are similar to those of CML, but the spleen is not so large and there is a general enlargement of the lymph nodes. Treatment is with chlorambucil or cyclophosphamide and patients often survive in reasonable health for several years; a few patients have lived for 20 years or more from the time the disease was first diagnosed and treatment begun.

See also the major article on **Oncology.**

leukoderma

A patchy deficiency of pigmentation of the skin, the patches often being milk-white. Leukoderma is another name for VITILIGO.

leukodystrophy

A group of disorders characterized by progressive degeneration of the white matter of the brain. They are due to an inborn error of metabolism with a breakdown in the enzyme systems concerned with the metabolism of lipids (fats or fatlike substances) in the nerve cells.

There is progressive destruction of the protective and insulating myelin sheaths of the nerve fibers, which usually begins in the back part of the brain and spreads more or less symmetrically throughout the white matter of the cerebral hemispheres.

Some forms of leukodystrophy begin in early childhood; there are also late childhood forms, which usually confine the child to a wheelchair in adolescence.

The symptoms include dementia, paralysis, generalized fits, speech difficulties, disorganization of movement and mental deterioration. There is no known treatment.

leukoplakia

Abnormal thickening and whitening of the tongue, the lining of the mouth, the lips, or the genital area. Affected areas may be yellowish-white and leathery. The lesions may be precancerous. By the time pain is present a lesion is usually advanced.

Leukoplakia is thought to be often caused by chronic irritation in the mouth. This may be due to tobacco, highly seasoned food, alcoholic drinks, excessive heat, trauma, the use of a particularly strong dentifrice (flavored toothpastes and tooth powders), jagged teeth, or dentures. Possible predisposing factors include coexisting syphilis, lack of vitamin A, and gonadal (sex-gland) deficiencies; approximately 65% of cases occur in men.

The first step in treatment is to remove the cause of the irritation. Good oral hygiene should be established. Faulty dentures should be corrected or sharp teeth dealt with. A mild alkaline mouthwash, such as equal parts of water and aluminum hydroxide (Amphojel), four times daily may be useful.

Early thin leukoplakia which fails to respond to conservative measures should be removed completely after a BIOPSY has been obtained. Larger lesions may have to be surgically removed in more than one operation. Regular reexamination of treated areas is advisable in case there is a serious recurrence.

Leukoplakia can also occur in the vulvar or vaginal area in women and on the penis in men. Again conservative measures such as control of any irritating discharge may be sufficient to effect a cure.

leukorrhea

An abnormal whitish discharge from the vagina which may occur at any age. It affects many women at some time.

The amount of normal vaginal secretions varies among women and in the same woman during the menstrual cycle. Excess mucus production may occur normally during pregnancy, as a result of sexual and emotional stimulation, and at the time of ovulation. Secretions are also increased just before and after menstruation.

In leukorrhea the abnormal vaginal discharge may just be excessive or it may be purulent (pus-filled) as the result of an infection by *Trichomonas vaginalis* (a protozoan—see TRICHOMONIASIS), *Candida albicans* (thrush—see CANDIDA), or other pathogens. A purulent discharge may also be due to disease of the cervix or uterus, senile VAGINITIS, or the presence of pessaries or other foreign bodies.

In treatment, hygiene of the genital area is important. A vinegar douche may be helpful. Sulfonamide creams may combat bacterial infections and metronidazole in treating Trichomoniasis. Postmenopausal inflammation of the vagina is usually controlled by local estrogen applications.

leukotomy

Another word for LOBOTOMY.

libido

A drive usually associated with the sexual instinct—that is, for pleasure and the seeking out of a love object. In Jung's original sense of the term, the energy designated "libido" was of a general kind, and applied to any instinctive force.

Freud maintained that in early life instinctive satisfaction is largely obtained from the individual's own body. As development proceeds, instinctive satisfaction is obtained increasingly from without, and the libido is directed toward external objects.

In the early oral and anal craving stages, guilt feelings are said to be established. In the so-called phallic stage, satisfaction is concerned with the genital zone. In the final stage, complete "object-love" is said to be possible.

lice

Three kinds of lice infect man; infestation with lice is known as *pediculosis*. The louse itself is a small wingless flattened insect.

Pediculosis capitis is due to the head louse and affects the scalp, though sometimes involves the eyebrows, eyelashes and beard. Infestation is particularly common in children, especially girls. The lice feed on blood from the scalp and are transmitted by direct contact of hair and by items such as combs, towels and headgear. The bites cause severe persistent itching and the lesions may become infected. The glands of the neck may sometimes enlarge.

Adult lice may be seen particularly around the back of the head and behind the ears. The small ovoid eggs, or nits, are easier to detect, as they are firmly attached to hair shafts. These hatch in 3 to 14 days. They may be removed with a nit comb and the scalp should be treated with benzyl benzoate, gamma benzene hexachloride, or malathion. Members of the same household should also be examined for infestation.

Pediculosis corporis is due to the body louse, which primarily inhabits the seams of clothing worn next to the skin and feeds on the skin. Under good hygienic conditions it is uncommon. The bites of the lice are seen as small red marks and itching leads to severe scratch marks. There may be secondary bacterial infection. Lesions are especially common on the shoulders,

HUMAN LOUSE

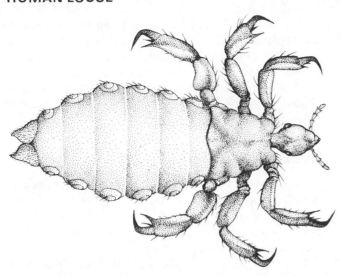

Human lice are small, wingless insects which spend their whole existence on man. They lay their eggs on hair, and spread from person to person by direct contact. The species of louse pictured above lives in hair or underwear and causes itching. More importantly, it transmits the microorganism which causes typhus.

buttocks and abdomen. Both the parasites and nits are easily found in clothing.

Laundering and hot ironing of seams will kill the lice. The skin should be rubbed with gamma benzene hexachloride. Lotions may soothe inflammation.

Nits remain viable in clothing for as long as one month, hatching when they are reexposed to body heat. Dissemination of lice occurs through contact with infested persons, clothing, or bedding.

Pediculosis pubis is caused by the crab louse, which invades the area of the genitals and anus and sometimes other hair regions. Infestation may be venereal or acquired from clothing, bedclothes, or toilet seats. Severe irritation, with scratch marks, occurs. Application of benzyl benzoate or gamma benzene hexachloride is an effective treatment. However, prolonged use of such chemicals should be avoided.

Lice are known to transmit typhus fever, relapsing fever and trench fever, but these infections are rare.

lichen planus

A fairly common benign inflammatory disease of the skin and the lining of the mouth, which often gives rise to itching. There are small discrete raised areas of skin which at times coalesce into rough scaly patches. The raised areas are angular and have a flat shiny surface of pink or violet hue.

Children are rarely affected. Certain drugs may produce an identical eruption. The initial attack persists for weeks or months and may recur intermittently.

The condition frequently affects the wrists, arms, legs and trunk, but is rarely seen on the face. Occasionally the lesions are generalized.

The cause of the disease is unknown. Sedation may be necessary in severe cases, but usually all that is required is the application of a soothing lotion. Hydrocortisone ointment may be administered.

lipodystrophy

A disturbance of fat metabolism in which the subcutaneous fat disappears over some regions of the body, but is unaffected in others.

In progressive lipodystrophy the loss of fat is confined to the upper part of the body above the pelvis. This is a rare disease of unknown origin in which the loss of fat occurs over time and is eventually complete. The subcutaneous fat of the buttocks and lower limbs is unaffected or may be increased. The general health of the patient remains unimpaired. There may be psychological disturbances resulting from the patient's abnormal appearance.

About 80% of cases are female. The onset tends to be early in life—in about half of all cases before the age of 10, and in about three-quarters before the age of 20.

Two endocrine abnormalities have been observed in a significant proportion of cases—HYPOTHYROIDISM and either established DIABETES MELLITUS or a high blood sugar level.

The loss of fat from the face, neck, upper limbs and trunk gives a superficial appearance of emaciation, but closer examination reveals the muscles to be normal in size. Occasionally cases are seen where the fat has left the lower limbs and is normal on the upper part of the body.

There is no treatment for lipodystrophy. Once established, the condition remains more or less stationary, although the life expectation is unaffected.

Localized lipodystrophy may occur in some diabetics where there is loss of fat at the site of repeated insulin injections.

lipoma

A soft round swelling or tumor composed of fat cells, occurring in the dermis or subcutaneous tissue. The fat tissue is enclosed in a fibrous capsule. Usually solitary, but sometimes multiple, lipomas vary in size from minute growths to huge masses weighing several pounds.

They are occasionally associated with endocrine and neurological disturbances, and in these cases probably result from disordered fat metabolism. They may occur from early age to advanced age, but from 40–50%

appear between the ages of 30 and 40, when the body begins to accumulate excess fat—at which time the incidence of these benign tumors is about twice as high in women as in men.

The majority occur on the neck, back, shoulders and abdominal wall; they are seen only rarely on the face, scalp, hands and feet. As a rule such lumps cause few symptoms, but in areas such as the inner surfaces of the thighs they may form pendulous masses.

Lipomas may also be associated with muscles or the larger joints. Internal lipomas, on the intestine for instance, are relatively uncommon.

Microscopically, a typical lipoma is similar to normal fat tissue. As lipomas usually expand without infiltrating adjacent areas, they are easily removed and seldom recur.

liposarcoma

An extremely uncommon malignant tumor composed of mutant fat cells. Liposarcomas rarely arise from lipomas. Unlike lipomas, they arise primarily in deeper structures and have a predilection for certain sites—particularly the thigh, leg and buttock.

Examples of liposarcomas have been recorded in children but they are uncommon in patients under the age of 20 and arise mainly in middle and later life. The frequency in males and females is about equal. Beginning as inconspicuous swellings, they have usually attained an appreciable size before they are diagnosed and treated. Treatment involves surgical removal of the tumor, including removal of sufficient adjacent tissue to discourage recurrence.

lithotomy

The removal of a stone, usually a bladder stone, through an operative incision. Stones (see CALCULUS) may form in the bladder or may enlarge there after being passed from the kidney. The main symptoms are pain, frequent urination and blood in the urine. An x-ray usually reveals the presence of the stone. It is removed by the introduction of a crushing instrument via the urethra, or, if too large and hard, by lithotomy—surgical incision into the bladder above the pubis.

The word also describes a position—the *lithotomy position*. The patient lies on the back with the thighs raised and the knees supported and held apart. The position is employed during childbirth, for gynecological procedures, and in operations on the rectum or anus.

livedo

A mottled discoloration of the skin. In *livedo reticularis* (or *marble skin*) there is a blue purplish appearance seen as a constant phenomenon or upon exposure of the skin to cold air.

It is a disorder involving spasm of an artery and is seen most frequently in a "fish net" pattern of the skin on the arms, legs, or trunk. The condition occurs as a primary disorder or secondary to an underlying disease.

The condition is benign: those who suffer from it should avoid the cold, and as far as possible avoid emotional stress.

liver disease

In order to understand the consequences of liver disease, it is first necessary to appreciate some of the normal functions of the organ—the largest in the body. They may be considered under three main headings: blood, food, and removal of "poisons."

Red blood cells stay in the circulation for 120 days on average and are then removed by the spleen and other tissues. Most of the HEMOGLOBIN from these cells is converted into bilirubin, which is then transported to the liver. Enzymes in the liver cells modify the chemical structure of bilirubin to make it soluble in water—a process called "conjugation." The conjugated bilirubin is secreted into the bile ducts and eventually passes to the intestines. Here bacteria convert the bilirubin into a number of pigments which form the coloring matter of feces.

The total level of bilirubin in the blood does not normally exceed 10 milligrams per liter; if this concentration doubles for any reason, bilirubin is deposited in the skin and whites of the eyes to produce the characteristic yellow appearance of JAUNDICE. There are numerous causes of jaundice and they do not all originate in the liver itself. Even the purely hepatic (liver) causes interfere with the processing of bilirubin at different stages. *Gilbert's disease* is a common harmless condition which runs in families and is marked by a mild, fluctuating jaundice due to inefficient transportation of bilirubin into the liver cells. Jaundice is almost universally found in newborn babies because their conjugating enzymes have a limited capacity.

HEPATITIS, inflammation of the liver due to viruses, alcohol, or drugs, reduces the number of functioning liver cells and blocks the bile ducts by tissue swelling.

The other functions of the liver concerned with blood are the manufacture of plasma proteins (particularly albumin) and factors which are necessary for blood clotting. Both these processes fail in chronic liver diseases such as CIRRHOSIS, when large numbers of cells have been destroyed. The major consequences of these failures are ASCITES (a collection of free fluid in the abdominal cavity) and easy bruising.

The portal vein carries nutrients from their sites of absorption in the small intestine to the liver, where they

THE LIVER

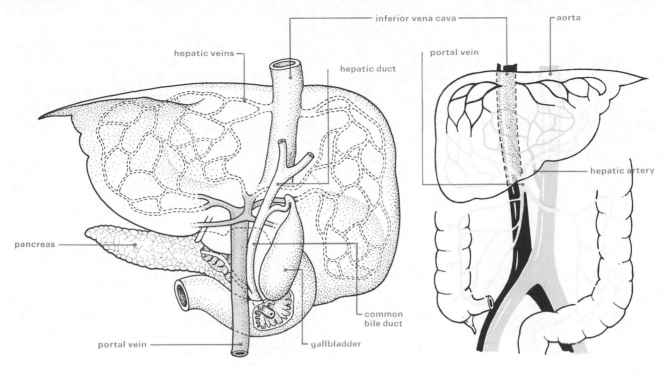

POSTERIOR VIEW OF THE LIVER

BLOOD SUPPLY OF THE LIVER

The liver develops in the embryo as an outgrowth of the intestine and always retains a close link with the digestive system. The portal vein drains blood from the intestine into the liver, where nutrients are utilized and toxic products removed. The liver also secretes bile which is then stored in the gallbladder; after a meal the gallbladder contracts, squeezing bile into the duodenum where it helps to absorb fats.

are extensively processed according to the body's needs. Carbohydrates and other foods are converted into glycogen by the liver. Glycogen is stored in many body cells and can be broken down into glucose (sugar) when energy is needed. GLYCOGEN STORAGE DISEASES are rare conditions in which glycogen stored in the liver or muscles cannot be broken down into glucose. Although the liver controls the level of glucose in the blood, significant disturbances are found only in severe liver disease. This is also true for protein handling—in patients with liver failure the buildup of ammonia and amino acids damages the brain and is an important cause of COMA.

Cirrhosis not only leads to the death of many liver cells but also distorts the "architecture" of the organ, blocking the blood flow through it. This leads to back pressure down the portal vein—*portal hypertension*—and the blood is forced to take alternative routes. The easiest but potentially most dangerous alternative is

through the veins around the esophagus. These become dilated and can eventually burst, leading to massive vomiting of blood (HEMATEMESIS). Drastic measures then have to be taken, and if the patient survives there is a great risk of brain damage.

The final major role of the liver is the removal of toxic substances from the blood. As mentioned above, some toxins (for example, ammonia) are derived from proteins in the diet; drugs are the other important group. The liver deals with many drugs in the way it does with bilirubin: it conjugates them into water-soluble substances which can be excreted in the urine. In patients with liver disease, drug therapy presents major problems and common drugs like diuretics (given to reduce the fluid load in ascites) can precipitate coma. Diets too must be strictly controlled with limited amounts of naturally salty foods and no added salt, and protein and fluid restrictions.

Primary cancer of the liver, HEPATOMA, is the most common cancer in Africa and the Orient, but accounts for only about 2% of all cancers in the United States. Preexisting cirrhosis is present in an estimated 70% of American patients and the prognosis is poor.

See also HEPATOMEGALY.

lobotomy

A neurosurgical operation (one form of PSYCHOSURGERY) in which association tracts between the prefrontal part of the cerebral cortex and the rest of the brain are destroyed. Also known as *leukotomy*.

The most obvious difference between a monkey's brain and a man's brain is the size of the frontal lobes, but it has proved very difficult to ascribe precise functions to the large areas of brain tissue lying in front of the motor area. Over the years it was noticed that those who had suffered brain injury involving the frontal part of the brain were liable to show less anxiety than normal, and paid less attention to normal social restraints, and in 1935 the Portuguese neurosurgeon Egaz Moniz introduced the operation of lobotomy in cases of extreme anxiety or emotional tension. But the consequent popularity of the operation, which was radical and relatively crude, led to many poor results and indeed tragedies.

With the advent of modern drugs effective in the treatment of anxiety, tension and other psychiatric states, the operation of lobotomy fell into disrepute. It is now performed only as a last resort in cases of intolerable suffering. Such operations are still somewhat unpredictable in their results.

lockjaw

A common name for TETANUS.

lumbago

An old-fashioned term used to describe an acute and severe pain felt in the lower part of the back for which no definite cause can be found. Treatment should be rest in bed, on a hard mattress, analgesics (painkillers, such as aspirin), and the local application of heat.

lung diseases

See PULMONARY DISEASES.

lupus erythematosus

A chronic skin disease, thought to be associated with an immunological disturbance, which manifests itself in two ways: one is confined to the mucous membranes and the skin, the other is a systemic disorder which may affect the skin.

Discoid lupus erythematosus affects patients of middle age, more commonly women than men. It starts as a red patch on the face or on other skin exposed to light, which slowly spreads to become a well-defined disk covered by gray scales. As over months or years the lesions spread the center atrophies and as it scars small blood vessels become prominent (TELANGIECTASIA). It seems that sunlight is an important factor in the development of the disease, and it is therefore important that patients should avoid direct exposure to the sun and use a barrier cream.

About 10% of those affected also develop *systemic lupus erythematosus (SLE)*—also known as *disseminated lupus erythematosus*—a progressive and potentially serious disease. It can affect nearly every organ in the body. Among the complications that may be seen are inflammation of the membrane lining the heart and the smooth membranous sac enveloping the heart, pleurisy, kidney lesions and disorders of the central nervous system.

Treatment recommended is the use of antimalarial drugs by mouth, such as quinacrine or chloroquine, but regular medical supervision is necessary because of toxic effects on the eyes.

lupus vulgaris

Tuberculosis of the skin. It is a slowly developing disease, fortunately now rare. When it does occur it often affects the face or neck. The tubercle bacillus invades the skin directly, or reaches it by spreading from underlying infected glands or joints, or via the lymphatics from a respiratory infection. It is more common in women than in men.

The shape of the lesion is always irregular and the surface may be covered with an adherent crust. The lesion may eventually ulcerate. The mucous membranes of the nose and mouth are frequently affected, and in these cases the ultimate effect (if the condition is left untreated) is serious deformity with scarring. The tongue when attacked has large painful fissures.

Antituberculosis drugs may have to be continued for many months.

lymphadenitis

Inflammation of lymph nodes in the LYMPHATIC SYSTEM.

Acute inflammation of the nodes occurs when there is infection nearby; they may swell to three times their normal size and be very painful. The patient may suffer chills and fever, but can be successfully treated with antibiotics.

Chronic lymphadenitis occurs when there is prolonged or repeated infection of the area from which lymph drains into the node: for example, chronic tonsillar or dental infection may cause chronic lymphadenitis of the neck "glands" and repeated infections of the foot may lead to lymphadenitis of the nodes in the groin. The nodes enlarge but may not be painful or cause fever. Treatment is directed at the chronic or repeated infection.

Sometimes lymphadenitis is caused by direct infection of the lymph nodes themselves, rather than by spread of infection from another site. Among the many conditions that can infect lymph nodes are tuberculosis, typhoid, infectious mononucleosis, measles and several parasitic diseases.

lymphangioma

A malformation—not cancerous—of the lymphatic vessels. It is usually present from birth.

The severity of a lymphangioma ranges from a simple dilatation of a lymph vessel to the formation of groups of thick-walled cysts in the skin. The most common sites are the neck and the limbs.

Diffuse lymphangiomas in the tongue cause *macroglossia* (large tongue) and in the lip *macrocheilia* (large lips). In the limbs they can cause a form of ELEPHANTIASIS (a gross swelling of the tissues of the lower extremities caused by obstruction of the lymphatic vessels).

Treatment of lymphangiomas is difficult. Although they are not malignant they do tend to infiltrate other structures and to recur after surgical removal.

In general, however, lymphangiomas are only a cosmetic problem. They can be more dangerous when they are large and cystic because there is a risk of sudden hemorrhage into the cyst (which would cause it to enlarge and perhaps compress a vital organ or structure, for example, the windpipe).

lymphangitis

Inflammation of a vessel in the LYMPHATIC SYSTEM.

It is caused by the spread of infection from the main site to the lymphatic vessels. Inflamed vessels may throb painfully; in many cases the patient also has a fever and chills. The infection can spread rapidly. Antibiotics are given to avoid the possibility of SEPTICEMIA.

lymphatic system

The vast network of vessels throughout the body (similar to the blood vessels) which transports a watery fluid known as *lymph*.

Lymph is formed from the clear fluid that bathes all tissues of the body and contains material that is too large to enter the blood capillaries. It also carries cells—LYMPHOCYTES—and other substances concerned with the IMMUNE SYSTEM.

The lymphatic system is a network of vessels which drain most of the body's tissues and return excess fluid from between the cells back to the bloodstream. During this journey the lymph fluid filters through lymph nodes, where any foreign particles such as bacteria are trapped.

THE LYMPHATIC SYSTEM

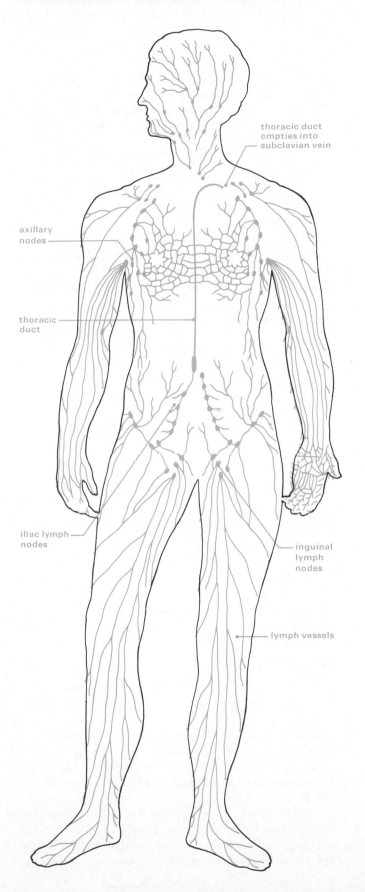

thoracic duct empties into subclavian vein

axillary nodes

thoracic duct

iliac lymph nodes

inguinal lymph nodes

lymph vessels

Tiny lymphatic vessels are found in all organs except the heart and brain. Protein, bacteria and other foreign particles enter the lymphatics, which unite to form larger vessels. Like veins, lymphatic vessels have valves to prevent a backflow of fluid. If for any reason a lymphatic vessel becomes obstructed, the buildup of lymph is called LYMPHEDEMA.

Eventually all the lymphatics drain their contents into two large ducts; from there the lymph reenters the blood circulation through veins at the base of the neck.

Lymphatics draining the small intestine (known as *lacteals*) have a function apart from clearing debris and defending the body: fat is absorbed from the small intestine into the lacteals and so eventually into the bloodstream.

The lymphatic system is interrupted at intervals by groups of glands known as *lymph nodes,* which have two main functions: (1) they have a role in immunity, producing both lymphocytes (defensive white blood cells) and antibodies; and (2) they also act as a second line of defense against infection by bacteria, filtering off and destroying any which bypass the inflammatory response at the site of infection. In the case of cancer cells, the lymph nodes act as a temporary but only partially effective barrier to metastasis (spread of cancer cells from one site to another—see CANCER).

When a lymph node is stimulated into activity, for example by infection, it swells and becomes painful. This swelling may be noticeable even before the infection itself is apparent (swelling of the "glands" in the neck during a throat infection is a common experience).

Apart from those in the back and sides of the neck, the main groups of lymph nodes are in the armpits and groin; either of these groups may be felt to swell and be painful during a limb infection. Other lymph nodes lie at the base of the lungs and around large veins in the abdomen and pelvis.

The tonsils and spleen are also composed of lymphatic tissue and are usually regarded as part of the lymphatic system.

lymphedema

Swelling of a limb, or limbs, caused by blockage of the flow of lymph through the vessels of the LYMPHATIC SYSTEM.

Initially the swollen limb "pits," that is, when pressed with a finger the depression remains—a finding known as *pitting edema.* Later the limb becomes hard and nonpitting and the skin and underlying tissues become thickened.

The condition is occasionally due to congenital abnormalities of the lymphatic vessels. In other cases the blockage of lymph flow is due to inflamed or fibrosed lymph nodes or vessels or to the removal of lymphatics

as part of the treatment of cancer. The lymphatics may also be blocked by parasites (as in some forms of ELEPHANTIASIS). While some relief may be given by elevation of the limb and the use of elastic bandaging or stockings, surgical removal of the thickened tissue from below the skin is the only curative procedure.

lymphocyte

A type of white blood cell. Between 20 and 50% of white blood cells in an adult are lymphocytes.

Lymphocytes play an important role in immunity, in producing antibodies and in recognizing "foreign" tissue. The so-called *B lymphocytes* produce antibodies which they release into the blood. The *T lymphocytes,* on the other hand, are processed in children by the thymus gland; they carry antibodies on their own surface and produce cellular immunity—for instance, in the rejection of transplants.

Large numbers of lymphocytes are found in patients with a chronic infection, both in the blood and commonly at the site of the infection. There may also be excessive numbers of these white cells in LEUKEMIA, but in such cases immunity is depressed because the lymphocytes are abnormal.

In certain rare disorders the number of lymphocytes is decreased, leading to poor immunity.

Normally lymphocytes are produced in the lymphoid tissues of the body (lymph nodes, spleen and tonsils); to a lesser extent they are also produced in the bone marrow.

lymphogranuloma venereum

A sexually transmitted disease caused by virus-like organisms of the genus *Chlamydia.* It is quite rare.

After infection, through sexual contact, there is an incubation period of 5 to 21 days. A blister then forms on the genital area, often unnoticed. It disappears and the infection spreads to the lymph nodes—which enlarge, soften and eventually break down. In women and in homosexual men the rectum may become inflamed. Fistulas (abnormal openings) may form and the rectum and anus may be permanently narrowed.

Elsewhere in the body the infection leads to fever, joint pains, skin eruptions and conjunctivitis.

Early treatment with an appropriate antibiotic (usually tetracycline) cures the condition and prevents the later complications. Pain over the enlarged lymph nodes can be relieved by hot compresses and analgesics.

lymphoma

A cancer of the lymphoid tissue.

There are several types of varying degrees of

malignancy, which can be distinguished by microscopic examination of a sample of tissue.

A technique known as *lymphangiography* may be used to detect the positioning and spread of a lymphoma. Radiopaque material is injected into a lymphatic vessel, which can then be seen on an x-ray together with any abnormalities.

Treatment of a lymphoma depends on its type, but is based on the usual anticancer measures of radiotherapy, chemotherapy and surgery.

Common forms of lymphoma are HODGKIN'S DISEASE and LYMPHOSARCOMA.

See also CANCER, LYMPHATIC SYSTEM.

lymphosarcoma

A type of lymphoma (cancer of the LYMPHATIC SYSTEM) mainly affecting middle-aged people and causing symptoms similar to chronic LEUKEMIA.

A lymphosarcoma may arise in any lymph node. Since the cancer spreads rapidly, by the time it is detected more than one site is usually involved. In later stages of the disease, malignant cells spill over into the bloodstream where they are found in large numbers—resembling the blood pattern of chronic lymphatic leukemia. The symptoms are similar: fatigue and loss of energy due to ANEMIA, and abdominal discomfort from the enlarged liver and spleen.

Treatment of a lymphosarcoma is by radiotherapy and chemotherapy, and remissions of the disease often last for several years.

BURKITT'S LYMPHOMA is a type of lymphosarcoma affecting children in tropical countries. There is very strong evidence to suggest that this cancer is caused by a virus (the Epstein-Barr virus which causes infectious mononucleosis). Treatment with a combination of anticancer drugs results in cure in as many as 70–80% of cases.

M

malabsorption

A term applied to a number of conditions in which normal absorption of nutrients is impaired. The consequences are disorders of the body due to deficiencies of substances necessary for health, and disturbed function of the intestines.

Failure to absorb fat from the intestine produces offensive pale stools larger than normal which tend to float in water; sometimes there is diarrhea with colic, sometimes constipation. If the malady involves failure to absorb carbohydrates, the abdomen becomes enlarged and uncomfortable and there is a frothy diarrhea. Various deficiencies may show themselves. In children and infants there is failure to thrive, and perhaps loss of weight.

The patients·are weak and may be anemic. Vitamins are lost: the consequence may be RICKETS, TETANY and a low level of calcium in the blood, or a dry skin and sparse hair, sore mouth and tongue, and various neurological signs. If there is a loss of water and salts there may be a low blood pressure, cramps, thirst and excessive formation of urine, with weakness and abnormalities of sensation.

Malabsorption occurs in many diseases; they range from conditions which block the lymphatic vessels draining the intestine to the operative removal of parts of the intestine or stomach; but the best known are CELIAC DISEASE, TROPICAL SPRUE, CROHN'S DISEASE, liver disease, chronic enteritis, infestation by worms, and the atrophy (wasting away) of the stomach that is part of pernicious ANEMIA. Diseases of the gallbladder and pancreas may produce malabsorption syndromes, as may the effects of radiation. In each case, treatment is directed at the underlying disease.

malaria

A parasitic infection occurring mainly in the tropics and subtropics.

Malaria is caused by a protozoan parasite of the genus *Plasmodium*, which requires two different hosts during its life cycle: man and mosquito. It is transmitted from man to man by the bite of an infected mosquito. The mosquito sucks blood from an infected person, taking in the parasite—which can then continue its life cycle within the mosquito. Later, when the mosquito bites another human, the parasites pass in with the insect's saliva.

Once inside man, the parasites continue to develop in the liver. From there they reenter the bloodstream and multiply inside red blood cells, causing them to rupture within two or three days. This rupture of the red cells is responsible for the characteristic chills, fever and sweating of malaria. Parasites released into the bloodstream when the cells rupture can enter other red cells, and the life cycle is repeated.

Four species of *Plasmodium* cause human malaria. Three of them (*P. vivax, P. falciparum* and *P. ovale*) repeat the cycle every 48 hours and produce symptoms every third day (tertian malaria); *P. malariae* repeats the cycle every 72 hours (quartan malaria).

Among other consequences of the parasitic infestation and rupture of blood cells are anemia, jaundice, an enlarged spleen, congestion of blood vessels in the brain, and kidney failure.

MALARIA

LIFE HISTORY OF *Plasmodium* PARASITE

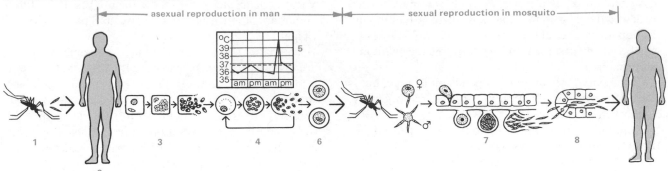

A female Anopheles mosquito (1) injects Plasmodium parasites into man (2); they develop in the liver (3) before reproducing asexually inside red blood cells (4). These cells periodically burst, releasing parasites which attack more red cells, causing fever (5). Some red cells become filled with sexual forms (6) which reproduce in the stomach of a mosquito (7) after it has sucked blood from the man. Infective forms then migrate to the mosquito's salivary glands (8), ready to enter the next victim when it bites.

Quinine was the classic antimalarial drug, but it has been largely superseded by less toxic drugs such as chloroquine and primaquine. Other drugs, such as proguanil and pyrimethamine, can protect against malaria if taken for two weeks before entering a malarious area and continued for a month after leaving it. The inhabitants of malarious regions need to take regular doses of drugs to protect themselves against the infection.

At a public health level, eradication of malaria is best attempted by attacking the mosquito in order to break the life cycle of the parasites. Partial success has been achieved by draining swamps and other breeding places and by the use of special insecticides (unfortunately, mosquitoes tend to develop resistance to these chemical agents). Despite prolonged efforts by the World Health Organization malaria is still a major public health problem in Africa and Asia.

Malaria may be seen in temperate areas since it can develop in a traveler after his return from the tropics. Symptoms may be delayed for weeks or even months. The parasite can also be transmitted directly from man to man by the transfusion of contaminated blood.

malignancy

The tendency of a disease to progress relentlessly to a fatal end. The term is generally used to refer to cancers as distinct from benign tumors—which, though they may grow in size, do not invade surrounding tissue, nor produce "seedlings" which can travel in the circulation and set up secondary growths (*metastasis*).

Microscopically, malignant tumors differ from benign tumors in that their structure is atypical and does not closely resemble their tissue of origin. There are varying degrees of imperfect differentiation of tissue; the poorer the differentiation, the more malignant the tumor.

The term may also be used to refer to the most dangerous form of a disease, such as when MALARIA caused by *Plasmodium falciparum* is called *malignant tertian malaria* to distinguish it from the benign tertian forms caused by *Plasmodium vivax* and *Plasmodium ovale*. *Malignant hypertension* is a severe form of high blood pressure that is rapidly progressive, usually accompanied by extensive damage to the blood vessels.

See also CANCER and the major article on **Oncology.**

malnutrition

The causes of malnutrition, or starvation, fall into two basic groups: the first includes poverty, famine, natural disasters and war; the second includes a number of diseases such as neurological conditions in which the patient cannot feed himself or cannot swallow food, cancer, malabsorption syndrome, and psychological disorders (see ANOREXIA NERVOSA).

The greatest cause of starvation is poverty, present in all the countries of the world, even the most well-developed; in less fortunate countries it is from time to time exacerbated by famine due to the failure of crops.

One of the recognized weapons of war is blockade, and now herbicides may be used to promote the failure of crops in hostile lands in order to starve the enemy into submission. But the last to be affected are the fighting men, and war means starvation for the women, children and aged.

A healthy man or woman can go without food for

MALNUTRITION

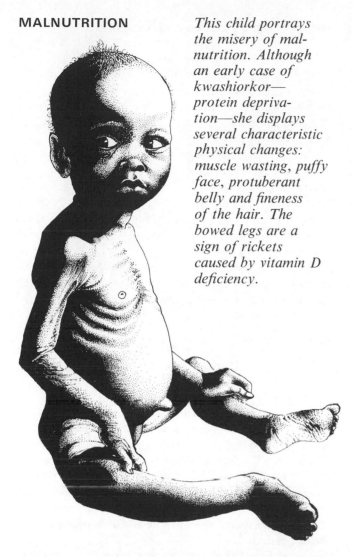

This child portrays the misery of malnutrition. Although an early case of kwashiorkor— protein deprivation—she displays several characteristic physical changes: muscle wasting, puffy face, protuberant belly and fineness of the hair. The bowed legs are a sign of rickets caused by vitamin D deficiency.

about two weeks with little effect except loss of weight, but he or she needs to have an adequate supply of water. The effects of prolonged undernutrition include swelling of the tissues (edema), most marked in the legs and sometimes in the abdomen, loss of weight and elasticity of the skin, low blood pressure, pulse and temperature, diarrhea, susceptibility to infection, anemia, apathy, and emotional instability.

Recovery depends on the restoration to normal of tissues which have become atrophic, particularly the tissues of the gut and the heart. Those with persisting diarrhea and a systolic blood pressure below 80 mm of mercury may die although there is a plentiful supply of food.

See also CACHEXIA, KWASHIORKOR, MARASMUS.

mammography

X-ray examination of the breast in the diagnosis of the cause of breast lumps; it is used as a screening test for BREAST CANCER.

A picture is obtained of the soft tissues of the breast in which any potentially cancerous areas may be seen. Mammography can detect cysts and tumors in the breast tissue while they are still too small to be readily palpated by a nurse or physician, so that it provides a means for the detection of early cancer.

Like any screening test, its cost has to be weighed against its accuracy, any potential dangers, and the value of detection. Tumors detected by mammography may be either benign or cancerous; further tests and often removal of the tumor may be needed before a firm diagnosis can be made. Breast cancer screening by mammography carries a very small risk since repeated x-ray examinations may themselves induce cancer. For that reason, current policy in the United States is for mammography to be used in screening only for women aged over 50 and for women in high-risk groups, such as those related to women who have had breast cancer. Studies such as the Health Insurance Plan project in New York have shown, however, that in these high-risk groups and in women over the age of 50 mammography can improve the detection rate and lower mortality from breast cancer.

mammoplasty

A cosmetic operation to enlarge or reduce the size of the breast or to restore its shape after a cancer operation.

Reduction mammoplasty consists of removal of tissue from the breasts when they are too large or heavy, followed by their cosmetic "reconstruction."

Augmentation mammoplasty is the opposite: enlargement of the breasts. Surgeons currently prefer to implant a sealed bag containing silicone or saline. The implant is placed into a pocket cut into the breast, and its size can be adjusted up or down after the operation. There is a small long-term risk of scarring and distortion of the shape of the breast, especially if the silicone leaks out of the implant. Mammoplasty is being used increasingly to restore the breast contours after surgical removal of a tumor by partial mastectomy. In such cases the surgeon usually excises most of the breast tissue, leaving the skin and if possible the nipple intact.

The volume of the breast may then be restored to normal either with a silicone implant or with a graft of fat or muscle taken from another part of the body. With such restorative surgery no form of artificial breast or padding is needed, and the fact that surgery has been performed may be unnoticeable even when the patient wears a bikini.

mania

A disordered mental state characterized by a mood change to excitement and elation. Often the mood swings between mania and profound depression—the *manic depressive psychosis.*

The sufferer becomes optimistic, overconfident and has a general feeling of euphoria. He becomes talkative yet flits from subject to subject and is easily distracted. He has little insight into his condition and will rarely admit that he is unwell.

The manic patient often gets into difficulties—for example, overspending, making rash promises or unwise business deals, or becoming violent when thwarted.

The severity of mania varies widely; in mild cases it is necessary to have an idea of the patient's previous personality to be sure of the diagnosis. Mild mania is known as *hypomania* and severe mania as *acute mania.* The extreme form is *delirious mania,* in which mental activity is so "high" that the patient's speech is incoherent and his constant restlessness and failure to sleep can lead to total exhaustion.

Acute mania is a medical emergency needing treatment with large doses of major tranquilizers such as chlorpromazine or haloperidol. The outlook for patients with recurrent attacks of mania (with or without depression) has been transformed by the discovery that regular treatment with *lithium salts* can prevent or reduce the severity of the episodes of mental abnormality. The dose has to be carefully adjusted to avoid toxic side effects (tremor, mental confusion and eventually coma); regular measurement of the blood content of lithium is an essential part of treatment.

See also the major article on **Psychiatry.**

Mantoux test

A test for tuberculosis.

The test consists of the injection of tuberculin, a protein derived from the tubercle bacillus, or a purified protein derivative of tuberculin, PPD. If the patient is (or has been) infected with tuberculosis a positive reaction occurs at the site of the injection within 48 to 72 hours. The tuberculin—being a "foreign protein" recognized by the body of a person who has experienced TB—evokes a delayed immune response in the form of a raised, red, itchy swelling.

The reaction may also be positive in a person who has never been infected with TB but who has previously been immunized against the disease by an injection of BCG (BACILLE CALMETTE-GUÉRIN) vaccine. Since a positive reaction may be due to a symptomless infection in the past, it is of little diagnostic help; but a negative response is close to certain proof that the individual concerned has not had TB and has no immunity to it. False negative reactions do occur in persons in poor health and with diseases such as HODGKIN'S DISEASE which affect the body's immune responses.

maple syrup urine disease

An inherited error of metabolism.

As with other metabolic abnormalities the condition is rare, is due to an enzyme defect, and is characterized by excretion of a recognizable substance in the urine—in this case one with a characteristic odor that gives the disease its name.

The patient cannot cope with certain essential amino acids (the "building blocks" of protein); therefore, a special diet is necessary in which these amino acids are contained in the minimum possible quantities. Normal food, especially food rich in protein, cannot be eaten without the risk of severe neurological disease and mental retardation.

The special diet has to be given as early as possible in infancy—as soon as the disease is diagnosed; survival might then be expected for many years.

marasmus (starvation)

Gross undernutrition; the condition caused by a deficiency of both calories and protein.

There is a spectrum of effects of protein-calorie malnutrition: when both are in short supply the result is marasmus; when protein is deficient in a diet adequate in calories, the result is KWASHIORKOR.

Marasmus is most commonly seen in children in the first year of life in Third World countries. There is marked retardation of growth, extreme wasting of muscles and general debility. Although the child remains alert and hungry, there is a risk of long-term mental deficit.

Unlike kwashiorkor, there are no hair changes or swollen abdomen.

Apart from shortage of food, the condition may be caused by poor digestion and absorption (for example, in prematurity), cystic fibrosis, or through mental illness.

Adequate feeding reverses marasmus.

Marburg virus disease

A rare hemorrhagic viral disease first associated with vervet monkeys imported from Africa. Also known as *green monkey disease.*

Marburg virus disease was first identified in an outbreak in laboratory personnel in Germany and Yugoslavia in 1967. Seven people died in this outbreak and a further three in a second episode in Johannesburg. Subsequently there has been a widespread epidemic in Zaire and the Sudan. The first symptoms are fever, headache and muscular pain, followed by nausea, vomiting and diarrhea. Bleeding from the nose and other body orifices may occur. The incubation period is believed to be from 4 to 9 days and the mortality rate in known outbreaks has been about 30%. Transmission of the disease is usually from infected tissues or body fluids, but airborne transmission (by droplet spray from the breath of an infected person) is also suspected. Treatment consists of "barrier nursing" and the administration of serum from a surviving patient.

Marfan's syndrome

A relatively rare inherited disease of connective tissue, in which the patient grows extremely tall and thin and is subject to various other abnormalities.

In addition to the effects on the skeletal system, the main signs of the disease occur in the eyes (the lens often becomes dislocated and the retina may become detached from the underlying tissues). The cardiovascular system may also be affected, manifest especially by the development of a progressive weakness in the wall of the largest artery (aorta).

Patients have exceptionally long bones, including the bones of the hand; this gives rise to an appearance known as *arachnodactyly* ("spider fingers"). The skeletal deformities are the most obvious feature of the condition: long arms and legs, flat feet, a narrow and pointed skull, deformities of the chest and an abnormally wide degree of joint mobility.

Patients who survive to adulthood may pass the disease on to their children.

marijuana

See CANNABIS.

mastectomy

Surgical removal of a breast.

The traditional theory about the progression of BREAST CANCER has been that the tumor arises in a single site, and, at an indeterminate time later, spreads outside the breast to form metastatic deposits. The first metastatic spread is thought to occur via the lymphatic drainage to local lymph nodes in the armpit or beneath the sternum (breastbone). Later spread of cancer cells may be by means of the blood circulation, leading to metastases in the bone, brain and liver. Thus, the logical way to cure breast cancer is to remove the affected breast and any involved lymph nodes in a mastectomy operation.

Around the beginning of the 20th century, Halstead and Meyer independently described their versions of the mastectomy technique. Both employed a *radical* approach in which the breast, the underlying pectoral muscles and the lymph nodes in the corresponding armpit were removed en bloc. Many women found this

to be a mutilating operation; in addition, it produced problems of arm swelling and shoulder immobility. Nevertheless, radical mastectomy is unsurpassed in terms of the number of patients with early breast cancer who survive for five years after operation and has been the mainstay of operative treatment for 75 years.

Although radical mastectomy statistically seems to offer the best chance for survival in early breast cancer, it is only marginally better than other less extensive operations. For this reason and to spare the patient unnecessary psychological suffering, radical mastectomy has been practiced far less in the past few years. A modified radical mastectomy, in which the pectoral muscles and the lymph nodes highest in the armpit are spared, is now probably the most common operation used in the United States. Some surgeons have gone a step further and only perform a *simple mastectomy,* leaving all the lymph nodes in place. The argument advanced for this operation is that the lymph nodes are a powerful natural defense against cancer spread: opponents point out that lymph nodes are often involved when they feel normal and anyway will have to be constantly checked after surgery.

If the breast cancer has already formed distant metastases or large lymph node deposits, mastectomy alone is ineffective. Various combinations of hormones, drugs and radiation therapy are then added to the surgical treatment. Many surgeons now believe that combination therapy should be applied even in early cases because it is likely that microscopic metastases are already present.

See also the major article on **Oncology.**

MASTECTOMY

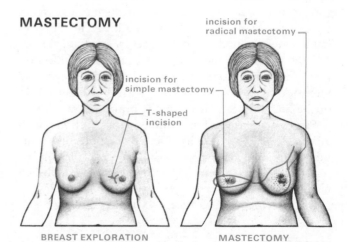

incision for
radical mastectomy

incision for
simple mastectomy

T-shaped
incision

BREAST EXPLORATION

MASTECTOMY

There are many techniques employed in breast surgery. The picture on the left shows the small T-shaped cut used for exploring the nipple region so that any suspicious lumps can be removed and examined microscopically. The right hand figure illustrates two types of mastectomy used in the treatment of breast cancer.

mastitis

Mastitis strictly means inflammation of the breast and its most important manifestations occur in the lactating woman. In one type the woman may have a raised temperature and congested, painful breasts. There is no pus produced and the inflammation is hormonal rather than infective in origin.

By contrast, in *acute suppurative mastitis* the breast becomes infected with *Staphylococcus aureus* or (less commonly) *Streptococcus pyogenes*. The bacteria gain access to the breast either via the ducts or through a crack in the nipple. If appropriate antibiotic treatment is not instigated, an abscess may form, resulting in considerable pain and possibly scarring of the breast.

Chronic mastitis is a term used to describe certain hyperplastic and cystic conditions of the breast. This group of diseases is also referred to as *mammary dysplasia, fibroadenosis* and *mastopathy*. The condition is extremely common and is caused by an imbalance in the hormonal cycle associated with menstruation. As a result the breast tissue feels more nodular than usual and may be tender. Inflammation plays no part in the cause and the major pathological changes are of fibrosis, cystic change, and increase in the number and size of breast lobules.

mastoiditis

A complication of middle ear infection. Infection reaches the middle ear from the throat, via the Eustachian tube. From the middle ear, infection may spread to the *mastoid air cells,* small air-filled cavities in the *mastoid bone* (which forms the bulge in the skull immediately behind the ear). In severe cases an abscess may be formed in the mastoid bone and the infection may then spread, with a danger that it may reach the interior of the skull to cause MENINGITIS (inflammation of the membranes that cover the brain).

Prompt treatment of middle ear infections with antibiotics is now usually effective in preventing this once common complication but surgery (*mastoidectomy*) may be required if infection becomes established in the bone itself.

See also the major article on **Otolaryngology.**

measles

A highly contagious viral disease (also known as *morbilli* and, in English-speaking countries, *rubeola*), common in childhood.

Before the introduction of active immunization, epidemics used to occur every two or three years. In affluent countries the illness mainly involves children aged three to five years and is usually mild; in underdeveloped countries, where nutrition is poor, children under two years are predominantly affected and there is a high mortality rate.

The measles virus is 150 millionths of a millimeter in diameter. Infected individuals shed the measles virus in droplet secretions from the nose, mouth, or throat for four to five days before their skin rash appears and for three to five days after the rash disappears—the time during which they can pass the infection to susceptible people.

The incubation period from exposure to the onset of symptoms is usually 10–14 days. The first symptoms are a fever, cough, runny nose, red and watery eyes, and general irritability. During the period just before the rash appears it may be possible to notice what are known as *Koplik's spots,* which resemble coarse grains of salt on a red background; these often appear on the mucous membranes of the mouth opposite the molar teeth.

The rash first emerges behind the ears and along the hairline, and quickly involves the whole face. It then travels downward to reach the feet on about the third day. Initially the rash consists of dusky-red spots, but these coalesce to form irregular blotches. After three days the rash begins to fade, the fever subsides, and the patient's condition rapidly improves.

Complications do occur and mainly involve the respiratory and central nervous systems. Secondary infection with bacteria leading to bronchitis or ear infection is relatively common; it should be suspected if fever persists, and is treated with antibiotics. More seriously, 1 in 1,000 cases develop a postinfectious encephalitis (inflammation of the brain) three to four days after the onset of the rash. It can vary from transient drowsiness to coma and death.

Active immunity against measles can be induced by giving a live attenuated virus vaccine by injection. Natural immunity due to the disease is lifelong but the duration of immunity conferred by vaccination is unknown.

See also the major article on the **Health Care of Children.**

megacolon, congenital

See HIRSCHSPRUNG'S DISEASE.

Meibomian cyst

Another name for CHALAZION.

melanoma

Malignant melanomas are tumors of pigment cells (melanocytes); they can arise either at the site of preexisting moles (pigmented nevi) or at apparently unblemished sites in the skin. Although such malignant transformation in a mole is very rare (1 in 1 million), any changes in shape, size, or pigmentation, or itching, ulceration or bleeding in a dark spot should arouse strong suspicion.

Early diagnosis and treatment of a malignant melanoma is vital because it spreads cancer cells to other sites and can be fatal. Malignant melanoma is responsible for 0.75% of all cancer deaths in the United States and nearly all the patients are over 30 years old. *Juvenile melanoma* is a term applied to a benign pigmented skin lesion in children; it is not a precursor of malignant melanoma. Factors thought to predispose to malignant melanoma are exposure to excess sunlight in the fair-skinned, x-rays, contact with tar and repeated trauma (e.g., shaving or rubbing) to a mole.

A definite diagnosis can only be made after examining a specimen of tissue microscopically. Surgery remains the most effective treatment for the early localized lesion.

During fetal development, melanocytes migrate from the primitive "neuroectoderm" to the eye and meninges (covering membranes of the brain) as well as to the skin. Malignant melanomas occasionally arise in these sites.

melena

The passage of black, tarry stools, indicative of bleeding from the upper gastrointestinal tract. It may occur independently of or in conjunction with hematemesis (the vomiting of blood). The altered color of the blood in melena is due to the action of gastric juice; if the hemorrhage originates below the small intestine, red blood may be passed with the stools.

In patients with melena, two basic questions have to be answered. First, how much blood has been lost? If less than 1 pint, the patient is unlikely to have generalized symptoms of shock, but larger quantities need to be replaced by blood transfusion. Second, what is the source of the bleeding? Melena can be due to swallowed blood from nose bleeds or dental extractions; however, the three most common sources of blood are peptic ulcer, gastritis (inflammation of the stomach lining) and varicose veins around the esophagus.

Other sources of upper gastrointestinal hemorrhage are esophagitis (inflammation of the esophagus) and cancer of the esophagus or stomach. In order to distinguish between these causes, it is usually essential to pass a fiberoptic endoscope through the mouth and into the stomach to visualize any lesions. Once the site of bleeding has been identified, it is possible to initiate the appropriate treatment for the patient.

Finally, it should be remembered that black stools can be caused by ingestion of iron, charcoal or bismuth.

memory

The ability to recall past experiences, ideas, or sensations.

In man, memory is an integral part of the mental processes of learning and thinking, and depends on perception, language, attention and motivation. Thus, memory is not only a complex process in itself, but is extremely difficult to study sensibly in isolation. Nevertheless, the problems of memory have been attacked at various levels by philosophers, psychologists, neurophysiologists and biochemists. In recent years the advent of computer science has led to the analysis of memory in terms of information storage.

The key steps which need to be explained by any theory of memory are: (1) how the information to be remembered is encoded by the brain; (2) how and where this coded information is stored; (3) how the information is retrieved from storage when required. Despite intensive research for many years, any ideas we have about these stages remain largely speculative.

Most psychologists think that human memory has two phases, usually referred to as *short-term memory (STM)* and *long-term memory (LTM)*. STM is operative for a few moments after new information has been received and is of limited capacity. This capacity or memory span was described by Miller (1956) as being of the "magic number 7 plus or minus 2." By this he meant that most people can remember 7 unrelated things, on average, which are presented to them together. The memory span is not limited by information content—7 random digits are remembered for a short time as well as the names of 7 presidents.

Unless the information transiently held in STM is consolidated and transferred to LTM, it is totally lost. However, information which has been properly learned tends to be forgotten bit by bit, over extended periods, if at all. To explain such accurate storage over many years, stable complex molecules such as nucleic acids and proteins have been suggested as the repositories for information in LTM, but this has not been proved. The exact sites of memory storage are also unknown, but lesions in the front part of the temporal lobes of the cerebrum are most often found to impair memory.

menarche

The time of the first menstrual period, at puberty. In temperate climates the average age of a girl at the menarche is about 13 years; it has fallen steadily during the 20th century, perhaps because of the general improvement in nutrition.

The timing of menarche is much influenced by genetic factors and body weight is also important. The natural variation in the age of onset is so wide that menarche is not considered to be abnormally delayed until it has failed to appear by the age of 17.

Normally, estrogen production by the ovaries gradually increases from 8 to 11 years and it becomes cyclical in nature about one year before menarche. Secondary sexual characteristics, such as breast development and pubic hair growth, also often precede the menarche. The initial menstrual periods tend to be irregular and painless (because ovulation does not occur). Nevertheless, their occurrence can be a frightening experience for the girl if she has not been psychologically prepared for her menarche.

In rare cases a girl experiences the symptoms of menstruation, but no menstrual blood is passed. This may indicate a vaginal obstruction due to an imperforate hymen ("maidenhead") which should be corrected surgically. True primary *amenorrhea,* a delay in the menarche beyond the age of 17, may be due to a malfunction or disease of the ovary, the pituitary gland or the hypothalamus. It may also occur in malnutrition anemia or in generalized debilitating disease. Precocious menarche may be a constitutional trait or may result from a hypothalamic disorder.

Ménière's disease

A disorder characterized by vertigo, deafness and tinnitus (ringing in the ears).

In about 50% of cases, unilateral deafness is the first symptom; this may have been present with tinnitus for several years without the patient seeking medical advice. However, the first attack of vertigo is profoundly disturbing to the patient and he feels that either he or his surroundings are spinning. Such an attack may last up to two hours and is often accompanied by vomiting.

The attacks of vertigo recur irregularly, but often every few weeks. During a period of remission the hearing and tinnitus may improve, but they become progressively worse with each attack. Ménière's disease tends to run its course over several years; the attacks tend to decline in severity and finally cease, but the patient is left with severe deafness.

The cause of Ménière's disease is unknown, but the major pathological change is an accumulation of excess fluid in the inner ear *(endolymphatic hydrops)* damaging the delicate nerve endings. Some believe that the chain of events which results in the excess of endolymph is triggered by stress. Treatment for Ménière's disease may be medical or surgical, but there is no definitive cure. Drug treatment largely comprises sedatives and antiemetics (to prevent vomiting) whereas the variety of operations practiced is surprisingly wide. Operation is rare, however; many patients have only mild and occasional attacks and require relatively little treatment.

See also the major article on **Otolaryngology.**

meningioma

A tumor of the meninges—the membranes which cover the brain and spinal cord. Meningiomas do not usually occur before middle age and are slightly more common in women than in men.

Characteristically, a meningioma is a single, large, lobulated tumor which is clearly separate from the underlying nerve tissue. They are classified pathologically as benign tumors in that they do not invade the adjacent brain, and do not spread to other parts of the body. However, meningiomas often infiltrate the overlying skull and a bony prominence can sometimes be felt on the head.

Although meningiomas are classed as benign, their presence within the skull or spinal canal displaces the normal tissue and can have serious consequences. *Spinal meningiomas* initially cause sensory symptoms such as pain, but can progress to complete paraplegia. Because meningiomas grow slowly, the brain can often adjust and accommodate tumors 2–3 cm in diameter with little or no evidence of a rise in intracranial pressure. When symptoms do occur they may include paralysis or weakness of limbs, convulsions, headache, impairment of speech, interference with vision and subtle mental changes.

Unless an intracranial meningioma can be removed surgically it may eventually be fatal. The new technique of computerized axial tomography (the CAT scanner) is very effective in displaying small meningiomas, and earlier diagnosis should improve the chances of successful surgery.

meningitis

The brain and spinal cord are covered by three membranes, known technically as the *meninges:* the *dura mater* (the outermost and toughest, in contact with the inner surface of the skull), the *arachnoid* (the middle membrane) and the *pia mater* (the innermost membrane, directly in contact with the surface of the brain). Meningitis means inflammation of these membranes, especially the arachnoid and pia mater.

Meningitis is most commonly caused by a bacterial or viral infection. The microorganisms can reach the meninges from the exterior (such as by means of a severe head wound), from the bloodstream (for example, from another focus of infection such as the upper respiratory tract), or (rarely) directly from the brain itself.

In the United States approximately 70% of all cases of acute pyogenic ("pus-forming") meningitis are caused by infection with any one of three species of bacteria: *Neisseria meningitidis* (or meningococcus), *Diplococcus pneumoniae* (or pneumococcus) or *Hemophilus influenzae* (meningitis caused by the last-named microor-

MENINGITIS

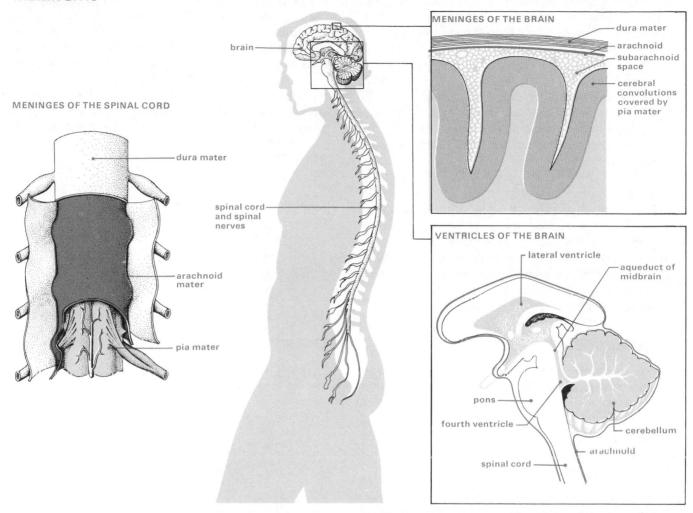

MENINGES OF THE SPINAL CORD

brain

dura mater

arachnoid mater

pia mater

spinal cord and spinal nerves

MENINGES OF THE BRAIN

dura mater
arachnoid
subarachnoid space
cerebral convolutions covered by pia mater

VENTRICLES OF THE BRAIN

lateral ventricle
aqueduct of midbrain
pons
fourth ventricle
cerebellum
arachnoid
spinal cord

The meninges are three layers of protective membranes which cover the brain and spinal cord. The subarachnoid space between the inner two layers contains cerebrospinal fluid (CSF). CSF is produced in the ventricles of the brain and flows into the subarachnoid space through openings in the fourth ventricle. Meningitis, inflammation of the meninges, results from bacteria and viruses multiplying in the CSF.

ganism is more common in children under the age of five). When any of these bacteria infect the lining membranes of the brain the meninges can become quickly inflamed and the space between the two innermost membranes (the "subarachnoid space"), which normally contains clear cerebrospinal fluid, becomes filled with pus. Pus is not usually formed in acute meningitis caused by a viral infection or the causative organism of tuberculosis (*Mycobacterium tuberculosis* or the "tubercle bacillus").

All forms of acute meningitis, regardless of their cause, give rise to a number of common symptoms

(although the symptoms of tuberculous meningitis are insidious rather than dramatic). Headache, increasing in severity, is usually the first symptom. The patient typically has a high fever and pronounced stiffness of the neck. As the disease progresses, the mental state of the patient can change from delirium through drowsiness to coma. Photophobia (extreme sensitivity of the eyes to light) and convulsions are also often experienced. A definitive diagnosis depends largely on a study of the cerebrospinal fluid, obtained by means of a lumbar puncture: insertion of a hollow needle between two of the lumbar vertebrae (in the lower part of the back) to the point where a sample of the fluid can be drawn off. The visual appearance of this fluid (cloudy or clear), its protein and sugar content, and the presence of bacteria—which can be stained and examined under the microscope for specific identification—are all important diagnostic evidence of meningitis. Confirmation of the diagnosis by bacterial culture of the cerebrospinal fluid takes about one or two days, but it is imperative to start treatment immediately.

Both the meningococcus and pneumococcus are

usually sensitive to penicillin; typical initial treatment involves the intravenous injection of benzyl penicillin (penicillin G) every four hours. Meningococcal meningitis responds particularly well to penicillin and this treatment, if it is given sufficiently early, should result in complete cure in the vast majority of cases. Pneumococcal meningitis is typically slower to improve and is occasionally associated with permanent neurological complications (such as impairment of hearing). This condition has a higher fatality rate in patients over the age of about 50. Meningitis caused by infection with *Hemophilus influenzae* can usually be cured in 90% or more of children by prompt treatment with ampicillin or chloramphenicol. There is no specific drug treatment available for viral meningitis, which comprises the majority of the remaining cases, but fortunately most patients make a full spontaneous recovery. Tuberculous meningitis usually responds well to specific drugs used in the control of tuberculosis.

See also the major article on **Neurology.**

meningocele

A protrusion of the covering membranes (meninges) of the brain or spinal cord through a defect in the skull or vertebral column. In the latter case the condition is also known as a *meningomyelocele.*

See also SPINA BIFIDA.

menisectomy

In the knee joint, the medial and lateral cartilages *(menisci;* singular, *meniscus)* are two crescent-shaped wedges of fibrocartilage interposed between the femur and tibia (the thighbone and shinbone, respectively). These menisci compensate for the incongruities in the shapes of the two bones and facilitate smooth movement at the joint. If one or other meniscus should be torn and displaced by injury, or if it is distorted by a cyst, then it is usually removed surgically (a procedure known as menisectomy).

Although the knee is principally a hinge joint, once it has been flexed it is possible for the tibia to be rotated or twisted. When the leg is bearing weight and the flexed knee is violently twisted, the meniscus can be torn. The torn and displaced fragment of cartilage can jam between the femur and tibia, "locking" the knee so that the leg cannot be straightened. Two-thirds of these cases involve the medial meniscus only. Such injuries are often incurred in sports, particularly football.

Initial treatment following injury may be nonsurgical and involve merely splinting the affected joint. However, a true tear does not heal satisfactorily because the cartilage has virtually no blood supply. Therefore, if the symptoms of pain and knee-locking persist,

menisectomy is indicated. With appropriate physical therapy, approximately 75% of patients regain complete functional efficiency of the knee joint (a "rim" of fibrocartilage regenerates from the margin of the excised meniscus). In cases where the diagnosis is not clear or where symptoms persist postoperatively, ARTHROSCOPY can be performed—in which a special optical instrument (arthroscope) is inserted into the joint cavity to permit direct inspection of the damage.

MENISECTOMY

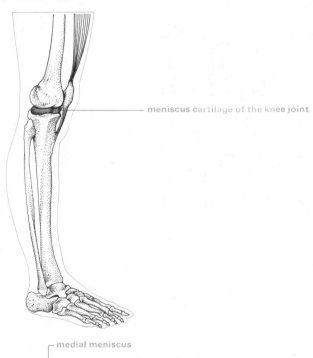

meniscus cartilage of the knee joint

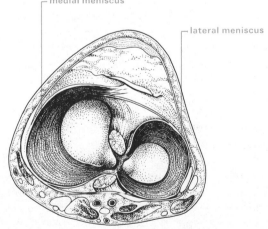

medial meniscus

lateral meniscus

A CROSS SECTION THROUGH THE RIGHT KNEE SEEN FROM ABOVE

The two meniscus cartilages in the knee transmit weight from the thigh to the lower leg. Cartilage injuries result from violent twisting of the knee; torn cartilages do not heal and have to be removed by a menisectomy operation.

menopause

The menopause (or "climacteric") marks the cessation of a woman's sexual cycles (menstruation) and may occur any time between the ages of 40 to 55 (although the onset is more commonly between the ages of 47 and 50).

The precise mechanism underlying the menopause is not fully understood, but it seems that the ovaries become unresponsive to the gonadotropic hormones (GONADOTROPINS) secreted by the pituitary gland at the base of the brain. Therefore, the blood level of circulating ESTROGENS falls significantly, resulting in many changes.

In the normal menopause the menstrual periods may be scant and infrequent before the final cessation. Heavy or irregular bleeding should always be investigated. Perhaps up to about 70% of menopausal women experience "hot flushes" (or "hot flashes"). These are produced by vascular disturbances and are characterized by a feeling of warmth in the face, neck and chest; they may be accompanied by blushing or sweating. It has been suggested by some medical experts that the symptoms may be related to increased secretion of FSH (follicle-stimulating hormone) by the pituitary gland, in the absence of the normal inhibitory feedback of ovarian estrogens; however, some physicians dispute this theory. Hot flushes typically last for only a few minutes at a time, but may occur several times a day. Vaginal dryness is also commonly associated with the menopause.

Apart from the physical changes of the menopause, many women experience psychological problems. Nervous tension and irritability are common. Adaptation is often extremely difficult to the idea of approaching old age, the end of childbearing and the diminution of family responsibilities. Some women become severely depressed.

Treatment to relieve some of the more troublesome symptoms of the menopause includes psychotherapy in varying degrees (to allay anxiety and alleviate depression) and hormonal replacement for the suppression of hot flushes. The lowest effective dose of estrogen is frequently prescribed to minimize possible side effects (such as coronary or cerebral thrombosis). Recent evidence has been presented which suggests that estrogen replacement therapy increases the risk of cancer of the uterus. Much more information needs to be collected and evaluated on this possible side effect, but all patients on long-term therapy should be closely supervised. It is doubtful if short-term therapy is at all dangerous.

Postmenopausal bleeding (vaginal bleeding which occurs a year or more following the onset of the menopause) must always be investigated.

menorrhagia

Menorrhagia means excessive or prolonged bleeding at the normal time of menstruation. It may occur in isolation or be associated with other disturbances in the menstrual cycle—such as *polymenorrhea,* where bleeding occurs with abnormal frequency. In menorrhagia, up to 180 ml of blood can be lost during each menstrual cycle and the woman can thus easily become anemic as a result.

Menorrhagia has many possible causes and should always be fully investigated by a gynecologist. Lesions in the pelvis which can give rise to this condition include FIBROIDS, POLYPS and ENDOMETRIOSIS. However, in many cases no specific cause can be found (classified as "dysfunctional bleeding"). This is possibly related to a disorder of the production and release of the hormones which control menstruation.

DILATATION AND CURETTAGE (D & C) is often the only way to establish the cause of menorrhagia. In addition to providing diagnostic information, it is frequently a curative procedure. Hormonal therapy with PROGESTINS (or, more commonly these days, with the oral contraceptive pill itself) is sometimes successful in controlling dysfunctional bleeding. In severe cases, HYSTERECTOMY (surgical removal of the uterus) is occasionally required.

menstruation

Menstruation is the normal monthly discharge of blood and cellular debris from the vagina which accompanies the periodic shedding of the lining of the uterus in nonpregnant women. By convention, the first day of menstruation is taken as "day 1" of the menstrual cycle (which is an average of 28 days long). It is only human females and other primates who menstruate; other mammals have an "estrous cycle" which is characterized by a period of "heat" when the sexual interest of the mature female is aroused.

In women the time of the first menstrual period (MENARCHE) is generally around the age of 13; the menstrual cycle continues (in the absence of pregnancy or certain other influences) until the MENOPAUSE.

Menstruation normally lasts for about four days, but can vary from approximately two to seven days. On average, 50 ml of blood are lost and at the end of a menstrual cycle all but the deepest layers of the uterine lining have been shed. The lining of the uterus is restored during the "proliferative" phase of the menstrual cycle, which lasts from about the 5th to the 14th day. This "endometrial proliferation" is stimulated by estrogen (secreted by a ripening ovarian follicle). One ovarian follicle develops during each cycle and its progress is controlled by two hormones—FSH (follicle-stimulating

THE MENSTRUAL CYCLE

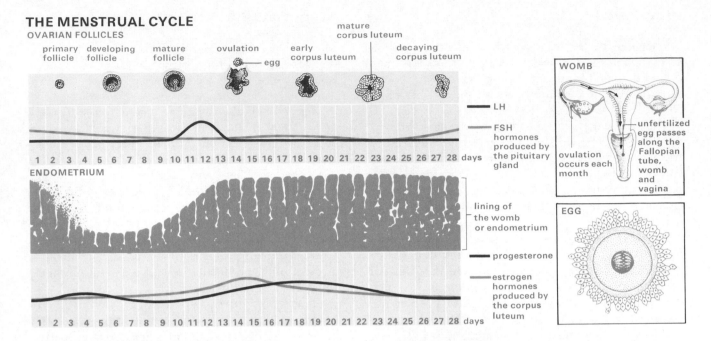

The human menstrual cycle is a monthly fluctuation in the state of the endometrium (lining of the womb), and depends on hormonal changes governed by the pituitary gland in the brain. Day 1 is the first day of menstruation, when the old endometrium starts to slough off. Although the length of the cycle can vary from 23 days to 35 days in normal women, ovulation nearly always occurs 14 days before the end of the cycle.

hormone) and LH (luteinizing hormone)—from the PITUITARY GLAND in the brain. At about the 14th day there is a burst of LH released from the pituitary gland, which causes the distended ovarian follicle to rupture and release an ovum (egg). This is the process of OVULATION and a simple (although rather unreliable) indicator of its occurrence is a temporary rise in the woman's body temperature. Menstruation without ovulation is painless and is common in young girls and at the menopause (and for a time following childbirth).

Shortly after ovulation the empty ovarian follicle is transformed into the corpus luteum, which secretes ESTROGENS and PROGESTERONE for the remainder of the menstrual cycle. This period is the "secretory phase" and the glands in the lining of the uterus become tightly coiled. If fertilization of the ovum has not taken place, the corpus luteum begins to decay on about the 24th day. The falling estrogen and progesterone levels lead to certain changes in the blood vessels of the uterine lining and menstruation occurs. If fertilization *does* take place, the corpus luteum enlarges and maintains the uterine lining in a suitable condition for the nourishment of the fertilized egg (and, thus, menstruation does not occur).

See also PREMENSTRUAL SYNDROME.

mental handicap

An umbrella term used to describe retarded intellectual development resulting in low intelligence, from whatever cause. It is either present at birth as a constitutional trait or it develops in childhood as a result of an environmental insult, such as trauma or infection.

Although there may be a clear-cut genetic cause for a person's mental handicap, it is always important to provide the optimal environment so that he can maximize his potential, however limited it may be. The deterioration of mental powers later in adult life is normally classified as *dementia* rather than as mental handicap, because a normal level of intelligence has been attained at some stage.

In order to understand the concept of mental handicap, it is first necessary to form a working definition of intelligence and to understand how it can be measured. Psychologists have defined intelligence in many different ways, but most would agree that it involves the individual's ability to adapt successfully to his environment and his capacity to learn and manipulate abstract ideas.

There is much controversy about the worth of intelligence tests, but they do provide a standardized means of comparing one person's mental capacity with that of the general population. Many tests are designed so that if the average intelligence quotient (IQ) is 100, then approximately 68% of the population will have an IQ between 85 and 115, and about 95% will lie between 70 and 130. In fact the distribution of intelligence among the population is not quite symmetrical: there are more people with IQs of less than 70 than there are gifted people with IQs above 130.

As a crude numerical measure, an IQ of less than 70 is often taken as the criterion for mental handicap, although this varies with the type of IQ test used. Obviously there is no clear-cut boundary between high-grade mental handicap and the lower levels of "normal" intelligence. Moreover, while subnormal intelligence is the essential factor in mental handicap, it is often the social incompetence and emotional inadequacy of the individual which present the greatest problems.

In the majority of cases, intellectual deficit is not associated with any known organic disease. However, many mentally handicapped people show physical signs of a brain defect and this is nearly always so in the most severely retarded. For practical purposes it is useful to grade mental handicap into three arbitrary groups—morons, imbeciles and idiots.

Morons have IQs of approximately 50 to 70 and constitute the largest class of mental defectives. They are often the children of parents who themselves are intellectually dull. Their constitutional disadvantage is often compounded by poor living conditions and inadequate parents. As infants they tend to lack curiosity and are quiet and well behaved. For this reason they are often undetected until they go to school, when their performance falls progressively further behind that of their peers. It is especially important to identify these children, because with special training they can be helped to lead independent lives. Unfortunately, many do not receive appropriate education and drift into unemployment and crime.

By contrast, imbeciles (with an IQ of approximately 20 to 50) are incapable of independence and are more likely to be diagnosed earlier because of associated physical abnormality. Developmental milestones are delayed and they typically show impulsive, infantile behavior throughout their lives. Parents of imbeciles usually have normal intelligence, and accept that their child will benefit from special education. Mongolism (DOWN'S SYNDROME) is by far the most common syndrome associated with this degree of mental subnormality.

Idiots constitute the lowest grade of mental handicap and are estimated to have an IQ below 20, although this is largely a meaningless figure. They are differentiated from imbeciles by the need to be constantly protected against common physical dangers. The majority of idiots are stunted in growth, have severe brain damage and may suffer from epileptic fits. Many are bedridden, speechless and do not survive childhood.

mental illness

The term "mental illness" covers problems of personality and sexual deviation, NEUROSIS, and the psychotic states of SCHIZOPHRENIA and DEPRESSION.

The nature, cause, diagnosis and treatment of mental illnesses are more controversial than is the case with diseases caused by bacteria or due to an obvious physical abnormality such as a tumor. Doctors not only disagree among themselves but also must contend with the theories (helpful or otherwise) of psychologists, philosophers, and even artists (some of whom insist that a mild degree of mental aberration is essential for the creative process). The fact that so many different views of mental illness are tenable only reflects our basic collective ignorance about many facets of the subject.

The major division among psychiatrists concerns the extent to which they regard mental illness as originating primarily in a structural or biochemical disorder in the brain and how much importance they attach to influences in infancy and childhood and to psychological reactions to conscious or unconscious stresses. These two basic approaches are not mutually exclusive—neurological and psychogenic influences may *both* be involved in most mental problems.

When it comes to treatment, psychiatrists also fall into one "camp" or the other. Those who believe in an organic cause of mental illness will treat their patients with the use of appropriate physical techniques, including drugs, surgical procedures and electroconvulsive therapy. Those who favor a "psychogenic" cause will lean toward various psychotherapeutic techniques—which are often expensive and time consuming. However, when specific, effective drug treatments are available—such as the use of lithium in manic-depressive psychosis—there is usually a consensus of opinion.

See also MANIA and the major articles on **Psychiatry** and **Psychotherapy.**

mercury poisoning

Mercury and its compounds may cause acute or chronic poisoning. Metallic mercury is not dangerously poisonous in very small doses: the child who bites through a clinical thermometer and swallows a few drops of the metal will probably come to no harm. However, mercury salts such as mercuric chloride may cause serious illness; they cause ulceration and chemical burning of the intestinal tract and, after absorption into the bloodstream, may damage the kidneys and nerves. Acute poisoning from an accidental or suicidal dose of a mercury salt causes vomiting, diarrhea, and kidney failure, which is the usual cause of death in fatal cases of mercury poisoning.

Chronic mercury poisoning is most often due to occupational exposure or to industrial pollution of the environment. It may cause mental disturbances, tremor, nerve damage leading to paralysis, and kidney failure. Mass outbreaks have occurred in the past 20 years:

MINAMATA DISEASE in Japan was due to contamination of fish by industrial effluent, and more recently in the Middle East there have been several epidemics of paralysis, especially in children, from the use for human consumption of chemically treated seed corn.

mesothelioma

A rare malignant tumor of the pleura and peritoneum—the membranous sacs lining the thoracic (chest) and abdominal cavities, respectively.

In 1960 a relation was established between mesothelioma and exposure to asbestos, particularly of the crocidolite or Cape blue fiber type. It was found that exposure to asbestos need only have been for one to two months to account for the development of a mesothelioma 20 to 50 years later. Thus, although protective measures are now taken against environmental pollution with asbestos, new cases of mesothelioma will still be presenting themselves at the end of the 20th century.

While radiation therapy occasionally prolongs survival in cases of *pleural mesothelioma,* most patients die within a year of diagnosis.

metabolism

This term, literally meaning "change," is used to refer to all the chemical and energy transformations that are carried out in an organism or in a single cell.

The first specific function of metabolism is to extract chemical energy from the environment. Higher plants and blue-green algae are photosynthetic: they can extract energy from sunlight and make use of carbon dioxide as their sole source of carbon. The cells of all higher animals cannot make direct use of solar energy or carbon dioxide; they derive energy by the chemical degradation of complex nutrients, principally into carbon dioxide and water. This chemical degradation, carried out in a complex series of individual *oxidation-reduction reactions,* is called *catabolism.*

Beside the complete catabolism of exogenous nutrients to yield energy, the body's metabolic processes have to convert foodstuffs into molecular building blocks and assemble them into the components of cells, such as proteins, nucleic acids and lipids (fats or fatlike substances). This synthesis of cellular macromolecules is called *anabolism.* Finally, some of these macromolecules have to be broken down for use or for excretion, as do drugs administered to the body.

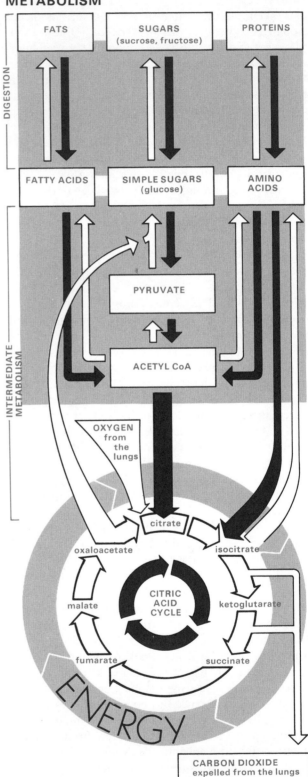

METABOLISM

The diagram shows the pathways of metabolism. Sugars, fats, and proteins are broken down into simple chemicals in the stomach and small intestine, absorbed into the blood and transported to the tissues; within each cell they are transformed into a key substance—"acetyl CoA." Then follows the "citric acid cycle," where controlled combustion with oxygen leads to the production of energy; carbon dioxide is released during this process.

The *basal metabolic rate (BMR)* is the amount of energy consumed by a person in a day in order to maintain essential bodily functions. In an average adult under conditions of mental and physical rest, the BMR is about 2,000 kilocalories/day; in order to carry out a sedentary job only about an extra 500 kilocalories are required. (A kilocalorie is also known as a *kilogram calorie, large calorie* or a *Calorie*—spelled with a capital C to distinguish it from the *small calorie* or *gram calorie*.) BMR is raised by anxiety but decreased in depression. Metabolic processes are sensitively regulated by hormones, and increased levels of epinephrine, norepinephrine and thyroid hormone raise the BMR.

The end products of digestion in humans are mainly amino acids, fat derivatives and sugars such as glucose. These digestive products are catabolized to simpler, intermediate molecules which constitute the common "metabolic pool." The intermediate molecules then either undergo anabolism into proteins, fats or carbohydrates or they may be further catabolized into hydrogen atoms and carbon dioxide. This final catabolism is carried out by a biochemical pathway known as the *citric acid cycle* and occurs in the specialized mitochondria of cells. The energy thereby liberated is not used directly by the cell, but stored in high-energy phosphate compounds, the most important being adenosine triphosphate (ATP).

See also the major article on **Nutrition.**

metastasis

The spread of cancer cells from one site in the body (especially at the site of a primary cancerous growth) to other parts of the body.

See CANCER, MALIGNANCY and the major article on **Oncology.**

migraine

The word migraine is derived from *hemicrania* (literally, "half head") which was introduced into medicine by Galen (A.D. 131–201). Unilateral headache is still regarded as the cardinal feature of migraine, although the diagnosis may be made in the absence of headache.

Classically, a migraine starts with visual disturbances. Jagged brilliant streaks of light (fortification figures) may be seen on one side; bright spots may obscure the vision, which may become blurred or even completely lost. This may be followed by numbness or pins and needles in the hands or face, and possibly transient weakness of a limb or of half the body. After 15 to 30 minutes these symptoms give way to a boring pain on one side of the head, which typically reaches a peak intensity after an hour or so and may persist for days.

The headache becomes throbbing in character and is often accompanied by nausea and vomiting.

The above is a description of "classical" migraine, but there are many variant forms. In "atypical" migraine, which is in fact the most common form, the headache with or without vomiting occurs in the absence of other symptoms. The characteristic feature of all migraine is that it occurs in attacks, separated by intervals of freedom. In addition, the headaches tend to last for several hours and may persist for days.

Migraine usually first appears around the age of puberty and recurs with gradually diminishing frequency through adult life. However, it may begin during early childhood or in middle age. Women are slightly more susceptible than men and it often runs in families. It is popularly believed to occur in intelligent, conscientious individuals and to be triggered by stress, but this view is an oversimplification. Sufferers from migraine are more prone to allergies, and it is not uncommon for attacks to be linked to certain dietary factors, such as red wine, oranges, cheese or chocolate.

An attack of migraine is believed to begin with spasm of the arteries, causing the visual and neurological symptoms, followed by arterial dilation, causing the headache. Ergotamine tartrate, a powerful blood vessel constrictor, is the basis of most antimigraine drugs. It should not be given to patients with vascular disease or during pregnancy (when the attacks usually cease anyway). Mild tranquilizers may reduce the severity and frequency of the attacks, and there are a number of drugs which may prove useful to a varying degree.

miliaria

Miliaria ("heat rash" or "prickly heat") is an acute itching eruption of the skin common among white people in hot summer weather or tropical and subtropical areas. The condition results from excessive sweating and blocked sweat glands.

Prolonged exposure to heat and moisture causes the skin to swell enough to block the openings of the sweat glands. Newly produced sweat is then deposited in the skin and not on it; this results in local irritation and the formation of minute blisters. Pimples may subsequently develop, inflammation leads to an itching sensation, and the affected area may become infected. Sites which tend to be involved are the chest, back, waistline, groin and armpits. The best treatment involves removal of the patient to a cooler, less humid atmosphere. Lotions, cold compresses and cool showers or tub soaks may also help. Any irritants—such as unsuitable clothing, medications and harsh soaps—should be avoided.

If fungal infections develop in the affected areas, they require separate treatment with antifungal ointments or other preparations.

Minamata disease

Another name for MERCURY POISONING; named after Minamata Bay, Japan, where one of the most notorious examples of industrial poisoning occurred between 1953 and 1958. In the outbreak scores of people died and hundreds suffered irreversible brain damage from eating fish containing an organic mercury compound, itself absorbed by the fish from industrial effluent discharged into the sea.

miosis

Constriction of the pupil of the eye. The pupil is controlled by the radial and circular muscle fibers of the iris. The iris is the pigmented, opaque part of the front of the eye; it functions in much the same way as the diaphragm of a camera. Constriction of the pupil (miosis) prevents light from passing through the more peripheral parts of the lens system, cuts down the amount of light reaching the retina and reduces distortion effects of vision known as chromatic and spherical aberration.

Drugs which constrict the pupil are used in the treatment of some eye diseases such as GLAUCOMA. Many drugs acting on the autonomic nervous system cause miosis as a side effect.

miscarriage

In a miscarriage (technically known as a *spontaneous abortion*) the fetus and associated placental membranes are delivered before the 28th week of pregnancy. At this early stage the fetus is not yet sufficiently developed to maintain its life functions outside the womb. The patient undergoes a miniature labor with dilation of the cervix and experiences some pain. The most common time for a miscarriage to occur is about the 12th week.

The cause of spontaneous abortion can often not be determined but the following factors can play a part.

Many early aborted fetuses have abnormalities. Maternal disease may be a cause, such as hypertension, kidney and heart disease, diabetes or thyroid abnormalities. Uterine and placental abnormalities, a "lax" cervix, severe vitamin deficiencies, or possibly violent exercise also tend to interrupt pregnancy.

A threatened miscarriage is indicated by bleeding and a little pain. If it progresses and the cervix becomes dilated, loss of the fetus becomes inevitable. If placental tissue is retained in an incomplete miscarriage there is a danger of hemorrhage and sepsis. Thus, prompt medical attention—usually including a DILATATION AND CURETTAGE (D & C)—following a miscarriage is essential.

See also ABORTION.

mites

Small organisms (technically known as *arachnids,* the group to which spiders belong), some of which burrow into the skin and cause irritation. They may transmit serious disease, and some varieties may cause allergic reactions such as asthma.

The human parasite *Sarcoptes scabiei* is the cause of SCABIES, an irritative skin disease. Scabies itching is intense, especially at night. The penetration of the mite (smaller than a pinhead) causes linear scratches, small blisters, or pimples. Scabies parasites are transmitted by direct contact and from shared towels and bed linen. The disease is also frequently acquired by sexual contact. Bathing and applications of gamma benzene hexachloride or benzyl benzoate are effective treatments.

House mice are responsible for passing on *rickettsialpox* in North America and Europe. Cases occur annually in New York City, where mice infected with RICKETTSIAE (microorganisms intermediate in size between bacteria and viruses) in apartment houses maintain the infection. Tetracyclines are used in treatment.

Mites living in house dust do not infect man directly, but their presence in the dust is an important cause of hypersensitivity and asthmatic reactions, especially in children. Removal of dust-laden mattresses may cause dramatic relief of symptoms.

mole

A blemish on the skin which may be present at birth or may develop subsequently. Moles are comprised of clusters of nevus cells, which are specialized epithelial cells containing the pigment melanin.

Moles may be small or large, flat or raised, smooth, hairy or warty. They vary in color from yellow-brown to black. A mole is also classified as a type of pigmented NEVUS.

Moles may rarely undergo malignant (cancerous) change to become malignant MELANOMAS. They can be classified according to where they arise and this gives some indication of the likelihood of malignant changes occurring. About a quarter of malignant melanomas do not develop from a preceding mole.

Intradermal or "common" moles—in which the melanin-forming cells are in the lower layer of the skin or dermis—are benign. They are elevated and often have a hair in them. These intradermal nevi need not be removed except for cosmetic purposes as they are not precursors of melanomas.

Another type known as *junctional nevi* arise from nevus cells at the junction between the outer layer of the skin or epidermis and the dermis. They may be flat and are deep brown or black in color. Though more susceptible to activation, only a small percentage become malignant. They do not require removal unless they show a recent change or are situated in the nail matrix, are the site of frequent trauma, or are on surfaces such as the lips, anus, penis or vulva. A sudden increase in size or color, or bleeding or ulceration, is an indication for surgical removal of junctional nevi.

In general, malignant melanomas develop more readily from moles on the lower legs and on mucous membranes than from those elsewhere. Pigmented moles subjected to constant irritation or trauma show a relatively high incidence of malignant changes.

During pregnancy a benign increase in mole size and color is common. Children tend to develop more junctional nevi than intradermal nevi, yet they rarely acquire malignant melanoma. Large speckled, flat, rough lesions on the exposed parts in the elderly resemble junctional nevi and are best removed surgically because of their potential for malignant transformation.

molluscum contagiosum

A viral disease of the skin, characterized by one or more discrete, waxy, dome-shaped nodules or tumors frequently with a central dimple.

The virus is probably transmitted by direct contact or by clothing or other items which have been contaminated with the virus; outbreaks are common in schools.

The condition is of little clinical importance once the diagnosis is known. In many cases the lesions disappear without treatment; if they persist they can be removed by a dermatologist with a curette or by electrodesiccation.

mongolism

Another name for DOWN'S SYNDROME.

Monilia

Another name for CANDIDA.

morning sickness

Nausea and vomiting of varying severity that occurs in pregnancy, usually in the early months. Morning sickness is a common symptom of pregnancy; as the name implies, it tends to occur in the early part of the day. It is seen in about half of pregnancies from about the end of the first month, usually ceasing by the end of the third month.

The symptoms begin with a feeling of nausea on arising. The expectant mother is often unable to retain her breakfast, but by midday the symptoms have disappeared and she feels well until the following morning. In some cases the condition evolves into prolonged bouts of vomiting with a resultant weight loss.

Most women with morning sickness can keep it under control by taking only small meals with generous amounts of fluid between meals. Nausea can sometimes be averted or minimized by getting out of bed slowly. Drugs not prescribed by the doctor should be avoided, if possible, but antinauseants and sedatives may be necessary in the more severe cases.

mosquitoes

Approximately 2,500 different species of mosquitoes have been identified. The bloodsucking habits of the females of a few of these species are responsible for transmitting various disease to man and other mammals. In obtaining their "blood meal," the females use their specially modified mouth parts to pierce the skin of their victims and suck up the blood.

The female mosquito first injects saliva containing an anticoagulant into the skin of its victim to prevent the blood clotting. It also injects a "sensitizing" agent, which may cause severe irritation in some people. Soothing lotions and creams may be applied to alleviate the itching.

As a mosquito feeds it may pass on various disease-causing (pathogenic) microorganisms from one person to another. Several diseases can be spread in this way—including MALARIA, YELLOW FEVER, FILARIASIS and DENGUE FEVER. In some cases the pathogenic microorganisms have evolved a highly complex life cycle using the mosquito as a "vector."

A large number of "arboviruses" are known to produce disease in man. Most of these are examples of a ZOONOSIS, accidentally acquired by man through the bite of an insect such as the mosquito. The diseases can be divided into three basic categories: (1) acute central nervous system diseases, usually with ENCEPHALITIS; (2) acute benign fevers, and (3) hemorrhagic fevers.

Of the mosquito-borne infections in the first category, *Eastern equine encephalitis* carries one of the highest mortality rates. Cases of it are recognized in the eastern and north central parts of the United States and adjacent Canada. Mosquitoes usually acquire the infection from wild birds or rodents.

Dengue fever comes within the second category. During the 20th century, epidemics have occurred in the southeastern and Gulf sections of the United States and elsewhere. The fatality rate is low. Mosquitoes can pick up the pathogenic viruses from patients from the day before the onset of the patient's fever to the fifth day of the disease; 11 days after the mosquito takes its "blood meal" it becomes capable of infecting another person.

In the third category, *hemorrhagic fevers,* comes yellow fever. Except for a few cases in Trinidad, W.I., in 1954 no urban outbreak has been transmitted by mosquitoes since the 1940s. Jungle yellow fever is present from time to time in mainland countries of the Americas from Mexico to South America.

The bite of a mosquito harboring infective larvae of a nematode parasite transmits the tropical condition known as filariasis.

Preventive measures against all these conditions involve keeping the mosquito at bay. They include control of mosquito breeding grounds, the use of residual insecticide sprays in homes and outbuildings, mosquito repellants for personal use, screens on doors and windows in homes or mosquito netting where screens are not practical, and sufficient clothing, particularly after sundown, to protect as much of the skin surface as possible against bites.

motion sickness

See TRAVEL SICKNESS.

multiple myeloma

A malignant growth of certain special cells in the bone marrow. It most commonly occurs in people over 40 and affects men twice as often as women. The condition may be accompanied by anemia, kidney damage and the overproduction of certain proteins and their constituent polypeptides.

The most common initial symptom is bone pain, often in a rib or vertebra. (The bones most frequently affected are the ribs, spine and pelvis.) There are multiple well-defined areas where bone is destroyed and replaced by certain closely packed cells which are active in the formation of antibodies.

Fractures in the ribs and long bones and collapse of the vertebrae may occur. X-rays may show general demineralization of the bones or characteristic punched-out lesions.

Anemia, from impaired production of red blood cells, is usual and *hemolytic anemia*—in which there is excessive destruction of red blood cells caused by antibody formation in the blood—may develop. Ultimately a decrease in the platelets in the blood and spontaneous bleeding is to be expected.

The excess plasma cells produce an abnormal protein. The disease gradually disseminates through the body, although a single lesion may be involved initially. The tubules in the kidney may become blocked by coagulated protein.

The drug melphalan may be used in treatment alone or combined with steroids. The pain from local involvement of bone can be relieved by radiotherapy. Transfusion may be required to correct anemia.

multiple sclerosis

A disorder of the brain, spinal cord and nerves, also known as *disseminated sclerosis.* In this condition destruction of the protective myelin sheaths (which insulate nerve fibers) occurs in patches throughout the central nervous system, giving rise to the formation of plaques. The cause is unknown.

The disease has been attributed variously to autoimmune mechanisms (when the body's own immune system turns against the patient—see AUTOIMMUNE DISEASE); to infection by a virus which has a prolonged incubation period before producing symptoms; to toxic agents; metabolic faults; and trauma and blood vessel lesions.

Symptoms of multiple sclerosis usually first appear in late teenage or early adult life. One or more parts of the body may become weak or paralyzed. Among other symptoms, there may be loss of sensation, blurred vision, and loss of control over the bowel and bladder. The patient's speech may be slowed and his or her emotions may be labile. The severity of the symptoms is likely to fluctuate over time with remissions and exacerbations. Onset is usually insidious, and the disease is slowly progressive.

In the early stages there is sometimes complete remission of symptoms, which may last for many years; but with recurrent episodes, remissions are likely to be less complete and the patient may suffer an increasingly permanent disability.

Initially there may be fleeting visual symptoms, or slight stiffness and unusual tiredness in a limb. Far later there is paralysis of the legs and poor coordination of arm movements. In many patients, however, the disorder fortunately remains mild and interferes little with ordinary life.

There is currently no specific cure, but wide claims have been made for a number of treatments. Spontaneous remissions make any treatment difficult to evaluate. Massage of weakened limbs and muscle training are of some benefit.

Prompt treatment of infections and an adequate diet with vitamin supplements, where necessary, are sensible measures. In the later stages of multiple sclerosis, good nursing will help in the prevention of bedsores. Steroids and other drugs are used to alleviate symptoms; for example, vertigo may be treated with chlorpromazine.

There is a definite geographical distribution of incidence; the closer the country is to the Equator, the lower the prevalence of the disease. In Mexico, for instance, the rate is only 1/30 of that in Denmark.

See also the major article on **Neurology.**

mumps

A contagious viral disease common among children which usually causes painful inflammation and enlargement of the salivary glands, particularly the parotid glands. There is fever, and swelling develops in front of the ears, making the chewing of food difficult. Also called *epidemic parotitis*.

In young children mumps is a relatively trivial illness, but if contracted after puberty it may affect the testicles and have serious complications.

The disease is spread by droplet infection through the respiratory tract. The incubation period is 12 to 28 days, but the great majority of children develop it about 18 days after exposure.

A child with mumps can usually be nursed at home. He is infectious until the swelling subsides. It is said to be impractical and unwise to try to prevent other children in the house from coming into contact with him. A child who has once had the infection is unlikely to contract it again because of the long-term immunity which develops.

The initial symptoms may be a high temperature, headache and sore throat which arise a few days before the characteristic swelling of the parotid glands, but the swelling is often the first symptom. It usually subsides within 7 to 10 days.

The virus occasionally invades tissues other than the salivary glands, notably the testicles, ovaries, pancreas and the meninges (membranes covering the brain and spinal cord). About a quarter of boys over 14 years of age having mumps develop inflammation of the testicles (orchitis) as a complication; this is rare in childhood. Serious consequences of orchitis are not as common as was once believed but may include permanent sterility.

Live mumps vaccine was introduced in the late 1960s

MUMPS

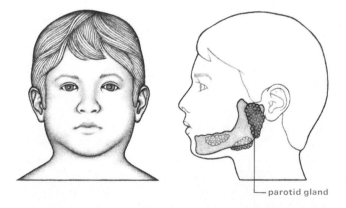

parotid gland

Mumps is one of the common viral diseases of childhood. The virus attacks the parotid gland in front of the ear, producing a painful swollen face.

and it may be useful in those who have reached puberty without contracting the illness, or for administration to younger children. The vaccine must not be given to pregnant women.

See also the major article on the **Health Care of Children.**

Munchausen's syndrome

A strange type of complaint named after the 16th-century Baron von Munchausen. He was a traveler, served in the Russian army, and was the reputed source of a collection of preposterous stories. The baron has been described as a proverbial liar. (One of the stories attributed to him relates that during a blinding snowstorm he tethered his horse to what he thought was a fence post. On awaking the next morning, he discovered that the horse was dangling from the top of a church steeple.)

His name was first used in the medical context in 1951 by Richard Asher, who described a patient suffering from the syndrome. Such people travel from one hospital or doctor to another telling untruthful stories about their medical condition, describing dramatic but false symptoms, or simulating acute illness. They may happily submit themselves for countless operations (having scars that bear testimony) or undergo what they know to be unnecessary medical investigations.

They often leave a hospital without notice (or payment) and resume their travels.

muscle

Tissue composed of fibers which have the power to contract. Muscles thus produce movements of the body. *Voluntary* muscle, also known as *striped* or *striated* muscle, is under the direct control of the will. *Involuntary,* or *smooth,* muscle is not under the control of the will. It is to be found in the heart, blood vessels, the walls of the stomach and intestines and in most internal organs. The heart is composed of partially striated muscle.

Voluntary muscles are activated and controlled by motor nerves, which reach them directly from the brain or by way of the spinal cord. If a motor nerve is cut or injured, the muscle or that group of muscles which it supplies is paralyzed, as impulses from the brain are interrupted.

An average fiber in a voluntary muscle is from 2–4 cm long. Under the microscope it has a banded or striped appearance. During contractions one set of filaments (composed of *actin*) pass down between another set (*myosin* filaments), and optically the lighter bands become reduced in size.

The immediate source of energy needed for contraction appears to be a substance known as *adenosine triphosphate,* but the ultimate source is carbohydrate and fat. Oxygen is used in the contraction process and **muscle fatigue and rigor are accompanied by the** production of lactic acid.

In *muscle strain,* overstretching occurs; there may be a sudden sharp pain at the site of injury and swelling.

Cramp (a painful sudden involuntary contraction of a muscle or muscles) is sometimes caused by poor coordination during exercise; by chilling, as in swimming; or by excessive loss of salt and body fluids from severe sweating, diarrhea, or persistent vomiting. Often the cause is not known.

In salt deficiency the patient should be given copious amounts of cold water to which a small quantity of salt has been added.

See also the major article on **Rheumatology.**

muscular dystrophy

A group of inherited diseases characterized by progressive weakness due to degeneration of muscles. They are thought to represent inborn errors of metabolism, although precise biochemical abnormalities have yet to be fully identified.

The pathological changes primarily affect the muscles responsible for body movement, but heart muscle may also be involved. There is variation in muscle fiber size, degeneration of fibers and an increase in connective tissue.

Onset is usually in childhood or adolescence. Wasting is symmetrical and slowly progressive. Remissions do not occur in muscular dystrophies. Similar cases frequently occur in the same family (in up to 50% of cases, another member of the direct family line is affected).

The condition usually begins centrally as opposed to in the muscles of the extremities; posture is typically disturbed, with the development of spinal curvature.

Two major variations have been described. In the *Duchenne* or "pseudohypertrophic" form only boys are affected. This form differs from other types in that wasted muscles are replaced by fat, giving the muscles a bulky appearance which contrasts with the weakness present. It usually starts at about the age of four or five. The muscles of the shoulder and pelvic girdle become enlarged, as do the calf muscles. This leads to a waddling gait and frequent falls. The child has a characteristic way of getting up from the lying position; he has to roll over onto his face, and then onto his hands and knees, from which he gradually stands up onto his legs. The shoulders are affected later.

In the other main type, the "facioscapulohumeral" or *Landouzy-Dejerine* form, both sexes are affected. It starts later in adolescence and commences in the face.

Weakness of the shoulder girdle is more prominent than leg weakness. Some patients with the condition are scarcely aware of the symptoms throughout a normal life span: in others, disabilities gradually increase. An affected child may lack normal facial expressions and be unable to raise his arms above his head.

Other forms and intermediate conditions exist. For instance, there is an arm and shoulder variety and a rarer form known as "distal myopathy." In this condition **weakness starts in the hands and spreads inward.**

There is no specific drug treatment for these diseases. Muscle-strengthening exercises, corrective surgery and the use of braces may be helpful in some cases.

See also the major article on **Rheumatology.**

myasthenia gravis

A form of muscle debility which is progressive and characterized by abnormal fatigue of voluntary muscle and rapid recovery after rest. It is a slowly progressive disease, usually encountered in adults and rarely seen before the age of puberty.

Myasthenia gravis affects both sexes. The highest incidence occurs in females between the ages of 18 to 25 and in men over 40. The condition is sometimes associated with HYPERTHYROIDISM as well as with excessive formation of tissue in the thymus gland in a high percentage of cases, or with a thymic tumor.

There is a disorder of conduction at the point where the nerves meet and activate the muscle cells. The muscles thus fail to respond to the signal from the nerve endings. Myasthenia gravis is thought to be caused by the failure of formation of the "neuromuscular transmitter" chemical acetylcholine.

The paralysis produced is normally minimal in the morning and worse at night. The disease most often affects the eyes, facial and shoulder girdle muscles and (less often) the legs.

Paralysis of the eye muscles leads to STRABISMUS (squint) and double vision. Drooping of the eyelids and weakness of the facial muscles cause the typical "myasthenic smile" and lack of expression. Gradual loss of the voice and difficulty in chewing or swallowing during the course of a meal are frequent complaints. Weakness of the arms may also be present.

Symptoms fluctuate in severity from day to day and remissions occur in about a quarter of the patients.

For treatment, tablets of neostigmine (a specific antidote), or the longer-acting pyridostigmine may be given. If weakness is severe, an intramuscular injection of neostigmine may be necessary in the morning and before meals.

Removal of the thymus gland is beneficial in about two thirds of cases.

See also the major article on **Endocrinology.**

mydriasis

Dilation of the pupil of the eye. Mydriasis occurs when the light falling on the eye decreases in intensity or when the lens focuses from a near object to a distant one. The widening pupil permits more light to fall on the retina and more to be seen in poor light.

Stimulation of sensory nerves may cause a dilation of the pupil. In conditions such as excitement, fear, pain, or asphyxia (which lead to the release of epinephrine from the adrenal glands), the pupils dilate, as they do when the sympathetic nerves to the eyes are stimulated. Certain drugs can produce mydriasis—for example, atropine, homatropine, cocaine and epinephrine. Alcohol intoxication has the same effect.

myelitis

1. A general term that means inflammation of the spinal cord.

Acute transverse myelitis is the name given to a syndrome which may be caused by a viral or bacterial infection; often the cause is undetermined. The symptoms are dramatic, as over the course of 48 hours there is complete loss of muscle power and sensation below the affected section of the spinal cord. Usually there is some recovery as the inflammation subsides; its extent is difficult to predict.

The term *myelitis* is sometimes used imprecisely by members of the medical profession to refer to a lesion of the spinal cord which is not caused by inflammation (in such cases the term *myelopathy* is more correct).

See also POLIOMYELITIS.

2. Inflammation of the bone marrow (see OSTEOMYELITIS).

myelocele

See SPINA BIFIDA.

myeloma

See MULTIPLE MYELOMA.

myiasis

Invasion or infection of a body area or cavity by the larvae (maggots) of flies. Many fly species have been implicated. Some are termed *obligate parasites*—that is, they cannot survive without involving humans in their life cycles. Others, known as *facultative parasites,* are capable of being free-living as well as acting as parasites. In a third category there is only chance invasion of human subjects.

Among those classified as obligate parasites are the human botfly, the rodent botfly and flesh flies. In the second category come the common screwworm fly, the bluebottle, other types of flesh fly and the stable fly. Examples in the final category are houseflies, cheese skippers and fruit flies.

Myiasis usually involves the skin or mucous membranes, especially those of the nasal passages and pharynx. Lesions in the skin may be shallow or deep, leading to "boils" containing the larvae.

In some infestations the larvae burrow deep and reach the membranes or cavities of the nose, pharynx, ear, eye and vagina, where they cause extensive damage.

Gastrointestinal myiasis arises from the accidental swallowing of larvae in contaminated foodstuffs, which may occasionally lead to invasion of the intestinal wall.

Surgical removal of deep-burrowing skin larvae may be necessary, but a more superficial type can be treated with an ethyl chloride spray or the application of ice (which kills the larvae before they are removed).

Larvae in a deep boil are best extracted surgically. Eggs of the screwworm fly, which is found in the southern United States, are laid in an open wound and can invade tissue extensively. The larvae are removed after swabbing the affected area with ether or chloroform in oil. Serious intestinal myiasis may be treated by vermifuges and purges.

myocardial infarction

A technical term for a "heart attack."
See also INFARCT/INFARCTION.

myocarditis

Inflammation of the muscular tissue of the heart. This sometimes serious condition may arise due to an unknown cause or may be a complication of a number of illnesses—such as rheumatic fever, scarlet fever, diphtheria or typhoid fever. Apart from being associated with bacterial, fungal or viral diseases (especially *Coxsackie virus B*), myocarditis may be due to toxic chemicals, alcohol, drugs or to electrical shock or excessive x-ray treatment.

The condition leads to circulatory disturbances and the patient may have a rapid, soft and often irregular pulse. Myocarditis may leave a residual effect on the efficiency of the heart after recovery. Once the condition is suspected, complete bed rest, sedation and continuation of therapy for any underlying illness may help to prevent a sudden exacerbation.

myoclonus

A spasm of muscle. It has been described as a sudden, nonrhythmic, nonpatterned twitching.

Normal individuals often experience an isolated myoclonic jerk or two in drowsiness or light sleep.

The term can be used to refer to such movements in a part of a muscle, a whole muscle or group of muscles, a limb, the trunk or the face. Myoclonus results from a paroxysmal discharge in the central nervous system.

This type of movement can be a characteristic of epilepsy. In such a myoclonic seizure the patient may experience muscular jerks of varying intensity, usually without an evident alteration in the level of consciousness. Myoclonic seizures are often associated with other types of seizure, however, especially those characterized by sudden loss of muscle power and sudden transient lapses of consciousness; they have a tendency to occur more frequently in the mornings or on going to sleep.

Progressive *familial myoclonic epilepsy* is an inherited degenerative disease beginning in childhood or adolescence, characterized by progressively worsening generalized myoclonic seizures and mental disturbances.

In the clonic stage of major general epilepsy there are a series of convulsive movements not only in the trunk and limbs but in the jaw and tongue, so that the tongue may be badly bitten or saliva may be lathered into foam. First aid treatment for a patient undergoing such a seizure is to put a knotted handkerchief or similar soft object between their jaws to protect the tongue. (However, the teeth must *not* be forced apart as serious damage may result.) Keep the patient's airway clear.

myoma

A benign tumor of muscle tissue. They most frequently occur in the smooth muscle wall of the uterus as spherical masses, in which case they are also referred to as *fibromyomas* or *fibroids*. They may arise in any part of the uterus from its top to the cervix (neck of the womb). Uterine myomas occur more frequently in blacks, are more common after the age of 30 and do not develop before the onset of menstruation (menarche) or after the menopause. They most frequently do not cause symptoms, but may be associated with infertility, abnormal menstruation, pain and other symptoms.

If the symptoms warrant, surgical removal of myomas may be performed (myomectomy). When continued fertility is not required, total hysterectomy (surgical removal of the uterus) may be performed.

Myomas may also occur elsewhere in the body—for instance in the stomach and small bowel, where they form masses in the walls. Here they are prone to ulceration and then cause blood in the feces and anemia.

myopia

An optical defect in which the image of distant objects is focused in front of the retina (the light-sensitive "screen" at the back of the eye) rather than directly on the retina. The result of this is that distant objects appear blurred, although near objects can be seen clearly. Also called *near-sightedness*.

In myopia it is an excessive length of the eyeball which gives rise to the focusing defect. This can be corrected for far vision with a concave lens (or a contact lens). Near objects can still be focused on the retina by inhibiting the normal reflex of accommodation of the lens.

MYOPIA

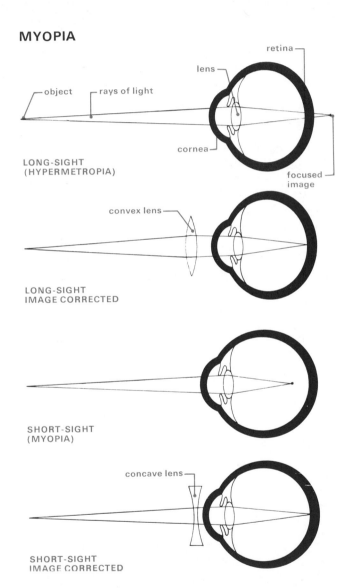

LONG-SIGHT
(HYPERMETROPIA)

LONG-SIGHT
IMAGE CORRECTED

SHORT-SIGHT
(MYOPIA)

SHORT-SIGHT
IMAGE CORRECTED

Myopia, or short-sight, can result either from an elongated eyeball or from a lens which is too powerful. The outcome as shown above is that rays of light are focused in front of the retina so that the image is blurred. Long-sight is the reverse optical error and usually results from the lens weakening with age. Both conditions can be corrected by wearing glasses with lenses of the correct strength.

The normal eye is so shaped that rays of light from distant objects are brought to an exact focus on the retina. Nearer objects are brought into focus by a contraction of the ciliary muscle, allowing the lens to become more spherical.

In the large majority of cases, myopia is simply a variation in the shape of the eyeball. The problem may get no worse after adolescence and a little reduction in the myopia may even take place in late middle-age. In some cases the eyeball may continue to elongate throughout life ("progressive myopia"), leading to a retinal degeneration or even to DETACHED RETINA.

Severely myopic eyeballs may in fact look large and even appear like those of someone suffering from HYPERTHYROIDISM.

Different types of myopia have been outlined by ophthalmologists. In *curvature myopia* the fault is due to excessive curvature of one of the refractive surfaces of the eye where the light path is normally deviated for focusing. The excessive curvature is usually present in the anterior surface of the cornea but sometimes it occurs in the lens.

Index myopia is due to an increase in the refractive index (a unit that indicates the light-refracting properties of a medium). This type of myopia usually refers to change in the lens, which may progress to a future development of CATARACT; but it may also refer to an increase in the refractive index of the aqueous humor of the eye as in IRITIS.

In the myope, then, a concave lens will push the focal point backward toward the backward placed retina, so as to allow clear distant vision. Since the curvature of the cornea is almost never exactly the same in all directions, this associated *astigmatism* (as it is known) may at the same time be corrected by giving the lens the appropriate added convexity or concavity.

See also the major article on **Ophthalmology.**

myositis

Inflammation of a muscle. The condition usually occurs in a voluntary, or striated, muscle. There is pain, tenderness and stiffness of the muscle and adjacent tissues and joints may also be affected. It may be secondary to trauma, infection, strain, poisons or exposure to damp or cold, but often occurs in older people for no known reason. When connective tissue is also involved the condition is often loosely known by the term "rheumatism." Myositis commonly involves the back, neck, shoulders, chest or thighs. If it affects the neck it may temporarily give rise to wry neck (TORTICOLLIS), in which the head cannot be turned, or may even be drawn downward to the shoulder on one side.

Onset of pain may be sudden and local muscle spasm is present in some cases. Fever is only evident if the condition is part of a general infection.

Fortunately, myositis tends to disappear in a few days, but occasionally it may become chronic or may recur at frequent intervals.

When diagnosing the condition the physician attempts to establish that myositis is not a manifestation of a more serious underlying disease.

Rest, heat, massage, analgesics (painkillers) and application of liniments are simple measures that can be employed to bring relief.

In *myositis ossificans* bone cells deposited in muscle continue to grow and form lumps. It may occur after a fracture—for example, in the elbow region. The type of exercise given to such an arm may affect the development of this condition and only prescribed active exercise should be performed initially.

Passive movements, such as those involved in massage, should be discouraged. With correct exercises and rest the calcified masses usually disappear.

See also the major article on **Rheumatology.**

myxedema

A condition caused by malfunction or surgical removal of the thyroid gland. Subsequent lack of circulating thyroid hormone in the body gives rise to a series of signs and symptoms, which represent a severe form of HYPOTHYROIDISM.

There is swelling of the face and limbs because of subcutaneous fluid deposition. This may particularly affect the area around the eyes and the hands and feet. The skin becomes dry and rough and there may be some hair loss. The patient exhibits slowness of action and thought and this mental dullness is accompanied by slow speech, with a voice which may become hoarse. Lethargy and weakness may be associated with slowed reflexes, a slow pulse, lowered metabolism and subnormal body temperature. The patient sometimes experiences poor tolerance to cold and (especially in the elderly) HYPOTHERMIA. The appetite may be poor, yet—in contrast—there is often a mild weight gain. Shortness of breath and constipation are not uncommon. About one third of patients suffer from high blood pressure, ANGINA PECTORIS and palpitations.

The condition may arise through primary disease of the thyroid or following removal of the gland in the treatment of thyrotoxic or malignant goiter. Iodine deficiency or circulating antithyroid antibodies may also be contributory factors.

Recovery is usually excellent with the administration of thyroxin or thyroid extract, which must be continued throughout life. The dose of thyroxin is increased by small amounts about every two weeks, as necessary. In older patients with heart disease the thyroid hormone level is increased slowly, since a rapid rise can precipitate angina pectoris and heart failure.

Each patient's therapy has to be tailored to his or her own particular needs.

When thyroid hormone deficiency occurs in infancy it may lead to CRETINISM, characterized by abnormal thickness of the neck, stunted growth and imperfect mental development.

Once diagnosed this condition requires immediate thyroid replacement therapy—ideally within the first three months of life—to avoid long-term damage.

Coma developing in a patient suffering from myxedema represents a medical emergency. It is more likely to occur in the elderly (particularly during a cold winter) if they are not receiving a satisfactory dose of thyroid extract. Treatment should be intensive but not hasty. The patient is cold to the touch, with a body temperature often below the range of a standard clinical thermometer. Vigorous rewarming should be avoided, the use of blankets being preferable. Triiodothyronine is given intravenously.

See also the major article on **Endocrinology.**

N

naturopathy

A system of health care which suggests that disease is provoked by violation of "Nature's Laws," and that the reparation of physical or psychological disorder depends entirely on the use of diet, massage, or special bathing procedures. The naturopath believes, not incorrectly, that health is the normal state of the human being, and, quite incorrectly, that it can invariably be maintained by "natural" foods alone.

While naturopathy may seem a reasonable philosophy for someone in good health, it may be dangerous in disease; few naturopaths, if any, have formal medical skills and may fail to recognize life-threatening and curable disorders such as tuberculosis. There is no scientific basis for the claims of naturopaths in healing.

nausea

A feeling of wanting to vomit, with a characteristic sensation that passes through the upper part of the abdomen.

The stomach normally contracts regularly to empty its contents into the duodenum and the small intestine. If this reflex action temporarily ceases and the duodenum itself contracts to prevent the stomach emptying, the effect on the individual is to experience nausea.

Nausea can thus be brought on by virtually anything that affects gastrointestinal function in any way, direct or indirect.

See also TRAVEL SICKNESS, VOMITING.

necrosis

The death of areas of tissue or bone surrounded by healthy parts.

Necrotic tissue is seen, at the simplest level, in the pustular content of even the smallest septic spot, where the yellow fluid discharged is composed of dead bacteria, the body's dead white blood cells, and skin cells that have failed to survive the ravages of an infective agent. Necrosis takes place even where infective agents are not present when any tissue is deprived of its blood supply: for example, in small areas of the heart muscle after a "heart attack," in the middle of tumors that have outgrown their blood supply and in areas of the body where GANGRENE (which is another name for a wide area of tissue necrosis) has occurred.

Where OSTEOMYELITIS occurs in bone there is necrosis of the bone cells (*sequestrum*) because the inflammation has caused the blockage or thrombosis of the minute arteries supplying these bone cells. In atherosclerosis the blood vessels may be partially blocked by fatty deposits (atheromas) and the blood supply to the peripheral parts of the lower limb may be insufficient to maintain nutrition of the tissues, so that necrosis—or gangrene—may occur in the toes. In frostbite, necrosis of the tissues may occur because the peripheral blood vessels have frozen.

neoplasm

An abnormal new growth of cells or tissues; tumor.

See CANCER and the major article on **Oncology.**

nephrectomy

Surgical removal of a kidney.

nephritis

Nephritis (inflammation of the kidney) falls into two principal groups: (1) PYELONEPHRITIS, a bacterial infection which spreads from the bladder and ureters and (2) GLOMERULONEPHRITIS, a noninfective disease usually affecting both kidneys.

See also KIDNEY DISEASES and the major article on **Nephrology.**

nephroma

A tumor involving kidney tissue. See KIDNEY DISEASES.

nephrotic syndrome

Many healthy young individuals are found to have protein in their urine at routine medical checks, especially if it is measured after a period of prolonged standing or exercise. However, some people lose an excessive amount of protein in the urine, so that the level of albumin in their blood is greatly reduced (hypo-albuminemia) and excess fluid collects in the tissues as EDEMA.

This triad of signs (heavy proteinuria, hypoalbumi-nemia, and edema) is known as the *nephrotic syndrome,* and is more common in childhood than in adult life. About 80% of the cases in young children result from "minimal change" pathology in the kidney. The prognosis for children in this group is excellent and nearly all of them make a rapid and complete recovery following treatment with corticosteroid drugs.

When the nephrotic syndrome occurs in a patient over about ten years of age, or if a younger patient shows additional signs such as blood in the urine or high blood pressure, it is necessary to obtain a small piece of kidney by a needle biopsy. When viewed under the microscope, this tissue might reveal changes characteristic of GLOMERULONEPHRITIS, DIABETES MELLITUS, AMYLOIDOSIS, or systemic LUPUS ERYTHEMATOSUS— all possibly associated with the nephrotic syndrome. Nephrotic patients with kidney lesions other than "minimal change" do not respond well to corticosteroid drugs. They are usually maintained on a diet high in protein and low in salt; diuretic drugs ("water pills") are used to control the edema.

See also KIDNEY DISEASES and the major article on **Nephrology.**

neuralgia

A term which implies pain arising along the course of a nerve, which may be severe, dull, or stabbing.

Usually nothing can be seen, but sometimes there is evidence of inflammation or damage to the sensory nerve affected—as in the neuralgia which may follow HERPES ZOSTER (shingles). SCIATICA, which is pain along the course of the sciatic nerve, is associated with interference with the nerve roots making up the nerve by a prolapsed or herniated intervertebral disk ("slipped disk") or by arthritic processes arising in intervertebral joints. Neuralgia in the hands may occur in the CARPAL TUNNEL SYNDROME.

Neuralgia is an imprecise term except when applied to *trigeminal neuralgia,* an affliction of the sensory nerve supplying the face (the Vth cranial nerve, or trigeminal nerve). This is a very severe intermittent pain on one side of the face, coming on in spasms which last less than a minute. During the attack the patient may show agonized contortions of the facial muscles which give the disease its alternative name, *tic douloureux* (see TIC). Treatment involves administration of drugs such as phenytoin sodium or carbamazepine. If these fail, it may be necessary to destroy the ganglion of the nerve inside the skull by injection or by open operation, procedures which are followed by total anesthesia of the face on the affected side. The disease is rare in patients below the age of 50, although it may occur in younger patients in association with multiple sclerosis.

Other patterns of facial neuralgia may occur, usually described as "atypical facial pain," including a neuralgia affecting the IXth cranial nerve (*glossopharyngeal neuralgia*). It is characterized by intermittent attacks of severe pain, usually beginning at the base of the tongue and radiating down the neck or to the ears. It is triggered by movements such as swallowing, chewing, sneezing, or sometimes just by talking. Treatment involves the administration of carbamazepine. Temporary or partial relief is sometimes obtained by the local application of an anesthetic to the throat. In severe cases surgical disruption of the nerve may be necessary.

See also the major article on **Neurology.**

neurasthenia

An outdated term, neurasthenia (Greek *neuron* = nerve, *asthenia* = weakness) was once commonly used to describe conditions characterized by marked mental and physical irritability with excessive fatigue. An inability to concentrate, impairment of memory and complaints such as "pressure in the head," "eyes ache with reading," palpitations, constipation and impotence would lead to a diagnostic label of neurasthenia.

It was common after a debilitating illness, particularly in the era before antibiotics and was especially applied to professional or intelligently curious patients who required an "explanation" for their symptoms of fatigue. Nowadays it would be considered a normal convalescent stage in which the patient recovers spontaneously and progressively with rest, or where no physical reason was detectable for the complaints—such as a psychoneurotic disorder, anticipating a depressive illness.

neuritis

The general term applied to disease of the peripheral nerves.

Degeneration of the nerve tissue occurs with consequent loss of sensation, impairment of muscular control and symptoms that vary from severe pain to tingling and "pins and needles" brought about by movement of the involved part of the body— particularly if the nerve is stretched. A single nerve or multiple nerves may be involved and the causes may be *infective* (as in diphtheria, tetanus, or leprosy), *mechanical* (as in compression, arthritis, or obstetric injury), *chemical* (as in arsenical poisoning or antibiotic sensitivity), *vascular* (as in arteriosclerosis, diabetes or myxedema), or *nutritional* (as in beriberi, alcoholism or porphyria).

The diagnosis is made by determining the character and distribution of the nerve's impairment. For example, *brachial neuritis* with pains in the whole arm and varied loss of sensation in the skin of the arm (in particular, pain when the muscles are compressed) follows the use of crutches that press on the brachial nerves in the armpit. Generalized neuritis in the diabetic, or the alcoholic, or the patient with malnutrition will affect most peripheral nerves.

Treatment is aimed at relief of the cause, if it is specific, combined with rest, physical therapy and analgesics (painkillers). Correction of dietary inadequacy achieves a cure of the neuritis where malnurition is the cause.

See also the major article on **Neurology.**

neurofibroma

A tumor of the connective tissue which forms the nerve sheath. It may occur as a single swelling and reach a considerable size; normally benign, the tumor may become malignant, but it usually gives rise to symptoms because it exerts pressure on neighboring structures—for example, the spinal cord or the nerve upon which it lies. A neurofibroma may be evident as a swelling in the skin; treatment of the solitary tumor is surgical removal.

Neurofibromas may occur in considerable numbers as part of VON RECKLINGHAUSEN'S DISEASE (or *multiple neurofibromatosis*). The tumors are associated with irregular brown pigmented patches on the skin (*café au lait* spots), and they represent a defect in the development of the supporting tissue of the nervous system. Where they give rise to symptoms they may require surgical treatment.

neurofibromatosis

Another name for VON RECKLINGHAUSEN'S DISEASE (also known as *multiple neurofibromatosis*).

neuropathy

In medical practice the terms *neuritis* and *neuropathy* are used almost interchangeably, but the implication of neuropathy is that a degenerative change has taken place in the nerve, or nerves, affected by either inflammation, injury, nutritional deprivation or toxic poisoning.

On microscopic examination the nerves show fragmentation of the nerve fibers, but in *generalized neuropathy* the lesions may begin in the nerve roots at the spinal cord. The manifestations are variable but include fluctuating pain that may be deep and aching, sharp, pricking, burning, or any combination of these qualities. Examination of the sensory abilities demonstrates impairment of all sensations but to different degrees; in *peripheral neuropathy* there is often a symmetrical "glove" or "stocking" pattern in the area deprived. Muscular weakness is also variable in severity and the affected muscles are flaccid with loss of the tendon reflexes. The skin of the affected area becomes thin and shiny and there may be excessive sweating in the area. All these manifestations reflect the disordered conduction pathway of the nerve supplying the distinct area.

One of the best examples of generalized neuropathy is that which occurs in the vitamin B_1 (thiamine) deficiency disease of beriberi, but in alcoholics and diabetics the same degrees of peripheral neuropathy are also seen. Metallic poisons—lead, mercury, silver, thallium—and chemicals such as trinitrotoluene, trichlorethylene, and carbon disulfide cause generalized and peripheral neuropathy. Rare inherited diseases may be progressive; but in general, once the cause is identified—if it is specific—correction is possible.

The management of neuropathy is mainly the control of pain and protection of the weakened muscles from stretching and excessive wasting (atrophy). Bed rest is recommended and aspirin or a stronger analgesic is used to control the pain. Heat from infrared lamps or warm baths is helpful. Splints and limb supports may be necessary to prevent deformity; when local muscular tenderness subsides, passive action, massage and other forms of physical therapy are advisable. A well-balanced diet should be maintained and, where undernutrition was responsible for the neuropathy, vitamin supplements may be prescribed. Recovery depends on the extent of the original damage.

See also the major article on **Neurology.**

neurosis

A neurosis is a personality disorder. Behavior traits, thought processes, emotional responses and some body functions may all be influenced by the neurosis. It is usually a maladjustment to the ordinary stresses and demands of life, but is often characteristically irrational.

Any neurosis may be traceable in origin to the early learning experiences of life and to childhood in particular, but the individual may suffer great conflict and discomfort in not being able to recognize his or her own failure to adapt to the anxiety that is the cause of their neurosis. Neuroses develop in the predisposed individual from childhood onward, and appear at the particular times of life when society and community living demand adaptation of the personality. For example, in adolescence when a sexual identity is being sought, in adult life when vocational demands or choice provoke stress, and in parenthood when adaptation of the role toward accepting responsibility for the dependence of others is a challenge—in all these common circumstances of life, neurosis is prone to occur in the insecure individual.

Neurosis is seen more commonly in females, particularly as a response to the stress of a career and the responsibilities of marriage and at the menopause, when adjustment to a new life is required. In elderly couples the approach of retirement can sometimes provoke neurosis. It rarely appears anew in the middle-aged individual who has not shown previous neurotic tendencies.

The incidence is estimated at about 3–4% of the normal population, but it is higher in the physically ill; at the University of Chicago Hospital, one survey found what they defined as neurosis present in 30% of patients. Of those rejected on medical grounds from the U.S. Armed Services, 20% had disorders complicated by the presence of neurosis.

Neurosis can commonly take the form of an exaggerated response to physical illness—because it threatens security. In answer to fear, and as a consequence of exposure to anxiety-arousing situations, neurosis can become phobic, obsessive, compulsive, hysteric or psychosomatic in its character. Recent thinking emphasizes the importance, in the development of neurosis, of an individual's feelings of loneliness and the shallowness of his or her interpersonal relations with other individuals. The neurotic person's expectations of helpers and physicians are often immature and demanding of immediate relief; they thus face a lifetime of disappointments and frustrations that compound the neurotic personality.

Acute and severe attacks may provoke psychosomatic symptoms that cause severe distress—*hyperventilation* (overbreathing) is one example; the *panic attack* with an irresistible sense of impending death is another. PHOBIAS with regard to crowds, open spaces, heights, dirt, or insects can be occupationally disabling, as can *compulsive neuroses* that involve ritual hand washing. *Genitourinary neurosis* can produce dyspareunia (pain experienced by a woman during sexual intercourse) or frigidity, dermatological expressions of neurosis may produce chronic skin rashes, gastrointestinal manifestations may include peptic ulcers or colitis, and in particular coronary ischemia (reduced blood supply to the heart muscle) is complicated by a cardiac neurosis that produces invalidism.

Diagnosis involves psychological testing and a careful medical history, which may require analysis to identify the cause. Treatment has to be skilled, prolonged and supportive. Psychotherapy and behavioral techniques can assist in adjustment; medication helps—usually with tranquilizers to resolve the acute phases. Cure is achieved in only about one third of cases, but the considerable success of professional supportive therapy may help the individual to adjust to life's demands, and largely overcome the personality disorder.

See also the major articles on **Psychiatry** and **Psychotherapy.**

neurotransmitters

Chemical substances that transmit nerve impulses between nerve cells.

The basic unit of the human nervous system is the nerve cell (neuron), which has a long extension called an *axon* that comes almost in physical contact with the receiving processes (dendrites) of other nerve cells. Across this microscopic gap (the "synapse") an electrochemical impulse is transmitted from the axon of one neuron to the dendrites of an adjacent neuron, or to a gland cell to cause secretion, or to a muscle to cause contraction. The transmission of the impulse is achieved by the release of neurotransmitters from special parts of the nerve cell membrane.

Neurotransmitters are not all identified chemically, but they include such substances as acetylcholine, norepinephrine, serotonin, glutamine and several other acids. The neurotransmitter is stored on one side of the synapse with the reactive site on the other side. The signal ceases when the neurotransmitter is chemically changed, diffuses away from the synapse, or is reabsorbed.

The neurotransmitter is vulnerable to drugs or toxins which modify its synthesis or action. Anything that interferes with its breakdown will cause prolonged action (as in TETANUS), while substances that delay its release have equally dramatic effects (as in paralysis due to curare poisoning). Many drugs act by their effect on neurotransmitters: for example, certain drugs used to control blood pressure.

nevus

A type of skin discoloration; a "birthmark."

It is due to an anomaly in the embryonic development of the skin, particularly affecting the blood vessels of the subcutaneous layer in small or wide areas. Nevi vary considerably in size and appearance. The most commonly recognized type is the "strawberry" birth mark. Others are the tiny star-shaped discoloration often called the "spider" nevus—commonly seen in adults— and the quite disfiguring "port wine stain" (*nevus flammeus*) that can occupy half the face of the newborn.

Nevi may appear at birth or soon after; occasionally they develop within the first two years of life. They affect all ethnic groups from the "blue" nevus of the Mongolian races to the "pale" nevus of the negroid. There is no known cause and the suggestion that nevi are intrauterine "pressure" marks is untrue. They affect the sexes equally, but are considered cosmetically less acceptable in the female.

Nevi may be single or multiple, faint in discoloration or very obvious. *Pigmented nevi,* containing an excess of melanin making them much darker than normal skin, may grow hairs that are thick, black and profuse. *Vascular nevi*—those containing blood vessels—deepen in color when a child cries or exercises, because the blood vessels are engorged with incomplete blood pathways. Nevi are usually demarcated at the border and rarely increase in size.

The "strawberry" birthmark usually disappears as the child grows, since deposits of subcutaneous fat tend to hide it. Such a nevus therefore requires no treatment.

NEVUS

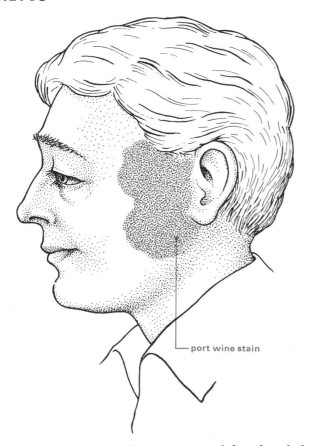

— port wine stain

A nevus, or birthmark, is an area of discolored skin which results from a congenital malformation of surface blood vessels. Certain types of nevus have descriptive names, such as "strawberry nevus" and the "port wine stain" illustrated here.

Pigmented nevi with hairs may also be left, to observe their possible fading or disappearance, but they may occasionally require surgical excision or other treatment—such as electrolysis, diathermy cauterization or "freezing." "Spider" nevi respond to electrolysis. There is no truly effective treatment for a port wine stain, but a cosmetician can prepare a special cream which matches the patient's skin to provide a means of concealing the disfigurement. In all cases the skilled advice of a dermatologist should be sought.

See also MOLE.

Niemann-Pick disease

An extremely rare disease, inherited as a recessive gene. It is characterized by a widespread accumulation of a particular kind of "fat" cells throughout the body, particularly affecting the tissues of the nerves, brain, spleen, liver and lymph glands.

The disease is seen in infants, who rarely survive beyond the sixth month. Mental retardation, spasticity, and convulsions occur and there is progressive wasting of the body with the appearance of jaundice. Diagnosis is confirmed by tissue biopsy. Most common among those of Jewish origin, it is also associated with inbreeding. There is no treatment, and only in a few cases does survival occur to late childhood. It occurs in equal sex distribution.

night blindness

A condition in which vision is fairly normal in good light but defective in dim light. The technical term is *nyctalopia.* It is primarily a symptom of severe vitamin A deficiency but also occurs in RETINITIS PIGMENTOSA, an inherited degenerative disorder of the retina.

The ability of the eye to adapt to varying degrees of light and dark depends on photoreceptors in the retina. One type of photoreceptor, the rods, mediate vision in dim light. They contain pigment known as rhodopsin or "visual purple," which is temporarily bleached by light. The speed of the eye's adaptability to dark depends on the speed with which rhodopsin is re-formed in darkness, which in turn depends on vitamin A.

If night blindness is due to vitamin A deficiency, treatment is by vitamin A replacement; if it is due to retinitis pigmentosa, there is no effective treatment.

See also VISION.

noma

A rare condition of progressive gangrene (necrosis) that affects children in the terminal stages of severe malnutrition. Also known as *cancrum oris* or *gangrenous stomatitis.*

It is almost unknown in the United States, although seen in Central and South America in areas of starvation and very poor hygiene. Noma may also occur in the genitalia of starving children, particularly in young girls, and may develop in any area of the body that has previously been attacked by infections.

It is caused by the invasion of *fusospirochetal* organisms and other bacteria in children whose resistance is markedly lowered by malnutrition and other infections. A green to black area develops characteristically on the gums and spreads until the ulceration denudes the jaw. The teeth loosen and fall out but pain, surprisingly, is rarely severe—probably because the sensory nerves are deprived of their function. The destruction of local affected areas, mouth, nose and cheek continues unabated unless treatment is initiated; death can result from septicemia and toxemia.

Treatment with penicillin arrests the disease immediately but the malnutrition must be corrected to prevent its recurrence. The damage done by noma is not naturally repaired except by scar tissue, and deformity results.

nonspecific urethritis (NSU)

Urethritis is inflammation of the urethra—the tube through which the bladder discharges urine; it passes from the neck of the bladder to the external genitalia. Urethritis can occur as an inflammation due to various known infective organisms, or as a result of trauma; but when bacteriological investigations fail to yield any positive results the inflammation is said to be *nonspecific*.

The symptoms are pain and a burning sensation on passing urine and urinary frequency. There is a urethral discharge, and the disease is confined to the age of the sexually active.

Nonspecific urethritis is more common in males; but as the urethra is anatomically longer in the male, it may be that it is underdiagnosed in females and many cases of "cystitis" in women may be cases of nonspecific urethritis. It develops 5–30 days after sexual intercourse and varies in the intensity of its symptoms. The condition may last for several weeks and its recurrence rate is high.

The cause, as the name implies, is unknown. Viruses, bacteria, funguses and other genital parasites, as well as allergies, have been blamed but proof of the actual cause is lacking. Diagnosis depends on the medical history and the absence in urine cultures, or urethral swabs—even after massage of the prostate gland in the male—of any positive bacterial growths. Tetracycline, an antibiotic, is an effective treatment but it may need to be taken in prolonged courses.

See also the major article on **Urology.**

nosebleed

Bleeding from the nose (known medically as *epistaxis*) is a common experience, usually as a result of trauma to the flexible cartilaginous area of the nose below the nasal bones (i.e., below the "bridge").

If minor trauma is the cause it is of little medical significance—for, with the correct first-aid treatment, it ceases quite quickly. It may occur spontaneously, however; sometimes due to hypertension in an older person, due to allergic rhinitis and excessive sneezing, due to cabin depressurization when flying, or alternatively due to "mountain sickness." When recurrent nosebleeds are experienced, examination may reveal the presence of nasal POLYPS. It is of no danger to the individual unless he is taking anticoagulants; although the quantity of blood lost in a nosebleed may seem to be considerable, it is rarely ever enough to warrant replacement by transfusion.

The correct treatment is to sit the sufferer up with the head held forwards. He is instructed to breathe through the opened mouth, and to grasp the soft part of his nose between his fingers and thumb to close the nostrils down onto the middle septum throughout its length. This pressure should be sustained until the bleeding stops. Thereafter no attempts to sneeze or blow the nose should be made for at least 48 hours.

Recurrent attacks require referral to a specialist for the affected blood vessel to be cauterized.

See also *Bleeding from the nose* in the **First Aid** section.

nyctalopia

The technical term for NIGHT BLINDNESS.

nystagmus

Rapid, rhythmic flickering movements of the eyeball. The movements may take place in a horizontal, vertical, rotatory, or oblique plane (or rarely in a combination of all planes). There are two main rhythms of movement: a "pendular" variety in which the movements in both directions are equal; and a "jerky" variety consisting of a slow movement in one direction followed by a rapid, jerky movement in the opposite direction.

Normal nystagmus occurs when a person is looking at scenery from a moving vehicle. Otherwise, the causes of abnormal nystagmus fall into three main groups.

The first group consists of defects in vision in which the eye does not receive sufficient visual stimuli for it to fix its gaze. The second group consists of disturbances of the elaborate mechanisms in the ear which help to maintain posture and which have nervous connections to the eye. The third group of causes of abnormal nystagmus consists of diseases of the nervous system.

Nystagmus does not usually produce symptoms but it may sometimes produce vertigo or double vision. Treatment depends on the cause.

obesity

The excessive accumulation of body fat. A person is generally considered obese when his weight is more than 20% above the average weight for people of his race and height. In children, age has also to be taken into account. Other causes of overweight, such as accumulation of fluid, or extremely well-developed muscles, should be excluded before an overweight person is said to be obese.

Another simple and commonly used method for assessing obesity is the measurement of *skinfold thickness* using calipers, since a large proportion of the fat stores are found just underneath the skin. There are also a number of sophisticated laboratory methods for measuring obesity which can be used to detect very mild cases of excessive accumulation of fat, or when very accurate measurements are required.

Weight reduction is usually attempted for aesthetic reasons, but there are essential medical reasons why it should be attempted. Obesity predisposes to conditions like diabetes mellitus, atherosclerosis, backache and osteoarthritis.

Most cases of obesity are caused by an energy input (in the form of the caloric value of food eaten) that is greater than energy expenditure. The excessive input is usually one that has gradually built up over a very long time. If such obese patients want to lose weight, this can be achieved only by caloric restriction. Often the excess calories have been taken in the form of carbohydrates, and reducing this aspect of the diet is helpful. Other reducing diets may involve eating small meals throughout the day rather than concentrating the same amount of food into two or three meals a day; yet others recommend avoiding all fat. Whatever the method, the general principle is to reduce the caloric intake below requirements; it is best to ensure that, in doing so, a balanced, nutritious diet is taken. Caloric requirements vary enormously from individual to individual, and the most suitable diet for a person may only be found by trial and error.

The greatest rate of weight loss usually occurs in the first week of a reducing diet, largely because of an accompanying fluid loss. This should be borne in mind, otherwise a person can be extremely disheartened when weight loss slows down after the first week or two. Since the fat has usually accumulated over a long period, it is unrealistic, and indeed unwise, to aim at a sudden weight loss. The rate of weight loss varies between individuals, but a target of an average weekly loss of one pound is reasonable.

The loss of weight achieved by dietary restriction should be accompanied by reeducation in sensible eating habits, so that the weight is not regained. Eating habits are often acquired in childhood, and the possibility of obesity in later life can be minimized by establishing sound eating habits in young children. And since a high proportion (up to 80–90%) of obese children usually remain fat as adults, obesity in childhood should not be dismissed lightly as "puppy fat."

Another way of adjusting the balance between energy input and output is to increase output by exercise. Considerable activity is required: estimates of the amount of exercise required for losing one pound of fat vary from running 50 miles to playing 100 holes of golf! If the increase in activity is sudden and unaccustomed, it may result in increased consumption of food. A moderate, controlled, regular increase in daily activity is helpful in losing weight.

Sometimes additional measures are required to assist in weight reduction. Drugs may be given that depress appetite or increase the utilization of energy. But because some have side effects, such as the possibility of addiction, and others lose their effectiveness in three or four weeks, drugs should be taken only in short courses and only as an adjunct to sustained dietary restriction.

Quite often there is an emotional problem behind the obesity, comfort being found in eating. If so, it is important to try to remove the emotional factor; psychotherapy may be required.

Very rarely surgery may be required. This may consist of removing a portion of the intestine so that absorption of food is impaired. Such extreme procedures are always reserved for serious cases, as they are not without their problems, which include diarrhea, nutritional effects on the liver and disturbances in mineral metabolism.

In a small proportion of cases, obesity may be due to hormonal disturbances or be associated with a number of congenital or hereditary disorders. These are usually accompanied by other symptoms and treatment should be directed at the underlying cause.

See also the major article on **Nutrition.**

obsession

A repetition of irrational thoughts, doubts, actions, or fears of which the sufferer is aware but which he cannot conquer, however hard he tries. One obsession may lead to another: for example, an obsession with contamination may result in repeated hand washing. The obsession drives the person to wash his hands repeatedly even though he knows they are already clean.

Obsession may be a symptom of several psychiatric disorders or of organic brain disease, or it may exist alone—in which case it is referred to as an *obsessional state*.

Treatment is essentially by PSYCHOTHERAPY, but if the symptom has led to anxiety, tension, or depression, appropriate drug therapy may be required.

occult blood

Small quantities of blood in feces which are not apparent to the eye and can be detected only by special laboratory tests.

If occult blood is detected it suggests that there is bleeding somewhere along the gastrointestinal tract, which will have to be investigated.

Since the bleeding may be only intermittent, the stools have to be negative for occult blood on several occasions before the physician can be fairly certain that there is no bleeding in the gastrointestinal tract. Blood from ingested meat (even if cooked) can give a positive result to the test; thus, the patient should go on a meat-free diet for about three days before the test.

See also the major article on **Gastroenterology.**

occupational diseases and disorders

A group of conditions, each of which is more common in people doing certain kinds of work, and is due to repeated exposure to one or more factors in the working environment.

When dealing with occupational disease, the most important aspect is prevention. The law plays a part, for example, by making regulations governing the safety standards of equipment, or specifying the maximum permissible concentrations of different types of dust particles in the work place. Workers themselves should take care to minimize exposure to any factor likely to cause an occupational disease. Those working in very noisy conditions should wear the ear protectors provided, or if they are exposed to irritant chemicals they should take care to wear all the protective clothing necessary, including gloves.

Newer and safer equipment is constantly being designed, and safer substitutes for material such as asbestos are being developed. Unfortunately, new developments often bring new and unforeseen hazards. More and more occupational diseases are being recognized, although many conditions may not be easily recognized as occupational diseases because of the long time they take to develop. A disease may sometimes appear several years after a person has ceased contact with the alleged causal agent.

The two most common types of occupational disease involve the skin and lungs.

Many skin rashes are caused by contact with irritants or are the result of allergic reactions. In both cases the effect is a skin inflammation known as *contact dermatitis*. Those due to allergy are commonly found in people who work with wet cement (the allergy being due to chromate), those who work with epoxy resins, or those in contact with vulcanizing agents in the rubber industry. Irritant dermatitis tends to be more common in certain industries, such as the coal mining industry, metal goods industry, leather industry, chemical and allied industries and the textile industry. Minute injuries such as those caused by particles of metal in cutting fluids are common sites of irritant dermatitis.

Lung disorders related to occupations (for example, PNEUMOCONIOSIS, SILICOSIS and ASBESTOSIS) occur when very fine dust particles in the environment pass through the body's physical defenses (e.g., hairs in the nostrils or cilia in the bronchi) to reach the air sacs of the lungs. There, over a number of years, they may induce a fibrous reaction which in some cases impairs breathing and produces chronic disability. In other cases they may produce no symptoms and be detected only on x-rays. Sometimes the lung may be affected by an allergic reaction (as occurs in FARMER'S LUNG and BIRD BREEDER'S LUNG) with symptoms that resemble those of ASTHMA.

Other well-known occupational diseases include *caisson disease* or *decompression sickness* (the BENDS) which occurs in deep-sea divers and tunnel workers in a compressed-air environment, and RAYNAUD'S DISEASE which has a particularly high incidence in those who handle vibrating tools such as pneumatic drills. People who work with animals or who handle animal products have to be careful to avoid infections such as BRUCELLOSIS.

Industrial poisoning was once a fairly common occupational disorder. It may be acute in nature, as with a leak of noxious fumes (e.g., ammonia) into the environment; or it may occur insidiously, such as occurs in LEAD POISONING—although this is less common now that many industries in which exposure to lead is likely take blood samples from their workers at regular intervals to test for the possible presence of lead.

Some cancers may be occupational hazards. For example, cancer of the scrotum was recognized more than 200 years ago to be an occupational disease of chimney sweeps. Scrotal cancer is still seen, mainly in those who work with cooling oils in the engineering industry. Cancer of the bladder was at one time quite common in those working with aniline dyes; some of these dyes are no longer produced, but cases have been reported in those working with other amines. There has recently been medical interest in investigating the incidence of liver tumors occurring in those working with vinyl chloride, and MESOTHELIOMA in those exposed to asbestos.

Oedipus complex

Excessive love of a boy for his mother, persisting into adolescence and beyond. It is named after the mythical Greek king who killed his father and married his mother.

Freud believed that an individual passes through a series of stages in his psychosexual development. It is in the "genital stage," between the third and sixth years, that an Oedipus situation is said to arise in boys, experiencing sexual desire for the mother but hostile and aggressive feelings toward the father. The corresponding situation for girls, who are said to be sexually attracted to the father, is the *Electra complex*.

Arrest of psychological development or regression to this stage of development is said to be responsible for an Oedipus complex in later life.

oliguria

An abnormal reduction in the amount of urine secreted.

onychia

Inflammation of the nail.

It usually results from PARONYCHIA (inflammation of the tissues surrounding the nail), caused by nutritional disturbances associated with inflammation in the matrix lying just underneath the nail bed.

The most common cause of the inflammation is trauma to the matrix. The nail is often lost but will regrow if the matrix is not permanently injured. If the matrix is chronically inflamed, the nail that forms is discolored and cracked.

Onychia is common among people whose hands have to be immersed in water for long periods. The skin around the nails is red, swollen and painful, while the nails themselves lose their natural gloss, become opaque and—in severe cases—may become loose and drop off.

onychogryphosis

Excessive growth of a nail into the shape of a claw or horn, with a horny texture.

It may occur in any nail but is most common in the toenails, especially on the big toes. The affected nail is thick, elongated, raised, green or black and the surface is irregular and opaque.

Onychogryphosis is usually seen in people who go about barefooted, although it can be caused by tight shoes. Trauma is said to be the usual cause. It may also

be seen in patients with peripheral NEURITIS, congestive HEART FAILURE, LEPROSY, ICHTHYOSIS, some hormonal disturbances, SYPHILIS, and after a STROKE. Sometimes it runs in families.

If there is an underlying cause it must be recognized and treated. Otherwise, attention should be paid to hygiene and shoe fitting. Hot baths and massage with warm olive oil or with hydrogen peroxide may help. Some doctors, though not all, believe that high doses of vitamin A are useful. Another treatment is to remove the nail, but it will grow again.

onychomycosis

Fungal infection of the nail. It is the most common inflammatory nail disorder and may be caused by a number of fungal species which are identified by examining nail scrapings in the laboratory.

Fungal infection is common in people whose resistance to infection is low, such as diabetics, or anyone taking corticosteroid drugs. It is also common in sufferers of PARONYCHIA (inflammation of skin around the nail), usually people whose work involves immersing the hands in water for long periods, or people with ingrowing toenails. (See INGROWING NAILS).

Onychomycosis is chronic but painless. The nail lacks luster and is opaque and brittle. It may show striations, have a "worm-eaten" appearance, or have a surface of heaped-up flakes. Paronychia of the surrounding soft tissues may cause pain and tenderness, with the exudation of serum or pus—especially if there is a superimposed bacterial infection.

Onychomycosis is treated with griseofulvin (an antifungal drug) applied to the nail or given by mouth. The treatment usually has to be continued for months or years and, even then, may not achieve a permanent cure. Filing the affected nails may shorten the course of the disease by removing infected nail. Sometimes the entire nail has to be removed. Any underlying condition should also be treated, as should any superimposed bacterial infection. Patients should keep the nails clean and dry and footwear should never be shared.

oophorectomy

Surgical removal of an ovary.

This operation was first performed in 1809 by Ephraim McDowell (1771–1830) of Danville, Kentucky, on a patient called Jane Crawford who suffered from a large ovarian tumor. It is pleasant to record that she got out of bed on the fifth day and made a complete recovery, despite the fact that the operation had been performed without anesthesia, and that she lived for a further 31 years.

The operation is carried out nowadays mainly (1) on

ovaries which are the seat of malignant disease, usually combined with removal of the Fallopian tubes and the uterus; (2) on ovaries involved in a widespread chronic inflammatory process; or (3) on ovaries almost completely destroyed by a large benign tumor. Usually in the case of a benign tumor every effort is made (especially in the younger patient) to preserve whatever functioning ovarian tissue is left; the ovary has such a good blood supply that it is able to heal quickly and retain normal function. If the ovary has to be removed in an older woman at or near the menopause, the other ovary and the uterus are often removed at the same time although the tumor may be benign, and HYSTERECTOMY in women past the menopause is often accompanied by oophorectomy.

Some malignant tumors of the breast are hormone-dependent, and it may be useful in the management of such a cancer to remove both ovaries. About 30% of patients, particularly those before the menopause, show a degree of remission of symptoms, some for a long time.

Removal of both ovaries may be performed in severe cases of ENDOMETRIOSIS, and is usually accompanied by removal of the uterus and as much of the abnormal endometrial tissue as possible. The operation induces an abrupt menopause, which is the desired effect in endometriosis and cancer of the breast; but in cases of oophorectomy where this effect is unwelcome, patients can be given the ovarian hormone estrogen.

ophthalmia neonatorum

CONJUNCTIVITIS in a newborn baby caused by infection with bacteria or viruses encountered in the mother's vagina during childbirth. The microorganism most commonly responsible is the gonococcus, the bacterium that causes GONORRHEA.

The infection causes a discharge from the eye in the second or third day of life; it rapidly progresses if the infection is not treated. The eyes become puffy, the conjunctiva becomes intensely red and thick, and the discharge runs down the cheeks in a constant stream. The cornea becomes hazy and ulcerated, which can lead to blindness.

Ophthalmia neonatorum was once a very common disease—affecting up to 10% of babies in some urban areas—and was a principal cause of blindness. It was controlled by silver nitrate drops instilled routinely into the eyes of every newborn baby, a practice that became universal and is still used in many places. Modern treatment of the infection, which is quite effective, is the administration of antibiotic injections and eyedrops.

Several organisms apart from the gonococcus can cause ophthalmia neonatorum. The disease is similar, but vaginal scrapings may be necessary to identify the organism and discover its antibiotic sensitivity. Genital

herpes, for example, is considered so dangerous in this respect that experts regard its presence in the mother as a justification or indication for a CESAREAN SECTION.

ophthalmoplegia

Paralysis or weakness of the muscles that control eye movements, together with dilation and contraction of the pupil. If there is only mild weakness, the earliest symptom is double vision. If the muscles are actually paralyzed, it may be obvious that the eye does not move in certain directions.

Ophthalmoplegia can be produced by any condition affecting the muscles themselves or the nerves that supply them. Head injuries, strokes, meningitis, encephalitis, brain tumors and diabetes are the usual causes. The condition also occurs in HYPERTHYROIDISM and MYASTHENIA GRAVIS. The treatment depends on the cause.

opium

Opium, the drug extracted from a particular species of poppy, is the source of morphine, heroin, codeine and other compounds used in medicine. In the past, crude opium was used to relieve pain and opium has been a drug of addiction for many centuries.

Taken by mouth or inhaled from a pipe, opium causes a feeling of contentment or euphoria, relieves pain and hunger, and eventually causes drowsiness and sleep. The dreams of the opium addict may be vivid and sometimes terrifying—as described by poets such as Samuel Taylor Coleridge and writers like Thomas De Quincey. However, the addictive potential of opium is so powerful that most regular users become addicts who are physically and mentally dependent on the drug.

The medicinal use of opium, mainly to relieve pain, led to the purification of its constituent alkaloids and crude opium is no longer used. Nevertheless, its derivatives—especially heroin—retain the powerful addictive properties, and their use is controlled by drug legislation in most countries.

See also ADDICTION, DRUG ABUSE.

orchiopexy

An operation to fix an UNDESCENDED TESTIS in the scrotum.

In the early embryo, the testes lie near the kidneys and usually descend into the scrotum by the time the child is born or a few weeks after (certainly within the first year). A testis that is not in the scrotum by the time a child is six will be most unlikely ever to produce spermatozoa. The operation to correct the undescended testis is therefore generally performed at least by the time the child is five

OPIUM POPPY
Papaver somniferum

seeds

flowering plant

seed pod

Opium is the dried juice of the unripe seed pod of the poppy Papaver somniferum. *The major constituent of opium is morphine but it also contains lesser amounts of other alkaloids.*

years old and if it is in any way possible much earlier.

If only one testis is undescended, the other should be able to produce enough sperm to maintain fertility; but there are other reasons for orchiopexy. If a testis remains undescended, an inguinal HERNIA is more likely to develop; there is a thirty-fold increase in risk of cancer in that testis; the testis is more likely to be injured or to undergo torsion (in which it twists on its stalk and cuts off its own blood supply—see TORSION OF THE TESTIS); finally, orchiopexy may be performed for cosmetic and psychological reasons.

Sometimes a parent may fear that his boy has an undescended testis when it is, in fact, a "retractile" testis. A retractile testis is one that withdraws up toward the abdomen easily; with careful manipulation it can be brought farther down into the scrotum, and usually stays down by the time of puberty.

The surgical procedure of suturing an undescended testis in the scrotum is also known as *orchiorrhaphy*.

orchitis

Inflammation of the testis.

Acute orchitis is usually the result of a generalized infection such as mumps, scarlet fever, or typhoid. In other cases it may result from the spread of infection from neighboring structures such as the epididymis, the seminal vesicles, or the prostate, or from other distant structures via the bloodstream.

The testis enlarges and there is severe pain in the scrotum, which is tender, red and swollen. The patient usually has a fever and a general feeling of being unwell (malaise). Severe acute orchitis may result in some wasting away of the testis (occasionally enough to cause sterility).

In treatment the scrotum is supported by a suspensory "bridge" and ice packs are applied during the acute phase. Analgesics such as aspirin and codeine will relieve pain; the infection itself is treated with appropriate antibiotics. If there is an abscess the pus has to be drained. Some physicians believe in giving corticosteroid drugs to relieve the inflammation; others make a small incision in the tough, inelastic covering of the testis during the very early stage of the disease. A few doctors prescribe female sex hormones in treating orchitis associated with mumps. If symptoms persist for more than a month, surgical removal of the testis may be necessary.

Chronic orchitis may be caused by syphilis; it is often unnoticed since it is painless. Tuberculosis is another cause of chronic orchitis; here the testis is hard and nodular and may be mistaken for a tumor. Once the diagnosis is confirmed by BIOPSY, an appropriate antibiotic can be given.

orgasm

The climax of sexual activity.

The normal response to sexual stimulation can be divided into four phases: excitement, plateau, orgasm and resolution. In the first two phases a number of physiological changes occur; these include not only changes in the breasts and genitals of both sexes but also flushing of the skin and a rising pulse rate and blood pressure.

During the *orgasmic phase,* which is the shortest of the four phases, there is intense physical activity: involuntary contractions of various muscles, thrusting movements of the pelvis, contraction of the anal sphincter (the muscular ring that controls the opening and closing of the anus), a further quickening of the pulse and breathing rate and a further rise in blood pressure. The female cervix dilates and the male ejaculates semen.

Orgasm is followed by the phase of *resolution* during

which there is a relaxation of sexual tension and a reversal of the physiological processes of sexual excitement. Restimulation of the woman during this phase may induce another orgasm, but in the man there is a variable refractory period during which re-stimulation does not produce another orgasm.

orthodontics

The branch of dentistry concerned with the study of the growth and development of the jaws and teeth and with the correction of irregularities of the teeth (such as abnormal alignment) and associated facial abnormalities.

Orthodontic treatment may be required for several reasons—in addition to the obvious esthetic and psychological value of regular, symmetrical teeth. Some positions of teeth may result in poor coordination of the chewing muscles, giving rise to symptoms in the joint between the jaw and the rest of the skull. If teeth are overcrowded the teeth and gums cannot be cleaned effectively (naturally or artificially), and the patient may become prone to gum trouble and CARIES ("cavities"). Finally, orthodontics may be required to facilitate other forms of dental treatment—such as the fitting of dentures, bridges or crowns and certain types of oral or dental surgery, or to hold erupted teeth in position so that later teeth can erupt in proper alignment.

The basic principle of orthodontic treatment is to apply pressure to the teeth to direct their growth into the position required. Teeth may be tipped, rotated or moved bodily. Some dentists exert a small pressure continuously, while others prefer stronger pressure with intermittent periods of rest.

Pressure is exerted by a variety of appliances, such as wires, braces, screws, wedges and rubber bands. Some can be attached entirely within the mouth, whereas others need "extra-oral" attachments by bands around the head or neck. Some are fixed, while others have to be removed and replaced by the patient for cleaning. Treatment usually has to be continued for months or even years, and several courses of treatment may be needed as a child grows.

There are limits to what orthodontics can achieve: it is not the solution to every speech defect or to all types of malalignment of the upper and lower jaws. Even so, children should be encouraged to persist with orthodontic treatment since good results are more likely while the jaws and teeth are still growing.

See also the major article on **Dentistry**.

orthoptics

The treatment of STRABISMUS (squint or cross-eye) by eye exercises. The treatment is given by an orthoptist, who is medically trained in all aspects of the diagnosis and treatment of strabismus.

The principle behind orthoptic treatment is the retraining of the eye muscles and the brain so that both eyes are used simultaneously to view objects. The brain may have to be retrained because some patients with strabismus overcome their double vision by learning to ignore images coming from one eye. This has to be "unlearned" and the brain taught to appreciate images from the eye it has previously ignored. The orthoptist works with a number of sophisticated instruments which can present pictures separately or together to one or both eyes.

Not all cases of strabismus can be successfully treated by orthoptic methods. Cases which are more suitable are those in which the degree of the cross-eye is not too severe, those in which vision in both eyes is still good, and those which have not appeared suddenly or before the age of two.

Although orthoptic treatment is more likely to be successful the earlier treatment is started, it requires a great deal of cooperation from the patient; thus, young children (under the ages of about five to seven) are not good candidates. Young children can, however, be given "preorthoptic" treatment designed to prevent further deterioration of the squint; occlusion, or covering the unaffected eye, thereby forcing the child to use the affected eye, is the basis of preorthoptic care and may have to be carried out for days or weeks at a time.

When proper orthoptic treatment is begun, the treatments must be frequent and continued for a very long time. The frequency of treatment (usually daily at the beginning) can be reduced over the course of treatment. Treatment is unlikely to be successful if the patient is over the age of about 20.

osteitis

Literally, inflammation of bone.

Inflammatory disease of bone is commonly due to infection and often affects the marrow as well, in which case it is known as OSTEOMYELITIS. The term osteitis tends to be used for a number of other bone disorders, not necessarily inflammatory in nature. Some are the result of biochemical derangements, while others are inherited or of unknown cause.

Osteitis deformans, also known as PAGET'S DISEASE, is of unknown cause. There is excessive bone destruction and subsequent spontaneous repair; the repair takes place in a disorganized fashion leading to deformities. Often there are no symptoms at first, but some patients suffer pain. Later the back may become hunched, the legs bowed and the skull enlarged; a waddling gait may develop and the bones fracture easily.

Complications include kidney stones (the calcium

coming from the destruction of bone) and bone deformities that may press on nerves and cause blindness or deafness. In a few cases, cancer of the bone may develop. A number of drugs are now available to suppress the excessive activity of bone.

Osteitis fibrosa cystica is a bone disease caused by the overactivity of the parathyroid glands (HYPERPARATHYROIDISM). The excessive amounts of parathyroid hormone remove calcium from the bone so that cystic demineralized areas develop throughout the skeleton. Symptoms range from back pain, joint pain and other bone pains to fractures, loss of height and a hunched back. Treatment involves correction of the parathyroid disorder which is often due to benign tumors in the gland. They can be removed surgically.

Syphilis, whether congenital or acquired later in life, can cause a type of osteitis. In children, inflammation of the bone, cartilage and periosteum (outer lining of the bone) may pass unnoticed because they produce no symptoms. In some cases, however, fractures may occur and pain may prevent the child from moving the limbs. In adults the bone involvement usually takes the form of localized areas of destruction by "gummata" (the characteristic syphilitic lesions).

Osteitis fibrosa disseminata and *osteitis condensans generalisata* are two rare bone disorders. The former is of unknown cause and is characterized by fibrous overgrowths in bone. The latter is an inherited condition in which the bone becomes very dense.

See also the major article on **Orthopedics.**

osteoarthritis

A degenerative disease of the joints, usually accompanied by pain and stiffness.

Radiography shows that over 80% of people between the ages of 55 and 64 show changes characteristic of the disease; of these, about 20% complain of symptoms. It causes a great deal of pain and discomfort to a large number of people of both sexes, although females tend to suffer more severely than males. The cause of the disease is not known, but it may be described as a degenerative disorder developing with age.

Many sufferers give a history of antecedent injury, sometimes many years before; any fracture or joint disease which results in injury to the joint cartilage or misalignment of the joint predisposes a patient to the development of the disease. The large weight-bearing joints of the lower limb are particularly affected, but osteoarthritis can also affect the fingers, elbows, shoulders and the vertebrae. Occupations involving the use of other joints may in time produce signs of the disease in unexpected places.

The basic change in the affected joints is loss of the *articular cartilage*, which normally protects the ends of

the bones and provides a smooth working surface for movement. The exposed ends of the bones become hard and shiny, and at their margins small spurs of bone develop known as *osteophytes*. The changes are evident in radiographs (x-rays) which show the osteophytes and narrowing of the joint space where the cartilage has been lost. The membranes lining the joint (synovial membranes) become thickened, and there may be an effusion of fluid into the joint which causes it to swell.

The patient suffers increasing pain on movement of the joint, and the joint becomes stiff. Usually the pain becomes worse as the day progresses, and the affected limb is difficult to use. In advanced cases of the disease, joint function may be lost and the muscles acting on the joint may waste (atrophy). Grating (crepitus) may be felt in the joint on movement. Where the fingers are affected, small swellings (Heberden's nodes) may develop beside the finger joints. As the disease progresses, the hands may become deformed. In the back and neck, degeneration of the intervertebral joints with osteophyte formation may involve the spinal nerves as they leave the spinal cord and produce neurological symptoms.

The treatment of milder cases includes reduction of body weight in those who are obese. As with all common diseases which are difficult to relieve, a large number of drugs are offered on the market, but most of them have in common an irritant action on the stomach which may provoke the development of a peptic ulcer. They must therefore be used with caution. The most useful drug is aspirin, but it too has undesirable side effects and cannot be used in all cases. Orthopedic surgery has in the last few years improved the treatment of severe cases with the introduction of artificial joints. It is now often possible to replace a painful diseased hip joint with success. In many cases the knee can be replaced, although the operation is not yet as uniformly satisfactory as a hip replacement.

See also the major articles on **Orthopedics** and **Rheumatology.**

osteogenesis imperfecta

A condition seen at birth or in infancy in which there is extreme fragility of the skeleton, leading to multiple fractures and deformities. Also known as *brittle bone disease* and *fragilitas ossium.*

The bones are brittle as the result of defective formation in fetal life. The cause is unknown, but the milder form of the disease, seen in infancy, sometimes tends to run in families. Infants with osteogenesis imperfecta may be born with multiple fractures of every bone in the body. The resulting damage to the brain and other organs usually leads to death within a few weeks.

When the disease is less severe, fractures occur after birth and fewer bones are involved. Healing usually occurs readily, but severe deformity may result. The skull is usually flattened and the sclera of the eyes is thin and bluish in color. Deafness due to OTOSCLEROSIS is common later in those who survive.

Diagnosis is made by clinical and x-ray examination. It is important, but sometimes difficult, for the physician to distinguish between osteogenesis imperfecta and the BATTERED CHILD SYNDROME, where fractures in a normal infant result from assault by a parent or guardian.

Osteogenesis imperfecta cannot be prevented, but fractures occurring in infancy can often be minimized by careful attention to the child. When fractures occur, their healing is aided by the usual orthopedic methods in an attempt to prevent deformity.

osteoma

A benign tumor composed of bone.

Osteomas are usually attached to normal bones, but they may also occur in other structures. They are commonly attached to the bones of the skull (including the sinuses) and the lower jaw, but they may occur anywhere in the body.

The cause of osteomas is not known. The common symptom is the presence of a hard, painless lump. Other symptoms may result from pressure of the tumor on nerves or other structures, but these symptoms are quite rare.

Osteomas are not malignant and probably only rarely change into a malignant OSTEOSARCOMA. Treatment of osteomas is surgical removal, but this is necessary only where there are troublesome symptoms, such as pain due to pressure, or for cosmetic reasons.

osteomalacia

A disease of adults, especially women, in which the bones are generally softened, due to the impaired deposition of calcium. The matrix (organic tissue) of the bones is normal or increased in quantity. In childhood, RICKETS leads to a similar softening of the bones and also to characteristic deformities in their development.

Osteomalacia is caused by lack of vitamin D as the result of dietary deficiency, malabsorption from the intestine, abnormal metabolism, or increased requirements for the vitamin during pregnancy. Lack of vitamin D leads, in turn, to decreased absorption of calcium from the intestine and abnormal calcium metabolism in the body.

Vitamin D is lacking from many basic diets, but it is synthesized in the skin (especially in white races) in response to sunlight. Natives of tropical countries who move to temperate climates or who remain indoors are thus particularly liable to osteomalacia. Vitamin D is malabsorbed in conditions such as celiac disease and abnormal metabolism occurs in kidney failure; osteomalacia is fairly common in these circumstances.

Osteomalacia causes bone pain and tenderness. True bone fractures may occur and *pseudofractures*—transverse translucent bands extending across the bones—are commonly seen on x-rays. The calcium deficiency also causes muscular weakness and loss of appetite and weight. Blood levels of calcium and other substances may help to confirm the diagnosis.

Treatment involves the administration of vitamin D or one of its synthetic analogues. Further treatment depends upon the underlying cause and on any complications.

Vitamin D deficiency can be and is prevented in most Americans by addition of the vitamin to dairy products; but osteomalacia is still quite common in the elderly, the poor and those with disease of the kidneys or small intestine.

See also the major article on **Orthopedics.**

osteomyelitis

An infection of bone and bone marrow.

Acute osteomyelitis is fairly uncommon in the Western world, but is still common in areas of poor health and nutrition—especially among children. There is severe pain and tenderness in the affected bone, and the patient rapidly becomes extremely ill with a high fever, drowsiness and dehydration.

Acute osteomyelitis is usually caused by infection with bacteria of the species *Staphylococcus aureus*. The main treatment is the administration of appropriate antibiotics, but in the absence of a rapid response it is also necessary to drain pus from the bone by drilling a hole in it—a surprisingly minor operation.

With rapid diagnosis and antibiotic treatment, most patients with acute osteomyelitis make a full recovery. There is a risk of death due to septicemia (blood poisoning) but this is slight in comparison with the major mortality before antibiotic treatment was available.

Chronic osteomyelitis may be a late result of acute osteomyelitis, it may follow an open fracture of a bone, or it may result from the presence of a foreign body (e.g., a bullet or a surgical plate). Here an area of bone is dead and infected (a *sequestrum*) and infection persists because antibiotics cannot reach the area in adequate amounts. The symptoms fluctuate, but include local pain and the discharge of pus. Deformities may result.

Treatment involves the removal of all dead tissue, surgical drainage, antibiotic treatment and the repair of any resulting bone defect. This treatment is usually lengthy, complicated and hazardous. It is not always successful, and the prognosis of chronic osteomyelitis is correspondingly uncertain. It may cause chronic ill-health and even require amputation of a limb, or it may be totally cured. Fortunately, however, it is a fairly rare disease.

osteoporosis

A disease in which the bones are generally thinned, due to a loss of organic matrix with a corresponding decrease in calcified tissue.

Starting around the age of 20, everyone's bones become progressively thinner with age. When this thinning proceeds faster than normal it leads to osteoporosis. The disease is common in old age, especially in women.

Osteoporosis also occurs in a number of other conditions at any age. These include complications following corticosteroid therapy, Cushing's syndrome, hyperthyroidism, acromegaly, rheumatoid arthritis, and other diseases leading to immobilization.

The disease may be symptomless, or it may cause pain—commonly in the back, ribs or limbs. Vertebrae may collapse suddenly, causing severe back pain; in any case, they contract gradually as the disease progresses, leading to a loss in height and increased curvature of the spine (kyphosis). Osteoporosis of the femur is the underlying cause of most hip fractures in the elderly.

The main treatment for pain is the administration of analgesic drugs. Support of the affected spine by a corset may also help, and physical therapy and exercises may aid the muscles of the spine in supporting the vertebrae and thus minimizing or preventing pain.

Osteoporosis that occurs as the result of another disease demands treatment of the primary disease. Corticosteroid therapy should be avoided or stopped if possible.

Specific therapies for osteoporosis include estrogens in women, androgens in men, calcium by mouth or intravenously, fluoride supplements and a diet high in protein and calcium. The range of treatments used shows that none is entirely satisfactory.

Osteoporosis itself does not shorten life expectancy; but fractures, especially of the hip, and underlying diseases may lead to premature death.

See also the major article on **Orthopedics.**

osteosarcoma

One of the most common types of malignant bone tumor.

Osteosarcomas may occur at any age, but are more common in children and young adults. They may also occur as a complication of PAGET'S DISEASE, typically in the 60s. They usually occur in the limbs, but may affect any bone.

The usual symptom is pain. Sometimes there is swelling and tenderness; occasionally the diagnosis is made only when the affected bone fractures.

Osteosarcomas are malignant, and the major spread of the cancer cells (metastasis) occurs in the lungs—which is the most frequent cause of death. X-rays are helpful in making the diagnosis and in determining whether metastasis has occurred.

Diagnosis demands BIOPSY of the tumor with immediate examination (by frozen section) of the sample. If the diagnosis is confirmed and there is no evidence of metastasis, the affected limb is amputated under the same anesthetic (or the affected part elsewhere in the body is widely excised). An alternative is to give a course of irradiation to the tumor, at the beginning of which it is biopsied. If there is no sign of spread to the lungs or elsewhere after three months the limb is then amputated. This avoids the amputation of a part in a patient who is likely to die from secondary spread in any case, but the results are not quite as good as those from the first approach. There is no effective treatment for metastases, although radiation may be palliative.

There is considerable variation in the aggressiveness of the tumors, but on average only 10–15% of patients will survive for five years after diagnosis, even with modern treatment.

See also CANCER and the major article on **Oncology.**

otitis externa

Inflammation of the outer canal of the ear. It is a common and usually trivial condition.

The ear is composed of four parts: the *pinna* is the part which projects from the head; the *outer ear* includes the opening and the canal to the eardrum; the *middle ear* is the section immediately beyond the eardrum; and the *inner ear* is the part furthest into the head.

Otitis externa affects the outer ear. Sometimes the pinna or the middle ear may be inflamed at the same time, depending on the cause, and the condition may be difficult to distinguish from OTITIS MEDIA (inflammation of the middle ear).

Otitis externa causes pain in the ear and a discharge from it. The pain may be severe and is usually worsened by movements such as chewing and yawning, but hearing is seldom affected.

Causes include foreign bodies in the ear, amateur attempts to remove them by excessive poking, moisture (for instance, if the ears are not dried after swimming), cosmetics, hair sprays, and allergy to drugs contained in eardrops. The ear is often infected with bacteria or fungi, but this infection is frequently a *consequence* of otitis externa and not the primary cause. It may lead to a painful boil in the outer ear.

Most cases of otitis externa resolve spontaneously without treatment, but a doctor should be consulted if the condition persists or grows worse for more than a day or two. The ear may be made more comfortable by moistened gauze or bland eardrops. Antibiotics may be required by mouth for an infected otitis externa. Drops containing antibiotics or other drugs may make the condition worse.

Otitis externa tends to recur, so the sufferer should try to discover the cause and avoid it in the future. Children with otitis externa should not swim until the condition is fully healed, and even then recurrence is common. Otitis externa caused by a fungus infection may take months of treatment to eradicate.

See also the major article on **Otolaryngology**.

otitis interna

Inflammation of the inner ear. Also called *labyrinthitis*.

The inner ear, or labyrinth, contains the organs of balance and of hearing, both of which may be affected by the spread of infection from the middle ear (see OTITIS MEDIA). The patient suffers from VERTIGO; if some hearing is retained, the condition is called *diffuse serous labyrinthitis*, but if hearing is totally lost, then the disease is called *diffuse purulent labyrinthitis*. The main danger is spread of infection to the meninges, the membranes covering the brain. Treatment is rest in bed with the administration of appropriate antibiotics, perhaps with the addition of cyclizine or prochlorperazine to relieve the vertigo.

Vertigo of sudden onset may occur without obvious infection or loss of hearing; this condition is called *infective labyrinthitis*, perhaps wrongly, as it is thought to be due to a virus infection of the nerve fibers running from the inner ear to the brain stem. In most cases the disease is self-limiting, with spontaneous recovery, but in a very few the patient later develops signs of MULTIPLE SCLEROSIS.

See also the major article on **Otolaryngology**.

otitis media

Inflammation of the middle ear (the part just behind the eardrum).

Acute otitis media is most common in infants and young children; about 20% of children under a year of age have at least one attack.

The middle ear is connected to the back of the nose by the Eustachian tube. In children the tube is short and wide and the lower end is easily blocked by enlarged ADENOIDS. Infection spreads freely from the nose and throat to the middle ear.

Acute otitis media can cause severe illness with fever, vomiting, diarrhea and failure to feed; in infants there is

often no reason for the parents to suspect that the ear is the site of infection. Older children usually complain of earache. Deafness may occur during the attacks, but usually resolves with treatment. The infection may give rise to complications such as meningitis or mastoiditis, although this is rare with current therapy.

The doctor examines the patient's ear with a simple instrument called an otoscope. In acute otitis media the eardrum is red, inflamed and swollen. In severe cases it may burst, or the doctor may incise it to relieve pressure ("myringotomy").

Acute otitis media usually responds rapidly to treatment with antibiotics—commonly penicillin—although many cases would resolve spontaneously within 48 hours or so. Analgesics are needed for the pain; soothing eardrops may also be helpful. In children, ephedrine nose drops help to reestablish drainage of the ear through the Eustachian tube. Successfully treated otitis media has no long-term complications. Recurrent attacks may occur, however, and sometimes removal of the adenoids is helpful in preventing them.

Chronic otitis media is usually the result of repeated attacks of acute otitis media. The eardrum is scarred, thickened and often perforated. The patient may be partially deaf in the affected ear, which usually discharges. The main risk is the development of a "cholesteatoma," an accumulation of debris which may erode bone and cause further damage to the ear and even to the brain. A cholesteatoma requires skilled surgical treatment.

Secretory otitis media ("glue ear") is a painless condition, most common in children, in which the middle ear fills with viscous fluid. This is usually the result of recurrent or untreated otitis media, but in a few cases the cause may not be known. The condition leads to deafness and there is a risk of permanent ear damage. Treatment involves long-term drainage of the ear by myringotomy or the insertion of tubes ("grommets") through the eardrum to drain the fluid.

See also the major article on **Otolaryngology**.

otosclerosis

A disease causing deafness which occurs in about 1% of the American population.

The disease is due to the abnormal formation of spongy bone in the inner ear which immobilizes the *stapes*, the innermost of the tiny sound-conducting bones in the middle ear. The amplification of sound, normally achieved by these small bones, is ruined.

Otosclerosis often runs in families as part of some rare disease complexes. Otherwise its cause is unknown.

Deafness usually starts in the teens or early twenties and is slowly progressive. It may remain static for many years or it may progress more rapidly for a period, especially in pregnant women. It usually affects one ear before the other, and is accompanied at first by a ringing sensation in the ear (tinnitus). The diagnosis is suggested by the results of hearing tests.

Otosclerosis cannot be prevented, but it can usually be successfully treated by surgery. The stapes is removed and replaced by a Teflon or wire substitute which restores the vibration characteristics of the chain of tiny bones. The operation is extremely delicate—these tiny ear bones are the smallest bones of the body—and carries a 2% risk of causing total deafness in the ear, but the other 98% of patients achieve greatly improved hearing within two to three weeks. It is impossible to predict which patients will become deaf, but most sufferers are prepared to accept the risk.

See also the major article on **Otolaryngology.**

ovarian cyst

A swelling of the ovary, containing fluid.

Ovarian cysts are very common, particularly in women between the ages of 30 to 60. They may be single or multiple and can occur in one or both ovaries. Most are benign, but approximately 15% are malignant.

Some ovarian cysts are related to a persistence of changes which take place in the ovary during every menstrual cycle. They may, for example, result from retention of a Graafian follicle (developing ovum) or a corpus luteum (old ovum)—structures which normally disappear with each cycle. Others, such as *dermoid cysts* or those seen in the STEIN-LEVENTHAL SYNDROME ("polycystic ovary"), are due to developmental abnormalities in the ovary. The cause of most cysts, however, is unknown.

Cysts may grow quietly and cause no symptoms until they are found on routine examination. On the other hand, they may become large enough to cause abdominal distension or even obstruct venous drainage, causing swelling of the legs. Malignant cysts may cause the general symptoms of cancer, such as loss of weight and wasting.

Bleeding may occur in some cysts and others may rupture. Both these complications are painful, as is twisting of a cyst (torsion), which may occur when the cyst is on a "stalk." These diagnoses may all be confused with acute appendicitis and other abdominal emergencies and may only become apparent on LAPAROTOMY (examination through an incision in the abdomen). A further possibility is infection in a cyst, which may cause pain and high fever.

Ovarian cysts are usually removed surgically to prevent further complications. The type of operation depends on the individual case but may include removal of the cyst alone or removal of the entire ovary (oophorectomy). Removal of both ovaries results in

sterility and an artificial MENOPAUSE; it is usually performed only in the treatment of ovarian cancer or in postmenopausal women. Ovarian cancer may require follow-up radiation or drug treatment, but surgery alone is sufficient for most ovarian cysts.

ovulation

The release of an ovum from the ovary.

Ovulation occurs around the middle of the menstrual cycle and is followed either by fertilization and pregnancy or, after 14 days, by MENSTRUATION. The ovum travels down the Fallopian tube to the uterus; if it meets and is penetrated by a male sperm cell during its journey down the Fallopian tube, the fertilized ovum becomes implanted in the wall of the uterus. There it

OVULATION

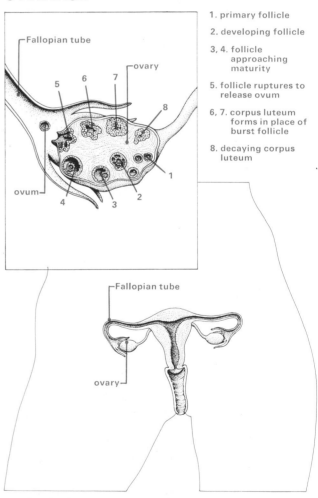

1. primary follicle

2. developing follicle

3, 4. follicle approaching maturity

5. follicle ruptures to release ovum

6, 7. corpus luteum forms in place of burst follicle

8. decaying corpus luteum

At birth the ovaries contain many primary follicles, each containing an immature ovum, or egg. After puberty, one of these follicles ripens and releases an ovum (ovulation) at the midpoint of each menstrual cycle. If the ovum is not fertilized, menstrual bleeding results.

grows and develops into a human embryo.

Ovulation depends on the secretion of hormones by the pituitary gland (at the base of the brain) which is itself under the control of the hypothalamus, the region of the brain concerned with basic sex drives, hunger and sleep. The *hypothalamic releasing factors* stimulate the secretion by the pituitary of follicle-stimulating hormone (FSH), which causes a single ovum to ripen and be released by the ovary. Fertility also depends on other pituitary hormones—luteinizing hormone and prolactin—which interact with the estrogen and progesterone secreted by the ovaries themselves.

Minor impairment of the hormonal cycle may be enough to suppress ovulation while not interfering with menstruation: a woman may have regular periods but be infertile because she does not ovulate. It is for that reason that the investigation of infertility may require careful measurement of hormone levels in the blood and urine and assessment of the woman's response to hormone treatment. When the cause of infertility is shown to be failure of ovulation, there is a good prospect of successful treatment: ovulation may be induced either by drugs such as clomiphene (which alter the hormone balance) or by specific hormone treatment.

oxygen

An odorless, tasteless gas (atomic weight 16) occurring free in the atmosphere, of which it comprises 20% by volume.

Oxygen is essential to most forms of life, including man. Man absorbs it from his lungs into the bloodstream. It is carried in combination with the HEMOGLOBIN in the red cells and discharged from there to the tissues. Oxygen is essential to the metabolism of every living human cell.

The human body can tolerate a lack of oxygen for only a very short time—the brain is the most sensitive organ and it is permanently damaged if its oxygen supply is cut off for more than about three minutes.

Oxygen therapy is necessary in various diseases of the lungs and heart, and "hyperbaric oxygen" (oxygen under pressure) has a role in the treatment of infections such as gas gangrene (see GANGRENE) and some cancers (in combination with radiation therapy).

oxyuriasis

Infestation with PINWORMS.

ozena

A disease of the nose characterized by a foul-smelling discharge of pus and the formation of crusts. Ozena occurs mainly in young adults, especially women.

The lining of the nose starts to waste away or atrophy ("atrophic rhinitis") and the whole cavity becomes larger than normal. The foul-smelling discharge is constantly produced; it cannot easily be removed by blowing the nose.

One cause of ozena is the prolonged abuse of locally applied decongestant drops or sprays, but in many cases the cause is not known.

No specific infection is present and antibiotic treatment is no help. Treatment consists of getting rid of the crusts and discharge by repeated nasal douching and the use of appropriate nose drops. The damage to the lining mucosa is irreversible and treatment may be required for life. Fortunately, the condition is very uncommon.

P

pacemaker

A device which controls the heart rate by the rhythmic discharge of electrical impulses. (This is technically known as an *artificial pacemaker*, since the term "pacemaker" also describes the group of specialized cells in the heart—the "sinoatrial node"—which generates the natural impulses that control the rhythmic beating of the heart.)

Pacemakers are most commonly used for the treatment of "heart block," where the ventricles beat slowly and may stop altogether. In such cases a pacemaker is usually required permanently. They are also used in other cardiac arrhythmias in which the heartbeat is abnormally slow or fast, in some patients after myocardial infarction ("heart attack"), and in some patients after cardiac surgery. Here the pacemaker may be required temporarily or permanently.

Heart muscle has the intrinsic ability to beat and should do so in a controlled way, the beat spreading from a point of stimulus through the whole heart. When heart muscle beats arrhythmically the control has evidently been lost, and the pacemaker is intended to replace it: each pulse of the pacemaker sets off a heartbeat.

The electrodes through which the impulses reach the heart may be on the outside surface of the heart ("external") or on its inside surface ("internal"). External pacemakers require surgical implantation while internal pacemakers can be maneuvered into the right ventricle of the heart via the veins.

Pacemakers are powered by batteries which may be outside the body if the device is temporary but must be implanted beneath the skin of the chest wall (to prevent

CARDIAC PACEMAKER

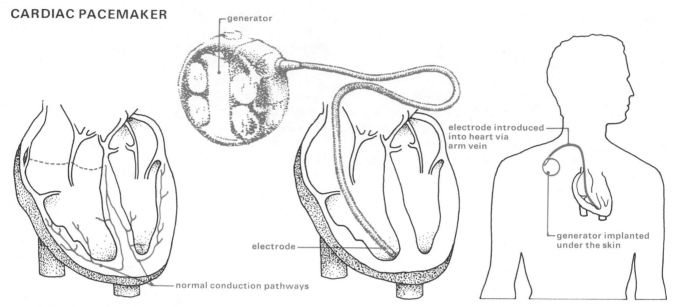

generator

electrode introduced
into heart via
arm vein

generator implanted
under the skin

electrode

normal conduction pathways

Heart disease sometimes involves the conduction pathways so that the pulse becomes dangerously slow or irregular. A cardiac pacemaker may then be inserted, temporarily or permanently, to correct the heartbeat.

infection) if it is permanent. Most permanent pacemakers have batteries which last about two years. Some new models last longer and (in the future) nuclear powered pacemakers may last for 20 years or more. A minor operation is required to change the battery box of the pacemaker.

The main complication of pacemaker therapy is its failure to function—due to battery failure, displacement of the electrode, or fibrosis around the electrode. It is also said that coming into the vicinity of poorly shielded microwave ovens or other microwave devices can interfere with the pacemaker's function. Other complications include infection in the blood or around the battery box, ulceration of the skin above the box and, rarely, perforation of the heart by the pacemaker.

Pacemakers are generally safe and effective. Their development during the last 20 years has completely changed the previously poor prognosis of many patients with heart block and other cardiac arrhythmias. Many patients in their 80s and 90s are now equipped with pacemakers.

See also BUNDLE BRANCH BLOCK and the major article on **Cardiology.**

Paget's disease (osteitis deformans)

A bone disease, first described by the English surgeon Sir James Paget in 1877. The affected areas of bone become thickened and soft and there is an increase in the total number of bone cells. It is quite common in old age,

especially in men, but rarely occurs in those under 50. The cause is unknown.

The spine is most commonly affected; other common sites for the disease include the skull, breastbone (sternum), pelvis and thighbones (femurs). The bone enlargement may lead to deformity: for example, bowed legs or an enlarged head (typically discovered by the need for an increased hat size).

The softened bones are often painful and prone to fractures. Enlargement of the skull may compress the nerves which pass through it, leading to deafness or other forms of nerve paralysis (occasionally including blindness). Affected bones have an increased blood flow which may ultimately lead to heart failure. If a patient with Paget's disease is immobilized he may develop increased calcium levels in the blood and urine, which may lead to urinary stones (see CALCULUS). Finally, a risk exists of the development of a type of malignant tumor (OSTEOSARCOMA) in the affected bones.

The pain does not always respond to standard analgesics ("painkillers"), and therapy sometimes requires the use of RADIATION THERAPY and corticosteroids. Although there is no cure for Paget's disease, a number of promising drugs have been used over the past few years which help to relieve pain and may arrest the progress of the disease. (These include the hormones calcitonin and glucagon, the diphosphonate drugs and mithramycin.) Further developments in treatment are likely within the next few years.

pain

A localized feeling of severe discomfort, occurring anywhere in the body and usually caused by disease or injury.

Pain is difficult to define accurately because it means

different things to different people at different times. Its subjective nature makes it hard to identify as an entity requiring treatment. Pain cannot be measured and the physician has to rely mainly on a combination of the patient's medical history and his own experience of pain in assessing its nature and degree and the need for treatment.

The mechanism by which pain is felt is not fully understood despite considerable research. It seems likely that pain results when the balance of nerve impulses entering the central nervous system from a particular area of the body is abnormal in a particular way. It is unlikely that pain is simply the result of the stimulation of specific receptors at nerve endings. The complexity of the origins of pain helps to explain the possible complexity of its treatment.

Pain may be caused by many types of disease, including trauma, infection, cancer, degenerative changes, ischemia (inadequate blood supply to an organ or part) and others. In addition, pain is commonly caused or modified by psychological factors; it may also occur as the result of physical factors which have not caused actual tissue damage—e.g. "gas pain" due to distention of the large intestine. Here it may be considered to be a warning of potential damage rather than a result of that damage.

The doctor evaluates a patient's pain by asking a number of questions relating to its localization, quality, intensity, time relations, modifying factors, physiological relations and any mental changes associated with it. As a result, it is often possible to make a more or less certain diagnosis of, say, ANGINA PECTORIS or MIGRAINE, without the need for further investigations. Many types of pain are not so easy to diagnose; in some cases the cause may never be found. Pain is not always felt at the point from which it arises—for example, pain from the diaphragm is often felt in the shoulder. This phenomenon is known as "referred pain."

Ideally, pain is treated by removal or treatment of its cause. This is not always possible and even when it is it may take time. It is thus frequently necessary to relieve the pain itself. This may be achieved in a large number of ways:

(1) *No treatment.* Most normal people have occasional twinges of pain in one site or another for which they do nothing. Such pain usually has no significance and disappears spontaneously.

(2) *Analgesic drugs* ("painkillers") are the most frequently used and abused treatment for pain. Mild analgesics including aspirin, propoxyphene hydrochloride (Darvon) and many others are taken in large numbers for headaches, menstrual pains, etc. Despite the potential hazards involved in their long-term use, many people take them as a habit. Narcotic analgesics (such as morphine, codeine, etc.) are very effective in the treatment of most severe pain, but they are addictive and their abuse is one of the major medical and social problems in North America today.

(3) *Local anesthetic drugs* are of value in preventing or relieving local pain where the affected area can be clearly identified and infiltrated or the relevant nerve "blocked" (as in dental surgery).

(4) *Other drugs* may aid specific types of pain—for example, antacids may relieve indigestion and some anti-inflammatory drugs relieve only arthritic pain.

(5) *Surface methods* of pain relief—including heat, cold, vibration, manipulation, electrical stimulation and chemical counterirritants—all have a place in relieving some types of pain.

(6) *Acupuncture* is an ancient Chinese method of pain relief, effective in some circumstances and now fashionable in the West.

(7) *Neurosurgery* on appropriate nerves, the spinal cord or the brain is occasionally necessary and effective for intractable pain.

In additon to the use of these techniques, patients with pain require psychological support and (particularly in rheumatic diseases) physiotherapy and occupational therapy may be helpful.

Where the cause is not clear or the underlying condition cannot be satisfactorily treated, pain relief is probably best achieved with the help of a physician who specializes in solving the problem of intractable pain—since he is likely to be most familiar with the range of possible techniques.

palsy

A less common word for PARALYSIS.

The term survives, however, in the description of particular types of paralysis.

BELL'S PALSY is a paralysis of the muscles of one side of the face, caused by damage to the facial nerve. This is commonly caused by a virus, and complete recovery frequently occurs.

CEREBRAL PALSY is a permanent disorder of movement associated with varying paralysis, caused by a defect or disease of the brain and typically occurring within the first three years of life. Affected patients are called "spastics" and they may also have sensory and mental handicaps. Cerebral palsy may be caused by infection or damage during development in the womb, during birth, or in infancy.

Erb's palsy and *Klumpke's palsy* are two types of paralysis resulting from damage to the nerves of the arm, usually occurring at birth. Also known as *brachial birth palsy.*

Bulbar palsy and *pseudobulbar palsy* both cause weakness of the muscles of the face, throat and tongue due to damage to the brain. They occur in adults and are usually progressive and incurable, with a poor prognosis.

"The Shaking Palsy" was Parkinson's original term for the disease now known as PARKINSON'S DISEASE (or *Parkinsonism*).

See also the major article on **Neurology.**

pancreas

A large gland situated at the back of the abdominal cavity, behind the stomach and between the duodenum and the spleen.

The pancreas has two main functions. As an *exocrine gland* it produces various enzymes necessary for digestion which flow through the pancreatic duct to the duodenum (the beginning of the small intestine). As an *endocrine gland* it produces hormones which are released into the bloodstream. These include insulin and glucagon, which are essential to normal carbohydrate metabolism, and also more recently discovered hormones related to digestion.

The pancreas may be damaged by infection, injury, tumor or alcoholism and such damage may lead to abnormalities of its endocrine or exocrine functions.

See also INSULIN, ISLET CELL TUMOR, PANCREATECTOMY and PANCREATITIS.

pancreatectomy

Surgical removal of the pancreas.

This is a major operation with considerable risk and it is only appropriate for carefully selected patients. The main reason for the operation is the presence of pancreatic cancer, but it may occasionally be required in the treatment of chronic pancreatitis, pancreatic cysts or following injury to the pancreas.

In some cases of cancer a better operation is pancreaticoduodenectomy, in which only the head of the pancreas is removed, together with a segment of duodenum. In many others the tumor is too far advanced for removal. A major hazard of pancreatic surgery is the leakage of digestive enzymes into the peritoneal cavity, where they can cause severe damage.

Patients who survive total pancreatectomy require insulin therapy for the resulting diabetes and oral therapy with pancreatic extracts to permit the normal digestion of food.

pancreatitis

Inflammation of the pancreas, which may be acute or chronic.

Acute pancreatitis is a disease in which the pancreas appears to "digest itself" due to the liberation of its digestive enzymes into the tissues. It may be provoked by infections (e.g., mumps), trauma, regurgitation of bile up the pancreatic duct, alcoholism and some vascular diseases. Patients have severe abdominal pain and rapidly become seriously ill. Intensive supportive treatment in the hospital is required, although there is no specific treatment.

Chronic pancreatitis may result from repeated attacks of acute pancreatitis or directly from alcoholism or disease of the biliary tract. It causes recurrent abdominal pain and MALABSORPTION, with fatty, offensive stools and, less often, diabetes.

Chronic pancreatitis is common in Western countries, including the United States, where alcoholism is a widespread problem. Treatment involves prohibition of alcohol, a low-fat diet, pancreatic enzymes by mouth and insulin if necessary, but the disease cannot be cured.

papilledema

Swelling and congestion of the "head" of the optic nerve (*optic disk*), at the back of the eye.

The optic nerve, which passes through the "optic foramen" (a tiny hole in the skull), is the pathway along

PANCREAS

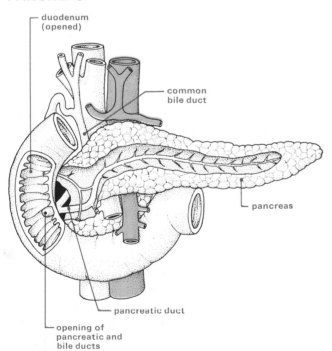

- duodenum (opened)
- common bile duct
- pancreas
- pancreatic duct
- opening of pancreatic and bile ducts

The pancreas is a digestive gland which lies behind the stomach and in front of the major abdominal blood vessels and the left kidney. It secretes digestive enzymes down the pancreatic duct into the duodenum where they break down proteins and fats. In addition it produces two hormones—insulin and glucagon.

which visual signals from the retina are transmitted to the specialized nerve centers for vision at the back of the brain. If the fluid pressure within the brain is raised above normal, which can result from various disorders within the brain or skull, the pressure change is transmitted along the optic nerve and through the retinal vein to the optic disk. The resulting swelling and pink congestion is visible through an ophthalmoscope (an illuminated instrument for examining the interior of the eye, especially the light-sensitive retina).

Papilledema may occur in one eye or in both, depending upon the extent of pressure change in the brain. It does not usually cause symptoms in itself, but may lead to diminished visual acuity (including blurred vision) when severe. Raised intracranial pressure may lead to headache and vomiting and, ultimately, to unconsciousness; thus, papilledema may provide the doctor with a useful clue in a patient with unconsciousness of unknown cause.

Papilledema is caused most commonly by severe hypertension (high blood pressure) and cerebral tumors. Other masses within the skull, such as an abscess or a hematoma (massive blood clot) may give an identical appearance. Other causes include severe ANEMIA, POLYCYTHEMIA, carbon dioxide poisoning (as in respiratory failure) and a rare but harmless condition of women known as "benign intracranial hypertension."

Papilledema must be distinguished from *papillitis*, in which the optic disk is inflamed and vision severely affected. This is often a complication of MULTIPLE SCLEROSIS. The distinction may require photography of the optic disk following an intravenous injection into a peripheral vein of fluorescein (a fluorescing dye).

Papilledema requires the urgent investigation and treatment of its underlying cause, but no treatment in itself.

papilloma

A basically benign tumor growing on a free surface of epithelium (the outermost layer of cells of the skin or a mucous membrane), commonly as a lobulated mass on a stalk. (Only rarely do they become malignant.) Papillomas, which include growths such as warts and polyps, are most often found on the skin and in the mucous membranes that line the intestinal and urinary tracts.

Papillomas may occur on any part of the skin and are especially common in the elderly. Usually they remain small, but occasionally reach the size of an egg or an orange. Papillomas are normally treated by cautery; the larger ones can be surgically removed by cutting through the supporting stalk.

Intestinal papillomas are most common in the colon and rectum, where they sometimes bleed and are associated with the excess mucus in the patient's stools. They may be single, of unknown cause, or multiple—a condition known as *familial polyposis coli*, which is inherited as a dominant trait. Such forms must be regarded as "premalignant," since malignant change is quite common. Single papillomas can often be removed by using a proctosigmoidoscope—a special instrument inserted into the lower part of the large intestine via the rectum; but multiple polyps are best treated by surgical removal of the affected portion of the bowel.

In the urinary tract, papillomas are most common in the bladder, although they can occur anywhere from the kidney to the urethra (the passage through which urine is voided). The cause is usually not known, but they are particularly common in those who have worked in the rubber industry and in smokers. All are potentially malignant, so all must be removed. In the bladder this is usually done by diathermy (therapeutic use of heat generated by high-frequency current) through a cystoscope (a special instrument for examining the interior of the urinary bladder). Recurrence is common and life-long regular cystoscopy and diathermy is usually necessary once the diagnosis is made.

See also POLYP.

Pap smear

See CERVICAL SMEAR.

paralysis

The loss of muscular function in a part of the body, caused by damage to the muscles themselves or to a part of the nervous system. Paralysis may vary in severity from affecting a single small muscle or nerve to affecting most of the body.

Disease of the muscles themselves leads more commonly to weakness than the total paralysis. However, the various forms of MUSCULAR DYSTROPHY, most of which occur in childhood, can progress to severe and eventually fatal paralysis. There is no effective treatment for these conditions.

Any block in the transmission of impulses from nerves to muscles may also result in paralysis. This occurs in MYASTHENIA GRAVIS, in BOTULISM and in some other types of poisoning (e.g., with "nerve gas").

The peripheral nerves may be injured directly or damaged by disease, including DIABETES, POLYARTERITIS NODOSA, CANCER, ALCOHOLISM, vitamin deficiencies, LEPROSY, PORPHYRIA and some drug reactions. This damage may lead to weakness or to total paralysis of the muscles supplied by the affected nerves.

The spinal cord may be damaged by a number of diseases, including POLIOMYELITIS, MULTIPLE SCLEROSIS and trauma. The pattern of the resulting paralysis depends on its cause. Complete division of the spinal cord results in PARAPLEGIA—complete paralysis of the legs and the lower part of the body, usually including bladder paralysis. If the spinal cord is damaged in the region of the neck the arms may be paralyzed as well as the legs—*quadriplegia.*

Brain damage may also result in paralysis. The most common cause here is a STROKE, caused by hemorrhage or thrombosis in the brain. The extent of the paralysis is variable, but the most common pattern is partial or complete paralysis of the arm and leg on one side—HEMIPLEGIA. Other causes include MENINGITIS, ENCEPHALITIS, SYPHILIS, brain tumors and impairment of cerebral blood flow. Transient paralysis (*Todd's paralysis*) may occur in part of the body following an epileptic attack.

Paralysis resulting from division of a major nerve tract in the spinal cord or brain is permanent and irreversible, but that resulting from other diseases may have a more variable prognosis. In some diseases, such as "acute infective polyneuritis" (the GUILLAIN-BARRÉ SYNDROME), more or less total paralysis may be followed by complete recovery if the patient survives. In some (e.g., strokes) the extent of recovery is extremely variable and in others (e.g., *motor neuron disease*) recovery is unknown.

Survival in paralysis depends upon the underlying disease and whether or not it affects the respiratory and heart muscles. Artificial ventilation may keep alive patients with some diseases (e.g., poliomyelitis or acute infective polyneuritis) until the paralysis improves or remits; patients may live for years, severely paralyzed, in an "iron lung" respirator.

All paralyzed patients require special care of the affected part of the body to prevent trauma and ulceration, especially if there is also sensory impairment ("sensory paralysis"). Most patients can be taught to overcome their disabilities partially by the clever use of their remaining normal muscles. Physical therapists and other rehabilitation workers have an essential role to play here. The existence of events such as the "Paraplegic Olympics" shows the extent to which many patients can be aided.

paranoia

A chronic personality disorder in which the individual develops systematized, sometimes permanent and mainly persecutory delusions in a setting of otherwise undisturbed thought and personality. Paranoia must be distinguished from *paranoid schizophrenia*, in which the same delusions occur but there is also disturbance of thought processes and personality and the occurrence of hallucinations.

Paranoid reactions are displayed by most people at one time or another in response to severe disappointment or humiliation. The reaction is the mistaken belief that the sufferer is the center of attention and that he is being talked about, usually in a critical way which invades his privacy and embarrasses him.

Paranoia is a state in which the patient experiences constant "paranoid reactions" and where these reactions cannot be dispelled by others. Suspicion and resentment of others arises and the patient takes innocent matters to be a direct attack on himself. He usually feels that his true worth is not recognized, and he often has grandiose ideas about what his true worth is.

Temporary paranoid reactions are fairly common and usually harmless—providing they are not associated with other thought disorders or personality changes—although they may be irritating for the family and colleagues of the sufferer. In contrast, true paranoia is relatively rare and can cause considerable annoyance and harm to innocent people outside the sufferer's immediate circle. It is not easy to treat, but is sometimes helped by PSYCHOTHERAPY.

See also the major articles on **Psychiatry** and **Psychotherapy.**

paraplegia

Paralysis of the lower limbs, often accompanied by dysfunction of the rectum and the bladder.

Paraplegia is usually caused by a lesion of the spinal cord; its extent is governed by the position and magnitude of the lesion. Complete severance of the spinal cord will lead to total paralysis of the legs and fecal and urinary INCONTINENCE. Lesser damage may affect the legs and leave the bladder and rectum function unimpaired. Recovery will sometimes take place if the damage to the cord is minimal, but lifelong paralysis is more often the result.

Care of the paraplegic patient should be designed to relieve the symptoms often associated with paralysis, such as pressure sores and urinary infections. As soon as possible a program of physical therapy and retraining should be started—if necessary, in a special center devoted to the care of paraplegics. The provision of special equipment will greatly ease the problems of incontinence and immobility. Many paraplegics, although confined to wheelchairs, live active and useful lives.

parasites

A parasite is an animal or plant which lives inside or upon another living animal or plant without extending any benefit to it in return for the advantages gained.

A large number of organisms find man an ideal place to live. Bacteria, viruses, fungi and protozoa are said to *infect* man, but worms and insects are said to *infest* him and are what is normally meant by the term *parasites*. They may be quite harmless, or may produce symptoms of disease.

In general it may be said that the hotter the country and the worse the standard of hygiene the more parasites flourish. Among the most common in temperate climates are lice, fleas and bedbugs. They are not usually important carriers of disease, but they are disagreeable. They can be controlled by the use of modern insecticides.

More harmful are worms, which range from the pinworm which is more of a nuisance than a threat to life, to the flatworm (trematode) of SCHISTOSOMIASIS which makes life miserable for more than 200 million people in tropical countries and is responsible for untold morbidity and mortality.

Strict attention to personal hygiene will ward off the attentions of most parasites; but those who are not accustomed to the conditions in less developed tropical and subtropical countries may inadvertently lay themselves open to infestation by worms. It is important to avoid uncooked or undercooked food, and to avoid bathing or wading in water which may be the haunt of the freshwater snail that harbors a stage in the development of the parasite which causes schistosomiasis. It is also sensible to wear shoes in wet land in the tropics, and to avoid drinking from village wells and rivers.

The average traveler is in no great danger of becoming infested with parasites, and those whose lives lead them into the remoter parts of the world are usually well informed about such dangers. Nevertheless, it is well to keep the possibility in mind.

The control of parasitic diseases is one of the great tasks of the future for the developing countries; it depends to a large degree on improving the standards of public and private sanitation.

See also FLEAS, FLUKES, LICE, MITES, PINWORMS, ROUNDWORMS, TAPEWORMS, TICKS.

paratyphoid fever

An acute generalized feverish disease caused by bacteria of the genus *Salmonella*.

Paratyphoid fever is so called because it resembles TYPHOID FEVER, but in most cases the symptoms are less severe and the course of the disease is less harmful.

The onset of the disease may be more rapid than in the case of typhoid fever, but the symptoms are much the same. The patient may complain of discomfort, lassitude and headache and suffer from insomnia as well as a high temperature. As in the case of typhoid fever, the fever may be more marked in the morning but the daily peak gradually rises until about the eighth day,

when it levels out. The patient feels restless, hot and uncomfortable; there may be pain in the abdomen which, however, is not as extreme as in typhoid fever. Rose-colored spots are common in typhoid fever, but less common in paratyphoid fever (although they may occur).

Prevention of paratyphoid fever is possible, not only through vaccination but also through the application of measures relating to public hygiene—including a pure water supply—that are common in advanced nations. Travelers to places where paratyphoid fever is still common, such as India, should consult a doctor about vaccination. The TAB vaccine incorporates protection against both typhoid and paratyphoid and is commonly given to children, but the immunity so gained is not permanent. It is prudent to boost the immunity before going to any country where paratyphoid fever exists.

Treatment consists of alleviating the symptoms as far as possible. Drugs such as aspirin to lower the fever may be given under medical supervision and antibiotics may be useful in shortening the period of illness. Caution must be exercised, however, for chloramphenicol—which is used with good effect against typhoid—may have serious side effects and may not be justified for the comparatively trivial paratyphoid. Ampicillin is usually effective.

The diet should be bland and nutritious, with little solid food being given while the gastrointestinal tract is irritated by the bacteria. Convalescence may be prolonged; as in typhoid fever, the attack cannot be regarded as over until six consecutive stool and urine specimens are found to be negative for the presence of the causative bacteria.

Parkinson's disease

A disease, especially of the elderly, characterized by tremor (the head and limbs of the patient shake) and stiffness (muscular rigidity). The patient is unable to initiate movements quickly and has a characteristic bowed posture and immobile face.

Parkinson's disease (also known as *Parkinsonism*) is associated with degeneration of nerve centers deep within the brain (*basal ganglia* and *brain stem nuclei*); these nerve centers are known to be closely linked with the control of posture and movement. The reason for the changes in the brain are not known, although a few cases of Parkinsonism are believed to be related to brain damage caused by toxic substances such as carbon monoxide or high concentrations of manganese. Others arise from the use of certain drugs but in these cases the signs and symptoms of the disease are reversible when the drugs are withdrawn. Some cases follow viral ENCEPHALITIS and Parkinsonism is a feature of the "punch-drunk" syndrome.

Recent research has drawn attention to the importance of *neurotransmitters* in Parkinson's disease. These are chemicals able to facilitate the transmission of impulses across the junctions between nerves. Sufferers from Parkinson's disease show depleted levels of one of these neurotransmitters, *dopamine*, normally found in marked concentrations in the basal ganglia and brain stem nuclei. Since the 1960s, treatment for Parkinson's disease has concentrated on remedying this deficiency.

The most important drug now used is *levadopa* (or *L-dopa*), which is the immediate chemical precursor to dopamine. As the neurotransmitter itself cannot be administered as a drug, because it cannot penetrate the blood-brain barrier, levadopa must be given to help the body make its own supply of dopamine. About one third of patients shows a great improvement of their condition when given levadopa and another third reports that their symptoms abate.

Some patients cannot take advantage of levadopa because of severe side effects, including nausea and vomiting. More sophisticated preparations, in which the side effects of the levadopa are countered by other drugs, are now being administered. Some patients, particularly those under the age of 50, who are resistant to drugs can be helped by *stereotaxic* brain operations designed to modify the functions of the basal ganglia. Another important element in Parkinson's disease is physical therapy, since any break in physical activity can be disastrous and lead to immobility. Approximately 300,000 patients in the United States suffer from Parkinson's disease. About 40,000 new cases occur each year.

See also *Drugs for Parkinson's disease* in the major article on **Drugs and Medicines.**

PARKINSON'S DISEASE

 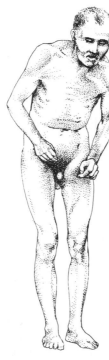

Patients with Parkinson's disease are characterized by muscle tremors affecting the head and extremities, staring eyes, an expressionless face, rigidity of some muscle groups and a slow gait marked by short shuffles. Often there is also an involuntary "pill-rolling" movement of the thumb against the first two fingers.

paronychia

A superficial infection of the epithelium beside a nail, usually a result of tearing a hangnail.

Paronychia is most often caused by infection with staphylococcus. It leads to cellulitis, which can be suppressed by hot applications. There is occasionally a tendency for the infection to burrow under the nail and so form an abscess. This can be painful as well as persistent; it is then necessary to make an incision for the purposes of drainage. The partial or complete removal of the nail may also be necessary. Among nail biters in particular, recurrence is common and it is possible for this comparatively superficial infection to cause severe disability. In diabetes, various fungi can cause chronic paronychial inflammations and similar lesions are sometimes seen in PSORIASIS and some kinds of PEMPHIGUS.

paroxysm

A sudden attack, usually of convulsions or tachycardia, or a sudden exacerbation of disease or a particular symptom, e.g., the pain in trigeminal neuralgia (see TIC).

pasteurization

The process by which milk and other fluid foods are sterilized.

Unlike boiling, pasteurization does not significantly affect the taste of milk. When Louis Pasteur, the famous 19th-century French scientist, was investigating problems of wine growers, he studied the process of fermentation. Arising from his discoveries, he realized that heating milk to a temperature well below the boiling point would effectively stop fermentation and so prevent milk from being spoiled. It also destroys disease organisms that would otherwise be passed on to human consumers, of which the most important is the tuberculosis bacillus (see TUBERCULOSIS).

Pasteurization is normally achieved by heating the milk for about 40 minutes at 140–160°F (60–70°C).

This destroys some of the vitamin C in the milk, but in a balanced diet this is not an important deficit.

patch test

A test to establish the cause of a contact dermatitis or other sensitivity reaction.

Since sensitivity reactions can be caused by a large number of substances to which the patient's body may be allergic, treatment can be properly planned only when the cause is known. To find out the cause, a small square of gauze is applied to the skin, usually on the upper part of the back. The gauze is impregnated with a purified extract of the suspected substance or substances. If, after about 48 hours, there is an allergic response to the substance under test, it can be assumed that the cause of the sensitivity has been identified.

See also the major article on **Dermatology.**

patent ductus arteriosus

A congenital heart defect in which the prenatal circulation of the blood persists after birth.

In a fetus, the blood is oxygenated through the placenta, as the lungs are immersed in fluid and are not used for breathing. In order to bypass the lungs, the circulation is augmented by the *ductus arteriosus*, which connects the left pulmonary artery with the aorta. Occasionally, the ductus arteriosus does not wither away after birth and instead remains *patent* (or open). The result is a mixing of the arterial and venous blood which can lead to failure to thrive, but in the last 25 years surgeons have found that it is possible to cure the condition by means of tying off the duct.

pediculosis

Infestation with LICE.

pellagra

A vitamin deficiency disease, caused by the lack of niacin (or nicotinic acid) in the diet.

Niacin is a substance found in association with the B vitamins, present in meat, eggs, vegetables and fruit.

Symptoms include digestive upsets, loss of appetite, irritability and headache. Skin involvement leads to redness (similar to a severe sunburn) on the parts exposed to the sun, which later become roughened and brownish. The symptoms recur each year and may eventually lead to paralysis. Treatment involves establishing a balanced diet, with supplements of niacin where necessary.

See also DEFICIENCY DISEASE and the major article on **Nutrition.**

pelvic inflammatory disease

The internal sexual organs of women are liable to be the seat of generalized infection. Although it was long accepted that the main cause of the inflammation was gonorrhea, this is now no longer universally held. It is rare for the gonococcus to be isolated in cases in which an abscess of the Fallopian tubes or ovaries has ruptured and other organisms are known to be involved in the disease, sometimes secondary to gonorrhea. Whether or not it is originally caused by gonorrhea, the inflammation apparently spreads up from the lower genital tract, involving first the Fallopian tubes and then the ovaries.

In most cases the ovaries are turned into a mass several times their original size. Even in cases where they do not have to be removed by surgery the outcome may be infertility. Some cases have been noted following the insertion of an intrauterine contraceptive device (IUD). Death has even resulted in some of these cases.

The symptoms begin with pelvic pain, which may be accompanied by lassitude, chills and low-grade fever. Abdominal and pelvic tenderness will be experienced, and there may be acute pain when an abscess has ruptured. Although the treatment of choice is the administration of appropriate antibiotics, surgery may be necessary to drain abscesses.

pemphigus

A group of diseases of the skin and mucous membranes characterized by the formation of blisters. It is thought that they may be autoimmune disorders, as during the active stages of the disease an immunoglobulin may be found in the circulating serum. (See AUTOIMMUNE DISEASE.)

Pemphigus vulgaris commonly occurs between the ages of 40 and 60. Large blisters suddenly form on the skin, perhaps after blistering has occurred in the mouth. The blisters tend to develop in crops about every three weeks, and may involve the throat, conjunctiva, anal canal and vulva. The natural course of the condition is deterioration after remissions, and the outcome without treatment may be fatal; but the disease responds to the use of corticosteroids.

In *pemphigus vegetans*, the areas of blistering do not tend to heal, but develop outgrowths of wartlike tissue in the armpits, groin, and around the mouth.

Pemphigus foliaceus is rarer; it involves the whole skin, with areas of redness and crusting which looks like exfoliative dermatitis. *Benign familial pemphigus* develops usually in adolescence in the armpits, groins, on the neck and around the anus. It is hereditary and passed on as an autosomal dominant. It tends to heal, but may recur.

peptic ulcer

An ulcer involving those areas of the digestive tract exposed to pepsin—acid gastric juice. The most common are those involving the stomach (GASTRIC ULCER) and the first portion of the duodenum (see DUODENAL ULCER).

See also ULCER and the major article on **Gastroenterology.**

pericarditis

Inflammation of the pericardium, the membrane surrounding the heart. It is usually secondary to inflammation elsewhere. Causes include pneumonia, tuberculosis, typhoid fever and rarely osteomyelitis; bacteria may gain entry through serious wounds of the chest.

Virus infections may give rise to pericarditis, among which are respiratory infections and infection with echo viruses and the Coxsackie B virus. Underlying infarction of the cardiac muscle may produce aseptic inflammation of the pericardium, and the membrane is affected in the cardiac reaction of rheumatic fever.

The main symptom is pain felt in the center of the chest, which may radiate to the neck, shoulders and upper arms; but the symptoms of the causative disease often predominate. In some cases there is an effusion of fluid into the pericardial sac sufficiently great to affect the action of the heart, and steps must be taken to aspirate the fluid through the chest wall. After some infections scarring may produce a constriction in the pericardium which can disturb the action of the heart.

perifolliculitis

The presence of an inflammatory infiltrate surrounding hair follicles. It frequently occurs in association with FOLLICULITIS.

Pustular perifolliculitis is a disease of the scalp which is not uncommon among business executives and may originate from stress. A few pustules appear on the head and cause intense itching.

Perifolliculitis abscedens et suffodiens is a chronic dissecting folliculitis of the scalp. Another form, *sycosis vulgans* (also known as "barber's itch"), covers the area of the face that is normally shaved.

The various forms of perifolliculitis are caused either by staphylococci or streptococci and may be treated with antibiotics.

periodontics

A branch of dentistry dealing with the study and treatment of diseases of the *periodontium*, the tissues investing (or "embedding") and supporting the teeth.

There are several classes of periodontal diseases. Under the heading of "inflammatory diseases" comes GINGIVITIS, which may be caused by bacteria, nutritional deficiencies, endocrine variations, herpes virus, or by metabolic errors. Also included is *periodontitis*, which may be due to calcified deposits or improper tooth anatomy and position.

"Dystrophic diseases" include *gingivosis*, which involves painful desquamation of the epithelium and degeneration of underlying connective tissue fibers; *periodontosis*, which leads to bone resorption along the side of the tooth; *periodontal atrophy*, which leads to exposure of the root surface on some or all of the teeth; and *hyperplastic periodontal conditions*, in which the periodontium grows in size, because of the side effects of drug therapy or other forms of irritation. Periodontists also treat periodontal trauma.

Much of the work of periodontists involves the removal of calcified deposits from around the teeth and their roots, a feature of several periodontal diseases. In addition, they perform operations for the removal of pockets of pus in the gums and undertake other soft tissue repairs.

Orthodontic aids are used to reposition migrating teeth; it has been shown that stretching and compression of the *periodontal ligament* (connective tissue which attaches a tooth to its bony socket) stimulates new tissue and bone formation. When a tooth is placed under strain by an orthodontic appliance, the periodontal ligament is compressed on the pressure side and

PERIODONTITIS

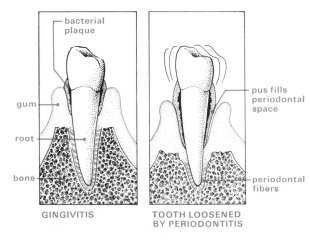

GINGIVITIS

TOOTH LOOSENED BY PERIODONTITIS

If gingivitis (inflammation of the gums) is not treated, bacterial plaque forms between the gums and the roots of teeth. The inflammation progressively destroys the periodontal fibers and bone which hold the teeth in place. Pus forms in the deep periodontal spaces (a condition called pyorrhea) and eventually the teeth fall out.

stretched on the other. Resorption of bone occurs in the area of compression. Thus, repositioning of the teeth is followed by an improvement in the status of the supporting tissues; the teeth become stable as new bone and periodontal ligament tissues grow.

See also the major article on **Dentistry.**

peritonitis

Inflammation of the peritoneum, the membranes lining the abdominal cavity.

Most acute cases are caused by the perforation of one of the hollow abdominal organs or by infection spreading from an inflamed organ. Occasionally in children no obvious source of infection is found. Peritonitis may remain localized, especially when it arises from inflammation of the gallbladder or the appendix, but in severe perforations—for example of a peptic ulcer or a gangrenous appendix—the whole peritoneal cavity may be involved. Peritonitis resulting from the perforation of a peptic ulcer is at first chemical, but soon bacterial infection spreads and the abdominal cavity becomes full of pus.

The main symptom of peritonitis is severe pain and tenderness of the abdominal wall, which becomes rigid. The patient may experience nausea and vomiting; soon the intestines become paralyzed and the abdomen distends. The pain makes the patient lie still with his legs drawn up. The temperature may be raised or may be subnormal, and the blood pressure may fall. The pulse is quickened and may be weak. In most cases a period of resuscitation with intravenous therapy and the administration of antibiotics precedes the operation necessary to drain the peritoneal cavity and treat the cause of the peritonitis. The postoperative course is likely to be stormy.

Tuberculosis of the peritoneum is now rare, but at one time it was a cause of chronic peritonitis and the adhesions (see ADHESION) which sometimes form after any case of peritonitis. Rarely peritoneal adhesions cause acute or chronic obstruction of the intestine, and may be relieved only by operation; but this in itself may set up further adhesions in patients who are apt to react in this way to disturbance of the peritoneum.

pernicious anemia

See ANEMIA.

personality

The sum total of all the characteristics of a person—including the mental, moral, physical and social qualities—as they are perceived by other people. The word may be used either in a popular sense, in which the meaning is simply linked to the type of person as seen by others, or in a psychological sense, in which the meaning is more complex and sometimes less obvious.

Psychoanalysts regard personality as the result of the interaction between instinct and the environment. Other schools of psychology and psychiatry have more complicated explanations, combining the effects of upbringing, heredity, experience and biochemical factors.

One of the most widely followed divisions is Jung's categories of extroverted and introverted personalities. The distinction in technical terms is that the extrovert directs his LIBIDO and instinctual energy toward the environment, whereas the introvert has weak instinctual energy and directs it inward toward himself. Most people combine aspects of both personality types, and the extreme examples of either can be instantly recognized by their behavior.

Personality may have no medical connotations at all. To describe a person as an "unpleasant" personality or a "miserable" personality is not to suggest that he or she is in any way mentally ill. On the other hand, there are various defects in behavior or lifestyle which are regarded widely as *personality disorders.* These are characterized by pathological trends in personality structure, with minimal subjective anxiety—in most cases manifested by a lifelong pattern of abnormal action or behavior, and not by mental or emotional symptoms.

Sociopathic personality disturbance, for instance, may be a pathological relationship between the patient and the society in which he lives, together with personal discomfort and poor interpersonal relationships. *Personality trait disturbance* is an inability to maintain emotional equilibrium in stressful situations.

Various mental disorders are often expressed in terms of personality. Sufferers will be categorized as *paranoid personalities* or *neurotic personalities* and there are also authenticated cases of *multiple personality,* which most authorities believe are delusional in character. In all these cases personality is distorted into an abnormal type by the underlying mental or emotional disorder.

Perthes' disease

A disease of the growth of ossification centers in children. The child begins to limp and complains of pain, often in the knee. Perthes' disease affects the head of the femur (thigh bone). Technical name: *oesteochondritis deformans juvenilis.*

The disease is of unknown origin and is usually experienced in three stages, each lasting about 9 to 12 months. In the first period, the head of the femur suffers from NECROSIS and degeneration. In the second period, revascularization (the return of blood vessels) takes place; in the final stage the bone is replaced by reossification. Boys between the ages of 4 and 10 are most often affected, and the prognosis may be good or the disease may lead to some permanent disability.

Treatment is usually limited to the avoidance of weight-bearing on the affected leg. It is rarely bilateral.

pertussis

The technical name for WHOOPING COUGH.

pessary

1. Any device placed in the vagina to support the uterus or to provide contraception. 2. Any form of medication (especially a vaginal suppository) placed in the vagina for therapeutic purposes.

petechiae

Minute hemorrhagic spots on the skin, ranging from the size of a pinhead to a pinpoint.

Petechiae are formed by the escape of blood into the skin or mucous membranes. They appear for a variety of reasons when there is a rupture in the junction between capillary and the artery from which it is fed. A large number of conditions and diseases exist which cause these ruptures.

Petechiae are a sign of many illnesses, ranging from Rocky Mountain spotted fever to measles, and from scarlet fever to smallpox. They can also accompany cerebrospinal meningitis and (especially in older people) they may be an external sign of vitamin C deficiency. Their appearance after surgery can be a sign of a fat embolism; the fracture of a long bone may lead to the same sequence of events.

In *hyperglobulinemic purpura*, petechiae appear in "showers" all over the body, but especially on the lower extremities. These attacks may be brought on by prolonged walking or standing, or by wearing constrictive garters or clothing.

Peutz-Jeghers syndrome

An inherited disease characterized by gastrointestinal POLYPS and the appearance of brown lesions on the lips, hands and feet.

The marks, which are not accompanied by any symptoms, usually appear when the patient is a child. The syndrome shows a great deal of variety in its other manifestations. The brown marks, which are pigmented macules, affect the inside of the mouth—including the gums and the palate—and the area around the nose. In addition to the skin symptoms, there are usually polyps in the stomach and intestines, which lead to abdominal pain and vomiting. In the majority of cases the polyps are most numerous in the small intestine, where they are usually benign; in the large intestine, stomach, duodenum and the rectum they may rarely become malignant.

Inheritance is by an autosomal dominant gene and either sex may be affected.

Peyronie's disease

A painful disease of the penis; also known as *fibrous cavernitis*.

With no known cause, plaques or strands of dense fibrous tissue develop around the *corpus cavernosum* (a cylinder of erectile tissue) of the penis. These cause a deformity, with the penis twisted to one side, and the patient may feel intense pain during an erection. The disease is sometimes associated with DUPUYTREN'S CONTRACTURE, in which there is a profusion of fibrous tissue of the palm, leading to contracture with permanent flexion of the fingers, especially the fourth or fifth. In addition to the unknown form of the disease, cases have been reported in recent years in which the patient had been taking the drug propranolol (Inderal) for heart disease.

The disease is benign and self-limiting, although effective treatment is very difficult.

phagocytosis

The destruction of bacteria by the leukocytes or white blood cells.

Phagocytosis is part of the process of the immune response, by which the body repels or consumes foreign bodies which threaten it. When a bacterium appears in the bloodstream, as long as the immune response is normal in the individual, it is immediately surrounded by leukocytes. The leukocyte is able to absorb the bacterium by smothering it and drawing it through its cell wall.

After digesting the invader, the leukocyte itself will usually die after undergoing a granular fatty degeneration and it is an abundance of dead leukocytes which collect together in an infected wound or an abscess as pus.

It is possible that the leukocytes initiate the process of digestion of the bacteria by secreting substances which are toxic to the invaders.

See also ANTIBODY/ANTIGEN, IMMUNE SYSTEM.

phantom limb syndrome

Following amputation of the whole or part of a limb, it is fairly common for the patient to feel that the part is still there.

The patient may experience feelings of touch, heat, cold and position in the phantom limb, but often the most serious problem is pain. A patient who has lost a hand may, for example, complain of pain in his thumb or at his finger tips.

Most cases of the phantom limb syndrome are mild and disappear within days or weeks of the amputation. Severe persistent pain may be relieved by applying stimuli such as vibration or heat to the amputation stump or by drug treatment. With modern methods of pain relief (see PAIN) the phantom limb syndrome can sometimes be successfully treated.

pharmaceutics/pharmacy/pharmacology

Pharmacy and *pharmaceutics* are alternative terms for the art and science of preparing and dispensing medicines. Pharmacy is also used to describe the place in which drugs are prepared and dispensed; *pharmaceutic* or *pharmaceutical* is used as a term for a medicinal preparation or drug.

Pharmacology is the study of the action of drugs on the living body and its biochemical systems.

Pharmacy is principally concerned with the accurate preparation and presentation of drugs. In the past, most medicines were prepared from their basic ingredients at the point of dispensing—by the physician or in the drugstores. While this is still true of some drugs, the majority are now formulated and prepared in bulk by the pharmaceutical industry. The pharmacist often simply dispenses already prepared drugs in the dosage and form prescribed by the physician or recommended by the manufacturers. However, pharmacists receive a full professional training and are capable of preparing many medicines from their basic ingredients, and of aiding patients in choosing appropriate self-medication.

Pharmacology can be divided into two areas: *basic pharmacology* and *clinical pharmacology*. Basic pharmacology is the study of the basic action of drugs on normal and abnormal living organisms at any level from bacteria to man, or on isolated biochemical pathways from these organisms. Pharmacologists working in this field may not be medically qualified—often a training in biochemistry and physiology is more relevant than a full medical training.

Clinical pharmacologists, however, are physicians with a special expertise and interest in the action of drugs in man. They have become increasingly important as the number of potent drugs available has multiplied over the past 30 years. All doctors must understand much about clinical pharmacology, but those with a special interest study details of drug actions and interactions with diseases and with each other. "Polypharmacy," the prescription of multiple drugs to the individual patient, while sometimes essential, runs the risk of causing interactions between drugs which may endanger the patient. These risks are a major field of current study for clinical pharmacologists.

See the major article on **Drugs and Medicines.**

pharyngitis

Inflammation of the pharynx, the common cause of sore throat. The pharynx is the passageway that connects the back of the mouth and nose with the larynx and esophagus and contains the tonsils.

Pharyngitis is a common component of upper respiratory infection, usually caused by viruses such as those of the common cold or bacterial infections (especially with *Streptococci*).

Chronic pharyngitis may be caused by heavy smoking or by the "postnasal drip" associated with allergic or other diseases of the nose. In debilitated patients, pharyngitis may be caused by thrush (*candidiasis*—see CANDIDA) or by several species of microorganisms that ordinarily cause no problems in those who are otherwise healthy. Some blood diseases (including leukemia) may sometimes cause pharyngitis.

Viral pharyngitis usually resolves spontaneously within a few days. No curative treatment is possible, but the sore throat may sometimes be relieved by gargles containing aspirin or other substances. Penicillin or other antibiotics are of no value in viral infections (but are necessary in streptococcal and other bacterial infections).

TONSILLECTOMY may be required for severe recurrent pharyngitis involving the tonsils.

Culture of microorganisms obtained by means of a throat swab can identify most of the dangerous causes of pharyngitis, but it is impracticable to perform this test on all patients with sore throats.

See also the major article on **Otolaryngology.**

phenylketonuria

A disease characterized by an inborn error of metabolism of the amino acid phenylalanine.

The disease is present from birth in affected individuals, although it is not clinically recognizable at first. Progressive mental retardation occurs from the age of a few weeks, and irritability and vomiting are early features. Dermatitis may occur at five or six months of age. Affected children are usually of fairer complexion than unaffected siblings. Untreated patients become so retarded that institutional care is usually required, and they frequently develop epilepsy.

The disease is inherited on a recessive basis: both parents are unaffected but carry the trait, and they have a one in four chance of producing an affected infant in each pregnancy. The incidence in the United States is about 1 per 16,000 live births.

The diagnosis can often be made by urine testing, but the most reliable method is to test a drop of the baby's blood within a few days of birth. This screening test is mandatory for all babies in most American states and commonly used elsewhere.

Treatment involves strict adherence to a low phenylalanine diet. A small amount of phenylalanine is required for normal growth, but no more than this must be consumed. Most normal foods contain phenylalanine, so the special diet involves considerable modifications. The diet should probably be continued for life, but this is not yet certain as it has only been in use for about the past 20 years.

In the future it is possible that "enzyme transplantation" from a normal individual (e.g., by partial liver transplantation) may be used to give normal phenylalanine metabolism to affected individuals.

pheochromocytoma

A tumor of the adrenal gland which causes hypertension (high blood pressure).

Pheochromocytoma is rare, accounting for less than 0.1% of all cases of hypertension, but it is important because it causes potentially lethal hypertension—which can usually be completely cured by surgery.

Some pheochromocytomas cause a persistent increase in blood pressure, but many lead to sudden attacks associated with the release of epinephrine and norepinephrine from the tumor. The hypertensive attacks may be associated with sweating, palpitations, headaches, anxiety and facial pallor or flushing.

A screening test for pheochromocytoma is performed on the urine of most patients with hypertension; positive results are confirmed by special blood, urine and radiographic (x-ray) tests.

Treatment is by surgical removal of the tumor, preceded by appropriate drug therapy.

Very few pheochromocytomas are malignant, but multiple tumors may occur. Removal of all tumor tissue usually cures the hypertension.

phimosis

Tightness of the foreskin of the penis, which prevents it from being drawn down over the glans (bulbous end of the penis).

Until the age of five it may be quite normal for the foreskin not to retract. Forcible attempts to retract the foreskin at this age may cause damage and even lead to true phimosis in later life. Above the age of five the foreskin normally will retract; if it does not, true phimosis exists.

PHIMOSIS

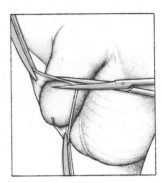

phimosis   circumcision

Phimosis is a tight foreskin which cannot be pulled back over the head of the penis. In boys under the age of 4 years, the foreskin normally adheres to the penis and should not be forced back during washing. Such attempts are likely to cause a true phimosis by scarring the foreskin. Phimosis is relieved by circumcision.

If phimosis at any age causes obstruction to the flow of urine, with "ballooning" of the foreskin, or if after puberty it interferes with normal erection of the penis, then CIRCUMCISION is required.

phlebitis

Inflammation of the wall of a vein, commonly associated with THROMBOSIS within the vein (see also THROMBOPHLEBITIS).

Phlebitis occurs most frequently in varicose veins in the leg, where it may be spontaneous or may follow trauma or infection. It may also occur elsewhere in the body in abnormal veins (e.g., hemorrhoids) or in normal veins. It may occur at the site of an intravenous infusion or injection or may be deliberately induced by "sclerosing agents" to cure varicose veins or hemorrhoids.

Symptoms vary from mild discomfort over the affected vein to severe pain associated with tenderness and swelling of the surrounding tissue and sometimes a high fever.

Treatment involves supporting and elevating the affected part to prevent painful swelling and movement. Elevation of the leg helps to drain blood efficiently through the deep veins, but a similar effect can often be obtained in the ambulant patient by the use of supportive elastic stockings or dressings. Infection may require antibiotic treatment. Aspirin-like drugs may help to suppress both the inflammation and the pain.

Most cases of phlebitis are harmless and resolve spontaneously. Pulmonary EMBOLISM occurs very rarely following *superficial venous phlebitis* in contrast to the high risk of this complication following *deep vein thrombosis*. Where phlebitis is associated with infection there is a risk of septicemia (blood poisoning), but this should be rare with adequate treatment.

phlebothrombosis

Thrombosis (clotting) in veins which are not inflamed. Compare THROMBOPHLEBITIS.

phlebotomy

Another name for VENESECTION—incision into a vein for the purpose of drawing blood; bloodletting.

phobia

A persistent excessive fear of an object or situation which is not of real danger. Examples include CLAUSTROPHOBIA (fear of confined spaces), AGORAPHOBIA (fear of being in the open), specific phobias (e.g., for spiders, mice, thunder or darkness) and social phobias (e.g., excessive anxiety in the presence of other people).

Phobias, especially specific phobias, may be isolated abnormalities in an otherwise normal person, or they may sometimes be a manifestation of underlying anxiety or depression of a more general nature. It is likely that many phobias may represent a prolonged response to an unpleasant experience in childhood, but the original stimulus is usually forgotten.

Phobias of all kinds are more common in women than in men, but most individuals have some degree of phobia for some situation.

Phobias produce three main kinds of response: (1) a subjective experience of fear for the object or situation; (2) physiological changes such as palpitations or blushing in response to it; and (3) behavioral tendencies to avoid or escape from it. Some truly phobic patients experience symptoms rarely because they avoid the feared situation, but most patients with a severe phobia ultimately seek treatment.

Patients with underlying anxiety or depressive states often benefit from drug therapy or psychotherapy, but most other phobias are resistant to these techniques. Here the most effective therapy is often "desensitization," a form of behavior therapy in which the patient is gradually taught to relax while imagining the feared object. An alternative technique is "flooding" or "implosion" therapy, in which the patient is confronted by the feared object or situation at once and encouraged to remain in contact with it until his anxiety disappears.

Therapy for phobias is not always successful, and "cures" are not always permanent, but most sufferers can be helped by current treatment. The understanding and patience of family and friends is essential.

See also the major article on **Psychotherapy.**

photophobia

1. Abnormal sensitivity of the eyes to light.

It is a feature of various conditions, including MIGRAINE, MEASLES, MENINGITIS, CONJUNCTIVITIS, IRITIS and KERATITIS. Photophobia may also be experienced by persons taking or addicted to certain drugs.

2. A morbid or irrational fear of light or of being in well-lit places.

physical therapy

The treatment of patients by physical methods and agents to treat or prevent disease, or to assist in rehabilitation and restoration of normal function following a disease or surgical operation.

Physical therapy is practiced to some extent by all who are involved in the care of patients, but those paramedical personnel who are specially trained in the field are known as physical therapists (or physiotherapists).

Physical therapy is usually carried out under medical supervision and prescribed by a doctor. The methods used include the following:

Therapeutic exercises for the limbs, abdominal muscles, chest muscles, etc. These are of value before and after any significant operation, in prenatal and postnatal care, in any patient who has been confined to bed by illness and (more specifically) in those with disabilities resulting from injury or disease. "Active" exercises are those carried out by the patient, but "passive movements"—made on the patient's body by the therapist—are of value in unconscious patients and some others, especially to prevent the development of muscle contractures.

Massage and *manipulation*, properly carried out, may be of value in a number of musculoskeletal diseases.

Movement in a pool of water (*hydrotherapy*) is easier for patients with many kinds of arthritis than movement in air, and this may help to strengthen muscles.

Heat therapy may aid in the restoration of joint and muscle function. Heat may be applied in a number of ways including lamps, pads, hot water and hot wax.

A number of other techniques including *ultrasound*, *electrotherapy*, etc., have special applications in different areas of medicine and may be administered by physical therapists. Many of these forms of therapy can be carried out anywhere, but some need the facilities of a well-equipped hospital department.

pica

The habit of eating substances which are not normally taken as foodstuffs; particularly the eating of clay, earth, charcoal, ashes, or paint off windowsills, cribs, etc.

Pica derives its name from the scientific name for one species of magpie, *Pica pica*—a bird which is traditionally believed to sample all available substances. The reason for the human habit is not known, but it is widespread—particularly in pregnant women and in children. It is linked to the cravings which pregnant women sometimes exhibit for inappropriate foods at inappropriate times (such as pickles and ice cream at midnight!).

Some work has been done to investigate the theory that the craving for clay and earth may be a sign of a lack of various nutrients. It is possible that pica is characteristic of individuals lacking iron and potassium; in some parts of India the habit (and perhaps this form of malnutrition) is so common that cakes of clay are sold in markets.

pinworms

The most common worm PARASITES of man in the United States, particularly among schoolchildren. The worm is also known as the "threadworm" (scientific name: *Enterobius vermicularis*, formerly known as *Oxyuris vermicularis*). The infestation they cause is known as *enterobiasis* or *oxyuriasis*.

The adult worms live within the human intestine. Females are about half an inch long; males are much smaller. Mature females crawl through the anus to the perianal skinfolds where they lay up to 10,000 eggs each, typically at night. This process usually causes intense itching at the anus (*pruritus ani*). Within six hours the eggs turn into infectious larvae. If swallowed by man these develop into adult worms in the small intestine and the cycle starts again.

The severe itching at the anus causes great discomfort and scratching, and it may lead to irritability and insomnia, but other symptoms are unlikely to be due to pinworms. In particular it is doubtful if they ever cause the abdominal pain or weight loss so often blamed on them. In females they may wander into the vagina, uterus, and Fallopian tubes, but serious consequences are very rare.

Transmission of the parasites occurs by self-infection from anus to mouth as a result of scratching in sleep or poor hygiene, by cross-infection from anus to hand to the hand of another individual, or by taking in eggs from dust in homes or classrooms.

The worms may be seen in the stools, or swabs may be taken from around the anus, using Scotch Tape which is then examined under the microscope.

Pinworms can be killed by drugs such as piperazine taken by mouth, but reinfection is extremely common and repeated treatment is often necessary. Although irritating, the infection is harmless; complications of

PINWORM (THREADWORM)

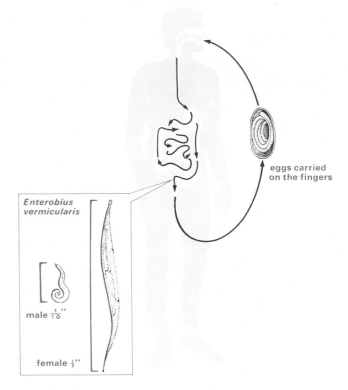

Enterobius vermicularis

male $\frac{1}{10}$''

female $\frac{1}{2}$''

eggs carried on the fingers

Enterobiasis, pinworm infection, is characterized by intense itching around the anus. This is due to the female worm migrating down the gut at night and laying eggs on the anal skin. Scratching contaminates the fingers with eggs, which are then carried to the mouth and ingested.

infection and treatment are very rare. When one member of a family is infected, all members of the family should be treated at the same time.

pituitary gland

A pea-sized endocrine gland at the base of the brain, which is enclosed within a bony cavity in the skull (the pituitary fossa) situated just above and behind the nasal cavity. The gland is connected to the hypothalamus of the brain by a thin stalk and divided into two parts, the *anterior* and *posterior* divisions (or lobes) of the pituitary gland.

The pituitary gland produces a number of hormones which influence the function of other endocrine glands and organs throughout the body. It was once described as "the conductor of the endocrine orchestra" of the body, but it has become clear in recent years that the anterior pituitary is itself strongly influenced by hormones released by the hypothalamus, which travel directly to it through special blood vessels. The hypothalamus in turn is influenced by a complex of factors including the rest of the nervous system and the concentration of various substances in the blood.

The anterior division of the pituitary gland (*adenohypophysis*) releases a number of hormones into the blood:

Growth hormone (SOMATOTROPIN) is necessary for normal growth, and has other metabolic actions. Deficiency in childhood leads to dwarfism; excessive production, usually caused by a tumor of the pituitary, leads to gigantism in childhood and ACROMEGALY in adult life.

Thyroid-stimulating hormone (*TSH*) stimulates the thyroid gland to produce thyroxine and triiodothyronine. The level of TSH in the blood is usually raised in MYXEDEMA and lowered in thyrotoxicosis (see HYPERTHYROIDISM) by a feedback effect of thyroid hormones on the pituitary.

Adrenocorticotropic hormone (ACTH) maintains normal activity in the cortex (outer portion) of the adrenal gland, stimulating the normal secretion of corticosteroid hormones.

Luteinizing hormone (also known as *interstitial cell-stimulating hormone*) and *follicle-stimulating hormone* regulate the secretion and activity of the testes and ovaries. Abnormalities of secretion may result in abnormal sexual characteristics and infertility.

Prolactin regulates milk production and breast development in pregnancy. Recently high levels of secretion have been recognized as a factor in some women with infertility, but the output from the pituitary can be diminished by drugs such as bromocriptine.

The posterior division of the pituitary gland (*neurohypophysis*) releases two hormones into the blood. Both are produced in nerve cells in the hypothalamus and pass through the stalk to the far end of the cells in the neurohypophysis:

Antidiuretic hormone (or *vasopressin*) acts on the kidneys to prevent excessive water loss in the urine. If the secretion is low due to hypothalamic or pituitary disease, DIABETES INSIPIDUS develops.

Oxytocin makes the uterine muscle contract in labor. Its role in men and at other times in women is less well defined.

The pituitary gland may be damaged by trauma to the head, by infections of various kinds and by tumors. Where deficiencies of hormones occur as a result, those produced by the "target organs" may often be used in treatment, rather than those produced by the pituitary itself which are difficult to obtain in large amounts.

ACTH is available in large amounts, however, and human growth hormone is used for the treatment of pituitary dwarfism. Oxytocin and antidiuretic hormone are synthesized and generally available.

See also HORMONES and the major article on **Endocrinology.**

PITUITARY GLAND

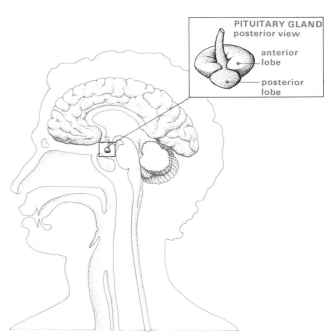

The pituitary, the master gland at the base of the brain, regulates much of the body's hormonal system. Its anterior lobe secretes hormones which stimulate many other glands to produce hormones of their own. Occasionally benign tumors grow in this anterior lobe and disturb the body's growth, its response to stress and other functions. The posterior lobe secretes only two hormones; the first acts on the kidney to retain body water and the second makes the womb contract in labor.

pityriasis rosea

A mild inflammatory skin disease, probably caused by a virus. It produces a characteristic skin rash and there are rarely any other symptoms. The disease is quite common in the United States, especially in winter.

The rash starts with a single flat red spot, an oval area about 1 inch across with a ring of tiny scales near its edge, usually on the front of the chest. After a few days smaller but similar oval patches appear, mainly on the chest and abdomen, but also sometimes on the back, upper arms and thighs. The number of patches ranges from a few to hundreds.

The patches increase in number for two or three weeks and the disease then resolves spontaneously over six to ten weeks. Itching is occasionally troublesome and may require treatment with a lotion such as calamine, but there are no other symptoms. Recovery is complete within ten weeks; there are no long-term effects and relapses or second attacks are very rare.

placenta

The afterbirth—the fleshy round pancake-like organ which is delivered shortly after the birth of the baby, and which is connected to the child by the umbilical cord. The child's blood flows through it until a few minutes after the birth.

When the baby is in the womb it receives all its nutrients and oxygen from the mother via the umbilical cord. It is the placenta which makes this possible. It develops on the inner wall of the womb at a very early stage of pregnancy, and remains firmly attached to the womb until just after the child has been born. The mother's blood passes through the wall of the womb and transfers its precious cargo of oxygen and food into the placenta, where the baby's blood picks it up before returning to the child via the umbilical cord.

There is ordinarily no actual mixing of the mother's blood with the baby's, but simply a transfer of oxygen and nutrients through the wall of the placenta (which lies in intimate contact with the wall of the womb).

The placenta is usually about 8 in. (20 cm) across and 1½ in. (4 cm) thick. It weighs about one sixth of the weight of the baby—ordinarily about 1 to 1½ lb. (450 to 700 grams). Because of its relatively small mass, it causes the mother little or no discomfort during its expulsion. After the umbilical cord has been tied off and cut by the obstetrician, the placenta is usually disposed of, unless there is some good reason to examine it for evidence of disease.

See also CHILDBIRTH and the major article on **Pregnancy and Childbirth.**

PLACENTA

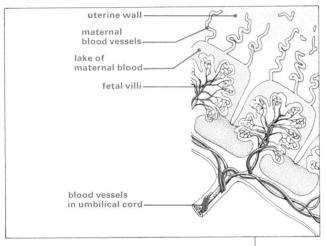

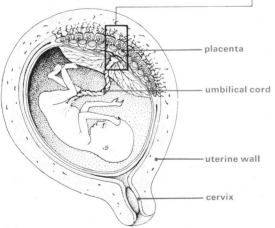

The placenta develops early in pregnancy and normally occupies an area high in the uterus. The maternal and fetal circulations do not mix, but are able to exchange nutrients and waste products across the placenta. Maternal blood is pumped into "lakes" which surround the villi containing delicate fetal blood vessels. The placenta also secretes hormones.

placental insufficiency

The situation in which a fetus fails to grow normally and becomes "small-for-date"—traditionally ascribed to inadequacy of the PLACENTA for the needs of the fetus. Such presumed *placental insufficiency* has been supported by the finding of a "gritty," calcified and sometimes partly damaged placenta at birth, and by studies on levels of hormones produced in part by the placenta.

In recent years, however, it has become clear that the state of the placenta at birth does not necessarily bear any relation to the state of the baby. Many normal and healthy babies are born with apparently "unhealthy" placentas and vice versa.

"Placental insufficiency" is thus often a misnomer for more complex problems affecting the mother or fetus, or both, rather than the placenta alone.

placenta previa

A PLACENTA positioned in the lower segment of the uterus, bridging or on the edge of the opening from the uterus into the vagina. The consequence is complication of late pregnancy and labor.

The major complication is bleeding, which occurs as the lower segment of the uterus dilates in late pregnancy—the placenta cannot stretch with it, so some degree of separation from the uterus occurs by tearing.

Placenta previa causes no symptoms until the bleeding begins, but this may be severe and of sudden onset. Placenta previa may be suspected earlier on clinical examination and confirmed by a number of radiologic, ultrasonic and isotopic techniques.

Bleeding is treated by rest and blood transfusion if necessary. If it persists or recurs, or if the fetus is in danger, immediate Cesarean section is required (see

CHILDBIRTH); otherwise, this may be delayed until 38 weeks of pregnancy. Normal delivery is rarely possible—the placenta would be delivered first and the baby would be in danger.

Placenta previa usually results from chance; subsequent pregnancies are very rarely affected.

plague

An infectious disease caused by the bacterium *Pasteurella pestis*. The disease is endemic in the western United States and in South America, China and parts of Africa.

The causative bacteria normally infect rodents and are carried by the rat flea. These may bite humans, especially when the host rats are dying of plague.

There are three forms of plague: *bubonic plague*, with general enlargement of lymph glands and a rash; *pneumonic plague*, with pneumonia due to organisms in the lungs which can be spread to others by coughing; and *septicemic plague*, where there is rapid spread of the organisms throughout the body in the blood.

The "Black Death" in the 14th century in Europe was due to plague. Epidemics are now fortunately rare and precautions can be taken to limit their spread, but the disease is still extremely dangerous and antimicrobial treatment is usually only effective if started within a few hours of onset. Treatment involves the administration of sulfonamides, streptomycin, chloramphenicol or tetracyclines.

plantar reflex

A reflex movement of the toes, especially the big toe, elicited by scratching the outside of the sole of the foot.

The normal reflex is downward movement of the big toe (flexion). An abnormal response is upward movement (extension) followed usually by flexion. Except in young babies the abnormal response (BABINSKI'S REFLEX) is an indication of neurological abnormality (upper motor neuron damage).

plantar wart

A wart occurring on the sole of the foot.

Like other WARTS, plantar warts are caused by a virus. They are common and contagious and are spread particularly by close contact with bare feet, e.g., in swimming pools and school locker rooms. Some individuals seem completely immune while others may develop large numbers of warts. Plantar warts, unlike most warts, are usually painful because pressure forces them into the foot.

There is no reliable treatment, but many are used. Warts can usually be removed by cautery, curettage or

the application of liquid nitrogen, and regular soaking of the feet in formalin. Special plasters and a number of other techniques are sometimes effective. In all cases recurrence is common; but, equally, the warts may disappear suddenly and permanently for no obvious reason.

plastic surgery

See the section on *Plastic surgery* in the major article on **Surgery.** See also COSMETIC SURGERY.

platelets

A component of the blood. Platelets (also known as *thrombocytes*) are colorless disks, much smaller than the red and white cells; there are approximately 300,000 per cubic millimeter of blood. They are not cells but cellular fragments, produced by large cells (*megakaryocytes*) in the bone marrow. They have a normal lifespan in the blood of about ten days.

The best understood function of platelets is their role in the formation of blood clots. They stick to the walls of damaged blood vessels and release substances which initiate the formation of a clot. They are not essential for all blood clotting, but a deficiency of platelets may lead to abnormal bleeding, especially in the skin (*thrombocytopenic purpura*).

Several diseases lead to a fall in the number of platelets in the blood. These include leukemia, aplastic anemia, cancer which has spread to the bone marrow, severe infections, collagen diseases and some cases of heart and kidney failure. In addition, some conditions (such as kidney failure) may impair the function of the platelets which do remain. Some patients develop a low platelet count for no obvious reason—a condition known as *idiopathic thrombocytopenic purpura*.

In POLYCYTHEMIA the platelet count can be greatly increased and add to the risk of thrombosis.

Platelets can be separated from blood and transfused into patients with a deficiency. The effect is temporary but may be of value if such a patient is bleeding or requires surgery.

Platelets are also involved in the formation of abnormal and dangerous venous thromboses and are also implicated in the formation of the fatty plaques ATHEROSCLEROSIS. Platelet function can be suppressed by drugs such as aspirin.

See also THROMBOCYTOPENIA.

pleural effusion

An abnormal collection of fluid in the pleural space.

The pleural space separates the membranes (pleura) covering the lungs, the chest wall and the diaphragm; it normally contains only a small amount of fluid which lubricates the surface of the lungs as they move with respiration. An abnormally large amount of fluid may accumulate in a number of conditions including cancer of the lung, breast or ovary, tuberculosis, pneumonia, pulmonary embolism, heart failure, cirrhosis and collagen diseases.

Small effusions may cause no symptoms. Large effusions, however, may cause severe shortness of breath and pain, especially if associated with PLEURISY.

Where possible treatment is directed at the underlying condition; but it is also often necessary to relieve breathlessness by aspirating the fluid through a needle. Examination of this fluid may also help to diagnose the cause.

The prognosis of pleural effusions depends upon the cause, but they are often recurrent and repeated aspiration may be necessary.

pleurisy

Inflammation of the pleura. The pleura is the membrane which covers the outer surface of the lungs and the inner surface of the thorax (chest). These two surfaces normally move on one another with respiration, being lubricated by a small amount of pleural fluid.

Pleurisy may occur in a number of conditions and in two forms: "dry pleurisy" and "pleurisy with effusion." (The causes of pleurisy with effusion are listed under PLEURAL EFFUSION). Dry pleurisy is pleural inflammation without significant effusion. It may be caused by conditions including tuberculosis, pneumonia, pulmonary infarction, chest injury, chronic kidney failure and primary viral infections.

The main symptom of pleurisy is sharp, stabbing chest pain, which is usually made worse by coughing or deep breathing. The patient often takes only short, grunting breaths; he usually has a fever and a painful cough. The physician can usually hear a characteristic sound—a "pleural rub"—when he listens with a stethoscope. If there is also a pleural effusion there may be additional findings and the patient may be severely breathless.

The immediate treatment of pleurisy usually involves bed rest and painkilling drugs.

The prognosis depends largely on the underlying cause. Pleurisy due to viral infection is usually benign and responds to supportive treatment, but recurrent attacks are quite common.

See also LUNG DISEASES and the major article on **Pulmonary Diseases.**

pleurodynia

See EPIDEMIC PLEURODYNIA.

PLEURISY

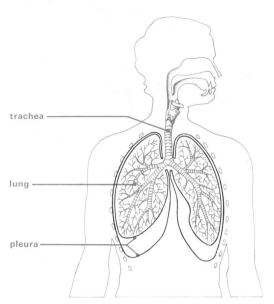

trachea

lung

pleura

The outer surface of the lungs and the inner surface of the chest wall are covered with shiny, lubricated membranes—the pleura. Pleurisy is the condition where the pleura are inflamed and no longer slide over each other smoothly.

pneumoconiosis

The inhalation of particular forms of dust, over long periods, can lead to changes in the lungs that are non-reversible. This disease is called pneumoconiosis. Mineral dusts, notably silica and asbestos, are the most common causes. Vegetable fiber dusts from sources such as hay and grass may cause what is known as "farmers' lung." Similar dusts to which workers are exposed during many years in the sugar cane and cotton industries can also lead to pneumoconiosis. In the U.S. the most common form is SILICOSIS.

The nasal passages and the lining of the respiratory passages usually prevent the absorption by the lungs of most dust particles. Minute particles inhaled over a period of at least five years may be constantly deposited in the smallest bronchial passages; silica, in particular, sets up an acidic response that leads to scar formation or FIBROSIS. The thickened lung tissue is then deprived of its distensibility and the symptoms of DYSPNEA (shortness of breath) coughing and wheezing on exertion and impaired respiratory function develop. X-ray studies confirm the diagnosis of mottling of the lungs with formation of scar tissue. There is no treatment.

Prevention of the disease requires effective ventilation in the industries of mining, stone-cutting, and sandblasting and the wearing of respirators and the suppression of dust by every means possible.

See also the major article on **Pulmonary Diseases.**

pneumonia

Inflammation of the lungs from bacterial, fungal, or viral infection or from chemical damage. The outflow of fluid and cells from the inflamed lung tissue fills the airspaces, causing difficulty in breathing and in severe cases the disease may be fatal.

The lungs are unusually open to infection, since the air inhaled with each breath always contains microorganisms. Their defenses include the filtration of air by the nose, the mucous lining of the air passages that traps dust particles and bacteria, and the IMMUNE SYSTEM operating within the lung tissues—the combination of antibodies and protective white blood cells (phagocytes). If these defenses are impaired by old age, by a virus infection such as measles, or by *immunosuppressive* drugs (given to prevent rejection of a transplanted organ) then pneumonia is more likely.

Before the antibiotic era the most common type of pneumonia was *lobar pneumonia*, due to one species of bacterium, the pneumococcus. Pneumococcal pneumonia is usually confined to one lung or one lobe of a lung, which is so heavily inflamed that it changes from a normal spongy, air-filled consistency to a heavy, "consolidated" state. Lobar pneumonia causes a high fever, often with delirium; if it is extensive, the lack of normal lung tissue means that oxygenation is inadequate and the patient becomes very short of breath and cyanosed and may lose consciousness. There may be associated inflammation of the membrane covering the lung and chest wall—PLEURISY—causing a sharp pain in the chest with each breath. The sputum coughed up may be bloodstained.

Before antibiotics lobar pneumonia was often fatal, especially when it affected both lungs (*double pneumonia*). Nowadays, however, penicillin typically produces a dramatic cure in up to 95% of cases.

In *bronchopneumonia* patches of inflammation and consolidation are scattered through the lungs. The symptoms are usually less dramatic than in lobar pneumonia, but again there will be cough, difficulty in breathing and fever. Bronchopneumonia may be fatal, especially in the elderly and in anyone weakened by another illness such as advanced cancer, and it is indeed a common cause of death in such diseases.

Bronchopneumonia may be due to bacteria such as Hemophilus, to mycoplasma, and to viruses. It is a common complication of influenza. Treatment with antibiotics is usually effective in the bacterial pneumonias, but there is still no effective specific treatment for viral pneumonias. However, the symptoms may be relieved by oxygen therapy and drugs to lower the temperature and relieve chest pain.

Pneumonia may also be due to chemical damage to the lungs from inhalation of gases such as sulfur dioxide

PNEUMONIA

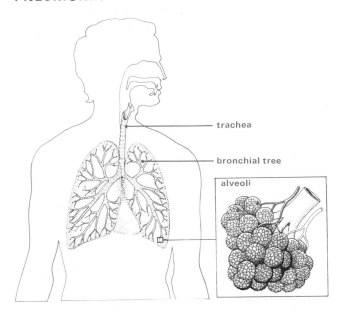

trachea

bronchial tree

alveoli

Pneumonia is inflammation of lung tissue usually caused by bacteria or viruses. Fluid and cells pour into the alveoli (air sacs) so that the air is excluded. Thus breathing is impaired, and pneumonia can be life-threatening in the very young and very old.

in industrial accidents, or from inhalation of vomit by an unconscious or semiconscious person. The treatment of chemical pneumonias depends on the removal of inflammatory fluid from the lungs by suction, anti-inflammatory drugs and oxygen therapy.

Some forms of pneumonia may be prevented by vaccination against the virus or bacterium responsible. Vaccines against influenza and the pneumococcus are available, and their use may be recommended in the elderly and patients with debilitating illness.

See also the major article on **Pulmonary Diseases.**

pneumonitis

Literally meaning inflammation of the lung tissue, pneumonitis occurs in the development of any infective invasion of the lower respiratory tract (such as PNEUMONIA). It is the initial stage where the cells of the lung in the alveoli (the air sacs or terminal passages) are swollen and infected and where the lining cells of the smaller respiratory passages leading to the alveoli are being attacked by infective organisms. In the absence of infection, pneumonitis can occur as a result of inhaling noxious gases or markedly subzero atmosphere (as in Arctic conditions) which paralyze the respiratory cilia (the hairlike processes that project from the lining of the larger air passages and propel mucus, dust particles, etc., away from the lungs). The symptoms are a painful cough which is initially dry and unproductive (no mucus or phlegm is coughed up) with pain on inhalation.

Treatment is directed at the underlying cause, if known. For example, antibiotics are usually effective in controlling a primary or secondary bacterial infection (although they have no effect on viral pneumonitis).

pneumothorax

The presence of free air or gas in the *pleural cavity*. (The pleural cavity is a narrow space between two layers of the *pleura*, the serous membrane that lines the chest cavity—*thorax*—and surrounds each lung.) When this occurs it may cause the lung to retract from the thoracic wall and provoke a collapse of the lung. The condition may be barely detectable or massive and threatening to life.

A superficial "blister" of the lung tissue may accidentally burst and allow the escape of inhaled air from within the lung (forceful increases in lung pressure may provoke this, as in blowing a trumpet or filling a balloon). Among the healthy it is most common in young adult life due to profound respiratory exertions and occurs more frequently in males. In those over 45, *spontaneous pneumothorax* (as this type is called) is usually associated with chronic EMPHYSEMA, ASTHMA, FIBROSIS, SILICOSIS and other chronic lung disease. *Traumatic pneumothorax* may occur when air enters the pleural cavity through a penetrating wound of the chest (e.g., a stabbing or gunshot wound).

The onset of a pneumothorax is painful on the affected side, with shortness of breath and a sense of tightness in the chest. No special treatment is necessary in less serious cases, apart from rest, as the air is absorbed into the tissues over a period of a week or more. In more severe cases of pneumothorax, surgical aspiration through a puncture of the chest wall may be immediately necessary. Full recovery is usual.

See also the major article on **Pulmonary Diseases.**

podiatry

The skills of foot care are practiced by those trained in podiatry (also known as *chiropody*.) Special schools may conduct training, examination and licencing (depending on the region of the country), but many surgeons practice podiatry as part of their patient care.

The skills are sought by those who have particular problems associated with the feet. PLANTAR WARTS (warts on the sole of the foot) may require attention by the careful removal of the hardened skin over the surface of the wart or scraping (curretting) it out followed by DIATHERMY to the base. Calluses (areas of hardened skin) may require similar but more gentle treatment. INGROWING NAILS frequently require prolonged atten-

tion to overcome the infection at the side of the nail until the nail grows correctly; surgical treatment may be required if other measures fail to overcome the problem.

Flat foot (technically known as *pes planus*), or reduction of the longitudinal arch of the foot, is another common cause of podiatric attention. It is often associated with some partial twisting or rotation of the foot. All children for the first two years after walking have "flat" feet, where the middle of the arch almost presses on the ground; but the choice of correct footwear with a heel and arch support in the shoe overcomes this. *Foot strain* in the middle-aged is commonly caused by stress on the longitudinal arch ligaments and sometimes by muscle weakening of the foot due to lack of adequate exercise. Foot-strengthening exercises and electrical stimulation of the affected muscles can overcome this, in addition to the use of appropriate arch supports in the shoe.

For the elderly person deprived (by arthritis, fragility or dizziness on bending) of the opportunity to maintain normal foot care, podiatric attention can be essential to prevent deformities occurring in uncut nails. Similarly, foot deformities due to OSTEOARTHRITIS, hallux valgus (inturning big toe) BUNIONS (thickened bursa on the big toe joint) are common in the elderly; podiatry becomes necessary for foot comfort and to permit normal physical activity and mobility. Diabetic patients require similar attention and care because of the hazard of foot infections in the elderly diabetic.

poisoning

The accidental (or deliberate) ingestion of substances that may be poisonous—in small or large doses—is an occurrence of increasing frequency. The incidence of poisoning in one form or another is rising annually throughout the developed world because of the availability of potent medicines and the cultural phenomenon of "overdosing," because of the frequency of the illicit use of drugs, and because of the ever-increasing number of toxic chemicals, gases and liquids employed in modern industry. Fortunately, because of the increase in sophistication in medical techniques for supporting life's vital functions during hospitalization, death from poisoning is not as common as it once was.

Poisoning can produce abdominal pains, vomiting, delirium, loss of consciousness, suppression of respiration and death. A multitude of other symptoms can also occur during this progression that are specific or characteristic to the noxious substance. The effects of some poisons (e.g., alcohol) are reversible; given time, the human body is capable of excreting them or biochemically changing them to substances that are less toxic. Others (e.g., lead) are accumulative in small doses and permanently stored by the body until they destroy vital functions. Still others (e.g., the toxic elements of FOOD POISONING) may be rapidly evacuated from the body, although survival and prompt recovery depends on the initial state of health of the individual.

In all cases the finding of an unconscious person must initiate the same "first aid" procedures; because of the danger to the unconscious victim of choking to death on inhaled vomit, he must be turned to the *recovery position*—lying prone, the head resting on a raised arm, the knees bent, and the mouth and face pointing sideways and down—while transport to the hospital emergency room is arranged. Should breathing cease, artificial "mouth to mouth" resuscitation should be undertaken. Providing the physician knows what has recently been ingested, the conscious patient may be encouraged to vomit, after which he should also be transferred to the hospital in the recovery position.

Identification of the poison may depend on finding medicine bottles or other substances near the victim, retaining a specimen of vomit for hospital laboratory analysis, or the questioning of relatives and friends. The physician can be greatly aided in the treatment of the poisoned patient by such information. Barbiturates (sleeping pills), opiates (morphine, cocaine, heroin), tranquilizers and antidepressants are the most common pharmaceutical agents used in deliberate overdosage or poisoning. The danger from these is *respiratory suppression*. Thus, delay in hospitalization can prove fatal—for only with the proper facilities can respiration be maintained until full recovery occurs.

Metallic poisons (such as cadmium, lead, mercury and other substances) are an industrial risk even though their effects may take many months or years before they are noted. Appropriate legislation can prevent or minimize these industrial hazards by requiring proper safeguards for worker protection. Herbicides and pesticides can be accidentally inhaled or absorbed through the skin in crop-spraying; the use of respirators and protective clothing prevent poisoning for those handling these substances. Poisoning by gas inhalation, (e.g., *carbon monoxide* car exhaust fumes) may be deliberate or accidental; it requires oxygen administration for recovery plus respiratory support. Children are particularly prone to accidental poisoning from medicines found in the home, the eating of poisonous berries, contact with household cleaners (especially lye, or Electro-Sol or other dishwasher detergents) or other household or agricultural chemicals that are unguarded or unsafely stored. In all circumstances, if it is suspected that the child has ingested or come into contact with poisonous substances, he must receive immediate hospital care. Small doses of poisonous substances that might not harm an adult may be lethal to a small child.

The prognosis for many cases is good. Some antidotes may be specific (as in barbiturate poisoning), but in general the prevention of death depends on maintaining respiration and sometimes on "washing out" the poison by DIALYSIS (the artificial kidney)—thus ensuring the victim's survival until the poison is excreted. Ingestion of caustic materials by children may require prolonged medical or surgical treatment.

See also LEAD POISONING, MERCURY POISONING, and *Poisoning* in the **First Aid** section.

poliomyelitis

Once called "infantile paralysis," poliomyelitis is an acute viral infection of the gastrointestinal tract that may attack the central nervous system to produce motor nerve paralysis. It has a worldwide distribution and in temperate zones occurs in epidemics in the summer months, being transmitted by dust and fecal contact—especially in areas of poor sanitation and hygiene. Artificial immunity can be provoked by the injection of the "killed virus" developed by Dr. Jonas Salk or by the oral administration of a "live attenuated (weakened)" virus vaccine developed by Dr. Albert Sabin. In the unvaccinated, susceptible person, the virus of poliomyelitis can be inhaled or ingested. The first symptoms may fall into any of three patterns: sore throat and fever, diarrhea, or aching in the limbs and back. These symptoms may resolve within three to five days (*nonparalytic polio*) or the virus may spread through the bloodstream to invade the central nervous system.

Signs of irritation of the covering membranes of the brain develop (stiff neck, PHOTOPHOBIA, headache) as well as painful muscular cramps and spasms. The virus causes most damage to the nerve cells controlling the muscles (the motor neurons) and within 48 hours there is obvious paralysis of the muscles. This may be limited to the muscles of the limbs or (bulbar polio) it may affect respiration and swallowing. Diagnosis is made clinically and by virus culture or determination of increases in the specific antibodies. Treatment involves hospitalization and nursing care to rest the affected muscles, and (if necessary) artificial maintenance of respiratory function (the "iron lung" machine). No medication is effective against the polio virus. The overall mortality rate is around 5%. Many patients recover with a return of some degree of muscle function, but a few remain severely or even totally paralyzed.

Prevention depends entirely on immunization. The live oral vaccine confers 100% gastrointestinal immunity to attack and by "boosters" prevents spread. A policy of infant immunization has virtually eradicated the disease from the United States and other developed countries, but booster doses are recommended every eight years in childhood and before foreign travel for adults, since polio is still a major public health problem in much of Africa, Asia, and Southern Europe.

polyarteritis nodosa

This rare disease is characterized by areas of inflammation that develop in the walls of blood vessels—both arteries and veins—which may be segmental, diffuse or discrete. The "node" of inflammation may result in NECROSIS of the blood vessel wall and the extent of the damage may vary from the ANEURYSM (blister) or rupture, to healing with FIBROSIS or THROMBOSIS. The cause is unknown for this disease of connective tissue, although allergic, infective, toxic, rheumatic and neurogenic causes have all, at times, been implicated. It more commonly attacks males, of all ethnic groups, in their 40s. Any blood vessel in the body may be affected.

Since the area of attack, the extent of the damage, and even the onset in stages may all vary there are no "typical" symptoms. Fever with drenching sweats, complaints of weakness, muscular pains and general fatigue are experienced while the disease is active; but the diagnosis can be made if minute but sore nodules are detected along visible blood vessels in the skin, tongue, retina or conjunctiva. Any organ in the body may be affected with consequent symptoms or disturbed function; in particular, NEURITIS (inflammation of a nerve or nerves) may occur. BIOPSY of skin or muscle may be necessary for the diagnosis; treatment is by administration of steroids (for example, prednisolone). The likelihood of recurrence is high.

polycystic kidney

This inherited disease, passed as a dominant gene to either male or female, causes dilation of the tubules in the kidney and leads to obstruction, infection, cysts and kidney failure (see KIDNEY DISEASES). Its manifestations may appear in infancy, or be delayed until adult life. The extent of the disease may vary, with the more severely affected cases occurring early in life. Cysts may also occur on blood vessels in other parts of the body. Progressive kidney failure occurs but may be delayed by continuous medical care that reduces infection, and death from UREMIA is prevented by DIALYSIS ("artificial kidney" machine) or a kidney transplant, when the disease has not seriously affected other organs.

polycythemia

Literally, an increase in the number of circulating red blood cells. Polycythemia may occur as a result of a demand on the body to produce more hemoglobin, in order to absorb more oxygen, in environments where the atmospheric oxygen is reduced—such as at high altitudes. Thus, healthy people living in the Andes, Rockies or other high mountainous areas may show "relative polycythemia" which is normal. New residents may develop *acute polycythemia* and initially experience "mountain sickness" with DYSPNEA, CYANOSIS, headache, vomiting and lethargy. But on their return to lower altitudes the symptoms disappear.

As a disease that is *not* an environmental adaption, it may occur in CUSHING'S SYNDROME, brain, liver and uterine tumors and in kidney disease, or spontaneously (*polycythemia vera*) as an overproduction of red cells by the bone marrow. This latter type of the disease is of high incidence in Jews, low in blacks, and men in middle or later life are more frequently affected than women. A ruddy engorged complexion, abdominal pain due to spleen and liver enlargement, headaches and bleeding from mucous membranes may occur. The diagnosis is made by blood tests and a biopsy of the bone marrow. Complications of the disease include THROMBOSIS and hemorrhages in the gastrointestinal tract. Treatment is by blood removal (phlebotomy) to balance the overproduction, and radioactive chemicals or cytotoxic drugs to suppress the bone marrow. Prognosis is a chronic recurrence over many years with ultimate anemia and cardiovascular or kidney complications which may lead to death.

polymyalgia rheumatica

Muscular pains throughout the body—appearing abruptly in the neck and shoulder muscles and spreading down the back to the buttocks and thighs—with stiffness, headache, fever, and loss of appetite and weight. Characteristically it attacks middle-aged and elderly persons and is more common in women over 60.

Laboratory tests such as ESR (ERYTHROCYTE SEDIMENTATION RATE) are helpful: a very high ESR is virtual confirmation of the diagnosis.

The course fluctuates with remissions and exacerbations but is usually self-limiting, with relief after a few months. The disability may be severe but bed rest and medication with anti-inflammatory agents or steroids will usually produce rapid relief. The symptoms may recur when treatment is stopped, but the prognosis (with treatment) is good and there is no long-lasting disability.

polyp

A polyp is an overgrowth of the "submucous" tissue, which pushes up its covering of mucous membrane to project (often from a stalklike connection) into the anatomical cavity or passage. Multiple polyps frequently occur in the nose, cervix and uterus; they are rarely malignant in these sites but cause symptoms due to obstruction or deformation of the anatomical cavity and excessive stretching of the mucous membrane. Chronic superficial infections predispose to their development and they are usually only seen in adults.

Patients with allergies or chronic RHINITIS are more prone to develop nasal polyps. Excess mucous formation, nose bleeds and loss of the sense of smell may occur, and the polyps are easily recognized on examination as glistening extrusions of the nasal lining. In the cervix or uterus, bleeding between menstrual periods is a possible sign of polyp development; some FIBROIDS of the uterus may resemble polyps in shape. Polyps may occur in the colon and rectum as a rare genetic trait (*familial adenomatous polyposis*) and appear in hundreds. Lower abdominal pain, loss of weight, diarrhea and the passage of mucus and blood in the stools may signal their development. This rare familial disease does show malignant change in a significant number of cases.

Polyps are mainly removed by surgery, cautery or dissection. Periodic medical examinations are necessary because polyps tend to recur. In the rare genetic disease of *colonic polyps*, surgical removal of the affected portion of the large intestine may be necessary.

porphyrias

The porphyrias are a group of very rare disorders usually caused by an "inborn error" of metabolism.

POLYPS

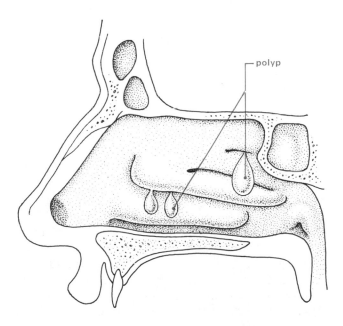

polyp

MULTIPLE POLYPS IN THE NASAL CAVITY

Nasal polyps are areas of the membrane lining the nose which become distended with excess tissue fluid and hang down into the nasal cavity. They are usually due to an allergy. Since they can cause nasal obstruction, they may have to be removed.

Porphyrins are complex chemical compounds which are normally produced as steps in the formation of *heme*, the red pigment which contributes its color to the hemoglobin in the red blood cells. In the porphyrias, a "block" is present at one of several sites in this chain of chemical reactions—resulting in an abnormal accumulation in the tissues of various types of porphyrin pigment. Their presence in excess in the tissues leads to their excretion in increased amounts in the urine and feces.

Symptoms of the porphyrias include excessive sensitivity to sunlight with blistering, pigmentation, and various types of skin eruption. Discoloration of the teeth and bones also typically occurs. Nerve damage from the toxic effects of the porphyrins on nerve fibers may occur with muscular weakness and paralysis, severe abdominal pain and other neurological symptoms. Psychological disturbances may occur with MANIA, delirium or coma; death may sometimes occur. Some cases, however, are very mild with only slight sensitivity to sunlight and no other symptoms.

The disease is familial and has, for example, been traced with some certainty in the British Royal Family from James I to his living descendants through the Hanoverian line.

Diagnosis is confirmed by the presence of porphyrins in the urine, which is often reddish ("port wine urine") or darkens on standing in the light. Excessive amounts are also present in the feces, where they can be identified by means of chemical tests.

Treatment is unsatisfactory, but patients must be protected from sunlight. Certain drugs may be used to control the psychological manifestations.

However, drugs such as barbiturate "sleeping tablets," which can precipitate an attack, must be avoided.

portal hypertension

See LIVER DISEASE.

postnasal drip

A trickling of mucus from the posterior portion of the nasal cavity onto the surface of the throat, usually caused by a common cold or an allergy (allergic rhinitis).

postpartum depression

Depressive reactions are fairly common in the first week after childbirth, with some 90% of women experiencing "fourth day blues." True depressive illness—with insomnia, tearfulness, irrational fears, irritability, guilt and psychic disturbances (which may include rejection of the baby and even infanticide in extremely severe cases)—is much more rare. But at least 15% of women experience some symptoms of depression within the first six months after labor.

Hormonal origins are suspected and menstrual irregularity is a frequent accompaniment; but environmental, social and sexual difficulties also predispose the woman to the development of postpartum depression. In addition, any emotional disorder prior to pregnancy is frequently magnified or exacerbated in the postpartum stage. (Depression following miscarriage or abortion is similar in its pattern.)

Suicide is extremely rare, but neglect of or physical harm to the baby is a common manifestation. The diagnosis is made by psychiatric specialists when family problems emerge that cannot be overcome by support from husbands, relatives and close friends. Treatment is essential; antidepressant medication is usually effective if administered in the early stages. Admission to a psychiatric hospital may be necessary in a very few cases; the woman is often advised to avoid further pregnancies. In addition, in severe cases, sterilization may be considered. Fortunately, however, most cases of postpartum depression are mild and transient.

posture

Modern man (*Homo sapiens*) evolved from primates who learned to walk on two feet (*Homo erectus*). Problems with posture have been a consequence ever since, for the human spine is not yet perfectly adapted to what is required of it. The multiple vertebrae of the spinal column are maintained in position, flexibly, by what are normally strong ligaments over which the spinal muscles lie.

Disease of the spinal column, congenital or acquired disorders of the spinal bones, and injury or weakness of the spinal ligaments or muscles can all result in compensatory postures—often leading to curvatures, pains or lack of flexibility. Normally, with the shoulders held back and the head upright looking forward, there are two natural curves in the spine (the sacrolumbar and the cervicothoracic) which look roughly like an "S" bend when viewed from the side and straight when viewed from the front or rear. If there is hip disease or leg shortening, then the pelvis tilts and the spinal column will curve laterally to compensate   a condition known as *scoliosis*. *Kyphosis* ("humpback" or "hunchback") is an excessive curvature due to disease, abnormal development, or injuries of the upper spine. *Lordosis* is exaggeration of the normal curve in the lower part of the back (the lumbar region) due to obesity, a heavy abdomen and lax muscles. Minor degrees of spinal deformity and postural abnormality are quite common.

Encouragement of habits of good posture in children is important, not only for a pleasing physical appearance but also to prevent the possible development

POSTURE

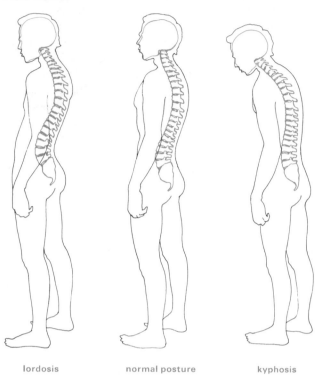

lordosis   normal posture   kyphosis

The illustration shows how the curvature of the spinal column determines posture, whether correct or incorrect. Abnormal postures such as lordosis and kyphosis are usually the result of laziness, and can interfere with the body's mechanisms for supporting weight. This can cause symptoms, for example, low back pain.

of permanent deformities. In the adult, *postural backache* due to lifting injuries, strain and sitting slouched (especially in poorly designed furniture) is the most common single reason for referral to an orthopedist (a medical expert on disorders of the bones and joints). The spinal ligaments loosen with childbirth, debilitating illness and obesity—particularly in tall individuals, who become prone to pain in the lower part of the back. Postural backache, which is worse on stooping, causes great and often recurrent distress. Treatment typically involves physical therapy (heat, massage and special exercises), manipulation of the lower parts of the spine, or the wearing of an external support (corset).

See also SPINAL CURVATURE and the major article on **Orthopedics**.

Pott's fracture

A fracture-dislocation of the ankle first described in 1769 by Percival Pott (1713–1788), a London surgeon.

POTT'S FRACTURE

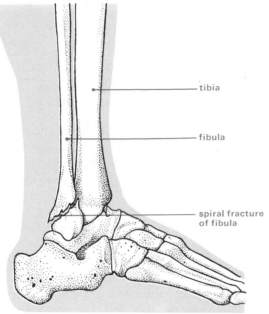

tibia

fibula

spiral fracture of fibula

Pott's fracture results from the foot being twisted violently outwards. The basic injury is a spiral fracture of the fibula, as pictured above, but in addition the inner side of the ankle may be damaged and the bottom of the tibia fractured.

(Pott had sustained such a fracture himself in 1756.) The fracture usually results from the foot being caught while the body is moving forward (for example, during walking or skiing). As a result the foot is twisted outwards, producing a spiral fracture at the lower end of the *fibula* (the bony prominence felt on the outer side of the ankle).

This type of fracture is treated by immobilization in a plaster cast from below the knee to the base of the toes; the cast is usually left in position for about three weeks. However, more severe torsion can pull a flake of bone from the inner side of the ankle and also fracture the bottom of the *tibia,* or "shin bone." In such cases, the bones have to be realigned under anesthesia and sometimes held in place with screws; the plaster cast is then left in position for up to three months.

preeclampsia

A rise in blood pressure during pregnancy, with PROTEINURIA (the abnormal presence of protein in the urine), weight gain and EDEMA. It occurs in some 10% of women, most commonly in young women during their first pregnancies, anytime after the 12th week up to and including labor and the immediate postpartum period.

Placental causes—by secretion or an excess of hormones that provoke hypertension; *immune response causes*—with antibody formation against the fetus or the placenta, thus affecting the kidney; *dietary causes; hormonal causes*, due to excess adrenal gland secretions, and *alterations in blood coagulability* have all been variously blamed; but the underlying mechanism remains unexplained.

Early detection is essential. Routine prenatal care with regular surveillance is the only way to detect and correct the abnormality. Untreated, the progressive rise in blood pressure threatens thrombosis of the placenta, which can lead to its premature separation, death of the fetus, and subsequent hypertensive coma in the mother.

Bed rest is required, in addition to a restriction of salt; antihypertensive drugs may be administered to counteract the rise in blood pressure. In the majority of cases this is successful, preventing *eclampsia* (the flagrant untreated condition); but, in some, premature labor by induction or Cesarean section is necessary. Recurrence in future pregnancies is less than 20%.

pregnancy

Conception, the fertilization of an ovum by a sperm, can occur in a woman from the menarche to the menopause, and takes place in one of the Fallopian tubes. Pregnancy occurs when the fertilized ovum moves down and implants on the wall of the uterine cavity—usually four or five days later; it lasts until labor takes place—on average, 40 weeks later. The initial signs of pregnancy are breast engorgement, blueness of the vagina and absence of the expected period. The early symptoms are nausea and frequency of urination. Tests to confirm the diagnosis are undertaken on a sample of urine to detect the excess of hormones that are only present from the second week after the expected period.

In the first three months the breast signs are the most obvious with enlargement of the areola (the dark ring of tissue surrounding the nipple) and prominence of the sebaceous glands around it. In the fourth month the uterus enlarges to be palpable above the pubis; therafter the abdominal swelling is plainly visible. Fetal movements are felt at this time by a woman experiencing her first pregnancy (20 weeks), a little earlier by those who have previously experienced childbirth. In the eighth month there is a "lightening" as the fetal head descends into the pelvic brim. The onset of labor in the ninth month is announced by a "show" as the mucous plug of the cervix is discharged into the vagina, after contractions of the uterine muscle have been experienced as regular cramplike pains.

The incidence of miscarriage (spontaneous abortion) is high, with as many as 20% of conceptions failing to implant, sustain their growth beyond the next menstrual period, or survive beyond the eighth week. The complications of any pregnancy after the 12th week include PREECLAMPSIA, anemia, premature delivery, and labor abnormalities. Congenital abnormalities have an incidence of one in every hundred live births.

The essence of medical care is the prevention of problems in pregnancy by ensuring, initially, good health in women of reproductive age and their immunization (if required) against diseases such as rubella and polio which can cause fetal abnormality. Antenatal care must be regular, commencing from the first month and involving periodic supervision, comparison of blood pressure, weight, hemoglobin and urinalysis to maintain maternal health. Surveillance of fetal health includes the detection of maternal antibodies to blood-group incompatibility, ultrasound visualization to monitor fetal growth rate, and AMNIOCENTESIS in the event of suspicion of certain fetal abnormalities. Medication for all pregnant women includes iron, vitamins and extra calcium as required, to prevent anemia and maternal deficiency diseases. The normal diet must be rich in protein, fat and vitamins, but controlled in carbohydrate to prevent excessive weight increase.

PREGNANCY

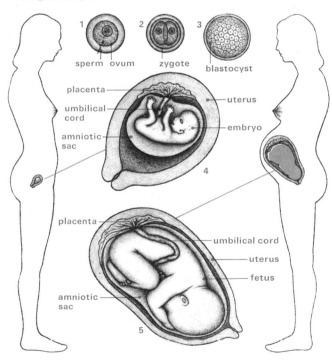

Conception occurs when a sperm fertilizes an ovum (1), and a zygote (2) forms. The zygote divides into many identical cells and becomes a blastocyst (3) which embeds itself in the lining of the uterus. During the first three months the embryo takes shape (4) with the appearance of all its major organs. In the last six months the fetus increases in size dramatically (5).

An average weight gain of 20 lbs. is associated with minimal complications; most of this is put on after the 20th week, but many women experience appetite variations in pregnancy—in particular, bizarre or obsessional tastes in the first three months. Constipation is a frequent problem in the later months, and hemorrhoids may be a complication; both need to be dealt with by dietary advice and appropriate medication.

Fetal position changes frequently in the last three months of pregnancy, but after the 32nd week the head should be entering the pelvis, the body uppermost (*vertex presentation*); safe delivery is compatible with other presentations but more liable to hazards in labor. Backache due to loosening of the ligaments in the last three months is also commonly experienced; but correct posture, exercise and antenatal relaxation goes far to avoid such problems and to prepare the woman for effective labor.

Pregnant women should avoid taking any drugs except under medical supervision, particularly during the first three months.

See also CHILDBIRTH and the major articles on **Pregnancy and Childbirth** and **Obstetrics and Gynecology**.

premature ejaculation

This is a common condition, on occasions, in perfectly normal males who are relatively inexperienced, or have had infrequent coitus and who are excessively stimulated—by accident or design—by their sexual partner.

It is the ejaculation of seminal fluid from the penis prior to the time at which it would have been desired. As such it may be a subjective judgment that it occurs prematurely, for if the achievement of the partner's orgasm is the criterion, then retention and delay of ejaculation will depend on the sexual partner's level of excitation (which is obviously variable).

Control over ejaculation is acquired with experience, though frequently denied initially to the young and inexperienced; but the level of psychic control varies with fatigue, fantasy and drugs such as alcohol. In middle age infrequency of coitus may cause the return of premature ejaculation and lead to sexual difficulties, particularly since with age the male becomes relatively less sexually demanding and the female often more. Masters and Johnson reported premature ejaculation as a problem, at some time, in at least 60% of marriages, and an experience that was common at least on some occasions in all men.

Treatment is necessary when it provokes marital problems and occurs with greater frequency after relative control over ejaculation had been established for some time. Isolated occurrences are compensated for by resumption of intercourse after a period of delay, to achieve a second orgasm; repeated occurrence may lead to *psychic impotence* as a compensation that prevents exposure to the risk, and so treatment becomes essential.

Medication has little to offer. Sexual counseling of both partners is recommended—in particular, instruction in the "squeeze" technique. After erection and just prior to the overwhelming desire to ejaculate the tip of the penis (glans) is firmly compressed—more effectively by the female—by fingers and thumb placed above and below the coronal ridge. This counteracts the reflex of ejaculation and may be repeated periodically when the desire to achieve orgasm returns. Effective control is reestablished in a high percentage of cases where this technique is mutually employed.

See also the major article on **Psychiatry.**

premenstrual tension

The condition of mental tension, irritability, headache, depression and a feeling of "bloatedness," with some evidence of EDEMA, that begins in the week prior to menstruation and resolves completely the day after a menstrual period's flow has begun.

It is a common condition which causes a good deal of distress to those affected by it—which includes women of all ethnic groups. It is *cyclical* in that it may occur before the menarche, after the menopause and even after a hysterectomy. Hormonal origins are the obvious cause, with water and salt retention as the consequence of a hormonal imbalance; but psychogenic causes play their part in initiating a behavioral response to physical changes in the body.

Conditions described as *psychosomatic* have been reported as being exacerbated in the premenstrual period—such as eczema, migraine and allergic responses. Various conditions not clearly associated with the menstrual cycle can also occur, such as admissions to psychiatric hospitals, suicides, accidents and misbehavior in schools—which are found to occur more frequently in the premenstrual period.

In severe cases, treatment is often effective with hormonal supplements of the progesterone type, with the initiation of anovulatory cycles by use of the oral contraceptive pill and with diuretics ("water pills") taken for the immediate premenstrual period.

priapism

When the penis remains erect, is painful, and despite the conclusion of sexual excitement does not subside, priapism exists. The erection may have occurred and been sustained without sexual excitement. The cause of priapism is most often THROMBOSIS in the veins of the prostate gland. It may occur as a result of leukemia or sickle cell anemia, and secondary deposits of cancer in the corpora cavernosa of the penis—leading to obstruction and thus unrelieved venous engorgement—may be responsible. Spinal injury and brain injury may lead to priapism due to interference with neurological control.

Anticoagulant therapy and sedation will often resolve the condition.

prickly heat

Another name for MILIARIA.

proctitis

Inflammation in the region of the anus or rectum.

There are a variety of causes of proctitis, but one which is causing particular concern to public health officials is that arising from GONORRHEA. This is a self-limited inflammatory disease of the rectum caused by infection with the gonococcus, leading to severe rectal burning and itching; it usually lasts less than a month. The condition is now more common than it used to be among male homosexuals, but it is also found in women with gonorrhea.

Treatment is aimed at relief of symptoms such as pain and itching. The gonorrheal form does not appear to respond to treatment, naturally regressing in most cases, but forms due to other organisms will be affected by antibiotic or steroid treatment in varying degrees. Constipation should be avoided as far as possible in patients with any form of proctitis. The affected area should be washed regularly and care taken to avoid harsh abrasion.

progesterone

Of the two major types of female sex hormones secreted by the ovary, progesterone is the main one of the progestogen group.

During the menstrual cycle, progesterone—in combination with estrogens—is secreted by the corpus luteum, which develops in the ovarian follicle after *ovulation*, and the decline of both hormones is associated with the onset of menstruation. Progesterone, like estrogen, thus maintains the uterus in a state of receptivity for the implantation of a fertilized ovum.

In early pregnancy the corpus luteum secretes progesterone, as does the developing placenta. Initially the greatest quantity comes from the corpus luteum, but by the tenth week of pregnancy placental secretion is fully established and rises steadily as pregnancy advances.

See also HORMONES and the major article on **Endocrinology.**

progestin

The name originally given to the crude hormone of the corpus luteum (which develops in the empty ovarian follicle after OVULATION) now known as progesterone. The function of this hormone is to prepare the uterus for the reception and development of the fertilized ovum by inducing secretion in proliferated glands.

The term progestin is now applied generally to *progestational agents*, a group of hormones secreted by the corpora lutea and the placenta. It is the synthetic analogues of these hormones that are the basis of the ovulation-inhibiting effect of the oral contraceptives.

Progestational agents are combined with estrogen to give the best protection from conception, together with the minimum of side effects such as breakthrough bleeding.

prognosis

A prediction regarding the likely course and outcome of a disease, disorder, etc., especially one based on the judgment of the attending physician.

prolapse

The "falling down" of any organ: usually applied to the uterus (womb) and the rectum.

Prolapse of the uterus is relatively common, particularly in elderly women. It is associated with the increasing lack of tone of the muscles and other supportive structures in the pelvic area in later life. This is often caused by injury to or overstretching of the pelvic floor in childbirth. Injury to the perineum (the bottom of the trunk of the body) and the vagina may contribute to the prolapse.

Prolapse of the "first degree" implies the presence of the cervix (neck of the womb) at the vaginal opening. In "second degree" prolapse the cervix protrudes through the vaginal opening; in "third degree" prolapse the entire uterus protrudes through the vaginal opening. In some cases no symptoms exist apart from the mechanical discomfort of the movement of the uterus; but there may be some feeling of "bearing down" or heaviness in the lower part of the abdomen and back.

Treatment is ideally by surgery in many cases. The laxness in the ligaments and muscles is taken up and the uterus replaced in its proper position. In women past childbearing age the more radical operation of removal of the uterus (hysterectomy) may be preferred. Another form of treatment in elderly women or those who are poor operative risks is the insertion of a hard rubber ring to take up the slack in the vagina and to support the neck of the womb.

In *prolapse of the rectum*, all the layers of the rectal wall may protrude through the anal opening, in which case it is called "complete prolapse." If only the mucous membrane protrudes it is known as a "partial prolapse." The latter is much more common, especially in old age. The protrusion is rarely more than one inch long.

Complete prolapse, which may contain coils of small intestine, is approximately six times more common in women than in men and is associated with repeated pregnancies and consequent weakening of the pelvic floor. Any condition that leads to straining at stool may lead to prolapse; these include chronic constipation and threadworm infection, but the most common cause is hemorrhoids ("piles"). Again, surgical treatment is necessary if the prolapse is not to recur. Attention must also be given to the predisposing causes.

prophylaxis

Prevention of disease or various measures which prevent the development and spread of disease.

proptosis

Abnormal protrusion of the eyeball. It may be bilateral or unilateral.

One-sided proptosis may be caused by inflammation within the orbit (the bony cavity that houses the eye), usually consequent upon infection of the air sinuses or puncture wounds of the tissue around the eye. There is pain, paralysis of the eye muscles, protrusion of the eyeball, malaise (a general feeling of being unwell) and fever. Treatment involves the administration of appropriate antibiotics.

Another cause of unilateral proptosis is the development of a tumor in the orbit. Dermoid cysts, meningiomas and tumors of the optic nerve may be implicated, as may tumors arising in the nasopharynx.

Proptosis is a feature of *thyrotoxicosis;* it may be present on one side or both. In this form of exophthalmos the white of the eye is exposed above the pupil, especially on looking downward. The cause is not known, but microscopy shows the tissues behind the eye to be edematous and fatty, often infiltrated by lymphocytes and leukocytes. In most cases of exophthalmos associated with thyrotoxicosis (*exophthalmic goiter*) the condition develops slowly and is relatively mild, but there are cases of sudden onset and rapid progression— known as *malignant exophthalmos*. This is accompanied by paralysis of the extrinsic muscles of the eye giving rise to double vision, with inflammation and swelling of the conjunctiva and swelling of the tissues around the orbit. It may become impossible to close the eyelids properly, so that the cornea is liable to become damaged and scarred. Treatment of the thyrotoxicosis in cases of exophthalmic goiter does not necessarily improve the condition; it may be advisable to close the eyelids by surgical operation in order to protect the cornea.

In all cases of exophthalmos of any degree of severity the operation of *orbital decompression*, in which the bone of the orbit is removed, may be necessary in order to preserve the eyeball and restore eye movement.

prostaglandins

Seminal fluid (semen) contains lipid-soluble substances which cause smooth muscle fibers to contract. When they were first isolated the active principles were called prostaglandins, from their origin. Since that time they have been found in many other tissues in the body, so that the name is to a certain extent misleading.

Prostaglandins stimulate smooth muscle, change the heart rate, affect the motility of the intestine, influence blood pressure, and cause the uterus to contract. They have been used to promote abortion in the first weeks of pregnancy. They also act upon hormones, antagonizing the action of epinephrine, glucagon, vasopressin and ACTH; it seems that they play a part in metabolic processes. They alter the stickiness of the blood platelets and prevent clotting in arteries.

So far over 20 different prostaglandins have been isolated, and research in the field is active. Among their possible uses, beside their use to induce abortion or labor at term, may be an application in depressing male fertility which could make a male contraceptive pill practical.

prostatectomy

Surgical removal of part or the whole of the prostate gland, which in men surrounds the urethra as it leaves the bladder.

Because of its position, enlargement of the prostate leads to difficulty in passing urine and ultimately to complete urinary obstruction. There are two common causes of prostatic enlargement; simple hypertrophy (or overgrowth) of the gland and the development of cancer.

Simple hypertrophy of the prostate is a complication of later life, which most commonly develops between the ages of 60 to 90. About 80% of men over the age of 80 suffer from its effects to some degree. The cause is unknown, but it never occurs in those who have been castrated. At first there may be difficulty in starting to urinate and increased frequency; later, as a result of congestion, the urethra may be completely blocked and urination becomes impossible. This is the state of acute retention. In some cases the process stops short of complete blockage, but as the patient finds it progressively harder to empty the bladder completely, it gradually distends and more urine remains in it after the patient urinates—thus producing the state of chronic urinary retention.

Similar symptoms are caused by cancer of the prostate. Diagnosis between the two is made by physical examination and by blood tests. Both causes of obstruction are dealt with first by catheterization.

If the enlargement of the prostate is benign, the surgeon will (if the physical state of the patient permits) proceed to remove the gland—either through the abdominal wall, which makes it easier to be sure that the gland has been removed entirely, or through an instrument passed into the urethra.

In cases of cancer many surgeons prefer to try to reduce the enlargement by the administration of estrogens, for the tumor is hormone-dependent. If difficulty in urination persists it may be necessary to performs a *transurethral prostatectomy*.

Cancer of the prostate is the third most common cancer in men, exceeded only by cancer of the lung and cancer of the large intestine.

prostatitis

Inflammation of the prostate gland.

The prostate can become inflamed for a variety of reasons, sometimes in association with the hyperplasia (excessive proliferation of normal cells) of the gland

PROSTATE GLAND

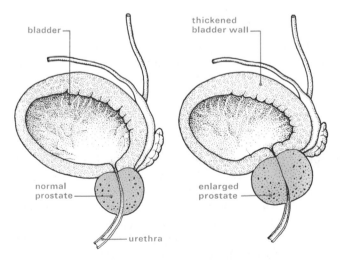

Some degree of prostatic enlargement is extremely common in men over the age of 45. In most cases it causes either no or only minor symptoms, but urination may be difficult because the urethra is obstructed. The bladder wall becomes thickened in its attempts to force urine past the obstruction, and there is also damaging back-pressure on the kidneys.

which occurs with increasing frequency among men over the age of 40. Many cases are nonspecific in the sense that there is no known cause although some follow infection with gonorrhea. Patients complain of slight fever and pain in the perineum (the area between the thighs) and in the lower part of the back.

While the probable infecting organism may be identified, the success rate for eliminating prostatic bacteria is low because antibiotics have difficulty in reaching the tissues of the gland.

Nonspecific granulomatous prostatitis is thought to be a severe reaction to the gland's own secretion which is retained. *Eosinophilic prostatitis* is a rare variation of the disease which is associated with bronchial asthma. A disease known as *malacoplakia* (often associated with a bacterial infection) is usually found in the urinary tract but also in the prostate. Other forms of prostatitis are associated with tuberculosis of the urinary tract, schistosomiasis (bilharziasis) and malignant disease.

Treatment involves drinking large quantities of liquids and emptying the bladder frequently and completely. It may be necessary for the patient to follow a course of antibiotics for many months to neutralize the organisms as they escape into the urethra.

See also the major article on **Urology.**

prosthesis

Any device used to replace a part, organ, or limb, usually taking over all or part of its function.

The most common prosthetic device (and the only one which the vast majority of the population are likely to need) is the *artificial denture* ("false teeth" or a "false tooth"). More than 50% of the American population over the age of 50 have dentures of some sort, either complete or partial, or have had teeth crowned.

The design of *artificial limbs* has been much improved in recent years. At one time an artificial leg was little better than the old-fashioned wooden leg; but the use of lightweight materials and improvements in articulation (joint movement) have now made it possible for amputees to pass undetected in company. The most recent advance is the development of artificial limbs which are controlled by nerve impulses fed from the stump of the natural arm. These prostheses look like a normal limb, and their internal power systems enable the user to pick up and manipulate objects.

A third common use of prostheses is in the treatment of ARTHRITIS. Replacement of the hip joint in cases of both rheumatoid arthritis and osteoarthritis is now commonplace, using stainless steel and plastic materials. As a result of the success of this type of operation, surgeons have gone on to design elbow, knee, shoulder, and finger joints which are now implanted in the hands of many patients with severe arthritis.

One of the most common reasons for open-heart surgery is the implantation of artificial valves in the hearts of patients whose valves are distorted or damaged from conditions such as RHEUMATIC HEART DISEASE.

Other prostheses in current use include acrylic lenses to replace those affected by CATARACT and artificial eyes, whose purpose is entirely cosmetic. An artificial larynx ("voice-box") is still under trial, and attempts are being made to miniaturize an artificial pancreas for use by diabetics. In the case of many complex internal organs, however, TRANSPLANTATION has so far proved more practicable than the development of mechanical prostheses.

proteinuria

A condition in which protein is present in the urine. Proteinuria is sometimes also known as ALBUMINURIA. This is not exactly correct, however, since both the blood proteins (globulin as well as albumin) may be present in the urine in this condition.

Presence of the proteins is often a symptom of serious disease of the kidney or heart. The detection of albumin in the urine may, in fact, be the earliest and most conclusive evidence of kidney disease. Heart failure leads to proteinuria as a result of the accompanying congestion of the kidneys. Patients are treated for the underlying disease.

prothrombin

A constituent of normal blood plasma which is essential for the clotting of blood.

prurigo

A chronic inflammatory eruption of the skin which is usually characterized by the formation of small whitish papules (small, solid, circumscribed elevations of the skin) accompanied by severe itching.

The eruptions characteristically begin early in life. There are two main forms: *prurigo mitis* (which is comparatively mild) and *prurigo agria* (which is severe). The condition may be permanent or it may come and go. In young children the nonpermanent form may be associated with problems of teething. The papules, which are deeply seated, are most prominent on the extensor surfaces of the limbs.

Summer prurigo is another name for *hydroa vacciniforme*, a skin disease usually affecting adolescent boys and young men; it appears in the summer on exposed parts of the body and fades in the winter. It is characterized by the formation of ulcers (on which crust may appear) and by vesicles. Following the onset of puberty, this disease gradually disappears.

pruritus ani/pruritus vulvae

An intractable itching in the region of the anus (*pruritus ani*) or the vulva (*pruritus vulvae*).

Pruritus ani is usually found in men and is quite common. It can be intensely irritating and should be treated if it reaches the point of acute discomfort. The first line of treatment is to find the cause of the pruritus and if possible remove it. One common cause is parasites, particularly PINWORMS, which lay their eggs around the anus and so cause itching. CANDIDA (thrush) infections also cause itching and invasion by yeasts can be another cause.

Both lack of cleanliness and excessive sweating can contribute, and the latter may be due to unsuitable underclothes which prevent proper evaporation. In the past woolen underwear was to blame, but now in many cases it is nylon and other synthetic fibers which are the cause of pruritus. A patient may also be sitting for long periods on plastic seats, either at home or at work, which would not give sufficient ventilation.

Some pruritus is undoubtedly caused by garments having been washed in harsh detergents; the enzyme detergents have been said to have been involved in some cases.

Discharges from the anus or the vagina, as in HEMORRHOIDS (piles) or VAGINITIS, can be a potent cause of itching.

Pruritus vulvae has similar causes, complicated by the fungus and yeast infections that the vagina is prone to, while the modern habit of wearing panty hose made of nylon has exacerbated the problem.

Patients should pay particular attention to personal hygiene. After the use of the toilet the perianal region should be cleaned with damp cotton wool and then dried. It is advisable for patients to avoid the use of detergents in washing their clothes, taking care to wash them only in soap powder. Underwear of synthetic material should be avoided, and cellular cotton garments substituted. Panty hose should be ruled out and patients should be encouraged to avoid plastic seats and sit on a sheepskin rug or something similar.

Calamine lotion is effective in soothing the itching and keeping the area dry. In cases of thrush infections, special ointments can be used. Some cases of pruritus ani and pruritus vulvae are psychological in origin and tranquilizers may be effective.

psittacosis

A disease (also known as *ornithosis* or *parrot fever*) caused by a strain of the microorganism known as *Chlamydia psittaci*, transmitted to humans by a variety of birds. It was first detected in parrots, thus the name—which is based on the Greek word for parrot. But it is now known that several species of birds harbor the microorganisms and can pass them on to man.

In man the disease usually takes the form of a pneumonia, with fever, cough and perhaps an enlarged spleen. It has been compared with typhoid in its manifestations, and may cause hepatitis, myocarditis, delirium and coma.

Domestic fowl have been implicated in outbreaks, and other birds involved include pigeons, parakeets, budgerigars, ducks, turkeys, pheasants and chickens. The organism is sensitive to tetracycline.

psoriasis

A skin disease, believed to result from a disturbance in skin enzymes, which affects between 1–2% of the population. The disease is associated with an increased turnover of epidermal cells and a dilation of the dermal capillaries. Some sufferers also have a form of arthritis and the skin lesions may be precipitated by mental stress.

Psoriasis is not contagious and the skin lesions can vary enormously. They can include chronic scaling plaques, ringed lesions, smooth red areas, acute pustules and droplike (guttate) lesions. Most often the condition becomes apparent for the first time in adolescence, but it is sometimes delayed until old age.

Oral corticosteroids are used to treat only two forms of the disease, those of severe *erythrodermic* or *generalized pustular* types. These should be treated in the hospital. In ordinary cases, a powerful peeling agent can be used to remove encrusted scales; the same agents, used with ultraviolet light and tar baths, can remove

PSORIASIS

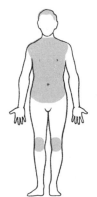

The center picture shows the characteristic skin changes in psoriasis—a clearly defined, red, raised plaque topped by silvery scales. These plaques are usually present over the elbows, knees and scalp, but may spread more extensively to involve the trunk and hands as illustrated here.

chronic thickened psoriatic plaques. Topical steroid creams and ointments can also be used, and antifungal agents applied if fungal infection supervenes.

Special therapy involving a mixture of coal tar and oils may be necessary to deal with thick psoriatic crusts on the scalp and betamethason lotion is useful. The face may be treated with an ointment of coal tar and salicyclic acid, coal tar treatment sometimes being combined with exposure to ultraviolet light or sunlight. The drug methotrexate (a cytotoxic preparation) has been used by mouth to control exacerbations of the disease.

Psoriatic patients often need support from their families and their family physicians, as the chronic nature and unsightly appearance of their lesions can cause depression. There is now some ground for encouraging patients with the idea that although the cause of psoriasis is still unknown, many of the symptoms can be alleviated by new methods of treatment. The complex biochemistry of the reaction may yield up its secrets to concentrated research in due course.

See also the major article on **Dermatology.**

psychiatry

The study and treatment of mental disturbances of all kinds.

At least 1% of any population is suffering at any one time from some form of mental disorder, and an estimated 10% will need treatment at some time in their lives. During the 20th century, classification of mental abnormalities has become more scientific and psychiatry has developed methods of treating them—ranging from chemotherapy to psychosurgery and from psychotherapy and psychoanalysis to electroconvulsive therapy.

Nowadays, although psychiatry set out in the modern era to deal with the psychoses (such as schizophrenia and manic-depressive illness), psychiatrists spend a great amount of their time dealing with neurotic patients, together with addicts and other "deviants." The environmental stresses of life are great enough in a significant minority of any population to cause anxiety, depression and behavioral disorders in patients who are not psychotic (that is, who do not suffer from serious mental disturbances).

Psychiatry has evolved into many groups whose rationale and methods are often mutually contradictory. It can be said in general that at one extreme are the psychiatrists who try to modify the behavior of their patients by altering their body chemistry, while at the other it is postulated that psychotherapy without drugs is the most likely course to be successful. In practice, few psychiatrists adopt an extreme position; a psycho-therapist, for example, will often prescribe tranquilizers to lower a patient's level of anxiety.

Psychiatrists are all medically qualified doctors, although there is nowadays a school of thought that maintains that a full medical training is unnecessary. In the United States there has already been some reduction in the amount of medical training required by a qualified psychiatrist, and the trend may be toward an even greater specialization.

See also the major article on **Psychiatry.**

psychoanalysis

The system of analyzing emotional patterns and developments in patients devised by Sigmund Freud (1856–1939), used to bring out valuable information from the unconscious mind and so make it available to manipulation by the conscious mind.

Psychoanalysis is now a widely accepted method of treating emotional disorders such as neuroses. Essentially, it consists of allowing the patient, usually lying on a couch to relax mind and body, to give free expression to his thoughts, ideas and fantasies. The analyst meanwhile adopts a neutral attitude, not making any judgment on anything that he is told, but encouraging the flow of words.

The object is to persuade the patient to go further and further back into his childhood and reenact his early emotional attitudes. It is hoped in this phase to release various infantile emotional tensions which, according to Freud's theories, can affect the whole of one's emotional development. Theoretically, once enlightenment about the cause of one's mental symptoms has been reached (such as hatred of one's father or guilt about sex), the symptoms should be relieved. Freud's theories were based on the concept that much of our later development is based on the experience of the first five years of life, thus the interest in the earliest memories.

The psychoanalytic theory is based on a threefold division of the human personality: the *id*, the *ego* and the *superego*. The *id* is the "instinctual self" which is concerned with the immediate discharge of energy or tension; the *ego* regulates the interactions of the person with his environment; and the *superego* is the "superior being" representing the moral aspects of personality or "conscience."

Freud postulated that there are two great groups of instincts that provide energy for the id. The first, serving the purposes of life, provide the energy known as *libido*. According to Freud, all activities of the mind are driven by the need to reduce or eliminate the tension caused by the painful impact of the life instincts. The second group of instincts, such as aggression, sadism, masochism and the urge to suicide, are in the service of *death*.

To protect itself from anxiety, the Freudian ego

develops many defense mechanisms and it is the task of psychoanalysis to break down the barriers that conceal these mechanisms, which often cripple the personality. However, one should point out that treatment is lengthy and very expensive, and overall results have not been particularly good—especially in comparison with the therapeutic usefulness of several new psychoactive drugs. Finally, it should also be noted that whereas Freud got the ball rolling, his theories have been greatly modified, and a whole subsequent superstructure of analytic theory is now in use.

See also the major article on **Psychotherapy.**

psychoses

Mental disorders of a severe kind in which there is an extensive disorder of the personality. They are usually more severe and more disabling than other psychiatric syndromes and are often accompanied by an inability to cope with reality.

One of the main psychoses is SCHIZOPHRENIA, a description given to a group of illnesses marked mainly by disordered thought processes. By-products of this disorder include difficulty in communication and in interpersonal relationships. About 25% of all admissions to state mental hospitals are for schizophrenia; since it is a chronic condition, schizophrenics make up about 50% of the hospitals' resident population. It is the major public health problem in advanced societies.

Affective disorders are those psychoses in which the main symptom is a severe disorder of mood. They include *involutional melancholia*, which is a major mental illness usually having its onset in women aged 45 to 55 and men aged 50 to 65. The main symptom is agitated depression and suicide is a real risk. Therapy commonly involves electric shock treatment and the administration of monoamine oxidase (MAO) inhibitors.

Outgoing, sociable people are at risk from *manic-depressive illness*, in which severe depression alternates with elation. PARANOIA is a term applied to a group of psychoses in which there are delusions of grandeur or of persecution, and which often respond to psychotherapy.

See the major article on **Psychiatry.**

psychosomatic illnesses

Disorders with physical symptoms that are thought to be caused by emotional factors. When modern medicine first began to evolve, developments led to an early belief that illness was mainly, if not entirely, physical in origin. With greater understanding of disease processes, it is now realized that the body (or *soma*) and the mind (or *psyche*) are intimately linked in ways that can lead to a wide variety of illnesses.

When a person is put under stress he may react *normally*, *neurotically* (when his defense against the stress becomes ineffective), or *psychotically* (when the alarm is misconceived or ignored). The fourth possibility is that he may react in a "psychophysiologic" way—the alert is translated into an effect on somatic systems, causing changes in body tissues (*blushing* is a simple example of how the emotions can have a physical manifestation). What is happening is that the physical changes are normal for the emotional states involved, but they are either too sustained or too intense. The individual may not be consciously aware of his emotional state.

An example which is widely known is the peptic ulcer. Tension in work or home can produce or exacerbate ulcers, although it is now believed that ulcer patients may also be genetically predisposed to the complaint by a chromosomal fault (which gives them too little of an enzyme which is necessary for a healthy stomach). Stress can be caused by such opposites as success and failure, puberty and aging, parenthood and conflict. Suppression of anxiety or rage may lead to cardiovascular problems and to "vascular headache."

Irritable colon (see IRRITABLE BOWEL SYNDROME) is now regarded as psychosomatic, but in these cases as well there may be a congenitally high sensitivity to parasympathetic stimulation. ULCERATIVE COLITIS, too, is a disease triggered by "psychic insult" in people who are often described as neat, orderly, punctual, conscientious and conforming. Asthma is a general description for a group of respiratory disorders, some of which are certainly psychosomatic in origin.

In general it may be said that some individuals seem to be predisposed by the nature of their personality structure to react to a difficult life situation which threatens their security not by adequate action but by emotional conflict. If the conflict is not discharged by action or speech, it persists and can create a state of acute or chronic emotional tension which seeks another outlet and leads to physical symptoms.

psychosurgery

Surgery of the brain designed to cure or alleviate symptoms of severe mental illness.

While "psychosurgery" is the generic term it is in effect a synonym for the main operation, *lobotomy*, in which the surgeon severs the connection between the frontal lobes and the rest of the brain.

There has been a great deal of controversy on the subject of psychosurgery. Some authorities maintain that it is unnecessary, ineffective and inimical to the civil rights of the patient. Advocates of psychosurgery maintain that in cases of very severe incapacitation lobotomy is the only treatment which brings relief.

On average, patients who undergo lobotomy have been incapacitated for ten years with intractable depression, anxiety and obsessional neurosis. Some have made suicide attempts. Psychosurgery is employed according to the supporters of the procedure only after other methods of treatment have failed to bring about any improvement over a long period, and only with the full and informed consent of the patient.

At one time the operation was done "freehand" by the surgeon, which had the disadvantage that the lesions which were produced were not always the same. Therefore the outcome could not be predicted on any organized basis.

Nowadays the *stereotactic* approach is employed. Orderly measurements of the connexions between the frontal lobes and the rest of the brain are taken by means of x-rays, thus locating the "target" area in three dimensions. Electrocoagulation is then brought about by the introduction of a thin probe into the brain, or radioactive "seeds" are planted to produce the same effect.

Except for removing brain tumors that are responsible for some forms of epileptic attacks (e.g. *temporal lobe epilepsy*), psychosurgery in any form is becoming an outmoded therapeutic approach.

psychotherapy

A method of treating a psychiatric disorder based mainly on verbal communication between the therapist and his patient.

The object is to cure or alleviate the symptoms of the disorder by making the emotionally disturbed patient feel better or helping him to learn to live more effectively. A feature of many types of psychotherapy is the patient's relief at being able to talk to a noncritical listener. Apart from being able to obtain relief through "confession," the patient may be able to experience the emotional discharge known as *abreaction* by recalling significant incidents and sensations that had been forgotten or repressed. It is also possible through psychotherapy to "desensitize" a patient by referring repeatedly to a disturbing topic and to clarify his own feelings by exploring them. Psychotherapy also relieves many patients of the burden of loneliness.

The role of the therapist is often to interpret and explain to the patient reasons for recurring patterns of behavior and so clear the way for an improvement in the patient's interactions with the environment and with others. Psychotherapy, which is normally carried out on the basis of weekly interviews, embraces PSYCHO-ANALYSIS, HYPNOSIS, hypnotherapy, conditioning and aversion therapy. *Group therapy*, while enabling patients to develop skills in interacting with others, and overcoming feelings of isolation and alienation, has the disadvantage of lack of confidentiality. It also leads to less individual attention being given to patients; but it is, nevertheless, a popular and growing form of psychotherapy. It has one sterling advantage—it is within the financial means of many patients.

See also the major article on **Psychotherapy.**

pterygium

A degenerative condition of the eye in which a triangular area of fleshy conjunctiva, usually on the nasal side, extends across the eye and on to the cornea. The base is toward the nose and the apex of the triangle toward the pupil. The apex is immovably united to the cornea, while it is firmly attached to the sclera throughout its middle portion, and merges with the conjunctiva at its base.

Pterygium is particularly common in windy, dusty climates, and it is believed that the degeneration takes place as a result of continual bombardment of the eye by dust particles.

The condition causes no known medical problems, but eye surgeons often remove the pterygium for cosmetic reasons as it is unsightly.

ptosis

Prolapse or drooping of an organ, often used to describe the drooping of an upper eyelid.

Paralysis of the third cranial nerve causes this condition in many cases, which may be congenital or acquired.

Ptosis adiposa is drooping of the eyelid caused by orbital fat coming forward into the lid owing to its atrophic (wasting) condition. In young children, *congenital ptosis* is due to malformation of the levator palpebrae superioris muscle, or to a defective nerve supply to the muscle. *Hysterical ptosis* is a drooping of the eyelid caused by a spasm of the orbicularis oculi muscle. *Mechanical ptosis* is due to the thickening and consequent increase of the weight of the upper eyelid which arises in diseases such as trachoma.

A fairly common experience is *waking* (or *morning*) *ptosis*, in which difficulty is found in raising an upper eyelid. This may be due to an early stage of *keratoconjunctivitis sicca*. In elderly people the condition is often caused by loss of orbital fat and lack of tone in the levator palpebrae superioris muscle. In some cases of trauma, particularly where the skull is fractured (as in automobile accidents), the levator muscle may be damaged and subsequently be unable to control the eyelid correctly. It is possible to correct the condition surgically, to some extent, by resecting the levator muscle; but the eye surgeon has to be careful not to raise the eyelid so high that the eye cannot be closed, and also to make it match the other lid as closely as possible.

puerperal fever

Blood poisoning (septicemia) caused by bacterial infection of the genital tract shortly after childbirth. The disease is also known as *puerperal sepsis* or *childbed fever*.

In the mid-19th century, deaths from puerperal fever were so common that women were afraid to have their babies in the hospital. The high death rates dropped sharply when doctors realized that they were caused by attendants carrying the infection from one patient to another. Strict observance of the rules of hygiene and the use of antiseptics greatly improved survival rates, but childbed fever remained a source of anxiety until the discovery of sulfonamides.

The raw surface of the womb left after separation of the placenta provides ideal circumstances for the growth of bacteria, and in puerperal fever the wound is colonized by *streptococci*, bacteria commonly found in the nose and throat of healthy persons. Nowadays any woman whose temperature rises above 100°F (38°C) in the 14 days after delivery will be treated with appropriate antibiotics. Septicemia after childbirth has become extremely rare.

pulmonary diseases

The exchange of gases between the air and the blood occurs in the lungs; oxygen is absorbed and carbon dioxide excreted. The process is essential for life.

Inspired air passes down into the lungs through the windpipe (trachea), which branches into right and left main bronchi and then divides into even smaller branches until the smallest (bronchioles) end in minute air sacs (alveoli), whose walls are one cell thick and in direct contact with the capillary blood vessels. Through the walls of the alveoli gaseous exchange takes place.

Disease can affect any of these structures and interfere with their vital functions.

An early sign of a lung problem is persistent coughing, which may be dry and irritating in the early stages and later produce sputum. The sputum may be stained with blood (hemoptysis), or may be clear, yellow, or greenish—according to the nature of the disease. Pain may occur on breathing because the membranes covering the lungs (the pleura) may be inflamed. Interference with the respiratory function of the lungs may produce breathlessness.

Diseases affecting the lungs are usually inflammatory infections or new growths. Infections may be viral or bacterial; not infrequently, virus infections such as influenza or measles are followed by a secondary bacterial infection. Inflammation of the air passages (bronchi) is called BRONCHITIS; inflammation of the substance of the lung is PNEUMONIA.

Because the air we breathe in cities is far from clean, the bronchi are subjected to continual irritation—which is worse in those who work in dusty surroundings or who smoke. It would appear that the worse the pollution of the air becomes the greater is the incidence of lung cancer.

Certain substances are more likely to produce malignant growths than others, among them being the tar contained in cigarette smoke. Continual smoking or exposure to polluted air, combined with liability to virus infections, often causes chronic bronchitis, which may proceed in time to EMPHYSEMA—a condition in which there is dilation and loss of function of the alveoli (air sacs of the lungs). This may also be found in association with ASTHMA, a disease of complex causation producing spasm of the air passages.

THE LUNGS

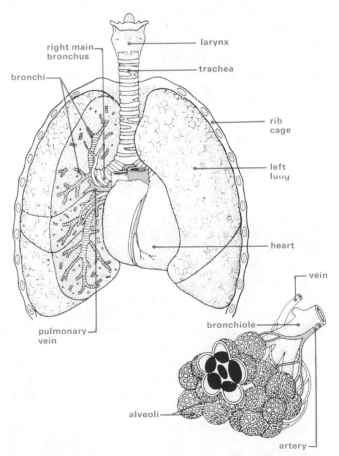

RESPIRATORY UNIT OF LUNG

The lungs are delicate and complex organs; their function is to allow oxygen to enter the bloodstream and to remove carbon dioxide. Respiration is impaired either when the bronchi are obstructed (for example by foreign bodies, cancer or inflammation) or the alveoli are diseased (emphysema, pneumonia or fibrosis).

Although cancer of the lung has become the most common form of cancer in men, two other lung diseases are now far less dangerous than formerly; pneumonia is usually susceptible to treatment with antibiotics, and so is tuberculosis.

See also the major article on **Pulmonary Diseases.**

pulmonary embolism

Blockage of one of the pulmonary arteries (those which take blood from the heart to the lungs) by a clot of blood, a clump of fat, or any other solid object. If one of the main pulmonary arteries is blocked the result may be collapse and sudden death. Less severe episodes of pulmonary embolism commonly cause chest pain associated with shortness of breath and the coughing up of bloodstained sputum.

By far the most common cause of pulmonary embolism is a blood clot carried by the bloodstream into the lungs from one of the veins in the legs. Blood clots are most likely to form in these veins as a result of prolonged bed rest or immobility; *venous thrombosis* in the calves and thighs occurs in as many as one third of all patients who have an operation under general anesthesia. The thrombus or clot goes unnoticed by the patient and eventually dissolves, but it may remain in the legs, causing localized pain and swelling, or (very occasionally) a fragment of the clot may become detached (at which point it is known as an *embolus*) and be swept up through the veins into the heart and so into the lungs.

Other sources of pulmonary embolism include fat globules after injuries causing bone fractures, and the formation of blood clots inside the heart after a coronary thrombosis ("heart attack").

Major pulmonary embolism is a medical emergency. Sometimes an immediate operation may be performed to remove the blood clot; more commonly treatment is given with anticoagulant drugs to prevent extension of the clot. The most effective treatment is preventive, and many surgeons now use anticoagulant drugs such as heparin as a routine to reduce the risk of venous thrombosis and pulmonary embolism in the postoperative period.

See also EMBOLISM/EMBOLUS.

pulpitis

Inflammation of the dental pulp (the soft vascular part in the center of a tooth). It may be *open* or *closed*, and there may be a number of causes, but in the main it is associated with dental caries ("cavities"). In *closed pulpitis*, where there is no break in the surrounding dentin, considerable pain may be experienced. *Open pulpitis* occurs when dental caries leads to a break in the dentin and exposure of the pulp, to which bacteria are attracted by local irritation.

Hyperplastic pulpitis is distinguished by exuberant proliferation of chronically inflamed dental pulp. It appears as a soft pink insensitive mass, which pushes through an aperture in the wall of the pulp cavity into a carious cavity.

Treatment involves correction of the underlying caries after first controlling any infection by appropriate antibiotics.

See also the major article on **Dentistry.**

pulse

The palpable and sometimes visible change in arterial pressure caused by the pumping action of the heart.

When the heart contracts, pumping blood through the arterial system, the arteries expand slightly during the increased blood flow. It is this periodic expansion which is felt when a finger is placed on an artery close to the skin surface. Normally, the *radial artery* (in the wrist) is used to take the pulse, but several others in the body and the limbs may also be used.

The pulse is a useful indicator of several aspects of health, disease and injury. It is usually said that the "normal" pulse rate is about 72 per minute, but in healthy individuals at rest it can vary anywhere between 50 and 100. While undergoing severe exercise, or while under mental stress, the pulse rate can go far above this range (even above 200) without harm.

The pulse rate is quicker in children than in adults and slows down progressively throughout life. When a patient is suffering from a fever the pulse rate is usually elevated. The absence of perceptible pulse is not a definite sign of death; a person suffering from disease or injuries may exhibit no pulse, and this startling fact does not always mean that the heart has stopped beating. Patients with heart disease often exhibit irregular pulse rhythms; irregularities and variations are a diagnostic aid in diseases of the heart and the arteries.

See also BLOOD PRESSURE.

purpura

A condition in which tiny red or purple spots appear on the surface of the skin, in mucous membranes and elsewhere, due to the escape of blood from the vessels.

Purpura appears either when the capillaries become more permeable or when there is a shortage of blood platelets, which normally seal off damage to the walls of the capillaries.

A variety of diseases and conditions cause purpura. It may follow an infection such as scarlet fever; it sometimes appears in wasting diseases; and it can be caused by toxic drugs or malnutrition. In addition, the signs and symptoms occur in what is known as *thrombocytopenic purpura*, when there is a shortage of platelets (THROMBOCYTOPENIA), and in *anaphylactoid purpura*, which is thought to be associated with an allergic reaction. *Henoch's purpura* is a form of allergic reaction in the walls of the intestine, and *Schönlein's purpura* is a form that affects the joints of young adults.

The symptoms of purpura are usually feverishness and lassitude, followed by characteristic spots on the trunk and limbs. The spots may change color from red to purple until they are nearly black, and finally disappear in much the same way as a bruise. The most serious form is *purpura hemorrhagica*, in which bleeding occurs from mucous surfaces in the nose and also in the mouth, digestive organs and womb, and may be fatal. Thrombocytopenic purpura responds to steroid drugs, but in some cases surgical removal of the spleen (splenectomy) may be necessary. Where purpura follows infection or other disease, treatment is directed at the underlying condition.

pus

A yellowish or creamy white collection of viscid fluid that often forms at the site of a wound or infection. It contains normal and damaged white blood cells and other cellular debris.

pyelitis

Inflammation of the pelvis of a kidney—the funnel-shaped expansion which collects urine formed in the nephrons and conveys it to the ureter (the passage from each kidney leading to the bladder).

Pyelitis alone is extremely uncommon, since almost invariably the main body (or *parenchyma*) of the kidney is also infected. Inflammation of both the pelvis and the parenchyma of the kidney is known as PYELONEPHRITIS. The term pyelitis is sometimes used loosely to mean pyelonephritis.

See also KIDNEY DISEASES and the major article on **Nephrology.**

pyelonephritis

Inflammation of the main substance (parenchyma) and pelvis of the kidney due to infection. It is a very common condition, females being more commonly affected than males. (Compare PYELITIS.)

The infecting microorganisms may reach the kidneys by means of the bloodstream or may travel upward from the bladder via the ureter and the lymphatic vessels around the ureters. The organisms which most commonly cause pyelonephritis are those found in the gastrointestinal tract.

Stasis or collection of urine in the bladder is an important factor which invariably predisposes to infection. This is why there are three peaks at which acute pyelonephritis is most common—in childhood, during pregnancy, and in the elderly. In childhood, major or minor degrees of urinary tract abnormalities may cause some degree of reflux of urine up the ureter when the bladder contracts to expel urine, and an attack of acute pyelonephritis may be the first sign that an abnormality exists. In pregnancy, the uterus compresses the ureters and causes stasis of urine. In the elderly, stasis is often caused by PROLAPSE of the uterus in the female and by enlargement of the prostate in men.

Other conditions which predispose to pyelonephritis include DIABETES MELLITUS, kidney stones and surgical procedures which require instruments to be passed into the urinary tract.

Pyelonephritis can be acute or chronic. An attack of pyelonephritis is characterized by fever accompanied by chills, pain in the loin, the need to pass urine very frequently and urgently, and burning pain at the urethra (the urinary outlet from the bladder) on passing urine. The last two symptoms on their own usually suggest infection of the bladder and infection of the urethra respectively.

Treatment consists of the administration of antibiotics. The urine will have to be examined in the laboratory to determine which microorganisms are responsible for the infection, so that the appropriate antibiotic can be given. Repeated laboratory examinations of the urine will have to be carried out on one or two occasions in the first few months after completion of a full course of antibiotics to ensure that the infection has been completely eradicated or that reinfection has not taken place. If the infection recurs, or another infection occurs, a predisposing cause for the infection must be sought.

Before kidney failure develops, the steps taken to prevent or delay further damage include vigorous treatment of any low-grade urinary tract infection (determined by laboratory examination of the urine) and thorough investigation to discover treatable conditions which predispose to pyelonephritis.

Compare GLOMERULONEPHRITIS. See also KIDNEY DISEASES and the major article on **Nephrology.**

pyoderma

Any of various pus-forming skin infections. The group of conditions known collectively as the pyodermas include: (1) IMPETIGO—a common, contagious, superficial, bacterial infection seen most often in children. The lesions vary from small to large blisters that rupture and release a honey-colored liquid. New lesions can develop very rapidly (within hours). Crusts form from the discharge. (2) *Ecthyma*—similar to impetigo, but it affects slightly deeper layers of the skin. (3) *Folliculitis*—which affects hair follicles anywhere on the body, including the eyelashes (to form a STY). (4) *Furuncle* (or boil)—a more extensive infection of the hair follicle involving deeper underlying tissues. (5) CARBUNCLE—an extensive infection of several adjoining hair follicles; the carbuncle drains with multiple openings on to the skin surface. (6) *Sweat gland infections*—not a common condition. (7) ERYSIPELAS—an uncommon infection caused by streptococcal bacteria; it results in a characteristic type of CELLULITIS (inflammation of the loose connective tissue under the skin) which appears as a red, warm, raised, well-defined plaque; blisters may form on the skin.

The general principles of treatment include: (a) administration of the appropriate antibiotic; (b) general isolation of the patient, with frequent change of clothing and bedding (towels should not be shared) and strict hygiene. (c) if the furuncle or carbuncle comes to a "head"—that is, when an abscess has formed with a definite point—the pus should be drained by an incision. (d) if pyodermas recur, investigations should be carried out to exclude diabetes (which makes a person prone to infections).

pyorrhea

Literally, "a copious discharge of pus." But the term is usually used to mean *pyorrhea alveolaris*—inflammation or degeneration of tissues which surround and support the teeth, including the gums, the bone surrounding the tooth socket, the ligaments around the bone and the *cementum* (the bonelike connective tissue covering the root of the tooth and assisting in its support).

Pyorrhea usually begins as gingivitis (inflammation of the gums) and progresses to periodontitis. The most common source of the infecting organism which causes gingivitis is bacterial plaque (microbial colonies found on the tooth surface). Gingivitis need not be infective in origin. It may be a sign of: (1) vitamin deficiency, (2) an allergic reaction, (3) a reaction to heavy-metal poisoning, (4) a reaction to drugs, or (5) leukemia. In addition, it may accompany pregnancy. Whatever the cause, inflamed gums often become secondarily infected.

The symptoms of gingivitis consist of redness, swelling, changes of contour, and bleeding of the gum. A cleft may form between the gum and the tooth in which food debris collects and the infection may become chronic. Treatment is by correction of the underlying cause, proper hygiene of the mouth, antibiotics, and sometimes extensive dental surgery.

When gingivitis spreads to produce periodontitis, there is deepening of the pockets between the gums and the teeth, loss of the supporting bone, loosening of teeth

and recession of gums. Dental treatment is required to eliminate local irritating factors, reconstruct gingival (gum) tissues, splint loose teeth or extract hopelessly decayed teeth.

See also ABSCESS.

pyrexia

The technical name for FEVER. The condition of an exceptionally high fever is known as *hyperpyrexia*.

Q

Q fever

An infection caused by the microorganism (rickettsia) *Coxiella burneti*, a parasite of cattle in which it produces mild or subclinical infections. These animals excrete the microorganisms in the milk or feces. Man becomes infected usually by inhaling dusts which have become contaminated by infected animal material; sometimes infection occurs by drinking infected milk, as the rickettsiae are relatively resistant to pasteurization.

After an incubation period of two to four weeks, symptoms may appear. These consist of fever, headaches, prostration and cough. X-rays usually show an inflammation of the lung, although the cough may be slight. Occasionally the heart may be affected, sometimes months after the original infection. The disease may be acute, or chronic and relapsing. Even in untreated patients, the infection is rarely fatal.

Prevention is by avoiding contact with infected cattle. If the disease develops, symptoms may be suppressed by the administration of tetracyclines, although the infection may not necessarily be eradicated.

See also RICKETTSIAE.

quarantine

The detention or limitation of freedom of movement of man (or domestic animals) who are apparently well but who have been in contact with a serious communicable disease (one that can be transmitted directly or indirectly from one individual to another). The reason for this is that such persons or animals may have become infected, although they have not yet shown signs or symptoms of the disease—that is, they are in the *incubation* stage of the disease, during which time they may be able to pass the disease on to unaffected others. To prevent this they are quarantined for the longest usual incubation period of the disease in question, by the end of which time it should have become clearer who are the ones who have been infected and who need to be isolated or nursed by *isolation* techniques.

Quarantine need not be carried out in the hospital. The person can be quarantined anywhere as long as he does not have unlimited contact with unaffected persons.

There are various degrees of quarantine. *Complete quarantine* means the quarantine of all persons who have been in contact with the communicable disease. With *modified quarantine*, it may be that only those who are likely to pass the disease on to particularly susceptible people are held in quarantine. For example, if children are particularly susceptible to the disease, child contacts of the case may be asked to stay away from school; or perhaps only those contacts who have no immunity to the disease have to stay away from school, since they are the ones most likely to have caught the infection and be "incubating" it.

The least strict form of quarantine is personal surveillance in which the contact's movements are not limited—except for the fact that health officials should be able to get in touch with him daily or at frequent intervals to ensure that he has not fallen ill.

The type of quarantine applied varies depending on the seriousness of the disease, the closeness of the contact with the disease, and the state of immunity of the susceptible people within the community.

quinsy

An abscess forming in the space around the tonsils (peritonsillar abscess). It is a complication of acute tonsillitis.

When a peritonsillar abscess forms, the sore throat of acute tonsillitis suddenly becomes severe on one side, there is an acute increase in the difficulty in swallowing and there may be spasm of the muscles around the jaw.

Treatment consists of antibiotics, bed rest, a light diet, plenty of fluids, and analgesics (such as aspirin). When the abscess is fully formed it may discharge itself, or it may require surgical incision and drainage. After the infection has subsided a TONSILLECTOMY may be considered to prevent recurrence.

R

rabies

A viral disease affecting animals (especially carnivores) characterized by irritation of the nervous system followed by paralysis and (in virtually every case) death.

The virus is found in the saliva of infected animals, which transmit the disease by their bites. The disease may also be spread if open wounds are contaminated by infected saliva. Also called *hydrophobia*.

Vaccination of dogs in the United States has controlled canine rabies. Most cases are the result of bites of infected wild animals such as skunks, foxes and bats. Infected animals may have the "furious" form of the disease (in which they become very agitated and aggressive) or the "dumb" form (in which change of habits or paralysis predominates). The diagnosis may require laboratory tests and examination of the nervous tissue of the animal obtained at autopsy.

In man the incubation period varies from approximately ten days to over a year, but most often it is from 30 to 60 days. The incubation period is shorter the more extensive the bite or the nearer the bite to the head. Once the first symptoms of rabies appear, the disease is inevitably fatal (although at least one documented case of survival exists).

The initial symptom in man consists of sensitivity of the area around the wound to changes in temperature. This is typically followed by a period of mental depression, restlessness and fever. The restlessness may increase to states of rage and violent convulsions. Attempts to drink result in spasm of the larynx ("voice-box") so that the patient eventually refuses to drink (becomes "hydrophobic"). Spasm of the larynx is also easily precipitated by mild stimuli such as a gentle breeze. The attacks of asphyxia produced by laryngeal spasm can lead to death. Death may also result from exhaustion and paralysis of the muscles that control respiration.

People working with animals should be immunized against rabies. Vaccination should also be started after a person is bitten by an animal suspected to be rabid. The animal should be confined and observed for symptoms of rabies so that the diagnosis can be confirmed and permit a prompt vaccination of the victim—a painful and prolonged procedure which is not always successful. The local wound should be thoroughly washed with soft medicinal soap.

No cure currently exists once the first symptoms are experienced. Supportive treatment is the best that can be offered.

radiation therapy

Treatment of disease by ionizing radiation or high-energy radiation. The radiation may be given in the form of a beam, or a radioactive material (such as radium or cobalt) may be contained in various devices which can be inserted directly into the tissues or into a body cavity. The radioactive material may also be given by injection into a vein or as a drink (radioactive phosphorus is usually given by injection or as a drink, and radioactive iodine given as a drink).

The most common condition for which radiation is used is CANCER. Some cancers respond well to radiation therapy alone; others are best treated with radiation therapy in conjunction with surgery or anticancer drugs (or both). When a cancer is too far advanced for surgery, radiation therapy can often help to relieve symptoms.

Radiation kills not only cancer cells, it can also have harmful effects on normal cells. But cancer cells are more susceptible because radiation acts best on cells that are dividing (multiplying) rapidly. The normal cells most commonly affected are those which are dividing rapidly—such as the skin cells, those lining the gastrointestinal tract and the bone marrow cells. Side effects of radiation are known as *radiation sickness.* Symptoms usually consist of diarrhea and vomiting, mouth ulcers, temporary loss of hair and anemia. The treatment is simply to reduce the dose of radiation (or to stop treatment). Recovery may be rapid, but in some cases recurrences occur even after the treatment has been stopped. Sometimes the inflammation that is produced around the site of treatment becomes chronic and causes symptoms later. Radiation to the abdomen, for example, may cause fibrotic reactions which lead to intermittent abdominal pains. Chronic inflammation of the LYMPHATIC SYSTEM produced by radiation to lymph nodes may impede the flow of lymph from the area drained and result in a form of ELEPHANTIASIS.

However, improvements in technique—which allow doses to be more accurately calculated, and which enable the radiation to be directed more specifically to the small area of tissues to be treated—have considerably reduced the frequency of side effects.

The other conditions for which radiation therapy is used include ANKYLOSING SPONDYLITIS, polycythemia vera (see POLYCYTHEMIA) and thyrotoxic goiter (see HYPERTHYROIDISM).

rash

A skin eruption which typically takes the form of red patches or spots and is often accompanied by itching. The rash may be localized in one part of the body or involve extensive areas. A rash may be the result of a number of conditions, including certain communicable diseases (such as measles or chickenpox).

Diaper rash is the dermatitis (skin inflammation) which occurs in infants on the areas covered by diapers and is due to irritation by wet or soiled diapers. A fungal infection (candidiasis or moniliasis) may be super-imposed in diaper rash; if it develops, antifungal treatment is required. In most cases, however, diaper rash can be controlled by keeping the diaper area dry and clean and by prompt changing of wet diapers.

MILIARIA ("heat rash" or "prickly heat") is a form of rash due to blockage of sweat ducts. The function of the sweat glands is to flood the skin surface with water for cooling. They become very active in hot weather. The constant maceration of the skin because of the moist environment around the sweat pores blocks the ducts, so that the part of the duct behind the blockage swells up.

An *allergic rash* usually appears as weals, which are well-defined elevated lesions caused by local accumulation of fluid in the tissues. It is the type of rash seen with insect bites or STINGS, allergies to food or drugs, or URTICARIA ("hives"). Drug eruptions, however, may take on a number of other forms ranging from a measles-like rash to sloughing off of the skin. The treatment for allergic rash is to stop contact with the agent causing the rash; if the eruption does not clear up, antiallergic agents such as antihistamines and cortico-steroids may be required.

Many *viral infections* produce a rash, which in some infections are fairly characteristic of the particular infection. In MEASLES and GERMAN MEASLES the rash usually starts around the ears or on the face and neck before spreading to the trunk and limbs. In mild cases, the limbs may be unaffected. In CHICKENPOX, the rash usually starts on the trunk and later spreads to the face and extremities; blisters soon form. In SMALLPOX, the rash first appears on the face and quickly spreads to the trunk and hands, forming fluid-filled blisters (pustules), or "spots." The fluid within the center of the spots turns to pus (which dries and forms scabs). In INFECTIOUS MONONUCLEOSIS, the rash is most prominent over the trunk.

Bacterial infections may also produce rashes; for example, secondary SYPHILIS is characterized by a transient skin eruption.

A rash may also be seen in the group of conditions known as the AUTOIMMUNE DISEASES. With lupus erythematosus, a "butterfly rash" may form (so named because of the typical pattern it forms across the bridge of the nose and over the adjacent areas of the cheeks).

See also the major article on **Dermatology.**

Raynaud's phenomenon

First described by Maurice Raynaud in 1862, Raynaud's phenomenon is most common in young women: first the fingertips (then the rest of the fingers) go white and cold, the fingers feel numb and may become stiff, and it is evident that their blood supply has temporarily been cut off. On recovery the blood comes slowly back to the fingers, which turn bright red and become painful.

The condition may be slight or severe; in severe cases small ulcers may form on the fingertips and the nails may be affected. If there is no underlying cause, the condition usually improves and in the end subsides. But in some cases the phenomenon is a complication of more widespread disease such as atheroma, scleroderma, or systemic lupus erythematosus; the "cervical rib syndrome" may include Raynaud's phenomenon, or it may be precipitated by the use of vibrating tools. It may also be an occupational disease (e.g., of butchers).

All sufferers should avoid cold hands, and they should avoid handling cold metal with bare hands. Attacks may be made worse by emotional disturbances, particularly anxiety. Treatment includes keeping the whole body warm as well as the hands and feet, and the relief of pain with analgesics. In severe cases it may be useful to block the sympathetic nervous supply to the affected limb, or to interrupt it by surgical operation. Patients may have to change their employment.

Recklinghausen's disease

See VON RECKLINGHAUSEN'S DISEASE.

rectal cancer

The most common cancer of the gastrointestinal tract, generally occurring in middle age but sometimes in the young. It may arise more often in those who have a family history of multiple polyposis, chronic ulcerative colitis, or simple rectal tumors, and the incidence increases with age.

The onset is often insidious, and the first sign may be bleeding from the anus or bloodstained stools which may lead the patient to think he has hemorrhoids (piles). The bowel habits change, constipation alternating with attacks of diarrhea. It may feel that the rectum is never entirely empty, and there may be a dragging dull discomfort. Pain develops with the growth of the tumor—which may reach a considerable size, filling the lower part of the abdomen. If the growth is neglected, partial obstruction occurs which leads to offensive diarrhea.

Providing that the condition is recognized early, surgical removal of the tumor offers a considerable hope of cure; it is therefore important that rectal bleeding should never be dismissed as being due to hemorrhoids without a proper medical examination—which will include a rectal examination and possibly endoscopy.

See also the major article on **Gastroenterology.**

rectocele

A pouch formed when part of the rectum protrudes into the vagina. It is the result of rupture (during childbirth) of the fibrous connective tissue that separates the rectum from the vagina. It may be due to a rapid delivery or to a difficult one. Sometimes the diagnosis is made soon after delivery, but usually symptoms do not appear until a woman is aged about 35 to 40.

Factors which affect the development of a rectocele include the condition of the tissues, the degree of damage, and persistent straining at stool. There is a vicious cycle here because one of the signs of a rectocele is constipation due to collection of feces in the pouch; this leads to straining, which further aggravates the herniation. Patients may complain of a sense of rectal or vaginal fullness and the constant urge for a bowel movement.

Treatment consists of good dietary habits to avoid constipation or straining at stool. Laxatives or suppositories may be necessary. Surgery is required to achieve a cure, the chances for which are good if subsequent vaginal delivery and straining at stool can be avoided.

reflex

A reflex is an involuntary action or movement which occurs in response to a stimulus. Examples of reflex actions are the quick closure of the eye when an object approaches it or when the eyelash is touched, or the sharp recovery of balance when a person begins to slip. There are also reflexes of which one may not be conscious; for example, the secretion of gastric juices at the sight of food, or the movement of the pupil in response to change in the intensity of light.

A reflex is brought about by the activity of the *reflex arc*. In its simplest form, the reflex arc consists of a nerve cell which acts as a "receptor" for the stimulus, and a nerve cell which acts as an "effector" for the reflex action. In addition there is a *reflex center* (the brain or the spinal cord). The nerve from the receptor brings the message from the receptor to the reflex center where it meets the nerve leading to the effector and passes the message on. Thus nerve cells in the retina (receptors) receive light (the stimulus) and pass the message on to the effectors (muscles which control the movement of the pupil).

Some reflexes can be conditioned—that is learned or modified. The classic example is the experiments with dogs conducted by the Russian physician and physiologist Ian Pavlov (1849–1936). A bell was rung whenever the dog was served food. The normal response to food is salivation. After a number of times, the dog salivated when the bell was rung without food being served at the same time.

Many reflexes may be tested during a general medical examination. When an appropriate stimulus is provided by the doctor, the reflex response is involuntary; any disturbance in the expected reflex thus affords an objective sign of disturbed neural function. One common test is the "knee jerk" reflex. This is commonly elicited by a firm tap with a rubber-headed mallet on the tendon just below the kneecap. The normal response is for the lower leg to jerk outward suddenly and then return to its former position.

Another fairly common test of neurological function is BABINSKI'S REFLEX, which is elicited by stimulating the sole of the foot (as by firmly stroking the sole with the blunt end of a key). In adults, the normal response is for the large toe and usually the other toes to "clench" or be drawn down; if the large toe extends instead of flexes, and the other toes fan out, it is a sign of some disorder of the nerve tract from the spinal cord to the brain (corticospinal tract).

See also the major article on **Neurology.**

Reiter's syndrome

A group of three conditions (also known as *Reiter's disease*): nongonococcal urethritis, arthritis and conjunctivitis. In addition to these three main disorders, the disease may include a number of other features such as balanitis, anterior uveitis, stomatitis, or thrombophlebitis. Sometimes the disease appears in a less complete form—that is, with one or two of the three main features, plus one or more of the other features.

The cause of the disease is unknown. Most cases are preceded either by an attack of dysentery or by sexual contact. The nondysenteric cases are thought to be of venereal origin. Although some organisms have been isolated from urethral or conjunctival discharges and from joint fluids in Reiter's disease, it is still not certain what their role is in causing the disease, which most commonly affects young men.

The arthritis usually appears about 10 to 14 days after the manifestation of dysentery or urethritis and affects mainly the large joints, often the knees and ankles. It may persist for months, whereas most of the other symptoms usually disappear within a few days or weeks.

The condition usually resolves on its own, but recurrences are common. The recurrent attacks tend to be milder than the first attack. Recurrent involvement, however, may lead to permanent changes.

There is no specific treatment, only treatment to relieve symptoms.

relaxation therapy

A form of behavior therapy which is used as a preliminary to "desensitization"—a technique of getting patients to overcome irrational fears which can lead to NEUROSIS. Desensitization works best when a subject is not anxious and tense. When a person is able to relax his muscles voluntarily, certain physiological changes occur (such as a slight reduction in the rate of the heartbeat, a slowed rate of breathing and a detectable diminution in the resistance of the skin to an electrical current). These changes are the opposite of those found in an *anxious* person. The voluntary relaxation of muscles has an overall calming effect which makes desensitization easier. The muscle relaxation has to be achieved voluntarily; paralyzing the muscles by using drugs does not produce the same effect.

The therapist first gets the patient to *contract* a group of muscles—for example, the muscles of the upper limbs—and then gradually trains the patient to *relax* these muscles. The patient is then taught how to relax other muscle groups—for example, the lower limbs, the neck, the face, the eye muscles, and so on—until he is able to relax all muscles in the body. There need not be a strict order in which one learns to relax muscle groups; the order varies with the therapist.

If a person has difficulty in relaxing muscles at will, HYPNOSIS or tranquilizing drugs may help.

See also DESENSITIZATION.

renal failure

See KIDNEY DISEASES.

resection

The surgical procedure of cutting out, especially the surgical removal of a segment or section of an organ.

respiration

The exchange of oxygen and carbon dioxide between the atmosphere and body cells. Oxygen combines with carbon and hydrogen furnished by food. These reactions generate heat and provide the living organism with energy for physical work as well as for the many other processes essential for life, such as digestion, growth and brain function. The carbon dioxide that is produced during respiration has to be eliminated; accumulation of carbon dioxide in the body disturbs body function by causing the tissue fluids to be too acid.

In an adult at rest the frequency of respiration is about 14 to 20 breaths per minute; children tend to breathe at a faster rate. Atmospheric air breathed in contains approximately 21% oxygen and 0.03% carbon dioxide. Air breathed out of the lungs contains approximately 14% oxygen and 5.6% carbon dioxide.

All the air in the lungs is not expelled with each breath. The amount of inspired air that actually reaches the lungs with each breath (during normal quiet breathing) is known as the *tidal volume;* it represents only about 1/18 of the total capacity of the lungs. The *vital capacity* is the amount of air the lungs can hold after trying to force out as much air from the lungs as possible and then taking the deepest possible breath.

The *residual volume* is the amount of air the lungs hold after trying to breathe out as hard as possible; it is impossible to empty the lungs of all their air in this manner, and approximately 1,200 cubic centimeters (cc) remain—compared with approximately 500 cc of air drawn into the lungs with each breath during normal breathing.

The act of breathing is accomplished by the action of the diaphragm (which moves down) and the muscles between the ribs (which expand the chest upward, outward and sideways). As air is drawn into the lungs (*inspiration*) the pleural cavity—the airless space between the lungs and the chest wall—becomes larger; this creates a suction effect on the lungs and causes them to expand. As the volume of the lungs increases, it creates a partial vacuum within the lungs; air rushes in through the nose, mouth (if open) and air passages to fill this space. Breathing out (*expiration*) is a passive action caused by the escape of air temporarily held in the lungs at a slightly higher pressure than the atmospheric air.

There are three components involved in the transport of oxygen and carbon dioxide between the cells and the external environment. Exchange of the two gases between the body cells and the atmosphere takes place in the lungs. Breathing consists of alternate acts of inspiration and expiration; during inspiration, atmospheric air is taken into the lungs while during expiration the air which is relatively poor in oxygen and rich in carbon dioxide is expelled into the atmosphere.

In the lungs, exchange of gases takes place by diffusion across the walls of the air sacs (alveoli); oxygen from inspired air diffuses across the lining of the air sacs and enters the circulation, while carbon dioxide moves in the opposite direction. The gases are transported between cells and the lung by the blood circulation.

Any disorder that affects transport of the gases can impair respiration and, if the impairment is severe enough, death occurs; death may be of the whole organism or localized, such as occurs in heart attacks (myocardial infarction) or STROKES when the blood supply to specific tissues is cut off. Other disorders which can affect transport of gases include nervous or muscular disorders which impair the movement of chest and abdominal muscles required for breathing, or disorders which affect the lining of the air sacs, such as PNEUMONIA or collapse of the lung (ATELECTASIS).

See also the major article on **Pulmonary Diseases.**

respiratory distress syndrome

Another name for HYALINE MEMBRANE DISEASE.

respiratory tract infection

The respiratory tract extends from the nostrils down to

RESPIRATION

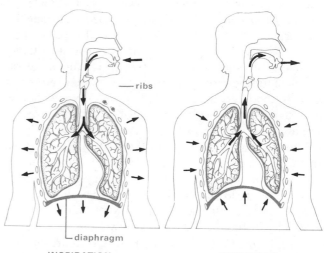

INSPIRATION   EXPIRATION

At rest, a normal adult breathes about 14 times per minute; oxygen enters the blood in the capillaries of the lungs and carbon dioxide is carried away in the expired air. Muscle action lifts the ribs and pulls down the diaphragm, so increasing the volume of the chest: the lungs expand, drawing in air through the nose or mouth. When these muscles relax, the lungs recoil, and air is expelled.

the air sacs in the lungs (pulmonary alveoli). Broadly speaking, the respiratory tract can be divided into the *upper respiratory tract* (above the larynx) and the *lower respiratory tract* (below the larynx). Infections (producing inflammation) of specific parts of the respiratory tract are known as RHINITIS (inflammation of the nasal passages); PHARYNGITIS (inflammation of the pharynx, or throat); LARYNGITIS (inflammation of the larynx, or "voice-box"); TRACHEITIS (inflammation of the trachea, or "windpipe"); and BRONCHITIS (inflammation of the bronchi or major air passages below the trachea). When the air sacs are affected the infection is known as PNEUMONITIS. Untreated infection of any part can spread readily to other parts.

The infecting microorganisms—usually bacteria or viruses—most commonly enter the respiratory tract by inhalation of infected droplets exhaled (or coughed or sneezed out) by someone with an existing respiratory tract infection. Sometimes a respiratory tract infection spreads from a previously localized infection in the mouth or is introduced from other parts of the body by means of the bloodstream.

The body has a number of defense mechanisms specifically designed to ward off or attack respiratory tract infections. The nostrils have lining hairs which act as filters for the air breathed in. There are also a number of "turbinates" in the nasal passages which have mucus-covered surfaces that act very much like "fly-paper" to trap irritants and infective organisms. (The turbinates—or *nasal conchae*—are intricately shaped and roughly parallel and horizontal bony ridges that separate the deeper airways on either side of the nose into three drainage channels—each of which is known as a *meatus*.) Furthermore, nasal secretions contain enzymes and antibodies which can kill or interfere with the growth and multiplication of some bacteria and viruses. Irritation of the nose and nasopharynx (the part behind the nose just above the roof of the mouth) also initiates sneezing, which expels irritants; similarly, irritation of the larynx or upper part of the trachea triggers the cough reflex. Lower down, the diameter of the air passages progressively diminishes so that the velocity of air is gradually reduced as it passes down the respiratory tract, allowing particles to fall out of the airstream and stick to the mucus-covered walls; these walls bear cilia (hair-like structures) on their surface. The cilia move in such a way as to sweep the mucus upward and out of the respiratory tract. Obstruction of the respiratory tract by a foreign body or by a tumor will prevent the mucus from being effectively swept upward. The action of cilia is also impaired by chronic inflammation, such as that associated with chronic bronchitis, the common cold and by some anesthetics. When the mucus is

RESPIRATORY TRACT INFECTION

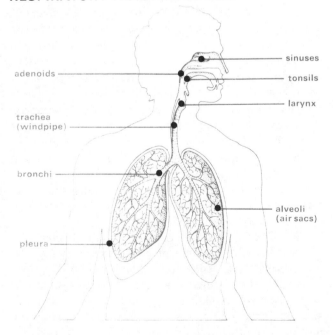

adenoids

sinuses

tonsils

larynx

trachea (windpipe)

bronchi

alveoli (air sacs)

pleura

Infections of the respiratory tract cover anything from the common cold to pneumonia. The illustration shows the possible sites of infection; symptoms may include cough, excess phlegm, chest pain and breathing difficulties.

abnormally thick, and thus unable to flow easily, infection is common.

A number of factors make a person more susceptible to respiratory tract infection; these include the extremes of age, debilitation by chronic illness, and DIABETES MELLITUS.

Symptoms of an infection of the respiratory tract depend primarily on the severity of the attack and on the site affected.

Treatment is primarily the administration of the appropriate antibiotic.

See also the major articles on **Otolaryngology** and **Pulmonary diseases.**

restless legs syndrome

A relatively common condition (of unknown cause) characterized by aching or burning sensations in the muscles of the lower limbs, accompanied by a desire to move the legs. Also known as *jittery legs syndrome* or *Ekbom's syndrome*.

The onset of symptoms typically occurs when the patient is resting, especially when in bed. After a period of restless shuffling, the patient may be compelled to get up and walk about to obtain relief. Except for occasional muscular cramps, there is usually no associated pain or any sign of disease in the muscles or nerves of the legs. Although no specific medical treatment exists to relieve the condition, many patients benefit from the administration of an appropriate tranquilizer just before bedtime.

resuscitation

The emergency measures performed to attempt to restore breathing and the heartbeat in someone who has apparently just died. There are three essential measures in resuscitation, most easily remembered by the letters *A* (keep the *airways* clear), *B* (restore *breathing*), and *C* (restore the *circulation*).

To prevent blockage of the airway by the tongue (which may have fallen back and obstructed the upper part of the airway), the patient's head should be tilted right back. If the airway is blocked by vomit, mucus, mud, or dentures it should be "hooked out" very rapidly with a finger.

If the patient is not breathing spontaneously, mouth-to-mouth breathing should be initiated at once. This consists of the first-aider taking a deep breath of air which is then immediately blown out into the patient's mouth, taking care to pinch the patient's nostrils at the same time so that the air blown in does not escape through the nostrils. This should be repeated about 12 times per minute.

If after the first three or four breaths the victim's color

has not improved, the pupils of his eyes remain very wide, and there is no detectable pulse or heartbeat, then CARDIAC MASSAGE is indicated. This procedure is also known as *external cardiac compression.*

External cardiac compression carried out by inexperienced people can fracture ribs and cause damage to internal organs. Sometimes the heart will start after a sharp thump on the chest and this should be attempted before external cardiac compression. When cardiac compression is given it must be accompanied by the continuation of artificial respiration.

See also *Resuscitation* in the **First Aid** section.

retention of urine

Inability to empty the bladder may be caused by obstruction of the urinary passages or by neurological disorders which disturb the neuromuscular mechanisms of urination. Retention of urine may be acute or chronic.

Obstruction to the outlet of the bladder may be caused by enlargement of the prostate gland in men, by benign or malignant tumors, fibrosis of the bladder neck, stones, blood clots, or pressure from outside by fibroids of the uterus or a pregnant uterus. The urethra may be obstructed by strictures (usually the result of previous infection or injury), stones, foreign bodies, or acute inflammation.

One of the most common causes of acute urinary retention is postoperative pain; other conditions disturbing neuromuscular reflexes are diseases of the spinal cord such as multiple sclerosis and tabes dorsalis (locomotor ataxia), tumors, injuries and inflammations. Hysteria may produce acute or chronic urinary retention, and in the elderly the bladder may not be emptied because of confusion and loss of awareness.

Acute retention is painful except in neurological disorders. The pain is felt above the pubis at the lower part of the abdomen; chronic retention is usually painless.

Treatment includes the use of catheters and operative relief of obstructions. In chronic conditions it may be necessary to introduce a catheter permanently; in some cases permanent drainage may be carried out through the lower part of the abdominal wall.

See also the major article on **Nephrology.**

retinitis

Inflammation of the retina, the light-sensitive lining at the back of the eyeball.

The retina forms the innermost of the three coats (tunics) of the eye. True inflammation of the retina rarely occurs on its own, but usually together with inflammation of the *choroid* (the middle coat)—a condition known as *chorioretinitis.* This may be caused by infections such as TUBERCULOSIS or SYPHILIS, or by parasitic infestations. Symptoms include blurring of vision, distortion of the size and shape of the image, and extreme sensitivity of the eye to bright light (photophobia). If the cause is known, specific treatment is administered; if not, corticosteroids may help.

All three coats of the eye may sometimes become infected with pus-forming (pyogenic) microorganisms. This can occur after injury, when a corneal ulcer perforates, or when the infection spreads from other parts of the body. This serious condition is characterized by intense pain and rapid loss of vision. Treatment is the administration of appropriate antibiotics.

Two degenerative (not inflammatory) conditions are also known as retinitis—RETINITIS PIGMENTOSA, and *retinitis proliferans.* The latter is a complication of diabetes mellitus and is characterized by the formation of masses of new blood vessels in the retina.

retinitis pigmentosa

An inherited disorder characterized by a slowly progressive degeneration of the retina of both eyes.

Symptoms may be noticed from early childhood, the earliest signs usually being defective night vision since the degeneration first affects the *rods*, which are receptors that mediate vision in dim light. Later the central field of vision becomes lost; this gradually progresses until (in some cases) total blindness occurs.

There is no effective treatment for retinitis pigmentosa. Genetic counseling may help to prevent the disease. About 90% of cases are inherited as an "autosomal recessive" feature, 9% as an "autosomal dominant" feature and the rest as "sex-linked."

retinopathy

Damage to the retina (the light-sensitive layer at the back of the eye) caused by disease of the blood vessels.

In advancing age the blood vessels in general become hardened and narrow (arteriosclerosis). In some people the condition may be severe enough to lead to small hemorrhages into the retina, but usually hemorrhages occur if the blood pressure is above normal and undue strain is put upon the aging blood vessels. These hemorrhages may produce defects in vision.

Malignant hypertension can bring about similar changes in younger people, for it produces widespread damage to the smaller arteries (arterioles) which leads to the formation of exudates and hemorrhages.

Retinopathy is one of the most serious complications of advanced diabetes mellitus; it is present in about 90% of cases of over 25 years duration, and is dependent on the duration rather than the severity of the disease. It can result in complete bilateral blindness in early adult life, but if the condition is diagnosed early enough it can be treated. It is therefore extremely important that all diabetes patients should have the retina examined at least once a year by an ophthalmologist.

See also the major article on **Ophthalmology.**

Rh (Rhesus) factor

Prior to 1940, it was thought that the ABO BLOOD GROUPS were the only groups of clinical importance, particularly in the area of blood transfusion. However, unexplained reactions occurred in patients when transfused with blood of their own ABO group. There had also been interest for many years in the fact that certain women were prone to bear children who were born jaundiced and anemic, who sometimes died soon after birth, or, in severe cases, who were stillborn.

Some parallel work with red cells from Rhesus monkeys involved the preparation of antibodies (agglutinins) capable of clumping or agglutinating Rhesus monkey cells. It was a surprising discovery that such agglutinins would react with 85% of human red cells (*Rhesus positive*) but not with the remaining 15% (*Rhesus negative*). Furthermore, women who had produced jaundiced or dead infants, as described above, were found to be invariably Rhesus negative while their husbands were Rhesus positive.

The conclusion from this work was that incompatibility within the Rhesus system was responsible for the abnormalities in these "Rhesus babies" suffering from *erythroblastosis fetalis* (a "hemolytic" disease of the newborn, characterized by enlargement of the liver and spleen, anemia and jaundice) and that transfusion of Rhesus negative patients with Rhesus positive blood was responsible for subsequent incompatibility reactions when further Rhesus positive blood was given. Understanding of the nature of the problem has led to good control of both transfusion reactions and Rh disorders of pregnancy and the salvage of many babies.

rheumatic fever

A once common disease of childhood and adolescence which today is less frequent. It occurs as a delayed complication of infection of the throat by bacteria known as *Group A hemolytic streptococci*. It is now known to be an example of an AUTOIMMUNE DISEASE, resulting from an allergic reaction following the release of poisonous substances (toxins) by the bacteria.

It occurs in about 1 in 50,000 children and affects the joints, heart, skin and (sometimes) the brain. The acute attack produces painful swollen joints, skin rashes, nodules in the tissues just beneath the skin, and fever. The effect on the heart is variable. There may be a persistently raised heart rate, minor irregularities in the heartbeat, or even acute congestive heart failure, but recovery is the rule. Damage to the heart valves may reveal itself many years later in RHEUMATIC HEART DISEASE with serious disturbance of cardiac function.

Treatment involves the administration of penicillin to clear up the streptococcal infection; cortisone-like drugs (steroids) and aspirin are used to relieve symptoms. Better and earlier treatment of streptococcal infections (and of rheumatic fever itself) has reduced the chance of subsequent heart problems.

rheumatic heart disease

A complication or end result of an attack of RHEUMATIC FEVER.

The interval between the original rheumatic fever (usually occurring in childhood or adolescence), and the appearance of symptoms of rheumatic heart disease may vary from a few years to many decades. Rheumatic fever attacks the heart muscle and the heart valves; while the damage to the heart muscle is usually repairable, changes in the heart valves may subsequently cause the cusps of the valves to become deformed or stick together at their margins. The heart valves most affected are the *mitral* and *aortic* valves. Two main types of defect can be produced: (1) narrowing of the valve opening with obstruction to the flow of blood (*stenosis*) or (2) *incompetence* and *regurgitation*, in which the valve fails to close properly and allows a reverse flow of blood.

Symptoms depend largely on the type of defect present and its severity. For many years the heart may continue to compensate for a defectively functioning valve; but shortness of breath on fairly severe exertion, occurring in a patient in his 20s or 30s, is characteristic of *mitral stenosis* in particular. *Aortic stenosis* is typically a complication seen later in life. *Incompetence* of the valves will also eventually produce symptoms; these may include increasing shortness of breath on exercise, palpitations, angina pectoris, attacks of shortness of breath on lying down at night, or fainting attacks.

Treatment involves first increasing the strength of the heartbeat with suitable drugs and the avoidance of overexertion. If the problem is severe, surgical repair of the valve or its replacement by a grafted or plastic valve may be required.

See also the major article on **Cardiology.**

rheumatism

A general term that indicates any of the various diseases of the musculoskeletal system characterized by pain and stiffness of the joints.

See ARTHRITIS, RHEUMATOID ARTHRITIS, OSTEO-ARTHRITIS and the major article on **Rheumatology.**

rheumatoid arthritis

A chronic inflammatory disease affecting the connective tissue of the joints. It has been found all over the world, although the incidence is considerably higher in temperate climates, and the symptoms are more pronounced in cold damp places.

Women are affected more often than men, and the usual age of onset is between 25 and 55. There is a slight genetic factor. The cause of the disease is not known; both autoimmune and infective factors have been implicated. It has been suggested that a "slow virus" infection may be a cause, and in many cases a rheumatoid factor (RF) is detected in the blood. It is an immunoglobulin, but is not thought to be the cause of the disease but rather to develop as a consequence of the disease.

The onset of rheumatoid arthritis is usually insidious, but in some cases it may be acute and accompanied by fever and loss of weight. In others, there may be malaise (a general feeling of being unwell) and fatigue for some weeks with pains and stiffness in the joints. In time arthritis appears, often beginning in the joints of the fingers and spreading to involve the wrists and elbows; less commonly the feet are first affected, with the disease spreading to the ankles and knees. The shoulders and hips may be involved. The joints become swollen, tender and hot, and all movement is painful. The joints are stiff, particularly in the morning and after rest. When the large joints of the shoulder and hip are affected, the resulting disability may be serious.

The joints of the spinal column may be affected, especially in the neck, and the patient may have pain and tenderness in the joint of the lower jaw just in front of the ear; this interferes with eating. Nodules may develop under the skin, and disturbances of the circulation are common in which the hands may sweat to an abnormal extent or may become cold and blue. Complications sometimes involve the chest, with the development of an effusion in the pleural cavity and even acute pneumonia. The lymph nodes draining the affected joints are often enlarged, and in about 5% of patients the spleen is also enlarged. Anemia is common, its severity being proportional to the severity of the disease; the eye may be inflamed or dry.

Diagnosis of the disease may be difficult, as the presence of rheumatoid factor is not entirely specific. The ERYTHROCYTE SEDIMENTATION RATE of the blood is raised, but again the finding is not specific. In a typical case, radiographic examination will show characteristic changes in the joints; these, with the polyarthritis and a positive test for rheumatoid factor, will make the diagnosis certain.

Treatment begins with rest, initially in bed (if necessary, with sedation). Anemia must be treated; as it responds poorly to iron given by mouth, a blood transfusion may be recommended. The diet must be good, possibly with vitamin supplements. In the acute phase of the disease the inflamed joints are fixed in light splints to prevent the development of deformity, but they must be put through a full range of movement at least twice a day, and the patient must try to prevent wasting of the muscles by carrying out isometric contractions at least 12 times an hour. As soon as active movement of the affected joints is possible, they must be exercised by graded movement; active exercises are then started, designed to rebuild wasted muscles.

A number of drugs may be used in treatment. The least expensive and most effective is aspirin, given daily in divided doses. About one-third of patients find that they develop indigestion, in which case it is possible to use special preparations of the drug. Other anti-inflammatory drugs are used such as indomethacin, phenylbutazone, flufenamic acid and ibuprofen, but they sometimes have adverse effects on the blood and the digestive system. Gold salts have been shown to produce symptomatic relief, but they have a number of serious adverse effects which mean that they must be used with caution under close medical supervision. Chloroquine is useful in chronic cases, but cortico-steroids are not advised for long-term treatment and are not used in short-term treatment except under special circumstances. They may be injected locally into inflamed joints to relieve pain. Penicillamine has proved useful in severe cases, but its place in treatment is not yet fully determined.

Surgery has a considerable part to play in the treatment both of acute cases and of the deformity that may result in chronic disease. In the acute stages where there is much pain and thickening of the synovial membranes, excision of the affected membrane may be most beneficial; in chronic disease, ARTHROPLASTY and tendon surgery may be employed in selected cases.

See also the major article on **Rheumatology.**

rhinitis

Inflammation of the mucous membrane that lines the nose (nasal mucosa). Rhinitis may be caused by the common cold virus (of which there are over 100 species) or by an allergic reaction to substances such as grass pollens, in which case it is a symptom of hay fever. Repeated attacks of acute rhinitis may lead to a chronic form. For a discussion of allergic rhinitis (hay fever) see the appropriate section in the major article on **Allergy and Immunology.**

ribonucleic acid

See DNA/RNA.

rickets

A disease of childhood resulting from deficiency of vitamin D, which leads to faulty or inadequate bone growth.

Vitamin D is essential to health because it aids the absorption of calcium from food and is also important for the incorporation of minerals into bone. Vitamin D is formed in the skin after exposure to sunlight and is also found in small amounts in milk and dairy products. Fish oils are rich in vitamin D. Many margarines are fortified with vitamin D, and so are most milks on the market, including dried milk. Cheap, monotonous diets often contain too little of the vitamin, particularly among the poorer sections of the community. A contributory factor to the development of rickets, especially in high altitudes, is that there is often insufficient winter sunlight to assist the natural formation of vitamin D in the skin.

Children suffering from vitamin D deficiency typically have softening and irregular growth of bones, swollen joints, distorted limbs, deformities of the chest and similar malformations. Many "cripples" of the past were actually people who had suffered as children from bone disease due to vitamin D deficiency and were grossly handicapped as a result. Although rickets is much less common in developed countries than it used to be, it is still seen in poorer areas—especially in inner cities where children see little sunlight.

When milk or margarine is fortified with vitamin D there is usually little need to supplement the diet with vitamin D. Synthetic forms of the vitamin are many times more effective in preventing rickets than the natural oils.

rickettsiae

Microorganisms intermediate in size between bacteria and viruses; like viruses, they grow within the cells, but like bacteria are sensitive to appropriate antibiotics. They are transmitted to man by the bites of certain arthropods—lice, fleas, ticks and mites.

In addition to infecting humans rickettsiae can infect small mammals such as rats, rabbits and squirrels—who may form a reservoir of infection. They produce the Typhus group of fevers including trench fever, murine typhus, louse-borne typhus, scrub typhus (TSUTSUGAMUSHI DISEASE), Q FEVER and ROCKY MOUNTAIN SPOTTED FEVER.

rigor mortis

The stiffening of the muscles that occurs after death as a result of changes in substances in the blood. It begins four to ten hours after death in the muscles at the back of the neck, spreads to the rest of the body in a few hours and lasts approximately two to four days.

ringworm

See TINEA.

RNA

See DNA/RNA.

Rocky Mountain spotted fever

A tick-borne typhus fever. There are a number of typhus fevers caused by infection with various species of RICKETTSIAE, which vary in the manner of their occurrence according to the nature of the insects spreading the infection and the mammals which form a reservoir for the rickettsiae. Rabbits, chipmunks, squirrels, rats and mice as well as dogs harbor the organisms responsible for Rocky Mountain spotted fever; the disease is spread to man by *Ixodes* ticks.

The disease shows a seasonal incidence, being prevalent from May to September, and occurs not only in the Rocky Mountains but in other parts of the United States and in other countries.

About 12 days after the tick bite the patient develops fever, with pains in the muscles and joints. The fever may rise high enough to produce delirium; there is a cough, and on the fourth or fifth day a rash appears. Between the 12th and 14th day the condition improves.

The disease is treated by the administration of chloramphenicol and tetracyclines.

rodent ulcer

A chronic, "gnawing" ulcer arising from a tumor known as a *basal-cell epithelioma*. The ulcer, usually on the face or nose of elderly people, is locally malignant but the cancer cells do not (like most cancers) spread to other parts of the body.

It may be excised by surgery, or may be treated by RADIATION THERAPY: the ulcer will often heal completely after a few exposures to radium.

rosacea

A chronic disease (formerly known as *acne rosacea*) affecting the skin of the nose, forehead, cheeks and chin. The skin is colored red or pink as a result of the dilation of capillaries (tiny blood vessels near the surface) and papules and pustules frequently develop.

In severe cases the condition may progress to *rhinophyma*, in which the nose is hugely swollen and deformed. A great deal of debate exists over the cause of rosacea. There is some evidence to link it with the excessive consumption of stimulants such as coffee, tea and alcohol; but it is more common in women over 40, so hormonal influences may be important.

Treatment typically involves the administration of oral tetracycline and application of cortisone ointments; more recently, the drug metronizadole has been found to be effective.

roundworms

The roundworm *Ascaris lumbricoides* is a human parasite found all over the world, especially in the tropics. Its life cycle is bizarre.

The human host swallows the eggs; larvae hatch out in the small intestine, make their way through the intestinal wall into the bloodstream and become lodged in the lungs. Here they pass through the walls of the capillary blood vessels into the air spaces of the lungs and wriggle up through the air passages into the throat (pharynx). They then make for the intestine again via the esophagus and on reaching the small intestine develop into adults. They may live in the intestine for a year.

ROUNDWORM

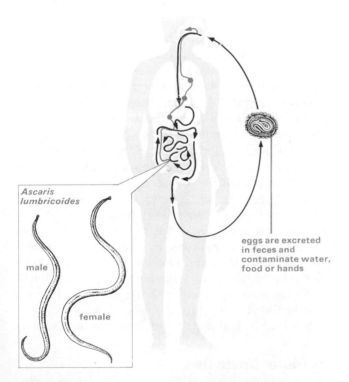

Ascaris
lumbricoides

male

female

eggs are excreted
in feces and
contaminate water,
food or hands

Ascariasis, infestation with the roundworm pictured above, is due to poor hygiene and is estimated to affect one quarter of the world's population.

If their numbers are few they may produce no symptoms; but if they are present as a heavy infection they produce a cough and spasm of the air passages as they pass through the lungs, and interfere with the absorption of food from the intestine. They may wander up the esophagus to emerge at the mouth or the nose, or may be vomited up, or passed from the rectum. They may entwine to form a ball of worms which obstructs the small intestine.

The most effective treatment is piperazine, given as piperazine citrate in a single dose from 500 mg for a child 1 year old to 3 gm for an adult. Thiabendazole may also be used.

rubella

Another name for GERMAN MEASLES.

rupture

See HERNIA.

S

salpingitis

Inflammation of a FALLOPIAN TUBE. The inflammation often arises from GONORRHEA, either immediately or months or years after the infection. Another kind of salpingitis is caused by streptococci or staphylococci bacteria, which may reach the Fallopian tubes following childbirth or abortion. The infection typically produces EDEMA in the mucous membrane which lines the tubes and a discharge of pus may leave the tubes and cause PERITONITIS or an abscess.

Among the consequences of salpingitis are sterility, as a result of the tubes becoming blocked so that ova can no longer reach the womb; and ECTOPIC PREGNANCY, in which the fertilized ovum does not reach the uterus but grows in the tube itself, eventually causing it to rupture—requiring emergency surgery.

Most early cases of salpingitis can be controlled by the administration of an appropriate antibiotic. In advanced or long-term cases, surgical incision and drainage or removal of the Fallopian tube may be needed.

See also the major article on **Obstetrics and Gynecology.**

sarcoidosis

A disease of unknown cause mainly affecting young adults; in many ways it resembles tuberculosis, but there is no evidence of any infective element. Many organs of the body can be affected by the disease; on examination they are seen to contain *granulomas* (tumor-like masses of granular tissue).

The lungs, eyes and skin may be involved as well as the lymphatic system, liver, spleen, heart, muscles and nervous system. In many cases there are no symptoms and the disease is discovered only by routine x-ray examination.

There is often no need for treatment in these cases and spontaneous remissions are common; steroid drugs may be effective in relieving any troublesome symptoms. Sufferers have a normal expectation of life.

sarcoma

A malignant tumor originating in connective tissues, bone or muscle.

Sarcoma is distinguished from the other main type of malignant tumor, *carcinoma* (which is composed mainly of cells similar to skin or mucous membrane). There are about 20 cases of carcinoma to every one of sarcoma. The most common sarcomas are the malignant bone tumors, some of which (such as *osteogenic sarcoma*) are especially common in childhood. A combination of radiation therapy and anticancer drugs may arrest the disease for long periods. In some cases surgery is needed.

See also CANCER and the major article on **Oncology.**

scabies

A skin disease caused by infestation with the parasitic "itch mite" (*Sarcoptes scabiei*). The disease is spread by close contact with infested persons.

The female of the parasite burrows into the skin, particularly on the front of the wrist, the sides and webs of the fingers, the buttocks, the genitals and the feet. Eggs are deposited in the small tunnels she makes, while the male remains on the surface of the skin.

The burrowing activities of the parasites cause intense itching and the original small blister-like lesions may be made much worse by scratching. Treatment will be successful only if all of the patient's close contacts and his family are treated for the disease. Various effective applications are now available, including benzyl benzoate emulsion, gamma benzene hexachloride cream, and monosulfiram in alcohol.

See also the major article on **Dermatology.**

scar

The mark (also known technically as a *cicatrix*) in the skin or an internal organ left by a healed wound, ulcer or other lesion.

Scar tissue consists essentially of fibers which, in the case of scars on the skin surface, are covered by an imperfect formation of cuticle. The fibrous tissue is produced by cells of connective tissue brought to the lesion by the bloodstream.

At first the scar is soft because the fibrous tissue is supplied with ample blood vessels, so that the scar appears more red than the surrounding skin. As fibers contract and harden, the scar loses its blood vessels and becomes whitish.

There is wide variation in the amount of scar tissue which appears, depending on the extent to which the wound is allowed to gape during the healing process. The smaller the distance between the edges of the wound, the less will be the amount of scar tissue. That is one of the reasons why it is considered essential to close a wound (either surgical or traumatic) with stitches to make the resulting scar as thin and as faint as possible.

In general, scars do not regenerate specialized tissue, such as the hair follicles and sweat glands of skin, although damaged muscles and nerves do regenerate specialized fibers in scars.

When large areas of skin have been damaged, as in burning, the resulting scars may contract so much that movement becomes restricted. In such cases plastic surgery is indicated, as it is for disfiguring facial scars.

scarlet fever

Some of the streptococci which cause sore throats produce a toxin (poison) which brings the skin out in a characteristic scarlet rash. This is most commonly seen in children of school age, who develop fever, a rapid pulse, headache, sore throat and perhaps abdominal pain and vomiting. After one or two days a rash starts on the neck, spreads to the chest and then covers the abdomen and the limbs. It leaves a pale area around the mouth which lasts for a few days, after which it fades. The skin becomes scaly, and the scales flake off. While the rash is present the tongue is covered with a white "fur" which peels off to leave the tongue red, with prominent papillae ("strawberry tongue").

In the last century scarlet fever (or *scarlatina*) was a serious disease, complicated by infection of the middle ear, rheumatic fever and inflammation of the kidneys. But with the advent of sulfonamides and penicillin its importance has declined. The streptococcus involved may be found in the throat or nose of healthy carriers.

See also the major article on **Infectious Diseases.**

schistosomiasis

A chronic illness caused by parasitic worms which live in the blood vessels around the liver and bladder. Schistosomiasis is one of the most important causes of ill health, lethargy and premature death in tropical

SCHISTOSOMIASIS

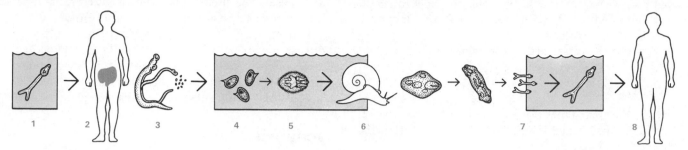

LIFE CYCLE OF *Schistosomatidae* FLUKES

Schistosomiasis affects 200 million people throughout the world. Infective larvae (1) abound in freshwater in many countries and penetrate the skin of bathers (2). They develop into flukes which enter the bloodstream and damage many organs. Adult flukes lay eggs (3) which are excreted into water (4) and hatch into miracidia (5). These penetrate a snail host (6) and change into thousands of larvae which are released into the water (7), where they can reinfect humans.

countries: worldwide more than 200 million people are infected.

The complex life cycle of the parasite starts with an infected person discharging eggs in the urine or feces. If the eggs reach fresh water in a lake, canal or irrigation ditch they hatch into *miracidia*, which may infect a particular form of snail. After multiplication inside the snail the *schistosomes* are released into the water as *cercariae*, and this larval form is highly infectious. The cercariae readily penetrate the skin of anyone swimming or wading in contaminated water for even a few minutes.

Once in the bloodstream, the cercariae migrate to the lungs; then, depending on their subtype, they move either to the veins leading to the liver or to veins around the bladder. Having reached the network of veins, the cercariae mature into adult worms: the male is about 2 cm long and the thinner, longer female lives in a cleft in the male's body. Schistosome worms may live for as long as 30 years and some varieties lay up to 3,000 eggs daily. The eggs penetrate the lining of the bowel and bladder and so are passed out of the body with the excreta.

Schistosomiasis may cause few or no symptoms, but when the infection is heavy the patient may pass blood in the urine or have repeated attacks of diarrhea. Weakness, lack of energy and repeated attacks of abdominal pain cause chronic ill health, eventually leading to failure of either the liver or kidneys.

Schistosomiasis can be treated by drugs which destroy the worms, but long-term control depends on public health measures—the life cycle of the parasite can be interrupted by providing safe disposal of sewage, backed up by the elimination of the snails from irrigation channels and watercourses.

See also the major article on **Healthy Living in a Hostile Environment.**

schizophrenia

A mental illness characterized by false beliefs, irrational thinking and a retreat from contact with the normal world. Over half the long-term patients in mental institutions have schizophrenia, which affects about 1% of the adult population of all countries.

The illness typically begins in adolescence; the onset may be abrupt or gradual. Early symptoms include hallucinations—especially the hearing of voices critical of current actions, with the patient discussed in the third person; *delusions*, typically of persecution (PARANOIA); and *flight of ideas*—rapid and apparently meaningless changes in the topic of conversation. Often the schizophrenic withdraws from his family and friends to spend hours and days on end in solitary silence. He may become convinced that his thoughts and actions are being controlled by outside influences. Among other common variants of schizophrenia are CATATONIA, in which the patient spends minutes or hours motionless and mute, often in a bizarre posture; and *hebephrenia*, with rapid swings in the emotional mood, incoherent speech, and outbursts of laughing and crying.

The cause of schizophrenia is unknown, but there is a genetic factor; the disease is found in 5% of brothers or sisters of schizophrenic patients and even more often in twins. There also seems to be an environmental factor— the first attack of schizophrenia may be provoked by emotional conflicts within the family. Despite enormous research efforts no one has yet found convincing evidence of an underlying chemical disturbance in the brain of schizophrenics.

Even so, there is an effective treatment; drugs of the phenothiazine group, such as chlorpromazine (Largactil) or trifluoperazine (Stelazine), reduce the length and severity of attacks of schizophrenia. Many patients with chronic schizophrenia are able to live in the community or with their families as long as they have regular drug treatment.

See also the major article on **Psychiatry**.

sciatica

Pain in the area of the body supplied by the sciatic nerve, including the buttocks, hip, back and outer part of the thigh, leg, ankle and foot.

It is caused by irritation of the spinal nerve roots which go to make up the sciatic nerve. The most common reason for the irritation is disease of the joint between the 4th and 5th lumbar vertebrae. The intervertebral disk—a cushion of cartilage between the vertebrae—may protrude and encroach on the space through which the nerve root passes (SLIPPED DISK), or the space may become narrowed by arthritic changes in the bones and ligaments of the joint. Rarely, sciatica is a symptom of a more serious disease of the lumbar part of the spine.

The pain down the leg is aggravated by straining, coughing, sneezing or bending and the part of the leg affected may become numb. The ankle reflex disappears, and the sensation produced by a pin prick is blunted. The muscles may be weakened and, in consequence, the foot may drop in severe cases. The lower part of the back is stiff and loses its normal contour (it becomes flat), while the muscles along each side of the spine go into spasm. Sciatica is usually accompanied by lower back pain, and raising the straight leg makes the pain in the back and the leg worse.

The first line of treatment is rest in bed: the bed must be firm, and in most cases this is best assured by putting boards under the mattress. Analgesics (painkillers, such as aspirin) are useful, as may be the local application of heat. Resistant cases may need physical therapy followed by special exercises and perhaps manipulation of the back.

Only in severe cases of demonstrable disk protrusion (slipped disk) is an operation advisable; but when the protruded disk is removed in a well-chosen case, the relief is usually immediate and lasting.

See also the major article on **Rheumatology**.

scleroderma

A rare disease which produces hardening of the skin, which becomes smooth, shiny and tight. The skin of the face may shrink so much that it becomes difficult to open the mouth widely; movement of the fingers is hampered and they may develop contractures.

The skin manifestations are part of a general systemic disturbance which affects the connective tissue of the intestine, lungs and kidneys, and may affect the heart. The cause of the disease is not known with certainty, but it is thought to be an immunological disorder.

Patients may survive for 20 years or more after the disease makes its appearance, usually in middle age, more often in women than men. There is no known effective treatment, but administration of corticosteroids may bring subjective improvement.

scoliosis

Scoliosis refers to an abnormal side-to-side curvature of the spine. It may involve the neck (*cervical scoliosis*), the chest region (*dorsal scoliosis*) or the small of the back (*lumbar scoliosis*). The main area of curvature will have secondary curvatures above and below it as a result of the body's attempt to maintain a more or less upright posture.

Scoliosis may be congenital, in which case it is associated with malformation of one or more vertebrae. Acquired forms of the condition occurring in later life are more common, however, and may result from disease of the bones of the spine or paralysis of the muscles which support the spinal column (*paralytic scoliosis*).

Paralysis of the muscles as a result of a disease such as poliomyelitis results in a loss of support to the spine from the muscles of the trunk. Scoliosis affecting one or the other side will then occur; if allowed to persist, it may result in secondary bony deformities.

The most common type of scoliosis has no detectable cause and the bones and muscles appear normal. The deformity is not usually severe in such cases, which are probably the result of prolonged habits of bad posture.

Special exercises are important in the treatment of the simpler types of postural scoliosis; but if bony deformity or muscle weakness is involved, surgical treatment or the use of various types of spinal supports may be necessary.

The prognosis for the simpler types is good but in more severe cases complete correction of the deformity may be impossible.

See also the major article on **Orthopedics**.

scotoma

A defect in the visual field that may be caused by a variety of disorders affecting the optic nerves. A "blind spot" may be one-sided or bilateral and sometimes not appreciated until full visual field testing is performed by an eye specialist.

Color scotoma may occur where certain areas of the retina are insensitive to color vision. They may be congenital, or acquired through damage to the nerve fibers brought about by optic neuritis—itself caused by a large number of conditions from anemia, disseminated sclerosis and diabetes, to tobacco, alcohol, chemical toxic agents and vitamin deficiencies. The treatment of the neuritis is directed toward the cause, and recovery is possible if the condition is not progressive.

See also the major article on **Ophthalmology.**

screening

The periodic examination of the body to determine the general state of health and to discover the development of any early signs or symptoms of disease.

Screening programs may involve individuals or entire communities exposed to special risks. It may be devoted to looking for one disorder of one part of the body—as in routine "Pap smears" of the cervix to assess any cellular change that may indicate early signs of cancer of the cervix, or routine chest x-rays of miners to detect early signs of silicosis. It may be devoted to an assessment of as many of the body's organs or systems as are amenable to standardized tests—sometimes called *multiphasic screening*—and be done as part of an annual or periodic physical. Presymptomatic testing, as in multiphasic screening, is thus a routine of some health care systems for communities (e.g., Kaiser Permanente clinics in California), and for others may perhaps only be offered as a preemployment examination by the employer's medical service. Most physicians nevertheless nowadays do some screening of their patients, although—because of the cost of the more complicated tests—in the majority of cases the screening will be undertaken only in the presence of preexisting symptoms (to help obtain an accurate diagnosis).

In a complete screening program, much of the testing may be done by specially trained nursing staff or technicians. It may involve all or any of the standard measurements of height, weight, skinfold thickness, chest expansion and abdominal girth. The vision will be tested, and a hearing test and dental examination may be included. Respiratory efficiency will be measured by a flow-meter and the blood pressure will be noted lying and standing. An electrocardiogram (ECG) will be taken at rest and after exercise, as well as a chest x-ray and perhaps a sputum analysis. The female's breasts will be palpated and MAMMOGRAPHY may be undertaken. In the man a rectal examination may be included to check for enlargement of the prostate gland; in a female the physician will perform a pelvic examination (vagina and uterus) and take a cervical smear. A urine specimen will be analyzed for the presence of sugar, protein or bacteria, and perhaps a specimen of stool will be examined for the presence of intestinal parasites or contagious organisms, where the medical history indicates a possible risk. Blood tests are given which indicate the hemoglobin level (abnormally low in anemia) and reveal the concentration of many chemical constituents of the blood (for example, an abnormal elevation in uric acid is diagnostic of gout). A blood count to determine the relative number of white cells, red cells and platelets per unit of blood, is also diagnostically useful—characteristic changes occur in various diseases, while a normal count is a good sign. Tests of liver and kidney function may also be performed.

In some community screening services, questionnaires have been used to gain some insight into individual psychological makeup and to attempt to identify those in need of follow-up. The value of screening is considerable, particularly if it is directed to those with special need or known vulnerability. Economically, however, it may be both expensive and time-consuming and may give a low yield of abnormality in well-cared for patients and communities.

See also the major article on **Preventive Medicine.**

scurvy

A condition caused by prolonged dietary deficiency of vitamin C (ascorbic acid), which man cannot synthesize. It is characterized by bruising of the dry scaly skin, bleeding gums (which are swollen and spongy), and delayed wound repair. Lassitude and weakness, anemia, loss of appetite, and internal bleeding may also occur. It was once an extremely common disease in seafarers deprived of fresh fruit and vegetables.

An average person needs 75 mg of ascorbic acid a day, and a normal diet contains an excess; but elderly persons may frequently suffer from deficiencies due to inadequate diet. Infant feeding with cow's milk alone may lead to scurvy. Scurvy can be cured by the administration of ascorbic acid (100 mg/day) within two weeks; a balanced diet must thereafter be maintained.

See also *The Sea Vitamin* in the major article on **Nutrition.**

sebaceous cyst

The sebaceous glands of the skin, which secrete *sebum*— a lubricant which helps maintain the health of the epidermis—are present throughout the surface of the body except for the palms and soles. They are most common on the head, shoulders and trunk. If the gland's outlet on the skin surface becomes blocked, the gland may continue to secrete and thus form a *retention cyst*, distended with sebum. Typically, it is a hemispherical swelling, firm and discrete. The cyst may proceed, if uninfected, to reach a considerable size.

Sebaceous cysts frequently become infected, discharge and collapse. If a cyst remains or poses a problem it can be surgically removed.

seizures

Sudden convulsions, usually caused by epilepsy, high fever (in children), poisoning, or hysteria.

Hysterical fits have a purpose, very often to gain sympathy, and never occur without an audience. The patient is not incontinent, never hurts himself, and "wakes up" quickly if painful stimuli are applied. The true epileptic fit (see EPILEPSY) is usually a very different matter.

The patient with *petit mal* (a form of epileptic attack) experiences a very quick and short loss of consciousness, which may amount to no more than a momentary silence or loss of attention. The patient is typically anxious to conceal what has happened—or may not realize anything has happened.

The patient with *grand mal* (the typical epileptic attack) often becomes unconscious, falls, shakes, is incontinent and may hurt himself—perhaps biting his tongue during the attack. He recovers consciousness slowly and cannot be aroused during the attack, even by painful stimuli. There are several different variations on this pattern.

In *focal* or *Jacksonian epilepsy* only a part of the body shakes and the patient may remain conscious, although such a seizure often goes on to a full-blown generalized convulsion. In *temporal lobe epilepsy* the features of the attack are varied and can be bizarre: the patient may suffer a dramatic change of mood, talk nonsense and experience hallucinations or feelings of DEJA VU (the sensation that what are in reality new experiences have happened to the patient before). After the seizure he may embark on acts at variance with his usual nature, for which he afterward has no recollection.

Children may develop convulsions as the result of a high fever; such seizures do not necessarily mean that the child is epileptic. They are rare in the first six months of life and after the age of five years are always generalized.

Simple fainting may be confused with epilepsy, for the patient may show minor twitching movements, and there are diseases such as diabetes mellitus which may produce loss of consciousness. Some middle-aged women suffer from a condition described as "benign episodic falling" in which the legs suddenly give way, possibly as a result of momentary interruption of the blood supply to the brain; such patients do not usually lose consciousness.

While a patient with known epilepsy has no need of medical attention each time he has a seizure, attacks occurring for the first time should always be referred to a doctor, who will be very grateful for a full and accurate description of the seizure.

See also *Seizures* in the **First Aid** section and the major article on **Neurology.**

senility

Progressive impairment of mental and physical functions, brought about by aging, may lead to a state of senility—characterized by mental deterioration.

In the early stages, mental versatility and the ability to maintain adequate intellectual performance during stress are reduced. Mental fatigue, anxiety and irritability increase with time. Speech becomes slower and impairment is noted in concentration, memory and time orientation. Dress and personal appearance are less tidy and appetite diminished. Alcohol and sedatives have an increased effect. Senile persons become increasingly self-absorbed and insensitive to the feelings and reactions of others; recall is delayed, calculation labored and there may be incomprehensible speech.

Some senile persons show restless overactive behavior and impulsive or inappropriate activity that can prove dangerous or hazardous to themselves. In the final stages, skills in performing even routine domestic tasks are lost, apathetic demeanor and behavior indicate an inability to communicate; there may be repetition of old familiar phrases that conceal the emptiness of the personality. Progressive impairment of mental ability often leads to fecal and urinary incontinence, an inability to walk and ultimately stupor and coma.

Senility is basically caused by diminished circulation of blood to the brain, in most cases as the consequence of progressive arteriosclerosis. Because the onset of this is variable, senility may occur over a wide age range. It must not be confused with depression, a condition common in old age, which may produce similar symptoms.

For more detailed information, see the section on *Senility* in the major article on **The Health Care of the Elderly.**

septal defect

See HOLE IN THE HEART.

septicemia

The presence and persistence in the bloodstream of pathogenic (disease-causing) bacteria. If the bacteria are not destroyed with the administration of an appropriate antibiotic, they can multiply and cause a massive infection of the body (systemic infection) possibly leading to death.

The signs and symptoms of septicemia usually include chills, fever, and the formation of pustules and abscesses.

The most commonly encountered bacteria that can cause septicemia are: *Enterobacter* species, *Escherichia coli*, *Klebsiella* species, *Meningococcus*, *Pneumococcus*,

Proteus species and *Staphylococcus aureus*. Less commonly encountered bacteria that can cause septicemia include *Pseudomonas aeruginosa, Staphylococcus epidermidis* and ß-*Hemolytic streptococcus*.

Also called *blood poisoning*.

serum sickness

When sera were widely used for the treatment of microbial disease, a number of patients developed reactions to the injections. These were usually reactions to foreign proteins from the animals in whom the sera had been prepared—the horse in particular—and often appeared days or weeks after the injection had been given.

Serum sickness produces swelling of the face, itching of the skin and severe joint pains and there may be nausea, vomiting and fever. It should be noted that very similar allergic reactions may occur in some patients given drugs or receiving blood transfusions.

The condition is now rare since most microbial diseases are now treated with antibiotics; sera prepared from human sources, less likely to cause allergic reactions, are widely available when their use is unavoidable.

The best treatment for serum sickness is the use of cortisone-like drugs (steroids), though antihistamines may also help. Response is usually rapid.

sex hormones

Chemical substances, secreted by the testis in the male and the ovary in the female, which determine sexual characteristics and function.

In the male the secretion of *androgens* (the most potent of which is *testosterone*) from the testis aid the development of the male sex organs, stimulate the secretion of semen, and are responsible for the masculine sexual characteristics.

In the female the secretion of *estrogen* and *progesterone* from the ovary stimulates the development of the breasts, the uterus and the external genitals, and maintains the menstrual cycle and the capacity of the woman for reproduction through pregnancy. In both sexes the sex organs (gonads) are under the control of the PITUITARY GLAND, which initiates their development at puberty and maintains their function in adult life.

Deficiencies of the sex hormones may occur where the glands themselves are abnormal, or where pituitary secretions are insufficient. In contrast, sexual precocity may be associated in either sex with tumors of the gonads, pituitary gland, or ADRENAL GLANDS.

Treatment with sex hormones is effective for identified deficiencies, but the tailoring of the dosage to the individual is essential and requires complicated biochemical analysis. Moderate supplementation is used in treating infertility, in either sex, and the menopause in the female; sex hormones are also sometimes used in the treatment of certain types of malignant disease.

See also HORMONES and the major article on **Endocrinology.**

sexually transmitted diseases

See VENEREAL DISEASE.

shock (cardiovascular)

Shock is the medical term for collapse due to inadequate circulation of the blood. Whatever the cause, the symptoms include pallor, sweating, nausea, restlessness, confusion, weakness and finally loss of consciousness. Shock may be caused by failure of the heart to pump sufficient blood through the body—because of, say, a CORONARY THROMBOSIS—by loss of blood as the result of hemorrhage (internal or external), by the plasma loss associated with severe burns, or by loss of body fluids from excessive vomiting or diarrhea (as in CHOLERA). Primary shock, or a faint, may be caused by the blood pooling in some veins and arteries which have suddenly lost their reflex tone; the consequent loss of consciousness is caused by impaired circulation to the brain.

When shock occurs the patient should be placed at rest, kept warm with light coverings, and the legs raised slightly to encourage the return of blood to the brain. Shock due to diminished circulatory volume—as in hemorrhage, trauma or dehydration—requires restoration of the volume to normal by the intravenous administration of fluids. The prevention of shock depends on the proper evaluation of the factors causing circulatory failure. The prompt initiation of therapy in cases of trauma, by teams of medical or paramedical personnel, has done much to save lives that would otherwise have been lost through irreversible damage to the heart, brain, or kidneys brought about through sustained circulatory collapse.

See also *Shock* in the **First Aid** section.

sickle cell anemia

Red blood cells contain the red pigment HEMOGLOBIN. In the majority of people, hemoglobin has a characteristic and unvarying structure and is referred to as *hemoglobin A* (or *adult hemoglobin*).

In certain people, a minute abnormality occurs in the chemical structure of the hemoglobin molecule, resulting in what is referred to as a *mutant hemoglobin*. These abnormal hemoglobin pigments are inherited from parent to child. Two forms of inheritance occur. The abnormal hemoglobin may be present in only one of the parents and the child can then only inherit a single dose and its cells will contain only a small proportion of the abnormal pigment. In such cases little harm will result. If both parents carry the abnormality, however, the child may inherit a double dose, causing the red blood cells to contain a large amount of the abnormal pigment. Serious illness may follow.

In many cases, fortunately, the clinical effects of even a double type of inheritance are minimal. In the case of the abnormal pigment referred to as *hemoglobin S* (or *sickle hemoglobin*)—which is common in persons from Africa or of African descent—the chemical abnormality present results in a tendency for the red blood cells to become distorted in a crescent shape ("sickle cells") if the level of oxygen in the arterial blood falls. This "sickling trait" can be identified by microscopic examination of the blood.

Sickle cell anemia refers to the double inheritance of hemoglobin S from both parents with large amounts of sickle hemoglobin in the cells. Even slight degrees of oxygen lack will result in a marked "sickling" change in the blood and consequent obstruction to the circulation in various parts of the body by masses of sickled cells ("sickle cell crisis"). During a sickle cell crisis (and, to a lesser extent, at other times as well), the sickle cells hemolyze (are destroyed and liberate hemoglobin into the surrounding fluid) in great numbers—sometimes enough to produce jaundice and to lower the red cell count seriously. Severe pain, dangerous organ damage and even death may result. Recovery is possible, however; with good medical care the patient may live a normal life, though crises may recur.

The single type of inheritance usually presents no symptoms.

See also ANEMIA and the section on *The Hematologist* in the major article on **Specialists You Seldom See.**

siderosis

A disease caused by the excessive inhalation of iron oxide dust. It is comparable initially to the effects of inhaling silica dust (which produces SILICOSIS).

Iron-ore miners and workers in the iron and steel industries are at special risk if they are unprotected by respirators. The condition causes less progressive lung damage than silicosis because the iron oxide particles do not provoke such an extensive fibrotic reaction (abnormal formation of fibrous tissue) in the lungs. The patient experiences breathlessness (DYSPNEA) and may cough up phlegm that is stained a dark color. Recovery, though with some permanent dyspnea that is not progressive, occurs when exposure to the dust-inhaling occupation ceases. There is no effective specific

treatment of the established case. Eradication depends on prevention.

Pulmonary siderosis is a rarity. More important is *hemosiderosis*, in which damage to the heart, liver and other internal organs is caused by an excess of iron in the body. It occurs most commonly as a complication of repeated blood transfusions for chronic anemias such as THALASSEMIA. The symptoms are similar to those of HEMOCHROMATOSIS, in which the accumulation of iron in the body is due to an inherited abnormality of iron metabolism.

See also PULMONARY DISEASES and the major article on **Pulmonary Diseases.**

sigmoidectomy

Surgical removal of the final descending part of the large intestine (colon), which joins on to the rectum. It is usually performed because of cancer (sometimes because of ULCERATIVE COLITIS) in that part of the colon.

See also COLOSTOMY and the major article on **Gastroenterology.**

silicosis

A disease of the lungs caused by the prolonged inhalation of fine particles of silica, which provoke a response of FIBROSIS (or permanent scarring) in the pulmonary tissues.

The most common form of silica is quartz, which is abundantly distributed in the earth's surface. Thus, miners, rock-cutters, sand-blasters and those who work in the ceramic and glass industries are especially exposed to the risk of silicosis. In the areas in the lung in which the particles accumulate, nodules of fibrosis develop; in advanced cases, both lungs may be heavily scarred. The mechanical and chemical irritant effects of silica are responsible. The characteristic feature of silicosis is loss of the normal elasticity of the lungs, so that breathing requires more effort.

The earliest symptom is shortness of breath on exertion (DYSPNEA); this may be followed by coughing, wheezing, and other features similar to bronchitis. There is a particular proneness to tuberculosis. Diagnosis is made by chest x-rays, which reveal the characteristic changes, although exposure to the dust over a period of 10 to 20 years may occur before symptoms are experienced. The changes in the lungs are irreversible and treatment is limited to the relief of symptoms. Prevention of the disease includes the use of efficient ventilation in modern industry, the regular use of respirators, and techniques of dust control.

See also PULMONARY DISEASES and the major article on **Pulmonary Diseases.**

sinusitis

The sinuses are cavities in the bones of the face and skull. They reduce the weight of the skull and add resonance to the voice. The largest are the *frontal sinuses* in the forehead and the *maxillary sinuses* in the cheeks. The maxillary sinuses communicate with the nasal cavity; because of extension of infections from the nose, these are the most liable to infection. The symptoms of pain and tenderness over them (frequently with a thick nasal discharge) are the classical signs of sinusitis.

Because the floor of the maxillary sinus lies directly above the first and second upper molars on either side of the upper jaw, abscess of the roots of these teeth can also extend upward and may drain into the sinus to cause a spread of infection. However, a complication arising from the common cold is the most frequent cause of sinusitis; obstruction of the normal sinus drainage by thickened mucus produces intense pain in the sinus itself as the fluid level rises. The affected side of the face may swell, as well as the lower eyelid. X-rays of the skull may reveal fluid that requires drainage.

Acute sinusitis may resolve rapidly with the administration of antibiotics and steam inhalations, which reduce the viscosity of the obstructive fluid. Chronic recurrent sinusitis may require surgical drainage and "sinus washout" to remove the accumulated pus. To achieve a permanent cure, it may be necessary to remove the lining membrane of the affected sinus surgically.

See also the major article on **Otolaryngology**.

SINUSITIS

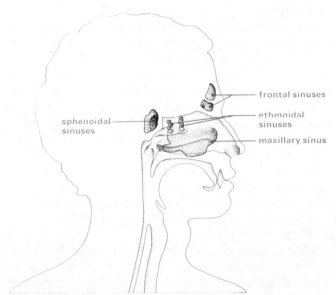

Sinusitis is caused by bacterial infection of the air sinuses which connect with the nose. It usually follows a head cold and causes a heavy feeling in the face and a blocked nose.

STRUCTURE OF THE SKIN

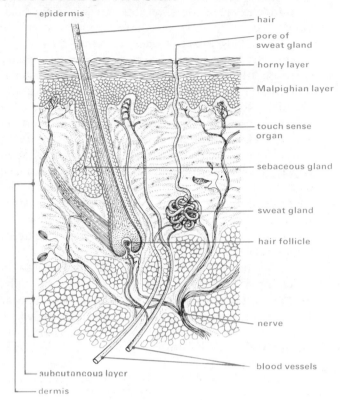

Skin encloses our entire body and provides a barrier against the entry of infection and the loss of tissue fluid. Although we think of skin as being extremely thin, the magnified section shown here reveals that it has many layers.

skin diseases

The skin may be affected by diseases which involve the whole body, but it is also especially vulnerable to external factors such as heat, radiation, and contact with chemicals and other irritants.

Structurally, the skin is divided into three rather distinct layers. The innermost (*subcutaneous*) layer serves as the receptacle for the formation and storage of fat and as a support for blood vessels and nerves which pass to the more superficial parts of the skin. It is also the layer in which the deeper hair follicles and the sweat glands originate.

The middle layer (*dermis*) consists of connective tissue which contributes to the support and elasticity of the skin. It is made up of a variety of cells which each have their own function—some to produce connective tissue, some to fight infection and so on. The dermis is also the layer in which sebaceous (oil-secreting) glands and the shorter hair follicles originate.

The *epidermis* is made up of layers of cells which form keratin (a tough protein substance which is found in hair, nails and other "horny" tissues), and cells which produce the pigment responsible for skin color (melanin). The epidermis constantly renews itself by shedding old layers as new ones are formed.

Any structure of the skin may be the primary structure affected by a particular disease; a malignant MELANOMA, for example, arises from the melanin-producing cells.

Exposure of the skin to the sun may cause burning and in pale-skinned persons prolonged exposure to strong sunlight increases the risk of skin cancer. Soap powders, solvents, dyes and cosmetics may all damage the skin, causing DERMATITIS. Some people develop an allergic sensitivity to metal (especially nickel) or other substances and are affected by a localized inflammation where the skin is in contact with the sensitizing agent (*contact dermatitis*).

Among the more common diseases are ECZEMA, in which the skin is reddened, weeping and intensely itchy; PSORIASIS, in which patches of silvery gray scales appear on the knees, elbows, and sometimes affect the whole body; thickening and roughening of the skin, as in LICHEN PLANUS; infection with bacteria and funguses, such as TINEA ("ringworm"); and a large spectrum of rashes associated with generalized infections, from measles to typhoid fever.

Identification of the cause of a skin disease often allows the irritant or the cause of an allergy to be removed. But even when the cause remains unknown (as in psoriasis), the symptoms can often be relieved by treatment with creams containing corticosteroid drugs, such as prednisolone or betamethasone. Sometimes the disease can be suppressed by drugs taken by mouth.

See the major article on **Dermatology,** and also ACNE, ALLERGY, BLACKHEADS, BLISTER, BOIL, BURNS, CARBUNCLE, CELLULITIS, CHILBLAIN, CORNS, DERMATOFIBROMA, DERMATOMYOSITIS, DERMATOSIS, ERYTHEMA, EXANTHEMA, FROSTBITE, HERPES SIMPLEX, HERPES ZOSTER, ICHTHYOSIS, INTERTRIGO, JAUNDICE, KERATITIS, KERATOSIS, KERATOSIS FOLLICULARIS. NEVUS. PAPILLOMA. PATCH TEST. PETECHIAE, PRURIGO, PRURITUS, RASH, RODENT ULCER, ROSACEA, SCABIES, SCAR, SCLERODERMA, SEBACEOUS CYST, STINGS, TATTOOING, TELANGIECTASIA, URTICARIA, WARTS, VITILIGO, XERODERMA.

sleep

A recurring state of inactivity accompanied by loss of awareness and a reduction in responsiveness to the environment. Unlike a coma, or unconsciousness caused by general anesthesia, a sleeping person can be easily aroused. Sleep is not a single state: electroencephalographic (EEG) studies, which measure the electrical activity in the brain, show that there are two basic alternating states.

The first is known as *nonrapid eye movement (NREM) sleep*, during which the heart and respiratory rates slow down, the muscles are greatly but not completely relaxed, and the eyelids remain quite still. This can be divided into four general states of increasing depth of sleep. If awakened during the NREM sleep, the individual may say that he was "thinking" at the time of waking up.

During *rapid eye movement (REM) sleep*, the eyeballs move jerkily under closed lids, the heart and respiratory rates quicken (but this is variable), and the muscles (especially the neck muscles) are completely relaxed. This is the stage during which dreams occur, and dreams are more likely to be remembered if the individual wakes up or is awakened during REM sleep. (See DREAMING).

On going to bed, drowsiness is followed by NREM sleep of progressively increasing depth. After about 90 minutes, REM sleep takes over; during this first cycle of sleep, the REM stage may last only about 5 to 10 minutes. There are also fewer eye movements in the first cycle. During a night's sleep there may be 4 to 6 cycles of sleep, each lasting 80 to 100 minutes; the duration of REM sleep increases with each successive cycle and may make up about 30 minutes of the later cycles.

The amount of sleep required by an individual and the pattern of cycles varies according to age. The young adult who has about 6 to 8 hours of sleep spends about 20–25% of the night in REM sleep. The baby, whose sleep cycle is short (about 40 to 45 minutes) spends about 50% of the sleep in REM sleep. In the elderly—in whom the total sleep time required gradually diminishes—the proportion spent in REM sleep also reduces gradually toward 20%.

Despite these general patterns of sleep, the amount required varies a great deal from person to person. The function of sleep is not entirely clear, but is thought to be a time which the body uses to catch up with the growth processes and repair. Some sleep is certainly required, but how much is difficult to say. Extreme sleep deprivation (used as one method of "brainwashing") can lead to hallucinations and paranoia. However, most people manage to adapt to smaller amounts of sleep deprivation; they may complain of irritability and loss of efficiency (but again it is difficult to quantify how much of this is caused by the loss of sleep and how much to *worry* about loss of sleep and lack of efficiency). When they do get a chance to catch up on the lost sleep, they do so not only by longer hours of sleep but also by spending a greater proportion of it in REM sleep.

Sleep disorders may be *primary*—the inability to fall asleep or stay asleep for very long (insomnia) or the abnormal tendency to fall asleep or have uncontrollable

SLEEP

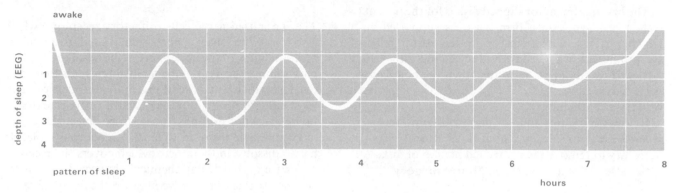

This diagram shows the fluctuations in the depth of sleep during a typical night as reflected by an EEG recording of brain waves. These waves change through stages 1 to 4 as the person becomes more deeply asleep. About every 90 minutes, the sleeper makes rapid eye movements (REMs); it is generally accepted that these coincide with periods of dreaming.

attacks of drowsiness in the daytime (narcolepsy)—or they may be *secondary* to various emotional or mental disturbances, chronic alcoholism, disease of the thyroid gland (hyperthyroidism), or brain disease.

The treatment of primary sleep disorders is the administration of the appropriate drug: stimulants (such as amphetamines) to control narcolepsy and sedatives or *hypnotics* (drugs that induce sleep) to control insomnia. It should be remembered, however, that it is unwise to take hypnotics for prolonged periods. Most of these drugs lose their effectiveness when used excessively and they may make the person psychologically and physically dependent on them. Withdrawal of most of these drugs may cause the individual to react by having more than usual amounts of REM sleep; this leads to vivid dreams, which then make the individual even more reluctant to stop taking hypnotics.

See also *Drugs for treating sleep disorders* in the major article on **Drugs and Medicines.**

sleeping sickness

1. Short for *African sleeping sickness* (see AFRICAN TRYPANOSOMIASIS). 2. Another name for ENCEPHALITIS LETHARGICA.

slipped disk

The intervertebral disks—which act largely as "shock absorbers" between the vertebral bodies and convey flexibility of the spine—may herniate, or "slip" forward or sideways, as the result of trauma (80% of cases), weakness of the retaining ligaments, or changes occurring in the fibrous consistency of the disk's outer wall. Typically, the disk "slips" while lifting a heavy weight with the body bent. The risk of a disk injury can be reduced by keeping the back straight while lifting. The condition is also known technically as *herniated disk*, *ruptured disk*, or *prolapsed disk*.

Protrusions of the lumbar disks (in the lower part of the back) are approximately 15 times more common than cervical (in the neck); thoracic disks (in the chest region) are rarely affected. Protrusion forward may impinge on the spinal cord or the nerves leading from it, so causing pain (SCIATICA), weakness, and numbness.

X-rays of the spinal area will usually show loss of disk space between particular vertebral bodies (but will not show the disk itself, which is not opaque to x-rays). Injection of a radiopaque dye (a myelogram) is required to define the precise extent of a disk's protrusion forward. Treatment depends largely on the severity of

SLIPPED DISK

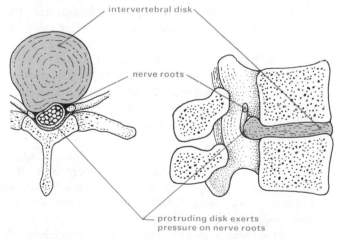

The picture shows a "slipped disk" where the fluid center of the disk herniates into the spinal canal. Such herniation results from excess strain or degeneration of the disk, and it presses on nearby nerves causing backache and pain in the legs.

the symptoms and the nature of the injury.

The first treatment for slipped disk is for the patient to rest in bed, lying on a firm mattress supported on a wooden base. Complete rest will often lead to relief of symptoms within a few days and to healing within a few weeks. If rest alone is ineffective, then the bones of the spine may be stretched apart by TRACTION, supervised by a physical therapist.

If these measures fail, or the symptoms recur on several occasions, then surgical treatment may be necessary to remove the protruded section of disk.

See also the major article on **Neurosurgery.**

smallpox

A highly contagious viral disease of man (also known as *variola* or *variola major*). At one time it was a major cause of death throughout the world.

Smallpox is characterized by a high fever of three or four days duration followed by a generalized skin eruption—consisting of crops of pink-red spots (1–2 mm in diameter) which typically appear first on the face and about the mouth. Within a few hours they begin to spread to the neck, arms and trunk. After a day or so the clear fluid in the center of the spots turns to pus, and this later dries to form scabs. The pustules (pus-filled sores) involve the deeper layers of the skin and after the crusty scabs fall off may leave pockmarks on the face or neck.

In people unprotected by vaccination, the mortality rate in epidemics has been as high as 20–40%. The disease is prevented by vaccination.

In 1921 there were over 100,000 cases in the United States; since 1953 no new cases have been reported. In 1958 over 250,000 cases were reported throughout the world—the majority on the Indian subcontinent. In 1977, for the first time, there were no reported cases of *variola major* anywhere in the world. However, cases of a less severe variant of smallpox (*variola minor*) continued to occur up to the late 1970s among the nomads in the remote desert regions of Somalia and near the borders of Ethiopia and Kenya. The World Health Organization hopes that both forms of smallpox will be extinct within a very few years.

No specific treatment exists for smallpox, although some relatively new antiviral agents have been tried with variable success. Only by means of vaccination against smallpox—which establishes artificial immunity—is protection ensured. Revaccination is necessary at intervals of three years or less to maintain a high level of immunity. Some countries require medical evidence of a smallpox vaccination before entry is permitted. Children with eczema are usually not vaccinated against smallpox, since there is a danger of the disease spreading from the vaccination site.

See also the major article on **Infectious Diseases.**

smell

The specialized nerve cells (olfactory receptors) which give rise to the sense of smell lie in a small patch of the mucosal lining of the upper part of the nasal cavity. This part is above the path of the main air currents that enter the nose with normal breathing, and odorous molecules must either diffuse up to the receptor cells or be drawn up by the act of sniffing in order to be detected.

To stimulate the sense of smell, an odorous molecule has to dissolve in the mucus which covers the receptor and set up a particular chemical change; this, in turn, electrically excites the nerve fibers of the main olfactory nerve.

Sensitivity to smell varies with the state of the nasal mucosa. It decreases during the common cold (especially if the nose is stuffy or runny), is impaired by smoking, and is increased in conditions of hunger. In general, females appear to have a slightly more acute sense of smell than males. Damage to nasal bones—in particular, fractures of the frontal base of the skull—may permanently impair the efficiency of the olfactory nerve; in some cases the sense of smell may be totally lost.

Discrimination between tens of thousands of different odor qualities is possible in the trained individual (for example, those who blend tea or prepare new types of

SMELL

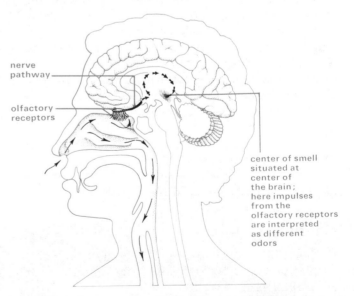

nerve pathway

olfactory receptors

center of smell situated at center of the brain; here impulses from the olfactory receptors are interpreted as different odors

Although our sense of smell is poorly developed compared with that of most animals, we are capable of distinguishing thousands of different aromas. Without it, our appreciation of food, our ability to enjoy numerous pleasant odors and our capacity to react to important signals from the environment—including dangerous fumes—would be lost.

perfumes). Physiological perception of smell may be based on the recognition of a limited number of *primary odors* (as is similarly true with the senses of taste and sight); varying intensities of stimuli from different combinations of odor molecules simultaneously and differentially excite large numbers of receptors.

smoking

Smoking affects health in three basic ways: (1) nicotine and other chemical constituents of tobacco smoke have an immediate effect on the body; (2) repeated exposure to smoke damages the lungs; and (3) regular smokers have a heightened susceptibility to heart disease and several common forms of cancer.

Nicotine is a brain stimulant, although habitual smokers often find it also has a calming effect. It speeds the heart, raises the blood pressure and reduces the appetite (many people find that they can skip a meal and have a cigarette instead).

The irritants in tobacco smoke narrow the air passages in the lungs. Smoke slows down the action of the hair-like cilia lining these passages, and so reduces the efficiency of the natural process of removal of inhaled dust from the lungs. Smoking also accentuates the normal loss of lung elasticity with age. These two effects account for the frequency of BRONCHITIS in smokers, who often accept a chronic cough as inevitable. In fact smokers are six times more likely than nonsmokers to die of bronchitis.

Smoking is a major factor in death from coronary thrombosis ("heart attack"). In men aged 40 to 55 who smoke, coronary attacks are three times as common as in male nonsmokers in the same age range—and sudden death from coronary disease is five times as common. As yet the mechanism by which smoking increases the risk of heart disease is unknown—so that claims that some cigarettes are "safer" than others cannot be justified.

Lung cancer is the best known disease associated with smoking: it is extremely rare in those who have never smoked; many studies have shown that the risk of the disease is proportional to the amount smoked. Smoking cigarettes carries a higher risk than smoking cigars or a pipe. Smokers also have a higher than average risk of bladder cancer, laryngeal cancer and stomach ulcers.

Taken together, the associations of smoking and disease make tobacco the single most important cause of death so far identified in Western society—which is why doctors in the United States and Britain smoke less than any other occupational or social group, and why their mortality rate from lung cancer has fallen.

snakebite

See *Snakebite* in the **First Aid** section.

sneeze

The respiratory tract, including the passages of the nose, is lined with specially adapted nerve cells (receptors) which are exposed on the surface of the mucous membrane. Stimulation of these receptors by noxious gases, irritant fumes, particles, microorganisms, or dust can result in an urgent stimulation of the brain's respiratory center. This produces a deep inspiration and a violent expiration so that particles can be literally exploded out of the respiratory tract. The sneeze is thus a protective mechanism.

somatotropin

The growth hormone; it is released by the anterior lobe of the PITUITARY GLAND.

The physiological effects of this hormone are numerous; they are associated not only with bone growth and cartilage extension, but the release of stored body fat and its conversion to energy, an increased rate in protein absorption by muscle cells—thus muscle development and growth—and an accelerated use of the body's glucose (sugar). The hormone itself is inextricably linked with the release and the effect of thyroid, adrenal and sex hormones.

Where pituitary disease or damage has occurred and somatotropin is deficient, growth is defective. Children born with a pituitary defect may grow very slowly (*pituitary dwarfs*), but if the condition is recognized early enough treatment with the hormone will permit them to reach a normal height. Excess growth hormone production during childhood causes *gigantism;* most of the famous giants had pituitary tumors. Excess growth hormone secretion caused by a tumor in later life produces ACROMEGALY; the condition can often be cured by treatment of the pituitary tumor, either surgically or by radiation therapy.

See also HORMONES and the major article on **Endocrinology.**

South American trypanosomiasis

Another name for CHAGAS' DISEASE.

spasticity

The special type of paralysis associated with damage to the nerve cells in the cerebral cortex (the upper motor neurones). Spastic paralysis occurs in stroke, cerebral tumors, and in multiple sclerosis, but the term is most often used in connection with the birth handicap spastic diplegia, cerebral palsy, or simply spastic paralysis. The neurological damage responsible for this type of paralysis is first noted in infancy, is nonprogressive and therefore assumed to be due either to birth trauma or defective development, being more common in prematurely born babies or in babies who sustain a cerebral hemorrhage. In particular, spasticity involves increased resistance to passive movement, exaggerated reflexes, spasms of the limbs and uncontrolled movements (ATHETOSIS). There is considerable variation in severity and in the defects (and, therefore, of muscular control), but it is important to remember that intellectual function and intelligence may not be impaired.

Approximately 25% of the infantile cases are mildly involved; another estimated 25% are severely affected, with loss of speech control and the development of seizures. There is no cure for what is essentially an irreversible defect of neurological control; but with physical therapy, bracing of limbs and the use of other appliances, considerable benefits can be achieved. Surgical intervention can be helpful to minimize deformities, and tendons can be transplanted so that the controllable muscles can achieve voluntary movement and overcome involuntary spasm. Drugs to overcome reflex spasticity are occasionally helpful but frequently sedate the intellect excessively. Survival prospects are nowadays excellent, provided the respiratory (breathing) mechanisms are not involved.

speculum

An instrument for examining body passages or canals.

The cone attachment of the *otoscope*, which is inserted in the ear to examine the eardrum, is a speculum. A *nasal speculum* is frequently a small flat-edged springed device that gently expands the nostrils so that the nasal passages can be examined. A *rectal speculum* is an illuminated cylindrical instrument with a removable tip which is withdrawn after insertion, so that the inside of the rectal canal can be examined in the diagnosis of disease of the rectum and nearby areas of the lower part of the large intestine. *Vaginal specula* are designed in various types and sizes. Some are single-bladed to pull the lower wall of the vagina downward to reveal the inside of the orifice, the upper wall and the front, or the cervix (neck of the womb); others are dual-bladed and open the vagina to reveal the deepest recesses and a larger area of the cervix. These are frequently used to obtain a "Pap smear" in diagnosing cervical cancer.

In all cases the instruments are sterilized prior to use. The recent development of inexpensive plastics, which are sterilized by irradiation, has led to the "disposable" speculum—which is used only once and then discarded.

speech

The use of sounds made by the mouth, tongue, and respiratory system to communicate specific thoughts from one person either to another or to many others.

The development of a spoken language is the most obvious difference between man and animals. Chimpanzees and other primates can be taught a language based on signs or pictures, but so far no animal has been taught to speak.

Speech develops slowly in the normal child. Between the age of 9 months and 5 years he learns a simple vocabulary and the basic elements of sentence construction, but the acquisition of full language skills takes the whole of childhood. Even in normal children there is great variation in the pace at which speech develops, but a child may be slow to speak because of low intelligence, extraordinary shyness, a physical defect such as deafness, or lack of stimulation in a deprived social environment. Speech defects such as lisps and stammering are more often due to psychological than to physical causes.

Once speech has been developed it may be lost again due to physical injury or disease of the larynx or tongue, or more commonly due to damage to the brain from a stroke (a cerebral thrombosis or hemorrhage), a tumor, or any other lesion.

When the loss or difficulty in speech is due to impairment of the control of the muscles used in forming the sounds the defect is termed *dysarthria*. One common example is the difficulty in speech associated with BELL'S PALSY, a temporary paralysis of the nerve supplying the muscles of the face. When the defect is in the brain centers concerned with language, the condition is termed *dysphasia* or *aphasia*. Loss of speech after a stroke may be due to either or both of these mechanisms; some recovery is usual and speech therapy may be helpful. Loss of speech in adult life may also be due to psychiatric disorders such as hysteria and catatonic schizophrenia.

spherocytosis

A condition in which red blood cells change in shape and become thick and almost spherical. It is a rare inherited disorder, found in northern European ethnic groups, with an incidence of 20 to 30 per 100,000 of the population.

The abnormal cells are unusually fragile, so that their life span is reduced, and the spleen usually enlarges owing to its role in destroying the defective cells. There may be no symptoms, or the high rate of cell destruction may cause a chronic anemia. Diagnosis of the condition, which is not usually obvious until adulthood, is made by a blood test. Treatment is by surgical removal of the spleen—which does not prevent spherocytes from still being made, but reduces the anemia and the incidence of complications from the increased rate of destruction of red blood cells (hemolysis).

SPEECH

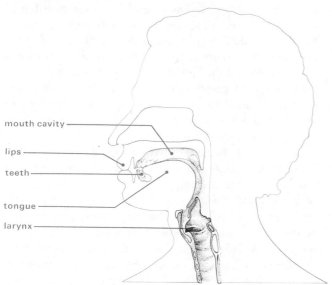

VOICE PRODUCTION

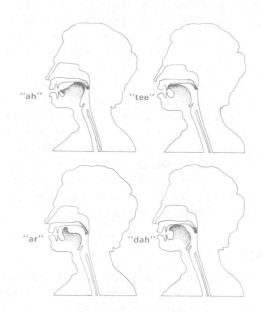

"ah"   "tee"

"ar"   "dah"

Vibrations of the vocal cords in the larynx produce the basic sound of the voice. The different elements of speech are produced by modifying the shape of the mouth cavity, position of the tongue, and the use of the teeth and lips.

sphygmomanometer

A device for measuring the BLOOD PRESSURE. Many types are in use, often bearing the names of their originators.

The most common instrument consists of an upright glass column filled with mercury and calibrated in millimeters. To this is attached, by a length of plastic or rubber tubing, an inflatable cuff designed to be wrapped around the patient's upper arm. Inflation of the cuff by compression of a rubber bulb applies pressure to the arm and the pressure in the cuff is recorded by the height to which the mercury rises up the calibrated glass tube (manometer).

When a STETHOSCOPE is applied over the main artery of the arm just below the cuff, the pulsation of the vessel can be heard. If the pressure in the cuff exceeds the highest pressure generated in the arteries with each heartbeat, no blood will pass through the artery and no sound will be heard. Lowering the pressure slowly, a point is reached at which the blood begins to flow through the vessel with each heartbeat but the vessel collapses again between beats and the flow ceases. The coming together of the vessel walls results in a sharp tapping noise, heard by the examining doctor, and the point at which this is first heard is described as the *systolic pressure*—the highest pressure generated by each heartbeat (see SYSTOLE).

Lowering the pressure still further, a point is reached

SPHYGMOMANOMETER

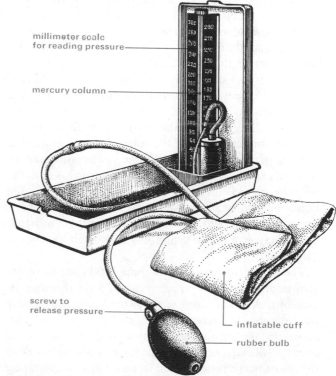

millimeter scale for reading pressure

mercury column

screw to release pressure

inflatable cuff

rubber bulb

The familiar sphygmomanometer is a simple but accurate device for measuring blood pressure. The cuff is wrapped tightly around the patient's arm and inflated to a high pressure by pumping the rubber bulb; this stops blood flow through the arm. The operator then slowly reduces the pressure and listens with a stethoscope over the artery for the sounds of the pulse. He records the levels of the mercury at which these sounds appear and then disappear.

where the blood flow becomes continuous but the individual heartbeats can still be heard as a softer tapping sound. The point at which this is first heard is described as the *diastolic pressure* (see DIASTOLE) and represents the steady pressure remaining in the arteries between heartbeats. Further reduction of the pressure results in the loss of all sounds in the stethoscope.

The final result of the measurement is recorded in millimeters of mercury pressure—often expressed, for example, as 120/80 (indicating a systolic pressure of 120 millimeters of mercury and a diastolic pressure of 80).

Modern variants of the instrument use direct-reading manometers or the pressure may be electrically recorded, but the underlying principle remains the same.

spina bifida

During the third and fourth weeks of embryonic life, the *neural groove*, which runs along the back of the embryo, fuses to form the *neural tube*. This tube is the forerunner of the central nervous system (the brain and spinal cord). Spina bifida results when closure of the neural tube is incomplete and is accompanied by a similar defect in the closure of the bony vertebral canal. The site most frequently involved is the lumbosacral region (at the bottom of the back), although higher regions are occasionally affected. Three varieties of spina bifida are recognized: *spina bifida occulta*, meningocele, and meningomyelocele.

Spina bifida occulta, the least severe form, results from incomplete fusion of the bony vertebral arch and is usually of no medical significance. The site may be marked externally by a tuft of hair, but often is detected only by chance on x-ray examination. Rarely, spina bifida occulta is accompanied by another spinal cord lesion such as a benign fat tumor, cyst or fibrous band. These may give rise to symptoms which can be relieved surgically.

The other two varieties of spina bifida are far more serious and involve the protrusion of a sac through the vertebral defect. In *meningocele*, the sac contains only the membranes which cover the spinal cord (the *meninges* or meningeal membranes); in the more common *meningomyelocele*, the sac contains spinal cord tissues or nerve roots as well as meningeal membranes. These forms frequently coexist with other congenital abnormalities, especially HYDROCEPHALUS (accumulation of fluid within the brain). Severe degrees of spina bifida may be incompatible with life, the baby being stillborn or only surviving a few hours. Neurological defects commonly found in those who survive include mental handicap, variable motor and sensory loss in the limbs, and impaired control of the muscular ring which controls the opening of the anus (anal sphincter).

The cause of spina bifida is unknown, but a woman who has had one affected child stands an increased risk of having another. It has recently become possible to diagnose meningocele and meningomyelocele before birth, by detecting increased levels of ALPHA-FETOPROTEIN in the amniotic fluid (which surrounds the fetus) so that the mother can be offered a therapeutic termination of pregnancy. A blood test for screening purposes is also available; at present its use is limited to women known to have a higher than average risk of giving birth to an abnormal child.

By 1954 it became possible to decompress hydrocephalus surgically, which dramatically cut the mortality rate in meningomyelocele. In addition, early repair of spinal defects was found to reduce MENINGITIS (inflammation of the meningeal membranes) and neurologic damage. Application of these new techniques has led to the survival of many severely handicapped children, while benefiting others enormously. However, neurosurgeons have been placed in a considerable ethical dilemma; many do not now operate on children with the most severe defects who, they think, would not have an acceptable quality of life despite surgery.

See also the major article on **Neurosurgery**.

spinal curvature

The human spine normally curves outward in the thoracic region, inward in the lumbar region and like an elongated "S" curves again in the sacrum to finish at the coccyx pointing downward and forward. Vertically, in correct posture, the uppermost cervical vertebra is directly in a gravitational line above the end of the sacrum. Abnormal curvature may be an exaggeration of the normal curves (KYPHOSIS), or extend laterally on either side of the vertical (SCOLIOSIS), or be a combination of both *kyphoscoliosis*.

Lateral curvature—scoliosis—is often associated with a compensatory twisting of the spine and may be due to congenital abnormalities of the vertebrae, bad posture in the child, paralytic disease affecting the muscles (such as POLIOMYELITIS) or pulmonary disease, particularly where the effects on one lung have caused contraction of the chest wall on that side. Cases which develop in puberty are recognized as more common in girls and require constant supervision involving serial x-ray examinations, physical therapy, exercises, spinal jackets and (if necessary) spinal fusion to prevent the development of permanent deformities.

Excessive convexity of the spine—kyphosis—may result from trauma (particularly mild compression fracture of a dorsal vertebra), from TUBERCULOSIS (now rare, but formerly known as Pott's disease of the spine) which erodes the vertebral bodies, and from secondary growths of a tumor.

ABNORMAL SPINAL CURVATURES

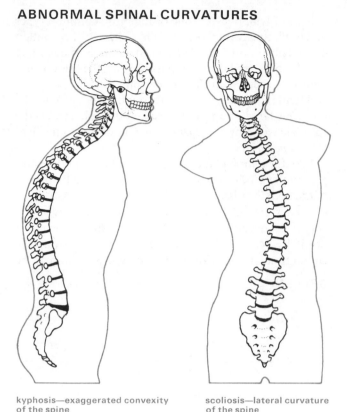

kyphosis—exaggerated convexity of the spine

scoliosis—lateral curvature of the spine

Illustrated above are two of the most common spinal deformities. Kyphosis, or "humpback," may result from poor posture (in which case it is often reversible) or from structural abnormalities in the vertebrae. Likewise, scoliosis may be postural, a congenital deformity or the result of a neurological disease such as poliomyelitis. The two deformities are sometimes combined in a condition called kyphoscoliosis.

ANKYLOSING SPONDYLITIS, by its production of rigidity in the lower spine, may cause an excessive curvature (as a compensation) in the cervical region. Paget's disease (see OSTEITIS) leads to a slow bending of the vertebra which, in the elderly, can also be a cause of kyphotic deformity. In the postmenopausal and the elderly, OSTEOPOROSIS can cause excessive spinal curvature as the result of weakening of the vertebral bodies. These disorders are less amenable to successful correction than those which first appear in the developing young.

See also POSTURE, SPINE and the major article on **Orthopedics.**

The spinal column (right) consists of 24 separate vertebrae plus two composite bones—the sacrum and coccyx. Our upright posture has led to the characteristic curvature of the column seen from the side, and means that the skull sits supported on a springlike structure.

SPINAL COLUMN

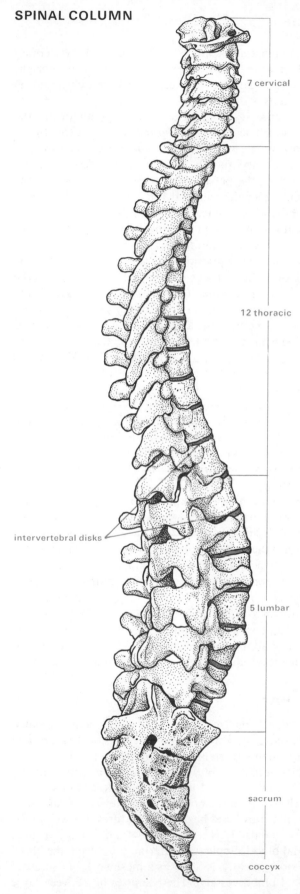

7 cervical

12 thoracic

intervertebral disks

5 lumbar

sacrum

coccyx

spine

The human spine consists of 29 bones (the vertebrae) which provide a stiff but flexible "backbone" for upright locomotion, and which encase the spinal cord and its nerve roots.

There are seven *cervical vertebrae* (supporting the skull and the neck), twelve *thoracic vertebrae* (providing anchorage for the rib case) five *lumbar vertebrae*—which are the largest—and five *sacral vertebrae* fused together (supporting the pelvis). The *coccyx* at the end of the sacrum is a small triangular bone; it is formed by fused and vestigial vertebrae, like a "tail." The two uppermost cervical vertebrae, which permit movement of the head, are called the *atlas* and the *axis*.

The spinal vertebrae are separated from each other by a disk of cartilage tissue (*intervertebral disk*). From the second cervical bone (axis) to the first sacral the vertebrae are held in close proximity by ligaments and muscles, which permit a limited range of bending and twisting while also protecting the spinal cord. Although the range of movements between the spinal bones is small, the somewhat elastic nature of the disks also permits them to be compressed. This ability to absorb compression stresses, aided also by the natural curvatures of the spine, means that the effects of the weight of the upright body and the impact of the feet—whether light (as in walking) or more heavy (as in running or jumping)—are smoothed out by this system of "shock absorption."

The anatomy of the spine is complicated in that each vertebral bone is different from another, but each has a thick and substantial *body* with extensions outward that form the protective arch for the nerves. Injury to the spine may be direct, causing fracture of one or other of these vertebral bodies, or excessive bending may cause a *compression fracture* of a vertebral body—in either case the pressure on the spinal cord can result in paralysis below that site. Deformities associated with disease, chronic bad posture or malignancy may occur and treatment is required at the first sign of abnormality.

spleen

An organ lying within the abdominal cavity, situated under the margin of the ribs on the left side. In shape and size it roughly resembles its owner's cupped hand.

The spleen resembles a large lymph gland in structure, similar to the glands found in the neck, armpits, groins and elsewhere in the body. It is, however, the largest of these structures and has special features not seen in the lymph glands. It is a vascular organ, having a large arterial blood supply. On entering the spleen, the blood flow slows greatly as it enters a meshwork of "sinuses" (dilated blood vessels). These sinuses lie between large masses of lymphocytes, one of the more common types of circulating white blood cells. Their walls contain other cells (known as *phagocytes*) capable of engulfing certain cells and foreign particles in the blood and removing them from the circulation.

After its slow passage through the spleen, the relatively large volume of arterial blood which enters the spleen leaves it by the *splenic vein* and passes to the liver via the *portal vein*.

Like the lymph glands, the spleen plays an important part in the production of the antibodies, which are part of the body's resistance to infection (see ANTIBODY). To a greater extent than the lymph nodes, however, the spleen is concerned with the removal of abnormal or normally worn out ("dying") blood cells from the circulation. Its function in antibody formation can be

SPLEEN

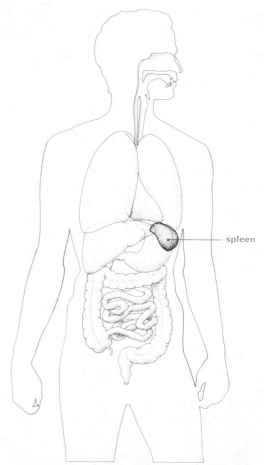

spleen

The spleen is an abdominal organ which lies underneath the lower ribs on the left of the body. It cannot be felt during a physical examination unless it has become enlarged by disease. It is frequently traumatized in automobile accidents and a splenectomy then has to be performed; removal of the spleen does not lead to any permanent disabilities in an adult.

readily taken over by the lymph nodes and removal of the spleen (following an injury, for example) is without serious effects except in very small children. In certain blood diseases, however, the spleen enlarges and removes blood cells more rapidly than usual from the blood; its removal may then be beneficial (SPLENECTOMY).

Enlargement of the spleen (SPLENOMEGALY) also occurs in a number of other conditions, including some infections, parasitic disorders, diseases of the liver and malignant tumors affecting the LYMPHATIC SYSTEM.

splenectomy

Surgical removal of the spleen. This organ lies under the margin of the ribs on the left side of the abdomen. The surgeon will approach it either by an incision made vertically on the front of the abdomen or by an oblique incision below the margin of the left rib.

The most common reason for removal of the spleen is accidental damage to the organ. This can occur on impact with the steering wheel in automobile accidents, as a result of blows to the abdomen, or as part of more widespread injuries received in a fall or other accident. Damage to the spleen—an extremely vascular organ— leads to a tear in its enclosing capsule; being soft and "friable," it does not lend itself to surgical repair and it is safer to remove it. Failure to do so may lead to dangerous hemorrhage within the abdomen.

The spleen may also have to be removed because it is diseased. This occurs commonly in malignant tumors of the LYMPHATIC SYSTEM and in HODGKIN'S DISEASE. It may then be removed as part of an exploratory operation on the abdomen designed to determine the extent of the disease before starting treatment. In certain blood diseases the spleen may remove red and white cells and platelets from the circulation at a sharply increased rate; surgical removal of the spleen may greatly alleviate these conditions. In other conditions, the spleen becomes abnormally enlarged (SPLENOMEGALY) and may cause the patient much discomfort, in addition to producing adverse effects on the number of circulating blood cells, and it may be removed for this reason.

Removal of a normal spleen is not considered to be a particularly dangerous operation, although if the organ is diseased or greatly enlarged the operation may be technically difficult and the risk increased. Except in very small children, removal of the spleen is not accompanied by an undue risk of adverse effects.

splenomegaly

Abnormal enlargement of the spleen, an organ lying in the abdominal cavity under the margin of the left rib and forming part of the LYMPHATIC SYSTEM.

A spleen of normal size cannot be felt by the doctor when examining the abdomen since it lies wholly beneath the rib margin. When checking for an enlarged spleen it can be felt more easily if the patient lies on his right side and takes a deep breath; descent of the diaphragm will then displace the spleen downward so that (if enlarged) it can then be felt protruding below the left rib margin.

Many different conditions may cause enlargement of the spleen. Enlargement occurs in some blood disorders (including the chronic leukemias) and a grossly enlarged organ may occupy much of the abdominal cavity. More common causes of enlargement, however, are certain infectious diseases; the detection of an enlarged spleen may be an important diagnostic finding in such conditions as INFECTIOUS MONONUCLEOSIS, TYPHOID FEVER and MALARIA.

splint

A rigid appliance for the immobilization of a part of the body's musculoskeletal system, or for the correction of a deformity.

It may thus be a simple slab of plaster of Paris, or acrylic, on the lower forearm and wrist to protect against excessive movements of an injured wrist bone or tendon—or a whole-body plaster jacket, also encasing part of the head, to secure immobility of a fractured spine. Following the correction of some bone injuries or joint disorders, plaster-impregnated bandages can be applied after wetting. They can be molded to the individual's needs, they set quickly and can be left on as long as necessary to secure healing. X-rays can be taken through them and they are easily removed by cutting, using special plaster shears or saws that oscillate and do not cut the skin.

When a plaster splint has been applied over a fresh fracture, a careful watch is necessary in case swelling of the limb in a close-fitting splint impairs the blood circulation. The period of greatest potential danger is from about 12 to 36 hours after injury; severe pain or swelling of the exposed limb beyond the splint is a sign for reassessment and perhaps splint removal and replacement, or merely splitting open the splint. In emergencies a splint can be made from any material—a piece of wood or a tree branch, or one injured limb can be splinted to another part of the body by binding (for example, the legs can be bound together or an arm can be bound across the chest). Inflatable splints—fitting like gloves over an injured limb, which then stiffen when inflated—are a relatively recent invention of great benefit to emergency services. Specialized splints (such as supports for the legs, back braces, or cervical collars) are "tailor-made," frequently from steel or inflexible plastic. Internal splints for fractures and deformities are achieved with metal plates and screws, or rods and nails; this method is used where external splintage would be unsatisfactory.

See also *Fractures* in the **First Aid** section.

spondylosis

A degenerative disorder of the spine which leads to narrowing of the spinal canal. It can occur in the cervical or lumbar area and leads to pressure on the spinal nerves or spinal cord.

Initially the cause can be trauma, which shows itself in middle life and old age to produce symptoms chiefly in those between the ages of 50 to 60. Degeneration of the nucleus of the intervertebral disk and the surrounding fibrous tissue leads to a reaction of the adjacent areas of vertebra. Variable calcified outgrowths from the vertebra may then protrude to press on the spinal cord, or occlude the spinal nerve's exit from the cord and so cause considerable neurological discomfort. This slow progression of disk degeneration followed by bony overgrowth of the spine may take place over many years and be the result of former sporting injuries, whiplash or trauma.

Commonly pain is the initial symptom, with some loss of comfortable spinal movement. Muscular weakness may occur in the specific areas supplied by the spinal nerves and, where spinal cord compression occurs, sensory deprivation over wide areas of the body (below the affected level) is experienced.

Diagnosis is by x-ray of the spine and myelography. Treatment consists primarily of rest by immobilization

CERVICAL SPONDYLOSIS

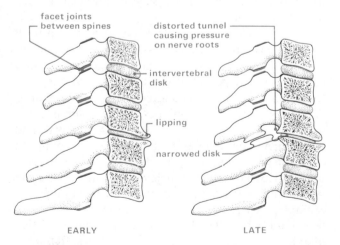

facet joints
between spines

distorted tunnel
causing pressure
on nerve roots

intervertebral
disk

lipping

narrowed disk

EARLY   LATE

Cervical spondylosis is simply osteoarthrosis of the spine in the neck and results from years of wear and tear. The intervertebral disks become narrowed and extra spurs of bone encroach into the spinal canal and nerve tunnels.

of the affected area of the spine, in a plaster or plastic jacket or collar. Surgery to relieve compression may be necessary in cases where paralysis is severe.

See also OSTEOARTHRITIS.

sporotrichosis

A fungus infection that may gain entry to the body through inhalation, ingestion or inoculation from a contaminated environment. The fungus exists in soil, peat moss, and decaying vegetation, and the disease is contracted mainly by laborers, farmers and florists. Outbreaks commonly occur in Mexico and Florida.

Pustules on the exposed skin enlarge and lead to involvement of the lymph glands, which themselves may ulcerate. Internal absorption of the organism produces the same lymph gland response and the disease, if untreated, may be fatal.

Diagnosis is made by blood tests and culture of the organism from the gland or pustule. Treatment is usually effective with antifungal medication, which may need to be continued for several weeks.

sprain

The incomplete tear of a ligament. Sprains are not serious injuries, but it is important to distinguish between sprains and complete disruption of a ligament, which may lead to subsequent instability of the affected joint. Complete tears are recognized by abnormal mobility of the joint, and the diagnosis may rest on radiological (x-ray) appearances.

The ligaments of the knee and ankle are most commonly sprained (the ankles more often than the knee), although it is not uncommon for the wrist to be sprained in a fall. The injury is often very painful and is accompanied by considerable swelling and bruising. Movement is painful.

At first the joint will probably be more comfortable if it is bandaged to limit movement and help keep the swelling down, but as soon as possible the joint should be moved and used.

See also *Sprains* in the **First Aid** section.

sprue

1. See TROPICAL SPRUE.
2. A term used to describe the adult form of CELIAC DISEASE; also known as *nontropical sprue*.

sputum

An adult in normal health secretes about 100 milliliters (ml) of mucus from the cells lining the respiratory tract each day. This is removed from the air passages by the action of the ciliated cells which line the trachea (windpipe), bronchi and bronchioles, and is not noticed.

Sputum is the word used to describe excess secretions which cannot be removed by ciliary action; it stimulates the nerve endings in the mucous membrane and sets up a cough reflex. It is the result of irritation or inflammation of the air passages, and may be classified under six headings; (1) *mucoid*, which is clear; (2) *black*, which contains dust, or cigarette and atmospheric smoke; (3) *purulent*, which contains pus; (4) *mucopurulent*, with mixed pus and mucus; (5) *bloodstained*, with streaks of clots of blood (hemoptysis); and (6) *rusty*, which is mucus mixed with small amounts of altered blood and is found mainly in association with pneumonia.

The appearance of blood in the sputum always requires medical investigation to rule out a potentially serious condition.

squint

Another name for STRABISMUS.

stammering

Stammering or stuttering is a disturbance of speech in which it is abruptly interrupted or certain sounds or syllables are rapidly repeated.

It is much more common in men than women and more common in left-handed or ambidextrous persons as well as in those who have attempted to become ambidextrous though originally left-handed. It occurs in up to 1% of schoolchildren, usually before the age of 10, and tends to run in families.

Whether speech is disturbed by repetition of sounds or syllables, or is interrupted completely because the patient "cannot get the word out," a degree of shame or embarrassment is usually present. Patients may thus often appear to have psychological problems or to be shy or withdrawn; but these features may be the *result* of the condition rather than its *cause*. Most patients who stammer or stutter do not have an underlying psychological disturbance.

Treatment involves speech training, the restoration of confidence and the overcoming of any psychological problems which may have arisen as a result of the disorder. A skilled speech therapist (or speech pathologist) will employ relaxation exercises, breathing exercises and carefully controlled speech exercises. A slow, "syllable-by-syllable" type of speech may be cultivated and confidence restored by singing or shouting words over which difficulty is experienced. Stressful situations are avoided until confidence returns. Tranquilizing or sedative drugs may be helpful. The enthusiastic encouragement of therapist and family plays an essential role.

Prognosis is good with proper treatment; the less the patient is disturbed by his speech problem, the better the outlook.

stapedectomy

A surgical procedure to correct one form of hearing loss.

Sound waves entering the outer ear cause the eardrum, between the outer and middle ear cavities, to vibrate. These vibrations are conducted across the middle ear cavity to the inner ear (where they are transformed into nerve impulses and sent to the brain) by a chain of three tiny bones (*ossicles*) which bridge the cavity of the middle ear.

In the condition of OTOSCLEROSIS there is formation of new bone at the point where the innermost ossicle (the *stapes*) fits into the *oval window*—a minute aperture between the middle and inner ears. The "footplate" of the stapes, normally free to move in the aperture and thus to transmit the vibrations to the inner ear, becomes fixed in position and sound-conduction deafness results.

STAPEDECTOMY

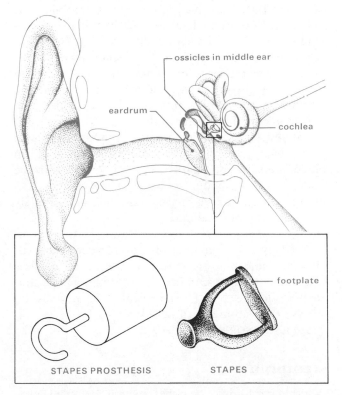

ossicles in middle ear

eardrum

cochlea

footplate

STAPES PROSTHESIS   STAPES

Hearing depends on the ability of the ossicles (little bones) of the middle ear to transmit sound. Occasionally, the footplate of the stapes becomes fused to the cochlea in a disease called otosclerosis. The resulting deafness can be cured by a stapedectomy operation, where the stapes is replaced a tiny stainless-steel piston.

Surgical removal of the stapes—*stapedectomy*—performed through an incision into the middle ear, is followed by re-establishment of the chain of conduction for the vibrations of the eardrum by means of a plastic or metal prosthesis (replacement part). The success rate of this operation in restoring a useful degree of hearing is about 80%.

The operation is not without potential complications, including total loss of function of the organ of hearing itself in the inner ear, perforation of the eardrum and damage to nerves in the vicinity of the middle ear. Dizziness may also occur but is usually temporary.

See also the major article on **Otolaryngology.**

starvation

In *acute starvation* the patient's intake of calories falls seriously below his normal energy requirements. Unless reduction in his physical activity can reduce these requirements to bring them within the calorie intake available, he must draw on his own tissues as an energy source.

Fat is the obvious energy storage tissue, having a high calorific value, but some protein must be mobilized as well to provide essential nutrients for certain tissues that require them. Loss of body weight occurs both from loss of fat and of muscle protein. There may be swelling of the tissues as the result of an accumulation of fluid in them, especially in the legs and feet, when standing.

When the last reserves of fat have been mobilized, the patient's condition deteriorates rapidly—since only essential protein-containing tissues can now be drawn on for energy supplies. Lassitude, weakness, a fall in blood pressure and death will soon follow. In some cases, dehydration due to water deprivation is also present; complete lack of water is much more rapidly fatal than starvation alone.

In *chronic starvation* the condition may be complicated by the symptoms of multiple deficiencies of vitamins, minerals and protein. Deficiency diseases which may then be seen include BERIBERI, PELLAGRA, SCURVY, RICKETS and the protein deficiency disease KWASHIORKOR. (See also MARASMUS.)

See also ANOREXIA NERVOSA.

steatoma

A term used to describe either a SEBACEOUS CYST or a LIPOMA.

steatorrhea

The condition of having an excessive amount of fat in the stools. It is common in most conditions that cause MALABSORPTION.

Stein-Leventhal syndrome

Abnormally large cystic ovaries with fibrosed capsules are found in about 1% of women; in some cases these findings are associated with AMENORRHEA, abnormal growth of hair, obesity and infertility, and the pattern is known as the Stein-Leventhal syndrome.

The disturbances are thought to be the effect of disordered steroid production in the ovaries, possibly following disturbed function of the pituitary gland and the hypothalamus.

It has been found that surgical removal of part of the enlarged ovaries is followed by renewal of menstrual flow, reversal of the masculinizing changes and restored fertility, but it is also possible to treat the condition with clomiphene (Clomid).

stenosis

The abnormal narrowing or constriction of a hollow passage or orifice (the entrance to a cavity or tube).

sterilization

Any surgical procedure which makes a man or woman infertile while leaving sexual desire and capacity unaffected. In men the operation is *vasectomy*, a simple procedure done under local anesthesia. The surgeon makes a small opening in the scrotum and cuts through each of the two *vas deferens* (the tubes connecting the testes to the base of the penis). After vasectomy there is no apparent change in sexual performance, but the ejaculated semen no longer contains spermatozoa (once the stores are used up, which takes a few weeks). There are no long-term effects on general health or on sexuality.

In women the most usual sterilization procedure is cutting or blocking the Fallopian tubes which connect the ovaries to the uterus. Only a minor operation is needed, for the surgeon can locate and divide the tubes through an incision only half an inch or so long, using an operating "laparascope"—a thin tube through which the interior of the abdominal cavity can be examined. Division of the Fallopian tubes does not have any apparent effect on the menstrual periods or on sexuality.

Sterilization is being used increasingly as an alternative to contraception by couples who have completed their families: it is safe and reliable and (unlike the use of oral contraceptives) carries no risk to general health. The procedures are not readily reversible: a man or woman who has been sterilized has only a small chance of being restored to normal fertility if the surgeon reconnects the separated tubes. However, successful techniques for reversal of sterilization are currently being developed.

STETHOSCOPE

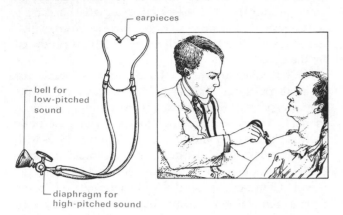

earpieces

bell for
low-pitched
sound

diaphragm for
high-pitched sound

The stethoscope is a very simple instrument which has been in use for many years, but still retains an important place as a diagnostic tool in modern medicine. Doctors use it to listen to the sounds from our hearts and lungs.

stethoscope

The common instrument used by a doctor to listen to the sounds made by a patient's heart or lungs (AUSCULTATION). It can also be used to listen to sounds produced in blood vessels in the limbs and the sounds produced by the movements of the intestines during digestion. Together with a SPHYGMOMANOMETER, it is an essential piece of equipment for taking the blood pressure.

The general shape of the stethoscope will be familiar. The chest piece, which is applied to the patient's chest wall, may be of two types. One is bell-shaped and open, the other (Bowles type) is flat and covered with a plastic or metal diaphragm. The chest piece is attached to a Y-shaped connector which transmits the sounds by means of two lengths of thick-walled rubber tubing to the ear pieces.

Modern variants include electronic detection and amplification of the sounds. A simpler type of instrument using only one ear piece is more efficient and convenient for obstetric use.

stings

Two major groups of stinging creatures exist, fish and other types of marine life and the venomous or biting *arthropods* (a phylum of invertebrate animals containing over 700,000 species, including the insects, spiders and crustaceans).

Among the marine group are the venomous fish that carry poisonous spines. These include the stone fish, scorpion fish, lion fish and the weever fish. These all inhabit shallow waters and lie concealed in sand or among rocks. Swimmers and skin divers may be stung by them and fishermen may be injured while removing them from nets and lines. Pain from their stings may be very severe, constitutional symptoms may occur and death may occasionally result. In the case of the stingrays, the fish carries the sting in its tail and drives it into the victim when disturbed.

Jellyfish can cause painful stings and both the Portuguese man-of-war group and the true jellyfish may produce severe pain, extensive rashes or even death. Jellyfish cannot of course "attack" man; contact with them occurs accidentally among swimmers and skin divers.

The stinging insects include the many varieties of wasps and bees. The effect of stings from bees and wasps depend on the patient's personal sensitivity. Lethal reactions are relatively rare. In the case of the potentially dangerous scorpion sting, the mortality rate may be as high as 5%.

In serious cases immediate medical aid should be urgently sought to combat shock; specific *antisera* are available in most cases. Symptoms of milder stings may be relieved by the administration of antihistamines, steroids, and painkilling drugs.

See also *Stings* in the **First Aid** section.

Stokes-Adams syndrome

See ADAMS-STOKES SYNDROME.

stoma

1. A small opening, pore, or mouth.
2. An opening created artificially between two body cavities or passages and the surface of the body (such as the surgical opening created by a COLOSTOMY).

stomach

The stomach lies centrally in the upper part of the abdomen and provides a receptacle for the immediate reception of food after it has been chewed and swallowed. Food enters the stomach at the *cardiac sphincter*, a valve-like ring of muscle at the lower end of the esophagus ("gullet") and leaves it by the *pylorus* (a similar structure at the lower end of the stomach) to pass to the duodenum and small intestine.

Between the cardiac sphincter and the pylorus, the upper and lower borders of the stomach (as it lies in the abdomen when the subject is erect) are referred to as the lesser and greater curvatures, respectively. The organ is also subdivided into an upper portion (above the entry of the esophagus at the cardiac sphincter) called the *fundus* and a lower portion (close to the pylorus) called the *antrum*. Between these lies the *body* of the stomach.

The stomach has a thick muscular coat and can

STOMACH

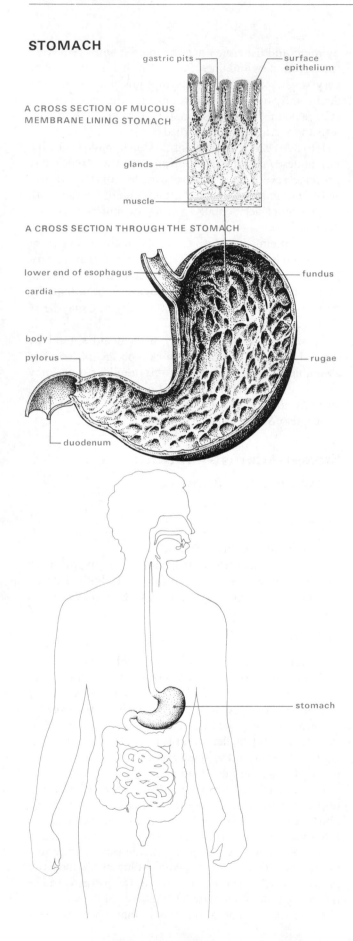

gastric pits — — surface epithelium

A CROSS SECTION OF MUCOUS MEMBRANE LINING STOMACH

glands

muscle

A CROSS SECTION THROUGH THE STOMACH

lower end of esophagus — — fundus

cardia

body

pylorus — — rugae

duodenum

stomach

contract to force food through the pylorus or, in vomiting, up through the esophagus. It is lined by a mucus-secreting membrane (the *gastric mucosa*), which is also responsible for the digestive secretions produced by the organ.

As its contribution to the digestive process, the stomach produces *hydrochloric acid* and an enzyme, *pepsin*, capable of breaking down protein in the presence of acid. The food, already broken up and partially digested by chewing and mixture with saliva, mixes with the acid and pepsin in the stomach and protein digestion begins—although no major absorption occurs in the organ. Contractions of the stomach wall, while the pylorus remains closed, mix the food thoroughly with the digestive juices. When digestion with pepsin is completed, the pylorus opens and allows the food to pass on into the duodenum—where it meets other digestive juices from the liver and pancreas.

Another very important secretion produced by the stomach wall is known as *intrinsic factor*. This substance is required for the normal absorption of vitamin B_{12} from the diet. In "pernicious anemia," thinning and degeneration of the mucosa occurs with loss of intrinsic factor secretion, failure of vitamin B_{12} absorption and the development of a characteristic type of ANEMIA as the result of lack of the vitamin.

See also the major article on **Gastroenterology.**

stomatitis

Inflammation of the lining membrane of the mouth (*oral mucosa*). It often involves the tongue as well and the patient complains of a sore mouth.

Many conditions can produce a sore and inflamed mouth. Scalding by hot fluids or burning by caustic ones, hot or spicy foods and damage from jagged teeth or ill-fitting dentures can all cause stomatitis.

Local infections which produce a sore mouth include CANDIDIASIS ("thrush") and infections with bacteria known as "Vincent's organisms." Some virus infections—including HERPES ZOSTER ("shingles"), CHICKENPOX and MEASLES—may involve the mouth. Prolonged antibiotic therapy, by altering the balance of normal bacteria which inhabit the mouth, can also produce stomatitis.

The stomach acts as both a reservoir for food and a site for its digestion. The interior of an empty stomach is marked by prominent folds (rugae) which are flattened out as the stomach expands after a meal. The surface of the body and fundus when seen under a microscope is marked by numerous small openings, the gastric pits. Digestive juices well up from these pits when the stomach is stimulated by food.

Certain vitamin deficiencies cause stomatitis. A prolonged lack of riboflavin and nicotinamide (in the vitamin B group) produces a characteristic clinical picture; SCURVY, the result of a lack of vitamin C, can produce swelling and hemorrhage in the gums. Vitamin B deficiency in "pernicious anemia" is accompanied by a sore mouth and tongue, which is also the case in patients with folic acid deficiency and iron-deficiency anemia. (See ANEMIA.)

Other blood disorders—including leukemia, agranulocytosis (loss of circulating white blood cells, sometimes as a side effect of drug therapy) and "aplastic anemia" (failure of production of all blood cells by the bone marrow)—may be accompanied by severe stomatitis, often with ulceration of the oral mucosa. A condition of unknown cause is *aphthous ulceration* (or *aphthous stomatitis*), in which recurrent crops of small ulcers ("canker sores") appear spontaneously on the oral mucosa.

Treatment of stomatitis is directed toward the underlying cause. Milder cases clear up spontaneously with antiseptic mouth washes or good dental hygiene and aphthous ulcers usually disappear spontaneously within a few days.

stones

See CALCULUS.

strabismus

The medical term for a "squint." The condition is most common in young children and several types are found.

In a patient with a squint the eyes do not (as in normal persons) remain parallel; one or the other eye diverges from the direction in which the gaze is directed. A tendency exists for one eye to become the "master eye" and, when the patient looks at an object, it is fixed by the master eye and the other is seen to be directed in a slightly different direction. Squints may thus be *divergent* if the squinting eye looks away from the line of the master eye ("wall-eye") and *convergent* if it looks toward the master eye ("cross-eye").

Squints may also be divided into the *concomitant* squints (commonly seen in childhood), in which an imbalance exists in the strengths of the paired muscles which move the eyeball, and the rarer *paralytic* squints, in which there is a complete or partial paralysis of one or more muscles in the affected eye.

The appearance of a squint may lead the patient to seek medical advice; double vision may occur, especially in paralytic squint. Squint in young children is an important condition, since the brain suppresses the image seen by the squinting eye; if correction of the squint is delayed the eye may become functionally blind (AMBLYOPIA). In such circumstances the child will never develop binocular vision.

Treatment of concomitant squint is either by eye exercises designed to strengthen the muscles whose power is deficient (*orthoptics*) or by surgery. Orthoptic treatment requires a long period of therapy and much cooperation from the patient, but may be helpful. Operative treatment involves the shortening of the affected muscles so that their contractions are able to balance the pull of their opponents.

See also the major article on **Ophthalmology.**

stress

Stress is a term used medically to describe pressure or physical force such as the compression of the lower teeth against the upper teeth during chewing or the forces acting on a joint during weight-bearing or during physical exercise. It is also used to refer to any influence that disturbs the natural equilibrium or internal environment of the body.

Such stress may be produced by physical injury, temperature changes, disease, emotional disturbances, or prolonged demands on physical or mental endurance. If the stress persists for too long or is too intense for the body's regulating mechanisms, one or more of the *stress diseases* may develop: these include mental disorders such as schizophrenia and physical conditions such as peptic ulcer, ulcerative colitis, hypertension, eczema, or asthma.

The ADRENAL GLANDS, which are two small endocrine glands situated on top of the kidneys, play a key role in regulating the body's response to stress by releasing their hormones into the blood circulation.

Epinephrine and *norepinephrine* (two hormones secreted by the adrenal glands) increase the heart rate and blood pressure, constrict the blood vessels in the skin and digestive system (thus diverting blood to the muscles), and encourage the release of glucose (sugar) from the liver stores to supply the body's energy demands. In other words, they induce changes in the body which prepare the animal for "fight" or "flight."

The adrenal glands also secrete the *corticosteroid hormones*, which play a major role in the body's response to infections and other diseases. They control the internal balance of sugars, fats and minerals and the incorporation of protein into the muscles. The interaction between the external stresses and the internal response by the adrenal glands help to determine whether the individual concerned remains healthy; prolonged stress will·eventually exhaust the internal reserves and precipitate some form of mental or physical ill health.

See also the major article on **Healthy Living in a Hostile Environment.**

stridor

Any harsh, high-pitched, rattling or "snoring" sound produced during respiration—either while awake or during sleep. It is fairly common in babies and young infants, in whom it may have no medical significance. Such prolonged (chronic) noisy breathing is frequently caused by the "floppiness" of the epiglottis, which may vibrate during breathing. (The epiglottis is a fleshy structure that covers the entrance to the larynx, or "voice-box," during swallowing to prevent food or liquid from entering the air passages.) In such cases there is rarely a danger of any obstruction of the baby's airways. In older children or adults, however, such breathing may be a sign of a serious disorder and requires prompt medical attention.

There are many causes of stridor, including the presence of an inhaled foreign body (see FOREIGN BODIES) or spasm of the vocal cords following the inhalation of irritant material or vomit. Acute infection can produce obstruction to the airway. Simple LARYNGITIS in a small child—in whom the airway is smaller and therefore more easily obstructed by swelling of its lining membrane—can produce the type of stridor commonly known as CROUP. DIPHTHERIA can also obstruct the airway.

In older patients, tumors of the larynx, windpipe or lungs may cause stridor. Treatment depends on the underlying cause. If the obstruction is severe and cannot otherwise be rapidly relieved, a temporary opening must be made into the windpipe below the obstruction (TRACHEOSTOMY) to provide an artificial airway. Croup in children often responds well to simple procedures such as increasing the water vapor in the air of the child's room by means of a vaporizer.

See also the major article on **Otolaryngology.**

stroke

The common name for a sudden paralysis or loss of sensation resulting from THROMBOSIS in or bleeding from one of the arteries supplying the brain (CEREBRAL HEMORRHAGE). Each year about half a million Americans have a stroke and there are approximately 200,000 deaths from this cause. The severity of strokes is

A stroke results from damage to brain cells, following a prolonged interruption to their blood supply. Each artery in the brain is responsible for nourishing a particular territory and the severity of a stroke depends on which vessel is involved. The general arrangement of nerve fibers means that when the right side of the brain is damaged, symptoms of paralysis and numbness affect the left side of the body and vice versa.

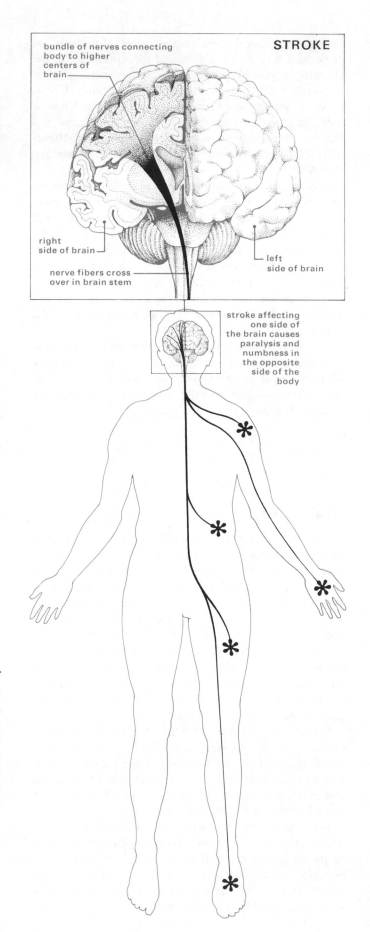

STROKE

bundle of nerves connecting body to higher centers of brain

right side of brain

left side of brain

nerve fibers cross over in brain stem

stroke affecting one side of the brain causes paralysis and numbness in the opposite side of the body

variable; sometimes the episode lasts only a few minutes, or less than 24 hours, with complete recovery (a "transient ischemic attack"). At the other extreme there may be sudden loss of consciousness progressing to death within a few hours. More typically, the onset of symptoms takes a few minutes, with gradual loss of power and feeling in an arm or leg.

The most common form of stroke is caused by thrombosis in one of the main blood vessels of the brain (the middle cerebral artery). The resultant partial or total paralysis affects one arm and leg (HEMIPLEGIA) and the facial muscles on the same side. If the right side is affected there may be loss of speech (*aphasia*) as an added disability. Other equally distinctive stroke syndromes, due to thrombosis in different arteries, may affect balance, vision, sensation, memory, or any other brain function. Loss of muscular control may occur without any effect on mental alertness or intelligence, and a stroke patient who has difficulty in speaking may retain normal understanding.

About 20–25% of patients who have a stroke die within hours or days. The outlook is worse with patients over 70 years of age and in cases in which there is loss of consciousness and profound paralysis. For those who survive the initial episode, however, there is a good chance of substantial recovery in the weeks that follow, especially in patients whose general health is otherwise good. There is no specific curative treatment for the common forms of stroke, but physical therapy can be very helpful in speeding the recovery of muscular power and control. More specific help may be needed with walking, speech, and the relearning of day-to-day tasks.

Little is known of the cause of stroke, except that there is a strong association with raised blood pressure (hypertension). Other predisposing factors are diabetes and any condition that makes thrombosis more likely (including use of oral contraceptives and POLY-CYTHEMIA). The best prospects of reducing the ill-health due to stroke lies in the detection and treatment of the conditions which increase the risk.

See also the major article on **Neurology.**

sty (hordeolum)

A common type of inflammation of the eyelid, often the upper lid. Each eyelash follicle is accompanied by a sebaceous gland, which secretes an oily material (sebum) that keeps the skin of the lids soft and pliable. Infection (usually with staphylococcal bacteria) starts in a sebaceous gland and spreads to the follicle of the eyelash. Swelling and redness are evident and considerable pain is felt at the margin of the lid. The infection may "come to a head" with a spontaneous discharge of pus.

Special treatment is not often required. If the

STY

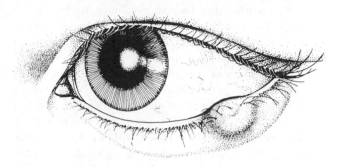

A sty is a bacterial abscess in the follicle of an eyelash. It appears as a localized red swelling on the upper or lower lid. The main symptom is pain, which can be helped by warm compresses.

condition is severe, however, treatment may include removal of the affected eyelash, the local application of penicillin ointment and hot fomentations to the eye. Administration of antibiotics by mouth or injection are rarely required.

In recurrent cases, a local source of infection (such as boils on the neck or face) should be sought (see BOIL). Inadequate personal hygiene may predispose to infection and certain general diseases such as diabetes (in which there is a special susceptibility to infection) must be excluded.

sudden infant death syndrome

The sudden and unexplained death of an infant during sleep. See CRIB DEATH.

suicide

The deliberate taking of one's own life, which accounts for less than 1% of all deaths in most Western countries. In contrast, so-called attempted suicide from an overdose of sleeping pills or tranquilizers is now one of the most common causes of hospital admission.

Most successful suicides are in persons suffering from severe DEPRESSION, in which the thoughts become dominated by irrational feelings of guilt and unworthiness. The high suicide rate in severely depressed patients justifies the opinion that the condition is a potentially life-threatening medical emergency warranting urgent treatment. Patients who refuse treatment may need close supervision if the risk of suicide is to be minimized. The belief that people who talk about suicide do not carry out their threats is false. Men are more likely to use violent means such as shooting, drowning or hanging; women commonly take an overdose of drugs, often combined with alcohol.

However, most people who take an overdose of drugs

are not suffering from depression and have no real determination to die. Indeed psychiatrists distinguish two separate conditions: *attempted suicide* and *parasuicide*, in which the suicidal gesture is a means of seeking attention at a time of emotional conflict. Parasuicide is most common in teenagers and young adults, women more than men, usually with some personality disorder and a past history of behavioral problems. In contrast, suicide occurs more commonly in middle-aged and elderly persons, with a preponderance of men. Many countries now have organizations (such as the Samaritans) which offer a 24-hour telephone counseling service for anyone contemplating suicide; many individual communities have "crisis lines" for the same purpose. The growth of these services has coincided with a fall in the numbers of deaths.

Anyone found having recently taken an overdose of pills should be taken to a hospital emergency room; loss of consciousness may develop quite suddenly in such circumstances, when immediate treatment may be needed.

sunburn

A reaction of susceptible skin to exposure to the ultraviolet rays of the sun. It can range from slight redness and tenderness to severe blistering. Sunburn is common among swimmers, skiers and outdoor workers (if unprotected).

Blonds are more susceptible than brunettes, although previous exposure and tanning of the skin gives some protection. The effect of exposure to sunlight is greatest when the sun is high in the sky (between about 10 am and 2 pm) and in midsummer. Reflection will also increase the effect—snow, water and sand reflect much of the burning wavelengths of sunlight. Scattered rays may also produce sunburn, even in the presence of haze or thin fog.

The symptoms of simple sunburn need no description; when sunburn is severe, however, there may be a marked constitutional disturbance with nausea, chills and fever and the symptoms may be mixed with those of heat stroke and HEAT EXHAUSTION. Sunburn may also bring on or aggravate other conditions, notably cold sores on the lips and a variety of skin disorders. However, ACNE and some other skin conditions may actually be improved by cautious exposure to the ultraviolet rays of the sun.

Treatment is usually limited to the application of cold compresses to the skin and the administration of emollient lotions to counteract dryness and painkilling drugs to relieve the discomfort. In severe cases, medical advice should be sought and admission to the hospital may even be necessary if the patient becomes ill.

Prevention is by avoidance of exposure to the sun when it is directly overhead or by graduated exposure so that protection is obtained by prior tanning of the skin. Certain drugs may increase the rate of tanning. "Sunscreen" lotions are available which may provide some degree of protection by helping to obstruct the ultraviolet rays responsible for sunburns.

sympathectomy

Surgical removal of part of the sympathetic nervous system.

In addition to the main components of the nervous system—the brain, spinal cord and the nerves of the trunk and limbs—two subsidiary systems exist: the *sympathetic* and *parasympathetic* nervous systems. These two systems have generally opposing effects and are concerned with bodily functions which are not under voluntary nervous control. They control the heart rate, the blood flow to organs and tissues, the secretions of the digestive juices, the movements of the intestinal tract, and sweating.

Among the important functions of the sympathetic nervous system is the control of the caliber (internal diameter) of the arteries, thus influencing the blood flow. The arteries have muscular walls which, when contracted, produce constriction of the vessels (*vasoconstriction*) and a consequent reduction in blood flow and increase in blood pressure. Stimulation of the sympathetic nerves increases vasoconstriction, while paralysis or surgical removal of the nerves produces the opposite effect (*vasodilation*).

When the blood supply to a limb (especially the leg) is poor because the blood vessels are narrowed by spasm (see RAYNAUD'S DISEASE), surgical removal of the sympathetic nerve supply to the limb often results in a great improvement in blood flow. This operation is referred to as a *sympathectomy*. In the case of the leg, it is performed by removing the sympathetic nerve ganglia which supply the legs. These are approached through an incision in the abdominal wall.

Sympathectomy may also be used to treat other forms of vascular disease, including hypertension which does not respond to drugs, and occasionally to relieve symptoms due to excessive sweating.

syncope

A temporary loss of consciousness due to an inadequate flow of blood to the brain; FAINTING.

synovitis

The inner surfaces of a joint are lined by a fine membrane, the *synovial membrane*. Inflammation of this membrane is referred to as synovitis.

Synovitis may be acute or chronic. It usually occurs as a result of disease affecting the joint as a whole. Thus *acute synovitis* occurs in cases of bacterial or viral infection of the joints, after injuries, and in conditions such as HEMOPHILIA in which hemorrhage into joints may occur. *Chronic synovitis* occurs in RHEUMATOID

SYMPATHECTOMY

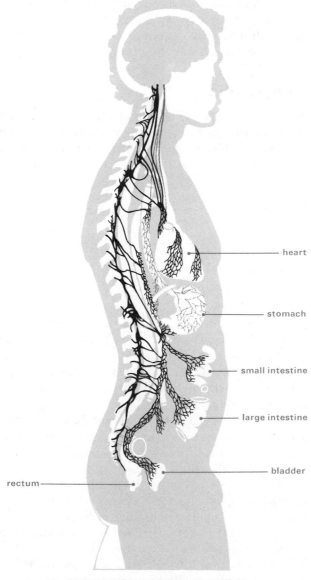

THE AUTONOMIC NERVOUS SYSTEM

The autonomic nervous system has two components—the sympathetic (black) and parasympathetic (gray)—both of which supply the internal organs. Sympathectomy is an operation, usually performed in the neck or the low back, to improve the blood flow to the arms or legs by cutting the sympathetic nerves to the blood vessels.

ARTHRITIS and in OSTEOARTHRITIS and in infection of the joints by tuberculosis. The presence of loose fragments of bone or cartilage in a joint may cause acute or chronic synovitis; it occurs in the condition of torn cartilage in the knee (see MENISECTOMY).

Treatment depends on the cause. In synovitis associated with rheumatoid arthritis, for example, generalized treatment of the primary disease is required; in osteoarthritis, drugs are administered for the relief of pain. In both these conditions, surgical treatment of the joint (including joint replacement operations) may be necessary. Infections are controlled with the administration of antibiotics. Loose fragments of bone or a torn cartilage in the knee will require surgical exploration of the joint.

See also the major article on **Orthopedics** and **Rheumatology**.

syphilis

The most serious of the sexually transmitted (venereal) diseases, which may prove fatal if not treated. It is caused by infection with the spirochete bacterium *Treponema pallidum;* the disease is transmitted only by sexual contact or (very rarely) by the transfusion of contaminated blood.

The first sign of syphilis, which appears after a silent incubation period of two to six weeks, is the *chancre*—a hard, painless ulcer on the penis, the female genitalia, or (more rarely) on the lips, tongue or finger. There is some swelling of the lymph nodes nearest to the chancre, which heals slowly in about one month. As the chancre heals, however, syphilis moves into its "secondary stage" with fever, a generalized rash (usually consisting of pale red spots), a sore throat and swelling of lymph nodes throughout the body. Occasionally the infection may inflame the brain coverings (*meningitis*), the membranes that invest the bones (*periostitis*) and the iris of the eyes (*iritis*). Even without treatment this stage will resolve after some weeks, leaving the individual apparently cured; but months or years later "tertiary" syphilitic lesions will appear. These may damage the heart valves or weaken the main blood vessels—causing stretching, swelling and eventually rupture of an artery. The brain and spinal cord may be affected, causing either insanity (*general paralysis of the insane*, or *GPI*) or loss of muscular coordination (*tabes dorsalis*). Indeed, tertiary syphilis may involve any organ and mimic virtually any other chronic disease.

Syphilis can be cured by a full course of treatment with penicillin. Inadequate treatment may only suppress the symptoms, however, and careful medical follow-up is needed to ensure that the infection has been eliminated. Furthermore while penicillin treatment will stop syphilis from progressing it cannot repair damage to the heart valves, nerves, or other organs caused by chronic infection.

An unnoticed syphilitic infection may be suppressed by a short course of antibiotics given as treatment for gonorrhea or any other venereal disease. However, tests on the blood will establish whether or not an individual has syphilis. Anyone who suspects they may have acquired a venereal disease should be examined and treated by an accredited clinic or specialist.

See also VENEREAL DISEASE and the major article on **Infectious Diseases.**

systemic lupus erythematosus

See LUPUS ERYTHEMATOSUS.

systole

The period when a chamber of the heart contracts and ejects blood. (DIASTOLE is the period when the heart muscle is relaxed and a chamber fills with blood.) During *atrial systole*, blood is pumped from the atria into the ventricles; this period corresponds to ventricular diastole. During *ventricular systole* the right ventricle pumps blood into the lungs where the blood becomes oxygenated while the left ventricle pumps blood into the aorta, and so around the rest of the body.

The term "systolic blood pressure" refers to the pressure in the large arteries during ventricular systole. *Asystole* means cardiac standstill or absence of a heartbeat. If it lasts more than four minutes, deterioration of brain cells begins.

See also BLOOD PRESSURE.

T

tabes dorsalis

A form of tertiary SYPHILIS, affecting men more frequently than women, which appears some years (5 to 20) after the primary infection.

Degeneration occurs in the sensory nerves, which originate in the spinal cord, producing impairment of sensation of temperature and pain and the loss of tendon reflexes. Bouts of acute severe paroxysmal pain ("lightning pains") develop in the legs or arms. Loss of the sense of pain and temperature occurs on the under side of the forearm and arm and spreads over the chest thorax. The abdomen is usually normal, but loss of sensation is again found over the legs.

The patient cannot tell where his legs are when his eyes are closed, and he has to keep his eyes open in order to maintain his balance. He develops a characteristic gait with the feet wide apart, and because he has lost sensation in the soles of his feet he picks them up high when he walks and stamps them down. The same loss of sensation leads to damage of the joints and painless ulcers on the soles of the feet. Sensation from the bladder may be lost, so that the patient suffers from painless retention of urine, and he may be constipated. In some cases there are attacks of acute abdominal pain, with vomiting (tabetic crisis), which may mimic an acute abdominal emergency.

The difficulty in walking gave the disease its alternative name, *locomotor ataxia*.

tachycardia

A marked increase in the rate of the heartbeat, which can be either sudden or gradual in onset. It may arise from some malfunction of the heart, from the action of a drug, from exercise, or from excitement or anger.

talipes

See CLUBFOOT.

tapeworms

Intestinal PARASITES found in virtually every animal species. The two common human tapeworms are acquired from infected pork and beef; a third variety is found in societies which eat infected raw fish. Man may also be parasitized by the larval forms of tapeworms, including some that affect other animals (such as dogs). Infestation of the body with tapeworms is known as *teniasis* (or *taeniasis*).

Infection with the pork tapeworm *Taenia solium* is acquired by eating undercooked "measly" pork, when one or more of the tiny cysticerci (the encysted larval forms of the tapeworm) becomes attached to the small intestine and develops into an adult tapeworm attaining a length of up to 4 meters. A single worm causes few symptoms, but multiple infestation may cause some loss of weight. For the whole of its 30-year life span the worm produces eggs which are excreted with the feces. These eggs are infectious for pigs—and for man. If they are swallowed and partially digested in the stomach, the eggs develop into *oncospheres* (the embryonic stage in which six hooks exist on the head or "scolex" of the tapeworm) which penetrate the intestinal wall and pass in the bloodstream to form cysts in the muscles, brain and other organs. This condition (known as *cysticercosis*) is by far the most dangerous aspect of tapeworm disease, for the cysts in the brain frequently cause epilepsy.

The beef tapeworm, *Taenia saginata*, is common in

TAPEWORM *Taenia solium*

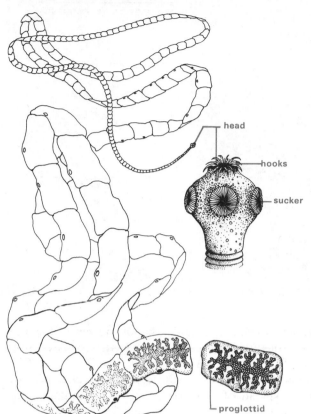

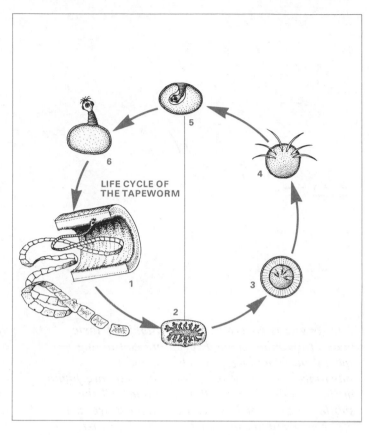

LIFE CYCLE OF
THE TAPEWORM

The adult form of Taenia solium, *the pork tapeworm, is only found in the gut of man, where it may reach a length of 4 m; it attaches itself by the hooks on its head (1). Segments full of eggs (2) are excreted in the feces, and embryos in the soil (3) are eaten by pigs. Encysted larvae (5) reproduce in the pig and develop into adult worms (6) after the human host has eaten infected pork that has not been properly cooked.*

countries where beef is eaten raw. Despite its length (5–6 meters or longer) it rarely causes serious symptoms and the eggs are hardly ever infectious for man, so that cysticercosis is not a problem.

The fish tapeworm, *Diphyllobothrium latum*, is the longest human tapeworm, reaching a length of up to 15 to 18 meters, although the average length is approximately 6 meters (20 feet). Unlike other tapeworms, its presence may lead to serious malnutrition, since the worm competes with its host for vitamin B_{12}; persons infected with the parasites may become profoundly anemic.

Tapeworms may be ejected from the intestines by treatment with special drugs such as quinacrine. The only treatment for cysticercosis is the surgical removal of any cysts causing symptoms.

Compare PINWORMS, ROUNDWORMS.

taste

Although the ancient Greeks recognized nine categories of taste, it is usual today to subdivide them into four—sweet, sour, salty and bitter. The sensation of taste is produced by minute taste buds situated on the surface of the tongue and palate in response to the chemical nature of various substances. Each bud is oval or round and consists of a large number of spindle-shaped cells. Although they appear identical, certain buds (distributed on the tongue in groups) are particularly sensitive to specific tastes. The taste buds at the tip are particularly sensitive to sweet substances, those on the edge to sour (acid) and salt and those on the back of the tongue to bitter substances. At the same time, there is evidence that all taste buds are sensitive in some degree to all four sensations. Chewing the leaves of certain Indian plants destroys the power to taste sweet and bitter substances, while allowing the tongue to recognize those that are salty and sour. This indicates that, although apparently identical, the taste buds have different nerve fibers for the different categories of taste.

Loss or reduction of the ability to taste may be brought about by smoking or the common cold. The once traditional practice of holding the nose while swallowing an unpalatable medicine also indicates that the sense of taste is intimately connected with the sense

TASTE

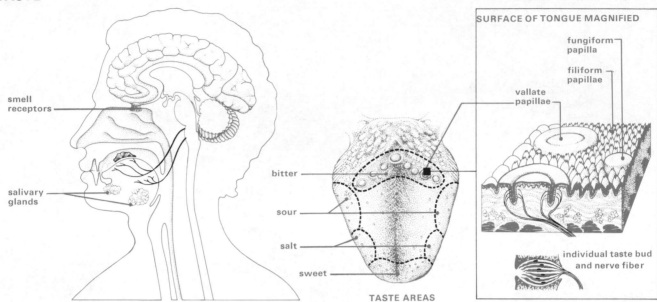

The tongue is covered with thousands of taste buds (tiny onion-shaped receptors containing special nerve endings) which respond to substances dissolved in saliva. The buds are found in the fungiform and vallate papillae. All the subtle flavors which we can distinguish are just different combinations of the four basic tastes—sweet, salt, sour and bitter.

of smell. An extremely acute sense of taste to certain substances can be developed—a fact used by wine-tasters or tea-tasters—although this ability tends to lessen after the passage of years. Many tastes are transmitted by the ordinary action of the substance on the tongue, as sensations on the skin are felt. Examples are the "astringent" taste of tannin and the metallic taste produced when a weak electrical current is allowed to pass through the tongue. All tastes produce a reflex flow of saliva, but the awareness of taste also depends to a large extent on such extraneous factors as smell, texture and appearance.

See also SMELL.

tattooing

A method of obtaining a permanent mark or design on the skin by puncturing and the introduction of color. It is of very ancient origin and is found worldwide, except in the darkest-skinned communities and in China. Various methods are used to produce tattooing, the most common being with needles and pigment, though small cuts with special knives are also used.

During the last 20 years tattooing has become increasingly popular among young people in the Western world. In unskilled hands, however, it can be dangerous and has been implicated as a possible cause of some forms of skin cancer. In 1961 the New York City administration severely restricted the practice because of the spread of HEPATITIS caused by contaminated instruments.

Tattooing can be erased only by the removal of the tattooed skin section and the grafting on of new skin.

Tay-Sachs disease

A rare disorder most often found in Ashkenazi Jews, which starts at about the age of six months and affects the nervous system. Victims of the disease, which is inherited as a recessive trait, show retarded physical and mental development, increasing paralysis and blindness, with eventual death by the age of about 18 months to four years.

About one in 30 Ashkenazi Jews carry the gene determining the disease—which is a disorder of fat metabolism—and as carriers can be detected by chromosome tests. They should be screened for the trait before starting a family.

telangiectasia

Small vascular malformations consisting of a group of dilated blood vessels (usually capillaries). They are sometimes seen in the skin in pregnancy, in old age, and in liver disease. The condition may be present at birth, in which case it usually disappears before the age of six.

In most cases the cause is unknown, although telangiectasias may be seen in ROSACEA and certain systemic diseases, such as SCLERODERMA.

temperature

In man and warm-blooded animals the temperature of the body remains almost constant despite the temperature of the surrounding environment. Human beings have a normal body temperature of about 98.6°F (37°C), but the body temperatures of many birds and mammals are somewhat higher. The body temperature of cold-blooded animals (amphibians, invertebrates and fish) varies greatly according to the degree of environmental heat.

Yet even in man the temperature can vary by 1–2°F during the day and is usually highest in the evening. This is probably because of the many movements of the muscles during daytime activity, the energy used being partly dissipated as heat. The intake and digestion of food also slightly increases the temperature of the body.

The temperature can vary in different parts of the body—the skin is about 0.5°F lower than the interior of the body or the natural orifices (e.g., the mouth and rectum).

If the body becomes overheated (for example, by exercise) the blood vessels of the skin dilate and sweat is produced. This evaporates and the cooling effect results in the reduction of the body temperature back to normal. When the surrounding atmosphere is very cold the body conserves body heat by contracting the smaller blood vessels especially those near the body surface. In old people and infants the body is less efficient in maintaining a constant temperature and both heatstroke and extreme loss of heat (HYPOTHERMIA) are more common in these age groups. Hypothermia is especially dangerous in the elderly since its onset may be insidious. An old person living in an unheated house in the winter may lose heat over several days and eventually pass into a fatal coma.

In disease the temperature of the human body may vary from about 90°F (32.2°C) to 110°F (43.3°C) for a time, but there is grave danger to life should it drop and remain below 95°F (35°C) or rise and remain at or above 106°F (41°C). In rare cases, patients have survived a drop in body temperature to below 80°F (26.7°C); indeed, one young patient recovered after a drop in body temperature to 69°F (20.6°C). (Unconsciousness typically occurs when the temperature of the body drops below about 80°F.) Prolonged high fever (hyperpyrexia) can cause irreversible damage to the brain.

The Fahrenheit scale is normally used in the U.S. and U.K.; in Europe the Centigrade (or Celsius) scale is preferred.

tenesmus

A constant desire to evacuate the bowel, although nothing is passed except mucus (occasionally mixed with blood). The condition is spasmodic and extremely distressing. It is likely to be encountered in such disorders of the large intestine as ULCERATIVE COLITIS, DYSENTERY, HEMORRHOIDS or tumor. It can occur when the lower bowel is packed with very hard feces or it may be provoked by fissure of the anus or by a growth. In young children tenesmus may be caused by the presence of worms in the bowel.

Relief of tenesmus depends on treatment of the underlying condition.

teniasis

Infestation of the body with TAPEWORMS.

tenosynovitis

Inflammation of a tendon sheath—in particular, one of the hand, wrist or ankle.

Tendons are white, fibrous bands of varying lengths which connect muscle to bone. They are very strong. Some tendons consist of round bundles of fibers while others are flat. Most tendons are encased in a sheath similar to the synovial membrane lining joint cavities; this ensures that the tendon glides smoothly over the adjoining bone when contracted.

Tenosynovitis is most commonly found in the wrist and hand and may be caused by bacterial infection following a wound. It may also occur as the result of RHEUMATOID ARTHRITIS or GOUT, or from gonococcal or tubercular infection. Tuberculous tenosynovitis is most common in the wrist.

Nonspecific tenosynovitis may occur as the result of repeated injuries where frequent and rapid movements of the wrist or ankle are involved. Initial treatment consists of rest and the application of heat. Should this fail, local injections of cortisone may be of value. In extreme cases it may be necessary to excise part of the synovial sheath.

See also the major article on **Rheumatology.**

teratogenesis

Literally "giving birth to an abnormality."

The term is used in connection with the production of a physically deformed fetus. This may be caused by the action of certain drugs taken during pregnancy or as the result of a maternal infection during pregnancy, of which the most likely is rubella (German measles).

The drug thalidomide, first used in Germany in 1958, is the best known example of a teratogenic drug. When it was taken by pregnant women (as a tranquilizer), it resulted in the birth of many children with serious physical defects, specifically the absence of limbs (phocomelia). The drug has now been withdrawn. Many drugs have not been adequately tested for teratogenic effects; for this reason, pregnant women are prescribed as few drugs as possible, even supposedly "familiar" ones.

If a pregnant woman catches German measles up to the sixth month of pregnancy it may affect the unborn child; it is estimated that in approximately 20% of such cases damage is done to the fetus. Should the mother go to full term and the child is born, the defects caused are varied and serious. They include retarded physical and mental development, brain damage, malformation of the heart, cataract and deafness.

testosterone

Testosterone is a male sex hormone—the most important of the group of hormones known as the *androgens*. This group is responsible for the development of internal and external sexual organs, and for the growth and maintenance of the secondary sex characteristics in the male. It is produced in the testicles and in a healthy young man the amount secreted is approximately 5 mg per day. Testosterone, in the form of testosterone propionate, is used in the treatment of *hypogonadism*—the failure to develop the secondary sexual characteristics associated with maturity. It is also used in the treatment of PROSTATITIS and certain deficiencies of testicular function.

In females it is sometimes used in the treatment of inoperable breast cancer. Though not a cure, it is of value in arresting the spread of the cancer from soft tissue to the adjoining bone, reducing pain and limiting bone destruction. Testosterone propionate is normally administered in the form of intramuscular injections, but methyltestosterone tablets are given by mouth.

See also HORMONES and the major article on **Endocrinology.**

tetanus

An acute infectious disease of the nervous system (also known as *lockjaw*) characterized by spasms of the voluntary muscles and painful convulsions. The cause of the disease is the action of the bacillus *Clostridium tetani* which was first isolated by a Japanese researcher, Kitasato, in 1889.

Spores of the bacillus are commonly found in earth, especially when it is contaminated with manure from horses or cattle. These spores may survive in the earth undisturbed for many years and may enter the body when a wound is contaminated with soil. However, the bacteria cannot multiply in the body in the presence of oxygen, so they grow only in dirty wounds or in dead, bloodless tissues around a deep wound. Once multiplication begins, however, the bacilli produce toxins which destroy the tissue around them, providing ideal conditions for further bacterial growth. The toxins also enter the nerves, spreading up the nerve fibers to reach the spinal cord, where they cause generalized muscle spasms.

The first sign of tetanus is stiffness felt around the site of the wound followed by stiffness of the jaw muscles, irrespective of the location of the wound. The spasms gradually extend to the muscles of the neck and eventually affect the muscles of the chest, back, abdomen and extremities. During such spasms the body may be drawn to the left or right, backward or forward, causing extreme pain and distress to the patient, who remains conscious throughout. In the early stages such convulsions are intermittent, but may be precipitated by any minor disturbance (such as the banging of a door or sudden exposure to bright light). The patient may eventually die from sheer exhaustion due to prolonged spasms.

The treatment of the illness consists of eliminating the infection by cleaning the wound and giving antibiotics, blocking the action of the toxin with specific antitoxins, and reducing the muscular spasms by means of sedatives, such as chlorpromazine or the barbiturates. In severe cases the spasms may be abolished altogether by the administration of muscle-paralyzing drugs such as curare. The patient will then need treatment in an intensive care unit, with artificial or assisted respiration, until the toxin is finally eliminated from the body.

TRACHEOSTOMY may be necessary in order to facilitate breathing in patients treated by paralytic drugs. This form of treatment has cut the mortality rate of severe tetanus from 90% or more to close to 10%.

Tetanus is one of the diseases (including polio and diphtheria) which are entirely preventable by immunization. If children are given tetanus vaccine at the same time as their immunizations against diphtheria and whooping cough (the "triple vaccine," DPT) they develop lasting immunity against the toxin. This immunity should be boosted with another shot of toxoid as part of the treatment of any dirty or ragged wound. If these precautions are followed there need be no fear of tetanus.

See also IMMUNIZATION and the major article on **Infectious Diseases.**

tetany

An affliction which causes spasms and twitching of muscles, particularly of the arms and hands. The elbows are bent and the fingers squeezed together. Sometimes the lower limbs are similarly affected and sometimes the face. (This condition should not be confused with TETANUS.)

Tetany is due to a fall of the ionic calcium content of

the blood and tissue fluids. It is most common in infants, where it may be associated with RICKETS, excessive vomiting or certain disorders of the kidney. It is also associated with malfunction of the parathyroid gland and with vitamin D deficiency. Tetany can also occur as the result of metabolic disturbances created by *hyperventilation* (one form of which is hysterical overbreathing).

Treatment involves the intravenous administration of calcium, normally as calcium gluconate. Parathormone is administered when tetany results from underactivity of the parathyroid gland.

tetralogy of Fallot

One of the most common congenital multiple defects of the heart. About a fifth of all cases of *cyanotic congenital heart disease* ("blue babies") are in this category. The four defects which make up the tetralogy are (1) interventricular septal defect ("hole in the heart"), (2) transposition of the aorta (the largest artery), (3) narrowing of the pulmonary artery, and (4) enlargement (hypertrophy) of the right ventricle of the heart.

A baby with these heart defects will grow slowly with repeated attacks of breathlessness. The CYANOSIS (blue coloration of the skin and lips) and shortness of breath are worse on exertion. If untreated, the child will develop swollen (clubbed) fingers and be susceptible to attacks of bacterial endocarditis and heart failure. However, surgery is widely and successfully used to improve the circulation through the pulmonary artery and to repair the heart defects, restoring the child to near-normal health.

See also the major article on **Cardiology.**

thalassemia

A group of inherited disorders affecting the red blood cells. The "heterozygote" has a form of the disease, *thalassemia minor*, which only produces mild symptoms of hemolytic disease; but the "homozygote" develops *thalassemia major*, a severe disease which is usually fatal in early adult life.

The disease probably had its origin by the shores of the Mediterranean, for it is most common in Sicily, Sardinia and Greece—although it has spread through northern India into Thailand and China.

Affected children may become jaundiced and develop enlargement of the spleen and liver. There is a family history of the disease. Firm diagnosis is made by examination of the blood, which in many cases contains abnormal red cells with a pale rim and a central spot of hemoglobin; an alternative name for the disease is therefore *target cell anemia*. There is no known cure, but palliative treatment is possible.

thermography

Variations of temperature over the surface of the body can be estimated by measuring infrared radiation.

Infrared waves are not visible to the eye, but an infrared camera will show the amount of radiation and therefore the amount of heat given off from a specific area of skin.

The heat given off by the skin is determined by the amount of blood passing through the local circulation and other known factors, so that variations in surface temperature may indicate an underlying abnormality. The technique is useful in SCREENING cases of suspected cancer of the breast where an underlying tumor may produce an area of increased temperature in the skin, and in estimating blood flow in limbs affected by circulatory disease.

The diagnostic accuracy of the method in detecting cancer of the breast is not very high, and its clinical use is therefore restricted.

See also the major articles on **Preventive Medicine** and **Examination, Diagnosis and Therapy.**

thirst

The instinctive craving for fluid. The sensation of thirst is felt as dryness of the throat and mouth; when there is a deficiency of water in the body, moisture evaporates quickly and immediately from these parts.

In the course of 24 hours the kidneys excrete about $2\frac{1}{2}$ pints of water, while the lungs and skin also lose considerable quantities. To make good this loss, fresh supplies of fluid are required, and thirst is the signal that this has become necessary. In particular, thirst arises from vigorous muscular exercise, owing to the loss of water by the excretion of sweat. Thirst also becomes intense when the body loses a considerable amount of fluid, as in hemorrhage or diarrhea.

Thirst is a common symptom in fever owing to increased body heat and sweating. The thirst which follows the intake of salt or sugar is an indication for the need of the dilution of these substances in the digestive tract and bloodstream. Excessive thirst (polydipsia) is also a feature of DIABETES INSIPIDUS.

thoracotomy

The operation of opening the thorax (chest), the necessary prelude to operation performed on the lungs and heart.

The scope of thoracic surgery has been immensely widened since World War II because of advances in the art of anesthesia, the development of the heart-lung machine, and the discovery of antibiotics. Operations that were technically impossible 40 years ago are now almost matters of routine. It is possible to remove whole lungs or parts of the lung, remove or reconstruct the esophagus, and operate on the arrested heart.

At the same time, the pattern of chest surgery has changed; originally, most chest operations were performed in the treatment of tuberculosis. Emphasis then shifted to the treatment of lung cancer, while now a great deal of time is devoted to heart surgery.

threadworms

Another name for PINWORMS.

thromboangiitis obliterans

A chronic and recurring vascular disease (also known as *Buerger's disease*) which affects the arteries and, to a lesser extent, the veins. A thickening appears in the lining membrane of the affected blood vessel and this progresses until the bore of the vessel becomes progressively reduced and finally obliterated (*obliterative endarteritis*). The disease may take months or years to reach this stage. The cause is unknown but it is definitely worsened by smoking, is much more common in men than in women and is seen more often in certain ethnic groups (young Jewish males are particularly susceptible).

The symptoms are those of a failing blood supply to the limbs, especially the legs, accompanied in some cases by reddened and painful areas over the veins. Symptoms of the failing blood supply are seen in the onset of pain on walking. This characteristically occurs in the calf of the leg after the patient has walked a certain distance, but disappears again rapidly on standing still (a condition known as INTERMITTENT CLAUDICATION). More prolonged pain may occur and there may be ulceration of the skin of the foot or leg; gangrene of the toes or foot may occur if the blood supply becomes seriously impaired.

Treatment is initially conservative (nonsurgical). Tobacco in any form is forbidden since it aggravates the condition. In severe cases, the development of a better circulation through unaffected tributaries of the vessels may be encouraged by a SYMPATHECTOMY operation—which causes dilation of those vessels remaining unobstructed.

Prognosis for life is good but amputation of toes, the foot or even the lower leg is possible if gangrene occurs.

thrombocytopenia

A condition in which there is a deficiency of *thrombocytes* (PLATELETS) in the blood, which gives rise to a number of diseases involving failure of the blood to clot adequately, including thrombocytopenic PURPURA.

Platelets are minute, colorless particles existing in the blood in great numbers, and one cubic millimeter of blood contains about a quarter of a million of them. When a blood vessel is damaged and blood escapes, the platelets fuse together at the site of the injury and so plug the breach. Thrombocytes also release the hormone *serotonin*, which causes the blood vessels to contract and again reduces the flow.

Insufficiency of platelets can result either from their underproduction in the bone marrow or from the destruction of existing platelets. Certain diseases which inhibit the production of white blood cells can also stop the production of platelets. This can happen through radiation, diseases of the bone marrow or leukemia. A deficiency may also arise through a massive transfusion of banked blood, for platelets do not remain viable in banked blood.

Underproduction of platelets may also occur on its own, and not as the result of another disease. In such cases it is known as *idiopathic thrombocytopenia*. This is rare, but is sometimes seen in children and premenopausal women.

Treatment, according to the type of thrombocytopenia involved, is either by drugs (prednisone), removal of the spleen, or by platelets transfusion. The last method is used only in extreme cases owing to the danger of the development of subsequent resistance to further treatment.

thromboembolism

The blockage of a blood vessel by a thrombus that has become detached from its site of origin.

See also EMBOLISM/EMBOLUS, THROMBUS/THROMBOSIS.

thrombophlebitis

Thrombosis (clotting) in veins is divided into two classes, depending on whether or not the wall of the affected vein is inflamed. If it is inflamed the condition is called *thrombophlebitis;* if it is not, the condition is known as *phlebothrombosis*.

In thrombophlebitis the clotting in the vein follows inflammation of its wall. The affected vein is red, tender, painful and hard. The clot sticks to the wall of the vein and there is little danger of it breaking away and producing an embolus. Infection of the vein may be a complication of varicose veins of the leg. It may have no obvious cause, or may be secondary to THROMBOANGIITIS OBLITERANS. Damage to the walls of varicose veins may be produced intentionally by the injection of sclerosing agents as part of a course of treatment, for in this way the varicose veins can be obliterated.

The treatment of thrombophlebitis is initial rest and analgesics (painkillers); elastic support may be comfortable. The affected leg should be used as soon as possible because walking improves the flow of blood through the veins.

See also PHLEBITIS, THROMBUS/THROMBOSIS.

THROMBOPHLEBITIS

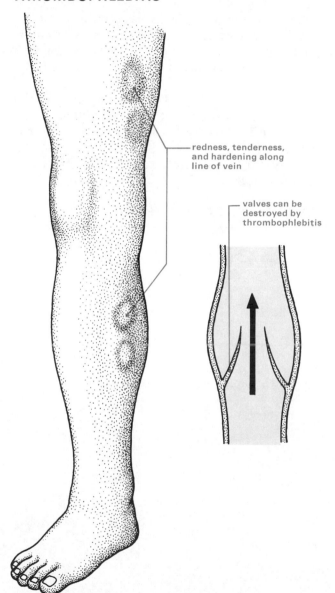

redness, tenderness, and hardening along line of vein

valves can be destroyed by thrombophlebitis

Thrombophlebitis (inflammation of a vein followed by blockage of the vein due to the formation of a blood clot) is usually marked by pain, heat and redness along the course of the involved vein. The illustration shows this process in the long saphenous vein of the leg. The condition is only dangerous if it extends into the deep leg veins from where pieces of blood clot can travel up to the lungs.

thrombophlebitis migrans

This is a condition in which symptoms of THROMBOPHLEBITIS occur in various parts of the body at different times. They may appear in the neck, abdomen, or pelvis as well as in the legs. Small red nodules, which are very tender to the touch, can be seen along the veins immediately under the skin.

This form of thrombophlebitis sometimes arises during the course of an infectious or malignant disease, but can also occur spontaneously for no apparent reason.

thrombus/thrombosis

A *thrombus* is a blood clot; *thrombosis* is the process of formation of a blood clot.

Normally, the inside walls of the blood vessels are smooth; although the blood readily clots when outside the vessels, it remains fluid in normal arteries and veins. If, however, the walls of the vessels are damaged by disease or injury, the blood clots as it comes into contact with the damaged area. This mechanism prevents blood loss in the case of injury, but in disease can lead to the formation of blockages inside the vessels.

Moreover, parts of the clot may break off and travel through the circulation until they are held up and so cause an obstruction to the passage of blood in places remote from the original clot. Pieces of clot which break off in this way are called *emboli*, and the blockage they cause when they become lodged in an artery is an *embolism* (see EMBOLISM/EMBOLUS).

It is possible for arteries to be completely blocked without causing too much disturbance as long as the part of the body affected has a rich blood supply, for the blood needed can still find its way to the tissues by means of bypasses (collateral circulation). If, however, there is no alternative circulation, the tissues normally supplied by the blocked vessel will die. The area of tissue so affected is called an *infarct*, and the process is known as an *infarction*. The effects of a thrombosis are therefore more serious in some parts of the body than others. Examples are (1) the heart, where thrombosis of a coronary artery (*coronary thrombosis*) may lead to the death of part of the heart muscle (*myocardial infarction*); and (2) the brain, where the collateral circulation is poor and a *cerebral thrombosis* leads to loss of function which is manifest by paralysis or weakness of the side of the body opposite to the side of the vascular blockage (see STROKE).

Arterial thrombosis is the end result of atherosclerotic disease of the vessels; but thrombosis of the venous system—commonly seen in the vessels of the lower limbs—may be caused by a number of conditions. Superficial thrombosis of the leg veins is not often of consequence, but thrombosis of the deep veins may be a dangerous condition as emboli may break off and become lodged in other parts of the body, notably the lungs.

Thrombosis of the deep veins occurs principally after childbirth and after surgical operations. It may also occur in women taking oral contraceptive pills and in elderly people confined to bed. If the development of deep vein thrombosis is suspected, anticoagulants are used to minimize the risk of the blood clots breaking off and traveling through the circulatory system.

See also the major articles on **Cardiology** and **Hypertension.**

thrush

A fungal infection of the mouth or throat characterized by the formation of white patches and ulceration of the affected tissues. It is caused by infection with *Candida albicans*, and the condition is known technically as *candidiasis*. See CANDIDA.

thyroid

The thyroid is an endocrine or ductless gland situated in the neck. It has two lobes, one on each side of the larynx, joined by an isthmus. Two *parathyroid glands* lie in each lateral lobe.

The thyroid gland affects the rate of body metabolism, the process by which energy is made available. This is done by the secretion into the blood of two HORMONES, *thyroxine* and *triiodothyronine*, which are produced from tyrosine and inorganic iodine. These hormones stimulate metabolism and increase the consumption of oxygen. They are also essential for normal development and growth.

Deficiency of thyroid hormone brought about by failure of the gland to develop, disease affecting it, or its surgical removal results in HYPOTHYROIDISM. Oversecretion of thyroid hormone results in HYPERTHYROIDISM. The controlling factor in thyroid activity is the *thyroid-stimulating hormone* of the anterior part of the pituitary gland.

Deficiency in the supply of iodine, normally present in the diet in the small quantities needed, causes the thyroid to enlarge and form a GOITER.

See also the major article on **Endocrinology.**

thyroidectomy

Surgical removal of the whole thyroid gland or part of it.

The main indication for the operation is in cases of *thyrotoxicosis* (see HYPERTHYROIDISM), where medical treatment with antithyroid drugs has failed, particularly in patients under 40. It is also indicated in the treatment

of goiters, where the size of the tumor is causing trouble. About nine-tenths of the gland is removed in operations for thyrotoxicosis, leaving that part of the gland which is in close relation to the parathyroid glands. In experienced hands the operation is safe, but is sometimes attended by complications ranging from damage to the "recurrent laryngeal nerve," which causes postoperative hoarseness, to tetany due to inadvertent removal of parathyroid glands.

Recurrence of thyrotoxicosis may occur in about 10% of cases; the occurrence of symptoms due to insufficiency of thyroid hormone (HYPOTHYROIDISM) is under 10%. Periodic medical checks are required after thyroidectomy.

The operation is also indicated in the treatment of cancer of the thyroid, but because of the radical operation needed the occurrence of complications may be higher.

See also GOITER, HORMONES and the major article on **Endocrinology.**

THYROID AND PARATHYROID

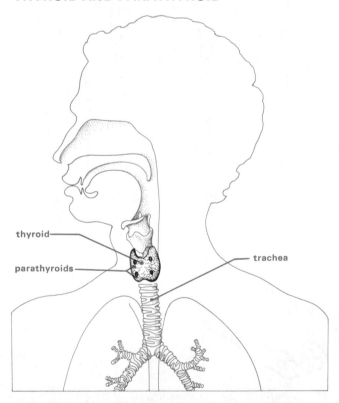

The thyroid gland lies in front of the trachea in the neck and secretes thyroxine, a hormone which controls the rates of many bodily activities. The four pea-sized parathyroid glands embedded within the thyroid secrete another hormone (parathormone) which is essential for maintaining correct levels of calcium and phosphorus in the blood.

thyroiditis

Inflammation of the thyroid gland. It is a relatively rare condition.

Acute inflammation of the thyroid gland may follow severe infections of the upper respiratory tract with streptococci, staphylococci, or pneumococci; subacute infection is thought to be caused by a virus, although definite demonstration of such a virus has not yet been possible. Chronic inflammatory change is found as a manifestation of autoimmunity in lymphadenoid goiter or HASHIMOTO'S DISEASE. The thyroid is enlarged, smooth and rubbery, and may be uncomfortable. Treatment involves the administration of thyroxine.

In focal thyroiditis similar changes are found. In cases of primary MYXEDEMA in the middle-aged or elderly the thyroid may be found to be very small, with its normal structure lost but small areas left showing the changes of chronic thyroiditis (*diffuse atrophic thyroiditis*).

thyrotoxicosis

A toxic state caused by HYPERTHYROIDISM.

tic

An involuntary movement or twitch of part of the body which is repeated time after time for no apparent reason.

A tic usually represents a movement which would be useful in its proper place, and at one time was made normally because of prevailing conditions. For this reason it is sometimes known as a *habitual spasm*. As an example, a tic of blinking may have come about originally as a result of poor eyesight. This may have been corrected by glasses, but the tic (or habit) of blinking may continue, particularly if the person concerned is of a nervous disposition.

A tic may be a sign of overwork or ill health, and is not usually present during sleep. The movement may be mild, such as blinking, coughing or sniffing, but whole limbs can be affected. The movements are generally sharp and quick, resembling the results of an electric shock. A tic may respond to psychotherapy.

Tic douloureux is spasm of the facial muscles due to paroxysms of pain in the trigeminal nerve; the condition is also known as *trigeminal neuralgia*. It may affect any one of the three parts of the face supplied by this nerve: the forehead and side of the head, the cheek and upper jaw, or the lower jaw. The paroxysms are extraordinarily painful, and even after the attack has subsided the site remains sore and stiff. Normally only one side of the face is affected. An attack may be precipitated by some minor shock, such as a draft or the eating of very cold food; but in some cases it occurs for no obvious reason. The condition typically occurs in people over the age of 50. Treatment may involve the surgical destruction of the ganglion of the trigeminal nerve.

See also the major article on **Neurology.**

ticks

Small PARASITES belonging to the spider class (arachnids) which depend on an intake of blood for their growth and development.

Ticks are found in the ground and in undergrowth and attach themselves to the skin of their victim, which may be animal or human. They do this by means of sharp and tenacious teeth and with a probe that sucks the blood into their bodies. Both male and female ticks engorge themselves with blood; the male usually remains unchanged during the process, while the female swells up and resembles a red or purple berry on the skin.

A large number of infections are carried by ticks including ROCKY MOUNTAIN SPOTTED FEVER, African tick typhus, and Queensland tick typhus. They can cause Texas fever in cattle.

Ticks cannot usually transmit infection to man unless they have been on the skin for several hours. In tick-infested areas, therefore, it is a wise precaution to examine the body thoroughly at least twice daily and remove any ticks found. The tick should *not* be rubbed off nor pulled off for fear of further damage to the skin

TICK

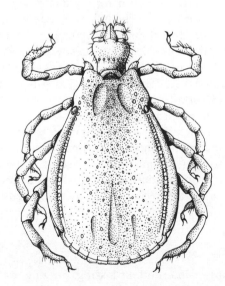

male brown tick *Rhipicephalus appendiculatus*

Ticks are blood-sucking arthropods which transmit harmful microorganisms to man when they bite. Diseases spread in this manner include tick-borne typhus, relapsing fever, and Q fever.

or tissue. It can either be removed by "drowning" with a heavy oil, such as salad oil or machine oil, or can be killed by carefully applying a lighted cigarette to its body. (See *Tick Bites* in the **First Aid** section.) The use of tick-repellent chemicals on skin and clothing reduces the risk of infection in tick-infested localities.

tinea

A group of common fungus infections of the skin, hair, toenails and fingernails caused by three types of fungus: *Microspora*, *Trichophyton* and *Epidermophyton*. The skin lesions tend to spread outward while the central part heals, thus creating the appearance of a ring. This gives the infection its common name of *ringworm*. The infection is also known as dermatophytosis.

Tinea capitis is ringworm of the scalp. It is found in children under the age of ten and is virtually never present after adolescence. There are a number of round scaly patches on the scalp from which the hair falls out.

Tinea cruris (popularly known as "jock itch") is ringworm of the crotch, seen mainly in young men. A red itchy patch of inflammation extends from the crotch down the inner side of the thighs for about two or three inches. It is most common in hot weather, and sweating athletes are particularly vulnerable.

Tinea pedis is the technical name for *athlete's foot*—an extremely common infection, most often occurring in young adults. It is so common that it affects about half the population at one time or another. The skin between the third, fourth and fifth toes becomes sodden and irritating and peels off. The infection may be found on other parts of the feet and may spread to the hands. In some cases the presence of athlete's foot produces skin changes in the hands, although the fungus cannot be demonstrated there. The fungus may also infect the nails (*tinea unguium*); it is one form of ONYCHOMYCOSIS.

Ringworm is spread by direct contact. Treatment is by local application of fungicidal preparations. The development of the antibiotic griseofulvin has made it possible to treat fungus infections orally; the drug is given in appropriate daily doses for about a month, but must be used with caution in patients sensitive to penicillin.

tinnitus

A constant or intermittent hissing, buzzing, or ringing noise in the ear. It may arise from a disorder of the nerves of the ear; it may also occur through blockage of the Eustachian tubes or excessive wax in the ears. Irritation of the auditory nerve may follow large doses of aspirin, quinine, or other drugs. Tinnitus is a common feature of MÉNIÈRE'S DISEASE, in which it is accompanied by gradually increasing deafness.

toilet training

The training of a child to control his bladder or bowel. There are no rigid methods of training, but it is worth keeping in mind a few guiding principles which apply to both bladder and bowel training.

The first is that normal development, maturation, and ability to learn vary enormously from child to child, and a child who is later than others in learning control should not be punished for his failure. Generally, however, the intervals between voiding increase gradually, so that by about the age of $2\frac{1}{2}$ years most children can hold their urine for about five hours.

Babies often empty their bladder or bowel after a meal, and may be conditioned to do so after the age of 2 to $2\frac{1}{2}$ months by placing them on the potty after a meal. It must be remembered that this is conditioning and not voluntary control. The conditioning may break down whenever there is a disturbance in routine, such as during teething. Moreover, if a child is punished for not using the potty he can become conditioned against it. Many children go through a stage of characteristic negativism after the age of one year, during which they rebel against being forced to do anything; over-enthusiastic efforts by anxious parents could result in the opposite effect to what is desired.

Voluntary control does not begin until after a child is about 15 to 18 months old. Often the first indication that a child has reached this stage is that, having passed urine, he can point this out to the mother. This goes on to his being able, on being asked, to say with reasonable accuracy whether or not he wants to void. Finally, he reaches the stage when he can say when he wants to go to the toilet. In the early part of this stage, the child cannot hold his bladder or bowel for very long once the desire to void has set in; if he is not given the opportunity to empty his bladder or bowel when he first announces it, the learning of control may be delayed.

On the other hand, a child soon realizes that a parent may drop everything he or she is doing to attend to his toilet needs, and may use this as an attention-seeking device. It may be difficult to distinguish between natural frequency of wanting to empty the bladder and attention-seeking. If it is due to the latter, the calls should be ignored except at what are thought to be suitable intervals. If it is not likely to be due to attention-seeking, the urine should be examined for evidence of an infection (cloudy urine, containing pus cells, or traces of blood).

In some cases voluntary control may be lost after it has been learned. This may be due to the child deliberately holding back the urine or stool when he is in the middle of an interesting game which he does not want to leave. Accidents may then occur, when he can hold his bladder or bowel no longer; they may be prevented by gently reminding the child who is engrossed in a game to go to the toilet.

See also BEDWETTING (ENURESIS).

tonsillectomy

Surgical removal of the tonsils. The indications for the operation have changed in recent years.

Most surgeons are unwilling to operate because difficulties with the tonsils usually resolve themselves with puberty—in girls rather later than in boys—and they confine themselves to operating only in cases of recurrent severe infection involving spread to the ears, or obvious cases of chronic infections which do not respond to medication. They are now inclined to perform adenoidectomy alone, because of middle-ear involvement, and omit tonsillectomy.

In adults it may be necessary to remove the tonsils when they are the seat of a new growth, or have been involved in a QUINSY. The operation is usually performed under general anesthesia for children up to the age of about 12; for teenagers and adults the surgeon may prefer local anesthesia. The most common complication is postoperative bleeding, which requires urgent treatment.

See also the major article on **Otolaryngology.**

tonsillitis

Infection of the tonsils, which are masses of lymphatic tissue lying on each side of the entrance to the throat at the back of the tongue.

TONSILLECTOMY

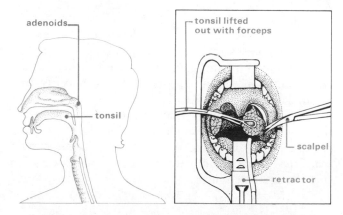

Tonsillectomy is most often carried out on children who have had frequent attacks of acute tonsillitis. The tonsils are removed under general anesthesia by cutting them off the side wall of the throat with a scalpel and lifting them out with forceps. Very often, the adenoids are removed at the same time.

The infection is very common, particularly in children, and is usually caused by a streptococcus. Very often the infection is self-limiting; but in many cases it spreads to involve the lymph glands which drain the tonsils, and a painful swelling develops behind the angle of the jaw.

Children can become quite ill and run a high temperature during an attack of tonsillitis; if prompt treatment is not obtained, some streptococci produce a toxin which brings out the skin rash of scarlatina (scarlet fever). There may also be abdominal pain and vomiting. Fortunately, however, this is a rare complication today, as prompt and effective treatment eliminates this risk.

The organisms causing tonsillitis are sensitive to antibiotics, and attacks of any severity can usually be controlled with penicillin. Occasionally, infection goes on to abscess formation; an abscess developing in the loose tissue around the tonsils is known as a quinsy. It may need surgical relief.

See also the major article on **Otolaryngology.**

torsion of the testis

While the fetus is still within the womb the testes are carried in the abdomen; but at birth, or soon afterward, they descend through the muscles of the abdomen into the scrotum. This is normally accomplished within a few weeks, but occasionally one of the testes fails to descend and surgical intervention may be necessary.

In their descent the testes bring with them their duct, the *vas deferens*, and various blood vessels—the whole forming the *spermatic cord.* In torsion of the testis a twisting of the gland compresses the blood vessels in the spermatic cord and so cuts off its blood supply. There is intense pain and tenderness of the testis, often accompanied by nausea and vomiting. Diagnosis may be difficult if the testis is still in the abdomen—as may be the case in infancy. However, torsion of the testis does not happen only during descent of the testes; it can also occur to a mature man as a sudden and devastating event that requires fast medical or surgical intervention if the testis is to be saved.

Occasionally the symptoms may be relieved by untwisting the spermatic cord; more often a surgical operation is needed. Delay may mean permanent damage to or loss of the testis. Whenever torsion has occurred an operation should be carried out on both testes to prevent recurrence.

torticollis

The medical name for *wryneck*, a condition in which the neck is bent to one side or the other. It may be either chronic or spasmodic.

In *chronic torticollis* the neck is permanently bent due

to shortening of one of the sternomastoid muscles. These are two large muscles, one on each side of the neck, which help to maintain the head and neck in an upright position and act rather like guy ropes. Shortening of the sternomastoid may be the result of injury at birth or later in life, but may also be inherited. It is not usually evident at birth owing to the shortness of the baby's neck, but if discovered will often respond to manipulation. If it does not respond and becomes definitely established, an operation may be required to divide the shortened muscle. Chronic torticollis may also arise from an inflamed gland pressing on the sternomastoid muscle, or from rheumatism.

Spasmodic torticollis is an involuntary twitching of the neck either to the left or right and is often a habit acquired in childhood. It is of nervous origin and can develop into the chronic state. It is extremely difficult to cure but may be relieved by psychiatric treatment.

TORTICOLLIS

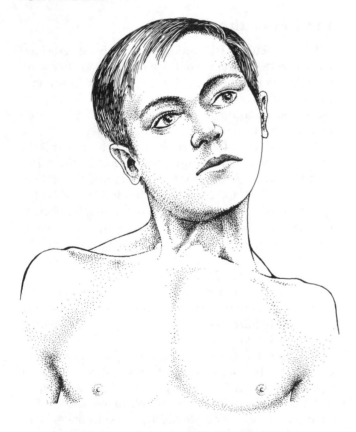

torticollis (congenital wry-neck) in a boy aged 14 years

Congenital torticollis usually affects babies who were breech presentations or difficult deliveries, but its exact cause is unknown. Fortunately, early correction either by repeatedly stretching the neck in the opposite direction or by surgery usually prevents this picture in a teenager.

tourniquet

A band placed tightly around a limb to control severe arterial bleeding. There are several kinds of tourniquets, but basically they consist of a wide band or pad placed around the limb, with an appliance or lever which tightens it enough to stop the flow of blood through a main artery.

Modern medical opinion has discouraged the use of tourniquets except (1) in special operative techniques where blood must be excluded as far as possible from the site of the operation, thus permitting delicate procedures; and (2) for the control of severe bleeding at the end of a limb which has been accidentally amputated and which is not controllable otherwise.

The use of tourniquets is no longer considered acceptable in first-aid work. Either it is inefficient or it will, as well as controlling blood loss, do much damage (because of the prolonged pressure) in the area applied.

See *Bleeding* in the **First Aid** section.

toxemia of pregnancy

Another term for PREECLAMPSIA. See also the major article on **Pregnancy and Childbirth.**

toxoplasmosis

An infection with a protozoan parasite, *Toxoplasma gondii*, which is common in both animals and man. Most human infections cause few or no symptoms, but infection during pregnancy may spread to the fetus causing serious damage to the brain or the eyes. This congenital toxoplasmosis occurs in about 1 in every 2,000 newborn infants.

Adult toxoplasmosis has assumed new importance in recent years since the disease may be a serious threat in patients whose natural immunity has been lowered by treatment with immunosuppressive drugs after transplantation and in patients given anticancer (cytotoxic) drugs.

Toxoplasmosis often responds to treatment with antimalarial and sulfonamide drugs, but suppression of the disease should be based on public health measures, since the source of human infection is animal excreta and contaminated meat.

tracheitis

Inflammation of the trachea ("windpipe"), the vertical tube extending down from the larynx to immediately above the heart, where it divides into two main *bronchi*, one extending to each lung.

Tracheitis causes pain in the upper part of the chest, accompanied by a dry painful cough. Often it occurs as a complication of a more general respiratory infection, such as influenza or bronchitis. The symptoms may be relieved by inhalation of steam, by cough syrups, or by antibiotics.

See also the major article on **Otolaryngology.**

tracheostomy

An operation in which the trachea ("windpipe") is opened from the front of the neck and a tube inserted to allow air to reach the lungs. It becomes necessary when the windpipe is obstructed or narrowed as the result of an illness such as diphtheria; or if the larynx has to be excised in the treatment of cancer. Tracheostomy is also necessary whenever the respiration has to be maintained artificially by a mechanical ventilator.

If the opening is made immediately under the chin and above the thyroid gland the operation is called *high tracheostomy*, and below the thyroid *low tracheostomy*. In practice the operation frequently involves cutting through the center of the thyroid gland.

The entry into the windpipe is made by cutting a vertical slit through the skin and fatty tissues of the neck. Tracheostomy tubes are then inserted, an outer tube first which remains in position, and an inner tube which may be removed or coughed out if, for example, it becomes blocked with mucus. The tubes are made of hard rubber or metal and a dressing is inserted between the outer tube and the wound. The entrance to the inner tube is protected by medicated gauze to act as an air filter.

TRACHEOSTOMY

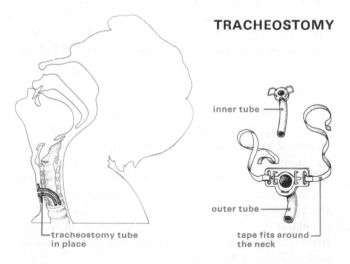

inner tube

outer tube

tracheostomy tube in place

tape fits around the neck

A tracheostomy is an opening made in the trachea (windpipe) through which a tube is inserted to create an emergency airway. The main indications for a tracheostomy are: (1) an obstruction in the larynx or upper respiratory tract, (2) an unconscious patient who needs to be attached to an artifical respirator for a considerable period.

Where blockage of the windpipe has taken place, and no other measures give relief, the operation should be performed as soon as possible and before the patient becomes *cyanosed* through lack of oxygen. If delayed until this point the operation may result in sudden cardiac failure and death.

When there is a permanent obstruction the tubes must be left in place. In other instances, such as diphtheria, the tubes are left in for three or four days and then removed, after which the wound will heal.

Patients with a permanent tracheostomy can learn to speak again by regurgitating air from the esophagus—*esophageal speech.*

trachoma

A disease, affecting over 400 million people in the world, which is the chief cause of blindness in tropical and subtropical countries. It is an infection of the conjunctiva by a virus-like microorganism belonging to the group *Bedsonia.*

As the infection spreads slowly through the conjunctival sac, scar tissue forms which distorts the eyelids and renders the cornea liable to ulceration and the formation of dense opacities. The disease is spread by contaminated flies and dirt and is clearly associated with poverty and poor hygiene.

The causative organism is sensitive to antibiotics, and research is being conducted to develop an effective vaccine.

traction

A technique used in orthopedics for treating fractures, straightening the spine, or for treating slipped disks.

When a bone has fractured the resulting inflammation and irritation around the fracture cause the muscles in the area and those attached to the bone to go into spasm. This may result in some overriding of the broken ends of the bone or in their being pulled into an unsatisfactory position. Untreated, the result would be shortening of a limb. Traction is applied by fixing weights and pulleys to the broken limb so that the bones are pulled into the correct alignment. Traction, skillfully applied, can overcome the effects of the muscles which have gone into spasm. Overzealous traction, on the other hand, may pull the fractured ends apart and so delay healing.

Patients with SCOLIOSIS, a type of spinal curvature, may also be treated by traction applied to the head and pelvis or to the spine and pelvis; the steady push and pull of the spine in the desired direction slowly results in some straightening.

Traction is commonly used for treating slipped disks in which the symptoms are thought to be due to pressure of the intervertebral disk on the nerves coming off the spinal cord; traction would then pull the two vertebrae apart on either side of the degenerate disk and allow it to slip back into place. However, there is no proof that this is how symptoms are relieved; some experts believe that traction relieves symptoms by enforcing bed rest.

Traction may also be applied by gravity. This is used, for example, in treating upper arm fractures, or congenital dislocation of the hip in children. With upper arm fractures the affected part is held in a wrist sling so that the weight of the upper limb pulls on the humerus (the bone in the upper arm).

Skin traction may also be used. With hip and thigh injuries, elastic devices may be applied around the upper thigh and traction exerted on the elastic by connecting it to weights which run over pulleys at the foot of the bed. Similarly, the weights may be connected to pins or wires inserted into the bone to which traction is to be applied.

See also the major article on **Orthopedics.**

transplantation

The surgical replacement of a diseased organ by a healthy one taken from another individual. The donor may be living (usually a close relative) or the organ may be removed from a body shortly after death.

Transplantation began with grafting of the cornea (the transparent layer at the front of the eye) as a treatment for some forms of blindness. When attempts were made to transplant skin, however, it soon became clear that the grafts survived for only a few days: the body's immune defenses *reject* grafts from another individual in the same way that they destroy invading bacteria. The bloodless cornea is the exception to this general rule.

Successful transplantation had to wait for the development of *immunosuppressive drugs*, which temporarily suppress this immune rejection reaction. As these became available, surgeons began the grafting of major organs—including the kidney, liver, heart and lungs. A major transplant operation will usually be considered only in cases of life-threatening illnesses, since the administration of immunosuppressive drugs has potentially dangerous side effects (it lowers the body's defenses against bacteria and viruses; serious infections are thus a risk during this period in transplant patients).

Experience worldwide with over 20,000 transplants, mostly of kidneys, has shown that many factors affect the chances of success. The best results have come when the grafted kidney has been taken from a volunteer who is a close relative (ideally, from the patient's own twin brother or sister). Just as successful blood transfusion depends on matching the blood groups of the donor and recipient, so does successful transplantation depend on close matching of the "tissue types." There are four sets of transplantation *antigens;* among the thousands of possible combinations, the best results come with a match of at least three of the sets. Such matching is most likely to be found within a family, but many transplant centers now use computer banks to select the best match among waiting patients when a kidney becomes available from a patient dying in the hospital. Other factors that affect success are the age of the patient, how many blood transfusions have been given, and the amount of immunosuppressive drugs that are needed. In the early years of transplant surgery another factor was delay between the death of the donor and removal of the organ. But now that the concept of BRAIN DEATH has become widely accepted, this is no longer a major problem.

Kidney transplantation is now a routine in many specialist centers. The operation is successful in about 70% of cases, and many patients are alive and well more than five years after surgery. If the grafted kidney is rejected or ceases to function it may be removed, and second or third transplants are by no means rare. Even so, the operation carries a substantial mortality rate from complications such as infection in the immediate postoperative period—but this is falling steadily in hospital centers with extensive experience in kidney transplants.

Transplantation of other organs has proved disappointing in comparison. Liver, lung and pancreas transplants have been attempted in only a few centers and the mortality rate in the 12 months after operation has been extremely high. The same is true of heart transplantation, with the exception of Professor Norman Shumway's unit in Stanford, California, where the success rate two years after operation is close to 50%.

trauma

A wound, blow or injury, whether physical or psychic.

The response to physical injury is inflammation (followed by healing) or death of the tissue at the site of the injury. Severe physical injury may also produce widespread effects beyond the site of the injury. Shock is an acute failure of the circulation due to a disturbance of the nervous control of the circulatory system or a loss of circulating fluid (such as when massive or prolonged hemorrhage occurs); severe shock may be irreversible, and death is then inevitable.

Special forms of injury include:

1. *Burns*—which may be thermal, electrical, chemical or radiation burns.

2. *High-temperature injuries*—which may be endogenous in origin (very high fevers: hyperpyrexia), or exogenous (as with burns or heatstroke).

3. *Low-temperature injuries*—which may be local (trench foot or immersion foot), due to long-continued

exposure to low but not freezing temperatures; and frostbite, due to exposure to freezing temperatures.

4. *Hypothermia*—the effect of exposure of the whole body to low temperatures.

5. *Crush injuries*—due to sudden prolonged external pressure on the tissue; damage to muscles or death of tissue from compression of blood vessels can lead to the release of a protein from the muscle known as myoglobin, which can lead to shock or kidney failure.

6. *Blast injuries*—due to an airblast which produces high pressure followed by low pressure from all directions, or to an immersion blast in water which produces high pressure followed by low pressure from all directions. These injuries could cause rupture, compression, or laceration of the internal organs.

7. *Radiation injuries*—may produce burns, dermatitis, tissue death, or the radiation may be stored to produce chronic damage. Conditions like leukemia may arise many years after exposure to high doses of radiation.

Psychic trauma is an emotional shock or disturbance that makes a lasting impression—for example, maternal deprivation or a broken home.

traveler's diarrhea

A brief attack (usually lasting one to three days) of DIARRHEA of uncertain cause. When it affects tourists it is also often referred to humorously as *Delhi belly*, *Rangoon runs*, *Tokyo trots*, *Montezuma's revenge*, *Aztec two-step*, and *la turista*.

Besides the diarrhea, there may be nausea, vomiting, rumbling noises in the abdomen and abdominal cramps. The severity varies, but most cases are mild.

Treatment consists of rest and a bland diet, starting with perhaps warm sweetened tea, fruit juices and strained broth, progressing to cooked bland cereals, gelatine and soft-boiled eggs. If the diarrhea persists after 12 to 24 hours, antidiarrheal agents such as kaolin may help. Antibiotics are generally avoided since they may adversely affect the intestinal flora and even prolong symptoms.

Most important is the prevention of the condition, especially when traveling to areas where the standard of hygiene is not too high. Drinking water and milk should be boiled, food should be fresh and well cooked, shellfish should be eaten with care, and fruit should always be peeled.

See also the section on *Drugs for diarrhea* in the major article on **Drugs and Medicines.**

travel sickness

Nausea or vomiting (or both) experienced when traveling in a car, ship, aircraft, train, etc. This is the result of the intermittent and erratic stimulation by the movement of the vehicle of the sensory receptors in the organ of balance in the inner ear.

The organ of balance, or equilibrium, is made up of a continuous system of passages (the semicircular canals) and chambers (the utricle and saccule) filled with a fluid called endolymph and containing sense organs. Movement or a change in position of the head causes movement of the endolymph, which stimulates the receptors. Nerves pass from these receptors to various parts of the nervous system. These connections with the nervous system serve to start off reflex movements which enable the individual to right himself when for some reason he is thrown off balance. However, some of the nerves also connect with the vomiting center in the brain.

Travel sickness may to some extent be a conditioned reflex, so that a person who expects to be sick is more likely to *be* sick; it may also be aggravated by psychological or emotional factors. Keeping oneself occupied is one method of attempting to prevent travel sickness. Tranquilizers or drugs which contain scopolamine or antihistamines may help to prevent travel sickness. They are best taken about an hour before the start of a journey. It must be remembered, however, that they can cause drowsiness; a person who has taken them for a short sea journey, such as on a ferry, should be careful not to drive while the drug still has its effect.

Other measures which help prevent the severity of an attack include adjusting the ventilation to get some fresh air, sitting with the head tilted back as in a dentist's chair, and having small but frequent meals rather than no meals.

tremor

A series of involuntary movements in one or more parts of the body produced by alternate contractions of opposing muscle groups. Tremor may indicate a disturbance in the *extrapyramidal system*—that is, in those parts of the brain and spinal cord involved in motor activities, especially the control and coordination of postural, static, supporting, and locomotor mechanisms. The disturbance may be due to a variety of causes.

Hunger, cold, physical exertion, fatigue, or excitement may produce a transient tremor which is of no special significance. It may also be present as a benign hereditary condition, which becomes apparent during or after adolescence and is found in several successive generations. Other diseases in which a tremor is quite characteristic are Parkinson's disease, hyperthyroidism, Wilson's disease, diseases of the cerebellum and multiple sclerosis. Tremor may be due to the effect of toxins (poisons) on the nervous system, the most common being alcohol; mercury poisoning also produces tremor.

It may also accompany emotional disorders such as anxiety states or hysteria.

The cause of the tremor may to some extent be identified by its characteristics and by the accompanying signs of the underlying condition which produces it. Tremors may be rapid and fine (the type usually seen in thyrotoxicosis) or coarse and slow (as in Parkinson's disease); they may occur at rest (as in Parkinson's disease) or be accentuated when an attempt at a voluntary movement is made (as in cerebellar disease), or they may appear when attempting to maintain the position of the affected part without support.

Treatment depends on the cause of the tremor. When it is due to toxic states, removal of the toxin is the treatment; when due to thyrotoxicosis, control of the hyperthyroid state should remove the tremor. The tremor of Parkinson's disease may respond in part to some drugs; tremor caused by anxiety and emotional disorders usually responds to sedatives, tranquilizers or antianxiety agents, but that due to multiple sclerosis does not respond to drugs. However, the patient can be taught certain postures and maneuvers which may reduce the tremor brought on by a particular movement.

trench mouth

Another name for VINCENT'S ANGINA.

trichomoniasis

Infection with a parasitic protozoan, *Trichomonas vaginalis,* which lives in the vagina and urethra of women and also in the urethra of men (in whom, however, it mostly causes no symptoms). Infection can be transmitted by sexual or other contacts.

Symptoms of an acute infection consist of the sudden onset of an intensely irritating discharge, which may be yellowish, greenish or frothy; the amount of the discharge varies. The vagina feels sore and there is usually pain during sexual intercourse. There may also be the urge to pass urine very frequently, associated with painful urination.

In chronic trichomoniasis, symptoms come and go, usually appearing around menstruation.

The diagnosis is made by examining the discharge under the microscope for the presence of the parasite. Treatment involves the administration of metronidazole (Flagyl) taken orally, or other drugs. Both the patient and her sexual partner (even if he is symptomless) should have the treatment.

Trichophyton

A genus of fungi that attack the hair, skin and nails. The disease they cause is known as *dermatophytosis.*

trigeminal neuralgia

See TIC.

trismus

A disturbance of the motor part of the trigeminal nerve (the Vth cranial nerve), which supplies both motor and sensory nerves to the face, teeth, mouth, nasal cavities, and the muscles of chewing. Irritation of the nerve produces spasm of the muscles around the jaw. Mild trismus results in a fixed grinning appearance known as *risus sardonicus.* In infants, the risus sardonicus may not be very apparent, and the first sign of spasm of the jaw muscles may be difficulty in feeding.

The most common cause of trismus is TETANUS. It may also occur in association with diseases of the mouth, such as dental abscesses, peritonsillar abscesses, or incomplete eruption of the wisdom teeth (third molars). Actinomycosis, which can cause widespread inflammation in the region of the jaw, may also cause trismus. So too may neonatal jaundice and rabies, conditions in which the nerves in other parts of the body are also easily irritated.

Treatment is directed toward the underlying disease. In severe cases intravenous feeds may be necessary. Sedatives and muscle relaxants may partially relieve the muscle spasm.

tropical sprue

A tropical disease of unknown cause, characterized by MALABSORPTION of fats, protein, vitamins, iron and calcium. Its clinical features include muscle wasting, anemia and diarrhea.

Treatment basically involves the initiation of a balanced diet high in protein (but with only normal amounts of fat) and the administration of folic acid, vitamin B_{12} and iron (in the presence of iron-deficiency anemia).

Nontropical sprue is a term used to describe the adult form of CELIAC DISEASE.

truss

A device for retaining in position a hernia which has been reduced into the abdominal cavity. It is most definitely *not* an adequate substitute for surgical repair, and in most cases the use of a truss should be discouraged. A truss is most commonly used for an inguinal hernia. Essentially, it consists of a pad joined to a belt made of various types of material, such as a leather-covered steel spring. The pad is positioned so as to cover the site of the hernia. In infants it is best to use a washable rubber truss.

A truss is usually used when a patient is not fit for surgery or refuses surgery. It is also used for babies with inguinal hernias, who are usually not operated on till they are about three months old.

To be effective, the wearing of a truss requires some degree of intelligence and perseverance on the part of the patient. The truss has to be put on with the patient lying down and the hernia completely within the abdomen; the truss is then applied with some pressure over the hernia site. A truss should fit properly and patients should be properly measured for their truss. The skin underlying the truss should be kept clean and powdered to prevent chafing.

trypanosomiasis

Any of various diseases caused by infection with protozoa of the genus *Trypanosoma*.

See AFRICAN TRYPANOSOMIASIS, CHAGAS' DISEASE (South American trypanosomiasis).

Tsutsugamushi disease

An infection caused by the microorganism *Rickettsia tsutsugamushi*. It is also known as *scrub typhus*, *mite-borne typhus*, or *tropical typhus*. The disease occurs mainly in the Asian-Pacific area bounded by Japan, India and Australia. It is principally a disease of small rodents, acquired by man through the bite of a mite infected with the causative microorganism.

The incubation period lasts from 6 to 21 days, after which there is a sudden onset of fever, chills, headaches and pains in the muscles and joints. At the same time, an ESCHAR develops at the site of the bite; it begins as a firm nodule about 1 cm in diameter, and becomes a blister which ruptures and is covered by a black scab. About a week after the fever starts, a rash appears. There may also be a cough which later becomes a pneumonitis. Other organs in the body may be involved. The heart muscle may become inflamed, the spleen may enlarge, and there may be delirium, stupor or muscle twitching.

Untreated, the fever usually lasts about two weeks, but with the appropriate antibiotics it begins to drop in about two days. The diagnosis has first to be made by examining blood and tissue for the Rickettsia, or by detecting antibodies which the patient produces against the organism.

Preventive measures consist of clearing the bush and spraying infested areas with insecticides to kill the mites, and the use of insect repellents.

tube feeding

The feeding of a patient through a tube which has been passed into the stomach, either by way of a nostril or through an artificial opening made into the stomach through the abdominal wall. Most of the tubes used now are made of plastic and come presterilized.

Tube feeding is required (1) in unconscious persons; (2) in persons who, because of neurological disease, may be conscious but unable to swallow; and (3) in persons in whom the esophagus is partially obstructed so that solids cannot be swallowed.

In a conscious person, the tube is usually introduced with the person sitting up comfortably in bed with the head supported. The nostrils are cleaned with absorbent cotton plugs soaked in a bland antiseptic. As the tube is passed in through a nostril the patient is encouraged to swallow it, if necessary by simultaneously sipping water. A conscious person may be very anxious when the tube is being passed, and may retch so that it becomes extremely difficult for the tube to reach the stomach. A mild sedative given beforehand, or some local anesthetic sprayed on the throat, may minimize the patient's anxiety and discomfort.

Once the tube has reached the stomach, the end protruding out of the nostril is taped to the patient's cheek. Food can then be syringed through the tube. The tube has to be checked frequently to see that it is functioning properly, is unblocked, and that its tip is still in the stomach. Blockage is checked by injecting air into the tube, while the aspiration of gastric juice will confirm that the tip is still in the stomach.

The tube is inserted directly into the stomach by means of a gastrostomy (the formation of an artificial opening into the stomach) when a patient is unable to swallow the tube, or when the obstruction in the esophagus is complete.

tuberculosis

An infection caused by the bacterium *Mycobacterium tuberculosis* (rarely it may be caused by *Mycobacterium bovis*, which normally infects cows).

Practically any organ in the body may be affected by the infection (which may be acute or chronic). The most common site of infection, however, is the lung. At one time, tuberculosis was a common cause of death all over the world, but with control of infection, antituberculosis immunization and chemotherapy, mortality due to tuberculosis has decreased dramatically in most developed countries.

Apart from the few cases in which the disease is spread across the placenta from mother to fetus, tuberculosis is acquired mostly by inhalation or ingestion of infected material in the form of droplets, dust, food and milk. Once the infection has set in, the disease may spread from its primary site—directly to adjacent structures, or it may be carried by the lymphatic system or bloodstream to distant sites.

Symptoms of tuberculosis include malaise (a general feeling of being unwell), lassitude, tiredness, loss of appetite, fever and night sweats. Other symptoms depend on the site affected. For example, with infection of the lungs there may be cough, sometimes with bloodstained sputum. An infection of the intestine (most commonly the small intestine) may produce a malabsorption syndrome, or intestinal obstruction. There may be a tuberculous meningitis, pericarditis, arthritis, and so on. Very often, the lymph glands draining an infected area enlarge, and it may be the enlarged lymph nodes which draw attention to the presence of an infection.

The infection may often be present for a long time without producing symptoms. Since the lung is the most common site of infection, in areas where tuberculosis is prevalent, persons in close contact with tuberculosis patients are sometimes screened for the disease either by chest x-rays or by a MANTOUX TEST.

Diagnosis is made by x-rays and examination of various body tissues and fluids for the causative organisms. Treatment consists of a combination of antibiotics, usually for at least six months. Sometimes surgery is necessary. Healing typically results in the formation of a scar at the site of infection. Sometimes organisms remain viable for a long time in the scar and become reactivated at a later date. In most cases the scar itself produces no symptoms; sometimes, however, the scar has some effects. For example, Fallopian tubes which have been infected may become fibrosed and thus produce infertility.

Immunization with BCG is believed to be at least partly effective in preventing tuberculosis in some people. Such an immunization, however, renders the patient permanently positive to tuberculin tests in the future, meaning that they cannot be used for diagnostic purposes.

See also PULMONARY DISEASES and the major article on **Pulmonary Diseases.**

twins

Two offspring produced in a single pregnancy.

There are two ways in which twins can be produced. Normally only one ovum, or egg, is fertilized. If two ova are fertilized at the same time, the result is a pair of *fraternal* (or *nonidentical*, or *dizygotic*, or *binovular*) twins, who may be as different from each other as any pair of siblings. If only one ovum is fertilized and the resulting embryo divides at a very early stage to produce two embryos, the result is *identical* (or *monozygotic*, or *monovular*) twins. Since the twins would have originally formed from the same ovum and sperm, identical twins would have the same genetic makeup: they would be of the same sex, have the same blood group, same build,

same color of eyes, and even the same pattern of hair whorls.

Twins occur in about 1 in 80 births. The tendency to having dizygotic twins is inherited, especially through the mother's side. Dizygotic twins also appear more

TWINS

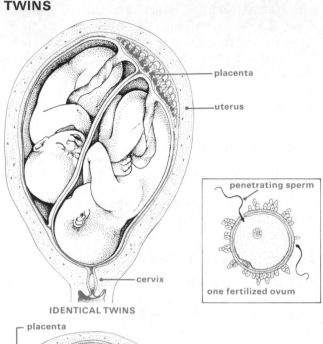

IDENTICAL TWINS

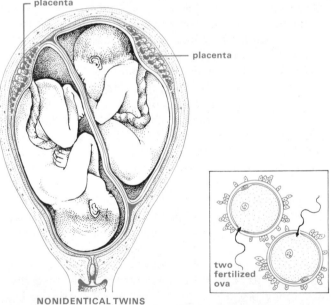

NONIDENTICAL TWINS

Identical twins are the result of a fertilized egg dividing into two identical cells which then separate and develop independently. Since both twins are derived from one sperm and one egg they are genetically identical. Nonidentical twins are no more genetically similar than ordinary brothers and sisters; they develop from two different ova (each fertilized by separate sperms) and have separate placentas.

frequently after the second pregnancy and with advancing maternal age; mothers of 35–40 are three times more likely to have twins than mothers under 20.

Twins have a higher perinatal mortality rate than single children. For a start, life in the uterus is more difficult, and twin pregnancies tend to be associated with more obstetrical complications. Twins are also more prone to fetal growth retardation; this may affect one twin more than the other if the distribution of blood supply to the two embryos is uneven. The difference in growth and development may persist after birth.

There is also a higher rate of mental subnormality, cerebral palsy and of congenital abnormalities in twins. Monozygotic twins may have a higher risk of certain tumors, such as Wilm's tumor, medulloblastoma, retinoblastoma and leukemia.

Less is known about the psychological development of twins, although they can certainly be quite different psychologically; even monozygotic twins reared in the same environment may have quite different psychological makeups. However, if one twin has schizophrenia the other twin—especially if he is an identical twin—has a higher risk of the condition.

Twins should be treated as individuals, each with their unique traits and abilities, and encouraged to develop apart. Otherwise emotional disturbances may develop later, especially if they have to be separated.

Siamese twins or conjoined twins are twins who at the time of birth are physically joined to each other at some part of the body.

typhoid fever

A bacterial infection acquired from food or water contaminated with particles of human sewage containing the causative microorganisms. The bacteria responsible, *Salmonella typhosa*, may be found in dairy produce such as milk and cream as well as in undercooked meats. The disease received its name because of the similarity of its symptoms to TYPHUS.

Typhoid fever used to be one of the most dangerous of the "enteric fevers" affecting adults. It remains a threat to health for people who travel to countries with inadequate sanitation, and there are still a few deaths each year among tourists returning to the United States from Europe, Africa and the Far East. The incubation period is from about 5 days to 5 weeks (usually 8–14 days) between the eating of contaminated food and the onset of illness.

Early symptoms include headache, loss of energy, and fever; cough is common and there may be nosebleeds. After 7 to 10 days the fever becomes steady, the abdomen is swollen and the patient may become profoundly weak, confused and delirious. In the second or third week a pink "rose-spot" rash appears; it is at about this time that serious complications may occur, including perforation or hemorrhage in the intestines. In most cases, however, the fever begins to subside at this time and slow recovery follows.

With early diagnosis and antibiotic treatment the course of the illness is cut short; chloramphenicol, co-trimoxazole, or ampicillin are effective in virtually 100% of cases. Even so, a few patients will recover to become symptomless "carriers" who pass typhoid bacteria in their excreta. These carriers are the source of further infections, especially if they are employed in the food industry.

Prevention of typhoid depends on good sanitation, proper hygiene among food handlers and the tracing and treatment of carriers.

Vaccination gives valuable protection for travelers outside the United States and northern Europe: a course of two or three injections is required, but the effect lasts for only one to two years, when a further booster dose will be needed.

See also the major article on **Infectious Diseases.**

typhus

Any one of three related infectious diseases caused by a species of rickettsia (microorganisms intermediate in size between bacteria and viruses), transmitted to man by human lice. First described clearly in 1490, it went on to kill more soldiers than died in battle in every major European war until the late 19th century; between 1918 and 1922 there were 30 million cases with a 10% mortality rate in Russia and Eastern Europe. Also known as *typhus fever*, the disease was prevalent whenever people were crowded together in conditions of poor hygiene.

The microorganisms which cause typhus can multiply in both lice and man. Lice acquire the infection by biting someone with typhus; the microorganisms then multiply inside the louse, eventually killing it—but not before it has had the chance to pass the infection on to another human.

The incubation period between infection and the onset of symptoms is about 14 days. The illness begins abruptly with fever and a severe headache; after three to four days a pinkish rash appears. Typically the high fever is accompanied by confusion and delirium; in untreated cases the mental state may become increasingly stuporous, with eventual coma and death. The mortality rate ranges from 10–50%, varying with the age of the victim and his previous health.

Early treatment with the antibiotic chloramphenicol or one of the tetracyclines is highly effective. A protective vaccine also exists, but prevention is essentially a matter of personal hygiene: the disease can be acquired only from infected lice.

U

ulcer

A defect in the surface of the skin or a mucous membrane exposing tissue normally covered by epithelial cells.

It may develop as the result of several factors, all of which interfere with the proper nourishment of the tissues. These factors include a poor blood supply, poor venous drainage leading to waterlogged tissues, infection, damage by physical agents such as heat and cold, continued pressure, malignant growths and disease of the nervous system leading to loss of sensation and repeated minor trauma. Examples are varicose ulcers, where the venous drainage is inadequate, syphilitic ulcers from infection, frostbite, RODENT ULCERS (which are the result of malignant growths of the skin) and BEDSORES. *Peptic ulcers* form in the stomach and duodenum as the result of loss of the ability of the mucous membranes to withstand the action of hydrochloric acid and pepsin, and occasionally as the

ULCERS

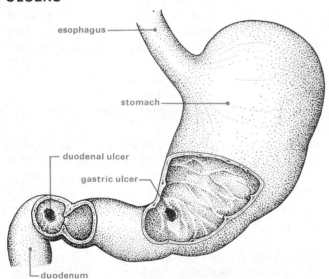

esophagus

stomach

duodenal ulcer

gastric ulcer

duodenum

TWO TYPES OF PEPTIC ULCER

Peptic ulcers are erosions in the lining of the digestive system caused by the action of gastric acid. Many factors—age, sex, occupation, diet, blood group—appear to influence one's likelihood of developing either gastric or duodenal ulcers. Both types of ulcer can usually be managed by drugs and dietary measures, unless complications necessitating surgery (such as hemorrhage or perforation) supervene.

result of a malignant growth (see DUODENAL ULCER and GASTRIC ULCER).

The treatment of an ulcer is by removal of the cause. Patients with varicose ulcers must elevate the leg as much as possible to promote venous drainage, areas liable to develop bedsores must be subjected to as little pressure as possible; malignant growths must be removed. In some cases plastic surgery is necessary, but treatment cannot hope to succeed unless the circumstances that originally led to ulcer formation are rectified. This is particularly true of varicose ulcers and peptic ulcers, for it is not easy to follow the regimes of treatment often required to heal and then to avoid ulceration, and relapses are frequent.

See also the major article on **Gastroenterology.**

ulcerative colitis

A nonspecific inflammatory condition of the large bowel (colon) of unknown cause; 75% of cases begin between the ages of 15 and 50. It is slightly more common in women than men, and appears to be more common among Jews.

It has been suggested that the disease has an immunological basis; certainly patients suffering from ulcerative colitis are liable to psychological disturbance.

The lining of the large bowel is ulcerated and liable to bleed, so that the symptoms include incessant bloody diarrhea as well as abdominal discomfort. The loss of protein may be severe enough to produce symptoms of protein malnutrition, and there may be anemia. Complications can occur: the bowel may bleed severely, chronic inflammation may produce a stricture of the intestine, and in some cases the intestine may suddenly distend (toxic dilation)—a condition that requires immediate surgical treatment. The wall of the bowel may perforate, producing PERITONITIS. The risk of developing a malignant growth is significantly greater than it is in the general population.

Diagnosis is based on the patient's medical history, and confirmed by endoscopy of the large bowel and a barium enema. Treatment is difficult; general measures include rest and the correction of any nutritional deficiencies. In severe cases, close collaboration of surgeon and physician is essential, for operative treatment may become needed urgently.

See also the major article on **Gastroenterology.**

ultrasound

A valuable technique for visualizing internal bodily organs, using inaudible (or ultrasonic) sound waves of a frequency of more than 20,000 cycles per second. These can be formed, like light, into a beam which will reflect from various "interfaces" in the body between structures which have different acoustic properties. The technique (also called *ultrasonography*) can be used to inspect organs or structures which will not show up on an x-ray photograph—for example, blood vessels, or gallstones in position in the gallbladder. It has the added advantage over x-rays of producing no radiation hazards, and is therefore extremely useful for monitoring the developing fetus in pregnancy.

The process is also particularly useful in estimating the position of midline structures in the skull (*echoencephalography*); in echoencephalography the midline structures reflect waves produced by a "transducer" held against the patient's head just above the ear; the time taken for the signal to leave the transducer and arrive back again is proportional to the distance from the transducer to the reflecting structures. Comparison of records taken from the left and right sides of the head will show whether the structures which should lie in the midline are indeed there, or whether they have been displaced to one side or the other.

About 6% of results are misleading, but the technique is very valuable because it does not disturb the patient and can be repeated frequently. In pregnancy the size and shape of the developing fetus can be estimated; moreover, as the beam of ultrasound is reflected from a moving surface a *Doppler shift* of frequency is seen in the reflected signal, so that the beating of the fetal heart can be detected from about the 12th week and the pulse rate counted.

The uses of ultrasound in medicine continue to be the subject of research and the technique is used increasingly in the investigation of blood vessel disease, as well as in the investigation of organs within the abdominal cavity.

See also the major article on **Gastroenterology.**

unconsciousness

The loss of consciousness, characterized by the inability to respond to sensory stimuli or to have subjective experiences. It may result from a blow on the head, the effects of a disease or disorder (such as the blockage or rupture of a margin artery within the brain) or be induced during general anesthesia.

The degree of unconsciousness may vary from FAINTING to deep COMA.

undescended testis

The development of the testis in the male fetus takes place inside the abdomen near the kidney. It descends into the scrotum before birth, but the descent may be imperfect.

There are three varieties of imperfect descent: (1) retractile testis; (2) incompletely descended testis; and

(3) ectopic testis. The retractile testis can be manipulated into the scrotum; it descends completely into the scrotum at puberty and requires no treatment, unless a hernia defect remains.

The incompletely descended testis lies somewhere along the normal path of descent; it may be in the abdomen, in the inguinal canal or at the neck of the scrotum. It cannot be manipulated into the scrotum and it will not descend at puberty. Such cases usually require operative treatment between the ages of 1 and 3. The affected testis is smaller than usual and there is virtually always an associated inguinal hernia.

The ectopic testis has wandered from the normal line of descent and lies somewhere near the inguinal canal, perhaps in the perineum or near the root of the penis. It is usually of normal size, but because of its abnormal position it is particularly liable to damage. Like the incompletely descended testis, it will not produce spermatozoa unless it is surgically replaced in its normal position in the scrotum by the time of puberty. If it proves impossible to replace the testis in the scrotum it should be removed, for ectopic and undescended testes—if left in their abnormal positions—are liable to develop tumors.

uremia

The abnormal accumulation in the body of substances normally excreted by the kidney produces a clinical state called uremia. The name was given to the condition

UNDESCENDED TESTIS

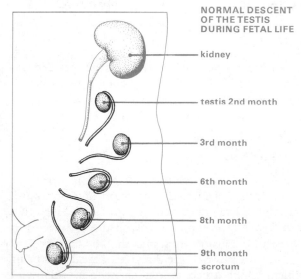

NORMAL DESCENT OF THE TESTIS DURING FETAL LIFE

— kidney

— testis 2nd month

— 3rd month

— 6th month

— 8th month

— 9th month
— scrotum

The downward migration of the testis in the fetus can become arrested at any point, trapping the testis in the abdomen. If it does not descend into the scrotum during early childhood, it should be brought down surgically, preferably before the age of three.

because an excess of the substance *urea* was detected many years ago in cases of kidney failure.

The condition is often of gradual onset. At first the patient becomes tired and is not able to concentrate properly. If the condition progresses, he becomes drowsy and confused. In addition to the lassitude the patient may be out of breath, nauseous and without appetite; he may experience abdominal pain or pain behind the sternum (breastbone). He is more susceptible to chance infection (particularly of the lungs and urinary tract) and may develop diarrhea. Neurological signs may include unsteadiness, weakness and numbness of the legs.

The manifestations of uremia are many, and can include psychological difficulties. On investigation many abnormal substances are found in the blood, and it is clear that kidney function is disturbed. The nature of the disturbance and the severity of functional loss must be determined, both by examination of the urine and special investigations of the kidneys and urinary tract. If possible the underlying disease is treated; but in some cases the function of the kidneys is so far impaired that the use of an artificial kidney machine is required, and a kidney transplant may have to be considered.

There are many conditions that may damage the function of the kidneys badly enough to produce uremia, some acute, others chronic. Although the precise reasons for the development of clinical uremia are not yet fully understood, it seems clear that it is produced by the retention in the blood of some of the products of protein metabolism.

See also the major article on **Nephrology.**

urethritis

Inflammation of the urethra (the passage that conveys urine from the bladder to the outside of the body).

See NONSPECIFIC URETHRITIS, URINARY TRACT INFECTION and the major article on **Urology.**

urethrocele

One form of genital prolapse in females, in which the whole urethra is displaced downward and backward. The displaced urethra is also often dilated. Like other forms of genital prolapse, it arises from damage to or weakness of the ligaments supporting the urethra—the most common cause of the damage or weakness being childbirth. Often it occurs together with a prolapse of the rest of the bladder, the combined condition then being known as a *cystourethrocele.*

The urethrocele may not form until many years after the initial damage. Usually symptoms do not arise till about the menopause when there is some degeneration of the muscles and connective tissue in the pelvis.

Symptoms include a feeling of discomfort or weakness in the vagina, especially after the patient has been standing all day. There may be urinary symptoms, especially stress incontinence, and a tendency to recurrent urinary tract infection.

Treatment involves supporting the prolapse with a pessary, which may relieve symptoms. An operation is required to cure the condition.

urinary frequency

The frequent passage of small amounts of urine.

Control of micturition (urination) in the normal adult is a complex act which is often disturbed in diseases of the central nervous system. Sensory nerves convey pain impulses and a sense of distension to the brain, where these sensations are interpreted. If as a result the person wishes to empty the urinary bladder, impulses travel downward to relax the sphincter muscles and contract the detrusor (expelling) muscles.

Frequency suggests inflammation of the urinary bladder (cystitis). This is most commonly due to bacteria entering the bladder through the urethra. About 50% of married women have a urinary infection at some time in their lives and hence suffer frequency.

Pregnancy distorts the shape of the bladder neck, which is another cause of frequency. PYELONEPHRITIS (bacterial inflammation of the kidney) may also give rise to the symptoms.

urinary tract infection

The urinary tract includes the urethra, bladder, ureters and the kidneys. It is prone to bacterial infection, particularly in women.

The most common organism causing infection is *Escherichia coli* (the "colon bacillus"), which normally flourishes in the large intestine. *E. coli* is often present in the urethra of healthy men and women, and it may be present in the urine without causing symptoms. Usually it causes inflammation when present in the urine in concentrations of more than 100,000 per milliliter; the urine becomes full of white and red blood cells, sometimes to such an extent that the appearance of the urine changes and the presence of blood is obvious. The patient has pain on urination, urinary frequency (especially noticeable at night), and develops a high temperature with shivering attacks (rigors) and complains of severe headache.

Diagnosis is made by examination of the urine for pus cells and red blood cells, and by culture and identification of the infecting organism. Sensitivity tests made on the isolated organism will indicate the appropriate antibiotic to be prescribed.

The incidence of urinary tract infection is fairly high

in children between the ages of 6 months and 4 years, possibly because of the risk of infection from diapers; the incidence then falls until there is a rise among young women of childbearing age, the frequency of infection being about 50 in 1,000. Young men are 10 to 20 times less likely to suffer from urinary infection. The reason for the greater incidence in women is that the urethra is shorter and infection is more likely to spread from the anus and vagina. Moreover, factors which are not fully understood render the pregnant woman especially liable to infection, and many women date a chronic urinary infection back to their first pregnancy.

It is said that infection of one part of the urinary tract means infection of all the structures making up the tract, but treatment with antibiotics will halt the disease even if it has spread from the bladder to the kidneys. Nevertheless, the disease is prone to recur, and in a number of cases infection of the kidney is found without the symptoms produced by bladder infection.

Factors which predispose to chronic urinary tract infection are the presence of stones, anatomical abnormalities and obstructions to the free flow of urine—which become increasingly common with age, with the development of prostatic hypertrophy (enlargement of the prostate gland) in men and uterine prolapses in women. After the age of 60, the incidence of urinary tract infections is about equal in both sexes.

Chronic or recurring urinary tract infections require investigation by the urologist, who will try to identify the factors causing repeated infection with a view to definitive treatment; but there are many cases where no abnormality can be found.

In uncomplicated cases of urinary tract infection, *E. coli* are responsible in up to 85% of cases. Other microorganisms which are also able to infect the urinary tract include *Klebsiella* species, *Proteus* species, *Enterobacter aerogenes* and *Pseudomonas aeruginosa*. Less commonly the causative microorganisms may include *Staphylococcus epidermidis, Staphylococcus aureus* and enterococci *(Streptococcus faecalis)*. In many cases these bacteria cause urologic problems only after catheterization of the urinary tract or following operations on the bladder or prostate gland. Indwelling catheters—i.e., those left in position in the bladder for prolonged periods—may set up an irritation that leads to bacterial infection.

URETHRITIS in men may be caused by infection with *Neisseria gonorrhoeae,* the microorganism which causes GONORRHEA. In such cases there may be a purulent (pus-filled) discharge from the tip of the penis. Specific antibiotic treatment usually clears up the infection within a short time.

See also BLADDER PROBLEMS, CYSTITIS, NONSPECIFIC URETHRITIS and the major articles on **Urology** and **Nephrology.**

urticaria

A skin eruption not unlike that caused by nettles; raised red-and-white patches on the skin, which cause great irritation, are seen mainly on the trunk and on the face. Also called *hives.* If the swelling extends to the throat (angioneurotic edema) there may be difficulty in breathing. The attack may subside in a few hours or may last several days.

Urticaria is an *allergic* reaction to certain protein foods especially fish or shellfish; to drugs, especially penicillin; and occasionally to insect bites or stings.

As in other allergic disorders, emotional stress and anxiety may be important factors; the condition tends to run in families. In severe cases treatment may be needed urgently, when injections of epinephrine or corticosteroids (such as prednisolone) give dramatic relief. Usually, however, itching may be allayed by antihistamines or by any of the many proprietary "antipruritic" lotions or ointments on the market. Preventive treatment may be given by the administration of *antihistamine* drugs, but the only certain way of eliminating the possibility of further outbreaks is for the factor causing the allergy to be identified and avoided.

See also the major articles on **Allergy and Immunology** and **Dermatology.**

URINARY TRACT INFECTION

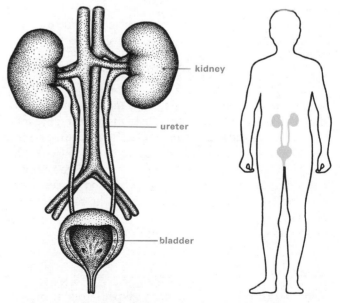

The urinary system is a common site of bacterial infection. Nearly all cases are "ascending" infections caused by bacteria from the anus entering the urethra and then moving up the urinary tract into the bladder. Women have considerably shorter urethras than men, and are therefore much more likely to be affected.

uterine neoplasms

A growth in the uterus which may be either benign (such as FIBROIDS) or malignant.

Fibroids are overgrowths of the muscle of the uterus; they may be quite small or may grow to weigh several pounds. They may form swellings on the outside of the uterus or within its cavity. Fibroids are found in up to 50% of black women but in only 20% of whites; they often increase in size during pregnancy. These tumors are usually painless and often unsuspected, but they may cause cramping pain, especially at the menstrual period; or they may cause pressure on other internal organs, such as the bladder, and so provoke frequency of passing urine. The most usual symptom, however, is MENORRHAGIA—an increase in the amount and duration of menstrual blood flow. The loss of blood may cause anemia. The only effective treatment of fibroids is surgical removal either of the growth (myomectomy) or of the whole uterus (hysterectomy).

Malignant tumors of the uterus include cancer of its body and cancer of the cervix (the neck of the womb). Cancer of the body of the uterus usually originates in its lining. There may be no symptoms or the growth may cause intermittent and irregular blood loss. For that reason, any unusual uterine bleeding should be investigated without delay. When surgical removal of the uterus is performed early in the disease the outlook is excellent: 75–90% of early cases of this cancer are cured by operation.

Cancer of the cervix is the most common form of cancer in women—and the most preventable, since the condition can be detected in its preliminary stage ·by examination of a sample of cells taken from the cervix ("Pap smear"). Wherever Pap smears have been used by women as a regular screening test, the death rate from the disease has fallen precipitously in the last 20 years.

The cancer starts as a small "ulcer" or bleeding point on the cervix, but spread may occur early on to lymph nodes in the pelvis. Treatment is surgical, sometimes backed up with radiotherapy. Again, the prospects for cure are good in cases treated early in the course of the disease.

See also the major article on **Oncology**.

uterus

The uterus (womb) is a pear-shaped hollow organ situated in the female within the pelvis between the bladder and the rectum. It is about 9 cm long, 5 cm wide and 3 cm thick. Its narrow neck (cervix) opens into the vagina. From each side of the upper portion, one of two Fallopian tubes connects with the ovaries. Underneath it is supported by ligaments attached to the muscular floor of the pelvis. The arrangement is such that the uterus can easily be displaced by pressure from adjacent organs.

In women between the ages of about 13 and 45, the interior lining of the uterus (endometrium) is shed every month (menstruation); a new lining is then grown to prepare for a fertilized ovum. When fertilization occurs the endometrium is no longer expelled, there is no menstruation, and the uterus begins to expand in order to accommodate and nourish the developing embryo.

The muscles which form the outside wall of the uterus have remarkable powers of adaptability and during pregnancy increase from 1 oz. (28 g) in weight to $2\frac{1}{4}$ lbs. (1 kg). After the birth of the child the uterus returns to its normal size within a few weeks and the process of the monthly shedding of the endometrium (menstruation) begins anew.

Owing to its structure and position, the uterus can suffer from downward displacement or PROLAPSE. Another common condition is the growth of benign tumors (FIBROIDS), but these can often be successfully removed.

See also UTERINE NEOPLASMS.

uveitis

Inflammation of the uvea (the pigmented, vascular layer of the eye, including the iris).

See also IRITIS.

vaccination

See IMMUNIZATION.

vaginal cancer

Primary cancer of the vagina is rare; it accounts for about 1% of all malignant growths of the female reproductive system. It is rarely present before the age of 45, and may be associated with carcinoma of the cervix (neck of the womb) or the vulva. Treatment is surgical with the aid of radiation therapy. The most common form of cancer involving the vagina is that which has spread from adjacent structures such as the rectum, bladder, or uterus.

See also CANCER and the major article on **Oncology**.

vaginismus

Spasm of the muscles surrounding the vaginal opening, resulting in painful intercourse (DYSPAREUNIA) or preventing penetration of the penis.

It may be due to anxiety, local tenderness, or an unduly small vaginal opening. The anxiety may arise from ignorance of sexual matters, fear of pregnancy, excessive modesty, dislike or distrust of a sexual partner, or dislike of the act of sexual intercourse itself; it may be allayed by psychiatric treatment. Local conditions producing tenderness can be treated as required. In most cases of vaginismus the cause is fairly clear, and the family physician can help a great deal.

vaginitis

Inflammation of the vagina, usually characterized by a vaginal discharge.

The inflammation may be due to a variety of causes, of which infection is the most common—especially that caused by the fungus *Candida albicans* (which produces candidiasis or "thrush"—see CANDIDA) and that by the parasite *Trichomonas vaginalis* (which produces TRICHOMONIASIS). Because the vagina is anatomically related to the cervix, cervical infections (such as that caused by gonorrhea) may also cause vaginitis. In children, vaginitis may occasionally be due to a pinworm infestation.

Foreign bodies are another cause of vaginitis in children. In adults, the types of foreign body most likely to cause vaginitis are pessaries inserted for the treatment of prolapse of the cervix, a tampon left behind after menstruation—either because it has been forgotten or because a second tampon has been put in without removing one already there. Vaginitis due to a foreign body causes an acute highly offensive discharge which usually responds well to the removal of the foreign body and, if necessary, to a slightly acid douche.

Chemical vaginitis is usually caused by the use of an unsuitable chemical for douching or for contraception. Often the chemical solution is too highly concentrated, or the patient is allergic to it. *Senile vaginitis* is seen in postmenopausal women, or premenopausal women in whom the ovaries have been removed or are not functioning. It is due to deficiency of the ovarian hormone estrogen. The lining of the vagina becomes smooth, thin, shiny and dry, and small hemorrhages may appear. The vagina normally has a slightly acidic secretion which helps protect it against infection; this protection is lost in senile vaginitis, which is treated by administering therapeutic amounts of the hormone.

See also the major article on **Obstetrics and Gynecology.**

vagotomy

The cutting of the two *vagus* nerves. It is often performed as part of the treatment for uncontrolled peptic ulcer, since stimulation by the vagus nerves is one of the main factors in secretion of the digestive juices (hydrochloric acid and pepsin) by the stomach. Patients with duodenal ulcers commonly secrete abnormally large amounts of hydrochloric acid; vagotomy results in a lower acid output and thus reduces the chances of further ulceration.

The vagus nerves begin in the brain stem, travel down the neck close to the jugular vein and then to the abdomen, where branches serve the various digestive organs. In their course, the vagus nerves also provide branches to the heart and lungs.

Vagotomy may be *complete* or *selective*, in which only some of the branches are divided, so reducing the likelihood of unwanted side effects such as diarrhea.

Valsalva's test

Antonio Mario Valsalva (1666–1723) was an Italian physician and Professor of Anatomy at the University of Bologna. He was among the first to recognize the importance of examining diseased organs after death, in an age when autopsies on human bodies were still largely illegal. He also studied the effects of deep breathing on the vascular system.

The *Valsalva test* (or *maneuver*) is the act of breathing out hard while the mouth and nose are held tightly closed, thus raising the pressure inside the chest. The rise in pressure inside the abdomen may help to empty the bowels or bladder. However, the return of blood to the heart is slowed, the heart itself slows, and the blood pressure rises. Straining to empty the rectum may, therefore, cause a dangerous rise in blood pressure in someone with vascular disease and precipitate a stroke or a heart attack.

valvotomy

Literally, "cutting a valve." The valves of the heart normally consist of two or three separate flaps (cusps) which are free to move as the valve opens and closes. As a result of disease (rheumatic fever, for example), the valve becomes inflamed and the cusps may become damaged or scarred and will subsequently stick together. The valve becomes narrowed and no longer functions normally, presenting a considerable obstacle to the free flow of blood (*stenosis* of the valve: *mitral stenosis*, or *aortic stenosis*, depending on which valve is affected).

To overcome the obstruction of the stenosed valve, the valve cusps are divided surgically (valvotomy) to allow freer movement and an unobstructed flow of blood. Alternatively, the diseased valve may be removed and replaced with a plastic substitute (prosthetic valve). The choice of operation depends on the severity of the damage to the valve cusps—although valvotomy is a technically simpler procedure than valve replacement.

varicocele

Enlargement of the veins of the spermatic cord. The condition occurs most often in adolescent males, who have a sensation that the affected scrotum feels like a bundle of worms. This may be accompanied by a dull ache along the cord and a dragging sensation in the groin. The condition usually requires no treatment.

varicose veins

The blood supplied to the limbs via the arteries is returned to the heart via the veins. While the pressure generated in the arteries by the heartbeat suffices to force blood through the smaller blood vessels to the tissues, no such pressure exists on the venous side of the circulation to return blood to the heart. The venous return is accomplished by a dual mechanism: the veins contain nonreturn valves which allow blood to flow only toward the heart, while the veins themselves are compressed by the contraction of the muscles with each movement of the limb. Blood is thus forced toward the heart and, having passed through the nearest valve, cannot return; further muscle contractions will force it further up the vein.

When this valvular mechanism becomes defective, the veins of the lower part of the leg become swollen by the pressure of the column of blood in the veins higher up the leg. This swelling eventually causes them to become dilated and knotted; they are then described as *varicose*.

In a minority of cases the condition may result from obstruction to the passage of blood up the veins. This may occur when a major leg vein undergoes THROMBOSIS, or when the flow of blood from the leg through the lower part of the abdomen is obstructed by pressure on the veins by a pregnant uterus or a tumor in the pelvis. In the majority of cases, however, the cause is incompetence of the valves in the veins (which may be hereditary).

Varicose veins are a relatively common condition. Many methods of treatment are used, including the use of elastic stockings or bandages to support the veins. The injection of various chemical substances into the veins will cause them to become thrombosed and in due course obliterated by scar tissue. Alternatively, they can be removed surgically (stripping) or tied off at a number of points.

Complications of the condition include the formation of varicose ulcers on the lower leg and a tendency to thrombosis in the dilated vein (superficial THROMBOPHLEBITIS) resulting in a painful, red swelling along the course of the vein.

VARICOSE VEINS

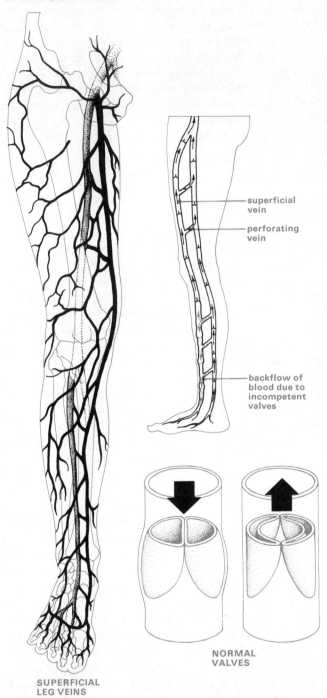

superficial vein

perforating vein

backflow of blood due to incompetent valves

SUPERFICIAL LEG VEINS

NORMAL VALVES

The veins in the legs are arranged into superficial and deep systems, connected by perforating veins. If the valves in the perforating or superficial veins leak, blood flows back down the superficial system causing dilated, tortuous vessels. Varicose veins may be symptomless or cause aching, swelling, eczema and ulceration, as they become distended, enlarged and twisted. Veins almost anywhere in the body can be involved, although those in the legs are most commonly affected.

vasectomy

The operation of cutting and tying the *vasa deferentia* (singular, *vas deferens*), the two ducts passing from the testicles to the seminal vesicles through the inguinal canal.

It is a simple operation rapidly gaining in popularity throughout the world as a means of sterilization of males who no longer want to father children, and can be carried out under general or local anesthesia. In the usual technique, small incisions are made in the scrotum through which the vasa are identified, cut and tied off. It is not the same as castration, for the testes are left undisturbed and functioning.

After the operation a store of sperm is left beyond the block, which means that the man will not be sterile until the live sperms have been ejaculated—a process which may take up to two months, during which another form of contraception is required. At the end of this period consecutive sperm counts are made; two or three negative results are obligatory before the operation can be considered successful. The patient himself will not notice any difference in his sexual activity, for most of the fluid ejaculated at orgasm comes from the prostate gland and seminal vesicles, which are untouched; the secretion of male hormone from the testicles continues without interruption, so that virility and sexual arousal and desire are not affected.

VASECTOMY

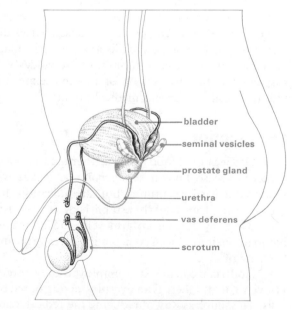

Vasectomy is a method of male sterilization carried out through a small incision in the scrotum. The vasa deferentia are cut and tied back, as pictured above, so that sperm can no longer pass from the testes to the urethra. Very few vasectomies can be reversed successfully.

It is technically possible to reverse the operation, but restoration of the continuity of the vasa deferentia does not always restore fertility.

vasoconstriction

The arteries contain muscle tissue in their walls; contraction of the muscular coat of a blood vessel, reducing its bore and the amount of blood that can flow through it, is referred to as vasoconstriction. It has a valuable physiological function in controlling the flow of blood through a tissue; however, under certain circumstances, an inappropriate constriction of the arterial supply to a tissue can cause serious problems.

The degree of contraction present in the muscular wall of an artery is under involuntary nervous control and is also affected by a number of physiologically active chemicals (HORMONES) circulating in the blood. It can also be increased or decreased by the action of certain drugs.

A common example of the effect of vasoconstriction is the marked variation in blood supply to the hands in hot and cold weather, allowing either extra heat loss (when the temperature is high) or reducing heat loss (when it is cold).

vasodilatation

While VASOCONSTRICTION refers to the contraction of the muscular wall of an artery, reducing its bore and the blood flow through it, *vasodilatation* is the relaxation of the muscular coat. This permits the vessel to increase in bore, thus also increasing the blood flow within it.

As with vasoconstriction, vasodilatation is under involuntary nervous control and is also affected by circulating drugs and physiologically active chemicals (HORMONES) in the blood. Common examples of vasodilatation are seen in the flushing of the skin of the face in response to embarrassment or excitement and the general increase in blood flow in the skin when the body is overheated—allowing more heat to be lost, especially from exposed areas such as the hands.

vegetarianism

The practice of abstaining from all flesh foods of animal origin and living mainly on vegetables. An extreme form of vegetarianism prohibits even the consumption of eggs, milk and dairy products because they come from animals. Upholders of this extreme practice are known (especially in Britain) as *vegans*, to distinguish them from ordinary vegetarians.

Vegetarianism is of extremely ancient origin and was advocated by Pythagoras in the 6th century B.C. During the period of the Roman Empire many religious sects opposed meat eating as a cruel and barbarous practice, as well as being contrary to such beliefs as the "transmigration of souls."

Modern vegetarianism dates from the 18th century, with such famous figures as Benjamin Franklin and Voltaire proclaiming its virtues. The first vegetarian association was formed in Manchester, England, in 1809; it was followed, from 1850, by the founding of similar societies in the United States and Germany. Because the majority of modern vegetarians do not belong to societies or associations, the total number in the United States is difficult to assess. An American Vegetarian Union was formed in 1949 and the American Vegan Society came into being in 1960.

Vegetarians who also eat eggs and dairy produce have no difficulty in obtaining the required dietary balance (especially of "high quality" proteins), for these foods contain adequate amounts of calcium, protein and B vitamins. Whether or not such a diet is more beneficial and hygienic than a diet containing meat remains a matter of argument. Vegetarian "propagandists" point to the tests made at Yale University and the University of Michigan in 1907 and 1909, respectively, in which it was suggested that vegetarians had far greater endurance and "staying power" than those who include meat in their diets. It is certainly a fact that during World War II, when the Allied blockade severely restricted the import of meat to Norway, the general health of the population improved.

Vegans find it more difficult to maintain an adequate diet, for the minerals and vitamins present in eggs and dairy produce must be replaced from vegetable sources. The diet must include nuts and whole-grain cereals and a wide variety of vegetables, otherwise there is a risk that mineral deficiency diseases may occur.

Probably the strongest argument for vegetarianism is that such a diet does not lead to the excessive formation of CHOLESTEROL in the blood. As there is a possible connection between this chemical (technically known as a *sterol*) and cardiovascular diseases, a growing number of physicians are of the opinion that a vegetarian diet may lower the incidence of these conditions.

See also the major article on **Nutrition.**

venepuncture

The puncture of a vein with a hollow needle. It is performed for the removal of a sample of blood or the injection or transfusion of drug solutions, blood or other fluids. It is most commonly performed, however, for the removal of blood samples for laboratory testing.

The most accessible veins for the purpose are those on the inner side of the elbow (antecubital fossa), although veins on the hand, wrist and (in small infants) the scalp and neck may be used.

Blood is commonly drawn with a plastic syringe attached to the needle.

Compare VENESECTION.

venereal disease (VD)

Disease transmitted by sexual intercourse.

The organisms responsible vary a great deal, but all depend on the warmth and moisture of the sexual organs for survival—for they die when the temperature drops much below that of body heat. SYPHILIS and GONORRHEA are the best-known venereal diseases, but the range also includes CHANCROID, LYMPHO-GRANULOMA VENEREUM, donovanosis (granuloma venereum, GRANULOMA INGUINALE), NON-SPECIFIC URETHRITIS (NSU), REITER'S DISEASE, genital warts, genital herpes (see HERPES SIMPLEX), TRICHOMONIASIS, genital candidiasis (see CANDIDA), MOLLUSCUM CONTAGIOSUM and pediculus pubis (see LICE).

Despite better diagnosis and treatment, venereal diseases have increased during the last 25 years. Changes in public attitudes toward sexual matters, widespread use of contraceptive pills, and the emergence of resistant strains of organisms seem to have contributed to the increase. But the diseases have always tended to spread because of ignorance, reticence and the fact that women may not notice symptoms.

When diagnosed in a man or woman the disease has probably already passed on to the sexual partner; it is therefore important that both should be treated to prevent reinfection. The potential consequences of the major venereal diseases, syphilis and gonorrhea, are so damaging that there is no room for false modesty. Any suspicion of the disease, or of possible exposure to infection, calls for urgent medical attention.

venesection

The "letting of blood" as a therapeutic medical procedure. Also known as *phlebotomy*. It was widely practiced in earlier centuries, but the indications for its use were far from clearly established. It was usually carried out by cutting an arm vein and allowing the blood to run into a basin (venesection literally means the "cutting of a vein").

In modern medicine, it is employed only rarely. In POLYCYTHEMIA there is an overproduction of red blood cells. The simplest way of reducing the red cell count is by the removal of blood, using a needle and a length of plastic tubing, usually 500 cubic centimeters at a time. In HEMOCHROMATOSIS, excessive amounts of iron accumulate in the body and, since iron can only be removed from the body in the form of the hemoglobin pigment in the red blood cells, venesection is the treatment of

choice. Blood donation also involves venesection.
Compare VENEPUNCTURE.

venogram

The veins, like most of their surrounding tissues, are readily penetrated by x-rays and therefore do not show up on an x-ray film (radiograph). To make them visible they must be injected with material which obstructs the passage of x-rays (a *radiopaque contrast medium*). If this is done, the veins will show up as light areas on the film—no blackening has occurred, as no rays can penetrate. Many such materials are available, most of them containing the heavy and radiopaque element iodine.

Liquids containing iodine compounds can be injected at any convenient site into a vein and a series of x-ray pictures taken as the radiopaque material is carried along the vein by the blood flow. Obstruction to the vein can thus be demonstrated. The technique is particularly useful in the diagnosis of THROMBOSIS of the leg veins.

ventricular fibrillation

The normal heartbeat is initiated by an electrical impulse generated in the walls of the upper chambers of the heart (atria). This impulse spreads to the remainder of the heart, producing a coordinated contraction of the muscular walls of first the atria, driving blood into the lower chambers (ventricles), and then of the ventricles themselves, driving blood out into the general circulation.

When a disorder of this regular series of events occurs, the heartbeat becomes irregular and the condition is described as a *cardiac arrhythmia*. (See ARRHYTHMIA.)

The most serious of the arrhythmias is VENTRICULAR FIBRILLATION. In this condition, the ventricles cease to contract regularly and instead show a rapid and uncoordinated contraction of all their muscle fibers without a recognizable rhythmic heartbeat. Since the effect of this is to prevent the heart from performing its normal pumping action, the circulation ceases immediately and—unless immediate measures are taken—sudden death will result. (See DEFIBRILLATION.)

Ventricular fibrillation can occur as a result of damage to the heart or its valves by drugs, infections, or interference with its blood supply via the coronary arteries (*coronary insufficiency*). Its greatest importance, however, is its occurrence as a complication of a *coronary thrombosis* (also known as a *myocardial infarction* or "heart attack")—where it is often the terminal event in sudden death.

Treatment is a matter of extreme urgency. If the situation cannot be remedied within two or three minutes, permanent or fatal damage to the brain from lack of oxygen may occur. Drugs are of limited value; the only effective treatment is to apply electrodes to the chest wall and give a short and controlled direct-current shock to the heart from a machine known as a *defibrillator*. This will lead to restoration of a normal heartbeat in a proportion of cases, although it may fail to do so.

While a defibrillator is being set up, maintenance of the blood circulation by means of closed cardiac massage and mouth-to-mouth artificial respiration is essential. If efficiently performed, it can greatly prolong the normal interval of two to three minutes between cessation of the circulation and BRAIN DEATH and will allow defibrillation to be performed even if the apparatus is not immediately available.

ventricular septal defect

See HOLE IN THE HEART.

verruca

The technical name for a wart.
See WARTS.

vertigo

A condition in which the subject feels dizzy, with a definite sensation of movement, and feels that he is or his surroundings are rotating in space. This last factor is an essential ingredient of true vertigo and distinguishes it from simple dizziness. It is often accompanied by nausea, headache or vomiting.

The loss of balance experienced in vertigo may be caused by motion (as in sea sickness), ear disease such as OTITIS INTERNA (labyrinthitis) or MÉNIÈRE'S DISEASE, damage to the acoustic (VIIIth cranial) nerve, cerebellar disease (the *cerebellum*, a major division of the brain beneath the back part of the cerebrum, is concerned with maintaining balance and coordinating muscular movements), or the effects of some drugs (such as streptomycin).

Sudden vertigo is one of the three characteristic symptoms of Ménière's disease (first discovered in 1861 by Prosper Ménière), the other two being fluctuating loss of hearing and tinnitus (a ringing sensation in the ears). Similar symptoms may sometimes occur, although less violently, after removing wax from the ear with a syringe. Vertigo may also be a symptom of certain stomach and digestive disorders, but in some people it is brought on merely by standing on a height and looking down.

While the attack lasts the patient should lie flat on his back and his collar and clothing around his neck loosened. Sedatives may be administered by a physician if the patient remains conscious. If attacks occur frequently, the patient should consult his doctor to find the cause and permit the appropriate treatment to be given.

Vincent's angina

A noncontagious infection of the gums and throat caused by either of two types of bacteria or a combination of both: a *fusiform bacillus* and a *spirochete*.

Symptoms include painful bleeding gums, excessive production of saliva and fetid breath. In the untreated disease, ulcers form on the gums and sometimes the throat, and the affected tissues may be covered with a gray membrane—the irritation or removal of which typically causes bleeding.

Both types of bacteria are found in healthy mouths, but are normally dormant. In cases of poor oral hygiene, poor general health, prolonged exhaustion, or nutritional deficiences the infection may suddenly establish itself. (This is the reason why Vincent's angina also has the World War I nickname of *trench mouth*.)

Treatment consists of cleansing the mouth and throat with appropriate antiseptic lotions, rest, and attention to the reestablishment of adequate nutrition and good general health. Antibiotics are not usually required.

viruses

Viruses are the smallest known infectious organisms; with certain exceptions, they are too small to be seen under the ordinary light microscope. They vary in size from 10–300 nanometers (nm) in diameter. The smallest virus is about $\frac{1}{100}$ the size of a bacterium, and about $\frac{1}{750}$ the size of a red blood cell. They are unable to live or multiply outside a host cell since most do not possess the means to synthesize protein.

Structurally, a virus consists of a core of nucleic acid (its genetic material) surrounded by a protein coat. This protein coat is antigenic—that is, it will cause the production of antibodies in the blood of the host; each type of virus has an antigenic property specific for its type. (See ANTIBODY/ANTIGEN.)

Viruses are classified according to the type of nucleic acid they possess and their appearance. The main groups of medically important viruses are the *pox viruses, adenoviruses, herpes viruses, papovaviruses, myxoviruses, rhabdoviruses, enteroviruses, picornaviruses, reoviruses arboviruses* (also known as *togaviruses*), and *arenoviruses*.

Most forms of life (animals, plants or bacteria) are susceptible to virus infection. Viruses affect the cells which they inhabit in several ways. They may kill the cell; they may transform the cell from a normal cell to a cancerous cell; or they may produce a latent infection, in

Viruses, seen here magnified many thousands of times by an electron microscope, have a wide variety of striking, even beautiful, geometric shapes. They are parasitic microorganisms which can only reproduce by taking over the genetic machinery of a host cell (animal, plant or bacterium).

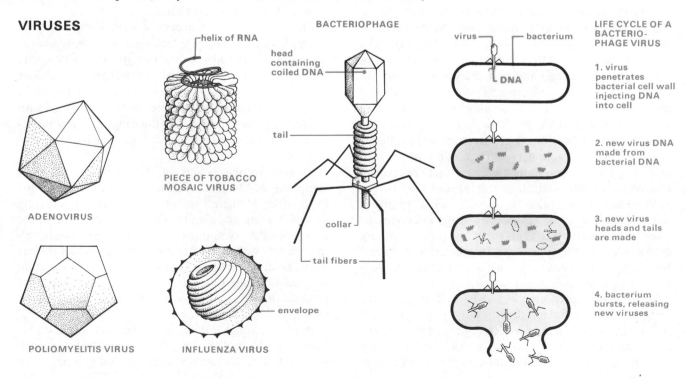

VIRSUSES

helix of RNA

PIECE OF TOBACCO MOSAIC VIRUS

ADENOVIRUS

POLIOMYELITIS VIRUS

envelope

INFLUENZA VIRUS

BACTERIOPHAGE

head containing coiled DNA

tail

collar

tail fibers

virus — bacterium

DNA

LIFE CYCLE OF A BACTERIO-PHAGE VIRUS

1. virus penetrates bacterial cell wall injecting DNA into cell

2. new virus DNA made from bacterial DNA

3. new virus heads and tails are made

4. bacterium bursts, releasing new viruses

which the virus remains in the cell in a potentially active state but produces no obvious effects on the functioning of the cell.

Most viruses are inactivated by heat (100°F for 30 minutes, or 212°F for a few seconds), but most are stable at very low temperatures (for example at −95°F). The effect of drying on viruses is variable. Ultraviolet radiation inactivates viruses, and so do oxidizing agents such as formaldehyde, chlorine, iodine and hydrogen peroxide; but chloroform and ether inactivate only those viruses which contain lipid. They are resistant to glycerol, which is sometimes used as a preservative to prevent bacterial contamination of virus suspensions.

Viruses are important causes of human disease. Most virus infections are mild and may go unnoticed by the patient, although the viruses may multiply in the body and be passed on to another susceptible person. In children, the elderly, and those who are debilitated, a viral infection that is normally mild can produce severe effects. Some virus infections (such as smallpox) are severe and have a high mortality rate.

Viruses usually enter the body via the respiratory tract by inhalation, but some enter by ingestion or by inoculation through skin abrasions. The disease produced may be systemic—for example mumps, in which the virus travels through the bloodstream and invades many organs and tissues—or it may be localized and invade only tissues near the site of entry, as in respiratory viral infections.

Unlike some bacteria, viruses do not produce toxins; they produce their effects directly by multiplication in the tissues.

The body attempts to protect itself against viral infections by producing *interferon*, a protein released from infected cells which, when taken up by other cells, renders them refractory to viral infection. The body can also produce antibodies to specific viruses; these antibodies may persist for several years.

Although there are a few drugs which exhibit a degree of antiviral activity, they act only against a few types of viruses. Most viruses are resistant to the antibiotics available. Prevention of viral diseases is by avoiding contact with infected persons or by vaccination where the specific vaccines are available.

See also IMMUNIZATION and the major article on **Infectious Diseases.**

vision

The structures concerned with vision are the eyes, optic nerves, and the occipital lobes of the brain.

Light enters the eye through the cornea, the transparent part of the outer covering of the eyeball which overlies the pupil. The pupil is the central aperture of the *iris*, the colored diaphragm which controls the amount of light admitted to the interior of the eye; it is capable of contracting so that the pupil enlarges when the intensity of the light is low. In conditions of high ambient light the pupil is small because the smooth muscle of the iris relaxes. The light reflex (or pupillary reflex) is controlled in the brain stem, and is sometimes affected in disease.

Behind the iris is the *lens* of the eye (also known as the *crystalline lens*), a transparent biconvex structure with the front curved slightly less than the back. Because it is elastic, its shape can be changed by the action of the *ciliary muscle* on the suspensory ligament which supports the lens; in this way the image of objects near the eye can be brought to a focus at the retina (see ACCOMMODATION). With age the elasticity of the lens decreases and the ability of the eye to bring near objects into focus fails; glasses for reading then become useful.

In later life the lens may become obscured by the development of a CATARACT, an opacity which interferes with vision. The image of objects falling on the lens is focused on the *retina*, which consists of receptors sensitive to light; they are of two kinds, called *rods* and *cones*.

There are about 120 million rods and about 6 million cones. Nerve fibers run from them to gather at the optic disk (the "blind spot") where they form the *optic nerve*, which passes from the eyeball to the brain. Behind the

EYE

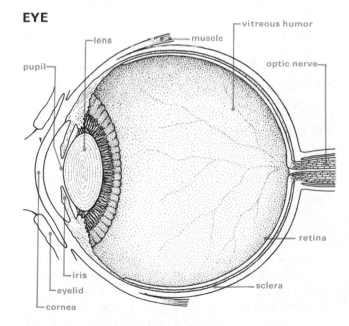

A CROSS SECTION THROUGH THE EYE

The eye is often likened to a camera because it has an adjustable lens and aperture (the pupil) with a light-sensitive film (the retina) behind. The optical images are encoded and transmitted along the optic nerve to the brain, where the simultaneous signals from both eyes are coordinated.

eyes the fibers of the optic nerves in part cross over at the *optic chiasm*, so that images entering the eyes from the right and falling on the temporal or outer side of the left retina and the inner or nasal side of the right retina are conducted to the left side of the brain (and vice versa).

If the shape of the eyeball is abnormal, objects cannot be brought to a sharp focus on the retina—a long eyeball produces short sight, while short eyeballs cannot produce a sharp image of near objects. Both conditions may be remedied by special glasses, as may aberrations of shape of the crystalline lens; if the eyeball is not truly spherical, parts of an image will not be in sharp focus at the retina, producing a defect in vision known as ASTIGMATISM.

Defects in the cones of the retina produce COLOR BLINDNESS, for they are thought to contain the three visual pigments. Rods contain only one pigment (rhodopsin), whose adsorption is greatest for blue-green light. The retina itself may be affected by disease resulting in DETACHED RETINA, hemorrhage or exudation—all of which obscure vision.

Behind the eye, disease may affect the optic nerve or the crossing of the nerves (optic chiasm) so that there are defects in the field of vision; disease may also interfere with the nerve fibers as they pass through the brain to the occipital cortex at the back of the cerebral hemispheres. Examination of these visual field defects is of great value to the neurologist, who can often (by consideration of the shape and site of the defects) localize brain lesions.

Finally, the movements of the eyeballs must be accurately coordinated. Each eyeball is moved by a complex of six external *ocular muscles* supplied by nerves arising in the brain stem. Interference with the central mechanism of coordination, with the nerves or with the muscles themselves, can result in DOUBLE VISION.

See also BLINDNESS, NIGHT BLINDNESS and the major article on **Ophthalmology**.

vitamins

A group of unrelated substances, occurring in many foods in small amounts, which are essential for growth, health and life.

Vitamins are generally divided into two broad groups—fat soluble (A, D, E, K) and water soluble (B, C). They were originally named after a letter of the alphabet, but some—such as vitamin B—have since been found to consist of a mixture of several substances. The individual constituents of vitamin B have been given distinctive names: *thiamine* (vitamin B_1), *riboflavin* (B_2), *nicotinic acid, cyanocobalamin* (B_{12}) and so on. The whole group of vitamin B constituents is usually referred to as *vitamin B complex*.

Some vitamins can be synthesized by the body; for example, vitamin D can be synthesized from cholesterol with the action of sunlight on the skin. Others, such as vitamin K, are synthesized by bacteria in the intestine. Still others, such as vitamin C, cannot be synthesized by man and have to be provided in the food we eat.

Each vitamin has a distinctive function, and deficiency of most any vitamin may produce a characteristic group of signs and symptoms. Deficiency may arise (1) because of an inadequate intake of the vitamin or its precursors; (2) because of factors which prevent its absorption or use; or (3) because of factors which increase requirements for the vitamin or promote its excretion from the body.

Excessive amounts of many vitamins (hypervitaminosis) can produce toxic symptoms.

Vitamin A is found mainly in fish-liver oils, liver, egg yolk, butter and cream; its precursors are found in green leafy and yellow vegetables. Vitamin A deficiency produces NIGHT BLINDNESS (nyctalopia), eye changes and thickening of the cells which cover internal and body surfaces such as the skin and the lining of the gastrointestinal and urinary tracts. There is also susceptibility to infections. *Hypervitaminosis A* may be acute, and causes increased pressure in the brain producing drowsiness, irritability, headaches and vomiting. Chronic vitamin A toxicity produces loss of hair, rough skin, cracked skin and lips, and later severe headaches, generalized weakness, bony ·changes and pain in the joints.

Vitamin D comes from the same sources as vitamin A. Its deficiency results in rickets or osteomalacia, while *hypervitaminosis D* causes loss of appetite, nausea, vomiting, thirst, the passage of large quantities of urine, weakness, nervousness, itch, impairment of kidney function and calcification in various tissues.

Vitamin E is found in vegetable oils, wheat germ, leafy vegetables, egg yolk and legumes (peas, beans, etc.). Its role is to maintain the stability of cell membranes; deficiency can lead to early breakdown of red blood cells.

A deficiency of vitamin K causes bleeding, while excessive amounts cause breakdown of red blood cells.

Vitamin B_1 is found in dried yeasts, whole grain, meat, legumes (peas, beans, etc.) and potatoes; deficiency produces BERIBERI.

Vitamin B_2 is found in milk, liver, meat and eggs; deficiency produces inflammation and ulceration of the skin, mouth, eyes and genital areas.

Niacin, or nicotinic acid, is found in the same foods which contain vitamin B_1; deficiency produces pellagra.

Vitamin B_6 comprises a group of related compounds which are involved in the metabolism of many tissue systems; deficiency does not usually produce characteristic symptoms, although a number of vague symptoms may occur which can be relieved by treatment with vitamin B$_6$.

Vitamin C (ascorbic acid) is found in citrus foods and green vegetables; deficiency causes SCURVY.

Folic acid is a B vitamin found in many animal and plant tissues. Deficiency is associated with malabsorption of food from the small intestine and megaloblastic anemia. Similarly, deficiency of vitamin B$_{12}$ (which is found in meat and dairy products) may produce megaloblastic anemia.

See also the major article on **Nutrition.**

vitiligo

A condition in which light-colored blotchy patches appear on the skin or hair as a result of the localized absence of the pigment *melanin*, the presence of which gives the skin its characteristic color. Also called *leukoderma*.

vomiting

The forcible ejection through the mouth of the contents of the stomach, brought about by a complicated reflex controlled by a vomiting center in the brain. Retching is the act of vomiting without the production of stomach contents.

The vomiting reflex can be set in motion by many different stimuli. Direct stimulation of the vomiting center occurs in meningitis, migraine, and the state of increased pressure within the skull caused by tumors or hemorrhage. This type of vomiting is not accompanied by nausea; it may also be caused by various drugs.

Many people vomit as the result of emotional shock—for example, at the sight of a bad road accident, or the perception of a disgusting smell; others vomit when unduly excited or anxious. Travel sickness is a problem for a number of people, particularly the young. It is caused by stimulation of the vomiting center by impulses arising in the inner ear.

The most common cause of vomiting is intestinal disturbance, when irritation brought about by over-distension or inflammation sets up the reflex through the vagus nerve—which serves both to carry stimuli to the vomiting center and to transmit the outgoing nerve impulses necessary for the accomplishment of the act.

The vomiting which often occurs during pregnancy—see MORNING SICKNESS—may be due to changes in hormone balance, but the cause is not definitely known; in many cases it is accompanied by anxiety or other emotional disturbances.

Vomiting in children may herald the onset of an infectious fever, while in babies it is often the result of injudicious feeding or the swallowing of too much air.

So many disturbances cause vomiting that it is not possible to generalize about the most effective treatment, which must depend on the treatment of the underlying condition. One danger of vomiting to excess, particularly in young children, is loss of water and salts from the body with consequent dehydration and imbalance of electrolytes. A more immediate danger is inhalation of vomit, which may occur in unconscious or semiconscious persons.

von Recklinghausen's disease

A hereditary condition (also known as *neurofibromatosis*) in which numerous "neurofibromas" are found all over the body. These are benign tumors that arise in the skin or in the fibrous tissue surrounding peripheral and cranial nerves. The neurofibromas may occur on any nerve. If superficial, they may be seen as nodules under the skin; if they develop around deeper nerves, they may not be noticed until they produce symptoms by pressing on adjacent structures.

The symptoms of the disease depend largely on the severity of nerve involvement. In many cases, where the peripheral nerves are affected, there may be no symptoms at all (except perhaps pain on pressure over the course of the affected nerve or nerves). However, if the cranial nerves or the roots of the spinal nerves are involved, serious disability may result—depending on the function of the damaged nerves. Associated tumors of the brain (although relatively uncommon) can be particularly serious; surgical removal of accessible tumors is usually attempted.

Aside from surgical intervention (where appropriate), no specific treatment currently exists for von Recklinghausen's disease. It is very rarely fatal; the major complications arise in those patients who develop a malignant degeneration of the affected tissues.

vulvitis

Inflammation of the vulva, the female external sexual organs excluding the vagina. The vulva consists of the labia majora, labia minora, clitoris, the urethral meatus and various glands. It may become inflamed as the result of many types of skin disorders.

Infections which may be involved include the herpes simplex virus (although only rarely herpes zoster), other viruses, and Trichomonas (see TRICHOMONIASIS). Infections by fungus and yeast organisms are often associated with pregnancy and diabetes. They lead to a beefy red appearance and severe itching. This particular type of infection can usually be controlled quickly and effectively with local applications of nystatin (Mycostatin).

It is also essential to control the underlying disease in cases of diabetes. *Molluscum contagiosum*, a viral disease of the skin, is noted in the vulval area and can be transmitted during sexual intercourse.

In general, dermatological problems such as psoriasis, seborrheic dermatitis and folliculitis often involve the vulva. Friction, allergies, or irritation can lead to "eczematoid dermatitis," which responds well to local hydrocortisone and antihistamines. INTERTRIGO may involve the labial folds. It is not uncommon for vulvitis to be initiated by vaginitis spreading to the vulva by the agency of an extensive discharge, with resultant severe vulvar edema and itching. Treatment is directed at the underlying cause.

W

warts

Small solid benign tumors that arise from the surface of the skin as a result of a virus infection.

Warts (or *verrucas*) are extremely common and in the vast majority of cases completely harmless, although they may be unsightly and irritating. A wart appears when the activity of the virus causes hypertrophy of the papillae of the skin. This results in the growth of a bundle of fibers from the skin's surface, capped by the horny cells that cover the cuticle. The mass of the wart is surrounded by a ring of thickened cuticle and the fibers can be seen particularly well when the wart has been growing for some time and has become abraded. The color of the wart is usually darker than the color of the background skin, but this is merely because dirt becomes lodged in the minute crevices between the fibers.

Warts are common in children, probably because of a lack of immunity to the causative virus. They often appear more thickly on areas such as the knuckles, the insides of the knees and the face—where the skin is more likely to be irritated. Adolescents and young adults often suffer from epidemics in schools and other institutions, such as military camps, where physical education and swimming may be conducted in bare feet. The wart transmitted in these cases, the *plantar wart* on the soles of the feet, can be painful because of the pressure of the body's weight during walking. Older people suffer from *senile warts* and there is a type of *soft wart* on the eyelids, ears and neck which can occur among people working with hydrocarbons.

Treatment of warts is usually accomplished successfully, where it is thought necessary, by the simple expedient of removing them by application of a freezing agent such as liquid nitrogen or carbon dioxide snow. Plantar warts unsuitable for this treatment may need surgical excision. Chemical agents for the removal of warts are now little used: their effects are slow and repeated applications are necessary.

Compare MOLES, NEVUS.

weaning

Teaching a baby to eat foods other than milk. In the past 30 years some nutritionists have argued that weaning can be started in the first month of life; others have urged that it should be delayed until the age of six months. This lack of any consistent expert advice is evidence that a baby will come to little harm whichever policy is followed.

So long as a baby seems content and gains weight satisfactorily on a milk diet there need be no hurry to wean him.

See also the major article on **The Health Care of Children.**

wheeze

A noise produced in respiratory diseases when the walls of the larger airways are in apposition and behaving like the reed of a toy trumpet.

Wheeze is frequently observed in patients with airway obstruction and is often worse in the morning, during and after exercise, and following a chest infection. A high-pitched wheezing is characteristic of acute asthma.

Although wheezing is diagnostic of chest disease and is one of the signs looked for by the doctor, it is also heard in normal people during a sudden violent expiratory effort.

See also PULMONARY DISEASES and the major article on **Pulmonary Diseases.**

whiplash injury

If an automobile is suddenly hit from behind, the head and neck, which are more mobile than the trunk, move violently forward and backward like the lash of a whip. The movement can damage the neck, or in violent accidents the spinal cord or even the brain.

A very common complaint even after minor collisions is stiffness of the neck. This usually wears off, but the injury can be severe enough to require the wearing of a collar to limit movement of the cervical spine until recovery is complete. Unfortunately, the effects of whiplash injury may take a long time to show themselves, and the development of "cervical disk syndrome" can sometimes be traced back to an accident that occurred some years before.

Headrests (or more properly, head restraints) fitted to car seats protect against these injuries by preventing the backward whiplash movement of the neck.

whooping cough

An infectious disease of the mucous membranes lining the air passages. Also called *pertussis*. It is mainly a disease of children, who achieve lifelong immunity after infection. Thanks to improved health care and vaccination programs, it is no longer the menace that it once was in heavily populated countries.

Whooping cough gets its popular name from the fact that the irritation of the upper respiratory passages causes convulsive bouts of coughing, followed by a peculiar indrawing of the breath. Children, particularly those under the age of one year, were once greatly at risk from whooping cough. In 1906 the causative organism, *Bordetella pertussis*, was isolated for the first time and in the last three or four decades vaccines of greater and greater efficacy have been prepared. The effect has been to make whooping cough a comparatively rare disease. In Massachusetts, for instance, there were over 10,000 cases in 1930 but only 27 in 1973. Some cases of brain damage to children who have been vaccinated have been reported, but authorities agree that the risk of this side effect is smaller than the risk of similar damage caused by the disease itself.

In cases where vaccination has not been performed, three stages of the disease may be expected to occur. The initial "catarrhal" stage is followed by the "spasmodic" stage—in which all the classical symptoms appear—and by the stage of decline. During the spasmodic stage the bouts of coughing and "whooping" last about 30 to 45 seconds and can be extremely distressing to a child.

The spasmodic stage may last four to seven weeks and in rare cases may leave behind side effects such as EMPHYSEMA or a liability to attacks of ASTHMA. Whooping cough is highly contagious. Where a case occurs it is wise to isolate the sufferer from other children, or even adults, who have not previously had the disease (or have not been vaccinated). The patient should be kept warm and restricted to bed until the symptoms abate. Spasms of coughing may be relieved by the administration of drugs such as phenobarbital.

Vaccination should be performed at as early an age as possible, with a reinforcing dose at a year to 18 months.

See also the major article on the **Health Care of Children.**

xeroderma

A disorder in which the skin is very rough and dry.

The most common form is also known as *ichthyosis*

simplex, in which large corrugated papery scales form on the skin (which is deficient in sebaceous glands and sometimes also in sweat glands). *Xeroderma pigmentosum* is a rare disease, usually appearing in childhood, in which the skin atrophies (wastes away) and contracts. It is associated with overexposure to harsh sunlight, but there is also a familial tendency. Sufferers have photophobia (abnormal sensitivity of the eyes to light) and the warty and "keratolytic" lesions of the disease quickly become malignant. The skin has the appearance of senility even in young patients.

x-rays

X-rays, discovered in 1895 by the German physicist Wilhelm Konrad Roentgen (1845–1923), have become one of the best-known aids to both diagnosis and treatment.

A standard radiograph (or "x-ray picture") is produced by placing the hand, for example, on a sheet of x-ray film enclosed in a light-proof envelope and exposing it to radiation from an x-ray tube. The bones, being resistant to the passage of x-rays (*radiopaque*), will appear on the film as a white unexposed area, while the soft tissues, offering no resistance (*radiolucent*), allow the film underlying them to be exposed and blackened by the rays. The result, in photographic terms, is a "negative" picture of the bones of the hand.

Since most soft tissues are radiolucent, their visualization requires special radiographic techniques; although the lungs, since they are air-filled, are so much more radiolucent than other tissues that the lung fields can be easily studied on a simple chest x-ray. A technique with wide applications, however, is to inject or give by mouth or otherwise introduce into the body a fluid contrast material which is opaque to x-rays. The upper part of the intestinal tract can thus be visualized on x-rays if the patient first swallows a suspension of barium sulfate (*barium meal*); to visualize the large intestine on an x-ray, a similar suspension can be given as an enema (*barium enema*).

Certain iodine-containing compounds can be injected into a blood vessel to allow x-ray visualization of the heart, arteries and veins (*arteriogram, venogram*). Similar material, on injection into the circulation, is rapidly excreted by the kidneys, allowing the kidneys to be visualized (*intravenous pyelogram*); by the same means the liver, gallbladder and bile ducts can be visualized (*cholecystogram*). Injection of iodine-containing material into the cerebrospinal fluid (around the brain and spinal cord) allows these structures to be seen on an x-ray (*myelogram*).

A new technique for soft tissue visualization is *tomography*. Movement of the x-ray tube during the exposure allows a plane of tissues to be examined in more detail, since there is no interference by tissues which lie above or beneath. This technique will reveal soft tissue structures not identifiable on a standard x-ray. A more recent development still is *computerized axial tomography (CAT scan)*. Here multiple tissue planes are viewed by tomography and the results are analyzed by an attached computer to build up a detailed picture of the soft tissue structures. This technique is applicable to the diagnosis of tumors and other lesions within the brain, liver, and other organs not easily visualized on x-rays by other means. (For more information on the CAT scan, see also the appropriate section in the major article **Examination, Diagnosis and Therapy.**)

X-rays are also widely used in the treatment of cancer. See the major article on **Oncology.**

Y

yaws

An infectious disease occurring in the hot moist tropics—especially in Africa, the West Indies and some parts of the Far East.

It is caused by a spirochete known as *Treponema pertenue*. The disease is also known as *frambesia* (from a French word meaning raspberry), because of the resemblance of the lesions to squashed raspberries. The first manifestation of yaws is an initial lesion of the skin, which is known as the mother yaw (or mamanpian). After this lesion has appeared, probably as a result of the transmission of the spirochete to the skin by various species of flies, or by direct contact with a sufferer, other lesions follow over the surface of the body. If the disease is left untreated more damaging lesions can occur, eroding both skin and bones.

The incubation period for yaws is two to four weeks, during which time the patient may experience a general feeling of being unwell (malaise) as well as pains, fever and a severe itching of the skin. A scaly eruption on the body and legs turns into the characteristic lesions with the appearance of lumps. Some of them may develop to be several inches in diameter and when the general level of health is low they may break down and form ulcers.

In most cases the lesions shrink slowly and eventually disappear after a few weeks or months. Yaws is one of the more important debilitating diseases of the tropics, especially in people who are malnourished or otherwise not in good health. It can be an especially severe disease when it occurs in combination with syphilis or tuberculosis. Since the introduction of antibiotics, however, its effect on the economic and social life of the

people of the tropics has diminished; penicillin has dramatic effects on the lesions by killing the infecting microorganisms. Prevention is by normal hygienic safeguards; spread of the disease can be checked by isolating sufferers.

yellow fever

An acute viral infection of the liver, kidneys and heart muscle transmitted by a female mosquito of the genus *Aedes*. It occurs in tropical Africa and parts of America lying between Brazil and the southern United States.

In the last century yellow fever killed so many workers engaged in constructing the Panama Canal that the French Panama Canal Company became bankrupt. During the Spanish–American war in 1900 a team of Army doctors—including Walter Reed—showed that the disease was transmitted by a species of mosquito known as *Aedes aegypti*. An efficient vaccine was eventually produced, giving up to ten years protection.

There is no known specific treatment for yellow fever. From about 3 to 14 days after being bitten by an infected mosquito the patient develops a headache, fever, and pains in the muscles. In a severe attack the temperature rises, the face becomes flushed and the mind confused. After two days the fever abates and confusion clears; but within 48 hours delirium may return, the pulse becomes slow and weak and the patient ceases to pass urine and becomes yellow as the infection spreads in the liver, kidneys and heart muscles. About one in five of those who develop jaundice die.

The control of yellow fever depends on strict control of the *Aedes aegypti*, which is a domestic mosquito breeding in pools of stagnant water and the water in the bottoms of old pots and pans and oil drums left near houses.

All travelers to places where the disease exists must be immunized at least ten days before they travel.

Z

zoonosis

Any disease shared by man and other vertebrate animals.

More than 150 zoonoses, carried by a variety of animals, are known; but modern medicine and veterinary science have been able to control many of them, or to ameliorate their effects. Even so, some of them still present a very real threat to human and animal life.

Examples of zoonoses are ANTHRAX, BRUCELLOSIS, PSITTACOSIS and RABIES.

Section III

The Complete Family Health Guide

Family Health Records

Record of Illnesses

ILLNESS	FAMILY MEMBER					REMARKS
	1	2	3	4	5	
Chickenpox						
German measles (rubella)						
Measles						
Mumps						
Whooping cough						
Convulsions						
Tonsillitis						
Strep infections						
Ear infections						
Influenza						
Rheumatic fever						
Urinary and kidney infections						
Skin diseases						
Other illnesses						

Allergies and Allergic Reactions

REACTION	FAMILY MEMBER					REMARKS
	1	2	3	4	5	
Asthma						
Hay fever						
Hives						
Insect bites						
Eczema						
Plants (Ivy, Oak, Sumac, etc)						
Foods						
Chemicals and household products						
Antibiotics						
Other medication						
Blood transfusions						

Immunization Record

IMMUNIZATION	FAMILY MEMBER					REMARKS
	1	2	3	4	5	
DTP (diphtheria, tetanus and whooping cough)						
Poliomyelitis						
Tetanus and diphtheria boosters						
Measles						
Mumps						
German measles (rubella)						
Other immunizations (influenza, typhoid, yellow fever, cholera, gamma globulin, etc)						

Hospitalizations

FAMILY MEMBER	REASON AND DATES			
1				
2				
3				
4				
5				

Emergency Telephone Numbers and Addresses

Hospital	
Police	
Fire Department	
Poison Control Center	
Pediatrician HOME	OFFICE
Doctor HOME	OFFICE
Neighbors, Relatives and Friends	
Husband	
Wife	

Examination, Diagnosis and Therapy Dr. John L. Roglieri and Dr. Robert Lewy

In general, 100 years ago physicians could diagnose a particular disease only by relying on what they could see, hear, or feel directly. Modern methods of examination, diagnosis and treatment have dramatically improved the ability of doctors to identify potentially life-threatening diseases and prescribe specific drugs to arrest and reverse their course. The following article discusses these fascinating advances.

In this section we shall discuss examination, diagnosis and some of the various therapies currently available. Analysis (or examination), diagnosis and treatment are very closely related in clinical practice. In the simplest cases they follow one another in order—that is, a series of diagnostic studies leads to diagnosis and prescription of the most effective known treatment. Then, monitoring the illness by repeated examination and laboratory tests helps confirm the accuracy of the diagnosis and the effectiveness of the therapy. In this simplest case, examination leads to diagnosis, which dictates therapy.

It is not at all unusual, however, for examination to be followed by therapy and then by diagnosis. When the examination suggests two equally likely diagnoses, the physician may prescribe the simplest possible medication or perform the safest therapeutic procedure to help clarify the diagnosis. Improvement in the patient's condition in such a "therapeutic trial" frequently provides a most important clue to the precise diagnosis (or a confirmation of it).

Much less commonly, a treatment may lead to an unsuspected second diagnosis which may then be confirmed through various laboratory tests. A widely recognized example is drug allergy. For instance, the use of penicillin for many common infections has caused "side effects" in some patients, either in the form of a mild skin rash or as much more serious complications. The diagnosis of penicillin allergy is confirmed in these patients by carefully injecting a very small amount of a diluted penicillin solution. The number of situations where treatment suggests a diagnosis which is then confirmed by tests appears to be growing as the selection of drugs available increases.

Because examination, diagnosis and therapy relate to each other in several ways, physicians must frequently conduct two, or even three, of these activities at the same time. The need for combining examination, diagnosis and therapy is especially important in hospitalized patients. With few exceptions, the reason for hospitalization is usually either the presence of a serious illness or the occurrence of symptoms that require major diagnostic studies. Fortunately, the diagnosis is relatively obvious for most life-threatening illnesses. On the other hand, diseases which require hospitalization for diagnosis frequently call for some partial treatment while the tentative diagnosis is being confirmed. The need for simultaneous diagnosis and therapy may arise from (1) worsening of the patient's condition, (2) the expense of hospitalization, (3) the cost, discomfort and inconvenience to the patient of drawn-out or repeated testing, or (4) the desirability of a "therapeutic trial."

EXAMINATION

In conducting a medical examination, the physician is given privileges by his patient which are highly unusual in a civilized society. He is permitted—in fact, he is expected—to ask the most probing questions relating to intimate aspects of the patient's personal life and to pursue answers to these questions in detail. At the conclusion of this brutally candid interogation, the physician routinely asks his patient to disrobe and to assume the most undignified of physical positions. No part of the patient's body is considered to be beyond the limits of the doctor's jurisdiction.

After every accessible body opening has been manually probed, the physician may seek greater penetration and exposure through the use of metal, plastic, or "fiberoptic" instruments. Specimens of every conceivable body fluid may be obtained through rubber tubes, or by means of metal or plastic cylinders introduced into veins, arteries and various body cavities. Finally, with the patient's informed consent, the physician or surgeon is empowered to render the patient unconscious (by means of a general anesthetic), depriving him of all his natural senses, and to remove tissue or even an organ from the unconscious patient.

Clearly, this extreme degree of confidence and trust placed in the physician must be deserved, respected and reciprocated. The physician must keep confidential all of the information obtained and must minimize the required invasions of the patient's most basic human rights. He is taught early in medical school to limit his

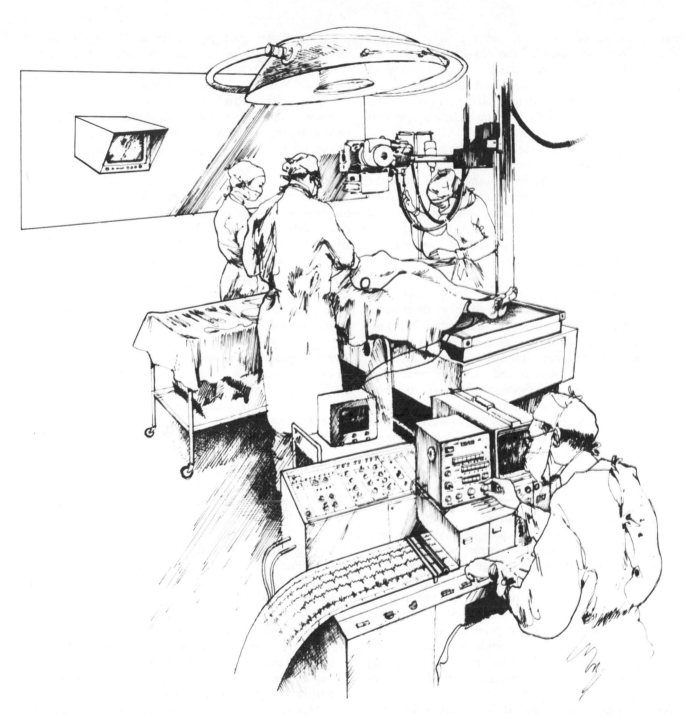

efforts to analyze and cure according to the fundamental rule: "First, do no harm!" In order to minimize the likelihood of harming his patient, the physician accumulates as much information as possible using the simplest available techniques.

In the following pages we shall consider the diagnostic process as it begins with the safest and least expensive steps and proceeds to those analytical steps that are more costly, difficult and complicated. The process begins with the patient's medical history, continues through the physical examination and concludes with laboratory tests and other diagnostic procedures.

Modern hospitals are fully equipped with sophisticated electronic equipment to monitor the vital signs (pulse, respiration and temperature) of patients undergoing surgery. In special cases it may also be desirable to record the electrical activity of the brain by means of an EEG.

Medical history

In most clinical situations, the medical history is the single most important component of the physician's evaluation. As it is often the first serious contact between the physician and a new patient, the typical interview—skillfully conducted—enables the physician to gain the confidence and trust of the patient, thereby forming an important basis for their relationship. At the same time, the physician is quickly able to determine the seriousness and urgency of the illness as well as the patient's apparent ability to cope with his disease.

In reviewing the patient's medical history, the physician makes mental notes regarding indications for special attention during the physical examination and the laboratory evaluation. Some physicians feel that a medical history will clearly reveal the final diagnosis in a majority of patients. Some senior clinicians teach that the diagnosis is *made* on the basis of the medical history, *confirmed* by physical examination of the patient and *quantified* by laboratory tests and x-rays.

There has been a recent trend on the part of some physicians to delegate all (or at least some) of the medical history-taking process to nonphysicians. Responsibility for taking the patient's history has been turned over to nurses, nurse practitioners, physician's assistants, non-professional (clerical) persons and even electronic computers. Many physicians are willing to delegate to others the gathering of routine patient data such as vital statistics, past injuries or operations, etc. They feel, however, that the "nonverbal clues" which the physician picks up during a personal interview with a patient necessitate that he himself should take the most important parts of a medical history.

Contents of the medical history

The basic elements of a medical history are widely standardized: the first series of items include "general identifying" data. Even your name, age, sex, marital status, occupation and race are not medically neutral. There are obviously sex-related diseases for which a member of the opposite sex is ineligible. Blacks, Jews, Mediterraneans, Scandinavians and other ethnic groups are each highly susceptible to certain diseases while seemingly almost immune to others. Marital status and occupation may imply certain lifestyle characteristics which could be medically suggestive.

The second category of medical history data is the "chief complaint." The chief complaint is the patient's answer to the question, "What brought you to the doctor's office?" Closely related to the chief complaint is the subsequent series of questions which elicits details regarding the "present illness." (Note that patients who visit their doctor for an "annual physical," a preemployment examination, or a "camp physical" have neither a chief complaint nor a present illness.) For patients whose visit to the physician is prompted by discomfort, the present illness is the most important part of the whole medical history. The precise nature of symptoms, their chronological development, related positive responses (as well as pertinent negative

ones) are all part of the present illness. When did you first notice the pain (or other symptom)? Has it been getting better or getting worse? Where does it start and where else does it go? What makes it feel better and what makes it feel worse? How has it affected your ability to function at work, at home, at play? Responses to these and similar questions (which are suggestive of possible diagnoses) are followed by further, more specific, questions in a "branching logic" fashion.

In seeking information on your family history the physician will ask the age and health status of your parents, brothers, sisters and other blood relatives, as well as the cause of death and age at death for those family members who are deceased. Inquiry will be made into the incidence within the family of infectious diseases (e.g., tuberculosis and syphilis), high blood pressure, alcoholism, drug abuse, mental illness, neuromuscular disorders, migraine headaches, bleeding disorders, heart disorders, diabetes, anemia, arthritis, allergy and so on.

Typical questions asked

Questions regarding your "social history" will include birthplace, education, marital history, military history, social and economic status and extent of use of cigarettes, alcohol, or drugs.

The physician will also want to know about your past medical history. Have you had any operations or sustained any injuries? Have you been hospitalized for any other reason? Have you had the usual childhood infectious diseases such as measles, chickenpox and mumps? Have you had any other infectious diseases as an adult? Venereal (sexually transmitted) disease? Have you been generally healthy all your life or have you rarely enjoyed good health? Finally, in an attempt to insure that no pertinent item of medical history has been omitted in any of the above categories, the physician will conduct a "review of systems"—asking about symptoms typically associated with each of the body systems.

(1) Skin. Have you had changes in skin color, sweating, rash, itching, easy bruising? Has there been change in the texture and distribution of your hair? Have you noticed any changes in your nails?

(2) Musculoskeletal system. Have you had swelling, aching, redness, tenderness or pain in any of your joints? Have you experienced any muscular weakness or loss of muscle control? Have you dislocated or sprained any joints? Have you broken any bones?

(3) Blood. Have you had swollen or tender glands? Have you ever been anemic? Have you ever had clotting difficulties?

(4) Endocrine system. Have you experienced any abnormal overall body growth or any recent change in the size of your hands, feet or head? Have you ever been told of thyroid problems or a goiter? Do you frequently feel more cold or warm than other people in the same room?

Do you have excessive thirst, appetite or frequent urination? Have you suffered from impotence, frigidity, or sterility?

(5) Head. Have you ever had a skull fracture, suffered a concussion, or had a serious head injury? Have you ever had a convulsion or a seizure? Have you ever lost consciousness? Have you experienced dizziness? Are you troubled by headaches (are they migraine, tension or other)?

(6) Eyes. Troubled by blurred vision or double vision? Do you wear glasses for reading? What was the date of your last eyeglass prescription? Are you colorblind?

(7) Ears. Troubled by difficulty in hearing or by ringing in your ears? Earaches?

(8) Nose. Do you have nosebleeds, sinus problems, or difficulty breathing through your nose?

(9) Mouth. Do you have an unusual degree of difficulty with your teeth or gums?

(10) Throat. Frequent sore throats or hoarseness? Have you had your tonsils removed?

(11) Neck. Do you have frequent stiff neck or swollen glands in your neck?

(12) Breasts. Have you ever had breast lumps, breast pain, discharge?

(13) Allergy. Do you suffer from asthma, hayfever, or hives?

(14) Respiratory system. Have you ever had pneumonia, tuberculosis, bronchitis, pleurisy, coughed up blood or had night sweats? Have you ever been awakened by shortness of breath or developed shortness of breath on lying down? Become short of breath when exercising? Noticed wheezing? Have chronic cough, if so, is it associated with coughing up sputum?

(15) Cardiovascular system (heart and blood vessels). Ever had a rapid or irregular heartbeat or palpitations? Do you have shortness of breath with exercise? Do you ever have chest pain? Do you ever have swelling in your feet, ankles, or legs? Have you been told of high blood pressure, heart murmur, or rheumatic fever?

(16) Gastrointestinal system (stomach and intestines). Have you experienced loss of appetite, loss of weight, nausea, vomiting, diarrhea, difficulty in digesting fatty food, or difficulty in swallowing? Have you ever noticed signs of blood in your stools? Vomited blood? Had unusually dark stools or "yellow jaundice"?

(17) Genitourinary system (genitals, kidneys, bladder and related structures). Have you ever noticed blood or pus in your urine, painful urination, excessive urination, any loss of urine, kidney stones? For women: at what age did your menstrual periods start? Have you had regular periods or have you ever been troubled by an excessive number of periods or excessive bleeding? Have you undergone the change of life (menopause)? At what age? Have you had any bleeding since the change? Have you had an abortion, miscarriage, or stillbirth? How many times have you been pregnant? Have you ever had complications? Have you ever had a venereal disease?

(18) Nervous system. Have you ever had weakness, paralysis, seizures or convulsions, loss of coordination, loss of pain sensation, loss of control of urine or feces (stools)?

(19) Mental illness. Have you ever had a "nervous breakdown" or been institutionalized? Have you ever been treated by a psychiatrist? Have you ever "heard voices"?

The above are typical leading questions and will be followed up by more detailed probing in the case of any positive response. On completion of the review of systems, the "complete" medical history has been taken. At this point the physician routinely asks the patient if he has any other points to mention or questions to ask. The stage has been set for the initiation of the objective evaluation.

Objective evaluation

The objective evaluation includes the physical examination, laboratory tests, x-rays and the results of any other specialized tests which may be required.

The nature and extent of the physical examination will vary with the medical circumstances. For example, a surgeon evaluating an adolescent for possible acute appendicitis will not be too concerned with the details of the neurological side of a complete physical examination. He will spend most if not all of his time in a thorough evaluation of the abdominal and pelvic areas. In the absence of such specialized circumstances, however, a thorough medical evaluation requires a complete physical examination.

Physicians develop a personalized routine approach to performance of the physical exam. In much the same way that a medical history is taken in the same order for every patient, the physician performs the parts of the physical examination in the same order so that no area is overlooked or forgotten. Many physicians accomplish this routine by beginning the examination at the head and working down to the patient's feet; others prefer to reverse the procedure.

Some important parts of the physical examination may be performed by the nurse or by the physician's assistant. Determination of your height, weight, blood pressure, pulse rate, body temperature and respiratory (breathing) rate will usually have been recorded before the physician sees you. He will therefore be able to rule out, or be made to consider, whether you are overweight, have high blood pressure, fever, an abnormal heart rate, or respiratory difficulty. These baseline data—together with the information from the medical history—will help direct special emphasis toward certain parts of the body during the physical examination. Similarly, any positive findings noted at the beginning of the physical examination usually suggest that a more detailed examination or special tests may be required to confirm the diagnosis.

In examining each part of the body, the physician makes use of four basic techniques: inspection, palpation, percussion and auscultation.

Inspection

The physician carries out a thorough visual examination of the body prior to manual examination.

Palpation

Palpation implies a "feeling" of the area; it is usually done with the pulps of the fingertips or the fingers and palms. Superficial palpation is essentially a gentle feeling of the skin and the tissues and organs immediately beneath the skin. Deep palpation is the more forceful technique used in attempting to define the outlines of organs (such as the liver or spleen) situated more deeply in one of the body cavities.

Percussion

We are all familiar with the technique of percussion: the physician firmly taps one of his fingers against a finger of the opposite hand which has been placed on the patient's body. The sound produced can provide evidence of any fluid or pus in a body cavity and aid in determining the size and consistency of underlying structures.

Auscultation

Auscultation signifies listening to the sounds of one of the body's functions through a stethoscope. The physician routinely listens to the sounds made by your heart, lungs and bowels; he may occasionally apply the stethoscope to other areas of the body for special purposes.

Some of the specific information the physician is looking for in his examination of each part of the body is described below.

Vital signs

The pulse rate, body temperature, respiratory rate and blood pressure comprise the data set known as "vital signs." The term is applied to these measurements because they represent bodily functions which are essential for life. They are closely monitored when a patient is seriously ill, as the signs are most likely to become quickly altered in the presence of acute illness.

A normal pulse rate averages between 60 and 100 beats per minute at rest for adults (higher for children and young adolescents). A resting pulse rate above 100 beats per minute always indicates abnormality. However, the pulse rate may be lower at rest than 60 beats per minute in adults who are vigorously athletic and in good physical condition.

The "normal" body temperature of 98.6°F (37°C) is an average figure for an adult, measured orally (with the thermometer held under the tongue for three minutes or so). Rectal temperatures are about 1° higher. Both temperatures may vary by as much as 1° in either direction

from individual to individual and within a single individual at different times of the day or under different conditions of exercise and rest.

The respiratory rate may vary between 10 and 20 breaths per minute in the adult; higher rates are normal under conditions of exercise and lower rates may sometimes occur during sleep.

Blood pressure varies widely from individual to individual and is affected somewhat by weight, sex and age. Blood pressure readings also vary from the sleeping state to wakefulness, from the sitting position to the lying position and sometimes (within a very small range) from arm to arm. A large or fatty arm may distort the blood pressure reading. The physician is especially on the lookout for elevations of blood pressure, since untreated high blood pressure (hypertension) may predispose patients to changes in the blood vessels which could cause a stroke, heart attack, or damage to the eyes or kidneys.

As for "low blood pressure" (hypotension), blood pressure readings lower than those normally expected do not usually represent an abnormality nor do they cause weakness, fatigue, or other symptoms. Low blood pressure is only abnormal when it occurs at the levels found in patients suffering from extensive bleeding, advanced heart disease, or serious blood-borne infections.

Height and weight

A physician normally records a patient's height only as a basic index to what the patient's ideal body weight should be. Ideal body weight is a specifically determined value based on insurance company experience in determining the highest weights (for each height, sex and body build) which have been maintained by their clients without experiencing health problems or disease earlier than would have been predicted. As with most cases of low blood pressure, being "underweight" is no cause for concern except in patients who are seriously ill with "body-wasting" diseases. Obesity, on the other hand (weight roughly 30% or more greater than ideal), appears to exert significant adverse consequences on health, especially by placing undue stress on many organs and joints.

Skin

Examination of the skin includes an assessment of color, moistness, elasticity, signs of easy bruising or bleeding and conditions such as rash, abnormal moles, unusual distribution of hair and abnormalities of the fingernails and toenails.

Head

The head is examined for signs of injury, abnormal hair growth or scalp conditions, and unusual facial features.

Eyes

The eyes are first examined externally by asking the patient

OPHTHALMOSCOPE

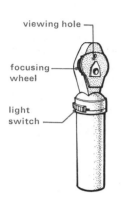

viewing hole
focusing wheel
light switch

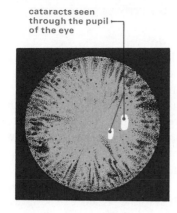

cataracts seen through the pupil of the eye

The ophthalmoscope consists of a light source, a system of mirrors, and interchangeable lenses, which enable doctors to examine the interior of the eye. Cataracts (opacities in the lens) are seen as spots. The ophthalmoscope is also helpful in diagnosing diseases in which the retina at the back of the eye undergoes characteristic changes—for example, hypertension and diabetes—and therefore has a part to play in a general medical examination.

to follow the examiner's finger or other object through a range of normal eye motion. The strength (or relative strength) of the six muscles controlling each eye is thereby assessed.

Internal examination of the eye is performed by means of the ophthalmoscope; this instrument projects a narrow beam of light through the outer lens of the eye, through the liquid interior of the eye and onto the retina and optic nerve at the back of the eye. The normally transparent lens becomes progressively opaque with the development of cataracts. The presence of a "mature" or completely opaque cataract may prevent the physician from making a further examination.

The retina is examined closely for signs of hemorrhage, abnormal development of blood vessels or an abnormal relationship between the optic nerve and the retina. Examination of the retina frequently provides clues to the presence and severity of generalized diseases such as high blood pressure, diabetes, or increased pressure on or within the brain.

When time permits, the examining physician will make a general determination of visual acuity—including peripheral vision—using either an eye chart, his fingers or some other object.

Ears

The ears are examined closely for signs of discharge, inflammation or scaling of the ear canal, the presence of an abnormal amount of wax and for signs of inflammation or an abnormal collection of fluid behind the eardrum.

Hearing acuity may be immediately assessed with the use of a wristwatch or a tuning fork.

Nose

The nose is examined for signs of a perforated or deviated nasal septum (the partition which separates the two sides of the nasal cavity) and for any signs of swelling or inflammation.

Mouth and throat

Close examination of the teeth and gums, as well as the texture of the tongue, precedes the physician's examination of the back of the mouth and upper throat. Saying "ah" opens widely the visually accessible part of your throat and raises the uvula (which dangles from the upper part of your throat) out of the way, providing a clearer view of the back of the throat and tonsils.

Neck

A chain of lymph glands (or lymph nodes) runs along the back of the neck, another along the front part of the neck and yet another under your lower jaw. Each of these groups of lymph glands are examined for signs of swelling, tenderness or change in texture.

When the physician puts his finger or fingers deep into the front part of your neck, he is feeling the "carotid pulse" in the arteries which provide the major part of the blood supply to your head and brain. His examination of the lower front part of your neck is performed to estimate the size and firmness of your thyroid gland. Your ability to turn your head fully to the left and to the right and upwards and downwards assures him that you have no serious disease in the cervical (neck) part of your spine and that you show no evidence of inflammation of your meninges (the membranes which cover the brain) by either infection or bleeding.

Breasts

Breasts are examined for unusual discharge or other abnormality of the nipples and for suspicious lumps. Many women have "fibrocystic changes" which give the breasts a lumpiness that makes abnormal masses difficult to feel. Many women will also experience changes in the size, fullness and "nodularity" of their breasts around the menstrual period. The determination that any breast lumps are due to fibrocystic change or to menstrual events should be made in consultation with your physician and should *not* be assumed to be harmless without his confirmation.

Heart

Examination of the heart may begin with a thorough visual inspection, since the heartbeat is frequently seen just below the left nipple when the patient is in the supine position (lying on his or her back). Signs of abnormal function may be seen across the chest wall and in the veins of the neck.

OTOSCOPE

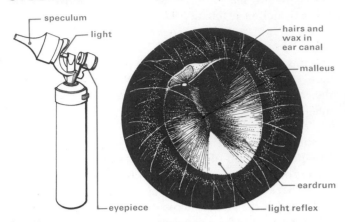

VIEW OF LEFT EARDRUM

Otoscopes are instruments for visualizing the eardrums. A healthy eardrum has a pearly appearance and strongly reflects light from the otoscope as a conical "light reflex." In middle ear infections, the eardrum looks red, a fluid level might be seen through it and the light reflex is absent.

After visual inspection, the physician will palpate (feel) the left side of your chest with his fingertips or palm to determine the location of the point where the heartbeat feels strongest. The location of this point gives him an approximate indication of the size of your heart; corroborating information is obtained by tapping (percussing) on the chest wall to determine the area of dull sounds reflected by your heart.

Finally, he will listen to your heart with his stethoscope—through which he hears first the sounds thought to represent the opening and closing of the heart valves. The quality and intensity of these sounds are considered an accurate guide to the functional status of the heart valves. He may also be able to detect sounds made by unusual turbulence created by the flow of blood through abnormal heart valves, as well as unusual sounds created by inefficient pumping (contraction) by the muscular wall of the heart.

Lungs

The sounds of air flowing through your lungs may be heard through the stethoscope at the front, top and sides of your chest as well as across your back. The nature of these sounds gives the examiner important clues to the volume of air moving in and out of your lungs and the degree of resistance to the normal flow. Abnormal accumulations of fluid, either within the lungs or between lungs and chest wall, also impart characteristic sounds.

Back

The general alignment and curvature of your spine may be quickly perceived by the physician as he runs his hand down your back. In looking for certain disease states he may gently punch the spine and the lower side areas of your back overlying your kidneys.

Abdomen

The physician examines your abdomen for surgical scars indicating previous surgery and for any extreme or taut protruberance which may suggest fluid within the abdominal cavity. At the upper right side of your abdomen he will palpate and percuss your liver to determine its size, texture and any tenderness. He may also probe his fingers into the upper left side of your abdomen to check for any enlargement of the spleen.

The lower part of the abdomen may yield significant clues to the presence of some abnormality within the pelvis as well as the abdomen. Through his stethoscope, placed on your abdomen, the physician can determine the degree of activity of your intestines.

Genitalia

The physician will look for swollen lymph nodes in the groin. In the male he will check the testicles for size, lumps and tenderness and will use his finger (as the patient coughs) to search for an unsuspected hernia. In the female the external genitalia are checked for abnormal bleeding, discharge or inflammation.

Internal (pelvic) exam

With the female patient appropriately positioned and draped, the examiner introduces a small instrument (speculum) into the vaginal canal, into which he shines an ordinary light or small flashlight. Progressing inward, he searches for signs of bleeding, discharge, inflammation, or abnormal dryness of the vaginal walls. At the back part of the vagina he can see the cervix (neck of the womb), which he examines for bleeding, discharge, color changes and abnormal growths. Using a small thin piece of wood, he will gently scrape the cervix to collect cells for a "Pap smear." (A small pool of secretions generally accumulates just below the cervix and specimens of this collection are also taken for microscopic cellular examination.) This test is effective in identifying cancerous or precancerous changes in the cervix at a very early time, when appropriate treatment can still be effective. (See also CERVICAL SMEAR.)

Introducing his rubber-gloved finger (or two fingers) into the vaginal canal, the physician will gently move the cervix in order to introduce a small degree of tension in the Fallopian tubes. Normally, this movement is not perceptible to the patient; in the presence of certain disease states, however, pain elicited by this maneuver may indicate the presence of infection.

Finally, with his inserted fingers on either side of the cervix and uterus, the physician will place his other hand on the surface of the lower part of the abdomen in an attempt to palpate between his two hands the entire uterus and the furthest part of the Fallopian tubes and the ovaries.

Rectal exam

Rectal examination will reveal the presence or absence of hemorrhoids ("piles"). In addition, approximately 25% of all intestinal tumors are generally found within reach of the examining finger. In the female the physician will be able to feel the patient's cervix or uterus through the front wall of the rectum. In the male patient the rectal examination enables the physician to determine the size, texture and any abnormal growth of the prostate gland. Small amounts of stool obtained from the physician's glove are tested for traces of blood.

Legs and feet

The legs and feet are examined for the presence of diminished blood circulation, accumulation of fluid (edema), or abnormal skin changes.

Neurologic examination

The neurologic examination is divided into four basic parts. Motor function, sensory function (sensation), mental status and function of the cranial and cerebellar nerves are all tested. *Motor function* merely means the patient's ability to use the muscles of the body with reasonable strength; it is tested by asking the patient to perform various movements of the head, trunk and limbs against resistance provided by the physician. *Sensory function* is determined by asking the patient to respond to touches by objects which are sharp, smooth, or of different temperature. *Mental status* is roughly assessed by determining the patient's general fund of knowledge regarding current events and recent history, and by asking him to perform several basic mathematical procedures such as simple addition and subtraction. The *cranial nerves* are each tested by specific function such as motion of the eyes, tongue, neck, shrugging of the shoulders, identifying odors, etc. *Cerebellar function* is appraised on the basis of tests of coordination such as walking a straight line (placing heel to toe), or touching one's nose and the physician's finger, and so on.

Additional tests

The above description of the various parts of the physical examination has been intended as a general guide. Your physician may perform additional tests under certain circumstances; in other circumstances, he may perform only a few of the above-mentioned tests. Further, the information which he seeks and its interpretation is much more extensive than has been described above and falls largely beyond the scope or intention of this book.

Having taken your medical history and completed the physical examination, the physician will frequently elect to order certain laboratory tests and x-rays to confirm his clinical impressions and to screen out other diseases which may not yet have become evident. We shall describe the routine laboratory tests, routine x-rays and other routine evaluative procedures and will make only brief allusion to more sophisticated tests which are sometimes required.

There has been (and continues to be) some controversy over the degree to which a physician should use tests in order to "rule out" the possibility of the presence of the early stages of an unsuspected disease. (See the major article on **Preventive Medicine**.) This issue arises because, for many diseases, there appears to be a lag between the time of the first detectable clinical or laboratory abnormality and the onset of symptoms. It has been suggested, therefore, that a system of "health maintenance" could be built upon periodic SCREENING of all individuals for as many diseases as might be detected by laboratory methods. While this approach has a very basic intuitive appeal to both physicians and healthy patients, it has come to be a sharply criticized method for two reasons.

The first basis of criticism is the remarkable cost of regular performance of such examinations on well patients when compared with the relatively low incidence of diagnosing a significant abnormality. In part, this great expense stems from the need for further investigation when an abnormality is detected during a screening test; subsequent, more sophisticated and more expensive confirmatory tests often yield negative results. The second major basis of criticism stems from the conviction of many physicians that the earlier treatment permitted by screening (as opposed to waiting until symptoms eventually appear) does not have a significant bearing on the ultimate outcome of the disease.

It has, therefore, become generally accepted medical practice that extensive "multiphasic screening" is reasonable only in patients who are medically "at risk" due to genetic, environmental, personal or socioeconomic factors. On the other hand, the alarming increase in the incidence of malpractice suits brought against physicians for failure to perform every conceivable screening test has encouraged many physicians to order an excessive number of tests and to practice "defensive medicine."

Despite this continuing controversy, there is widespread agreement on the value of the performance of a certain minimal set of baseline screening tests on all patients. It is to these tests, to be described, that we apply the term "routine." Because differences remain in the beliefs of individual physicians, your own physician may choose not to perform one or more of the tests described.

Blood count

A complete blood count includes determination of the hematocrit, hemoglobin, red cells indices, white cell count and white cell differential count. The hematocrit and hemoglobin are measures of the red blood cell content per unit of BLOOD. The red blood cell indices describe the size and shape of the red blood cells. The white blood cell count is an indication of the number of white blood cells in a given volume of blood. The differential white blood cell count describes the distribution of each type of white cell and the total white blood cell count.

Hematocrit and hemoglobin
The hematocrit and hemoglobin are abnormally low in various types of anemia and may be abnormally high in the presence of chronic lung disease. The white blood cell count may be high or low in the presence of infection or leukemia and may be somewhat elevated by various inflammatory diseases. The differential white blood cell count helps to differentiate between the various diseases which may raise or lower the total number of white blood cells in the circulating blood.

Urinalysis
The density (specific gravity) of the urine gives important information regarding the ability of the kidneys to excrete a concentrated urine and also provides insight into the state of hydration or dehydration of the patient. Abnormal coloration of the urine frequently indicates liver disease, kidney disease or infection. Clarity of the urine will obviously also be decreased in the presence of blood or pus.

The acidity of the urine is routinely measured and tests are made for the detection of abnormal amounts of sugar or trace amounts of blood. The urinary sediment is closely examined under the microscope for the presence of red blood cells, white blood cells, bacteria and abnormal solid elements. (See also URINARY TRACT INFECTION.)

"SMA 6" and "SMA 12"
These are the most widely used of the nonspecific screening tests and are known by their trade name, implemented by the Technicon Auto Analyser Company which labeled the system *Sequential Modular Analysis (SMA)*.

Routine blood counts no longer have to be made by looking under the microscope. This information, plus an analysis of other blood constituents, can be made automatically and within seconds by placing a blood sample in a modern blood chemistry machine (illustrated above). The information is printed out on a strip of paper, which can easily be attached to the patient's medical records.

The SMA 6 test includes determinations of the electrolytes sodium, potassium, chloride and bicarbonate and of serum glucose (sugar) and blood urea nitrogen (BUN). Almost as widely used as the SMA 6 is the SMA 12—which, in addition to measurement of uric acid, protein, albumin, creatinine, cholesterol and glucose levels, includes determination of the ions of calcium and phosphorus and the enzymes LDH, alkaline phosphatase, the pigment bilirubin and the enzyme SGOT.

Collectively, the SMA 6 and the SMA 12 are designed to detect a wide spectrum of disease and disorders representing the individual failure or combined failure of many organs. The ability to make all of these measurements rapidly and simultaneously may entail some sacrifice in accuracy of some of the determinations. Because each of these components varies from day to day within an individual patient—and because of the possibility of some loss of accuracy—it is not uncommon for a "screened" patient to have one or more of these values reported as abnormal on an initial screening test, to be followed within a relatively short space of time by a negative repeat confirmatory test.

Electrocardiogram (ECG)
Most physicians recognize the value of a baseline ECG in people under the age of 40 who do not have symptoms or other evidence of heart disease. The electrocardiographic changes which do represent real (potentially serious) diseases are frequently subtle and only discernible when the recent ECG record is compared with a previous recording.

Thus, it is helpful to have a baseline tracing on all patients, especially for those who (because of one or more risk factors) have a greater propensity to develop serious cardiac disease. Most general internists and family physicians will include at least one electrocardiogram in the medical record of all patients beyond young adulthood.

Chest x-ray
Until recently, the incidence, threat and fear of tuberculosis motivated most state health departments to insist that any patient admitted to a hospital be given a chest x-ray prior to admission. Happily, the incidence and prevalence of tuberculosis have lessened in recent years; with improved nutrition, sanitation and general socioeconomic status, its ability to sweep quickly through large populations has also decreased. The development of effective medications has also greatly reduced the seriousness of the disease in an individual patient once it has been contracted. Accordingly, many states have relaxed their requirement regarding routine chest x-rays. Nevertheless, the low cost, safety and general medical value of the chest x-ray have caused most physicians to continue to include it in a routine evaluation. (See also PULMONARY DISEASES and the major article on **Pulmonary Diseases**.)

In addition to defining with some degree of precision the

shape and size of the heart, the chest x-ray reveals important data regarding the functional capability of the lungs and the degree (if any) of imbalance between the pressures developed in and by the heart and those sustained in the blood vessels of the lungs. The early detection of lung cancer has not been among the benefits of routine chest x-rays. Such cancers tend to be relatively far advanced and sometimes have even spread to distant parts of the body before they become obvious on an x-ray.

Nonroutine radiological studies and other procedures

The nonroutine studies include plain films, contrast studies, scans and tomography. (See also *The Radiologist* in the major article on **Specialists You Seldom See.**)

Plain films

This technique is used for all nonroutine x-rays of various parts of the body which are visible on the x-ray film without the injection of "radiopaque" substances (contrast substances opaque to x-rays), radioactive elements, or other trace materials. These studies are not performed on a routine basis, but are done in response to rather specific complaints.

For example, an x-ray of the hand, arm, leg, ankle or spine will be performed when the patient complains of either acute severe pain or injury to one of those areas. Similarly, multiple views from diverse angles will be made of the abdomen in the case of acute abdominal distress and of the skull in cases of injury to the skull or in cases of suspected brain tumors.

Contrast studies

This term is used to describe x-rays taken of bodily parts not ordinarily visible on plain films. To make the outline of the parts visible, a contrast in density must be achieved by introducing a radiopaque substance.

For example, the well-known gastrointestinal (GI) series for the detection of a suspected peptic ulcer involves the patient's swallowing a thick solution containing barium sulfate (called a "barium meal"), which provides a dense white outline on the x-ray film of the path of the radiopaque material through the upper gastrointestinal system—i.e., the stomach, duodenum and small intestine. The outline of the large intestine is made visible by first administering a barium enema. (See BARIUM MEAL/BARIUM ENEMA.)

In preparation for x-rays of the gallbladder, the patient will take (for several days beforehand) a radiopaque substance in tablet form which is concentrated by the gallbladder.

A more rigorous form of the contrast study involves the injection of a radiopaque substance directly into a major blood vessel or into the heart itself. In some such instances,

The fluoroscope permits the radiologist to observe an image of the internal organs in motion on a fluorescent screen. For example, if the patient swallows a special mixture opaque to x-rays (barium meal), defects or obstructions in the esophagus, stomach or small intestine can be detected as the mixture moves through them.

one is interested in the heart or the major vessels themselves in a search for obstruction to the normal blood flow. In other studies, the radiologist watches for distortion of the normal arterial or venous distribution pattern occasioned by the rapid and deforming growth of a tumor or of pockets of blood.

Scans

Many different substances are used for the class of tests known as scans. Some of these are mildly radioactive forms of the same chemicals normally processed or concentrated by the organ under study. The fate of these radioactive substances, as traced by radiation counters, produces important information regarding the rate of metabolism of these substances and the size, shape and activity of the organ or organs under study.

Tomography

In its original form, tomography consisted of attempts to define a radiologic abnormality more precisely by making x-ray photographs of the abnormality from several different perspectives in different planes. The development of tiny integrated circuits (electronic components) and the ensuing miniaturization of computers facilitated the recent rapid evolution of this process into the new technique known as *computerized axial tomography (CAT scanner)*.

The development of computerized axial tomography (the CAT scanner) is a revolutionary diagnostic advance. It is now possible, without injecting contrast material, to obtain x-rays of parts of the body that were formerly inaccessible to conventional x-ray techniques. The scanner takes x-ray pictures from different angles, which the computer builds up into a three dimensional-image.

Without introducing any radiopaque substances or radioisotopes into the body, the CAT scanner compiles and integrates multiple sequential views of an organ (or even of the whole body) through a full 360°. The computer part of the machine coordinates, integrates and interprets this vast amount of data into clear, crisp images of high resolution which clearly demonstrates abnormalities of a size imperceptible to earlier generations of machines. Further, the procedure may be performed on an outpatient basis, thereby obviating the need for hospitalization.

Theoretically, the development of the CAT scanner should save many dollars not only for individual patients but in the costs of overall health care. However, the study has become so popular and its use so widespread that it has, paradoxically, come to add many dollars per year to the total health care cost in the United States. It is likely that the CAT scanner will come to be more appropriately and advantageously used as its costs and limitations come to be as widely recognized as its advantages.

Ultrasound procedures

In ULTRASOUND procedures, sound waves from an emitting source are aimed at the organ or organs to be studied. The reflected sound waves are recorded and automatically transformed into an image. The technique (which is not unlike sonar) is totally painless and in fact imperceptible to the patient being studied.

These procedures—which are also known as "echo studies"—have been widely applied to many parts of the body, although they are most commonly used to study the heart and brain. In the brain, *echoencephalography* indicates the presence or absence of a shift of the structures which are normally found in the midline. Such a shift suggests the presence of a tumor or unusual bleeding on the side from which the structures are being displaced. In the heart, *echocardiography* detects accumulations of fluid between the heart and its lining sac (the pericardium). It also provides useful information regarding the functioning of heart valves. Increasing use has made of ultrasonography in the detection of pregnancy—especially in the early identification of multiple gestation (twins, triplets, etc.).

Endoscopy

ENDOSCOPY refers to the insertion into one of the body's natural openings of a rigid metal or flexible "fiberoptic" illuminated tube for the purpose of examining organs, cavities or other internal structures. (See also the major article on **Gastroenterology.**)

The simplest such instrument is the *anoscope*, a short plastic or metal instrument used to examine the anal region for hemorrhoids or fissures. A slightly longer instrument, the *sigmoidoscope*, measures about 10 inches and enables the examiner to look beyond the anus and rectum into the lower part of the large bowel. Sigmoidoscopy is useful in the search for a tumor or POLYPS and frequently provides diagnostic confirmation of suspected inflammatory diseases of the bowel. Through the instrument, the physician may remove a polyp or a small piece of intestinal tissue for microscopic examination (BIOPSY).

Similarly, a *bronchoscope* (inserted through the mouth) permits inspection of the vocal cords, larynx, trachea (windpipe) and the main part of the bronchus. In addition to the advantages of direct examination of these internal structures, the physician may remove "washings" or "brushings" for microscopic studies of cells in the diagnosis of a suspected tumor. Similar materials may be removed for culture in the case of suspected tuberculosis or other infection. When appropriate, the bronchoscopist may also remove a small section of tissue for study in the laboratory. Finally, the instrument may be used by the physician to remove a plug of mucus or similar substance which may be obstructing one of the bronchi.

Examination of the esophagus and stomach is possible through a flexible *gastroscope*. This instrument is especially helpful in cases where it is important to determine the site of bleeding in the upper part of the gastrointestinal tract.

Each of these forms of endoscopy has become increasingly valuable in recent years due to the development of fiberoptic technology. This is based on the ability of flexible interwoven strands of glass (or plastic) to channel light around corners. In other words, light from a source external to the patient's body directly illuminates the structures at the end of a long tube—no matter how many twists and turns are imposed on the tube during its passage through the internal conduits of the body.

Centesis

It may be diagnostically advantageous at times to remove all or some abnormal fluid from body cavities for examination. The general term for this procedure is *centesis;* the region of the body or the nature of the fluid further characterizes the name of the study. For example, *thoracentesis* is the removal of fluid from the thorax (chest).

In performing such procedures the skin and the area immediately below the skin are deadened by the introduction of a local anesthetic agent (not unlike the Novocain used by your dentist). Then a thin hollow needle is inserted through the skin into the cavity and fluid is withdrawn. When the procedure is performed for diagnostic purposes, a small amount of fluid will suffice. However, in cases where an abnormal accumulation of fluid interferes with vital bodily functions (such as breathing), the physician may remove up to a liter (2.1 pints) or even more in a slow and cautious manner. The most frequent causes of such accumulation are congestive heart failure, tuberculosis, other infection, or a tumor.

The similar removal of fluid from the abdominal cavity is called *paracentesis.* As in the case of the thorax, fluid removed from the abdomen is examined for traces of blood, pus, bacteria, red blood cells, white blood cells and evidence of abnormal concentrations of chemicals or enzymes.

Amniocentesis is the withdrawal of fluid from the amniotic sac (which surrounds the fetus in the womb). This fluid is most frequently drawn in order to complete chromosomal studies when the likelihood of a serious genetic disorder is high.

Arthrocentesis, the removal of abnormal fluid from an affected joint, gives important information regarding the differentiation between injury, inflammation and infection of the joint.

Biopsy

At times, fluid alone will not provide adequate material for diagnostic study. The physician must then remove small amounts of solid tissue. The removal of such specimens of tissue for microscopic analysis is called BIOPSY. While it may be performed on any tissue in which abnormality is suspected, the most common sites for biopsy are the liver, kidneys, skin, muscles, cervix and any area of abnormal growth. In one form of biopsy—*needle biopsy*—the procedure is very similar to that for centesis, in that the area is locally anesthetized and a small hollow needle is introduced. The principal difference is that the biopsy needle is introduced into a solid tissue where the centesis needle is placed in a fluid-filled cavity. Certain tissues—for example the bone marrow—may be studied by either simple aspiration (drawing out of fluid) or biopsy.

Arthrography

Arthrography is an x-ray technique in which a radiopaque substance is injected into a joint. It is frequently used to highlight torn cartilage or other disruptive changes in the joint.

Cardiac catheterization

A technique involving the passing of a catheter (a flexible tube) into one or more of the heart's chambers. It is done for various reasons, including the collection of blood samples, detection of abnormalities and determination of the blood pressure within the heart itself. In the evaluation of heart disease due to abnormalities of the valves, for example, it is frequently useful to determine the pressure which exists in each of the heart's chambers—and by calculation, the pressure difference across each of the heart valves. The sensitive instrument used to detect and measure pressures in this manner (called a transducer) is attached to the catheter.

Pulmonary function tests

Simple tests of lung function are performed by having the patient inhale deeply and then exhale forcefully into a tube attached to a machine which records the total volume of air exhaled as well as the rate at which the air has been expelled. This is a useful test in screening for early evidence of respiratory disease. With certain refinements, these tests can also be useful in distinguishing between several different types of lung disease.

Mammography

This x-ray examination of the female breasts remains somewhat controversial. Malignant tumor of the breast is not a rare disease; since recovery appears to be related to early diagnosis and treatment, the concept of periodic x-ray examination to detect any malignant change at the earliest possible time has great appeal. On the other hand, the test has been challenged on the basis of its accuracy (sensitivity vs. specificity), cost and the relatively high doses of radiation which accumulate as the test is repeatedly performed.

Critics contend that regular self-examination of the breasts, coupled with periodic checks by the physician, will provide as much information as mammographic screening. Improvements in technology which lower the cost of the test and decrease the level of radiation required to perform the test may blunt some of the arguments against regular use of mammography—at least for those women who are at higher risk for the development of BREAST CANCER due to family history or other factors.

Special neurologic procedures

Lumbar puncture

More widely known as a "Spinal tap," this is a procedure in which a small needle is introduced into the space between the spinal cord and its innermost covering membrane ("subarachnoid space"), usually in the lower part of the back, after the area has been infiltrated with a local anesthetic. Cerebrospinal fluid is then withdrawn and examined for the presence of white cells, red cells, the levels of protein and sugar, bacteria and other elements. In addition, the pressure of the fluid before and after removal of the sample is diagnostically helpful. In certain disorders, the introduction of air into the space normally filled by cerebrospinal fluid will help provide further diagnostic information.

Myelography

This involves x-rays of the spinal cord following the introduction of a radiopaque substance into the subarachnoid space. This technique is frequently used to confirm the diagnosis of herniated intervertebral disk (SLIPPED DISK).

Electroencephalography (EEG)

Electroencephalography involves recording the brain's electrical activity, measured externally through the scalp.

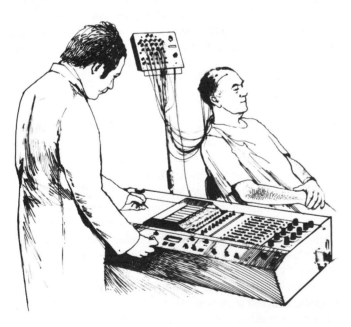

The electroencephalogram (EEG) provides a tracing of the electrical activity of the brain as detected through electrodes pasted to the scalp. Abnormal tracings can help provide diagnostic evidence of several problems, such as epilepsy, tumors, or the site of other brain damage.

As many as 12–14 electrodes (small metal clips at the end of tiny wires) are attached to the scalp for this recording. In most cases it is helpful to measure electrical activity during sleep as well as during wakefulness. When the monotony of the test and the quiet of the room do not induce sleep in the patient being tested, medication may be administered to induce sleep. Abnormal electrical activity may be found in certain disorders of the sleep/wake cycle, epilepsy (and other seizure disorders) or tumor. (See also EEG.)

Newer diagnostic tests are being developed at a very rapid rate; many of these newer procedures are used only in very specialized circumstances.

DIAGNOSIS

I earlier pointed out that examination, diagnosis and therapy are closely interrelated parts of medical care. Medical care consists largely of the coordination of these three activities. The process is a continuous one in which the physician conducts an ongoing examination, "fine tuning" his diagnosis while administering (and observing the effects of) therapy.

The art of medical judgment consists of achieving the most effective balance between these three processes. In so doing, the physician continuously seeks and uses additional information, such as changes in symptoms, new signs and findings from repeated physical examinations, and reactions to therapy (favorable and unfavorable). In this chapter I will describe some of the physician's thinking as he works this information into a diagnosis.

Taking the patient's medical history

My approach to diagnosis in a new patient begins "at first sight." The patient's height, weight, age, race, sex, speech and walk all provide a great deal of information. In addition to helping me to come to know the patient as a person, these characteristics frequently give early clues to an underlying medical condition. After a warm, friendly and hopefully reassuring greeting, I begin the interview by asking "general identification" questions regarding occupation, marital status and home situation. As we proceed through the rest of the medical history, the patient's description of his medical problems (symptoms) will soon begin to suggest several possible diagnoses. In order to distinguish between these alternative diagnoses, I ask more specific and detailed questions regarding signs and symptoms that are more common in one disease and less common in the other.

For example, chest pain may be caused by several life-threatening diseases or may be a part of a minor illness which will get better without treatment in a few days. Two or three questions—"Is it made better or worse by taking a deep breath? Is it made better or worse by exertion? Is it made better or worse by moving your arms?"—will help me to distinguish between the very serious medical problems and the less threatening ones. By the time the medical history taking is complete, I have a good indication as to whether or not we are dealing with a serious disease or a relatively minor illness. At this point, we have also probably been able to narrow down the hundreds of possible diagnoses to just two or three which are *most likely*. This is what doctors call the "differential diagnosis."

The physical examination

In performing the physical examination then, I shall pay particular attention to those parts of the body which are most likely to provide further clues which will help to distinguish between the few diagnoses that are still being considered.

It is especially useful to be able to bring on the symptoms of which the patient complains. For example, if chest pain is caused by moving the arm in a certain way, it is useful to move the patient's arm in that manner. In addition to helping me to localize the source of the pain, I can watch the patient's face for an indication as to whether the pain is excruciating or simply bothersome. Finally, at the completion of the history and the physical examination, we should have arrived in most cases at a point where a single diagnosis has become obvious or only two or three real possibilities remain. Standard tests will usually help to confirm the diagnosis.

When the diagnosis is unclear

However, for a very small number of patients we still may be struggling for a diagnosis even after completion of the medical history, the physical examination and the standard battery of tests. The so-called "fever of unknown origin," is an example of such a diagnostic problem. At this point in the advanced stages of diagnosis, I have three options: time, tests and treatment.

The role of time in diagnosis

The passage of time is, of course, inevitable and so time is always a factor in diagnosis no matter what else we may be doing. What I mean by "time" as an option in diagnosis is the use of time for close observation of the patient (usually in the hospital) while we perform no further tests and use no specific treatment. A few days of cautious patience may enable the patient to make a spontaneous recovery.

In such instances, we will have learned that the disease was relatively harmless and was self-limited, although we may not have established a precise diagnosis. On the other hand, within a few days there may occur some new symptoms or new physical findings which will help to clarify the diagnosis.

Choice of tests and treatment

As for further tests, the list of available tests is extensive and seems to grow each year. The tests which I may order range widely in degrees of pain and other discomfort as well as in expense and risk to the patient. For these reasons, I attempt to minimize inconvenient and expensive tests while judiciously using time and observation. As for treatment, the use of the "therapeutic trial" has been described in earlier pages. Potential treatments range from safe and simple medications to those which have greater likelihood of side effects. Some drugs tend to give an early indication of their effectiveness or ineffectiveness while others may take months or a year or more to show positive results. If a diagnosis can be clarified by the use of a safe and simple drug, I do not hesitate to prescribe that drug.

For example, in children it may be difficult to distinguish between a diagnosis of acute rheumatic fever and a diagnosis of acute rheumatoid arthritis. In acute rheumatic fever, aspirin will usually relieve fever and joint pains very rapidly (often within 24 to 48 hours). In fact, if there is not complete relief of all joint symptoms within 48 to 72 hours, the diagnosis of acute rheumatic fever becomes much less likely. The much more gradual improvement seen in children who have acute rheumatoid arthritis and are given aspirin is very helpful in distinguishing between these two diseases.

The medical checkup

Fortunately, the above-described steps in advanced diagnosis are ones which will be taken in relatively few patient/physician encounters. Most meetings between patients and their doctors occur because of relatively minor problems such as colds and sore throats, where the diagnosis is quite obvious. Another frequent reason for visiting the doctor's office is for a "checkup" when the patient is well and has no symptoms. Of course, a complete checkup consists of a full medical history, a thorough physical examination and a few standard tests. The difference is that the physician is not attempting to arrive at a single diagnosis. Rather he is considering the full range of potential (rather than actual) diseases which will be important to this specific patient.

At the conclusion of the checkup, the patient will be advised of his or her potential medical problems and will be encouraged to make changes in lifestyle which may ward off or minimize those potential problems. Examples of such lifestyle changes include exercise, weight loss, reducing or eliminating the use of cigarettes and alcohol, the use of seat belts, etc.

In summary, the physician will make great efforts to arrive at a single diagnosis in the presence of active disease but will usually settle for more general conclusions in the absence of active disease. In either case he will use the patient's medical history to provide a broad base for his diagnostic analysis: the physical examination helps to narrow down this broad base, and laboratory tests and x-ray studies help confirm the diagnosis.

THERAPY

In this chapter we will discuss many of the modes of treatment available to the physician. The physician can select from a wide choice of therapies such as surgery, medical therapy (including the administration of various drugs, antibiotics, HORMONES, and dietary modifications), or PYSCHOTHERAPY. The choice of a particular therapy is dependent upon many factors. In most instances the diagnosis determines the therapy. For many conditions only one correct mode of treatment exists. An inflamed appendix, for example, can be "cured" only by its surgical removal. For other conditions, though, more than one therapy may be appropriate. The choice of therapy may then depend not only upon the diagnosis but also upon such secondary factors as the training and experience of the physician or the stage of advancement of the disease.

SURGERY

There are many different types of surgical specialists, each dealing with a particular aspect of surgery.

Surgery can be divided into three common phases: (1) the preoperative phase, (2) the operative phase and (3) the postoperative phase. The preoperative phase consists of evaluation and treatment required to prepare the patient for surgery. The operative phase includes the anesthesia and the operation itself. The postoperative phase includes the care and follow-up treatment required to insure recovery after surgery. (See also the major article on **Surgery.**)

Although each surgical procedure is preceded by a preoperative evaluation and followed by postoperative care, the nature of each phase will vary with the type of surgery. It is possible to divide surgical procedures into three major types: (1) emergency surgical treatment, (2) major elective surgical procedures and (3) minor elective surgical procedures.

Emergency surgical procedures consist, for the most part, of the treatment of accident victims and BURNS. The accident victim presents special problems. No history of the patient may be available and there may be little time for an extensive preoperative evaluation. Multiple injuries involving several body systems may require immediate emergency treatment.

Major surgical procedures are performed in a hospital, usually under general ANESTHESIA. They can be either emergency procedures or procedures which were planned in advance. Whenever possible, it is advantageous both to the patient and to the physician to be faced with a planned

procedure. A major advantage of a planned operation is the time available for preoperative evaluation and adequate preparation.

The following guide outlines what a patient may expect on entering a hospital for emergency surgical treatment.

Emergency surgery

The first principle in managing the trauma patient is to remove any obstruction to breathing. If necessary, this is done by relieving any airway obstruction either by means of suction or by intubation—that is, placing a tube into the trachea (windpipe) through the mouth. Or, if that is not possible, it may be necessary to perform an emergency TRACHEOSTOMY. Once an airway has been established, attention must be paid to establishing a proper fluid balance and to treating SHOCK. Lost blood must be replaced by BLOOD TRANSFUSION—either with properly cross-matched blood or with a suitable plasma volume expander. At this point it is necessary to treat the initiating causes of shock.

An examination must be made for fractures, head injuries, and blood in the chest or abdomen. Fractures are immobilized with temporary splints as soon as possible. The patient's blood circulation is stabilized, the blood volume restored, and adequate urinary output established before further treatment is given. Once these emergency techniques are performed, an operation may be needed to control bleeding or reduce fractures.

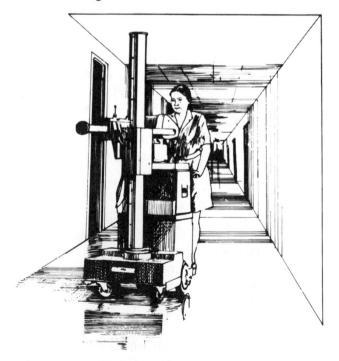

The heavy patient load at all modern hospitals makes portable x-ray units, such as the one illustrated above, a highly useful diagnostic tool.

Head and neck injuries

There are several types of trauma that produce particular problems. Head and neck injuries may be difficult to diagnose since it is often impossible to obtain a meaningful history from the patient. However, most patients with serious head injuries are admitted to the hospital for further observation—especially to determine if there has been any bleeding within the brain.

Neck injuries sustained as the result of traffic accidents may result from direct trauma or from an injury during sudden deceleration ("whiplash" injuries). These injuries may often be overlooked in the presence of more obvious injuries to the head, chest or abdomen. Furthermore, the comatose (unconscious) or confused patient is not easy to examine for neck stiffness or pain. The patient with a stiff neck without any obvious motor or sensory impairments has his neck immobilized in a plastic collar. If there has been displacement of one or more vertebrae in the neck (cervical vertebrae), traction is applied. Patients with known sensory or motor impairment are placed in traction immediately.

Chest injuries

These may involve the chest wall, heart and lungs. Rib fractures, which may interfere with effective breathing and lead to lung collapse and pneumonia, can be treated by the injection of a local anesthetic or by strapping the chest wall with tape or elastic bandages. If several ribs or the sternum (breastbone) are fractured in more than one place the chest wall may not be able to expand normally during breathing. In such cases the fractured segments are usually secured with internal wires and plates.

PNEUMOTHORAX occurs when air enters the chest cavity from an injured lung or, less commonly, through penetrating injuries. Pneumothorax may impair effective breathing, in which case it can be treated by inserting a chest tube connected to a water-sealed drain; when suction is applied, it promotes reexpansion of the lungs and restores effective breathing. Less severe forms of pneumothorax may require no treatment, as the air will be naturally reabsorbed within a few days of so.

Abdominal injuries

These can result either in bleeding within the abdominal cavity from the rupture of a solid organ or in PERITONITIS, an inflammation of the lining of the abdominal cavity. Every patient with abdominal trauma must be reexamined frequently. Open penetrating injuries—such as those caused by a bullet or a knife—require immediate surgical investigation (exploratory laparotomy), to determine major sites of injury, control hemorrhage, or reverse shock (circulatory collapse).

Burns

Minor burns which constitute less than 10% of the total body area, and which are located on the trunk or extremities, can often be treated on an outpatient basis by merely cleaning the wound and applying topical dressings. Patients with more extensive burns must be hospitalized.

As with all emergency patients, an adequate airway must be assured for the patient—if necessary by means of an emergency tracheostomy. Fluids are then administered intravenously to minimize or prevent burn shock. The wound is cleansed with soap and water and dead tissue and other debris are removed. Topical antibacterial agents and dressings may then be applied. Severe wounds may require skin grafting. (See also *Burns* in the **First Aid** section.)

Elective surgery

The surgeon admitting the patient for an elective operation will write routine orders for his patient. These orders are used to convey to other members of the surgical team (nurses, physical therapists, or technicians) exactly what the surgeon wants done for his patient.

Included is a record of the admitting diagnosis necessary to alert the hospital staff to the kind of care the patient needs and the complications that may arise. Any dietary requirements are also listed, based on the patient's overall condition and the present surgical problem. For example, patients without teeth, or with poorly fitting dentures, who cannot chew solid foods would be on a soft or liquid diet. A patient with a chronic illness who may have lost weight and appetite may need frequent small feedings of high caloric value. If a patient is so debilitated that he cannot take food voluntarily a small tube can be passed through the nose into the stomach and feedings of a liquefied high-calorie food can be dripped in continuously. Many patients with particular diseases, such as heart disease or diabetes, will also require specific diets.

The orders should include a general guide to activity recommended; as a general rule the maximum activity compatible with the patient's conditions is permitted, as inactivity may lead to complication such as blood clots or wasting of the muscles. Vital signs—including pulse, blood pressure and respiratory rate—are usually not recorded more often than once a day unless the patient is critically ill or his condition is changing.

Preoperative medication and preparation

Most patients are anxious before an operation and an appropriate sedative is often ordered. Elderly patients are frequently bothered by constipation and the authorization to administer a mild laxative may also be included in the orders. Any currently used medications are continued unless contraindicated by the surgical problem or its proposed treatment. Currently used medications may include: cardiac drugs, diabetic drugs, antihypertensive drugs, antibiotics, tranquilizers and antacids. Vitamins—particularly the B and C vitamins—are especially necessary for the debilitated patient prior to operation. The B vitamins are essential in metabolizing carbohydrates and vitamin C is essential in wound healing; since there are no great body stores of B or C vitamins they need to be provided daily.

A daily bath is good for all patients, with special attention to the area of the planned incision. Many elderly patients and those of any age who smoke or who may have chronic lung disease are at increased risk for general anesthesia. Several techniques, such as intermittent positive pressure breathing, may help improve lung function prior to the operation.

Before any major operation an evaluation must be made of kidney, heart and lung function. Generally, for a young individual with no personal or family history of kidney disease who is undergoing an elective procedure, a routine analysis of a urine specimen is a sufficient screening examination. The routine analysis includes a test for specific gravity, pH (degree of acidity or alkalinity), glucose, protein, acetone, and the possible presence of traces of blood. If there is any abnormality in the urine, additional tests of kidney function may be necessary.

A careful medical history and a physical examination are the most important measures in assessing the cardiac status of the patient preoperatively. Past history of multiple "strep throats," rheumatic fever, scarlet fever, or fever associated with painful swollen joints may suggest potential rheumatic heart disease. A past or current history of use of cardiac medications or complaints of symptoms such as progressive shortness of breath, or shortness of breath on exertion, chest pain, or episodes of palpitations may suggest heart disease. A routine chest x-ray should be examined for possible enlargement of the heart or unusual calcification of the heart valves. If a careful medical history and physical examination have revealed no significant findings, no further evaluation of heart function is usually necessary for patients under 40 years of age.

For those patients over the age of 40, or any patient with suspected heart disease, additional tests may be ordered to supplement the information gained from the history or physical examination. The electrocardiogram (ECG) will provide information on the rate and rhythm of the heart, increased heart size, or evidence of past heart attacks (myocardial infarctions).

Pulmonary evaluation

Evaluation of the lungs and breathing function is mandatory prior to a major operation. Respiratory insufficiency implies an inability of the lungs to exchange gases adequately to meet the needs of the body during effort. Although respiratory insufficiency may be compensated for by decreased physical activity, a stress such as an operation may produce respiratory failure.

The most common sign of respiratory distress is shortness of breath on exertion (DYSPNEA). Nonpulmonary causes of shortness of breath, such as heart disease or metabolic disturbances, must be recognized and treated. The medical history and physical examination can disclose chronic cigarette smoking, exposure to irritating chemicals, occupational hazards, or a previous history of fungal disease of the lungs, tuberculosis, chronic bronchitis, or other chronic lung diseases.

Routine chest x-rays provide valuable information regarding pulmonary hypertension, acute and chronic lung disease, EMPHYSEMA and pulmonary fibrosis. The "cough test" will help to identify patients with chronic bronchitis. When asked to cough voluntarily, these patients often precipitate a self-sustaining attack of coughing. The "match test" is a simple screening measure that will help to identify patients with diminishing lung capacity. The patient is asked to blow out an ordinary match held approximately six inches from his mouth; patients who cannot pass this match test should have formal testing of their pulmonary function.

Exercise tolerance is important in preoperative assessment. A degree of shortness of breath induced by climbing three flights of stairs is a good indicator of respiratory function. Patients who cannot climb three flights of stairs without resting should also have formal tests of pulmonary function to evaluate their degree of respiratory sufficiency.

The healthy patient who has no signs or symptoms of pulmonary disease, who does not have a chronic cough, who can pass the match test and who can climb three flights of stairs, does not have any functional impairment of respiratory function. The smoker or the patient with a chronic cough who cannot pass the match and exercise tests should be prepared for anesthesia by using deep breathing exercises and coughing exercises and by avoiding tobacco.

Anesthetic pre-medication

Drugs, usually in combinations, are given prior to a general anesthetic to achieve one or more of the following effects: mild sedation, deep sedation, tranquility, pain relief, reduction of salivary secretions, and inhibition of nausea and vomiting.

Preoperative preparation of the bowel

If the patient is to have a general anesthetic the fecal contents of the colon (large bowel) must be cleaned out or evacuated the night before the operation. The principal reason for this is to prevent uncontrolled defecation. Enemas are used for patients who cannot defecate spontaneously (see ENEMA.)

Fluids

Fluids and electrolytes (substances, such as various salts) are essential for normal physiologic function. Since there will be an interval just prior to, during and just after the operation in which the normal intake of fluids and electrolytes cannot be maintained, supplementary fluids and electrolytes are given intravenously. To maintain the patient in a basal state a total of approximately 2,000–2,500 ml of water is required per day in addition to several salts—such as sodium, potassium, calcium and magnesium.

Additional imbalances may also be present and these will need to be corrected. Imbalances can be produced by excessive vomiting, diarrhea, burns, or sweating. A large variety of standard fluid and electrolyte solutions exists. In addition, the physician has the option of modifying these to suit the patient's exact individual requirements.

Preoperative orders

These are written a day before the planned operation. Usually for a period of at least eight hours preoperatively nothing is permitted to be taken by mouth. This allows the patient's stomach to empty, reducing the risk of vomiting and aspiration of vomitus into the lungs during the induction of general anesthesia. Solid foods are typically discontinued after the evening meal and liquids discontinued after bedtime the night before the patient is to undergo the operation.

A bath is given from head to toe, including a shampoo with an antibacterial soap. If the patient is unable to evacuate the bowels spontaneously, an enema may be required; the patient should urinate before leaving for the operating room. No medications should be taken by mouth by the patient during the few hours immediately prior to surgery; if the medications are required, their route of administration should be changed to intramuscular or intravenous.

Anesthesia

The selection of an anesthetic agent depends upon several factors, but the safety of the patient is always the primary concern. To determine which anesthetic is most suitable, the following facts are considered: the condition of the patient, the particular mechanism of action of the anesthetic, the site and type of surgical procedure to be performed, the training and background of the person who is to administer the anesthesia and the training and requirements of the surgeon.

Postoperative phase

After a surgical procedure all orders must be rewritten. As the patient's condition changes and improves postoperatively, orders are revised daily. This generally involves increasing the diet and activity and decreasing medication. The orders will include a record of what was done during the operation; this informs the staff of the nature of the operation so they can anticipate the kind of care which may be needed and the potential complications to watch for.

Postoperative orders will include an assessment of the patient's vital signs. Vital signs are recorded every half hour for the first few hours after an operation and then less often as the patient's condition stabilizes. The patient's post-

operative diet is dependent upon the type of operation and the type and duration of the anesthesia. In general, it takes several days for bowel function to return to normal. Usually one or two days after anesthesia a diet is started with liquids; if they are tolerated for one or two meals, a regular diet may then be given.

The patient's activity will depend upon the operation performed, the type of anesthetic used, and the duration of anesthesia. Most patients having a general anesthetic and an operation involving a major organ system will be at bed rest the afternoon or even the night after the operation. Beginning in the evening, or certainly by the next morning, they should be up walking with assistance; they should then progressively increase their activities with each day. Inactivity can lead to complications, such as the formation of blood clots. Recently there has been a trend toward increasing early ambulation postoperatively.

In the early postoperative period the patient will need to be turned and told to cough. This helps prevent the accumulation of secretions in the chest and the possible development of lung complications such as pneumonia. After some surgical procedures, certain drains or tubes may be temporarily left in the body. The drains are placed to prevent the accumulation of fluids or to promote the escape of fluids which have already accumulated. Since the drain is a "foreign body" and will cause the production of a small amount of irritation as long as it is present, it should be removed as soon as possible. Nasogastric tubes are placed to remove food and gas present in the stomach or to prevent the accumulation of swallowed air in the bowels.

Postoperative complications

For the great majority of patients undergoing surgery there are no postoperative complications. However, a very few may unfortunately have one or more of the following postoperative complications.

Fever

FEVER is the most common symptom of a postoperative complication. Generally, fever following an operation is produced in response to both infectious and noninfectious diseases. Minor elevations of body temperatures which occur transiently in the postoperative period may be related to food losses and an altered metabolic state during the operative procedure. Any postoperative elevation of the body temperature which is one degree above normal or which lasts more than two days may be significant and diagnostic studies will usually be undertaken to determine the cause.

Fever that appears after the fourth postoperative day is commonly caused by wound infection. The location of the operative wound is important because tissue resistance to infection varies. Surgical wounds at the head and neck rarely become infected because of their excellent blood

supply and their tendency to heal rapidly. Elderly patients with ARTERIOSCLEROSIS ("hardening of the arteries") and obese patients may have an abnormally decreased blood supply in the area of the operative wound, leading to an increased incidence of wound infection. Inspection of the wound discloses extreme tenderness and redness around the borders. Treatment includes adequate drainage and appropriate antibiotic therapy.

Thrombophlebitis

THROMBOPHLEBITIS, an inflammation of the veins of the extremities, may occur any time during the postoperative period. Symptoms include fever, tenderness and swelling of the involved extremities. Localized thrombophlebitis may be associated with the prolonged presence of an intravenous needle, but it rarely produces fever. Prolonged bedrest predisposes to thrombophlebitis of the lower extremities. A helpful measure has been the use of tight surgical stockings, which decreases pooling of blood in the legs. For patients who require prolonged bedrest postoperatively, it is helpful to insure at least some motion of the lower extremities to promote blood flow.

Pneumonia

PNEUMONIA caused by bacterial infection may be treated

The intensive care unit of a modern hospital contains electronic monitoring devices that alert the specially trained medical personnel to possible emergencies following a major operation, such as a cardiac arrest (sudden stopping of the heart).

by the administration of appropriate antibiotics.

Aspiration pneumonia is a type of pneumonia caused by breathing in secretions into the lungs. This occurs most often in debilitated patients, those under the influence of alcohol, or in patients undergoing general anesthesia who vomit and then breathe the vomitus into the lungs. No measures are completely successful in preventing vomiting or regurgitation during anesthesia.

A small percentage of patients will aspirate a small amount of gastric contents during general anesthesia. Aspiration pneumonia is then caused by a response to chemical irritation.

The best prevention for aspiration pneumonia prior to general surgery is to keep the patient fasting for at least 12 hours prior to the operation.

Pulmonary embolism

PULMONARY EMBOLISM is a fairly common and dreaded postoperative complication. The embolus usually originates as a blood clot in the veins. Factors which promote blood clot formation are pooling of the venous blood, any condition that makes the blood tend to clot more readily than usual, and any injury of the lining of the veins. Other factors which predispose to pulmonary embolisms are injuries to a lower extremity, heart failure, obesity, advanced age, or any previous history of phlebitis.

Once the diagnosis has been established, the administration of anticoagulant drugs is the most common therapeutic measure. Because of the relative frequency with which pulmonary embolisms occur postoperatively, it has recently been recommended that low doses of anticoagulants be given to all patients before operating. The results of recent studies have shown that this may be a reasonably effective technique.

See also *Drugs to prevent blood clotting* in the major article on **Drugs and Medicines.**

Recent trends in surgical therapy

Several recent trends in surgery are of great importance and concern to the patient. One of them is the trend toward reducing hospital stays for surgical procedures. The impetus for this movement has arisen out of a general need to decrease the tremendous costs of surgical care. Not only has the postoperative recovery period been greatly reduced, but early ambulation has been encouraged.

In order to decrease the length of hospital stays for surgical procedures much of the preoperative diagnosis is done on an outpatient rather than an inpatient basis. With the advent of preadmission testing the patient can have his preoperative evaluation done as an outpatient and enter the hospital either on the day of the scheduled operation or the night before.

Another significant trend in this direction has been the development of ambulatory surgical centers where patients can be operated on and then go home the same day. "One-day surgical centers" have been shown to be generally safe; however, patients for such procedures have to be carefully selected.

Another major concern in surgical care relates to the question of unnecessary surgery which may be performed. It has been found that "surgical utilization" rates differ in different regions of the country and in populations with different methods of payment. In general it seems that surgical rates are higher where there are more physicians. Surgical rates are also higher where there are more hospital beds and where "fee for service" payment is used rather than a prepaid system. Recently a subcommittee of the U.S. House of Representatives held hearings on the cost and quality of surgical care. This committee alleged that over two million unnecessary operations were performed in 1974 which resulted in 11,900 deaths and almost $4 billion in unnecessary expenses. Although this study has been criticized severely, there may indeed be some validity to it.

One attempt to reduce the amount of unnecessary surgery involves a presurgical screening program. This program was first tried in 1972 and calls for the second opinion of a Board-certified surgeon to determine the advisability of the proposed operation. The primary referring physician makes the recommendation for surgery and then sends the patient to another Board-certified surgeon who may or may not confirm the opinion for the desirability of surgery. The advantages to the patient and his family are many in that the program may offer a decreased surgical risk.

It may also offer an advantage to the patient in that the added discussion between the consultant and his physician may alert the physician to any undetected disorder. Furthermore, there are definite financial advantages in that the cost of an average surgical hospitalization in 1978 was $1,654.00, whereas the average surgical consultation fee was $33.00. However, since no follow-up study has yet been made on those patients whom the consultant had *not* recommended for surgery to find out what eventually happened to them, there is little evidence to indicate that this program may indeed have long-term beneficial effects. Nevertheless, at this point it seems to the patient's advantage where possible to have a second surgical opinion.

MEDICAL THERAPY

The exact definition of "medical therapy" is somewhat difficult. However, a traditional and useful distinction is made between surgical and medical therapy—neither of which includes those specialized treatment modes which are in the province of the psychiatrist and clinical psychologist. But a surgeon does not always have to cut into a patient in the course of his work, nor does a physician always have to prescribe drugs. In fact, most family physicians are qualified to perform certain types of surgery (such as suturing together the edges of a wound) and surgeons frequently prescribe drugs and other treatment modes. In the wide field of medical science there is an inevitable overlapping of specialties.

It is obvious that medical therapy primarily involves the diagnosis and treatment of diseases and disorders by means other than cutting away or repairing diseased organs and tissues. In the majority of cases the physician will prescribe one or more pharmaceutical products in the course of his chosen treatment. In addition, the physician—whether or not he is in general practice or a specialist or subspecialist—can make use of a wide range of other established or experimental therapeutic modes, including those which at one time were considered unorthodox (such as ACUPUNCTURE or HYPNOSIS).

The management of five commonly occurring diseases—heart disease, hypertension, infectious diseases, diabetes and cancer—will be discussed as examples.

Coronary heart disease

Coronary heart disease (or atherosclerotic cardiovascular disease) is a general term that refers to a long-term chronic disease process involving narrowing of the coronary arteries—the blood vessels which supply nutrients to the heart muscle.

Angina pectoris

When the coronary arteries are narrowed to such a point that they can no longer supply an adequate amount of blood to the heart muscle, a painful condition called ANGINA PECTORIS typically results. The pain is usually described as "squeezing" or "vicelike" and is felt behind the sternum (breastbone); it rarely lasts longer than a few minutes and may or may not radiate up toward the neck or down the left arm. It is commonly relieved with rest—which is a diagnostically significant factor. Angina usually and typically occurs with increased activity; it may also occur after heavy meals or be triggered off by undue psychological stress.

Angina pectoris is associated with a long-term build up of fatty plaques within the coronary arteries, which narrow their internal diameter and limit the blood flow. There is little that medical science can do at present to change that chronic disease process. Therapy is directed at reducing the frequency and severity of attacks. Since exercise is one of the most common precipitating factors, the patient should be instructed to avoid any activity that produces chest pain; however, mild forms of exercise that do not precipitate anginal attacks are encouraged. A twice daily short walk on level ground is excellent. Angina is often more severe during very cold, windy or hot and humid weather. Walking up an incline of 15 degrees doubles the work of the heart. If anginal attacks are frequently precipitated by activity, stopping and resting will usually produce rapid relief.

Tension and anxiety are common precipitating causes of angina. Treatment of the underlying anxiety by the administration of tranquilizers is an important part of therapy. Smoking has definitely been associated with an increased risk of coronary heart disease; nicotine in the cigarettes may induce a constriction of the coronary blood vessels and aggravate preexisting angina. Thus, patients should be strongly encouraged to discontinue smoking. The obese patient should be placed on a diet designed to achieve a steady loss of weight until return to the ideal body weight. Large meals and heavy bedtime snacks should be discouraged since they may precipitate an anginal attack. Tea and coffee may be allowed in moderate quantities unless they interfere with sleep or produce chest pain or abnormal heart rhythms.

Cholesterol in the disease process known as ATHEROSCLEROSIS has been widely discussed. Most data from the current epidemiologic studies do suggest that cholesterol is associated with an increased risk of coronary heart disease. There are no unequivocal data to indicate that lowering the blood levels of cholesterol will reverse an established atherosclerotic change. Nonetheless, it is still prudent to recommend that all angina patients reduce their intake of dietary fats. Saturated fats should be limited to one-third to one-half the total fat intake; the dietary fat intake should be reduced to half the usual levels of 60 grams.

See also CHEST PAIN and the major articles on **Cardiology** and **Fitness and Health.**

Drug therapy for angina

The nitrites are the first line of drug therapy against angina pectoris and are most effective in relieving the chest pain. The nitrites cause a general dilation of the coronary arteries and thus permit an increase in the flow of blood to the heart muscle. It is not clear whether the relief of anginal pain is due to this action or to their action in reducing the actual workload of the heart.

Glycerol trinitrate (or nitroglycerin) is dispensed in tablets, taken by dissolving a tablet under the tongue. Tablets dissolve within 20 seconds and produce relief of pain usually within two to three minutes. Unfortunately, there are some unpleasant side effects which may be associated with the use of nitroglycerin. These include a sensation of warmth, flushing, occasional throbbing headaches, and varying degrees of dizziness.

Nitroglycerin should be taken as soon as possible after the onset of an attack of angina pectoris. The drug may also be used prophylactically (before engaging in activity likely to produce pain) to prevent the onset of an anginal attack. Relief is usually achieved within two to three minutes. However, if pain continues the drug may be repeated up to five times at intervals of five minutes. With rest and this regime, if the chest pains continue it is unlikely that the attack is merely angina but is likely to be more serious—a myocardial infarction ("heart attack").

Nitroglycerin is relatively inexpensive, it can be easily carried, it has a relatively long duration of action and is convenient to take. Recent evidence has shown that the "shelf life" of nitroglycerin is relatively short, probably no greater than one month. Since it is very sensitive to light, no more than a month's supply of tablets should be purchased at one time and tablets should be dispensed and kept in dark brown bottles to minimize the entry of light.

Besides the relatively short-acting nitroglycerin there are also several long-acting nitrates which are widely used to help reduce the frequency of attacks of chest pain. These drugs are usually given orally, although they can also be dissolved under the tongue for more rapid effect. Isosorbide dinitrate (Isordil) is available in 5 mg sublingual tablets and 10 mg and 40 mg sustained-action tablets for oral administration. These oral tablets may be taken prophylactically during the course of the day and night to prevent or lessen frequency of chest pain.

See also *Drugs for angina pectoris* in the major article on **Drugs and Medicines.**

Other therapeutic measures for angina

For those patients who have not responded to the initial treatment of angina pectoris—including weight control, rest, cessation of smoking, and the use of nitroglycerin and long-acting nitrates—another newer medication known as propranolol hydrochloride (Inderal) is available. Propranolol produces its major effects in angina by decreasing the contractile force of the heart. As such, it may have severe unwanted effects, especially in an already debilitated person; but in those selected cases where it is used, propranolol has shown remarkable improvement in reducing the frequency of angina attacks. It decreases the heart rate, cardiac output, arterial pressure, and the work of the left ventricle. The drug is thought to be beneficial in angina by improving the balance between available oxygen and cardiac work. Side effects with propranolol are usually minor: nausea, fatigue, dizziness, and rarely a rash.

Myocardial infarction

A myocardial infarction (a "heart attack," or coronary occlusion) is an acute medical emergency caused by the sudden complete blockage of one of the coronary arteries (which supply nutrients to the heart muscle). It is a late manifestation of the chronic disease process of ATHEROSCLEROSIS. Although the best hope for reducing the death rate due to myocardial infarction may lie in prevention, prevention may not be relevant for millions of Americans each year who will have a heart attack.

Since the heart (like all muscles) requires oxygen, a blockage of one of the arteries which supplies the heart with vital oxygen will shortly produce injury and death to the affected area of the heart muscle. Although medical science can do little to change this underlying disease process, therapy has been successful in reducing the death rate due to the many complications which arise secondary to a blockage of the coronary arteries. Since a great majority (as high as 50%) of deaths due to myocardial infarction occur within minutes of its onset, rapid medical therapy is essential. It is this sense of urgency that has given rise to the development of mobile coronary care teams; they have been successful in reducing the death rate from acute myocardial infarction.

Coronary care units

Over the last decade many medical centers have established special coronary care units in the hope of significantly reducing the death rate from heart attacks by providing constant electronic monitoring of the heart rate and rhythm, constant nursing and medical care, and the immediate availability of the necessary equipment for the treatment of cardiac complications. Patients may remain in such units for the first critical five to seven days of their illness when complications are most common. The data from such centers show that there is a definite decrease in the death rate from complications due to abnormal heart rates following acute myocardial infarction. Evaluation of the effect of the coronary care unit on the overall death rate is difficult, however, because of the problem of comparing the care and treatment of patients from one center with those of another. Some centers have reported as much as a 30% reduction in their overall mortality rate because of the coronary care unit.

The seconds and minutes following the blockage of a coronary artery are critical. It is at this time—when the heart muscle is being deprived of its oxygen supply—that the heart may set up centers of abnormal electrical discharge which can cause a deviation from the normal pattern of cardiac electrical activity which may produce dangerous ARRHYTHMIAS (irregular heart action). Arrhythmias occur in up to 90% of patients with acute myocardial infarction and have accounted for up to 40% of deaths. Therefore, early treatment is directed at reducing or eliminating these dangerous arrhythmias. Since cardiac arrhythmias can occur in other conditions, in addition to following myocardial infarction, a more complete discussion of the treatment of cardiac arrhythmias will follow later in this article.

Recovery following myocardial infarction

After the initial phase of treatment has passed and the danger of arrhythmias subsided, the goal of therapy is to provide an adequate period of rest so that the heart muscle can heal itself. On the average this process requires six weeks. The part of the heart muscle that has been damaged will eventually die and be replaced by scar tissue; the process is similar to the production of a wound on the skin and the gradual formation of a scab which will be replaced by scar tissue. The size and location of the damaged heart muscle and ensuing scar tissue are also of major importance. Since the heart must function as a muscle, if a large segment of it—especially a large segment of the left ventricle (the large hollow chamber that contracts to force blood out of the heart into the arterial system)—has been damaged, the heart can no longer function effectively as a pump. If the heart cannot adequately pump the volume of blood necessary to meet the body's requirements, another serious complication of myocardial infarction occurs—*congestive heart failure*. This may also double the death rate from myocardial infarction. Since it may occur in conditions other than myocardial infarction, congestive heart failure will be discussed in greater detail later in this article.

Although healing may take six weeks or more, the length of hospitalization is usually three to four weeks. The initial five to seven days are in the coronary care unit. It is during this period that the danger of cardiac arrhythmias is

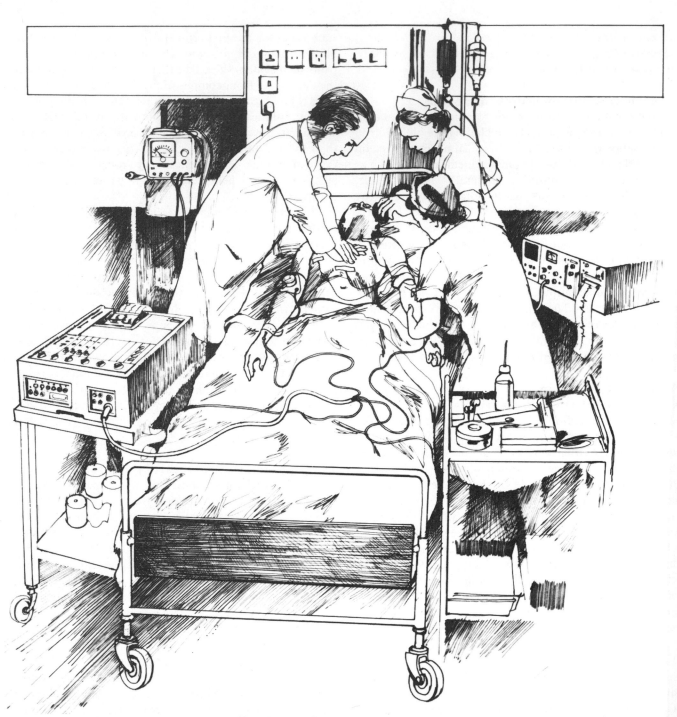

The patient shown above has just suffered a cardiac arrest (sudden stopping of the heart). The physician is performing the first emergency procedure of "closed chest compression," in which the breastbone is pressed down with the heel of the hand (once each second) with enough force to depress it 1–2 in.

greatest and it is in the coronary care unit that these can be treated most effectively. As the danger of arrhythmias subsides, the patient is removed from the coronary care unit to an intermediate unit where he may still be monitored but where he is allowed more activity. After

several days here, he may then be moved to a regular hospital bed. The goal of this phase in therapy is to promote and provide a program of graduated activity which will prevent or minimize the possibility of further complications and promote healing.

Most physicians feel that patients will do better if allowed to sit in a bedside chair for short periods several times daily. This is probably preferable to complete bed rest because of the greater physical and mental comfort and easier breathing; however, strict bed rest is usually enforced for the first five to seven days, especially during the time when the patient may be in the coronary care unit. Longer periods of complete bed rest can lead to increasing complications with urinary retention, constipation, pneumonia and pooling of the venous blood in the extremities which may lead to PHLEBITIS and ultimately a pulmonary embolism. Gradually increasing ambulatory activity is allowed after three to four weeks, depending on the patient's progress. The resumption of former activities in the postconvalescent period is also dictated by the clinical course. Although some patients may never return to their previous routine, many are back at work within six months following a heart attack.

Other therapeutic measures for myocardial infarction

Oxygen and the control of pain are other therapeutic measures. In the early phases, or when the heart muscle is being deprived of sufficient oxygen, oxygen administration is usually indicated. Indeed, oxygen is often administered routinely during the first 24 hours or so to the patient who has just suffered a myocardial infarction. Pain is almost universally present during this phase and may foster severe anxiety. It is treated promptly with adequate doses of effective drugs—usually the opiates, particularly morphine. Demerol is slightly less effective but is also commonly used.

Diet, bowel care and adequate sedation are other ancillary therapeutic measures. For the first few days after the heart attack the diet should be liquid or soft, low in salt and fat and easily digestible. To avoid producing or contributing to cardiac arrhythmias, very hot or cold liquids are not given during the first few weeks. As the patient improves and appetite increases, a more liberal diet is allowed. For the patient at bed rest, constipation is an almost constant problem and if possible should be prevented or relieved by the routine administration of stool softeners. Also, some patients are not able to use a bedpan and for these patients there is less emotional stress if they are allowed a bedside commode. Since the period following a myocardial infarction produces great anxiety, adequate sedation is essential.

The use of anticoagulants in the treatment of patients with acute myocardial infarction is still controversial; many large-scale studies have shown conflicting results. However, most physicians generally agree that giving drugs to reduce the possibility of the formation of blood clots will not significantly affect the course of the myocardial infarction; however, they may be effective in preventing complications secondary to the infarction or to bed rest.

Congestive heart failure

This term is used to describe the inability of the heart to pump a sufficient quantity of blood to meet the body's needs. As a result, blood may pool (or congest) in certain organs, particularly the lungs. Congestive HEART FAILURE may occur in any type of heart disease. It commonly occurs as a result of long exposure to uncontrolled high blood pressure and after severe myocardial infarctions.

In the case of a severe infarction in which a large area of the heart muscle—particularly part of the left ventricle—has been rendered inoperative, the heart can no longer produce sufficient pumping action to meet the body's needs. Basic therapeutic measures directed for congestive heart failure do not alter the basic disease process, but are directed toward improving the circulation. Rest and diet are two major elements of therapy. Rest is important for two reasons: (1) resting reduces the workload of the heart; and (2) rest in bed produces a fluid loss which is beneficial.

An important part of therapy is the restriction of salt intake. The average American diet without salt restriction contains anywhere from 6–15 grams of salt daily, with an average of 10 grams. This value can be reduced to 4–7 grams by merely restricting the use of additonal salt at the table; it can be reduced to 3–4 grams by further restricting salt during cooking. Most patients with congestive heart failure can be managed on a 2 grams salt diet. Diets with more severe salt restriction offer little therapeutic advantage as a rule and are highly unpalatable and generally difficult to follow outside of the hospital setting. As an adjunct to limiting salt intake, fluid intake should be kept under 3,000 milliliters daily.

Drugs used in the treatment of congestive heart failure

In addition to the general measures for treating congestive heart failure discussed above, two major types of drugs—digitalis and diuretics ("water pills")—provide the mainstay of pharmacologic therapy for congestive heart failure. Digitalis is one of the oldest known drugs and originally came from the foxglove plant. The main pharmacologic effect of digitalis is to increase the force of the heart's contraction: the increased force of contraction results in complete emptying of the heart, permitting an improvement in the mechanical efficiency of the heart muscle. As the circulation improves with the improved pumping action, the heart rate slows slightly; there is also a direct effect by digitalis on slowing the heart rate. These improvements result in an increased volume of blood and a reduction in venous pressure.

Digitalis

Although the effects of digitalis can be life-saving, the most serious disadvantage with the drug is that its therapeutic dosage is uncomfortably close to its toxic (poisonous) dosage. Thus, unless close supervision is constantly maintained, toxic symptoms and manifestations can occur; recent studies have shown that many patients receiving digitalis have experienced or will experience one or more toxic manifestations. The most common of these are gastrointestinal symptoms and cardiac irregularities. Gastrointestinal symptoms—such as nausea, vomiting, diarrhea, abdominal pain and loss of appetite—are early symptoms. They may be followed by more serious alterations in cardiac rhythm caused by irritability of the heart muscle. Other less common symptoms include headache, drowsiness, disorientation, confusion, blurred vision, yellow vision, and seeing white halos around dark objects. Very uncommonly, skin rashes may also be attributed to toxic doses of digitalis. (See also *Drugs for heart failure* in the major article on **Drugs and Medicines**.)

The response to digitalis varies widely and can be influenced by several factors. Until recently there has been no test available to assist the physician in planning the adjustment of the digitalis dose and he had to rely solely on the clinical status of the patient and his response to treatment. Within the last several years a very sensitive blood test has become available for measuring the levels of digitalis in the circulating blood and has proved to be useful in adjusting the dosage of digitalis and in looking for early indications of excess digitalis. In any case, close monitoring of all patients on digitalis is mandatory.

Digitalis preparations can be administered orally, intramuscularly, or intravenously. Except in emergency situations, such as life-endangering arrhythmia or acute pulmonary edema, the oral route is preferred. Prior to therapy a control electrocardiogram (ECG) must be available, because administration of digitalis may induce changes in the electrical activity of the heart. Since some preparations of digitalis are excreted relatively slowly from the body, it is important to know if the patient has had digitalis in the preceding two or three weeks. If it is not known whether or not the patient has recently taken digitalis, smaller doses of rapidly acting preparations are usually given. Some patients are less tolerant of the effect of digitalis than others and therefore require smaller doses; such is the case in elderly debilitated patients. Also, smaller patients require less of the drug than larger patients.

Diuretics

Diuretics, commonly known as "water pills," promote the excretion of fluid by the kidneys. They are useful in the treatment of a variety of diseases associated with the abnormal retention of salt and water. In congestive heart failure they are useful in the control of excess fluid. However, the administration of diuretics constitutes secondary treatment; digitalis, salt restriction and reduced physical activity, when indicated, are the prime methods of therapy.

Diuretics must be used properly because numerous water and electrolyte abnormalities may result from their improper administration; the most serious and common complication following diuretic therapy is the loss of the essential mineral potassium. The condition of extreme depletion of potassium in the circulating blood (hypocalcemia) may result in severe cardiac arrhythmias, especially in those patients who are also taking digitalis. There are a variety of diuretic agents, each one having a particular function and each one acting at a particular site in the kidneys. (See *Diuretics* in the major article on **Drugs and Medicines**.)

Cardiac arrhythmias

Cardiac arrhythmias occur commonly following acute myocardial infarction ("heart attack"). Certain of them can be life-threatening. For example, when the ventricular rate is greater than 180 per minute, approximately half of all patients will develop vascular collapse (shock)—which requires prompt and precise treatment. Other arrhythmias may contribute to congestive heart failure by impairing adequate filling of the left ventricle; these also require prompt therapy. Others may be less serious but may be early signs of more serious arrhythmias to come.

Appropriate therapy of all cardiac arrhythmias requires correct diagnosis. Once the diagnosis is made, the type of arrhythmia, the severity of the clinical situation, the ventricular rate, the age of the patient, the previous administration of digitalis or other cardiac drugs, will determine the exact type of therapy. The correction of any underlying abnormality—such as low blood pressure, low oxygen, or preexisting electrolyte imbalances—may occasionally terminate a cardiac arrhythmia without the need for specific therapy. The two major types of therapy available to treat cardiac arrhythmias are the antiarrhythmic drugs and *cardioversion*.

Antiarrhythmic drugs

In order to understand the mechanism of action of many of the antiarrhythmic drugs a brief description of the electrical conduction system of the heart is necessary. Very simply, the heart can be considered as four chambers: a left and a right *atrium* and a left and right *ventricle*. The atria pump blood to the ventricles. The ventricles pump blood to vital body organs: the right ventricle pumps blood to the lungs and the left ventricle pumps blood into the arterial system to the rest of the body, including the brain. It is easy to see why rhythm disturbances involving the left ventricle may be a threat to life. Rhythm disturbances involving the atria are not usually life-threatening, although they may contribute to congestive heart failure and thus reduce the efficiency of the heart as a pump. (See also *Drugs to regulate the heart rhythm* in the major article on **Drugs and Medicines**.)

Electrical impulses which coordinate the pumping action of the heart originate in the PACEMAKER, a specialized part of the heart muscle embedded in the wall of the right atrium, and spread via a conduction system to the ventricles.

Quinidine is used as an antiarrhythmic drug to slow the ventricular rate; it has a direct effect on the electrical conduction system and slows the rate of conduction.

Quinidine is also useful in lowering the electrical excitability of irritated heart muscle. Since a major pharmacologic effect of the drug is to slow electrical conduction velocity, quinidine has proved most useful in the treatment of premature atrial contractions. Most common side effects of quinidine are diarrhea, nausea and vomiting; in some patients a ringing in the ears, salivation, headache and visual disturbances may occur.

Procainamide (Pronestyl) has many cardiac actions similar to those of quinidine; it is most commonly used for the treatment of premature ventricular contractions or other ventricular arrhythmias. Procainamide may be given orally or intramuscularly if immediate effects are required. Common side effects include nausea, vomiting, fever, rashes and loss of appetite. A syndrome resembling LUPUS ERYTHEMATOSUS has been described following sustained use of procainamide. A severe drop in blood pressure, which may occur after rapid intravenous administration, is probably the most serious immediate toxic effect of Pronestyl.

Lidocaine (Xylocaine), administered intravenously, is perhaps the drug most widely used to treat ventricular arrhythmias. Its prompt and effective use is credited with preventing many deaths due to ventricular arrhythmias after acute myocardial infarctions.

Diphenylhydantoin sodium (Dilantin), a drug commonly used to control seizures, is also effective in the treatment of certain cardiac arrhythmias, particularly those due to excess digitalis. The drug can be administered orally or intravenously for rapid effect.

Cardioversion

Some arrhythmias, unless treated, can be rapidly fatal. In seriously ill patients with these particular rhythm disorders, electrical cardioversion of the arrhythmia may be life-saving. Examples include patients with *ventricular tachycardia*, where the ventricles beat too rapidly for effective action, or those with VENTRICULAR FIBRILLATION, where the heart muscle beats out of phase.

Two electrical paddles are placed on the front of the chest wall and an electrical current is applied until a normal rhythm ensues. Adverse effects are few; they include muscle soreness and irritation of the skin at the electrode sites. These unpleasant effects are inconsequential in view of the countless times cardioversion has been used to restore normal heart rhythm in patients where drugs would not have had time to be successful. Cardioversion is usually applied as an emergency procedure; however, it may be used in certain cases where drug therapy has failed.

Hypertension

Hypertension refers to an abnormal elevation of the BLOOD PRESSURE. Generally, blood pressures greater than 140/90 are considered abnormal. Although blood pressures

usually rise with age, it is possible to consider diastolic blood pressures from 90–110 as mild elevations, from 110–130 as moderate, and more than 130 as severe hypertension (see DIASTOLE). These general divisions are important in the approach to therapy.

Since the treatment of hypertension requires long-term therapy, establishing an accurate diagnosis is essential. Except in emergencies, where immediate treatment is essential, the diagnosis should be confirmed by repeated blood pressure examinations, as an isolated blood pressure reading which is abnormally high may be relatively meaningless. If the pressure remains elevated after repeated blood pressure readings, the physician attempts to discover any underlying and hopefully correctable cause.

The second goal of the diagnostic procedure is to assess any damage that the hypertension has caused to various organs, such as the kidneys, heart, or blood vessels. In severe or moderate hypertension which has been complicated by kidney or cardiovascular damage, immediate treatment is necessary. The more severe the hypertension the more the prognosis can be improved with therapy.

Treatment of hypertension

Antihypertensive treatment must first lower the blood pressure immediately and then maintain it at or near normal levels over prolonged periods. In severe or moderate hypertension with no complications, the goal of therapy is to prevent complications from developing; very good evidence exists that treatment does reduce the possibility of complications. In cases of mild hypertension, treatment

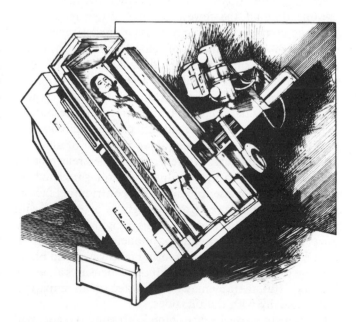

Specialized x-ray procedures (such as myelography or bronchography) may require equipment such as that illustrated above, in which the patient is placed on a remote-controlled tilting table.

has been shown to be effective in preventing the effects of advanced ATHEROSCLEROSIS. Rapid control of the blood pressure can almost always be achieved, especially in the hospital. Maintenance of that control at or near normal levels once the patient is home has proved far more difficult.

Patients nearly always question the necessity of taking drugs for prolonged periods when they feel well. In addition, many of the antihypertensive drugs produce unpleasant side effects. Thus the burden of educating patients about the necessity of taking drugs for long periods when they do not appear to be ill is placed upon the physician.

Patients with severe uncontrolled hypertension, especially those with complications, usually require hospitalization. Hospitalization for two to three weeks is usual when therapy is initiated, although longer periods may be required; in less severe forms of hypertension, therapy is almost always started on an outpatient basis.

Choice of drugs to treat hypertension

There is no one standard drug or standard dosage that is applicable to all patients. Every patient must have his or her treatment individualized. Adjustment of dosage and medication may take up to several weeks. Often one drug may not be sufficient to control the blood pressure. A second drug that may lower the blood pressure, usually by a different mechanism, is then prescribed. Judicious combinations of drugs make it possible to obtain effective control of high blood pressure with the least possible side effects. As with all types of medical therapy, the smallest possible dose of the fewest possible drugs required to maintain control of the blood pressure is desirable.

Although good control of blood pressure is rarely achieved with a single drug, the thiazide diuretics—unless contraindicated—are usually the first drugs prescribed in an antihypertensive regime. Although they are potent drugs, the thiazides are usually prescribed first because of their relatively unimportant side effects. In addition, their antihypertensive activity is additive to those of all other antihypertensive drugs. However, it must be remembered that before drug treatment of hypertension is initiated, an attempt must be made to control the contributing factors of high blood pressure. Excess weight is associated with high blood pressure and a serious weight-loss program must be started. In addition, moderate restriction of dietary salt is often enough to bring mildly elevated blood pressure to within normal levels; if these measures alone are not successful, therapy may be instituted on an outpatient basis—usually with the thiazides.

If after two weeks the blood pressure is not well controlled another medication may be added. It may take several weeks to adjust both medications to achieve an optimum level of control. In moderate hypertension, where the blood pressure is initially at a higher level, therapy may

be started with two drugs rather than one. Patients with severe or complicated hypertension usually require the intramuscular injection of drugs, where control of blood pressure may be obtained within a matter of hours or days. Usually hospitalization is required for this type of therapy.

See also *Drugs for high blood pressure* in the major article on **Drugs and Medicines.**

Treatment of infectious diseases

Antibiotics are extremely effective in the treatment of bacterial infections, but they have no effect whatsoever on viral infections. Viral infections can only be treated through supportive care (relief of the symptoms of the disease). Adequate supportive treatment of infectious diseases requires the proper nutrition and the intake of an adequate quantity of fluids. Depending on the clinical situation, other measures of importance include rest, the proper drainage and evacuation of pus, or removal of foreign bodies. (See the major article on **Infectious Diseases.**)

Fever is one sign of an illness or disorder and as such does not itself usually require treatment—unless the fever is sufficiently high to produce complications involving either the central nervous system or the cardiovascular system. A rapid rise of body temperature, especially in children, may lead to febrile convulsions and sufficiently high temperature in the elderly may lead to disorders of the blood circulation. These two examples are definitely indications for treatment. Significant discomfort is also a valid indication for lowering elevated body temperature, although care must be taken not to obscure the underlying cause of the fever. The routine administration of aspirin or other drugs which reduce fever is generally discouraged.

Diagnosis and treatment

Clinical and laboratory findings should be used to obtain a specific diagnosis of the infection. Once a specific diagnosis is made the proper therapy can be initiated, which may include the selection of an appropriate antibiotic. Viral infections, unless complicated by bacterial infections, should not be treated with antibiotics. Fever alone is not an indication for antibiotic treatment. In certain critically ill patients the administration of two or more antibiotics may be justified to obtain additive effects, to treat infections due to multiple organisms, or to prevent the emergence of resistant forms of the infecting organism.

The duration of antibiotic therapy varies with the type of infection and the response to treatment. The administration of an antibiotic should not usually be discontinued sooner than three to five days after the patient's body temperature returns to normal; in any case, the physician's instructions should be followed to the letter. A minimum of five days of antibiotic treatment is recommended for any infection. (See also *Drugs to treat infections* in the major article on **Drugs and Medicines.**)

Use and abuse of antibiotics

The inappropriate use of antibiotics is strongly condemned for two reasons. First, inappropriate antibiotic usage promotes the emergence of resistant strains of bacteria. It is generally accepted that development of resistant strains of bacteria is directly related to the duration and extent of use of the antibiotic. Each one of the antibiotics available is potentially dangerous for some people. The most severe toxic reaction, which is sometimes fatal, is known as an *anaphylactic reaction,* and may affect some people who have become allergic to any drug. This has been observed with the use of penicillin, more commonly following an injection rather than oral administration. To minimize the risk of a reaction a previous drug history should always be obtained.

Antibiotics can also cause other side effects, including gastrointestinal disorders, cramps, or sore mouth. These reactions may result in the suppression of normal bacteria found in the gastrointestinal tract.

Women on prolonged doses of broad-spectrum antibiotics may be subject to an overgrowth of fungi which can cause a distressing vaginal itch. A few antibiotics have such toxic effects that their usefulness is limited; such antibiotics should be prescribed only in cases of a life-threatening illness for which no effective substitute drug is available. Examples of toxic antibiotics include *chloramphenicol,* which may injure the bone marrow irreversibly, and *streptomycin,* which may cause deafness and permanent loss of balance.

In spite of the potential complications which can result from antibiotics, they should be prescribed when indicated. In addition to the indications above for treating bacterial infections, antibiotics may be used in certain preventive situations. For example, streptococcal infection is treated quickly so that more serious complications may not occur. Another recognized prophylactic use of antibiotics is when surgery or dental work is performed in patients who already have rheumatic heart disease or may have congenital heart disease. In these cases bacteria may be released into the blood and eventually lodge on a diseased heart valve and produce infection of the valve or lining of the heart (bacterial endocarditis). It is known that after any operative procedure these transient "showers of circulating bacteria" can be eliminated by the prophylactic use of antibiotics. However, the prophylactic use of antibiotics does not include preventing complications which might result from minor illnesses such as the common cold.

Diabetes mellitus

Diet is the major element of diabetic therapy. All other treatment is based upon the degree of diabetic control that can be achieved with a diet. The degree of control is generally a reflection of the severity of the diabetes, the age of the patient at the onset of the disease, and the body weight. Patients who contract diabetes before 15 years of age are generally considered as *juvenile* or *brittle* diabetics. These diabetic patients are more unstable so that small increases or decreases in metabolic activity may provoke a severe rise or drop in the blood level of sugar (HYPER-GLYCEMIA or HYPOGLYCEMIA). Most adult patients who contract diabetes are far more stable, in that slight changes in carbohydrate metabolism do not alter their diabetic control significantly. Most cases of adult-onset diabetes can be adequately controlled by diet alone.

The aims of diabetic management include the correction of the metabolic abnormalities first with diet and then, if necessary, with drugs. Implicit in this is an attainment and maintenance of ideal body weight. Treatment of diabetes is designed to prevent the complications associated with the disease. (See DIABETES MELLITUS.)

In a very high percentage of patients with adult-onset diabetes obesity can be managed solely with a low-calorie weight-reduction diet. Marked increase in carbohydrate tolerance may occur as weight is lost. For those patients who require additional therapy, the oral hypoglycemic (blood-sugar lowering) agents provide satisfactory control in most older patients with adult-onset stable diabetes. These drugs are unlikely to be effective in those patients who require higher doses of insulin and in those with juvenile-onset diabetes. Insulin is generally reserved for the juvenile diabetic or those not responsive to diet and oral hypoglycemic agents. Many patients with mild diabetes, who do not ordinarily require insulin, may require short courses of insulin therapy during periods of acute major stress, such as surgery or illness. Approximately a third of all diabetics require insulin regularly.

Importance of diet control

Since diet is the basis of all treatment of diabetes, a stable dietary intake is essential. In calculating a proper diet, the patient's age, sex, activity and present and ideal body weights are relevant factors. In the obese patient with a moderate elevation of blood sugar (glucose), weight reduction may be all that is required for satisfactory control. In the obese individual with more severe elevations of glucose a more controlled diet is necessary. In this case the standard exchange list adopted by the American Diabetes Association and the American Dietetic Association are commonly used. In this plan all food is divided up into six groups. Food of a particular group in stated portions (or "exchanges") contains approximately the same amount of carbohydrate, protein or fat as any other food in that group. The patient is directed regarding the number of exchanges to take from the various lists. In this way the patient's daily intake of these major dietary elements can be calculated. A proper diet calculation should take into account total caloric intake, total carbohydrate intake, total protein and total fat intake per 24 hours.

A large number of dietetic foods are commercially available. These are usually significantly more expensive than corresponding non-dietetic foods. Calorie-free carbonated drinks are permissible. Some of the other diabetic foods, although they may be sugar-free, do contain significant food value and cannot be consumed in addition to the diet, but may be substituted for other foods.

See also *Drugs for diabetes* in the major article on **Drugs and Medicines.**

Insulin therapy

Insulin is required in the juvenile (or brittle) diabetic and in those patients unresponsive to diet and oral hypoglycemic agents. Most commercial insulin is a mixture of beef and pork insulins and is injected to simulate the natural actions of insulin that the diabetic patient lacks. Insulin preparations are of three different types:

(1) Regular insulin, which is short-acting; it is given in acute situations such as for severe infections or during surgery when the patient's food intake and carbohydrate metabolism is variable. It may also be used in combination with longer-acting insulins for routine management.

(2) Intermediate insulin, known as NPH or Lente; this may be used alone and is administered once daily, 30–45 minutes before breakfast. This may provide adequate control in most stable adult diabetic patients.

(3) The long-acting insulins; these are rarely used alone. Hypoglycemic reactions following the administration often occur during sleeping hours.

New patients presenting with severe diabetes are usually hospitalized to gain control of their diabetes and to educate them about proper insulin therapy. In new patients, the course of therapy usually begins with regular insulin before each meal. Once an estimate is made of the amount of regular insulin required, a switch may be made to an intermediate preparation. For less severe forms of diabetes, treatment may be started with a small amount of an intermediate preparation. Further adjustments are made as dictated by response.

Insulin requirements may be increased under the following circumstances: an increased food intake, weight gain, pregnancy, or decreased exercise. Certain disease conditions—such as acute infections or hyperthyroidism—may increase insulin requirements. Thyroid medication, epinephrine and thiazide diuretics may increase insulin requirements. During periods of decreased physical activity or mild infections small increases in insulin dosage generally allow for adequate control.

The following factors decrease insulin requirements: decreased caloric intake, weight reduction, or increased physical activity. Kidney disease or abrupt termination of any of the above-mentioned drugs may also decrease insulin requirements.

Adverse reactions

The most dangerous complication of the use of insulin results from taking an excessive amount of the drug; this may produce hypoglycemia (low blood sugar). Prolonged repeated bouts of hypoglycemia may cause serious consequences, including permanent brain damage. Patients on insulin should be taught to recognize the symptoms of hypoglycemia (such as light-headedness and dizziness) and should carry some kind of sugar with them at all times. More severe reactions require the intravenous administration of glucose followed by oral carbohydrates to prevent recurrent hypoglycemia. Other reactions related to insulin include certain skin reactions, which may occur during the first few weeks of therapy. Complications related to the injection, such as a hardening of the skin at the injection site, may be avoided by rotating injection sites. A small number of patients are allergic to insulin and have a variety of mild and local reactions. Very rarely, severe and general reactions may occur. These may be prevented by switching to an insulin preparation without added protein (such as Lente) or by using insulin from a different animal.

Chemotherapy of malignant diseases

There are three major methods available for treating malignant diseases: surgery, ionizing radiation (such as x-rays) and chemotherapy (the use of special cytotoxic drugs). Since in disseminated cancer (where the cancer cells have spread to various parts of the body) there are relatively few cures, treatment is directed at control of the disease. When surgery and radiation are impractical, chemotherapy can control the disease in many cases. Chemotherapy may result in the relief of symptoms, longer survival of the patient, and regression of the tumor. (See the major article on **Oncology.**)

All the chemotherapeutic drugs are extremely toxic. They are toxic to all cells but the principle of their use is that they have a greater effect on cells that are dividing rapidly: thus they selectively affect cancer cells since these divide more rapidly than normal cells. It is this "selective toxicity" that is the underlying principle of chemotherapeutics. Before a decision can be made to treat a patient with one of these cytotoxic agents, a complete diagnostic evaluation must be undertaken. The various chemotherapeutic agents are designed to have more or less specific activities against a single type of cancer. Every attempt must be made to establish the site of origin and the type of malignancy to best choose the proper chemotherapeutic agent.

Drugs used in cancer chemotherapy

Well-nourished ambulatory patients are best suited for cancer chemotherapy; a debilitated patient with advanced malignancies may not tolerate the toxic effects of the chemotherapy. If one agent fails to control the disease there

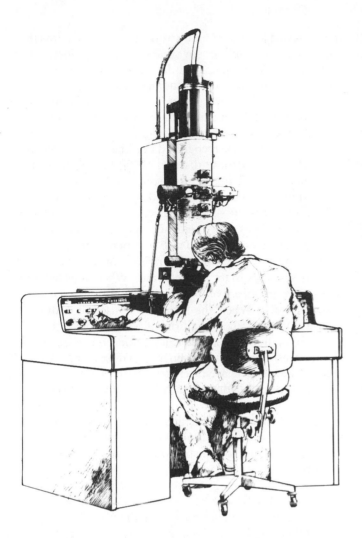

The electron microscope (illustrated above) is an important tool in medical research and has proved to be especially valuable in the field of cancer research. It is capable of a magnification (as seen on enlarged photographs) more than 500 times that of a standard compound light microscope.

may be time to use another agent or a combination of agents. The field of chemotherapy is constantly and rapidly changing; thus, no attempt will be made to review all the chemotherapeutic agents or combinations of agents that are currently used. The following discussion will introduce the clinical use of a few well-accepted drugs.

The *alkylating agents* can interfere with cell division, produce chromosomal damage and mutation, and also suppress normal immune responses; they are extremely toxic to tumor cells. These agents can be divided into the *nitrogen mustards*, the *ethylenimines* and the *alkyl sulfonates*. The nitrogen mustards are given intravenously. Modifications of the drug have been made in attempts to allow oral administration and to decrease its toxicity. The drug is most useful in disseminated HODGKIN'S DISEASE. It may be used with or without radiation and is highly

effective in providing relief from compression of vital structures which may be subject to pressure from a tumor around the neck. Nausea, vomiting, diarrhea and weakness are common side effects.

Chlorambucil (one of the nitrogen mustards) is used most often in chronic lymphocytic leukemia and may also be beneficial in Hodgkin's disease. Its greatest toxicity is in suppressing the bone marrow. *Cyclophosphamide* (another of the nitrogen mustards) is used to treat acute and chronic leukemia, Hodgkin's disease and may be beneficial in cases of bronchogenic carcinoma. Cyclophosphamide is well-absorbed orally; the toxic side effects are primarily related to the blood system, with abnormally low white blood cell counts being the main side effect. Other toxic effects include loss of hair after three or more weeks of treatment (in about 30% of patients); nausea, vomiting, dizziness and liver toxicity may also occur. Melphalan (also a nitrogen mustard) is useful in the treatment of multiple MYELOMA. Its toxicity is similar to that of the other alkylating agents. The alkyl sulfonates, such as busulfan, are useful in the treatment of chronic leukemia. Toxic effects include a general suppressive effect on the bone marrow, loss of hair, nausea, vomiting and diarrhea.

Another class of chemotherapeutic agents are known as the *antimetabolites*. This group of drugs interferes with the synthesis of the essential cell components by competing with natural substances. In general, they have their greatest toxicity in tissues which are very active—such as those composed of active cancer cells. *Folic acid antagonists* compete for an enzyme known as folic reductase, thereby interfering with the synthesis of a necessary enzyme important in vital metabolic functions. The most commonly used folic acid antagonist is *methotrexate*, which is very useful in the management of acute leukemia in children; remission rates of up to 47% have been reported. The toxicity of methotrexate includes bone marrow depression, ulceration of the gastrointestinal tract and the oral cavity, hemorrhage and loss of hair.

Another group of drugs useful in chemotherapy of malignant disease are the *vinca alkaloids*. These drugs are active in impairing cell division and thus are more toxic toward active cancer cells than normal cells. They are useful in the treatment of Hodgkin's disease and in some acute leukemias of childhood. The vinca alkaloids are extremely toxic and may induce neurologic symptoms such as loss of the tendon reflexes, headaches and convulsions.

Role of hormone therapy

Hormones play a role in treatment of certain tumors, especially those that depend upon hormonal action. The *androgens* (male hormones) are useful usually late in the treatment of metastatic breast cancer in women who are premenopausal or less than five years postmenopausal. The *estrogens* are the hormones of choice in the treatment of metastatic breast cancer in women more than five years postmenopausal. *Progesterone* hormones have been used in patients with advanced cancer of the endometrium (the lining of the uterus).

HORMONE THERAPY

HORMONES are the internal secretions produced by the ductless (or endocrine) glands throughout the body. These glands secrete their hormones directly into the bloodstream in response to certain stimuli. In general, hormones act either to increase or decrease various chemical reactions of the body. Although a hormone may have one main action, it can also affect a wide variety of other chemical reactions.

Hormones have regularly been used to treat those endocrine disorders where there is a deficiency of the naturally produced hormones. Diabetes, for example, is an endocrine disorder caused by a lack of insulin. Insulin—which was first isolated from a dog pancreas in 1922—has revolutionized the treatment of diabetes and has prolonged the life of many diabetic patients. Although the major action of insulin is carbohydrate metabolism, insulin also affects the metabolism of protein and fat.

Thyroid hormones

Thyroid hormones were first isolated in 1915 and have been used to treat such conditions as cretinism and *myxedema*, both of which are attributable to thyroid deficiency. The thyroid gland hormones control many of the important regulatory activities of the body, including temperature regulation and oxygen consumption. However, as with all hormones, their effects are widespread and thyroid hormones may also affect reproduction, growth and development and exert an influence on the cardiovascular and nervous system.

Adrenal cortical hormones

The adrenal steroid hormones are produced by the outer layer (cortex) of the adrenal gland. Although more than 40 different types of hormones have been identified, the steroid hormones have two major functions. The *mineralocorticoid* group controls mineral content of many body fluids, particularly the sodium and potassium content. The *glucocorticoid* group controls different aspects of metabolism, including carbohydrate, fat and protein metabolism. The first use of the adrenal hormones was to treat *Addison's disease*, a rare disorder resulting in a wasting or atrophy of both adrenal glands and a deficiency of adrenal hormones.

However, shortly after the main glucocorticoid adrenal hormone—cortisone—was synthesized in 1946, it was used in a radically different way. In the first nonendocrine use of cortisone, the drug was given to a number of patients severely crippled with *rheumatoid arthritis*. The results were dramatic. Patients were relieved of pain and tenderness in their affected joints and many were able to move joints that had been immobilized for years. It was evident that cortisone was not replacing a deficiency, but was acting in another way to decrease an inflammatory process.

Cortisone was soon found to cause symptomatic improvement in an amazing number of disease conditions. While the steroid hormones became known as "wonder drugs," it also became recognized that the steroids were not a *cure* for any of these diseases. Nevertheless, the anti-inflammatory activity of cortisone is widely useful in alleviating inflammatory and allergic diseases such as rheumatoid arthritis, rheumatic fever, lupus erythematosus, nephrosis, sarcoidosis, ulcerative colitis and asthma. When incorporated into ointments they are useful in relieving inflammation and itching in many types of allergic skin disorders and eczema. When injected into joints they are effective in relieving symptoms of bursitis and tendonitis. When the hormone is used as a drug to treat a nonendocrine condition rather than as a replacement for a hormonal deficiency, side effects are more common, especially when given in high doses for prolonged periods. Side effects are rarely seen with occasional use of steroids. The most common adverse effect is salt retention leading to fluid retention and high blood pressure. Other serious complications include peptic ulcer, decreased resistance to infection, thinning of the bones and changes in mood. Long-term administration of cortisone leads to an impairment of the body's ability to produce its own cortisones. Because of these and other serious complications, chronic use of steroids should be limited to those diseases which seriously impair normal well-being and activity and for which no alternative treatment is available.

Female sex hormones

The female sex hormones, estrogen and progesterone, are used in a wide variety of both endocrine and nonendocrine conditions. Oral contraceptives, consisting of differing formulations of synthetic female sex hormones, rapidly became a very widespread means of birth control.

The first successful report of fertility control by an orally administered agent appeared in 1956 and ushered in a "contraceptive revolution." More than 8 million women regularly take the "pill." Although oral contraceptives are undoubtedly one of the most effective means of birth control, recent evidence suggesting long-term complications raises questions regarding the ultimate effects of such mass medication. Two types of oral contraceptive are in use today—combination pills containing estrogen and progestogen, and the low dose progestogen-only pill. The combination pills inhibit ovulation by suppressing the actions of the pituitary gland. Newer pills contain significantly lower amounts of hormone than earlier pills and are equally effective. The low dose progesterone pill does not interfere with normal ovulation, but rather seems to affect the viscosity of the cervical mucus so that sperms cannot penetrate it.

Like all other hormones, the female sex hormones have a wide range of actions. When used for other than simple replacement purposes, side effects and complications can occur. A number of relatively minor adverse effects are commonly associated with the oral contraceptives—such as breakthrough bleeding, enlargement of the breasts, changes in skin complexion, and changes in liver function and glucose tolerance. Headaches and changes in visual disturbances may also be observed.

A number of more serious complications are suspected but not yet definitely proved. Oral contraceptives have been linked with a higher incidence of thrombo-embolic phenomena such as pulmonary embolism and heart attacks. A recent study showed that women over age 40 taking the pill have a greater incidence of heart attacks than women not taking the pill, though the increased incidence appears to be limited to smokers. A relationship between oral contraceptives and cancer is the subject of much discussion. Although as yet there is no proven link between the oral contraceptives and cancer, many studies are continuing in this field.

In addition to their use in oral contraceptives, the estrogens are widely used in other conditions—such as menstrual irregularities, menopausal disturbances and postmenopausal osteoporosis (a thinning of the bones). They are useful in the late treatment of cancer of the prostate gland, and breast cancer. Although estrogen may be useful for short-term treatment of many conditions due to estrogen deficiency, one study has linked the long-term administration of postmenopausal estrogen to higher rates of cancer. Many physicians feel that the use of estrogen for osteoporosis is without a sound basis.

See also *Oral contraception* in the major article on **Family Planning** and *Hormonal drugs* in the major article on **Drugs and Medicines.**

Summary

We have presented a broad and basic overview of the principles of medical examination, diagnosis and therapy to help readers understand some of the physician's tools and to appreciate both the extent and the limitations of his capabilities. It is obviously not intended to be exhaustive, nor to provide insights into specific medical situations, nor to serve as a guide for the patient's critical evaluation of the work of his physician.

Until that unlikely day when human behavior—including response to illness—can be fully characterized both scientifically and mathematically, the practice of medicine will continue to be an *art* as well as a science.

Preventive Medicine

Dr. Robert Lewy

The term "preventive medicine" describes all types of activity aimed at the avoidance, prevention, or early detection of disease (when it can often be treated more successfully). The following article outlines the major concerns of this important service of medical science.

Role of prevention in health care

Despite the sensible supposition that prevention is good for health, preventive medicine has unfortunately been relegated to a very low level among national health priorities. According to one recent estimate, expenditure for preventive health care amounted to approximately 2% of total health expenditure.

Although it would make good sense to prevent as well as treat illness, the role of prevention in health care remains controversial. What exactly can be prevented? How? What is the role of the physician in preventing disease? Are periodic physical exams worthwhile? If so, how often? How beneficial are mass screenings for specific diseases?

A great deal of research is being directed at providing answers to these complex problems. What seems to be emerging is an improved concept of the "annual checkup" that identifies specific preventive measures for specific age groups. Included in this streamlined checkup are certain specific testing procedures designed to identify risk factors or the early onset of disease. In addition, emphasis is being placed upon education and counseling procedures designed to influence an individual's health-related behavior.

Disease prevention can be classified into at least two main categories: primary and secondary prevention.

Primary prevention

This refers to those measures taken to change the environment of the person to prevent disease from ever occurring. It is the most desirable and effective form of preventive medicine. If disease can be prevented from occurring, the need for prolonged and perhaps only partially successful therapy may be eliminated. Preventive medicine's most dramatic successes have occurred as a result of primary preventive tactics. As a result of primary prevention, many communicable diseases (those spread from one person to another) have been eradicated or controlled. In most developed countries which have taken advantage of primary preventive tactics, epidemic diseases such as SMALLPOX, CHOLERA, TYPHOID FEVER, DIPHTHERIA, POLIOMYELITIS and TUBERCULOSIS have virtually disappeared. This is so because most communicable diseases can be traced to a single organism which, when identified, may be prevented from causing disease in protected people

The chronic degenerative diseases, which are so prevalent today, may not be as amenable to primary preventive tactics as are the communicable diseases. Chronic diseases are more often the result of multiple causes, many of which may be social in nature. Habits associated with a particular lifestyle are major contributors to many chronic diseases. Although there is no simple primary preventive technique which can as yet prevent many chronic diseases, much is known about the risk factors which predispose to such conditions. Some of the chronic diseases can be averted or their effects minimized by controlling these risk factors.

Secondary prevention

This refers to the detection of disease through SCREENING tests even before signs or symptoms of a disease appear. The basic purpose of a screening test is to separate from a large group of apparently healthy persons those with a high likelihood of having a given disease. A satisfactory screening test must first uncover a disease for which early treatment can lead to a cure or at least improve the quality or the period of survival. A screening test must also be simple to perform, accurate and relatively inexpensive. Although there continues to be a great deal of controversy over which conditions to screen for, it seems clear that only a limited number of conditions exist which meet all the criteria for a satisfactory screening test. These conditions will be covered in a later section.

Automated "multiphasic screening tests," brought about by recent technological advances, make it as easy and inexpensive to analyze a dozen or more laboratory tests as one. There is a great deal of controversy surrounding the actual usefulness of the information derived from these tests. The mere availability of these tests, of course, does not guarantee their usefulness. Although some experts feel that the use of multiphasic screening can be justified on the basis of serving as an "entry point" to the health care system, others feel that the limited impact of multiphasic screening cannot justify its widespread adoption as a screening tool.

Identifying and dealing with risk factors

An important aspect of health maintenance is the identification of risk factors and the prescription of measures which will result in the reduction of those risk factors. A "risk factor" is a condition which has been found on the basis of large scale epidemilogical studies to precede a certain disease. Many times, if the risk factor can be modified or eliminated, the chance of that disease developing will be lessened. During the 1960s, the concept of health maintenance became widely accepted and contributed to the rising popularity of the Health Maintenance Organizations (HMOs) of the 1970s. Health Maintenance Organizations emphasize disease prevention through early detection. Results from one large HMO have conclusively demonstrated a favorable impact of screening on decreased disability rates, increased work time and fewer days spent in a hospital. The appeal of health maintenance lies in its protection against diseases whose signs and symptoms have not yet appeared.

The following discussion will be limited to those preventive services which can be supplied by a personal physician. Although there is still a great deal of controversy surrounding any exact schedule of preventive health services, many leading authorities agree that, in general, the services described—when performed on a periodic basis—are beneficial. The following guide is not intended to represent an exact schedule of health maintenance procedures, because no single universal schedule currently exists or meets the needs of any single person exactly. Rather, it is intended to represent a general approach to personal health maintenance.

Preventive services

The following primary and secondary preventive services, if properly used, could have a positive impact on present and future health. Undoubtedly, many of the procedures described may be modified or replaced by newer ones. Different populations may also require alternative or additional procedures to those recommended. Nevertheless, these screening tests are meant to complement—not replace—the continuing care of a skilled physician.

Childhood and adolescence

Primary and secondary health services in childhood and adolescence are intended to minimize the risks of disease and trauma and to insure normal growth and development and the acquisition of good health habits. Although most persons pass through the period of childhood and adolescence without any serious problems, many are known to be handicapped, many show signs of poor nutrition (including obesity, anemia and retarded growth) and many are not properly immunized. Since the foundation of many adult diseases, both organic and functional, are laid down at this time, this is the ideal period in which to build good health habits.

Primary preventive services for infants and preschool children are provided mainly through parental education. Parents of these children should be counseled about sound practices in child rearing. Also to be stressed are nutrition, the recognition of signs and symptoms requiring early medical attention and the dangers of household accidents and poisons.

Physical growth

A simple record of height, weight and head circumference is usually adequate. The *rate* of gain is as important as any single measure. Measurements of length and weight are indicated every six weeks during the first six months of life, every three to six months through the age of two years and once a year from ages two through five. The head circumference, which is a sensitive indicator of brain growth, should be measured at six-week intervals until one year of age. These measurements are usually compared with standard growth charts.

Vision

Defects of eyesight are among the most common handicaps of childhood. Up to 10% of preschool children and up to 30% of school-age children may have some type of vision impairment. Since many of these conditions may be corrected if detected early, effective screening is of utmost importance. Vision screening can detect eye muscle imbalances, amblyopia ("lazy eye") and significant refractive errors. These conditions, particularly amblyopia, should be detected as early as possible in order to insure adequate treatment.

Hearing

Approximately 10% of young schoolchildren have a hearing impairment; in about 1% of these, the impairment will be found to have an identifiable cause. Although no useful screening test exists for the newborn, hearing can be screened as early as four months.

Cardiovascular

Cardiovascular screening in infancy is primarily meant to identify the 3–7 cases of congenital HEART DISEASE per 1,000 live births. Since up to one third of all deaths from congenital heart disease occur in the first month of life, early evaluation is necessary. Cardiovascular screening in children over two years of age must also include a measurement of blood pressure. Although hypertension (high blood pressure) continues to be a leading public health problem among adults, recent evidence has shown that high blood pressure may begin early in childhood.

Blood pressure measurement should be included as part of the routine examination of all children.

Orthopedic (bones and joints)

CONGENITAL DISLOCATION OF THE HIP, which occurs in two to five children in every thousand, can usually be identified within the first few days of life. Early treatment can eliminate future significant complications. Screening for hip dislocation should be continued until six months of age.

Blood

Iron-deficiency anemia is a common childhood condition for which screening is justified. However, since the prevalence of anemia correlates with socioeconomic status, the screening interval must be planned individually for each child. Up to 20% of children from poor homes may be anemic at one year of age, while only 4% of children from more advantaged homes will be anemic. Screening is usually indicated at six months of age and again at one and two years of age. Anemia becomes less common between the ages of three and five and the need for screening is therefore diminished.

Public health authorities are now recommending the routine screening of the entire newborn population for a variety of hereditary metabolic diseases. Early presymptomatic detection will prevent later unfortunate complications. Many states now require screening by a simple blood test for PHENYLKETONURIA (PKU), even though it may affect only 1 child in 16,000. Routine urine testing in newborns is also recommended for another rare disorder, *galactosemia*. This is an inherited metabolic defect in which the baby cannot convert galactose (a sugar present in milk) to glucose; as a result, the baby cannot tolerate milk in any form.

Urine

A complete urinalysis is recommended to detect unsuspected cases of DIABETES MELLITUS, KIDNEY DISEASE (via the spilling of protein into the urine) and symptomless URINARY TRACT INFECTIONS, particularly in girls, at least once before age five.

TB testing

Although the incidence of TUBERCULOSIS (TB) has decreased sharply, routine skin testing for tuberculosis is still recommended. The incidence of tuberculosis is higher among the urban indigent population. Black children have up to ten times the tuberculosis rate of white children. In these high-risk groups *tuberculin skin testing* should be performed annually from age one until age five. It may be performed less often in groups with a lower risk of TB.

Lead poisoning

Screening for LEAD POISONING is recommended for children between the ages of 18 months and five years who live in older, dilapidated homes (often equipped with lead water pipes or walls and woodwork painted with a lead-based paint, which may flake off and be ingested by infants). Up to 20% of children under age five who live in substandard housing may have early signs of LEAD POISONING. The disease can be treated if it is detected at an early stage.

Immunizations

All infants should receive immunizations against: DIPHTHERIA, TETANUS and pertussis (WHOOPING COUGH), given as a combined "DPT" shot; polio, given orally; MEASLES, MUMPS and rubella (GERMAN MEASLES), given as a combined "MMR" shot. To be effective, some immunizations need to be repeated. A common schedule starts at two months of age, when all infants should receive (at bi-montly intervals) a series of three DPT shots together with a series of three doses of oral polio vaccine. At approximately 15 months of age a combined shot is recommended to protect against measles, mumps and rubella. Booster shots of DPT and booster doses of polio vaccine are recommended at 18 months and four to six years of age. At 14–16 years, booster shots against diphtheria and tetanus are recommended.

Adult preventive health services

Since over 75% of all deaths in the U.S. are due to chronic diseases, effective preventive measures could significantly reduce this death rate. It is safe to say that *the average life expectancy of U.S. males could be extended by seven to nine years if the present knowledge of disease prevention were fully applied.* Those chronic diseases that lend themselves most suitably to prevention are coronary HEART DISEASE, hypertension and its complications (see the major article on **Hypertension**), certain forms of CANCER—particularly lung cancer, BREAST CANCER, large-bowel cancer and cervical cancer—and CIRRHOSIS of the liver. Accidents are another leading cause of death which can be significantly reduced through primary prevention.

The best method of primary prevention is simply common-sense living. Tobacco should be avoided. Regular exercise in adequate amounts should be obtained. The diet should limit the intake of sugar, saturated fats and CHOLESTEROL.

Many disease processes, if detected early enough, can be prevented through prompt treatment. Screening procedures to detect these diseases should be part of routine medical care. Application of these screening procedures could hopefully reduce by 50% all major disabilities, all hospital days and even many deaths in adults under age 70.

Complete history and physical examination

A complete history and physical examination should

certainly be performed at least once during the early adult years. A complete examination at this time will identify areas of future risk and serve as a baseline of medical data which can later be used for comparison.

Smoking history

Cigarette smoking, one of the major contributing factors to premature deaths, is linked with such diseases as coronary heart disease, STROKE, cancer of the lung, cancer of the oral cavity, cancer of the esophagus, cancer of the bladder, chronic BRONCHITIS and EMPHYSEMA. It is clear that stopping smoking reduces the risk of virtually all of these conditions. Recent data suggest that the physician may play a significant role in increasing a patient's motivation to stop smoking. Several newer techniques of behavior modification may also prove effective.

History of alcohol abuse

Alcohol abuse is an extremely common problem that not only affects middle-aged persons but also seems to affect young adults and even teenagers. Several screening tests have been developed to assist the physician in identifying alcohol abusers. With treatment, the eventual outlook is good for up to 20% of alcohol abusers with a stable emotional background. It is recommended that appropriate questions concerning drinking habits or the use of a more formal screening test be performed at least at intervals of five to ten years. (See also ALCOHOL/ ALCOHOLISM.)

Use of seat belts

Automobile accidents account for approximately 45,000 deaths annually in the United States and rank as the leading cause of death among young adults. The regular use of seat belts could save thousands of lives yearly. Although the need for seat belts is obvious, less than 40% of adults and less than 10% of children under age five are properly restrained. (See also *Balance sheet of risks* in the major article on **Healthy Living in a Hostile Environment.**)

Physical examination

Blood pressure

At least 15% of the adult population has blood pressure greater than 160/95, a conservative definition of hypertension (high blood pressure). Another 15% may have borderline hypertension. Since hypertension is a major risk factor of two of the leading causes of deaths, heart disease and stroke, it warrants periodic and frequent screening. Adults should have their blood pressure checked at least every two years.

Weight

OBESITY, defined in this case as more than 20% above ideal body weight, increases the risk of death by 50%. Although diagnosis presents no difficulty, it is difficult to establish and maintain a long-term effective weight-control program. The personal physician can play a supportive role in aiding the patient to follow dietary restrictions necessary to reach and maintain an ideal weight for that individual. All adults should have their weight measured and compared with tables of ideal weights (listed according to height, basic body build and sex) at least every four years.

Breast examination

BREAST CANCER is one of the leading causes of death in women over age 30. An effective screening program based on breast self-examinations and physician examination can result in early diagnosis and treatment, and thus significantly reduce breast cancer mortality.

Women should be taught the techniques of monthly breast self-examination. In addition, it is desirable that the personal physician perform this examination about once each year. While the use of routine MAMMOGRAPHY remains controversial, it has been shown to aid in the detection of early breast cancer in women over the age of 50.

Pap smear

The Papanicolaou smear or test ("Pap smear" or "Pap test")—named after the Greek-American physician and cytologist George N. Papanicolaou (1883–1962)—is an inexpensive and reliable test for detecting cancer of the cervix (neck of the womb). Cancer of the cervix is a slowly progressive disease that requires approximately five to ten years to become invasive. It is a curable disease during the preinvasive states.

At the present time there is some controversy over how often women should have a Pap smear. As a minimum, all women over age 20 (especially as sexual activity increases) should have a Pap smear every other year indefinitely; women over the age of 30 should have a Pap smear annually. Certain women at higher risk may require further or more frequent screening. (See also CERVICAL SMEAR and the major article on **Oncology.**)

Tonometry

Tonometry is one method of diagnosing the presence of GLAUCOMA—an abnormal elevation of pressure inside the eye which, if untreated, may gradually lead to blindness. It is a condition that occurs in as many as 2% of those over the age of 40. (See also the major article on **Ophthalmology.**)

Tonometry is the most widely used screening test to measure the pressure within the eye. Although it is simple to perform, painless and inexpensive, it unfortunately is not a particularly good *screening* test. Up to 60% of those with glaucoma may have normal pressure readings and will be falsely reassured. In addition to tonometry, the presence of glaucoma can be determined by checking visual fields and by examining the retina (the light-sensitive layer at the back of the eye). Since no single diagnostic test is sufficient, tonometry plus an examination of the retina is recommended for adults over age 40 every year to detect early cases of glaucoma.

Laboratory tests

Serum cholesterol

An association exists between increased levels of blood serum cholesterol and an increase in coronary heart disease. Although average serum cholesterol levels in the United States are higher than elsewhere, a cholesterol level over 275 milligrams per cent is usually considered "elevated." Screening is necessary because high levels of cholesterol in the blood produce no symptoms.

Diet and drug therapy can lower cholesterol levels; this lowering is associated with a reduced risk of coronary heart disease. Serum cholesterol is measured on a sample of venous blood. Because early treatment can reduce morbidity and mortality associated with abnormally high levels of cholesterol, all adults should have their cholesterol levels measured at least every four years.

Venereal disease research laboratories (VDRL)

SYPHILIS occurs mostly in young and middle-aged adults. Untreated persons with syphilis have a 20% decreased life expectancy, but the disease is curable in the primary and secondary stages. There are several reliable, inexpensive tests for determining the presence of syphilis. A "serologic test" of the blood should ideally be performed at least every five years until age 60.

Culture for gonorrhea

The incidence of gonorrhea is rapidly increasing. Often, particularly in women, the disease is symptomless until very late in its course. Untreated cases of gonorrhea may lead to severe complications, including sterility. A new culture technique can detect the presence of the micro-organisms responsible for gonorrhea and should be included as a routine screening procedure for all women.

Stool for occult blood

Colorectal cancers are one of the leading causes of cancer deaths. Most people with early cancers of the lower bowel have very small amounts of blood in their stool; however, even microscopic amounts of blood in the stool can be readily detected by means of a simple test. Usually a minimum of two stool specimens are obtained and examined. All adults over the age of 40 should have yearly examinations for blood in their stool.

Hemoglobin

Nutritional anemia (iron-deficiency anemia) is a relatively common condition which often contributes to less than optimal functioning. It can be quickly detected by means of a simple blood test which reveals the level of HEMOGLOBIN (the oxygen-carrying pigment of the red blood cells). Many physicians therefore recommend that such a test be performed at least every two years.

Urine

A complete laboratory analysis of a specimen of urine (urinalysis) may be helpful in detecting unsuspected cases of diabetes, kidney disease, or urinary tract infections. It may be included along with other laboratory tests.

Immunizations

Adults should routinely have booster shots for diphtheria and tetanus every ten years. In addition, since INFLUENZA can appear in those over the age of 65, especially in those people who are burdened with chronic diseases, all adults over 65 should have routine annual influenza immunizations.

Conclusion

I have discussed some of the tests, procedures and techniques which play an important role in a comprehensive program of preventive medicine. The effectiveness of such a program naturally requires the mutual cooperation and understanding of both the patient and the family physician.

Some of the screening tests—such as the Pap smear—are absolutely essential to detect potentially life-threatening diseases in their early and more easily treatable stages. A combination of all of the tests and procedures mentioned— or at least an intelligent selective choice of the most important ones for a particular patient—can help identify medical risk factors and permit the initiation of treatment or a modification in the patient's lifestyle which is essential to maintain good health.

Medical History Checklist

The topics listed here are likely to be covered when a physician in general practice first consults with a new patient. The patient's answers to questions about these matters gives the physician information which can be extremely helpful in diagnosing a specific complaint, in prescribing treatment to ward off potential problems, in recommending clinical tests, or in giving plain old-fashioned good advice based on his experience.

A doctor takes an oath, the famous Hippocratic Oath, which binds him to protect the secrecy of personal data. The courts also respect the confidentiality of the information a patient gives his doctor. The more frank and complete a patient can be when he or she answers questions on these subjects, the more likely the physician can help the patient.

General:

Age
Marital Status
Recent Travel

Reason for coming to Physician
Chief Complaint
Symptoms of Present Illness

Family History:

Allergic Disorders
High Cholesterol
Hypertension (High
  Blood Pressure)
Hypoglycemia
Tuberculosis

Heart Disease, or Premature
  Heart Attacks
Stroke
Diabetes Mellitus
Malignant Disease (Cancer, Leukemia)
Mental Disorders or Seizures

Personal History:

Alcohol Intake
Drugs
Diet

Smoking
Coffee or Tea
Exercise

General Lifestyle:

Sleep
Tolerance for Pressure
Sex Life

Fatigue
Depression

Medications:

Vitamins
Drug Allergies
Blood Pressure Pills
Hormones
Cortisone
Cough Mixture
Appetite Suppressants
Birth Control Pills
Tranquilizers
Narcotics

Aspirin
Heart Medication (Digitalis)
Blood Thinners
Water Pills
Iron
Laxatives
Thyroid Pills
Sleeping Pills
Antihistamines

Past Health:

Childhood Diseases
Hospitalizations

Operations
Irregularity in Function of Body
  Systems

Psychotherapy

Dr. Arlene N. Heyman

Psychotherapy is an important means of treating certain types of emotional or mental disorders. The following article discusses some common problems that may be solved by psychotherapy, the techniques used by the therapist or psychoanalyst, and what outcome the patient undergoing analysis can expect.

In the general practice of psychiatry, that branch of medicine which deals with the healing of the mind (psyche), many kinds of therapy are included. Some of them—drug therapy, electroshock, sex therapy—were alluded to in an earlier section (see the major article on **Psychiatry**). This section will discuss another mode of treatment—the management of mental illness through PSYCHOTHERAPY and in particular PSYCHOANALYSIS. But before arriving at a decision about treatment, a considerable number of factors must be taken into account; a whole process must be set into motion.

In most branches of medicine, treatment decisions occur late in the process: first, a person must define himself or herself as a patient; then he or she must determine how to choose appropriate help in evaluating the problem; then a careful analysis must be done consisting of history taking, examination, perhaps certain tests; a diagnosis is arrived at; treatment follows last. The intelligent layperson considering psychiatric help is bound to have certain questions about the process which will be set in motion.

(1) How is he or she to decide if care is needed at all?

(2) If the decision is made, how does the layperson find a properly qualified expert to make an evaluation? Especially in big cities, a wide variety of people call themselves "therapists" and they are not necessarily psychiatrists, psychologists or social workers. How can one judge anyone's competence?

(3) What goes on in a consultation? What is the therapist looking for? What might the prospective patient look for?

(4) What goes into the decision of choice of treatment? How is it determined if a patient ought to be engaged in psychotherapy or if something else—drugs, hypnosis, relaxation exercises—would be more effective?

(5) If the most appropriate treatment is psychotherapy, then what kind of psychotherapy? Psychoanalysis? (What is that?) What about weekend "cures," marathons and encounter groups? Are they valid forms of psychotherapeutic treatment?

(6) What can the patient in psychotherapy expect? What is the process like? How long does it last? And what can one anticipate getting from it in the end?

Essentially this section is designed to answer these questions. Its purpose is to help the intelligent layperson figure a way through the "confusing woods" of psychiatry so that he or she may locate treatment that will be useful. Of all the psychiatric treatment modalities, psychoanalysis and related forms of psychotherapy are perhaps the ones least understood—not only by the layperson but by physicians in other medical specialties as well. This section closes with a discussion of those procedures.

Why one might seek help

People usually go to a psychiatrist when all else has failed. They have tried battling it out themselves first—using will power, exercise, talking to friends, praying. Sometimes they have been to physicians and had "work-ups" for gastrointestinal problems, cardiac problems, backaches, headaches; sometimes they have been to several medical specialists. Often these patients have been given prescriptions for sleeping pills or tranquilizers, but these have not provided lasting relief or adequate relief.

Warning signs and symptoms

In the end, people usually go to a psychiatrist because they feel demoralized. Something is going on in them which, despite heroic efforts, is out of their conscious control. They are suffering from various symptoms—anxiety which seems somehow out of proportion to the given stimulus; a "gray feeling" of depression and hopelessness even though their objective situation in life is not overwhelmingly bad; phobias which exclude them from some of life's pleasures; or rituals that make a torment of everyday routine activities (e.g., going to bed must be done in a certain way, taking a bath, getting dressed). People who suffer from such symptoms usually recognize them as due to something "mental," although they don't know what. Other symptoms the sufferer does not immediately think of as psychological—bodily discomforts and pains for which the physician can find no physical cause or permanent medical remedy because while they are clearly *physical* symptoms—upsets of stomach and digestion and excretion, skin eruptions, headaches, backaches, sleeplessness—their cause is *psychological*. Sexual difficulties—problems with erection, with orgasm—fall into this category. All of these signs and symptoms betray their psychological origin in one way or another: people notice that they get headaches when they're annoyed or that they have diarrhea before

At some time or another almost everyone has experienced a sense of hopelessness or a short period of crippling depression. People usually decide to seek the help of a psychiatrist or psychotherapist when, despite all their efforts to come to terms with their problems, symptoms persist and the need for outside help is recognized.

making public appearances or that they can reach orgasm alone but not in lovemaking.

General unhappiness with life

Besides seeking help to alleviate distressing symptoms—behaviors or feelings or selective inabilities that the person finds alien to him but stuck on him somehow like burrs on a dog's ears, stuck past the point of shaking off on his own—a person might see a psychiatrist because of displeasure or distress at the way life is turning out. He or she notices trends which do not seem accounted for merely by chance: he never falls in love, or if he falls in love, he seems to do so only when there is no possibility it will come to anything. She is always working at a job far below her abilities and when it looks as though she might get a promotion, something always happens so that she finds herself quitting. He notices that he can never be boss, never be the one in charge; or he notices that he can never *not* be boss, never be the one *not* in charge. In these situations a person often feels at first that he has no "luck," that fate is against him. Later he sometimes recognizes that he must be

contributing in some way to his own repeated failures, that his fate is somehow in himself. It is as though there were some particular pattern, some design that he is compelled to repeat with whatever materials come to hand; he never recognizes it as the same design until it is finished, whereupon he finds himself feeling dreadful in the same old way. Such a person is in the grip of a *repetition-compulsion;* he has an unconscious psychological problem which he re-enacts now in this situation, now in that. He thinks that he is behaving freely, making choices, but everything always turns out in the same way.

Feeling like an "outsider"

Other people come to a psychiatrist because they have acquired a sense that there is something basically "awry" with them, something about their character which diminishes the range of their emotional responses and usually limits them to only one kind of underlying feeling. Often they have not been aware for most of their lives of anything unusual or stereotyped about their way of being and sometimes they have felt no special discomfort about it. In fact, the difficulty may have been called to their attention by others, or they may have grown aware of it through comparing themselves with others. Such a person may come to a psychiatrist because he realizes that he never feels close to anyone. Or he notices that there is no spontaneity in his life, that he feels and sometimes even looks like a robot, that his relationships are all mechanized and distant. Or he sees that he has a chronic sense of suffering, that he tends to complain and depreciate himself, that he seems to annoy people with his constant need for reassurance and that he ends up by angering them—the last thing he wants. Psychiatrists call such difficulties *character pathology*—unconscious psychological conflicts that have resolved themselves not in a troublesome symptom like a backache or an anxiety attack, nor in a repetitive way of living out one's life in the world, but into a seemingly permanent character type. The person has beaten himself into a certain peculiar shape.

In general, then, people go to a psychiatrist because they are acting or feeling or suffering in some way typical of them which is not wholly the outside world's responsibility. What they experience because of poverty cannot be treated by a psychiatrist, nor what they experience because of a society's racism or sexism or political oppression. On the other hand, if a person feels that he is in some way colliding with the outside world—that he is keeping himself poor or that she is not taking advantage of the career opportunities that *are* available to her or that in some secret part of her she believes that women *are* inferior beings, then that becomes a problem to be approached psychologically.

Of course not all psychic suffering calls for psychiatric intervention. Life is full of tragedy, and what one feels at a husband's death is not usually a cause for consultation— although it may be if one feels nothing or if mourning becomes endless. In such cases, counseling may restore the person's *ability* to grieve. And sometimes, in a crisis, one simply needs someone to talk to and there isn't anybody else.

Being dependent on others

So far we have been discussing *why* one would go for help. There are many people who have problems which might be amenable to therapy but they consider seeing a psychiatrist unacceptable. Some feel there is something "weak" about it, that they are putting themselves in a position of being dependent on another and that such dependency is intolerable. In fact, we are *all* dependent on one another— on our surgeon, on the electric power company, on the shoemaker. The goal of psychiatric intervention is to lessen "crippling" kinds of dependencies—to make the patient stronger, more in control of himself or herself—and, in the end, to eliminate the need for the psychiatrist. However, there are some people whose need *not* to accept help of any kind is so passionate that it overrides all logical considerations; they cannot even give therapy a try. Often such a person is fighting off an equally passionate unconscious wish to be tended to, to be passive—a wish he finds wholly unacceptable. This fight usually occurs on other battle-grounds as well, the proposed trip to the psychiatrist being just one of them. Often the person is a "man's man," who has a strong need to demonstrate his virility, who delivers swift retribution for real and imagined slights; he is a battler. The anxiety which underlies these traits might well be lessened with treatment, if he were able to bring himself to go.

Making the decision to seek help

Some people do not consult a psychiatrist from fear of social stigma. Now the social status of seeing a psychiatrist varies very much from community to community. In some of the big metropolitan centers, or at least in some circles in the big metropolitan centers, it is socially acceptable—note such movies as *Annie Hall* where seeing a psychiatrist is simply a part of everyday life like playing tennis. In other parts of the country, and in many small towns, this is certainly not the case. If you live in an area where your neighbors regard getting psychiatric help as a sign of being "crazy," then you might not want to tell anyone or else you might simply lie. There are many parts of our lives which we don't share with the neighbors. Because they realize that a history of psychiatric consultation might be held against them, many people of sound judgment and morals deliberately conceal the fact that they have seen a psychiatrist on college or job application forms.

Some people are afraid to go to a psychiatrist because they are worried that they will end up in a hospital. In fact, in most states a person can be admitted to a hospital *against his will* only if he is actively homicidal or suicidal or is unable to care for himself (it is not enough to have suicidal thoughts—everyone has suicidal thoughts at one time or another). Most psychiatrists consider hospitalization only in extreme situations where real danger exists, and it is a decision which should be made by doctor and patient *together*. If hospitalization is called for, then usually it will be of short duration. Most insurance companies (for instance, Blue Cross-Blue Shield), pay for only 30 days of inpatient care. In the state hospitals, which take people with no insurance, or after their insurance has run out, the fashion nowadays is to return people to the community as quickly as possible. (There is considerable controversy about whether this is always in the patient's best interest.) At any rate, if despite all these safeguards a person feels that he is being confined without cause, he ought to call a lawyer; if he can't afford a lawyer, he ought to call legal aid—which provides lawyers without cost.

People who are involved in antisocial activities (who are often in trouble with the law) and people who are obviously disturbed (who walk the streets in outlandish outfits talking to themselves and picking things out of garbage cans)—these two groups rarely consult a psychiatrist of their own free will. Their families often feel tormented and helpless and do not know where to turn. While it is difficult and sometimes impossible to help people who do not want to be helped, there is occasionally a secret part of the most defiant or apathetic human being which longs for an alliance with another person. Should the family find it impossible to induce the prospective patient to take the first step on his own, then a relative may want to make an appointment himself with a pyschiatrist to discuss the problem.

And this holds true in general: if a person has doubts about whether he or a family member might be benefited by psychiatric help, then he might want to have a consultation to clarify that very issue.

Where to go and to whom

Having decided that something ails him, the layperson is faced with the problem of what kind of help to seek. He is in the position of someone who, after waiting awhile, decides there is no doubt he has a pain in his abdomen which is not going away. The issue becomes what to do next. What both people want—the one who feels his psychic life is disordered and the one who feels his physical life is disordered—is someone with broad experience to make an appropriate assessment of the problem. Analysis and diagnosis must come before treatment. The patient who has a physical problem of which he doesn't understand the origin ought to go to the best-qualified physician for a consultation—such as a specialist in internal medicine (an *internist*), who has knowledge of the broad range of medical possibilities. With an undefined pain in the abdomen, one does not go first to a surgeon. The purpose of the consultation is to allow the physician to do an appropriate preliminary analysis—listen to the patient's history; perform a physical examination covering certain prescribed maneuvers to elicit the state of well-being or ill-functioning of the different organ systems (gastrointestinal, cardiac, and so forth); draw blood samples for analysis, take x-rays or do whatever tests he or she feels appropriate to complement the findings; and then, from all this material, come to a tentative diagnosis. With this in mind, the internist can outline the possible courses of treatment for the patient and make appropriate referrals— to a surgeon, a gastroenterologist, etc. This initial evaluation may take several visits or it may result in an immediate recommendation depending on the difficulty of elucidating the problem or "presenting complaint."

A similar situation holds true in psychiatry. The person feels that some particular aspect of his life is disturbed. He doesn't know why; he doesn't know if other aspects of his life, which seem all right to him, may not be implicated as well. He doesn't see the "total picture," he doesn't know what it means, and he doesn't know what the best form of treatment is. So he also needs to go for a consultation.

To whom should he go? His problem is the same as if he had a physical complaint of unknown origin. And the solution is the same. For a diagnostic consultation, the patient needs to find someone with the broadest range of expertise, who can recognize the whole spectrum of psychiatric illness, make a complete analysis of the problem, outline the appropriate treatment possibilities

Heavy drinking may be one sign of a deep-seated emotional problem. Psychotherapy can sometimes be of value to the cooperative alcoholic by helping him to understand and cope with an underlying feeling of desperation or inadequacy.

and make a referral if necessary. If a well-qualified internist is the best person to fill this function for the other branches of medicine, who is the person to see if the problem is psychological?

Qualifications of a psychiatrist

Who are the people working in psychiatry and in the allied mental health professions? What kind of training do they receive?

A *psychiatrist* is a person who has completed medical school, in most cases done an internship, and then done three years of specialization in psychiatry—a "residency." The quality of different residencies varies considerably as does the scope of skills taught. The best residency programs are designed to give the doctor broad experience: under supervision, he or she works in a psychiatric emergency room and on a psychiatric inpatient ward; consults on medical wards when poeple with physical illness develop related (or unrelated) psychic difficulties; learns to administer drugs and electroshock therapy; and sees outpatients in psychotherapy. The doctor may also have had some personal psychotherapy, although this is not a requirement for finishing a residency program.

A year after completing an approved residency—approved by the American Psychiatric Association—the psychiatrist becomes "Board Eligible." He or she may take comprehensive examinations which evaluate competence in general psychiatry and neurology. This is especially relevant for psychiatrists who work with hospitalized patients or who have a general psychiatric practice where many patients require drug treatment or have concomitant organic difficulties. In the past relatively few psychiatrists chose to become Board Certified; now more are doing so although they are still in the minority.

Psychoanalytic practice

Another kind of certification which some psychiatrists seek out is awarded by the American Psychoanalytic Association. To obtain this kind of certification requires many additional years of training, training which is especially helpful in working with patients who do not require hospitalization or drugs—that is, patients whose difficulties fall within the nonpsychotic realm, and who would be benefited by certain "talking" therapies, specifically psychoanalytically oriented psychotherapy or psychoanalysis. There are two major kinds of post-residency training available—training in child psychiatry, which usually entails two years of working exclusively with children and training in psychoanalysis.

Psychoanalysis, which will be discussed in detail in the section Range of therapies, is the longest, most intensive kind of treatment and one applicable only in certain cases. The theory underlying psychoanalytic practice, however, is an explanation of the functioning of the human mind. It is a theory which has broad applicability both in the understanding of a wide range of psychological problems and in the shaping of a wide range of different kinds of treatment. For example, there are individual, group and family therapies which are called "psychoanalytically oriented"—because they are based on psychoanalytic insights; in fact, with the exception of behaviorist therapy, it is difficult to find a treatment modality which is not an offshoot of psychoanalysis.

Now there are many different psychoanalytic institutes in the United States where a psychiatrist may pursue training, and these institutes vary greatly in quality and rigor. The American Psychoanalytic Association evaluates psychoanalytic institutes and certifies some of them; it is the only organized accrediting group which guarantees certain standards. Any psychiatrist who graduates from an institute certified by the American Psychoanalytic Association has the following credentials: besides having completed acceptable residency training, he or she has attended five years of classes in psychoanalysis, has analyzed a certain minimum number of patients under supervision, and has gone through a personal psychoanalysis of many years' duration. The purpose of this analysis is to free the analyst of psychological difficulties, not only so that he can live better but also so that there will be as little interference as possible with his helping his own patients.

Psychologists

Among the nonmedical professionals in the field of mental health, those who will concern us here are psychologists and social workers.

Psychologists differ from one another in their level of training and their areas of expertise. The most highly trained have PhD degrees.

Of these, psychologists with doctorates in clinical psychology have expertise most relevant to doing psychotherapy, as distinguished from psychologists with doctorates in experimental, school, or developmental psychology whose training is geared to other ends. Beyond their Bachelor's degrees, clinical psychologists have studied three years of academic coursework including testing and have done some clinical work under supervision. They then do a year's intership in which they obtain more clinical experience; finally they write a PhD dissertation.

Like medical schools and residency programs, graduate schools and internships vary in quality and scope. Like psychiatrists, psychologists are not required to undergo a personal analysis. After they have received their degree and spent additional years doing supervised work with patients, they are eligible for state certification. Some clinical psychologists go on for postgraduate psychoanalytic training; however, there is no accrediting organization comparable to the American Psychoanalytic Association which certifies their institutes. Some few psychologists with superb qualifications are admitted to institutes which are approved by the American Psychoanalytic Association.

Social workers

It is more difficult to categorize the training of social workers, since this varies greatly in emphasis from school to school. Some programs are clinical and teach social workers therapeutic techniques; others do not. Social workers are not required to have personal treatment. A year or two after receiving a Master's degree, social workers can take an exam to be certified by the National Association of Social Workers. Some go on for psychoanalytic training, but there is no accrediting agency to establish the caliber of these institutes. With rare exceptions, social workers are not admitted to institutes approved by the American Psychoanalytic Association.

The aforementioned people are legally entitled to call themselves psychologists or social workers because of their credentials. There are many other people who call themselves therapists or psychoanalysts who have no credentials whatsoever. It would be wise to stay away from such people.

Seeking the best qualifications

For a diagnostic interview the best-qualified person to see would be a psychiatrist who is also a psychoanalyst graduated from an institute approved by the American Psychoanalytic Association. There are many psychiatrists without analytic training who can do the job as well and who will make a referral to an analyst if that is indicated. The difficulty comes in identifying those psychiatrists without having special inside information. Board certification attests only to academic competence. And membership in the American Psychiatric Association indicates the completion of an approved residency, that there are three other doctors who have written lettters of recommendation, and that the member has paid his yearly dues. Both are pluses in choosing a psychiatrist; but as with similar certifications in other branches of medicine, neither is geared to attest to the doctor's character or ethics in the most thoroughgoing sense or to the intactness of the doctor's own personality. These are crucially important in long-term intensive psychotherapies, where the doctor's human resources are heavily taxed. For these reasons a psychoanalyst accredited by the American Psychoanalytic Association remains the best choice. Such a person has the broadest skills and the most certified ones. He or she will do a consultation of one or several sessions, make an evaluation, come to a diagnosis, and make an appropriate referral—to another psychoanalyst, to a psychiatrist who is doing other forms of therapy, to a clinical psychologist or to a social worker. He may also refer you to an internist.

One finds such a person by consulting the catalogue of the American Psychoanalytic Association, available at most medical school libraries, or by writing to the American Psychoanalytic Association (One East 57th Street, New York City, 10022). They will supply you with the names of whoever is accredited in your vicinity.

If there is no one accredited in your city or state, the next best solution is to get the catalogue of the nearest medical school and call the senior people in the department of psychiatry for consultation. Chances are good that those engaged in teaching psychiatry will have a high level of competence.

With no psychoanalyst and no medical school in your area, consult the biographical dictionary of the American Psychiatric Association, or write to the Association (1700 Eighteenth Street, N.W. Washington, D.C.). (There is probably a branch in your state as well.) The member's credentials can be examined in his or her biographical sketch.

In the end, of course, no system is foolproof. As with internists, lawyers and clergymen, "impeccable credentials" are not the whole story. Despite their rigor, even approved psychoanalytic institutes are not always successful in weeding out people who lack certain human characteristics necessary for doing psychoanalytic treatment: an ability to take the passive position—to sit still and listen; an ability to "feel" the other's unconscious and not to confuse it with one's own; an ability to examine one's own reactions and separate out those that come from one's own neurotic difficulties and those that the patient is repeatedly trying to elicit in all people; an ability to observe certain ethical norms—that one does not gratify oneself sexually or socially with one's patients and that one unremittingly observes confidentiality. Certainly no person

> Choosing a good psychoanalyst may at first appear to be an insurmountable problem. However, a list of psychoanalysts who practice in your area may be obtained from the nearest medical school or from the catalogue of the American Psychoanalytic Association. It is important, in the end, to select one with whom you feel comfortable.

ought to enter into treatment with a therapist who lacks these qualities. If the patient has serious doubts, it may be advisable to see more than one doctor for initial consultations or to see the same doctor several times before reaching a decision.

How much does psychotherapy cost?

So far we have been working on the assumption that the layperson can afford to pay for private treatment or at least for private consultation. Average fees range between about $25 and $60 an hour, with some psychiatrists charging a flat rate and others taking into account the patient's financial situation. It is important to check your medical insurance policy; many people have, under their major medical policy, coverage for outpatient psychiatry. It varies greatly in amount, from some policies that pay nothing to others that pay up to approximately 80% of fees. Some of these policies pay fees only to psychiatrists while others pay for psychologists as well. Obviously it is important to know which kind of policy you have.

People who have Medicare or Medicaid can also usually follow the above set of recommendations, making clear to whomever they speak just which policy they have. Some psychiatrists accept Medicare payments, some accept Medicaid, and some accept neither.

If you have no money but there is an accredited psychoanalytic institute in your area, call and they will evaluate you to see if you need analysis; if so, they will often give you a candidate in training (that is, a full-fledged psychiatrist or psychologist who is at least half-way through his analytic training) who will see you at what you can afford: anywhere from nothing an hour to $15 or $20. (If you can afford more than that, you will usually be referred to someone in private practice.) If there is no institute in your vicinity, call the medical school and ask for a referral to their clinic; here you will see psychiatrists in training, who are under experienced supervision.

Failing all this, write to the American Psychoanalytic Association and the American Psychiatric Association; explain where you are, what your financial problem is, and see what they suggest. All of the preceding recommendations have been made assuming the prospective patient has time to think things through. In an emergency situation, one goes to an emergency room. As there are *physical* emergencies so there are *psychiatric* emergencies—someone's life is in danger or someone *feels* his life is in danger. Once the emergent situation is controlled, one can then again approach the situation in a more leisurely consultative manner.

What goes on in a consultation

Assuming that one goes to a person with broad training, then the shape of the consultation ought to be determined by the nature of the presenting complaint. In psychiatry the presenting complaint is (in the largest sense) the whole patient. One looks at the patient—dress, bearing, nails, gait. The doctor invites the patient to talk and then sees how he does so, if he does so, how he relates to the doctor, how much he can tell the doctor. Often within the first five minutes the doctor has a rough idea of whether the picture he is seeing falls into the realm of psychosis or not and whether such a picture could be caused by physical illness. If these are possibilities, then the doctor gets active and asks questions in a manner similar to that of the internist. Typical questions might include: When did this start? Have you ever had it before? Did you notice that you also felt this and this? Does anyone in your family have this? Again there are a number of psychotic conditions that the psychiatrist has in mind—major DEPRESSION, SCHIZOPHRENIA, manic-depressive illness (see MANIA)—and he is asking questions to see if this illness conforms to one of those patterns.

He may run through some verbal tests with the patient, ask the patient to subtract or remember certain items for five minutes or to interpret proverbs. These are part of a "mental status exam" which helps the doctor decide, among other things, if the physical functioning of the brain

has been in any way impaired—which might be the case in organic illness. The doctor may then take the patient's temperature and blood pressure and do a physical exam himself, or he may make a referral to an internist or a neurologist or to a psychologist for extensive formal testing.

When the problem is physical illness or a clear-cut case of major depression, schizophrenia, or manic-depression, the psychiatrist can frequently make a rough diagnosis in one interview and suggest a course of treatment or make a referral. The psychiatrist may rapidly rule out these possibilities (just as the internist can often tell immediately if he is faced with an emergency or not, and if it is of a gastrointestinal nature or a cardiac nature). If so, then the consultation goes in another direction. The patient is questioned very little. The questions that are asked are

The stresses of modern life can sometimes be so emotionally disabling that the affected individual decides to seek professional help. In many cases the initial consultation will help patient to view his or her problem in its proper perspective.

often of an open-ended nature: "Tell me something about your childhood." Sometimes no questions are asked at all; there may be no need. If the person talks without great difficulty and the overall character of the illness is clearly a neurotic one—that is, one where the person has bothersome symptoms or troublesome life patterns, but where he is at the same time functioning in the world (in his job and in his human relations)—then the physician's purpose will be to interfere with the patient as little as possible, so that he can pick up the data in a relatively unadulterated way. He wants to see how the patient tells his story, how the patient relates to the physician. From this he will get a hint of what unconscious forces may underlie the story and how the patient relates to other people in his life. In short, a physician doing a consultation where it seems clear that the patient is in the neurotic realm will restrict the possible influence of his personality on the patient, especially if he plans to treat the person himself: he will not be lavishly warm; he will probably not tell jokes; and he may not even answer all questions. Of course, at the same time he ought not to be cold or "clipped." Either of those extremes—ingratiating behavior or rudeness—may represent intrusions of the psychiatrist's own personal difficulties into his work.

Once it is clear that the diagnosis is in the neurotic or near-neurotic realm, the psychiatrist looks for a number of factors which will determine whether the best treatment is psychoanalysis or psychotherapy that is psychoanalytically oriented or some other form of therapy—that is, he is looking at the soundness of the whole psychic system; and he is looking to see if the current conditions in the patient's life are conducive to a long, arduous, contemplative kind of treatment. These decisions may take longer to make (several consultation sessions) and sometimes the doctor has to begin a treatment, go on with it for a few months, and then change it if it seems inappropriate. This, of course, happens in all branches of medicine.

At some point in the consultation the psychiatrist will tell you what he thinks the matter is. It is a rare psychiatrist indeed who—in telling what the matter is, if the problem falls within the neurotic realm—will say more than that. Rarely is the patient told that he has an "obsessive-compulsive neurosis" or a "hysterical neurosis" or a "narcissistic character disorder." Most neuroses are *mixed*—they show a little of this and a little of that; the therapist will not know the proportions or even many of the ingredients until the therapy is well under way. While it may at some point be useful for the therapist to conceptualize his patient's difficulties in such terms in his own mind, such diagnoses offered to the patient are extraneous factors that may distort his treatment—much as the intrusion of the analyst's full everyday personality would be a distortion. The reasons for this will become clear in the discussion of the psychoanalytic process. On the other hand, if the diagnosis is major depression,

schizophrenia, organic brain syndrome, manic-depressive illnesses (illnesses for which the appropriate treatment is supportive therapy and physical intervention—drugs, hospitalization, physical work-up), then there is no general reason not to give the patient a specific diagnosis.

The psychiatrist will in the end make a referral or, if he is experienced in treating the type of illness the patient has, he will offer the option of continuing. Usually he will openly discuss fees. Discussion of fees and hours is not only of course a necessary precondition for continuation of therapy; it also provides additional data for the treatment process. (The way the patient handles, or avoids handling, time and money is typical of him and is derived from unconscious processes.)

Range of therapies

As the nature of the illness to some extent shapes the consultation, it should almost wholly determine the nature of the treatment. (In all branches of medicine, choice of treatment may be affected by financial considerations; it is always affected by the availability of properly trained personnel. In the best of all possible worlds, these limitations would not exist.) In internal medicine, a patient who has an ulcer must be treated with therapy designed especially for that condition; anything else is malpractice. At the same time, there may be a number of possible approaches in the treatment of an ulcer—some of them determined by the nature of the ulcer (ulcers are very different one from another), some of them determined by the patient's life situation, and some of them true options; there may be several equally valid therapeutic approaches.

In psychiatry, for example, there is a range of treatment for what is loosely called "depression." But as ulcers are very different if you know them well, so depressions are very different and the treatments differ radically. The type of depression where one has lost 30 pounds, awakens every morning at 5 a.m. ruminating, believes one has committed a crime and deserves to be punished, thinks incessantly about suicide—that kind of depression is usually treated with drugs, and sometimes with electroshock. The kind of depression where the patient continues to go about her business, working, making love, etc.—but all the joy has gone out of things and the patient doesn't feel like getting up in the morning and has the sense that she is really dreary and pitiful and loathsome, although she doesn't exactly know why—for *that* kind of depression, some form of psychotherapy may be called for. *Which* kind would depend upon many factors, but most likely drugs would be of no use. The feelings people have following the death of a loved one do not constitute a depression at all, or not usually.

Many factors must be taken into account, therefore, in making a diagnosis. There is no "cookbook" approach to it; even what I have said in the above paragraph is oversimplified—sometimes a person who has a depression amenable to psychotherapy rather than drugs also has a symptom of early morning awakening and sometimes he has lost weight as well. Thus, determining the diagnosis and recommending a mode of treatment are complicated decisions. The therapist needs considerable training and experience to make them well and they can rarely be made long distance. The doctor needs to see the patient.

The group approach

It follows from all of this that *encounter groups* or *est* or *meditation weekends* are not treatments. Numbers of people are taken together irrespective of what ails each individually and are then exposed to a given philosophy, a way of viewing the world, a particular approach to human relations. Often conventional taboos are broken—strangers talk to each other about intimate matters, weep in front of each other, grow angry with each other, touch each other; words that are not normally used in "polite company" are used lavishly.

In certain "treatments," one is subjected to "brainwashing" or "breaking-down" techniques—such as not being allowed to use the toilet for eight-hour stretches and being called demeaning names.

Some people find these experiences exciting and exhilarating, others find them frightening, some find them childish. As with any other experience in life—reading a book, attending a sermon—it may make for lasting change in a person, for good or for ill. (There have been reports of people having psychotic episodes after some of these "weekend cures.") Or, as with most other experiences in life, it may affect a person temporarily and then he continues about his business unchanged. The point is that encounter groups or *est* are experiences; they are not treatment because they are not based on careful individual evaluation. They are at best educational experiences applied *en masse*, without concern for individual needs.

What then is meant by the "range of therapy" in psychiatry? There is a spectrum of treatment just as there is a spectrum of illness. Where the person's functioning is most interfered with, where he cannot take care of his business or go about his daily activities, there treatment must be most interventionist, supportive, active. The physician is standing in for the patient's judgment and synthesizing capacities, for his reason. Drugs, hospitalization, or electroshock therapy may be called for. In psychotherapy, rather than *uncovering* unconscious meanings the therapist is often *covering up* the unconscious and trying instead to show the patient the everyday significance of things in the world. He is offering advice, being himself, doing whatever he can. In cases where a person is well able to take care of himself from day to day but is displeased with certain aspects of his life or bothered by symptoms—there, treatment would be least interventionist, least supportive, and most "analytic." That is, hospitalization

or electroshock would be useless and the administration of drugs a rare and temporary event. Less attempt need be made to mask symptoms, since they are not wholly disorganizing, and more attention can be paid to undergoing them and dissolving them through personality change.

Psychoanalysis and "psychoanalytically oriented" psychotherapy

The internist to whom you go with a gnawing pain in your abdomen has in mind a certain way of understanding physical life: he or she has a picture of how the organs in the body relate when all is going well and at the same time an overall idea of the multiplicity of ways in which disorder may express itself. In a consultation, the doctor evaluates the patient's particular complaints against this "backdrop." The best internist's understanding has certain weak places in it because of the state of medicine: there is no understanding of the causes of some diseases although the medical expert recognizes the symptoms and sometimes has a mode of treatment; other times there is an understanding of the cause but no mode of treatment. In other words, for a number of illnesses there is not a perfect fit between theory and practice. For instance, medical science has a sufficient understanding of the process of cancer to be able to say that deranged cells multiply wildly and that certain environmental factors—asbestos inhalation, smoking—seem to cause derangement in cells.

Medical specialists also have a number of measures they take against deranged cells: the surgeon cuts them out, the internist prescribes certain drugs and the radiologist provides x-ray treatment to kill them off. With some cancers the treatment is not effective and with all of them the treatment tends to kill off healthy cells as well.

In the case of cancer, it is obvious that theory and practice are in some respects lacking and that they do not always dovetail. No one understands what triggers off derangement in the individual cell. (How does *smoke* do it? Does it interact with the DNA? If so, how?) No one knows the precise combination of factors which triggers off the rapid multiplication of cancer cells in a given case; and no one knows how to reverse the process. Doctors do much better with ulcers and best with pneumococcal pneumonia, where the specific cause *is* known and effective therapy is available.

When a psychiatrist sees a patient he, too, has in his mind a certain way of understanding mental life. He or she has a knowledge of how the "organs" of the psyche function together in health as well as an overall picture of the various ways they malfunction in mental illness. Because of the state of psychiatry, some mental or emotional illnesses are understood relatively well both from the point of view of the cause and the treatment. In others, the therapist has a better understanding of the cause than of the treatment, or vice versa.

Theory versus treatment of mental illnesses

Generally speaking, psychiatry does not have a thorough-going coherent understanding of PSYCHOSES. What we have are various theories of the causes and various kinds of treatment, some of them excellent in that they work. But there is not enough "fit" between theory and treatment. Thus, electroshock and antidepressants are more or less curative for *episodes* of major depression; but it is not clear *why* they are curative, because there is no wholly satisfying explanation of the causes of depression, one which would account for the success of two such different kinds of treatment. Manic-depressive illness is well controlled by lithium and some types of schizophrenia respond to antipsychotic medication. In each of these illnesses much is known and many patients can be cured or helped significantly, but the situation is nowhere as clear-cut as it is with the diagnosis and definitive treatment of, say, pneumococcal pneumonia.

In the range of neurotic illnesses, however, the psychiatrist has a coherent way of viewing cause and treatment. He is not always fully successful, any more than the internist is always fully successful in treating ulcers or pneumonia or rheumatic heart disease.

Role of psychoanalysis

A psychiatrist understands the symptoms or presenting problems of a patient—the inability to reach orgasm or maintain an erection, anxiety on taking exams, persistent thoughts that one's child will be hurt in some way—as having unconscious meaning(s) individual to that particular patient and usually out of the patient's awareness. If the psychiatrist considers that it is appropriate and no other treatment will be effective, he or she will enter into an agreement with the patient that the two of them will engage in a known procedure—*psychoanalysis.*

The purpose of psychoanalysis is to elucidate the meaning of those difficulties over a period of time and by elucidating them, free the patient of them. In psychoanalysis the patient usually comes four or five time a week at set times, lies on a couch, and tries to say everything that goes through his mind—whatever it is and in whatever order it comes. That is, he stops attending to the usual requisites of polite conversation—coherence, logic, goal orientation, and a good deal of censorship—and tries instead to associate freely, to say one thing and then the next thing that occurs to him and then the next thing.

The "rules" of conversation are conscious rules: they are intended to exclude the irrelevant, the embarrassing, the unacceptable. The patient, however, has difficulties caused by matters out of his conscious awareness, matters which he in some way excludes without knowing he's excluding them. Relaxed on the couch, the psychiatrist behind him

and thus out of his way (the process is not on the face of it a "dialogue"), the patient tries to exclude nothing. The psychiatrist listens and from his knowledge of human mental processes determines what is excluded over a long period of time that one would ordinarily expect, or what is included markedly and repeatedly and insistently that one would ordinarily not expect. (The importance of the psychiatrist himself being analyzed so that his perceptions are relatively undistorted is here evident.) He notes that the patient never has an unkind thought about anybody and that the patient never has a thought about his psychiatrist at all that isn't altogether flattering. Or he notes that whenever the patient becomes involved with a woman he seems to expect that she will not prove trustworthy and that the patient is moreover very reluctant to tell the analyst about his involvement.

Dialogue between patient and analyst

The analyst mentions his observations to the patient and the patient says what comes to mind about that, says what

> Often just being able to talk freely with a psychoanalyst will help relieve the anxieties and frustrations of a patient—especially those who find it hard to confide in friends. But when deep-seated problems must be overcome, the dialogue between the patient and analyst is indispensable. It helps both to "decode" what the patient reveals.

he felt while the analyst was speaking, then goes on. The analyst may at some point be able to connect for the patient his current lack of trust or his exclusion of all derogatory thoughts with certain other ways the patient thinks and feels, and with certain earlier experiences. The patient says what he thinks about that, and he goes on. A process is activated which is both intellectual and emotional, in which the patient feels and reflects on how he feels. The analyst continues to attend to impediments in the free flow of the patient's associations ("resistance") and to the way the patient relates to the analyst ("transference"). The analyst slowly comes to understand this patient's relationships with other people through the patient's relationship with him. Of course, the analyst tries not to let his own idiosyncracies and personal preferences intrude for the same reasons he keeps his physical presence and facial expressions out of the way—by sitting out of view—in order that the patient may project onto the analyst whatever unconscious distortions he brings to *all* relationships.

These unconscious ideas and ways of behaving toward other people (derived from these ideas) have usually governed the patient's entire life. They go back very far to ways he got on with his parents as a child, to fears he had about them and to intense wishes that he had toward them. The fears were distorted and terrifying—consider the overwhelming response a child has to nightmares—and the wishes seemed impossible to fulfill or wrong, and all fears and wishes were pushed out of his mind. The patient was then no longer consciously aware of them but they still affected behavior or *could* affect behavior if a situation came along which in some way touched off those earlier fears and wishes. They would be embodied in symptoms that the patient didn't understand and that seemed to have no relation to the current situation. They would be embodied in repetitive behavior patterns out of awareness. They would be embodied in character traits.

Decoding what the patient reveals

The shared job in analysis, at some point, is to decode these manifestations, relate them to earlier fears and wishes, show their inappropriateness to the current situation and possibly also to the earlier situation. That is, the child often was not perceiving things accurately or was perceiving them in an exaggerated or distorted way. Instead of being excluded from consciousness—seen as overwhelming or crazy and ridiculous, or an act of fate—the behaviors and what they derive from can be included as a part of the self, seen in all its relations. Once everyone is seated at the "peace table," negotiations can begin and chances are better to work out a new arrangement.

This takes a long time. At first the patient understands nothing. Then he catches a glimpse and then more than a glimpse; but still he doesn't believe it. Then the patient starts to see himself doing the same thing here and here and now here, and it is eventually revealed to him that the very same or similar elements underlie the reasons for his current problem or unhappiness. And then after a long time the patient comes to believe that perhaps this is all true. After a longer time the truth becomes fuller and inescapable and the information begins to be assimilated.

The process is one in which two people work together in complementary ways. The analyst does not know the details of the patient's life but he knows about the wishes and fears that all people have; he knows it intellectually and he knows it emotionally from his *own* analysis. The patient knows the details of his life but he does not know all of them—some he has "forgotten"—and he does not know what these details mean to him. One part of the patient is busy keeping things *out* of awareness while the other part is working with the analyst to let things *in*. How long this process takes is a highly individual issue. Each analysis moves at its own pace because each patient's "stride" is different. While no analyst can tell the patient how long his analysis will take, the patient can be sure that lifelong difficulties will not be whisked away in a matter of months.

Psychoanalytic psychotherapy

For *psychoanalytic psychotherapy* the situation is somewhat different. The therapist will use psychoanalytic theory (namely that current difficulties are based on unconscious wishes and fears arising in another time and place, that the patient will to some extent recreate in his relationship with the analyst relationships of another time and place, and so forth) to clarify or order things in his own mind. But he will depart from classical psychoanalytic *technique* for a variety of reasons. Besides such "extra-analytic" reasons as the patient's not being able to afford to come often enough or not wanting to, the analyst may decide to alter some of the traditional conditions of analysis because of the "systemic integrity" of the patient or his life situation. For example, lying on a couch with the analyst out of sight can be very disorienting for some people. The emotional distortions that nearly everyone in such a situation produces about the character of the analyst, and which the analyst and patient use together to understand the nature of the patient's human relationships, may come to seem to the patient simply "the truth" about the analyst. Such a patient, who has trouble distinguishing between his fantasies about the analyst and the objective qualities of him, may be better helped if he sits in a chair and sees the analyst in front of him at all times. With such a person, whose functioning is seriously awry, the therapist may need to point out certain aspects of reality, give advice, be supportive. Sometimes the patient's "psychic equipment" is so weakened that he will need this type of help not merely for a short interval but—like the patient in heart failure—for a lifetime.

Or a person who is usually functioning well across the board may come to see a psychiatrist because of a specific life crisis which created certain symptoms—a broken marriage may lead to anxiety attacks, a mastectomy may lead to severe depression. Sometimes the therapist is able to help resolve these issues satisfactorily in weeks or months and the patient then goes about his business. At other times the patient comes to feel that those issues are related to other basic personality traits that he would like to alter. In such cases "classical" psychoanalysis may then be entered into.

What can one expect?

It is very difficult to generalize about the outcome in psychotherapy, since the aims and technique vary so much according to the problems of the patient. Psychotherapy is not "one thing"; at one end of the spectrum it approaches psychoanalysis, and at the other end it is as goal directed as a lesson in a class.

Psychoanalysis, on the other hand, is a well-established procedure. If the patient has been properly selected for it, and the analyst knows his or her work, then one can expect a certain outcome. In the short run the patient can expect to continue suffering. That is, the patient will temporarily continue to go through what he has gone through in the past—except that now he will go through it with both himself and his analyst trying to understand it. The analyst does not attempt to comfort the patient, because that would do no good in the long run; he attempts to understand with the patient, to analyze, not to block difficulties but to allow them to emerge and be fully visible. In the long run, patient and analyst work together to free the patient from his cramped life patterns and symptoms, to expand his freedom to work and to love. No one is changed beyond recognition and no one is given talents that he or she didn't have to begin with (although some people discover talents they didn't know they had). The hope is that, in the end, the patient will be able to use more of himself, to enjoy more of himself, to "own" more of himself and to become more liberated and controlled through a new awareness and understanding of his problems.

Guide to Home Nursing Care

Marceline Meyerriecks R.N., B.S.N.

Surprisingly few people know how to care at home for a sick child or adult, a handicapped person or a chronically ill patient. Modern techniques of home nursing care will make it easier both on the person who has to do the caring and on the patient.

At some time, nearly every family faces the problem of caring for the sick at home. Those needing nursing care may be the chronically ill, the handicapped, the elderly, bedridden patients requiring total care, a family member recuperating from an illness that required hospitalization, or one who has an illness that is temporary but incapacitating.

Health-related groups and social agencies in the community that serve families in caring for the sick at home make it possible for some patients to remain at home and for many who are hospitalized to go home earlier. The responsibility of care for a patient with a long-term illness, however, rests essentially with the family.

Basic nursing knowledge and skills can be learned to give good nursing care to the sick. The basic principle of nursing is service to others, given with the desire to lessen pain and discomfort and assist the patient in every way for the recovery of health.

No two illnesses are alike, and no two patients are alike. However, certain nursing fundamentals apply in the care of any sick person. It is taken for granted that the doctor has confidence in the ability of the home nurse to give competent care, and that the home conditions are such that necessary medications and treatments can be given as ordered. Specific manual and observational skills can be learned by anyone, but all factors of nursing care must be considered—the emotional aspects, personal hygiene, the environment, nutrition, elimination, comfort, medications and treatments, observation, precautions if an infectious disease occurs and proper rest. Each factor will be discussed to help the home nurse give successful home nursing care.

Preparation

If you know in advance that home care of an invalid may extend over several weeks or longer, plan the room in advance. Consider first the comfort of the patient and his need for rest and quiet. Some rearranging of bedrooms may

be necessary and a bathroom should be reasonably close by. It is desirable to see that the patient has a comfortable, firm mattress with a waterproof cover; a night stand large enough to hold books, magazines and tissues; a sturdy lamp and a night light; a call bell; and a nearby waste basket lined with a plastic bag.

Try to think ahead about the patient's needs. Comfortable chairs located near the bed are handy both for the patient and for visitors. Keep the room as uncluttered as possible. If it is located a distance from the kitchen or your own bedroom, either buy an inexpensive call bell or set up a glass and spoon at the bedside; a spoon tapped on a glass, or the call bell (even if not often used), lessens the patient's sense of isolation and gives assurance that help will arrive when summoned.

Glaring lights are troublesome to ill people. If the light is too harsh, draw the shades when necessary; but don't keep the room in semidarkness. Let the sunshine in. The room should be aired daily. If the patient is ambulatory (able to get up and walk about), let him leave the room; then air his room thoroughly, change the bedding and finally close the windows and let the room return to normal temperature before the patient reenters.

Medications

The importance of a daily record cannot be stressed enough. Use a notebook. On the front page, write the name and phone number of the doctor, the pharmacy and the hospital. Then list all medications prescribed for the patient, including the date first prescribed and the times and dosage ordered. On the following pages, for each day, write down the medications, times and dosage. Leave room for other observations, which will be discussed later.

The medicine the physician prescribes for the patient is intended to help him, but to obtain its greatest benefits, with the fewest problems, you should know how to use it correctly. For every prescription medicine you give, you should know the following: the purpose of the medicine; how it is administered; the best time of day to give it; how much to give; how to store it; which foods, beverages, activities or other medications should be avoided; extra measures that may be necessary; how to recognize unwanted effects and how to cope with them.

Always ask the physician the reason why a particular medicine is being prescribed. For example, is it to control high blood pressure, relieve pain, help remove excess fluids, treat an infection, induce sleep, relieve the symptoms of arthritis, control depression, treat a stomach disorder, relieve the symptoms of coughs and colds, induce muscle relaxation or treat a heart condition? What *is* it for? By understanding the reason why a particular medicine is prescribed the home nurse can be more helpful, both to the patient and the doctor. For example, the doctor would undoubtedly agree that it would be ridiculous to wake up a patient late at night to administer a medication if the home nurse knew that the drug being given was prescribed to induce sleep! On the other hand, an antibiotic may have to be administered according to a strict schedule if its full therapeutic benefits are to be obtained.

Keep the patient's medications together in a safe place, away from children and away from the patient. Know the "five rights of medication"—The Right Medication, The Right Patient, The Right Dosage, The Right Time and The Right Method of Administering.

On your daily record sheet, cross off the name of the medication after it is given; if it is not taken, circle the time. Write down the reason why it was not taken—if it was refused by the patient, not retained (vomited), if the patient was weeping or nauseous. Observe the patient. Is the pain medication effective? Does the patient vomit the medication each time it is given? Are there any visible side effects? Notify the physician promptly.

Be prepared with a list of questions when you call the doctor and also be prepared for any questions he may ask you; listen carefully to his answers and write them down.

At times of illness, the reassurance provided by familiar surroundings is often of more help than modern hospital care. Basic nursing skills can be quickly mastered to care for every need of the patient at home. The psychological support of the family can be a crucial factor in aiding the patient's return to full health and activity and the regaining of self-confidence.

The doctor is not always available to come to the phone, but his office staff are trained to answer many of your questions. If they cannot be answered immediately, the office staff will obtain the patient's chart and your call will be returned by the doctor or his nurse as soon as possible.

Bed rest

Bed rest for the patient, prescribed by the doctor, is a form of treatment which is often as important as medication, and without which the medication can sometimes do little good. The doctor is responsible for determining the duration of bed rest and whether or not it should be partial or complete. There are times when enforced mobility is vital in the prevention of complications. Even on complete bed rest, exercises to help maintain good circulation and muscle tone can be done. Encourage the patient to wiggle his toes, rotate his ankles in a circular motion, flex the knees and elbows, shift position in bed, take two or three deep breaths every hour, stretch the back, bend the neck and move the head from side to side. Care of the helpless, bedridden patient will be discussed later in this section, as will the care of a sick child for whom bed rest is ordered but almost impossible to maintain.

Nutrition

Nutrition is important in maintaining health, and doubly important when recovering from an illness. It is the doctor's responsibility to determine which diet his patient is allowed. It is the home nurse's responsibility to have the meals attractively served, using foods the doctor allows. When getting diet restrictions or special diets, be sure to have the doctor or nurse answer any of your questions. Ask for sample diet lists, including what to do and what not to do.

When a regular diet is recommended, let the patient pace his own intake and let his appetite be the guide in offering him food. Everyone knows the anxiety of having a sick family member whose appetite is listless, but it is better for the patient to retain his intake rather than to be pushed beyond his limits and lose it by vomiting. Fluids should be offered frequently but in small amounts. As a rule, don't hurry the mealtime; let the patient feed himself, if possible.

Many people do not like to eat alone. If it is impractical or impossible for the patient to join the family for at least one meal a day, have someone in the family join the patient, even if it's only to have a cup of tea at his bedside.

Hygiene

Only the acutely ill will need to be washed by the home nurse. If a patient can do no more than wash his hands and face, he should be urged to participate as much as possible; it is a mild form of exercise and assists the regaining of self-

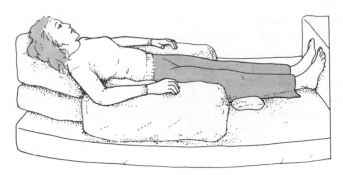

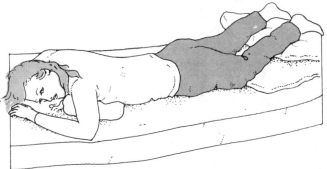

Correct posture and the use of pillow supports as illustrated here are necessary for the comfort of every patient confined to bed.

reliance. If the patient is ambulatory but needs assistance, prepare in advance all the equipment he needs for self-care. For example, draw his bath water, help in undressing and assist him into the tub. It is best to keep the bathing as brief as possible. Avoid drafts. Oral care and hair care may be given in the bathroom at the same time. After the bath, wrap the patient in a warm robe or blanket and have him sit in a comfortable chair while you change the sheets and straighten the bedding.

Think ahead and combine as many activities as possible into this time, so that when the patient returns to bed he may rest uninterrupted for a few hours. A word of caution: as patients recover from an illness, they overestimate their ability to cope with the activities of daily life. Nature will quickly let them know the limitations of their strength. Be nearby in case your assistance is needed during any phase of attempted independence on the part of the patient.

Cleanliness is important to the welfare and comfort of the patient. It keeps the patient and bedding free from perspiration and body discharges and protects other family members from possible infection. Careful washing of your hands before and after giving nursing care is a basic precaution against the spread of infection.

I have seen patients meticulously cared for with the exception of clean hair and scalp. If the patient does not have a fever there is no reason why a shampoo cannot be given in draft-free room, followed by quick drying with an electric hair drier.

Women feel better if their hair is set in rollers and kept brushed and combed in their customary manner; the application of makeup and a touch of perfume or hand lotion add the finishing touches both in appearance and morale. Men should be kept cleanshaven if that is their daily habit. Deodorants and powder may be applied for comfort. Encouraging the patient to take an interest in his or her appearance can be a valuable therapeutic aid.

Pulse, breathing and temperature

Pulse, respiratory rate and temperature are all useful indicators of the patient's condition. The pulse is the throbbing caused by the heart as it forces blood through the arteries; respiration is the act of inspiration and expiration, the exchange of air and carbon dioxide in the lungs. Rate and rhythm of pulse and respiration and the temperature vary somewhat with age, sex, body size and physical and emotional activity. Usually, as the body temperature rises, both the pulse and respiration rates increase.

Procedure: Have a clock or watch with a second hand and locate the pulse by placing the fingers (not the thumb) on the palm side of the patient's wrist between the tendons and the wristbone. When you are sure you have a good location and feel the beating pulse, look at the clock and start counting. Thirty seconds is long enough; multiply by two for pulse rate. Count the patient's respirations; you are more likely to get an accurate count if the patient is unaware that you are counting. Count the number of times the chest rises for 30 seconds and multiply by two. Record both the pulse and respiratory rate on your daily record, noting the time they were taken.

For an accurate reading, the thermometer must be kept under the tongue for at least three minutes. Do not take an oral temperature immediately after the patient has had hot or cold food or fluids. Take the temperature in the rectum when it cannot safely be taken in the mouth. In some cases it may be necessary to take the temperature in the axilla (armpit); the thermometer should be left in position for at least five minutes to give an accurate axillary reading. A rectal temperature should not be taken right after the patient has had an enema as the temperature will not be correct.

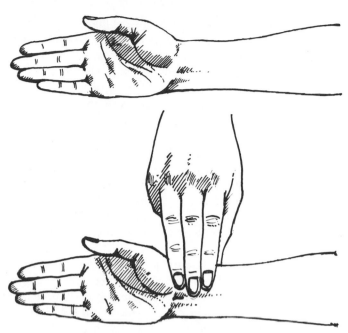

This diagram shows the correct way of feeling a patient's pulse at the wrist. Fingertips, not the thumb, should be used and it is important to count the beats accurately for exactly 30 seconds. Multiply the result by 2 to get the pulse rate.

A thermometer should always be held by the top, opposite the bulb end. To read, hold the thermometer in your right hand, with the bulb ending pointing left. Rotate the thermometer slowly until you see a clear line in the glass; the numerical readings will be along the side. In a

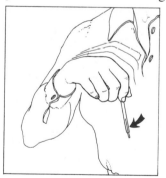

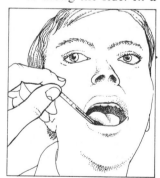

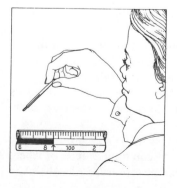

To take a patient's temperature, the mercury must first be shaken down. It is then placed under the tongue for 3 minutes with the mouth closed. Remember that hot or cold drinks consumed beforehand will cause false readings.

good light, see where the mercury, or red fluid, stops. Long lines on a thermometer designate degrees and short lines designate two tenths of a degree.

After taking the temperature, wash the thermometer in cool (never hot) water, shake down with a brisk wrist movement to bring the mercury down to about 95°F and store in a safe, cool place.

Elimination

The number, frequency and consistency of bowel movements should be noted. Any changes in color or consistency should be reported to the doctor. Diarrhea is characterized by frequent, watery stools and may be caused as a response to medications, infection, emotional strain, viruses or poisonous foods; it is one of nature's ways of removing noxious substances from the body. It may cause serious dehydration very quickly, especially in young children and the elderly; severe or persistent diarrhea should be reported to the doctor. After an episode of diarrhea, cleanse the patient and the area. Bed rest is indicated until symptoms have subsided.

Stool softeners may aid in relieving constipation. Lessened physical activity may change customary elimination habits. Do not give strong laxatives.

Urine: the amount, odor, color, and frequency should be noted.

Vomitus or other body discharges, however unpleasant, must be checked and reported. When a bedridden patient vomits, turn his head to the side to prevent aspiration (breathing in the vomitus inadvertently). When vomiting occurs, wait awhile and then offer very small amounts of water. If this is tolerated, give water, tea or ginger ale in increasing amounts about every half-hour. The best course to follow when starting to give solid foods is to offer small portions of bland, fat-free foods and progress to a full diet that the patient wants and enjoys.

If vomiting is persistent, withhold fluids. Report the color, character and frequency to the doctor. When any body discharge is unusual, save a specimen in a clean household container for the doctor to examine.

The sick child

Children and adults may experience the same illness quite differently, in large part because of the anatomical, physiological and psychological differences. Anatomical differences are obvious. Physiologically, a child may be more susceptible to certain diseases and the probability of lasting harm may be greater. Any condition that causes loss of body fluid—for example, diarrhea or fever—quickly alters a child's body chemistry.

Reaction to illness differs in various age groups. Since the infant or toddler cannot tell you how he feels or where the pain is located, he must be observed closely. Any

behavior indicating pain should never be ignored. Sudden changes in the condition of a young child, given his inability to express how he feels, are warning signals for the home nurse to be constantly on the alert.

Children are sensitive to suggestion and the mother who is apprehensive and alarmed creates similar feelings in the child. The child's attention span is short but intense and can often be shifted from his bodily discomfort to something pleasant. Response to endeavors to amuse a child should not be regarded as evidence that the cause of pain or discomfort has abated.

Once the acute stage of an illness is over, the child must not be allowed to feel that he is alone in his difficulties. This does not mean that a family member must constantly be with him, but rather that he should be made to feel secure in knowing someone will come when he cries or calls for help.

Medications don't always taste good and skill is needed to persuade children to take some types of them. For a very young child the taste may be disguised by crushing pills or emptying capsules in applesauce or jelly. In general, put the medication in the first teaspoonful only, then follow with the unmixed portion of the food. Older children should be told truthfully that the taste is unpleasant, but that the medication is necessary for them to get well. The best approach is positive, calm, kind and firm: there should be no implication by word, tone of voice or manner that there is any doubt in your mind about his taking the medication. Sometimes, the child would rather take the medication himself, rather than having it given to him. Let him. Never, never hold a child's nose or force medication into his mouth, for he may aspirate it into the lungs and suffer severe complications! If the medication is immediately vomited, the physician should be notified. He should also be notified if the child's cooperation cannot be obtained and medication is not taken.

Your doctor will tell you if a special diet is needed. Otherwise, a regular diet is given. Small, attractive portions should be offered—a large plate, loaded with food, often "turns off" any listless child. Let the child set his own pace and let him feed himself; don't let your own anxieties show by insisting that he eats all foods served. Once a child is balky, and once a mother becomes worried or angry, he becomes less inclined to eat. It is better to add nourishment between meals than to attempt to overfeed the patient at regular mealtimes.

When bed rest is ordered, a very young child may need his mother very close by and may need to be held almost continuously. A rocking chair serves two needs: it gives the mother a needed rest, of sorts, and the rocking motion and the security of being closely held lulls a sick child into needed sleep.

Older children can be kept occupied with coloring books, games, television and visits from friends and family. Children have amazing recuperative powers. If it's just too much of a problem keeping them in bed, ask the doctor if some ambulation around the home is allowed. The doctor will usually allow the child to extend his activities to whatever his illness can tolerate.

Everyone has a point of exhaustion—even mothers. The emotional and physical strain of caring for a sick child can be overwhelming and temporary relief from the pressure may be necessary. Other family members can and should help. Take care of yourself and try to have adequate nutrition and rest. The sick child is your priority at this time; other household duties will have to wait and other family members will have to understand the situation.

Good posture and body mechanics

Posture is the relationship of the various parts of the body. Good posture for the patient and the home nurse is necessary to prevent strain, fatigue, discomfort or injury. Body mechanics is the way the body moves. It is important for the welfare of the patient—whether he is in bed, in a wheelchair or able to walk—that awareness be given both to his posture and to his body mechanics. When the home nurse practices good body mechanics and good posture, there is less expenditure of energy. When working with a bedridden patient, stand with your feet comfortably apart, one foot forward. Stand close to the work area, flexing hips and knees when stooping or bending. Use the longest and strongest muscles of the legs and arms when moving or lifting. Move a bed patient by turning and sliding, since this requires less effort than lifting.

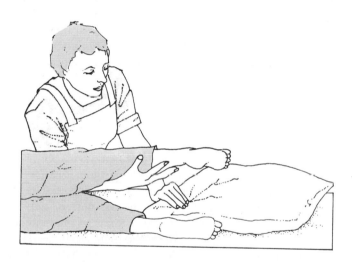

If a patient is unable to move himself in bed, the home nurse can change his position without unnecessary strain to himself and without causing discomfort or injury to the patient. It is a mistake to permit an immobile patient to remain in one position for any length of time. Sick people have the tendency to prefer one position, either because it alleviates pain or just out of habit. Prolonged immobility causes fatigue, loss of muscle tone, decreased circulation to pressure points (which often results in bedsores, or decubitus ulcers), and an increased likelihood of muscle contractures and joint stiffness.

Assistance is needed to move an immobile patient up in bed. Facing the bed, flex the patient's knees; one person places his or her arms (palms up) under the patient's neck across under the shoulders to the opposite shoulder. The other person places his or her arms under the patient's buttocks and thighs. On signal, they slide the patient toward the head of the bed. A "draw sheet" is most often used, which is simply a folded sheet placed under the patient, extending from shoulders to knees; it is used for pulling the patient up in bed and for turning him. It is easier to move a patient with a draw sheet because the weight of the patient is more evenly distributed. After a patient has been moved with a draw sheet, always make sure it is pulled taut and tucked in so that no wrinkles remain under the patient.

A paralyzed patient should be cushioned as shown here so that pressure is taken off the skin over bony prominences such as elbows and heels. A pillow placed between the ankles is particularly valuable. It is still necessary to turn the patient at least once every 3 hours around the clock and this can be done most easily by using a draw sheet.

To turn a patient onto his side, first move him to the side of the bed opposite to the one where he will finally lie. If you are alone, place both hands, palms up, under the head and shoulders of the patient and pull toward you, pulling and turning at the same time. Working in steps, pull and turn in like manner the lower back and hips, and flex the patient's knees. Look at the patient. Does his body look comfortably arranged? Does the position seem awkward? Have pillows ready to help support the patient as you work; inexpensive throw cushions are useful for this, for they are a convenient size. Flex the patient's upper knee. Straighten the lower leg. A small pillow between the patient's knees and ankles helps to maintain the position and relieve pressure. Make small adjustments for comfort and good posture, with the body—the trunk—in line with the head. If the patient is very heavy, it is easier to move the heaviest part of the body—the hips—toward you first. Get used to using a draw sheet for moving the patient and always flex knees and thighs before turning; put the patient's arms either folded on his chest or straight on his abdomen before turning. Before leaving the patient, check to see that he is not lying on an arm, or that, in turning, the downward ear is not doubled over. Adjust the patient's hair so that it is free from tension. Many patients, especially stroke victims, may be acutely uncomfortable from some minor problem and unable to communicate their discomfort to you.

Just as bed rest is a form of treatment, self-help has a beneficial effect on the morale of the patient. The patient who is not totally immobile should be encouraged to do as much as possible for himself. The amount of activity allowed, even in bed, will vary according to the patient's condition. Most doctors want their patients to do as much for themselves as possible, including changing their own position and posture.

Bedridden patients and problems of elimination

If the patient must stay in bed, either because of immobility or because of the doctor's strict orders, the home nurse needs to provide a bedpan. When a bedpan is to be used, keep it in a convenient place, keep it covered when not in use, and place it in an area away from possible contamination. Besides the usual bedpans, there are child-sized bedpans and a small, slanted bedpan called a "fracture pan." Before giving a bedpan to a patient, be sure its seat is dry. A sprinkling of talcum powder greatly eases the discomfort of friction caused when the pan is placed and removed. If the patient can help, let him. Flex his knees and lift his hips off the bed during placement. Turn back one cover of the bedding for easier access to the patient, but try to keep him covered as much as possible, to prevent both chills and embarrassment. A pillow placed under the small of the patient's back helps maintain better alignment and

This illustration shows how a bedridden patient can be helped onto a bedpan. If the patient is very heavy or completely unable to help, it may be necessary for two nurses to lift him or her joining hands underneath the knees and behind the shoulders.

raising his head and shoulders with pillows prevents an awkward posture.

If possible, leave the patient alone. Most people require privacy at this time. When elimination is completed, remove the bedpan, cleanse the area, cover the bedpan and remove it from the room. The patient who cannot aid in placement of the bedpan needs to be turned onto his side, facing away from the nurse. Place the open side of the bedpan against the buttocks, depressing the mattress down as much as possible, then with a pulling, turning motion, turn the patient onto his back. To remove the patient from the bedpan, hold the pan firmly on the mattress and roll the patient off, again facing away from the nurse. Remove the pan from the bed and give personal care as needed; leave the patient dry, clean and covered. Examine the contents of the pan for color, consistency and amount and note the frequency of bowel movements. Dispose of the contents and cleanse the pan, first in cold water then in hot soapy water. Always hold a bedpan by the side and never by the open end (which is the front of the pan) or by the closed end tip (which goes directly under the patient).

Dry the pan, cover it, and put it back in its customary place. Nothing is more maddening than to have a hurry call from a patient and to have to scurry around trying to find the bedpan. Have all family members who participate in home care follow the same routine as to where equipment is kept and replaced.

If the patient can tolerate getting out of bed, the use of a commode is more effective. It requires less energy than using the bedpan and the body position is more normal. The procedure used is the same as getting a patient from the bed to a bedside chair. As in all procedures, plan ahead, have supplies within reach, and be aware that the nurse's responsibility is to provide the assistance needed by the patient. A urinal for males should be kept within reach if the patient is able to use it. A urinal must be emptied after each voiding. Note the color, odor, clarity and amount of urine voided and record this information on your daily notes. If the urine is tested for sugar and acetone, the test must be done on a freshly voided specimen and the results recorded.

The incontinent patient

Incontinence is the medical word for loss of control of the bladder and bowels. This happens frequently in elderly people who have loss of sensation in the area. Some handicapped people, particularly those with paralysis below the waist, cannot control elimination. Incontinence is difficult for both the patient and the home nurse. The doctor may be able to give specific suggestions regarding diet and bladder or bowel training. If the patient is aware of the problem, he typically feels humiliated and depressed; thus the home nurse must be careful not to show annoyance, disgust or impatience. It is a very difficult problem and the nurse must constantly bear in mind that the patient cannot help it, no more than can a tiny infant.

A "Foley catheter" may be inserted by the visiting nurse or the doctor. Get specific instructions for the care of the catheter insertion area, the bedside drainage bag and the proper method of taping to the leg to prevent trauma. If a patient has been in the hospital with a Foley catheter, often the bladder can be trained to hold a certain volume of urine before voiding. This is done by clamping the catheter, first for short durations, then gradually extending the time. This should only be done on doctor's orders, for the danger of urinary tract infection is always present. The patient's condition may be such that this type of training will not be effective but it is worth inquiring about the possibilities, especially if the patient has an almost constant dribble of urine.

Protection of the bed with a waterproof mattress cover is necessary. A waterproof flannel-covered rubber sheet, or plastic sheeting placed under the draw sheet, saves changing the entire bed each time. Adult-sized "diapers" are available from some rental services; however, if the patient is alert and oriented, the use of the adult diaper can be emotionally devastating. Literature on bladder training can be obtained from the U.S. Government Printing Office, Washington, D.C.

The patient will need special skin care because the skin comes in contact with the urinary and bowel discharges. Change the patient and wash and dry the contaminated areas immediately. Sprays, deodorizing powders and wicks help to eliminate odors. Bladder training involves following a routine which, once established, must be followed throughout the entire day and night. Factors that determine the success of training will be amount, frequency and kind of fluid intake and the regularity of the patient's attempts to void. Bowel training is easier to establish, since the diet helps to control the regularity of the bowel movements. Stool softeners help prevent constipation. Some patients may be stimulated with a glycerine suppository. Do not use enemas or laxatives unless ordered by the doctor, since the body quickly becomes dependent on the stimuli from them and will not evacuate stools in a normal manner.

Bedsores

If the patient is elderly, immobile or suffering from inadequate protection, prevention of bedsores is another difficult problem for the home nurse. Bedsores (also known as *pressure sores* or *decubitus ulcers*) are caused by prolonged pressure, especially on the bony prominences of the body—the base of the spine, shoulder blades, heels, elbows and hips. Dampness, wrinkles in bedding, crumbs, all contribute to skin and muscle destruction.

Special air-filled mattresses, which alleviate pressure, can be rented from surgical supply houses. Synthetic sheepskin, which is washable, also helps. The only really effective way to prevent bedsores is to reposition the patient, at least every three hours, around the clock—turn more frequently if possible. Dry, taut sheeting and cleanliness are essential. Foam padding on the bed under pressure spots is an aid.

No aids can obviate the need for frequent repositioning of the patient. Turn the patient on his right side and put pillows under his back for support. After two or three hours, turn the patient on his back in a flat position; then two or three hours later turn him on his left side, propping again with pillows for support. Keep good body alignment in mind. The heels and elbows most frequently become sore from friction caused by constant contact with the bedding. Heels may be elevated off the sheet by placing a small pillow or rolled-up towel under the ankles. Small soft flannel rolls under the elbows protect them.

If a bedsore develops despite careful nursing, notify the doctor, as there are several treatments that can aid in healing the painful sore. The skin is typically raw and red and easily becomes a source of infection and discomfort to the patient.

Bed baths

Only helpless, critically ill, or very young patients need to be washed by the home nurse.

Skin care is essential to clean and refresh, to aid in circulation, to aid in elimination of waste given off by the skin, and to provide exercise (even if only passively).

Fever increases the secretions through the pores of the

skin. Tepid or cool sponge baths are often ordered by the doctor to reduce fever. Do not use iced water or chilled alcohol as they will only make the patient shiver—and the body's reaction to a chill is to increase its temperature. When giving a tepid or cool bath for fever reduction, do only one area at a time, gently sponging. Uncover one area—for example, the left arm; sponge lightly, then let the arm dry. Pay special attention to the axilla (armpit): leave a cool wet washcloth there while the rest of the arm and shoulder are being washed. After drying, cover lightly and go to another area.

The skin of an elderly person tends to be very dry. Avoid using soap as much as possible and don't leave the soap in the bath water; keep it in a soap dish and use it only on the washcloth for the axilla and genital areas.

Giving a bed bath requires, once again, thinking ahead, assembling equipment and good organization. Choose a time that is convenient for you and for the patient. Nowhere is it written in stone that a bath must be given in the morning, in the evening or even daily. Prepare the patient by telling him you are going to give him a bath. Even unresponsive patients should always be told when they are going to be subjected to any procedure. Have the room warm and free from drafts. Avoid exposing the patient; keep a light cover over him to avoid embarrassment.

The nurse's attitude will be reflected in the patient's response. Encourage the patient to do as much as possible. Consider the fundamentals of safety, comfort, efficiency and effectiveness. Start with oral care. If the patient is unable to participate, the home nurse can brush the teeth and give sips of cool water as a mouthwash. Have a small basin and tissues nearby. Brush and comb the hair. Remove the patient's gown or pajamas. Place a towel under the head and under each area as you work. Avoid using a saturated washcloth, and do not use soap except where necessary. Avoid dragging a towel across any part of the skin. Pat the skin dry. Protect the bedding with towels or newspapers. Rinse and dry each area before proceeding.

After the neck and shoulders, wash the arms and hands; place the patient's hands in the basin and clean the nails carefully. Immersion in the warm water is the only way to get hands really clean; it is usually a lifelong habit and psychologically makes the patient feel cleaner. Change the bath water. Next, wash the legs, one at a time, keeping the other covered. Inspect the skin throughout the bathing procedure for redness, swelling, sores or any changes. Immersing the patient's feet in the basin (one at a time)—with the knee flexed and the foot placed flat in the basin—is of tremendous comfort to the patient, although it need not necessarily be done at each bathing.

Change the bath water, then wash the patient's trunk, rinse and dry; then wash the abdomen, rinse and dry. Turn the patient and wash the back in long firm strokes. When washing a feverish patient, care must be taken to avoid

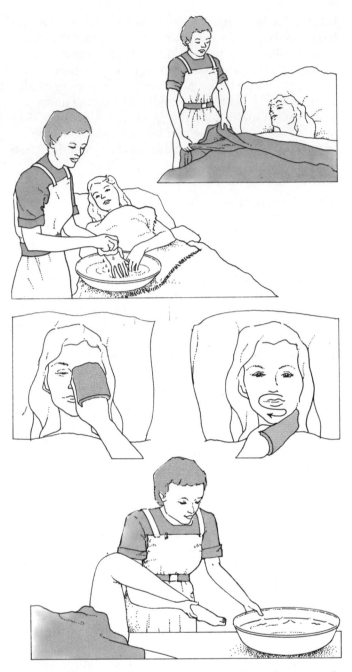

Patients should always be encouraged to do as much for themselves as possible, but the seriously ill will need a nurse to wash them. When cleaning the patient's face, the nurse should always wash from the center out towards the hairline, and wipe around the mouth in an S motion. Before immersing the patient's hands or feet in water, always check that it is at a comfortable temperature.

infection. Always wash the genital area from front to back. Always test the temperature of the water, as patients may be easily burned or chilled and they are more sensitive to extremes; what may seem reasonable to the nurse is not always the right temperature for the patient. They will usually react by pulling away from the stimulus if the water is too hot or too cold.

Some patients resent their loss of independence and find it difficult to accept bed bathing. Others regress and seem to enjoy dependence. Insist that the patient participate in his daily care if he is able—even if it is only to the extent of washing his face and brushing his teeth.

Now that the patient is all clean and dry, loosen the bedding on all sides and leave a blanket over the patient for warmth and protection. Gather fresh linen to make the bed. Roll the bedridden patient to one side of the bed, adjust his arms and legs so that he is comfortable and move the pillow to that side of the bed. Have a fresh, clean pillow ready for later repositioning. With the patient on his side, roll all bedding lengthwise onto the unoccupied side of the bed; roll as close and as tightly to the patient's back as possible. It is assumed that the bed has a waterproof mattress cover. If the cover is damp, wipe it dry with a towel and place a fresh sheet lengthwise on the bed, centering it with a folded roll near the patient. Tuck in the top, then the outer edges, keeping it wrinkle-free and tucking in the sides fully under the mattress. Next, fold a large sheet in half and place it on top of the bottom sheet, centering it so that it goes approximately from the shoulders to the hips of the patient. This is your draw sheet.

Follow the same procedure of tucking in along the outer edge of the mattress and making a flat roll next to the patient's back. To prevent fresh sheets from being dampened by wet sheets from the bed bath, place towels between the soiled sheets and the fresh sheets. Now roll the patient over or have him turn to the other side. There will be a hump in the middle of the bed, so tell the patient to expect it as he rolls over. Try to keep the top cover loose so that when the patient turns, the top cover does not get under his body. With the patient on the clean side of the bed, remove the soiled pillow and place a fresh pillow under his head.

Since the soiled bedding is all loose, it may be removed quickly and easily in one deft sweep. Pull the clean bottom sheet and draw sheet toward you, starting in the middle. Pull as taut as possible and tuck in all around. Reposition the patient and help him put on a fresh gown or pajamas. Put on a fresh top sheet over the light covering first; then, while holding the top sheet securely, withdraw the light covering and add fresh blankets as needed. This may all sound very complicated, but it really isn't; with good organization and practice, the necessary skill and efficiency are easily acquired.

A final retouch of the hair, some deodorant, perhaps a little perfume—and always a *smile*—complete a job well done. Keep in mind that the top sheet and blankets should be loose at the bottom of the bed. There are different ways to allow for looseness. A vertical pleat may be made in the center, or an extra fold made near the foot of the bed; before tucking in the top sheet and blanket, allow for freedom of motion with no restriction. A tight, taut upper cover may look nice and neat, but the patient's comfort has priority over appearance.

Getting out of bed

After a patient has been bedridden for a time, even for a relatively brief period, he will most likely require assistance in getting out of bed. The doctor's orders should be strictly followed about when the patient is to be allowed out of bed, how often and to what extent. As the patient convalesces he will usually regain strength to increase his movements in bed. Assist the patient in sitting up in bed first; place your arm, palm up, across his shoulders and upper back and help him to the sitting position. Gradually he will be able to sit up in bed unaided. Don't be discouraged if the patient's progress seems slow; the nurse must realize that the patient may be depressed by a less than rapid recovery of strength. By all means encourage the patient to do all he can for himself; but assist him in his efforts, and don't belabor or belittle him on a day when *you* think he could be doing more than he is capable of doing physically or emotionally. Take for granted that he will have good days and bad days. As his strength returns, the patient will do more for himself; the nurse will be at his side, giving less physical support and more moral support.

The advantages of getting out of bed are numerous and very important. It improves the morale of both the patient and his family, actively involves muscles and improves their tone, gives the back a chance for improved circulation and improves breathing. The appetite is stimulated, since the patient may eat his meals in a more normal position and feel more socially acceptable.

Use of proper body mechanics is the most important aspect of helping a patient out of bed and into a chair. Again, think ahead and prepare for what is needed. Have a comfortable chair ready. A blanket spread over the entire chair is a good idea; it can be later wrapped around the patient's shoulders, body and legs for warmth and may be more comfortable than a robe, especially for the first few times out of bed. The chair should be firmly placed facing the foot of the bed, with one arm touching the bed. If in any doubt about your ability to assist the patient alone, have another family member work with you.

First, get the patient up in bed and let the legs dangle over the edge. Wait a few minutes. Watch for dizziness or any change in facial color. Let the patient adjust to the change in position. Stand directly in front of the patient in case he suddenly falls forward. Have a good steady stance with one foot forward. Be prepared for any sudden swaying or pitching forward—or backward. After the patient has overcome any dizziness he may feel, allow him a few more minutes to feel secure. Put your hands, thumbs up, under the patient's armpits. Make sure you are directly facing the patient and have him place his hands on your hips or shoulders for support. Help the patient to come to a full standing position, with your legs and knees directly in front of him. Let the patient stand erect for a moment then sidestep with the patient to the chair, continuing to give full support. Have the patient put the back of his legs against the front of the chair so that he gets a sense of orientation to the placement of the chair. Lower the patient into the chair, bending your knees and hips in preparation for the shift of weight. Wrap the blanket around the patient and place his feet on a low hassock or footstool if it adds to his comfort.

The patient should be watched for signs of fatigue. Sometimes the first time out of bed is for a very limited period, perhaps only ten minutes. Be prepared in advance for assistance in getting the patient out of bed and in returning him quickly to bed if he shows evidence of extreme weakness or fatigue. Do not extend the time limit, especially during the first few times out of bed. If the doctor orders one half-hour, make it exactly 30 minutes, not 45 minutes, since extending the time may do more harm than good. Some doctors may order "as tolerated"—and that means the *patient's* tolerance, not yours.

While the patient is out of bed, the nurse may air the bed, freshen the bed linen, brush the patient's hair, give oral care—anything—but the nurse must stay in the room with the patient. This is of the utmost importance. Patients can either fatigue quickly and fall out of the chair or decide they have had enough of you telling them what they can and cannot do and decide to go back to bed by themselves. Since they overestimate their own strength, a disastrous fall to the floor can be avoided if you stay in the room with them. If a patient is confused or disoriented, two people are definitely required to get the patient in and out of the bed. A restraint, called a Posey Belt, is available from surgical supply firms, and is the most effective and safest way to help keep a confused patient in a chair. No restraints are entirely foolproof and the nurse or a member of the family is the best protection.

Helping the patient back into bed is as much work as getting him out of bed, sometimes more, for he may be fatigued and less able to give any help. Have the patient flex his knees and push forward to the edge of the chair, using his arms to push himself to the upright position. The nurse stands facing the patient, lifting up as he pushes up. Sidestep to the bed. Assist the patient to the sitting position on the bed. Supporting his legs by one arm under the knees, and the shoulders with one arm across the back of the shoulders, swing the patient into a lying position. Cover and make the patient comfortable; note his reaction and how well he tolerated the entire procedure.

For convalescing patients, the first few times out of bed are very tiring. It's a lot of work for them at this stage of recovery. Helping the patient to walk requires only supportive assistance. Using the same technique of getting the patient out of bed and onto his feet, start walking alongside. Let the patient set the pace; take only a few steps

Helping a person to sit up in bed is an easy procedure, providing it is done properly as shown above. Your left arm should raise the patient's shoulders and he or she should lift him or herself at the same time by pulling on your right shoulder.

and give as much assistance as needed while you assess the patient's ability. Many patients find it more helpful to lean on your extended arm rather than being given support in any other manner. Let the patient verbalize and exchange ideas with you concerning the best management techniques. Encourage good posture. Patients tend to flex the spine and walk bent over; get them to stand tall with the head up—which is not only good for morale, but good for the muscles and circulation as well.

Many of these nursing skills are needed in the care of the helpless patient or in the care of the patient with long-term illness or disability. A difficult problem to face is the occasional realization that (realistically) the patient may never regain the ability to care for himself. Partial self-care may deteriorate to a point of complete dependence. As long as the patient can participate in even minimal self-care, encourage him to do it; give him enough time to complete a task and don't get impatient. The activity, no matter how slowly or clumsily it may be accomplished, has real meaning for the patient. You could undoubtedly do the same thing for the patient in a matter of moments, but you may be denying the last shred of self-reliance left to him.

Feeding the patient unable to feed himself

Prepare the patient for the food service by first explaining what you are going to do. Wash the patient's hands and, of course, your own. Prop the patient up into a sitting position or at least insure that his or her head and shoulders are elevated. Test the food for temperature, since very young children and the elderly cannot tolerate food which is too hot. They may be burned and unable to tell you. The wrist test, similar to the testing of the temperature of a baby's bottle, is an old tried and true test. Place a drop of food on the inner aspect of your wrist. If the drop doesn't feel too hot, then it is of a satisfactory temperature. Taking a sip of the food—soup, tea, mashed potatoes, etc.—is not sanitary, is not a reliable test and is not recommended.

Put a bib or towel across the patient's chest under the chin and have a dry washcloth or tissues ready. Elderly patients may have some difficulty swallowing; soft or pureed foods, offered in portions of half a teaspoonful, are the easiest for them to swallow. Don't hurry the mealtime but try to keep the food warm and palatable. Liquids should be offered in frequent small amounts. It is easier to handle one or two tablespoonsful of a liquid (consomme, soup, tea, creamed soups, etc.) if it is given in a very small glass. Less mess and less waste.

Patients may prefer drinking through straws, which enables them to set their own limits of intake. Remove the tray when the patient is finished, because it is a mistake to think that maybe the patient will eat a little more later if you leave the tray at the bedside; nothing looks less appetizing than cold, leftover food on a messy tray. Wash the dishes immediately afterward and, to save time, reset the tray with essentials for the next meal and cover with a clean napkin or dish towel. The home nurse will, by trial and error, soon learn what may be best in caring for the patient. Record the time of feeding, the amount taken and the patient's reaction.

Home treatments

Simple treatments are often given by the home nurse on doctor's orders. The exact purpose of the treatment is varied, but all are aimed at helping the patient get well, or making him more comfortable. Some treatments prevent more serious problems, such as the danger of spreading infection from one source to another. Heat and cold applications are commonly used home remedies. Heat

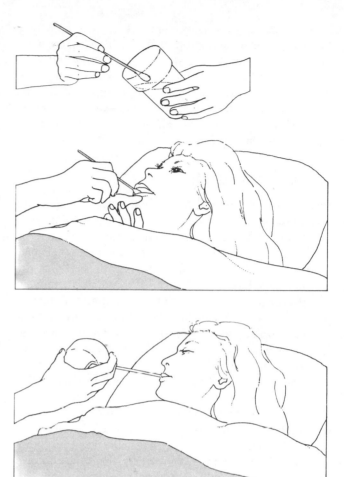

It can be an uncomfortable and degrading experience for an adult patient to be fed unless it is carefully and skillfully done. Soft or pureed foods given in small portions by teaspoon are often the easiest to swallow. It is much more pleasant for a patient to regulate his or her own intake of fluid through a straw, rather than be helped with a cup.

applications help to relax muscles, ease tension, relieve pain, increase circulation and provide warmth. Cold applications help to reduce the body temperature, reduce inflammation, relieve pain and control bleeding.

You must be aware that ill people are apt to be especially sensitive to heat—particularly moist heat, which is more penetrating and conducts faster than an application of a dry heat. Heat treatments are varied. The electric pad, the heat lamp, a hot water bottle, hot baths, hot irrigations, enemas and moist compresses. Whenever in doubt, keep in mind that what seems quite hot to you is probably much too hot for the patient.

A hot water bottle should be only two-thirds filled with water. Before filling, push the air out of the bag to make it more flexible; it will then fit the contours of the body more closely. Secure the stopper tightly, dry the exterior of the bag and wrap in flannel or soft material; never place the rubber bag directly on the patient's skin.

Moist compresses are best prepared using pieces of wool cloth placed in hot water, wrung out tightly and then placed on the afflicted area. If the patient is allergic to wool, cotton may be used. The hot moist compress should be loosely applied and then covered with a waterproof plastic wrap. Be sure to extend the edges of the wrap past the compress, since a damp bed is a chilly bed.

Caring for wounds

Before changing dressings on a wound, have a paper bag open and ready for disposal of soiled dressings. Don't ever put them on the bed, the bedside table, the floor, a chair or any other place that happens to be handy. Have the paper bag ready and place the soiled dressing promptly in the paper or plastic bag. After the soiled dressing is removed, follow the doctor's instructions as to irrigations, ointments or any care ordered. Wash your hands thoroughly with hot soapy water and apply a clean (preferably sterile) dressing.

If you notice any skin breakdown from constant application and removal of adhesive tape, you might try a nonallergic paper tape, which is available in pharmacies. The frequency of changing dressings will depend largely on the amount of drainage from the wound; if a dressing is dry and intact, leave it alone unless ordered otherwise. Excessive changes of the dressing may lead to more infection and more damage to the skin from the adhesive tape. If you are unsure about any part of the procedure, ask the doctor or the public health nurse.

Nursing care of the handicapped

Nursing care focuses not on what is lost but what remains, and the regaining of the patient's fullest potential. The patient must be motivated by encouragement and self-will to regain as much of his physical and emotional activity as is possible.

A basic human need is to be independent. The individual's sense of self-esteem and dignity are based on a need for independence. The home nurse should be aware that the psychological needs of the patient may vary in degree from time to time and she should be flexible in adjusting to the patient's particular needs at particular times. Community resources may be available. Call the social worker at your local hospital or call the visiting nurse agency; they usually have "resources lists" available and can be of inestimable help in finding out where you can get medical, surgical or rehabilitation care, supplies or advice. Your doctor will tell you what active or passive exercises may be appropriate.

Rehabilitation is often a slow process. How the patient reacts emotionally toward his rehabilitation will depend on his own hopes and the amount of love and support he receives from his family. Emotional problems, feeding problems, bedsores, elimination problems and immobility may be expected.

In an area where a patient is paralyzed there is usually no sensation. The handicapped person has to practice and develop skills which we take for granted; allow him time to develop these skills. Such patients have to think consciously about the effort involved in retraining muscles, and they have to summon up the energy to make those muscles work for them. They need time. The home nurse should schedule a generous amount of time so that the exercises are not rushed and should give assistance only when the patient absolutely needs it. When a patient is trying an exercise for the first time, he may need assistance to succeed in the task. Give encouragement, instructions and supervision. Where he has tried and become tired, offer the patient minimal assistance.

The disabled person should be encouraged to wear normal daytime clothing. Constantly wearing pajamas, bathrobe and slippers tends to lead to withdrawal from normal living and keeps the patient in the "invalid role." Give the handicapped person his clothing and place it in the order in which it will be put on. Start with the affected side first, then let the patient finish the job to the best of his ability. Clothing that is one size larger than the patient usually wears is easier to place. Simple clothing, with large buttons and button holes, velcro adhesive snaps, loose elastic belts, zippers either in front or back and dresses which button down the front all help to avoid frustration.

It may be difficult for the nurse to stand by and be an encourager and assister, rather than a "doer." If the patient expects to regain partial independence he must be an active participant in his own care. Start the dressing in the bed or a chair with arms. Use your community resources. You are not alone in dealing with any disabled patient. Your physician, the hospital or community social worker, the visiting nurse service, public health nurses, the American Red Cross, the nationwide chapters of organizations with special interests in certain types of patients can all help you. Pamphlets and other literature may be obtained from the American Cancer Society, the American Heart Association, the National Society for Crippled Children and Adults and the U.S. Department of Health, Education and Welfare. Many pharmaceutical companies have free publications that are good guides to home care. The role of the home nurse is different when caring for a patient with a long-term illness than when caring for one with a short-term convalescence period. Seek out help.

Professional help

Although the physical, emotional and financial burden may be primarily your responsibility, involve others in your family and the community in participating in the care of the patient. Total involvement by the home nurse leads to fatigue, mentally and physically, to the detriment of herself and other members of the family. Before the home nurse reaches the point of total despair, the employment of a professional registered nurse should be considered. Many families can cope with the daytime care of a patient and feel they only need the services of a night nurse. The situation may be reversed, however; the physical care of the patient needed during the day may be too demanding. A daytime nurse would relieve you for other household or business duties, and you may feel capable of coping with the patient during the evening and nighttime hours.

When you decide that a registered nurse is needed, call a Nurse Registry. Ask for 12-hour duty nurses. Ask for references. Ask to see her license. Ask about payments (how much, how often). If at all possible, try to have continuity. Every nurse has a different personality, a different background, and if the patient is alert and well-oriented, it is difficult to adjust to a different nurse each day. Of course, nurses have "relief nurses" to cover them on their days off, but if possible try to have the same relief nurses, too.

When the nurse comes into your home, she is there because she is a trained professional. Don't interfere with her ways of working. You know the patient's likes, dislikes, schedule, original illness and present status and she will want to know them. Give her an orientation tour—the sickroom, the bathroom, the kitchen, where she may go to relax for a few minutes, the doctor's phone number, where family members may be reached when absent, the linen closet and where medicines and clean clothing are kept. The patient may resent not having the home nurse entirely devoting all her time to him. Usually, however, if told ahead of time that a registered nurse is coming to relieve you, and that this is necessary for his care and comfort, the patient will welcome or at least accept the fact.

If you employ around-the-clock nurses, one nurse should be in charge. The day nurse will call the doctor when necessary. She is a trained observer. She may also want a professional medical report from the doctor when she starts on the case. The competency of a registered nurse is difficult for the layman to evaluate; obvious responsibilities and functions may be observed—in addition to overall neatness and efficiency. These include cleanliness of the incontinent patient, administration of all medications and the charting of the patient's blood pressure, pulse, temperature and respirations.

Often it is the judgment of the nurse not to disturb a sleeping patient right on the dot of midnight to give medication. She may have given it at eleven, or she knows that the patient usually awakens at one and will give it to him then. Don't hover around and try to run the show. She's a professional, getting paid to take care of the patient so that you can get some rest. When a nurse works in a home it is expected that meals will be served to her and that you will relieve her for coffee or tea breaks and be considerate of her in every way. If she has suggestions to improve the care of the patient and needs supplies, the family should provide them. Make up a schedule of nursing coverage for both day and night, with nurses' names and their home telephone numbers. If the patient's condition deteriorates to the point where hospitalization is needed, the registered nurse can accompany the patient to the hospital and continue caring for the patient there, if necessary.

Summary

An illness may continue over a prolonged period. The home nurse needs to plan for the care of the patient, for her own personal needs and for the care of her family and home. The involvement of all members of the family in the day-to-day care of the patient gives everyone an opportunity to share in part of the work. Keep the daily record of the patient's schedule of activities, medications, treatments, intake and output where all members of the family can refer to it when necessary. Common sense and good judgment, safety, cleanliness and comfort are the fundamentals of nursing.

The home nurse can learn to give good care effectively. Special techniques and devices, properly applied, can make the care of the patient easier for you as well as for the patient. Always keep in mind that the patient's *psychological* health is as important as his *physical* health. Use all resources available in your community. They will give assistance and help the family to give the best possible care.

The Health Care of Children

Dr. Lenore S. Katkin

The modern pediatrician is an expert in diagnosing and treating diseases and disorders of childhood. The following article not only discusses the current medical treatment for a wide range of conditions that commonly affect infants and children, but provides valuable information on choosing a doctor, normal patterns of growth and development of children, nutrition in childhood and nursing a sick child.

Since the second half of the 19th century, physicians have come to recognize that infancy, childhood and adolescence are unique stages in the growth and development of human beings. With this awareness has come the realization that this population merits specific health care considerations, usually provided by pediatricians or family physicians who are knowledgeable about young patients. The common goal is to provide comprehensive health care for each child so that satisfactory growth and development is achieved, health is maintained, and impaired health is restored by proper diagnosis and therapy. Parents, too, must come to understand that the practice of pediatric medicine is not merely a "miniaturization" of adult medical practice, but rather a specialized health science encompassing all the basic scientific disciplines as well as the socioeconomic factors which affect the child and his environment.

For the first several years, parents are the primary health advocates for their children. They must assume responsibility for scheduled medical visits to insure periodic evaluation of the child's health and make sure that regular immunizations are given against infectious diseases. Parents may also sometimes need counseling in child-rearing practices.

How to choose a physician for your child

Pediatricians are physicians who have acquired a special interest and knowledge of the health needs of infants, children and adolescents by virtue of an extensive training in these areas after completion of formal medical education. Along with pediatricians there are many family physicians who, in the course of their training to provide for the health needs of complete families, have acquired sufficient expertise to deal with the health needs and problems of children. Basically, it is these physicians—together with specialists in pediatric nursing—who provide the bulk of primary medical care for children today.

How a parent chooses a physician for a child is dependent upon many factors. In certain areas, where the number of physicians or clinics is limited, then the decision is a simple one. Where a choice of medical resources exists, however, the decision is usually arrived at in a much more complicated manner.

Ideally, the first-time parent should choose a pediatrician a short while prior to the actual birth of the child. This pediatrician is frequently recommended by another physician, such as the mother's obstetrician, or by friends or relatives. A meeting prior to the baby's birth allows the parents to assess the physician's attitude without any urgency imposed by the infant's immediate medical needs. It is assumed that the physician has been educated and trained in the health requirements of children, that he therefore has a sincere interest in children and is a personal advocate for them, and that he (or, of course, she) is comfortable in the management of their illness. What the prospective parent needs to evaluate is how this physician relates to them. It is usually advisable for both parents to meet the physician at this initial visit, unless circumstances make this impossible. But I would not recommend that prospective grandparents, no matter how eager, be present at this initial interview. Questions relating to scheduling of visits, office practices and routines, and fees are appropriate to this discussion. In addition, parents need to know when it is best to call for routine questions, the procedure to obtain aid in an emergency, and what provisions the physician has for medical coverage when he is away or otherwise unavailable. Many physicians have a routine "telephone hour" to answer necessary but nonemergency questions. Some physicians include nurse practitioners as part of the expanded health team. The parent should ask about and understand the role of these "health care extenders."

Similarly, parents of older children who relocate into a new community should meet the new pediatrician prior to the acute illness of any one child. This again allows for a nonharried interview and assessment of the relationship between the health provider and the family—both parents and children.

If this relationship does not appear to be completely satisfactory, and if there is another source of health care in the community, then by all means carry the investigation further. Ideally, the relationship between the child and the physician—as well as between the parents and physician—should be one of mutual respect and affection.

We assume that a children's physician is well trained and, equally, that he or she has a sincere interest in children and is comfortable with them.

The roles of parents and physicians in health maintenance

The physician, the parents and ultimately society as a whole have a responsibility to promote healthy child growth and development, and to eliminate hazardous physical and environmental conditions which could be deleterious to this goal. The parent is the prime nurturer of the child, the primary "role model" for the child, and the child's primary stimulus for growth and development. The parent is not only responsible for the basic needs of food, clothing and shelter, but also for the basic health needs as determined by current medical practice regarding immunization and health-screening programs for diseases of infancy and later adult life.

Along with the pediatrician, parents should be made

aware of the major health problems of adult life. Four causes—heart disease, cancer, stroke and accidents—are responsible for the majority of deaths in developed nations. Heart disease, arthritis, rheumatism, back and hip disorders, and hypertension (high blood pressure) are responsible for approximately 40% of all nonfatal adult disabilities. Behavior problems, school and job failure, marital discord, unwanted pregnancy, venereal disease, and violence are major problems. Therefore, a high priority must be given to what can be done in childhood to prevent these conditions.

The major factors which we identify as the contributing entities in the above conditions—e.g., nutritional deficiencies and excesses, the abuse of tobacco and alcohol, and the lack of attention to safety—have their origins in infancy or childhood. For instance, there is good evidence to suggest that babies and children who are chubby in their early years are more likely to be obese adults. The risk of adult disease is also due in great part to heredity. The identification of individuals who have a genetic risk of a disease is now recognized as an important responsibility of pediatric medicine. Parents must be educated so that they may give guidance to their children regarding preventive measures and healthy life styles.

Normal growth and development

Is my child growing and developing normally? This is a common question of concern to parents. Physicians are obviously also concerned about this area; indeed, the usual visit begins with the taking of the child's height and weight. These are duly recorded on a growth chart, which serves to show the parent and physician the pattern of each child's physical achievement. Thus, disparities between height and weight can be noted and discussed. Parents should be reassured that a child is growing and gaining weight normally, even in the face of what the parent considers an inadequate food intake. It is usually only when a marked change occurs that some explanation must be sought. The physician is primarily concerned with changes in the growth *pattern*, since deceleration of the growth rate is one of the most sensitive and best screening tests for the early detection of some types of illness in children.

The development assessment of the young child is an ongoing activity each time the child comes to the pediatrician's office. The physician not only interviews the parent, but also observes the child and watches the parent and child interact. Parents and physicians are equally concerned about delays or deviations in motor development, communication skills, intellectual development, relationships with other children, the ability to play, and the ability to comply with the expectations of adults. When the pediatrician asks whether the baby smiles, sits, pulls to standing, walks alone or says words, he is gathering developmental data. When he watches the parent interact-

ing with the child he gains additional impressions. Additional questions are frequently asked about the child's daily routine—such as feeding habits, naps, interaction with other adults or older siblings—in order to obtain a clearer picture of the child and his family.

Many physicians use a developmental checklist such as the parent-answered Denver Prescreening Developmental Questionnaire (reproduced overleaf) to routinely check a child's progress. If the child is suspected of being slow, the physician may employ further checks (such as the Denver Developmental Screening Test) to judge the child's developmental status. If a significant delay is suspected, a referral to a pediatrician with special training in developmental diagnosis (or to a developmental neurologist or developmental psychologist) is indicated.

Parents frequently compare their baby's progress with that of other children, their own or their acquaintances. Questions about the appropriateness of a child's activity should be asked should the occasion arise; however, parents should understand that there is an approximate age range when children develop the ability to perform each social, motor and adaptive function. Whereas one baby may walk alone at 9 months, another may not do so until 15 months. Although early speech is often associated with high intelligence, there are many gifted adults who did not speak until quite late by "normal" standards. A great deal of observation and data must go into the judgment and decision about whether or not a developmental or intellectual problem exists.

Current immunization practices

Most clinicians and health care providers rely on the IMMUNIZATION guidelines established by the American Academy of Pediatrics in their *Report of the Committee on the Control of Infectious Diseases*. Although there is some variation of immunization schedules among physicians, there is general agreement about the necessity of immunization against the common childhood illnesses of DIPHTHERIA, pertussis (WHOOPING COUGH), TETANUS, POLIOMYELITIS, MEASLES, MUMPS and rubella (GERMAN MEASLES). After the primary series of immunizations, which are given during the first and second years of life, booster doses of certain antigens are recommended at stated intervals during later childhood and adolescence.

Some vaccines have side effects which are usually predictable, mild and self-limited. Occasionally a more severe adverse reaction may occur. The incidence of side effects and adverse reactions, however, must be contrasted with the risks of the disease. Parents should discuss with the health personnel administering the vaccines the nature and frequency of side effects. At the next visit, parents and patients should report any unusual reaction. Where abnormal reactions do occur—such as a very high temperature, or severe local redness or swelling—repeat vaccination with the same agent should be avoided. If there are compelling reasons for repeating the vaccination, fractional doses should be used.

Children should not be immunized in the face of an acute, febrile illness. Certain youngsters who have *immunodeficiency disorders*, or who are taking medications which suppress the immune system, should not be immunized. In addition, children who are allergic to eggs, chickens or ducks should not receive vaccines which are grown on chick or duck embryos; these include vaccines against influenza, yellow fever and rabies (duck embryo rabies vaccine). Measles, rubella and mumps vaccines are grown on chick or duck *fibroblast tissue cultures* which do not contain egg albumin or yolk components, and therefore are considered safe for allergic individuals.

Passive immunization (with gamma globulin) is used to provide temporary immunity when active immunization is not available (as in the case of viral hepatitis) or when active immunization has not been given prior to exposure (as in tetanus or rabies). Either standard immune serum globulin or special human immune serum globulin for specific illnesses is used. Passive immunization is not always effective and the duration of action may be short or variable. (See also IMMUNE SYSTEM.)

Immunization schedules should be recorded by both the physician and the parents. Too often parents rely only on the physician's records and do not have an accurate record of their own. The record should indicate not only the date of administration, but also the type of vaccine used and the amount given. Immunization records are necessary throughout childhood and even into later years.

Nutrition in childhood

The first major concern of parents, after the initial assurance that a newborn is normal and healthy, is what and how to feed and nourish the infant. This concern should remain throughout infancy, childhood and adolescence because it is during these crucial years that the child's diet is modified to meet the needs for normal growth and development. While malnutrition and vitamin deficiencies were the major concerns of the first half of this century, we are now increasingly aware that *overnutrition* can be as harmful to good health and longevity as is *undernutrition* and vitamin deprivation. The obese child is as much a concern as the child who "fails to thrive."

Like the adult, the child constantly expends energy, largely in the form of heat and work; this process goes on whether he is asleep or awake, although it is least rapid during periods of quiet sleep and much greater during periods of physical activity. To maintain energy balance, food is assimilated for use as energy. The energy value of foods is usually expressed in calories, which in nutrition work are referred to as *kilocalories* (or large calories). The different foodstuffs when burned in the body have approximately the following energy equivalents: 1 gram of fat yields 9 calories, 1 gram of protein yields 4 calories and 1 gram of carbohydrate yields 4 calories.

The calorie requirements of a growing child must not only provide the energy for *basal metabolism* (the energy requirements of the body at rest), bodily activity and growth, but also energy for the processes of digestion and excretion. The quantity of food willingly accepted by an infant is determined to a large extent not only by calorie requirements for maintenance and growth, but also by attitudes of the parent as well as the infant's age, sex, size and general state of health. In addition, the "caloric density," digestibility and nutritional adequacy, as well as the taste and consistency of the food offered, have relevance. (See also the major article on **Nutrition.**)

Breast versus bottle feeding
With the increasing safety and convenience of formula feeding since World War II, the decision whether to feed by breast or bottle has been left largely to the mother. In the 1940s approximately 65% of infants in the United States were breast fed. By 1960, less than 25% were fed in this manner. From 1930 to the middle 1940s BREAST FEEDING was most common among the lower social classes; by the early 1960s this was reversed so that it is now more common in upper social class mothers. Populations most likely to breast-feed their infants today include college students, physicians and health food enthusiasts.

The advantages of breast feeding are worthy of review and consideration. These are: (1) breast feeding is safer; (2) it provides a food superior from the nutritional point of view; (3) it is more convenient; and (4) it is of psychological value to the mother and to the infant.

It is important for the nursing mother to know that the amount of milk varies with the needs and demands of the child. Complete emptying of the breast is the strongest stimulus to the production of milk; a hungry infant will therefore soon increase his milk supply. Conversely, when the supply is overabundant the breast is incompletely emptied and within a few days the quantity secreted falls off. It is also important to note that a mother's ability to nurse is not affected by the season of the year, her age, the number of children, or the size of her breasts. It *is* affected, however, by her general state of health and well-being, her diet and her emotional or psychological state. The effect of emotional stresses on the secretion of milk is very striking. Worry, fatigue, anxiety, or any prolonged emotional reaction tends to reduce the secretion of breast milk.

The mother who cannot or who chooses not to breast feed is readily reassured that there are a variety of milk preparations available to assure the optimum growth and development of the newborn infant. The most basic formula consists of evaporated milk, water and carbohydrate in the form of sugar, corn syrup or dextro-maltose. Most recent is the introduction of what are known as

3 - 4 MONTH

DENVER PRESCREENING DEVELOPMENTAL QUESTIONNAIRE

Please read each question carefully before you answer. Circle the best answer for each question. YOUR CHILD IS NOT EXPECTED TO BE ABLE TO DO EVERY-THING THE QUESTIONS ASK.

| Child's Name |
| Date |
| Birthdate |

YES - CHILD CAN DO NOW or HAS DONE IN THE PAST
NO - CHILD CANNOT DO NOW, HAS NOT DONE IN THE PAST or YOU ARE NOT SURE THAT YOUR CHILD CAN DO IT.

R   - CHILD REFUSES TO TRY
NO-OPP - CHILD HAS NOT HAD THE CHANCE TO TRY

© Wm. K. Frankenburg, M.D., University of Colorado Medical Center, 1975.

3 month check - Answer 1 through 10

1. When your baby is lying on his back, does he move each of his arms as easily as the other and each of his legs as easily as the other? Circle NO if your child makes jerky or uncoordinated movements with one or both of his arms or legs.   YES   NO   R   NO-OPP

2. When your baby is lying on his back, does he look at you and watch your face?   YES   NO   R   NO-OPP

4 month check - Answer 3 through 12

3. Does your child make sounds such as gurgling, cooing, babbling, or other noises except crying?   YES   NO   R   NO-OPP

4. When your child is on his back, does he follow your move-ment by turning his head from one side to facing directly forward?

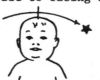

YES   NO   R   NO-OPP

5. When your child is on his back, does he follow your move-ment by turning his head from one side <u>almost all the way</u> to the other side?

YES   NO   R   NO-OPP

6. When you smile and talk to your baby does he smile back at you?   YES   NO   R   NO-OPP

7. When your baby is on his stomach on a flat surface can he lift his head <u>off the bed or surface</u> like the picture below?

YES   NO   R   NO-OPP

8. When your baby is on his stomach on a flat surface can he lift his head <u>45°</u> like the picture below?

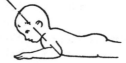

YES   NO   R   NO-OPP

9. When your baby is on his stomach on a flat surface can he lift his head <u>90°</u> like the picture below?

YES   NO   R   NO-OPP

5 - 8 MONTH

DENVER PRESCREENING DEVELOPMENTAL QUESTIONNAIRE

Please read each question carefully before you answer. Circle the best answer for each question. YOUR CHILD IS NOT EXPECTED TO BE ABLE TO DO EVERYTHING THE QUESTIONS ASK.

YES - CHILD CAN DO NOW or HAS DONE IN THE PAST
NO - CHILD CANNOT DO NOW, HAS NOT DONE IN THE PAST or YOU ARE NOT SURE THAT YOUR CHILD CAN DO IT.

Child's Name

Date

Birthdate

R   - CHILD REFUSES TO TRY
NO-OPP - CHILD HAS NOT HAD THE CHANCE TO TRY

© Wm. K. Frankenburg, M.D., University of Colorado Medical Center, 1975.

10. Does your baby laugh out loud without being tickled or touched?　　　　　YES　　NO　　R　　NO-OPP

5 month check - Answer 11 through 20

11. Have you seen your baby play with his hands by touching them together?　　　　　YES　　NO　　R　　NO-OPP

6 month check - Answer 12 through 21

12. When your child is on his back, does he follow your movement from one side all the way to the other side?

YES　　NO　　R　　NO-OPP

13. Does your child hold his head upright and steady? Circle NO if his head tends to fall to either side or to his chest.　YES　　NO　　R　　NO-OPP

14. IT IS IMPORTANT THAT YOU FOLLOW INSTRUCTIONS CAREFULLY AND ANSWER THE QUESTION FROM YOUR OBSERVATIONS. Do NOT place the pencil in the palm of your child's hand. Touch a pen or pencil to the back or tips of your baby's fingers. Does your baby grasp the pencil for a few seconds?

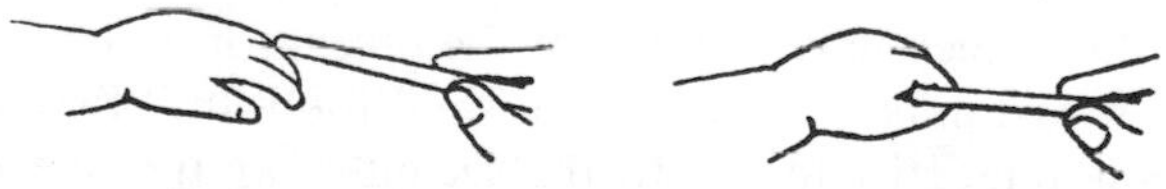

TRY THIS　　　　　NOT THIS

YES　　NO　　R　　NO-OPP

7 month check - Answer 15 through 24

15. When your child is on his stomach on a flat surface, can he lift his chest using his arms for support like the picture to the right?

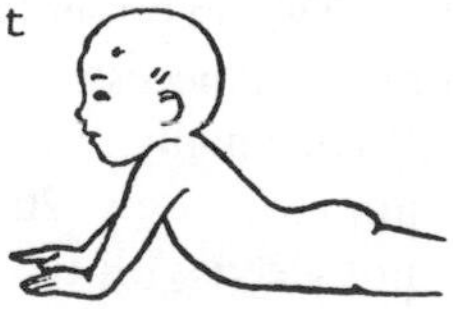

YES　　NO　　R　　NO-OPP

16. Does your baby ever make happy high-pitched or squealing sounds which are not crying?　　　　　YES　　NO　　R　　NO-OPP

17. Has your baby rolled over at least two times, from his stomach to his back or back to stomach?　　　　　YES　　NO　　R　　NO-OPP

18. Have you ever seen your child smiling at crib toys, pictures or pets when he is playing by himself?　　　　　YES　　NO　　R　　NO-OPP

8 month check - Answer 19 through 28

19. Does your child focus his eyes on small objects the size of a pea, a raisin or a penny? Circle NO if he does not focus.　YES　　NO　　R　　NO-OPP

20. Is your child able to pick up a toy if it is placed within his reach?　　　　　YES　　NO　　R　　NO-OPP

Breast feeding is not only safer but has a psychological value for mother and child.

"humanized milks"—cow's milk modified to resemble breast milk in the proportions of protein, carbohydrate and fat, and which requires only the addition of water. These are most commonly known under the trade names of Similac, Enfamil, S.M.A. and Bremil. Several are reinforced with vitamins. When properly diluted they have the same caloric and nutritional value as breast milk.

When feeding a baby a bottle, it is common practice to warm the food to approximately 100°F by placing the bottle in warm water for a few minutes. The temperature of the milk may be tested by pouring a few drops upon the inner surface of the wrist, where it should feel warm but not hot. However, warming the feeding is not a real necessity, since infants fed cold formulas seem to thrive equally well. Ordinarily, it should take an infant approximately 20 minutes to finish a feeding. He should not sleep with the nipple in his mouth. He should be fed in such a manner as to keep the nipple full. Sometime during the feeding (and again after it) the infant should be held upright over your shoulder and patted·on the back to allow him to bring up any air he might have swallowed during the feeding.

There are special artificial formulas for infants with specific medical problems relating to allergy, inborn errors of metabolism, or the inability to digest and utilize the normal nutrients because of intrinsic gastrointestinal disorders.

Vitamins

In technically advanced countries vitamin deficiency diseases are relatively uncommon. In recent years vitamins as food supplements have been commercially exploited; today vitamins are commonly added to all foods from cereals to candy. Rather than supplementing each item in the human diet to make it a complete food, it is more important to *balance* the diet by eating a *variety* of foods. Nevertheless, in infancy it is appropriate to provide supplementation for vitamins A, C and D where they are not artificially added to the infant's formula. In addition, fluoride should be introduced in early infancy to those children who reside in areas where there is a lack of fluoride in the drinking water. By the second year of life it is assumed that the child is eating a balanced diet, and added vitamins are not required, although fluoride supplementation may be continued on the recommendation of the pediatrician or dentist.

Solid foods

Market research data concerning infants in the United States in 1970 indicate that more and more infants are being fed solid foods at an earlier age. This is at a time when nutritionists examining the problems of obesity, atherosclerosis and cardiovascular disease are encouraging a *delay* in introducing solid foods at least into the second half of the first year of life. Although the early introduction of solid foods is well tolerated, it is probably not necessary for the nutritional needs of the child. Advocates of early solid feedings point out that the child should become accustomed to a variety of foods and should depend less on milk and in fact be weaned from the bottle or the breast by the end of first year. It is known that some children kept on the bottle or the breast for an undue length of time will often refuse all solid food until they are finally weaned.

In the second year the diet of a healthy child should consist of milk, breadstuffs, cereals, vegetables, fruit juices, fruit, meat and eggs. Usually, not more than a pint of milk is required per day. The child's appetite is a fairly satisfactory guide to the quantity of food he requires. Parents should bear in mind that different quantities of food may be eaten at different times, and should not force children to eat foods they strongly dislike.

Obesity

OBESITY in childhood is probably more frequent than the number of overweight children who come for treatment would indicate. Many parents are inclined to overlook obesity in a young child, or indeed to look upon it as a desirable attribute. Several studies have indicated that obese adolescents and children had been obese during infancy, and that a majority of obese adolescents and children do indeed become obese adults.

Along with excessive eating, the obese child shows a definite avoidance of physical activity compared with his slimmer peers. Since prevention of obesity is clearly preferable to treatment, it seems desirable to avoid obesity during infancy and childhood. This should be done by cutting back on the caloric intake of the infant deemed to be overweight for his height and body frame. In the older child, dietary restriction should be combined with increased physical activity. Sometimes it is preferable to retard or arrest the rate of gain until the child "grows up to his weight." It must be recognized that along with the problem of obesity, the concurrent psychological and social problems of the child and his parents must be considered.

The obese child must have help in finding new sources of personal satisfaction and self-respect; otherwise the simple restriction of food will be useless.

Screening for health

Health promotion starts during the prenatal period. The newborn is the product of a gestation which reflects the genetic strengths and weaknesses contributed by the parents as well as the strengths and weaknesses of the environment. Prenatal SCREENING can begin in the womb for genetic factors responsible for a number of pathologic states which can profoundly affect the infant's quality of life. Rapid advances in prenatal diagnosis allow informed decisions to be arrived at by the prospective parents, the genetic counselor and the obstetrician. (See AMNIO-CENTESIS.)

The screening process is extended to the newborn infant in the hospital nursery for the possible presence of inherited disorders ranging from SICKLE CELL ANEMIA to PHENYLKETONURIA to glucose-6-phosphate dehydrogenase (G-6-PD) deficiency. The last is an inherited enzyme deficiency which predisposes some children and adults to episodes of anemia. Each of these conditions may seriously affect children and adults unless recognized and treated early. In the very near future, routine screening for abnormal fat or lipid profiles which might lead to atherosclerosis and cardiovascular disease in the adult will also be routine, as will be screening for congenital HYPOTHYROIDISM. During infancy and childhood the screening process continues. Yearly HEMOGLOBIN and hematocrit determinations are performed to detect anemias. Routine urinalysis is carried out to detect inapparent infections of the urinary tract or systemic illness such as nephritis (inflammation of the kidneys) or diabetes. In addition, an annual skin test for tuberculosis is performed. With an increasing awareness of the threat of undetected hypertension in the adult, routine BLOOD PRESSURE determinations should be part of the physical examination of all children over the age of three.

Finally, all children should have ear and eye tests at least prior to entrance into school. VISION screening should detect myopia or near-sightedness, far-sightedness, strabismus or squint, amblyopia (non-use of one eye) and color perception. Audiometry should pick up a gradually acquired or subtle hearing loss which may interfere with normal function and learning.

Fever is often the first sign of an infectious illness in children, but needn't always be treated.

Dental care

It is frequently the physician who recognizes serious tooth decay or malocclusion (misalignment) of teeth and therefore urges the parent to seek dental help for the child.

Up to now, we have discussed the parents' and physician's role in health maintenance. It is equally important to consider the needs of the sick child and the impact of childhood illness on the rest of the family. This is especially true in this age of working mothers and surrogate parents. Not only does the illness of a child cause anxiety about the outcome and effects of the illness, but it also frequently means a rearrangement of working schedules, child care arrangements and the need for all involved with the care of the sick child to know about medications, therapeutic routines, and the specific medical resources of the family regarding routine and acute episodes of illness.

Common symptoms of illness

It is necessary, particularly for the inexperienced parent, to know not only how to discuss the common signs and symptoms of illness, but also how to report them to the concerned medical person. Parents must ask themselves several questions: is it serious or minor? What are the signs and symptoms? What should we do right now? Is it contagious? Should we wait and watch? Should we call the doctor? The fact that a child "has something" does not always mean that you have to do something about it, much less call the physician. But it is important to know when and how to care for a child at home, when to call the physician, and what to say when you do call. Most physicians have a specified "telephone hour" when calls for routine problems are expected and accepted. This allows them to interrupt the daily routine of the hospital and office, and all of us do make provisions for these calls. However, in a true emergency or acute situation, call the physician *at once*—regardless of the time of day or night!

Fever

Often the first sign of infectious illness is fever. It is important to note that 98.6°F is not a magic number and that body temperature does vary slightly with the time of day, the environment and the physical activity of the child. In addition, if a *rectal thermometer* is used the temperature will register about 1°F higher than when using an oral thermometer (by mouth). The best time to take a temperature during the course of an illness is early in the morning or late in the afternoon.

If the child looks acutely ill, is unresponsive, or wavers between periods of normal awareness and deliriousness, call your physician at once. Occasionally, a child may manifest a febrile convulsion—that is, trembling, rigidity and loss of consciousness with a sudden rise in temperature. These episodes are usually short-lived and leave no untoward effects, but they are understandably most anxiety-provoking to parents and do merit immediate medical evaluation of the child. Although low-grade fevers may accompany even the most simple of illnesses, a fever which lasts more than two to three days also merits medical evaluation or at least consultation over the telephone.

Many parents mistakenly think that if they reduce the temperature prior to the child being seen by a physician the diagnosis will be obscured. It is important to begin to reduce a high fever when it develops even before medical care is being sought, if only to make the child more comfortable. Most children tolerate low-grade fevers very well, and probably no intervention is needed for a temperature below 102°F.

At present, aspirin and acetaminophen (Tylenol or Tempra) are highly effective antipyretic (fever-reducing) drugs. You should consult your physician about which preparation to use and the exact dosage for your child, but the table opposite gives a reasonable dosage schedule to be repeated three or four times a day.

Other measures to lower temperature include: (1) the removal of warm clothing and bed clothes, to expose as much of the body surface as possible; (2) lowering the room temperature to 65–68°F; and (3) maintaining hydration by offering fluids such as tea, juices and carbonated beverages. Sponging with tepid water is frequently effective. This is best done by sitting the child in the sink or bathtub and wetting him down completely rather than applying wet cloths to the forehead or the arms or legs. There is some

Age	Aspirin (1¼ grains)	Tylenol (elixir)
< 1 year old	½ tablet	½ teaspoonful
1 year old	1 tablet	1 teasponful
2 years old	2 tablets	1 teaspoonful
3 years old	3 tablets	1 teaspoonful
4 years old	3½ tablets	1½ teaspoonfuls
5 years old	4 tablets	1½ teaspoonfuls
6 years old	4 tablets	1½ teaspoonfuls
Over 6	1 *adult* tablet	2 teaspoonfuls

question as to whether adding alcohol to the water enhances cooling. I would advise against this, since the alcohol fumes frequently make the child groggy.

Crying, irritability and change in activity

Illness in young infants is very often not manifested by a fever. They may become sluggish, inactive and have a diminished appetite. Frequently the quality of the cry changes and they cry feebly or whimper. Sometimes a usually content baby or infant will cry interminably or become irritable when moved or carried. Any child acting unusually sick is reason to call the physician, even if the symptoms are vague. You should call even if you are merely concerned and cannot explain why. A good physician respects the judgment of a concerned parent.

Upper respiratory illnesses

Upper respiratory infections are the most common childhood illnesses; they are usually mild and can be treated at home. Unfortunately, there is no way to prevent the common cold and virtually no method by which its course can be shortened. Thus, therapy is directed at relief of the symptoms. Symptomatic therapy may include only efforts to relieve the mild malaise and discomfort associated with a cold plus attempts to keep the nasal passages open and relieve the symptoms of a persistent runny or stuffed nose. Relief of the mild systemic symptoms may be relieved by the administration of aspirin or Tylenol in the dosages previously discussed.

Nasal obstruction sufficient to interfere with eating and sleeping is particularly a problem in the very young infant. This may be partially relieved by humidification. A vaporizer in the room often will make the child feel more comfortable and breathe more easily. I prefer cold mist vaporizers to the hot steam models for two reasons. First, the cold mist variety is safer if an older infant or toddler should happen to pull the unit down upon himself. Many serious burns have been caused by the hot steam variety. Second, if the child shares a bedroom with the parents or an older sibling, it is much more comfortable for all concerned to sleep in a cool moist room as opposed to a hot steamy one. An infant nasal aspirator, available at most pharmacies, is also useful to help remove some of the nasal mucus and relieve obstruction to the child's breathing.

Finally, the use of decongestants such as $\frac{1}{8}$% phenylephrine (Neo-Synephrine) in each nostril before feeding often helps. In older children $\frac{1}{4}$% phenylephrine may be used. Such nasal vasoconstrictors should not be used for more than three or four days because rebound swelling and dependence may occur.

Recurrent colds are particularly upsetting to parents. However, over 100 different viruses can produce the common cold and it is important for parents to understand that the infection cannot be prevented or treated with antibiotics or by removal of the tonsils or adenoids, and that colds are not associated with any immunological deficiency. In addition, they are not induced by chilling and are not related to allergy. Six separate upper respiratory infections per year are about average for the preschool child. As children approach their teens they usually decrease to two or three per year.

Occasionally a foul-smelling discharge from the nostril may indicate a foreign body in the nose. Parents should be particularly suspicious if the discharge is one-sided and persistent and the child does not look ill. You should not attempt to look for or remove a foreign body at home. This should be done in an adequate medical setting with proper light and instruments and frequently with sedation or mild anesthesia.

(See also the major article on **Otolaryngology**.)

Tonsillitis and pharyngitis

Most episodes of tonsillitis or pharyngitis (sore throat) are caused by viruses and resolve, like the common cold, with only supportive measures. In some instances an acute sore throat combined with fever and swollen glands in the neck may indicate a bacterial infection caused by the streptococcus and usually referred to as a "strep throat." Frequently, streptococcal pharyngitis or tonsillitis is accompanied by vomiting and abdominal pain. The only definitive method of diagnosis is to make a throat culture which the physician usually processes in his own office (but may send it to a local or state laboratory). Since culture results are usually valid in 24–48 hours, many physicians will withold definitive antibiotic therapy until the results are known.

INFECTIOUS MONONUCLEOSIS, long thought to be a disease of adolescents and young adults, is now known to occur in early childhood as well and frequently may mimic the tonsillitis and pharyngitis caused by other viruses or by streptococci.

(See also the major article on **Otolaryngology**.)

Otitis media (middle-ear infections)

OTITIS MEDIA, or infection of the middle ear, is usually caused either by a primary bacterial infection or by an initial viral upper respiratory infection with a secondary bacterial infection. The child typically complains of pain and has a fever. The young infant may indicate pain by head shaking, or tugging or batting at his ear, but there may be only the constitutional signs of fever, irritability and vomiting. Young children are especially predisposed to infections of the middle ear because the anatomy of the Eustachian tube (which leads from the middle ear to the back of the pharynx) is shorter and straighter than in the older child and adults, and because drainage is frequently blocked by the adenoid tissue normally found surrounding the Eustachian tube. In addition, the young infant or child with otitis media spends much of his time lying down, which further diminishes drainage from the middle ear.

All cases of acute otitis media require treatment with an antibiotic, a nasal decongestant, and medication to relieve the pain of the first few hours. Usually the pain subsides after the first few hours of treatment, but aspirin or Tylenol is useful. Warm glycerin containing 5% phenol (Auralgan) may be used as eardrops, and often heat in the form of a hot-water bottle provides satisfactory relief of pain.

Ideally, all patients with acute otitis media should be reexamined seven to ten days after the start of therapy. This is to make sure that the infection is subsiding and responding to therapy. Pain and fever should usually be relieved in 24–48 hours; if not, the child should be reexamined. If there is a recurrence a few days after the discontinuation of therapy, further antibiotic therapy with higher doses and of longer duration may be indicated.

Serous otitis media is a condition in which uninfected or mucoid material accumulates in the middle ear. It is usually accompanied by a temporary but significant hearing loss and is therefore a trying condition for the parents, the child and the physician. The first step in treatment is to look for an underlying problem, such as allergy, which might be amenable to simple measures. If there is significant enlargement of the adenoid tissue surrounding the Eustachian tube and also causing nasal obstruction, surgical removal of the ADENOIDS may be considered.

The child should undergo periodic audiograms, or hearing evaluations, to determine the extent of a hearing deficit, if any. In addition a long course of an oral decongestant-antihistamine preparation may be used. Where there is a prolonged, handicapping hearing loss, the child may be referred to a specialist who can insert small plastic tubes through the ear drum and thus drain and ventilate the middle ear. This procedure may not be definitive, but it will provide improved hearing—which is the major concern in this condition.

(See also the major article on **Otolaryngology**.)

Lower respiratory infections

Lower respiratory infections include those involving the larynx and adjacent airway (trachea)—"croup" syndromes—and those involving the larger airways (bronchi), the smaller airways (bronchioles), and the lung's small air sacs (alveoli). We refer to these inflammations, respectively, as laryngitis (or laryngotracheobronchitis), bronchitis, bronchiolitis and bronchopneumonia. Lower respiratory infections usually show up as coughs, wheezes and breathing difficulties, with or without accompanying fever. If your child suddenly has trouble breathing, it is important that you remain calm and reassuring while you seek appropriate medical help. (See also the major article on **Pulmonary Diseases.**)

Coughing, unless persistent or severe, is not necessarily a bad sign. Rather, it is nature's way of getting rid of mucus and foreign matter in the respiratory tract. However, coughing which is accompanied by a high fever or rapid respirations is usually a signal that an infectious process is taking place, and medical treatment should be sought.

A word about COUGH medication is in order here. Most over-the-counter cough preparations contain an expectorant with or without a decongestant and an antihistamine. While these do no harm, they are probably no more beneficial than keeping the child properly hydrated with warm, soothing beverages such as tea and honey. For the child with spasmodic exhaustive coughing, who is unable to rest or sleep, a specific cough suppressant is indicated. These are usually substances containing codeine or dextromethorphan and must be prescribed by a physician.

Laryngitis and laryngotracheobronchitis (croup)

Acute inflammations of the larynx (voice box) and the adjacent trachea (upper airway) are characterized by hoarseness and coughing and frequently associated with high-pitched or harsh breathing (STRIDOR). This is particularly significant in infants and younger children since the younger child has a smaller airway to start with and is thus more affected by narrowing in the presence of inflammation.

Infection is the most common cause of this condition, usually viral. This is particularly true of the influenza and *parainfluenza* viruses. Bacterial infection is sometimes significant and requires prompt treatment with antibiotics. In underdeveloped countries, or areas in which immunizations are not carried out, DIPHTHERIA is also a cause of this syndrome. (See also LARYNGITIS.)

A child who develops CROUP should be immediately placed in a well-humidified atmosphere. At home this may be accomplished by running hot water from the shower and faucets, and, for longer periods, using a steam vaporizer or cold mist nebulizer. The output of the vaporizer or nebulizer should be concentrated by a sheet tent or canopy placed about the head of the child. Again, I would caution about accidental burns from a hot-steam vaporizer.

Syrup of ipecac, if available, may be useful in breaking the spasm of the larynx, which causes the croup. This

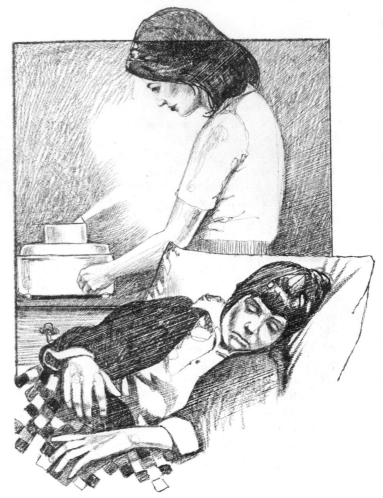

Humidifying the air with a vaporizer or nebulizer helps in both croup and bronchitis.

should be used in the appropriate or recommended dosage according to the age of the child. Usually this is one drop per month up to the age of two years, and then a teaspoonful in older children. Vomiting may occur; thus, the child should be maintained in an upright position and observed after the administration of the drug.

Anxiety and agitation frequently accompany this type of respiratory obstruction. The physician should be called with the onset of these symptoms; occasionally he may recommend hospitalization for further therapy and observation. In very severe cases intubation of the airway or a TRACHEOSTOMY (surgical incision into the airway) is required to circumvent the obstruction and allow the child to breath more easily.

Many youngsters tend to have recurrent croup with each upper respiratory infection. In approximately 15% of cases there is a strong family history of croup. These croup-prone children do tend to outgrow the condition as they get older and the airway becomes larger.

Acute bronchitis

Inflammation of the lower airways is usually caused by infection with one of the numerous viruses that may involve the entire respiratory tract. Bacteria are rarely involved as secondary invaders, and routine administration of antibiotics has not usually been found to be helpful in foreshortening the course or decreasing the severity of these infections. They are usually characterized by a persistent mucus-producing cough, sometimes accompanied by fever. (See also BRONCHITIS.)

Although antibiotics may be prescribed on the remote possibility that there is a superimposed bacterial infection, the usual measures relied upon are those that provide symptomatic relief—that is, humidification of the surrounding air, decrease in activity that promotes coughing, and fluids to keep the secretions in the lower airways moist so that they may be readily coughed up. Cough medicines probably make no difference to the duration of the illness.

Bronchiolitis
This is a respiratory illness caused by an inflammatory process which narrows the caliber of the smaller respiratory passages. It is usually a disease of early infancy, with almost 90% of the patients being less than one year of age. Most cases are caused by infectious agents, the majority of which are viruses. The disease occurs particularly in winter epidemics and early spring outbreaks.

Because of the inflammation of the smaller branches of the respiratory tree, more air gets into the air sacs (alveoli) than gets out; with this trapping of air, wheezes may be heard and the patient is seen to have difficulty breathing out. There is an increase in the rate and effort of respiration, and in young infants this may be fatiguing to the point of irritability and unwillingness to eat.

The treatment for this illness is largely symptomatic, with fluids and humidified air. Very ill infants should be taken to the hospital, where oxygen therapy may be added to the increased humidity, and intravenous fluids may be administered to the infant who is too tired to drink and eat normally. If the child is treated at home, small, frequent feedings are probably easier to handle. Antibiotic therapy is not indicated except where there is clear evidence of an overlying bacterial infection (indicated by an elevated temperature) or abnormally high white blood cell count.

Pneumonia
The vast majority of bronchopneumonias in children over the age of one month and under the age of four years are viral. The symptoms of high fever, rapid breathing and cough may occur in all pneumonias, viral or bacterial, and therefore are not useful in determining whether antibiotics should be used. Chest x-rays, blood counts, and cultures of the blood and sputum may help clarify the underlying cause of the infection and determine which, if any, antibiotics will be effective.

Most youngsters with bronchopneumonia may be treated at home with appropriate medications, fluids and humidification provided by "cold mist." Very young infants or children with respiratory difficulty should be admitted to the hospital for closer observation and more intensive therapy. (See also PNEUMONIA.)

Common neurological problems

Among the common neurological problems which concern parents, head injuries, convulsions and headaches probably rank foremost. These are anxiety-provoking situations for both the child and the parent.

Head injuries
It is the rare child who has survived childhood without sustaining a significant bump or blow to the head. Although accurate statistics are not available, the majority of children who suffer such injuries do not require hospitalization and probably only a fraction of them are ever seen by the family physician or the pediatrician. Yet it has been estimated that over 200,000 children are hospitalized each year for the evaluation or treatment of head injuries and approximately 5-10% of these cases do exhibit neurological signs.

There are three basic mechanisms responsible for head injury: (1) the head may be struck by a relatively small, rapidly moving object; (2) the head which is stationary may suddenly be accelerated; (3) the head which is moving may suddenly be decelerated. The first mechanism results in a tearing of the tissues and the others cause damage to the contents of the skull by movement of the brain against the bone and by tearing small arteries and veins. Any and all of these injuries can result in symptoms which are of medical concern.

Concussion
The term CONCUSSION refers generally to a definite loss of consciousness, but in the pediatric age group there are many injuries which are followed by lethargy, pallor, confusion and vomiting which may last for several hours. Any of these signs or symptoms following a head injury requires medical evaluation, followed by close observation for intracranial bleeding and control of vomiting. Thus any child who exhibits any of the previously described signs or symptoms following a head injury should be seen by a physician. Hospitalization is usually recommended for any child who has had a definite period of unconsciousness or in whom the postinjury symptoms last more than two hours. Observation in the hospital is concerned mainly with the level of consciousness of the patient, and incidentally with changes in pulse, blood pressure and respiration. The patient is usually not fed by mouth until the vomiting stops, and then is advanced to a clear liquid diet and finally to a normal diet. The total observation for a simple concussion is usually overnight or for 24 hours if the vomiting is controlled and the patient

remains alert and responsive.

More serious injuries to the brain are associated with prolonged and sometimes permanent neurological deficits. These are usually accompanied by a longer period of unconsciousness and specific neurological signs and symptoms. These children require intensive therapy to maintain adequate respirations, body temperature, blood pressure, etc. There is no doubt that these youngsters require hospitalization and expert medical management.

Skull fractures

Skull fractures may be relatively insignificant or extremely worrisome depending upon their location and whether or not they are simple and *linear* in nature or whether or not they are *depressed* and impinging upon the brain substance coverings. Linear fractures which occur in the area of the forehead are usually of no clinical significance. On the other hand, a fracture which crosses a major artery, or is in a significant area, must be treated with respect and a period of hospitalization is usually indicated. Fairly wide or large fractures also demand special attention. A depressed fracture is one in which several fragments of bone press on the brain substances or coverings. Obviously these require neurosurgical intervention. (See also the major article on **Neurosurgery.**)

Scalp injuries

A word about scalp injuries or lacerations. These are very common and, because the scalp is well supplied with blood vessels, cause profuse bleeding, much to the concern of the parent. Except for very small lacerations, most of the larger ones should be surgically cleansed and closed with sutures. They rarely become infected; antibiotics are not routinely used unless the laceration is very extensive or a considerable amount of time has elapsed before the wound could be closed surgically.

Seizures or convulsions

Convulsive disorders are quite common in childhood and may occur in a variety of conditions, some of which are quite benign. There is no doubt, however, that SEIZURES— by their very nature—cause great anxiety to both patients and parents.

A significant number of youngsters will have convulsions associated with a rapid rise in body temperature. Frequently, the parents or other members of the family have had similar occurrences. These episodes usually begin in children over the age of nine months and before the age of five years. For the most part they are very brief and are associated with an infection such as tonsillitis or otitis media (middle-ear infection). Most physicians will perform a lumbar puncture after the first febrile seizure to make sure that there is no serious infection of the nervous system such as MENINGITIS or ENCEPHALITIS.

After the child has been without fever for a week or more, an EEG, or electroencephalogram (brain wave test), is performed to make sure that there is no underlying abnormality. When the results of all tests are normal, we assume these are simple febrile seizures with an excellent prognosis. Although no therapy is needed, other than keeping temperature down in subsequent infections, these children should be observed throughout early childhood. If the convulsions occur more frequently than four times a year, or if other symptoms develop, then a diagnosis consistent with a seizure disorder is made and specific anticonvulsive medication is started.

If your child should have a seizure, there are several aspects of general care you should know about. First, the patient should be allowed to remain in the place where the seizure occurred until the active spell has subsided. He should be placed in such a position that he cannot harm himself by knocking his body against hard or sharp objects. Tight clothing, especially around the neck, should be loosened or removed.

Should a child suffer a seizure in bed, he should be observed so that he does not fall to the floor. Guard rails or boards should be placed at the side of the bed. All pillows should be removed to prevent possible suffocation. If possible, the child should be kept on his side so that mucus and saliva will flow freely from the mouth; in the event that vomiting occurs, the vomitus will also be expelled rather than aspirated into the lungs (a potentially very serious condition).

If the child is biting his tongue or cheek, a firm blunt object such as a folded leather belt or a leather glove can be inserted between the teeth. All prolonged major seizures require prompt medical attention.

The child with a seizure disorder requires the ongoing supervision of a physician. There is an ever-increasing variety of medications which can control these spells and provide for a normal, active life for the child. (See the major article on **Drugs and Medicines.**)

Petit mal is a form of epileptic seizure characterized by a momentary loss of consciousness and a cessation of activity. These are sometimes referred to as "absence" or "lapse" attacks, since they usually last for only 5 to 15 seconds. Just as abruptly, the child recovers his senses and resumes his activity as if nothing happened. Sometimes children have semipurposeful movements such as snapping the fingers, patting movements or walking around in circles. Attacks may vary from an occasional episode to hundreds per day. The child's mental development is usually unaffected and the neurological findings on examination are completely normal. The diagnosis is confirmed by a characteristic pattern on the EEG. Although these attacks tend to decrease with time and frequently disappear in the late teens, they do warrant specific therapy which is now available.

See also EPILEPSY and *Seizures in children* in the **First Aid** section.

Headaches

Headaches are common in children. While a significant number may be MIGRAINE or "tension" headaches, other causes may include fever or specific illness such as sinusitis, allergy, or emotional disorders. Children with migraines are very much like adults who have symptoms of blurred vision, "spots" before the eyes, nausea, vomiting and severe discomfort. Most functional headaches respond to rest and routine analgesics such as aspirin or acetaminophen. True migraines frequently require more specific therapy. A child who has persistent or unusual headaches should receive medical attention.

Heart disease

It is beyond the scope of this section to discuss specific heart diseases in childhood. If a child is receiving routine ongoing medical care, congenital heart defects will be recognized and treated in early infancy and childhood. However, some mention should be made of *murmurs*, which are heart noises caused by the normal turbulence and vibration of the pumping heart and which usually do not indicate present or future heart disease. They are frequently called "functional murmurs," or "innocent murmurs," which is a better term to describe a phenomenon heard in the examination of at least 30% of normal children.

With age and increasing thickness of the chest wall, the murmurs become harder to hear and are therefore easily detected in only 15–20% of teens or adults. It is important for parents to understand that such children are normal in every way, and should not be restricted from any activity.

At present there are many sophisticated methods to study and diagnose the child with true heart disease. These should be carried out by a competent cardiologist in a medical setting where a complete plan of diagnosis and therapy may be established.

(See also HEART DISEASE and the major article on **Cardiology**.)

Abdominal pain

Recurrent abdominal PAIN is a common complaint in pediatric practice; it has been estimated that 1 in 10 school-age children suffer at some time with the problem. Yet an organic cause for this condition is found in less than 10% of the patients.

Abdominal pain is more likely to be significant if it is sharply localized and constant, especially if it occurs during the night and awakens the child from sleep. Fever, vomiting, loss of appetite or loss of weight should alert the parent to consult a physician. Many children have brief episodes of abdominal pain with infectious diseases such as tonsillitis or bronchitis. This type of pain will subside as the infection resolves.

See also APPENDICITIS/APPENDECTOMY.)

Some children are genetically predisposed to constipation or trapping of gas in the intestine; they may complain more often of abdominal discomfort and pain. Medical treatment of the underlying condition will usually help. A significant number of youngsters have a psychogenic cause for their abdominal pain, especially those who may be anxious about interfamily problems or who may be having school or learning difficulties. With an appreciation of the problems—which may involve parents, siblings or peers—the abdominal symptoms usually subside.

Infantile colic

This is a vague symptom complex of early infancy in which the baby appears to have intermittent periods of abdominal pain for which no organic reason can be established. The baby has periods of extreme fussiness associated with clenching the fists and flexing the legs; there is associated belching, passing of gas, and stomach rumbling. The passage of gas is frequently accompanied by temporary relief. Colic usually starts at the second to fourth week of life and persists to the third or fourth month.

Treatment of infantile colic usually involves changes in techniques of feeding and careful burping at the end of the meal. Changing of formulas is useless except in rare cases of milk allergy or specific intolerance to lactose (the sugar in milk). Occasionally drugs are used, but these should be prescribed by the physician. An old wives' remedy of 10 to 15 drops of an alcoholic beverage in 2 ounces of sweetened warm water will sometimes afford relief of symptoms, as will a warm bath or heating pad applied to the abdomen.

Rashes and dermatological complaints

Because they are readily visible, SKIN DISEASES can be very distressing to both parents and patients. The skin is a complex "organ"—a protective wrapping which not only keeps in vital fluids and solutes, but also keeps out noxious environmental substances. It has multiple functions of absorption, secretion, respiration, temperature regulation and pigment formation. The skin frequently reflects the state of well-being of the entire patient. (See also the major article on **Dermatology**.)

A child's skin is an ever-developing organ and matures along with the rest of the child. In infants the *epidermis* layer is thin and particularly susceptible to irritation and infection. Sweating is scanty in the young infant and the young child's skin is more prone to blistering from trauma or infection. During adolescence the skin becomes thicker and the sebaceous (oil-secreting) glands become more active, leading to a higher incidence of ACNE or seborrhea.

It is important to know that inflamed or denuded skin loses much of its protective function. Parents should not use home remedies that will irritate or further inflame the skin. Soothing compresses, baths and lotions are safe until medical help is obtained.

Itching is perhaps the most common and least tolerated of symptoms. Further scratching, rubbing or chafing causes greater inflammation and more discomfort, with a greater likelihood of secondary infection and possible long-term scarring. Sometimes antihistamines and a mild analgesic such as aspirin will give some relief. Soothing and cooling agents, even a tepid bath, will often help. Irritants such as bubble bath, wool clothing and strong laundry products should be avoided. If there are signs of secondary infection, a physician will usually prescribe appropriate topical or systemic antibiotics. Calamine lotion is widely used to relieve itching, particularly in cases of poison ivy and related rashes.

Open wet dressings with mild astringents (such as Burow's solution) are frequently used for compresses applied to inflamed areas. Baths containing starch (such as Linit starch), oatmeal, or specific lubricating substances such as Alpha-Keri are also useful. The use of creams, ointments, tars and topical antibiotics should be discussed with a physician.

Many lesions of childhood are now treated chemically with good results. Warts, acne cysts and psoriasis lesions can often be successfully treated by a dermatologist.

Skin rashes may be a manifestation of so many different conditions that it is hard to generalize over the telephone. The physician will usually want to see the rash in question unless it is a long-standing chronic condition. A rash and fever or other signs of systemic illness should warrant immediate medical attention.

(See also *Drugs for skin and local disorders* in the major article on **Drugs and Medicines**.)

The kidneys and urinary tract

The watchful physician always pays careful attention to the condition of the urinary system. Due to its complicated development, a high incidence of hidden anomalies may occur which are only evident after repeated infection or specific investigation. Periodic urinalyses are most important in the routine annual care of children. The physician will usually obtain a sample of urine for bacteriological culture whenever there is fever without a definite cause.

After a URINARY TRACT INFECTION is diagnosed and treated adequately, predisposing anatomical defects should be looked for. To this end the physician may request a special x-ray study of the kidneys called an intravenous pyelogram (IVP) and a voiding cystogram. These studies will delineate the kidneys, ureters, bladder and the urethra and reveal any serious underlying malformation. Additional urologic investigations are indicated if the x-ray studies disclose significant abnormalities, or if the child continues to have recurrent infections despite what on x-ray films appears to be a normal genitourinary system. The purpose of this investigation is the early detection of surgically correctable anatomical defects; institution of appropriate therapy follows the diagnosis.

The prevention of chronic infection is a most important goal in order to prevent hypertension and chronic kidney failure in the adult.

Diseases of the kidney substance itself (nephritis or nephrosis) require specific medical surveillance and management. (See KIDNEY DISEASES.)

Enuresis is the inappropriate voiding of a normal stream of urine beyond the age at which one would expect normal voluntary urinary control. Usually this occurs somewhere between two and four years of age. Daytime control is attained before nighttime control. Enuresis can be primary (that is, there never having been a period of dryness) or secondary. Secondary implies a period of dryness preceding the recurrence of urinary incontinence. Nocturnal enuresis is exceedingly common, usually occurring in children with a familial predisposition (see BEDWETTING).

There are many causes—physiological, neurological and emotional—which have been proposed for this condition. However, it is generally recognized that there is no single factor responsible. Once the pediatrician has ruled out an organic cause for this condition, parents are left with the assurance that even without treatment, one out of seven patients achieves a spontaneous cure each year. At present therapy includes behavior modification with rewards for dry nights, an alarm bell system and in some instances medication. It should be pointed out that no matter what method used, most children (75%) are cured after a period of about five years.

Allergy in childhood

It is estimated that between 15 and 25% of Americans suffer from some kind of allergy. Allergy can affect many different areas of the body, and the result may be chronic disability and discomfort. In children we see atopic dermatitis, allergic rhinitis, allergic conjunctivitis, bronchial asthma and gastrointestinal upsets. Less frequent are SERUM SICKNESS (which is a generalized systemic reaction), specific hypersensitivity to physical factors such as cold or heat and specific drug or substance allergies.

The genetic factors in allergy are complex. There is firm evidence that children who suffer from allergies have a positive family history of allergy. When both parents are allergic there is a greater than 50% probability that the child will be allergic; when only one parent is allergic there is a greater than 35% chance that a child will be allergic.

Most physicians tend to treat mild to moderate manifestations of allergy with oral antihistamine medication and nasal decongestants. If these measures fail, or the lower respiratory tract becomes involved (as in bronchial asthma), then additional therapy in the form of DESENSITIZATION (or *hyposensitization)* or corticosteroids are considered.

Desensitization therapy consists of identifying which substances cause the clinical symptoms. These are determined by a series of skin tests. Over a period of time, small amounts of these substances are injected in order to build up specific circulating antibodies, which in effect allows the patient to build up a tolerance to the offending substance. This therapy usually continues over several years in order to achieve the maximum effect.

When a child is allergic to dust, the physician will recommend "dust-controlling" the bedroom where the child sleeps. This entails removing woolen carpeting, upholstered furniture, stuffed toys, heavy draperies, etc. The child sleeps on a foam rubber mattress, uses a Dacron or foam rubber pillow and synthetic fiber blankets. The room should be kept well dusted and vacuumed. Pets should be kept out of the bedroom, if not out of the house.

Children with bronchial asthma are maintained on a regimen of bronchodilator drugs as well. Older children may also be able to use inhalation therapy in the form of packaged metered aerosols. All of these drugs require medical supervision.

Treatment of *atopic dermatitis* involves topical therapy, and general symptomatic relief in the form of wet dressings for open weeping lesions; antibiotics may be administered to treat specific infections. Topical corticosteroids are used under the direction of a physician, who will prescribe what is appropriate from the wide variety of such preparations currently available. The use of systemic corticosteroids is generally avoided, but in acute situations these are often used for the short term. Elimination of foods such as eggs, wheat and milk may be tried, but a specific food allergen is rarely found. Specific immunotherapy or hyposensitization for atopic dermatitis is generally unsuccessful and therefore is rarely attempted. Although this condition is usually outgrown, there are some adolescents and adults for whom this is a lifelong problem.

See also the major article on **Allergy and Immunology.**

Accidents and injuries

Though childhood deaths have declined dramatically owing to advances in medical science and public health measures, there has not been a significant decline in deaths and permanent injuries caused by childhood accidents. The majority of injuries in children in all age groups are sustained at home. However, motor vehicle accidents rank first among those that are fatal to children from birth to 14 years of age. Significantly, more small children are killed inside the vehicle than outside. Deaths from fire burns and explosions are also significant, as are falls from heights (e.g., unprotected windows or fire escapes), and constitute a major health hazard for preschool children. Accidents occur more frequently in boys than girls and are more frequent in the summer than in the winter. Four times as many accidental deaths occur in teenage boys as in girls of the same age.

Developmental sequences that children go through from birth to maturity determine in part the types of accidents that are more apt to occur at specific times. A small infant may roll over or propel himself from an open crib, a bed, or dressing table. At the time of crawling there is a tendency to put foreign objects in the mouth and the ingestion of poisonous substances or dangerous objects becomes a hazard throughout early childhood. As the child becomes increasingly mobile, the ability to climb, further explore and pull and grasp for objects brings about falls, burns, scalds, electric shocks and injuries from toppling furniture or objects. As the child further matures, intense preoccupation with play makes him inattentive in street traffic or in the water.

It is our responsibility as parents and physicians to modify the environment so that it is safer for children. Thus we are concerned with seat belts, safety glass for doors, nonflammable material, safe toys, safe play areas and supervised recreation. We must protect, educate and legislate to create a safer environment. The pediatrician, with his special knowledge of child development, can provide guidance about how to avoid the types of accidents most likely to occur at a specific stage of childhood.

Poisoning

In the United States each year more than two million poisonings occur, almost half occurring accidentally in children under five years of age. In many cases of POISONING, parents not in tune with their child's development neglect to put household agents in a safe place, or leave prescription drugs or household remedies (such as aspirin) in the sight and reach of children. Many poisonings can be avoided if the following warnings are heeded:

1. **Keep all drugs, pesticides and potentially poisonous household chemicals out of the sight and reach of children and stored away from food.**
2. **Do not store poisons or inflammable materials in food containers or bottles.**
3. **Lock up all dangerous substances.**
4. **Never tell children that medicine is candy.**
5. **Purchase less toxic household products (read the label) and when possible buy only those agents and drugs that are in safety containers or fitted with safety closures. Always reseal safety closures, and never transfer the contents into other bottles or containers.**

If, despite all precautions, a toxic agent is ingested, every effort should be made to identify the poison. Every family should have the number of the regional Poison Control Center and call it immediately. They will usually be able to advise you as to what is in the substance and what measures should be taken. If you rush your child to an emergency room or a physician's office, take the container or bottle.

If a poison is ingested, the stomach should ordinarily be emptied as quickly as possible. However, never make a child vomit if he is comatose or if he has ingested a corrosive product such as lye or a petroleum distillate. Each home should have syrup of ipecac which may be administered in a dose of two to three teaspoonfuls. This dose can be repeated in 15 to 30 minutes if the first dose has been ineffective. To facilitate vomiting, give the patient a glass of fluid after the first dose of ipecac. If syrup of ipecac is not available, give the child a drink of water and then gag the child by inserting a finger down his throat or stroke the back of the throat with a blunt object.

Further therapy in the hospital includes lavage of the stomach and the administration of an antidote where indicated. Depending upon the type of poison ingested, the child may be admitted to the hospital for further observation and supportive therapy.

(See also *Poisoning* in the **First Aid** section.)

Symptoms of chronic illness

During the course of providing child health care it is the pediatrician who recognizes aberrations in a child's normal growth and development, with possible underlying illness. Growth failure is often a major clinical manifestation of chronic illness. In some instances the primary disease process is not suspected or diagnosed until the physician and the parent recognize poor weight gain and growth. Kidney disease, gastrointestinal malfunction, congenital heart disease, hematological (blood) illness, asthma and cystic fibrosis may all inhibit growth. This is to be differentiated from the congenitally small child who continues to remain small but who is consistently growing along his own growth path and is otherwise normal and healthy.

In addition to the delayed growth processes, the appearance of secondary sexual characteristics, menarche (the first menstrual period) and appropriate skeletal development may also be delayed.

You and your child's doctor

It is important that parents interpret accurately and clearly their perception of the child's illness or complaints. When presenting an acute illness there are several points to be made. How long has the child been ill? When did the temperature elevation occur? How high is the temperature? Is the child having any difficulties speaking, breathing, walking? Is his general level of activity normal or decreased? Is he in pain? Does he look pale or flushed? Has there been vomiting or diarrhea? If you report these findings to the pediatrician it enables him to make a significant judgment about the degree of the child's illness.

When dealing with a chronic complaint it is equally important to document when the problem started, what events may have preceded it, what significance it has on the child's daily living pattern, etc. This is particularly important for younger children. Older children and adolescents are usually their own best historians.

Diagnostic procedures

Many routine diagnostic procedures—such as simple blood tests, white blood cell counts, urinalysis and simple x-rays—can be performed in the physician's office or the outpatient department of the local hospital. More complicated tests, hormone assays, or complicated sophisticated radiological studies (such as computerized axial tomography, or CAT scans) are more readily performed in a hospital setting. Where 24-hour urine collections are required on an untrained young child, this also must be performed in the hospital.

If you as a parent have any questions about the reason behind various tests, they should be expressed to the physician. Frequently, parents do not understand the need for many x-rays or blood tests. No physician wants to expose the child to unwarranted studies or unnecessary discomfort.

Nursing a sick child at home

Nursing a sick child at home is easier if the parent fully understands the needs of the child and the requirements of the physician. Most sick children regulate their own activity—that is, the acutely ill child *chooses* to lie quietly in bed, as does the child who is in pain. A child who feels better may be happier sitting in a chair and taking his meals at the table. Understand the reasons for medications or treatments and explain pleasantly but firmly that these are necessary for the child's well-being. It is much easier to measure medications into a small paper cup and offer them to the patient rather than run after a toddler with a full teaspoon. Unpleasant medication may be administered in fruit juices or syrups, while tablets may be embedded in a teaspoonful of applesauce.

It is important to ask the physician when the child can resume normal activity and return to school. With an older child, it is important to discuss this together in the presence of the physician so that there is no misunderstanding. Be specific about asking when the patient can return to participation in sports and other strenuous activities.

(See also the major article **Guide to Home Nursing Care.**)

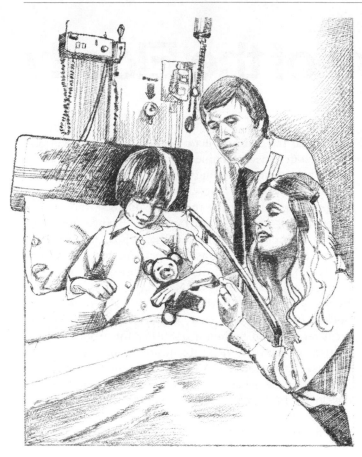

Most hospitals have now recognized the importance of liberal visiting hours for parents.

The child in the hospital

Many hospitals offer preliminary guided tours for the youngster who is scheduled for an elective admission. These tours introduce the child to the physical setting, the operating room, the anesthetic mask and the staff.

For the child admitted with an acute illness, the hospital can be a frightening experience. Most hospitals now have liberal visiting hours for parents. Many provide a simple chair-bed for parents to spend the night. During the early days of an illness, this is usually reassuring to both the child and the parent. But as the child recuperates the parent may come to realize that "hospitals are not for sleeping" and that it is a good idea to go home in the evening and come back refreshed and better able to provide care for the child. Another consideration must be other children at home, who should not feel left out and abandoned by the parent in favor of the child in the hospital.

Parents must strike a happy balance between helping the child and hindering the staff providing nursing and medical care. Parents may usually accompany the child to the X-Ray Department and other diagnostic areas of the hospital, but most parents are uncomfortable in the face of procedures such as changing a dressing or inserting an intravenous tube, and probably would do better to wait nearby while such procedures are being performed.

In many hospitals there is a primary nurse working together with a team of physicians who know the child. These personnel will answer questions and give information if asked at intervals. But obviously they cannot be distracted from their duties all day long. Therefore a parent should request a brief interval with these people and get a comprehensive report for the day. Parents have questions about diagnostic studies and therapies. These should be posed to your child's doctor and nurses, not to any hospital personnel who pass by, since conflicting and nonspecific information can only confuse you.

Hospitals can be awesome and overwhelming to many families. There are always nonmedical personnel, such as social workers and administrators, who can help with problems and answer questions. If your child will have a prolonged stay, it is advisable to seek out such people.

Finally, in this day of educational awareness, many older children are disturbed about missing school work. If the child is able to do school work, it is advisable to speak to the school authorities and bring in assignments. Some hospitals have part-time teachers who can help.

The Health Care of the Elderly

Dr. Thomas Kalchthaler

At some time of life, most everyone faces the problem of how to care for aging relatives or friends. The following article dispels many common myths about aging and the elderly, and explains the physical and psychological changes that occur as one grows older.

Geriatrics is the branch of medicine which is involved with the medical, psychiatric and social problems of late life. *Gerontology*, on the other hand, is the science or study of the aging process. It includes the biological, social and psychological aspects of the aging process. As a result of prejudice and disinterest, it has not been until the last century that either geriatrics or gerontology developed as legitimate "foster children" of medicine and science.

History of geriatric medicine

It has been recorded that Hippocrates defined "old age" as beginning at the surprisingly *young* age of 56. During his study and practice of medicine, he collected and recorded many exact observations on the elderly. Among them were the facts that older persons apparently have a decreased need for food and an increased incidence of respiratory problems, arthritis, cataracts and urinary problems. Hippocrates recommended that old people should live a life of moderation, although he advised active involvement with life. He warned against withdrawal and retirement. Aristotle felt that "inward heat" was necessary for life and that the aging process was a gradual loss of this. In the second century, Galen defined old age as a state somewhere between illness and health. In his treatise *Gerocomica*, he reconciled the "humors" of Pythagoras with the "inner heat" of Aristotle. He urged that the aged body be kept warm and moist through the frequent use of hot baths and the generous ingestion of wine.

During the 13th century, Roger Bacon (1214?–1294) looked upon old age as a disease process. Bacon, however, was the first to suggest correcting poor vision with magnifying lenses. Until the end of the 15th century, all works on old age generally dealt with hygiene. During the Renaissance, anatomy flourished and cadavers were dissected for the first time. Under the watchful eyes of Leonardo da Vinci (1452–1519), anatomical differences between the young and old were noted. From the 16th to the 18th centuries man was variously described as either a chemical compound or likened to a machine. Aging was considered the end product of either "auto-intoxication" or a well-designed machine simply running down.

It was not until the end of the 18th century and the beginning of the 19th that scientific papers on aging began to appear with increasing regularity. In 1850, the medical specialty of geriatrics surfaced in France with the establishment of large "chronic disease hospitals," such as the one at Salpetriere. It was at Salpetriere that Jean Martin Charcot (1825–1893) gave his insightful and inspiring lectures on old age. In 1912, Nascher—who is considered by many to be the "Father of Geriatrics"—founded the Society of Geriatry in New York; interestingly, he had great difficulty in finding a publisher for a book he had written on geriatrics (a problem not totally unknown to medical experts today!). Along with an increased impetus in geriatric medicine, a growing interest in gerontology developed. In 1945, the Gerontological Society was formed in the United States; in 1950, an International Gerontological Society was established.

Geriatrics in the 20th century

Since World War II, programs in gerontology have flourished in the United States. Many superb multidisciplinary centers of gerontology have been established through the financial assistance of the Federal government. These centers are primarily involved with research and education. In addition, many community colleges have established elective courses in gerontology. Unfortunately, geriatrics has lagged far behind gerontology. In a recent survey conducted in Westchester County, New York, 50% of all physicians who participated had had no significant contact with geriatric medicine in their medical education, and 70% of all general practitioners, family practitioners and internists had none. In a similar survey done at several medical schools, most medical students desired at least an exposure to geriatrics; few felt that their present knowledge was adequate. Until recently, many medical educators denied that physicians needed to understand normal aging before developing the expertise to care for elderly patients. In addition, little credence had been given to the now well-established fact that disease processes are altered by aging and that the presentation, diagnosis and treatment of disease processes in late life are quite different from those of young and mid-life. Health care delivery systems designed to meet the needs of an aging population are only now beginning to develop.

The recognized "graying" of America and the example of model geriatric programs, both in the United States and abroad, have stimulated a reawakening of health care educators to the needs of the elderly; they have come to accept their responsibility to provide educated physicians and systems of health care to meet these needs. Since the 1960s several medical residency training programs in geriatrics have been established. The National Institute of Aging, a division of the National Institute of Health, has recently been established to provide medical leadership in research, education and training. At present at least 13 training programs provide some exposure to geriatrics. There is now some interest in integrating gerontology and geriatrics into the curriculum of several medical schools.

It's only a beginning. But at least these important areas are receiving more attention at the primary level of medical education.

What is aging?

Aging involves those changes which occur in any cell or organ system as a function of time, independent of disease. Disease, on the other hand, is a *pathologic* or abnormal state found in any cell, organ or organ system in a unit of time or extending over many units of time. Unfortunately, many people do consider aging to be a pathologic state or

The "graying" of America is considerably more noticeable in the warm southern states.

disease process. Aging is neither a disease process nor the result of multiple disease states. If a cure were found for atherosclerosis and cancer, the average human life span would undoubtedly increase to 90 or 100 years. The life survival curves would merely become rectangular, with a precipitous drop after the age of 90 or so. Aging and death, like birth and maturation, are part of the normal life cycle.

Biological theories of aging

Of the many different theories of cellular aging, the *biological clock* demonstrates the most promise. This theory states that manifestations of senescent changes are the result of the "playing out" of the genetic program which contains specific information (or "aging genes") that code for the senile changes preceding the demise and death of the organism. In the early 1960s, Hayflick and Morehead found that when certain normal human embryonic cells (called *fibroblasts*) were cultured, they underwent 50 doublings or cell divisions and then died. This finite number of cell divisions could not be explained on the basis of culture techniques or the particular culture medium used. Furthermore, when these cells were frozen with liquid nitrogen and later reconstituted, the total number of cell doublings again equalled 50. When fibroblasts were taken from skin and lung tissue of adult human volunteers, these cells would undergo only 14 to 29 cell divisions—depending on the age of the adult. From this it was concluded that there is an inverse relation between the age of a human donor and the ability of the cell to reduplicate in culture media. Subsequent studies have shown that a correlation exists between the mean maximum number of cell reduplications in culture media and the mean maximum life span of the particular organism. Although the results of these experiments were certainly intriguing, what happens in cell cultures (*in vitro*) does not necessarily happen in life (*in vivo*). Further studies done by Hayflick and others have established that the "pacemaker" of cellular aging is located not outside the individual cell but within the nucleus of that cell. In addition to cell division, other metabolic functions and cell constituents—which may either increase, decrease, or remain the same—may be under the control of the "playing" genetic code. Thus, within the cellular genetic code is the information which probably programs normal cellular aging. Similar cells in different species of organisms may "age" at a different rate, just as different cells within the same organism may "age" at a different rate.

Other theories of aging include aging as *random deterioration* and aging simply resulting from *gene exhaustion*. It has been proposed that aging is caused by random events called "aging hits," which occur with a constant probability per unit of time throughout life. These "hits" alter the chromosomes within the nucleus of the cell and cause aging. This "somatic mutation" is not widely held to be a satisfactory explanation of the aging process. Others have suggested that with increasing time the body falsely recognizes part of itself as "foreign" and produces antibodies against itself; the destruction caused by these antibodies is postulated to result in aging. Alternatively, the body may contain antibodies against itself. With time those factors which are suppressing these antibodies become weakened and, again, these antibodies produce the results leading to aging and death. There is some evidence that aging may be associated with problems of self-recognition and the production of *auto-antibodies*.

The third major theory of random deterioration is that of *free radical reactions*. "Free radicals" are molecules that are unstable and are found in all living matter. These free radicals produce random oxidative reactions and multiple deleterious changes in biologic systems. Aging is the end result of the changes produced by free radicals. The theory of gene exhaustion suggests that, with time, genetic material can no longer be reduplicated. Reduplication may be hindered by depletion or abnormalities of elements found within the cell. Inadequate protein-synthesizing enzymes have also been indicated as a possible explanation for aging. Obviously much research is needed in understanding aging on a cellular basis.

Anatomical concomitants of normal aging

Although the "pacemaker" for aging may be the cellular "biological clock," aging also occurs anatomically and physiologically. Stature decreases somewhat as a function of aging. Researchers have noted a statistical decrease in height for each 20-year interval past maturity. The rate of decrement, 1.2 cm/20 years, has been found to be constant between sexes and in both blacks and whites. This loss of height occurs primarily in the spinal column and results initially from thinning of the intervertebral disks and later from diminution of bone height.

Long bones do not shorten with age, nor does bowing of the long bones of the lower leg occur. As a result, the ratio of arm span to height changes with age and is the reverse of that of infancy and childhood. Shortened stature is further accentuated by flexion of hips and knees, a posture many elderly persons assume in order to stabilize balance. *Dorsal kyphosis* ("humpback") frequently results from the changes occurring in the vertebral column. To compensate, the neck may be held in extreme extension to improve balance and allow for better vision. The chest itself may decrease in diameter by 2 to 3 cm with age. This decrease is most marked in the lower portion of the chest, giving it a "barrel-shaped" appearance. This appearance may be the result of the muscles of respiration on weakened demineralized ribs.

Although obesity—provided that being grossly overweight is not associated with hypertension, elevated blood

Decline in organ function, thinning hair, wrinkles and change in body contours are inevitable.

cholesterol, or coronary artery disease—may not militate against survival, few obese people survive to a truly advanced age. Many people continue to gain weight in their 50s and 60s, but generally do not retain their body contours. Most fat tends to be deposited on the abdomen and hips, with little or no increase in other areas such as the face, arms and legs. The female breast also decreases in size and contour with age. This wasting includes both subcutaneous fat and glandular elements. Soft tissue tumors, which are entirely benign, may be mistaken for breast cancers. This redistribution of body fat, while rounding some contours, markedly accentuates others. These include the hollows of the eyes, armpits and the spaces between the ribs. These accentuated hollows may give many old people a "bony" appearance, which is not altered by increased caloric intake.

Body hair tends to decrease with age. In addition to a gradual thinning, graying and receding hairline in a "V" configuration, there may also be a gradual loss of axillary (armpit) and pubic hair. Women may develop coarse chin hair and both men and women may lose hair on their legs. Men frequently retain arm hair.

Wrinkles may be the delight of some plastic surgeons—for the challenge presented in removing them—but they are a plague for those elderly persons who are especially concerned with maintaining a youthful appearance. With the loss of facial fat (and muscle enlargement secondary to use), facial wrinkling develops. Wrinkling of the forehead begins in the 20s and progresses in the 30s and 40s. "Crow's

feet," radiating from the lateral aspect of the eye, also begin appearing at this time. Nasal folds may become more pronounced and grooves may develop between the lower lip and chin in the 50s and 60s. Multiple fine wrinkles of the upper and lower lips, radiating from the border of the lips, may also develop in the 60s. Two prominent lines coursing up the neck on either side of the midline may also appear in the 50s. Frequently, with loss of teeth, there is a significant reabsorption of bone from the upper and lower jaw which can produce a marked infolding of the mouth. This infolding decreases the distance between the chin and nose and accentuates or proportionately elongates the nose.

Arcus senilis, a white band found around the outer edge of the cornea, can be present at any age but is more commonly found in late life. When present in young and mid-life, it may be a marker of underlying coronary artery disease. The lower eyelids may become puffy with age as a result of herniation of fat into this area. With age, there may also be a loss of fat behind the eye giving the eyes a sunken appearance and drooping of the upper eyelid. Occasionally, this sagging of the upper eyelid may hinder vision and require surgical correction. Cataracts, the most frequent cause of loss of vision in late life, increase with age.

A gradual reduction in lean body mass begins at around the age of 40. Although the extent of this reduction may vary between sexes and races, and may be partly related to the level of activity, it nevertheless occurs. The loss occurs primarily in skeletal muscle, organ systems and the brain. With age, there is also a gradual change in body composition. At the age of 25, body composition consists of approximately 14% fat, 61% water, 19% cell solids and 6% bone minerals. At the age of 70, body composition changes to approximately 30% fat, 53% water, 12% cell solids and 5% bone minerals. Progressive decrement is the rule in late life. This decrement is not secondary to disuse, but more likely is the result of both decreased cell division and decreased cellular function.

Physiologic concomitants of normal aging

With aging, there occurs a decline in organ function (which is quite independent of disease). Whether or not these changes in organ function are a reflection of what is occurring at the cellular level can only be speculative at this time. What is clear is that organ function declines in a fairly predictable fashion; this decline can either be hastened by disease or (to a degree) retarded through such preventive means as rest, proper nutrition and exercise. It is important, however, to understand that these age-related decrements in organ function do not significantly impair the lifestyles of most elderly persons. They primarily affect the reserve capacity of the organ system and the ability to handle and withstand stress—not the ability to maintain equilibrium or perform those functions which are nec-

The physical changes of aging need not mean a significant impairment of lifestyle.

essary to maintain life. Cardiac function, for example, decreases slightly with age, but in spite of this decrease healthy elderly persons may lead a very comfortable and fulfilling life. However, stress such as severe pneumonia, or trauma such as a fractured hip, may tax the cardiac reserve and could precipitate an episode of congestive heart failure. Aging then decreases the reserve capacity of the body to withstand insults to it which at an earlier age could have been tolerated with greater ease.

The brain
There is a progressive decline in brain weight with age, particularly after the 50s. Many conflicting studies have been reported about brain cell or neuron loss during life. In neither man nor animals have there been sufficiently well-controlled studies for any generalization to be safe. The brain itself does decrease in size and weight with age. This decrease is most marked in the frontal area and involves flattening or shrinking of the "hills and valleys" found on the surface of the brain (cerebral *convolutions* or *gyri*). Several of the chambers located within the brain (cerebral ventricles) may also enlarge with age. Externally the coverings of the brain thicken, become fibrotic and may calcify. Microscopic and electron-microscopic changes of the brain are virtually endless. Generally, as in the other organ systems, there is gradual accumulation of a peculiar brown pigment. Characteristic "neurofibrillatory tangles" occur with the brain cells and increase in number with age. Another characteristic finding is the presence of *senile plaques*, composed of degenerated tissue found between brain cells. These lesions are uncommon before the age of 50 to 60. When seen earlier they are frequently associated with *presenile dementia* or mental confusion. There is a significant reduction in cerebral blood flow and metab-

olism with aging; however, no direct correlation exists between cerebral blood flow and metabolism and intellectual impairment in the elderly.

The speed at which impulses are conducted through nerves becomes somewhat reduced after the age of 40 to 50. Anatomical, microscopic, metabolic and physiologic changes occur within the normal aging brain. Psychometric (psychological) testing has also revealed age-related functional changes. It is imperative to recognize that not every elderly person is confused; nor is it true that if an individual lives long enough, he will become confused. Intellectual integrity is compatible with old age despite the age-related changes which occur in the normal brain.

Vision
It has been estimated that blindness due to aging would only become inevitable if people lived to the age of 120 or 130. It is certainly true, however, that visual acuity decreases with aging. This occurs partially as a result of cumulative damage to the transparent portions of the eye. Other changes which occur in vision as a result of normal aging include: (1) a decrease in visual fields; (2) an increase in the amount of time it takes for the eye to adapt to the dark; (3) an increase in the minimum amount of light necessary to see; and (4) a decrease in the ability to see in dim light.

The density and pliability of the lens and the axis of the cornea change with age. In addition, the mechanism responsible for reabsorbing ocular fluid becomes less efficient with age and may in part be responsible for the increased frequency of chronic noncongestive glaucoma in late life.

Hearing
There is a progressive decrease in the ability to hear well with age. This is a result of a decrease in the ability to distinguish between different sounds and an increase in the minimum loudness which can be heard.

Pitch depends on frequency, or the number of vibrations per second. Old people first lose the ability to hear very high pitches. Speech discrimination—the ability to recognize spoken words—is affected most severely by age.

The heart
In the absence of disease, heart weight remains relatively constant after about the age of 25. The lining of the heart, the *endocardium*, becomes diffusely thickened with age from fibrosis (the formation of fibrous tissues). The valves and valve leaflets, particularly of the aortic and mitral valves, become thickened and may undergo calcification. On examination under a microscope an age-associated accumulation of pigment and atrophy of heart muscle fibrils can be noted.

Physiologic measurements document that with advancing age the heart becomes a less effective and efficient pump, working against a gradient of increasing resistance—the result of age-related changes which occur in the blood vessels (arteriosclerosis and atherosclerosis). Normal control mechanisms regulate cardiac output to meet the demands of the body. In youth the heart can vary its output fivefold to sixfold. It is the *cardiac reserve*, the ability to react to stress, which is lost in late life. The cardiac output of healthy elderly persons is sufficient to support usual activities; it is not, however, sufficient to tolerate either severe acute stress or prolonged stress. It is for this reason that surgery, infection, trauma, or blood loss can precipitate heart failure in an older individual who is otherwise healthy.

The lungs

The front-to-back diameter of the chest increases slightly with age. Other age-associated changes include: (1) the development of abnormal curvatures of the spine; (2) demineralization of the backbone and ribs; (3) calcification of rib cartilage; (4) decrease of rib mobility; and (5) partial contraction of the muscles of respiration. Microscopic dilation of air spaces occurs and the lung stiffens and becomes more rigid. The blood vessels supplying the lung also become less elastic and resistant to increases of blood flow. The cough reflex and force of cough may also diminish with age. Additionally, other mechanisms by which the airways of the lungs are cleared of debris become less efficient. The end result is similar to that in the cardiovascular system: normal aging of the lung will not hinder the routine activities of late life. However, the "pulmonary reserve" is greatly diminished. This diminution places the elderly at high risk of either pulmonary complications or respiratory failure in the event of stress.

The kidney

The kidney performs the following three necessary functions: (1) *volume control:* the kidneys allow the body to maintain a certain fluid volume despite ingestion of fluids and fluid loss through sweating, breathing and defecation; (2) *elimination of toxic elements:* toxic elements, whether ingested or produced by the body itself, are removed by the kidneys; (3) *acid base balance:* as in any living organism, acids and bases are both ingested and produced; maximum cell and organ function occur only if the acids and bases are closely balanced.

Age-related kidney changes are manifested by a reduction in the weight and mass of the organ: kidney weight decreases by an estimated 30% from youth to advanced old age. (This corresponds to a general decrease in size and weight of all organs.) Microscopically, there is a decrease in the number and size of individual filtering units (nephrons), an increase in the spaces between cells and an increase in the supportive tissue structure of the kidneys.

The permeability of cell membranes may decrease and the blood supply may become less rich with aging. The ability of the aged kidney to maintain acid-base balance, to control fluid volume and to remove toxic substances from the body is maintained throughout life. However, with age the ability to respond to extreme acid or base loads, volume overload (or volume depletion) and to filter out unusually large amounts of toxic substances is decreased. As in other organ systems, the aged kidney can maintain equilibrium but cannot adequately respond to severe challenges.

The gastrointestinal tract

The gastrointestinal tract comprises the mouth, esophagus ("gullet"), stomach, small intestine, large intestine, rectum and anus. Associated structures include the liver, gallbladder and pancreas. The gastrointestinal tract performs the functions of digestion of food, absorption of nutrients and elimination of waste. Secretions of the salivary glands, necessary for digestion, decrease with age and there is a diminution in the acuity of the senses of taste and smell. Teeth become worn and lost for many reasons as individuals grow older. Tooth loss through *caries* ("cavities") is largely avoidable. Dentures are not an inevitable concomitant of aging and can be avoided by lifelong good dental hygiene.

One of the most crucial functions of the gastrointestinal tract is the absorption of nutrients. Factors influencing absorption include changes in bowel motility, blood flow, the degree of digestion, the effectiveness of the absorbing surface and the efficiency of transport mechanisms. To a degree, anatomical changes in the aging gastrointestinal tract affect all factors related to absorption. However, the results of some studies suggest that the rate of absorption and not the quantity absorbed may change with age. The pancreas, liver and gallbladder also demonstrate anatomical and functional changes as the result of normal aging; but these age-related changes are compatible with normal functioning and are similar to alterations in all other organ systems.

The endocrine system

The endocrine system consists of a glandular network located throughout the body. It is closely controlled by its own feedback system. This network includes the following: (1) pituitary gland; (2) thyroid gland; (3) parathyroid glands; (4) pancreas (the islets of Langerhans, which secrete insulin); (5) adrenal glands; (6) ovaries; and (7) testes (testicles).

The secretions of these glands are extremely important in maintaining the physiologic equilibrium of the body. With normal aging a decrease occurs in both gland size and gland function. The delicate balance maintained by this organ system, however, is not affected. As with other organ systems within the body, the reserve capacity of the endocrine system is affected—that is, its ability to react and to withstand stress is diminished. A severe infection, a heart attack, or some other serious illness can easily disrupt the ability of this system to maintain normal blood pressure, normal blood sugar levels, or normal body temperature. Diabetes and thyroid disorders are *not* part of normal aging.

Psychosocial concomitants of normal aging

Twenty million Americans—nearly 10% of the total population—are over the age of 65. Under present mortality rates, by the year 2000 this population can be expected to increase to about 26 million and possibly 35.5 million under reduced mortality rates. This segment of the American population has expanded from 8.1% in 1950 to 10% in 1975 and may approach 13% by the year 2000. This rapid growth cannot be explained on the basis of increased longevity, but simply by the fact that more people are surviving to late life. Since 1929, the number of remaining years of life after age 65 has increased by an average of only six years. Decreased infant mortality and better health care for the young and middle aged better explain this burgeoning of the elderly population.

Men versus women
Women are more likely to survive into late life than men. There are approximately 1.3 women for every man over the age of 65. This fact is also reflected in the marital status of the elderly. More elderly men than women are married, 59% compared with 20%. 71% of all women over the age of 65 are widowed compared to 34% of men.

Where they live
The elderly, particularly those of minority groups, most often live in decaying central city areas, with decreasing numbers living in rural or other urban areas. 70% of the elderly own their own homes; however, approximately 19% of the 16 million housing units where senior citizens live may be classified as substandard housing. Old people tend to live in old housing not only because of lower rents, but also because of a reluctance to move to different neighborhoods.

More than three-fourths of all housing occupied by the elderly was built prior to 1940. As a result of urban renewal and the development of expressways and shopping centers, the metropolitan areas in which the elderly live are under constant threat of demolition and the residents are under constant threat of relocation. Low-rent public housing specifically designed for the elderly is insufficient to meet even the present demand, much less the demand of the next quarter century. However, this form of housing has demonstrated remarkable growth since 1960, when there were just over 18,000 housing units designed for the elderly. By 1972, this type of housing had increased to almost 350,000 units. In the same period, nonprofit sponsored elderly housing projects have also grown proportionately. In 1972, 66% of all low-income elderly housing units were located in projects that were age segregated.

Public housing has gone far beyond merely providing safe and secure shelter. Many public housing projects provide on-site congregate facilities, such as a central dining room and food services, social and recreational services and medical care through "satellite" clinics. In addition to low-cost public housing units, there has also been an increase in the number of retirement communities or villages and an increase in congregate living facilities such as adult homes. Although low-rent public housing, retirement villages and congregate living facilities may well be criticized for further segregating society by age, many studies have documented the increase in quality and quantity of life, and independence for those elderly able to obtain such housing compared with people of similar ages living in either unsafe or unplanned housing. The elderly feel more secure in a protected environment with their own peer groups and least secure in an urban area with a heterogeneous population where community relationships are poor, perceived environmental protection is poor, and the socioeconomic level depressed.

Income

Poverty
Poverty is a concept which frequently engenders feelings of guilt in an affluent society. Poverty is either denied, or rationalized by such terms as "relative deprivation" or "geographical poverty pockets." In fact, 20% of the population of the United States falls below its own poverty level and one-fifth of all poor are elderly.

Poverty, as defined by the United States Department of Agriculture, is a restriction of income to cover only essential needs. Since the average person spends one third of his income on food, the poverty level is determined by multiplying the cost of a 30-day supply of groceries by three. Anyone whose monthly income falls below this level is defined as living in poverty. In 1973 the poverty level for a single person was considered to be an annual income of $2,650. Even with the slightly higher purchasing power of the dollar in 1973, it is difficult to conceive of anyone subsisting on this amount; yet 20% of the elderly lived on less.

Source of income
Mandatory retirement and "agism" (discrimination against the elderly) have excluded most elderly persons from the job market. In addition, in most cases their personal resources and sources of income are limited. Retirement benefits such as social security, public pensions and private pensions account for an estimated 46% of all income. Employment earnings for those fortunate enough

Over one quarter of the elderly live alone or with nonfamily. Nearly half live close to their children.

to have a part-time job account for 29%. Income from assets, public assistance, veterans' benefits and gifts from families accounts for the remaining 25% of income. Most elderly persons do not enter late life or retirement impoverished, but become impoverished as a result of their retirement. They simply outlive their resources.

Double jeopardy

Those elderly persons who belong to minority groups may live in multiple jeopardy as a result of racism, chauvinism, and agism. Widows and single women are particularly disadvantaged. In 1970, 51% of elderly women living alone fell below the poverty level; 70% of black elderly Americans have incomes below $3,000 per year, and 50% have annual incomes less than $2,000. According to the Senate Special Committee on Aging, the statistical likelihood of poverty for elderly minority groups is twice as great as for the elderly white population, and four times as great as for the total population (of all ages). The plight of the aged widow, the aged single woman, and the aged minority member is grave.

Priorities

In a country which is capable of spending billions of dollars on defense, space exploration and foreign aid, the elderly are seemingly forgotten. France spends 7% of its gross national product on aiding the elderly. Britain spends 6.7% of its gross national product on services and subsidies to the aged. The United States spends only 4.2% of its gross national product on goods and services for elderly Americans. Certainly a reordering of priorities is needed. Most people of advanced age are not looking for a handout or for something they have not earned. Today's elderly have survived two world wars, a devastating depression, in addition to periods of inflation and recession. Most have been productive members of society. They have served their country and supported and educated their families. All they request now is to live their remaining years with dignity.

Crime

Contrary to popular belief, the elderly are less often the victims of crime than any other segment of the population over age 12. In a recent survey by the U.S. Department of Justice, *Criminal victimization in the United States*, it was noted that for the age group 65 and over, the rate of victimization was 4.4 per thousand. This compares with 10.0 in the 35 to 49 age group and 31.3 in the 20 to 24 age category. Researchers found that age, sex, race and city size were important determinants for fear of crime among the aged. Those over age 65 were more likely to report fear of crime than those less than 65. Women are far more likely to express fear then men. Blacks are generally more afraid of crime than whites. Residents of large cities tend to be more fearful of victimization than people in smaller towns and rural areas. It has been noted that elderly people who live in cities tend to be alienated from their communities, have the greatest fear of criminal victimization, are distrustful of police, and depend on isolation and apartment security devices to provide for their safety. Residents of retirement communities experience personal security, identify with their communities, have more social contacts, and depend on the physical structure of the community and the private security agency to provide for their safety. Although the incidence of criminal victimization of the elderly is lower than in other age groups, the resulting fear of crime significantly affects the quality of life and leads to further isolation and withdrawal among the elderly.

Health status

With advancing age, unfortunately, poor health often accompanies diminished income. Almost all elderly persons report at least one chronic condition or impairment. For many, the chronic disease or illness does not impair either their lifestyles or their daily activities. However, almost one in five with a chronic disease is incapacitated and one in three is partially limited in his activity level. The most frequently reported debilitating chronic diseases are cardiovascular (21.8%), arthritis and rheumatism (20.7%), and visual problems (9.5%). In comparison to the rest of the population, those elderly who are able to secure health care have, per capita, more physician visits per year, consume more medications, are hospitalized more frequently with longer hospital stays, and have significantly greater proportions of their incomes diverted to health care. Approximately 30% of the health care cost is now borne by the older person.

Medicare, which is only an insurance system, partly succeeded in helping the elderly finance the cost of health care, but also inflated the cost of care. Medicare failed by not providing a health care delivery system designed to meet the unique health care needs of the elderly. *Medicaid*, a second government health financing system, is particularly important to the indigent elderly. Medicaid completely covers the cost of physician, hospital, home and long-term care. However, the 60–70% of the elderly who are middle-class cannot avail themselves of Medicaid and are the group most hurt by the high cost of medical care.

Participation in the political system
Although the elderly compose only 10% of the total population, according to the Bureau of Census, they cast 16% of the votes (or every sixth vote in the 1976 election). Future elderly will not only compose a larger segment of the population, but they will conceivably be better educated. They may also be more affluent and vocal. If this minority group organizes itself, it will have a profound influence in determining policies particularly affecting its own welfare.

The "family-intergenerational contact"
The majority of elderly persons (67%), contrary to popular belief, live either in or within their own families; 28% live alone or with nonfamily. Only 5% live in long-term care facilities. Of those living in a family unit, over a third live with either married or unmarried children and brothers and sisters; nearly half of all elderly persons live within a 30-minute distance of one or more of their children. Altogether, 75–80% of old people with children live with their children or within 30 minutes of at least one of their children. Most see their children on a weekly basis. Again, from a third to nearly two-thirds of those living alone report staying with children overnight during the previous year. Contacts with brothers and sisters are more frequent among those persons who lack children or who do not see their children weekly or daily.

In addition to physical proximity and frequent contact, adult children and their parents support each other to a remarkable degree both in illness and in health. Approximately half of all old people give assistance to their children and grandchildren, including money as well as housekeeping services. Approximately two-thirds receive help from their families, including either occasional financial support or other gifts. In illness, four-fifths depend either on spouses, children, or other relatives for help with housework, meals and shopping. Contrary to popular belief, only a small minority depend either on social services or others for assistance. Evidence suggests that social services tend to complement rather than replace informal community and family associations and that they tend to reach those in genuine need.

Family structure among the elderly depends chiefly on marital status. Married elderly prefer to maintain separate households from their children. Widowed elderly are more likely to be found living with a child, more frequently a daughter. Single nonmarried elderly or widowed childless elderly persons are more likely to live either alone or with siblings, when available. Family relationships remain the most enduring social contacts of the elderly.

Satisfying relationships between the elderly and their children do not appear to be dependent on geographical proximity, but are related to communication between parents and children. The better the elderly parents' health, the better the relationship between parent and child. The better the elderly parents' attitude toward aging, the better the relationship between elderly parents and their adult children. Poor family relationships are a significant factor in the institutionalization of the elderly parent. Most old people (70%) live in a family structure which extends over several generations and which offers emotional, social, financial and physical assistance. It is only when these resources have been exhausted that the elderly either seek or come to the attention of the social services, which either help develop community supports or seek placement for the individual in a long-term care facility.

Marriage
Marriages in late life demonstrate as much flux, stress and diversity as young and mid-life marriages. Generally, the expectations found in older marriages consist of care during illness, household management and emotional gratification. Some degree of deterioration is found in up to one third of elderly marriages. Variables affecting marriages over a long period were found to be environmental influences, physical and mental health, and the particular historical period in which the marriage is found.

Children and grandchildren frequently serve as bonds for marriages in stress (as they do in young and mid-life marriages). For many, marriage becomes supportive and more acceptable than the unknown. A common difficulty in older marriages is the disruption caused by the physical or emotional illness of either spouse. Patterns of dominance may shift in old age, with the wife assuming a more active and responsible role. But ascendance to dominance may be shortlived and unrewarding. Mutuality and equality throughout life may be a better pattern and carry over to a more consistently mutual relationship in old age.

Grandparents
One of the more satisfying and fulfilling roles for many is that of being a grandparent; 70% of older people have living grandchildren and 32% are great grandparents. Often the relationship between grandchild and grand-

parent is far more positive than the relationship between parent and child of earlier generations. Grandparents frequently have more time, patience and interest for grandchildren than they had for their own children simply because they have been relieved of the stresses, demands and roles of young and mid-life. On the other hand, for those elderly persons who did not particularly enjoy the role of being a parent, it would seem unlikely that they would find the role of grandparent uniquely fulfilling.

Mental health and aging

The true incidence of psychiatric disorders in late life is unknown. It is difficult to determine not only because of confusing classification systems but also because of the problem of truly objective criteria in establishing a diagnosis. In 1971, the American Psychological Association estimated that at least three million elderly (15% of all elderly) were in need of mental health services. Most would agree that this estimate is conservative. Depression is the most common "affective disorder" found in an aging population. Various researchers have projected anywhere from a 10–65% incidence in late life, and it seems to increase with advancing age.

The depressions of the aged have been divided into three groups: neurotic or situational depressions, endogenous depressions, and the depressions which occur in the course of senile and arteriosclerotic dementia. These categories are not mutually exclusive, nor are they comprehensive. Other terms used to describe depression include psychotic, neurotic, primary, secondary, bipolar, unipolar, involutional. This confusion over and diversity in nomenclature is probably a result of limited knowledge in the cause and "pathophysiology" of depressive illness. Impressive gains, however, have been made in the study of the chemical content and metabolism of the brain in different depressive disorders. That depression is a real problem in late life is reflected by the increased rate of suicide, particularly among elderly Caucasian men. White men over the age of 85 have a higher incidence of suicide than any other group by age, sex and race.

The clinical presentation of depression frequently differs from the classic loss of appetite, weight loss, insomnia and early morning waking. Most elderly persons will deny depression on questioning, but will present with apathy, withdrawal, self-depreciation, psychomotor retardation or a host of hypochondriacal complaints. The diagnosis is often missed and the patient labeled either a "crock" or merely senile. Tragically, the prognosis for treated depression in late life is quite good and is often smoother than for a younger population. Most elderly persons respond well to a relief of environmental stress, antidepressants, or occasionally electroconvulsive therapy. Rarely is prolonged psychotherapy indicated.

(See also the major articles on **Psychiatry** and **Psychotherapy**.)

Religion and death

It can only be speculated whether or not today's elderly are more religious than younger age groups or whether they are more or less religious than previous generations of elderly persons. Religion when viewed in terms of providing a meaning for existence, a value for life, and an opportunity to worship as a community, does have a meaningful role for many older people. Those with strong religious beliefs have a more positive attitude toward life, aging and death. Those with few religious convictions, or none, tend to have the most difficulty in adjusting to the inevitability of aging and death.

For many elderly people, organized religion provides opportunities for social participation, e.g., missionary activity, bake sales, sheltered workshops, visitations and pilgrimages. Many also look to their ministers, rabbis, and pastors for guidance and counseling in resolving problems peculiar to late life and accepting its peculiar disabilities. Unfortunately, many clergymen find working with the elderly depressing, unrewarding and (like physicians and others) are quite "agist" in their attitudes. Hopefully, education and exposure will alter these attitudes.

Longevity

Within the aging population there exists a "subpopulation" of individuals characterized by unusual health and vigor well into advanced late life. Researchers have termed this the *longevity syndrome*. Among factors found common to this group of elderly persons are advanced education and a life characterized by varied and diffuse interests and hobbies. Most had come from smaller communities, were independent in attitude, and had developed a lifestyle of active interests and the capacity to entertain themselves rather than be dependent on others for their entertainment. All had a joy of life. They were attuned to their times, spent little time reminiscing, and had less of a generational gap than many in mid-life. All had a lifestyle of curiosity, self-fulfillment, and self-sufficiency.

Successful aging is an art associated with a lifestyle cultivated since childhood.

Many had developed new pursuits and interests at age 85 or older. Most were married or had been married at some time. Most had led a life characterized by moderation, not only in nutrition, exercise and rest but also in the use of alcohol and tobacco. Most did have some religious beliefs, but none had been zealous in their beliefs or in the exercise of a particular religious tradition. All accepted death as an inevitability but none spent considerable time contemplating their approaching demise. General health was good and few took any medications routinely. Interestingly, a family history of longevity was not a constant in their histories. Whether good health promoted the lifestyle or the lifestyle promoted health and longevity could not be ascertained.

In an 11-year prospective study completed by the National Institutes of Health, medical, biochemical and socio-psychiatric variables were assessed in an attempt not only to gain insights into the aging process but also to determine predictors of survival. The population studied included 47 men with a mean age of 70. The behavioral factors which best predicted survival were the mental status and the organization and complexity of daily behavior. The physical variables which were most accurate in predicting mortality were the systolic BLOOD PRESSURE and weight. Systolic hypertension and low body weight were associated with an increased mortality rate. When both behavioral and physical variables were analyzed together, two factors emerged as the most reliable predictors of survival. They were the complexity and organization of a typical day in the subject's life and the habit or absence of cigarette smoking.

The average human lifespan, unaffected by disease, may well be 90 to 100 years. Successful aging, aging in terms of quality and quantity, is an art. It is an art that is not learned or acquired in late life. It is associated with a lifestyle that begins with childhood. Aging and death should be the culmination of a successful existence.

Senility

Normal aging

Mental confusion is not part of normal aging. It is not a normal concomitant of aging nor can all individuals who reach advanced age necessarily expect to become mentally impaired. It has been estimated that 15% of people 65 to 75 years old and 25% of those 75 and older (or some four million people in the United States) are confused to some degree. Some degree of mental confusion is manifested by an estimated 60% of institutionalized elderly patients.

With normal aging, the capacity for abstract thinking does not necessarily decrease and in some individuals may actually increase. Likewise, problem-solving ability does not necessarily decrease with age. However, the amount of *time* required to solve problems may increase. In addition, the older individual may be less flexible in his problem-solving behavior and may have difficulty in accepting new approaches to problem solving. However, in approaching problems he does bring with him a wealth of experience acquired through the years. The net result is that no generalizations can be made about the mental capacity of the elderly.

Intelligence was objectively evaluated in a group of community elderly over a seven-year period using what is known as the Wechsler Adult Intelligence Scale. The areas tested included vocabulary, similarities, digital span, and block design. Over the seven-year period only digital span demonstrated a statistically significant decrease. Further analysis revealed that neither age nor the initial level of health or scores obtained on the Wechsler Adult Intelligence Scale were related to test-score changes over time. When types of intelligence are examined, however, changes do occur.

Researchers have subdivided intelligence into "fluid" and "crystallized" intelligence. *Fluid intelligence* purportedly reflects functioning of neurological structures which increases until maturation of the brain is completed. This generally occurs during adolescence followed by a gradual decline. Fluid intelligence is needed for problem-solving tests such as figural relations and matrices. *Crystallized intelligence* is thought to reflect cultural assimilation. Assuming adequate health, crystallized intelligence is felt to increase steadily during adult life and is evaluated by means of tests which evaluate verbal comprehension. It is through the exercise of fluid intelligence that crystallized intelligence increases throughout life. With the postulated age-related decline in fluid intelligence, secondary to the structural changes which occur with normal aging, the increments of crystallized intelligence decrease throughout life. It is important, however, to realize that crystallized intelligence.*does* increase throughout life. Only the size of the increments decrease. In particular, word vocabulary may demonstrate constant improvement as one ages.

Clinically, nonpathological forgetfulness is frequently observed in late life. Many elderly persons compensate by developing elaborate written lists as a memory aid. Memory itself may be recent or remote. The physician most often finds *long-term memory* intact but with deficits in *recent memory*. By the use of testing methods emphasizing the ability to recall and recognize items, researchers found greater decrements in long-term recall than immediate or short-term recall. Visual short-term recall also appears to be affected more than verbal short-term recall. Further research has suggested that the deficit is not in the acquisition or "encoding" nor in the retrieval (remembering) of information but in its actual storage. Neuroanatomists have recently linked this deficit to the depigmentation of a certain structure called the *hippo-campus*, located in the midbrain.

Problem-solving ability is essential for successfully coping with one's environment. It is through problem-solving mechanisms that obstacles met in daily living are

The pace of urban life creates difficulties for all of us—but especially for the elderly.

resolved or overcome. Reasoning and information gathering are important components of problem solving. The efficiency of reasoning appears to decline sometime after about the age of 36. This decrease in efficiency is thought to be related to a decrement in the gathering, storing and use of new information. When subjected to tests, the elderly are found to be more distracted by irrelevant data than younger individuals. More appropriately, there may be some decrease in problem-solving ability with age. This decrease, however, may be compensated for by reducing irrelevant or distracting stimuli or information and by allowing greater time for the problem-solving process. It is also known that the elderly tend to be more cautious and take fewer risks in their problem solving. Through these compensatory mechanisms, most elderly persons are quite capable of dealing with the problems of everyday living.

A common fallacy is that "you can't teach an old dog new tricks." It is possible through training to produce a significant increase in intellectual performance in the elderly. Surprisingly, training appears not only to improve the performance of a specific task but tends to spill over or generalize in broader areas. The fact that *any* training results can be obtained working with the elderly suggests that intellectual changes associated with aging are not necessarily irreversible. The intellectual deterioration found in late life may be partially the result of the role society has forced upon the elderly. The role which society may have encouraged is one of dependency, helplessness

and withdrawal rather than independence, involvement and competence.

Personality also appears to be altered by age. Although there are no gross changes in personality, certain aspects or attitudes do change with age. By administering "personality scales" on a cross section of the population, it was found that youth showed openness to *feeling*, middle-age showed openness to *ideas*, and the elderly showed a balanced openness to *both feelings and ideas*. The results of additional studies have demonstrated that *caution* advances with age. The elderly are less likely to become involved in certain tasks unless the probability of success is relatively high. Compared with other age groups, they are also less likely to raise their level of aspiration following success. This behavior may be a defense mechanism protecting them from developing a more negative "self-concept" than the one most elderly persons already have.

Senility (or *organic brain syndrome*) can be defined as a decrease in the intellectual and functional ability of an individual to such an extent that he can no longer cope effectively with his environment. Traditionally, the intellectual functions which correlate with effective behavior include judgment; orientation to time, person and place; memory, recent and remote; arithmetic ability; reasoning; and emotional stability. By experience, most physicians have found that loss of recent memory is usually the first finding to appear in the symptom complex designated the organic brain syndrome. Loss of recent memory includes more than simple forgetfulness, which can be quite common in the elderly, and is usually compensated for by written lists and reminders. Loss of recent memory refers, for example, to the complete inability to recall what one had for lunch, or a conversation which may have occurred half an hour earlier. The last intellectual function to disappear is loss of personal identity, manifested by the inability to recall one's own name. This is usually seen only in the most severe or far advanced cases of the organic brain syndrome.

Acute reversible senility

The causes of the organic brain syndrome can be approached by empirically dividing the syndrome or symptom complex into those cases which occur suddenly and those which have a slower, insidious onset or have been evident for a prolonged time. The cause of sudden confusional states (acute organic brain syndromes) include the following: (1) medications; (2) infections; (3) anemia; (4) electrolyte imbalance (abnormalities of blood chemistry); (5) elevated or low blood sugar (*hyperglycemia* or *hypoglycemia*); (6) kidney failure; (7) stroke; (8) cardiac dysfunction (heart disease); (9) pulmonary insufficiency; (10) liver decompensation; (11) overactive or underactive thyroid gland (*hyperthyroidism* or *hypothyroidism*); (12) malnutrition; (13) psychiatric disorders; (14) loss of vision; (15) loss of hearing.

Medications are probably the most frequent cause of sudden or acute organic brain syndromes. Many elderly persons self-prescribe and ingest multiple nonprescription drugs such as "cold remedies," arthritis pills, sleeping potions, and laxatives. Most of those elderly able to obtain health care frequently "shop" for physicians as one might an automobile mechanic. Each physician may prescribe a different medication. Elderly people also tend to be collectors and amass multiple drugs in their medicine chests, simply because they never or rarely discard any of their medications once the problem for which they were taking the drug has resolved. Those living in close proximity to each other, such as in housing complexes for senior citizens, may share their medications with each other, particularly if their complaints are similar. Finally, many physicians may often prescribe either too many different drugs in confusing patterns of self-administration, inappropriately high doses, or drugs which may interfere with or potentiate the effects of each other. In the elderly, in particular, certain drugs may be as life-threatening as life-saving.

Pneumonia, urinary tract infections, appendicitis, and other *infectious disorders* can present as confusional states rather than with the traditional hallmarks of infection such as fever, cough, burning on urination or abdominal pain. The diagnosis can be missed unless the physician thoughtfully and thoroughly searches for it. *Anemia*, whether secondary to blood loss (such as in cases of peptic ulcer or diminished production of red blood cells) can cause a confusional state in the elderly. The most common cause of anemia in the elderly is chronic deficiency of iron in the diet. This may be related to dietary preferences or the inability to purchase, prepare or digest the proper foods. It may also be secondary to chronic blood loss associated with peptic ulcer disease, the effects of medications such as aspirin, or cancer of the colon. Other common deficiencies in the elderly which result in decreased blood production are folic acid and Vitamin B_{12} deficiency. *Blood sugar abnormalities* are commonly seen in diagnosed or undiagnosed diabetics. Insulin and oral diabetic agents can profoundly and dangerously lower the blood sugar in the elderly, particularly in those with erratic eating habits. Likewise, an infection or any other cause of stress (such as the loss of a loved one) may throw a previously "controlled" diabetic out of control and precipitate a confusional state which may progress to coma. Abnormalities of blood chemistry involving sodium and calcium (electrolyte imbalance) may be secondary to a multitude of causes but can nevertheless cause confusional states in older people.

In the elderly, disease processes of specific organ systems rarely present with classic symptoms. Less than an estimated 40% of the elderly complain of chest pains while having a heart attack. Similarly, those elderly suffering from congestive heart failure or irregular heartbeats may manifest abnormal or even bizarre behavior rather than complain of shortness of breath or dizziness. Individuals experiencing "small strokes" (*transient ischemic episodes*) may become confused and 24 hours later may be unable to recall the episode. Dysfunction of other organ systems such as lung, liver, and kidney, again may assume unusual presentations in late life.

Thyroid disorders resulting in either increased or decreased production of thyroid hormone can be mistaken for either depression or organic brain syndromes in the elderly. *Malnutrition* is probably more common among the aging population than is recognized. For not completely understood reasons, it may lead to a progressive confusional state indistinguishable from senility. Finally, *psychiatric disorders*, most commonly depression, may be misdiagnosed and the individual needlessly institutionalized for life. Other psychiatric disorders (such as paranoia) may result from loss of vision secondary to cataracts or loss of hearing caused by impairment of sound conduction by the bones of the middle ear or some disorder of the nerve pathways in the inner ear. Appropriate treatment would usually involve either a cataract extraction or a hearing-aid rather than "psychotropic" medication or institutionalization.

Confusional states resulting from the above-mentioned causes may be completely or partially reversible. It is important that families, relatives, or friends do not automatically accept sudden or rapidly progressive changes in behavior as senility, but instead seek health care from a competent physician. It is encumbent on the physician to obtain a careful medical history of the patient, perform a thorough physical examination and order appropriate laboratory tests to exclude reversible causes of confusional states in the elderly.

Chronic irreversible senility

Chronic irreversible confusional states (termed "chronic organic brain syndromes") usually have a very insidious onset and frequently are not even recognized by families until some precipitating event—such as a fractured hip resulting from an avoidable fall, or a needless apartment fire—emphasizes the limited intellectual capacity of a parent, relative or friend. Although the classification of causes frequently changes as knowledge of disease process increases, the following are considered the more common causes of chronic organic brain syndromes: (1) Alzheimer's disease; (2) multi-infarct dementia; (3) Creutzfeldt-Jakob's disease; (4) post-traumatic dementia; (5) normal pressure hydrocephalus; (6) toxic encephalopathy.

Alzheimer's disease is a disease of possibly multiple causes, occurring usually in the fifth to seventh decades of life (40s to 60s), characterized clinically by a very insidious onset leading eventually to a severe confusional state. When first seen by the doctor, the patient typically manifests severe forgetfulness involving recent memory.

There is a gradual waning of the ability for abstract thinking, including the ability to perform simple calculations, solve everyday problems and exercise judgment. Paranoid behavior may develop. The individual finally becomes disorientated to time, person and place. At postmortem examination, the brain is usually shrunken in size, with decreased weight, and the chambers of the brain (ventricles) are abnormally dilated. On microscopic examination there is a marked diminution in the number of brain cells (neurons). Research has suggested that this disease may be caused by a transmissible agent (such as a slow-growing virus) or a gradual accumulation of a metal (such as aluminum) in the brain. Undoubtedly more causes of this unfortunate disease will be uncovered as researchers and clinicians learn more about it. Unfortunately, at present no treatment is specific for this disease process and prevention is not possible.

Multi-infarct dementia is commonly seen in elderly patients who have evidence of generalized arteriosclerosis ("hardening of the arteries"). There is often evidence of a decreased blood supply to the lower extremities (termed *peripheral vascular disease*), a decreased blood supply to the coronary arteries (which supply the heart muscle), and a

> Certain mental changes commonly occur with advancing age and almost come to be expected by the elderly person and his or her family. But a few patients experience a dramatic and progressive confusional state, representing one of the "chronic organic brain syndromes."

decreased blood supply to other organ systems of the body, such as the brain and kidneys. Characteristically, these people or their families will give a history of intermittent confusional states alternating with periods of lucidity. These intermittent confusional states have been termed "small strokes" (or *transient ischemic episodes*). As these episodes become more frequent and the periods of lucidity become shorter, total resolution or total recovery may not occur and the individual will begin manifesting loss of recent memory, loss of ability to reason or calculate, and may show marked errors of judgment. Focal areas of the brain are destroyed and replaced by supportive elements of brain tissue. There is some evidence that the frequency of these "small strokes" can be decreased by the effect of aspirin on the blood's clotting system. Treatment at best is poor and nonspecific.

Post-traumatic dementia is commonly seen in former prize fighters (who have become "punch drunk") and individuals who have sustained severe head injuries (such as victims of automobile accidents or muggers). Especially in cases of repeated trauma there is a gradual decrease in

intellectual prowess and the patient's behavior may become both bizarre and aggressive. Treatment is supportive and major tranquilizers (such as the phenothiazines) may be needed to control behavior.

Creutzfeldt-Jakob's disease is a rapidly progressive disorder characterized by dementia, muscular spasticity or rigidity and difficulty in walking. A slow-growing transmissible virus has been identified as the causative agent. Treatment is supportive, although the disease has an unfavorable prognosis.

Normal pressure hydrocephalus is a relatively rare (and recently described) clinical disorder characterized by difficulty in walking, incontinence and mental confusion. It can be associated with the after-effects of stroke, encephalitis, brain trauma, brain tumor, an irregular blood vessel in the brain or a narrowing of one of the channels connecting the chambers (cerebral ventricles) of the brain. Diagnostic tests reveal progressive dilation of one or more ventricles. In selected cases, shunting of cerebrospinal fluid away from the ventricles has resulted in clinical improvement. Enthusiasm for the procedure, however, has been waning because of the lack of uniform success and the risks associated with it.

Confusional states that result from the ingestion, injection, inhalation, or absorption of toxic substances (with the exception of alcohol) are relatively rare in late life. Alcohol is toxic to the brain and may cause irreversible cell death, particularly in the midbrain; 10% of all alcoholics are over the age of 60. Approximately 2–10% of the elderly are alcoholic and can be grouped into two distinct populations. They are the young alcoholic who has survived into late life and the elderly alcoholic who has escalated his drinking habits either in late mid-life or in late life. Of the former, the majority have resolved their problem of alcohol abuse and are in relatively good health. The latter, the elderly alcoholic who has commenced his alcoholism in late life, is generally in poor health, has multiple medical problems and has an increased incidence of "mixed" dependencies (on both drugs and alcohol). Interestingly, the older alcoholic has a better response to therapy than the younger alcoholic.

Confusional states secondary to acute alcohol abuse may take the form of DELIRIUM TREMENS or a withdrawal state characterized by agitation, excessive perspiration, tremors, rapid pulse and an elevated temperature. Chronic confusional states secondary to alcohol abuse may be seen in different but related medical syndromes. One is characterized by confusion, disorientation, loss of memory and a tendency to confabulate (make up stories). The mortality rate in untreated cases can be high. Recovery, following treatment, is slow and often incomplete. Residual mental defects may be severe enough to require chronic institutionalization. A second type of chronic confusional state is characterized by the sudden onset of paralysis of eye movements, difficulty in walking and disturbances in the state of consciousness. Frequently both are seen in association with each other.

Alcohol may also damage the peripheral nerves and may cause foot drop, weakness, paralysis, tingling sensations, excessive pain, or loss of sensation (particularly in the lower extremities). In severe cases the upper extremities may also be affected. Peripheral nerve damage may be seen independently or in association with both clinical syndromes. With abstinence there may be some return of function. Other substances which can be toxic to the brain, but which rarely affect the elderly, include arsenic, lead, manganese, mercury, and carbon monoxide.

Role of society

Some gerontologists have suggested that in some individuals the development of an organic brain syndrome may be a defense mechanism in which the psyche withdraws from an increasingly hostile world. Although this may be a simplified explanation, certainly environment does play a role in the development of chronic confusional states. In those societies (such as Soviet Georgia) in which age is considered an asset, not a liability, organic brain syndromes are rare. In such societies the elderly are esteemed for their wisdom; they continue to be productive members of the workforce, and they participate in the decision-making processes of their villages.

Since medical care was underdeveloped in this area, it may be argued that survival of the fittest occurred. Those who might have become mentally or physically infirm had died at an earlier age from natural selection. Only the fittest survived into advanced late life. Also, in such societies as Soviet Georgia the mentally or physically infirm are not allowed to marry or reproduce. The "gene pool" in this way has also been preserved. In practice, however, environment does play an important role in mental health and the development of chronic confusional states. Forced retirement, loss of income, loss of peer respect, prestige, and companionship can hardly insure successful aging in any society. Forced dependency does not encourage fulfillment of lifetime aspirations. The scenario of mandatory retirement, poverty, chronic disease and disability is repeated too often for anyone to deny its existence.

Medications and the elderly

Drug tolerance

Old people tolerate drugs unpredictably. In addition to an almost 20-fold variability in drug response, determined genetically, old people may react adversely to drugs for multiple reasons. Elderly persons have a smaller lean body mass through which an administered drug is distributed. Thus a given dose may result in a significantly higher blood level in an older than in a younger person.

Normal aging produces a gradual diminution of the functions of the kidneys, liver and lungs which may not be evident clinically nor shown by laboratory tests. This gradual diminution in organ function may lead to decreased metabolism and excretion of many drugs commonly used to treat an elderly population. Drug absorption is variable in any population. In the elderly this variability may be increased by age-related changes in the absorptive surface of the gastrointestinal tract. Following absorption, most drugs are bound in some degree to plasma proteins. With aging there is also a decrease in plasma binding proteins. This decrease results in elevated levels of unbound drugs, their most active form.

Finally, the ability of the aged organ to respond may be variable. It is well known, for example, that barbiturates which are normally used for sedation may cause extreme agitation in the elderly; the brain's reaction is the exact opposite to the predicted and desired response (sedation). The same may be true in many or all organ systems. Fortunately, for many drugs, methods have been developed to determine the amounts of drug in the bloodstream and thus to help determine therapeutic versus toxic levels.

Multiple medications

Problems of the effects of drugs in late life are further compounded by multiple drug administration to the elderly. Most elderly persons have from one to three chronic medical problems needing treatment for which they receive on the average three to six different medications. As the number of medications increases, the number of possible drug interactions also increases dramatically. These may either dangerously potentiate the desired effects of the drug or nullify them.

Many elderly take medicines as many as nine times a day for a number of chronic medical problems.

Undesired side effects of drugs may also be potentiated by drug interactions. The greater the number of medications and the number of times they are taken each day, the greater the risk of drug error or side effects. Many elderly persons may be prescribed three different drugs, one to be taken twice a day, a second to be taken three times a day, and a third to be taken four times a day. The least number of drugs should be prescribed in the simplest pattern of self-administration. In the elderly, there *is* a role for combination drugs (drugs which contain two or more active ingredients, which often exert more than one type of therapeutic effect). Through the use of combination drugs, the total number of pills may be reduced and the risk of drug error or side effects may also be reduced appreciably.

Reducing medication errors

Elderly patients who are hospitalized for acute and often life-threatening medical and surgical problems are occasionally treated with potentially dangerous drugs and frequently complicated dose regimes. On the day of discharge they are often given a handful of prescriptions with no adequate explanation of the drugs they are taking or their potential side effects. Clinical research has documented that drug errors *can* be reduced with self-medication programs. Prior to discharge the patient is instructed in his medications and tested to determine his understanding. Dosage regimes are then developed which the patient can reliably follow and methods of administration established.

Pharmacies and the elderly

The elderly are the largest consumers of drugs, receiving annually over 225 million prescriptions, including almost 180 million for mood elevators and depressants. Yet many pharmacies, as a result of recent legislation, will dispense only containers with safety caps. These safety caps may protect the pediatric population but only make it more difficult for the geriatric population. Elderly persons with fingers crippled by arthritis, limbs paralyzed by strokes, and memories which are frequently failing, often do not have the mental or physical dexterity to manipulate these containers.

Directions for administration, giving the number of pills to be taken at what intervals, are typed on small labels pasted on the container. Since visual acuity decreases with age while the incidence of cataracts, diabetes and glaucoma increase, many elderly persons simply cannot read the directions on the medicine container.

Psychosomatic complaints

Although it is not well documented, it would seem that psychosomatic complaints increase with age. Since our present society is a "drug culture" which expects a cure for every complaint, patients are not satisfied unless their physician prescribes a medication for their complaints. In the elderly, there is a real role for the administration of *placebos* (unmedicated preparations which patients believe to contain medically active ingredients). Many studies have demonstrated that placebos are effective in the management of psychosomatic complaints. Insomnia, musculo-skeletal complaints and anxiety respond to placebos as well as to sleep medications, muscle relaxants and tranquilizers.

Role of drug therapy

There is no drug which will combat aging. Drug therapy, when used appropriately, can relieve many of the symptoms of chronic disease and thus add both quality and quantity to remaining years. The elderly have special therapeutic needs and exhibit unique responses to drugs. A careful assessment of symptoms and an evaluation of the known responses of the elderly to a proposed drug must be weighed before initiating treatment. In prescribing for the elderly, it is wise to remember Napoleon's words, "I do not want two diseases—one nature made, one doctor made."

Long-term care

Long-term care is a loosely organized system of services to assist those in need to reach and maintain their highest level of health and psychosocial functioning. It encompasses such diverse areas as homemaker services, home health aides, hot meal programs, "meals-on-wheels," transportation, community mental health programs, social services, nursing, physical therapy, occupational therapy, and domiciliary care such as adult homes, foster home care and nursing home care.

Nursing homes

A nursing home may well be thought of as a conglomerate of the above-mentioned services organized within a fixed geographic location to provide services primarily to those elderly who, for various reasons, can no longer be supported in the community.

Nursing homes constitute a diverse and heterogeneous group of institutions whose only common denominator is that of being licensed. With the passage of Medicare and Medicaid legislation in the mid-1960s, nursing home stock became "glamour stock" and the United States experienced a rapid expansion of the nursing home industry. In 1974, there were over 22,000 nursing homes and health-related facilities in the country, with a total bed capacity of over 1,200,000; 10% were government owned, 17% not-for-profit, and 73% proprietary. In 1975, $9 billion was spent on nursing homes, in which 4–5% of the population over the age of 65 resided.

Services rendered by nursing homes can be broadly grouped into four major categories: (1) hotel services; (2) personal care services; (3) nursing, medical and rehabilitative services; and (4) psychosocial services.

Hotel services include housekeeping, laundry, dietary

and maintenance services. Personal care services include assistance with the activities of daily living such as washing, dressing, eating, and frequently ambulating (assisting the patient while he or she walks). These services are usually delivered by nurses' aides and nursing assistants. Nursing, medical and rehabilitative services are comprised of such traditional services as those found in most hospitals, including physical therapy, occupational therapy and speech therapy. Psychosocial services include social services, recreational therapy and religious care.

Nursing homes essentially deliver two broad levels of care: skilled nursing care and intermediate or health-related care. These levels of care have been defined and developed by the major "third-party" reimbursers of care, Medicare and Medicaid. Skilled nursing care—the higher level of care provided by a nursing home—consists of the monitoring of specific disease processes, such as unstable diabetes mellitus, congestive heart failure and chronic obstructive lung disease. It includes the provision of services which must be delivered by or under the supervision of a registered nurse, such as tracheostomy care, colostomy care, care of pressure sores, and aspiration of the upper airways. Rehabilitative services such as physical therapy, occupational therapy and speech therapy are also included.

Individual functional disabilities such as mental confusion, incontinence, and the inability to walk or transfer from bed to wheelchair, are either not recognized as disabilities in some states or relegated to a "point system" evaluation which has been shown to have as many drawbacks as advantages. Intermediate or health-related care consists of providing such personal care services as assistance with dressing, washing, eating and ambulating. Few or no skilled nursing services are offered or are readily available except for the distribution of medications and monitoring of vital signs such as blood pressure, temperature, pulse and respiration. Reimbursement determines staffing patterns. Since third-party reimbursement is considerably less for intermediate or health-related care, the ratio of staff to residents (in terms of nurses and nursing assistants and other health providers) is considerably less in the intermediate care nursing homes and in those homes offering more than one level of care.

Patient population

At present, 5% of the population over the age of 65 are institutionalized in nursing homes. This figure in a sense is misleading. Various studies have shown that at least one in five individuals over the age of 65 will die in a nursing home. Consequently, although at any one time only 5% of the elderly population is institutionalized in a nursing home, the actual prevalency rate for this segment of the population is 20%. Similarly, a 20-year study of 207 normal aged persons found that their total chance of institutionalization sometime before death was about one in

The ratio of nursing aides to patients is crucial to the quality of nursing home care.

four. Not only has death become increasingly "institutionalized," but the risk of death is also greater for the institutionalized elderly when compared with their age-matched cohorts. In 1972, the mortality rate for persons over age 55 was 3.9 deaths per 100 persons. In comparison, the death rate per 100 resident-years of care in the nursing home population was eight to ten times higher than for the general population.

Factors precipitating nursing home placement

Psychosocial factors increasing the need for institutionalization include living alone, being unmarried, being separated, having no children (or few children), and being female. Sex can be considered a risk factor simply because women more often live alone, have never married, or are separated or have fewer surviving children. Interestingly, in contrast to the prevalence rate, the total chance or risk of institutionalization does not increase with age.

Psychosocial factors which affect the chances of being accepted for institutionalized care include financial resources, level of education and race. Better education affecting nursing home accessibility can be explained by its association with greater income. The easier accessibility for whites to nursing home care, however, cannot be entirely explained by their higher educational level or greater financial resources. Paradoxically, more institutionalized elderly persons are financially disadvantaged. Institutionalization itself rapidly depletes financial reserves so that after a variable period of time most institutionalized elderly find themselves bankrupt.

Role of physical disability

Chronic disease rarely precipitates institutionalization. Almost all elderly persons have at least one chronic illness or impairment; for many, the chronic disease or illness does not impair either their lifestyles or their ability to care for themselves. However, almost one in five elderly persons with a chronic disease is to some degree incapacitated and one in three is partially limited in his level of activity.

The most frequent debilitating chronic conditions are cardiovascular disease (21.8%), arthritis and rheumatism (20.7%), and visual problems (9.5%). Functional disability resulting from chronic disease, however, does precipitate institutionalization. Functional risk factors include mental impairment and physical disability resulting in loss of ambulation and fecal and urinary incontinence. By far, incontinence more than any other functional disability overwhelms both family and community resources and necessitates institutionalization.

Mentally impaired and "wheelchair-independent" elderly can be supported in the community. Incontinent elderly persons, possibly because they are frequently also mentally impaired, can rarely be supported in the community either by caring families or by community service organizations such as the Visiting Nurse Service.

Choosing a nursing home

Various considerations have been suggested to families by both researchers and community organizations in selecting an appropriate nursing home for parent or relative. Among these have been the size of the facility, its ownership, its resources (in terms of physical therapy, occupational therapy and speech therapy), the ratio of nurses and aides to patients, the levels of care available, and the physical environment of the nursing home. Ownership appears to be a debatable factor. Some researchers have produced studies demonstrating that a "voluntary" nursing home will generally provide superior care; others have stated that no correlation exists between ownership and quality of care. Obviously the selection of an institution cannot be based on ownership alone. A larger institution would be more likely to have greater resources to support ancillary services such as physical therapy, occupational therapy, speech therapy, and social services, and a well-developed recreational therapy program.

It can also be argued that the larger the facility the more impersonal the care becomes, and the less responsive persons involved in the supervision of care become to the individual needs of the patients, residents and families. If all other factors are held constant, the ratio of nurses and nursing aides to patients emerges as a crucial factor. The fewer the nursing staff, regardless of training or intent, the more the quality and individuality of care will suffer. Adequate staffing, particularly in nurses' aides, is crucial to quality care and patient satisfaction.

Studies have also shown that facilities which offer more than one level of care provide care of a higher quality than those offering only one level of care. Closed medical staffs, in which a fixed group of physicians provide all medical care, were found to be more responsive and to provide a higher quality of care than open medical staffs (in which any physician who desires can provide patient care). Finally, physical environment as a single variable is an important factor in resident satisfaction. It is more pleasant to live in a modern, well-designed, barrier-free, clean environment than to live in a not-so-new, poorly designed, poorly maintained environment.

Important factors, then, in selecting a nursing home are size, levels of care available, resources, staff-to-resident ratio, organization of medical staff and physical environment. More practically, most nursing homes which have been established for some time will have developed a reputation both within the community and among other professional organizations, such as hospitals. *Investigate and determine that reputation.* Visit the institution to which application is being made more than once. Comparison between an announced and unannounced visit can be very informative. Finally, examine the displayed documents which give both the federal and state rating of the facility. Institutionalization is not a pleasant development in anyone's life. However, it can be made safer and more palatable if the institution which meets the *applicant's needs* is selected rather than selecting the institution which forces the applicant to meet his or her own needs.

Role of nursing homes in organized systems of health care

In time nursing homes will become a more integral part of a more highly organized system of health care for the elderly and the disabled. Several different models have been suggested. One model proposes that nursing homes develop a comprehensive system of services which would be available both to institutionalized and community elderly. These institutions would offer multiple levels of care including skilled nursing care, extended care for those recovering from an acute illness, intermediate care, and domiciliary care for those primarily in need of housing and minimal supportive services (such as laundry, dietary and housekeeping services). Along with these multiple levels of care, nursing homes would develop needed medical, nursing, social and restorative resources. These resources would be shared with the community elderly through day hospitals, outpatient geriatric clinics, home care programs and "psychogeriatric" programs.

An alternative proposal has been that individual nursing homes develop according to a *medical* model, a *social* model, a *rehabilitative* model, or a *psychiatric* model.

The *medical model* would be similar to the chronic disease hospitals found in Britain and some other countries. Its purpose would be to care for those individuals who have serious and irreversible heart disease,

Even good nursing homes can be depressing.

lung disease, and various malignancies. The *rehabilitative model* would be located fairly close to an "acute care" hospital. Its purpose would be to make available extensive rehabilitative medicine and restorative nursing to those elderly persons who have incurred such acute but reversible or partially reversible problems as hip fracture, stroke, congestive heart failure and pneumonia. The *psychiatric model* would be developed to manage the long-term psychiatric patient and also to diagnose and treat reversible psychiatric problems in late life.

The *social model* is conceptually similar to present adult homes and domiciliary care facilities. These facilities would offer a structured environment and essentially "hotel-like" services to those elderly who could no longer provide these services for themselves in the community. Both the proposed "comprehensive" model and the "fractionated" model have inherent problems. The comprehensive model would result in large monolithic institutions which could become impersonal and nonresponsive to both the institutionalized elderly and the community elderly. In addition, health care, supportive services and institutional care, rather than occurring in the community, may be far removed from the community. Few elderly persons have either a single medical problem or psychosocial problem; most have multiple medical, social and psychiatric problems. The fractionated model could split up health care, social services and supportive services to a greater extent than at present. Obtaining needed health care, social and supportive services could become more difficult and more distant with such a system. Limiting institutional size and properly distributing and locating comprehensive

geriatric centers may be a method of resolving current problems and preventing future problems.

Alternatives to institutional care

During the past several years there has been increasing interest in alternatives to institutional care. This interest is a result of spiraling costs of institutional care, rapid expansion of the population over age 65, and realization that many of the services provided by the nursing home can be provided in the community at far less cost and with greater comfort and safety to the person in need.

One study (performed in Monroe County, New York) found that 30% of all elderly persons receiving care were receiving more care than they needed, while 25% of elderly persons in need of care were receiving no care or assistance. In another study of nursing home residents, it was found that approximately half of the residents needed little assistance with activities of daily living, and that half were mentally alert. More than 50% of the residents' time was spent doing nothing and most of the rest in personal care or socializing.

Associated with nursing home placement or relocation is the phenomenon of "transfer trauma." Among those elderly persons relocated in a new and unfamiliar environment there is an associated increase in the incidence of accidents, acute medical and psychiatric illnesses, and death. Despite the good intentions of the individual seeking placement for parent, spouse or relative, nursing home placement is not a benign event in an elderly person's life. Indeed, it can be an extremely depressing experience.

Alternatives to institutional care being considered include day hospitals, day care centers, home care programs, and "outreach" programs.

Day hospitals, pioneered primarily by the British, incorporate the services provided by the convalescent unit or hospital into a "9 to 5" day. The patient is picked up at his residence by a vehicle designed for the handicapped and brought to the day hospital for however long his particular therapy or therapies require. While there, he is served a warm meal and attention is given to his multiple problems. Day hospitals have allowed for earlier discharge of patients from acute care and convalescent centers and prevented regression of functional ability after discharge.

Day care, similar in concept, delivers more supervision in terms of recreational therapy and socialization than actual restorative techniques such as physical therapy or occupational therapy. Day care permits families caring for a mentally or physically impaired parent to continue their normal eight-hour working day and yet still be able to care for their parent evenings, nights and weekends. Since in increasing numbers both spouses work, day care fulfills a very real need.

Many homebound elderly persons who are unable to leave their apartments or homes are in need of medical, nursing, restorative or social services. *Home care* can fulfill this void by providing these needed services in the home, thus obviating or at least delaying the need for institutional care. In several cities, *outreach programs* have been developed which seek out those in need of care before an acute crisis precipitates the need for institutionalization.

Since most of the programs described are funded by grants, they are limited in scope and duration. Today, little is available in permanent funding or existing reimbursement to support these needed programs. It could well be that providing alternative services may not actually decrease the absolute number of institutionalized elderly persons as much as increase the number who actually receive appropriate supportive services.

Healthy Living in a Hostile Environment

Dr. Tony Smith

Ever since the Industrial Revolution man has contributed relentlessly to the health risks of all forms of life—especially his own—by polluting the air we breathe and contaminating our rivers and oceans. In addition, man's environment has been adversely affected by a wide variety of other factors. The following article discusses these health risks and what is being done to minimize them.

Until the present century few people thought about the effects of their way of life on their health. True, a few favored places such as the French Riviera acquired a reputation as having healthy climates, while there were equally obvious disease hazards for slum dwellers and the workers in hundreds of dark satanic mills during the Industrial Revolution. Yet most people—rich or poor—ate the food available, drank the water, breathed the air and lived out their lives wherever they might be. Their existence was essentially natural and disease and death were accepted with relative indifference.

Only very recently have people begun to expect to live out a full life span. As they have done so, environmentalists have also begun to look at the causes of disease and have started to question the medical consequences of atmospheric pollution, synthetic foods, contamination by industrial wastes and radioactive fallout.

Almost every aspect of modern life can affect health: the place a person is born, where he chooses to live, his job, his food, drink, transport, his hobbies, his addictions and his temperament. Many of these influences are unalterable. No one can choose his parents, yet life expectancy appears to be more closely linked to parental life spans than any other single determinant. Other factors are avoidable, however, given adequate knowledge and an appreciation of the relative risks. Once informed of the dangers of cigarette smoking or of driving without a seat belt, a person is free to make his own choice.

But what of other, less clearly defined and less well publicized hazards of the 20th-century life style? What are the effects of climate, pollution and the stresses and strains of city dwelling—with its violence, noise and packaged foods?

Before the advent of modern drugs, physicians placed great faith in the healing qualities of a "healthy" climate: invalids were sent on long sea voyages and tuberculosis sanatoria were built high in the Swiss mountains. Altitude, humidity, sunlight and variations in temperature do all affect health. Part of the variation in disease and death rates in a large country such as the United States and between the North and South of Europe is due to geographical factors.

Changes in altitude have little effect in themselves until the decrease in atmospheric pressure is so marked that the intake of oxygen through the lungs is reduced. These extreme conditions are found only in mountain ranges such as the Andes and Himalayas. Even so, the body can slowly acclimatize to the thin air by an increase in the number of red cells in the blood. In addition to its effect on respiration, the combination of cold and high altitude reduces fecundity; conceptions are fewer and complications of childbirth more common at high altitudes. Indeed, that was said to be the reason for the Spaniards' decision in 1535 to move the capital of Peru from the Andean city of Janja to Lima, on the coast. Even today in

these regions pregnant women are often advised to return to sea level to have their babies to reduce the risk of miscarriage or early infant death. The variations in temperature and humidity characteristic of Northern Europe and the Northern United States—especially the combination of cold and damp in the winter months—increase the frequency and severity of respiratory diseases: the common cold, asthma and bronchitis. Rapid changes in atmospheric pressure may precipitate an attack of asthma, especially when a steep fall in pressure accompanies a sudden influx of a cold air stream. Humidity affects the secretion of mucus in the nose and lungs, and the low humidity in many air-conditioned and centrally heated buildings may encourage the spread of respiratory disease.

Sunlight not only warms and cheers us: its ultraviolet rays have a specific disinfectant action, killing bacteria and viruses. In addition, skin exposed to sunlight can synthesize vitamin D, thus reducing to some extent the intake required in the diet. Some of the benefits of a sea voyage or a vacation on the coast come from the high intensity of solar energy reflected by water and sand, so that two hours sunbathing on a beach may be equivalent to eight hours in an inland park.

Some of the geographical variations in disease remain mysteries. One of the most serious congenital defects of the brain and nervous system is SPINA BIFIDA, in which faulty embryonic development of the spine and spinal cord leads to a baby being born with paralysis of the lower half of the body and often with some degree of mental defect. In Britain as a whole spina bifida affects 3 in every 1,000 pregnancies, but the rate is twice as high in the north and west as in the south and east, and these defects are eight times as common in South Wales as in Japan. Nor is the rate consistent from one generation to another: between 1950 and 1970 in Scotland the rate more than doubled and then returned to the earlier low level. No explanation has yet been found for these variations despite intensive research and a plethora of theories ranging from an association with blighted potatoes to a link with malnutrition in the mother's infancy. Fortunately, it is now possible to detect the condition early enough in pregnancy for the mother to be offered the chance of clinical abortion of the affected fetus.

An equally mysterious variation is seen in the incidence of MULTIPLE SCLEROSIS, the progressive paralyzing disease of the nervous system that attacks teenagers and young adults. Multiple sclerosis is most common in Northern Europe and the Northern U.S.A., where it affects about 1 in 5,000 of the population. In Southern Europe and the Southern states of America the rate is only 1 in 20,000. In Africa and Central America it is almost unknown (except among migrants who left Europe as teenagers).

Even more puzzling are the enormous differences in the common varieties of cancer from country to country. For example, breast cancer is rare in Japan, but stomach cancer is common. When Japanese people move to California, however, the incidence of cancer in this group changes to the American pattern within two generations.

Explanations of some of the variations in the incidence of cancer are being discovered. The high rate of liver cancer in Southern Africa is associated with a fungal infection of cereal crops.

Another possibility (under current investigation) is that variations in cancer may be linked with high or low concentrations of trace elements such as cobalt or chromium in the soil—especially in regions such as Southern China, where high rates of esophageal cancer are found both in man and poultry.

Minerals, soil and water

While the influence of trace elements and minerals on the incidence of cancer may be speculative, there is no doubt about their importance for general health. The best-known example is the thyroid disease found in regions where the soil lacks iodine. The hormones produced by the thyroid gland control the rate of the chemical reactions within every cell in the body; the thyroid is, in effect, the thermostat which regulates the energy output of muscles and other organs. Too little thyroid activity leads to physical and mental sluggishness; too much, to a nervous overexcitability. Iodine is an essential ingredient of these hormones, but since iodine salts dissolve easily in rainwater they have long been washed out of the soil in mountainous and old glaciated regions (such as the Alps, the Himalayas and the Andes). In such regions the lack of iodine may lead to a characteristic form of mental deficiency, cretinism, and to swellings in the neck (goiters) caused by overgrowth of the thyroid in an attempt to compensate for the lack of iodine.

The remedy is simple: iodine is added to the diet (in the form of iodized table salt) and both goiters and cretinism have become fairly rare except in the most remote mountainous regions.

Disease due to excessively high concentrations of minerals is less easily combated. Campaigners against the fluoridation of water supplies to prevent dental decay base part of their objections on the occurrence of bone disease in regions of India where the soil and water naturally contain very large amounts of fluoride (40–100 times the concentration of artificially fluoridated water supplies). In these areas the inhabitants develop disabling overgrowth of the bones of the spine and the pelvis and discoloration of the teeth.

In urban communities, in countries such as Britain and the United States, the most obvious variable in the mineral content of the diet is that due to the hardness or softness of the water supply. Hard water (so-called because a hard scale forms inside kettles and pots used to boil it) contains calcium and magnesium carbonates and sometimes chlorides and nitrates as well. Housewives prefer soft water because it lathers easily when used for washing. Central heating engineers like it because it does not block pipes and boilers with scale. Unfortunately, for some reason as yet undiscovered, cities with a hard-water supply have a lower incidence of heart disease (especially CORONARY THROMBOSIS) than those with soft water. Indeed, it has been calculated that a community which switches from a hard-water to a soft-water supply increases its frequency of coronary thrombosis by about 15%. Equally unexplained is an effect on pregnancy: women living in soft-water regions give birth to a higher proportion of babies with serious defects of the brain and spine, and infant mortality is raised in such regions.

Soft water has one further drawback: if the household water pipes are made of lead there is a risk of lead poisoning. This hazard has been recognized comparatively recently, and tests in cities such as Glasgow have shown that the combination of a soft-water supply and old tenement housing may lead to the domestic water containing substantial quantities of lead. The lead content of the water is rarely high enough to cause serious poisoning (with anemia and damage to the nervous system) but biochemical tests on children in these parts of Glasgow have shown that many have raised concentrations of lead in their blood; medical experts in the city believe that this hidden lead poisoning may affect the children's mental development.

Part of the problem in interpreting these associations between health statistics and soft water is that they may possibly have a historical explanation. In the 18th and 19th centuries heavy industries grew up in regions with good supplies of soft water for steam power, although any link between poor health and soft water is inevitably obscured by the known association of poor health with industrial overcrowding. However, the balance of evidence suggests that the effect is real. High mortality rates from heart disease are found in soft-water regions from Japan to England, and the advice of health experts to community waterworks departments is now firmly against softening water supplies.

Water impurities

Whatever the chemical makeup of the water supply, most Western city dwellers can safely assume that their drinking water is otherwise pure. In much of the world, however, water is not necessarily safe to drink. Much of the improvement in health in the industrial West in the 19th century came from sanitary reforms—the provisions of city sewers and closely supervised water supply systems. Unfortunately, most rapidly growing cities in developing countries do not have comprehensive sewers. For the foreseeable future much of the world will have to rely on water supplies of doubtful purity, and waterborne diseases such as cholera will remain common. Western travelers to Africa and Asia should continue the precautions of their grandparents and drink only boiled or bottled water.

Another set of waterborne hazards for the traveler are the parasitic diseases such as SCHISTOSOMIASIS that may be acquired by swimming or bathing in contaminated water. Schistosomiasis is one of the world's great killing and crippling diseases and causes chronic ill health in hundreds of millions of people. It is caused by parasitic blood flukes (a type of trematode worm) which penetrate the skin of any part of the body submerged in water and then make their way to the blood vessels of the intestines and bladder. Schistosomiasis parasites are to be found in fresh-water lakes in much of Africa and Asia and even in parts of the Caribbean. The only safe rule is never to swim or wade in fresh water in a tropical country.

Air pollution

Throughout the great manufacturing centers of Europe and North America, the years after World War II saw a dramatic improvement in atmospheric pollution. Smoke-blackened Sheffield, the German Ruhr and other steel cities (such as Pittsburgh) cleaned up their factory processes and then removed a century of grime from their buildings. The switch from coal to oil and gas for domestic heating brought further benefits; cities such as London now have twice as many hours of winter sunlight as in the 1930s. Paradoxically, the cities with the worst problems of pollution are those with the most favored climates: viewed from the California coastal mountains, both Los Angeles and San Francisco are curtained by the hazy smog that results from the action of sunlight on nitrogen oxides and hydrocarbons in vehicle exhaust fumes. Peroxyacetyl

Exhaust fumes are a major source of air pollution.

nitrate, the major pollutant in smog, is highly irritant to the nose and eyes and also toxic to crops.

In much of the world the exhaust fumes from motor vehicles have replaced factory smokestacks as the leading source of atmospheric pollution. In a country the size of the United States, 100 million tons of carbon monoxide are discharged from exhausts into the atmosphere each year. Carbon monoxide is a lethal gas if inhaled in high concentrations, and even small amounts can cause headaches and other symptoms. Exhaust fumes also contain lead (although the amounts have been reduced by legislation controlling or eliminating the proportion of the "antiknock" compound tetraethyl lead put into gasoline) and motor vehicle exhausts cause substantial lead pollution—especially around major highway intersections and overpasses where there is a high density of fast traffic. (There is already widespread use of unleaded gasoline.)

Without doubt these pollutants are absorbed by city dwellers—especially by taxidrivers, traffic police, attendants at filling stations and others whose work brings them into prolonged contact with heavy traffic. However, while industrial pollution by coal has been firmly linked with respiratory illness, there is far less convincing evidence that pollution by automobile exhausts is a direct threat to health.

The malignant reputation of the soot and sulfur dioxide characteristic of coal smoke is fully justified. In the winter of 1952, in London, the combination of weather conditions and heavy pollution from household fires as well as factories led to a build-up of smoke-polluted fog which lasted four days. In those four days alone the death rate in London doubled: an estimated 4,000 people died as a direct effect of the smog. Similar isolated catastrophic events have occurred in industrial areas of the United States and Europe. But most deaths from industrial pollution are less spectacular. Britain is one of the most densely populated industrial countries; for most of this century the combination of dirty air and a cold, damp climate gave the British the highest death rate from bronchitis in the world. Clean-air legislation has cleaned up the industrial cities in the last 20 years and the death rate from bronchitis has declined in parallel (it is still high, however, largely because so many British men are heavy cigarette smokers).

Throughout the world there remains a close connection between the amount of smoke in a community's air and the frequency and severity of chest illnesses. No such connection has been established for vehicle pollution. Carbon monoxide, the most obvious toxin, is absorbed by the red pigment in the blood cells—but the amount of carboxyhemoglobin in the blood of a nonsmoking taxidriver or policeman on the beat has been shown to be less than that of a regular cigarette smoker living on a relatively nonpolluted farm. Exhaust fumes seem to raise the blood carboxyhemoglobin content by no more than 3%, at which level there is no evidence of harmful effects.

Similar results have come from studies of the effects of pollution by the lead content of exhaust fumes. Without doubt people living close to urban highways do absorb some lead from the atmosphere; but the amounts found in their blood are low compared with the concentrations found in families living close to lead chemical factories and smelters. Everyone has traces of lead in his blood: there is some lead in food, in the air and often in drinking water. While no universal agreement exists on the safe upper limit for blood lead concentrations, most authorities put it at 36–40 micrograms per 100 ml. Levels close to this limit have been found in children living in city areas affected by industrial pollution, but not as a result of pollution by road traffic alone.

How safe is our food?

Man is what he eats, and perhaps the most challenging problem facing medical research is the extent to which major killers such as heart disease and cancer are the result of the modern Western diet.

Most of us know that we should not eat too much food rich in animal fats or too much sugar. What, however, of food additives—the preservatives, flavoring agents and artificial coloring put into supermarket food? Part of the explanation for the growing popularity of "organic" and "health" foods is that they are believed to be free from chemical pollutants.

Natural or home-grown foods may in fact contain just as many dangerous chemicals as synthetic products. Indeed, the purpose of many additives is the prevention of spoiled food by chemical, bacterial or fungal decay. For example, foods such as butter, meat and some cereals may go rancid if not eaten quickly—a familiar problem for housewives of earlier generations. The process is slowed by refrigeration, but a more effective method is the addition of an antioxidant such as ascorbic acid. Not only do antioxidants preserve flavor, they also prevent the denaturation of the fat-soluble vitamins A and E. Indeed, one possible explanation for the gradual decline in frequency of stomach cancer in the West is that antioxidants may prevent food contaminants such as polycyclic hydrocarbons from causing malignant changes in the cells lining the digestive tract. Food preserved with antioxidants not only tastes more wholesome but is probably less harmful to health than natural foods unless they are absolutely fresh.

Unfortunately, there is not such a good case for the use of other food preservatives. Nitrates are widely used as fertilizers and find their way into vegetables, and both nitrates and nitrites are also used as meat preservatives. Nitrites can react with other common food constituents to form compounds called nitrosamines; a similar reaction may occur when meat is fried. These nitrosamines have been shown to cause cancer in laboratory tests on

In general, the less processed, the better it is.

animals—although as yet there is no proof of any connection between human cancer and the nitrosamine content of the diet. There is, however, some evidence that cancers of the digestive organs are found more often in meat eaters than in vegetarians, and government agencies are taking steps to reduce the permitted concentrations of nitrites in meat.

The most widespread traditional preservative is salt. Salting and pickling with or without spices are well-established and effective ways of preventing decay in meat, fish and vegetables—but salt is also the only preservative proved to be harmful to health when used in excessive quantities. There is a close association between the amount of salt in a community's diet and the prevalence of heart disease and high blood pressure. Indeed, the first effective treatment of high blood pressure was a low-salt diet. A tiny amount of salt is an essential ingredient of the diet, but the overuse of added salt—either directly at the table or in the form of salted condiments—is one factor predisposing to heart disease and should be discouraged.

What about smoking and drying, equally traditional techniques? The wood smokes used to preserve fish and meats contain chemicals known to be capable of causing cancer in tests on animals, but there is no convincing evidence of any link between any human cancer and the amount of smoked fish or meat in the diet.

Chemicals are also added to food as coloring agents; some are synthetic dyes and others are based on plant extracts. Both in North America and Europe the use of colorings is closely controlled by law, and all dyes in current use have been tested by prolonged administration to animals. Many traditional coloring compounds have been banned as a result of these tests, and those remaining may be assumed to be free from any substantial risk.

Flavorings are not so straightforward. Perhaps the best known is monosodium glutamate—a natural constituent of many cereal proteins. Monosodium glutamate adds flavor to otherwise tasteless dishes and is widely used in soups and stews. Large amounts are used in Chinese cooking, and a few unlucky individuals react to it with an unpleasant combination of flushing, sweating and speeding of the heartbeat giving a sensation of palpitation. This "Chinese restaurant syndrome" is, however, no more than a relatively mild allergic response: sufferers simply have to learn to avoid foods rich in monosodium glutamate. There is nothing to suggest that regular consumption of monosodium glutamate is otherwise dangerous to health.

Sugar is perhaps the most common flavoring. The most striking change in the Western diet in the 20th century is the growth in the contribution of sugar to the total calorie intake. One hundred years ago the average British or American adult consumed about 2 lb. (1 kg) of sugar in the course of a year; now he eats 2 lb. a week and sugar accounts for about one fifth of the intake of energy from food. Weight for weight, sugar is a marvelous supplier of energy: the calorie content of 2 lb. of sugar is equivalent to that of 12 lb. of potatoes. Not surprisingly, heavy sugar eaters consume a much smaller volume of food than do people on a predominantly vegetarian diet. This decline in bulk is thought to be partly responsible for some of the "diseases of civilization." There may be more specific grounds for reducing the sugar content of the diet in illnesses such as diabetes, and the growth in sugar consumption has been paralleled by the use of artificial sweeteners to give foods and drinks a sugary flavor without the undesirable high-calorie content. Best known of these are saccharin and the cyclamates, but both have been alleged by some experts to be possible causes of cancer. The U.S. Food and Drug Administration banned the use of cyclamates in 1970 after tests had shown that rats fed on the sweetener (in high doses for prolonged periods) developed cancer of the urinary bladder. More recently similar results have been reported in tests of saccharin on rats. Against these objections—based on laboratory tests in abnormal conditions—must be set the results of human experience. Diabetics use far more artificial sweeteners than the rest of the population, but there appears to be no significant increase in bladder, kidney or other cancers in diabetics. If there is any risk to health from the use of artificial sweeteners, it would seem to be so small as to have escaped current medical detection.

Doubts about the wholesomeness of supermarket foods are not confined to anxieties about preservatives, colorings and artificial flavorings. Another big question mark hangs over the factory farming techniques used to produce many foodstuffs. What are the effects of the fertilizers, in-secticides and other chemicals that have transformed agricultural methods in the last 20 years? Investigations began when it became apparent that organochlorine pesticides such as DDT are virtually indestructible. Once sprayed on crops they are incorporated into the bodies of herbivorous animals and subsequently into the carnivorous animals that eat them, along the whole food chain. In the mid-1950s, animals (especially birds) at the end of these chains were shown to have absorbed large amounts of DDT. Some became sterile in consequence: falcons and some species of eagles were threatened with extinction.

> **The potential danger to health of spraying crops with DDT and certain other insecticides and chemicals was not known until many years after they came into general use. Government regulations provide safeguards for testing new chemicals designed for use as fertilizers or pesticides, although no guarantee exists to prevent the occasional poisoning of both animals and man.**

Fortunately, man is less susceptible than birds of prey to the harmful effects of DDT, although the results of tests in all parts of the world show substantial amounts in human fat. As a result of public concern in the 1960s, use of DDT and other pesticides became much more closely controlled. Since then, monitoring has shown a steady decline in pesticide concentrations in both human fat specimens and those taken from animals. The control of pesticides has led to a proliferation of controls on other potential contaminants—fruit sprays, ripening agents and virtually all agricultural chemicals. While it is impossible to guarantee that no harm will come from their use, the current safeguards do ensure that all new chemicals used in food production are tested by long-term feeding to animals. There are still occasional disasters, for no system can protect against every possibility. One outbreak of paralysis and nerve damage in the Middle East, for example, was traced to the inadvertent use in bread making of grain that had been treated with mercury to protect it against mold (it had originally been intended for planting, not for human consumption). In general, however, the watchdog agencies set up to protect the consumer have been given the necessary powers and the U.S. Food and Drug Administration has now tested many thousands of chemicals used in agriculture and the food industry.

Yet, despite this reassuring umbrella of governmental controls, there seems little doubt that some human cancers are linked to our food. Sir Richard Doll (the British physician whose research first proved an association between lung cancer and cigarette smoking) has argued that 80% of the common cancers will eventually be proved to have external causes. This effect is shown by the enormous variations, described earlier, in the frequency of various types of cancer in different parts of the world. As noted, the high frequency of stomach cancer among the Japanese people does not persist when they move to the United States and begin eating American food. Within one or two generations their susceptibility to cancer has become the same as that of native Americans. While trace elements may play a part in these geographical variations, cultural differences in diet seem more likely to prove responsible. Among the many theories offered to explain the remarkable decrease in stomach cancer in affluent countries in the 20th century are the decline in damage to the stomach lining from abrasive irritants (such as uncooked grains and nuts) and changes in methods of food preservation and cooking, as well as changes in the makeup of the diet. Overeating appears to increase the cancer risk: overweight individuals in all societies seem to be more prone to cancers of all kinds.

City stresses

When historians look back on the 20th century they will undoubtedly view the transition from rural to city life as one of its greatest social changes. Within two or three generations, developed and developing countries have seen their populations leave the land and villages for the cities. Is this change inherently unnatural and unhealthy, as is sometimes alleged? How much truth is there in the Arcadian belief that mankind can be content only in a simple rural environment? How harmful are the noise, overcrowding, highrise housing, social isolation and the competitiveness of city life? Noise—from aircraft, traffic, industrial machinery and pop music—invades the privacy of every city dweller. Much of the protest it has evoked is based on a conviction that noise can be harmful to health. Prolonged exposure to very loud noise does damage the ears; some heavy industries, such as shipbuilding, are notorious for the deafness found in men who have spent their working lives in occupations such as riveting. Boilermakers, scalers, propeller shapers and others are today supplied with special ear protectors in an attempt to minimize damage to the ears. Electronically amplified pop music can approach the noise levels found in industry and some loss of hearing has been found in both pop musicians and their fans. Experts do not suggest, however, that there is any serious risk to hearing from exposure to noise from traffic or aircraft. Complaints from people living close to airports and urban highways are based on the cumulative, wearing effect of such noise on the nerves. One team of London psychiatrists has claimed that admissions to mental hospitals are more frequent in areas close to the airport than in otherwise comparable areas less affected by aircraft noise, although the differences are small and other research workers have not confirmed the association. Many people who live close to airports, however, gradually come to tolerate the noise.

Animals kept in overcrowded conditions are more susceptible to illness, their fertility declines, and they become restless and aggressive—but these effects become apparent only with extreme degrees of congestion. Sociologists who allege that the crime, violence and other problems found in overcrowded urban areas are explicable in the same biological terms are, however, on uncertain ground. There is no evidence that mental illness is found more often in persons living in overcrowded conditions, nor is there any consistent relation between personality disorders in children and the size of their families. However, some research in Hong Kong in the 1970s has suggested that although crowding by families is relatively harmless there is some strain from repeated interaction with strangers in large apartment houses and similar dwellings.

People may not like living in highrise housing projects—as their gradual abandonment by architects shows—but, again, there is little evidence that residents of such housing are any less healthy than other apartment dwellers. One widely reported study of servicemen's families living in Germany showed that those in highrise apartments consulted their doctors more often than those living in houses. The former group seemed to have more neurotic disorders, more respiratory illnesses and more menstrual problems. These differences have not been found by other research teams, however, and most medical experts now discount any real health hazard from living in highrise apartments. (After all, the *penthouse* is generally accepted as a highly desirable town residence!)

What about the social isolation of city life? Do the close family connections in a village community provide support that is lacking in the anonymity of a city? These questions have proved very difficult to answer.

Firstly, city dwellers may not have the emotional support of an extended family, but neither do they have to put up with the social and family pressures inevitable in a closed community. Secondly, alcoholics, schizophrenics and dropouts seem to gravitate to cities—in particular, they often congregate in depressed city areas—so that any comparison of town and country has to take account of this drift. Even so, psychiatrists have studied the problem in depth and found that throughout the world major mental illnesses have a remarkably consistent incidence. Around 0.5%–1% of the rural and city populations of countries as diverse as China, Brazil, the United States and Sweden develop schizophrenia, suggesting that environmental factors are of relatively minor importance. Even strict ascetic sects such as the Hutterites (who live in enclosed, self-sufficient agrarian communities) have the same incidence of psychotic illness as that found in urban slums.

Mental illness is not the only measure of stress. What evidence there is linking stress with ill health suggests that it precipitates *physical* disease. Disorders of the digestive system (stomach ulcers, ulcerative colitis, and other colonic diseases), coronary thrombosis, eczema and asthma are all thought to be aggravated by anxiety. Research in the United States has shown that the most stressing life events are loss of a job or a change in working conditions, marital conflicts, death of a member of the family and minor infringements of the law such as traffic offenses. Whether or not such stresses are more characteristic of city than rural life is questionable. For example, perhaps the single most stressing event is the death of a husband or wife; within six months of such a bereavement the survivor's risk of dying is raised by as much as 40%. Nearly 5% of men aged 45 or more die within six months of the death of their wives, most commonly from heart disease. Morale has a striking effect on survival. Many elderly people manage to stay alive until their 80th, 90th or 100th birthdays only to die within a few days of having passed the landmark—an example of an "artificial goal" that seems to spark the will to live.

Stress in the working environment, such as the "rat-race" found in competitive industries, may act as an adverse life event. High-pressure work schedules do not, however, seem inherently harmful to health: the danger comes from a combination of these pressures and discontent or depression. A CORONARY THROMBOSIS is much more likely in a middle-management executive who has been passed over for promotion than one who has just been given a new district to reorganize.

These stresses should, moreover, be seen in perspective. They are far less important than the better known, familiar precipitants of heart disease in middle age: overweight, too little exercise and too much smoking.

Internal pollution

What of the voluntary "internal pollution" of man's natural environment by alcohol, tobacco and other drugs of potential addiction?

Alcoholism has become one of the most important causes of physical and mental disintegration in middle age in most Western societies; it is also a major factor in causing accidents on the road and in industry, the breakup of marriages and behavior problems in children. Furthermore, regular drinking which falls short of alcoholism may nevertheless cause serious disease of the stomach, liver and heart. It has only recently been discovered that heavy drinking during pregnancy may affect the development of the unborn child.

How much does the incidence of alcoholism in a country depend on external factors? In practice there are enormous variations among Western countries which reflect differences in social customs and affluence. In Europe, the French have the worst alcoholism problem: 10% of the adult population suffer from the physical or mental effects of excessive consumption, while as many as 50% of all hospital admissions are alcohol-related: traffic accidents,

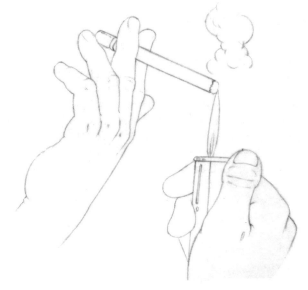

Among professional men, smoking has declined.

liver disease, etc. (Britain, in contrast, has only 1% of its adult population seriously affected by alcohol addiction.) While some of the factors responsible for this difference may be social and racial, there is no doubt that the root cause is the much higher per capita consumption of alcohol in France—largely related to the low price of alcoholic drinks and their availability at all hours of the day and night. Countries such as Sweden and Norway, which tax alcohol punitively and also restrict the retail outlets, may not suppress alcoholism completely but they do reduce its frequency to very low levels. Similar variations are seen between different states (and even counties) in the United States, with their very different liquor laws.

A similar pattern is seen with tobacco consumption. In most Western countries both tobacco and alcohol have become relatively cheaper in the past 20 years (that is, their cost has fallen as a proportion of the average weekly wage). Even so, tobacco consumption is to some extent price-related: studies in Britain have shown that every 1% rise in the cost of cigarettes causes an immediate 0.5% fall in consumption (although the effect may not be permanent). These cost effects have been confused by two conflicting social changes. Before World War II, cigarette smoking was predominantly a male habit: few women smoked heavily (and few poorer women had the money to do so). Experience in wartime factories, mirrored in contemporary films, led to a surge in the popularity of smoking among women; the proportion of women smokers gradually approached that of men. More recently, the publication in the mid-1960s in the United States and Britain of medical reports linking cigarette smoking with lung cancer, heart disease and bronchitis has discouraged smoking—but, as yet, this effect has been largely restricted to men in the professional classes.

Cannabis (marijuana), heroin and other drugs are subject to the same interaction between social, legal and financial restraints. Where there are neither financial nor legal barriers to access to a drug its use tends to grow to proportions that cause social disruption. Every technically advanced country has found it necessary to control the consumption of alcohol (and the most easily available alternatives) by some form of taxation and often by restrictive legislation as well. The proportion of the population that develops addiction depends as much on the severity of these taxes and controls as it does on the personalities of the individuals concerned.

Radioactivity

While public disquiet about radioactivity reached its peak at the time of the nuclear testing in the 1950s and early 1960s, there are still justifiable anxieties about both fallout from nuclear explosions and the potential hazards of nuclear-fueled power stations and ships. Radiation is known to cause some forms of cancer, especially leukemia, and it may damage the sex glands and increase the risk of abnormal births.

Radioactivity is not a complete novelty as an environmental hazard. In all human history man (and other animals) has been exposed to radioactive emissions from three sources. The Earth's crust contains radioactive minerals (the best-known is pitchblende, the source of Marie Curie's radium). These minerals include both radioactive elements such as radium and radioactive isotopes (variants of a slightly different atomic weight) of common elements such as potassium. The intensity of the radiation absorbed by any one individual depends on where he lives and varies from 25 millirads a year in London to 4,000 millirads in parts of India. (A *rad* is the standard unit of an absorbed dose of radiation.) Cosmic rays from outer space contribute another small fraction of the background radiation to every part of the Earth's surface. These rays are largely absorbed by the denser part of the atmosphere but their intensity is much higher in the stratosphere (from about 6 to 15 miles above the Earth's surface), where they may be a hazard to the crews of supersonic aircraft. About one-fifth of the "natural" radiation comes from radioactive elements which have been incorporated into bones and muscles. A tiny fraction (0.012%) of the potassium in the body is the radioactive isotope potassium-40, which contributes another 20 millirads a year to the total dose absorbed by each individual. The "background" dose from all sources is about 100 millirads.

It is the "internal" radioactivity that is dangerously affected by testing nuclear weapons. Such explosions disseminate radioactive particles throughout the atmosphere, which become dissolved in the rainwater as "fallout." Some of the radioactive elements formed by nuclear explosions, such as strontium-90, remain potentially dangerous for many years. (The time taken for a

newly formed radioactive element to disseminate half its radioactivity is termed its "half-life." Strontium-90 has a half-life of 28 years.) The radioactive isotopes are absorbed by the soil and become incorporated into plants and later animals, so that in time they find their way into human bodies as part of the "internal" radioactivity.

How much, then, have nuclear tests increased the amount of radioactivity in the environment? The total dose from all nuclear explosions up to 1968 was calculated by the United Nations Scientific Committee on the Effects of Atomic Radiation as equivalent to a dose of 110 millirads (in the northern temperate zone and measured on the same basis as the figures quoted for natural, background radiation). However, most experts now believe that half the total radioactivity released by these tests has now been disseminated; and there have been very few tests since 1968—although the Chinese tested a nuclear device in 1977 which sent a cloud of radioactive debris drifting around the world.

Before the effects of this radiation on health can be estimated, account has to be taken of the other man-made sources. Most important of these is the use of x-ray techniques in medicine. Few people now go through their lives without having x-ray films taken of their chest, teeth, or bones. Ten years ago the annual number of x-ray examinations done in a country such as Britain had reached the same total as the population (since most people admitted to the hospital have more than one x-ray examination, the proportion of the population actually examined in any one year is only about 10%). The average dose per person per year may now have reached 240 millirads in countries such as the U.S.A. with widely used and highly developed radiological services—more than twice the total of natural background radiation. However, averages are of little help in this context. The most potentially dangerous x-ray examinations are those which could affect the sex glands (ovaries or testes); young men who suffer multiple injuries in motorcycle accidents are at particular risk.

Finally, nuclear power plants need to be taken into account. Occasional leaks of radioactive material from electricity generating stations have caused localized increases in radiation and subsequent tests have shown an increase in the amount of radioactivity in the bodies of local inhabitants. Again, the amounts have been small.

The harmful effects of radiation are not in dispute. Firstly, both x-rays and nuclear explosions can cause cancer—as first became apparent in early research scientists working with radium. Since then it has become clear that the use of x-rays to treat some forms of spinal arthritis and skin complaints increases the incidence of leukemia in the patients treated. Similarly, patients with tuberculosis whose treatment included repeated x-ray examinations have been shown to have an increased incidence of breast cancer. In both examples the interval between the irradiation and the development of cancer has been as few as 2 years or as many as 30 years later.

The Japanese survivors of the atomic bombs dropped on Hiroshima and Nagasaki in 1945 have shown that same pattern: leukemia and a large range of other cancers have continued to occur more frequently than normally in the survivors.

The second type of damage caused by radiation is *genetic* damage. Experiments on animals have shown that when cell nuclei are exposed to radiation the chromosomes may be affected, causing mutation—so that when the cell divides the progeny are different from the parent cell. Irradiation of the sex cells in either males or females may be expected to cause genetic mutations; the offspring of irradiated animals have a high incidence of deformities and other abnormalities. The same effect is inevitable in men, women and children exposed to radiation, but so far there is little evidence of serious results. Even in Japanese survivors of atomic bombing, the only suggestion of genetic damage is a slight shift in the proportions of male and female births; there has been no increase in the incidence of abnormal births. On the other hand, inhabitants of regions with very high levels of natural radiation from radioactive minerals *do* have a slight excess of congenital abnormalities.

Overall, the effects of weapon testing, medical use of x-rays and radioactive isotopes—and even occasional disasters at nuclear power stations—seem unlikely to do more than fractionally increase the background radiation to which the world's population is exposed. At worst, such an increase might raise the frequency of some forms of cancer and speed up the natural process of evolution by natural selection. On present evidence, however, neither effect is likely to be substantial.

Self-poisoning

The great Canadian physician William Osler (1849–1919) observed that man differs most from the lower animals in his apparent need to take medicines. Certainly every culture has its medicine men, and even in our "over-doctored" society there is still an insatiable demand for drugs for self-medication.

Possibly the greatest sales of these over-the-counter medicines are for painkillers such as aspirin. One man in every 50 and one woman in 10 take aspirins every day of their lives—for the symptomatic relief of headache, arthritis, rheumatism and even as a sort of tonic for tiredness. Most of the widely advertised painkilling tablets and powders are based on aspirin. The tons of these drugs taken annually, without widespread ill effects, indicate that they are remarkably safe. There are, however, two important risks from the use of these analgesics. Firstly, the mixture of alcohol and aspirin can cause serious internal bleeding; a high proportion of people admitted to the

hospital with loss of blood from the stomach admit to having taken the combination shortly beforehand. Anyone with a tendency to indigestion (and certainly anyone known to have a stomach or duodenal ulcer) should use one of the relatively safer alternatives to aspirin. Secondly, long-continued regular use of some analgesic mixtures may damage the kidneys.

Second only to self-medication with analgesics comes dosing with purgatives—drugs, mixtures and powders taken to relieve "constipation." Many people have a mistaken belief that daily bowel action is essential for health; but such regularity is rarely compatible with the modern low-residue Western diet. Laxatives will certainly hurry along the bowel action, but they do nothing to affect the underlying cause of most intestinal bowel complaints—the lack of "bulk," or residue, in the diet. Unfortunately, long-continued use of powerful purgatives may damage the muscles of the intestinal walls and, in extreme cases, may disturb the internal chemistry of the body—loss of potassium may cause irregularity of the heartbeat and kidney disorders.

Tranquilizers

Although not available legally without a prescription, tranquilizing drugs such as diazepam (Valium) and chlordiazepoxide (Librium) and antidepressants such as amitriptyline (Elavil) are taken by vast numbers of people, often with little or no medical supervision. Only too often someone prescribed tranquilizers by his doctor will pass them on to a friend who seems upset or miserable. The danger of such casual use of drugs lies not in addiction—they are remarkably nonaddictive—but in their effect on driving and other skilled behaviors. Control of a machine (indeed, any activity requiring good muscular coordination and close mental concentration) is impaired to some extent

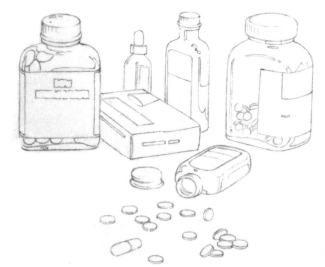

Excessive and unsupervised use of drugs and medicines has become a real danger to millions of people.

by all tranquilizers and other drugs acting on the brain. Particularly dangerous in this respect is the combination of tranquilizers (or sleeping pills) with alcohol, yet many people seem unaware that there is any risk in taking "nerve pills," having a drink or two and then setting off to drive a car.

Overdosage

The popularity of self-medication and the near-universal availability of tranquilizers has led to an accumulation of bottles of tablets in almost every household in the Western world. This may well be the root cause of one of the most troublesome modern epidemics—overdosage with drugs. In Britain, for example, the single most common cause of admission to the medical wards of hospitals is acute poisoning from a self-administered overdose of drugs. The same is true in most Western countries. Few of these overdoses are lethal: most are taken by teenagers after a quarrel with parents or with a lover. The intention is rarely suicidal. Indeed, many psychiatrists no longer label such actions attempted suicide, preferring terms such as "parasuicide" or simply self-poisoning. Tragically, however, the gesture may sometimes be fatal: the combination of drugs with alcohol may have unpredictable effects. Individuals seriously intent on suicide will usually succeed, but the frequency of "parasuicidal" gestures would almost certainly be reduced if drugs were less readily available for impulsive self-poisoning.

Balance sheet of risks

Disturbing as the hazards of radioactivity or the unsensed dangers of trace elements may be, their effects on health are minor compared with the more familiar dangers of Western life. In reality, the most important single cause of death among children and young adults in Europe and North America is road accidents. Half of all deaths in men aged 15–24 are due to traffic accidents, mostly as drivers or passengers in cars or on motorcycles. (Children and older adults are more often killed as pedestrians.) Factors known to influence the numbers of these deaths include speed limits, use of seat belts by motorists, the vigor of drinking-driving laws and the density of traffic. It is not surprising that Sweden comes low on the list, with its strict control of drivers and sparsely populated countryside.

In North America the second major cause of death in young men is homicide: indeed, in some cities (such as Baltimore), gunshot fatalities have overtaken road accidents as the principal cause of death in young black men. Most of these fatal shootings occur in family quarrels rather than in the course of crime; only 10% are associated with armed robbery or shootings by police officers. Accidents may also be a substantial threat to life in some high-risk occupations.

Top of the list comes diving in the North Sea oilfields, where an average of 10 of the total workforce of 1,000 divers die each year from accidents while working on the seabed 600 ft below the surface. Coalminers and deep-sea fishermen, the traditional high-risk occupations, have an accident rate that is only one-twentieth that of the divers— and it is getting lower year by year with improved safety measures.

In contrast, accidents associated with leisure and sporting activities are becoming more common. Among the most tragic of these are drownings in home swimming pools, so common in the southern and western parts of the United States and in Australia. Research in Brisbane, Australia, has shown that most such drownings occur in children aged less than five and that accidents are virtually confined to pools without a guard-fence.

Drowning is also a substantial cause of death in people using water for recreational purposes— swimming, sailing, canoeing and fishing. As more and more people have moved out of the cities into the mountains and open country for their leisure, there has been a corresponding rise in death rates from exposure, from falls while mountain climbing and from hazardous sports such as hang-gliding.

Dramatic as these deaths may be—largely because they are sudden and often in young fit men and women—they remain small in total numbers compared with deaths on the roads. All accidental deaths account for less than 3% of the total in Western societies. The great killing *diseases* remain heart disease, stroke and cancer. The only environmental factors generally proved to be of importance in their causation, other than industrial hazards, are tobacco and alcohol.

Nutrition

Professor John Yudkin

We have never before had such an abundance of food, nor have we had to choose between so many bewildering forms and preparations. We have never needed sound and scientific advice on the basic principles of nutrition so much as we do today.

One of the ways we get confused about nutrition is that we get more and more involved in detail, so that we find it more and more difficult to see the general pattern of what we should be eating, and why. So I shall start with some very general ideas, and some very brief and superficial notes about nutrition; after that, I shall elaborate on what I have said in more detail. It may be that some of the questions you may have early on will be answered later. I cannot promise, however, that all your possible questions can be answered, since—as in all sciences—there are still many things we don't know about nutrition, even though there is already a vast amount that we do know. But the important practical point I hope to show you is that, even without a great deal of expert knowledge, it is not too difficult for anyone to learn general rules about how to "eat for health."

It is not so common nowadays to hear old ladies say, "I don't believe in all this about vitamins and proteins; I brought up all my children on plain wholesome food without bothering about such things." What they said has in fact an important element of truth; that we have been brainwashed into thinking that good nutrition is difficult to achieve, if not impossible, with just food alone. Some special pills or special fortified preparations in addition are widely believed to be essential for good nutrition.

Let us start at the beginning, and forget for a while the current discussion about dietary fiber, polyunsaturated fats and vitamin supplements. A good beginning is to ask how it is that all wild animals—and, for that matter, the human race—have managed to survive all the millions of years of evolution by choosing their food themselves, and without having the advice of professors of nutrition! A simple but not very illuminating answer is that we have a "food instinct" that guides us to eat correctly. But if this is so, how does it come about that there are now so many people around with nutritional problems?

One important answer is that, taking the world as a whole, the major reason why people eat badly is poverty—not only in the deprived countries of the Third World, but also among the less fortunate individuals in the wealthy countries. But not all bad nutrition is caused by poverty; many of us whose choice of an excellent diet is not limited by money nevertheless do not choose well.

If you think for a moment, this less than ideal choice comes about because we are tempted to take very enjoyable food and drinks of little nutritional value, instead of those of high nutritional value which, although palatable enough, are nevertheless not quite so tempting.

There are, then, two main factors that determine what foods we eat. Firstly, the food must be available—available not simply in the store, but also within our financial resources. Secondly, we eat what we do because we *like* it: a reason that is obvious enough to ordinary people, but often seems to be forgotten by professional nutritionists.

If you now ask again why animals, in their ordinary wild environment, eat healthy nutritional diets, we have to say that they eat what they like, and in doing so they eat what they *need*. This was true for the human animal too, when he also gathered and hunted his food. But it is no longer true because of our ability (especially during the last hundred years or so) to make foods that are more and more attractive, but less and less nutritious. I hasten to say that it is not, as some writers seem to suggest, because of a deliberate policy of food manufacturers to produce malnutrition in their customers. It is simply that we, the customers, demand that our foods be very palatable, and the food manufacturer, like any other manufacturer, responds to our demands, as does the cook in the kitchen. We insist on buying foods and drinks because we like their taste, and we show no interest in their nutritive value. What then do we expect the food manufacturer to do?

But what do we mean by the "nutritive value" of foods? We can answer this question by looking at what our body needs from food, and how the mixture of foods that we eat—that is, our *diet*—supplies these needs.

Imagine that the body is a car. A very special sort of car, since it begins very small, no bigger than the simplest Volkswagen, and ends up as an elaborate Cadillac. And all the time, or most of the time, it runs excellently, with no worn tires and no rust, and is able to go fast or slow, or stand still, just as you want it to.

Fruit and vegetable produce from our farms and orchards is an elemental basis of good nutrition.

Energy, growth and maintenance

In order to do all this, the car has to be supplied not only with fuel but also with lubricating oils for the engine and transmission, distilled water for the battery, and constant replenishment of all the parts that are slowly but constantly wearing out or corroding or breaking off. It also has to supply whatever is necessary for the growth from the VW into the Caddy. Now imagine that (when you go to get your gasoline) there are several pumps that supply a mixture of gasoline with some of the items needed for growth and for making good "wear and tear." One of the pumps provides gas and also, say, lubricating oil mixed together with the gas; but the car we are imagining has the facility of *separating* these items and sending them to the parts of the car that need them. Another pump may provide gas together with some steel, chromium and aluminum that are needed for the maintenance of the engine, chassis and body of the car. All of the pumps, we shall suppose, provide gasoline; some provide little else, while others provide a range of those items needed to keep the car in good repair and help it to get "big and strong."

Our bodies also need fuel to keep them going, in addition to several other items for growth and replacement. And growth, incidentally, not only to transform a 7 lb. baby into a 120 or 140 lb. adult woman or man, but growth too for the baby inside the womb of a pregnant woman, as well as the growth of the baby after birth through the milk that the nursing mother supplies—if at all possible—during the first few months of its separate life.

These necessities for our bodies are contained in food, which thus has to serve two purposes: providing fuel and also providing material for increasing and renovating the body's tissues.

Apart from the moisture that practically every food contains, the solid part is made up mostly of one or more of three sorts of materials: *carbohydrate*, *fat* and *protein*. Starch and sugars are carbohydrates. Starch is found in bread and in potatoes. The most common sugar is what we simply *call* sugar, but the chemist calls it *sucrose*. It is found in the sugar bowl, in candy and in ice cream and soda pop made with sugar—foods and drinks that we find so "delicious." Other sugars are *glucose* and *fructose* (found with a little sucrose in fruits) and *lactose* (found in milk). Lard, beef dripping, butter, margarine and oil such as peanut oil and corn oil are largely fat. Proteins—of which there are very many sorts—are virtually never seen on their own, unless they have been extracted and purified (for example, casein from milk). Otherwise you find them with fat or with carbohydrate or with both. Meat always has fat with the protein, even if it is lean meat; while milk, peanuts, peas and beans have fat and carbohydrate with protein.

Let me throw in here one important point of language. You often hear people speak of "carbohydrate" when they mean bread or potatoes, or "protein" when they mean meat or fish or peas. This is as silly as saying "bricks" when you mean "house," or "steel" when you mean "car." Carbohydrate, protein and fat are not foods; they are *constituents* of foods.

The body's fuel

Except for the small proportion that has to be retained for growth, carbohydrate, fat and protein are used as fuel—the carbohydrate and fat more or less directly, and the protein in a roundabout sort of way. They release energy when they are burned (oxidized) in the body. This is carried out in a very controlled manner, so that only tiny amounts of energy at a time are released exactly where required—for moving the muscles that let us write, or shake hands, or walk, or moving the chest so that we take in the air used for burning the fuel and let out the air that contains the carbon dioxide released when the fuel is burned. The energy also keeps the heart beating—about 70 times a minute, 60 minutes an hour, 24 hours a day, 365 days a year, for say 70 years.

As well as such obvious needs, the body also requires energy for "putting together" various constituents from food in order to repair the wear and tear of the tissues. The total activities of the burning of the fuel, the breaking down of the tissues in wear and tear, and their reconstitution of the wear and tear—all these activities are chemical reactions that together are called *metabolism*. As a result of this process heat is released; that is how we keep warm. The average daily diet of adults contains about 300 g (11 oz.) of carbohydrate, about 125 g ($4\frac{1}{2}$ oz.) of fat, and about 100 g ($3\frac{1}{2}$ oz.) of protein.

For restoration of wear and tear, and for necessary growth, special and very specific constituents of the food are required. These body-building constituents are mostly needed in quite small amounts. The only exception is protein, of which we need something like 50 g ($1\frac{3}{4}$ oz.) a day. The other body-building constituents are the mineral salts and vitamins, some of which we need in amounts of a gram or so a day and others in amounts of—believe it or not—only a few millionths of a gram a day.

Food for energy

You will have noticed that when a room is full of people it gets warm very quickly. This is because the average adult produces the equivalent of more than 100 watts of energy, so that 15 people in a room are producing as much heat as a two-kilowatt electric heater. Energy can be measured in any one of several units (e.g., watts, footpounds or calories) and it is customary to measure the energy used by the body as calories. Strictly speaking, it is measured in *kilocalories*, the calorie itself being only a tiny unit. Instead of saying that the average person uses, for instance, 2,750,000 calories a day, we say that he uses 2,750 kilocalories. At

Energy is constantly being consumed by the body, which gives off heat in the process. The average adult radiates the equivalent of more than 100 watts—which is why an overcrowded and unventilated room can be insufferably stuffy.

least that's what we ought to say, but we have got into the habit of saying calories instead. But because I am a scientist, I am going to be fussy and use kilocalories (*kcal* for short) when I talk about a particular amount of energy, and calories when I talk of energy in general (whenever I *remember*, that is!).

When we use the energy-releasing food components in the body, we get nearly 4 kcal from oxidizing a gram of carbohydrate, 9 kcal from a gram of fat and 4 kcal from a gram of protein. From the average sort of diet we would get 1,200 kcal from 300 g of carbohydrate, 1,125 kcal from 125 g of fat, and 400 kcal from 100 g of protein—a total of 2,725 kcal. We might also be getting some energy from alcohol: burning 1 g of alcohol releases 7 kcal, so a couple of ounces of Scotch, which contains something like 20 g of alcohol, will release 140 kcal.

It is usual to say that foods "contain" so many calories, but this only means that if all the carbohydrate, fat and protein (and alcohol) is in fact burned up in the body, that number of calories would be released. If, however, your rate of metabolism (and thus the rate of releasing calories) is *less* than the rate at which you are taking in calories from your food, then *not* all the food will be metabolized. What is left over will be turned by the body into fat.

Conversely, if your rate of using calories is *more* than your rate of taking in calories from food, you will have to burn some of the fat stored in your body to make up the calorie shortage. As you have no doubt realized, I have just touched on the problem of gaining weight or losing weight. We shall look at this in more detail later on.

Digestion

Nothing that you eat or drink can do you any good until it has been absorbed from the small intestine into the blood.

Once there, it will be carried around the body to every organ and tissue and cell so that it can be used. The absorption through the intestinal wall can only happen if the food components are present in quite small molecules. But since much of it is originally present as large molecules, they have to be broken down to small ones. This is the process of *digestion*.

Starch is gradually digested to a small sugar called maltose, and then to another "smaller" sugar called glucose. This process begins when you chew food, since saliva contains a substance (a digestive enzyme) that starts the process. Try chewing a piece of bread for a minute or two before swallowing it, and you will notice that it gradually becomes sweet. Not only maltose but also ordinary table sugar (sucrose) and milk sugar (lactose), though quite small, are not absorbed until they are digested to smaller sugars. Sucrose is digested to glucose and fructose, and lactose to glucose and galactose.

Since all the reactions in the body take place in a watery solution, the fats which are not soluble in water present a special problem. This is overcome by breaking up the fat in the alimentary canal into tiny droplets, which, although by no means single molecules of fat, are nevertheless so small that the enzymes in the watery fluid surrounding each droplet can get to work on it. The breaking up of fat into droplets—making it into an emulsion, like cream—is done in the same way as you remove the fatty stains on your clothes by means of a detergent. The "detergent" in the alimentary canal is found in the *bile*, which is made in the liver, stored in the gallbladder and released into the first part of the small intestine when fatty food has been eaten. The emulsified fat is then digested into glycerol (glycerine) and fatty acids.

There is a range of fatty acids that are different in size and in actual make-up from one another. From a nutritional point of view, there are two or three important things we need to know about them. One we have already dealt with: the fatty acids, and the glycerol, can be burned (oxidized) to release energy; or alternatively, if they are not needed for energy, they can be put together again and added to the fat store in the body. Secondly, while they are all composed of atoms of carbon and hydrogen and a little oxygen, some of them have all the hydrogen they can carry; others have room for more hydrogen. The former are called "saturated fatty acids" and the latter are called "unsaturated fatty acids." When they are still combined with glycerol, they are called saturated or unsaturated fats. If they can take up a lot of hydrogen, they are called polyunsaturated fatty acids ("PUFA") or fats. The more saturated a fat is, the more solid it is at ordinary temperatures; conversely, the more unsaturated it is, the more liquid it is—so that, at ordinary temperatures, it is an oil.

There has been a lot of talk in the last few years about the possibility that "hard" (saturated) fats in the diet tend to produce heart attacks, while "soft" (polyunsaturated) fats or oils tend to prevent heart attacks. Again, this is something we shall have to deal with in more detail later.

There are perhaps 20 or 30 important fats which in their make-up are different from one another—because of the different sorts of fatty acids that are joined to the glycerol or because of the rather different ways they are joined. There are perhaps half a dozen important carbohydrates, different also because of the different "units" that go to make up their molecules and their different size. At the other extreme, there are thousands of different proteins. This is because they are all very large molecules, each made of hundreds of units called *amino acids* (the "building blocks" of protein. And there are 20 or so different amino acids.

If that sounds complicated, let me give you an analogy. Let us suppose that the different amino acids are like the 26 different letters of the alphabet. Now look at a paragraph in a book; some consist of perhaps only 200 or 300 letters, some perhaps as many as 5,000 or more letters. Although each paragraph will have the same letters, they will differ in the number of each of the 26 letters—and, of course, in the order in which they are printed. There is an almost infinite number of different paragraphs that can be made out of the same 26 letters. In the same way, there are thousands of different proteins that can be made from the 20 different amino acids.

The proteins in your food are needed to make the proteins in your body during growth and the repair of wear and tear. These body proteins go to make up not only the main part of the structure of the different cells but also those substances, the enzymes, that regulate all the vast range of chemical processes that we have called metabolism.

During digestion, the proteins in the food are broken down into their individual amino acids, which are then absorbed into the blood and carried to all the cells of the body. These cells, constantly losing part of their own protein, now pick out the appropriate amino acids that are in the blood and use them to rebuild their own lost proteins.

So a part of the food proteins is used to replace the same amount of body proteins that have been broken down and oxidized. The food proteins that are now left over are also oxidized so that the *total* amount that is oxidized is the equivalent of the *total* amount of proteins in the food. (This is why I said earlier that the proteins of the food are oxidized in "a roundabout sort of way.")

Of the 20 amino acids that proteins contain, the body can manufacture 12—but not the remaining eight. These eight are called the *essential amino acids;* growing children cannot make an additional one fast enough for their needs, so for them there are nine essential amino acids.

Not every protein contains all of the eight or nine essential amino acids, just as not every single paragraph contains, say, the letter "r" (although it is, in fact, difficult to write many words without that letter). So while it is true that the body as a whole needs all the essential amino acids because of the need to make so many different sorts of body protein, individual foods will have a much smaller range of proteins, and some of them may not have every one of the eight essential amino acids, or may have only very little of one or more of them.

Thus, not all of the proteins in food are equally useful to the body, because they may or may not have an adequate amount of the essential amino acids. On the whole, the proteins in animal foods (such as meat, fish, eggs and milk) have a better assortment of amino acids, and so have a higher "biological value" than do the proteins in vegetable foods like cereals, peas and potatoes. But this is not an invariable rule. The animal protein *gelatin* is not very good; on the other hand, *soya bean* protein is almost as good as many animal proteins.

But in practice you do not really have to worry about the biological value of individual proteins. This is because the "poor" proteins do not all lack the same amino acids. We eat a mixture of different foods, so that an amino acid missing from one of their proteins will almost always be present in one of the other proteins. There is a second reason: a greater *quantity* of protein can make up for a poorer *quality*. For example, if you were taking the perfect "protein mix," you would need about 40 g ($1\frac{1}{2}$ oz.) a day. But if the protein mix you are actually taking has only half the needed amount of one of the essential amino acids in 40 g, it would still be adequate if in fact you were taking not 40 g but 80 g of total protein a day. (And not very many people are taking less than 80 g a day.)

The mineral elements ("The salts")

We can now look at the mineral elements you need. The best known is *sodium*, which comes mainly as common salt (sodium chloride). We do not need more than approximately 2 g of salt a day, unless we are living in a very hot climate or unless we are undertaking very strenuous physical work and losing salt in perspiration. Most of us take much more than we need (around 10 or 12 g a day), and we all know people who take much more than this, sprinkling salt on almost anything that is put in front of them. These large quantities of salt almost certainly play a part in causing high blood pressure, so it would be a good idea if we restrained ourselves from using the saltshaker so much.

Another mineral element that we need in about the same quantity is *potassium*. This is found especially in cereals, fresh vegetables, fresh or dried fruits and fresh fish and poultry. It is impossible to go short of potassium in the diet; deficiency occurs mainly in certain illnesses and as a result of drug action (particularly the use of certain diuretics).

Most of the sodium in the body is outside the cells and most of the potassium is inside. They are largely responsible for the way in which the body's water is distributed (inside and outside the cells, and the proportion in these compartments). In addition, the sensitivity of the tissues—for example, the response of the muscles of the limbs and the heart to particular stimuli—depends among other things on a correct balance of sodium and potassium.

The amount of *calcium* we need is about half a gram a day, although growing children need more, and pregnant and nursing mothers considerably more. This is because most of the calcium is needed for building teeth and bones; that also explains why the richest food sources of calcium are milk and cheese. Calcium is also needed for blood clotting, to make sure you do not go on losing blood from a small scratch. Many people believe that calcium is needed to prevent their nails from splitting. This is nonsense. Your nails are made of *keratin*, the same protein that makes your hair and the horn of the rhinoceros.

The element *phosphorus* exists in the body almost entirely as *phosphate*. About 80% of the body's phosphate is present in the bones and teeth, compared with about 99% of the body's calcium. The rest is found in many parts of the body—in the nuclei of all the cells (including the genetic material DNA), in the blood where it helps to prevent the blood from getting too acid or too alkaline and in the cells themselves, where it takes part in the chemical reactions that constitute the body's metabolism.

We need something like a gram or so of phosphate in our food, and it is virtually impossible to get less. Every single food we take, except sugar and liquor and refined fats and oils, provides phosphate; human deficiency is quite unknown.

Magnesium is an essential element which is also so abundant in our foods that dietary deficiency is unknown. For example, magnesium is found in all vegetable foods including cereals. It is needed for the action of many of the body's enzymes; like potassium, most of it is inside the body's cells.

Iron is chiefly used for making *hemoglobin*, the red coloring matter of the blood which is used to carry oxygen to the tissues. Some iron is also found in virtually every cell in the body, where it helps in the process of oxidation and energy production from the fuel materials that come from food. Iron is needed especially in growing children, in premenopausal women (because of the blood lost during menstruation) and during pregnancy (when hemoglobin must be produced for the developing fetus). Pregnant women need approximately 25 milligrams a day, while it is possible that healthy adult men (or women after the menopause) can manage with very little iron, although it is customary to put their requirements at some 10 or 15 milligrams a day.

If the diet contains too little iron, the result will be anemia—that is, an inadequate amount of hemoglobin in the blood. Such people will then be pale, tire easily and get short of breath on exertion. But let me say at once that the converse is not true; many people get tired easily and are short of breath, and many, many more look pale. This often has nothing whatever to do with the amount of hemoglobin in the blood. So do not be persuaded to take iron tablets for your "anemia" unless your blood has actually been examined and shown to have too little hemoglobin; if it is short of hemoglobin, moreover, your doctor will have to make sure whether it is due to iron lack or to some other cause.

Iron is found especially in meat, but also in green vegetables. White bread is often enriched with iron, as well as with some vitamins. The iron in bread and vegetables is not very well absorbed; you will get more out of meat, especially out of liver and kidney. There is some iron in blackstrap molasses and in dried fruits such as raisins, but much less than in meat; moreover, these foods supply very little of the proteins and vitamins that you find in foods such as meat.

There are several other mineral elements that the body requires in quite small quantities and which occur in these small quantities in ordinary diets. They are called "trace elements," but the term is a little muddling. As we saw, we need something like 500 milligrams a day of calcium; we need only about one-eighth of 1 milligram of iodine, so it is reasonable to talk of iodine as a trace element. On the other hand, we need about 10 milligrams a day of iron, and probably about the same amount of zinc, yet iron is not called a trace element whereas zinc is.

Before I tell you a little about some of the better known trace elements, let me say quite categorically that the diet of no one in any Western country has ever been shown to be lacking in any trace element except iodine.

Iodine is needed to make the hormone of the thyroid gland, which helps us to control the general metabolism of the body. If the diet is lacking in iodine, the thyroid gland in front of the neck, which is usually not visible, becomes enlarged—a condition that is called *simple goiter*. It is as if the gland gets bigger in order to try and make enough of the hormone with its limited supply of iodine. If the deficiency is so severe that it impairs the manufacture of enough hormone, thyroid deficiency develops (which in infants is called *cretinism* and in adults *myxedema*). Treatment with small amounts of iodine cures this, and even cretinism if it is begun early enough.

Simple goiter used to occur commonly in certain areas, for example the inland mountainous areas in the United States, in the Swiss Alps and in central England (where it was known as "Derbyshire neck"). It is now much less common, partly because of a wider distribution of such iodine-rich foods as fish and partly because in many countries iodized salt is available.

Zinc has been known for several decades as being an essential component of several body enzymes. Only during the past ten years or so, however, has deficiency of zinc been identified—firstly in Iran, and then in Egypt and other countries of the Middle East. It shows itself as stunted growth, failure to reach sexual maturity and the presence of severe anemia. The deficiency condition improves rapidly when zinc salts are prescribed.

Fluoride is a chemical compound (of the element fluorine) about which there is a great deal of disagreement. This is not only about whether or not it should be added to our domestic water supplies, but whether it should be classed as an essential dietary constituent. Certainly it occurs naturally in our food and (at least to some extent) in the water we drink in some places. The amount in water varies enormously, supplying very little indeed or as much as 3 or 4 milligrams a day. A "typical" Briton drinking several cups of strong tea a day can easily get another milligram or so of fluoride a day. (For a more complete discussion, see *Fluoride and fluoridation* in the major article on **Dentistry**.)

> The maximum benefits from drinking fluoridated water are obtained in children before eruption of the permanent teeth, although partial benefits occur at any age. In addition, fluoride solutions applied directly to newly erupted teeth can reduce the incidence of tooth decay by up to 40%.

Very small quantities of fluoride are found in the bones and teeth. There is no doubt that making sure of an adequate fluoride supply—for example, by seeing that there is about one part per million in the public water supplies—considerably reduces dental decay in children. In spite of the many statements to the contrary, there is absolutely no evidence that this amount has any ill effects; there are very many natural water supplies that contain as much fluoride or more, and no harm comes to the people who use them. However, water that contains high natural amounts of fluoride (more than four or five parts per million) tends to produce teeth that are mottled. This does not occur in areas where the water contains one part per million of fluoride.

The vitamins

At any given moment there are many thousands of different chemical substances undergoing interrelated changes inside the body which, altogether, add up to the process of living. Almost all of these substances can be made from a few simple materials that come from the protein, carbohydrate and fat in the food we eat. But the body cannot make every one of the vast number of chemical substances in the body. Obviously, it cannot make the mineral elements such as sodium, calcium, iron

and so on. It cannot make all the amino acids, as we saw; it needs eight of these, or nine in a child, to be supplied ready made. Finally, it cannot make a dozen or so chemical substances that act, in different ways, to keep the host of chemical reactions going. These are the *vitamins*, which also have to be supplied in the diet.

The vitamins are substances with chemical structures that vary from being relatively simple to quite complex. They are required in quite small amounts to insure health—or, indeed, in many instances to prevent death. The amounts needed vary from as much as 30 milligrams a day (one-thousandth of an ounce) for vitamin C, to as little as 3 micrograms a day (one ten-millionth of an ounce) for vitamin B_{12}. Thus, 1 oz. of vitamin C is roughly enough for three people for a year, whereas 1 oz. of vitamin B_{12} will be enough for 30,000 people for a year.

It so happens that some of these substances can be made by some species of animals, but not others. A good example is a substance that, for now, I shall call *ascorbic acid*. All animals need it in their bodies, and almost every sort of animal makes it very readily. So ascorbic acid, for these animals, is simply one of the very many materials that are being made in their bodies all the time. But for you and for me, and for a very few other species, ascorbic acid has to be supplied in the diet—and so it is a vitamin (vitamin C).

Someone once described sugar as the substance that makes tea or coffee bitter if you don't put any in. Similarly, you can say that a vitamin is a chemical substance in our foods that makes you ill when you don't have it. When vitamins were first discovered, they were given letters of the alphabet, since little or nothing was known about their composition. Later, they were isolated from the foods one by one; still later they were analyzed chemically so that they can be (and nowadays often are) manufactured in the laboratory or factory. As a result, many of the vitamins are now known by their chemical names, although sometimes we stick to the old letters. For example, we still usually speak of vitamin A, although the biochemist calls it *retinol*; we speak of vitamin D rather than use the somewhat daunting *cholecalciferol*. On the other hand, most people now talk of *thiamine* rather than vitamin B_1, and many talk of *riboflavin* rather than vitamin B_2. But we need not worry about this. Language is for communication; so long as people know what you mean, it doesn't matter if you say vitamin E or *tocopherol*.

Here then is a short description of each of the vitamins: what happens when they are not there, which foods you find them in, how likely it is that you can be short of them, whether you can have too much and any special features that one or other vitamin has.

The "Adek" vitamins

Vitamin A is found in some fatty foods; liver is the richest source. Some livers are so rich that their oils (such as cod liver oil) have all the vitamin A you need for a day in a teaspoon (halibut liver oil has as much in two or three drops). There is some vitamin A in milk, and since it is in the fat of the milk it is in butter and in cheese (e.g., Cheddar cheese) made from whole milk.

All animals need vitamin A. You might ask how herbivorous animals get theirs, since vitamin A is found only in animal foods and not vegetable foods. The answer is that one of the components of the coloring matter of green leaves is a substance called *carotene*, which can easily be changed into vitamin A in the body. Carotene is also found in some fruits and in some root crops (as the name suggests, it is found in carrots).

The first effect of not having enough vitamin A or carotene in the diet is an inability to see very well in the dark. You have no doubt noticed that, when you go into a dark room or into a street at night after having been in a well-lit room, you don't see very well at first. Gradually, however, your vision improves and this is called "dark adaptation." In this process there is an increase of a substance in the retina called *visual purple* when little or no light falls on the retina; the more of this you can make, the more sensitive your eyes are to very poor illumination. Visual purple is made from vitamin A; if you are short of the vitamin, you will inevitably be short of visual purple and so have poor dark adaptation.

If vitamin A deficiency is more prolonged, or more severe, other ill effects occur. The skin becomes dry and rough, as do soft membranes such as the lining of the lungs and (perhaps) the urinary and genital passages. In particular, the surface of the eye becomes dry and rough. These changes in the eye and soft tissues make them more likely to become infected with bacteria that are on the body—but ordinarily kept at bay by the secretions of the tissues, or by the constant slight amount of tear fluid that moves over the eye surface. If the eye becomes infected, it may lead to the obstruction of the cornea (which covers the pupil), and result in blindness. It is said that today there are still 20,000 or more new cases of blindness occurring each year in children in India because of shortage of vitamin A— a shortage that need never exist if the children were to eat the green vegetables that are readily available. Here is a good example of how nutrition overflows from the laboratory and clinical sciences into the social sciences; how can the knowledge of what people *should* eat be translated into behavior in regard to what they *do* eat?

It is possible to take too much vitamin A, though not of carotene (which is converted too slowly into the vitamin for this to reach high concentrations). But if you are thoughtless enough to eat a sizable portion of polar bear liver, which is a very rich source of vitamin A, you might well find that you have very severe headaches, you may vomit and your skin may peel just as it does a day or two after you have been too much in the sun. Occasionally, overzealous mothers have made their children ill by giving

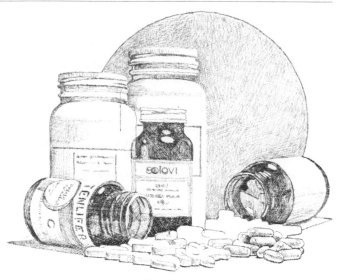

In most cases we get all the vitamins we need in our daily diet and under normal circumstances the ritual consumption of vitamin supplements and heavily vitamin-enriched foods is unnecessary.

them too much cod liver oil or some other rich source of vitamin A. Presumably they think that if a little is good for you, more must be better. Since the rich sources of vitamin A are almost always very rich in vitamin D as well an excessive amount can result in too much of either vitamin, depending on their relative amounts.

Now that I have touched on vitamin D, let me continue with it, if for no other reason than that (as we saw) some foods are rich in both vitamins. This is particularly true of liver and liver oil, but both vitamins also occur in milk and butter.

Like vitamin A itself, vitamin D does not occur in vegetables; unlike vitamin A, however, there is nothing in these foods that can be converted into vitamin D. But there is nevertheless a second source of vitamin D other than food. This is because it can be manufactured in the skin when it is exposed to sunlight, or more strictly to the ultraviolet rays of the sun. It can also be made by irradiating with ultraviolet light a chemical rather like vitamin D, and this is the material that is usually used when milk and other foods are fortified with vitamin D. Vitamin D in the diet is needed by infants and young children whose rapidly growing bodies do not receive reasonable amounts of sunlight. This would apply especially to babies in smoky cities, in temperate climates, or even to babies—and adults too—in sunny climates where custom dictates that they stay indoors most of the time. Adults who get even small amounts of sun on their skins need little if any vitamin D in the diet, provided it contains enough calcium.

The disease best known as being associated with lack of vitamin D is RICKETS. It is now very much less common than it was, even as short a time ago as the 1930s. Rickets is usually seen in babies between six months and two years. Since vitamin D is involved in helping the absorption and utilization of calcium from food, the bones become soft, so that the legs are bent, producing bowlegs or knock-knees; the arms may also be bent. The head seems enlarged, and the forehead is especially prominent. There is swelling of the wrists and perhaps of the ankles with a similar enlargement at the ends of the bony ribs as they approach the breastbone—so giving the appearance known as the "ricketic rosary." Usually, the abdomen is swollen, and the baby is subject to frequent respiratory infections.

The bony deformations tend to heal, even without treatment, as the child grows older; but sometimes there is permanent deformity (for example, of the pelvis). When rickets was common, the pelvic deformity in girls often resulted later in difficulty during childbirth.

Deficiency of vitamin D also occurs in adults, especially in women where there is a combination of vitamin D deficiency, calcium deficiency and frequent pregnancies. This condition, called OSTEOMALACIA, is seen today chiefly in the Far East, although it seems to be not so common as it used to be. It leads to considerable deformity of the body, affecting not only the limbs (especially the legs) but also the spinal column and the pelvis, and often leads to an inability to walk and finally death. The severe sort of osteomalacia I have just described is basically unknown to the Western countries, but there is a mild condition in the elderly in which the bones becomes less dense and thus less strong. As a result, they tend to fracture after a fall that would cause no bone damage in younger people. This condition is called OSTEOPOROSIS, and no one is quite sure why it occurs. Several causes have been suggested, however: a prolonged slight deficiency of calcium, or a change in hormone balance, or a mild shortage of vitamin D, or a combination of two or more of these. If, as seems likely in some instances, vitamin D shortage really is involved, then the condition is at least partly an example of mild osteomalacia.

The gap between the amount of vitamin D that is enough, and the amount that is too much, is narrower than it is for any other vitamin. When infants are given too much, they first begin to lose their appetite and so do not grow very well. If the high intake continues, bony deposits begin to appear in the kidneys, arteries and other soft tissues; ultimately, death may occur.

There are two other "fat-soluble" vitamins—vitamins E and K—that are found dissolved in the oily or fatty constituents of food. The richest source of vitamin E is the germ of cereal, so that wholemeal bread (which includes the germ) has a fair amount of the vitamin. On the other hand, there is some vitamin E in many ordinary foods, so that it is impossible for anyone to have a diet without at least some vitamin E.

In animals that have been fed special diets in the laboratory in which sources of vitamin E have been omitted altogether, several conditions developed, depending on the species of animals studied. In rats, a particular sort of sterility occurred. The deficient female rat mates in the ordinary way, becomes pregnant and carries her litter for about 14 days out of the normal 21 or 22 days. But at that time the fetuses die and are dissolved and "reabsorbed" by the mother. (The technical name for this sort of pregnancy is *resorption gestation*.)

The male rat is affected only by more severe deficiency. This produces sterility because of the failure of the rat to produce sperm.

Other animals are affected differently. Rabbits lacking vitamin E become paralyzed because of muscle wasting. In chickens, the tissues become waterlogged because of edema, and the blood vessels of the brain tend to break and so cause brain damage.

Since vitamin E was discovered half a century ago, there have been innumerable claims about what it can do in human beings. It has been supposed that it can cure, or prevent, heart disease, or one or two of the rare muscle diseases that affect children, or sterility in men or women. The fact is that there is no satisfactory evidence that taking preparations of vitamin E does any of these things.

The claims that are still being made are based on observations such as that a woman who has had two or three miscarriages and is then given vitamin E carried her next pregnancy to term. This does not always happen, though, and when it does it must be remembered that even without any treatment women often have an uneventful pregnancy after two or three miscarriages.

Some people even have the extraordinary notion that, because vitamin E deficiency in female rats affects the outcome of their pregnancies, taking vitamin E tablets will make their sex life more active, more satisfying and more interesting. This is about as logical as saying that the reluctant bull can be induced to mate if the cows were to wear false eyelashes, put on a new shade of lipstick and dab a touch or two of Chanel No. 5 behind each ear.

If however in spite of what I say you think it worthwhile to take preparations of vitamin E, you at least have the

Vitamin E has been hailed as a "wonder drug" with numerous curative and preventive powers, but there is no satisfactory evidence to support these claims.

consolation that you are only wasting your money; unlike vitamins A and D, you will most probably suffer no ill effects, since it seems that you cannot take too much vitamin E.

Vitamin K is found in almost every vegetable food, and, though to a much lesser extent, in meat and other animal foods too. Experimental diets with too little of this vitamin lead to bleeding from a slight scratch or other damage, and animals may die from the consequent hemorrhage. There are substances that counteract vitamin K, so that they will produce a deficiency even if the amount of the vitamin in the diet would ordinarily be enough. One of these substances, "Warfarin," which is used as a rat poison, can be said to make the rats bleed to death because of an induced deficiency of vitamin K. Similar substances are used in medicine if it is thought necessary to reduce the clotting power of the blood, that is, in people who are liable to thrombosis. Those who take such "anticoagulants" are monitored at regular intervals so as to check that the clotting power ("coagulability") of the blood is not so much reduced as to produce a danger of uncontrolled bleeding. If it is judged that this is likely, it can be counteracted by giving some extra vitamin K.

Vitamin K deficiency in the diet is virtually impossible to find in the adult. On the other hand, it does seem to occur sometimes in the newly born infant. Partly this is because there is little in the baby's body when it is born, and partly because babies are born with no bacteria in their gut. After a few days, the gut becomes very much a home for vast numbers of bacteria, and one of their activities is the manufacture of vitamin K; at this stage, babies need very little vitamin K in the diet. Some doctors prescribe vitamin K routinely to newly born babies, and it has even been prescribed routinely to mothers just before childbirth. Other doctors are inclined to look out for early signs of bleeding, and only then give the vitamin.

The "B" vitamins

The remaining vitamins are water soluble. Several of them are contained in what is sometimes called the *B complex*, or the *vitamin B complex*. The reason for this is that, in the early days, it was shown that there are some foods, especially yeast and liver, that are particularly good at protecting people from a disease called beriberi, or even curing it. It was thought that there was one vitamin in these foods, and it was given the name water-soluble B, and later, vitamin B. But it soon became clear that there were other constituents that were necessary for the proper growth of animals in foods like liver and yeast, yet these remained when the antiberiberi vitamin had been destroyed. Eventually, several different constituents were identified in these foods. However some research workers thought that they were describing a new vitamin when in fact they were describing the new property of an already identified one. As

a result, there is a vitamin B_2, but no vitamin B_3 or B_4 or B_5; a vitamin B_6, and after that vitamin B_{12}.

Vitamin B_1 is the one that prevents or cures beriberi, as we saw. It is now more commonly known as *thiamine*. Beriberi used to be common especially in the countries of the Far East where the main food was polished rice. The vitamin is chiefly in the germ and outer layers of cereal foods, and little is left if rice is milled and polished. Although the vitamin also occurs in many other foods, especially in animal foods, the diets of some of the poorer populations consist largely of the polished rice with very little else.

Beriberi affects both the circulation and the nervous system. It leads to heart failure and swollen limbs from edema, and to a loss of sensation in the limbs and paralysis. When the former symptoms predominate, the condition is called *wet* beriberi; when the latter predominate, it is called *dry* beriberi. If beriberi is untreated, the outcome may be fatal.

Mild beriberi is characterized by poor appetite, vague stomach pains and constipation, a rapid pulse, perhaps some swelling of the feet and a diminished sensitivity of the limbs to touch or pain.

Beriberi is not so common as it used to be. This is partly because several countries where it was common—the Philippines for instance—have laws that require the addition of vitamin B_1 and some other B vitamins to polished rice. This would not be necessary if people ate rice that was only lightly milled, but just as most people in the West prefer white bread to wholemeal bread, so many people in the rice-eating countries like their rice highly polished. An alternative is to boil the rice for a short time before milling; in this process of "parboiling," much of the thiamine and of the other B vitamins that are present in the germ and outer layers of the rice pass into the central part of the grain, so that after polishing the rice is not so bereft of these vitamins. Again, eating parboiled rice is a matter of taste and custom, and people that are not used to it do not readily take to parboiled rice.

Niacin, another of the B vitamins, is also found especially in liver and yeast, and to a lesser extent in the grain of cereals and in meat. Yet the disease pellagra with which niacin deficiency is associated is particularly found in areas where the staple diet contains a great deal of corn (maize). We shall see in a moment why this is so.

Pellagra was especially common in the Mediterranean countries, in parts of Southern Africa, and before World War II in Southern United States. The skin becomes dark, rough and thickened; there is abdominal discomfort with diarrhea. If the disease is prolonged it leads to mental disturbances, especially irritability and depression. If untreated it can lead to death.

The disease has virtually disappeared from the Southern states, following an improved standard of living and much less dependence on corn as a major item of diet. The vitamin in foods and in the body is not niacin itself, but a chemical derivative called niacinamide. Nothing seems to happen if you take a lot of this "amide," but niacin itself (which is often the form in which it occurs in vitamin pills and enriched foods such as cornflakes and bread) can cause uncomfortable, though not serious, symptoms if taken in large quantities. The effects are flushing and perhaps palpitations, which clear up quickly when the vitamin concentrate is no longer taken.

The reason why the disease pellagra is associated with corn diets is threefold. Firstly, corn contains little niacin, although in fact rather more than does wheat. Secondly, the body can make additional niacin from one of the amino acids, tryptophane, but the protein in corn contains only small quantities of tryptophane. Thirdly, cereals as a whole, but corn in particular, contain a material that holds on to the niacin so that much of it fails to be absorbed from the alimentary canal into the blood. Incidentally, this binding effect is eliminated by cooking corn in the presence of lime, and this is why Mexicans rarely suffer from pellagra; the white powder is added to corn meal before it is made into tortillas, which are the main way Mexicans eat their corn.

> **Pellagra, a disease caused by a gross deficiency of niacin in the diet, is characterized by the classical "3-Ds"— dermatitis, diarrhea and dementia. Among the mental disturbances associated with this disease are general confusion, irritability, depression and delirium.**

Riboflavin is still sometimes called vitamin B_2. A diet that has too little riboflavin leads especially to changes in the eyes, lips and skin. The eyes become itchy and sensitive to the light. The lips become raw and red and painful cracks develop at the corners of the mouth. The skin most affected is in the groin, where it becomes thick, inflamed and irritated.

It is said that mild symptoms of *riboflavin deficiency*, either alone or together with the signs of pellagra, are the most common forms of vitamin deficiency in the world as a whole. Nevertheless, if it does occur, it is not in itself very serious; the symptoms very rapidly clear up when riboflavin is given, or better still when the diet is improved with riboflavin-containing foods.

Vitamin B_{12} is found only in animal foods, although it can be extracted from some sorts of mold. An excellent source is liver, as with other B vitamins, but it is not found in yeast. Other good sources are milk and meat. Ordinary dietary deficiency is rare; it has however been reported in vegetarians who take no animal food at all (known in Britain as "vegans"). Nowadays, vegans are able to get the

vitamin as a by-product from special extracts of molds that have been used to produce antibiotics.

Although primary deficiency is so rare, secondary deficiency of vitamin B_{12} is well known. It is the disease pernicious anemia, which comes about because of the absence of a substance in the stomach that reacts with vitamin B_{12} and allows it to be absorbed. The effect is a very severe form of anemia, because the vitamin is needed for the production of the red cells of the blood. In addition, there gradually develops a disease of the nervous system, with numbness and tingling, weakness of the limbs and especially an inability to maintain balance. Untreated, pernicious anemia commonly ends in death.

Until vitamin B_{12} was identified in the late 1940s, people with pernicious anemia had to eat large amounts of liver regularly. We now know that this contains so much vitamin B_{12} that enough gets absorbed even without the stomach substance. Today, when the vitamin can be obtained pure, injections of quite tiny amounts are enough to cure the disease. As with insulin for diabetes, injection of vitamin B_{12} is needed regularly, but 1 milligram a month is usually enough, since the body requires only 3 or 4 micrograms (thousandths of a milligram) each day.

Of the other B vitamins, only three are worth a mention: folic acid, vitamin B_6 and pantothenic acid. Folic acid deficiency leads to a special sort of anemia. It occurs commonly and in severe form in the poor countries of the tropics. In the better-off countries, it is rarely seen in children or men, or in most women, except that it occurs in mild or moderate form in a fair number of women during pregnancy. The vitamin is found mainly in green leaves, and like all the other B vitamins also in liver. There is not much in meat, milk or fruit.

Vitamin B_6 deficiency produces very different effects in different animals: dermatitis (inflammation of the skin) in rats, anemia and paralysis in pigs, and convulsions in dogs. The very rare deficiency in human beings also results in convulsions. This occurs not because there is too little vitamin B_6 in the diet, but because of some obscure abnormality in metabolism.

Many claims have been made that taking vitamin B_6 will prevent or cure human disease, notably schizophrenia and arthritis. There is absolutely no acceptable evidence that vitamin B_6—or indeed any vitamin or other nutritional supplement—will do anything to improve these conditions. The amount of the vitamin that we get is quite adequate, since it occurs in most of the foods we eat.

Pantothenic acid is another vitamin that is found in many foods, and deficiency in man occurs very rarely indeed, if at all. During World War II, some of the prisoners in the Far East suffered from a condition called the "burning feet syndrome," which may have been in part caused by a deficiency of pantothenic acid. In black or brown rats, a diet that is deliberately made to contain no pantothenic acid results in their fur becoming gray. So you

No tonic, vitamin, pill or other substance has yet been developed which can restore missing hair or reverse the graying that often comes with age.

may see pills or other tonics that promise—or suggest—that they will restore the dark color that your hair may originally have had. Do not believe it, because it is not true.

The "Sea vitamin"

The fact that in America an Englishman is known as a "limey" comes from the earliest days of the discovery of vitamin C. A very elegant nutritional experiment was carried out in about 1750 by a Scottish ship's surgeon, Dr. James Lind, who was horrified by the vast number of sailors who on long voyages developed scurvy, from which many of them died. On one such voyage, he gave small groups of sailors with scurvy a variety of treatments; the only ones who were rapidly cured were those receiving lemon juice. In the usual unhurried way of British officialdom, it was not until another 40 years had passed that the British Navy issued lemon juice, and later lime juice, as part of the standard ration, and this continued right up to 1945. The number of sailors with scurvy in the British Navy fell from nearly 1,500 in 1780 to a single case in 1806.

The chemistry of vitamin C is quite simple; it was worked out in the 1930s, and the vitamin given the chemical name of ascorbic acid. Since that time it has been manufactured very cheaply and in large quantities by the pharmaceutical industry. It occurs naturally, and in an identical form, in all fruit and vegetables, although in widely varying amounts. There is quite a lot in citrus fruits, strawberries and raspberries, but much less in grapes, plums and most varieties of apple. Similarly, there is more in leafy vegetables than in beans and peas. Potatoes have a modest amount—more when newly harvested than after months of storage—but they can provide a fair proportion of what the

average person needs, since many people eat several ounces of potatoes virtually every day.

Full-blown scurvy is rare today. It occurs in special circumstances, such as in mentally deranged persons with bizarre eating habits who refuse to take any fruit or vegetables, or in individuals living alone, usually in poverty, who do not bother to include fruit or vegetables in their diets.

Scurvy begins with what has been neatly described as "irritability and uncalled-for argumentativeness." Then the gums begin to swell and bleed, and the teeth may fall out. Small spots appear under the skin because of bleeding capillaries which have become weakened. There may also be bleeding into the joints, which become very painful. People with scurvy, even in the mild stages, are rather more susceptible to infection.

Guinea pigs belong to one of the very few species of animal that, like man, need vitamin C. When put on a diet with no vitamin C, they develop a condition very similar to human scurvy and they become *very* susceptible to infection. In guinea pigs, this almost always results in respiratory disease, beginning with coughs and sneezes that rapidly lead to pneumonia and perhaps death.

It was this effect in guinea pigs, and the somewhat increased susceptibility to infection of people who have scurvy, that has led to the idea that one of the major functions of vitamin C is to increase the body's resistance to coughs and colds. It was also the beginning of the current widespread belief that enormously large doses of vitamin C—of 2,000 or 3,000 milligrams (2 or 3 g) or more—will help to cure or prevent colds. This is very much more than the 30 milligrams a day recommended by the British as being perfectly adequate, or the 45 milligrams a day recommended in America. These recommendations have not been taken out of thin air, but are based on very careful consideration of a vast amount of research. You really do not need these huge quantities of vitamin C, I am quite sure.

Do you need vitamin supplements?

Many people believe that they must take, every day, supplements of vitamins, minerals or proteins, or a mixture of these. They think that many of the foods we eat have been deprived of these nutrients, either because of modern ways of farming or because of what happens in the food factory. Again, many people think that, if a little vitamin is "good for you," a lot must be better.

But the nutritional value of crops grown with organic fertilizers is no different from that of crops grown with chemical fertilizers. Preserving by canning does very little to the nutritional value of the food put in the cans, and freezing does even less. The way food is prepared in the kitchen is of far greater importance in determining, for example, how much vitamin C is left in vegetables.

Again, if you have enough of a vitamin, or a mineral or protein, then you have enough. Pouring two quarts of oil into your car engine if it needs only one quart does not improve its performance; at best it is a waste, and at worst the excess can cause damage to one or other of the sensitive parts of your car.

It may be true that your diet is not as nutritious as it could be, but that will be because you yourself have pushed nutrient-poor foods into it and so pushed better foods out. And if your diet *is* poor, are you sure you know what nutrients are on the low side, and by how much? You cannot turn a bad diet into a good diet by sprinkling it with a few pills containing a mixture of vitamins and so on that the manufacturers have found to be convenient enough or inexpensive enough to go into their preparations.

A sensibly chosen diet will have all the nutrients you need and will not be made better by adding some concentrates to it. There is some evidence that some people, sometimes, can marginally reduce the number and severity of colds by taking an extra few milligrams of vitamin C a day. This will only be if they have been eating very little fruit or vegetables, and the slight improvement they may achieve will come just as well with 20 or 30 milligrams a day as it will from taking 2,000 or 3,000 milligrams or more that lots of people have been persuaded are necessary.

Vitamin A deficiency, as we saw, results in poor night vision. But if you see poorly in the dark, the chances are very small indeed that it is due to deficiency of vitamin A. It may be simply that you are not as young as you were or that, as with other bodily functions, some people see better in dim light than others. Vitamin B_1 deficiency can lead to poor appetite; it is most unlikely that this is why you are sometimes off your food. Nutrition is to do with food, not pills or extracts. For millions of years man has survived by eating foods; the most important reason why people eat badly is either because they cannot get the foods they want, or—especially recently—because the foods they *want* are not always the foods they *need*.

You remember that I said that one of the important reasons that determines what we eat is that we eat what we like. I then went on to point out several times that we now have available a large number of foods and drinks of poor nutritional value, which we take because they are so very attractive and tasty. As a result, it is no longer true that food instinct directs us to good nutrition as it did in the days when, like all other animals, our foods were selected from what we found in our environment. In those times, eating what we *liked* was the same as eating what we *needed*; this is no longer true. We shall come back to this later.

Is it good for you?

One of the most common things people want to know about a food is whether it is "good for you." Partly they mean, "Does this food have special and perhaps unique properties: making the hair grow, curing arthritis or improving the function of the liver?" Partly they mean, "Does this food contain a good assortment of nutrients in reasonably high amounts?" As to the first, what they are really asking is whether the food has some sort of drug action.

Only a very few foods and beverages come into this category, and they are not the ones that most people are thinking about. The most common are the drinks that contain either caffeine or alcohol. You find caffeine in tea, coffee and cola drinks; since by itself it contributes neither calories nor nutrients, it cannot properly be classed as a food. Alcohol, on the other hand, does provide calories (energy); if it is in distilled spirits such as whiskey or vodka or brandy or gin, there will be no nutrients, whereas beer and hard cider do contain a little of some nutrients.

But foods do not contain the sorts of drugs that would do anything at all for your hair or your joints or your liver. This is just as well: you would need to take such drugs in particular and carefully measured amounts, just as you take the medicines given to you by your doctor. But you do not know how much of the imaginary ingredients are contained in the foods, nor is there any way of finding out, since no one has ever identified what these active substances are supposed to be. So if these "good for you" items really did work, it would be just as sensible to eat them for these drug effects as it would be to take aspirin in unknown amounts and at some odd times in order to keep you from developing a headache.

Now let us look at the "good for you" foods in terms of nutrients. The amount of protein, or vitamin A, or iron, or whatever that you will get out of the food, depends not only on whether there is a large amount in one ounce; just as important is how many ounces you are likely to eat and how often. My favorite example is parsley, which everyone tells you is a rich source of vitamin C. A quarter pound of parsley has about three times as much vitamin C as there is in a medium sized orange. Now please be good enough to get a quarter of a pound of parsley, and tell me honestly whether you are likely to eat this amount during the next ten years. Even if you are a parsley addict, you will—I am sure—not eat as much as an *ounce* a year, and this will give you as much vitamin C as you would get by putting a drop or two of orange juice into your mouth each day.

Honey and cider vinegar are two examples of food which people seem to imagine have both properties: some special ingredients in the nature of drugs, and high nutrient value. No one has identified what the drugs are that they contain, nor what they are supposed to do; they are simply supposed to be "good for you." As to nutritional value, honey contains such small amounts of vitamins and minerals that you would need to eat a pound or more each day to get the quantity that you would get from a tiny piece of bread and cheese. The only difference between cider vinegar and apple juice is that some of the sugar from the apple has been turned into acetic acid. Otherwise it has the same mineral content as does apple juice, and rather less of the vitamins.

Let me here put in another special food, just for luck: *sea salt*. Look up what it contains. You will see that its chief claim is that, while it is mostly ordinary salt, it also contains small quantities of potassium. If you switch from using ordinary salt to using nothing but sea salt in all your foods, you will get an extra 30 milligrams or so of potassium a day. You normally take at least 2,000 milligrams of potassium a day, and no one has ever been know to take too little.

Here are some sensible rules you should use before choosing a food that is said to be especially good for you.

1. Take no notice of any claim that it is good for your kidneys, or for your lungs, or for your left small toe.
2. Make sure you really are short of the nutrients the food is supposed to supply.
3. Even if the food is "the world's most concentrated source of vitamin B_{99}," ask yourself how much of it you are going to take every day.
4. Will it give you anything else that is worthwhile, or will it, like honey, come with a vast number of extra calories that are almost certainly just what you *don't* need?
5. Are you sure you cannot get the same nutrient just as easily from other foods that are far cheaper, and just as palatable?

Brown is beautiful

I must say a little about white bread versus brown. And I don't mean simply "brown bread," but bread made of *100% extraction flour*—that is, flour milled from the whole wheat including all the germ and all the bran.

Wholemeal bread has more of the B vitamins and more iron than white, unless the white has been enriched. It also has more roughage (dietary fiber) from the bran, but only a little more protein.

From the criteria I mentioned earlier, you would really need the additional vitamins and minerals from wholemeal bread only if your diet consisted largely of nonenriched white bread, making up say 60% or more of your total diet. In addition, the remaining diet would have to consist of nutrient-poor foods with little or no meat or fish or eggs or fruit and vegetables. But if you are *not* eating large quantities of bread, as well as a poor mixture of foods in the rest of your diet, you are not going to go short of nutrients.

That leaves the dietary fiber. There has been a lot of talk recently about the greater amount of this that you get out of wholemeal bread. But when you look closely at all the amazing things that are claimed for it, there are really very few effects that have been substantiated. One is that if you have true constipation, and not the imaginary constipation that so many people have talked themselves into, then it is possible that a switch from white bread to wholemeal bread could cure you. Secondly, if you suffer from that uncomfortable disease of the colon called *diverticulitis*, then a branny sort of bread could help to relieve your symptoms. Thirdly, apart from these two effects that, for some people, are distinct advantages to be gained from eating wholemeal bread, there is one distinct disadvantage. The fiber reduces the ability of the intestine to absorb some nutrients, although if the rest of the diet is pretty good, this will not deprive you sufficiently to produce a nutritional deficiency. One nutrient that is affected is protein, so that although 110 g (4 oz.) of wholemeal bread may contain say 9.5 g of protein compared with 9.0 g in white bread, the fiber interferes with its absorption, and you end up getting about the same amount of protein from both sorts of bread. Again, several of the mineral elements, including calcium, iron and zinc, are not so well absorbed if there is more fiber in the diet.

Having said what the dietary fiber in wholemeal bread will do, let me tell you what it does *not* do. In spite of the claims to the contrary, changing from white bread to wholemeal does *not* reduce your appetite, so it will not help to control your overweight. It does *not* reduce the cholesterol concentration in the blood, so even if you believe this is important it will do nothing to reduce your chances of getting a heart attack.

I am not at all sure that I have convinced you with what I have said; after all, there is a great deal of publicity for wholemeal bread or for bran from all sorts of interests, as well as from those who are certain that somehow or other wholemeal bread is an entirely natural food that man has been destined to eat from the very beginning of his existence. The fact is of course that, in evolutionary time, bread is a very recent introduction to man's diet. But whether you accept my views or not, please do not say that I told you not to eat wholemeal bread. If you like it, eat it; all I say is that it will not do the miracles that have been claimed for it.

Sweet and dangerous

Curiously enough, although many people have convinced themselves that white bread is harmful, few have properly appreciated the harm that can come from eating sugar. I shall talk about white sugar first, then we can see whether brown or raw sugars are any better.

Firstly, most people do not realize how much sugar we now eat. For millions of years, the extracted sugar that is in our sugar bowls and in the many manufactured foods was quite unknown. Even only 200 years or so ago, the average amount of this sugar eaten in America and in Britain was something like 4 lb. a year, and about the same quantity of the "natural" sugar present in the fruit and the vegetables in our diets. Nowadays, there has been only a relatively small increase in what you might call "natural" sugar, but we now take an average of 100 lb. or more of extracted sugar. Between two thirds and three quarters of this, incidentally, is not bought as such, but it is bought in manufactured foods such as candy, chocolate, cookies, ice cream and sodas. During the same period, when there has been this enormous increase in sugar consumption, there has been a reduction in the amount of starch in our diet to about the same extent.

During the past ten years or so, a number of research workers in different countries have compared the effects, both in laboratory animals and in human subjects, of two diets either with starch or with sugar. Sugar produces an increase in the blood in the amount of cholesterol, triglyceride (neutral fat), uric acid and at least two hormones, insulin and cortisol. It produces a diminished glucose tolerance—that is to say, a dose of glucose taken by mouth causes an abnormally high and prolonged rise of the glucose in the blood; this is the main characteristic of diabetes. The insulin that circulates in the blood has much less effect on the metabolism of the body's tissues than does the insulin on normal tissues; this too is a common feature of diabetes. The blood clots more easily. The liver and the kidney are enlarged; the kidney and the retina of the eye undergo abnormal changes in the same sort of way as they do in diabetes.

These effects of sugar suggest that it is involved not only in producing diabetes but also in producing coronary heart disease. There are many abnormalities associated with coronary heart disease. They include those that I have mentioned as being produced by sugar: a low glucose tolerance, an increase in triglyceride as well as an increase in cholesterol; an increase in clotting power in the blood; an increase in uric acid and an increase in the insulin and cortisol in the blood.

I shall say more about the role of sugar in heart disease and diabetes a little later, but whether or not I can convince you, you do not have to be persuaded that sugar and the sugar-rich foods and drinks have a lot to do with producing overweight and dental decay. Ask any formerly overweight person about sugar and obesity; ask any dentist about sugar and dental decay.

You may believe that all these adverse effects only happen with unrealistically large quantities of sugar. This is in fact not so. Though the average amount of sugar is something like 100 lb. a year or a bit more, which is something like 5 oz. a day, I can assure you that there are many people who take much more than this. Indeed, the average consumption of boys of 16 or 18 is twice the national average, and we have found many people of all ages who take 12 oz. a day or even more.

Many people who do accept that sugar is harmful believe that this applies only to white refined sugar, because the refining process has removed important nutrients. Unrefined raw sugar does contain very tiny amounts of some minerals and vitamins. If you closed your eyes to the fact that it also contains a great deal of dirt and rubbish, and

perhaps a selection of bacteria, molds and lice too, your consumption of 1 oz. of raw sugar would contribute toward your daily needs of iron 5%, of calcium 2%, of thiamine 1%, and of riboflavin 0.5%. One oz. of the brown sugars (such as Barbados or Demerara) would give you less of these vitamins and no iron or calcium at all.

But I should be happy if you told me that you would give up all white sugar and foods and drinks made with it, and take only raw or brown sugars. Since very few manufactured foods are made with these sugars, you would end up taking far less sugar than most people do.

Diet and heart attacks

I touched on the problem of coronary heart disease when I talked about sugar, but there is more that we need to know about it. From the many articles that have been written and talks that have been given, you have almost certainly got the idea that, although there is some disagreement about why people get heart attacks, there are some things that are certain. Among these you would most likely include the importance of reducing particular sorts of fats in the diet and the number of eggs that you eat.

In fact there are very few things that are entirely certain about heart disease, and research scientists and doctors are still strongly debating such matters as the role of the diet. Almost all those who have studied the problem agree that heart attacks have become much more common in well-off Western countries during the last 50 or 100 years; that they are much commoner in these countries than in the poorer countries of Africa, Asia or South America; that women before the menopause are less affected than men of the

Experts tend to agree that the risk of heart disease is increased by lack of exercise, overweight and cigarette smoking.

same age, and that there is not one single cause of the disease but several. Most research workers would say these causes include smoking cigarettes, being physically inactive and being overweight.

But apart from overeating in general, there is the common belief that an important cause is eating too much of the so-called *saturated fats* (from meat and dairy produce) and eating too little of the soft vegetable fats (like corn oil or specially prepared margarines). The chief reasons for this belief are that in the wealthier countries, fat consumption—especially saturated fat consumption—has gone up at the same time as the disease has become more common, and that the countries where heart disease is common are those with a higher consumption of saturated fat. Moreover, the populations in the countries with more heart disease have a higher amount of cholesterol in the blood and changing the amount of fat or type of fat in the diet changes the amount of cholesterol in the blood.

More recent research suggests that cholesterol is not the best blood constituent to measure as an indication of whether a person is likely to have a heart attack; a better constituent seems to be one called High-Density Lipoprotein (HDL). But we don't yet know much about how the diet affects HDL in the blood, and especially we don't know whether, if it does, it also affects the risk of developing coronary disease.

But many research workers believe that there are already enough reasons to recommend that you should eat less fat altogether, that you should change some of the saturated fat for *polyunsaturated fat* (PUFA) and that you should restrict the number of eggs, because they have a lot of cholesterol. But the belief that dietary changes will reduce your chances of getting a heart attack is not shared by large numbers of serious and knowledgeable workers, who have spent just as much time on study and research.

The most commonly rejected part of the dietary recommendations are those referring to the cholesterol intake. Many researchers do not believe that eating more than three or four eggs a week leads to a significant increase in the amount of cholesterol in the blood, or even if there is a slight increase that it would in itself make a heart attack more likely. I myself do not believe that fat in the diet has anything to do with coronary disease, and this view is shared by quite a number of important research workers.

The main reasons why I believe dietary fat or cholesterol is not important are that I think the most logical view of the underlying cause of coronary heart disease is a disturbance of hormone balance. This would explain why there are so many changes in coronary disease; it would also explain why coronary disease is linked with diabetes and other diseases. Some people think that the basic cause of coronary disease is an excessive amount of insulin in the blood, but since several hormones interact with each other, it could well be a different one, for example, one of the sex hormones. I say this because a characteristic of coronary

disease is that young women are far less likely to get a heart attack than are men of the same age. They lose this comparative immunity after the menopause, when there is a change in the balance of their hormones.

As far as I know, changes in the sorts or amounts of dietary fat do not affect the amount of insulin—or any other hormone—in the blood. On the other hand, the causes of coronary heart disease that are agreed—physical inactivity, cigarette smoking and obesity—do affect the amount of insulin, and so does a high consumption of sugar.

But whether or not you are convinced that sugar is one of the causes of heart disease, there are several other reasons why we should reduce our sugar consumption. If it also reduces the chances of getting a heart attack, this is simply an added bonus, but of course a very important one.

On the other hand, if you want to do something about fat, there is certainly no harm in reducing the total amount you eat, or reducing the meat and dairy fat, except that a diet low in fat is not very palatable. I am not at all sure, however, about the safety of increasing the polyunsaturated fats. Firstly, most margarines contain no more PUFA than does butter; you must check the label. Secondly, I am less and less inclined to accept without question foods that have been chemically changed by the manufacturer, and there are many changes that occur in the factory in turning the (unspecified) mixture of fats and oils into margarine. Thirdly, I think in principle one should not introduce new foods into man's diet if this can be avoided. The ability to consume large quantities of polyunsaturated fat is very recent indeed, since it depends on highly sophisticated technology for growing the seeds and other sources from which the oil is extracted, for extracting it efficiently, and for purifying it so that it does not get rancid. But if you have been persuaded about dietary fats and heart disease, remember that it is only one of the factors you should do something about. Keeping an eye on your weight, not smoking cigarettes and not being as sedentary as many of us nowadays are, will all help you to avoid falling a victim to this modern epidemic.

The "No-gimmick way" to deal with overweight

The term "overweight" is in one sense misleading. What we really are concerned about is too much fat in the body. But since it is difficult to measure body fat in people, we usually content ourselves with weighing them. If they weigh more than we think is appropriate, we assume it is fat. We should remember, however, that occasionally the overweight is due to something else: to very well-developed muscles (for instance, in an all-round wrestler), or to water (fluid). But fluid can account for only a few pounds of overweight in an ordinary healthy person; for example, in some women a few days before menstruation. More than 2 or 3 lb. of water (or perhaps up to 5 lb.) can be retained only in someone who is ill—particularly with an illness that requires the administration of a steroid hormone such as cortisone, or something as serious as kidney disease or heart failure.

An excess of fat, as we saw, can only come about if the calories in the food we eat have been more than the calories being used up. We can get rid of fat by eating less, by being more active, or by a combination of the two. I find it difficult enough to persuade people to eat less, but even more difficult to persuade them to be more active. By more active, incidentally, I mean a *constant effort to do more*—walking upstairs, leaving the car in the garage—and not simply a weekly round of golf, or even the twice weekly game of tennis or squash.

There have been thousands of "diets" for overweight. Most of these are clearly ineffective, or why should there be new ones virtually every day? The best way to begin is to make up our minds what it is we need. We need a way of eating that not only provides us with fewer calories but one that is also permanent. The approach that so many people go in for is to have alternate periods of losing weight on a diet and gaining it when they go back to their ordinary eating: the rhythm method of girth control.

> Despite the extravagant and nearly magical claims of manufacturers of products designed to aid in weight loss, the only sensible answer remains to cut down on the quantity of food we constantly place in the "hole" just beneath our nose!

To adopt a diet that we stay with for the rest of our lives, we need a new way of eating, and this must be both nutritious and sociable. We need to reduce the calories without reducing the protein or the vitamins and mineral salts, and we need to be able to eat with our friends and family without having to prepare or buy special foods.

But before I go on, let me make two points. Firstly, I do not like to use the word "diet." Most people think of diet as a special and temporary way of eating. A diet is something you "go on," so you look forward to the day when you "come off."

Secondly, if we are to eat differently from the way that made us fat in the first place, then it is bound to be a less attractive way than we are now eating. For what we are now eating represents the amounts and sorts of food we like best, even if we are pretending to be dieting. We must therefore begin by making up our minds that, at least to begin with, we are going to have some sort of restriction. You will notice that I said "at least to begin with" the diet will be less attractive—this is because much of the way we now eat is a bad habit that we can gradually lose. It is no use

doing what some of my overweight patients did, saying that they "must have this" and they "can't possibly give up that"—saying, in fact, that they would keep to any diet I gave them, provided it lets them eat exactly as before.

One way in which calories can be reduced is simply to eat the same foods as before, only less. This is possible, but it has two disadvantages. First of all it reduces the nutrients in the diet as well as the calories, and there is no reason to suppose that fat people are eating such a nutritious diet that they can afford to reduce its nutrient content. The second disadvantage is that simply eating less of all the usual foods will result in a constant feeling of hunger and frustration, as well as a temptation to eat more.

A better way is to reduce especially the carbohydrate-rich foods, and more particularly those that are sugar-rich. This has several advantages. Firstly, many of these foods have little or nothing in the way of nutrients, and even starch-rich foods like bread and macaroni are relatively poor in nutrients when compared with the calories they have. The second advantage is that it will be a healthier diet because it will avoid the harmful effect of sugar. Thirdly, meat and fish, eggs and cheese, butter and cream and green vegetables, which have no carbohydrate or only very little, are more satisfying, so that it usually turns out that one does not eat more fat and protein to make up for eating less carbohydrate. In fact, cutting the carbohydrates sufficiently, to 50 g or 60 g a day instead of the usual 300 g or so, allows one usually to eat as much as one likes of those other foods. Many people imagine that it is impossible to eat "as much as you like" of them, and yet lose weight. But "as much as you like" is not "an infinite amount," but just what it says; you stop eating when you have had as much as you like. Thus, the low carbohydrate diet is low in calories just because it is low in carbohydrate and has no more fat or protein.

Now that we have surveyed the nutrition scene, however superficially, we can make some general comments about how to choose a diet that is nutritious, satisfies our bodily needs and also helps us to keep fit and slim. The underlying principle for doing this is to get back as far as possible to the foods that were chosen by man over millions of years of evolution, before he gave up hunting and gathering his food, and began first to grow and later to manufacture his food. For many reasons, we cannot revert entirely to foods that we can get by hunting them, or picking them from a tree or a bush or digging them up from the ground. But we can avoid many foods that are made from extracting and mixing foods, and so changing them that they would not be recognized by a thawed-out caveman who had been frozen into the ice since the last Ice Age. So I *do not* mean that we should avoid canned meat or frozen vegetables. I *do* mean that we should avoid the sorts of food I have mentioned so often, most of which are rich in carbohydrate and many of which are rich in sugar. Then we shall find that our food instincts are quite capable of guiding us to an excellent diet.

Learning what foods not to eat is perhaps more important to good nutrition than knowing which foods are good for health; it is easy to instill the wrong attitudes in children by offering them an abundance of candy and "junk" food.

Food instinct is not enough

During the ten years or so before World War II an American pediatrician, Dr. Clara Davis, carried out an experiment that makes the point about food instinct more clearly than anything I can say. She took several babies around six months old, and let them choose their own food. They could take whatever they wanted, and however much they wanted. Dr. Davis found that over the next four years or so, they grew at least as well, and were at least as healthy, as other children being brought up under the most careful supervision, and being fed according to the most expert knowledge of the nutritional needs of children. When she summarized her results in 1939, she pointed out why children did so well when allowed to choose their own food by "instinct." It was not simply that they were offered all the foods we know are good foods (fruit, vegetables, meat, milk, fish, eggs) but that they were *not* offered any of the wrong foods—no candy or chocolate, no cakes or cookies or pastries, no ice cream or sodas.

We can now see that the rules for a good diet are more to do with what we should *not* eat than with what we *should* eat. I am not therefore telling you the sort of thing that you so often hear, that "you should eat at least two portions each day from the following four food groups"—or five or seven or whatever.

Provided the good foods are available and provided you are not diverted by those very tasty foods that have been made specially to tempt you, your food instinct will see to it that you choose a good mixture of foods with all the nutrients you need and without the components that can harm you.

Simple rules for good nutrition

Remember that it is not only *foods* that are tempting, but *drinks* too. The easiest thing to avoid is the sugar-laden mixer drink. Use the low-calorie tonic, or dry ginger ale or bitter lemon, all of which have no added sugar. Although I know I can't stop you taking alcohol if you really can't do without, I do not accept the excuse that you drink only because it is socially necessary. If that is the real reason, you can carry a glass around at parties with club soda rather than with gin and tonic. In general, it is amazing what you can do if you are convinced that it is important, and I don't suppose that there is anything more important than your health.

If you want more specific advice about what you should or should not eat, I can summarize much of what I have said by making groups of foods, but different from those that you commonly see. My three groups are those foods that you should try to avoid altogether, those that you should eat moderately and those that you can eat as much of as you like. You may think that it does not help if I say "you can eat moderately" when I don't say what moderately is. The reason is that only *you* can judge the amounts, and the way to judge is by keeping an eye on your weight.

Group 1. Avoid these items as much as you possibly can: (1) Sugar in your coffee or tea, in sodas, or on your breakfast cereal; (2) Alcoholic drinks; (3) Sugar-coated breakfast cereal; (4) Cookies; (5) Candy and chocolate and desserts; (6) Prepared, canned or frozen foods in which sugar is the first or second item in the list of ingredients. You do not need to worry if it is the third or later item. You do not *need* any of these sugary items. They do you no good and you will soon learn that you can do without their attractive taste.

All this does not mean that you have to make a nuisance of yourself with friends who have gone to a lot of trouble to prepare some special dish. By all means have a small portion, but don't use "social occasions" as an excuse for frequently eating something you can mostly avoid if you really want to.

Group 2. These items should be taken in moderation: (1) Bread; (2) Crackers; (3) Macaroni; (4) Rice; (5) Corn; (6) Breakfast cereal.

With items from Group 3, these will make up your calories to what you need, but you must see that they don't exceed what you need. If you are overweight, you should limit the quantities of these starch-rich foods.

Group 3. Take as much as you like of these foods, unless you develop a passion for one or more of the asterisked items (7, 8 and 9): (1) Meat; (2) Fish; (3) Eggs; (4) Milk; (5) Green vegetables; (6) Root vegetables; (7) Cheese*; (8) Fruit*; (9) Potatoes*.

If you have carefully avoided items in Group 1, and cut down to some extent on those in Group 2, your weight should get to what it should be. If, however, you need to lose a bit more, then you must cut down the Group 2 items more. If you still feel you need to get rid of a few more pounds, then you will have to limit whichever of the three asterisked items in Group 3 you may be overeating. The limits you should aim at each day are not more than 1 oz. of hard cheese, or 2 oz. of cottage cheese, 8 oz. of fruit, two medium sized potatoes.

If you are eating more than is right for you, you will be overweight. You must remember, though, that it is not only your diet that can affect your weight. A lot of people who are very inactive—and that goes for so many of us nowadays—will find it difficult to lose the last few pounds even it they keep to the eating rules that I have drawn up. So if you need to lose more in spite of doing the right thing about your eating, then you have either to get up off that chair more often, or you've got to go hungry by eating *less* than the rules otherwise allow. The choice is yours.

Alphabetical list of most popular brand name drugs with their generic equivalents

Brand Name—*Generic Component(s)*

Achromycin-V—*Tetracycline*
Actifed—*Tripolidine and Pseudoephedrine*
Actifed-C Expectorant—*Tripolidine, Pseudoephedrine, Codeine and Glyceryl Guaiacolate*
Aldactazide—*Spironolactone and Hydrochlorothiazide*
Aldactone—*Spironolactone*
Aldomet—*Methyldopa*
Aldoril—*Hydrochlorothiazide and Methyldopa*
Amoxicillin (Generic)
Ampicillin (Generic)
Antivert—*Meclizine*
Apresoline—*Hydralazine*
Atarax—*Hydroxyzine*
Atromid-S—*Clofibrate*
Azo Gantrisin—*Sulfasoxisole and Phenazopyradine*

Bactrim DS—*Trimethoprim and Sulfamethoxazole*
Benadryl Cap./Tab.—*Diphenhydramine*
Benadryl Elixir—*Diphenhydramine*
Benedectin—*Doxylamine and Pyridoxine*
Bentyl—*Dicyclomine*
Butisol Sodium—*Butabarbital*

Chlor-Trimeton Tab.—*Chlorpheniramine*
Compazine—*Prochlorperazine*
Coumadin—*Warfarin*

Dalmane—*Flurazepam*
Darvocet-N 100—*Propoxyphene and Acetaminophen*
Darvon—*Propoxyphene*
Darvon Compound 65—*Propoxyphene, Aspirin, Phenacetin and Caffeine*
Diabinese—*Chlorpropamide*
Dilantin Sodium—*Diphenylhydantoin or Phenytoin*
Dimetapp Expectorant—*Brompheniramine, Phenylephrine and Phenylpropanolamine*
Diuril Oral—*Chlorothiazide*
Donnatal—*Phenobarbital and Hyoscyamine*
Drixoral—*Dexbrompheniramine and Pseudoephedrine*
Dyazide—*Triamterine and Hydrochlorothiazide*

E.E.S.—*Erythromycin ethyl succinate*
Elavil—*Amitriptyline*
Empirin Compound—*Aspirin, Phenacetin and Caffeine*
E-Mycin—*Erythromycin*
Enduron—*Methyclothiazide*
Equanil—*Meprobamate*
Erythrocin—*Erythromycin ethyl succinate*
Erythromycin (Generic)
Esidrinx—*Hydrochlorothiazide*

Fiorinal—*Aspirin, Phenacetin, Butalbital and Caffeine*
Fiorinal/Codeine—*Aspirin, Phenacetin, Butalbital, Caffeine and Codeine*
Flagyl—*Metronidazole*

Gantrisin—*Sulfisoxazole*

Hydrochlorothiazide (Generic)
Hydropres—*Reserpine*
Hygroton—*Chlorthalidine*

Ilosone—*Erythromycin Estolate*
Inderal—*Propranolol*
Indocin—*Indomethacin*
Isopto-Carpine—*Pilocarpine*

Brand Name—*Generic Component(s)*

Keflex—*Cephalexin*
Kenalog-Derm.—*Triamcinolone*
Kwell—*Gamma Benzene*

Lanoxin—*Digoxin*
Larotid—*Amoxicillin*
Lasix—*Furosemide*
Librax—*Chlordiazepoxide*
Librium—*Chlordiazepoxide and Clidinium*
Lidex—*Fluocinonide*
Lomotil—*Diphenoxylate and Atropine*
Lo-Ovral—*Ethinyl Estradiol and Norgestrol*
Lotrimin—*Clotrimazole*

Macrodantin—*Nitrofurantoin*
Marax—*Theophylline, Aphedrine and Hydroxyzine*
Mellaril—*Thioridazine*
Meprobamate (Generic)
Monistat-7—*Miconazole*
Motrin—*Ibuprofen*
Mycolog—*Neomycin and Triamcinolone*

Nalfon—*Fenoprofen*
Naprosyn—*Naproxen*
Nembutal—*Phenobarbital*
Neosporin—*Polymyxin, Neomycin and Gromicidin*
Nitrobid—*Nitroglycerin*

Omnipen—*Ampicillin*
Orinase—*Tolbutamide*
Ornade—*Chlorpheniramine and Phenylpropanalamine*
Ortho-Novum 1/50-21—*Norethindrone and Mestranol*
Ortho-Novum 1/80-21—*Norethindrone and Mestranol*
Ovral—*Norgestrel and Ethinyl Estradiol*
Ovulen-21—*Ethynodiol and Mestranol*

Parafon Forte—*Chlorzoxazone and Acetaminophen*
Pavabid—*Papaverine*
Pen-Vee-K—*Penicillin*
Percodan—*Oxycodone, Aspirin, Phenacetin and Caffeine*
Periactin—*Cyproheptadene*
Persantine—*Dipyridamole*
Phenaphen/Codeine—*Codeine and Acetaminophen*
Phenergan Expectorant—*Promethazine Hydrochloride*
Prednisone (Generic)

Quibron—*Theophylline and Glyceryl Guaiacolate*

Serax—*Oxazepam*
Sinequan—*Doxepin*
Slow-K—*Potassium Chloride*
Stelazine—*Trifluoperazine*
Sumycin—*Tetracycline*

Tagamet—*Cimetidine*
Thorazine—*Chlorpromazine*
Tylenol-Codeine—*Codeine and Acetaminophen*

Valisone—*Betamethasone*
Valium—*Diazapam*
Vibramycin—*Doxycycline*
V-Cillin K—*Phenoxymethyl Penicillin*

Zyloprin—*Allopurinol*

Drugs and Medicines

Part of this article deals with various categories of drugs and how they are used. The following table will help the reader to locate these categories. To find a specific drug and the indications for its use, the reader should consult the general index at the back of the book.

Drugs and Medicines

Dr. Judith K. Jones

Drugs are among the most powerful tools available to doctors today. They can successfully combat life-threatening diseases and bring relief to sufferers from innumerable disorders. For most of us, taking drugs and medicines prescribed by the doctor or bought over the counter is a common experience. Yet few of us are aware of why drugs are prescribed, how they work, and what potential dangers they represent.

Definitions of drugs and medicines

Drugs and medicines can be defined in terms of several characteristics: their use, their origins and their actions, both helpful and harmful. In very general terms, a drug or medicine is any substance or mixture of substances which is taken into the body for the purpose of improving one's physical or mental condition. This, then, also includes vitamins and hormones as well as the more conventional drugs. Conversely, any drug (especially if taken in excessive amounts) may be likely to cause side effects or poisoning. Some traditional poisons have medical applications, such as curare, the poison used by South American Indians on their arrows, which is a very useful drug to induce muscle relaxation during general anesthesia in the controlled setting of a surgical operation. From another viewpoint, antibiotics often act as a "poison" to bacteria but do not affect the host (ourselves). Similarly, many cancer drugs act as "poisons" to the tumor and may also be somewhat toxic or "poisonous" to human organs but are used because their overall benefit to the cancer patient is greater than the risk they entail.

In the past, medicines were usually mixtures of many plants and mineral substances, prescribed in Latin by physicians and deciphered and made up by pharmacists into elixirs, powders or ointments that were often strange smelling and tasting. Some of these unusual concoctions contained ingredients still seen in drugs today, but many of these old medicines appear to have been effective as much through patients' expectations of good results as from anything else. (We now call this phenomenon a *placebo* effect—from the proven capacity of patients to benefit even from a harmless, nondrug preparation provided they believe that it will do them good.)

Today we live in an entirely different era of drugs and medicines. Rarely are prescriptions written in Latin and rarely does the pharmacist himself prepare the mixtures, except for some elixirs. Instead, most medicines are manufactured in large quantities (often as single chemical entities) in the form of tablets, capsules, time-released particles, creams, suppositories and liquids for oral use or injection. Their exact contents are very carefully measured and standardized. Production, distribution and availability of each type of drug is controlled by legislation dating back to the first half of this century, although new laws continue to be made. Nowadays, before a drug is introduced on the market, it must meet stringent standards of safety and effectiveness, since it may be used by millions. To determine whether it does meet these requirements, it is first tested in many animals and later in human volunteers and persons with specific diseases which the drug is designed to treat.

Where do drugs come from?

Drugs and medicines come from many different sources. In ancient times, "medicines" were made from mixtures of extracts of plants, certain animal material (such as horns) and occasionally from mineral sources. In fact, many of our drugs are still derived from plants (for example, the quinine used to treat muscle cramps and quinidine used to control abnormal heart rhythms both come from the bark of the cinchona tree). Likewise, animal glands (and other material) such as the thyroid gland and the pancreas are still the major sources of certain drugs such as thyroid and insulin. Minerals, such as calcium and iron supplements, still come from natural mineral sources. Since it was discovered that the simple bread mold produced the invaluable antibiotic penicillin, living fungi continue to be important sources of drugs—primarily antibiotics and some of the drugs used in cancer therapy. In fact the fungi are much more efficient at making these drugs than our own chemical sources and so continue to be used. Finally, some drugs (such as Valium and Librium) are chemically synthesized from organic chemicals; this process represents a major source of our medicines at present.

How are drugs named?

Drug names are often confusing to patients as well as their physicians since there are many thousands of entities. Most drugs begin as a basic chemical substance (such as penicillin, tetracycline or prednisone)—or a combination of two or more chemical substances—which is produced by several manufacturers. These companies then sell these drugs directly to pharmacists or hospitals under generally accepted, less technical chemical names—called *generic* names. Alternatively, the manufacturers will apply a trade or *brand* name to their product to differentiate it from the same generic product manufactured by other companies. Thus, tetracycline may be sold by its generic name, *tetracycline hydrochloride*, or by one of its trade names, such as *Achromycin*. Some manufacturers sell only generic products, both to pharmacists and other companies which apply their own brand names. Other drug manufacturers only sell their products under a trade name, although they may be available by a generic name from other manufacturers. Often, a single generic name of a drug will have several trade names. All of this contributes to the confusion and, in general, the trend is toward more common use of generic names (although in some cases these are more difficult to pronounce than the trade names).

When a pharmaceutical company spends several hundred thousand dollars or more on the development of a new drug, it is understandable that the cost of research and development is a gamble against the profits should the drug prove to be effective and acceptable to the Food and Drug Administration (the governing body for approval of all new drugs in the United States). When the drug is approved for general clinical use by doctors, it is ordinarily sold under its brand name (although it may be prescribed under its generic name). The patent obtained by the original pharmaceutical manufacturer guarantees it the sole right to sell the drug for a given number of years—although it may grant a license for any other pharmaceutical manufacturer to make and sell the drug under a different brand name. When the patent expires any pharmaceutical manufacturer may make and sell the drug—either under a new brand name or under the generic name only.

As an example, for many years the well-known tranquilizer *meprobamate* (generic name) was available only from its original manufacturer and sold under the name of *Miltown* (brand name). Today, however, the patent has expired and the drug is available on prescription either under its generic name or about a dozen different brand names (including not only Miltown, but also Equanil, Bamadex, Pathibamate, Deprol, Kesso-Bamate and Milprem). (See *The cost of drugs* in this section.)

Drugs in current society

Drugs in current society fall into three general groups: prescription drugs, over-the-counter drugs and illicit drugs.

Prescription drugs are distinguished by the fact that they require the authorization and supervision of a physician for their use. This authorization is usually given in the form of a written prescription which is made after a physician or dentist has determined that a person has a specific condition that will benefit from taking a specific drug. The prescription is an official document which indicates the name of the drug, the dosage, the quantity of the drug to be issued under that prescription and very specific instructions for its use.

The over-the-counter drugs comprise more than 300,000 different entities which are available to the public over the counter in drugstores and markets. They are very widely used and include such common entities as aspirin, Tylenol, milk of magnesia, Maalox, vitamins and other similar drugs. The over-the-counter drugs have caused some confusion because many people do not consider them as drugs—although, like prescription drugs, they also can cause side effects and drug interactions (usually at a much lower rate of incidence and less risk of potentially serious effects, which is the reason they are available more freely over the counter).

The final group of drugs, the drugs that especially lend themselves to abuse, has also played a significant role in our society, particularly in the last 20 years. The specific drugs of abuse have varied over time. They include drugs that are also used as prescription drugs (such as barbiturates, morphine and Demerol) in addition to drugs which are virtually never used in prescription (such as LSD or mescaline). This area remains a subject of considerable controversy and is beyond the scope of this section.

Drug actions

All drugs have a variety of actions when taken. A classical example of this, as illustrated in Figure 1, is aspirin. When aspirin is taken, it can relieve pain, and it can also reduce fever if either symptom is present. In addition to these effects, it can relieve inflammation to a certain extent, and it

Figure 1

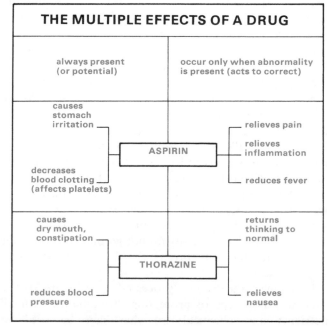

also affects the function of certain blood clotting elements called *platelets*. If taken frequently, aspirin can cause stomach irritation and even ulceration. Aspirin often produces all of these effects, but in most cases it is given in order to achieve one or another of its effects, its other actions being disregarded.

Another drug, used in psychiatric patients, provides a similar example (Figure 1). This drug, called Thorazine, is specifically used to correct disorders of thinking, as in schizophrenia. However, it also causes sedation and decreases blood pressure, which are effects sometimes desired after surgery. Furthermore, it decreases nausea, but is rarely used for this. Finally, it also causes constipation, although this predictable effect is usually viewed as a side effect. Again, in most cases this drug is used for one or two of these effects and the other effects are disregarded or considered as side effects.

Drugs are frequently defined or classified according to their action. Thus aspirin is often classified as a pain reliever or analgesic, although it has other effects; but in special cases it is classified as an anticoagulant or a drug to prevent clotting. In general, it is necessary to consider drugs and medicines in terms of both their intended action and uses and their other, sometimes undesirable, effects.

The journey of a drug through the body

If a drug is taken into the body, where does it go? It is useful to consider the journey of a drug through the body since this journey often determines how long a drug acts and how strongly it acts. There are many ways in which a drug can get into the body. The most common way is usually through the mouth, although it is often given by injection—either into a vein, into a muscle, or sometimes just under the skin. Likewise, it can be introduced into the lungs, as is the case for general anesthetics. It can also be introduced into the lungs as an aerosol or a spray as well as into the rectum as a suppository (where it is absorbed into the bloodstream at that site). If a drug is taken by mouth, it goes through the stomach—which often contains food and almost always contains strong hydrochloric acid. Many drugs will begin to dissolve here, even before they pass along into the intestines. As they dissolve, they pass through the walls of the stomach or intestines and are carried out into the bloodstream directly to the liver (see Figure 2). When drugs are given by other methods they enter the bloodstream directly and can go to their site of action first and secondarily to the liver. Some drugs (such as creams or ointments) are for direct use on the skin or in the eye. These drugs usually do not go into the body, but they can enter the body through the bloodstream if used in large amounts.

In the liver, the drug is "processed" (see Figure 3). The liver acts as a type of processing "roundhouse" for all nutrients and chemicals so they can be used or

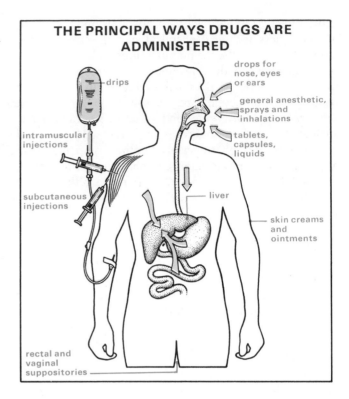

Figure 2: *the principal ways in which drugs can be given. They can be taken orally, injected directly into the bloodstream, breathed into the lungs, introduced as suppositories, or applied locally as drops, sprays, ointments and creams. Those that enter the bloodstream (either directly, by injection, or indirectly by absorption), are transported to the liver, where they are metabolized (see Figure 3).*

eliminated from the body. Through the long history of evolution, man has developed a very sophisticated liver which can process the many complex chemicals present in plants and other foodstuffs. Some of the chemicals in the substances we eat are toxic (poisonous). The liver converts these by a process called *metabolism* to less toxic substances which can be eliminated or used by the body. Most drugs arriving at the liver are partly metabolized to other substances at this "first stop." Sometimes the metabolized drug is more (sometimes less) active than the original drug. Obviously, if a person has a liver disease (such as hepatitis) this metabolic function may be affected. This is why people with liver disease sometimes require lower doses of the drugs they take.

In the liver the drug may "hop onto" a carrier protein—as shown in Figure 3. This protein acts as a carrier in the bloodstream by which the drug can get to various organs, although some drugs will travel "freely" in the bloodstream to all organs of the body. Once a drug reaches its site of action (Figure 4) it can attach to a protein molecule on a cell in the organ in which it acts. This protein is called a *receptor*. At this point the receptor is changed and the

HOW THE LIVER METABOLIZES A DRUG

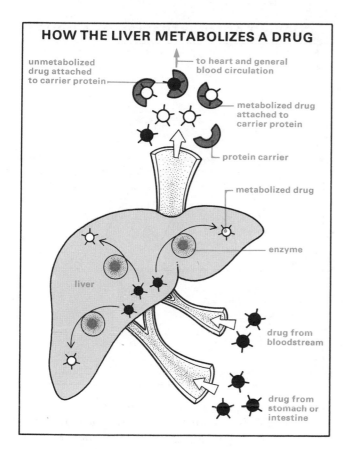

Figure 3 *The liver is a great chemical factory and is equipped with special enzymes capable of transforming the chemical structure of almost any substance they encounter. Most drugs active in the body dissolve in fat, but not in water, and therefore they are not soluble in urine. The liver changes such drugs into water-soluble substances by combining them with another chemical so that they can then be excreted by the kidneys. Apart from metabolizing drugs, the liver also manufactures "carrier" proteins which bind to drug molecules and carry them around the circulation.*

action of the drug takes place, sometimes by changing the function of the cell or muscle. At the end of this journey, the drug reenters the bloodstream and is eliminated, usually through the kidneys and the urine. Some drugs are eliminated through the bile into the intestines and pass out in the stools. If there is kidney failure, the drug cannot leave the body and this accounts for the practice of using smaller doses and allowing longer intervals between doses of drugs to prevent accumulation.

Variability of drug effects

Not only do drugs have a variety of effects, but the magnitude of these effects likewise vary. There are many factors which cause this variation in magnitude.

DRUG ACTION AND EXCRETION

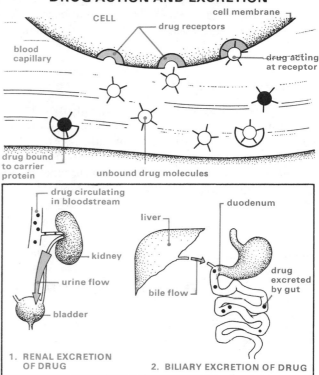

Figure 4 *(above) shows the site of drug action, where drug molecules bind to receptors on a cell membrane. Many drugs are transported around the circulation bound to "carrier" proteins, but it is only the free or unbound drug molecules which are active at the cell receptors. The lower drawing depicts the two main routes by which drugs are excreted from the body after a period in the circulation. Most drugs are extracted from the blood by the kidneys and excreted in the urine, but the liver secretes some into the bile for excretion in the feces.*

Dose

The dose greatly determines the effect of a drug on the body. For example, a very tiny dose of a tranquilizer might have very slight sedating effects; the larger the dose, the greater the sedation until sleep is induced or even unconsciousness. The effective therapeutic dose of a particular drug is usually standardized, although in fact there are often variable responses to the same amount of drug. Dose sizes of drugs vary greatly— from grams (as in many antibiotics) to millionths of a gram (as in the synthetic thyroid preparations). The effective dose of any drug is usually established by extensive testing—first on animals and then on humans.

It is important to note that the dose of any two drugs, even those with similar actions, should not necessarily be compared as to size or magnitude of effect. For example, five milligrams (one thousandth of a gram equals one milligram) of Valium is often just as strong and effective a sedative as one hundred milligrams of phenobarbital. The dose of any particular drug only relates to the amount *of that particular drug* found to be effective.

Frequency of dosing

The effect of a drug is also often dependent upon how frequently it is taken. The frequency of taking drugs was once determined arbitrarily in many cases, so that drugs were taken three to four times a day in divided doses—although this was often based on the fact that the effective drug appeared to wear off in six to eight hours.

Currently, however, there is a trend toward measuring the amount of drug in the blood at various times. This measurement in some cases relates directly to the magnitude of its effect. It also permits a calculation of the

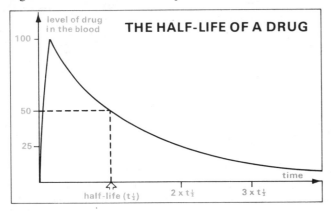

Figure 5 *The half-life ($t\frac{1}{2}$) is the time taken to clear one-half of the quantity of the drug from the body; this determines how frequently the drug should be administered. The half-life is not always the same for a particular drug but varies from person to person. However, most drugs have half-lives of between 8 and 24 hours.*

drug's half-life ($t\frac{1}{2}$)—see Figure 5. The half-life of a drug is the length of time it takes for the body to eliminate half the drug from the body. If a drug is taken every half-life, relatively constant amounts of drug are present in the body and the level of drug in the bloodstream can be maintained at the "therapeutic level"—see Figure 6. The major discovery of these studies was that many drugs which are frequently taken in divided total daily doses three or four times a day (such as Dilantin, Zyloprim and Elavil) have half-lives of more than one day; therefore, they can be taken only once daily (in the full daily dose) and have a similar effect.

Changes in absorption and excretion

Furthermore, various changes in the absorption or excretion of a drug can significantly affect the magnitude of

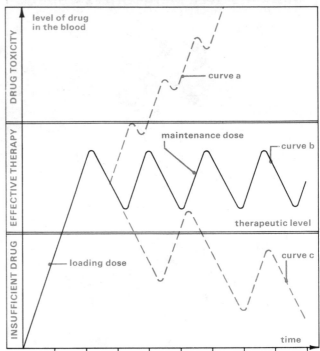

Figure 6 *shows why the timing of drug administration is crucial to successful therapy. The effect of most drugs depends on their concentration in the bloodstream. In order to establish the correct level of drug in the blood (the "therapeutic level"), one large "loading dose" is given initially, followed by smaller "maintenance doses." Curve (b) shows the ideal result of this technique, where the amount of drug in the bloodstream remains at the therapeutic level. Curve (a) demonstrates that if maintenance doses are given too frequently, an excess of the drug builds up, leading to toxic effects. Curve (c) shows that if the maintenance doses are not given often enough, the amount of the drug in the blood soon falls, thereby ceasing to be effective.*

effect. For example, food in the stomach will often interfere with the absorption of some drugs, but not with others. The antibiotic ampicillin is poorly absorbed with food, whereas a similar antibiotic, Amoxicillin, is easily absorbed with food. This will greatly affect the level of the drug in the blood. Conversely, diarrhea—where the drug may move very rapidly through the gastrointestinal tract—may prevent absorption and likewise decrease the amount of drug that gets into the bloodstream. Similarly, increased drug levels can be caused by slower elimination. For example, a failure of the kidneys also causes accumulation of the drug, as shown in Figure 7. (The kidneys are the primary means by which drugs are eliminated.) This is often a very important factor in determining the dose of the drug and how often it is taken.

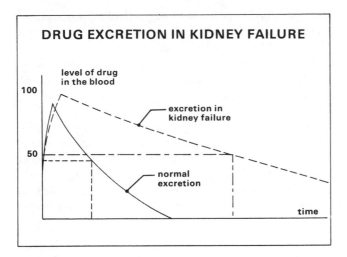

Most drugs are excreted from the body in urine. **Figure 7** *compares the time taken for a normal person to clear a dose of drug from his bloodstream with the much longer time needed by a patient who has kidney failure, and produces very little urine.*

The effect of disease

The effect of any given drug also varies with the presence of disease. For example, if a person has a fever, both aspirin and Tylenol will tend to bring the fever back down to normal; but in a person with a normal temperature, these drugs will not significantly lower the body temperature. In a person suffering from disordered perception of reality, as in schizophrenia, the use of the drug Thorazine will tend to normalize the thinking process, but the same drug will not significantly affect the thinking of a person in touch with reality.

The effect of age: drugs in children

The prescribing of medicine for children presents certain problems—especially where infants are concerned—because their reactions to drugs tend to differ from those of adults. The liver, which metabolizes drugs in an adult body, may not be completely developed in an infant and thus cannot process drugs properly. In some cases this can lead to poisoning. Drugs can also have an opposite effect on children to that which they have on adults. A classical example is the drug Ritalin, which is used to calm hyperactive children; in adults it can produce hyper-activity. These factors, plus the fact that the amount of drug needed to produce an effect in a child is smaller, make the use of medicines in children a very specialized subject.

The effect of age: drugs in the elderly

The elderly, likewise, have special responses to drugs in some cases. Just who belongs in this classification is debatable, since physiologic aging does not necessarily relate to one's exact age in years. Nevertheless, when aging becomes apparent it is associated with a gradual change in response to drugs. One factor that contributes to this change is the gradual decline in efficiency of the kidneys for eliminating wastes—and, therefore, drugs. This is one of the reasons for the need to use lower doses of drugs in elderly people in some cases. Since this change does not often take place at the same rate in everyone, individual dosage adjustment may often be needed.

The use of various sedative and tranquilizing drugs (such as chloral hydrate, Valium, Librium, Dalmane or Seconal) by elderly people can be problematic for two reasons. First, as noted above, these drugs may be eliminated more slowly, and if given on a regular basis they may accumulate and cause excess drowsiness. Second, some elderly persons (like children) may experience excitement rather than sedation with some of these drugs. The reason for this is not known, but it can cause confusion since often the response is to give more sedative!

Genetic factors which influence drug action

Genetic differences between people can also influence a drug's effect. For example, some persons ("rapid acety-lators") can more rapidly metabolize the antituberculous drug INH and certain sulfa drugs, as well as the antihypertensive drug Apresoline (hydralazine). In some cases this can significantly influence the effective dose since the rapid metabolism may decrease the amount of available drug in the body. Another example are those individuals who are more sensitive than others to doses of "tricyclic antidepressant drugs," such as Elavil, Tofranil and Sinequan. Studies have shown that equal doses given to several people would result in different levels of the drug in their blood. However, identical twins had very similar blood levels, which suggests that at least some of the differences were due to genetic factors in dealing with the drug in the body. These genetic causes of variable drug effects are just beginning to be studied and defined, but in the future they may become well accepted factors in determining the exact dose administered in each individual. Some individuals have genetic traits which can make common drugs harmful, although fortunately this is relatively rare. People with the rare metabolic disease called PORPHYRIA, for example, cannot take phenobarbital and certain related sedative drugs because of the severe reactions these drugs produce. Likewise, approximately 13% of the black population and a certain percentage of persons of Mediterranean origin have a deficiency of a certain enzyme (called G6PD) which makes them partic-ularly susceptible to drugs used to treat malaria (prima-quine), some sulfa drugs and the drugs Furadantin and Macrodantin used to treat bladder infections. When any of these drugs are taken by persons with this deficiency, their blood cells begin to break down, and they may develop fever, anemia and discomfort. Fortunately, the presence of this enzyme deficiency can be detected by a simple blood test and the problematic drugs avoided. In many other cases the genetic differences which cause these effects cannot be anticipated, although further research into this problem may increase the chances of doing so in the near future.

Drug interactions

When two or more drugs are taken together, there is a certain likelihood of these drugs interacting to produce an increased, decreased or entirely new effect from either one or both of the drugs taken separately. This type of action is termed a drug interaction and in some cases can be very significant. For example, when the anticoagulant drug Coumadin interacts with vitamin K in the liver, the two drugs cancel each other out.

The placebo effect

Another factor which strongly influences the way in which a drug will affect a person is the so-called *placebo effect*. In Latin the word placebo means "I will please." In medical terminology, the word generally refers to a pill or other treatment which by itself has no chemical activity or druglike effect on the body. Frequently, it is a pill made of sugar or lactose. When a placebo is given, it may in fact bring about certain changes in the patient's condition simply because the patient or the doctor, or both, *expect* it to cause a change. These changes are called the placebo effect. Placebos are most often used in studies of drugs to ascertain the effects of the real drug. This is highly important since many people have marked responses to placebos. For example, most mild pain-relieving drugs are tested against a placebo (usually in a double-blind test where neither the doctor nor the patient knows which is the real drug) for the ability to relieve mild pain. It is significant that 20–40% of people receiving the placebo will also experience pain relief! Further, if the study checks for side effects, it is frequently found that people may experience nausea, vomiting, itching of the skin or even rashes after taking the placebo! This is why the placebo effects of a drug must be subtracted from the final result of a drug test to determine the actual pharmacologic effect of the drug.

Why do people experience effects from a placebo? The primary reason lies in the *expectation*, both of the patient and of the therapist. For example, if a person has a headache, he frequently will experience relief even if the pill is completely inactive. If this expectation of relief is further enhanced by the enthusiastic expectation of effect by the doctor prescribing the pill, it is even more likely to achieve relief.

The placebo effect tends to be particularly noticeable in connection with drugs used for pain, sedation, tranquilization or other consciously experienced sensation. It is much less noticeable when the anticipated effect is not directly perceived, as in the case of antibiotics or heart medication, although even in these cases there are sometimes placebo effects.

Occasionally a chemically inactive substance is administered when the physician feels that relief (often of mild anxiety) may be obtained as readily by the placebo effect of *anticipated* relief as by an active (and possibly harmful) drug. This is sometimes effective and is often done to protect the patient from chronic use of sedatives or pain relievers—not to "fool" the patient.

Problems with drugs: side effects

Any drug is likely to have effects on many parts of the body. Some of these effects are desired, some are of little consequence and some are not desired and are usually termed side effects. A side effect (or adverse effect) in one setting, however, may be a desired effect in another. There is considerable public and medical concern over side effects and adverse drug reactions. It is contended by some that these are a significant cause of hospitalization and of problems during hospitalization and in recent years various frightening statistics have been cited in the popular press.

However, some of the figures have represented general conclusions drawn from small studies; whether or not these are really accurate has been questioned. One recent large study of drug reactions in eight hospitals over a period of several years, including more than 20,000 patients, indicated that the rate of adverse reaction was not as high as previously thought. The controversy, nevertheless, continues, and this fact makes no less significant the adverse reaction in a particular individual.

Pinning down what is and what is not a genuine reaction to any drug is not always easy. Just because a symptom occurs after taking a drug does not necessarily mean the drug caused that symptom. It may, for example, represent a placebo side effect or a totally separate problem. On the other hand, it sometimes happens that a side effect such as headache and nausea is ascribed to the underlying disease while the drug as a cause is missed. In such cases a simple discussion with the physician about whether a particular sign or symptom could be caused by a drug might clarify this situation early on and save valuable time and discomfort for the patient.

Indeed, when a side effect is suspected the doctor should always be consulted. In some cases administration of the drug will be stopped—not only to prevent further reaction, but also as a test to see if the effect goes away. In other cases the side effect may be treated directly or even anticipated, as when antacids are given during treatment with aspirin or cortisone to prevent the gastric (stomach) irritation that is so often a side effect of these drugs.

In general, unwanted side effects of drugs are classified into two main categories:

1. The known and predictable side effects of the drug which often can be anticipated and either accepted, prevented or treated. For example, most diuretics (drugs which increase the secretion of urine) cause potassium loss; this undesirable effect can be anticipated or looked for and controlled with potassium supplements.

2. The second type of side effects is not as predictable since these occur in only a small percentage of persons receiving certain drugs. These reactions can include so-called idiosyncratic reactions or allergic reactions. The idiosyncratic reactions may or may not be truly allergic reactions but may also relate to the genetic makeup of individuals in the way they handle a particular drug. The unpredictable type of reaction is much more difficult to anticipate, since it may occur in only one out of 10,000 or 100,000 persons and may not be discovered before the drug is released for use. In contrast to the first category of reactions, these unwanted reactions cannot necessarily be prevented but their possible occurrence is usually noted and considered in the "cost-benefit analysis" of the prescribing of any drug.

Some confusion exists with regard to the understanding of a true allergy to a drug versus a nonallergic side effect. It is important to note that most allergic reactions to drugs involve either a rash, hives, itching, localized swelling or (more severely) wheezing and a true "anaphylactic" reaction where there is difficulty in breathing. Fever is also sometimes a manifestation of allergy. Some of the most common drugs to cause this are penicillin and related antibiotic drugs. Conversely, although called "allergies," many reactions are simply related to predictable effects of the drug, the most common example being the nausea and vomiting which occur in many persons who take morphine or the constipation that occurs in persons who take codeine. These are not allergic reactions but relatively predictable side effects of the drug. There are still other effects which are more difficult to determine. For example, certain types of jaundice which occur with drugs such as Thorazine or the antituberculous drug INH represent a true allergic reaction, whereas other types of jaundice caused by drugs are not.

Long-term versus short-term adverse effects of drugs

The short-term adverse effects of drugs usually occur within the period of time the drug is taken. A greater concern exists about those side effects which occur long after the drug has been discontinued. A relatively uncommon example of this is the allergic reaction called *serum sickness*, which causes joint pains and fever and occurs several days or weeks after a drug such as penicillin has been discontinued. Another example is the apparent predisposition to develop cancer as much as 10 to 20 years after taking certain very potent anticancer drugs. Whether other drugs have this potential is as yet undetermined but most drugs are screened for this.

The potential effects on the unborn child of drugs taken during pregnancy are of great concern. Since the *thalidomide* tragedy there is a much greater and more widespread awareness of the potential danger of drugs taken during pregnancy, especially during the first 8 to 12 weeks of pregnancy when the development of vital fetal structures is taking place and thus can be adversely affected. Thalidomide, which was originally prescribed in Europe as a sedative, was found during the early 1960s to produce—when taken by a pregnant woman during this critical period—deformities in development of the arms and legs of unborn infants.

Unfortunately, partly because of the time lag between the critical developmental period early in pregnancy (often before pregnancy is discovered or even strongly suspected) and the birth of the infant, it has been difficult to identify the factors or drugs which have caused developmental problems in the fetus. Collecting exact information on the relationship between drugs and malformations also presents problems. For example, animal studies do not relate specifically to what occurs in humans. Certain drugs can affect fetal development only at one critical time during pregnancy but are otherwise not harmful. Other drugs are thought to be harmful throughout the pregnancy or for longer periods of time. The antibiotic tetracycline can affect bone and teeth development, and thus is not prescribed during pregnancy at all and is contraindicated during most of childhood for the same reason.

The effects of excessive alcohol consumption and cigarette smoking may also affect developmental progress of a fetus at several stages. The most difficult factor is that adverse effects produced by any agent seldom occur all of the time. In fact, a drug which is known to cause adverse effects may only do so 5–20% of the time or even less. Again, this makes tracing the relationship between cause and effect very difficult.

Still a further problem is that the harmful effect of a drug taken during pregnancy may not be easily discovered for some time. This would be the case, for example, with adverse effects on mental or neurologic development. A different—and classical—example of this type of problem is the DES or diethylstilbestrol problem. For a period beginning in the late 1940s, women who had threatened miscarriages were given the synthetic female hormone diethylstilbestrol to prevent this. Some 13 to 16 years later a small percentage of the female children born to these mothers had developed cancer of the vagina—a form of cancer that was previously very rare. Only very careful detective work on the part of pathologists who became suspicious about the increased rate of this cancer revealed the connection with DES. Not surprisingly, this discovery has increased the concern about drugs in pregnancy to an even greater extent. The state of knowledge about this subject will continue to be limited since adequate testing can frequently not be carried out. However, the general rule of obstetricians has been to have pregnant women avoid most drugs during pregnancy—except vitamins, iron and a few drugs which may be essential to the mother's health, such as hormones like thyroid or insulin. Use of any drug during pregnancy is usually carefully supervised because of concern about the danger.

The major problem still lies not with women who are *aware* of their pregnancy but with those potentially pregnant women who are taking very teratogenic (fetus-deforming) drugs such as tetracycline. Clearly, any woman of childbearing age who is currently having sexual relations and may become pregnant must exercise great caution where drugs and medicines of all kinds are concerned.

Factors increasing the likelihood of drug reactions

Certain conditions seem to increase the likelihood of drug reactions. The longer certain drugs are taken, for example, the more likely they may be to cause side effects—although this is not always the case. Likewise, a higher dose of the drug may cause more side effects than a lower dose. A person who has already had an allergic reaction (such as a rash or swelling of various areas or wheezing) to one or more drugs is more likely to have an allergic reaction to another drug, particularly if that one is chemically related to the drugs that have produced allergic reactions in the past. A classical example of this is the fact that if a person is allergic to penicillin, he will most likely also be allergic to ampicillin, carbenicillin, dicloxacillin and other related penicillin-type drugs. Finally, the greater number of drugs a person takes, the more likely he is to experience side effects—not only because of the individual effect of multiple drugs but also because with several drugs there is a greatly increased possibility of drug interactions (for example, a "synergistic" effect may exist where one type of drug taken at about the same time as a second type of drug will greatly increase the possibility of side effects with the latter drug).

Avoiding drug reactions

In general it is a good rule for each individual not only to be aware of but also to carry a list of those drugs which he or she is taking or those which in the past have caused reactions. In our highly mobile society, visits to unfamiliar clinics, doctors or emergency rooms are a fairly frequent occurrence and specific information about a patient's drug history is often very helpful. A simple list of drugs on a 3 ×

5 card carried folded in a wallet will often suffice; alternatively, wearing a metal bracelet carrying this information is also helpful.

The risk versus benefit consideration

In the ideal setting, all drugs would be optimally effective and carry no risk; but, in fact, very few drugs are totally free of occasional unwanted side effects. Some drugs have a greater potential for producing side effects than others. Thus, the prescribing of a drug by a physician is usually the result of a careful calculation of the benefits to the patient—that is relief of symptoms or cure of disease—versus the risk and cost to the patient. This consideration is closely related to the seriousness of the disease and the seriousness and frequency of the side effects. *It is never a simple calculation.*

For example, in the treatment of arthritis the benefits of a higher dose of aspirin (which produces effective relief of both pain and inflammation at a relatively low cost) must be weighed against its disadvantages and risks (hearing disturbances, gastric upset, bleeding or ulceration). A much more difficult calculation is called for with the use of anticancer drugs. In this case, the possibility of their prolonging of life must be weighed against their potentially serious side effects, the need they entail for frequent and costly medical supervision, and sometimes their very high cost.

Clearly, the decision as to whether the benefits of taking a drug outweigh the risks can be difficult, and the problem is often complicated by a lack of sufficient information about the statistical likelihood of effects or the statistical likelihood of both beneficial and adverse effects.

Accordingly, a projection is generally made in which relative safety is the primary priority (more than or equal to the effectiveness of the drug and more than equal to the cost). All of these factors must be considered—not only on a short-term basis, but (if the drug is to be used for many years) over a prolonged period. This, in some cases, can change the cost versus benefit analysis.

The cost of drugs

Many drugs today are fairly expensive. Some people, in fact, must pay a dollar a day or more for their drugs; when these drugs are taken for months or years, it can cause a heavy financial burden.

What determines the cost of a drug? In general, the cost of a drug to the patient is based on the cost of research and development, manufacturing, advertising, packaging, shipping and pharmacy handling. But the price of an individual drug on a prescription is not necessarily related to any of these factors.

Frequently drugs are developed by one company and then produced and manufactured by that company under a drug patent which gives it exclusive rights to make and market the drug for 17 years. The price of a drug in that category may in some cases reflect the actual factors noted above. However, once the 17 years have elapsed, the particular company holding the patent no longer has exclusive rights to the drug; thus, it may be produced and manufactured under its generic name as well as under new trade names. A good example is the drug Librium whose patent is now expired and which is available under its generic name, chlordiazepoxide. In the case of many generic drugs there are three or more companies selling the drug under different trade names. Tetracycline hydrochloride is available under the generic name *or* as Achromycin, Robitet, Sk-Tetracycline and Retet. Ampicillin (the generic name) is available under that name as well as under the brand names Supen, Amcill, Omnipen, Polycillin, Penbritin, Pen. A, Principen and Pensyn. This multiplicity of brand names for one generic name creates confusion for prescribing, but the drug industry argues that it allows for healthy competition in the drug market. It also has an effect on the price of drugs in some cases as a result of this competition.

A company will usually spend money in promoting their brand name product, and this cost is usually added to the basic cost of the drug. This means that in general, trade name drugs are more expensive (sometimes by several times) than their generic equivalent. This being so, many consumer groups have advocated that the generic drugs be used in preference to brand-name drugs to save money. However, there are several factors which complicate this apparently straightforward approach. In the first place, many companies with brand name products have argued that their drugs are more carefully tested and regulated than their generic equivalents. Indeed, it has been found that several products containing the same generic drug may be absorbed very differently so that one may produce definite effects and another none at all. This has raised the entire issue of *bioavailability* (how much of the drug can be absorbed by the body to produce an effect due to various differences in manufacturing practices) and led to stricter requirements on the part of the Food and Drug Administration for each manufacturer to prove that its drug, in fact, is available to the body in equivalent amounts.

In the long run, the argument of drug companies that their brand-name products represent better quality control may tend to counteract generic prescribing—although this generalization about quality may or may not apply, as almost every drug company has been subject to drug "recalls" at some point.

Another factor which has confused the assumption regarding lower-priced generic drugs relates to the generic substitution law in many states. This law allows pharmacists to substitute one brand of a generic drug for another if the pharmacist deems this necessary for reason of better quality, lower price or stock supply. Thus, a prescription for erythromycin tablets in 250 milligram strength might be filled with large, red, round tablets (Ilotycin), large, blue-green tablets (Robimycin), or large, peach-colored tablets (E-Mycin), or a variety of other products. Any would contain the prescribed amount of erythromycin, and the effect would in all probability be the same—although the cost of the various brands might vary considerably. The drug supplied may or may not be the least expensive type.

If the physician simply wrote the brand name on the prescription, any equivalent erythromycin could be substituted at this pharmacist's discretion.

The cost of a drug, whether it is under a generic or brand name, can vary depending on additional factors. Prescriptions for a large number of pills or capsules are usually less expensive. Each prescription does include a handling fee for the pharmacist so that the more prescriptions needed, the more handling fees need be paid. Although smaller, private pharmacies may have higher prescription prices than larger, chainstore operations, this is not always the case. Further, private pharmacies may also offer certain convenient extra services, such as home delivery, "drug profiles," counseling on the effects of drugs and so forth. Many states require that pharmacies post their drug prices so that persons who take drugs over long periods of time (such as persons with high blood pressure) may check prices at various sources and even report their findings back to the physician if they wish to aid in obtaining lower-cost drugs.

Another factor which influences the cost of prescriptions only affects those on government health plans, such as Medicaid and Medi-Cal (California's Medicaid program). In these plans there are certain allowances for prescriptions as long as the drugs are on the list of drugs approved. However, if the drugs are not on this list the patients must either pay for their prescriptions themselves or obtain a special request justifying the use of their particular drug before qualifying for their allowance. Since a limited number of allowances is available, the size of individual prescriptions is usually larger—a factor which has created some problems where drug abuse is a possibility.

In summary, how does one get the best quality drug at the most reasonable cost? First, it is helpful to indicate to the doctor a preference for generic-named drugs in maximum quantity (100 to 200 pills is customary) if they must be used for long periods. This is based on the generally valid assumption that, in most cases, generic drugs are equivalent and are less expensive than their brand-name counterparts. There are some exceptions to this case when the question of abuse or deterioration of the drug (such as nitroglycerin) is a factor. The doctor may have objections, both to prescribing a generic equivalent and to prescribing in quantity, but it should generate a useful dialog to determine a satisfactory compromise.

Second, in addition to comparing prices at various

pharmacies, it is wise to consider the quality of the service those pharmacies provide. A good pharmacist, whose thorough training equips him to provide useful information about differences between drugs and advice about "over-the-counter" drugs may be well worth some extra charge. Keep in mind, however, that the *size* of the pharmacy alone is no guarantee that it is better than, say, your local corner drugstore.

Regulation of drugs

Finally, a general comment about the regulation of the manufacturing, sale and prescribing and use of drugs is in order. Over the last 70 years the Food and Drug Administration has gradually developed a series of regulations which deal with how drugs can be used. From 1938, it has been required that the *safety* of drugs be established. Since 1962 (when the so-called Kefauver Amendments were added) the *effectiveness* of drugs also had to be established. Certain other drugs, such as aspirin, which were in use before the stricter laws governing the testing of drugs were passed, were not required to be tested as stringently due to a "grandfather" clause relating to their presumed safety as demonstrated by many years of use.

These Food and Drug Administration requirements for safety and effectiveness have long been the subject of controversy. On the one hand, there is a real fear that another thalidomide (the "sleeping pill" which produced deformities in many unborn babies) tragedy will occur if every drug is not carefully tested. On the other hand, such testing takes much time and delays introduction of many promising drugs. This has led to a frequently expressed concern that the American public is being deprived of good and useful drugs that are available in many other countries because the Food and Drug Administration requirements are too strict. There is no simple solution to this controversy, although new legislation may be on the horizon.

At the present time, the Food and Drug Administration affects every aspect of drugs, beginning from the original testing of new chemicals right up to the manufacture and indications for use and their actual distribution. The primary goal is that of protecting the consumer and maintaining a high standard of drugs used in the United States.

The labeling on all prescribed drugs and over-the-counter drugs has become the "bottom line" for many of the actions of the FDA. Thus, in prescription drugs this labeling includes all of the actions of the drugs, as well as the indications for their use, the usual dosage, their known or suspected side effects, and precautions. In the past this has been used primarily by doctors, but in recent years a greater concern for the enlightenment of the consumer has been felt, and at present there is a move toward providing

this labeling for consumers as well (as is already available in the case for over-the-counter drugs). A patient "package insert" is currently available for all estrogen drugs and will most likely be available in the near future for a variety of other drugs, particularly where the risk versus benefit considerations of their use are particularly complex and require a very careful dialog between doctor and patient.

In the following section are described a variety of drugs in general terms. These drugs are categorized according to their primary use; the reasons for their use are described together with the most common drugs in each section.

CATEGORIES OF DRUGS AND HOW THEY ARE USED

I Drugs for the relief of pain or inflammation

Pain is often our first indication that something is wrong—sometimes serious, often not. Relieving the pain can sometimes be sufficient therapy. In some types of disease, relieving pain is the only therapy possible. Drugs that relieve various types of pain or discomfort can be generally grouped into three categories, which overlap somewhat:

A. Drugs for moderate to severe pain, primarily narcotic drugs
B. Drugs for mild pain such as headaches
C. Drugs which can relieve both pain and inflammation, usually of joints

Before considering these drug groups, it will be helpful to review the subject of pain and the principles underlying the methods used to relieve it.

Pain can be defined as a perception of discomfort due to irritation, chemical stimulation or stretching of a pain nerve ending. Pain nerves are located throughout the body (except inside the brain) and send signals indicating pain to the brain where they are registered and perceived. In some cases the brain can send return signals back to the body, usually to the muscles, which can initiate withdrawal from the pain (see Figure 8). Prevention or relief of pain can best be accomplished in several ways. We all know, for example, that the total perception of pain in major surgery can be eliminated by general anesthesia—which simply puts the perceptive organ, or the brain, to "sleep." Perception of localized pain, such as that experienced during dental work, can be similarly avoided by preventing the initiation of signals by pain nerves in the region by using local anesthetics, such as procaine, or Xylocaine. In rare cases of chronic pain, the pain nerves themselves can be cut, usually near the spinal cord. These methods of preventing or relieving special kinds of pain do not involve the drugs and medicines we normally use and are not discussed further in

PAIN PATHWAYS

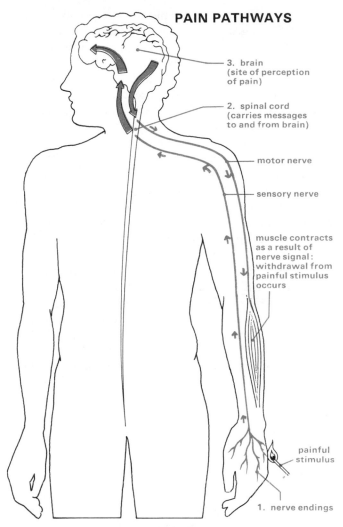

3. brain
(site of perception
of pain)

2. spinal cord
(carries messages
to and from brain)

motor nerve

sensory nerve

muscle contracts
as a result of
nerve signal:
withdrawal from
painful stimulus
occurs

painful
stimulus

1. nerve endings

Figure 8 *Pain is a vital mechanism, causing us to withdraw from potentially dangerous stimuli. The illustration above shows in diagram form an everyday "withdrawal reflex" from a painful stimulus—in this case fire. Pain may also result from internal disease, in which case simple withdrawal is not possible. However, the pain pathway can be interrupted at various points to produce relief:*
(1) at the site of the pain, for example by anti-inflammatory drugs such as aspirin or by an injection of local anesthetic;
(2) in the spinal cord, by surgically cutting the pain fibers (only in cases of continual severe pain);
(3) in the brain, by general anesthesia or narcotics (such as morphine).

this section. (See also PAIN.)

For most types of pain, the means of relief is to remove or eliminate the cause of the pain or, alternatively, to decrease the sufferer's perception of the pain. The pain of red, swollen, inflamed joints can be relieved in part by drugs that decrease inflammation, such as aspirin (as discussed below). The perception of pain from a joint that is not inflamed, however, can only be relieved by a drug that changes the person's perception of what he describes as pain.

The subject of pain and its relief is very complex because of considerable variation of pain perception between individuals and the difficulty of objective measurement. For example, the pain of an ordinary headache may vary from a dull ache to a sharp shooting pain to a "band" of pain felt around the head. One reason for this variation is that the cause of headache pain actually differs and may include muscle spasm, injury, hangover, sinusitis, eye fatigue or a true migraine headache. The duration and severity of the pain may also vary. Acute (temporary) and chronic (continual and recurring) pain are often perceived in different ways.

An important additional reason for variation in pain relates to the many psychological factors which affect the *perception* of pain. These include the emotional impact of the pain (if the pain raises the question of cancer or heart attack, it will always be very noticeable until the suspicions are disproved), and they include the presence or absence of other distracting factors—as when one suddenly dismisses a headache at the beginning of a long-awaited party. Just as the pain is influenced by all these factors, so the effects of any drug are designed to change perception of the pain. Of course, the effectiveness of any drug is partly dependent upon the *expectations* of the person taking it and the expectations of the doctor prescribing it. For example, a tablet or capsule that someone strongly believes will work will be effective more frequently, even if it is only a "sugar pill" (a *placebo*, with no chemical effect) than a pill believed to be useless in the first place. This placebo effect—caused by expectation rather than a true chemical or pharmacologic effect on the body—often leads physicians to prescribe placebos to "cure" nonexistent ailments. It is a predictable phenomenon, as demonstrated by the fact that 20–40% of patients with mild pain can get relief from a placebo if they in fact believe it is a pain-killing drug. This factor makes the evaluation of pain medicines fairly difficult, especially when only mild pain is involved.

Analgesics
Most drugs for relief of pain act primarily to alter the perception of pain and are called (as a group) *analgesics*. Three major categories of analgesics are considered here, with examples.

1. Narcotic analgesics or drugs for severe pain
   Examples:
   a. Single drugs: codeine, morphine, Demerol
   b. Combination drugs: aspirin with codeine, acetaminophen with codeine, Empirin with codeine, Percodan
   These drugs are primarily used to relieve moderately

severe or severe pain. All the narcotics are very similar to morphine in their actions, although they may differ in strength or length of action. Along with an analgesic effect, they also produce *euphoria* (a sense of intense joy or elation), and this in part predisposes to their potential for abuse. Further, if these drugs are used repeatedly the user becomes tolerant to their effects, and higher doses are required. This is not a major problem in some illnesses, such as terminal cancer, but can be of concern in less serious ailments where long-term use is not desired. In a person who is tolerant to a narcotic, suddenly stopping the drug can cause "withdrawal symptoms" such as marked nervousness and cramps, indicating a physical dependence upon the drug. These symptoms are rapidly relieved when the drug is once again taken; thus, a cycle can develop in which it is difficult to discontinue the drug permanently. The presence of tolerance and physical dependence are indications of "addiction" to the narcotic.

Despite the hazard of addiction, the potent narcotic analgesics remain highly valuable drugs when used carefully and only when needed for relief of severe pain. Because of the addiction potential, however, this class of medications is restricted in its use and distribution in hospitals and pharmacies according to regulations established by the U.S. Drug Enforcement Agency.

Narcotic analgesics often have certain side effects, which include marked constipation, depression of coughing and respiratory function (which is usually only significant when there is serious lung disease or when other depressants are being administered), occasional nausea and vomiting and (less commonly) rashes, itching or mental changes.

Many narcotics, but especially codeine, are combined with nonnarcotic analgesics (see below), and these are very commonly used for pain relief—partly because prescribing them is less strictly regulated at present. Whether the effects of these analgesics are in fact addictive is not known, but the potential exists.

All narcotics can interact and add to the effect of other sedative drugs and alcohol to cause increased drowsiness and depression of breathing. This represents a definite hazard in some cases.

2. Nonnarcotic pain relievers
    Examples:
    a. Single drugs: aspirin, acetaminophen (Tylenol), Darvon
    b. Combination drugs: Equagesic, Fiorinal, Norgesic, Empirin, Anacin, Alka-Seltzer
Although a very large number of products for relief of mild to moderate pain are available both over-the-counter and by prescription, it is important to point out that they are generally composed of one or more of three basic components, all of which can relieve mild pain: *aspirin*, *acetaminophen* and *phenacetin* (which is converted in the

body to acetaminophen), or the Darvon group of drugs. One of the most commonly used analgesics, aspirin, relieves both mild pain and inflammation; it also has other effects, such as decreasing fever and preventing some blood clotting. Its use has waned in recent years because it often causes stomach upset (or even bleeding) and is a frequent cause of drug overdose, especially in children. Conversely, acetaminophen (Tylenol) has increased in popularity because it does not cause stomach irritation; however, although it can reduce fever, it has no effect on inflammation and is probably more hazardous in overdose than aspirin. Finally, the Darvon group of drugs (generic name: propoxyphene) is more closely related to the narcotic pain relievers but is still a very mild pain reliever. It differs from the other two mild pain relievers in that it can be obtained only by prescription and is considerably more expensive. It has no effect on fever or inflammation but does occasionally cause stomach upset.

These drugs are often combined with each other or with small amounts of the mild stimulant caffeine (whose effect is unclear in the combination) and sometimes smaller amounts of codeine or tranquilizers; but the relative contribution of each agent in these combinations is seldom known. Frequently, the drugs are essentially equivalent except for their cost and packaging, although it can be reasonably argued that both of these latter factors increase the psychologic expectation of greater effect.

3. Drugs for pain with inflammation and antiarthritic drugs
    Examples:
    Single drugs: aspirin, Indocin, Butazolidin, Motrin, Tolectin, Naprosyn, Nalfon
The word *inflammation* is a general term which applies to the occurrence of swelling along with pain and often external redness. Inflammation is a complex response of the body to various noxious stimuli (such as insect stings), local infections or abscesses, injury (such as wounds or broken bones), burns and chronic diseases (such as rheumatoid arthritis or gouty arthritis). In all of these, the area affected becomes red, swollen and painful. The treatment of inflammation often involves eliminating the cause through a means other than medication—for example, draining an abscess or treating an infection.

However, some types of inflammation, particularly arthritis, are fairly consistently relieved by the anti-inflammatory drugs. The term *arthritis* applies to diseases that affect the joints of the body and cause chronic pain, and often swelling and eventual destruction of joints. Some types of arthritis are associated with acute inflammation in several joints. The most common of these are rheumatoid arthritis and gouty arthritis. Both diseases have courses which vary so that there are "flare-ups" alternating with asymptomatic periods of no discomfort.

Several drugs exist which are effective in treating the

acute flare-ups by slowing the inflammatory process and relieving pain and sometimes even preventing their occurrence. Except for aspirin, most of these drugs tend to relieve pain more by helping to relieve the inflammation that causes the pain than by changing perception of the pain. Some drugs are more effective for certain diseases than others. For example, *colchicine* exerts a dramatic effect in helping to decrease inflammation in gout but has virtually no effect in the other diseases.

Several new anti-inflammatory drugs have been put on the market in recent years. Although these newer drugs have been shown in short-term studies to be equal in effect to aspirin in relief of chronic arthritic pain, they are far more costly and share many of the side effects of aspirin and the other anti-inflammatory drugs. The primary side effect that all of these drugs exhibit is that of gastric irritation and ulceration, although some (such as aspirin and Butazolidin) tend to be more likely to do this than others such as Motrin or Naprosyn. There are other side effects of some of the more potent drugs, such as the induction of certain abnormalities of the blood as occasionally occurs with the long-term use of Butazolidin. (Periodic studies of blood samples of patients receiving Butazolidin are necessary to detect the development of such adverse reactions and permit early modification of therapy.)

II Drugs for treating sleep disorders and problems with anxiety, mood or thought

Medication used for treating anxiety or disorders of sleep, mood or thought make up the most commonly prescribed group of drugs in the United States. Although sedative and tranquilizing substances (not the least of which is alcohol) have been used worldwide for centuries, it is only since the 1950s that a wide range of drugs for treating "nervous disorders" has become available. Development of these more sophisticated drugs has allowed the treatment of a broader spectrum of disorders, although the origins of these disorders and the mode of action of the drugs themselves often remain mysterious. Indeed, there is a vast diversity in the chemical structures of the various compounds used to threat insomnia, anxiety and various emotional or mental conditions.

Drugs in this category fall into two major classes:

1. Those used for mild, self-limited problems which are part of the normal stress of life; these include sedatives, tranquilizers and "sleeping pills."
2. Those used for more disrupting disturbances that seriously interfere with day-to-day behavior; these include the major tranquilizers for thought disorders and the antidepressants and lithium for disabling problems of mood.

Minor tranquilizers or antianxiety agents

Examples: Atarax, Equanil, Librium, meprobamate, phenobarbital, Serax, Tranxene, Valium, Vistaril

Minor tranquilizers, also called "antianxiety agents," are part of the most frequently prescribed drug group, along with sleeping pills. In fact, Valium is the most prescribed medicine in the United States. Since the introduction of Valium and the very similar Librium, the percentage of the population taking such medication has sharply increased, as the result of many factors.

Minor tranquilizers, sleeping pills and sedatives have very similar effects—their differences are related more to dosage and use than to actual pharmacologic activity. For example, Dalmane (which is prescribed for sleep) is not significantly different from Valium or Librium (which are usually prescribed as tranquilizers).

One group of antianxiety agents, the *benzodiazepines,* includes the related drugs Librium, Valium, Serax and Tranxene. The important differences between various tranquilizers and sleeping pills include their potential for abuse, death when taken in an overdose, and drug interactions. The benzodiazepines appear to have the lowest potential for all these problems. Conversely, the barbiturate group—including phenobarbital, Seconal, as well as the nonbarbiturates Quaalude and Doriden (which are more commonly used as sleeping pills)—has high potentials for all of these and requires very judicious use.

Another group of drugs, the *antihistamines*, has significant sedative effects in certain individuals, although their actions differ from other drugs in the antianxiety or tranquilizing group. Since they are relatively safe, antihistamines (such as Atarax and Benadryl) are often used both as tranquilizers and sleeping pills; antihistamines have long been major components of the over-the-counter sleep preparations.

All of the antianxiety drugs decrease the feeling of anxiety and often allow calmer, though altered, perception of life at lower doses. The effect of any drug dose appears to vary considerably among individuals. For example, 5 milligrams of Valium (the usual antianxiety dose) may calm one person, put another to sleep, make a third feel dizzy and have no effect on a fourth. Occasionally these drugs can actually *excite*—especially children or the elderly—but most people are tranquilized at this dose. At higher doses, especially when taken at night, these drugs can help induce sleep; however, the sleep is different from unassisted sleep, and, with habitual use, real sleeping and dreaming time may decrease (as discussed below).

The major side effect in using mild tranquilizers is drowsiness, which is often a function of dose. This can be a useful effect if the drug is used at night. A small percentage of persons taking these drugs also experience confusion, disorientation or even vertigo.

All of the antianxiety drugs share characteristics which can make them hazardous in certain settings:

1. They can depress breathing in persons with significant lung disease (asthma or emphysema) or when taken in excessive dosage.
2. They are "additive" to one another and to alcohol in producing sedation and depressing breathing (this explains the accidental deaths due to the intake of slightly excessive amounts of sedatives with alcohol).
3. They can be habit forming. Once a habit is established, not only is it difficult to stop, but withdrawal symptoms can follow a sudden drug stoppage. In mild cases this may only mean nightmares or some anxiety for several days; but in more severe cases, seizures can result.

Mild tranquilizers are often prescribed for use two to four times a day; in many cases, however, this may be excessive or unnecessary. First, anxiety is often transient and may require only occasional doses rather than continuous use. Second, drugs such as Valium, Librium and phenobarbital stay in the body for long periods so they often can be taken just once a day or less frequently.

Sleeping pills

Examples: Butisol, chloral hydrate, Dalmane, Doriden, Nembutal, Quaalude, Placidyl, Seconal

Most tranquilizers can be used as sleeping pills and vice versa (as noted in the previous section). However, drugs such as chloral hydrate or Dalmane are more commonly prescribed as sleeping pills, even though in lower doses they have essentially the same effects as the "daytime" tranquilizers or antianxiety agents.

Before some recent studies of sleep characteristics, sleeping pills were routinely administered in hospitals and nursing homes and frequently prescribed for use at home for treating common insomnia. Our greater understanding of sleep has questioned the wisdom of using sleeping pills routinely, however. These studies of brain waves showed that normal sleep consists of several stages, numbered 0 to 4. After going to sleep there is a stepwise descent from 0 to 4 then back and forth through three or more cycles. Dreaming usually occurs after return to stage 1, and since it is accompanied by rapid movements of the eyes under closed lids it is called *rapid eye movement* (or REM) *sleep.* REM sleep appears to be important because anyone deprived of REM sleep for long periods may become irritable, anxious or even hallucinate. In fact, many sleeping pills tend to change the normal sleep cycle. For example, certain barbiturates (such as Seconal) tend to suppress REM sleep—see Figure 9. Drugs like Dalmane or chloral hydrate do not affect REM sleep but eliminate stage 4 sleep. Studies of long-term users of sleeping pills indicate that not only do they skip REM sleep but they tend to wake up several times during the night! The meaning of the results of these and other studies needs to be clarified, but they certainly indicate that *sleeping pills do not produce normal sleep.* Because of this, most doctors have become more selective in prescribing sleeping pills.

THE EFFECT OF BARBITURATES ON SLEEP PATTERNS

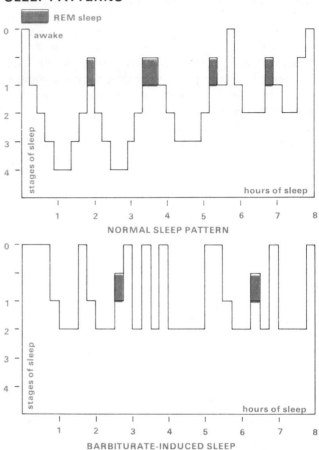

Figure 9 *EEG recordings of brain waves have shown that the depth of sleep normally fluctuates throughout the night. In the upper diagram a typical pattern is shown varying from Stage 0 (awake) to stage 4 (deeply asleep). At about 90-minute intervals, the sleeper has periods where his eyes move quickly from side to side (Rapid Eye Movement sleep) and these probably coincide with dreaming. If a person is repeatedly awakened whenever he is starting REM sleep he becomes anxious and irritable. The lower diagram shows how barbiturate drugs alter the sleep pattern and reduce REM sleep in particular. However they do not produce the adverse psychological effects which would be expected from sleep deprivation.*

Another factor promoting caution in the use of sleeping pills is the significant problem of abuse with many of these drugs, particularly the barbiturates—such as Seconal, Nembutal—and other drugs such as Quaalude. The prescribing of many of these drugs has been restricted in a manner similar to that of the narcotics. A third concern with sleeping pills is their use in suicide attempts, particularly in certain age groups.

The therapeutic approach to insomnia is changing—because, like pain, it is often a *symptom* of other physical and mental problems. Sometimes it reflects depression; when this emotional problem is treated sleep improves. Other times insomnia may be a transient reaction to specific life stresses and will disappear in time. Although sleeping pills are still helpful in some situations for short-term assistance, their use will hopefully be more selective in the future.

Major tranquilizers

Examples: Haldol, Mellaril, Navane, Prolixin, Sparine, Stelazine, Thorazine, Trilafon

The group of drugs called major tranquilizers, or "antipsychotic drugs," must not be confused with the more commonly used minor tranquilizers or antianxiety agents (such as Librium or Valium, discussed previously). Major tranquilizers, although they have the ability to cause sedation, have a broader range of pharmacologic effects and stronger adverse reactions—so they are used only in specially controlled situations for treating disorders of thinking.

True major tranquilizers came into being in the early 1950s, revolutionizing the care of severely disturbed patients. Using these drugs enabled many persons to return to a relatively normal life. This is because one of the major actions of these drugs is to return thinking processes to normal. The effects are frequently dramatic in patients with severe thought disorders who have hallucinations or a loss of contact with reality (as in schizophrenia or certain types of neurologic diseases). Although the major tranquilizers do not always eliminate the need for other types of therapy, they have wide usage. Often the most effective treatment for thought disorders involves a major tranquilizer in combination with psychiatric or social therapy.

The major tranquilizers are promoted by the drug companies and sometimes prescribed by doctors for treating anxiety problems which do *not* involve disorders of thinking. Although the sedative effect of these drugs does help in these cases, it is very questionable whether such potent drugs are needed. These drugs are also occasionally prescribed for the treatment of other disorders (such as the use of a related drug, Compazine, to relieve nausea).

The major tranquilizers work by acting on nerve endings in the brain and elsewhere in the body. There is a wide variation in response to these drugs and a corresponding wide variation in the effective dose. These drugs stay in the body for a long time, so when used over long periods they are often taken only once daily (sometimes skipping the drug on weekends to prevent accumulation). These drugs are often used selectively because of the variety of side effects, some of which are predictable, others not.

Almost all major tranquilizers can sometimes produce undesirable neurological effects, the most common being symptoms resembling Parkinson's disease. These symp-

toms include hand tremors, rigidity of the arms and legs and a masklike facial appearance. (They are often treated with a standard drug used in treating Parkinson's disease, such as Cogentin.) Other neurological effects occur but are less predictable and less frequent but can be severe. Because of these effects, these drugs are prescribed very selectively, with frequent medical checks. Other common side effects that can occur with these drugs include lowered blood pressure, dry mouth, constipation and change in bladder function. Less commonly, these drugs can cause liver abnormalities, or jaundice, rashes and a decrease in the number of circulating white blood cells (which can predispose to infection). If an allergy develops to one type of major tranquilizer, an agent with a different chemical structure (such as Haldol) is usually substituted. The occurrence of these side effects again emphasizes the need for careful medical follow-up.

One major tranquilizer is now combined with a "tricyclic antidepressant," and the two products (Triavil and Etrafon) are frequently used in the treatment of various types of depression with anxiety. For several reasons there is considerable question whether this combination has any appropriate use. The response to both types of drugs is highly variable and seldom can a fixed combination provide the proper dose of each. Furthermore, certain side effects of both drugs are additive so that in most cases the administration of one or the other drug alone is preferable.

Antidepressants and lithium

Examples:
a. Tricyclic antidepressants: Elavil, Sinequan, Tofranil.
b. Lithium: Eskalith and Lithane

Variations in mood from temporary elation to depression occur normally at times in almost everyone. In some people, however, the degree and duration of moods may be exaggerated. When a person sees himself and his life in a totally negative way, the mood can lead to an inability to work and occasionally to severe depression or even suicide. However, such a state is almost always temporary and after a time the mood lightens. In some, the mood may lighten to the point of elation, which can be so excessive that a person thinks he can achieve things well beyond his means or capacity. While all of these moods are experienced occasionally, when a person has longstanding, repeated excessive mood changes it interferes with day-to-day activities and relationships and therefore requires treatment.

One type of recurrent depression is called *unipolar endogenous depression*, while fluctuation from depression to marked elation is generally called *manic depression*, a "bipolar" state. Although serious longstanding "problem moods" are treatable with specific medication, in some cases these drugs are used to treat relatively minor mood problems (especially depression). Many life changes, such as the death of someone close, can cause depression; but unless there is a history of recurrent serious depression, these passing episodes usually resolve spontaneously—many times even before drugs could take their full and sustained effect (which often takes more than two or three weeks).

Until the 1960s, the treatment of serious depression included the administration of stimulant drugs such as *amphetamines* (which, when eventually discontinued could cause even worse depression), electroshock therapy and another class of drugs in occasional use called *monoamine oxidase inhibitors*. The last group of drugs include Parnate and Nardil, which are also rarely used to treat high blood pressure. The use of these drugs has decreased because of their potential ability to cause very serious drug interactions with certain kinds of food (such as certain types of cheese, red wine and brewer's yeast), occasionally causing severe hypertension.

Fortunately, a group of drugs related to the major tranquilizers (e.g. Thorazine) was introduced shortly after the monoamine oxidase inhibitors. Called "tricyclic antidepressants" (because of their chemical structure), they are currently the most useful drugs in the treatment of serious depression.

A major difficulty with these drugs is that they may take up to three weeks to exert their full effect. This factor is compounded by the fact that when first given they may have unpleasant side effects—including dry mouth, difficulty in urinating, sleepiness, blurred vision or constipation. In short, a depressed person starting to take these drugs may actually feel worse and must be strongly supported until they begin to exert their therapeutic effect. At the time the antidepressant effect takes hold, however, side effects tend to become less bothersome.

The sedative effect of tricyclic antidepressants is often put to good use. As these drugs tend to stay in the body for more than a day or two, they are often taken at night when they can also promote sleep. In addition to the temporary side effects noted above, these drugs can occasionally affect heart rhythm so their use in persons with heart disease requires careful observation.

When mood swings tend more toward marked elation (*mania*), alternating with mild or severe depression, a mineral salt called *lithium carbonate* is extremely useful in allowing patients to function normally. When using this preparation, however, dosage and blood levels must be carefully monitored since excessive doses can be hazardous. When excessive doses are reached, a patient may develop tremors and serious gastrointestinal problems. Further, lithium may interact with certain diuretics (drugs which increase the secretion of urine by the kidneys), and these are usually not taken together. Other drugs, such as the major tranquilizers or antidepressants, are sometimes used in treating the manic phase, but responses are highly individualized; again, this type of therapy requires very strict medical supervision.

III Drugs for heart and vascular disorders

Cardiovascular disease in the United States is a major cause of hospitalization and a principal contributor to the need for continued medical care. Thus, it is not surprising that many of the most frequently prescribed drugs come into the general classification of cardiovascular drugs, which fall into a large number of categories. To look at this group of drugs and what they do, it is necessary to consider briefly what the cardiovascular system is, how it works and how drugs can affect it.

The term *cardiovascular* refers to the heart plus the associated blood vessels, which include the arteries, veins and the tiny vessels (capillaries) that form a connecting link between the arteries and veins (Figure 10). Under normal

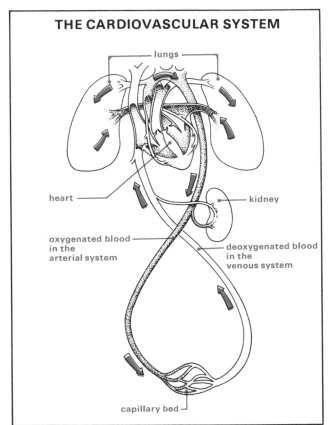

THE CARDIOVASCULAR SYSTEM

lungs

heart

kidney

oxygenated blood in the arterial system

deoxygenated blood in the venous system

capillary bed

Figure 10 *The cardiovascular system, the heart and blood vessels, is responsible for circulating the blood around our bodies. The heart is actually a double pump which feeds two circulations. First is the pulmonary circulation to the lungs where blood is oxygenated. Then it returns to the heart before being pumped into the arteries of the systemic circulation. These arteries eventually branch into tiny capillaries through which blood flows slowly, giving up oxygen to the tissues and carrying away their waste products. This deoxygenated blood then returns to the heart through the veins.*

conditions, the cardiovascular system can be considered as a closed system of tubes (blood vessels) with a pump (the heart) to move the blood through these tubes. The main purpose of this system is to deliver oxygen (which is picked up when the blood passes through the lungs) and nutrients by way of the arteries to the capillaries, where the oxygen and nutrients pass across the capillary walls to the tissues. Further along, the capillaries empty oxygen-depleted blood into the veins. The venous blood carries waste products and carbon dioxide back to the lungs, where it picks up more oxygen and is conveyed to the heart for another cycle. The ability of this system to give efficient blood flow to the tissues is not unlike that of a mechanical pumping system. It is related to the efficiency of the pump (the heart), the size and openness of the blood vessels or tubes, and the pressure in the system—which is a function of the strength of the heart's contraction as well as the stiffness of the arterial walls and the volume of fluid in the system. This system is very finely attuned but flexible—so it is able to adapt quickly to many situations, such as exercise and stress. But if damage occurs to the system, either from disease or injury, there can be several problems and several different types of drug may have to be administered to return the system to normal. These drugs fall into various general categories.

A. Drugs for heart failure

Examples: Digoxin, digitalis, Lanoxin, and diuretics

If the heart is not getting enough oxygen due to clogged arteries serving the heart muscles (coronary arteries), the heart may not function as efficiently as it should or contract as well as it had in the past. This can result in *heart failure*. This means that the heart is failing to do its job efficiently, not that it has failed completely. Except when the pumping action of the heart fails suddenly (as in an acute coronary occlusion or "heart attack") the changes are small. Often inefficiency results when the heart muscle fails to get enough oxygen because of a blocked coronary artery (which carries blood and oxygen to the heart itself). At other times there is too much blood for the heart to pump or too much resistance in the vascular system for the heart to pump against efficiently. The heart will also pump ineffectively if it beats too rapidly or irregularly, as in the case of an irregular heart rhythm (*arrhythmia*).

When the heart pumps ineffectively, a signal goes to the kidneys to retain water in order to maintain an adequate pressure in the circulatory system. This protective system is useful in such acute situations as shock, but it can also place a heavy load on the pumping efficiency of the failing heart. The heart cannot pump all of the extra fluid, which then tends to accumulate in the legs (as *peripheral edema*) or in the lungs (as *pulmonary edema*). Meanwhile, the heart beats more rapidly. In very severe cases this heart simply cannot get enough blood and oxygen to certain tissues and they tend to have a purplish or bluish tinge.

Reduced blood circulation helps explain some of the symptoms of heart failure, including shortness of breath with light exercise—since the heart cannot supply the body with enough oxygen. At night the lungs can become congested with fluid and cause breathlessness. Swelling of the feet and legs occurs as does the sensation of the heart beating rapidly (*palpitations*). All of these predictable symptoms *can* indicate a failing heart, although a thorough medical evaluation is essential for a definite diagnosis.

Since one acute problem is the presence of excess fluid in the lungs and elsewhere in the body, initial treatment of heart failure often involves use of diuretics (or "water pills") to reduce the load on the heart or the total fluid volume in the closed vascular system. Often this alone will relieve many of the symptoms, but the specific causes of heart failure must be treated if possible. For example, if the heart has been pumping irregularly, then regulating the rhythm will help ease the problem. Similarly, if the heart has been pumping against high pressure, relief of the high blood pressure (*hypertension*) will also help. Occasionally, in severe heart failure, blood pressure and work for the heart are decreased by dilating the blood vessels and thus decreasing the work for the heart. Further, a defective heart valve obviously affects the heart's ability to pump so that surgical repair or replacement of a valve can sometimes improve functioning.

Sometimes, however, treatment of the specific causes of heart failure are not sufficient, and the heart must be treated directly to improve its performance. In 1775 an English physician, William Withering (1741–1799), found that a local country woman could treat a condition of edema called "dropsy" with a herbal tea from the foxglove plant. Dr. Withering made good use of this chance observation and introduced the foxglove component, digitalis leaf, to modern therapy as the primary drug for heart failure. The administration of *digitalis*, or its purified derivative (*digoxin*), continues to be a major means of therapy in heart failure. These drugs can overcome heart failure by actually increasing the strength of the heart contraction; in addition, they improve the heart rate if it is rapid and irregular, which occurs in a fairly common abnormal rhythm called *atrial fibrillation*.

B. Drugs to regulate the heart rhythm

Examples: Inderal, Pronestyl, quinidine, Xylocaine, Dilantin

The closed circulatory system functions less efficiently if the heart beats irregularly. The heart's muscle fibers are connected to an elaborate "wiring" or conduction system (the *pacemaker*) which transmits electrical signals throughout the heart muscle to coordinate its regular contractions. These signals occur about 72 times per minute and start at the top of the heart, run through the middle and spread out through the heart walls. If the heart is damaged (as in a heart attack) or stressed (as in heart failure), conduction can be affected and the rhythm changed. If the conduction system is blocked, heart conduction can slow; conversely, a type of "short-circuiting" can take place whereby the signals bypass the organized conduction system and fire more rapidly—sometimes irregularly, sometimes not. When normal conduction becomes disrupted, the resultant abnormal rhythmic beating of the heart is called an *arrhythmia*. The drugs used to treat this condition are known as antiarrhythmia drugs, and they come from a wide variety of unrelated classes. In general, however, the action of all of these drugs is to correct the abnormal rhythm.

Certain types of arrhythmia are only partially responsive to drugs and include a block of rhythm, causing the heart to go too slowly. In this case, the condition is temporarily responsive to drugs but often requires placement of an artificial pacemaker.

C. Drugs for angina pectoris

Examples: Inderal, Isordil, Nitro-Bid, nitroglycerin, Sorbitrate

The function of the heart as an effective pump is also related to its own blood supply through the *coronary arteries*. If these arteries become clogged with arteriosclerotic plaques, the blood and oxygen supply is decreased and if the pump must work harder (as in exercise or stress), this lack of oxygen can cause pain in the heart, called *angina pectoris*. On a longer-term basis, a chronic lack of oxygen to the heart can gradually cause weakening of the heart muscle and heart failure. An acute blockage in one of the coronary arteries results in a heart attack or a "coronary" (*coronary thrombosis*). Angina attacks, which are characterized by chest pains, usually below the breastbone (sternum), may persist for months or years before obstruction, heart attack or heart failure occur. These cannot be predicted, however, and a person with angina pectoris should be under the direct care of a physician.

Traditional drugs used to treat angina pectoris help prevent the attacks in two ways: (1) by opening up or dilating the coronary arteries to the heart (thought to be the way in which nitroglycerin acts) and (2) by decreasing the work the heart must do (and, therefore, the need for oxygen).

The most commonly used drugs in treating angina pectoris belong to the family of medications related to nitroglycerin, which is a drug taken under the tongue or on a paste on the skin. Another type of drug used to treat angina pectoris is exemplified by Inderal (propranolol), which decreases the work the heart must do and thus decreases the incidence of angina pectoris. It is usually taken on a regular basis, although discontinuation must be done with caution in persons with severe heart failure. It is usually not used in persons with severe asthma or those who have had previous heart failure.

Patients with angina pectoris will frequently be put on a general program for the treatment of heart disease which includes changes in diet, smoking and drinking habits and exercise as well as special medication. Each program is ideally individualized and supervised, with the physician reviewing the patient's progress or status on a regular basis. It is difficult to judge if successful treatment results from medication or the change in physical and dietary habits—especially when the primary cause of the attacks is stress.

D. Drugs which decrease blood clotting

Examples: heparin, Coumadin, aspirin

When the heart is functioning less effectively, the blood flow in the closed cardiovascular system may be less efficient. The tendency toward sluggish flow is greatest in the return system of veins, with an increased likelihood of clotting within the vessels (*thrombosis*). There are also many other causes of thrombosis that do not directly relate to failure of the cardiovascular system. If clots which are formed travel to the lungs through the veins, they can cause a *pulmonary embolus*, which can affect the heart and the exchange of oxygen in the lungs. To prevent further formation of these clots, drugs called *anticoagulants* are used. These include heparin, which is usually used in the hospital setting intravenously as well as the oral drug Coumadin. And a third group of drugs called *antiplatelet drugs*, which includes aspirin and Persantin. These drugs all act to prolong the time it takes blood to coagulate (clot), and thus, they help to *prevent* clot formation. None of these drugs actually dissolves clots which are already formed.

In the most common situation in which anticoagulants are used (to prevent the progression of clots in the leg or clots moving to the lungs), the patient is usually hospitalized and given intravenous injections of heparin. After several days the *oral* anticoagulant, usually Coumadin, is administered.

When anticoagulants are taken there needs to be very close medical supervision, and doses must be highly individualized and adjusted (if necessary) during therapy. The effectiveness of anticoagulation varies from individual to individual and even from time to time in the same person. Laboratory blood tests measuring the time it takes for blood to clot before and after administration of anticoagulants are used to determine the amount of drug the person must take to produce adequate results without risking complications. These laboratory tests are extremely important and must be performed on a regular basis as long as the drug is taken.

The most common side effect of anticoagulant drugs is uncontrolled bleeding, but this is usually treated rapidly if the physician is notified following any evidence of minor bleeding.

Many drugs taken for completely unrelated conditions can greatly increase or decrease the degree of effects of the oral anticoagulant Coumadin. Physicians and pharmacists are aware of these interactions, but they must be consulted beforehand and advised whenever any change in drug regimen is planned. The anticoagulant action of Coumadin can also be affected by large amounts of vitamin K (taken in food or multivitamin preparations).

The ability of aspirin and related drugs to prevent clotting (especially the type associated with strokes and heart attacks) by affecting one element of the blood, called *platelets*, has recently received attention, and these drugs are currently being tested for their therapeutic value. Their effect on clotting is much less marked than the Coumadin type of drug, so the potential hazards noted above do not generally apply.

E. Drugs for high blood pressure

Examples: Aldactone, Catapres, Diuril, Esidrex, HydroDIURIL, Inderal, Lasix, Salutensin

When the heart contracts, or beats (called *systole*), it must pump against both the pressure of the arterial walls and the volume of blood in the closed vascular system. If the arteries are constricted, as is often true in a condition of high blood pressure (hypertension), the heart must pump harder than normal to generate sufficient pressure to get blood to all the organs and tissues. If the heart is already weakened, the need to generate further pressure puts it under even greater strain.

High blood pressure is one of the most common health problems in modern society, and many drugs are used to treat it.

The normal blood pressure in human arteries is a ratio, usually less than 140 over 90 mm of mercury (mercury pressure is an arbitrary scale). The upper figure, 140, is called the *systolic* pressure and indicates the force of the contracting heart (systole) as well as indirectly the "openness" and strength of the arteries (Figure 11). The

VARIATIONS IN BLOOD PRESSURE

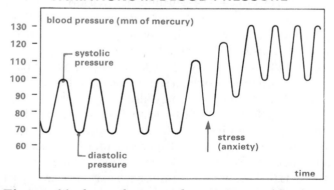

Figure 11 *shows the normal variations in blood pressure within the arteries. With each heartbeat the pressure rises from a diastolic level (maintained by the elastic artery walls) to a systolic level as the heart pumps blood into the arteries. In a state of anxiety, the blood pressure rises because the heart beats more quickly.*

lower pressure, 90, is called the *diastolic* pressure and is the pressure when the heart momentarily relaxes (diastole) between beats; only the stiffness of the wall, the size of the arteries and the volume in the system determine the diastolic pressure. Since the heart beats about 72 times per minute, in a person with a blood pressure of 140/90, there is a pressure of 140 in the system 72 times a minute as the heart beats and a pressure of 90 between each beat.

Hypertension occurs when the heart contracts with more force or when the arteries become smaller in diameter, usually due to constriction of the muscular walls of the arteries. It can also occur when there is more fluid (or blood volume) in the system. A pressure of more than 140/90 in persons below the age of 60 about 160/95 in older persons (when taken on more than one occasion) is usually considered evidence of hypertension. The higher the pressure, the greater the potential problem. The reason why high blood pressure can be harmful is that, over periods of months or years, this "pounding" type of pressure eventually damages small arteries and the organs that they supply—especially the brain and the kidneys. Also, of course, it affects the heart itself, since it has to pump against the higher pressure and do more work. Like any mechanical system that must work hard, it will eventually wear out, and the heart and the kidneys can fail and strokes can occur. Thus, the control of high blood pressure is a preventive measure to avoid this potential damage.

One of the major determinants of blood pressure is the degree of contraction in the arterial blood vessels, which is controlled by many regulating substances in the body as well as the nervous system. For example, blood pressure can rise as the result of an increase of activity in the sympathetic nervous system, which releases a substance called norepinephrine, or noradrenaline (similar to epinephrine, or adrenaline). This causes the arteries to constrict more tightly, thus increasing the necessary force of heart contractions to pump blood to the organs and tissues. Under stress which may sometimes relate to periods of increased blood pressure, this system is also activated. When this occurs, many people are aware of the heart pounding or may have headaches, although generally they cannot directly experience the increased blood pressure. Many types of medicines—including general stimulants, appetite suppressants or decongestants or drugs used to treat asthma or allergies—have similar effects on the arteries and can aggravate high blood pressure. They can also interact with drugs used to treat high blood pressure.

The majority of antihypertensive drugs can be classified into three general categories. The first comprises the *diuretics*, which are usually the first drugs to be prescribed; they also represent the mainstay of therapy in many cases because they actually promote the effect and benefit of other drugs. Examples of these include HydroDIURIL and

Lasix. Diuretics act to decrease the volume in the system by causing a loss of excess water (often manifested as swelling of the feet, or edema) and salt. They also may dilate or enlarge the blood vessels to some extent and decrease the blood pressure by this mechanism. By virtue of these effects, they are widely used alone to treat mild cases of hypertension and in combination with other drugs in more severe cases. (See *Diuretics* later in this section.)

The second group of drugs used to treat hypertension consists of the *sympathetic-blocking drugs.* Reserpine, Aldomet, Ismelin, Catapres and propranolol are included in this category. Since the sympathetic nervous system can raise blood pressure by increasing the forcefulness of the heart's contractions (as well as forcing constriction of the blood vessels), these drugs usually act both to decrease the heart's contracting force and to dilate blood vessels. The sympathetic nervous system originates in the brain and affects many other functions, such as bladder and sexual functions. This fact explains many of the side effects seen with these drugs that block the system, which include drowsiness, depression, change in sleep or dreaming patterns, diarrhea and change in sexual appetite. Since there is considerable variability in this system from person to person, dosage and side effects also vary widely.

The third category of drugs, the *vasodilators* or "blood vessel relaxing agents"), acts primarily on the blood vessels to relax their walls and thus decrease pressure in the system. The drug Apresoline (hydralazine) and prazosin (Minipress) are the only drugs in this category for oral use available in the United States at this time. Other vasodilators are used intravenously in emergency treatment. The effectiveness of these drugs is dependent upon the physical position of the patient. Thus, if a person stands suddenly, much of the blood will go to the lower part of the body, decreasing the supply of blood to the head and causing faintness. This is called *postural hypotension* (temporary low blood pressure caused by a sudden change in position). It usually resolves within minutes, although one type of readjustment is for the heart to beat rapidly and harder to increase the blood pressure (which can be a bothersome side effect). Postural hypotension can be controlled in part by sympathetic-blocking drugs, so these are often used in combination with vasodilators. In addition, patients taking these drugs are usually instructed to move more slowly.

High blood pressure is often treated with a combination of all of these drugs. One of the major problems in treatment of hypertension is the requirement for a number of drugs per day so that many patients fail to take their medications and continue to have hypertension—which may eventually lead to stroke, kidney failure or heart failure. One approach to this multiple drug problem has been the production of "combination drugs" for high blood pressure, so that one tablet contains drugs from two or all three categories of drugs discussed above.

Unfortunately, the establishment of an effective antihypertensive regimen often takes considerable adjustment to an individual drug; using combinations when initiating or changing therapy complicates this effort. Once a therapeutic regimen is established, however, the combination preparations may be useful, even though they are considerably more expensive.

Another approach is to find drugs that are effective for a relatively long time, so that they need be taken only once or twice daily. In some cases this is possible, especially in the treatment of mild hypertension. In more severe cases, however, drugs must often be taken two or three times a day.

F. Drugs for preventing and treating arteriosclerosis

Examples: Atromid-S, Cyclospasmol, Hydergine, nicotinic acid, Pavabid, Vasodilan

Finally, one of the major causes of cardiovascular problems comes from the formation of arteriosclerotic plaques in arterial blood vessels. *Arteriosclerosis* describes the condition in which deposits of fat, cholesterol and calcium build up on the inner walls of arterial blood vessels. Eventually, this can lead to partial or complete obstruction of these vessels, cutting off the vital blood and oxygen supply to the tissues. If the affected arteries serve the heart, angina pectoris can occur. Similar obstruction of arteries to the head can cause strokes, while obstruction of arteries to the legs can cause gangrene and loss of a leg if not treated.

The buildup of these fat-filled plaques is believed to occur over many years, with some evidence that the process starts in the early 20s. The process may often continue unnoted until a catastrophic event occurs—such as a heart attack or stroke.

There is much controversy about the factors that cause this insidious buildup, but several so-called risk factors have been identified. These include elevated levels of fatlike substances in the blood (such as cholesterol and triglycerides), the presence of diabetes, a history of heavy smoking, a history of high intake of animal fats in meat and milk products, a history of high blood pressure and, in some cases, a history of high sugar intake. Certain types of personality characteristics may also play a role.

A family history of early death from heart attack or stroke appears to increase the likelihood of problems of arteriosclerosis. The medical approach to this problem has been both preventive and therapeutic. There are indications that the preventive approach may have an impact on certain groups where there is a decreasing incidence of arteriosclerotic disease. This reduction has been attributed to various factors, the most prominent being the lower animal fat and cholesterol diet advocated for years by many heart associations and cardiologists. In fact, the true reasons are not known.

Preventive drug therapy has been aimed at decreasing

the amount of substances (such as cholesterol) available to make up the plaque. These efforts have been questionably successful, although a number of drugs do reduce blood fats (lipids). One of the most commonly used is Atromid-S. Other drugs prescribed have included nicotinic acid, Choloxin, estrogens and drugs which prevent the absorption of fat and cholesterol from the bowel, such as Questran (cholestyramine). Thus far, however, none of these drugs has been shown to be especially effective except in certain specific disorders of fat metabolism. In the meantime, evidence continues to suggest that careful dietary regulation at an early age may play a key role in prevention.

A second approach to arteriosclerosis has been an attempt to prevent plaque formation and further obstruction which comes from formation of small clotlike material on the plaques. One of the common contributors to such a clot is the type of blood cell called a *platelet*. When several platelets stick to a plaque they can increase the obstruction. A group of drugs undergoing extensive tests are the "antiplatelet drugs" (including aspirin and Persantin), which decrease the stickiness of the platelets and thus the likelihood of clot formation. The usefulness of these drugs remains to be proved, but the small doses that seem necessary are relatively safe and suggest a safe approach to some arteriosclerotic problems. Some physicians also use the blood thinner Coumadin; because of its many problems in use and interactions, however, it is usually reserved for more active clotting problems.

Other approaches to the treatment of arteriosclerosis may be resorted to once there has been an occurrence of angina pectoris, a heart attack, a warning stroke or poor circulation in the legs. If the arteriosclerotic plaques are within larger blood vessels, they may be able to be surgically removed or bypassed with the insertion of a section of an artificial artery or vein. Drug therapy, on the other hand, is directed at opening (dilating) the arteries to improve circulation. Nitroglycerin has long been used to dilate the coronary arteries (which supply the heart). Other drugs prescribed for opening up arteries elsewhere (which are somewhat more controversial) include Pavabid, Cerespan, Persantin, Cyclospasmol, Vasodilan and Hydergine. All of these have demonstrated an ability to dilate some blood vessels when tested in laboratory animals; a number appear to be active only when injected. Few studies demonstrate that the drugs taken orally can have much effect in arteriosclerosis, although they are widely used and have relatively few side effects. However, they are often expensive.

IV Diuretics ("water pills")

Diuretic drugs are sometimes referred to popularly as "water pills" because they promote the loss of water (as well as salts) through the kidneys into the urine. They are the mainstay in the treatment of high blood pressure and heart failure, but are also used to treat edema (swelling usually of the feet or legs but sometimes of the face, hands or abdomen), kidney disease and liver disease (such as cirrhosis). Diuretics have two related effects. The primary therapeutic effect is that of causing loss of unwanted water; the second effect is that of a loss of salt (*sodium chloride*, the same as common table salt). In many illnesses the kidneys tend to retain water and salt in the body; diuretics act on the kidneys to block this effect. Certain diuretics also cause loss of the essential salt or mineral *potassium chloride*, which must be replaced either through the diet or by means of a dietary supplement. Other diuretics (such as Dyazide, Aldactazide, Aldactone and Dyrenium) do *not* cause loss of potassium and are called "potassium-retaining diuretics." These are not always considered the drugs of choice because of other effects on the body's salt balance.

Diuretics are commonly classified as *thiazide* type, *potent* diuretics or *potassium-retaining* diuretics. Thiazide diuretics are named after their chemical class, which relates them to the sulfa drugs and the oral antidiabetic drugs. The most commonly prescribed diuretic, *hydrochlorothiazide* (HydroDIURIL or Esidrix) is also included in many combination antihypertensive drugs and combination diuretics (such as Dyazide and Aldactazide).

Major side effects of thiazide diuretics include a tendency to increase the blood sugar in those predisposed to diabetes and to increase the uric acid content in the blood (which can produce gout). They all can cause an excessive loss of water, potassium or sodium chloride. Thus, long-term therapy with any of the diuretics usually requires occasional checks of blood values for sugar, uric acid and potassium. Occasionally they can cause rashes or muscle cramps.

The potent diuretics include Lasix (furosemide) and Edecrin (ethacrynic acid). Although Lasix is sometimes used in the routine treatment of high blood pressure or heart failure, the potent diurctics are usually reserved for treatment of severe edema—since they can cause a loss of considerably more water and salt than the thiazide diuretics. The potent diuretics share the same side effects as the thiazides, but they can also rarely cause hearing problems (particularly if used with other drugs that can affect nerves of hearing, such as streptomycin or gentamicin).

The potassium-retaining diuretics, Dyrenium and Aldactone, are similar to thiazides but weaker. Because they do not cause potassium loss (thus eliminating the need to take extra potassium) they are often combined with a stronger thiazide diuretic such as Aldactazide (Aldactone plus hydrochlorothiazide) and Dyazide (Dyrenium plus hydrochlorothiazide). Although sometimes useful, they can be associated with some loss of kidney function and retention of too much potassium. Such combinations are usually more costly than hydrochlorothiazide.

The fourth kind of diuretic, Diamox, is essentially reserved for use in the treatment of glaucoma, partly because resistance to its effects develops rapidly and because it is not very strong. It is used in the treatment of glaucoma to reduce the pressure in the eye, but it is preferably taken only intermittently.

V Drugs for gastrointestinal disorders

Few persons can go through life without suffering some symptoms of nausea, vomiting, constipation or diarrhea. Consequently, there are an astounding number of preparations available by prescription or over the counter to relieve such symptoms. Frequently, the ailments associated with these symptoms are benign and self-limiting; sometimes they signal more serious problems such as ulcers, colitis and even cancer. Most drugs used for gastrointestinal complaints primarily attempt to relieve the symptoms, with variable degrees of success; they can seldom affect the underlying cause, especially if it is serious or chronic. Sometimes dysfunction of the digestive or gastrointestinal (G.I.) tract may be a reaction to stress, so that a queasy stomach or episodes of diarrhea may be common symptoms of anxiety. Nonetheless, any of the gastrointestinal symptoms, if recurrent, usually requires medical evaluation to rule out serious causes. Many preparations used or prescribed for G.I. troubles act to *relax* the digestive tract muscles—the antispasmodic and antidiarrheal drugs. Many others aim to alter the actual content of the intestines and help to normalize function. Gelusil neutralize stomach acids; laxatives and some antidiarrheals, such as Kaopectate, change the bulk and content of the intestines and help normalize its function. Few of these drugs are for long-term use since benign conditions often disappear after changes in the diet or relief of stress. Specific types of disease and the drugs used for problems of the digestive tract are discussed in the next three sections.

A. Drugs for nausea, stomach upset and ulcers

Examples: Antivert, Bentyl, Compazine, Gelusil, Maalox, Mylanta, Pro-Banthine, TUMS

Nausea (the sensation of stomach upset) and vomiting can be due to a variety of causes. If these can be identified, they can be treated or prevented by relatively specific measures. Nausea can be due to a wide variety of problems, some as general as "gastrointestinal flu." Frequently a sensation of nausea or stomach upset can be due to irritation of the stomach lining because of an ulcer, or when a strong, irritating medicine is taken, for example, liquid potassium, high doses of theophylline (a drug for asthma), or aspirin. In these cases direct treatment of the ulcer with antacids (see below) or preventing the irritation by diluting the medication with food or water may help avoid the symptoms.

Another occasional local cause of nausea or stomach distress may be overdistension or overfilling of the stomach with food or, not uncommonly, air that has been swallowed. Once considered, this seldom calls for drugs.

Vague stomach upset or vomiting is sometimes due to increased contraction of the muscles of the stomach, which can often give a sensation of a "knot in the stomach," hunger pangs or nausea. This can, of course, be due to an ulcer or other local irritation, but often is associated with increased stomach contractions linked to stress. Although the exact mechanism is not known, these symptoms can often be relieved by antacids or by antispasmodic drugs such as Pro-Banthine or atropine—which act directly either on the stomach or on the nerve to the stomach to decrease and slow contractions of the stomach and bowel. Because these, as well as some symptoms of ulcer, are frequently associated with stress reactions, there are a number of antispasmodic drugs which are combined with tranquilizers, such as phenobarbital in Donnatal and Librium in Librax. Although extremely widely used, there is considerable question about these fixed combinations directed at two relatively *different* problems which need individual attention and dosing.

Many people become nauseated after eating certain foods. People with a tendency to have gallbladder disease may become nauseated after eating fatty foods, rich sauces or butter, or sometimes corn and cabbage. Others experience symptoms of intolerance and upset to a wide range of foods, such as spicy foods, coffee or dairy products. Although prevention is the key factor in this type of nausea, antacids will often, but by no means always, help.

Frequently nausea and vomiting are due to irritation of four separate areas in the brain, including the vomiting center, an area called the "chemoreceptor trigger zone" and the "vestibular apparatus" in the inner ear, which is often affected in motion sickness or Ménière's disease. A number of drugs (such as codeine, morphine and certain anticancer drugs) directly affect these brain centers to cause vomiting. Fortunately, there are also a number of drugs that will stop or prevent nausea and vomiting due to these causes. Some of the most effective drugs for motion sickness are the various antihistamines (see *Antihistamines*) which act on the vestibular area. These include meclizine (Antivert, Bonine), Dramamine, Benadryl and hydroxyzine (Atarax, Vistaril). Nausea and vomiting due to stimulation of the other areas in the brain are sometimes helped by the antihistamines, but are also prevented with major tranquilizers such as Thorazine, Compazine or Phenergan, which are very effective. An antispasmodic drug, scopolamine, is effective against most types of central vomiting.

A peptic ulcer is a common specific cause of stomach upset and occasionally of pain, nausea and vomiting. An ulcer is essentially a breakdown in the mucus-covered lining of the stomach or the duodenum (which connects the stomach to the small intestine). This breakdown of the tissue, which can be the size of a dime or much larger, can cause pain, spasm and bleeding. Ulcers can be very serious as heavy bleeding usually requires hospitalization and sometimes surgery. For this reason, early treatment at the first sign of an ulcer is essential.

The proper treatment of ulcers has long been a subject of debate in medical circles, but at present it is felt that regular antacid therapy is of greater importance than a rigid diet in most cases. Although authorities still differ overall, most agree that coffee, alcohol and large amounts of spicy foods are not helpful.

The stomach is essentially a "bag" of hydrochloric acid in which food begins to be broken down by the strong acid and by an enzyme, pepsin, produced in the stomach. Any ulcer in this environment will be aggravated by the acid and enzyme; therefore, the primary goal in therapy is to neutralize the acid as continuously as possible with antacids. If an antacid is given and the stomach empties slowly, acid will be neutralized longer, which may justify the addition of an antispasmodic drug, such as Pro-Banthine.

> **Millions of Americans routinely take antacids to combat the unpleasant effects of overeating and taking just one or two too many drinks the night before. However, the routine use of any drug—regardless of how harmless you think it to be—is never a good idea unless it is done on the advice of your doctor and under continuing supervision.**

Antacids come in a wide range of compositions, tastes and prices. Most antacids contain one or more of the following salts: magnesium, calcium or aluminum. Because magnesium salts usually cause diarrhea when taken alone (for example, milk of magnesia is an antacid, but is more commonly used as a laxative!), and calcium and aluminum salts cause constipation on their own, the majority of antacids are made up as mixtures to avoid both side effects. Often, however, this is not the case and some experimenting with several antacids may be necessary to prevent constipation. Sodium bicarbonate is an effective antacid but cannot be used on a regular basis because it is absorbed and could cause problems with retention of the salt and alkali.

There are a large number of antispasmodic drugs available, most of them acting as "anticholinergic drugs" to block signals to the vagus nerve (which increases acid secretion and contraction of the stomach). These antispasmodic (anticholinergic) drugs act elsewhere in the body, so that together with effects on the stomach they may cause dryness in the mouth, blurring of vision and difficulty with urination at higher doses. Since a person can seldom feel effects of medication on the stomach, the presence of a dry mouth is usually a good indication that the drug is working. Usually these drugs are taken before meals or at bedtime, or both. The bedtime dose may be most useful since it can help retain the antacid taken at night in the stomach (which it slows down) and decreases the need for antacids in the middle of the night. Antispasmodic drugs may cause retention of urine in men with prostate trouble, so they are used with caution, if at all, in elderly men. They can also counteract the drugs used in glaucoma, so are likewise used cautiously in that condition.

B. Drugs for constipation

Constipation, commonly defined as difficult, infrequent evacuation of the bowel, has been a preoccupation of advanced societies for years. For a long time, daily evacuation of the bowels was believed to prevent virtually all disease, but we can now be absolutely certain that good health does not require regular bowel movements at fixed times. Normal bowel function can range from three bowel movements a day to three a week or even less.

The last few decades have seen a dramatic decrease in the routine use of cathartics by the medical profession, but self-prescribed laxatives still enjoy widespread use by the general public, and a large majority still remain "bowel conscious." This is confirmed by the availability of more than 700 different laxative products, on which over $400 million is spent annually. General misconceptions about normal bowel function and extensive advertising by pharmaceutical manufacturers contribute to the overuse, misuse and abuse of self-prescribed laxatives.

Simple constipation most frequently results from the wrong sort of diet, insufficient intake of liquids, sometimes a change in habits because of travel and perhaps insufficient exercise. Laxatives are rarely indicated for relief of simple constipation: relief can be achieved by changing to a better quality diet which includes foods with a higher fiber content, by drinking more fluids, and by responding promptly to the urge to evacuate the bowels.

The terms laxative, cathartic and purgative are often confused: all three describe agents that act to bring about a bowel movement, but these agents differ in degree of action. A *cathartic* is slightly more active than a *purgative*, but the two terms are relatively interchangeable since both types of agent rapidly produce bowel evacuation and a definite change in stool consistency (often watery feces). These actions are less pronounced in the case of a *laxative*, although a sufficiently large dose of laxative can produce a cathartic effect.

Laxatives can be classified into several groups: (1) bulk-forming laxatives; (2) stimulant laxatives; (3) saline laxatives; (4) lubricants (mineral oil) and (5) stool softeners.

Bulk-forming laxatives promote bowel movement by

increasing the mass of the stool and by softening the stool through their ability to attract and hold water within it. The increased bulk of the stool usually increases the frequency of bowel movements. These laxatives are generally not absorbed from the intestines and do not appear to have any influence on the absorption of nutrients from food. They are considered the safest laxatives, although an adequate fluid intake is necessary. A bulk-forming laxative may take from one to three days to have an effect, so that to maintain a consistent result, it should be taken three or more times a week.

Bulk-forming laxatives come from two main sources. The least costly source is crude dietary fiber, including bran, whole fruits, leafy vegetables, raw carrots and wholegrain breads. Most others are made from semi-synthetic cellulose derivatives, such as psyllium (obtained from Plantago seed), and methylcellulose. They include Dialose, Effersyllium, Hydrocil, Metamucil and Serutan.

Stimulant laxatives increase the wavelike (peristaltic) contractions of the intestinal musculature which pushes the bowel content along in the direction of the wave. They also cause more fluid to enter the intestine—which in itself will stimulate increased peristalsis.

The potency of different stimulant laxative products varies greatly according to the response of the individual. A bowel movement usually occurs after about six hours. Stimulant laxatives should be used only occasionally and never more than daily for one week to relieve simple constipation. If stimulant laxatives are used for a long period, normal bowel function can be lost and the individual may become dependent on the drug for bowel evacuation.

Noticeable side effects of these laxatives can include intestinal cramps and burning, diarrhea and depletion of body water (dehydration). In general, this group of laxatives is considered the least desirable because of the unpleasant side effects and the tendency to alter bowel function after extended use. Examples include Dulcolax, Senokot, Fletcher's Castoria and Feen-a-Mint.

Saline laxatives, such as milk of magnesia, are chemical salts that hold water within the intestine and so indirectly stimulate peristalsis. A bowel movement usually occurs within one or two hours with a sufficient dose of the laxative. Saline laxatives can be regarded as safe and effective only when used occasionally. Continuous use for more than a week can cause side effects due to dehydration or loss of essential minerals.

Lubricant laxatives (mineral oil) are a colorless, tasteless mixture of liquids that have enjoyed popular use. Whether mineral oil lubricates the intestinal tract is unknown, but the oil softens the stools and promotes their easier evacuation. Mineral oil preparations are nonirritating and only slightly absorbed. The usual dose is one or two tablespoons taken at bedtime on an empty stomach. With proper and careful use, mineral oil produces few side

effects, but these laxative preparations should be strictly reserved for very occasional use.

Stool softeners are the most developed laxatives. Their detergent action facilitates the penetration of intestinal fluids (primarily water) into the stool, which is softened and so more easily passed out of the bowel. The effects are apparent only one to three days after ingestion. For beneficial and consistent effects, stool softeners therefore need to be taken at least three times a week, although not for long, continuous periods. These laxatives should be used only occasionally for simple constipation and, in any event, no more than daily for one week.

The most frequently prescribed laxatives—dioctyl sodium sulfosuccinate (known by the brand names Colace, Doxinate and Peri-Colace or as D.S.S.)—are stool softeners.

C. Drugs for diarrhea

Examples: Donnagel-PG, Kaopectate, Lomotil, paregoric

Diarrhea can be defined as the passage of bowel movements with increased frequency and with increased water content. Normal bowel movements contain approximately 60–70% water, but in the case of diarrhea, they contain up to 80–95% water. When diarrhea occurs, there is usually an increased movement of the circular muscles of the bowel walls, which in wavelike contractions (peristalsis) "rushes" food and fluids through the gastrointestinal tract. This prevents their proper digestion and absorption into the body and accounts for the increased fluid and undigested food particles in the stools.

Causes of diarrhea include bacterial and viral infections, parasite infestations, diseases of the intestine (such as ulcerative colitis) and hormonal disturbances, to name just a few. Diarrhea is often accompanied by loss of appetite, abdominal cramps due to the contractions of the bowel and trapped gas, and nausea and vomiting, which is also usually due to the increased contraction of the muscles in the gastrointestinal tract. Diarrhea can also occur due to an irritant in the bowel—this can signal a serious ulcer, or even tumor, which is one of the reasons diarrhea should be evaluated if it persists for more than two to three days.

Another reason why persistent diarrhea requires medical attention is that it can cause significant loss of water and salt from the body (dehydration). This is particularly true of infants and elderly persons. Diarrhea may also prevent absorption of certain drugs, such as oral contraceptives or anticonvulsants, so that loss of their effects can occur. The experience of diarrhea is quite uncomfortable, unsociable and often embarrassing, so that immediate symptomatic relief is often sought.

Antidiarrheal products act to decrease diarrhea in two general ways. One type of product (which includes drugs such as Kaopectate) acts to increase the bulk of the stool, and also possibly absorbs some of the toxins contributing to the increased movement or irritability of the bowel. Another type of drug (such as Lomotil) tends to act directly on the bowel muscle and decreases contraction, thus slowing the movement of material through the gastrointestinal tract. These drugs all provide symtomatic relief and do not usually affect the cause of the diarrhea. They are most effective in the mildest forms of diarrhea.

Prolonged use of an antidiarrheal preparation without identification of the underlying cause may result in serious complications. For this reason, symptomatic relief of undiagnosed diarrhea for more than two or three days is not recommended and proper examination by a physician is then advisable.

VI Hormonal drugs

Hormones are given for two general purposes. First, they are used as replacement therapy to provide normal hormone levels when a gland has been removed (as when the thyroid is removed) or is malfunctioning (as in diabetes, where the pancreas cannot produce enough insulin). In general, hormones are given in doses similar to those normally produced in the body and at the time they are normally secreted (for example, cortisone is released by the adrenals in the morning, so it is usually given then). Replacement therapy makes up for deficient thyroid, adrenal, ovarian (estrogen and progesterone), testicular (androgen or testosterone) and pancreatic gland secretions. The parathyroid hormone is not usually given, but since it regulates calcium metabolism, calcium is prescribed instead. The most common hormone deficiencies are those of thyroid, insulin and female hormones.

The second type of hormone therapy involves use of the hormone in higher than usual doses (pharmacologic doses), as a drug. Synthetic hormones resembling cortisone, such as prednisone, are most commonly used in this way. Many uses of estrogen, including oral contraceptives, also fall into this category (see *Oral contraceptives; Estrogens and progestogens used in hormone therapy*). This type of therapy does tend to interfere with normal gland function because of the feedback cycle; therefore the monitor in the brain registers high hormonal levels and generates signals to the pituitary gland and to the primary glands to decrease their function. For example, the ovaries get smaller when oral contraceptives are taken. So when these hormones are stopped, it may take weeks or months for the ovaries to return to normal function.

A. Drugs for thyroid disorders
Examples: Cytomel, Proloid, Synthroid, Tapazole, thyroid

If an excess of thyroid hormone is produced (hyperthyroidism), a person may feel continually warm, sweaty, shaky and experience diarrhea, nervousness, palpitations and changes in the skin or hair. The most usual treatment is

by radioactive iodine therapy or surgery. Occasionally certain drugs are used either prior to surgery or alone in an attempt to control the disease. If surgery is planned, iodine or iodine solution is sometimes prescribed together with one of the antithyroid drugs, either propylthiouracil or Tapazole (methimazole). Occasionally, when the symptoms are very severe, the drug propranolol (Inderal) or guanethidine (Ismelin) has been administered for short periods to decrease the palpitations and nervousness.

The condition where there is undersecretion of thyroid hormone, due to either removal of the gland or decreased function, is called *hypothyroidism*. This condition, with lower amounts of thyroid hormone, can result in slowed metabolism, which can cause lethargy or tiredness, increased sensitivity to cold, constipation and dullness or dryness of the skin or hair. When this is discovered, usually by measuring levels of thyroid hormone in the blood, thyroid is given as replacement therapy. If true deficiency is established, it is usually taken for life. For many years, the source of thyroid hormone was the dehydrated thyroid glands of cows or pigs, and thyroid pills were the primary drug used. Although the amount of thyroid hormone present was tested, the actual amount tended to vary from lot to lot. Thus, when the purified hormone *thyroxine* (used in Synthroid) became available more recently, it quickly became the preferred form.

Thyroid therapy has unfortunately found use in many programs for weight loss since the thyroid hormone increases metabolism and the rate of use of foodstuffs. In all cases except where true deficiency of hormone has been found by blood tests, the use of such therapy is inappropriate and can cause problems, especially if there is a risk of heart disease.

B. Drugs for diabetes
Examples: DBI, DBI-TD, Diabinese, Orinase, regular insulin, Tolinase

Diabetes mellitus is a complex disease associated with two major abnormalities. First, it is characterized by high levels of blood sugar (hyperglycemia) and changes in the use of foodstuffs due to either a lack of (or an inability to use) the hormone insulin, which comes from the pancreas gland. Second, it is characterized by an abnormality of tiny blood vessels throughout the body, which over long periods produce abnormalities of many organs and parts—such as the eyes, kidneys and nerves.

Two very general types of diabetes exist which differ considerably in their severity, their treatment and age of onset. "Classical" diabetes is associated with a partial or complete lack of insulin, usually starts (often abruptly) before age 30 or 40, and requires insulin therapy. For this reason it is often termed "insulin-dependent diabetes." It is also called "juvenile-onset diabetes" because it often starts in the teenage years or earlier. This type is more likely to be associated with a very serious condition called *ketoacidosis* (usually requiring hospitalization) which may occur with stress, infection or inadequate insulin therapy.

The other and much more common type of diabetes—often termed "maturity-onset diabetes" or "adult-onset diabetes"—is not necessarily associated with an absolute lack of insulin, but rather a dysfunction of the pancreas in releasing insulin or an inability of the body to use the insulin properly. It is more often seen in persons over age 40 and more frequently in overweight persons. Only 10–20% of persons with this type of diabetes actually require insulin, and sometimes only when they become otherwise ill. Most people with this type of diabetes can be treated by diet and weight loss, although a few may need oral antidiabetic drugs as well. People suffering from this type of diabetes seldom "get out of control" with ketoacidosis and seldom require hospitalization for their diabetes except for late-stage complications such as foot ulcers and arteriosclerosis.

The specific goals in treatment generally relate to those factors which cause problems and complications in diabetes. These include: (1) prevention of "spilling" excess sugar in the urine by use of diet or insulin or antidiabetic drugs; (2) prevention of infection by avoidance of exposure, adequate vaccination and special care with hygiene; (3) prevention of excess lowering of blood sugar (hypoglycemia) and (4) prevention of the arteriosclerosis and vascular changes associated with many of the longer-term problems, such as foot ulcers and arterial blockage.

There is considerable argument over whether there should be close control of the amount of sugar in the blood or not, although most experts agree that continual spillage of sugar in the urine is not desirable.

Most diabetics are taught to check their urine for sugar using tablets (Clinitest) or paper strips (Diastix or Tes-Tape). They are also sometimes asked to check for acetone (an early sign of ketosis) with Ketostix, Acetest or Keto-Diastix. In persons with insulin-dependent diabetes, urine testing may be done frequently; it is usually checked less often in most adult-onset diabetics. Clinitest tablets can give a false positive result in the presence of certain drugs, such as high doses of vitamin C (more than one gram per day) or the antibiotic Keflex, so other tests (such as Tes-Tape or Diastix) must be used.

Prior to the discovery of insulin in the 1920s, the outlook for persons with insulin-dependent diabetes was very bleak. Therefore, the discovery that this protein hormone could be extracted from the pancreas of pigs and cows for treatment was a great medical advance. There have been many refinements since, and insulin is now available in several forms, primarily differentiated by onset and length of action. The short-acting "regular" insulin is commonly used when treatment is first started and to give control during stress or illness, usually in the hospital. For chronic or long-lasting therapy, such intermediate-acting forms of insulin as NPH or Lente are used, which (depending on the individual) often require only one injection a day.

Insulins are now available in three concentrations: U-40, U-80 and the newer, more concentrated U-100 form. Because of some confusion over the various concentrations of insulin, it is usually being recommended that all diabetics convert to the standard form, U-100 insulin, which has specially measured syringes. In the future, this will help avoid errors or confusion associated with differing concentrations.

In the early 1960s, the introduction of a new group of drugs (some chemically related to sulfa drugs and thiazide diuretics) promised the potential of *oral* therapy ("oral hypoglycemics") for diabetics which would eliminate the need for insulin in many cases. Two general types of drug were introduced: the *sulfonylureas* which include Orinase (tolbutamide), Tolinase (tolazamide), Diabinese (chlorpropamide) and Dymelor (acetohexamide), which act to enhance the action or secretion of insulin; and the *biguanides*, including phenformin (DBI) which acts on the metabolic processes to decrease resistance to insulin action. These agents were used very widely in the 1960s, especially in older patients before it was generally appreciated that elevation of blood sugar appears to be an accompaniment of the aging process and does not always need treatment. It was often found that these drugs were not useful for true insulin-dependent diabetics, *but only for maturity-onset diabetics.*

In the 1960s, a large study of these drugs was undertaken to see if they were indeed more effective and safer than diet alone and insulin and diet. The results of the study have been the source of a great controversy in medicine since their publication. The study suggested that the drugs were no more, and possibly less, effective in preventing the long-term complications (stroke, heart attack and arteriosclerosis) of diabetes than other traditional therapy. Many have criticized the design of the study and its findings are still argued, but it did cause many physicians to look critically at their prescription of these drugs and generally to limit use to a select group of persons who could not (or would not) control their diet or could not take or did not require insulin. The *biguanides* (phenformin, or DBI) have been particularly criticized. Although effective in lowering blood sugar, they are also associated with producing a special complication called *lactic acidosis*, which requires more careful scrutiny by the physician. In general these drugs are used as therapy in addition to a well-regulated diet. In the absence of food, they can also cause a low blood sugar, or hypoglycemia. The government announced an orderly withdrawal of DBI from the market.

C. Oral contraceptives

Examples: Brevicon, Demulen 21, Enovid, Loestrin, Lo-Ovral, Micronor, Modicon, Norinyl, Norlestin 21, Ortho-Novum, Ovral, Ovulen 21

Oral contraceptives (the "pill") have been taken by

women in the United States since 1960. Although there are several types of contraceptive pill, the most common and most reliable is the type containing a combination of two synthetic female hormones, an *estrogen* and a *progestogen*. This combination-type pill, if taken regularly as directed, is almost 100% effective in preventing pregnancy.

The female menstrual cycle is regulated by several hormones and by interactions between these hormones. Among them are estrogen and progesterone (to which the synthetic progestogens are related) which are produced in the ovaries. The production of these hormones and of the ovum, or egg, released by an ovary each month, is stimulated by hormones from the pituitary gland, located at the base of the brain. Once the supply of ovarian hormones reaches a certain level, the supply of the pituitary hormones is depressed, working in a "feedback" system.

The minute amounts of additional estrogen supplied by oral contraceptives inhibit the production by the pituitary of the hormone that stimulates the growth, in the ovary, of the follicle containing the egg. The progestogen inhibits another pituitary hormone that triggers ovulation—the release of the egg. With no ovulation taking place, conception is impossible.

> **Most women who take oral contraceptives are now aware of their potential dangers—such as the possibility of increasing the risk of blood-clot formation. Because various formulations of the "pill" often have different effects on different women, your doctor may find it desirable to change the brand you have been taking if you experience any troublesome or annoying side effects.**

If by some remote chance an egg is produced, additional safeguards will stop a pregnancy. The progestogen contained in the pill has the effect of thickening the mucus in the cervical canal so that sperm cannot enter the uterus. Yet another function of the pill is to alter the lining of the uterus so that it would not be receptive to a fertilized egg in any case.

The estrogen-progestogen pill is taken for 21 days (sometimes a day more or less, according to the brand), usually starting on day 5 of the menstrual cycle. (The first day of bleeding is counted as day 1.) The pill is then stopped for a week. Within a few days of stopping the pill, menstruation begins. The amount of bleeding may be less than in a normal period, a fact which explains why women on the pill are less likely to suffer from iron deficiency than women who do not take the pill. Many women who have had irregular periods in the past may experience improvement in regularity, and some women with acne find that the condition improves after they begin taking the pill.

Women taking the combined estrogen-progestogen pill have reported a variety of side effects, including increased weight, depression, reduced sexual desire, cramps in the legs and dryness in the vagina. If contact lenses are used, after use of the pill for several months the eyes can become dryer and more sensitive to the lenses. Each individual may react differently to different contraceptives.

There are many possible adverse effects of taking oral contraceptives. The most serious of these is the risk—a relatively low risk—of thrombosis. Thrombosis is the formation of a blood clot (thrombus), usually in the deep veins of the leg or in the pelvis. If the clot moves to the lungs (where it is called a *pulmonary embolism*) it may cause death. In rare cases, another type of thrombosis may occur (in the blood vessels supplying the brain) to produce a stroke. In women over the age of 35, the risk of side effects is sufficiently large for many doctors to recommend alternate methods. These side effects include gallbladder disease and heart attacks (especially in heavy smokers).

Although the theory has not been conclusively proved, it is now believed that the estrogen in the pill may be the cause of this risk. Accordingly, doctors now tend to prescribe contraceptives containing the *minimum effective dose* of estrogen (0.05 micrograms or less), although whether this does in fact decrease the risk is not yet clearly proven.

Some women, however, are at risk from taking *any* amount of additional estrogen. These include women who have had a thrombosis, those with some heart conditions and those with past or present liver disease. For these women, another kind of contraceptive may be prescribed. One possible alternative is a pill containing only a progestogen. This pill is taken every day, instead of just for three weeks of the cycle, and it must be taken at the same time every day; whereas the estrogen-progestogen pill is effective even if 36 hours elapse between taking one pill and the next. The effectiveness of the progestogen pill depends mainly on its building up the sperm-deflecting mucus in the cervical canal; it apparently does not prevent ovulation. Even if the pill is taken every 24 hours, there is still a slightly greater risk of pregnancy than with a pill containing estrogen and a progestogen. There are also some side effects, notably irregular and heavy periods.

D. Estrogens and progestogens used in hormone therapy

Examples: DES, Estradiol, Premarin, Provera

Although the oral contraceptives have enjoyed wide use for the last decade or so, female hormones also have been widely used in other circumstances, the most common being estrogen for treatment of postmenopausal symptoms. For example, Premarin (an estrogen preparation marketed almost exclusively for this purpose) is one of the most frequently prescribed drugs of any type. The wisdom of this widespread use is now being questioned, due to increased awareness of potential problems with long-term use of the estrogens. Clearly written brochures on the benefits and risks of such medication have been ordered by the government to be given with each prescription. Such leaflets should be carefully read. If you have any further questions, discuss them fully with your doctor.

The female menopause is a period of time occurring between the mid-40s to early 50s when the ovaries begin to lose their ability to produce estrogens and progesterone. Thus ovulation and menstrual periods usually become irregular, less frequent and finally cease. As the level of female hormones decreases, the feedback system through the brain and pituitary results in increased levels of the "tropic hormones" (FSH and LH). This process may occur over months or years. The same situation occurs, but more abruptly, when ovaries are removed surgically. The symptoms, which may or may not occur, are believed to be related to those changing levels of hormone in the blood.

The symptoms experienced in the menopause vary considerably in frequency, severity and duration. In addition to changes in menstrual periods, there are often symptoms of "hot flushes" or flushing, depression or irritability and mood changes, especially in the early stages. As menopause progresses, there are reduced secretions in the vagina, which may produce irritation during intercourse and predispose to bladder irritation. Approximately 25% of women (usually white women) experience loss of bone (called osteoporosis) and may be more susceptible to fractures, especially of the spine.

Estrogen therapy for postmenopausal symptoms is usually given in a cyclic fashion—that is, for three to four weeks—followed by a week off the drug, since this somewhat resembles a normal cyclic sequence, and it may be less likely to predispose to uterine cancer if taken in this way. Common estrogen preparations used include Premarin, conjugated estrogens and Estinyl. Some physicians will add a progesterone-like drug at the end of the cycle, to more closely resemble the normal cycle, but the real value of this remains unclear.

Estrogens are also used for other purposes. For example, they can be used to regulate irregular menstrual cycles, treat a disease called endometriosis and prevent pregnancy after rape (DES has been approved for this use). They are also used in two specific types of cancer therapy: cancer of the breast in certain postmenopausal women and cancer of the prostate in men.

Estrogens may have a variety of side effects and these are discussed in detail in the section on *Oral contraceptives.*

E. Steroids or cortisone-like drugs

Examples: Decadron, Medrol, prednisone

Cortisone and related steroids resembling the hormones produced by the adrenal gland were introduced as "miracle" drugs for arthritis in the 1950s. Subsequent experience reveals that the miracle had a very high price in the form of severe side effects. The cortisone-like drugs (called *corticosteroids,* or simply *steroids*) have now gained wide use, but their proper role remains controversial.

The paired adrenal glands, located above each kidney, are stimulated by the hormone from the pituitary gland, ACTH, to secrete several steroid hormones: cortisone, hydrocortisone and small amounts of male and female hormones, as well as certain other hormones. The corticosteroid hormones are classified in terms of two types of activity: *glucocorticoid* activity, the ability to affect sugar (glucose) metabolism; and *mineralocorticoid* activity, the ability to affect levels of the minerals sodium and potassium. Cortisone and hydrocortisone each exhibit some of both activities, which relate to their uses and side effects when used as medication. Many synthetic steroid hormones are produced that have similar activity to the natural hormones (cortisone and hydrocortisone) and, as in the case of prednisone, are more frequently used.

The corticosteroid hormones are used both as "replacement therapy" when the adrenal glands are not functioning (as in Addison's disease) and in higher doses for drug therapy in a variety of diseases. In replacement therapy, the naturally occurring hormones are most commonly used. In drug therapy, such synthetic corticosteroids as prednisone, methylprednisolone (Medrol) or triamcinolone (Kenalog) are used, partly because of their lower mineralocorticoid effect resulting in fewer problems of salt retention, edema and potassium loss.

Corticosteroids have a broad spectrum of effects on the body, some of which can be very helpful in treating diseases, and some of which can cause severe unwanted side effects and reactions. The primary useful effects are associated with the "glucocorticoid" activity. They include suppression of inflammation (redness and swelling of an area), which is useful in treating such diverse conditions as poison ivy and poison oak, ulcerative disease of the colon (ulcerative colitis) and various types of acute arthritis.

In many cases, corticosteroids are used without a clear understanding of exactly how they work, although they are clearly known to be successful. These drugs have nevertheless been used in the treatment of a very wide variety of acute and chronic diseases. The list is long: rheumatoid arthritis; certain collagen diseases (such as lupus erythematosus); certain types of chronic hepatitis; such serious widespread skin diseases as psoriasis; acute severe bronchial asthma and blood diseases such as leukemia. In addition, they have been tried for treating shock and certain neurologic diseases (such as multiple sclerosis), where their effectiveness is a matter of debate.

The many significant adverse effects of these hormones used in high doses are clearly related to both the dose and duration of time given. Thus, a few days of even relatively high-dose therapy will not often cause problems. But beyond one to two weeks, problems invariably begin to appear. The glucocorticoids, in excess dose, usually cause a variety of metabolic changes. So, for example, the blood sugar often increases (which can bring out diabetes in those predisposed), and the deposits of body fat become gradually redistributed—the face often gets rounded ("moon face") and fat is often deposited on the back of the neck ("buffalo hump") and in the abdominal area. There is usually a weight gain, although this is partly due to the "mineralocorticoid" effects of salt and water retention.

As in the case of other hormones, a high level of adrenocorticosteroid hormone signals the master gland, the pituitary, to decrease release of ACTH, the tropic hormone that stimulates the adrenal gland to produce the steroid hormone. If a steroid is given at high levels for a long time, the adrenal gland gradually shrinks due to a lack of stimulation, and after a time stops working. Therefore, once corticosteroids have been taken for longer periods (greater than two to three weeks) they must be *gradually* withdrawn to allow the adrenal gland to recover. This withdrawal can be done in a variety of ways. If steroids, such as prednisone, have been taken for months or years, it may take several months to completely discontinue administration of the drug safely. A person on corticosteroids for long periods should wear appropriate identification since in time of stress (an auto accident or surgery), he or she may need extra steroids to prevent serious complications.

Corticosteroids are given by mouth, by injection, as enemas (to treat ulcerative colitis), in the eyes (to treat inflammation) and are applied to the skin (steroid creams and ointments are one of the most frequently used dermatologic drugs). Recently, they have been used as aerosols (Vanceril, or beclomethasone) in treatment of chronic asthma. They are used locally by injection into joints or into other inflamed areas such as large acne lesions. The overall principle has been to use corticosteroids locally when possible, and in high doses only for short periods. The pituitary gland hormone ACTH (adrenocorticotropic hormone), which stimulates the adrenal gland to produce steroids, is sometimes administered by injection in place of the corticosteroid hormones. It also is used to test the adrenal gland for its level of functioning. Except when used as a test, it is usually less preferable than the actual hormone.

In summary, corticosteroid hormones have occasional use as replacement therapy but extremely wide use as drug therapy for many ailments of many organs. The problems with the drug emphasize the critical need for careful cost versus benefit analysis whenever long-term use is considered.

VII Stimulants and drugs for weight loss

Examples: amphetamines, Dexedrine, Dexamyl, Ionamin, Ritalin, Tenuate

The only method of losing weight safely and maintaining the reduced weight is to reduce one's intake of calories by eating less and adhering to a balanced diet low in starches, sweets and fats. "Crash" diets or radical diets may achieve a sudden weight loss, but they fail to establish a healthy pattern of food intake needed for maintaining the reduced weight. This kind of diet is almost invariably followed by an overeating spree and, consequently, a weight increase.

Many drugs have been used in the treatment of obesity. None has been shown to be consistently effective in producing long-lasting weight loss. Some are very hazardous.

A group of drugs frequently prescribed in reducing programs are the *anorexiants* (or *anorectics*). They include the amphetamines and other drugs which resemble amphetamines. Their name, anorexiants, is derived from the medical term *anorexia*, which means loss of appetite; they can cause a loss of appetite for a period of a few days to several weeks. It is important to realize that the drug itself has no direct effect on body weight; what it does is to stimulate the central nervous system in such a way as to make you want less food. Soon, however, the body will develop a tolerance for the drug. As the appetite-suppressant effect wears off, the person taking the drug will resume his or her former eating habits—unless he or she has, in the meantime, resolutely established a restricted diet. In other words, an anorexiant might help to *launch* a diet, but it will not do the *work* of dieting for the person hoping to lose weight.

The amphetamines are particularly dangerous in terms of their potential for psychologic dependence. Widespread abuse of these drugs in recent years has led to their being classified by Federal law as restricted drugs. The number of amphetamines prescribed by doctors and the number kept in stock by pharmacists must be reported and must not exceed certain limits. By law, package inserts on amphetamines must at present bear the following warning:

> Amphetamines have a high potential for abuse. They should thus be tried only in weight reduction programs for patients in whom alternative therapy has been ineffective. Administration of amphetamines for prolonged periods of time in obesity may lead to drug dependence and must be avoided.

It should be noted, however, that the U.S. Food and Drug Administration would like to ban the use of amphetamines in weight-control programs; this may be forthcoming.

The use of diuretics in reducing programs can be hazardous, because they deprive the body of necessary minerals (such as potassium). They have no place in legitimate weight-reducing programs.

Preparations containing thyroid hormone are often used inappropriately by weight-control clinics; they speed up the metabolism of the cells and so cause the body to burn up more calories. These drugs should be used only when the person is suffering from hypothyroidism and not for simple weight control.

Another hormone often used in reducing clinics in the

U.S. is human chorionic gonadotropin (HCG) a product of the placenta similar to a pituitary hormone. Its weight-reducing properties—if any—have not been clearly established. Most clinics giving HCG injections also put their patients on a very low-calorie diet, which will in itself cause a weight loss. When the treatment is stopped the patient often quickly regains the lost weight.

To sum up, *drugs have very limited usefulness in weight-reduction programs.* A balanced, low-calorie diet is the only sure, safe way to lose weight.

VIII Drugs for asthma and lung disease

Examples: Aarane, Alupent, Bricanyl, Bronkosol, Elixophyllin, Intal, Marax, Quibron, Tedral, theophylline, Vanceril

Most drugs used to open the airways of the lungs act on the muscles in the bronchial tubes and are called *bronchodilators.* They include epinephrine, theophylline, Tedral, Marax and Isuprel. It is now believed that most of these drugs achieve their results by regulating the amount of a hormone-like substance called "cyclic AMP" in the bronchial muscles.

An increase of cyclic AMP in these muscles causes them to relax. When the substance is used up, the muscle tends to contract again. One group of bronchodilators acts to increase the production of cyclic AMP and so relax the muscles. These are drugs related to adrenaline (epinephrine), such as ephedrine, Brethine and Alupent. If these drugs are used continually, the body may develop resistance (or tolerance) to their effects and they will become less useful. They can also have adverse effects including an increased heart rate, palpitations, high blood pressure, trembling and dizziness.

Another group of bronchodilator drugs acts in a preventive way by inhibiting the breakdown of cyclic AMP in the bronchial muscles, This preventive action has the same result as the increased production of cyclic AMP caused by the first group of drugs; it raises the level of cyclic AMP and so helps the muscles to relax. This second group of drugs includes theophylline and others resembling it, such as aminophylline and Choledyl. Adverse effects of these drugs include rapid heart rate, loss of appetite, nausea and vomiting.

Bronchodilators can be taken in a number of ways. Most of them are available in inhalers, which permit small droplets of the drug to be inhaled through the mouth into the bronchial tubes. This is probably the quickest but not necessarily the most efficient way to get the drug where it is needed. Bronchodilators are also given orally, by injection and even as rectal suppositories (in the case of theophylline).

Another group of drugs acts by preventing broncho-constriction from occurring in the first place. For example, in the case of allergic asthma—asthma caused by an allergic reaction—some antihistamines and other drugs such as Intal will block the constrictive action of histamine on the muscles and reduce the severity of an attack. However, they are not effective against all substances causing an allergic reaction.

In cases of severe asthma one of the cortisone-like drugs (such as prednisone) may be prescribed. These drugs are thought to act partly to increase the effect of the bronchodilator drugs and also possibly to prevent recurrent attacks of the disease. They belong to a group of drugs called steroids. Prednisone is usually taken orally, either for a short period with a dose tapering off gradually or on a long-term basis in a low dosage. Another type of steroid recently put on the market (Vanceril) is adminis-tered by inhaler.

It is important to remember that the immediate causes of bronchoconstriction can vary considerably. A person can be breathing completely normally, and then come in contact with something that causes his bronchial airways to close suddenly. Naturally, the wheezing and difficult breathing which result can be alarming, and it is important that he be prepared for it—by learning from his doctor how to use the drugs that have been prescribed for him, how long they take to act, and exactly how much and how often they should be used (excessive use of either inhalers or oral drugs may cause more harm than good and make subsequent therapy more difficult).

IX Drugs to treat infections

Examples: Achromycin-V, Ampicillin, Amoxil, Azo Gantrisin, Bactrim, Chloromycetin, penicillin, Polycillin, Erythrocin, erythromycin, Gantanol, Gantrisin, Garamycin, Robitet, Septra, sulfasoxisole, Sumycin, Laratid, Macrodantin, Mycolog, Mycostatin, Pediamycin, tetracycline, Vibramycin

Simply stated, an infection is the invasion of the body by pathogenic (disease-causing) microorganisms, including bacteria, viruses, protozoa or fungi. These organisms cause infections that can be local, such as a boil on the skin or pneumonia in the lungs, or general, as is common with typhoid, mumps or malaria, where many parts of the body are affected. The symptoms and damage resulting from an infection are caused both by the organism's invasion of tissue and the response of the body's defense system. The most common signs of infection are inflammation (pain, heat, redness, swelling and sometimes pus production), and often fever.

Not all microorganisms produce infections, and even those that can do not do so all the time. Those bacteria better at breaching the body's defense mechanisms are more likely to cause disease and are described as virulent. It is also true that the fewer bacteria present, the lower the likelihood of infection. This is why it is advisable to cleanse and cover open wounds or cuts. Location of the bacteria also affects their ability to cause infection. Under normal circumstances, with good standards of hygiene, the bacteria in the air, on the skin and in the mouth and intestine, are harmless. Individual response to potential invaders differs according to the state of the body's defense mechanisms, including natural antibodies and those that result from vaccination, plus white blood cells called phagocytes, which "eat" foreign organisms. When infection does occur, more phagocytes are produced and travel through the bloodstream to the site.

Some individuals have a decreased resistance to infection because of frequent bouts with diseases or due to certain drugs that reduce the effectiveness of the body's defense system. Included in this group are persons with kidney or other organ transplants, and those receiving anticancer or cortisone-like drugs. Exposure of such individuals even to small numbers of pathogenic organisms may cause infection.

Treatment of infection through medication aims to decrease the number of microorganisms or eliminate them without significantly harming the "host" (the infected person). By this means, the host can recover or continue to fight the few remaining organisms. Treating infections in people with very low resistance (as in persons with cancer) is much more difficult, and direct aids to the body's defenses, such as extra white blood cells, may be necessary.

> When taking antibiotics it is essential to follow your doctor's instructions to the letter. If you stop the therapeutic course just because you are feeling better and the infection seems to be resolved, there is a possibility that not all of the bacteria will have been destroyed by the antibiotic. Those that survive may not only begin to multiply again in the body, but some may have become resistant to the antibiotic. Also, taking more of an antibiotic at one time than your doctor prescribes can cause potentially serious side effects.

Antibiotics: their sources and functions

Medication used to treat infections caused by microorganisms (microbes) are called *antimicrobial drugs*, among which are antibiotics and sulfa drugs (discussed later). Antibiotics are themselves produced by microorganisms; they can be obtained from molds or other microorganisms and are then purified or modified for therapeutic use. For centuries, certain moldy materials were known to be useful in treating local infections such as boils. But not until 1928 did Alexander Fleming discover that the mold *Penicillium notatum*, growing accidently in a bacterial culture, could kill bacteria. Following this chance observation, the active substance was identified and called *penicillin*.

Antibiotics are among the most frequently prescribed

drugs today after sedatives and tranquilizers; they account for up to one third of some hospital pharmacy budgets. They can be used both to treat and prevent bacterial infection, but they are essentially ineffective against viruses and only effective against some parasites and fungi. Antibiotics may be *bactericidal* (killing the bacteria) or *bacteriostatic* (stopping bacterial multiplication). They act in conjunction with the body's defenses to overcome infection, but in serious infections, their timely help is essential to redress the balance in favor of the host and provide a chance to recover.

Some antibiotics are very specific; they kill some kinds of organisms, but not others. Infections that occur commonly, such as "strep throat," local infections of the hands and feet or gonorrhea, are known to be sensitive to particular antibiotics. For example, strep throat is almost always treated with penicillin, except in persons who are allergic to penicillin, when erythromycin is usually used. But in many infections, bacteria are collected from an infected source, such as the throat or urine, *cultured*, and tested for their *sensitivity* to a range of antibiotics (a procedure often abbreviated to "C and S"). In this way, the antibiotics most likely to be effective can be identified.

Antibiotics are given systemically by injection and orally, as well as locally on the skin, in the eye and other places. Many common antibiotics, such as tetracycline, are not well absorbed into the bloodstream if taken with food; thus, most oral antibiotics should be taken on an empty stomach. When taken orally, many of these drugs may cause diarrhea because the antibiotic affects some of the bacteria in the intestines. This effect is not usually a major problem, but in certain cases—for instance with clindamycin (Cleocin)—diarrhea can be a serious problem and any occurrence should be discussed with a doctor.

Antibiotics for treating infections are usually taken for at least five days, and more often for eight to ten days. *Completion of the course of treatment is most important*, even though one often feels better, with a normal temperature, after two or three days. If the medication is not all taken, any surviving, temporarily subdued bacteria may later cause a relapse. Worse, the bacteria may develop a partial immunity to that particular antibiotic making future treatment more difficult.

Antimicrobial drugs other than antibiotics

Certain antimicrobial drugs cannot be obtained from molds or other organisms. Apart from the means of production, the reasons for using these drugs, their mode of action, and the duration of therapy are the same as for antibiotics. Sulfa drugs (properly called *sulfonamides*), first used clinically in 1935, were derived from dyes produced in Germany in the early 1900s.

Sulfa drugs enjoyed wide use against bacterial infections and provided the first effective method of treating certain diseases, such as gonorrhea and bacterial meningitis and (most notably) pneumococcal pneumonia. But, for a variety of reasons, their use declined with the advent of penicillin and the subsequent development of other antibiotics. Many sulfa drugs (notably Gantrisin) are still widely used in the effective treatment of infections of the bladder and urinary tract.

Sulfa drugs, including co-trimoxazole, are usually taken in the form of rather large pills washed down with lots of water, since the drug has a slight tendency to recrystallize, which could cause damage in the kidney. This precautionary measure is always important, although the problem is less common with some newer sulfonamides.

Very few drugs are effective in treating viral infections. The only preparation with any wide use is idoxuridine (Stoxil), and that only for a particular type of eye infection. Considerable research is being carried out to find clinically useful antiviral agents, and hundreds of chemicals, both naturally produced and synthetic, are being tested. Unfortunately, many doctors are under pressure to "prescribe something" when patients come in with valid complaints, such as chest colds. Antibiotics are usually prescribed, although *they have absolutely no effect on the virus.*

Fungal infections within the body are fortunately uncommon and are extremely difficult to treat; but those on the skin or nails or in the vaginal region are susceptible to direct treatment. Such local fungal infections tend to persist or recur, and in many cases treatment must continue for lengthy periods. For example, griseofulvin, the oral antibiotic used to treat fungal infection of the nails, often needs to be taken for six months to a year. Tolnaftate (Tinactin), one of several antifungal drugs applied locally to treat common fungal infections of the skin (such as athlete's foot), commonly needs to be used regularly for 10 to 14 days to assure success. Other antifungal drugs, including the antibiotic nystatin (Mycostatin), are discussed further in the section on *Drugs for skin and local disorders.*

X Drugs for coughs and colds

Examples: Actifed, Afrin, Ambenyl Ex., Benylin Cough Syrup, Drixoral, Naldecon, Neo-Synephrine nasal spray, Novahistine, Ornade, Phenergan, Singlet, Sudafed, Tuss-Ornade

There are literally hundreds of drugs available by prescription or over-the-counter for treatment of the symptoms of colds and related problems such as hay fever and sinusitis. *None of the drugs cures colds, or shortens their duration, but some can relieve the symptoms.* Many of the drugs, especially combination products, are directed to some or all of the symptoms. Therefore, it is useful to define the symptoms and see how they can be relieved by the multitude of remedies.

The common cold is undoubtedly man's most wide-spread affliction, a source of general inconvenience and loss of work. Unfortunately, partly due to the fact that colds are caused by viruses (and no drugs are known to cure most viral illnesses), the successful prevention, cure, or even shortening of colds, is somewhere in the future. The much publicized role of vitamin C in preventing or curing colds is still argued, and its usefulness unresolved. Likewise, antibiotics (such as penicillin) have no effect on the true common cold due to a virus. For the present, therapy is aimed at relieving the very typical symptoms, which may vary in severity from person to person or from one episode to another.

Characteristically, the symptoms of a cold start with either the fairly sudden onset of sneezing and runny nose, or a tickling sensation or sore sensation at the back of the throat. This is sometimes followed by fever, headache, general aching, a husky voice or laryngitis, sore throat and often (a few days later) a cough. The symptoms may continue for as long as 7 to 14 days. A closer look at the types of symptoms will clarify why certain drugs are included in the medications commonly used. It is important to note that certain other disorders—especially hay fever, vascular rhinitis or allergic sinusitis—have many similar symptoms and are often treated with the same drug.

Sneezing and a runny nose that is also stuffy are usual symptoms of a cold, but are also present in hay fever, or allergic rhinitis, or sinusitis. These symptoms are due to the increased fluid and mucus production and swelling of the lining of the nose and the sinuses—hollow cavities which branch out from inside the nose above and below the eyes. There are actually three kinds of drugs which are used to relieve these symptoms: (1) decongestants, (2) anticholinergic drugs and (3) antihistamine drugs.

The sensations of a stuffy nose, blocked ears (due to swelling of the eustachian tubes extending from the back of the throat to the ears) and congested sinuses are due to swelling of mucous membranes in this area. The swelling in turn is due to dilation of blood vessels caused by either the cold or allergic reaction. Sometimes blood vessels will dilate from other causes, but that produces the same symptoms. Decongestants act to constrict the blood vessels, which decreases the swelling. These blood vessel constricting drugs, or *vasoconstrictors*, are found in nasal sprays such as Afrin or Neo-Synephrine and are also found in many of the cough/cold medicines such as Actifed, Sudafed, Allerest, Dimetapp or Ornade. The common decongestant component of these mixtures includes such drugs as ephedrine, pseudoephedrine, phenylephrine, phenylpropanolamine, naphazoline and oxymetazoline, to name a few. Most of these decongestants are effective, but they have some drawbacks. If they are used repeatedly, they begin to lose their effectiveness and greater amounts may be needed. Also, since they do cause constriction of all blood vessels in the body, they often raise the blood pressure and increase the heart rate somewhat. This is not usually a serious problem unless the person has high blood pressure or is taking drugs for high blood pressure, in which case it is worthwhile consulting a physician.

When the nose and sinuses are affected in a cold or allergy they respond by producing more fluid and mucus. If this is due to an allergy, it may involve the release of histamine. For this reason, antihistamine drugs such as methapryrilene, doxylamine, pyrilamine, brompheniramine, chlorpheniramine and diphenhydramine are found in a variety of cough/cold medications and may be helpful in drying the secretions. However they also cause drowsiness. In the absence of allergy, as in the common cold, secretions can be decreased if an *anticholinergic* drug (such as atropine or belladonna alkaloid) is used. Since most antihistamine drugs also have anticholinergic effects, which enable them to work on the common cold, they are the drugs usually preferred. The majority of cough/cold preparations do have either antihistamines or anticholinergic drugs in them.

Most persons with a cold develop a cough, often several days later. This symptom is a protective reflex which occurs in all persons to clear the bronchial tube of any foreign material, including mucus. In some cases, the airways are simply irritated and the cough is a reflex response. Drugs for coughs may act in two separate and sometimes opposite ways: (1) simply to suppress coughing or (2) to loosen or help liquefy the mucus in the lungs (called an "expectorant" effect). The expectorant may either decrease or increase coughing! By increasing the amount of mucus it actually stimulates coughing; on the other hand, it can reduce coughing by decreasing irritation from drying mucus. Cough suppressants, for their part, can act either locally in the bronchial tubes to prevent irritation, or in the brain to prevent the cough reflex. Codeine is one of the most effective cough suppressants known, but other cough suppressants also include the nonnarcotic drugs dextromethorphan (Romilar) and diphenhydramine, which is the antihistamine Benadryl. Although these medications are effective, the suppression of a protective cough which helps get rid of mucus and prevents obstruction is only indicated when coughing becomes repetitive and very bothersome. Coughs should only be suppressed for short periods.

The majority of cough medicines contain one or more drugs which are included for their expectorant effect—ability to liquefy thick mucus or phlegm to help with its elimination. Drugs which are used for this effect include terpin hydrate, glyceryl guaiacolate, benzoin, camphor, menthol and iodides. Unfortunately, although the theory of expectorant action is good, it has been difficult to determine whether any of these drugs really functions in quite this way. Since the problem has been recently emphasized, promoting an FDA review of cough and cold medicines, it may be that this issue will be clarified in the near future. In the meantime, it is likely that most cough syrups with expectorants will continue to be used in the hope that they relieve some symptoms—although simply drinking adequate fluids may be sufficient to give the same expectorant effect. Whether the extra drug is worth the expense remains to be seen.

Not uncommonly, a patient afflicted with a cold will experience one to two days of feeling tired, and may have headache, muscle aches or back pains, which are fairly typical of most other infectious illnesses. The major useful additional drug for the cold sufferer is one which reduces the pains and fevers, if any. The most commonly used drugs, which in fact do both, are aspirin and acetaminophen (Tylenol). One or the other of these may also be included in some cough/cold medications such as Phenaphen with codeine. Frequently, these drugs (aspirin or acetaminophen) are the only ones really needed for treating most colds, taken with lots of fluids and adequate rest.

XI Antihistamines

The term antihistamine refers to a class of drugs available over the counter or by prescription, which have a variety of uses, including counteracting some symptoms of allergic reactions, relieving itching in skin eruptions (especially those due to allergy), treating anxiety and decreasing nausea and vertigo due to motion sickness.

The numerous uses stem from the variety of pharmacologic effects that these drugs share. The most important is their ability to block the effects of histamine, a substance released by the body in allergic-type reactions. Histamine can cause nasal stuffiness, itching and redness of the skin and local swelling. Antihistamines are more effective when used prior to, or in anticipation of, an allergic reaction, or when used in a continuing allergic reaction, as in hay fever or allergic sinusitis.

Antihistamines may also cause varying degrees of drowsiness. The effect is sufficiently common that certain antihistamines (such as Atarax or Vistaril and Benadryl) are used as antianxiety or sleeping medication. In other situations, however, drowsiness constitutes a troublesome side effect, which can interfere with concentration, driving and operating machinery. Another unwanted effect of over-the-counter cough and cold remedies containing antihistamines to reduce nasal secretions is that they may do harm by drying the lining of the nose and upper respiratory tract. Not only can this lower the body's defenses against infection, but an actual increase of congestion can result.

Finally, antihistamines (especially Dramamine and Antivert) act on the brain to decrease nausea and vertigo associated with motion sickness and certain disorders of the inner ear, such as Ménière's disease.

Despite this wide assortment of effects, antihistamines are relatively safe drugs—bearing in mind that they can cause allergic reactions, that the drowsiness may be bothersome and that the sedation is additive to other sedatives, tranquilizers and alcohol. Antihistamines are generally inexpensive, especially in single generic ingredient forms, but are somewhat more expensive in combinations such as Orinade or Dimetapp.

XII Vaccines

Vaccines are not medicines, but they are given to almost every individual in the United States at one time or another and are a vital part of maintaining good health.

Vaccines and "antiserums" are used to build immunity against infectious diseases caused by bacteria or viruses.

Two kinds of immunity can be produced. In *active immunity*, the vaccine stimulates the body to make antibodies against the bacteria, the toxins produced by bacteria or the virus. If a person is then exposed to the infection, a protective mechanism already exists in the body to fight the disease. This immunity can last many years (as the 7–10 years with tetanus toxoid) or a very short time, as with influenza vaccines.

Passive immunity is obtained when the serum containing antibodies from another person or animal (called antiserum) is given after exposure to the infectious disease to prevent severe effects of the disease (as in rabies) or to counteract the toxin (as in botulism or tetanus). This type of immunity is very short in duration and is only given after the person has been exposed to the disease or toxin.

There are several types of vaccines. Some bacterial vaccines are made from small amounts of killed whole bacteria or from the toxins produced by bacteria (in which case the vaccine is called a *toxoid*). Vaccines for viral infections are commonly made from live viruses, which have been greatly modified in a laboratory so that they do not produce disease but do signal the body to produce antibodies to fight the harmful virus. This is why, in certain cases, mild symptoms are experienced—as when measles or mumps vaccine is given. In other cases, killed viruses are used.

There are some very general facts about vaccines or antiserums that are important to understand fully. In recent years, it has been found that some persons have failed to receive certain vaccines, such as measles or polio, and this has resulted in some outbreaks of these diseases which might have been prevented. For this reason, it is very important for everyone to have a record of their immunizations.

The majority of common vaccines are given in early infancy and childhood according to a recognized schedule. These include diphtheria and tetanus toxoid and pertussis (whooping cough) vaccine which are usually combined as DPT. The vaccine for all three polio viruses is given orally (but should not be given when suffering from diarrhea). Measles, rubella (German measles) and mumps virus vaccines are also preferably given in early childhood. Since diphtheria and pertussis are primarily childhood diseases, the only common vaccine which needs renewal in adulthood is tetanus toxoid, which should probably be renewed with a booster every 10 years. Further, if a person has a cut or wound associated with obviously dirty material such as rusty metal, there may be a need for passive immunization with tetanus antitoxin or tetanus immunoglobulin, depending on the number of previous tetanus immunizations and the type or age of the wound. The only other types of vaccination necessary in adulthood, except those needed when traveling to areas where contagious diseases are endemic, come when a person such as a hospital worker is exposed to a disease, such as polio.

The general recommendation for influenza vaccination is that the only persons who need it are those susceptible to severe effects from the illness, such as elderly people or those with severe lung disease (emphysema, or chronic bronchitis) or diabetes mellitus.

The principle of preventive therapy in stimulating the body to create its own immunity is old, but continues to be a very promising area of medical research. In the future we may well see vaccines or other drugs which cause greater immunity for the hepatitis virus, the common cold and other common viruses. Immunotherapy is also being studied in treating cancer, but its usefulness is not yet known.

XIII Drugs for skin and local disorders

Examples: Aristocort Derm., Cordran, Cortisporin, Flagyl, hydrocortisone cream, Isopto Carpine, Kenalog Derm., Lidex, Mycolog, Mycostatin, Neosporin Eye Drops, Synalar, Valisone

Many external or local problems are highly visible, disfiguring or uncomfortable, and a wide variety of preparations are made for application to the skin or body orifices, mostly to produce a local effect. There are literally hundreds of drugs used for local disorders, of which several rank among the most commonly prescribed medicines.

The most widely used topical (local) medications are the corticosteroid creams and ointments such as Valisone, Synalar, Cordran, Lidex, T.A.C. (triamcinolone) and hydrocortisone. These applications, which have a cortisone-like effect, are drugs of choice in many skin disorders with symptoms of inflammation and itching such as eczema, dermatitis and psoriasis. Because of their rather dramatic effect on some skin ailments, indiscriminate use of these products on every skin lesion has led to occasional problems with longer-term use. Some of the corticosteroids applied to the skin are the same as those given orally or by injection (for example, hydrocortisone and triamcinolone).

Topical corticosteroids seem to work better on moist skin, so moistening the skin is advisable before application.

This has also led to development of the "occlusive dressing." In conditions where steroids must be applied for many days, they are more effective if the area is covered with plastic wrap to seal in the moisture. This procedure is regularly used in the treatment of psoriasis. Long-term use of such topical corticosteroid creams often results in sufficient absorption of the drug to cause corticosteroid side effects and to decrease normal activity of the adrenal gland. The cost of many such trade name preparations is very high, but equally effective preparations are available by generic name.

> **Corticosteroid creams and ointments are widely prescribed for the treatment of various local disorders of the skin. However, because they are extremely potent drugs, continual application can cause side effects; long-term use should therefore always be under the close supervision of your family doctor.**

In contrast to antibiotic creams and ointments, local antifungal preparations such as nystatin (Mycostatin), candicidin (Candeptin), miconazole (Monistat) and Tinactin (tolnaftate) appear to be relatively effective applied locally. Because fungi are very persistent, the primary rule for treating fungus infections is to use a preparation regularly for the prescribed period, usually 10 days or more. Sensitization to these preparations is relatively low.

A specialized group of local antimicrobial preparations include creams or suppositories for *vaginal infections.* These occur most frequently in association with the use of birth control pills, but also through using antibiotics like tetracycline or with diabetes. They may also occur without any obvious cause as a result of changes in the vaginal pH (acidity/alkalinity) and to a multiplication or "flare-up" of the normal bacteria residing in the vagina. Under these conditions there is often a white discharge, with itching and burning. Vaginal discharge may be due to fungus infections, bacteria, Trichomonas or venereal disease, such as gonorrhea. The cause should be diagnosed by a physician or at a family planning clinic. If a fungus or Candida infection is diagnosed, it is usually treated with antifungal creams like Mycostatin (nystatin), candicidin (Candeptin) or Monistat (miconazole). If it is due to Trichomonas, treatment will be with an oral drug, Flagyl (metronidazole), sometimes with treatment of the woman's partner if it is recurrent. If the problem is due to neither, it is probably a bacterial infection. In this case, and if gonorrhea has been ruled out, vaginal creams containing sulfa drugs (such as AVC Cream, Sultrin Cream and Vagitrol) are frequently prescribed, although failure to use them for the prescribed course is a common mistake. Many gynecologists believe wearing cotton underwear and

normalizing the acidity of the vagina with simple vinegar douching may help eliminate the problem.

An unrelated local problem is pain, as in cuts, sunburns and other minor superficial wounds. One of the most common treatments involves the use of drugs called *local anesthetics.* The Novocain (procaine) and Xylocaine used by dentists to prevent pain are examples. Benzocaine is a common local anesthetic sold for relief of pain such as sunburn (Solarcaine). Many of these local anesthetics do not act on intact skin but may on burned skin or abrasions. The major concern about their use is the tendency for some local anesthetics (such as benzocaine) to cause allergic reactions. The general rule is to discontinue use if the condition worsens.

There are a large number of medicines which are used directly on the eye. Most of these preparations act locally, on the pupil, cornea or lids, but they can sometimes be absorbed into the system and produce side effects. A variety of preparations are used. Antibiotics, in combination (as Neosporin eye drops) or alone, are often used to treat local infections or corneal scratches. Some corticosteroids are also used, with and without antibiotics. These are controversial, because although they are essential in preventing corneal scarring in some cases, they can worsen the condition when applied to virus lesions, as in herpes of the eye. They can also predispose to fungal diseases of the eye if used for long periods.

Another common use of eye drops is in the treatment of glaucoma. Glaucoma is a disorder which causes a block of normal fluid flow in the eye and can increase the pressure in the eye. This in turn can cause increased pressure on the retina and optic nerve and cause blindness. Local drugs, such as pilocarpine (Isopto Carpine) can relieve the pressure. Oral drugs, especially the diuretic Diamox, are also used to decrease this pressure.

Some factors are very important when medicines for the eye are considered. First, it is very important to keep the droppers sterile to prevent infections. Second, if different medicines are applied to each eye it is very important to have all of them marked to avoid confusion.

The ear canal is a limited area where a few drugs are applied only to treat local infections or skin disorders. Since the eardrum closes the canal and forms a barrier, medicines do not usually reach the middle or inner ear by this route. If the eardrum is not intact, eardrops should generally be avoided. The most commonly used ear preparation is Cortisporin—a mixture of a steroid and antibiotics.

XIV Drugs for migraine

Examples: Bellergal, Cafergot, ergotamine
True migraine headaches are often confused with other types of severe headaches, which are due to stress or tension. Tension also appears to precipitate true migraines

in some people. Migraines are specific kinds of headaches, which may be preceded by a feeling (called an "aura") that the headache is about to occur. Migraines often occur on one side of the head and may be accompanied by a loss of appetite, nausea and vomiting, and transitory visual changes. They may last for hours or days. Migraine headaches are associated with constriction of some of the arteries to the head (which may produce the aura), followed by relaxation of the arteries, which produces the severe pain. However, the reason this occurs is not known. Symptomatic treatment of mild migraine often involves the same analgesics (pain-relieving medicines) used for other headaches, like aspirin or Darvon. But if the headache is severe, narcotics may be required to end the attack. The regular use of narcotics, even codeine, should be avoided because of the potential for addiction.

The most specific drug treatment for true vascular or migraine headaches is ergotamine (Ergomar, Gynergen) taken at the first warning of an attack. It may be given by injection, taken by inhaling, dissolved under the tongue or swallowed; in the presence of nausea or vomiting, the rectal suppository is effective. Ergotamine—a drug derived from *ergot*, prepared from the fungal parasites which cause a disease of rye plants—acts to constrict the arteries and possibly prevents the relaxation (pain) stage. Ergotamine is also combined with caffeine (in Cafergot) as well as with other drugs for sedation, nausea or to relieve pain (Cafergot P/B, Midrin, Bellergal, Wigraine, Migral). Caffeine appears to increase ergotamine absorption from the stomach, but the value of any such ingredients varies and has been questioned. Because there is a tendency for resistance (or tolerance) to develop, regular use of ergotamine to prevent attacks may hinder effective treatment of an acute attack.

Sansert (methysergide) has been found to prevent recurrent attacks of migraine if taken regularly. However, its use is usually discontinued at intervals due to serious side effects, which can result in extensive scar formation around the kidneys, lungs or heart. It is always used under careful medical supervision.

XV Drugs for seizures or convulsions

Examples: Clonazepam, Dilantin, Mebaral, Mesantoin, phenobarbital, primidone, Valium

When certain parts of the brain are disturbed by injury, high fever, damage from a stroke or tumor or from a congenital defect, there is the possibility that a seizure may occur. The seizure results from a brief disorganization of the brain's electrical impulses, which can be measured by an electroencephalogram (EEG). Physically, seizures range from localized twitches or arm movements to rigidity of one side or of the entire body (grand mal seizures), or by a sudden fall to the floor (akinetic seizures). The most common type of seizure has no known external cause and is

called *idiopathic epilepsy*. The majority of persons with seizure disorders can, with proper treatment, function quite normally.

There are only a few drugs suitable for treating epilepsy, and they are geared to the type of seizure being prevented. Only in rare cases, where seizures persist, must the seizure itself be treated by intravenous injection of drugs such as Valium or Amobarbital.

Epilepsy is treated with drugs from three chemical groups: the *barbiturates*, such as phenobarbital, methylbarbital (Mebaral), primidone (Mysoline); the *hydantoins*, Dilantin (phenytoin), mephenytoin (Mesantoin) and the *succinimides*, Zarontin, Celontin and Milontin.

By far the most commonly used anticonvulsant drugs are Dilantin and phenobarbital. Treatment for epilepsy is often started with one of these two anticonvulsant drugs, and the dose adjusted to prevent seizures. If one drug in normal dosage is not effective alone, the other may be taken at the same time, depending on the type of seizure. Although childhood idiopathic seizures do not require life-long therapy, those occurring in adulthood, such as after head injury, may. This requires initial physical and psychologic adjustment to therapy, but once stability has been achieved should represent no major problem. Use of both drugs mentioned can lead to adverse effects. In most cases, however, the drugs are well tolerated; but if they are stopped suddenly, especially phenobarbital, a seizure called *status epilepticus* (a series of fits) may occur, requiring diazepam (Valium) administered intravenously.

XVI Drugs for Parkinson's disease

Examples: Artane, Cogentin, L-dopa

Parkinson's disease (or Parkinsonism) is a brain disorder with a characteristic set of signs and symptoms, all or some of which may be present. These include tremor of the hands, feet and sometimes the head, which is greater at rest; rigidity of the arms and legs; slowness of movement; loss of facial expression; a tendency to drool and mental deterioration. Often these symptoms may be very mild and progress very slowly. This set of symptoms may be seen not only with Parkinson's disease but also commonly as a side effect of therapy with major tranquilizers such as Thorazine.

The symptoms seem to be due to damage or degeneration of a specific part of the brain. In cases not related to drugs, Parkinson's disease is due to deficiency of a substance in the brain called *dopamine*. This substance and another (acetylcholine) balance each other, making body movement smooth and coordinated. When there is not enough dopamine, acetylcholine is assumed to cause the symptoms. These facts form the basis for drug therapy in Parkinson's disease: medication to either increase dopamine levels or block the effects of acetycholine.

Until the last few years, only one group of drugs was

available, the acetylcholine-blocking or *anticholinergic* drugs, the most commonly used being Artane (trihexyphenidyl) and Cogentin (benztropine). These are prescribed for types of Parkinson's symptoms and are the only drugs effective in cases due to major tranquilizer usage. They are used to treat mild Parkinsonism, though their effect tends to grow weaker with continued use.

Treatment of Parkinson's disease was changed considerably several years ago with the introduction of levodopa or "L-dopa" (Dopar) which is converted into dopamine by the body. Initially hailed as the therapeutic answer to Parkinson's disease, levodopa's side effects have caused it to be reserved for more difficult cases. Nonetheless, it has considerably widened the possibilities of treatment, allowing many persons to function normally (despite some side effects) for much longer. A refinement to levodopa therapy was the addition of *carbidopa* in a combination product (Sinemet), decreasing side effects.

A third useful drug was introduced as an antiviral agent called amantadine (Symmetrel). It is now used alone in the treatment of mild cases of Parkinson's disease, or in combinations of the other two types of drugs, although it is only effective in some cases.

Treatment of mild cases frequently is initiated with an anticholinergic drug (for example, Artane or Cogentin) or amantadine, often in conjunction with therapy aimed at exercising muscle function and decreasing stress or tension. Levodopa or Sinemet is later added or substituted after gradual withdrawal of other drugs.

There is still much to be desired in improving the therapy of Parkinson's disease, particularly with respect to the frequency with which the drugs must be taken and reducing their side effects. But the fact that drugs can often correct very minute biochemical abnormalities in the brain brings some hope for development of more specific medication for this and related disorders in the future.

Fitness and Health

Dr. Tony Smith

In the last few decades we have had a virtual epidemic of heart attacks, stroke and other circulatory diseases. Most people now understand the importance of physical fitness in protecting against these serious illnesses and improving the quality of life. This article explains why fitness is so important and discusses some of the ways you can set about achieving it.

Exercise: the cult of the 80s

If Cole Porter were alive today he might have re-written his classic "Let's Do It" with reference to jogging rather than falling in love. Everyone in the public eye—from TV stars to politicians—seems to have bought a track suit and running shoes and to be out in the park early in the morning. Nearly 20 million Americans now ride bicycles; millions more play tennis and swim. The Chinese get up early to run around the block or to perform military-style exercises in their public parks. Even the relaxed and sedentary British have begun to take an interest in exercise, with 12,000 participants in a run around Hyde Park in September 1978 (sponsored by the *Sunday Times*).

Most of the impetus for this surge of interest in physical fitness has come from claims by enthusiasts that physical exercise not only promotes health but also protects against disease—especially against CORONARY THROMBOSIS ("heart attacks").

A healthy lifestyle does seem to make people feel better: even the most committed armchair baseball fan will admit to enjoying fresh air and exercise when on vacation. Indeed, many fitness fanatics claim that regular exercise can become as addictive as smoking or drinking, and that a week spent out of town and away from the swimming pool causes a real physical longing for the opportunity to "get the muscles moving again." Yet many men and women in their late 20s, 30s, or more, find that they have stopped taking exercise because they have been too busy. With their time split between work, making a home, raising children and building a social life there may have been little opportunity for physical recreation. They have become physically unfit in the same gradual, involuntary way that they have gained too much weight (and returning to fitness requires the same kind of consistent effort as dieting).

The importance of being physically fit

Does it matter? Is physical fitness anything more than a fashionable cult for the average suburb-dweller with his car, his power tools for the garden and workshop, and his battery-powered golf cart?

The medical experts are for once agreed on this question. There is no doubt that lack of exercise is an important factor in the cause of coronary heart disease, which is the most important single cause of death in middle age in Western society. Exercise is not the only factor: smoking may well be more important—and diet, an individual's genetic inheritance from his parents, blood lipids (fats or fatlike substances, of which the best known is cholesterol), high BLOOD PRESSURE, obesity and emotional stress have all been shown to be relevant. However, when account has been taken of all these other variables, exercise can still be shown to protect against heart disease.

First of all, there is a mass of evidence that sedentary workers have more heart disease than do men whose work entails regular physical activity. One of the best-known research studies was done more than 20 years ago by Professor Jerry Morris in London. He looked at the staff of the famous red double-decker buses and compared the health of the drivers, who spent their days sitting in their "cabins," and the conductors, who had to climb the stairs to the upper deck scores of times every day. Not surprisingly, the drivers were found to have 50% more heart attacks than the conductors. However—as critics were quick to point out—among other factors may have been the men's health at the start of their jobs and the effect on the drivers of the mental stress of steering a massive bus through dense traffic.

These objections could not, however, be leveled at Dr. R. S. Paffenbarger's vast study of longshoremen in San Francisco. He assessed the amount of physical work done by different men and was able to divide them into two groups on the basis of their energy expenditure. Over a 16-year period of study there were 291 deaths from coronary disease; the frequency of these deaths was one third greater in the less active group—and the difference remained substantial even when account was taken of other factors such as smoking and blood pressure.

Regular exercise and heart disease

Next, there is equally good evidence that leisure-time activity influences death from heart disease. At the ultimate extreme, exercise enthusiasts have contended that no regular marathon-runner has ever died of coronary disease. Few of us, however, are sufficiently dedicated to run 26 miles—even once. At a more mundane level, New York doctors studied 55,000 men who enrolled in the New York Health Insurance Plan. They were classified on the basis of their energy expenditure at work and in their leisure time into light, moderate and heavy activity groups. During the 16 months of the study, 301 of the men had coronary attacks. The mortality rate in the light activity group was 49%—more than three times the 13% mortality in the men whose daily activities included heavy exertion.

Equally convincing differences were found in London by Professor Morris again. He recorded the leisure-time activities of 17,000 government office workers and

Most people now appreciate the importance of physical fitness in maintaining health and improving the quality of life.

classified these into vigorous exercise (swimming, hill climbing, cutting down trees, heavy digging, or building in stone) and light exercise (golf, home decorating, lawnmowing, carpentry). During the follow-up period, 232 of the men had heart attacks—and these were found to be only one third as frequent in men who took vigorous exercise as in those who did not.

Large-scale postmortem studies of men dying of conditions other than heart disease have confirmed the protection given by regular exercise: men whose occupations involved physical labor have less coronary disease than do sedentary workers. Again the picture is seen at its clearest in marathon runners; one man who died of cancer at the age of 70 was Clarence de Mar, who won the Boston marathon on seven occasions. His coronary arteries were

The results of careful scientific studies show that men who regularly devote their leisure time to some form of vigorous physical activity (such as hill climbing or heavy digging—above) are up to three times less likely to suffer a heart attack than those whose leisure-time activity includes only light exercise (such as carpentry or playing golf—right).

virtually free of fatty deposits or atheroma (see ATHEROSCLEROSIS) and were more than twice the average diameter of men of his age.

Simply because these research studies have concentrated on men is no reason for women to believe they are immune to coronary disease. Between the ages of 45 and 64 one quarter of all deaths in women are from heart disease, and in older women the proportion is even higher. The risk factors are just the same as in men—smoking, overeating, lack of exercise, and raised blood pressure—with the addition of a small but significant risk from the use of oral contraceptives.

Other factors associated with heart disease

Simply because there are so many other factors, it has been argued that exercise may be linked only indirectly with heart disease and that there may be no true association. Health fanatics, the argument runs, not only go out running; they also tend to be nonsmokers, near vegetarians and underweight. This possibility was considered in several of the later research investigations. People employed in the London civil service, for example, were known to be very similar in social background, in financial status and in their material possessions. Those who took a lot of vigorous exercise were found to be no different from the rest in their physical or mental makeup—exercise was as frequent in the tall as in the short and in the heavy as in the light.

What is still far from clear, however, is the mechanism by which exercise protects against coronary disease. There is some evidence that regular vigorous exercise affects the metabolism of fats and so alters the proportions of different fat-consuming compounds in the bloodstream.

Cholesterol

Such an effect might be expected, since regular exercise is known to consume fat as well as other sources of energy—as is obvious by the fact that exercising can help to shed excess weight. However, so long as research workers used the blood CHOLESTEROL levels as their measure of circulating lipids they were unable to show any convincing effects. Some reports claimed that exercise lowered the cholesterol; others found that it did not.

High-density lipoproteins may protect against heart disease

More recent research, however, has shown that a better biochemical measure of susceptibility to coronary disease is the proportion of high-density and low-density forms of lipoproteins (emulsified compounds of cholesterol, triglycerides and protein). A relative excess of high-density lipoproteins (HDL) and a relative lack of low-density lipoproteins (LDL) seems to protect against heart disease—and this is, in fact, the composition of lipoproteins found in people who take regular exercise. Furthermore, a change in the ratio of HDL to LDL can be shown to occur during the course of an exercise program.

Blood pressure

Exercise also has some effect on the blood pressure. High blood pressure (hypertension) is known to be linked with heart disease (and also with STROKE). Trained sportsmen and women have lower blood pressures than the rest of the population, and several research studies have shown that the systolic (upper) and diastolic (lower) blood pressure may be lowered by about 10 points by exercise programs. Surprisingly, there is no consistent effect on body weight: often it seems that exercise leads to an increased appetite that compensates for the raised expenditure of energy.

Since the cause of serious and fatal heart attacks is usually THROMBOSIS in a coronary artery, exercise might be expected to have an effect on blood clotting; there is some prolongation of the clotting time and an increase in the rate at which small clots are dissolved by the bloodstream. Again, these effects are not striking.

Emotional stress and heart disease

Overall, then, exercise seems to have a small but distinctly beneficial action on many of the physical processes known to be of importance as causes of heart disease. Possibly it may also have important psychological effects, for the link between emotional stress and heart disease is one of the most perplexing aspects of coronary disease.

Doctors find that among the 50 million Americans who take no exercise there are many who claim that physical fitness is of less importance than peace of mind. There is a popular stereotype of the hard-driving executive, working a 14-hour-day with only snack meals taken in the office, who is heading for an early grave. The concept was first given medical backing by the work of Friedman and Rosenman, who popularized the idea of the "Type-A" personality. Their studies showed a typical pattern of behavior in many men who had suffered a coronary thrombosis. These "coronary-prone" characteristics included ambition, competitiveness, aggressiveness, haste, impatience, restlessness, alertness and hurried movements.

The Type-A individual (previously discussed) talks rather than listens, constantly interrupts with impatient "Yes, yes, yes" comments and demands high-speed activity and instant responses from all of those around him. Usually he or she smokes heavily, drives aggressively, honks impatiently in traffic jams, swears at other drivers and accelerates away from intersections only to brake hard at the next stop sign. At weekends he is not content to relax with his family; he will either play sports competitively or find some other outlet (such as gambling) for his energy.

Without doubt there is some truth in the Friedman-Rosenman theory and it has been validated in several careful studies. Type-A behavior is a risk factor for coronary disease (after other factors, such as smoking, are taken into account, the risk is thought to be doubled in Type-A individuals) and it increases the risk of a second heart attack among men who have already had one. This difference is true even in closed, ascetic communities such as Trappist and Benedictine monasteries. Yet there are some highly active, driving personalities who seem to exhaust all their subordinates while they, themselves, remain in robust good health.

"Life events" and heart disease

A partial explanation has come from research into the effects on health of mental stress associated with the individual and his occupation—and with unexpected crises known to psychologists as "life events." Life events first came into prominence in the context of heart disease in the late 1960s, when several investigators reported that men who had had a MYOCARDIAL INFARCTION (another technical term for a "heart attack") often expressed dissatisfaction with their work, their families and their lifestyles. More detailed studies showed that in the six months or so preceding their heart attack many of these men had gone through one or more stressing experiences.

One of the pioneer researchers in this field, Professor Richard H. Rahe of the U.S. Navy Medical Neuropsychiatric Research Unit (San Diego, California) gathered data on life events from 4,000 servicemen. He found that the most stressing events were death of a husband or wife, divorce, or marital separation; death of a close family member; detention in jail; major personal injury; loss of a job and, finally, a major change in financial status. Rahe allotted these events (and many others) points on a rating scale, and found that in men who had a major illness the mean score in the preceding year was 164, while in healthy men the score averaged only 72. When the life event scoring system was applied to men admitted to the hospital in Stockholm following a heart attack, there was clear evidence that the score had risen progressively year by year for about three years before the heart attack. Many of the stresses had developed at work, especially conflicts between the men and their supervisors.

The other well-authenticated association between emotional stress and heart disease is the so-called "heartbreak death" that occurs in survivors of married couples after the death of one partner. In the first six months after the death of a husband or wife there is a greatly increased risk of a heart attack in the surviving spouse. Nearly 5% of widowers aged over 45 die within six months of their wives, mostly from coronary disease. Many old people die shortly after major anniversaries such as 90th or 100th birthdays—as if the emotional strain of achieving the milestone had drained their systems.

Emotion, exercise and health

How does emotion have such a profound effect on the heart? In the 18th century the British surgeon John Hunter (1728-1793), aware that he had coronary disease, was said to have declared that his life was "at the mercy of any fool who shall put me into a passion"—and proved his point by dropping dead during an angry committee meeting.

All middle-aged men and most middle-aged women in Western cultures have some coronary disease (probably as a result of their high-calorie, high-fat diets). The extent of the atheromatous thickening of their coronary arteries is highly variable, however. There is growing evidence that one of the factors responsible for this variability is the interaction of emotion and exercise.

Man is provided by nature with a quick response system to cope with physical dangers—the saber-toothed tiger in his caveman days, the bolting horse more recently. In the face of danger the brain responds through the sympathetic nervous system, releasing two hormones—epinephrine (adrenaline) and norepinephrine (noradrenaline). The surge of these hormones through the circulation speeds the heart rate and increases blood flow to the muscles and away from the skin (causing the pallor seen in intense fear). The lungs work faster, priming the circulation with oxygen, and reserves of sugars and fats are released into the bloodstream to provide the muscles with the fuel they will need for combat—or for flight at top speed, if that seems the better option.

Unfortunately for Western man, most of the stresses and dangers that now confront him do not call for a vigorous sustained physical response. The quarrel with a foreman is unlikely to end in a fight; the frustrations of traffic jams, the apprehension of job interviews, and the excitement of gambling—all of these stresses have the same biological results, an increased secretion of epinephrine and norepinephrine and so an increase in the amounts of sugars and fats in the bloodstream. When these fuel supplies are not used up by the muscles they stay in the circulation and form fatty deposits on the blood vessels.

One explanation for the beneficial effects on health of regular exercise is that it provides a means of "burning off" the excess fats and sugars that have accumulated during episodes of emotional stress. The same theory helps to explain why someone who responds angrily and emotionally to day-to-day frustrations and irritations may be at higher risk of a heart attack.

Answers to some commonly asked questions

Confusing as the picture may be, the arguments in favor of exercise have proved convincing enough to persuade millions of middle-aged men and women to take it up. These newcomers to physical training have many questions to ask. What sort of exercise should they take? How much is enough? How often? And how regularly—does it matter, for example, if jogging is abandoned in the dark, wet winter months?

These question are best answered by looking at our knowledge of the nature of physical fitness and the effects of training. A healthy individual's ability to perform physical tasks—such as running, climbing stairs, walking around a golf course, or playing tennis—depends, firstly, on the condition of the muscles he uses and, secondly, on the condition of his heart and lungs.

Keeping the muscles in trim

Muscle power is usually determined during youth and declines relatively slowly; at the age of 65, muscular strength is still 80% of the maximum at the age of 25. Both muscle bulk and strength do decline with age and with disuse, however. At its most extreme the effects of disuse on the muscles can be dramatic. Someone in good physical trim who breaks a leg skiing or in a traffic accident, and who has to spend two or three weeks in bed, will find that his muscles become weak and flabby even in that short time.

Physical therapists will do their best to slow this deterioration; but despite their efforts the patient will find walking difficult when he is first allowed out of bed, and he will take months to recover his previous stamina. The explanation is that muscles thrive on work. Regular contraction of muscle fibers against a load—the sort of exercise done by weight lifters, shot-putters and other "heavy" sportsmen—increases muscle bulk as well as muscle strength. This "work hypertrophy" is very obvious in professional sportsmen: soccer players have massive thighs, while in tennis professionals one arm is often noticeably bulkier than the other.

Not surprisingly, then, anyone who takes up jogging, tennis, or some other sport after years following a sedentary lifestyle will find that his muscles fatigue easily and that they cannot produce the power asked of them. Yet even someone who is totally out of condition may be able to produce a massive muscular effort for a few seconds, but usually he will not be able to sustain this effort.

Energy consumption of muscles

Muscular work requires energy and the source of energy in the body is the oxidation ("burning") of sugars. In strenuous exercise, such as running at top speed, the rate of consumption of energy is so high that the body cannot supply enough oxygen to the muscles. The anaerobic (literally, "airless") exercise can be sustained for a few seconds—perhaps as much as a minute—but no longer. The chemical wastes (mostly lactic acid) accumulate in the muscles, causing them to ache; a second critical factor is the speed of release of sugars from the stores in the muscles. Once the intense exertion is over, the heart and lungs continue to work hard for some minutes to compensate for the relative lack of oxygen: in physiologists' terms the muscles have built up an "oxygen debt" which has to be repaid.

The amount of anaerobic work that the muscles can do, and thus the maximum size of the oxygen debt, gives an index of physical fitness. Both decline with age. Both can be increased with physical training; indeed, measurement of the size of the oxygen debt is a good measure of the effects of training.

In less strenuous exercise, such as jogging or swimming, someone who is fit can continue at the same pace for long periods—sometimes for several hours. Here the energy consumption by the muscles is balanced by the intake of oxygen from the lungs and the exercise is described by physiologists as "aerobic." As long as the metabolism remains aerobic there is no accumulation of waste products such as lactic acid and thus no pain.

Why, then, does the unfit jogger find that he has to pause for a rest after only a hundred yards or so? There are two limiting factors. Firstly, the rate at which the muscles can use oxygen to convert sugars into energy varies with fitness, and one of the effects of training is to increase oxygen uptake by the muscles. While the muscular energy comes from *aerobic* metabolism there will be few symptoms of fatigue. However, if the energy required to fuel the exercise is greater than can be provided aerobically the muscles will move over to anaerobic metabolism, with its attendant build-up of lactic acid, oxygen debt and—consequently—pain and exhaustion.

The second limiting factor is the supply of oxygen and sugars to the muscles by the heart and lungs. In many cases these "cardiorespiratory" factors are more important than any flabbiness of the muscles. The lungs lose some of their elasticity with aging; their efficiency may also be reduced by chronic structural disease such as EMPHYSEMA and by functional disorders such as ASTHMA. In medical examinations, lung function may be assessed by measuring the volume of air they can contain or (more usually) the amount of air that can be breathed out and the speed of air flow. These indices of lung function all show a regular decline with age; but there are reversible factors, too,

Swimming at a moderate pace is an example of "aerobic" exercise—where oxygen intake from the lungs is sufficient to balance energy expenditure. A fit person can sustain such an effort for long periods, whereas "anaerobic" exercises (e.g. sprinting)— where the body cannot supply enough oxygen to the muscles—can only be sustained for short bursts. The amount of anaerobic work the muscles can do is an indication of one's fitness.

especially the effects of smoking and of the chronic BRONCHITIS so commonly associated with it.

No matter how good the lungs, the transport of oxygen to the muscles depends as much or more upon blood flow. At rest the heart pumps out about 5 liters of blood each minute. During vigorous exercise a fit young adult can raise this "cardiac output" to as much as 30 liters a minute. The volume of blood pumped out by the heart depends on two variables: the amount pumped in each beat (the *stroke volume*) and the number of beats each minute (the *heart rate*).

In common with other physical characteristics, the maximum cardiac output declines with age—but, again, the rate of this decline can be slowed by physical training.

The effects of training

What, then, are the effects of exercise on the muscles, heart, and lungs? Clearly this depends on the activity chosen and on the motivation of the individual concerned.

In anyone under the age of 50, the muscles should be in reasonably good condition even if no exercise has been taken for many years. Of course someone who has spent 20 years commuting by car between his television set and his office cannot expect to go for a five mile walk without suffering aches and pains in his legs. But he will certainly be in better shape than someone who has spent the last two weeks in bed and even a few days of graduated practice will get the muscles back into trim.

Isometric exercises and muscle tone

If the objective is an increase in muscle bulk (as in the case with a body-building course, for example) the best form of exercise is *isometric,* in which the muscle fibers are contracted and relaxed without any change in their length. The classic body-building pose in which the fingers of the two hands are interlocked and the arm muscles tensed is a typical isometric exercise. However, since only relatively small muscle masses are exercised at any one time, isometric exercises make few demands on the heart and lungs. Moreover, what effect there is on the heart is undesirable since vigorous isometric exercises can raise the blood pressure substantially.

Importance of regular exercise on the heart and lungs

For anyone primarily concerned with overall physical fitness, the ideal exercise is one which involves as many muscles as possible. Walking, running, jogging, swimming and, indeed, almost any outdoor sport fulfills these requirements. In addition to increasing muscle bulk, regular exercise also improves the use muscles can make of the oxygen circulating in the bloodstream. As a result, someone whose muscles are trained can do more aerobic work and so is less easily fatigued than someone who is untrained.

Unfortunately, the restoration of the heart and lungs to reasonable fitness after years of indolence takes rather longer than does toning up the muscles. Someone who starts jogging or running after a long layoff will very soon find his heart racing and his lungs crying out for more air. The body's capacity for physical work declines at about 1% per year from the age of 20 onwards. This decline can be slowed by attention to physical health, but its reversal is less easy. However, a trained 65-year-old man may have the same work capacity as an untrained man in his mid-30s. If exercise is to have its most beneficial effect on the heart and lungs, they need to be working at near their maximum capability.

While there are many elaborate ways of measuring this capability, the simplest and most convenient means of assessment is to record the pulse rate.

The pulse rate

The pulse rate is simply the pressure wave transmitted with each heartbeat along all the arteries throughout the body. The wave moves quickly—at about 15 feet per second—and may be detected wherever there is a large artery close to the surface of the body—for example, at the wrist, in the throat, on the upper surface of the foot and in the groin. Anyone embarking on an exercise program should learn to take his pulse at the wrist, by placing the first and second fingers flat on the inner surface of the wrist.

Practical experience with exercise programs at the City Gymnasium in London (sponsored by the British Medical Research Council) has shown that the safe maximum for the pulse during exercise can be calculated from a man's age and his physical condition. The basic guide is that the pulse should not be allowed to rise over 200 minus the age in years—so that a 50-year-old has a maximum of 150 and a 30-year-old a maximum of 170. However, someone who is totally unfit should add another 20-30 onto his age for the first few weeks of his training program.

The pulse, then, provides a natural monitor of the rigorousness of the exercise to be taken. Whether it is running, swimming, tennis or whatever, the novice should take his or her pulse at the end of 1, 5, 10 and 20 minutes and compare it with the target. If the rate is too high then the pace of the exercise should be slackened; if it is too slow then more effort is needed. Each week the maximum rate may be increased slightly; after a month it can be set at the level of 200 minus age.

The pulse also gives a guide to the effects of exercise in improving physical fitness. If after one month of running around the park the pulse rate at the end of the circuit is 150, then by the end of another month a circuit at the same speed will probably raise the pulse to only 120 or so. Top class middle and long distance runners often have phenomenally slow pulse rates when in peak condition: the great Finnish runner Nurmi and the contemporary New Zealander Walker both had resting pulse rates below 40.

Duration of exercise

How long should exercise be continued? Again there is no clearcut answer, but the pulse rate will provide a guide. So long as the pulse rate comes down steadily week by week after the same amount of exertion—say a 20-minute jogging session—then the exercise is having a training effect. Obviously the fall in the pulse rate cannot continue indefinitely; soon it will "plateau out." But as long as it stays at the low rate then all is well. Sadly, even a week or two taking it easy and missing out an exercise will be reflected in a rise in the pulse rate when exercise is resumed. In practice most people find that 40-60 minutes a week is the minimum to maintain themselves in reasonable condition, best divided into 3 sessions of 20 minutes.

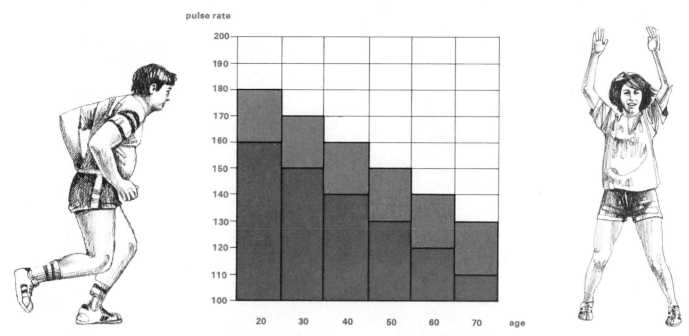

pulse rate

The safe maximum pulse rate depends on a person's age and physical fitness. The above chart gives a basic guide for each age group (colored bars). People who are very unfit should set a lower limit (gray bars) before starting a fitness program until their physical condition improves.

Exercise at home

Not everyone is willing to take exercise outdoors. People of all ages may be seen out jogging, but the idea may not appeal to residents of inner cities with dense traffic and no public park within an easy distance. Swimming comes close to the ideal exercise, but not everyone has regular access to a pool.

Exercise can be taken perfectly well at home. Probably the best known series of indoor exercises is the *BX fitness plan* developed by the Royal Canadian Air Force and proved by tens of thousands of satisfied fitness enthusiasts over the past 20 years.

The principle of the BX system is that it is progressive, building up from a very easy routine to a much more demanding one. The program for men is graduated into five phases with five exercises in each phase. The time required is only 11 minutes each day, yet the exercises will tone up all the muscles in the body as well as the heart and lungs. The first five minutes are spent on bending and stretching exercises and the final six minutes on running and jumping. In phase one, each of the bending exercises is done slowly—about ten repetitions in a minute—but in the later phases this is gradually built up to 30-35 repetitions, still within one minute. The length of time recommended for buildup to phase five varies from three months for men in their 20s to six or more for a man aged 40.

The program for women is basically similar, but there are ten exercises and only three phases. Again, all muscle groups are included and the pace at which the exercises are speeded up is carefully controlled. The BX system is only one of many systems that can provide healthy exercise at home, without the need for displaying your athletic prowess to the entire neighborhood (if that is your wish). Ideally, however, a combination of *both* indoor and outdoor exercise is more likely to result in a significant improvement in muscle tone and physical fitness.

Exercises of the kind just outlined have been proved highly effective in improving physical fitness. Just as with running or swimming, the pulse rate provides a natural monitor of progressive improvement. Within two or three months of starting the program many more of the exercises can be completed in the same time.

The gymnasium and health club

Some people find it easier to conform to an exercise program if they join a health club and carry out a daily or three-times-weekly session in a gymnasium. Certainly there may be psychological advantages to being a member of a group, and the skilled supervision of an athletic coach may be helpful in pacing and varying the exercise routine. Many people enjoy swinging dumbbells, weight lifting, and even gymnastics on apparatus such as bars and "horses." Without doubt, one of the drawbacks of an indoor exercise program is that it can become monotonous; in those circumstances the solution may lie in swimming or in finding a sport such as squash, handball or racquet ball that can maintain fitness while also providing mental stimulation.

Exercise and slimming

Most people who take up exercise in middle life assume that it will help them to lose weight. Often they have an

Sports such as squash, handball or racquet ball can provide a welcome alternative to the potential monotony of a gymnasium fitness program.

unpleasant surprise as they discover the effect of outdoor exercise on the appetite. Nutrition experts are agreed that the dominant factor determining optimum calorie intake is physical activity, and there is no escaping the need to fuel exercise with calories.

The crucial question for each individual is whether the calories consumed by exercise exceed the total contributed by the extra food eaten. Sitting or standing still, an average woman burns up 2 calories a minute; an average man burns up 2.5 calories. Brisk walking raises these figures to 6 and 7.5 calories a minute, respectively, and running may double them again. "Weight Watchers" put the same facts in simple terms: getting rid of the calories in a doughnut requires about 29 minutes of walking or 8 minutes of running. Clearly, the longer and more regular the exercise sessions, the more likely the calorie balance is to be negative—leading to loss of weight. Furthermore, the value of exercise lasts for some time after vigorous exertion: the body continues to burn up extra calories for as long as four hours.

Again, the benefits start to flow once the exercise level is raised from light to vigorous: the results of research studies have shown that the relaxation and relief from tension associated with regular, moderate to vigorous exercise tends to reduce feelings of nervous hunger between meals and so reduces the urge to eat.

Aches, strains and common injuries

Everyone has a story to tell of a jogger who snapped a tendon on his second outing. It would be shortsighted to deny that most new recruits to exercise programs suffer aches, pains and sometimes worse disasters in their early days. What are the most frequent hazards?

The most common injuries associated with running are blisters, strained and pulled muscles, tendon injuries, "shin splints," joint disorders and fractures. Anything more than a minor injury needs assessment by a physician; self-medication may be dangerous and lead to worsening of the damage to muscles and joints.

Blisters

Blisters are almost inevitable when soft skin suddenly sustains a physical battering that it has not experienced for many years. The feet are less likely to give trouble if they are provided with a *single* layer of socks inside well-fitting, soft running shoes. If blisters do develop, check the fit of the shoes; often a blister on the heel is due to friction from shoes that are too loose or have a rigid rim. Treatment is simple: soak the feet in warm water and apply a protective bandage. There is no evidence that the skin can be "hardened" by immersion in salt water or any other folk-remedy.

Strains and tears

The muscles often become strained or torn when the physical tension in the muscle causes shearing of some of the fibers. The runner feels a sudden intense pain in the calf or thigh and within a few seconds he will be able to feel a tender, hard swelling due to bleeding into the muscle from the damaged fibers. Sometimes the bleeding is severe enough to cause discoloration of the skin.

The immediate treatment of a muscle tear involves resting and relieving the inflammation in the damaged muscle. Often a cold compress (cloth strips soaked in ice water and placed over the painful region) will ease the pain. Anything more than a minor strain should be treated by rest and elevation for at least 48 hours. When (as is usually the case) the injury is in a leg, the limb should be kept flat or raised on a pillow in the bed. The muscle may be given support by a strapping applied by a physical therapist or nurse.

Forty-eight hours after injury a start should be made on exercises designed to maintain the full range of movement in the affected limb and to strengthen the muscle groups affected. But a delay of four to six weeks may be needed before a full return to exercise is safe. Expert advice should be taken on the timing of the return to full activity after anything but a very minor muscle tear.

Tendon injuries

Tendon injuries are caused in the same circumstances as muscle tears: the force exerted is too great for the fibers in the tendon. By far the most common injury of this kind is a partial rupture of the Achilles tendon at the back of the ankle. The pain is usually out of proportion to the severity of the damage, but occasionally the rupture is complete or nearly complete. Again, the injury should be examined by a physician or other health professional, since a complete tear of the tendon will require surgical repair. Minor tears of a tendon are treated in the same way as muscular tears.

Joint injuries

Inexperienced joggers and gymnasts often "turn" their ankles or twist their knees, causing severe pain and swelling of the affected joint. Joints are surrounded by a fibrous capsule, enclosing the cartilaginous joint surfaces and containing the lubricating (synovial) fluid. Parts of this capsule are thickened to form ligaments which maintain the bones in correct alignment. If these ligaments have become weakened from lack of exercise they are more likely to give way under strain. In their early weeks of exercise, new joggers should be wary of running over uneven surfaces—which may put an unexpected strain on the joints.

If a ligament is strained or ruptured, the joint will usually swell as the result of the accumulation of fluid within and around the capsule. Sometimes, as with a muscular tear, there may be discoloration of the skin from bleeding into the tissue. Treatment is basically the same as for a muscular tear: a cold compress for immediate relief followed by rest and a support bandage. If symptoms are severe, expert advice should be obtained; if a ligament has parted, or if there has been damage to the bone, the joint may need to be immobilized in a cast.

"Shin splints"

Shin splints is the name given by runners to severe pain in the front of the lower legs, just alongside the shinbone (tibia). The pain is experienced after a few minutes running and gets steadily worse, eventually forcing the runner to halt. The cause is swelling of the muscle groups in the narrow compartment at the front of the leg. This swelling prevents blood circulating in the affected muscles, thus creating a vicious circle.

Such pain is usually a transient symptom during a progressive exercise program. Provided the pain is recognized as a warning to ease off the intensity of exercise, it is unlikely to lead to serious complications. But if the runner insists on continuing, some of the muscle fibers may be damaged from the reduction in their blood supply. Very occasionally the condition becomes chronic, when surgical treatment may be necessary to relieve the pressure on the muscles.

Stress fractures

Stress fractures may occur in bones, without any direct physical injury, as a result of repeated movement. The best

People who embark on a program of physical fitness can expect some aches and minor injuries. These can include blisters on the soles of the feet, torn tendons, swollen, torn or strained muscles, injured joints, frostbitten extremities and even sore nipples!

known of these "fatigue fractures" is the *march fracture* commonly reported by military recruits in their early days of training. Pain just behind the toes is due to a hairline crack in one of the thin metatarsal bones in the foot. The pain may not be dramatic, but it is persistent and made worse by exercise. Once the condition is recognized (which will require an x-ray examination of the foot) treatment is straightforward: the bone will heal if the foot is rested and supported by strapping.

A similar fatigue fracture may occur in the fibula, the smaller of the two bones in the lower leg. Again the fracture will heal provided that the injured limb is rested; often a cast will be applied to the leg.

Other injuries

Since the start of the jogging craze in North America, some unexpected hazards have been reported in medical journals. Joggers (of either sex) may develop sore nipples owing to friction against their shirts: the treatment advised is protective strapping of the nipples. In cold weather, frostbite may occur in exposed parts such as the ears; there have also been reports of frostbite of the genitals.

Exercise and heart disease

What is the chance that jogging or some other exercise will precipitate a heart attack? Newspaper and radio and TV stations are quick to draw attention to incidents in which a jogger or swimmer suffers a fatal coronary thrombosis. However, with 40-50 million Americans taking regular exercise such events are inevitable by sheer chance—just as a few unfortunates happened to die within hours of vaccination in the 1977 "Swine flu" scare.

In fact, exercise now forms a central part of the rehabilitation of patients recovering from heart attacks. All the evidence points in the same direction: a graduated exercise program will hasten the physical and psychological recovery of a coronary patient.

Even so, anyone over the age of 35 who has taken no vigorous exercise for several years should arrange for a medical checkup before starting on a fitness program. If there are any signs of unsuspected heart disease, high blood pressure, or any other condition that might make exercise hazardous, the program may need modification.

The "anticoronary" lifestyle

Exercise is not a panacea guaranteed to prolong active life. No exercise program can compensate for unhealthy activities, such as overeating or heavy smoking. Anyone who is concerned about his or her health, and in particular about avoiding premature heart disease, needs to take account of all the known avoidable risk factors. Even if other members of the family have had heart attacks, there is no need for a defeatist attitude. In such circumstances there is almost invariably an identifiable cause of this susceptibility to coronary disease. It may, for example, be an abnormality in the blood lipids or high blood pressure. Abnormalities of this kind can be treated and the risks of a heart attack occurring are significantly reduced.

For most people in apparent good health the avoidable risk factors are well enough known. They include cigarette smoking, lack of exercise, emotional stress and overeating. The avoidance of emotional stress is mainly a matter of attitudes—of reassessing priorities, so that contentment and job satisfaction are rated higher than promotion or financial success.

Exercise may provide a key to the control of stress. The very decision to embark on a program of regular exercise should be evidence of a wish to improve physical health; psychological health obviously goes with it. There is little point in a Type-A personality fitting a 30-minute gymnasium session into an already hectic day. The anticoronary lifestyle is based on *moderation*—in diet, in consumption of alcohol, in smoking and in work and recreation. An unusually heavy daily work schedule is incompatible with this lifestyle, as is any occupation that causes recurrent anxiety, discontent and depression.

Choice of exercise

The choice of exercise should follow the same approach. A teeth-gritting determination to spend 20 minutes daily doing pushups is unlikely to last more than a week or two. The men and women who have made exercise a valued and indispensable part of their daily lives are those who have found their physical activities intrinsically rewarding. One man may choose to cut and split wood; another may prefer to swim every morning before breakfast. Possibly several alternatives will need to be tried before the answer is found, but the search is worthwhile.

Exercise is not just a passing cult, like skateboarding or canasta. Millions of Americans have found out for themselves that it may transform and improve the quality of their lives.

Pregnancy and Childbirth

Dr. Gordon Bourne and Dr. David N. Danforth

Pregnancy and childbirth are perhaps the only natural and normal conditions for which we consult the doctor as a matter of course. Our ancestors took it for granted that "nature" alone would see them through the whole process. Mostly it did, sometimes—tragically—it did not.

Today, the discomfort, pain and risk of pregnancy and childbirth have been enormously reduced both for the mother and child. The modern obstetrician can call upon a sophisticated array of tests and procedures to meet any difficulty. Dangerous conditions can be detected and treated before they become a real threat to the mother or child. But despite everything that doctors and hospitals now have to offer, it is important to remember that the active cooperation and wholehearted participation of the mother and her family remains a most essential element in the process of childbearing and the period that follows. Most of us today have children by choice, so it is more important than ever that women—and men—should understand what happens in pregnancy and childbirth.

Duration of pregnancy

The average duration of the normal pregnancy is 266 days from the date of conception. Fertilization (and therefore conception) usually takes place on the 14th day of a normal 28-day menstrual cycle. Pregnancy, if it is calculated from the first day of the last menstrual period, thus lasts for 280 days—which is the same as 40 weeks, or nine calendar months.

The easy method of calculating the expected date of delivery is to subtract three months from the date of the first day of the last menstrual period and then to add seven days. For example, if the last period was on June 20th, subtracting three months brings the date to March 20th; adding seven days brings the expected date of delivery to March 27th. This calculation is dependent upon a normal 28-day menstrual cycle in which OVULATION has occurred naturally on the 14th day. If the menstrual cycle usually lasts for *less* than 28 days, then ovulation will occur *earlier* in the cycle; thus, the expected date of delivery has to be earlier. On the other hand, if the normal menstrual cycle lasts for 31 or 35 days then ovulation will occur, respectively, three or seven days later. The expected date of delivery would then have to be *advanced* by three or seven

days, respectively. Most women will deliver within one week of this calculated date.

The average duration of pregnancy is not influenced by age, height, color, race, or climatic conditions. However, on average, multiple pregnancies do have earlier expected delivery dates than single pregnancies.

Ovulation

Ovulation is the production of an egg (ovum) by the ovary. The egg is produced 14 days before the onset of the next menstrual period. Its production is not related to the previous menstrual period and it is entirely fortuitous that ovulation occurs on the 14th day of a 28-day cycle. The ovum lives for approximately 18 hours after it has been shed from the ovary.

Fertilization

Fertilization is the union of a sperm with the ovum. Only one sperm can fertilize the ovum.

A normal ejaculation may contain up to 500 million sperms. It is most likely that up to one million sperms, or even more, may obtain access to the uterus and to the outer part of the Fallopian tubes. They will survive in the female genital tract for up to 72 hours. Although only one sperm is capable of fertilizing the ovum, it is probable that the presence of several sperms is necessary before the fertilizing sperm can actually gain access to the ovum itself.

Sexual intercourse which takes place any time after the 10th day of a 28-day cycle is therefore capable of fertilizing the ovum that is produced on the 14th day. It takes approximately 40 minutes for the sperms to migrate from the cervix (neck of the womb) through the uterus and up to the outer end of the Fallopian tube. If sexual intercourse occurs 24 hours *after* ovulation, then pregnancy is impossible in that particular menstrual cycle because, as previously noted, the ovum dies approximately 18 hours after it has been released from the ovary.

Implantation

The fertilized ovum is gently conducted down the Fallopian tube to the uterus. This journey normally takes seven days, during which time it develops sufficiently to embed in the lining of the uterus—a process it achieves by means of *chorionic villi* that have developed on its outer surface.

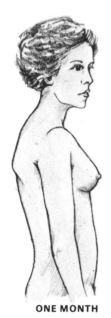 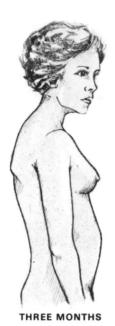 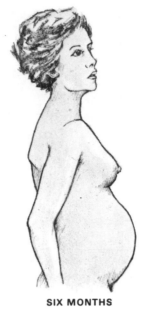 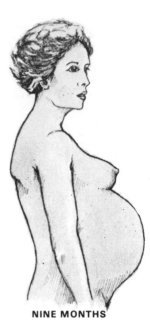

ONE MONTH　　**THREE MONTHS**　　**SIX MONTHS**　　**NINE MONTHS**

The first signs of pregnancy are the absence of periods, morning nausea and water retention. Breasts usually enlarge slightly and become tender. the skin becomes warm and the mother enjoys a "glow" caused by increased hormone levels. Her girth will not increase before three or four months.

The middle of pregnancy sees rapid fetal growth with corresponding maternal enlargement. Fetal movements are usually felt at around the 5th month. The mother's circulation and pulse rate increase. Toward the 9th month the enormous womb may make breathing shallow and large meals uncomfortable.

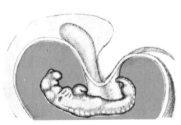 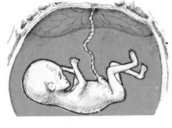  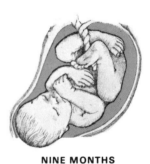

ONE MONTH　　**THREE MONTHS**　　**SIX MONTHS**　　**NINE MONTHS**

The fetus grows from a single cell, increasing its weight about 6 billion times. At two months, the baby's heart is beating and its limbs and some of its bones have formed.

At about three months, the placenta have developed and the fetus weighs 1 oz. (30 g). At seven months it weighs $2\frac{1}{4}$ lbs. (1 kg) and during the last two months it trebles in size.

The newly implanted ovum now receives all its nutrition from the mother via the uterus and will continue to grow until the 40th week of pregnancy or delivery.

Determination of sex

All human cells contain 44 chromosomes plus two sex chromosomes, making a total of 46 in all (23 pairs). The first 44 chromosomes are found in both males and females and affect the development of the structure and function of the body and are responsible for all hereditary characteristics. The sex chromosomes of the normal female cell are both X chromosomes; they are responsible for all the

female characteristics and are designated as XX. The normal male cell contains two sex chromosomes: one is an X chromosome and the other is a Y chromosome; they are therefore designated as XY.

The ovum consists of 22 chromosomes plus one sex chromosome which *must* be an X chromosome. Each sperm contains 22 chromosomes plus one sex chromosome which may be *either* an X or a Y chromosome. If a sperm containing an X chromosome fertilizes an ovum, then the ovum will contain XX sex chromosomes and the product of conception will be female. If sperm containing a Y chromosome fertilizes the ovum, then the subsequent cell will contain XY sex chromosomes and the product of

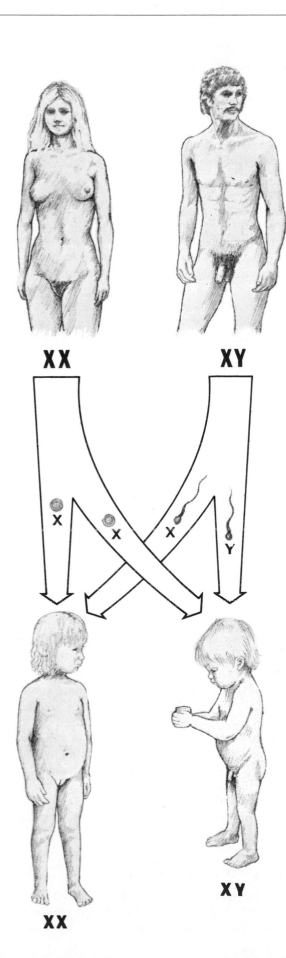

of this conception could therefore only be a male child.

The sex of the child is therefore determined by the male sexual partner. Some people believe that the internal environment of the woman's reproductive organs may in some way favor either "male" or "female" sperms, but the present state of our scientific knowledge is quite definite that the mother cannot influence the selection of sperms containing X or Y chromosomes, and that the mother therefore has no part in determining the sex of her child.

Development of the embryo

At the time of fertilization the "pregnancy" (product of conception) consists of a single cell. This soon divides into two, then four, then eight and then 16. By the time the fertilized ovum arrives in the uterus on the seventh day after fertilization, it consists of a sphere of cells surrounding a small fluid sac in which a number of cells have started to differentiate into what will eventually become the fetus itself.

The cells surrounding the sphere are known as "chorionic cells" and are responsible for the active embedding of the embryo within the lining of the uterus itself. They are subsequently responsible for the secretion of a hormone called *chorionic gonadotropin*, which in turn stimulates secretions from both the pituitary and the ovary that are essential for the continuation of pregnancy. Chorionic gonadotropin is the substance that is measured by modern biochemical pregnancy tests.

4th week

By the end of the fourth week after the first day of the last period the developing embryo is just large enough to be seen with the naked eye (if it were outside the womb).

5th week

At the end of the fifth week (or 35 days after the last period) the embryo measures about 2 mm in length and the cells within the newly formed amniotic sac are beginning to take shape into the major component parts of the fetus. Both the spine and rudimentary nervous system are just recognizable.

6th week

At the end of the sixth week the head, chest and abdominal cavities can be recognized. The rudimentary brain is completed and the spinal column and spinal cord are properly formed. The limb buds have appeared at the

From each parent a baby inherits 22 "body" chromosomes plus one sex chromosome (46 in all). The sex chromosome carried in the ovum is always X, that in the sperm either X or Y. The combination of these determines the baby's sex: XX chromosomes result in a female child. XY in a male.

corners of the body. The heart, which has been forming within the chest cavity, is commencing to beat and a rudimentary circulation is forming.

The face has not yet taken shape but small depressions indicate where the eyes and ears will develop. The mouth and jaw are also beginning to form.

7th week

By the end of the seventh week the limb buds have grown considerably and are recognizable as arms and legs, at the ends of which small clefts slowly begin to separate into fingers and toes. The heartbeat is circulating newly formed blood cells throughout the body, the intestines are almost completely formed and the liver and kidneys are developed but are small and not yet capable of functioning. The brain and spinal cord have grown rapidly and (with the exception of the nerves to the limbs) are almost complete. The head is forming rapidly, but is bent forward upon the chest. The situation of the eyes and ears are now obvious. The length of the fetus at this stage is approximately 1.3 cm.

8th week

The head of the fetus is large in proportion to the body. The face is beginning to assume recognizable characteristics. The limbs have developed and now possess joints and the first very small movements have begun.

12th week

The head has now assumed a more rounded form, but it is still bent forward on the trunk. The facial characteristics are easily recognizable. All the essential organs of the fetus are formed and the majority of them are beginning to function. The limbs are growing rapidly and their various components are easily recognizable. Fingers and toes, however, are still not completely separated.

Both the internal and external genital organs are developing. The length of the fetus at this stage is approximately 6.5 cm and it weighs about 18 g.

16th week

By the end of the 16th week the limbs and their constituent joints are properly formed. Vigorous movements continue but are rarely felt by the mother until slightly later in pregnancy. The fingers and toes are normal and fingernails and toenails have developed. The head remains relatively large but its characteristics—especially that of the face—are easily recognizable.

Primary sex characteristics continue to develop and the sex of the fetus is now obvious. The whole body is covered with a fine downy hair (lanugo). The eyebrows and eyelashes are growing. The fetus is approximately 6 in. (16 cm) in length and weighs 5 oz. (135 g).

24th week

The fetus continues to grow. The vital organs are now sufficiently mature for it to survive for a short while if delivered prematurely. Independent life, however, would not be maintained for long because the lungs are inadequately matured. All the organs are now properly formed and the remainder of the pregnancy is designed for growth and maturation. The fetus is now approximately 13 in. in length and weighs $1\frac{1}{4}$ lbs.

32nd week

The child is now perfectly formed and its head is in proportion to its body. The entire skin is covered with *vernix caseosa*, which is a greasy adherent cheese-like material over the whole of the baby's skin protecting it from becoming waterlogged by its continued immersion in the amniotic fluid.

The baby remains relatively thin, but some subcutaneous fat has been deposited and more will be deposited over the next few weeks to give the child the normal chubby appearance of a newborn infant.

Its length at this stage is approximately 16 in. and its weight $3\frac{1}{2}$ lbs.

36th week

The baby is now almost fully mature and has more than a 90% chance of survival if delivered. The last of the major fetal organs to mature are the lungs; their possible lack of maturation is the main reason why an infant delivered at this stage might fail to survive.

A great deal of subcutaneous fat has been deposited. A large amount of vernix still covers the baby's skin. The child has assumed its permanent position within the uterus and if it is the first pregnancy the head will probably have engaged within the mother's pelvis.

40th week

The average pregnancy lasts 280 days or 40 weeks, as previously noted, but because this is an *average* there will be some babies that mature between the 38th to the 40th week and others that mature between the 40th and the 42nd week. However, the vast majority will mature and deliver themselves within one or two days of the 280th day (see CHILDBIRTH).

The mature baby has a large quantity of subcutaneous fat, most of which has been deposited during the previous ten weeks. Most of the *lanugo* (fine downy hairs that cover the body of the fetus) has disappeared, together with a large percentage of the vernix, but this remains and is particularly thick in most of the skin creases (especially the armpits and groin).

Development of the placenta

The PLACENTA (or "afterbirth") is formed from the chorionic cells that surround the original sphere of cells when they embed in the uterus on the seventh day after fertilization. As the pregnancy grows, the placenta develops into an organ in the shape of a flattened disk measuring approximately 7 in. in diameter and $1\frac{1}{2}$ in. in thickness. Its weight is approximately $1\frac{1}{2}$ lbs., or about one sixth of the baby's weight. The placenta is responsible for the selective transfer to the fetus of oxygen and other necessary substances as well as removal from the fetus of its waste products. Everything that the fetus requires for its growth and maturation must pass through the placenta.

The maternal and fetal circulations are entirely independent. The fetal blood circulates from the fetus into the placenta and returns to the baby. The maternal circulation arrives at the uterus by way of the uterine artery and leaves it by the uterine veins. At no stage do the circulations of the fetus and the mother mix.

Occasionally a few cells do escape from the fetal circulation into the maternal circulation. The escape of these cells is a normal phenomenon and may occur intermittently throughout pregnancy. An increased number of fetal cells may gain access to the maternal circulation during labor or at the time of delivery; it is the escape of these cells that is responsible for the RH (RHESUS) FACTOR and other types of sensitization.

Umbilical cord

The blood is carried from the fetus to the placenta and back again by way of the umbilical cord, which usually measures about 20 in. in length and about $\frac{3}{4}$ in. in diameter. It contains two arteries and one vein.

The membranes

The membranes consist of two very thin structures called the amnion and the chorion. They lie in the inner surface of the uterus during pregnancy and are responsible for forming the bag within which the water or amniotic fluid is contained ("bag of waters"). The most important function of the membranes is to maintain and keep the amniotic fluid within the cavity of the uterus. If the membranes rupture, then the amniotic fluid will drain away—which will inevitably result in uterine contractions and the termination of the pregnancy. This should normally occur either immediately before or during labor at term; but if it occurs at any stage during pregnancy then labor usually follows within 48 hours. In some instances, especially if the baby is not mature, it may be desirable to attempt to prevent labor after the membranes have ruptured; medications are available for this purpose.

Amniotic fluid

Throughout its whole development and growth, the baby is surrounded by amniotic fluid (which is contained within the amniotic membrane) formed in the very early stages of the development of the human embryo.

In the early stages of pregnancy the size of the amniotic cavity is larger than required by the small fetus, therefore affording it complete freedom to move and develop. This freedom continues until about the 30th week of pregnancy, when the baby has a tendency to become fixed in a longitudinal position within the uterine cavity.

Approximately 1 liter (2 pints) of amniotic fluid is present at the 36th week of pregnancy, after which the amount of fluid gradually diminishes until the expected date is reached. The quantity of amniotic fluid is thereafter reduced more rapidly, so that by the 42nd week there may be only 100-200 ml of fluid remaining.

Functions of amniotic fluid

The amniotic fluid provides a liquid environment in which the fetus can develop and exercise in complete freedom. It prevents pressure upon the developing fetus from the muscular walls of the uterus. Its constituents vary as pregnancy advances and as the requirements of the fetus change. The fetus swallows some fluid and this enables it to develop its swallowing and breathing mechanisms. The amniotic fluid functions as a shock absorber which is so efficient that it is virtually impossible to damage the fetus itself as a result of indirect or even direct injury.

Amniocentesis

By examining a sample of the amniotic fluid in early pregnancy, certain congenital and other abnormalities of the fetus can be detected. The sample is obtained by AMNIOCENTESIS: a thin hypodermic needle is passed into the uterus through the abdominal wall (a general anesthetic is not required). Investigation of the baby's cells found in the sample can reveal abnormalities such as DOWN'S SYNDROME—(mongolism) or SPINA BIFIDA.

Amniocentesis can be performed early enough to be able to offer the mother a therapeutic abortion in the event of a serious fetal abnormality. Later on in pregnancy, amniocentesis can be used to estimate the chances of survival of a baby born prematurely—either accidentally or by induction. In particular, the condition of a baby with severe Rhesus problems can be monitored.

Every amniocentesis carries a very small risk of stimulating premature labor or miscarriage and rarely, damage to the baby or placenta. Although these complications are unusual amniocentesis is not carried out routinely, but is only advised in specific situations.

The fetal heart

The fetal heart begins to develop during the sixth week of pregnancy and the fetal circulation is established by the end of the seventh week. The movements of the fetal heart can be detected by ultrasonic scan (see ULTRASOUND) at the end of the seventh week. They can usually be heard with an ordinary stethoscope at about the 20th week of pregnancy.

The speed of a baby's heart varies from about 120 to 160 beats per minute and sounds very fast when it is heard for the first time.

Early pregnancy

Absence of menstrual periods (amenorrhea)
Failure of the period to commence at the usual time is generally the first sign of pregnancy. A missed menstrual period in any woman exposed to the possibility of pregnancy should be assumed to be due to pregnancy until proved otherwise. Other causes of AMENORRHEA include stress, strain, psychological upset and severe illnesses as well as climatic changes and travel. Some women do not have a period while they are taking a contraceptive pill.

Partially suppressed periods occasionally occur in early pregnancy if the level of hormone produced by the ovary is inadequate to suppress completely the menstrual period. In this circumstance a small amount of uterine bleeding may take place. The amount of loss is usually less and of a shorter duration than normal. However, the woman may naturally interpret this bleeding as a normal period when she is in fact pregnant. This explains why occasionally women "have their dates wrong" and go into labor a month earlier than expected.

Nausea
Nausea, a sensation of feeling that you are about to vomit, is very common during the first three months of pregnancy and may even be the first symptom noticed by some women. The NAUSEA tends to be more severe in the early morning, although it can occur at any time of the day, and is usually specific not only to each person but also to each pregnancy. Because it occurs most frequently in the morning it is known as MORNING SICKNESS.

Nausea is usually provoked by unpleasant smells, the smell of fried or frying food and frequently by cigarette smoke. It can be relieved by raising the level of blood sugar, which is best accomplished by taking small frequent meals. These should not contain a large quantity of sugar— because a high concentration of glucose in the stomach will itself increase the amount of nausea—but should consist of a drink of tea or milk together with a piece of unbuttered toast or a plain cracker.

Nausea can be helped by the doctor's assurance and the symptoms can be controlled by careful attention to diet. For those who find it too severe, there are some medications which can be taken safely during early pregnancy and which will at least relieve the symptoms even if these are not completely eliminated.

Nausea usually diminishes in severity after the 10th week

of pregnancy and typically decreases quite dramatically after the end of the 13th week.

Vomiting
Vomiting in early pregnancy is usually associated with severe nausea but may occur spontaneously. VOMITING is more frequent in the early morning and it usually relieves a fairly severe degree of nausea. However, vomiting may occur at any time of day.

Excessive vomiting, known as *hyperemesis gravidarum*, may require treatment in the hospital. Such excessive vomiting is not harmful to the woman or her fetus providing it is properly treated. Any woman who is sick more than three or four times a day should consult her doctor.

Early morning sickness can usually be controlled by careful diet, resting quietly on waking and taking a small drink of some bland fluid (such as sweetened tea) and a cracker or some dry toast. Butter and other fats should be avoided. For the rest of the day the diet should consist of small and frequent meals, avoiding fats and an excessive intake of concentrated sugar. The intensity of vomiting may vary from day to day, but can be expected to decrease spontaneously after the end of the 10th week and normally ceases completely at the end of the 14th week.

Urination
One of the early signs of pregnancy is an increase in the frequency of urination, most noticeable at night. This is not associated with any discomfort. The frequency tends to persist throughout pregnancy and becomes worse especially after the baby's head is engaged in the pelvis (see URINARY FREQUENCY).

Constipation
Constipation is an early symptom of pregnancy and is a result of the action of the hormone progesterone upon the intestine, which reduces its motility.

CONSTIPATION is best treated by increasing the amount of roughage (dietary fiber) and maintaining an adequate fluid intake.

Taste
Alterations in taste are among the earliest symptoms of pregnancy which some women will recognize even before they miss their first period. Such a taste is characteristic for each individual and is usually described as "metallic." It may be associated with a dislike of cigarette and tobacco smoke, as well as alcohol (especially red wine), coffee, fat and occasionally meat.

Skin changes
Changes in the skin are not very common during early pregnancy but some women do complain of dry skin and spots on the face (especially around the mouth). The dry

skin may persist throughout pregnancy, although the spots will usually disappear at the end of the 13th week.

Breast changes
The premenstrual fullness normally present in the breasts continues when the period does not appear; within a matter of days the symptoms become even more marked. The breasts are full, tender and more sensitive than usual, especially in the region of the nipples. There may also be a sensation of tingling. The breasts enlarge quite slowly at first, but by the end of the sixth week there is a very appreciable change in their size. There is also an increase in superficial veins over the breasts and the nipples may enlarge and become more prominent.

"Quickening"
The baby begins to move at about the sixth or seventh week of pregnancy. The baby's movements are not normally felt by a woman having her first baby until between the 18th and 20th week of pregnancy, or in a subsequent pregnancy between the 16th and 18th week.

Diagnosis: pregnancy tests
The only sure method of diagnosing early pregnancy is by means of a pregnancy test, because in early pregnancy a woman does not undergo sufficient physical changes for clinical examination to detect pregnancy with accuracy. Pregnancy tests are usually performed upon urine by the use of an immunological technique in which the hormone chorionic gonadotropin is made easily detectable. The test is simple, takes about two minutes and is accurate in about 99% of cases. It does not normally yield positive results until about 10 days after the first suppressed period.

More sensitive tests can demonstrate the presence of a pregnancy-specific hormone in the blood of the pregnant woman even before she has missed her period. At present, however, these are research investigations and are not generally available.

X-rays
X-rays are no longer used for the diagnosis of early pregnancy.

Ultrasonic scan
The rapid development of ULTRASOUND as a diagnostic tool throughout pregnancy has been remarkable. Sound waves in the frequency range of 2.5 MHz (2.5 million cycles per second) are generated in an electronic transducer. This ultrasonic energy can pass through fluids and solids but not through gases and are therefore capable of outlining structures deeper in the body.

Ultrasound will demonstrate the enlarged uterus and the pregnancy sac within it as early as the seventh week of pregnancy. It will also define the movements of the fetal

heart at the end of the seventh or early in the eighth week of pregnancy. Thereafter it may be used to monitor certain aspects of the uterus and its contents, such as the number of fetuses, the position of the placenta, the size of the uterus and the presence and size of any pelvic tumors as well as certain more defined aspects of the fetus—such as its overall size, its rate of growth, the size of its head, certain abnormalities, its position and (by implication) its general welfare.

Antenatal care
The importance of good antenatal care cannot be emphasized too strongly. The whole basis of modern obstetric management is the early recognition and the prevention of both minor and major complications. A visit to your doctor as soon as you know you are pregnant is essential.

Continued supervision throughout pregnancy is one of the best forms of preventive medicine known to modern medical science. The outcome of a pregnancy for both the mother and her child will be directly related to the quality of antenatal care. The best results can only be obtained with the enthusiastic cooperation of the pregnant woman herself. (See also the major article on **Obstetrics and Gynecology.**)

Rest
The amount of rest required by any individual varies with many personal factors. You should have sufficient rest during pregnancy so that you do not feel overtired. The ideal is ten hours rest every day, but if this is not possible you should get as close to it as circumstances permit.

A certain amount of lethargy and tiredness is normal in early pregnancy. There is no point in trying to fight it. You can either give in to it and rest, in which case you will feel much better, or try to resist it with the inevitable result that you become bad-tempered and even more tired.

Sleeping during pregnancy
The natural tiredness of early pregnancy usually results in sound sleep. Occasionally, however, worry, apprehension or other reasons may cause sleeplessness—in which case you should discuss it with your doctor. In late pregnancy the physical problems of a large abdomen may make sleep somewhat difficult. Most obstetricians agree that sleeping pills should be avoided if possible, but it is better to have a good night's sleep with a mild and safe sleeping pill prescribed by your doctor than to fail to sleep altogether and be a neurotic wreck the next day.

Exercise in pregnancy
Most people understand "exercise" to mean physical activity above their normal daily duties. This is not strictly true. Most women have a home to look after and either a

job to do or other children to take care of; these duties in themselves require a considerable amount of work and exercise. There is no reason why a woman progressing through a normal pregnancy should not continue with her normal household duties. If complications arise then her activities may be restricted by her doctor.

For a pregnant woman who is going out to work there is a world of difference between being a shorthand typist and being in retail sales. Women who are accustomed to a certain amount of physical exercise—or sports such as tennis, golf, cycling, or swimming—may continue during pregnancy providing the pregnancy progresses normally. You must, however, avoid undue exertion which could produce tiredness and exhaustion.

There is really no limit to the amount of walking you may do during pregnancy, nor is there any harm in swimming, so long as overtiredness is avoided. Exercises and occupations that involve a high risk (such as riding horses or skiing) should be avoided. Skin diving is also best avoided during pregnancy.

Diet

A proper diet is extremely important in pregnancy. Even though you may be overweight to begin with, your daily caloric intake should never be restricted to less than 2,200 calories. Special emphasis should be given to protein intake, which in pregnancy should amount to at least 1 g of protein per kg ($2\frac{1}{4}$ lbs.) of body weight. Meat, eggs, cheese, fish, and skim milk are excellent sources of protein, and each meal should include at least one of them.

Alcohol

Excessive amounts of alcohol have been shown to be injurious to the developing fetus; it is thus important that alcoholic intake be restricted to not more than two drinks per day. The baby probably tolerates this amount without damage, but it is really preferable that alcohol be either entirely eliminated during pregnancy or restricted to an occasional cocktail or glass of wine.

Travel during pregnancy

If you have a good, stable, normal pregnancy, then there is no harm if you have to travel. However, you should not travel over long distances unless it is essential and you should always consult your doctor before undertaking a long journey. The majority of airlines will not accept pregnant women as passengers if they are more than 35 weeks pregnant.

Teeth

Care of the teeth during pregnancy is of the utmost importance. You should visit your dentist as soon as you know you are pregnant and must be scrupulous about your oral hygiene during pregnancy.

Sexual intercourse during pregnancy

There is no reason why normal sexual intercourse should not continue throughout a normal pregnancy until labor begins. There are, however, some exceptions. Any woman who has suffered a previous miscarriage ought to avoid sexual intercourse for the first 14 weeks of pregnancy and any woman who has suffered from recurrent miscarriages should discuss the problem with her doctor.

Any threat to miscarry or bleeding at any stage in pregnancy must automatically result in cessation of sexual activity until the doctor advises that it may be resumed.

Frigidity

Lack of sexual desire, or FRIGIDITY, sometimes occurs during pregnancy and may continue for the whole of the pregnancy. This is a normal phenomenon and should be treated with gentle understanding. A normal sexual appetite will return.

Smoking in pregnancy

Most people agree that smoking should be discouraged at any time, and this is certainly true during pregnancy. Women who smoke a large number of cigarettes have smaller babies than do nonsmoking pregnant women, although it is probably smoking after the 16th week of pregnancy that has the greatest effect and which may cause both mental and physical retardation of the unborn infant.

Bathing

Pregnancy need not alter your previous habits. Bathing or taking a shower is not contraindicated during normal pregnancy. A word of warning, however, is that the bath should not be too long or too hot. There is always a tendency toward fainting, especially in early pregnancy, and if you get up too quickly from a long hot bath you can quite easily feel dizzy or even faint.

Douching

Douching is not advised during pregnancy, but there is no objection to a woman using a bidet (which are much more common in Europe than in the United States) at any stage of pregnancy unless she has suffered from some vaginal bleeding, the waters have ruptured, or she is in labor.

For those women who insist on douching daily, then the use of antiseptic solution should be avoided and only plain water used.

The abdomen

The secret of preserving your figure is the control of the amount of weight you gain during pregnancy. If you do not gain more than 22 lbs. throughout your pregnancy, then there is every chance that your abdomen will return to normal after the baby is born. Your muscles and skin will be just as good as they were before you became pregnant, providing you do not have a multiple birth. Stretch marks, however, may be caused by increased levels of the hormone progesterone during pregnancy rather than overweight, and there is no guarantee that these will disappear.

There is no need to wear an abdominal support unless you are accustomed to doing so prior to the onset of pregnancy. The care of the skin of your abdomen should be similar to thè care of the rest of the skin of your body. Massaging oil into the abdominal skin every night will not prevent stretch marks, but is nevertheless worthwhile because it helps to keep the skin in good condition.

Warning or symptoms of danger

There are ten major groups of symptoms which might occur during pregnancy and they merit serious attention. They do not indicate a disaster, but they should be considered seriously and reported to the doctor either immediately or as soon as is reasonably possible. The first five listed below should be reported immediately, while the second five may be reported at the earliest convenient time, usually within 24 hours.

1. Vaginal bleeding
If vaginal bleeding occurs in the first 28 weeks of pregnancy it indicates that the pregnancy is unstable and that there is a threat of miscarriage (spontaneous abortion). If the amount of bleeding is slight, then you should go to bed and the doctor can be notified as soon as is reasonable; but if the bleeding is heavy or associated with pain, you should go to bed at once and notify the doctor immediately. Any bleeding after the 28th week of pregnancy may indicate the onset of labor: notify your doctor immediately.

2. Severe continuous abdominal pain
The onset of severe continuous abdominal pain should be reported to your doctor at once. It is emphasized that this is related to *continuous* and not to intermittent pain.

3. Breaking of the "bag of waters" or rupture of the membranes
When this happens the onset of labor usually follows fairly rapidly. It is therefore important to notify your doctor or the hospital immediately so that arrangements can be made for your urgent admission.

4. Misty, difficult, and blurred vision
In the second half of pregnancy these may be a symptom of PREECLAMPSIA or raised blood pressure; if they persist you should go to bed and notify your doctor at once.

5. Continuous severe headache
Headache that is not relieved by aspirin or other simple headache remedies may also be a symptom of preeclampsia or raised blood pressure. It is emphasized that this type of headache continues for several hours and does not respond to the usual remedies. A headache which is felt as a pressure on the top of the head is not usually significant.

Symptoms not so urgent as the above five include:

1. Fever
A rise in temperature to 101°F usually merits some form of active treatment.

2. Frequency and pain on urination
This usually indicates a URINARY TRACT INFECTION and should be treated as soon as convenient.

3. Swelling (edema) of the hands, face and ankles
This may occur at any stage of pregnancy and is frequently associated with preeclampsia, raised blood pressure or excessive weight gain.

4. Absence of fetal movements
Babies frequently stop moving for quite long periods during pregnancy and it is fairly common for a baby not to move for several days between the 20th and the 24th week of pregnancy or to stop moving for up to 24 hours during the latter part of pregnancy. If, however, your baby has not moved for 48 hours the doctor should be notified.

5. Excessive vomiting
Excessive vomiting may occur during the first 14 weeks of pregnancy. If it becomes so severe that no fluid or food can be retained then the doctor should be notified. During the last three months of pregnancy some women will vomit occasionally; but repeated, recurrent, or severe vomiting is unusual and should be reported as soon as possible.

X-rays
X-rays of the abdomen and pelvis should be avoided during pregnancy if possible. There are certain indications which make an x-ray necessary. X-rays of other parts of the body may be required, but before these are taken you should inform the doctor of your pregnancy.

Drugs in pregnancy
Generally speaking, all drugs should be avoided during pregnancy except those that have been specifically permitted and prescribed by your doctor. If you are contemplating pregnancy and are taking routine drugs such as tranquilizers or sleeping tablets, then you should certainly ask your doctor about them before you embark upon a pregnancy.

"Heartburn" (pyrosis)
Heartburn is not to be confused with simple indigestion. It is a searing, burning sensation felt in the lower part of the chest just beneath the breastbone, frequently associated with bringing up or regurgitating small quantities of very acid fluid.

If heartburn becomes a constant or serious problem, you should notify your doctor. It is caused by the regurgitation of acid from the stomach into the lower part of the esophagus and will be treated by alkali. Swallowing large quantities of a strong alkaline mixture will correct the gastric acidity, but only for a short while. The proper treatment is to take a *small* quantity of alkali to neutralize the stomach contents and to continue with the small quantity of alkali over a prolonged period.

Heartburn may be worse at night when you are relaxed and lying flat in bed. A simple remedy is to raise the head of the bed or to sleep with three of four pillows.

Vaginal discharge

Vaginal discharge may occur throughout pregnancy as a result of the increased blood supply to the vagina and cervix (neck of the womb). The term "discharge" is intended to mean the passage from the vagina of a simple clear mucoid or white discharge without any soreness, pain, or irritation. This occurs normally during pregnancy. Sometimes, however, the discharge becomes yellow and offensive, usually because of a mild infection. If this happens you should report it when you next see your doctor.

Vaginal irritation

Irritation in the vagina is nearly always associated with the irritation of the vulva (the external female genitals). A mild discomfort may be felt in the early stages of pregnancy and is usually transient. The most common reason for the severe irritation is a fungal infection (see CANDIDA). If this should happen it is easily and simply treated by using a fungicidal cream or other preparation. If you have had a fungal infection during pregnancy you should keep a reserve of the fungicide available, since the infection has a way of recurring at a later date for no apparent reason.

Shortness of breath

Many women complain of intermittent shortness of breath at all stages of pregnancy. But it is more common toward the end of pregnancy when the enlarging uterus pushes the abdominal contents upward underneath the ribs and thus forces the diaphragm upward into the chest. This causes inefficient breathing and shortness of breath on the slightest exertion.

Shortness of breath may occur at night while lying flat; it can easily be remedied by propping the head and shoulders on two or three pillows.

Most women find that sitting in a low chair is uncomfortable and makes shortness of breath worse; sitting in a higher chair gives much better support and makes breathing much more easy.

Fainting

Most women feel faint on some occasion during early pregnancy and a few may actually faint. The feeling of faintness results from a lowering of blood pressure which occurs when blood is allowed to "pool" in the legs after prolonged standing or other inactivity. It can usually be prevented by not standing still or, alternatively, by gentle movement and exercising of the feet and legs.

A feeling of faintness may also occur when you suddenly stand from a sitting position. Most pregnant women rapidly appreciate the circumstances which make them feel faint and learn to avoid them. If, however, you do feel faint, you should either sit down or take several deep breaths in rapid succession. This will restore the blood pressure to normal and the faint feeling will be relieved.

Pigmentation

Pigmentation of the nipple and the areola (the dark ring of tissue surrounding the nipple) commences at about the 14th week of pregnancy. The amount and area of pigmentation will vary from person to person. It is more obvious in women who have dark hair than in those who have fair hair and skin.

The *linea nigra* is a dark line that develops down the center of the abdomen commencing at about the 14th week of pregnancy. This will gradually fade after the end of pregnancy and disappear completely in about six months. Pigmentation of the nipple and areola, however, tends to remain.

Some pregnant women develop the characteristic "butterfly mask of pregnancy," where there is distribution of pigmentation over the nose and cheeks rather like the wings of a butterfly. It may also occur on the forehead. It has no special significance and will always disappear after the end of pregnancy. No attempt should be made to bleach it because not only will this not work but the surrounding skin will be bleached—thus making the mark even more obvious.

Costal (rib) margin pain

This pain is situated in the lower border of the chest wall. It usually occurs toward the end of pregnancy, is more common on the right than on the left, and is caused by compression of the lower ribs by the enlarging uterus as it pushes up under the ribs, forcing them together. This results in pain in the lower ribs.

The pain tends to be more severe when sitting. There is little that can be done to relieve it, other than to avoid sitting in a slumped or slouched position. The pain is always relieved at the time of delivery.

Ligament pain

This is a specific pain or discomfort caused during pregnancy by the stretching of the ligaments that support the uterus. The pain usually develops between the 16th and 20th week and is felt low down in the right side of the abdomen. It is recognized as an aching, dragging, nagging pain—usually more severe on standing after a period of sitting down. There is no specific treatment. It will not do the baby any harm and usually disappears spontaneously after about eight weeks.

Edema (swelling) of the ankles and feet

Part of the natural weight gain of pregnancy is due to retention of water within the body. If the amount of water retained becomes excessive, then certain parts begin to swell; in pregnancy this usually happens in the feet and ankles.

The edema or swelling usually disappears during the night when the feet are raised, but reappears during the following day. Severe swelling may be associated with quite a lot of discomfort in the lower part of the legs and ankles.

Management of edema of the ankles is difficult except by continuous bed rest, but it may be controlled to a certain extent by careful dietary methods or by the careful administration of diuretic drugs; these must be taken only under the direction of your doctor. If edema of the feet remains severe, or there is an accompanying rise in blood pressure, then admission to the hospital for further observation or treatment may become necessary.

A certain amount of swelling of the fingers seems to occur during pregnancy for which there is no known reason. However, edema of the fingers during the later stages of pregnancy causes rings to become excessively tight and this is usually associated with fluid retention. The treatment is similar to that for edema of the feet.

Incompetent cervix

An incompetent cervix will cause miscarriage at about the 20th week of pregnancy. In this condition the canal of the cervix has usually been previously damaged and it dilates quite painlessly—with the result that the "bag of waters" protrudes and rupture of the membranes occurs. This is followed quite rapidly by a relatively painless labor and spontaneous delivery of the fetus.

The treatment for incompetent cervix is the insertion of nonabsorbable sutures (stitches) around the cervix at about the 14th week of pregnancy. This procedure has a success rate in excess of 75%.

Ectopic pregnancy

An ECTOPIC PREGNANCY is one in which the fertilized ovum implants outside the cavity of the uterus, most frequently in the Fallopian tube. It inevitably gives rise to pain and bleeding and is surgically removed.

Antepartum hemorrhage

Antepartum hemorrhage is the term given to bleeding from the vagina after the 28th week of pregnancy. It may fall into one of three main categories:

(1) *Incidental antepartum hemorrhage.* This is bleeding that occurs from the genital tract as the result of small ulcerations or injury, or—most commonly—at the time of

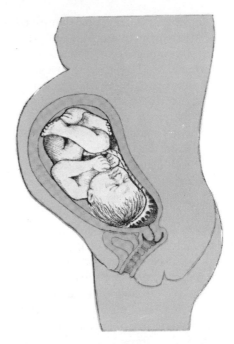

In placenta previa, the placenta (afterbirth) lies over the neck of the womb. This often necessitates Cesarean delivery, especially if the placenta lies centrally over the cervix, as otherwise heavy bleeding may occur when labor begins.

the onset of labor.

(2) *Placenta previa.* This is a condition in which the placenta, instead of being attached to the upper part of the uterus, is attached to the lower part in the region of the lower uterine segment and cervix. When the placenta is attached in this segment of the uterus, bleeding will inevitably occur either before or at the time of the onset of labor. This results in separation of a small portion of the placenta with the resulting brisk but painless bleeding. There are several degrees of PLACENTA PREVIA, varying from *marginal* (in which very little bleeding will occur and normal delivery can be anticipated) to *central* (in which severe bleeding is bound to take place and delivery must be by CESAREAN SECTION.

(3) *Accidental hemorrhage.* This is a comparatively rare condition (ABRUPTIO PLACENTAE) in which the placenta is normally implanted in the upper part of the uterus but detaches from it prematurely and results in vaginal bleeding. Accidental hemorrhage is also associated with continuous and severe abdominal pain. The uterus will contract and become extremely hard. This is a dangerous condition which requires urgent admission to the hospital.

Hydramnios

Hydramnios means the presence of an excessive amount of fluid within the amniotic cavity ("bag of waters"). In most cases there is no recognizable cause and no accompanying abnormality. However, some cases are associated with a twin pregnancy, diabetes, and preeclampsia—as well as with congenital abnormality of the infant. The uterus enlarges to a size much greater than normal and the abdominal girth increases rapidly and to a greater size than is normal. The rapid or extreme enlargement of the uterus can cause quite a lot of distress to the mother and may occasionally be extremely painful.

The treatment is usually confined to the symptomatic relief of pain, discomfort and the inability to sleep.

X-ray of the abdomen or ultrasonic scan is justified to exclude congenital abnormality.

Preeclampsia

PREECLAMPSIA is a condition which is specific to pregnancy and in which at least two of three classic symptoms are present: (1) a raised blood pressure; (2) swelling of the feet, ankles or hands; and (3) protein in the urine. The cause of preeclampsia is still unknown, despite an extensive amount of research. One of the major aspects of the care of the pregnant woman in the antenatal clinic is always directed toward the prevention or early detection of preeclampsia.

The real danger of preeclampsia is to the unborn child, because it certainly increases the risk to the fetus both before and during labor.

Preeclampsia itself does not do any lasting harm to the pregnant woman if she is properly and efficiently treated. After delivery, the edema will subside, the blood pressure will gradually return to normal (although it may take several months) and the kidneys will gradually resume their normal function. Untreated preeclampsia, however, may develop rapidly into *eclampsia,* which is a very dangerous condition.

Eclampsia

Eclampsia is a condition in which a woman who is suffering from preeclampsia suddenly develops convulsions or fits. The convulsions last for approximately one minute and are followed by a period of unconsciousness.

Eclampsia typically occurs in late pregnancy, but may begin during labor or even after delivery. It is generally preceded by very severe headache, visual disturbances, irritability and abdominal pain. The blood pressure rises to an unacceptably high level. The condition must be treated with the utmost speed.

Prevention is the keynote and one of the many advantages of careful medical supervision during pregnancy has been the early recognition and adequate treatment of preeclampsia, which in turn has virtually eliminated eclampsia itself.

Placental insufficiency

Placental insufficiency is a condition in which the placenta either does not grow normally or, having grown, does not then function normally. This results in slow or delayed growth of the fetus. Placental insufficiency causes an inadequate oxygen supply to the fetus and there is also a reduction in the ability of the placenta to remove waste products from the fetus itself. Such a "dysmature" placenta can provide only a restricted supply of materials and nutrition—with the result that the fetus develops normally, but conserves its resources by growing very slowly. Such a slowly growing fetus is a baby at high risk, because the placenta will eventually no longer be able to supply the basic requirements—the result is that the baby becomes short of oxygen and may even die.

Recognition of placental insufficiency is one of the important aspects of modern antenatal care. Extensive tests of placental function will be undertaken for any woman in whom the condition is suspected; early induction of labor may be indicated to prevent the infant from dying in the uterus. Selective delivery by Cesarean section may also be required.

Anemia

The prevention of ANEMIA is one of the most important aspects of antenatal care. Dilution of the blood is a normal phenomenon in pregnancy. The circulating blood volume increases by approximately 33% during pregnancy and it is most important that this dilution should not result in anemia. It is therefore routine practice to provide pregnant women with iron supplements to maintain their HEMOGLOBIN level.

The increase of circulating blood volume during pregnancy is necessary so that the increased requirements (especially of the uterus and breasts) may be satisfied without any detriment to the mother's brain or other vital organs.

The symptoms of anemia are slow in onset and are recognized only when the anemia has become established and even then only gradually. They include tiredness, lethargy, lack of energy and inability to perform ordinary daily duties. Color and whiteness of the skin eventually make the diagnosis obvious.

The main predisposing causes of anemia are a history of previous anemia, iron deficiency, folic acid deficiency and minor infections (especially those involving the urinary tract). The prevention of anemia, or its correction if it becomes established, involves the elimination of all the predisposing factors.

Hypertension (high blood pressure)

A rise in BLOOD PRESSURE is a serious complicating problem in pregnancy. The blood pressure is always expressed as two figures, such as 120/80 ("one twenty over eighty"), measured in millimeters of mercury. The higher figure represents the *systolic* blood pressure (see SYSTOLE), which is the pressure reached within the blood vessels at the height of a heartbeat—when the heart contracts and pumps blood out into the arteries — and varies considerably with exercise, fatigue, excitement and emotion. The lower figure represents the *diastolic* blood pressure (see DIASTOLE), which is the minimum level to which the blood pressure falls between heartbeats; this is of greater significance because it varies only as a result of some fundamental change in the circulation.

Hypertension during pregnancy is said to exist when the diastolic blood pressure reaches 90 or more while resting.

Hypertension can predispose to placental insufficiency or to preeclampsia and may result in a baby that is small, "dysmature," or one that may even fail to survive. One of the main objects of antenatal care is to prevent or detect hypertension during pregnancy so that appropriate steps may be taken to prevent damage or harm to the developing fetus.

The fetal position

The lie

The "lie" of the baby refers to the way in which the fetus is lying in the uterus.

Longitudinal lie. In this position one end of the baby is lying over the pelvic brim or is engaged within the brim of the pelvis itself. In early pregnancy the baby can lie in any position and is free to move at will inside the uterus. At about the 28th week it begins to assume a longitudinal lie, with one end lying immediately over the pelvic brim. In 98% of pregnancies the lie is longitudinal.

Oblique lie and transverse lie. In approximately 2% of all pregnancies the lie is *oblique*, with the lower part of the body just above the mother's groin, with the baby's spine lying obliquely in relation to the mother's spine—or the baby lies *transversely,* with its spine at right angles to that of the mother.

Obviously, a baby in neither an oblique nor a transverse lie can be delivered normally. The majority of oblique lies, however, are converted into longitudinal lies when labor commences. Unfortunately, a baby lying in a transverse position cannot be delivered vaginally. If this position persists the delivery will have to be performed by Cesarean section. This, however, is a very rare complication.

Position of the baby
When a baby is in a longitudinal lie it may have the head in the lower part of the uterus, and thus lies over the pelvic brim. Or the bottom (*breech*) may be the part of the baby which is related to the pelvic brim. If the head is presenting it is known as a *cephalic* presentation; 96% of all longitudinal lies present by the head.

Breech presentation
The remaining 4% of babies lie with the breech or bottom presenting. This may be the normal position for a baby to present until about the 32nd week of pregnancy. At this stage the vast majority of babies rotate from a breech presentation to cephalic presentation. This is done spontaneously; the reason why they do this and the mechanism whereby it is done are not understood.

External cephalic version
If a baby is lying as a breech presentation at the 33rd or 34th week of pregnancy, it is a comparatively easy procedure to rotate the baby by exerting gentle pressure on

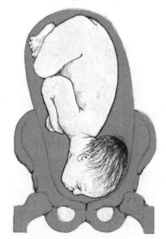

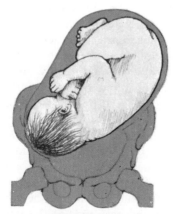

NORMAL (CEPHALIC) PRESENTATION

BROW OR FACE

BREECH

OBLIQUE LIE

The normal presentation, i.e. the baby's position relative to the cervix, is head down with chin on chest. In "brow" (or "face") presentation the baby's neck is extended, and labor may be delayed.

Cesarean section may be required; this is also usually the case for breech presentation (bottom first) and sometimes for the oblique lie, although this often corrects itself when labor begins.

the front of the mother's abdominal wall and thus to rotate the baby from a breech to a cephalic presentation.

Labor

Cause of labor
The precise reason why labor begins is not known, although there is an increasing amount of evidence to indicate that the fetus produces a hormone which leads to the onset of labor and thereafter controls the course of labor.

The mechanism of labor
Stage one, or the first stage of labor, is measured from the onset of labor to full dilation (opening up) of the cervix. *Stage two* is from full dilation of the cervix to complete delivery of the baby. *Stage three* is from completion of the delivery of the baby to completion of the delivery of the placenta ("afterbirth").

First stage of labor
The first stage of labor is designed to shorten the cervix and then to dilate the cervical canal so that the head (which is the widest part of the body) can pass through the cervix without causing damage or injury. The lower part of the uterus and the cervix can then return to normal after delivery has been completed and thus allow the uterus to prepare itself for a subsequent pregnancy.

The beginning of labor is indicated by the onset of regular painful uterine contractions. These may begin initially in the lower part of the back, recurring every 20 or 25 minutes. The frequency of contractions gradually increases and the discomfort spreads from the back to the lower part of the abdomen. When contractions are occurring every 15 minutes, the discomfort spreads over the entire abdomen and the uterus will be felt contracting strongly at approximately 10-minute intervals.

The uterine contractions continue for approximately 50 seconds; in between contractions the uterus relaxes completely. Gradually the contractions become more frequent and more forceful, so that toward the end of the first stage of labor they will last for approximately one minute and occur about every three minutes. The first stage of labor lasts between 4 to 18 hours in a woman having her first baby; it may last from half an hour to 12 hours in a woman having a second or subsequent baby.

The signs of the onset of labor are (a) the onset of powerful, regular uterine contractions; (b) rupture of the membranes; and (c) the passage of a small quantity of blood (the "show"). When uterine contractions are occurring every 15 to 20 minutes and have become regular, then labor has commenced.

A mucous plug (*operculum*) lies within the cervical canal protecting the cavity of the uterus throughout pregnancy and is usually dislodged as soon as the cervix is fully effaced

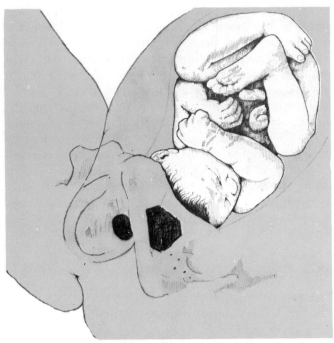

When the cervix is fully dilated, the baby's head passes transversely through the bony arch of the pelvis before turning to face downward. As the nape of the neck passes under the arch the head moves upward and backward (chin moves away from chest).

or "taken up." The mucous plug may be expelled and appear before the onset of actual labor, especially if a lot of backache has been experienced. Usually, however, it comes away early in the first stage of labor and can be easily recognized as a lump of thick, fairly solid, clear sticky mucus which may occasionally be tinged with a small amount of blood.

The "show"
The passage of a small quantity of blood is one of the most common signs of the onset of labor.

The "bag of waters"
Occasionally the bag of waters, lying in front of the baby's head, ruptures; this is one of the first signs of the onset of labor. This is recognized by a gush of clear water from the vagina. The membranes may rupture before the onset of labor, in which case labor will commence shortly afterward—or the membranes may break during the course of labor.

Second stage of labor
At the onset of the second stage of labor the uterine contractions undergo a subtle but definite change and are associated with the desire to push or bear down. This expulsive desire is at first present only at the height of a contraction, but gradually becomes more noticeable so

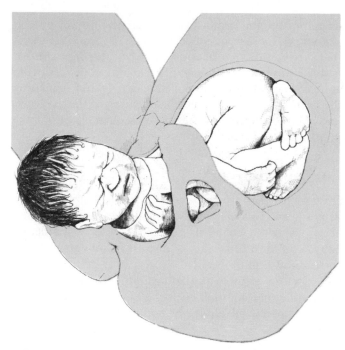

After the baby's head is born, it turns to the side without assistance (restitution). The upper shoulder dips under the arch, followed by the other shoulder, body and arms, pelvis and legs.

that eventually it lasts throughout a uterine contraction. The uterine contractions continue once every minute or perhaps every two minutes and last for approximately one minute. The baby's head descends down the birth canal and eventually emerges to be delivered, followed very rapidly by the limbs and trunk.

As soon as the baby has been delivered, the respiratory passages will be aspirated and any mucus removed to permit the baby to breathe. The umbilical cord is then clamped and the baby is now free to live an entirely independent existence. Plastic clamps are then placed on the umbilical cord to prevent any subsequent bleeding.

Usually within a few seconds of delivery of the baby's head, and certainly within a few moments of completion of delivery, he takes his first breath. As soon as he does this he rapidly turns from a dusky gray or blue to a brightish pink color. Breathing is at first somewhat irregular and may be accompanied by a powerful splutter, but within a few seconds (or minutes at the most), regular respirations are established and are rapidly followed by the first cry.

Third stage of labor

The third stage of labor extends from the delivery of the baby to the delivery of the placenta ("afterbirth"). In anticipation of the third stage of labor, an injection is usually given to hasten contraction of the uterus and thus speed the expulsion of the placenta. The uterus contracts powerfully and within a very short time the placenta is delivered. The entire process of labor is thus completed.

Painkilling drugs (analgesics)

These fall into three main groups: analgesic drugs given by mouth or injection; inhalation analgesia; and conduction analgesia.

Analgesic drugs. Mild analgesics may be given in the early stages of labor and even sedatives may be given to induce sleep if labor is slow during the early part of the first stage. Subsequently, drugs such as meperidine (Demerol) may be given by injection to alleviate pain.

Inhalation analgesia. Nitrous oxide and oxygen may be used as required.

Conduction analgesia. Epidural analgesia is an injection of anesthetic into the "epidural space" of the spinal cord which is given in the lumbar region (the small of the back) to induce complete relief from pain. *Sacral epidural analgesia* involves the injection of anesthetic into the lower end of the spinal area (sacrum). These methods of analgesia are gaining in popularity and in the majority of instances result in a completely painless labor. They do, however, require very expert and careful administration and can be conducted only by anesthesiologists who have been specially trained in the technique.

Pudendal block is an injection into the "pudendal nerve" in the lower back area of the pelvis. It may be used to relieve pain or discomfort during actual delivery without affecting the discomfort of the uterine contractions themselves.

Maternal and fetal monitoring

The safety of both mother and baby during the course of labor depends greatly on the attention paid to the heartbeat of the baby and to the duration, frequency and quality of the maternal uterine contractions. If the progress of the labor is slowed, the baby's health may suffer; this will be shown by a rise in the fetal heart rate with intermittent decelerations. This condition is known as FETAL DISTRESS. Similarly, any holdup in the labor may threaten the mother as well. In such conditions as *obstructed labor,* the uterus will not contract properly (with a possible risk of dangerous uterine rupture) and this is also usually accompanied by fetal distress.

The subtle changes preceding these events can be detected by recording the baby's heartbeat rate and the uterine contractions. Formerly these recordings (every 15 minutes in some cases) were performed manually by a nurse in attendance, listening with a fetal stethoscope and feeling sets of uterine contractions. This is very tedious work, and errors can occur—especially if the fetal heartbeat is faint. Far more accurate (and less tiring) is the continuous recording of these data by machines, either externally or internally.

In *external monitoring* two little disks are attached to the mother's abdomen. One disk emits a small beam of sonic waves directed onto the baby's heart. Reflected sound waves from the heart are picked up and recorded as heartbeats mapped out on a paper trace. Subtle deflections in the heart rate (usually as fast as 160 beats per minute) can be detected; these provide an early warning of fetal distress, so that any action can be taken as early as necessary. The second disk will record the quality and frequency of the uterine contractions. Thus the obstetrical team can see at a glance if the labor is slowing down, e.g., due to uncoordinated uterine function, or contractions of insufficient strength. Sometimes maternal movements dislodge the external monitors, and so when the amniotic sac has been breached (when the "waters have broken"), *internal monitors* are usually applied.

These consist of a small electrode attached to the fetal head to record the electrical impulses of the heart—which travel throughout the whole body, like an electrocardiogram in the adult—and a small length of sterile pressure-sensitive tubing inserted into the uterine cavity to record the contractions on the same trace.

Episiotomy

This is the name given to the operation in which the perineum (the tissue between the vulva and anus) is cut or incised to facilitate the delivery of the baby's head, either because the tissues of the perineum are too rigid or the vaginal entrance is too tight to allow the baby's head to pass through without tearing the tissues.

Opinions are divided not only as to whether EPISIOTOMY should be undertaken but even as to which particular episiotomy technique should be performed. Modern obstetric opinion tends toward the performing of episiotomy on more frequent occasions. The reason for this is that an episiotomy incision can be properly sutured (stitched) following delivery and thus return the perineum and the vaginal entrance to a state closely approximating the normal, whereas uncontrolled tearing of the tissues or undue stretching may result in subsequent laxity of the perineum and vaginal entrance.

Forceps delivery

Obstetric forceps are used to facilitate the delivery of the baby's head. This may be required if there has been some delay during the second stage of labor, or if the mother or baby has shown some sign of distress or intolerance. The correct and skillful use of the forceps for delivery of the baby does not result in any damage either to the baby or to the mother; indeed, their correct and opportune use is to the very definite advantage of both mother and child.

Cesarean section

CESAREAN SECTION is the operation by which the baby is delivered at operation by incising the mother's abdomen and also the uterus so that the baby is delivered artificially through the abdomen. The uterus and abdomen are surgically repaired very carefully so that subsequent babies may be delivered either by the normal vaginal route or by a repeat Cesarean section. As many as four or even six babies may be delivered by Cesarean section.

Although this operation is extremely safe, it does entail more risk than a simple vaginal delivery. Consequently, it is performed only when it is considered to be in the best interests of the mother and baby.

Family Planning
Infertility, contraception, sterilization and abortion

Dr. Graham H. Barker

This article reviews in depth the whole field of family planning. It is divided into four parts: the first section, Infertility, explains what can be done to help couples who experience difficulty in having a child; the second, Contraception, offers full and objective information on the various methods of birth control available; the third deals with Sterilization, and the fourth discusses the controversial subject of therapeutic Abortion.

INFERTILITY
Introduction

Many married couples today, especially those with major diverting interests such as business or academic careers, have made a conscious choice to remain childless rather than bring up children in a half-hearted manner. For the majority of couples, however, raising a family remains the major reason for marriage.

When a couple find that they are unable to produce children, great strains may be placed on them; frequently, these are insurmountable and can lead to failure of the marriage. The investigations into the causes of the infertility must therefore be carried out with both sympathy and tact. The causes must be clearly understood so that blame is not unfairly apportioned to either partner, or guilt unnecessarily felt.

Before infertility can be understood, a certain knowledge of the normal processes leading to conception and pregnancy is necessary (these are extensively covered elsewhere—see FERTILIZATION and the major article on **Pregnancy and Childbirth**). Briefly, for conception to occur, fertile spermatozoa must be deposited at the cervix during sexual intercourse (or, on rare occasions, by artificial insemination) at around the time a fertile ovum is produced by the ovary. The ovum travels slowly down the Fallopian tube awaiting the arrival of the sperm. When

the spermatozoa reach the ovum, one of them may penetrate it. This is the process of fertilization. The fertilized ovum now travels down the Fallopian tube and embeds itself in the lining of the uterus, where it will grow into an *embryo* and later, a *fetus*. Successful fertilization therefore depends on the timing of sperm deposition—this must coincide with the production of an ovum. The points of failure in this essentially simple process are many, but fortunately today medical science is able to overcome a large proportion of them.

Normal difficulties

Couples vary greatly in the speed with which they are able to conceive. Many women are able to conceive in the month following the discontinuation of contraceptive precautions. However, a large number of couples may wait sometimes two to five years or even longer before a child is born, despite both of the partners being entirely normal. In addition to the normal variation between couples and individuals, a person's fertility varies during different stages of his or her reproductive life. In general, a woman's fertility decreases as she approaches the menopause and the readiness with which she can conceive at the age of 45 is usually much less than when she was 25. In men the pattern is less well established; many men are capable of fathering children in the upper age extremes of life.

Many couples who have not used any form of contraception during their married life are surprised by the pattern in which their children are born. For example, their children's ages may be 10, 8 and 3 years and they will maintain that no conscious form of contraception was used between second and third children and none after the birth of the last child. In more extreme cases, a woman might have two or three children before the age of 30, use no contraception thereafter, and be more than a little surprised to find she is pregnant at the age of 40 or even older.

The "luck factor"
It is obvious, therefore, that the ability to produce children depends upon more than just physiological competence; it

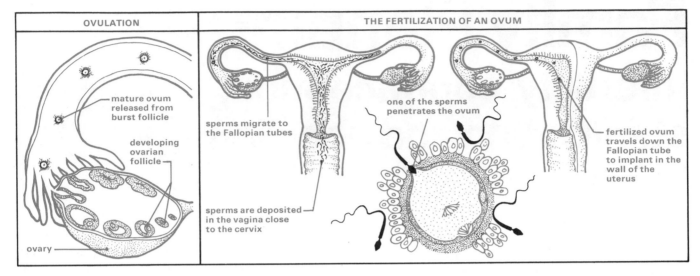

OVULATION	THE FERTILIZATION OF AN OVUM

mature ovum released from burst follicle

developing ovarian follicle

ovary

sperms migrate to the Fallopian tubes

sperms are deposited in the vagina close to the cervix

one of the sperms penetrates the ovum

fertilized ovum travels down the Fallopian tube to implant in the wall of the uterus

The diagram above shows the normal sequence of events that are necessary for conception to occur. At ovulation (left) a ripe egg cell or ovum is released from the ovary and begins to travel slowly down the Fallopian tube toward the uterus. During sexual intercourse, sperm cells are deposited in the vagina in the seminal fluid ejaculated by the man; they then travel up through the uterus to the Fallopian tubes to meet the ovum. Fertilization occurs when one of the sperms penetrates the ovum, after which the fertilized egg continues its journey to the uterus, where it attaches itself to the uterine lining.

requires a combination of correctly timed physical and hormonal events, a suitable mental attitude by both partners, and many other poorly understood factors—which, until they are explained by scientific analysis, can only be described as "luck." It cannot be denied that after exhaustive tests at the most skilled medical centers in the world, there are couples who are deemed to be normal in every way and—despite trying very hard for many years—are incapable of producing a child. For these couples the "luck factor" obviously represents some as yet undiscovered piece of biological information. This may provide some justification for a continuing "fertility rite" (such as the throwing of rice at weddings), even in the most sophisticated, civilized societies.

Psychological factors

The psychological aspects are clearly important. Much has been written concerning the need for harmony within the couple's relationship. It is well known that emotional trauma can in some cases reduce a woman's fertility, at the extreme of which is AMENORRHEA (absence of menstruation)—as frequently seen in young women who undergo major changes or upsets in their lives. The girl who goes away to college or moves to a new environment may frequently stop her menstrual periods spontaneously for

three or four months or even longer. This in itself is extremely worrying, particularly if there is a fear of pregnancy, and these anxieties may be compounded and prolong the amenorrhea.

Marital discord may delay conception in quite simple ways, such as the interruption of the normal timings and frequency of intercourse, and in some couples the concealed unwillingness by one partner to start a family may have subconsciously affected the speed of conception. While most accept the need for a sympathetic mental attitude in both partners, the exact definition of this is liable to conjecture; therefore, when found to be deficient, it is frequently difficult to treat, even by expert counseling.

When is medical investigation necessary?

A line must be drawn between those couples who are entirely normal and experience acceptable delays in producing children, and those who are in need of medical investigation and possible treatment. This line will vary from couple to couple and many other factors must be considered. The couple in their late 30s perhaps will require tests after one year of trying for pregnancy. A couple aged 21 or thereabouts might well be encouraged to spend at least two years or even longer before undergoing infertility tests.

As a rough guide, many doctors would be reluctant to investigate couples who have been unsuccessful in producing a child within less than two years of trying to conceive when their relationship has been normal. This is an extremely important point. Many couples realize that they may not be infertile after all when an examination of their relationship reveals that, for instance, over the past two or three years—with business trips, vacations and other activities—they might have been together for only a few months each year. Frequently, intercourse may not have taken place at the crucial mid-cycle fertile time.

One of the most easily cured cases of infertility that I have had to treat was that of a woman who worked as a night supervisor, married to a man who worked as a policeman on day shifts. A simple change of occupation by the woman, so that she worked in the day and slept with her husband at night, quadrupled their frequency of intercourse and the woman became pregnant after three months, despite "trying" for three years previously!

Primary or secondary infertility

It is frequently helpful to know whether either partner has fathered or mothered a child either in that relationship or previously. Having had one or more children by a previous relationship does not necessarily exonerate one of the partners. However, it does indicate that one partner (or both) was at one time capable of producing children and this may be important during investigations.

A man or a woman who was previously capable of having children might well acquire diseases (such as mumps in men, or pelvic infection in women) which subsequently render them unable to have children. Infertility investigations can be misdirected if one of the partners refuses to undergo tests on the basis that he or she has already produced a child by a different partner.

Requirements for normal conception

As a rough guide, it can be assumed that the life of an individual sperm is about 48 hours. The female ovum (egg) released or caught in the Fallopian tube by the fimbriae (finger-like projections) is probably viable for 18 hours or more. Most women ovulate at mid-cycle time, although this varies slightly from woman to woman. Under optimum conditions intercourse should therefore take place around the 12th or 13th day of the cycle, with the first day being counted as the onset of bleeding at the start of the normal menstrual period. Abstinence from both intercourse and masturbation will allow the male partner to increase his sperm count; many experts recommend that a serious attempt at conception around the mid-cycle point should be preceded by two or three days of such abstinence, and suggest that high frequency of intercourse—such as two or three times per day—renders the sperm numbers beneath optimum for conception.

Sperm counts

Several points must be made about sperm counts. The first is very simple: men with low sperm counts may not have trouble fathering a child, and men with high sperm counts may be sterile. These are exceptions to a generalization that if the sperm count falls beneath 60,000,000 per ml of ejaculate, a man may well have difficulty in becoming a father, and that a man with more than that number will on the whole have little difficulty. In addition to the number of

sperm, the *quality* of the sperm is also extremely important. In particular, a large proportion of sperm seen under the microscope should be fully motile and there should be a low proportion of abnormal shapes. It cannot be overemphasized that this is a generalization. But it is accepted that if a low sperm count is found in a man while the female partner has been shown to be normal following her infertility tests, then he is likely to be the cause of the couple's difficulties in producing children.

Sperm counts of less than 60,000,000 per ml (termed *oligospermia*) are not uncommonly found in men who have had difficulty in becoming fathers. There is obviously more to this problem than just low numbers of sperms, and the quality of the individual sperm or the fluid in which it is situated may be more important. Occasionally, a man will be found to produce no sperms at all (*azoospermia*). (See the section on *Male Infertility*.)

The life of spermatozoa can be extended by storage in cold conditions, and "sperm banks" have already been established. In men who are to undergo either surgery or drug treatment which is likely to render them sterile afterward (such as those used for treating tumors of the testis) the stored sperms can then be used for artificial insemination (see AID/AIH) in the future. There are also one or two centers which will store sperm for those men undergoing vasectomy (voluntary male sterilization) in case they should wish to have a further child in the future. Much study and research has been given to the question of which sperms will produce a male infant and which will produce a female. Various systems of centrifugation have so far failed to produce a method of dividing sperm so that the sex of a child can be predetermined.

Failures of technique

It is necessary for the spermatozoa to be deposited at the neck of the womb (cervix) during intercourse. Spermatozoa deposited at the front of the vagina can occasionally work their way through the vagina and impregnate the woman, although this is much less likely than if the spermatozoa are deposited high inside the vagina. It is usually necessary, therefore, that the sexual technique results in the correct placing of spermatozoa. In cases where the man is unable to do so, such as in the early discharge of semen before entering the woman (premature ejaculation), fertility is likely to be impeded.

A gynecologist investigating a couple complaining of infertility would insure that intercourse is satisfactory—without necessarily going into every small detail; occasionally, abnormalities of sexual technique have explained some cases of infertility. Successful technique is checked by means of the postcoital test (see later) and it is necessary to exclude the possible abnormalities at the outset. Strange as it may seem to most people, the abnormalities can include the deposition of spermatozoa in the umbilicus (navel) instead of the vagina, and occasionally couples have practiced rectal intercourse without necessarily considering this to be incorrect.

Failure of penetration is the most common difficulty of technique. The management of premature ejaculation usually requires the assistance of a skilled sex therapist, and frequently requires a programmed course of instruction in which stages of the sexual act are built up to enable the man to increase his control of ejaculation. Simple discussion of the problem with a third party often relieves the anxiety this sexual failure produces and improvement of the problem frequently stabilizes a marriage or relationship as well as enhancing fertility.

Effects of the woman's internal environment on sperm

The spermatozoa are happy in an environment which is slightly alkaline. The pH of the normal cervical secretion at the neck of the womb is between 7 and 8; this is suitable for prolonging the life and activity of the male seed. The vagina, however, in order to minimize the incidence of infections, has secretions which are acid; its pH is between 4.5 and 5. Thus, spermatozoa deposited low in the vagina remain active for only a short time under these acidic conditions.

The spermatozoa are constructed and stored in the testes of the man within the bag of skin known as the scrotum. Production depends on their rate of use. During ejaculation the spermatozoa are conducted up a small muscular tube known as the *vas deferens* and during their journey they receive juices from a pouch called the *seminal vesicle,* and from the *prostate gland.* The normal seminal fluid is slightly alkaline (pH 7.5) and in this the spermatozoa will remain alive for up to 48 hours. In a more acid medium they become very active but do not live as long. Research shows that in the acidic vagina they do not live longer than 10-12 hours, whereas in the cervical mucus produced at the time of ovulation they may survive for up to 72 hours; those that reach the Fallopian tubes shortly after intercourse appear to survive there for about 48 hours.

In laboratory experiments it has been shown that the spermatozoa rapidly line up along the interface between the seminal fluid and the normal mucus from the cervix at the time of ovulation. Penetration into this cervical secretion occurs in columns. Infections around the cervix at this time may cause a discharge of pus which can form a barrier which the spermatozoa are unable to penetrate. Research has suggested that in some women antibodies are developed against their husband's sperm, and semen collected from the cervix of such women shows only dead sperms.

Although failure of the woman to have an orgasm is not usually a cause of infertility, it is possible that in such circumstances there is less cervical secretion.

After the spermatozoa enter the uterus, the contractions of this muscular organ conduct them to the Fallopian tubes—entering on either side of the top of the uterus. The spermatozoa find their way along these tubes where, in one of the tubes, the ovum is awaiting their arrival. Although many spermatozoa surround the ovum, their heads pressed hard against the cell membrane, only one will enter the ovum and its chromosomes fuse with those of the egg and cause fertilization. It is believed that while penetrating the cervical mucus a chemical change takes place inside the sperm cell which enhances its chance of entering and fertilizing the ovum.

Male infertility

Unfortunately, society has been slow to differentiate between male infertility and impotence. For this reason many men are unwilling to undergo tests for infertility, although they are happy that their wives should be extensively investigated. It must be emphasized therefore that a man who is potent—that is, who has no difficulty in sustaining an erection of the penis—may well have an ejaculate which contains insufficient or abnormal spermatozoa and thus renders him less than normally fertile or infertile. It is essential that a man's fertility should be established as early as possible during investigations into why a couple cannot conceive, before subjecting the woman to more complex tests which may involve a general anesthetic and consequently a small but significant risk.

MALE REPRODUCTIVE ORGANS

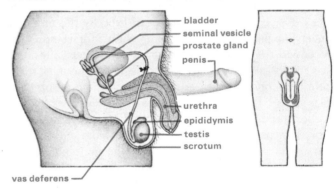

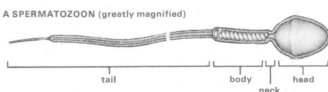

A SPERMATOZOON (greatly magnified)

The small quantity of fluid ejaculated for a man's penis at orgasm consists principally of secretions from the seminal vesicle and prostate gland and up to 500 million or more spermatozoa produced in the testes. A high percentage of malformed sperms, abnormally low numbers of sperms and sometimes the complete absence of live sperms in the seminal fluids are all possible causes of infertility.

Semenalysis

Historically it has been assumed that if a couple are infertile it is because the woman is "barren." In the light of more recent knowledge, *both* partners should be tested at the outset and no man should be ashamed to come forward for *semenalysis*. In this simple test the man collects the ejaculate in a sterile container following masturbation (or it is collected during intercourse) and this is examined with a microscope within two to four hours of collection. It is helpful if the man has abstained from intercourse for two or three days before this collection. In a normal collection the quantity of the ejaculate may vary between 2 and 6 ml and will have an alkaline pH as mentioned before. The number of spermatozoa should be over 60,000,000 per ml, and 80% or more of the spermatozoa should be actively motile.

A search is made for abnormal cells and spermatozoa may be noticed with double heads, double tails or short tails. The normal count contains less than 20% of abnormal forms. The size of the individual cells is also noted and it does not matter if all the cells are large or all small, but a specimen that contains cells of different sizes may well be associated with lower than normal fertility.

Causes of low sperm counts

There are many causes for azoospermia (no sperms produced) or oligospermia (scanty numbers) and some of these may be due to congenital abnormalities. Just before birth in the normal male fetus, the testes (which are developed in the abdominal cavity) descend through the inguinal canal of the groin down through into the scrotum, which is a bag held outside the body. The temperature in the scrotum is slightly lower than that of the rest of the body, and this enhances sperm production. In some cases one, or both, of the testes fails to descend completely (see UNDESCENDED TESTIS). Retention of the testes in the abdominal cavity is frequently associated with infertility. The retained testes are, incidentally, more likely to undergo malignant changes than those properly descended into the scrotum.

It is believed that the production of sperm is reduced if the temperature of the testes is raised—such as in wearing thick underwear, or too frequent hot bathing, or in the presence of a varicocele (an abnormality of the testicular veins which leads to high blood flow through the testis and therefore a rise in the temperature of the scrotum). Living at high altitudes for long intervals has also been shown to interfere with the production of spermatozoa. Disease of the testis—such as mumps and bacterial infections such as gonorrhea and syphilis—can sometimes produce sterility, but by no means in every case. Sperm production may also be unsatisfactory if the man is an invalid or leads a sedentary existence, without proper exercise.

Absolute definitions of the requirements to improve sperm production are difficult to delineate and there is much that is surrounded by folklore. It has been popular in the past to recommend that men who are less than normally fertile should take more exercise; some doctors have recommended an early morning run in the doubtful hope of improving sperm production. Success of this treatment is difficult to evaluate.

If semenalysis shows repeated low sperm counts then a man should be seen by an expert in a genitourinary department, where some improvement in the sperm count may be possible by various measures. Recently sperm counts have been improved by the use of hormonal drugs, but much research still remains to be done. The man with persistent azoospermia may well be advised to consider adoption of a child or artificial insemination by donor (see AID/AIH). In some of oligospermia, collections of ejaculates have been made and artificial insemination with the husband's amalgamated ejaculates has been performed.

Investigation of the woman

Causes of female infertility

A woman may be unable to conceive because of congenital abnormalities of her uterus, Fallopian tubes or ovaries. In other cases, despite having normal pelvic organs, she may be unable to produce an ovum (failure of ovulation) or her pelvic organs may have become altered by disease.

Congenital problems

Rarely the uterus or ovaries (or both) may not have developed normally and may be unusually small or completely absent. This will usually result in a failure of menstruation. In rare cases where the ovaries are abnormal or very poorly developed, the female may well have menstruated for a few times, but never experienced anything like normal periods.

Failure of ovulation

It is possible in some cases for a woman with normal menstrual bleeding to fail to produce an ovum each cycle. After the ovum is released from the ovary, the lining of the womb becomes enlarged and produces secretions which will enable a fertilized ovum to implant. At the same time the woman's normal basal body temperature rises about 0.5–1°F (about 0.5°C) and remains slightly higher in the second half of the menstrual cycle than in the first half if ovulation has occurred normally. In addition, in the second half of the cycle, the ovary will produce a hormone called progesterone in preparation for the expected development of a fetus; this can be detected by a blood test.

In any woman with lengthened menstrual cycles or infrequent periods, ovulation is less likely to occur than in one who menstruates normally. It must be emphasized that this is only a generalization and women who ovulate maybe three or four times a year, instead of the normal 12, may well have no difficulty at all in conceiving. However, the woman who never ovulates will not conceive.

Another important point is that during breast feeding the majority of women do not have periods and cease to ovulate until the baby is weaned. (About a third of women who are lactating—producing milk—begin to menstruate before the child is weaned and in these cases pregnancy can occur.) The inhibition of ovulation is achieved by the production of an hormone called prolactin from the pituitary gland at the base of the brain. In a few cases of women complaining of infertility, a high level of prolactin in the blood is discovered, despite the fact that they are not nursing a child. This condition of *hyperprolactinemia* prevents ovulation; it may be caused by a tumor of the pituitary gland, although some women have raised prolactin levels without such a tumor. A proportion of these women will produce small amounts of breast milk without being pregnant. If a tumor is found this must be treated immediately, but in cases of hyperprolactinemia without a tumor, normal levels of prolactin can be restored by treating the woman with a drug called bromocriptive. This is frequently accompanied by restoration of fertility and subsequent pregnancy.

The Fallopian tube

The Fallopian tube is more than just a simple funnel to conduct the egg from ovary to womb. In the normal woman at the time of ovulation, the finger-like extremity of the Fallopian tube is close to the surface of the ovary, so that when the egg is released it finds easy entry into the Fallopian tube. Inside the lining of the Fallopian tube are little cells with hairs called cilia, which are able to waft the egg along the tube to meet the spermatozoa at a slight expansion of the tube near the womb. This movement is also assisted by squeezing of the smooth muscle in the tube wall.

During this time the ovum is nourished by the lining cells of the Fallopian tube. Obviously, destruction of this delicate lining by infection or other disease processes will cause infertility, as will destruction of the tube itself. In cases of partial damage to the lining of the Fallopian tube, the ovum which has been fertilized may be unable to move down into the womb and the pregnancy develops in the tube. This is a potentially very serious condition called an ECTOPIC PREGNANCY; treatment requires a surgical operation to remove the developing embryo and the affected tube.

In normal women, ovulation occurs at monthly intervals from alternative ovaries. Thus, the woman with only one tube will have only six chances of conception per year instead of the usual twelve. In the past, if a Fallopian tube was removed, surgeons often removed the ovary on the same side as well in order to insure that ovulation occurred on the side of the remaining tube every month. It has been discovered, however, that ovulation can in some circumstances take place on the opposite side and the egg still find

its way to the remaining Fallopian tube. Providing the remaining tube is healthy, there is no reason why a woman with only one tube will not conceive, although the speed of conception may be less than a woman with functioning tubes and ovaries on both sides.

Abnormalities of the uterus

Congenital abnormalities of the uterus, Fallopian tubes and vagina occasionally contribute to a failure to conceive. In particular, the double uterus with or without a divided (septate) vagina may inhibit conception and require surgical correction. A septate vagina may cause pain during intercourse and prevent satisfactory penetration by the man.

Occasionally the womb may be distorted by the growth of benign tumors known as FIBROIDS. These may require surgical removal. About four out of every five women have wombs which are normally pulled forward (anteversion). It was thought in the past that women whose wombs pointed backward (retroversion) were less fertile, and frequently operations were performed (with varying success) to correct this condition. Serious infections of the womb lining (ENDOMETRITIS) caused by diseases such as tuberculosis may destroy the lining to such an extent that it is unable to receive the fertilized ovum and implantation is impossible.

Endometriosis

In this condition, which usually affects women between the ages of 30 and 40 (especially those who have not previously conceived), reduced fertility is usually experienced. These women have collections of endometrial cells—similar to those found in the lining of the womb—scattered about in little clumps in various sites (usually the pelvis). Particularly common is endometriosis involving the ovary and the space between the womb and the rectum. Like the cells in the lining of the womb, these abnormally placed endometrial cells are subject to hormonal influences, and enlarge at the time of the menstrual cycle. These cell conglomerations may enlarge and bleed, causing "chocolate cysts."

Various theories have been put forward to explain the appearance of these abnormally placed cells. It would seem likely that these cells have traveled up the Fallopian tubes from the womb and have been deposited inside the abdominal and pelvic cavities by passing through the Fallopian tubes. However, such cellular deposits have been found throughout the body, including in some rare cases the lungs and even the elbow; the theory of "retrograde menstruation" outlined above would not explain this entirely.

It is not fully understood how these endometriotic deposits influence fertility. But like the normal lining cells of the womb, these deposits secrete powerful hormones and chemicals, in particular PROSTAGLANDINS, which may well influence the ovum after it is released from the ovary. Treatment of the endometriosis, if successful, frequently improves fertility.

General conditions

In women who have undergone excessive dieting the severe reduction in body weight can cause the periods to cease (weight-related amenorrhea). In its severe form, ANOREXIA NERVOSA, the periods are completely absent. Weight-related amenorrhea or oligomenorrhea (scanty periods) among dieting young women is not uncommon. The condition is easily treated by encouraging the woman to eat sufficiently to return her weight to that at which her periods ceased.

In animals a diet deficient in vitamin E leads to sterility, but there is no evidence that deficiency of this vitamin occurs in women. In particular, there is no evidence to suggest that taking excessive amounts of vitamin E will improve fertility at all. Chronic alcoholism or addiction to drugs such as morphine or heroin tends to decrease ovarian activity. In many severe disorders of the endocrine glands—such as severe diabetes, thyroid abnormalities, or insufficiency of the adrenal glands—there may be amenorrhea or failure of ovulation. Exposure to excessive x-rays or radioactive materials is a rare cause of infertility.

Medical history

When a woman is investigated for infertility, the doctor will want to establish her present and past state of health. In particular he will be interested in any previous infections—such as tuberculosis or infections inside the abdomen or pelvis, such as peritonitis from an appendix abscess. In an appendix abscess, infection may have caused adhesions around the Fallopian tubes, and thus cause some blockage. Or the tubes may have been damaged by the nearby infection. The woman may have had previous pregnancies which ended in a miscarriage, and subsequent fever following this miscarriage may well have indicated that there had been some infective process in either the womb or the Fallopian tubes—thus producing subsequent sterility. Such an infection is more likely to occur in the so-called "backstreet abortion," in which unsterile instruments were used.

The doctor will ask about the nature, duration and type of periods the woman has experienced. The time at which the periods commenced (menarche) is important; if this was delayed it may suggest some congenital abnormality. The woman with light and rather scanty periods which are irregular or separated by long intervals (such as six to eight weeks) is less likely to be ovulating as frequently as a woman whose periods are moderate in volume and occur regularly every 28 days. Periods that are painful are often an indication that ovulation occurs. This is most easily understood by recalling that when a girl of 11 or 12 begins

to menstruate her first periods are usually painless, since they are not accompanied by ovulation. When ovulation begins, periods may become painful to a variable degree. (However, the absence of pain during periods does not indicate that ovulation is not occurring—many women who ovulate normally and regularly experience quite painless periods throughout their lives.)

A gentle inquiry is usually made to see if sexual intercourse is satisfactory and whether there are any abnormal strains on the relationship. The woman who cannot relax and enjoy her sexual relationships often becomes tense and anxious, which may increase as the stress of not conceiving becomes greater. It has been suggested that this may produce spasm of the womb, and possibly the Fallopian tubes, thus preventing normal function.

Whether this mechanism operates or not, and how important it is if it does, is not entirely clear; many doctors today do not share this theory. However, it is occasionally found that when a woman decides to adopt a baby because she has been unable to conceive herself, she becomes pregnant within a short time of the adoption—as the acquisition of the adopted baby frequently relaxes the couple in both mind and body. In addition, a large proportion of women investigated for infertility frequently conceive after investigations have begun—as they relax in the knowledge that something positive is being done.

Examination of the woman

Usually those congenital abnormalities which would be apparent on general examination of a woman (such as failure of secondary sexual characteristics) are detected and investigated long before the woman complains of infertility. A careful examination of the abdomen frequently reveals scars of operations not previously discussed. In particular, the scar of an appendectomy may be revealed (the occasional problems this produces have already been mentioned). It is not uncommon for the pain of Fallopian tube infection (salpingitis) to mimic appendicitis, and these women are operated on only to find inflamed Fallopian tubes and a normal appendix. The appendix is usually removed at this time, but the woman may not fully appreciate that the pain was caused by salpingitis rather than appendicitis, and the salpingitis may have subsequently damaged the lining of the Fallopian tubes.

A bi-manual vaginal examination will confirm the presence and position of a normal-sized womb and the presence of normal-sized ovaries. Any abnormalities of the womb or ovaries, as previously mentioned, may require treatment—such as the removal of fibroids, or the correction of a double uterus. In cases where the male partner has been unable to penetrate the female, an intact hymen (maidenhead) may be the cause; this can be removed by a simple operation.

If there has been severe salpingitis, the Fallopian tubes will be abnormally enlarged and possibly tender. All the female pelvic organs are mobile in health. If the womb is immobile this may be due to previous infections or possible endometriosis. The marriage may not have been consummated as the result of anxiety causing excessive spasm of the vagina (vaginismus). This may be helped by reassurance and the passage of progressively larger vaginal dilators in a programmed course over weeks or months.

Establishment of ovulation: temperature charts

A simple method of checking that a woman is ovulating is to ask her to keep temperature charts. These are simple daily recordings of her body temperature taken at the same time every day, usually on arising from sleep. She should not drink coffee or tea, smoke, or even clean her teeth before taking her temperature, as these measures can affect the readings.

In a normal menstrual cycle, as mentioned before, the temperature will usually fall slightly just before ovulation, followed by a rise of $1°F$ ($0.5°C$) after ovulation. This rise is sustained until the onset of menstruation. If conception occurs during the cycle the temperature will remain elevated and menstruation does not usually occur (it is possible that after conception a woman might experience a slight scanty period before they cease completely). Temperature is usually recorded for three or four cycles, and the woman is also asked to record the dates on which intercourse took place. After this record is complete the investigating doctor will have an idea of (1) whether the woman shows signs of ovulation; (2) whether intercourse is taking place at the right time in the cycle; (3) whether intercourse is too frequent or insufficient; and (4) an idea of the patient's interest in the subject overall!

Inadequately kept temperature charts may require further discussion with the doctor to insure that a woman is keen to conceive and to be investigated. Very occasionally a woman will have embarked on infertility investigations when, either consciously or subconsciously, she has no real desire to conceive; she may have been pressured by the husband, who may not be aware of her lack of desire for a child.

Further tests for ovulation

In cases where there is doubt whether ovulation occurred or not, there are some further simple tests that can be performed. These are made during the second half of the cycle, after which it is hoped that ovulation will have occurred. The first test consists of examining a small drop of the mucus from the neck of the womb; this is easily obtained during a vaginal examination. Under the microscope a characteristic appearance will be seen if ovulation has occurred. Secondly, a blood sample taken around day 21 will show a raised level of progesterone (as discussed before). Thirdly, a small piece of the lining of the womb (endometrial biopsy) may be taken relatively painlessly without any form of anesthetic. An expert pathologist will be able to report that ovulation has taken place if he sees that the lining of the womb has become secretory, and ready to receive any fertilized ovum.

Postcoital test

This simple test yields much information and is usually performed early during investigations for infertility. The couple are asked to have sexual intercourse, preferably at the ovulation phase of the woman's menstrual cycle, and the woman is given a medical examination within four to six hours. Mucus from the neck of the womb is obtained with a small wire loop and examined immediately under the microscope; if numerous motile sperms are seen, the result is normal. If only dead sperms are seen and yet the results of the semenalysis are normal, the implication is that the cervical mucus is hostile to the spermatozoa—because of the quality of the mucus, infection, or possibly because of antibody formation.

If no sperms are seen, the test is repeated. If successive postcoital tests do not reveal the presence of any sperms at all, doubt is cast over the sexual technique, suggesting perhaps a failure of penetration. On several occasions where no sperms have been seen it has been discovered on further questioning that following intercourse the woman has leaped up and performed vigorous vaginal douchings with water. This procedure of immediate activity, with or without douching, is used in some underdeveloped countries as a feeble contraceptive. However, it does occasionally explain infertility in some women who might not have considered this as a contributing factor to their difficulty in conceiving.

If ovulation has been confirmed and the results of postcoital tests are normal (with male infertility having been excluded), the investigations progress to more complex procedures.

Special tests and procedures

1. Insufflation of the Fallopian tubes

If gas is blown under gentle pressure up through the womb, it will escape into the abdominal cavity along the Fallopian tubes, providing they are not blocked. A simple test to see if the Fallopian tubes are open is performed by placing a small tube into the cervix and releasing a gentle stream of carbon dioxide. This gas is chosen so that it will be absorbed quickly into the bloodstream without adverse effects. As the tubes are muscular there is always a slight resistance to the flow of the gas; but the carbon dioxide should flow through at a steady rate. Occasionally a stethoscope placed on the abdomen just over the ends of the tubes can detect the bubbling of gas. If both tubes are blocked, gas will be unable to pass. In the presence of tubal spasm there will be intermittent passage of gas.

Unfortunately, if one tube is blocked it is unlikely that insufflation will indicate which tube this is, and so the information obtained from insufflation of the Fallopian tubes is rather limited. For this reason it has been superseded by laparoscopy (see below).

2. The Hysterosalpingogram

This is essentially similar to the insufflation, but instead of using carbon dioxide gas a water-soluble fluid is used which is opaque to x-rays. Thus, as the fluid is injected up into the womb, an outline is shown on a moving x-ray film. Gradually the womb will fill with the dye and then the fluid will enter the tubes up to the ovary end. Any abnormalities in the shape of the womb will be revealed, as will blockage of the Fallopian tubes.

Some gynecologists perform this examination without a general anesthetic, but many find a general anesthetic kinder to the patient. This procedure is of definite help if a uterine abnormality is suspected. Not infrequently pregnancy follows a hysterosalpingogram, and it may be that a small blockage (such as by a plug of mucus, or fine adhesions) is cleared by the passage of the oily contrast fluid.

3. Laparoscopy

Laparoscopy is an investigation which yields a great deal of information. The investigating doctor will see at first hand the uterus, Fallopian tubes and ovaries. He will be able to watch the passage of a blue dye through the tubes out into the pelvic cavity. He will also be able to observe the state of the pelvis and the other abdominal organs (such as the bladder and rectum)—specifically, to detect any signs of previous infection and to look for the presence of endometriosis.

The operation is performed under general anesthesia and a very small incision (about 1 cm long) is made just beneath the umbilicus. After the bladder has been emptied, a thin hollow needle is inserted into the abdominal cavity; a gas, either carbon dioxide or nitrous oxide, is then gently passed through the tube to inflate the abdomen. After about 3 liters of gas have been passed, the abdomen will be distended—leaving a large space between the front abdominal wall and the intestines and pelvic organs.

When this has been achieved a laparoscope (which is like a small telescope with an internal lighting system) is inserted into the abdominal cavity through the small incision, after removal of the inflating needle. The woman is then tipped on the operating table with her head down and feet raised. This causes the bowel to slide away from the pelvic organs, thus providing a better view of the uterus, ovaries and Fallopian tubes. The doctor will then visually inspect the pelvic organs; a second doctor will pass a colored fluid up along the cavity of the uterus and out through the Fallopian tubes (as in the case of a hysterosalpingogram).

Through the laparoscope the first doctor will see the actual passage of the dye through both tubes. He will notice if one tube is open and the other closed, or whether there is complete blockage of both tubes. As the dye passes along

To obtain a hysterosalpingogram a radiopaque liquid is injected through the cervix; obstructions in the uterus and the Fallopian tubes can thus be detected on moving x-ray film. In the left-hand example the uterus is normal and the Fallopian tubes are open—there is some spillage of the fluid at the ends of the tubes around the ovaries. In the right-hand picture, however, both Fallopian tubes are shown to be blocked close to the uterus.

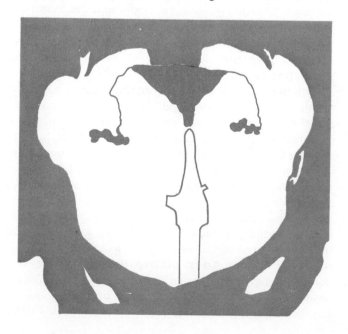
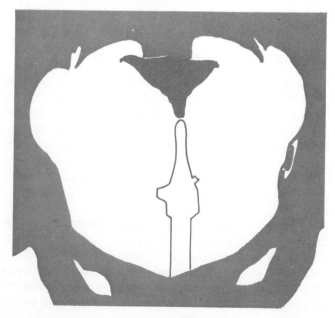

Laparoscopy is a technique for direct visual examination of the pelvic organs. The abdominal cavity is first inflated with gas passed through a hollow needle and the patient is tilted so that the intestines move away from the pelvic organs (left); the laparoscope is then inserted, allowing the doctor to inspect the uterus, ovaries and Fallopian tubes (right).

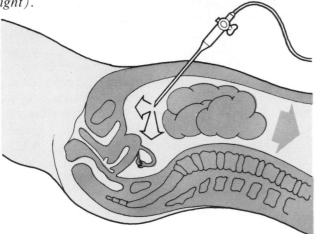

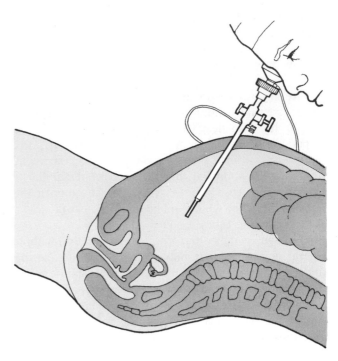

the tube there is a slight discoloration of that tube and the doctor may confirm where any blockage has occurred, although confirmation of the site of a blockage is best performed by hysterosalpingogram.

A major advantage of laparoscopy is that the condition of the uterus and tubes can be observed directly and the feasibility of subsequent operations to improve fertility can be assessed at that time. In particular, the presence of endometriosis may well be established and congenital abnormalities discovered. At the end of the procedure the laparoscope is removed and all the gas is drawn out (aspirated). The abdominal wound is held together with a small stitch; the whole operation usually takes only about 15 minutes.

Treatment of female infertility

If pelvic examination or laparoscopy reveals the presence of an abnormality, it can usually be corrected. For example fibroids may be removed, or a fixed retroverted uterus may be corrected if it is thought to contribute to the infertility. Endometriosis may well need treatment. In some cases the treatment consists of surgical removal or electrocautery of the endometriotic deposits or by the production of a "pseudo-pregnancy" by the continuous administration of progestogen and estrogen.

There are numerous side effects from continuous hormone administration; although the menstrual periods are usually suppressed, "breakthrough" bleeding is quite common. This can be distressing, since treatment usually takes six to twelve months. Recently, however, considerable success has been achieved in the treatment of en-

dometriosis with an antihormone preparation, which does not give rise to these problems.

If ovulation has not occurred, or occurs very infrequently, laparoscopy will reveal the state of the ovaries. In rare cases the ovaries may be replaced by multiple small cysts called "polycystic ovaries." In this condition the ova fail to mature and treatment may take the form of surgical removal of a wedge of ovary.

"Fertility drugs"

If ovulation does not occur in the presence of normal healthy looking ovaries, then it may be possible to stimulate ovulation by the use of hormones. One example is the synthetic drug clomiphene (which is an antiestrogen); another is the hormone normally produced by the pituitary gland to stimulate the release of an ovum—follicle-stimulating hormone or FSH.

Clomiphene is usually used when the patient's FSH level (as measured by urinary output) is found to be normal. Its exact mode of action is uncertain, but it appears to stimulate the pituitary gland to produce FSH, and to enhance the normal effect of FSH in stimulating ovulation.

However, when the patient's production of FSH is low, this hormone can be administered by injection to replace the body's lack.

An active extract containing FSH can be prepared from human pituitary glands. Obviously the supply of this material is very limited, and it is not usually available for routine clinic work. An extract from the serum of pregnant mares is commercially available, but antibodies are quickly developed against it so that it provides only a short effect. However, large amounts of the hormone are obtainable

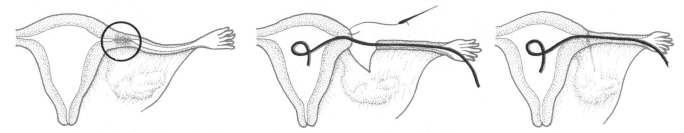

A blocked Fallopian tube can sometimes be corrected surgically, especially if the blockage is close to the uterus, as shown above. The blocked section (left) is removed and a tubal splint (fine nylon catheter) is passed through the tube into the uterus (center) before the shortened tube is sutured onto the uterus (right). The tubal splint maintains the normal tubal canal and can be removed easily through the cervix (neck of the womb) once the healing process is complete.

from the urine of postmenopausal women. The reason for this is that at the menopause a woman's ovaries become inactive and the pituitary gland produces more and more follicle-stimulating hormone in an effort to get the unresponsive ovaries to produce an egg. Thus, high levels of the hormone are found in the urine of these women. This human postmenopausal FSH is given by daily injections, usually for five days.

The patient's excretion of the female hormone estrogen is measured daily by a 24-hour urine sample or a blood test. If there is no response the dose is progressively increased on subsequent days until an adequate response is shown by the rise in female hormone excreted in the urine. This is usually accompanied by the injection of a substance called human chorionic gonadotropin (HCG), which also enhances an early pregnancy. This treatment is not without risks, and the response of a particular dose of these hormones varies greatly from patient to patient. In each case the response must be measured by careful daily analysis of the urine or blood tests. If excessive doses are used it can produce multiple ovulation, with multiple pregnancy as a possible result. The rapid change from being a woman who has considered herself infertile for several years to being the prospective mother of triplets or quads can be overwhelming, the usual reaction being a mixture of extreme elation and shock!

Tubal surgery

When the Fallopian tubes are damaged (for example following infection) they usually become blocked. The lining of the tube may be destroyed and unable to function properly. However, in the majority of cases damaged tubes are usually *blocked* tubes. The hysterosalpingogram will give an indication of where a tube is blocked, but no real indication is given of the length of blockage in an individual tube. Laparoscopy will reveal the condition of the tube and

whether or not there is any chance of improving tubal function by microsurgery.

Surgery to remove a portion of a diseased tube in the middle and join the two ends is possible, but by no means always successful. However, a much higher success rate is achieved in cases where the blockage lies close to the uterus. Cutting out this diseased portion and rejoining the tube to the uterus (see illustration) is frequently successful—providing that the rest of the tube is un-damaged and that the remaining length of tube is sufficient to allow the fimbriae to reach the ovary to pick up the released ova.

During all forms of tubal surgery, careful attention is paid to the prevention of bleeding and infection both during and after the operation—since these procedures can cause further adhesions and tubal blockage. Even when the tubes have been successfully reimplanted into the uterus, and have been shown by subsequent tests to be open, the cells lining the tube may well have been damaged and fertility impaired.

When all has failed

Out of a group of couples complaining of infertility a large proportion will conceive while undergoing tests. Another group will be helped by the procedures mentioned, such as the induction of ovulation or tubal surgery. However, there will be a small group for whom medical science is at present unable to provide the solution to their fertility problem.

For the man with azoospermia or the woman with completely damaged tubes, the confirmation that they will not have children of their own frequently brings to an end a long period of doubt, mistrust and anxiety. Once the position has clearly been established and the uncertainty ended, arrangements can be made for the adoption of a child if desired. As mentioned before, artificial insemination of a woman by her husband, especially with pooled semen collections, has been offered in certain situations. Artificial insemination by donor semen is more controversial.

The future

Extreme excitement was generated around the world in 1978 with the birth in Britain of the first "test-tube baby." This may well herald a new chance for many women to conceive. It is a great sadness that a woman with perfectly functioning ovaries and a normal uterus is unable to conceive because her Fallopian tubes are blocked and the egg cannot make its two-inch journey down to the uterus. Drs. Steptoe and Edwards were able to remove a ripe ovum from their patient's ovary, using a laparoscope and micropipette, and fertilize that ovum with her husband's semen. The resulting embryo grew for a few days in a special nutrient fluid and then was sucessfully implanted into the mother's womb, where it continued to develop normally.

The difficulty in this process has been the successful implantation of the microscopic fertilized ovum, because at the first menstrual period the fertilized ovum is usually shed along with the menstrual fluid. But this technique is especially significant, since the results of tubal surgery are frequently disappointing—despite very skilled teams operating for many hours using complex microsurgical techniques. It is hoped that as the expertise of the "test-tube baby" process becomes more widely available, many women who had resigned themselves to infertility may well be delighted to find themselves one day in an antenatal clinic.

CONTRACEPTION

The importance of contraception

Despite the ease with which contraceptive precautions can be obtained in Western countries, the number of unwanted pregnancies which are either aborted or go to term for adoption is still enormous. It may be that a small proportion of these were initially wanted but changed circumstances, such as marital break-up, later made the pregnancy undesirable. However, the majority of unwanted pregnancies are entirely unplanned. Surprisingly, even people who are well aware of the risk of becoming pregnant often seem to have the attitude that "it will never happen to me." Unwanted pregnancies occur even in intelligent girls who have access to adequate contraceptive facilities. For many women, anxiety about family planning procedures and contraceptive precautions is often compounded by false information passed on by friends and relatives. These fears may discourage a woman from seeking the advice she needs.

While ideally responsibility for contraception should be shared between the male and female partners, in most cases the price of failed or ignored contraceptive procedures is paid largely by the woman. In a happy understanding relationship, the responsible male can be relied upon to take his full share of contraceptive precautions if necessary. However, where the relationship is less well founded or more casual, the woman cannot leave this important matter to chance.

Pregnancy and childbirth still involve risks to the mother's health, despite all the facilities of modern medicine. Although they are relatively small today, there can be no justification for these risks if the pregnancy is unwanted. Similarly, a therapeutic termination of pregnancy carries a risk of psychological problems, and—despite all precautions that doctors can take—a slight danger of medical complications. Therefore, no one should regard the availability of abortions as a failsafe against carelessness in contraception. Furthermore, it is generally agreed that no one has the right to bring a child into the world without accepting full and personal responsibility for its upbringing, education and general wellbeing.

As a population becomes better nourished and more healthy in general, the reproductive years of the women of that society become longer. In the Western world girls are becoming sexually mature at an earlier and earlier age, and today most girls have reached puberty by the age of 13 or 14; most will continue to menstruate until they are around the age of 48–50 years. (In developing countries the reproductive span is much less.) It follows that most girls become capable of reproduction long before their mental, social and economic status suggests they should bear a child. While sex education distributes more and more information about contraception, the one great barrier yet to be overcome is to convince every girl that it *can* happen to her. A typical situation is for a young couple to have intercourse without adequate contraceptive protection, or maybe use the safe period or withdrawal method, and to "get away with it" for several months or even longer. Their success makes them bolder and that visit to the doctor or family planning clinic for more effective contraceptive precautions is delayed until the inevitable pregnancy occurs. It is vitally important that all those exposed to a risk of an unwanted pregnancy should seek adequate contraceptive advice from a qualified person at the earliest opportunity.

Of course, throughout the world there are many millions of people, particularly Roman Catholics, who do not use "artificial" methods of contraception (such as the condom, diaphragm, intrauterine device, spermicides or the oral contraceptive pill) because of religious objections. The safe period (or "rhythm method") is the only method of birth control available to such people. Unfortunately, however, this method (which is discussed below) is not 100% reliable, and the stark fact is that if you do not wish to use artificial contraception—for whatever reason—the only *certain* way of avoiding pregnancy is to refrain from sexual intercourse.

In the past it has been maintained by some that by publicizing contraceptive information, or by making contraceptives easily available, one is encouraging promiscuity. It must be remembered that whereas social attitudes may change, sex and indeed promiscuity have been extremely popular throughout the ages. Even in prudish Victorian England the number of unwanted pregnancies was staggering. Contraceptive advice is not therefore likely to encourage promiscuity or extramarital intercourse, but aims to insure that unwanted children are not brought into the world; also that women should not undergo potentially life-threatening procedures such as therapeutic abortion, and that as far as possible gynecologists and their nurses will not be called upon to perform these operations.

Withdrawal method

In this method of contraception (also called *coitus interruptus*) the male withdraws his penis from the vagina before ejaculation takes place. It has the advantage of not requiring any physical contraceptive precaution, involves no risk to either the man or woman, and still remains popular among the general population. The overwhelming disadvantage is that it often renders intercourse unsatisfactory and unfulfilled, and frequently fails when the man either withdraws too late or not at all. In addition, a small amount of fluid, usually from the prostate gland, is discharged from the penis before the main part of the ejaculate. This may contain spermatozoa, and the woman can therefore get pregnant even though the man withdraws before ejaculation. She can even get pregnant when the man does not actually enter her—a surprisingly frequent occurrence among high school children, and one which demonstrates the importance of obtaining effective contraceptive precautions before any sexual relations take place. The withdrawal method is *not* reliable and is not recommended as a means of contraception.

The "safe period" (or "rhythm method")

A woman is only capable of conceiving at the time of ovulation. For most women ovulation occurs in the middle of the menstrual cycle. Many women therefore are able to avoid conceiving by abstaining from intercourse during the mid-cycle, e.g., between the 10th and 18th days. This method is also popular, particularly in countries where more active contraceptive precautions are not encouraged or are prohibited by canon law. It can be a suitable method for women in the late reproductive years whose fertility is considerably reduced anyway. However, the method is not reliable for women who do not ovulate exactly at the midpoint of the cycle each month, and in women who have irregular periods. Reliability can be slightly improved by the use of temperature charts or spermicidal pessaries.

The sheath, or condom

Apart from abstinence, this is the form of contraception most widely used throughout the world. A lubricated latex rubber sheath is drawn onto the erect penis. The entire ejaculate is held within the condom and spermatozoa

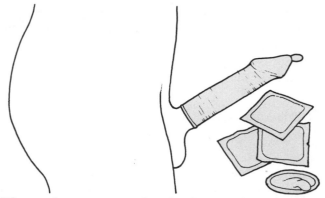

The condom consists of a thin latex rubber sheath drawn over the erect penis before intercourse. The seminal fluid is retained in the reservoir at the end.

cannot escape into the vagina. Soon after ejaculation the condom is carefully withdrawn from the vagina. Care should be exercised when removing the condom from the penis to prevent spill of the ejaculate near the vagina or introitus (opening). Occasional failures do occur with this method, especially if the condom is not applied properly, if it is not worn in the earlier phases of coitus, or because it slips from the penis after ejaculation. Probably the greatest cause of failure in this method is that, in the heat of the moment, the condom is not put on, and there is no contraceptive protection from a condom left in a jacket pocket. The efficiency can also be improved by lubricating the condom with a spermicidal jelly, i.e., a jelly containing chemicals which will kill any sperm on contact.

The condom has many advantages as a method of contraception. It is reliable if used correctly, it does not cause any risk to the man or woman, and it also provides a barrier between the penis and the vagina and cervix. In this way it can help to prevent the transmission of venereal disease (although it is not foolproof by any means); it has also been suggested that limiting the contact of the cervix with the penis and seminal fluid may reduce the stimulation of cervical cancer. The main disadvantage is that although they are made of very thin latex rubber, sheaths do cause some loss of sensitivity and many men—and indeed women—find that this is unacceptable. Some might argue that the interruption of sexual activity to apply a condom is also undesirable. In casual relationships, and in those where the male partner is not as trustworthy as he might be, the great disadvantage of the sheath is that it is dependent upon male responsibility, and this is grossly lacking in some cases.

Spermicides

There are a variety of spermicidal preparations available today. Pessaries, foams or films containing spermicidal compounds may be placed in the vagina before intercourse. By themselves they are relatively unsafe and should not be relied upon for protection; however, they are useful in conjunction with other forms of contraception, such as the intrauterine device, diaphragm or condom, to increase reliability. Again there is no risk to either the man or woman from the use of spermicides.

Hormone injections

It is possible to prevent ovulation by the injection of hormones, mostly progestogen. The usual injections are given intramuscularly and may give protection for between one and three months. There are many disadvantages to this method, one being the irregular menstrual bleeding which may occur and the loss of regular menstrual cycles. However, hormone injections can be used where short-term contraception is required and other methods are unsatisfactory, or in situations where more straightforward contraceptive precautions are not indicated, such as in severe mental deficiency or markedly disturbed psychiatric patients.

The diaphragm or Dutch cap

This method is reliable if it is used correctly and every time. The diaphragm consists of a round thin flexible ring across which is stretched a thin latex rubber film or diaphragm with a slight bulge. They are made in various sizes; a doctor will measure a woman and fit the correct size. When properly in place the diaphragm lies at an angle in the vagina with the back part of the rim fitting closely behind the neck of the womb (cervix) and the soft rubber diaphragm covering the neck of the womb completely. The front part of the diaphragm rim lies behind the pubic bone. Before insertion the woman checks for minute holes in the rubber by holding it up to the light. She then smears the whole of the diaphragm, on both surfaces, with spermicidal cream and then inserts it. When the diaphragm is correctly in place the neck of the womb is covered by spermicidal cream and there is a seal around the rim which prevents the spermatozoa from getting to the cervix. The diaphragm is inserted before intercourse and should not be removed for at least 6 hours afterward, so that the spermicide will kill any spermatozoa before it is removed. There is also a smaller device called the *cervical cap,* which is a small cup-shaped rubber cap fitting directly over the neck of the womb. This is less effective because it is difficult for the woman to place it accurately in position and in some cases it can be dislodged during intercourse.

Advantages and disadvantages

There are many pros and cons with the diaphragm. On the plus side it is reliable if used correctly and involves no risk to either woman or man. After careful instruction it is easy for the woman to insert, and when properly fitted the woman is unaware of its presence in the vagina. It is

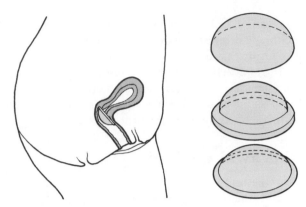

The diaphragm or Dutch cap is always used in conjunction with a spermicidal cream; it must be correctly inserted into the vagina before intercourse to cover the cervix and left in position for 6 hours afterward.

popular among women in the later reproductive years where frequency of intercourse may not be so high as in 20-year-olds, or where other methods of contraception, such as the contraceptive pill, become more hazardous with age. It is a well tried and popular method—it is said that Cleopatra used a diaphragm made from a lemon skin.

The main disadvantage of the diaphragm is that it must be inserted before intercourse; some spontaneity may be lost if events are interrupted by the insertion of a diaphragm. Most pregnancies resulting "from" the diaphragm occur because it has not been used rather than through failure of the diaphragm itself. The diaphragm must be inserted accurately and a small proportion of women are completely unable to do this; when a diaphragm is prescribed great care should be taken to insure that a woman is completely able to insert the device correctly. There is a slight decrease in sensitivity which some men and women find unacceptable. The device is checked regularly at intervals by a family planning specialist to insure that the good fit is maintained. The size of the diaphragm may need to be changed after a woman has had a child or after she has undergone significant weight increase or weight loss, as these events may alter the shape required.

The intrauterine contraceptive device (IUD or IUCD)

It has been known for centuries that objects placed in the uterus decrease fertility. It is said that Arabs traveling on long caravan trains put pebbles in the wombs of their camels to prevent them from becoming pregnant and thus unable to carry the necessary heavy loads. Interest in this form of contraception was revived earlier this century with the popularization of the Graafenberg ring. This was a small gold ring, similar to a wedding ring, which was inserted into the uterine cavity. Being gold the ring was inert and not liable to corrode or to cause a reaction by the

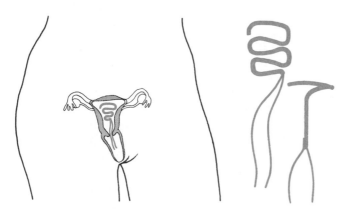

The IUD or coil is available in a variety of shapes; once correctly inserted into the uterus, it can usually be left in position for several years. The nylon string protruding through the cervix is to aid removal and to check for its presence.

body. This was moderately successful, but the idea was slow to catch on. It is interesting to note that the German gold used contained a significant proportion of copper. Interest in IUDs returned after World War II, particularly with recent development of plastic technology. Present day IUDs (or coils) consist of a small flexible plastic device which, before insertion, is drawn into a very narrow plastic tube the size of an average drinking straw. This tube is gently inserted up through the hole in the neck of the womb (the *cervical os*) and with a small plunger the outer tube is withdrawn leaving the IUD to uncurl inside the uterine cavity. A length of nylon string is attached to the device to aid removal. The string hangs down through the cervix into the top of the vagina when the IUD is in place. Although no one is certain exactly how the coil works, it is assumed that it prevents a fertilized ovum from implanting in the wall of the uterus.

A tremendous variety of shapes has been employed in an attempt to find an effective but comfortable, problem-free shape. It has been shown conclusively that the contraceptive efficiency of an IUD depends upon its overall surface area. Thus although on the whole the smaller the coil the more easy it is to insert and wear, the less efficient it becomes in preventing a pregnancy. This problem was overcome by increasing the surface area with a small coil of copper around the basic plastic shape. It is also thought that the copper in such devices enhances its contraceptive properties. It was also important to obtain a shape which was not only comfortable to wear and easy to insert but which would be retained inside the womb. The womb is a muscular organ and can very effectively expel unwanted contents by coordinated muscular contractions. In addition, any intrauterine device must be completely sterile on insertion and inert once inserted, or infection will result. All of these problems have been largely overcome with modern IUDs. However even these are not 100% efficient: although a device may be inserted correctly, retained

properly and checked regularly, there is a small failure rate associated with each different type of IUD.

Fitting an IUD
Before inserting an IUD the doctor will examine the woman to check that the uterine shape is normal. The cervix is visualized with the use of an ordinary vaginal speculum as in the taking of a routine CERVICAL SMEAR. The IUD loaded in its little tube is gently inserted into the uterus through the cervical os. In some women the uterus is very mobile and the doctor may grasp the cervix with a small pair of forceps to steady it, but the whole procedure should involve only minor discomfort and a slight period-like pain as the device passes through the cervical os. This mild pain usually persists for 24–48 hours after insertion, and can be relieved with minor analgesics such as aspirin or acetaminophen. There may be a few spots of bloods passed shortly after insertion. The first period after an IUD has been inserted is frequently more heavy than usual, but thereafter the periods usually settle down to normal or only slightly heavier than usual. Most devices can be left in place for several years, even up to ten or fifteen years in some cases. The smaller devices dependent upon the copper coil of wire lose their contraceptive efficiency after about two years and are usually replaced after this length of time.

Removing an IUD
Removing or changing an IUD is relatively easy and painless. After passing an ordinary vaginal speculum, the doctor will grasp the string at the top of the vagina and pull the device gently out of the womb. Occasionally, the IUD has moved within the uterine cavity, causing it to lie awkwardly and thus prevent easy removal. Under these exceptional circumstances, the device is removed under general anesthesia. The cervix is dilated a little to allow the coil to be grasped with long thin forceps.

Failure of the IUD
The likelihood of failure of an IUD can be minimized by regular checkups. The woman herself can check for the presence of the string at the top of the vagina at frequent intervals, and she can visit her doctor at longer intervals for overall checks. If there are episodes of cramplike pains at any time after the device has been inserted, the woman should also seek medical advice to check that the coil is still inside and has not been forced out.

Pregnancy with an IUD in place
If a pregnancy occurs with the device in place, the woman will be at a higher risk of miscarriage. However, if miscarriage does not occur, the baby will be unaffected and will grow normally to term. When a pregnancy occurs with the coil inside the uterus and the woman wishes to continue with the pregnancy, the doctor will examine the cervical os. Occasionally, the device will be found to be partly out of

the womb. The doctor may be able to remove gently a partially extruded coil without disturbing the pregnancy and thus minimize the risk of subsequent miscarriage. On the whole, however, pregnancies with coils inside the womb proceed quite normally. The device is usually found plastered to the back of the PLACENTA and does not usually enter the amniotic sac; despite rumors, this makes the chance of the baby holding the coil in its hand at delivery most unlikely! Frequently a woman has stated that she is pregnant with the coil inside the womb and after the baby and placenta have been delivered, there is no coil to be found—the implication being that the woman had not checked her coil and had in fact become pregnant because the coil was not inside the womb.

Problems associated with the IUD
On rare occasions, during insertion of an IUD the device will be pushed through the wall of the uterus; this may sometimes occur with the soft uterus of a woman who has recently given birth. Also rarely, a properly fitted IUD will bury its way through the uterine wall and end up in the peritoneal cavity of the abdomen. Perforations like these usually cause crampy abdominal pains, and a misplaced IUD can be checked with x-rays (because all IUDs are radiopaque) and/or the use of ULTRASOUND. A displaced IUD can be removed by a minor operation—occasionally using a laparoscope and forceps technique.

It has been suggested that in exceptional cases an IUD has increased the risk of pelvic infection and even ECTOPIC PREGNANCY (a pregnancy which develops anywhere outside the uterus—particularly in the Fallopian tube). However, since to some extent ectopic pregnancy and in particular pelvic infections are relatively common in young women, it is difficult to implicate the IUD if it has been properly inserted under sterile conditions.

Indications for removal
As mentioned, the first period after insertion of an IUD is usually heavier than the woman expects normally. Thereafter periods should settle down to normal. In a small proportion of women the length and volume of their menstruation is significantly increased, and they may request the removal of the device. Occasionally, IUDs are removed because of persisting period-like pains. Frequently, a change of coil alleviates the pain, suggesting that the previous coil's position inside the womb was unsatisfactory. Most IUDs take a few weeks to settle down completely, but it must be stressed that the great majority of women experience no problems after having a coil properly inserted. Naturally enough, those women who have had problems with an IUD are usually more vociferous than those who are quietly happy with theirs.

Advantages of the IUD
The IUD has many advantages; the device need not be thought about after being properly inserted and the woman is extremely well protected at all times; the spontaneity of sex is not impaired, as in some of the barrier methods, e.g., condom or diaphragm. Providing the IUD is properly inserted and regularly checked, there is no risk to either man or woman. (Occasionally, the string will be taken up inside the womb; if a very short length of the string, which is similar to fishing line, protrudes through the cervix, it can cause a pricking sensation on the man's penis. This is easily remedied by pulling the string down a short distance to its proper length of about $1\frac{1}{2}$ in. where it lays down flat and is completely imperceptible to the man.) An IUD is usually easier to fit after a woman has had one baby, or more, because the neck of the womb is slightly open. However, the device is also quite easy to fit in a proportion of women who have not had a child. Frequently, a woman who has had her first child will want a gap between the next of, say, two to three years. This is an ideal situation in which to have an IUD; it can be fitted after the birth of the first baby, say, at the postnatal check, and then removed after two years. In such women, the small failure rate is usually no problem. An IUD is also useful in women during the latter years of their reproductive time, e.g., the over 35s who have finished their families; many such women may not wish to be sterilized, and doctors may be reluctant to prescribe the pill because of their age.

Oral contraception

The oral contraceptive pill was introduced as long ago as 1958; the type most widely used is a tablet containing synthetic estrogen and progestogen hormones, taken for three weeks out of every four. During the week when the tablets are not taken "withdrawal" menstrual bleeding occurs. While it is still not completely understood how oral contraceptives produce their effects, the basic principle is that the hormones contained in the pill interfere with the normal hormonal feedback system by which the hypothalamus in the brain and the pituitary gland control the menstrual cycle. In response to the presence of these "extra" hormones in the blood, the pituitary ceases to produce two hormones—one necessary for the growth and maturation of the ovum inside the ovarian follicle, and another which triggers ovulation. No egg is released, and conception is therefore impossible. However, even if ovulation should occur, other actions of the pill will prevent pregnancy. Progestogen acts to keep the mucus around the cervix viscid; this inhibits the easy passage of spermatozoa. In addition, some forms of progestogen cause a slight change in the lining of the womb which may also interfere with the implanation of a fertilized ovum.

Another less widely used form of oral contraception consists of taking continuous progestogen in the so-called "mini pill." This is taken every day and although ovulation

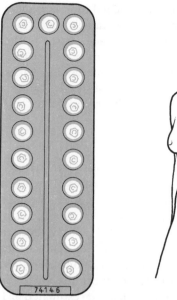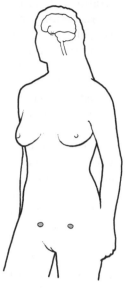

The combined estrogen-progestogen contraceptive pill inhibits the release of hormones from the pituitary gland in the brain. These are necessary to encourage maturation of the ovum in the ovary.

does not seem to be inhibited, it probably acts by causing increased viscosity of the mucus around the cervix.

When first introduced, oral contraceptives contained relatively large amounts of hormones, but nowadays much smaller doses are applied, which are just as effective, but have fewer side effects and problems—since most of these are dose-related. If taken regularly at approximately the same time each day, e.g., every morning or evening, the "pill" will provide almost complete contraceptive protection—it is certainly by far the most reliable method of contraception (excluding sterilization) currently available. Failures have been reported in women who were taking certain antibiotics concurrently, or who suffered episodes of excessive diarrhea and vomiting, which can prevent adequate absorption and utilization of the hormones by the body. In these situations, of course, extra precautions are required if intercourse takes place.

When to start
On which day of the cycle to start the pill is a matter of slight debate. Most women take their first combined estrogen-progestogen pill on the fifth day of their period (day one being the first day of bleeding), but some are advised to commence on the first day. Whatever day is recommended by the prescribing doctor, the couple should use extra contraceptive precautions for the first monthly cycle while the pill takes effect.

If you forget a pill
If one pill is forgotten then taking two the next day usually provides adequate protection, even in low dose pills, *but if*

more than one pill is omitted extra contraceptive precautions should be used for the rest of the cycle. Discontinuing the pill in the middle of the cycle will produce a withdrawal bleed.

After childbirth
After the birth of a baby, a woman who wishes to take oral contraceptives and breast feed is usually advised to take the progestogen-only "mini pill," as the use of an estrogen combined pill will inhibit milk formation. Most postnatal women are advised to commence on the "mini pill" if they so wish as soon as they are ready to commence intercourse; they should not wait for the first period to occur, as a large proportion of women can ovulate even though they are still breast feeding.

In cases where the woman wishes to bottle feed, the combined estrogen-progestogen pill may be used; the doctor may advise beginning the pill immediately or may suggest the woman waits until her first period and begins on the first or fifth day of that period. It must be remembered, however, that during the early months after childbirth ovulation is a very real possibility; precautions must be used until the pill is commenced *and has taken effect.* Far too many women have ignored this advice and have conceived very quickly after giving birth, believing that they would be protected by breast feeding, and have continued into the second pregnancy without having menstruated after having the first baby.

Side effects of the pill
It is difficult to assess the side effects produced by oral contraceptives. On the one hand, any odd symptom that happens to occur may be ascribed to the use of oral contraceptives by patients (and indeed doctors and nurses) who may have religious or other grounds against contraceptives in general, and the pill in particular; and some symptoms may be a reflection of the woman's subconscious objection to the interference with her normal fertility—even though she realizes the need for contraception. On the other hand, it is certainly true that the larger-dose pills can produce side effects such as headache, nausea, facial pigmentation, fluid retention, weight increase, discomfort in the breasts, intermenstrual "breakthrough" bleeding and, occasionally, depression or irritability. Usually these symptoms improve after two or three cycles, and since most of them are due to the estrogen component of the tablets, the modern tendency to use a lower dose of estrogen has reduced greatly the incidence of side effects. Periods are usually more regular and the menstrual loss is frequently much less, with relief from painful periods in many cases. The effect on libido can be variable, but in most women the relief from fear of pregnancy allows them to enjoy sexual intercourse without constraint. Occasionally, varying the brand of pill used can sometimes improve libido if, indeed, it was depressed by oral contraception.

Some women who have had problems with side effects using the combined contraceptive pill have switched to progestogen-only "mini pill" with some success. For the majority of women, the control of periods is inadequate for them to be satisfied with this form of contraception. After a few cycles, breakthrough bleeding frequently occurs and the periods may degenerate into irregular, spasmodic bleeds. This is, of course, no problem during breast feeding when the woman does not usually menstruate. However, when breast feeding is discontinued most women change from progestogen-only to the combined pill, which controls their periods much better. However, some women, particularly in Scandinavian countries, opt to use the "mini pill" initially. The failure rate with the progestogen-only pill is slightly higher than with the combined preparation, but many women who are unable to take the combined preparation because of side effects have found the "mini pill" perfectly satisfactory.

The enormous number of women in the Western world who are currently taking oral contraceptives quite happily is a great testimonial to their efficiency.

Who should and who should not take the pill?

Before prescribing oral contraception the doctor will screen the patient for diseases which might increase risks associated with taking the pill. In particular, doctors are reluctant to prescribe if there is any history of venous thrombosis (clotting), severe diabetes, liver disease, or indeed any other serious medical problems which need to be evaluated. Women who have had scanty or very irregular periods may, after investigation, be deterred from taking oral contraception. Also, some women who wear contact lenses may find slight difficulty when taking the pill. This is due to a change in the curvature of the cornea of the eye which can occur when taking the pill. The reasons for this change are not well understood, but in any case the proportion of women so affected is quite small; most often there is no problem with wearing contact lenses and taking oral contraception. In short, therefore, a doctor will be reasonably happy to prescribe oral contraceptives to a young woman who has been relatively fit all her life, is not suffering, or has not suffered, from serious medical problems, whose periods are reasonably regular and who appears to be ovulating normally.

The pill and young girls

How soon after puberty can the pill be prescribed to a girl? The only *medical* limitation is that the pill cannot be given until the doctor is sure that periods are relatively normal in frequency and duration—i.e. *at least* 9 months to a year after the start of menstruation. The pill does not appear to inhibit the development of those secondary sexual characteristics which may not yet be complete (i.e., hip and breast size). Sometimes the pill is prescribed to young adolescent girls to relieve painful periods. The ethical considerations of prescribing the pill to young adolescents for contraception are more complex, and individual doctors will vary in their approach. Perhaps the most important criterion remains that any girl after the age of puberty who is having sexual intercourse without an express wish to become pregnant needs contraceptive advice, and the pill is the only method that is, for all practical purposes, 100% reliable.

The pill and blood clotting

The risk of a venous thrombosis (see THROMBOSIS/THROMBUS) is about ten times greater in women who use oral contraceptives than in other women of comparable age. Among women aged 16 to 40 who are not using oral contraceptives about 1 in 20,000 will be admitted to hospital each year with some form of venous thrombo-embolism. Among those who use oral contraceptives about 1 in 2,000 will be admitted. The mortality attributable to the use of oral contraceptives has been estimated at 1.3 per 100,000 for healthy women aged 20–34 and 3.4 per 100,000 for women aged 35–44. It should be remembered that such a risk over one year's treatment amounts to very much less than the risks involved in a pregnancy, whether it ends in abortion or goes to full term. However, the enhanced risk of venous thrombosis in those over the age of 35 has led many doctors to dissuade women of that age or over from using oral contraception. Nevertheless, each case must be examined on its merits, and if there is no other alternative a woman over 35 may well be prescribed the pill (although barrier methods—condom or diaphragm—and IUD are more frequently recommended in this age group).

Discontinuing the pill

Ovulatory cycles usually return as soon as the oral contraception is stopped, but in a few women absence of periods may occur and persist for several months. Spontaneous return of normal menstruation is the rule, but where absence of periods is prolonged, the new drugs designed to induce ovulation have been frequently used with success. However, problems with ovulation after discontinuing the pill are less likely to occur in women who had normal ovulatory cycles before taking the pill; this is why doctors may be reluctant to prescribe the pill for women whose periods are scanty or irregular.

There is no limit to the length of time the pill can be taken. Many women have exceeded five continuous years and even longer, and periods have returned spontaneously on discontinuing the tablets. If there are any doubts, seek the advice of the prescribing doctor, as medical opinion may vary on this point. Certainly women have on occasion discontinued oral contraception for a month or two to see if their menstrual cycles return to normal; while this is very reassuring, unwanted pregnancies have occurred because of inadequate precautions when the pill, with all its reliability, is discontinued—even for a short time.

STERILIZATION
Introduction

There is as yet no method of sterilization for either a man or a woman which can be reversed with any guarantee of certainty. Thus it must be emphasized that all forms of sterilization available today must be regarded as final. This statement must be qualified somewhat in the light of recent successes with reversal of more modern sterilization techniques, but when sterilization is contemplated it should be thought of as a permanent impairment of fertility. If there are any significant doubts remaining in either partner sterilization should be avoided.

Sterilization offers many benefits, especially for those who have had problems with other forms of contraception such as the pill or IUD and have decided that their family is complete. In the case of a second marriage, or if children are lost, perhaps in automobile accidents or through disease, the initial decision that no more children are desired may be changed. However, many couples do arrive at a decision that, come what may, they will not have more children, and women especially may reach a time in their lives where they decide that should they marry again, even perhaps a dozen times again, they would not have further children.

The choice whether the man or the woman in a relationship should be sterilized is difficult. The operation of sterilization is, in general, a smaller procedure for a man than for a woman. However, a man's reproductive life frequently extends from puberty until death and he may be able to father children in a second or subsequent marriage quite easily, even in advanced years. The woman, on the other hand, will have decreased fertility after the age of 40 and is unlikely to desire children much above that age. It can therefore be an easier decision for a woman to be sterilized in her middle 30s, with perhaps five or ten years of fertility curtailed, than for a man to be vasectomized at a similar age with a possible 35 years of fertility in front of him. Finally, of course, it is the woman who must bear the pregnancy, delivery and usually, most of the work of bringing up the infant; she may well come to a more permanent conclusion that after, say, two or three children, enough is enough, whether her partner wishes for more children or not. Thus advice concerning sterilization can only be given after considerable discussion in the presence of both partners to insure that the pros and cons of sterilization are explained, that both partners are really in agreement with it, and that much discussion has taken place between the partners on the subject.

Sterilization of the very young, for example, women in their early 20s, cannot be dogmatically categorized. In certain cases where all other contraceptive measures have failed and a large number of therapeutic abortions and/or children have resulted, sterilization is occasionally performed (after considerable discussion), but each case must be considered on its merits and gynecologists in particular vary with their approach. Although much shopping around between doctors is sometimes necessary before a woman, say who is unmarried, or has chosen her career instead of children, may obtain a sterilization, she may well benefit from the different opinions and advice she receives, so that when the operation is performed by a sympathetic doctor she will have had considerable counseling beforehand. The sterilization of mentally deficient patients in institutions is a highly controversial subject; but it must be pointed out that sexual irresponsibility in these patients, who are often warm, outgoing and gregarious, can be a very difficult problem indeed for those looking after them.

Male sterilization (vasectomy)

Male sterilization is performed by interrupting the tubes which conduct spermatozoa from the testes on their way up to the penis; these tubes are the *vasa deferentia* (singular: *vas deferens*)—hence the name of the operation, *vasectomy*. It is a relatively simple operative procedure taking about 20 minutes and is usually performed under local anesthetic. The skin above each vas deferens at the top of the scrotum is "frozen" with local anesthetic and the tube divided surgically on both sides. In order to prevent the tubes repairing themselves the ends are usually brought back on each other and tied down in the form of a blind loop. Reversal by joining the cut ends of the vas deferens is occasionally possible but no guarantee of success can ever be given beforehand. As some spermatozoa may be already awaiting delivery in the ejaculate the first groups of semen passed after vasectomy may well contain spermatozoa; semenalysis is performed after vasectomy and it is usual to wait until at least two clear ejaculates are produced before pronouncing the man "safe."

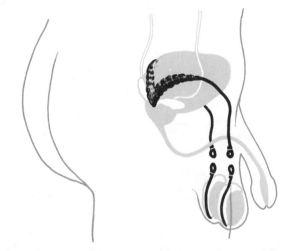

Vasectomy is a minor operation to cut and tie off the vasa deferentia—the tubes that conduct sperms from the testes to the urethra. This is done through a small incision close to the top of the scrotum.

The big question surrounding vasectomy is what effects it may have on the sexual powers of the man afterward. The answer is, in general, no change. The volume of the ejaculate, which is usually between 2 and 6 ml, is not affected by the absence of spermatozoa. Most of this fluid comes from the seminal vesicles and prostate gland higher up along the tube so that the ejaculate appears unchanged. However, it does not contain spermatozoa. Ability to obtain and maintain erection is completely unaltered. The spermatozoa, which are usually produced according to demand, are simply not produced. There is thus no great buildup of spermatozoa awaiting release from the testes.

Can it fail?

There is a very small failure rate associated with this, and indeed all sterilization procedures, but inadequate operations are usually detected by the persistence of spermatozoa in the semenalysis taken afterward. Very rarely the vas deferens will be able to recanalize spontaneously. Infrequently, bleeding into the scrotum following this operation causes large bruising around the groin and testicles. This usually subsides spontaneously with rest and a scrotal support.

Recent research has shown that ultrasonic irradiation of the testes can produce temporary male infertility for several weeks, but this method has not so far proceeded further than the research stage. Considerable research is also geared to male contraceptive pills.

Female sterilization

The usual method of female sterilization is by cutting and tying the Fallopian tubes. In this way the female ova are prevented from entering the uterus. This can be performed at an open operation whereby a small incision is made in the lower abdomen and the tubes are cut and tied off. This requires a general anesthetic and a short stay in the hospital. Recently more and more use has been made of the laparoscope. (For a full description of the use of the laparoscope, see the section on *Infertility*.) The laparoscope is inserted into the abdomen and the pelvic organs are inspected. A second small probe is inserted, and each Fallopian tube is grasped with an electrocautery; this destroys a small section of the tube by heat coagulation. The safest and most modern sterilization technique, however, which is superseding the cutting and tying and heat coagulation methods, consists of placing small clips, one on each tube. This is also performed using a laparoscope and a special "gun" to position the clips or rings (see illustration). Clip and ring sterilizations such as these are safer because there is no danger of damaging the bowel or other vital structures. The body does not reject these clips or rings, which are quite inert. The whole procedure takes a very short time, usually about 15 minutes. The scar left from laparoscopic sterilization is minimal and the operation does not require more than a short while in the hospital and is sometimes performed as a day-case.

It must be noted that general anesthesia and laparoscopy do involve risks for the woman, and this must be weighed against the desirability of sterilization and the risk of having unwanted pregnancies.

Possibility of reversal

A significant advantage of the ring or clip method over both *formal tubal ligation* (cutting and tying the Fallopian tubes) and heat coagulation of the tubes is that only a small portion of the tube is destroyed. The clips or rings are placed close to the uterus and if a subsequent reversal is requested it is a relatively simple procedure to excise the affected centimeter of clipped or ringed tube and reimplant the otherwise undamaged tubes. (See Tubal surgery in the *Infertility* section.) Reversal cannot be guaranteed, but it is more likely to succeed in this way than if the entire tube or greater part of it has been destroyed by heat coagulation, or has been divided near the fimbrial, finger-like end.

The most modern methods of female sterilization consist of blocking off the Fallopian tubes by the application of rings or clips. This can be performed through a very small abdominal incision using a laparoscope and a special attachment.

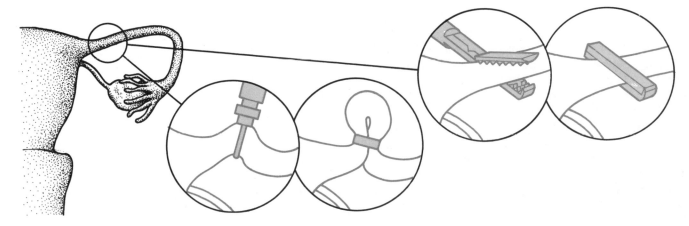

Sterilization should never be performed with any thoughts of reversal, but a significant proportion of women do apply for reversal. For this reason every effort is made to perform an effective sterilization with the minimum possible destruction of the tube.

Failure

It must be remembered that every operation for sterilization has a small failure rate. Even when tubes are tied at open operation, including after a Cesarean section, there are still failures, albeit in very small numbers. In front of the Fallopian tubes are two very similar looking tubes called the round ligaments; these help to anchor the uterus, rather like the guy lines of a tent. It is not difficult, even for the most skilled operator, to divide these tubes or apply clips or rings to them in difficult sterilizations, instead of the actual Fallopian tubes. The application of clip or rings by the laparoscopy method has the smallest failure rate, but this averages around two per thousand.

Sterilization at Cesarean section

Occasionally, sterilization is performed at Cesarean section, and although this has the advantage of combining the two procedures under one anesthetic, it does require a difficult exercise of judgment at the time. The tubes are usually ligated after the baby has been delivered and the uterus has been sewn up. During this time a pediatrician will have a chance to assess the baby's health. In cases where there is any doubt at all, sterilization is usually deferred, but even a baby who looks very healthy at delivery and a few minutes after delivery can develop problems in the neonatal period, or even in the first year of life. For this reason many surgeons now tend to delay sterilization until a few months, at least, after the delivery, and perhaps perform it with one of the modern laparoscopic techniques, which involves only minimal disruption of the mother's routine.

Psychological and physical effects

Sterilization can in a few cases profoundly alter a woman's attitude toward sexual activity, and her loss of fertility may cause (again, in a very few cases) bouts of depression. In unusual cases such poststerilization depressions have been relieved by reversing the operation—even though there is no desire for further children. With proper preoperative counseling the number of women regretting sterilization can be kept to a minimum, and if any doubts exist before a sterilization is performed the operation should be deferred. There are no physical after-effects of the operation; any subsequent weight increase, increased energy or similar symptoms are not attributable to the actual procedure itself. However, many women freed at long last from the fear of pregnancy may well overeat as part of the healthy subconscious celebration after this burden has been relieved. There are no hormonal changes

associated with sterilization and eggs continue to be produced, but they are unable to make contact with spermatozoa and degenerate. The periods similarly continue. Recently attention has been drawn to the small increase in the volume and length of the menstrual periods following sterilization. This is difficult to assess, because frequently women have been on oral contraception before sterilization and had their periods artificially lightened by the pill. When they discontinue the pill following the operation the periods return to their normal volume and length, which may be considerably greater than when they were on the pill. However, recent work has suggested that sterilization may disturb the internal circulation of such hormones as PROSTAGLANDINS, and this may contribute to the occasional increase in period volume and length. This is, however, an uncommon complication. The majority of women who are sterilized following satisfactory discussion notice no change in their lives or in their menstrual periods, and greatly benefit from the permanent relief from the fear of pregnancy—particularly those who have been advised not to become pregnant on medical grounds.

Contraception and sterilization: conclusions

I would hope that from what has been written above, it is realized that a couple should select any particular method of contraception only after many factors have been taken into consideration. It is pointless for a doctor to fit every woman who attends his consulting rooms, say, with an IUD. It would be equally ridiculous to recommend the sheath for a couple in whom the male partner was completely untrustworthy. If intercourse is frequent and pregnancy would be a relative disaster, then only oral contraception or sterilization can be recommended with any measure of safety. Contrast this situation with a woman of, say, 44 years of age who expects to enter the menopause in a few years' time and who has intercourse three to four times per month. Oral contraception in this situation is rather like taking a roadroller to crack a nut, and a simple barrier method such as the sheath, or even an IUD would be more appropriate. Similarly, a woman with very scanty periods who might only menstruate three or four times a year, and whose fertility may well be impaired anyway, would probably be better advised to use a barrier method of contraception rather than interfere with her marginal menstruation by using oral contraceptives.

It cannot be overemphasized, however, that in balancing the risks of one form of contraception against another, the overriding factor is the risk of an unwanted pregnancy which may be a physical or psychological disaster for the woman, and a possible disaster for the unwanted child brought into the world unnecessarily. Unfortunately, there is no completely ideal form of contraception; those which are relatively safe have higher failure rates than those which involve a minor risk to the woman. Experimentation with "morning-after-pills" and male oral contraception is currently taking place and this may produce some improvement in the current situation.

The widespread availability of contraceptive precautions has led some groups to consider their advertisement and distribution to be encouraging promiscuity. It is the unfortunate experience of most of us who have had to assist with unwanted pregnancies that thoughts of contraception rarely precede thoughts of sexual relations. In a great number of unfortunate cases thoughts of contraception appear too late, if at all. It is hoped that current liberal attitudes toward sex will soon be accompanied by better sex education to encourage more responsible attitudes toward contraception, and that no couple should take the risk of bringing a child into the world unless they are prepared to offer it security until it can take proper care of itself.

ABORTION

Spontaneous abortion (or miscarriage)

For a variety of reasons, a substantial proportion of all pregnancies end in miscarriage. If the fertilized ovum is grossly abnormal the embryo will not develop. However, if there is only a minor abnormality the early embryo may develop for a time only to be later rejected by the body in the form of miscarriage (or *spontaneous abortion*). In this the womb contracts, the cervix opens and the embryo along with its membranes is expelled from the uterus (this is accompanied by some bleeding).

It is known that over half of the fetuses from miscarriages have chromosomal and other abnormalities. However, in a large number of cases doctors are unable to say exactly why a woman may have miscarried; but the process of miscarriage is thought to be a system of "quality control" to reduce the possibility of an abnormal baby developing further. This system is not foolproof, however; occasionally, abnormal babies proceed to term and ultimately are born with deformities ranging from very mild to major life-threatening types.

Therapeutic abortion

When a miscarriage or abortion is induced by surgical or medical means for the benefit of the woman or her existing children, this is termed a "therapeutic abortion." Throughout the ages women have found themselves in situations where they do not wish to carry on with a pregnancy and in nearly every society throughout the world therapeutic abortion has been practiced. The many primitive attempts to procure a therapeutic abortion are well documented—such as drinking excessive alcohol, bathing in alcohol, violent exercise, trauma to the abdomen and the drinking of various herbal beverages—all with varying degrees of failure for the most part.

Dangers of unskilled abortion

If the early fetus in its protective amniotic fluid is disturbed sufficiently, the uterus will contract and expel both fetus and placenta. Thus abortionists of the past have introduced objects, such as knitting needles or noxious fluids (like soapy water) through the cervix into the uterus where the growing fetus is attacked. Labor-like uterine contractions begin after a few hours and the uterine contents are expelled. The whole process in unskilled hands is fraught with many dangers. Firstly, the object introduced into the uterine cavity may well carry infective bacteria if unsterile. Secondly, the uterus may not expel all the contents completely and the residue remains inside the womb where it provides an excellent medium for the growth of introduced bacteria. Thirdly, the inadequately emptied uterus may bleed profusely. Fourthly, during the abortion process the muscular uterine wall may be damaged by the instrument used and this may cause massive bleeding in some cases.

Any introduced infection may cause a severe inflammatory process which may cause sterility in later life, such as by blocking the Fallopian tubes. Even more tragically the infection may be overwhelming and completely uncontrollable, even with powerful antibiotics, and the woman may die. Any retained products of conception will prevent the successful clamping down of the uterine muscles, thus preventing the normal arrest of uterine bleeding that usually follows a complete abortion. Furthermore, there is very little oxygen inside the uterine cavity and this will encourage the growth of those bacteria which can survive in such "anaerobic" conditions.

One group of bacteria is called *Clostridia*, which survive in little protective spores. On being introduced to an anaerobic condition with plenty of dead tissue around (such as in an incomplete abortion), the spores will germinate rapidly and produce bacteria. These bacteria are sensitive to modern antibiotics; if an infection is treated quickly, recovery is the usual course. However, these clostridial bacteria secrete a powerful toxin which is spread throughout the body by the bloodstream, and may cause gas GANGRENE of the muscles and total body shock with kidney failure and lowered blood pressure—frequently within a few hours. There is no complete treatment for these toxins and once they are released, despite intensive medical treatment, the woman frequently dies. Thus the principles of a therapeutic abortion involve the maintenance of complete aseptic precautions in the actual operative technique, such as the use of sterile instruments, the complete emptying of the uterus of all the products of conception, the prompt treatment of any infections should they occur, and the replacement of any blood loss.

Before more liberal attitudes allowed women to seek abortions performed by competent doctors, women were exposed to all the risks of a "backstreet abortion." If the woman was lucky the abortion would be complete; the not-so-lucky ran the gauntlet of septic abortion with possible sterility in the future or even death. The legacy of the illegal abortionist was frequently a young woman on the mortuary slab.

How safe is legal abortion?

The very real dangers accompanying illegal or unskilled abortion have been discussed above. However, even when performed legally by skilled surgical teams, abortion (like any other surgical procedure) involves risks to the patient's health. In addition, there may be complications following the operation (these are discussed later in this article).

Nevertheless, recent research studies indicate that legal abortion is a relatively safe procedure. The risk of death as a result of legal abortion is in fact substantially less than that involved in a pregnancy which proceeds to term. Enormous numbers of legal abortions are performed each year—in the four-year period from 1972–1975 over 3 million were carried out in the United States alone. The crude death rate for this period was 3.2 per 100,000 abortions—falling from 4.1 in 1972 to 2.6 in 1975. To give some idea of the relative safety of legal abortions, these figures can be compared with the numbers of deaths arising from complications of pregnancy and childbirth, which over the same period were estimated at 12.4 deaths per 100,000 live births.

By far the most important risk factor in legal abortion is the duration of pregnancy—the later the abortion is performed, the greater the risk to the woman. It is estimated that the death rate for abortions performed at 16 weeks' duration is over 30 times higher than for those performed at 8 weeks or less, and the falling death rate from 1972–1975 is attributed principally to the tendency of women to seek earlier abortions.

Early therapeutic abortion

Menstrual regulation
The ease with which a uterus can be emptied of its contents depends largely on the duration of the pregnancy. As the placenta and fetus continue to grow it becomes more difficult to remove both completely.

Most pregnancy tests require a gestation period of about six weeks from the last menstrual period before they will be effective in recording (by means of a urine sample) whether or not conception has occurred. Before this time, a woman who suspects she may have conceived and requires a therapeutic abortion may undergo a *menstrual regulation* (or *menstrual curettage*) during her period. This consists of introducing a small piece of suction tubing into the womb; the menstrual contents, and hopefully the fertilized ovum, are gently sucked out. This can be performed without general anesthesia and causes only a minimum of discomfort.

Vacuum aspiration
However, most women who request an abortion do so after a urine pregnancy test has become positive and they have missed one or two periods—usually at around six to eight weeks of gestation. At this stage the removal of the fetus, placenta and membranes requires more firm scraping (curettage) and this is usually performed under general anesthesia.

The cervix (neck of the womb) is dilated from its usual tiny opening to a width sufficient to allow the introduction of a metal or plastic tube (such as the Karman catheter, which is soft plastic, or the Bierra, which is a steel tube). The top of the tube is fashioned into a spoonlike shape which allows the operator to scrape the products of conception from the muscular uterine wall. The tube is connected to a high-pressure vacuum source by thick rubber tubing. As the products of conception are scraped from the uterine wall they are sucked out through the vacuum tubing and collected in a reservoir for later confirmation that the pregnancy has been terminated and that the uterus should then be empty.

During this process, or just before, a drug called ergometrine is given to the patient intravenously; this encourages the uterus to contract, thus closing the uterine blood vessels and preventing excessive bleeding. This system of *vacuum aspiration* is usually performed up to about the 11th or 12th week of gestation.

Late abortion

After about the 11th or 12th week of gestation it is impossible to terminate a pregnancy by means of vacuum aspiration. The technique of late abortion usually involves inducing the uterus to expel the fetus (as in a miscarriage). The "abortifacient" (any substance which is used to induce an abortion) is introduced into the womb mixed with the normal amniotic fluid; labor usually begins a short time afterward. Various substances have been used. Currently, very concentrated solutions of urea, saline, or mixtures of the natural substance prostaglandin (SEE PROSTAGLANDINS) are injected into the uterus using a long thin needle. This process does not require general anesthesia. A local anesthetic is used to "freeze" a small area of skin just beneath the umbilicus (navel) and the needle is introduced through the muscles of the abdomen into the enlarged uterus. When a good communication with the amniotic fluid is obtained the abortifacient is injected.

Another means of inducing a late abortion is by inserting a small soft rubber tube through the cervix up to the outside of the fetal membranes. Prostaglandin solution is then injected into the womb (outside the membranes) at regular intervals.

In all these methods, labor begins a few hours after the first injection; the normal uterine contractions of labor can be augmented by administering oxytocin (a hormone naturally secreted by the pituitary gland to stimulate the uterus to contract during labor) through an intravenous drip, as is common practice in slow normal labors. The uterine contractions increase to a frequency sufficient to expel the fetus and placenta, which is usually complete in about 8 to 12 hours.

Another means of emptying the contents of the uterus is *abdominal hysterotomy*. This operation is a miniature Cesarean section and can be performed at any stage of pregnancy. Under general anesthesia an incision is made into the abdomen and the womb is exposed. An incision is then made into the womb and the fetus, placenta and membranes are removed. Similarly, to encourage uterine contractions and reduce bleeding, an injection of ergometrine may be administered. The fetus is usually extracted alive and if of advanced gestation may live for a few minutes or even hours.

Indications for abortion

A small proportion of women will be advised to have their pregnancies terminated because of medical conditions of the mother or suspected or confirmed abnormalities of the fetus. These conditions are not absolute and much depends upon the individual judgment of the obstetrician. However, termination of pregnancy is occasionally advised when the mother has a severe heart disease, tuberculosis, severe diabetes, severe kidney disease or severe psychiatric illness.

If a pregnant woman has never before had rubella (German measles) and has not been vaccinated against it, she must be extremely cautious about avoiding those who have the disease. The dangerous period is especially during the first three months of pregnancy—a period which carries a high risk of congenital defects being caused in the baby—but it is thought that the risk continues throughout the duration of pregnancy.

In pregnancies where there is a suspected congenital abnormality such as mongolism (DOWN'S SYNDROME) there are several means of confirming this; if confirmed, termination of pregnancy may be advised. In particular, SPINDA BIFIDA may be indicated by blood levels or amniotic fluid levels of a substance called ALPHA-FETOPROTEIN. Amniotic fluid is easily obtained by a process called AMNIOCENTESIS; this consists of passing a thin needle through the abdominal wall into the womb, from which a small amount of the fluid is extracted.

Examination of this fluid might also reveal chromosomal abnormalities which may indicate that the baby's normal development may be impaired.

Nonmedical reasons

Other reasons for abortion include the recognition that for some women giving birth might damage their physical or mental health and might also prejudice the physical and mental well-being of existing children in the family. Most Western countries have interpreted these criteria in a liberal way to insure, as far as possible, that every child born stands a good chance of being wanted—and therefore will have a reasonable chance of being brought up in a satisfactory family and social environment.

In the Western world large numbers of therapeutic terminations of pregnancy are performed each year, despite the relative ease of obtaining contraception and family planning advice. In the United States, an average of over 750,000 legal abortions were performed annually in the first half of the 1970s. The women requesting termination of pregnancy for nonmedical reasons range in age from those at the beginning of their reproductive life to those at the very end of it. Women of 40 years or more may, to their great surprise, find themselves pregnant by "accident" after reducing or even discontinuing previous contraceptive precautions. The shock of starting a family again, perhaps after the existing children have left school—combined with the increased risk of mongolism if the mother is over 40—frequently induces them to seek a termination of pregnancy. In the middle range of a woman's reproductive life, marital and other troubles with relationships may possibly induce a woman to undergo termination of pregnancy—such as those pregnancies conceived extramaritally or those that occur in the face of impending divorce. Occasionally, termination of pregnancy may be requested because conception followed a failure of contraceptive measures such as a burst sheath (condom) or (in a small number of cases) occurred even with an intrauterine contraceptive device in place.

The younger age group, who form the majority of requests for termination of pregnancy, are of a mixed nature. Unwanted pregnancies occur in the brightest of academic girls as well as in those who have become pregnant through utter ignorance. Young women who request termination of pregnancy have often been reluctant to seek satisfactory contraceptive measures, such as the contraceptive pill, for fear of discovery by their parents or friends; it frequently takes a pregnancy to jolt them into taking adequate precautions in the future.

A further big proportion of young women who request terminations lead unhappy, depressed lives and have endured much social and familial turmoil in the past. In the case of the very young (such as those aged 13 and 14), pregnancy may have occurred as the expressed wish of a precocious young couple, who only come to realize the implications of such an early pregnancy after conception has taken place.

Counseling

Before agreeing to perform a termination of pregnancy, a gynecologist will want to know the circumstances of the woman requesting it. With this knowledge he will be able to advise the woman on the problems and risks of a termination of pregnancy and also inform her of various alternatives to abortion, such as the support of several interested organizations. The woman should be encouraged to seek as much advice as possible from social workers, family, religious adviser, etc., before making the decision to have an abortion. If after obtaining as much advice as possible the woman decides to terminate her pregnancy, she will be less likely to regret the decision later than if she visits a doctor one day and has the operation almost at once without serious thought and advice.

Abortions are frequently the result of failed contraceptive precautions. In these cases every effort should be made to discuss with the gynecologist future methods of contraception, and no woman should leave the doctor's care without having discussed all the various possibilities, and if appropriate she should have some equipment such as the contraceptive pill or intrauterine device to prevent a further unwanted pregnancy.

It has been popular in the past to occasionally offer a woman a sterilization at the time of the termination of pregnancy. If a woman genuinely does not wish for any further children, this is acceptable and frequently helpful. However, the pregnant woman is not in the most advantageous position to consider both termination of her pregnancy as well as the termination of her fertility, and many practitioners would perform the therapeutic abortion and then allow some time to elapse before discussing the possibility of sterilization.

Problems following an abortion

As already mentioned, infection at the time of or soon after a therapeutic abortion may require intensive antibiotic therapy and usually hospitalization. A small proportion of women with infections of the womb and Fallopian tubes will become infertile—depending on the severity of the infection and the speed of treatment. It cannot be emphasized too much, therefore, that all therapeutic terminations of pregnancy should be performed in completely sterile conditions by skilled operators—with adequate facilities should troubles occur.

Occasionally, during curettage the uterine wall is punctured and considerable bleeding may result. When this occurs an incision is made into the abdomen and the tear in the uterine wall is repaired with sutures. In extreme cases where the uterus is beyond repair or bleeding is excessively severe, a hysterectomy is performed (surgical removal of the womb). This is fortunately rare. Most terminations of pregnancy are performed under general anesthesia and modern techniques have reduced the risk of anesthetic problems—such as chest infections, severe reactions and even death.

Women who have had a late termination of pregnancy are given special attention in antenatal clinics to insure that the cervix remains closed throughout any subsequent pregnancy. If there are signs that the cervix is opening up (such as at 16 to 18 weeks gestation) then a form of "purse-string" suture is usually inserted to close the cervix and thus maintain the pregnancy. Just before term these sutures are removed to allow labor and delivery to proceed normally.

Psychological and psychiatric problems

It is known that a proportion of women who request termination of pregnancy are emotionally disturbed. Termination of pregnancy should not necessarily be refused women who might be so disturbed, but in managing these patients extra care is required to observe any worsening of symptoms—in particular, if there is any significant risk of suicide.

A varying proportion of patients who undergo termination of pregnancy experience guilt feelings for a considerable time afterward. This may or may not be associated with clinical signs of depression. It is thought that this may be manifest in the high proportion of women who have "rebound pregnancies"—that is, who become pregnant again within a short time after the termination (usually less than one year).

Feelings of guilt and regret may be heightened by pressure from religious feelings, family resentment, and anti-abortion literature. It is therefore essential that before a woman undergoes termination of pregnancy she should have had the benefit of expert counseling to point out, on the one hand the problems of facing an unwanted pregnancy and bringing up an unwanted child, perhaps in adverse social and economic conditions, and on the other hand the possible physical and emotional complications of a termination. At the end of a sufficient discussion, if the woman feels that termination of pregnancy is the most appropriate course of action, then she will be able to reflect on this judgment and—if necessary—receive support during the early period following abortion.

Questions and Answers

Dr. Michael Hastin Bennett

Much of a doctor's time is devoted to answering patients' questions. Here is a carefully chosen selection of 250 typical questions, based on the author's wide experience as a specialist and general practitioner. They are arranged under general headings for easy access.

CHILDHOOD ILLNESSES

adenoids—immunization—immunization and the sick child—premature babies and illness—a child's development—fevers—treatment of fevers—convulsions—chickenpox—chickenpox and shingles—measles—the difference between measles and German measles—bacterial and viral infections—urinary tract infections—diagnosing urinary tract infections—sore throats

Q. *What are adenoids? Why are they sometimes removed?*

A. Masses of lymphoid tissue, also known as the *nasopharyngeal tonsils,* on the back wall of the throat above the level of the soft palate. They can become enlarged by infection and block the back of the nasal cavity, leading to mouth breathing, snoring and SINUSITIS. Moreover, they may block the inner end of the auditory tube—which leads from the middle ear to the nasopharynx—so that the eardrums are drawn in and the child's hearing is affected.

The middle ear may become infected, and after repeated attacks (treated with antibiotics) fluid may collect there. Children usually grow out of the tendency to infection and enlargement of the adenoids by the age of eight (as with the tendency to tonsillitis), but in some cases the symptoms caused by enlargement of the adenoids are severe enough to indicate their removal.

When faced with a troublesome case of recurrent infection of the middle ear (otitis media), many surgeons today prefer to remove the adenoids but leave the tonsils. In other cases both the adenoids and tonsils are removed during the same operation, especially if they are both the seat of disease.

Q. *Now that diphtheria and polio are so rare is it worth having my child immunized?*

A. Yes. Only by maintenance of child immunization will these diseases be kept at bay—they are still common in many other countries.

Immunization against diphtheria, tetanus and whooping cough is usually carried out in the third, fourth and fifth months of life; at the same time, polio vaccine should be given. Immunization can be undertaken as early as the sixth week, but is probably more effective at the later age. Immunization schedules can be varied at the discretion of the doctor. Booster doses are given at intervals to maintain levels of immunity, and are required at least when the child reaches school age and again at puberty—although the booster injection for whooping cough is omitted after the child enters school. Children can be immunized against measles, mumps and German measles (rubella) during the second year.

Q. *Should immunization injections be given if my child is not well?*

A. No. Immunization is postponed if a child is ill—for example, with a cold or a sore throat. It does not matter if booster doses are postponed for a few weeks until the child is in good health again.

Q. *My baby daughter was born prematurely. Is she particularly liable to illness?*

A. Children do need special care during the first year or so of life if they have been born prematurely, or if the delivery has been complicated, or if they are unusually small. However, once she has reached a weight of 10–12 lbs. she is at no greater risk than any other baby of the same weight.

Q. *How can I tell if my baby is developing normally?*

A. The developmental milestones are fairly obvious, although they are not absolute. Children vary in their development and may not follow the average pattern.

At about the age of six weeks the baby will fix his eyes on moving objects, move all his limbs, smile and respond to sudden noises. At about the age of six months he will turn to look at a rattle, sit up, grasp objects, watch a ball rolling along, and first place his weight on his legs. At 18 months he will retrieve the ball, understand simple requests and simple words, drink from a cup, walk, and play with toys. He has a small vocabulary, and has often been toilet trained as far as his bowels are concerned. By three years he can dress and undress, talk, is often dry and clean both night and day, can run and stand on one leg and is ready to play with other children.

Q. *Why do children get fevers?*

A. A raised temperature is usually the result of a bacterial or viral infection. Many microorganisms contain compounds called *pyrogens,* which act on the heat-regulating mechanism of a part of the brain known as the hypothalamus. Localized bacterial infections, such as boils, may not give rise to a fever as long as the infection is contained by the body's natural defense system. If the bacteria overcome this defense system and invade the bloodstream, then a general fever usually develops. Small children up to the age of five become feverish very easily; a minor digestive upset may be enough to raise the temperature for a few hours. Only if the fever persists is it a cause for concern.

Q. *Should I try to reduce a fever?*

A. A rise of body temperature probably stimulates the immune response (see IMMUNE SYSTEM). Unless it is very high (above 102°F/39°C), or lasts for a long time, it is best not to try to bring it down, but rather to treat the cause. Children with a high fever may go into convulsions and become delirious; they also quickly become dehydrated. High fevers may be brought down by sponging the child's body with tepid water and the use of cooling fans. The doctor may prescribe chlorpromazine or phenobarbital, which provides valuable sedation. Always encourage a child with a fever to drink as much fluid as possible.

Q. *If my child develops convulsions during a high fever, does it mean that he is liable to epilepsy?*

A. No. Many children who have had convulsions during a high fever show no ill effects afterward, and they certainly do not develop epilepsy. Your doctor

may recommend an electroencephalogram (EEG) after convulsions, but in nearly all cases the tracings of the brain waves will be within normal limits.

If your child should develop convulsions, remember that he may vomit and may hurt himself by striking hard objects. Try to keep his head turned to the side to prevent the breathing in of vomit, and remove anything nearby that may hurt him. If it is necessary to restrain his movements, be very gentle and avoid any force. The convulsions will soon be over, and it is more important to stay with the child than to run for help.

Q. *How long does the rash last in chickenpox? Can it leave scars?*

A. Usually the fluid-filled blister-like elevations on the skin (vesicles) persist for about a week, then the scabs that subsequently develop drop away. It is important to discourage the child from picking or scratching the blisters or scabs, for scarring may follow if they become infected with bacteria. Calamine lotion is useful to relieve the itching and frequent bathing helps prevent infection. In general, an attack of chickenpox in childhood is very unlikely to leave scars.

Q. *Has chickenpox anything to do with shingles? My grandfather had an attack of shingles when my small son had chickenpox, and the doctor said that the two diseases were the same.*

A. The same virus causes both chickenpox and shingles; one type of infection usually affects children, the other older people. In most cases where the two diseases are coincidental, the adult with shingles transmits the virus to a child who then develops chickenpox. But from time to time an adult will develop shingles after being in contact with a child with chickenpox. Most adults with shingles have had chickenpox as a child, so that it appears that the virus lies dormant in the nervous system for years before being reactivated; but it is not known what sort of stimulus is needed to make the virus attack a sensory nerve root.

Q. *Should I have my child immunized against measles? Is it a dangerous disease?*

A. Measles is unpleasant but not dangerous unless complications develop, and the risk of these depends to a large extent on the general health of the child. The most common are lung infections—bronchitis and pneumonia—and infection of the middle ear (otitis media). These are treated by antibiotics. In about one out of every thousand cases, following an attack of measles, inflammation of the brain (encephalitis) develops due to hypersensitivity of the nervous system to the measles virus. Small as this risk may be, it is enough to tip the balance in favor of immunization with a live attenuated (weakened) measles vaccine.

Q. *How do I tell the difference between German measles and measles?*

A. Measles is a much more severe disease than German measles (rubella), and the child's constitutional upset is much more obvious. Also, the incubation period in measles is shorter—10 to 14 days compared with 14 to 21 days for German measles. German measles is really important only because an attack affecting a woman during pregnancy may produce congenital abnormalities developing baby.

In measles, the child has a runny nose, red eyes, a cough, and feels miserable for a few days. The temperature is high and there may be diarrhea. Two or three days after the onset of the illness the rash appears as small red patches behind the ears and along the hairline. It spreads onto the face, then onto the trunk and finally involves the arms and legs. The separate red spots join together to form large irregular patches, which in about three days begin to fade. They take up to a week or more to go away entirely.

You may be able to see at the beginning of the infection, before the rash appears, small white spots inside the mouth on the mucous membrane which look like little grains of salt. They are most common where the lower gum meets the inside of the cheek and are called *Koplik's spots.* They disappear when the skin rash develops.

In rubella, or German measles, the earliest evidence of illness is not so obvious, and the rash may be the first sign of the disease. Although the throat and nose may be sore and there may be a mild inflammation of the eyes, the temperature does not rise to such a high level as it does in measles. In some cases there is enlargement of the lymph glands behind the ears. The rash starts, like measles, on the face and then spreads to the trunk and limbs. It starts as very small pink spots, which are not as dark as the spots in measles. In general, the spots in German measles begin to fade much sooner than in measles. In measles, the rash takes a week to fade, whereas in German measles it begins to fade within 48 hours (though it too may last for up to 7–10 days).

There are other rashes which can be confused with measles and rubella. It is evident that this happens because from time to time one hears of people who are said to have had measles or rubella more than once, which is not possible. One attack confers immunity for life. Drug reactions can sometimes be mistaken for measles, especially if penicillin has been given for a respiratory infection, and it is possible to make the reverse mistake and attribute the rash of measles to the effect of penicillin given during the first stages of the illness. In most cases, however, the course of the disease is clear to the doctor, and the most obvious distinctions between rubella and measles are the time the rash lasts and the severity of the illness.

Q. *Is there any practical difference between bacterial and viral infections? What are the most common diseases caused by bacteria and viruses?*

A. The most common infectious fevers caused by bacteria are diphtheria, whooping cough, scarlet fever, typhoid fever, paratyphoid fever and meningococcal meningitis. The common viral infections are chickenpox, measles, German measles, mumps, infectious mononucleosis, influenza and some epidemics of vomiting and diarrhea. Smallpox is a virus infection; so is the common cold. The incubation period of virus diseases tends to be longer than that of bacterial infections; the approximate times are:

Up to 7 days
 Meningococcal meningitis
 Diphtheria
 Scarlet fever
10 days to 2 weeks
 Whooping cough
 Smallpox
 Measles
 Typhoid and paratyphoid fever
2 weeks to 3 weeks
 German measles
 Chickenpox
 Mumps

Bacteria are likely to be sensitive to appropriate antibiotics; the whooping cough bacterium may be an exception, although in the laboratory it is sensitive to chloramphenicol, ampicillin and tetracycline. Viruses are not affected by antibiotics, but in cases where primary infection by a virus is followed by secondary bacterial infection—as in bronchopneumonia or otitis media or measles—antibiotics are very valuable.

Q. *Is it true that little girls often develop urinary tract infections?*

A. The incidence of URINARY TRACT INFECTION in children under four years is about 1% in girls and 0.3% in boys. In about half the cases there is no abnormality of the urinary tract, and if the condition is treated properly no harm results in later life. But in some cases there is an underlying cause which may be an *anatomical* abnormality (such as being born with double ureters or having a blockage of the urinary tract) or an abnormality of *function* leading to reflux of urine from the bladder into the ureters (the tubes which carry urine from the kidneys to the bladder). Children with recurring attacks of urinary infection should be examined for the possible presence of these abnormalities so that they can be treated.

Q. *How can I tell if my child has a urinary tract infection?*

A. It may not be obvious, especially in children under the age of one. The only signs may be fever (perhaps with convulsions), failure to gain weight, or vomiting. In children up to the age of five with urinary tract infection, about a third complain of pain on urination or urinate more frequently than usual. Fever is a fairly constant sign, and there may be pain in the abdomen. An accurate diagnosis can often be made only on examination of the urine under the microscope and by bacterial culture.

Q. *My doctor diagnosed an infection of my baby's throat, but she never showed any signs of a sore throat—she only had a high temperature. Did I miss something I should have noticed?*

A. No. Children under the age of four years very rarely seem to show signs of discomfort in the throat, even when they have a fairly severe infection. They are usually taken to the doctor because—in addition to a fever—they have been vomiting and have abdominal pain. They may say they have difficulty in swallowing or pain in the throat if they are asked specifically about these things.

(For more information on childhood illnesses, see the appropriate sections in the major article on **The Health Care of Children.**)

HEADACHES AND MIGRAINE

causes of headaches—migraine in children— migraine and visual disturbances— hypertension and headaches—anxiety and headaches—headache after a blow on the head—depression and headaches—neuralgia

Q. *What is the most common cause of headache?*

A. There is no easy answer. Headaches are one of the most common complaints a doctor has to deal with, and in many cases he finds it hard to be sure of the diagnosis. Somewhere around 90% of women and 80% of men will have a headache of some sort every year; in one analysis of cases in a family practice, pain in the head was the tenth most common complaint.

Headaches are often referred to as "migraine," but this is a moderately well-defined condition and probably the diagnosis in many cases is made on insufficient grounds. The salient features of migraine are that it is usually one-sided, sometimes follows disturbances of vision which may be described as flashing lights or blurring, and is frequently accompanied by nausea and vomiting. It may be associated with changes in mood. Although it has been said that migraine occurs more often in intelligent people, this is probably not true; it is more likely to be true that these people consult their doctors more frequently.

Q. *Can children get migraine?*

A. Not usually in the classic form. But children may be subject to attacks of headache and vomiting which are almost certainly related to migraine. At first the pattern of the malady may not be recognized. But the diagnosis becomes clear if attacks of severe headache recur at intervals varying between once or twice a month to once or twice a year and are accompanied by abdominal pain and vomiting (which can be disabling). It is often found that there is a family history of migraine, and adults who suffer from migraine often remember that they were subject to this kind of episode in childhood. Fortunately both adult migraine and the "cyclical vomiting" of children are improved a great deal by medical treatment.

Q. *Can the visual disturbances in migraine result in permanent damage to the eyesight?*

A. No. If a "migraine headache" is accompanied by permanent alteration of vision, then the diagnosis is wrong and the headache is due to another cause.

Q. *I often suffer from headaches. Could they be due to high blood pressure?*

A. Not necessarily. In assessing any patient complaining of headaches the doctor will take the blood pressure. But, although headache can be a feature in hypertension, the relationship between blood pressure and headaches is not clear. Patients known to have a high blood pressure may never be affected by headaches, while others complain of headaches from time to time. In a number of cases headaches are due to anxiety generated by a diagnosis of hypertension.

Q. *Are my headaches likely to be due to anxiety?*

A. Possibly. Many recurring headaches are related to anxiety, especially in women. In some people it is thought that emotional upset may bring about spasm of the muscles surrounding the outside of the skull, which may produce pain in the head. It has also been thought that emotion can result in dilation of the cerebral blood vessels, and it is known that such dilation will produce a headache—this is probably the mechanism in the headache of a "hangover." However, it is clear that such explanations cannot cover a large number of headaches related to anxiety, and the mechanism remains obscure. Headaches also occur in association with depression; as with headaches related to anxiety, they usually respond to treatment directed toward the underlying condition.

Q. *Is it normal to have a headache for several days after a blow on the head?*

A. Yes. A severe blow on the head is often followed by a headache for a few days or even longer. Very rarely this may be a sign of damage inside the head, such as a *subdural hematoma*—the formation of a blood clot between the brain and its outermost covering membrane, the *dura mater*. But in most cases the headache clears up over the course of a week. Sometimes a persistent headache seems to be related to the progress of a legal action—for example, following a traffic accident.

Q. *I've been feeling tired and depressed and have begun to have headaches. Could I be suffering from anemia?*

A. You could be. A simple blood count will show if you are in fact anemic. Not many patients with anemia complain of headache; a more likely diagnosis is depression, which saps the energy and is often accompanied by headaches. If, however, the headache is localized to the front of the head above and behind the eyes, a possible cause is sinusitis—which, if chronic, can produce a general feeling of being unwell (malaise) in addition to localized discomfort.

Q. *What exactly is neuralgia? Can it be a cause of headaches?*

A. Neuralgia is the word used to describe pain originating in a nerve; its character is stabbing, with aching discomfort felt between the paroxysms of pain. In the head the nerve most commonly affected is the "trigeminal," which transmits sensation from the face and the upper part of the head. *Trigeminal neuralgia* can hardly be described as a headache; it is too painful and sharp in its paroxysms, which affect the side of the face as well as the side of the head. There are other less common types of neuralgia which affect the face, but almost always discomfort described as headache is far removed from the pain of neuralgia.

(See also the major article on **Neurology**.)

NEUROLOGICAL PROBLEMS

loss of memory after a blow on the head—skull fractures—blood clot on the brain following an accident—brain hemorrhage in young people—dizziness in old age—recovery after a stroke—sciatica—how to deal with epileptic seizures—hereditary transmission of epilepsy—fainting and epilepsy

Q. *I had an accident a few weeks ago in which I was hit on the head so hard that I was unconscious for six hours. I can't remember the accident at all and would like to know whether I will ever be able to remember what happened.*

A. You may never remember exactly what happened, although as time passes the gap in the memory becomes shorter. It is not understood why the memory for the most recent past events is lost in these cases, while events which happened a few hours before the accident remain clear. But it is evident that the more severe the blow, the longer the period of lost memory.

Q. *I was quite surprised to be told that a fracture of the skull may be an unimportant injury. Can this really be true?*

A. Yes it can. Some fractures of the skull, particularly of the lower part, the base, are very important because they can involve vital structures and can open up a communication between the inside of the skull and the nose or the ear through which infection can pass. Open fractures are important for the same reason, and depressed fractures, where a piece of bone has been driven inward, nearly always affect the brain lying below. A number of fractures of the top, or the vault, of the skull, without displacement of the bone, run across blood vessels and damage them, but the remainder are not of much consequence except that they show the amount of violence applied to the skull. In themselves, they don't need any treatment and don't have any after-effects.

Q. *My grandfather was in an automobile accident, and hit his head fairly hard but didn't lose consciousness for more than a minute or two. But he began to have headaches, which got worse, and six weeks afterward he suddenly became confused and had to have a brain operation. We were told he had a clot of blood on the brain. Why did it take so long to develop? Shouldn't they have operated on him right after the accident?*

A. There are two main types of blood clot that can press on the brain after a blow on the head. One has immediate effects, but the other, as you have seen, takes a long time to show itself. The first type is called an *extradural hemorrhage*, the second type a *subdural hemorrhage*. The first forms outside the membranes covering the brain, the second forms inside them.

The first kind of hemorrhage is caused by bleeding from an artery in the region of the temple, and the usual pattern is that the victim starts to regain consciousness normally after the accident but within a matter of hours relapses into unconsciousness again. In a case like this the operation has to be carried out at once. People who have lost consciousness after a blow on the head should be observed in a hospital for the first 24 hours for this reason.

In the second type of clot, the bleeding is from the veins, and it takes days or weeks to develop to such a size that it shows itself. To all intents and purposes recovery from the accident, which may be quite a mild injury, is normal at first. But as time goes on headaches may begin, which get worse and may be accompanied by attacks of confusion and sleepiness and perhaps slight weakness in the limbs. It is hard to recognize the condition, and it is usually not until the first vague signs and symptoms become definite that it can be diagnosed and the blood clot relieved by surgery. It's not possible to predict if a subdural hemorrhage is going to form after an accident and it's impossible to carry out an operation to stop one from developing. All the doctor can do is remain alert to the possibility, especially in older people, and like your doctor act quickly if the suspicions are confirmed.

Q. *I have just heard that a friend of mine who is only 32 years old has had a brain hemorrhage. I thought this only happened to older people.*

A. There is a form of brain hemorrhage, called a *subarachnoid hemorrhage* which can occur in younger people. It happens because of an abnormality in the blood vessels of the brain which has been there since birth, either an aneurysm, which is a local swelling on an artery, or an arterio-venous malformation, which is roughly like a birthmark on the skin. These conditions are not common, but as they develop over the years the fragile vessels may give way and cause bleeding within the membranes that cover the brain or actually into the tissues of the brain.

Q. *Since I passed my 70th birthday, I have had attacks of dizziness, especially when I look up. Am I in danger of having a stroke?*

A. Attacks of dizziness as you get older can be due to a number of reasons, including high or low blood pressure, low blood sugar, and disease of the inner ear, but in your case it is probably due to a combination of hardening of the arteries and osteoarthritis of the bones of the neck. Both of these conditions are obviously associated with getting older. The trouble is that osteoarthritis causes small spurs of bone to grow from the bones of the spine which can press on the two arteries running up through the vertebrae of the neck. When your neck is straight, there is no interference with these arteries, which go to supply the lower part of the brain; but when you tilt your head back to look up, the neck extends and the bony spurs press on the arteries, which lack their earlier elasticity, so that the blood cannot run freely up to the brain and you become dizzy. This doesn't mean that you are likely to have a stroke, and you can avoid the unpleasant attacks by being careful about tilting your head backward.

Q. *What are the chances of recovery after a stroke? My father had one recently and has still not recovered his speech.*

A. A stroke is caused by a clot in one of the blood vessels supplying the brain, or by a hemorrhage in the same area. The centers for speech are on one side of the brain only, in the case of a right-handed person on the left side, in a left-handed person on the right side. When the stroke occurs, the functioning of the brain is disturbed not only in the part directly affected but all around it as well, because the brain tissue reacts by swelling. This means that the effect is worse at first than you might expect from the actual damage that has occurred. The brain tissue around the area recovers, and function returns, but this takes some time.

Recovery from a stroke may take many months, and during this time it is very important that the affected limbs should be kept moving; otherwise they will stiffen, and when the paralysis recovers they will be far less useful than they should be. It is easy for an active person who has had a stroke to become anxious and depressed, particularly if they cannot speak properly, so they need continual support and encouragement— and you must remember that although people who have had a stroke may not be able to express themselves clearly, this does not mean that their intelligence has altered. It may not be possible to achieve complete recovery from a stroke, but the amount of recovery possible is sometimes astonishing as long as active treatment is continued and the patient is helped by an optimistic and confident attitude all around. It is not easy sometimes for the family to keep going in the face of such a severe illness, but your perseverance can secure the return of your father to a happier life.

Q. *What is sciatica? Is it always caused by disk trouble? What is the best treatment for it?*

A. Sciatica is pain in the leg extending downward from the buttock to the foot, and is caused by pressure on or irritation of the sciatic nerve. The most common cause is damage to one of the intervertebral disks, but the same symptoms may be due to arthritis or to a blood clot or tumor affecting the spine or spinal cord. When the cause is a herniated ("slipped") disk the best treatment is still rest for a few days, as it is for any kind of back trouble that comes on suddenly. You should be on a hard bed, with boards under the mattress, and you can generally expect the pain and discomfort to go within three weeks.

In many cases of low back pain the exact cause may never be found, and the best treatment may remain a matter of opinion. When there is pain down the leg and your doctor has found enough evidence on examination to make a tentative diagnosis of a herniated intervertebral disk, the condition is well enough understood to make the proper course of treatment clear. A first attack means that you have to rest in bed in most cases, but after recovery the main thing is to be careful about your posture. As far as possible, your back should be straight rather than bent, since it is bending forward that puts a strain on the intervertebral disks. Stooping forward to work, or bending down from the waist to pick things up, sitting slumped in a chair or over a desk are all things which can make your back worse. So can long bouts of sitting, such as the kind you

often get in an airplane or car trip. If you can, get up frequently and walk around to relieve the pressure on the disks that comes from the weight of your head and upper body. Very often a small folded towel placed just at the natural curvature of the spine between you and the back of your seat will help a lot. The main value of the spinal corsets that are still recommended in some cases is to remind you to keep your back straight, since they can do little to support the spine itself. The main thing for your posture is to maintain the natural curve of the spine as much as possible in every situation.

Q. *I have a brother-in-law with epilepsy. What should I do if I see him having a seizure?*

A. Most epileptics take drugs to control the seizures, and you wouldn't know they were suffering from epilepsy unless they told you. Uncontrolled seizures are very alarming to see for the first time, but the only real dangers are that the epileptic may be injured in falling or in striking something during the convulsions. The tongue sometimes gets bitten and this has to be watched out for. In time the epileptic will recover consciousness and return to normal.

Often the first warning that a seizure is about to occur is a sensation that lasts for a very short time before consciousness is suddenly lost, and the epileptic falls down. At first the person becomes very stiff, and may give a cry as the air is expelled from the lungs. Breathing stops and the person may actually begin to turn blue, since the spasm lasts for anything up to half a minute. For the next half-minute or so the general spasm subsides into jerking movements of the whole body including the face. During the attack there may be incontinence.

When the jerking movements stop, the state of consciousness becomes lighter, and usually full consciousness comes back in a matter of minutes— although it may take up to an hour in rare cases. All you can do to help is to make sure that the epileptic is moved away from anything that could cause an injury, and to stay with the person until full consciousness comes back. Remember that the most distressing thing about a seizure to an epileptic is the attention and disturbance it causes.

Q. *I've had epilepsy since I was very young, but it's controlled very well by anticonvulsant drugs. I would like to marry and have children, but what are the chances that they will be epileptic?*

A. If an epileptic is married to a nonepileptic, the chances are slightly greater that their children may be epileptic than the children of a marriage of two nonepileptics. Unfortunately the chances of two epileptics having epileptic children are quite high, and such married couples should take medical advice and go into the whole thing very carefully before they become parents. The best thing is to be absolutely open about such matters, and to talk about your fears to your future marriage partner and your doctor.

Q. *Is a fainting attack connected with epilepsy? I've always had a tendency to faint, and I'm worried that I might one day have a seizure.*

A. Fainting is not connected with epilepsy. You faint because of a sudden loss of blood flow to the head, but an epileptic seizure comes from an abnormal focus of activity in the brain.

In a simple faint—which is usually brought on by an emotional shock, pain, or fear—the attack develops while a person is standing up, and never when they are lying down or walking. It can also come from standing or sometimes sitting in a stuffy or hot room. The basic mechanism is a pooling of blood in the lower part of the body which upsets the balance of the circulation, so that the heartbeat becomes slow and the circulation to the brain is less than normal. There is a feeling of faintness or weakness, nausea, sweating, and clouding of consciousness, which usually develops slowly enough to prevent a sudden fall, but may result in collapse. As soon as the head is at the same level as the rest of the body the circulation returns to normal and recovery is quick. Although there may be some stiffening of the muscles, and even twitching of the limbs, there are no generalized convulsions as there are in epilepsy, and there is no incontinence. If these are the sort of attacks you sometimes have, you don't have to worry that you have epilepsy, or that they may develop into seizures.

(See also the major articles on **Neurology** and **Neurosurgery**.)

SLEEP

amount of sleep—depth of sleep—dreams— function of sleep—age and length of sleep— causes of insomnia—sleeping pills—unusually long sleep

Q. *How much sleep do I need to stay healthy?*

A. There is no "required" amount of sleep, but it is true to say that those who sleep regularly for less than three

hours almost invariably complain. The hours of sleep taken by healthy people vary from about five to ten, with the majority of people sleeping for seven to eight hours. It is very unlikely that anyone gets too little sleep to maintain health, but there is no doubt that a bad night's sleep is followed by subjective feelings of tiredness during the day. In general one takes the view that if a patient complains of lack of sleep then the matter needs investigating. Insomnia is not dangerous, nor has it any long-term effects.

Q. *What is the difference between deep sleep and light sleep?*

A. The difference shows in the electrical activity of the brain. Electroencephalographic (EEG) records taken during sleep show that there are various stages of brain activity. The first stage, drowsiness, is followed by stage two in which sequences of fast waves occur between the sequences of the slow waves characteristic of stage one. Slow waves follow in stages three and four. The stages run together and later stages may give way to an earlier one in a pattern described as the "orthodox sleep cycle." Each cycle lasts for about an hour and a half, and is followed by a period of REM (or "rapid eye movement" sleep), during which the eyes move rapidly under closed lids; it is thought that most dreams occur during REM sleep, which takes up about a quarter of a night's sleep.

Q. *Very often I do not seem to dream at all. I have heard it said that we need to dream to remain sane. Is this true?*

A. No. In fact some research workers have claimed that depressed patients who are awakened whenever they enter the period of REM sleep have actually shown an improvement in their mental state.

Q. *Why do we have to sleep at all?*

A. No one really knows for certain. The physiological processes which occur during sleep are very poorly understood. The blood pressure falls, the rate of breathing becomes slower and the pulse rate falls by about 10%. Muscle tone lessens, and so does the activity of the kidneys. The body temperature falls slightly and is at its lowest at about 4 o'clock in the morning. Other physiological changes have been noted, but are not illuminating. It seems likely that sleep is necessary as a period for growth and the regeneration of body cells, since the secretion of growth hormone (somatotropin) occurs almost exclusively during sleep.

Deprivation of sleep eventually results in overwhelming sleepiness. Irritability, lack of concentration and slowness of thought develop; if the deprivation lasts long enough, delusions may follow, with hallucinations and paranoia. Lack of sleep has never, as far as is known, proved fatal. The only explanation of the need for sleep that science at present has to offer is that we sleep because we must!

Q. *Does age make any difference to the amount of time we sleep?*

A. Yes. The time we spend asleep gets less as we get older. After birth a baby sleeps for most of the day and night, but it soon develops a "diurnal rhythm" and sleeps for about 16 hours a day. By the time it is five years old it may sleep for about ten hours daily; the time spent asleep diminishes until as an adult it varies between five and ten hours with the majority of people sleeping between seven and eight hours. By the age of 70 this falls to an average of about six hours.

Q. *What are the common causes of insomnia?*

A. One of the most common causes is discomfort, such as that associated with arthritis or a peptic ulcer. Sometimes lying in a certain position will produce uncomfortable sensations in a limb, particularly if the circulation is poor or if there are degenerative changes in the lumbar or cervical spine associated with sciatica or CERVICAL SPONDYLOSIS. Other common causes are anxiety and depression, a change of surroundings, or an alteration of routine. Anxiety may lead to the production of a vicious circle, where the original cause of insomnia is reinforced by anxiety over loss of sleep.

Q. *Should I ask my doctor for sleeping pills if I can't sleep? Or can I treat myself?*

A. If insomnia is becoming a problem, you should see your doctor so that he can try to find a cause for it. He may prescribe sleeping pills, but if he finds an underlying cause—and there very often is one—it is obviously more logical to treat this than to treat the symptom. It is too easy to get into the habit of relying on hypnotics (sleep-inducing drugs); except in illness or old age it is a particularly bad habit. If you wake up during the night, or find it hard to fall asleep, it is better to try to read a bedside book until you fall asleep naturally than it is to reach out for a pill. Remember that the more you worry about losing sleep, the more sleep you lose.

Q. *I can never get my husband to wake up in the morning. He sleeps for about 12 hours if I let him. Is this abnormal?*

A. No. Some people—about 2% of the population—sleep regularly for 10 hours, and many adults can sleep for 12 hours at a stretch. There are conditions (such as *narcolepsy*) in which abnormal sleep occurs, but the sufferer is liable to fall asleep at any time, and usually complains of attacks of weakness. If your husband sleeps long in the morning, it may be useful to remember the old saying that an hour of sleep before midnight is worth two afterward.

EYE PROBLEMS

sticky eyelids—bloodshot eyes—conjunctivitis—object in the eye—chemical burns—stys—shingles and eye involvement—glaucoma—cataracts—"floaters"

Q. *When I wake up in the morning I find it difficult to open my eyes, because the lids are stuck together. Should I wash my eyes?*

A. No. The usual cause of stickiness of the eyelids is conjunctivitis, in which the white of the eye is usually redder than normal. In such cases it is not advisable to irritate the eyes further by washing them. Ask the doctor to look at them; he will frequently prescribe medicated eyedrops. Babies often have sticky eyes, and the "nasolacrimal duct" becomes blocked so that tears cannot be led away into the nose and the eyes weep. Antibiotic eyedrops usually clear the condition.

Q. *I have suddenly developed a very bloodshot eye. It does not seem to hurt; is it a sign of eye disease?*

A. Not necessarily, although if the condition persists you should see your doctor. Painless hemorrhage into the conjunctiva is not uncommon; although it looks alarming it is usually of no consequence. In time the blood will be absorbed and no ill effects will follow.

Q. *I have an attack of conjunctivitis. Should I wear an eyepatch?*

A. It is better not to cover the eye in cases of simple conjunctivitis, for the action of closely covering the eye encourages the growth of the invading organism. It is better to wear dark glasses. In general, the eye should only be covered when it has been injured.

Q. *If I get something in my eye, what is the best way of getting it out?*

A. If the object is lying on the colored part of the eye (the iris or pupil), don't attempt to remove it yourself; you should get immediate medical help. This part of the eye is important to vision—don't risk damage through inexperienced handling. If the object is lying in the white part of the eye, you can try to dislodge it yourself, or have a friend try, using a clean handkerchief moistened and rolled into a point. If it doesn't come out easily, don't keep trying to remove it, but see the doctor; the object may be embedded, and you could damage the eye by trying too vigorously to get it out. If you think you have had something fly into your eye, but cannot see it and the pain continues, you should go and ask your doctor to look at your eye within 12 hours. Don't rub your eye if you think there may be anything in it.

(See also *Object in the eye* in the **First Aid** section.)

Q. *What do I do if a chemical splashes in my eye?*

A. Wash out the eye at once with water. Speed is the most important thing; although it may be messy, it is better to put your head under the nearest faucet than to try to find an eyecup when you cannot see properly.

Q. *What is the best treatment for a sty?*

A. A sty is an abscess in the small glands associated with the eyelashes. Usually it "comes to a head" and discharges in a day or two; it can be encouraged to do this by the application of a spoon covered with absorbent cotton and a bandage soaked in water as hot as you can bear it. If the infection persists, medical advice is needed.

Q. *My mother has an attack of shingles which involves her eye. Is the damage likely to be permanent?*

A. The danger in herpes zoster ("shingles") involving the eye is scarring of the cornea, but this is not inevitable. The eye is most commonly affected when herpes spreads to the side of the nose, but providing the condition is recognized quickly and treated at once the eyesight may not be affected.

Q. *I have been told that I have glaucoma and have been given eyedrops. Will I have to have an operation?*

A. It depends largely on the severity of the condition. Glaucoma is a condition in which the pressure inside the eyeball is greater than normal. Eyedrops containing a drug to reduce the pressure are used in the treatment of cases of mild or moderate severity, and in many cases the pressure will remain within safe limits as long as the drops are used. Regular follow-up will show how successful the treatment is; but even if in time the pressure rises, the operation for glaucoma is well understood and effective. It is important to see your doctor regularly for follow-up even after a successful operation, because sometimes the unaffected eye will in time show signs of increased pressure.

Q. *I am developing a cataract in the eye, but I have been told that I must wait before I can have an operation. Why is this?*

A. A cataract is an opacity in the lens of the eye, and the operation involves removal of the lens. Vision is corrected afterward by special glasses. But the eye, although able to see well, has a smaller field of vision and things look larger than they did before operation. The combination of normal vision in the good eye and the new kind of vision in the eye with the lens removed is unsatisfactory. As long as one eye is functioning well enough to be of practical value, it is usually advised that the operation should be postponed until the vision in the good eye is in turn diminished, for cataracts are very often bilateral.

However, it is not advisable to leave a fully developed cataract for too long, for in some cases an "over-ripe" cataract will set up a serious inflammation. In general the aim is to provide vision adequate for the patient's needs; to avoid unbalanced vision between the eye without a lens and the eye still with a lens, and to avoid allowing a cataract to become "hyper-mature." In some cases—especially of cataract following injury in younger people—contact lenses are very valuable. Recently, successful attempts have been made to replace the natural lens with an artificial lens, especially in elderly persons. Such "lens implants," as they are known, are positioned permanently inside the eye. However, the operation is far from routine and does involve a certain risk if the lens shifts position (which can injure the eye).

Q. *I can see fine black threads floating in my field of vision, especially when I look at a white background. Does this mean I may lose my sight?*

A. No. Although these "floaters" can be distracting, they are in most cases not important and in time they disappear. They are particularly common in near-sighted people. If they appear suddenly for the first time, or increase in number, you should ask for the opinion of an ophthalmologist.

(See also the major article on **Ophthalmology**.)

EAR AND HEARING PROBLEMS

loss of hearing—deaf children and
intelligence—ringing in the ears—pressure
pain in the ears—ear disease and giddiness

Q. *I seem to be going deaf. Should I get a hearing aid?*

A. You may not need one. The most common cause of deafness is merely excessive wax in the ear, but to establish its presence for certain you need a medical examination. It is not wise to try to remove the wax yourself (except by using special drops designed for the purpose) and you should not try to clean your ear out with absorbent cotton on a stick because it is too easy to damage the passage to the eardrum and the drum itself. It is even easier to damage the drum in an infant because the external passage is much shorter than it is in an adult.

Diseases which affect the hearing range from infections to degenerative change in the auditory nerve, with middle-ear disease more likely to affect the young and nerve deafness occurring in later life. Temporary deafness may occur if the tube connecting the middle ear with the inside of the nasopharynx is blocked, usually as the result of a common cold. This type of mild deafness resolves itself in a few days or weeks. Progressive deafness starting in fairly early adult life may be due to OTOSCLEROSIS; in such cases there is very often a history of deafness in the family. It is possible to improve the hearing in otosclerosis, in selected cases, by operative treatment (stapedectomy). Progressive deafness starting late in life is usually the result of *presbyacusia* (senile nerve deafness). Here the best treatment is by hearing aids, but it is often difficult to persuade the elderly that they need one.

Remember that an increasingly common cause of deafness is exposure to loud noise. If you work with tools or machinery that produce loud noise, or listen regularly to highly amplified music, there is a danger of progressive hearing loss. In the first case, you should get protective coverings for your ears; in the second you would be well advised to modify your tastes.

Q. *If a baby is born deaf, will it affect his intelligence?*

A. Not in itself. Children who are born totally deaf do not speak, but there is nothing wrong with their organs of speech nor necessarily with their intelligence. Although it needs extreme patience and skill to help such children, the results are extremely rewarding. Children with a lesser degree of hearing loss are sometimes thought to be lacking in intelligence until it is realized that in fact they cannot properly hear what is said, and so miss a great deal of instruction. As simple a measure as bringing them up to the front of a classroom can make all the difference. Hearing tests should be performed as a routine during the first five years of life, particularly if the child has been subject to ear infections, and should always be performed in the case of a child who shows signs of a behavior disorder or who is backward at school.

Q. *I have lately begun to hear a high-pitched noise in my ears. Does this mean that I am going to go deaf?*

A. No, the odds against that happening are very high. The name given to the sensation of noises in the ear is TINNITUS. There are many causes; some are trivial, such as taking too many aspirin, but others are associated with inner-ear disease. In many cases tinnitus may be no more than a nuisance—though it is difficult to treat satisfactorily. Your doctor will be able to reassure you that nothing sinister is wrong much more easily than he will be able to stop the noise. Tinnitus is also an early symptom of an ear disorder called MÉNIÈRE'S DISEASE.

Q. *Why do I get pain in my ear if I am in an airplane which is descending?*

A. The lower end of the tube connecting the middle ear with the nose and throat acts as a valve, so that when an airplane is ascending the air in the middle ear expands and escapes; but when pressure increases on descent, the flap valve prevents air reentering the middle ear and a pressure differential builds up between the middle ear and the air outside. This is the cause of the pain. The rate of descent of civil aircraft planes is normally regulated so that the pressure differential in a healthy ear never becomes marked enough to produce pain. But if a passenger is suffering from a cold, which tends to block the nasopharyngeal end of the tube, or if the rate of descent is abnormally high, the resulting pain may be quite severe. Frequent swallowing, yawning, moving the lower jaw and tipping the head back helps to open the end of the tube. The use of a nasal decongestant spray may also be helpful.

Q. *Can disease of the ear cause giddiness?*

A. Yes, that is a possible cause. The organ of balance is in the inner ear. Infection of the middle ear can spread as far as the inner ear to produce VERTIGO, but this is not common. In some cases vertigo is caused by wax blocking the outer ear, blockage of the Eustachian tube (which connects the middle ear with the nose and throat), OTOSCLEROSIS and Ménière's disease—the latter two being more serious causes. It is possible to make a person giddy by introducing very cold water into the outer ear canal, and rarely a foreign body stuck firmly in the outer canal of the ear will make a child feel giddy.

NOSE PROBLEMS

sinusitis—nasal decongestants—hay fever—nosebleeds

Q. *I suffer from sinusitis. Exactly what are the sinuses and why is it so painful when they become infected?*

A. This is another example of a pressure differential in an enclosed air space causing pain. The paranasal air sinuses are spaces contained within the bones of the skull above and below the eyes; normally they communicate freely with the nasal cavity. If the openings between the nose and the sinuses are blocked, usually as the result of infective swelling of the mucous membranes, the air in the sinuses is absorbed into the bloodstream and the pressure falls. The pain in SINUSITIS is caused both by the local infection and by the partial vacuum which develops.

Treatment is directed both toward the eradication of the infection and the establishment of communication with the nose. Steam inhalations, with the occasional use of nasal decongestants, usually free the blockages, and the infection is controlled with the administration of antibiotics. In cases of chronic infection of the nose, or of longstanding allergic conditions affecting the nose, POLYPS—protrusions of the nasal mucous membrane—may form and block the nose and the openings of the sinuses. These require surgical removal.

Q. *Are nasal decongestants useful in keeping my nose from running?*

A. They do work. But unless you have a particular reason, such as the necessity to make a journey by air when you have a cold, you should not use nasal decongestants except on medical advice. The reason is that the overuse of these "vasoconstricting" drugs usually prolongs stuffiness and may even lead to a spread of infection from the nose to the sinuses. It is better to relieve the symptoms by steam inhalations. The use of nasal decongestants by patients being treated for high blood pressure (hypertension) with certain drugs—the "adrenergic blocking agents," which sometimes produce nasal congestion as a side effect—may lead to a potentially dangerous rise in blood pressure.

Q. *Is there any effective treatment for hay fever?*

A. It is difficult to treat hay fever (allergic rhinitis) successfully. There are three main lines of treatment: oral antihistamines, specific desensitization based on skin tests, and the continued use of cromoglycate, an agent which is inhaled to prevent attacks of asthma. The drawback to the use of antihistamines is their well-known sedative effect, and the fact that they enhance the effect of alcohol. The drawback to desensitization lies in its expense, and in that the treatment does not always provide long-lasting effects; because it is based on the sometimes unreliable results of skin testing, it is not even always effective. The use of cromoglycate requires inhalation of the drug six times a day, as the treatment is prophylactic (preventive). In exceptional circumstances steroid therapy may be suggested, but the condition has to be very severe before this course of treatment can be justified.

Q. *My son sometimes suffers from nosebleeds. What is the best way of stopping them?*

A. Get him to sit up with his head bent forward, and then make him pinch the soft part of his nose between his fingers and his thumb. He should breathe through his mouth; the blood may run from his mouth and can be caught in a basin, or he can sit over the basin. Pressure should be kept up for fully five minutes. This will seem a long time, and will be uncomfortable, but in most cases continuous pressure will be successful.

The usual site of bleeding is near the front of the nose, and pressure will induce the clotting of blood in the vessels. When bleeding has stopped, your son should not blow his nose for at least 12 hours. If he should feel faint, it is better to stop the treatment and let him lie down until he feels he can safely sit up—rather than to try to keep him upright. Remember that a little blood goes a long way in producing bloodstains, and that bleeding from the nose is rarely dangerous.

If simple pressure for five minutes does not stop the bleeding, it may be necessary for your doctor to identify the bleeding area by examining the interior of the nose. He can then apply direct pressure to the ruptured blood vessel, pack the nose, or—in the case of recurrent bleeding—coagulate the bleeding point.

SORE THROATS

antibiotic treatment—tonsillectomy—infectious mononucleosis—quinsy—difficulty swallowing—laryngitis

Q. *Should sore throats be treated with antibiotics?*

A. In general they should not. Sore throats may be the result of infection by viruses or bacteria (especially the streptococcus); in most mild cases the infection is self-limiting, lasts only a few days before recovery, and leaves no ill-effects.

Clinically, it is almost impossible to tell what type of infection is present; if a definite diagnosis is required a throat swab will have to be taken and the micro-organisms cultured. Until this is ready (and it takes time), the prescription of a specific antibiotic is impossible. However, most doctors go by the severity of the infection and if the patient is really ill (with a high temperature and headache) or if there are signs of a spread of the infection (such as earache or enlarged glands in the neck) they will prescribe a broad-spectrum antibiotic. It is not sensible to take antibiotics for a sore throat without a doctor's advice because there is the possibility of producing resistant organisms by the indiscriminate use of antibiotics, and also the possibility of inducing sensitivity in the body. *Excessive use of antiseptic lozenges may in itself make the throat sore.*

Q. *My son suffers from recurrent sore throats. Should he have his tonsils removed?*

A. It is not advisable to remove children's tonsils except for well-defined reasons, and the same advice holds good for adults. Most doctors believe that there has in the past been too much willingness within the medical profession to advise tonsillectomy, although this was understandable when antibiotics were not available. Now, when the medical treatment of infected tonsils and infection of the ear is so much more effective, the usefulness of surgery has diminished. In its place it is still essential, but the indications are far fewer.

Q. *Can a sore throat cause infectious mononucleosis?*

A. No. The reverse is true. INFECTIOUS MONO-NUCLEOSIS is a virus disease, mostly affecting young adults, in which the lymphoid tissue of the body is involved. One of the early symptoms is a sore throat, as the lymphoid tissue of the tonsils is affected. This is part of the disease and not the *cause* of it.

Q. *Can swollen tonsils cause choking?*

A. Very rarely. If greatly swollen by infection, the tonsils can partly obstruct the airway, but they do not stop the flow of air completely. The tissues around the tonsils may become severely swollen if an abscess develops in the tissues surrounding the tonsils (quinsy); in such cases it is difficult to swallow and talk. This painful condition is more often seen in adults than children and needs immediate medical treatment. It is possible to see the affected tonsil displaced toward the middle of the throat, and the soft palate is swollen. Antibiotics and surgery—either to drain the abscess or to remove the diseased tonsil—bring relief.

Before immunization against diphtheria was a routine, some cases of "tonsillitis" were in fact cases of DIPHTHERIA. In this disease a membrane forms over the tonsils; if the infection affects the larynx, the airway may become obstructed and urgent TRACHEOSTOMY (the surgical formation of an airway directly through the throat into the windpipe), is indicated. Diphtheria is now rare, but it still exists. There is little doubt that relaxation of the strict routine of immunization would allow the disease to spread again.

Q. *One of the difficulties I have when my child has a sore throat is that he will not swallow. Is there anything I can give him to help him to eat?*

A. The main object in treating a small child who has difficulty in swallowing is to persuade him to *drink* enough. In most cases you don't have to worry that he is not getting enough to eat; a few days without solid food will do no harm. However, a few hours without enough to drink can be serious. It is often possible to give ice cubes (flavored, if necessary) to the child to suck, and any cold drink he likes should be at his bedside. Sometimes a fizzy drink goes down better than a still one, but it is not necessary to put sugar in the drink with the idea of keeping up the level of nourishment.

As long as he has enough water, however he takes it, the child will come to no harm; when he is ready, he will ask for something to eat. This should at first be soft food, and it may take a little time before he is back on a normal diet. It is better to give too much to drink than too little; the mouth should never be dry, nor should the amount of urine passed be obviously less than normal.

Q. *I have had an attack of laryngitis and don't seem able to throw off the hoarseness. Should I gargle, or is there anything else I can do?*

A. Persistent hoarseness after an attack of laryngitis is usually caused by overuse of the voice. The only sensible way of treating it is to stop talking, because as long as the inflamed vocal cords are used they will stay swollen. Steam inhalations may help, perhaps with the addition of compound tincture of benzoin. Persistent misuse of the voice may result in the formation of small nodules on the vocal cords, which may require surgical treatment. Hoarseness without any obvious cause is a strong indication to seek your doctor's advice.

(See also the major article on **Otolaryngology**.)

COUGHS

morning coughs—persistent nighttime coughing in children—cough mixtures— whooping cough—chest pain and coughing— bloodstained sputum—coughing in heart failure

Q. *Is a cough in the morning normal?*

A. No. It may be caused by smoking or a respiratory disease. If you begin to cough in the morning, and you are a smoker, it is a sign that you are smoking too much. If the cough begins to get worse it is time to see your doctor for an examination. Cough resulting from an upper RESPIRATORY TRACT INFECTION should disappear within three weeks.

Q. *My child has been coughing, particularly at night, so that we have all lost sleep. Is there anything that I can do to stop it?*

A. Children at the age when they start to go to school, or attend a play group, very often develop a persistent cough. Sometimes they have had signs of a tendency to allergic reactions, such as eczema, or there may be a family history of some allergic disorder. If this is so, it is worth trying to identify a precipitating factor—animals (for example, cats) or even plants in the home. Sometimes they have had an acute respiratory illness treated by antibiotics, or are subject to recurrent attacks of upper respiratory tract infection.

It is important to have your doctor examine the child, although in many cases no signs of disease will be found. Usually it is not sensible to suppress a cough if it brings up sputum; but in cases where the cough is dry and irritating, and nothing has been found in the way of allergic factors, it is best to use a simple cough syrup and perhaps a mild sedative such as promethazine hydrochloride. Steam inhalations are very useful with or without the addition of a liquid inhalant.

The tendency to night coughing will pass, but while it lasts the attacks are very wearing both to a child and its parents.

Q. *What is the best cough mixture to take for a cough which has troubled me for some time? I find my chest feels tight and I cannot free my lungs properly.*

A. While it is sensible to try to treat a simple cough yourself, there comes a time when you should ask for your doctor's opinion—generally speaking, when you have been suffering from a productive (sputum-producing) cough for more than two weeks.

Coughs can be caused by a large number of conditions, ranging from a simple cold to heart failure, but a common cause of a prolonged productive cough is BRONCHITIS. In its acute stage, bronchitis should not last more than two or three weeks, and it can be treated successfully. But if it is made worse by cigarette smoking, or by atmospheric pollution, or by a combination of these factors—such as may occur in people living in industrial surroundings—it may progress to chronic bronchitis, which in turn leads to considerable respiratory disability.

Another common cause of persistent cough is excessive nasal discharge, caused by chronic infection or irritation of the nasal membranes. The discharge can drip down the back of the nose into the throat and so give rise to a cough. Often this kind of cough is worse at night, when the position of the head in sleep encourages "postnasal drip." Large numbers of preparations are on the market for the relief of coughs and tightness of the chest, but the best are usually the simplest. It has been found that the most effective medicine for loosening sputum is a solution of salt in hot water, of a strength just below that producing nausea. But it is doubtful whether many people would prefer this to a proprietary expectorant mixture of less efficacy but much more agreeable flavor.

Q. *Is there any way of relieving whooping cough?*

A. The cough in an uncomplicated case of whooping cough can last for a long time—several weeks after the end of the acute phase of the illness—and treatment presents a difficult problem. There is no easy answer, but it is important to remember that the attacks of coughing, which often occur in the middle of the night and are accompanied by considerable distress and vomiting, leave the child surprisingly well. Treatment involves mild sedation, the use of a simple cough syrup, and the inhalation of steam or a medicated vapor. You may think your doctor is doing nothing, and just being reassuring, but believe him. The child will recover, although the parents may be exhausted.

Q. *I have had a bad cough and now have a pain in the chest. Could this be caused by coughing?*

A. It is possible to cough hard enough to break a rib, and it is certainly possible to develop a muscular pain in the chest wall through severe coughing. Very often such a pain will raise suspicions of PLEURISY, but the pain in pleurisy is characteristic—sharp, stabbing and produced by the act of breathing so that full movement of the chest is impossible and short shallow breathing develops. Patients suffer from pleurisy usually as a complication of pneumonia and they are very ill. It is possible for pleurisy to follow injury to the chest wall, or it may be a complication of a cancer of the lung; but in such cases the diagnosis has usually become obvious before pleurisy develops.

Q. *I have had a bad cold and cough and noticed on one occasion that my sputum was bloodstained. Should I go to my doctor, or could it have been caused by my cold?*

A. You should go to your doctor; but the bloodstained sputum could have been caused by the cold. There are many causes for this; some are serious, but not all. It is not possible for you to make the diagnosis yourself. In the case of serious disease such as tuberculosis, prompt treatment could make all the difference. It is very important that a correct diagnosis is made by your doctor as soon as possible.

Q. *Why do elderly people with bad hearts sometimes start to have fits of coughing and breathlessness in the middle of the night?*

A. In HEART FAILURE the lungs become engorged with blood because of the poor circulation, and the exchange of gases in the lungs between the air and the blood is inadequate. Moreover, the normally elastic lung tissue becomes stiff and the lungs move less easily, so that the act of breathing becomes more difficult and a conscious effort has to be made. When people with heart failure lie down, the blood moves from the legs and the abdominal organs into the chest and head, and the state of the lungs deteriorates because of the increased blood volume.

The patient with heart failure therefore finds it easier to breathe when sitting up, and when he goes to bed finds it more comfortable to lie with the upper half of the body propped up on pillows. During the night he tends to slip down in the bed and gradually the lungs become engorged. By the time that the discomfort has become bad enough to wake him up, fluid has exuded into the air spaces of the lungs and he finds himself very short of breath. The exuded fluid makes him cough and the sputum may be stained with blood.

Usually the attack can be relieved by sitting him up and opening the window so that there is an obvious supply of fresh air—anxiety plays an important part in the distress caused by acute breathlessness (dyspnea). Only by propping the patient up securely when he goes to sleep can the attacks be prevented; in extreme cases, sufferers may prefer to sleep in a chair. If they do, the legs should not be allowed to hang down for they will become swollen.

PNEUMONIA

coughing in pneumonia—exposure to cold—crisis and lysis—antibiotic therapy

Q. *Does a person with pneumonia always have a cough?*

A. A cough is not always a prominent feature in the early stages of pneumonia. Pneumonia often shows itself by producing a high temperature quickly. The patient, particularly if under five years old, may feel very ill, shiver, possibly have an abdominal pain and be short of breath. Older patients often complain of severe headaches before they cough or feel any discomfort in the chest. They may complain of the headache so bitterly that the doctor only learns that they have a cough by asking direct questions.

Q. *How can exposure to cold make people more likely to develop pneumonia?*

A. It is thought that exposure to cold makes it easier for the pneumococcus and other bacteria which are often present but harmless in the upper part of the respiratory tract to make their way into the lower reaches of the respiratory passages, where they multiply and set up a spreading infection. Between 20–40% of people harbor pneumococci in their throats, although some are not of the type which can cause infection. Types which can cause pneumonia are found more often in the throats of people who are suffering from a cold.

Q. *We have had a case of pneumonia in the family and my grandmother told me that there used to be a time called the "crisis" when the patient suddenly recovered. This does not seem to happen now. Why?*

A. When the infection is overcome by the body's natural defense system, some high fevers will suddenly drop and the temperature will stay within normal limits. This drop is called the *crisis*. Other fevers fall more slowly and they are said to resolve by *lysis*. Since the advent of antibiotics, few fevers are left to recover naturally. Most are treated with a view to destroying the invading microorganisms by the use of the appropriate drug, which either prevents the bacteria from multiplying (*bacteriostatic* action) or actually kills them (*bacteriocidal* action). Consequently, the natural pattern of fever is rarely seen today.

The disease that usually resolved by crisis in the days before antibiotics was pneumonia; typhoid fever typically resolved by lysis. Pneumonia is far from the killing disease it once was, now that it can so easily be treated by antibiotics. Perhaps one of the most striking changes in medicine in the last 40 years is the fact that a promptly treated case of pneumonia may last only as long as a common cold and be little more debilitating.

Q. *My child developed a bad case of measles and the doctor said he had pneumonia. He treated him with antibiotics. Surely measles is a virus infection, and I understand that viruses are not susceptible to antibiotics. Why was this antibiotic treatment necessary?*

A. Most cases of pneumonia, even those which occur in the course of a virus disease like measles or influenza, are caused by secondary invasion of the lungs by bacteria. While it is true that viruses themselves are not affected by antibiotics, the bacterial invaders are vul-

nerable. That is why pneumonia following a virus infection is usually treated with antibiotics.

(See also the major article on **Pulmonary Diseases.**)

CHEST PAIN AND HEART DISEASE

pain of indigestion—pain of heart disease—angina pectoris—onset of angina pectoris—pain of pleurisy—heartburn—sudden death from a heart attack—hearing one's heart at night—"skipped heartbeats"—rapid heartbeat—swollen ankles and heart disease

Q. *I have been told that pain in the lower part of the chest on the left side is more likely to be due to indigestion than heart disease. Is this true?*

A. Roughly speaking this may be true. Pain in the chest, particularly in the lower left side where the heart lies, is one of the most common complaints that a doctor has to deal with. Many patients with this problem are worried that they have heart disease.

A large number of pains arise from the muscles of the chest wall and the ribs; providing that the patient can give a clear account of the nature of the pain the diagnosis is often obvious. Indeed, it is sometimes easier to make a diagnosis by listening carefully to what the patient has to say than by examining him. If you ask the doctor's advice about a pain in the chest try to get a clear idea in your mind of the nature of the pain, when it comes on, what makes it worse—taking food, for example, or going for a long walk—and be ready to answer his questions, which may go into detail.

If your doctor is in any doubt about the nature of your pain he will usually take an electrocardiogram (ECG), but do not jump to the conclusion that if he does you certainly have heart disease. It is only one of the investigations that may be necessary before a definite diagnosis can be made; since it is an easy one, and can be done in the office, it may almost be regarded as a routine.

Q. *What sort of pain in the chest is characteristic of heart disease?*

A. It is usually described as a tight or crushing sensation, sometimes as burning, choking, or as a heavy numbness; it is rarely said to be stabbing or throbbing. It occurs in the left side of the chest and may spread to the neck, the left arm and in some cases the right arm, or around the chest. It may be felt in any of these places without involving the chest and it is characteristically brought on or made worse by exercise or strong emotion, exposure to cold or eating a large meal. The chest wall over the heart is not tender, nor are movements of the arms painful. The pain usually goes away in a short time unless it has been caused by an acute obstruction of the arteries of the heart (the *coronary* arteries). The natural tendency for anyone feeling such a pain is to keep still, and this is the best thing to do.

As you see, there can be so many variations in the nature and site of pain caused by a poor blood supply to the heart that often the doctor cannot be sure—without special investigations—that the discomfort is associated with heart disease.

Q. *I suffer from angina pectoris. Is it sensible to try to take exercise?*

A. In general you should stop short of producing pain, but it is certain that exercise within reason can improve the state of the heart muscle and is advisable. Always take your doctor's advice on the degree and extent of exercise, however, especially after the age of 40.

Q. *Is it possible to develop angina pectoris without exertion?*

A. Most people with angina suffer pain only after making a physical effort. But in some cases the pain is produced by emotion more than by exercise; in others the pain may come on for no obvious cause. In these cases (which are not common) the diagnosis may be difficult.

Q. *I am told that I have had an attack of pleurisy. But the worst pain was in my shoulder, not my chest. Why?*

A. If the pain of PLEURISY is caused by inflammation of the membranes lining the chest wall, the pain is felt in the chest wall at the site of the inflammation. If the inflammation is in the membranes separating the lungs from the diaphragm, the pain is felt either in the shoulder or in the abdomen. The reason for this is that the central part of the diaphragm develops in the neck region of the fetus and is supplied by the "phrenic nerve," which originates in the neck and runs in the fully developed individual through the chest to the diaphragm (being made up of nerve fibers derived from the third, fourth and fifth nerve roots arising from the

neck or cervical portion of the spinal cord). Fibers from these nerve roots also make up the nerves supplying the skin over the shoulder; when the sensory fibers of the phrenic nerve are stimulated by painful conditions of the central part of the diaphragm the pain is felt as if it came from the shoulder.

There are a number of similar instances of pain originating in internal organs being felt in different parts of the body which share the same basic nerve supply. Sometimes this "referred pain" can be misleading.

Q. *I sometimes feel a gripping, burning sensation behind my breastbone which seems to involve my arms, but it has nothing to do with exercise and in fact comes on worse when I lie down. I am told it is heartburn. Does it have anything to do with my heart?*

A. Although such a pain is called "heartburn," it has nothing to do with heart disease; it is the consequence of trouble in the lower part of the esophagus. It is usually made worse by bending forward and by lying down, and is particularly liable to come on after a heavy meal in the evening when you go to bed.

The pain has been produced experimentally by distending the lower end of the esophagus and by introducing acid resembling the acid normally found in the stomach; it seems to be due to regurgitation of the stomach contents into the esophagus. It can occur during pregnancy and in people who are overweight, particularly in middle age and later. It is often found in association with a HIATUS HERNIA, where the upper part of the stomach is displaced upward through the opening in the diaphragm through which the esophagus passes. This opening can become abnormally enlarged, especially after the age of 60.

Reduction of weight, avoidance of large meals, and the use of antacids reduce the incidence of heartburn, which characteristically is intermittent. An attack at night is often relieved by getting out of bed and walking about.

Q. *We have recently had the unfortunate experience in the family of a doctor telling my uncle that his heart was healthy two days before he suddenly died of a heart attack. Was there any way of telling that it was going to happen?*

A. Most doctors have experienced similar unfortunate occurrences in their practices. It is one of the reasons why so much attention has been paid to research into the chemical analysis of blood in suspected cases of heart disease. Great progress has been made in identifying various factors which make heart disease more likely to occur and in finding preventive treatment. Nevertheless, it remains true that there are many cases of sudden death from heart attacks in which the victim has been in apparently normal health, and at autopsy there may be little evidence of arterial disease.

Q. *I sometimes wake up in the night and I hear my heart beating very hard. Is this normal?*

A. If you lie with your ear on the pillow and listen carefully you can often hear your heartbeat; in the middle of the night, when everything is quiet, once you have picked up the beat it may be difficult to disregard it. The easiest way is to change position, remembering that if you lie on your left side you are more likely to be conscious of the action of the heart. The more you listen and "feel" for the action of your heart the more you will be conscious of it. But undue perception of the heart's action is not a symptom of heart disease; it is more likely to indicate a state of general anxiety.

Q. *My heart seems to skip beats sometimes. Is this anything to worry about?*

A. It is quite common for this to happen occasionally and such irregularities normally have no significance. They are most likely to be associated with exhaustion, too much tea or coffee, acute infections, or smoking to excess, and may be accompanied by a sinking sensation or a feeling of "butterflies" in the chest. It sometimes happens when one is suddenly alarmed. If it happens often and is disturbing you must ask for your doctor's opinion; he will be able to recognize the rare case in which the skipped beat is medically significant.

Q. *There are times when my heart seems to beat much more quickly then normal. Is this important?*

A. In general it is true to say that persons with heart disease do not complain of disorders of rhythm or "pace" of the heartbeat, but rather of symptoms such as pain and breathlessness. Most people aware of irregularities of heart action (sometimes called *palpitations*) have nothing to worry about.

Most of us are conscious of a quickened pulse when we are excited, anxious, or undertaking physical exertion. But there is a condition called "paroxysmal tachycardia" in which the pulse rate doubles, and there may be discomfort in the chest or a choking sensation

accompanied by acute awareness of the rapid beating of the heart. The condition comes on suddenly and disappears just as quickly. Apart from the resulting limitation of activity and mild breathlessness, it is harmless. However, if you find the attacks distressing, or if they last for a long time, your doctor will be able to give you advice on ways of cutting them short and perhaps prescribe drugs which will prevent them occurring frequently.

It is important to emphasize that most people who are conscious of the action of their heart, or who consciously experience irregularities of pulse rate, have nothing serious to worry about. Those who are in fact suffering from heart disease very rarely come to the doctor with such symptoms. Doctors find that they are more likely to be associated with anxiety, emotion, increasing age, lack of exercise and excessive smoking.

Q. *My ankles tend to swell toward the end of the day, especially when it is hot. Is this a sign of heart disease?*

A. It is normal for the ankles to swell to some degree at the end of the day if you have been standing a lot and walking little; this tendency is made worse by wearing a tight girdle. The same thing happens if you have been sitting still with your feet hanging down for a long time, as they might be during a long plane flight. The experience of taking your shoes off for comfort at the beginning of the flight and being unable to put them on again at the end is well known. The reason is that drainage of blood from the legs depends a great deal on movement of the muscles, which helps the flow of blood up through the veins; if the legs are still, the force of gravity tends to make the blood pool in the feet and ankles so that fluid collects in the tissues.

The remedy is to loosen tight clothes and to walk about from time to time; or, if you have to stand in the same place, stand on tiptoe a few times every now and then. If you can lie down with your legs well raised the swelling will go quite quickly. If there is anything wrong with the veins of the legs, swelling of the ankles occurs more easily; the same is true if you are overweight.

Although the ankles do swell in HEART FAILURE, there are usually other more obvious and distressing symptoms which bring a patient to the doctor. But in the elderly, whose circulation is often not all that it once was and who are liable to sit still for long periods, recurrent swelling of the ankles may sometimes be almost taken for granted—when it should draw attention to a slowly failing heart.

As always, if you are in doubt, it is advisable to ask for your doctor's opinion and not wait for any length of time "to see if it gets better." If the swelling of the ankle or foot is limited to one side, unless you know of a recent injury to that limb, you should not wait at all.

(See also the major article on **Cardiology.**)

VARICOSE VEINS AND VARICOSE ULCERS, BLOOD CLOTTING IN THE VEINS

varicose veins and ankle swelling—causes of varicose veins—treatment of varicose veins—when to start treatment—is treatment always necessary—bleeding from varicose veins—blood clots in varicose veins—blood clots in deep veins—itching—varicose ulcers

Q. *Do varicose veins make the ankles swell?*

A. Not necessarily. Most cases of mild varicose veins look unsightly but do not interfere much with the circulation. Severe cases indicate failure of a number of the one-way valves which normally control the flow of blood from the surface veins to the deeper veins of the legs. This means that blood stagnates or pools in the varicose veins and also that blood can be forced from the deep veins of the leg out into the superficial veins with a consequent rise of venous pressure. The drainage of blood from the ankles and lower parts of the legs is then inefficient and fluid is liable to collect in the tissues. Moreover, the skin becomes stained and less able to heal readily, so that a small wound or scratch may lead to the formation of an ulcer.

Therefore, if you have marked varicose veins, and the skin begins to be discolored or your ankles and legs begin to swell, it is important to ask your doctor's advice on treatment before the changes go too far and you are faced with the problem of a varicose ulcer.

Q. *What are the causes of varicose veins?*

A. Venous blood normally drains from the legs through two sets of veins—surface and deep. The surface veins lie just under the skin and are connected to the deep veins through a number of communicating veins. The deep veins lie inside a layer of firm fibrous tissue which surrounds and contains the muscles of the leg, and the veins are surrounded and supported by the muscles. Both the veins which lie under the skin and the deep veins are furnished with one-way valves, which allow the blood to flow upward toward the heart. When the muscles surrounding the deep veins contract inside their envelope of fibrous tissue the veins are compressed and the blood within them is driven upward—the only way it can go—against the force of gravity.

The surface veins are not subject to the pumping action of muscular contraction, but the blood within them flows through the communicating veins to refill the empty deep veins. The efficiency of this mechanism depends on the integrity of the one-way valves present in the deep, surface and communicating veins. The valves may become incompetent in surface and communicating veins because of a hereditary tendency or because the veins become engorged and stretched. It then follows that the length of vein below the incompetent valve cannot clear itself of blood, and in turn becomes stretched until the next valve in the series is damaged and the process continues. Incompetence of the valves in communicating veins is particularly likely to set up this train of events, and in looking at a network of varicose veins you may see prominent swellings where the incompetent veins lie.

Engorgement of the veins of the leg is encouraged by standing still, or sitting with the legs hanging down, particularly if the edge of a chair obstructs the flow of blood in the veins behind the knee. If you have to stand up for long periods at a time it is worth exercising your legs (if possible) by walking about every now and then, or by standing on tiptoe; the contraction of the calf muscles then pumps the blood out of the legs. During pregnancy the veins become engorged but it is difficult to relieve the pressure, so that varicosities often develop.

Varicose veins may also develop because of incompetence of the valves of the deep veins of the leg after THROMBOSIS. If the clots "recanalize," the new channels lack valves. Engorgement of the surface veins is caused initially by the blocking of the deep veins by a clot. When the deep-vein thrombosis begins to recover (because new vascular channels are formed through the obliterated veins) the pumping action which normally drains blood from the surface veins into the deep veins is no longer present, so that varicose veins develop.

Q. *Is it always possible to treat varicose veins?*

A. Some varicosities form after a deep-vein thrombosis—when the blood no longer finds adequate drainage through the deep veins of the leg and therefore flows through the surface veins, which consequently become swollen. In these cases it is not possible to remove or obliterate the surface veins, for they offer the only way that venous blood can drain from the leg.

Q. *When should I ask for treatment for my varicose veins?*

A. Pain in the legs and swollen ankles after a day's work is good reason to see your doctor, and the development of large and unsightly varicosities is an indication for treatment—as are eczema above the ankles, the formation of an ulcer, and bleeding from the veins.

Q. *Is it necessary to have varicose veins treated if they are not painful? I only have a few.*

A. No. If you can put up with their appearance they will not do you any harm, but many people do undergo treatment for cosmetic reasons. If the varicosities are extensive you should ask for your doctor's advice, for they may in time impair the drainage of venous blood from the leg.

It is better to have them treated before the tissues of the lower part of the leg are affected by the accumulation of fluid which could impair their vitality.

Q. *Is bleeding from varicose veins dangerous?*

A. A damaged varicose vein can bleed alarmingly fast and be very frightening. It can, however, be easily controlled by elevating the leg above the level of the body; this is done by lying the patient flat and raising the leg until the bleeding stops. You should then apply firm pressure to the bleeding area, using a pad and bandage. The same technique applies to bleeding from a varicose ulcer.

Q. *Is the formation of a blood clot in a varicose vein dangerous?*

A. Not usually; if the vein becomes red, tender and swollen, it means that a clot has formed inside the vein. Unless there is a suspicion of infection, the use of antibiotics is not necessary and the condition will resolve with conservative (nonsurgical) treatment. Support with elastic bandages and a certain amount of rest will help relieve the discomfort, but it is not necessary for the leg to be rested completely.

One of the recognized treatments for varicose veins is the injection of substances to produce clotting inside the veins and subsequent bandaging to prevent the clot becoming "recanalized." A naturally occurring clot may well have the same effect—the obliteration of the offending vein. The danger of THROMBOSIS (clotting) of the veins is that the clot may release fragments which are carried in the circulation to become lodged in the lungs (or, rarely, elsewhere) and interfere with vital functions. But this is true only of clots forming in the deep veins of the leg; it does not happen when the clots

are on the surface, as they are when they form in varicose veins.

Q. *How could I tell if I had a blood clot in a deep vein?*

A. While a thrombus (blood clot) in the surface veins of the leg makes the vein red and tender (and is obvious), a clot in the deep veins cannot be seen. It reveals itself by producing tenderness in the part of the limb affected, often the calf, and the surface veins may become more prominent than usual. The ankle may swell and there may be a slight rise in body temperature and pulse rate. If he is in doubt, your doctor may perform specific tests to confirm the presence of a clot.

The treatment of deep-vein thrombosis is different from that of a clot in a surface vein; it involves the use of anticoagulant drugs, which may have to be continued for some time. Fortunately, clotting in the surface veins is much more common than deep-vein clotting, which does not often occur except after surgical operations, debilitating illnesses and in old age (when the limbs tend to lie immobile). It may also occur after childbirth. There is an increased risk of venous thrombosis in women who take the contraceptive pill and the use of oral contraceptives should be discontinued well before any surgical operation.

Q. *Why does the discolored skin caused by varicose veins sometimes itch?*

A. Diseased skin often itches. It seems that damage to the skin short of the degree necessary to cause pain results in the release of histamine into the tissues, which probably stimulates nerves in the sensory network closely related to those which carry the sensation of pain, particularly burning pain. These are the "C" fibers of the sensory nerves. As well as the release of histamine, the presence in the tissues of certain enzymes concerned with the breakdown of protein produces the itching associated with eczema. It may be the latter process which gives rise to the itching associated with varicose veins; but the practical importance is that itching provokes scratching, and this damages the skin enough to start varicose ulcers.

Older people are, in general, more liable to develop an itching skin—possibly because the glands which normally lubricate the skin surface dry up. The danger of ulcer formation is increased because ARTERIOSCLEROSIS diminishes the arterial blood supply to the skin, especially at the junction of the lower third of the leg with the upper two-thirds—the usual site of a varicose ulcer.

Q. *What is the best treatment for varicose ulcers?*

A. There is no easy way to get rid of a varicose ulcer once it has become established. The one certain way to induce it to heal is bed rest; but it may need a period of two or three weeks before the ulcer responds, and this may not be convenient. Nevertheless, most doctors know cases where a few weeks in bed could have averted months of inconvenience caused by an ulcer that will not heal.

If an ulcer does give trouble it is best—if at all possible—to rest in bed with the leg slightly elevated. The reason is that ulceration takes place when the tissues are waterlogged by the accumulation of tissue fluid that forms when the drainage of venous blood is inadequate, and normal healing processes are impeded. While the leg is lower than the rest of the body this condition will continue; the local swelling produced by the ulcer further interferes with healing, so that a vicious circle is set up.

If the leg is kept higher than the rest of the body, as it will be if you lie down and put it up on a pillow, then the leg will drain under the influence of gravity and the tissues will lose the excess of tissue fluid—thus returning to a comparatively healthy state in which healing can take place. If it is impossible to take the time to rest in bed, the return of blood from the veins of a leg with severe varicosities can be aided by the use of supporting bandages put on firmly after a night's rest, when the condition of the leg is at its best. The elastic bandaging must be firm to do any good and must cover the leg from the base of the toes all the way to the knee. It is possible to use specially prepared adhesive bandages when an ulcer is active; these, after firm application, are left in place for some days.

No local treatment by itself can heal a varicose ulcer; the first requirement is efficient drainage of blood from the veins to reduce the accumulation of fluid in the lower part of the leg; it is only when this has been accomplished that local treatment can hope to be helpful. When the ulcer has healed the leg will continue to need support from elastic bandages or an efficient elastic stocking. If possible, the varicose veins which caused it should be treated according to your doctor's advice.

STOMACH AND INTESTINAL PROBLEMS, ULCERS

belching—gastritis—nighttime indigestion—
"ulcer personality"—symptoms of peptic
ulcers—treatment of peptic ulcers—healing of
ulcers—tests for ulcers—perforation

Q. *I suffer from the embarrassing trouble of belching. Is there any way I can control it?*

A. Yes, it is possible. Most of the gas present in the stomach and the intestines arrives through the mouth, swallowed with food or drink or because of an unconscious habit. This habit is called *aerophagy* and is quite common. It usually occurs in people who are tense and anxious and swallow their meals quickly, and they may also suffer from indigestion pains.

If you think you may be troubled by aerophagy, the best way to demonstrate it to yourself is to hold a cork between your teeth for an hour or more so that you cannot swallow air. You may then find that the troublesome belching has disappeared. It is not practical to try to cure the condition this way, but you should watch your tendency to swallow air and try to relax and eat your meals regularly and slowly.

Q. *What is meant by gastritis?*

A. In the past, the term gastritis was used to mean conditions in which a patient complains of symptoms resembling those of a peptic ulcer, but the results of x-ray investigations prove to be negative. Since the more widespread use of endoscopy (by means of which the physician can actually see the internal lining of the stomach through an optical instrument passed into the stomach via the esophagus) it has been realized that the term is imprecise. The appearance of the stomach lining does not necessarily bear any relation to the symptoms.

Two forms of gastritis are generally described—acute and chronic. In the acute form, which may exist in the absence of symptoms, the lining of the stomach is congested and it may bleed from eroded areas. Associated nausea and vomiting may be alarming because the vomit is bloodstained. The condition can be brought on by excessive indulgence in alcohol, by taking aspirin tablets, by swallowing chemicals such as acids or alkalis, and by infection of the gastrointestinal tract. In most cases the symptoms disappear and the stomach returns to normal in a couple of days; but if there is excessive bleeding, treatment in the hospital may be necessary.

Chronic gastritis is found fairly commonly and the number of cases increases with age. Again, there may be no symptoms and the reason for its development is obscure—except that it is said to occur more often in heavy smokers. It is often found that those with chronic gastritis suffer from iron-deficiency anemia, and it is a characteristic feature of pernicious anemia. It is also thought that cancer of the stomach is more likely to develop in persons with chronic gastritis. The importance of the condition is that its appearance will lead the physician to look out for diseases related to it. Special treatment for the condition itself is rarely needed.

Q. *I often have indigestion at night, especially after a good meal. Antacids don't seem to help much; is there anything else I can do?*

A. Pain in the upper part of the abdomen or the lower part of the chest is often caused by a PEPTIC ULCER, but can also be caused by irritation of the lower part of the esophagus by regurgitated stomach contents. This is more likely to occur when you lie down after a heavy meal. The pain or discomfort is usually described as "burning" and is often called "heartburn"—although it has nothing to do with the heart.

The tendency for food to regurgitate is greater as one gets older and heavier. It also happens when the capacity of the abdominal cavity is reduced by the enlargement of the uterus in pregnancy, from about the 20th week onward. One of the characteristic features of the discomfort is that it is relieved by getting out of bed and walking about. This is a mechanical effect, as the stomach and its contents then tend to fall back into the abdomen.

Heartburn is occasionally accompanied by regurgitation of food as far up as the mouth, where it tastes bitter and acid. Usually the discomfort of heartburn can be avoided by taking smaller, dry meals and keeping away from alcohol, hot strong coffee and highly spiced food. Loss of surplus weight is advisable. If you have to eat a large meal at night, you may find it better to sleep propped up in bed, or to raise the head of the bed. Antacid tablets dissolved slowly in the mouth are better than liquid antacids. Pain caused by a peptic ulcer may come on in the night, but in contrast it is usually relieved by eating a few crackers and drinking a glass of milk.

The diagnostic picture may be obscured because heartburn can occur in association with a peptic ulcer, but the pain and discomfort are often severe enough to make it unreasonable to describe them as simple indigestion.

Q. *Is there such a thing as an "ulcer personality?"*

A. Peptic ulcers (i.e., gastric and duodenal ulcers) are commonly thought to be prevalent in people who lead anxious lives, but there is no real evidence that stress produces ulcers, or that they are more likely to occur in anxious people. The actual cause of peptic ulcers is not clear, but there are several factors which may be implicated. One is genetic; ulcers do run in families, to the extent that some families tend to develop gastric ulcers, other families duodenal ulcers. Chronic gastritis may lead to ulcer formation and may be brought on by excessive cigarette smoking or drinking very hot coffee or tea, or straight alcohol.

Women, during the reproductive period of their lives, seem to be far less likely to develop ulcers than men; peptic ulcers are extremely rare during pregnancy. Ulcers are thought to be twice as common in men as in women. In Japan, gastric ulcers (involving the lining of the stomach) are much more common than duodenal ulcers, (involving the lining of the first section of the small intestine), while in other countries (such as the United States) the reverse is true. Missing meals or taking hurried, irregular meals may encourage the development of a peptic ulcer; those with blood group O have been shown to be particularly prone to suffer from ulcers. Some drugs, such as aspirin, can damage the stomach lining and lead to ulceration.

Q. *What is the most common symptom of a peptic ulcer?*

A. The most important symptom is pain, and often it is the only one. The pain is felt in the center of the upper part of the abdomen under the ribs and is influenced by meals. A duodenal ulcer causes pain when the stomach is empty ("hunger pain"); the pain is relieved as a meal is eaten. A gastric ulcer tends to be painful about half an hour to an hour after a meal. Sometimes the pain of a duodenal ulcer seems to be in the lower part of the abdomen, or goes to the back; it may, however, be felt in the chest.

Attacks of pain caused by an ulcer are subject to remissions and the pain may be absent for some weeks or months, very often returning during the winter. Pain seems to be dependent on inflammation of the ulcer and not merely on its presence, for painless ulcers can be found during endoscopy. When the ulcer is inflamed it is sensitive to the action of stomach acid and the pain can be relieved by antacid mixtures or tablets. It is probable that pain can also be produced by spasm of the muscular walls of the stomach or duodenum. Vomiting may also occur in some patients. It tends to occur in people with severe pain, and brings relief; it may be the sign of scarring and narrowing of the duodenal end of the stomach, with consequent obstruction to the passage of food and enlargement of the stomach.

Q. *Can medical treatment alone really cure peptic ulcers?*

A. There have been considerable advances in the medical treatment of ulcers. In particular, the use of the drug cimetidine, has given relief to many people with ulcers that are difficult to control by other means. Unless certain complications are found, it is always better to give medical treatment a reasonable trial; but it remains true that over a third of ulcer patients are likely to have recurrent trouble. It is important to emphasize that symptoms may disappear before the ulcer has completely healed; some ulcer patients thus give up before the course of treatment has been completed. It is essential to follow your doctor's instructions to the letter if medical treatment is to succeed.

Q. *Do gastric and duodenal ulcers ever get better by themselves?*

A. Most peptic ulcers do heal spontaneously. Rest, perhaps mild sedation, attention to diet and the use of antacids give relief in most cases; cigarette smoking retards healing. The dangers of stomach ulcers lie in their complications, for both duodenal and gastric ulcers are liable to perforate and give rise to PERITONITIS, may bleed quickly and cause massive hemorrhages, or may bleed slowly over a period of time and produce anemia. If there is chronic ulceration in the duodenum (the first part of the small intestine), in time it becomes scarred and its opening may become narrow to the extent that the passage of food is impeded. The condition is known as *pyloric stenosis* and leads to enlargement of the stomach, nausea and vomiting.

Malignant changes sometimes occur in gastric ulcers; these changes can only be diagnosed by means of specific investigations. These considerations make it foolish to try to cure ulcers by yourself, or to ignore ulcer symptoms in the hope that the condition will get better by itself. It is far better to ask your doctor's advice—even though he may prescribe simple remedies which, you may think, you could have adopted for yourself.

Q. *What are the special tests usually used in the investigation of peptic ulcers?*

A. Analysis of stomach secretions can be made on specimens withdrawn from the stomach through a tube passed by way of the nose or mouth through the esophagus—which, although uncomfortable, is not as unpleasant as it sounds. After the first specimen has been obtained, one of a number of stimulants to the secretion of acid may be given so that the function of the acid-secreting cells can be checked.

One commonly used stimulant is pentagastrin, which is injected into the skin; following injection, the secretions are collected over a given period and the acid output estimated. People with peptic ulcers usually have a high acid level, (those with cancer of the stomach have a normal or low level). The test is particularly useful in cases of pernicious anemia, where there is little acid secretion and an absence of the "intrinsic factor" normally secreted by the stomach (without which the essential vitamin B_{12} cannot be absorbed), but it is not of absolute diagnostic value in cases of peptic ulcer.

Of greater value is *endoscopy,* which makes possible visual inspection of the inside of the stomach. This procedure has become practical since the introduction of fiberoptics, for the instrument now used is flexible, and only just over 1 cm in width. It carries a channel through which a BIOPSY can be taken of the lining of the stomach, and an attachment for a camera so that photographic recordings of the appearance of the interior of the stomach can be made. Endoscopy is particularly useful in cases where x-ray investigation has proved inconclusive.

Plain x-rays of the abdomen are not very useful in the investigation of stomach ulcers, for only the air in the stomach can be visualized. However, if the stomach is filled with a substance opaque to x-rays its outline can be fully seen. The substance used is barium, which blocks the passage of x-rays and is therefore seen as a white outline on the negative x-ray film. If the patient under investigation swallows a liquid containing barium sulfate the progress of the barium can be followed through the esophagus into the stomach, where it defines the outline of the stomach wall—demonstrating the pattern of the ridges into which it is folded and any defects ("filling defects") caused by the presence of an ulcer. The barium is followed through the stomach into the duodenum; any delay is apparent and deformity of the duodenum caused by ulceration can be recognized.

The combination of contrast radiography and endoscopy is capable of producing extremely accurate diagnoses of diseases of the stomach and duodenum, and while the procedures are not entirely comfortable they are extremely safe and easily endured.

Q. *What is a perforation?*

A. Stomach (gastric) or duodenal ulcers can, when severe, perforate the wall of the organ in which they lie. When they do, the sudden discharge of food and acid into the cavity of the peritoneum produces acute abdominal pain and shock which reduces the patient to immobility. He is obviously very ill and in pain; the diagnosis is usually clear although in some cases there may be little history of indigestion. The treatment is surgical; an incision is made into the abdomen as soon as possible and the hole in the stomach or duodenum is sewn up. In some cases the leak may be small and slow and an abscess may form, sealed off by the omentum (the fatty apron which hangs down in the front of the abdominal cavity).

The results of operative treatment are good, especially in younger people. After a successful operation, ulcer symptoms may vanish for up to a year, although subsequent definitive surgical treatment may be recommended.

ABDOMINAL PAIN

childhood abdominal pain—appendicitis—
chronic appendicitis—causes of abdominal
pain—when to call the doctor—colic—
adhesions—abdominal pain of shingles

Q. *I have a child of seven who sometimes says he has a pain in his stomach which is bad enough to prevent him from going to school. Is it just nerves, or is it likely to be anything more serious?*

A. It is not uncommon to find children between the ages of three and ten who suffer from recurrent attacks of abdominal pain, associated with a headache and even vomiting. The pain is felt around the navel, but it is difficult to get the child to describe it exactly. There is no fever, but he may look ill and pale. The condition has something in common with migraine. Parents of such children may have had a similar pattern of illness in their childhood, and others suffer from migraine as adults.

As the problem is often associated with anxiety or excitement, and may develop in the morning before school, the child may be thought to be just trying to avoid his classes. By the age of ten years such pain typically disappears. However, one potential danger is that once an "emotional" cause for the pain has been diagnosed, a more serious condition—such as appendicitis—may at first be overlooked. In most cases, however, it is obvious to the doctor that the pattern of illness is different.

Q. *Is appendicitis more dangerous in children than in adults?*

A. The danger of appendicitis in young children is the speed with which the condition develops. The basic signs and symptoms of appendicitis are well known: the pain at first usually centers around the navel, then it travels to the right lower part of the abdomen (where the appendix lies). The first pains may be very sharp and intermittent; then, as the condition develops, the pain becomes continuous. There may be nausea and vomiting, with diarrhea or constipation. At first the body temperature and pulse rate are not significantly altered, but in time the pulse becomes faster (although the temperature does not rise to any marked degree). The breath is often foul and the tongue coated.

In children, however, these classical signs of appendicitis may not be clear-cut. The illness is more general, the fever higher, vomiting more common and the pain more diffuse. The appendix lies higher in the abdomen in children than in adults, and the omentum—the fatty membrane which lies at the front of the abdominal cavity and wraps itself around areas of inflammation within the abdomen—is shorter and smaller. There are a number of other conditions which can confuse the diagnosis—perhaps the most common being acute inflammation of the lymphatic glands of the abdomen, which may be accompanied by inflammation of the tonsils. Where there is any doubt your doctor will usually advise the surgical removal of the appendix, for it is better to remove a normal appendix than to leave one which may be inflamed.

Q. *Can pain in the abdomen which comes and goes be due to chronic appendicitis?*

A. Acute inflammation of the appendix can eventually become chronic if the appendix is not removed. The wall of the organ becomes damaged, so that parts of its inner lining can bulge through the muscle layers to form pouches (diverticula) which—if infected—again produce the signs and symptoms of acute appendicitis. In some cases the hollow interior of the appendix is blocked by the effects of acute inflammation, and secretions which normally escape into the blind pouch at the beginning of the large intestine (cecum) accumulate to swell the appendix gradually until in time the scarred wall may give way. This condition is called a *mucocele*.

It is doubtful whether the appendix can ever be the seat of chronic infection unless there has been a previous acute infection. Although a diagnosis of chronic appendicitis without the history of an acute attack is sometimes made, removal of the organ in such cases often fails to cure the symptoms and examination of the removed specimen shows it to be normal.

Q. *What is the most common cause of severe abdominal pain?*

A. Gastroenteritis—inflammation of the stomach and intestines—caused by infection; in the majority of cases the cause of the infection is not identified. The pain, which is sharp and intermittent and usually felt all over the center of the abdomen, comes on suddenly and is associated with vomiting and diarrhea. There may be a fever and often the victim complains of feeling giddy, cold and sweaty. In most cases the condition is self-limiting and of little medical significance; it typically improves quickly and often disappears within 48 hours. But the effects may be more severe in the very young and the very old, who may lose too much water and essential salts (electrolytes) and pass into a state of dehydration and biochemical imbalance.

In general, no special treatment is needed for otherwise healthy people except a fluid diet with plenty to drink. If the diarrhea persists a kaolin mixture is useful.

Q. *How long should I wait in a case of sudden pain in the abdomen before calling the doctor?*

A. There is no hard and fast rule. In many cases the patient is obviously ill from the start of the attack and you will be in no doubt that he needs immediate medical attention. In the event of acute gastroenteritis the diagnosis is often clear, because the sharp pains are accompanied by vomiting and diarrhea—which typically last only a short time, after which the condition quickly improves. In other cases, such as appendicitis, the pain will at first often be vague; but it builds up until the sufferer is unable to go on with what he or she is doing and has to lie down.

If the pain persists for long you should seek medical attention; abdominal pain persisting for more than six hours is usually caused by a condition of surgical importance. This is often true of pains which make the patient lie still as opposed to those which are eased by sitting up or moving about. In general, if you are in any doubt call your doctor.

Q. *What is colic? How does it differ from other abdominal pains?*

A. Colic is a severe pain which is caused by spasmodic contraction of the muscle in the wall of a hollow organ, such as the intestine. As the force of the contraction increases so does the pain—which reaches a peak and then dies away again, often leaving a dull ache. Colic can be produced by infections or by obstructions—such as a stone blocking the duct which carries bile from the gallbladder, or a kidney stone blocking the ureter (the tube through which urine passes from the kidney to the bladder). The colic resulting from inflammation of the intestines is caused by interference with their normally rhythmic contractions (which become unsynchronized and overly strong).

The coming and going of pain makes colic different from the steadier pain which follows inflammation of the peritoneum (the membrane which lines the abdominal cavity). While the inflammation is limited to the membrane covering the affected organ, the pain is felt diffusely in the abdomen—often centering on the navel. But when the inflammation begins to reach the membrane covering the inside of the abdominal wall, the pain becomes localized and much sharper and is felt over the organ affected. For example, in the case of the appendix it is felt in the lower right part of the abdomen; in the case of inflammation of the gallbladder, it is felt in the upper right part of the abdomen. The muscles over the site of inflammation become rigid and pressure on the abdominal wall is painful.

The pain resulting from the perforation of a peptic ulcer is caused by irritation of the peritoneal membrane by the material leaking out, and it is sudden and severe. As the leakage continues the pain becomes more diffuse and may be bad enough to interfere with breathing. Although the onset of this pain is as dramatic as the colic caused by obstruction of the ureter or the bile ducts, it does not vary in intensity. Even though the pain of colic is sudden and severe, in general it does not call for such urgent surgical treatment as the pain of a perforation or inflammation within the abdomen.

Q. *I had an appendectomy some years ago; since then I have had abdominal pains from time to time, which I am told are due to "adhesions." What does this mean?*

A. In the course of any abdominal operation the surgeon obviously must handle the intestines; this is sometimes followed by a tendency for the normally smooth membranes covering the abdominal organs and the inner walls of the abdomen to stick together (adhere) where they have been disturbed. The tendency is greater where these membranes—the *peritoneal membranes*—have been inflamed by an infection within the abdomen. The abdominal organs are continually moving in relation to each other as we breathe, walk about and change position, and the intestines are in continual motion with waves of muscular contraction passing down their walls. Adhesions between organs thus interfere to a greater or lesser extent with the natural order of things.

At their worst, adhesions involving the intestines can cause obstruction by kinking the intestines or forming a pocket or ring in which a portion of the intestine can be trapped. At best, only vague discomfort is felt. It is true that there is a temptation to blame "adhesions" for a number of postoperative maladies for which the cause is not immediately obvious. But there is no doubt that adhesions do occur and are difficult to treat, because any operation for their relief is liable to be followed by further adhesions in those people who are prone to their formation. Operation for the relief of adhesions is therefore best reserved for those patients in whom the adhesions have caused partial or complete obstruction of the intestine.

Q. *My father recently developed a severe pain in his abdomen on the right side, and the doctor thought he had gallbladder disease. A few days later he broke out in shingles in the same place. Is there some connection between shingles and disease of the gallbladder?*

A. No, but it sometimes happens that the pain of early shingles is severe enough to mimic disease of an internal organ, and it can be almost impossible to distinguish between the two. While the blisters of an attack of shingles are unpleasant, they do not (except when they involve the eye) cause much harm. The great problem with shingles is control of the pain both of the immediate attack and afterward when the rash has gone.

The early application of a 5% solution of idoxuridine to the blisters and a course of the drug amantadine have been helpful in reducing the pain to the level where it can be controlled by ordinary painkillers. If shingles attacks the face and involves the eye, there is a danger of subsequent infection and scarring of the eye which may cause blindness. At the first signs of an attack of shingles in the face and forehead it is very important to seek medical attention.

KIDNEY STONES AND GALLSTONES

how kidney stones form—treatment of kidney stones—avoiding recurrence of kidney stones—gallstones—complications of gallstones—nonsurgical treatment of gallstones—gallbladder cancer associated with gallstones—inflammation of the pancreas associated with gallstones

Q. *Why do stones form in the kidneys?*

A. There are a number of factors thought to be responsible for the formation of stones in the kidneys and bladder, but the exact mechanism is unclear. Infection is usually thought to be a common cause, but infection alone is unlikely to form stones. Other factors are involved. Most stones contain calcium, the most common stones being made up of a combination of calcium phosphate, calcium carbonate and magnesium ammonium phosphate. This type of stone is found in association with infection by bacteria which change urea to ammonia, thus altering the acidity of the urine to a level at which phosphates are less soluble.

The concentration of the urine is an important factor in the formation of stones; they are more likely to form in hot climates where a great deal of water is lost by sweating and the urine is therefore scanty and highly concentrated. Certain stones contain uric acid, and may occur in patients with GOUT where the level of uric acid in the blood is high. Others are made of oxalate; they are said to occur especially in people who eat a great deal of rhubarb or spinach, both of which foods have a high content of oxalate. The normal person excretes a certain amount of oxalate in the urine, but the concentration of oxalate does not bear any consistent relationship with the formation of oxalate stones. There are other rarer stones made of cystine and xanthine which may be found in association with disorders of the metabolism of these substances.

The presence of a foreign body, such as a catheter left in place for a long time, makes stone formation likely—especially if there is a urinary tract infection.

Q. *Is surgery the only possible treatment for kidney stones?*

A. Small stones often pass from the kidney through the ureter into the bladder and thus to the exterior, producing an attack of colic as they do so. However, if they become lodged in the urinary passages they may have to be removed surgically. Some large stones which form in the kidneys may be too big to pass down the ureter; in many cases they produce only an ache in the flank. However, they may be responsible for continuing bacterial infection of the urinary tract and cause damage to the kidney with loss of its normal function. In such cases surgical removal of the stones is necessary.

Stones which stay in the bladder (or those which form in the bladder) produce pain, lead to infection and sometimes make it difficult to pass urine. In suitable cases they can be crushed and washed out by the use of a special instrument passed into the bladder through the urethra.

Q. *I have had an attack of sharp abdominal pain caused by a kidney stone which passed naturally.*

Is there anything I can do to avoid another attack?

A. Your doctor will undoubtedly have performed tests to make sure that you are not suffering from any conditions such as a high blood level of uric acid or chronic infection of the urinary tract which could make the further formation of stones likely. But in many cases nothing can be found. If the stone passed was an oxalate stone, it is sensible not to eat foods which are rich in oxalates (the main two items you should avoid are spinach and rhubarb). In the case of uric acid stones (as in gout) the foods to avoid are sardines, sweetbreads, liver and kidneys. It is not practical to try to avoid food containing phosphates, but it may be useful to maintain urine on the acid side by the use of daily doses of ammonium chloride. In all cases it is very important to keep the urine dilute, and the intake of water should be enough to produce a daily output of about three quarts of urine. This is especially necessary for those who live or work in hot conditions, and lose an excessive amount of water in the sweat.

Q. *Do gallstones form in the same way as kidney stones?*

A. As in the case of kidney stones, the mechanism underlying the formation of gallstones is not well understood. The same factors appear to be present—infection, the physicochemical properties of the bile, and metabolic abnormalities. Most gallstones are made up almost entirely of CHOLESTEROL, which is precipitated out of solution if its concentration in the bile rises or the amount of bile salts falls. Infection is thought to result in the loss of water and bile salts, thus making the conditions more favorable for the formation of stones, which may take place around a nucleus of dead bacteria. Gallstones are usually multiple and in addition to cholesterol contain a mixture of calcium phosphate and carbonate, bile pigment, protein and iron. Some stones are made of cholesterol alone and are much larger than the mixed stones. They may be as much as 4 cm in diameter and are solitary. A few stones are made up solely of bile pigments, but these are very small (about 5 mm in diameter). Stones made of cholesterol do not show up in x-ray plates, nor do pigment stones. About 10% of mixed stones contain enough calcium to show up on an x-ray.

Q. *Are gallstones dangerous?*

A. In a good number of cases gallstones cause no symptoms. If they pass out of the gallbladder into the duct carrying bile to the duodenum (the first part of the small intestine) they may form an obstruction and cause an attack of gallbladder colic, accompanied by acute infection of the gallbladder. If they pass far enough down the duct to block the flow of bile from the liver, the result may be JAUNDICE—with yellow discoloration of the skin and the whites of the eyes, dark urine and the passage of light-colored feces. Although jaundice and infection of the gallbladder are potentially serious conditions, in the majority of cases they can be treated successfully.

Infection of the gallbladder is treated with antibiotics and antispasmodic drugs are given by injection. In selected cases it will be necessary to remove the gallbladder surgically when the acute attack has resolved, but there are cases in which the surgeon will advise immediate operation; each case must be decided on its merits and in the light of the surgeon's experience. In general, if tests demonstrate the presence of gallstones, it is better to have them removed surgically.

Q. *I have heard that it may be possible to dissolve gallstones without an operation. Is this true?*

A. In some cases this is possible. Cholesterol stones are likely to be formed if the concentration of cholesterol in the bile is high and the amount of bile salts low. This ratio can be altered by treatment with a drug such as chenodeoxycholic acid or ursodeoxycholic acid. While these drugs will not affect stones which show up on x-ray plates (for they contain too much calcium), they do have an effect on "radiotranslucent" stones, providing that the gallbladder function is normal. If the size and type of stones are suitable, treatment with these drugs may be of great benefit; but their action is slow, extending over months rather than weeks, and if they are withdrawn the stones may recur.

Q. *Is it possible to have cancer of the gallbladder?*

A. It is possible, but it is rare. Those cases that do occur are nearly always found in association with gallstones, so that it is thought likely that somehow the presence of gallstones may encourage the development of cancer. This is another good reason for having gallstones removed surgically even though they may only be producing mild symptoms.

Q. *I had an uncle who nearly died of inflammation of the pancreas, and the doctor said that the inflammation was caused by gallstones. How could this come about?*

A. The association of disease of the gallbladder and bile ducts with acute inflammation of the pancreas is well known, and usually the patient is middle-aged or elderly. The bile duct joins up with the duct leading from the pancreas (through which the secretions of that gland pass into the upper part of the small intestine); any obstruction of the common duct will shut off the flow of both bile and pancreatic juice.

Such an obstruction can be caused by a gallstone or by scarring brought about by chronic inflammation of the bile ducts. If it occurs, bile can flow the wrong way into the pancreas and the ducts inside the pancreas can burst. There follows the escape of pancreatic secretions into the body of the organ, which becomes swollen as the digestive enzymes secreted by the pancreas attack the tissues. There is increasing abdominal pain and a degree of shock with a rapid pulse. It is possible for the pancreatic secretions to escape from the damaged pancreas and attack the fatty tissues related to it, resulting in PERITONITIS.

Many patients with this disease survive, although intensive hospital treatment is usually necessary—which may include an exploratory surgical operation to confirm the diagnosis. In some cases the acute attack is followed by chronic pancreatitis, but most chronic cases start gradually. They may also be associated with gallbladder disease and gallstones, but some cases are associated with chronic alcoholism. The pain can be severe and the condition is a serious one, which may call for extensive biochemical tests, x-rays and endoscopy. Surgical treatment may provide the only means of relief.

BOWEL PROBLEMS

changes in bowel habits—constipation—children and laxatives—constipation in pregnancy—coated tongue and constipation—constipation and diarrhea in the elderly—diarrhea in children—antidepressants and constipation—penicillin and diarrhea—diarrhea caused by stress—irritable bowel syndrome—ulcerative colitis—pinworms and diarrhea—blood in the stools—hemorrhoids—when to see the doctor—painful bowel movements—embarrassment when consulting your doctor—pain the the rectum—dark stools—fistulas—colostomy

Q. *I used to be quite regular in my bowel movements, but during the last few weeks I have noticed that my habits have changed; I seem to be getting constipated. What should I do?*

A. This may just be caused by a change of diet or perhaps a change of circumstances. If your bowel habits change for any length of time it is important that you see your doctor.

Q. *I have always been troubled by constipation. Is there any way I can overcome this without taking laxatives?*

A. Most people are brought up to consider that at least one bowel movement a day is necessary for good health, but this is not exactly true. The frequency of bowel motions can vary a great deal between one individual and another—from two or three a day to one every other day or even less.

There used to be a theory that the presence of feces in the rectum could in some way be poisonous and lead to "autointoxication," but this is not so. It can be uncomfortable, but the anxiety caused in some people because they have not had a bowel movement is far more upsetting than the fact that they have not.

There are many reasons why bowel movements become irregular in the absence of any disease, ranging from the hurry to get to work in the morning and the consequent neglect of a set routine, to disagreeable or unfamiliar surroundings which impair any attempt to move the bowels.

The first requisite for regularity is a set routine. The first meal of the day normally sets up a reflex in the digestive tract which results in the passage of feces into the rectum. If this is neglected, water is absorbed from the feces and the residue becomes smaller—thus diminishing the stimulus to defecate and making it more difficult to have a bowel movement. It is important to drink enough water during the day to insure that the stools are of normal size—dehydration can be one cause of constipation.

If bowel habits have deteriorated so far that a set routine and attention to the intake of water fail to work, it is sometimes useful to increase the bulk of the stools by eating bran (up to four tablespoonfuls a day of miller's bran). The most important single thing is to stop being anxious. If you are in good health, irregularity of the bowels will not hurt you; you are better off if you let your body act naturally than if you take any of the countless laxatives urged upon you every day by the pharmaceutical industry.

Q. *My little boy, who is two years old, is very constipated. Should I give him a laxative?*

A. No. It is better to ask the advice of your doctor, for there may be a reason for his constipation such as a painful condition of his anus; or he may be rebelling against bowel training for some other reason. It is not wise to start the use of laxatives without medical advice at any age, let alone the age of two.

Q. *Is it normal to be constipated during pregnancy?*

A. Yes. This may be due to both the effect of the enlarged uterus on the lower bowel, and a reduction in the activity of the smooth muscle of the intestinal tract caused by changes in the hormone balance during pregnancy. Very often it can be avoided by increasing the amount you have to drink during the day, or eating more fresh fruit. If you have to take a laxative, ask your doctor to recommend one that is suitable to take during pregnancy.

Q. *Is a coated tongue a sign of constipation?*

A. Too much importance has been put on the appearance of the tongue as a sign of constipation. The coating on the tongue is made up of food particles, dead bacteria and the scales which are discarded from the surface of the membrane covering the tongue. If the tongue is not moved in speaking, or it is dry and nothing has been eaten, the coating appears thicker—as it does first thing in the morning. The flow of saliva, the passage of food and drink, chewing and speaking, all change the appearance.

While it is true that the tongue is an important part of the body to the physician in his examination of a patient, the changes he is looking for as signs of disease do not include coating of the tongue as a sign of constipation (pronounced coating is more likely to be a sign of fever or severe loss of appetite). The tongue may be badly coated even when the patient is in good health.

Q. *I have to take care of my elderly grandmother and I have some difficulty with her because she seems to be constipated at times and at others she suffers from diarrhea. Is there anything we can do to help her?*

A. It is not uncommon for the elderly to become constipated, for with age the muscle tone and the movements of the intestines may be diminished. If this happens and a mass of feces builds up in the lower bowel, the intestinal tract becomes irritated and partially obstructed; it is possible for liquid bowel contents to leak past the mass of retained feces. The resulting diarrhea is called "paradoxical diarrhea," and it is important to understand what is happening because

medicine designed to control the diarrhea will only make the condition worse. The proper treatment is an enema and evacuation of the mass from the rectum. Once this has been done, bowel motions should return to normal. But it may be necessary to repeat a gentle enema occasionally, or use the mildest laxative.

Q. *My children suffer attacks of diarrhea from time to time. When should I call the doctor?*

A. As a general rule it is sensible to call the doctor if you are in doubt, but diarrhea is very common among children. If a baby has diarrhea, you must remember that it is losing water and essential salts fast. The danger is dehydration; this can occur quickly. Except in the mildest case it is wise to ask for the doctor's advice if the condition does not clear up within a matter of hours. With older children the danger is not as great, but it is still present.

Diarrhea in children is often the sign of a disease that does not primarily affect the intestines, such as acute tonsillitis, and young children do not always complain of a sore throat; but they do appear to be ill and commonly have a fever. In any case, do not wait for more than two days; if the child's condition has not improved with simple measures within 48 hours—a fluid diet with plenty to drink, and rest—it is best to seek medical attention. It is not wise to give medicine to children except on a doctor's advice.

Q. *I have been under treatment for depression, and I find I am becoming constipated. Could it be caused by the drugs my doctor prescribed?*

A. Yes, it very well could be. The "tricyclic" group of antidepressants, which are commonly prescribed, have as a side effect an action on the movements of the intestines. You may also notice that you have a dry mouth, which is sometimes so pronounced as to make it hard to swallow. It is also true that depression itself can encourage constipation and the action of the antidepressive drugs can compound a natural tendency. The action of the drugs is too valuable to take constipation as an indication to stop treatment; in such circumstances it is justifiable to use a suitable laxative, which your doctor will prescribe. Your bowels will return to normal when the therapeutic course of drugs has been successfully completed.

Q. *I was given penicillin for a sore throat and developed diarrhea. Is this common? Do many drugs have this effect?*

A. Penicillin, ampicillin and tetracyclines can all upset the intestines in this way. Other commonly used drugs that can have the same side effect are magnesium trisilicate (used to treat stomach trouble), guanethidine (used to treat high blood pressure) and some anti-inflammatory drugs (such as indomethacin) used in the treatment of arthritis and allied conditions. Many other drugs can have the same effect, some because of a sensitivity reaction in susceptible people.

Q. *If I find myself under stress, I tend to get diarrhea. Can I do anything about it?*

A. Unfortunately, there is not very much you can do. However, there are drugs which have a calming effect on the motility of the intestines. One of these can be prescribed by your doctor in cases of acute diarrhea, and could be useful if you knew that you were going to undergo a stressful time.

Diarrhea is often present in anxiety states, where it can be a distressing symptom; it is also found in cases of overactivity of the thyroid gland (hyperthyroidism), one of the symptoms of which is undue anxiety. If you do find yourself unduly anxious, or tend to worry about things more than you should, it is worthwhile talking to your doctor about the problem.

Q. *I have been told that I have an "irritable bowel syndrome," which causes me a good deal of discomfort and diarrhea. Is it likely to get better?*

A. This condition may be caused by a number of factors, but it is never diagnosed if there is any permanent damage to the bowel; there is therefore always the likelihood that it can improve. The factors involved are very often emotional, and the condition varies with your emotional state, becoming worse if stress is greater. The disease can be precipitated by an attack of food poisoning, or by a course of antibiotics; these cases are more likely to recover than those in which no precipitating stimulus can be found. It is also possible to induce the condition by the habitual use of laxatives.

The fear of cancer is at the back of many people's minds who suffer from this disease. This, in itself, may cause enough anxiety to prolong the condition, but the fears are groundless—it does not have anything to do with cancer, nor is it a "precancerous" state.

Control of an "irritable bowel" depends to a large extent on the control of the emotional factors involved. The treatment is largely directed toward this end, with symptomatic treatment of the diarrhea by the administration of drugs such as diphenoxylate or codeine. The abdominal discomfort can be relieved by increasing the bulk of the stools (with a suitable diet or the use of bran) and by taking a drug such as dicyclomine hydrochloride, which reduces the spasm of the smooth muscles in the walls of the bowel.

The condition may relapse after an apparent cure, but with sympathetic and efficient treatment most patients can come to terms with their disability.

Q. *Has the irritable bowel syndrome anything to do with ulcerative colitis? Can one lead to the other?*

A. Ulcerative colitis is a separate condition in which there are distinct and recognizable changes in the lining of the bowel, absent in the irritable bowel syndrome—which is not liable to turn into this more serious disease. The cause of ulcerative colitis is not understood, although it has been suggested that it is an immunological disorder. It does not appear to be caused by a bacterial or viral infection, nor infection with protozoa. It is, like the irritable bowel syndrome, affected by psychological factors; but it is not clear whether they are among the causes of the condition or are a consequence of it.

Q. *Can pinworms cause diarrhea?*

A. No, they do not cause diarrhea; but they can collect in the appendix and give rise to the symptoms of appendicitis.

Normally, a pinworm infection is more of a nuisance than a danger, because the irritation around the anus caused by pinworms is often enough to interfere with sleep. An attack of diarrhea will carry away with it a large number of the worms and may well reduce the infestation.

Drugs used to treat pinworm infections are administered with a gentle laxative in order to clear out the bowel properly; they should thus be used with caution if a child with pinworms is also suffering from an attack of diarrhea.

Q. *Is blood in the stools a symptom of serious disease?*

A. The most common cause of bleeding from the rectum is hemorrhoids ("piles"), which is not a serious condition. You should see your doctor rather than try to treat the condition yourself, although there are a number of "cures" on the market. Some people are so frightened by the appearance of blood in their stools that they delay going to the doctor in case he finds that they have cancer, but it is most unlikely that he will. Even if he does find that the blood loss is a sign of a more serious condition, the sooner it is diagnosed the better, for early treatment is likely to be successful.

Q. *Is it possible to treat hemorrhoids with suppositories?*

A. It is quite possible to treat hemorrhoids by using appropriate suppositories, but do not try to do it without advice from your doctor. Depending on what he finds, he may recommend suppositories, a course of injections, or in severe cases an operation. Surgical treatment is reserved for cases in which the hemorrhoids "come down," or protrude from the anus. They may be easy to replace, in which case it is possible that injection treatment may be successful; or they may be permanently protruding, in which case they are liable to become infected and cause a great deal of discomfort and pain. It is in such cases that surgery is recommended after the inflammation has receded.

In most cases of any severity, certainly if bleeding has been troublesome, your doctor will recommend a course of local injection, which are quite painless; only in mild cases will he advise suppositories, with a diet designed to keep the bowels regular and the stools soft. Hemorrhoids are always made worse by constipation or diarrhea.

Q. *I have suffered from hemorrhoids for a long time. They never gave me much trouble until a few weeks ago when they began to protrude and became very painful. The condition now seems to have improved. What should I do if the same thing happens again?*

A. Even if the hemorrhoids are not painful now you should see your doctor, for the same thing may well happen in the future. The immediate treatment for such a condition is rest in bed after the hemorrhoids have been returned inside the anus. This may not be easy and in some cases it may even require a light anesthetic, but it is not wise to let the condition stay as it is. The sooner the prolapsed hemorrhoids are returned, the sooner the pain and swelling will be relieved. Left to themselves they may become infected and badly inflamed, because the spasm of the anus reduces and may even cut off their blood supply.

Q. *I have developed considerable pain during bowel movements and there seems to be a bruise in the area, with a painful small swelling. Is this a sign of hemorrhoids?*

A. There is a condition called *external hemorrhoid,* which strictly speaking is not true hemorrhoids. True hemorrhoids are dilated veins lying inside the anus; external hemorrhoid is caused by the rupture of a small vein in the tissues next to the anus, with the formation of a blood clot—thus the appearance of a bruise. The only danger of the condition is that the affected area may become infected. In many cases no treatment is needed, but in some it is advisable to have the clot removed by a minor operation which can be performed under local anesthesia.

Q. *I find it very embarrassing to have to go to my doctor with this sort of trouble, but I have had such severe pains during bowel movement that I have become constipated. Is it likely to be serious?*

A. Although it may appear embarrassing to you, you must remember that to a doctor these troubles are viewed in much the same way as mechanical faults in a complicated machine; the doctor's office is not a place for false modesty. There are a number of conditions which could give you pain; if the pain is bad enough to interfere with the proper working of your body you should ask your doctor's advice, although the condition is not likely to be a serious one.

The most common reason for such a pain is a fissure or crack in the skin which lines the anal canal, and while it will respond quickly to treatment it will not easily go away by itself.

Q. *What could be the cause of a very severe pain I feel from time to time in my rectum? It is not associated with bowel movement, but it is bad enough to wake me up at night.*

A. There is a condition called *proctalgia fugax* (which usually affects men) that causes sudden severe pain in the rectum and may spread up into the abdomen. The pain is like a cramp and may be accompanied by faintness and sweating. The exact cause is not understood—the Latin name is only descriptive and means a "fleeting pain in the rectum"—but it does not seem to be associated with any serious disease Nevertheless, you should see your doctor about it, for the diagnosis can only be made in the absence of any signs of disease that could otherwise account for the pain. He will examine you to assure himself that you are not suffering from any other condition.

Q. *After an attack of indigestion I was found to be anemic; my doctor told me that I had been bleeding from an ulcer of the stomach. Although my stools were dark, I never saw any blood. Why is this?*

A. If an ulcer bleeds, the blood passes through the intestines and its color is altered by the action of the digestive juices and the bacteria present in the intestinal tract. Instead of being red and recognizable as blood, it becomes black. Dark stools are not always the sign of bleeding in the intestinal tract; the color can be influenced by food and drink (for example, red wine will discolor the stools) but there are chemical tests (usually performed in the hospital) that are performed to detect the presence of blood. These tests require a period of careful dieting before they are done, to make sure that they are not influenced by what has been eaten.

Q. *What is a fistula? How does it cause boils beside the anus?*

A. The most common kind of fistula is a passage formed between the intestines and the skin; fistulas may also occur from the bladder, or they may be internal. The cause of these abnormal passages is usually inflammation or sometimes a tumor. The fistula you ask about is a communication between the lower part of the rectum and the skin beside the anus. It usually forms as the result of an abscess in the tissue spaces beside the anus. The abscess can be drained by making an incision into the skin. However, if the abscess bursts and discharges into the anal canal, the track may not heal up. Infection may cause a very painful inflammation under the skin beside the anus. The collection of pus that forms is not really a boil, since it lies deeper than the skin (a boil is an infection in the skin). A simple incision will not cure the trouble; a more thorough surgical operation is required before the possibility of further infection can be prevented. Various tests may be advised before the operation, as some cases of fistula are a sign of a tuberculous infection or of an inflammatory condition of the intestine called CROHN'S DISEASE.

Q. *A relative of mine recently had an operation for obstruction of the bowel, and came out of hospital with a colostomy. She was told that in time it would be necessary to have another operation to repair it, and that she did not have cancer. She is staying with us and we would like to know the truth. Aren't colostomies used only in cases of bowel cancer?*

A. No. A colostomy is an artificial opening made between the large intestine and the exterior of the abdominal wall; it is used when a part of the bowel has had to be removed or when it is necessary to bypass a section of the bowel that has become infected and inflamed. In your relative's case, it seems fairly clear that the original obstruction was caused by inflammation of the wall of the bowel, probably as the result of diverticulitis—which is a condition that will recover when the bowel is rested. It has nothing to do with cancer.

The operation of restoring a colostomy is relatively simple, and she will be inconvenienced with the nuisance of a colostomy for only a short time. Even a permanent colostomy can be little more than a minor disability; there are many people who lead active and normal lives with such an artificial opening. It is certainly not true that the operation of colostomy is used only in the treatment of cancer.

HERNIAS

treatment of hernias—types of hernia

Q. *I have had a hernia for some years and I wear a truss. It seems now that the truss does not control the hernia and I have a pain in the groin—especially when I walk. Is a hernia dangerous? Should I have my doctor look at it?*

A. Hernias are quite common, especially in the groin. They develop either as the result of a slight congenital abnormality or because the muscles of the abdominal wall become weak. They are sometimes first noticed after a muscular strain, or they may gradually form a swelling—often in young people. Of themselves, hernias in the groin are not dangerous; the potential danger arises if they contain a small portion of the intestine, which under certain circumstances may become trapped. If this happens, and the hernia cannot be pushed back into the abdomen, the intestine can swell so much that it becomes blocked, the blood supply becomes cut off and gangrene may even result.

It is not possible for a truss to cure a hernia; the only treatment is surgical, and it is better for people who are fit enough to have the operation to undergo what is a safe and well-understood operation than to take the risk of a strangulated hernia. Trusses are reserved for those who, for one reason or another, are not fit for surgery.

Q. *Can a hernia occur in places apart from the groin?*

A. The most common type of hernia affects the groin. But, especially in women, it is possible for a hernia to form in the top of the thigh, just under the fold of the groin. These *femoral hernias* cannot be controlled by a truss and are more liable to trap a part of the intestine than those that occur in the groin. They produce discomfort and swelling low in the groin, and these signs call for medical advice at once. A hernia can occur at the umbilicus (navel); these are usually found in babies in whom the muscles of the abdominal wall are weak and the umbilicus does not close properly at birth. They usually resolve spontaneously in time; only a few require surgical treatment. Another type of hernia may develop at the site of a surgical incision in the abdominal wall, especially in the middle line in people who are overweight. These "incisional hernias" may become quite large and cause partial blocking of the intestines, but they are not often dangerous—although they are uncomfortable and unpleasant. Some can be repaired by surgery, but others are best controlled by a special corset or other surgical support. Finally, hernias may occur internally, especially through the diaphragm (the muscle separating the lungs from the abdomen). These *hiatus hernias* are one common cause of HEARTBURN.

SKIN AND SCALP CONDITIONS

warts—ointments—antihistamine ointments— corticosteroid ointments—skin creams—skin complaints and emotional disturbances— dermatitis—photosensitivity and sunburn— sunbathing and skin cancer—psoriasis—PUVA treatment—dandruff—acne—impetigo—boils— recurrent boils—vitiligo—athlete's foot— ringworm of the scalp—ringworm transmitted by animals—scabies—head lice

Q. *How are warts formed and what is the best way of getting rid of them?*

A. Warts are caused by a viral infection of the skin; they may occur anywhere, although they are commonly seen on the hands and the soles of the feet, where they are painful because they become embedded in the skin. Warts will often disappear by themselves if left alone; but it is impossible to say when, so that many forms of treatment (including "charming" and hypnosis) can appear to some people to be successful. Persistent warts are best treated either by freezing or by surgical removal

Q. *What is the best ointment for a skin irritation?*

A. It depends on the cause of the irritation, but it is said that 99% of skin diseases can be treated with half-a-dozen drugs. If you are trying to treat a skin condition yourself because you think it is too trivial to worry your doctor with, use only simple remedies such as a cold water compress or calamine lotion. The skin is very sensitive, especially when it is inflamed, and the application of antiseptics of other chemically irritating compounds is liable to make a simple condition considerably worse. If you are not successful with a simple remedy it is better to ask for your doctor's advice. Minor skin conditions are more likely to recover if left to themselves. And remember that scratching the skin is bound to make the condition worse.

Q. *I have used an antihistamine ointment on a skin rash which I am sure is caused by an allergic reaction. Since I understand that histamine is involved in the reaction, why doesn't it work?*

A. Although on theoretical grounds there are a number of skin conditions that should respond to the action of antihistamines, the fact is that they are disappointing when used in an ointment. Given by mouth they do help to relieve an itchy skin, particularly at night when the irritation is usually at its worst. They must be used with caution during the day, however, as they can interfere with the alertness and concentration needed in driving or operating machinery.

Q. *Is it true that the use of corticosteroid skin ointments can be dangerous?*

A. The local application of corticosteroids quickly suppresses inflammation of the skin and the effects can be dramatic. In the past this sometimes led to the overuse of these drugs and the use of compounds in concentrations that were too strong. In time it became clear to doctors that prolonged application of potent corticosteroids could result in a thinning of the skin, markings called "striae" in moist areas, and on the face eruptions around the mouth or severe acne. Moreover, if corticosteroids alone are used on bacterial or fungal infections they distort the natural appearance of the disease so that it becomes very difficult to recognize and treat effectively.

A great deal of fuss has been made of the complications following the use of corticosteroids on the skin, and to a certain extent there has been an overreaction. But it remains true that these compounds, used with good medical judgment, represent an enormous advance in the treatment of many skin conditions.

Corticosteroid creams should only be used on advice and under constant medical supervision.

Q. *How important are creams in keeping the skin in good condition?*

A. A normal skin needs only to be kept clean and dry. Despite the vast number of preparations sold to improve or maintain the condition of the skin, (particularly the face) and the advertising that supports their sale, the best way of cleaning the skin is to use plain soap and water, and to rinse it off with clean water. Too much washing can damage the skin—a fact well known to anyone who has to do the housework—because it leads to excessive dryness and loss of water from the keratin.

Some skins are more liable to become dry than others. As the keratin becomes dehydrated it becomes brittle, so that the skin cracks painfully (usually over the finger joints). The simplest remedy is plain petroleum jelly, for a thin film put on while the hands are still moist will stop the loss of water from the surface.

A dry skin is especially common in old age. The simpler skin preparations are the best, for it is easy to produce sensitivity reactions—especially in older people, who should be particularly careful to use only plain soap and water-based creams without perfume.

Q. *Can skin complaints be caused by emotional disturbances?*

A. Skin specialists sometimes say that the skin is the "mirror of the soul." It is true that the condition of the skin can affect the emotions and that the emotions can affect the condition of the skin. Obvious examples are blushing and the sweating caused by acute anxiety. The skin is the "organ" through which we feel outside contacts, pleasant or unpleasant, and it is the part of the body seen by other people. It thus plays an important part in the appearance we present to the world at large and in our perception of that world.

The only skin *disease* that is clearly produced by emotional disturbance is called *dermatitis artifacta,* which is the result of self-inflicted damage—such as that caused by superficial cigarette burns or the application of chemicals. The patient scratches the injuries to enlarge them and keep them active; often the doctor can only recognize the condition because it does not fit any naturally occurring disease pattern, and treatment is invariably ineffective. Once it has been recognized it becomes clear that it is the result of hysteria, although in most cases the patient will deny having any emotional disturbance.

Apart from this curious condition, it is difficult to say that emotional problems can actually cause skin diseases, but they certainly affect the progress of an existing problem—just as a skin disease, especially one which disfigures the appearance, may have a profound effect on the mind. It is sometimes difficult to realize just how much a few pimples on the face of an adolescent can destroy self-confidence, and every doctor knows how young people who suffer from acne are far more conscious of their appearance than people who look at them. If this is so, then how much more distressing it is to suffer from a truly disfiguring disease of the skin which changes the attitude of people who cannot help showing some signs of revulsion.

Most skin diseases are not "catching," but it is difficult to make this known to a large majority of people. Probably many "lepers" of ancient times did not have leprosy, but a benign disfiguring condition such as PSORIASIS. They were nevertheless banished to leper colonies, and much the same reaction prevails today—although we know that in the present state of medical knowledge virtually no one with a contagious disease walks about freely to the danger of others. Those afflicted with an obvious skin disease often cannot disregard the effect that their appearance has on people around them, however well balanced they are emotionally, and it is no wonder that their distress may play a large part in the progress of their disease.

Q. *What exactly is dermatitis?*

A. Dermatitis is a word used to describe a pattern of changes in the skin which can be caused by a number of different stimuli and can present varying appearances, although the basic processes are the same. One form of dermatitis is commonly called *eczema,* a Greek word meaning "boiling over" or "breaking out." There is a confusion in medical terms here, but the majority of doctors prefer to refer to dermatitis, dividing it into two basic groups called *exogenous* and *endogenous,* according to whether the cause comes from outside the body or from within. The importance of this is that if the disease is caused by an outside factor it may be cured and subsequently avoided by identifying the factor and keeping away from it. Exogenous dermatitis can further be divided into allergic and irritant groups according to the nature of the precipitating factor; endogenous dermatitis is divided into groups according to the appearance of the skin and the part of the body in which it occurs. Exogenous dermatitis is also called *contact dermatitis,* because it is caused by contact with external agents.

The course of an uncomplicated, untreated case of dermatitis (and it can get better spontaneously at any stage) follows a definite pattern. At first the blood vessels of the skin dilate and the skin becomes red. Fluid then collects and small blisters form, which burst and "weep." The fluid dries and crusts are formed. In time the excessive formation of fluid stops and the skin, which has become thicker, begins to scale and may split. At any point in the process, usually during the "weeping" stage, the area may become infected with bacteria. This is more likely to happen if the skin is scratched. Scratching can also result in the development of chronic dermatitis, with thickening of the skin and pigmentation (or, in dark-skinned people, loss of pigment).

Although in contact dermatitis the skin is affected at the actual site of contact with the irritating factor (for example, an identification bracelet made of nickel), eruptions may occur at sites elsewhere in the body—such as the fronts of the elbows or the skin of the face. Among the materials which can irritate the skin or cause allergic reactions are nickel, rubber and synthetic rubber, cosmetics, dyes, dust, soap powder and detergents, oil, cement, poison ivy, and various materials used in making clothes. The list is very long and even includes substances used in the preparation of ointments and creams for use in the treatment of dermatitis. Fortunately, not everyone is sensitive to the same materials, although very many people during their lives develop a transient patch of dermatitis at some time or other. It is one of the most common complaints to bring a patient to the doctor.

Q. *Is photosensitivity the same as sunburn?*

A. No. Photosensitivity means an abnormal response to exposure to ultraviolet light. It can happen because the skin is sensitized to light, because it lacks the normal protection of pigmentation, and for no identifiable reason. Conditions which sensitize the skin to the action of ultraviolet light are the PORHPYRIAS, a group of diseases affecting the biochemistry of heme, which is part of the compound hemoglobin (the blood pigment), and the action of various drugs including tetracyclines, sulfonamides, chlorpromazine, thiazide diuretics and the antibiotic nalidixic acid (which may be used in the treatment of urinary tract infections).

Exposure of a photosensitive skin to sunlight may result in redness and blistering, with subsequent peeling. Some chemicals can produce photosensitivity if they are applied to the skin—in particular, oil of bergamot (used as an essential oil in formulating cosmetics), preparations containing tar, and other compounds used in making soaps and deodorants called halogenated salicylanides.

Sunburn is a normal skin reaction to excessive exposure to sunlight. After a long time in the sun, the short ultraviolet waves bring about photochemical reactions in the skin that result in reddening, pain, swelling and waterlogging of the skin; 24 hours later blisters may form, which later burst. The skin scales as it recovers and the irritation may be intense. If sunburn is severe, it may be accompanied by fever, headache and a general feeling of being unwell (malaise), or even by a serious state of shock and a very high temperature. If this is the case it may be necessary to use corticosteroids during treatment by injection, but milder cases can be helped by the local application of corticosteroid creams. Very mild cases will not need such active treatment, but calamine lotion is useful.

After an attack of sunburn you should be careful how you expose yourself to the sun again. Although the temptation is to go out before the redness has gone, it should be resisted—especially if you are fair-skinned. There are effective preparations on the market for screening the skin from ultraviolet light, which last for about eight hours, but don't forget that you should apply some again after you go swimming.

Q. *Can sunbathing cause skin cancer?*

A. Normal sunbathing will not cause skin cancer. There is a condition called "actinic keratosis" found in people above the age of 60 who all their lives have been engaged in work that exposes them to the sun; it can also be found in fair-skinned people working in the tropics. The condition is characterized by a number of raised patches covered by dry hard scales, colored yellow, brown or almost black. They occur on the face and on the backs of the hands and forearms; if they are left untreated, about 20% may eventually become malignant. They are treated by surgical removal or by application of a drug known as 5-fluouracil. Normal sunbathing, unless you have a skin that is abnormally sensitive to light, is harmless.

Q. *Is psoriasis hereditary? I have suffered from it for some years, and I wonder if my children are likely to get it.*

A. There is some evidence that psoriasis may run in families. But the disease is so common, particularly in colder countries, that it has proved difficult to demonstrate a definite hereditary pattern; as many as two in every hundred white people may develop the disease at some time or other. It usually comes on between the ages of 15 to 30, but it can appear later (rarely earlier).

The severity of the disease varies a great deal, as do the remissions which occur in over one-third of cases;

some people are clear for years, others only for months, while others never have remissions at all. The disease remains poorly understood; but it is not infectious, does not endanger the general health, and does respond to treatment—although the treatment may be prolonged in the presence of recurring attacks, for no cure is permanent.

The worst effects of the disease are on the self-confidence, for it takes a strong character to live with a possibly disfiguring skin condition.

Q. *What is PUVA treatment?*

A. PUVA stands for "Psoralen and Ultraviolet light A." It has been known for a long time that exposure to sunlight is very beneficial in cases of psoriasis, which are usually much better in the summer than the winter. Psoralen, a drug which can be taken by mouth, has the action of sensitizing the skin to ultraviolet light so that its effect is increased. Ultraviolet light can be divided into two classes according to its wavelength. UVB is the ultraviolet light which produces sunburn; it is therefore not used in treatment.

When UVA is directed onto the skin from a special ultraviolet light, psoralen enters into a reaction with the skin cells which apparently blocks the process which produces psoriasis. A course of PUVA involves four sessions a week, and may last for a month. There may be remissions, and it may be necessary to undergo further courses of therapy once or twice a week for longer periods after the initial course. During the treatment the skin becomes deeply tanned, which may be a pleasant side effect of therapy.

Q. *I am troubled by dandruff. Is there any special preparation I can use to get rid of it?*

A. Useful lotions contain selenium sulfide and should be used twice a week for the first two weeks and then once a week until the condition is controlled—usually within about two or three weeks. After that the special lotion can be used when necessary. Before applying the lotion the hair should be washed with soap and water rather than a detergent shampoo.

If the condition is severe you should seek medical advice. There are other scalp conditions that can be mistaken for simple dandruff. Of itself, dandruff is not very important—about 60% of people are affected to a greater or lesser degree—but those who are liable to have it badly are also liable to bacterial skin infections and to develop acne. Their skin is sensitive to chemicals and they may have to avoid industrial employment where they come into contact with irritating substances.

Q. *I am 18 years old and for a long time I have had acne. How long will it be before it eventually clears up?*

A. Acne is caused by blockage and infection of the sebaceous glands—the glands that secrete the natural oils of the skin. One of the effects of the hormonal changes at puberty is that these secretions become thicker and stickier, and the skin pores become blocked, forming blackheads. If the blocked glands become infected they form red, swollen pimples.

There is at present no fast, certain cure for acne; so it is not surprising that there are scores of acne lotions and creams on sale in drug stores, and many different recommended diets. Some individuals find that certain foods such as chocolate or fried foods make their acne worse, but only trial and error will show whether this is true for you. Sunlight is sometimes beneficial. It is also usually helpful to wash the affected areas frequently using mild soap and water.

If your acne is very troublesome and unsightly your doctor may consider prescribing a course of the antibiotic tetracycline, which often reduces the severity of the inflammation, though it does not affect the underlying cause of acne. In most cases, however, the condition of the skin begins to improve without specific treatment within a year or so of the onset of the acne.

Q. *There has been an outbreak of impetigo at my son's school. Exactly what is this and how can I avoid the risk of the infection spreading to my other children?*

A. Impetigo is a bacterial infection of the skin which is spread by direct contact with an infected person or contaminated articles. Strict attention to cleanliness, the use of separate washcloths and towels, and care in not touching the affected skin will keep the infection away from the rest of the family while it is being treated.

The infection normally responds quickly to antibiotics; the application of antibiotic creams will help prevent the spread of the infecting organisms. There is no need for the infected person to be isolated, but it is better to keep children away from school until they have fully recovered.

Q. *Can boils spread from one person to another?*

A. No, because a boil is the end result of a local infection of the skin; it forms as the infection is overcome. The pus that discharges from a boil is composed of dead bacteria, dead white blood cells and tissue fluid, as well as a number of living bacteria. It is infective, but the boil itself is not.

Q. *I have been plagued by boils which come and go. Is there any way I can prevent this?*

A. The treatment of recurrent boils is difficult and can be disappointing. It is important to establish that you are not suffering from any general disease that encourages the formation of boils (such as diabetes). If nothing has been found, then it is necessary to search for a place on your body which harbors the infecting organism. The most common areas are the nostrils, the armpits and the inner sides of the thighs. Your doctor may take swabs from these areas for bacteriological examination. If organisms of the type that can cause recurrent boils are found, treatment with an appropriate antibiotic can be started. It is usually continued for some weeks and may be combined with the use of hexachlorophene soap or ultraviolet light therapy.

Q. *I have a number of fairly large white patches on my skin, which make it embarrassing to wear a bathing suit. Can anything be done about it?*

A. This skin disorder is called vitiligo and it is quite common. The reason for it is not precisely known. It is thought to be associated with a disorder of the immunological mechanism which results in prevention of the formation of pigment by the pigment cells of the skin. The actual texture of the skin is quite normal, but the hair in an affected area may turn white.

The condition is liable to affect people of any age or sex and it is often first noticed in the summer when the rest of the skin is tanned. It is possible for it to recover spontaneously to some extent, but it takes a long time and the recovery may be incomplete. It is, however, possible to use corticosteroids in the treatment of vitiligo; some effect will be achieved in about 20% of the patients so treated. Corticosteroid ointment or cream is used for a minimum of three months, but only under medical supervision. The other drug used in the treatment of this condition is psoralen, which acts on the pigment cells of the skin, causing them (when exposed to the action of ultraviolet light) to produce more melanin, the dark pigment of the skin. If the patch of discoloration is small, psoralen can be applied as an ointment, but if large the drug is taken by mouth. Two hours after the drug has been taken the skin is exposed to a dose of ultraviolet light (as in the PUVA treatment for psoriasis). If the treatment is not effective it is still possible to stain the skin itself; a commonly used agent for this purpose is dihydroxyacetone.

Q. *I have athlete's foot, which I think I picked up in a swimming pool, and I cannot get rid of it. Is there any cure?*

A. Athlete's foot is one of a group of fungus infections of the skin commonly called ringworm—the technical name being TINEA. Athlete's foot (or *tinea pedis*) usually occurs in the moist skin between the toes. It may be extremely difficult to cure completely. The condition usually persists between the third, fourth and fifth toes, and resists the application of fungicidal creams and ointments. About one in two people suffer from the infection at some time or another, but one of the curious things about it is that "cross-infection" in families is rare.

Once the condition is established, and if it fails to respond to local applications—there are many, ranging from benzoic and salicylic acid to clotrimazole—you should pay close attention to the general hygiene of your feet. Shoes should be light and loose fitting, socks should be changed at least once a day (as should stockings or tights) and if the feet sweat they should be washed as often as possible, drying carefully between the toes. The more the feet are exposed to the air the better. The drug griseofulvin may be given by mouth to try to eradicate infection of the feet, but it is usually recommended only in cases of severe infection. It must be used with caution in patients who are sensitive to penicillin.

Q. *Is ringworm of the scalp infectious? Why is it called ringworm, as I am told it has nothing to do with worms?*

A. Ringworm of the scalp is not infectious, but it is contagious—that is, it is spread by contact. It is best treated by taking the drug griseofulvin by mouth for about four or five weeks, or until there have been no signs of the fungus on microscopic examination for two weeks. The infection is usually controlled quickly. The disease is spread by contact. Thus, combs, hairbrushes, and similar items used by an infected person should be thrown away and the bed linen boiled.

The reason that fungus infections of the skin are called ringworm is that they start as a small patch and spread out—so that the advancing edge of the infected area leaves behind it a center of healing skin, making a mark like a ring. Before it was known that the infections were caused by a fungus they were thought to be caused by small worms.

The Latin name for diseases of the skin caused by fungus infections is *tinea,* which means a gnawing worm, and that for ringworm of the scalp is *tinea capitis.*

Q. *Can you catch ringworm from animals?*

A. Yes. Children can develop ringworm from contact with cats or dogs, and farm workers from contact with cattle. Usually, ringworm caught from animals lasts a shorter time than ringworm caused by fungi that only infect man, although the initial reaction is more severe. There are also some infections that can be picked up from contaminated soil.

Q. *Is scabies dangerous?*

A. No. It is a very uncomfortable disease, because the scabies mite lives in the outer layer of the skin, where it lays its eggs in short burrows. In doing so, it produces a substance which sensitizes the skin; after two or three weeks the presence of a mite or its eggs produces intense itching. This is characteristically worse at night and causes active scratching which, while it may dislodge the mite and its eggs, may also result in a secondary infection of the skin by bacteria.

Fortunately, the condition is readily recognized and treated, but the itching does not disappear at once. This sometimes makes people think that the infection is still present and they treat themselves again with an anti-scabies lotion—which may not be advisable, for the lotions themselves can cause an irritation of the skin.

Q. *I have heard scabies called a venereal disease. Is that true?*

A. In a certain sense, scabies can be described as a venereal disease because the mite which causes the disease is passed on only by prolonged close contact in warm conditions, so the easiest way to pick up the disease is to share a bed with an infected person. It is not necessarily transferred during the sexual act in the way that true venereal diseases are. But it is true that the skin most likely to be affected is that around the sexual organs.

Q. *I know that some serious diseases are spread by lice. Do head lice spread disease?*

A. The fever spread by lice is typhus, but head lice in ordinary conditions do not spread disease. It is only when large numbers of people live together in insanitary surroundings that outbreaks of typhus occur. Epidemics occur especially in winter, in time of war, or after a great civil disaster. Since the availability of insecticides that can control lice, the threat of typhus has decreased.

Ordinary head lice that children sometimes catch at school do not cause any other disease, though they are disagreeable and scratching can lead to bacterial infection of the scalp. Once they have been identified, they are easily controlled by lotions containing gamma benzene hexachloride or a 0.5% solution of malathion. Their eggs laid on the hairs close to the roots—the "nits"—can be removed with a fine comb.

(See also the major article on **Dermatology.**)

REACTIONS TO FOOD

allergic reactions of food—childhood allergies—seafood poisoning

Q. *What sort of food is liable to produce allergic reactions?*

A. The most common foods are hen's eggs, cow's milk, fish, wheat and various vegetables and fruit. It is also possible that substances in food (such as a trace of penicillin in milk) or substances used to preserve food may in some cases cause an allergic reaction. It may be very difficult to identify the food at fault, even though extensive tests are performed. People who suspect they suffer from a food allergy should keep a record of what they eat, the time of the meal and any reactions that appear afterward. A complete record kept over a prolonged period may give a clue which can be followed up with various tests.

In one such test the food which is implicated as the cause of the problem may be served to the patient disguised—although this test must not be performed if the allergic attacks are severe. Again, a diet omitting the suspected food may be tried; records kept of meals eaten and reactions observed may confirm suspicions. Skin tests can also be performed, but the results can be misleading; foods which are known to cause a general reaction when eaten may not cause a skin reaction.

It is essential to remember that allergies to certain foods may be important in other contexts; certain immunizing injections are prepared on an egg medium, ACTH injections may be prepared from cattle, and insulin injections may be prepared from the pancreas of pigs. Such injections may precipitate severe reactions in those sensitive to eggs, beef or pork, so that it is wise to make sure that your doctor knows of any food allergies you may have.

Q. *As a child I used to be allergic to eggs, but I have found that I can now eat them without* *trouble. Is it common to grow out of a food allergy?*

A. It does happen that people who had an allergy to certain foods as children grow out of it. Children are more likely than adults to suffer from food allergies; the fact that you could not eat a certain food as a child does not mean that you will never be able to enjoy it. It is not, however, possible to "desensitize" yourself by taking small quantities of the offending food by mouth. Attempts can be made to desensitize patients by injections of food allergens; unfortunately, however, these are not always successful.

Q. *Is poisoning by seafood particularly dangerous? I have heard that in Japan it is not uncommon for people to die as the result of eating fish.*

A. In Japan, the amount of fish eaten is greater than in most other countries—about 10% of their food supply comes from the sea. Fish are most often rendered poisonous by certain protozoa or algae that they feed on. One fish in particular, a Puffer fish, is very dangerous to eat. It contains a poison called tetradoxin, which acts on the central nervous system and causes paralysis of the muscles in a very short time.

Many other fish are poisonous, either naturally or because toxins can be formed in them by bacterial action after the fish die; tuna fish and mackerel have been reported as causing moderately mild symptoms including headaches, itching and hives in this way. The livers of dogfish, rays and sharks may be poisonous, and there are fish called clupeoids in the Pacific which are so poisonous that if eaten they can cause death within the hour. Outbreaks of shellfish poisoning have occurred because the fish have eaten a protozoan organism called *Gonyaulax catanella,* which contains a toxin that acts on the heart, the blood vessels and the nervous system. But if you avoid eating unfamiliar fish, and if you make sure the fish you do eat is fresh, seafood is no more dangerous than any other food.

VENEREAL DISEASE

transmission of gonorrhea—complications of gonorrhea—gonorrhea and sterility—gonorrhea and syphilis—hereditary syphilis—other venereal diseases

Q. *In my youth while I was in the Navy I contracted gonorrhea, which was treated straight*

away. I have had no trouble for ten years, but could I pass the disease on to my wife?

A. As you had medical treatment at once there is little doubt that you were cured; once cured you cannot pass the disease on to anyone else.

Q. *I have heard that one of the results of an attack of gonorrhea can be difficulty in urination—not because of pain, but because of narrowing of the urinary passage. Is there any way of preventing this?*

A. Narrowing of the urinary passage in the penis was at one time a late consequence of infection, but since the introduction of antibiotics it is only rarely seen—and then only in cases where treatment of the disease has been neglected. After an adequate course of treatment, begun at the first signs of the disease, there is virtually no chance that this condition (called a stricture) will develop.

Q. *Can an attack of gonorrhea lead to sterility?*

A. Properly treated, gonorrhea has no effect on a man's fertility; he is likely to seek treatment early in the course of the disease because of the obvious discharge and pain he experiences on urination. In the case of women, however, the situation is different and the discharge may pass unnoticed; indeed, at least half of the women who become infected have no symptoms at all. This is obviously a very serious matter, for in about 10% of cases infection travels up the genital tract to the Fallopian tubes and ovaries, causing SALPINGITIS, which is a common cause of infertility. Early diagnosis and treatment will prevent these grave complications.

Q. *Is it true that you can contract both gonorrhea and syphilis at the same time?*

A. Yes. In a way this may be fortunate, for the signs of gonorrhea—especially in men—call attention to the possibility of infection with syphilis, which in such cases is detected early. In cases where syphilis is the only infection, the first sign (the syphilitic sore or chancre) develops about three weeks after exposure to the disease, while the first signs of gonorrhea develop in a matter of days.

Q. *Can an attack of syphilis before marriage be passed on from parents to their children?*

A. Adequate treatment of the first stage of syphilis will always protect you from the late stages of the disease, and it is only in cases where treatment has been neglected that the late effects can develop and infection be transmitted unknowingly. Negative blood tests can be believed, for they are very sensitive; the blood tests required before marriage have nearly wiped out the possibility of syphilis being passed on to legitimate children. If you have had this disease it is very understandable that you should be anxious, but as long as you were treated properly and your blood tests are negative you may be confident that it is behind you.

Q. *Are there any other venereal diseases besides gonorrhea and syphilis?*

A. There is a disease called *nonspecific urethritis,* which causes a discharge and pain on passing urine; it is less dangerous than the two venereal diseases you mention, but if you have these symptoms, you cannot be sure that it is *only* this disease without the proper tests.

Nonspecific urethritis can be passed on as a venereal disease, although it can also develop in other ways; it is a great deal more common in men than in women. It may affect the eyes, joints and other organs, but two thirds of people affected recover within three months. The disease can recur, but the first attack is usually the worst. Tetracyclines are the drugs used to treat the inflammation of the urinary passages, whereas penicillin is the drug used to treat gonorrhea and syphilis.

A number of other less common infections (such as *chancroid* and *lymphogranuloma venereum*) can also be transmitted by sexual contact.

(See also VENEREAL DISEASE and the major articles on **Urology** and **Obstetrics and Gynecology**.)

URINARY PROBLEMS

bedwetting—urinary incontinence—blood in the urine—cystitis—abnormal substances in the urine—bladder papillomas

Q. *My daughter aged 7 is still wetting her bed at night. Could she have something wrong with her bladder?*

A. Bedwetting at night is a very common trouble; doctors can find nothing to account for it in most children. It is important to investigate the kidneys and bladder in children who persistently wet the bed, especially girls, because infection of the urinary tract is quite frequent and could be the underlying reason. Other tests can be undertaken, including x-rays, if there is any doubt about the health of the urinary tract.

Psychological difficulties may account for bedwetting, but this is not very common; in most cases the likely explanation is that there is some delay in the development of a function which is poorly understood. From a practical point of view, there are a number of possible lines of treatment—which include the use of a buzzer which signals when the bed is wet so that the child can get up to go to the bathroom (thus building up a conditioned reflex) and the drug imipramine which changes the sleep pattern. In any case, the child must not be blamed for something which is not her or his fault, for feelings of guilt will only make the condition worse. Nearly all children become dry at night in time, but it may not be until they have reached their teens that they cease to have occasional accidents.

Q. *I find that I sometimes wet myself if I cough, or even if I sneeze. What is wrong? Can it be cured?*

A. This is a condition that sometimes occurs in women who have had children, in which the muscles and ligaments that support the womb and bladder have become stretched. The womb falls out of position and both the bladder and the rectum may bulge into the wall of the vagina. This state is called a prolapse. It can be cured by surgery and the results are good.

Q. *I have been passing blood in my urine; is it a sign of cancer?*

A. There are a number of reasons for passing blood-stained urine; the most common cause in women is infection of the bladder and kidney. In men, urinary tract infection is a frequent cause, but men are also liable to pass blood because of an enlarged prostate or infection of the prostate. Simple tumors of the bladder can cause bleeding, as can kidney stones; blood may also be seen in the urine after an injury to some part of the urinary tract.

Though cancer is low on the list of causes, the presence of blood in the urine is always a sign that you should seek medical attention.

Q. *I have attacks of discomfort from time to time and have to pass urine more often than usual. I am told I have cystitis, but treatment does not seem to cure it, and I wonder if there could be something more serious wrong with me?*

A. Cystitis is a very common cause of discomfort or pain on passing urine, and it can become chronic—that is, it is never completely cured and tends to flare up from time to time. In some cases there is an underlying cause, such as kidney stone or an abnormality in the urinary tract, but in other cases no such trouble can be found.

In all cases where the disease recurs a full examination of the urinary system should be performed—including x-rays and possibly inspection of the inside of the bladder through the cystoscope—as well as a full gynecological examination. Cystitis in which no underlying cause can be found is far more common in women than in men; it occurs even in young girls, as well as in women who have had children. In people over the age of 60, both sexes may be affected.

Although it may seem that treatment in your case is not effective, you should consult your doctor when you get an attack, and it is important that he should examine you from time to time. It may happen that the underlying cause becomes clear after a while; in any case he will be able to detect and deal with any complications that may occur. In some cases it is possible to prevent attacks by taking drugs such as mandelamine regularly, or by taking small doses of antibacterials; but you should not try to treat yourself nor should you take it for granted that nothing effective can be done, and therefore neglect the condition.

Q. *I am, as far as I know, in perfect health, but I have just been turned down for life insurance because something abnormal was found in my urine. What should I do?*

A. When insurance doctors find an abnormality in the urine they usually tell your doctor, although they cannot give him the reason why they decided you were a bad risk. The most common abnormalities found in the urine are the presence of sugar or albumin. You should go to your doctor for him to check the results of the tests and to investigate the reason for the trouble.

Q. *I have had treatment for a bladder papilloma and have been told to return in six months for a checkup. Do these tumors always recur? Can they become cancerous?*

A. Most of these tumors, which are sometimes loosely called "warts," are not dangerous. But they have to be examined through the cystoscope at regular intervals and if necessary treated by touching them with an electrode carrying a coagulating current. Sometimes such papillomas may undergo a cancerous change

which will make it necessary to use radiation therapy, but regular medical follow-up will insure that the changes are seen by the surgeon in plenty of time for the treatment to be effective.

MALE GENITOURINARY PROBLEMS

difficulty in urinating—removal of the prostate gland—effects of removal on virility—treatment of prostate cancer—enlarged prostates and cancer—circumcision of adolescents—genital development—undescended testis—varicocele—mumps and sterility—epididymitis—hydrocele—"triple testicles"—torsion of the testis—warts on the penis—bruising of the testicles

Q. *I am 56 years old and have noticed lately that I have to get up at night to urinate and I have a little difficulty in starting. Is this beginning of prostate trouble? Will I have to have an operation?*

A. You are indeed describing the early features of prostate enlargement, which affects many men between the ages of 60 and 80—about 80% of men over the age of 80 suffer from the condition to some extent. The prostate gland lies just below the urinary bladder and it is about the size and shape of a chestnut. Its secretions form a part of the seminal fluid in which spermatozoa are carried when they are ejaculated at orgasm. Normally the gland begins to shrink slightly from the age of 40 onwards; but in some cases it undergoes a process called benign enlargement, the cause of which is not known—although it may be associated with a change in the balance of the male hormones.

The disease certainly cannot be the result of absence of the male hormones, for it never occurs in eunuchs. Nor is it the result of over-indulgence in sexual activities, nor abstinence, nor (as some men fear) of venereal disease. When the prostate starts to enlarge it may press on the urethra (the passage between the bladder and the penis) or part of the gland may enlarge upwards and form a projection in the floor of the bladder just next to the internal opening of the urethra. In this way the bladder is irritated and the passage of urine becomes obstructed, at first mildly but in time in some cases quite seriously, so that it may become very difficult or even impossible to empty the bladder.

Not all cases of an enlarged prostate require surgical treatment; it depends a great deal on the severity of the obstruction and each case must be treated as a separate problem. Your doctor will wish to examine you thoroughly, and he may very well decide to observe the progress of your condition before he is able to advise you whether or not you should consider having an operation.

Q. *Is the operation for removal of the prostate gland serious? Is it possible to have it done without abdominal surgery?*

A. The standard operation for removal of the prostate is a major procedure which involves opening the abdominal wall, and carries the small but inevitable risks associated with any abdominal operation. In some cases, the symptoms can be relieved by a much simpler procedure ("transurethral resection") in which the portion of the gland causing obstruction to the flow of urine is removed through a cystoscope. The choice between the two procedures has to be made after assessment of the individual patient and his general health.

Q. *Does an operation for removal of the prostate gland affect a man's virility?*

A. No, it makes no difference to the virility or to the sex drive, but it may affect the amount of fluid ejaculated at orgasm because much of it is composed of the secretions of the prostate gland. After some operations in which the excretory ducts (vasa deferentia) are tied to prevent the possibility of infection reaching the testes, there may be a loss of fertility.

Q. *Why is it that a prostate gland which is enlarged by a simple swelling is removed, while one that is cancerous is not?*

A. The trouble is that cancer of the prostate gland is rarely diagnosed until the growth has spread too far for it to be practical to remove it entirely—for it does not enlarge the gland in the way that a simple swelling does. Fortunately, it has been found that cancer of the prostate can be kept under control in many cases by the administration of large doses of estrogenic hormones; if difficulty in urinating occurs, part of the prostate can be removed through the cystoscope.

Q. *Does simple enlargement of the prostate gland ever turn into cancer?*

A. No, the two conditions are quite separate. A large

number of cancers of the prostate gland never give trouble during life, and are only found at autopsy. It has been estimated that about 80% of prostate glands removed at autopsy from men over the age of 90 can be shown to contain cells that have undergone cancerous changes involving only a small part of the gland.

Q. *My son, who is 15, was not circumcised as a baby; last week his foreskin became rolled back and he had great difficulty in replacing it. Could this happen again, and if so, should he be circumcised?*

A. This condition, when the foreskin rolls back and cannot be replaced, is called *paraphimosis*. The danger is that the tip of the penis may swell up because the tight foreskin impairs the circulation to such an extent that an anesthetic may be needed to replace it. If this happens again, and it may, your son should consider circumcision, which is not dangerous although it is uncomfortable and has to be performed under a general anesthetic.

Q. *My boy is at the age of puberty and his voice has broken, but he came to me very worried that his penis is not the right size. I think his development is quite normal; what should I tell him?*

A. Many boys at the age of puberty, and some men beyond it, are secretly worried that their genital organs are not properly developed and have remained small. It is often very difficult to persuade them that all is well. It may be necessary to take him to your doctor, who may have a better chance of making him believe that he is normal. In only a few cases are the sexual organs underdeveloped; in most, it is the imagination that is at fault. In any case, it may be worthwhile pointing out that the size of the genital organs bears no relation to a man's virility.

Q. *My boy was born with one testicle undescended. Will this interfere with his fertility? Are we likely to have the same trouble with future children?*

A. For reasons which are not understood, the testicles sometimes fail to descend from the region of the kidneys (where they develop) into the scrotum. Normally they take up their final position shortly before birth, but they may be held up in the abdomen, in the groin, or at the entrance to the scrotum. In some cases the testicle is drawn into a position removed from the normal path of descent and it may lie at the root of the penis, behind the scrotum, or even at the top of the thigh. The trouble is that a testicle in the wrong place will not produce sperm, probably because the temperature is too high. The temperature of the testicles in their proper place in the scrotum is about 2°C below the temperature of the body; it is only at this lower temperature that the production of sperms proceeds normally.

It is important to bring imperfectly descended testicles down into the scrotum by means of a surgical operation for two reasons. The testicle will produce healthy sperm only if the operation is performed, and if it is left undescended there is a small but definite risk of cancer developing in it. If it proves impossible to operate successfully, the testicle is best removed. Even so, the remaining testicle will be fertile—and it is perfectly possible for a man to have children in the absence of one testicle. Thus, you need have no worries about your son's fertility, and there is no evidence to suggest that any other children you may have will be affected in the same way.

Q. *I have a condition called a varicocele, which I am told is a kind of varicose vein affecting the testicles. I have been advised to have an operation because the condition may affect my fertility. Why is this?*

A. As explained in the previous answer, the testicles do not function correctly if they are at the wrong temperature. It is thought that the enlargement of the plexus of veins around the affected testicle raises its temperature (because of the increased flow of blood) and that this is sufficient to affect the formation of sperms.

The operation is a satisfactory one and is not dangerous, so that it is worthwhile having it carried out even if the varicocele is not particularly uncomfortable.

Q. *We have a child with mumps. My husband has never had mumps and he is worried in case he catches the disease, for we have heard that an attack of mumps in a grown man might result in sterility. Is this true?*

A. In about a quarter of the cases of mumps in adult men a testicle is affected. Usually only one testicle becomes inflamed, however, and while this is most painful and unpleasant it does not have the effect of making a man sterile. One testicle is quite sufficient to maintain a high level of sperm production. It is quite probable that your husband will not catch mumps, for

many people have the disease in childhood without knowing it. This is shown by the frequent finding of a positive "complement fixation test" in people who have never apparently had the disease. However, in view of his anxiety, the best course would be for him to be given an injection of immune globulin, which will protect him against infection for several weeks—well beyond the time your child will be infectious.

Q. *I have had a very painful swelling of my right testicle, which my doctor treated successfully with antibiotics. I was told I had epididymitis. Is it infective? Could I infect my wife?*

A. No. Although the disease is caused by a bacterial infection, you cannot infect your wife unless the disease was caused by gonorrhea, and your doctor would have diagnosed this and told you. The common infecting organisms in an acute epididymitis do not behave in the same way as the organisms that cause venereal disease. They probably reach the epididymis through the bloodstream or by direct spread through the excretory ducts of the testicles from the urinary passage (urethra). Your doctor will have tested your urine to make sure that you have not been suffering from a urinary infection. There is no fear that your fertility will have been affected.

Q. *My father in later life had a swelling of his testicle which was diagnosed as a hydrocele, but six months later he had to have his testicle removed because it had become cancerous. I have had a small swelling of the testicle for a few years, and now my doctor tells me that I have a hydrocele. Am I likely to develop cancer?*

A. No. A hydrocele, which is quite common, is usually a simple collection of fluid in the membranes surrounding the testicle—sometimes the result of an injury but often unexplained. They cannot become cancerous, but a secondary hydrocele can be formed if there is an underlying tumor of the testicle. In your case, since the swelling has been there for a few years, it must be a simple hydrocele. In any event, your doctor will have examined your testicle when he made the diagnosis and will have satisfied himself that there is nothing wrong.

There is no reason to suppose that cancer of the testicle is hereditary, and it is far less common than simple hydroceles.

Q. *I know it sounds unlikely, but I have met a man who says he has three testicles. Is this possible?*

A. No. It does sometimes occur that men claim to have three testicles, but the third always turns out to be a cyst of the epididymis or a cyst associated with the spermatic cord.

Q. *I have heard that it is possible for the testicles to become twisted in some way. Should I wear an athletic support to prevent this?*

A. It is possible for the testicle to become twisted on the spermatic cord, but it is rare for it to happen. Most cases occur in teenage men and are caused by a minor anatomical abnormality. Torsion of the testis may happen at any time, even during sleep, and it is accompanied by acute pain and swelling. If medical attention is sought quickly the testicle can be untwisted during a minor surgical operation but if it is left for more than about eight hours the testicle will be irreversibly damaged. The condition is not uncommon; unfortunately, wearing an athletic support will not prevent it.

Q. *I seem to be developing warts on my penis. I have not exposed myself to the risk of venereal disease, but could I have picked up an unpleasant disease somehow?*

A. Warts on the end of the penis do occur, and they are almost always simple and comparable to warts anywhere else on the body—they are probably caused by a virus. They do not mean that you have an unpleasant disease, and they can be treated in the same way as other simple warts under medical supervision. There are, however, warts called *condylomata lata* which grow on the penis as part of a venereal infection. They are a manifestation of secondary syphilis and are very infectious. If you have any doubt that you might have exposed yourself to infection during the past six months you must go to your doctor at once.

Q. *I accidentally suffered a severe blow on the testicles a few weeks ago. The pain has now gone, but there still seems to be some thickening. Will it go, or have I suffered some permanent damage?*

A. After a severe blow anywhere there is bound to be bruising; this is especially true of the loose tissue around the testicles and spermatic cord which is rich in blood vessels. In some cases a small collection of fluid, called a hydrocele, develops in the membranes around the testicle. The bruising and consequent thickening of the tissues will go without leaving any ill effects, but the hydrocele may persist and need treatment.

GYNECOLOGICAL PROBLEMS

late start of menstruation—late menopause—estrogen therapy—premenstrual tension—painful periods—removal of an ovary and fertility—IUDs and future pregnancy—miscarriages—Trichomonas—bleeding between periods—curettage—hysterectomy and depression—erosion of the cervix—ectopic pregnancy—fibroadenomas—cystic mastitis—breast cancer (predisposing factors)—injury and breast cancer—investigating breast lumps—breast screening clinics—different ways of treating breast cancer—breast abscess

Q. *My daughter has not started to menstruate, although she is 15. Is there anything wrong with her?*

A. The normal young girl should start menstruating before the age of 17; after that age there may be something wrong. The average age at the onset of menstruation is 13.5 years. There appears to be a trend toward earlier starting, but there is a great deal of variation. The difficulty about a girl who starts to menstruate later than her friends is that she begins to feel that there is something wrong with her; she tends to become self-conscious and to lose her confidence, so that she needs a great deal of support during this difficult time. She might be helped by the reassurance of your family doctor, who will be able to examine her for the remote possibility of hormonal imbalance. If he finds nothing wrong, he will explain to her that she is just the same as many other girls in starting her periods late.

Q. *At what age does the menopause usually happen? I am 52 and still have periods.*

A. The age beyond which menstrual bleeding is thought to be abnormal is 60, but the menopause usually occurs well before that age—at about 50. About two years before the menopause the length of the cycle usually increases and there is some irregularity. A considerable variation exists in the ages both of the onset and cessation of menstruation, and you are well within the normal range. About 10% of women do not experience the menopause until after the age of 55.

Q. *What are the arguments for and against the long-term use of estrogens during the menopause? I have been advised not to use them, but some of*

my friends have told me that they have made a great difference in their lives.

A. As you know, there is a great deal of argument on this subject. The arguments given against the use of estrogens over long periods are that they may cause overgrowth of the lining of the uterus and increase the risk of cancer; that they may favor the development of fibroid growths in the uterus; that they may produce irregular bleeding and lead to difficulty in diagnosis of the cause; and that they may increase the risk of THROMBOSIS of the veins.

In favor of the use of estrogens it is argued that they remove the unpleasant symptoms of the menopause; that they are contraceptive and preclude the risk of a late pregnancy; that they stop the rise of blood cholesterol at the menopause which brings with it the risk of heart disease; that they prevent the menstrual irregularities which accompany the menopause; that they counteract the softening of bones and withering of the genital organs that may follow the drop in the level of the sex hormones; and that if mixed therapy is used (that is, a combination of estrogens and progestogens) it may actually reduce the risk of cancer of the uterus.

It is not easy to strike a balance between these arguments, and much research is underway to help doctors make their judgment. Individuals vary a great deal; what may help one may be dangerous for another. You must trust your own doctor to prescribe what is best for you in the light of his understanding of your own special requirements. Temporary use of hormones may be all that is necessary rather than a long-term course.

Q. *I always feel miserable and on edge before my period. I have been told that it is just "nerves" and that I ought to be able to cope with what is a normal phenomenon. I have tried hard, but it seems to be impossible to overcome my feelings. I am not at other times a nervous woman; is it not true that there are bodily changes at this time that could account for my trouble?*

A. There is no doubt that about 1 in 16 women suffer emotional changes before the menstrual period, and that as many as 3 out of 5 women feel "swollen." The suicide rate rises among women just before the menstrual period. They are also more liable to have accidents and hospital admissions are more frequent. This is true all over the world; it means that the physical changes that accompany menstruation must have a profound effect on the emotional state.

Unfortunately, the reasons for this are poorly understood. One result is that the subtle and obscure physical causes are disregarded and the obvious emotional upsets are taken at their face value. However, it is possible for a doctor to help his female patients a great deal even if his treatment is directed only toward the relief of the symptoms rather than to setting right the unknown underlying processes.

Q. *For centuries women have been experiencing discomfort or actual pain in connection with their periods, yet I am told that the reasons are not understood. Is there still no way of dealing with this problem?*

A. There are more ways than there used to be, but there is no getting away from the fact that no general cure exists. Pain associated with menstruation affects a very large number of women; in one survey, 12% had severe pain and another 35% had moderate pain. The pain can be divided into two major classes, primary and secondary.

Primary pain is the most difficult to deal with since it has no obvious cause. It seems to be connected with the cycle of ovulation, and in some cases it is relieved by suppressing ovulation with oral contraceptives. At one time it was thought that the underlying reasons could be emotional, but there is plenty of evidence to show that this is not so, although the pain is liable to produce emotional upsets for obvious reasons. Doctors can use a number of therapeutic approaches, according to the needs of each patient. It is worthwhile asking for medical advice rather than resigning yourself to days of reduced efficiency and pain every month.

Secondary pain may be easier for the doctor to deal with. The term is used to describe pain coming on after some years of pain-free periods, and it may be due to a disturbance which he can diagnose and treat. In all cases of painful periods it is important that a full gynecological examination be made, but there are still a large number of women who do nothing about period pain and accept it as the age-old "curse."

Q. *What is the possibility of having children after one ovary has been taken away? I have been advised to have an ovarian cyst removed, and I understand the ovary may be in danger.*

A. Providing that the Fallopian tube which carries the egg into the womb is in a normal state, there is no reason why one ovary should not be quite sufficient for successful conception and pregnancy. The operation may not involve removing the ovary from which the cyst is growing, for it is possible in many cases to dissect the cyst free and leave the major part of the ovary intact. But this does depend on the nature of the cyst, as your gynecologist probably explained to you. He will not know for certain until he actually performs the operation. If he is able to leave the greater part of the ovary intact, the risk of another cyst growing is very small—in fact, almost nonexistent. You should not have the operation postponed for fear of diminishing your chances of having children in the future.

Q. *Because contraceptive pills did not agree with me, I have had a coil fitted. Will it interfere with my future chances of having children?*

A. No. It has been demonstrated that intrauterine contraceptive devices (IUD or IUCD) do not interfere with the normal functioning of the ovary, or indeed with fertilization of the ovum. The way in which they work is not clear, but they appear to prevent the fertilized egg from becoming implanted in the womb. It follows that when the IUD has been removed, and there is no longer any interference with implantation, the pregnancy will go ahead normally for the IUD leaves no damage behind it after removal. About 60% of women conceive within the first three months after removal of the device, and about 90% conceive within the year.

Q. *I started to bleed after about two months of pregnancy and lost my baby. I was told that it was not wise to try to prevent the threatened miscarriage because it probably meant that the baby was abnormal. Does this mean that in the future I might have an abnormal baby?*

A. No. Even if the reason for the miscarriage was that the baby was abnormal, you are in no more danger of having an abnormal child in the future than any other normal woman. There is little doubt that the majority of aborted fetuses are abnormal, and many doctors take the view that it is unwise to try to prolong a pregnancy threatened in its early stages unless there are very special reasons for doing so. However, if a pregnancy that has been in danger in its early stages does continue successfully, there is no increased risk that the child will prove to be abnormal.

Q. *I have been worried by a white discharge and irritation in the vagina. My doctor tells me that I have an infection with* Trichomonas, *and that my husband should be treated as well as myself. I find it difficult to tell my husband, since I am afraid it could be some sort of venereal disease.*

A. Trichomonas infection can be passed on by sexual intercourse, but (in contrast to the true venereal diseases such as syphilis and gonorrhea) most cases are not acquired by sexual contact. The tiny parasite responsible, a protozoan called *Trichomonas vaginalis*, is found in the human vagina. It can give rise to an unpleasant discharge and much irritation. *Trichomonas* may also survive in the male genital passages without producing any discomfort; if your husband is not treated at the same time as you he may reinfect you and start the disease over again.

Q. *Is bleeding between periods serious? Could it mean cancer?*

A. Although it should be taken seriously, bleeding between periods by no means always indicates the presence of cancer. There are two main causes— hormonal imbalance or some abnormality near the surface of the vagina, the neck of the womb or the womb itself. Although this could be a tumor, it is more likely to be benign than malignant. Bleeding of this kind has to be investigated thoroughly, and sometimes this may involve a diagnostic curettage and examination under anesthesia.

Q. *What is the purpose of curettage?*

A. This is a minor operation to remove of the contents of the uterus by use of a special instrument, the curette. In order to introduce the curette into the uterus the neck of the womb has to be dilated through the vagina. The operation is therefore usually called a "D and C"—dilatation and curettage. It is done under an anesthetic and is performed both for diagnostic and therapeutic reasons. For example, a curettage may have to be performed after a miscarriage if the doctor thinks that parts of the placenta or the fetus have remained behind, or when there is an abnormality of the membrane lining the uterus, such as a polyp or overdevelopment of the cells. The operation is not painful and it does not interfere with future pregnancies.

Q. *I am 40 years old and, because of fibroids, I have had a hysterectomy. Although the operation was successful, I found that I was very depressed when I came out of the hospital, and I can't seem to shake it off. Could this be caused by some hormonal disturbance, like the depression that some women have at the menopause?*

A. When you have a hysterectomy for fibroids the

ovaries are not removed; although you obviously can't have periods after the operation, the ovaries continue to function just as they did before. This is different from the situation at the menopause, when the ovaries are ceasing to ovulate and the hormonal balance is changed. Many women feel much better than they have for a long time after they have had a hysterectomy, but others for no apparent reason become depressed. In all probability this reaction reflects the fact that a very special organ has been removed which is basic to a woman's life, and represents her essential femininity.

Although your doctor can help a great deal in treating your depression, he obviously cannot change your emotional reaction to the operation. In time this will go and then you will begin to feel the benefits of the operation—which are very real. You don't have to worry about experiencing a premature menopause or worry that your appearance will in some way be changed. It is more likely that although you are still depressed you are looking better than you did before the operation.

Q. *I have been told that I have an erosion of the cervix. Is there any danger that cancer is associated with this condition?*

A. No. Erosion of the cervix has nothing to do with cancer and the condition is not precancerous. The term "erosion" is actually misleading, since it suggests that something has been worn away—which is far from the truth. Erosions are in fact areas where the cells that cover the vaginal part of the neck of the womb have been replaced by cells that normally line the inner canal leading from the neck of the womb into its body. When they are seen through an instrument called a vaginal speculum they appear to be bright red and raw, and they may produce an increased vaginal discharge.

Erosions are found in healthy young girls and in women who have had no children, but they are most common during and after pregnancy. Very often they clear up in the months after childbirth, but sometimes they have to be treated by cauterization—a minor procedure performed without an anesthetic. Erosions may sometimes become infected, but apart from the increased vaginal discharge they cause no trouble.

Q. *My sister suddenly got very sick recently and had to have a serious operation for an ectopic pregnancy. Can this happen to anyone?*

A. An ectopic pregnancy is one in which the fertilized ovum has become implanted somewhere other than in the lining of the uterus—most often in the wall of one of the Fallopian tubes. The tube is liable to rupture, and this leads to sudden profuse bleeding into the abdominal cavity—followed by shock, pain and collapse. It can happen to anyone, although there are factors such as previous inflammation of the Fallopian tubes (salpingitis) which make it more likely.

Sometimes an ectopic pregnancy can be diagnosed before it ruptures the tube. The early signs of pregnancy may be present—a missed period, morning sickness, discomfort or enlargement of the breasts—accompanied by pain in the lower part of the abdomen and possibly pain during sexual intercourse. A pregnancy test will usually be positive. If an ectopic pregnancy is suspected, examination of the tube through an instrument called an endoscope may confirm the diagnosis. An immediate operation to remove the affected tube will prevent serious bleeding.

Not all ectopic pregnancies cause severe bleeding, since the fertilized ovum may die and be expelled into the abdominal cavity, or may cause slow bleeding into the Fallopian tube. This is more likely to happen if the ovum has become implanted in the outer end of the tube, near the ovary. The rupture usually follows if there is implantation further down the tube, near the junction of the tube and the uterus.

The incidence of ectopic pregnancies varies a good deal according to the general prevalence of salpingitis, but in one series of patients studied the proportions were 300 normal pregnancies to one ectopic.

Ectopic pregnancies may also occur in women fitted with a contraceptive coil, but the risk is very small.

(See also the major article on **Obstetrics and Gynecology.**)

Q. *I had a lump removed from my breast, which I was told was a simple tumor called a fibroadenoma. I am still a little anxious about the whole thing. Could this kind of tumor turn into a cancer?*

A. No, simple fibroadenomas do not turn into cancers even if they are left in the breast. Most of them occur in women between the ages of 20 and 35 years, and they may fluctuate in size with the menstrual cycle and enlarge during pregnancy. As a rule they are removed as soon as they are noticed to establish that they are not cancerous. If you have been told by your doctor that the tumor removed from your breast was benign, you can be absolutely confident that it has nothing to do with cancer.

Q. *I suffer from a condition called cystic mastitis,*

and I can feel more than one lump in my breast. It really worries me that I might develop something more dangerous than mastitis without being able to notice it. Could this happen?

A. Even though cystic mastitis is not a precancerous condition, your doctor will want to examine you periodically to make sure that there are no persisting lumps in your breast. If there are, he will investigate them either by aspiration (taking some cells out with a needle), if he thinks the swelling is cystic, by MAMMOGRAPHY (a low-dosage x-ray) or in some cases by taking a biopsy. There is very little risk that you might develop anything more serious, and if you do, there a number of ways of detecting it which will determine whether another biopsy is needed. Since you have already had your attention drawn to the state of your breasts, you are more likely to notice any change in their condition than the average woman.

Q. *Is it true that cancer of the breast is less likely to develop in women who have had children? What other factors are involved?*

A. Cancer of the breast is about twice as common in unmarried as in married women, and more common in women who have had one child or no children at all than in those who have had several. The earlier the pregnancies, the greater the protection seems to be. Whether or not the infants were breast fed seems to make little difference. Women who have had their ovaries removed are about half as likely to develop cancer of the breast as the rest of the population, which is further evidence that hormonal balance has something to do with the disease. Some breast cancers are sensitive to female hormones, so the removal of the ovaries, the adrenal glands, and in some cases the pituitary gland, can influence the course of the disease. Treatment with antiestrogen drugs can have the same effect.

Not all malignant tumors of the breast appear to be dependent on hormones; in some cases this kind of treatment is ineffective.

Another factor in the occurrence of breast cancer is an immediate family history of the disease.

There is some evidence that environmental factors, including diet, may influence the likely occurrence of the disease. One study showed that it was only a quarter as likely to occur among Japanese women as among American women. But when immigrants from Japan settled in California, over a time the rate among the new generations rose until it was nearly that of the native population. Such facts, and many others, suggest lines for research; but it remains sadly true that we still

do not know a great deal about this—the most common type of cancer to affect women—nor do we yet know of any way to prevent it.

Q. *Can an injury to the breast cause cancer?*

A. No, there is no evidence to suggest that it can. It is more likely that an injury to the breast will cause a woman to examine her breast and find a lump which has escaped her notice up to that time. Sometimes an injury will cause severe bruising, with damage to the fatty tissue of the breast which results in the formation of a lump; this does not lead to the development of cancer.

Q. *When I noticed a small lump in my right breast my doctor advised me to have it removed at once. But he would not say whether it was likely to be cancer. Isn't it possible to tell whether a lump is cancerous without operating?*

A. There are a number of diagnostic procedures your doctor can use to investigate a suspicious lump in the breast: mammography—a low-dosage x-ray; or xero-radiography, another special kind of x-ray; or thermography, which analyzes heat from the tissues. The lump may also be assessed by ultrasound scanning. He may use a needle to remove some cells for analysis. Nevertheless, in a large number of cases it is not possible to tell for certain the nature of a lump in the breast without removing it and looking at it under a microscope. The great majority of lumps that are removed are harmless, but the fact that your doctor advised you to have an operation means that he is too experienced to take anything for granted. A BIOPSY of this kind is naturally worrying to any woman, but the important thing in these cases is above all to catch any malignant tumor—if it is that—at an early stage of development so that treatment has every chance of being successful.

Q. *At what age should I start attending a breast screening clinic?*

A. Screening clinics which use mammography and other diagnostic techniques for the early detection of breast cancer have been established throughout the Western world, but there is still a conflict of medical opinion about their value. On present evidence regular screening is of proved value to women over the age of 50 and to those with relatives who have had breast cancer. Its value for younger women is less certain; and there is a very small risk that the x-rays used for screening may themselves lead to cancerous changes in later life. On balance, the current advice from cancer advisory groups is to delay regular screening until you are 50.

Q. *Two of my friends developed cancer of the breast, but the treatment they had was very different. Isn't there a standard treatment for this disease?*

A. Doctors have a number of techniques for dealing with cancer of the breast, and in most cases a combination of approaches is used. There can be no standard treatment, because each case is different. The doctor chooses his method according to the needs of each case, and often he will not be able to make his mind up until the actual operation when he can see the situation clearly.

Q. *In my last pregnancy I had a breast abscess. It healed up, but is there going to be any permanent effect?*

A. No, an abscess in the breast is the same as an abscess anywhere in the body; once the infection has been controlled and the abscess has healed it won't cause any further trouble.

STARTING A FAMILY

waiting time for conception—checks for ovulation—fertility drugs—best time for intercourse—best position for intercourse— causes of infertility—VD and sterility— consulting the doctor—examination: which partner?—tests on the man—treatment of the man—age and fertility—sterilization: which partner?

Q. *I am getting married later this year and my husband and I want to start a family as soon as possible. How long do most couples have to wait?*

A. Couples trying to start a family take a very variable time to achieve successful conception. About 25% are lucky and the wife becomes pregnant within the first or second month; 60% are fortunate in the first six months, 80% within a year, and 90% within 18 months. Not until two years have elapsed should a childless couple think about consulting their doctor to ask for his help in the diagnosis of any potential problem.

For a woman to become pregnant there must first of all be normal ovulation (the release of an egg cell (ovum) from the ovary) and transport of the ovum from the ovary to the uterus through the Fallopian tube. Secondly, there has to be normal cyclical development of the lining of the uterus and normal hormone secretion to encourage the growth of the fertilized ovum and allow it to become firmly implanted. Thirdly, of course, there must be adequate insemination by a sufficient number of healthy sperm cells, and lastly, the ovum and sperm have to meet at the right time (fertilization).

Q. *How can I tell if I am ovulating normally?*

A. Although there is no guaranteed method, the most important indication of regular ovulation is a regular normal menstrual cycle. The entire cycle should last about four weeks, and menstrual bleeding should last between three or four days in sufficient quantities to make it necessary to use two or three daily changes of tampons or sanitary napkins. Irregular periods suggest irregular ovulation; scanty periods, or no periods, may indicate that ovulation is not taking place at all. Normally, the body temperature rises about 0.5°C (1°F) at the time of ovulation and continues at this level until menstruation.

Ovulation takes place during the middle of the menstrual cycle—that is, about 14 days before the expected beginning of the next period. Unfortunately, it is not always easy to interpret a record of daily temperatures kept throughout a cycle and irregularities may make the pattern misleading. However, your own doctor will explain how to keep a temperature chart; for many women this is a fairly reliable indication of the time of ovulation.

Special tests can help shed light on the nature of ovulation problems. These include taking a sample of tissue from the lining of the uterus (which shows characteristic changes about a week after ovulation) and hormone analyses which show a rise in the blood levels of progesterone during a normal menstrual cycle.

Q. *What can be done if I am not ovulating normally?*

A. Hormonal "fertility" drugs such as clomiphene and follicle-stimulating hormone (FSH) may be used to stimulate ovulation. Clomiphene is given daily for five days and in suitable cases ovulation occurs in well over 50% of the women treated. The drug has to be used under close medical supervision because it can produce complications such as enlargement of the ovaries and multiple pregnancies. There is also an increased risk of spontaneous abortion after the use of clomiphene—the rate may be as high as 20%. A course of five days of FSH, followed by a single dose of human chorionic gonadotropin (HCG), can be given to stimulate ovulation. During the course of treatment laboratory tests are necessary to check the concentration of estrogen in the blood or urine.

Q. *Is there any special time in the month when my husband and I should have intercourse to make conception more likely?*

A. Yes. If your menstrual cycle is 28 days (which is not the case with all women), then the fertile period is likely to be between the 10th and the 17th days of the cycle, counting from the start of the periodic bleeding. The period of time during which the ovum can be fertilized after release from the ovary is about 24 hours; sperm cells retain their capacity to fertilize an ovum for about 48 hours after ejaculation. Since it is not often possible to know the precise time of ovulation (although temperature charts can be of help) it is advisable for you and your husband to have intercourse three or four times a week during the fertile period if you wish to conceive.

Q. *Is there any particular position for intercourse which will aid conception?*

A. Not necessarily. But it is possible that with some couples the semen is more likely to be deposited nearer to the neck of the womb (cervix) if the face-to-face position is used, with the woman's legs flexed at the hip, or if the man enters from behind. But, in general, the position is not likely to make any significant difference.

Q. *I have regular periods, so I must be ovulating. What other reasons are there that could keep me from getting pregnant?*

A. There are a number of disorders, both in men and women, which can lead to difficulty in becoming pregnant. In women they include abnormalities of the cervix, the result perhaps of chronic inflammation or extensive damage caused to the cervix during childbirth, or the presence of POLYPS. It is also thought that in some cases there may be a factor in the secretions of the glands of the cervix which make the sperm cells ineffective. A simple gynecological examination will usually reveal any disorders of the cervix. A *postcoital test* can be performed which will show whether the woman's cervical secretions are incompatible with the

sperm cells. If this turns out to be the case, it is often possible to remedy the situation.

FIBROIDS lying under the lining of the uterus can prevent successful conception, but more commonly the problem lies in some disorder of the Fallopian tubes. A Fallopian tube is not only the pathway guiding the ovum into the uterus, but also the site where fertilization takes place and the fertilized ovum first begins to divide. Also within the Fallopian tube, certain changes are thought to take place which enable a sperm cell to penetrate the ovum and fertilize it.

In normal conditions, sperm cells (spermatozoa) reach the Fallopian tubes about 30 minutes after ejaculation. But of the hundreds of millions of sperm cells deposited in the vagina, only a few reach the ovum—only one of the sperm cells is normally responsible for fertilization. It is thus easy to see how a disorder of the tubes can lead to low fertility or infertility.

The most common problem in this respect is distortion of the tube by adhesions, which impede or prevent the collection of the ovum from the ovary after its release. Adhesions can be caused by infection of the peritoneum (the membrane that lines the abdominal cavity and covers its internal organs)—for example, as a complication of appendicitis or some other pelvic inflammation—or infection of the tubes themselves (SALPINGITIS) following childbirth, gonorrhea or tuberculosis, or a previous ECTOPIC PREGNANCY. The condition of the tubes can be assessed by your gynecologist following the results of specific tests. These may include *insufflation* (filling the tubes with carbon dioxide or another gas to see if they are obstructed), a *hysterosalpingogram* (x-ray of the uterus and Fallopian tubes after injection of a radiopaque liquid) or *laparoscopy* (direct examination of the tubes with the use of a special instrument known as a laparoscope). Past disease of the tubes does not necessarily result in sterility, and adhesions and blockages of the tubes are in many cases successfully treated surgically.

Recent work has demonstrated conclusively that it is possible for the ovum to be removed from the ovary, fertilized outside the body, and implanted into the uterus to produce a normal pregnancy—thus bypassing diseased and blocked Fallopian tubes. However, the techniques involved demand special laboratory skills and experience and this is not yet a routinely available procedure.

Q. *Can venereal disease produce sterility?*

A. Yes, it is possible. In the case of a woman, gonorrhea can result in damage to the Fallopian tubes. In a man, blockage of the tubes which carry the sperm cells to the exterior may arise from a complication of gonorrhea (as well as from tuberculosis or other infections that involve the testes or the prostate gland).

Q. *I have been told that when there is a problem becoming pregnant, both partners should see the doctor. Is it important that we should see him at the same time, or should one of us be examined first? If so, should it be the wife or the husband?*

A. In general, the husband is examined first. It has been found that up to 40% of barren marriages are caused by conditions that affect the man. Since it is much easier to investigate the male than the female partner (and much less expensive) the husband's sperm is usually examined first for evidence of an infertility problem.

Q. *Is there any way we can tell which of us has a fertility problem without going to the doctor?*

A. No, only if there is some obvious cause. In most cases it is far better to ask for your doctor's advice. He will look for defects in the formation of sperm or in the passage of sperm from the testes to the vagina. *Semenalysis* (examination of the seminal fluid under a microscope) will show whether or not sperm cells are present in sufficient amounts, and, if they are, whether or not they are normally formed and motile (capable of the appropriate degree of movement).

Inadequate sperm formation may be caused by failure of the testes to descend normally (see UNDESCENDED TESTIS), atrophy (wasting) of the testes following mumps, malformation of the veins of the spermatic cord (VARICOCELE) and overexposure to radiation. Impotence and low fertility are not related; an impotent man (that is, one who is unable to achieve an erection of the penis) may well be fertile, although artificial insemination techniques may be required to enable his wife to conceive. In contrast, men well able to take part in sexual intercourse may be sterile.

Q. *Is analysis of the sperm cells the only useful test in examining the male partner?*

A. No, it may be that your doctor will recommend a BIOPSY of both testicles in order to study the process of formation of the spermatozoa. The procedure is relatively simple, and specimens can be obtained either through a hollow needle or through a very small incision in the skin. Doctors can also find out whether the level of gonadotropins (sex hormones) are too low. Hormone therapy may remedy the deficiency.

Q. *Is any other form of treatment likely to help my husband start a family?*

A. That depends on the cause of the fertility problem, which a thorough medical examination should be able to reveal. For example, if the tubes that carry the sperm cells from your husband's testes are blocked, it may be possible to remove the obstruction surgically. Varicoceles may be treated by a relatively simple operation. Unfortunately, the use of hormone therapy is not always successful.

In about 30% of fertility problems all tests and examinations give normal results, so no logical treatment is possible. But doctors can never be certain that complete and permanent sterility exists.

Q. *What is the relationship between age and fertility?*

A. Women are most fertile at about the age of 24. After the age of 30, the level of fertility begins to diminish and conception after the age of 50 is very rare.

Men may remain fertile until they are much older; in fact, there is a recorded case in which the father was 94 years old. But men are also most fertile at about the age of 24, and fertility gradually declines after that.

(For further information on the problems of starting a family and what can be done to help childless couples, see the section on *Infertility* in the major article on **Family Planning.**)

Q. *My wife and I have decided that our family is complete; rather than rely on contraceptives we think one of us should be sterilized. Which should it be?*

A. There can be no general answer to this question, because the problem of voluntary sterilization is so complex—involving emotional, physical and moral questions. The operations of vasectomy and ringing or clipping the Fallopian tubes are of comparable severity, but the latter does require a general anesthetic and therefore carries a slightly higher risk. Neither method of sterilization can be reversed with any degree of certainty if the patient later regrets the operation.

The operation in the female does not interfere with the function of the ovaries, nor does the operation in the male interfere with virility; but there is always the risk that a loss of fertility may carry with it a degree of psychological trauma. It is not so likely that this could happen in the case of older people, but if you still have, say, ten years of reproductive life ahead of you, you do run this risk. In the future it may be possible for the operation of vasectomy to be successfully reversed; if this does become a practical possibility, your question then has an obvious answer—the male should be sterilized. Until the time that surgeons can accomplish this without fail, your decision is not one which can be made without a great deal of thought over a long time. You will find it very valuable to talk the matter over with your doctor. You may find it advisable to try one of the modern methods of contraception, perhaps a coil, before you finally make up your minds.

BREAST FEEDING

advantages of breast feeding—breast size—sufficient feeding—how long should one breast feed—formulas

Q. *What are the advantages of breast feeding?*

A. First, most women enjoy it and derive a great deal of satisfaction from BREAST FEEDING their babies. The other advantages are that breast milk is nutritionally and chemically balanced, it is cheap and easily available, and is always at the right temperature. Breast milk is sterile and contains immune substances which help to protect the baby from infections such as gastroenteritis. The act of breast feeding brings the mother and infant together in a way which offers very real psychological advantages; and breast-fed babies have fewer illnesses in the first year of life.

Q. *I have small breasts. Is this likely to make breast feeding difficult?*

A. No. The size of the breasts has nothing to do with the success or failure of breast feeding. Inverted nipples may make breast feeding difficult, but they can often be drawn out during pregnancy. During the first two or three days after delivery only colostrum ("first milk") will be secreted by the breasts, and they may become painfully swollen. Gentle milking of fluid from the breasts will help; if the nipples become painful and develop fissures, they will recover if the affected breast is rested for a day or so while manual milk expression is continued.

Q. *How do I know if my baby is getting enough milk?*

A. If your baby is content after feeding and gains weight satisfactorily, she is being properly fed. All babies show a slightly different demand for food; there is no hard-and-fast rule. In general, they become hungry and need feeding about every three or four hours, but the demand may be irregular. Nursing usually lasts about 20 minutes at a time. If your baby is not getting enough she will show that she is hungry by restlessness and crying and will not gain weight. It is always possible to supplement breast feeding by giving formula after the breast has become exhausted.

Q. *How long should I continue to breast feed my baby?*

A. Normally breast feeding should continue for about four to seven months; some mothers breast feed their babies for as long as a year. Even if you cannot continue for the full four months, it is better to start breast feeding than to put your baby on a bottle from the start.

Q. *Will my baby suffer if I can't breast feed him?*

A. No—provided you take reasonable care over the preparation of his formulas. There are a large number of mothers who for one reason or another find it impossible to breast feed their babies—or choose not to. Modern formulas are very satisfactory. A baby who seems unhappy on such a formula, providing that it is being prepared correctly, is usually protesting against the amount he is being given, or the fact that the rubber nipple has a hole which is too small or too large, rather than the formula itself. The average requirement at a feeding is 5 fluid ounces for every 2 pounds of body weight. Within reason, the baby should be allowed to set his own timetable for feeding.

DRUG EFFECTS

penicillin reactions—aspirin reaction—other drugs and skin reactions—side effects of drugs—body weight and drug doses—drugs in pregnancy—doctors and new drugs—amphetamine treatment of hyperkinetic children

Q. *I am sensitive to penicillin and develop a skin rash if I take the drug. Are there any other drugs I should be careful not to take?*

A. Penicillin sensitivity is unfortunately a common condition, but it does not necessarily mean that you are sensitive to other types of drugs. Since penicillins are made under different names you have to be careful that an antibiotic is not a member of the penicillin family, although the name may not suggest that it is. If you ever change doctors, make certain that your new doctor is aware of your sensitivity to penicillin. It is also a good idea to wear a "medical alert" bracelet or carry some other means of conveying this information in the event that you should ever require emergency medical treatment (where penicillin might be inadvertently administered).

Q. *I have had a skin reaction after taking aspirin. I can see that it is not worth continuing to take aspirin if it upsets me when there are other drugs which will have just as good an effect. But is it always worth giving up taking an effective drug just because it causes a rash?*

A. Yes, because the skin reaction may be only one manifestation of hypersensitivity. Allergic reactions to drugs are more likely to occur in children than in adults, and in women more than men. People who have had trouble with allergic reactions in the past are especially liable to drug rashes, and the use of a number of complex drugs at the same time also increases the possibility of trouble.

Once a person has become sensitized to a drug, reactions can occur after very small doses. A first drug reaction usually takes between one and three weeks to develop, but subsequent reactions to the same drug are evident in a matter of hours. Skin reactions to drugs include itching, urticaria (hives), blistering, and contact dermatitis. Other body reactions may damage the liver and kidneys and affect the blood. Fever and joint pains may also occur.

The decision to continue taking a drug that is known to be causing immunological reactions is a serious one; it should be taken only when there is no other drug that can be used and then only in cases when the drug is likely to save life.

Q. *What drugs are most liable to cause skin reactions?*

A. There are a great number of complex drugs that can cause reactions—ranging from antibiotics (especially penicillin) to laxatives. Not all drug reactions are allergic. Some people are abnormally sensitive to certain drugs and normal doses produce all the symptoms of an overdose. Other people show an unpredictable reaction to certain drugs, which is different from the usual effect and is described as an *idiosyncratic reaction*.

The majority of drug reactions, however, are thought to be allergic. Drugs that commonly cause skin reactions include barbiturates, phenylbutazone, procaine, salicylates, penicillins, sulfonamides, phenothiazines (major tranquilizers), benzothiadiazines (diuretics), iodides, bromides, gold, quinine, mepacrine, chloroquine and phenolphthalein. This list is by no means exhaustive; almost any drug can produce a skin reaction of almost any type.

Q. *Why do so many modern drugs seem to have side effects? Isn't it possible to make drugs that don't affect the rest of the body?*

A. Most drugs act on the cells of the body to modify their activity in a particular way. Unless the drug can be applied directly to the cells on which it is supposed to act (as in the case of drugs applied to the skin, for example), it has to be introduced into the whole system, which means that it is bound to reach all the cells in order to get to the ones it is designed to act on. Cells with different functions can carry out these functions by using a common mechanism, so that any drug which modifies this common mechanism can produce different effects in different organs. The subject is an extremely complicated one, bound up with the study of the intricate chemical and physical processes of life and disease. Continual efforts are made to find new drugs that act specifically on certain cell functions, but very few out of the thousands of compounds that are tested are acceptable. Progress in the last 30 years has been remarkable, and more new drugs have been introduced in this time than in the whole period since drugs were first made synthetically over 100 years ago.

Q. *Is the dose of a drug affected by body weight?*

A. Firstly, the effects of drugs given in the same dose to similar people may vary a considerable amount. In most cases, the doctor will start with a standard dose of a drug, and in many cases this will be satisfactory. If necessary, he will alter the dose until he succeeds in producing the effect he wants. In the case of some drugs he will judge the effect by his own observations, but with other drugs he has to rely on blood tests to estimate the right dose. Body weight is only one factor in determining the right dose. Once the drug has been absorbed, it has to pass through the liver where further chemical reactions take place. The speed of these reactions depends on how long you have been taking the drug, any other drug you may be taking, and on factors such as your alcohol consumption. The form in which the drug has been supplied is also important.

Different drugs given at the same time may interfere with each other's absorption, and after absorption they may interfere with each other's action. One example is the interaction between aspirin and indomethacin, which may both be given for arthritis: aspirin stops the absorption of indomethacin. Another example: the absorption of the important antibiotic tetracycline is impaired by milk, antacids and iron preparations.

Q. *Are there any drugs which can safely be taken by an expectant mother to stop morning sickness? Are all drugs dangerous during pregnancy?*

A. Since the tragic discovery in 1961 that a seemingly safe tranquilizer called thalidomide produced terrible congenital deformities in children born to mothers who had taken it, most doctors advise that no drugs should be taken by a pregnant mother, especially in the first three months of pregnancy. This is the period during which the fetus takes shape as a human being. Certain drugs are known to be more dangerous than others, but most drugs pass readily across the placenta from the mother to the fetus, and all doctors are well aware that any drug given to an expectant mother is also given to her baby. You should therefore avoid taking any drugs during pregnancy, even such common ones as aspirin, except those prescribed by your doctor.

Q. *When I went to my doctor to ask if I could try a new drug for migraine which had been reported to be very effective he was reluctant to let me have it, because he had no first-hand knowledge about it. Isn't this kind of attitude a little too conservative? It seems to me that with the rapid advance of knowledge a doctor should always be alert to new drugs and ready to use them.*

A. All doctors try to be alert to the possibilities of new drugs and methods of treatment, but they must offer real advantages. Doctors are always being urged by the pharmaceutical industry, and sometimes by patients, to try new remedies, to use a wide range of drugs and to be "up to date." If this were carried to the extreme, it would mean the doctors could never thoroughly know and understand the actions of all the medicines they prescribe. Under these circumstances the likelihood of ineffective treatment and unwanted side effects is greater than if doctors keep to the range of drugs they know well. Most doctors will try to have a really good

knowledge of one or two drugs in the different major classes, and use a particular preparation of them. And they try to follow the basic rule of prescribing that the fewer the drugs prescribed, the safer. This may sound a little unadventurous to the person who's anxious to "try something," but the doctor's first obligation is not to injure the patient—a very ancient medical maxim that is more than ever applicable today.

Q. *My boy, who is now 8, was a real behavior problem in school; he didn't seem to be able to learn anything and gave us all no end of trouble. He was diagnosed as hyperkinetic, and he's being treated with amphetamines. I thought that these drugs were used to "pep people up," that they were dangerous, and that they could lead to addiction. Is this treatment going to make him into an addict?*

A. No. The effects of amphetamines used to treat hyperkinetic children are very different from the effects you might expect. People who abuse amphetamines—or "speed"—take it because it makes them feel alert, full of energy and excited. It also helps to overcome sleepiness and fatigue on a short-term basis. Unfortunately, all these effects tend to be accompanied by a loss of judgment, and when the dose is high it may cause hallucinations and delusions. People who abuse amphetamines have to keep raising the dose to get the full effect.

When amphetamines are given to children with symptoms of hyperactivity the effect is different. The reason is thought to be that children with the hyperkinetic syndrome react to multiple stimuli in their environment without being able to discriminate and therefore are unable to concentrate on any task in hand. Increased arousal of the central functions of the brain by amphetamines enable normal control to be established, so that automatic responses are damped down and sensory input, kept down to its more normal level, is less distracting. The lack of concentration, poor attention span and impulsive behaviour are all changed for the better, so that the high level of activity falls and the child is able to behave more normally and benefit from school. In other words, the drug enables the thoughtless hyperkinetic child to think what he or she is doing.

(For more information on drug actions and effects, see the major article on **Drugs and Medicines.**)

Section IV

First Aid

First Aid

Dr. Alexander S. Playfair

Table of Contents

INTRODUCTION

This section will not teach you enough to turn you into a generally efficient first aider. It cannot do this any more than your car manual will make you a good mechanic. But it certainly can help you and the person you are treating in an emergency. It will guide you to achieve the three important aims of first aid:

1. To keep the patient alive
2. To prevent his condition from worsening
3. To relieve anxiety, pain and discomfort.

Of course not every injury threatens life, but every one can be aggravated by bad handling and every one creates some degree of psychological tension.

You must remember that first aid is FIRST aid only, consisting of measures to be taken before a nurse or doctor attends to give "second aid"—that is, treatment proper. Your care will insure that the patient is in the best possible condition when the professional takes over.

Throughout, stress will be placed on the use of improvised material as well as on items available from a carefully prepared home first-aid kit. Experience shows that all too often such a kit is just not available when the need arises.

Use this section of the book for reference and let the index help you. But also read through it so that when the emergency arises the ground will be familiar. Some parts are so important, describing urgent actions, that you should study and learn them right now. They are:

Bleeding
Burns
Unconsciousness
Epilepsy
Electric shock
Road accidents
Resuscitation

You should also read the section on shock carefully.

Finally, why not enroll as a student in a first-aid class; spend some productive hours deepening knowledge and experience by learning with a group under a qualified teacher? Your telephone book will give the number of the local Red Cross unit from which you can inquire.

WOUNDS

When there is no heavy bleeding first aid is simple. You apply a clean dressing firmly and this pressure will control any slight bleeding present.

If the injury involved a blow which could have caused a fracture *do not move the damaged part* until you have safeguarded it (see *Fractures*).

1. Get your patient sitting or lying down.
2. Wash your hands (if at all possible).
3. Protect the wound temporarily by keeping it covered with a clean dressing or swab.

   Wash not the wound itself but the skin around the wound with soap and water on just damp pieces of absorbent cotton or clean cloth like a handkerchief. Do this in separate strokes all around, wiping from the wound edge and away from it (see Figure 1). Use a fresh piece of absorbent cotton or fresh surface of cloth for each wipe.

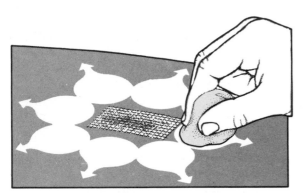

Figure 1 *Use separate strokes and wipe away from the edges when cleaning the area around a wound.*

4. Cover the wound and the washed area with clean material like gauze (from a freshly opened package).
5. Put a thick pad of absorbent cotton or suitable cloth over the material.
6. Bandage the whole firmly (but not tightly). Be careful that the knot of your bandage does not lie over the wound.

   Alternatively, safety pins can be used. Each turn of the bandage should overlap the preceding one by about two thirds of its width.
7. If the wound is a severe one, keep the part at rest (for example put an arm in a sling; see Figure 17).
8. If necessary use antishock measures (see *Shock*).

What to use as dressing

Note that in first aid we do not use antiseptics; this is reserved for treatment proper (i.e., "second aid").

The best cover for the wound is white gauze from a freshly opened package. Failing this, a clean handkerchief or small smooth towel will serve. But handle it carefully— hold it by one corner, let it fall open; then, still handling only by corners, refold it so that what was the inner aspect (unexposed to germs since it was ironed and put away) becomes the outer surface which goes onto the wound.

For the pad you can use absorbent cotton or a thickly folded handkerchief, small towel or even something like a clean sock. The bandage can be improvised from a stocking, necktie, small towel or scarf; use safety pins if it is impracticable to knot it.

Your first-aid kit, however, may contain more suitable items. The quite small superficial wound can be dealt with by ready-prepared *self-adhesive dressings:* the protective layer is partly peeled off the front so that the gauze pad now exposed can be applied without being touched by the fingers.

For larger wounds the prepared sterile dressing is ideal. Taken from its individual package it consists of gauze and pad in one, already attached to its bandage (see Figure 2).

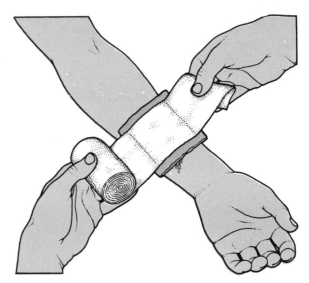

Figure 2 *Ready-prepared dressings, available in individual packages, are useful for larger wounds.*

When something is embedded in the wound

Leave it there. Loose dirt or gravel lying on the surface certainly can be gently brushed away with a clean cloth. But anything stuck in, whether it be a sliver of broken glass or even a knife, should not be moved. The deep point may be lying against an important structure like a large blood vessel or nerve, ready to be damaged by an unplanned pull.

How then to cope? Let your first covering layer lie loosely folded over the object. Then build around this projection a thick firm trough of padding so that the embedded object is deeply protected within it (see Figure 3). This trough will now receive the pressure of the bandage.

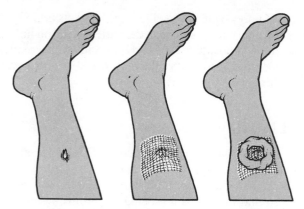

Figure 3 *Do not attempt to remove an object embedded in a wound, but cover with a protective ring of padding before applying a bandage.*

The *ring pad* is a device which can sometimes be used for making this trough. Take a large handkerchief, small towel folded into a thin band or something like a stocking. Make a circle of the right size with one end. Now twist the long free end in and out until it is all used up. You end with a quite firm, fairly thick circle with a small hole in the middle (see Figure 4).

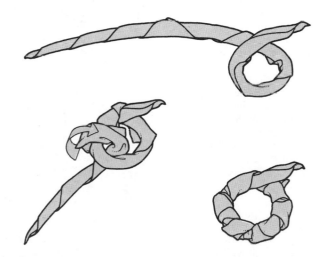

Figure 4 *A ring pad can be improvised from a handkerchief, stocking or even a small towel.*

The tetanus risk

Tetanus (lockjaw) can develop from many wounds, especially if they are contaminated with soil or road dust or if they come from animal bites and if they are deep. The germs are often found in soil or agricultural areas and they thrive on enclosed airless conditions in the tissues. Make sure your patient gets medical advice on being protected against this risk. Following a wound, protection against the development of the disease can be provided by injection of tetanus antitoxin.

Eye wounds

Do not attempt any cleaning with soap and water. Bandage a smooth pad over the eye. If movement hurts the eye it could be wise temporarily to put both eyes at rest by covering the good eye as well since the two eyes move together.

For particles in the eye see *Object in the eye*.

Chest wounds

A penetrating wound of the chest wall can be devastatingly dangerous. As the patient breathes in, air may enter not only through his mouth and windpipe but also through the wound itself. From this point it does not enter the lung but fills up the space between lung and chest wall (see Figure 5).

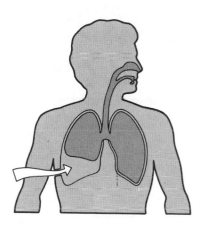

Figure 5 *In a penetrating chest wound, air may fill the space between the lung and chest wall.*

During expiration the loose tissues at the wound tend to close up like a valve flap. At each breath in, more and more air (which cannot get out) fills up that side of the chest. Air under tension compresses and flattens the lung and places an extra burden on the working of the heart. The quicker the wound is sealed, the better.

1. Immediately close the opening in the chest wall with the palm of your hand (see Figure 6). Keep it there while:
2. you have someone prepare as quickly as possible a thick pad (towel, handkerchief) to replace your hand; if alone with the patient, you will have to use your free hand to accomplish this.
3. Bandage this firmly in position to seal off the hole. Use wide bandages, folded towels, stockings or, if available, elastic adhesive strapping. The urgency to close the wound overrides the need to clean the skin around it.
4. Lie the patient *toward the injured side.* This helps by leaving the good side unhindered to do the breathing for both sides. It also reduces the risk of any coughed up blood flowing over into the good lung. If the

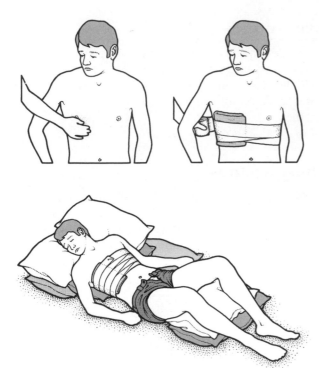

Figure 6 *First seal the chest wound with your palm; after applying a thick bandage, lay the patient toward the injured side; this helps breathing.*

patient becomes short of breath do not let him lie flat, but have him propped up (by blankets or pillows), seated half upward. Breathing becomes easier in an upright position.

Abdominal wounds

Muscles of the abdominal wall are directed mainly from top to bottom (rib cage to pelvis). Their fibers are under some tension like taut rubber bands. If some of them are cut, the hole will tend to widen as the cut ends pull away. This can be avoided if the tension is reduced by "folding" the patient so as to bring pelvis and rib cage nearer to each other.

Lay the patient down with head and shoulders a little

Figure 7 *Use pillows, blankets, jackets, etc., to raise the patient's legs; this relaxes the abdominal muscles and relieves pressure on the wound.*

raised and knees bent, using pillows or blankets (see Figure 7). A good alternative is to have the patient lying on his side in this "folded" position. His head is now low; any vomit he may bring up will flow out of the mouth and he is protected against inspiring it into his windpipe.

BLEEDING

Blood at any wound tends to clot, thereby forming a "stopper" to close up the bleeding vessels. However, for this to happen bleeding must be stopped or sufficiently slowed so that the clot is not being constantly swept away as fast as it tries to form. Simple, slight bleeding will respond this way if the area is treated like a wound with a firmly bandaged pad over a dressing.

However, when bleeding is severe the situation is urgent and attempts at sterility or cleanliness may have to be sacrificed for speed.

General rules

1. At once use your hand either to press hard over the bleeding area or to pinch the wound edges together with fingers and thumb. This pressure must be maintained ten minutes.

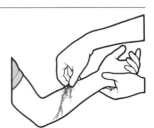

2. Meantime lay the patient down. Whenever possible elevate the bleeding area as this helps a little to reduce the blood flow in it. But be careful not to move a part which may be fractured.

3. As soon as possible replace the hand pressure with that of a firm pad held down by a tight bandage. If, as is likely, orthodox dressings and bandage are not immediately available use what is at hand: socks, handkerchiefs, ties, belt, stockings. *Never leave the wound without any pressure at all.* If you are alone with the patient this may mean keeping one hand on him while you use the other to reach for anything suitable, including clothing.

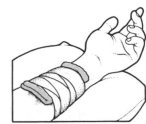

4. Watch the bandage carefully. If it shows blood still oozing through do not remove it but apply more pressure over it with further padding and bandage. In exceptionally difficult cases this may have to be done several times so that the dressing becomes very bulky. Control will generally be achieved.

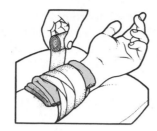

Apply the necessary antishock measures (see *Shock*). Get medical aid or call an ambulance immediately.

Scalp bleeding

Elastic fibers in the scalp tend to pull the wound open so that bleeding is profuse. Furthermore, the vessels come to any point in the scalp from all around it, so that local pressure can prove disappointing. In that case a ring pad (see Figure 4) around the wound with very firm bandaging over this may succeed.

Bleeding about the ear, nose or eye

A blow on the head may transmit its force around the skull and cause a fracture at the base of the skull. This may show up as bleeding from the ear, bruising around the eye, or bleeding from the nose (see Figure 8).

Regard any such bleeding, however slight, with suspicion and obtain medical advice as rapidly as possible (see also *Head injury*).

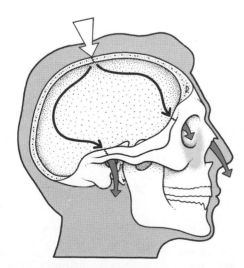

Figure 8 *Bleeding around the ear, nose or eye can result from a blow on the head. Any sign of such bleeding demands urgent medical attention.*

The Ear. The amount of blood to flow out is not likely to be dangerous in itself. But if there has been a blow fracturing the base of the skull (see Figure 9), there now is an open pathway for bacteria from the ear canal to move into the skull cavity and infect the brain.

DO NOT plug the ear; this would allow blood to collect and clot in the canal, forming a nutrient medium in which bacteria rapidly multiply. Instead, let the blood escape by laying the patient down toward the injured side. Lightly cover the whole ear with a dressing and bandage, which will protect against dirt but allow blood to flow out.

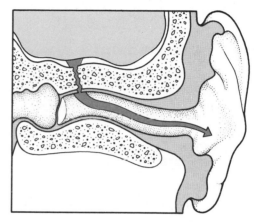

Figure 9 *Bleeding from the ear may be due to a fracture at the base of the skull.*

The Nose. If bleeding follows a blow to the top of the head, consider the possibility of a fracture at the base of the skull. If it follows a blow on the nose, then the nose may be fractured and need treatment but the bleeding is likely to stop soon.

Most nosebleeds happen when a vessel just inside the nostril bursts because of engorgement with inflammation, because of raised blood pressure or because of finger scratching within the nostril. Sit the patient up. Let him pinch the *whole lower soft part* of the nose between his finger and thumb for *ten minutes without letting go.* Some blood may yet flow down the back of the throat; it will do no harm and can be gently spit out. The patient sits with the elbow of the pinching arm on a table, a bowl in front of him and a towel around his neck. Let the window be open to avoid a hot atmosphere which encourages the vessel to enlarge.

If this does not work try a second bout of ten minutes. Tell the patient not to sniff or blow his nose, which could dislodge the clot.

Bleeding tooth socket

Bleeding can begin copiously a few hours after a tooth extraction. Sit the patient up in the same way as for the nosebleed victim. He bites hard on a thick pad of gauze or absorbent cotton bridging over the area of the missing tooth (but not packed into the socket, which could be injurious). The pad will tamp down to a smaller size as it gets wet, so it should start out quite big. The biting pressure is maintained for at least ten minutes, the patient resting his chin hard on his cupped hand, the elbow on the table.

Cut tongue bleeding

The patient sits at a table with his elbow on it. He puts out his tongue and holds the bleeding area firmly within the folds of a handkerchief between thumb and forefinger for at least ten minutes.

Bleeding from cut palm

The patient makes a tight fist over a thick pad in the palm. The whole hand is firmly bandaged in this clenched position (with the thumb *outside* the bandage).

Bleeding from the lungs

Blood may be coughed up as a single streak from the effort of a heavy cough. However, it must never be ignored because it could have a more serious cause. The patient ought to get his doctor's opinion at the first convenient opportunity.

Heavier and more alarming bleeding shows up as bright red blood which *may* be frothy because it is mixed with air. The matter is extremely urgent. Put the patient at rest and *get medical help at once.*

If you know which side the blood is coming from, lay the patient on the affected side. This is because blood may be coughed up from the affected lung; if the patient is lying on the good side, some of this blood may flow back down the air passages into the good lung. Always place the patient so that he is lying with the affected side facing downward.

Bleeding from the stomach

This can arise from irritation of the stomach lining by certain drugs (e.g., aspirin), or from an ulcer or tumor. See the table below for first-aid action.

BURNS

Injury from burns is far more than surface destruction. It is the heat spreading into the deeper tissues and remaining there which does the greatest harm likely to leave permanent scarring and disability. In particular the liquid part of the blood, the plasma, oozes in very large amounts from the blood vessels of the area. Some of this which reaches the surface we see in blisters. But the volume lost from within the circulation is certainly more than that which fills the blister; a great deal swells up the burned tissues. A severe burn which has destroyed skin surface leaves no "roof" to contain the blister and considerable seepage may proceed from this open raw area. There is therefore a high risk of shock developing (see *Shock*).

The first-aid approach is one of countering this process by rapidly cooling the burned area.

If clothes are on fire

Seize the first available thing with which to smother the flames; thick curtain or towel, a rug or even your coat

Bleeding from the stomach

Speed of bleeding	Slow	Fast	Very fast
FEATURES	Almost hidden; the blood passes into the bowels. It may (by action of digestive changes) color the stools black.	Blood accumulating in the stomach is digested to a black mass, like coffee grounds, which may be vomited.	Fresh looking blood is vomited before it has time to change color.
PATIENT'S CONDITION	In time could become anemic and weak.	Feels ill and often nauseated with discomfort or pain.	Weak and shocked.
ACTION TO TAKE	Consult a doctor as soon as possible.	Put the patient to bed and get medical advice at once. Give nothing by mouth.	A severe emergency needing urgent hospital help. Apply antishock measures (see *Shock*). Give nothing by mouth.

which you pull off fast. Wrap it over the flames, pressing down to exclude air.

The panic-stricken child may be running around, thus fanning the flames and making things worse. Get him on the floor so that the burning surface is uppermost with the flames rising away from his body. As you apply the smothering material, do this, if you can, from his head and toward his feet so that flames are directed away from his head (see Figure 10).

Now pull away any bits of clothing which may yet be smoldering, but nothing that is adhering to the skin. Leave untouched that which is burned but extinguished; it may be stuck to the skin.

Adults and older children should be taught that when no help is available they should STOP, DROP to the floor, and ROLL to smother the flames.

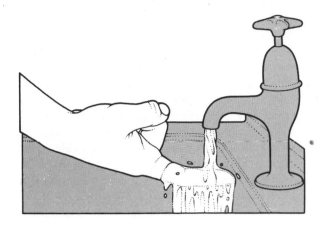

Figure 10 *Use a coat, towel, drape or anything handy to smother burning clothes, pressing down to exclude air; direct the flames away from the head.*

Treating the burn

1. Immediate cooling. Apply cold water at once and liberally (see Figure 11). A burned hand or arm is plunged in a bucket or sink of water. A simple fingertip burn can be held under running water.

A large area of the body, or a part such as a face, cannot easily be plunged in water. Get a thick pad made by something like a folded towel; soak it in cold water and place it over the whole burned area. As this pack tends to dry out and become warm you should repeatedly remoisten and reapply. (One thing you do NOT do is to put the patient in a cold bath. This is too upsetting.)

This wet cooling action gives great relief of pain, and you maintain it for ten minutes. If after this the patient still feels much pain continue for another ten minutes.

Figure 11 *Cool the burned area immediately by immersing in cold, preferably running, water.*

Ordinary cold water gives best results; ice packs or iced water are less efficient.

Even if you reach the patient some 15 to 20 minutes after the burn it is still wise to apply cooling.

2. Dress the burn. If there are any possibly constricting items in the area (rings, garters, bracelets) remove them carefully before swelling creates more problems. Pin on a dry dressing of the cleanest available material to cover the whole burned area as a protection against infection. Bandage firmly but not tightly. Where an arm or leg is involved, encasing the limb in a pillowcase is an excellent improvisation. Keep it elevated, as this reduces the swelling—DO NOT use any creams or antiseptics.

3. Antishock treatment is important (see *Shock*). When the burn is extensive and there may be delay in getting the patient to the hospital, we can break one of the rules: if he is conscious and if he is showing no signs of vomiting get him to drink, to compensate for the fluid and salts lost with the plasma. Prepare tepid water with half a teaspoonful of salt and a quarter of a teaspoonful of baking soda to each pint. He takes half a glass of this in slow sips every 15 minutes. Prompt medical attention is essential however, since extensive burns are life-threatening.

Blisters

If blisters have formed your first-aid measure is not to disturb them: include them under the dressing.

However, when the burn is so slight that medical aid is not necessary but the blister is large enough to be a nuisance if left projecting, you are justified in giving "second aid" by puncturing it. Clean the whole area gently and thoroughly with soap and water or a suitable antiseptic solution. Sterilize a long needle by boiling it in water for ten minutes. Pour away the water without taking the needle from the container and let it cool. Holding only the blunt end, pierce the base of the blister at two diametrically opposite points; gently press it down with sterile or clean material to squeeze out the fluid; apply a dressing and bandage.

Chemical burns

Caustic materials on the skin need immediate washing away with a long-continued, copious but gentle stream of water until you are certain that none remains.

Chemicals in the eye have the extra problem that the patient in pain tends to keep his lids tightly shut. They have to be gently opened to let the water flow over the eyeball and under the lids. Lay him down on the affected side so that the washings do not stream into the other eye or over the rest of his face.

SPRAINS

The sprained joint has had its ligaments and fibers overstretched and partly torn by a sudden forceful movement: for example the inward wrenching of an ankle.

A cold compress is helpful if applied immediately, as it helps to reduce the pain and swelling. Soak a thick pad of material (a folded small towel or a large handkerchief) in cold water; wring it out so that it is just comfortably wet; bandage it on closely with some open-weave material. Keep the joint elevated and at rest. After about 20 minutes the compress can be discarded and you move on to the next stage of support.

Firm support: absorbent cotton or thick pads applied around and interleaved with firm bandaging (a crepe or elastic bandage is useful here). Or you can closely apply firm cushioning by bandaging a cylinder of rolled-up thick material about the joint (see Figure 12).

Be careful not to make the whole so tight that it occludes the blood supply. This risk is greater at the front of the elbow and back of the knee where the vessels run close to the skin. Warn your patient to ease the bandage if the part beyond becomes cold, numb or puffy.

A severe sprain may be difficult to distinguish from a fracture. Whenever there is doubt, the line to take is quite definite: treat it as if it were a fracture.

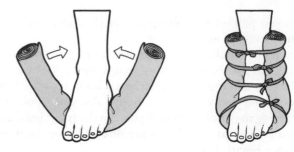

Figure 12 *A roll of thick material can be used to provide support for a sprained ankle joint.*

FRACTURES

The great point about fractures is to suspect them when they are likely—that is, when the patient has received a blow or crush over an area with underlying bone (which is practically anywhere except the abdomen). Some fractures can be severe without showing much or any deformity or disability or even without causing severe pain.

Some fractures may not happen at the point which received the blow. The power of a fall onto the outstretched hand may travel up the arm to jerk and break the collarbone near the shoulder. A falling person may land heavily on the heel and break not the ankle but the thighbone near the hip; this is especially likely in the elderly.

First-aid management

The general rules are extremely straightforward:

1. Warn the patient not to move. And warn bystanders not to move him. The general tendency of the solicitous but uninformed is to try to pick up a fallen victim.

2. Stop any severe bleeding (see *Bleeding*).

3. Dress any wound at once (see *Wounds*), but take care not to move the fracture area. Even a hastily improvised cover is important to minimize the risk of bacteria reaching the fracture.

It may seem that so far you have done nothing specific for the fracture itself. But you have already achieved a lot. You have protected the patient against blood loss and against infection. And by his immobility you have made sure broken bone ends do not become more displaced and do further tissue damage around them.

4. Immobilize the fracture. (If, however, you expect medical or ambulance help to be rapidly available it is wise to do no more and to leave it to the experts.) You immobilize by applying a splint. In some cases you can improvise a splint out of slabs of wood, cardboard, or even magazines and newspapers: a good splint to immobilize an injured forearm, elbow and wrist can be made from a magazine or thick newspaper, tightly rolled and then padded and bandaged. However, the best and ever present splint is the patient's own body: good leg against injured leg or chest wall against injured arm.

Principles of immobilization

Do not move the injured part if you can avoid it. Aim to immobilize not only the fracture area or the whole bone but also the joint at either end of the bone. Bring the good side (for example, the other leg) as a splint alongside the injured one. Between the two parts insert padding (wool, folded towels, scarves) to fill up hollows or prevent chafing where bumps lie against each other. Secure the injured part to the good part firmly enough to prevent movement, with real or improvised bandages. Avoid placing a bandage where you suspect the fracture to be, and tie the knots off on the good side (see Figure 13).

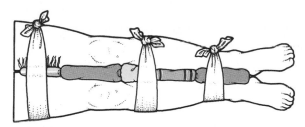

Figure 13 *A fractured leg can be immobilized by splinting it against the good one. Towels, scarves, or similar material can be used as padding.*

Lower jaw fracture

Give primary attention to the problems of the patient who may not be able to speak or swallow while his mouth is filling with blood or saliva. His tongue may have slipped back to obstruct the airway if the damage is severe: in that case keep the jaw forward with your fingers hooked over the teeth. If artificial respiration is needed you will have to use an alternative to the mouth-to-mouth method.

Clear his mouth gently. If he is conscious and his general condition is good, let him sit leaning forward to allow fluid to drain away. If the injury is severe or he is unconscious put him in the Recovery Position (see Figure 24). Throughout, support the jaw until you get your firmly applied bandage to do this (see Figure 14).

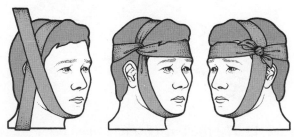

Figure 14 *A fractured lower jaw should be immobilized by a bandage tied as shown above.*

Collarbone fracture

The patient has pain in the shoulder and is likely to support the elbow on the injured side to relieve the pull of the arm on the broken bone. Maintain this support as you apply a sling.

The sling is made from a triangular bandage (its long side about 60 inches) or can be improvised from scarves or towels (see Figure 15).

In the absence of these, improvisation can be made by pinning up a sleeve or the turned-up lower edge of a jacket.

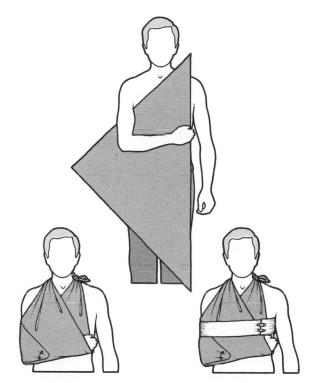

Figure 15 *Use a triangular bandage as a sling to relieve the pull of the arm on the broken collarbone. Keep the forearm sloping slightly up, secure with a knot over the good shoulder and a safety pin near the elbow. A wide bandage to hold the upper arm against the chest completes the immobilization.*

Rib fracture

In simple cases the main feature is painful breathing, not extremely severe, and the fracture tends to heal easily. No special first-aid treatment is needed, except that sometimes the patient gets relief by having the arm of the affected side in a sling. However a physician should be consulted.

For more severe injuries of the chest wall see *Wounds*.

Upper limb fracture

If the elbow can be bent without pain
Put padding in the armpit, and apply a sling, preferably

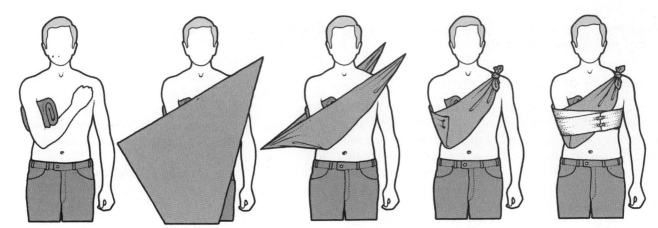

Figure 16 *To immobilize a fractured upper limb: put thick padding (wool, rolled-up towel) in the armpit and against the chest. Carefully bring the arm to the side of the chest with the hand toward* the opposite shoulder. Then apply a sling, using a triangular bandage as shown, or improvising. Give further support by firm broad bandaging of the upper arm to the chest wall.

using a triangular bandage as shown in Figure 16.

If the elbow cannot be bent

Keep the limb straight and secure it by three broad bandages to the side of the body. This patient should travel on a stretcher.

Pelvis fracture

Allow the patient to lie on his back in the position he finds most comfortable. If he wishes to bend the thighs and knees (thus relaxing the pull of muscles on the broken bones) let him do so and support the bent knees with pillows or rolled blankets under them.

If he has a long wait or difficult travel to face, then you should immobilize with two broad, overlapping bandages firmly round the pelvis, padding between the legs, a figure-of-eight bandage around the ankles and bandaging around the knees.

Take great care since a fractured pelvis may be accompanied by severe internal damage, by a fracture of the thighbone or by a fracture of the spine.

Leg and thigh fracture

Immobilize the leg and thigh as shown in Figure 17:
1. Bring the good leg alongside the injured one.
2. Put padding between the legs.
3. Tie a figure-of-eight bandage around the ankles.
4. Bandage the knees together.
5. Bandage just below the fracture site.
6. Bandage around the thighs.

Foot fracture

Carefully and gently remove the patient's shoe and sock; cradle the whole foot and ankle in a pillow or folded blanket firmly bandaged around it, to act as splint. Keep the leg elevated (on pillows or a folded blanket), as this helps to reduce the swelling.

Spine fracture

You must take the suspected fracture of the spine extremely seriously. The ringlike bones of the vertebral column surround the spinal cord; if a disrupted bone fragment were to move against or into the spinal cord it could cause permanent paralysis or loss of feeling to some part of the body, sometimes very extensively. This calamity might not have happened at the time of the fracture itself but improper handling of the patient might cause the bone to shift.

Suspect a fractured vertebra after any forceful fall or blow followed by pain in the neck or back. Immediately tell the patient not to get up, but to lie still. And make sure no bystander tries to move him—it is essential to wait for trained experts to get him on the stretcher.

While you wait, cover him with blankets or coats to keep him warm.

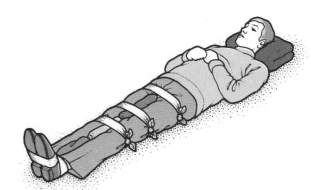

Figure 17 *The fractured leg and thigh are immobilized by bandages around the ankles, knees and thighs, with padding between the legs.*

The mechanics of the spine are such that any "folding up" or bending forward of the vertebral column could push a piece of broken bone against the spinal cord. When it comes to getting this patient on a stretcher, the ambulance attendants may tie his legs together and go through a special lifting routine which keeps him straight and stretched. Or they may use a specially designed stretcher which can slide under him and allow him to be lifted and carried in the position in which he lies.

However, if he is unconscious and at risk from choking through the falling back of his tongue (see Figure 23) this caution to avoid movement does not preclude gentle and careful bending backward of the head at the neck to open his airway. In some circumstances you may use an improvised splinting collar to keep his neck protected (see *Road accidents*). But do not move him into the Recovery Position.

You may be in the unhappy position of having to move the patient from an urgently dangerous situation (fire, exposed mountain slopes, water immersion). If time allows, get three or four helpers who will share the support of the patient evenly so that he can be lifted without folding or twisting his body or turning his head. One helper should cradle the head between his palms with outstretched fingers extending to the shoulders. Lift together at a prepared signal; carry him the minimal distance compatible with safety and lower him to a firm surface still in the same position.

Skull fracture

See *Head Injury*.

DISLOCATIONS

The features of a dislocation are very much like those of a fracture. As a first-aider you do not face the problem of making the exact diagnosis. Treat it like a fracture. In any case many dislocations do not happen alone, but are accompanied by some bone breakage in the joint area.

SHOCK

In first-aid terms shock refers not to emotional upsets but to a physical condition, a failure of the heart and circulation which follows severe injuries. It is caused by a loss of blood fluid. In *severe hemorrhage* the reduced amount of blood in the body results in a weakened heartbeat and inadequate supply of oxygen and other chemicals to all the tissues. In particular the brain is sensitive to this lack; the centers in the brain which automatically regulate respiration, blood pressure and heart action no longer work adequately. In this way, even if the bleeding is controlled, a vicious circle of increasing failure may have been set in action (see Figure 18). With

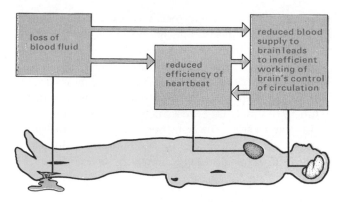

Figure 18 *The vicious circle of developing shock is sparked off by severe blood loss.*

large *wounds and bruises* there may be extensive blood loss deep within the tissues. Although still inside the body, it has escaped from the blood vessels; it is stagnating and taking no part in the circulation. *Fractures* of large bones involve damage not just to the bones themselves but also to the muscles and other organs which are packed around the bones, causing disruption of blood vessels and loss of blood from the circulation. Burns themselves can create blood loss in an extensive, if more disguised way by dilating the blood vessels of the injured area, and making them "porous" so that the plasma—the liquid component of the blood—oozes out copiously (see Figure 19).

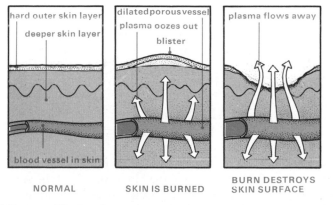

Figure 19 *By damaging surface tissue and dilating underlying blood vessels, burns can cause extensive loss of plasma and lead to shock.*

The patient in shock

One who has suffered any of these injuries in a severe way is therefore at risk of developing shock: a low blood volume, a failing heartbeat, a poor flow of what blood remains circulating, and inadequate nutrition to all parts of the body—specifically to brain, heart and lungs. This steadily worsening condition could be described as a "running down of life forces."

The badly shocked patient is pale, cold, sweating; his pulse and his breathing are fast and weak. he feels faint, nauseated, thirsty. He may become restless or irrational and eventually comatose and unconscious. In this stage, first aid is of minimal help; he needs the full technique of hospital treatment, including a blood transfusion.

We must realize that immediately after the injury he may still appear tough and resistant, but that inside him the machinery of shock has been set in motion. How long it will take for him to show the signs depends on such factors as his original strength and the rate and amount of blood loss. It may be a matter of a few minutes or several hours.

Preventing shock

As first-aiders we cannot treat fully developed shock. But we can prevent or minimize its development. Happily the actions for this are very simple. Unhappily their very simplicity often makes the first-aider overlook them. Take these measures seriously and act on them even if your patient seems in fairly good shape—do not wait for him to deteriorate.

1. Stop bleeding at once (see *Bleeding*).

2. Ensure rest and position. Treat the patient where he is. Do not transport him unless you are in a danger area (fire, fumes, collapsing building). In a traffic-laden road have someone divert the cars.

Loosen tight clothing (belts, suspenders, collars, corsets). Keep the patient laying down with his head low and his legs raised some 1 to 2 ft.; this gradient helps a little to send blood to the heart and brain.

Have him on his side to safeguard his airway (see Figures 20 and 24). However, beware of moving a patient who may have a fracture—especially if his back is involved. In some cases it is best to keep him in the position in which you have found him.

3. Keep him warm with loose coverings of blankets or coats (see Figure 21). See that he is protected from heat loss both above and below the body. But do *not* add electric blankets or hot water bottles. The extra heat might improve his color by dilating the blood vessels of the skin, but that would mean drawing away toward the surface a large volume of blood from the depths of the body where it is needed for the essential organs of life.

4. Relieve discomfort. Reducing both pain and mental anxiety plays a great role in warding off shock. First aid does not permit giving medicine or tablets without medical authority. But the immediate dressing of wounds and immobilization of fractures are important pain relievers. Talk to your patient with calm confidence, explaining your actions as reassuringly as possible. Answer any questions as accurately as you can, dwelling on the positive and comforting aspects only. Tactfully but firmly clear away any agitated or demoralizing bystanders (see Figure 22). Give them things to do which take them off the scene.

Never whisper to others near your patient and remember

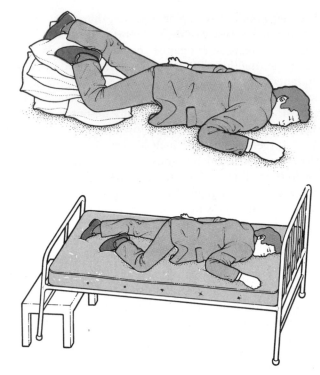

Figure 20 *Lay the patient on his side in the Recovery Position and raise the legs to send blood toward the brain. See also Figure 24.*

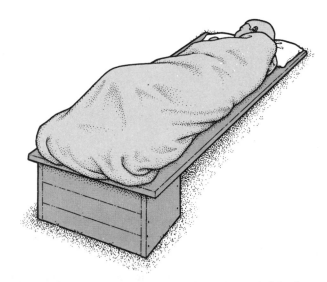

Figure 21 *Cover the patient loosely with blankets or coats to prevent undue heat loss.*

that an apparently unconscious man may be able to overhear what is said near him. Guard your speech.

5. Give nothing by mouth. Do not give hot tea or coffee. The patient may vomit. Anything he brings up may then be aspirated into his windpipe and choke him, especially if he is comatose or later under anesthesia for emergency surgery. If he is thirsty you can relieve this by giving him a rolled up and moistened handkerchief to suck.

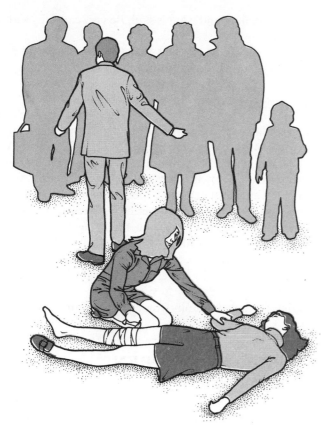

Figure 22 *Try to keep away any bystanders who could be distressing to the patient—and remember that an apparently unconscious person can often hear what is said by people nearby.*

Brandy or whisky are dangerous as they can dilate skin vessels and draw blood away from the body depths.

Even a single cigarette can have a deleterious effect by reducing the oxygen capacity of the blood and by reducing the blood supply to the heart muscle.

UNCONSCIOUSNESS
The risk of suffocation

Your first-aid problem with an unconscious patient is not to find out why he is in this condition, but to protect him from the very real risk of choking. Abnormal unconscious-

ness (as distinct from sleep) allows no protective reaction from the patient if his airway gets blocked—blood, vomit or even saliva in the mouth may run into the windpipe of a man lying on his back. Dentures can become misplaced and cause blockage.

However, it is the patient's own tongue which forms the greatest threat. Attached by its base to the jaw bone, the tongue is free to move backward and forward.

It is a muscle and like all muscles loses tone and becomes limp in the unconscious person. Were he to be lying on his back, the flaccid tongue could easily fall against the back of the throat and block the air entry to the windpipe (see Figure 23).

You can counter these hazards by:
1. Clearing the mouth.
2. Pulling his jaw forward and bending his head right back—actions which pull the tongue away from the back of the throat.
3. Positioning him with his head low to one side, so that any fluid in the mouth can flow out.

Action on the unconscious person

1. Is he breathing? If not begin resuscitation at once (see *Resuscitation*).

2. Is he trying to breathe but failing because he is choked? Immediately sweep a finger deeply all around his mouth to clear out any material lying there. Bend his head back as far as it will go and keep it thus. (This carries the calculated risk of aggravating any damage to his neck, but that risk is small and the risk of death from choking is high). Generally the neck movement is enough and the additional clearance by pushing the jaw forward is not needed.

3. Stop any bleeding (see *Bleeding*).

4. Check for possible fractures (unless the nature of the case excludes their likelihood). You want to move him into a safe position, but you must be sure that you do not

Figure 23 *To avoid the risk of suffocation, bend the unconscious patient's head back and pull his jaw forward: this simple measure prevents the flaccid tongue from blocking air entry to the windpipe.*

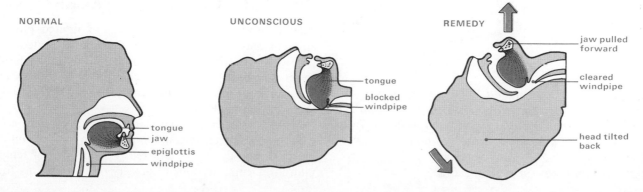

NORMAL   UNCONSCIOUS   REMEDY

tongue
jaw
epiglottis
windpipe

tongue
blocked
windpipe

jaw pulled
forward
cleared
windpipe
head tilted
back

first have to immobilize a broken bone (see *Fractures*). It is difficult to detect a fracture in a person who is normally dressed and unable to respond to touch or to questions. However, you do your best by palpating (feeling) carefully but firmly all over without moving any part. Unless you can see a gross deformity you have to be guided by feeling for irregularities, comparing the knobs and contours of both sides.

5. Put the patient in the Recovery Position—the name given to the position, with the patient lying on his side, which ensures free breathing and the flowing out of any fluid coming into the mouth (see Figure 24).

First empty his pockets and take off any wristwatch. Tuck his near hand and arm against his trunk and the foot on the other side over the nearer ankle. Now kneel at his side. Put one hand protectively over his face as you pull on his hip with the other hand, rolling him toward you.

6. Dress any open wounds (see *Wounds*).

7. Take antishock measures (see *Shock*).

Do not reserve the Recovery Position for the unconscious only. You will wisely use it for those who might become unconscious, the severely wounded, those who have head injuries, the poisoned or those who have just been afflicted with a stroke. It is not only a safe position, but a comfortable and relaxing one.

If the patient smells of alcohol this is no reason to think he is unconscious because of intoxication. The drink may have had nothing to do with his condition. Or it may be only an indirect factor, such as having made him fall and damage his skull.

Remember that a man who appears to be senseless may yet hear and understand what is said. Be very cautious with your speech.

Finally, it should be obvious that you never attempt to give anything to drink to someone who is unconscious.

FAINTING

If your patient is feeling faint and still conscious, help him to lie down at once. Raise his legs if you can, loosen any tight clothes and get him covered. Ask him to relax and to take deep breaths slowly. The attack generally eases and the patient wants to struggle up. Do not let him do so until you are sure his color and strength are back to normal. Then let him change slowly from the lying to the erect position. Give him a drink of water.

Where lying down is not possible, as in the auditorium of a theater, tell the patient to bend down low, with his head between his legs.

If he has fainted away fully, treat him as for unconsciousness (see *Unconsciousness*).

SEIZURES IN CHILDREN

Often such seizures occur as the child is developing a feverish infection. The nervous system of small children not only has less efficient body heat control but also is more sensitive to high temperatures.

The child, who may have seemed out of sorts and with poor appetite suddenly goes unconscious and stiff with head held back and eyes rolled up. This is not the time to rush to telephone the doctor. Stay with the child; he needs your help during the fit.

Turn him into the Recovery Position (see Figure 24), and clear any fluid from his mouth. If he seems very feverish remove his clothes and reduce his temperature by an electric fan, by fanning with sheets or paper, or by gentle sponging with cold water. You aim not to bring the temperature back to normal but only to reduce it a degree or two—that is, to below the level which initiated the fit.

Now dry the young patient and cover him. By now he probably is conscious. This is the time to send for medical help.

BREATH-HOLDING ATTACKS

The small child over one year old of limited physical strength may use a psychological game presented as a physical move when he is frustrated and cannot get adults to let him have his own way. He holds his breath and consciously or subconsciously enjoys the concern caused to those in charge of him.

He interrupts crying and forceful breathing with a full expiration and gets more and more blue in the face, until he may lose consciousness and fall. It is a form of temper tantrum. Demonstrations of anxiety or punishments from

THE RECOVERY POSITION

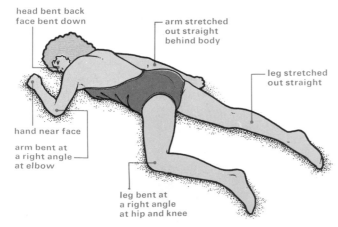

head bent back
face bent down

arm stretched out straight behind body

leg stretched out straight

hand near face

arm bent at a right angle at elbow

leg bent at a right angle at hip and knee

Figure 24 *Everyone should know how to put a patient in the Recovery Position. In this position the injured person can breathe freely, and fluids such as blood or vomit can escape from the mouth, lessening the risk of choking. Your knowledge of this maneuver could save a patient's life.*

the grown-up serve only to reinforce his behavior.

The attack can be interrupted if the adult both appears to be unconcerned and does something unusual which astonishes or interests the child. Not every parent can suddenly stand on his or her head and sing (which would be an excellent move) but immediately turning your back on the child and jumping noisily clapping your hands or slamming a door could be effective (see Figure 25). He will stop his act to see just what is happening.

You then go to him in a friendly way and divert his attention by finding something pleasant to occupy his mind. But you do not give in to the original demand.

EPILEPSY

As there are several forms of epilepsy, and attacks tend to vary with the individual, only an "average" type will be described. This is the "grand mal" form with loss of consciousness and jerking. The following table outlines its various stages and the first-aid action you should take.

Rarely a patient has a succession of epileptic fits, following each other rapidly. This is a dangerous situation which needs immediate help from a doctor.

Stage	Possible duration	First-aid action
Attacks usually come without warning. However, some sufferers get a brief premonition accompanied by hesitation and pallor.	A very few seconds	Immediately have the patient lie down.
Most lose consciousness and fall very suddenly. They are silent but a few give one brief cry as they fall. They lie still and rigid, often with limbs extended and head bent back. The mouth is clenched, the breath is held and complexion is blue.	30 to 60 seconds	Loosen tight clothing. Guard the airway by positioning the head (see Figure 23).
Still unconscious, the patient begins twitching and this passes into hard sharp jerking of muscles. These convulsions may knock the limbs against nearby furniture or walls, may make the patient bite his tongue or be incontinent of bladder and wet himself. His mouth may fill with frothy saliva.	20 to 60 seconds	Do not try to restrain the jerking but quickly push aside furniture or pack a buffer (cushions, rolled up towel or coat) between limb and surface knocked. Clear froth from the mouth. Remove false teeth if you can. Place a *soft* article (handkerchief pad) in the corner of the mouth to prevent the teeth injuring the tongue. Continue to guard the airway.
The jerking ceases and the patient lies unconscious and relaxed.	2 to 5 minutes	Turn the patient into the Recovery Position (see Figure 24), but be wary lest he has sustained a fracture in his fall.
Recovering consciousness the patient is at first dazed, then fully aware of what has happened.		Do not let him rise too soon. Let him rest and sleep. Check for signs of injury from the fall. If the attack happened in the street or away from home you should send the patient to the hospital by ambulance.

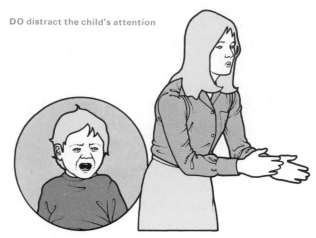

DON'T get upset or angry   DO distract the child's attention

Figure 25 *Attacks of breath holding are best dealt with by distracting the child's attention rather than by showing signs of anger, anxiety or concern.*

HYSTERICAL ATTACKS

Hysteria is a physical expression of a mental anguish. Society is more prone to sympathize with a bodily than with a mental disturbance. An unhappy patient may chronically or suddenly hate his frustrations, his work, his relations. The office worker may be rebelling against a mode of life from which he wants to escape, the housewife may feel imprisoned by her home tasks.

What may seem an unimportant event may trigger off the attack. A screaming and shouting session could be apposite, but would receive little pity. The cry for help, the advertisement of unhappiness is disguised as a demonstration of acute or chronic illness which is likely to create sympathy.

The hysterical man or woman is not deliberately pretending. He has no true understanding of the mechanism at play and believes genuinely in the truth of his symptoms. He is frightened by them.

An acute hysterical attack can take many forms. The patient says he cannot breathe (while breathing hard all the time), that he is paralyzed (while moving), that he has uncontrollable shaking (while interrupting the movements as he speaks). He may collapse and moan but become normal as he assesses a change in the situation by the arrival of a newcomer. He may appear unconscious but be noted to follow the actions of bystanders or to have a good firm muscle tone; an arm lifted and let go does not fall back flaccidly but is kept held up and gently lowered by the patient.

Treatment depends on realizing that:

1. *The patient is "advertising."* The more public he has the more he will want to advertise. Clear away all bystanders whose presence only encourages the performance to continue.

2. *The patient is frightened.* Do not scold him, do not slap him, do not throw water over him. Speak to him very firmly but also reassuringly. Do not say that his symptoms are false. Tell him that however unpleasant they may be they are transitory and will rapidly disappear.

3. *The patient feels lost and confused.* Give him no requests or suggestions but very definite instructions. Explain that if he lies or sits down and has a drink of water (or coffee or tea) the symptoms will ease.

You may have to reassure overanxious friends and relatives that your hard attitude is no sign of cruelty but a definite attempt to help. If in any doubt, however, play safe and get medical advice.

In any case, once the attack is over, a doctor is needed to help the patient to recognize and deal with the real sources of his trouble.

STROKES

A stroke is the loss of function of some part of the brain caused by an interruption of its blood supply. The blood vessel in that area may have ruptured or it may have become blocked by a clot. The old alternative term "apoplexy" has been replaced by that of "cerebrovascular accident."

The results of a stroke depend on the part of the brain involved and the speed with which this disruption to its circulation occurred. Minor weakness of some part of the body, poor arm or leg action, altered speech, loss of bladder control, paralysis of one side of the body, difficulty in swallowing, or total unconsciousness—any one of these can happen. If you suspect that your patient has just had a stroke, be cautious. It may be progressive. The victim who finds that his hand grasp has become inexplicably weak and clumsy may be at the beginning of a mishap which rapidly worsens to make a leg and arm functionless.

Unless he cannot be moved, do not keep the stroke patient dressed and sitting. Get him resting in bed and call for medical help. Watch him carefully to see if his state worsens. In severe cases he should be placed in the Recovery Position (see Figure 24) until the doctor arrives.

OBJECT IN THE EYE

Tell the patient to stop rubbing his eye—which almost certainly he has been doing, making the irritation worse.

Wash your hands. Moisten the corner of a clean handkerchief and roll it into a point. You will use this to touch and lift out the object.

Seat the patient in a good light and stand behind him, bending his head up against you. This keeps his head firm and gives you a clear vision of the eye.

The object may lie on the white part of the eye. If the attempt to pick it off fails to move it, it is probably embedded. Do not try again. If the object is anywhere within the colored circle (see Figure 26), you should leave it alone. This area is important to vision and could be damaged by inexperienced handling. Cover the eye with a clean pad and let a doctor deal with it.

Generally the object has moved under one or other lid, often into the corner. Look under the lower lid. The patient looks up while you evert the lid, pulling it down by the pressure of two fingers (see Figure 27).

To look under the upper lid, have the patient look down while you evert the lid over a matchstick held across the "hinge" of the lid (see Figure 28). Grasping the edge of the lid firmly is less uncomfortable for the patient than if you try a light and slippery hold.

OBJECT IN THE EAR

Do not attempt its removal as this could be dangerous without special training and instruments.

The only exception is a very fine thread or an insect, which can be intensely irritating to the patient. Lay the patient down with the ear uppermost and pour in a little tepid water or olive oil. Be very careful not to overheat the fluid. The insect will float to the top and can be wiped away.

The method is more likely to succeed if you pull the top of the ear lobe up and back; this straightens out the external ear canal.

If there is any chance that the eardrum is perforated do not pour the fluid in; it could pass into and harm the middle ear.

OBJECT IN THE NOSE

Children in "experimental" moods often push objects up the nostril. A bean or pea tends to absorb moisture and swell and then be very difficult to dislodge.

Never try poking the object out from the depths, you would only drive it in further. Let a doctor, using special forceps, deal with it.

A small object can sometimes be expelled by careful nose blowing. Avoid hard blowing, however, which might cause painful air pressure inside the nose and sinuses. If there is any problem, see your physician at once.

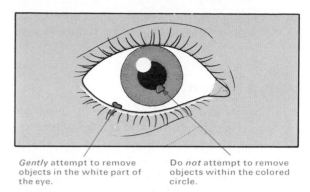

Gently attempt to remove objects in the white part of the eye.

Do *not* attempt to remove objects within the colored circle.

Figure 26

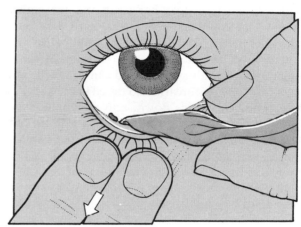

Figure 27 *Using two fingers, gently pull down the lower eyelid while the patient looks up.*

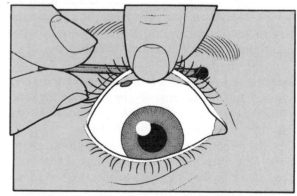

Figure 28 *Carefully pull up the upper eyelid as the patient looks down. A matchstick can help you to grip the lid as shown.*

CHOKING

Air entry into the windpipe may be blocked by:

1. An object at the back of the throat (solid food, dentures, mud).

2. The tongue in the unconscious may also block (see *Unconsciousness*).

3. Compression from outside (cord, strangulation, hanging).

4. An object within the windpipe itself.

The victim reacts by hard coughing attempts to expel the object. Muscles in the windpipe tend to tighten around and hold it.

First-aid action

1. Open the patient's mouth widely; with your finger, feel deeply for anything at the back of the throat and scoop it clear.

2. The object may be too deep for you to reach. If the patient's condition is good and he is coughing well, advise him to breathe deeply and very slowly: this helps to relax the spasm of the windpipe.

If the obstruction does not clear and the patient is becoming blue and weak, give several hard slaps between his shoulder blades. In the case of an adult patient, this is best done when he is standing up; if he is unable to stand, roll him over onto his side. A child can be held bent face downward over your forearm and raised knee. A very small child can be held upside down: grip the ankles and feet firmly with one hand, and give the slaps with the other.

3. If the patient has lost consciousness and is limp, give mouth-to-mouth artificial respiration. In his state the windpipe spasm is now relaxed and your air can pass around the object without appreciable danger of driving it further down.

Abdominal thrust for total obstruction

Sometimes trying to swallow a badly chewed lump of food results in total obstruction. The struggling patient is quite silent, unable to speak or cough and there is no whistling sound of any air moving in the windpipe.

Thrusting hard on the upper abdomen, between the navel and the lower end of the breastbone may give a popgun result, forcing air from the lungs up the windpipe to propel the object up and out. This procedure is known as the *Heimlich maneuver* (see Figure 29).

Press the upper part of the abdomen hard, inward and upward. One thrust may succeed, but several may be needed. You may have to give artificial respiration after this (see *Resuscitation*).

If the patient vomits after this procedure immediately turn him on one side and clear his mouth.

You must get medical advice after the rescue: rarely some internal damage may occur from the thrust. The risk of this is minimized by the correct positioning of your hands.

HANGING

As you rescue the patient, relieve the pull on his body by supporting his legs. Control his fall as the cord is cut, and ease the tight band around the neck. You may have to give artificial respiration (see *Resuscitation*).

THE HEIMLICH MANEUVER
(abdominal thrust for choking)

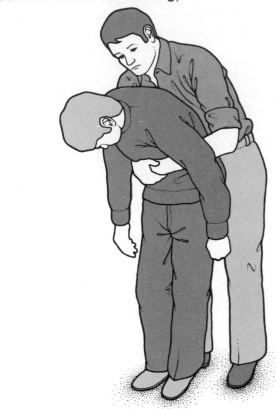

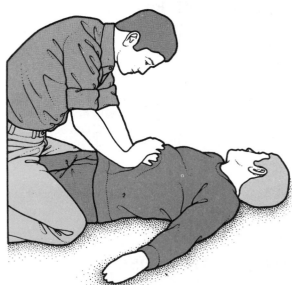

Figure 29 *This maneuver can save lives and should be learned by everyone.* **If the patient is standing or sitting:** *wrap your arms around his waist from behind. Put one fist with its thumb edge on the upper abdomen: your other hand clutches the fist. Thrust hard, inward and upward.*
If the patient is lying down: *get him quickly on his back. Kneel astride his hips. Thrust with the heel of one hand covered by the other hand.*

ASTHMA

In an asthmatic attack three main things happen to the tubes which form the airways of the lungs: (1) the airway tube tenses and contracts; (2) its lining becomes much thicker; and (3) this lining secretes thick mucus. All these narrow and block the tube, causing wheezing and a very difficult passage of air.

There are three likely "trigger" factors which can set this off in the asthma-prone patient: allergy, infection and emotion. However the attack may have begun, the emotional factor plays a large part; discomfort, anxiety and fear cannot help but build up in the victim who finds his breathing progressively more obstructed.

Your first-aid contribution will be to get the patient to relax physically and mentally and to position him to help the mechanics of breathing. A calm attitude of confidence, with advice clearly given, helps greatly.

If he has any tablets or inhalers prescribed for such attacks make sure he uses them. But be certain this is done according to the doctor's instructions and do not let him take overdoses.

Let in fresh (but not cold) air and loosen tight clothing. Do not let him crouch forward. Tell him to hold his back upright, either sitting or standing. He must relax all other parts of the body (limbs, neck, face).

Advise him to concentrate breathing movements from the lower part of the chest and waist level. Most patients struggle to move the upper part of the chest, with poor results.

HEART ATTACKS

"Heart attack" is a term which covers many types of sudden failure of the efficient beating of the heart muscle. For the first-aider there are two main forms: coronary occlusion and acute congestive failure.

Coronary occlusion

The heart muscle gets its blood supply from its own vessels, the coronary arteries, and not from the blood within its chambers. If one of these vessels suddenly becomes blocked by a clot, that part of the heart muscle which the vessel serves is deprived of blood and this is felt as pain—although the underlying mechanisms responsible for the pain are not fully understood.

As a rule this pain is extremely severe, like a tight vice gripping the chest, and it may spread to the neck, shoulder or arm. The patient collapses, is pale or blue, breathless and sweating, with a fast weak pulse. Sometimes he loses consciousness. Death may result.

However, please note that coronary occlusion can occur with pain of lesser severity and no marked evidence of shock. Such an attack may be mistaken for a digestive upset. The symptoms may be minor but the threat to the heart is nevertheless very real. For safety, in case of doubt, assume the worst.

If the patient loses consciousness check whether the heart is beating. If it is not proceed immediately to resuscitation (see *Resuscitation*). But never try heart compression if the heart is still beating, however weakly or irregularly.

If the patient is conscious bear in mind that anxiety or fear produce body chemicals which can be extremely detrimental to the functioning of the heart muscle. Give sympathy with an attitude of calm confidence which can help to reassure.

Send for medical aid, with oxygen if possible. Let the doctor (but not the patient) realize the degree of emergency you suspect.

Put the patient at full rest, with clothing loosened. If his breathing is difficult he should be sitting up, propped on a bed rest with pillows. Otherwise he should be lying down. If he is sweating mop his face dry. Keep helpers from fussing or crowding him, which could add to his anxiety. Have the room warm but let in fresh air.

Acute congestive heart failure

In this case a fatigued or "worn" heart muscle is suddenly unable to propel blood adequately. There results congestion of blood in the lungs, whose air sacs become filled with plasma (the liquid part of blood) and some red cells which ooze from the lung vessels.

This can happen as the patient is asleep. He wakes up very breathless, with a "bubbly" chest, each breath making a wet sound, different from the hard wheeze of asthma; he may cough up pinkish frothy fluid. He is distressed but not shocked, nor in pain.

Sit him supported in an upright position; be calm and reassuring, allow in fresh air, and immediately send for a doctor; this is the best you can do.

RESUSCITATION

Resuscitation consists of restoring life to someone who is near death because:

1. His breathing has stopped; but his heart is still beating; you give artificial respiration.

2. His breathing and his heartbeat have stopped; you have to give both artificial respiration and heart compression.

Note that the heart can beat for a short time after breathing has ceased, but that if the heart has stopped so has breathing. So you never give heart compression alone but have to combine it with artificial respiration.

Resuscitation may be needed:

—after asphyxia
—after drowning
—after electrocution

—after some heart attacks when the beat stops
—after some forms of poisoning which affect the nervous control of heart and lungs, or the ability of the blood to carry oxygen.

> **When resuscitation is needed you must act very fast; however, never jump to wrong conclusions. It is harmful to try it on someone who has "collapsed" but is still concious, or on the unconscious man who is breathing. Your efforts would interfere with the still active respiratory and cardiac work of the victim.**

Summary of method

Airway: position the patient so as to get his airway clear
Breathing: breathe the air from your lungs into his mouth, which will fill his lungs with air.
Circulation: if his color does not now improve and his pulse is absent you add heart compression.

Airway—very rapidly:
1. Turn the patient on his back.
2. With one finger scoop into his mouth to check for and clear any blocking matter, such as slipped dentures, mud or vomit.
3. Cupping one hand under his neck and lifting it slightly, tilt his head back as far as you can. With the palm of the other hand pinch the lower end of his nose shut; this will prevent air blown into his mouth from escaping through the nose (see Figure 30).

If the mouth has not fallen open move your hand from the neck to pull at the lower jaw and so open the mouth. Be careful not to let your fingers impede the lip area where your mouth will settle and not to let the edge of your hand press on the victim's throat.

All these operations, described here in detailed steps, are really done in one quick movement.

Breathing
1. Take a deep breath in.
2. Open your mouth wide and seal it over and around the patient's mouth (see Figure 31).
3. Breathe out into the patient, steadily and fully—but not violently. You should see his chest rise as air enters his lungs.
4. Lift your head away from the patient, turning it toward his chest which now you should see sinking as the air comes out. At the same time you take another breath in.

As soon as the patient's lungs have emptied repeat stages 2, 3 and 4. Timing therefore is by the rise and fall of the

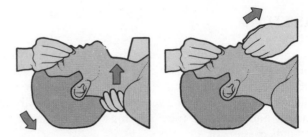

Figure 30 *With one hand under the patient's neck, tilt his head back; pinch nostrils shut. Then pull the lower jaw to open his mouth.*

Figure 31 *Breathe in; seal your mouth over and around the patient's mouth. Then breathe out steadily and fully into the patient's mouth.*

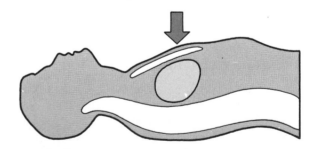

Figure 32 *In cardiac compression, depressing the breastbone squeezes the heart against the spine, forcing blood into the circulation.*

chest. However, *give the first five breaths rapidly* so as to build up the patient's oxygen quickly. After that you maintain the natural rate.

Do not blow hard. This could damage the patient's lungs or fill his stomach with air or make him vomit. If he vomits, turn his head to one side and clear his mouth at once.

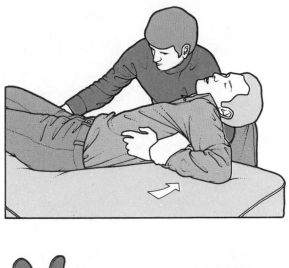

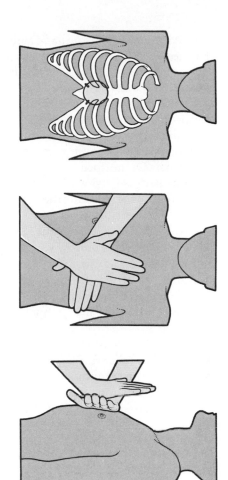

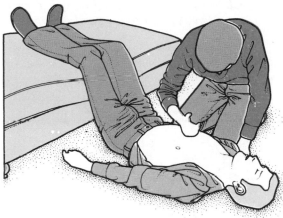

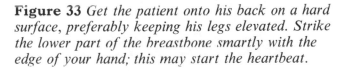

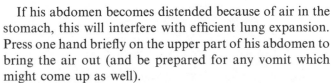

Figure 33 *Get the patient onto his back on a hard surface, preferably keeping his legs elevated. Strike the lower part of the breastbone smartly with the edge of your hand; this may start the heartbeat.*

Figure 34 *It is vital to apply pressure at the correct point—the lower part of the breastbone. Press with the heel of one hand crossed by the heel of the other, keeping the fingers clear of the chest.*

If his abdomen becomes distended because of air in the stomach, this will interfere with efficient lung expansion. Press one hand briefly on the upper part of his abdomen to bring the air out (and be prepared for any vomit which might come up as well).

Whenever you have had to interrupt breathing into the patient, resume with the first five quick breaths.

Circulation

If artificial respiration is successful, the oxygen you breathe into the patient is distributed around the body by his bloodstream and his color improves. However, if after the first five quick breaths there is no improvement this indicates that the oxygen is not being carried around, because there is no circulation of the blood—that is, the heart is not beating. In addition to the unchanged color, two other features can confirm this:

—you cannot feel a pulse beat at the neck or wrist
—the pupils of his eyes are widely dilated

You must now at once turn to giving cardiac compression. The principle is to depress the breastbone (sternum) against the heart (see Figure 32). This pushes the heart against the backbone and squeezes blood from it into the circulation. By continuing this rhythmically you are giving an artificial heartbeat.

Sometimes the nonbeating heart muscle can be activated by a sharp blow over it on the chest wall.

Acting fast, your technique now is:

1. Get the patient onto a hard surface. If he is on a soft couch or mattress pull him carefully to the floor. If possible keep his legs on the bed or get them raised (see Figure 33), *but do not do this if it delays the next steps.*

2. Give two hard smart slaps with the edge of your hand onto the lower third of the breastbone. This might start the heartbeat. If it does not, proceed to heart compression.

3. Kneel by the patient. Positioning your hands is very important: pressure has to be at the lower third of the

breastbone. Put the "heel" of one hand here and cross it with the "heel" of the other hand. But make certain that only the "heel" is pressing. Keep the fingers well up and off the chest wall (see Figure 34). This reduces the risk of damage to ribs and to internal organs.

4. Rock forward smoothly, keeping your arms straight, to thrust down firmly (not jerkily)—depressing the breastbone against the heart; it can move down as much as 2 inches. Do not bend your elbows; let the weight of your body do the work (see Figure 35).

5. Rock back to release the pressure: the breastbone will rise again.

6. Repeat steps 4 and 5 rhythmically to give one compression a second, checking by your watch. Keep your hands in position all the time.

But you must alternate artificial respiration with heart compression. Give five compressions and immediately follow by one long breath, then five compressions again and so on (see Figure 36).

If you have a helper, let one of you attend to the heart. The other, kneeling on the other side by the patient's head, watches and waits to give one mouth-to-mouth respiration as soon as the five compressions are over—the moment that the chest has flattened the first helper begins compression again.

How long should you continue?

Carry on resuscitation until a physician arrives or other professional help is at hand to advise. A doctor may pronounce the patient dead, or—hopefully—the patient may begin to breathe for himself.

When the patient does breathe spontaneously this may be feeble or irregular. If necessary, add an occasional small breath from yourself.

Once his own breathing is good put him in the Recovery Position (see Figure 24). Remain by him, watching closely in case he fails and you have to resume resuscitation.

Get him to the hospital as soon as possible.

Resuscitating children

Small children. Use the mouth-to-mouth-and-nose method, sealing your lips around both mouth and nose (see Figure 37). Blow only just enough to let the chest rise. The natural rise and fall of the chest is likely to be higher than in adults, about 20 to 30 a minute. Heart: use only one hand or two fingers (see Figure 38). Increase the rate to 80 a minute.

Babies. Respiration—give gentle puffs only. The rate is likely to be 30 or 40 a minute. Heart: press in the center of the breastbone (not the lower part). Use only one finger (Figure 39). Increase the rate to 100 a minute. It is essential not to use undue force when resuscitating babies and infants, as this could cause damage.

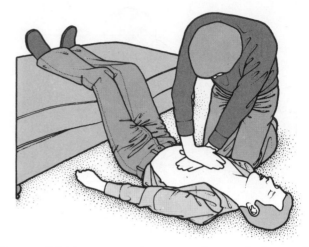

Figure 35 *Keep your arms straight; rock forward to thrust down firmly onto the breastbone.*

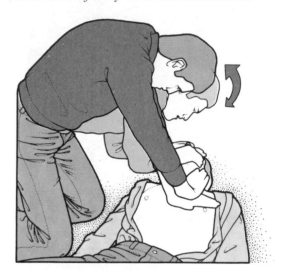

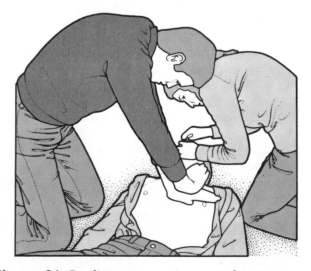

Figure 36 *Cardiac compression must be given alternately with artificial respiration. Always give five compressions followed by one long breath, whether you are acting alone or have a helper.*

Figure 37 *When resuscitating small children, seal your lips around the child's mouth and nose.*

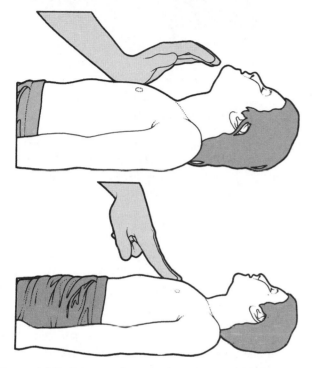

Figure 38 *Use one hand only or two fingers to perform cardiac compression on small children.*

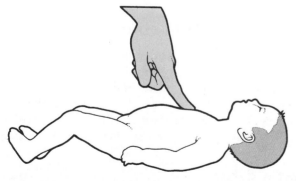

Figure 39 *For babies, use only one finger.*

IMPORTANT
Resuscitation is best learned in first-aid classes under a qualified instructor. It should be practiced on a manikin or dummy only. You must never practice on someone else.

ELECTRIC SHOCK

1. When the patient is in contact with electricity

Do *not* touch him: you too may receive an electric shock or even be electrocuted. *Pull the plug out at once.* If this is not possible: *wrench the plug free by the insulated cord, or turn off the power.* If this is not possible: *use a dry nonconducting material to push or knock the patient from his contact* (see Figure 40).

Never use metal. Use a wooden stick, a thick cushion, a rapidly folded coat, a chair, a wooden pole.

You may have difficulty and need to use traumatic force if the patient is holding an object live with alternating current (AC). This type of current puts the muscles in spasm so that the victim's hand clutches firmly.

Figure 40 *Never touch a patient in contact with electricity; disconnect the power immediately.*

WARNING
Where very high voltage is involved (some industries, power stations, high tension towers, etc.) you must *NOT* attempt the rescue. This electricity can leap across gaps and hit the approaching first-aider. Keep at least 20 yards away. All you can do is to notify the authorities at once. No rescue is possible until the current has been cut off. In any case, the chance of the patient's survival is extremely small.

2. When the patient is clear of contact

He can safely be touched. This applies also to those who have been hit by lightning.

The electric current can have:
—thrown or knocked down the victim
—burned deeply, damaging blood vessels
—caused unconsciousness
—stopped respiration and heartbeat by its action on nerves and brain centers

You may have to initiate resuscitation immediately. Be on your guard for fractures and wounds from the patient's fall. Remember that a small skin burn can be a mark of extensive damage inside.

Put to rest and keep a close watch on any patient who has received a severe electric shock if he has not lost consciousness or if he appears to have recovered. He may collapse later.

HEAD INJURY

Damage to the cranium (the upper part of the skull) can threaten the brain in several ways:

Infection. A wound of the scalp may lead to a fracture of the bone (not always exactly underneath it). The route is then open for bacteria to gain entrance to the brain.

A blow on the upper part of the head may fracture the base of the skull, on which the brain is resting. Bleeding or watery discharge (cerebrospinal fluid) from the nose or ear might result, with the risk of infection reaching the brain through the ear or nose.

Concussion. A blow on the head may give a general "shaking up" of the brain and knock out the victim. He becomes *instantly unconscious.* But if no other damage has occurred he will return to full consciousness—sometimes within seconds, sometimes within hours.

Compression. Pressure on the brain is an extremely serious matter because its soft tissues are very vulnerable and because it is tightly encased in the hard structure of the skull. Unlike organs elsewhere (e.g., the intestines in the abdomen) there is no room for displacement or an increase in size. Relatively minor changes of configuration give major pressure effects with marked consequences on the central nervous system.

Compression following injury can happen in one (or several) of three ways:

1. From depressed bone in a skull fracture.
2. From bleeding within the skull.
3. From the general swelling of brain tissue. This makes the brain fit even more tightly within the skull. It drives the brain stem downward to jam into the bony hole at the back of the base of the skull, where the medulla oblongata leaves the cranium to become the beginning of the spinal cord (see Figure 41). The brain stem contains nerve centers controlling such life functions

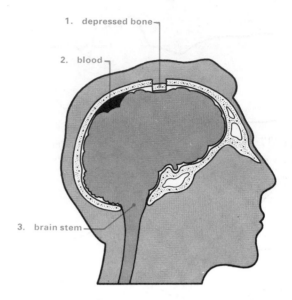

Figure 41 *After injury, compression may result from (1) depressed bone, (2) bleeding inside the skull, or (3) pressure on the brain stem due to swelling. The effects are potentially very serious.*

as circulation and respiration. Subjected to pressure it may fail in its work.

Unlike concussion, which gives immediate unconsciousness, compression develops gradually. It may take minutes or hours for its effect to show, the patient gradually becoming comatose before passing into unconsciousness.

One feature which sometimes (not always) shows is the result of pressure on the cerebral nerve which controls the action of the muscles of the iris, the colored ring which surrounds the dark pupil of the eye. As a consequence the pupils of the eyes may be unequal. If such a sign arises after head injury it is of grave significance.

Compression following concussion

It can easily happen that after a head injury the patient is knocked out immediately from concussion and then apparently recovers ("lucid interval") before being overtaken by compression which also has resulted, and sinking back into unconsciousness. Be on your guard: the victim who comes to after concussion may yet be in danger.

First aid

1. Treat unconsciousness according to the important principles outlined in the section on *Unconsciousness.*

2. Dress wounds very meticulously.

3. Beware of other injuries, including fractures—especially fractures of the spine (see *Fractures*). Check for these as best you can before you move your patient. If in doubt, do not move him but watch his airways carefully.

4. If you see blood or fluid from nose or ear suspect

a fractured base of the skull. Keep the patient in the Recovery Position (see Figure 24), unless other circumstances like a fractured spine forbid you to move him. Lay him on the side of the affected ear or nose, to allow the fluid to run away. Do not plug the ear but cover it with a protective dressing. If the nose is involved, warn the patient not to blow it for the act may drive contaminated fluid toward the fracture site and the brain.

5. Get medical help as rapidly as you can.

POISONING
Swallowed poisons

Act according to this plan. The numbers refer to the notes which follow.

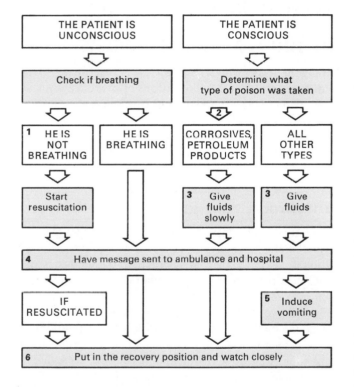

(1) Some poisons inhibit the respiratory control centers of the brain. Others may interfere with the blood's capacity to carry oxygen. A patient may have become asphyxiated on vomit, and the airway need clearing (see Figure 24).

(2) *Corrosives* are chemical substances which can burn. You find them in some domestic cleaners, bleaches, rust removers, toilet bowl cleaners, and in car batteries. They include strong acids (e.g., sulfuric, nitric, hydrochloric) and alkalis (e.g., ammonia, caustic soda) which may leave marks and stains on the face and lips, or where they have splashed on clothes.

On being swallowed they grossly damage the back of the throat and the esophagus. Inside the stomach they do equal harm. Were the patient now to vomit, some of the corrosive

would travel back into the mouth and aggravate the injury. Worse still, the stomach wall—weakened by the corrosive, and subjected to the convulsive movements of vomiting—might perforate, letting the poison leak into the abdominal cavity.

Petroleum products like gasoline or kerosene have a characteristic odor. As they are swallowed their fumes pass into the air passages and so to the lungs where they can cause great inflammation—a chemical pneumonia. A return journey by vomiting would repeat this damage.

Therefore, in both these categories—corrosives and petroleum products—you do not want the patient to vomit.

(3) *Give fluids* to dilute the poison: four glasses of milk or water to an adult, two glasses to a child. But this you do to the *conscious patient only; never give anything by mouth to an unconscious person.*

The victim of a corrosive poison takes half this dose only: two glasses for the adult and one for the child. He must take it in slow sips; too much too fast may cause vomiting. In any case, after corrosive poisoning it will be difficult and painful to swallow.

(4) *Getting hospital admission* must be done quickly. It is wiser for you to remain with and attend to your patient and to delegate to someone else the message sending. He must tell the sex and age and exact address of the patient, the poison suspected and the probable amount taken. Let him also explain what first aid is being given and whether or not the patient has vomited. He may be given advice on further action pending the arrival of the ambulance.

(5) *Induce vomiting* only to the conscious patient who has not taken a corrosive or a petroleum product. The best way to make him vomit is to rub against the back of his throat with your finger or with the blunt end of a spoon.

Please note that you do *NOT* give salt. Not only is salt an inefficient emetic but also it can be harmful in large doses. Some premises where poisoning is a possible hazard may keep *syrup of ipecac* as an emergency emetic; the provision of this and instructions as to dosage should come through a doctor. Many doctors urge that every family should keep a supply in their medicine chest.

Keep a sample of the vomit to send with the patient to the hospital if there is time.

The most important thing to do is to get the patient to hospital quickly: your attempts to induce vomiting must not delay this.

(6) *The Recovery Position* (see Figure 24) is necessary for any poisoned patient after you have taken other measures. The victim who has been conscious or recovered consciousness may suddenly become unconscious and start to vomit.

Always stay closely by the patient in case his condition worsens. A would-be suicide, frustrated by his failure to kill himself, may make another attempt unless watched. Where you are suspicious of suicide or homicide you should call the police, and try not to handle surrounding articles.

Try to obtain a sample of any vomit and also any containers (even if empty) from which the poison may have come; send these to the hospital with the victim.

Gas poisons

Carbon monoxide from incomplete burning of fuels, especially gasoline, is the most likely poison in this category. Car engines running in a closed garage or with an exhaust leaking into the inside of the car are a common source, as are poorly burning coal fires with inadequate ventilation. In industry other gases, such as carbon tetrachloride, may escape in poisonous amounts. In a house fire poisonous gases may be present in a smoke-filled room.

If you have to rescue someone from a gas-filled area, take a deep breath and hold it before going in. The first thing to do is to get the victim out into the fresh air; if it does not cause delay, you should also switch off the car engine and open (or break) the windows.

As soon as you are clear of the gas, check the victim's airway. If he is not breathing give artificial respiration. If he is breathing and conscious, advise him to take deep and slow breaths.

Agricultural poisons

Some pesticides can be dangerous, not only when swallowed but if invisible droplets are inhaled after the chemical has been used as a spray. Also any droplets settling or liquid splashing onto clothes and skin could be absorbed into the body.

Massive doses will produce fast and obvious poisoning. A more hidden situation is that in which the poison gradually builds up after recurrent exposure to smaller concentrations. Symptoms may develop slowly and moderately and then suddenly become severe and dangerous. The time factor may vary from minutes to days.

These symptoms are not very specific and at their onset could suggest influenza. The patient has a headache, is sweating, thirsty and nauseous. He is abnormally tired. Impaired action of nerves and muscles may lead to dimmed vision and to difficulty in breathing with tightness of the chest. Eventually his breathing and heartbeat could fail.

Your first-aid treatment may thus begin with suspecting the exposure in its early stages. Stop the patient from working; put him at complete rest.

Carefully remove contaminated clothing (put it in a plastic bag, working with gloves, if you can). Wash his skin very thoroughly. Irrigate his eyes with water if they could have been contaminated. He may need artificial respiration.

If he is conscious let him drink sweetened water to which you have added a pinch of salt.

The containers of the pesticide may carry special instructions concerning emergency treatment of the poisoning. But get medical help quickly.

Poisonous contact plants

Poison ivy, poison sumac and poison oak can—within a couple of hours or days after contact—cause rashes and blisters.

Take off the patient's clothes and wash his skin with copious changes of soap and water. The irritation comes from a plant resin which the patient, by scratching and manipulation, may have carried from the original exposed areas of contact (hands, wrists, face, ankles) to other parts of his body.

In mild cases a simple soothing lotion (e.g. calamine) may then be enough; but some attacks are severe, with a raised body temperature, and need medical help.

THE DRUG ADDICT IN CRISIS

Helping the addict who is having a severe reaction to a drug is a difficult problem. Manifestations of overdosage are so varied from drug to drug and (for each drug) from individual to individual that only the broadest outline can be given. Here we consider not the basic state of addiction but the sudden crisis which can arise from self-administration.

Stimulants

Stimulants such as amphetamines ("speed") in large doses can make the taker behave very like the irresponsible, irrational alcoholic. He is energetic, loquacious, over-active. Very rarely marijuana (cannabis) can give a similar reaction.

The thing to do is to treat him like the drunken man who is behaving badly. Keep friendly with him, keep talking to him, be amenable as far as possible. Do not leave him alone at any time but keep with him and, if you can, get someone to be with you or at least close at hand and within call for help. The effect wears off with time and the addict can then be handled more easily.

Hallucinogens

Someone under the severe effect of drugs like lysergic acid (LSD, "acid") can be in danger—and so could those alongside him. The victim becomes psychotic, with the most bizarre ideas and behavior. He might pass through a phase of fear amounting to panic. You must constantly speak to him; be comforting and reassuring, although this may be difficult to achieve.

He might have self-destructive impulses and do almost anything, like trying to jump out of a high window. He might have delusions of being attacked or ill-treated and then could be violently hostile and attack you.

Be on your guard, seek help, and use whatever force is reasonable, but only when his safety or your self-defense makes it necessary. Calling an ambulance for his removal to the hospital might be a necessary solution.

Depressants

Depressants such as barbiturates slow down a person's reactions considerably. These drugs depress and eventually induce sleep. The takers may easily be involved in traffic accidents.

Barbiturates may first briefly put the victim into a state of overactive excitement. This does not last long, and he is likely to collapse quite suddenly. At this point his life is in danger. Put him in the Recovery Position (see Figure 24) and arrange to have him sent to the hospital. If depressants have been combined with alcohol the situation is particularly perilous.

On the other hand, *withdrawal symptoms* in a drug addict can be accompanied by delirium and convulsions which need immediate medical aid. Guarding the victim's airway (see *Unconsciousness*) is your principal task.

Narcotics

Addicts often take morphine and heroin by injection into a vein, first dissolving the powder or tablet in water. One danger lies in the way these drugs depress respiration. The collapsed addict with an overdose could cease breathing and need artificial respiration.

Another major threat is the risk the addict runs from his self-administered intravenous injection. An embolism (the blockage of a vessel) by some of the inadequately dissolved preparation can damage part of the heart, brain or lung and cause death. First aid can help little, but you must try the general principles of resuscitation (see *Resuscitation*).

Withdrawal symptoms of these narcotics can cause real distress. They develop gradually and can become very severe.

An addict who has accustomed himself to more or less regular doses and who, for some reason, cannot get one when it is due will soon develop a craving and will become generally anxious and restless. Some hours later symptoms like yawning, sneezing and watering of the eyes and nose will appear. In about 24 hours these worsen. He sweats; his temperature and pulse rate are increased; his skin may itch; he is nauseous. Though he feels very tired and hungry he can neither sleep nor eat. This may be followed by abdominal cramps, vomiting, diarrhea and severe prostration.

Eventually he will recover but he will have been through a very high degree of mental and physical suffering. Reassure and support the patient but do all you can to dissuade and prevent him from seeking out more of his drug for self-treatment (unfortunately, this advice usually falls on deaf ears). Medical help is needed as early as possible. Very often a dose of morphine or heroin *substitute* is given as effective alleviation.

INSECT STINGS

The only real dangers from insect stings are:

1. Infection at the sting site. A doctor may advise antibiotics.

2. Some insects can transmit diseases.

These two potential dangers are relatively long-term features and not factors involving first aid.

3. More immediate is the chance that the patient has acquired, from past stings, a hypersensitivity to the insect's venom. He may rapidly develop an allergic reaction with pallor and collapse. Some people, like beekeepers, who are exposed to this risk keep antihistamine tablets to take immediately in case of emergency—however, the serious case needs rapid medical attention and treatment by injections.

The usual insect sting is only a minor matter of pain and inconvenience.

If, as with bees, the sting is still embedded in the skin try to remove it with tweezers—which you apply low down against the skin (see Figure 42). Were you to press your forceps higher up the sting, this could inject into the skin some of the venom still left in it. Apply an antihistamine cream, smoothing it gently into the skin.

TICK BITES

The tick often remains attached to the skin. The sooner you get it off the better. Do not pull; this would leave part of it still embedded.

Either: (1) "drown" it by covering with a heavy oil like salad oil or machine oil. If it does not separate at once leave the oil over it for half an hour and then slowly, carefully, remove its body with tweezers;

Or: (2) light a cigarette and apply the glowing end to its body; it should now fall off (see Figure 43).

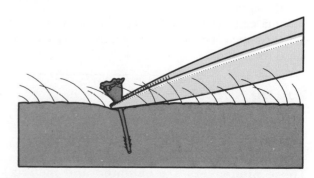

Figure 42 *To remove a bee sting, apply tweezers low down against the skin.*

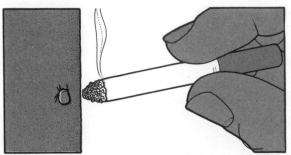

Figure 43 *One method of removing a tick attached to the skin is to apply a lighted cigarette to its body, taking care not to burn the skin.*

SNAKEBITES

Snakes vary so much in habitat and potential harmfulness that only general rules can feature here. Seek expert advice in your locality, preferably *before* any snakebite has happened.

If possible, kill the snake. Keep the body to show the doctor to help him assess specific treatment needed.

Immediately lay the patient down; let him be at rest. Wipe away from the bite area any venom lying on the skin. Wash the area thoroughly with soap and water. Mop it dry (do not rub). Put on a clean dressing.

Immobilize the bitten area as if it were fractured. This reduces the speed of flow of venom into the patient's circulation.

Give any pain-relieving tablets you may have. This justifiably breaks the rule of not giving medicines in *first-aid* treatment. Pain can be very great. So can fear. Your patient may be convinced that all snakebites are fatal. They are not and terror (not too strong a word) may be a great factor affecting his general condition. Very strong reassurance is a great help. In the few cases where snakebite proves fatal, death generally does not happen quickly, but one or two days after the incident. Get the patient to the hospital by ambulance or car. Keep the bitten area as low as possible. If circumstances force the patient to walk, let him do this slowly and gently.

Send a telephone message ahead to the hospital, so that preparations may be made.

In some cases shock and respiratory difficulty occur. Watch the patient's breathing. You may even have to give artificial respiration.

> **YOU DO NOT**
> — **suck the wound area.**
> — **apply chemicals to it.**
> — **cut into it.**
> — **apply a tourniquet.**
> **These maneuvers are outdated and ineffective. They may do more harm than good.**

SCORPION AND SPIDER STINGS

These can give intense pain and skin damage. Some can cause general symptoms of collapse, sweating, nausea and vomiting—it is rare for them to be fatal.

Treat as for snakebites (see above).

FROSTBITE

In severe cold the blood vessels of the skin narrow as the result of a reflex action and exposed areas blanch and may be at risk of gangrene. Parts especially threatened are extremities like fingers, toes, nose, ears and chin. The condition worsens if partial thawing is followed by a recurrence of frosting and you must take great care to avoid this.

The affected skin is "devitalized" and must be treated gently. *It should never be rubbed.*

Treatment of frostbite

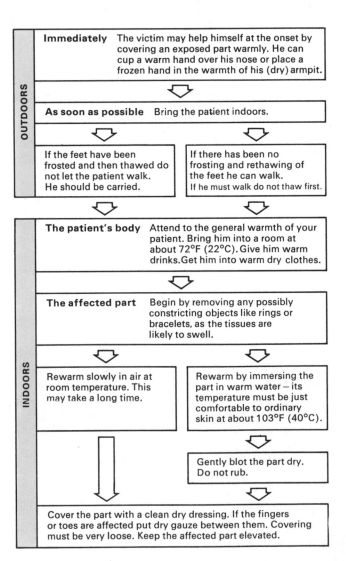

Immediately	The victim may help himself at the onset by covering an exposed part warmly. He can cup a warm hand over his nose or place a frozen hand in the warmth of his (dry) armpit.	
As soon as possible	Bring the patient indoors.	
If the feet have been frosted and then thawed do not let the patient walk. He should be carried.		If there has been no frosting and rethawing of the feet he can walk. If he must walk do not thaw first.
The patient's body	Attend to the general warmth of your patient. Bring him into a room at about 72°F (22°C). Give him warm drinks. Get him into warm dry clothes.	
The affected part	Begin by removing any possibly constricting objects like rings or bracelets, as the tissues are likely to swell.	
Rewarm slowly in air at room temperature. This may take a long time.		Rewarm by immersing the part in warm water – its temperature must be just comfortable to ordinary skin at about 103°F (40°C).
		Gently blot the part dry. Do not rub.
Cover the part with a clean dry dressing. If the fingers or toes are affected put dry gauze between them. Covering must be very loose. Keep the affected part elevated.		

OUTDOORS / INDOORS

EXPOSURE TO COLD

Severe exposure to cold may have a devastating effect on the body, especially on the heart muscle. The general result is a progressive slowing up of the patient, who may become clumsy with poor judgment developing into mental confusion. From drowsiness he may pass into coma. He is at risk of dying of heart failure. Act as follows:

1. Give resuscitation if this is needed (see Resuscitation). Check very carefully that there is no breathing or pulse detectable. Attempts at heart massage on a heart which is still beating, however slightly, can be extremely harmful.

2. Put the patient at complete rest. Do not let him struggle on.

3. Transport him into a warm room or shelter. If there is no shelter and you have to treat him outside, shield him as best you can within a tent or by setting up a screen of poles, clothes or blankets to protect against the wind.

4. Give him warm drinks if he is conscious. Cocoa or hot chocolate is very suitable. Let him take this slowly. NEVER give him alcohol, which would make him lose more heat by dilating the skin blood vessels.

5. Replace wet and cold clothes by warm dry covers. A plastic sheet incorporated in these would help the body to retain heat. A great deal of heat can be lost from the head; make sure that it is within the covering, with only the face exposed. Two blankets can be used to cover the patient effectively as shown in Figure 44.

Sometimes you can use a sleeping bag; it may be possible to include within a warm companion to contribute further heat.

Rapid rewarming by putting the patient in a bath of about 103°F (40°C) is sometimes used, but under domestic circumstances this is best reserved for cases of sudden and relatively brief immersion, as in icy water. Where the patient has cooled slowly, the gradually altered body chemistry and heart muscle may not be able to cope with changes brought about by a sudden return to warmth.

ACCIDENTAL HYPOTHERMIA

This name is given to a dangerous condition of very low body temperature which may arise in the home in an almost unsuspected way. In very cold weather and where rooms are inadequately heated the occupants can gradually cool, down to a temperature of 95°F (35°C) or below. In extreme cases the temperature can reach below 86°F (30°C).

The extremes of age are particularly prone to this mishap. The small baby, paradoxically, has a relatively large body surface from which to lose heat: he is not active

USING TWO BLANKETS TO COVER THE COLD PATIENT

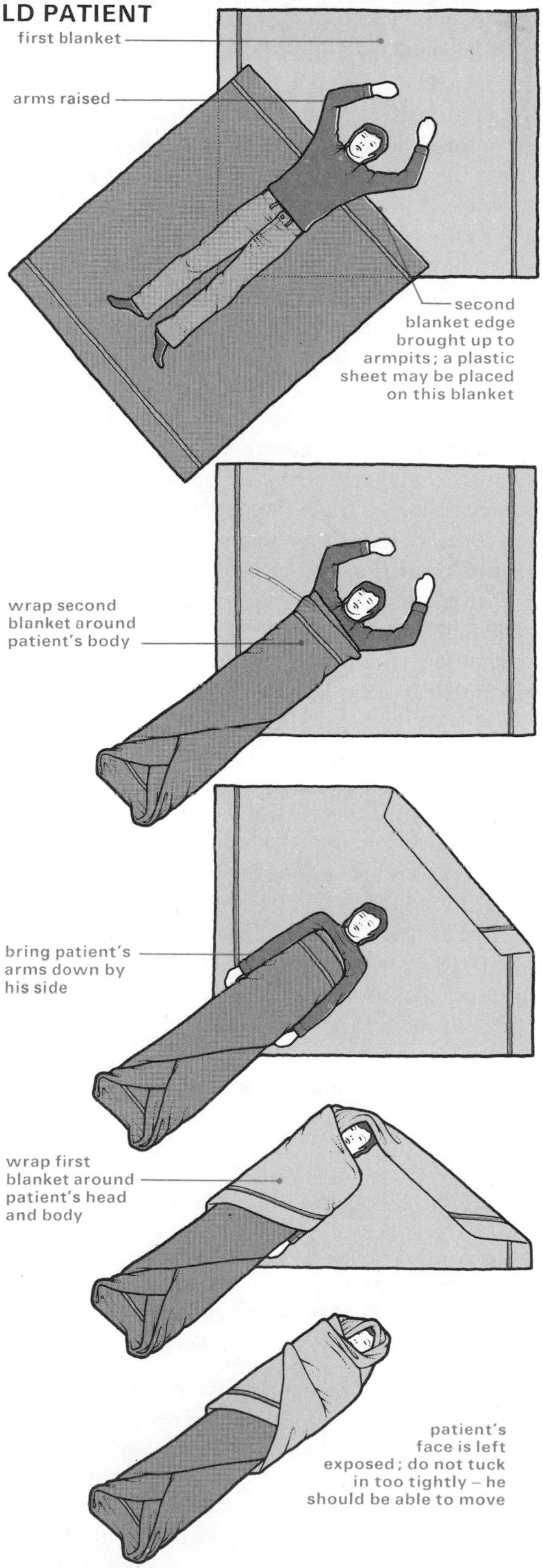

first blanket

arms raised

second blanket edge brought up to armpits; a plastic sheet may be placed on this blanket

wrap second blanket around patient's body

bring patient's arms down by his side

wrap first blanket around patient's head and body

patient's face is left exposed; do not tuck in too tightly – he should be able to move

Figure 44 *Use two blankets as shown to cover the patient who has been exposed to cold.*

and does not produce much body heat by muscle action as he lies in his crib, his temperature-regulating mechanism is not yet fully developed and if his covers slip off he cannot pull them back.

Compared with younger people, the elderly have a slightly lower body temperature; their blood vessels are narrower: they move less in sleep; their thyroid glands (which help to produce body heat) are less active. In addition many are taking sleeping tablets or tranquilizers which can have some temperature-lowering effect.

Thus one can find these patients having gradually slipped into a deeply cold state, often overnight while asleep. They are very drowsy or even in coma, icy to touch (even under the blankets) and their pulse and respiration are slow and poor in volume. The skin is puffy and pale (but sometimes rosy in babies).

You must *not* try rapid rewarming for this might lead to circulatory collapse. Have the patient lie in bed fully (but loosely) covered, including the head. Do not warm the bed (for example, never use an electric blanket), but *warm the room*. If they are conscious give them warm drinks, but never alcohol.

You should get immediate medical advice; some of these patients urgently need hospital admission.

HEAT EFFECTS

Perspiring as we become hot is one of our protective methods against becoming overheated. As it evaporates, sweat fluid carries heat out of the body. This effect helps to maintain normal body temperature.

Effective as it is, this mechanism has one disadvantage: the sweat carries with it a fair concentration of salts which are natural components of the body chemistry. A deficiency of these salts causes weakness and, sometimes, severe cramps.

This is the simple background to understanding the two main ways overheating can affect us.

HEAT EXHAUSTION	HEAT STROKE
This can attack someone who has perspired heavily after long exertion or on a very hot day.	This can happen in a very hot region of jungle type where the atmosphere is windless and very humid.
The body loses an excessive amount of water and salts.	There is a breakdown of the sweat-producing mechanism: sweat is unable to evaporate into the atmosphere, which is already saturated with water vapor. The air temperature may be higher than that of the patient.
Thanks to the sweating, the patient's body temperature is normal or only slightly raised.	The body, unable to lose heat, becomes extremely hot. The body temperature may rise to 107°F (42°C) or more.
He feels faint, exhausted and sometimes nauseated.	The patient is restless, confused and may become unconscious.
His skin is moist and may be pale.	His skin is hot, dry and red.
His pulse is fast and feeble.	His pulse is fast and forceful.
He may develop cramps.	
First Aid	**First Aid**
Get the patient into a cool area and let him lie down.	Quickly get the patient into the coolest place, indoors if possible.
Loosen his clothing and raise his feet.	Remove his clothing.
Give him fluids with salt to drink: one TEAspoonful of salt per glass. Fresh fruit juice is excellent for this. Let him drink slowly—half a glass every 15 minutes.	Now cool him down by sponging his body with cold or tepid water, and by fanning him vigorously. Do not aim to bring his body temperature to normal, but only to lower it by 2–3°F.
Recovery is likely to be good, but it is wise to get medical advice.	This condition can be mortally dangerous and you need medical help urgently.

ROAD ACCIDENTS

Deal with the accident by a threefold program.
1. The urgent patient.
2. The urgent situation.
3. The other patients.

1. The emergency patient

Just as soon as you are at the scene of a car crash check whether or not anyone needs help for severe bleeding (see *Bleeding*) or asphyxia (see *Choking*).

As far as possible, treat the patient where you find him. Tell any other injured passengers to remain where they are and that you will help them very shortly.

Always look over nearby low walls or hedges for a victim who might have been thrown there.

2. The urgent situation

The situation could indeed be full of risk. A road that is partially obstructed as the result of an accident and which still bears approaching traffic is full of hazards.

—No one must smoke because of the chance of escaping gasoline.

—If there is any fire or smoldering put it out at once with the fire extinguisher which you should be carrying in your car. If fire persists then you must try to get the occupants out quickly.

—Switch off the ignition key and turn out the lights of any car involved.

—Put on the emergency brake. If it does not work and the car is on a hill get something, such as a box or a rear seat, jammed up behind a wheel.

—Get your car parked well out of the way, off the road if you can, to leave room for police and rescue services. This is for you and your car's safety and to leave a clearing for the rescue services. At night have your headlights shining on the scene.

—Set warnings for drivers of approaching cars. Put a flare or a red reflector at least 200 yards on either side, or have a lookout signaling with a flashlight, a white scarf, or even a newspaper.

—Send a message for the police and an ambulance by one or even two messengers. Write out what is to be telephoned. Give the exact location, the number and type of casualties and whether or not any are trapped.

It may seem as if all this is spending too much time away from the patients waiting in the car. Experience has shown that these moves avoid extra damage.

3. The other patients

Now you can return to attend to patients with less urgent injuries. Carefully examine all persons involved and treat them where they are.

The person who is making a fuss or much noise is unlikely to be badly injured; he will usually respond to strong reassurance.

Beware of the unconscious victim in his seat. His neck (a possible fracture) and his airway are the most vulnerable parts. Wipe his mouth free of any fluid. Support his jaw, gently pull the trunk forward and get his head supported on his own hands against the wheel or the dashboard.

You can protect his neck and his airway at the same time by improvising a stiff collar out of a stocking or tights and a folded newspaper. Bend this into a curve and carefully slide it under his jaw and around the neck; tie the free ends of the stocking or tights firmly at the back (see Figure 45). You could have such a collar ready prepared in your car first-aid kit.

Often you will find that the small or average sized dressing is useless when you try to cover wounds. Wounds

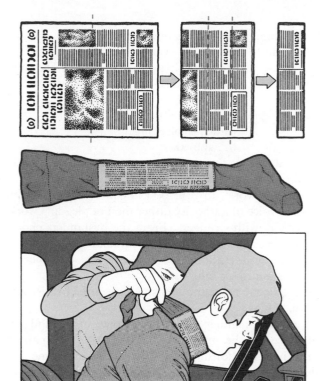

Figure 45 *Using a rolled-up newspaper and a stocking or tights, make a stiff collar to support the victim's jaw, thus keeping his airway clear.*

resulting from traffic accidents often tend to be big ones and your kit should contain really large items.

It is wise not to take an accident victim to the hospital yourself; wait for the ambulance. Your ordinary looking car may be held up in a traffic jam. And you will be in great difficulties if the patient collapses while you travel.

In any case you should not try to extricate patients from a smashed car. Leave this to the experts. Using special equipment they may have to remove large sections of a wrecked car to be able to get the victim out without doing him further harm.

FINALLY: If you come upon an accident scene where rescue services are already in operation, do not stop; this could impede their work. Pass very slowly and carefully.

Matters of priority

When facing any event with one or several accident victims you must have a method of approach. Do not automatically tend the nearest patient, but begin with a quick assessment of the whole situation.

There may be an immediate further risk at the scene. Walls may threaten to collapse, there may be fast-moving traffic, or there may be a fire or gas hazard. You may have to remove the patient(s) speedily and gently instead of following the rule of treating on the spot.

Survey the injured quickly. Decide which patient urgently needs your help and go to him. Call out to the others to remain still where they are, adding that you will soon attend to them. Also, warn bystanders who are not first aiders not to try to lift up any of the victims. They may have a fracture, which could be made worse with improper movement.

Priority goes to resuscitation needs
         to heavy bleeding
         to asphyxia

With due care, put the unconscious patient in the Recovery Position (see Figure 24).

While you work, do your best to control any gathering crowd. A voice of authority rather than of pleading works wonderfully with strangers. From the bystanders choose someone to send a message for an ambulance; this must be very definite, detailing the address, the number of casualties and their injuries.

Get someone to clear away any dangerous debris, such as broken glass.

Your calm manner, your appearance of method and confidence can be invaluably reassuring to the patient. Establish a relationship with him. Get his name and address; give him your name. Always speak to him as you work, showing sympathy and explaining in advance anything you are about to do.

If some of his property is lying about, look after it and let him know you are doing so.

As you deal with injuries remember to think of the hidden wound and the unsuspected fracture.

And never forget the importance of preventing shock (see *Shock*).

YOUR FIRST AID BOX

Where do you keep it? The bathroom is not the best place for it. It should avoid steamy atmospheres; it should always be immediately accessible; it should be out of the reach of children; it should be in a zone frequently occupied by the people of the house or apartment and easily seen by guests. In the upper shelves of a cupboard of the hall or of a dry area of the kitchen is satisfactory.

What sort of box? It should be both roomy and portable, and made of metal or plastic with a tight-fitting lid which is easily opened by an adult. Label it very clearly.

What should it contain? Since it is for domestic use, we can presume that it will often be called upon for minor treatments which do not need a doctor. Therefore it will go a little beyond *first* aid and venture a little into *second* aid, that is simple home treatments.

Instruments:
    Tweezers.
    Scissors (kept for this purpose only).
    Thermometer.
    Safety pins.

Medicine:
    Acetaminophen or soluble aspirin tablets.
    Simple antiseptics like cetrimide or chlorhexidine in suitable dilution ready for use, or in stronger form with the instructions on diluting carefully marked on the bottle. Ask your doctor or pharmacist.
    An antiseptic cream for spreading on dressings.

Dressings:
    White gauze.
    Absorbent cotton.
    Paper tissues.
    2-inch and 3-inch wide plain bandages.
    Ready-to-apply sterile dressings, each packed singly in its protective covering. These are obtainable in various sizes.
    2-inch and 3-inch wide adherent dressing strips, which can be cut to size for covering simple wounds.
    1-inch wide adhesive strapping.

The above will cover most needs. It is better to keep to a few standardized items than to have a large mixed collection which can confuse. Items like absorbent cotton and gauze should be in small intact packs: once they have been opened they should not be put back for further use later.

Anything you use from the box you should replace with new items as soon as possible.

Index

Figures in **bold** indicate main entry.

A

B

C

D

E

F

G

H

I

N

O

U

W

Y

Z

X